# THE Bible Knowledge Commentary

## An Exposition of the Scriptures by Dallas Seminary Faculty

### OLD TESTAMENT

Based on the *New International Version*

EDITORS

# John F. Walvoord
# Roy B. Zuck

VICTOR BOOKS®

A DIVISION OF SCRIPTURE PRESS PUBLICATIONS INC.
USA CANADA ENGLAND

13  14  15  16  17  18  19  20   Printing/Year  95  94  93

Library of Congress Catalog Card Number: 85-50328
ISBN: 0-88207-813-5

# Contents

## Charts and Diagrams (for Maps, see page 6)

## Maps (for Charts and Diagrams, see page 3)

# Preface

*The Bible Knowledge Commentary* is an exposition of the Scriptures written and edited solely by Dallas Seminary faculty members. It is designed for pastors, laypersons, Bible teachers, serious Bible students, and others who want a comprehensive but brief and reliable commentary on the entire Bible

Why another Bible commentary when so many commentaries are already available? Several features make this two-volume set a distinctive Bible study tool.

First, *The Bible Knowledge Commentary* is written by faculty members of one school—Dallas Theological Seminary. This commentary interprets the Scriptures consistently from the grammatical-historical approach and from the pretribulational, premillennial perspective, for which Dallas Seminary is well known. At the same time, the authors often present various views of passages where differences of opinion exist within evangelical scholarship.

Second, this is the first two-volume commentary to be based on the *New International Version of the Holy Bible* (1978 ed.). The NIV is widely accepted as a translation that faithfully renders the biblical text into clear modern-day English. *The Bible Knowledge Commentary* thus becomes immediately useful as a companion to one's personal Bible study.

Third, this commentary has features that not all commentaries include. (a) In their comments on the biblical text, the writers discuss how the purpose of the book unfolds, how each part fits with the whole and with what precedes and follows it. This helps readers see why the biblical authors chose the material they did as their words were guided by the Holy Spirit's inspiration. (b) Problem passages, puzzling Bible-time customs, and alleged contradictions are carefully considered and discussed. (c) Insights from the latest in conservative biblical scholarship are incorporated in this volume. (d) Many Hebrew, Aramaic, and Greek words, important to the understanding of certain passages, are discussed. These words are transliterated for the benefit of readers not proficient in the biblical languages. Yet those who do know these languages will also appreciate these comments. (e) Dozens of maps, charts, and diagrams are included; they are placed conveniently with the Bible passages being discussed, not at the end of the volume. (f) Numerous cross references to related or parallel passages are included with the discussions on many passages.

The material on each Bible book includes an *Introduction* (discussion of items such as authorship, date, purpose, unity, style, unique features), *Outline, Commentary,* and *Bibliography.* In the *Commentary* section, summaries of entire sections of the text are given, followed by detailed comments on the passage verse by verse and often phrase by phrase. All words quoted from the NIV appear in boldface type, as do the verse numbers at the beginning of paragraphs. The *Bibliography* entries, suggested for further study, are not all endorsed in their entirety by the authors and editors. The writers and editors have listed both works they have consulted and others which would be useful to readers.

Personal pronouns referring to Deity are capitalized, which often helps make it clear that the commentator is writing about a Member of the Trinity. The word Lord, as in the NIV, is the English translation of the Hebrew YHWH, often rendered *Yahweh* in English. *Lord* translates *'Ădōnāy.* When the two names stand together as a compound name of God, they are rendered "Sovereign Lord," as in the NIV.

The consulting editors—Dr. Kenneth L. Barker and Dr. Eugene H. Merrill on the Old Testament, and Dr. Stanley D. Toussaint on the New Testament—have added to the quality of this commentary by reading the manuscripts and offering helpful suggestions. Their work is greatly appreciated. We also express thanks to Lloyd Cory, Victor Books Reference Editor, to Barbara Williams, whose careful editing enhanced the material appreciably, to Production Coordinator Myrna Jean Hasse, to Jan Arroyo, and other people in the text editing department at Scripture Press, who spent many long hours keyboarding and preparing pages for typesetting, and to the several manuscript typists at Dallas Theological Seminary for their diligence.

This two-volume commentary is an exposition of the Bible, an explanation of the text of Scripture, based on careful exegesis. It is not primarily a devotional commentary, or an exegetical work giving details of lexicology, grammar, and syntax with extensive discussion of critical matters pertaining to textual and background data. May this commentary deepen your insight into the Scriptures, as you seek to have "the eyes of your heart . . . enlightened" (Eph. 1:18) by the teaching ministry of the Holy Spirit.

This book is designed to enrich your understanding and appreciation of the Scriptures, God's inspired, inerrant Word, and to motivate you "not merely [to] listen to the Word" but also to "do what it says" (James 1:22) and "also . . . to teach others" (2 Tim. 2:2).

*John F. Walvoord*
*Roy B. Zuck*

# Editors

**John F. Walvoord,** A.B., M.A., Th.M., Th.D., D.D., Litt.D.
Chancellor and Minister at Large
Professor of Systematic Theology, Emeritus
Dallas Theological Seminary

**Roy B. Zuck,** A.B., Th.M., Th.D.
Chairman and Professor
of Bible Exposition
Editor, *Bibliotheca Sacra*
Dallas Theological Seminary

# Consulting Editors

*Old Testament:*
**Kenneth L. Barker,** A.B., Th.M., Ph.D.
Executive Director, NIV Translation Center
(A Ministry of International Bible Society)
(Formerly Chairman and Professor of
Old Testament Studies, 1968–81,
Dallas Theological Seminary)

**Eugene H. Merrill,** A.B., M.A., M.Phil., Ph.D.
Professor of Old Testament Studies
Dallas Theological Seminary

*New Testament:*
**Stanley D. Toussaint,** A.B., Th.M., Th.D.
Chairman and Senior Professor of Bible Exposition
Dallas Theological Seminary

# Contributing Authors*

**Walter L. Baker, A.B., Th.M.**
Associate Professor of World Missions
*Obadiah*

**Craig A. Blaising, B.S., Th.M., Th.D., Ph.D.**
Professor of Systematic Theology
*Malachi*

**J. Ronald Blue, A.B., Th.M., Ph.D.**
Chairman and Professor of
World Missions
*Habakkuk*

**Sid S. Buzzell, B.S., Th.M., Ph.D.**
Senior Pastor, Heritage Church,
Aurora, Colorado
(Formerly Assistant Professor of
Christian Education, 1974–77, 1979–84,
Dallas Theological Seminary)
*Proverbs*

**Donald K. Campbell, A.B., Th.M., Th.D., D.D.**
President
Professor of Bible Exposition
*Joshua*

**Robert B. Chisholm, Jr., A.B., M.Div., Th.M., Th.D.**
Professor of Old Testament Studies
*Hosea, Joel*

**Thomas L. Constable, A.B., Th.M., Th.D.**
Director of D.Min. Studies
Professor of Bible Exposition
*1 and 2 Kings*

**Jack S. Deere, A.B., Th.M., Th.D.**
Associate Pastor,
Vineyard Christian Fellowship,
Anaheim, California
(Formerly Assistant Professor of Old
Testament Studies, 1976–87,
Dallas Theological Seminary)
*Deuteronomy, Song of Songs*

**Charles H. Dyer, A.B., Th.M., Th.D.**
Dean of Enrollment Management
Associate Professor of Bible Exposition
*Jeremiah, Lamentations, Ezekiel*

**Gene A. Getz, A.B., M.A., Ph.D.**
Adjunct Teacher in Pastoral Ministries
Pastor, Fellowship Bible Church, North
Plano, Texas
Director, Center for Church Renewal,
Plano, Texas
*Nehemiah*

**Donald R. Glenn, B.S., M.A., Th.M.**
Chairman and Professor of Old
Testament Studies
*Ecclesiastes*

**John D. Hannah, B.S., Th.M., Th.D., Ph.D.**
Chairman and Professor of Historical Theology
*Exodus, Jonah, Zephaniah*

**Elliott E. Johnson, B.S., Th.M., Th.D.**
Professor of Bible Exposition
*Nahum*

**F. Duane Lindsey, A.B., B.D., Th.M., Th.D.**
(Formerly Registrar and Assistant
Professor of Systematic Theology, 1967–91,
Dallas Theological Seminary)
*Leviticus, Judges, Haggai, Zechariah*

**John A. Martin, A.B., Th.M., Th.D., Ph.D.**
President, Central College, McPherson, Kansas
(Formerly Dean of Faculty and Professor
of Bible Exposition, 1978–90,
Dallas Theological Seminary)
*Ezra, Esther, Isaiah, Micah*

**Eugene H. Merrill, A.B., M.A., M.Phil., Ph.D.**
Professor of Old Testament Studies
*Numbers, 1 and 2 Samuel, 1 and 2 Chronicles*

**J. Dwight Pentecost, A.B., Th.M., Th.D.**
Distinguished Professor of Bible Exposition,
Emeritus
*Daniel*

**John W. Reed, A.B., M.A., M.Div., Ph.D.**
Chairman and Professor of Pastoral Ministries
*Ruth*

**Allen P. Ross, A.B., Th.M., Th.D., Ph.D.**
Associate Professor of Biblical Studies,
Trinity Episcopal School for Ministry,
Ambridge, Pennsylvania
(Formerly Chairman and Professor of
Old Testament Studies, 1975–89)
*Genesis, Psalms*

**Donald R. Sunukjian, A.B., Th.M., Th.D., Ph.D.**
Pastor, Westlake Bible Church Austin, Texas
(Formerly Associate Professor of Pastoral
Ministries, 1979–87,
Dallas Theological Seminary)
*Amos*

**Roy B. Zuck, A.B., Th.M., Th.D.**
Chairman and Professor
of Bible Exposition
*Job*

*All authors are either present or former members of the faculty of Dallas Theological Seminary.

# Abbreviations

## A. *General*

| | | | |
|---|---|---|---|
| act. | active | n., nn. | note(s) |
| Akk. | Akkadian | n.d. | no date |
| Apoc. | Apocrypha | neut. | neuter |
| Aram. | Aramaic | n.p. | no publisher, no place of |
| ca. | *circa*, about | | publication |
| cf. | *confer*, compare | no. | number |
| chap., chaps. | chapter(s) | NT | New Testament |
| comp. | compiled, compilation, | OT | Old Testament |
| | compiler | p., pp. | page(s) |
| ed. | edited, edition, editor | par., pars. | paragraph(s) |
| eds. | editors | part. | participle |
| e.g. | *exempli gratia*, for example | pass. | passive |
| Eng. | English | perf. | perfect |
| et al. | *et alii*, and others | pl. | plural |
| fem. | feminine | pres. | present |
| Gr. | Greek | q.v. | *quod vide*, which see |
| Heb. | Hebrew | Sem. | Semitic |
| ibid. | *ibidem*, in the same place | sing. | singular |
| i.e. | *id est*, that is | s.v. | *sub verbo*, under the word |
| imper. | imperative | trans. | translation, translator, |
| imperf. | imperfect | | translated |
| lit. | literal, literally | viz. | *videlicet*, namely |
| LXX | Septuagint | vol., vols. | volume(s) |
| marg. | margin, marginal reading | v., vv. | verse(s) |
| masc. | masculine | vs. | versus |
| ms., mss. | manuscript(s) | Vul. | Vulgate |
| MT | Masoretic text | | |

## B. *Abbreviations of Books of the Bible*

| | | | | |
|---|---|---|---|---|
| Gen. | Ruth | Job | Lam. | Jonah |
| Ex. | 1, 2 Sam. | Ps., Pss. (pl.) | Ezek. | Micah |
| Lev. | 1, 2 Kings | Prov. | Dan. | Nahum |
| Num. | 1, 2 Chron. | Ecc. | Hosea | Hab. |
| Deut. | Ezra | Song | Joel | Zeph. |
| Josh. | Neh. | Isa. | Amos | Hag. |
| Jud. | Es. | Jer. | Obad. | Zech. |
| | | | | Mal. |

| | | | | |
|---|---|---|---|---|
| Matt. | Acts | Eph. | 1, 2 Tim. | James |
| Mark | Rom. | Phil. | Titus | 1, 2 Peter |
| Luke | 1, 2 Cor. | Col. | Phile. | 1, 2, 3 John |
| John | Gal. | 1, 2 Thes. | Heb. | Jude |
| | | | | Rev. |

## C. *Abbreviations of Bible Versions, Translations, and Paraphrases*

| | |
|---|---|
| ASV | American Standard Version |
| JB | Jerusalem Bible |
| KJV | King James Version |
| NASB | New American Standard Bible |
| NEB | New English Bible |
| NIV | New International Version |
| RSV | Revised Standard Version |

# Transliterations

## Hebrew

### Consonants

| | | | | |
|---|---|---|---|---|
| א — ’ | ד — $\underline{d}$ | י — $y$ | ס — $s$ | ר — $r$ |
| ב — $b$ | ה — $h$ | כ — $k$ | ע — $‘$ | שׂ — $ś$ |
| ב — $\underline{b}$ | ו — $w$ | כ — $\underline{k}$ | פ — $p$ | שׁ — $š$ |
| ג — $g$ | ז — $z$ | ל — $l$ | פ — $\underline{p}$ | ת — $t$ |
| ג — $\underline{g}$ | ח — $ḥ$ | מ — $m$ | צ — $ṣ$ | ת — $\underline{t}$ |
| ד — $d$ | ט — $ṭ$ | נ — $n$ | ק — $q$ | |

*Daghesh forte* is represented by doubling the letter.

### Vocalization

| | | | |
|---|---|---|---|
| בָה — bâh | בָ — bā | בֹ — bo[1] | בֱ — bĕ |
| בוֹ — bô | בֹ — bō | בֻ — bu[1] | בְ — b |
| בוּ — bû | בֻ — bū | בֶ — be | בָה — bāh |
| בֵי — bê | בֵ — bē | בִ — bi[1] | בָא — bā’ |
| בֶ — bè | בִ — bī | בַ — bă | בֵה — bēh |
| בִי — bî | בַ — ba | בׇ — bŏ | בֶה — beh |

[1] In closed syllables

## Greek

| | | | | | |
|---|---|---|---|---|---|
| α, ᾳ — $a$ | | ξ — $x$ | | γγ — $ng$ | |
| β — $b$ | | ο — $o$ | | γκ — $nk$ | |
| γ — $g$ | | π — $p$ | | γξ — $nx$ | |
| δ — $d$ | | ρ — $r$ | | γχ — $nch$ | |
| ε — $e$ | | σ, ς — $s$ | | αι — $ai$ | |
| ζ — $z$ | | τ — $t$ | | αυ — $au$ | |
| η, ῃ — $ē$ | | υ — $y$ | | ει — $ei$ | |
| θ — $th$ | | φ — $ph$ | | ευ — $eu$ | |
| ι — $i$ | | χ — $ch$ | | ηυ — $ēu$ | |
| κ — $k$ | | ψ — $ps$ | | οι — $oi$ | |
| λ — $l$ | | ω, ῳ — $ō$ | | ου — $ou$ | |
| μ — $m$ | | ῥ — $rh$ | | υι — $hui$ | |
| ν — $n$ | | ‘ — $h$ | | | |

# An Overview of Old Testament History

CREATION

**Genesis**

JACOB MOVED TO EGYPT 1876

**Exodus**

(430 years)

EXODUS AND WILDERNESS WANDERINGS 1446

**Lev., Num., Deut.**

(40 years)

ISRAEL CROSSES JORDAN 1406

(7 years)

CONQUEST COMPLETED 1399

**Joshua**

(ca. 49 years)

JUDGES BEGIN ca. 1350

**Judges & Ruth**

(ca. 299 years)

SAUL RULES 1051

---

SAUL RULES 1051

**1 Samuel**

(40 years)

DAVID RULES 1011

**2 Samuel & 1 Chron.**

(40 years)

SOLOMON RULES 971

**1 Kings 1–11 & 2 Chron. 1–9**

(40 years)

KINGDOM DIVIDED 931

**1 Kings 12– 2 Kings 17**

ISRAEL

(209 Years)

ASSYRIA CONQUERS ISRAEL 722

JUDAH

**1 Kings 12–2 Kings 24 & 2 Chron. 10–36**

(345 Years)

BABYLON CONQUERS JUDAH 586

BABYLONIAN EXILE

(70 years)

TEMPLE REBUILT 515

(85 years)

OLD TESTAMENT CLOSES ca. 430

# Biblical Weights and Measures

| BIBLICAL UNIT | | AMERICAN EQUIVALENT | METRIC EQUIVALENT |
|---|---|---|---|
| **WEIGHT** | | | |
| talent | (60 minas) | 75 pounds | 34 kilograms |
| mina | (50 shekels) | 1 1/4 pounds | 0.6 kilogram |
| shekel | (2 bekas) | 2/5 ounce | 11.5 grams |
| pim | (2/3 shekel) | 1/3 ounce | 7.6 grams |
| beka | (10 gerahs) | 1/5 ounce | 6 grams |
| gerah | | 1/50 ounce | 0.6 gram |
| **LENGTH** | | | |
| cubit | | 18 inches | 0.5 meter |
| span | | 9 inches | 23 centimeters |
| handbreadth | | 3 inches | 7 centimeters |
| **CAPACITY** | | | |
| **Dry Measure** | | | |
| cor [homer] | (10 ephahs) | 6 bushels | 220 liters |
| lethech | (5 ephahs) | 3 bushels | 110 liters |
| ephah | (10 omers) | 1/2 bushel | 22 liters |
| seah | (1/3 ephah) | 7 quarts | 7.3 liters |
| omer | (1/10 ephah) | 2 quarts | 2 liters |
| cab | (1/18 ephah) | 1/2 pint | 0.3 liter |
| **Liquid Measure** | | | |
| bath | (1 ephah) | 6 gallons | 22 liters |
| hin | (1/6 bath) | 4 quarts | 4 liters |
| log | (1/72 bath) | 1/3 quart | 0.3 liter |

The information in this chart, while not being mathematically precise, gives approximate amounts and distances. The figures are calculated on the basis of a shekel equaling 11.5 grams, a cubit equaling 18 inches, and an ephah equaling 22 liters.

# GENESIS

## Allen P. Ross

## INTRODUCTION

Genesis is the book of beginnings; it provides a dramatic account of the origins of mankind and his universe, the intrusion of sin into the world, the catastrophic effects of its curse on the race, and the beginnings of God's plan to bless the nations through His seed.

Most of the books of the Bible draw on the contents of Genesis in one way or another. Apart from this, however, Genesis' subject matter and the unembellished way in which it is written have captivated the minds of biblical scholars for ages.

As with biblical truth in general, this book has been a stumbling block for many who have approached it with preconceived notions or antisupernatural biases. But for those who recognize it as the Word of God, whom they seek to serve, Genesis is a source of comfort and edification. And by them, the questions and difficulties of the book are approached differently.

**The Titles of Genesis.** The Hebrew title of the book is the initial word *bᵉrēʾšîṯ*, translated "in the beginning." The English title "Genesis" was derived from the Greek translation of *tôlᵉḏôṯ*, the key word of the book. In Genesis 2:4a, the Septuagint translation is, "This is the book of the *geneseōs* of heaven and earth."

**The Authorship of Genesis.** Both Scripture and tradition attribute the Pentateuch to Moses. This was enough to satisfy most people in the synagogue and the church for ages that Genesis, the first book of the Pentateuch, could be safely ascribed to Moses.

Indeed no one would have been better qualified to write the book. Since "Moses was educated in all the wisdom of the Egyptians" (Acts 7:22), his literary skills would have enabled him to collect Israel's traditions and records and to compose the work. His communion with God at Horeb and throughout his life would have given him direction for this task. Genesis provided the theological and historical foundation for the Exodus and the covenant at Sinai.

Critical scholars, however, deny the Mosaic authorship of both Genesis and the rest of the Pentateuch. This is not a recent view; early in the Christian era theologians vacillated between Moses and Ezra as the author of the Pentateuch. But the modern view that the Pentateuch was compiled from various sources seems to be the product of rationalistic skepticism. Benedict Spinoza (A.D. 1632–1677) believed that the Pentateuch was written by Ezra, who utilized a mass of traditions (including some by Moses).

The first attempt at a documentary theory of Pentateuchal origins was made in 1753 by Jean Astruc (1684–1766). He promoted the idea that Genesis was composed from two major and several minor documents. Over the next 124 years scholars debated and developed that idea until finally Julius Wellhausen (1844–1918) restated the documentary approach forcefully and meticulously in 1877.

Wellhausen divided the Pentateuch into four literary sources, represented by the letters, J, E, D, and P. The "J" material (named because of its preference for the name Yahweh [Jehovah]) was supposedly written in the Southern Kingdom about 850 B.C. It was personal, biographical, and anthropomorphic. It included prophetic-like ethics and theological reflection. "E" (named because of its preference for Elohim [God]) was written in the Northern Kingdom about 750 B.C. It was more objective, less concerned with ethical and theological reflection, and given more to concrete particulars.

According to this view as elaborated by subsequent scholars these two documents were combined around 650 B.C. by an unknown redactor or editor. The result was "JE."

The composition was completed by "D" and "P" material. "D" was composed under Hilkiah around 621 B.C. as part of Josiah's reforms. This Deuteronomic school was also responsible for reworking the Books of Joshua through Kings. The "P" source (Ezra and the Holiness Code known as H), dated anywhere from 570 to 445 B.C., is said to be concerned with the origins and institutions of the theocracy, genealogies, rituals, and sacrifices.

What brought about this approach was an analytical study of the text that observed apparently irreconcilable difficulties. The critical scholars observed changes in the divine names (Yahweh vs. Elohim). They could not reconcile parallel stories (e.g., the endangering of Sarah told in Gen. 12:10-20 and chap. 20). Furthermore, linguistic differences showed up that seemed to coincide with other peculiarities of different sources (e.g., J might use Sinai, and E Horeb). Finally, diverse theological ideas seemed to harmonize with the various emerging sources.

This documentary theory, being highly developed and deceitfully plausible, has deceptively captured the scholarly world for decades. For further information, see R.K. Harrison, *Introduction to the Old Testament.* Grand Rapids: Wm. B. Eerdmans Publishing Co., 1966; Umberto Cassuto, *The Documentary Hypothesis;* and H. Wouk, *This Is My God.* Garden City, N.Y.: Doubleday & Co., 1959. pp. 312-20. J. Skinner's book, *Genesis* (International Critical Commentary. Edinburgh: T. & T. Clark, 1910), is an example of how this theory wrongly influences the exegesis of Genesis.

Criticism of the documentary theory must certainly begin with its antisupernaturalist base. Proponents of the view subjected the Bible to criticism as if it were merely a human book and therefore unreliable. The approach of the theory was anthropomorphic and evolutionary (i.e., the monotheism seen in Gen. was of human origin and gradually evolved from primitive states). Hegelian dialecticism was employed to show how teaching evolved till it reached its final form of "truth."

Apart from its fundamental presuppositions that undermine revelation, the approach is fraught with problems. One is the lack of unanimity concerning the four sources (J, E, P, D) and which passages belong to each of them. Another problem is the subjectivity involved. Too often circular reasoning appears. For example, a passage would be assigned to J because it frequently used the Hebrew word *yālad* ("to bear, to generate"); therefore, it was argued, *yālad* is peculiar to J. Though the approach claimed to be analytical it too often evaded, emended, or deleted a text when it contradicted the system.

Archeological discoveries have contributed material that not only calls into question the criteria of the documentary hypothesis, but also lends coloring to the Pentateuchal literature in its early setting. In the land of Canaan, Ugaritic literature (ca. 1400 B.C.) shows widespread use of cultic terms (attributed to P), poetic clichés, rare words originally considered late "Aramaisms," a variety of divine names and compound names, as well as repetition in style. The recent discovery of the Ebla tablets in Syria also provides very early documentation of names, places, and ideas presented in the Pentateuch (cf. Giovanni Pettinato, *The Archives of Ebla.* Garden City, N.Y.: Doubleday & Co., 1981).

Farther east the Nuzi tablets discovered in 1925 and the Mari tablets brought to light in 1933 record many customs and laws that are comparable to those reflected in the patriarchal narratives in Genesis.

Though these and many other contributions from archeology do not "prove" the existence of the patriarchs or the early date of the narratives, they do fit rather well with the Pentateuchal material and the manner in which the narratives are presented in Genesis. With the ever-increasing archeological finds there is less and less reason for a later date for the material.

Form criticism, pioneered in Old Testament studies by Hermann Gunkel, recognized the antiquity of the traditions (e.g., that Genesis 1–11 must be compared with the Sumerian-Akkadian literature of the third and second millennia B.C. and that the patriarchs would be strangely out of place against an Assyrian background of the first half of the first millennium). Form criticism sought to determine the genre, structure, setting, and intention of each literary unit *behind* the extant material in order to reconstruct the original unit and to relate the texts to the people in ancient Israel.

This method isolates the literary units, often following the arrangement of the JEDP sources. It then identifies the form (or genre) of the unit (e.g., blessings, oaths, hymns, legends, etc.) and compares common motifs, common vocabulary, and common structure. It then seeks to state the setting for the unit in the life of ancient Israel in order to determine its original intent. In order to do this the form critic must often seek to determine how the unit was transmitted.

Gunkel listed six kinds of narratives in Genesis which reflected an early poetic, oral stage of the material (Hermann Gunkel, *Genesis*. Göttingen: Vandenhoeck und Ruprecht, 1922). They are: (a) etiological (e.g., a narrative explains why man is sinful), (b) ethnological (e.g., a narrative explains why Canaan was enslaved), (c) etymological (e.g., a narrative explains a well-known name such as Babel), (d) ceremonial (e.g., a narrative explains the Sabbath), (e) geological (e.g., a narrative explains salt near Sodom), and (f) a group of unclassified types.

Form criticism has produced much that is valuable in Old Testament studies. In general, it takes a more cautious view of the text, often being concerned with the final, fixed form of the text as a part of the study. Its emphasis on literary types and ancient oral tradition point out Israel's ancient literary development.

However, form-critical scholarship is often plagued with the same weaknesses as the documentary approach. The presupposition that the literature developed naturally rather than supernaturally leads to false conclusions: that Israel's monotheism developed out of polytheism, that miracles were later explanations of early events, and that the records may not tell the real history.

The idea that sagas existed as distinct oral literary units before they were collected may be correct in some cases, but it would be difficult to prove. The idea that these oral traditions were edited and embellished as they reached their final form is problematic. Too often the

critical interpretation considers this embellishing to be an extensive reshaping and reinterpreting of the tradition. Consequently much of form-critical exegesis is concerned with reconstructing the original tradition—a procedure that is often quite subjective and probably impossible.

However, the emphasis in form criticism on the literary units, the types of literature, the structure, and the setting in the life of ancient Israel are important for exegesis. Exegesis is concerned with the final form of the biblical text, not with possibly preliterary stages of the traditions. (For further information, see Gene Tucker, *Form Criticism of the Old Testament*. Philadelphia: Fortress Press, 1971.)

Out of form criticism a number of emphases in the study of the Pentateuch developed. Most notable has been traditio-historical criticism. Several scholars criticized the old literary analytical approach (JEDP) from various perspectives. They believed that a complete analytical approach was needed—one that took into account oral tradition, comparative mythology, and Hebrew psychology—for the purposes of discovering the formation and transmission of Israelite tradition in its preliminary stage.

Though the subjectivity prompted by such an approach has led to a great diversity among the critics, the essential elements in the theory are as follows: The story was transmitted from memory at the preliterary stage; it was accompanied by an interpretation; it was reformulated in accordance with various forces (perhaps, e.g., a Canaanite etiology, or a redemptive motif in the period of the monarchy). The cycles of stories were next redacted into a literary unit by a creative editor. The collections of stories then became normative for faith in the postexilic period.

The two long-developing, contemporaneous tradition collections that traditio-historical criticism posits are the P and the D collections. The former is largely Genesis through Numbers; it centers on the Passover in which the Feast is historicized. The D work is Deuteronomy through 2 Kings. So even though literary sources of the old documentary approach are rejected, a similar source analysis is maintained. Too often the history of the tradition is considered more important than the tradition itself.

Traditio-historical criticism places too much emphasis on oral tradition. No doubt there was oral tradition, but it was usually accompanied by written documents (Kenneth A. Kitchen, *Ancient Orient and Old Testament*, p. 136). Archeological evidence relevant to Palestine (E. Nielsen, e.g., draws also on Hindu and Old Icelandic materials [*Oral Tradition*. London: SCM Press, 1954]) emphasizes the great care taken in copying documents in the ancient world (see W.F. Albright, *From the Stone Age to Christianity*. Garden City, N.Y.: Doubleday & Co., 1957).

The emphasis on comparative mythology presupposes that Israel's religion was comparable to the pagan religions. Similarities exist, but essentially Yahwism (Israel's worship of the true God, Yahweh) is distinct. Following this approach, one is left without an explanation of the origin of the Hebrew faith.

Finally, concentration on the supposed reformation of traditions lacks scientific control, a fact evidenced by the lack of agreement over the reconstructions. Reconstructions indeed are often the products of critics' predispositions.

Though many contributions to the study of the Old Testament have been made by these approaches, they all fail to place a proper emphasis on the final form of the text, the canonical shape of the biblical material. If one could trace these levels of development with certainty—which he cannot—and if one used sources to explain difficulties, he would still be left with the question as to why the material was recorded in the form in which it now exists.

Consequently more emphasis is now being placed on the present shape of the text. Repetition, diversity of style, variation of vocabulary, and the like, are often considered proof of the unity of the text by scholars following a modified structuralism or rhetorical criticism.

The traditional view that Genesis (and the Pentateuch) possesses unity and is the work of Moses has not been destroyed. On the contrary, the evidence points more and more to the antiquity and unity of the work. This is not to say that the present form of the book has not been edited by subsequent writers whose

work was guided by the Holy Spirit's inspiration; it does affirm that widespread reshaping of the accounts is unfounded and unnecessary. Any reshaping of the traditions of Genesis would have been done by Moses under divine inspiration, with the result that the book reports actual events and gives correct theological interpretations of them.

**The Nature of Genesis.** Much of the discussion regarding the historicity and origin of Genesis is related to a consideration of the nature of its contents, especially the primordial events recorded in chapters 1–11.

*1. Is Genesis myth?* Many writers describe the contents of Genesis as myth or attribute its origin to myth. Mythological literature seeks to explain the origins of things in symbolic forms. Myth records so-called "sacred history" rather than actual history; it reports how reality came into existence through the deeds of gods and supernatural creatures. It purports to establish reality, the nature of the universe, the function of the state, and the values of life (cf. J.W. Rogerson, *Myth in Old Testament Interpretation*. New York: Walter de Gruyter, 1974).

Pagan literature that records supernatural activities such as Creation, the Flood, and other divine interventions in man's world are often compared with Genesis. Some scholars envision a wholesale borrowing of such mythologies by Israel, with a subsequent demythologizing (removal of pagan elements) to make them satisfactory for Yahwism. But when Semitic mythology is correctly understood, it is clear that this was not possible.

Myths were not merely symbolic language or reflections of primitive mentality. They were ancient man's expression of his view of reality. At the center of a myth is its doctrine of correspondence (e.g., the god dies; therefore vegetation dies). Consequently ritual based on sympathetic magic was enacted to ensure the vital forces of life and fertility.

The Old Testament makes a radical break with this philosophy of the ancient world. One does not do justice to the Old Testament by saying that Israel borrowed myth, or used mythological language to describe its faith. To the Hebrew, an absolutely sovereign God brought them into existence as a nation. Their concept of time was not cyclical but eschatological; their ritual at the temple was not cosmic and magical but an enactment of their redemption; and their concept of space was not limited to the primeval world but was actualized in history. In a word, reality to Israel was within her concept of history (Brevard S. Childs, *Myth and Reality in the Old Testament*. Naperville, Ill.: Alec R. Allenson, 1960, p. 13).

Therefore Genesis is not myth. The Hebrew faith was a radical departure from the characteristic mythical thought of the pagans. James Barr says, "The main battle of the Hebrew faith is fought against the confusion of human and divine, of God and nature" so prevalent in pagan myth ("The Meaning of 'Mythology' in Relation to the Old Testament," *Vetus Testamentum* 9. 1959:3). If the Old Testament preserves any vestiges of myth, it is to show that such were done away with in Yahwism. Gerhard Hasel says that Genesis employs certain terms and motifs, partly taken from theologically incompatible predecessors and partly chosen in deliberate contrast with comparable ancient Near Eastern concepts, and uses them with a meaning that is consonant with and expressive of faith in Yahweh. It represents a parting of the spiritual ways brought about by a deliberate antimythical polemic which undermined the prevailing mythological views ("The Polemic Nature of the Genesis Cosmology," *Evangelical Quarterly* 46. 1974: 81-102). Thus the Old Testament in general and Genesis in particular are a cemetery for lifeless myths and gods.

2. *Is Genesis etiology?* The narratives of Genesis have also been classified as etiologies, stories that explain some given phenomenon, a topographical, ethnological, cultic, or customary reality (see S. Mowinckel, *Tetrateuch-Pentateuch-Hexateuch*. Berlin: Verlag Alfred Töppelmann, 1964, p. 81; and Brevard S. Childs, "The Etiological Tale Re-examined," *Vetus Testamentum* 24. 1974:387-97).

If the etiological narrative is the tradition and not simply a motif, that is, if it is a primary etiology, then doubt is cast over the historicity of the event. John Bright correctly observes that it is impossible to prove that an etiology is the creative force of the tradition (*Early Israel in Recent History Writing*. London: SCM Press, 1956, p. 90). The narratives no doubt record actual events. If there is an etiological element added in the use made of the tradition, it is usually responsible for a single detail or application of the story. To say a story explains why something exists is one thing; but to say a story employs some mythical episode to form the tradition is quite another.

Etiological motifs do occur in general in the Bible, especially in Genesis which explains the beginnings of many things. But these narratives cannot be referred to as etiological tales that came into being to answer certain questions.

3. *Is Genesis history?* All this raises the question of the historicity of the accounts. Scholars have been unwilling to use the term "history" unless it is adequately qualified as distinct from modern philosophies of history. Norman Porteous explains, "The fact that Israel's religious traditions made frequent reference to supernatural interventions is usually enough to make the historian look askance at them and assume that the actual course of events must have been very different" ("The Old Testament and History," *Annual of the Swedish Theological Institute* 8. 1972:22).

For many, the evidence of events from Genesis is not reliable as history. Without outside sources to verify the events, historians must depend on the biblical records themselves. Even the many findings of archeology, though confirming the cultural setting of the events, do not actually *prove* the existence of an Abraham or a Joseph. So critical scholars hesitate to designate Genesis as factual history.

However, one must remember that the Bible is a unique Book. Genesis was not intended to be a mere chronicle of events, a history for history's sake, or even a complete biography of the nation. It is a theological interpretation of selected records of the ancestors of Israel. As with all histories, Genesis explains the causes behind the events—but its causes are divine as well as human. Because it is part of the revealed Word of God, and not merely human history comparable to ancient pagan mythologies, both the events and the explanations are true.

For the Israelites some of the basic questions about life were answered within this theological interpretation of the events of their history. These events were recognized as integral parts of the God-planned and God-directed course of history, extending from Creation to the last days. In between this starting point and finishing point is biblical history. Thus faith was an essential part of understanding national and international events.

At the heart of this biblical history was God's covenant. It began with election—God chose Israel through Abram. God's people could look back and see what God had done, and on the basis of that they could look forward to the fulfillment of the promises. Even though promise and fulfillment were predominant motifs of the biblical history, obedience to the covenant was uppermost in the minds of the narrators. So the events of the past were recounted for apologetic, polemic, and didactic reasons.

The fact that Genesis is a theological interpretation of ancient events does not destroy its historicity. As Porteous says, "It would seem reasonable to suppose that interpretation is a response to something that demands interpretation" ("The Old Testament and History," p. 107). E.A. Speiser says that while the material may not be history in the conventional sense of the term, "it cannot be set down as fancy. The author retells the events in his own inimitable way; he does not invent them. What is thus committed to writing is tradition, in the reverent care of literary genius. Where the tradition can be independently checked, it proves to be authentic. This much has been evident for some time in respect to a number of incidental details. It now turns out that the main framework of the patriarchal account has been accurately presented" ("The Biblical Idea of History in the Common Near Eastern Setting," *Israel Exploration Journal* 7. 1957:202). For evangelicals, of course, it comes as no surprise that the biblical narratives prove to be authentic.

*4. Is Genesis tradition?* Many biblical scholars prefer to describe the Genesis narratives as "traditions" or "sagas" (which should have been used instead of

"legends" in translating Gunkel's book *The Legends of Genesis*). By these terms they mean the people's recollections of historical events. In this view historicity is not endangered; it is just not assured. Gerhard von Rad says that saga is more than history because God, not man, is the subject (*Genesis*. Philadelphia: Westminster Press, 1961, p. 31).

Conservative scholars do not share this hesitancy to regard the narratives as true. Certainly the primeval accounts and genealogies could have been brought from Mesopotamia by the ancestors. To these would have been added the family records of the patriarchs. All the traditions—oral and written—could have been preserved in Egypt by Joseph along with his own records. Moses could then have compiled the work in essentially the form in which it exists today, being preserved from error and guided in truth by the divine inspiration of the Holy Spirit (Kenneth A. Kitchen, "The Old Testament in Its Context: 1," *Theological Students Fellowship Bulletin* 59. 1971:1-9). So whether the narratives are called traditions or history, they record God's true revelation and therefore correspond with what actually happened.

Genesis is the first book of the Torah, the five Books of the Law. It may be best to classify the work as "Torah literature." It may not be legal literature specifically, that is, laws and commandments, but it lays the foundation for the Law. It is a theological interpretation of the historical traditions behind the formation of the covenant with Israel at Sinai. Throughout Genesis one may discern that Moses was preparing his readers for the revelation of the Law. It is in this that Genesis conveys its didactic nature.

But the material in Genesis is closely related to wisdom literature as well, especially in the Joseph narratives. The emphasis in the book on God's blessing for those who walk in faithful obedience suggests many parallels with the Books of Wisdom, as will be observed. Genesis, then, is a unique book but it is also a book that is like the rest of the Bible in many ways. It is here that theology and history begin.

**The Literary Composition of Genesis.** Genesis is a literary unity, arranging the traditions from the past according to "accounts" (*tôlᵉdôt* in Heb.) which develop the motifs of blessing and cursing. Also it presents the historical basis in tradition for the election of and covenantal promises to Abraham and his descendants.

*1. The purpose of Genesis.* Genesis supplies the historical basis for God's covenant with His people. This can be traced through the entire Pentateuch, for, as Moses Segal states, "*The real theme of the Pentateuch is the selection of Israel from the nations and its consecration to the service of God and His Laws in a divinely appointed land.* The central event in the development of this theme is the divine covenant with Abraham and its . . . promise to make his offspring into the people of God and to give them the land of Canaan as an everlasting inheritance" (*The Pentateuch: Its Composition and Its Authorship and Other Biblical Studies,* p. 23, italics his).

Within the development of this theme, Genesis forms an indispensable prologue to the drama that unfolds in Exodus. As a literary and explanatory pendant to the summons to go forth from Egypt to the Promised Land, Genesis demonstrates that such a command was in fulfillment of a covenant with Abraham and Isaac, and with Jacob, the founding father of those tribes. Wilhelm M.L. DeWette stated that Genesis was the foundation of the theocracy, showing that the people of God were gradually separated from others because their whole history was penetrated by a clear and constant plan of divine government of the world, to which individual circumstances were subordinated (*A Critical and Historical Introduction to the Canonical Scripture of the Old Testament,* trans. Theodore Parker. 2 vols. Boston: Charles C. Little & James Brown, 1850, pp. 1-22).

The outworking of the divine plan begins with sovereign Creation, and develops toward the selection of Israel in the man Abraham. Genesis 1–11 appears to be designed to explain "the reason for setting apart the worship of God in the world of a special people, Israel, in a special land, Canaan" (Segal, *The Pentateuch,* p. 28).

Two opposite progressions appear in this prologue: (a) God's orderly Creation with its climax in His blessing of man, and (b) the totally disintegrating work of sin with its two greatest curses being the Flood and the dispersion at Babel (Derek Kidner, *Genesis,* p. 13). The first progression demonstrates God's plan to bring about perfect order from the beginning in spite of what the reader may know of man's experience. The second progression demonstrates the great need of God's intervention to provide the solution for the corrupt human race.

The moral deterioration of mankind was connected with the advance of civilization; and when it was corrupted beyond repair, it had to be destroyed by the Flood. Yet even after the new beginning, vices were also multiplied and human insolence had far-reaching effects. It was not for a group but for all mankind. Arrogance and ambition in the race brought universal dispersion.

Consequently Genesis has taken these events and constructed a theological picture of man's revolt against his Maker and its terrible consequences. These narratives, woven into the prologue of Genesis, precede Abraham in time and prepare the reader for him. Rebellious man is left looking for a solution to his dilemma.

The whole of the primeval history may be described as continuous punishment and gracious provision. Yet with rebellious humanity cursed through dispersion around the world, the reader wonders about God's relationship to the cursed race. After the judgment at Babel, when people scattered throughout the world, was God's relationship with the human race broken?

That is the question intended by the whole plane of primeval history. Only then is the reader ready for the election and program of blessing through Abraham (Gen. 12–50). The moral deterioration of mankind dispersed over the earth led to the election of a people who would serve as a source of blessing for all humanity. This was done by focusing on one man and his seed. God's saving will was extended to the scattered nations through one who was loosed from his tribal ties among the nations and made the founder of a new nation, the recipient of promises reaching even beyond Israel. Only with Genesis 12:1-3 does the significance of the universal preface to saving history become understandable, and only with this prologue does 12:1-3 become fully clear (von Rad, *Genesis*, p. 148).

**2. The motifs of Genesis.** The entire Book of Genesis turns on the motifs of blessing and cursing. The promised blessing would give the seed to the patriarchs and the land to the seed; the cursing would alienate, deprive, and disinherit the seed. Later, prophets and historians expanded these motifs and applied them to future events. It is no surprise that these motifs seen throughout the Scriptures drew on the book of beginnings. Blessing and cursing envelop man from his beginning.

In the Old Testament the verb "to curse" means to impose a ban or a barrier, a paralysis on movement or other capabilities (H.C. Brichto, *The Problem of "Curse" in the Hebrew Bible*. Philadelphia: Society of Biblical Literature and Exegesis, 1963, p. 217). Such power belongs only to God or an agency endowed by Him with special power. Anyone could imprecate; but imprecation is strongest when it invokes supernatural power. The curse involves separation from the place of blessing or even from those who are blessed. The prologue of Genesis (chaps. 1–11) preeminently portrays the curse from the very first sin to the curse of Canaan.

On the other hand the verb "to bless"—being the great benediction word of the Bible—basically means "to enrich." Here too God is its source, even when man offers it. As used in Genesis, the promise of blessing is largely concerned with offspring in the land of Canaan (Claus Westermann, *Blessing in the Bible and the Life of the Church*. Philadelphia: Fortress Press, 1978, pp. 18-23). The promised blessing included prosperity with respect to fertility (of both the land and the patriarch). The blessing reflected divine approval; therefore it was ultimately spiritual. The contrast between blessing and cursing reflects man's obedience by faith or disobedience by unbelief and describes God's approval or disapproval in a graphic form.

**3. The structure of Genesis.** The structure of Genesis is marked by an initial section and then 11 sections with headings. The major structural word is *tôlᵉdôt* ("these

are the generations of . . . "). It is a feminine noun from *yālaḏ* (from the causative form of the verb "to bear, to generate"). The noun is often translated "generations, histories," or "descendants." Francis Brown, S.R. Driver, and Charles A. Briggs explain it as "account[s] of men and their descendants" (*A Hebrew and English Lexicon of the Old Testament*. Oxford: Clarendon Press, 1972, p. 410). The NIV translates it "account."

This word has been traditionally viewed as a heading of a section. According to this view the book has the following arrangement:

1. Creation (1:1–2:3)
2. *Tôlᵉdôt* of the heavens and the earth (2:4–4:26)
3. *Tôlᵉdôt* of Adam (5:1–6:8)
4. *Tôlᵉdôt* of Noah (6:9–9:29)
5. *Tôlᵉdôt* of Shem, Ham, and Japheth (10:1–11:9)
6. *Tôlᵉdôt* of Shem (11:10-26)
7. *Tôlᵉdôt* of Terah (11:27–25:11)
8. *Tôlᵉdôt* of Ishmael (25:12-18)
9. *Tôlᵉdôt* of Isaac (25:19–35:29)
10. *Tôlᵉdôt* of Esau (36:1-8)
11. *Tôlᵉdôt* of Esau, father of the Edomites (36:9–37:1)
12. *Tôlᵉdôt* of Jacob (37:2–50:26)

The views on this arrangement vary. For example, Speiser takes *tôlᵉdôt* as a heading in all places except 2:4; 25:19; and 37:2. In these places he suggests it means "story" or "history" and that it refers to the preceding not the following narrative (*Genesis*, p. xxiv). Skinner, however, doubts that this word could be used in reference to what preceded; he says that it served as a heading (*Genesis*, pp. 39-40).

As stated earlier, since *tôlᵉdôt* is derived from *yālaḏ* ("to bear, to generate") it refers to what is "brought forth." This formula word for Genesis, then, marks a starting point, combining narrative and genealogy to move from the one point (*tôlᵉdôt*) to the end (the next *tôlᵉdôt*). It is Moses' means of moving along the historical lines from a beginning to an ending, including the product or result of the starting point. S.R. Driver explained that the word referred to "the particulars about a man and [his] descendants" (*The Book of Genesis*. London: Methuen & Co., 1904, p. 19).

Some do not agree with this traditional approach that each *tôlᵉdôt* is a heading. P.J. Wiseman and R.K. Harrison suggest that these are similar to the colophons on clay tablets and refer to the *preceding* material in the narrative (Wiseman, *New Discoveries in Babylonia about Genesis*. London: Marshall, Morgan & Scott, 1937, p. 8; Harrison, *Introduction to the Old Testament*, p. 548). They think the Genesis traditions were recorded on clay tablets and finally collected into the present form of Genesis.

Wiseman argues that the Genesis *tôlᵉdôt* are like the Babylonian colophons in that each contains a title, date of the writing, serial number, and statement of the completion of a series (if it completes one), and the scribe or owner's name (*Creation Revealed in Six Days*. London: Marshall, Morgan & Scott, 1949, p. 46).

This view is unconvincing, however. The colophons on the tablets are not like the *tôlᵉdôt* of Genesis (see, e.g., Alexander Heidel, *The Babylonian Genesis*. 2nd ed. Chicago: University of Chicago Press, 1963, pp. 25, 30; A. L. Oppenheim, *Ancient Mesopotamia*. Chicago: University of Chicago Press, 1964, pp. 240-1). In the cuneiform tablets each title is a repetition of that tablet's first line and not a description of its contents. Also the owner's name seems to refer to the present owner, not the original owner. Moreover, the Akkadian equivalent of *tôlᵉdôt* is not used in the formula.

If the Genesis *tôlᵉdôt* are references to what had immediately preceded the phrase, then the statement in Genesis 5:1 should have come at 4:16, at the end of the story of Adam and not later after the intervening material in 4:17-26. Another passage that would be improbable as a concluding form is 10:1, the *tôlᵉdôt* of the sons of Noah. But it is unlikely that it concludes the Flood and the curse, especially in view of 10:32. Besides these problems of harmonization is the difficulty of having the story of Abraham preserved by Ishmael (the *tôlᵉdôt* of Ishmael would be the colophon concluding that preceding history), having Isaac keep Ishmael's archives, Esau those of Jacob, and Joseph those of Jacob.

Nowhere in the Old Testament does *tôlᵉdôt* clearly refer to what has preceded; in every place it can and often must refer to what follows (e.g., in Ruth 4:18 the word looks forward to Perez's line, and in Num. 3:1 the *tôlᵉdôt* of Aaron and Mo-

ses cannot refer to the preceding census in Num. 1–2). In Genesis when the *tôlᵉdôt* are taken to refer to the following sections, these *tôlᵉdôt* fit nicely.

Also Genesis 2:4 includes a heading for the following section. Wiseman himself avows that 2:1-3 forms a natural conclusion for the Creation account. Genesis 2:4a would then be the heading and 2:4b would be the beginning dependent clause (much like the beginning of the *Enuma Elish*: "When above . . . "). This structure is similar to 5:1, as seen in these two verses:

"These are the *tôlᵉdôt* of the heavens and the earth when they were created. When Yahweh God made earth and heaven . . . " (2:4, author's trans.). "This is the book of the *tôlᵉdôt* of Adam. When God created man . . . " (5:1, author's trans.).

The fact that "Yahweh God" is used throughout 2:4–3:24 also leads one to connect the contents of that passage with the title in 2:4. (However, evidences of some tailpieces—expressions other than *tôlᵉdôt*, which are virtually colophons—in Gen.—*do* exist in 10:5, 20, 31-32. Also 25:16 concludes vv. 12-16; 36:19 concludes vv. 1-19; 36:30b concludes vv. 20-30; and 36:43 concludes all of chap. 36.) The *tôlᵉdôt* heading introduces the historical result of an ancestor and could be loosely rendered, "This is what came of . . ." or "This is where it started from" (with reference to the following term) (M.H. Woudstra, "The *Toledot* of the Book of Genesis and Their Redemptive-Historical Significance," *Calvin Theological Journal* 5. 1970:187). In Genesis 2:4, then, *tôlᵉdôt* introduces the historical result of the cosmos, and 2:4–4:26 presents what became of the heavens and the earth. What follows, of course, is the story of the Fall, the murder of Abel, and the development of sin within civilization. The story does not present another Creation account; instead, it carries the account from the point of the climax of Creation (reiterated in chap. 2) to the corruption of Creation by sin. This is "what became of it."

When the crucial passages in the Old Testament are looked at in this way, this definition is the most satisfactory. The term cannot be restricted to mean a "genealogy" because the contexts are frequently more than that. Nor does the word depict only biographies or histories, because the narratives certainly do not follow that through. The narratives depict what became of "so and so" in the details relevant to the purpose of Genesis. The *tôl'dôt* of Terah is not about Terah, but is primarily concerned with what became of Terah, namely, Abraham and his kin.The *tôl'dôt* of Isaac has Jacob at its center, with other parts relating to Esau. The *tôl'dôt* of Jacob traces the family from him through the life of Joseph. The name following the *tôl'dôt* is usually the starting point, not the central character, in the narrative. So in this commentary the phrase will be translated, "this is the succession from. . . ."

Two additional observations may be made about the material in each succession section. One is that in the tracing of each line there is also a narrowing process. After the new beginnings with Noah, the writer supplied the *tôl'dôt* of Shem, Ham, and Japheth. But immediately afterward, the *tôl'dôt* of Shem is selected. The next *tôl'dôt* is that of Terah, a descendant of Shem. This account is concerned with the life of Abraham. The line then narrows to Isaac, the son of Abraham, but the *tôl'dôt* of Ishmael, the line not chosen, is given first. The same development holds true of the next generation; before the *tôl'dôt* of Jacob is developed, Esau is dealt with.

A second observation is that the material within each *tôl'dôt* is a microcosm of the development of the Book of Genesis itself, with the motifs of blessing and cursing playing a dominant role. Within each of the first several *tôl'dôt* is a deterioration to cursing until 12:1-2, where the message moves to the promise of blessing. From this point on there is a constant striving for the place of blessing, but still with each successive narrative there is deterioration, for Isaac and Jacob did not measure up to Abraham. Consequently at the end of Genesis the family is not in the land of blessing but in Egypt. Kidner expressed this development by stating the "man had traveled far from Eden to a *coffin*, and the chosen family far from Canaan to *Egypt*" (*Genesis*, p. 224).

**The Development of the Message of Genesis.** The *tôl'dôt* headings are "the very fabric around which the whole of Genesis has been constructed" (Woudstra, "The *Toledot* of the Book of Genesis," pp. 188-9). Each *tôl'dôt*, explaining what became of a line, shows a narrowing and a deterioration in the development of the theology of blessing.

*1. Creation.* The first section (1:1–2:3) is not headed by a *tôl'dôt*, and logically so. Being the beginning, there is no need to trace what became of Creation. Rather, its own heading in 1:1 depicts the contents of the chapter. The significance of the section is that the work is wrapped in divine approval and blessing over the fulfillment of the plan. Animal life (vv. 22-25), human life (v. 27), and the seventh day (2:3) were all blessed specifically. This trilogy is important to the argument: man, made in the image of God, enjoying sovereignty over the creatures of the earth, and observing the Sabbath rest of God, had a blessed beginning.

*2. The* tôl'dôt *of the heavens and the earth.* In this section (2:4–4:26), Genesis reports what became of the cosmos. The section begins with a description of the creation of Adam and Eve and traces their sin, God's curse on sin, and the expansion of sin in their descendants. No longer at rest, mankind experienced flight and fear, making his way in the world, surviving, and developing civilization. As if in answer to the blessings of Creation, this passage supplies a threefold cursing (of Satan [3:14], of the ground because of man [3:17], and of Cain [4:11]).

Yet in this deteriorating life there is a token of grace (4:15) and a ray of hope (man began to call on Yahweh).

*3. The* tôl'dôt *of the book of Adam.* Here too in this central genealogy of the line from Adam to Noah man's downward drift is seen (5:1–6:8). The section begins with a reiteration of Creation and concludes with God's intense displeasure over man's existence. Genesis 5:1-2 recalls the Creation with the use of *bārak* ("to bless"); verse 29 records the birth of Noah as a token of grace for comfort from the curse with the use of *'ārar* ("to curse"). The blessing that began the race was enshrouded by the notice of all of the descendants' deaths. One exception to the curse of death (Enoch) provides a ray of hope that the curse was not final.

4. *The tôl°dôt of Noah.* This section (6:9–9:29) is one of judgment (curse) and blessing in that God promised never again to curse the ground like this (8:21). Nevertheless the story of Noah begins with his finding grace and ends with his cursing Canaan.

Yet in this section there is a new beginning out of a watery world, parallel in many ways to chapter 1: the destruction of a violent world in chaos, the gracious provision of redemption so that man can sail into the new world, the appearance of dry land for a fresh beginning, the Noahic Covenant, and blessing on Noah and his sons (parallel to that for Adam). Here the race began anew, and from this beginning point the blessing motif becomes more prominent in antithesis to the cursing. Shem was blessed.

5. *The tôl°dôt of the sons of Noah.* As the population expanded in line with Noah's worldwide oracle, the direction of the book turned to the nations. The writer consistently developed the message that man's bent is toward ruin and chaos. This section begins with the fruitful population from Shem, Ham, and Japheth, but ends with the explanation of the origin of the nations by the dispersion at Babel (10:1–11:9). It is a stroke of genius to put such a climactic story at the end, especially when it precedes it chronologically. This leaves the reader looking for the answer to man's continual decay. It prepares him for the promised blessing.

6. *The tôl°dôt of Shem.* Predicated on the world view of the expanding race in the previous section, this section (11:10-26) forms another transition in the book, narrowing the choice from the line of Shem to Abram. This list traces the line from Noah to Abram within the blessings of prosperity and posterity (whereas chap. 5 traced the line from Adam to Noah and the Flood). God would not leave the world to an expanding and divided population under the curse without hope; He would select a man and build a nation that would provide blessing for the earth. Anyone knowing of Abraham would immediately catch the significance of this

tôl°dôt that spans the sections of dispersion and promised blessing (11:10-26).

7. *The tôl°dôt of Terah.* Whereas chapters 1–11 generally portray man's rebellion, chapters 12–50 detail God's bringing man into a place of blessing. This section (11:27–25:11) tells what became of Terah, the last man on the list (11:32). The story traces his son's life and becomes the key to the book as well as the Old Testament plan for blessing. God promised Abraham, who was blessed above all, a nation, the land, and a name. The narrative develops the account of his growth in obedient faith.

8. *The tôl°dôt of Ishmael.* This section (25:12-18) explains what became of Ishmael since his was not the line God had chosen. The writer dealt with Ishmael's line before returning to the chosen line.

9. *The tôl°dôt of Isaac.* In explaining what became of Isaac, the son of promise, this section records the story of Jacob, his son, the struggle within the family, and the emergence of the people of Israel (25:19–35:29). The promises in 12:2 begin to unfold. The blessing given to Abram was now uniquely transferred to Jacob (chap. 27). Jacob also developed in faith, but he was crippled in the process. He was not the man his grandfather was; yet Israel was "born."

10. *The tôl°dôt of Esau.* Once again Genesis continues the development from Isaac. Yet before discussing the *tôl°dôt* of the son of succession, this section (36:1-8) discusses Esau, the brother from whom Jacob stole the birthright and the blessing. The nation that came from Jacob would frequently encounter their relatives, the Edomites, descended from Esau. This section accounts for three of Esau's wives and his five sons.

11. *The tôl°dôt of Esau, father of the Edomites.* Another accounting of the development from Esau is added because of the great significance of Edomite, Amalekite, and Horite chieftains (36:9–37:1).

12. *The tôl°dôt of Jacob.* What became of Jacob? His sons became the founding fathers of Israel's tribes (37:2–50:26). This narrative is concerned with the life of

Joseph and the move of Jacob's family to Egypt. In essence, the narrative relates why God's people were in Egypt and how they were related to the promised blessings. In Canaan the family had deteriorated to the point of merging with the Canaanites. To preserve the line of blessing, God moved amazingly through the evil will of Joseph's brothers to bring him into power in Egypt. When the land of promise was cursed with a famine, blessing was provided through Joseph's power and wisdom. However, the book closes in anticipation of another visitation of blessing from God.

*Conclusion.* Because Genesis is the foundation of the rest of the Pentateuch, the Book of Exodus goes back to God's remembering His covenant with Abraham: "God heard their groaning and He remembered His covenant with Abraham, with Isaac, and with Jacob. So God looked on the Israelites and was concerned about (lit., 'took notice of') them" (Ex. 2:24-25). In fact the final events and the closing words of Genesis anticipate the Exodus: "God will surely come to your aid (lit., 'take notice of you') and take you up out of this land to the land He promised on oath to Abraham, Isaac, and Jacob" (Gen. 50:24). This statement was reiterated by Moses when he took the patriarch's bones out of Egypt (Ex. 13:19).

Therefore Genesis gives Israel the theological and historical basis for her existence as God's Chosen People. Israel could trace her ancestry to the patriarch Abraham, whom God had elected out of the dispersed nations, and to whom God had made the great covenantal promises of posterity and land.

Because of the importance of lineal offspring (the first promised blessing) much space is devoted to the family concerns of the patriarchs, such as their wives, sons, heirs, and birthrights and blessings. After Jacob's oracle (Gen. 49), the Pentateuch spans four centuries. So Genesis stands as a statement of the birthright of the tribes of Israel as they labored in Egypt and then were called to leave it.

Recognizing that they had indeed become the great nation promised in the blessing to Abraham, they would realize also that there was no future in Egypt, or in Sodom, or in Babylon. Their future was in the land that had been promised by divine oath, the land of Canaan.

The contents of Genesis would assure the Israelites that God had promised them such a future, and that He was able to fulfill His promises. Over and over again the book tells of God's supernatural dealings in the lives of the ancestors to bring Israel to this point. Certainly the God who had begun a good work would complete it (Phil. 1:6). If the people would recognize that they owed their existence to sovereign election and blessing, they would respond in obedience. Genesis is well suited, then, for Moses' task of drawing Israel out of Egypt.

**The Theology of Genesis.** Genesis is written with the presuppositions that God exists and that He has revealed Himself in word and deed to Israel's ancestors. The book does not argue for the existence of God; it simply asserts that everything exists because of God.

The subject matter of the theology in Genesis is certainly God's work in establishing Israel as the means of blessing the families of the earth. This book forms the introduction to the Pentateuch's main theme of the founding of the theocracy, that is, the rule of God over all Creation. It presents the origins behind the founding of the theocracy: the promised blessing that Abraham's descendants would be in the land.

Exodus presents the redemption of the seed out of bondage and the granting of a covenant to them. Leviticus is the manual of ordinances enabling the holy God to dwell among His people by making them holy. Numbers records the military arrangement and census of the tribes in the wilderness, and shows how God preserves His promised blessings from internal and external threats. Deuteronomy presents the renewal of the covenant.

In the unfolding of this grand program of God, Genesis introduces the reader to the nature of God as the sovereign Lord over the universe who will move heaven and earth to establish His will. He seeks to bless mankind, but does not tolerate disobedience and unbelief. Throughout this revelation the reader learns that "without faith it is impossible to please God" (Heb. 11:6).

# OUTLINE

# COMMENTARY

## I. The Primeval Events (1:1–11:26)

### A. The Creation (1:1–2:3)

The account of Creation is the logical starting point for Genesis, for it explains the beginning of the universe. These verses have received much attention in connection with science; this is to be expected. But the passage is a theological treatise as well, for it lays a foundation for the rest of the Pentateuch.

In writing this work for Israel, Moses wished to portray God as the Founder and Creator of all life. The account shows that the God who created Israel is the God who created the world and all who are in it. Thus the theocracy is founded on the sovereign God of Creation. That nation, her Law, and her customs and beliefs all go back to who God is. Israel would here learn what kind of God was forming them into a nation.

The implications of this are great. First, it means that everything that exists must be under God's control. The Creation must be in subjection to the Creator. Forces of nature, enemies, creatures and objects that became pagan deities— none of these would pose a threat to the servants of the living God.

Second, the account also reveals the basis of the Law. If indeed God was before all things and made all things, how foolish it would be to have any other gods before Him! There were none. If indeed God made man in His image to represent Him, how foolish it would be to make an image of God! If indeed God set aside one day for rest from His work, should not man who is walking with God follow Him? The commandments find their rationale here.

Third, the account reveals that God is a redeeming God. It records how He brought the cosmos out of chaos, turned darkness into light, made divisions between them, transformed cursing into blessing, and moved from what was evil and darkness to what was holy. This parallels the work of God in Exodus, which records His redeeming Israel by destroying the Egyptian forces of chaos. The prophets and the apostles saw here a paradigm of God's redemptive activities. Ultimately He who caused light to shine out of darkness made His light shine in the hearts of believers (2 Cor. 4:6) so that they become new creations (2 Cor. 5:17).

**1:1-2.** These verses have traditionally been understood as referring to the actual beginning of matter, a Creation out of nothing and therefore part of day one. But the vocabulary and grammar of this section require a closer look. The motifs and the structure of the Creation account are introduced in the first two verses. That the universe is God's creative work is perfectly expressed by the statement **God created the heavens and the earth.** The word *bārā'* ("created") may express creation out of nothing, but it certainly cannot be limited to that (cf. 2:7). Rather, it stresses that what was formed was new and perfect. The word is used throughout the Bible only with God as its subject.

But 1:2 describes a chaos: there was waste and void, and **darkness was over the surface of the deep.** The clauses in verse 2 are apparently circumstantial to verse 3, telling the world's condition *when* God began to renovate it. It was a chaos of wasteness, emptiness, and darkness. Such conditions would not result from God's creative work (*bārā'*); rather, in the Bible they are symptomatic of sin and are coordinate with judgment. Moreover, God's Creation by decree begins in verse 3, and the elements found in verse 2 are corrected in Creation, beginning with light to dispel the darkness. The expression **formless and empty** (*tōhû wābōhû*) seems also to provide an outline for chapter 1, which describes God's

bringing shape and then fullness to the formless and empty earth.

Some have seen a middle stage of Creation here, that is, an unfinished work of Creation (v. 2) that was later developed (vv. 3-25) into the present form. But this cannot be sustained by the syntax or the vocabulary.

Others have seen a "gap" between the first two verses, allowing for the fall of Satan and entrance of sin into the world that caused the chaos. It is more likely that verse 1 refers to a relative beginning rather than the absolute beginning (Merrill F. Unger, *Unger's Commentary on the Old Testament.* 2 vols. Chicago: Moody Press, 1981, 1:5). The chapter would then be accounting for the Creation of the universe as *man* knows it, not *the* beginning of everything, and verses 1-2 would provide the introduction to it. The fall of Satan and entrance of sin into God's original Creation would precede this.

It was by the Spirit that the Lord God sovereignly created everything that exists (v. 2b). In the darkness of the chaos **the Spirit of God** moved to prepare for the effectual creative word of God.

**1:3-5.** The pattern for each of the days of Creation is established here. There is (a) the creative word, (b) the report of its effect, (c) God's evaluation of it as "good," (d) at times the sovereign naming, and (e) the numbering of each day. Regarding the word **day** (*yôm*) several interpretations have been suggested. (1) The days of Creation refer to extended geological ages prior to man's presence on earth. (2) The days are 24-hour periods in which God *revealed* His creative acts. (3) They are literal 24-hour days of divine activity. In favor of the third view is the fact that the term *yôm* with an ordinal (first, second, etc.) adjective means 24-hour days wherever this construction occurs in the Old Testament. Also the normal understanding of the fourth commandment (Ex. 20:11) would suggest this interpretation.

God's first creative word produced **light.** The elegance and majesty of Creation by decree is a refreshing contrast with the bizarre creation stories of the pagans. Here is demonstrated the power of God's word. It was this word that motivated Israel to trust and obey Him.

The light was natural, physical light.

Its creation was an immediate victory because it dispelled **darkness. Light** and **darkness** in the Bible are also symbolic of good and evil. Here began God's work which will culminate in the age to come when there will be no darkness (Rev. 22:5). Israel would know that God is Light—and that the Truth and the Way are with Him. In the darkness of Egypt (Ex. 10:21-24) they had light; and in the deliverance they followed His light (Ex. 13:21).

**1:6-8.** On **the second day** God separated the atmospheric **waters** from the terrestrial waters by an arching **expanse, the sky.** This suggests that previously there had been a dense moisture enshrouding the earth. God's work involves making divisions and distinctions.

**1:9-13. Dry** land with its **vegetation** was formed on **the third day. Vegetation** is part of the ordered universe of the true **God.** There is no cyclical, seasonal myth to explain it. **God** started it, once and for all. Moreover, while pagans believed in deities of the deep as forces to be reckoned with, this account shows that **God** controls the boundaries of the **seas** (cf. Job 38:8-11).

**1:14-19.** Day four included the sun to rule (**govern,** v. 16) **the day** and the moon and **the stars** to rule **the night.** Either these were created with apparent age, or they had been previously created and were then made visible on the earth on days one and two when **God** separated light from darkness and waters above from water below.

These heavenly bodies were to **serve as signs** for **seasons and days and years** (v. 14). These terms, as well as "day" and "night" in verse 5, are meaningless without the existence of the sun and the rotation of the planets.

In astrology unbelievers use stars and planets for guidance, but the Bible says they merely display the handiwork of **God** (Ps. 19:1). What folly to follow astrological charts of the Babylonians or worship the sun god in Egypt; rather, one should trust the One who made these objects in the heavens. However, many humans repeatedly reject the Creator to worship the Creation (Rom. 1:25).

**1:20-23. The great creatures of the sea** and the air were **created** on **the fifth day.** In this section (v. 21) is the second use of *bārā'* ("created"; cf. v. 1). Great creatures of the deep, worshiped as dragons and monsters in the ancient world, were nothing more than creations by Almighty **God.** Moreover, fertility of life comes from the blessing of the true **God** (v. 22).

**1:24-31.** Day six was Creation's climax for it included mankind. Though **man** was the last creature mentioned in the account, he did not evolve; he was **created.**

Human life was created **in** (lit., "as," meaning "in essence as") **the image of God** (v. 27). This **image** was imparted only to humans (2:7). "Image" (*ṣelem*) is used figuratively here, for **God** does not have a human form. Being in God's image means that humans share, though imperfectly and finitely, in God's nature, that is, in His communicable attributes (life, personality, truth, wisdom, love, holiness, justice), and so have the capacity for spiritual fellowship with Him.

God's purpose in creating human life in His image was functional: man is to **rule** or have dominion (1:26, 28). God's dominion was presented by a "representative." (Egyptian kings later, in idolatry, did a similar kind of thing: they represented their rule or dominion by making representative statues of themselves.) However, because of sin all things are not under man's dominion (Heb. 2:8). But Jesus Christ will establish dominion over all the earth (Heb. 2:5-8) at His second coming.

God pronounced His blessing on the **male and** the **female:** they were to **be fruitful and increase in number.** In Genesis, to be blessed was to be enriched and fertile. Such marvelous decrees of **God** would be significant for Israel, that was God's representative on earth. She would enter the land of promise and would expect God's continued blessing.

**2:1-3. The seventh day** was the day of rest, the Sabbath. The structure of verses 2 and 3 in the Hebrew is well ordered in its clauses with parallel emphases on the adjective **seventh.** The number "seven" often represents the covenant (the verb "swear" is related etymologically); thus it is no surprise that the Sabbath became the sign of God's covenant at Sinai (Ex. 31:13, 17).

**God blessed the seventh day and made it holy** (sanctified it) because it commemorated the completion or cessation of His creative **work.** God's Sabbath rest became a predominant motif of Scripture. Here before the Fall it represented the perfect Creation, sanctified and at rest. After the Fall this rest became a goal to be sought. The establishment of theocratic rest in the land, whether by Moses or by Joshua at the Conquest, demanded faith and obedience. Today believers enter into that Sabbath rest spiritually (Heb. 4:8-10) and will certainly share in its full restoration.

The account of Creation, seen through the eyes of the new nation of Israel in Moses' day, had great theological significance. Out of the chaos and darkness of the pagan world God brought His people, teaching them the truth, guaranteeing them victory over all powers in heaven and earth, commissioning them to be His representatives, and promising them theocratic rest. So too it would encourage believers of all ages.

*B. The succession from the creation of the heavens and the earth (2:4–4:26)*

1. THE CREATION OF THE MAN AND THE WOMAN (2:4-25)

**2:4a.** This section (vv. 4-25), as indicated in verse 4a, traces **the account of** (what became of) **the heavens and the earth when** (*bᵉyôm,* lit., "in the day," an idiom for "when") **they were created.** What became of Creation is that sin entered and devastated it.

**2:4b-7.** In the creation of Adam the contrast is striking: against the background of a time when there was no life, no growth, no rain, no one to till the ground, God took great care in forming man. The arrangement in these verses includes a title (v. 4), three circumstantial clauses beginning in the Hebrew with "when" ("when" **no shrub . . . had yet appeared,** "when" **there was no man to work the ground,** "when" **streams . . . watered the . . . ground**), and the verb beginning the narrative (**and** [He] **formed**). This mirrors chapter 1 (title, 1:1; circumstantial clauses, 1:2; and the first of the narrative verbs, 1:3).

The repeated emphasis on **the LORD God** is significant (2:4-5, 7-9, 15-16, 18-19, 21-22). The sovereign Creator ("God") of chapter 1 is also the covenant-making Yahweh (**LORD**). Thus Israel would know that her **LORD** had created everything,

and that *He* had formed mankind by special design.

The work of the Lord in creating human life involved both fashioning **from the dust** and inbreathing. The word **formed** (from *yāṣar,* 2:7) describes the work of an artist. Like a potter shaping an earthen vessel from clay, so **God** formed man from clay. Man was made by divine plan; also he was made from the earth. He is "earthy" in spite of subsequent dreams of being like God (3:5). The Hebrew for **man** (*'ādām,* whence "Adam," 2:20) is related to the word for **ground** (*'ādāmâh;* cf. 3:17).

God's breathing **the breath of life** into man transformed his form into **a living being** (lit., "a living soul"). This made man a spiritual being, with a capacity for serving and fellowshiping with God. With this special Creation in mind, the reader can see the significance of the Fall. Since the Fall, regeneration by the "inbreathing" of the Holy Spirit is essential in order for people to enjoy fellowship with God.

**2:8-10.** Mankind was placed in a perfect setting. The **garden** provided the arena for man's test of obedience. The description of the lavish garden (v. 8) and the **trees** (v. 9) and **river** in it (v. 10) leads up to the commandment: man could enjoy it all but he must not eat from the one forbidden tree (v. 17).

Whereas God had possibly created trees with the appearance of age (1:12), the trees in the garden were others that had grown later (2:9). Among those trees in the garden was one that produced life (**the tree of life**) and another that produced knowledge (**the tree of the knowledge of good and evil**), or at least eating from them did. This "knowledge" was experiential. "Good and evil," a merism for the things that protect life and that destroy life, would be experienced if the forbidden fruit were eaten (v. 17). The potential for catastrophe was great if they in self-confident pride (hubris) overstepped their bounds and attempted to manipulate life. The tree of life, on the other hand, was apparently a means of preserving and promoting life for Adam and Eve in their blissful state. These trees were **in the middle of the garden,** apparently close to each other; they provided the basis for the testing to come.

The trees (v. 9), the river (v. 10), and

the precious gold and gems (vv. 11-12) in the garden will also be in the new earth in its eternal state. The new Creation will be endowed with all these elements (Rev. 21:10-11, 21; 22:1-2), thus indicating that paradise will be restored in the new earth.

**2:11-14.** These verses, a long parenthesis, describe the richness of the then-known world. The garden was probably in the area of the Persian Gulf, judging from the place names in these verses. If the geography of that area was the same after the Flood as before, then **the Tigris** (lit., *Hiddeqel*) and **the Euphrates,** the **third** and **fourth** rivers, can be identified. The first of the four rivers, **Pishon,** was in **Havilah,** in north-central Arabia, east of Palestine. The second river, **Gihon,** was in **Cush,** probably not Ethiopia but possibly the land of the Cassites (*kaššu* in Akk.) in the mountains east of Mesopotamia.

**2:15-17.** Man's purpose is to provide spiritual service, as the carefully selected words indicate: he was placed (*nûaḥ*, "set to rest") **in the Garden . . . to work it** (*'ābad,* "to serve") and to **take care of it.** Whatever work he did was therefore described as his service to **God.**

Verse 16 includes the first use in the Old Testament of *ṣāwâh,* the major verb for "command." God's first command to man concerned life and death, good and evil. As with all God's subsequent commandments, there were positive blessings and negative prohibitions. All earthly goods and pleasures were at man's disposal, except this one **tree** which was forbidden. The Hebrew wording in verses 16-17 states the command in strong terms: **man** could **eat** freely from all the other fruit, but if he ate from the forbidden **tree** he would **surely die.**

Once again the primary lesson is related to the people of God under Moses. God prepared mankind with a specific design and gave them the capacity for moral responsibility. He set them **in the Garden** to be obedient servants, warning that before them was life or death, depending on whether they obeyed the commandment. Deuteronomy 30:11-20 set forth for Israel all the instructions parallel to the motifs of Genesis 2:8-17: obedience to the commandments of God results in life and blessing.

**2:18-25.** This section records the cre-

ation of the first woman and the institution of marriage; so it says much about the mainstay of Israel's society. God intended husband and wife to be a spiritual, functional unity, walking in integrity, serving **God,** and keeping His commandments together. When this harmony is operative, society prospers under God's hand.

Adam was **alone** and that was **not good;** all else in Creation was good (cf. 1:4, 10, 12, 18, 21, 25). As man began to function as God's representative (naming the animals [2:19-20] represented his dominion over them; cf. 1:28), he became aware of his solitude (2:20). **God** therefore put him to **sleep** (v. 21) and created Eve from his **flesh** and **bone** (vv. 21-23).

God decided to **make a helper suitable** (lit., "a helper corresponding to him," or "a corresponding helper") **for** the man (v. 18). "Helper" is not a demeaning term; it is often used in Scripture to describe God Almighty (e.g., Pss. 33:20; 70:5; 115:9, where it is trans. "help" in the NIV). The description of her as "corresponding to him" means basically that what was said about him in Genesis 2:7 was also true of her. They both had the same nature. But what man lacked (his aloneness was not good) she supplied, and what she lacked he supplied. The culmination was **one flesh** (v. 24)—the complete unity of man and woman in marriage. Since Adam and Eve were a spiritual unity, living in integrity without sin, there was no need for instruction here on headship. Paul later discussed that in relationship to the order of Creation (1 Cor. 11:3; 1 Tim. 2:13).

The words *'al-kēn* (**for this reason,** Gen. 2:24) are used frequently in Genesis. If the words in verse 24 were spoken directly by God to Adam, then the verb "leave" must be translated as the future **will leave** (as in the NIV). But if God said those words through Moses, they should be translated in the present tense: "that is why a man leaves. . . ." The implication is that marriage involves one male and one female becoming "one flesh." Their nakedness (v. 25) suggests that they were at ease with one another without any fear of exploitation or potential for evil. Such fellowship was shattered later at the Fall and is retained only in a measure in marriage when a couple begins to feel at ease with each other. Here the nakedness, though literal, also suggests sinlessness.

## 2. THE TEMPTATION AND THE FALL (CHAP. 3)

**3:1-7.** These verses provide both the record of the historical Fall of man and the archetypal temptation. This passage is a perfect case study of temptation, for sin cannot be blamed on environment or heredity.

Genesis 1–2 recorded what God said; **now the serpent** (the devil, Rev. 20:2) spoke. The word of the Lord brought life and order; the word of the serpent brought chaos and death. Truth is older than falsehood; God's word came before Satan's lies.

Genesis 3:1 is connected with 2:25 by a Hebrew wordplay: Adam and Eve were "naked" (*'ărûmmîm*); and the serpent **was more crafty** (*'ārûm,* "shrewd") than all. Their nakedness represented the fact that they were oblivious to evil, not knowing where the traps lay, whereas Satan did and would use his craftiness to take advantage of their integrity. That quality of shrewdness or subtleness is not evil in itself (indeed, one of the purposes of the Bible is to make believers so, according to Prov. 1:4, where *'ārmâh,* shrewdness, is trans. "prudence"). But it was used here for an evil purpose.

The tempter was a serpent (Satan in the form of a snake), thus suggesting that temptation comes in disguise, quite unexpectedly, and that it often comes from a subordinate (someone over whom one should have exercised dominion; cf. Gen. 1:28). Also there may well be a polemical element here, for the serpent was worshiped by pagans. Their symbol of life was in fact the cause of death. Divinity is not achieved (the promise of Satan here; 3:5) by following pagan beliefs and symbols. That is the way of death, not of life.

Eve either did not know God's command very well or did not want to remember it. By contrast, Christ gained victory over Satan by His precise knowledge of God's Word (Matt. 4:4, 7, 10). (See the chart "Satan's Temptations of Eve and of Jesus," near Matt. 4:3-11.) Eve disparaged the privileges, added to the prohibition, and weakened the penalty—all seen by contrasting her words (Gen. 3:3) with God's original commands (2:16-17). After Satan heard this, he blatantly negated the penalty of death that God

had given (3:4). Satan is a liar from the beginning (John 8:44), and this is his lie: one can sin and get away with it. But death is the penalty for sin (Gen. 2:17).

The tempter also cast doubt over God's character, suggesting that **God** was jealous, holding them back from their destiny (3:5). They would become **like God** when they ate—and God knew that, according to Satan. So Satan held out to them the promise of divinity—**knowing good and evil.**

With this the work of Satan was finished. The woman was then left to her natural desires and physical appetites. The word for **desirable** (*neḥmād,* v. 6) is related to a word that appears later in the command, "You shall not covet" (*taḥmōd,* Ex. 20:17). Physical practicality (**good for food**), aesthetic beauty (**pleasing to the eye**), and the potential **for gaining wisdom**—to be "in the know"—these draw a person over the brink once the barrier of punishment is supposedly removed.

The results, of course, were anticlimactic. The promise of divine enlightenment did not come about. They both ate and saw, but they were spoiled by so doing. They were ill at ease with one another (mistrust and alienation) and they were ill at ease with God (fearful and hiding from Him). Satan's promises never come true. Wisdom is never attained by disobeying God's Word. Instead the fear of the Lord is the beginning of wisdom (Prov. 1:7).

**3:8-13.** The remainder of this chapter falls into three sections: (a) the confrontation with **the LORD** in which the two sinners, hearing Him, feared and **hid . . . among the trees** (vv. 8-13); (b) the oracles of the Lord in which new measures were given to the serpent, the woman, and the man (vv. 14-19); and (c) the clothing by the Lord as a provision for the new order (vv. 20-24).

The effects of sin are punishment and provision. Whereas **the man** and the woman had life, they now had death; whereas pleasure, now pain; whereas abundance, now a meager subsistence by toil; whereas perfect fellowship, now alienation and conflict.

The motifs in chapter 3—death, toil, sweat, thorns, the tree, the struggle, and the seed—all were later traced to Christ. He is the other Adam, who became the curse, who sweat great drops of blood in bitter agony, who wore a crown of thorns, who was hanged on a tree until He was dead, and who was placed in the dust of death.

**3:14-19. God** spoke **to the serpent** (vv. 14-15), to Eve (v. 16), and **to Adam** (vv. 17-19). God's words to the serpent included (a) the announcement that the snake, crawling and eating **dust,** would be a perpetual reminder to mankind of temptation and the Fall, and (b) an oracle about the power behind the snake. God said there would be a perpetual struggle between satanic forces and mankind. It would be **between** Satan **and the woman,** and their respective **offspring** or "seeds." The "offspring" of the woman was Cain, then all humanity at large, and then Christ and those collectively in Him. The "offspring" of the serpent includes demons and anyone serving his kingdom of darkness, those whose "father" is the devil (John 8:44). Satan would cripple mankind (**you will strike** at **his heel**), but *the* Seed, Christ, would deliver the fatal blow (**He will crush your head**).

Then God told the **woman** that she would have **pain** in bearing **children,** and that she would be mastered by her **husband** whom she desired. Because Eve's **desire** probably refers in this context to her prompting Adam to sin, it is better to translate the verse "Your desire *was* for your husband." Having overstepped her bounds in this, she would now be mastered by him.

God then told Adam that he would experience great pain in scratching out a livelihood (3:17-19). (**Painful toil** translates the same word used in v. 16 for the woman's pain. This word occurs only three times in the OT, in vv. 16-17 and 5:29.) Death will be his end—he will **return to the ground** ('ă*ḏ*āmâh; a gracious provision in view of the suffering), and he will **return** to **dust** and become the serpent's prey again (cf. 3:14). So much for ambitions for divinity! Man may attempt to be like God, but he is dust.

These punishments represent retaliatory justice. Adam and Eve sinned by eating; they would suffer in order to eat. She manipulated her husband; she would be mastered by her husband. The serpent destroyed the human race; he will be destroyed.

God also made gracious provisions. Mankind will die and not live forever in this chaotic state, and children will be born (v. 16) so that the human race will endure and continue. Ultimate victory will come through Christ, the Seed (Gal. 3:16) of the woman (cf. Gal. 4:4, "born of a woman").

No matter how hard people try to do away with male dominion, agonizing labor, painful childbearing, and death, these evils will continue because sin is present. They are fruits of sin.

**3:20-24.** Adam's faith and God's provision are noted in these verses. God would save them and ensure that they would not live forever in this state. Adam's faith is seen in his naming **his wife Eve** (lit., "living"). Thus Adam was looking to the future and not primarily to death. Eve's faith is seen later (4:1) when she named her firstborn Cain because he was from the Lord.

All God's dealings with people as sinners can be traced back to this act of disobedience by Adam and Eve. **God** is a saving God, however, and the fact that He **clothed . . . Adam** and Eve testifies to that. An animal was sacrificed to provide **garments of skin,** and later all Israel's animal sacrifices would be part of God's provision to remedy the curse—a life for a life. The sinner shall die! (Ezek. 18:20; Rom. 6:23) Yet he will live if he places his faith in **the Lord,** who has provided a Substitute. The skin with which God clothed Adam and Eve perpetually reminded them of God's provision. Similarly in the fullness of time God accepted the sacrifice of Christ, and on the basis of that atonement He clothes believers in righteousness (Rom. 3:21-26).

### 3. THE ADVANCE OF SIN IN CAIN'S MURDER OF ABEL (4:1-16)

The subject of chapter 4 is the spread of godless society. Here is man in rebellion against God—man who did not obey and who destroyed the godly and denied his responsibility and culpability for it. The ungodly here are portrayed as living on in the world (with a protective mark of grace; cf. comments on v. 15) without being saved. Their sense of guilt was eased by their cultural development and their geographical expansion.

Under Moses' leadership Israel would move into a world of cultures. Civilizations with music, art, industry, and enterprise would be on every side.

These would be antagonistic to Israel, and would help cause God's people to reject the sacrifices and live as cursed people. Israel needed to be warned against such arrogant opposition.

In the story of Cain and Abel the seed of the woman met the seed of the serpent (3:15). Cain fell to the prey of the crouching evil and eventually went out to form a godless society, rejecting God's way. The "way of Cain" (Jude 11), then, is a lack of faith which shows itself in envy of God's dealings with the righteous, in murderous acts, in denial of responsibility, and in refusal to accept God's punishment.

**4:1-5.** **Cain** and **Abel** were played off against each other, reversing the subjects clause after clause. In fact, the entire chapter contrasts them: Cain is mentioned 13 times in verses 1-16. Seven times Abel is mentioned, and three other times "brother" is substituted. Rightly the Apostle John saw murder as a sin against one's brother (1 John 3:12, 15).

The nature of rebellious man unfolds in the person of **Cain** who had an auspicious beginning as the child of hope. But the narrative lines him up with the curse; he **worked the soil** (lit., ground, *'ăḏāmâh,* Gen. 4:2; cf. 3:17). **Abel,** however, seems to be lined up with man's original purpose, to have dominion over life (cf. 1:28); he **kept flocks.** These coincidental descriptions are enhanced with their actions in worship. **Abel** went out of his way to please God (which meant he had faith in God, Heb. 11:6), whereas **Cain** was simply discharging a duty. Abel's actions were righteous, whereas Cain's were evil (1 John 3:12). These two types of people are still present.

Cain's lack of faith shows up in his response to God's rejection of his offering of fruit (Gen. 4:5). Rather than being concerned about remedying the situation and pleasing God, he **was very angry.**

**4:6-7.** **Cain** was so **angry** he would not be talked out of his sin—even by God. Eve, however, had to be talked *into* her sin by Satan; but Cain "belonged to the evil one" (1 John 3:12). It is as if he could not wait to destroy his brother—a natural man's solution to his own failure.

God's advice was that if Cain would please God by doing **what is right,** all would be well. **But if** not **sin** would be **crouching** (*rōḇēṣ* is used here in the figure of a crouching animal) **at his door,** ready to overcome him. Sin **desires to have** Cain (these words show God's interpretation of "desire," the same Heb. word, in Gen. 3:16), but Cain could have the mastery over it. Here is the perpetual struggle between good and evil. Anyone filled with envy and strife is prey for the evil one.

**4:8-16.** After murdering **his brother** (v. 8) **Cain** repudiated responsibility for it (v. 9) and claimed that God's punishment (cropless soil and wandering, vv. 10-12) was too severe (v. 13). God graciously protected him by some **mark** or sign that would be a deterrent to an avenger (v. 15—nowhere is the nature of this "mark" clarified), but God condemned him to a life of ceaseless wandering (v. 12). This was his curse, to be banished from God's **presence** (v. 14). But **Cain** defied that curse by living in a city **in the land of Nod** (lit., "wandering"), **east of Eden** (v. 16).

Several Mosaic motifs were founded here: (1) Sacrifices should be offered to God from a heart of faith, and should be the best of the livestock, the firstborn (v. 4). (2) Israelites had responsibilities to their brothers—they were each others' keepers and must not kill one another. (3) Homicidal blood polluted the land, crying out for vengeance—spilled blood raised its voice of accusation (v. 10). (4) Blood revenge was averted by God through protective care, just as later removal to a city of refuge would avert an avenger. (5) Punishment for guilt was at the foundation of Israel's theocracy. (6) Life without God is a dangerous life without protection. (7) Sometimes the elder was rejected in favor of the younger, turning the normative societal custom around.

### 4. THE SPREAD OF GODLESS CIVILIZATION (4:17-26)

The narrative now traces the line of Cain to its full development. What becomes of a society that rebels against God and leaves the land of blessing in angry defiance of His laws and His sacrifices? In this case it prospers. But the righteous should neither envy the wicked nor follow their way of life (Pss. 49; 73). God allows them to prosper in their earthbound way. They produce music, weapons, agricultural devices, and cities—culture. It is their only recourse in a bitter, cursed world.

Not so are the righteous. Some who traced their lineage to Seth, the replacement of Abel, began to make proclamation in the name of the Lord. These—and Noah, and Abram, among others—declared the truth to their generations. Some people—though only a remnant—do not go overboard in living an affluent "good life" but are concerned with things spiritual. Israel should trace her ancestry to Enosh (Gen. 4:26), in spirit and in fact.

**4:17-18.** Cain's family began in Nod (v. 16). The name "Nod" (*nôd*) is related to the words for "restless wanderer" (*nā' wānād*, v. 14). It was the land of fugitives from God. Here Cain fathered a child, **Enoch,** and **named a city** after him. (No doubt Cain's **wife** was a daughter of Adam; cf. 5:4.)

**4:19-24.** The seventh from Adam through Cain was **Lamech** (probably a contemporary of the righteous Enoch, also seventh from Adam, 5:3-21). Lamech altered the plan of God and **married two women.** His family produced musical instruments (**the harp and flute**) and implements (**tools out of bronze and iron**) to make life enjoyable.

But in spite of this prosperous good life, evil was advancing ominously. **Lamech** slew a youthful warrior who wounded him and demanded greater leniency in any vengeance that might come his way than that afforded to **Cain** (4:24). **Lamech** boasted about the murder (the word **killed** in v. 23 is *hārag*, "to slay, to slaughter," the same word used of Cain's murder of Abel, vv. 8, 25). So here is a picture of an affluent society defying God and His laws, seeking pleasure and self-indulgence. Into this world Israel (and later the church) would come as a kingdom of priests to proclaim God's righteousness.

**4:25-26.** In strong contrast with this godless society were the righteous. In the line from **Seth** there was faith. **Seth** himself was a provision from **God,** according to Eve's statement of faith. In the days of **Enosh,** Seth's son, **men began to call on** (better, "proclaim") **the name of the LORD** (*Yahweh*).

## C. The succession from Adam (5:1–6:8)

A new *tôlˁdôt* begins here, with the dual purpose of linking the history of the early people to the story of Noah and of showing the result of sin. In fact it answers a problem raised in the preceding section. If in spite of sin there is progress, civilization, and prosperity, what about the curse? The answer is that despite people's aspirations, they die.

1. THE GENEALOGY FROM ADAM TO NOAH (CHAP. 5)

The genealogy in this chapter is a "vertical" list, showing descendancy from Adam through Seth to Noah. The Cainites' genealogy in chapter 4 had 7 generations (from Cain to Jubal); this genealogy has 10 (from Adam to Noah). Both lists end with three sons coming from the final name on the list (Jabal, Jubal, Tubal-Cain [4:20-22]; Shem, Ham, Japheth [5:32]). In each list only one man spoke—Lamech in the Cainite list (4:23-24), and a different Lamech in the Sethite list (5:29). The Cainite Lamech was taunting the curse (4:24), whereas the Sethite Lamech was moaning under the curse, looking for comfort from his son Noah (5:29).

Both the biblical record and the Sumerian King List from Mesopotamia attest to the longevity of the ancient people. Apparently the environment before the Flood enabled people to live longer. Certainly this could have been part of God's plan to fill up the earth (cf. 1:28).

**5:1-2.** This chapter begins with a reiteration of the creation of man **in** (or, "as") **the likeness** ("resemblance," a synonym of "image"; cf. 1:26-27) **of God.** One cannot miss the emphasis on the blessing of the image (**He blessed them**) at Creation. But with that in mind the chapter then traces the result of sin, death.

**5:3-32.** God's **image** in **Adam** was then reproduced in **Seth,** Adam's **son.** The capacities and qualities of a parent are passed on to his children by natural reproduction.

Besides providing the link between Adam and his times and Noah and his, this chapter has a motif that cannot be missed—**and then he died** (vv. 5, 8, 11, 14, 17, 20, 27, 31). If one were in doubt whether the wages of sin is death (Rom. 6:23), he need only look at human history.

In Enoch's case, the statement was not made—as it was with the other males in this genealogy—that he lived so many years and then died. Instead he **walked with God** (Gen. 5:22, 24). "Walk" is the biblical expression for fellowship and obedience that results in divine favor. Enoch's walk lasted **300 years.** No doubt his walk would have continued, but **God took him away** (v. 24)—he did not die. Such a walk was commanded of Israel (Lev. 26:3, 12) and of the church.

Genesis 5 includes the etymology of the name of **Noah** (v. 29), whose life would be the dominant force in the sections to follow. **Lamech** named his son **Noah,** hoping he would bring **comfort** to them from the curse (v. 29; cf. "painful toil" and the ground's curse in 3:17). "Comfort" is not the meaning of "Noah," but the words sound the same. Lamech had no idea how God would turn these words around and fulfill the wish in His own way (cf. comments on 6:5-8), but he did have high hopes for his boy. Thus a second glimmer of hope appears in this chapter of death. Enoch escaped the curse of death, and Noah would comfort those under the curse.

### 2. THE CORRUPTION OF THE RACE (6:1-8)

This section's details have been the subject of endless debates, often leaving the obvious untouched. It must be remembered that it is part of the _ṯôlᵉḏôṯ_ beginning in 5:1. Whatever view one takes of the details, it is clear that these verses show how wicked the human race had become, and that death was its ongoing punishment.

**6:1-4.** Many have suggested that **the sons of God** were the godly line of Seth and **the daughters of men** were the Cainites. But this does not do justice to the terminology or the context. Others view the "sons of God" as angels (as in Job 1:6), who cohabited with women on earth. This, however, conflicts with Matthew 22:30.

The incident is one of hubris, the proud overstepping of bounds. Here it applies to "the sons of God," a lusty, powerful lot striving for fame and fertility. They were probably powerful rulers who were controlled (indwelt) by fallen angels. It may be that fallen angels left their habitation and inhabited bodies of human despots and warriors, the mighty ones of the earth.

It is known from Ezekiel 28:11-19 and Daniel 10:13 that great kings of the earth have "princes" ruling behind them—their power is demonic. It is no surprise that in Ugaritic literature (as well as other nations' literature), kings are described as divine, half-divine, or demi-gods. Pagans revered these great leaders. Many mythological traditions describe them as being the offspring of the gods themselves. In fact *bn'lm* ("sons of the gods") in Ugaritic is used of members of the pantheon as well as great kings of the earth. In the Ugaritic legend of the Dawn, the chief god of the pantheon, El, seduced two human women. This union of a god with human women produced *Šḥr* ("Dawn") and *Šlm* ("Dusk") who seem to have become goddesses representing Venus. Thus for the pagans, gods had their origin in copulation between gods and humans. Any superhuman individual in a myth or any mythological or actual giant would suggest a divine origin to the pagans.

Genesis 6:1-4, then, describes how corrupt the world got when this violation was rampant. It is also a polemic *against* the pagan belief that giants (**Nephilim;** cf. Num. 13:32-33) and **men of renown** (Gen. 6:4) were of divine origin, and that immortality was achieved by immorality. The Canaanite cult (and most cults in the ancient Near East) included fertility rites involving sympathetic magic, based on the assumption that people are supernaturally affected through an object which represents them. Israel was warned to resist this because it was completely corrupt and erroneous.

The passage, then, refutes pagan beliefs by declaring the truth. **The sons of God** were not divine; they were demon-controlled. Their marrying as many women as they wished (possibly this is the origin of harems) was to satisfy their baser instincts. They were just another low order of creatures, though powerful and demon-influenced. **Children** of these marriages, despite pagan ideas, were not god-kings. Though **heroes** and "men of renown," they were flesh; and they died, in due course, like all members of the human race. When God judges the world—as He was about to— no giant, no deity, no human has any power against Him. God simply allots one's days and brings his end.

**6:5-8.** God's words concerning the human race are filled with pathos. People's **wickedness** was **great,** and **every inclination** (better, "plan," *yēṣer*) of their hearts **was only evil** continually (cf. 8:21, "every indication of his heart is evil from childhood"). God had made man by design (*yāṣar*, "to form by design"; 2:7), but man had taken that capacity given to him and produced evil alone. There is hardly a stronger statement in the Bible about the sin of mankind. This passage gives insight into Jesus' explanation that "before the Flood people were eating and drinking, marrying and giving in marriage" (Matt. 24:38)—seemingly a harmless statement until its context is studied. In addition man was "corrupt" and "full of violence" (Gen. 6:11, 13).

The wordplays in verses 5-8 are striking. God "repented" (KJV) that He had made man because the sin of the race **filled** Him **with pain.** The words "repented," "pain," and "made" go back to chapters 3 and 5. Lamech longed for comfort (*nāḥam*), from the *painful* toil under the curse (5:29). Now God "repented" (*nāḥam*, **was grieved,** NIV) **that He had made man** because human sin *pained* Him (6:6). This is why pain was brought into the world—God was grieved with sin. But now God, rather than comforting man, "repented" after making him. This gave an ironic twist to Lamech's words. God determined to destroy them all. ("Repented" does not suggest that God changed His mind, for He is changeless [Mal. 3:6]. Instead, it means that God was sorrowful.)

Even though swift judgment would fall because God's Spirit would not always shield (*dûn*; "shield" is better than NIV's "contend with," Gen. 6:3) mankind, the judgment would be delayed 120 years (v. 3). During this time Noah was "a preacher of righteousness" (2 Peter 2:5).

Noah was a recipient of God's grace and therefore was spared from the judgment (in contrast with those who aspired to immortality). In the time of Moses, Israel would know they were chosen of God and should walk in righteousness. They, as God's people, would meet the Nephilim, the Anakites (Num. 13:33), and the Rephaites (Deut. 2:11; 3:13; Josh. 12:4) when they entered the land. But Israel should not fear them as demigods.

God would judge the corrupt world for its idolatry and fornication. And in the latter day the wicked will suddenly be swept away by judgment when God will establish His theocratic kingdom of blessing (Matt. 24:36-39).

## D. The succession from Noah (6:9–9:29)

### 1. THE JUDGMENT BY THE FLOOD (6:9–8:22)

God judged the wicked with a severe and catastrophic judgment in order to start life over again with a worshipful covenant. In the midst of the Flood, in which the sovereign Lord of Creation destroyed the world Noah, God's servant and a recipient of grace, sailed through to the "new creation" and worshiped God.

Why would God bring such a Flood? There are several reasons: (1) God is sovereign over all creation and frequently uses nature to judge mankind. (2) The Flood was the most effective way of purging the world. It would wash it clean so that not a trace of the wicked could be found. The dove would not find a place "to set its feet" (8:6-9). (3) The Flood was used by God to start a "new creation." The first Creation with Adam is paralleled here by the second with Noah. Much as the dry land appeared from the receding waters (1:9), so here the waters abated until the ark came to rest on Ararat (8:4). When Noah was finished with the ark God commissioned him to be fruitful and multiply (9:1) and to have dominion over the earth (9:2), just as He had told Adam (1:26, 28). Noah planted a garden (9:20), whereas God planted a garden for Adam and Eve (2:8). But sin had tarnished the race. Adam and Noah are contrasted: whereas Adam's nakedness was a sign of righteousness (2:25), Noah's was one of degradation (9:21) and he ended up cursing his grandson Canaan (9:25-27).

The motifs in 6:9–8:22 are significant. First, God is shown to be the Judge of the whole earth. In a word He made distinctions between the righteous and the unrighteous, the clean and the unclean. What was clean was for God.

A second motif is that God made provision for the recipients of His grace. Thus the warning is that those who claim to be grace-receivers should walk with God in righteousness, being separate from sinners.

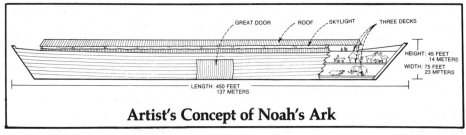

GREAT DOOR    ROOF    SKYLIGHT    THREE DECKS

HEIGHT: 45 FEET
14 METERS
WIDTH: 75 FEET
23 MFTERS

LENGTH: 450 FEET
137 METERS

## Artist's Concept of Noah's Ark

A third motif had significance for Israel. As God judged the world in Noah's day and brought Noah through the Flood, so He judged the wicked Egyptians and brought Israel through the waters of the Red Sea to worship and serve Him. Instructions for that worship were distinctly spelled out in Leviticus. It is not surprising that many terms used here (Gen. 6:9–8:22) also appear in Leviticus.

It was expedient that that generation of sinners die so that all others might be warned of the coming wrath of God. However, Noah escaped through the judgment to a new age; catastrophe does not interrupt God's program.

The Flood narrative points up God's power and freedom over His creation. The Flood reveals God's deadly anger over sin. The Flood shows that God's gracious redemption is meaningful in light of judgment, and that His grace is not to be taken lightly. The cause of God's judgment is stressed—the monstrous acts of sin performed in their habitual courses. In this the Genesis Flood is distinct from pagan accounts (e.g., *Atraḥasis* and *Gilgamesh*); the Babylonian *Gilgamesh* account explained that the gods brought the Flood because of noise humans made.

So basically chapters 6–9 answer the question, What is the end of man? Can he get away with pursuing life immorally and enjoying the pleasures of this world with reckless abandon? Is this life final or preparatory? God's judgment makes the answer clear. But the expense seems so great. This judgment seems harsh. No word about the terror of the lost is mentioned, though Noah must have felt it. The Flood shows the extent to which God will go to help bring about holiness and rest on the earth. It is here that the godly find encouragement—in God's plan for good to triumph ultimately over evil. Only one other event shows that

holiness among people is the object for which God will sacrifice everything else—the crucifixion of His Son.

The narrative divides into three sections: the commission to Noah to build the ark and preserve life (6:9–7:5), the destruction of all flesh outside the ark by water (7:6-24), and the sacrificial worship by Noah after the Flood (chap. 8).

a. *The commission to Noah*
   *(6:9–7:5)*

**6:9-13.** In contrast with the reason for the Flood in the Babylonian account (the caprice of the gods because of man's noise), the biblical record presents the Flood as a distinctly moral judgment. The human race had become so **corrupt** (vv. 11-12) and **full of violence** (vv. 11, 13) that God's wrath would **destroy** all flesh, except **Noah,** who **walked with God** (v. 9), and his family (v. 18).

**6:14-18.** The deliverance was to be by means of **an ark,** a flat-bottomed rectangular vessel **450' long, 75' wide, and 45' high,** with a displacement of some 43,300 tons (Merrill F. Unger, *Archaeology and the Old Testament*. Grand Rapids: Zondervan Publishing House, 1954, pp. 59-60) and three **decks.** (The sketch is one artist's concept of how the ark may have looked.) The ship in the Babylonian tradition was of cubical construction and was five times as big as Noah's ark. Genesis alone preserves the description of a seaworthy vessel.

**6:19–7:5.** Into this **ark** Noah was to take **all** kinds of animals to preserve life on earth. A distinction was made very early between **clean** and **unclean** animals. To preserve life **Noah** had to take on board **two of every kind** of **animal,** but for **food** and for sacrificing he had to bring **seven** pairs of each **kind of** clean **animal** (7:2, marg.). The distinction between **clean** and **unclean** animals became a major point in the Levitical order (Lev. 11:2-23).

## Chronology of the Flood

| | | Event | Date | Reference |
|---|---|---|---|---|
| Waiting in the ark 7 days (7:7, 10) | 1. | Noah entered the ark | Month 2, day 10 | 7:7-9 |
| | 2. | *7 days later:* Rain began falling | Month 2, day 17* | 7:10-11 |
| Water continued for 150 days (7:24) | 3. | *40 days later:* Heavy rains stopped | Month 3, day 27 | 7:12 |
| | 4. | *110 days later:* Prevailing waters receded and the ark rested on an Ararat mountain | Month 7, day 17* | 7:24; 8:4 |
| Water receded in 150 days (8:3) | 5. | *74 days later:* Tops of mountains visible | Month 10, day 1* | 8:5 |
| | 6. | *40 days later:* Raven sent out, and a dove sent out and returned | Month 11, day 11* | 8:6-9 |
| | 7. | *7 days later:* Dove sent out again and returned with a leaf | Month 11, day 18* | 8:10 |
| | 8. | *7 days later:* Dove sent out a third time and did not return | Month 11, day 25 | 8:12 |
| | 9. | *22 days later:* Water receded | Month 12, day 17 | 8:3 |
| Earth dried in 70 days | 10. | Noah saw dry land | Month 1, day 1* | 8:13 |
| | 11. | Land completely dry, and Noah exited the ark | Month 2, day 27* | 8:14-19 |

377 days

1 year and 17 days in the ark

*Dates specified in the Scriptures; other dates are implied.

b. *The destruction of all flesh outside the ark (7:6-24)*

**7:6-20.** After all preparations had been completed, **the Flood** came. On the one hand there was a torrential **rain** for **40 days** and **nights** (vv. 11-12). On the other hand there were corresponding gigantic upheavals and shiftings of the earth's crust which caused the oceans' floors to rise and break up their reservoirs of subterranean waters (v. 11; cf. Unger, *Archaeology*, p. 61). As a result, the whole earth was flooded in the disaster (v. 19). No doubt the surface of **the earth,** the manner of life, and the longevity of life were changed by this catastrophe.

**7:21-24.** Everything **living . . . on the earth** (outside the ark) was destroyed. Only marine life survived. Sin had infected every aspect of life, and

nothing short of a new beginning would suffice. Thus it will also be at the end of this Age (Matt. 24:37-39).

c. *Noah's sacrificial worship (chap. 8)*

**8:1-3.** The heavy rains lasted 40 days (7:4, 12), but the waters continued on for 110 days (cf. 7:24, "The waters flooded the earth for 150 days"; KJV has "the waters prevailed"). The 40 days were part of the 150 days, with apparently lighter **rain** falling (or subterranean water upheavals continuing for another 110 days; see the chart "Chronology of the Flood").

**8:4-19.** **The ark** rested in **the mountains of Ararat** 150 days after the rains began. Assyrian records may identify such a name in Armenia of eastern Turkey, but the precise location remains unknown. After it was clear that the earth was suitable for habitation, the eight people and all **the animals** left **the ark.** This was 377 days after they had entered it (cf. 7:11 with 8:13-14). The theme of "rest" seems to be quite strong throughout the story. The ark rested (v. 4); at first **the dove could find no place to set its feet** (v. 9; lit., "could not find a resting place for its feet"). When the ark came to rest on Ararat, this was more than a physical landing on dry ground. It was a new beginning; the world was clean and at rest.

**8:20-22.** Leaving the ark, **Noah** made a sacrifice to God, which was a **pleasing aroma** to Him. The people of God are a worshiping people, as Israel would learn, and that worship was to take the form of giving God some of the best of what was His. The redeemed of the Lord offer Him the praise of their lips (Heb. 13:15), the best of their possessions (Prov. 3:9), and the willingness and humility of their spirits. Noah received God's grace, walked with God in obedience and righteousness, was preserved from judgment, entered a new age with people's wickedness temporarily removed, and responded with worship and sacrifice.

After Noah made the sacrifice, God promised **never** to **curse the ground** in this way again. The continuity of seasons is evidence of God's forbearance.

2. THE COVENANT WITH NOAH (9:1-17)

**9:1-4.** God instructed Noah to **be fruitful and increase in number and fill the earth** (vv. 1, 7) just as He had told Adam (1:28). And Noah, like Adam, was to have dominion over animals (9:2; cf. 1:26, 28). Also both were given food to eat (9:3; cf. 1:29; 2:16) with one prohibition (9:5-6; cf. 2:17).

**9:5-7.** With Noah's new beginning came a covenant. It was necessary now to have a covenant with obligations for mankind and a promise from **God.** Because of the Flood's destruction of life people might begin to think that God holds life cheap and assume that taking life is a small matter. This covenant shows that **life** is sacred and that **man** is not to destroy **man,** who is made **in the image of God.**

In essence, then, this covenant was established to ensure the stability of nature. It helped guarantee the order of the

world. People would also learn that human law was necessary for the stability of life and that wickedness should not go unchecked as it had before. So human government was brought in.

**9:8-17.** That this **covenant** (vv. 9, 11-13, 15-17) is cosmic and universal (**every living creature,** vv. 10 [twice], 12; **all living creatures,** vv. 15-16; **all life,** vv. 11, 15, 17) is seen from the **rainbow** God gave as a **sign** (vv. 12-13, 17). When it arches over the horizon after a rainfall it is an all-embracing sign of God's faithfulness to His work of grace. Signs remind participants in a **covenant** to keep the stipulations. In the rainbow God, who is omniscient, perpetually reminds Himself (repeated in vv. 15-16) **never** to **flood** the whole world again (vv. 11, 15). Since no rain had fallen before the Flood (2:5), no rainbow was needed. Now when clouds clear, light refraction shows this marvelous display. The rainbow arcs like a battle bow hung against the clouds. (The Heb. word for rainbow, *qešeṯ*, is also the word for a battle bow.) Elsewhere in the Old Testament God referred to judgment storms by using terms for bows and arrows.

The bow is now "put away," hung in place by the clouds, suggesting that the "battle," the storm, is over. Thus the rainbow speaks of peace. In the ancient Near East, covenant treaties were made after wars as a step toward embarking on peace. Similarly God, after judging sin, made a **covenant** of peace. Israel certainly would be strengthened to see in the skies again and again God's pledge that He keeps His promise of grace. But certainly it also reminded the faithful in Israel that God's judgment was completed for that age. Judgment will come once again in the end times (Zech. 14:1-3; Rev. 19:15) before there can be complete millennial peace and rest (Rev. 20:6). So Genesis 9:8-17 anticipates that in the end Israel will beat her swords into plowshares (Isa. 2:4; Micah 4:3). In the meantime life goes on in a new order; the divine will of forbearance, "common grace," is at work until that end.

3. THE CURSE OF CANAAN (9:18-29)

This passage has several interpretive problems that have always plagued Bible scholars. It is important to remember the purpose of the book, for this passage has direct reference to the nature and destiny of the Canaanites, Israel's antagonists.

**9:18-23.** Those **who came out of the ark** are identified, with the special note that **Ham was the father of Canaan.** From Noah's three **sons** descended all the world's **people.** The descendants of **Shem** were the Shemites from whom Abraham descended (cf. 10:21-31; 11:10-26).

**Noah,** "the man of the earth" (as the rabbis translated the words **a man of the soil**), began **to plant a vineyard.** Though **wine** is said to cheer the heart (Jud. 9:13; Ps. 104:15) and alleviate the pain of the curse (Prov. 31:6), it is also clear that it has disturbing effects. Here Noah lay **drunk** and naked in **his tent.** Intoxication and sexual looseness are hallmarks of pagans, and both are traced back to this event in Noah's life. Man had not changed at all; with the opportunity to start a "new creation," Noah acted like a pagan (cf. Gen. 6:5; 8:21).

The basic question concerns what **Ham,** Noah's youngest son, did (9:22, 24) and why Noah cursed Ham's "son" Canaan (vv. 25-27). Many fanciful ideas have been proposed. The rabbis said Ham castrated Noah, thus explaining why Noah had no other sons. Others claim that Ham slept with his mother, thus uncovering his father's nakedness, and that Canaan was the offspring of that union. Others have said that Ham was involved in a homosexual attack on his father. But the Hebrew expression here means what it says: **Ham . . . saw his father's nakedness** (v. 22). He was not involved with Noah sexually, for in that case the Hebrew would be translated "he uncovered (causative form of *gālâh*) his father's nakedness." Instead Noah had already **uncovered** himself (*wayyitgal*, reflexive form, v. 21), and **Ham** saw him that way.

To the ancients, however, even seeing one's father naked was a breach of family ethic. The sanctity of the family was destroyed and the strength of the father was made a mockery. Ham apparently stumbled on this accidentally, but went out and exultingly **told his two brothers,** as if he had triumphed over his father.

So what seems to be a trivial incident turned out to be a major event. Noah's oracle (vv. 25-27) showed that the na-

tures of his three sons would be perpetuated in their descendants.

In all but one of the verses in Leviticus 18:6-19, Moses used the causative form of the verb *gālâh* to refer to the Canaanites' (Ham's descendants) "uncovering" another's nakedness (rendered in the NIV, "have sexual relations"). This euphemism reports the actual licentious and repulsively immoral behavior of the descendants of Ham (cf. Lev. 18:3). Ham's disposition toward moral abandon thus bore fruit in the immoral acts of his descendants, the Canaanites.

**9:24-29.** Because of this incident **Noah** prophesied about his sons' descendants. He began with the direct words, **Cursed be Canaan!** However, Noah was not punishing Ham's son for something *Ham* did. Instead, Noah's words referred to the nation of Canaanites that would come from Ham through Canaan. Ham's act of hubris could not be left without repercussions. A humiliation in like measure was needed, according to the principle of retributive justice. Ham had made an irreparable breach in his *father's* family; thus a curse would be put on his *son's* family. It has been suggested that Ham may have attempted to seize leadership over his brothers for the sake of his own line. This would be similar to other ancient traditions about a son replacing his father. But if he did his attempt failed, and his line through Canaan was placed not in leadership over other clansmen, but under them (v. 25).

Noah's oracle predicted that the Canaanites would be in servitude to the Shemites and Japhethites (vv. 26-27). But this was because the Canaanites lived degrading lives like Ham, not because of what Ham did. The point is that nationally, at least, drunken debauchery enslaves a people. This is why, in God's program to bless Israel, the Canaanites were condemned. They were to be judged by God through the Conquest because their activities were in the same pattern and mold as their ancestor Ham.

The enslavement of Canaanites is seen in many situations in the history of the Old Testament. Such a case turned up fairly soon; the Canaanites were defeated and enslaved by eastern kings (chap. 14). Another example was the Gibeonites who later under Joshua became wood choppers and water carriers for Israel's tabernacle (Josh. 9:27). If the subjugation of Canaan to Japheth's line is to be carried to the extreme, as *'ebed* (**slave,** Gen. 9:26-27) sometimes implies, then it would go no further than the Battle of Carthage (146 B.C.) where the Phoenicians (who were Canaanites) were finally defeated. But Noah's words seem to be more of a general than a specific prophecy, that the line of **Shem** will be blessed and the line of Ham in **Canaan** will be cursed.

This blessing-cursing motif is crucial in Genesis. The Canaanites would have to be dispossessed from their place by Israel under Joshua in order for blessing to come on Shem (v. 26) and for the Japhethites to dwell **in the tents of Shem** (v. 27). This meant that the Japhethites would live with the Shemites on friendly terms, not that the Japhethites would dispossess the Shemites. So verses 24-29 actually set the foundation for Israel's foreign policy in the land (Deut. 20:16-18).

E. *The succession from the sons of Noah (10:1–11:9)*

1. THE TABLE OF NATIONS (CHAP. 10)

**10:1.** This table of nations gives a survey of the descendants of **Noah's three sons.** God had told them to "fill the earth" (9:1). But later their descendants' moving out and filling the earth (11:1-9) was divine judgment on a rebellious people.

This table appears to represent the known tribes of the earth. Seventy descendants of Noah's sons are listed, including 14 from Japheth, 30 from Ham, and 26 from Shem. And these are cleverly arranged into patterns.

The basic framework of the table is the *b^enê* ("the sons of") motif (the Heb. *b^enê* occurs 12 times, in vv. 2-4, 6-7, 20-23, 29, 31-32). Other times, however, the chapter uses *yālaḏ* ("he begot"), which seems to suggest that these were interpretations given to the *b^enê* table. These *yālaḏ* sections (beginning in vv. 8, 13, 15, 21, 25-26), in line with the idea of the *tôl^eḏôṯ*, trace the significant developments of personages within the structure of the table. (The NIV renders the *yālaḏ* verb "was the father of" in vv. 8, 13, 15, 26, "was the ancestor of" in v. 21, and "were born to" in v. 25.) Of special note are verses 15-19, in which Canaan's descendants are traced (vv. 15-18) and even the

boundaries of the Promised Land are given (v. 19). The writer was apparently using an ancient table to clarify which of Noah's descendants would experience blessing and which ones would experience cursing. Most of the *yālaḏ* ("he begot") sections pertain to the Canaanites or the Hamites, the tribes close to Israel. To see which neighbors would face blessing and which ones cursing, Israel need only consult this table.

The table of nations is a "horizontal" genealogy rather than a "vertical" one (those in chaps. 5 and 11 are vertical). Its purpose is not primarily to trace ancestry; instead it shows political, geographical, and ethnic affiliations among tribes for various reasons, most notable being holy war. Tribes shown to be "kin" would be in league together. Thus this table aligns the predominant tribes in and around the land promised to Israel. These names include founders of tribes, clans, cities, and territories.

The table shows which peoples in the ancient world shared in the blessing and cursing motif. The table also stresses how they spread out and replenished the earth, though not in obedience. They all came from one, Noah, and were therefore one people; but some were closely related and others were distant. The table also shows the plight of the human race, scattered across the face of the earth and living according to their own cultural and linguistic affiliations. Wars and conflicts inevitably result from this arrangement.

**10:2-5.** The descendants **of Japheth,** numbering 14, were given first. These were northern people, remote from Israel. **Gomer** represented the Cimmerians, thought to be of the same stock as the Scythians. **Magog** was the land of Gog, between Armenia and Cappadocia (Ezek. 38:2; 39:6; see the map "The World of Jeremiah and Ezekiel" in Introduction to Jer.). The name represented Scythian hordes southwest of the Black Sea. **Madai** represented the Medes east of Assyria and southwest of the Caspian Sea. **Javan** was the general word for the Hellenic race, the Ionians of western Asia Minor. **Tubal** and **Meshech** were northern military states. They might have been located in Pontus and the Armenian mountains. **Tiras** may refer to the seafaring Pelasgians of the Aegean coasts.

From these seven, seven more were

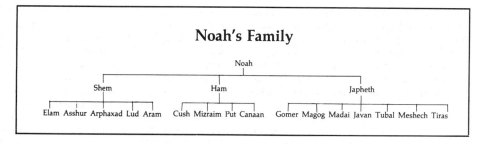

## Noah's Family

Noah

- Shem
  - Elam Asshur Arphaxad Lud Aram
- Ham
  - Cush Mizraim Put Canaan
- Japheth
  - Gomer Magog Madai Javan Tubal Meshech Tiras

derived. Three northern tribes came from **Gomer: Ashkenaz** (related to the Scythians), **Riphath, and Togarmah** (distant northern tribes).

**The sons of Javan,** two geographical names and two tribal names, were all kin to the Greeks. **Elishah** was Alashiyah or Cyprus. **Tarshish** was a distant coast in Asia Minor. **The Kittim** also dwelt on Cyprus. The "Dodanim" (NIV marg.) may have lived in Dodona, Greece (unless "Dodanim" is a textual variant for **Rodanim** [Rhodes]; cf. 1 Chron. 1:7).

These northern tribes did not figure predominantly in Israel's history, but occur frequently in prophetic writings (Ezek. 27; 37–39).

**10:6-7.** The descendants **of Ham** (vv. 6-20) formed the eastern and southern peoples of Mesopotamia.

The Cushites (descendants of **Cush**) settled in south Arabia, and in present-day southern Egypt, Sudan, and northern Ethiopia. They became mingled with Semitic tribes dwelling in the same region; hence there is repetition of some of the names in other lines. **Seba** was in Upper Egypt. **Havilah** ("sand-land") could refer to northern and eastern Arabia on the Persian Gulf or the Ethiopian coast. **Sabtah,** ancient Hadhramaut, was on the western shore of the Persian Gulf. **Raamah and Sabtecah** were in southern Arabia.

**Sheba** was in southwest Arabia (cf. the queen of Sheba, 1 Kings 10:1-13), and **Dedan** was in northern Arabia. Some of the people in these ancient kingdoms traced their lineage to Joktan from Shem (Gen. 10:29). So there was a mixing in the settlement.

**10:8-12.** Inserted in this table of nations is the story **of Nimrod.** This is the first "begot" (NIV, **was the father of**) section (cf. comments on v. 1) and forms a major stylistic break from the tribal names preceding it. Attempts to identify

or date Nimrod have proven unsuccessful. Because his name seems to be connected with the verb "to rebel" (*mārad*), tradition has identified him with tyrannical power. He was the founder of the earliest imperial world powers in **Babylon** and **Assyria.** The table simply presents him as **a mighty hunter,** a trait found commonly in Assyrian kings. He was founder of several powerful cities. The **centers** he established became major enemies of Israel.

**10:13-14.** Another "son" of Ham was **Mizraim,** or Egypt. Mizraim developed into (*yālad*) tribes that ranged from North Africa to Crete. The placing of **the Philistines** in this connection represents migration, not lineage (similar to Israel being "from" Egypt). The Philistines migrated **from** their Aegean homelands through Caphtor into the Delta of Egypt and finally to Palestine. This, however, appears to refer to an earlier group of Pelasgo-Philistine tribes, distinct from those in the 13th century B.C.

**10:15-20.** The final Hamite line that was significant for Israel was **the Canaanite** group. Once again the listing employs "begot" (*yālad*) to list the cities and tribes of peoples living in the Promised Land. **Sidon** was the predominant Phoenician city. **Hittites** (*ḥēt*, "Heth") is problematic, but may refer to a pocket of Hittites from the early movements of tribes. The **Jebusites** dwelt in Jerusalem. **Amorites** was a general reference to western Semites, but here points to a smaller ethnic group in the mixed population of Canaan. The other seven Canaanite tribal names are less problematic; they were tribes that settled in Lebanon, Hamath on the Orontes River, and all through the land. Their listing is significant after the passage pronouncing the curse on Canaan (9:25-27).

**10:21-31.** The descendants from **Shem** are recorded last. Elamites, de-

scendants of Shem's first son **Elam,**
dwelt in the highlands east of Babylonia.
**Asshur** was the name of the region and
people of Assyria, where Nimrod, a
Hamite, had founded several cities (v.
11). **Arphaxad** resided northeast of Nineveh. **Lud** was the Ludbu of the Assyrians. Perhaps Lud was a shortened form
of Ludda, possibly another name for
Lydia (in what is now western Turkey).
**Aram** was an ancestor of the Aramean
tribes in the steppes of Mesopotamia. His
descendants (v. 23) are not well known.

The line then traces **Arphaxad** to
**Eber** and his sons, using "begot" (NIV,
**was the father of**) to introduce this
embellishment.

The note on Eber's son **Peleg**—that
**in his time the earth was divided**—
seems to pinpoint the Babel experience
(11:1-9). The verb *pālag* is used in the Old
Testament to describe division into languages. So the Babel event occurred five
generations after the Flood.

The table then turns to trace the
tribes from Peleg's **brother . . . Joktan**
(10:26-29), most of whom **lived** in the
Arabian peninsula. Israel would find ancient blood ties with these 13 tribes of
Joktanites in the desert.

**10:32.** Here is a colophon-type ending, reminding the readers that all families came from Noah, but some were of
special interest for the nation Israel.

2. THE DISPERSION AT BABEL (11:1-9)

This passage explains how the nations came to be scattered across the face
of the ancient world. It is a message of
judgment: what they prided themselves
in became their downfall, and what they
feared the most came on them (cf. Prov.
10:24a).

The account is structured in antithetical parallelism and chiasm. Everything that mankind proposed in the first
half (Gen. 11:3-4) was disposed of in the
second (vv. 5-9), almost an undoing or
reversal of their activity, even to the extent of parallel expressions. The narrative
hinges on the central fact, "the LORD
came down" (v. 5).

One of the problems in this passage
is its connection with chapter 10. At the
beginning of chapter 11 the whole world
is of "one language" and one vocabulary.
But chapter 10 has already divided the
nations according to peoples and

tongues. "Territories," "clans," "nations," and "languages" occur three
times, though not always in the same
order (10:5, 20, 31). Probably 11:1-9 explains how the arrangement in chapter 10
came about. Genesis often goes outside
the chronological order to arrange the
material thematically. The exact chronology is only hinted at in the expression
about Peleg: "In his time the earth was
divided" (10:25).

**11:1-4.** The sin of the Shinarites
(people in **a plain in Shinar**) appears to
be immense pride. They said, **Come, let
us build ourselves a city, with a tower
that reaches to the heavens, so that we
may make a name for ourselves.** This
was open rebellion against God, an independence of God. Humility is often
equated with trust and obedience, and
conversely pride is related to independence and disobedience. Here the people
came together to strengthen themselves
and in pride to make a reputation for
themselves lest they **be scattered over the
face of the whole earth.** This appears to
be in direct opposition to God's command to spread out and fill up the whole
earth (9:1).

**11:5-9.** Their desire to enhance their
unity and strength had potential for the
greatest evil, according to the Lord's
evaluation: **If . . . they have begun to do
this, then nothing they plan to do will
be impossible for them.** Thus what they
would not do in obedience (viz., scatter
over the earth, v. 4) He did for them in
judgment (v. 8).

No doubt Shinar (v. 2) refers to the
area of Babylon, because the passage culminates (v. 9) in a name play: **Babel**
(*bābel*) sounds similar to the verb **confused** (*bālal*). Written Babylonian accounts of the building of the city of Babylon refer to its construction in heaven by
the gods as a celestial city, as an expression of pride (*Enuma Elish* VI, lines 55-
64). These accounts say it was made by
the same process of brick-making described in verse 3, with every brick inscribed with the name of the Babylonian
god Marduk. Also the ziggurat, the step-
like tower believed to have been first
erected in Babylon, was said to have its
top in the heavens (cf. v. 4). This artificial
mountain became the center of worship
in the city, a miniature temple being at
the top of the tower. The Babylonians

took great pride in their building; they boasted of their city as not only impregnable, but also as the heavenly city, *bāb-ili* ("the gate of God").

The account in Genesis views this city as the predominant force in the world, the epitome of ungodly powers, in a word, the "anti-kingdom." Thus the record in verses 1-9 is polemical in that it shows God's absolute power in His swift judgment. What the people considered their greatest strength—unity—He swiftly destroyed by confusing **their language** (v. 7; cf. v. 9). What they considered their greatest fear—scattering (v. 4)—came naturally on them (**the LORD scattered them . . . over all the earth**, v. 8; cf. v. 9). What they desired most—to make a name for themselves (v. 4)—ironically came to pass, for they became known as "Babel." Then **they stopped building the city** and were scattered abroad.

This narrative provides a fitting conclusion for the primeval events. It describes the families of the earth hopelessly scattered throughout the then-known world. There was then no record of a mark for the fugitive (cf. 4:15), no rainbow in the clouds (9:13), no ray of hope or token of grace. This leaves the reader looking for a solution. After a connecting genealogy (11:10-26), that solution is provided: out of the scattered nations God formed one nation which became His channel of blessing. So God was not done with the human race. This chapter simply prepares the reader for His work.

Certainly there is much more here than an account of what happened to explain the table of nations (chap. 10). If Moses simply wanted to trace the development of God's program, he could have done it straightforwardly. But his wordplays, repetitions, characterizations, and moralizations—all with the *tôrâh* ("law"), the ethical standard, in mind—teach a lesson.

Israel was called out of Egypt to be God's theocracy. Israel was to be established as the unified people of God, known around the world. The one simple requirement of them was that they obey. If they would do so, God would establish them firmly. But if they lifted their heads in pride and rebelled against God, they too would be scattered across the face of the earth. As it turned out, Israel followed the same disastrous

course as the Babylonians.

The theme of pride here, then, is important. God puts down those who exalt themselves in pride. Scattering (with its wars and conflicts) is better than unified apostasy. God's plan will be accomplished, if not with man's obedience, then in spite of man's disobedience.

The undoing of Babel was cleverly explained by Zephaniah, whose terms certainly retraced this event, anticipating the great unification in the millennial kingdom, when everyone will speak one pure language and worship in God's holy mountain, being gathered from the nations into which they have been dispersed (Zeph. 3:9-11). The miracle at Pentecost (Acts 2:6-11) was a harbinger of that yet-future event.

### F. The succession from Shem (11:10-26)

**11:10-26.** This genealogical record traces the line from Noah's son **Shem** to **Abram.** Earlier Moses had traced the families of the earth that came from Noah's three sons (chap. 10), explaining how they came to be scattered around the earth (11:1-9). Here he directed attention again to the Shemites.

The genealogy of **Shem** is a "vertical" genealogy designed to show legitimate ancestry. This type was often used in the ancient world to establish the authenticity of a king or a dynasty. The list in verses 10-26 shows the straight line of Shem, who was blessed, to Abram, thus authenticating God's handing down the blessing to Abram.

Some have argued that the names in the genealogical lists in chapters 5 and 11 are contrived, with the names selected (from among others not listed) to show symmetry (e.g., each list ends with reference to three sons, 5:32; 11:26), but this view cannot be substantiated by consistent exegesis. To show "gaps" in the genealogy, one must posit ellipses: "X lived so many years and begot [the line that culminated in] Y." Such ellipses are hard to prove. Moreover, gaps are not possible in two places in the list (Shem was the son of Noah, and Abram was the son of Terah). Thus verses 10-26 seem to present a tight chronology.

The main contribution of this passage is the linking of Abram with the line from Shem. The ancestry of Israel lies here. Interesting archeological material

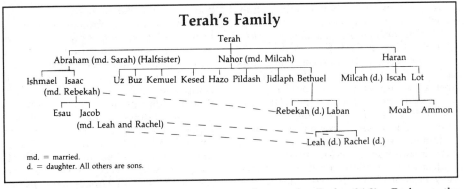

## Terah's Family

Terah

Abraham (md. Sarah) (Halfsister)      Nahor (md. Milcah)      Haran

Ishmael Isaac    Uz Buz Kemuel Kesed Hazo Pildash Jidlaph Bethuel    Milcah (d.) Iscah Lot
(md. Rebekah) —

Esau Jacob                       —Rebekah (d.) Laban      Moab   Ammon
(md. Leah and Rachel) — — — — — — — — —

— — — — — — — — — — —Leah (d.) Rachel (d.)

md. = married.
d. = daughter. All others are sons.

shows that many of these names are preserved in place names around Haran.

Unlike the genealogy in chapter 5, the list in 11:10-26 does not tally the total number of years of each person and does not close each section with the words "and he died." Genesis 5:1–6:8 stresses death before the Flood; 11:10-26 stresses life and expansion even though longevity was declining. The mood of chapter 11 is different, then, from the earlier genealogy. This is because verses 10-26 trace the lineage of Abram—who was to be blessed by God—back to Shem, the son of Noah who was blessed by God (9:26).

## II. The Patriarchal Narratives (11:27–50:26)

### A. The succession from Terah (11:27–25:11)

The story of Abraham, which begins here, is under the heading of the name Terah. As noted earlier (see *Introduction,* "3. The Structure of Genesis") what follows after *tôlᵉdôt* are the "particulars" about the family from Terah—this is what became of Terah in his son Abram. It began with Terah's move to Haran and continued with the move on to Canaan by Abram, the recipient of the promise. Terah's story is completed when Abram finally had a son, who would carry forward the line and the blessing.

1. THE MAKING OF THE COVENANT WITH ABRAM (11:27–15:21)

### a. The journey of Terah (11:27-32)

**11:27-32.** This brief section accounts for the three sons of **Terah,** and their marriages. (See the chart "Terah's Family.") It also accounts for Lot, Abram's nephew, who figures prominently in the narratives about Abram.

Terah was an idolater, worshiping

other gods (Josh. 24:2). Perhaps the home of Terah was originally in **Haran** because many of Terah's ancestors' names are similar to place names in the land of Aram where the city of Haran was located. If so, then the family had migrated southeast approximately 600 miles to **Ur,** capital of Sumer, where Terah's youngest son **Haran** was born and (Gen. 11:28) **died.** God's call to Abram (12:1) initially came in Ur, and the family then moved back to **Haran** and **settled there** (11:31), where Terah **died** (v. 32). Because that was not the Promised Land, Abram moved on to Canaan, where God appeared and confirmed the location.

### b. The call of Abram (12:1-9)

In this narrative the direction of the book changes. This passage records how God called Abram out of a pagan world and made astounding promises to him, promises that later became part of the formal Abrahamic Covenant.

The passage also points up the faith of Abram, and teaches that faith obeys God. Abram was middle-aged, prosperous, settled, and thoroughly pagan. The word of the Lord came to Him—though it is not known exactly how—and he responded by faith and obediently left everything to follow God's plan. That is why he is the epitome of faith in the Bible (cf. Rom. 4:1-3, 16-24; Gal. 3:6-9; Heb. 11:8-19; James 2:21-23).

The religio-historical point of the passage certainly is the call of Abram to found a new nation. Israel would learn by this that her very existence was God's work through a man who responded by faith and left for Canaan. It would be a message to convince Israel of the divine call they were facing, and their need of faith for their move from Egypt to Canaan.

**12:1-3.** Verses 1-3 record God's call to **Abram,** and verses 4-9 record Abram's obedience. The call had two imperatives, each with subsequent promises. The first imperative was to get out (**Leave your country . . . go to the land,** v. 1), and the second imperative was to be a blessing. (The second imperative, in v. 2, is imprecisely rendered in many versions, including the NIV, as a prediction, **you will be a blessing.** But lit., it is, "Be a blessing.") His leaving started a chain of reactions. If Abram would get out of Ur, God would do three things for him, so that he could then be a blessing in the land (the second imperative); and he had to be that blessing so that God would do three more things for him. This symmetry should not be missed, for it strengthens the meaning. Abram's calling had a purpose: his obedience would bring great blessing.

Three promises were based on God's call for Abram to leave his land: (a) **a great nation,** (b) a blessing for Abram, and (c) a great **name** (v. 2). These promises would enable him to "be a blessing" (the second imperative, v. 2). Based on this obedience were God's three promises to: (a) **bless those who** blessed him, (b) **curse** anyone who would treat him lightly, and (c) bless the families of the **earth** through him (v. 3). To bless or curse Abram was to bless or curse Abram's God. Unfortunately God often had to use other nations to discipline His people because, far from being a blessing to the world, they were usually disobedient. The third promise takes on its greatest fulfillment in the fact that Jesus Christ became the means of blessing to the world (Gal. 3:8, 16; cf. Rom. 9:5).

The idea of faith is stressed in these passages. Abram was told to leave several things—his "country," his **people,** and his **father's household** (Gen. 12:1). But he was told nothing about the land to which he must go. His departure required an unparalleled act of faith.

The themes of blessing and cursing are heightened here. In fact this is the central passage of the Book of Genesis. Here begins the program that was so desperately needed in chapters 1–11 (a purpose of which was to show that this blessing was needed). This was the call; Abram responded to it by faith. The ensuing promises were formulated later, under covenant conditions (15:8-21).

**12:4-9.** The narrative reports simply that **Abram** obeyed. His obedience is recounted in two ways, corresponding to the two imperatives in verse 2. He **left** (v. 4), and he was a blessing (vv. 5-9). **In Haran** many **people** (lit., "souls") were **acquired** by **Abram** and his family (v. 5). This "getting of souls" may refer to proselytizing, that is, to Abram's influence on some Haranites to follow Yahweh. Then in **the land of Canaan** he built altars **at Shechem** (v. 6) and **east of Bethel** (v. 8). At this second location he **called on the name of the Lord,** that is, he made proclamation of Yahweh by name (cf. 21:33; 26:25). Luther translated this verb "preached"; he was not far off. God thus had a witness in the midst of **the Canaanites,** who **were then in the land.** In fact the mention **of the great tree of Moreh** (lit., "teacher") is significant in connection with this. The Canaanites had shrines in groves of oak trees, and Moreh may have been one of their cult centers.

At Shechem, Yahweh **appeared to Abram** to confirm His promise and to reward Abram's faith: **To your offspring I will give this land** (12:7). Abram arrived in the land and God showed it to him. But it would be given to his descendants, not to him. Indeed, when Abram died his only real estate was a cave he had bought for his family's burials (23:17-20). After God confirmed His promise, **Abram** abode in the land, waiting for the promise. But the Canaanites had all the good, fertile land; **Abram** had to journey by stages **toward the** great and terrible **Negev** (12:9), a barren desert south of Canaan.

For Israel the call of their great patriarch demonstrated that their promises were from God, promises of a great nation, a land, divine blessing, and sovereign protection. Yahweh's appearance and confirmation (v. 7) proved that Canaan was their destiny. But God demanded a response by faith if this generation were to share in those promised blessings. Faith takes God at His word and obeys Him.

*c. The sojourn in Egypt (12:10-20)*

This sojourn has much more to it than a simple lesson in honesty—though the story certainly warns against the folly

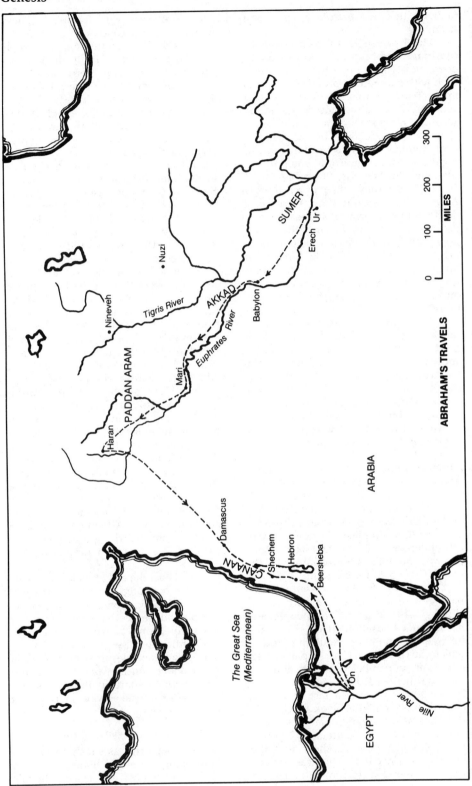

ABRAHAM'S TRAVELS

of deceit. The claim that she is "my sister" occurs three times in the patriarchal narratives (v. 13; 20:2; 26:7). Critics say these occasions refer to the same event. However, in the second instance Abram explained that this was their policy wherever they went (20:13) so it is not surprising that he repeated this lie.

One cannot miss the deliberate parallelism between this sojourn of Abram in Egypt and the later event in the life of the nation in bondage in Egypt. The motifs are remarkably similar: the famine in the land (12:10; 47:13), the descent to Egypt to sojourn (12:10; 47:27), the attempt to kill the males but save the females (12:12; Ex. 1:22), the plagues on Egypt (Gen. 12:17; Ex. 7:14–11:10), the spoiling of Egypt (Gen. 12:16; Ex. 12:35-36), the deliverance (Gen. 12:19; Ex. 15), and the ascent to the Negev (Gen. 13:1; Num. 13:17, 22). The great deliverance out of bondage that Israel experienced was thus already accomplished in her ancestor, and probably was a source of comfort and encouragement to them. God was doing more than promise deliverance for the future nation; it was as if in anticipation He acted out their deliverance in Abram.

In relation to the message of the book, Genesis 12:10-20 is significantly placed right after Abram's call and obedience. In this story Abram was not walking by faith as he had been in the beginning, but God had made promises to him and would keep them. Abram was not the only patriarch who had to be rescued rather ingloriously from such difficulties.

**12:10-13.** Abram's scheme, born out of fear, turned against him, and God's promise to him was thrown into jeopardy. Only God could rescue **his wife** so that the promise to Abram might be fulfilled. **Abram,** faced with **a famine,** decided to go **to Egypt** to sojourn (a temporary stay—**to live there for a while**—without plans to settle). Other famines in Palestine are mentioned in 26:1 and 41:56. One cannot fault him for this, except that there is no indication Abram was operating in faith. The bedouin scheme he concocted was to speak a half truth about his sister-wife. This was a subtle way to salve his own conscience. She was indeed his **sister** (actually a half-sister; cf. 20:12), so he conveyed to the

Egyptians only what he wanted them to know. His motive was undoubtedly based on fratriarchical society laws (cf. Laban, 24:29-61). In enemy territory a husband could be killed for **his wife.** But if Abram were known as her brother, someone wanting her would have to make marriage arrangements with him, which would possibly give him time to react in his own interest.

**12:14-16.** The ironic twist to the story came when someone wanted Sarai, someone who need not bargain for her, namely, **Pharaoh.** The very words of **Abram** ("so that I will be treated well," v. 13) came back on him for Pharaoh **treated Abram well** because of **beautiful** Sarai, and **Abram** got very wealthy. (Cf. a later Pharaoh's good treatment of Abraham's great-grandson Joseph, 41:41-43, and of Abraham's grandson Jacob, 45:16-20.) But this bound **Abram** to an obligation from which he was not able to deliver himself. His scheme nearly lost him his wife, and without Sarai his promised blessing would be doomed.

**12:17-20.** But the LORD plagued residents of the Egyptian palace with **serious diseases.** Divine intervention alone could deliver **Sarai** from Pharaoh's harem unharmed. With that deliverance came a royal rebuke (vv. 18-19) and expulsion from the country (v. 20). The Egyptians were a superstitious people, and any such plague would be ominous to them. Pharaoh's **orders** for **Abram** to leave (**Take her and go!**) parallel the words of God's call to Abram ("Leave your country . . . and go"; v. 1), but Pharaoh's words were said in dishonor.

Certainly one can see in this story how God delivered the patriarchal family from the Egyptians by means of plagues, and how that mirrored the future Exodus experience. But this first deliverance was made necessary because of Abram's deception. In spite of the trouble Abram caused for himself, God was faithful to His word and did not let the foolishness of this man throw His plan into jeopardy. Abram probably felt that the easiest way *out of* danger was to manipulate deceptively. But such scheming put him *in* danger and jeopardized the promise. God's servants should trust Him completely and not resort to self-directed schemes.

At first Abram prospered as a result

of his deception. It is true that he got rich, but all those riches could have diverted him from retaining Sarai, the one person who was needed for fulfilling the promise. Moreover, it is generally assumed that Hagar was acquired during this Egyptian stay. In "giving away" his wife, Sarai, Abram may have acquired Hagar, who later became his slave-wife (16:1-2).

Moses would have his readers learn of God's gracious protection of His plan through divine intervention and deliverance. He would also have them learn of the folly of trying to deliver themselves from difficulties by means of deceptive schemes.

*d. The separation from Lot (chap. 13)*

Faced with a problem of survival because of their many possessions (v. 6) and ensuing strife (v. 7), sheiks Abram and Lot had to separate, one going one way and the other another. One might have expected that Abram, the recipient of God's promise, would have exercised his right and chosen first. But he magnanimously offered the first choice to Lot. Lot made his choice purely on the human level, satisfying himself with the fat of the land. Abram's decision to let Lot choose first was undoubtedly a choice made by faith, with Abram not looking on things temporal, but on things spiritual, that is, God's promise.

Chapter 13 shows how faith solves strife. One might say that generosity is a sign of faith in God's promises, for faith does not selfishly seek one's own desires, but is generous, magnanimous, and self-denying.

**13:1-7.** Verses 1-4 provide the setting for the story, but that setting is a story in itself. It is one of conflict in the midst of God's blessings. The first few verses stress the return of **Abram** to **the place** where he had been at the beginning. Here one cannot help but see the emphasis placed on **earlier** and **first** ("formerly") in describing his return to the land (vv. 3-4). Back in the land, Abram renewed his worship and proclamation of **the LORD** (*Yahweh*) at **an altar** (cf. 12:8).

Rather significant to this section is the stress on the wealth of **Abram** (13:2, **very wealthy in livestock and in silver and gold**) and on that of **Lot** who traveled with him (v. 5, **flocks and herds and tents**). They had both greatly prospered. **Lot** specifically is singled out as having tents, a fact to be developed later.

But in the midst of the land, with **Canaanites and Perizzites** around them, **quarreling** broke out (v. 7). (The Perizzites were one of several tribes living in Palestine, usually listed with the Canaanites; cf. 34:30; Deut. 7:1; Jud. 1:4; 3:5.) **The land could not** sustain Abram and Lot dwelling **together,** because the Canaanites held the best parts, so these two men's servants had to scrap for water and food in the rest. When faced with this dilemma, a strife (*rîḇ*) broke out. (This Heb. word was later used to describe legal controversy in Israel.)

**13:8-13.** Abram's solution to the strife was magnanimously to give **Lot** the first choice. Here is irony, for one might expect **Abram** to cling to what was promised to him and tell Lot to go find his own place.

Abram's cautionary note—**Let's not have any quarreling** (*merîḇâh,* related to the word *rîḇ*)—must have struck a responsive note in the hearts of Israel when later they read this in conjunction with what happened at Meribah (Ex. 17:1-7). In that wilderness there was no water to drink and the people strove with Yahweh so that Moses smote the rock. Thereafter, Massa ("testing") and Meribah ("quarreling") became ominous names because the people out of unbelief provoked Yahweh and were sent to wander in the wilderness until they died (Ps. 95:8-10). Their selfishness exhibited unbelief (Ps. 95:10) so that they did not enter the land (Ps. 95:11). Here too Lot's choice was totally selfish; so he left Abram and went off toward **Sodom** (Gen. 13:12). God's warning (Ps. 95:8-11) was almost like Abram's warning (Gen. 13:8).

The motivation for this concern must not be missed—they were **brothers,** that is, relatives (v. 8). Their common bond shared over such a long period of time was to **Abram** something worth saving. To keep that intact, separation seemed the only possibility.

The **land** again became prominent. Abram offered Lot the choice of the whole land that rightfully belonged to him, Abram. **Lot looked up** (lit., "lifted up [*nāśā'*] his eyes") **and saw** (*rā'âh*); cf. v.

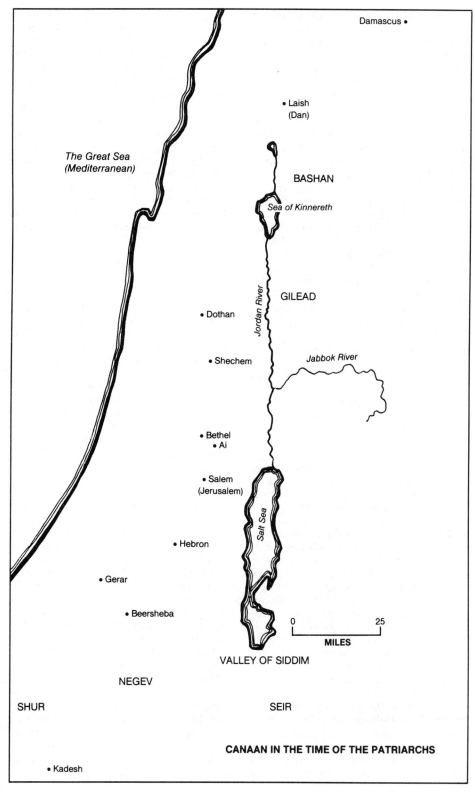

**CANAAN IN THE TIME OF THE PATRIARCHS**

14) **the whole plain** (circle) **of the Jordan** Valley. This valley was lush and fruitful, **well watered, like the garden of the LORD.** (**Zoar** was a small town in the plain to which Lot and his family would flee, 19:18-22. Before that it was called Bela, 14:2, 8.) This may be a solemn reminder of the first look on such a garden land with intent desire (3:6). But certainly an ominous note is struck in the temporal clause—**before the LORD destroyed Sodom and Gomorrah**—as if to say that what appealed to **Lot** was to be short-lived. Without a concern for Abram, Lot made the choice, the greatest mistake of his life.

Lot **pitched his tents** next to **Sodom,** where **the men** were **wicked . . . sinning greatly** before the **LORD.** Later chapter 19 clarifies their wickedness.

**13:14-18.** This third section in this chapter provides the solace: Yahweh confirms His promise. The strong break in the narrative is marked by (lit.) "Now Yahweh. . . ." Verses 14-17 explain why **Abram** could give **Lot** the choice of all the land—Abram had the sure promise of God. He had the sense that in God he had abundant possession. Knowing that God's promise was genuine, Abram was indifferent to what Lot would choose. A person who has the promise of God's provision does not have to cling to things.

In verses 14-17 Abram is contrasted with Lot. Lot had been active in taking what he thought was best. Now Yahweh reworded the ideas, instructing Abram with several commands. Abram was told to **lift up** (*nāśā'*) his **eyes . . . and look** (*rā'âh*, v. 14; cf. v. 10), which Lot did on his own. Abram was waiting for God to **give** him the land; Lot just took it. God restated that He would give **the land** to Abram as a possession. Better that God give it than that someone take it. God also told Abram his descendants would be as numerous as **the dust of the earth** (cf. 22:17; 28:14). He then was invited by God to **walk through . . . the land** and see his possession. Chapter 13 closes the way it began, with Abram settling down (this time **near the great trees of Mamre;** cf. 14:13, **at Hebron,** 22 miles south of Jerusalem) and making **an altar to** Yahweh.

Hardly any other chapter in the Bible describes faith so marvelously. Here was the patriarch as a genuine believer in and worshiper of Yahweh—whose faith functioned in a conflict. Lot, walking by sight, chose on the basis of what appealed to him. His choice was self-seeking and self-gratifying. But such a choice became dangerous and short-lived, for all was not as it appeared to be on the surface. **Abram,** on the other hand, walking by faith, generously let Lot choose first. Abram was unselfish, trusting God. He had learned that it was not by his own plan that he would come into the possession, or by jealously guarding what was his. He acted righteously and generously. One who believes that God is pledged to provide for him is not greedy, anxious, or covetous.

*e. The victory over the Eastern kings (14:1-16)*

The record of the battle of the four kings against the five is interesting, for it is part of the outworking of God's promise to make Abram great and to bless those who blessed him and curse those who cursed him (12:3). Chapter 14 describes a typical "international" skirmish in the ancient world in which powerful nations formed a coalition to plunder and subjugate areas near the border of the land promised to Abram.

**14:1-12.** In an effort to put down a rebellion (v. 4), **four** powerful Eastern **kings** invaded the Jordan Valley near **the Salt Sea,** that is, the Dead Sea (v. 3), defeating all the forces in the region (vv. 5-7), plundering the **five** Jordanian kings (vv. 8-11), and taking Lot captive (v. 12).

Archeology is most helpful in understanding the background of this chapter. The kings have not been identified, but their names fit the types from the ancient Near East of this period, especially the Mesopotamian kings. (The name Arriyuk, similar to **Arioch,** was found at Mari; **Kedorlaomer** fits the name Kudur; and Tudhalia, mindful of **Tidal,** is attested in early Hittite literature.) Moreover, the gathering of city-states ("nations") in military service was common.

The locations of many of the areas and cities are also now known. **Shinar** (cf. 10:10) is another name for what later became known as Babylonia. **Elam** (cf. 10:22) was east of Shinar. But the locations of **Ellasar** and **Goiim** remain unknown. **Sodom . . . Gomorrah . . .**

**Admah . . . Zeboiim** and **Bela (that is, Zoar;** cf. 19:22)—the cities of the five kings who rebelled against **Kedor-laomer**—were near the Salt (Dead) Sea. **Ashteroth** and **Karnaim** (14:5) were in Hauran, ancient Bashan, east of the Sea of Kinnereth. **Ham** was in eastern Gilead, south of Bashan. **Shaveh Kiriathaim** was east of the Dead Sea, and **the hill country of Seir** was southeast of the Dead Sea, in the area later known as Edom. **El Paran** was modern Elat, on the Gulf of Aqaba. **Kadesh** and **Tamar** were southwest of the Dead Sea. The route of the conquerors was well known in antiquity, being designated as "the king's highway" (Num. 20:17; 21:22). Those **four kings—Kedorlaomer . . . Tidal . . . Amraphel,** and **Arioch** (Gen. 14:9)—went down the eastern side of the Jordan, turned around in the Arabah (the rift valley south of the Dead Sea), went up to Kadesh, over to Tamar, and then to the region of **Sodom and Gomorrah** in the **Valley of Siddim** (vv. 8, 10). The five cities of the plain apparently were close together at the southern end of the valley (Unger, *Archaeology and the Old Testament*, pp. 114-8). The four kings looted Sodom and Gomorrah and captured Lot.

**14:13-16.** Hearing of the invasion and of the capture of Lot, **Abram** mustered his **318 trained men** and together with his allies (v. 13) pursued and defeated the invaders in a night attack. He pursued them all the way to **Dan,** the future northern border of the Promised Land (140 miles from Abram's home in Hebron). Dan was then named Leshem (Josh. 19:47) or Laish (Jud. 18:29). **During the night** Abram pursued them on to **Hobah,** another 100 miles north of Dan, and **brought back . . . Lot and his possessions** and family **and other** captives. This was a striking victory for the patriarch over four leading kings who had previously conquered such an extensive portion of Transjordania and the area south of the Dead Sea.

**Abram the Hebrew** (*'ibrî,* Gen. 14:13) was now recognized as a clan leader. This is the first occurrence in the Bible of the word "Hebrew." Though the term "Hebrew" is not to be equated with the later group of marauding soldiers known as the "Habiru," it may be etymologically related. In fact Abram's military activity in this chapter shows that this

meaningful designation fits. He was thus a force to be reckoned with among the nations.

Lot's dwelling in Sodom was the means of Abram's being drawn into the conflict. Abram was dwelling in Hebron (13:18), but had a covenant with **Mamre the Amorite** and his brothers **Eshcol and Aner** (14:13; cf. v. 24). Here this covenant worked in favor of Abram, for these Amorites, who allowed him to dwell with them, had to fight with him. When the term "Amorite" is used alone, it refers to western Semitic peoples living in Transjordanian kingdoms and the hill country of Palestine. These Amorites were a small ethnic group, not the large wave of Amorites who poured into both ancient Sumer and the West.

Abram was the general, and the victory was attributed to him (v. 17). But this does not fully explain the triumph. Later Melchizedek attributed the victory to God as part of God's blessing on the patriarch (v. 20). God was working through the life of Abram in accord with His promise. When invaders plundered the land and stole **his** troublesome **relative,** Abram instinctively sprang into action.

Israel would thus learn that God would give His Chosen People victory over enemies that plundered the Promised Land. This must have encouraged God's people in the times of the Judges and in later invasions. Of course faith in and obedience to God were prerequisites to victory.

In the Old Testament, warfare was actual and physical; but it was also spiritually significant in relationship to faith. According to the New Testament, a Christian's battle and weapons are spiritual, and God's promises are eternal. Using military figures of speech, Paul portrayed Christ's death as a victory (Eph. 4:8) in which He conquered sin, death, and the grave. Christ's gifts are spiritual gifts for His servants to use in service. With these spiritual gifts and armed with spiritual weapons, Christians are to champion righteousness, truth, and equity (Eph. 6:10-19). God gives His people victory over the world in accord with His promises to bless and to curse, using His servants who know His high calling and who can use the weapons of spiritual warfare with skill.

*f. The blessing by Melchizedek (14:17-24)*

**14:17-21.** This is one of the most fascinating encounters in the Old Testament. Two kings met **Abram** on his return from the battle, and they could not possibly have been more different. In contrast with the wicked city of **Sodom** and its ruler Bera (v. 2), who also was undoubtedly wicked, was **Melchizedek king of Salem** (i.e., Jerusalem, Ps. 76:2), **a priest of God Most High** (Gen. 14:18). Melchizedek's name (which means "king of righteousness") suggests a righteous ruler who was God's representative. (Some Bible students believe Melchizedek was a theophany, an appearance of the preincarnate Christ.)

Melchizedek is the only person whom Abram recognized as his spiritual superior. **Abram** accepted blessing from him (v. 19), and Abram paid him **a 10th** (a tithe) of all he had (v. 20). **Abram** did this deliberately, in full awareness of what he was doing. It shows how unthreatened and humble Abram was, even after a victory. He recognized that God's revelation was not limited to him. While the reader's attention is focused on Abram carrying the whole spiritual hope of the world, there emerged out of an obscure Canaanite valley a man nearer to God than Abram was, who **blessed Abram.** That valley was **the Valley of Shaveh** (v. 17), possibly the Kidron Valley near Jerusalem (cf. 2 Sam. 18:18).

The arrangement of Abram's confrontation is chiastic: (*a*) **the king of Sodom** met Abram (Gen. 14:17), (*b*) the king of Salem met Abram (v. 18), (*b'*) the king of Salem blessed Abram (vv. 19-20), (*a'*) **the king of Sodom** offered Abram a deal (v. 21). The fact that the offer from the king of Sodom came after Melchizedek's blessing helped Abram keep things in perspective.

**14:22-24.** **Abram** swore before **the Lord, God Most High, Creator of heaven and earth** (cf. v. 19), that he would take **nothing** that belonged to Sodom, lest **the king of Sodom** take credit for making **Abram rich.**

This incident was a test of Abram's faith after a great victory. Bera, Sodom's king, offered a most appealing deal. But Abram, knowing what he did about the king of Sodom, felt that keeping Sodom's loot which he captured would make him

subject to Bera. He wanted something far more enduring than possessions and wealth; he wanted the fulfillment of God's miraculous and enduring promise. Faith looks beyond the riches of this world to the grander prospects God has in store.

Abram knew that he would become more prosperous, and he knew who was blessing him. He intended to receive everything from God and **not even a thread** from Sodom. Obedient believers frame their lives so that for all success, joy, comfort, and prosperity they depend on God—but their faith is like Abram's, deeply rooted and growing stronger rather than brief and weak. The king of Sodom was obviously a wicked man over a wicked empire; Abram discerned that dealing with him might be dangerous. Abram could have reasoned that God was seeking to bless him by means of this offer. But he could not bring himself to equate the blessing of God with the best that Sodom had to offer.

Melchizedek is an important figure in the Bible. Preceding Abram, he was not a Levitical priest. When David, the first Israelite king to sit on Melchizedek's throne, prophesied that his great Descendant, the Messiah, would be a priest forever after the order of Melchizedek (Ps. 110:4), David looked beyond the Levitical priesthood which would be done away with. The Book of Hebrews demonstrates how Jesus Christ in His death fulfilled the Levitical order and began a better high priesthood. In referring to Melchizedek as the perfect type of Christ, the writer of Hebrews capitalized on Melchizedek's anonymity: in a book (Gen.) filled with genealogies and ancestral notations, this man appeared without family records (Heb. 7:3). Melchizedek is remembered as a high priest. Because Abram paid tithes to Melchizedek, the order of Melchizedek is superior to Levi, who descended from Abram (Heb. 7:4-10).

*g. The cutting of the covenant (chap. 15)*

After Abram's rescue of Lot and blessing from Melchizedek, the Lord formally made a covenant with Abram, thereby confirming the promise given earlier (12:2-3). God warned, however, that there would be a long period of enslavement (15:13).

**15:1-3.** Before God made the covenant, He set aside Abram's fear and doubt by a word of assurance: **Do not be afraid. I am your Shield.** When **the LORD** promised **Abram** that his **reward** would be **great,** the patriarch immediately asked **what** he would receive since he was **childless.** This shows his faith. His vision was not blinded by Bera's offer (14:22-24); **Abram** still had only one hope, the original promise God had given (12:2-3). His concern was expressed by a marvelous word play on his household servant's origin: this **Eliezer of Damascus** (*Dammeśeq*) is the possessor-heir (*ben meśeq,* lit., "son of possession") of **my estate** (15:2). It is as if Abram was stressing to God that "the omen is in the nomen"—a mere **servant** would become his **heir.**

**15:4-6.** But **the LORD** strongly answered, **This man** (not even using Eliezer's name) **will not be your heir.** Instead **a son coming from** Abram's **own body** would be his **heir.** God then showed Abram **the stars,** pointing out that Abram's **offspring** would be just as innumerable (cf. 22:17; 26:4). The word by which God created the stars would also guarantee Abram's seed.

**Abram believed** (lit., "believed in") **the LORD and He credited . . . to him . . . righteousness.** This foundational truth is repeated three times in the New Testament (Rom. 4:3; Gal. 3:6; James 2:23) to show that righteousness is reckoned in return for faith.

Genesis 15:6 provides an important note, but it does not pinpoint Abram's conversion. That occurred years earlier when he left Ur. (The form of the Heb. word for "believed" shows that his faith did *not* begin after the events recorded in vv. 1-5.) Abram's faith is recorded here because it is foundational for making the covenant. The Abrahamic Covenant did not give Abram redemption; it was a covenant made with Abram who had already believed and to whom righteousness had already been imputed. The Bible clearly teaches that in all ages imputed righteousness (i.e., salvation) comes by faith.

**15:7-10.** In the solemn ceremony in which **the LORD** made a binding covenant with **Abram,** God assured him of the ultimate fulfillment of His promises (vv. 7, 18-21). God also declared that there would be a long 400-year period of enslavement for Abram's descendants (vv. 13-16).

Obeying God's instructions, **Abram** severed in **half** (v. 10) three animals— **a heifer, a goat, and a ram** (v. 9)— and also brought **a dove and a young pigeon.**

**15:11-16.** Just then sudden horror must have come on **Abram,** for unclean **birds of prey** swooped **down on** the offering animals—obviously an evil omen. God's announcement of Israel's enslavement (vv. 13-14) clarified the meaning of the attacking birds. The word **mistreated** (*'ānâh,* v. 13; cf. 16:6) is the same word used in Exodus 1:11-12 to describe Egypt's oppression of Israel. Egypt, like birds of prey, opposed the covenant, but ultimately the covenant will be fulfilled. Later, in Moses' day when the Israelites were in Egypt, they could count the years and see that **400 years** had elapsed (from the time of Jacob's entry into Egypt in 1876 B.C.; cf. the chart "Chronology of the Patriarchs," near Gen. 47:28-31) and their time of deliverance from slavery was at hand (**they will come out**). Exodus 12:40 and Galatians 3:17 state that the Egyptian bondage was 430 years (from 1876 to 1446). Apparently, then, Genesis 15:13 and Acts 7:6, with their references to 400 years, are using rounded figures (see comments on Acts 7:6 and Gal. 3:17).

God is just, and wished to permit **the sin of the Amorites** to be **full** before He would judge them (Gen. 15:16). (See comments on the Amorites at 14:13-16.) God would tolerate their sins until Israel under Joshua conquered Palestine. Thus the fulfillment of the promises to Abram involves a retributive judgment on the inhabitants of the land of Canaan. Abram's seed would get the land—but not one hour before absolute justice required it. God had much to do before fulfilling His promise—including disciplining His nation to make it fit for receiving the promise. Abram's seeing this in advance was horrible—like watching birds of prey.

**15:17-21.** Then after sunset God revealed Himself in connection with the image of an oven (**smoking fire pot**) and a **torch,** two elements that were connected with sacrificial ritual in the ancient world. These images are part of the "burning" motif that describes God's zeal and judgment in the world. Fire represents the consuming, cleansing zeal of Yahweh as well as His unapproachable holiness, which are interrelated (cf. Isa. 6:3-7). In the **darkness** (Gen. 15:17) **Abram** saw nothing else in the vision except these fiery elements that **passed between the pieces** of the slaughtered animals. Thus the holy God was zealous to judge the nations and to fulfill His covenantal promises to Israel. He came down and **made** (lit, "cut") a formal treaty (**a covenant**) **with Abram** (the Abrahamic Covenant). Since God could "swear" (confirm the covenant) by none greater, "He swore by Himself" (Heb. 6:13). In other words this was a unilateral covenant. So its promises are absolutely sure.

God even specified the geographical boundaries of Israel's land—**from the river of Egypt** (Wadi el-Arish, not the Nile River) **to the great river, the Euphrates.** Israel has never possessed this land in its entirety, but she will when Christ returns to reign as Messiah. The Canaanite tribes listed (Gen. 15:19-21) were dispossessed later in the Conquest.

For Abram God's message was clear: in spite of the prospects of death and suffering (enslavement in bondage), his descendants would receive the promises, for God assured it. So Israel could be encouraged by this at the Exodus as well as in subsequent times of distress, even during the Babylonian Captivity. God's solemn covenant assures the Chosen People of the ultimate fulfillment of His promises in spite of their times of death and suffering.

Israel would also notice the parallel touch at the beginning of this narrative. (Cf. "I am the LORD [*Yahweh*] who brought you out of Ur," v. 7, with Ex. 20:2: "I am the LORD [*Yahweh*] your God who brought you out of Egypt.") This assured Israel that in spite of opposition and bondage God would judge their enslavers and fulfill His promises.

This passage encourages New Testament believers as well. God affirms solemnly that He will fulfill His promises concerning salvation and all the blessings that pertain to that life (cf. 2 Peter 1:3-4); despite opposition, suffering, and even death, He keeps His promises.

## 2. THE PROVISION OF THE PROMISED SEED FOR ABRAHAM WHOSE FAITH WAS DEVELOPED BY TESTING (16:1–22:19)

This cycle of narratives presents the struggle Abram the patriarch underwent while he was waiting for God's promises to be fulfilled. At times he stumbled, but eventually his faith was proved.

### a. The lack of faith and the birth of Ishmael (chap. 16)

As Abram's faith was developed and tested, delay was seen in the fulfilling of God's promise. In moments of weakness there are suggestions of alternative plans—plans not characterized by faith. Human efforts to assist in the fulfilling of divine promises complicated the matter. Later Israel too would learn that when she tried to do things without God, those things would get complicated.

**16:1-6. Sarai** was barren so by all human calculations the heir of the promise could not come through her at all. This set in motion some dubious activities by Abram and Sarai. **Abram** learned, however, that God's promise was not to be fulfilled in this way.

In the legal custom of that day a barren woman could give her maid to **her husband** as a **wife,** and the child born of that union was regarded as the first wife's child. If the husband said to the slave-wife's son, "You are my son," then he was the adopted son and heir. So Sarai's suggestion was unobjectionable according to the customs of that time. But God often repudiates social customs.

Sarai's plan, with Abram's approval, turned sour, however, after the **Egyptian** slave girl, **Hagar,** became **pregnant.** Hagar **began to despise** Sarai. Both women may have wondered what would become of Abram's seed. Would Hagar have it? Because of the conflict between the women, **Sarai** blamed **Abram** for the problem. He told her to handle it in **whatever** way she wished. Sarai then **mistreated** ('*ānâh*; see comment on this word in 15:13) **Hagar so** that **she fled** (16:6).

Now Abram, who like Adam followed the wrong advice of his wife (3:17), was caught weakly in the middle.

**16:7-16.** The story has both a dark side (Sarai mistreated her maidservant) and a bright side (**the Angel of the LORD** communicated with **Hagar** in **the desert**).

There is no problem seeing what went wrong in the dark side of the story. When the way of faith (which involves patient waiting) was abandoned and the way of human calculation was taken, Abram was caught up in a chain of causes and effects that would trouble him for years to come. (Ishmael became the ancestor of the Arabs, who are still hostile to the Jews.)

The Angel of the Lord **found** the maidservant in the desert at **a spring . . . beside the road to Shur** (cf. 25:18) on the way to her homeland, Egypt. This is the first reference in the Old Testament to "the Angel of the LORD" (lit., "the Angel of Yahweh"). This Angel is identified with Yahweh in 16:13, as well as in 22:11-12; 31:11, 13; 48:16; Judges 6:11, 16, 22; 13:22-23; Zechariah 3:1-2. And yet the Angel is distinct from Yahweh (Gen. 24:7; 2 Sam. 24:16; Zech. 1:12). Thus "the Angel of the LORD" may refer to a theophany of the preincarnate Christ (cf. Gen. 18:1-2; 19:1; Num. 22:22; Jud. 2:1-4; 5:23; Zech. 12:8).

After asking **Hagar** two questions (**Where have you come from, and where are you going?**) God gave her two sure words: one was hortatory—return **and submit** (Gen. 16:9), and the other was promissory—she would give birth to a boy (vv. 10-12). She called God **the One who sees me** (v. 13), and to commemorate the event she named the well at that (unknown) location **Beer Lahai Roi** ("well of the living One who sees me"; cf. 24:62; 25:11).

Often in Genesis popular etymologies capture the message. These are rhetorical devices that draw from the account the explanation of names. Thus the name was a mnemonic device for remembering the events and their significance. In this passage two popular etymologies form not only the climax of the section but the point of the whole unit. God Himself named the boy **Ishmael,** which He then explained: **for the LORD has heard of your misery** (16:11). Clearly He meant this primarily for Hagar, but it was also meant for Abram and Sarai.

The other naming was Hagar's referring to God as "the One who sees" after her, that is, looks out for her. So in these two names is a world of theology: God hears and God sees. This spot would afterward become holy, a place where God

could be found providing for and hearing the cries of His people.

The names provide the message: God spoke in direct revelation, and Hagar responded in faith. God *sees* distress and affliction, and He *hears*. Sarai should have known this. Since God knew Sarai was barren, she should have cried out to the Lord. Instead she had to learn a lesson the hard way—from the experience of a despised slave-wife who, ironically, came back with a faith experience. How **Abram** must have been rebuked when **Hagar** said God told her to name her son **Ishmael,** "God hears."

In great distress (here Sarai's barrenness) one must turn to the Lord because He hears the afflicted, sees them in their need, and will miraculously fulfill His promises. They cannot be turned by human intervention. Giving children to the barren is God's work (Ps. 113:9). Later Leah also knew that God heard her affliction, for she named Reuben and Simeon to reflect that (Gen. 29:32-33). Sarai still had a way to go in her faith.

So God provided for the pregnant woman who was thrust out into the desert. God promised that Hagar would be a matriarch—her son would become the father of a great tribe of **wild,** hostile people (cf. 25:18), living in the Arabian desert (25:12-18). But they would not be the promised seed; they would only complicate matters. Sarai's sin caused the origin of the Ishmaelites, a harvest that is still being reaped. In fact Joseph, Sarai's great-grandson, was later taken to Egypt by the Ishmaelites (37:28).

The lesson was clear for Sarai, Abram, Hagar, Israel, and for Christians: God's servants are to trust His Word and to wait for its fulfillment, enduring patiently till the end. It becomes increasingly clear in Genesis that any person or any nation that owes its existence to divine election should live by faith. Human efforts will not help. But the good news for God's people is that the living God sees and hears.

*b. The promise of a seed confirmed by a name and a sign (chap. 17)*

This chapter records (a) God's assurance of His promises by changing the names of Abram (vv. 1-8) and Sarai (vv. 15-18), (b) God's instituting circumcision as the sign of the covenant (vv. 9-14), (c)

God's sure word on the promises' fulfillment through Sarah (vv. 19-22), and (d) Abraham's compliance (vv. 23-27).

God is dominant in the first three sections: He promised Abram a son and named him Isaac, He renamed Abram and Sarai to reflect that promise, and He instituted the sign.

**17:1-8.** God's promises to **Abram** grew more and more magnificent. As **God Almighty,** He was fully capable of accomplishing all His promises. (This is the first OT occurrence of the title "God Almighty" [*'ēl šadday*], which is used several times in Gen. [17:1; 28:3; 35:11; 43:14; 48:3; cf. 49:25]. Some scholars suggest that *šadday* is related to the Akk. word *šadû* that means breast or mountain or both. [Some words describing parts of the body were also used for geographical descriptions; e.g., "mouth" of a river, "foot" of a mountain.] So *šadday,* when used of God, refers either to His ability to supply abundantly ["the Abundant One"] or to His majestic strength ["the Almighty One"].) Now, **God said . . . you will be the father of many nations** (17:4; cf. "a great nation," 12:2), and **kings will come from you** (17:6; cf. v. 16). And, God said, the **covenant** will be **everlasting** (v. 7). Also the **land of Canaan,** which Abram would possess (15:7), would be **an everlasting possession** of Abram's descendants.

The patriarch's name change was crucial. The name **Abram** (17:5), meaning "exalted father," harked *back* to Terah (11:27) and implied that Abram came from royal lineage. But in Hebrew the name **Abraham** (*'abrāhâm*) sounds similar to "**father of** a multitude" (*'ab hāmôn*) of **nations** (17:4-5). His new name implied a look *ahead* to his **descendants.**

One can well imagine that Abram was hurt by the suppressed smiles on the faces of his men when he told them to call him Abraham, meaning the father of a multitude of nations—**when** he was **99 years old** (vv. 1, 24). Yet Abraham knew that God had not deceived him. His new name and his wife's new name were perpetual reminders of God's sure word. Every time someone addressed him he would recall God's promise, until finally Isaac, the child of promise, would call him "abba" (father).

**17:9-14.** The other confirming sign (cf. "confirm" in v. 2) was circumcision.

This one applied to all males who shared the promise. Circumcision was practiced elsewhere in the ancient Near East, but here it achieved a new meaning. It too would remind **Abraham** and his **descendants** of the **everlasting covenant** (v. 13; cf. vv. 7, 19). By this symbol God impressed them with the impurity of nature and with dependence on God for the production of all life. They would recognize and remember: (a) that native impurity must be laid aside, especially in marriage, and (b) that human nature is unable to generate the promised seed. They must be loyal to the family. Any Israelite who refused to be cut physically in this way would be **cut off** (separated) **from his people** (v. 14) because of his disobedience to God's command.

Elsewhere Scripture refers to circumcision as a symbol of separation, purity, and loyalty to the covenant. Moses said that God would circumcise the hearts of His people so that they might be devoted to Him (Deut. 30:6). And Paul wrote that "circumcision of the heart" (i.e., being inwardly set apart "by the Spirit") evidences salvation and fellowship with God (Rom. 2:28-29; cf. Rom. 4:11). One must turn in confidence to God and His promises, laying aside natural strength. Unbelief is described as having an uncircumcised heart (Jer. 9:26; Ezek. 44:7-9).

**17:15-18.** God announced that **Sarai** was to be called **Sarah.** This new name, though involving only a slight change and meaning "princess," was fitting for one whose seed would produce **kings** (v. 16; cf. v. 6). Hearing this, **Abraham . . . laughed** because it seemed incredible that a barren **90**-year-old woman could give birth to a **son.** Abraham had assumed that his descendants would come through **Ishmael.**

**17:19-22.** Yet **God** assured him that she would **bear . . . a son** whose name would be **Isaac,** meaning "he laughs" (v. 19). His name would be a constant reminder that a word from God was laughed at. **Ishmael** was not forgotten, however, for God said he would have many descendants also. Even the number of Ishmael's sons—**12**—was predicted. Their names are recorded in 25:13-15.

**17:23-27.** However, **Abraham,** having received God's word about Isaac, immediately obeyed God's command about circumcision, thus reflecting his faith in

God's word. Abraham was **circumcised** at the age of **99** . . . **Ishmael** at **13**, and **every male in** the patriarch's **household,** whether **born** there or **bought from a foreigner, was** also **circumcised.**

*c. The promise of the seed confirmed by visitation (18:1-15)*

**18:1-8. Three men** visited **Abraham near the great trees of Mamre** at Hebron (cf. 13:18; 14:13) to confirm the time of the fulfillment of the promise. These three were **the LORD** (18:1, 10, 13; cf. comments on "the Angel of the LORD," 16:7) and two angels. Though one is justified in seeing lessons here about hospitality, the angels certainly did not visit Abraham for the purpose of teaching him this. Why did the Angel of the Lord approach Abraham in this manner? Why did He not use an oracle, a vision, or a voice? Possibly He meant it as a test for both Abraham and the Sodomites. The moral states of Abraham and Sodom may have been indicated by their different treatments of strangers. Abraham's peaceful, quiet visit contrasted greatly with Sodom's outbursts of brutality and inhumanity (cf. chaps. 18–19).

But more likely Abraham's visitors meant to convey intimate fellowship. To eat together was important for fellowship, peace offerings, and treaties. When the Lord was ready to specify the fulfillment of the covenantal promise, He came in person and ate in Abraham's tent. Nothing could more significantly communicate their close relationship. **Abraham . . . hurried** to **them** (18:2), **hurried** back to **the tent** (v. 6), **ran to the herd** (v. 7), and his servant **hurried** (v. 7); Abraham **bowed low** before them (v. 2); he had **water** brought to **wash** their **feet** (v. 4); he served them freshly baked **bread** (v. 6), a **choice . . . calf** (v. 7), **curds and milk** (v. 8), and he **stood** while they were eating (v. 8; cf. vv. 1-2). All this suggests that he perceived who his visitors were.

**18:9-15.** After the meal one of the angelic visitors announced that a **son** would be born to **Sarah** in a **year.** This Angel of the Lord was clearly the Lord Himself (cf. 16:7). The thought seemed ludicrous to **Sarah** and she **laughed** in her heart. The Lord's reply rebuked the woman: **Is anything too hard** (better, "marvelous") **for the LORD?**

Basically this account is a call to believe that God can do the impossible. He confirmed His promise by a personal visit—and ate with them—to announce that the **time** was at hand. It was the annunciation of a humanly impossible birth. When something as incredible as this is declared, the human response is consistent: like **Sarah,** people are taken off guard, **laugh,** and then out of fear deny that they laughed (18:15). But God knows human hearts and that Christians often do stagger at what He says He can do.

Is a child from a dead womb too marvelous for the One who called all things into existence? It is no laughing matter. He can do it. Nothing is incredible for those in covenant fellowship with the Lord because nothing is too difficult for Him.

*d. The intercession of Abraham for the people of Sodom (18:16-33)*

The predominant theme of this narrative is justice. It grows out of the preceding verses (vv. 9-15). Certainly God is able to do whatever He chooses to do, but will it be just? The answer is evident, as shown by His replies to Abraham's appeals.

**18:16-21.** This is the Lord's soliloquy about His judgment on the cities of the plain, with the major city being **Sodom.** Interestingly God had a double motivation for revealing His plan: (1) **All nations** would **be blessed through** Abraham; therefore God told him that one city (Sodom) was to be removed before it had a chance to be blessed through him. (2) Abraham was to teach his offspring righteousness and justice (**what is right and just,** v. 19) **so that** they might enjoy God's blessings.

Since **the outcry** of people **against** the **grievous** sins of **Sodom and Gomorrah** was **so great,** the Lord went to see if it was that **bad.** (Of course in His omniscience He knew the sins of Sodom and Gomorrah, but He wanted to demonstrate His justice to them.) If the sin of those people was "complete," they would be judged.

**18:22-33.** Would God **sweep away the righteous with the** unrighteous? **Abraham** was convinced there were **righteous people** in Sodom—he did not pray merely for Lot—so he appealed for Sodom on the basis of God's justice.

Abraham's great character is revealed by his intercession. He prayed that all in the cities—**the wicked** as well as **the righteous**—be spared **for the sake of the . . . righteous** (v. 23). Earlier he had personally rescued these people in battle (14:16). Now he pleaded for them with the same boldness, perseverance, and generosity with which he had fought for them. Abraham's "bargaining" with God jars some readers. But Abraham's prayers, though audacious, were made with genuine humility and profound reverence. It was for justice that he pleaded: deliverance for Sodom if there were as few as **50. . . . 45. . . . 40. . . . 30. . . . 20,** or even **10** righteous people **there** (18:24-32). He was not trying to talk God into something against His will (Lot's prayer for Zoar, however, was quite a contrast, 19:18-23).

Thus the theme of justice predominates: those who will enjoy God's blessing (a) will teach justice (18:19); (b) may intercede for just judgment to preserve the righteous; and (c) know that God may preserve the wicked for the sake of the righteous. Certainly Israel learned from this that God is a righteous Judge, that righteousness exalts a nation (cf. Prov. 14:34), and that righteous people help preserve society (cf. Matt. 5:13). These truths should have been as great a concern to Israel as they were to **Abraham** who turned them into compassionate intercession.

*e. The judgment of the cities of the plain (chap. 19)*

This chapter records God's judgment on a morally bankrupt Canaanite civilization, but it also provides a severe warning against others becoming like them: it was difficult to get Lot out of Sodom, and Sodom out of Lot's family.

Lot was an upright citizen, hospitable and generous (vv. 2-3), and a leader of the community. Actually he was a judge, for he "was sitting in the gateway of the city" (v. 1; cf. v. 9). Judges usually sat by the city gates, public places (cf. Job 29:7, 12-17) where legal and business transactions were finalized (cf. Gen. 23:18). As a judge Lot sought to screen out the wickedness of his townfolk and to give advice on good living. He knew truth and justice, righteousness and evil. He was "a righteous man" (2 Peter 2:7-8).

Yet in spite of his denunciation of their lifestyle, he liked the good life of Sodom's society. He preferred making money off its citizens to staying in the hills (cf. Gen. 13:10-11) where there would be no filthy living but also no "good life."

The hour of truth came with the visitation from on high. Lot seemed godly and pure, but he was hypocritical. His words were not taken seriously (19:14). The "saint" at first pitched his tent near Sodom, but later Sodom controlled his life. He was moral, for he opposed sodomy and homosexuality; he knew great evil when he saw it. But ironically he was willing to sacrifice his daughters' virginity to fend off the vice of Sodomite men (v. 8). He escaped judgment by the grace of God, but his heart was in Sodom. His wife was too attached to the city to follow the call of grace, and his daughters had no qualms against having sex with their drunk and naked father (vv. 30-35).

As long as the Lord left Lot alone, he would seek to profess faith while at the same time living in Sodom. Ultimately he could not have both. Sodom would have destroyed him if the Lord had not destroyed Sodom.

**19:1-14. The two angels** (cf. 18:2, 22) were reluctant visitors to **Lot.** In spite of Lot's hospitality, they preferred to lodge **in the square.** But when the angels were in Lot's **house. . . . all the men . . . of the city . . . surrounded the house.** They wanted to **have sex with** (lit., "to know," i.e., sexually) Lot's visitors. They wanted homosexual relations with these two who they thought were men. As angels, they apparently were handsome. The men's vileness was matched, surprisingly, by Lot's hypocrisy, for he was willing to give them his virgin **daughters** (19:8). To protect one's guests was part of hospitality, but this was going too far! Lot's pleas for righteousness (v. 7) were now wasted as the Sodomites saw a different side of their **judge** (v. 9). He might as well have mocked. The angels then **pulled Lot back into the house,** made the **men** outside **the door** blind, and told Lot to **get . . . out** because they were **going to destroy** the city. When Lot told this to his two daughters' fiancés, they did not believe him.

**19:15-22.** Early in the morning the **angels** literally had to drag **Lot** from the city (v. 16). **The LORD,** of course, **was** being **merciful** in sparing Lot for Abraham's sake (cf. 18:23; 19:29). But even after he was delivered, **Lot** wrung a concession out of the angels. He wanted to go to the **small** town of **Zoar,** which means "a little one" (vv. 18-22). (Before that it was known as Bela, 14:2.) But this scene would always remind Israel of Lot, lingering and halting, being dragged to safety. Why do some of God's people fall in with the corrupt world rather than willingly flee a society destined for destruction?

**19:23-29.** With **burning sulfur** the Lord **overthrew** the wicked **cities and the entire plain** in a great destruction (vv. 24-25). Some have suggested that deposits of sulfur erupted from the earth (cf. the "tar pits," 14:10), and then showered down **out of the heavens** in flames of fire (cf. Luke 17:29). **Lot's wife** gazed **back** intently and was changed into **a pillar of salt,** a monument to her disobedience. The **dense smoke** (19:28) Abraham saw was caused by the burning sulfur (v. 24). Though **God** judged the sinners in **the cities of the plain,** He also **remembered Abraham,** that is, God remembered his request (18:23-32) and saved **Lot** from **the catastrophe.**

**19:30-38.** This closing section records the incident of Lot's **two daughters** in a mountain cave. **Lot** had been **afraid** to flee to the mountains (v. 19) so he went instead to **Zoar** (v. 22). But now, ironically, he **left Zoar** for **the mountains** and **lived in a cave** (v. 30). What a contrast with the "progressive civilization" (Luke 17:28) of the city of Sodom, which he had left.

Thinking their chances for remarrying were slim (Gen. 19:31), the two daughters, whose fiancés were killed in the holocaust of Sodom, took turns getting their father drunk and having sex with him (vv. 32-35). Their acts of incest show Sodom's influence on them. They gave birth to boys, **Moab** and **Ben-Ammi,** whose descendants were the **Moabites** and **Ammonites** (vv. 36-38), perennial enemies of Israel. "Moab" sounds like the words "from father," and "Ben-Ammi" means "son of my kinsman." These etymologies perpetuated for Israel the ignominious beginning of these wicked enemies.

Four major motifs are in this chapter:

God's swift judgment on the vile Canaanites, Lot's close attachment to the wicked society, God's merciful sparing of Lot from the doom, and "the rebirth of Sodom" in the cave.

Through these, Israel could see that if God judges a people severely, He is righteous because of their great evil. She also could learn of the folly of becoming attached to the wickedness of Canaan.

How should one live, then, knowing how God dealt with the Canaanites? The lesson is quite clear: "Do not love the world or anything in the world. . . . [for] the world and its desires [lusts] pass away" (1 John 2:15, 17) under the judgment of God. It is dangerous and folly to become attached to the present corrupt world system because it awaits God's swift and sudden destruction.

Jesus referred to Genesis 19:26 to warn of the destruction to come on unbelieving Israel: "Remember Lot's wife!" (Luke 17:32) When Christ returns, people should not look back as she did (Luke 17:30-31). If an unbeliever craves the best of this world he will lose both this world (since it passes away) and life in the next world (Luke 17:33-37).

Jesus also said that if the miracles He did in Capernaum had been done in Sodom, the Sodomites would have repented (Matt. 11:23). As it is, "it will be more bearable for Sodom on the day of judgment" than for the cities of Galilee (Matt. 11:24). This signifies that God judges according to knowledge, and that judgment greater than physical destruction awaits sinners.

*f. The deception of Abraham before Abimelech (chap. 20)*

This story records God's providential protection of His people, but its emphasis is on purity, specifically the preservation of Sarah's purity. For the fulfillment of the promise, marriage is important: participation in God's promised blessings demands separation from worldly corruption.

Sinfulness and weakness of faith created a threat to the promised blessing. It is a sad commentary on one's lack of faith if God has to deliver him again and again.

**20:1-7.** Earlier God delivered Abram from Egypt with plagues after he lied about Sarai being his sister (chap. 12).

Here **Abraham** again told the same lie about **Sarah** (20:2) to **Abimelech king of Gerar,** out of fear (v. 11). Later Isaac did the same thing with another Abimelech! (26:1-11) **Gerar** was near the coast about 12 miles south of Gaza and about 50 miles south of Hebron, in the land of the Philistines (21:34). When Abimelech **took** Sarah, **God** warned him by **a dream** (20:3) and by the barrenness of his wife and slave girls (vv. 17-18) that she was **married.**

There is a fitting wordplay here. Abraham had prayed that the righteous would not be *destroyed* with the wicked (18:23-32). Now Abimelech's words echoed the same concern: **Lord, will You destroy an innocent nation?** The rebuke of this expression would have been forceful for Abraham.

So when Abimelech assured God of his **clear conscience** in the matter, **God** told him to **return** Sarah and to have Abraham the **prophet** (*nābî*, the first occurrence of this word in the OT), God's spokesman, **pray for** Abimelech. Only the patriarch's prayer saved the king's life.

God did not rebuke Abimelech, but He certainly gave him the sternest of warnings: he should not commit adultery because it was a capital offense (20:7). The wording clearly anticipates the same command in the Decalogue (Ex. 20:14). God made Abraham and Sarah one so that they might produce a godly seed. This was basic to the covenant.

Both deliverances of the patriarch preserved the purity of Sarah and kept the promise intact. The first incident (Gen. 12), however, was outside the Promised Land and reflected more clearly the life-and-death struggle of the nation in Egypt as God would later save them and deliver them. The second incident (chap. 20) was in the land and was an event in which God protected their marriage and thereby His promise. God controls birth; He miraculously intervenes; He opens and closes wombs (vv. 17-18). No mere human potentate can thwart God's plan.

**20:8-18.** Though God did not rebuke Abimelech, **Abimelech** did rebuke **Abraham.** The king spoke of the **great guilt** Abraham's action brought on him (v. 9) and he spoke to Sarah of his (Abimelech's) **offense against** her (v. 16). He

sensed that his plan to take her into his harem was wrong. So he made amends by giving the patriarch livestock (**sheep and cattle**; cf. 21:27) and **slaves** (20:14), allowing him to **live** in his **land** (v. 15), and giving Abraham (whom he called Sarah's **brother!**) **a thousand shekels of silver** (v. 16).

God's preventing the destruction of Abraham's marriage by adultery reinforced the fact that the Israelites should not destroy their marriages by adultery. Here the stress was also on the protection from intermarriage with pagans. To take the wife of another man is a life-and-death issue. God punishes such a sin.

So the message was clear: God did not want Israel to intermarry with pagans—especially when adultery or divorce was involved. Israel seldom remembered this (Mal. 2:10-17).

*g. The birth of Isaac and the expulsion of Ishmael (21:1-21)*

**21:1-7.** God provided the child of promise **to Abraham** and to **Sarah . . . at the very time God had promised** (cf. 18:10). They responded in faith by (a) naming him **Isaac** (21:3), (b) circumcising him according to the covenant (v. 4; cf. 17:9-14), and (c) praising God for this amazing fulfillment (21:6-7).

The name Isaac ("he laughs") is cleverly explained in this passage. **Sarah said** that **God** gave her **laughter** (v. 6), that is, joy. Her laughter of unbelief (18:12) was now changed to rejoicing through the provision of her son. **Everyone who** would hear **about this** would **laugh,** that is rejoice, **with** her. But Ishmael turned her laughter into a ridiculing mockery (see comment on 21:9) of God's work.

**21:8-13.** God used this incident of Ishmael's **mocking** Isaac to drive out the child Ishmael and **Hagar** (v. 10), for they would be a threat to the promised seed. The word "mocking" is *mᵉṣahēq* ("laughing or jesting"), from which comes "Isaac" (*yiṣhāq*). Earlier Sarah had mistreated Hagar (16:6); now Hagar's son was mistreating Sarah's son. Earlier Sarah caused pregnant Hagar to flee (16:6); now she caused Hagar and her 16- or 17-year-old **son** to flee. (Abraham was 86 when Ishmael was born [16:16], and 100 when Isaac was born [21:5], and Isaac **was** probably **weaned** [v. 8] at age 2 or 3.) When **Abraham** became **distressed** because of Sarah's request to oust Hagar and Ishmael, **God** assured Abraham that Ishmael would have a future because **he** too was Abraham's **offspring** (vv. 11-13).

The two emphases (vv. 1-13) then are these: the birth of Isaac (in which the naming commemorated the fulfillment and the circumcision confirmed the covenant), and the expulsion of Ishmael as the removal of the threat. Once the promised child was received, Abraham and Sarah, rejoicing in God's miraculous provision, had to avoid any possible threat to Isaac's inheritance. Because God chose one son, His choice had to be protected. Abraham and Sarah had to expel Ishmael.

**21:14-21. The Angel of** the Lord met **Hagar in the desert** (vv. 17-18) as before (16:7), and provided **water** from a **well** (21:19) as before (16:14). **God told Hagar,** as He had told Abraham, that from Ishmael would come **a great nation** (21:18; cf. v. 13). Ishmael **lived in the desert . . . became an archer** (v. 20; cf. 16:12), and married an Egyptian (21:21). **The Desert of Paran** is in the northeast portion of the Sinai peninsula.

Paul's use of this account is marvelous (Gal. 4:21-31; see comments there). Ishmael was born by the flesh through "the slave woman" (Gal. 4:29-30). Isaac was born by the promise and was the heir. One represented bondage at Sinai, the other freedom when the promise finally came. When Christ, the seed, came, the old was done away. Now that the promise has come, believers are co-heirs with the promised Seed by adoption through God's grace. To go back under the Law would be to undo the fulfillment of God's promise. Those adopted by the Seed become seeds and are set free from the bondage of the Law (Gal. 5:1). Just as Ishmael and Isaac were in conflict (Gal. 4:29), so the flesh and the Spirit do not harmonize. The flesh struggles against the Spirit, often mocking it (Gal. 5:16-18). Therefore believers are to "get rid of the slave woman and her son" (Gal. 4:30), that is, to remove the threat of the flesh and "live by the Spirit" (Gal. 5:16).

*h. The covenant at Beersheba (21:22-34)*

The striking feature about this passage is the explanation of the name of Beersheba, the home of Abraham. This name will always reflect the covenant the patriarch made with the residents of the land, which enabled him to dwell there in peace and prosperity.

**21:22-34.** The word *šāba'* ("to swear or take an oath") occurs three times in the passage (vv. 23-24 [**swear**], 31 [**swore**]); the numerical adjective *šeba'* (**seven**) occurs three times as well (vv. 28-30); the name *bᵉ'ēr šāba'* ("well of seven" or "well of the oath") also occurs three times (vv. 31-33). Certainly the stress is on the significance of the **oath** (v. 31) between **Abraham** and **Abimelech,** a fact commemorated by Beersheba's naming. *Šāba'* is clearly the key to the passage. Later Israel would learn about the solemnity of oaths and treaties.

The story fits well in the context that builds up to the sacrifice of Isaac in chapter 22. The birth of Isaac was clearly promised (18:1-15), and in Abraham's deception (chap. 20) Abimelech learned that God's hand was on this man (cf. 21:22). Then the promised seed was born and the rival was expelled (vv. 1-18). Now (vv. 22-34) a covenant was made that allowed **Abraham** to settle in the land in peace and **Abimelech** to share in the blessing. All this built slowly to the test in chapter 22, each chapter showing the completion of different phases of the promises.

The story in 21:22-34 reveals that the patriarch was blessed of God, and that some pagans recognized God's blessings. The motif of the **well** appears again (cf. 16:14; 21:19). God provided water—a symbol of blessing—out of the wilderness, out of the barren land, out of the rock. Abimelech realized this, and after the controversy over his servants' seizure of the well (v. 25), the **two men made a treaty** so that the pagan king could share in the blessing (cf. 12:1-3).

In making the treaty (covenant) **Abraham** gave **Abimelech** both **sheep and cattle** (21:27; cf. the reverse in 20:14), including **seven ewe lambs** (21:29-30). These secured Abraham's legal right to dwell in the land in peace, and legally forced Abimelech to recognize that **this well** at **Beersheba** belonged to Abraham (vv. 30-31). The patriarch thus secured by treaty his right to the well, that is, God's provision of blessing.

Significant is the fact that Abraham **planted a . . . tree** there and sojourned there many days (vv. 33-34), indicating

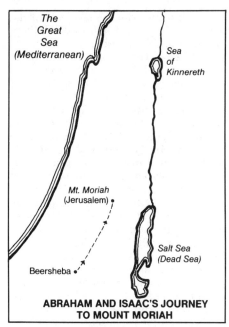

The Great Sea (Mediterranean)

Sea of Kinnereth

Mt. Moriah (Jerusalem)

Salt Sea (Dead Sea)

Beersheba

**ABRAHAM AND ISAAC'S JOURNEY TO MOUNT MORIAH**

his faith and security. To plant a tree in Beersheba presupposed a constant supply of water, and indicated a determination to stay in the region. God would bless with well water, and Abraham would stay settled in the land. Dwelling under one's tree was a sign of peaceful security (Zech. 3:10).

The passage certainly anticipated Israel's future peaceful coexistence in the land with other tribes who would respond to the message of peace and desire to share in the blessing.

A subtle rebuke, however, is found in the story (cf. Abimelech's rebuke in Gen. 20:9-10). Abimelech pressed for the treaty so that Abraham would **not deal falsely with** him (21:23). All Abimelech knew of this man was that (a) God blessed him (v. 22) and (b) he was deceptive (v. 23). This tragic contradiction called for a binding treaty.

Likewise, Israel was to keep her oaths and avoid falsehood. Today believ-.ers should speak the truth without using oaths (Matt. 5:37; James 5:12). Truthful and faithful dealings that preserve such peaceful relations enhance the work of God.

**The Philistines** (Gen. 21:32) settled in Palestine en masse around 1200 B.C. However, some sea traders settled on the coast of Palestine as early as Abraham, who lived 2166–1991 B.C.; see the chart

"Chronology of the Patriarchs," near 47:28-31.

*i. The testing of Abraham's faith (22:1-19)*

**22:1-2.** The greatest test in the life of **Abraham** (**God tested** him) came after he received the promised seed following a long wait. The test was very real: he was to give Isaac back to God. As a test it was designed to prove faith. And for it to be a real test, it had to defy logic; it had to be something Abraham wanted to resist.

God had told the patriarch to send Ishmael away (21:12-13), and now He told Abraham to sacrifice Isaac. Abraham had willingly sent Ishmael away, but he would not want to kill Isaac.

It is one thing to claim to trust God's word when waiting for something; it is quite another thing to trust and obey His word after it is received. This was a test of how much Abraham would obey God's word. Would he cling to the boy now that he had him, or would he still obey and return him to the Lord? In other words how far would Abraham go in obedience? Did he really believe that God would still keep His word and raise the seed of promise?

There are obvious connections with God's earlier words to Abraham to get out and go to the land God would show him (12:1-3). But in this subtle reminder of the original call God also reminded him of the fulfillment, which made the test so hard: **Take your son, your only son Isaac** ["laughter"] **whom you love** (22:2). The command to **sacrifice** his own son **as a burnt offering** would have undoubtedly seemed totally unreasonable (even though child sacrifice was known in Canaan). How then could God fulfill the promises He made earlier (12:1-3), to say nothing of Abraham's emotional loss of his only son, born to him so late in life?

**22:3-8.** Abraham's response was staggering—he gave instant, unquestioning obedience. He even got an **early** start! However, the three-day journey (v. 4) was probably silent and difficult. The distance from Beersheba to Mount Moriah was about 50 miles (see the map "Abraham and Isaac's Journey to Mount Moriah").

When he **saw the place in the** region of Moriah (v. 2; later the temple mount; 2 Chron. 3:1) he took only **Isaac** and had the two **servants** stay behind. His statement, **We will worship and then we will come back** (Gen. 22:5), is amazing. All Abraham knew was that (a) God planned the future around Isaac, and (b) God wanted him to sacrifice Isaac. He could not reconcile the two, but he would obey anyway. That is faith. In response to Isaac's question **Where is the lamb?** Abraham again revealed his faith: **God Himself will provide** (v. 8; cf. v. 14). Isaac was brought "from the dead" twice—once from Sarah's dead womb, and again from a high altar (cf. Heb. 11:17-19).

**22:9-14.** God's intervention—so dramatic and instructive—showed that He never had intended **Abraham** to go through with the sacrifice (child sacrifice was not to be practiced in Israel) but that it indeed was a test. **The Angel of the LORD** (cf. comments on 16:7) stopped Abraham just as the patriarch **took** in his hand **the knife to slay** Isaac! Now God knew that Abraham would hold nothing back and that he did in fact **fear God.** To fear God means to reverence Him as sovereign, trust Him implicitly, and obey Him without question.

A true worshiper of God holds nothing back from God but obediently gives Him what He asks, trusting that He will provide. The key idea of the entire passage is summarized in the name Abraham gave to the **place:** Yahweh Yir'eh, **The LORD will provide** (or, "see"; v. 14). The explanation is, **On the mountain of the LORD it will be provided** (or, "seen," yērā'eh, v. 14; cf. v. 8). This is the basis of a truth often repeated in the Old Testament: the Lord was to be worshiped in His holy mountain by the nation. "Three times a year all the men [of Israel] are to appear [yērā'eh, 'be seen'] before the Sovereign LORD" to worship Him, bringing their offerings and sacrifices (Ex. 23:17; cf. Deut. 16:16). The Lord would see (rā'âh) the needs of those who came before Him, and would meet their needs. Thus in providing for them He would be "seen."

In naming the place Abraham of course was commemorating his own experience of sacrifice to the Lord. But an animal (**a ram**—not a lamb; cf. Gen. 22:8—**caught . . . its horns** in a thornbush) was provided by God's grace as a substitute for the lad in the offering (v.

13). Later all Israel would offer animals to the Lord. Worship involved accepting God's sacrificial substitute. But of course in the New Testament God substituted His only Son for the animal, and the perfect Sacrifice was made. John certainly had this in mind when he introduced Jesus as "the Lamb of God, who takes away the sin of the world!" (John 1:29)

Yet the main point of Genesis 22:9-14 is not the doctrine of the Atonement. It is portraying an obedient servant worshiping God in faith at great cost, and in the end receiving God's provision. Abraham did not withhold his son. Similarly Paul wrote that God "did not spare [epheisato] His own Son, but gave [delivered] Him up for us all" (Rom. 8:32). A form of the same Greek word is used of Abraham in the Septuagint: "Thou hast not spared [epheisō] thy beloved son" (Gen. 22:12).

This reveals the greatness of Abraham's faith; he was willing to obey God by sacrificing his son. It also reveals the greatness of Isaac's faith in submission; he had everything in the world to live for but willingly followed his father's words, believing that God would provide a lamb.

**22:15-19.** God again confirmed His covenant with **Abraham** (cf. 15:5, 18-21; 17:3-8). His **descendants** would be **numerous** like **the stars** (cf. 15:5; 26:4), like **the sand on the seashore** (cf. 32:12), and "like the dust of the earth" (cf. 13:16; 28:14). God then added another element: Abraham's **descendants** would be victorious over **the cities of their** Canaanite **enemies.** This was done by Joshua in the Conquest.

The lessons about true worship are timeless: (1) Faith obeys completely the Word of God. (2) Faith surrenders the best to God, holding nothing back. (3) Faith waits on the Lord to provide all one's needs. But God does not provide until personal sacrifice has been made. True worship is costly. This was always so for Israel when they brought sacrifices. Those offerings were supposed to be given in faith so God would provide all the needs of each willing worshiper.

3. THE TRANSITION OF THE PROMISES TO ISAAC BY FAITHFUL ABRAHAM (22:20–25:11)

From this point on, Abraham's task was to prepare for receiving future blessings through Isaac.

**65**

### a. The report of Nahor's family (22:20-24)

**22:20-24.** Reports came from the East that the family of **Nahor,** Abraham's brother (cf. 11:27-29), was expanding. Among those born was **Rebekah,** the future wife of Isaac (cf. 24:15, 67). She was a daughter of **Bethuel,** the youngest of Nahor's eight sons by **Milcah** (Nahor's niece). (See the chart "Terah's Family" near 11:27-32.) This record is included here even though one would expect it closer to chapter 24. But it serves as a tie-in with chapter 23, which records Sarah's death and burial. In burying Sarah, **Abraham** ignored his ancestry, not going back to Paddan Aram for her burial.

### b. The purchase of the Cave of Machpelah in the land (chap. 23)

**23:1-4.** Abraham's purchase of a burial cave "near Mamre" (v. 19; cf. 13:18; 14:13; 18:1) was occasioned by the death of **Sarah,** who **lived to be 127.** (Isaac was 37 at the time, 17:17.) This was the first indication that a transition was underway. After mourning for his **wife** at **Hebron** (23:2) **Abraham** bargained for a portion of land with **a burial site.**

This incident includes many similarities with Canaanite and Hittite laws. (See James B. Pritchard, ed., *Ancient Near Eastern Texts Relating to the Old Testament.* Princeton, N.J.: Princeton University Press, 1955, pp. 188-96, par. 46 on feudal obligations for the whole field, par. 47 for gifts that nullify feudal obligations, as well as pars. 48 and 169.) Other laws from Ugarit (in Syria) are also relevant to this event. The owners of the field were **Hittites** (vv. 3, 5, 7, 10, 16, 18, 20). Even though the great Hittite Empire (Josh. 1:4) never extended down this far, pockets of Hittites could have settled here and kept their customs even though speaking a Semitic language. Also even though the written Hittite laws were dated later than these events, those laws could have been oral traditions before they were put in writing.

**23:5-20.** Abraham was held in high regard by the people around him: **You are a mighty prince among us** (cf. 20:6-11).

In this legal transaction **Abraham** wanted to purchase only **the cave** owned by **Ephron** (23:9), but Ephron wanted to sell the whole **field.** When **Ephron** said he would **give** the field and **the cave** (three times in v. 11), he did not mean it was free. This was bedouin bargaining—giving for giving. Though **Abraham** did not want the whole **field,** he was willing to take it (vv. 12-13) at a high price (**400 shekels of silver**) to get the cave (vv. 15-16). The transaction was then finalized **in the presence of all the Hittites** at the city **gate,** the place of legal and business dealings (cf. 19:1).

In this **cave** was buried not only **Sarah** but also Abraham (25:9), Isaac and his wife Rebekah, and Jacob and Leah (49:29-31; 50:13).

The point of this event was to ensure that the cave and field would be Abraham's possession. He was not presumptuous. In faith he bought the land, taking nothing from these people (cf. 14:21-24). It was important then where people buried their dead; burial was to be done in their native land. Thus there was no going back. Though **Abraham** was **an alien and a stranger among** the people (23:4), his hope was in the land.

When Abraham bought this cave, he was renouncing Paddan Aram, that is, northwest Mesopotamia (cf. 25:20). This had just been brought to the reader's attention (22:20-24) indirectly by mentioning the relatives of Abraham who remained in Mesopotamia (cf. 11:27-31).

Canaan was now Abraham's new native land. But interestingly the only part of the Promised Land Abraham himself ever received he bought, and that was a burial cave. This first property of the patriarchs—a cave—bound them to the Promised Land. This was a real "occupation" of the land. There would never be a return to Mesopotamia. Later patriarchs would also die and be buried with their ancestors in Canaan.

Abraham knew he could not exhaust God's promise, so he made plans for the future. By buying the land for his dead, he was forced to realize that God's promises do not end with this life. God will do far more than He has done in this life, which is the hope of all who die in faith.

The promise of the land is one of the major themes in Genesis. But so is death. Death entered by sin and ruined the race. The deaths of patriarchs and saints are brutal reminders that people are sinners. Death brings out mourning. But death in this passage was also a basis for hope. In life the patriarchs were sojourners; in death they were heirs of the promise and "occupied" the land.

The patriarchs and others died, not receiving the promises; yet they died in faith (Heb. 11:39-40). It was not God's plan to give them the promised rest without the participation of New Testament believers. A Sabbath-rest yet remains; yet those who believe enter into it even now and will fully realize it in the future (Heb. 4:8-10). The point is that God's promises to those in the faith are not exhausted in this life. As Abraham in hope bought a grave site in the land, so believers today have a hope beyond this life. The time of death—when one's natural inclination is to mourn as the world mourns—should be the time of a believer's greatest demonstration of faith, for the recipient of God's promises has a hope beyond the grave. Jesus Himself referred to Abraham when discussing the resurrection with the Sadducees (Matt. 22:31-32). God's promises demand resurrection!

*c. The acquiring of a wife for Isaac (chap. 24)*

This event emphasizes the providential working of God in the circumstances of His faithful servants. The key idea in the passage is in the word *ḥesed*, "loyal love" or "loyalty to the covenant"—from both God's perspective and man's. ("Kindness," NIV's trans. of *ḥesed* in vv. 12, 27, 49, does not convey the full meaning of the word.)

The Lord providentially ensured the fulfillment of His promise by guiding Abraham's servant in acquiring a bride for Isaac. The chapter divides into four sections:

(1) The commission. 24:1-9. Abraham, confident in the Lord's promise, had his chief servant . . . swear an oath to find a wife for Isaac from Abraham's native land, 450 miles away. Eliezer's putting his hand under the patriarch's thigh (cf. 47:29) was a solemn sign that if the oath were not carried out, the children who would be born to Abraham would avenge the servant's unfaithfulness.

(2) The trust. 24:10-27. Eliezer (15:2) trusted the LORD to grant him specific leading. He prayed that Isaac's future bride would give him and his camels . . . water to drink. To water 10 thirsty camels involved much work, for camels guzzle great amounts of water. At the town of Nahor in Aram Naharaim (northwest Mesopotamia, 24:10; cf. 25:20) he received a precise answer to his prayer. In gratitude he gave the girl some expensive jewelry—a gold nose ring weighing a beka (half a shekel, i.e., 1/5 ounce) and two gold bracelets weighing 10 shekels (4 ounces). He asked if there was a room at her father's house in which to stay overnight. Again she revealed her kindness by offering him not only a place to stay but also food for the camels.

(3) The success. 24:28-59. Laban invited Eliezer and his men in. Eliezer then recounted to Rebekah's family his mission and God's providence and gained their permission and blessing to take her to Isaac. In that society a woman's brother gave his sister in marriage, which explains why Laban, Rebekah's brother, was the negotiator in this marriage contract.

(4) The completion. 24:60-67. Rebekah returned with Eliezer to Isaac . . . in the Negev, and became Isaac's wife when Isaac was 40 years old (25:20; Abraham was then 140).

In these four sections four participants were acting in *ḥesed*: Abraham in preparing for the future, Eliezer in carrying it out, God in performing it, Rebekah in responding to it.

In God's providence and His *ḥesed* ("loyal love") He sovereignly worked through the circumstances of those who lived by faith. This hidden causality of God is stressed in chapter 24 in three ways:

1. God was the sole cause of all the events in the story. Eliezer's words, "The LORD has led me" (v. 27; cf. v. 48), are the motto. This is true throughout all the Bible. Even Laban, Rebekah's brother (v. 29), recognized this was the Lord's doing (vv. 50-51).

2. God was deliberately behind the scenes, directing the acts. So this event in Abraham's life was similar to Ruth's experience (Ronald M. Hals, *The Theology of the Book of Ruth*. Philadelphia: Fortress Press, 1969). The narrative in Genesis 24 records no word from God, no miracle, no prophetic oracle; it does not even restate the Abrahamic Covenant. This event is unique in Genesis; yet it is realistic for believers today. The anticipatory role of faith, expressed in personal

prayer, looks for outward evidences of God's working and is predominant because God is not *visibly* active.

3. The story reveals more than God's providence. It is also part of the development of His plan to bless mankind. Many potential mishaps were avoided: the servant could have failed (vv. 5-8), the "sign" could have been missed (vv. 14, 21), Laban might have refused (vv. 49-51), or Rebekah might have been unwilling (vv. 54-58). God steered through all the potential hazards and then put all the parts together.

While one marvels at God's providence in this event, human responsibility was also evident. The servant faithfully carried out his assignment. (1) He was loyal to his holy commission to further God's program to bless mankind. (2) He trusted God implicitly, looking in prayer to God's leading. (3) Covenant loyalty was his predominant motivation (vv. 9, 12, 27, 49). (4) He praised God even before his assignment was completed (vv. 27, 48-49). This praise is an important part of the story. Many expositors pass over it as repetitious. But that is the point: It is such a marvelous story it has to be repeated.

So the choice of a bride for Isaac was God's. The sign confirmed it. Laban recognized it. Rebekah complied with it. They who do the will of God, prayerfully and obediently, are led by God (Prov. 3:5-6).

### d. The death of Abraham (25:1-11)

With this report the life of Abraham came to a close and God's blessing was transferred to Isaac, his "only" son (22:2).

This passage includes four sections: (a) the births of other sons to Abraham (25:1-4), (b) the safeguarding of Isaac's inheritance (vv. 5-6), (c) the death and burial of Abraham (vv. 7-10), and (d) the blessing of Isaac (v. 11).

**25:1-4.** When **Abraham** married **Keturah** is unknown, but the verb **took** and the adjective **another** suggest it was after Sarah's death. (Actually **Keturah** was a concubine, 1 Chron. 1:32.) That would mean there was a maximum span of 37 years for the births of Keturah's six sons. (Abraham was 138 when Sarah died, and he died at 175.) Tribes in **Sheba and Dedan,** in Arabia (Gen 25:3), as well as

the Midianites (v. 4), came from Abraham. This was in fulfillment of God's promises to Abraham that he would become great (12:2) since so "many nations" look to him as their ancestor (17:4).

**25:5-6.** **Abraham** loved all these boys; **he gave** them **gifts.** But they and their descendants may possibly have posed a threat to **Isaac.** So Abraham **sent them away** as he had done with Ishmael (21:8-14). He sent them **to the land of the East,** thus preserving Isaac's primacy and his right as Abraham's heir.

**25:7-11.** While **Isaac and Ishmael** together **buried** their father (who had **lived 175 years**) in **the cave** where **Sarah** was buried (cf. 23:19), Ishmael's presence may have posed a possible threat to Isaac's rights, now that their father was dead. But God's blessing rested on Isaac.

**Isaac** was then living at **Beer Lahai Roi.** This was a place where God was known to respond. God had heard Hagar there and had delivered her (16:14). And Isaac meditated there when waiting for his future wife (24:62). Thus Isaac lived at a special place, a place where God had answered prayer.

When Abraham by faith sent away all his other sons, he provided for transferring his blessing to Isaac who waited on the Lord. Abraham would be gone, but God's program would continue. No leader of the covenant is indispensable, for God's program to bless the world will continue to grow and expand from generation to generation. Each of God's servants must do all he can to ensure the ongoing of God's work, but the work is bigger than any individual.

## B. The succession from Ishmael (25:12-18)

**25:12-18.** Ishmael too was a **son** of Abraham, so God told what became of him and his line (**the account** [*tôlᵉdôt*] **of . . . Ishmael**) before returning to the chosen line, the succession of Isaac. Ishmael had 12 **sons,** as God had predicted (17:20), and died at the age of **137.** His sons lived in the Arabian peninsula **from Havilah** (in north-central Arabia) **to Shur** (between Beersheba and Egypt). The Ishmaelites **lived in hostility toward all their brothers,** a fulfillment of God's words to Hagar (16:12).

## C. The succession from Isaac
### (25:19–35:29)

After briefly mentioning Ishmael's line (25:12-18), the narrative returned to the chosen line through Isaac. "This is the account (*tôlᵉdōt*) of . . . Isaac," 25:19). The first section (25:10–28:22) records Isaac's prosperity and Jacob's struggle for the right to it—events within the land of promise. Chapters 29–32 relate Jacob's blessing in his sojourn out of the land of promise, and chapters 33–35 his return to the land and possible corruption of the land.

1. THE TRANSFER OF THE PROMISED
   BLESSINGS TO JACOB INSTEAD OF TO ESAU
   (25:19–28:22)

### a. The oracle at the birth of the twins (25:19-26)

This account of the births of Esau and Jacob is a fitting introduction to the following chapters, for their struggle for supremacy manifested itself even before their births (cf. Hosea 12:3).

**25:19-20. Rebekah,** Isaac's wife, was also his cousin (cf. 24:15). Similarly Nahor had married his niece (11:29). (See the chart "Terah's Family," near 11:27-32.) Isaac's marriage to Rebekah thus tied him to Abraham's native country and family, and to the Arameans in northwest Mesopotamia (cf. 24:10), later known as Syria.

**25:21-23.** God supernaturally provided a son for **Isaac.** Like Sarah, **Rebekah** was **barren** (v. 21) even though God promised that nations would stem from Abraham! In contrast with Abraham (16:1-4), Isaac **prayed,** and God responded. This shows that births were sometimes supernatural provisions. Later, Rachel, Jacob's wife, was also temporarily barren (29:31).

But there was conflict in Rebekah's womb (25:22). When **she went to inquire** about this from **the Lord,** she received a prediction from Him: **Two nations,** that is, twin progenitors of two nations, were struggling **in her womb** and **the younger** would triumph (v. 23). Indeed the Israelites (Jacob's descendants) and the Edomites (Esau's descendants) fought continuously. God's election of Jacob the younger over Esau the older was against the natural order.

**25:24-26.** The parents observed the strange situation, and in view of God's oracle they commemorated the event by giving them appropriate names.

The first of the twins was **red** and **hairy,** like a little animal, **so they named him Esau.** The mention of "red" anticipated the future rugged nature of Esau (vv. 27-34).

Fascinating wordplays were used to describe the first twin. The name Esau (*'ēśāw*) has a loose connection with the word "Seir" (*śē'îr*), the early name for Edom to the southeast of the Dead Sea, where Esau later lived (32:3; 36:8). The Hebrew word "red" (*'aḏmônî*) is related to the word "Edom" (*'ĕḏôm*; cf. 25:30); and "hairy" (*śē'ār*) is similar to "Seir." Those words were carefully chosen to portray in the lad the nature of Edom, a later arch rival of Israel.

The second twin was born **grasping Esau's heel** (v. 26). In view of the oracle the parents had received (v. 23) it seemed appropriate to give this child a name that would preserve the memory of this event. The name **Jacob** (*ya'ăqōḇ,* meaning "may He [God] protect") was selected because of its connection in sound and sense to the noun "heel" (*'āqēḇ*). The verb *'āqaḇ* means "to watch from behind." But as with Esau, so Jacob's name would take on a different sense later in life as his deceptive nature became evident. His name also meant "one who grabs the heel" or "one who trips up." So the twins' births had great significance for later events in their lives.

God's fulfillment of His promise to Abraham was carried out by His election of Jacob (later, the nation Israel). At the same time, on the human side, prayer was necessary (v. 21). God's promise is not carried out except through faith in His supernatural work. God later gave Israel, His elect nation, the promise. But it would not come without Israel's struggle.

From the outset the birth of the nation of Israel was supernaturally superintended. Paul noted that before the twins' births the younger was chosen over the elder (Rom. 9:11-12). God often reverses man's natural order, for His ways are not man's ways.

### b. The purchase of the birthright from Esau (25:27-34)

Sadly, things of great spiritual value are often handled in profane or crafty ways. Some people treat spiritual and eternal things with contempt, for they see them as of no value. And others, though regarding such things highly, make the higher cause serve themselves through craft and manipulation. Esau and Jacob are examples of both types.

**25:27-34.** Jacob and Esau developed in accord with their initial characteristics. Esau, "the red man," was overcome by his physical appetite for **red stew** (v. 30) and sold his birthright. And Jacob, "the heel-grabber," cunningly overtook his brother and gained the **birthright.**

Though Jacob was not righteous, he was not in this instance deceptive. He was open and obvious, but he was unscrupulous. He must be given credit for knowing what was of value and going after it. Esau, however, was totally "godless" ("profane," KJV; Heb. 12:16.)

This passage too includes several important wordplays. Esau was **a skillful hunter** (lit., "a man knowing game" [ṣayiḏ], **a man of the open country**; Gen. 25:27), but he could not find game this time (v. 29). His father **loved** him because of his own **taste for wild game** (ṣayiḏ, v. 28). Thus Esau's nature and occupation were favored by **Isaac** because of the satisfaction of his palate. Both Isaac and Esau made choices because of this.

Jacob was **loved** by Rebekah (v. 28), partly because of the oracle (v. 23) which she probably mentioned often. And he **was a quiet man, staying among the tents** (v. 27). But ironically Jacob was the craftier hunter, baiting his trap for the hungry "animal." One day he **was cooking** (lit., "boiling," wayyāzeḏ) **some stew** ("vegetable soup," nāzîḏ, v. 29) made of lentils (v. 34). These words reflect by sound the word for "game" (ṣayiḏ, vv. 27-28). But also the verb zîḏ ("to boil") speaks of Jacob's presumption, for it means "to be exalted or presumptuous." Thus the boiling soup portrays a man whelming up over his bounds.

As the firstborn, **Esau** had the **birthright** and Jacob had the **stew.** But in the exchange, Esau received the **stew** and Jacob the birthright. But **Esau despised his birthright** (v. 34), for what could it do for him if he died of starvation? (v. 32)

**Jacob,** the second-born, then had the **birthright.** The calculating, quiet man who recognized the spiritual value in the

birthright manipulated his profane brother into giving it up. Perhaps knowing the oracle (v. 23), Jacob had been waiting for this opportunity. However, God later made Jacob realize that His promises are not acquired in this way (cf. his grandfather Abraham's manipulating, 16:1-6).

Certainly the profane nature of Esau was a warning for Israel. It is wrong to sacrifice spiritual provisions to satisfy one's physical appetites. This is a question of priorities. Easu saw only food; and he did whatever was necessary to get what he wanted (cf. Eve and the food on the tree, 3:6).

**Esau** is portrayed as emotional: he was fainting and gasping (**famished,** 25:29), gulping (suggested by the Heb., v. 34), and then despising (v. 34). In this instance he was not a skillful hunter; he was more like an animal he had trapped with bait. To live on this base level, to satisfy one's appetites, inevitably leads to a despising of spiritual things.

**Jacob,** though an indoorsman, was a better hunter than Esau. He too craved—but something worth craving. Once he had grabbed by the heel; now he pressed the matter harder. But danger lies even in such spiritual ambition. Believers should seek things of spiritual value, but they should avoid the devices of the flesh. After Jacob was later purged of his human expedience, however, he became a capable servant, for his priorities were then correct.

*c. The prosperity of the Abrahamic blessing enjoyed by Isaac (26:1-33)*

**26:1-5.** Some have supposed that this story of **Isaac** in **Gerar** with **Abimelech** was confused in tradition with the occasions when **Abraham** was in **Egypt** (12:10-20) and in Gerar with Abimelech (chap. 20). But the repetition of motifs is deliberate; it shows that the blessing was passed on to Abraham's descendants. Isaac's parallels to **Abraham** here are numerous: (a) **a famine** (cf. 12:10); (b) a plan to go to Egypt (cf. 12:11); (c) the stay in Gerar (cf. 20:1); (d) out of fear calling his wife his "sister" (cf. 12:12-13; 20:2, 11); (e) the wife's beauty (12:11, 14); (f) Abimelech's concern about committing adultery (20:4-7); and (g) Abimelech's rebuke (20:9-10). The Abimelech in 26:1 was probably not the same Abimelech as in chapter 20, for the events were about 90 years apart. It is not impossible that Abimelech was a title (like Pharaoh or Caesar), for Achish (1 Sam. 21:10) was also known as Abimelech (cf. title to Ps. 34). Similarly, Phicol (Gen. 26:26) might be a title, though there is no evidence for this. Or Phicol may simply be a namesake of the earlier Phicol (21:22, 32).

Abraham was now gone. He was dead! What would happen to God's promise to him? Very simply, the promise would continue right on after his death. Chapter 26 stresses by rhetorical devices that the promise continued to **Isaac.**

The basic idea in 26:1-11 was that the descendants of the obedient servant Abraham would be blessed because of him, but they too had to exercise faith in order to enjoy the promised blessings. Genuine faith in God's promises engenders a fearless walk with Him; but to cower in fear endangers the blessing and makes a mockery of faith.

The obedience of one man brought blessings to his descendants. The Lord gave the Abrahamic promises to Isaac (God's presence, His blessing, possession of **the land,** and posterity **as numerous as the stars**; cf. 12:2-3; 15:5-8; 17:3-8; 22:15-18; 28:13-14). All this, God said, was **because** Abraham **obeyed Me** (lit., "obeyed My voice") **and kept My requirements, My commands, My decrees, and My laws.** These are standard terms in the legal literature of the Old Testament. Israel would immediately see Torah (Law) terminology in the record of Abraham, and would be prompted to keep the Law. Abraham learned that true faith obeys God's words.

**26:6-11.** Isaac in **Gerar,** like his father, deceived **Abimelech** and was rebuked by the pagan **king** who knew that the penalty for adultery was **death** (vv. 10-11). This legal note also would remind Israel of the importance of preserving marriage for the future of their nation. When that mainstay goes, a society crumbles (if Isaac's marriage would have ended, there would have been no Israelite society).

But the interesting thing is the word play on Isaac's name. After deceiving **Abimelech** into thinking **Rebekah** was his **sister,** Isaac was seen **caressing** her (*mᵉṣaḥēq,* v. 8). This participle is a play on

the name **Isaac** (*yiṣḥāq*), but it also reminds one of Ishmael's mockery (*mᵉṣaḥēq,* 21:9). The choice of words is interesting. It is as if Moses was writing that Isaac's lapse of faith—going to Gerar and calling **his wife** his **sister**—made a mockery of the great promise embodied in his name. In fact **Isaac** made a mockery of **Abimelech** by the deception. "Caressing" his **wife** was a mockery to **Abimelech,** whom he had tried to deceive. **Isaac** should have taken more seriously the covenant promises just given (26:2-5).

So Isaac, like Abraham, received God's great promise, but in fear he deceived Abimelech and made a mockery of the promised blessing. Fear mocks faith; faith boldly laughs in triumph. But a person who truly believes God's promises obeys His statutes, precepts, and commands.

**26:12-22.** **Isaac** sojourned in the land, enjoying divine prosperity (his **crops** flourished and he **became rich**). But **the Philistines,** envious of his wealth, filled Isaac's **wells** with dirt.

Again wells provide a dominant motif: they are tangible evidence of divine blessing (cf. Abraham's dispute with the Philistines over a well, 21:25, 30). No matter where **Isaac** dug, and no matter how often **the Philistines** stopped up **the wells,** he **reopened** old dirt-filled wells (26:17). God's blessing on Isaac could not be hindered.

Driven away by the Philistines, Isaac **encamped in the Valley of Gerar,** and continued his search for water. He faced opposition there too; the Gerarites claimed that **the water** from two of the three wells Isaac dug was theirs. The names he gave the three wells reflect not only his struggle but also his triumph: **Esek** ("dispute") and **Sitnah** ("opposition") reflect the conflict over two wells, and **Rehoboth** ("room") represents the **room** provided by **the Lord.** Isaac refused to fight back. He continued to relinquish one well after another until the Philistines in frustration let him alone.

**26:23-25.** After Isaac moved to **Beersheba,** God **appeared to him,** confirming again the Abrahamic Covenant (vv. 23-24). **Isaac** responded as did his father, by building **an altar** and proclaiming Yahweh's **name** (cf. 12:7-8; 21:33).

**26:26-33.** Once the conflict over the

wells was settled, **Abimelech** requested that he and Isaac make **a treaty.** Just as an earlier Abimelech acknowledged that God was with Abraham (21:22), so this Abimelech acknowledged that God **was with** Isaac. **Isaac** named the well there **Shibah** ("oath" or "seven") for they made a treaty by **an oath** (26:28-31, 33) similar to the earlier treaty Abraham made when he named the city **Beersheba** (21:23-24, 31). That treaty was necessarily renewed with Isaac. God's blessing was on the seed of Abraham; Isaac was the rightful heir.

No matter how much opposition came to thwart it, the blessing would thrive. Other nations would recognize that God's hand was on the seed of Abraham and would seek **peace** with Israel if they were to share in the blessing.

### d. The failure of Esau (26:34-35)

**26:34-35.** Esau's marriages to two **Hittite** women (**Judith** and **Basemath**) were a **grief** to his parents. This note demonstrates how unfit Esau was for God's blessing, and how foolish was Isaac's later attempt to bless **Esau** (27:1-40). Esau later married a third wife, Mahalath (28:9).

### e. The deception of Jacob for the blessing (27:1-40)

God expects His servants to carry out their spiritual responsibilities by faith. Unfortunately faith is not always present and then matters become complicated. This chapter portrays an entire family attempting to carry out their responsibilities by their physical senses, without faith. This is the familiar story of how Jacob got the blessing of his father Isaac through deception. It is a story of the fragmenting of a family over spiritual matters!

All participants were at fault. Isaac knew of God's oracle to Rebekah (25:23) that the elder would serve the younger; yet he set out to thwart it by blessing Esau! Esau, agreeing to the plan, broke the oath he had made with Jacob (25:33). Rebekah and Jacob, with a just cause, each tried to achieve God's blessing by deception, without faith or love. Theirs would be the victory, but they would reap hatred and separation for Rebekah never saw Jacob again! So the conflict between Jacob and Esau was greatly

deepened by Jacob's pursuit—he wanted what belonged to the firstborn, the blessing. Yet the story is not just about Jacob. He alone did not destroy the family; parental preference did.

**27:1-4.** SCENE 1 (*Isaac and Esau*)— Issac offered to bless **Esau.** Important notes are given here about Isaac's **weak** eyesight and **old** age. Moreover, stress is placed on the love he had for **wild game** and **tasty food** (cf. 25:28, 34). His palate governed his heart. But Isaac's point was that he intended to **give** Esau his **blessing.** Here was a dilemma for Rebekah that prompted her to action.

**27:5-17.** SCENE 2 (*Rebekah and Jacob*)— **Rebekah** sent **Jacob** into action to stop **Isaac.** Rebekah seemed certain she could duplicate the taste of meat from wild **game** with goat's meat (v. 9). But **Jacob** was not so sure he could deceive his father. After all, Jacob said, if Isaac touched him, Isaac would know the difference between Esau's **hairy** skin and Jacob's **smooth skin.** Jacob had no guilt— only fear—regarding the plan. But the **blessing** was in danger and all must be risked, including even the possibility of **a curse** on **Rebekah** (vv. 12-13). So **Jacob** did as **his mother** told him. **Rebekah** even had **Jacob** put on some of Esau's **best clothes!**

**27:18-29.** SCENE 3 (*Jacob and Isaac*)— Jacob deceived **his father** and obtained the blessing. Prodded by his mother **Jacob** lied twice to his father, first, about his identity (**I am Esau,** v. 19), and second, that **God** had given him **success** (in hunting, v. 20). Three times the old man voiced his suspicion (vv. 20, 22, 24). But deceived by his senses of touch (vv. 16, 23) and smell (v. 27), **he blessed** Jacob, thinking he was **Esau** (vv. 27-29). The blessing included prosperity in crops (v. 28), domination over other nations and his brothers (cf. v. 37), cursing on those who **cursed** him, and blessing on those who **blessed** him (v. 29).

**27:30-40.** SCENE 4 (*Esau and Isaac*)— Soon **Esau** came home and pleaded for a **blessing** from **his father.** When Esau brought in his **food,** emotions ran high. **Isaac trembled violently** over what had happened and **Esau** was very **bitter** and angry (v. 34). **Isaac** knew he had been tampering with God's plan and had been overruled; there was no going back now. **Esau** began to realize the true nature of

Jacob—twice he had "overreached" or **deceived** Esau, by taking his **birthright** (25:27-34), and now by taking his **blessing.** All that was left was a **blessing** for a profane person (27:39-40). **Esau** would not enjoy **the earth's** riches or heaven's **dew** (cf. v. 28). The Edomites, Esau's descendants, would live in a land less fertile than Palestine. Also Esau would **live** by force, be subservient to Jacob, and be **restless** (cf. Ishmael, 16:12).

So in a sense Rebekah and Jacob won, though they gained nothing that God would not have given them anyway; and they lost much.

Yet God would work through their conniving. Their activities only succeeded in doing what God's oracle had predicted. God's program will triumph, often in spite of human activities.

The story is one of parental favoritism, which tore their family completely apart. The story is also an account of spiritual insensitivity. All the natural senses play a conspicuous part—especially the sense of taste in which Isaac prided himself, but which gave him the wrong answer. Reliance on one's senses for spiritual discernment not only proves fallible, but often fouls up life unduly.

Most importantly, however, the story is about deception. Jacob's only hesitancy was his fear that he would be cursed instead of blessed (27:12). At least he realized such actions would place God's promise in jeopardy. Jacob later would learn that blessings are given by God, not gained by deceit.

### f. The flight of Jacob (27:41–28:9)

**27:41-46.** This passage begins the transition to the Laban stories. Because of his deception **Jacob** had to flee from home. But the occasion introduced the motif of his taking **a wife** from his relatives in the East. Whereas Isaac had remained in the land while Abraham's servant had gone to find and fetch his wife (chap. 24), Jacob's journey was necessitated by the imminent danger of being killed by his angry **brother** (27:41-42). Moreover, God would deal with Jacob severely under the hand of **Laban,** his uncle. Indeed, the sojourn out of the land in several ways parallels the later sojourn of Jacob's family in Egypt.

**Rebekah** told **Jacob** about Esau's anger, and urged him to go immediately to

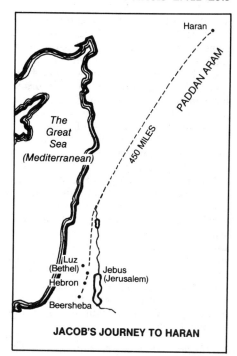

**JACOB'S JOURNEY TO HARAN**

her **brother** Laban **in Haran.** Again deceiving her husband for the sake of her son, she expressed disgust with her two **Hittite** daughters-in-law, Judith and Basemath (v. 46; 26:34-35) and urged **Isaac** to let **Jacob** get a wife from her own people. In that way Jacob could flee with Isaac's blessing (cf. 28:1).

**28:1-5.** Again **Isaac** blessed **Jacob** and told him, **Do not marry a Canaanite woman.** The Canaanitish people were a mixed breed—they incorporated dozens of groups and clans into their society by treaties and marriages. The family of Abraham would resist such mixing (cf. Abraham's refusal to give Isaac a Caananite wife, 24:3). The reason for marrying within the clan was a desire for maintaining purity of the line and being loyal to one's family. The surest way to lose tribal distinction was to intermarry with people of mixed elements. Moses' telling the Israelites again and again that their ancestors resisted marriage to the Canaanites certainly sounded a note of warning. To marry Canaanites would destroy the purity of the line, to be sure, but more importantly it would destroy the purity of the Israelites' faith.

Before Jacob departed, Isaac gave him the pure and legitimate blessing. There was no holding back now; **Isaac**

73

specifically passed on to **Jacob** the blessing **God** had given both **Abraham** and Isaac. Isaac reiterated the blessing from **God Almighty** (*ʾēl šadday;* see comments on 17:1) pertaining to prosperity and **the land** (28:3-4; cf. 15:5, 18-20), and urged his son to go **to Paddan Aram.** Those inheriting the blessings of the Abrahamic Covenant were not to endanger those blessings by intermarriage with Canaanites. Spiritual purity should be maintained in all generations.

**28:6-9.** In a contrasting anticlimax **Esau,** trying to please **his father,** married a descendant of **Abraham** through **Ishmael. Mahalath, a daughter of Ishmael,** was thus a cousin of Esau. Ironically the unchosen son of *Isaac* married into the unchosen line of *Ishmael!* So Esau tried to better his marital reputation by marrying a third wife (cf. 26:34). Esau had no understanding of the Abrahamic Covenant and its purity. He was still living on the human level.

*g. The promises of the covenant confirmed at Bethel (28:10-22)*

Jacob's vision at Bethel was based on God's pure grace. God appeared to Jacob to assure him of His promise of blessing and protection, prompting in Jacob a marvelous worshipful response in which he vowed loyalty. This passage (a) answers the question of whether the Lord was also the God of Jacob, and (b) shows how Jacob's outlook was dramatically changed.

**28:10-15.** Jacob, stopping **for the night** on his way to his Aramean Uncle Laban at **Haran** in Paddan Aram (cf. 25:20; 28:2), dreamed of **angels** on a **stairway** extending **to heaven.** The point of the story is that God was present with Jacob **wherever** he went. This was symbolized by the "ladder," explained in words by God (vv. 13-15), and recognized in faith by Jacob (vv. 20-22). God reiterated to Jacob the covenant made with Abraham and Isaac, promising him **the land . . . descendants** as numerous as **the dust** (cf. 13:16; 22:17), and universal blessing through him (cf. 12:2-3; 15:5, 18; 17:3-8; 22:15-18; 35:11-12). God also promised to protect and be with Jacob while he was out of the **land** and to see that he returned.

**28:16-22.** Jacob's worshipful response included (a) having fear before the LORD, (b) erecting a memorial **stone . . . pillar,** (c) consecrating the stone by anointing the **top** of it with **oil,** (d) naming the **place Bethel** ("house of God") to commemorate the event, (e) making **a vow** in which he expressed for the first time his faith in the Lord (**the LORD will be my God**), and (f) promising to tithe (v. 22). All these enhance the central idea of God's protecting presence.

Several motifs pertaining to later Israelite customs are established here in Jacob. The most notable is the memorial at Bethel. Later the conquering Israelites would reckon this to be a holy place where God could be "seen."

Another motif here is tithing (as with Abram in 14:20). To give a tithe was an act whereby a person acknowledged that everything he had belonged to God. Faith outwardly recognizes this fact in token form.

Also Jacob's vow was an important element in this event. He vowed that **if God** would protect him, provide for him, and **return** him to his homeland, **then** this place would become a major worship center for Him. Vows were important later to Israel.

Moreover, standing stones also become important from this point on. These are different from altars. Memorials were set up to recall divine visitations so that others might learn about God when they would ask, "What do these stones mean?" (Josh. 4:6)

The presence of these important religious motifs stress the point that an anonymous "place" became a major worship center for Israel. The parallel structure between the two sections (Gen. 28:10-13 and 16-19) shows that the worship was a response to the vision. For example, "head" is repeated, first for Jacob's **head** on the stone (v. 11), then for the top (lit., "head") of the stairway (v. 12), and then for the top of the pillar (v. 18). Another wordplay occurs with the word "standing"; first, the Lord **stood** at the top of the stairway (v. 13), and the stone was **set . . . up** (lit., "stood up") as a memorial (v. 18). These parallels show that Jacob's miniature altar represented the vision.

God's promise to be with His people is a theme repeated throughout Scripture (e.g., God said to Isaac, "Do not be afraid, for I am with you," 26:24). The assurance of God's presence should bring about in every believer the same response of worship and confidence in **Jacob.** This is the message from the beginning: God by grace visits His people and promises them protection and provision so that they might be a blessing to others. They in turn were to respond in faith, fearing Him, worshiping Him, offering to Him, vowing to Him, and making memorials for future worshipers at such places.

This event at Bethel then was archetypical of Israel's worship, patterned after—and indeed named after—her patriarch Jacob.

2. THE BLESSING OF JACOB IN HIS SOJOURN (CHAPS. 29–32)

These chapters display how God kept His promise and blessed Jacob abundantly. They also show how God disciplined the patriarch in the process.

a. *The meeting of Rachel and the deception by Laban (29:1-30)*

**29:1-6.** The structure and the content of this passage reflect the significance of the Bethel experience. **Jacob** had been fleeing from Esau; now he was looking for a bride. This change in purpose was due to God's promise given him at Bethel. His quest now was the fulfillment of part of that promise, namely, the seed, while Jacob was outside the land. Moreover, Jacob's spirit was now magnanimous and unselfish. He had a new outlook.

Significantly Jacob's meeting of Rachel parallels his father's meeting of Rebekah (chap. 24). Certainly Laban, Rebekah's brother, would have remembered how God had led Eliezer. Yet this narrative, unlike chapter 24, does not emphasize divine leadership; but it is implied. Here was a man who received a marvelous vision. He knew God's plan to bless him and lead him. So Jacob hastened on his mission (**continued on his journey** is lit., "picked up his feet"). He "happened" onto a spot where **a well** was located; it "happened" to be near **Haran,** where **Laban** lived (29:5), and Laban's **daughter Rachel** just "happened" to be coming to the well (v. 6). This timing was the work of the loving sovereign God who was leading all the way (cf. 24:27). The fact that the meeting

took place at a well is significant because a well was often associated with God's blessing (cf. 16:13-14; 21:19; 26:19-25, 33).

**29:7-14.** When Jacob **watered Laban's** flocks, a note of anticipation was there: subsequent chapters (30–31) show how **Laban** and his flocks prospered in Jacob's presence (cf. 12:2-3). In contrast with Laban's lazy shepherds (29:7-8) **Jacob** was generous, zealous, and industrious (v. 10). He had a mission, a quest. That burning goal implanted by previous experience drove him to succeed.

Kissing of relatives (vv. 11, 13) was a proper greeting. In calling **Jacob** his **own flesh and blood** (v. 14), **Laban** possibly was adopting **Jacob,** his nephew, as a son.

**29:15-30.** Jacob's joyful prospect of marrying **Rachel** turned, by Laban's deception, into a nightmare. In **Laban . . . Jacob** met his match and also his means of discipline. **Jacob** had deceived his own brother and father, and now was deceived by his mother's brother! Twenty years (31:38) of drudgery, affliction, and deception lay ahead. Through **Laban** he received his own medicine of duplicity. But Jacob's tenacity shows that he counted these as minor setbacks. God took him, developed his character, turned the fruits of his deception into blessing, and built the promised seed, the nation of Israel.

Jacob's plan was to **work . . . seven years** to have **Rachel** as his wife. Those **seven years** of work passed quickly for Jacob **because of his love for her** (29:20). Interestingly the wives of each of the first three patriarchs were beautiful: Sarah (12:11), Rebekah (24:15-16), and Rachel (29:17).

When the time came for the wedding **feast** (vv. 21-22), hearts were merry and spirits high. But in the night **Leah,** Rachel's older sister, was substituted. This was a masterpiece of shameless treachery—unloved **Leah** given to a man in love with **Rachel.**

Jacob's anger was to no avail. Now, as the object of trickery, he would understand how Esau felt. **Laban** offered a technicality of local custom: **it is not** right to marry **the younger . . . before the older.** Those words must have pierced **Jacob!** In his earlier days he, the younger, had deceptively pretended before his father to be the older brother (chap. 27). If

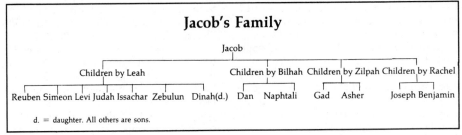

**Jacob's Family**

Jacob

Children by Leah — Children by Bilhah — Children by Zilpah — Children by Rachel

Reuben Simeon Levi Judah Issachar Zebulun Dinah(d.) — Dan Naphtali — Gad Asher — Joseph Benjamin

d. = daughter. All others are sons.

social convention were to be set aside, it should be by God, not by deception. Laban's stinging words were left without any comment; the event was simply God's decree against **Jacob.**

The Bible demonstrates over and over the principle that what a man sows he reaps (Gal. 6:7). Some have called this irony or poetic justice, but it is more than that. It is divine retribution in which there is often a measure-for-measure turn of affairs. God orders the affairs of people to set things right. With **Jacob** this deception was perfectly fitted; it was divine punishment to bring his own craftiness before his eyes. He had deceptively presented himself to his father under the guise of Esau the firstborn; now **Leah** the firstborn was deceptively introduced to him under the guise of **Rachel** the younger! After his initial reaction Jacob recognized the deception for what it was and accepted it. **He finished out** the **bridal week** (Gen. 29:27; cf. **week** in v. 28) at the end of which he was given **Rachel** (two wives in seven days). (Each daughter was given a **servant girl** as a wedding gift, a custom common in that society. **Leah** was given **Zilpah**, v. 24, and **Rachel** received **Bilhah**, v. 29; cf. 30:4-13.) Then Jacob **worked . . . another seven years,** which he owed **Laban** in return for **Rachel** (29:30; cf. 31:38, 41).

Unfortunately **Jacob** was not the only believer who needed a **Laban** to discipline him.

b. *The expansion of the promised seed in the births of the tribal ancestors (29:31–30:24)*

The desire for affectionate approval often leads down dangerous paths. The contest of childbearing between Rachel and Leah shows just such a struggle within a family. The story is about the craving of human beings for love and recognition, and the price of thwarting it.

**29:31-35.** In his family relationships

Jacob still sowed some bitter seeds. He was cool to **Leah,** his unwanted wife; God, as well as Leah, was aware of it. **Rachel,** like Sarah and Rebekah before her, **was barren** (v. 31; cf. 16:1; 25:21).

Leah's first four sons were born in rapid succession; and this must be contrasted with the long waits of the earlier fathers. The story of these births is sad, but in them, as in the chapter as a whole, God is recognized as the One who gives life in spite of human efforts.

Leah named her firstborn **Reuben** (*rᵉʾûḇēn*), indicating that **the LORD** had **seen** her **misery** (*rāʾâh bᵉʿŏnyî*). Another wordplay joins it: **Now at last my husband will become attached to** (*yᵉʾĕhāḇanî*) **me.** This naming showed her hope but also her consolation and faith. Jacob never saw her affliction, but God did (cf. "Beer Lahai Roi," lit., "the well of the living One who sees me," 16:14; 24:62; 25:11).

**Simeon** was so named **because the LORD heard** (*šāmaʿ*) that Leah was **not loved.** "God heard" was her testimony in faith to His provision (cf. "Ishmael," which means "God hears," 16:15).

**Levi** was named for her hope that her husband would become attached (*yillāweh*) to her, but it was not to be.

**Judah** was her consolation; she would be satisfied to **praise** (*ʾôḏeh*) **the LORD,** for Judah means "let Him be praised." Leah exhibited genuine faith during her great affliction.

**30:1-8.** Rachel's sons through **Bilhah** do not reflect the faith Leah had. **Rachel** felt wronged over her barrenness. Her effort to have **children** through her **maidservant** reflects Sarah's similar attempt with Hagar (16:1-4). The names of the two sons born to Bilhah reflected Rachel's bitter struggle and feeling of victory. The name **Dan** is explained by the word *dānannî*, **God has vindicated me,** that is, He now had corrected Rachel's wrong, her barrenness. The name **Naph-**

tali reflected her **great struggle** (*naptûlê*) which, she said, "I fought" (*niptaltî*) **with my sister** (30:8).

**30:9-13. Leah** responded by offering **Jacob** her **maidservant Zilpah,** to whom **Gad (fortune)** and **Asher** ("blessing") were born. **Leah** saw that with God's help she was prospering.

**30:14-21. Reuben,** Jacob's firstborn, **found some mandrake plants,** supposedly aphrodisiacs, and **Rachel** felt they would work for her (vv. 14-15). Thus Leah **hired** Jacob with the plants and had a son **Issachar.** Issachar is explained by *śᵉkartîkā* ("my hire," KJV). The name of Leah's **sixth son. . . . Zebulun,** has the double significance of dowry or "gift" as well as "honor"; **Leah said God** gave her Zebulun as a **gift** and her **husband** would **treat** her **with honor.** Thus Leah's hopes never left her. Then **Dinah,** a **daughter,** was born to her.

**30:22-24.** Finally **Rachel** gave birth to **Joseph** (*yôsēp̄*) but not by the mandrakes. This shows that births are given by God, not manipulated by people. Joseph's name, like Zebulun's, had a double meaning. She **said, God has taken away** (*'āsap̄*) **my disgrace;** and **she** prayed that He would **add** (*yōsēp̄*) **another son.** Finally Rachel was jubilant, looking in faith for a second child from God.

This passage (29:31–30:24) is a combination of small narratives, accenting the puns on Jacob's sons' names. Each name was interpreted by Leah or Rachel to reflect concrete family conditions at the price of the pious substance which they had as testimonies to God as the Giver of Life.

Certainly the passage shows how God prospered Jacob and started to make from him a great nation. All Israelites could thus look back and see their ancestry in Jacob and in the conflict of the women. As brothers the sons of Jacob, who became "Israel," were not to become envious like their mothers.

To Israel these narratives were more than interesting little stories. The rivalry that appears here explains much of the tribal rivalry that followed. But Genesis is clear: God chose the despised mother, Leah, and exalted her to be the first mother. The kingly tribe of Judah and the priestly tribe of Levi trace back to her, in spite of Jacob's love for Rachel and her son Joseph.

*c. The expansion of Jacob's possessions at the expense of Laban (30:25-43)*

This is an unusual story of Jacob's acquiring wealth. This clever man outwitted another opponent, or so it seemed. But Jacob's victory owed more to God than he might have realized at the time.

**30:25-36.** When **Jacob** appealed to **Laban** for permission to go home, **Laban** bargained for him to stay (vv. 27-28, 31). Here was oriental diplomacy—two bedouin leaders cautiously on their guard as they negotiated. Laban stated he had **learned by divination** that God had prospered him because of **Jacob.** He may have looked for omens, or may have simply perceived. **Dark-colored** sheep were an omen for good, and perhaps an inordinate amount of them spoke of this (v. 32). **Jacob** agreed that God had **blessed** Laban (v. 30). Thus Jacob proposed a plan by which (ostensibly) he would gain little. He would receive as **wages** for his work the black and multicolored goats— the rarer kind—and **speckled** and **spotted** sheep which would be born. **Laban** thought this over and quickly closed the deal (v. 34). He could see only advantages for himself.

Jacob's plan was most risky. Nevertheless he was looking out for his own interests, hoping to prosper from this.

But Laban's ploy added to the risk. For greater security, Laban immediately **removed all** the animals of abnormal color, giving them to **his sons** and not to Jacob. And as an additional precaution he placed **a three-day journey between** them. Thus he was seeking to ensure that **Jacob** would have a difficult time acquiring a large herd.

**30:37-43.** God blessed **Jacob** in an unusual way. Here there is a wordplay on the name **Laban** for as Jacob peeled back **the bark** on the sticks and exposed the **white** (*lābān*), he saw his **flocks** grow. He played the Laban game and won—he outwitted "Whitey."

Clearly, as Jacob later admitted (31:7-12), God intervened to fulfill the expectations Jacob had in the **branches. The peeled branches,** placed in **the watering troughs,** appeared to make his animals reproductive as they mated in front of the troughs. In addition, **Jacob** used selective breeding by mating **the stronger** animals for himself and **the weak** female goats and sheep for **Laban.** But this was not the only time God's part in Jacob's success was much greater than it seemed to an observer.

So **Jacob** was greatly prospered (30:43) in fulfillment of God's promise at Bethel, and at the expense of Laban, who now received in part the recompense due him. A fascinating struggle developed between Jacob and Laban. Laban's injustice and artifice preceded Jacob's project, just as Isaac's attempt to bless Esau had earlier prompted Jacob's deception. In both cases the attempt to defraud Jacob was actually overcome by Jacob. Afterward, however, **Jacob** viewed his real gain as divine blessing, though he had to accept the effects (fear and danger) of his craftiness.

*d. The flight from Laban and the protection by God (chap. 31)*

It is a testimony to the blessing of God that Jacob prospered with Laban and that Jacob returned unharmed to his homeland. This proof of divine protection and prosperity should help lead God's people to live by faith.

**31:1-16.** Jacob left for Canaan for two interrelated reasons. First, animosity by **Laban's** sons was growing against Jacob, and **Laban's** mood was dangerous (vv. 1-2). Perhaps God stirred up the nest. Second, God told **Jacob** to return to his own **land** (v. 3). Here was a divine call to leave for the land of promise.

Jacob gave a marvelous speech to his two wives, who met him at his request **out** in **the fields** (vv. 4-16). But this was more than self-defense. He wanted to take with him a willing family, so he attested to God's leading and provision. He now must keep the vow he made at **Bethel** (28:20-22). The response of both women was in faith as well (31:14-16). Laban had exploited his daughters' **wealth** and had lost their good will. So they were willing to leave their father.

**31:17-21.** So the flight ensued, but it was more risky than **Jacob** had hoped because **Rachel stole** Laban's **household gods** (lit., "teraphim," figurines of deities). This shows the pagan influence in Laban's family. A wordplay shows Rachel to be a true "Jacob," for there were parallel thefts: he stole away and she stole the gods. Perhaps she told herself she deserved them since **Laban** had

turned the tables on her in the name of custom and had deprived her of her right to marry first. Whatever the reason, her hardheaded self-interest almost brought disaster. To have the teraphim may have meant the right to inheritance (it did mean this according to the Nuzi tablets of the 15th century B.C.); it certainly meant Laban was without what he thought was his protection.

This is why Laban pursued Jacob. It was one thing for Jacob to take his flocks and family; but his gods too? Perhaps Jacob would try to steal back to Haran someday and claim all of Laban's estate. (Failing to find the gods, Laban later, vv. 43-53, made a treaty to keep this troublesome man out of his territory.)

**31:22-35.** In the **seven**-day pursuit to **Gilead,** east of the Jordan River, just as **Laban** was catching up with **Jacob,** he was warned by God **in a dream** not to speak **good or bad** to Jacob. Without this decisive act of God **Jacob** might not have brought anything home with him.

In the controversy between **Jacob** and **Laban** legal jargon was used to describe their civil suit. In the first "strife" (*rîḇ*; cf. v. 36) or accusation **Laban** claimed that **Jacob** had robbed him (vv. 26-27, 30)—but he presented himself as a hurt father (v. 28) and a baffled avenger (v. 29). When **Laban** demanded that **Jacob** return the teraphim (**gods**), Jacob put the death penalty on **Rachel** unknowingly (v. 32).

But **Laban** was then deceived by **Rachel** (vv. 33-35). She put the idols in **her camel's saddle** and sat on the saddle **in her tent.** Apparently **Laban** never dreamed that a woman would dare take a chance to contaminate the idols. But what a blow this was to the teraphim— they became "nothing gods," for a woman who claimed to be unclean sat on them (vv. 34-35; cf. Lev. 15:20).

**31:36-42.** The second "strife" or accusation came from **Jacob.** (The words **took Laban to task** are lit., "had a strife or controversy [*wayyāreḇ,* related to the noun *rîḇ,* 'strife or accusation'] with Laban.") Laban, the prosecutor, now became the accused. Ignorant of Rachel's theft of the idols, Jacob angrily made a devastating counterattack. He recounted the hardships he had undergone for **Laban** for **20 years** (cf. 29:27-30), taking financial losses while caring for his **flocks**

during **the heat** of the **day** and **the cold at night. The fear of Isaac,** the God Isaac feared, was **with** Jacob and God had **seen** his **hardship** and hard work.

**31:43-55. Laban** suggested they **make a covenant** (i.e., a treaty) for a boundary **between** them (vv. 44, 52). **Laban** instigated it, for Jacob neither needed it nor cared for it!

**Jacob** set up a tall **stone** and then **piled** a **heap** of **stones** around it. **Laban** called them by the Aramaic name **Jegar Sahadutha,** but **Jacob** called them the Hebrew **Galeed. Laban** explained that the name means a **heap** of **witness** but he added the Hebrew name **Mizpah** ("watchtower"), entrusting God to **watch** over them. The stipulations were that Jacob would not harm Laban's **daughters** (v. 50) and that Jacob and Laban would stay apart (v. 52).

In expressing the stipulations of the agreement, **Laban** used many words to cover up his untrustworthiness. The undependable man was trying to convey that Jacob was a slippery character who had to be bound by a whole series of stipulations. Laban tried to terrify Jacob as though he were ungodly and needed to be threatened. He even appropriated the heap of stones (**this heap and . . . this pillar** *I* **have set up,** v. 51, italics added), the monument Jacob had made.

Both the boundary settlement and the wives' rights show that Laban and Jacob wanted to confirm the status quo. But the treaty also marked a break with the East for the family of Israel. This border treaty marked out the frontier **in the hill country** of Gilead.

In their last confrontation God appeared to Jacob (v. 3) and to Laban (v. 24) in dreams for the purpose of separating them. The entire event was complicated by earthly, selfish interests, such as Rachel's theft of the idols and Laban's self-seeking animosity. Interestingly at the end God Himself was invoked to watch between them (v. 49).

This account later had great significance for Israel: God would deliver and protect Israel as He brought them back to the land from Egypt. Here Israel would see God's victory over idols and idolaters, God's use of dreams for deliverance and protection, and the boundary by which God would keep His people apart from her enemies. All this became

important for later Israelite-Aramean relations (Laban was an Aramean, or Syrian, 25:20).

*e. The preparation for Esau (32:1-21)*

**32:1-2.** God prepared **Jacob** for meeting Esau by giving the patriarch a vision of angels. Jacob had just left Laban and was about to return to the land and face Esau once again. At this point God's invisible world openly touched Jacob's visible world.

The encounter is described with striking brevity. Four Hebrew words report the meeting: **the angels of God met him.** Jacob then **named** the place **Mahanaim,** possibly meaning "two camps." He must have seen the camp of angels as a source of comfort to his own camp as he prepared to reenter the land.

A comparison with Jacob's earlier encounter with angels at Bethel (28:10-22) when he left the land proves most instructive. The expression "the angels of God" occurs only in 32:1 and in 28:12 in the Old Testament. The Hebrew *pāga'* with *b^e* occurs in 28:11 ("reached") and in 32:1 ("met"). *Zeh* ("this") is used four times in 28:16-17 and is an important reference in Jacob's response in 32:2. (Cf., e.g., "This is the gate of heaven," 28:17, with **This is the camp of God!** 32:2) In both cases Jacob interpreted what he had seen before naming it (28:17; 32:2), and in Hebrew the identical expression is used in the naming of both places (28:19; 32:2). And finally *hālak* and *derek* ("to go on one's way," i.e., "to take a journey") are used in 28:20 and 32:1.

Obviously the two passages are correlated. What took place at the naming of Bethel on Jacob's way out of the land now took place at the naming of Mahanaim on his way back into the land. His glimpse of the angels of God assured him once again of divine protection accompanying him. And the angels welcomed him on his return to the land of promise. This reassurance came at a time when Jacob sorely needed it.

When God's work is involved, the conflict is spiritual, not physical. This was true for Jacob, it was true for Israel, and it is true today. No human effort can be sufficient for these things. The source of defense and the means of victory come from God's ministering angels.

**32:3-8.** Prompted by the idea in the

vision, **Jacob sent messengers** to **Esau** in **Edom.** (The Heb. word for "angels" also means "messengers.") Many key ideas and wordplays are in this section. **Jacob** had just seen the angels (God's messengers) and now he sent his own messengers to **Esau.** He had recognized the angels as "the camp (*mahǎnēh*) of God," he had named the place *mahǎnāyim* (v. 2), and then (out of **fear** of **Esau** who was **coming** toward him with **400 men**) he **divided** his family **into two groups** or camps (*mahǎnôt*).

**32:9-12.** Out of fear **Jacob prayed** to be delivered. Doubtless he recalled Esau's threat to kill him (27:41). Jacob still would fear, but he would see that God would deliver him from his **brother.** In fact Jacob's deep fear shows up in every section of this passage, even in his prayer.

Jacob addressed God as the **God of my father Abraham** and **of my father Isaac,** and reminded **God** of His command for him to return to his **country** and of His promise to bless him. God wants people to remind Him of His word when they pray. This is a motivation to faith. Jacob then confessed his unworthiness of God's **kindness and faithfulness** and material blessings. He had the correct attitude in prayer—total dependency on God. Jacob petitioned God to be delivered from **Esau** because the younger twin was scared. Then he repeated the promise God had made to him about his **descendants** becoming as numberless as **the sand of the sea** (cf. 22:17). All this should have built Jacob's confidence, but his guilt and fear completely controlled him at this point.

**32:13-21.** To appease **Esau,** Jacob took a portion of his blessing and prepared **a gift** (*minhâh*) for **Esau.** A *minhâh* was often given to a superior to gain his favor. **Jacob sent Esau . . . goats,** sheep, **camels,** cattle, and **donkeys**—550 animals in all, not counting the **young** camels! He thought these five herds sent separately would impress Esau and **pacify him** (v. 20). Jacob had to learn later, however, that God would have delivered him without such **gifts.** So too the nation would need to learn that deliverance comes by faith in God, and not by giving tribute to the enemy.

This passage closes with a significant wordplay in verse 21 that shows how contrary this gift was to the vision (v. 1) that assured him of protection: The **gifts** (lit., "gift," *hamminhâh*) **went on ahead of him, but he . . . spent the night in the camp** (*bammahǎneh*).

### f. The blessing at Peniel (32:22-32)

Before Jacob entered the land of promise, he was met by God who both crippled and blessed him. This event was an important turning point in the patriarch's life.

To understand the purpose of the account several features must be noted. First, the wrestling occurred when Jacob was at the threshold of the land of promise, for the Jabbok River in Gilead flows into the Jordan River from the eastern frontier (vv. 22-24). Second, Jacob became and was named Israel (v. 28). His new name was not merely linked to the narrative; it is explained by it. Third, the account is linked to a place name, Peniel, given by Jacob in response to his being named (v. 30). Fourth, the story includes a dietary restriction for the people of Israel (v. 32). This taboo then became a custom in Israel, but was not made part of the Mosaic Law. Orthodox Jews still refuse to eat the tendon of the hindquarter of animals.

The emphasis of the narrative is certainly on the wrestling; but its purpose was the changing of Jacob into Israel. One cannot ignore the context of Jacob's life here. The connection is strengthened by the plays on the names. At the outset (vv. 22, 24) are *ya'ǎqōḇ* ("Jacob"), the man; *yabbōq* ("Jabbok"), the place; and *yēʾāḇēq* ("he wrestled"), the match. These attract the Hebrew reader's attention immediately, because of the similarity of the consonants *y*, *q*, and *b* in the words. Before Jacob (*ya'ǎqōḇ*) could cross the Jabbok (*yabbōq*) to the land of blessing, he had to wrestle (*yēʾāḇēq*). He was to try once more to trip up an adversary, for at this point he was met by Someone wishing to have a private encounter with him, and he was forced to fight.

**32:22-25.** Before **Jacob** could cross **the Jabbok** River after his family, servants, and **possessions. . . . a Man** attacked and fought **with him.** No details of the fight were given, for it was just the preamble to the most important part, the dialogue. Yet the fight was real and physical.

The word 'îš ("a Man") reveals nothing about His identity. But this is fitting, for the "Man" later refused to reveal Himself directly (v. 29).

The fact that the match lasted **till daybreak** is significant. For the darkness symbolized Jacob's situation. Fear and uncertainty seized him. If Jacob had perceived that he was to fight God, he would never have engaged in the fight, let alone have continued all night.

On the other hand the fact that the wrestling lasted till daybreak suggests a long, decisive bout. In fact the Assailant did not defeat **Jacob** till He resorted to something extraordinary.

At last the Assailant **touched** Jacob **so that his hip** went out of joint. The point is clear: the Assailant gave Himself the advantage. Jacob, the deceitful fighter, was crippled by a supernatural blow. In a word, like so many of his rivals, Jacob now encountered Someone he could not defeat.

**32:26-29.** Nevertheless, though crippled and unable to win, **Jacob** clung to his Assailant for a blessing. Then both the identity of the Assailant and the significance of the fight dawned on Jacob. Once he realized who his Assailant was (v. 28) **Jacob** held on resolutely, pleading for a blessing. It is significant that in response to Jacob's request for a blessing **the Man asked . . . What is your name?** When one remembers that in the Old Testament one's name is linked to his nature, the point becomes clear: Jacob's pattern of life had to be radically changed! In saying his name, **Jacob** had to reveal his whole nature. Here the "heel-catcher" was caught, and had to confess his true nature before he could be **blessed.**

The blessing took the form of a new name—**Israel.** This name probably means "God fights," as the popular etymology signifies. The explanation was then given that **Jacob** had fought **with God and with men.** It is easy to comprehend his having fought "with men" but that he fought "with God" is more difficult to understand. Throughout Jacob's entire life he had been dragging God's blessing out under all circumstances for his own use, under "his own steam." He was too self-willed and too proud to let the blessing be given to him.

So "God fights" was now his name.

This meant, first, that God chose, because of the patriarch's stubbornness and pride, to fight against him. Second, it meant that God would fight for Israel.

Jacob's new name would remind him and others of this fight in which he had **overcome.** These words were full of hope to the Israelites. If one could contend successfully with God, he could then win the battle with man. Thus the name "God fights" and the explanation that Jacob had "overcome" obtained the significance of a promise for the nation's forthcoming struggles.

**32:30-32.** Jacob named **the place Peniel** ("face of God") **because** he had seen **God face to face** and had been **spared.** As before (28:19; 31:47; 32:2), he named the place to commemorate the event. However, "no one has ever seen God" (John 1:18). For an explanation of this alleged contradiction see comments on Exodus 33:11, 20; John 1:18.

God had come as close to Jacob as possible—He had laid hands on him. The idea is not **and yet** he was spared, but rather "*and*" his life was spared. He had prayed for deliverance (Gen. 32:11), using nāṣal ("Save me"), the same word he used later (nāṣal, "spared," v. 30). Jacob's prayer for deliverance was answered by God in this face-to-face encounter and blessing.

When God touched the strongest sinew of the wrestler, it shriveled, and with it Jacob's persistent self-confidence also shriveled. His carnal weapons were lame and useless; they failed him in his contest with God. What he had surmised for the past 20 years now dawned on him: he was in the hands of the One against whom it is useless to struggle. After this crippling touch, Jacob's struggle took a new direction. Now crippled in his natural strength he became bold in faith.

Jacob was not the only one whom God encountered in this manner. Moses was met by God when he had not yet complied completely with God's will (Ex. 4:24). Jacob's encounter was at the frontier of the land promised to the seed of Abraham. God, the real "Proprietor" of the land, opposed his entering as "Jacob." In his self-will and his own strength he could never enter the land.

The point of the story for the new nation of Israel that would come from

Egypt into the land of promise is clear: Israel's ultimate victory would come not by the usual ways by which nations gain power, but through the power of the divine blessing. Self-sufficiency is incompatible with the work of God in any age. Faith alone overcomes the world.

3. THE RETURN OF JACOB AND THE DANGER OF CORRUPTION IN THE LAND (CHAPS. 33–35)

a. The reconciliation with Esau (33:1-17)

Jacob's long-expected meeting with Esau was a marvelous event. God so turned Esau's heart that he was eager to be reconciled with his brother. Earlier Esau had cared nothing for his birthright (25:32-34), and he cared little for old grudges now. Jacob, relieved because of Esau's lack of hostility, had to admit once again that more was due to God's intervention than he had realized.

**33:1-7.** Jacob still showed weakness and fear when he met **Esau.** He lined up his **children** and wives in order of their importance to him, with **Rachel and Joseph in the rear,** the safest place.

The contrasts between the two brothers, as they met after 20 years, are interesting.

Jacob **bowed down to the ground seven times** in homage (v. 3), thus halting on his way toward Esau. **Esau,** however, eagerly **ran to meet Jacob and embraced him . . . kissed him,** and **they both wept.** What a change is made when "God fights" in His way. In talking with Esau, Jacob constantly referred to himself as **your servant** or "his servant" (vv. 5, 14) and to his brother as "my lord" (vv. 8, 13-15) whereas **Esau** simply called **Jacob** "my brother" (v. 9). This contrasts with their father's blessing when Isaac made Jacob Esau's lord (27:29). Jacob definitely approached Esau cautiously and humbly, in an effort to ward off any possible retaliatory spirit.

**33:8-11.** Jacob pressed **Esau** to accept the gift of 550 animals (cf. 32:13-15). When Esau hesitated to accept the livestock, Jacob insisted. He said, **Accept this** (lit., "my") **gift** (*minḥātî*, the same word he used in 32:13). Then Jacob added, **Accept the** (lit., "my") **present** (*birkātî*). The word "present" comes from *bārak*, "to bless." By using *birkātî*, **Jacob** showed that he was deliberately wanting to share

his blessing with **Esau,** trying to soften his earlier actions.

Jacob's explanation, that seeing Esau's **face** was **like seeing the face of God,** showed he knew this deliverance from harm by Esau was of God. At Peniel Jacob had seen the face of God and was delivered (32:30). Having lived through that, he then survived Esau. Thus Esau's favorable reaction was God's gracious dealing.

**33:12-17.** Jacob cleverly avoided traveling with **Esau.** He led Esau to think that he needed to travel slowly because of his young **children** and **young** animals, and that he would meet with Esau at **Seir.** But Jacob headed in the opposite direction—north **to Succoth,** east of the Jordan River and north of the Jabbok River, instead of south to **Seir!** He may have been wise to avoid Edom, but he did not need to deceive his brother again.

Thus miracles were worked in Jacob and Esau. In **Jacob,** God brought about a spirit of humility and generosity. **Esau** was changed from seeking revenge to desiring reconciliation. These changes were proof that God had delivered Jacob in answer to his prayer (32:11).

b. The settlement at Shechem (33:18-20)

**33:18-20.** These verses form a sort of epilogue to Jacob's sojourn outside the land. He returned in peace and camped near **Shechem,** directly west of the Jabbok River and about 20 miles from the Jordan **in Canaan.** This is where Abram first camped when he arrived in Canaan (12:6). Shechem was between Mount Ebal and Mount Gerizim.

**Jacob,** like Abram, purchased a portion of the land and there, like Abram, Jacob **set up an altar** (12:7) **and** named **it El Elohe Israel** ("El is the God of Israel"). In this way he acknowledged that the Lord had led him all the way back to the land.

The following chapters shift the focus onto Jacob's children. His arrival back in the land and his establishing of the altar are the culmination of Jacob's "Laban experience." In this chapter Jacob named two more places (cf. Bethel, 28:19; Galeed, 31:47; Mahanaim, 32:2; Peniel, 32:30). Succoth ("shelters") was named because of the sheds he built for his livestock (33:17), and the name of the altar commemorated the significance of God's relationship to Israel, Jacob's new name. God had prospered and protected him as He had promised.

### c. The defilement of Dinah (chap. 34)

Once Jacob settled in the land, the threat from the Canaanites became a problem. The story is a tangled skein of good and evil, as are all the patriarchal narratives. To Israel this would certainly be a warning against the defiling effect of interrelations with Canaanites, even by deception. Israel was not supposed to intermarry with Canaan or make treaties with them. But the passage also warns against even going to visit the daughters of the land (v. 1). Moreover, covenantal agreements must not be made in a sham (v. 13), for the name of Israel was at stake in the land (v. 30). For this, Simeon and Levi (v. 25) were passed over in the blessing with the birthright (49:5-7).

**34:1-4.** Dinah, Jacob's only **daughter** (30:21), **went out to visit the women of the land.** This action loosened a stone that caused a landslide. Jacob had made a commercial connection with Shechem (33:19), but Dinah's step toward social interaction had serious complications. Avoidance of the Canaanites would have been much safer.

**Shechem . . . the ruler of that area,** lay with her and **violated** ('ānâh, "to afflict, oppress"), that is, raped **her.** After a woman was debased in this way, she had no expectancy of ever having a valid marriage. **Shechem,** however, **loved the girl** and wanted her to be his **wife.**

**34:5-7.** Jacob's response to Dinah's situation was most unusual. **When he heard that** she **had been defiled** (ṭimmē', "to pollute") **he kept quiet about it** till **his sons** got **home.** His sons, however, were incensed, for **a disgraceful thing** (lit., "folly," nᵉbālâh) had been done **in Israel.** (This is the first mention of the nation by this name.) Such a sexual evil was infamous, incriminating a whole community, something **that should not be done.** While the sons **were filled with grief and fury,** Jacob was passive and could not pull things together. Perhaps if Dinah were his daughter by Rachel rather than by Leah, he would have acted differently.

**34:8-12.** The Canaanites approached with a proposal. Old **Hamor,** Shechem's father, made a diplomatic speech: great advantages would be gained by both sides from an agreement to **intermarry** (vv. 8-10). He poignantly offered Israel **the land** (v. 10). But God, not the Canaanites, would give it. Hamor's later appeal to his fellow citizens showed that he was deceptive all along, hoping only to take over Jacob's possessions (v. 23). No good would come to Israel from trusting the defiling Canaanites. **Shechem** then offered to pay Jacob and Dinah's **brothers** whatever **price for the bride** they suggested, trying to buy his way out of trouble.

**34:13-24.** The brothers (not Jacob!) refused such a treaty because, they said, **Shechem** was **not circumcised,** and intermarriage **would be a disgrace** (ḥerpâh, "a reproach, a scorn"). (These words—"not circumcised" [this word in Heb. also suggests being impure] and "a disgrace"—describe the Canaanites well.) So the brothers planned for Shechem's outward conforming to circumcision, but of course this was not a true covenant. They, like their father, dealt **deceitfully** (v. 13). They apparently assumed that **Shechem** and **Hamor** would never **consent** to their **males** being **circumcised** as a condition for intermarriage. But the Canaanites accepted the proposal and had **every male** in town **circumcised,** not only so that **Shechem** could have **Dinah** but also so that they could subtly acquire all the Israelites' **livestock** and other **property.**

**34:25-31.** The outworking of the plot was tragic. **Simeon and Levi** (and no doubt their households) slaughtered the Canaanite males **while** they were **in pain** from the circumcision and still weak from healing. The brothers then rescued **Dinah** and plundered **the city** and **the fields** for the Shechemites' property, livestock, **wealth,** and **women and children.** This all struck fear into **Jacob,** for it could bring serious repercussions on him and his family. But the brothers simply **replied, Should** Shechem **have treated our sister like a prostitute?**

Later the nation of Israel was instructed to avoid defilement with the Canaanites. Israel's foreign policy was to destroy them completely before they could defile the Israelites (Deut. 20:16-18).

In this story the instinct of **Simeon and Levi** was correct, but because of their unbridled passion they were later passed over in Jacob's blessing (Gen. 49:5-7). Moreover, a deceptive covenant was not to be dangled before the pagans. On occasion, however, God used a Simeon and a Levi, and a Jehu (2 Kings 10:11-14, 17-31), as His instruments of judgment.

### d. The return to Bethel (35:1-15)

Two themes run through chapter 35: completion and correction. It is a story of completion because Jacob was back home in the land of promise, with all his family and all his wealth; victory was won, the goal achieved, and the promise fulfilled. But it is also a story of correction, for the family had not completely held to the walk of faith: idols had to be buried and Reuben had to be dealt with.

**35:1.** The first 15 verses record Jacob's return to **Bethel,** about 15 miles south of Shechem, as the completion of his vows. Those vows, made earlier at Bethel, included making Yahweh his God, making Bethel God's house, and pledging to tithe to God (28:20-22). God called Jacob to return to the land (28:13-15; 31:3), but his pilgrimage took a long time. God had to remind Jacob of his forgotten vows. Apparently his indifference to those vows provided the occasion for Dinah's defilement by Shechem (chap. 34). Jacob should have traveled on to Beersheba, his parents' home (28:10), without stopping at Shechem.

**35:2-5.** To complete his vows, there had to be a sanctification process. Jacob's family had to remove all their idols, **the foreign gods.** God permits no rivals; He allows only single loyalty and no magical charms. All this purification (getting rid of idols, washing themselves, and changing their **clothes**) was instructive for Israel, who later would need such a consecration when they entered the land of promise (Josh. 5:1-9).

After burying the idols (and earrings, apparently associated with the idols in some way, possibly as fetishes) at **Shechem . . . Jacob** and his family **set out** for Bethel. People in surrounding **towns,** apparently having heard of the massacre at Shechem (Gen. 34:25-29), feared Jacob.

**35:6-8.** Arriving back in **Bethel** (which used to be called **Luz,** 28:19), Jacob **built an altar** there as God had told him to do (35:1). Meanwhile **Deborah,** the **nurse** of Rebekah, Jacob's mother,

**died.** This death seemed to indicate that another stage in the patriarchal narratives was ending. The naming **Allon Bacuth** ("oak of weeping") commemorated the weeping over this old nurse, buried under an **oak** tree. Interestingly Jacob's wives' idols were also buried under an oak, back in Shechem (v. 4).

**35:9-15.** At Bethel **God** confirmed the promise He had made there earlier (32:28). Jacob's name-change to **Israel** was proof of the promised blessing. God's reference to Himself as **God Almighty** (*'ēl šadday;* cf. comments on 17:1) was also an assurance that His promise would be fulfilled (cf. 28:3). Now that the patriarch was back in the land of promise, the promise of the **nation** ("seed"), **kings,** and **the land** was once again confirmed (cf. 12:2-3; 15:5, 18; 17:3-8; 22:15-18; 28:13-14). Jacob's actions here are almost identical with those in his earlier Bethel experience: setting up **a stone pillar,** pouring **oil on it,** naming **the place . . . Bethel** (cf. 35:6-7, 14-15; 28:16-19). And both times **God** promised **Jacob** many **descendants** in the land (28:13-14; 35:11-12). But here He added that kings would be included in Jacob's offspring.

### e. The completion of the family and the corruption of Reuben (35:16-29)

**35:16-20.** Once in the land the family was completed by the birth of Benjamin. (Interestingly 11 of Jacob's 12 sons, progenitors of the nation's 12 tribes, were born out of the land in Paddan Aram, 29:31–30:24.) Now **Rachel** died in **childbirth.** Her death was the second transitional death in chapter 35 (cf. v. 8).

The name **she** gave the child, **Ben-Oni** ("son of my sorrow") would not do for the lad. Jacob renamed **him Benjamin** ("son of my right hand"). Jacob turned this occasion of sorrow into triumph and victorious prospects. In addition, he wanted to give a good name to the child who was the answer to Rachel's prayer (30:24) for a second son (the name Joseph, *yôsēp,* is from *yāsap,* "to add").

This section also signifies that Israel, once in the land, would continue to flourish under God's blessing. **Jacob set up a stone pillar** (cf. his other pillars: 28:18; 31:45-47; 35:14) over her grave between Bethel and **Bethlehem.** (**Ephrath** was an older name for Bethlehem; cf. "Bethlehem Ephrathah," Micah 5:2. Also cf. Ruth 4:11; 1 Chron. 2:50-51.)

**35:21-22.** The *tôlᵉdôt* ("account") of Isaac draws to a close in verses 21-29 with several short reports. The first describes Reuben's breach of Jacob's family by incest with **Bilhah,** Jacob's **concubine** and Rachel's servant by whom he had two sons, Dan and Naphtali (30:3-8). Reuben's transgression took place near **Migdal Eder** between Bethlehem and Hebron. It is possible that **Reuben,** Jacob's eldest, was trying to replace his father as patriarch prematurely by this pagan procedure. But in so doing, he *lost* his inheritance (his birthright; cf. 49:3-4; 1 Chron. 5:1-2). This act was noted by Jacob who in Genesis 35:21-22 was twice called **Israel.** (Cf. 32:28; 35:10. And note his silence when he heard of the rape of his daughter Dinah, 34:5.)

**35:23-26.** A second report lists the **12 sons** who became heads of the 12 original tribes. (See the chart "Jacob's Family" near chap. 29.) This was another assurance that the promises of God are good. The list provides a firstfruits, as it were, of the tribes that would become the great nation.

**35:27-29.** The chapter's last report is of the death of **Isaac,** who **lived 180 years.** This is the third transitional death recorded in chapter 35 (cf. vv. 8, 18). Isaac was then living near **Hebron,** farther south in Beersheba (cf. 28:10). **Jacob** and **Esau** united to bury him. Perhaps this was the first time the two brothers met since their departure (33:16-17).

In the events of chapter 35, Jacob learned that while his return to Canaan was a completion of promises, he could not be complacent for it was also a new beginning. Deborah, Rachel, and Isaac all died, marking the end of an era. Reuben relinquished his right to inherit a blessing (cf. 49:3-4); sin was dealt with. Idols had to be buried and everyone had to be consecrated in order for Jacob's vow at Bethel to be completed. The nation had to be complete with 12 sons (tribes) in the land. During this great transition faith in God had to be revitalized so that His covenant could be carried forward. For this reason this chapter emphasized Jacob's vows and God's promise.

### D. The succession from Esau (36:1-8)

This chapter is complicated and difficult, the details quite baffling. The *tôlᵉdôt* of Isaac (25:19–35:29) has closed, so the book discusses the successions from his sons, following the custom of wrapping up the history of the unchosen line (chap. 36) before going to the chosen (chap. 37; cf. chap. 4 with chap. 5; 10:1-20 with 10:21-31; 21:8-21 with 22:1-18).

**36:1-8.** These verses give the *tôlᵉdôt* **of Esau.** He had three wives: **Adah . . . Oholibamah,** and **Basemath.** Since two of these wives' names are not the same as those listed earlier (26:34; 28:9), either the others had died or he favored these three among his six or the two took different names.

Oholibamah was a great-granddaughter of Seir the Horite, whose descendants were living in Edom when Esau went there (36:20, 25). From these three wives **Esau** had five **sons.**

The narrative stresses two elements. First, Esau's sons **were born** in the land (**Canaan,** v. 5) before he moved to **Seir** (v. 8). This contrasts sharply with Jacob, whose children were born *out of* the land, and who then moved *into* the land. Second, **Esau** was **Edom.** In fact all through the chapter the reader is reminded of this. Certainly Israel would understand the import of this because she often struggled with the Edomites (cf. Obad.), Esau's descendants (Gen. 36:43).

The wording in verse 7 is striking. One thinks of Lot: **the land** was not able to bear **both** of **them** because their herds were so **great** (cf. 13:5-6). Esau, like Lot, left for the East and greener land (cf. 13:8-12).

### E. The succession from Esau, father of the Edomites (36:9–37:1)

**36:9-19.** The latter part of chapter 36 (vv. 9-40) also begins with *tôlᵉdôt* (**the account,** v. 9; cf. v. 1), though most see this as a minor division within the account that traced what became of **Esau.**

The sons of Esau also had sons. Thus Esau had 5 **sons** and 10 **grandsons** (either literal descendants and/or tribes founded by them). (Esau had 11 grandsons if **Korah** [v. 16] is included. The Heb. MT lists him here but not in v. 11 or in 1 Chron. 1:36. Perhaps he died soon after becoming a chief. Or perhaps the word Korah in Gen. 36:16 is a scribal error, picked up by dittography from the Korah in v. 14.) In the Hebrew, each of the 10 grandsons and 3 of the sons—13 in all —was called a "chief" (*'allûp,* vv. 15, 17-18), a head of a tribe. A picture of Esau as an overlord was emerging (cf. vv. 40-43).

**36:20-30.** These verses list **the sons** (i.e., sons, grandsons, and granddaughters) **of Seir the Horite,** inhabitants of the land. These sons were probably aboriginal Edomites conquered by Esau (Deut. 2:12). Seir's 7 **sons** (Gen. 36:20-21) became **Horite chiefs** (cf. v. 29) and from those came 20 "sons" or "daughters" (i.e., tribes). One of Esau's wives was **Oholibamah,** a great-granddaughter of Seir (cf. vv. 2, 14, 18, 25; Seir gave birth to Zibeon, v. 20, who bore Anah, v. 24, whose daughter was Oholibamah).

**36:31-39.** It is not certain how the kings of Edom were related to Esau, but they were **kings who reigned in Edom,** and "Esau . . . is Edom" (v. 8). The organization of the clans in Edom apparently paralleled that in Israel. They ultimately chose a king from one of their tribes and carried on a line of succession from him. Whether or not the line of eight kings mentioned here extends beyond the time of Jacob and Esau is unclear. The point is comparative, though: there were kings in Edom **before any Israelite king reigned** (v. 31).

**36:40-43.** These verses list the names of the **chiefs** who **descended from E-sau . . . according to their** families, after their places, and by their names. **Esau** was thus a great, powerful overlord: the **father of the Edomites** (v. 43) over **clans and regions** (v. 40), with 11 chiefs descended from him. Isaac's promises to Esau were thus being fulfilled: and by being away from Jacob he was shaking the "yoke" of his brother from his "neck" (27:39-40).

**37:1.** In dramatic contrast with the expanding, powerful Esau, **Jacob** was dwelling **in the land** of the sojournings of **his father . . . the land of Canaan.** Unlike Esau, Jacob had no "chiefs" or kings (35:11) yet, no lands to govern, and no full tribes. He was a sojourner. Delitzsch pertinently remarked that secular, worldly greatness comes swifter than spiritual greatness (*A New Commentary on Genesis,* 2:238). A promised spiritual blessing demands patience and faith. Waiting while others prosper is a test of one's faithfulness and perseverance.

## F. The succession from Jacob (37:2–50:26)

The story of Joseph in Egypt forms a unique literary unit in the Book of Genesis. The fact that there are repeated elements in the narratives does not prove that the material was handed down in two differing traditions as many critical scholars suggest. Repetition is the hallmark of Hebrew style; it serves to heighten the message, giving it a multiple emphasis.

One example of repetition is the analogy between the Jacob and Joseph stories. Both cycles of narratives begin with the father being deceived and the brothers being treacherous (chaps. 27; 37). Both cycles include a 20-year period of separation, with the younger brother in a foreign land. (For Jacob see 31:38. As for Joseph, he was 13 years in Potiphar's house and in prison—from age 17 [37:2] to age 30 [41:46]—and after 7 years of abundance his brothers came to Egypt, 41:53-54; 42:1-2.) Both conclude with a reunion and reconciliation of the brothers (33:1-15; 45:1-15). As God had worked out matters to a proper resolution with Jacob, He would do the same with his son Joseph.

The Joseph stories also were instructive for Israel. As Joseph spent years in bondage in Egypt before being delivered, so the descendants of Jacob would be in bondage there and would then be delivered from it. For Joseph the discipline would test his faith; for the nation the stay in Egypt would be for their preservation and discipline.

In the record of Joseph's life are several cycles of events: three sets of dreams, four sets of parallel relationships (Joseph and his family, Joseph and Potiphar's household, Joseph and the prisoners, Joseph and Pharaoh's household), two episodes in a pit-prison that involve false accusation and the use of his clothing for proof, and repeated visits to Egypt by his brothers. These cycles form the structure of the *tôlⁱdôt* ("account") of Jacob (37:2).

The narratives differ in tone from the preceding material in Genesis. The emphasis here seems to be closely related to the wisdom literature of Proverbs and Ecclesiastes, including incidental comments and the major point that Joseph was a wise ruler (Gen. 41:39).

The theme of suffering as a test of character is predominant, both for Joseph and his brothers. Though Joseph was righteous he was not kept from suffering. He was preserved by his faith through it. In the end Joseph could acknowledge that God meant it all for good (50:20). The Bible's wisdom literature assures the faithful that God brings good out of evil and suffering. Though the wicked may prosper for a time, the righteous hold fast to their integrity because there is a higher, more enduring principle of life (cf. the Book of Job). The wise recognize that the Lord God is sovereign over nature and the nations, and that He righteously orders the affairs of His people. At times God's ways seem unfair and paradoxical, but if endured by faith they bring blessings to the righteous.

1. THE SELLING OF JOSEPH INTO EGYPT (37:2-36)

a. The dreams of Joseph (37:2-11)

**37:2-4.** After the heading introduces this section as the last *tôlᵉdôt*, **the account of Jacob,** the story of Joseph begins. **Joseph** is introduced as an obedient **17-year-old** son who **brought** back a **bad report about** his half **brothers** (he did not bring a bad report about his full brother Benjamin). The substance of this report is not given. Though doing this has never been popular, it shows that Joseph was faithful as a servant. Naturally **his brothers . . . hated him** for this.

The lad was also honored by Jacob who gave him **a richly ornamented robe,** probably a multicolored tunic. This seems to signify that Jacob favored him above the rest with the intent of granting him all or a larger portion of the inheritance. For **Joseph** was the firstborn of Rachel, Jacob's loved wife (30:22-24). Yet Jacob should have remembered what parental favoritism does to a family. It had separated him from his loving mother (27:1–28:5), and it would separate Joseph from Jacob.

**37:5-11.** God confirmed Jacob's choice of his faithful son by two dreams. God's revelation was given in different forms in the Old Testament. He used dreams when His people were leaving or outside the land, that is, in the lands of pagans. In a dream God had announced to Abraham the Egyptian bondage in the first place (15:13); in a dream God promised protection and prosperity for Jacob

in his sojourn with Laban (28:12, 15); and by two dreams God predicted that Joseph would rule over his family.

The **brothers . . . hated** Joseph **all the more** (37:5, 8) and were **jealous of him,** but Jacob pondered the matter (v. 11). He knew how God works; he was well aware that God could select the younger to rule over the elder, and that God could declare His choice in advance by an oracle or a dream.

The scene of the first **dream** was agricultural (v. 7). There may be some hint here of the manner in which Joseph's authority over his brothers would be achieved (cf. 42:1-3). His **sheaf** of **grain** was **upright while** their **sheaves . . . bowed down to** his. The scene of the second **dream** was celestial (v. 9). **The sun, the moon, and 11 stars** bowed **down to** him. In ancient cultures these astronomical symbols represented rulers. The **dream,** then, symbolically anticipated the elevation of Joseph over the whole house of Jacob (Joseph's **father,** the sun; his **mother,** the moon; his 11 **brothers,** the stars, v. 10).

Sensing that **Joseph** was to be elevated to prominence over them, the envy and hatred of his brothers is understandable. However, their reaction in contrast with Joseph's honesty and faithfulness demonstrated why Jacob's choosing him was proper. God's sovereign choice of a leader often brings out the jealousy of those who must submit. Rather than recognize God's choice, his brothers set on a course to destroy him. Their actions, though prompted by the belief that they should lead, shows why they should not have led.

b. The sale of Joseph (37:12-36)

**37:12-17.** The occasion for selling **Joseph** came when he obediently went to his brothers **near Dothan** (v. 17) to inquire about their welfare. In spite of the hatred **Joseph** knew they held for him, he complied with his father's wishes. From Jacob's home in **the Valley of Hebron** (v. 14) north to **Shechem** (v. 12) was about 50 miles, and Dothan was another 15 miles north. One may wonder if they had taken their flocks to **Dothan** with the hidden agenda of checking out the land of Shechem, whose ruler had raped their sister Dinah (chap. 34).

**37:18-24.** The brothers devised a

plot to kill **that dreamer** in order to prevent **his dreams** from being fulfilled. Before, they plotted to kill many Shechemites in revenge for their sister (34:24-29); now, by contrast, they plotted to **kill** their own brother!

**Reuben,** trying to gain an opportunity to restore **Joseph** to Jacob, persuaded his brothers not to commit such a crime. Reuben suggested they **throw** Joseph alive **into** a **cistern.** Then Reuben thought he could go **rescue him** later. So the **brothers . . . stripped** the lad of his tunic and threw him into a dry cistern to die.

**37:25-28. Judah** then prompted his brothers to **sell** Joseph to passing **Ishmaelites** on their way **from Gilead . . . to Egypt.** Ishmaelites were descendants of Abraham by Hagar (16:15) and the Midianites (37:28) descended from Abraham by his concubine Keturah (25:2). The term **Ishmaelites** became a general designation for desert tribes, so that **Midianite** traders were also known as Ishmaelites. **Joseph** was treated harshly by his brothers; but being sold for **20 shekels** (8 ounces **of silver**) and taken **to Egypt,** he was preserved alive.

**37:29-35.** The theme of deception again surfaced in the family; here Jacob was deceived once again—this time by his own sons! The sons **dipped** Joseph's tunic in goat's **blood** to deceive the patriarch into thinking that Joseph was dead, **devoured** by a **ferocious animal. Jacob** mourned greatly over the loss of his beloved **son** (tearing one's **clothes** and wearing **sackcloth** [coarse animal skins] were signs of grief and mourning; cf. 44:13; Job 1:20; 16:15) and **refused to be comforted.** Thus everyone shared in suffering for this treachery.

**37:36.** The sad scene in Hebron (cf. v. 14) contrasts with a note that **Joseph** was **sold** to **Potiphar . . . Pharaoh's . . . captain of the guard.**

This is a story of hatred and deception. The brothers tried to improve their lot with their father by wicked means. Jacob himself had attempted something similar with his father. The brothers would have to learn, however, as did Jacob, that God does not continue to give His blessings to those who do such things. Their use of goat's blood is ironic, for the skins of a goat were used by Jacob to deceive his father (27:16). Jacob's sin of years before had come back to haunt

him. The brothers' attitude would also have to be changed by God, or there would be no nation.

Here then is the beginning of the suffering of Joseph, the obedient servant. God would test his character through the things he suffered, so that he could then be exalted.

2. THE CORRUPTION OF JUDAH'S FAMILY AND CONFIRMATION OF GOD'S CHOICE (CHAP. 38)

A bizarre event seems at first glance to intrude on the story of Joseph. However, it served an important purpose in Genesis. It confirmed God's plan of selecting the younger over the elder, despite how others attempted to contravene it.

**38:1-5. Judah,** who had suggested that the brothers sell Joseph to the Ishmaelites (37:26-27), then **left** and stayed in **Adullum** (about 15 miles northwest of Hebron) and **married** a **Canaanite** woman. They had three sons, **Er . . . Onan,** and **Shelah.** This marriage to a Canaanite almost ruined Judah's family. Intermarriage with the Canaanites had been avoided earlier (chap. 34), but not here. This account of assimilation with the people of the land helps one understand why God settled His young nation in the safety of Egypt for its growth.

**38:6-11. Judah's** first son **Er** died because he **was wicked.** By the custom of the levirate (from Latin *levir,* "husband's brother") law of marriage, the second son, **Onan,** was to marry **Tamar,** the widow of his **brother,** and raise up **offspring for** his brother. However, **Onan** repeatedly used that law for sexual gratification. He took advantage of the situation, but refused the responsibility that went with it. So God took his life too.

In view of the situation, **Judah** refused to give his third **son Shelah** to **Tamar,** Er's widow. Shelah was not yet grown up (and even later when he was, Judah still refused; v. 14).

**38:12-23.** Thus the family's future was placed in jeopardy. **Tamar** felt she would have to take matters into her own hands if she were to be granted the rights of the levirate custom. This system was later codified by Moses for the sake of preserving the name of the deceased (Deut. 25:5-10).

When the time seemed right, Tamar

## Chronology from Solomon Back to Joseph

| Years (B.C.) | Events |
| --- | --- |
| 971<br>− 4 | Beginning of Solomon's reign |
| 967 | Fourth year of Solomon's reign (1 Kings 6:1) |
| − 1 | Year to adjust for the fact that the fourth year of Solomon's reign was actually the fourth *full* year of his reign (but into the fifth year of his reign calendarwise) |
| 966 | Year the temple construction began |
| +480 | Years from the Exodus to Solomon's beginning to build the temple (1 Kings 6:1) |
| 1446 | Year of the Exodus from Egypt |
| +430 | Years the Israelites were in Egypt (Ex. 12:40) |
| 1876 | Year Jacob and his family moved to Egypt (after 2 years of famine; Gen. 45:6) |
| + 2 | Portion of the seven-year famine before Jacob moved to Egypt (Gen. 45:6) |
| 1878 | Year the seven-year famine began |
| + 7 | Years of abundance (Gen. 41:47) |
| 1885 | Year Joseph was taken out of prison and made second-in-command (at age 30; Gen. 41:46) |
| + 13 | Years Joseph was in Potiphar's house and in prison |
| 1898 | Year Joseph was sold to Egypt (at age 17; Gen. 37:2, 28) |

deceptively lured her **father-in-law** Judah into an immoral union with a temple **prostitute,** or so he thought (Gen. 38:15, 21). In **pledge** that he would **send a goat** for payment, he left his **seal** (which hung suspended from a **cord** around his neck) and his **staff** with her. When he tried to retrieve them through **his friend Hirah** (cf. v. 1), the girl was nowhere to be found. Again Jacob's family experienced deception—this time by **his** Canaanite **daughter-in-law!**

**38:24-26.** **Judah** lacked integrity (v. 16), and now he was seen to be a hypocrite. When **Tamar** was reported to be **three** months **pregnant,** he condemned her **to death** as a prostitute. Then she proved by the **seal . . . cord, and staff** that he was the guilty partner. Tamar had won the right to be the mother of Judah's children, though in a deceitful way. Her action was desperate and risky.

**38:27-30.** This final part of the story provides the significance of the whole account. God gave Tamar twins, and the line of Judah continued because of her. But in the birth of the **boys** an unusual situation occurred, paralleling the births of Jacob and Esau. After one twin's **hand** came out the other made a breach and was born **first,** so he was rightly named **Perez** ("breach"). Then the second twin was named **Zerah** ("scarlet ") because of **the scarlet thread** the **midwife** tied **on his wrist.** It is as if the oracle concerning Jacob's ruling over his older brother (27:29) was being relived in the line of Judah. What was so significant was the connection with Judah's dealing with Joseph (37:26-28). He and his brothers sold their younger brother into Egypt, thinking they could thwart God's design that the elder brothers would serve the younger Joseph. Yet in Judah's own family, despite his attempts to hinder Tamar's marriage, God's will worked out in a poignant confirmation of the principle that the elder would serve the younger. The line of promise would carry on through Perez (cf. Matt. 1:3), for God's program

89

cannot so easily be set aside.

3. THE RISE OF JOSEPH TO POWER IN EGYPT (CHAPS. 39–41)

*a. Joseph's temptation by Potiphar's wife (chap. 39)*

**39:1-6a.** After the important digression in the family history of Judah (chap. 38), the narrative returns to **Joseph** who had **prospered** under God and had become the **attendant** or steward over Potiphar's **household. Potiphar** was **captain of the guard** for Pharaoh. This Pharaoh was probably Sesostris II (1897–1879 B.C.). (See the chart "Chronology from Solomon Back to Joseph.") Joseph's presence was also the means of God's **blessing** on **Potiphar.**

**39:6b-10.** Yet God tested **Joseph** with Potiphar's **wife** to see if he was obedient. When she tempted **handsome** Joseph, he refused to go **to bed with** her for that would be a **sin against** both **God** and his **master.** He then deliberately and wisely sought to avoid her daily advances by refusing **even** to **be around her.** His refusal was strengthened because he was convinced that God had called him to a special task—he had seen evidence of that in his rise from slavery. If one is to fulfill God's plan, he cannot sin against the God who will bring it about.

**39:11-20a.** Potiphar's **wife,** humiliated by Joseph's refusal of her, fabricated a lie to accuse Joseph of assaulting her. **She** showed to **her household servants** and then to Potiphar the garment that Joseph left when he fled from her persistent advances. This was the second time Joseph's clothing was used to bring a false report about him (cf. 37:31-33). In both cases he had been serving faithfully. But in both cases Joseph ended up in bondage.

**39:20b-23.** **Joseph** prospered in **prison** by God's favor. As a result, the jailer **put Joseph in charge of** the **prison.** Joseph had prospered under God in Potiphar's house and was put in charge, and here again he prospered under God and was put in charge. Four times, this chapter affirms, **the LORD was with Joseph** (vv. 2-3, 21, 23).

This chapter shows that Joseph was a faithful servant of God. With the dreams of prosperity in his memory (37:6-7, 9) he remained loyal to God rather than yield to temptation at the first glimpse of his rise to power. Wise rulers recognize that allegiance to God is the first requirement of an ideal king. Israel too would learn that she should remain faithful to the Lord in spite of the consequences, which included the suffering of the righteous.

This story is similar to the advice given frequently in Proverbs by King Solomon. It is folly to yield to the temptations of a flattering woman or man and ruin all prospects of a life of service to God. The way of wisdom is to consider the cost of sin. Joseph did not yield to temptation because he was convinced God had something marvelous for him to do. Joseph would not throw away God's blessings for the pleasures of sin. Nor was he troubled because he suffered for his faithfulness. God would ultimately honor him as He had promised.

*b. Joseph's interpretation of the prisoners' dreams (chap. 40)*

That Joseph did not lose faith in God's promise is proved by his willingness to interpret dreams. He was still convinced that God's revelation in his two previous dreams (37:5-7, 9) would be fulfilled.

**40:1-8.** In **prison** two servants of **Pharaoh**—his **chief cupbearer** and his **chief baker**—each **had a** troubling **dream the same night. Joseph** noticed their sadness and agreed to **interpret** their **dreams.** He understood their **dreams** to be from **God** and realized that God was beginning to work His will through two more dreams.

**40:9-15. Joseph** interpreted the dreams of the two servants of Pharaoh. **The chief** cupbearer's **dream** had a favorable interpretation. His dream reflected his profession, but with accelerated activity. The dream of the **three** vine **branches** of ripening **grapes** signified that **Pharaoh** would **lift up the head** of this man, that is, **restore** him to service **within three days.** To this, **Joseph** added the request that the man **remember** him and seek his release from **prison.**

**40:16-19.** The **dream** of the **baker** was not favorable. His dream also reflected his profession, but in it **birds were eating** the **bread** he was carrying in **three baskets** on his head. To the disappointment of the baker, **Joseph** explained that

**Pharaoh** would also **lift** up his head within **three days,** but it would be execution by hanging after which **birds** would **eat** his **flesh.**

**40:20-23.** The interpretations proved to be true, for in three days Pharaoh on his **birthday . . . restored the . . . cupbearer** but executed the **baker. Joseph,** however, was forgotten in prison.

Yet the significant fact for Joseph was that he was correctly interpreting dreams. He did not misunderstand God's revelations to him by dreams. He might not have understood his imprisonment, but he was encouraged in his faith. The **cupbearer . . . forgot him,** but God did not. In this hope Joseph had a persistent faith. His faith was not destroyed by his circumstances.

*c. Joseph's interpretation of Pharaoh's dreams (41:1-40)*

God then used two dreams to elevate Joseph from the misery of prison to the splendor of the court. Joseph had proven himself faithful to God and therefore fit for service.

**41:1-8.** Pharaoh's two dreams caused him great distress, especially since none of the **wise men of Egypt** could explain them (v. 8). God used an Israelite slave to confound the wisdom of Egypt. Later in the days of Moses another Pharaoh would be at the mercy of God's power.

Egyptian coloring is evident in these dreams. **Cows** like to stand half-submerged in the Nile **among** its **reeds** in refuge from the heat and the flies. They then come **up out of** the water for pasture. The troubling part of the first dream was that seven **ugly and gaunt** cows came up and devoured the **seven . . . fat cows.**

The **second dream** carried a similar message: **seven** plump ears **of grain . . . on a single stalk** were swallowed up by seven **thin and scorched** ears of **grain** that sprouted **after them.**

**The magicians** belonged to a guild expert in handling the ritual books of magic and priestcraft. However, they could not **interpret** Pharaoh's **dreams.** A later guild of wise men in Babylon also would be unable to interpret a king's dream, and God would use another Hebrew slave, Daniel, to show that no matter how powerful a nation might be, it is still not beyond God's sovereign control (Dan. 2).

**41:9-27. Joseph** was summoned from prison when the **cupbearer** remembered that **Joseph** was gifted in interpreting **dreams.** Yet when Joseph stood before Pharaoh (**shaved,** as was the Egyptian custom, and in a fresh change of **clothes**) he declared that the interpretation was with **God** alone (cf. 40:8). After **Pharaoh** recounted both dreams (41:17-24; cf. vv. 1-8), Joseph reiterated this conviction as he explained that **God** was making known **to Pharaoh what He** was **about to do** (vv. 25-27).

**41:28-32.** Both dreams predicted that **seven years** of plenty would be followed by **seven years of** severe **famine.** Furthermore, Joseph explained that because **the dream** came in **two** versions it signified that it was of **God,** and would be carried out **soon.** During God's dealings with him several things must have been on Joseph's mind: his own two dreams (37:5-7, 9), his two imprisonments (37:36; 39:20), the two dreamers in prison (40:5-23), and now Pharaoh's two dreams.

**41:33-36.** God's revelation demanded a response. So Joseph advised **Pharaoh** to choose a **wise man** who would oversee storing 20 percent of **the grain** during each of the **years** of plenty for the coming **years of famine.** Wisdom literature teaches that wisely planning ahead is a basic principle of practical living.

**41:37-40.** The **man** whom **Pharaoh** recognized as capable for such a task was **Joseph** in whom was **the Spirit of God.** Centuries later Daniel was chosen to be the third highest ruler in Babylon for the same reason (Dan. 5:7, 16).

Joseph had been faithful over all the little things God sent him; now he would become ruler over all the land of Egypt under **Pharaoh.**

*d. The exaltation (41:41-57)*

**41:41-46.** The **signet ring** Pharaoh gave **Joseph** was a ring with a seal used for signing documents. When the seal was impressed on a soft clay document which then hardened, it left an indelible impression of the ruler's seal and so carried his authority. Pharaoh also **dressed** Joseph in **linen** clothes and a **gold** neck **chain,** made him **second in command** to Pharaoh, and **had him ride** in the second **chariot** so all the people could do homage to him. As a token of Joseph's new status, **Pharaoh** gave him a wife, **Asenath,** from the priestly family **of On** (a city which was a center of sun worship seven miles north of Cairo and also known as Heliopolis). He also gave Joseph an Egyptian name, **Zaphenath-Paneah** (the meaning of which is unknown). **Joseph was 30** at the time of his installment, 13 years after he was sold by his brothers (cf. 37:2). Joseph's position gave him opportunity to travel extensively across **Egypt.** (Ps. 105:16-22 speaks of Joseph's imprisonment, release, and rise to power.)

**41:47-52.** Pharaoh's dreams were then fulfilled. **The land produced** abundant, even immeasurable crops for **seven years,** and **Joseph** gathered them into storage **in the** Egyptian **cities,** exercising absolute authority throughout the land.

In spite of his success, he did not abandon his Israelite heritage. He gave his two sons characteristically Hebrew names. **Manasseh (forget)** signified that **God** had **made** him forget the misery of his separation from his family. **Ephraim (fruitful)** signified that **God** had **made** him fruitful **in the land** of Egypt.

**41:53-57.** Joseph's wisdom bore fruit, for **the seven** good **years** were indeed followed by **seven years of** severe **famine,** and **the Egyptians** and people in other **countries** as well went to **buy grain** from the storehouses throughout Egypt.

At last **Joseph** was in power in **Egypt.** God's revelation to him by dreams was being fulfilled.

4. THE MOVE TO EGYPT (42:1–47:27)

The following narratives show that God used the famine to bring Israel into Egypt under the rulership of Joseph. The nation would remain there some 400 years, as God had prophesied to Abram (15:13). Israel could take comfort that in spite of her bondage God would someday enable her to triumph over Egypt.

a. The first visit of the brothers to Egypt (chap. 42)

**42:1-5.** The famine was widespread; it was in **Canaan** too. So **Jacob** sent **his sons** down to **Egypt** to **buy** food—all his sons except **Benjamin,** for he did not want to lose Rachel's other son. His refusal to send this lad reveals what Jacob had come to suspect. Joseph's fate had

not come to light, but the brothers' characteristics were known to the old man. Perhaps they would **harm** Benjamin as well.

**42:6-17.** Recognizing his brothers, **Joseph** tested them by accusing them four times of being **spies** (vv. 9, 12, 14, 16). He was handling them roughly (vv. 7, 30), but underneath his severity was affection, as the later reunion makes clear. Ironically the **brothers** were speaking to a person they thought was dead (**one is no more;** v. 13).

Their presence in Egypt confirmed the truth of his dreams, but not their fulfillment. Joseph knew that all the family must come to Egypt under his rulership. He demanded that **one of** them bring their little **brother** as proof that they were not **spies.** Retaining them in **prison** was an interesting turn of events, since the brothers had previously put Joseph in a "cistern-prison."

**42:18-24.** After a three-**day** custody of the brothers, **Joseph** altered his plan and suggested keeping only **one . . . in prison** while the other nine returned. He retained **Simeon** (v. 24) while the others returned home to Canaan with **grain.** If they would not return with their **youngest brother,** Simeon would be killed. A taste of retribution began to awaken feelings in the brothers, feelings that Joseph's cries for mercy (v. 21) and Jacob's tears (37:34-35) had failed to awaken. They sensed that having to bring Benjamin back to Egypt against the wishes of their father would be punishment for their having sold Joseph. Since Jacob was still **distressed,** now *they* were in distress. As they spoke, they were unaware that **Joseph** understood **them** for **he was using an interpreter.** Seeing their sense of remorse touched Joseph and **he turned away** and wept (cf. 43:30; 45:2, 14; 50:1, 17).

**42:25-28.** As a further means of striking the fear of God (cf. vv. 18, 28, 35) into his brothers, **Joseph** had their **silver** (with which they had purchased **grain**) put into their sacks. Whether he meant the money to be discovered on the way home or at home, its initial shock was effective. The sense of guilt already aroused made the group quickly see the hand of God in the governor's action. So the question, **What is this that God has done to us?** was, as far as it went, a fruitful reaction to trouble. They apparently felt that Joseph would accuse them of theft, which would support his contention that they were spies.

**42:29-38.** When they arrived home in **Canaan,** the nine brothers told **Jacob** what **had happened.** Jacob, grieved because he thought another son was dead (**Simeon is no more**), refused to let **Benjamin** return. **Reuben,** the eldest, sought to assure **his father** that he would bring Benjamin back. This is ironic since Reuben had failed to prevent the loss of **Joseph** (37:21-22). **But Jacob refused to let Benjamin go.** He said if something happened to his youngest, he would sorrow the rest of his days, just as he had said when he heard of Joseph's "death" (37:35).

Joseph's tests were important in God's plan to bless the seed of Abraham. God planned to bring the family to Egypt so that it would grow there into a great nation. But it was necessary that the people who entered Egypt be faithful to the Lord. It was necessary that the brothers be tested before they could participate in God's blessing. Joseph's prodding had to be subtle; the brothers must perceive the hand of God moving against them so that they would acknowledge their crime against Joseph and their previous unbelief in his dreams. But one test was not enough; there must be two.

*b. The second visit of the brothers to Egypt (chap. 43)*

**43:1-7.** The **famine** continued and Jacob's family needed more **grain.** This time, however, Benjamin had to go with them to **Egypt. Judah** reminded his **father** that without Benjamin their long trip to Egypt would be in vain. Jacob was, of course, reluctant; his scolding (**why did you** tell **the man you had another brother?**) was an effort to escape the decision he dreaded to make. Yet he must release Benjamin so they could return to Egypt. Otherwise they would all die from starvation.

**43:8-14. Judah** broke the deadlock with a warmly personal initiative, offering to take **the blame** if Benjamin were not returned. Judah (Jacob's fourth son; 29:31-35) succeeded where Reuben had failed (42:37), and Benjamin went down to Egypt with his brothers. Interestingly Judah was the one who had come up

with the plan to sell Joseph to Egypt (37:26-27). Now he had to negotiate with his father in order to get Benjamin to see Joseph.

Jacob suggested that they take some of their **best products . . . to the man as a gift,** including **balm . . . honey . . . spices and myrrh . . . pistachio nuts, and almonds.** Apparently these delicacies were not available in Egypt (cf. 37:25). They also took **double the amount of silver,** returning what they had found in their money pouches before. Jacob resigned himself to the high risk involved in possibly losing a third son—first, Joseph; then Simeon; and now perhaps **Benjamin** too.

**43:15-30.** The brothers **hurried** to **Egypt.** When they arrived, they were taken to Joseph's **house.** They **were frightened,** thinking they were going to be captured. When they told **Joseph's steward** about the **silver** they found in their **sacks** when returning from their **first** trip, the steward told them not to **be afraid** because their **God** had **given** them that money. Perhaps Joseph had talked with **the steward** about the true God.

**Simeon** was returned **to them** (v. 23), and a **noon** meal was prepared for Joseph's 11 guests. When **they presented** their **gifts** to **Joseph . . . they bowed down before him** in fulfillment of Joseph's dream (37:7). Joseph, seeing his brother **Benjamin,** could not hold back his tears of joy. Benjamin, of course, was his full brother; the others were half brothers. As before when he talked with the 10 (42:24), **he went** aside **and wept.**

**43:31-34.** At the dinner, Joseph demonstrated something ominous to them. The mysterious accuracy of the seating (**from the firstborn to the youngest**) would increase their uneasy sense of exposure to divine intervention.

Yet in all the events of this visit the brothers were confronted with gracious dealings from God through this "Egyptian" (vv. 16, 27, 29, 34). The chapter is a foretaste of future things for, as Joseph said later (45:5), God sent him down before them to provide for them in the midst of famine.

*c. The testing of Joseph (chap. 44)*

**44:1-13.** Joseph, already brilliantly successful in creating tensions during their two visits, now produced his master stroke. He tested their concern for Benjamin in order to get them to recognize their evil. If they failed this test, if they had no compassion for this second son of Rachel, then they would have no part in the fulfillment of the promises. God could start over again and make Joseph into a great nation if the others proved unworthy (cf. Ex. 32:10).

The test involved the men's **silver** in their **sacks** (as had been done on the first return trip) and placing Joseph's own silver **cup** in Benjamin's **sack** and then pursuing them to arrest Benjamin. **When** the **steward . . . caught up with them** and accused them of theft, he deliberately created tension among them by opening the sack of **the oldest** first **and ending with the youngest.** He knew, of course, that the silver **cup** was **in Benjamin's sack.** The sudden threat to Benjamin was like a sword thrust through their hearts (cf. Solomon's plan, 1 Kings 3:16-28). All the conditions were present for another betrayal when Benjamin was accused. Yet this time their response shows how well the chastening had done its work. **They tore their clothes** in grief (cf. Job 1:20), a response which they had earlier caused their father to make over Joseph's loss (Gen. 37:34).

**44:14-17.** The **brothers** returned and bowed again before **Joseph** (v. 14; cf. 37:7; 43:26, 28). **Joseph** probably did not actually use **divination** in discovering their treachery (44:5, 15). He may have simply referred to it to enhance his brothers' awe of him. **Judah,** again the spokesman, confessed that **God** had found out their iniquity and declared that they were all Joseph's **slaves. But Joseph** announced that as the steward had said (v. 10), only the "guilty" one would be his **slave.** The others could return home.

**44:18-34.** Judah interceded for **the boy**; his lengthy plea to be imprisoned in place of Benjamin is among the finest and most moving of all petitions. It demonstrated his concern for his **father** who would surely **die** if Benjamin did not **return** with them (vv. 31, 34; cf. 42:38).

Thus the brothers demonstrated that they had repented of their sin against their brother Joseph ("God has uncovered your servants' guilt," 44:16). Also they demonstrated concern for their **father** and their **youngest brother** Benjamin. So Joseph then (45:1-15) made him-

self known to them and brought them and their families to live in Egypt where there was food (45:16–47:12).

*d. The reconciliation of the brothers with Joseph (45:1-15)*

**45:1-8.** With a burst of emotion **Joseph** revealed himself **to his brothers.** This (v. 2) was the third of five times **he wept** over his brothers (42:24; 43:30; 45:14; 50:17; cf. 50:1). They were stunned by the news, unable to speak for fear that **Joseph** might kill them. In this passage strong feelings and sound spiritual judgment and argument complete the work of reconciliation which till now had called for severe testing. It had been the task for a wise man, and over an extended period of time Joseph accomplished the task marvelously.

Joseph explained that **God** had sovereignly brought him to **Egypt** to prepare for their deliverance from **famine.** His words form a classic statement on providential control. **God sent me ahead of you** (45:5). **It was not you who sent me here, but God** (v. 8; cf. v. 9). The certainty that God's will, not man's, is the controlling reality in every event shined through as the basis for reconciliation. No doubt Joseph had consoled himself many times with this principle of faith. He who is spiritual can perceive the hand of God in every event, and therefore is able to forgive those who wrong him.

**45:9-13.** Joseph then instructed his brothers to **hurry back** without **delay** (cf. **quickly** in v. 13 and cf. 43:15) to Jacob and inform him of Joseph's power (as "ruler of all Egypt," 45:8, and **lord of all Egypt,** v. 9) and **honor** in all the land of **Egypt** (vv. 9, 13). The whole family must move to Egypt and **live in the region of Goshen,** a fertile area in the Nile Delta (cf. comments on 47:1-12), to dwell under Joseph's rule, because God had prepared the way through all the circumstances.

**45:14-15.** Finally the **brothers** were reunited, first Joseph and **Benjamin,** then **all** of them. Those were emotion-filled moments, filled with **weeping** (cf. 42:24; 43:30; 45:2) and then conversation. Their previous hatred and jealousy of Joseph (37:4, 8, 11) was now gone.

*e. The moving of the family (45:16–47:12)*

**45:16-24.** Instructions were given to the brothers to bring Jacob's entire family to **Egypt. Pharaoh** himself instructed them to **return,** offering them **the best of the land of Egypt,** providing **carts** for transporting the family members back (cf. 46:5), and promising them **the best of all Egypt.**

**Joseph** gave his brothers elaborate **provisions for their journey,** including **clothing,** food and, for Jacob, **the best things of Egypt.** As they left, Joseph told **his brothers** not to **quarrel on the way.** This was not a time for accusations and recriminations. It was a time for joyful reunion. Yet he knew that they could fall out on the way home.

**45:25-28.** At first **Jacob was stunned** with unbelief at his sons' report that **Joseph** was **alive.** But then, hearing their story and seeing what all **Joseph had sent** him, **Jacob** was **convinced** and immediately decided to make the move and see his **son.**

This royal invitation to Jacob, the old patriarch near the end of hope, and to the 10 brothers burdened with guilt, was a turning point in their lives and a fulfillment of God's prediction (15:13-16) that they would go into isolation in a foreign country and multiply without losing their identity.

**46:1-7.** Years before, Abram had gone to Egypt during a famine in Canaan (12:10). Now Abram's grandson Jacob and 11 great-grandchildren (not counting Joseph who was already there) were moving there. **God** comforted **Jacob** in his move **to Egypt.** Leaving Hebron (cf. 37:14) his first stop was **Beersheba,** where he sacrificed **to the God of . . . Isaac.** Beersheba was where Isaac had lived and where Jacob left to escape Esau's anger (28:10).

Then Jacob received **a vision** from the Lord in the **night.** The Lord reiterated the promise that He would **make** his family **a great nation there** in Egypt, and He also stated that He would **bring** that nation **back again.** God had told Isaac not to go to Egypt (26:2), but now He told Jacob **to go.** This vision, which comforted the patriarch, would also encourage the nation of Israel when Moses would exhort them to leave the land of Egypt and return to Canaan to receive God's promises.

**46:8-27.** Included in the account of the move **to Egypt** is a listing of Jacob's **descendants.** In verse 26 the number of

descendants is said to be **66,** whereas the number in verse 27 is **70.** The first number represents those who traveled with Jacob to Egypt, and the second number includes the children and grandchildren already in Egypt. The following tabulation shows how these two figures are determined:

Leah's children and grandchildren (v. 15) 33

Zilpah's children and grandchildren (v. 18) 16

Rachel's children and grandchildren (v. 22) 14

Bilhah's children and grandchildren (v. 25) 7

———

70

Dinah (v. 15) + 1

———

71

Er and Onan (who died in Canaan; v. 12); Joseph and his two sons, already in Egypt (v. 20) -5

Those who went to Egypt with Jacob (v. 26) 66

Joseph, Manasseh, Ephraim, Jacob (v. 27)+ 4

Jacob and his progeny in Egypt (v. 27) 70

It is from these 70 (which included Joseph's two sons born in Egypt, vv. 20, 27; cf. 41:50-52) that the nation of Israel would grow. (In the early church, Stephen referred to 75 members in Jacob's family; see comments on Acts 7:14.)

**46:28-34.** Finally, after 22 years (see the chart "Chronology from Solomon Back to Joseph," near 39:1-6a), **Joseph** and **Jacob** were reunited. Their response was one of mutual joy. Once again Joseph **wept** (cf. 42:24; 43:30; 45:2, 14-15) and understandably so. The last time Joseph saw his father was when Joseph was 17 (37:2). Jacob was satisfied to see his son **alive,** for he was the one designated as the heir, the one whom God had chosen to rule over the family. So this was more than a family reunion; it was a confirmation that God's promised blessing was intact.

**Joseph** encouraged them to stress before **Pharaoh** that they were cattle raisers, not sheepherders, because **the Egyptians** detested the latter. Joseph, as usual, was eager not to upset Egyptian custom and preference (cf. 41:14; 43:32). However, five of the **brothers** did not respond with the same diplomacy (47:3).

## Chronology of the Patriarchs

| 2166 B.C. | 2066 | 2006 | 1991 | 1915 | 1898 | 1886 | 1876 | 1859 | 1805 |
|---|---|---|---|---|---|---|---|---|---|
| (100 years) | (60 years) | (15 years) | (76 years) | (17 years) | (12 years) | (10 years) | (17 years) | (54 years) | |
| Abraham was born | Abraham died (at age 175; Gen. 25:7) | | | | | | | | |
| | Isaac was born (when Abraham was 100; Gen. 21:5) | | | Isaac died (at age 180; Gen. 35:28) | | | | | |
| | | Jacob was born (when Isaac was 60; Gen. 25:26) | | | | Jacob moved to Egypt (at age 130; Gen. 47:9) when Joseph was 39 | Jacob died (at age 147, 17 years after he moved to Egypt; Gen. 47:28) | | |
| | | | Joseph was born | Joseph was sold into Egypt (at age 17; Gen. 37:2, 28) | | | | Joseph died (at age 110, Gen. 50:26; therefore he was born in 1915) | |

**47:1-12.** Pharaoh gave Jacob's family **the best part of the land,** namely, **Goshen** (cf. 45:10), even giving some of the **brothers** oversight of his **own livestock** (47:6). Goshen is not referred to in ancient Egyptian writings, but the name it bore in later times was **the district of Rameses** (v. 11; cf. Ex. 1:11). This, plus the fact that it was fertile and near to Joseph at court, suggests that it was near the eastern part of the Nile Delta.

When **Jacob** was **presented** before **Pharaoh,** the patriarch acknowledged his troubled life of **130** years. To him it had been a **pilgrimage.** When **Jacob** both entered and left, he **blessed Pharaoh.** It is interesting to think of the Israelites in a foreign land, a country with a different culture, in which the patriarch wished God's blessing on the **Pharaoh!**

*f. The wisdom of Joseph's rule (47:13-27)*

**47:13-27.** **Joseph** proved to be a wise administrator in the land of **Egypt,** so that under his authority the people were saved from starvation and **Pharaoh** prospered. The ruler by now was Sesostris III (1878–1843 B.C.).

In selling **food** to **the people** during **the famine** that was **severe,** Joseph accepted **money** and livestock (**horses . . . sheep . . . goats . . . cattle, and donkeys**) as payment, and finally the entire **land** of **Egypt** itself except **the land of the priests.** Once the land belonged to **Pharaoh . . . Joseph** instructed the people to plant **seed,** which he gave them. His only stipulation was that **Pharaoh** must receive **a fifth** of all the produce. In a word, the people survived but they (except **the priests**) were **in bondage to Pharaoh.**

However, in the land **of Goshen** the **Israelites** prospered and multiplied **greatly.**

So God blessed His people according to the promises He made to Abraham. They were fast becoming a great nation. Moreover, God blessed Pharaoh because he had blessed the seed of Abraham with the best of Egypt. Later in the time of Moses, when another Pharaoh oppressed Israel, God dealt harshly with the Egyptians.

5. THE PROVISION FOR THE CONTINUATION OF THE PROMISED BLESSING (47:28–50:26)

In this final section of the book the narratives look to the future of Abraham's seed.

*a. The blessing of Ephraim and Manasseh (47:28–48:22)*

Out of Jacob's long career, the writer of the Book of Hebrews selected this blessing of Joseph's sons by the patriarch as his great act of faith (Heb. 11:21). It was his reaching out for the continuation of God's promise in the face of death. Ironically this is the very thing he had once accomplished by deception (Gen. 27). Once more the blessing would be given to the younger, but this time there was not scheming or bitterness. It was an act of faith.

**47:28-31.** **Jacob lived in Egypt 17 years** (cf. v. 9) to the age of **147.** (Abraham died at the age of 175 [25:7-8] and Isaac at 180 [35:28].) If the year of Jacob's move to Egypt was 1876 B.C. (see the chart "Chronology from Solomon Back to Joseph" near 39:1-6a) then Jacob died in 1859. His birth, 147 years earlier, would have been in 2006 B.C. (see the chart "Chronology of the Patriarchs"). At the end of his life Jacob exhorted **Joseph** to **swear** that he would **bury** him **where** his **fathers** had been **buried** (cf. 49:29-33). He referred, of course, to the Cave of Machpelah which had been purchased by Abraham (chap. 23). Wanting Joseph to affirm that he would carry through on his **promise,** Jacob asked his son to **put** his **hand under** Jacob's **thigh** (cf. comments on this custom at 24:1-9). Even as he neared death Jacob (here called **Israel**) **worshiped.**

**48:1-4.** **Jacob,** ill but sitting **up in bed,** rehearsed how **God Almighty** (*'ēl šadday;* cf. comments on 17:1) had **appeared to** him **at Luz,** which Jacob renamed Bethel, and had promised him the blessing of an innumerable people in the **land as an everlasting possession** (cf. 28:10-22). The words of this promise had provided the patriarch with hope through all his pilgrimage, just as they would quicken hope in the nation that sprang from him. They had the sure word of God.

**48:5-7.** Jacob gave the birthright to Joseph by elevating **Ephraim and Manasseh,** Joseph's **sons** (41:51-52), to the rank of firstborn sons, thus giving a double portion to Joseph. They thus replaced **Reuben and Simeon,** Jacob's first two sons, born to Leah (cf. 1 Chron. 5:1-2). The recognition of Joseph's sons would have an effect on the apportioning of the land of promise years later in the days of Joshua (Josh. 16–17). Jacob's elevation of the sons of Joseph was prompted by his recollection of **Rachel,** his favorite wife, who **died in the land of Canaan** (cf. Gen. 35:16-20).

**48:8-14.** When **Joseph** presented his two **sons** to the aged patriarch, the blessing was pronounced. Like Isaac, Jacob gave this blessing when his eyesight was **failing.** But in the blessing **Israel** crossed his hands so that **his right hand** was **on Ephraim's head** and **his left** on **Manasseh's . . . even though Manasseh,** the **firstborn,** would normally have been blessed with the right hand. This was Jacob's decision in spite of Joseph's direction. **Joseph,** like so many others, expected God to work in a certain way, but found that He is often pleased to work differently and sometimes even unconventionally. But faith recognizes that God's ways are not man's ways. It took Jacob a lifetime of discipline to learn that fact. But he learned it, and now he blessed the younger over the elder. For four consecutive generations this reversed pattern was followed: Isaac over Ishmael, Jacob over Esau, Joseph over Reuben, and Ephraim over Manasseh.

**48:15-20.** In his blessing on **Joseph,** Jacob used a threefold invocation of **God** (v. 15): (a) the God who was in covenant with his **fathers Abraham and Isaac** (a fact that steadied Jacob's faith many times, 28:13; 31:5, 42; 32:9; 46:3), (b) the One **who** had **been** his **Shepherd** (cf. 49:24; Ex. 6:6; Ps. 23:1; Isa.59:20) all the way, and (c) **the Angel** (cf. comments on Gen. 16:7) who **delivered** him **from all harm.** The Hebrew word *gā'al,* translated "delivered," expressed the protection and reclamation Jacob experienced from trouble. With these remarkable descriptions of God, Jacob prayed for God's gracious blessing on the **boys.** Here one catches a glimpse of Jacob's faith.

**When Joseph saw** that **his father** was blessing Ephraim over Manasseh, he protested. **But** Jacob's words, **I know, my son, I know,** expressed the confidence of his faith: he was blessing according to the divine plan, not according to normal custom. He had learned that in spite of what man attempted to do **God** had blessed him, the younger. This he now carried forward to Joseph's sons. Years later **Ephraim** became a leading tribe in the Northern Kingdom, much superior to the tribe of **Manasseh,** as Jacob had predicted.

**48:21-22.** Convinced that **God**

would **take** them **back to the land** of promise, Jacob said that a double portion belonged to Joseph. The NASB rendering of verse 22a is preferred: "And I give you one portion more than your brothers" (cf. NIV marg.). The Hebrew word for "portion" is *šekem*, a wordplay on the name of the town Shechem. Later Joseph was buried in Shechem (Josh. 24:32) as a sign that he possessed this bequeathed land. Jacob apparently had conquered this portion of land **from the Amorites** (hill-country Canaanites), though this is the only mention of such a conquest in the Bible, and had dug a well there (cf. Sychar, John 4:4-5).

### b. The oracle of Jacob concerning the tribes (49:1-28)

A fundamental principle in God's economy is that the lives and natures of the patriarchs affected their descendants. God works out the manifold destinies of His people in accordance with their moral distinctions. Genesis 49 gives a glimpse into such a program of God. This chapter includes the last of the several great sayings of destiny in Genesis— blessings, cursings, judgments, and promises. Jacob, in faith and as God's covenantal instrument, looked forward to the conquest and settlement of Israel in the land of Canaan, and then beyond to a more glorious age.

God gave His people this prophecy to bear them through the dismal barrenness of their experiences and to show them that He planned all the future. For Jacob's family, the future lay beyond the bondage of Egypt in the land of promise. But the enjoyment of the blessings of that hope would depend on the participants' faithfulness. So from the solemnity of his deathbed Jacob evaluated his sons one by one, and carried his evaluation forward to the future tribes.

**49:1-2.** In calling **his sons** to his bedside, **Jacob** said he would tell them **what** would become of them in the **days** ahead. His words, then, were a deliberately chosen prophetic oracle.

**49:3-4.** Jacob heaped praise upon **Reuben,** his **firstborn,** which collapsed when he announced that Reuben had **defiled** his father's **couch,** clearly a reference to Reuben's adultery with Jacob's concubine Bilhah (35:22). Reuben was entitled to leadership and a double inheri-

tance (1 Chron. 5:1-2), but because he had the ungoverned impulse of boiling water (**turbulent as the waters**) he would fail in leadership. In the time of the Judges (Jud. 5:15-16), the tribe of Reuben was characterized by irresolution.

**49:5-7.** **Simeon and Levi** were men of anarchy (**violence**) and not justice, men of uncontrolled **anger** and **fury,** with disregard for men and animals. Here was God's moral judgment on their slaughter of the Shechemites (34:25-29). God distinguishes holy war from vengeance. Both tribes were later scattered (49:7). Simeon was largely disintegrated (with its land inside that of Judah; Josh. 19:1, 9), but Levi was afforded an honorable dispersion because it was the priestly tribe (Josh. 21).

**49:8-12.** In this oracle Jacob predicted a fierce lionlike dominance of **Judah** over his **enemies** and over his **brothers** who would **praise** him. A wordplay was made here on the name Judah which means "praise" (cf. 29:35, NIV marg.). The oracle pivots on the word **until** (49:10b). When the Promised One who will rule the nations appears, the scene will become an earthly paradise. These verses anticipate the kingship in Judah culminating in the reign of Messiah (cf. the tribe of Judah, Rev. 5:5), in which **nations** will obey Him.

The NASB renders the third line of Genesis 49:10, "Until Shiloh comes." Many sources, including the Targum (Aram. paraphrase of the OT), see "Shiloh" as a title of the Messiah. However, the Hebrew word *šîlōh* should be rendered "whose it is," that is, **the scepter will not depart from Judah . . . until He comes** whose it (i.e., the scepter) is (or as the NIV puts it, **to whom it belongs**). Similar words in Ezekiel 21:27, "until He comes to whom it (the crown, Ezek. 21:26) rightfully belongs" were addressed to the last king of Judah.

With the coming of Messiah there will be paradise-like splendor. Kidner says that every line of Genesis 49:11-12 "speaks of exuberant, intoxicating abundance: it is the golden age of the Coming One, whose universal rule was glimpsed in [v.] 10c" (*Genesis*, p. 219). For Judah, grapevines will be so abundant that they will be used for hitching posts; **wine** will be as abundant as wash water. In Judah, people's **eyes** will be red or bright from wine and their **teeth** will be white from drinking much **milk.** These are picturesque ways of describing the suitability of Judah's territory for vineyards. Such opulence will be evident in the Millennium (Isa. 61:6-7; 65:21-25; Zech. 3:10).

**49:13-15. Zebulun** would be enriched by seaborne trade (though it did not actually border the Mediterranean; cf. Josh. 19:10-11). Like a strong **donkey,** the tribe of **Issachar** would be **forced** to work for others. Issachar, located in the fertile broad **pleasant** plain of Esdraelon, was often subject to invading armies.

**49:16-17. Dan** shows another disparity between calling and achievement (cf. vv. 3-4). Dan was to **provide justice** ("Dan" means "judge"), but the tribe chose treachery, like a snake **by the roadside.** In the time of the Judges the first major practice of idolatry appeared in the tribe of Dan (Jud. 18:30).

**49:18.** Jacob then interjected a request for **deliverance** by the LORD. He may have been indirectly reminding his sons of their need for dependence on the Lord (if he needed it, certainly they did too). Or he may have been expressing his desire to enjoy the messianic hope, when he would be delivered from all trouble and grief (cf. "redemption" in Anna's desires, Luke 2:38).

**49:19-21.** Three of the six Hebrew words in verse 19 are a play on the name Gad ("attack"): **Gad will be attacked by** a raid of *attackers,* **but he will attack.** The verb *gādad* means "to break into" or "to attack." Border raids were often experienced by the tribes settled east of the Jordan River (e.g., 1 Chron. 5:18-19).

Asher would be fertile and productive, providing rich **food.** That tribe settled along the rich northern coast of Canaan. **Naphtali,** like **a doe,** would be a **free** mountain people. Deborah sang of the people of Naphtali risking their lives "on the heights of the field" (Jud. 5:18). That tribe settled northwest of the Sea of Kinnereth (Galilee).

**49:22-26.** This oracle treats **Joseph** more lavishly than any of the others, for here the main blessing lay (cf. 1 Chron. 5:1-2). Jacob took up the promise of fruitfulness from the name of Joseph's son Ephraim (which means **fruitful**) and lavished the promise of victory (Gen. 49:23-24a) and prosperity (v. 25b) on Joseph's two tribes. Victory in battle was experi-

enced by Joshua, Deborah, and Samuel, all of the tribe of Ephraim, and by Gideon and Jephthah, both of Manasseh's tribe. In these verses are several marvelous titles for God—the **Mighty One of Jacob . . . the Shepherd** (cf. 48:15), **the Rock of Israel . . . your father's God . . . the Almighty** (*šadday;* cf. *'ēl šadday* in 17:1)—the One who ensures **blessings** from the **heavens above** (i.e., rain for crops) from **the deep . . . below** (i.e., streams and wells for water), and from **the breast and womb** (i.e., abundant offspring). Jacob bestowed on Joseph the **greater** blessings because he was **the prince among his brothers** (cf. 41:41).

**49:27-28.** The oracle about **Benjamin** describes a tribe violent in spirit: **a ravenous,** devouring **wolf** (cf. the cruel Benjamites in Jud. 20, and Saul, a Benjamite, in 1 Sam. 9:1-2; 19:10; 22:17).

These oracles serve a purpose in the book similar to that of Noah's oracles about his sons (Gen. 9:24-27). Both look ahead prophetically to the destinies of the sons at the end of their respective ages—Noah in the primeval days and Jacob in the patriarchal.

*c. The death and burial of Jacob (49:29–50:14)*

**49:29-33.** Once more the subject of a patriarch's grave became important as Jacob instructed Joseph to **bury** him **with** his **fathers** in **Canaan,** not in Egypt (cf. 47:29-30). That is where his hope was. At **the Cave . . . of Machpelah** (purchased by **Abraham,** 23:3-20) near Hebron were buried **Sarah** (23:19), **Abraham** (25:8-9), **Isaac** (35:27-29), **Rebekah** (Isaac's **wife,** 49:31), and **Leah** (Jacob's first wife, v. 31).

So **Jacob** died after 147 years (47:28) of struggle; his sorrow came to an end. Infirmities, he had many; sins, not a few. But Jacob had an unquenchable desire for God's blessing. He had a deep piety that habitually relied on God in spite of all else. In the end he died as a man of genuine faith. He learned in his life where the real blessings came from, and he fought with God and man to be privileged to hand them on to his sons.

**50:1-6.** After weeping on his father's dead body (cf. Joseph's other occurrences of weeping: 42:24; 43:30; 45:2, 14; 50:17), **Joseph** instructed that Jacob's body be **embalmed** for burial in typical Egyptian fashion. The **embalming** period was seldom less than a month and normally took **40 days.** The Egyptians mourned for Jacob 70 days—two and one-half months—just two days short of the normal time of mourning for a Pharaoh. This showed the great respect the Egyptians had for Joseph. After the time of **mourning, Joseph** asked **Pharaoh** and got permission to go **bury** his **father** in the Cave of Machpelah in **Canaan.**

**50:7-9. Joseph** led a huge procession, including Egyptian **dignitaries . . . Joseph's** family and **brothers,** and charioteers, to Canaan to bury his father. This was Joseph's first time back in his homeland in 39 years (he had been in Egypt 22 years before Jacob moved there and Jacob had lived there 17 years). Centuries later the children of Israel would leave Egypt again, taking with them the bones of a patriarch, Joseph himself. Here, however, the sojourn into the land of promise was temporary; the grave was a claim to the land of promise. God had promised Jacob that He would return him to the land and that Joseph would bury him (46:4).

**50:10-14.** Along the way the **mourning** of the bereaved for **seven** days at a **threshing floor. . . . near the Jordan** River gave rise to naming the place **Abel Mizraim,** meaning "meadow (*'ābēl*) of Egyptians," but by a wordplay it suggests "mourning (*'ēbel*) of Egyptians." **The Canaanites** recognized that this was a great event. The trip back to Egypt was the fourth time the majority of the brothers made that journey to Egypt, and it was Joseph's second trip.

d. *The reassurance of the fulfillment of the blessing (50:15-26)*

**50:15-21.** Now that Jacob **was dead,** the **brothers,** fearing that **Joseph** would deal harshly with them for their **wrongs** (cf. 45:3), pleaded for forgiveness. Once again (cf. 44:33) they referred to themselves as Joseph's **slaves** (cf. 37:7). **But Joseph** (after weeping; cf. 42:24; 43:30; 45:2, 14; 50:1) reassured them (twice saying, **Don't be afraid,** vv. 19, 21; cf. 43:23) that all that had happened was part of God's plan to bring about the fulfillment of the promised blessing (cf. 45:5, 7-9). Joseph also promised again to **provide for** them (cf. 45:11), and he **spoke kindly to them.**

**50:22-26. Joseph** also **died** in the land of **Egypt.** Like his father before him, he made **his brothers** promise that his **bones** would be taken **out of** the **land** of Egypt at the great deliverance (vv. 24-25; cf. Ex. 13:19; Josh. 24:32; Heb. 11:22). This deliverance, he reassured them, would take place when **God** would visit them to fulfill His promises to their fathers.

Joseph lived to see his great-great-grandchildren by Ephraim and his great-grandchildren by Manasseh. Placing them on his **knees** at their **birth** was a gesture signifying they belonged to him (cf. Job 3:12). Then Joseph died at **110** and, like Jacob, was **embalmed.** (Abraham lived to be 175 [25:7]; Isaac, 180 [35:28]; and Jacob, 147 [47:28].) The Book of Genesis closes with the promise of **the land** yet unfulfilled but with the expectation of a visitation from on high. The words of Joseph, given twice, amazingly summarize the hope expressed throughout the Old Testament as well as the New: **God will surely come to your aid** (50:24-25). So the company of the faithful would wait in expectation for that visitation of the promised Seed, the Messiah, who will bring the curse to an end and establish in reality the long-awaited blessing of God.

# BIBLIOGRAPHY

**Commentaries**

Bush, George. *Notes, Critical and Practical, on Genesis.* 2 vols. New York: Ivison, Phinney & Co., 1857. Reprint. Minneapolis: Klock & Klock Christian Publishers, 1981.

Cassuto, Umberto. *From Adam to Noah: A Commentary on the Book of Genesis.* Vol. 1. Translated by Israel Abrahams. Jerusalem: Magnes Press, 1961.

_____. *From Noah to Abraham: A Commentary on the Book of Genesis.* Vol. 2. Jerusalem: Magnes Press, 1964.

Davis, John J. *Paradise to Prison: Studies in Genesis.* Grand Rapids: Baker Book House, 1975.

Delitzsch, Franz. *A New Commentary on Genesis.* Translated by Sophia Taylor. 2 vols. Edinburgh: T. & T. Clark, 1899. Reprint. Minneapolis: Klock & Klock Christian Publishers, 1978.

Dods, Marcus. *The Book of Genesis*. The Expositor's Bible. London: Hodder & Stoughton, 1892.

Jacob, Benno. *The First Book of the Bible: Genesis*. New York: KTAV Publishing House, 1934.

Kidner, Derek. *Genesis*. The Tyndale Old Testament Commentaries. Downers Grove, Ill.: InterVarsity Press, 1967.

Leupold, H.C. *Exposition of Genesis*. 2 vols. Grand Rapids: Baker Book House, 1942.

Phillips, John. *Exploring Genesis*. Chicago: Moody Press, 1980.

Speiser, E.A. *Genesis*. The Anchor Bible. Garden City, N.Y.: Doubleday & Co., 1964.

Stigers, Harold G. *A Commentary on Genesis*. Grand Rapids: Zondervan Publishing House, 1976.

Thomas, W.H. Griffith. *Genesis: A Devotional Commentary*. Grand Rapids: Wm. B. Eerdmans Publishing Co., 1946.

Westermann, Claus. *Genesis*. Neukirchen Vluyn: Neukirchener Verlag, 1976.

Wood, Leon J. *Genesis: A Study Guide Commentary*. Grand Rapids: Zondervan Publishing House, 1975.

**Special Studies**

Cassuto, Umberto. *The Documentary Hypothesis and the Composition of the Pentateuch*. Translated by Israel Abrahams. Jerusalem: Magnes Press, 1961.

Fokkelman, J.P. *Narrative Art in Genesis*. Assen, Amsterdam: Van Gorcum, 1975.

Kitchen, Kenneth A. *Ancient Orient and Old Testament*. Downers Grove, Ill.: InterVarsity Press, 1966.

Livingston, G. Herbert. *The Pentateuch in Its Cultural Environment*. Grand Rapids: Baker Book House, 1974.

Lowenthal, Eric I. *The Joseph Narrative in Genesis*. New York: KTAV Publishing House, 1973.

Segal, Moses Hirsch. *The Pentateuch: Its Composition and Its Authorship and Other Biblical Studies*. Jerusalem: Magnes Press, 1967.

Vos, Howard F. *Genesis and Archaeology*. Chicago: Moody Press, 1963.

Westermann, Claus. *The Promises to the Fathers: Studies on the Patriarchal Narratives*. Translated by David E. Green. Philadelphia: Fortress Press, 1980.

# EXODUS

## John D. Hannah

## INTRODUCTION

**Title.** The name of the second book in the Hebrew Bible is *wᵉʾēlleh šᵉmôt* ("these are the names"), the first phrase in the book. Sometimes it is shortened to *šᵉmôt* ("names"). The English title *Exodus* ("a going out") transliterates the title in the Septuagint, which named the book for its central focus, the departure of the Israelites from Egypt. However, the book covers more than that event. The departure from Egypt is described in 13:17–15:21, but the book also describes the circumstances of Jacob's family before the Exodus, the journey from Egypt to Sinai, and some of the events that Israel experienced there.

**Author.** Scholars are divided over the authorship of the Book of Exodus. Skeptical scholars submit the text to detailed, analytical investigation with the presupposition that Mosaic authorship is unlikely and the date for the writing of the narrative is quite late.

Liberal scholars approach the book in one of three ways. First, scholars after Julius Wellhausen attempt to isolate the literary origins of the book, assuming three sources over a lengthy time span. This is commonly known as the documentary approach or JEDP theory (but there would be no "D" source in Ex.). (Cf. "The Authorship of Gen." in the *Introduction* to Gen.) Second, the form-critical approach attempts to discover in the text small literary units through an understanding of the history behind the forms. In this way these scholars attempt to determine the date of the original writing of the book. Third, the traditionalist-critical school argues for a long, oral transmission of the accounts, though the exact recovery of the accounts is unlikely. These three approaches are similar in their basic assumptions: Moses probably did not write the book, the exact nature

of the events is difficult to determine, and the date of compilation is late.

Evangelicals believe that the book was written by Moses sometime during his stay near Mount Sinai or shortly thereafter. Support for this view is that the Bible explicitly witnesses to this fact.

The Bible clearly states that Moses had the ability to have undertaken such a task ("Moses was educated in all the wisdom of the Egyptians," Acts 7:22).

The Book of Exodus explicitly verifies Mosaic authorship. God commanded Moses to write the events of Joshua's military encounter with the Amalekites ("Write this on a scroll," Ex. 17:14). Also Moses wrote the communication the Lord gave him on Sinai ("Moses then wrote down everything the Lord had said," 24:4). This recording was called "the Book of the Covenant" (24:7). On Mount Sinai the Lord told Moses, "Write down these words" (34:27) and Moses "wrote on the tablets the words of the covenant" (34:28).

Statements in other portions of the Pentateuch also verify Mosaic authorship. According to Deuteronomy 31:9, "Moses wrote down this Law [for] . . . the priests." The statement in Deuteronomy 31:24 is clear; "Moses finished writing in a book the words of this Law from beginning to end."

Other books of the Old Testament witness to the Mosaic authorship of Exodus. David charged Solomon to obey God's "laws and requirements, as written in the Law of Moses" (1 Kings 2:3). Ezra read from "the Book of the Law of Moses" (Neh. 8:1). Also the Pentateuch is called "the Book of Moses" (Neh. 13:1).

Jesus accepted the Mosaic authorship of Exodus. Jesus introduced a quotation of Exodus 20:12 and 21:17 with the words "Moses said" (Mark 7:10) and a quotation of Exodus 3:6 by the words

# Exodus

"Have you not read in the Book of Moses" (Mark 12:26).

**Date.** The date of the Exodus, the date of Jacob's entrance into Egypt, and the date of the writing of the Book of Exodus have all been debated by biblical scholars.

*1. The date of the Exodus.* Some scholars date the Exodus in the 13th century B.C. (ca. 1290, in the reign of Rameses II) while others date it in the 15th century B.C. (1446, in the reign of Amenhotep II).

Support for the early date comes from the biblical record and archeological evidence. First, in 1 Kings 6:1 the time between the Exodus and the beginning of Solomon's temple construction (in the fourth year of his reign) was 480 years. Since the fourth year of Solomon's reign was 966 B.C., the Exodus was in 1446. Also in the time of Jephthah (ca. 1100 B.C.) Israel had been in the land for 300 years (Jud. 11:26). Therefore 300 years plus the 40 years of the wilderness sojourn and some time to conquer Heshbon places the Exodus in the middle of the 15th century.

Second, archeological evidence from Egypt during this period corresponds with the biblical account of the Exodus (see Merrill F. Unger, *Archaeology and the Old Testament*. Grand Rapids: Zondervan Publishing House, 1954, pp. 140-5; and Gleason L. Archer, Jr., *A Survey of Old Testament Introduction*. Chicago: Moody Press, 1964, pp. 215-6). For example, though Thutmose IV succeeded his father, Amenhotep II, Thutmose was not the eldest son. (The eldest son was killed by the Lord on the night of the first Passover, Ex. 12:29.) Amenhotep II (1450–1425 B.C.) repressed insurgents in the early part of his reign. Semites were forced to make bricks (cf. 5:7-18). Several of the Pharaohs of Egypt's 18th dynasty (ca. 1567-1379 B.C.) were involved in building projects in northern Egypt. "Since Eighteenth Dynasty Pharaohs were very active in Palestinian campaigns, it would seem reasonable that they would have established garrisons and store cities (cf. 1:11) somewhere in the Delta regions to facilitate movement between Syro-Palestinian sites and Egypt itself" (John J. Davis, *Moses and the Gods of Egypt*, p. 27).

Third, events in Palestine about 1400 B.C. correspond with the Conquest under Joshua. Archeological evidence suggests that Jericho, Ai, and Hazor were destroyed about 1400. One scholar has concluded, "All the accredited Palestinian artifactual evidence supports the literary account that the Conquest occurred at the time specifically dated by the biblical historians" (Bruce K. Waltke, "Palestinian Artifactual Evidence Supporting the Early Date of the Exodus," *Bibliotheca Sacra* 129. January-March, 1972:47).

Arguments for a late date of the Exodus (ca. 1290) are answerable. First, advocates of the late date refer to the enslaved Israelites being forced to build the "store cities" of Pithom and Rameses (1:11). Archeological evidence, it is argued, suggests that these cities were built in the reign of Rameses II (ca. 1304–1236 B.C.), who then would have been the Pharaoh at the time of the Exodus. However, those two cities were built at least 80 years before the Exodus. (Moses, 80 years old at the time of the Exodus, 7:7, was not born until after the events recorded in 1:11.) This would place the building of Pithom and Rameses *before* the rule of Rameses II.

This means that the city of Rameses could not have been named for the monarch. How then is the reference to Rameses to be explained? Rameses may have been a common name during the time of the Hyksos kings of Egypt (1730–1570 B.C.) Rameses means "begotten of Ra [Re]," the Hyksos' sun god. Also the name of the city was originally spelled Raamses (Heb., *ra'amsēs*; cf. ASV, NASB) whereas the Pharaoh's name was spelled Rameses or Ramesses (*Ra-mes-su*).

Second, advocates of the later date for Exodus argue that conditions in the Transjordan area do not coincide with an early date for the Exodus. Archeologist Nelson Glueck found no evidence of settlements in Edom, Moab, and Ammon from 1900 to 1300 B.C. Therefore Moses could not have encountered strong opposition there until later (in the 13th century).

Two replies may be given to this argument. Settled populations need not have existed at that time; the Edomites, Moabites, and Ammonites may have simply had military control of those territories though they were semi-nomads. Commenting on Numbers 20:14-17

Unger noted that "there is nothing in the passage which would demand a developed urban life in Edom or require the building of stout fortresses" (*Archaeology and the Old Testament,* p. 151). Also Glueck's methods have been questioned by other archeologists and more recent findings suggest that some settlements were in the area, particularly at Tell Deir 'Alla (H.J. Franken and W.J.A. Power, "Glueck's *Explorations in Eastern Palestine in the Light of Recent Evidence,*" *Vetus Testamentum* 21. 1971:119-23).

Third, late-date Exodus advocates argue that archeological evidence points to widespread destruction in Palestine in the 13th century but not in the 15th century. However, with the exception of Jericho, Ai, and Hazor, Joshua's military tactics did not involve destruction of the cities conquered (cf. Josh. 11:13). Waltke notes, "Other historical events could account for these layers of destruction; namely, the raids into Palestine carried out by Merneptah of Egypt circa 1230 B.C. or the raids of the People of the Sea circa 1200 B.C. by the Israelites in their continuing seesaw struggle with the Canaanites during the time of the Judges" ("Palestinian Artifactual Evidences," pp. 35-6).

2. *The date of Jacob's entrance into Egypt.* If the date of the Exodus is 1446 B.C. then certain biblical notations help establish other important dates. Since the duration of the wilderness sojourn was "430 years to the very day" (Ex. 12:40-42), Jacob moved to Egypt in 1876. (See the chart "Chronology of the Patriarchs," near Gen. 47:28-31.)

3. *The date of the writing of the Book of Exodus.* The journey from Egypt to the Sinai wilderness took exactly three months (Ex. 19:1-2). It would seem logical that Moses composed the book during or shortly after the encampment at Sinai (1446 B.C.). Thus the book covers events that occurred sometime before Moses' birth in 1526 (chap. 2) to the events surrounding Mount Sinai (1446).

**Purpose and Themes.** The central events in the Book of Exodus are the miraculous deliverance of Israel from Egyptian bondage and God's establishing the theocratic nation under Moses by means of a new "constitution," the Mosaic Covenant (19:3-19). Unger notes, "The aim of the Book of Exodus centers in the great experience of redemption and the constitution of Jacob's posterity as a theocratic nation at Mount Sinai. God, connected heretofore with the Israelites only through His covenant with Abraham, confirmed to Isaac and Jacob, now brings them to Himself nationally through redemption. As the Chosen People through whom the Redeemer was to come Jehovah also places them under the Mosaic Covenant and dwells among them under the cloud of glory" (*Introductory Guide to the Old Testament.* Grand Rapids: Zondervan Publishing House, 1951, p. 196).

Thus the Book of Exodus is a connecting link between the origin of the people in God's promise to Abraham (Gen. 12:2) and the beginning of the theocratic kingdom under Moses. The people of promise were miraculously redeemed from servitude and placed under the Mosaic Covenant so that they might become "a holy nation" (Ex. 19:6), an avenue of blessing to the Gentiles (Gen. 12:3; cf. "a light for the Gentiles," Isa. 42:6). The Book of Exodus, then, stresses redemption and consecration.

### Historical Background

1. *The history of Egypt before the Exodus.* Ancient Egypt stretched a distance of about 550 miles from Aswan (ancient Syene), the first cataract on the Nile, northward to the Mediterranean Sea. This area included the narrow Nile Valley (from Aswan to Memphis) and the Delta, the broad triangle from Memphis to the sea. South of Aswan was the ancient land of Cush. The name "Egypt" is from Greek (*Aigyptos*) and Latin (*Aegyptus*), forms of the ancient Ha-ku-ptah, an earlier name for Memphis, the capital city just north of Cairo. When Memphis was the capital, foreigners used it as a designation for the entire nation. The native population referred to it as Ta-meri ("the beloved land") or Kemet ("the black country," a name reflective of the fertile soil along the Nile).

Ancient Egypt's history is divided by scholars into three periods: predynastic (ca. 3500–3100 B.C.), protodynastic (ca. 3100–2686 B.C.), and dynastic (2686–332 B.C.). In the predynastic period an agricultural population along the Nile progressively became more sedentary. The emerging civilizations of Upper (southern) and Lower (northern) Egypt were united by Narmer, the first Pharaoh of Upper Egypt, thus marking the beginning of the protodynastic period. This period included Egypt's first two dynasties.

The dynastic period from 2686 to the conquest of Egypt by Alexander the Great in 332 included 29 dynasties. Dynasties 3-6 (ca. 2686-2181 B.C.) were characterized by rapid progress in culture and technology. In those years, called the Old Kingdom period, the great pyramids were constructed, and the Pharaohs ruled from Memphis with a strong absolutist government. The First Intermediate Period (dynasties 7-11; 2181–1991) was a time of decline. Then came the Middle Kingdom (dynasty 12; ca. 1991–1786) in which the nation enlarged its borders with the capital at Thebes. Centralized rule was reestablished under Amenemhet I, founder of the flourishing 12th dynasty.

The 12th dynasty was Egypt's golden age of art and craftsmanship, in which her prosperity was restored. In this affluent era Joseph emerged as prime minister of Egypt, and Jacob and his sons sojourned in Egypt (1876 B.C., Gen. 46:6).

Then came the Second Intermediate Period (ca. 1786–1567), comprising dynasties 13-17. In the 13th and 14th dynasties Egypt declined. In the 15th and 16th dynasties Egypt was subjugated and ruled by the Hyksos, a people of mixed Semitic-Asiatic descent. Because of superior military technology, the Hyksos—using iron chariots and Asiatic bows—dominated the land for a century and a half from Avaris in the Nile Delta. The Hyksos were gradually displaced beginning about 1600 when Seqenenre II, prince of Thebes, rebelled. The history of Jacob's descendants during the Hyksos period is obscure (cf. Unger, *Archaeology and the Old Testament*, pp. 130-5).

Under Ahmose I of Thebes the New Empire period (ca. 1567–1220; dynasties 18-19) commenced, resulting in one of the most brilliant periods in Egyptian history. Egypt emerged as an international power and extended her influence beyond the Euphrates River. During the 18th dynasty the events of the Book of Exodus took place. This was a time when a new wave of Egyptian nationalism had supplanted the older Hyksos tolerance of foreigners. The Egyptians embarked on empire-building as a means of defense, pushing their borders into Palestine. Apparently not wanting to eradicate the Semitic population already settled in Egypt, the Egyptian Pharaohs used them as slave labor for building defense projects and royal palaces.

*2. The history of Egypt near the time of the Exodus.* Amenhotep I ruled in the newly centralized government from 1546 to 1526 (actually begun by his father Ahmose I) and was succeeded by Thutmose I (who ruled ca. 1526–1512). Moses was born (ca. 1526) in this king's reign (or at the end of the reign of Amenhotep I). This king's famous daughter, Hatshepsut, may have been the royal princess who discovered Moses along the Nile. When Thutmose II (1512–1504) died, Thutmose III was very young. So his stepmother, Hatshepsut, contrived to make herself ruler starting in 1503. (Thutmose III is considered king from 1504 to 1482 though Hatshepsut "coreigned" with him to 1482.)

During Hatshepsut's brilliant reign Egypt experienced prosperity. In these years Moses spent his youth in the royal court. After Hatshepsut's death in 1428 Thutmose III ruled alone till 1450. Thutmose III liquidated the entire royal court and attempted to obliterate Hatshepsut's name from monuments in the land. At that time Moses probably found the court of Egypt inhospitable and fled to Midian. Thutmose III became a powerful kingdom builder, extending his empire to include Syria.

Thutmose III was succeeded by Amenhotep II (1450–1425), the Pharaoh of the Exodus (1446). Unlike his warring father, Amenhotep II seems to have suffered military reverses because he was not able to carry out extensive campaigns. His weak war efforts may have resulted from the loss of all or most of his chariots, in the waters of the Sea of Reeds. The so-called "Dream Stela" of Thutmose IV records that the god Harem-akht told the young prince in a dream that someday he would be king. If Thutmose IV had been the eldest son, proof of his throne-right would have been unnecessary. It is logical, therefore, to assume that he was a younger son, not the oldest son, of Amenhotep II. This accords with the statement in Exodus 12:29 that the eldest son of Pharaoh died the night of Israel's first Passover.

Thus Thutmose III was the Pharaoh of the oppression and Amenhotep II was the Pharaoh of the Exodus. Egyptian history after the New Empire Period and up to Greek rule included the late New Kingdom (dynasty 20, ca. 1200-1085) and the Third Intermediate Period (1085–663 B.C.; dynasties 21-25) and the Late Period (663–332 B.C.; dynasties 26-31).

*3. The site of the Exodus.* The route Israel followed out of Egypt has occasioned much debate. Complicating the issue has been the inaccurate translation of the Hebrew *yām sûp* as Red Sea instead of Sea of (Papyrus) Reeds. The area is somewhere between the Gulf of Suez and the Mediterranean Sea, along the line of the present Suez Canal where there are many marshy lagoons and lakes.

Two views are held as to the possible site of the Exodus. The "northern view" places the Exodus at a lagoon bordering the Mediterranean Sea, and the "southern (or 'central') view" places the Exodus south of Succoth near Lake Balah or Lake Timsah. God led the Israelites away from the well-traveled and fortified trade route that progressed northward ("the road through the Philistine country, though that was shorter," 13:17) into the desert to avoid contact with Egyptian militia. The northern view assumes that Mount Sinai is in the vicinity of Kadesh Barnea. The evidence, however, favors the placement of the Sinai in the peninsula's southern portion.

The Israelites left Rameses and traveled to Succoth, about 30 miles southeast (Ex. 12:37; Num. 33:5). Near Succoth, the Israelites were miraculously delivered from Amenhotep II's chariot army. Also favoring the "southern view" is the fact that the Desert of Shur (Ex. 15:22), where Israel went after crossing the Reed Sea, is directly east of Succoth. Another factor is that Lake Balah and Lake Timsah can be affected by strong east winds in the way described in 14:21. (See the map "Possible Route of the Exodus," near Num. 33:1-5.)

# OUTLINE

I. The Redemption of God's People from Egypt (chaps. 1–18)
   A. The oppression of Israel in Egypt (chap. 1)
      1. The setting: Israel in Egypt (1:1-7)
      2. The oppression: Israel under the Pharaohs (1:8-22)
   B. The deliverer of Israel from Egypt (chaps. 2–4)
      1. The birth and protection of Moses in Egypt (2:1-10)
      2. The escape of Moses to Midian (2:11–4:17)
      3. The return of Moses to Egypt (4:18-31)
   C. The struggle of Moses with Pharaoh in Egypt (5:1–12:36)
      1. The confrontations of Moses with Pharaoh (5:1–7:13)
      2. The judgments of God on Egypt (7:14–12:36)
   D. The deliverance of Israel from Egypt (12:37–18:27)
      1. The flight in Egypt toward the sea (12:37–13:22)
      2. The crossing of the Red (Reed) Sea (chap. 14)
      3. The praise by Moses and Miriam for deliverance (15:1-21)
      4. The journey to Mount Sinai (15:22–18:27)
II. The Revelation to God's People at Sinai (chaps. 19–40)
   A. The covenant of God with His people (chaps. 19–31)
      1. The setting for the revelation of the Law (chap. 19)
      2. The Decalogue (20:1-21)
      3. The Book of the Covenant (20:22–24:11)
      4. The ceremonial regulations (24:12–31:18)
   B. The failure and restoration of God's people (chaps. 32–34)
      1. The breaking of the covenant by Israel (32:1–33:6)
      2. The renewal of the covenant by God (33:7–34:35)
   C. The construction of the tabernacle (chaps. 35–40)
      1. The preparation for the construction (35:1–36:7)
      2. The building of the tabernacle (36:8–39:31)
      3. The completion of the

tabernacle (39:32-43)
4. The assembling at the tabernacle (40:1-33)
5. The dwelling of God with His people (40:34-38)

# COMMENTARY

The Book of Exodus divides into two sections. The first section (chaps. 1–18) deals with the plight and deliverance of Jacob's descendants from the oppressive policies of Thutmose III and Amenhotep II; the second section (chaps. 19–40) deals with the worship of the redeemed nation. The first delineates God's mighty deliverance; the second, their preparation for quiet, obedient submission in worship.

## I. The Redemption of God's People from Egypt (chaps. 1–18)

Moses described the plight of Israel in Egypt, the rise of a deliverer (himself), and the struggles with Pharaoh's obstinate heart which resulted in a miraculous deliverance of the nation Israel through the Sea of Reeds and their safe arrival at Mount Sinai.

### A. The oppression of Israel in Egypt (chap. 1)

1. THE SETTING: ISRAEL IN EGYPT (1:1-7)

**1:1-5.** These verses provide a connecting link between the patriarchal period described in the last chapters of Genesis and the events in Exodus. God providentially protected the children of **Jacob** (also called **Israel**) and increased their **descendants** from a small group to a large segment of the population in Egypt.

Leah's six **sons** are listed in the order of their birth; from **Reuben** through **Zebulun** (cf. Gen. 35:23). **Benjamin,** the son of Jacob's second wife Rachel, is mentioned next but **Joseph,** Rachel's firstborn, is not listed because he **was already in Egypt. Dan and Naphtali** were the sons of Rachel's maidservant Bilhah (Gen. 35:25), and **Gad and Asher** were the sons of Leah's maidservant Zilpah (Gen. 35:26). The males who **entered Egypt** with Jacob numbered **70** (cf. Gen. 46:27; Deut. 10:22; cf. comments on Acts 7:14 where the number is said to be 75).

**1:6-7.** Jacob's descendants increased: **The Israelites were fruitful and multi-**plied greatly and became exceedingly numerous (cf. Acts 7:17). Several generations separated Levi from Moses (cf. comments on Num. 26:58-59) so that the time from Joseph's death (Gen. 50:26) to the growth of the nation as described in Exodus 1:7 was probably little more than 100 years. The adult males in the Exodus totaled 600,000, not counting women and children (12:37), so the total Israelite population at that time may have been about 2 million. No wonder **the land** (i.e., Goshen, Gen. 45:10, in the southeast Delta) **was filled with them.** According to God's promise to Abraham (Gen. 12:1-3) a large nation had emerged. They had yet to receive a land (Gen. 15:18-21) and a "constitution" (the Mosaic Law).

2. THE OPPRESSION: ISRAEL UNDER THE PHARAOHS (1:8-22)

Moses discussed two forms of oppression in the reign of a Pharaoh in Egypt's 18th dynasty: slave labor (vv. 8-14) and child extermination (vv. 15-22). God used these practices of the Pharaoh to stir up the people of God to desire deliverance from Egypt.

*a. The imposition of slavery (1:8-14)*

The logic of the new king is stated (vv. 8-10) and also the policy that resulted from his reasoning (vv. 11-14).

**1:8-10.** The **new king . . . did not know about Joseph.** The identity of this Pharaoh is uncertain but possibly he was Ahmose I, founder of the 18th dynasty, or more likely, Amenhotep I (1545–1526) or Thutmose I (1526–1512; see "Historical Background" under the *Introduction*). If "did not know about Joseph" means "had no appreciation for Joseph's character or achievements," this suggests that the new monarch came after the Hyksos oppression. In the wave of Egyptian nationalism (which included a hatred of the Hyksos) all Semites, including the Hyksos and the Israelites, may have been treated with suspicion. This Pharaoh voiced two reasons for his concern: the alarming increase in the number of **the Israelites** and the fear of their aligning politically with a foe in time of **war.** The words **deal shrewdly** imply a policy that would check their increase and exploit their labor potential.

**1:11-14.** So **forced labor** was established throughout the Delta area with

Hebrews being required to build the royal **store cities** of **Pithom and Rameses. Oppressed** (*ʿānâh*) is the same word God used in Genesis 15:13 (where it is trans. "mistreated") when He predicted the Egyptian bondage. This slavery in Egypt was like being in an "iron-smelting furnace" (Deut. 4:20). In spite of the Egyptians' ruthless treatment of **the Israelites,** God prospered them numerically. This caused greater consternation for **the Egyptians** and an increase in the Israelites' workload.

### b. The extermination of children (1:15-22)

**1:15-16.** Enslavement was only partially effective so Pharaoh decided to enact a more aggressive policy, namely, infanticide. It must not be thought that the Israelites had only two **midwives** (lit., "those who help to bear"). Most likely, because of the vast number of Israelites, these two women were the chief administrators of an organization of midwives. The king's instructions were explicit; male babies were to be killed and female infants kept alive. **The delivery stool** (lit., "two stools") refers to the custom of mothers delivering their babies while sitting on two stones.

**1:17-19.** However, **the midwives,** fearing **God** (cf. v. 21) more than the laws of an earthling, though a monarch (cf. Acts 5:29), **did not** obey the command. So they (Shiphrah and Puah, Ex. 1:15) were called in to answer for their misconduct. These **midwives** answered that the Hebrew wives delivered so quickly that **before the midwives** could **arrive,** the babies were already delivered. Apparently this implies that the baby boys were hidden by their parents so that it was impossible for Shiphrah and Puah to kill them. The answer seems illogical; actually the midwives may have simply responded slowly to house calls. Evidently Pharaoh did not punish them for their inability to effect his policy.

**1:20-21. God** blessed the Israelites in general with increased fertility (cf. v. 7), and bestowed mercy on Shiphrah and Puah in particular. God's purpose in granting the increase seems to have been to stir the ire and fear of the Egyptians so that they would more severely discomfort God's people and thus cause them to desire deliverance. So immediate blessing effected a negative action that later precipitated a larger future blessing.

**1:22. Pharaoh** then enacted an open, more aggressive policy to stem the Israelites' numerical increase. Failing to limit the growth of the people secretively through Hebrew midwives, Pharaoh commanded **his** own **people** to police the decree. So the oppression against the Israelites deepened, but as God's people were suffering under this subjugation, God prepared a deliverer.

### B. The deliverer of Israel from Egypt (chaps. 2–4)

#### 1. THE BIRTH AND PROTECTION OF MOSES IN EGYPT (2:1-10)

**2:1-2.** Notice of Moses' birth is commented on briefly. Obviously Pharaoh's decree (1:16, 22) jeopardized Moses' life. The names of Moses' parents are not given here but in 6:20 it is learned that his father was Amram and his mother Jochebed, Amram's aunt. This Levite couple had two other children: Miriam (15:20) and Aaron (6:20). Aaron was three years older than Moses (7:7). Assuming that the Exodus occurred in 1446 and since Moses was 80 years old at that time (7:7), he was born in 1526 B.C. at the beginning of the reign of Thutmose I (1526–1512) or at the end of Amenhotep I's reign (1545–1526). Moses' parents defied Pharaoh's decree and hid the baby (cf. Acts 7:17-20). The infant was named not by his parents but by an Egyptian princess (Ex. 2:10).

The **child** was **fine** (v. 2), that is, beautiful and healthy. Stephen said Moses "was no ordinary child" (Acts 7:20); so did the writer to the Hebrews (Heb. 11:23). Acting by faith in God's ability to solve their problem, Moses' parents **hid him,** not fearing the king's edict. But after **three months** it was no longer safe to keep him at home.

**2:3-4.** Moses' mother Jochebed decided to hide **the child in** a **basket** along the Nile River **among the** dense **reeds.** She wove **papyrus** stems into a boxlike structure and then **coated** the exterior **with tar and pitch** (cf. "pitch" on Noah's ark, Gen. 6:14) before placing it in the marsh. Ironically Jochebed, putting her son into the Nile, was in one sense obeying the Pharaoh's edict to "throw" baby boys into the river! (Ex. 1:22)

Jochebed had the baby's **sister** Miriam stand **at a distance.** Was this a preconceived plot on Jochebed's part, hoping that someone would find and protect the child? Perhaps so for the mother's instruction to Miriam **to see what would happen to him** and Miriam's question to Pharaoh's daughter (2:7) suggest planning on the mother's part.

**2:5-9.** God's providence is clearly evident in His care of the infant, for miraculously the child was restored to his own parents. Who was **Pharaoh's daughter**? If the monarch at that time was Thutmose I, she may have been his daughter Hatshepsut. Perhaps **the basket**-boat was not fully hidden from sight, because the princess **saw** it (though her curiosity may have been aroused by hearing the infant crying).

When Pharaoh's daughter **opened** the box the infant's cries evoked her compassion (**she felt sorry for him**). At that precise moment Miriam offered to secure a **nurse** among **the Hebrew women.** In a vivid display of God's control over events, Moses' **mother** was reunited with her child—which was legally sanctioned in the home despite Pharaoh's edict (1:22)—and she was even remunerated for her services! (2:9) Interestingly several women were involved in the events surrounding Moses' birth: the midwives' fear of God and their disobeying Pharaoh's orders; the defiance of Moses' mother; the compassion of the Egyptian princess, Pharaoh's own daughter; and the availability of Moses' own sister. In verses 1-10 all the women are anonymous.

**2:10.** After Moses' earliest years he was returned **to Pharaoh's daughter** as a member of the royal household (cf. Acts 7:21-22). He was adopted and **named** by her and raised as **her son.** He "was educated in all the wisdom of the Egyptians" and was a powerful speaker (Acts 7:22). But later he repudiated that Egyptian heritage, refusing "to be known as the son of Pharaoh's daughter" (Heb. 11:24-25).

Some say that the name **Moses** (*mōšeh*) was a Hebrew word and that Hebrew was understood by the Egyptians. Others say "Moses" was an Egyptian name, like "Mose" in Thutmose or Ahmose. Cassuto (*A Commentary on the Book of Exodus*, pp. 20-1) suggests the term is Egyptian meaning "son" or "is born" though in sound *mōšeh* was a pun

on the Hebrew verb *māšâh*, "to draw out" (**I drew him out of the water**).

Once again Pharaoh's efforts to exterminate the male Hebrew population were thwarted. The child was protected in a reed basket as it floated helplessly in the Nile and then by the instantaneous affection, ironically, of Pharaoh's own daughter. In God's sovereignty He kept the infant safe from Pharaoh's edict and even made the child a member of the royal family!

**2. THE ESCAPE OF MOSES TO MIDIAN (2:11–4:17)**

*a. The cause of Moses' escape (2:11-14)*

**2:11-14.** The events described in these verses took place 40 years after Moses' birth (cf. Acts 7:23); the year was about 1485 B.C. in the reign of Hatshepsut (see "Historical Background" in the *Introduction*). By this time Moses was highly educated (Acts 7:22) and probably spoke fluently in both Egyptian and Hebrew.

**Moses** protected one of his oppressed brethren by killing **an Egyptian** and hiding his body **in the sand.** Moses thought that in protecting his fellow Israelite his people would realize he was their deliverer (Acts 7:25). He thought **no one** saw him but apparently the Israelite whom Moses had protected had told what he did. For **the** very **next day** when Moses intervened in the **fighting** of **two Hebrews,** one of them referred to Moses' having **killed the Egyptian** (cf. Acts 7:24-28). Moses then feared that word of this murder was already widespread and would reach Pharaoh.

*b. The place of Moses' escape (2:15a)*

**2:15a.** When Pharaoh heard of the murder **he** in anger (Heb. 11:27) **tried to kill Moses.** Perhaps this Pharaoh was Thutmose III who was reigning with Hatshepsut. **Moses fled** eastward and lived among the nomadic Midianites. The founder of these people was **Midian,** a son of Keturah, wife of Abraham, who sent them "to the land of the east" (Gen. 25:1-6). The Midianites lived in southeastern Sinai and northwestern Arabia on both sides of the Gulf of Aqaba. This desert land differed greatly from Goshen in Egypt.

*c. The marriage of Moses (2:15b-22)*

**2:15b-22.** One day in Midian while

Moses was sitting **by a well** he met the **seven daughters** of Reuel (elsewhere called Jethro, 3:1; 18:1), **a priest of Midian.** Moses' benevolent act, protecting the daughters while they were securing **water,** was the third incident in which he sought to deliver others from harm (cf. 2:12-13). These incidents anticipated his future role as his nation's deliverer. This heroism on his part caused the girls' **father** to invite **Moses** (whom they called **an Egyptian,** perhaps because of the way he was dressed) to dine with his family. Moses subsequently married Reuel's **daughter Zipporah** (which means "little bird") and to them was born a son **Gershom,** whose name means "expulsion" or "resident alien there." It is probably related to the Hebrew verb *gāraš*, "to drive out or banish" (cf. 6:1). He was a child of Moses' banishment, that is, a child born while **Moses** was **an alien in a foreign land.**

For 40 years (Acts 7:30) Moses undertook the toilsome life of a sheepherder in the Sinai area, thus gaining valuable knowledge of the topography of the Sinai Peninsula which later was helpful as he led the Israelites in that wilderness land.

### d. The call of Moses (2:23–4:17)

(1) The cause of Moses' call. **2:23-25.** The deceased **king** (v. 23) is probably Thutmose III, the Pharaoh of the oppression (1504-1450 B.C.), who was followed by Amenhotep II (1450-1425). During Moses' 40 years in Midian the Israelites continued to suffer under the servitude of the Egyptians (1:11). Hearing their anguish **God** thought of **His covenant** promises to **Abraham** (Gen. 12:1-3; 15:18-21; 17:3-8), **Isaac** (Gen. 17:21), and **Jacob** (Gen. 35:10-12). In His compassion **God** considered the plight of **the Israelites.** He **looked on** them (cf. Ex. 3:7, 9) **and was concerned about them** and decided to intervene. Exodus 2:24-25 is a hinge in the narrative. Suppression, slavery, and death were dominant themes in 1:1–2:23. Now deliverance and triumph will be major emphases. God in His sovereign power was ready to act in accord with His promises to deliver and preserve His people.

(2) The call of Moses (3:1–4:17). These verses, which record God's call to Moses on Mount Horeb, may be divided into five parts: circumstances (3:1-3), con-

frontation (3:4-10), consternation (3:11-15), instructions (3:16-22), and complaints (4:1-17).

**3:1-3.** These verses present the *circumstances* of Moses' call by God. After 40 years of training in the courts of Pharaoh, **Moses** now neared the end of another 40 years of his life as a shepherd. Leading his father-in-law's **flock** in search of grassland, Moses approached Mount **Horeb** (another name for Mount Sinai; cf. 19:10-11 with Deut. 4:10). Why **his father-in-law** is here called **Jethro** instead of Reuel (cf. Ex. 2:16, 18) is uncertain. Perhaps Reuel thought his daughter's marriage to Moses, an Egyptian raised in the royal family, brought him (Reuel) prestige so he changed his name to Jethro, which means abundance or superiority. Moses' reference to Horeb as **the mountain of God** (cf. 4:27; 18:5; 24:13) probably reflects his estimation of that mountain after the events that took place there later.

Interestingly Moses' communication from God here (3:1-3) is at the same mountain where God later gave him the Law (19:20; 24:13-18; cf. 3:12). There Moses' curiosity was engaged by **a bush** that was aflame but was **not** burned **up. The Angel of the LORD** (v. 4) is the Lord (cf. comments on Gen. 16:9). **Fire** was a symbol of God's presence, seen later when He descended upon Mount Sinai (Ex. 19:18).

**3:4-10.** In this *confrontation* with **Moses,** God commissioned him to deliver His **people** from **Egypt** (v. 10). Aware that it was **God** who was calling him, **Moses** responded, **Here I am.** The same response was given God by Abraham (Gen. 22:11), Jacob (Gen. 46:2), and Samuel (1 Sam. 3:4). God told **Moses** to remove his **sandals** (cf. Josh. 5:15) in a gesture of worship. The **ground** was **holy** not by its nature but because of God's presence. When **the LORD** identified Himself to Moses as **the God of** his ancestors (**Abraham . . . Isaac . . . and . . . Jacob;** cf. Ex. 3:15-16; 4:5) **Moses** covered **his face,** fearful of looking **at God** (cf. comments on 33:11, 20; John 1:18).

God then told Moses He was aware of the plight of His **people** (Ex. 3:7, 9; cf. 2:24) and that He planned **to rescue them from** Egypt. The result of His concern is captured in the words **I have come down** (3:8), an idiom describing divine intervention. God would (a) deliver them from Egypt and (b) take them to **a good and spacious land,** unlike the Midianite desert.

The phrase **a land flowing with milk** means that Canaan was ideal for raising goats and cows. Feeding on good pastureland the goats, sheep, and cows were full of milk. Flowing with **honey** means that the bees were busy making honey. Milk and honey suggested agricultural prosperity. This is the first of numerous references in the Old Testament to the "land flowing with milk and honey" (cf. v. 17; 33:3; Lev. 20:24; Num. 13:27; 14:8; 16:13-14; Deut. 6:3; 11:9; 26:9, 15; 27:3; 31:20; Josh. 5:6; Jer. 11:5; 32:22; Ezek. 20:6, 15).

This land then was occupied by **Canaanites, Hittites, Amorites, Perizzites, Hivites, and Jebusites** (cf. Ex. 3:17; 13:5; 23:23; 33:2; 34:11).

In Genesis 10:15-18 all of these are listed except Perizzites, along with several other peoples who descended from Canaan, son of Ham and grandson of Noah. In the Abrahamic Covenant (Gen. 15:18-21) God mentioned five of the six groups of Exodus 3:8, along with five others (cf. seven in Deut. 7:1).

Canaanites is the more general term. Hittites were probably pockets of people who immigrated from the north. Amorites were the same as the Amurru of northern Mesopotamia (cf. comments on Gen. 14:13-16). Perizzites were perhaps village-dwellers or nomads. Hivites were possibly in northern Palestine and beyond (Josh. 11:3; Jud. 3:3). Jebusites lived in the hill country (Num. 13:29) of and around Jebus, later known as Jerusalem (Josh. 15:8).

God then told Moses how He would bring about the deliverance of His people. He would use Moses, not in his own strength (Acts 7:25) but by divine enablement. God said, **So now, go. I am sending you.** Interestingly while God promised the people two things (deliverance from Egypt and entrance into a new land), He commissioned Moses to accomplish only the first. God knew Moses would not enter the Promised Land (Deut. 32:48-52).

**3:11-15.** That **Moses** was shocked by God's words (vv. 7-10) is evident by his *consternation.* He found the command hard to believe. Immediately Moses ob-

jected to God's command because of his lack of ability (v. 11) and his lack of authority (v. 13). Moses doubted his ability to confront the new **Pharaoh** (Amenhotep II) successfully and to lead the nation out. **God** responded to this objection with two promises: the assurance of His personal presence (**I will be,** v. 12; cf. comments on v. 14, **with you**) and the promise of Moses' return to Mount Horeb (**you** [pl., referring to Moses *and* the people] **will worship God on this mountain**).

The purpose of the deliverance was that Israel might "worship God." This purpose is stated frequently in Exodus (4:23; 7:16; 8:1, 20; 9:1, 13; 10:3, 7-8, 11, 24, 26; 12:31). The Hebrew word for "worship" is the same word for "to be a slave" (*'ābad*). Israel had been slaves (*'ābōdîm*) of Egypt (6:6), and was in slavery (*'ābōdāh*, 2:23) in Egypt ("the land of slavery," lit., "the house of slaves," *bêt 'ābādîm*, 13:3, 14; 20:2). Having served as slaves to the Egyptians, Israel was now to serve the Lord, worshiping Him as His subjects.

In Moses' second objection he felt the Israelites would challenge his assertion that God had **sent** him to deliver them. **God** told **Moses** to tell them, **I am who I am** (*'ehyeh 'ăšer 'ehyeh,* 3:14; cf. "I will be," *'ehyeh,* v. 12) and **I AM** (*'ehyeh*) **has sent me to you** (v. 14). This One said He would be with His people in their time of trouble and need. *'Ehyeh* is probably a wordplay on Yahweh (LORD) in verse 15. Thus, the name Yahweh, related to the verb "to be," probably speaks of God's self-existence, but it means more than that. It usually speaks of His relationship to His people. For example, as Lord, He redeemed them (6:6), was faithful to them (34:5-7), and made a covenant with them (Gen. 15:18).

The word **also** (Ex. 3:15) points to a second reply to Moses' second objection (the first reply is in v. 14). The always-present God had demonstrated His character in the past to the **fathers** (patriarchs; cf. vv. 6, 16; 4:5) and that willingness to look over His people tenderly is an abiding attribute. He is **to be remembered** by that **name forever.** Perhaps Moses knew of God as the distant Sovereign but not as the immanent God who cares for and loves His chosen ones. Both of Moses' objections (3:11, 13) were answered with lessons on the nature and character of God (vv. 12, 14-15).

**3:16-22.** After being apprised of the nature of his mission (vv. 7-10) and of his God (vv. 11-15), Moses received *instructions*, details about how to accomplish the task. The instructions relate to the elders (vv. 16-17), the king (vv. 18-20), and the Israelites (vv. 21-22). God told Moses to **go** to **the elders** (leaders and counselors) in **Israel** and tell them of the theophany, the appearance of **God** in the bush and His message of concern (**I have . . . seen what has been done to you;** cf. 2:24; 3:7) and of His plan to deliver them **out of . . . Egypt** and **into** Canaan (cf. v. 8 and comments there). With **the elders** Moses was to approach Amenhotep II. The phrase **the God of the Hebrews** was later used by Moses when he spoke to Pharaoh; it is a term polytheistic people could understand (cf. 5:3; 7:16; 9:1, 13; 10:3).

Moses and the elders were simply to request permission to leave **Egypt** for a short trip (**three-day journey**) for religious purposes. He deliberately said nothing about them returning.

God told Moses (3:19-20) that Pharaoh would **not** respond to his request except by divine imposition. (God's **mighty hand,** suggesting His firmness and strength in action, is also referred to in 6:1 [twice]; 13:14, 16; 32:11; Deut. 4:34; 5:15; 6:21; 7:8, 19; 9:26; 11:2; 26:8.) But God would perform **wonders** (the 10 plagues) to persuade Pharaoh to **let them go.**

The plagues on Egypt would cause **the Egyptians** to be **favorably disposed toward** the Israelites so that when asked **the Egyptians** would give **silver . . . gold,** and **clothing** (cf. Gen. 15:14b; Ex. 12:35-36) to the Israelite women (and men, who are mentioned in 11:2). God's people were **not** to leave **empty-handed;** perhaps this was partial compensation for the 400 years of slavery. Later the gold and silver were used in constructing the tabernacle (35:5, 22).

**4:1-17.** Again (cf. 3:11-15) **Moses** voiced *complaints* about his assignment because of his sense of personal inadequacy. The detailed instructions in 3:16-22 may have heightened Moses' anxieties about his new role, so he posed two more objections: his fear that his compatriots would repudiate his authority (4:1)

and his lack of eloquence (v. 10). God patiently and gently dealt with Moses' apprehensions. Fear that the Israelites might not believe God had appeared to him is reasonable because God had apparently not appeared to the Israelites for 430 years, the length of the sojourn in Egypt. The Lord's answer to the doubtful deliverer was to enable Moses to perform three supernatural tasks, two immediate (vv. 3-5, 6-8) and one in the future (v. 9).

The first of the signs to Moses was the turning of his shepherd's **staff** into **a snake** and **back into a staff.** Grabbing a snake **by its tail** was normally a dangerous thing to do! To follow the Lord's directive took courage and faith. Because snakes symbolized power and life to the Egyptians, God was declaring to Moses that he would be able to overcome the powers of Egypt. This miracle, God said, would cause the Israelites to **believe that** He, **the God of** the patriarchs (cf. 2:24; 3:6, 15-16) had spoken to Moses.

The second sign was **his hand** becoming leprous and its healing. This disease, though perhaps not the same as what is today called leprosy, was prevalent in Egypt and was considered incurable. Moses had run in fear from the snake (4:3). Now he must have been horrified when he withdrew his smitten **hand** from his garment. But then he was probably filled with reverential awe when it was suddenly cleansed. This **sign,** God said, might be more effective with the people than the first one (v. 8). Thus Moses' fear that no one would believe he was commissioned by God was placated.

The third sign would be Moses' miraculous ability to turn **water from the Nile** into **blood** (v. 9). The Egyptians regarded the Nile River as the source of life and productivity. So Moses' showing the people that he had power over the Nile would prove that God had given Moses ability to overcome the Egyptians. Later Moses performed these miracles before the Israelites (vv. 29-30) and as God predicted (vv. 5, 8), the people believed (v. 31). Interestingly the first plague was similar to the third sign: When Aaron hit the Nile River with his staff the water turned to blood (7:17-21).

Moses' fourth complaint was his supposed lack of eloquence and oratorical skills (4:10-17; cf. 6:12, 30). **Slow of** speech and tongue means lacking in fluent speech. Apparently **Moses** was downplaying his abilities because Stephen said he was "powerful in speech" (Acts 7:22). God's initial reaction to Moses' objection was to remind him, by a series of questions, that **the LORD** determines man's abilities or disabilities. Then God repeated His brief commission (**Now go**; cf. Ex. 3:10). Though assured of God's enabling power (**I will help . . . you**; cf. 4:15) the magnitude and difficulty of the talk frightened him.

When **Moses** suggested God get a replacement (v. 13) God became angry. (Cf. five other references to God's anger: 15:7; 22:24; 32:10-12.) Why was God angry? Probably because He perceived that Moses was speaking more out of disobedience than fear. So God told Moses He would let his **brother** speak for him (4:14-16; cf. 7:1). And yet this spokesman for Moses would one day make a golden calf (32:1-5) and become a lying spokesman (32:22-24). God then said He would **help both of** them **speak** before Pharaoh and **the people** (4:15-16; cf. v. 12; 7:1-2). Moses was told to **take** the **staff** that had become a snake (4:2-4) as a means for achieving the wonders that were to follow (cf. 7:9-10). In 4:20 it is called "the staff of God."

3. THE RETURN OF MOSES TO EGYPT (4:18-31)

*a. The preparation for the return (4:18-23)*

**4:18-23.** Moses asked **Jethro** for permission to return to his **people in Egypt** because he was concerned for their welfare. **Jethro** granted him leave with his blessing. **The LORD** had revealed **to Moses** that in his 40-year sojourn in Midian those who had sought his life, no doubt including Thutmose III, were **dead** so he need have no fear of reprisal. He **took** with him **his wife** (Zipporah, 2:21) **and sons.** His first son was Gershom (2:22; cf. 18:3) and the second son, named later, was Eliezer (18:4). Perhaps Eliezer was born after God appeared to Moses (3:1-17), when Moses had returned to Jethro.

Then God told **Moses** about his future ministry **before Pharaoh** (4:21-23). Moses would demonstrate God's **power** to Amenhotep II. **But,** God said, it would be of no avail because He would **harden** Pharaoh's **heart, so** he would refuse to **let the people** of God **go.** On numerous occasions in Exodus God is said to have hardened Pharaoh's heart. To some people God's hardening seems to preclude Pharaoh's exercise of his own will. But Pharaoh also hardened his own heart (7:13, "became hard"; 14, "unyielding"; 22, "became hard"; 8:15, 19, "was hard"; 32; 9:7, "unyielding"; 34, "hardened"; 35, "was hard"; 13:15, "stubbornly refused," another Heb. word meaning "hardened"). The first two references to God's hardening Pharaoh's heart (4:21; 7:3) were actually *predictions* that He would do it in the future. Then in the next seven references Pharaoh is said to have hardened his own heart (7:13-14, 22; 8:15, 19, 32; 9:7) *before* God is said to have hardened it (9:12; 10:1, 20, 27; 11:10; 14:4, 8). God's first hardening came after the sixth plague. Pharaoh hardened his own heart six times by his refusals. Then later he hardened it again in response to the seventh plague, and God hardened his heart after each of plagues 8-10. God confirmed Pharaoh's defiant willful obstinance by then judicially hardening his heart (cf. Deut. 2:30; Josh. 11:20).

Repentance is a gift from God (Acts 5:31; 11:18; 2 Tim. 2:25) that He grants to some by His grace, though in His infinite love He desires that all be saved (1 Tim. 2:4; 2 Peter 3:9). God uses people to fulfill parts of His plans, which is Paul's understanding of Pharaoh's obstinance (Rom. 9:17-18). In God's infinite wisdom He raised up this Pharaoh for that occasion so that in his rebellion against God he might be an instrument for God's glory. Since Pharaoh's heart would remain calloused, it was ultimately necessary to compel him by the last of the plagues, the death of the firstborn. Amazingly Moses told him this right at the beginning (Ex. 4:22-23). Egyptians prized their firstborn sons, treating them as special. Strikingly Israel is God's son (cf. Hosea 11:1) and therefore sacred to Him.

Another factor in God's hardening of Pharaoh's heart is that it was a reversal of an Egyptian belief. Egyptians believed that when a person died his heart was weighed in the hall of judgment. If one's heart was "heavy" with sin, that person was judged. A stone beetle scarab was placed on the heart of a deceased person to suppress his natural tendency to confess sin which would subject himself to judgment. This "hardening of the heart" by the scarab would result in salvation for the deceased.

However, God reversed this process in Pharaoh's case. Instead of his heart being suppressed so that he was silent about his sin and thus delivered, his heart became hardened, he confessed his sin (Ex. 9:27, 34; 10:16-17), and his sinfully heavy heart resulted in judgment. For the Egyptians "hardening of the heart" resulted in silence (absence of confession of sin) and therefore salvation. But God's hardening of Pharaoh's heart resulted in acknowledgment of sin and in judgment.

### b. The circumcision of Moses' son (4:24-26)

**4:24-26.** The circumcision of Moses' son (either Gershom or Eliezer) seems strange. In his years in Midian **Moses** had neglected to obey God's command (cf. Gen. 17:10) to circumcise one (or both?) of his sons. So God **was about to kill** Moses, perhaps by causing him to be gravely ill. **Zipporah** reluctantly circumcised her son with **flint** and then God healed His prophet. Her touching **Moses' feet** with the **son's foreskin** was possibly a symbolic act of substitution, in which obedience was seen as replacing disobedience. Zipporah called Moses **a bridegroom of blood.** The meaning of this phrase is unknown, but some say it was used in a derogatory way to suggest that she did not favor the rite. (Yet she did it to save her husband's life.) Others propose that she saw in the act a sort of redemption by which the blood of the youngster restored Moses to the Lord and also to her as a new bridegroom.

At this time Zipporah and the sons may have returned to Jethro (18:2-3). Moses' sudden illness was a warning that he must obey God wholly and fulfill his mission. Also this incident follows up the emphasis in 4:22-23 on sons (Pharaoh's son, and Israel as God's son).

### c. The meeting with Aaron and the people (4:27-31)

**4:27-31.** As God had indicated (vv. 14-17) the meeting with **Aaron** was cordial. They met at Mount Horeb (Sinai, **the mountain of God;** cf. 3:1; 18:5; 24:13), where **Moses** had seen the burning bush. **Moses told Aaron** about their newly appointed task (4:28). To authenticate his commission Moses **performed** miracles

**before the people** (as indicated in vv. 8-9, 28) and explained God's concern for **their misery** (cf. 2:24-25; 3:7, 9) and His plan to deliver them from Egypt (cf. 3:8, 10, 17). In response the people **believed** that **Moses** was sent by God (thus allaying Moses' fears; cf. 4:1) and they **worshiped** God for His merciful care.

### C. The struggle of Moses with Pharaoh in Egypt (5:1–12:36)

In this lengthy section Moses recorded his attempts to gain the release of God's people from Amenhotep II's domain. God's leader faced not only the torrid anger of the Pharaoh but also the dissatisfaction and distrust of his own people. The section has two parts: (a) the confrontations of Moses with Pharaoh along with a description of the actions of the Israelites (5:1–7:13) and (b) God's judgments on Egypt, commonly called the plagues (7:14–12:36).

#### 1. THE CONFRONTATIONS OF MOSES WITH PHARAOH (5:1–7:13)

Moses demanded the release of his people from Egypt on two occasions (5:1-5; 7:10-13). Each time (as the Lord had previously indicated, 4:21) Pharaoh refused to permit their freedom.

##### a. The initial confrontation (5:1–6:27)

Moses spoke to Pharaoh, who then increased the Israelites' workload (5:1-14). Then Moses was disquieted by his people who believed he was the cause of their added oppression (5:15–6:9).

(1) The plea of Moses. **5:1-4.** This must have been a dramatic meeting! As emissaries of God, **Moses and Aaron,** both in their 80s, confidently faced **Pharaoh,** whom his people considered a god. Their request is stated in verse 1 and expanded in verse 3; Moses and Aaron asked for permission to undertake **a three-day journey into the desert to offer sacrifices to the LORD** (cf. 3:18).

Pharaoh reacted in three ways: (1) He repudiated **the God of Israel** as having no authority (5:2). (2) He was calloused to the possibility of any harm that might come on the Israelites for disobeying their God (vv. 2-3). (On the title **the God of the Hebrews** see comments on 3:18; also cf. 7:16; 9:1, 13; 10:3.) (3) He was concerned for his own loss of **labor** productivity (5:4-5). This Pharaoh (probably Amenhotep II) viewed the Israelites as a commodity and their services as valuable, whereas the Pharaoh of 1:8-10, 22 (perhaps Ahmose) wanted to exterminate them.

(2) The added workload from Pharaoh. **5:5-14.** The hardness of Pharaoh's heart is evident in the words **that same day** (v. 6). Immediately he set about to make the burden of the Israelites more oppressive. Pharaoh's argument seems to be that people in bondage dream of freedom only when they have excessive free time or are allowed to idle away valuable time (**they are lazy**; cf. v. 17). To solve this problem he told the slave-masters to **require** the **same** quota **of bricks** but no longer to help the people by bringing the **straw.** Straw was mixed with clay and sand not so much as a binding agent but to cause the clay to be more durative. Pharaoh's orders were carried out (vv. 10-13) but the work was so much more demanding and time-consuming that the daily **quota of bricks** could not be met. As a result **the Israelite foremen** over their own people **were beaten** by Pharaoh's **slave drivers** who demanded that they comply with Amenhotep II's directives.

(3) The pleas of the Israelite foremen. **5:15-19.** As a result of these oppressions **the Israelite foremen** sought an audience with **Pharaoh** to complain about his unreasonable demand. But the foremen's meeting with Pharaoh was unproductive. Three times they stressed the loyalty of the Israelites (**your servants,** vv. 15-16). They argued that the failure to meet the assigned quota of brick production arose from their need to collect **straw,** a job previously assigned to Egyptians. But **Pharaoh** insisted that they were **lazy** (cf. vv. 8-9). The **foremen** recognized that Pharaoh was not going to change his orders.

(4) The accusation against Moses (5:20-23). **5:20-21.** The foremen's words to Moses and Aaron were poignant (vv. 20-21) and Moses was just as stark with God (vv. 22-23). Why **Moses and Aaron** were **waiting** for the foremen is unknown, but the men's harsh words are clear. The people had been severely oppressed before Moses' return, but this added pressure was simply too much to bear. The meaning of the word **stench** (v. 21) must be understood metaphorically

as "scorned or condemned." Earlier Moses had told the king that God's judgment might fall on the Hebrews if they were not permitted to worship in the wilderness (v. 3), but here the foremen complained of *Pharaoh's* **sword.**

**5:22-23.** Moses immediately turned to the Lord in a lament. He agreed with the foremen that the latest oppression of the Israelites resulted from his confrontation with **Pharaoh.** He now questioned God for sending him to do it. Moses' query was motivated by a heavy heart, not distrust of God, though his language (**You have not rescued Your people at all**) is abrupt.

(5) The reassurance of Moses (6:1-9). **6:1.** Moses sorrowed because his demand for freedom ironically had *increased* his people's burden, not eased it. So **the Lord** comforted and reassured his messenger, speaking to Moses twice (indicated by the word "also" in v. 2).

In the first statement (v. 1) God again told Moses what He would **do to Pharaoh,** whereas in the second statement He reviewed His promises to His people (vv. 2-8). God assured Moses that He would indeed deliver His people. He was arranging circumstances so that Pharaoh would let them go and would even compel them to do so. All this would be **because of** God's **mighty hand** (see comments on 3:19; also note "outstretched arm" in 6:6). **Drive them out,** or "expel them," translates $y^e g\bar{a}r\check{s}\bar{e}m$ from the verb $g\bar{a}ra\check{s}$ (cf. comments on the name of Moses' son Gershom [$g\bar{e}r\check{s}\bar{o}m$] in 2:22).

**6:2-5.** Then **God** reminded Moses of His character as revealed in His name Yahweh (cf. 3:14). The words **I am the Lord** occur four times in 6:2-8. As the Lord, Yahweh, He is **with** His own and is always faithful and true to them.

Why did God say that **by** His **name** the **Lord** He had **not** made Himself **known to** the patriarchs? Was not God known by the name Yahweh to the patriarchs **Abraham . . . Isaac,** and **Jacob?** Yes, He had been (e.g., Gen. 13:4). But He mainly appeared to them **as God Almighty** ($'\bar{e}l\ \check{s}adday$), the One who provides or sustains (cf. comments on Gen. 17:1). He had not displayed Himself to the patriarchs *primarily* by the name Yahweh. So in Exodus 3:14 God meant that now He was revealing Himself to Moses not only as Sustainer and Provider, but also as the Promise-Keeper, the One who was personally related to His people and would redeem them (cf. comments on 3:14-15).

**6:6-8.** God then told Moses to put aside his broken spirit and feelings of inadequacy and return to the people. Seven times in these three verses God said **I will,** thus emphasizing that He is the promise-keeping God. The "I wills" cluster around three promises: deliverance from Egypt (v. 6: **I will bring you out . . . I will free you . . . I will redeem you),** possession of the **people** as His **own** (v. 7), and the gift of the **land** (v. 8). Further the passage begins and ends with the same declaration, **I am the LORD.** The people's deliverance would become the basis of a covenantal relationship which would result in their being in **the land.** These verses present a cameo of Israel's history from the release from Egypt to the Conquest under Joshua. God's redeeming them **with an outstretched arm** (v. 6) meant that His power would be evident (cf. Deut. 4:34; 5:15; 7:19; 11:2; Ps. 136:12; Ezek. 20:33). And the **uplifted hand** (Ex. 6:8) was a gesture used when making an oath (as it still is today; cf. Gen. 14:22; Deut. 32:40; Neh. 9:15; Ps. 106:26; Ezek. 20:5-6, 15, 23, 42; 36:7; 44:12; 47:14). Moses' sagging spirit was again buttressed by a revelation of God's character and purposes.

**6:9.** With renewed vigor **Moses** returned to his people with God's words, **but** the burden of their oppression caused them **not** to **listen.** Tragically they forgot their initial response to Moses and Aaron (4:31).

(6) The recall of Moses to Pharaoh. **6:10-13.** Again God told **Moses** to **go** to **Pharaoh** and tell him to release **the Israelites.** Moses hesitated, his zeal dampened by the people's response (v. 9). Since he did not have power to influence his own people, how could he persuade **Pharaoh?** He must have thought that his lack of success with the people was caused by his lack of oratorical ability (cf. 4:10). **I speak with faltering lips** (cf. 6:30) is literally, "I am circumcised of lips" (cf. NIV marg.), that is, morally unclean and incapable. This objection was answered by the Lord's command—this time to both **Moses and Aaron**—to lead the people **out of Egypt.**

(7) The genealogy of Moses and Aar-

**Moses' Ancestry from Abraham**

Abraham
Ishmael   Isaac
          Esau   Jacob
                 Levi
          Gershon  Kohath  Merari
Amram  Izhar   Hebron   Uzziel
Aaron   Moses   Miriam

on. **6:14-27.** This passage puzzles some readers because it seems to be an unnatural insertion into the narrative. However, the genealogy was placed here to identify Moses and Aaron more precisely because of the prominent position they were assuming as representatives of the people before the Egyptian state. Verses 26-27, which close this passage, tie this unit with verse 13 and explain why the genealogy is given: **It was this same Moses and Aaron** (v. 26; repeated in v. 27), and **they were the ones who spoke to Pharaoh** (v. 27).

The title **These were the heads of their families** (v. 14) is repeated but with slightly different wording at the end of the genealogy (v. 25). **The** clans **of Reuben** and **of Simeon** were mentioned (vv. 14-15) in order to get to **Levi,** Jacob's third son and Moses and Aaron's ancestor. Levi's **sons** are mentioned in verse 16 and his other descendants in verses 17-19. Moses and Aaron's father **Amram,** their uncles, and cousins, and Aaron's family are chronicled in verses 20-25. The Amram in verse 20 is probably not the **Amram** in verse 18 (**sons** in v. 18 may be descendants). See the chart "Moses' Ancestry from Abraham" and the comments on Numbers 26:58. (Since 430 years lapsed from the time Levi moved with his brothers and his father Jacob to Egypt in 1876 to the Exodus led by Moses in 1446, more than two generations had to occur between Levi and Moses.) Thus Moses and Aaron were established as being in the tribe of Levi and the Amramite branch of the Kohath clan.

Though Aaron's family is traced to his sons and his grandson **Phinehas** (Ex.

6:23, 25), Moses' marriage is not mentioned. Perhaps this is because his wife Zipporah was not a Hebrew. As stated, verses 26-27 highlight the purpose of this genealogical digression—to focus on Moses and Aaron's pedigree and thus their authority to lead the people from Pharaoh's grasp. In verses 20 and 26 **Aaron** is mentioned before **Moses** because Aaron was older (cf. 7:7). But in 6:27 Moses' name precedes Aaron's because the major responsibility of the Exodus was his.

### b. The second confrontation (6:28–7:13)

(1) God's renewed command to Moses (6:28–7:7). **6:28-30.** When God confronted **Moses** this time, a discourse resulted that is much like His first summons to Moses to speak to Pharaoh. In addressing Moses God began with the words **I am the LORD**; the ever-present One who cares for His people and fulfills His promises (cf. 3:14-15; 6:2, 6-8). Again **Moses** complained that **Pharaoh** would not respond because of Moses' lack of eloquence (cf. 4:10 and comments on 6:12).

**7:1-5.** After hearing Moses' words about his inadequacy (6:30) God again told him to obey. **Moses,** God said, would seem **like God to Pharaoh** (cf. 4:16), probably because of the plagues God would miraculously perform through him. Also **Aaron** would **be** his **prophet** (*nābî*, i.e., one who speaks for another; cf. 4:16). The brief message to Pharaoh was to be the same as before (7:2; 5:1; cf. 3:10, 18; 6:11). Several things would result (7:3-5). In spite of Aaron's eloquence and Moses' ability to verify their authority with supernatural **signs,** God would **harden Pharaoh's heart** (see comments on 4:21). Pharaoh's hardness would result in God's **mighty acts of judgment** (the 10 plagues) **on Egypt** (7:8-12:36), which in turn would lead to Israel's release (7:4) and to the Egyptians' acknowledging that He is Yahweh (**the LORD,** v. 5).

**7:6-7.** **Moses and Aaron** obeyed **the LORD.** The ages of the two major figures are given. **Moses was 80** and **Aaron 83.** Often in the Old Testament the age of a prominent figure is given when a major event was about to occur (cf., e.g., Gen. 16:16; 17:24-25). After 40 years in the wilderness wanderings Moses died at age

120 (Deut. 34:7) and Aaron at 123 (Num. 33:38-39).

(2) Moses' command to Pharaoh. **7:8-13.** Knowing that **Pharaoh** would question Moses and Aaron's authority (cf. 5:1-2) and would challenge them to **perform a miracle,** God instructed them about using their credentials. Moses was to tell **Aaron** to **throw** his **staff . . . down before Pharaoh and it** would **become a snake** (cf. 4:2-4). But when they did this Pharaoh's **magicians** duplicated the feat **by their secret arts,** probably miracles empowered by Satan, not merely some sleight-of-hand trickery. Satan is able to perform "all kinds of counterfeit miracles, signs, and wonders" (2 Thes. 2:9) that deceive (2 Thes. 2:10; Rev. 13:11-15; cf. Matt. 24:24). Perhaps two of these men were Jannes and Jambres, who "opposed Moses" (2 Tim. 3:8).

The conjurers were also able to duplicate the turning of water to blood (Ex. 7:22) and the appearance of the frogs (8:7), the first two plagues. However, **Aaron's staff**-snake consumed those of the magicians, thus demonstrating God's superior power.

**Moses and Aaron,** emissaries of God, confronted the emissaries of Satan, the gods of Egypt, and their magicians. Each of the judgments to follow smashed some aspect of Egypt's religious life (i.e., Satan's domain), culminating in the death of their heir-god, Amenhotep II's firstborn son. The God of Israel triumphed over the powers of darkness. As God had predicted (4:21; 7:3; cf. v. 22; 8:15, 19) **Pharaoh's heart** was not enabled to heed the message and demonstrate repentance by releasing the people (7:13). God demonstrates His absolute sovereignty over mankind by using them as He pleases; some, like Moses, to honor Him and others, like Amenhotep II, to dishonor Him. Both kinds of people bring glory to God though it is beyond man's finite ability to understand how this can be.

### 2. THE 10 JUDGMENTS OF GOD ON EGYPT (7:14–12:36)

Ten judgments were poured out on the Egyptians. These judgments, commonly called plagues, may be grouped in three units of three plagues each, with a 10th culminating in judgment. The 1st, 4th, and 7th judgments, at the beginning

## Warnings, Usages of Staffs, and Pharaoh's Responses to the Plagues

| Plagues | Warnings | Uses of Staffs | Pharaoh's Responses |
|---|---|---|---|
| *First cycle* | | | |
| 1. Nile turned to blood | Warning—to Pharaoh at the Nile in the morning (7:15-18) | Aaron's staff (7:19) | Did not listen to the request that the Israelites be released (7:22-23) |
| 2. Frogs | Warning—to Pharaoh probably in his palace (8:2-4) | Aaron's staff (8:5-6) | Agreed to let the people go if the frogs were taken away (8:8) |
| 3. Gnats | No warning | Aaron's staff (8:16-17) | Refused to listen to his magicians' suggestion (8:19) |
| *Second cycle* | | | |
| 4. Flies | Warning—to Pharaoh at the Nile in the morning (8:20-23) | No staff used | Suggested the Israelites sacrifice in Egypt (8:25) |
| 5. Death of livestock | Warning—to Pharaoh probably in his palace (9:1-5) | No staff used | Refused Moses' request (9:7) |
| 6. Boils | No warning | No staff used | Refused Moses' request (9:12) |
| *Third cycle* | | | |
| 7. Hail | Warning—to Pharaoh in his palace in the morning (9:13-19) | Moses' staff (9:22-23) | Promised to let the Israelites go if the rain and hail were stopped (9:28) |
| 8. Locusts | Warning—to Pharaoh probably in his palace (10:3-6) | Moses' staff (10:12-13) | Offered to let only the men go (10:11) |
| 9. Darkness | No warning | (Moses' hand; perhaps the staff was used; 10:21-22) | Agreed that the people could go but not their animals (10:24) |
| *Culminating judgment* | | | |
| 10. Death of the firstborn | Warning—to Pharaoh probably in his palace (11:4-8) | | Urged the people to go! (12:31-32) |

of each cycle of three, are introduced by the words, "in the morning" (7:15; 8:20; 9:13). The 1st three (blood, frogs, and gnats) were loathsome; the 2nd three were bothersome (flies) or painful (death of livestock and boils on people and animals); and the 3rd three were "natural" plagues (hail, locusts, darkness). The 3rd plague ends with the defeat of the magicians (8:19), the 6th with their inability to stand before Moses (9:11), and the 9th with the separation of Moses and Pharaoh (10:28).

In plagues 1-3 Aaron used his staff (7:19; 8:5-6, 16-17) and in plagues 7-9 Moses used his staff (9:22-23; 10:12-13, 21-22; though 10:21-22 mentions only Moses'

hand, the staff may have been included). No staff was used by either man in plagues 4-6.

The 10 plagues may have occurred over a period of about nine months. The 1st occurred when the Nile rises (July-August). The 7th (9:31) was in January, when barley ripens and flax blossoms. The prevailing east winds in March or April in the 8th plague (10:13) would have brought in locusts. And the 10th plague (chaps. 11–12) occurred in April, the Passover month. By the plagues God was judging the gods of Egypt (of which there were many) and showing Himself superior to them (12:12; 18:11; Num. 33:4). See the chart "The Plagues and the

## The Plagues and the Gods and Goddesses of Egypt

| Plagues | References | Possible Egyptian Gods and Goddesses of Egypt Attacked by the Plagues* |
|---|---|---|
| 1. Nile turned to blood | Exodus 7:14-25 | Hapi (also called Apis), the bull god, god of the Nile; Isis, goddess of the Nile; Khnum, ram god, guardian of the Nile; and others |
| 2. Frogs | 8:1-15 | Heqet, goddess of birth, with a frog head |
| 3. Gnats | 8:16-19 | Set, god of the desert |
| 4. Flies | 8:20-32 | Re, a sun god; or the god Uatchit, possibly represented by the fly |
| 5. Death of livestock | 9:1-7 | Hathor, goddess with a cow head; Apis, the bull god, symbol of fertility |
| 6. Boils | 9:8-12 | Sekhmet, goddess with power over disease; Sunu, the pestilence god; Isis, goddess of healing |
| 7. Hail | 9:13-35 | Nut, the sky goddess; Osiris, god of crops and fertility; Set, god of storms |
| 8. Locusts | 10:1-20 | Nut, the sky goddess; Osiris, god of crops and fertility |
| 9. Darkness | 10:21-29 | Re, the sun god; Horus, a sun god; Nut, a sky goddess; Hathor, a sky goddess |
| 10. Death of the firstborn | 11:1–12:30 | Min, god of reproduction; Heqet, goddess who attended women at childbirth; Isis, goddess who protected children; Pharaoh's firstborn son, a god |

*Some gods and goddesses had more than one function or area of responsibility. Also in ancient Egyptian religion many of the gods and goddesses who were worshiped in one city or location and/or at one period of time were believed to have assimilated the gods and goddesses of other areas and time periods. Their religion was thus often complex and at times even contradictory.

Sources: *Encyclopaedia Brittanica*, under the word "Egypt"; Lionel Casson, *Ancient Egypt* (New York: Time-Life Books, 1965); Pierre Montet, *Egypt and the Bible* (Philadelphia: Fortress Press, 1968).

Gods and Goddesses of Egypt."

Also the plagues may have been designed to oppose and show up the impotency of the Pharaoh. Pharaoh's people considered him the god Horus, son of Hathor. Hathor's father was the god Amon-Re. The plagues also showed the Pharaoh and the Egyptians that He is the Lord (Yahweh; Ex. 7:5, 17; 8:10, 22; 9:14, 16) and showed Israel the same truth (10:2).

Pharaoh's response to each of the plagues is interesting. After the 1st one he would not even listen to the request for the Israelites' release (7:22-23). In the 2nd plague he agreed to let the people go if the frogs were taken away (8:8). In the 3rd plague he refused to listen to his magicians' suggestion (8:19). In response to the 4th plague he first suggested that the Israelites sacrifice in the land (8:25). Later he agreed to let them go but not far (8:28) and then backed down on his promise (8:32). Again after the 5th and 6th plagues he refused the request (9:7, 12), but after the 7th he promised to let them go (9:28) if the rain and hail would be stopped, but again he backed down (9:35). In the 8th plague he offered to let only the men go (10:11) and even admitted his sin (10:16), and in the 9th he said the men, women, and children could go but not their animals (10:24). After the 10th plague he actually urged them to go! (12:31-32) Psalms 78:46-51; 105:28-36 refer to several of the plagues as evidences of God's power and care.

*a. Plague 1: Nile turned to blood (7:14-25)*

This passage, on the first of the plagues, can be divided into three parts: God's instructions to Moses and Aaron (vv. 14-19), the miracle through Moses and Aaron (vv. 20-21), and the resultant action of Pharaoh and his people (vv. 22-25).

**7:14-19.** God instructed **Moses** to meet **Pharaoh . . . as he** went **out to visit the Nile.** The Nile, considered the source of Egypt's livelihood, was regarded as a god. When the Nile flooded its banks in July and August it inundated the soil, thus making it possible for the people to grow bountiful crops. At that time the Pharaohs officiated at ceremonies commemorating the blessings brought by the river. Perhaps Moses interrupted Pharaoh during one of these special occasions of celebration (cf. 8:20).

**Moses** was to inform Pharaoh of the reasons for the judgment. (On **the God of the Hebrews,** 7:16; cf. 3:18; 5:3; 9:1, 13; 10:3.) Pharaoh had failed to recognize the true God (7:16), which explained the nature and ramifications of the coming judgment (vv. 17-18). The judgment would fall on **the river,** its tributaries, and even the smallest common receptacles (v. 19).

**7:20-21.** As **Aaron** through Moses' direction held **his staff** over **the Nile** the awful judgment occurred—**the water** turned to **blood.** Some commentators have suggested that the water did not literally become blood, but simply became reddish in color. Cassuto suggests that this red color came through "minute fungi and other red vegetable matter, or tiny insects of reddish hue" (*A Commentary on the Book of Exodus,* p. 98). This, however, is not warranted, nor does it explain the suddenness of this miracle or the extensiveness of death to the fish. Though the chemical makeup of the red substance is unknown, to the Egyptians it looked and tasted like blood. The dead fish in the river caused it to stink (v. 18; cf. smell **bad,** v. 21). Since the Nile was

so vital to Egypt's agriculture and economy, this miracle was alarming. Several Egyptian gods were associated with the Nile including Hapi, Isis, Khnum (see the chart "The Plagues and the Gods and Goddesses of Egypt"). Also the yearly miraculous rebirth of Osiris, a god of the earth and vegetation, symbolized the flooding of the Nile. Other gods supposedly protected fish in the Nile. Since the Egyptians believed the Nile was Osiris' bloodstream it is remarkable that **the Nile** was turned to **blood** (Davis, *Moses and the Gods of Egypt,* p. 94).

**7:22-25.** Pharaoh's **magicians,** however, were able to duplicate this miracle, so he hardened his **heart** toward God.

If all the water became blood, where did the magicians obtain water to duplicate the feat? The answer seems to be in verse 24: the waters in the Nile were stricken but not the natural springs or waters filtered through the soil. The people had to abandon the Nile in order to have water to **drink.** This fouling of the Nile lasted **seven days** (v. 25). Some say this means seven days intervened between the first plague (of one day) and the second plague. However, since intervals are not stated between any of the other plagues, it seems better to assume that the first judgment lasted seven days.

*b. Plague 2: Frogs (8:1-15)*

**8:1-4.** God told **Moses** to return **to Pharaoh** with an ultimatum to release the Israelites or face further judgment, this time **frogs.** (**If you refuse** also is stated in 9:2; 10:4.) **Frogs** were normally abundant in **the Nile** after the waters receded in December, but the people would not have expected them in August. The frogs would normally stay near the Nile but now they left the Nile, invading **the houses** (8:3), courtyards, and fields (v. 13) probably because of the dead fish in the Nile. The Egyptians regarded frogs as having divine power. In the Egyptian pantheon the goddess Heqet had the form of a woman with a frog's head. From her nostrils, it was believed, came the breath of life that animated the bodies of those created by her husband, the great god Khnum, from the dust of the earth. Therefore **frogs** were not to be killed.

God said He would cause another of their deities to be a curse to them, not a help. These sacred animals would multiply and infiltrate people's bedrooms. This is ironic since the frog-goddess Heqet was believed to help women in childbirth. Here the frogs entered people's kitchens and even crawled on the people themselves (vv. 3-4).

**8:5-7.** Following God's instructions, **Moses** commanded **Aaron** to enact the judgment (v. 5), which he did (v. 6). In the first three plagues Aaron used his staff (7:19-20; 8:5-6, 16-17), and in plagues seven and eight Moses used his own staff (9:23; 10:13). Again the Egyptian **magicians** were able to duplicate the feat (cf. 7:22), but ironically they increased their own distress! (8:7)

**8:8-11.** Here the narrative shifts to **Pharaoh** who apparently did not want his magicians to repeat the plague but to remove it. He turned to **Moses and Aaron** for help, which showed that his knowledge of the God of the Hebrews had improved (cf. 5:2). He sought divine aid, being so distressed that he was willing to grant Moses his wish. **Moses** allowed the king to set the timetable for relief from the plague, but Moses wanted him to know the reason: **so that** he would **know there is no one like the LORD . . . God** (8:10). **Pharaoh** asked that **Moses** pray the next day for relief from **the frogs.**

**8:12-15.** Moses prayed and God caused the plague to subside the next day. The carnage of frog carcasses caused a stench throughout the land (**the land reeked of them**). **But . . . Pharaoh** reneged on his promise.

*c. Plague 3: Gnats (8:16-19)*

**8:16-19.** Unlike the previous two plagues, this one came without warning. This was also true of the sixth and ninth plagues. This may have been because of Pharaoh's false promise of release (vv. 8, 15). The judgment was sudden. **Aaron struck the dust** with his **staff,** and flying, biting insects covered man and beast. The Hebrew word for **gnats** is *kinnîm,* which occurs only here in the Old Testament. It may mean gnats or perhaps mosquitoes. The statement **the dust will become gnats** may be a way of saying the gnats were unusually numerous.

This plague may have been an attack against Set, god of the desert. Also it may have been directed against the Egyptian

priesthood. The priests prided themselves in their purity with their frequent washings and shavings, and their wearing of linen robes. Here the Lord polluted the religionists with pesky insects.

**The magicians,** unable to duplicate this miracle, admitted that it was God's doing (**This is the finger of God**; cf. 31:18; Deut. 9:10; Ps. 8:3; Luke 11:20). **As the LORD had** indicated (cf. Ex. 7:3) **Pharaoh** remained obstinate and unrepentant (cf. "just as the LORD had said," in 7:13, 22; 8:15).

*d. Plague 4: Flies (8:20-32)*

**8:20-24.** This fourth plague begins the second cycle of three judgments; this is evident by the phrase **in the morning** (v. 20; cf. 7:15; 9:13). Like the first three plagues, these three were restricted to the Egyptians (**I will deal differently with the land of Goshen, where My people live,** 8:22). This showed that God made **a distinction between** the Israelites and the Egyptians (cf. 9:4; 11:7), marking His people for deliverance and the others for judgment. This would further demonstrate God's sovereignty and power.

The Lord instructed Moses to **confront Pharaoh** once again by the Nile (cf. 7:15) about releasing the Hebrews. If Pharaoh refused, **swarms of flies** (8:21) would be sent on **the Egyptians** and in their **houses.** The flies may have been attracted to the decaying frogs. **Dense swarms of flies** (v. 24) is literally, "a heavy or oppressive swarm." These flies may have been the dog flies known for their painful bites. They may have represented Re, a prominent Egyptian deity. Or the flies may have been *Ichneuman* flies, who depicted the god Uatchit.

**8:25-32.** Smarting under the cumulative weight of the judgment of four plagues, **Pharaoh** was willing to suggest a compromise. The Israelites, he said, could **sacrifice to** their **God,** but in Egypt, not in the desert. This compromise was unacceptable to **Moses.** He explained that their animal **sacrifices** would **be detestable** in Egypt. This may have been because the Egyptians considered sacred the bull which represented the god Apis or Re and the cow which represented their goddess Hathor. **To the Egyptians** this would be blasphemy and would result in rioting.

Pharaoh's second compromise was

to allow them to go only a short distance into **the desert** (v. 28). Accepting this compromise **Moses** sternly warned **Pharaoh** not to be practicing deceit as he did earlier (vv. 8, 15). This was a remarkable—even daring—statement since Pharaoh was supposed to be the model of justice and truth.

**Moses left Pharaoh,** thinking that the monarch might keep his word. So as **Pharaoh** had asked, Moses **prayed** for relief from the plague. But again **Pharaoh** changed his mind and refused to keep his word.

### e. Plague 5: Death of livestock (9:1-7)

**9:1-4.** Again **Moses** demanded the release of the Israelites. (On **the God of the Hebrews**; cf. 3:18; 5:3; 7:16; 9:13; 10:3.) If Pharaoh refused, Moses said, **the hand of the Lord** (cf. 3:19; 6:1) would **bring a . . . plague on** their domesticated animals: **horses . . . donkeys . . . camels . . . cattle . . . sheep . . . goats.** With dead frogs throughout the land and with swarms of flies spreading germs, this pestilence, so destructive to animal life, may have been the infectious disease known as anthrax. This would have been in January when cattle were led out to pasture after the Nile inundation subsided. This plague would have been economically distressing for the Egyptians. Also many animals were sacred (cf. 8:26), particularly, as stated earlier, the bull which represented the god Apis or Re, and the cow which represented Hathor, the goddess of love, beauty, and joy. Hathor was depicted in the form of a woman with the head (or sometimes only the horns) of a cow. Also Khnum was a ram-god. The animals of **the Israelites,** the object of God's mercies, would not be affected by the plague (9:4; cf. 8:22-23; 11:7).

**9:5-7.** The plague·occurred as **the Lord** predicted: **all the livestock of the Egyptians died. Pharaoh** investigated Goshen to see if any of the Israelites' **animals . . . had died.** Even though he saw that God had indeed made a distinction (v. 4), he still refused to repent.

But if all the cattle died in this plague, how can one explain the presence of animals later in verse 10 and of livestock in verses 20-21? Two explanations are possible: (1) The word "all" (v. 6) may be employed hyperbolically, as a

figure of speech for a large quantity without meaning the totality of the livestock. (2) Perhaps a better explanation is that the plague killed all the animals **in the field** (v. 3) but not those in shelters.

### f. Plague 6: Boils (9:8-12)

**9:8-12.** Like the third and ninth plagues, this one was not announced to **Pharaoh.** This plague, the first to endanger human life, resulted in open sores (**festering boils,** vv. 9-10) on the bodies of **men and animals.** Moses' tossing **soot from a furnace** may have been a symbolic act, like his and Aaron's use of their staffs in several plagues. **The Egyptians,** fearfully aware of epidemics, worshiped Sekhmet, a lion-headed goddess with alleged power over disease; Sunu, the pestilence god; and Isis, goddess of healing. Yet these deities could not deliver the people and animals from their torments. **The magicians** of Egypt were again helpless (cf. 8:18) because they were similarly afflicted (9:11) and found their own deities powerless. Yet **Pharaoh** persisted in willful obstinance (v. 12).

### g. Plague 7: Hail (9:13-35)

This judgment commences the third cycle of the plagues. These three plagues (seven, eight, and nine) were more severe than the previous ones and are described in more detail. This seventh plague resulted in great economic duress. Clearly the abilities of several Egyptian gods were again being challenged. Nut, the sky goddess, was not able to forestall the storm; and Osiris, the god of crop fertility, could not maintain the crops in this hailstorm; nor could Set, the storm god, hold back this storm.

The lengthy section describing this plague includes four things: the instructions to Moses (vv. 13-19), the destruction of the plague (vv. 20-26), Moses' discourse with Pharaoh (vv. 27-32), and the impenitence of Pharaoh (vv. 33-35).

**9:13-19.** Again **Moses** was to see Pharaoh **early in the morning** (cf. 7:15; 8:20). The reason for the impending judgment was again Pharaoh's unwillingness to release God's **people. Pharaoh** had failed to recognize the worth of **the God of the Hebrews** (cf. 3:18; 5:3; 7:16; 9:1; 10:3). He would not admit that **there is no one like** Him **in all the earth.** Though God had been gracious in not displaying the full fury of His wrath (9:15), this **plague** would teach them something of His **power**. In fact God said this was why He had **raised . . . up** Pharaoh (cf. Rom. 9:17, 22). God was about to demonstrate His power by a **hailstorm** of huge proportions, without historic precedent (Ex. 9:18; cf. v. 24). Yet in His grace God told the king to have **livestock** (cf. comments on vv. 5-7) and people brought under **shelter**. In Egypt cattle were usually outdoors from January to April, before the summer heat set in.

**9:20-26, 31-32.** Hearing of Moses' forewarning, some of the Egyptians believed God's **word** through Moses and responded appropriately.

**The LORD** brought destruction on the Egyptians as He had predicted, though the hail (and rain, vv. 33-34) did not fall on **the Israelites** in **the land of Goshen** (v. 26). **Men and animals** were killed by the **hail,** and crops were demolished. However, the phrase **everything growing in the fields** (vv. 22, 25) is qualified by the statements in verses 31-32. "Everything" refers to those crops about to be harvested, namely, **flax** (used in making linen cloth), and **barley. Wheat and spelt** (an inferior type of wheat) were unaffected. Flax and barley blossomed in January and were harvested in March-April. Wheat and spelt ripened about a month later (in April) and were harvested in June-July. (See the chart "Calendar in Israel," near 12:1.) So this plague may have occurred in February.

**9:27-30, 33-35.** Such an awe-inspiring display of omnipotence brought an unqualified repentance from **Pharaoh** (**I have sinned,** v. 27; cf. 10:16). Acknowledging that God is **right** (9:27), he consented to release the Israelites (**I will let you go,** v. 28). **Moses** promised to ask God to stop the plague, though he recognized that Pharaoh's repentance was superficial and merely self-seeking (v. 30).

Since the plague was raining murderous hail through Egypt, except in Goshen, how could Moses move about so freely? Again the plague was probably in the fields (cf. v. 3) and selective in what it destroyed (viz., people, animals, trees, flax, and barley). **Moses** was correct (cf. v. 30); though the true God was gracious in bringing this holocaust to an end, **Pharaoh** remained calloused against Him.

*h. Plague 8: Locusts (10:1-20)*

This record of the eighth plague can be divided into four sections: the instructions to Moses (vv. 1-6), the discourse with Pharaoh (vv. 7-11), the destruction by the locusts (vv. 12-15), and the humbling and hardening of Pharaoh (vv. 16-20).

**10:1-6.** This plague reveals another purpose for the judgments. Besides humbling Pharaoh and bringing about Israel's deliverance, the plagues showed *Israel* God's power, which they were to **tell** to their **children and grandchildren.** By these **signs** Israel would **know that** God is **the LORD** (Yahweh).

If Pharaoh refused **to humble** himself **before** God, then God would bring a terrible locust infestation. **Locusts,** flying by the millions, can completely devastate miles of crops (cf. Joel 1:2-7; Amos 7:1-3), eating leaves and even tree bark. Much of a city's or a nation's food supply from crops can be wiped out completely in minutes or hours.

What the previous plague of hail did not destroy—wheat and spelt (9:32), fruit (10:15), and other field vegetation (10:12, 15)—would now be devoured. Like the frogs (8:3-4) and flies (8:21, 24), the locusts would enter people's **houses.** Like the hail (9:18) the locust invasion was unprecedented in Egypt (10:6; cf. v. 14).

**10:7-11.** Such extensive economic disaster caused **Pharaoh's officials** to realize that retaining their slaves was not worth the price: **Egypt,** they said, **is ruined.** So **Pharaoh** succumbed to Moses' general petition and said **Go** (v. 8). Though **Moses** never said he would return the people, Pharaoh sensed they would be gone permanently if they took all their family members, **flocks, and herds** (v. 9). This, he said, was **evil.** So he introduced another compromise (cf. 8:25, 28): **Have only the men go** (10:11). **Moses and Aaron,** unwilling to settle for this compromise, were expelled (*gāraš;* cf. comments on 2:22; 6:1) from the court.

**10:12-15.** As a result of Pharaoh's impiety and stubbornness, God told **Moses** to **stretch out** his hand (cf. 9:22; 10:21) **so that locusts** would come. He extended **his staff** and **an east wind** blew **all . . . day.** Some say "east wind" means "fierce wind" because normally winds blow across **Egypt** from the south. However, this interpretation is strained because later (v. 19) Moses referred to a west wind which carried the **locusts** into the Red Sea (lit., "Sea of [Papyrus] Reeds"; cf. NIV marg. and comments on 14:2). The devastation was beyond imagination; their numbers were so massive that **the ground . . . was black** (10:15). **All . . . Egypt** was affected. **Egypt** was deprived of her natural beauty with tragic economic, social, and theological consequences. Nut, the Egyptian sky goddess, could not control these locusts and Osiris, god of crop fertility, could not prevent the destruction of the crops.

**10:16-20. Pharaoh** again repented of his sin (cf. 9:27) and pleaded for relief, but his actions revealed an impenitent heart. In response to Moses' petition God relented of this judgment and Pharaoh again impiously repudiated his promise.

*i. Plague 9: Darkness (10:21-29)*

**10:21-23.** Like the third and sixth plagues this ninth judgment came without warning. When Moses extended **his hand** (cf. 9:22; 10:12-13), the land was draped with a thick cloak of **darkness . . . for three days,** except in the land of Goshen. The exact nature of the **darkness** is uncertain, but since Goshen was spared it could not have been an eclipse of the sun. Some interpret **darkness that can be felt** (10:21) to mean a massive sandstorm with its darkness and heat that would cause people to seek shelter. With the land bare from the loss of crops by hail and locusts, a sandstorm, possibly flowing from the south in March, would have been unusually fierce.

This plague was aimed at one of the chief Egyptian deities, the sun god Re, of whom Pharaoh was a representation. Re was responsible for providing sunlight, warmth, and productivity. Other gods, including Horus, were associated with the sun. Nut, the goddess of the sky, would have been humiliated by this plague (as well as by the plagues of hail and locusts).

**10:24-29.** In his misery **Pharaoh summoned Moses and said** he was willing to let him leave with the people, but not with their **flocks and herds.** This was Pharaoh's fourth attempted compromise (cf. 8:25, 28; 10:11). These animals, if retained, would help replenish Egypt's loss of animal life in the fifth and seventh plagues. **But Moses** was uncompromis-

ing to the minutest degree (**not a hoof is to be left behind**). He insisted that the people had been called to **worship** and therefore they would not leave behind any animals of sacrifice.

In belligerence **Pharaoh** ordered **Moses . . . out of** his presence. **Moses** calmly **replied** that he would **never** return **before** him **again.** However, this seems to be contradicted by the confrontation Moses and Aaron had with Pharaoh later (12:31). This can be explained by understanding Moses to have said (in 10:29) that, because of Pharaoh's raging, Moses would not go to him in mercy with a word from God. In other words, if Moses saw Pharaoh again, it would be to announce unavoidable judgment or it would be at Pharaoh's request to grant Moses and the Israelites permission to leave the land.

*j. Plague 10: Death of the firstborn (11:1–12:36)*

From the three cycles of three plagues, the land lay in ruins. God had demonstrated His mighty power by showing up the impotence of the gods of Egypt. And by devastating that powerful nation economically, He struck fear into the hearts of her populace. He had caused the Egyptians to be eager for the removal of the Israelites though Pharaoh was yet to be humbled. The 10th plague would bring great sorrow to *every* Egyptian family with children. This plague would result in the release of God's people.

(1) The announcement of the last plague (chap. 11). **11:1-3.** After **one more plague,** God said, **Pharaoh** would release his slaves without any reservations (cf. 8:25, 28; 10:11, 24). Up to then **Moses** did not know how many plagues would befall the nation of **Egypt.** In light of their soon-coming deliverance the Israelites were to request **silver and gold of the Egyptians,** who apparently were more kindly **disposed** to them than was Pharaoh (cf. 3:21-22; 12:35-36). Even **Moses himself was highly** esteemed **by Pharaoh's officials** (probably because of the miracles they had seen) **and by the people.** This helps explain why the Egyptians gave some of their expensive jewelry to the Israelites.

**11:4-8.** Like plagues three, six, and nine this 10th one came with no warning to Pharaoh and with no opportunity for him to repent beforehand. Possibly these verses continue the confrontation between Pharaoh and Moses in 10:24-29. The judgment was specific: in **every** Egyptian family the **firstborn son** would **die** in the middle of the night—**from the** poorest of the poor (**the firstborn son of the slave girl**) to the royal household (**the firstborn son of Pharaoh**). A firstborn son received special honor and a Pharaoh's son, heir to the throne, was even considered a god. The **wailing** over the loss of sons would be unprecedented.

Why would God bring such a calamity on the Egyptians? It must be remembered that God is sovereign over all human affairs. People's prosperity or judgment is not because of God's favoritism or lack of it but because He desires to accomplish His will on earth. Since He alone is holy, He has the right to use and dispose of mankind as He wills. Anything God does is right because He is God! (Ps. 115:3) Also one must remember that the Egyptians were polytheists, worshiping many idols and false gods. Refusing to worship the true God, they became objects of His judgment (cf. Rom. 1:18-23).

The goddess Isis, the wife and sister of Osiris, supposedly protected children. But this plague showed her to be totally incompetent to do what the Egyptians trusted her for!

In this great plague the Israelites would lose no one. In fact at midnight **not a dog** would **bark** (lit., "not a dog will sharpen its tongue"). That is, no dog would growl or bite because no harm would come to God's people. By this special treatment of the Hebrews, **Egypt** would know that God favored **Israel** (cf. Ex. 8:23; 9:4). Therefore Pharaoh's **officials,** who after eight plagues urged their king to release the Israelites (cf. 10:7), would directly urge Moses to take his people away.

In several of the other confrontations **Moses** gave Pharaoh opportunity to release the people as a means of warding off the announced plague. Not so this time. The plague would come; *then* Pharaoh would let the people go. Moses' angry pronouncement was final. Never again would he confront **Pharaoh** with the option to repent (cf. comments on 10:28-29). In the previous plagues Moses

and Aaron had a part, but not in the final judgment; this was to be the work of God alone.

**11:9-10.** These verses summarize Pharaoh's recalcitrant spirit (God had said **Pharaoh will refuse to listen,** cf. 7:22). This refusal led to God's **wonders** being displayed in an idolatrous land and to the Lord's hardening of the ruler's **heart** (cf. comments on 4:21).

(2) The celebration of the first Passover (12:1-28). Rather than focusing on the confrontations of Moses with Pharaoh, the narrative now shifts to Moses and the people of Israel. This passage has two parts: the Lord's instructions to Moses concerning the feast (vv. 1-20) and the observance of the festival (vv. 21-28).

**12:1-2.** First God told **Moses and Aaron** about the time of the Passover. This feast was to mark a new age in the history of Israel (**the first month, the first month of your year**). Though the events in this chapter occurred in the seventh month according to the civil year (which began in September-October) this is the first month in Israel's religious calendar. This month is called Abib (lit., "fresh young ears" of, e.g., barley). This was when barley was to be harvested (March-April). With a new calendar the Israelites were to receive a new identity as the favored people of the true God.

After Israel was taken into captivity the names of 4 of the 12 months were given Babylonian names, and April was called Nisan (cf. Neh. 2:1; Es. 3:7), which means "early" or "start." (See the chart "Calendar in Israel.")

**12:3-6.** The phrase **the whole community of Israel** (cf. v. 6) is used here for the first time in the Old Testament to refer to the nation. The word suggests a new beginning. The celebration of Passover was centered in homes. **On the 10th day of** the **month** (March-April) **each** Israelite family was to select **a lamb** or a goat (*śeh,* the word trans. **lamb,** can mean either a young sheep or goat; cf. v. 5). If a family was **small** and not able to eat an entire animal, arrangements could be made to **share** the meal with another family. The animal was to be a one-**year-old** male **without** blemish. Four days later (on **the 14th**) each animal was to be killed **at twilight.** This meant either between sunset and dark or between 3 and 5 P.M. The latter time period is probably

# Calendar in Israel

| Gregorian Calendar | Jewish Calendar | Farming Year | Special Days |
|---|---|---|---|
| March-April | Month 1: *Nisan* (Early name: Abib) | Latter rains Barley harvest Flax harvest | 1. Nisan 14: *Passover* (Ex. 12:1-11; Lev. 23:5) 2. Nisan 15-21: *Unleavened Bread* (Lev. 23:6-8) 3. Nisan 21: *Firstfruits* (Lev. 23:9-14) |
| April-May | Month 2: *Iyyar* (Early name: Ziv) | Dry season begins | |
| May-June | Month 3: *Sivan* | Early figs ripen Vine tending | 4. Sivan 6 (50 days after Firstfruits): *Pentecost* (Lev. 23:15-22) |
| June-July | Month 4: *Tammuz* | Wheat harvest First-ripe grapes | |
| July-August | Month 5: *Ab* | Grape harvest | |
| August-September | Month 6: *Elul* | Dates and summer figs | |
| September-October | Month 7: *Tishri* (Early name: Ethanim) | Early rains | 5. Tishri 1: *Trumpets* (Lev. 23:23-25) 6. Tishri 10: *Day of Atonement* (Lev. 16; 23:26-32) 7. Tishri 15-21: *Tabernacles* (Lev. 23:33-36) |
| October-November | Month 8: *Marchesvan* (Early name: Bul) | Plowing Olive harvest | |
| November-December | Month 9: *Kislev* | Grain planting | 8. Kislev 25: *Dedication* (Hanukkah) (John 10:22) |
| December-January | Month 10: *Tebeth* | Latter rains | |
| January-February | Month 11: *Shebat* | Almond trees blossom | |
| February-March | Month 12: *Adar* | Citrus fruit harvest | 9. Adar 13-14: *Purim* (Es. 9:26-28) |

correct because it would allow more time for slaughtering and preparing the animal, which would be needed later when many sacrifices would be offered at the sanctuary.

**12:7-11.** In these verses instructions are given on how to observe the Passover. Though the feast was observed in each Israelite home, their united and simultaneous worship would help weld them together as a single community (cf. v. 3). **The blood** of the animals was to be placed on **the doorframes of the houses,** the animal **meat roasted,** and the people were to **eat** it **with bitter herbs and bread . . . without yeast.** The slaying of the animals (instead of the Israelites' firstborn sons, v. 13) and the sprinkling of blood prefigured the substitutionary death of Christ. He is "our Passover Lamb" (1 Cor. 5:7), "a Lamb without blemish or defect" (1 Peter 1:19; cf. John 1:29). His own sacrifice is the means whereby individual believers escape the horrors of spiritual death.

Bitter herbs (probably endive, chicory, dandelions) symbolized sorrow or grief (cf. Lam. 3:15) for past sin, or the Israelites' bitter experience of oppression in Egypt. The bread without yeast symbolized their leaving in haste (Ex. 12:11, 39; Deut. 16:3). The **meat** was to be roasted, not eaten **raw** as some pagans did. The people were to eat the entire meal quickly while dressed ready for travel (on the **cloak tucked into** the **belt,** see comments on "Brace yourself like a man," Job 38:3; 40:7).

Thus under the protection of shed blood, the congregation was to be reminded of cleansing from sin (cf. Heb. 9:22) and that they were sojourners in a strange land. **It is the LORD's Passover** means the Passover lamb was for the Lord (cf. "a festival to the LORD," Ex. 12:14).

**12:12-14.** God said that **on** the very **night** (at midnight, 11:4; 12:29), after the Israelites had eaten the Passover lambs with herbs and bread, He would kill the **firstborn** son and animal in every Egyptian family (cf. 11:5; 12:29-30). The purpose of this final plague was like the others: to **bring judgment on all the gods of Egypt** (cf. Num. 33:4), thus showing that God is **the LORD.** Pharaoh's eldest son and successor supposedly had divine properties. Min, the Egyptian god of re-

production, and Isis, the goddess of love who attended women at childbirth, were judged as impotent by this climactic plague and catastrophe.

The sprinkled **blood** on the Israelites' **houses** provided protection from death when God destroyed the Egyptian firstborn. From the verb, **pass over** (*pāsaḥ*) comes the noun that designates the feast, the Passover (*pesaḥ*). As the blood of an animal was the means of deliverance and of escaping death, so Christ's blood is the means of redemption for believers (Rom. 5:9; Eph. 1:7).

The Passover was to be observed annually (**for the generations to come**) as a **lasting ordinance** (cf. Ex. 12:17, 24; 13:10). Other annual events and feasts and Levitical regulations were also called "lasting ordinances" (e.g., 27:21; 28:43; 29:9; 30:21; Lev. 16:29, 31, 34; 23:14, 21, 41). The Passover was **a festival** to **the LORD** (cf. Ex. 5:1; 10:9).

**12:15-20.** God then gave instructions for **the Feast of Unleavened Bread** as a national celebration of Israel's redemption from Egypt. The Passover and the Unleavened Bread feasts were so closely connected that the two were often considered as one feast (cf. Luke 2:41; 22:1; Acts 21:3-4, and see comments on Luke 22:7-38; John 19:14). The Feast of Unleavened Bread was to be **for seven days** (Ex. 13:6-7), from the 15th to the 21st of the **month** (Lev. 23:6; Num. 28:17). Of course **no** bread with **yeast** (leaven) was to be eaten on the Passover either (Ex. 12:8). Homes were to be cleansed of **yeast** (vv. 15-16), a symbol of sin (1 Cor. 5:8). The absence of yeast suggested that those who were under the safety of shed blood were free from the corruption of sin before a holy God. If anyone ate **anything with yeast** in those feast days he would be **cut off from . . . Israel** (Ex. 12:19), that is, excluded from the camp, separated from covenant rights and privileges, possibly resulting in death. Also on the **first** and **seventh** days of the feast the people were to gather together for special services. And **no work** other than **food** preparation was to be done all week. Like the Passover, the Feast of Unleavened Bread was to be **a lasting ordinance** (v. 17; cf. v. 14) to benefit forthcoming **generations.** Together the Passover and Unleavened Bread feasts were an "ordinance" to be obeyed (vv. 14, 17, 24) and a "ceremony" to be observed (vv. 25-26). And the Passover was a "festival" (v. 14) involving a "sacrifice" (v. 27). Verses 19-20 repeat the instructions in verses 15-16, perhaps for emphasis.

**12:21-28.** Moses now gave **the elders** instructions (vv. 21-23) for **the Passover** similar to those that the Lord gave Moses (vv. 3-11). **The blood** to be placed on the doorframes (v. 7) was to be applied with **a bunch of hyssop,** a common bushy plant that grows on rocky surfaces. It was widely used in Israel's rites of purification (cf. Lev. 14:4, 6, 49, 51-52; Num. 19:6, 18). **The destroyer** (cf. Heb. 11:28) who killed the firstborn may have been the Angel of the Lord (the preincarnate Christ; cf. comments on Gen. 16:9) or an angel. Then God's people were told to be sure to **observe** the Passover in **the land that** God had **promised** to give them. Also they were to teach its meaning to their **children** (Ex. 12:26-27; cf. 13:14-15). **The people,** grateful for their soon-to-come deliverance from centuries of slavery, **worshiped** the LORD. Then they carried out His commands.

(3) The destruction by the plague (12:29-36). The lengthy instructions about the Feasts of the Passover and Unleavened Bread added to the suspense that led to the climax in which judgment fell on the Egyptian firstborn (vv. 29-30), and the Israelites were released (vv. 31-36).

**12:29-30.** The 10th plague is described as to its time (**midnight**), extent (every **firstborn;** cf. 4:22-23), and effect (**loud wailing;** cf. 11:6). Great sorrow gripped the nation as God destroyed the favored sons of families in every stratum of society, from royalty to political **prisoner** (cf. 11:5). This presents a vivid reminder of the fury of God against sinners and the awful price that sin exacts. Obviously "a mighty hand"—God's—had compelled Pharaoh to let His people go! (3:19)

**12:31-33.** In response to the tragedy, **Pharaoh** released the Israelites that same **night** without any restrictions. He even *demanded* that they **leave.** God had predicted, "He will let you go" (3:20; 6:1). Amazingly the Pharaoh, who was considered a god, was now humbled to the point of asking that **Moses and Aaron. . . . bless** him (cf. 8:28). He wanted to be under Yahweh's blessing, not the curse of His plagues. Even the Egyptian people

urged the Israelites to leave quickly for fear they too would **all die.**

**12:34-36.** The Exodus happened so quickly that **the people took** unleavened bread **dough;** they had no time to make bread (v. 39). The plagues, evidencing God's power, so **favorably disposed** the **Egyptians** toward **the Israelites** that they were willing to do anything to hasten their departure, even giving away valuable jewelry and **clothing** (cf. 3:21-22; 11:3). This fulfilled God's promise to Abraham about his descendants' captivity (Gen. 15:13-14). From the Egyptians they received some "wages" for their 400 years of servitude.

### D. The deliverance of Israel from Egypt (12:37–18:27)

This section delineates the Exodus of the Hebrews from their leaving Rameses to their arrival at Mount Sinai three months later. Through the sprinkling of blood the Israelites had been delivered from death (12:13); now they were about to be rescued from bondage with a view to leading lives of holiness and worship.

1. THE FLIGHT IN EGYPT TOWARD THE SEA (12:37–13:22)

**12:37-42. From Rameses,** where apparently the people were concentrated (cf. 1:11), they **journeyed** to **Succoth,** present-day Tell el-Maskhutah near Lake Timsah. The number of Israelite **men** was **about 600,000** (in 38:26 and Num. 1:46 the exact figure is 603,550). With **women and children,** the number of Israelites was about 2 million. With them were non-Israelites of an undesignated number, apparently a variegated group (a "rabble," Num. 11:4). In the wilderness they caused the Israelites to complain against Moses.

En route the people **baked . . . unleavened bread** (cf. Ex. 12:34). Moses concluded this section about the beginning of the Exodus with a historical notation, a reminder of God's faithfulness, and a call to remembrance. The length of Israel's time **in Egypt** is here said to be **430 years** (cf. Gal. 3:17), while other passages state that it was 400 years (Gen. 15:13, 16; Acts 7:6) and "about 450 years" (Acts 13:20; cf. comments there). Apparently the total time in Egypt was 430 years (from 1876 B.C. to 1446 B.C.; cf. comments on Acts 7:6; Gal. 3:17). The fact of God's care over His people on the **night** of the Exodus should be remembered. Since He **kept vigil** over **them** they should **keep vigil to honor** Him. They were told to be careful and vigilant because He is.

**12:43-51.** At Succoth, **Moses and Aaron** were given **regulations** about celebrating **the Passover** (vv. 43-51) and instructions for the dedication of the firstborn (13:1-16). The several regulations for the Passover were apparently necessitated by the non-Israelites who joined the Exodus and had identified with the religion of the Hebrews. If a man did not identify with the covenant promises by the rite of circumcision he could not **celebrate** the **Passover** (12:44, 48-49). The feast was to be centered **in the** home and observed by the entire **community** (cf. vv. 3, 6, 19).

**13:1-16.** After an introductory statement about the Israelites' **firstborn** (vv. 1-2), who were to be dedicated for the service of **the Lord** (since they were spared in the 10th plague), **Moses** addressed **the people** again about the Passover and the Unleavened Bread feasts (vv. 3-10), and then returned to the subject of the **firstborn** (vv. 11-16).

Again **Moses** reminded the people of the importance of the day of their deliverance (cf. 12:24-27) from **the land of slavery** (lit., "slave house") by God's **mighty hand** (cf. comments on 3:19) **into the land of** promise. (On **the Canaanites** and other groups mentioned in 13:5, see comments on 3:17; and on the **land flowing with milk and honey** see comments on 3:8). This victorious event was to be remembered annually in the **ceremony** of the **seven**-day **festival** of **Unleavened Bread.**

Like the Passover (12:26-27), the Feast of Unleavened Bread had great educational value in the home (13:8-9). The feast was **like a sign on** their **hand** or **forehead,** that is, it was a continual reminder of God's mighty deliverance from **Egypt.** Some orthodox Jews today interpret that passage (and Deut. 6:8; 11:18) literally and bind passages of the Law (viz., Ex. 13:2-10; Deut. 6:4-9; 11:13-21) on their arms and foreheads in small pouches, so-called phylacteries, though this was probably not God's intention.

Once in the land of promise (Ex. 13:11), the **firstborn** sons and male animals were to be dedicated **to the Lord** (cf. v. 2; Num. 18:15). Animals were included because "they too benefited from the redemption which God provided in the 10th plague" (Davis, *Moses and the Gods of Egypt,* p. 154). Since donkeys were considered ceremonially unclean animals (Lev. 11:2-4) they could not be sacrificed, but they could be redeemed (*pādâh,* "to buy back for a price") by lambs sacrificed in their place. Of course since human sacrifice was unacceptable the Hebrews' **sons** were also to be "redeemed." This too would have teaching value in the home (cf. Ex. 12:26-27; 13:8). The Egyptian **firstborn** were slain, in judgment, and the Israelite "firstborn" were either slain (the animals) in substitutionary **sacrifice** or redeemed (the **sons**). Like the Feast of Unleavened Bread (vv. 7-9) the consecration of the firstborn was a sign and **symbol,** a reminder of God's powerful deliverance (v. 16). Both were reminders of God's gracious deliverance from the land of bondage.

**13:17-22.** The shortest route to the land of Caanan was **through the** territory of the Philistines in the direction of Beersheba and the Negeb. It led along the Mediterranean Sea, the military road of the Egyptians. But the route chosen by **God** was southeastward toward the Sinai to avoid possible military confrontations with Egyptian guards who might encourage the people to **return to Egypt.** The exact location of the desert road is uncertain but it probably led to the Bitter Lakes (see the map "Possible Route of the Exodus," near Num. 33:1-5). **Armed for battle** probably means organized for march rather than equipped with armor, bows, and arrows for warfare.

Moses had heard of Joseph's request that his **bones** be taken from Egypt (cf. Gen. 50:25), so he honored that request. Later Joseph's bones were buried at Shechem (Josh. 24:32). Stephen indicated that the remains of other sons of Jacob were taken there also (Acts 7:15-16; see comments there).

After some time at **Succoth** the Israelites journeyed to **Etham** (see the map "Possible Route of the Exodus," near Num. 33:1-5). Supernaturally guided by a **pillar of cloud** in the daytime, which became **a pillar of fire** at **night,** the Israelites apparently traveled some distance every day. Besides guiding them, the cloud, symbolizing God's presence, assured them of His goodness and faithfulness. (There was one cloud, not two; cf. Ex. 14:24.) The people were brought to **the edge of the desert** (cf. Num. 33:6).

### 2. THE CROSSING OF THE RED (REED) SEA (CHAP. 14)

#### a. The encampment by the Red (Reed) Sea (14:1-4)

**14:1-4.** After the Israelites had traveled for some days in a southeasterly path and camped awhile at Etham, **the LORD** told **Moses** to **tell** the people **to turn back** to **Pi Hahiroth between Migdol and the sea** and **opposite Baal Zephon** (cf. Num. 33:7). These cities were east of Rameses. This change in direction would have led **Pharaoh** to **think the Israelites** were confused. As a result of God's hardening of his **heart** (cf. comments on Ex. 4:21) Pharaoh would attempt to enslave the people again and then God would demonstrate His awesome power through another great judgment.

**The sea** is called the Red Sea in 10:19; 13:18; 15:4, 22. "Red Sea" ( yām sûp) is literally, "Sea of [Papyrus] Reeds." Several reasons indicate that this is farther north than the northern tip of the Gulf of Suez (the northwestern "finger" of the Red Sea between Egypt and the Sinai Peninsula): (1) The Gulf of Suez has no reeds. (2) The northern tip of the Gulf of Suez is much farther south than Pi Hahiroth and Migdol. (3) The area where the Israelites camped was marshy but this is not true of the land west of the Gulf of Suez. (4) From "the sea" the Israelites went east or southeast into the Desert of Shur (15:22), also called the Desert of Etham (Num. 33:8), in the northwestern part of the Sinai Peninsula. Possibly, then, the sea that the Lord dried up for the Israelites was Lake Balah (see the map "Possible Route of the Exodus," near Num. 33:1-5).

#### b. The pursuit by the Egyptians (14:5-9)

**14:5-9.** Realizing the implications of the release of the Hebrews (**we . . . have lost their services**; cf. 1:14) **Pharaoh and his** officers were determined to prevent the escape. Though the Israelite men numbered over 600,000, Pharaoh was apparently encouraged by their seeming in-

decisiveness and by his own superior military prowess. Pharaoh was probably informed immediately of the Israelites' departure from Rameses on the 15th day of the month. But no doubt he did not react immediately because the Egyptians were involved in burying and bemoaning their dead (cf. Num. 33:3-4) and because Moses had repeatedly referred to "a three-day journey" (Ex. 3:18; 5:3; 8:27). Later, realizing the Israelites' departure was not temporary, he got together **600 . . . chariots,** charioteers, **and troops** and caught up with the Israelites **near Pi Hahiroth.**

#### c. The cry of the people and the faith of Moses (14:10-14)

**14:10-14. As** Pharaoh's charioteers and armed troops **approached,** fear struck the encampment. They were trapped between the Red Sea (lit., "Sea of [Papyrus] Reeds"; see comments on v. 2) before them and a vicious foe behind them. The reaction of the Israelites here was much the same throughout the book (cf. 5:21) in times of duress and fright. Though they **cried out to the LORD,** they had no confidence He could help. Quickly forgetting the past, they bitterly accused **Moses** of deceiving them by leading them into **the desert to die. . . . Didn't we say . . . in Egypt, Leave us alone; let us serve the Egyptians?** Moses, recognizing that fear was distorting their memories and arousing their passions against him, sought to reassure them that **the LORD** would deliver them by fighting **for** them (cf. 15:3; Neh. 4:20; Ps. 35:1) as they remained firm in confidence. Surprisingly, as they came to their greatest moment of deliverance, the people of God were full of distrust and fear.

#### d. The parting of the Red (Reed) Sea (14:15-22)

God communicated His intentions to Moses (vv. 15-18), the angel of God protected the Israelites (vv. 19-20), and they crossed on dry land (vv. 21-22).

**14:15-18.** God told **Moses** He would miraculously deliver the people **through the sea.** Moses only needed to **raise** his **staff . . . over the sea** and **the water** would **divide** and the floor of **the sea** would be **dry ground.** Pharaoh's charioteers would foolishly pursue the Israelites into the sea. There, as with the plagues, God would demonstrate His power and **glory** in the destruction of the Egyptian military. **The Egyptians,** God said, **will know that I am the LORD.**

**14:19-22. Then the angel of God,** perhaps a theophany (cf. comments on Gen. 16:9) or an angelic messenger, moved **from** the **front** of the Israelites to the rear to protect them from the charging Egyptians. The angel shifted from guide to guardian! All through that night **the pillar of cloud,** which **also** had **moved** to the rear to be between the two camps, brought such darkness that military advance was impossible for the Egyptians. **That night** God was performing another miracle: splitting **the sea** (cf. Ps. 74:13) by **a strong east wind** and drying the sea floor (cf. Pss. 66:6; 106:9). The sea was deep enough (cf. Ex. 15:5) that later it drowned the Egyptians (14:28). While the wind kept the sea floor dry and the sea split, the Israelites walked **through the sea** (cf. v. 16; Ps. 78:13). The passageway may have been wide in order to allow about 2 million people and their flocks and herds to walk through. This was a miraculous wind!

God's deliverance of Israel from Egypt pictures His mercy in delivering all His people from bondage. In a mighty display of His power He freed Israel.

*e. The destruction of the Egyptians (14:23-31)*

**14:23-28.** As **the Egyptians pursued** the Israelites into the dry sea bed, **in the morning watch** (sometime between 3 A.M. and dawn) **the LORD** slowed their progress and they were panic-stricken. According to Psalm 77:16-19 God caused a rainstorm, lightning, thunder, and an earthquake. Perhaps the rain quickly soaked the sea floor, which caused **the wheels of their chariots** to **swerve.** There was also the noise and buffeting of the wind that was banking the waters. **The Egyptians** sought to escape, realizing that the God of the Hebrews (**the LORD**) was **fighting for** Israel (cf. Ex. 14:14). **At daybreak the sea** water **went** together again and **the Egyptians** were **swept . . . into the sea** (lit., "thrown downward"). The crashing walls of **water** crushed the Egyptians in the sea so that **not** a single soldier **survived.**

**14:29-31.** God delivered His people **through . . . dry** land, while He de-

stroyed **the Egyptians** in the sea; their dead bodies floating ashore were a grim reminder of the awesome **power** of God in judgment. As a result **the Israelites . . . feared** and trusted **the LORD.** The people often fluctuated between trust and complaining, between belief and unbelief (4:31; 5:21; 14:10-12, 31; 15:24; 16:2-4; 17:2-3).

3. THE PRAISE BY MOSES AND MIRIAM FOR DELIVERANCE (15:1-21)

The groaning and crying of the Israelites (14:10-12) turned to worship as they were led by Moses (15:1-18) and his sister Miriam (vv. 19-21) in triumphal praise to the Lord.

*a. The praise by Moses (15:1-18)*

This poem of praise has three main sections (vv. 1-6, 7-11, 12-16) and a conclusion (vv. 17-18). At the end of each section certain words are repeated: "Your right hand, O LORD" (v. 6); "who is like You?" (v. 11) "until . . . people . . . pass by" (v. 16).

**15:1-6.** In the first section the theme is immediately stated—the destruction of the Egyptian army in **the sea** (v. 1; cf. v. 4). Moses acknowledged the great **strength** (v. 2; cf. v. 13) and **power** (v. 6; cf. v. 16) of the only true **God** in bringing about such an awesome deliverance (**salvation**). For that reason Moses said God caused him to rejoice (**He is . . . my song**).

**15:7-11.** This second section details the crushing of the Egyptians by God. These verses stress the mighty power of God (**the greatness of Your majesty,** v. 7) in controlling the elements and in using them to destroy His adversaries. **The blast of Your nostrils** (v. 8) refers to the wind that parted the sea, and the words **You blew with Your breath** (v. 10) refer to the wind that collapsed the billowed water; these are poetic anthropomorphisms. The Egyptians, confident of victory (v. 9), arrogantly charged against Israel, but in the minutest expense of divine energy God utterly destroyed them (**they sank like lead;** cf. v. 5, "they sank . . . like a stone"). Recognition of God's mighty works led Moses to extol the Lord's uniqueness: **Who is like You?** (Cf. Pss. 35:10; 71:19; 77:13; 89:6; 113:5; Micah 7:18.) No one is like Him **in holiness** and **glory.**

**15:12-18.** Then Moses described the consequences of Israel's deliverance by such a great God. As a result of this marvelous triumph by His **right hand** (cf. v. 6) God in His **unfailing love** (*ḥeseḏ,* "loyal love") would then lead His own into His **holy dwelling** in the Promised Land. Another result was that other nations would fear Israel, especially those lands Israel was about to enter. The greatness of Egypt had been effaced, her land ravished, her people left in mourning, and her army destroyed. Other nations, hearing of the power of the Israelites' God, would cower in fear. **People of Philistia,** mentioned first, would have been some of the first ones to have heard of the Red (Reed) Sea crossing. **Edom** was located south and east of the Dead Sea, and **Moab** was immediately north of Edom. According to Joshua's account of the Conquest, the Canaanites had a predisposed fear of the Israelites (cf. Deut. 2:25; Josh. 2:9-11, 24; 5:1).

Moses' triumphal song includes the assurance (Ex. 15:17) that God would **bring** His people into the Promised Land and to Jerusalem, **the mountain of** God's **inheritance,** where His presence would be evident in **the sanctuary.** Moses also affirmed the fact that **the LORD will reign** over His people **forever.** God is to be praised for what He did in effecting a mighty deliverance, for what He was then doing in preparing the land for conquest, and for what He will do in His eternal reign.

### b. The song by Miriam (15:19-21)

**15:19-21.** Though at first glance verse 19 may seem to be misplaced in the narrative, it purposefully repeats the reason for such joyful praise—the defeat of the Egyptian army in **the sea** (cf. v. 1) and the deliverance of **the Israelites.** This verse has three clauses each ending (in Heb.) with the word **sea. Miriam** (cf. Num. 12:1-2) is the first woman in the Bible to be called a **prophetess.** Micah suggested that she, along with Moses and Aaron, had a significant leadership role in Israel's wilderness wanderings (Micah 6:4). Since Moses was 80 years old and Aaron was 83 at the time of the Exodus (Ex. 7:7), Miriam was probably in her 90s because she was a young girl when Moses was born (2:4, 7-9). She and **the women** with her danced **with tambou-** rines (cf. 1 Sam. 18:6) as she **sang** a joyful reply to Moses' song of God's triumph over the Egyptians (cf. Ex. 15:21 with v. 1).

### 4. THE JOURNEY TO MOUNT SINAI (15:22–18:27)

Having been miraculously redeemed from bondage, God's people were full of praise. But now they faced the wilderness. Would the joy of deliverance and the knowledge of their God give them inner strength to face the trials that lay before them? This section of the book describes the travels of the people from the Red (Reed) Sea to Mount Sinai, a three-month journey (19:1). The rest of the book (chaps. 19–40) describes God's dealings with the people during the encampment there.

### a. The provision of water at Marah (15:22-27)

**15:22-26.** Leaving the lakes region the Israelites entered **the Desert of Shur** in the northern part of the Sinai Peninsula. That desert was also called the Desert of Etham (Num. 33:8). Traveling southward the Israelites went **three days . . . without . . . water** until **they came to Marah** (probably present-day Ain Hawarah). But **they could not drink the water** there **because it was bitter.** So they complained **against Moses.** This response is amazing in light of their recent deliverance and triumphal songs of worship. They were so privileged; yet hardship quickly induced them to impugn **Moses** (cf. Ex. 14:10-12; 16:2; 17:3; Num. 14:2; 16:11, 41).

The sight of undrinkable water greatly discouraged **the people,** but God responded mercifully to Moses' prayer and made **the water** drinkable (Ex. 15:25). The **wood** that Moses tossed **into the water** did not have a magical effect on the **water;** it was simply a symbolic act in anticipation of God's working a miracle (like Moses lifting his staff over the sea, 14:16).

Then the Lord gave the people a simple principle: obedience brings blessing, and disobedience brings judgment. The **diseases** (cf. Deut. 7:15; 28:60) may refer to the plagues, or more likely, to boils (cf. Deut. 28:27) common to the Delta region of Egypt. The sweetening of the water with a branch was another of God's miracles for keeping His people safe. Today the oasis at Ain Hawarah has only bitter water.

**15:27.** From Marah the people went **to Elim,** probably Wadi Gharandel about seven miles south of Marah, where there was abundant **water** and shade as is true today. **There were 12 springs and 70 palm trees at Elim.** Exactly how long the people **camped there** is not stated. Perhaps Moses' knowledge of the region helped the people locate Elim.

### b. The provisions in the Desert of Sin (chap. 16)

(1) The provision of bread and quail (16:1-20). **16:1-12.** From the Desert of Shur (15:22) the Israelites one month later (cf. 12:6) entered **the Desert of Sin . . . between Elim and Sinai.** As the people continued toward Sinai, the Lord provided several things for them, including bread (16:4) and quail (v. 13; cf. vv. 8, 12). As the journey lengthened into weeks the supply of bread (cf. 12:34) must have been depleted, so that the redeemed people again murmured **against Moses** (cf. 15:24). The lack of bread caused the people to forget their horrible plight in Egypt, to think only of the food they had **in Egypt** (cf. Num. 11:5), and to impugn the motives of their leader. As with the people's complaint for water at Marah, **the LORD** immediately responded by giving them **bread from heaven** (which they called "manna"; see comments on Ex. 16:31). The bread came early **in the morning** (vv. 8, 12-13)—actually during the night (Num. 11:9)—and melted in the heat of the day (Ex. 16:21). Each day the people were to **gather** only **enough** bread **for that day.** This meant they would have to trust **the LORD** to bring the food each morning! **On the sixth day they** were to **gather** enough for that day and the next, since the bread would not come on the seventh day (v. 5; cf. v. 26). **Moses and Aaron** rebuked the people for their **grumbling against** them (v. 7) and **the LORD** (v. 8) and reassured them of His provision for their need, which provisions would cause the **community** to **know** that He is **the LORD** their **God** (v. 12).

**16:13-20.** That very **evening** God miraculously provided **quail** in response to the people's request for meat (v. 3; cf. Num. 11:31-32, which refers to a different occasion; Pss. 78:27-28; 105:40). In the fall this small game bird, similar to pheasant

and grouse, migrates south from Palestine and Arabia to Central Africa, and in the spring it returns. Egyptian art depicts people catching the birds in hand nets.

**The bread** (cf. Ex. 16:4, 12) came with the **dew.** When the dew was gone, **thin flakes** were on the desert. Never having seen this before, the people asked, **What is it?** (See comments on "manna" in v. 31.) Because it was sent from heaven the Psalmist Asaph referred to it as "the bread of angels" (Ps. 78:25). God told them to **take an omer** (about two quarts; see the chart "Biblical Weights and Measures" before the Book of Gen.) **for each person . . . in** his **tent,** which **the Israelites** obediently **did** (Ex. 16:17). However, some of them, failing to obey the next instruction, **kept** some **of it** till **morning.** Because of their lack of faith God caused their bread to spoil.

(2) The provision of a Sabbath rest for the people. **16:21-30.** This is the Bible's first mention of the Sabbath. After His six-day work of Creation God rested on the seventh day (Gen. 2:2-3). The Hebrew words "seventh" and "rested" are similar. Later God's command for the Israelites to rest on the Sabbath became part of the Decalogue (Ex. 20:8-11). Following the Lord's orders (16:4) most of the people **gathered** only enough bread for each day, and **twice** the amount **on the sixth day** because **the seventh day** was to be **a day of rest** (v. 23; cf. v. 26), **a holy Sabbath to the LORD** (cf. v. 26). No bread would be given on that day, but part of the bread of the sixth day was to be baked or boiled to preserve it for **the seventh day.** Disregarding God's instruction (v. 23) **some of the people went out on the seventh day to gather** the bread. Lack of faith in God's Word is disobedience. **The LORD** in His displeasure asked them, **How long will you refuse to keep My commands and My instructions?**

(3) The provision of a memorial of God's grace in the wilderness. **16:31-36. The people . . . called the bread manna** (mān hû', "what is it?" cf. v. 15). It was in thin flakes (v. 14), **white like coriander seed** (an herb), looked like resin (Num. 11:7, perhaps meaning it was light-colored and/or sticky), and it **tasted like honey wafers.** It also had the taste of "something made with olive oil" (Num. 11:8). Some writers have suggested that the manna was a sweet-tasting excretion

left by insects on the twigs of tamarisk trees in June and July. However, manna was provided year-round, on the ground, and the tamarisk excretion does not spoil within 24 hours.

Then God told **Moses** to keep **an omer of manna,** about two quarts (or **1/10 of an ephah,** Ex. 16:36), in **a jar** as a reminder of God's goodness for future **generations.** The manna was to be placed **in front of the Testimony** (v. 34). "The Testimony" refers to the two tablets of the Law (25:16; 31:18; 32:15; 34:29) which were in "the ark [of the covenant] of the Testimony" (25:16, 21) in the most holy place. The Hebrew word (and the corresponding Akk. word) for "Testimony" may have been a technical term to designate covenant stipulations. For a discussion of whether the manna was kept in the ark, as Hebrews 9:4 suggests, or in front of it see comments on 2 Chronicles 5:10.

**The LORD** continued to supply manna **until** the nation **came to** Gilgal, where they began to eat the products of the land (Josh. 5:12). The manna in the ark was a perpetual reminder of God's loyalty to His people in supplying their needs. Jesus, referring to the Israelites' manna (John 6:31, 49, 58), called Himself "the true [spiritual] Bread from heaven" (John 6:32), "the Bread of God . . . from heaven" (John 6:33), "the Bread of life" (John 6:35, 48), and "the Living Bread . . . from heaven" (John 6:51). Everyone who believes in Him, He said, would have eternal life (John 6:33, 51, 58).

### c. The provisions at Rephidim (chap. 17)

This chapter records two additional provisions by God for His people: water (vv. 1-7) and victory in battle (vv. 8-16). God was demonstrating that He is capable of nourishing and sustaining His own.

**17:1-7.** After the nation left **the Desert of Sin. . . . they camped at Rephidim.** (But they also camped at Dophkah and Alush before Rephidim, Num. 33:12-14.) Rephidim is traditionally thought to be present-day Wadi Refayld near Jebel Musa, the supposed site of Mount Sinai.

Parched from their journey and finding **no water** in the oasis, **the people** again complained against **Moses** and blamed him for taking them **out of Egypt**

(cf. Ex. 16:3). This was worse than their murmurings of distrust at Marah (15:24) or in the Desert of Sin (16:2), for here they even **quarreled with Moses** (17:2) and were about **to stone** him (v. 4). Such quarreling, Moses said, was putting **the LORD to the test** (v. 2), that is, they were challenging **the LORD** or trying His patience (v. 7) rather than trusting Him.

But God was patient with His disobedient and grumbling people. He told **Moses** to take . . . **the staff with which** he had **struck the Nile** River (7:20) and to **strike** a **rock at Horeb** (17:6). This "staff of God" (4:20; 17:9) was a symbol of power; holding it was a sign of dependence and trust in God. Though Horeb is another name for Mount Sinai, Israel did not camp at Sinai until later (19:1). However, "Horeb" can also mean the Sinai region. Rephidim was close to Sinai so that the mountain slopes reached there. In Moses' striking the rock, the Lord was pleased to satiate His thirsty people with an abundant supply of **water.** So the Lord provided for them through another miracle. Because the people had tested the Lord there, **Moses** called **the place** by two names: **Massah** ("testing") **and Meribah** ("quarreling").

**17:8-16.** At Rephidim the Lord also gave His people a military victory. **The Amalekites** were nomads in the desert south of Canaan (cf. 1 Sam. 15:7; 27:8). They were descendants of Esau through Eliphaz (Gen. 36:12). They apparently were attempting to dislodge the Israelites from this pleasant oasis and to secure their territory from intrusion. In this crisis **Moses** called on **Joshua,** who is mentioned here for the first time. Though Joshua entered into battle with zeal, the victory was secured in a unique fashion in order to demonstrate God's power. Moses' holding **the staff of God** (cf. Ex. 4:20) above his head with both **hands** symbolized Israel's total dependence on the power of God. When Moses lowered his hands, a picture of lack of dependence, the enemy was **winning.** With the assistance of **Aaron and Hur** Moses' hands **remained** uplifted and a great victory was secured. (Hur is mentioned only here; 17:12; and in 24:14; 1 Chron. 2:19-20; the Hur mentioned in Ex. 31:2; 35:30; 38:22 is probably another person. Still another Hur, a Midianite king, is referred to in Num. 31:8; Josh 13:21.)

The defeat of **the Amalekites** was something God wanted **Joshua** to remember. The Amalekites remained a persistent, harassing enemy of Israel (cf. Num. 14:45; Jud. 6:33; 1 Sam. 14:48; 15:7; 27:8) until they were finally destroyed by King David (1 Sam. 30). **Moses** commemorated the victory in his day by building **an altar** which he named **the LORD is my Banner.** An interesting sidelight is that Exodus 17:14 includes the first mention in the Bible of the writing of official records, though Moses did keep some type of a diary of the sojourn (Num. 33:2). God proved Himself faithful in preserving and protecting His people.

*d. The provision of wise counsel for Moses (chap. 18)*

The story of Jethro's visit contrasts with the Amalekite confrontation. One came to fight, the other to seek knowledge; with one there was war, with the other judging or mediating for peace; with one, Moses' hand grew heavy, with the other his work was too heavy. The chapter has three sections: the setting for the visit of Jethro (vv. 1-6), the praise of Jethro (vv. 7-12), and the advice of Jethro (vv. 13-27).

**18:1-6.** Hearing of the Exodus, **Jethro, Moses' father-in-law** (cf. 4:18; also known as Reuel, 2:18), visited **Moses** when Israel was camped at Rephidim **near** Sinai (see comments on 17:16 regarding Horeb and Sinai), **the mountain of God** (18:5; cf. 3:1; 4:27; 24:13). **Jethro** apparently had followed the affairs of his son-in-law with interest so that when the Israelites camped at Rephidim Jethro determined to see him. Jethro came also to reunite his grandsons **Gershom** ("banishment"; cf. comments on 2:22) and **Eliezer** ("my God is help") and daughter **Zipporah** with Moses, for Moses had apparently **sent** them back to Jethro after they had started for Egypt. Though the reason for that action is not stated, Moses may have wanted to protect them from the horrors of the Egyptian bondage. So now, several months later, Moses was reunited with his family.

**18:7-12.** Moses' meeting with Jethro was marked by gestures of respect (**bowed down**) and gratitude (**kissed**) as they greeted each other. **Moses** rehearsed the many exciting events that had occurred since he returned to Egypt,

particularly **how the LORD** delivered **them.** Delighted with this wonderful news, **Jethro** responded, **Praise be to the LORD.** Jethro then gave the marvelous testimony that he knew **that the LORD,** the God of Israel, **is greater than all other gods.** Convinced of Yahweh's superiority, **Jethro** offered **sacrifices** to show his respect for **God.** The **burnt offering** was totally consumed by fire but fellowship offerings (**other sacrifices**) were part of a communal meal which Jethro shared with Israel's leaders possibly in making a covenant or peace agreement. The scene is one of jubilant praise and fellowship, but Jethro's true spiritual condition is not explicitly stated. He returned to Midian (v. 27), either as a convert to the true God or perhaps continuing as a priest for the idolatrous Midianites. His later words to Moses seem to suggest that he now feared God ("may God be with you," v. 19; "select . . . men who fear God," v. 21; "God so commands," v. 23).

**18:13-23.** Jethro observed that much of Moses' time was taken up in answering disputes and inquiries as the **judge** of **the people,** who sought through him (their prophet, Deut. 34:10) to know **God's will.** Because of this work overload which **Moses** was trying to do all by himself (**Why do you alone sit as judge? . . . You cannot handle it alone,** Ex. 18:14, 18) Jethro warned that Moses would become overexhausted. Also the **people** would be worn out (v. 18), waiting for their turns to present their cases.

Wisely, Jethro urged **Moses** to delegate some of his responsibilities. But Moses was to continue teaching the people the **laws** of God (cf. v. 16) and how **to live** before Him and to appoint spiritually and morally qualified **men** as judges to implement the keeping of the Law (vv. 20-21). They were to be "wise . . . respected . . . and leading men" in their tribes (Deut. 1:13, 15). **Moses** was to **be the people's representative before God** (Ex. 18:19) and their teacher but most judicial matters were to be given to others. As **officials over thousands, hundreds, fifties, and tens** (words used of those in military rank) they were to serve in various levels of civil courts to hear cases of varying degrees of importance.

**18:24-27.** Accepting his father-in-law's advice, **Moses** apparently implemented the judicial court system after the

## The Mosaic Covenant Compared with Suzerainty Treaties

| Parts in the Near Eastern Suzerainty Treaties | Given on Mount Sinai | Given in the Transjordan | Given in Canaan |
|---|---|---|---|
| Preamble | Ex. 20:2a | Deut. 1:1-4 | Josh. 24:1-2a |
| Historical prologue | Ex. 20:2b | Deut. 1:5–4:43 | Josh. 24:2b-13 |
| General stipulations | Ex. 20:3-17 | Deut. 4:44–11:32 | Josh. 24:14-15, 23 |
| Specific stipulations | Ex. 20:22–23:33 | Deut. 12:1–26:15 | |
| Deposit and periodic reading | Ex. 25:16, 21 | Deut. 31:9-13, 26 | Josh. 24:25-26a |
| Invocation of witnesses | | Deut. 30:19; 31:28 | Josh. 24:22, 26b-27 |
| Curses and blessings | Lev. 26 | Deut. 27–28 | Josh. 24:19-20 |
| Vassal's oath of allegiance | Ex. 24:3 | | Josh. 24:16-18, 21, 24 |
| Solemn ceremony | Ex. 24:4-11 | | |

Law was given at Mount Sinai (Deut. 1:9-15; cf. Horeb in Deut. 1:6). If so, then possibly Exodus 18:24-26, about the later implementation of the plan, was included in the narrative here to complete the story about Jethro's advice. Occasionally Old Testament writers treated subjects topically rather than in strict chronological sequence.

## II. The Revelation to God's People at Sinai (chaps. 19–40)

The Israelites arrived at Mount Sinai where they remained throughout the rest of the events recorded in Exodus 19:1–Numbers 10:10. They were at Sinai 11 months and 6 days—from the 15th day of the third month of their first year of travels (cf. Ex. 12:2, 6, with 19:1) to "the 20th day of the second month of the second year" of their travels (Num. 10:11). There Moses received from God the Law with its many instructions for worship by the redeemed people.

### A. The covenant of God with His people (chaps. 19–31)

God had redeemed His people from Egypt, "the land of slavery" (13:3, 14;

20:2; cf. comments on Deut. 5:6), through the sprinkling of blood (Ex. 12) and by the marvelous deliverance through the Red (Reed) Sea (Ex. 14). Now He brought them to Sinai where He entered into a covenant with them. The Law was the nation's "constitution" for their theocratic state under their great God, Yahweh.

1. THE SETTING FOR THE REVELATION OF THE LAW (CHAP. 19)

The Mosaic Covenant or "contract" is similar in form to the suzerainty treaties of the Near Eastern kings with their vassals. Many of the parts of those treaties were included in God's Mosaic Covenant with His people. Apparently this was a common literary structure in those days. (See the chart "The Mosaic Covenant Compared with Suzerainty Treaties.") Here God is the absolute Sovereign and His people were the vassals.

*a. The encampment before Mount Sinai (19:1-2)*

**19:1-2.** Exactly three months **after** the Exodus from **Egypt,** the Israelites **entered the Desert of Sinai** and **camped** by **the mountain,** Mount Sinai. The term "desert" does not always mean a dry wasteland but sometimes uninhabited grazing country. The exact location of Mount Sinai is unknown, but traditionally it is identified as Jebel Musa in the southern portion of the Sinai Peninsula. This is the same as the mountain of God (cf. 3:1; 4:27; 18:5; 24:13), also called Horeb, where God appeared to Moses in a burning bush.

### b. The benefits of the covenant (19:3-6)

**19:3-4.** As the Israelites were camped by Sinai, **Moses went** on **the mountain** and there God spoke to him about the pact He would ratify with the **people (Jacob** and **Israel** were synonyms for the nation).

God compared His delivering the people out of **Egypt,** across the Red (Reed) Sea, and to Sinai to His carrying them **on eagles' wings** (cf. Deut. 32:10-11). When young eagles are learning to fly, the mother eagle flies under them with her wings spread out to catch them.

**19:5-6.** This proposal made by God (**My covenant**) would give Israel an exalted position among the **nations** in view of their acceptance of God's righteous standards. If they accepted and obeyed the covenant stipulations, God promised to make them His **treasured possession** (cf. Deut. 7:6; 14:2; 26:18; Ps. 135:4; Mal. 3:17). They would be His own people, highly valued by and related to Him. Also they would become **a kingdom of priests,** that is, each member of the nation with God as his King would know and have access to Him and mediate on behalf of each other as did priests. Also they would be **a holy nation,** a nation morally pure and dedicated entirely to the service of God. God redeemed Israel so that she might be in touch with and separated to Him.

### c. The preparations for the covenant (19:7-25)

**19:7-15.** Moses then informed **the elders of** Israel and **the people** about God's covenant and His plan to possess them uniquely. **The people** heartily **responded** by promising to obey His laws strictly. In anticipation of the covenant God ordered **the people** to separate themselves from impurity and to **consecrate** themselves to God. The three-day purification ritual included washing their garments and abstaining from **sexual** intercourse. Also during the three days no person **or animal** was to contact **the mountain** or he or it would **be put to death.** Such careful preparation underscored the significance of the event that was about to transpire. The God of the heavens was about to make a covenant with His people. Unlike pagan deities who supposedly dwelt in the mountains, the God of Israel descended from heaven (1 Kings 8:30, 49) to the mountains to converse with His people. Only when summoned by the blast of a **ram's horn** (cf. Ex. 19:16, 19) were the people to go toward **the mountain** (v. 13).

**19:16-25.** Then on **the third day** of preparation the **God** of heaven descended to **Sinai** in a display of power and majesty. God demonstrated His holiness and awesomeness; little wonder that the people **trembled,** standing **at the foot of the mountain** (v. 16; cf. 20:18). The people heard crashing **thunder** and **a very loud trumpet blast** (cf. 19:13); they saw flashing **lightning. . . . fire,** and dense billowing **smoke** as from a smelting **furnace;** and they felt the **mountain** trembling in a violent earthquake. The "black cloud" of smoke brought "darkness" to the sky (Deut. 4:11; cf. Ex. 20:21).

Only **Moses** (19:20) and **Aaron** (v. 24) were permitted on the mountain; **the priests** and **the people** were to stand before it. If they in curiosity saw the **Lord** they would perish (cf. comments on 33:11, 20; John 1:18). Though the Levitical priesthood had not yet been established, the elders (Ex. 3:18) or some young men (24:5) served as priests. **Moses** made three trips to the mountaintop and back (19:3, 7; vv. 8-9; vv. 20, 25). These instructions vividly reminded the people of the immeasurable chasm between the divine and the human, as well as the miracle of divine revelation.

### 2. THE DECALOGUE (20:1-21)

One of the great events in the history of Israel, and perhaps in the history of all mankind, is the giving of the Law. The Law was not given so that the Israelites by keeping it could attain righteousness (Rom. 3:20a; Gal. 3:11). A righteous standing (justification) before God has always been only by faith (trust) in God (Gen. 15:6; Rom. 4:3, 22; 5:1; Gal. 2:16; 3:6, 21). The Law functioned to show the

Israelites their sinfulness (Rom. 3:19-20b; 7:7) in contrast with God's standards of holiness and righteousness, and to condemn mankind. The Mosaic Law in Exodus has three parts: the Decalogue (Ex. 20:1-21), the Book of the Covenant with civil and religious ordinances (20:22–24:11), and ceremonial regulations (24:12–31:18).

*a. The introduction to the Decalogue (20:1-2)*

**20:1-2.** The Ten Commandments (in 34:28 "Ten Commandments" is lit., "Ten Words"), the hub of all of Israel's religious and civil laws, has two parts. The first four commandments pertain to the relationship of the Israelites with God, and the other six deal with social relationships within the covenant community. Before giving these 10 stipulations, **God** in the preamble spoke of His unique relationship with His people (**I am the LORD your God,** 20:2a) and in the historical prologue He briefly summarized what He had done for them (**brought you out of Egypt . . . the land of slavery,** v. 2b; cf. 13:3, 14; Deut. 5:6; 6:12; 7:8; 8:14; 13:5, 10). Centuries before, God had led Abraham out of Ur (Gen. 15:7); now He led Abraham's descendants out of Egypt.

The Ten Commandments are an excellent summary of 10 divine rules for human conduct. They might be called rules of (1) religion, (2) worship, (3) reverence, (4) time, (5) authority, (6) life, (7) purity, (8) property, (9) tongue, and (10) contentment.

*b. The first commandment (20:3)*

**20:3.** The first of the Ten Commandments is that Israel was to worship the one true God. Worshiping false **gods** would be setting up rivals to Him (**before Me** may mean "in opposition to Me" as well as "in My presence") and thus overlooking His uniqueness (cf. vv. 22-23). Unfortunately Israel often disobeyed this very first command by worshiping the idols of other nations. This eventually resulted in her being exiled to Assyria and Babylonia.

*c. The second commandment (20:4-6)*

**20:4-6.** The worship of God was to be spiritual, not material. Israel was forbidden from worshiping idols (v. 3) and also from making images of God. **Idol** is *pesel,* "carved wood or stone," from *pāsal,* "to

carve." Later (34:17) "cast idols" made from molten metal were forbidden too. Since God is spiritual no material representation can possibly resemble Him. To make an idol of God like something in the sky (sun, moon, stars), **or on the earth** (animals), **or in the waters below** (fish, crocodiles, or other sea life) was forbidden because God is **a jealous God** (cf. 34:14; Deut. 5:9; 6:15; 32:16, 21; Josh. 24:19), that is, He is zealous that devotion be given exclusively to Him. His uniqueness (Ex. 20:3) requires unique devotion. Absence of such dedication is sin and has its effect on future generations. Those who thus are influenced to **hate** God will be punished by Him. By contrast He is loyal (**showing** *ḥesed,* "loyal **love**") to those who **love** Him and who show that love by their obedience (cf. 1 John 5:3).

*d. The third commandment (20:7)*

**20:7. The name of . . . God** should be honored and protected. The Israelites were not to use His name for any idle, frivolous, or insincere purpose (such as speaking His name when taking an oath with no intention of keeping it, Lev. 19:12). People should not use His name for selfish or evil purposes (cf. Ps. 139:20; also see comments on Deut. 5:11), thereby seeking to usurp His authority.

*e. The fourth commandment (20:8-11)*

**20:8-11.** A day of solemn worship of God should be kept weekly. Keeping **the Sabbath Day . . . holy** means to separate it, **the seventh day,** from the other six as a special day **to the LORD.** People are to work in **six days** and worship on the seventh. This contrasted with the Israelites' slavery in Egypt when, presumably, they had no break in their daily routine. The basis for this commandment is God's creating the universe **in six days** and resting **on the seventh** (Gen. 2:2-3; Ex. 16:23). This was not to be a day of slothful inactivity but of spiritual service through religious observances. For the violation of this command God imposed on Israel the death penalty (Ex. 31:15; Num. 15:32-36). In the present Church Age the day of worship has been changed from Saturday to Sunday because of Jesus' resurrection on the first day of the week (cf. Acts 20:7; 1 Cor. 16:2).

*f. The fifth commandment (20:12)*

**20:12.** Commandments 5-10, the second portion of the Law (vv. 12-17), deal with one's relationships to others. All the commandments include a negative except the fourth (the last in the first group) and the fifth (the first in the second group). The fifth commandment enjoins respect (**honor**) of parents. It implies obedience and submission to them (cf. Eph. 6:1-2). The promise of longevity that accompanies the command (**live long**) refers to duration as a nation in covenant relationship with God (**in the land the LORD your God is giving you**) rather than a lengthened lifespan for each obedient individual. Cursing one's parents, tantamount to repudiating their authority, was a capital offense (Ex. 21:17; Lev. 20:9; Prov. 20:20).

*g. The sixth commandment (20:13)*

**20:13.** To help preserve society and because people are made in God's image (Gen. 9:6), the Israelites were commanded **not** to take another person's life by **murder** (*rāṣaḥ,* "to slay").

*h. The seventh commandment (20:14)*

**20:14.** This commandment is directed toward protecting the sanctity of the home (Heb. 13:4; see comments on Gen. 2:24; Matt. 19:1-12), the fundamental building block of society. The marital vow is a holy commitment that should **not** be violated by sexual unfaithfulness under any circumstances. **Adultery** (*nā'ap*) refers to infidelity on the part of either men or women (Lev. 20:10).

*i. The eighth commandment (20:15)*

**20:15.** This command was given to encourage the respect of others' property. This too is an important element in a stable society. It is closely related to the 10th commandment.

*j. The ninth commandment (20:16)*

**20:16.** This command concerns bearing **false testimony against** someone that would cause him unjustified injury. Keeping this law helps maintain stability in a society by protecting individuals' reputations.

*k. The 10th commandment (20:17)*

**20:17.** This is a general safeguard against many other sins, particularly commandments six through nine. Israelites were **not** to long for, desire earnestly, or lust after what legitimately belonged to others.

These commandments are the fundamental statements of a good and wholesome society as ordered by the holy and righteous God. Though believers today are not under the Law (Rom. 6:15), they are under obligation to abide by the holy standards represented in the Ten Commandments. Nine of the Ten Commandments are repeated in the New Testament with added stipulations that are even higher than those in Exodus 20:3-17. The one not repeated is the command to keep the Sabbath; yet the first day of the week is to be set aside for worship in commemoration of the Savior's resurrection.

*l. The people's response (20:18-21)*

**20:18-21.** The response of **the people** gathered before **the mountain** was one of **fear** and awe (cf. 19:16). Recognizing the mighty power and majesty of God, they wanted to hear of Him *through* **Moses**— not directly lest God destroy them. **Moses** assured them that the purpose of this display of God's power and holiness was **to test** their reaction to Him. **Fear of** Him would help curb their disobedience. Tragically Israel soon lost this fear of Him (Ex. 32)—a frequent theme in her history.

3. THE BOOK OF THE COVENANT (20:22–24:11)

God applied and elaborated on the Decalogue in its civil and religious implications for the nation. This section is called "the Book of the Covenant," based on that phrase in 24:7.

*a. Statutes concerning worship (20:22-26)*

**20:22-26.** God gave the nation regulations about their worship of the true God and the building of **an altar.** He had come **from heaven** to Mount Sinai (19:20) to give the Ten Commandments. Now (20:22–23:19) He elaborated on many of those 10. The command to worship God alone, not other deities (20:23), and the caution against making carved or molten idols **of silver or . . . gold,** re-emphasizes the first and second commandments (vv. 3-4).

On **an altar** the people were to offer **burnt offerings and fellowship offerings,** which would result in His **name** being **honored** and their lives being blessed. Reference to a single altar indicates that God intended that worship should be centralized in one place. The altar was to be unadorned by craftsmanship; it was to be **of earth** (i.e., of natural stones; cf. Deut. 27:5-7), and without steps so the priests would not be indecently **exposed.** Altars with elaborate craftsmanship and elevated platforms with staircases were common in the worship of false deities.

*b. Statutes concerning the care of servants (21:1-11)*

**21:1-6.** The subject of verses 1-11 is regulations governing the rights of male (vv. 1-6) and female (vv. 7-11) **Hebrew** slaves. Among the Israelites a person could sell himself and his wife into slavery due to poverty or debt (Lev. 25:39; Deut. 15:12; 2 Kings 4:1; Neh. 5:5), but the servitude was to be limited to **six years** (Ex. 21:2). Thus it was indentured service. Further, a **master** was obligated to provide for his **servant** on his release (Deut. 15:13-14). If a male **servant** wanted to remain in permanent servitude his request was to be validated by **the judges** and then one of his ears was to be pierced **with an awl,** to symbolize willing service (Ps. 40:6). A female servant could do the same (Deut. 15:17).

**21:7-11.** Female slaves were treated differently. Many times female slaves were concubines or secondary wives (cf. Gen. 16:3; 22:24; 30:3, 9; 36:12; Jud. 8:31; 9:18). Some Hebrew fathers thought it more advantageous for their daughters to become concubines of well-to-do neighbors than to become the wives of men in their own social class. If a **daughter** who became **a servant** was not pleasing to her master she was to **be redeemed** by a near kinsman (cf. Lev. 25:47-54) but never sold **to foreigners** (Ex. 21:8); she could also redeem herself. If she married her master's **son** she was to be given family status (v. 9). If the master married someone else he was required to provide his servant with three essentials: **food, clothing,** and shelter (**marital rights** probably means living quarters, not sexual privilege).

*c. Statutes of capital offense (21:12-17)*

**21:12-17.** These verses enumerate four crimes that required the death pen-

alty: premeditated murder (vv. 12, 14; cf. the sixth commandment in 20:13 and Gen. 9:6); physical violence against parents (Ex. 21:15); kidnapping (v. 16; cf. Deut. 24:7); and verbal abuse of parents (Ex. 21:17; cf. the fifth commandment in 20:12 and note Lev. 20:9). Allowance was made for unintentional, accidental deaths (Ex. 21:13). A "guilty" person could escape to one of the six cities of refuge after Israel was in the land (Num. 35:6-34; Deut. 19:1-13; Josh. 20). Because of the importance of the home its sanctity was guarded, parents protected, and children controlled; disrespectfulness was to be dealt with in the same way as murder.

*d. Statutes concerning physical injury (21:18-27)*

Regulations concerning several civil deviations are given that were not severe enough to merit the death penalty.

**21:18-19.** In a physical **quarrel** the injured party, whether or not the injury was premeditated, was to be given compensation for his **loss** of work **time** (while he was walking **around outside with his staff**) and for medical expenses.

**21:20-21.** Slaves were not to be treated cruelly by their masters, though they were considered **property.** If a master beat his **slave . . . and the slave** died, the master was to **be punished** (but probably not by death). However, **if the slave** soon recovered, no punishment was to be exacted (for apparently homicide was not intended); the loss of a slave's work was his master's loss.

**21:22-25. If . . . a pregnant woman** delivered her child prematurely as a result of a blow, but both were otherwise uninjured, the guilty party was to pay compensation determined by **the woman's husband** and **the court.** However, **if there** was **injury** to the expectant mother or her child, then the assailant was to be penalized in proportion to the nature of severity of the injury. While unintentional life-taking was usually not a capital offense (cf. vv. 12-13), here it clearly was. Also the unborn fetus is viewed in this passage as just as much a human being as its mother; the abortion of a fetus was considered murder. A person's physical loss by **injury** was to be punished by a similar loss to the offender (vv. 24-25), the law of retaliation (cf. Lev. 24:19-20;

Deut. 19:21). This law was designed to *restrict* the exacting of punishment to what was equitable.

**21:26-27.** The law of retaliation, however, did not apply to a master who injured his **servant.** Any permanent maiming of a slave would result in his being legally freed (the master **must let the servant go free**).

*e. Statutes concerning culpable neglect (21:28-36)*

**21:28-36.** Here statutes were given for cases involving injury through negligence. First, God gave regulations concerning injuries inflicted by animals (vv. 28-32). **If a bull** gored someone **to death,** the animal was to be killed. However, if the animal had a **habit** of violently attacking people **and the owner** did nothing to prevent it and someone was killed, **the owner** (as well as **the bull**) was to **be put to death.** He could avoid the death penalty if he could come up with financial compensation **demanded** by the dead person's relatives. If a **slave** was killed by a **bull,** the animal's owner had to remunerate the slave **owner** by paying **30 shekels of silver** (cf. Matt. 26:14-15), apparently the price of **the slave.**

Second, in the event of animal loss due to someone's negligence (e.g., in not covering **a pit**—perhaps used to collect rainwater—to prevent an animal falling in), the guilty party was required to render full compensation for the loss of the **animal** (Ex. 21:33-34). This regulation was important because animals were important property of the Israelites.

Third, **if a** bull killed someone else's **bull,** the loss was to be shared **equally** between the owners by selling **the live** bull and splitting the money (v. 35). **However, if** a man knowingly neglected to pen his goring **bull, he must** then **pay** for the **dead** bull.

*f. Statutes concerning thieves (22:1-4)*

**22:1-4.** These regulations deal with the theft of animals. These verses expand on the eighth commandment (20:15). If a person stole and then killed or sold someone's **ox** or **sheep** he must compensate for (**pay back,** *šālēm,* "to repay a legal obligation"; cf. 2 Kings 4:7; Joel 2:25) the loss by returning the same kinds of animals. Here again was retribution in kind. But **five head of cattle** had to be

paid for the loss of one **ox,** and **four sheep** for the loss of one **sheep.** No doubt this heavy compensation effectively deterred animal theft. **If,** however, **the stolen animal** was still **alive,** the remuneration was less but still costly (Ex. 22:4).

**If a thief** burglarized in the night and was killed by the owner of the house, then the defendant was **not guilty of murder. But if** the burglar was killed during the daytime the houseowner was guilty of homicide. (Apparently the day thief could be seen and help could more easily be obtained.) The Mosaic code sought to protect human life, even that of criminals. The **thief** was either to compensate for the crime with his own material wealth or to be sold into slavery.

*g. Statutes concerning property damage (22:5-6)*

**22:5-6.** If the grazing rights of a farmer were violated by another man's **livestock** or **if a fire** destroyed another's crops, the offender had to **make restitution** from his own fields. **Thornbushes** often burned easily and thus helped spread field fires quickly. The Mosaic code strongly affirmed the right to both life and property.

*h. Statutes concerning safe-deposits (22:7-13)*

**22:7-13.** In the ancient Near East there were no banks, so personal property was sometimes given to a **neighbor** for protection. The one who received someone's valuables (**goods,** clothing, or animals) **for safekeeping** was responsible for them. If personal valuables were lost and no **thief** was **found,** the one who kept the goods had to prove **before the judges** that he did not steal them or he had to make restitution by paying **double** (vv. 7-9). If an **animal** in safekeeping was **injured** or lost, the one taking care of it had to give evidence that he was not negligent or he had **to pay** for the loss (vv. 10-13).

*i. Statutes concerning borrowing (22:14-15)*

**22:14-15.** When **an animal** was borrowed, the borrower was responsible for its safekeeping. If **the owner** was not present when the animal was **injured** or died, the borrower had to pay for the loss; he was responsible. **But if the owner** was present then **the borrower** was not culpable. If an animal was rented and injury occurred then the owner's compensation was the rent **money.**

### j. Statutes concerning sexual seduction (22:16-17)

**22:16-17.** These statutes elaborated the seventh commandment (20:14). Unmarried and unbetrothed daughters in Israel were considered part of their father's property; consequently the loss of a daughter's virginity diminished her value and therefore compensation was due to the father. The seduction of a girl who was betrothed resulted in stoning for both parties (Deut. 22:23-24). If an unengaged **virgin** submitted to seduction **the male was to pay the bride-price** and marry her. Normally the parents of a girl were paid a fee at the time of betrothal which ratified the engagement (cf. Gen. 34:12; 1 Sam. 18:25). **If her father** did not want his daughter to marry the fellow, the man was **still** obligated to **pay** the **bride**-money.

### k. Statutes concerning idolatrous customs (22:18-20)

**22:18-20.** The three sins mentioned in these verses merited the death penalty; they anticipated Israel's struggle against the worship of idols. The first deals with female practitioners of sorcery (telling the future or controlling others by demonic power; see comments on Deut. 18:9-12 and on Dan. 2:2); the second is bestiality (cf. Lev. 20:16; Deut. 27:21) which figured prominently in Canaanite Baal worship (cf. Lev. 18:23-24); and the third deals with sacrificing **to any god other than** the true One, **the LORD** (cf. Ex. 20:3-5).

### l. Statutes concerning the care of the needy (22:21-27)

**22:21-27.** Various laws for the protection of the underprivileged were included because God cares for them (**I am compassionate,** v. 27). Foreigners were to be treated benevolently because the Israelites themselves had been **aliens in Egypt** (v. 21; cf. 23:9). Also they were **not** to **take advantage of** people without fathers or husbands because they were already without protection (22:22-24). Mistreatment of them would arouse God's **anger** and the guilty parties would lose their lives.

Grain was to be left behind for widows and orphans during harvest (Deut. 24:19-21) including the edges of fields (Lev. 19:9-10). The helpers were to be given special hospitality at feasts (Deut. 16:11-14), to receive a special tithe every third year (Deut. 14:28-29; 16:12-13), and to be allowed to plant crops in others' fields during the sabbatical year (Ex. 23:11-12).

Also for Israelites in financial need, loans were to be **interest**-free (22:25-27; cf. Lev. 25:35-38; Deut. 15:7-11; 23:19-20). If a loan was made to a poor person, some valuable possession of his, usually a **cloak,** was normally given to the creditor **as a pledge** of repayment. His cloak, however, had to be returned to him **by sunset** to give him comfort at night (cf. Deut. 24:10-13; Job 22:6).

### m. Statutes concerning reverence (22:28-31)

**22:28-31.** In the previous verses (vv. 21-27) the needs of people low on the social scale were discussed. This passage (vv. 28-31) deals with rules concerning those higher on the social scale. Neither the name of **God,** the supreme Ruler, nor the name of a human leader was to be cursed. Israel was always to remember that **the firstborn of** her **sons** and animals belonged to God (cf. 13:2, 12). Sons were to be dedicated to God when they were eight days old and redemption money was to be paid (13:13). The firstborn of the **cattle** and **sheep** were to be sacrificed.

Animals killed by carnivorous **beasts** were **not** to be eaten by Israel because the blood had not been drained and through it they would have contact, though indirectly, with the unclean animal that killed it. Israel's inward holiness was supposed to be accompanied by her being physically separate from every form of uncleanness.

### n. Statutes concerning legal justice (23:1-9)

**23:1-9.** These admonitions, which expand the ninth commandment (20:16), deal with the need for impartial justice in lawsuits. The Israelites were to bear a true witness in legal cases. Israelites were **not** to **pervert justice by** being influenced by **the crowd** or even by **favoritism to** the **poor.** The words **enemy's** (23:4) and **someone who hates you** (v. 5) probably mean "a legal adversary"; an Israelite was to be kind even to the animals of someone with whom he had a legal disagreement. Denying **justice to** the **poor** because of their social status (v. 6; cf. v. 3), giving **false** testimony in court that results in an **innocent** person's **death** (v. 7), accepting **a bribe** (payment for favoritism in court, v. 8; cf. Deut. 16:19—this was a common problem in the ancient Near East), and oppressing **an alien** (cf. Ex. 22:21; perhaps 23:9 refers to court cases) were all forbidden.

*o. Statutes concerning the Sabbaths (23:10-13)*

**23:10-13.** The Lord then instructed Israel concerning the sabbatical year (vv. 10-11) and the Sabbath Day (vv. 12-13), instructions that expanded the fourth commandment (20:8-11). The sabbatical year reminded Israel that God owns the land and that it was theirs merely as a trust (Lev. 25:23). Also the sabbatical year provided for **the poor,** who could glean from the **fields.**

By resting **on the seventh day** man and animals could **be refreshed** for another six days of work. This section (Ex. 23:13) ends with a general admonition to obey God's commands and a warning not to recognize the existence of any **other gods** by mentioning their **names.**

*p. Statutes concerning annual festivals (23:14-19)*

**23:14-19.** Here God gave instructions for three agricultural festivals to be held annually: (a) **the Feast of Unleavened Bread** in **the month of Abib** (March-April), about the time of the barley harvest; (b) **the Feast of Harvest** in the spring at the beginning of the wheat harvest (cf. 34:22) when **the firstfruits of the crops** were to be given to the Lord, and (c) **the Feast of Ingathering** in early autumn (September-October; cf. the chart "Calendar in Israel," near 12:1).

The first of these great agricultural feasts was a memorial to the hasty Exodus from **Egypt** (cf. 12:15-20). The second feast, in which two loaves made of new grain were presented to the Lord (Lev. 23:15-21), was also called the Feast of Weeks (Ex. 34:22) because it was celebrated seven weeks (50 days) after the Feast of Unleavened Bread. In the New Testament (Acts 2:1; 20:16; 1 Cor. 16:8) it is called the day of Pentecost. The third festival, the Feast of Ingathering—at **the**

end of the agricultural or civil **year**—was also called the Feast of Tabernacles or Feast of Booths (Lev. 23:33-36; Deut. 16:13-15; 31:10).

These were constant reminders to Israel of God's provisions for His people. So **three times a year** (Ex. 23:14, 17; 34:23) **all** adult males in Israel were supposed to worship at the tabernacle (or later, at the temple) with grain and animal offerings. When an offering was consumed on the altar it had to be without **yeast.** Only **the best of** the crops' **firstfruits** were to be given to the Lord.

The prohibition against cooking **a young goat in its mother's milk** (23:19; cf. 34:26; Deut. 14:21) may have been because of religious practices in which the Canaanites cooked goats in their mother's milk in a fertility rite. God did not want His people to partake of anything related to idolatrous worship. Or the prohibition may have been against the inhumane treatment of young goats. In the Feast of Ingathering (Ex. 23:16b) the Israelites may have been tempted to follow the common bedouin practice of cooking the meat of young goats in goat's milk, whereas the young goats should have been left with their mothers. In other words, perhaps the prohibition meant that the Israelites were not to take what was intended to promote life (goat milk) and use it to destroy life. This stipulation may be the basis for the present Jewish custom of not mixing milk products with meat.

*q. Epilogue: A promise about the Conquest of the land (23:20-33)*

The section on the ordinances (beginning at 20:22) has a comforting promise about God's directing His people into the Promised Land wherein the laws just enumerated would be practiced. It contains promises of cursings for disobedience and blessings for obedience, similar to those in Leviticus and Deuteronomy.

**23:20-26.** First the Lord stressed the need for obedience. The **angel** (vv. 20, 23) may have been a special guardian angel for Israel (perhaps Michael, Dan. 12:1) or, more likely, the Lord Himself or the preincarnate Christ (cf. Gen. 24:7 with Gen. 24:27; and see comments on Gen. 16:9) because of His ability to forgive. God promised to guide His people in the days before them; specifically, of course, the guidance would come through Moses and Aaron. When the people arrived in Canaan God promised to **wipe . . . out** her enemies (on the peoples named in Ex. 23:23 see comments on 3:8). And the Israelites were to destroy the Canaanites' idols and **sacred stones** (cf. 34:13; Deut. 7:5; 12:3). Possibly these stones were male fertility symbols. Worshiping and obeying God would result in their having health, longevity, and bounty.

**23:27-30.** God also promised to give the Israelites the land gradually. Their enemies, terrorized by God, would be confused and would retreat. Like running to escape the sting of a **hornet,** they would flee in fear and panic (cf. 15:15; Num. 22:3; Josh. 2:9-11, 24; 5:1; 9:24). Some Bible students, however, take the reference to "the hornet" literally. Others say it refers to the Egyptian army.

The Conquest would take longer than a **year;** in fact Joshua's Conquest, which did not wipe out all the enemies, took seven years (1406-1399 B.C.). If God had given them the land all at once rather than **little by little** (cf. Jud. 1) **the land would** have **become desolate** and overrun by **wild animals** before Israel could settle in and cultivate it.

**23:31-33.** Then the Lord prescribed the borders of the Promised Land. **The Red Sea** in this case is the part of the Red Sea now known as the Sea of Aqaba (probably to form the nation's southeastern boundary). **The Sea of the Philistines** would be the western boundary (the Mediterranean Sea), **the desert** the southern boundary, and the **Euphrates River** the northern (or northeastern) boundary. This territory was occupied during the time of Solomon (1 Kings 4:21) though much of it was not fully under Israel. Pockets of the enemy still lived in the land as vassals to Israel (cf. Deut. 11:24 and see comments on Deut. 1:7). Yet the presence of these enemies **in the land** was a constant menace to Israel, as God had predicted. Joshua 9:3-15 records a violation of God's command **not to make a covenant** or treaty (cf. Ex. 34:12) **with** any of the foreign peoples in the land of Canaan. Failure to **drive . . . out** the enemy (23:31) would result in their causing Israel to sin primarily through their idolatry. Israel's later history certainly proved this to be true.

*r. The confirmation of the covenant (24:1-11)*

The covenant stipulations—including the Decalogue and the ordinances—whereby the people of Israel were to be regulated as the people of the true God had been given. It now remained for the people to ratify the pact.

**24:1-4a.** God summoned **Moses** before Him with **Aaron,** Aaron's two eldest sons **Nadab and Abihu** (cf. Lev. 10), **and 70 of the elders** (leaders) of the people, though the men, all 73 of them, except for **Moses** were to keep their **distance** (cf. Ex. 19:12-13, 24) from **the LORD** out of respect for His majesty and holiness. Moses went to the top of the mountain, the 73 other leaders were on the mountain but not at the top, and the people were below at the foot of the mountain.

God was now ready to confirm the Mosaic Covenant with His people. **Moses** rehearsed before **the people all the LORD's words and laws** (20:22–23:33), called "the Book of the Covenant" (24:7). After hearing these laws the people heartily submitted themselves to obey them (cf. 19:8) and **Moses . . . wrote down** God's commands.

**24:4b-8.** Then Moses prepared the people for the ratifying of the Law. First Moses made **an altar at the foot of** Mount Sinai and erected **12 stone pillars** to represent Israel's **12 tribes.** Since the Levitical priesthood had not yet been organized, **young Israelite men** (perhaps the dedicated firstborn, 13:1-16), and **Moses** served as priests and **offered burnt offerings and . . . fellowship offerings to the LORD.** In the ratification ceremony **Moses** sprinkled **blood . . . on the altar** (24:6) and on the people (v. 8) who had heard Moses read **the Book of the Covenant** and had promised once again to **obey** it (v. 7; cf. v. 3). This is the only time in the Old Testament when *people* were sprinkled with blood. Possibly the people were sprinkled in the sense that the stones which represented them (v. 4) were sprinkled. (On the relationship of obedience and sprinkling of blood see comments on 1 Peter 1:2.) The sprinkled blood, then, symbolized the legal transaction between God (represented by the altar, Ex. 24:6) and the people (represented by the stones). Israel was thus ceremonially set apart through blood **(the blood of the covenant)** as the people of the true God. Later the New Covenant, established by Jesus, was also ratified by blood, His own (Luke 22:20; 1 Cor. 11:25-26).

**24:9-11. Moses . . . Aaron,** Aaron's two eldest sons, **and the 70 elders . . . went up** the mountain to confirm and ratify the covenant before God. Since no one can see God and live (see comments on 33:11, 20; John 1:18), they probably **saw the God of Israel** in the sense that they had a vision of Him in which they discerned who He is. Apparently the sight was so grand and awesome that their eyes saw only below **His feet.** The splendor of God looked like **sapphire** (cf. the throne of sapphire in Ezek. 1:26). Then they **ate** a meal before Him. It was common to symbolize the ratifying of a covenant with a meal (cf. Gen. 26:30; 31:54; Luke 22:15-20).

### 4. THE CEREMONIAL REGULATIONS (24:12–31:18)

The Mosaic Covenant had been confirmed (24:1-11) and Israel was then a theocracy, a government or commonwealth under God. Having been redeemed from bondage by God and now in a covenant under His laws, God's people were then enlightened as to the proper way to worship Him. So Moses was called into God's presence to receive the Decalogue in stone along with other commands (24:12) and he returned 40 days later (31:18; 34:28). In that period of time God communicated to Moses the form of Israel's worship. The tabernacle was to become the focus of Israel's worship of God. This lengthy section (24:12–31:18) deals with ordinances pertaining to the sanctuary and priestly ministry—ceremonial laws that undergirded the covenant.

*a. The context of the disclosure of the ceremonial law (24:12-18)*

**24:12-18. Moses** was summoned before God **on the mountain** to receive **the tablets of stone, with the Law** (the Decalogue, 20:2-17; cf. 34:28) **and commands** related to Israel's worship. God had given Moses the Decalogue earlier but now it was inscribed in stone.

The leadership of the people was temporarily delegated to **Aaron and Hur** (cf. 17:10, 12) while **Moses . . . with Joshua** proceeded up Sinai, **the mountain of God** (cf. 3:1; 4:27; 18:5). Joshua, first mentioned in 17:9, became increas-

ingly more prominent (cf. 33:11). Perhaps Joshua went up the mountain only partway.

A **cloud,** representing God's glory (cf. 19:16), heralded the approach of God to meet Moses. God's **glory. . . . covered the mountain** and there after **six days** God communed with **Moses from within the cloud.** To the people below, God's **glory . . . looked like a consuming fire** (cf. 19:18). While there **40 days** Moses ate and drank nothing (cf. Deut. 9:9).

*b. The instructions for the tabernacle (chaps. 25–27)*

The tabernacle was important to Israel's national life; it symbolized God's dwelling among His people (25:8; 29:45) and was the place where He would meet with the leaders (29:42) and the people (29:43). God's glory was manifest in the tabernacle (40:35). Also it was the newly established theocracy's visible center for the worship of God. The tabernacle prefigured Christ, who is said to have "tabernacled" (John 1:14) or dwelt among His people.

The tabernacle (Ex. 25:9) was referred to by several names: sanctuary, meaning a sacred place (25:8); tent (26:7, 11-14, 36), because of its tentlike structure; Tent of Meeting (27:21), signifying its structure and purpose; and tabernacle of the Testimony (38:21; cf. Acts 7:44) and Tent of the Testimony (Num. 9:15), meaning the place where the two tablets of the Law (the "Testimony"; cf. Ex. 31:18 and see comments on 16:34) were kept (i.e., in the ark, in the most holy place; cf. 25:16, 21). See the sketch "Plan of the Tabernacle." Some Bible scholars think that the tabernacle was V-shaped like a tent with a ridge pole and sloping roof. However, the Scriptures make no mention of a ridge pole. Also the gabled roof would increase the measurement of the roof beyond the width of 15 feet so that the curtains over the roof and sides would not adequately cover the gold-covered boards. Therefore the traditional flat-roofed view of the tabernacle seems preferable.

(1) The gathering of materials. 25:1-9. The LORD described to **Moses** the materials to be assembled for building the **tabernacle.** The Israelites were to bring a voluntary **offering . . . from each** person **whose heart** prompted **him to give.**

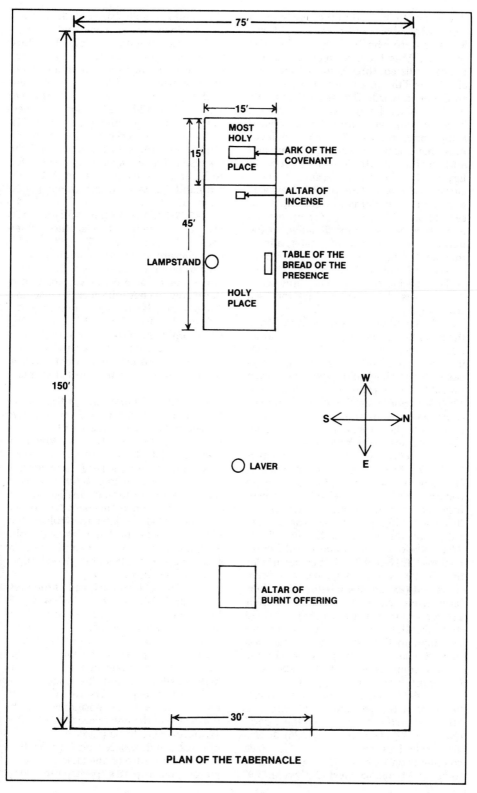

**PLAN OF THE TABERNACLE**

The metals to be used in the construction were **gold, silver, and bronze.** Gold was listed first probably because it is the most precious. After the three metals four materials are listed: three colors of **yarn** and also linen. **Fine linen** translates *šēš*, from an Egyptian word. "Egypt excelled in the production of linen, especially twined linen, where every thread was twisted from many strands. The Hebrew slaves must have learned many Egyptian arts and crafts . . . during their stay in Egypt" (R. Alan Cole, *Exodus: An Introduction and Commentary,* p. 189). Next was **goat hair, ram skins . . . and hides of sea cows.** "The sea cow (*dugong dugong*) is a herbivorous mammal native to the Red Sea and the Gulf of Aqaba, and to this day the bedouin make sandals from its skin" (Ronald F. Youngblood, *Exodus,* p. 114; see Ezek. 16:10, where the word "leather" is the same as that for "sea cow" in Ex.).

The **wood** of **acacia** trees, common in the Sinai Peninsula, is good for construction purposes. Other items to be brought included **olive oil . . . spices,** and precious **stones.** The gold, silver, and linen probably came from the Egyptians (cf. 12:35-36). Some of the other materials could have been from spoils in Israel's defeat of the Amalekites (17:8-16) or through trade with bedouins.

(2) The ark and the atonement cover (25:10-22). The previous section (vv. 1-9) closed with God's injunction to Moses to construct the tabernacle and its furnishings according to His instructions. (Chaps. 35–40 report Moses' careful execution of these plans.) Exodus 25:10–27:21; 30:1-6 give the details of those directions (cf. Heb. 9:23-24). Several articles of furniture within the tabernacle were described (Ex. 25:10-40) before the tabernacle itself (chap. 26) because of their greater importance; the tabernacle served to protect the furniture. The most important item in the tabernacle is described first. It was the only piece within the second compartment of the tabernacle (the most holy place).

**25:10-16.** The ark was called **a chest,** "the ark of the Testimony" (v. 22), and "the ark of the covenant of the LORD" (Num. 10:33; Deut. 10:8; 31:9, 26). It was also "called by the name" of God (see comments on 1 Chron. 13:6). The ark was to be a rectangular chest (2'3" wide, 3'9"

long, and 2'3" high, based on the cubit as 18") made **of acacia wood** and overlaid inside and out **with . . . gold.** The chest was to be mounted on **four** legs and was to have four **rings** for two **gold**-covered **poles** by which the **ark** would be carried. In the chest Moses was to place the two stone tablets, with the Decalogue (or **Testimony**) written on them (Ex. 25:16, 21), which he was to receive on the mountain (31:18). According to Hebrews 9:4-5 the ark also contained a jar of manna (cf. Ex. 16:33 and see comments on 2 Chron. 5:10) and Aaron's rod (see comments on Num. 17:10).

**25:17-22.** A **cover** (KJV, "mercy seat") was to be mounted over the golden chest. The chest lid (2'3" x 3'9")—with **two cherubim** (pl. of "cherub") facing **each other** on the lid—was to be made of a solid **piece** of **pure gold.** Apparently these golden **cherubim** were to resemble winged angels in God's presence (cf. 1 Sam. 4:4; Pss. 80:1; 99:1; Isa. 37:16). **Cherubim** were also woven into the curtains that covered the tabernacle itself (Ex. 26:1-6) and into the curtain between the holy place and the most holy place (26:31-33).

Of crucial importance is that **above the** atonement **cover between the two cherubim** God would **meet with** His people. There on the Day of Atonement (Lev. 16:1-20) the high priest sprinkled blood on the lid (*kappōreṯ,* "covering"). The blood then covered (*kāpar,* "to cover, make atonement for"; cf. Ex. 30:10) Israel's sin. The atonement cover symbolized for Israel what was later accomplished by Christ, who as the Lamb of God (John 1:29) made atonement for sin (Rom. 3:25; Heb. 9:11-14) by His shed blood (Eph. 1:7; 1 Peter 1:18-19).

(3) The table of the bread of the Presence. **25:23-30.** A **table,** 1'6" wide, 3' long, and 2'3" high, was to be made **of acacia wood** (like the ark, v. 10), covered **with . . . gold** and was to be carried by gold-covered **poles** in the same manner as the ark. A frame about 3" wide (**a handbreadth**) around the edge of the table would keep objects from falling off. On the table, to be positioned on the north side of the holy place (26:35; 40:22), 12 loaves were to be placed in two piles of 6 each and replaced on each Sabbath (Lev. 24:5-9). Also on the table were to be placed golden **plates** (perhaps for carry-

ing the loaves), and ladles . . . pitchers, and bowls for drink offerings. The bread was called the bread of the Presence (KJV, "showbread") because it was placed in God's presence (before Me). This table, with its 12 loaves which perhaps represented the 12 tribes of Israel, pictured the fellowship and communion of God with His people. The priests' eating of the bread (Lev. 24:9) demonstrated that spiritual fellowship supports spiritual life.

(4) The golden lampstand. 25:31-40. The lampstand (menôrâh, hence the Eng. word "menorah" for a Jewish candelabrum) was to be the most ornate piece of furniture in the tabernacle. Its decorative flowerlike cups, buds, and blossoms were formed from one solid piece of gold (vv. 31, 36). On each side of an upright shaft were three branches extended upward (v. 32). Each branch had three . . . almond flower-shaped cups (v. 33), and the center shaft had four such cups (v. 34). At the top of the center shaft and each of the six branches was a lamp (v. 37). The seven lamps in the lampstand provided light in the tent (v. 37).

The lampstand, which was to burn continually, was serviced by the priests in the morning and at sunset (27:20-21; Lev. 24:3-4). The amount of gold required for this piece of furniture and its accessories—wick trimmers and trays (perhaps for oil)—was a talent, which was about 75 pounds (cf. NIV marg.). As the lampstand provided light for the priestly functions before God, so Christ today is the Light of the world (John 8:12), who reveals the way to God (John 14:6, 9).

(5) The curtains for the tabernacle (26:1-14). 26:1-6. Chapter 26 focuses on the tabernacle that protected the three pieces of furniture (and also the altar of incense described in 30:1-10). The portable building was 15' by 45' (see the sketch "Plan of the Tabernacle") with a wooden framework at the sides, top, and back. Over the top and back of the structure were placed 10 curtains which served as a large tent. The tabernacle with its overarching tent was surrounded by a large courtyard (27:9-19).

The 10 curtains were made of linen and brilliantly colored (blue, purple, and scarlet) yarn (cf. 25:4), and were embroidered with cherubim (cf. comments on 25:18). The curtains were each 6' wide and 42' long.

When the long edges of 5 of the curtains were joined together the newly formed curtain measured 30' by 42'. With the next set of 5 curtains, the 10 together (fastened by 50 gold clasps on the edge of each of the adjoining two sets) measured 60' by 42'.

The 60' width (10 curtains each 6' wide), then enabled the curtains to cover the top of the tabernacle (45' long) and the back (15' high). The 42' (the length of each curtain) extended over the top of the tabernacle (15' wide) and down each side (15' high) to within 18" (one cubit) of the ground.

26:7-13. Over the colorful curtains that hung within the tabernacle (vv. 1-6), forming its walls, ceiling, and back with an exquisite tapestry, hung another set of curtains. These 11 curtains were made of goat hair, a black weather-resistant material still used today by bedouins in tent-making. They were longer than the inner curtains (45' rather than 42'), so that they touched the ground on the tabernacle sides (v. 13). This hid from view the brilliant colors of the inner curtains and the costly pieces of furniture in the tabernacle.

26:14. Five of the goat-hair curtains were to be joined together like the inner curtains, and the other six goat-hair curtains in the same way. When the two sets were joined together (by bronze clasps, v. 11) the length was 66'. This covered the length of the tabernacle (45') and the back (15' high). Of the remaining 6', three were folded over at the front (v. 9) and three were at the back (v. 12). Over the goat-hair curtains were placed two other curtains: ram skins dyed red and the hides of sea cows (see comments on 25:5). No dimensions are given for these coverings. They were probably placed over the goat-hair curtains; this is still the custom of some bedouins today.

(6) The frame for the tabernacle. 26:15-30. Apparently the "walls" of the tabernacle were not solid but consisted of wooden upright frames forming a trellised construction over which the curtains were draped. If the walls had been solid the colorful curtains could not have been seen from inside the tabernacle. Each frame was 15' high, suggesting the height of the tabernacle, and 2' 3" wide.

The width of each frame apparently extended outward from the inside of the tabernacle. Josephus wrote that the frames were 3" thick (*The Antiquities of the Jews* 3. 6. 3). If so, then the upright frames were about 2' apart.

The **two projections** on each frame were like tenons that fit into the **silver bases** or mortices. Forty-eight frames were used altogether, **20 . . . for the south side . . . 20** for **the north side. . . . 6** for the **west** (back) side, and an extra one at each corner for additional strength. The frames were also secured by a series of 15 **crossbars** (**5 on each of** the two sides and 5 at the back) that fit through **gold rings** horizontally (vv. 26-30). These bars were to be overlaid **with gold.** The center bar on each side was to extend the full length; apparently the other bars were shorter.

(7) The inner and outer curtains (26:31-37). Two curtains were to be made: one that separated the holy place from the most holy place (vv. 31-35) and one at the entrance into the tabernacle (vv. 36-37).

**26:31-35.** The inner **curtain** was to be made of brilliantly colored **yarn** and **linen,** like the 10 curtains over the tabernacle, with rich embroidery of **cherubim.** Hung on **gold hooks on four posts (overlaid with gold** and in **silver bases**; cf. vv. 18-21), **the curtain** divided the tabernacle into two sections. In the inner court, **the most holy place,** was placed **the ark** and its **cover** (cf. 25:10-22). In the outer section, **the holy place,** was **the table** (i.e., of the bread of the Presence; cf. 25:23-30) and **the lampstand** (cf. 25:31-39). Also in the holy place, though not mentioned till later (30:1-10) was the altar of incense.

**26:36-37.** The **curtain** at the tent's **entrance** was to be of the same materials as the inner curtain, but apparently without the cherubim embroidery. Also the **bases** for the golden posts were to be **bronze,** not silver (cf. v. 32), because this curtain would be part of the exterior that had bronze throughout. This curtain was supported by **five posts,** not four as with the inner curtain (cf. v. 32). With more posts in the 15' opening, the spaces for entering the tabernacle itself were narrower than the spaces between the four posts at the entrance into the most holy place.

(8) The altar of burnt offering. **27:1-8.**

In giving instructions about the tabernacle God progressed from within (the ark and the atonement cover) outward to the courtyard outside the tabernacle.

In the courtyard was **an altar** called "the altar of burnt offering" (30:28; Lev. 4:7, 10, 18) and "the bronze altar" (Ex. 38:30). Unlike the altar of incense (30:1-10), this was an altar for animal sacrifices. It was to be made **of acacia wood,** was 7½' **square** and 4½' **high,** with **a horn** (a projection that looked like an animal horn) **at each of the four corners,** overlaid **with bronze.** The **utensils** with it were to be **of bronze** also (27:3). The horns were to be covered with blood at the consecration of the priests (29:1, 10-12; Lev. 8:14-15; 9:9) and on the Day of Atonement (Lev. 16:18).

The **grating,** or **bronze network,** placed on a **ledge** within and **halfway up the altar** (a little more than 2' up) helped reinforce the altar and may have been the place where the animal meat was cooked. **Poles** were also to be overlaid **with bronze** and **inserted into** bronze **rings** at the altar's corners for use in carrying **the altar.** The bottom half of the **altar** was to be **hollow** but it may later have been filled with small stones, not with earth as some suggest, with the fire being built on the rocks. The exact location of this **altar** is not given but it was "at [just inside] the entrance to the tabernacle" (40:29). The basin was between it and the tabernacle (30:18). This **altar** illustrates the fact that one can approach God only through sacrifice; only by sacrifice is sin atoned for. On this altar—the first object a worshiper saw in the tabernacle courtyard—sacrifices for sin were continually being made. The ultimate Sacrifice was Jesus Christ (Heb. 10:1-18).

(9) The courtyard. **27:9-19. The tabernacle** complex was rectangular in shape (75' x 150', vv. 9, 13, 18) with an outer wall made of **linen** curtains supported by or hung on **20 posts on the south side. . . . 20 on the north,** and **10 on the west end,** all set in **bronze bases** and having **silver hooks** (for hanging the **curtains**) set in **bands** (vv. 10-11, 17). The posts were about 7½' apart, and the curtains were kept tight by bronze **tent pegs** (v. 19).

The **east** entrance was 30' wide because the **curtains** at each side of the entrance extended 22½' (75' − 22½' −

22½' = 30). **Three posts** helped support the curtains on each side of the entrance. Those posts were about 7½' apart.

Like the curtains at the entrance to the holy place (26:36) and to the most holy place (26:31-33) the curtain at the courtyard **entrance** was also to be made of colorful **yarn** and fine **linen**. The curtain to the holy place was to be hung on five posts (26:36-37) but this curtain was to be hung on **four** posts (27:16). The height of the surrounding curtain wall was 7½' (27:18). This was high enough to prevent casual onlookers from peeping in; yet it was only half the height of the tabernacle itself so that the tabernacle could be seen.

(10) The oil for the lampstand. **27:20-21.** To supply **light** in the tabernacle the lampstand with its seven **lamps** (cf. 25:31-39) required a continual provision of olive **oil.** The Israelites were to provide this oil so that the priests could **keep the lamps burning** continuously as **a lasting ordinance** (cf. comments on 12:14). As already stated, **the Testimony** refers to the Ten Commandments on stone kept in the ark of the covenant. The lampstand, being in the holy place, was therefore **in front of** the ark, though a curtain separated the two compartments of the tabernacle.

*c. The instructions concerning the priesthood (chaps. 28–29)*

Having described the tabernacle and its furniture, the Lord then instructed Moses concerning the priesthood that was to preside over the nation's religious life. The priests were to minister in the tabernacle complex in a variety of ways: burn incense on the golden altar twice daily, maintain the lampstand and the table of the bread of the Presence, maintain and offer sacrifices on the altar of burnt offering, and bless the people. In addition they presided over civil cases (e.g., Num. 5:5-31; Deut. 19:17; 21:5), instructed the people in the Law (Deut. 17:9, 11; 33:8, 10), and gave encouragement in times of war (Deut. 20:2-4).

(1) The garments for the priesthood (chap. 28). **28:1.** The **priests** who were to officiate in the ministry of the tabernacle were **Aaron** and **his four sons.** Later **Nadab** and **Abihu** died under God's judgment (Lev. 10:1-2) so that the Aaronic priesthood continued through his two younger sons: **Eleazar** who succeeded his father as high priest (Num. 3:4) **and Ithamar.**

**28:2-5.** The **garments for** the high **priest** were set apart from common clothing to elevate the office (**to give him dignity and honor;** cf. v. 40) and to serve as a constant reminder of God's holiness. The garments, to be worn only when the priests served in the tabernacle (35:19), were to be made by fine craftsmen (28:3) and of the same materials (**yarn and fine linen**) as the curtains of the tabernacle (cf. vv. 6, 8, 15, 33, 39, 42) along with **gold** (v. 5; cf. vv. 6, 8, 22, 24, 26-27, 36) and precious stones (vv. 17-20). The six pieces of the priest's attire, listed in verse 4, are detailed in the remainder of the chapter.

**28:6-14.** The **ephod** was probably a sleeveless outer garment that covered the priest's upper body. Apparently it had **two** parts, a front and a back, that were **fastened** on **two shoulder pieces** with straps (**braided chains**) of **gold** with mounted **onyx stones** (v. 9) and held to the body with a belt at the waist (v. 8). On **the two** onyx **stones** were to be engraved **the names of** Israel's 12 tribes (6 . . . on each stone, v. 10) so that as **Aaron** entered the tabernacle he would **bear** Israel's **names . . . before** God (v. 12).

**28:15-21.** The high priest's **breastpiece** was to be made of the same cloth as **the ephod** (cf. v. 6). It was to be 9" (**a span,** which was half a cubit) **square** with 12 **precious stones in gold . . . settings** mounted in **four rows** of 3 stones each. On each stone was to be **engraved** the name of one of the tribes **of Israel,** probably in the same sequence as the names on the engraved onyx stones (vv. 9-10).

**28:22-28.** The breastpiece was attached snugly over the ephod by four gold **chains. Two** of the chains were slipped through **gold rings** at the upper corners **of the breastpiece** and attached to the ephod's **shoulder pieces.** The **other** two gold chains were slipped through **gold rings** at the lower **corners** of the breastpiece and attached to the side seams of **the ephod** and tied . . . **with a blue cord . . . to the waistband.**

**28:29-30.** The breastpiece (**over his [Aaron's] heart** occurs three times in these verses) was to serve **as a continuing memorial before the Lord.** Another purpose is indicated in **the Urim and the Thummim,** which were **the means** by which the priests made **decisions for the Israelites** (cf. v. 15). The breastpiece was "folded double" (v. 16) to form a kind of pocket for the Urim and Thummim.

The "Urim" and "Thummim," which mean "lights" and "perfections," are referred to in Numbers 27:21; 1 Samuel 30:7-8 (the "ephod" suggests the Urim and Thummim); Ezra 2:63; Nehemiah 7:65. They were means of seeking from God through the priest answers to questions and crises beyond human perception.

Apparently the Urim and Thummim were two stones. How they were used in determining God's will is unknown, but some suggest the Urim represented a negative answer and the Thummim a positive answer. Perhaps this view is indicated by the fact that Urim (*'ûrîm*) begins with the first letter of the Hebrew alphabet, and Thummim (*tūmmîm*) with the last letter. Others suggest that the objects simply symbolized the high priest's authority to inquire of God, or the assurance that the priest would receive enlightenment ("lights") and perfect knowledge ("perfections") from God.

**28:31-35.** Under **the ephod** the high priest was to wear a **blue** sleeveless **robe** that hung below his knees and was reinforced at the **collar.** It was to be seamless with **pomegranates** (either hanging like bells on the hem or embroidered on the robe) and **gold bells** on **the hem.** The tinkling bells would allow the people to hear the high priest when he ministered in **the holy place. The sound of the bells** assured the people of God's mercy in allowing a priest to minister on their behalf. Only a priest properly attired could enter the holy place. Disregarding these instructions would result in death (cf. v. 13).

**28:36-38. The turban** of the priest was to be made of linen (v. 39). The most obvious feature of the turban was **a plate of pure gold** engraved with the words HOLY TO THE LORD. This expression of Israel's need for purity before God was attached to the **front of the turban** (and over **Aaron's forehead**) with **a blue cord.** This engraving was a "sacred diadem" (29:6; 39:30; Lev. 8:9). As representative of the people, he bore their **guilt** when

presenting their **gifts. . . . to the LORD.**

**28:39-42. The tunic of fine linen** was a long white coat worn beneath the robe of the ephod (Lev. 8:7). (On **the turban,** also made **of fine linen,** see comments on Ex. 28:36-37.) **The sash** was a wide belt worn around the waist of the priest, which hung down at the ends. Even these items would add **dignity and honor** (cf. v. 2) to the **priests** and thus help increase the people's appreciation for them and for God. When they were fully attired they were to be consecrated (cf. chap. 29).

**28:43.** Because God is holy, the priests were to approach Him with dignity and care. Otherwise they would **incur guilt and die** (cf. v. 35). **Aaron and his sons** were to dress appropriately when they entered the tabernacle (**the Tent of Meeting**) or approached **the altar** (presumably the altar of incense) to serve before the Lord.

(2) The consecration of the priesthood (chap. 29). Verses 1-37 of this chapter, repeated in Leviticus 8, include God's instructions to Moses for his installing the priests for service.

**29:1-9.** God told Moses to **take a young bull . . . two rams. . . . bread . . . cakes and wafers** and to enter the tabernacle courtyard and there meet **Aaron and his** four sons. After the priests' ceremonial washings (v. 4), Moses was to put the high-priestly **garments** (described in chap. 28) on **Aaron.** Also Aaron was to be anointed with **oil . . . on his head** (cf. 30:22-33), symbolizing his appointment by God for special service. The **sons** of Aaron were not to be anointed with oil but were to be dressed in priestly garb, which included **tunics . . . headbands,** and **sashes** (cf. 28:40).

**29:10-14.** After Aaron and his sons would be consecrated a variety of sacrifices were made, using the items Moses was commanded to assemble (vv. 1-2). Each of the three animal sacrifices was handled differently. First a **bull** (v. 10) was sacrificed as **a sin offering** (v. 14). Placing one's **hands on** the animals' heads (v. 10; cf. vv. 15, 19) signified identification. The priests identified with the animals who died in their places. In this way the priests acknowledged their own sinfulness and need of blood cleansing (cf. Lev. 17:11; Heb. 9:22).

**Some of the . . . blood** was placed

on the horns of the altar of burnt offering and some was poured at its base. The bull's internal organs were to be burned on the altar and the rest of the animal was to be burned outside the camp.

29:15-21. The second sacrifice, that of one of the two rams, was to be a burnt offering (v. 18). Unlike sacrifices that were consumed by the worshiper and the priests, the burnt offering was to be entirely consumed on the altar. The ram's blood was sprinkled on all sides of the altar and the ram was to be cut in pieces and washed.

The third animal to be sacrificed was the other ram. Its blood was placed on the right ears, right thumbs, and right big toes of Aaron and his sons, signifying that they were cleansed and dedicated to God. Blood on the ear may have symbolized dedication to the hearing of God's Word, blood on the thumb may have pictured holiness in doing God's work, and blood on the toe may have spoken of walking carefully in the service of God. The rest of the blood of the second ram was sprinkled on the altar . . . sides and on the priests and their garments with anointing oil.

29:22-28. Some of the second ram's organs, a loaf of bread, a cake, and a wafer were to be given to Aaron and his sons . . . as a wave offering to the LORD. The wave offering was waved, not from right to left, but back and forth toward the altar and the priest, symbolizing that the offering was being given to God. Then those items were burned on the altar. The breast of the ram was to be a wave offering eaten by Aaron and his sons (v. 26). When someone brought a fellowship offering, the animal's breast and thigh were always to be eaten by the priests. In this way the Israelites contributed to the work of the LORD.

29:29-30. First, at a seven-day consecration service Aaron's high-priestly garments were to be given to the son who would succeed him and passed on to succeeding generations. Only the high priest was to be given such an elaborate ceremony.

29:31-34. Second, instructions for eating parts of the ram for the ordination (the second ram; cf. v. 22) at the entrance to the tabernacle were repeated. The ram and the bread in this case were a communal meal that was of such a sacred nature

that any leftovers were to be burned.

29:35-37. Third, the consecration service for the priests was seven days with a bull offered each day as a sin offering. (Nothing is said about repeating the offering of the rams.) For seven days . . . the altar was to be atoned and consecrated for holy service by means of sacrifices.

29:38-41. Fourth, brief reference is made not to the priests' installation service but to the daily burnt offerings in the tabernacle service. Two lambs were to be sacrificed (one in the morning and one in the evening) accompanied each time by a grain offering (flour and oil) and a drink offering (wine). Thus the daily offerings contained basic parts of the people's daily diet: meat, flour, oil, and wine. These daily offerings (as well as the dedicatory sacrifice of the two rams, vv. 18, 25) were pleasing . . . to the LORD. Similarly Christ's sacrifice of Himself on the cross was "a fragrant offering and sacrifice to God" (Eph. 5:2).

29:42-46. Fifth, the passage ends with a statement about the importance of the daily burnt offerings in Israel's daily life. It was there that God promised to meet with His people. Fellowship with God is on the basis of blood shed for sins. When the priests were consecrated and serving the LORD then God would dwell with them and they would know that He is the LORD their God. God's condescending to dwell in a tent speaks of the depth of His concern for His people.

d. The instructions concerning the tabernacle service (chaps. 30–31)

(1) The altar of incense. 30:1-10. Perhaps this piece of tabernacle furniture is described here and not in chapter 25 because of the altar of incense's association (30:1-6) with the rituals to be performed on it (vv. 7-10). The basic material for this altar was the same as the other furniture inside the tabernacle: acacia wood overlaid with gold. It was comparatively small (1½' square and 3' high). Like the altar of burnt offering (27:1-2) it had horns. And like the altar of burnt offering, the table of the bread of the Presence, and the ark of the covenant, it had poles in gold rings, for carrying it.

The altar was placed in front of the curtain leading to the most holy place, in which was positioned the ark of the Testimony (cf. comments on 25:22). In Hebrews 9:3-4 the altar of incense is considered part of the most holy place. Apparently this was because on the Day of Atonement the high priest took incense from this altar into the most holy place (Lev. 16:12-13).

Aaron was instructed to burn . . . incense on this altar twice daily when he attended to the lamps on the lampstand. The ingredients in the incense are described in Exodus 30:34-38. Incense may be symbolic of prayer (Ps. 141:2; Luke 1:10; Rev. 5:8; 8:3-4). Aaron was to make no other offering on this altar. Once a year on the Day of Atonement he was to make atonement for the altar (i.e., to cleanse and reconsecrate it) by sprinkling bull's and goat's blood on the altar's horns (Lev. 16:18-19; as well as on the atonement cover, Lev. 16:14-17).

(2) The half-shekel offering. 30:11-16. Whenever a census was taken (e.g., Num. 1) each Israelite 20 years old or more was to pay a tax to help maintain the tabernacle and services. This tax was considered a ransom (Ex. 30:12) because its payment guaranteed protection from plagues. This helped motivate each male to pay. It was also considered an atonement, a covering for sins.

When counted, each adult male, whether rich or poor (v. 15), was to pay a half shekel, one-fifth of an ounce. A "gerah" was a Babylonian weight. The shekel was silver (cf. 38:25-26 and comments there). This practice became the basis of the later temple tax (Neh. 10:32, though the amount then was reduced to one-third of a shekel) that became an annual tax in the time of Christ (Matt. 17:24).

(3) The basin. 30:17-21. The basin (KJV, "laver"), the last piece of tabernacle furniture, is described here because of the emphasis on its use rather than on its construction. It was to be of bronze, not silver or gold, because it belonged in the sanctuary courtyard between the bronze altar of burnt offering and the entrance to the tent (cf. 40:30). When officiating in the tent or before the altar the priests were required to wash their hands and feet. If they failed to do so they would die. This too was to be a lasting ordinance (see comments on 12:14).

The laver symbolized the need for purity through cleansing from defilement. Thus while there was ritual cleansing at the altar, the priests also needed cleansing from actual defilement. The altar speaks of salvation through a sin offering; the basin speaks of sanctification which is progressive and continual.

(4) The anointing of oil. 30:22-33. Here God instructed Moses in the making of oil (vv. 22-25) for anointing the tabernacle, its furnishings (vv. 26-29), and the priests (v. 30). Its formula was as unique as the product was holy: about 12½ pounds of myrrh, 6¼ pounds of . . . cinnamon, 6¼ pounds of cane, 12½ pounds of cassia (from the fragrant bark of a tree), and about four quarts of olive oil. When mixed, these would make a fragrant blend. The use of oil in consecrating the priests was mentioned in 29:7. Because of its sacred nature this special oil was not to be used for any purpose other than those stated in 30:26-30.

(5) The incense. 30:34-38. Special incense was to be prepared by mixing equal amounts of three spices (their exact identity is unknown) and frankincense (a clear resin from the frankincense tree). Salt was to be added to the mixture to give forth a white smoke, and to add to the fragrance. Salt, in fact, was to be added to all the offerings (Lev. 2:13). The incense was to be placed in front of the Testimony (i.e., the ark), which probably means that it was to be burned on the altar of incense (Ex. 30:1-10) which was in front of the curtain to the most holy place. This incense, like the anointing oil, was exclusively for tabernacle use (cf. vv. 32-33).

(6) The appointment of craftsmen. 31:1-11. Having given Moses the directions for constructing the sanctuary as well as instructions for its service (chaps. 25–30), the LORD now appointed the artisans who were to do the construction work. Bezalel was appointed by God to have general oversight of the project and Oholiab (31:6) was to be his assistant. One was of the tribe of Judah, and the other of the tribe of Dan. Both were skilled craftsmen (vv. 3, 6) by divine gift, which was true of all the craftsmen appointed to the project. Bezalel had numerous abilities; he could work well with precious metals and also do masonry and woodwork.

In verses 7-9 the articles to be made by the craftsmen are listed. In verse 10 woven garments, not mentioned before, are included with the other **sacred garments.** Some think that these woven garments were undergarments for winter. The craftsmen were also to **make** the **oil** (30:22-33) and **incense** (30:34-38).

(7) The remembrance of the Sabbath. **31:12-18.** In the midst of His instructions on the work to be performed, God reminded **Moses** that obedience is also a religious duty. **The Sabbath** was the **sign** (vv. 13, 17) of the covenant that made Israel a theocracy. It was a test of the nation's commitment to God; failure to keep it a **holy** day would result in **death** (i.e., separation from the community which would probably result in death). This command, as stated in the Decalogue (20:8), was based on God's resting after His work of Creation in six days (31:17). Because the nation was in a **covenant** relationship with Him, the people were to do as He had done. **The Sabbath** marked Israel out as God's people. Observing the Sabbath showed that the Israelites were set apart (i.e., holy) to God.

Now God's instructions **to Moses** given **on Mount Sinai** (24:12) concerning the tabernacle and its priestly ministry were complete. The Decalogue (the Ten Commandments; also called **the Testimony** because they testify of God's standards), were somehow inscribed by God on **two . . . tablets of stone.** God's **finger** (cf. 8:19; Deut. 9:10; Ps. 8:3; Luke 11:20) may suggest that this was God's doing. According to Moses' account in Deuteronomy 9:12-16 the Lord informed him that the people had become "corrupt" and "stiff-necked," by casting an idol in the shape of a calf. Within 40 days they broke their commitment to keep what **God** had already commanded (Ex. 20:4).

## B. The failure and restoration of God's people (chaps. 32–34)

### 1. THE BREAKING OF THE COVENANT BY ISRAEL (32:1–33:6)

#### a. The idolatry of the people (32:1-6)

**32:1.** While **Moses** was experiencing spiritual triumph **the people** of God plummeted to a low point spiritually. God had repeatedly manifested His power and compassion, but they were soon forgotten. Repeatedly in the Book of Exodus the Israelites reacted with insensitivity and rebellion to God's marvelous displays of His goodness.

The people became fearful because of Moses' delay (he was on **the mountain** 40 days, 24:18) so they went to **Aaron,** their temporary leader (24:14). Assuming that Moses would not return to guide and comfort them (**We don't know what has happened to him**), they asked for a substitute or surrogate **who will go before us.** In suggesting that Aaron **make** them **gods** they were not asking for gods to replace Yahweh but for a visible, tangible object to follow.

**32:2-4.** Granting their request, **Aaron** suggested **the people** give him their **gold earrings** (probably acquired from the Egyptians on the day of Exodus, 12:35-36), which he then melted **into an idol cast in the shape of a calf.** Some commentators have suggested that this represented the Egyptian bull-god Apis, but this seems unlikely because Apis was not worshiped as an image. Even so, the bull symbolized fertility and sexual strength. This explicitly violated the second commandment (20:4-6; cf. 20:23), which the people had already received from God verbally through Moses.

Perhaps the people considered the calf-idol an image of God. Since only one idol was made, the word **gods** (32:1, 4, 8, 23, 31) may refer both to the idol *and* to God whom it supposedly represented. It seems unlikely that **Aaron** would attribute the Exodus to anyone but the true God.

**32:5-6.** **Aaron** then made **an altar,** and the next day in **a festival to the LORD. . . . the people** offered **burnt offerings and . . . fellowship offerings.** But then their activities led to **revelry** (cf. 1 Cor. 10:7; ṣāḥaq suggests immorality). This violated the seventh commandment (Ex. 20:14). Singing and dancing were included (32:18-19) and they were "running wild" (v. 25). Immorality often accompanies idolatry (Rom. 1:22-24). Yet they supposed they were worshiping the true God!

#### b. The intercession of Moses (32:7-14)

**32:7-10.** While **Moses** was on the mountain, God told him the **people** had **become corrupt** (v. 7) and **stiff-necked** (v. 9), that is, stubborn and unresponsive (cf. 33:3, 5; 34:9; Deut. 9:6, 13; 10:16; 31:27). In His **anger** God refused to claim the people as His own or even to claim that He delivered them from Egypt (*your* people, whom *you* brought up out of Egypt, Ex. 32:7; cf. *these* people, v. 9). After telling **Moses** what they had done (v. 8), God said that He would punish their rebellion by destroying them and that He would build a new nation beginning with Moses (**I will make you into a great nation,** v. 10).

**32:11-14.** **Moses** reversed God's reference to Israel as his people (v. 7) and called them *Your* people (cf. 33:13). Then Moses pleaded for mercy on two bases: his testimony to **the Egyptians** (32:12) and God's promises to the patriarchs (v. 13). Such a destruction would vindicate Pharaoh and the gods of **Egypt** and would cause the Egyptians to mock the true God. Further, God would be viewed as One who breaks promises. He said He would make the descendants of **Abraham, Isaac, and Israel** (Jacob) innumerable (Gen. 15:5; 22:17a; 26:4a; 28:14; 32:13) and would take them into the Promised **Land** (Gen. 15:18-21; 22:17b; 26:4b; 28:13; 32:13). Moses recognized that the people had sinned so he did not seek to justify their actions. As a result God **relented** of His threatened course of judgment. The word "relented" does not mean that God changed His mind but that He embarked on another course of action. The Hebrew word *nāḥam* suggests relief or comfort from a planned, undesirable course of action. God is not inflexible; He responds to individuals' needs, attitudes, and actions.

*c. The anger of Moses (32:15-29)*

**32:15-18.** As **Moses** descended **the mountain with the two tablets of the** Decalogue (cf. 31:18) he rejoined **Joshua,** who apparently was partway up the mountain (cf. comments on 24:13) and was not aware of what the Israelites were doing. Joshua thought that **the camp** was under military attack. However, **Moses** knew from what God told him that the people were **singing** and were involved in drunkenness and immorality.

**32:19-20.** In **anger** Moses at the foot of the mountain did four things. First, he smashed **the tablets** of the Law, symbolizing the people's **breaking** of the covenant. Second, he **burned** the idol, reduced **it to powder,** spread it on **water** (a mountain stream, Deut. 9:21), and **made the** people **drink it.** By this action he demonstrated both the powerlessness of

the calf-idol and God's wrath. Though the burning would not have demolished the gold idol, it was smashed till it was crushed into tiny **pieces.** Drinking it symbolized that the people had to bear the consequences of their sin.

**32:21-24.** Third, Moses summoned **Aaron** to give an account of what had taken place. Aaron's excuse was as ludicrous as the people's actions. He blamed the **people** (vv. 22-23) and then in a lie he suggested that the idol "just happened": **I threw it into the fire, and out came this calf. Aaron,** however, had actually shaped the idol himself (v. 4). God was so angry with Aaron that He was ready to kill him (Deut. 9:20).

**32:25-29.** Fourth, **Moses** judged the unrepentant. Moses rallied before the camp all who had not been involved in worshiping the calf. **The Levites** responded as a group. These were commanded to **go . . . through the camp** and kill any who persisted in idolatry. **Three thousand** Israelites were killed by swords. Others, however, died by a plague (v. 35). After completing this gruesome task the Levites were **set apart to the LORD.** Later they were assigned the responsibility of carrying the tabernacle (Num. 1:50-53).

*d. The renewal of intercession by Moses (32:30-35)*

**32:30-35.** Though the major instigators of the plot were put to the sword (except for Aaron, for whom Moses interceded, Deut. 9:20) **Moses** recognized that the nation as a whole shared the guilt. Therefore he again entreated **the LORD** for **atonement for** their **sin. Moses** told God that if He refused to **forgive** His people he would prefer to have his name removed from **the book** God had **written** (Ex. 32:32). Some say this was the book of life (Rev. 20:15; 21:27) that lists believers' names but, more likely, it was the census of the people. Moses' statement probably indicated he was willing to die a premature death (but not suffer eternal torment in hell). He did not want to be associated with a sinful, unforgiven people. Rejecting Moses' offer, God promised to **punish** the sinners (by premature death). Some died of **a plague** (Ex. 32:35) and all fighting men (except Joshua and Caleb) died later in the desert (Deut. 1:35-36; 2:14). Yet God said Moses would lead the nation (the younger generation) to the land promised them (Ex. 32:34). (On God's **angel** see 33:2.)

### e. The humiliation of the people (33:1-6)

**33:1-6.** God then told **Moses** that he **and the people** should go on toward the Promised **Land.** This was in response to Moses' prayer (32:13). By **an angel** (cf. 32:34 and comments on 23:23) God would defeat their enemies (see comments on those groups in 3:8) and they would proceed **to the land flowing with milk and honey** (see comments on 3:8). The people were distressed that God had said, **I will not go with you.** They were promised His protection and guidance by an angel, but not His personal presence. Otherwise, God said, He would be inclined to **destroy** them. However, based on Moses' prayer in 33:12-16, God did agree to go with them (v. 17). In remorse **the people** did not wear their **ornaments** (rings, necklaces, bracelets, anklets, etc.).

### 2. THE RENEWAL OF THE COVENANT BY GOD (33:7–34:35)

### a. The privileged position of Moses (33:7-23)

In contrast with the strained relationship between Israel and the Lord, Moses experienced intimacy with Him. These verses evidence that unique relationship in two connected sections.

**33:7-11.** Moses was intimate with God in the **tent** he erected **outside the camp.** There people could go to inquire **of the LORD,** apparently for spiritual guidance. This tent, though it was not the tabernacle, was also called **the tent of meeting.** When **Moses** entered **the tent, the pillar of cloud** (cf. 13:21) hovered at its **entrance.** The size and contents of this tent are not known, but it reminded **the people** that their sin was an alienating force in their relationship with God. They could worship God but from a distance (33:10); He was outside their community.

God **would speak to Moses face to face, as a man speaks with his friend** (v. 11), that is, clearly and openly. Moses' speaking "face to face" with God does not contradict the fact that he was not allowed to see God's face (v. 20) as "face to face" is a figurative expression suggesting openness and friendship (cf. Num. 12:8; Deut. 34:10; and comments on John 1:18). **Joshua** stayed in **the tent,** perhaps to care for it in some way when **Moses would return to the camp.**

**33:12-23.** Moses also evidenced an intimate fellowship with God through His spiritual concerns. These verses may be divided into three sections each introduced by the words **Moses said** (vv. 12, 15, 18). Moses first wanted to know the Lord's intentions for His people. God had told Moses to **lead** the **people,** but without God's presence **Moses** was concerned. God knew Moses **by name,** that is, Moses belonged to God. So Moses wanted to continue to learn God's **ways** and enjoy God's grace (**favor**). Moses interceded on behalf of the **nation** by reminding God that they were His **people** (cf. vv. 13, 16; 32:11). In response the Lord reversed His threat not to **go with** them (cf. 33:3, 5) and to **give** them **rest** (v. 14).

Moses' second request was for confirmation that the Lord would indeed go with His **people** (vv. 15-17). Absence of God's **presence** with them in their journey to the Promised Land would pose serious problems for their and God's reputations. So again God agreed to Moses' request, assuring Moses that He was **pleased with** him (v. 17; cf. v. 16).

Third, **Moses** asked to see the **glory** of God (v. 18). This request was fulfilled as God allowed Moses to have a deeper vision of His **glory** (33:19-23). Proclaiming God's **name** (v. 19, His revealed character) to Moses, God allowed him to see His **goodness** (v. 19) and His **back,** but not His **face** (cf. 3:6 and see comments on 33:11; John 1:18). This passage demonstrates that while people truly can know God, they can never know Him exhaustively.

### b. The renewal of the covenant (chap. 34)

The Lord gave Moses new stone tablets of the Decalogue, declared His glory to Moses as the inaugurator of the Mosaic Covenant, and enumerated the demands that stem from the covenant relationship. Other covenant renewals are recorded in Deuteronomy 5:2-3; 29:1; Joshua 24:25; 2 Kings 23:21-27.

(1) The second tablets of stone. **34:1-4.** The tangible token of God's unique relationship with Israel was **the two stone tablets** with the Ten Commandments, which **Moses** had broken (32:19). Once again **Moses** was to ascend **Mount**

**Sinai,** taking with him two tablets **chiseled . . . like the first ones.** As before, he was to go alone. This obviously indicates that God was about to renew His covenant with Israel.

(2) The revelation of God to Moses. **34:5-9.** On the mountain **Moses** experienced a new vision of the glory of God as Testator of the covenant. In fulfillment of His promise (33:19), God revealed **His name** (His character) to Moses. God told Moses that His name Yahweh (**the LORD**) means that He is a God of compassion, grace, loyalty (*ḥesed*, **love,** twice in vv. 6-7), **faithfulness** (*'ĕmet*, "reliability"), and forgiveness. This information adds to what was said earlier about His name (cf. comments on 3:13-14). Yahweh is the name that suggests God's relationship with His people. Some or all of these attributes of God are cited seven other times in the Old Testament (Num. 14:18; Neh. 9:17; Pss. 86:15; 103:8; 145:8; Joel 2:13; Jonah 4:2).

Within the display of His grand benevolence is the attribute of justice that necessitates His punishing any person who violates His righteous character (**He punishes,** Ex. 34:7). On God's punishing **children . . . to the third and fourth generation** see comments on 20:5.

In response to this disclosure of God's character **Moses . . . worshiped** Him, then pleaded for His mercy for such **a stiff-necked people,** as God had called them (32:9; 33:3, 5). Moses also asked that God again promise to **go with** them (cf. 33:3, 12, 14), thereby renewing His promise to dwell among His people and own them as His **inheritance** (cf. Deut. 4:20).

(3) The renewal of the covenant (34:10-28). **34:10-11.** These verses are a preamble or introduction to the terms of the covenant which follow in verses 12-28. God promised to renew the Mosaic Covenant and to work mightily through them, to display **wonders** (cf. "wonders" in 3:20) so that other **people** would see **how awesome** are God and His **work.** Those wonders would include His driving out the people living in Palestine (see comments on those groups in 3:8). But this Conquest was conditioned on Israel's obedience to God.

**34:12-17.** God had revealed His character (vv. 5-7) and promised His presence and power (vv. 10-11). The covenant obligation to obey, given in detail in chapters 21-23, was now (34:12-18) given in summary form. This code is essentially what was previously given in "the Book of the Covenant" (24:7) though 34:12-28 is more harsh than the first because of Israel's recent sin (chap. 32).

One of the major purposes of these regulations was to keep Israel from idolatry, an unthinkable practice in a theocracy. Israel, however, had already fallen into idolatry. To **make a treaty** (cf. 23:32) with a people implies the acceptance of **their gods,** and this was to be avoided. Strong action was to be taken against idols: **altars** were to be broken, **sacred stones** (cf. Deut. 7:5; 12:3), possibly male fertility symbols, smashed, and **Asherah poles** cut **down.** In their pagan worship Canaanites erected poles in honor of the goddess Asherah, consort of Baal (also see comments on 2 Chron. 14:3). Because Israel had fallen into idolatry (Ex. 32) the instructions here (34:12-13) were more inclusive than those in 23:24.

The Mosaic Covenant was the basis of God's theocratic rule over His people. Therefore since He alone is God He tolerates no rivals (cf. 20:3). It is in this sense that **God is jealous** (cf. 20:5).

Making **a treaty** with idolaters would lead to involvement in their sacrificial communal meals (34:15), to intermarrying their **daughters** (many of whom were spiritual and/or physical prostitutes **to their gods;** cf. Hosea 4:13-14), and even to making molten images (Ex. 34:17; cf. 20:4) as they had already done with the gold calf (32:4). Tragically Israel did not heed these warnings and they did in fact become involved in worshiping the Canaanites' and others' false **gods.** Ultimately this led to Israel being exiled.

**34:18-26.** Having described the forms of worship Israel must avoid (vv. 12-17), God reminded Israel to worship Him actively through the designated holy feasts. The three major feasts are enumerated (vv. 18, 22) with the promise that celebrating them properly would result in God's giving them the **land** of promise and keeping it safe (v. 24).

**The** seven-day **Feast of Unleavened Bread** was to be observed (cf. 12:15-20; 23:15) in **Abib** (March-April), the month of the Exodus, and **the firstborn** were to be dedicated to the Lord (34:19-20; cf. 13:12-13; 22:29-30). These two were associated because of the link between the 10th plague (death of the Egyptians' **first-born**) and the Exodus.

Before mentioning the second and third feasts (34:22), God reminded Israel of her obligation to **rest** on the Sabbath (cf. 20:8) even including Sabbaths in the busiest times of the year (**plowing season and harvest**). The harvesting season was mentioned because it led naturally to the next two annual feasts, both pertaining to harvests. **The Feast of Weeks,** also called the Feast of Harvest (23:16) and the Feast of Pentecost, was to be celebrated 50 days after the Feast of Unleavened Bread. This second feast was at the beginning **of the wheat harvest.**

**The Feast of Ingathering,** also an agriculturally related feast, was to be celebrated at harvesttime **at the turn of the year** (cf comments on 23:16). **All the men** of Israel were supposed **to appear before the . . . Lord** (34:23) for these three feasts (which later meant traveling to Jerusalem to the tabernacle or the temple). These pilgrimage feasts bound the nation together in religious worship. God promised that while the men were away from home worshiping the Lord, He would protect their **land.**

This passage includes other instructions: two additional regulations about the Feast of Unleavened Bread—the avoidance of **yeast** and the consumption of the entire **Passover** meal (34:25; cf. 23:18)—the law of **the firstfruits** (related to the Feast of Weeks), and the prohibition against cooking **a young goat in its mother's milk** (see comments on 23:19).

**34:27-28.** As with the giving of the Book of the Covenant the first time, **Moses** was to **write down** the commands (cf. 24:4). After **40 days,** the length of the first sojourn on Mount Sinai (24:18), **Moses** received **the tablets** of stone containing **the Ten Commandments,** the sign of **the covenant.** The Ten Commandments (34:28) were in addition to **these words** (v. 27). Unlike the previous 40 days, the people this time did not become infatuated with idolatry.

(4) The glory of God on Moses. **34:29-35.** In contrast with the anger and holy indignation that **Moses** evidenced when he returned with the first set of **tablets** (32:19), this time **his face** radiated with the glory of God (cf. 2 Cor. 3:7), but he was unaware of it. This made the

people **afraid** of **him,** but he encouraged them to listen as he told them the stipulations of the renewed covenant.

Apparently the people told **Moses** his face shone because he then covered it with **a veil** (*masweh,* a word used only here—in Ex. 34:33-35—in the OT; cf. 2 Cor. 3:13). But in **the Lord's presence** Moses took off **the veil** (cf. 2 Cor. 3:18).

## C. The construction of the tabernacle (chaps. 35–40)

With the covenant renewed, the construction of the tabernacle was essential. Most of the material in chapters 35–40 about the construction of the tabernacle is similar to God's instructions to Moses on the mountain (recorded in chaps. 25–31), except that most of chapters 35–40 records in the past tense Moses' and the people's carrying out God's commands. However, the order of the subject matter differs slightly in these two major sections of the book. The book concludes with the record of God's condescending to dwell in His glory among His people (40:34-38).

Comments on these last chapters of Exodus are comparatively brief because they have been discussed already. Chapters 35–40, however, are not needless repetition; they stress two important truths: (a) the faithfulness of God, who dwells among His people in spite of their failures, and (b) the obedience of Moses in carrying out God's instructions (cf. 25:9). Seven times in each of the last two chapters the words "as the Lord commanded Moses" (or "as the Lord commanded him") occur (39:1, 5, 7, 21, 26, 29, 31; 40:19, 21, 23, 25, 27, 29, 32). Moses was indeed a faithful servant (Num. 12:7; Heb. 3:5).

1. THE PREPARATION FOR THE CONSTRUCTION (35:1–36:7)

a. The reiteration of Sabbath observance (35:1-3)

**35:1-3. Moses** had **the whole Israelite community** (cf. v. 4 and comments on 12:3) assemble so he could give them the Lord's instructions. Verse 2 of chapter 35 repeats almost word for word the command in 31:15. Since the Sabbath was the sign of the covenant God made with Israel (31:16-17), its observance was crucial. Moses' words to the people about the **Sabbath** occur here at the beginning of chapters 35–40, not at the end as in God's instructions in chapters 25–31. This is because Israel had demonstrated a tendency to disobey. If the covenant were to be maintained, instructions about the sign of the covenant had to be obeyed. Also because of the people's excitement in constructing the tabernacle, it was important that worship not be neglected even in doing worshipful work. The prohibition against **a fire . . . on the Sabbath** (35:3) is a corollary to the order not to **work** (v. 2) by cooking food (cf. 16:23).

b. *The gathering of materials (35:4-29)*

**35:4-9.** As **Moses** continued his address to Israel, he urged the people to gather from their possessions the things needed for making the tabernacle (cf. 25:1-9). These materials, to be given voluntarily (whoever **is willing**; cf. 35:21, 29), were **an offering for the Lord.**

**35:10-19.** Then Moses called for workers (**all who are skilled among you**) to make the various furnishings, utensils, and priests' **garments.** The order in which these items are listed is the same as the order in which they are discussed in 36:8–39:31.

**35:20-29.** The people willingly committed themselves to the project by offering their goods and services. Whereas 25:3 referred to the need for **gold . . . silver,** and **bronze,** a point is added here (35:22) that **gold jewelry** was **brought. Women** were involved not only in bringing offerings (vv. 22, 29) but also in spinning **yarn . . . linen,** and **goat hair.**

c. *The appointment of Bezalel and Oholiab (35:30–36:1)*

**35:30–36:1.** This section is similar to 31:1-11. A new element in this description is the statement about **the ability** of **Bezalel** and **Oholiab . . . to teach others** (35:34). This passage (35:30–36:1) stresses the **skill** of the many workmen.

d. *The commencement of the work (36:2-7)*

**36:2-7.** Bezalel and Oholiab took oversight of the project with **every skilled person to whom the Lord had given ability** (v. 2; cf. v. 1) **and who was willing to . . . work.** Again (cf. 35:21, 29) the emphasis is on the willingness of the people to participate with labor and materials. In fact **the people** brought so many materials—even **more than enough**

—that they had to be **restrained.** An inventory of materials brought is included in 38:21-31.

2. THE BUILDING OF THE TABERNACLE (36:8–39:31)

a. *The construction of the tabernacle structure (36:8-38)*

**36:8-38.** The sequence of constructions differs from the order of the injunctions in chapter 26. Here the making of **the tabernacle** itself is recorded first, whereas in the earlier instructions three pieces of furniture in the tabernacle are described first (chap. 25). What is not included in 36:8-38 is the information in 26:12-13 about the hanging of the additional length of goat-hair curtains. Otherwise the accounts are nearly identical.

There were four components in **the tabernacle** structure: (a) the **linen** and **yarn. . . . curtains** that draped the sides and formed the ceiling (36:8-13; cf. 26:1-6); (b) the **curtains of goat hair . . . ram skins,** and **hides of sea cows** (36:14-19; cf. 26:7-14); (c) the wooden-trellised **frames** on the **north** and **south** sides and back end of the structure (36:20-30; cf. 26:15-25) with **crossbars** to hold the framework together (36:31-34; cf. 26:26-29); and (d) the two entrance curtains, one to divide the tabernacle's interior into two chambers and one at the entrance (36:35-38; cf. 26:31-37).

b. *The construction of the tabernacle furnishings (37:1–38:8)*

**37:1–38:8.** Six furniture items are discussed: (a) **the ark** with its atonement cover (37:1-9; cf. 25:10-22); (b) **the table of acacia wood,** that is, "the table of the bread of the Presence" (37:10-16; cf. 25:23-30; 39:36); (c) **the lampstand** (37:17-24; cf. 25:31-39); (d) **the altar of incense** (37:25-28; cf. 30:1-10), with the **anointing oil and . . . incense** used with the incense altar (37:29; cf. 30:22-28); (e) **the altar of burnt offering** (38:1-7; cf. 27:1-8); and (f) **the bronze basin** (38:8; cf. 30:17-21).

The descriptions in 37:1–38:8 add one additional fact to the previous passages; the bronze basin was made **from the mirrors** (of polished bronze, not glass) **of the women who served at the entrance to the Tent of Meeting.** Here the phrase "Tent of Meeting" probably refers to the tent that Moses erected outside the encampment after the covenant was abrogated and before it was renewed (cf. 33:7-11). Elsewhere, of course, "Tent of Meeting" refers to the tabernacle (e.g., 40:1, 12, 22, 24, 26, 29-30, 34-35).

### c. The construction of the tabernacle courtyard (38:9-20)

**38:9-20.** This section is a duplication of 27:9-19 with no additional information.

### d. The inventory of the tabernacle construction (38:21-31)

**38:21-31.** This passage has no parallel in chapters 25–31. Now that the work had begun, an inventory of **the materials** contributed was compiled **by the Levites under . . . Ithamar,** Aaron's youngest son. The statistics reveal the grandeur and expensiveness of Israel's center of worship. The materials included a little over a ton of **gold** (38:24), almost four tons of **silver** (vv. 25-28), and about two and one-half tons of **bronze** (vv. 29-31; cf. NIV marg.).

Figuring a half shekel as about one-fifth an ounce and a talent as 75 pounds the silver (**100 talents and 1,775 shekels**) totaled 603,550 half-shekels. This means each of the **603,550** males **20 years** of age and older paid exactly a half-shekel as specified for the "census offering" (30:11-16). (See the chart "Biblical Weights and Measures" before the Book of Gen.) Though the tabernacle's outer covering (of hides of sea cows) may have made **the tabernacle** look the color of a bedouin's tent, the richness of the metals signified to Israel the holiness, glory, and majesty of God who dwelt among them. His "house" suggested He was well able to provide lavishly for His own.

### e. The preparation of the priests' garments (39:1-31)

**39:1-31.** These verses correspond generally with God's instructions to Moses in chapter 28. The priestly **garments** included **the ephod** (39:1-7; cf. 28:6-14), **the breastpiece** (39:8-21; cf. 28:15-30), **the robe of the ephod** (39:22-26; cf. 28:31-35), miscellaneous **garments** (39:27-29; cf. 28:39-43), and the **engraved** headband (39:30-31; cf. 28:36-38). Since chapters 35–40 generally deal only with the tabernacle's construction and not with the functions in the sanctuary, this section (39:1-31) makes no mention of the Urim

and the Thummim (cf. 28:30). Other minor differences are that the "breastpiece for making decisions" (28:15; cf. 28:29) is simply referred to in 39:8, 15, 19, 21 as **the breastpiece.** The **plate** of **gold** that was worn as a headband by the high priest (28:36-38) is here called **the sacred diadem** (39:30-31). Also mention is made in verse 3 that the fine threads **of gold** worked into the **yarn** and **linen** of **the ephod** were **hammered out** of **thin sheets of gold.**

### 3. THE COMPLETION OF THE TABERNACLE (39:32-43)

**39:32-43.** When all the parts and **furnishings** of the central sanctuary and the **garments** were **completed** the people **brought** them **to Moses** for his inspection and blessing (v. 43). Recognizing that the craftsmen had meticulously followed the Lord's instructions, **Moses** put his approval on all their work. The order of **the tabernacle** parts and its furnishings is almost identical with that in 35:10-19 and in 36:8–39:31. **All** this was **done . . . as the LORD had commanded Moses** (39:32, 43; cf. vv. 1, 5, 7, 21, 26).

### 4. THE ASSEMBLING AT THE TABERNACLE (40:1-33)

This section has two parts that are similar in form to the relationship of chapters 25–30 and 35–39. In 40:1-16 the Lord gave Moses instructions about the arrangement of the various parts of the tabernacle and verses 17-33 record that those instructions were carried out.

**40:1-16.** These instructions deal with three matters: (a) the physical arrangement of the sanctuary from the interior to the exterior parts and the **courtyard** curtains (vv. 1-8); (b) the consecration (setting aside for holy use) of **the tabernacle and everything in it** (vv. 9-11), and (c) the washing, dressing, and anointing of the priesthood (**Aaron and his sons**) to **serve** God and the people in the sanctuary (vv. 12-16).

**The tabernacle** was erected (v. 1) about a year after the Exodus from Egypt: **on the first day of the first month** (v. 2), "in the second year" (v. 17). The Exodus occurred on the 14th day of the first month (12:2, 6, 33-34). Since the people arrived at Sinai three months after the Exodus, they were at Sinai eight and one-half months. Part of that time (at least 80 days) Moses was on the mountain (40 days, 24:18; and another 40 days for the covenant renewal, 34:28). So perhaps about six and one-half months were involved in gathering the materials and constructing the tabernacle. Those months were from about mid-September to late March.

**40:17-33.** These verses record the careful setting **up** of **the tabernacle** in response to the Lord's instructions (vv. 1-15). Verses 17-33 elaborate more on the statement made in verse 16 that **Moses** did as God commanded. Seven times in this chapter **Moses** is said to have done exactly **as the LORD commanded him** (vv. 19, 21, 23, 25-26, 29, 32). **The Testimony** (v. 20) placed **in the ark** refers to the two tablets of stone (16:34; 31:18). Of particular interest in this passage is the fact that **Moses** appears to have ministered as a priest until Aaron was installed: **Moses . . . burned . . . incense** (40:27) on the golden **altar** of incense and he **offered . . . burnt offerings and grain offerings** on **the altar of burnt offering.**

5. THE DWELLING OF GOD WITH HIS PEOPLE (40:34-38)

**40:34-38.** God's promise ("I will dwell among the Israelites and be their God," 29:45) was fulfilled as **the glory of the LORD filled the tabernacle. The cloud,** symbolic of the Lord's presence, had filled the temporary tent outside the camp only on occasions (33:7-11). Now, however, it came to fill **the tabernacle.** In fact even **Moses,** who had seen something of God's glory (33:18-23), was now unable to **enter** the tabernacle.

**The cloud** that had guided the Israelites when they set out from Succoth (13:20-22) now dwelt among them to lead them to the land of promise (40:36-39). As **the cloud lifted** the people would travel. If it stayed over the tabernacle **but** was not lifted **from above** it, the nation did not travel. The sovereign God of heaven had taken a people in slavery, delivered them in power, made a covenant with them, and established them into a theocracy, a nation under God on earth. The sign of the covenant was the Sabbath, and its regulations (stipulations) were the Law which included the Ten Commandments and various civil and ceremonial ordinances. The book ends on a strong positive note: God was

with the nation, and He was guiding them on to the Promised Land.

# BIBLIOGRAPHY

Bush, George. *Notes on Exodus.* 1952. Reprint (2 vols. in 1). Minneapolis: James & Klock, 1976.

Cassuto, Umberto. *A Commentary on the Book of Exodus.* Translated by Israel Abrahams. Jerusalem: Magnes Press, 1967.

Cole, R. Alan. *Exodus: An Introduction and Commentary.* The Tyndale Old Testament Commentaries. Downers Grove, Ill.: Intervarsity Press, 1973.

Davies, Gwynne Henton. *Exodus.* Torch Bible Commentaries. London: S.C.M. Press, 1967.

Davis, John J. *Moses and the Gods of Egypt.* Grand Rapids: Baker Book House, 1971.

Honeycutt, Roy L., Jr. "Exodus." In *The Broadman Bible Commentary.* Vol. 1. Nashville: Broadman Press, 1969.

Huey, F.B., Jr. *Exodus: A Study Guide Commentary.* Grand Rapids: Zondervan Publishing House, 1977.

Hyatt, J. Phillip. *Exodus.* New Century Bible. Greenwood, S.C.: Attic Press, 1971. Reprint. Grand Rapids: Wm. B. Eerdmans Publishing Co., 1980.

Keil, C.F., and Delitzsch F. "Exodus." In *Commentary on the Old Testament in Ten Volumes.* Vol. 1. Reprint (25 vols. in 10). Grand Rapids: Wm. B. Eerdmans Publishing Co., 1982.

Lange, John Peter. "Exodus." In *Commentary on the Holy Scriptures, Critical, Doctrinal and Homiletical.* Vol. 2. Reprint (24 vols. in 12). Grand Rapids: Zondervan Publishing House, 1980.

McGregor, James. *Exodus: With Introduction, Commentary and Special Notes.* 2 vols. Edinburgh: T. & T. Clark, 1909.

Pfeiffer, Charles F. *Egypt and the Exodus.* Grand Rapids: Baker Book House, 1964.

Ramm, Bernard L. *His Way Out.* Glendale, Calif.: G/L Publications, Regal Books, 1974.

Youngblood, Ronald F. *Exodus.* Everyman's Bible Commentary. Chicago: Moody Press, 1983.

# LEVITICUS

## F. Duane Lindsey

## INTRODUCTION

The Book of Leviticus was the first book studied by a Jewish child; yet is often among the last books of the Bible to be studied by a Christian. However, a book referred to about 40 times in the New Testament should be of great significance to every Christian. Apart from the question of the typological significance of the Levitical sacrifices, the Book of Leviticus contains extensive revelation concerning the character of God—especially His holiness but also His electing love and grace. Also it provides many rich lessons concerning the holy life that God expects of His people. Many New Testament passages, including some key concepts in the Epistle to the Hebrews, cannot be evaluated properly without a clear understanding of their counterparts in the Book of Leviticus.

**The Titles of the Book.** The title "Leviticus" comes from the Greek *Leuitikon*, an adjective used by the translators of the Septuagint as the title of the book because it pertains to priestly ceremonies and institutions. This may seem to be a strange title since the Levites are mentioned only once in the book (25:32). But since the Aaronic priests were from the tribe of Levi and the sacrificial system which they administered is generally referred to as Levitical, the name is justified. The title was carried across as "Leviticus" in the Latin Vulgate from which the English title was taken. The Hebrew title is simply *wayyiqrā'*, "and He called" (the first word in 1:1).

**Authorship and Date.** Though the author is not specifically identified in the book, Moses should be accepted as its author for these reasons: (1) Since the contents of the book were revealed to Moses at Sinai (7:37-38; 26:46; 27:34) and mostly to or through Moses (1:1; 4:1; 6:1,

8, 19, 24; 7:22; 8:1; etc.), he is most likely the one who recorded these divine revelations. (2) The book is the sequel to Exodus (cf. comments under Lev. 1:1) which specifically claims Mosaic authorship (Ex. 17:14; 24:4, 7; 34:27-28; cf. Deut. 31:9, 24). (3) Jesus affirmed its Mosaic authorship when referring to the law of cleansing from "leprosy" (Matt. 8:4; Mark 1:44; cf. Lev. 14:2-32). Thus Leviticus was written by Moses probably shortly after the composition of Exodus in the second half of the 15th century B.C.

Liberal viewpoints that deny Mosaic authorship and date much of the book, at least in its present form, in the period after the Exile (fourth century B.C.) have been satisfactorily answered by numerous conservative scholars (e.g., R.K. Harrison, *Leviticus: An Introduction and Commentary*, pp. 15-26; B.K. Waltke, "Leviticus," *The Zondervan Pictorial Encyclopedia of the Bible*, 3:913-20).

**Historical and Theological Setting.** The historical and theological context of the Book of Leviticus is implied in the opening and closing verses of the book (1:1; 27:34; cf. 7:37-38). *Historically,* Leviticus was the sequel to Exodus, for the Levitical sacrificial system was a divine revelation to Israel given through Moses as a part of the covenant obligation at Sinai. The book opens: "The Lord called to Moses and spoke to him from the Tent of Meeting" (i.e., the tabernacle). Thus the legislation contained in Leviticus follows the historical narrative concerning the construction of the tabernacle (Ex. 25–40) and precedes the next major historical narrative of the numbering of the Israelite tribes for the decampment from Sinai (Num. 1–4). The intervening exceptions are the historical narrative of the ordination of the priests (Lev. 8–10) and the brief interlude in 24:10-13.

*Theologically* the Levitical sacrificial system was instituted for a people redeemed from Egypt and in covenant relationship with their God. Thus sacrifice in Israel was not a human effort to obtain favor with a hostile God but a response to the Lord who had first given Himself to Israel in covenant relationship. Yet whenever sin or impurity, whether ethical or ceremonial, disrupted this fellowship, the individual or the nation (whichever was the case) renewed covenant fellowship with the Lord through sacrifice, the particular sacrifice depending on the exact circumstance of the disruption. This approach to God through sacrifice could, of course, be purely dedicatory or communal if no disruption had taken place, but this seems to have been the exception rather than the norm (see comments under "The Significance of Old Testament Sacrifice").

**Contents and Literary Genre.** The Book of Leviticus deals with the worship of Israel—its sacrifices, priesthood, laws rendering a person unclean and so disqualifying him for worship, and various special times and seasons of worship. It also contains many regulations pertaining to daily living and practical holiness, both ethical and ceremonial. The literary genre of Leviticus is legal literature, including both apodictic law (laws expressing necessary conduct: "You shall [not]. . . ." e.g., 26:1-2) and mostly casuistic law (laws expressing case decisions: "If [such is done] . . . then [such will result] . . . " e.g., 4:3). Through these literary forms within the historical framework of the covenant between the Lord and Israel, God chose to reveal certain truths about sin and its consequences, and about holiness of life before God.

**Theme and Structure.** The theme of Leviticus is the Israelite believer's worship and walk before the holy God. By way of application this theme is significant for Christians today (cf. 1 Peter 1:15-16). The theme verse is Leviticus 19:2: "Be holy because I, the LORD your God, am holy" (cf. 20:26; etc.).

Leviticus is the book of holiness (*qādôš*, "separateness"; cf. 20:26). While much stress is placed on ceremonial holiness, wherein persons, animals, or objects are set apart from profane use or cultic pollution for the service of God, such holiness is ultimately symbolic of

and foundational for ethical holiness (11:44; 19:2). God Himself is separate from all that is sinful and profane (morally holy) as well as transcendent above all His Creation (majestically holy). God, who was present in the midst of His people Israel (26:11-12), demanded that they be holy (20:22-26).

The structure of the book corresponds with its theme. Chapters 1–16 deal basically with worship before a holy God, while chapters 17–27 relate primarily to the daily walk in holiness before God and people. (See the following outline and comments at the beginnings of various sections in the *Commentary*.)

**The Significance of Old Testament Sacrifice.** Under the Law *sacrifice was given by God as the only sufficient means for Israelites to remain in harmonious fellowship with Himself.* It is noteworthy that the revelation of the sacrificial system through Moses did not include the revelation of any typical significance of the sacrifices. It did, however, spell out clearly the principle of atonement through a substitutionary sacrifice (see comments on 1:4; 17:11). Another important factor is the distinction between two relationships which an Israelite had/could have with God: (a) a corporate relationship with God as a theocratic nation (cf. Ex. 19–20), and (b) a personal relationship with God based on individual regeneration and justification by faith. While ideally these two relationships should have been coextensive, nevertheless it appears that throughout Israel's history (except possibly immediately after the Exodus) there was only a remnant of true believers, and that a large number of the people (often the vast majority?) were merely going through the form of worshiping the Lord without genuine faith in Him.

The traditional view that the sacrifices only "covered" sin fails to do justice to *the real forgiveness that was granted by God* (Lev. 4:20, 26, 31, 35; 5:10, 13, 16, 18; 6:7). That sacrificial atonement merely "covered" sin without in some sense removing it finds no support in the etymology of the Hebrew word for "atonement" (see comments on 1:4). Rather, sacrificial atonement involved the actual removal of the guilt and punishment for the particular sin(s) involved. The broad scope of the sacrifices on the Day of Atonement (cf. discussion on chap. 16) extended this principle to include "all the people" (v. 33) and "all their sins" (v. 22), that is, "all the sins of the Israelites" (v. 34). The complete forgiveness of the Israelites' sins for the past year is further described in terms of cleansing from sin in verse 30.

Nevertheless Levitical sacrifices (as well as genuine prelevitical sacrifices) had a number of limitations. First, *the sacrifices were limited in their moral efficacy.* Since empty ritualism was never an acceptable option to God, a truly acceptable sacrifice must have been *prompted by genuine faith and moral obedience to the revealed will of God* (26:14-45, esp. v. 31; Pss. 40:6-8; 51:16-17; Prov. 21:27; Amos 5:21-24; Heb. 10:5-10; 11:4, 6). Sacrifices that were not brought in faith were perhaps sufficient at times for restoring ceremonial cleanness and meeting civil requirements (e.g., the restitution connected with the guilt offering), but did not really please God because they were empty formality. It is noteworthy that the object of faith was not the typology of the sacrifices (see next section of this *Introduction*) or a consciousness of the coming Redeemer, but God Himself. Of course, the content of faith increased to correspond with progressive Old Testament revelation concerning the coming of the Lamb of God as the ultimate "guilt offering" (Isa. 53:10).

Second, with the possible exception of the Day of Atonement ritual, *the sacrifices were limited in scope to certain kinds of personal sins.* Theologically they did not atone for the sin nature, or for the imputed sin of Adam. Nor did they even include willful acts of sin which were committed in defiance of God (cf. Num. 15:30-31, and comments on Lev. 4:1-2). Therefore *Levitical sacrifice was not a complete and final scheme whereby all forms of sin could be removed.* It was mainly concerned with sins of ignorance, accident, carelessness, and omission, including sins of ritual defilement and misdemeanors that violated property rights. Sins for which there was no individual sacrifice were those done in defiance of the Lord and His commands—willful violations of the Ten Commandments (except minor violations of the eighth and ninth commands), willful disregard for ceremonial regulations, and any other violations of covenant relationship between Israel and the Lord. Such sins could be immediately forgiven only on the basis of unqualified grace in response to faith and repentance (cf. Pss. 32; 51). Otherwise they awaited the cleansing of the Day of Atonement ritual.

Third, *the sacrifices were limited in purpose to the covenant preservation and renewal of a redeemed people.* The Levitical sacrifices were a part of the worship of a redeemed people in covenant relationship with their God. Corporately, and perhaps for the most part individually, the occasion of the slaying of the Passover lamb and the application of its blood to the doorposts in Egypt were outward expressions of inward faith that signaled the regeneration and justification of individual Israelites. The subsequent sacrificial system dealt ideally with worship and covenant renewal, not initial salvation. It was comparable to the New Testament believer's experience of 1 John 1:9, not to the sinner's experience of John 3:16. Nevertheless it is obvious that as a new generation of Israelites came to the age of accountability, they needed to express faith for regeneration and justification before they could worship God acceptably and seek to maintain fellowship with Him. This might have occurred on any number of occasions, including the annual Passover commemoration with its attendant explanations. In some cases it might have occurred when the young Israelites brought their first sin offerings with a true understanding of what they were doing and with faith in their forgiving God.

Fourth, except for the Day of Atonement ritual, *the sacrifices were limited in scope and duration to one sin per sacrifice.* The forgiveness granted was real though temporary (in the sense that each sin required another sacrifice). Thus while God accepted the sacrifices for the removal of guilt in the case of the sin being dealt with, such temporary stays of divine wrath did not result in the permanent purging of a person's conscience (Heb. 10:2).

Fifth, *the efficacy of sacrifice was not inherent in the animals sacrificed or in any or all parts of the sacrificial ritual.* God provided atonement and forgiveness in view of the all-sufficient sacrifice that Jesus Christ would offer on the cross. Christ's death was "a sacrifice of atonement" by which God paid in full for the forgiveness which He had extended before the Cross (Rom. 3:25). In other words, *the Levitical sacrifices were validated in the mind of God on the basis of Christ's death* as the one truly efficacious Sacrifice for all sin, the Lamb of God who was slain from the foundation of the world (Rev. 13:8; cf. 1 Peter 1:19-20). The efficacious value of the sacrifices was therefore derivative rather than original. It is in this sense that the author of Hebrews asserts, "It is impossible for the blood of bulls and goats to take away sins" (Heb. 10:4). Nevertheless the benefits experienced by the Old Testament believers were just as real as the clothing which is worn by a 20th-century credit-card purchaser whose account has not yet been paid in full.

By way of summary, the Levitical sacrifices were efficacious both for restoring the covenant relationship and (when offered in faith) for the actual forgiveness of particular sins, but this efficacy was derivative, needing to be validated by the one all-sufficient sacrifice of Christ on the cross.

Though the sacrifices were limited in scope and purpose, their spiritual value was also pedagogical in teaching Israel about the right way to approach a holy God: "First of all, sin had to be dealt with; the appropriate offering (sin or guilt) had to be made. This was closely linked with a burnt offering that followed it immediately (with its accompanying cereal offering as stated in many cases) and thus completed the self-committal (2 Chron. 29:31) that qualified the suppliant(s) for the last stage of the liturgy. The crowning phase was the presentation of [additional] burnt and peace offerings, the former including both the voluntary gifts of individuals and the calendrical offerings symbolizing the constant devotion of the people as a whole, [and] the latter representing the communal experience in which the Lord, the priest, and the worshiper . . . all had a share" (A.F. Rainey, "Sacrifice," *The Zondervan Pictorial Encyclopedia of the Bible*, 4:203).

To summarize the theology of the ritual procedure (consult comments under various offerings in Lev. 1–7), it can be noted that when an Israelite worshiper laid his hand on the animal victim, he identified himself with the animal as his substitute. When done in faith, this accomplished a symbolic transfer of his sin and a legal transfer of his guilt to the animal victim. God then accepted the slaughter of the animal (this acceptance was symbolized by the burning on the altar) as a ransom payment for the particular sin which occasioned it (or for the sins of the past year in the case of the nation on the Day of Atonement), thus diverting God's wrath from the sinner and (ultimately) to Christ on the cross, so that God granted real forgiveness to the sinner who brought the sacrifice to Him in faith.

**Typology and the Book of Leviticus.** Biblical typology has probably suffered as much at the hands of its friends as at those of its enemies. A defense of the hermeneutics of typology is beyond the scope of this *Introduction*. However, since a suggested typological interpretation is given at the end of each of the five Levitical sacrifices (see comments after 1:17; 2:16; 3:17; 5:13; 6:7) and after the annual festival calendar (chap. 23), a few comments are in order concerning biblical typology. A type may be defined as an exceptional Old Testament reality which was specially ordained by God effectively to prefigure a single New Testament redemptive truth. Because of its divine institution and its role in the forgiveness of sins under the Mosaic economy, the Levitical sacrificial system and the place and times of worship associated with it are especially fertile ground for the recognition of types. However, those who seek to interpret types must always remember: (a) to give proper attention to the historical reality, noting especially its symbolic and redemptive significance to Old Testament believers and its subsequent continuation, commemoration, and influence on future generations of Israelites until its fulfillment in the antitype; (b) to locate the chief point(s) of resemblance between the type and its antitype, and not to press the interpretation beyond these points; (c) to relate the understanding of the typical significance to New Testament believers, not to Old Testament believers; and (d) to interpret in the light of the established doctrines of Scripture rather than attempting to establish a doctrine on a type.

# OUTLINE

I. The Way of Approach to God by Sacrifice (chaps. 1–16)
   A. The laws concerning sacrifices (chaps. 1–7)
      1. General sacrificial regulations for the people (1:1–6:7)
      2. Additional sacrificial regulations for the priests (6:8–7:38)
   B. The inauguration of the priesthood and sacrificial system (chaps. 8–10)
      1. The ordination of Aaron and his sons (chap. 8)
      2. The commencement of the public sacrificial system (chap. 9)
      3. The consequences of priestly ceremonial deviation (chap. 10)
   C. The laws concerning uncleanness (chaps. 11–15)
      1. The laws of food and clean and unclean animals (chap. 11)
      2. The law of childbirth (chap. 12)
      3. The laws for infectious skin diseases and mildew (chaps. 13–14)
      4. The laws of uncleanness from human discharges (chap. 15)
   D. The law of the Day of Atonement (chap. 16)
      1. Introduction (16:1-2)
      2. The preparation of the high priest and the animals for the ceremonies (16:3-5)
      3. A summary statement of the ceremonies (16:6-10)
      4. A detailed description of the ceremonies (16:11-28)
      5. The institution of the Day of Atonement as an annual ceremony (16:29-34)
II. The Walk of Holiness before God by Separation (chaps. 17–27)
   A. The laws for sacrifice and eating meat (chap. 17)
      1. Introduction (17:1-2)
      2. The requirement to kill domestic animals at the tabernacle (17:3-7)
      3. The requirement to offer sacrifices at the tabernacle (17:8-9)
      4. The prohibition against eating blood (17:10-12)

5. The application of these requirements to hunting game (17:13-16)
   B. The laws for covenant morality and nonconformity to pagan practices (chaps. 18–20)
      1. Laws restricting sexual relations (chap. 18)
      2. Laws promoting practical holiness before God and man (chap. 19)
      3. Laws requiring capital punishment (chap. 20)
   C. The laws for priestly and sacrificial holiness (chaps. 21–22)
      1. Personal restriction for priestly service (chap. 21)
      2. Sacrificial regulations for sacred offerings (chap. 22)
   D. The laws concerning the appointed feasts of the Lord (chap. 23)
      1. Introductory command (23:1-4)
      2. The spring festivals (23:5-22)
      3. The fall festivals (23:23-43)
      4. Concluding summary (23:44)
   E. Ceremonial and moral regulations (chap. 24)
      1. The daily and weekly ministry in the Tent of Meeting (24:1-9)
      2. An incident of blasphemy and the divine law based on the case (24:10-23)
   F. The laws concerning special years (chap. 25)
      1. The sabbatical year (25:1-7)
      2. The Year of Jubilee (25:8-55)
   G. The covenant blessings for obedience and curses for disobedience (chap. 26)
      1. Introductory summary of the fundamentals of the Law (26:1-2)
      2. The blessings for obedience (26:3-13)
      3. The curses for disobedience (26:14-45)
      4. Concluding summary (26:46)
   H. The law of vows, gifts, and tithes (chap. 27)
      1. Vows pertaining to people and animals (27:1-13)
      2. Dedication of houses and lands (27:14-25)
      3. Other dues and gifts (27:26-33)
      4. Conclusion (27:34)

## Rituals for Levitical Offerings

| | DEDICATORY | | | COMMUNAL | EXPIATORY | |
|---|---|---|---|---|---|---|
| | BURNT | GRAIN | DRINK | FELLOWSHIP | SIN | GUILT |
| REFERENCES | (Lev. 1:3-17; 6:8-13) | (Lev. 2; 6:14-23) | (Num. 15:1-10; Lev. 23) | (Lev. 3; 7:11-36) | (Lev. 4:1-5:13; 6:24-30) | (Lev. 5:14-6:7; 7:1-10) |
| PRESENTATION: Selection of Offering | Bull (1:3), male sheep (1:10), male goat (1:10), or dove or young pigeon (1:14) | Grain or barley could be prepared in one of five ways: 1. Basic flour with oil; incense mixed with the part burned on the altar 2. Oven-baked cakes/wafers mixed or served with oil 3. Griddle-baked cakes, with oil 4. Pan-baked cakes 5. If *firstfruits*: crushed heads of new grain | With a bull—½ hin With a ram—⅓ hin With a lamb—¼ hin (Note: one hin = ca. 1 quart) | Bull, lamb, or goat, male or female (3:1, 6, 12) (In the freewill offering, minor imperfections were permitted in animal, 22:23) | 1. Young bull (for priest or nation) 2. Male goat (for tribal leader) 3. Female goat or lamb (for layperson) 4. Dove, young pigeon (for poor person) 5. Flour (1/10 ephah) (for very poor) | Usually a ram (a male lamb in the case of a cleansed leper or defiled Nazirite) |
| LAYING ON OF HANDS | 1:4 (except for bird) (see under "Sin offering") | | | (3:2, 8, 13—see "Burnt offering") | Sinner's identification with animal or subsequent symbolic transfer of sin and legal transfer of guilt | Confession (Num. 5:7) apparently accompanied by laying on of hands |
| SLAYING OF ANIMAL | Done by worshiper except that a bird was killed by the priest (cf. 1:15) | | | At sanctuary entrance (see "Burnt offering") | 1. At sanctuary entrance for priest/nation 2. North of altar for others (see "Burnt offering") | North of altar (Lev. 7:2) |
| PREPARATION OF OFFERING | Skinning, dismembering, washing (cf. 1:6, 12, 16-17) | Worshiper normally prepared it in advance. Priest separated a memorial portion for burning on the altar | | | | |

**SACRIFICIAL RITUALS** — **Worshiper's Actions**

**SACRIFICIAL RITUALS — Priest's Actions**

| | DEDICATORY | | | COMMUNAL | EXPIATORY | |
|---|---|---|---|---|---|---|
| | BURNT | GRAIN | DRINK | FELLOWSHIP | SIN | GUILT |
| MANIPULATION OF BLOOD | 1. Blood caught in a bowl and splashed against sides of the altar (1:5, 11) 2. Bird's blood drained out on side of the altar (1:15) | | | Blood caught in a bowl and splashed against sides of the altar (3:2, 8, 13) | Ritual varied according to the position of the worshiper (but involved "splashing" rather than "sprinkling" of blood), the occasion of sacrifice, or the type of animal (e.g., different if a bird) | Blood caught in a bowl and splashed against the sides of the altar (7:2) |
| INCINERATION ON ALTAR | All the animal burned on the altar (1:8-9, 12-13, 15, 17) | Memorial portion burned on the altar by the priest (all was burnt if it was the priest's own offering) | Entire libation poured out to the Lord at the sanctuary (Num. 28:7) | Choice viscera (including "fat tail" of sheep) burned on altar | Choice viscera burned on the altar | Choice viscera burned on the altar |
| DISTRIBUTION OR DISPOSAL OF CARCASS — Priest's dues | Skin (7:8) | Accompanying burnt offering; the priest ate unburned portion | | Breast of animal was to be "wave offering" and eaten by priests | Priest received carcass of offering by leader or layperson | Priest received carcass |
| Worshiper's portion | None | Accompanying fellowship offering: the worshiper ate unburned portion, but a small portion went to the priest | | Communal meal for the worshiper's family at proper time and place | | |
| Remainder | Bird's crop to ashpit (1:16) | | | Remainder burned | Carcass burned outside the camp for priest or nation | |

# Other Features of Levitical Offerings

| | DEDICATORY | | | COMMUNAL | EXPIATORY | |
| --- | --- | --- | --- | --- | --- | --- |
| | BURNT | GRAIN | DRINK | FELLOWSHIP | SIN | GUILT |
| OCCASION | Voluntary worship; certain prescribed rituals and calendrical offerings | An auxiliary offering accompanying burnt and always accompanying fellowship offerings; could be sin offering for the very poor | An auxiliary offering normally accompanying burnt or fellowship offerings, but never with sin or guilt offering alone | THANK OFFERING: for unexpected deliverance or blessing already granted / VOTIVE OFFERING: for blessing or deliverance granted in answer to prayer which had accompanying vow / FREEWILL OFFERING: to express thankful devotion without regard to specific blessing | Unintentional sin against divine command by an individual or the entire nation | Misappropriation or denial of rightful due to God or man, normally assessable in monetary compensation |
| DISTINCTIVENESS | Wholly burned on the altar (Lev. 1:9) | As a nonbloody offering, it accompanied bloody offerings | Wine was probably a deliberate substitute for blood of pagan libations | Most parts eaten before the Lord by the worshiper (and his family) | (See "Occasion" above) | Sacrifice (see "Occasion" above) was usually accompanied by compensation plus fine to wronged party |
| OLD TESTAMENT THEOLOGICAL SIGNIFICANCE | Signified the worshiper's act of total dedication to God | Signified dedication of everyday life to God in recognition of His covenant mercies | | The worshiper recognized the meat eaten as a token of God's covenant faithfulness | Provided atonement and forgiveness for specific unintentional sins where no restitution was involved | The ram was for expiation, accompanied by payment of restitution to the wronged party |
| TYPOLOGY | Christ died as the Lamb of God in complete dedication to the accomplishment of God's will | Christ's perfect person is associated with His sacrificial death | | Christ's death is the basis of fellowship with God and other believers | Christ died as a satisfactory substitutionary sacrifice to provide the forgiveness of sins | Christ's death atones for the damage or injury caused by sin |

## Special Sacrificial Rituals

| | | DEDICATORY | | | COMMUNAL | EXPIATORY | |
| --- | --- | --- | --- | --- | --- | --- | --- |
| | | BURNT | GRAIN | DRINK | FELLOWSHIP | SIN | GUILT |
| Consecration | 1. Of priests (Ex. 29; Lev. 8) | Ram | | | Ram for the ordination | Bull (special ritual) | |
| Consecration | 2. Of temple (2 Chron. 29) | 70 bulls, 100 rams, 200 male lambs | | | Numerous bulls, sheep, and goats | Seven bulls, seven rams, seven male lambs, seven male goats | |
| Deconsecration | Fulfillment of Nazirite vow (Num. 6:14-17) | Year-old male lamb | Regular grain offering, special bread offering | | Ram | Year-old ewe lamb | |
| Purification rituals | 1. Broken vow (Num. 6:9-12) | Dove and young pigeon | | | | Dove and young pigeon | Year-old male lamb |
| Purification rituals | 2. Cleansing of leper (Lev. 14:12-20) | Year-old male lamb (dove or pigeon for poor) | Grain offering | | | Year-old ewe lamb | Year-old male lamb (plus log of oil) |
| Purification rituals | 3. Man (15:14-15) or woman with hemorrhage (15:29-30) | Dove or young pigeon | | | | Dove or young pigeon | |
| Purification rituals | 4. Woman after childbirth (12:6-8) | Year-old lamb (or dove or pigeon) | | | | Dove or young pigeon | |
| Other | 1. Jealousy ritual (Num. 5:15-26) | | 1/10 ephah barley meal, no oil or incense (Note: one ephah = 1/2 bushel, ca. 8 quarts) | | | | |
| Other | 2. Priest's daily grain offering (Lev. 6:19-23) | | 1/10 ephah fine flour | | | | |
| Other | 3. Sin offering of very poor (5:11-13) | | | | | 1/10 ephah fine flour (no oil or incense) | |

SPECIAL RITUALS

# COMMENTARY

Leviticus is a literary expression of God's desire that His holiness be reflected in the life of His covenant people Israel. This is seen in the two spheres of Israel's periodic worship and daily walk. Though there is substantial overlapping between these two spheres, they are reflected generally in the two major divisions of the book: (a) "The Way of Approach to God by Sacrifice (chaps.1–16)" and (b) "The Walk of Holiness before God by Separation (chaps. 17–27)."

## I. The Way of Approach to God by Sacrifice (chaps. 1–16)

This first major division provides a handbook on sacrifice for both the people and the priests (chaps. 1–7), records the great ceremonial events which inaugurated the Aaronic priesthood and the sacrificial system (chaps. 8–10), prescribes detailed regulations concerning such matters as diet and disease lest potential worshipers become ceremonially unclean (chaps. 11–15), and presents the features of the great Day of Atonement whereby the priesthood and the nation could restore and maintain fellowship with a holy God and continue to worship His indwelling Presence in a holy sanctuary (chap. 16).

### A. The laws concerning sacrifices (chaps. 1–7)

This divine revelation through Moses is virtually a procedure manual for offering the five basic sacrifices on the altar. The *main portion* of this handbook on sacrifice (1:1–6:7) is addressed "to the Israelites" (1:2; 4:1). It contains general regulations written from the viewpoint of the persons bringing the sacrifices, and outlines the rituals to be performed by both the worshipers and the officiating priests. A *supplementary section* of the handbook (6:8–7:38) consists primarily of additional regulations about sacrificial rituals for the priests, particularly concerning the disposal (primarily by eating) of various parts of the sacrifice. Thus this supplement is addressed through Moses to "Aaron and his sons" (6:9, 24). But the appendix in 7:22-36 is again addressed "to the Israelites" (vv. 22, 28). The five basic sacrifices are thus introduced twice, each sacrifice being treated both in the main section addressed to the people and in the supplementary section addressed to the priests. (See the charts "Rituals for Levitical Offerings" and "Other Features of Levitical Offerings.") On the difference in the *order* in which the sacrifices are treated in these two sections, and in other Old Testament lists, see comments under 6:8–7:38.

While Leviticus 1–7 records the most systematic statement of the individual sacrificial rituals, other passages further prescribe or describe the various sacrifices in actual contexts of worship. Numbers 28–29 (cf. Lev. 23; Deut. 16) prescribes the public sacrifices during the annual national festivals. (See chart on "Calendrical Offerings" at Num. 28.) Special rituals are also prescribed for such occasions as consecration (e.g., Lev. 8), deconsecration (e.g., Num. 16:14-17), and purification (e.g., Lev. 14:12-20; 15:14-15, 29-30). (See chart on "Special Sacrificial Rituals.")

1. GENERAL SACRIFICIAL REGULATIONS FOR THE PEOPLE (1:1–6:7)

Though this section presents the sacrificial regulations from the viewpoint of the people offering the sacrifice, yet as a schoolteacher must constantly refer to the student handbook to implement policy regarding his students, even so the priests would have diligently studied this section addressed to the people in order to perform their sacrificial rituals properly.

The five sacrifices described here are the burnt, grain, fellowship, sin, and guilt offerings. This is *not* the order in which the sacrifices were usually offered, but is rather a logical or didactic order, grouping the sacrifices by conceptual associations (see introductory note to 6:8–7:38). Thus the grain offering is presented after the burnt offering which it normally accompanied (e.g., Num. 15; 28–29) and before the fellowship offering which it always accompanied (e.g., Lev. 7:12-14; Num. 15:3-4). The sin and guilt offerings are grouped together because they have a number of similarities and are prescribed for designated situations requiring remedy.

The first three offerings are frequently called the "sweet savor offerings" (a better term is "pleasing aroma offerings") because the portion burned on the altar produced "an aroma pleasing to the LORD" (Lev. 1:9, 17; 2:2, 9, 12; 3:5, 16). Correspondingly the sin and guilt offerings are usually called "nonsweet savor offerings," but this is not a biblical expression and is contradicted by the fact that the portion of the sin offering burned on the altar is called "an aroma pleasing to the LORD" (4:31). The Lord received on the altar as much of the sin offering as of the fellowship offering (i.e., the "fat," cf. 3:3-4; 4:31), both of which are designated as "an aroma pleasing to the LORD" (3:5; 4:31). Therefore this expression seems to denote that portion of *any sacrifice* consumed on the altar, and so should not be used as a basis of classification.

Another classification of the offerings has been to call the first three voluntary and the last two nonvoluntary (i.e., required). These terms are somewhat more accurate, except that there were numerous occasions, particularly with regard to the special purification rituals (e.g., 14:12-20) and the annual festivals (cf. Num. 28–29), when burnt, grain, and even fellowship offerings were required, not voluntary (cf. Num. 6:14, 17; Deut. 16:10-12, 16-17).

A more satisfactory approach classifies the burnt and grain offerings as *dedicatory*, the fellowship offering (and its subsidiary offerings—thanksgiving, votive, and freewill) as *communal*, and the sin and guilt offerings as *expiatory* (but the concepts of atonement, forgiveness, and propitiation are present in all the offerings to one degree or another; cf. comments on Lev. 1:4).

*a. The law of the burnt offering (chap. 1)*

**(1) Introduction (1:1-2). 1:1.** Both the historical and theological contexts of the Book of Leviticus are implied not only in this introduction but also in the concluding summary which closes the handbook on sacrifice (7:37-38; see also *Introduction*). The details of the sacrificial ritual were prescribed when **the LORD called** (emphasizing the importance and solemnity of the revelation) **to Moses and spoke to him from the Tent of Meeting** (i.e., the holy place of the tabernacle). Thus the handbook of sacrifice follows the historical narrative concerning the construction of the tabernacle (Ex. 25–40) and precedes the next historical narrative

of the ordination of the priesthood (Lev. 8–10). The remainder of the Book of Leviticus records further revelation concerning Israel's worship and walk before the holy God. The historical narrative does not resume (except for 24:10-13) until the numbering of the Israelite tribes for the decampment from Sinai (Num. 1–4).

**1:2.** This verse forms a transition to the law of the burnt offering by referring to **an offering** (*qorbon*, "that which is brought" to God—a general term covering all sacrifice) **from either the herd** (i.e., a bull, vv. 3-9) **or the flock** (i.e., a sheep or goat, vv. 10-13). With the addition of birds (vv. 14-17), this provides the formal outline of the law of burnt offering (see also 6:8-13), the animals of the offering being listed in a descending order of value.

Several general observations about the burnt offering are noteworthy: (1) The burnt offering (*ʿōlâh*, "that which goes up," 1:3, 10, 14, probably so called because the sacrifice all "went up" in smoke to God) was distinct in that it was totally consumed on the altar (vv. 9, 13, 17) except for the hide (7:8) or the crop of a bird (1:16). (2) It was also called "an offering by fire" (vv. 9, 13, 17) or a "whole burnt offering" (*kālîl*; cf. Deut. 33:10; 1 Sam. 7:9; Ps. 51:19). (3) It was probably listed first because it was the oldest designated (Gen. 8:20) and the most frequent form of Israel's sacrifice. (4) In actual practice it was often preceded by a sin or guilt offering (see comments on Lev. 6:8–7:38). (5) The kinds of animals offered and the details of the ritual closely parallel those of the peace offering (chap. 3). (6) Like all Levitical sacrifices, the underlying purpose of the burnt offering was to secure atonement for sins (1:4; cf. Num. 15:24-25), though its more immediate purpose was to express total dedication to the Lord. (7) While the burnt offering was prescribed for the nation on a daily (Ex. 29:38-42; Num. 28:3-8), weekly (Num. 28:9-10), and monthly basis (Num. 28:11-15), and as a part of the sacrifices offered on numerous annual festival occasions (cf. Lev. 23; Num. 28–29), and for individuals at purification or other ceremonies (e.g., Lev. 14:12-20; 15:14-15, 29-30; Num. 6:9-12), it also could be brought voluntarily by an individual either as a separate offering of dedication (including an offering in fulfillment of a vow or a freewill offering, Lev. 22:17-20) or as an offering in a series after a sin offering (14:19-20; 15:14-15). (See also concluding summary after 1:17 and the *Introduction* ["The Significance of Old Testament Sacrifice"].)

(2) A burnt offering of the herd (1:3-9). The ritual of the burnt offering, like all the Levitical sacrifices, significantly involved the worshiper in the sacrificial procedure, for he performed the acts of presenting the animal, the laying on of hands, slaughter, skinning, dissecting, and washing. But all ritual procedures involving contact with the altar were reserved for the priest, including the manipulation of blood, the arrangement of the wood, and the appropriate parts of the sacrifice for incineration on the altar. The total ritual was performed by the priest in the case of a bird, or if the sacrifice was for himself or the nation.

**1:3.** The worshiper presented the animal **at the entrance to the Tent of Meeting.** Some interpreters limit the term "entrance" to the gateway of the outer court, but since "the Tent of Meeting" was the tabernacle proper, its entrance was probably the entire forecourt, particularly the areas adjacent to the altar of burnt offering. Probably all animal sacrifices were slaughtered on the north side of the altar. This location could be identified specifically as "at the north side of the altar" (e.g., v. 11), or more generally as "in front of the Tent of Meeting" (3:8) or "before the LORD" (1:5; 3:7), or even "at the entrance to the Tent of Meeting" (3:2). However, the actual presentation of the sacrifice probably took place at the actual entrance or gateway to the outer court before the priest, worshiper, and animal moved to the area north of the altar to enact the sacrificial procedure.

When the worshiper presented his animal, the priest would examine the animal to be certain that it met the following *individual characteristics*: (1) It had to be perfect, without spot, blemish, disease, or deformity (1:3, 10; see the list of disqualifying blemishes in 22:17-25; cf. Deut. 15:21; 17:1; an exception allowed a deformed limb for a freewill offering, Lev. 22:23). (2) The **burnt offering,** like most other offerings, had to be a **male** (but female animals were allowed for fellowship offerings, 3:1, 6, and were re-

quired in the sin offerings of the common people, 4:28, 32; 5:5-6). (3) Though a sacrificial animal might vary in age from one week (22:26-27) to probably three years, many of the sacrificial rituals specify a yearling. As to *general characteristics*, all Levitical offerings were (a) ceremonially clean (cf. chap. 11), (b) utilitarian and usable for common food, (c) domesticated (wild game could be eaten but not sacrificed, Deut. 14:4-5), and (d) costly, in relation to the domestic wealth of the Israelite. In short, God required the highest quality possible in line with the means of the worshiper.

**1:4.** Following the presentation of the victim was the laying on of hands. The worshiper was **to lay** (or "press") **his hand on the head of the** animal so that it would **be accepted on his behalf to make atonement for him.** The word translated "to lay his hand on" means "resting or supporting oneself" on the animal. Through this act the worshiper identified himself with the animal as his substitute.

The concept of sacrificial atonement was not limited to the sin and guilt offerings, for the burnt offering is clearly designated to make atonement (*kipper,* intensive form of *kāpar*) for the worshiper. There are two major views on the etymology of the verb *kipper.* It is (a) an Arabic verb *kafara,* meaning "to cover," or (b) one of two Akkadian homonyms— *kapāru*—meaning alternately "to wipe off" or "to smear" (cf. Harold R. Cohen, *Biblical Hapax Legomena in the Light of Akkadian and Ugaritic.* Missoula, Mont.: Scholars Press, 1978, pp. 53-4, n. 8). Numerous evidences, including the poetic parallelism in Jeremiah 18:23 between *kipper* and another Hebrew verb (*māḥâh,* "to wipe out, blot out"), support the second view. A third option suggested by a number of authors (cf. Leon Morris, *The Apostolic Preaching of the Cross.* Grand Rapids: Wm. B. Eerdmans Publishing Co., 1955, pp. 142-52) traces the significance of *kipper* to the Hebrew noun *kōper,* "ransom." But since the etymology of *kōper* is apparently an Akkadian word related to *kapāru,* this should not be regarded as a third possible *etymology* but a significant word in determining the *usage* of *kipper*—"to make atonement." Thus the actual usage in ritual passages allows for either nuance of the Akkadian *kapāru,* either "to wipe off" or "to smear" (e.g., the blood was sometimes smeared on the horns of the altar, as in Lev. 16:18, or the offense was regarded as "wiped off," i.e., cleansed and removed; cf. 16:10, 19).

The related Hebrew word *kōper*, "ransom," supports the conclusion of Morris that in ritual usage *kipper* acquired the technical meaning—"to accomplish reconciliation between God and man" (p. 148), particularly through offering as a ransom price a substitute for the object of divine wrath (p. 152). In Old Testament usage it is apparent that the atonement or reconciliation involved not only expiation of the sin but also propitiation of the divine Lawgiver. Though the offense had to be expiated, more significantly the sacrifice was required because the personal relationship between God and man had been disrupted. So expiation had the effect of making propitiation—turning away divine wrath by a satisfactory, substitutionary sacrifice.

**1:5.** In the next step, the worshiper was **to slaughter the young bull before the Lord.** Since the burnt offering of a sheep or goat was slaughtered "at the north side of the altar" (v. 11), this was evidently the case also with the bull, "before the Lord" simply being a general term applicable to any place in the forecourt which obviously included "the north side of the altar" (see comments under v. 3). The verb "to slaughter" is a technical term for sacrifice. The *death* of the animal victim was (theologically speaking) the most significant phase of the sacrificial ritual since the life poured out in death (symbolized by "blood" in 17:11) is what effects atonement.

The next step in the ritual passed to the priest who caught **the blood** in a bowl as the animal was slain and then splashed it **on all four sides** of the altar of sacrifice. This was done, at least in later times, by throwing it against two opposite corners of the altar so that blood splashed on all sides.

**1:6-9.** The person who was **to skin the burnt offering and cut it into pieces** was the worshiper, not the priest (cf. v. 12). He was also **to wash the** animal's **inner parts** (v. 9) **and** hind **legs** (i.e., those portions defiled by excrement), while **the priest** arranged **the wood** (v. 7) and then **the pieces** of the animal, **including the head and the fat** (v. 8, more carefully defined in 3:3-4 in the case of

the fellowship offering where only the fat was burned), on the fire on the altar. The instruction for the priests **to put fire on the altar** (1:7) is difficult to understand since at the ordination of the priests (chaps. 8–9), the national festivals (Num. 28–29), and numerous individual occasions sin offerings were offered before burnt offerings, so the fire would already be burning. In fact the fire was not to be allowed to go out between the daily morning and evening sacrifices (Lev. 6:12-13). Perhaps the expression is a general one to indicate priestly responsibility to care for the fire. The uniqueness of the burnt offering is made evident in that the priest was **to burn** the animal in its entirety **on the altar.** That the **burnt offering** was **an aroma pleasing to the Lord** is an anthropomorphic expression indicating the Lord's approval and acceptance of the completed sacrifice.

(3) A burnt offering from the flock. **1:10-13.** In the case of **a burnt offering** of a sheep or goat, the same individual characteristics (**a male without defect,** v. 10; cf. v. 3) and the same ritual procedure, though not spelled out in as much detail (cf. vv. 3-9), were in effect. The only additional clarification is that the **slaughter** was to be **at the north side of the altar** (v. 11; cf. comments on vv. 3, 5). Ingenious suggestions have been proposed as to the significance of this location, but probably it was simply the most vacant area adjacent to **the altar.**

(4) A burnt offering of birds. **1:14-17.** The offering of **a dove or a young pigeon** was permitted for the poor in the case of a burnt offering or a sin offering (5:7), and was prescribed for certain purification offerings (15:14-15, 29-30; Num. 6:10-11). The small size of the bird required a simplification of the sacrificial ritual so that all was done necessarily by **the priest.** According to Rashi (cited by Norman H. Snaith, *Leviticus and Numbers,* p. 32), the priest wrenched **off the head** of the bird with his fingernail close to the nape, through the neckbone, the windpipe, and the gullet. Then the **blood** was **drained out** to the last drop beside **the altar. The crop with its contents** was cast aside on the ashpit and then the bird which had been partially torn **open** was burned **on the altar** as **an aroma pleasing to the Lord** (cf. Lev. 1:9).

The *distinctiveness* of the burnt offering was that the entire animal (except for the hide or the crop of a bird) was wholly burned on **the altar** (v. 9). This signified the worshiper's act of complete dedication or surrender to God in association with the sin (or guilt) offering in the process of atonement (cf. 2 Chron. 29:27-28). In a **burnt offering** God received everything and the worshiper received nothing.

The *typology* of the burnt offering is that while all of the animal offerings pointed forward to the death of Christ, the burnt offering typified Christ's death not so much as bearing sin as accomplishing the will of God; Christ was the Lamb of God given in complete dedication to the accomplishment of God's will, as indicated in Hebrews 9:14: "Christ . . . offered Himself unblemished to God" (cf. Eph. 5:1-2; Phil. 2:8; Heb. 10:5-7).

*b. The law of the grain offering (chap. 2)*

The grain (or cereal) offering (*minḥāh*, which outside the Levitical system could refer to any gift or offering; cf. Gen. 4:3-5; Jud. 6:18; 1 Sam. 2:17) was normally a coarsely ground cereal (either wheat or barley), mixed with olive oil and topped with frankincense. The grain offering was to be free of yeast and honey (Lev. 2:11), but was to be salted like all offerings for the altar (v. 13). A grain offering could be offered by itself as a distinct sacrifice (e.g., vv. 14-16; 6:14; Num. 5:15). However, its more common use was as an accompaniment to either a burnt or a fellowship offering. It always accompanied fellowship offerings (Lev. 7:12-14; cf. Num. 15:4) and normally accompanied burnt offerings, especially the calendrical offerings (Num. 28–29).

Another supplemental offering not mentioned in Leviticus 1–7 but explained in Numbers 15:8-10 was the drink offering (consisting of wine or strong drink) which was poured out to the Lord "at the sanctuary" (Num. 28:7). This oblation was offered along with the grain offering which accompanied a burnt or fellowship offering. The quantity of both the grain offering and the drink offering was fixed according to the type of sacrificial animal which it accompanied (cf. Num. 15:2–10).

However, grain offerings were excluded from the burnt offerings for the high priest and the people in the special atonement ritual on the Day of Atonement (Lev. 16:3, 5, 24). Special rituals which prescribed the grain offering included (a) purification rituals after the termination of a Nazirite vow (Num. 6:15, 19) or after the purification of a leper (Lev. 14:10, 20-21, 31); and (b) the "jealousy ritual," which used one-tenth of an ephah of barley meal without oil or frankincense (Num. 5:15, 18, 25-26). The wave offering of firstfruits which consisted of two leavened loaves baked from the flour of new grain (Lev. 23:16-17) was not technically a grain offering since it was not offered on the altar (2:12). The use of one-tenth of an ephah of flour without oil or frankincense as a sin offering by the very poor (5:11-13) was not technically a grain offering but a sin offering.

The law of the grain offering (chap. 2; cf. 6:14-23) is subdivided according to different methods of preparation: one unbaked (2:1-3), three baked (vv. 4-10), and the special crushed and roasted grain offering of firstfruits (vv. 14-16).

(1) A grain offering in unbaked form (2:1-3). The ritual order for the grain offering involved four steps: (a) The worshiper prepared the offering (vv. 1, 4-7), and (b) presented it, probably in a bowl (cf. Num. 7:13), to the priest at the sanctuary (Lev. 2:2, 8); (c) the priest separated a handful as a memorial portion (vv. 2, 9, 16), and (d) burned this portion on the altar, "an aroma pleasing to the LORD" (vv. 2, 9).

**2:1.** The basic **grain offering** was to consist **of fine flour** (rather coarse by modern standards) mixed with **oil and incense** (the addition of the latter was all that distinguished the preparation of the grain offering from normal food preparation).

**2:2.** **The priest** took the grain offering from the worshiper and separated **a handful of the fine flour and oil, together with all the incense, and** burned it **on the altar** as **a memorial portion**—a token that the whole was given to God. When a grain offering was brought by a priest, the entire offering was burned on the altar (6:22-23). The grain offering was described in the same terms as the burnt offering: **an offering made by fire, an aroma pleasing to the LORD** (cf. 1:9, 13, 17).

**2:3.** In contrast with the burnt offering, which was totally consumed on the altar (cf. 1:9), **the rest of the grain offer-**

**ing** was given to the priests for food (or when it accompanied a fellowship offering, portions went to the priest [7:12-14] and the leftovers became a part of the fellowship meal eaten by the worshiper and his family [cf. 7:15-27]), for it was **a most holy part** of that offering. The phrase "most holy," as applied to a Levitical sacrifice, was a technical expression indicating those portions of an offering (whether a grain, fellowship, sin, or guilt offering) which were to be eaten only by qualified members of the priesthood.

(2) A grain offering in baked form (2:4-10). **2:4-7.** Using the normal cooking utensils and methods of food preparation (except that incense was added to the portion burned on the altar; cf. v. 2), the worshiper prepared either oven-baked **cakes** or **wafers . . . mixed** or **spread with oil** (v. 4), or crumbled griddle-baked cakes **mixed** and spread **with oil** (vv. 5-6), or pan-fried cakes mixed with **oil** (v. 7). This variety of three utensils and four types of bread was apparently designed to encourage worshipers to bring their offerings whatever their economic or social circumstances.

**2:8-10.** The ritual procedure for a baked **grain offering** was the same as for an unbaked offering (though no mention is made of incense). **The priest** burned **the memorial portion . . . on the altar** and retained **the rest** for food (with the exceptions noted under v. 3).

(3) Additional instructions regarding the grain offering (2:11-16). **2:11-13. Yeast** and **honey** were prohibited from all grain offerings. The **offering of the firstfruits** (cf. 23:16-17) allowed these, but it was not technically a grain offering, that is, one **offered on the altar as a pleasing aroma.** However, **all** the **offerings** for the altar were to include **salt,** apparently symbolic of Israel's covenant relationship with God (**the salt of the covenant of your God**), which was the foundation of the Levitical sacrificial system. Since **salt** was regarded in the ancient Near East as not being destructible by fire, "a covenant of salt" seems to refer to an eternal covenant (Num. 18:19; 2 Chron. 13:5).

**2:14-16.** Special instructions are needed for the **grain offering of firstfruits** offered at harvesttime. It consisted of **crushed heads of new grain roasted in the fire,** with **oil and incense** added, and

the normal **memorial portion** burned on the altar, the remainder no doubt going to **the priest.**

As a vegetable product (in contrast with animal) the *distinctiveness* of the **grain offering** was the absence of any blood ritual, though this offering was normally associated with burnt or fellowship offerings involving blood sacrifices. Since the grain offering involved the Israelites' normal food and cooking methods, it may have symbolized the dedication of everyday life to God and perhaps the recognition of God's provision of daily needs. Especially in the form of a firstfruits offering, it constituted a recognition of God's covenant mercies and an affirmation of loyalty to **the LORD** of the covenant who had brought Israel into their land (Deut. 26:9-10).

The *typology* of the grain offering pictures the person of Christ and points up the substitutionary value of His death on the cross. This is illustrated in the normal conjunction of the grain offering with the burnt or fellowship offerings. It may be that the fine flour speaks of His perfect, well-balanced humanity, the oil pictures the Holy Spirit who overshadowed Him at the Incarnation, the frankincense points to the moral fragrance of His person, and the absence of yeast (leaven) illustrates His separateness from sin. Beyond this, it is interesting that even the image of grain falling into the ground and "dying" to bring forth fruit was used by Jesus to illustrate His death (John 12:23-24).

*c. The law of the fellowship offering (chap. 3)*

The Hebrew words translated in the NIV as "fellowship offering" (*zebaḥ šᵉlāmîm,* always in the pl. except in Amos 5:22) has traditionally been translated "peace offering." G.J. Wenham says that the translation "fellowship" is "simply a guess based on the nature of the party [communal meal] after the sacrifice" (*The Book of Leviticus,* p. 76) and prefers the traditional translation of peace offering. Since the Hebrew concept of peace includes health, prosperity, and peace with God, R.K. Harrison aptly translates it "a sacrifice of well-being" (*Leviticus: An Introduction and Commentary,* p. 56). Perhaps a combination of both ideas, "well-being" (from the meaning of the word) and "fellowship" (from the distinctive feature of the communal meal after the sacrifice), identifies the fullest significance of this offering.

The law of the fellowship offering (cf. Lev. 7:11-36) is the third of the so-called "pleasing aroma offerings" (see comments under 1:1–6:7). It does parallel the burnt offering not only in the selection of sacrificial victims (except for the exclusion of birds, the inclusion of female animals, and the allowance of a deformed limb in the case of a freewill offering) but also in the major part of the ritual procedure. Though no mention is made of the fellowship offering making atonement, this might be implied in the normal laying on of a hand, the slaying of the animal, the manipulation of the blood (cf. 17:11), and the incineration of the fat parts on the altar (virtually identical with the ritual of the sin offering which is the most explicit atoning sacrifice).

At any rate, the presentation of a fellowship offering was conditioned on a worshiper's having first met the requirements of expiation (through a sin or guilt offering) and dedication (through burnt and grain offerings). The proper classification for the fellowship offering and its subcategories (thanksgiving, votive, and freewill offerings) is that of communal offerings because of the communal meal which climaxed the sacrifice. This was a time of rejoicing before the Lord (Deut. 12:12, 18-19; 27:7; 1 Kings 8:64-65) in which the worshipers, their families, and a Levite from their community (and also the poor during the Feast of Weeks, Deut. 16:11) shared a major portion of the sacrificial meal, perhaps as God's token to them of all the benefits of their covenant relationship with Him. The regulations regarding this meal are not given in the handbook to the worshiper but rather in the supplement for the priests (cf. comments on Lev. 7:11-36).

The fellowship offering was primarily an optional sacrifice. The Feast of Weeks (Pentecost) was the only annual festival for which fellowship offerings were prescribed (23:19-20). But they were also prescribed for certain special ceremonies of covenant initiation (Ex. 24:5) or renewal (Deut. 27:7), and consecration (Ex. 29:19-34; Lev. 8:22-32; 9:8-21; 1 Kings 8:63; etc.) or deconsecration (fufillment of a Nazirite vow, Num. 6:14, 17). Examples of other occasions at which fellowship offerings were sacrificed: (a) a successful military campaign (1 Sam. 11:15), (b) the cessation of famine or pestilence (2 Sam. 24:25), (c) an acclamation of a candidate for kingship (1 Sam. 11:15; 1 Kings 1:9, 19), (d) national spiritual renewal (2 Chron. 29:31-36), (e) an annual family reunion (1 Sam. 20:6), and (f) harvesting of the firstfruits (Ex. 22:29-31; 1 Sam. 9:11-13, 22-24; 16:4-5). A freewill offering was the minimum sacrifice that could be brought for the three annual holy convocations (Ex. 23:16; 34:20-24; Deut. 16:10, 16-17; 2 Chron. 35:8; Ezra 3:5).

Three subcategories of the fellowship offering (Lev. 7:12-16) suggest occasions or motivations for bringing this sacrifice: (1) A *thanksgiving offering* (*tôḏâh*, "confession" or "acknowledgment") was the most common type (7:12-15; 22:29), almost synonymous with the fellowship offering itself (cf. 2 Chron. 29:31; Jer. 17:26; 2 Chron. 33:16). It was brought as an acknowledgment to others of God's deliverance or blessing bestowed in answer to prayer (Pss. 56:12-13; 107:22; 116:17-19; Jer. 33:11). (2) A *votive* ("vow," NIV) *offering* (Lev. 7:16) was a ritual expression of a vow (cf. 27:9-10), or the fulfillment of a vow such as the deconsecration of a Nazirite (Num. 6:17-20). Though usually a fellowship offering, it could also be a burnt offering (Lev. 22:17-20). The votive offering should not be confused with the *tôḏâh*, or thanksgiving offering, that was brought as an acknowledgment of God's deliverance in response to a petition or lament psalm with its "vow of praise" (cf. Ronald B. Allen, *Praise! A Matter of Life and Breath*. Nashville: Thomas Nelson Publishers, 1980, pp. 38-9). (3) A *freewill offering* was brought to express devotion or thankfulness to God for some unexpected blessing (7:16; 22:18-23). A burnt offering could also be brought as a freewill offering (22:17-20).

The formal structure of the law of the fellowship offering, like that of the burnt offering, was determined by the types of the animals sacrificed. The exclusion of a sacrifice of birds may be accounted for on the basis that their small size disallowed an apportioning which would leave anything for a communal meal after burning even a small portion on the altar. (Even in the case of the sin offering of a bird, the priest received no portion for his allotment.)

(1) A fellowship offering from the herd (3:1-5). **3:1.** Unlike the burnt offering, **an animal from the herd** brought as **a fellowship offering** could be either **male or female** (i.e., a bull or a cow). The **animal** had to be **without defect** (cf. 1:3; 22:17-25).

**3:2.** The ritual of the fellowship offering paralleled that of the burnt offering up to the point of the use and distribution of the pieces of the dissected animal. These identical procedures were four: (a) the presentation of the animal by the worshiper, (b) the laying on of the worshiper's **hand,** (c) the worshiper's slaying of the animal **at the entrance to the Tent of Meeting** (i.e., in the forecourt north of the altar of burnt offering), and (d) the manipulation of **the blood** by the priest who splashed the blood **against the altar on all sides.** In the case of the fellowship offering the laying on of his hand probably included the worshiper's explanation of why he was bringing the offering, whether an acknowledgment of declarative praise in answer to prayer, or the testimony of the fulfillment of a vow, or a freewill thanksgiving at harvesttime, and so on.

**3:3-4.** The worshiper's preparation of the **offering** (skinning, dissecting, and washing) also apparently followed the same procedure as the burnt offering, but the ritual diverged in terms of the portions of the animal which the priest incinerated on the altar. Only **the fat that covers** the intestines, **both kidneys with the fat around them,** and **the covering** (long lobe) **of the liver** were burned on the altar (cf. the more physiological description of these parts by Harrison, *Leviticus,* p. 57). Since "the fat" was apparently synonymous with the best (cf. Gen. 4:4; 45:18), it may symbolize the dedication of the worshiper's best and deepest emotions to God.

**3:5.** The fat of the fellowship offering was burned **on the altar** by the priest **on top of the burnt offering,** that is, on the ashes of the continual burnt offering from the morning sacrifice, or perhaps on the smoldering remains of the same worshiper's burnt offering which preceded his fellowship offering. This fat, like the whole burnt offering (cf. 1:9, 13, 17) and

the memorial portion of the grain offering (cf. 2:2, 9), was **an aroma pleasing to the Lord,** symbolizing God's acceptance of the sacrifice.

(2) A fellowship offering from the flock (3:6-16). **3:6-11.** In the case of the offering of **a lamb** (v. 7) the flexibility of the fellowship offering is again seen in the acceptability of either **a male or female without defect** (v. 6). The ritual was the same as when offering a bull or cow except that **the entire fat tail** (v. 9) was included in **the fat** incinerated on **the altar.** The principal breed of sheep in Palestine was the oriental fat-tailed sheep (*ovis laticaudata*) which has several extra caudal vertebrae to support the body fat stored in the tail, which in mature animals can weigh between 22 and 33 kilograms (48-73 pounds) (Harrison, *Leviticus,* p. 59).

The indication in verse 11 (also v. 16) that the fat of the fellowship **offering** was burned **on the altar as food** should not be taken in the primitive pagan sense that worshipers shared meals with the Lord (cf. Ps. 50:12-13). **The Lord** received the fat on the altar in the case of the sin (Lev. 4:8-10, 19, 26, 31, 35) and guilt offerings (7:4-5) when no communal meal was involved.

**3:12-16.** The fellowship **offering** of a **goat** apparently allowed either male or female victims and followed the same procedure as the lamb except for the fat tail.

(3) Summary prohibition. **3:17.** Based on the summary principle at the climax of verse 16—"All the fat is the Lord's"—**a lasting ordinance** was set forth for all Israelites: **You must not eat any fat or any blood.** This ordinance is reaffirmed in 7:23-27 in greater detail with the punishment for violation being direct divine judgment. Harrison explains dietary reasons for the prohibition not to eat fat (*Leviticus,* p. 58).

The *distinctiveness* of the fellowship offering was in the communal meal which the worshiper and his family ate before the Lord (cf. 7:15). It was essentially a voluntary act in which the worshiper accepted the meat from God as a token of His covenant faithfulness and gave God acknowledgment or thankful praise for His past blessings bestowed, whether in answer to prayer, or granted unexpectedly, or the normal blessings such as a good harvest.

The *typology* of the fellowship offering pictures the fellowship that the New Testament believer has with God and with other believers on the basis of Christ's death on the cross (1 John 1:3). This is one phase of Christ's "making peace through His blood, shed on the cross" (Col. 1:20). In fact, "He Himself is our peace" (Eph. 2:14).

*d. The law of the sin offering (4:1–5:13)*

The sin offering (4:1–5:13) and the guilt offering (5:14–6:7) were clearly distinguishable offerings though they had some definite similarities. Traditionally called the "nonsweet savor offerings," this description is not fully adequate in view of 4:31 which indicates that the fat of the sin offering was burned "on the altar as an aroma pleasing to the LORD." (See comments under "1. General sacrificial regulations for the people [1:1–6:7].") The sin and guilt offerings are best described as expiatory offerings.

The same special rituals of consecration, deconsecration, and purification which required a burnt offering first required a sin offering. Also one male goat was required as a national sin offering on each day of all the annual festivals, but not with the daily, weekly, or monthly burnt offerings.

(1) Introduction. **4:1-2.** Prefaced by a formula of divine revelation—**The LORD said to Moses,** a clause not repeated till 5:14 (thus supporting a unity of theme in 4:1–5:13)—this introduction identifies the occasion of the sin offering—**When anyone sins unintentionally and does what is forbidden in any of the LORD's commands.** The word "when" (*kî*) introduces a broad, general statement in which the main clause of the sentence was omitted since the requirements varied from case to case, depending on the theocratic status of each offending sinner (4:3, 13, 22, 27).

The general act of sin which occasioned a sin offering was qualified in two respects: it was done "unintentionally," and it was against "any of the LORD's commands" (it could include sins of omission as well as commission; cf. Num. 15:22-23). Whatever specific acts these expressions and the examples to follow referred to, it is clear that for defiant sin (Num. 15:30, lit., "with a high

hand")—that is, sin with a set purpose of being disobedient to God—no sacrifice could be brought by an individual (but cf. comments under Lev. 16 on the Day of Atonement rituals). Therefore David, for example, threw himself on the mercy of God after his sin with Bathsheba which he confessed was rebellion against God (Ps. 51:1, 3, 16-17).

More specifically, the sin offering was for sins committed "unintentionally" (*bišgāgâh*, "in ignorance"). Though this term sometimes clearly refers to sins of ignorance or inadvertence (Lev. 4:2, 22, 27), it was also used of manslaughter (Num. 35:11, 15; cf. Josh. 20:3, where the act is further defined as "without premeditation" [NASB]). The contrast in Numbers 15:22-31 is simply between sins committed with a defiant attitude toward God and His Law and those done nondefiantly. Therefore the term *bišgāgâh* is broad enough to include all sins not done in a spirit of rebellion against the Lord and His covenant stipulations— whether sins of ignorance (Lev. 4), sins without conscious intent (chap. 5), or intentional but nondefiant sins (Num. 15:22-29). It was for such sins that the sin offering was prescribed.

The structure of the law of the sin offering (i.e., the primary ritual portion, Lev. 4; cf. 6:24-30) is divided according to the status of the offerer (priest, congregation member, ruler, or ordinary person). Also the variety of acceptable sacrifices is presented in descending order of value— a bull for the priest (4:3) or nation (v. 14), a male goat for a tribal leader (vv. 22-23), a female goat (v. 28) or lamb (v. 32) for a common person, two birds for a poor person (5:7), and even an offering of flour for the very poor (5:11-13). The difference in sacrifices did not depend on the nature of the sin but on the social and/or economic status of the sinner. The supplementary information in chapter 5 regards certain offenses requiring the sin offering (5:1-6) and concessions for the poor (5:7-13).

(2) The sin offering for a priest (4:3-12). **4:3.** Actually **the anointed priest** was the high priest who alone was anointed on the head (8:12). As the people's representative to God, his **sin** would bring **guilt on the people.** He was then to **bring to the LORD a young bull without defect as a sin offering.** It is noteworthy

that the same Hebrew word (*ḥaṭṭā't*) means both "sin" and "sin offering."

**4:4.** The ritual of the sin offering followed the same general pattern as the other offerings, but with distinctive features in the details pertaining to the manipulation of blood and the distribution or disposal of portions of the carcass. Thus the sacrificial victim was presented **at the entrance to the Tent of Meeting,** and after the laying on of hands, was slaughtered **before the Lord,** no doubt at the north side of the altar (cf. v. 33, "at the place where the burnt offering is slaughtered").

**4:5-7.** The manipulation of the blood in the sin offering ritual followed one of three basic procedures, depending on the theocratic position of the worshiper. The procedure for the high priest (vv. 5-7) or the whole Israelite community (vv. 16-18) was more elaborate than the second and modified procedure for a tribal leader (v. 25) or an ordinary member of the community (v. 30). A third and most elaborate procedure was followed in the special Day of Atonement ritual (16:6-19). In striking contrast was the simple procedure for the sin offering of a bird for a poor person (5:9).

For the sin of the high priest (4:5-7, and similarly for the nation; cf. vv. 16-18), the **priest** carried the **blood . . . into the Tent of Meeting** (commonly called the holy place, v. 5), dipped **his finger into the** bowl of **blood and** sprinkled (a technical sacrificial term meaning "to sprinkle or splash") **it seven times before the Lord, in front of the curtain of the sanctuary** (the veil separating the most holy place from the holy place), smeared **some of the blood on the horns of the altar of fragrant incense,** and then returned to the outer court where he poured out **the rest of the bull's blood** at **the base of the altar of burnt offering.** This latter act apparently had no sacrificial significance and was simply a means of disposing of the rest of the blood.

**4:8-10.** The incineration of the fatty parts on **the altar of burnt offering** paralleled that of the **fellowship offering** (cf. 3:3-4).

**4:11-12.** The disposal of the carcass followed two types of ritual, depending on whether the sacrifice was for the priest (or even the whole community which he represented) or for others. The priest was not permitted to eat the flesh of his own (or the community's) sacrifice (6:30), so all portions which were not burned on the altar (**all the rest of the bull**) were disposed of by taking them **outside the camp to a place ceremonially clean** (a ritual **ash** heap) where they were burned **in a wood fire.** Though the disposal of the carcass is not mentioned in the case of a leader (cf. 4:26) or an ordinary person (cf. vv. 31, 35), it is clearly stated in 6:26 that it was given to the officiating priest as food to be eaten in a holy place. Though no mention is made of atonement and forgiveness for the sinning priest, these were no doubt granted under the same conditions as for the people (cf. 4:20, 26, 35).

(3) The sin offering for the whole Israelite community. **4:13-21.** Corporate, national, theocratic sins were common throughout Israel's history (e.g., Num. 14). Sometimes these were unintentional, so that a sin offering was required (e.g., Num. 15:22-26). The nation was represented by **the elders of the community** who presented **a young bull as a sin offering,** laid **their hands on the bull's head** and **slaughtered** it **before the Lord.** The rest of the ritual was identical to that of the sin offering of the **priest:** the manipulation of **blood** (Lev. 4:16-18), the incineration of the fat **on the altar** (vv. 19-20), and the disposal of the carcass **outside the camp** (v. 21). The results of this **sin offering** were **atonement** and forgiveness (v. 20).

(4) The sin offering for a leader. **4:22-26.** After a tribal **leader** or clan representative (*nāśî*, "a lifted-up one"; cf. Ex. 16:22; Num. 34:18) sinned **unintentionally,** he was to bring **a male goat without defect.** The ritual procedure diverged at the point of the manipulation of blood, for instead of taking blood into the tabernacle, **the priest** simply took **some of the blood . . . with his finger and put it on the horns of the altar of burnt offering,** pouring **out the rest . . . at the base of the altar.** After the incineration of the fatty portions **on the altar,** the officiating **priest** received the flesh of the sacrifice for food for himself and his family (cf. Lev. 6:26, 29). When this procedure was followed in faith, the leader's sin was atoned for and he was **forgiven.**

(5) The sin offering for a member of the community. **4:27-35.** Like his leader,

a common person had to bring a sin offering for his unintentional sin, either **a female goat without defect** (v. 28) or **a lamb . . . a female without defect** (v. 32). The entire sacrificial ritual for either animal was identical to that of **the sin offering** of a leader (cf. vv. 22-26). It is significant that **the fat** burned on **the altar** was **an aroma pleasing to the LORD,** highlighting God's acceptance of the sin offering which resulted (when brought in faith) in **atonement** and forgiveness (vv. 31, 35).

(6) Three kinds of offenses requiring a sin offering (5:1-6). The relationship of verses 1-13 to their context has been debated by scholars. Some begin the law of the guilt offering with these verses. Others regard verses 1-13 as a transition between the sin and guilt offerings which they view as virtually the same. However, there are numerous reasons for recognizing the clear distinction between these two offerings. For example, the animal victim here was to be "a female lamb or goat" (v. 6), corresponding to the typical sin offering (4:28, 32), whereas the guilt offering called for a ram (5:15, 18; 6:6). The payment of an additional compensation, which was the distinctive feature of the guilt offering, was not involved here. The sacrifice discussed here is clearly called a "sin offering" (5:6-9, 11-12). Therefore verses 1-13 should be regarded as a supplementary section concerning the sin offering.

The first section (vv. 1-6) gives illustrations of four sins requiring the sin offering. All four cases involve sins resulting from negligence or perhaps even forgetfulness, and fall into the general category of unpremeditated, unintentional sins (though *bišḡāḡâh* does not occur in vv. 1-6).

**5:1.** In this instance **a person** who **does not speak up when he hears a public charge to testify** may have withheld information through negligence.

**5:2-3.** Two examples are given of accidental ceremonial defilement, through contact with a dead animal (v. 2; cf. 11:24-28, 30-40) and by contact with **human uncleanness** (5:3; cf. chaps. 12–15).

**5:4.** The final instance pertains to a **thoughtlessly** spoken **oath to do . . . good or evil** (a merism for "anything at all"), perhaps a vow to do something that was immediately forgotten.

**5:5-6.** Once an offender in such a case became conscious of his guilt, he was responsible to **confess** his sin and to **bring to the LORD a female lamb or goat . . . as a sin offering.**

(7) The sin offering concessions for the poor (5:7-13). **5:7-10.** A poor person who could not **afford a lamb** for a sin offering was **to bring two doves or two young pigeons . . . one for a sin offering and the other for a burnt offering.** This sacrificial ritual was similar to the ritual for a bird as a burnt offering (cf. 1:14-17) except that the priest sprinkled **some of the blood of the sin offering against the side of the altar.** Presumably the bird was burned on the altar in the same manner as the burnt offering (1:16-17). The second bird was offered **as a burnt offering in the prescribed way,** the end result being **atonement** and forgiveness.

**5:11-13.** An extremely poor person who could not even obtain the two birds for a **sin** and burnt **offering** was granted the concession of bringing **a 10th of an ephah,** about two quarts, **of fine flour for a sin offering.** In contrast with the fine flour brought as a grain offering (cf. 2:1-3), which was primarily a dedicatory offering, he was **not** to **put oil or incense on it, because it was a sin offering. The priest** burned **a memorial portion . . . on the altar** just as with the grain offering. The result of the offering was **atonement,** and he was **forgiven.** The remainder of the flour was given to the officiating **priest, as in the case of the grain offering.** This one instance of a bloodless sin offering—granted it was burned **on the altar on top of the** (bloody) **offerings** (5:12)—may have been in the mind of the author of Hebrews who wrote, "The Law requires that *nearly* [emphasis added] everything be cleansed with blood" (Heb. 9:22).

The *distinctive purpose* of the sin offering was to atone and provide forgiveness for specific unintentional or nondefiant sins where (in contrast with the guilt offering) no restitution was involved. God accepted the slaughter of the animal as a ransom payment for the particular sin which occasioned it, thus diverting His wrath from the sinner and (ultimately) to Christ on the cross.

The *typology* of the sin offering emphasizes the death of Christ as a satisfactory substitutionary sacrifice to provide the forgiveness of sins (2 Cor. 5:21; Eph. 1:7). Identification with Him through personal faith leads to the practical experience of this forgiveness.

### e. The law of the guilt offering (5:14–6:7)

The guilt offering was required whenever someone committed a "violation" (5:15, *ma'al*)—an act of misappropriation or denial to another (whether God or man) of his rightful due (cf. Num. 5:12, 19; Josh. 7:1; 22:20; 2 Chron. 26:16, 18; 28:22-23). When a sin could be assessed for monetary compensation, the offender had to bring not only the ram for the guilt offering but also compensation in property or silver, plus a 20 percent fine (Lev. 5:16; 6:5). The examples given in this section pertain to unintentional misappropriation of sacred property (5:14-16) and service (cf. 14:12, 24), suspected transgressions of divine commands (5:17-19), and the violation of others' property rights (6:1-7; cf. 19:20-22; Num. 5:6-10). It is apparently beside the point that some of these sins were unintentional (cf. comments on Lev. 4:1-2), since the sins listed in 6:2-5 were obviously intentional sins against man, though not defiant sins against the Lord (cf. Num. 15:30). Thus the common occasion of the guilt offering was an offense that caused damage or loss whether unintentional or deliberate, and either against God or against man.

(1) The guilt offering for unintentional violation of sacred property (5:14-16). **5:14-15.** The first category of sins requiring the guilt offering pertained to unintentional **violation** or misappropriation of **the Lord's holy things.** This could refer to the improper use of sacrificial flesh eaten by worshipers after a fellowship offering; misuse of the "most holy" portions of the grain, sin, or guilt offerings which were reserved for the priests alone (2:3, 10; cf. 22:14-16); failure to present to God due gifts of sacrifices, tithes, firstfruit offerings, or things dedicated to God (cf. chap. 27); failure to fulfill dedicatory vows (Num. 6:11-12); or deprivation of service due to the Lord (cf. Lev. 14:24). The prescribed animal for a guilt offering was usually **a ram . . . without defect** (5:15, 18; 6:6), but a male lamb in the case of a cleansed leper (14:12, 21; a bird was allowed in the case

of the poor, 14:30), or in the reconsecrating of a defiled Nazirite (Num. 6:12). This ram had to be **of the proper value in silver**—according to Jewish tradition, worth at least two shekels.

**5:16.** The **restitution** in compensation for the violated property plus a 20 percent fine was in addition to the sacrifice of **the ram.** Since the sin in this case was against the Lord, the restitution was made to His representative, **the priest.** The sacrificial ritual is not described here, but is summarized in 7:1-6. The results of the guilt offering included **atonement** and forgiveness.

(2) The guilt offering for suspected transgressions of divine commands. **5:17-19.** These verses seem to refer to a more positive transgression of **any of the Lord's commands,** whereas verses 15-16 dealt with numerous unintentional sins. The phrase **though he does not know it** could refer to an act committed unknowingly, but which one later felt **guilty** about. Wenham (*Leviticus*, pp. 107-8) concludes that the offerer only suspected he had transgressed because of his guilty conscience but could not be certain. Perhaps this is why the separate compensation payment and its fine were apparently not required in this case.

(3) The guilt offering for violation of property rights. **6:1-7.** Whereas 5:14-19 pertained to violations against "the Lord's holy things" (5:15) and "the Lord's commands" (5:17), 6:1-7 relates to defrauding another person though this is also recognized as being **unfaithful to the Lord.** The **sins** listed in verses 2-3 seem to relate to types of embezzlement, theft, **extortion,** and failure to return **lost property** (cf. Num 5:6-10). In such cases, since the violation was against human **property** rights, the **restitution** payment and fine were given **to the owner on the day** the offender presented **his guilt offering** (Lev. 6:5). If the offended party was no longer living and had no surviving relative, the restitution and fine were paid to **the priest** (cf. Num. 5:8-10). Again, the result of the guilt offering was **atonement** and forgiveness (Lev. 6:7).

The *distinctive feature* of the guilt offering was the restitution payment and fine to the wronged party, either man or God. The **ram** of the **guilt offering** was not part of the restitution but was an expiation for the sin before God.

The *typology* of the guilt offering stresses that aspect of Christ's death which atones for the damage or injury done by sin. Isaiah foresaw the death of Christ as "a guilt offering" (Isa. 53:10).

## 2. ADDITIONAL SACRIFICIAL REGULATIONS FOR THE PRIESTS (6:8–7:38)

This section supplements the handbook on sacrifice (1:1–6:7) and contains additional administrative details about the sacrificial ritual for the priests, especially the procedure for the distribution and disposal of the flesh and other parts of the sacrifice which were not burned on the altar. Whereas the major section on sacrifice was addressed "to the Israelites" (1:2; 4:2), this section (except for the appendix, 7:22-38) is addressed to "Aaron and his sons," that is, the priests (6:9, 25). The primary concern of the section is to identify which persons, places, and portions were acceptable to God as sacrificial meals.

Since the same five offerings are treated, there is some overlap with 1:1–6:7, and only new features are pointed out. A.F. Rainey has clearly demonstrated that the Old Testament sacrifices were listed in three different orders ("Sacrifice," *The Zondervan Pictorial Encyclodpedia of the Bible*, 4:201-3): (1) *The didactic order* (burnt, meal, fellowship, sin, and guilt offerings) was followed in 1:1–6:7. (2) *The administrative order* (i.e., inventory order: burnt, meal, sin, guilt, and fellowship offerings) was followed in 6:8–7:38 (cf. Num. 7:87-88). This order reflects the relative frequency of the sacrifices (if the expiatory offerings—sin and guilt—are grouped together), as well as the differences in disposing of the parts of the sacrifice. The burnt offering, mentioned first, was wholly consumed on the altar; the meal, sin, and guilt offerings were partially consumed on the altar and partially consumed by the priests; the fellowship offering, mentioned last, was partially consumed on the altar, partially consumed by the priests, and partially consumed by the worshiper and his family in a communal feast. (3) *The procedural order* in which the sacrifices were actually offered (sin and/or guilt, burnt, grain, and fellowship offerings) is obvious in numerous passages such as Leviticus 8:14-32 (cf. Ex. 29:10-34); Leviticus 14:12-20; 15:14-15, 29-30; Numbers 6:16-17 (con-

trast the administrative order in Num. 6:14-15); 2 Chronicles 29:20-35.

### a. Priestly regulations for the burnt offering (6:8-13)

**6:8-13.** Since no part of a burnt offering was eaten by priest or worshiper, this brief section treats only the responsibility of the priests in the proper care of the ashes and fire on the altar.

**Throughout the night** the embers of the evening **burnt offering** were **to remain on the altar** and the altar **fire** was to **be kept burning.** In the **morning,** wearing **clothes** appropriate to each task, the priest was to **remove the ashes** from **the altar** and then dispose of them in a **ceremonially clean** place **outside the camp.**

The priests were responsible to keep **the fire** burning **on the altar** at all times.

### b. Priestly regulations for the grain offering (6:14-23)

**6:14-18.** These verses add little to the procedure outlined in chapter 2. The words **most holy** (6:17) indicate sacrificial flesh that could be eaten only by the priests (**any male descendant of Aaron,** v. 18). (The burnt offering, which was not to be eaten, was never said to be "holy" or "most holy.")

**6:19-23.** The priest's **regular** (i.e., daily; cf. Heb. 7:27) **grain offering** was not mentioned in Leviticus 2. It was to be prepared by the "heir apparent" of the **anointed** (high) **priest** (6:22) and offered **half . . . in the morning and half in the evening** (v. 20). Since a priest was **not** to eat his own offering, it was to be **burned completely** on the altar (v. 23).

### c. Priestly regulations for the sin offering (6:24-30)

**6:24-30.** This paragraph outlines (a) the procedure by which the flesh of **the sin offering** was to be consumed by **the priest** (v. 26) and his **male** relatives (v. 29); (b) the ritual for reconsecrating clothing accidentally touched by sacrificial **blood** or utensils touched by sacrificial **meat** (vv. 27-28); and (c) the restriction against eating the flesh of the **sin offering** of the priest or the community (identified by the ritual of taking **blood . . . into the Tent of Meeting,** v. 30).

## d. Priestly regulations for the guilt offering (7:1-6)

**7:1-6.** A fuller presentation of the sacrificial procedures is given here than in 5:14–6:7. **The place** of slaughter (7:2) parallels that of **the burnt offering** (at the north side of the altar, 1:11). The ritual procedure for the manipulation of **blood** (7:2) and the incineration **on the altar** (vv. 3-5) parallels that of the fellowship offering (chap. 3). The eating of the sacrificial flesh (7:6) parallels that of the sin offering (cf. 6:26, 29).

## e. Priests' summary of expiatory and dedicatory offerings (7:7-10)

**7:7-10.** This paragraph mentions the first four offerings (**sin . . . guilt . . . burnt,** and **grain**) and summarizes what **the priest** received from each. Cooked grain offerings went to the officiating **priest** (v. 9) whereas uncooked grain offerings were shared by **all** the priests (v. 10).

## f. Priestly regulations for the fellowship offering (7:11-21)

The distinctive feature of the fellowship offering was its accompanying communal meal. Since the priests' regulations pertained primarily to the distribution of the flesh of the sacrificial animals, it is natural that many details of this meal are found only here.

**7:11-15.** In the case of a thank offering—the most common kind of fellowship offering (cf. 22:29-30)—the **sacrifice of thanksgiving** (7:12; cf. comments on chap. 3) was to be accompanied by **one of each kind** (7:14) of three unleavened grain offerings (described in v. 12). Since the offerings were **without yeast,** the priest apparently offered "a memorial portion" on the altar accompanying the fat of the animal of the fellowship offering (cf. 2:9, 11-12). Then **the** officiating **priest** retained the rest for his allotment (7:14). However, the **offering with cakes of bread made with yeast** (v. 13) was apparently for the communal meal rather than for the officiating priest. The priest's portions of the fellowship offering are explained in verses 28-34. The portion of **the meat of** this **fellowship offering of thanksgiving** that was for the communal meal had to **be eaten on the day** of the offering (v. 15). The participants in the communal meal were the worshiper and

his family. A Levite from his community and the poor (who could afford no fellowship offering of their own) could be included (Deut. 12:12, 18-19). This meal had to be eaten at a divinely appointed place (Deut. 12:6-26).

**7:16-18.** However, in the case of a fellowship offering for **a vow** or **a freewill offering . . . anything left over** could **be eaten on the next day.** But any leftovers beyond the second day had to be **burned up.** To eat **any meat** on **the third day** disqualified the entire offering and made the violator subject to divine punishment. (For the special ritual of a fellowship offering at the deconsecration of a Nazirite, see Num. 6:13-20.)

**7:19-21.** (Cf. 19:5-8.) The general rule for eating **meat** was that both the **meat** and its eater had to be **ceremonially clean. Anyone** ceremonially **unclean** (cf. chaps. 11–15; 22) who ate **any meat of the fellowship offering** was to **be cut off from his people** (i.e., through death; cf. 7:21, 25, 27; 17:4, 9; 18:29; 19:8; 20:8, 17-18; 22:3; etc.).

## g. Appended regulations addressed to the Israelites (7:22-36)

(1) The prohibition against eating fat or blood. **7:22-27.** The principle set forth in 3:17 is now expanded. Eating **fat** from a clean animal, whether it died of natural causes or was slain by a wild animal (7:24) or was slaughtered as a sacrifice (v. 25), was prohibited on penalty of direct divine judgment (**be cut off from his people**). The rest of an animal not used for sacrifice could be eaten, but since this resulted in temporary uncleanness (11:39-40; 17:15), it was preferably given to a non-Israelite (Deut. 14:21). The fat of such an animal could **be used for any other purpose** besides food, such as lighting, polish, or other household purposes. The second prohibition pertains to eating meat from which **blood** was not drained (cf. 1 Sam. 14:33). The threatened penalty again was divine judgment.

(2) The priests' share of the fellowship offering. **7:28-34.** This paragraph supplements verses 11-21 on the communal meal shared by a worshiper and his family. As with other offerings (except the burnt) the priest received designated portions for food. **The breast of the fellowship offering** was to be waved **before the LORD as a wave offering.** Jewish

scholars interpreted this as a sideways action, dedicating the offering to the Lord. On the other hand they regarded the "heave offering" (KJV; NIV translates **contribution,** v. 32, and **regular share,** v. 34) of **the right thigh** (v. 32) as an up-and-down motion. **The right thigh** was given to **the** officiating **priest** (vv. 32-33) whereas **the breast** was given to the whole body of priests (v. 34) and their families—"sons and daughters" (Num. 18:11-12).

(3) Summary of the priests' share of the offerings. **7:35-36.** These verses appear to summarize the entire section of 6:8–7:34. Immediately after their installation into priestly service, the **priests** began to receive **their regular share for the generations to come.**

*h. Conclusion to the laws concerning sacrifices (7:37-38)*

**7:37-38.** This concluding paragraph probably refers back to the entire first seven chapters of the book, which included both the handbook on sacrifice addressed to **the Israelites** (1:1–6:7) and the additional regulations addressed to the priests (6:8–7:36). The administrative order of listing the sacrifices was followed since this order was just followed in the priestly regulations. The addition of **the ordination offering** (which probably refers to the special fellowship offering of a ram, 8:22-29) anticipates chapter 9 which records the ordination of Aaron and his sons. The reminder that these regulations are those **which the LORD gave Moses on Mount Sinai** points out that the sacrificial system was part of the covenant obligation given at Sinai (cf. 1:1).

**B. The inauguration of the priesthood and sacrificial system (chaps. 8–10)**

These chapters, along with 24:10-23, contain the only purely narrative portions of Leviticus (cf. comments on 1:1). In order to approach God, a Jewish worshiper needed not only an offering (chaps. 1–7) but also the mediation of a priest (cf. Heb. 5:1-4). Thus the institution of the priesthood to conduct the sacrificial ritual was the next step in implementing Israel's communion with the holy God. God had already ordained a hereditary priesthood through Aaron and his descendants (Ex. 29:9).

**1. THE ORDINATION OF AARON AND HIS SONS (CHAP. 8)**

Leviticus 8 is a narrative *description* which fulfilled and presupposed a knowledge of the Mosaic *prescription* recorded in Exodus 29; hence there is a close parallel between these two chapters.

*a. The preparation for the ordination service (8:1-4)*

**8:1-4.** The formula of divine revelation (**the LORD said to Moses**) not only marks the beginning of a new section but also indicates Moses' continuing role as the covenant mediator (chaps. 8–10). **Moses** received a twofold divine command: (a) **Bring Aaron and his sons** along with the accoutrements needed for the ordination (8:2), **and** (b) **gather the entire assembly** (probably a body of elders representing all Israel; cf. 9:1) **at the entrance** (forecourt or enclosure) of the tabernacle (8:3). Moses' obedience (he **did as the LORD commanded**) sets the normal literary pattern of command-obedience repeated throughout these chapters (except in 10:1-3).

*b. The investiture of Aaron with the clothing of the high priest (8:5-9)*

**8:5-9.** **Moses** first washed **Aaron and his sons . . . with water** probably at the bronze basin or laver (cf. Ex. 30:17-21), and then clothed **Aaron** with the garments of the high priest. The high priestly garments were a uniform calling attention to Aaron's mediatorial function or office rather than to his individual personality (Ex. 28:1-39; 29:5-6; 39:1-26 explain the high priest's clothing).

*c. The anointing of Aaron and the tabernacle with oil (8:10-12)*

**8:10-11.** Moses consecrated **the tabernacle and everything in it,** and also **the altar** of burnt offering and **the** bronze **basin** by sprinkling them with **the anointing oil** (cf. Ex. 30:26-29; 40:9-11). The recipe for the anointing oil, and the prohibition against its secular use, were given in Exodus 30:22-25, 31-33.

**8:12.** Moses then **poured some of the anointing oil on Aaron's head . . . to consecrate him** (cf. Ex. 29:7; 30:30; 40:13). The purpose of these anointings was to set apart the tabernacle (Lev. 8:10), the various articles of sacred furniture (vv.

10-11), and the priest who ministered in the sanctuary (v. 12) as most holy to the Lord (cf. Ex. 30:29).

### d. The investiture of Aaron's sons with priestly clothing (8:13)

**8:13.** In accordance with the Lord's command, **Moses** also put the priestly garments (cf. Ex. 28:40-43; 29:8-9) on each of **Aaron's** four **sons** (Lev. 10:1, 6; cf. Ex. 6:23).

### e. The offering of sacrifices for the consecration of the priest (8:14-29)

Moses then performed the sacrificial tasks prescribed for the priest (chaps. 1–7) while Aaron and his sons assumed the role of ordinary Israelites bringing their sacrifices. Both this narrative (8:14-29) and the prescription in Exodus 29:10-34 list the sacrifices in their procedural order (cf. comments on 6:8–7:38).

**8:14-17. The bull for the sin offering** was **presented** first (cf. Ex. 29:10-14), **and Aaron and his sons laid their hands on its head.** Since Aaron was not yet ordained to represent Israel in a mediatorial priestly function, this sin offering must have been on behalf of Aaron and his sons, rather than the people of Israel. Also the basic purpose of this sin offering was **to purify the altar** by consecrating **it to make atonement for it.** The ritual of this sin offering generally follows that established in Leviticus 4:3-12 except that here the blood was smeared on **the horns of the altar** of burnt offering rather than on the altar of incense (4:6-7). As usual, with a sin offering for a priest, the remaining **hide,** carcass, and **offal** were **burned up outside the camp.**

**8:18-21.** Moses next offered **the ram for the burnt offering** (cf. Ex. 29:15-18) according to the prescribed ritual (Lev. 1:10-13), except that **Moses** apparently performed all the stages of the ritual other than the laying on of **hands.**

**8:22-29.** The final offering in the sequence was a fellowship offering called **the ram for the ordination** (cf. Ex. 29:19-28). The ritual generally corresponds with that prescribed for the fellowship offering (Lev. 3:6-11; 7:28-34). The most obvious difference, of course, was the use of the blood by **Moses** in smearing **some of** the ram's blood **on the lobe of Aaron's right ear, on the thumb of his right hand, and on the big toe of his**

**right foot,** and likewise on **Aaron's sons. Moses** also **sprinkled** some of this **blood** on **Aaron** and his **sons** and their clothes (8:30).

A unique procedure occurred when Moses placed **the fat** of the ram with its **right thigh . . . in the hands of Aaron and his sons** (vv. 25-27). This seemed to symbolize in the eyes of all the people the sanctity of the office to which the priests had been appointed. On top of this **wave offering** which was burned **on the altar** (v. 28) was placed **a cake of bread, and one made with oil, and a wafer** taken **from the basket of bread made without yeast** which had been prepared for this occasion (v. 26). **The breast** of the **ram,** which was **Moses' share** of the offering as the officiating priest, was **waved . . . before the** LORD and apparently retained by Moses for food (cf. Ex. 29:26).

### f. The consecration of Aaron and his sons with anointing oil and sacrificial blood (8:30)

**8:30.** This consecration by **Moses** was prescribed in Exodus 29:20-21 (cf. Lev. 8:23-24).

### g. The seven-day ordination confinement of Aaron and his sons (8:31-36)

**8:31-32. Moses** instructed **Aaron and his sons** to **eat** the rest of the ram of ordination, along with the remainder of **the bread from the basket of ordination offerings** and then to **burn up** the leftovers.

**8:33-35.** Aaron and his sons were required to stay in the forecourt of **the Tent of Meeting day and night for seven days** to complete their **days of . . . ordination.**

**8:36.** The chapter is summarized with a statement of the obedience of **Aaron and his sons** to **everything the** LORD **commanded through Moses.**

### 2. THE COMMENCEMENT OF THE PUBLIC SACRIFICIAL SYSTEM (CHAP. 9)

This description of the formal inauguration of the whole Israelite sacrificial system resembles the prescription for the Day of Atonement ritual since on both occasions sacrifices were brought for both the priests and the people. However, here the people's fellowship offerings replaced the scapegoat ceremony, making this a feast instead of a fast.

### a. The prescription for the offerings for Aaron and the people (9:1-4)

**9:1-4.** With the ordination of **Aaron and his sons** completed, he was instructed to commence his priestly duties of offering sacrifice, first for himself and then for the people (cf. Heb. 9:7). **The 8th day** clearly refers to the day after the 7 days of Aaron's ordination confinement (8:33-35). According to the Jewish talmudic tradition, the preceding week of priestly ordination began on the 23rd day of the 12th month so that this 8th day of the ordination ceremonies was identical with the 1st day of the 1st month mentioned in Exodus 40:2, 17 when the tabernacle was erected. So **Aaron** immediately began his priestly duties by offering the first of the sacrifices of the tribal leaders on 12 consecutive days (Num. 7:10-88; cf. Bernard J. Bamberger, "Leviticus," in *The Torah: A Modern Commentary,* 3:65-6). In spite of the initial offerings on behalf of Aaron and his sons (Lev. 8:14-29) and their subsequent daily sin offerings during the 7 days of confinement (Ex. 29:35-37), it was still necessary for Aaron to present for himself both a **sin offering** and a **burnt offering** (Lev. 9:2). The people (represented by the **elders**) were to present animals for "sin," "burnt," **grain,** and **fellowship** offerings (vv. 3-4). The whole sacrificial system was placed in its theological context in the reason given by Moses for these offerings: **For today the LORD will appear to you** (cf. v. 6). God instituted sacrifice so that His Chosen People might, in spite of their innate sinfulness, have access through atonement to Him as the holy God, and that He might dwell among them and be their God (cf. the significant passage, Ex. 29:42-46).

### b. The preparation for the offerings (9:5-7)

**9:5-7.** After instructing **the entire assembly** (apparently synonymous with "the elders" of v. 1), **Moses** delegated his priestly functions to **Aaron** by inviting him to begin the sacrifices (**Come to the altar and sacrifice**).

### c. The description of Aaron's offerings (9:8-14)

**9:8-14.** Assisted by **his sons** (who assumed the role of ordinary worshipers so far as the sacrificial ritual was concerned), **Aaron** offered a **calf as a sin offering for himself.** Since Aaron had sinned previously by making a golden calf (Ex. 32), it is ironic that he now offered as his first sin offering a calf as if to atone for that sin. The ritual described follows that prescribed in Leviticus 4:3-12 except that the blood was smeared again (cf. 8:15) on **the horns of the altar** of burnt offering instead of on the altar of incense. Likewise, Aaron offered his own **burnt offering** (cf. 8:18-21).

### d. The description of the offerings for the people (9:15-22)

**9:15-22.** By offering a **goat for the people's sin offering** (v. 15), a calf and a lamb (cf. v. 3) for their **burnt offering** (v. 16) with a **grain offering** (v. 17), and **the cow and the ram** for their **fellowship offering** (v. 18), Aaron offered virtually all the kinds of sacrificial animals (except birds which were concessions for poor people) that were presentable under the sacrificial system. Aaron's benediction on the people at the completion of the sacrifices (v. 22) is linked in Jewish tradition with that in Numbers 6:24-26.

### e. The appearance of the divine glory (9:23-24)

**9:23-24.** After **Moses and Aaron . . . went into the Tent of Meeting** (whether for Moses to instruct Aaron, or for Moses to identify him in the eyes of the people as the one to serve in the sanctuary, or for them to commune with God) and **came out** to bless **the people . . . the glory of the LORD appeared to all the people.** Thus the designed purpose of sacrificial approach to God (cf. vv. 4, 6) was accomplished. This visible and glorious manifestation of the Lord's **presence,** along with the supernatural **fire** that fully **consumed** the already partially burned sacrifices **on the altar,** indicated His approval of the sacrifices.

### 3. THE CONSEQUENCES OF PRIESTLY CEREMONIAL DEVIATION (CHAP. 10)

On the very first day of his high priestly ministry, Aaron had to face the tragic deaths of his two eldest sons. Whereas in chapters 8–9 obedience to divine directives ultimately led to fire from God consuming the sacrifices in gracious approval, in chapter 10 ignorant or presumptuous action without divine directive resulted in fire from God consuming the violators in immediate·judgment.

### a. The ceremonial deviation and immediate deaths of Nadab and Abihu (10:1-3)

**10:1-3.** The two eldest **sons** of **Aaron** (cf. Ex. 6:23; 28:1; 1 Chron. 6:3), either through ignorance or presumption, **offered unauthorized fire before the LORD, contrary to His command.** This incident interrupted the regular pattern of the previous two chapters in which everything was done in accord with the commands of the Lord (cf. Lev. 8:36). It is not stated what made their offering of incense "unauthorized" ("strange," KJV). Perhaps they used coals in **their censers** that came from elsewhere than the altar (cf. 16:12) or they may have offered at the wrong time of day (Ex. 30:7-9). It may even be that they sought to go into the most holy place, and so usurped the prerogative of the high priest on the Day of Atonement (cf. Lev. 16:12-13). The command prohibiting the priests from drinking "wine or other fermented drink" (10:9) may suggest that drunkenness was a possible factor in their sin. In any event, they acted contrary to God's will and their immediate judgment by God was a dramatic example of what it meant to be "cut off from his people" (cf. Num. 15:30). "The moral of the story" as summarized by Moses is that those who have the privilege of being nearest to God must bear special responsibility to exemplify His holiness and glory.

### b. The removal of the bodies of Nadab and Abihu (10:4-5)

**10:4-5.** In obedience to Moses' command two **cousins** of Aaron carried the bodies of **Aaron's** two sons **outside the camp,** like the useless parts of sacrificial animals.

### c. The regulation of mourning for Nadab and Abihu (10:6-7)

**10:6-7.** In obedience to Moses' command, **Aaron and his** two remaining **sons—Eleazar and Ithamar—**refrained from the usual signs of mourning and grief, though all others were permitted to mourn for Nadab and Abihu. This was in harmony with the later prohibition against having the high priests take part in any of the funerals of their relatives (21:10-12).

### d. The reassurance from the Lord to Aaron to continue in his high priestly duties (10:8-11)

**10:8-11.** Only here in the Book of Leviticus is it said that **the LORD** spoke directly **to Aaron** without the mediation of Moses. The prohibition against **wine or other fermented drink** was probably aimed at keeping their minds clear to fulfill their priestly duty of distinguishing **between the holy and the profane, between the unclean and the clean,** and so being prepared to **teach the Israelites** the rules revealed from God **through Moses** as well as to make decisions about difficult cases (cf. Deut. 17:9-11). The priests' task to teach the Israelites the way of holiness prepared the setting for the instructions in Leviticus 11–15.

### e. The command of Moses about the normal disposition of sacrificial portions (10:12-15)

**10:12-15.** **Moses** instructed **Aaron and his remaining sons** about those portions of the sacrifices that were given to them for food (cf. 6:26; 7:12-15).

### f. The anger of Moses regarding the deviant disposition of the carcass of the sin offering (10:16-18)

**10:16-18.** **Moses** became **angry with Eleazar and Ithamar** when he discovered they had **burned up** the entire carcass of the people's **sin offering** (cf. 9:15) instead of eating it as prescribed (**since its blood had not been taken into the holy place,** 10:18; if the blood had been taken into the holy place, then the carcass would properly have been burned "outside the camp," 4:12, 21).

### g. The satisfaction of Moses with Aaron's explanation (10:19-20)

**10:19-20.** Aaron's explanation for his sons' behavior (in which he apparently shared) seems to link the tragedy of Nadab and Abihu (**such things as this have happened to me**) with these irregularities in the **sin offering** procedure. **Aaron** asked his brother, **Would the LORD have been pleased if I had eaten the sin offering today?** Apparently he either had a genuine fear of eating what was "most holy" (v. 17) in the wake of his sons' deaths, or he was confused by grief and inadvertently mishandled the sacrificial procedure. If so, this would seem to be a case in which he should have brought his own sin offering for a ritual violation, though this is not indicated. In any event, Moses **was satisfied** with Aaron's explanation.

## C. The laws concerning uncleanness (chaps. 11–15)

The concepts of "unclean" and "clean" are not equivalent to "physically dirty" and "spic and span" (Bamberger, "Leviticus," p. 101), or are they directly related to sterility or contagion in a hygienic sense, though there were several degrees of ritual contagion. While the laws relating to uncleanness providentially had many good hygienic results, this was not their primary purpose. The distinction between unclean and clean was not even a matter of "sinful" and "unsinful," for much of the ritual defilement came about through accident, illness, physical processes, and other actions that were proper and even commendable (Bamberger, "Leviticus," p. 102.)

Actually there were three ritual states—holy, clean (pure), and unclean (impure). Thus ceremonial cleanness was merely a neutral state between the impure and the holy (cf. Wenham, Leviticus, pp. 18-25). The intent of the laws of uncleanness was essentially theological and religious—to set forth obedience to the laws of Israel's covenant Lawgiver because He had ordained them. However, this does not preclude a divine rationale in the selection of unclean and clean animals, including hygienic reasons in at least some cases.

One of the tasks of the priests was to teach the people to distinguish "between the unclean and the clean" (10:10-11). Thus it was important to have divine revelation on the subject of ceremonial uncleanness in relation to diet (chap. 11), disease (chaps. 13–14), and other forms of physical uncleanness (chaps. 12; 15). Because these chapters relate to matters involving such responsibilities of the priests, they are addressed to both "Moses and Aaron" (11:1; 14:33; 15:1).

### 1. THE LAWS OF FOOD AND CLEAN AND UNCLEAN ANIMALS (CHAP. 11)

This chapter (almost identical to Deut. 14:3-20) contains most of the Levitical dietary legislation (cf. Lev. 17).

### a. The definitions of clean and unclean animals (11:1-23)

Why did God disallow certain animals for food? Was it merely an arbitrary test of religious obedience? Certain hygienic considerations were no doubt part of the reason, at least in the providence of God (Harrison, Leviticus, pp. 124-6, gives an elaboration of this view). But the primary reason seems to have been theological—to teach symbolically Israel's status as the holy (separated) people of God. It is striking that the two major chapters on unclean foods are either introduced (Deut. 14:1-2) or concluded (Lev. 11:44-45) with an affirmation of Israel's election to be a holy people of God. The threefold classification of animals into unclean, clean, and sacrificial seems to parallel the division of mankind into unclean (those excluded from the camp of Israel), clean (ordinary Israelites when not defiled), and the priesthood (those who offered sacrifices in the sanctuary; Wenham, Leviticus, p. 170).

The major concepts of this chapter are these: (1) Unclean animals were not to be eaten, though no punishment is stated for violation of this command. (2) All dead animals, whether unclean or clean (unless ritually slaughtered at the tabernacle), rendered those who touched their carcasses ceremonially unclean, but this was only temporary if they washed in water and waited till evening. (3) Household articles touched by certain carcasses were also unclean (cf. vv. 32-38).

**11:1-8. Animals that live on land** are one of the three major groupings of animals (cf. Gen. 1:20-25). Clean and therefore edible animals from this group are listed in the parallel passage in Deuteronomy 14:4-5: the ox, sheep, goat, deer, gazelle, roe deer, wild goat, ibex, antelope, and mountain sheep. All others were inedible and unclean. Only the first three of these, being domesticated, were sacrificial animals. Only those land animals were clean which are cloven-hoofed and chew the cud. **The camel** (Lev. 11:4), **the coney** (i.e., rock badger, v. 5), and **the rabbit** (v. 6) were unclean because none of them has **a split hoof** (vv. 4-6). For example, a camel has a pad of tissue on the bottom of its foot which prevents it from being a cloven hoof. It is true that the coney and rabbit do not "chew the cud" in the modern scientific sense, but their jaw movements and thoroughness in chewing fell within the empirical significance of the Hebrew phrase. On the other hand, **the pig** (probably the wild boar) was disqualified because it **does not chew the cud.**

**11:9-12.** The second group was the animals **living in the water.** Only fish which **have** both **fins and scales** could be eaten. All other seafood was **detestable** (a stronger word for "unclean," v. 12) and could not be eaten.

**11:13-23.** The third group included flying creatures, both **birds** (vv. 13-19) and **flying insects** (vv. 20-23). Twenty species of birds (including **the bat** which is not strictly a bird) were forbidden. These are apparently birds of prey (which would thus violate the fundamental prohibition against eating flesh with blood in it; cf. chap. 17). Though not named, clean birds that could be eaten were doves, pigeons, quail, and sparrows. The only edible flying insects were four species of locusts (11:22).

### b. The defilement from dead animals (11:24-40)

**11:24-28.** Touching the dead **carcass** of any unclean land **animal**—including **those that walk on their paws** (lit., "hands," v. 27), for example, cats, dogs, and bears—rendered a person ceremonially **unclean** and so required washing and waiting until **evening.** The concept of being **unclean till evening** not only prohibited participation in worship but also restricted movement within society.

**11:29-38.** A special group of land **animals . . . move about on the ground** (lit., "swarm," i.e., occur in swarms and move about in haphazard fashion). The same Hebrew word is translated "insects" in verse 20. In fact, "swarmers" may fit into any of the three major groups of animals, whether they move on land, in water, or in the air. All such creatures were **unclean** and if they were found **dead** inside a household vessel or if their **carcass** touched any **article,** the article was **unclean** till destroyed or purified. An exception was made in the case of **a spring or a cistern** (v. 36) perhaps because of the dire need for water sources.

**11:39-40.** Even the carcasses of clean animals rendered a person who touched

them **unclean** and in need of the wash-and-wait procedure (ritual bathing and waiting **till evening** to be ceremonially clean; cf. comments on vv. 24-28).

### c. Summary and theological conclusion (11:41-47)

**11:41-47.** The whole set of food laws is summarized by the repetition of selected examples (vv. 41-43). As God's people were to distinguish between **clean** and **unclean** animals, so **God** had distinguished between them and other nations. These food **regulations** were to serve as a perpetual reminder of the holiness of God and His grace in choosing Israel (v. 45).

### 2. THE LAW OF CHILDBIRTH (CHAP. 12)

### a. The period of postnatal uncleanness (12:1-5)

Since childlessness in ancient times was a great misfortune (e.g., Gen. 15; 1 Sam. 1) and sometimes even a judgment of God (Lev. 20:20; Deut. 28:18), it may seem strange that childbearing would render a mother unclean, especially for such a long period of time (40 to 80 days). However, it was not the birth itself (the baby was not considered unclean) but the postnatal discharge of blood (Lev. 12:5, 7) that made the mother ceremonially unclean. The rationale behind this may have been that a bleeding or discharging body was considered to lack wholeness, and so was unclean (cf. Wenham, *Leviticus,* p. 188). Another suggestion is that such discharges contained dead matter (Harrison, *Leviticus,* p. 161).

**12:1-5.** If a **woman** gave **birth to a son,** she was **unclean for 7 days** (v. 2), followed by an additional **33 days** before she could **be purified** (v. 4). In the case of a daughter each period of time was twice as long (**two weeks** plus **66 days,** v. 5). It was only during her 7- to 14-day period that she was contagiously **unclean** (i.e., **as she was unclean during her monthly period,** v. 2; cf. 15:19-24), but she was still individually unclean for the remainder of the time and could not enter **the sanctuary** until the 40 or 80 **days of her purification were over.** The reason she was unclean for a longer period for a girl is not stated, but perhaps a postnatal discharge lasted longer in the case of a girl, or perhaps the reason was that the child would someday be subject to uncleanness associated with female discharges and childbirth.

### b. The purification offerings after childbirth (12:6-8)

**12:6-8.** Having a baby was not a sin but instead was the fulfillment of a divine command (Gen. 1:28). Thus the need of a **sin offering . . . to make atonement** was only a matter of ritual purification. In order to be pronounced **ceremonially clean** (12:7), the new mother offered **a year-old lamb for a burnt offering and a young pigeon or a dove for a sin offering** (v. 6). If she was a poor person, she brought **two** birds, **one** each **for a burnt offering** and **a sin offering.** Mary, the mother of Jesus, qualified for this concession (Luke 2:22-24).

### 3. THE LAWS FOR INFECTIOUS SKIN DISEASES AND MILDEW (CHAPS. 13-14)

Chapters 13–14 pertain to the diagnosis, treatment, and ceremonial cleansing of infectious skin diseases in people (13:2-46; 14:1-32) and spreading mildew both in clothing and similar articles (13:47-58) and in houses (14:33-53). This peculiar grouping together of such diverse contagions is explained in that they are all designated by the Hebrew word ṣārā'aṯ (traditionally trans. "leprosy") which is sufficiently broad to cover any form of spreading surface discoloration or flaking whether in humans or in objects subject to mold or mildew. The problem in translating this Hebrew word is illustrated by the fact that in one instance the NIV translated it with the whole compound phrase: "infectious skin diseases and mildew" (v. 57).

The abnormality of all these conditions would disrupt the wholeness necessary for Levitical worship and so render the infected persons or objects unclean. The Hebrew word for the skin diseases described in these chapters must be much broader than Hansen's disease (leprosy), but the question is whether or not it ever means "leprosy." The question cannot be answered with certainty. Modern medical opinion seems to be agreed that leprosy (Hansen's disease) is *not* the skin disease dealt with in these chapters. Some interpret archeological evidence to discount the possibility of widespread leprosy in the ancient Near East (see S.G. Browne, *Leprosy in the Bible.* London: Christian Medical Fellowship, 1970). One scholar has identified the following skin diseases in chapter 13—psoriasis (vv. 2-28), favus (vv. 29-37), and vitiligo (leucodermia, vv. 38-39; E.V. Hulse, "The Nature of Biblical 'Leprosy' and the Use of Alternative Medical Terms in Modern Translations of the Bible," *Palestine Exploration Quarterly,* 107. July–December, 1975:87-105; cf. Wenham, *Leviticus,* pp. 194-7).

On the other hand Harrison believes that Hansen's disease should definitely be *included* in the generic term ṣārā'aṯ (*Leviticus,* pp. 136-9). Possibly advanced forms of leprosy are not described in chapter 13 (cf. NIV marg.), since apparently the chapter discusses early diagnosis. People with advanced leprosy would be in isolation outside the camp.

### a. The diagnosis and treatment of human skin disease (13:1-46)

**13:1-46.** A stereotyped description is given of most of the 21 cases (not types) of skin disease mentioned in this section: (a) a preliminary indication of symptoms (e.g., vv. 2, 7, 9, 12, etc.); (b) a priestly inspection or reinspection (e.g., vv. 3, 10, 13, 15, etc.); (c) a statement of specific symptoms as viewed by **the priest** (vv. 3, 11, 13, 15, etc.); (d) the priest's diagnosis, whether **unclean** (vv. 3, 8, 11, 15, etc.) or **clean** (vv. 6, 13, 17, 23, etc.); (e-1) if diagnosed as **unclean,** the **isolation** treatment of verses 44-46 must follow (cf. v. 11b); (e-2) if the initial inspection is inconclusive, a **seven**-day quarantine may be imposed (e.g., vv. 4, 21, 31) to be followed by another inspection (vv. 5, 26) and diagnosis or in some cases a second week of quarantine (e.g., vv. 6, 33).

This section can be outlined as follows: (a) introduction (v. 1), (b) the first **skin disease** test series (vv. 2-8), (c) the second **skin disease** test series (vv. 9-17), (d) the third test series for skin diseases in scars (vv. 18-23), (e) the fourth test series for skin diseases in burns (vv. 24-28), (f) the fifth test series for skin diseases in scalp or beard (vv. 29-37), (g) identifying a ceremonially clean skin disease (vv. 38-39), (h) the relationship of skin diseases to baldness (vv. 40-44), and (i) the treatment of those diagnosed as ceremonially unclean (vv. 45-46) (cf. Wenham, *Leviticus,* p. 194).

The priest did not function as a doctor to prescribe medical treatment. He functioned more like a public health officer who isolated a person with a contagious skin disease. Whether this contagion was merely ceremonial or was also hygienic is beside the point of this comparison. The patient was basically left to natural (or supernatural) healing processes to cure his condition, during which time he was isolated **outside the camp** (v. 46) in a condition of mourning with the responsibility to warn any passerby that he was **Unclean!** (v. 45) The significance of this isolation was not only to prevent possible physical contagion but also to symbolize the person's separation from the holy camp of Israel where the Lord was dwelling (Num. 5:1-4; cf. Deut. 23:10-14).

*b. The diagnosis and treatment of mildew in clothing and personal articles (13:47-59)*

**13:47-59.** Like infectious skin diseases, mold and mildew can disfigure the outside surface of certain articles, causing them to flake or peel. This section contains three cases in which mildewed articles are diagnosed as unclean (vv. 47-52, 53-55, 56-57). When clothing or similar personal articles were **contaminated with mildew** (v. 47), they were to be **shown to the priest** (v. 49) who would **isolate the affected article for seven days** (v. 50), after which, **if the mildew** had **spread,** it would be labeled as **unclean** (v. 51) and had to **be burned up** (v. 52). If **the mildew** had **not spread** (v. 53), the article would **be washed** and isolated **another seven days** (v. 54), after which it would still be regarded as **unclean** and burned up unless **the mildew** had **faded**—then only **the contaminated part** was torn **out** and burned (v. 56), and the rest of the article **washed again** to **be clean** (v. 58). The entire regulation is summarized in verse 59.

*c. The ritual cleansing of a person cured of an infectious skin disease (14:1-32)*

After a person who had been isolated as unclean outside the camp of Israel had become cured (either by natural causes or in answer to prayer; cf. Num. 12:13), he could be readmitted to fellowship within the holy nation and could again draw near to worship the holy God at the Tent of Meeting. This readmission and ritual cleansing involved two stages:

(a) a two-bird ritual outside the camp (Lev. 14:3-7) followed by a ceremonial washing (v. 8), and (b) a series of sacrifices in the sanctuary eight days later (vv. 10-20; the alternate sanctuary ritual for a poor person is given in vv. 21-32).

**14:1-2.** This introduction identifies **Moses** as the mediator of these regulations for **ceremonial cleansing.**

**14:3-7.** The two-bird ritual **outside the camp** (cf. vv. 49-53 where the same ritual was used to "make atonement" for a house) bears a resemblance to the two-goat ritual on the Day of Atonement (cf. 16:7-9, 15-19). Wenham (*Leviticus,* pp. 208-9) thinks the **two live clean birds** represented a healed Israelite, as established by the **one** bird's **blood** being sprinkled on **him.** The slain bird would then symbolize the death he had just escaped, and the released bird symbolically carried away the polluting skin disease. It may also represent the life within the community to which the person was reintroduced. The **cedar wood, scarlet yarn, and hyssop** (14:4, 6), which are not explained but are associated with purification elsewhere in the Old Testament (e.g., Num. 19:6; Ps. 51:7), were to be dipped with **the live bird . . . into the blood of the** slain **bird** (Lev. 14:6), and used to **sprinkle the one to be cleansed.** After the person was pronounced **clean . . . the live bird** was to be released **in the open fields.**

**14:8a.** To symbolize his cleansing from pollution, **the person** then washed his clothing, shaved **off all his hair,** and bathed (cf. v. 9).

**14:8b-9.** Next, the cleansed person spent a **seven**-day period in semi-quarantine in **the camp** but **outside his tent. On the seventh day** he repeated the washing and shaving procedure (**head . . . beard,** and **eyebrows!**).

**14:10-11.** The sacrificial rituals for atonement and purification began **on the eighth day** when **the priest** presented the cured and cleansed person with his offerings to **the Lord.** This special ritual involved offering all four types of mandatory sacrifices (guilt, sin, burnt, and grain; see comments on chaps. 1–7 for additional explanation besides that which follows). The scope of these offerings and the use of both blood and **oil** are more reminiscent of the ordination service of Aaron and his sons (chap. 8) than of any other ritual.

**14:12-18.** The sacrifice of the **guilt offering** consisted of a **male** lamb. The allowance of this young ram instead of a full-grown ram (chap. 5) possibly was to reduce the cost as much as possible since the pollution incurred was not necessarily the person's fault (cf. Num. 6:12 for a parallel situation in the accidental breaking of a Nazirite vow). A **guilt offering** was normally expected after a person defrauded either God or man (cf. Lev. 5:14–6:7). Perhaps the person isolated outside the camp was viewed as having deprived God of due worship and service. Or he may have suspected that his disease was the result of an unidentified sin, and so required a guilt offering (5:16-19; the absence of the 20% compensation suggests this option).

The unusual features about this guilt offering were smearing **some of the blood . . . on the lobe of the right ear . . . on the thumb of his right hand, and on the big toe of his right foot** (14:14; cf. 8:23-24), and sprinkling **oil . . . before the LORD seven times** and putting some oil **on top of the blood** on the person's right ear, thumb, and toe (14:17), with **the rest of the oil** put on his **head.** The result of this entire series of rituals was to **make atonement for him before the LORD.**

**14:19-20.** The sacrificial procedure was completed with **the sin offering** (the one ewe lamb, v. 10) and **the burnt offering** (v. 19, the other male lamb of v. 10), accompanied by **the grain offering** (v. 20).

**14:21-32.** An alternative sacrificial ritual was prescribed as a concession for the **poor.** The ritual is the same as that just described (vv. 10-20) except that **two doves or two young pigeons** (v. 22) were substituted for the lambs of the **sin** and **burnt** offerings, thus also reducing the quantity of flour needed for the **grain offering** which was, however, usually offered along with the birds of the sin and burnt offerings.

*d. The diagnosis, treatment, and cleansing of mildew in houses (14:33-53)*

**14:33-53.** This section is really an extension of the law concerning clothing and personal articles (cf. 13:47-59), which apparently included the materials from which tents were made. This extension concerns houses made of **stones** and **clay** (14:42), and would be in effect after the Israelites entered **the land of Canaan** (v. 34). The procedures of the diagnosis, treatment, and cleansing of permanent houses were similar to those for persons or garments, including quarantine periods (v. 38). For treatment, the infected portions of the house were removed and replaced (vv. 39-42). **If the mildew** recurred, the whole **house** had to be destroyed (vv. 43-45). But if the treatment was successful, the house was purified with a two-**bird** ritual similar to that for a cured person (vv. 48-53; cf. vv. 3-7).

*e. Summary (14:54-57)*

**14:54-57.** These verses conclude **the regulations** for ṣāraʻaṯ—**infectious skin diseases and mildew** (cf. introduction to chaps. 13–14).

4. THE LAWS OF UNCLEANNESS FROM HUMAN DISCHARGES (CHAP. 15)

This chapter defines four cases of ceremonial pollution, a chronic case and a periodic case for males and a chronic case and a periodic case for females. All four cases probably refer to discharges from the sexual organs (though some interpreters think vv. 2-12 refer to hemorrhoids). For possible reasons why such discharges were considered defiling, see comments on 12:1-5.

*a. The purification of a man's chronic discharge (15:1-15)*

**15:1.** The formula of divine revelation is addressed again to both **Moses and Aaron** (cf. 11:1; 13:1; 14:33).

**15:2-12.** The chronic or long-term male **discharge** described in this section was probably gonorrhea. The major concern was the man's ceremonial **uncleanness** and its consequences because other persons and objects he contacted became not only ceremonially unclean but also secondary sources of further uncleanness, for example, his **bed** (pallet, vv. 4-5), his chair (v. 6), his person (v. 7), his spittle (v. 8), his saddle (v. 9), and anything **under him** (subject to contact from his discharge, v. 10). In this sense, his uncleanness was more infectious than that from skin disease (chaps. 13–14) or from unclean animals (chap. 11) which were limited to direct contact. However, since a **man** with a chronic **discharge** was not isolated outside the camp (cf. 13:45-46), his uncleanness was apparently less serious (though more ritually infectious) than that associated with skin disease. A probable conclusion to be drawn from this is that the purpose of the uncleanness codes was not primarily hygienic but religious and theological.

**15:13-15.** The appropriate rite of purification after the cessation of the discharge was a **seven**-day waiting period, after which the **man** bathed and washed **his clothes. On the eighth day he** made **atonement** by presenting the least expensive offering—**two doves or two young pigeons . . . the one for a sin offering and the other for a burnt offering.**

### b. The purification of a man's periodic discharge (15:16-18)

**15:16-18.** The second case pertaining to males was the periodic discharge of **an emission of semen,** whether possibly a nocturnal emission or one during intercourse. For this case, no sacrifice was required and the uncleanness was removed by a simple wash-and-wait (**till evening**) procedure (cf. comments on 11:24-28). It is noteworthy that while the normal sexual process between husband and wife (15:18) made **both** partners ceremonially **unclean,** it did not make them sinful—no guilt was involved and no sacrifice was required. So the chronic discharges which required a sin offering were not necessarily related to personal sin.

### c. The purification of a woman's periodic discharge (15:19-24)

**15:19-24.** The third case pertained to the ceremonial uncleanness resulting from the **regular flow of blood** during a woman's **monthly period.** Though this was a periodic rather than a chronic discharge (cf. vv. 25-27), the woman was considered unclean for **seven days,** in the same sense as a man who had a chronic discharge with the attendant possibilities of secondary pollution (cf. vv. 2-12). Since sexual intercourse was forbidden during a woman's period (18:19; 20:18), 15:24 probably means that if a woman's period commenced while she was having intercourse with her husband, he would be unclean like her and would also be a source of secondary pollution (as in vv. 2-12).

### d. The purification of a woman's chronic discharge (15:25-30)

**15:25-27.** However, in the fourth case, a woman's chronic **discharge** outside the **period** of menstruation resulted in extended uncleanness for her until the **discharge** ceased. The description of the discharge is broad enough probably to include a number of causes. The secondary pollution regulations were again in effect (v. 27). A woman in a thronging crowd who was healed by Jesus had such a chronic discharge (Mark 5:25-34; Luke 8:43-48). In view of the Levitical secondary pollution regulations, no wonder she was disturbed when Jesus revealed her presence to those who were jostling her!

**15:28-30. On the eighth day** after the cessation of her discharge, a woman was to bring **two** birds for **sin** and **burnt** offerings just as a man with a chronic discharge would do (vv. 13-15).

### e. Summary (15:31-33)

**15:31-33.** These verses state the purpose of this law—**so they will not die in their uncleanness for defiling My dwelling place, which is among them**—and relist the regulations (vv. 32-33).

## D. The law of the Day of Atonement (chap. 16)

The annual Day of Atonement was the one fast day (see comments on v. 29; cf. Acts 27:9) among Israel's annual feasts (cf. Lev. 23). Additional instructions are given in other passages (Ex. 30:10; Lev. 23:26-32; 25:9; Num. 29:7-11), but Leviticus 16 contains the fullest explanation of its ritual.

Wenham indicates, "The main purpose of the Day of Atonement ceremonies is to cleanse the sanctuary from the pollution introduced into it by the unclean worshipers (cf. 16:16, 19) . . . [so as] to make possible God's continued presence among His people" (*Leviticus,* p. 228). It is true that the cleansing of "the most holy place, the Tent of Meeting, and the altar" (v. 20) was a theologically significant feature of the Day of Atonement which appeared to be accomplished by the blood manipulation ritual of the slain goat for the people (vv. 15-19). But the completion of the sin offering with the live goat ritual involved a substitutionary carrying away of the people's sins (v. 22) which were identified as "all the wickedness and rebellion of the Israelites—all their sins" (v. 20), so that they "will be clean from all [their] sins" (v. 30). Of course Aaron and his household were the initial objects of the atoning sacrifice's special rituals (vv. 6, 11-14). So the special atonement ritual averted the wrath of God for all the sins of the people for the past year.

The comprehensiveness of the sins atoned for by the Day of Atonement ritual was staggering. One might expect that certain sins would be excluded—either those already expiated by individual sacrifices or those defiant sins for which there was no individual sacrifice and for which the prescribed punishment was capital and/or "cutting off" from the people (cf. comments under 17:3-7). But no such limitation is evident in chapter 16. The one apparently limiting factor to the efficacy of this national Day of Atonement for the individual was a proper heart attitude of penitence and faith, which was also true of the individual sacrifices (cf. *Introduction:* "The Significance of Old Testament Sacrifice").

## 1. INTRODUCTION (16:1-2)

**16:1.** This verse places the instruction concerning the Day of Atonement in a specific historical context. **The Lord spoke to Moses** (cf. 1:1; 4:1; etc.) **after the death of the two sons of Aaron who died when they approached the Lord.** Nadab and Abihu were consumed by fire from the presence of the Lord because they approached Him in an unauthorized manner (10:1-2). By contrast chapter 16 sets forth the *proper* occasion, manner of self-preparation, and prescribed ritual by which the high priest was to approach the Lord and *not* die.

**16:2.** God did not reveal priestly prescriptions directly to **Aaron** and his sons but rather spoke through **Moses.** The prohibition to ''come not at all times''(kjv) **into the most holy place** is indicated by the context to be a limitation to come only on this one annual occasion. Thus the NIV gives the proper sense, that Aaron was **not to come whenever he** chose. To enter **behind the curtain** would have exposed the high priest to the presence of the Shekinah glory of God **in the cloud over the atonement cover** of **the ark** (cf. Ex. 25:10-22, esp. v. 22; 40:34-38). The **atonement cover**

("mercy seat," kjv) obviously functioned as a cover for the ark, but the Hebrew word *kappōret* (related to *kipper,* "to make atonement," see comments under Lev. 1:4) suggests a "place of propitiation," a meaning suitable to the Greek word *hilastērion* (trans. "sacrifice of atonement" in Rom. 3:25). (See the diagram "Plan of the Tabernacle" near Ex. 25.)

## 2. THE PREPARATION OF THE HIGH PRIEST AND THE ANIMALS FOR THE CEREMONIES (16:3-5)

**16:3-5.** In preparation for the Day of Atonement ritual, the designated animals were to be brought to **the sanctuary area**: for the high priest and his family—**a young bull for a sin offering and a ram for a burnt offering,** and for the **Israelite community . . . two male goats for a sin offering and a ram for a burnt offering.** The high priest first bathed **himself with water;** then, in order to show his servant status before the Lord, dressed in simple **linen** clothing—shirt, shorts, **sash,** and **turban**—garments even plainer than those of an ordinary priest (cf. Ex. 39:27-29).

## 3. A SUMMARY STATEMENT OF THE CEREMONIES (16:6-10)

**16:6-10.** Before a more detailed description of the Day of **Atonement** rituals, an overview is given of the major features of the ceremonies: (a) the sin offering of a **bull** for the high priest **and his household** (cf. vv. 11-14, 24-25, 27); (b) the sin offering of **two goats** for the people, including the selection by **lot** of **the scapegoat** (vv. 7-8) and the sacrifice of **the goat whose lot falls to the Lord** (cf. vv. 15-19, 24-25); and (c) the ritual of **sending** the **scapegoat** into the wilderness (cf. vv. 20-22).

## 4. A DETAILED DESCRIPTION OF THE CEREMONIES (16:11-28)

### a. The sin offering of the high priest (16:11-14)

This paragraph explains the steps in the blood-sprinkling ritual of the bull slaughtered by the high priest "for his own sin offering" (v. 11). This ceremony resembles the ritual given in 4:3-12 for the ordinary sin offering of the high priest, the difference being in the *place* where the blood was sprinkled. Rather than in front of the curtain and on the incense altar (as in 4:6-7), the blood here was taken into the most holy place and sprinkled on "the front of" and "before the atonement cover" (16:14).

**16:11.** The purpose of the high priest's **sin offering** was **to make atonement for himself and his household.** The high priest himself had to be cleansed from the pollution of **sin** before he could function as a mediator to offer "the sin offering for the people" (v. 15).

**16:12-13.** The high priest was to enter the most holy place three times, the first time with **a censer full of burning coals from the altar** of burnt offering on which coals he was to burn **incense** prepared especially for use in the tabernacle (cf. Ex. 30:34-36). This apparently created a **smoke** screen to prevent his gazing at the Shekinah glory of God's presence over **the atonement cover,** thus averting divine wrath on himself.

**16:14.** Aaron was to enter a second time behind the curtain with **some of the bull's blood** which he was to **sprinkle . . . on the front of the atonement cover,** and then **seven times before the atonement cover** (either on the front of the ark or on the ground). The use of the rest of the bull's blood is indicated in verses 18-19.

*b. The sin offering of the people (16:15-17)*

**16:15.** The sin offering of the people consisted of "two male goats" (v. 5), one of which was selected by lot to be the Lord's goat and one to be "the scapegoat" (v. 8). This selection procedure is passed over here since the summary explanation (vv. 7-8) was adequate. The scapegoat is again the subject of verses 20-22, but first the high priest was instructed to **slaughter the** Lord's **goat for the sin offering for the people** and to manipulate the blood within the most holy place (his third entrance therein) **as he did with the bull's blood** (cf. v. 14).

**16:16-17.** The same ritual was to be enacted in **the Tent of Meeting,** perhaps through the sprinkling of blood seven times before the altar of incense, and then by smearing blood on the horns of this altar (as indicated in Ex. 30:10). The combined blood-sprinkling ritual (in the most holy place and in the Tent of Meeting) is said not only to make **atonement for** the high priest, **his household, and the whole community of Israel** (Lev.

16:17) but also to make "atonement for the most holy place, the Tent of Meeting, and the altar" (v. 20; cf. v. 16). Thus the purpose of the sin offering was to provide an atonement for Israel by cleansing the place of God's dwelling from the pollution of the people's sins. Alternately, it may be that the animal was slaughtered to make atonement for them and the blood was sprinkled to purify the sanctuary. God's dwelling place needed to be cleansed **because of the uncleanness and rebellion of the Israelites, whatever their sins have been** (v. 16).

*c. The cleansing of the altar (16:18-19)*

**16:18-19.** Not only was the most holy place and the rest of the Tent of Meeting to be symbolically cleansed from the pollution of Israel's sins, but also **the altar that** was **before the** LORD was to be cleansed. Though some scholars have identified this as the altar of incense (e.g., Harrison, *Leviticus,* p. 173), it more probably refers to the altar of burnt offering which is elsewhere described as "before the" LORD" (cf. 1:3, 5, etc.; cf. Wenham, *Leviticus,* p. 401). This cleansing was accomplished by putting a mixture of **some of the bull's blood and some of the goat's blood . . . on all the horns of the altar,** and sprinkling **blood on it** (either on the top or on the sides) **seven times** (16:19). The purpose of this action was **to consecrate it from the uncleanness of the Israelites.**

*d. The dispatch of the scapegoat into the wilderness (16:20-22)*

**16:20-22.** It is significant that the high priest *finished* **making atonement for the most holy place, the Tent of Meeting, and the altar** before he brought **forward the live goat** on whose head he was **to lay both hands . . . and confess over it all the wickedness and rebellion of the Israelites—all their sins—and put them** symbolically **on the goat's head.** Though some scholars maintain that already-atoned and already-forgiven sins were placed on the goat's head, it is clearer to understand that the effect of the people's sin on the sanctuary had been cleansed by the blood-sprinkling ceremony but that sending the live **goat away into the desert** (as a part of the sin offering) made atonement in the sense of cleansing the Israelites from their sins.

The identification of the live goat as a "scapegoat" (vv. 8, 10, 26) needs clarification since the Hebrew *'ăzā'zēl* (found only in these verses in the OT) has been translated in at least four ways: (a) as a reference to the goat itself—an "escape goat" or "goat of departure"; (b) as a proper name, Azazel, referring to the powers of evil, or to a desert demon, or even to Satan, so that the sins of Israel were sent back to their ultimate evil source; (c) as a term meaning "rocky precipice" (or some similar place), from which the goat was pushed over backward to kill it; and (d) as an abstract term meaning "complete destruction, entire removal," or the like (cf. C.L. Feinberg, "The Scapegoat of Leviticus 16," *Bibliotheca Sacra*, 115. October-December, 1958:320-33; Carl Schultz, *Theological Wordbook of the Old Testament*. Chicago, Moody Press, 1980, 2:658-9). A survey of scholarly opinion merely reinforces the uncertainty of the exact etymology and usage of this term. However, the significance of the goat's function in bearing away the people's sin into the wilderness is clearly set forth in chapter 16.

*e. The cleansing of the high priest and the incineration of the burnt and sin offerings (16:23-25)*

**16:23-25.** After the high priest removed and left his **linen garments** in the **Tent of Meeting,** he bathed (to assure ceremonial purity) **and put on his regular garments** of high priestly splendor for the incineration ritual. He then sacrificed **the burnt offering** of a ram (v. 3) **for himself and the burnt offering** of a second ram (v. 5) **for the people** along with **the fat of the sin offering** (apparently referring to both the bull of the high priest and the goat of the people). It is noteworthy that it was now the burnt offerings that made atonement for himself and the people (cf. 1:4). Apparently the supplemental sacrifices of Numbers 29:8-11 were offered next in the Day of Atonement ceremonies.

*f. The cleansing of other participants and the disposal of the remainder of the sin offerings (16:26-28)*

**16:26-28.** Continued ceremonial cleanness both of the participants and of the sanctuary itself is preserved by (a) the cleansing of **the man who releases the** goat into the desert, (b) the burning of the **hides, carcasses, and offal** of **the bull and the goat for the sin offerings** in a place **outside the camp,** and (c) the cleansing of **the man** who disposed of these.

5. THE INSTITUTION OF THE DAY OF ATONEMENT AS AN ANNUAL CEREMONY (16:29-34)

**16:29-34.** This Day of **Atonement** ritual was to be repeated annually **on the 10th day of the seventh month** (Tishri, October-November). Apparently the ceremonies were considered ineffective in themselves if they were not accompanied by genuine penitence on the part of the people, who were to **deny** themselves (usually understood to include fasting, Isa. 58:3, 5; cf. Lev. 23:27, 32; Num. 29:7) **and not** to **do any work** since the day was to be **a Sabbath of rest.** The significance of the ceremony is summarized in Leviticus 16:33-34, and its annual observance reaffirmed in verse 34, along with the historical statement that the ritual of the first Day of Atonement **was done, as the LORD commanded Moses.**

The Book of Hebrews uncovers the fulfillment of the typical sacrifices of the Day of Atonement by pointing out that Christ's sacrifice for people's sins, when He died on the cross, was not annual but once for all (Heb. 9:11-12, 24-26; 10:12).

## II. The Walk of Holiness before God by Separation (chaps. 17–27)

### A. The laws for sacrifice and eating meat (chap. 17)

This chapter is somewhat supplementary to chapters 1–7 since it explains the significance of blood in the sacrifices (17:11) and also treats other related matters already discussed (cf. 7:26-27; 11:39-40). It relates not to the role of the priests (though they are included in the introduction, 17:2) but to potential mistakes of laymen regarding sacrificing and eating meat.

1. INTRODUCTION (17:1-2)

**17:1-2.** A new section of the book is here indicated by the typical introductory formula, **The LORD said to Moses** (cf. 1:1; 4:1; 6:1; 7:28; 11:1; 15:1; 16:1-2; 18:1-2;

19:1-2). These particular commandments of the Lord (17:2) are each introduced by the phrase "Any Israelite" (vv. 3, 8, 10, 13) thus giving a fourfold division to the chapter.

## 2. THE REQUIREMENT TO KILL DOMESTIC ANIMALS AT THE TABERNACLE (17:3-7)

**17:3-7.** The prohibition is directed against the killing of animals without offering them to the Lord. When this legislation was enacted in the wilderness of Sinai, not only did the Israelites have a staple diet of manna, but also domesticated female animals were probably considered too valuable for their milk and dairy products to be eaten with any regularity as food. Thus the word **sacrifices** is probably meant in the broad sense of any slaughter of **a cow, a lamb, or a goat,** thus ruling out nonsacrificial slaughter entirely until they settled in the land of Canaan where the logistic difficulties of being spread throughout the land required a modification of this regulation (Deut. 12:20-28).

While still in the desert, those who desired to eat the meat of domesticated animals first had to offer them as **fellowship offerings** (Lev. 17:5; cf. 7:11-34). This not only assured that the needs of the priests were met but also prevented the possibility of offering **sacrifices to the goat idols** (perhaps a reference to a form of idolatrous goat worship which was practiced in the eastern delta of Lower Egypt; cf. Harrison, *Leviticus,* p. 180). If an animal could be slaughtered only in the sanctuary, then a person guilty of offering a pagan sacrifice could not excuse himself by claiming he was only killing it for food. The penalty for violating this prohibition was to **be cut off from his people** (17:4, as with all violations in this chapter: vv. 9-10, 14; cf. Ex. 30:33, 38; Lev. 7:20-21; 20:17-18; Num. 15:30-31). This penalty probably designated impending direct divine destruction rather than judicial execution by human agency (cf. Wenham, *Leviticus,* pp. 241-2), though possibly it could refer to banishment by God from the nation.

## 3. THE REQUIREMENT TO OFFER SACRIFICES AT THE TABERNACLE (17:8-9)

**17:8-9.** This requirement is similar to the preceding one but more clearly specifies one **who offers a burnt offering or sacrifice** of a fellowship offering elsewhere than at **the Tent of Meeting.** The reasons for this prohibition were probably the same as in the preceding paragraph, and the penalty for nonconformity was the same—the violator was **cut off from his people.**

## 4. THE PROHIBITION AGAINST EATING BLOOD (17:10-12)

**17:10-12.** Of the seven prohibitions in the Pentateuch against eating blood (Gen. 9:4; Lev. 3:17; 7:26-27; 17:10-14; 19:26; Deut. 12:15-16, 23-24; 15:23), this one (Lev. 17:10-14) is the clearest and provides the underlying rationale. Verse 11 gives two reasons for the prohibition against eating blood: (1) **The life of a creature is in the blood** (blood is inherently necessary to maintain animal life, so its blood is virtually identified with its life); therefore to refrain from eating blood is to show respect for the sanctity of life. (2) **The blood . . . makes atonement for one's life** (God has chosen sacrificial blood as the ransom price for a person's life, so the life of a substitute is given up in death); therefore to refrain from eating blood is to show respect for its sacredness as a vehicle of atonement. The fact that God said, **I have given it to you to make atonement for yourselves on the altar,** rules out the view that blood was inherently efficacious. Its atoning value was only because God had "given it" for this purpose; He had chosen it as a fitting symbol of the reality of atonement and forgiveness. Again, the penalty for violating this prohibition was being **cut . . . off from his people** (cf. comments on v. 4).

## 5. THE APPLICATION OF THESE REQUIREMENTS TO HUNTING GAME (17:13-16)

The subject now changes from the blood of domestic animals suitable for sacrifice to the blood of clean game caught in the hunt. Since wild game was not acceptable for sacrifice (it cost the worshiper nothing), only the prohibition against eating blood was applicable, not those regarding slaughter at the Tent of Meeting. (It would have been difficult to chase a wild antelope or gazelle into the sanctuary court before killing it!)

**17:13-14.** The disposition of the blood of clean wild animals (**drain out**

the blood and cover it with earth) was later expanded to include domesticated animals after they were no longer required to be slaughtered in the sanctuary for sacrifice (cf. Deut. 12:15-16, 22-24).

**17:15-16.** After a person has eaten from an unclean carcass (not from an unclean animal, but from a clean animal **found dead or torn by wild animals**), he **must wash his clothes and bathe with water** and wait **till evening** to be ceremonially **clean** again (cf. comments on 11:24-28). The probable reason that eating from such a carcass resulted in uncleanness was that it would not have had all its blood properly drained (cf. 1 Sam. 14:32-35; Ezek. 4:14; 44:31; Acts 15:20). In addition, merely touching a carcass was also polluting (cf. Lev. 11:39-40). This regulation was later modified by the restriction that such dead animals could be eaten only by resident aliens or foreigners (cf. Deut. 14:21), but an earlier statement, "Throw it to the dogs" (Ex. 22:31), should be taken literally, not applied to the aliens.

## B. The laws for covenant morality and nonconformity to pagan practices (chaps. 18–20)

### 1. LAWS RESTRICTING SEXUAL RELATIONS (CHAP. 18)

Chapter 18 sets the stage for the remainder of the Book of Leviticus. Not only does it introduce the important theme of Israel's responsibility to the holy God to be His holy people, and so to be distinct from the pagan nations (cf. the important introductory [vv. 2-5] and concluding [vv. 24-30] statements), but also the structure of this chapter resembles the covenant treaty form common in the ancient Near East (cf. K.A. Kitchen, *The Bible in Its World: The Bible and Archaeology Today.* Downers Grove, Ill., Inter-Varsity Press, 1978, pp. 81-5): (a) preamble—"I am the LORD your God" (Lev. 18:2), (b) historical retrospect—"Egypt, where you used to live" (v. 3), (c) basic stipulation—"obey My laws" (v. 4), (d) promise of blessing—"will live by them" (v. 5), (e) detailed stipulations (vv. 6-23), and (f) curses for disobedience (vv. 24-30). (Also see the chart "The Mosaic Covenant Compared with Suzerainty Treaties" near Ex. 19.) The specific prohibitions in Leviticus 18 are based on the principles of the sanctity of marriage and the need for stability in family life. The promotion of sexual license in pagan culture and cultic prostitution in pagan religion, especially among the Canaanites, was opposed to these principles.

### a. Introduction to covenant morality (18:1-5)

**18:1-5.** The phrase **I am the LORD your God** forms a preamble within the covenant treaty form of chapter 18. But in its other five occurrences in the chapter (vv. 4-6, 21, 30) it is more a motivation for keeping particular laws. An almost identical phrase introduces the Ten Commandments (Ex. 20:2; Deut. 5:6). Thus the exhortation to avoid the customs of other nations (specifically **Egypt** and **Canaan,** Lev. 18:3) grows out of the person of **God** and Israel's covenant relationship with Him. God's integrated system of physical and spiritual laws to provide a happy and meaningful life for Israel as His redeemed people is summarized as His **decrees and laws.** The motivation for keeping these laws is stated clearly—**the man who obeys them will live,** that is, enjoy life, **by them.**

Obedience to God's laws produces in His people happy and fulfilled lives (cf. 26:3-13; Deut. 28:1-14). For example, the marital and sexual restrictions in Leviticus 18 constitute one basis for a stable and happy family life. (However, an unregenerate or legalistically minded person experiences only the curse of the Law; cf. Gal. 3:10.)

### b. Prohibitions against incestuous unions (18:6-18)

**18:6-18.** The general principle of this section is given in verse 6: Do not **have sexual relations** (the Heb. uses a euphemism trans. lit., "to uncover the nakedness of") with **any close relative** other than your spouse. The primary thrust of the passage is to forbid illicit marriages, as the prohibition against adultery was assumed (cf. v. 20; but contrast Harrison, *Leviticus,* p. 186). Also assumed is the prohibition against marrying a non-Israelite (forbidden in Deut. 7:3-6; cf. 1 Kings 11:1-2). However, if a non-Israelite (as Ruth) converted to the Lord, marriage was permissible.

The following regulations can be gleaned from this section. A man could not marry his **mother** (Lev. 18:7) or his

**sister** (or half sister; first degree of consanguinity according to modern genetics, v. 9). Prohibition of marriage to one's daughter was assumed and so not mentioned (cf. Gen. 19:30-38). Nor could he marry his granddaughter (second degree of consanguinity, Lev. 18:10) or his **aunt** (father's or mother's sister, vv. 12-14). Also forbidden were marriages to a widowed wife of a close blood relative, that is, a man's stepmother (v. 8), half-sister (v. 11), aunt by marriage (v. 14), **daughter-in-law** (v. 15), sister-in-law (v. 16), step-daughter (v. 17), and step-granddaughter (v. 17). The apparent reason behind these prohibitions against marriage to those with such an in-law relationship was that they had become "one flesh" (Gen. 2:24) with the blood relative, and so were regarded as a part of the larger family unit (cf. Wenham, *Leviticus,* pp. 254-8, for specific examples of some of the more difficult identifications).

### c. Prohibitions against Canaanite sexual deviations (18:19-23)

**18:19.** See 15:19-24; 20:18; 2 Samuel 11:4.

**18:20.** Adultery in the Old Testament is described as **intercourse** between a married or betrothed woman and a man other than her husband. It did not include intercourse between a married man and a single woman, which was a lesser crime (Ex. 22:16-17; Deut. 22:28-29).

**18:21. Molech** was the national god of the Ammonites (1 Kings 11:7; cf. 2 Kings 23:10; Jer. 32:35). Child sacrifice by burning (2 Kings 3:27; Deut. 12:31; 18:10) is probably in view here (cf. the severe punishment in Lev. 20:2-5), though the context supports Snaith's interpretation that it refers to the dedication of **children** as cult prostitutes (*Leviticus and Numbers,* p. 125).

**18:22-23.** Also forbidden were homosexuality (cf. Gen. 19; Lev. 20:13; Jud. 19:22; Rom. 1:26-27; 1 Cor. 6:9) and bestiality (cf. Ex. 22:19; Lev. 20:15-16; Deut. 27:21).

### d. Concluding warning against disobedience to covenant stipulations (18:24-30)

**18:24-30.** This section functions like the curse section of a covenant treaty. Because of the things just described (esp. vv. 19-23), God had programmed the extermination of the Canaanites. Disobedient Israelites would suffer the same punishment as their predecessors. The graphic personification, **the land vomited out its inhabitants** (vv. 25, 28) shows how **detestable** (vv. 26, 29-30) these practices are in God's sight. The chapter closed as it opened: **I am the Lord your God.**

### 2. LAWS PROMOTING PRACTICAL HOLINESS BEFORE GOD AND MAN (CHAP. 19)

"The diversity of material in this chapter reflects the differentiation of life. All aspects of human affairs are subject to God's laws" (Wenham, *Leviticus,* p. 264). The holiness of God (v. 2) is the bedrock supporting the practical holiness promoted by these laws. Though the specific rationale behind some of the commands (e.g., v. 19) may not be clear to a modern interpreter, the ethical commands of this chapter are not arbitrary but are based on the just, humane, and sensitive treatment of the aged, the handicapped, the poor, the resident alien, the laborer, and others. These commands even reach behind mere outward behavior to inward motivation (cf. vv. 17-18). It is also noteworthy that the basic principles of the Ten Commandments are incorporated into chapter 19, though not in the same order and not always with the same emphasis. The phrases "I am the Lord" and "I am the Lord your God" punctuate the chapter 16 times, marking off most of its paragraphs.

### a. Introduction (19:1-2)

**19:1-2.** This chapter is not addressed to a few ascetics but to **the entire assembly of Israel,** the whole nation. The underlying motivation for holiness is expressed in what can be considered the motto of Leviticus—**Be holy because I, the Lord your God, am holy.** This statement weds ethics to theology forever. Human morality must ultimately rest on the unchanging nature of God. "Every biblical statement about God carries with it an implied demand upon men to imitate Him in daily living" (R.E. Clements, "Leviticus," in *The Broadman Bible Commentary,* 2:51). God called Israel to be a holy nation (Ex. 19:6).

### b. Religious requirements (19:3-10)

**19:3-4.** Honoring parents and the Sabbath summarizes the whole Law and illustrates that holiness begins in the home. A child who learns to **respect** (lit., "fear," as in v. 14) **his mother and father** is also likely to "fear God" and to flee from **idols or . . . gods of cast metal.**

**19:5-8.** This regulation pertains to the proper disposition of the meat of **fellowship** offerings (cf. 7:15-20). The severity of the penalty (**cut off from his people,** 19:8) indicates the seriousness of this ritual's offense.

**19:9-10. The gleanings** in the corners of fields and the fallen **grapes** in vineyards were to be left **for the poor** (23:22; Deut. 24:19-22; cf. Ruth 2).

### c. Good neighborliness (19:11-18)

**19:11-18.** This series of prohibitions is directed at promoting harmony and holiness between Israelites (**your neighbor,** vv. 13, 15-18), but the command to **love your neighbor as yourself** (v. 18; cf. Matt. 5:43; 19:19; 22:39; Mark 12:31, 33; Luke 10:27; Rom. 13:9; Gal. 5:14; James 2:8) is expanded in Leviticus 19:34 to "Love him [the resident alien] as yourself."

The regulations promote honesty, so that God's reputation will not be tarnished (vv. 11-12), nonexploitation of the weak, the laborer, and the handicapped (vv. 13-14), **justice** in the courts of law for both **the poor** and **the great** (vv. 15-16), and a behavior toward all that is motivated by genuine love (vv. 17-18).

### d. Various regulations (19:19-37)

**19:19.** This section (vv. 19-37) is marked at both the beginning and end by **Keep My decrees.** The forbidden mixtures (v. 19) suggest that man was not to confuse what God had made distinct.

**19:20-22.** According to the next chapter, "If a man commits adultery with another man's wife," they "must be put to death" (20:10). However, the **man** and the **slave girl** in these verses were **not to be put to death** since she was still legally a slave **who** had **not been ransomed or given her freedom.** Nevertheless there had to be **due punishment** (perhaps damages to be paid either to her owner or her **promised** fiancé), and **a guilt offering** was required for **atonement.**

**19:23-25.** The firstfruits of a **fruit tree** were to be given to the Lord in its **fourth year** as **an offering of praise to the Lord,** so the skimpy harvests of the first **three years** would not be presented to God. Besides crops (Ex. 23:19; Lev. 23:10; Deut. 26:1-15), the firstfruits law also covered animals (Ex. 34:19-20; Deut. 15:19) and children (Ex. 13:2; Num. 8:16-18).

**19:26-31.** These prohibitions seem to relate to pagan religious customs which should be avoided, including pagan mourning rites (vv. 27-28), cultic **prostitution** (v. 29, in contrast with proper worship of **the Lord,** v. 30), and necromancy (v. 31).

**19:32-34.** On the positive side **respect** and love should be shown **the aged** (v. 32) and each resident **alien** (vv. 33-34).

**19:35-36.** Street-market honesty exemplifies the practical holiness expected by **the Lord.** (Cf. Deut. 25:13-16; Prov. 11:1; 16:11; 20:10, 23; Amos 8:5; Micah 6:11; and see comments on Hosea 12:7.)

**19:37.** This summary is reminiscent of 18:4, 30.

### 3. LAWS REQUIRING CAPITAL PUNISHMENT (CHAP. 20)

Chapter 20 supplements and reinforces chapter 18, emphasizing the punishments for various offenses. Whereas the laws in chapters 18–19 are addressed to would-be offenders and prohibit specific actions, those in chapter 20 are addressed to the community and explain the punishments for specified crimes. Except for verses 19-21, the crimes identified in this chapter receive the death penalty (cf. Ex. 21:12-17). Though seemingly harsh, this was essential to prevent sin from infecting the community life of God's people. The gravest public sins against life, religion, and the family were those which carried the maximum penalty of death, such as premeditated murder (Ex. 21:12; Num. 35; Deut. 19), kidnapping (Ex. 21:16; Deut. 24:7), adultery (Lev. 20:10; Deut. 22:22), homosexuality (Lev. 20:13), blasphemy (24:13-16, 23), idolatry (Deut. 13:6-10), and persistent disobedience against authority (Deut. 17:12; 21:18-21).

The method of inflicting the death penalty is twice specified as stoning (Lev. 20:2, 27) and once as burning (v. 14, understood by Jewish tradition as hot lead being poured down the throat!). The most severe expression of the death penalty, however, is found in verses 3, 5-6 (cf. vv. 17-18)—"I will cut him off from his people." This expression of direct divine judgment seems, in this case at least, to be mediated by the criminal execution process of verse 2—"The people of the community are to stone him." Wenham suggests that the divine cutting off is in addition to the judicial sentence since it implies separation from the people even after death (*Leviticus*, p. 278; cf. pp. 242, 285).

### a. Religious sins deserving capital punishment (20:1-6)

**20:1-6.** The section on **Molech** worship (vv. 1-5) is an expansion of 18:21. The sin of necromancy (20:6) was also prohibited in 19:31.

### b. Exhortation to holiness (20:7-8)

**20:7-8.** Even in the midst of this list of capital crimes, **God** graciously extended exhortations to covenant morality, motivated by His own holiness.

### c. Family sins deserving capital punishment (20:9-21)

**20:9-21.** On the death penalty for persistent disobedience to parents (v. 9), compare Exodus 21:17. Leviticus 20:10-17 basically parallels 18:6-23 except for the addition of the punishment (and the prohibition against intercourse during a woman's menstruation; cf. 15:19-20). The penalty in 20:19-21 is not clear.

### d. Exhortation to holiness (20:22-26)

**20:22-26.** The exhortation and warning of verses 22-24 are similar to those in 18:24-30. The addition regarding the **distinction** between the **clean and** the **unclean** (20:25) is related theologically to the fact that God had **set** Israel **apart from the nations** (vv. 24, 26), and they were to **be holy** because He is **holy** (v. 26).

### e. A religious sin deserving capital punishment (20:27)

**20:27.** See verse 6 and 19:31.

## C. The laws for priestly and sacrificial holiness (chaps. 21–22)

### 1. PERSONAL RESTRICTIONS FOR PRIESTLY SERVICE (CHAP. 21)

### a. Introduction (21:1a)

**21:1a.** If God's holiness was a foundation and motivation for holiness on the part of the entire assembly of Israel (cf.

19:2), how much more would it be for **the priests** who ministered at the altar (21:1-9) and especially the high priest who stood as the mediator between men and God (vv. 10-15).

### b. Restrictions on mourning and marriage for ordinary priests (21:1b-9)

The sons of Aaron were given numerous personal prohibitions to promote priestly purity.

**21:1b-4.** The priests were to avoid ceremonial uncleanness arising from contact with the dead **except** in the case of **a close relative** (a blood relation within his own household, not one **related to him by marriage** [v. 5]; the NIV marg. trans., "He must not make himself unclean as a leader among his people," is defended by Harrison, *Leviticus*, p. 208, but not Wenham, *Leviticus*, p. 290). But this permission to touch the body of a close relative was not allowed in the specific case of Nadab and Abihu (10:3-7), probably because their deaths were a divine judgment.

**21:5-6.** Like all Israelites (19:27-28; cf. Deut. 14:1), the **priests** were to avoid pagan mourning customs. Such association with pagan practices would render them unholy and would **profane the name of their God**, making them unfit **to present the offerings** at the altar.

**21:7-8.** For the same reasons the **priests** were to avoid marrying prostitutes and divorcees, but could marry a widow (contrast v. 14). Obviously the reputation of a priest's wife could reflect on her husband's fitness to minister in **holy** things. The motivation and means of holiness are found in the divine pronouncement, **I the LORD, who makes you holy,** that is, the Lord, your Sanctifier, **am holy.** The threefold repetition of this (or a similar) phrase marks off the three major sections of this chapter (cf. vv. 15, 23).

**21:9.** Not only the reputation of a **priest's** wife (vv. 7-8) but also that of his **daughter** affected his fitness for priestly service. Such prostitution (either cultic, at a pagan shrine, or noncultic) required the death penalty (**burned by fire**).

### c. Restrictions on mourning and marriage for the high priest (21:10-15)

**21:10-12.** Stricter standards were expected of **the high priest,** distinguished above his fellow priests by **the anointing oil poured on his head** and his high priestly garments. So he was not to **make himself unclean, even for his father or mother** (v. 11, contrast v. 2). Nor could he show the normal marks of grief (e.g., tearing **his clothes,** v. 10), let alone practice pagan customs (v. 5). Verse 12 means he was not to **leave the sanctuary** for funerals, not that he was to live there.

**21:13-15.** The high priest was given an absolute restriction against marrying a nonvirgin, including **a widow** (not a restriction for ordinary priests, v. 7). This was a safeguard to assure that her first child (the next potential high priest) was really his own, and so of priestly lineage.

*d. Restrictions regarding physically defective priests (21:16-23)*

**21:16-21.** Physically defective or **deformed** priests were not allowed to function as priests by offering sacrifices. The abnormalities listed are probably examples rather than a complete list (cf. a comparable list of animal defects in 22:20-25). The ceremonial wholeness of the Levitical system found physical expression in wholeness and normality (cf. Wenham, *Leviticus,* pp. 23-5, 169-71).

**21:22.** But handicapped priests were assured of their share not only of **the holy food** (the priests' portions of the fellowship offerings), but also from **the most holy food** (the priests' portions of all standard offerings).

**21:23.** This summary stresses again the role of **the LORD,** the Sanctifier.

*e. Conclusion (21:24)*

**21:24.** This conclusion indicates that **Moses** obeyed God's command (v. 1, "Speak to the priests"), obviously in the presence of **Aaron** and **all the Israelites.**

2. SACRIFICIAL REGULATIONS FOR SACRED OFFERINGS (CHAP. 22)

*a. Introduction (22:1-2)*

**22:1-2.** Again **the LORD** gave **Moses** regulations for **Aaron and his sons** concerning **respect** for **the sacred offerings,** probably a broad term to cover all priestly dues, including tithes, firstfruits, and sacrifices (cf. Num. 18:8-19). Meal, sin, and guilt offerings could be eaten only by males of the priestly order (Lev. 6:16, 26; 7:6); other sacred offerings could be shared by their households. The real is-

sue is that the priests were **not to profane** the **holy name** of the **LORD** through misuse of what the people offered to Him.

*b. Restrictions on the eating of sacred offerings by priests (22:3-9)*

**22:3-9.** Ceremonial uncleanness prevented a priest from either offering or eating a sacred offering. The punishment for priestly noncompliance was severe— he was to be **cut off from** God's **presence.** Some sources of ceremonial uncleanness that prevented a priest from eating the sacred offerings were **an infectious skin disease** (cf. chaps. 13–14), **a bodily discharge** (cf. chap. 15), and contact with **a corpse** (cf. 11:39). The reminder for priestly compliance again stressed the holiness of God and His design to promote holiness in His people (22:9).

*c. Restrictions on the eating of sacred offerings by non-priests (22:10-16)*

**22:10-13.** The regulations are clarified concerning who may eat a **sacred** meal. The **priest's family** could, but who was considered a member of the priest's family? Apparently any permanent member of his household qualified, including **a slave** (v. 11) or a widowed or divorced **daughter** without **children** who returned to the household (v. 13). However, this did not include a **guest** or **hired worker,** who were not permanent residents (v. 10), or a **daughter** who lived with her husband's household (v. 12).

**22:14-16.** The procedure for unwitting violation of these regulations (**if anyone eats a sacred offering by mistake**) was to **make restitution to the priest . . . and add** a 20 percent penalty. The **payment** (v. 16) may refer to this restitution or it may refer to a ram for a guilt offering (cf. 5:14–6:7). **The priests** were responsible to oversee the eating of **sacred offerings** to prevent such violations (22:15-16).

*d. Restrictions and limitations concerning sacrifices (22:17-30)*

**22:17-21.** The section regarding personal disqualifications of individual sacrificial animals begins with a general statement regarding **burnt** and **fellowship** offerings.

**22:22-25.** The prohibition of **deformed** or defective sacrificial animals is explained in terms similar to those that precluded priests from offering sacrifices (21:18-20). This is probably intentional. Wenham argues that the sacrificial **animals** are "the priests of the animal world," that is, as the Gentiles are symbolized by unclean animals, and Israel by clean animals, the priests are symbolized by sacrificial animals (*Leviticus,* p. 290; cf. p. 170). The one exception that allowed an animal with certain defects as an offering was in the case of **a freewill offering** (22:23).

**22:26-28.** Limitations are also given concerning young sacrificial animals. They were not an acceptable offering before **the eighth day,** nor were they to be slaughtered **on the same day** as their "mothers."

**22:29-30.** A reminder is given regarding the time limitation for eating a **thanksgiving** offering. **It must be eaten that same day** (cf. 7:15).

*e. Concluding covenant declaration (22:31-33)*

**22:31-33.** This conclusion emphasizes both divine holiness and divine grace (**who brought you out of Egypt**; cf. comments on Deut. 4:20) as a motivation for holiness in the lives of God's people (cf. 18:24-30; 19:36-37; 20:22-26).

*D. The laws concerning the appointed feasts of the Lord (chap. 23)*

The Levitical system incorporated both individual and national occasions of sacrifice and worship. Much of chapters 1–7 assumed the individual occasions of sacrifice. Chapter 23 is structured around the national annual festivals of Israel. Though other passages give greater detail on some of these appointed times of meeting (e.g., the Passover in Ex. 12–13 and the Day of Atonement in Lev. 16), chapter 23 is the most complete account of the feasts from the viewpoint of their interrelationships within the annual festal calendar of Israel. The regulations of this chapter are given from the viewpoint of an ordinary worshiper. Numbers 28–29 treats the same feasts (no mention is there made of the sheaf of the first grain of barley harvest as in Lev. 23:9-14) more from the viewpoint of the priests by giving a detailed schedule of these special offerings. Once Israel entered the land of Canaan, the three great feasts of the year

(the Feast of Unleavened Bread accompanying Passover, the Feast of Harvest or Weeks, and the Feast of Ingathering or Tabernacles, as seen in Ex. 23:14-17; 34:18-25; Deut. 16:1-16) were to be occasions of pilgrimage to the central sanctuary by "all" male Israelites. Thus the basic Hebrew word for *feast* (*ḥag*; e.g., Lev. 23:6, 34, 39; Deut. 16:16; 2 Chron. 8:13) includes the idea of a pilgrimage and can be aptly translated "pilgrim feast" (cf. Wenham, *Leviticus,* p. 303). Another Hebrew word (*mô'ēd,* "appointed meeting, set time") occurs in the plural form four times in Leviticus 23, and each time is translated as "appointed feasts" (vv. 2, 4, 37, 44).

The exact number of annual feasts listed in this chapter is a matter of debate. Assuming a distinction between Passover and Unleavened Bread, (vv. 4-8) and not counting Firstfruits (vv. 9-14) as a separate feast, there are six feasts. A more natural division of the calendar as well as the structure of the chapter groups the annual feasts into (a) the *spring (and early summer) festivals* (that of Passover and Unleavened Bread including the barley sheaf ceremony [sometimes called Firstfruits but actually not a separate feast], followed 50 days later by the Feast of Weeks), and (b) the *fall festivals* of the seventh month (Trumpets, Day of Atonement, and Feast of Tabernacles).

1. INTRODUCTORY COMMAND (23:1-4)

**23:1-4.** In this chapter **the LORD** instructed His people to reserve certain dates in their appointment books (as it were) for national public worship and sacrifice. The Hebrew word *mô'ēd,* (pl., *mô'ădîm;* NIV "appointed feasts") can refer to a *place* of meeting (as in *'ōhel mô'ēd,* the Tent of Meeting) but here means an appointed *time* of meeting (vv. 2, 4, 37, 44). The reference to the **Sabbath** (v. 3) is somewhat parenthetical since all the rest of the chapter deals with annual festivals rather than the weekly Sabbath. Its mention is perhaps a reminder of the whole sabbatical system of which the weekly and annual festivals were only a part (see chap. 25). For an Israelite, the weekly Sabbath was a time of rest (Ex. 20:8-11; cf. Gen. 2:1-3) and a time to recall his redemption from Egyptian bondage (Deut. 5:15; Lev. 23:43).

## 2. THE SPRING FESTIVALS (23:5-22)

After the introduction, chapter 23 divides into two sections, each of which concludes with the phrase, "I am the LORD your God" (vv. 22, 43). These two divisions are each subdivided into two sections identified by the statement of institution, "This is to be a lasting ordinance for the generations to come, wherever you live" (vv. 14, 21, 31, 41).

### a. The Passover and Feast of Unleavened Bread (23:5-14)

**23:5.** The LORD's **Passover** was to be sacrificed **at twilight on the 14th day of the first month** (Abib, later called Nisan) to commemorate Israel's departure from Egypt (Deut. 16:1-7), particularly the redemption when the death angel passed over Egypt and spared the firstborn in homes where the doorposts were spattered with the blood of the Passover lamb (Ex. 12:1–13:10). The first anniversary of the Passover was observed at Sinai (Num. 9:1-5) but it was not celebrated again till Israel camped at Gilgal across the Jordan in the Promised Land (Josh. 5:10-12).

**23:6-8.** The LORD's **Feast of Unleavened Bread** was to begin on the morning after the Passover lamb was sacrificed and to last **for seven days (the 15th** through the 21st). It was so called because it commemorated the hasty flight from Egypt when God told Israel not to leaven their bread (Ex. 12:14-20). **The first** and last days of this week were to be a time of **sacred assembly** (a holy convocation) when **no regular work** (i.e., occupational work such as farming or trading) was to be done. On this occasion it seems likely that the absence of leaven signified discontinuity between Israel's new sustenance from God and her old sustenance, the bread of Egypt. The continuity was broken because God did not allow the Israelites to continue the normal leavening process (using a lump from an old loaf as **yeast** for the new **bread**).

**23:9-14.** This paragraph is regarded by many as the third distinct appointed feast in this chapter. (Barley was no doubt the sheaf to be waved because this feast occurred in March-April, when barley was first harvested. Wheat was not ready for harvesting till later, in June-July.) It prescribes a distinct ceremony (waving a **sheaf** of barley **before the LORD**) on a specific day (**the day after the Sabbath** [v. 11], normally understood as the 16th, following the rest day on the 15th [but some scholars place the wave sheaf on the 21st, e.g., Wenham, *Leviticus,* p. 304]), yet it seems more natural to regard this day as a special part of the Unleavened Bread celebration which was in progress at the time. After the Israelites entered the land, this **sheaf of grain** (the **first** grain of the barley **harvest**) was to be waved by **the priest** as a dedication offering before the Lord. A special **burnt offering** of a yearling **lamb** (v. 12), along with a double-portioned **grain offering** and an oblation **of wine** (v. 13), was to be made to the Lord as a part of this dedication. The Israelites were restricted from partaking of the barley harvest in any way until **this offering** was made. The statement instituting **a lasting ordinance** (v. 14) appears to unite the eight-day celebration of Passover/Unleavened Bread/barley firstfruits.

### b. The Feast of Weeks (23:15-22)

The Feast of Weeks (cf. Num. 28:26; Deut. 16:10) was known in New Testament times as the day of Pentecost (Acts 2:1; Gr. *pentēkostē,* "50th," from which comes the Eng. "Pentecost") because it was celebrated seven weeks plus 1 day (50 days) after the wave offering of the barley sheaf during the Feast of Unleavened Bread (Lev. 23:15-16). It was also called the Feast of Harvest (Ex. 23:16; cf. 34:22) and "the day of firstfruits" (Num. 28:26). As an early summer agricultural celebration at the end of the wheat harvest (cf. Ex. 34:22), it was both distinct from and yet related to the previous firstfruits of barley. The designated time lapse of 50 days links together this firstfruits offering at the end of early summer wheat harvest with that of the preceding firstfruits offering at the beginning of the spring barley harvest. No such time sequence is specified to link these celebrations with the fall festivals which were simply introduced as occurring on designated days in the seventh month (cf. Lev. 23:23, 27, 34). Of the three major feasts (cf. Deut. 16:1, 3, 6; Lev. 23:42-43), only the Feast of Weeks is not identified in the Old Testament with some prior occasion in Israel's history that it commemorates. Jewish tradition, however, supplied such an occasion by relating it to the day Moses was given the Law of God on Mount Sinai.

**23:15-17.** Following the identification of the time elements in this feast (vv. 15-16a), the key feature of presenting **an offering of new grain to the LORD** is explained as bringing **two loaves** of *leavened* bread **as a wave offering of firstfruits to the LORD.** This is the one time in the year when leavened bread was brought to the Lord, though none of it was burned on the altar. The bread was leavened by placing in the dough a lump of leaven (i.e., sourdough) from bread of the preceding barley harvest, thus reemphasizing the close connection between the barley and wheat harvests, and the festivals associated with them.

**23:18-20.** The offerings at this feast —more elaborate than those at the Feast of Unleavened Bread (cf. v. 12)—consisted of a burnt offering of **seven male lambs . . . one young bull, and two rams,** with an appropriate amount of **grain offerings and drink offerings,** a sin **offering** of **one male goat,** and a **fellowship offering** of **two lambs.** Portions of these lambs along with **the bread of the firstfruits** (cf. v. 17) were to be **a wave offering** given to the officiating **priest** as his share for performing the ceremony.

**23:21.** This festival **day** was specifically marked as **a sacred assembly** when **no** occupational **work** was to be done. The Feast of Weeks, along with those linked with it (vv. 4-14), was to be celebrated as **a lasting ordinance for the generations to come.**

**23:22.** This reminder to leave **the gleanings** of **the harvest . . . for the poor** at first seems to be misplaced from a more legislative context. However, the omission of reference to the vineyard and grapes (contrast 19:1-10), which were harvested later in the year before the Feast of Tabernacles, made it an appropriate **harvest** motto at the end of the barley and wheat harvests. As the priests' needs were met by the sacrificial meat (cf. 23:20), so the needs of the poor were met by leaving the gleanings for them in the harvest fields (cf. Deut. 14:27-29; 16:11).

## 3. THE FALL FESTIVALS (23:23-43)

The final three "appointed feasts of the LORD" all occurred in the seventh month (Tishri, October-November), marked the end of the agricultural year, and anticipated the two rainy seasons to begin the new year. This same month became the beginning of the new year in the civil calendar adopted in postexilic times.

### a. The Feast of Trumpets (23:23-25)

**23:23-25.** Silver trumpets were blown on the first day of *every* month (Num. 10:1, 10) but **trumpet blasts on the first day of the seventh month** were probably a special reminder of the approaching Day of Atonement (cf. Lev. 23:26-32). The Feast of Trumpets was **a day of rest, a sacred assembly** on which **no** occupational **work** was to be done and on which special offerings were to be presented **to the LORD** (cf. Num. 29:1-6).

### b. The Day of Atonement (23:26-32)

**23:26-28.** The Day of Atonement was on **the 10th day of the seventh month.** The major features and sacrificial details of this great day have already been given (cf. 16:1-28; Num. 29:7-11). The emphasis in Leviticus 23 is on how an ordinary Israelite was to observe the day. Verses 26-28 summarize the overall features of the day: **Hold a sacred assembly and deny yourselves, and present an offering made to the LORD by fire. And do no work.** Not only the special offerings of the atonement ritual (16:3-28) but also designated festival offerings (Num. 29:8-11) were to be offered at the sanctuary. The prohibition to do no work was absolute (cf. Lev. 23:30-31). In contrast with the prohibition against occupational work (e.g., v. 7), this prohibition appears to forbid even minor household chores such as lighting a fire or cooking (cf. Ex. 16:23-30; Num. 15:32-36).

**23:29-31a.** The meaning of **deny himself** (cf. v. 32) probably includes fasting and possibly other penitential exercises such as wearing sackcloth and ashes (Isa. 58:3, 5). The penalty for violating the rule to deny oneself and to abstain from all **work** was severe—to **be cut off from his people,** which was seen as a direct judgment from God (**I will destroy from among his people**).

**23:31b-32.** The importance of this day as **a lasting ordinance** (cf. v. 21) is affirmed and its character as **a Sabbath of rest** reiterated.

### c. The Feast of Tabernacles (23:33-43)

**23:33-34.** The **Feast of Tabernacles** was the final and most important feast of the year, lasting **for seven days** (from **the 15th** through the **21st of the seventh month**). This feast functioned not only as an agricultural thanksgiving at the end of the fall fruit harvest (v. 39, and so was called the "Feast of Ingathering," Ex. 34:22; Deut. 16:13-15), but also as a commemorative celebration of God's protective care during the 40-year period in the wilderness between Egypt and Canaan when Israelites lived in tents (thus the name Feast of Tabernacles, or "booths," Lev. 23:43).

**23:35-36.** On both **the first day** and **the eighth day** (the concluding day of the annual feasts following the **seven days** of the Feast of Tabernacles), the Israelites were to **hold a sacred assembly** and were to do **no** occupational **work.** The **offerings** to be brought were the most elaborate and impressive of the entire year (cf. Num. 29:12-38).

**23:37-38.** This parenthetical section indicates that the scheduled festival **offerings** for the **feasts of the LORD** (cf. Num. 28–29) were to be in addition to the weekly **offerings** (**those for the LORD's Sabbaths**) and the voluntary **offerings** of individual worshipers (e.g., **freewill offerings**). They were also in addition to the special monthly new moon **offerings** (Num. 28:11-15; 29:6; etc.).

**23:39-43.** Following the digression in verses 37-38, the calendar of the Feast of Tabernacles was restated (v. 39) and the particulars of the thanksgiving festivities announced (vv. 40-43). The **choice fruit from the trees, and palm fronds, leafy branches and poplars** may have been used in constructing the **booths** in which the people were to **live** for **seven days** as a reminder of the tents they lived in when they first came **out of Egypt.** The importance of this **festival** is indicated by the statement, **This is to be a lasting ordinance.** The divine pronouncement, **I am the LORD your God,** concludes this section on the feasts of the seventh month (cf. v. 23).

### 4. CONCLUDING SUMMARY (23:44)

**23:44.** In obedience to God's command (v. 2), **Moses announced to the Israelites the appointed feasts of the LORD.**

The annual cycle of the appointed feasts of the Lord is regarded by many as *typical* of God's future program for Israel as a nation. The interrelated spring and early summer festivals are thought to typify the events of Christ's First Advent: (a) the death of Christ on the cross as the Passover Lamb (1 Cor. 5:7), (b) the believer's holy walk and complete break from the old life, pictured by the absence of leaven (1 Cor. 5:7-8) (others think the unleavened bread pictures the sinless humanity of Christ), (c) the resurrection of Christ as prefigured by the firstfruits of the barley harvest (1 Cor. 15:20-23), and (d) the advent of the Holy Spirit as a fulfillment of the Feast of Pentecost (Acts 2; cf. Joel 2:28). The break in the festival calendar before the fall festivals suggests the present interadvent period during which Israel's messianic King is in heaven. The fall festivals prefigure events associated with His Second Advent: (a) Israel's future regathering at the end of the Tribulation period (Feast of Trumpets; Matt. 24:29-31), (b) Israel's national conversion at the Second Advent based on the death of Christ at the First Advent (Day of Atonement; Heb. 9:23-28; Zech. 12:10–13:1; Rom. 11:26-27), and (c) Israel's blessing by God on the millennial earth (Feast of Tabernacles, Zech. 14:9-20).

## E. Ceremonial and moral regulations (chap. 24)

### 1. THE DAILY AND WEEKLY MINISTRY IN THE TENT OF MEETING (24:1-9)

Two subordinate articles of furniture in the Tent of Meeting's holy place involved Aaron and his sons in daily and weekly ministry—the daily maintenance of the lamps of the pure gold lampstand (vv. 2-4) and the weekly preparation and replacement of "the bread of the Presence" (Ex. 25:30) on the table of pure gold (Lev. 24:5-9).

The transition from the festival calendar which climaxed in the magnificent Feast of Tabernacles (23:33-43) to the mundane maintenance of the lesser articles of furniture in the Tent of Meeting is difficult to explain but certainly illustrates the New Testament believer priest's faithfulness to God in the daily routine of life and not just during spiritual mountaintop experiences. Perhaps the purpose of this seeming digression (before matters pertaining to the holy calendar resume in chap. 25) was to dispel the notion that God's presence might be limited to special occasions of worship, since both articles of furniture were closely related to the continual presence of God in Israel's midst. Between the great festival occasions, unbroken daily fellowship in the Tent of Meeting was to continue without interruption.

*a. The daily care of the lampstand (24:1-4)*

**24:1-4.** The golden **lampstand** was described by Moses as to its design (Ex. 25:31-39), its construction (Ex. 37:17-24), and its placement (Ex. 40:24-25). The fuel for its lamps was to be **clear oil of pressed olives** (cf. Ex. 27:20-21; it was purer and of better quality than boiled olive oil), which was to be provided in such a way **that the lamps** would **be kept burning continually** since they provided the only light in the holy place.

*b. The weekly care of the table (24:5-9)*

**24:5-9.** The **bread** set **on the table of pure gold before the LORD** was called "the bread of the Presence" (Ex. 25:30). This paragraph supplements the account in Exodus 25:23-30 (cf. Ex. 37:10-16) which says little about the bread itself. **The bread** consisted of **12 loaves,** apparently of considerable size based on their recipe (Lev. 24:5), and so were probably placed in two piles (NIV, **two rows**). **Incense** was placed on the table beside the bread to be burned on the altar as **a memorial portion** (cf. 2:2, 9, 16) each **Sabbath** when the old bread was replaced and given to the priests as **their regular share.**

2. AN INCIDENT OF BLASPHEMY AND THE DIVINE LAW BASED ON THE CASE (24:10-23)

This brief narrative section (which along with chapters 8–10 comprise the only purely narrative portions of Lev.) is a reminder that the legislation of Leviticus was given in a specific historical context to meet particular historical situations.

*a. Blasphemy by a half-Israelite (24:10-12)*

**24:10-12.** A **son** of a mixed marriage (**an Israelite mother and an Egyptian fa-** ther) quarreled with **an Israelite** and **blasphemed the name of the** LORD **with a curse.** Apparently his sin was not merely uttering the covenant name of the Lord (*Yahweh*), but misusing the Lord's name in a curse (Ex. 20:7). Because of uncertainty regarding either his status under the Law as a resident alien or the exact punishment for his sin, **they put him in custody until the will of the** LORD **should be made clear to them.** This is one of four such cases where Moses had to await further divine revelation before a situation could be properly handled (cf. Num. 9:6-14; 15:32-36; 27:1-11).

*b. The revelation of God in the matter (24:13-22)*

**24:13-14.** In this case of blasphemy God Himself pronounced the sentence, capital punishment by stoning (cf. 1 Kings 21:10, 13; Matt. 26:65-66; Acts 6:11-15; 7:54-58). **All those who heard** the man blaspheme were **to lay their hands on his head,** either as a witness against him or to rid themselves of any guilt incurred in merely hearing the blasphemy (cf. Wenham, *Leviticus,* p. 311). The **entire assembly** was **to stone him,** a procedure that is not clearly described in the Old Testament (see the suggestion of Harrison, *Leviticus,* pp. 221-2).

**24:15-16.** The divine law based on this case is specified to apply equally to **an alien or native-born** person. Those aliens who lived in Israel and so enjoyed certain covenant blessings were not to repudiate the Author of that covenant.

**24:17-22.** This digression prescribed other situations which applied alike to Israelite and alien, another connecting link being the application of the death penalty in the case of murder (vv. 17, 21). The so-called *lex talionis* (law of the talon [lit., claw or hand]—**fracture for fracture, eye for eye, tooth for tooth**) indicates that a punishment should be gauged by the offense (cf. Ex. 21:23-25; Deut. 19:21; but cf. Matt. 5:38-39). Except in the case of killing someone, the restitution may have been understood in the sense of equivalent compensation.

*c. The execution of the blasphemer (24:23)*

**24:23.** The **Israelites** obeyed the Lord's command as mediated by **Moses** and **took the blasphemer outside the camp and stoned him.**

## F. The laws concerning special years (chap. 25)

### 1. THE SABBATICAL YEAR (25:1-7)

**25:1-7.** Much as people were to work six days and then rest on the **Sabbath,** so **the land** on which they lived was to be worked **for six years** (v. 3) and then allowed to **rest** on **the seventh** or sabbatical **year** (v. 4). No sowing, pruning, reaping, or harvesting was to be done during that seventh year (vv. 4-5). Any spontaneous yield of **the land** could be consumed for **food** by anyone (not just the owner), but there was to be no organized harvest and no selling of the produce to others (vv. 6-7; cf. Ex. 23:11). So for one-seventh of the time landowners and the landless were on an equal footing in living off the land. Thus the sabbatical year brought a cessation of all normal agricultural activity. A second purpose of that year is given in the supplemental passage (Deut. 15:1-11), the canceling of all debts. Also a freeing of slaves occurred at this time (Deut. 15:12-18; Ex. 21:2-6; but also see comments on Lev. 25:39-55).

### 2. THE YEAR OF JUBILEE (25:8-55)

The land of Israel was God's property and His people were its tenants (v. 23). Therefore the people's land ownership (understood in this sense) was not to be exploited for the enrichment of some and the impoverishment of others (see comments on vv. 23-24). Indebtedness might separate some land from its owner, either through the sale (really lease) of the land (vv. 14-17), or by the owner selling himself as a slave (vv. 39-55), or both. But the land was not to be deeded away in perpetuity. There were several ways in which the land might be reacquired or redeemed (see vv. 23-28). The same principles applied to release of a Hebrew from slavery so that he might return to his land (vv. 41, 48-55).

### a. Regulations for the observance of the Jubilee (25:8-22)

**25:8-13.** Every seventh sabbatical year (i.e., every 49th year) was to be followed by a Year of Jubilee (*yôbēl*, perhaps originally meaning "ram" or "ram's horn," taken from the horn blown to announce the year, but the LXX took it to mean "release") which (though appar-

ently begun on the first day of the seventh month) was officially announced by a **trumpet** blast **on the 10th day** (i.e., **the Day of Atonement,** v. 9). (For the inclusive-reckoning view according to which the 50th year was actually the 49th, see R. North, *The Sociology of the Biblical Jubilee*. Rome: Pontifical Biblical Institute, 1954, pp. 109-12; for the "leap year" view that the Jubilee was a short year only 49 days in length inserted into the seventh month of the 49th year, see Wenham, *Leviticus*, p. 319.)

The motto for the year was to **proclaim liberty** (i.e., release) **throughout the land** with the primary purpose of getting **family property** and the family back together again (vv. 10, 13). This meant that all property (except in walled cities, cf. vv. 29-30) was to be restored to its original owners (i.e., tenants, cf. v. 23), and all Hebrew slaves were to be released to return to their family property. Also, as during the preceding sabbatical year, the land was to enjoy a second straight year of rest (vv. 11-12; cf. vv. 4-7).

**25:14-17.** While selling **land** was not ideal, it was sometimes necessary. Then it was to be done fairly, the price computed **on the basis of the number of years since the Jubilee,** that is, computing **the number of years left for harvesting crops** until the next Jubilee would return the land to its original owner. In other words **what** one was **really selling** was **the number of crops,** a limited lease on the land paid in full in advance.

**25:18-22.** God's blessing **in the land** was promised for obedience to His **laws,** both freedom from want and freedom from war (v. 19; cf. 26:3-13; Deut. 28:1-14). This was particularly applied to the obvious fear an Israelite would have in the face of two successive years of neither planting nor harvesting his crops (Lev. 25:20). God promised an abundant harvest **in the sixth year,** sufficient to carry over **until the harvest of the ninth year comes in.**

### b. The relation of the redemption of property to the Jubilee (25:23-38)

**25:23-24.** **The land** of Israel did not belong to the people, for God was the great Landowner who allotted a portion of **the land** to each tribe and family (cf. Num. 32; Josh. 13–20). This theological principle underlies the basic instructions of Leviticus 25. God's gift of the use of the land to the people was rooted in the Abrahamic Covenant (Gen. 15:7; 17:8; 24:7; Ex. 6:4; cf. Lev. 20:24; 25:2, 38; Deut. 5:16). The provision **for the redemption of the land** is contained in the following verses.

**25:25-28.** A Hebrew who **becomes poor** and so must sell **some of his property** to survive should be helped by his **nearest relative** (*gōʾēl*,) who should **redeem** or buy back the land (cf. Ruth 3:12–4:6; Jer. 32:7-12), or perhaps he would later be able to **redeem it** himself, **the value** to be determined with reference to the date of **the Jubilee** (cf. vv. 16, 50-53). Otherwise, as a last resort, **it** would **be returned** to him in **the Year of Jubilee.**

**25:29-34.** Two exceptions are mentioned concerning the redemption of property. The Jubilee release did not apply to **a house in a walled city,** and one could not be redeemed more than a **year after its sale.** The second exception pertained to **Levites** (mentioned only here in the Book of Leviticus, though the priests, of course, were Levites) who **always** had **the right to redeem their** city property, which was also covered by the release of **the Jubilee.**

**25:35-38.** Pride should not keep a man from treating a **poor** countryman with as much hospitality as he would show **an alien or temporary resident.** Nor should **interest of any kind** be taken from a poor person (vv. 36-37), God's generosity to His people being their example.

*c. The relation of the redemption of slaves to the Jubilee (25:39-55)*

Though slavery was permitted under the Mosaic Law with certain restrictions, even Gentile slaves were given some protection, such as rest on the Sabbath (Ex. 20:10; Deut. 5:14) and prohibition of mistreatment (Ex. 21:20-21; Deut. 23:15-16). As God's servants the Israelites were not to be enslaved to any other master (Lev. 25:55). Yet a poor Hebrew might have to enter a type of temporary slavery, a situation more humane than 19th-century debtors' prisons. Hebrew slaves had broader rights than Gentile slaves and so a Hebrew's master's power over him was more restricted (vv. 39-43). This was in keeping with the slave's sta-

tus as a servant of the Lord.

**25:39-43.** A Hebrew slave was **to be treated as a hired worker** rather than as a **slave** (cf. v. 43). Both **he and his children** who were born in the master's household were **to be released** in the **Year of Jubilee. They** were **not to be sold as slaves** to others. According to Exodus 21:1-11 and Deuteronomy 15:12-18, a Hebrew slave could be released after six years of service, but it is not clear how this correlated with the release of the Jubilee.

**25:44-46.** Gentile **slaves** were exempt from these restrictions, so they were **slaves for life** and could be willed **as inherited property.**

**25:47-55.** Whether purchased by a fellow Israelite (vv. 39-43) or a resident **alien** (vv. 47-53), a Hebrew slave could be redeemed by laws similar to the **redemption** of property (cf. vv. 23-28). Ideally, a relative would free him by paying off the debt which forced him into slavery (vv. 48-49). Or if he prospered he could **redeem himself.** If neither of these measures was possible, he would **be released in the Year of Jubilee.**

**The Year of Jubilee** is not mentioned in the Old Testament outside the Pentateuch. There is no direct biblical evidence regarding its observance in Israel's history, but if its practice was normal, there might have been no occasion to mention it. On the other hand, the apparent failure of Israelites to keep the sabbatical years during the monarchial period (cf. 26:34-35, 43; 2 Chron. 36:20-21) suggests that the Jubilee might also have been violated.

## G. The covenant blessings for obedience and curses for disobedience (chap. 26)

It was common to conclude vassal treaties in the ancient Near East with a section on blessings for obedience and curses for disobedience (see Wenham, *Leviticus*, pp. 29-31, 327). Other passages relating the blessings and curses of the Mosaic Law include Exodus 23:22-33; Deuteronomy 28; Joshua 24:20.

### 1. INTRODUCTORY SUMMARY OF THE FUNDAMENTALS OF THE LAW (26:1-2)

**26:1-2.** Total commitment to **God** alone and avoidance of all forms of idolatry and false worship were to be manifested positively by observing the **Sab-**

baths (cf. 23:3) and reverencing the **sanctuary** (cf. 17:1-9).

### 2. THE BLESSINGS FOR OBEDIENCE (26:3-13)

#### a. The gift of rain and abundant harvests (26:3-5)

**26:3-5.** Unlike the repeated conditional clauses about disobedience (vv. 14, 18, 21, 23, 27), the condition of obedience is introduced only once for the entire blessings section (v. 3). The first blessing includes the promise of seasonal **rain** and the resultant exceedingly abundant **harvest** of **crops** and fruits with attendant plenty and peace.

#### b. The gift of peace in the land (26:6-10)

**26:6-10.** Divine protection from both **savage beasts** and **the sword** (invading armies) would result in **peace** without fear, a plentiful **harvest,** and divine blessing in fulfillment of the Abrahamic Covenant (cf. Gen. 17:7-8).

#### c. The gift of God's presence (26:11-13)

**26:11-13.** God's continued presence in the midst of Israel as He manifested His glory in the tabernacle was a further blessing for covenant faithfulness (v. 11). **God** even promised to **walk** with His **people** as He did with the patriarchs of old (cf. Gen. 5:22, 24; 6:9; 17:1; 24:40; 48:15). God's proclamation of His past deliverance of Israel in the Exodus closes this section on blessings (Lev. 26:13).

### 3. THE CURSES FOR DISOBEDIENCE (26:14-45)

As is typical with ancient Near Eastern vassal treaties, this section on curses is much more extensive than the blessings section, though there are clear parallels between the two sections (cf. Wenham, *Leviticus,* p. 328, n. 5).

The conditional clause, "If you will not listen to Me" (and similar phrases) introduces five paragraphs in this section (vv. 14, 18, 21, 23, 27), each followed by a series of "I wills" which proclaim divine discipline on Israel (vv. 16, 18, 21, 24, 28). See the chart "The Covenant Chastenings," near Amos 4:6.

#### a. Distress from illness, famine, and defeat (26:14-17)

**26:14-17.** The divine discipline for disobedience and **covenant** unfaithfulness brought physical and mental **dis-eases,** stolen crops, and defeat by enemies.

#### b. Drought and bad harvest (26:18-20)

**26:18-20.** God vividly expressed the result of failure to obey Him—**I will punish** (i.e., discipline) **you for your sins seven times over** (a round number for complete or full punishment). The reference to **the sky above** being **like iron** and **the ground beneath . . . like bronze** pictures the hardened crust of ground not soaked by rain (cf. Deut. 28:23).

#### c. Dread of dangerous animals (26:21-22)

**26:21-22.** Continued disobedience would result in multiplied divine discipline in terms of affliction **seven times over.** The desolation of the land, with **wild animals** running rampant, would result in further desolation.

#### d. Disease following desolation by enemies (26:23-26)

**26:23-26.** If God's people under such discipline would **continue to be hostile toward** Him, He would **be hostile** and **bring** a **sword** of vengeance (cf. Jud. 2:11-15) on them because of their **breaking of the covenant.** A divinely sent **plague** and oppression by **enemy hands** would result in further famine.

#### e. Devastation and deportation from the land (26:27-39)

**26:27-39.** In His **anger** God would **punish** Israel finally in dispersion and deportation from **the land.** This would begin with such horrors of war as cannibalism (v. 29), vast slaughter of people and destruction of **cities** and **sanctuaries** (vv. 30-31), and desolation of the **land** (v. 32). (On the high places see comments on Num. 33:52.) Dispersion **among the nations** would follow (Lev. 26:33). As a result **the land** would **enjoy its Sabbath years** which **it did not have during** the years of Israelite disobedience to God's laws concerning the sabbatical year (vv. 34-35; cf. 25:1-7). **Those** who would survive the slaughter would live in fear and ultimately **perish . . . in the lands of their enemies** (26:36-39).

#### f. The prospect of repentance and the promise of restoration (26:40-45)

**26:40-45.** The bleak prospect described in verses 14-39 is bathed in a ray of hope by God's gracious promise, **But if they will confess their sins . . . then . . . I will remember My covenant with . . . Abraham, and I will remember the land** (vv. 40-42). Though Israel would break this covenant (cf. v. 25), yet God would not break His **covenant with them** (v. 44). In His covenant faithfulness He will someday fulfill His **covenant** with Abraham (cf. Gen. 12:1-3) by blessing a repentant generation of Jews in the land of Israel. Though Israel has been divinely disciplined by numerous deportations and dispersions, the blessings of the Abrahamic Covenant with the Jewish nation in the Promised Land in perpetuity await fulfillment in the millennial kingdom after the Second Advent of Christ (cf. Amos 9:11-15; Rom. 11:25-27).

4. CONCLUDING SUMMARY (26:46)

**26:46.** This conclusion is reminiscent of verse 3 and identifies **Moses** as the mediator of this divine revelation given when Israel was camped at **Mount Sinai.**

## H. The law of vows, gifts, and tithes (chap. 27)

Since the exact connection of this with the preceding chapters is ambiguous, some have viewed it as a later addition to the book, or at least an appendix. However, the subject of vows does relate directly to the curses in chapter 26 since people are more likely to make rash vows in times of dire distress. Rash vows are, of course, warned against in Scripture (cf. Ecc. 5:4-5; Deut. 23:21-23; Prov. 20:25), and the high price on the commutation of vows of persons here (Lev. 27:3-7) would also discourage spontaneous vows. The subjects of vows (including those pertaining to sacrificial animals), gifts, and tithes for the sanctuary are closely related and so are appropriately grouped together in this final chapter of a book that began with sacrifices offered at the sanctuary.

1. VOWS PERTAINING TO PEOPLE AND ANIMALS (27:1-13)

a. Vows of persons (27:1-8)

**27:1-8.** The continuity of this final chapter with the rest of the book is indicated by the continued identification of **Moses** as the covenant's mediator. This first paragraph regulates the fulfillment of **a special vow to dedicate persons to**

the LORD by legislating monetary payment to the sanctuary treasury according to a system of **equivalent values.** The other option was direct fulfillment of the vow by service or worship in the sanctuary (as in the case of Hannah's vow to dedicate her son Samuel, 1 Sam. 1:11; cf. 2 Sam. 15:8; Ps. 116:14-18). A person could be redeemed by payment in **silver according to the sanctuary shekel** (cf. Lev. 27:25; 5:15).

The payments (27:3-7) varied according to the general characteristics of age and sex but apparently did not take into account individual characteristics such as health and earning power. Verse 8 allows reduced amounts for the **poor.** Since the 50-shekel evaluation placed on an adult **male** was equivalent to about 50 months' wages, this system tended to discourage rash vows!

b. Vows of animals (27:9-13)

**27:9-13.** Regulations were given regarding vows to give animals **to the** LORD, whether **an animal that is acceptable as an offering** or **one that** was **not acceptable as an offering.** Acceptable animals could not be redeemed by money or other animals, but animals not suitable for sacrifice (regardless of the reason) could be redeemed by paying the amount of the priest's appraisal plus 20 percent. If not redeemed, an animal apparently went to **the priest.**

2. DEDICATION OF HOUSES AND LANDS (27:14-25)

a. Dedication of houses (27:14-15)

**27:14-15.** A **house** (apparently in a walled city; cf. 25:29-31) could be dedicated **to the** LORD (set apart as **holy,** to be used by the priests). It could be redeemed with the standard 120 percent payment.

b. Dedication of lands (27:16-25)

**27:16-21.** The dedication of **family land** was more complicated, being correlated with the laws of **the Year of Jubilee** (cf. 25:23-38). The system of evaluating land began with the cost of **the amount of seed required** to plant it for 49 years, and then was discounted **according to the number of** harvests left **until the next Year of Jubilee** (27:17-18). Redemption required payment of the adjusted evaluation plus 20 percent (v. 19). Failure to redeem the land by the Year of Jubilee resulted in permanently forfeiting its title to **the priests** (vv. 20-21).

**27:22-25.** However, leased land (i.e., **not part of** one's **family land,** v. 22) would automatically **revert to** the original owner in **the Year of Jubilee,** so if a leasee dedicated it **to the LORD . . . its value** had to be established and paid to **the priest** on the **day** it was dedicated. Verse 25 clarifies the standard weight of silver in **the sanctuary shekel.**

3. OTHER DUES AND GIFTS (27:26-33)

*a. The dues of the firstborn (27:26-27)*

**27:26-27. Firstborn** animals **already** belonged **to the LORD** (Ex. 13:2; 34:19-20) and so could not be specially dedicated. But the firstborn of **unclean animals** could be redeemed (cf. Ex. 34:20).

*b. The irrevocable dedication by ḥērem (27:28-29)*

**27:28-29.** Anything irrevocably given **to the LORD** (*ḥērem,* "that which is placed under the ban," a term sometimes used in a "holy war" regarding the extermination of defeated enemies; cf. Num. 21:2; Deut. 7:2 [NIV marg.]; 1 Sam. 15:3-21; see comments on Josh. 6:21) could not be **redeemed** or **ransomed.** Such vows were probably normally limited to national contexts and would not be made by individuals.

*c. The dues of tithes (27:30-33)*

**27:30-33.** Tithes of **the land** could be redeemed by paying the standard 120 percent evaluation, but tithes of animals could not **be redeemed.**

4. CONCLUSION (27:34)

**27:34.** Typical of numerous sections of the book, the chapter closes with a reference to the divine Author, the covenant mediator, the location (implying the time of encampment at **Mount Sinai**), and the recipients of its commands.

# BIBLIOGRAPHY

Bamberger, Bernard J. "Leviticus," *The Torah: A Modern Commentary.* Vol. 3. New York: Union of American Hebrew Congregations, 1979.

Bonar, Andrew. *A Commentary on the Book of Leviticus.* 1852. Reprint. Grand Rapids: Baker Book House, 1978.

Clark, Samuel. "Leviticus." In *The Holy Bible . . . with . . . Commentary.* Vol. 1, part 2. 1877. Reprint. Grand Rapids: Baker Book House, 1981.

Clements, Ronald E. "Leviticus." In *The Broadman Bible Commentary.* Vol. 2. Nashville: Broadman Press, 1970.

Coleman, Robert O. "Leviticus." In *The Wycliffe Bible Commentary.* Chicago: Moody Press, 1962.

Erdman, Charles R. *The Book of Leviticus.* Westwood, N.J.: Fleming H. Revell Co., 1951.

Goldberg, Louis. *Leviticus: A Study Guide Commentary.* Grand Rapids: Zondervan Publishing House, 1980.

Gordon, Robert P. "Leviticus." In *The New Layman's Bible Commentary.* Grand Rapids: Zondervan Publishing House, 1979.

Harrison, R.K. *Leviticus: An Introduction and Commentary.* The Tyndale Old Testament Commentaries. Downers Grove, Ill.: Inter-Varsity Press, 1980.

Keil, C.F., and Delitzsch, F. "The Pentateuch." In *Commentary on the Old Testament in Ten Volumes.* Vol. 1. Reprint (25 vols. in 10). Grand Rapids: Wm. B. Eerdmans Publishing Co., 1982.

Kellogg, Samuel H. *The Book of Leviticus.* 1899. Reprint. Minneapolis: Klock & Klock Christian Publishers, 1978.

Kurtz, J.H. *Sacrificial Worship of the Old Testament.* Translated by James Martin. 1863. Reprint. Grand Rapids: Baker Book House, 1980.

Rainey, A.F. "Sacrifice and Offerings," *The Zondervan Pictorial Encyclopedia of the Bible.* 5 vols. Grand Rapids: Zondervan Publishing House, 1975.

Schultz, Samuel J. *Leviticus.* Everyman's Bible Commentary. Chicago: Moody Press, 1983.

Snaith, Norman H. *Leviticus and Numbers.* The Century Bible. London: Thomas Nelson and Sons, 1969. Reprint. Greenwood, S.C.: Attic Press, 1977.

Wenham, Gordon J. *The Book of Leviticus.* The New International Commentary on the Old Testament. Grand Rapids: Wm. B. Eerdmans Publishing Co., 1979.

# NUMBERS

## Eugene H. Merrill

## INTRODUCTION

The Book of Numbers takes its English name from the Septuagint which calls it *Arithmoi*, "Numbers." The reason for this is that the book contains many statistics such as tribal population figures, the totals of the priests and Levites, and other numerical data. The Hebrew name is *bᵉmiḏbar*, the fifth word in the book, and means "in the desert of."

**Authorship.** Universal Jewish and Christian tradition attributes the Book of Numbers (along with the rest of the Pentateuch) to Moses, though little in Numbers explicitly confirms it (cf., however, 33:2; 36:13). Even critical scholars admit that Numbers is an inseparable part of the Pentateuch though, as is well known, they deny its Mosaic authorship. Moses is certainly the principal figure in the book and throughout he is a participant in and eyewitness to most of its major events. Without the subjective and circular arguments employed by most source critics and redaction critics it is unlikely that any view of authorship other than Mosaic would ever have occurred to most readers. For a discussion of the authorship of the Pentateuch see the *Introduction* to Genesis.

**Date.** The last verse in the Book of Numbers states, "These are the commands and regulations the LORD gave through Moses to the Israelites on the plains of Moab by the Jordan across from Jericho" (36:13). This implies that the journey through the wilderness had been completed and that Israel was about to enter the land of Canaan. Crossing the Jordan occurred 40 years after the Exodus (cf. Josh. 5:6), an event to be dated 1446 B.C. So the Book of Numbers must be dated about 1406, obviously before Moses' death which also took place in that year. (The date 1446 for the Exodus is based on

1 Kings 6:1 which says that Solomon commenced the construction of the temple in his fourth year, 966 B.C., which was 480 years after the Exodus. See the comments on that passage.)

**Purpose.** The Book of Numbers seems to be an instruction manual to post-Sinai Israel. The "manual" deals with three areas: (a) how the nation was to order itself in its journeyings, (b) how the priests and Levites were to function in the condition of mobility which lay ahead, and (c) how they were to prepare themselves for the conquest of Canaan and their settled lives there. The narrative sections, of which there are many, demonstrate the successes and failures of the Lord's people as they conformed and did not conform to the requirements in the legislative, cultic, and prescriptive parts of the book. The fact that the book covers the nearly 40-year period from the giving of the Law at Sinai till the eve of the Conquest points to its character as history. But it is more than a recording of history. It is history with the purpose of describing the Lord's expectations and Israel's reactions in a unique period, an era when the nation had God's promise of the land but had not yet experienced its fulfillment.

## OUTLINE

I. Preparations for Travel (1:1–10:10)
   A. The order of the tribes (chaps. 1–2)
   B. Instructions to the Levites (chaps. 3–4)
   C. Cleansing and consecration (chaps. 5–6)
   D. Tabernacle service (chaps. 7–8)
   E. Passover instructions (9:1-14)
   F. The accompaniment of the Lord (9:15–10:10)
II. The Journey to Kadesh Barnea (10:11–14:45)

A. The departure from Sinai (10:11-36)
B. The rebellion of the people (chap. 11)
C. The rebellion of Miriam and Aaron (chap. 12)
D. Spying out the Promised Land (chaps. 13–14)
III. The Journey to the Plains of Moab (15:1–22:1)
A. The rehearsal of the covenant statutes (chap. 15)
B. The rebellion of Korah (chap. 16)
C. The vindication of Aaron (chap. 17)
D. The roles and privileges of the priests and Levites (chap. 18)
E. The laws of purification (chap. 19)
F. The journey in the Desert of Zin (chap. 20)
G. The journey to Moab (21:1–22:1)
IV. The Moabites and Balaam (22:2–25:18)
A. The plight of Moab (22:2-4a)
B. The invitation to Balaam (22:4b-20)
C. The journey of Balaam (22:21-35)
D. The oracles of Balaam (22:36–24:25)
E. The idolatry of Israel (chap. 25)
V. Final Preparations for Entering Canaan (chaps. 26–36)
A. The provisions for inheritance (26:1–27:11)
B. Succession to Moses (27:12-23)
C. Laws concerning offerings (chaps. 28–29)
D. Laws concerning vows (chap. 30)
E. God's judgment on the Midianites (chap. 31)
F. The inheritance of the Eastern tribes (chap. 32)
G. Resumé of the journey from Egypt (33:1-49)
H. Final instructions about conquest and inheritance (33:50–36:13)

# COMMENTARY

## I. Preparation for Travel (1:1–10:10)

### A. The order of the tribes (chaps. 1–2)

1. THE SOLDIERS (1:1-46)

**1:1-16.** After the making of the covenant and the giving of the Law at **Sinai,** the Lord instructed **Moses** to **take a cen-** sus of all the tribes of Israel by **clans and families** (v. 2). This enumeration of militarily fit males only and from **20 years** (v. 3) of age and older was commanded **on the first day of the second month of the second year after** the Exodus (v. 1). This was exactly one month after the tabernacle was erected at Mount Sinai (Ex. 40:17). **One man from each tribe** was to assist Moses (Num. 1:4); their 12 **names** appear in verses 5-15.

**1:17-46.** After careful research of clan and family records, qualified males **20 years** of age and older were singled out and **counted** (vv. 17-19). The numbers from the tribes were as follows:

| | | |
|---|---|---|
| **Reuben** | **46,500** | (v. 21) |
| **Simeon** | **59,300** | (v. 23) |
| **Gad** | **45,650** | (v. 25) |
| **Judah** | **74,600** | (v. 27) |
| **Issachar** | **54,400** | (v. 29) |
| **Zebulun** | **57,400** | (v. 31) |
| **Ephraim** | **40,500** | (v. 33) |
| **Manasseh** | **32,200** | (v. 35) |
| **Benjamin** | **35,400** | (v. 37) |
| **Dan** | **62,700** | (v. 39) |
| **Asher** | **41,500** | (v. 41) |
| **Naphtali** | **53,400** | (v. 43) |
| Total | 603,550 | (v. 46) |

The order of the listing of the tribes appears to have little significance except that the same groupings are evident in the arrangement of the tribes in their encampment around the tabernacle (2:2-31). Comparison with the sons of Jacob in Genesis 29–30 shows that **Reuben** and **Simeon,** the first two tribes in the Numbers list, were the two oldest sons of Jacob by Leah (Gen. 29:31-33). **Gad,** however, was the first son of Jacob by Zilpah, Leah's handmaid (Gen. 30:9-10). **Judah** was Jacob's fourth son by Leah (Gen. 29:35), **Issachar** the fifth (Gen. 30:17-18), and **Zebulun** the sixth (Gen. 30:19-20). **Ephraim** and **Manasseh** were, of course, **the sons of Joseph,** Jacob's first son by Rachel (Gen. 30:22-24). **Benjamin** was the second son by Rachel (Gen. 35:16-18). **Dan** was the oldest son of Jacob by Bilhah, Rachel's handmaid (Gen. 30:4-6), **Asher** the second son by Zilpah, Leah's handmaid (Gen. 30:12-13), and **Naphtali** the second son by Bilhah (Gen. 30:7-8). Levi, third son by Leah, is not listed in the Numbers census because the Levites were exempt from military service.

The list here in Numbers varies

somewhat from the traditional order (e.g., as in Gen. 46:8-25, though Gen. 49:3-27 is different still) especially in the placement of Gad. The order of the names in Numbers 26:5-50 is identical to that in chapter 1 except that the later list places Manasseh before Ephraim.

A greater difficulty lies in the immense numbers themselves. The total of 603,550 agrees with the figure given in Exodus 38:26 and approximates the number of men who participated in the Exodus (Ex. 12:37 has 600,000). With women and children the total must have reached several million for those counted in the Numbers census included only able-bodied **men 20 years** of age and older. The problem from the human standpoint is obvious: how could millions of people have gotten organized, maintained their cohesion, and traveled through deserts, frequently on narrow routes and difficult terrain? The answer does not lie in the possibility of text corruption, for the large figures prevail throughout the accounts.

One suggestion is that *'elep,* translated "thousand," should be understood as a social unit such as a clan or family (cf. Jud. 6:15; 1 Sam. 10:19; Micah 5:2; etc.). This then might be a technical term suggesting a much smaller actual number. In such a case the total for Reuben, for example (Num. 1:20-21), would be 46 **clans** plus 500 individuals rather than 46,500. If Reuben's clans were 100 men, his total would be 4,600 plus 500 non-clan individuals or 5,100 in all. The major objection to this view is that the grand total for the tribes is 603,550 which, by this system, would mean 603 clans plus 550 individual men. When all the **clans** of the tribes are added up, however, they come to a total of 598 plus 5,550 individuals. This cannot be harmonized with the biblical figures.

A second suggestion is that *'elep* in an unvocalized Hebrew text could be read *'allûp,* "chief" or "commander." Then in Reuben's case the number would be 46 *'allûp*s plus 500 men. The grand total would be 598 *'allûp*s plus 5,550 men. But this again cannot be squared with the Bible's own total of 603 plus 550. It seems best then to take the facts and figures literally and to view the movement and provision of this vast host as a part of the Lord's miraculous provision.

## 2. THE LEVITES (1:47-54)

**1:47-54.** The **Levites** were not to be counted in this **census** for they were exempt from military service in the sense of bearing arms. This is implied in the fact that they were set apart for the service of **the tabernacle and all its furnishings.** Only they could erect and dismantle it; any others who touched it would die (v. 51; cf. 1 Sam. 6:19-20; 2 Sam. 6:6-7). Morever, the **Levites** pitched **their tents** adjacent to **the tabernacle,** and the other tribes in the outer perimeter (Num. 1:52-53; cf. chap. 2).

## 3. THE REMAINDER OF THE PEOPLE (CHAP. 2)

**2:1-9.** The LORD addressed the matter of the arrangement of the **camp** for the anticipated years of journey to Canaan. The nation was to have a set procedure of encampment and march in order to insure efficiency of procedure. The arrangement was to consist of four groups of three tribes each, one group on each side of the tabernacle. The tribe of Levi was to be divided by its major clans and placed immediately around the tabernacle. (See the sketch "Arrangement of the Tribal Camps" and the list "The Israelite Tribal Line of March.")

**Banners** (*'ōtōt,* v. 2) or flags identified the individual families, and a **standard** (*degel,* vv.2-3) identified each three-tribe division. The three tribes **on the east** of the tabernacle were **Judah.** . . . **Issachar,** and **Zebulun** (vv. 3-9), with **Judah** the leader of the **divisions** (v. 9). The leader of Judah, **Nashon son of Amminadab** (v. 3), appears in later genealogies in the messianic line (cf. Ruth 4:20; Matt. 1:4). The tribes in this group represent the fourth, fifth, and sixth sons of Jacob by Leah (see comments on Num. 1:17-46). The east was the orientation of the tabernacle so the Judahite division led the moving procession.

**2:10-17.** To **the south** was the division **of Reuben** with its affiliated tribes **Simeon** and **Gad. Reuben** and **Simeon** were the first and second sons by Leah. Levi was the third son but that tribe could not make up part of the Reuben division because of its religious duties. So **Gad,** the oldest son of Leah's handmaid, was aligned with Reuben. This **division** followed that of Judah in the march.

Next in order was the tribe of Levi which would proceed according to its

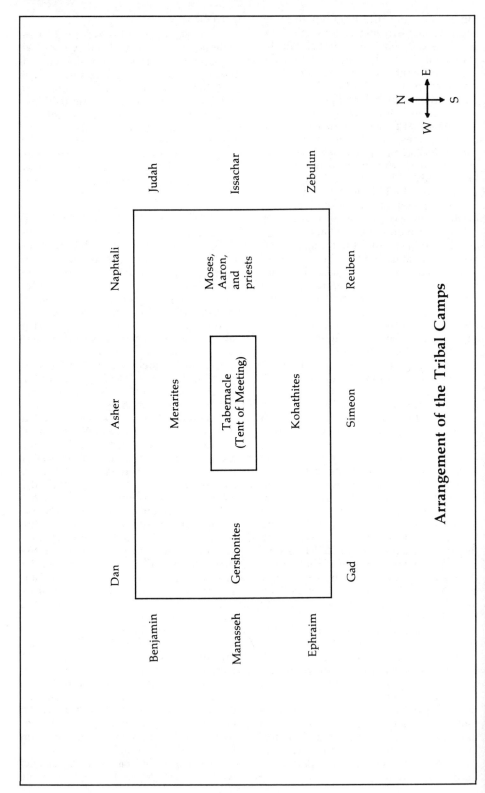

**Arrangement of the Tribal Camps**

## The Israelite Tribal Line of March

1. Judah
2. Issachar
3. Zebulun

4. Reuben
5. Simeon
6. Gad

Tent of Meeting and Levites

7. Ephraim
8. Manasseh
9. Benjamin

10. Dan
11. Asher
12. Naphtali

own clan divisions (v. 17; cf. 3:21-38).

**2:18-24.** To **the west** was the **division** of **Ephraim** and its sister tribes **Manasseh** and **Benjamin.** These three tribes traced their ancestry to Jacob through his wife Rachel. They followed the Levites in the journeyings.

**2:25-34.** Finally, to **the north** was the **division** of **Dan** and its related tribes **Asher** and **Naphtali. Dan** and **Naphtali** were the sons of Rachel's handmaid whereas Asher was the second son of Leah's handmaid.

A certain rationale may be seen in the arrangement of the tribes on ancestral grounds, with the exception of **Asher.** But with the grouping of the Rachel tribes together and the elimination of Levi there is hardly any other place for Asher to fit, so the overall pattern does appear to reflect maternal origins.

### B. Instruction to the Levites (chaps. 3–4)

1. THE LEVITES' RELATIONSHIP TO THE PRIESTS (3:1-13)

**3:1-4.** Chapter 3 refers back to the Lord's revelation to **Moses on Mount Sinai** concerning **the family of Aaron and Moses** (cf. Ex. 28–29). **Aaron,** the high priest, had had four **sons** who were to assist him and succeed him in the sacred office. But two of these four, **Nadab** and **Abihu,** died as the result of an arrogant deviation from authorized priestly procedure (see comments on Lev. 10:1-2). This

left the other two sons of Aaron, **Eleazar and Ithamar,** who served with their father. Since only Aaron and his direct descendants could serve as priests (Ex. 28:1; 29:9; 40:15) it was impossible for them to attend to all Israel's religious needs by themselves. So the entire tribe of Levi was selected to undertake religious responsibilities short of actual priestly ministry. Since Aaron was a Levite this meant that all the priests were Levites but not all the Levites were priests.

**3:5-10.** The specific task of the Levites was to do **the work of the tabernacle** (vv. 7-8). They could not approach **the sanctuary** itself (v. 10). This reference to the sanctuary (the Heb. says only "anyone else who draws near" and does not explicitly mention the sanctuary) clearly outlines the limitations of **the Levites**—they could not serve as priests by offering sacrifices or by performing other functions *in* the tabernacle.

**3:11-13.** The reason for the selection of the tribe of Levi is reviewed here. Since **the Lord** had spared **the firstborn** of Israel's children and animals in the 10th plague, He now had claim on **the firstborn** as His own possession. In lieu of the firstborn, however, the tribe of Levi was substituted (see comments on Ex. 13:1-16). The implementation of this principle of substitution is described in Numbers 3:40-51.

2. THE LEVITES' ASSIGNMENTS (3:14-39)

**3:14-26.** At last the Levites were also numbered in preparation for their order of encampment and service. All the males **a month old or more** must be tallied (v. 15). They were divided into three clans according to their affiliation with the three sons of Levi—**Gershon, Kohath, and Merari** (v. 17). The Gershonites were subdivided into the **Libnites and Shimeites** who altogether numbered **7,500** males (vv. 21-22). They camped **on the west** and **were responsible for the care of the tabernacle** cloths, hides, and **curtains** including **the curtain** that surrounded the outer **courtyard.**

**3:27-32.** The Kohathites consisted of the subgroups of the **Amramites, Izharites, Hebronites, and Uzzielites,** which had **8,600** males (vv. 27-28). Amram was the father of Aaron and Moses (26:58-59; cf. Ex. 6:16-20). To **the Kohathites,** who camped **on the south,** fell the responsibility for the tabernacle's holy objects (Num. 3:31). Their **leader** was **Eleazar, son of Aaron, the** high **priest** (v. 32).

**3:33-37. The Merarites** were divided into **the Mahlites and the Mushites** and numbered **6,200** males. Camped **on the north side,** they were put in charge of the wooden framework **of the tabernacle** and all the fastenings and other gear related to the framework.

**3:38. Moses and Aaron and his sons** camped on **the east** side **of the tabernacle.** Their responsibility was **the care of the sanctuary,** which implies overall supervision since everything else is covered in the assignments to the other three Levitical groups.

**3:39. The total number of Levites . . . was 22,000** whereas the total reached by adding up the figures in verses 22, 28, and 34 is 22,300. The 22,000 figure cannot be a rounding off since the 22,273 firstborn of Israel outnumbered the Levites by 273 (v. 46). The most satisfying solution is to suppose that the excess 300 were themselves the firtborn of the *Levites* who obviously could not serve to redeem the firstborn of Israel (cf. comments on vv. 40-51).

3. THE LEVITES' SUBSTITUTION FOR THE FIRSTBORN (3:40-51)

**3:40-51.** In compensation for His having spared the **firstborn . . . males** of Israel at the time of the Exodus, **the LORD** declared that all the **firstborn** of men and animals should belong to Him (see comments on vv. 11-13). This would not involve their deaths, but their lifetime service. A further development of this principle was the arrangement whereby the tribe of Levi would be given in service to the Lord as a substitution for all **the firstborn** of the other tribes.

The number of Levites to offer this vicarious service was 22,000 (v. 39) whereas the **firstborn males** in all Israel amounted to **22,273** (v. 43). This meant that there were insufficient Levites. Therefore, the **273 firstborn Israelites** without Levitic redemption had to be redeemed in another way. The solution was to exact **five shekels for each** of the 273 (v. 47), a total of 1,365 silver two-ounce shekels (more than 170 lbs., worth several thousand dollars in present-day currency).

The objection is frequently raised

that 22,000 male Levites from the age of one month and older is fewer than one would expect in light of the statistics from the other tribes. Two points are raised to support this objection: (1) Manasseh had the fewest of the others at 32,200 (2:21) and these were just males from age 20 and higher. However, the low population of Levi may simply mean that, for whatever reason, the tribe had not been as productive as others. Other figures about the tribe (e.g., 8,580 men from 30 to 50 years of age, 4:48) agree with the 22,000 population.

(2) Also some argue that the 22,273 firstborn of the 12 tribes was an unreasonably small number since the total population of Israelite men 20 years of age and older was 603,550 (cf. 1:46). This would yield a ratio of only about 1 to 27. However, the firstborn of Israel most likely refers only to those who were born after the tribe of Levi was established as a sacerdotal unit. The original statement concerning the firstborn (Ex. 13:11-13) clearly indicates that the implementation of the command was not retroactive to the Exodus but would come into effect in the future. That is, only **the firstborn** males who were born between the time of the Exodus and the setting apart of Levi about two years later (Num. 1:1) would be counted. So a total of 22,273 would be in line for that period of time since there could hardly be more than that number of families that would give birth to their first sons during that time.

4. THE MOVING OF THE TABERNACLE (CHAP. 4)

**4:1-3.** For the Levitical ministry described here, a Levite was to be between **30** and **50 years of age.** The purpose of counting Levite males from the age of one month and older (3:39-41), then, was purely for the sake of the redemption of the firstborn of Israel. The age of 30 for the minimum age of priestly service was still the custom centuries later (cf. comments on Ezek. 1:1). However, the Levites could and did serve in various capacities at younger ages (Num. 8:24). What was involved in this account was the heavy **work** of transporting the tabernacle and all its accoutrements.

**4:4-20.** First, **the Kohathites** were to be employed. To **Aaron and his sons** fell the awesome task of lowering the veil (**the shielding curtain,** v. 5) and placing it over **the ark** along **with hides** and cloths (vv. 5-6). The reasons were (a) to guard the holy ark from the gaze of human eyes (v. 20) and (b) to protect it from the elements. They were to do the same with **the table of the Presence** ("the table of showbread," v. 7, KJV) with all its vessels, the **lampstand** (v. 9), and **all the** other **articles used** in tabernacle worship (v. 12). They were to clean the great **bronze altar** of burnt offering of its **ashes** and cover it and its utensils with a **cloth** and **hides** (vv. 13-14). To all these heavy objects Aaron and his sons were to attach the appropriate carrying **poles** (vv. 6, 8, 11, 14) or frames (vv. 10, 12).

When all had been prepared by the priests the remaining Levitical **Kohathites** were to transport the above-named furnishings, being extremely careful **not** to **touch** any of the objects lest **they . . . die** (v. 15; cf. vv. 19-20). **Eleazar . . . the priest** was to supervise the entire procedure and to see that the oils, **incense,** and grains were properly handled (v. 16).

**4:21-28. The Gershonites** were charged with transporting the nonwooden parts of the tabernacle and outer court, including coverings, **curtains . . . ropes,** and other related **equipment.** This was under the supervision of **Ithamar . . . the priest.**

**4:29-33.** The wood and metal parts of the tabernacle complex were delegated to **the Merarites. Ithamar** was supervisor of this part of **tabernacle** transportation as well as the nonwooden parts (cf. v. 28).

**4:34-49.** The total number of Levites involved in this work was **8,580** (v. 48)— **2,750** Kohathites (v. 36), **2,630** Gershonites (v. 40), and **3,200** Merarites (v. 44).

## C. Cleansing and consecration (chaps. 5–6)

### 1. THE CEREMONIALLY UNCLEAN (5:1-4)

**5:1-4.** The Lord reminded the people of His holiness and of their need for holiness if they were to live near His dwelling place. In the Old Testament covenant, the community's spiritual holiness was linked to and symbolized by physical, bodily holiness and by proper interpersonal relationships. So anyone who contracted an illness that rendered him ceremonially unclean could not fellowship with the Lord at the tabernacle or with his human associates. This included

an infectious skin disease (not only leprosy; cf. NIV marg.), a bodily **discharge of any kind** (e.g., menstrual or seminal emissions), and the contamination resulting from contact with **a dead body.** (For a full description of various kinds of uncleanness and their treatments, see comments on Lev. 12–15 and Num. 19.)

### 2. THE LAW OF RECOMPENSE (5:5-10)

**5:5-10.** In line with the spirit of the Law which regarded sin against one's fellowman as sin also against God (cf. Ps. 51:4), the Lord here introduced the principle of recompense. The offender who wronged **another** person **in any way** must **confess** that **sin** and also **make full restitution** for it plus 20 percent. This obviously refers to losses that could be measured in monetary terms (cf. Lev. 6:1-7 for details). **But if** the offended party was no longer alive and had **no close relative to whom** restitution could **be made . . . the restitution** was to be given to **the LORD . . .** along with a **ram** which was required as a guilt-offering of **atonement** (cf. Lev. 5:15; 6:6; 7:1-10). This type of offering was actually given to **the priest** for him to eat (Lev. 7:6-7). Similarly **the sacred contributions** an Israelite might make voluntarily were to go to **the priest** for his use (Lev. 2:9-10).

### 3. THE ACCUSATION OF ADULTERY (5:11-31)

**5:11-15.** In the covenant community of Israel adultery, like ceremonial uncleanness and trespass against one's brother or sister (v. 6), was symptomatic of unfaithfulness to the Lord. It therefore could not be tolerated as either a breach of the relationship of husband and wife (Ex. 20:14) or as the expression of covenant infidelity (Ezek. 16). If a man suspected his wife of adultery he was to **take** her before **the priest** whether he had proof or not (Num. 5:11-15). Since adultery also was a sin against God the appropriate offering of **barley flour** was to be taken to the priest and offered before the Lord. The purpose of the offering was **to draw attention to guilt** (v. 15). (How this was done is explained in vv. 18, 25-26.)

**5:16-18.** To start the ritual for ascertaining guilt **the priest** presented the woman **before the LORD** (i.e., before the tabernacle), took **water** specially blessed or set apart for such cases, and mixed it with **dust from the tabernacle floor.** He then loosened the woman's **hair** and placed the barley **offering in her hands . . . while he** held the **water** jar in his hands. Though the scene so far suggests the magical procedures of pagan trials by ordeal, magic itself is expressly forbidden in the Old Testament (e.g., Deut. 18:9-13). So this ordeal ritual must be understood in terms of the symbolical value of its elements. The barley represents the offering appropriate to judgment, especially since it was not to be mixed with oil or incense (Num. 5:15; cf. Lev. 2:1-2; 5:11-13). The water mixed with dust was **holy** (Num. 5:17) because it was in a holy vessel (perhaps the bronze basin, Ex. 30:18). The dissolving of the dust in the water may well relate to the eating of dust by the serpent, who had been cursed by the Lord in the Garden of Eden (Gen. 3:14). If the accused woman proved to be guilty she, like the serpent, could expect the **curse** of God as well. The loosening of her hair, while not a token of her immorality (since that had not been proved), nevertheless reflects the seriousness of the accusation and the presumptive guilt attested by the husband's "feelings of jealousy" (Num. 5:14).

**5:19-31.** When all was ready, **the priest told the woman** she would not be cursed if she were innocent but would be cursed if guilty. She was to reply, **So be it.** If she was guiltless no ill effect (**harm**) would follow her drinking of **the bitter water,** the water mixed with dust. If she was guilty, on the other hand, her guilt would be manifest by the wasting **away** of her **thigh** and the swelling of **her abdomen.** This **curse** clearly refers to some physical disorder which would render the woman sterile (vv. 27-28). After the woman had taken the oath (v. 22), the ink with which the curses were written was rinsed off the **scroll** and into the jar of dust and **water** (v. 23). That is, **the woman** must now symbolically "eat her words." She then was to **drink the** potion while **the priest** offered the barley to **the Lord** (vv. 24-26). If guilty, she suffered the penalty of the **curse.** If innocent, she came through unharmed with her child-bearing capacity intact (vv. 27-28). In either case the **husband** was absolved of guilt for if the wife was **innocent** he had acted only because he had

been affected by a feeling of **jealousy** over which he had no control (vv. 29-31).

The physical manifestations of guilt were not inherent in the properties of the liquid mixture itself or, as stated earlier, could they be attributed to magic. More likely it was a matter of a psychosomatic reaction caused by genuine guilt or innocence, a reaction prompted by one's conscience and the convicting work of the Holy Spirit.

### 4. THE LAW OF THE NAZIRITE (6:1-21)

**6:1-12.** The counterpart to cleansing (chap. 5) is consecration (chap. 6). Priestly, Levitical service was the exclusive privilege of those who belonged to the tribe of Levi but the Lord here instituted a provision whereby any **man or woman** of Israel who wished could take **a vow** before **the Lord** to consecrate himself for a stated period of time to serve God. Occasionally such a vow would be made by parents on behalf of their children, as in the case of Samuel (1 Sam. 1:11), but ordinarily it was an act of devotion taken voluntarily by an adult.

A person who thus decided to consecrate himself was called **a Nazirite** (from *nāzar,* "to dedicate"). For the duration of his period of consecration he had to **abstain from . . . fermented** beverages and all other products of the vine (Num. 6:3-4); he could not shave **his head** (v. 5); and he could **not** come in contact with a corpse (vv. 6-8). To do so would violate the vow which was symbolized by his long hair (v. 7). If, however, he inadvertently came near a dead body he had to undertake a long ceremony of **cleansing** in which **his head** would be shaved on **the seventh day,** and **on the eighth day** he had to offer **two doves or two . . . pigeons. . . . one as a sin offering and the other as a burnt offering** (vv. 9-11; cf. Lev. 5:7-10). Then he could resume his period of consecration.

**6:13-17.** When one's time of consecration was **over,** the Nazirite was to take to the tabernacle **a year-old male lamb . . . for a burnt offering,** a year-old ewe **lamb . . . for a sin offering,** and **a ram . . . for a fellowship offering.** These, accompanied by **grain offerings and drink offerings and a basket of** unleavened **bread . . . made of fine flour** and oil and **wafers spread with oil,** constituted the formal announcement of his termination of **Nazirite** dedication. **The sin offering** was to atone for any sins unwittingly committed during the period of consecration (cf. Lev. 5:1-6). **The burnt offering** was to symbolize complete surrender to the Lord (cf. Lev. 1:10-13). And the **fellowship offering** was to speak of the fact that the Nazirite and **the LORD** were in perfect harmony (cf. Lev. 3:6-11; 7:11-14).

**6:18-21.** After this **the Nazirite** was to cut his **hair** and cast it on the altar on which **the fellowship offering** had been made. This offering of hair represents, perhaps, the commitment of the entire Nazirite experience to the Lord. It symbolized to the devotee the blessing of God, from whom all blessings come.

Finally **the priest** was to take **the ram** of the fellowship offering, place its choice parts and bread in the **hands** of the Nazirite, and offer the meat and bread to **the LORD.** The **wave offering** means the material was presented as a sacrifice to the Lord and to His servant the priest. So **the priest** and the offerer participated in a common meal (cf. Lev. 7:28-34). Only then could **the Nazirite** once more **drink wine** and, presumably, do all the other things forbidden to him while the vow was in effect.

5. THE LAW OF THE PRIESTLY BLESSING (6:22-27)

**6:22-27.** In pronouncing God's favor on the people, the priest was to use a formula for blessing. This beautiful blessing may be only a model, as the so-called "Lord's Prayer" is a model for prayer, but its purpose is clear: it communicates the desire of **the LORD** to invest His people with His **name.** The name of the Lord is tantamount to the Lord Himself so that this blessing becomes a petition that God might live among His people and meet all their needs. He alone can **bless** His people, **keep** them, look on them with favor (**make His face shine** and **turn His face toward** them), **be gracious to** them, **and give** them **peace.**

*D. Tabernacle service (chaps. 7–8)*

1. OFFERINGS OF THE LEADERS (CHAP. 7)

**7:1-9.** This chapter points retrospectively back to a month earlier when **the tabernacle** had just been completed and dedicated. In preparation for the move from Sinai to the Promised Land **the trib-**al **leaders** brought to the Lord **gifts** of **six wagons and 12 oxen.** These, they said, were to be at the disposal of **the Levites** to help them in their **work** of transporting the tabernacle and its contents (vv. 4-5). Moses therefore distributed the **oxen** and **carts** as follows: **two carts and 4 oxen to the Gershonites** (v. 7), **four carts and 8 oxen to the Merarites** (v. 8), **but none to the Kohathites** (v. 9) because they were to bear the sacred objects **on their shoulders** (cf. 4:15). Failure to do this later brought great grief to David and his servants when the ark was transported from the house of Abinadab to Jerusalem (2 Sam. 6:3; cf. 2 Sam. 6:7-8). The Merarites needed more carts and oxen than the Gershonites because they had to carry the heavy wooden and metal framework of the tabernacle (cf. Num. 4:31-32).

**7:10-17.** Each of the 12 tribal leaders (cf. 1:5-15) **brought . . . offerings for** the **dedication of the altar.** The word for leader is *nāśî*, meaning "elevated one." The **first** to bring **his** gifts **was Nashon,** leader **of Judah.** His contribution, in addition to the carts and oxen (7:3), consisted of a **silver plate** of **130 shekels** weight (worth ca. $260 at $5 per ounce), a **silver sprinkling bowl** of **70 shekels** (ca. $140), each of which was **filled** with **flour** and **oil;** a **gold ladle** of **10 shekels** ($1,800 at $450 per ounce) **filled with incense;** a **young bull,** a **ram,** and a yearling **male lamb,** all for **burnt** offerings; a **male goat for a sin offering;** and **two oxen, five rams, five male goats, and five** yearling **male lambs,** all for **fellowship** offerings.

**7:18-83.** All the remaining tribal leaders brought identical gifts, each on consecutive days. The 12 days spanned by these offerings most likely commenced with the 1st day of the first month of the second year since the Exodus (Ex. 40:17) and continued through the 12th day of that month. The order of their coming with their gifts corresponds exactly with the arrangement of the tribes around the tabernacle (cf. Num. 2:3-31).

**7:84-89.** The presentations of the 12 **leaders** (vv. 12-83) were summarized and totaled. The pleasure of **the LORD** at the generous spirit of the tribal leaders may be suggested by His communication to **Moses** in the tabernacle's most holy place **between the two cherubim.**

## 2. LIGHTING THE LAMPS (8:1-4)

**8:1-4.** After the offerings of the lay leadership (the 12 tribal leaders, chap. 7) were discussed, attention was turned to the priest's role in the service of the tabernacle. In addition to their sacrificial functions, clearly understood so that they did not require elaboration here, the priests were to attend to the setting and lighting of **the seven lamps.** Each lamp had six arms or branches (Ex. 25:31-40). They were to be set up so that they would cast their **light** forward and illuminate **the area in front of** them. This particular instruction had not been communicated to the priests previously.

## 3. CONSECRATION OF THE LEVITES (8:5-26)

**8:5-7.** The third major element of Israel's leadership, **the Levites,** now came to the forefront. To be qualified to attend to the holy ministry for which they were set apart, they had to go through a ritual **cleansing** (vv. 6-7) and then had offerings made on their behalf (vv. 8-19). The cleansing consisted of the sprinkling of **water,** probably that referred to in connection with the ashes of the red heifer (chap. 19). The second step in the cleansing was cutting all the hair on **their** entire **bodies.** This may not mean shaving, as the NIV says, for the usual Hebrew word for **shave** is *gālâh* but the words here are *'āḇar ṭa'ar 'al,* "bring a razor on." This seems to mean trimming the hair, not shaving it off completely. These two steps (sprinkling and trimming) represent outward purification.

**8:8-11.** The inward cleansing, as always, was to be accompanied by the offering of sacrifices. The animal to be slaughtered, **a young bull,** indicates that this was a burnt offering (Lev. 1:3-9). The **second young bull** was **a sin offering** made for unwitting sin (see Lev. 4:1-12). When all was ready **the Levites** (probably their representatives) were presented to the people, representatives of whom were to **lay their hands on** the Levites as a sign that the community was investing them with their authority to represent them in **the work of the LORD.** Then the priests were to offer **the Levites** to the LORD as a kind of living sacrifice.

**8:12-19.** Next **the Levites** placed **their hands on the heads of the** sacrificial animals, transferring to them their own sense of both guilt and commitment. The reason for setting **the Levites apart** was that they were to serve as substitutes for **the firstborn** of all **Israel** who rightfully belonged to the Lord because He had redeemed them from death in the 10th plague **in Egypt** (vv. 15-18; cf. comments on 3:11-13). Since **the Levites** were the Lord's it was His prerogative to give them **as gifts to Aaron and** the priests so they might care for the tabernacle and its precincts and so deliver the secular community from the danger of coming into direct contact with the holy things of God (8:19; cf. 1:53).

**8:20-26.** With all this done, **the Levites** went to the tabernacle to commence their ministry (vv. 20-22). This aspect of their work, compared with transporting the tabernacle and its furnishings, could be undertaken when they were **25 years** of age rather than 30 (v. 24; cf. 4:3). They could continue to serve up to **the age of 50** when they would **retire** but could return as assistants to the younger men (vv. 25-26). These limitations insured that **the Levites** would serve the Lord in the prime years of their lives.

## E. Passover instructions (9:1-14)

**9:1-8.** These instructions were given **in the first month of the second year after** the Exodus, just after the completion of the tabernacle (Ex. 40:17) and before the taking of the census (Num. 1:2) which was on the first day of the second month. In fact it must have been before **the 14th day of** the first **month** since that was the appointed time for **the Passover** (9:3; cf. Ex. 12:1-16).

The reason for new **Passover** instructions was to address the problem of any who for some reason might be unable to **celebrate** the festival at the designated time. Specifically, in this situation some of the people were ineligible to take part because they had become **ceremonially unclean** by having come in contact with **a dead body.** When those people pressed **Moses and Aaron** on the matter, **Moses** sought direction from **the LORD.**

**9:9-14.** God's answer was that **any of** them who were unable to participate in the festival because of uncleanness or even because they were **on a journey** could do so on the **14th day of the second month,** one month later than the prescribed date, observing it precisely as if it were carried out at the regular **time.**

Another (and new) stipulation to Passover observance pertained to someone who was eligible and available to take part in the festival but refused to do so. Such a one must be excommunicated from the community and **bear the consequences of his sin** (v. 13). The foreboding tone of this warning suggests that the excommunication meant death.

Finally, **an alien living among** them could participate fully in the **Passover** (cf. Ezra 6:20-21) if he had met the qualifications which, though not listed here (Num. 9:14), were well known to Israel. They consisted of proselyte conversion symbolized by circumcision (Ex. 12:48).

### F. The accompaniment of the Lord (9:15–10:10)

#### 1. THE PRESENCE OF THE CLOUD (9:15-23)

**9:15-23.** This passage anticipates God's guiding the people by **the cloud** night and day as they made their journey to Canaan. The cloud was the manifestation of the very person and presence of the Lord (Ex. 40:34-38). When **the cloud** moved on, it represented the movement and leading of God; when **the cloud settled** over **the tabernacle** it represented His stopping and settling. **Sometimes** the time of rest was **long** (Num. 9:19) but at other times **the cloud** remained **only** for **a few days** or a night and then moved on the next **day** (vv. 20-21). Whatever the situation, the nation moved in response to the divine direction (v. 23).

#### 2. THE BLOWING OF THE TRUMPETS (10:1-10)

**10:1-7.** In order for the people to know precisely when and how to move (cf. 9:15-23), it was necessary to devise a system of signals. This consisted of the blowing of **two** specially made silver **trumpets** whose purposes were both to signal the gathering of the people and to announce their continued march. **When both** were blown all the people were to **assemble . . . at the entrance to** the tabernacle (i.e., at the east side). When **only one** was **sounded** only the clan **leaders** were required to be present. With still a different call, or perhaps pitch, the trumpets would announce the departure of the eastern division of tribes (cf. 2:3-9). And a **second** call would alert the tribes **on the south** (9:6; cf. 2:10-16). Presumably the western and northern divisions also had their own signals.

**10:8-10.** The blowing of **the trumpets** was the responsibility of **the priests.** Even after the wilderness journey was over and the tribes were settled in the land **the trumpets** would be blown, particularly in war. The role of the priests in combat and the Lord's promise to respond to the trumpets suggests that His people were to be involved in holy war. That is, they were to fight the battles of **the LORD who,** of course, would lead the way against His **enemies** and guarantee success (v. 9; cf. Josh. 6:12-21). The priests were also to blow the trumpets at the times of the major **feasts** (Passover, Weeks or Pentecost, and Tabernacles) and the **New Moon festivals** on the first day of each month (Lev. 23, esp. v. 24). This use of **the trumpets** was not so much to announce these various festivals as to invoke and celebrate the presence of God among His people on those special occasions. They would each be **a memorial** for the people before **God,** a kind of reminder of His guidance and blessing in the past, particularly in the wilderness.

### II. The Journey to Kadesh Barnea (10:11–14:45)

#### A. The departure from Sinai (10:11-36)

**10:11-13.** On the 20th day of the second month of the second year after the Exodus, only 20 days after the beginning of the instructions to Israel about their move from **Sinai** (1:1), the Lord lifted **the cloud** of His glory **from above the tabernacle.** They had been at Sinai for almost a year (cf. Ex. 19:1 with Num. 10:11). This appearance of God's glory coincided with the end of the delayed Passover celebration (9:9-12). In a sense it repeated the leading of the Lord after the Exodus and the original Passover (Ex. 12:51; 13:21). The immediate destination was **the Desert of Paran,** a vast stretch of barren land that crossed the whole north-central part of the Sinai Peninsula, but there would be several intermediate stops (cf. Num. 11:3, 34-35; 12:16).

**10:14-28.** The order of march had been prescribed earlier by the Lord (2:3-31). The **Judah** division led the way (10:14-16). Following their departure, the Gershonite and Merarite Levites dismantled **the tabernacle** and **set out** after Judah. Next the **Reuben** division proceeded (vv. 18-20), followed by the Kohathite Levites, who carried the ark and the other sacred furnishings of the tabernacle. They departed later so that the Gershonites and Merarites would have enough time to erect the tabernacle in its new location before the Kohathites arrived (v. 21). The division of Ephraim followed the Kohathites (vv. 22-24), and finally the division of Dan brought up the rear (vv. 25-27). Apparently this was the unvarying pattern of their journeyings from then on (v. 28).

10:29-32. Meanwhile, before the trek to Paran commenced, Moses invited his brother-in-law Hobab to accompany him to the land of promise. The identity of Hobab is debated since his name seems to be an alias for Reuel . . . Moses' father-in-law (cf. Jud. 4:11, NIV marg.). To complicate matters Reuel is also known as Jethro (Ex. 2:18; 3:1). To address the second matter first, no particular problem exists in Moses' father-in-law being known as both Reuel and Jethro. Jacob, for example, was also called Israel, and Joshua was otherwise known as Hoshea (Num. 13:16). As for the identity of Hobab, he was clearly a son of Reuel and therefore Moses' brother-in-law. Why then does Judges 4:11 in some translations describe Hobab as the "father-in-law" (ḥōṯēn) of Moses? The answer is that the Hebrew root ḥtn is not always a reference to a father-in-law but can refer to any "in-law" relationship. For example, ḥāṯān occasionally means "son-in-law" (e.g., Gen. 19:12, 14; Jud. 15:6; 19:5), though certainly Hobab was not Moses' son-in-law. Perhaps the best solution is that Reuel (Jethro) had died (he is not mentioned after Ex. 18:27, i.e., about two years earlier than this reference to Hobab). Hobab, a brother of Zipporah, Moses' wife, would then have assumed the patriarchal role in the family and would play the role of Moses' father-in-law from the standpoint of the prevailing custom. In addition, the last that is said of Reuel is that he returned to his own land (Ex. 18:27) and yet Hobab was here at Sinai with Moses. In light of all these factors it is reasonable to distinguish Hobab from Reuel and to identify Hobab as Moses' brother-in-law, precisely as Numbers 10:29 says.

Moses' interest in taking Hobab was not merely to enable Hobab to participate in the blessings of the Promised Land. Moses was also interested in benefiting

from Hobab's familiarity with the desert routes ahead of them (vv. 31-32). Later accounts suggest that Hobab was persuaded to go and that he became an ancestor of certain Israelite tribal units (Jud. 1:16; 4:11).

10:33-36. The first leg of the journey from Sinai lasted three days. The travel was undertaken only in the daylight hours; at night the cloud and the ark rested along with the people. As an indication of the warlike nature of the journey, a foretaste no doubt of the military conquest which lay ahead, Moses would lead the people in a battle cry in which the presence and conquering power of the LORD were invoked (v. 35; cf. Ps. 68:1). When the day's march was over he would entreat the LORD to abide among His people through the night.

## B. The rebellion of the people (chap. 11)

11:1-3. After the three-day journey just described (10:33-36) the people began to complain in the hearing of the LORD. The reference to His hearing them is anthropomorphic language used, no doubt, to suggest that their complaining was not inward and quiet. Indeed, it was so loud it reached the very heavens! In reaction the LORD in His anger . . . consumed many of the rebels with fire. (The Heb. word for "the camp" suggests people who were encamped, not merely a place of encampment. Therefore people were consumed.) This fire is doubtless a metaphor to describe the fiery anger and judgment of God in whatever form it might take, though obviously it might have been a literal fire. So impressive was the Lord's punishment that the people named that part of the campsite Taberah ("burning"). This did not become a normal place name, however, as its omission from the later itinerary lists clearly shows (33:16-17).

11:4-9. No sooner had the wrath of God diminished than the rabble among the people began to crave other food, particularly what they had become used to in Egypt. All they had now, they said, was manna. The "rabble" ('ăsapsūp, "collection," occurring only here in the OT) were the "mixed multitude" of non-Israelites who left Egypt with Israel in the Exodus. The normal word to describe this element is 'ēreḇ, literally, "mixed company" (Ex. 12:38; Jer. 25:20; Neh.

13:3; etc.). (For a description of the manna, **like coriander seed** and **resin,** see the comments on Ex. 16:31-36.) Here in Numbers, Moses added that the **manna** was prepared for consumption by being **ground** or **crushed** and then **cooked . . . in a pot or made . . . into cakes.** Apparently the people differed in their feelings about its taste for, according to Exodus 16:31, it **tasted like** wafers made with honey whereas here it is said to have the flavor of **something made with olive oil.** In any event the blandness of the manna compared with the spicy food of Egypt prompted a wholesale rebellion against Moses and the Lord.

**11:10-15.** Moses' reaction was to ask **the LORD why** He was bringing **this trouble on** him. The Lord, not **Moses,** had created Israel as a **people** and had brought them into the wilderness. Since this was so, **Moses** could not and should not bear the responsibility for them (**I cannot carry all these people by myself**). If the Lord would not relieve him, Moses asked God if he could be **put . . . to death.**

**11:16-20.** The Lord's response was neither to allow **Moses** to die nor to take the leadership of Israel from him. Instead God created a structure of subleadership to enable Moses to delegate responsibility. God told Moses to select **70 . . . elders** of Israel, men of good reputation, on whom would be placed the same **Spirit** who rested on and empowered Moses (cf. Ex. 18:21-26; Acts 6:3). Then **the LORD** commanded **the people** to prepare for the next day **when** He would give them so much **meat** they would get sick of it (Num. 11:18-20). For a **month** they would gorge themselves till the meat would come **out of** their **nostrils.** This is probably hyperbolic language but it effectively communicates the truth that those who reject the perfect purposes of God find the alternatives nauseous and undesirable.

**11:21-23.** **Moses** found the Lord's promise to send **meat** in such quantities to be incredible. Moses thought that even all the **flocks and herds** of Israel and **all the fish of the sea** would be inadequate for the **600,000 men** of Israel and their families **for a . . . month.** But **the LORD** replied that He was more than able to do as He said and **Moses** would **see** the results with his own eyes.

**11:24-29.** Before this came to pass, however, **Moses** selected **70 . . . elders and** gathered **them** about the tabernacle (cf. v. 16). **Then the LORD** appeared in **the cloud . . . took of the Spirit that was on** Moses, and placed that **Spirit on the 70.** As a result they began to prophesy, **but** only this one time (lit., "and they did not add"). All that was necessary was for their ministry to be publicly authenticated so the whole community could see that they possessed the same spiritual qualifications and authority as Moses himself. Prophesying here does not refer to prediction or even to proclamation but to giving (in song or speech) praise and similar expressions without prior training (see the comparable experience of Saul in 1 Sam. 10:9-11). This prophesying could be done only in response to the special visitation of **the Spirit.**

To show that the bestowal of the Spirit was an act of God unrelated to Moses' presence, **the LORD** placed **the Spirit** on **two men . . . Eldad and Medad,** who **had** not joined the others at the tabernacle (Num. 11:26). They began to prophesy which so surprised the assembly **in the camp** that the people sent a messenger to **Moses** to inform him of it. **Joshua,** when he heard, became greatly disturbed and asked **Moses** to forbid this "unofficial" prophesying. Moses correctly interpreted Joshua's concern as one for Moses' unique character as mediator of God's blessing, but chided Joshua with the fervent wish that **all** God's **people** might share such a measure of God's **Spirit** with him.

**11:30-35.** After the 70 had been selected and properly validated **the LORD** sent a strong **wind . . . from the sea** that blew uncounted numbers of **quail** across **the camp.** The normal flight pattern of these quail to this day is northeasterly, from the interior of Africa. The wind must have been from the southeast, a most unusual phenomenon, and **drove** the birds northwest across the Sinai. Moreover, the Lord caused them to fly **about three feet above the ground** so the people could easily capture them or club them to the ground. This seems much better than the commonly held impression that the quail were piled up in a layer three feet thick **a day's walk in** every **direction** from the camp. The problems in such a scenario are obvious. For two days and a **night** the overflight continued till every gatherer had accumulated at least **10 homers** (ca. 60 bushels, NIV marg.) of **quail.** Soon after the people began their orgy of lustful gluttony **the** LORD unleashed His wrath **against** them **and** sent **a severe plague** that killed many of them. The reason for this is clear in the statement that **the place** where this happened **was named Kibroth Hattaavah** ("graves of craving") **because there they buried the people who had craved other food.** Their sin was, in effect, a rejection of the Lord and His bountiful provision in favor of an unbridled appetite. As Paul later said of the enemies of Christ, "Their god is their stomach" (Phil. 3:9). No doubt terrified by their experience there, the people moved on **to Hazeroth** (possibly present-day 'Ain Khadra), just south of the Desert of Paran.

## C. The rebellion of Miriam and Aaron (chap. 12)

**12:1-3.** After Israel settled down at Hazeroth (11:35), **Miriam and Aaron,** Moses' elder siblings, **began to** challenge his authority, ostensibly because **he had married a Cushite** woman. This challenge came either **because** he had married the woman and therefore in their eyes destroyed his credibility, or because they were disillusioned with his leadership for other reasons and used the marriage as an excuse. The marriage itself could not be criticized unless it were a case of bigamy (for which there is no evidence) for the Cushites were not among those whom Israelites might not marry (Ex. 34:11, 16). The Cushites were not necessarily a different color since people of that name existed in early times in Arabia as well as Cush proper (what is today southern Egypt, Sudan, and northern Ethiopia). Possibly Miriam, who apparently led this part of the challenge, saw in Moses' new wife a threat to her own standing as the major female figure in Israel's leadership.

The real reason is clear from Miriam and Aaron's question, **Has the** LORD **spoken only through Moses?** Envy, perhaps simmering for a long time, now came to the surface. And the writer (**Moses** himself) made the remarkable statement that such envy was totally uncalled for since he was not arrogant but was, in fact, **more humble than anyone else on the face of the earth.** This statement is often adduced as evidence that Moses could not have written the Book of Numbers for he would not have boasted of his own humility. On the contrary, the declaration concerning his humility is the strongest possible support for the traditional view that Moses wrote Holy Scripture as an inspired penman. Only one led by the Holy Spirit could make such a statement about himself, probably against his own natural inclination.

**12:4-8.** At that point **the** LORD Himself intervened and took up the defense of His servant **Moses.** He called **all three** to Himself at the tabernacle where He **summoned Aaron and Miriam.** The order of the names is significant here for though Miriam may have initiated the insubordination, Aaron evidently fostered this attitude. In a poetic address (see the poetic format in the NIV) **the** LORD reminded them that though His normal way of revelation to **a prophet** was by **visions** and **dreams,** He spoke to **Moses** in an absolutely unique way—**face to face.** The phrase "face to face" (cf. Deut. 34:10) is an anthropomorphism meaning that God spoke to Moses without mediation. This is because Moses was **faithful in all** God's **house** (Num. 12:7; cf. Heb. 3:2), a reference to Moses' faithful performance of his role as covenant mediator between God and Israel. How this was done precisely cannot be determined, but it appears from several passages that Moses actually heard the voice of the Lord and saw His glory (e.g., Ex. 19:16-19; 24:17-18; 34:5-11). God spoke **clearly** to Moses **and not in riddles.** He did not accommodate Himself to Moses through metaphors and other figurative devices because Moses entertained such a personal relationship with God that he could understand heavenly utterances.

Yet Moses could not and did not look upon the person of God Himself for no one can do this and live (Ex. 33:17-23) for God is a Spirit (John 4:24). **He** saw only **the form of the** LORD, but even this was a privilege extended to no other man. The "form" refers to a likeness or a representation of the Lord, not the very shape. It is perhaps what is meant by the "back" of the Lord (Ex. 33:23). So privileged was Moses in his access to God that the Lord asked how Aaron and Miriam could dare **speak against . . . Moses.**

**12:9-16.** The LORD then reached out in **anger** and struck **Miriam** with a loathsome skin disease. At once **Aaron turned . . . to Moses** and sought his intervention before the Lord. It must have seemed ironic for the high priest to need priestly intercession. So **eaten away** was Miriam's **flesh** that she looked to Aaron like a partly formed fetus **coming** to an ill-timed birth.

**Moses** too, out of both fraternal love and intercessory obligation, appealed **to the LORD** for immediate healing. But Miriam's offense was serious because she had led an insurrection against God's choice servant and covenant mediator. If she had merely suffered the disgrace of being spat on **in the face by her father** she would have had to remain **outside the camp for seven days.** Surely she must remain **outside** at least that long for having committed such a serious breach of propriety. Spitting in one's face expressed contempt (cf. Deut. 25:9). The Lord expressed His contempt for Miriam's presumption by afflicting her with a horrible skin disease. In line with ceremonial law, which required a diseased person to remain **outside the camp for seven days** (Lev. 13–14), **Miriam** was forced to do so. Only after that did **the people . . . move on** from **Hazeroth** (cf. Num. 11:35) to **the Desert of Paran.**

## D. Spying out the Promised Land (chaps. 13–14)

1. THE SELECTION OF THE SPIES (13:1-16)

**13:1-16.** At last the tribes of Israel reached the Desert of Paran where they camped for a long time, probably in the great oasis of Kadesh (v. 26). Kadesh, though technically in the Desert of Zin, is here located in **the Desert of Paran** because Zin was a subdivision of the great Paran wilderness (cf. 27:14; Deut. 32:51).

Here **Moses** instructed **each . . . tribe** to supply a spy **to explore the land of Canaan.** Each of these **leaders** is listed with his tribal affiliation (vv. 4-15). Of special interest in light of further developments are **Caleb,** the representative of **Judah** (v. 6), and **Hoshea,** the man chosen from **Ephraim** (v. 8). For reasons not entirely clear, **Moses** changed **the name** of **Hoshea** (hôšēa', "salvation") to **Joshua** (yᵉhôšūa', "Yahweh is salvation").

2. THE SENDING OF THE SPIES (13:17-25)

**13:17-20.** The route of the explorers was north from Kadesh **through the Negev and on into the hill country.** The Negev (lit., "south") refers to all the desert of southern Canaan, especially the area from Beersheba south. The hill country consisted of the mountains of Judah, north to the hills of Ephraim, and all the way to the heights of Galilee. In Moses' time the hill country was populated primarily by the Amorites, and the plains and valleys by the Canaanites (cf. comments on v. 29). The mission of the spies was clear: to determine the nature of **the land** itself and ascertain the strengths and weaknesses of its inhabitants (vv. 18-20). The reason for the route Moses suggested was probably his intention to attack and penetrate **Canaan** from that direction. There certainly was no plan originally to enter the land from the east through Jericho. That was not only far off the main Egyptian access to Canaan but it involved the hazard of passing near the heavily fortified defensive positions at Jericho and Ai.

**13:21-22.** The itinerary taken by the explorers began in **the Desert of Zin** and extended **as far** north **as Rehob** at **Lebo Hamath** (probably modern Lebweh, 14 miles northwest of Baalbek). Hamath was an important Aramean city in the great Central Valley known as the Beq'a. Lebo Hamath was at the lower part of that valley which began just north of the Sea of Galilee.

On the way back, the 12 leaders passed through **Hebron,** a city **built seven years before Zoan in Egypt.** Zoan, otherwise known as Tanis, was built by the Hyksos when they overran northeastern Egypt about 1730 B.C. The reason for this apparently irrelevant information may be the fact that Hebron later became the inheritance of Caleb (Josh. 14:23-25) and even later than that David's capital when he reigned over Judah (2 Sam. 2:1-4). In Moses' day, however, Hebron was the home of the Anakites, a tribe of giants (Num. 13:33; Deut. 9:2) who would prove to be implacable foes of Israel for years to come (Josh. 15:13-14).

**13:23-25.** Near Hebron was the **Valley of Eshcol** ("cluster") where the spies **cut** a great **cluster of grapes** so heavy that **two** men had to carry **it** suspended from **a pole between them.** They also took

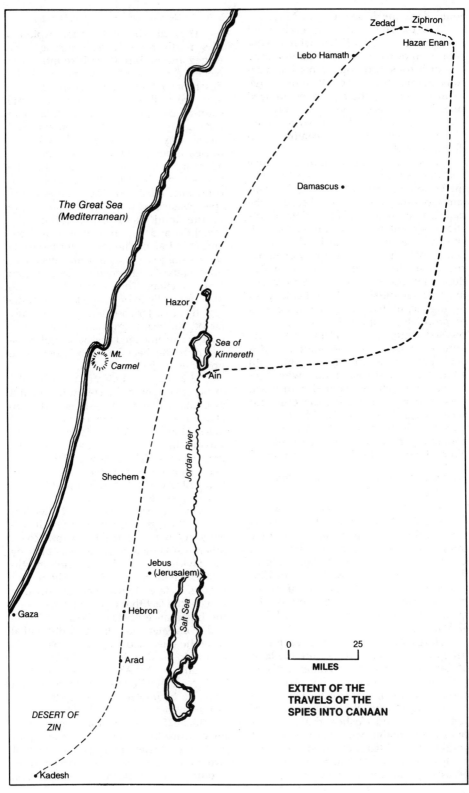

The Great Sea
(Mediterranean)

Zedad

Ziphron

Hazar Enan

Lebo Hamath

Damascus

Hazor

Sea of
Kinnereth

Ain

Mt.
Carmel

Jordan River

Shechem

Jebus
(Jerusalem)

Gaza

Hebron

Salt Sea

Arad

0        25

MILES

**EXTENT OF THE
TRAVELS OF THE
SPIES INTO CANAAN**

DESERT OF
ZIN

Kadesh

samples of **pomegranates and figs** and at last, after **40 days** of searching out **the land,** returned to Kadesh. The reason for the time being precisely 40 days was probably to compare this relatively brief period with the 40 years of wandering to which they would shortly be sentenced (cf. 14:34).

### 3. THE REPORT OF THE SPIES (13:26-33)

**13:26-29.** As soon as the travelers arrived **at Kadesh** they made their report. Demonstrating the produce they had carried back, they certified that Canaan indeed was **a land** flowing **with milk and honey. But** the negative side of their report was their observation that **the cities** were **fortified and very large** and **the people . . . powerful,** whether **the Amalekites of the Negev** (cf. Ex. 17:8-16); **the Hittites, Jebusites, and Amorites of the hill country;** or **the Canaanites** along the Mediterranean coastal plain and **the Jordan** Valley. The Canaanites were the indigenous population of Canaan. The Amorites had entered Canaan from northeast Aram (Syria) sometime before 2000 B.C., had driven the Canaanites out of the hill country, and took their place there. The Hittites originated in central Anatolia (modern Turkey) about 1800 B.C. and slowly spread south and southeast, probably identifying with the Amorites in Canaan. Nothing is known of the Jebusites except that they were centralized in Jerusalem and were also considered an Amorite group (Josh. 10:5). They remained in control of Jerusalem till 400 years after Moses, when David drove them out, captured the city, and made it his capital, in 1004 B.C. (2 Sam. 5:6-10).

**13:30-33.** This reference to the cities and people of the land occasioned a divided opinion among the spies. **Caleb** urged **Moses** to **go up** at once **and take . . . the land** because he was confident they could **do it. But** 10 of the spies (all except Joshua and Caleb, 14:6-9, 30), discouraged the people and pessimistically maintained that the task of conquest was impossible because of the unfavorable odds. The **Nephilim** (this word occurs only here and in Gen. 6:4; see comments there) were **of great size;** and the Anakites (cf. Num. 13:22), who descended from the Nephilim, were also "strong and tall" (Deut. 9:2).

### 4. THE RESPONSE OF THE PEOPLE (14:1-10A)

**14:1-4.** Unfortunately **the people** accepted the majority assessment and began to protest **to Moses** that they would have been better off to have **died in Egypt or** the **desert** than at the hands of the Canaanites. It would **be better** even now, they said, to **choose a** new **leader** and make their way **back to Egypt.**

**14:5-10a.** On hearing this, **Moses and Aaron fell** prostrate (**facedown;** cf. 16:4, 22, 45; 20:6; 22:31), no doubt in earnest supplication, while **Joshua** and **Caleb** reaffirmed their appraisal of **the land** and their confidence that **the LORD** would deliver it and its **people** into their hands. But all this was to no avail as the people even discussed **stoning them.**

### 5. THE REACTION OF THE LORD (14:10B-12)

**14:10b-12.** In the midst of this crisis **the LORD appeared** in His **glory . . . at the** tabernacle (v. 10b). He asked how much longer He could be expected to tolerate the people's **contempt** and unbelief. The remedy, God said, was to **destroy** the **nation** and **make** Moses the founder of a new and **greater** one.

### 6. THE PRAYER OF MOSES (14:13-19)

**14:13-19.** As tempting as the Lord's offer (v. 12) might be to some, Moses' love for his people and for the integrity of the Lord's reputation led him to reject it and seek God's forgiveness of the **people.** He reasoned that **the Egyptians** would view God's destruction of Israel as His inability to keep His promise to redeem them and give them **the land** as a possession. Furthermore, the Egyptians would repeat this to the Canaanites and other **nations** with the result that even they would mock God's impotence. The only action **the LORD** could take, **Moses** said, was to manifest His great power by **forgiving** the **people** even though they would have to suffer His punishment in some way. The basis for this forgiveness would be God's **great love** (ḥesed, "covenant faithfulness or loyal love").

### 7. THE JUDGMENT OF THE LORD (14:20-45)

**14:20-25.** God's promises are sure and steadfast and He had promised to save Israel and give them Canaan as an everlasting inheritance (Ex. 6:6-8). So it is obvious that His threat to destroy Israel and begin anew with Moses was as much

## Supplementary Grain and Drink Offerings

| Burnt and Freewill Offerings | Supplementary Offerings |
| --- | --- |
| All offerings | 2 quarts of flour mixed with 1 quart of oil |
| Lamb | 1 quart of wine |
| Ram | 4 quarts of flour mixed with 1¼ quarts of oil and 1¼ quarts of wine |
| Bull | 6 quarts of flour mixed with 2 quarts of oil and 2 quarts of wine |

Note: One ephah = ½ bushel, about 8 quarts
One hin = about 1 quart

a test of Moses, the covenant mediator, as it was anything else. God therefore pledged to forgive the people but pronounced that the entire adult generation which had participated in the Exodus and had witnessed all the other great **signs** and wonders He had performed on their behalf would never **see the land** of promise. The people had **disobeyed** and **tested** Him **10 times,** the Lord said (Num. 14:22). This could be a literal number but, more likely, it means a great many times (cf. comments on Job 19:3). The exceptions were **Caleb** (Num. 14:24)) and Joshua (v. 30) because they obeyed the Lord without reservation. Not even Moses is mentioned for the omniscient Lord foresaw his future disobedience regarding the rock and water (20:12).

Then, as part of the judgment, the Lord instructed Moses and Israel to resume the journey from Kadesh but not toward **the valleys** where **the Amalekites and Canaanites** lived. They now had to take the long and circuitous **route** toward **the Red Sea,** a route that eventually would end at the Plains of Moab, east of Jericho. The Red Sea here refers to the eastern arm of that sea, known today as the Gulf of Aqabah.

**14:26-35.** In elaborating further on the judgment, **the Lord** said that He would grant the Israelites their wish— they would die in the **desert** (vv. 29, 35; cf. v. 2). Their **children,** however, would be spared and with **Caleb** and **Joshua** would **enter** Canaan (vv. 30-32). Even this would not come to pass till **40 years** had come and gone because the people had to **suffer for** their **sins** (v. 34). This

illustrates the fact that sin may be forgiven but its consequences may endure and preclude God's otherwise intended blessings. Further, children sometimes must bear the *results* of their parents' sins (v. 33; cf. Ex. 20:5; Deut. 24:16). This does not contradict Ezekiel 18:1-3, 13-18 because Moses was referring to material and physical aftereffects whereas Ezekiel spoke of individual responsibility and culpability for sin and its spiritual results.

**14:36-45.** As a token of the certainty of impending judgment, the 10 spies who brought back a negative **report** and undermined the people's morale **were struck** by **a plague** and **died.** This so impressed the people that they then resolved to forget their fears and undertake the Canaanite conquest at once (vv. 39-40). But it was too late for they could no longer claim the presence and protection of **the Lord** (vv. 41-43). With characteristic obstinance they rejected Moses' counsel and without **Moses** and **the ark** pressed the attack in the **hill country** (v. 44). Not surprisingly, **the Amalekites and Canaanites** launched a counterattack and severely defeated Israel (cf. Deut. 1:41-46), driving them **all the way to Hormah,** some eight miles southeast of Beersheba.

### III. The Journey to the Plains of Moab (15:1–22:1)

*A. The rehearsal of the covenant statutes (chap. 15)*

1. THE OFFERINGS TO BE MADE (15:1-31)

**15:1-16.** Because the adult generation of Israel had been sentenced to die in the desert it became necessary for the younger ones to understand the requirements of their covenant relationship. Nothing was more central to this than the presentation of **offerings** for they represented the tributes that this vassal people must bring to their Sovereign as tokens of their covenant loyalty (Ex. 23:14-19; Lev. 1–7; Deut. 12:1-13). The "Supplementary Grain and Drink Offerings" chart summarizes the offerings discussed in Numbers 15:3-12. These **burnt** and **freewill offerings** were not sin or guilt offerings, since their form and content were invariable (Lev. 4:1–6:7); these were votive, **fellowship**, and thank or praise offerings (Lev. 1–3). All the people of Israel were enjoined to make these offerings whether they were **native-born** or **alien** (Num. 15:13-16).

**15:17-21.** The second set of regulations pertains to the offering of the firstfruits of harvest. **When** the people entered **the land** of Canaan and began to enjoy its produce, they were to show their devotion to **the Lord** by presenting to Him **a cake** baked **from the first** cutting of the grain.

**15:22-29.** The third category concerns **sin** offerings. These were made in atonement for the failure to keep any of the Lord's commandments unwittingly; that is, by unintentional neglect or omission. When **the whole community** was collectively guilty, they were to **offer a young bull** as a **burnt offering . . . along with** the **prescribed** accompanying offerings of **grain** and **drink,** and a **goat** as the **sin offering.**

The difference between the regulations here and those pertaining to the sin offerings in Leviticus 4:13-21 is that here the sins were of omission while those in Leviticus were of commission. Moreover, this passage in Numbers requires the offering of both a bull as a burnt offering and a male goat as a sin offering while Leviticus mentions only the bull as a sin offering. The reconciliation perhaps lies in the fact that in Numbers the bull as a sin offering was presupposed and was augmented by another bull offered as a burnt offering. The goat is mentioned with the bull but only in anticipation of the sin offering to be made for the individual ruler (not specifically mentioned here) who sins unwittingly. Leviticus also prescribes a male goat for the sin of the ruler (Lev. 4:22-26) so there is really no conflict. As for an ordinary individual citizen, his sin of omission required the **offering** of a **female goat** (Num. 15:27-29) precisely as stipulated in Leviticus 4:27-31.

**15:30-31.** The last regulation deals with a case of defiant sin, committed knowingly and deliberately. Such sin is described as blasphemous because it was an arrogant act of insubordination, a challenge to the lordship of Yahweh and His covenant demands. Anyone guilty of this kind of sin **must be cut off from his people.** As elsewhere, this means both excommunication and death (cf. Gen. 17:14; also see comments on Lev. 7:20; 17:4).

2. THE EXAMPLE OF A COVENANT-BREAKER (15:32-36)

**15:32-36.** As a possible illustration of defiant sin (cf. vv. 30-31), the narrator relates the story of **a man . . . found gathering wood on the Sabbath Day.** Since **it was not clear** that he had done so as a premeditated violation of the Sabbath Law, he was **kept** under arrest till **the Lord** rendered the verdict: **the man must die.** He was then taken **outside the camp and stoned** to **death.** This anecdote clearly interprets what was meant by defiant sin (vv. 30-31) and being "cut off" from the community.

3. TASSELS AS A MNEMONIC DEVICE TO REMEMBER THE LAW (15:37-41)

**15:37-41.** To **remember** the commandments **of the Lord** the **Israelites** were to wear **tassels on the corners of their garments with a blue cord** attached to **each tassel.** These tassels (cf. Deut. 22:12) would serve as visual aids to help them **remember to obey all** His **commands.** The Hebrew word for tassel is ṣîṣiṯ, possibly from a root word meaning "blossom." Perhaps this tassel was in the form of a flower or petal which, for reasons unclear now, symbolized the covenant bonds which linked **the Lord** to His people.

*B. The rebellion of Korah (chap. 16)*

1. THE CHALLENGE TO MOSES' UNIQUE AUTHORITY (16:1-3)

**16:1-3.** At some unidentified place and time in the desert wanderings, **Korah,** a Levite, and **Dathan and Abiram,**

of the tribe of Reuben, began to lead an uprising **against Moses.** They recruited **250** of the top **leaders** of Israel as collaborators. The tribal affiliations of the two main conspirators (Levi and Reuben) show that this was a rebellion against both the religious and political leadership of Moses. Thus **Aaron** the high priest also became an object of their attack.

Their discontent centered on the allegation that Moses and Aaron were unjustified in setting themselves over all the people since, by virtue of Israel's being **the LORD's** covenant **community,** all of them were equally **holy** and capable of being leaders. What they had neglected to point out was that the Lord Himself had appointed Moses and Aaron to their offices.

### 2. THE JUDGMENT OF THE LORD
(16:4-40)

**16:4-7.** Overcome by this opposition to his (and the Lord's) leadership, **Moses . . . fell** on his face (cf. 14:5; 16:22, 45; 20:6; 22:31). Then, assured by the Lord, Moses declared that on the very next **morning the LORD** would make clear His mind in the matter by allowing the divinely authorized leader to approach His holy presence. In preparation, **Korah and** his **followers** were to **take censers** and **put fire and incense in them.** Then they were to go near the tabernacle to await the Lord's response. The rebels had claimed Moses and Aaron had "gone too far" in usurping leadership (16:3), but Moses said Korah and the **Levites** with him had **gone too far** in their rebellion!

**16:8-11.** Moses then chided **Korah** with the reminder that he and his fellow **Levites** were already highly favored by **God** for having been selected from among all Israel to minister at the **tabernacle.** Not content with that great privilege, they aspired to the office of priest as well. But such aspiration was not a challenge to **Aaron;** it was rather an assault on the sovereign pleasure of **the LORD** Himself. He had plainly delegated the office of priest to the Aaronic family and that family only.

**16:12-15.** Moses then called for **Dathan and Abiram . . . but they** refused to obey. They claimed they had trusted Moses in vain in the past. All he had done

was bring them **out of** one **land flowing with milk and honey** (Egypt) and had failed to lead them into the other (Canaan). Their only hope was death **in the desert. Will you gouge out the eyes of these men?** they asked. This meant that Moses' hope to blind the people to his true intentions would fail.

Frustrated and **angry,** Moses turned **to the LORD** and asked Him not to **accept** the rebels' offerings, probably the incense to be offered the next day (cf. v. 7). Their accusations against him were unfounded, **Moses** said, for he had never profited as leader at their expense, not even taking **so much as a donkey from them.** Like Nehemiah, he did not demand the privileges a leader would normally expect (cf. Neh. 5:17-19).

**16:16-27.** Again **Moses** asked **Korah** and **250** cohorts **to appear** at the tabernacle the next day. **Aaron** too would be there and altogether they would contest the issue of the legitimate priesthood. Next day they all gathered as instructed and presented their **incense to the LORD** before the tabernacle. **The glory of the LORD** then **appeared** and **the LORD** advised **Moses and Aaron** to step aside so He could destroy Korah and the entire **assembly.**

As on a similar occasion (14:13-19) **Moses,** the covenant mediator, **and Aaron** appealed to **God** not to annihilate the whole nation for the sin of a few (16:22). The unusual title of God, **God of the spirits of all mankind,** occurs only here and in 27:16. It refers to God's omniscient understanding of all people. Surely then, Moses argued, God, who knows the hearts of everyone, knew that **only one man** (Korah the instigator, who led others with him) sinned.

**The LORD** therefore admonished **the assembly** to separate from **Korah** and his colleagues and not even **touch anything belonging to them** because they and all they had were objects of His wrath. So the people **moved away,** leaving **Korah, Dathan, and Abiram** and their families alone before God.

**16:28-35.** Moses then issued the guidelines of the contest. If the rebels should live on and **die** of old age, the nation would **know** that Moses had no special call from God. **If,** however, **the LORD** should do **something** unique— open **the earth** and swallow Korah and the others—the people would **know** that Moses' leadership was from God and that Korah had acted presumptuously and sinfully.

**As soon as** the conditions had been spelled out, **the ground . . . split apart and** Korah, his friends, their families, **and all their possessions** disappeared from sight. The earth then came together again, concealing the evidence that they had ever existed. Terrified by all this, the assembly of **Israelites . . . fled** for their lives lest **the earth . . . swallow** them as well. A **fire** then destroyed **the 250 . . . offering the incense.**

The fact that the wives and children of Korah, Dathan, and Abiram were included in the awful judgment of God (vv. 27, 32) illustrates again the Old Testament principle of family solidarity and the collective punishment if not guilt of the offspring of those who sin against God (Ex. 20:5-6; 34:6-7; Josh. 7:16-26). Since, however, each individual was accountable for his own sin only (cf. Deut. 24:16), one must conclude that the families of Korah, Dathan, and Abiram collaborated some way in their rebellion (cf. Josh. 7:22-25).

**Grave** (Num. 16:30, 33) is a translation of šeʾōl which can also refer to the place of the departed dead generally. It is therefore occasionally understood as "the underworld" or as "hell" (cf. Gr. hadēs). Here, however, nothing more is in view than the fact that the earth opened up a great crevice which became in effect a mass grave.

**16:36-40.** After this awesome display of His wrath, **the LORD** commanded **Eleazar . . . the priest** to gather up **the censers** which had been in the hands of the 250 rebels, for in the act of their having been presented before the Lord **the censers** had **become holy.** Even though those who used them were sinners **the censers** themselves had been created or set apart ("holy" means set apart) for worshiping the Lord. Further, the incense censers would become **holy** again to **the LORD** by being hammered **into** sheets (of **bronze,** v. 39) which would overlay the altar. In this way they would serve as a continual reminder (**a sign**) of what had happened that day. The people must never forget that only **a descendant of Aaron** could stand **before the LORD** in the holy office of priest.

### 3. THE RESULTANT POPULAR REBELLION (16:41-50)

**16:41-50.** Rather than achieving the expected end, however, the exhibition of the Lord's wrath only led to more complaining by the people. As they pressed their **opposition** against **Moses and Aaron . . . the LORD** again **appeared** in His glory at the tabernacle, told **Moses** to step aside, and once more threatened to destroy the nation (cf. 14:10-12; 16:21). Again, in abject humility and deference, Moses and Aaron prostrated themselves before the Lord.

This time, however, **Moses** undertook measures to forestall the divine judgment. He urged **Aaron** to **take** his **censer** and rush into the midst of **the assembly** of Israelites and there seek God's atoning grace. But when **Aaron** arrived he found the **plague**—evidence of God's wrath—**had already** begun and that many were **dead.** Nevertheless he **offered the incense.** By the time **the plague stopped . . . 14,700 people** had **died. Then Aaron returned to Moses** at the tabernacle.

Since incense was symbolic of prayer (Ex. 30:8; Ps. 141:2; Luke 1:10; Rev. 5:8; 8:3-4), Aaron in effect was appearing among the people to intercede in prayer for them. It must have been clear to all that one censer in the hand of a man of God far excelled 250 in the hands of that many sinners.

### C. The vindication of Aaron (chap. 17)

**17:1-9.** Because **Aaron's** priestly authority had been challenged (chap. 16) **the LORD** now showed all the people that Aaron still retained that authority to the exclusion of all other claimants. So the Lord told **Moses** to **get** a staff **from the leader of each** tribe and **write** that leader's **name** on it. Aaron was also to write his **name** on the tribal **staff of Levi.** Then all 12 staffs were placed in the tabernacle **in front of the Testimony** (the most holy place) where the Lord would **meet** Moses and cause **the staff** of the legitimate priestly tribe to **sprout** like a tree.

**Next day Moses entered the** tabernacle **and saw that** the **staff** of Aaron **had not only sprouted but had budded, blossomed, and produced almonds.** When this irrefutable evidence was presented to the tribal leaders and the people, all they could do was silently acquiesce in the Lord's vindication of Aaron.

**17:10-13.** So they might not forget what they had learned, **the LORD** directed that **Aaron's staff** be retained **in front of the Testimony** (the most holy place) **as a sign** (cf. 16:38). **This** would remind them not to grumble and question the Lord's ways of leadership. Characteristically the people overreacted and assumed that the presence of the staff would forever endanger anyone who even came close to **the tabernacle.** On the position of Aaron's staff see comments on 2 Chronicles 5:10.

### D. The roles and privileges of the priests and Levites (chap. 18)

**18:1.** Probably in light of the account of rebellion against the Aaronic priesthood just related (chaps. 16–17), this chapter is a reminder and amplification of the priests' and Levites' responsibilities. Only to the priests did the task of ministry at the tabernacle belong, at least as it pertained to **offenses against the sanctuary and . . . against the priesthood.** These difficult words mean more than priestly intercession; they also include the sins of the priests and Levites themselves in respect to their ministering the holy things of God at the tabernacle. For the office of priest included the awesome task of handling the sacred instruments in the tabernacle and following the divinely appointed rituals of the infinitely holy God.

**18:2-7.** Though most **Levites** were not priests and therefore could not enjoy every priestly privilege, they were permitted limited functions as assistants to the priests. The parameters of their ministry included everything except handling the tabernacle **furnishings** and **the** great **altar** of burnt offering. Otherwise **both** priest and Levite would **die** (v. 3); such lack of responsibility by the priests would invite God's **wrath . . . on the** people (v. 5). Other than those limitations, the Levites could be in contact with the tabernacle and its services. The priests had a heavy burden but God had given them the **Levites . . . as a gift** (cf. 3:9) to assist them in every way consistent with the previously listed job specifications.

**18:8-11.** In return for their service to the Lord the priests and Levites would receive from Him a **portion** of **the offer-**ings** which the people **presented** in worship. Specifically they would retain **all the** parts of the sacrifices not consumed on the altar by **fire,** for those, by their very consumption, were understood to belong to God. In most sacrifices the part burned to the Lord consisted of the fat and the internal organs such as the kidneys and livers (see, e.g., Lev. 3). Because these were **most holy offerings,** they could be eaten only by the priests and the **male** members of their families (cf. Lev. 6:18, 29; 7:6). But all family members could partake of **the wave offerings** (Num. 18:11; cf. v. 8). These were the same as the so-called fellowship offerings (cf. Lev. 7:11-18).

**18:12-19.** In addition to the preceding, the priests and their families could also take for their own use **the firstfruits** of Israel's **harvest** including **olive oil . . . wine, and grain** (v. 12). Though given to **the LORD** as an offering (cf. Deut. 26:1-11) these **firstfruits** were not consumed on the altar but were turned over to the priests. The same was true of **everything . . . devoted to the LORD** (cf. Lev. 27:1-33). Next were included the firstborn **offspring** of **man and animal.** Those of man and **unclean animals** were redeemed for **five shekels of silver** (ca. 2 ounces). This amount was paid by the offerer to the priest in lieu of the actual sacrifice of the firstborn (cf. Num. 3:44-51). The firstborn of clean animals, however (i.e., **of an ox, a sheep, or a goat**), were to be given **to the LORD** and slaughtered as **an offering** to God. The **meat** was not burned on the altar as a normal sacrifice, however, but was given to the priests.

All these provisions **from the holy offerings** for the priests were signs of God's covenant blessings to them. Their **share** was **an everlasting covenant of salt.** This probably is a metaphor to speak of its durability. As salt keeps its flavor so the Lord's covenant will forever be in force (cf. 2 Chron. 13:5). Salt was also sprinkled on grain offerings (Lev. 2:13), perhaps as a token of the covenant relationship.

**18:20-24.** Turning to another aspect of priestly and Levitical service, **the LORD** told **Aaron** that the priests and **Levites,** though they had **no** territorial **inheritance,** would have a greater one—**the LORD** Himself. This meant that **the Le-**

vites would receive **tithes** from the people as their source of income and in compensation for their service at the tabernacle. Since **the Israelites** as a whole could not approach the tabernacle, **the Levites** would represent them there.

**18:25-32.** Similarly **the Levites** themselves were to **tithe** of their income and **present** that to **the Lord**. This **tithe** was to be **grain or** grape **juice** (v. 27). It was to be considered as though they themselves had raised it (v. 30). It also must be the **best . . . part** of what they had (vv. 29-30, 32). The Levitical tithe would go directly to **the priest** (v. 28) and be retained at the tabernacle as a holy offering to the Lord (vv. 29-30). The remainder could be eaten and imbibed **anywhere** the Levites chose because it was not the priest's but theirs alone. When they took the people's tithes and in turn paid their own tithe of it to the Lord, they would be using the people's gifts as God intended and would therefore be free of blame before God (v. 32).

### E. The laws of purification (chap. 19)

In Israel certain experiences or contacts rendered a person ceremonially unclean. This was because all of life was regarded as essentially religious or as having religious significance. Moreover, life was inextricably bound up with symbolism. For example, skin diseases implied uncleanness because they typified or symbolized sin. Miriam's having been struck by such an affliction made her unclean but it also clearly attested to her sin of rebellion (12:9-15). Similarly Naaman's disease was symptomatic of his sinful condition. When he was healed he recognized that only the Lord of Israel was God (2 Kings 5:15).

Contact with the dead was an especially contaminating experience because of the obvious association of physical death with spiritual death (Gen. 2:17; Deut. 30:15, 19; Rom. 6:23). Therefore some means of purification must be provided for those who came into contact with dead bodies so they might be able to associate freely and without impediment with the Lord's living community. The purpose of Numbers 19 is to explain how contamination could occur and what must be done in each case to effect ceremonial cleansing.

**19:1-2.** As usual, purification involved vicarious sacrifice so the community must provide **a red heifer without defect or blemish . . . that** had **never been** put to work in plowing. Though this was a sin offering (v. 9), it was different because its purpose was not expiatory. Its purpose was not to remove sin itself, but to remove the contamination of sin which death represented. A red animal perhaps symbolized the blood. The fact that it was to be unbroken suggests that it must be well and whole, strong in every way—a pure and pristine animal fit to accomplish the sacred role for which it had been selected.

**19:3-8.** After **the priest** officiated at the slaughter of the heifer **outside the camp** (to represent the physical removal of the impurity from the people), he sprinkled **some of its blood . . . seven times toward the** tabernacle. This indicated that the offering was being made to the Lord. Then **the heifer** was totally consumed by fire, along with **cedar wood, hyssop, and scarlet wool**. These three materials were also used in the ritual of purification of skin disease (Lev. 14:1-9). Cedar was chosen because it is evergreen and aromatic, the hyssop because of its application of the blood at the Exodus (cf. Ps. 51:7; Ex. 12:22), and the scarlet wool because it symbolizes the blood itself.

The ashes of all these and the heifer were mixed and served as the agent by which cleansing could take place (Num. 19:9). When the ritual was completed **the priest** and his assistant (v. 8) would be **unclean** just by virtue of preparing the ashes of purification. In a paradoxical way, the handling of holy things made him who did so ceremonially unclean (cf. Lev. 16:26-28). This is because these objects became invested with the uncleanness which they were to remove.

**19:9-13.** When only **the ashes** remained, **a man** must **gather** them and store them **in a . . . clean place outside the camp**. They would then be ready **for use in the water of . . . purification**. Purification was necessary for anyone who touched a **dead body** and was therefore **unclean for seven days**. Such a person was required to **purify himself with the ash-water on the third** and **seventh** days; otherwise he would remain unclean. If he approached the **tabernacle** when he was ceremonially **unclean**, he would **be**

cut off from Israel, that is, put to death (cf. Lev. 15:31).

**19:14-16.** This same uncleanness would apply to an individual who even entered **a tent** in which someone had died. The effect of death was so pervasive that it corrupted **open** containers in its proximity. Contact outdoors with a corpse or with **human** bones or graves also brought impurity.

**19:17-22.** The ritual of cleansing consisted of mixing **ashes** and **water** in **a jar** and applying this mixture with a branch of **hyssop** (a shrub with medicinal properties) to the areas or objects affected by a death. **The unclean person** must then be sprinkled **on the third and seventh days,** after which he washed **his clothes** and bathed himself.

Failure to follow this procedure rendered the **unclean** party unqualified to approach the tabernacle on pain of death (**cut off from the community,** v. 20). He who officiated in the **cleansing must also wash his** clothing (and bathe) as must anyone who merely touched the sacred **water. Anything . . . an unclean person** touched became **unclean** and communicated that uncleanness to **anyone** else who came in contact with it (cf. Hag. 2:13).

### F. The journey in the Desert of Zin (chap. 20)

1. THE DEATH OF MIRIAM (20:1)

**20:1.** Within **the first month** of the 40th year after the Exodus the tribes **arrived . . . at Kadesh** (modern 'Ain Qedeis) where **Miriam died and was buried.** Though there is no reference to events between the second year—the year when Israel was sentenced to wander for 40 years (14:34; cf. 10:11)—and the death of Miriam, it is certain that she died in the 40th year because the next dated event is the death of Aaron at Mount Hor (20:27-28), which occurred (33:38) "on the first day of the fifth month of the 40th year after the Israelites came out of Egypt." The "first month" in 20:1 then must be understood in that context since the narrative of chapter 20 cannot accommodate anything much shorter or longer than three or four months. The reference to Kadesh does not mean that Israel arrived there for the first time, since they had already sent the spies out from there (12:16; 13:26). It

means simply that they returned to Kadesh on this occasion.

2. WATER FROM THE ROCK (20:2-13)

**20:2-13.** Though Kadesh was normally a well-watered oasis, when Israel arrived there this time they found it dry. So they began to argue **with Moses** in their characteristic way (Ex. 17:1-2; Num. 14:2-3; etc.) and rebuke him for bringing them **out of Egypt to this** barren **place.** As he had done in the past, **Moses** sought the Lord's counsel, falling **facedown** (cf. 14:5; 16:4, 22, 45; 22:31) in supplication. **The LORD** told him to **take** his **staff** in hand and **speak to that rock** and it would gush forth enough **water** for all the people **and their livestock.** The rock in question was probably one from which springs ordinarily flowed and from which they had drunk many times in the past. This is not the rock Paul referred to (1 Cor. 10:4) for Paul spoke of a "spiritual rock" which provides "spiritual drink." That spiritual rock, Paul said, was the presence of the preincarnate Christ Himself.

The Lord told Moses only to *speak* to the rock for its flow must not be attributed to his own efforts but to the Lord's miraculous provision. **Moses,** however, at the breaking point of his endurance and patience (he called the people **rebels**), drew attention to his own authority as covenant mediator by striking **the rock twice with his staff.** The **water** came because of God's beneficent grace, but because **Moses and Aaron** had drawn attention to themselves rather than trusting in **the LORD** they were denied entrance to **the** Promised **Land.** The principle here is clear: "From everyone who has been given much, much will be demanded" (Luke 12:48). A lesser man than Moses might not have suffered such divine displeasure and denial. So striking was both the miracle and its aftermath that the place was called **Meribah** ("quarreling").

3. EDOM'S DENIAL OF PASSAGE TO ISRAEL (20:14-21)

**20:14-17.** After the Israelites brief stay at **Kadesh,** Moses was eager to press on to Canaan. He had obviously given up any ideas of entering from the south because of the defeat Israel had already experienced from that quarter (14:44-45).

He therefore requested permission from **the king of Edom** to take the famous **king's highway** (20:17), a route that passed from the Red Sea (Gulf of Aqabah) north to Damascus via the Edomite city of Sela (later known as Petra). **Moses** appealed to Edom as a **brother** (v. 14) because the Edomites were descendants of Esau, Jacob's brother (cf. Gen. 36:6-8). Moses then reviewed Israel's history from the time of Jacob's descent to **Egypt** to the present moment (Num. 20:15-16), an account, he said, with which the king of Edom was already familiar (v. 14). Then Moses promised that if Israel were allowed to pass through Edomite **territory** they would stay strictly on the road and would not eat or **drink** at Edom's expense (v. 17).

**20:18-21.** The request fell on unfriendly ears. The king of **Edom** denied passage on the king's highway which passed through narrow mountain defiles and could easily be defended and barred against access (cf. Obad. 1-4). Again Moses pleaded, this time offering to **pay for** any **water** they might **drink**. Once more the entreaty was rejected and as a show of the seriousness of his resistance Edom's king sent out troops to intercept Israel. Discouraged, **Israel turned away.**

4. THE DEATH OF AARON (20:22-29)

**20:22-29.** Departing **from Kadesh,** Israel arrived at **Mount Hor,** probably Jebel Harun, a short distance northwest of Petra. This implies, no doubt, that though Moses had abandoned any plans to take the easier route along the king's highway he now determined to go north up the Arabah fault to the southeast corner of the Dead Sea, thus bypassing **Edom** to the east.

After they climbed **Mount Hor. . . . Aaron died** on **the mountain.** His priestly **garments** and office were transferred to **his son Eleazar.** The death was necessary as Aaron had been precluded from entering Canaan because of the incident at **Meribah** (vv. 12, 24). Nevertheless **the whole community . . . mourned for him** for **30 days.** Later they mourned Moses' death in Moab for 30 days (Deut. 34:5, 8).

### G. The journey to Moab (21:1–22:1)

1. VICTORY OVER ARAD AT HORMAH (21:1-3)

**21:1-3.** Arad was an important Canaanite city about 20 miles east-northeast

of Beersheba (see the map "Possible Route of the Exodus," near 33:6-8). Perhaps the **king of Arad** interpreted Moses' move from Kadesh to Mount Hor as a threat to his own security, particularly since he had **heard that Israel was coming along the road to Atharim** (site unknown). So the king **attacked** Israel and took some prisoners. Moses then vowed **to the LORD** that if He would **deliver** the Canaanites over to him he would **totally destroy their cities.** The word "destroy" (*hāram*) means he would devote them to the Lord as a kind of offering or tribute, thus keeping nothing for himself or the others (cf. comments on the related noun *hērem* in Josh. 6:21). **The LORD** answered, and Israel **destroyed** many Canaanite **towns.** To commemorate God's faithfulness they called the region **Hormah,** "destruction." Probably the reference to Hormah in Numbers 14:45 reflects the incident here.

2. THE POISONOUS SERPENTS (21:4-9)

**21:4-5.** Once again **Moses** could see the impossibility of penetrating Canaan from the south. Apparently he even gave up his plan to go north through the Arabah and, led by the Lord, undertook a circuitous route **around** the eastern frontier of **Edom.** This would explain why he led Israel **from . . . Hor along the route to the Red Sea** (the Gulf of Aqabah). **The people** must have been frustrated by this change so they began to complain not only about that but also about **the desert,** lack of **water,** and **food** (i.e., manna).

**21:6-9.** In anger **the LORD sent** poisonous **snakes among them** and **many** of **the people . . . died.** They urged **Moses** to intercede before God for them, which he did. He then relayed instruction from **the LORD** that all those **bitten** should **look** on **a bronze snake** which he constructed and placed high on a **pole.** Those who **looked at** it were healed. This involved a look of faith (cf. John 3:14-15).

3. THE CIRCUIT OF MOAB (21:10-20)

**21:10-13.** The route Israel took is difficult to reconstruct since many of the places named can no longer be identified. **Oboth** must be located in connection with the more complete itinerary of chapter 33. There Zalmonah and Punon are listed between Hor and Oboth (33:41-43). The route seems to be east of Edom because Punon (or Feinan) evidently was the site of copper mines in that region. The material for the bronze snake may also suggest a proximity of copper deposits. Oboth most likely was at the northern end of the Arabah, north of Punon. This is supported by the fact that the tribes turned north after paralleling the Edomite hill country in a southerly direction (Deut. 2:1-3). The next place mentioned is **Iye Abarim** (Num. 21:11; cf. 33:44), **in the desert** on the east side of **Moab** but otherwise unidentified. **From there** they traveled on to **the Zered Valley** which then formed the border between Moab and Edom. The Zered River flows into the Dead Sea at its southeast curve. They next moved north through Moabite territory to **the Arnon** River, **the border . . . between Moab and the Amorites** to the north (21:13). The Arnon empties into the Dead Sea about halfway along its eastern shore.

**21:14-15.** The Israelites' successful journey through Moab to that point was celebrated in a poem originally found in a no-longer extant text, **the Book of the Wars of the LORD.** The first line of the poem is now incomprehensible unless **Waheb** is a place name. Perhaps the quatrain is saying that the Lord had enabled Israel to take Waheb, a place **in Suphad,** along with the river and wadi systems **(ravines) along the** Moabite **border. Ar** (or el Misna') was a city in the northern part of Moab about 10 miles south of the Arnon (22:36; cf. Deut. 2:9, 18).

**21:16-20.** Leaving the eastern Arnon Valley the people moved **on to Beer** ("well"), so called because God miraculously provided a **well** for them there. The poem **about the well** (vv. 17-18) lyrically recounted that blessing. Moving still northward, alongside **the desert** (v. 18b), they came **to Mattanah** (or Khirbet el-Medeiyinah), **Nahaliel,** and **Bamoth** (eight miles south of Heshbon) and finally arrived at the foothills of **Pisgah.** Pisgah was a few miles due east of the northeast edge of the Dead Sea, almost to the Plains of Moab across from Jericho. At last Israel seemed to be on the verge of invasion and conquest of the Promised Land.

4. THE DEFEAT OF SIHON (21:21-32)

**21:21-25.** The plains of Moab must have been a contested territory (v. 26)

because they apparently were under Amorite control at this time though normally they belonged to Moab. In any case, Moses requested permission of **Sihon king of the Amorites** to journey through his **country** by way of **the king's highway.** He promised Sihon, as he had the king of Edom (cf. 20:17), that he would pass peacefully and would take no food or **water** from the Amorites (cf. Deut. 2:26-29). **Sihon** refused, however (cf. Deut. 2:30), and instead launched an attack **against Israel** at **Jahaz,** a few miles southeast of Pisgah. **Israel** defeated the Amorites (cf. Deut. 2:31-37) and claimed all of Sihon's territory **from the Arnon** River on the south **to the Jabbok** on the north. The eastern part of the Jabbok turned south, forming the extent of the Amorite holdings, while **the Ammonites** lay to the east of the Jabbok, toward the desert. The Ammonites' land was spared **because their border was fortified** and they were related to Israel through Lot (cf. Gen. 19:36, 38; Deut. 2:19). So Israel took all the Amorite **cities . . . including** Sihon's capital **Heshbon,** some 25 miles east of Jericho.

**21:26-32.** This defeat of **Sihon** was poetic justice since all this land south to the Arnon had originally belonged to the Moabites and had been stolen by Sihon. **Sihon's** former conquest had also been immortalized in poetry (vv. 27-30). The poets sang about the destruction of **Ar of Moab** by Sihon who evidently had **rebuilt** Heshbon and made it his chief city. He had then marched south against the Moabites, the **people of Chemosh** (the principal Moabite god), and had taken them **as captives.** Everything had been destroyed by **Sihon,** from **Heshbon** in the north **to Dibon** in the south, including places in between such as **Nophah** (site unknown) and **Medeba** (7 miles south of **Heshbon**). According to this interpretation Moses had used an Amorite poem ironically to describe Israel's destruction of **the Amorites.** In other words a boastful Amorite song celebrating their victory over the hapless Moabites now was sung by Israel to celebrate her victory over **the Amorites.** Israel's major conquest was followed by her expelling the Amorites from **Jazer** (or Khirbet Jazzir), about 15 miles northwest of Heshbon. So **Israel settled in the land of the Amorites.**

5. THE DEFEAT OF OG (21:33–22:1)

**21:33–22:1.** The land just north of the Jabbok River was under the control of **Og,** another Amorite **king.** The area was otherwise known as Gilead and **Bashan,** from south to north respectively. When Og heard of Israel's march north he met them **at Edrei** (or Der'a), an important city about 40 miles east-southeast of the Sea of Kinnereth. The LORD intervened for His people again, and Og and his troops were defeated and annihilated (cf. Deut. 3:1-11). So Israel controlled and occupied all the Transjordan between Mount Hermon (Deut. 3:8) and the Arnon River and east as far as the land of the Ammonites. This done, they moved unimpeded **to the plains of Moab** in preparation for the assault on Canaan (Num. 22:1).

## IV. The Moabites and Balaam (22:2–25:18)

### A. *The plight of Moab (22:2-4a)*

**22:2-4a.** When **Balak,** Moab's king, **saw** what **Israel had done to the Amorites** he and his people were **terrified** and looked about for some kind of solution to what he perceived to be inevitable destruction at Israel's hands. Because the Midianites were living in Moab at the time they too felt themselves to be in peril. The fears of Balak were actually in vain, for **the Moabites,** as kinsmen of Israel (cf. Gen. 19:26-37) like the Ammonites, were exempted from the attacks of Israel. In fact the Lord had explicitly revealed through Moses that Israel must assiduously avoid any harmful contact with the Edomites (Deut. 2:5-6), Moabites (Deut. 2:9), and Ammonites (Deut. 2:19). Even the Midianites were distantly related to Israel (Gen. 25:1-4), and so presumably they had nothing to fear.

### B. *The invitation to Balaam (22:4b-20)*

**22:4b-5.** Balak knew that Israel was far too powerful to defeat militarily so he decided to employ a famous diviner (cf. 24:1; Josh. 13:22), **Balaam son of Beor,** to invoke curses on Israel. Balaam was from **Pethor,** a city on **the River,** probably the Euphrates. Possibly Pethor was not far from the great city of Mari, discovered in 1933 in the Euphrates Valley. The discovery of a vast number of cuneiform tablets at Mari, beginning in 1933, re-

vealed among other things the existence of a complex cult of prophets and seers whose activities precisely resemble those of Balaam. The fact that he undoubtedly represented the prophetic customs and practices of Mari and vicinity makes possible a better understanding of Balaam's narrative in Numbers.

**22:6-8.** One power attributed to these prophets was that of pronouncing curses on intended victims. These curses would of course be couched in such qualified language that they were bound to come to pass one way or the other. **Balak** therefore asked Balaam to **come** to Moab and **curse** Israel at least to the extent that she would be weakened enough to be defeated. He acknowledged that Balaam had the reputation of pronouncing blessings and curses that worked. When **Balaam** received the delegation sent to him he said they must **spend the night** there while he sought to determine the will of the LORD. Such an inquiry coming from a pagan prophet might seem surprising. But in keeping with the pagans' general spirit of broad-mindedness and their recognition that a people's own gods had the greatest power over them for bad or good, Balaam attempted to establish contact with Israel's God.

**22:9-12.** In gracious condescension and in anticipation of His blessing on His own people, the Lord appeared to the diviner and warned him **not** to heed Balak's instructions to **curse** God's **blessed** people. The appearance of the **God** of Israel to unbelieving prophets and kings was not unique to Balaam. God revealed himself to Abimelech king of Gerar in Abraham's time (Gen. 20:6-7), to a Pharaoh in dreams (Gen. 41:25), to Nebuchadnezzar in a dream and visions (Dan. 4:1-18), and to others. As the sovereign God He rules and overrules in prophetic revelation as well as in all other areas of life. He therefore accommodated Himself to the crass manipulations of an Amorite diviner, though in the end God showed Himself to be the divine "Manipulator."

**22:13-20.** Convinced by the warning from the Lord **Balaam** told **Balak's** messengers to return without him **for the** LORD had forbidden him to **go.** Undaunted, **Balak sent . . . more distinguished** representatives, who reiterated his request and sweetened it with the promise of a handsome honorarium. Again **Balaam** refused to go because, he said, even a massive amount of **silver and gold** would not be sufficient (cf. 24:13) to persuade him to attempt the impossible—contravene the purposes of Yahweh, Israel's **God**. But **Balaam** said he would inquire of **the Lord** once more. This time **the Lord** granted Balaam permission, not to curse His people but to **go** to Moab so that He might reveal Himself gloriously through Balaam.

### C. The journey of Balaam (22:21-35)

**22:21-28.** Next day **Balaam** set off for Moab on **his donkey** but the Lord **was . . . angry** with him and appeared as **the Angel of the Lord** to block his path. The Lord had already given Balaam permission to go (v. 20) so this resistance was not against his going but against his unspoken motive or intention (he "loved the wages of wickedness," 2 Peter 2:15), which was obviously contrary to God's will (cf. Num. 22:32b, 34-35). The Angel of the Lord was a manifestation of the presence of **the Lord** Himself, that is, He was a theophany. This is clear from the fact that He frequently was equated with Deity and that He was offered and accepted worship, something absolutely forbidden to ordinary angels (see comments on Gen. 16:7; and cf. Gen. 18:1-2; 22:14-18; Ex. 3:1-6; Josh. 5:13-15; Jud. 6:20-22; 13:17-23; etc.).

When the donkey saw the Angel she left the roadway and went **into a field.** Balaam beat her, and she went **back** to the road only to meet **the Angel** again in **a narrow** passage **between two . . . walls.** Frightened, **she pressed . . . Balaam's foot against** one of the walls, for which she received a second beating. Finally the procession **moved on** to a **place where** the path was so narrow that the donkey could neither move past the Angel, who blocked the way, nor **turn** to either side. **She** therefore **lay down.** Once more the prophet **beat** the beast which suddenly spoke (by the Lord's miraculous enabling) and asked why she had been beaten those **three times** (cf. "three times" in Num. 22:32-33).

Balaam seems to have registered little surprise at this turn of events. The reason undoubtedly was that as a pagan diviner he may have heard such things before. Much of the success of such practitioners of the occult lay in the demonic inspiration of the prophets themselves or of the victims with whom they dealt. The serpent, for example, could speak because it was the incarnation of Satan (Gen. 3:1). Jesus cast demons out of a human being and allowed them to inhabit a herd of swine. Though there is no record of the demons speaking through the swine, the demons could and did identify with the animal world (Luke 8:26-39). So it is likely that Balaam, in his involvement with the spirit world, had experiences in the past with talking animals. But this time **the Lord,** not Satan or a demon, caused the animal to speak.

**22:29-35.** Balaam's only reaction was anger. He had been publicly humiliated and if he **had a sword,** he said, he **would kill** the donkey on the spot. But **the donkey** replied that since she had never done such things before there must be a hidden explanation for her behavior. **Then the Lord** opened Balaam's eyes—gave him spiritual perception—so he could see **the Angel** in the path, **standing** with a drawn **sword.** At this, Balaam **fell** on his face and heard **the Lord** rebuke him for having come on a **reckless** mission. This implies that Balaam's intentions were not in line with the Lord's wishes. Balaam was alive even then only because **the donkey** had seen the Angel and **turned** aside. **Balaam** therefore acknowledged his sin in opposing **the Lord** and not seeing divine direction in the donkey's behavior. He offered to return home to Pethor, but **the Lord** told him to **go** provided he spoke **only what** God commanded (cf. v. 20).

### D. The oracles of Balaam (22:36–24:25)

1. THE PREPARATION FOR THE ORACLES (22:36–23:6)

**22:36-38.** When **Balak** king of Moab finally met **Balaam,** he scolded him for having taken so long in arriving. He asked if Balaam had doubted his ability to pay. (**Am I really not able to reward you?**) The prophet replied only that he was **now** there **but** could **speak only what** God put **in** his **mouth.**

**22:39–23:6.** The two then went to **Kiriath Huzoth** (location unknown) where the divination rituals commenced. These frequently involved sacrifices as well as examining the animals' internal organs, a practice known as hepatoscopy or augury. The following **morning** they ascended **Bamoth Baal** ("the heights of Baal") **from** where they could see a **part of the people** of Israel. Bamoth Baal was probably a mountaintop overlooking the plains of Moab. Its association with Baal suggests that it was a high place where Canaanite cultic functions were carried out. **Balaam** asked Balak to **build . . . seven altars** there where **seven bulls and seven rams** could be sacrificed, **a bull and a ram** for **each altar** (cf. 23:14, 29-30). There is no biblical instruction or precedent for what Balaam did, so presumably the sacrifices were part of a pagan ritual. After the offerings were made **Balaam** went off by himself to elicit a revelation from **the LORD.** Balaam was still seeking to cooperate with the God of Israel even though his methods were not sanctioned in Israel's Law. And **God met with him** and gave him **a message** which he was to repeat **to Balak.**

### 2. THE FIRST ORACLE (23:7-12)

**23:7-12.** Balaam's first of four major oracles consists of a brief statement of how he happened to be there and what he had been instructed to do (v. 7). He then asked how it was possible to **curse** Israel, the people whom **God** had blessed (v. 8; cf. Gen. 12:1-3). **Balaam** said that he could look down from his lofty vantage point and see these blessed ones **who live apart and do not consider themselves one of the nations** (cf. Deut. 32:8-10). They were like **dust in number** (cf. Gen. 13:16), and to be identified with them in life or **death** was a blessing of God (Num. 23:10). Balaam almost seemed to wish that he were one of God's people. Balak's reaction to the oracle was predictable, since **Balaam** had hardly cursed Israel (v. 11). But Balaam could only reiterate that he **must . . . speak what the LORD** had put **in his mouth** (v. 12; cf. 22:38; 23:3).

### 3. THE SECOND ORACLE (23:13-26)

**23:13-24.** This time **Balak** moved the **place** of divination to another site, to **the top of Pisgah** (v. 14; cf. 21:20). Here they erected **seven** more **altars and offered** seven more bulls and seven more rams. Again **Balaam** went to a solitary place to commune with **the LORD** and again he returned **to Balak** with a **message** (23:15-17). The oracle consists of an introductory statement (vv. 18-20) in which **Balak** was told directly that the immutable **God** of Israel had promised to bless His people Israel and would not **change His mind.** Balaam, moreover, had just been given **a command to bless** and in the face of God's unbreakable commitment to Israel, Balaam had no power to do otherwise.

Balaam then said that because of the Exodus **out of Egypt** (cf. 24:8), Israel had supernatural prosperity (no **misfortune** or **misery,** 23:21a), the Lord's presence (v. 21b), and supernatural power (v. 22b).

**The shout of the King** must be understood as a militaristic threat, implying that the Lord is a Warrior who leads His hosts to victory (cf. Josh. 6:5, 20; Ps. 47:5; Jer. 4:19; 49:2). Such power renders **sorcery** and **divination** harmless. All that remains is for the nations to look on **Israel** and marvel at God's protecting grace (Num. 23:23). "Sorcery" (*naḥaš*) pertains to the use of omens. In the ancient Near East these were determined by observing animal entrails, smoke, oil patterns in water, birth defects, unusual phenomena of weather or the heavens, and a host of other things. Diviners, by studying these materials or movements, attempted to relate them to history and, by extrapolation, to the future. "Divination" (*qesem*) perhaps has a little more emphasis on casting lots than does sorcery (Ezek. 21:21; cf. comments on Deut. 18:14). Rather than being overcome, Israel **like a lion** would arise and utterly destroy her enemies (cf. Num. 24:9).

**23:25-26.** In abject dismay, **Balak** pleaded with **Balaam** to speak **neither** cursing **nor** blessing, but **Balaam** reminded him that he was powerless in the hand of **the LORD**—he could **do** only as he was told.

### 4. THE THIRD ORACLE (23:27–24:14)

**23:27-30.** For a third and final time **Balak** set the stage for **Balaam** to **curse** Israel. Superstitiously **Balak** felt that a move to a new location might create the proper environment for the cursing to take place. They arrived then at **the top of Peor,** a mountain near the town of Beth Peor (Deut. 3:29; 4:46), close to Israel's encampment in the plains of Moab. There once more they prepared the **seven altars** and sacrifices (cf. Num. 23:1-2, 14) necessary for the ritual of divination.

**24:1-3a. Balaam,** having understood by now the futility of **sorcery** against the people God had determined to **bless,** forsook his usual techniques and **looked out** over the host of **Israel** arranged in its prescribed tribal order. Then, invested with **the Spirit of God . . . he uttered his** third **oracle.** This coming of the Spirit no more proves that Balaam was a true prophet than the coming of the Spirit on Saul (see comments on 1 Sam. 10:6, 10-11) or the disciples (John 20:22) made them prophets of the Lord. There is a difference between the Spirit's coming on individuals to empower them supernaturally and His coming into them to abide (see comments on John 7:39).

**24:3b-7.** This third message **of Balaam** commenced with the prophet's testimony that now (perhaps for the first time) his **eyes** and ears had been **opened** to the truth **of God** and that he had received **a vision** concerning God's purposes for Israel. He next described **Israel** as a **beautiful** and vast host spread out across the wasteland like oases, verdant and fruitful. He prophesied that Israel would produce **abundant water** (symbolic of future prosperity) and would enjoy the blessing of a benign and powerful monarchy. Many scholars say the reference to **Agag** is anachronistic since this Amalekite king first appears in the story of Samuel and Saul, more than 300 years after Balaam (cf. 1 Sam. 15:8). It is more likely, however, that Agag was either a title such as Pharaoh or that a long line of Amalekite kings bore the name Agag. Parallels to this may be seen in Abimelech (Gen. 20:1-2; 26:1) and Jabin (Josh. 11:1; Jud. 4:2). The prophecy that Israel would have **a king** is in line with earlier revelation (Gen. 17:6; 35:11; 49:10).

**24:8-9.** Balaam next reviewed God's redemptive and protective work on Israel's behalf (cf. 23:22) and repeated that Israel was **like a lion** which one dare not arouse (cf. 23:24). Balaam concluded with an affirmation: **May those who bless you be blessed and those who curse you be cursed!** By this statement Balaam knowingly or unknowingly repeated God's promise to Abraham and the patriarchs concerning Israel's special redemptive role (Gen. 12:3).

**24:10-14.** At last **Balak** saw clearly that **Balaam** would not or could not **curse**

Israel, so **Balak** dismissed him without payment for his services. **Balaam** expressed no surprise at this and in fact said again that no amount of money could have made a difference in undoing the will of God (cf. 22:18). He would go **back** to his home, he said, but first he had one more, unsolicited word from God concerning Israel and Moab.

5. THE FOURTH ORACLE (24:15-19)

**24:15-16.** Balaam's fourth prophecy begins as the third one did—with a recognition that true understanding comes only from God (cf. vv. 3-4). The pagan mentioned three names or epithets of God: **God** (*'ēl,* "the powerful One"), **the Most High** (*'elyôn,* "the uplifted One"), and **the Almighty** (*šadday,* "the abundant One" or "the Almighty One"; cf. comments on Gen. 17:1). All these names were familiar in the ancient Near East and did not refer exclusively to the Lord of Israel. But the context of the **Balaam** oracles indicates beyond question that he was referring only to the Lord. The Lord had caused him to fall **prostrate** and in that posture to have his spiritual **eyes . . . opened** to God's truth.

**24:17.** The truth Balaam saw concerned primarily **a star** and **a scepter** that would originate in **Israel** in the future. Since poetically the star is parallel to the scepter, the star must also refer to royalty. This has now been strikingly confirmed in prophetic texts from Mari which describe various kings by the epithet "star." The connection of this prophecy to that **of Jacob,** in which he predicted that a ruler over Israel would come from Judah (Gen. 49:10), is unmistakable. Balaam went on to predict that this king **will crush the foreheads of Moab, the skulls of all the sons of Sheth.** The word translated "forehead" (*pē'âh*) is usually rendered "side" or "border," but it can mean forehead (as in Lev. 19:27; 21:5; Jer. 9:26, NIV marg.; 25:23, NIV marg.). With the verb "crush" (*mahaṣ*) *pē'âh* almost certainly should be rendered "forehead." The parallel word "skulls" translates the word *qodqōd* ("skull"). (The MT has the obscure *qarqar,* a word that appears only here and has no clear meaning.) The validity of this proposal is supported by Jeremiah 48:45c, "It burns the foreheads [*pē'âh* as in Num. 24:17] of Moab, the skulls [*qodqōd*] of the noisy boasters."

Also the Hebrew for "the noisy boasters" in Jeremiah 48:45 is literally, "the sons of uproar" (*b<sup>e</sup>nē šā'ôn*), not "the sons of Sheth" (*b<sup>e</sup>nē šēṯ*) as in Numbers 24:17. "Sheth" is of dubious etymology but perhaps, with Jeremiah, it suggests confusion or turmoil. In both Numbers and Jeremiah, "turmoil" (*šēṯ*) or "uproar" (*šā'ôn*) is parallel to Moab and therefore is a way of describing the Moabites as a people in an uproar. This may allude to all the terror and dread Moab felt when Israel camped in her plains (22:3).

**24:18-19.** **Edom** also was threatened with conquest by Israel. **Seir** was another name for Edom as the parallel construction indicates (cf. Gen. 32:3; Deut. 2:4). Balaam said **a ruler** would **come** from Israel **and destroy the survivors of the city.** This city is probably Sela, Edom's capital, known later as Petra. Fulfillment of these prophecies about Moab and Edom have already come to pass in some respects (cf., e.g., 1 Kings 11:15-18) but they still have prophetic overtones. Moab and Edom must yet suffer the judgment of the King of Israel, Jesus Christ (cf. Isa. 15–16; 21:11-12; Jer. 48; 49:7-11; Obad. 15-18, 21).

6. THE FINAL ORACLES (24:20-25)

**24:20.** **Balaam** also had a word concerning **Amalek.** He had previously mentioned Agag (v. 7), the Amalekite king. These references to Amalek indicate that these people lived among the Moabites. The Amalekites also had attacked Israel just after the Exodus (Ex. 17:8-16) and so were placed under the judgment of the Lord (cf. 1 Sam. 15:1-3). They were **first among the nations** in the sense that their ancestry could be traced back to Esau, making them an ancient people (cf. Gen. 36:16).

**24:21-22.** Next Balaam addressed **the Kenites** and told them that even though they had a secure **dwelling place** they would be taken **captive** by the Assyrians. The Kenites were identical to or a part of the Midianite peoples. Moses' brother-in-law Hobab was described earlier as a Midianite (10:29) but Hobab's father and thus Hobab were Kenites (Jud. 1:16). Their territories were primarily in the desert areas of the Arabian Peninsula and Sinai.

The reference to **Asshur** (Assyria) is a prediction of the conquests of the west

by Tiglath-Pileser III and Shalmaneser V. Though the Kenites are not mentioned in the period 745–722 B.C. when these captivities occurred, there is no reason to doubt that they made up a part of the great host of prisoners taken by the Assyrians. Mention of the Assyrians as early as Balaam (ca. 1400) is no problem either since by then the Middle Assyrian Kingdom period was under way and Assyria was on the way to becoming a mighty international power. (See the chart "Kings of Assyria in the Middle and New Assyrian Kingdoms," near Jonah 1:2.)

**24:23-25.** Finally Balaam looked far into the future and spoke of the coming of the **ships** of **Kittim** which would destroy **Asshur and Eber.** Many scholars think that Kittim refers not only to Cyprus specifically but also to all western Mediterranean maritime powers generally, particularly Rome (Jer. 2:10; Ezek. 27:6; Dan. 11:30). This remarkable prophecy found fulfillment in the overthrow of Asshur, which represented Mesopotamia and Persia, and Eber, which was the original name for the Hebrews, or Israelites. Later Rome did indeed incorporate the vestiges of the Assyrian Empire as well as Israel within its universal domination.

Having completed his mission, **Balaam . . . returned** to his homeland (in Pethor, Num. 22:5, in Mesopotamia).

### E. The idolatry of Israel (chap. 25)

**25:1-9.** Though Balaam had been unsuccessful in cursing the people of Israel, he evidently managed to play a role in their seduction by **the Baal** cult at **Peor** (cf. 31:16; Rev. 2:14). When **Israel was in Shittim,** immediately east of the Jordan River where they camped before crossing the river (Josh. 2:1), Israelite men engaged **in sexual immorality with Moabite women.** This was an integral part of the Canaanite fertility rites (cf. Deut. 23:17-18; 1 Kings 14:22-24) and was practiced in connection with the regular services of their temples (Num. 25:2). The physical, carnal aspects of this idolatry tempted the Israelites and led them into the spiritual apostasy of **worshiping . . . Baal.** So serious was this breach of covenant, especially when Israel was on the threshold of the land of promise, that **the**

LORD commanded **Moses** to **take** serious action—**all the** guilty individuals involved must die.

While Moses was delivering this verdict, **an Israelite man** (Zimri, v. 14) was brazen enough to bring **a Midianite** cult prostitute (Cozbi, v. 15) **right** into the camp. **Phinehas son of Eleazar,** a **priest,** was so incensed at this bold and open sin that he **took a spear . . . followed the Israelite into** his **tent,** and impaled **both** the man and his partner with it. This **stopped the plague,** evidently implied in the statement about God's **anger** (v. 3), but not before **24,000** people **died.** This incident at Baal of Peor is also referred to in Deuteronomy 4:3-4; Psalm 106:26-29; Hosea 9:10; 1 Corinthians 10:8.

First Corinthians 10:8 says 23,000 people died in this incident, whereas Numbers 25:9 has 24,000. This apparent discrepancy can be explained by Paul's mention of "one day," with the understanding that another 1,000 may have died on another day or days. Or 24,000 may have included the leaders, whereas 23,000 did not.

**25:10-13.** The LORD then told **Moses** that because **Phinehas** had been courageous in stemming the evil and had manifested great **zeal** on behalf of the Lord, **he and his descendants** would receive **a covenant of peace.** This is defined as **a lasting priesthood.** Such a promise had been made to Aaron and his sons (Ex. 29:9) but not specifically at that time to Aaron's grandson Phinehas. This suggests that the office of priest would now be channeled through Phinehas and not any other grandson of Aaron (cf. 1 Chron. 6:4-15).

**25:14-18.** The names of **the Israelite** and **Midianite** culprits, **Zimri** (a **Simeonite**) and **Cozbi,** appear here probably to emphasize that the matter was public and careful investigation was made of the particulars. Another reason might be to explain the great reduction in the Simeonite male population between the first census (59,300, 1:23) and the one after this incident (22,200, 26:14). If mainly Simeonites had been involved in the immorality and idolatry it would account for much of the difference in the totals. Also the identity of the woman is stressed in order to explain Israel's subsequent action of decimating the Midianite population (25:16-18; cf. 31:1-24).

## V. Final Preparations for Entering Canaan (chaps. 26–36)

### A. *The provisions for inheritance (26:1–27:11)*

1. THE NUMBERING OF THE 11 TRIBES (26:1-51)

**26:1-51.** The original generation of Israelites who left Egypt had died or would have done so by the time of the Conquest. Therefore it was necessary for the second generation to be counted in preparation for the military engagements which were shortly to take place in Canaan. This **census,** like the original one (1:20-46), pertained only to men **20 years** of age and older who were fit for military service. The four **clans of Reuben** totaled **43,730** (26:5-7). The clan of **Pallu** was singled out for special mention because **Dathan and Abiram,** the rebels who **died** with **Korah** (16:1), were from that clan (26:8-11).

The five **clans of Simeon** totaled **22,200** (vv. 12-14). This was the smallest population of all, a fact readily explained by Simeon's involvement in the Baal of Peor idolatry (25:14-15). The seven **clans of Gad** amounted to **40,500** men (26:15-18). The three major **clans of Judah** and the two subclans of **Perez** numbered **76,500** (vv. 19-22). The descendants **of Judah** listed here were actually from his one surviving son **Shelah** and his two illegitimate sons **Perez** and **Zerah** (cf. Gen. 38:5, 11, 26-30). **Er and Onan . . . died in Canaan** (cf. Gen. 38:6-10) and left no offspring. The four **clans of Issachar** totaled **64,300** men (Num. 26:23-25), and the three of **Zebulun** added up to **60,500** (vv. 26-27). The two major **clans** and six minor **clans of Manasseh,** a **Joseph** tribe, amounted to **52,700** men (vv. 29-34). The reference to **Zelophehad son of Hepher** (v. 33) anticipates the later instruction concerning the inheritance by **daughters** of a man who **had no sons** (27:1-11).

The three principal clans and one subsidiary **clan of Ephraim,** the other Joseph tribe, totaled **32,500** (26:35-37). The tribe of **Benjamin** consisted of five main clans and two minor ones, with their total of qualified males being **45,600** (vv. 38-41). **Dan** claimed only one clan, **Shuham,** and totaled **64,400** (vv. 42-43). There were three **clans** and two subclans in **Asher** with a total of **53,400** (vv. 44-47). Finally **Naphtali,** made up of four **clans,**

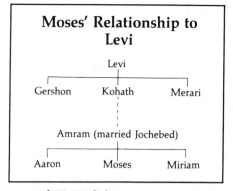

## Moses' Relationship to Levi

```
                    Levi
        ┌────────────┼────────────┐
    Gershon        Kohath        Merari
                     ┊
            Amram (married Jochebed)
        ┌────────────┼────────────┐
    Aaron          Moses         Miriam
```

counted **45,400** fighting men (vv. 48-50).

The grand **total** for all **Israel** (except Levi) was **601,730** (v. 51). This compares favorably with the sum of 603,550 38 years earlier (1:46). Despite the fact that the older generation was not counted, the Lord had made the younger generation prosperous and fruitful so that they could enter Canaan at full strength.

### 2. THE CASTING OF THE LOTS (26:52-56)

**26:52-56.** The census completed (vv. 1-51), the time had come to assign the tribal allotments on the basis of the population figures. The casting of lots (cf. Josh. 14:2) would not decide the size of the respective territories then, but only where the tribes would settle in Canaan. If a tribe were large it would have a large area but only the **lot** would decide whether it would be in the north, central, or south. These lots (*gôrāl*, sing.) were most likely the Urim and Thummin of the high priest (cf. Ex. 28:30).

### 3. THE ASSIGNMENT OF LEVI (26:57-65)

**26:57-62. The Levites** had **no inheritance** along with the other tribes (v. 62) because of the nature of their commitment and service to the Lord (cf. 3:11-13; 18:23-24). Therefore **they were not** numbered in the census **with the other** tribes. The Levite census included the three main **clans**—the Gershonites, Kohathites, and Merarites—and five subclans. The Libnites descended from Gershon (3:18), the Hebronites from Kohath (3:19), the Mahlites and Mushites from Merari (3:20), and the Korahites also from Kohath (16:1).

A Levitical line of particular importance to Moses, of course, was that of **Amram,** a descendant of **Kohath** (v. 58). **Amram's wife was Jochebed,** a descen-

dant of Levi, who **bore Aaron, Moses, and . . . Miriam.** (See the chart "Moses' Relationship to Levi.") This seems to suggest that Moses was a great-grandson of Levi (Levi—Kohath—Amram—Moses), but for chronological reasons this is impossible. Levi moved to Egypt when he was about 50 and Moses departed when he was 80 (Ex. 6:16-20; 7:7). The sojourn in Egypt lasted 430 years, however; so it is evident that Amram was not in the next generation after Kohath but was a later descendant (see comments on 1 Chron. 6:1-3).

The priestly aspect of the Levitical lineage appears next (Num. 26:60-61), with the information that **Aaron was the father** of four sons, two of whom—**Nadab and Abihu**—died because of ritual impropriety (cf. Lev. 10:1-2; Num. 3:4). **Eleazar and Ithamar,** of course, served as priests with Aaron (3:4). The total number of **male Levites a month old or more** was **23,000** (26:62). This compares with 22,000 in the first census 38 years earlier (3:39).

**26:63-65.** Of those **Israelites** (excluding the Levites) who were **counted** in the earlier census **in the Desert of Sinai** (cf. 1:19) only two were now alive, **Caleb . . . and Joshua.** All others had died **in the desert** because of their rebellious spirit (cf. 14:26-31).

### 4. THE INHERITANCE OF FAMILIES WITHOUT SONS (27:1-11)

**27:1-4.** When it came time to allocate the territory to the tribes, clans, and families, a problem arose in connection with the family of **Zelophehad** of the tribe of **Manasseh** (cf. 26:33). Zelophehad had **died,** not in the Korah incident but for a **sin** he himself had committed. He had **left no sons** (27:3), but he had five **daughters** (v. 1). Since the allocations were made to male family heads, the family and **name** of Zelophehad would pass into extinction since they would have no land within the tribe.

**27:5-11. Moses,** baffled by this unique situation, inquired of **the LORD,** who authorized him to grant the **daughters** of Zelophehad **an inheritance** along with the others. This became a precedent and with it were given other guidelines. **If a man** died with neither **son** nor **daughter . . . his brothers** must receive **his inheritance. If he** had **no brothers,**

# Calendrical Offerings

| | | BURNT | GRAIN | DRINK | FELLOWSHIP | SIN |
|---|---|---|---|---|---|---|
| **DAILY SERVICE** (Ex. 29:38-42; Num. 28:3-8) | | One male lamb morning and evening = "regular burnt offerings" | 1/10 ephah fine flour + 1/4 hin olive oil (with each lamb) | 1/4 hin fermented drink (with each lamb) | | |
| **WEEKLY SABBATH** (Lev. 23:3; Num. 28:9-10) | | Two male lambs (+ "regular burnt offerings") | 2/10 ephah fine flour + oil (+ daily offerings) | "drink offering" (+ daily offerings) | | |
| **MONTHLY NEW MOON** (Num. 28:11-15) | | Two young bulls, each + ----------> One ram + ------> Seven male lambs each + ----------> (+ "regular burnt offerings") | 3/10 ephah fine flour/ oil + -------------> 2/10 ephah fine flour/ oil + -------------> 1/10 ephah fine flour/ oil + -------------> (+ daily offerings) | 1/2 hin wine 1/3 hin wine 1/4 hin wine (+ daily offerings) | | One male goat |
| **ANNUAL** | **PASSOVER/ UNLEAVENED BREAD FESTIVAL** (Lev. 23:4-14; Num. 28:16-25) | *After Passover each day for seven days:* Two young bulls each + ----------> One ram + ------> Seven male lambs each + ----------> *On second day after Passover:* One male lamb (extra) + --------> (+ "regular burnt offerings") | 3/10 ephah fine flour/ oil + -------------> 2/10 ephah fine flour/ oil + -------------> 1/10 ephah fine flour/ oil + -------------> 2/10 ephah fine flour/oil + -------> + a sheaf of first-fruits as a wave of-fering (+ daily of-ferings) | 1/2 hin wine 1/3 hin wine 1/4 hin wine 1/4 hin wine (+ daily offerings) | | *Each of the seven days:* One male goat |
| | **FEAST OF WEEKS** (Pentecost) (Lev. 23:15-21; Num. 28:26-31) | Two young bulls each + ----------> One ram + ------> Seven male lambs each + ----------> (+ "regular burnt offerings") | 3/10 ephah fine flour/ oil + -------------> 2/10 ephah fine flour/ oil + -------------> 1/10 ephah fine flour/ oil + -------------> + wave offering of two loaves of new grain (+ daily offerings) | 1/2 hin wine 1/3 hin wine 1/4 hin wine (+ daily offerings) | Two male lambs as a wave offering | One male goat |
| | **FEAST OF TRUMPETS** (Lev. 23:22-25; Num. 29:1-6) | One young bull + --------------------> One ram + ------> Seven male lambs each + ----------> (+ monthly and "regular burnt offerings") | 3/10 ephah fine flour/ oil + -------------> 2/10 ephah fine flour/ oil + -------------> 1/10 ephah fine flour/ oil + -------------> (+ monthly and daily offerings) | 1/2 hin wine 1/3 hin wine 1/4 hin wine (+ monthly and daily offerings) | | One male goat |
| | **DAY OF ATONEMENT** (Lev. 16:1-28; 23:26-32; Num. 29:7-11) | One young bull + --------------------> One ram + ------> Seven male lambs each + ----------> *Atonement ritual:* One ram (for high priest) One ram (for nation) (+ "regular burnt offerings") | 3/10 ephah fine flour/ oil + -------------> 2/10 ephah fine flour/ oil + -------------> 1/10 ephah fine flour/ oil + -------------> (+ daily offerings) | 1/2 hin wine 1/3 hin wine 1/4 hin wine (+ daily offerings) | | One male goat *Atonement ritual:* One bull (for high priest) Two male goats (for nation) (one for scapegoat ritual, Lev. 16:7-10) |
| | **FEAST OF TABERNA-CLES** (Booths) (Lev. 23:33-36, 39, 43; Num. 29:12-38) | Days Bulls Rams Lambs 1 13 2 14 2 12 2 14 3 11 2 14 4 10 2 14 5 9 2 14 6 8 2 14 7 7 2 14 8 1 1 7 (+ "regular burnt offer-ings") | with →matching grain + ----> offerings fol-lowing pattern above (+ daily offerings) | matching drink of-ferings following pattern above (+ daily offerings) | | One male goat each day for eight days |

Note: No guilt offerings were included in any of these regularly scheduled calendrical offerings. On guilt offerings see Leviticus 5:14-6:7.

One ephah = 1/2 bushel, about 8 quarts.     One hin = about 1/2 quart.

his uncles were next in line. And if he had no uncles, **the nearest** of kin **in his clan** would become heir. So this ad hoc solution to a problem became translated into a permanent **legal requirement for** Israel.

### B. Succession to Moses (27:12-23)

**27:12-17. Moses** and **Aaron** had disqualified themselves from entering **the land** of promise when they had failed **to honor** the Lord by striking the rock at **Meribah** in **the Desert of Zin** (20:12). Aaron had already died (20:27-29) but **the Lord** now allowed **Moses** a glimpse of Canaan from afar. From the summit of a **mountain in the Abarim range** he beheld the vista to the west. This mountain was Nebo (Deut. 32:49), just across from Jericho.

Rather than lapsing into self-pity as a lesser man might have done, Moses expressed his concern that Israel have a good leader to take his place. He implored **the God of the spirits of all mankind** to select this leader. This unusual title of God (occurring only here and in Num. 16:33) refers to God's omniscient understanding of everyone, which guaranteed the wisdom of His choice. The leader, Moses said, should be like **a shepherd** who would **lead** Israel, his **sheep, out and . . . in.**

**27:18-23.** The Lord's response was immediate: **Take Joshua son of Nun.** This Spirit-filled man, who had already demonstrated his qualities and capabilities (Ex. 17:8-10; 24:13; 33:11; Num. 11:28-29; 14:30, 38), was an ideal successor to **Moses.** His appointment must be public, however, so the **community** would know Joshua was entitled to the same respect as Moses and was to have **some of** Moses' **authority.**

After Moses laid his **hand on him** thus commissioning him, **Joshua** was to **stand before Eleazar the priest** to symbolize the relationship that the two would enjoy from then on—**Eleazar** would reveal the will of God through **the Urim** (cf. Ex. 28:30) and Joshua would carry out God's directives. **Moses** then carried out these instructions.

### C. Laws concerning offerings (chaps. 28–29)

**28:1-8.** On the eve of the conquest and occupation of Canaan it was necessary that the younger generation be instructed concerning the offerings appropriate for the settled, agricultural way of life they would soon be living. (See the chart "Calendrical Offerings.") The first of these were the daily burnt **offerings.** These had already been legislated **at Mount Sinai** (v. 6; cf. Lev. 1 and comments on Ex. 29:38-46, where the reasons for their presentation were given). These daily offerings were a token of tribute by the vassal people to their sovereign **Lord** who met them in a unique way at the tabernacle.

**28:9-10.** The second category of offerings pertained to **the Sabbath Day.** Though the **Sabbath** itself had been set apart (Ex. 20:8-11), this is the first instruction given concerning Sabbath ritual. It consisted of **regular burnt** offerings, just described, plus **two lambs a year old** with their accompanying **drink** and **grain** offerings.

**28:11-15. On the first** day of each **month** the community was to **present** an enhanced **burnt offering** in addition to the regular one just described. This must consist of **two young bulls, one ram, and seven male lambs a year old, all without defect. With each** animal there must be an appropriate **grain offering** and **drink offering.** Also the **New Moon** festival was to include the offering of **one male goat . . . as a sin offering.** Earlier the Lord had instructed that the blowing of trumpets be an integral part of the New Moon festivities (10:10).

**28:16-25.** The regulations pertaining to the **Passover** elaborate on facts given earlier (Ex. 12:3-11; Lev. 23:5-8). **On the 14th day of the first month** (i.e., Nisan) the Passover **lambs** were to be slaughtered. Beginning **on the 15th day** and continuing **for seven days** (through the 21st) was the Feast of Unleavened Bread (cf. Ex. 12:15-20). The first of these seven days was a Sabbath and that day and each of the following six days required the same offerings as those of the New Moon (Num. 28:18-22, 24; cf. vv. 11-15) plus Sabbath offerings (vv. 9-10). These offerings were **in addition to the regular** daily **burnt** offerings (v. 23) for the remainder of the week. The last of the seven days (v. 25) also was considered a Sabbath and presumably required the same offerings as the first day.

**28:26-31. The Feast of Weeks** (cf.

Lev. 23:15-21) required Sabbath observance (Num. 28:26) and the offering of the same sacrifices as the New Moon Festival (vv. 27-30). In addition were the firstfruits of the **grain** which was the underlying reason for the festival (see comments on Lev. 23:15-21).

**29:1-6. The first day of the seventh month** was New Year's Day. Accompanying the blowing of **trumpets** was the **offering of one young bull, one ram, and seven male lambs** and a **male goat.** These were **in addition to the monthly** (i.e., New Moon) sacrifices (cf. 28:11-15), since this was no ordinary New Moon festival. Also the usual morning and evening **burnt offerings** were to be made.

**29:7-11.** The Day of Atonement, **on the 10th day of the seventh month,** was a Sabbath which required the same offerings as the New Year's festival except for the New Moon elements. Along with the **male goat as a sin offering,** however, the regular **sin offering for atonement** (see comments on Lev. 16) was to be made.

**29:12-40.** The Feast of Tabernacles, which lasted from **the 15th day of the seventh month** through the 22nd day (cf. Lev. 23:34), required a great number of sacrifices because it celebrated the end of the yearly harvests and was an expression of thanksgiving to God. The first day was a Sabbath on which **13 young bulls, 2 rams, and 14 male lambs a year old, all without defect,** were presented. With each bull, ram, and lamb there was to be the appropriate **grain offering** (Num. 29:14-15), though no drink offerings were explicitly mentioned for the first day (except what went with the regular burnt offering each day, v. 16). The **male goat** for **a sin offering** was mandatory, however, as was the **regular** daily **burnt offering.**

**On the second day** (vv. 17-19) everything was the same as the first except that **12** (not 13) **young bulls** were offered and the appropriate **drink offerings** were also included. On each successive day the number of **bulls** was reduced by one (vv. 20-31) till **on the seventh day** there were **7 bulls** (v. 32). This total of 7 bulls on the seventh day certainly has symbolical significance, perhaps as an expression of perfection.

**The eighth day** of the Feast of Tabernacles was the occasion for another Sabbath (v. 35) on which were offered the same sacrifices as on New Year's day (vv. 1-6) with the exception of the New Moon elements, but with the addition of **drink offerings.** All these festivals were to be carried out with their appropriate **offerings** besides the presentation of votive and **freewill offerings** (v. 39; cf. 15:1-12).

### D. Laws concerning vows (chap. 30)

As was pointed out in regard to the Nazirite custom (6:1-12), an individual could make a vow to the Lord to do something or perhaps to abstain from something for a designated period of time (see comments on Lev. 27). The purpose of Numbers 30 was not to specify what kinds of vows might be made or how they were to be undertaken or abrogated but only to teach how important it was that they be kept.

**30:1-8.** If an individual made **a vow** (*neḏer,* a promise to do something) or **a pledge** (*'issār,* a promise not to do something), he must keep it without equivocation (vv. 1-2). If an unmarried daughter made such a promise without contrary counsel from **her father,** she must keep it (vv. 3-4). **If her father** forbade **her,** however, her promise was null and void (v. 5). If she were married, **her husband** would bear the same kind of authority over her in such matters (vv. 6-8).

**30:9-16.** A **widow** or divorcee must stand by her **vow** in the same way as a man (v. 9). If a **husband** waited for a period of time after his wife made **a vow,** he must bear any **guilt** involved in nullifying it (vv. 10-15). That is, after an indeterminate period the vow was in force and could be abrogated only by an appropriate sin offering (Lev. 5:4-13).

### E. God's judgment on the Midianites (chap. 31)

**31:1-6.** The Lord's last assignment **to Moses** was carrying out His **vengeance on the Midianites.** The reason obviously was Midian's role in Israel's apostate behavior at Baal of Peor (cf. 25:16-18). This was holy war as the presence of **Phinehas . . . the priest** with the **12,000** fighting **men** attested. Holy war differed from other kinds in that **the LORD** Himself led the army (hence the presence of the priest and **articles from the sanctuary**). The result was to be total annihilation of all living things and the devoting of all

## The Israelites' Dividing of the Midianite Animal Spoils (Num. 31:25-47)

| | Sheep | Cattle | Donkeys | Totals |
|---|---|---|---|---|
| The soldiers' portion (1/2 of the total) | 337,500 | 36,000 | 30,500 | 404,000 |
| Minus the portion to the Lord (1/500 of the soldiers' portion) | −675 | −72 | −61 | −808 |
| Soldiers' portion (net amount) | 336,825 | 35,928 | 30,439 | 403,192 |
| The people's portion (1/2 of the total) | 337,500 | 36,000 | 30,500 | 404,000 |
| Minus the portion to the Lord (1/50 of the people's portion) | −6,750 | −720 | −610 | −8,080 |
| People's portion (net amount) | 330,750 | 35,280 | 29,890 | 395,920 |
| Total | 675,000 | 72,000 | 61,000 | 808,000 |

material properties to the Lord (cf. Deut. 20:16-18; Josh. 6:15-19).

**31:7-12.** The campaign **against** the Midianites was successful and resulted in the death of **every man** (i.e., every Midianite soldier). These included **the five** Midianite **kings** and the Prophet **Balaam** who obviously had returned from Pethor at some time to affiliate with the Midianites. The **towns** and **camps** of Midian were also destroyed and their **plunder** retained for the Lord. However, the **women and children** were spared as were the animals (v. 9).

**31:13-18.** When **Moses** met the returning army he **was angry** when he saw the Midianite survivors. **The** Midianite **women,** he said, should have died because they were directly culpable in Israel's sin at Baal of **Peor.** All the women except the virgins were then sentenced to death along with **all the boys.** This insured the extermination of the Midianites and thus prevented them from ever again seducing Israel to sin. Reference to Midianites in later history (e.g., Jud. 6:1-6) no doubt implies either a different clan or family from those in Numbers or the possibility that some escaped God's vengeance. The virgins were spared because they obviously had had no role in the Baal of Peor incident nor could they by themselves perpetuate the Midianite peoples. Nonetheless, strict application

of the rules of holy war dictated that they too should have been killed (Deut. 20:16), so it was only a concession by Moses that allowed them to live.

**31:19-24.** In the act of slaughtering the Midianites many Israelites had become ceremonially unclean so they, their prisoners, and **everything made of leather, goat hair, or wood** had to be cleansed by the proper rituals (cf. chap. 19). **Anything that** could survive **fire (gold, silver, bronze, iron, tin, lead)** could be **purified** by **fire** and **the water of cleansing.** Flammable materials, however, were to be purified by the **water** only.

**31:25-47.** All captives and goods were then to be divided according to a strict formula. On the dividing of the Midianite **spoils** see the accompanying chart. In addition to these extensive animal spoils, the soldiers took **16,000** virgin women out of **32,000** and gave **32** over to **the Lord** (vv. 35, 40). These 32 women must have functioned somehow as slaves to the priests or tabernacle (cf. 1 Sam. 2:22).

**31:48-54.** When a count was then made of the soldiers, **not one** was **missing!** The commanders of the troops were so grateful for this miraculous deliverance that they brought a freewill **offering** of **gold** ornaments **to the Lord.** They did this **to make atonement,** which likely means they recognized that the lack of casualties was an act of divine grace beyond anything they deserved. The total weight of their offering was **16,750 shekels** (ca. 420 pounds [6,720 ounces], worth several million dollars in current United States economy). All this was **brought . . . into** the tabernacle **as a memorial for the Israelites before the Lord** (vv. 51-54). That is, it was a tribute to His faithfulness and blessing (cf. 1 Chron. 18:11; 2 Chron. 15:18).

## F. The inheritance of the Eastern tribes (chap. 32)

### 1. THEIR REQUEST FOR INHERITANCE (32:1-5)

**32:1-5.** The tribes of Reuben and Gad were especially blessed with **large herds and flocks** and so desired to remain in the Transjordan because of the suitable pasturage, especially in **Jazer and Gilead.** Jazer was a settlement (perhaps modern Khirbet Jazzir) about seven miles west of Rabbath Ammon, in the great southern plateau of Gilead (cf. 21:32). Gilead refers to the more northern part. The leaders of these two tribes requested that they be allowed to settle there because of their needs and because **the land** had now been **subdued** and was ready for occupation. The places in 32:3 which can be identified all lie between the Arnon River to the south and the Jabbok to the north.

### 2. THE PREREQUISITE FOR THEIR INHERITANCE (32:6-32)

**32:6-15.** Moses' initial reaction to Reuben and Gad's request was unfavorable because he was afraid that their unwillingness to cross the Jordan and dispossess the Canaanites would undermine the morale of the other tribes who might also want to stay where they were. Their **fathers** (i.e., ancestors), he said, had done this very thing when they listened to the report of the spies and lost heart about the Conquest. This had caused the Lord to be angry (v. 10), and He caused that generation to die in the wilderness (cf. 14:1-35). Now, **Moses** said, they wanted to repeat the sin of their **fathers** and bring God's **anger** on **Israel** again.

**32:16-32.** To this Reuben and Gad responded that they had no desire to evade responsibility for the Conquest west **of the Jordan.** They would therefore provide **pens** for their **livestock** and fortification to protect their wives **and children** and would then join their brothers in the conquest of Canaan (vv. 16-19).

**Moses** assented to this plan and said that if they did all they were promising they could have the Transjordan as their inheritance (vv. 20-22). **But if** they failed **to do** so, they would **be sinning against the Lord** and their **sin** would surely **find** them **out** (i.e., the appropriate punishment for that sin would eventually be meted out). Again the **Reubenites** and **Gadites** affirmed their promise (vv. 25-27; cf. vv. 16-19, 31-32). **Moses** then outlined all these arrangements and pledges **to Eleazar . . . and Joshua.** He said **if the Gadites and Reubenites** crossed over the river to help their brothers they could have **Gilead as** a **possession**; otherwise, they must **accept** their inheritance **in Canaan** along with the rest (vv. 28-30). Once more the **Reubenites** and **Gadites** committed themselves to do all that they had promised (vv. 31-32; cf. vv. 16-19, 25-27).

### 3. THE ALLOCATION OF THEIR INHERITANCE (32:33-42)

**32:33-38.** Moses allotted to Reuben, Gad, **and the half-tribe of Manasseh** (first mentioned here in Num. as part of the Transjordanian tribes) the areas that had formerly belonged to the Amorite kings **Sihon** and **Og** (cf. 21:21-35). Sihon had ruled in the southern part (Gilead) and Og in the north (**Bashan**). **The Gadites** rebuilt **cities** in southern Gilead from **Aroer** on the Arnon River to the south to **Jogbehah,** 10 miles northwest of Rabbath Ammon to the north. The Reubenite cities were generally from **Heshbon** west and southwest to the Jordan and the Dead Sea. So Reuben was more or less a west-central enclave within Gad.

**32:39-42.** The half-tribe **of Manasseh** consisted of the clan **of Makir** and the **Gilead** clan (cf. 26:29). Their territory, to the north of Gad and Reuben, consisted of a cluster of settlements named **Havvoth Jair** ("settlements of Jair") after a **descendant** of Manasseh (cf. Deut. 3:13-15). Another descendant, **Nobah, captured Kenath and** vicinity and renamed **it Nobah after himself.** Kenath was in Bashan, about 60 miles due east of the Sea of Kinnereth.

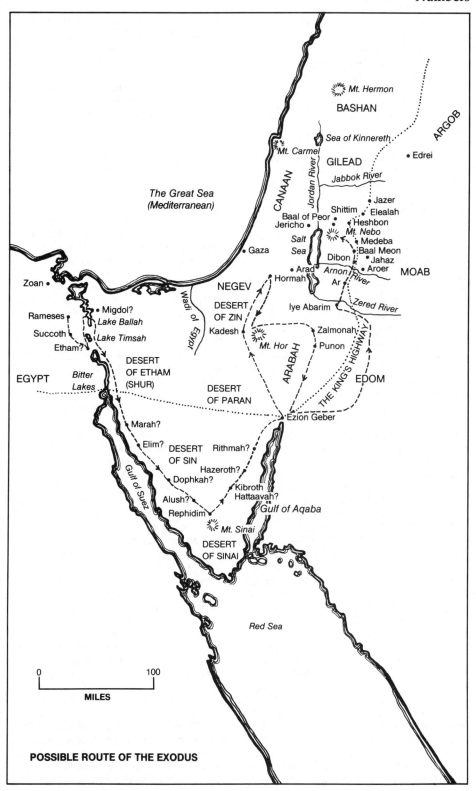

**POSSIBLE ROUTE OF THE EXODUS**

## G. Resumé of the journey from Egypt (33:1-49)

**33:1-5.** Among the records **Moses kept at the LORD's command** was a complete itinerary of the **journey** of Israel from **Egypt** to the plains of Moab (see the map "Possible Route of the Exodus"). It is impossible to know if this list is absolutely comprehensive or notes only the places considered important in their travels. Also most of the place names can no longer be identified or correlated with modern names and places. They **set out from Rameses** (perhaps a later name for Tanis, the Hyksos city, Ex. 1:11; 12:37) in the Egyptian Delta on **the day after the** first **Passover** (Nisan 15) and made their first encampment **at Succoth.** This first stop was perhaps the present Tell el-Maskhutah, about 40 miles southeast of Rameses.

**33:6-8.** They next went to **Etham, on the edge of the desert** (cf. Ex. 13:20). They **turned back** north **to Pi Hahiroth . . . east of Baal Zephon,** and **Migdol** ("tower"), where they **camped.** Here the Israelites seemed to be trapped by the Egyptians between **the sea** and **the desert.** Apparently they suddenly headed east or southeast, crossing one of the bodies of water (*yām sûp,* "Reed Sea" or "Sea of [Papyrus] Reeds,") mistakenly called the Red Sea; see comments on Ex. 14:2) along the way (cf. Ex. 15:22). After **three days . . . they camped at Marah** in the **Desert of Etham** (or Shur, Ex. 15:22). Marah cannot be located precisely.

**33:9-13.** From **Marah** they **went to Elim** (cf. Ex. 15:27), site unknown, and on to the shore of **the Red Sea.** From there they journeyed to **the Desert of Sin** in the central part of the Sinai Peninsula, arriving on the 15th day of the second month (Ex. 16:1), one month after they left Egypt. Leaving this encampment they **arrrived at Dophkah,** now unknown, and **Alush,** also unknown.

**33:14-32.** From there the Israelites went to **Rephidim** (cf. Ex. 17:1–19:2), and then moved to **the Desert of Sinai** at the southern tip of the peninsula. After about 11 months there (cf. Ex. 19:1; Num. 10:11), during which time God gave them the Mosaic Covenant, they traveled on to **Kibroth Hattaavah** (of unknown identification today), a three-day journey from Mount Sinai (10:33; 11:34). The route next took them to **Hazeroth** (cf. 11:35–12:16),

of unknown location, and then to **Rithmah** named only here. All the stations mentioned in verses 19 through 32 likewise cannot be identified with any certainty.

**33:33-39. Jotbathah** may be Tabeh, seven miles south of Elath on the western shore of the Gulf of Aqabah. **Abronah** is unknown but **Ezion Geber** is the famous port on the Gulf of Aqabah (cf. 1 Kings 9:26). From Ezion Geber Israel moved on to **Kadesh, in the Desert of Zin** (Num. 33:36). This is Kadesh Barnea (modern 'Ain Qedeis; cf. Deut. 1:2) as opposed to many other places named Kadesh. The nearly 100-mile distance from Ezion Geber northwest to Kadesh must have taken several days. At Kadesh Moses' sister Miriam died, just before Israel entered the Promised Land (cf. comments on 20:1). At or in the vicinity of Kadesh, Israel spent about 38 years between the revolt against Moses (Num. 14:26-35) and the movement on to **Mount Hor** (33:37; cf. 20:22). There at Mount Hor **Aaron . . . died** at the age of 123 **on the first day of the fifth month of the 40th year after** the Exodus (33:38-39). Since Moses died that same year at 120, he was three years younger than Aaron (Deut. 1:3; 34:5-7).

**33:40-49.** While Israel was at Mount Hor **the king of Arad** heard of their plan to journey to Atharim (cf. 21:1) and so attacked them. Israel retaliated, however, and destroyed several **Canaanite** towns (21:3). They then went on to **Zalmonah,** perhaps es-Salmaneh, about 25 miles south of the Dead Sea. Next they arrived at **Punon** (or Feinan), 15 miles southeast of Zalmonah, in the Arabah. From there they went to **Oboth,** of unknown identification. Though not stated in Numbers the Israelites apparently went south from Punon to Ezion Geber and then east and north *around* Edom "along the desert road of Moab" (cf. 21:4; Deut. 2:8). **Iye Abarim,** the next station, was **on the border of Moab,** probably near the headwaters of the Wadi Zered. Israel next traveled on to **Dibon Gad** (or Dhiban), just north of the Arnon River (cf. 21:11-13).

Their next stop was **Almon Diblathaim,** perhaps about 10 miles north of Dibon, and then they **camped in the mountains of Abarim, near Nebo.** Nebo (Jebel Nabba) is apparently a peak, also known as Pisgah (cf. Deut. 34:1), in the cluster of the Abarim Mountains. Finally the Israelites arrived in **the plains of Moab** "across from Jericho" (Num. 33:50). Because of the size of their camp the Israelites filled all the area **from Beth Jeshimoth to Abel Shittim,** a distance of about six miles south to north.

## H. Final instructions about conquest and inheritance (33:50–36:13)

### 1. DESTRUCTION OF THE CANAANITES (33:50-56)

**33:50-56.** In Moses' final address **to the Israelites,** he instructed them to **drive** the Canaanites **out . . . of the land,** to **destroy all their . . . images and . . . idols,** and to **demolish all their high places.** "High places" (*bāmôt*) were hills on which Canaanite altars and shrines were placed, possibly so the worshipers of Baal and other gods might have more ready access to them. When this was done Israel was to **take possession of the land and settle in it** in accord with God's promises (cf. Gen. 13:17; 17:8; Ex. 6:2-5; etc.). This was to be done according to God's previous instruction that **larger** tribes be given more **land** (cf. Num. 26:53-56). Failure to **drive out the people of the land** would result in their being a continuous **trouble** to Israel, and would eventually result in Israel's expulsion from Canaan (cf. Josh. 23:13; 2 Kings 17:7-20).

### 2. BOUNDARIES OF THE LAND OF PROMISE (34:1-15)

**34:1-5.** The territory assigned to Israel was to have precisely defined borders. To the south the line was to extend **from the end of the Salt Sea** (the Dead Sea) westward **south of Scorpion Pass** (perhaps Naqb es-Safa, about 20 miles southwest of the Dead Sea) to the Desert of **Zin** and to **Kadesh Barnea,** 65 miles southwest of the Dead Sea. From there the border extended northwesterly **to Hazar Addar** (4 or 5 miles away) and **Azmon** (3 miles away). There it joined **the Wadi of Egypt** (Wadi el-Arish) and continued northwestward to **the** Mediterranean **Sea,** about 50 miles south of Gaza.

**34:6-9.** The **western** border was the Mediterranean (**the Great Sea**). The **northern** border extended from the Mediterranean near **Mount Hor** (Ras Shak-

kah?), not the Mount Hor where Aaron died (33:38) but a northern peak about 10 miles north of the Phoenician city of Byblos. The border ran eastward **to Lebo Hamath** (cf. 13:21), about 50 miles north of Damascus, on to **Zedad** (northeast of Lebo Hamath about 30 miles) and **Ziphron** (10 miles farther east), and ended **at Hazar Enan,** 70 miles northeast of Damascus.

**34:10-15.** The **eastern** border commenced in the north at **Hazar Enan,** went south to **Shepham** (site unknown), **Riblah** (70 miles north of Damascus), and on to **the east . . . of the Sea of Kinnereth** (later called the Sea of Galilee; see comments on Josh. 11:2) and on to **the Salt Sea.**

This marked the areas assigned to **the nine and a half tribes** only, since **Reuben . . . Gad, and the half-tribe of Manasseh** had already been assigned their allotments in Transjordan (cf. Num. 32:33-42).

### 3. OFFICIALS TO SUPERVISE THE ALLOTMENTS (34:16-29)

**34:16-29.** The responsibility for overseeing the distribution of **the land** fell to **Eleazar the priest and Joshua** (cf. 27:22), who in turn selected a **leader from each** of the 12 tribes to assist them. Of the list of **names** given here (34:19-28) only **Caleb,** mentioned first, is otherwise known (cf. 13:6; 14:30; etc.).

### 4. INHERITANCE OF LEVI (35:1-5)

**35:1-5.** The tribe of Levi, whose inheritance was the Lord (cf. 18:20) and the ministry of the tabernacle (cf. 18:21), did not receive a tribal allotment. Yet **the**

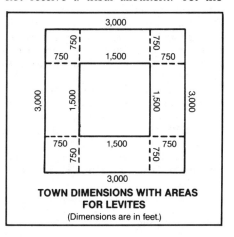

**TOWN DIMENSIONS WITH AREAS FOR LEVITES**
(Dimensions are in feet.)

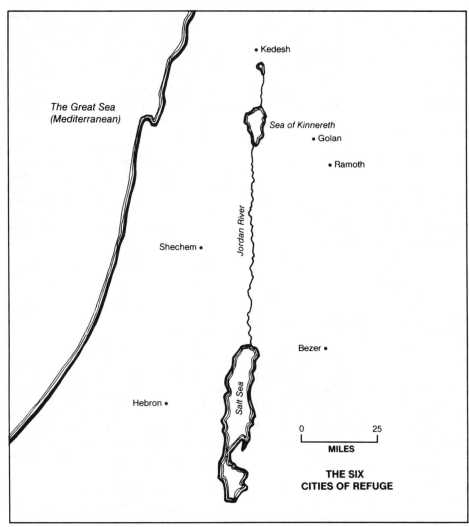

The Great Sea
(Mediterranean)

• Kedesh

Sea of Kinnereth
• Golan

• Ramoth

Jordan River

Shechem •

Bezer •

Salt Sea

Hebron •

0          25

**MILES**

**THE SIX
CITIES OF REFUGE**

**Levites** had to receive some land and goods so that they could function in a practical way among the tribes. The solution was the appointment of **towns** throughout the land where **the Levites** could be widely distributed and from which they could serve **the LORD** and Israel (cf. Lev. 25:32-34; Josh. 21:1-42). These towns would also incorporate the surrounding **pasturelands.** The properties were to extend out from the city walls **1,500 feet** and **measure 3,000 feet** on each **side.** These measurements probably are to be taken as an average, based on a town whose walls were 1,500 feet x 1,500 feet.

The pasturelands then actually extended 750 feet out from the city walls on each side. Some of the cities would be

larger and some smaller and certainly not all would be square but these proportions could still be used as a guideline.

5. LAWS CONCERNING MURDER AND REFUGE (35:6-34)

**35:6-15.** The total number of **towns** allocated to the tribe of Levi was **48.** Six of these would **be cities of refuge** to which manslayers might **flee.** These 48 **towns** were to be assigned fairly from all the tribal territories—more from the larger tribes and fewer from the small ones. If a person committed an accidental homicide, he was to flee to one of the **cities of refuge** to escape **the avenger** and thus live to stand **trial. Three** of these **cities of refuge** would be east of the Jordan (Josh. 20:8) and **three** to the west (Josh. 20:7).

(See map "The Six Cities of Refuge.") There anyone accused of manslaughter could find sanctuary among **the Levites.**

**35:16-21.** If an individual should strike another with an **object** that could be considered lethal—such as a piece of **iron** (v. 16), **stone** (v. 17), or wood (v. 18)—and the victim died, the perpetrator would be considered **a murderer** by virtue of the implement he used. In such a case he had no recourse to a city of refuge but might be hunted down by **the avenger** and **put . . . to death** (v. 19; cf. Ex. 21:12, 14). **The avenger** would be a member of the victim's family who had the responsibility of acting for society in avenging the murder by taking the murderer's life (cf. Gen. 9:5-6; Deut. 19:6, 12). The same fate awaited anyone who killed another with premeditation, that is, after having given prior evidence of hostility toward the victim (Num. 35:20-21).

**35:22-29.** However, if a person killed another purely by accident by shoving him, throwing **something at him,** or dropping **a stone on him,** he could find sanctuary in any one of the cities of **refuge** (cf. Ex. 21:13) till the matter could be adjudicated between **the assembly** of Israel **and the avenger.** If indeed it turned out that the case were one of manslaughter and not murder, the accused would be allowed to return **to the city of refuge** where **he** was to **stay** till **the high priest** died. If the **accused** went **outside . . . the** city before that time he could be slain by **the avenger** with impunity. **The death of the high priest** must have symbolized a cancellation or remission of the manslayer's sin.

**35:30-34.** In any case of homicide there needed to be **witnesses** to the act in order for guilt to be established; **one witness** alone was not enough (cf. Deut. 17:6; Matt. 18:16). Moreover, **a murderer** could not merely pay a fine (**ransom**) or otherwise redeem himself—he **must** die (Num. 35:31). Likewise a manslayer who had been confined **to a city of refuge** could not pay a monetary compensation (**ransom**) in lieu of his confinement (v. 32). The reason for such strict measures was the fact that **bloodshed** in murder **pollutes the land** and the only "cleansing" agent was **the blood of** the murderer himself (Gen. 4:10; 9:6). It was not fitting that Israel and **the LORD,** who

lived in Israel's midst, should occupy a polluted **land.** So blood vengeance was not an option but a theological necessity.

6. INHERITANCE OF DAUGHTERS WHO MARRY (CHAP. 36)

**36:1-12.** In previous instructions **Moses** had decreed that **the inheritance** of a man who died without sons must go to the daughters. This had arisen out of a specific situation involving the **daughters** of **Zelophehad,** a descendant of the Manassehite clan of Gilead (cf. 27:1-11). The question now arose as to the disposition of the properties of such daughters who married **men from other . . . tribes.** Would that land and property **be taken** from Manasseh and belong to those other tribes? Would it remain with another tribe at the time of **the Year of Jubilee?** The Year of Jubilee, occurring every 50 years, required the return of all purchased and mortgaged properties to their original owners (cf. Lev. 25:8-17). Presumably, however, this would not occur in the case of properties which had been lost to a clan by marriage. **Moses** concurred and, to prevent such a loss of tribal lands, commanded that **Zelophehad's daughters** (and others in similar situations) **marry** only within their father's **clan.** In this way each **tribe** of Isra-**el** would maintain its territorial integrity (Num. 36:7-9). **So Zelophehad's daughters. . . . married their** paternal **cousins,** thus preserving **their inheritance** within their own **clan** (vv. 10-12).

**36:13.** The Book of Numbers closes with the summary statement that all the foregoing record was communicated to **Moses** by the LORD **. . . on the plains of Moab** (cf. 22:1). Without question, this statement says that the Book of Numbers is the very Word of God through His servant Moses.

# BIBLIOGRAPHY

Binns, L. Elliott. *The Book of Numbers.* Westminster Commentaries. London: Methuen & Co., 1927.

Bush, George. *Notes, Critical and Practical, on the Book of Numbers.* 1858. Reprint. Minneapolis: Klock & Klock Christian Publishers, 1981.

# Numbers

Honeycutt, Roy L., Jr. *Leviticus, Numbers, Deuteronomy*. Layman's Bible Book Commentary. Nashville: Broadman Press, 1979.

Jensen, Irving L. *Numbers, Deuteronomy*. Bible Self-Study Series. Chicago: Moody Press, 1970.

Keil, C.F., and Delitzsch, F. "The Fourth Book of Moses (Numbers)." In *Commentary on the Old Testament in Ten Volumes*. Vol. 1. Reprint (25 vols. in 10). Grand Rapids: Wm. B. Eerdmans Publishing Co., 1982.

Lange, John Peter. "Numbers." In *Commentary on the Holy Scriptures, Critical, Doctrinal and Homiletical*. Vol. 3. Translated by Philip Schaff. Reprint. Grand Rapids: Zondervan Publishing House, 1980.

Noorditzij, A. *Numbers: Bible Student's Commentary*. Grand Rapids: Zondervan Publishing House, 1983.

Noth, Martin. *Numbers: A Commentary*. Philadelphia: Westminster Press, 1968.

Snaith, N.H. *Leviticus and Numbers*. Rev. ed. New Century Bible Series. Greenwood, S.C.: Attic Press, 1977.

Sturdy, John. *Numbers*. The Cambridge Bible Commentary. New York: Cambridge University Press, 1976.

Wenham, Gordon J. *Numbers: An Introduction and Commentary*. Downers Grove, Ill.: InterVarsity Press, 1981.

# DEUTERONOMY

## Jack S. Deere

## INTRODUCTION

**Title.** The English title Deuteronomy stems from the Septuagint's mistranslation of Deuteronomy 17:18, "this repetition of the Law." The Septuagint translated those words *deuteronomion* (lit., "second Law"), which were rendered *Deuteronomium* in the Vulgate, Jerome's fourth-century Latin translation of the Bible. The Hebrew title of the book is *'ēlleh haddᵉbārîm* ("these are the words") in keeping with the Hebrew custom of often titling a work by its first word(s) (see 1:1). This Hebrew title is a more apt description of the book for it is not a "second Law," but the record of Moses' sermons on the Law.

**Date and Authorship.** The Mosaic authorship of Deuteronomy was almost universally held by both Jews and Christians until the rise of liberal criticism in the 19th century. Liberal scholars have never agreed on who they think wrote the book except that most agree it was not Moses. Most critics say it was written in the seventh century B.C. One of their reasons for this date is the discovery of "the Book of the Law" in the temple in Josiah's reign (2 Kings 22). Many critics assumed that "the Book of the Law" referred to Deuteronomy and that it had been written in the name of Moses as a pious fraud, then placed in the temple so that at its "discovery" it could be used to effect the reforms Josiah later carried out.

Another reason given for a late date of Deuteronomy is God's command for Israel to have a central sanctuary (Deut. 12:1-14). This was thought to be a thinly disguised reference to Jerusalem and a polemic against worship at the "high places." Critics argued that neither Jerusalem nor high places were prominent during the Mosaic period.

A third reason critics say Deuteronomy was written in the seventh century is

that some material in the book was obviously post-Mosaic (e.g., chap. 34, which records Moses' death).

A fourth argument used for a late date and against a Mosaic authorship is that Deuteronomy includes several predictions of the Dispersion and subsequent regathering of Israel (4:25-31; 28:20-68; 29:22-28; 30:1-10; 32:23-43).

On close examination, however, none of these four arguments is decisive. It is impossible to know whether "the Book of the Law" discovered in the temple in Josiah's reign was the entire Pentateuch, the Book of Deuteronomy, or a portion of either. If it were Deuteronomy, it does not follow that "the Book of the Law" was a pious fraud "planted" in the temple to effect a reform. Law codes were often laid aside or ignored in the ancient Near East and it is entirely possible that this could have happened with a portion or all of the Pentateuch. This would be especially likely in view of the two kings Manasseh and Amon, who preceded Josiah and promoted idolatry in the temple! Also the production of "pious frauds" was virtually unknown in the ancient Near East. The parallels cited by the critics come from the much later Greco-Roman period.

Concerning the command in Deuteronomy 12 for a central sanctuary it ought to be observed that nowhere in the book is Jerusalem mentioned. If Deuteronomy were a forgery for the purpose of effecting reform by eradicating the high places in favor of the centralization of worship at Jerusalem, it is almost unthinkable that Jerusalem would not be mentioned. Furthermore, it is doubtful that a forger would have left 27:1-8 in the book if the centralization of worship at Jerusalem was his main concern, for these verses contain a command to build an altar on Mount Ebal and offer sacrifices there and to write the Law on stones there.

Concerning the post-Mosaic additions it is clear that certain editorial comments were added after Moses' death (in addition to chap. 34, other examples are 2:10-12, 20-23; 3:13b-14). However, the presence of these additions does not prove that Moses did not write the bulk of Deuteronomy, nor do they do violence to the verbal inspiration of the Bible (see comments on 2:10-12).

The argument arising from the presence of predictions concerning the Dispersion and regathering of the nation originates from a bias against supernatural predictive prophecy. So it may be concluded that there is no substantial reason for not taking Deuteronomy for what it claims to be, the words of Moses to the nation at the end of the 15th century B.C. as Israel was about to enter the Promised Land.

**Structure.** Deuteronomy follows the pattern of the vassal treaties typical of the second millennium B.C. When a king (a suzerain) made a treaty with a vassal country the treaty usually contained six elements: (a) a preamble, (b) a historical prologue (a history of the king's dealings with the vassal), (c) a general stipulation (a call for wholehearted allegiance to the king), (d) specific stipulations (detailed laws by which the vassal state could give concrete expression to its allegiance to the king), (e) divine witnesses (deities called to witness the treaty), and (f) blessings and curses (for obedience or disobedience to the treaty). See the chart "The Mosaic Covenant Compared with Suzerainty Treaties" near Exodus 19.

Deuteronomy approximates this structure, for 1:1-4 constitutes a preamble; 1:5–4:43 a historical prologue; 4:44–11:32 a general stipulation; chapters 12–26 specific stipulations; and chapters 27–28 blessings and curses. (Of course Yahweh, being the only true God, did not call on other deities to witness the treaty.) These correspondences and others are given specific attention in this commentary. These parallels with the form of vassal treaties of the second millennium B.C. also argue for an early date for the Book of Deuteronomy.

**Purpose.** Though Deuteronomy follows the vassal treaty form, in general it is more sermonic in nature. Moses was preaching the Law to Israel to impress

God's Word on their hearts. His goal was to get the people to renew the covenant made at Sinai, that is, to make a fresh commitment to the Lord. Only by unreservedly committing themselves to the Lord could the people hope to enter the Promised Land, conquer its inhabitants, and then live in prosperity and peace.

The fact that Israel was soon to enter the Promised Land is indicated by almost 200 references to the "land" in Deuteronomy (1:7). Moses repeatedly urged the people to "take possession" of the land (1:8), encouraging them not to be afraid of the enemy (1:21). Israel was to realize that this was their "inheritance" from the Lord (4:20) for God had given it to them by "oath" (4:31) as promised to their "forefathers" (1:35). They were to "remember" (4:10) what God had already done for them, and to "obey" Him (4:30), "fear" Him (5:29), "love" Him (6:5), and "hold fast" to Him (10:20). (The words in quotation marks each occur frequently in Deuteronomy; the references in parentheses show where comments are made on those words.)

# OUTLINE

# COMMENTARY

## I. Introduction: The Historical Setting of Moses' Speeches (1:1-4)

### A. *The speaker, audience, and location (1:1)*

**1:1.** The reference to Deuteronomy as **the words** of **Moses** reminded the readers that though the book was a covenant renewal document it was not a *lifeless* legal contract. "The words" of "Moses" suggest that the book's contents were given in a series of strong sermons to the wandering people.

Moses was eminently qualified to speak for God. He was more than Israel's human Lawgiver. He was the founder of Israel's religion and mediator of the covenant at Sinai (see comments on chap. 5). He was Israel's first prophet (34:10). Though God called Abraham a prophet (Gen. 20:7), Israel did not then exist as a nation. Through Moses, God set such a high standard for the people that all subsequent prophets lived under his shadow, never attaining to it, until the coming of the Lord Jesus Christ (cf. comments on Deut. 18:15-19; 34:10-12). Not surprisingly the New Testament authors mentioned Moses more frequently than

any other Old Testament person. So Deuteronomy is essentially a series of sermons by the greatest Old Testament prophet.

Moses' words were addressed **to all Israel,** an expression used at least 12 times in the book. Its frequent occurrence emphasizes the unity of Israel which was brought about by God's mighty deliverance of the nation from Egypt, and by her acceptance of His covenant at Sinai. They were uniquely God's people, the only nation on earth that had as its "constitution" the Word of God. Moses' words, then, had a special importance for every Israelite.

Except for **Jordan** and **the Arabah,** the exact locations of the place names given in 1:1 are not known with any certainty. The Arabah is the large rift valley that extends from the Sea of Kinnereth (later the Sea of Galilee) in the north to the Gulf of Aqaba in the south. Israel was not yet in the Promised Land, but was perched at its entrance (cf. v. 5) as they received Moses' final instructions.

### B. *The date (1:2-4)*

**1:2.** The references in verses 2-3 to time serve two functions. First, they place the revelation of God squarely in history. Second, the pathetic contrast of the **11 days** (v. 2) with the 40 years (v. 3) serves as an ominous reminder of the consequences of disobeying God. The Israelites turned an 11-day journey—**from Horeb** (another word for Mount Sinai; cf. Ex. 34:2, 27 with Deut. 5:2) **to Kadesh Barnea,** the first site for entering into the Promised Land from the south—into a 40-year wandering in the wilderness before they came to a second potential site for entering the land. From Horeb to Kadesh Barnea was only about 150 miles (see the map "Possible Route of the Exodus," near Num. 33:1-5).

The warning was implicitly sounded: do not be slow to believe God again. Unfortunately for Israel, they never fully heeded this warning. As Stephen pointed out centuries later (Acts 7:39, 51), the Israelites had always been slow to believe God.

**1:3. In the 40th** and final **year** of Israel's wilderness wanderings **Moses** gave his speeches, words **that the LORD** (Yahweh) **had** given him. Moses acted on the authority of his God. In the Old Testament, God was addressed as Yahweh when the writers wanted to stress the personal nature of the One who enters into covenant with people and imposes His moral will on them (cf. comments on Ex. 3:13-14). Therefore Yahweh is the normal designation for God when His dealings with Israel are in view.

Sometime after the close of the Old Testament canon (the end of the fifth century B.C.) the Jews developed a superstition about pronouncing the name Yahweh and began to pronounce it with a rough equivalent of the vowels for Adonai ("Lord or Master") when reading the Scriptures publicly. This was an unfortunate loss for the saints. Christians today no longer address God as Yahweh in their prayers because God's personal revelation of Himself is fully realized in Jesus Christ (Heb. 1:1-2). Now Christians know God even more personally as their Father (John 14:6; 20:17; Rom. 1:17; 8:15; 1 Cor. 1:3), a designation only infrequently used of God in the Old Testament. The authority behind Moses' first speech (in Deut. 1:5–4:43) was Yahweh, Israel's personal God.

**1:4.** The historical background to Moses' first speech is made complete with the note about the defeat of two kings, **Sihon** and **Og** (cf. Num. 21:21-35; Deut. 2:26–3:11).

## II. The First Address by Moses: Historical Prologue (1:5–4:43)

Like the great Hittite suzerainty treaties of the second millennium B.C., Deuteronomy includes a historical prologue. As in those treaties the benevolent acts of mighty kings for their vassals were given, so God's gracious and mighty acts for Israel are recalled (1:5–3:29). A king in a suzerainty treaty, on the basis of his benevolent acts, exhorted his people to be completely loyal to him. Similarly God exhorted the Israelites to faith and obedience (4:1-41).

### A. The review of God's mighty acts between Horeb and Beth Peor (1:5–3:29)

1. THE FIRST ATTEMPT TO ENTER THE PROMISED LAND (1:5-46)

a. The beginning at Horeb (1:5-18)

**1:5.** When **Moses** expounded these words, Israel was **east of the Jordan**

**in . . . Moab.** The word **expound** is significant for it means that Moses did all he could to make God's Word clear to the Israelites. The word *bā'ēr* is used only here and in 27:8 (where it is rendered by the adverbs "very clearly") and in Habakkuk 2:2 ("make it plain"). Basically the verb means "to dig" (e.g., to dig a well; "well" is *bᵉ'ēr*).

In the course of these speeches Moses sought in various ways to instill an obedient spirit in his audience. He used the threat of judgment, the promise of reward, and appeals to God's graciousness to seek to accomplish that goal. The word translated **Law** actually means "instruction," not merely a body of laws in the modern sense. It is instruction in how to walk with God.

**1:6-8.** The first words of the speech, **the Lord** (Yahweh) **our God,** have a particular emphasis in the Hebrew sentence and set the tone for the entire speech. In fact in Deuteronomy the words "the Lord our God" occur almost 50 times. Yahweh is the sovereign Leader of Israel's history. When the covenant was ratified and the revelation at Sinai (**Horeb;** cf. v. 2) completed, He directed the nation to Canaan. The boundaries (v. 7; cf. 11:24; Ex. 23:31) go beyond the territory that Israel ever actually possessed. Though David's and Solomon's empires extended to **the Euphrates** River (cf. 2 Sam. 8:3; 1 Kings 4:21), many of the peoples in that territory were subjects only by paying tribute; they were not conquered by Israelites so the land was not fully possessed by them. (On **the Amorites** see comments on Gen. 14:13-16; Ex. 3:8.) **The western foothills** in Canaan were toward the Mediterranean Sea next to **the seacoast. The Negev** was the extensive desert area west and southwest of the Dead Sea.

God's command (Deut. 1:8) to **take possession** (by conquest) of so vast an area should not have shocked His hearers. The promise of that same **land** had been given in a covenant hundreds of years earlier **to Abraham** (Gen. 15:18-21; 17:7-8), and reiterated to **Isaac and Jacob** (Gen. 26:3-5; 28:13-15; 35:12). These three patriarchs are mentioned seven times in Deuteronomy (Deut. 1:8; 6:10; 9:5, 27; 29:13; 30:20; 34:4). Moses left no doubt about the nature of this promise. It was gracious and it was permanent. When the Lord seals His promise with an oath (**swore**; cf. 1:35) He will never change that plan (cf. Ps. 110:4).

So from Abraham on to the nation at Moses' time each Israelite was to realize that he stood in the line of God's inviolable promise. The command to "take possession" (which occurs 18 times in Deut.: 1:8, 21, 39; 2:24; etc.) directed Israel's attention to more than the land. They were to be encouraged to fight for the land, realizing that it was already given to them through the Lord's covenantal faithfulness. This emphasis on the "land" is unusually strong in Deuteronomy, for this word occurs almost 200 times.

**1:9-18.** If the nation had any doubt about God's intention or ability to fulfill His ancient covenant with Abraham she had only to look at her present condition. Israel had become so numerous that they were like **the stars in the sky** (v. 10). This, of course, was one thing God had promised Abraham and Isaac (Gen. 15:5; 22:17; 26:4; Ex. 32:13). The nation's growth thus proved both God's intention and ability to fulfill His original promises to Abraham. Moses was confident God would continue to **increase . . . and bless** them, for they had the same Lord as their ancestors. **The God of your fathers** is a common title of **the Lord** in Deuteronomy (cf. Deut. 1:21; 4:1; 6:3; 12:1; 27:3). The words "the Lord your God" (1:10) occur over 250 times in Deuteronomy, no doubt to affirm to Israel that her God is not some dead pagan god but is Yahweh, the living Lord who made a covenant with her.

The fulfillment of this particular promise, however, had caused a problem. The nation had become **too** large for Moses to govern effectively (vv. 9, 12; cf. Ex. 18:13-27), so he had to appoint military leaders (**commanders**), **officials** (perhaps scribes or administrators), and **judges** (Deut. 1:15-16). The recording of these events is not incidental or parenthetical to Moses' discourse. The concern shown in the choice of **wise and respected men** (v. 15; cf. v. 13) and the command for fairness (**judge fairly,** v. 16) and absolute impartiality in **judgment** (v. 17; cf. 16:19; Prov. 18:5; 24:23) made it clear that the point of the Conquest was for Israel to establish righteousness and holiness in the Promised Land and ulti-

mately in the entire world (cf. Deut. 28:1, 9-10, 13). It took faith for Israel to conquer the land, but it also took faith for them to administer justice in the land, for here too they would encounter opposition.

### b. The failure at Kadesh Barnea (1:19-46)

**1:19-21.** As the first step toward conquering the land the Israelites had to travel **through** the **vast and dreadful desert** (cf. 8:15; 32:10), a journey from Horeb to Kadesh Barnea of more than 100 miles over an essentially waterless wilderness. This first step was perhaps designed by **God** to create a hunger in their hearts for the fruitfulness and beauty of the Promised Land. It also gave **God** the opportunity to demonstrate His fatherly love for them and His ability to protect them in a hostile environment (cf. 1:31). Both motivations—hunger for the land and confidence in God's love and power—were necessary if they were to accomplish the goal ahead of them. Moses' command to the people **not to be afraid** (another emphasis in Deut.: vv. 21, 29; 3:2, 22; 7:18; 20:1, 3; 31:6, 8; cf. Josh. 1:9; 8:1) shows that he realized the enormity of the task to **take possession** (cf. Deut. 1:8) of **the land** of **the Amorites,** but he was also aware of the sufficiency of their **God** for that task.

**1:22-25.** The second step involved sending out **12 men, 1 . . . from each tribe,** as spies into **the land.** Though the people initiated this plan (vv. 22-23), the Lord agreed to it (Num. 13:1-2). It was therefore not an act of unbelief initially but rather a wise step in the necessary preparations for battle. When the spies returned, part of their report was encouraging. The land was unusually fruitful (Deut. 1:25; Num. 13:23-27). **The Valley of Eschol** (lit., "cluster of grapes") was located near Hebron (cf. Num. 13:22-23) and even today that area is famous for its grapes. For this reason it was called **a good land,** a phrase used 10 times in Deuteronomy (1:25, 35; 3:25; 4:21-22; 6:18; 8:7, 10; 9:6; 11:17) to encourage Israel to undertake the Conquest. Moses did not explicitly mention the second half of the spies' report here, but their description of the land's inhabitants was so terrifying that almost all the people were discouraged (Num. 13:28-33).

**1:26-33.** In their fear the Israelites exaggerated about the size of the cities in Canaan, saying they were walled up to the sky. The most terrifying feature of the spies' report seems to have been the mention of the presence of the Anakites (v. 28) in Canaan, traditionally identified as an ancient clan of giants (cf. Num. 13:32-33). Out of cowardice the people rebelled and grumbled against the LORD (cf. Ex. 15:24; 16:2; 17:3). This illustrates how deliberate, defiant sin corrupts one's view of God. The people claimed, the LORD hates us, and said He delivered them from Egypt only to destroy them by the hands of the Amorites. Israel had reasoned in a similar way in the wilderness (Ex. 16:3; 17:3). Their description of the people (stronger and taller than we are) reveals that they thought their task was impossible for both themselves and God.

Moses, on the other hand, who was not in rebellion against the Lord, had the same set of facts as the people but interpreted those facts differently. God did not hate His people; He loved them with the tender love a father has for his helpless little son (Deut. 1:31). All the people needed to do was to look back into their recent past when God miraculously delivered and sustained them in their desert journey. Furthermore, the people need not be afraid (v. 29; cf. v. 21) because the Lord did not intend to destroy them but to fight for them (v. 30; cf. 3:22; 20:4).

Ironically Moses reminded the people that God, by means of the pillar of fire by night and . . . cloud by day (cf. Ex. 13:21) had even acted as a spy for them. The Hebrew word tûr (search out, Deut. 1:33), is the same word used in Numbers 13:2-25 of the spies' activity! Moses, in contrast with the people, relied on the Word of God and his experience of God in history, allowing these two realities to interpret his circumstances and control his response to the news of the Anakites.

The people's obstinate refusal to be encouraged by God's working for them in the past makes this passage an eloquent testimony to the fickleness of human hearts. A few "experts" (10 of the 12 spies) were able to overturn the facts of God's unmistakable providential care. It is hard to imagine the stupidity of the Israelites' unbelief. Yet people today

ought to be warned. The perverse vacillation displayed here is not uniquely Israelite. James needed to warn his Christian readers—who after the crucifixion and resurrection of the Lord Jesus never had cause to doubt God's love or power—not to approach their God with a vacillating spirit (James 1:5-8).

1:34-36. The introduction of God's judgment by the phrase When the LORD heard what you said suggests God's omniscience (for the people actually grumbled secretly in their tents, v. 27). Also the declaration of His devastating judgment on that generation (v. 35) clearly presupposes His omnipotence. He had sworn (affirmed by oath; cf. 4:31) to Israel's forefathers to fulfill the Abrahamic Covenant (1:8). The word "forefathers" occurs 21 times in Deuteronomy to stress Israel's relationship to the covenant promises through the three major patriarchs. God also swore to exclude every warrior (cf. 2:14) of the rebellious generation from the Promised Land with only Caleb (1:36) and Joshua (v. 38) excepted (Num. 14:36-38). The covenantal promises to Abraham were not invalidated by this act of judgment. The descendants of Abraham would still be given the good land, but it would be given to a more obedient generation. The covenant belongs to Israel, but only an obedient Israel will enjoy the covenant. The exemption of Joshua and Caleb from judgment clearly illustrated this point. Caleb, for example, followed the LORD wholeheartedly (cf. Josh. 14:8-9, 14).

1:37-38. God's judgment even extended to Moses. God was indignant with and disappointed in Moses (as revealed in the words with me also, emphatic in Heb.; cf. 3:26; 4:21). When Moses said that he was forbidden to enter the Promised Land because of you he was not laying the ultimate blame for his judgment on the people. Rather the people's grumbling caused him to sin too. So his assistant Joshua (cf. Ex. 24:13; 33:11) would lead the people into the land.

1:39-40. The people apparently used their children as an excuse for not attempting to enter the land. Verse 39 is important for more than revealing the rationalizing effects of unbelief, for God seems to acknowledge a so-called "age of accountability" of children. Apparently children are not held accountable by God until they are aware of the difference between **good** and **bad**. However, nowhere does the Bible state what that age is.

The children were not held responsible for their parents' cowardice but were assured **possession** of **the land,** whereas the parents were sent back to **the desert** (cf. 2:1) to die. The author of Hebrews later pointed to the wilderness strewn with the corpses of this generation as a grim reminder of the consequences of a believer's lack of confidence in God's power (Heb. 3:16-19).

**1:41-46.** When the devastating judgment was announced to the people they realized the enormity of their sin and responded with an immediate confession (**We have sinned against the LORD**) and a readiness to go to battle immediately. **But** then it was too late, for **God** had already sworn to judge them.

The insincerity of their confession was made evident in a second act of rebellion. The fickleness of the people is again underscored. They rebelled at first out of cowardice and unbelief in the Lord's ability to fight for them. They **rebelled** a second time in **arrogance** (v. 43) thinking they could win the battle without His help. Their defeat by **the Amorites** who **chased** them **like a swarm of bees** in **the hill country** (cf. v. 41b), made it plain that they were under the resolute and inescapable judgment of their God (cf. Num. 14:40-45). The exact location of the city of **Hormah** is not known, but it was in the Negev, the southern portion of Canaan, later assigned to Judah (Josh. 15:30) and then to Simeon (Josh. 19:4; cf. Jud. 1:17). **Seir** was an early name for Edom (Gen. 32:3; Deut. 2:4-5, 8, 12, 22, 29).

The people **wept** over their defeat but God would not change His mind and let them enter the land.

2. A NEW BEGINNING: THE JOURNEY
THROUGH THE TRANSJORDAN (2:1-25)

a. *The journey from Kadesh Barnea to Mount Seir (2:1-8)*

**2:1.** The words **a long time** designate the 40 years of wandering through the wilderness (cf. "many days," 1:46). In spite of this 40-year judgment of that ungrateful and rebellious generation God had not given up His people, for Moses could still say **the LORD had directed me.** God was still guiding the nation through

His Prophet Moses and had not abandoned His plan to give them the land of Canaan for their home.

**2:2-7.** God then told Moses to leave the **hill country** (west of Seir or Edom) and go through **Seir,** the home of Esau's **descendants** (cf. Gen. 36:8-9). God warned Israel to avoid fighting with them. This likelihood of **war** may have been because of the scarcity of rainfall in that area (only about five inches annually). A large contingent of people moving through Seir could easily deplete the Edomites' store of water. Therefore God told Israel **to pay** for whatever they ate and drank in order to avoid hostilities. (The Edomites, in fact, refused to grant the Israelites right of passage, Num. 20:14-21.)

These careful instructions show that the Israelites were not free to try to conquer any territory they wanted. Rather, God had promised them a definite land, and the war they would wage in order to conquer Canaan had a moral character to it (thus OT scholars have referred to it as a "holy war"; see comments on Deut. 7). These instructions as well as the clause **I have given Esau the hill country of Seir** (2:5) show that the Lord is sovereign over all lands and all peoples. This sovereignty should have encouraged the Israelites to enter Canaan and fight with courage. For since God honored the right of Edom—and also Moab (vv. 8-9) and Ammon (vv. 19)—to possess their land, how much more would He honor Israel's right to possess Canaan, which was guaranteed to them by His covenantal oath to the patriarchs! The Lord's protective care of Israel in the **vast desert** for **40 years** (v. 7) also motivated them to obey His immediate instructions.

**2:8.** Instead of going through **Seir** (Edom) up **the Arabah Road** to the southern part of Canaan, the Israelites traveled north **along the** east side of Edom (cf. comments on v. 29) up through **Moab** (cf. v. 18). (See the map "Possible Route of the Exodus," near Num. 33:1-5.) **Elath** is a later name for **Ezion Geber,** a seaport at the Gulf of Aqabah.

b. *The journey past Moab and Ammon (2:9-25)*

**2:9-13.** After God's command to treat **the Moabites** (the city of **Ar** was in

Moab), Lot's **descendants** (Gen. 19:36-37), as carefully as the Edomites (Deut. 2:4-6), a post-Mosaic editor inserted an explanatory note (vv. 10-12). Though it is impossible to determine precisely when verses 10-12 were inserted, verse 12 indicates that it was after the initial conquest of the land. Editorial notes in the Pentateuch do no harm to the doctrine of biblical inspiration (see "Date and Authorship" in the *Introduction*). Inspiration refers to the final product rather than to the manner of writings. The original texts of Scripture are "God-breathed" (2 Tim. 3:16), and therefore contain no errors, for God cannot lie (Titus 1:2). The Holy Spirit superintended the work of editors just as He did the historical research of Luke (Luke 1:1-4) so that the final words of the text, though obtained by different methods, are the words intended by God. It was this final text (including editorial insertions) that Jesus Christ pronounced perfect (e.g., Matt. 5:18; John 10:35).

On **the Anakites** (Deut. 2:11) see comments on 1:28. The **Rephaites** were an ancient tribe known for their tall stature (also mentioned in Gen. 14:5; 15:20; Deut. 2:20; 3:11, 13; Josh. 12:4; 13:12; 17:15; 1 Chron. 20:4). **The Moabites called** the Rephaites **Emites,** which means "terrors" or "dreaded ones." The **Horites** may have been the non-Semitic Hurrian people who lived in scattered groups in Palestine, Syria, and Mesopotamia. They occupied **Seir** before **Esau** moved there (Gen. 14:6; 36:8-9, 20) and **drove them out.** The fact that the Moabites could dispossess these **strong . . . numerous, and . . . tall** people underscored Israel's cowardice and faithlessness, who even with God's help shrank back from these same people (cf. Deut. 1:28; Num. 13:28, 33). These explanatory notes leave the impression that no enemy is invincible. If the Moabites could drive out the Anakites (Emites) and if Esau's descendants could expel the Horites, then surely God could give Canaan to Israel. This puts God's command to **cross the Zered Valley** in Moab (Deut. 2:13) in a fresh light.

**2:14-15.** Moses again reminded his audience of the terrible judgment that his own rebellious generation had suffered (1:35, 39). He made it clear **that** the **entire generation of fighting men** (cf. 2:16) did

not die of natural deaths during the previous **38 years** in the wilderness. The fact that **the Lord's hand was against** a people often meant that He sent a destroying pestilence against them (cf. Ex. 9:15; 1 Sam. 5:6-7, 9, 11; 6:3, 5, 9; 2 Sam. 24:17). Also the first part of Deuteronomy 2:15 should be rendered, "The Lord's hand was against them to panic [or confuse] them." The verb for "panic or confuse" (*hāmam*) is used for the divinely inspired panic that God sent on many of Israel's enemies so that they became too confused or terrified to fight competently.

Thus because of their rebellion against the Lord this first generation of Israelite warriors actually found *themselves* objects of God's "holy war." They left the protective care of His hand in their arrogant rebellion only to find that hand turned against them as they endured painful deaths outside the Promised Land. By reminding the people of this, Moses said in effect that God is faithful to His promises and His threats, and has the power to execute both.

**2:16-19.** God had told Israel not to molest Esau's descendants (vv. 4-5) or the Moabites (v. 9); now He said the same about **the Ammonites.** Israel was not to attack **the Ammonites** for they, like the Moabites, were Lot's **descendants** (cf. Gen. 19:36-38).

**2:20-23.** Verses 20-23 are another editorial insertion (cf. vv. 10-12). The Ammonites' destruction of **the Rephaites,** called **Zamzummites,** and Esau's descendants' destruction of **the Horites,** are attributed ultimately to God. For as Paul later wrote, it was He who set the times and boundaries for all the peoples of the earth (Acts 17:26). Even **the Avvites** living **as far** west **as Gaza** were destroyed by another people. **Caphtorites** is probably an early name for the Philistines, who came **from Caphtor,** another name for Crete.

**2:24-25.** God's command to dispossess **Sihon the Amorite king** of the city **of Heshbon** is another illustration of God's sovereignty over all **nations. The terror and fear** God would **put** in those **nations** constituted an essential "weapon" for Israel in this war and the Conquest (cf. Ex. 15:15; 23:27; Num. 22:3; Josh. 2:9, 11, 24; 5:1; 9:24).

3. THE CONQUEST OF THE TRANSJORDAN
(2:26–3:29)

a. The defeat of Sihon
(2:26-37)

This section (cf. Num. 21:21-35) describes the beginning of Israel's conquest of the land, a war that had been delayed for 40 years.

**2:26-29.** Moses recalled his peaceful offer **to Sihon,** an offer that had several things to commend it to the Amorite king. Moses promised they would not leave **the main road,** and therefore no plunder of the crops need be feared. The Israelites had already passed through the territories of Edom and Moab without war (v. 29). The Edomites had refused the right of passage to the Israelites (Num. 20:18-21). Probably the Edomites allowed Israel to pass by on their eastern border though they refused to let them pass through the middle of their territory. Moses also told Sihon that Israel's ultimate destiny was not the territory of Sihon but was on the other side of **the Jordan** in **the land the Lord** was **giving** them.

**2:30-37.** Sihon rejected this peaceful offer. The Hebrew verbs used to express the "hardening" of Sihon's mind and will (**heart**) can mean that the Lord "confirmed" what was already in Sihon's heart, namely, his arrogance against **the Lord** and His people Israel (cf. comments on Ex. 4:21 on the hardening of Pharaoh's heart). Sihon's arrogant refusal was a sure sign that he had just thrown away his one chance of survival. Since God controls all of history, Moses could say that **the Lord our God delivered him over to us.**

**Completely destroyed** (Deut. 2:34) translates ḥāram, "to give over [to the Lord] often by total destruction" (see NIV marg. and comments on Josh. 6:21). In Deuteronomy ḥāram also is used in 3:6; 7:2; 20:17. See chapter 7 for a discussion of the question of the morality of killing the total population—**men, women, and children.** The statement that **not one town was too strong for us** was a sharp reminder to the Israelites. The Hebrew sentence literally reads "not a town was too high for us." The high walls of the Canaanite cities terrified the first generation of Israelite warriors (1:28) so that they disobeyed the Lord's **command** to enter **the land.**

b. The defeat of Og (3:1-11)

**3:1-7. Bashan** was a little farther north than the Israelites needed to go to reach their point of entry into the Promised Land. However, in defeating **Og** on the north they were protecting their right flank when they turned to cross the Jordan. **Edrei,** where the battle began, was about 30 miles east of the southern tip of the Sea of Kinnereth (Sea of Galilee). God's command for Israel to battle Og (**Do not be afraid;** cf. comments on 1:21) rested on two assurances: God had **handed him over to** Israel, and Israel had recently gained victory over **Sihon.** Again God was credited with the outcome of the battle (3:3; cf. 2:30-31). And as in the case of Sihon's cities (2:32-36), Og's **60 cities** (with **high walls,** 3:5; see comments on 2:36) could not restrain the Israelite warriors. The **region of Argob** (3:4) was another name for Bashan or was a part of Bashan. It was known as the land of the Rephaites (v. 13). The trust of Israel's soldiers in the word of their God contrasts with the unbelieving warriors referred to in 1:28. On the total destruction of the inhabitants (3:6) see the comments on ḥāram in 2:34 and those on chapter 7.

**3:8-11.** These verses summarize the conquest of the territory controlled by the two Transjordanian Amorite **kings,** Sihon and **Og.** The Israelites needed the encouragement of repeated reminders of God's past faithfulness to them. Two aspects of this summary particularly heartened the Israelites. First, these verses stress the extensive nature of the Israelite conquest: **from the Arnon Gorge** to **Mount Hermon (called Sirion by the** Phoenicians of Sidon and called **Senir by the Amorites**). Second, Og was one of the last **of the Rephaites** the Israelites would face in battle. Og's iron **bed** was probably his coffin (sarcophagus, NIV marg.), which measured 6 feet wide by 13½ feet long.

c. The distribution of the conquered land (3:12-22)

**3:12-17.** The Transjordan was divided among the tribes of Reuben, Gad, and **the half tribe of Manasseh.** (See the map "Land Allotted to Israel's Tribes," near Josh. 13.) Reuben received the Moabite **territory** from the **Arnon Gorge** to Heshbon. Gad was given the southern **half**

... **of Gilead** from Heshbon to the Jabbok River. To the half tribe of Manasseh went the northern part **of Gilead** and **also . . . Bashan,** which was east of the Sea of Kinnereth (later named the Sea of Galilee; see comments on Josh. 11:2). **Og** was over this northern part of Gilead and Bashan. **Jair, a descendant of Manasseh,** was singled out for special mention (Deut. 3:14) because of his courage in capturing **the whole region of Argob** in Bashan (cf. v. 4; Num. 32:41). As a result the area **was named after him.** Likewise, **to Makir** (Deut. 3:15), a subtribe of the tribe of Manasseh, was given the rest of **Gilead** because they conquered that territory (Num. 32:34-40).

**3:18-20.** Numbers 32 records the request of two and one-half tribes for the Transjordan. They had acquired a large number of cattle and sheep (cf. Num. 32:1) and this region was especially well suited for raising cattle. At first Moses was angry at their request, fearing another defection like that at Kadesh Barnea (Num. 32:6-8, 14-15). But when the warriors of the tribes promised to **cross over** the Jordan and fight till all Israel had won her land, Moses granted their request. Since the time for battle was drawing near, the tribes east of the Jordan needed this reminder of their prior commitment (Num. 32:16-19). They could leave their new homes and family without fear because **the LORD** had **given** them **this land.** They could cross over the Jordan River and fight fearlessly for their **brothers** and then return to their families.

**3:21-22.** These two verses are a transition from the distribution of the land (vv. 12-20) to Moses' loss of leadership (vv. 23-29). Moses had reminded his audience that the time for the conquest of Canaan was near (vv. 18-20). Yet **Joshua,** not Moses, would lead the people in that conquest. By encouraging Joshua here Moses himself was obeying God's command (1:38; 3:28). Moses' firm assurance that **the LORD** had acted like a warrior for Israel in the past and would do so in the future greatly encouraged Israel's future leader. Joshua need **not be afraid** (cf. comments on 1:17). Moses' words also represented a major theme in Deuteronomy's historical prologue: the battle belongs to Yahweh (**the LORD your God . . . will fight for you;** cf. 1:30; 20:4; also note 2:24-25, 31, 33, 36; 3:2-3).

### d. Moses forbidden to enter the Promised Land (3:23-29)

**3:23-25.** God had made it clear to Moses that he would not be permitted to enter the Promised Land because of his unbelief at the waters of Meribah (Num. 20:12). However, in Moses' mind a new turn of events was indicated by his statement **You have begun to show to Your servant Your greatness.** This probably refers to the Lord's omnipotence revealed in the conquest of Sihon and Og, Transjordan's two Amorite kings, rather than to the events of the Exodus from Egypt. Since God let Moses take part in conquering the Transjordan, he may have thought the Lord intended to rescind His earlier prohibition about his not entering Canaan. Therefore this seemed an opportune time for him to ask God about his going in after all to **see the good land** (cf. comments on Deut. 1:25).

The question in 3:24 beginning with **For what god** does not imply that Moses believed in the existence of other gods. It is a rhetorical question, one of the ways the Old Testament expresses the incomparability of the Lord. He is totally unique in His attributes; no one compares with Him.

**3:26-29.** God **would not listen to** Moses, that is, He would not grant his request. In fact the Hebrew sentence implies that Moses had kept on asking God for permission, and that God became "furious" (an intensive form of *'ābar*) with him (NIV has a milder word, **angry;** cf. 1:37; 4:21). This conversation reveals something of the intimacy of Moses' relationship with God. It also heightens the feeling of tragedy in the experience of a man who devoted his life to fulfilling God's promise for Israel but knew he would never see its completion. But Moses could at least **look at the land** from the peak of Mount **Pisgah.**

Since Moses could not lead the people across Jordan, God reminded him of his responsibility to prepare **Joshua** for leadership. Joshua's succession to leadership is an important theme in Deuteronomy. This is the third time it has been mentioned in only three chapters (1:38; 3:21, 28). By merely repeating God's words on this subject to the people, Moses was encouraging Joshua and showing the people that Joshua was their next leader.

## B. An exhortation to obey the Law and resist idolatry (4:1-43)

### 1. THE PURPOSE OF THE LAW (4:1-8)

**4:1-2.** The words **Hear now** introduce the practical conclusions to be drawn from Israel's experience in the wilderness. Because of the Lord's faithfulness, mercy, and judgment displayed in her recent history, the nation was responsible to obey His **decrees and laws** unconditionally. "Decrees" may refer to permanent rules of conduct, statutory laws which are immutable, while "laws" may refer to case laws, decisions handed down by judges. It was crucial that Moses **teach** Israel this Law, for the motive clause **so that you may live and . . . take possession of the land** indicates that a full enjoyment of life is based on obeying God's Law. Israel must **not add to** it and thereby weaken its power, as the Pharisees and later Christian legalists would do. Nor must Israel **subtract** anything **from it** to accommodate the willfulness or weakness of human nature.

**4:3-4.** Moses referred to the incident **at Baal Peor** in Moab to illustrate from the Israelites' own history that their very lives depended on obeying God's Law. At **Baal of Peor** all the Israelites who entered into spiritual and physical adultery with the Moabite women were either put to death by the sword or died in a plague (24,000 died in the plague). On the other hand **all . . . who held fast to the LORD** lived. This incident is also mentioned in Numbers 25:1-9; Psalm 106:28-29; Hosea 9:10.

**4:5-8.** One purpose of the Law was to give the Israelites a full life as they obeyed God (vv. 1-4). In verses 5-8 another purpose of the Law is revealed: to make Israel morally and spiritually unique among all the nations and thereby draw other nations to **the LORD.** In contrast with all other nations Israel was not to be distinguished by her natural resources, wealth, or military might, but by her moral skill and close relationship to God, both of which would come from her obeying her moral constitution. If Israel would obey the Law she would be the envy of all nations. They would see her as (a) being **wise and understanding,** (b) having a **God** who is **near** her, and (c) possessing **righteous decrees and laws.**

### 2. THE PURPOSE OF THE EXPERIENCE AT HOREB (4:9-14)

**4:9.** The solemn admonition to **be careful** (an admonition that occurs numerous times in Deut.) and to **watch** implies that the Israelites constantly faced the danger of falling into a sin which would have brought them to the brink of annihilation as a nation. That sin was idolatry (vv. 15-31). The nation could become idolatrous in two related ways. The depravity of the human mind is so great that the great deeds of God for His people (e.g., the Exodus and giving of the Law at Horeb) might **slip from** their hearts if they did not constantly remind themselves of God's mighty works.

Or second, through laziness or apathy parents might fail to **teach them to** their **children** and thus their children would become idolaters. Deuteronomy lays great stress not on the priests or other religious leaders, but on the parents as the ones responsible for their children's spiritual education (vv. 9-10; 6:7, 20; 11:19; 31:13; 32:46). God trusts His great events of revelation, such as His giving the Law at Sinai, to faithful stewards who must never **forget** them and who must pass them on to their children. (Not forgetting is another emphasis in Deut., occurring in 4:9, 23, 31; 6:12; 8:11, 14, 19; 9:7; 25:19.)

**4:10-14.** The experience **at Horeb** was designed to produce a fear of **God** in the hearts of **the people** so that a covenant between them and **the LORD** could be possible. In the Old Testament the fear of God is more than awe or reverence though it includes both. Fearing God is becoming so acutely aware of His moral purity and omnipotence that one is genuinely afraid to disobey Him. Fearing God also includes responding to Him in worship, service, trust, obedience, and commitment. That day on Horeb God's *omnipotence* was displayed in the **fire . . . black clouds . . . deep darkness,** and the voice of God that thundered from the heavens. His *moral purity* was displayed in His **Ten Commandments,** called **His covenant.**

From this experience the Israelites should have learned to fear God as a Person who is *spiritual* (**you . . . saw no form;** cf. v. 15; **there was only a voice**) and as a Person who is *transcendent.* This latter point was pressed home by the fact that **He commanded** the Israelites **to fol-low** His commandments, **decrees, and laws** (which Moses would **teach** them, vv. 1, 14). The giving of the Law that day thus taught the nation that their God was a spiritual Person who could not be manipulated but instead imposed His moral will on *them*. They brought away no images of God from Horeb on that day; God gave only **two stone tablets** (probably each tablet was complete with all Ten Commandments, in keeping with ancient Near Eastern practice to have duplicates of such covenant documents). Thus in contrast with all the religions of the ancient Near East the Word of Israel's God became the foundation of their religion.

3. THE PROHIBITION AGAINST IDOLATRY
   (4:15-24)

**4:15-20.** Moses spelled out one of the implications contained in the experience at Horeb. Since the Israelites **saw no form** (cf. v. 12) of God on that **day** they were never to attempt to represent Him with any form. The religions of the ancient Near East worshiped idols in the shapes of various creatures mentioned in verses 16-18. Israel was never to limit her God in this way for it would call His transcendence into question and it would make them **corrupt** (cf. v. 25).

The worship of astral deities was also common in the ancient Near East. The **sun** was worshiped as the god Re or Aten in Egypt, and in the new land to which the Israelites were going astral worship was also common. (E.g., the city of Jericho was dedicated to the worship of the moon god.) The Israelites were not to let themselves **be enticed** (v. 19) **into** the worship of the luminaries (cf. 17:2-5) which **God** has provided for **all the nations under heaven.**

Another reason Israel was to denounce all forms of idolatry is that she was taken **out of Egypt,** an idolatrous land where the images of dozens of false gods were worshiped. (The fact that Israel was taken out of Egypt is mentioned about 20 times in Deut.) In slavery to Egypt, Israel's condition was like being in an **iron-smelting furnace.** But **now** Israel was God's **inheritance,** that is, His own unique possession (cf. 9:26, 29; Pss. 28:9; 33:12; 68:9; 78:62, 71; 79:1; 94:14; Joel 2:17; 3:2; Micah 7:14, 18).

**4:21-24.** Though Moses knew he **would not . . . enter** the Promised Land **(the good land;** cf. 1:25) he still desired it. So again he mentioned God's displeasure with him (cf. 3:26-27), and reminded the Israelites that he would not be there to enforce the prohibition against idolatry. However, **the LORD** would enforce the command. Like **a consuming fire** (4:24) He would purify what is precious (just as fire purifies precious metals) and destroy what is worthless. As **a jealous God** (cf. 5:9; 32:16, 21; see comments on 6:15) He will not allow another to have the honor that is due Him alone (Isa. 42:8; 48:11). Therefore Israel needed to **be** extremely **careful** to remember the **covenant** (cf. Deut. 4:9).

4. THE PREDICTED DISPERSION (4:25-31)

**4:25-31.** After the strong warning against idolatry (vv. 15-24) Moses spelled out the consequences of neglecting that warning (vv. 25-31). **After** the Israelites had been **in the land a long time** and had become secure they might forget the Lord and their need to trust Him alone. They would then be easily seduced into idolatrous **worship,** which would **corrupt** them (cf. vv. 15-16) and provoke God's **anger.**

Moses invoked **heaven and earth as witnesses** because of their permanence and unchanging character in contrast with the fickleness of human hearts. This certain judgment would take two forms, a dispersion **among the . . . nations** with a great loss of life (v. 27) and a giving over to idolatry (v. 28). This prophecy was fulfilled in the Assyrian and Babylonian Captivities, but its greatest fulfillment came in the dispersion of Israel after she rejected Jesus Christ.

The **later days** (v. 30) may refer to any time after the initial dispersions, but their ultimate reference is to the time when the Lord Jesus will return to earth to establish His 1,000-year kingdom (Rev. 20:4). At that time a repentant Israel will finally **seek the LORD . . . look for Him with all** her **heart and . . . soul** and will **obey Him.** (In Deut., Moses repeatedly stressed the need for wholehearted devotion to the Lord by the words "with all your heart and with all your soul"; see Deut. 4:29; 6:5; 10:12; 11:13; 13:3; 26:16; 30:6, 10.) Israel's final return to her Savior will be due not to any goodness of their human hearts, but rather to her **merciful God.** The Hebrew word translated "merciful" (*raḥûm*) refers to the tender compassion of a mother toward her helpless infant. So even if Israel forgets her God **He will not abandon** His morally helpless children because He has the tender compassion of a mother and because He made an inviolable **covenant with** Abraham and **confirmed** it **to** Isaac and Jacob (Gen. 15:18-21; 17:7-8; 26:3-5; 28:13-15; 35:12) **by oath** (mentioned 16 times in Deut.). Since God will not **forget** His covenant (Deut. 4:31) neither should Israel (v. 23).

5. THE COMMAND TO KNOW THAT THE LORD ALONE IS GOD (4:32-40)

**4:32-34.** Having spoken of the future ("later days," v. 30), Moses then spoke of **the former days**—from Creation to Sinai. Israel had had a totally unique experience of her **God.** No **other** nation could claim to have **heard the voice of God speaking out of fire.** No other nation could point to a god who had **created** it by redeeming it from a stronger **nation.** Furthermore, the true origin of this historical redemption was not open to various explanations. The voice of God, the **miraculous signs and wonders** (cf. 6:22; 7:19; 26:8; 29:3), **great and awesome deeds** (e.g., the plagues, the pillar of fire, the parting of the Red Sea, manna), and other phenomena made it clear that it was **God** who redeemed the Israelites. And He did so in a show of power and strength (**by a mighty hand and an outstretched arm**; cf. 5:15; 7:19; 11:2; Ps. 136:12; Ezek. 20:33-34).

**4:35-38.** The purpose of this miraculous deliverance was to enable the Israelites to **know,** not simply by their intellect but in their experience, **that the LORD is God** alone. The experience of hearing **from heaven . . . His** awesome **voice** and **on earth** seeing **His great fire** (at Sinai, Ex. 19:16-20) was not primarily aimed at instructing their minds, but rather at the **discipline** of their moral nature. It was meant to instill a spirit of submission and to quell the natural inclination of the human heart to arrogance. The experience of His voice and the fire, then, was designed to give them more than the content of His commandments. It was designed to make them fear to disobey those commandments. The rea-

son the Lord had taken such care to give Israel this extensive moral education was that **He** had **loved** their **forefathers** and had promised in a covenant to love **their descendants.** Because of that love He delivered them from **Egypt** (cf. Deut. 4:20), a nation stronger than Israel. And He would drive out from Canaan **nations . . . stronger than** Israel. Also He would give that **land** to Israel as her **inheritance** (cf. comments on v. 21).

**4:39-40.** In light of such electing grace and such unique revelation the Israelites were to **acknowledge** that **the LORD is God** alone (cf. v. 35) and to **keep His decrees and commands.** Only in doing these two things would the Israelites find prosperity and **long** life **in the land** (cf. 5:33; 6:2). The words **so that it may go well with you** occur eight times in this book, undoubtedly to emphasize this motive for obedience (4:40; 5:16; 6:3, 18; 12:25, 28; 19:13; 22:7). The idea that righteousness lengthens life and sin shortens it is common in the Old Testament (Prov. 3:1-2, 16; 10:27).

6. THE THREE TRANSJORDANIAN CITIES OF REFUGE (4:41-43)

**4:41-43.** This may be an editorial note placed here between the first and second addresses because at that time Moses had designated these **three cities east of the Jordan** as cities of **refuge.** They were **Bezer . . . Ramoth,** and **Golan** (see the map "The Six Cities of Refuge," near Num. 35:6-34). The significance of these **cities** will be discussed in the comments on Deuteronomy 19:1-13 (cf. Ex. 21:12-13; Num. 35:6-28; Josh. 20).

## III. The Second Address of Moses: Covenant Obligations (4:44–26:19)

In the suzerainty treaties of the second millennium B.C. the section after the historical prologue set forth the obligations of the vassals to their great king. This section containing the covenant obligations or stipulations was usually divided into two parts. The first part was a general exhortation to the vassals, encouraging total allegiance to the king or suzerain. The second part consisted of specific obligations or laws detailing how vassals were to express their complete fidelity to the suzerainty. The arrangement of Moses' second address seems to follow the same order as that of the suzerainty treaties. Moses began this speech by recalling the foundational experience at Horeb (4:44–5:33). This short section is followed by the call to total allegiance (chaps. 6–11). The speech then has an exposition of the Law that explains how the Israelites were to express their commitment to the Lord in the details of everyday life (12:1–26:15). The speech concludes with a declaration of commitment by the people and the Lord (26:16-19).

## A. Recapitulation of the Law at Horeb (4:44–5:33)

### 1. THE SETTING OF THE SECOND ADDRESS (4:44-49)

**4:44-49.** Moses set before the people God's instruction (*tôrâh,* the word rendered **Law,** means instruction) in how to walk with Him. If the Israelites were to prosper individually and nationally they had to obey **the stipulations** of the covenant expressed in the form of **decrees and laws.** These were originally given three months after the Israelites **came out of Egypt** (cf. Ex. 20:1-17; 21–23). Thus Deuteronomy is not a new covenant but the renewal of a covenant previously made. But it was repeated **east of the Jordan** River **near Beth Peor.** For details relating to **Sihon** and **Og** see comments on Deuteronomy 2:26–3:11.

### 2. THE CALL TO OBEDIENCE (5:1-5)

**5:1-5.** The solemn formula **Hear, O Israel** indicates that what follows (**the decrees and laws;** cf. 4:45) is not incidental but absolutely necessary for the survival of Israel as a nation. When **Moses . . . said** that **the LORD our God made a covenant with us at Horeb** and **not with our fathers,** he was teaching the Israelites that this covenant was meant to govern the living, not the dead. Moses had the right to say this for he was the mediator of the **covenant. The LORD spoke** with Israel **face to face** from **the mountain** of Sinai but did so through Moses (Ex. 19:9).

### 3. THE TEN COMMANDMENTS (5:6-21)

**5:6-7.** Verse 6 is crucial for understanding not only the first commandment but also the other nine. The Ten Commandments were given to a people already redeemed (**brought out . . . of**

Egypt), to enable them to express their love for and have fellowship with the holy **God.** (In Deut., Egypt is frequently called **the land of slavery:** v. 6; 6:12; 7:8; 8:14; 13:5, 10; cf. Ex. 13:3, 14; 20:2.) The Decalogue was never given to enable them to achieve justification, for that has always been granted freely through faith (cf. Gen. 15:6; Rom. 4). The Law was never designed to give people salvation.

Also since **the LORD** had taken the initiative in Israel's redemption the people were obligated to acknowledge His right of sovereignty over them and to bow to that sovereignty. The first commandment, **to have no other gods before Me,** called for a submission of every area of one's life to the rule of God. The phrase "other gods" is a technical term for pagan gods which of course existed in the form of idols and in the minds of their worshipers, but were not real.

**5:8-10.** The second commandment did not prohibit art in Israel (as the making of the tabernacle demonstrates), but rather the making of **an idol** to represent the Lord. The danger in this practice was twofold. First, since other nations used idolatry to express their devotion to their gods there was always the danger that the worship of **the Lord** could be contaminated by idolatrous forms of worship. Second, any attempt to represent **God** in any form from the natural world would have called into question the sovereignty of the One who cannot be limited by anything. As **a jealous God** (cf. 4:24; 32:16, 21; see comments on 6:15), He does not share His sovereign position with any other.

At first glance 5:9b may seem to contradict Ezekiel 18:20. However, the phrase **those who hate Me** must certainly refer to **the children,** not to **the fathers.** Children who hate the Lord will be punished. Rebellious God-hating parents often produce children **to the third and fourth generation** who also hate God (cf. Ex. 20:5; 34:6-7).

**5:11.** To **misuse** God's **name** means literally, "to lift it up to or attach it to emptiness." This command forbids using God's name in profanity but it includes more. The third commandment is a directive against using God's name in a manipulative way (e.g., His name is not to be used in magic or to curse someone). Today a Christian who uses God's name flippantly or falsely attributes a wrong act to God has broken this commandment.

**5:12-15. The Sabbath Day** was a gift of **God** to Israel. According to Exodus 20:11, Israel was to observe a **day** of rest each week so she could commemorate God's Creation of the world in six days and His rest on the seventh day. Thus Israel's observance of the **Sabbath** was a testimony to her belief in the personal, transcendent God who created the world. This belief was a doctrine unique to the ancient Near East. In Deuteronomy the reason for observing the Sabbath is not the Creation of the world, but the redemption of Israel from **Egypt,** which in effect was the creation of Israel as a nation. (The command **remember,** zākar, occurs 14 times in Deut.; the NIV has the command "remember" two additional times—4:10; 11:2—though the Heb. there has a different word. On God's **mighty hand and an outstretched arm,** see Deut. 4:34; 7:19; 11:2.) So by observing **the Sabbath** before her pagan neighbors Israel was expressing her faith in the personal God who created both the world and her as a nation.

This is the only one of the Ten Commandments not repeated in the New Testament, and Paul argued against enforcing it (cf. Rom. 14:5-6; Col. 2:16-17). The day of worship was changed in the early church to the first day of the week, in commemoration of Christ's resurrection. The temporary nature of the command regarding the Sabbath is due to the fact that it served as a "sign" of the Mosaic Covenant (cf. Ex. 31:12-17). After the Mosaic Covenant was done away with there was no longer a need for its "sign." In its place Christians have the Lord's Supper as the "sign" of the New Covenant.

**5:16.** To **honor** one's parents means to value or prize them highly. Children living at home express this by obeying their parents. This commandment was critical for the existence of the nation: **that you** (pl.) **may live long** (cf. 6:2; 11:9; 25:15; 32:47) **and that it may go well with you** (pl.) **in the land.** Parents, especially fathers, rather than the religious leaders, were to pass the covenant values to their children.

**5:17. Murder** means to take someone's life illegally. Since man was created by God and in His image, man should **not** take another human's life apart from

divine permission. (This commandment, therefore, did not prohibit capital punishment or engaging in war, both of which were regulated by laws in the Torah.)

**5:18.** The marriage relationship should reflect a believer's relationship to God. Therefore extramarital sex (**adultery**) was forbidden. Though the seventh commandment does not refer explicitly to premarital sex, the Pentateuch prohibits it elsewhere (e.g., Gen. 2:24; Ex. 22:16; Deut. 22:13-29). An Israelite who would be unfaithful to his or her partner would also be unfaithful to the covenant of God and would be inclined to go after other gods.

**5:19.** Many Bible scholars think that this eighth commandment (against stealing) refers primarily to kidnapping (cf. 24:7). It is probably more accurate, however, to view the command as a general prohibition against stealing, which would include kidnapping.

**5:20.** Though this commandment had its primary application in law courts, it could also seem to rule out gossip against one's **neighbor.** The sixth through ninth commandments thus acknowledge a person's right to his life, home, property, and reputation.

**5:21.** To **covet** means "to lust for another's property." It was different from the other commandments in that it did not deal with a specific act, but rather with an emotional, psychological sin. Therefore the breaking of this commandment could not be prosecuted in a law court. Yet "lust for another's property" often led to the breaking of the sixth through the ninth commandments. This was the point Jesus was making in His exposition of commandments six and seven (Matt. 5:21-32). It may have been possible for someone to keep the first nine commandments but no one could have avoided breaking the 10th at some time. In this respect the 10th commandment is the most forceful of all, because it made people aware of their inability to keep God's Law perfectly. And this awareness threw them back to depend on God's grace and mercy.

4. THE MEDIATORIAL ROLE OF MOSES (5:22-33)

**5:22.** This verse emphasizes the divine origin of the Ten **Commandments**

and the awe-inspiring setting in which they were given (**fire . . . cloud,** and **deep darkness;** cf. Ex. 19:18; 20:21).

**5:23-27.** The leaders' request for a mediator grew out of their encounter with their holy and majestic **God.** The experience at Horeb impressed on them a sense of their own moral inadequacy and morality (**we will die**) and their responsibility to obey **God** (**we will listen and obey**).

**5:28-29.** Though **the LORD** approved of the people's response, He hinted that they would not carry through with their good intentions. (On fearing God, see comments on 4:10.)

**5:30-33.** Again the divine origin of the Law is stressed. The people heard the Ten Commandments and then were dismissed **to their tents.** What Moses was about to tell them—all God's **commands, decrees, and laws,** beginning with chapter 6 (cf. 6:1)—was also from **the LORD** just as were the Ten Commandments. Their obedience to all that Moses was about **to teach them** was critical, for their prosperity **in the land** would depend on it (cf. 6:3, 24).

### B. The great commands and warnings (chaps. 6–11)

Having reminded his audience of the basic foundation, the Ten Commandments, which they heard at Horeb, Moses turned to details of the Law which they did not hear because they were afraid of the voice of God (cf. 5:25-27). Accordingly chapters 6–11, which may be called "the great commands and warnings," deal with the personal nature of the covenant relationship. Here the details relating to the total commitment of individuals to the Lord are discussed.

### 1. THE COMMAND TO LOVE THE LORD (CHAP. 6)

#### a. Promised blessings of obedience (6:1-3)

**6:1.** The legislation in chapters 6–11 may be viewed as an expression of one great command, namely, to "love **the LORD** your God with all your heart . . . soul, and . . . strength" (6:5). Therefore obedience on the part of the Israelites demonstrated that they loved **God.** Jesus laid down a similar principle for Christians (cf. John 14:21).

**6:2-3.** The Law was given so that the people could express their reverence

(**fear;** cf. comments on 4:10) for and obedience to **the LORD** in a concrete manner. (The need to **obey** Him is stressed repeatedly in Deut.) By fearing and obeying Him they would find prosperity (on the words **so that it may go well with you,** see comments on 4:40) and a **long life** in their new land (cf. 4:10; 5:33) which flowed **with milk and honey** (see comments on Ex. 3:8).

#### b. The command and its importance (6:4-9)

**6:4.** This verse has been called the *Shema,* from the Hebrew word translated **Hear.** The statement in this verse is the basic confession of faith in Judaism. The verse means that **the LORD** (Yahweh) is totally unique. He alone is **God.** The Israelites could therefore have a sense of security that was totally impossible for their polytheistic neighbors. The "gods" of the ancient Near East rarely were thought of as acting in harmony. Each god was unpredictable and morally capricious. So a pagan worshiper could never be sure that his loyalty to one god would serve to protect him from the capricious wrath of another. The monotheistic doctrine of the Israelites lifted them out of this insecurity since they had to deal with only one God, who dealt with them by a revealed consistent righteous standard. This confession of monotheism does not preclude the biblical doctrine of the Trinity. "God" is plural (*'ĕlōhîm*), possibly implying the Trinity, and **one** (*'eḥād*) may suggest a unity of the Persons in the Godhead (cf. Gen. 2:24, where the same word for "one" is used of Adam and Eve).

**6:5.** To **love the LORD** means to choose Him for an intimate relationship and to obey His commands. This command, to love Him, is given often in Deuteronomy (v. 5; 7:9; 10:12; 11:1, 13, 22; 13:3; 19:9; 30:6, 16, 20). Loving Him was to be wholehearted (**with all your heart**) and was to pervade every aspect of an Israelite's being and life (**soul** and **strength**).

**6:6-9.** God's people were responsible to meditate on **these commandments,** to keep them in their **hearts.** This enabled them to understand the Law and to apply it correctly. Then the parents were in a position to **impress them on** their children's hearts also. The moral and biblical education of the **children** was accomplished best not in a formal teaching period each day but when the parents, out of concern for their own lives as well as their children's, made God and His Word the natural topic of a conversation which might occur anywhere and anytime during the day (v. 7).

The commands to **tie them** and **write them** were taken literally by some later Jewish readers. However, the commands are probably emphasizing symbolically the need for the continual teaching of the Law (cf. Ex. 13:9, 16).

### c. The warning about prosperity (6:10-19)

**6:10-12.** The LORD was about to give the Israelites "instant prosperity" in their new **land.** But there is an inherent danger in prosperity, for when a person prospers he tends to **forget** God (cf. Prov. 30:7-9). It was at the height of his own prosperity that David committed his greatest acts of unfaithfulness (2 Sam. 11).

**6:13-19.** When they would come into this prosperity the Israelites were to be all the more careful to **fear** Him (see comments on 4:10) and to **serve Him.** The command to swear (**take . . . oaths**) by the **name** of the LORD reinforces the instruction to fear Him, for one swears by the God he fears, that is, by the God under whom he is responsible to fulfill his oaths. If they would forget God (v. 12) they would almost certainly **follow other gods,** for God created people not only with the *capacity* to worship but with the *need* to worship. And this act of unfaithfulness would result in judgment since **the LORD . . . is a jealous God** (cf. 4:24; 5:9; 32:16, 21). This means He is *zealous to protect what belongs to Him alone.* Jealousy in this sense is ethically right. Jealousy in the sense of envy for another's possessions or privileges is, of course, wrong.

Moses envisioned another sin to which the Israelites might be tempted in the new land, that of testing **the LORD** (6:16). This implies that at times the people would face hardship **as they did at Massah** (cf. Ex. 17:1-7) where they lacked water and thought they would die of thirst. Rather than trusting God in this trial they tested Him by complaining and quarreling. In the future the Israelites were to remember this embarrassing incident. They were to know that if they obeyed His **commands . . . stipulations,**

**and decrees** (cf. Deut. 4:44; 6:1, 20), doing what is right and good, then no matter what hardship they might encounter it would **go well with** them (cf. v. 3).

### d. The transmission of the covenant (6:20-25)

**6:20-25.** Once again Moses reminded his audience of the crucial need to pass on the covenant values to their children. The situation presented here concretely illustrates the command in verses 6-9. Moses envisioned a home where the Word of God is discussed openly as a part of everyday life. When a young **son** asked about **the meaning of** the Israelite Law his father was to use the following pattern in explaining it to him. First, the Israelites were in bondage **in Egypt** (v. 21a). Second, God miraculously delivered the Israelites (v. 21b; cf. 4:20) and judged the Egyptians (6:22). Third, this marvelous work was in accord with His ancient promise to the patriarchs (Abraham, Isaac, and Jacob) to build a nation of their descendants in **the land** of Canaan (v. 23; cf. Gen. 15:18-21; 17:7-8; 26:3-5; 28:13-15). Fourth, God gave His Word in the form of **decrees** so that the Israelites **might always prosper** (cf. Deut. 5:33) by obeying it and fearing **God** (cf. 4:10; 6:13). Near the beginning of this chapter, Moses stressed the need of parents to love Him with their total being. Now as the chapter closes Moses indicated that one aspect of loving (and thus obeying) God is to pass that same love for Him on to their children.

### 2. HOLY WAR (CHAP. 7)

### a. The command to destroy the inhabitants of the land (7:1-5)

**7:1-2.** The **seven nations** mentioned here are representative of the inhabitants of **the land** of Canaan (cf. Gen. 15:19-21). God listed six of these seven nations in His call to Moses (Ex. 3:17), all except the **Girgashites,** who (like **the Hittites . . . Amorites** and **Jebusites**) were descended from Canaan (Gen. 10:15-16). The point of Deuteronomy 7:1-2 is that Israel was to **destroy** *all* the nations within the borders of Canaan (see comments on these groups in 20:17).

The command to destroy **them totally,** that is, men, women, and children, has often been thought of as unethical for a loving God. However, several points must be kept in mind concerning these people. First, they deserved to die for their sin (9:4-5). Studies of their religion, literature, and archeological remains reveal that they were the most morally depraved culture on the earth at that time.

Second, they persisted in their hatred of God (7:10). Had they repented, God would have spared them as He spared the Ninevites who repented at the preaching of Jonah. Yet repentance seemed to be out of the question for these people.

Third, the Canaanites constituted a moral cancer (cf. 20:17-18; Num. 33:55; Josh. 23:12-13) and even one of them—even a child left alive—had the potential of introducing an idolatry and immorality which would spread rapidly among the Israelites and bring about the destruction of God's own people.

Fourth, two mitigating factors may be mentioned. In some ways the death of a Canaanite child could have been a blessing. For if the child died before reaching the age of accountability it is likely that his or her eternal destiny would have been made secure in heaven. The second factor to remember is that one day Jesus Christ will return to slaughter the unrepentant wicked on the earth (though nothing is said about His killing children), and that "holy war" will make Israel's holy war look pale by comparison (2 Thes. 2:5-10; Rev. 19:11-21).

So there is no dichotomy between the God of the Old Testament and the God of the New Testament. In both testaments He is revealed as a loving and righteous God. The command to engage in holy war is, of course, not applicable today since at the present time God is not working through one nation to set up His kingdom on the earth. But Christians today should learn from this command that they should be as ruthless with sin in their own lives as Israel should have been against the Canaanites.

**7:3-5.** The command against intermarriage assumes something about human nature. Paul stated the principle well: "Don't you know that a little yeast works through the whole batch of dough?" (1 Cor. 5:6) Marriage to an unbelieving Canaanite meant disaster for an Israelite's faith. Moses reminded the people (Deut. 7:4b) that **the LORD's** righteous sword cuts both ways. The Canaanites were being judged for their wickedness;

if the Israelites joined them in wickedness they would also join them in judgment. Therefore everything—even the Canaanites' religious objects—which might arouse the slightest curiosity about false worship, was to be totally eradicated. The **sacred stones** (cf. 12:3; Ex. 23:24; 34:13) were possibly male fertility symbols and the **Asherah poles** were wooden poles in honor of the goddess Asherah, the consort of Baal. Similar commands were given in Exodus 34:11-15; Numbers 33:50-52; Deuteronomy 12:2-3.

*b. The basis of the command (7:6-11)*

**7:6.** The basis for the command to destroy the Canaanites lay in God's election of Israel. The word translated **chosen** means "to be chosen for a task or a vocation." God had selected Israel as His means of sanctifying **the earth.** Thus they were **holy** (set apart for God's special use) and were **His treasured possession** (cf. 14:2; 26:18; Ps. 135:4; Mal. 3:17; see comments on Ex. 19:5). Since the Canaanites were polluting the earth, and since they might endanger Israel's complete subordination to the will of the Lord, they either had to repent or be eliminated. And as stated, for 400 years they had refused to repent.

**7:7-8.** God's election of Israel was never to become a source of pride for the nation. For God did not find any intrinsic merit in her which motivated Him to **choose** her. In fact her small size originally would have served as a hindrance to her election. On the positive side Moses offered two reasons for God's choice of Israel. First, **the LORD loved** Israel. Ultimately this divine love is a mystery since it was not motivated by any goodness in the nation. Second, He chose them **because** of an **oath He swore to** Israel's **forefathers** (cf. comments on 1:35), Abraham, Isaac, and Jacob. The Lord had promised the patriarchs that their descendants would be a mighty nation and inherit the land of Canaan (Gen. 17:7-8; 26:3-5, 24; 28:13-15), and He would always be faithful to His Word (cf. Heb. 6:13-18). For that reason **He brought** Israel **out . . . from the land of slavery** (cf. Ex. 13:3, 14; 20:2; Deut. 5:6; 6:12; 8:14; 13:5, 10).

**7:7-11.** Moses meant for the Israelites to draw two conclusions from God's choice and redemption of them. First, the

LORD alone **is God.** He is able to control history, to raise up nations, and to bring them down. Second, **He is the faithful God.** The **thousand generations** is a proverbial expression meaning "endlessly" or "forever." Though He will never abandon **His covenant of love** (cf. v. 12) **to** Israel, rebellious individuals within the nation will be judged for their sin just as His enemies in other nations (**those who hate Him**) are judged by Him. **Therefore** each individual Israelite needed to be careful **to follow** His **commands.**

*c. The reward for obedience (7:12-16)*

**7:12.** This verse summarizes verses 12-16. **If** the nation is obedient to the Lord she will experience His covenantal **love.** Though God will not abandon the **covenant** because of His promises to the patriarchs (**forefathers;** cf. vv. 8, 13; see comments on 1:35) the people could forfeit the *blessings* of the covenant through their own disobedience.

**7:13-15.** For their obedience, God promised the blessing of fertility of human, animal, and plant life in Israel. The Israelites could also count on freedom from **the horrible diseases** that were common **in Egypt** (possibly including boils; cf. 28:27, 60; Ex. 15:26).

**7:16.** The Israelites' obligation in entering the land was to **destroy all the peoples** within the borders of Canaan (cf. vv. 1-2). If Israel would not do so, they would become ensnared by them and **their gods** (cf. Ex. 34:12-14) and as a result would not experience the blessings just mentioned (Deut. 7:13-15). Verse 16 naturally led Moses to the exhortation recorded in verses 17-26.

*d. An encouragement to holy war (7:17-26)*

**7:17-26.** Moses knew the hearts of his fellow Israelites. He remembered how 40 years earlier the Anakites had made their hearts melt (1:26-28). So he concluded this part of his speech (on holy war) by setting the battles in proper perspective. The Israelites were to concentrate not on the strength of their enemies but on the greatness of **the LORD.** They had seen the miraculous defeat of **Pharaoh** by **miraculous signs and wonders** (the 10 plagues). These were performed by God's strength, His **mighty hand and outstretched arm** (cf. 4:34; 5:15; 11:2). Israel could expect to see history

repeated in the destruction of the Canaanites (**the LORD your God will do the same,** 7:19).

God would cause Israel's enemies to run from her in battle as if they were attacked by swarms of hornets (cf. Ex. 23:28; Josh. 24:12). (Some say the reference to **the hornet** is to be taken literally; others say it refers to the Egyptian army.) The enemies were in fact fearful of Israel (Ex. 15:15; Num. 22:3; Josh. 2:9-11, 24; 5:1; 9:24). He would throw Israel's enemies **into great confusion** (Deut. 7:23), that is, a divinely inspired panic would engulf the Canaanites and render them helpless in battle (v. 24). All this would happen according to a well-conceived plan (**little by little,** v. 22) so that the land would not be depopulated too quickly and overrun by **wild animals.**

The Israelites could be assured of this glorious victory if only they had the faith to begin the battle and afterward the discipline to **destroy** the idols left behind with the **silver and gold.** Otherwise the Israelites would find themselves trapped by idolatry and *they* would become the objects of the Lord's holy war. The Canaanites' idols, some of them suggestive of sexual perversions, were **detestable to** God. So His people were to **detest** them too, for the images were designated (**set apart,** *ḥērem;* see comments on Josh. 6:21) **for destruction.**

3. A WARNING AGAINST A SPIRIT OF INDEPENDENCE (CHAP. 8)

*a. An exhortation to remember the wilderness (8:1-6)*

**8:1.** This introductory verse reminded the Israelites again that the gifts of life and fertility in **the land . . . promised** by God did not come automatically to believers but were by-products of obedience. The wilderness experience was designed to produce both obedience and faith in the nation. The people were told to **be careful** (cf. 4:9) **to follow every command** from God.

**8:2-3.** When Moses said that God tested the Israelites **in order to know what was in** their hearts he was using an anthropomorphism. God, of course, already knew what was in their hearts. The point is that their obedience or disobedience had to be proven in history.

**God led** them into **the desert** where they had no alternative but to trust Him or to murmur against Him. In the desert they could not produce their own food but had to depend on God for food and thus for their very lives. When Moses reminded them that they did **not live on bread alone** he meant that even their food was decreed by the **word** of God. They had **manna** because it came by His command. It was therefore ultimately not bread that kept them alive but His word! "Bread alone," that is, bread acquired independently of His word, could not keep them alive.

This was why Jesus refused Satan's temptation to turn the stones into bread when He was in the wilderness (Matt. 4:3-4). Jesus knew that God had not decreed those stones for His food, and also that His Father would provide food apart from the Son's working of a miracle at the suggestion of Satan (cf. Matt. 7:9).

**8:4-6.** The LORD disciplined Israel by making her depend on Him for everything: food, water, and **clothes.** Since all these were provided by His decree the only logical response was to **observe** (obey) **the commands of the Lord,** following **and revering Him.** "Revering" translates a word that means fearing, that is, fearing to disobey the One who is so powerful and holy.

*b. An exhortation not to forget God (8:7-20)*

**8:7-9.** In contrast with the severity of the wilderness these verses describe the abundance of Israel's new **land.** It was abundant in **water** (essential for crops as well as for sustaining animal and human life); in agricultural produce including grains (**wheat . . . barley**), fruits (grapes, figs, **pomegranates**), **oil** from **olive** trees, and **honey**; and in minerals. (**Iron** and **copper** have been discovered in **the hills** south of the Dead Sea.) The people then would **lack nothing** (cf. Ps. 23:1).

**8:10-18.** Moses then spelled out the danger inherent in abundant prosperity. Whereas in the wilderness they had to depend on **God** for the necessities of life, their newfound prosperity might conceal their need for the same dependence. Moses prescribed a sure antidote for this danger: **praise the LORD your God.** In fact failure to praise Him for His blessings was a step toward forgetting God and then disobeying **His commands.**

An Israelite who ceased to praise the Lord sincerely would find that his **heart** had **become proud** (v. 14) in his abundance (vv. 12-13; cf. Hosea 13:6). He would **forget** (cf. Deut. 8:11, 19; see comments on 4:9) the miraculous deliverance of Israel from **Egypt . . . the land of slavery** (cf. 5:6; 6:12; 7:8; 13:5, 10; Ex. 13:3, 14; 20:2) and the wilderness (cf. Deut. 1:19; 32:10) **with its venemous snakes** (cf. Num. 21:6-7) **and scorpions.** (This is the only reference in the Pentateuch to scorpions in the wilderness wanderings.) Such a person who did not remember God's provisions of **water** (Ex. 15:25, 27; 17:5-7) and **manna** (Ex. 16) **in the desert** would be inclined to credit his own ability (**my power** and **strength**) for his **wealth,** when in reality it was as much a gift from God as the water **out of hard rock** had been in the wilderness. The provision of manna was a **test,** to see if Israel would depend on the Lord's word (cf. comments on Ex. 16:4). Such dependence is humbling (cf. Deut. 8:3). The people could avoid pride in their wealth and strength if they would constantly remember **the LORD** and the lesson of the wilderness: all of life is a gift from God and nothing is possible apart from Him (v. 18).

**8:19-20.** Just as failure to praise **God** would lead to forgetting Him, so forgetting Him would lead to worshiping **other gods.** That in turn would result in certain destruction (death). If Moses' audience wanted an example of national destruction all they needed to do was to remember **the nations the LORD destroyed,** namely, the kingdoms of Sihon and Og (2:26–3:11).

4. A WARNING AGAINST A SPIRIT OF SELF-RIGHTEOUSNESS (9:1–10:11)

*a. The conquest of Canaan not due to Israel's righteousness (9:1-6)*

**9:1-3.** Moses remembered the people's shock when they heard the original report of the 12 spies concerning the size, strength, and number of the inhabitants of Canaan (Num. 13:26–14:4). He did not want them to be surprised again or to underestimate the enormity of the task that lay before them. Therefore he emphasized that from a purely military and human point of view their victory was impossible. The enemy had superior strength, fortifications (**large cities** with high **walls**), experience, and numbers.

And they had gained a terrifying reputation: **Who can stand up against the Anakites?** (On the Anakites see comments on Deut. 1:28.)

Though the Canaanites had all these things in their favor, they were doomed before the battles began. Just as in the desert **the Lord** went before the Israelites in a pillar of cloud and fire so now He would go before the Israelite army as **a devouring fire** to **destroy** the enemy. This principle is stated in Proverbs 21:31: "The horse is made ready for the day of battle, but victory rests with the Lord." But God's people could not remain passive. In faith they had to begin the battle and to **annihilate** the enemy with the strength God would supply **as** He **promised.**

**9:4-6.** After experiencing the magnificent victories of the Conquest it would have been easy for the Israelites to have become proud. It would have been even easier for them to have become spiritually proud after meditating on the divine favor God gave them in those victories. In each of these three verses Moses warned against the danger of developing a self-righteous spirit by telling them that their victories were **not** a result of their **righteousness.**

In fact Moses gave three reasons why Israel would be victorious in the Conquest. First, the **wickedness of these nations** (vv. 4-5) was so great that it demanded God's judgment. He is the God of Israel but He is also the God of all nations. They are all accountable to Him. Second, God would give Israel victory because He had sworn this to the patriarchs (cf. comments on 1:8; note Gen. 15:13-21 which speaks of both God's judgment of the wicked Amorites and the promise of the land to Abraham).

Third, **the Lord** was giving the **land** as a pure gift of grace, for the Israelites were a **stiff-necked people,** stubborn and unresponsive (Deut. 9:6; cf. v. 13; 10:16; 31:27). Later Moses pointed out that the Israelites actually deserved to be destroyed (9:13-14) rather than blessed with the gift of the land. So Israel should never develop a self-righteous attitude because of her victories in the Conquest. Those victories would be due to her enemies' wickedness, God's promise, and God's grace.

*b. A recital of Israel's rebellious history (9:7–10:11)*

(1) The golden calf (9:7-21). **9:7-14.** This section and what follows (v. 22–10:11) are a well-argued commentary on the meaning of the statement "you are a stiff-necked people" (9:6). The emphatic exhortation, **Remember this and never forget,** underscores the absurdity of Israel ever supposing that the land was given them as a reward for their righteousness. Moses used one incident from their past, the worship of the golden calf, to illustrate that Israelite history has nearly always been one of rebellion (v. 7) against God's grace. This incident (Ex. 32), perhaps more than any other until that time, illustrates Israel's sinfulness on the one hand and God's grace on the other. While Moses was fasting for **40 days and 40 nights** on Mount **Horeb** (Sinai; cf. Deut. 1:2) and therefore was completely dependent on God, the **people** were feasting. While Moses was receiving the Ten **Commandments (the tablets of the covenant,** 9:9, 11) **by the finger of God** (see comments on Ex. 31:18), the people were breaking several of them by worshiping the golden calf (see comments on Ex. 32:6). As **the Lord** had given **the covenant** to Moses, the **people** had **become corrupt** and **turned away quickly** (Deut. 9:12). Even God Himself proclaimed that the people were **stiff-necked** (v. 13). Their rebellion was so great that He wanted to **destroy** the **nation** and start all over with Moses (cf. Ex. 32:9-10).

**9:15-21.** These verses record Moses' reaction to the people's sin. The fact that he mentioned they **had turned aside quickly** (cf. v. 12, "turned away quickly") emphasized the people's fickleness and the gravity of their sin. When Moses broke **the two tablets . . . to pieces before** the people he graphically illustrated what they had done to their covenant with **the Lord.** They had violated their agreement with Him (Ex. 24:3). Therefore **the Lord** had the right to do away with the covenant of Law made at Sinai.

The second thing Moses did was fast and pray **for 40 days and 40 nights** (Deut. 9:18; cf. v. 25; 10:10). In the Old Testament it was normal for people to fast in times of repentance (cf. Jud. 20:26; 2 Sam. 12:16; 1 Kings 21:27; Neh. 1:4). His fasting demonstrated his unity with the nation and his horror at their **sin.** Their **evil** had provoked God **to anger** (Deut. 9:18-20). The words **the LORD listened to me** suggest that Moses prayed. The contents of his prayer are recorded in verses 26-29. Only in verse 20 does the Old Testament record that Moses also **prayed for Aaron,** thus saving his life too. Moses' total destruction of the golden calf—called in satire **that sinful thing of yours**—put the gold of the idol beyond recovery. (See comments on Ex. 32:20.) Moses' demolishing the idol also illustrated that the people themselves deserved total destruction. Only God's grace invoked by Moses' intercession saved the people.

(2) Other rebellious incidents (9:22-24). **9:22.** This verse suggests that Moses could have continued indefinitely reciting other rebellious acts of Israel which angered **the LORD.** For the incident **at Taberah,** where the people complained about their hardships, see Numbers 11:1-3; **at Massah,** where the people complained about no water, see Exodus 17:1-7; **and at Kibroth Hattavah,** where Israel complained about the manna, see Numbers 11:31-34.

**9:23-24.** After God displayed His grace in the incident of the golden calf by not destroying the nation, one might have expected a significant change in the people's hearts. But again they collectively **rebelled against** their **God** by refusing to go up **from Kadesh Barnea** and begin the battle for **the land.** So Moses was completely justified in concluding that at every significant turn in their history the Israelites had **been rebellious.** Christians too need to beware of the danger of rebelling against God as did Israel (1 Cor. 10:1-12) by failing **to trust Him or obey Him.** They are every bit as much indebted to God's grace as were the Israelites of the wilderness generation.

(3) Moses' petition. **9:25-29.** The content of Moses' intercessory prayer is placed here rather than at verse 19 where at first glance it would seem more appropriate. It is probably here because of the words in verse 24. If the people had been so rebellious from their very inception why did not God do away with them? This prayer offers an answer to that question.

These verses record one of the model prayers in the Old Testament. The men-

tion of the **40 days and 40 nights** recalled Moses' fasting (v. 18) and indicated his sincerity as well as his understanding of the situation's gravity. He was totally concerned with God's glory and reputation on the earth. He did not plead for Israel on the basis of any merit of hers. Rather he "reminded" God that Israel was His **own inheritance** (cf. v. 29 and see comments of 4:20). Therefore in the light of His promise to the patriarchs (**Abraham, Isaac, and Jacob;** cf. 9:5; see comments on 1:8), God's destruction of Israel would call into question His ability to fulfill His promise (9:28). This prayer contained no self-seeking on Moses' part. Instead it was out of concern for God's reputation and a desire for Him to demonstrate once again His grace by forgiving **the stubbornness . . . wickedness,** and **sin** (v. 27) of God's **people,** His **inheritance,** whom He delivered **out of Egypt** by His **power** (cf. v. 26) and **outstretched arm** (see comments on 4:34).

(4) The acceptance of Moses' petition (10:1-11). **10:1-5. The LORD,** acting on Moses' request not to destroy the people, rewrote the Ten Commandments on **stone tablets.** This indicates that God did annul the prior covenant, concluded in Exodus 24:3. Probably each of **the two tablets** contained a complete copy of **the Ten Commandments.** This was normal in establishing the ancient Near Eastern suzerainty treaties to which Deuteronomy has been previously compared. As God instructed him, Moses made a **wooden chest** or ark (cf. Ex. 25:10-16) in which he then placed **the tablets.** This construction was done, of course, in connection with building the tabernacle (Ex. 37:1-5; 40:20-21).

**10:6-9.** These verses may be an editorial insertion (cf. comments on 2:10-12). When Israel was at **Moserah. . . . Aaron died.** According to Numbers 20:28; 33:38 Aaron died on Mount Hor. Probably Moserah was the district where Mount Hor was located.

The mention of Aaron's death indicates that the Lord also granted Moses' plea at Horeb years before to spare Aaron's life. **Eleazar,** Aaron's third **son,** became the high **priest** (Deut. 10:6) and the Levites were given specific responsibilities in relation to the tabernacle (v. 8). For other details relating to **the Levites** see the comments on 18:1-8.

**10:10-11.** When Moses was **on the mountain** a second time (vv. 1-5) for **40 days and nights** (cf. the first time, 9:9), he was involved in fasting and intercession for Israel (9:18, 25). Agreeing **not . . . to destroy** the nation, God told Moses to **lead the people on** to **possess the land.**

5. A CONCLUDING EXHORTATION TO TOTAL COMMITMENT TO THE LORD (10:12–11:32)

a. *An exhortation to love the Lord because of Israel's election (10:12-22)*

**10:12-13.** These verses are an introductory summary to the general exhortation in verses 14-22. Having shown the impossibility of self-dependence (chap. 8) and the impossibility of spiritual pride in light of her rebellious history (9:1–10:11), Moses called Israel to exercise her only option for survival: total commitment to **the LORD.** This is seen in the several infinitives used: **to fear** (cf. comments on 4:10), **walk . . . love . . . serve,** and **observe.** Such commitment was **for** their **own good** (cf. comments on "go well with you," 4:40).

**10:14-15.** The LORD is enthroned in **the heavens,** and therefore is not a part of Creation but is sovereign over all of it. Besides creating the universe, He *owns* it and **all the nations on the earth.** But He specially **loved** the patriarchs, and selected them to be intimately related to Him. **And He chose . . . their descendants,** that is, He called them to be His witnesses. So the first reason Israel was to love the Lord is that He had initiated a relationship of love with this rebellious nation. The same principle is true of God's relationship with believers today (Rom. 5:8; 1 John 4:10).

**10:16-18.** The proper response to their election by the sovereign Lord was to **circumcise** their **hearts** (cf. 30:6). An uncircumcised heart means a will that is hardened against God's commands. It is another way of saying the person is **stiff-necked** or stubborn (cf. 9:6, 13; 31:27). Thus the command to circumcise their hearts assumes that human hearts are naturally rebellious and need correction. Though human hearts are slow to change, Moses warned the nation that no bribe or anything less than an inward transformation could satisfy **the LORD,** who is **the great God.** God's treatment of the helpless (**the fatherless . . . the wid-**ow, and **the alien**) further illustrates His absolutely just character (showing **no partiality**) and highlights His requirement for Israel to be just.

**10:19-22.** The mention of the alien in verse 18 recalls God's great deliverance of Israel with **great and awesome wonders** (v. 21) from being **aliens in Egypt** (v. 19; cf. Ex. 23:9). Therefore the Israelites were to **fear . . . serve,** adhere to (cf. **hold fast to** in Deut. 11:22; 13:4; 30:20), and **praise** Him. As a further encouragement to be faithful to **the LORD,** Moses called the people's attention to the fact that He had already fulfilled part of the promise to Abraham by multiplying their number like **the stars in the sky** (cf. Gen. 15:5; 22:17; 26:4). On the question of whether **70** Israelites moved to **Egypt** (Ex. 1:5) or 75 (Acts 7:14-15) see comments on the Acts passage.

b. *An explanation to love the Lord because of His powerful deeds (11:1-7)*

**11:1.** Once again Moses laid special stress on the inseparability of love and obedience (cf. 6:5-6; 7:9; 10:12-13; 11:13, 22; 19:9; 30:6, 8, 16, 20). The ultimate test of an Israelite's love for God was whether he obeyed Him (cf. John 14:15). In Hebrew the command to **love the LORD** means to choose Him for one's most intimate relationship and then to express that choice in obedience to His revealed will.

**11:2-7.** All of Israel's history had been guided by the Lord for the purpose of motivating them to love Him unreservedly. **The discipline of the LORD** refers to God's moral education of His people. Because of the waywardness of the human heart, diligent and drastic measures were needed to quell that waywardness. So God sent Israel "to school" in **Egypt** so that she might learn of His **majesty** and power (**mighty hand** and **outstretched arm;** cf. 4:34; 5:15; 7:19) and respond with grateful obedience for her deliverance from **Pharaoh.** Israel was given distinct **signs** (11:3; the 10 plagues) so that she might understand her experience. The incident at **the Red Sea** (lit., "Sea of [Papyrus] Reeds"; cf. comments on Ex. 14:2) and the consequent **lasting ruin** brought on the Egyptians (Deut. 11:4) could be explained only by God's miraculous deliverance and judgment.

After the Egyptian experience the

Lord then sent His children "to school" **in the desert** for 40 years. Here their moral education was further refined as they had to depend on Him totally for all their needs. The vague reference **what He did for you** (v. 5) recalled God's miracles for His people in the wilderness, including the water from the rock (Ex. 17:1-7), the manna, and the quail (Ex. 16).

God's discipline, however, was not always positive. In the Exodus experience the people learned about God's grace and power, and in the desert they learned of His providential care. Then in the rebellion of **Dathan and Abiram** (Num. 16) Israel learned about God's holiness. Had it not been for Moses' intercession, the Lord would have "put an end to" the entire nation (Num. 16:45) for their grumbling unbelief (Num. 16:41).

Moses exhorted the people to learn from their past, for God had constructed their history with a didactic purpose. The stress on **your own eyes** and the double mention of the **children** not seeing the events of this period (Deut. 11:2, 5) hint at the parents' responsibility to set an example of obedient living for their **children** and to pass on the truths learned from these experiences.

c. *An exhortation to obey God's commands because success and longevity in the land depended on it (11:8-25)*

**11:8-9.** Moses wanted the people to draw an important conclusion from his brief review of their history (vv. 1-7). Since God had designed Israel's past experiences to bring about her moral education, it should have been plain to the nation that their experiencing the Lord's grace or judgment depended on their moral behavior. Therefore they could prosper in **the** new **land** only by observing (obeying) **all** God's **commands. The strength** of the Israelites was directly related to their obedience. So the supernatural ability to conquer enemies stronger than they and the ability to **live long in the land** (cf. 4:40; 5:16; 6:2; 25:15; 32:47) was ultimately a question of ethics, not military skill. (On the **land flowing with milk and honey,** words occurring frequently in Deut., see comments on Ex. 3:8.)

**11:10-15.** Mentioning the contrasts between the Promised **Land** and **Egypt**

might have been prompted by the reference to Dathan and Abiram (v. 6). These men had referred to *Egypt* as "a land flowing with milk and honey" and complained that Moses had not given them anything better (Num. 16:12-14). However, **the land** of Canaan had far more potential for agriculture. Whereas the people in Egypt had to depend on irrigation, God's people would have **rain from heaven,** for He watches over the **land** year-round. But this **rain,** unlike irrigation, did not depend on human ingenuity or skill, but rather on the will of Israel to **obey the commands** of the rain's Giver. This involved loving and serving Him (cf. Deut. 10:12). The **autumn . . . rains** (also called the early rains) come in September-October, and the **spring** rains are in March-April (cf. Joel 2:23). Those rains begin and end the rainy season. The rains are necessary to help crops and trees grow, including **grain** (wheat, flax, and barley), grapevines (**wine**), olive trees (**oil**), and **grass in the fields.**

**11:16-21.** Through Moses, God again warned Israel against worshiping **other gods.** This was appropriately related to verses 13-15, because many of the gods worshiped in Canaan were fertility deities, that is, gods of grain, oil, rain, etc. Unless the people of Israel were extremely **careful** (see comments on 4:9) they could easily be **enticed** by their pagan neighbors to enter into the sensual worship of these deities. It would simply be a matter of transferring their trust in **the Lord** for the fertility of their land to one or more of those false gods. And this worship, which was divorced from the realm of ethics and which emphasized ritual sex, was so appealing to human hearts that careless and morally undisciplined Israelites would be drawn into its fatal web.

The wrath of God expressed in famine (**He will shut the heavens**) could be avoided by abstaining from worshiping false gods. This was ironic, for Israel's attempt to guarantee rain by worshiping Canaanite gods would result in God's *withholding* rain!

However, their will to avoid this sin was so weak that it could only be sustained by diligent attention to the words of Moses concerning divine grace and deliverance as well as sin and judgment. They were to **fix** those **words . . . in** their **hearts** (cf. 6:6) **and minds.** (On attaching those words to their **hands** and **foreheads,** see comments on 6:8.) Only by letting God's words invade every area of their lives and homes and by diligently teaching **them to** their **children** (cf. 6:7) could the nation hope to escape the seduction of false **worship** and find permanent prosperity **in the land** of promise given by the LORD on oath to their **forefathers** (see comments on 1:35).

The same principle applies to Christians today. Commitment to know and obey the Scriptures keeps believers from contemporary forms of false worship (cf. 2 Tim. 3:1-9 with 2 Tim. 3:14-17). Therefore Paul exhorted all Christians to "let the Word of Christ dwell in you richly" (Col. 3:16).

**11:22-25.** At this point in his speech Moses turned from the theme of longevity in the land to the successful conquest of the land. The people were **to love the LORD** (cf. 6:5). Obedience to the specific commands was essentially an expression of one's love for God (cf. 11:1). And consistent allegiance to Him (**hold fast to Him;** cf. 10:20; 13:4; 30:20) was an evidence of love.

In return for their obedience **the LORD** would grant Israel supernatural success against superior (larger and stronger) enemy armies. He would put a **terror and fear** in their enemies so that they could not fight successfully against Israel. Rahab's words to the spies, "I know that the LORD has given this land to you and that a great fear of you has fallen on us" (Josh. 2:9), are one example of the fulfillment of this promise (cf. Ex. 15:15-16; Deut. 2:25; 28:10; Josh. 2:11, 24; 5:1). Had Israel continued to obey God faithfully, her boundaries would have been enlarged (Deut. 11:24; cf. comments on 1:7) to fulfill the promise made to Abraham (Gen. 15:18). But because of Israel's disobedience the fulfillment of **the whole land** promise is still future.

*d. The blessings and curses on Mount Ebal and Mount Gerizim (11:26-32)*

**11:26-32.** For details on this see the comments on chapters 27–28. Verses 26-32 of chapter 11 form a fitting conclusion to this section of Moses' speech. Once again he emphasized that the history of Israel would be determined by her ethical relationship to **the LORD.**

*C. The code of specific laws (12:1–26:15)*

1. THE INTRODUCTION (12:1)

**12:1.** The decrees and laws that follow in this section of Moses' speech (12:2–26:15) were not meant to be exhaustive. Moses intentionally did not repeat many of the details and laws recorded in Exodus and Leviticus. Deuteronomy is law preached (or better, "instruction"; see comments on 1:5). Moses was setting a quality of living before the nation rather than an exhaustive law code that covered every detail of life. The specific laws in this section were given to help the people subordinate every area of their lives to **the LORD,** and to help them eradicate whatever might threaten that pure devotion.

These laws were given with the Promised Land specifically in mind: **be careful** (cf. comments on 4:9) **to follow** these commands **in the land.** Because God's Word is certain of fulfillment, Moses could tell the Israelites on the plains of Moab, still outside the boundaries of the Promised Land, that the Lord had **given** them **the land.** So with the sure gift of the land in mind the people were to listen carefully to these **decrees and laws.** (On the title, **the God of your fathers,** see the comments on 1:11; cf. 1:21; 4:1; 6:3; 27:3.)

2. THE LAW OF THE SINGLE SANCTUARY (12:2-28)

*a. The command to destroy Canaanite worship centers (12:2-4)*

**12:2-4. Mountains** and **hills** were particularly significant in some of the religions of the ancient Near East for many deities were thought to have originated there and to live there. The **spreading tree** was also significant for the Canaanite worship of fertility deities. The **sacred stones** (cf. 7:5; Ex. 23:24; 34:13) were possibly male fertility symbols and the **Asherah poles** (cf. Ex. 34:13; Deut. 7:5; 16:21) were wooden symbols of the fertility goddess Asherah, Baal's consort. **The idols** (*pāsîl*) were probably in stone.

The complete destruction of these cultic objects was intended to remove the temptation to worship their deities and to stop polluting the pure **worship** of **the LORD** with pagan rituals and objects (12:4). The Lord would not tolerate a partial commitment. By destroying these cultic objects and centers the Israelites could express their total allegiance to Him. Also the Israelites could show that they did not believe in the existence of the Canaanite deities and therefore had no fear of "retribution" from them.

### b. The instruction about where to worship (12:5-7)

**12:5.** When Israel entered the Promised Land, **God** would **choose** a **place . . . to put His name** (cf. vv. 11, 21; 14:23-24; 16:2, 6, 11; 26:2) that is, He would choose a site for the tabernacle, the **place** where God and the people would meet (cf. Ex. 33:7-11). This command did not mean that the tabernacle would always stay in the same place, for it was moved at God's command. The ultimate fulfillment of this command came centuries later when God let David move the tabernacle to Jerusalem where his son Solomon built the temple. The command for a single sanctuary promoted or emphasized three things: the unity of God (i.e., He is One, not many), the purity of the Israelites' worship of the Lord, and the people's political and spiritual unity.

**12:6.** The **burnt offerings** (Lev. 1), to be brought to the place of worship, were to be completely burned on the altar. They were given at various times to express the worshiper's total dependence on the Lord. The word translated **sacrifice** (*zebaḥ*) refers to a sacrifice given as an expression of appreciation, and it involved a communal meal. It may have been given as a thank offering (Lev. 7:12-15; 22:29-30) for something specific God had done for a worshiper. Or it may have been offered as a votive offering to fulfill a vow made to the Lord (Lev. 7:16-17; 22:18-23). Or it may have been offered as a **freewill** offering in which the person thanked God (Lev. 7:16-17; 22:18-23) but not necessarily for anything specific. (On **tithes** see comments on Lev. 27:30-32 and Deut. 14:28. On the law of **the firstborn** see comments on 15:19-23.) The **special gifts** (lit., "what is lifted up in the hand") were for the priests.

**12:7.** An Israelite "worship service" would be characterized by joy (**you and your families shall eat and shall rejoice**) if they lived faithfully in the new land for they could count on the Lord's abundant blessing. "Rejoicing" in the Lord's presence occurs several times in Deuteronomy (vv. 7, 12, 18; 14:26; 16:11; also note 16:14-15).

### c. The instruction about when to worship (12:8-14)

**12:8-9.** Earlier in Israel's wilderness experience, **the Lord** instructed Moses to command the people not to slaughter a cow, sheep, or goat without first bringing the animal to the entrance of the tabernacle to present it as an offering to Him (Lev. 17:1-4). God had two reasons for this. First, the prohibition was designed to keep the Israelites from worshiping as pagans (Lev. 17:5-9). Second, it was to keep worshipers from eating the blood of the sacrifice (Lev. 17:10-13). **Everyone** does **as he sees fit** may imply some laxity on the people's part in observing the prohibition (Lev. 17:3-4). Or Moses may have meant that there had been some confusion as to how to apply the original prohibition. The following legislation, however, removes any ambiguity about the eating and sacrificing of meat.

**12:10-14.** The offerings (**burnt offerings . . . sacrifices . . . tithes . . . special gifts,** and vows, etc; see comments on v. 6), whether of flesh or grain, could be offered only at the tabernacle (cf. vv. 17-18), **the place the Lord** would **choose as a dwelling for His name** (see comments on v. 5). These acts of worship were to be times of joy (v. 12).

### d. The instruction about what to offer in worship (12:15-28)

**12:15-16.** Wild game **animals** and animals acceptable for sacrifice could be eaten without taking them to the central sanctuary as long as they were not slaughtered for offerings. Since such an animal was not intended for sacrificial worship it did not matter whether the partakers of the meal were **ceremonially unclean** or **clean.** (The ceremonial laws, found mainly in Lev., were not of a moral nature, but were designed to teach the people truths about the nature of God, their human natures, and their relationship to God. For example, the ceremonial laws in Lev. 12 regarding childbirth do not imply that the bearing of children is ethically wrong.) The prohibition against eating an animal's **blood,** however, was still in force (see comments on Deut. 12:23).

**12:17-19.** For a second time (cf. vv.

12-13) Moses warned the people that anything intended for use in worshiping **the** Lord could only be eaten at the future site of the central sanctuary. In this way purity in worship was protected. Again Moses spoke of worship as a time of joy (cf. v. 12). Since **the Levites** had no tribal allotment of land (10:9; 12:12), they lived in **towns** among the tribes (v. 18; 14:29; 16:11). The people were to provide for them (cf. 14:27).

**12:20-28.** The permission to eat **meat** not intended for use in worship without bringing it to the sanctuary was repeated here (cf. vv. 15-16) but with some added details. Modern readers may find this repetition a bit tedious. But it should be remembered that Deuteronomy was originally presented in sermonic form to Israel. Normally repetition is important in the learning process, but it is doubly important in oral presentations as the audience does not have the opportunity to "read" over something missed the first time.

The earlier prohibition (Lev. 17:1-12) against eating **meat** without offering it first at the tabernacle was only meant to apply while the Israelites were in the wilderness, when their "homes" were near the religious sanctuary. Now the people were about to move into the Promised Land where the majority would live **too far away from** the central sanctuary to bring all **meat** there. So permission was given to **slaughter** and **eat** animals at home for "secular" meals.

Yet the permission was given in such a way that the original intent of the command (Lev. 17:1-12) was preserved. There the prohibition was aimed at preventing the pollution of worship by Canaanite ritual, and at preventing the Israelites from eating **the blood** of the animals. Here Moses warned against eating **the blood** whether the animal was killed at home (Deut. 12:23-25; cf. v. 16) or at the sanctuary (v. 27).

**The blood** symbolized life (**the blood is the life,** v. 23). By refraining from eating blood the Israelites demonstrated a respect for life and ultimately for the Creator of life. Also as Leviticus 17:11 indicates, the blood is a ransom price for sins, so blood is sacred and should not be consumed by people. Moses also preserved the original intent of Leviticus 17:3-4 by again insisting that all offerings

to the Lord be given at the central sanctuary (Deut. 12:26-27; cf. vv. 11, 17-18). **The blood** was to **be poured beside the altar of** burnt offering.

The New Testament has abrogated the Law of the single sanctuary because each Christian has become a sanctuary, a "temple of the living God" (2 Cor. 6:16). However, the eternal principle expressed in the Law of the single sanctuary is still in force for God still demands purity in worship (John 4:24) and the unity of His people (Phil. 2:1-5).

Each of three sections in this chapter concludes with the admonition to **be careful** in carrying out the instructions (Deut. 12:13, 19, 28; also note vv. 1, 30). This is one of many emphases in Deuteronomy, given perhaps because the people tended to be careless and negligent.

3. THE REPRESSION OF IDOLATRY (12:29–13:18)

a. *Avoidance of pagan cultic practices (12:29-32)*

**12:29-30.** Once again Moses drove home the need to avoid all contacts with pagan cultic practices. This sin was offensive for two reasons. First, it would come in the wake of the Lord's grace, that is, after **the** Lord would **cut off . . . the nations** before them. In spite of such divine grace simple curiosity can lead believers to be ensnared (cf. 7:26) by idolatrous practices. This graphically depicts the depravity of the human heart and the fragile nature of the human will's commitment to the holy God. No wonder Moses again urged his people to **be careful!** (cf. comments on 12:28)

**12:31-32.** The second reason for the offensive nature of pagan worship is the depth of the abominations into which they lead. **In worshiping their gods,** pagans **do all kinds of detestable things the** Lord **hates.** The worst of these "detestable things" was child sacrifice. This practice of burning **their sons and daughters in the fire** as sacrifices was frequently associated with the worship of the Ammonite god Molech (Lev. 18:21; 20:2-5; 2 Kings 23:10; Jer. 32:35). God's penalty for child sacrifice was death (Lev. 20:2-5). Yet despite this Solomon built a high place for worshiping Molech on the Mount of Olives (1 Kings 11:7), and both Ahaz (2 Chron. 28:3) and Manasseh (2 Kings 21:6) sacrificed their own children in fire. The practice of child sacrifice is listed as the culminating reason for the exile of the Northern Kingdom of Israel in the eighth century B.C. (2 Kings 17:6, 17). Thus a simple curiosity about evil religious practices eventually led to the destruction of a nation. The same warning is repeated by the Apostle Paul. "For it is shameful even to mention what the disobedient do in secret" (Eph. 5:12).

### b. The solicitation to idolatry by a false prophet (13:1-5)

**13:1-5.** After the general prohibition against involvement in pagan worship (12:29-31) Moses discussed three ways in which the temptation to idolatry was likely to come: through a false **prophet** (13:1-5), a loved one (vv. 6-11), or "revolutionaries" who had been successful in leading an entire town into apostasy (vv. 12-18).

Miraculous signs alone were never meant to be a test of truth. Miracles happen in many religions because Satan uses false religions and false prophets to deceive the world (cf. 2 Cor. 11:13-15; Eph. 6:11; Rev. 12:9). So Moses warned the people that the standard for truth must never be **a miraculous sign or wonder** (or other areas of human experience). The standard of truth is the Word of God.

A prophet's or a dreamer's prediction may come true. But if his message contradicted God's commands, the people were to trust **God** and His Word rather than their experience of a miracle. If human experience seemed to contradict God's clear teachings the Israelites were to bow in submission to God's **commands,** for His Word is truth (cf. John 17:17).

The Israelites were to view each solicitation to idolatry as a test of their love for **the LORD.** Though there was always the danger that they might succumb to a temptation, with each successful resistance to sin their faith in and love for Him would grow stronger (cf. James 1:2-4). They were to **love . . . follow . . . revere . . . obey . . . serve,** and **hold fast to Him** (cf. Deut. 10:20; 11:22; 30:20). The **death** penalty for a false **prophet** was appropriate for if he would successfully seduce people into idolatry he would bring them under God's judgment (cf. 7:26). Killing a false prophet was a way to **purge the evil from** Israel. The need

to maintain national purity was emphasized by Moses, for the command, "You must purge the evil," occurs nine times (13:5; 17:7, 12; 19:19; 21:21; 22:21-22, 24; 24:7).

### c. The solicitation to idolatry by family members or friends (13:6-11)

**13:6-7.** Perhaps the most tragic and painful of all situations which Moses could envision was a temptation to idolatry by a loved one. He showed he understood the depth of the tragedy as he deliberately described the various relationships involved with endearing terminology: **your very own brother . . . the wife you love** (lit., "the wife of your bosom"), **or your closest friend.** Often friends try to influence each other. Unlike the preceding case in which false prophets openly attempted to seduce the people into idolatry (vv. 1-2), this temptation was offered **secretly** and individually. The absurdity of the temptation is heightened by Moses' explanation of the **other gods.** They are **gods that neither you nor your fathers** (ancestors) **have known.** Moses did not mean that the people had not known about these gods intellectually, but they had not known them experientially. These "other gods" had done nothing for Israel and never would because they did not exist.

**13:8-10a.** The person who was being tempted should respond first by not yielding to the temptation (**do not yield**). The command not to **listen to him** may have meant not to give in to his plea that his ways be kept secret. Since the temptation came through a loved one the tempted person would naturally feel compassion or **pity** and would probably be inclined to cover up the sin of his loved one (**shield him**). But here again God's commands were to rule over human feelings and experiences. The tempted person was to expose his loved one and in fact to **be the first in** stoning **him to death** (cf. Zech. 13:3). By casting the first stone the accuser was testifying to the truth of his testimony. The participation of the rest of the community then showed their allegiance to the Lord and their resolute hostility toward anything that might endanger that allegiance and turn them **away from the LORD.**

**13:10b-11.** The result of such a severe action would be that **all Israel** would

**hear** about this extraordinary devotion to the Lord **and be afraid** to disobey Him (cf. Acts 5:11). This is precisely what Moses was demanding of the people—an extraordinary commitment (superseding all other intimate relationships) to the God who had shown extraordinary grace to the nation (**who brought you out of Egypt, out of the land of slavery**; cf. Ex. 13:3, 14; 20:2; Deut. 5:6; 6:12; 7:8; 8:14; 13:5). This passage may have been in Jesus' mind when He demanded a similar commitment of His followers (cf. Matt. 10:34-39; Luke 14:26).

### d. The destruction of an apostate town (13:12-18)

**13:12-13.** The situation Moses envisioned here was perhaps the most potentially dangerous for the nation as a whole. Certain **wicked men** may lead a whole **town astray.** The men's wickedness is highlighted by the fact that they deceived **one of the towns the LORD** would give to Israel.

**13:14-18.** The punishment of this sin was to be so drastic that before any action was taken the truth of the report must be confirmed by a thorough investigation. If the report was confirmed, then the **town** was to be treated like a Canaanite city: set aside for complete destruction of **people** and **livestock** (on *ḥāram,* **destroy it completely,** see comments on 7:26; Josh. 6:21). The fact that **all its plunder** was to be destroyed, and that it was **never to be rebuilt,** precluded any greedy or illegitimate motivations by those who were to carry out its destruction. Obedience to this command would bring about a moral cleansing of the land and a spiritual renewal. Then in **mercy** and **compassion . . . the LORD** would prosper the people by increasing their **numbers, as He promised on oath** (cf. 4:31).

For the most part Israel failed to apply the commands of this chapter. This failure resulted in both the Northern Kingdom and later the Southern Kingdom being exiled. The commands of this chapter are not directed to Christians, because they do not live in one nation ruled by God; that is, the New Testament church is not a theocracy. However, church discipline should be exercised (Matt. 18:15-17; 1 Cor. 5) and there is a sin that leads to death (1 John 5:16-17; cf. Heb. 10:26-31).

### 4. LAWS REFLECTING THE HOLINESS OF THE PEOPLE (CHAP. 14)

To be "a people holy to the LORD" (v. 2) meant being a people set apart to God for His use. In the preceding section (12:29–13:18) Moses stressed the need for the nation in her worship to be set apart from all pagan nations. In chapter 14 Moses turned his attention to the everyday affairs of life and called for a distinctive lifestyle that would reflect Israel's unique position among all the nations.

### a. Prohibition of pagan mourning rites (14:1-2)

**14:1-2.** When Moses called the Israelites **children** (lit., "sons") **of the LORD your God** he was not referring to the new birth or regeneration. Rather he meant Israel's special privilege as the one nation **on the face of the earth** which had an intimate relationship with **the LORD.** All other nations were to come to the Lord through the ministry or testimony of the nation Israel. Because of this, Israel, **a people holy** (set apart) **to the LORD,** was to demonstrate her holiness before the other nations. A unique nation, Israel was God's **treasured possession** (cf. 7:6; 26:18; Ps. 135:4; Mal. 3:17; see comments on Ex. 19:5).

The other nations had peculiar and superstitious beliefs about dying and the dead. Some even worshiped dead spirits. The precise significance of the rituals mentioned here (Deut. 14:1)—laceration and shaving the head **for the dead**—is unknown today. But cutting oneself was a sign of mourning (cf. Jer. 16:6; 41:5; 47:5; 48:37).

However, it is clear that these practices reflected beliefs about the dead that conflicted with faith in the Lord, the ultimate Source of life. Therefore when a loved one died, the Israelites were to demonstrate their faith in the Lord by refraining from these pagan practices. Today Christians may demonstrate even greater faith when a believing loved one dies (cf. 1 Thes. 4:13-18).

### b. Clean and unclean food (14:3-21)

The precise meaning of these laws has been a source of debate since pre-Christian times. Perhaps the most popular modern explanation of the laws is that certain animals were prohibited for *hygienic reasons.* Commentators point out that pork may be a source of trichinosis and that the hare is a carrier of tularemia. However, several lines of evidence make this explanation improbable: (1) Jesus declared that all foods should be considered clean (Mark 7:14-23). This was reconfirmed in a heavenly vision granted to Peter (Acts 10:9-23) since the disciples seemed to have missed the point of Jesus' earlier declaration. It is difficult to believe that God was concerned about the health of His people in the Old Testament, but abandoned that concern in the New Testament. (2) Eating some of the "clean" animals may represent a greater danger to health than some of the "unclean" ones. (3) No hygienic reasons are given as motives for observing the law of the clean and the unclean. And the Old Testament does not state that the Israelites considered the unclean animals dangerous to their health.

A second popular interpretation of the prohibition of unclean animals for food is that they were used in *pagan cultic rites.* Evidence for this is that the unclean animals are said to be "detestable" (Deut. 14:3). The same Hebrew word is used elsewhere in Deuteronomy of idolatry and other pagan practices (7:25; 12:31). Also some unclean animals (e.g., pigs) were widely used in pagan rituals. However, this explanation clarifies so little of the data that it is not too useful. And one may adduce counter examples. For instance, the bull, a common symbol in the religions of the ancient Near East, was permitted as food for the Israelites.

A third explanation is that the clean and unclean animals were *symbolic* of good and evil in the human realm. This explanation became extremely subjective and even fanciful by earlier interpreters of the Old Testament. For instance, some held that chewing of the cud (14:6-8) represented the faithful believer who meditated on the Law. Others taught that the sheep (v. 4) was clean because it served as a reminder that the Lord is His people's Shepherd. This symbolic interpretation should be rejected since it is divorced from the controls of grammatical historical exegesis, and therefore is impossible to validate. However, a symbolic interpretation may be essentially correct if it is applied comprehensively under strict exegetical controls to all the ceremonially clean and unclean animals here.

The animals are divided into three classes: Those that live on land, those that live in the water, and those that live in the air. It has been suggested that certain animals in each group provide the standard for that class; any deviation from that standard renders the animal unclean. For example, the unclean birds are birds of prey that eat flesh without draining the blood and/or are carrion eaters, whereas clean birds are presumably those that eat grain. This, some suggest, symbolizes the two classes of people: Gentiles who eat animal blood and animal flesh that they find already dead (v. 21), and Israelites who refrain from both. However, the standard for each class is sometimes difficult to discern.

A fourth explanation is that the distinction between clean and unclean animals is purely arbitrary, that is, God made the distinctions so that Israel might have a way of expressing her unique relationship to Him, even in relation to food. Of these four explanations either the third or fourth one is preferable. If the clean and unclean animals symbolize the human realm (third explanation) then the food laws serve a double function. They were pedagogical illustrations to Israel of her relationship to God and the nations, and they reminded her of her uniqueness as a theocratic nation.

**14:3-8.** The exact identities of some of **the animals** and birds listed in verses 3-18 is uncertain. The animals in this first group are those that walk on land. **Any animal** could be eaten if it had **a split hoof divided in two and . . . chews the cud.** Ten such animals are listed in verses 4-5. Those that meet only one of these criteria were considered **ceremonially unclean.** These included **the camel, the rabbit,** and **the coney** (the rock badger; cf. NIV marg.), and **the pig.** The lists are obviously representative rather than exhaustive.

**14:9-20. Creatures** that swim in the sea could be eaten if they have **fins and scales.** Others could not be eaten for they were **unclean.**

Creatures that fly, the third classification, were subdivided into birds (vv. 11-18), and insects (vv. 19-20). As mentioned previously the unclean birds—21 of them are listed—are birds of prey and/or eaters of carrion. **Flying,** swarming **insects** were **unclean,** but others (e.g., the locust, cricket, and grasshopper) were **clean** insects (v. 20).

**14:21.** The prohibition against eating meat of an animal, bird, or insect found **already dead** was probably intended to prevent defilement from consuming blood, for the dead animal would not have had its blood drained properly. Other people could **eat it** but Israel was a distinct **people, holy to the LORD.**

The prohibition against cooking a **young goat in its mother's milk** possibly reflects a Canaanite fertility rite, though the interpretation of the Ugaritic text which is said to support this view is conjectural. Perhaps the prohibition meant that the Israelites were not to take what was intended to promote life (goat milk) and use it to destroy life (see comments on the parallel passage, Ex. 23:19; cf. Ex. 34:26).

In conclusion, all these food laws would have reminded Israel of her unique status before God. No Israelite could eat without realizing that in every area of his life he was to be consecrated to God. Likewise an Israelite's diet served as a testimony of his relationship to the Lord in the presence of Gentiles. As stated earlier, in the New Testament God abolished the food laws of the Old Testament (Mark 7:14-23; Acts 10:9-23). However, Christians should demonstrate their unique relationship to God by the purity of their lives. Christians may demonstrate their faith and unique relationship with the Lord by offering sincere thanks at mealtimes to God, the Creator and Provider of all food (1 Tim. 4:3-5).

### c. The law of the tithe (14:22-29)

**14:22-23.** The regulations about **the tithe** of the crops and livestock—which were to be eaten in a meal of fellowship at the central sanctuary—were connected to the preceding food laws (vv. 3-21). Eating the tithes in the Lord's **presence** was another way in which the Israelites were to express their unique relationship to and dependence on the Lord in reference to their food. (Regarding **the place** God would **choose as a dwelling for His name,** see comments on 12:5; also cf. 12:11; 16:2, 6, 11; 26:2.) Their diet was restricted not only in what they could eat but also in how much of their food they might keep for themselves. The law of the tithe, with its provision for the care of

the poor (14:28-29), also anticipated the following legislation (15:1-18) concerning debtors, slaves, and other impoverished people.

God emphasized the absolute necessity for the Israelites to tithe: **Be sure to set aside a 10th.** Previously Moses had indicated that the Israelites' tithes were to go to the Levites (Num. 18:21-32). Now Moses added a new feature to the legislation about the tithe. The Israelites were to take part of their tithe to the central sanctuary, and eat it there in a common meal before **the LORD.** Or this may be a second tithe (a 10th of the remaining 90%), part of which was to be eaten at the sanctuary with the remainder given to the Levites serving there (cf. Deut. 14:27). This experience was designed to teach them **to revere** (lit., "fear"; cf. 4:10) **the LORD** their **God always.** As they ate this meal before Him with priestly instruction they would be acknowledging that their food (and thus their very lives) depended not on their agricultural skills but on the Lord's blessing. So they would learn to fear Him, for only by obeying Him would they continue to eat and live in prosperity.

**14:24-27.** Some people would be living **too . . . far away** from the future sanctuary to make it practical to herd or **carry** their **tithe.** So they could sell their **tithe** of produce and livestock **for silver.** Then they could travel to the central sanctuary and there **buy . . . cattle, sheep, wine, or . . . fermented drink or** whatever they wished and **eat** and drink it there in God's **presence.** (Cf. another concession in 12:20-25.)

Both "wine" and "fermented drink" were permissible here in even an act of worship to **the LORD.** The Hebrew word for "wine" is *yayin,* which sometimes means an intoxicating beverage and other times means a nonintoxicating drink. The Hebrew word for "fermented drink" (*šēkār*) is often rendered "strong drink" in some translations (e.g., KJV, NASB, RSV). This is misleading because it suggests that *šēkār* refers to distilled liquor. But the process for distillation was not used in the Near East until the seventh century A.D. The "fermented drink" was probably a kind of beer (this is the usual NIV trans.), brewed by the ancient Egyptians and Akkadians, and therefore low in alcohol content. (However, wine [*yayin*] drunk in excess can be intoxicating; cf., e.g., Isa. 5:11; Prov. 20:1; and drunkenness is sin.)

Presumably one family could not eat all its tithe, so the remainder was to be given to **the Levites** at the sanctuary. In this way the Levites were provided for since they had no land **inheritance of their own.**

**14:28-29.** Every third year the second tithe (cf. comments on vv. 22-27) was not to be taken to the sanctuary but was to be used to feed **the Levites** and less fortunate members of society. **The aliens** were foreigners who lived with the Israelites. Though those foreigners were to be treated fairly, they did not share all the privileges of Israelite citizenship. **Widows** and their children (**the fatherless**) were also given special consideration (cf. 24:19-21; 26:12-13).

If the Israelites obeyed this command to share, then they could always expect to live in a prosperous society and could be generous, for **God** would **bless** them **in all the work of** their **hands.** Tithing is not commanded in the New Testament. Yet believers in the Church Age still indicate by their giving that God supports and cares for them. Christians are to give "generously," knowing that they "will also reap generously" (2 Cor. 9:6; cf. 2 Cor. 9:7-9; 1 Cor. 16:1-2).

5. THE YEAR OF RELEASE (15:1-18)

*a. The cancellation of debts (15:1-11)*

**15:1.** The sabbatical year or year of release was also commanded in Exodus 23:10-11 and Leviticus 25:1-7. However, while these verses stated that in the seventh year the land was to lie fallow without any crops being planted they did not mention the cancellation of **debts.** Only here did Moses prescribe this requirement. **At the end of every seven years** is a Hebrew idiom which means "during the seventh year." The law of cancellation is stated in Deuteronomy 15:1 and explained in verses 2-11.

**15:2-6.** The words **cancel the loan** could mean the loan was to be completely eliminated. Or they could mean it was to be canceled only during the seventh year. That is, payment could not be demanded in the seventh year, but after the seventh year the loan would still have to be repaid. In favor of this second view is the fact that during the seventh year

when the land was to lie fallow an **Israelite** debtor would not have the means to repay his debt, but in the next six years he would. (The debts of a foreign businessman—i.e., **a foreigner** but not a "resident alien"; cf. 14:29—were not canceled. This was because he did not let his land lie fallow or suspend his normal source of income for a year as the Israelites did.)

In spite of this argument, however, it is more likely that the debt was canceled completely and permanently. Several points favor this: (1) This view is more consonant with the generosity the Lord had expressed toward Israel. (2) It is more consistent with the statements in 15:9-11. (3) The practice of canceling the entire debt permanently in the seventh year was evidently meant to prepare the Israelites for the extravagant practices commanded for the Jubilee (50th) Year in which each one was to receive back "his family property" (Lev. 25:8-17). (4) Permanent cancellation of debts would help prevent poverty (Deut. 15:4a; cf. comments on v. 11). (5) The potential for incredible wealth in the land of Israel also argues for the permanent cancellation of debts. Israel had the opportunity to be the richest and most prosperous nation on the face of the earth (**He will richly bless you,** v. 4b; cf. v. 6a). This prosperity would be due not to any technological achievement on her part, but because of her wholehearted commitment to **God: if only you fully obey the** Lord **your God and are careful to follow all these commands** (v. 5). Moses' statement, **you will lend to many nations but . . . borrow from none,** was, in effect, a promise of world sovereignty (**you will rule over many nations**).

**15:7-11.** Moses left the realm of law for a moment to appeal to his fellow Israelites' hearts. The law of debt cancellation (vv. 1-6) was intended to instill a spirit of generosity within the Israelites and thus a freedom from the love of money and things. Therefore a calculating Israelite was guilty of sin if he refused a loan for a **poor brother** (v. 7; cf. **needy brother,** v. 9) out of fear that it might not be repaid since **the seventh year** was **near.** Being **hardened or tightfisted** meant he was not trusting **the** Lord to **bless . . . all** his **work.** Solomon may have been meditating on these words of

Moses when he wrote, "One man gives freely, yet gains even more; another withholds unduly, but comes to poverty" (Prov. 11:24). Moses summarized the attitude the Israelites should have toward those in need: **be openhanded** (Deut. 15:8, 11). The sad confession, **there will always be poor people in the land,** is perhaps a tragic foreshadowing of Israel's refusal to obey the Lord fully (v. 5).

#### b. The freeing of servants (15:12-18)

**15:12-15.** Sometimes a person unable to pay his debts would sell himself as a servant to his creditor. If the size of his debt meant he must work for **six years,** he was to be freed **in the seventh year.** This did not correspond to the year of debt cancellation (vv. 1-6), but was the seventh year of that person's work as a servant. The LORD had previously made it clear that six full years of a person's life were enough to make up for defaulting on a loan (cf. Ex. 21:2). However, in Deuteronomy Moses added that the employer must do more than free the servant; he must also **supply him liberally** with livestock, grain, and wine in accord with the way **the LORD** had **blessed** him.

After six years the servant would have little or nothing, so to **send him away empty-handed** would have jeopardized his freedom all over again. Obedience to **this command** would serve the valuable purpose of reminding employers of the grace God had shown Israel in redeeming her from **Egypt** (cf. Deut. 24:18, 22). It would remind them that their own welfare also depended on that grace.

**15:16-17.** Moses also provided for a **servant** who had become too attached to a family to leave it. The employer was to pierce the servant's **earlobe** with **an awl** to indicate he was the man's **servant for life** (cf. comments on Ex. 21:5-6).

**15:18.** Moses offered a double motivation to one who was perhaps too greedy **to set** his **servant free.** In fairness he should realize that it would have cost him at least **twice as much** if he had hired someone for **six years.** Second, if in faith he would obey the command to release his servant, **the LORD** would **bless** him in **everything** he would **do.** This promise of blessing in return for obedience is stated often in Deuteronomy, four times in this chapter alone (vv. 4, 6, 10, 18).

6. THE LAW OF FIRSTBORN ANIMALS (15:19-23)

The law regarding firstborn animals may have occurred here in Moses' sermon because, like the laws of canceling debts and releasing servants, it involved giving up one's possessions. This law was first recorded in Exodus 13:11-15. It was pedagogical: sacrificing firstborn animals reminded the Israelites of their redemption from Egypt when all the firstborn Egyptian sons died. It was an occasion for the Israelites to teach their children about God's redemption of their nation.

According to Exodus 22:29-30 the firstborn were to be sacrificed on the eighth day after birth. Firstborn animal sacrifices were also used to help support the priests (Num. 18:15-18).

**15:19.** In Israel's livestock **every firstborn male** was to be completely **set apart for the LORD.** Its owner received no benefit on his farm from the animal; **firstborn . . . oxen** were not to plow; **firstborn . . . sheep** were not to be shorn. (Goats are also mentioned in Num. 18:17.)

**15:20.** Annually (presumably during one of the annual feasts; cf. 6:16) the young firstborn animals were to be taken to the central sanctuary to be sacrificed. The sacrificed animals were then eaten there in a communal meal with one's **family.**

**15:21-23.** An imperfect firstborn **animal** was not acceptable as a **sacrifice** (cf. 17:1), so it was to be treated like a game animal (cf. 12:15; 14:4-5)—eaten at home but not sacrificed. As stated previously (12:16, 23-24) **the blood** of such animals was not to be eaten.

7. THE PILGRIM FESTIVALS (16:1-17)

The festivals mentioned here were the three great annual feasts which all male Israelites were supposed to attend (v. 16). If possible their families were to go along (cf. vv. 11, 14, see comments on v. 16). These feasts were so important to Israel's religious life that after the Dispersion some Jews residing far from Palestine still attended one or more of the festivals whenever possible (cf. Acts 2:9-11, the Feast of Weeks or Pentecost). Attending these feasts gave the Israelites opportunity to acknowledge the Lord as their Deliverer and Provider. It also gave them opportunity to express their faith in the Lord as they left their families in God's care to journey to the sanctuary. These festivals demonstrated that worshiping God should be a joyful experience in which the participants gratefully share in the bounty of His blessing (Deut. 16:11, 14-15; cf. 12:7, 12, 18; 14:26).

### a. The Passover (16:1-8)

**16:1-2.** The most detailed instructions for **the Passover** are in Exodus 12:1-28, 43-49. The word "Passover" (*pesaḥ*) comes from the verb *pāsaḥ* meaning "to pass over." This feast commemorated the **night** the Lord "passed over" the blood-sprinkled houses of the Israelites, sparing the lives of their firstborn people, and putting to death the firstborn Egyptians and their livestock. The lives of Israelite firstborn people and livestock were protected by the sacrificial blood. As a commemorative rite the Israelites were to use **the Passover** to teach their children about God's miraculous deliverance from **Egypt** (Ex. 12:26-27).

The Passover was celebrated on the 14th day of **Abib** (March-April). Originally the Passover **sacrifice** was from the **flock,** either a year-old sheep or goat (Ex. 12:5). The words **or herd** (cattle) mean that Moses widened the choice. Or perhaps the sacrifice from the herd was to be offered in the seven-day Feast of Unleavened Bread (Deut. 16:3) immediately after the Passover. At any rate lambs became the traditional Passover sacrificial animals. The animals were sacrificed "at twilight" (see comments on Ex. 12:6).

Gentiles were excluded from the Passover feast unless they had become proselytes (Ex. 12:43-49). Each year Passover was observed a month later for those unable to partake of the feast during **Abib** because of ceremonial uncleanness or absence on a journey (Num. 9:6-12).

**16:3-4.** The Passover was immediately followed by the **seven**-day Feast of **Unleavened Bread,** so in effect the two actually constituted one festival (cf. Luke 2:41; 22:7; Acts 12:3-4; see comments on Luke 22:7-38; John 19:14). Eating **bread** without **yeast** commemorated the **haste** with which the Israelites had to leave **Egypt** (Ex. 12:33-34). This would help them **remember** their quick **departure from Egypt.** As **bread of affliction** it also symbolized the Israelites' slavery in

Egypt. None of **the meat** sacrificed in **the evening of the first** feast **day** (the Passover lamb) was to be left over to eat the next **morning.** It was to be burned (Ex. 12:10), perhaps suggestive of the sacrifice's sacred nature.

**16:5-8.** The first **Passover** had been observed in the homes of the individual Israelites. But later after the central sanctuary was built (**the place** where God's **name** would dwell; cf. 12:5, 11; 14:23; 16:2, 11; 26:1, 15), the Passover could be observed only there. This may have symbolized Israel's birth as a nation at the Exodus, a nation meant to be a family with God as her Head. Even though "twilight" may have meant 3 to 5 P.M. (see comments on Ex. 12:6) that could still be called **in the evening when the sun** was beginning to go **down.**

After roasting and eating **the Passover** animal the people were to **return to** their **tents,** the temporary homes of those who had come to the central sanctuary for the celebration. In the New Testament Jesus Christ was identified as the Passover Lamb sacrificed for believers (1 Cor. 5:7; also cf. John 19:36 with Ex. 12:46b). By applying the blood of Christ to themselves, that is, trusting in Him who died in their place for their sin, Christians are spared from eternal death.

### b. The Feast of Weeks (16:9-12)

**16:9.** The name Feast of Weeks was given this festival in light of Moses' command to **count off seven weeks from the time** they **began to** harvest the **grain** in March-April. This would mean the Feast of Weeks was in late May or early June. It was also known as the "Feast of Harvest" (Ex. 23:16) and the "day of firstfruits" (Num. 28:26). Later it was given the title "Pentecost" based on the Septuagint's translation of the "50 days" (Lev. 23:16).

**16:10-12.** The Feast of Weeks was a celebration of God's rich provision for His people. Therefore each **freewill** (voluntary) **offering** was to be **in proportion to** one's **blessings** from the LORD (cf. v. 17; 15:14). Paul may have had this standard of giving in mind for Christians rather than a system of tithing when he directed the Corinthian Christians to give as each one "may prosper" (1 Cor. 16:2, NASB).

This feast was to be a time of joy and

sharing. Since **the** L<small>ORD</small> had been "generous" with the Israelites they were to be generous with others, especially with the less prosperous members of their society (cf. Deut. 14:21; 16:14; 24:19-21). Appropriately the Holy Spirit was given to New Testament saints during the Feast of Pentecost (Acts 2). This symbolized the end of the Old Testament system of worship and the beginning of the New (see comments on Acts 2:4). It also pointed to the fact that God's greatest provision for a Christian's daily living is the gift of the Holy Spirit. (On the admonition **follow carefully** see comments on Deut. 31:12.)

*c. The Feast of Tabernacles (16:13-17)*

**16:13. The Feast of Tabernacles** was so called because the Israelites, after the fall harvest (Lev. 23:39), were to live for one week in tabernacles or "booths" (Lev. 23:42) constructed of tree branches and foliage (Lev. 23:40). It was also called the "Feast of Ingathering" (Ex. 23:16; 34:22). It began on the 15th day of the seventh month (Lev. 23:34, 39), the month of Tishri (September-October). The fact that it was called "the L<small>ORD</small>'s Feast of Tabernacles" (Lev. 23:29), and also simply *"the* feast" (Ezek. 45:25) may indicate that this autumn festival became the greatest of the three Israelite pilgrim feasts.

**16:14-15. Joy** (v. 15) was to characterize this festival, which was also true of the Feast of Weeks (vv. 10-11). The people were to **be joyful** in God's provision, but also (as Lev. 23:42-43 indicates) they were to rejoice in their deliverance from Egypt. The week of living in booths was to recall the journey through the desert after the nation had come out of Egypt. Thus the autumn festival celebrated the formation of the nation through God's grace and His continuing support of her, right up to the moment of the festival.

**16:16-17.** In a summary Moses reminded the Israelite **men** of their obligation to go **three times a year** to **appear before the** L<small>ORD</small>. This did not mean, of course, that a man's family members were not to take part in the feasts. The ideal was for all family members—along with servants, Levites, aliens, the fatherless and widows—to join in the celebration (cf. vv. 11, 14). **Each** man was to **bring a gift** because the keynote of each of the festivals was the joyful expression

of thanks for God's rich spiritual and material blessings experienced in the past and the present. The gifts to **the** L<small>ORD</small> were to be proportionate to the people's blessings (cf. v. 17; 15:14).

8. THE INSTRUMENTS OF THEOCRACY (16:18–18:22)

The preceding sections (12:1–16:17) were mainly concerned with laws related to the worship of the Lord by His people. This section (16:18–18:22) deals with the responsibilities of the officials to maintain pure worship within the Promised Land and to administer justice impartially.

*a. Judges and officials (16:18–17:13)*

**16:18-20.** At this time in his sermon Moses did not specify *how* **judges and officials** would be appointed. In the wilderness Moses at first had been the only judge of the people. But when the judicial burden became too great for him he appointed "leading men" of the **tribes** as military leaders ("commanders"), officials, and judges (1:15-18; cf. Ex. 18). Probably these men were the chief elders in each tribe. So the judges appointed in each city were probably taken from that city's council of elders (the elders functioned as a judicial body; cf. Deut. 19:12).

The "officials" were probably assistants to the judges, probably functioning as clerks. These leaders were to **judge the people fairly** (lit., "righteously"; cf. 1:17; Prov. 18:5; 24:23). Their verdicts were to conform to the righteous standards set forth in the Word of **God** (which meant at that time the five books of Moses). They were **not** to **pervert justice.** This implies that God had given them a heavenly pattern for their actions toward each other. If their actions did not conform to this pattern, those actions were to be changed or punished. Any nonconformity to the pattern of justice was a perversion.

Nor were they to **show partiality** (lit., "do not recognize faces"). Ideally the judges were to treat each person as though they had no prior knowledge of him or her. Accepting **a bribe** was obviously wrong for it perverted (**blinds** and **twists**) the ability of judges to act in fairness to the parties in the litigation.

Moses summed up the requirements for the judges and officials with an emphatic command to **follow justice and**

**justice alone** (lit., "righteousness, righteousness you must pursue!"). These words imply that impartial justice could be an elusive goal because of the weakness of human nature. Therefore it was absolutely essential that the standard set forth in the Law be followed precisely. Their lives and prosperity (Deut. 16:20) depended on their establishing impartial justice in the Promised **Land.**

**16:21–17:1.** The first responsibility of the judges was to prevent impure worshiping practices in the land. Anything that might lead to syncretism (accommodating worship of the Lord to pagan systems of worship) was prohibited. This included **any wooden Asherah pole** (symbolic of Asherah, goddess of fertility and consort of Baal) or **a sacred stone,** a stone pillar symbolic of male fertility (cf. 7:5; 12:3; Ex. 34:13).

To take a defective **sacrifice to the LORD** (Deut. 17:1; cf. 15:21) was to bring something into the sanctuary that was foreign to the worship of **God,** just as Asherah poles and sacred stones were foreign to genuine worship. Such a sacrifice was **detestable to** the Lord. To offer less than the best to God was to "despise" His name (Mal. 1:6-8). Offering a less-than-perfect sacrifice was, in effect, failing to acknowledge Him as the ultimate Provider of all that is best in life. Also it was a failure to acknowledge the vast gulf that exists between the perfectly holy God and sinful people.

The priests were normally responsible to maintain pure worship at the sanctuary (i.e., no fertility symbols or defective sacrifices), but the ultimate responsibility rested with the judges. If the priests failed, it was necessary for the judges to intervene.

**17:2-7.** The judges were also to see that false worshipers were executed. One who **worshiped other gods** deserved capital punishment because his act threatened the nation's very existence. Astral worship was also forbidden (cf. 4:19) for it honored inanimate creation rather than the living Creator. The execution could take place only after it had been proved by a thorough investigation. To insure against a capricious execution **two or three** independent **witnesses** were required. **One witness** was inadequate (cf. 19:15) because if he lied no one would be able to prove or disprove it.

**The witnesses** were to **be the first** in the execution. So if their **testimony** was later proved false, they in effect would have committed murder and would be liable to execution. The whole community (**all the people**) would then join in the execution, thereby demonstrating their rejection of other gods (17:3) and their commitment to the Lord. Such idolatry was an **evil** to be purged **from** the people (cf. v. 12; see comments on 13:5).

New Testament churches have a similar responsibility to keep themselves pure. A Christian offender should be "cut off" from his local church's fellowship if a thorough investigation proves his sin and he is unwilling to repent of it. If he is a genuine believer he will not lose eternal life. But he will suffer loss on earth and receive less reward in heaven (Matt. 18:15-20; 1 Cor. 3:10-15; 5; 1 Tim. 5:19).

**17:8-13.** Moses made a provision for future judges in the Promised Land similar to that provided for judges in the time of the wilderness wanderings (1:17). If a judge felt a case was **too difficult for** him to decide, he could take it to a central tribunal (consisting of **priests** and the officiating chief **judge**) to be established at the future site of the central sanctuary (**the place the LORD** would **choose**). **The decisions** of the tribunal would be final. Any rebellion against the tribunal was considered "contempt of court" and was a capital offense. This made the rule of justice paramount in the land and helped prevent anarchy.

*b. The king (17:14-20)*

After Moses and Joshua died, the people were to be governed by judges and priests. However, this system did not provide Israel with any semblance of a strong central government. It could only work if the leaders (the judges and the priests) *and* the people were committed to following the Lord. The Book of Judges records the sad failure of the people and the leaders in this system. Moses anticipated that failure by including this law in reference to the future king. One may ask why God allowed the priests and judges to fail. Or why did not God institute the monarchy immediately? The answer, at least partly, is that He was preparing the nation to appreciate the gift of the monarchy.

**17:14-15.** After Israel could no longer tolerate her unique position of being without a king, she would ask for and receive **a king.** Verses 14-15 speak of the king's qualifications, verses 16-17 of his behavior, and verses 18-20 of his education. The king was to have two qualifications. First, he had to be chosen by **the LORD.** Later history made it clear that prophets, speaking on God's behalf, would declare His choice (e.g., Samuel's support for Saul, 1 Sam. 9–12, and then for David, 1 Sam. 16; Nathan's support of Solomon, 1 Kings 1). The people could **be sure** that God would place no one on the throne whom He had not gifted to be **king.** Therefore if a king failed, the reason for his failure would not lie in his lack of ability but in his moral life. Second, the king **must be** an **Israelite.** An Israelite raised from childhood in the traditions and Scripture of Israel would be a far better choice than **a foreigner** to protect the purity of Israel's religion.

**17:16-17.** Three things about the behavior of **the king** were singled out. The prohibition against acquiring **great numbers of horses** meant that on human terms the king's army, composed mainly of infantry, would be significantly weaker than an enemy's army with many chariots and cavalry. Yet this was precisely the point. An obedient Israelite king was to depend not on military strength but on **the LORD** alone. God had already demonstrated His ability to crush a large superior chariot army (Ex. 14–15). Acquiring horses would mean the people would be going **to Egypt,** where many were available. Returning to the nation's former land of slavery was unthinkable.

The prohibition against taking **many wives** was given because many kings married foreign women to form political alliances. If the king followed the Lord he would not need political alliances. Also foreign wives would cause **his heart** to **be led astray** to worship their idols.

The prohibition against **large amounts of silver and gold** was intended to keep the king from developing a sense of independence and a lust for material wealth (cf. Prov. 30:8-9). All three prohibitions, then, were designed to reduce the king to the status of a servant totally dependent on his Master, the Lord. The tragedy of ignoring these commands is seen in Solomon who broke all three pro-

hibitions (1 Kings 10:14-15, 23, 26-28; 11:1-6).

**17:18-20.** The *education* of a king consisted of his copying, reading, and following **carefully** the **Law and these decrees,** that is, the entire Book of Deuteronomy (not just this small section of vv. 14-20). This would insure a right spirit within the king (i.e., humility and obedience) and a **long** dynastic succession.

### c. The priests and Levites (18:1-8)

The tribe of Levi was divided into three families (Gershonites, Kohathites, and Merarites). Each division originally had different responsibilities regarding the tabernacle (Num. 3–4). The Kohathites were further divided into those who were descendants of Aaron and those who were not (Josh. 21:4-5).

Only the descendants of Aaron were permitted to serve as priests (Num. 3:10). They are generally referred to as "the priests" or "the sons of Aaron" (Num. 10:8). The rest of the tribe, those not serving as priests, were designated as Levites. Thus priests were a minority in the tribe of Levi.

The Levites served as ministers to the priests (Num. 18:1-7; 1 Chron. 23:28-32), and in general as teachers of the Law in Israel (Deut. 33:10a; 2 Chron. 17:8-9). The priests officiated at the tabernacle and also had other duties. They served as judges (Deut. 17:8-9), guardians of the scroll of the Law (17:18; 31:9), teachers of regulations concerning skin diseases (24:8), and assistants to Moses in the covenant renewal ceremony (27:9).

**18:1-2.** Unlike the other 11 tribes, none of the **Levites** including **the priests** was given an **allotment** of land to settle and cultivate. However, 48 cities were set aside for the Levites (Num. 35:1-8; Josh. 21:1-42). **The priests** (and the Levites who assisted them at the central sanctuary) were to be sustained by the people's **offerings made to the LORD.** The Levites who did not assist at the central sanctuary were to be sustained by gifts from the people (Deut. 14:28-29; 16:10-11).

**18:3-5.** The people were responsible for supporting **the priests** who officiated at the central sanctuary. The priests were to receive parts of bulls and **sheep** that were sacrificed, **the firstfruits of . . . grain, new wine, and oil, and the first wool.** This was because **God** had **chosen**

Aaron and his **descendants out of all** the **tribes to stand and minister in the** LORD's **name,** that is, on His behalf.

The New Testament broadened the priesthood to include all Christians (1 Peter 2:9). The reason for this is that Jesus Christ by virtue of His ministry, death, and resurrection superseded the Aaronic priesthood of the Old (Mosaic) Covenant and became the High Priest of the New Covenant (Heb. 2:17-18; 4:14–5:10; 6:19–7:28). Every Christian has come into the family of Jesus (Heb. 2:10-13) and therefore into Jesus' priestly line.

**18:6-8.** If a Levite wanted to go to the central sanctuary to **minister** there **in the** Lord's **name** (on His behalf), he was permitted to do so and to receive equal support along with the other **Levites.** This does not imply that this Levite would minister as a priest as some have suggested. The Levites were to *assist* the priests (1 Chron. 23:28-32). **Even though** a Levite had **received money from the** prior **sale of** his **family possessions** (cf. Lev. 25:32-34) before moving to Jerusalem, he was to receive support for his work at the sanctuary. Paul restated this principle for the New Testament church (1 Cor. 9:14; 1 Tim. 5:17-18).

### d. The prophets (18:9-22)

**18:9-14.** In these verses all the forbidden practices—called **detestable ways** (cf. v. 12) **of the nations** in the land—dealt with either foretelling the future or magic. By the use of magic one attempted to manipulate or force the "gods" into certain courses of action. Child sacrifice was mentioned here because it was used either as a means of foretelling or as magic to manipulate certain events.

All these practices are forbidden because they divorce life from morality. Several factors make this clear: (1) The future was "determined" by one's moral behavior, not by magical manipulation. (2) Using magic to manipulate one's circumstances was in essence a futile attempt to flee from the Lord's ethical laws which promoted life and blessing. (3) The use of magic and **divination** (vv. 10, 14) was a refusal to acknowledge the sovereignty of **the** LORD. (4) Reliance on these practices indicated a corresponding failure to trust **the** LORD with one's life. People who are knowledgeable of the occult and demon possession quickly point

out that the practices mentioned in verses 9-14 have led many into satanic bondage.

**Divination** (vv. 10, 14), from the verb *qāsam,* "to divide," means to give false prophecy or seek to determine the will of the gods by examining and interpreting omens. (*Qāsam* is also used in Josh. 13:22; 1 Sam. 6:2; 28:8; 2 Kings 17:17; Isa. 3:2; 44:25; Jer. 27:9; 29:8; Ezek. 13:6, 9, 23; 21:21, 23, 29; 22:28; Micah 3:6-7, 11; Zech. 10:2.) **Sorcery** (*'ānan,* Deut. 18:10, 14; cf. Lev. 19:26; 2 Kings 21:6; Isa. 2:6; Micah 5:12, "cast spells") is the attempt to control people or circumstances through power given by evil spirits (demons). To interpret **omens** is to tell the future based on "signs" such as the movements of birds, fire, or rain. **Witchcraft** (*kāšap*) involves practicing magic by incantations. One who **casts spells** is literally "one who ties knots" (*ḥābar*), thus one who binds other people by magical mutterings. A **spiritualist** is one who supposedly communicates with the dead but who actually communicates with demons. One **who consults the dead** may mean the spiritist's attempt to contact the dead to gain advice, information on the future, or help in manipulation.

Such **detestable practices** were one reason the Lord used Israel to destroy the Canaanites. Therefore it was understandably **detestable** for an Israelite to become involved in those things. By avoiding them the Israelites would be **blameless** of their terrible sins.

**18:15-19.** In contrast with the dark magic of Canaanite diviners, witches, and spiritists, Israelites were to **listen to** the Lord's **prophet.** The Israelites could be sure that a "line of prophets" would follow in succession after Moses because of their original request **at Horeb** (Sinai) that **God** speak to them through Moses as a mediator (cf. 5:23-27). Each prophet God would **raise up** would be an Israelite, and because the true **prophet** would only speak the **words** of **the** LORD, the people were obligated to obey (**listen to**) those **words.**

The ultimate **Prophet like** Moses (18:15, 18) is Jesus Christ—the One who spoke God's words and who provides deliverance for His people. Not even Joshua could be compared to Moses, for since Moses "no prophet has risen in Israel like" him (34:10) with such power before men and intimacy with God. However distinguished a future prophet's role might be in Israel, none would be like Moses until the Mediator of the New Covenant, Jesus Christ, came. Moses set the standard for every future prophet. Each prophet was to do his best to live up to the example of Moses until the One came who would introduce the New Covenant. During the first century A.D. the official leaders of Judaism were still looking for the fulfillment of Moses' prediction (cf. John 1:21). Peter said their search should have stopped with the Lord Jesus (Acts 3:22-23). (Other early and clear predictions of the Messiah may be found in Gen. 49:10-12; Num. 24:17-19.)

**18:20-22.** Since the people were to obey God's **prophet** without question (v. 19), to prophesy falsely was in effect to usurp the place of God. For this the false **prophet** was to **be put to death.**

Two tests could be used to determine whether a prophet was speaking God's words. First, the prophet's message had to be in accordance with God and His Word. If he spoke **in the name of** (on behalf of) **other gods** then he contradicted the objectively revealed Word of God and was therefore a false prophet (cf. 13:1-5). Second, his prophecy must **come true.** If neither of these conditions was met, then no matter how powerful the would-be **prophet** seemed to be, the people were **not** to **be afraid of him** or of any reprisals he might predict against them.

9. THE CITIES OF REFUGE AND CRIMINAL LAW (CHAP. 19)

*a. Three cities of refuge for manslaughter (19:1-13)*

**19:1-3.** Moses had previously **set aside . . . three cities** in the Transjordan (4:41-43). Since he knew that **the LORD** would not let him cross the Jordan River and enter the Promised Land with Israel, he now instructed the nation to set aside three more cities of refuge in accord with God's original instructions (Num. 35:9-34). The cities of refuge were to be equally spaced throughout the land (**build roads to them and divide into three parts the land**) so that they might be easily reached by **anyone who kills a man.** (See the map "The Six Cities of Refuge," near Num. 35:6-34.) The word translated

"kills" (*rāṣaḥ*; cf. Ex. 20:13) means "to take life without legal sanction." It could refer to murder when life was taken intentionally or to manslaughter done unintentionally.

**19:4-7.** These cities were to be "set aside" (v. 2) to prevent any further calamity from arising from a tragic situation. Only a person who killed **his neighbor unintentionally, without malice** (v. 4) could **flee to one of these cities and save his life** (v. 5). These cities offered protection from an **avenger of blood.** The word translated "avenger of blood" is *gō'ēl*. A *gō'ēl* was essentially a "family protector." He was a "near kinsman" (traditionally understood as the nearest male relative) responsible for redeeming (buying) a relative out of slavery (Lev. 25:48-49), for redeeming a relative's property (Lev. 25:26-33), for marrying a relative's widow and raising up children in the name of the deceased (Ruth 3:13; 4:5-10), and for avenging the death of a relative (Num. 35:19-28). One who killed his neighbor unintentionally (e.g., by an **ax . . . head** that accidentally flew **off** the handle **and hit** and killed **his neighbor**) had to stay in the city of refuge until the death of the current high priest. The elders of that city were obligated to protect him from the avenger of blood (Num. 35:25). If the person guilty of manslaughter left the city before the high priest's death then the avenger could kill him "without being guilty of murder" (Num. 35:27). The **cities** of refuge taught Israel how important life is to God. Even though a man had killed his neighbor accidentally he still had to give up a large measure of his freedom for an extended period of time.

**19:8-10.** If the Israelites had been faithful in following **the LORD** fully, then He would have enlarged their **territory** to the boundaries **promised** in the Abrahamic Covenant (Gen. 15:18-21). (On the Deuteronomic emphasis on **forefathers** see comments on Deut. 1:35.) In that case **three more cities,** a total of nine, would have been needed to prevent the **land** from being defiled with **innocent blood.**

The plural **these laws** (19:9) is literally, "this command." By using the singular Moses was emphasizing the unity of the Law; it is all one and to be obeyed in its entirety. But he also was pointing to the fundamental requirement of the Law, namely, **to love the LORD your God** (a theme stated repeatedly in Deut.—see comments on 6:5). The Law was given so that Israel might have a means to express her love for Him. In the Church Age Christians express their love for the Lord by obeying Jesus' commands (John 14:21).

**19:11-13.** A city of refuge could not provide sanctuary for a murderer. He was to be returned to **his town** and killed by **the avenger of blood** (see comments on v. 6). If the nation was to prosper under God's blessing Israel could not **show** the murderer **pity.** This sin **of shedding innocent blood** was to be purged from the nation.

### b. Displacing a boundary marker (19:14)

**19:14.** It is not clear why Moses placed this law about the **boundary stone** between the legislation about the cities of refuge (vv. 1-13) and the false witnesses (vv. 15-21). Moving a **neighbor's** boundary stone was equivalent to stealing his property. According to extrabiblical literature this was a widespread problem in the ancient Near East (cf. Job 24:2). Apparently it became widespread in Israel (Deut. 27:17; Prov. 22:28; 23:10; Hosea 5:10).

### c. The law of witnesses (19:15-21)

**19:15.** Moses laid down the principle that more than **one witness** was necessary **to convict a man** of a **crime** (cf. 17:6). This principle was to act as a safeguard against a false witness who might bring an untruthful charge against a fellow Israelite because of a quarrel or out of some other impure motive. By requiring more than one witness—at least **two or three**—greater accuracy and objectivity was effected.

**19:16-20.** Inevitably in some cases there would be only one witness. A single witness still was obligated to bring a charge against the offender. However, such a case would be taken to the central tribunal of **priests** and **judges** (cf. 17:8-13) for trial. **If** on investigation the testimony was found to be **false** then the accuser (a **malicious witness,** 19:16, and **a liar,** v. 18) received the punishment appropriate for the alleged crime. When the fate of the false witness became known in Israel it would serve as a great deterrent against giving false testimony in Israel's

courts. Violating the ninth commandment (Ex. 20:16) was another **evil** to be purged from the nation (cf. Deut. 19:13 and see comments on 13:5). Modern sociological theories which maintain that punishment, particularly capital punishment, does not deter crime contradict the biblical understanding of human nature.

**19:21.** The law of retribution, known in Latin as the *lex talionis,* was previously given in Exodus 21:23-25 and Leviticus 24:17-22. This law was given to encourage appropriate punishment of a criminal in cases where there might be a tendency to be either too lenient or too strict. The law codes of the ancient Near East did provide for the maiming of a criminal (e.g., gouging out an eye, cutting off a lip, etc.). With one exception (Deut. 25:11-12) Israelite law did not explicitly allow such mutilation. Apart from this one instance, therefore, only the first part of this law, **life for life,** was applied to indicate that punishment ought to fit the crime (punishment in kind). Thus a slave who lost his eye was freed (Ex. 21:26). The *lex talionis* also served as a restraint in cases where the punisher might be inclined to be excessive in administering punishment. Jesus did not deny the validity of this principle for the courtroom, but He denied its usage in personal relationships (Matt. 5:38-42). There should be no personal retaliation or revenge.

### 10. REGULATIONS FOR HOLY WAR (CHAP. 20)

### a. The command not to fear a superior enemy (20:1-4)

**20:1.** Similar principles for battle and legislation on holy **war** were given earlier (2:24–3:11; 7) and the subject was addressed again later in Moses' speech (21:10-14; 23:9-14; 24:5; 25:17-19). Israel was never to fear an enemy's **horses and chariots . . . because** the outcome of a battle would never be determined by mere military strength (cf. Isa. 31:1-3; Hosea 14:3). The command **not to be afraid of them** was based on the fact of God's faithfulness. He had already been proved faithful to the nation in bringing her **up out of Egypt.** In times of adversity believers today ought also to recall God's past faithfulness to them for this helps alleviate fear in their present circumstances.

**20:2-4.** The role of **the priest in battle** was not only to care for the ark, which symbolized the Lord's presence with Israel's **army,** but also by God's Word to encourage the soldiers to be strong in faith. A lack of trust in God's ability to fight for them (cf. 1:30; 3:22) would affect the strength of their will, that is, they could easily become **faint-hearted.** If a weak will was not controlled by faith from the very first, it would lead to fear, terror, and even **to panic before** their **enemies.** So if the soldiers failed to listen to the priest they would become fearful and experience defeat.

### b. Those exempted from military service (20:5-9)

**20:5.** The priests were responsible for encouraging the army by God's Word (vv. 2-4). **The officers** were responsible for making sure that **the army** was composed of qualified men. However, the most qualified were not necessarily those most gifted for battle. They were rather the men most committed to the Lord and free from any distractions that might dampen their spirits for battle. Therefore for humanitarian reasons as well as for the morale of the army **anyone** who had **built a new house and not** begun to "use" (this sense of the Heb. word *ḥānak* is preferable to **dedicated**) it was granted an exemption.

**20:6.** The same exemption was granted to **anyone** who had **planted a vineyard and not begun to enjoy it.** This particular exemption could last up to five years (cf. Lev. 19:23-25).

**20:7.** A man engaged to be **married** was also exempt from military service. The length of the exemption for a newly married man was one year (24:5). These exemptions (20:5-7) bring one of the basic purposes of holy war into sharp focus. Though it was waged as a punishment for the wickedness of the Canaanite population (see comments on chap. 7), it was also fought so that Israel might have a land in which to live a stable and peaceful life—building homes, planting crops, and raising families under God's rule. Since God was fighting for Israel it was not necessary for the war to take total priority over all domestic functions.

**20:8-9.** Whereas the previous exemptions had been granted for compassionate reasons, the exemption of a **faint-hearted** soldier was given for reasons of army morale. Since the best **army** was the one most committed to the Lord,

anything or anyone who might affect the faith and confidence of the Israelite troops was to be removed. Cowardice here was reckoned to be a spiritual problem. Since there was no court-martial, **the officers** removed a faint-hearted soldier before he had opportunity to defect in battle and/or cause other soldiers to become **disheartened too.** Moses' instruction that the officers **appoint commanders over** the army implies that Israel's army was not yet permanently organized with officers of every rank.

### c. Israel's foreign policy (20:10-18)

**20:10-15.** Moses then gave instructions for Israel's foreign policy (vv. 10-18). The people **at a distance** (v. 15) included those **nations** outside Canaan but within the extensive territory promised to Abraham and his descendants (Gen. 15:18-21). The command **make** a city's **people an offer of peace** meant to offer them a vassal treaty. In this way the city acknowledged the sovereignty of Israel's God and of Israel. If **a city** became a vassal to Israel, then her people were to become **forced** laborers (cf. Josh. 9). But if a **city** refused terms of **peace, the men** were to be executed and **everything else** was to be taken **as plunder for** the Israelites. Apparently then **the women** and **children** had opportunity to be introduced to Israel's religion (also see comments in the third paragraph under Deut. 20:16-18).

**20:16-18.** But inside Canaan absolutely nothing was to be spared. Six nations are listed in verse 17 as representing all the nations living in Canaan. **The Hittites** were from Anatolia (Turkey) but some early migrants had settled in Canaan (e.g., Ephron the Hittite in Gen. 23). The **Amorites** were hill-dwellers (cf. comments on Gen. 14:13-16). Their origin is uncertain (they are first referred to in ancient texts of the third millenium B.C.). **Canaanites** was a general term for the inhabitants of Palestine. The **Perizites** were perhaps village-dwellers or nomads. The **Hivites** were possibly in northern Palestine by the Lebanon mountains (Josh. 11:3; Jud. 3:3). The **Jebusites** lived in the hill country (Num. 13:29) of and around Jebus, later known as Jerusalem (Josh. 15:8). Another nation not mentioned here but included in Deuteronomy 7:1 (see comments there) are the Girgashites, whose locality is unknown.

These people were so degenerate and committed to evil that unless they were completely destroyed, they could easily influence (**teach**) the Israelites to follow their detestable ways in idolatry (cf. 18:9-12).

The women in the nations mentioned in 20:10-15 (i.e., from the Aramean culture) were not as degenerate as those from the Canaanite culture. Also Aramean women adopted the religions of their husbands. Abraham, for example, insisted that his servant get a wife from the Aramean culture for Isaac and not a Canaanite woman (Gen. 24). Thus the women and children of those nations could be spared. But one only needs to remember the influence of Jezebel who brought her husband Ahab under the worship of Baal to see the destructive effects of marriage to a Canaanite wife.

### d. Prohibition against destroying fruit trees (20:19-20)

**20:19-20.** In the ancient Near East military powers punished their enemies by indiscriminately laying waste to the land. This practice made no sense in relation to the land of Canaan for it was to become Israel's own possession. Why should Israel cut down **trees** whose **fruit** she could eat? And why should **trees,** that were not **men,** be besieged? Even in lands outside Canaan the practice was to be avoided because it showed a lack of respect for God's creation and an infatuation with the harsh and excessive use of destructive power.

### 11. MISCELLANEOUS LAWS (CHAPS. 21–25)

### a. An unsolved murder (21:1-9)

**21:1-9.** If a man was **found slain,** either as a result of murder or manslaughter, the **elders and judges** of the central tribunal (17:8-13) were to summon **the elders of the town nearest the body.** With **the priests** (presumably also from the central tribunal) before them **the elders of** that **town** were to **break the . . . neck** of a young **heifer** and **declare** their innocence.

Breaking the heifer's neck symbolized that the crime deserved capital punishment, and the washing of the elders' **hands over the heifer** symbolized their innocence in the matter. This ritual dem-

onstrated how extremely valuable God considers life. For even though no murderer was found, the land and the people both incurred **the guilt of shedding innocent blood.** The animal sacrifice, accompanied by the petition of the elders, made **atonement,** that is, turned the wrath of God away from the people.

### b. Family laws (21:10-21)

(1) Marrying a captive woman (21:10-14). **21:10-11.** An Israelite was permitted to marry **a beautiful woman** from **the captives** of a particular battle. This assumes the battle in question was against one of "the cities that are at a distance" (20:15), not a city within the borders of Palestine. Therefore the prospective **wife** would not have been a Canaanite woman (cf. the prohibition against marrying a Canaanite man or woman, 7:1, 3-4).

If an Israelite soldier genuinely desired one of the captives he could have her only through marriage. This helped protect the dignity of the women captives and the purity of the Israelite soldiers. Israelites were not to rape, plunder, or otherwise mistreat captives as other armies of the ancient Near East did.

**21:12-14.** A soldier's marriage to a foreign captive could not take place immediately. The prospective wife was first prepared psychologically for her new life as an Israelite. This was accomplished by her shaving **her head,** trimming **her nails,** having a change of **clothes,** and mourning for her parents for one **month.** The mourning may indicate either that **her father and mother** had been killed in battle or that she was now separated from them by her new marriage. The other rituals mentioned may also have symbolized her mourning for cutting herself off from her former life.

The full month allowed the captive woman a proper amount of time for mourning, and it also gave the prospective **husband** opportunity to reflect on his initial decision to take her as his **wife.** For with a shaved head she would be less attractive.

The phrase **If you are not pleased with her** may refer not to some trivial problem in their relationship, but to the new wife's refusal to accept her husband's spiritual values. In this case the husband could dissolve the marriage by giving up all rights over her. By forbidding him **to treat her as a slave,** even though she was **dishonored** through the divorce, the woman still retained a measure of dignity. This law underscored the value of human life; it contrasted with the terrible treatment of war captives common throughout the ancient Near East.

(2) The right of the firstborn. **21:15-17.** Monogamy was always the divine ideal for marriage in the Old Testament (Gen. 2:20-24). Polygamy, though practiced by some, never appears in a positive light in the Old Testament; the Bible never describes a truly happy polygamous marriage. One reason was that one of the **wives** would always be loved more than the **other**(s). The husband was forbidden in this case to follow his feelings and disregard the Law. His **firstborn** son must be given the **double share of** the father's inheritance even though he was **the son of his** father's **unloved wife.**

(3) A rebellious son. **21:18-21.** An extreme violation of the fifth commandment, "Honor your father and your mother" (5:16), was to be punished by **death.** In view here was not an occasional lapse into disobedience but a persistent rebellion against one's **father and mother** even after the parents had warned their **son** of the consequences of his **rebellious** actions. The son was ultimately rebelling against the Lord's authority and therefore attacking the foundations of the covenant community. The legislation here was not cruel nor did it give parents a right to abuse their children.

The **son** was to be taken **to the elders at the gate** (i.e., the place where the Law was administered; cf. 22:15; Josh. 20:4; Job 29:7). **The elders** were required to make an impartial judgment. The son was not judged for being **a profligate and a drunkard,** but for being **rebellious.** His self-indulgent living and drunkenness were simply examples of his rebellion against parental authority. **All the men** (rather than the parents) were required to **stone** the son if the charges were proved correct. Again mention is made of the deterrent effects of capital punishment: **All Israel will hear of it and be afraid** (cf. Deut. 13:11; 17:13). No record in the Bible or in extrabiblical literature has come to light which indicates that this punishment was ever carried out. The fear of death apparently deterred Jewish sons

from being **stubborn** rebels.

### c. Various laws (21:22–22:12)

(1) A hanged corpse. **21:22-23.** Hanging a criminal **on a tree** was not for the purpose of putting him **to death.** Rather, *after* he was executed for **a capital offense . . .** his **body** was hanged on a tree as a warning to all who saw it not to commit the same offense. The criminal was **under God's curse** not because his body was **hung on a tree** but because he had broken God's Law by committing a crime worthy of death. Therefore **his body** was not to be left **on the tree overnight.** This text was used by the Apostle Paul (Gal. 3:13) to support the doctrine of Christ's penal substitutionary death for sinners. Christ's being under God's curse (cf. comments on Mark 15:34) enabled Him to redeem "us from the curse of the Law."

(2) A fellow Israelite's livestock. **22:1-4.** The law about lost livestock was a concrete expression of the eternal moral principle to "love your neighbor as yourself" (Lev. 19:18), and to "do to others what you would have them do to you" (Matt. 7:12). The regulation in Deuteronomy 22:1-4 refers not primarily to taking someone else's lost animal but rather to the natural tendency to **ignore it** because of the extra time and labor involved in restoring it. If the animal's owner lived far away or was unknown, the finder could take it home till the owner came **looking for it.** The same was true of a lost **cloak** and other items that were found.

The same principle was to be applied in the case of a **fallen** animal (v. 4). Today this law would apply in any circumstance where a believer is tempted "not to get involved" with someone else's needs (cf., e.g., James 2:15-16; 1 John 3:17).

(3) Transvestism. **22:5.** The adoption of **clothing** of the opposite sex was forbidden because it obscured the distinction of the sexes and thus violated an essential part of the created order of life (Gen. 1:27). It was also perhaps associated with or promoted homosexuality. The same Hebrew word translated **detests** (*tôʿēbâh,* lit., "a detestable thing"; KJV, "an abomination") is used to describe God's view of homosexuality (Lev. 18:22; 20:13). Also some evidence exists that

transvestism may have been connected with the worship of pagan deities. Since this law was related to the divine order of Creation and since **God** detests **anyone who does this,** believers today also ought to heed this command.

(4) Birds in the nest. **22:6-7.** Many have suggested that this law was given to teach the Israelites compassion or reverence for parental relationships by using an object lesson from the animal world. However, the fact that the Israelites were permitted to **take the young** bird seems to militate against that view. More likely, Moses was teaching the Israelites to protect this food source. By letting **the mother** bird **go** they could anticipate the production of more young in the future. Obeying this stipulation, like obeying many others, would result in blessing (**it will go well with you;** cf. 4:40; 5:16; 6:3, 18; 12:25, 28; 19:13).

(5) A parapet. **22:8.** The roof of a **house** in the ancient Near East was used for a variety of purposes. Making **a parapet** on one's **roof** would help prevent someone from falling **from the roof.** This then was an opportunity to "love your neighbor as yourself" (Lev. 19:18) by being concerned about his safety. It also emphasized again the value of human life.

(6) Prohibition against mixtures. **22:9-11.** The reason for these prohibitions against planting **two kinds of seed** in a field, yoking together **an ox and a donkey** for plowing, and weaving **wool and linen . . . together** is uncertain. They may have had a symbolic function in teaching the Israelites something about the created order. Or the mixtures mentioned in these verses may reflect certain pagan cultic practices.

(7) Tassels. **22:12.** The significance of this instruction about **tassels** is not explained here, but its meaning is made clear in Numbers 15:37-41. The tassels were to serve as a reminder of the Lord's commands and Israel's obligation to obey them.

### d. Marriage violations (22:13-30)

**22:13-21.** This law was meant to enforce premarital sexual purity and to encourage parents to instill within their children the value of sexual purity. The law might be misused, however, by an unscrupulous husband against his wife

for personal reasons, or perhaps to recover the bride-price he originally paid to **the girl's father.** If such a husband charged that his **wife** was not **a virgin** when they were married then **her parents** were obligated to produce proof of her virginity. The evidence was to be a **cloth,** a bloodstained garment or a bedsheet from the wedding night. Records from various cultures in the ancient Near East refer to this kind of evidence being made public.

If the parents offered such evidence of her virginity before marriage then **the man** making the false charge was to be whipped (the probable meaning of the word **punish,** v. 18) and fined **100 shekels of silver** (about two and one-half pounds; cf. NIV marg.). Apparently this was double the original bride-price (v. 29 seems to indicate that 50 shekels was the usual bride-price). The fine was given **to the girl's father** because he too was slandered by the accusation which called into question his desire or ability to pass on to his children God's values regarding sexual purity. Also his daughter was given **a bad name.** Support for the **wife** (and perhaps also the legal right of her firstborn child) was protected by the forfeiting of the man's right ever to **divorce** his wife (v. 19).

On the other hand if the husband's charge could not be disproved, then the wife was to be stoned at **the door of her father's house.** This harsh punishment was not only intended for the sin of fornication (**being promiscuous**) but also for lying to her prospective husband and presumably for implicating her father in the deception. This **evil** too was to be purged from the nation (cf. vv. 22, 24; see comments on 13:5).

**22:22.** Though the death penalty was to be administered for sexual unfaithfulness in marriage (cf. Lev. 20:10), the precise manner in which it was to be carried out was not specified. In Mesopotamia an adulterous couple was bound and thrown into the water (Code of Hammurabi, Law 129), though no extant court records from Mesopotamia indicate that this penalty was ever enforced. The official leaders of Judaism in Jesus' day interpreted the penalty to mean death by stoning (cf. John 8:5) but later Rabbinic tradition prescribed death by strangulation. How frequently this penalty was enforced is unknown. (On the seriousness of the sin of adultery see comments on Deut. 5:18.)

**22:23-27.** **A virgin pledged to be married** was to be treated like a **married** woman. It was assumed that the sexual union which took place **in a town** was not rape (vv. 23-25) but adultery (i.e., the girl gave her consent). If it had been a case of rape her screams **for help** would have been heard whether or not she could have been rescued. If the assault occurred **out in the country,** then the betrothed **girl** was given the benefit of doubt and **only the man** was put to death (vv. 25-27). Rape was considered as serious as murder and therefore **deserving** of **death.**

**22:28-29.** A **man** who raped an unbetrothed **virgin** was forced to **marry** her (after paying the bride-price of **50 shekels** to her **father**) and had to forfeit the right of **divorce.** This protected, to a degree, the girl's honor and assured her (and her child if she became pregnant from the rape) permanent support. This stipulation may also have served as a deterrent against rape since the man would have to live with that woman for the rest of his life.

**22:30.** Rather than referring to adultery, this verse probably refers to a man marrying his stepmother after his father died. Such a marriage would have been regarded as incestuous (cf. Lev. 18:8).

*e. Exclusion from the assembly of the Lord (23:1-8)*

**23:1.** **The assembly of the Lord** probably referred here to the people gathered together for religious purposes. Therefore this law and the laws in verses 2-8 dealt with the exclusion from Israel's "worship service." These laws seemed to have had a certain ceremonial character. Like the laws of uncleanness (e.g., Lev. 12–15) they did not exclude an individual because of his own specific moral sin. Rather they had a pedagogical or symbolic function. Furthermore exclusion from the "worship service" did not prevent an individual from believing in the Lord and receiving the gift of eternal life.

Israel's history demonstrates that these laws (in Deut. 23:1-8) were never meant to be applied legalistically without regard for the circumstances of each individual who may have wished to worship with Israel. Excluding an **emasculated**

male may refer to a person who intentionally had himself castrated for pagan religious purposes. At any rate this regulation was probably never meant to exclude a eunuch committed to obeying the Lord (Isa. 56:3-5). However, some say this law *was* meant to exclude all eunuchs regardless of the reason for their castration. If so, then the law probably reflected the fact that a eunuch could no longer choose to have children with God's help. Something of the image of God in the man had been destroyed. The law would therefore have symbolically taught the need for worshipers to be perfect before God, as the sacrifices offered to God were to be without physical defects.

**23:2.** **Born of a forbidden marriage** is the translation of a single rare Hebrew word whose meaning is uncertain. (*Mamzēr* is used in the OT only here and in Zech. 9:6 where it is used figuratively of foreigners.) Traditionally it has been taken to refer (in Deut. 23:2) to a child of illegitimate birth (cf. NIV marg. and NASB). Possibly, however, the term refers to the child of an incestuous relationship, the child of a cult prostitute, or the child of a mixed marriage (i.e., an Israelite married to an Ammonite, Moabite, Philistine, or others). Again the stringent punishment inflicted on such a person would help deter Israelites from entering this kind of marriage.

**23:3-6.** **Ammonite** and **Moabite** people were not allowed to attend Israel's religious gatherings because of their treatment of Israel during the wilderness period. The had refused **bread and water** to Israel and through Balak the Moabites **hired Balaam** to **curse** Israel (Num. 22:2-6). (Nor was Israel to make **peace . . . with them,** Deut. 23:6.) Also the Moabites and Ammonites were descended from the incestuous unions of Lot and his daughters (Gen. 19:30-38). These facts confirm that from their very beginning they had been and would continue to be against **the Lord** and His people. The treatment of Ruth, however, by Boaz along with other Israelites of Bethlehem demonstrates that this law was never meant to exclude one who said, "Your people will be my people and your God my God" (Ruth 1:16). Isaiah seemed to have held a similar interpretation (cf. Isa. 56:3, 6-8) but perhaps those verses in Isaiah apply only to the end times.

**23:7-8.** The treatment of the **Edomite** people was more lenient since they were descended from Esau (Gen. 36:40-43), Jacob's brother. The harsh treatment of Israel by the **Egyptian** people was overlooked because of Israel's long sojourn there and perhaps also because of the initial positive treatment given to Joseph and his family when they first entered Egypt (Gen. 37–50).

### f. Uncleanness in the camp (23:9-14)

**23:9-14.** Verses 1-8 dealt with the need for maintaining the purity of the religious assembly. Verses 9-14 are concerned with the purity of the war **camp.** The **nocturnal emission** of a man, though not in itself morally wrong, rendered him ceremonially **unclean** for all the next day. Likewise the command to bury one's **excrement** (v. 13) did not deal with a moral area. Apparently this law also was ceremonial in nature. By regularly observing these regulations Israelite soldiers were reminded of the Lord's holiness and omnipresence. Even in a person's most private moments the holy **God** was with him, observing his behavior.

### g. Various laws (23:15–25:19)

(1) Escaped slaves. **23:15-16.** The slaves in view here were not Israelites. They were people from other countries who came to seek sanctuary (**refuge**) in Israel. The command **not** to **hand him over to his master** went against the normal practice in the ancient Near East. In fact treaties in the ancient Near East included the provision that escaped slaves and other fugitives be returned. Therefore this law may have served to remind Israel that their treaty was with the Lord and they did not need any political alliance with another nation. Or possibly since **a slave** had been oppressed unjustly, this law **not** to **oppress** a fugitive slave was meant to remind the Israelites of their former status as slaves in Egypt.

(2) Prostitution (23:17-18). **23:17. Temple** prostitution was common in the religions of the ancient Near East. The prohibition here was probably intended to prevent a foreign religion being practiced by Israelites, and to keep the worship of the Lord from being contaminated by temple prostitution. The later history of Israel is replete with examples of her failure to observe this command

(cf., e.g., 1 Kings 14:24; 15:12; 22:46; 2 Kings 23:7; Hosea 4:14).

**23:18.** The words for prostitutes here indicate that prostitution in general was in view, not specifically temple prostitution. The word for **female prostitute** is *zônâh* and the word for **male prostitute** is *keleḇ* (lit., "dog"). A **vow** was not to be paid with money obtained from this sinful practice. The payment of a vow allowed an Israelite to express his gratitude for God's gracious provision in his life. Therefore to use money God did not provide in order to pay a vow was insincere and hypocritical. No wonder it was detestable to the LORD. (Other detestable things included idolatry, offering sacrificial animals with defects, and dishonesty; cf. the word "detestable" in 7:25-26; 12:31; 13:14; 14:3; 17:1, 4; 18:9, 12 [twice]; 20:18; 24:4; 27:15; 29:17; 32:16; and the word "detests" in 22:5; 25:16.)

(3) Lending and charging interest (23:19-20). **23:19.** The parallel passages (Ex. 22:25; Lev. 25:35-37) make it clear that the **brother** who was borrowing **money** was an Israelite (cf. Deut. 23:20) who had become poor or was in severe need. He was not borrowing money to engage in a capitalistic endeavor. To charge a poor brother **interest** would only worsen his condition and would also feed the greed of the one wealthy enough to lend.

**23:20.** An **Israelite** was permitted to **charge a foreigner interest** since he was not a member of the covenant community or an alien within the Promised Land. Probably the "foreigner" was a merchant and the loan sought by him would have been for business purposes.

(4) Vows. **23:21-23.** This law stressed the need for the Israelites to be completely honest before their **God** and to be careful in their verbal commitments to Him. The **vow** in view was one that was made **freely** by a worshiper. Once made it had to be kept (cf. Prov. 20:25; Ecc. 5:4-5) as **the LORD** kept His promises to Israel.

(5) Eating in a neighbor's fields. **23:24-25.** This law, like those in 22:1-4, gave a concrete expression to the principle of loving one's neighbor as oneself. A traveler was given the right to refresh himself from a **vineyard** or **grainfield,** but **not** the right to carry **grapes** away with him or to harvest in the field. Since the Lord had been gracious in providing

for the farmer, he in turn should be gracious to a stranger traveling through his land.

(6) Divorce and remarriage. **24:1-4. Divorce** was widespread in the ancient Near East. However, the Old Testament always regarded divorce as a tragedy (cf. Mal. 2:16). The commands in Deuteronomy 24:1-4, then, were given to regulate an already existing practice. The **something indecent,** which a husband might find in his wife, cannot refer to adultery for which the penalty was death (22:22). Nor can the indecency refer to the wife's premarital intercourse with another man for which the penalty was also death (22:20-21). The precise meaning of the phrase is unknown. If a man found something indecent, the **certificate of divorce** he wrote was apparently given to the woman for **her** protection under the law. **If** after being divorced she remarried and then **her second husband** divorced her or died, **her first husband** was not permitted to remarry her since **she** had **been defiled.** The word translated "defiled" was also used to describe a man who had committed adultery (Lev. 18:20). So the use of this word to describe a woman who had been divorced and remarried to the same man suggests that divorce was viewed in a negative light even though Moses permitted it. A remarriage to her former husband would be tantamount to a legal adultery and therefore **detestable** to **the LORD** (see comments on "detestable" and "detested," Deut. 23:18). The purpose of this law seems to be to prevent frivolous divorce, and to present divorce itself in a disparaging light. Jesus' interpretation of this passage indicated that divorce (like polygamy) went against the divine ideal for marriage (see comments on Matt. 19:3-9).

(7) A new marriage. **24:5.** Like the preceding law (vv. 1-4) this one also emphasized the importance of marriage and the family. It was considered rather heartless to send a **recently married** man **to war** (cf. 20:7). If he were killed in combat he would probably have no posterity to preserve his name in Israel (on the significance of this see 25:5-10). Also a newly married man was **to be free** of other responsibilities in order to have time to adjust to and **bring happiness to** his **wife.**

(8) Pledges. **24:6. Millstones** were used daily in homes to grind grain in preparing meals. To take both or **one** of these as collateral **for a debt** would in effect deprive a man of his daily bread (**livelihood**) and therefore contradict the spirit of generosity which should have motivated the lender in the first place.

(9) Kidnapping. **24:7.** Apparently the crime of **kidnapping** was common in the ancient Near East for it was also mentioned in the law codes of Mesopotamia and the Hittite Empire. Since the kidnapper was depriving his victim of his freedom (by taking **him as a slave or** selling **him**), **the kidnapper** was to be punished by death—as though he had taken the victim's life. This was another of several crimes deserving capital punishment. On the purging of **evil,** see comments on 13:5.

(10) Skin diseases. **24:8-9.** The Hebrew word translated **leprous diseases** referred to a broad range of skin diseases, not exclusively to leprosy (NIV marg.). Instead of repeating the legislation concerning these diseases Moses referred the people to his original instruction (**what I have commanded** the **priests**) in Leviticus 13–14. Motivation to obey this ceremonial legislation was furnished by **Miriam** who because she opposed Moses was struck with leprosy (Num. 12).

(11) Collecting a pledge (24:10-13). **24:10-11.** The dignity of the borrower was preserved by prohibiting the lender to enter **his house** and take anything he might want **as a pledge.**

**24:12-13.** If the borrower was so **poor** that all he could offer as a **pledge** was **his cloak** (which served as a blanket at night) then the lender was to **return** it before nightfall (cf. Ex. 22:26-27; Job 22:6). By acting in this manner the lender was loving his neighbor as himself.

(12) Paying workers. **24:14-15.** A **hired man who** was **poor** needed to be paid **his wages each day,** not weekly or monthly. The clause, he **is counting on it,** seems to indicate that he needed to be paid each day in order to provide food for himself and his family. It would have been easy for a wealthy employer to withhold the poor man's wages. But the employer was to remember that Israel was at one time oppressed by Pharaoh until she cried out to the Lord (cf. Ex.

2:23; 3:9). Likewise if the poor man should **cry to the** Lord the employer might find himself judged as Pharaoh was.

(13) Responsibility for guilt within the family. **24:16.** Though personal responsibility was the norm in the law codes of the ancient Near East, in some cases a son was permitted to **be put to death** in place of his father (e.g., Code of Hammurabi, Law 230), though again (cf. comments on 22:22) no court records indicate that this was ever enforced. Moses forbade such a practice: **each is to die for his own sin** (cf. comments on Num. 14:26-35). It was true, however, that a father who rebelled against the Lord might influence his descendants to do the same (see comments on Deut. 5:9).

(14) Treatment of the alien, fatherless, and widow (24:17-22). **24:17-18.** Aliens, **the fatherless,** and widows (cf. vv. 19-21) could easily be oppressed in the courts and by the wealthy. But needy people in Israel were to be treated with love and **justice** (cf. 10:18-19; 27:19) especially in light of Israel's former oppression by Pharaoh and her deliverance from **Egypt** (15:15; 24:22). If the nation failed to act righteously in this regard God might judge them as He did Pharaoh. On taking a widow's **cloak . . . as a pledge** see comments on verses 12-13.

**24:19-22.** This law to **leave** some grain (barley and wheat), **olives,** and **grapes** made it possible for aliens, **the fatherless,** and widows to glean during harvesttime (cf. Lev. 23:22). In this way the needy were not reduced to the humiliation of begging or seeking welfare. They could still work for their food. Also farmers were given opportunity to express their gratitude to **the** Lord for His abundant provision and His love for poorer members in the covenant community.

(15) Prosecuting criminals. **25:1-3.** When two people had **a dispute** they could not settle by themselves, they were to let **the judges . . . decide** which one was **innocent** and which one was **guilty.** The primary intent of this law was to regulate corporal punishment. After a case was decided in **court. . . . the guilty man** was to be **flogged in** the **presence of the** presiding **judge** who was to see that the penalty was carried out justly. The dignity of the guilty man was preserved

to a degree by **not** allowing **him** to be beaten (probably with a rod; cf. Ex. 21:20) **more than 40** times. The Code of Hammurabi (Law 202) permitted 60 **lashes** and later Assyrian laws permitted between 40 and 50 **lashes.** By New Testament times the Jews had settled on 39 lashes as a safeguard against going over 40 (2 Cor. 11:24). It has often been said that Jesus' scourging consisted of 39 lashes, but since He was scourged by the Romans and not by the Jews the number of lashes He received is not known. Sometimes the Romans were excessively cruel in their scourging.

(16) Working oxen. **25:4.** The command **not** to **muzzle an ox while it is treading . . . grain** (on a threshing floor to break up the grain stalks for winnowing) stressed kindness and fairness to the animals that helped a person earn his daily bread. Paul's use of this verse (1 Cor. 9:9) did not imply that God did not care about oxen. Paul meant that if God cares about a working ox, how much more He cares about human laborers, especially those laboring for His kingdom (see the comments on 1 Cor. 9:9-10).

(17) Levirate marriage (25:5-10). **25:5-6.** In only one kind of circumstance was marriage to a close relative permitted. Marriage to a divorced or widowed sister-in-law was forbidden (Lev. 18:16) unless the following conditions were met. The **brothers** must have been **living together** (i.e., they inherited their father's property jointly), and the deceased **brother** must have died **without a** male heir. If both of these conditions were met, then levirate (from the Latin *levir,* "brother-in-law" or **husband's brother**) marriage was to take place. Levirate marriage thus would provide a male heir who in turn could care for the parents in their old age and prevent the alienation of family property.

Furthermore **the first son** born from the levirate marriage was given the deceased brother's **name . . . so that his name** would **not** be **blotted out from Israel.** In this way even though a man died before the Lord fulfilled the covenant promises made to Abraham and his descendants (Gen. 15:5, 18-21; 17:19; 22:17-18; 28:13-14; 35:12) he could participate, in a sense, in the glorious future of Israel through *his descendants.*

**25:7-10.** If a widow's **brother-in-law** refused to **fulfill** his **duty**—either through greed (not wanting to share the family inheritance with his sister-in-law) or through dislike of his sister-in-law— she could tell **the elders of his town** about it. She could then remove **one of his sandals** and **spit in his face.** These actions would show her strong disapproval of his refusal. This embarrassment to him, along with the stigma of being known for his refusal, illustrates how God used social pressure to motivate His people to obedience.

(18) Stopping a fight. **25:11-12.** This is the only instance in the Law where physical mutilation served as punishment for an offense (see comments on 19:21). Israel's restraint here contrasted with other ancient Near Eastern law codes which provided for a wide range of physical mutilations depending on the crime committed (e.g., in Assyrian law a man on the street who kissed a woman who was not his wife had his lip cut off with a sword). The command in 25:11-12 was probably intended to protect both womanly modesty and the capacity of a man to produce heirs. This second purpose probably helps explain why this law is placed here immediately after the instructions about levirate marriages (vv. 5-10). This is the fourth time in Deuteronomy Moses told the people to **show . . . no pity** in executing punishment for wrongdoing (cf. 13:8; 19:13, 21).

(19) Differing weights. **25:13-16.** The Israelites were to be totally honest in their business dealings. They could well afford to be so since it was ultimately **the Lord** who would withhold or give prosperity to them. Thus honesty in business was a way of proclaiming one's faith in the Lord's ability to support him and give him **long** life. The theme of **honest** and dishonest **weights . . . measures,** and "scales" is common in the Old Testament (Prov. 11:1; 16:11; 20:10, 23; Amos 8:5; Micah 6:11; see comments on Hosea 12:7). On the promise of long life **in the land,** see Deuteronomy 5:16; 6:2; 11:9; 32:47.

(20) The destruction of the Amalekites. **25:17-19. The Amalekites** were a nomadic desert tribe ranging from Sinai northward to upper Arabia (cf. 1 Sam. 15:7; 27:8). Their genealogy is traced to Amalek, son of Eliphaz and grandson of Esau (Gen. 36:12). The reference to "the whole territory of the Amalekites" (Gen. 14:7) is purposely anachronistic. Two specific battles with the Amalekites were mentioned in the Pentateuch (Ex. 17:8-16; Num. 14:39-45), but Deuteronomy 25:17-19 seems to indicate a series of hostilities that are not mentioned elsewhere. The unprovoked attacking of the weak, sick, and helpless Israelites **lagging behind** evidenced the cruelty and cowardice of the Amalekites as well as their lack of **fear of** Israel's **God.** Since the Amalekites had shown no mercy to Israel, they were to receive none. Israel was to **blot out the memory of Amalek from under heaven.** More than 400 years later David defeated the Amalekites (2 Sam. 1:1), but they were not completely wiped out till about another 300 years later in Hezekiah's day (1 Chron. 4:41-43). The strong command **Do not forget!** is the last of nine such commands in Deuteronomy (cf. comments on Deut. 4:9).

12. TWO LITURGICAL CEREMONIES (26:1-15)

*a. Liturgy for the presentation of the firstfruits (26:1-11)*

**26:1-4. When** Israel had **taken possession** (cf. comments on 1:8) of **the** Promised **Land** they were to celebrate two rituals. Since legislation had already been given regarding the tithe every third year (14:28-29) it seems that these two rituals accompanying the offering of the firstfruits (26:2-11) and the tithe "in the third year" (vv. 12-15) were meant to be practiced only once, the one after Israel's first harvest and the other after being in the land three years. They were given in order to celebrate Israel's transition from a nomadic existence to a settled agricultural community, made possible by the Lord's blessings.

The first ritual consisted of taking **the firstfruits** (i.e., the initial produce of the harvest; cf. Lev. 23:9-14) to **the priest** at the central sanctuary. The declaration by the offerer, **I declare today . . . that I have come to the land,** was a testimony to the Lord's faithfulness in bringing the nation into the land He had promised. In this way at the very beginning of their new life each one in the entire nation had the opportunity to come before **God** individually and confess his or her faith in Him. **The priest** was to **take the basket** (Deut. 26:4; cf. v. 2) of firstfruits, apparently speak some words, and then give it back to the worshiper.

**26:5-10.** The second part of the ritual was a more elaborate confession of the Lord's faithfulness (vv. 5-10a) followed by another presentation of **the basket** (v. 10b). The confession highlighted both God's faithfulness and the miraculous nature of Israel's preservation.

**A wandering Aramean** referred to Jacob, who was each Israelite's **father,** or rather, ancestor. When Abraham left Ur, he settled for a while in Haran, a city in Aram in upper Mesopotamia (Gen. 1:28-32). Abraham moved on to Canaan but some of his relatives stayed on and became known as Arameans. Both Isaac and Jacob married women from this Aramean branch of the family. Thus Jacob could also be called an Aramean. The word translated "wandering" usually meant "perishing" or "ailing." Jacob was already 130 years old when he **went down into Egypt** after which he lived only 17 more years. The **few people** in his family numbered 70 (Gen. 46:27).

Though the **Egyptians mistreated** the nation Israel, it still grew. **God** answered the cry of His oppressed people by miraculously delivering them **out of Egypt** by His **mighty hand** and **outstretched arm** (see comments on Deut. 4:34) which included His using **miraculous signs and wonders** (cf. 4:34; 6:22; 7:19; 26:8; 29:3).

Though powerful nations lived in Canaan, Israel would possess this **land flowing with milk and honey** (cf. 26:15 and see comments on Ex. 3:8). In short, the confession underscored God's miraculous working at every turn in their history.

**26:11.** After centuries of suffering and waiting, it was appropriate that every family along with all the needy in Israel **rejoice** over the abundant blessings provided by the **LORD.**

*b. Liturgy for the presentation of the tithe after the first three years (26:12-15)*

**26:12.** As stated in the comments on verses 1-4 this **tithe** may have been a one-time offering made after Israel's first three years in the land.

**26:13-15.** The confession to be made in connection with the offering of the tithe consisted of a positive statement (v. 13), a negative statement (v. 14), and a prayer for blessing (v. 15). Since this tithe was distributed in the towns and since there is no mention of the central sanctuary this confession was probably to be made in people's homes. The background of the negative statements in verse 14 is obscure but it may have related to Canaanite religious practices. The offerer was to indicate that he had **not eaten any of the** tithe **while . . . in mourning, nor** set any of it aside **while he was unclean, nor . . . offered any of it to the dead.**

The prayer for blessing (v. 15) on the **people** and **the land** emphasizes Israel's dependence on the Lord and God's grace. He is so transcendent that He dwells in **heaven,** but at the same time He is so near to His people that He hears their prayers on earth. (On the **land flowing with milk and honey** cf. v. 9, and see comments on Ex. 3:8.)

*D. A declaration of commitment (26:16-19)*

These four verses conclude Moses' explanation of the Law (5:1–26:15) by calling for a total commitment to the Lord and His commands, and also by affirming God's commitment to Israel. This section may also be viewed as a formal ratification of the covenant between the Lord and Israel even though the word "covenant" does not appear in these four verses. Israel accepted and affirmed her covenantal responsibilities and the Lord affirmed His promise to exalt an obedient Israel over all the nations of the earth.

1. ISRAEL'S RESPONSIBILTY (26:16-17)

**26:16-17.** Israel was to devote herself to obey **carefully** and unreservedly (**with all** her **heart** and **soul;** see comments on 6:5) the Lord's **decrees and laws.** The words **you have declared** were a technical statement in the treaty language of the ancient Near East. It meant that Israel formally accepted the terms of the Lord's covenant and acknowledged her responsibility to **obey** them.

2. THE LORD'S RESPONSIBILITY (26:18-19)

**26:18-19.** With the same treaty terminology (**has declared;** cf. v. 18) the

LORD formally acknowledged His obligation to Israel, to be her God, and to make her **His** most valued nation on earth. The reiteration of Israel's responsibility (**you are to keep all His commands**) reminded Israel that her special status of honor depended on her obedience to Him. To be the Lord's **treasured possession** (cf. 7:6; 14:2; Ps 135:4; Mal. 3:17; see comments on Ex. 19:5) meant that He would exalt Israel **high above all the nations** (cf. Deut. 28:1). Through disobedience and rebellion, generation after generation of Israelites forfeited their right to be exalted over the nations. But Isaiah wrote that Israel's rebellion would not continue forever, for **the LORD** will raise up a generation of faithful Israelites in the future who will enjoy God's grace in a golden age of blessing (Isa. 60–62). That age is commonly called the Millennium.

## IV. The Third Address of Moses: Covenant Renewal Commanded and the Declaration of Blessings and Curses (27:1–29:1)

A new address is signaled by the mention of Moses in the third person (27:1). Moses had not been mentioned in the third person since 5:1, at the beginning of his second address (5:1–26:15). Moses had explained the general requirements of the Lord's Law (chaps. 5–11) and the specific details of that Law (12:1–26:15). Throughout Israel's history it would be necessary to call the nation to renewals of covenant commitment and obedience. These renewals would take place at significant points in her history, such as in preparation for entering the Promised Land (chap. 27), at the dedication of Solomon's temple (1 Kings 8), and during a change of leadership (Josh. 24; 1 Sam. 12).

So Moses gave directions for a ceremony for the covenant renewal that were to be followed when Israel entered the Promised Land (Deut. 27). Then Moses turned his attention back to the people in the plains of Moab and set before them the blessings and curses of the covenant (chap. 28). Treaties of the ancient Near East usually placed a section of blessings and curses toward the end (see "Structure" in the *Introduction*). The blessings were promised for faithfulness to the treaty and the curses were threatened for disobedience to the treaty.

## A. Covenant renewal commanded (chap. 27)

### 1. THE WRITING OF THE LAW AND THE OFFERING OF SACRIFICES (27:1-10)

#### a. The writing of the Law (27:1-4)

**27:1.** The reference to **Moses and the elders** probably emphasized the leadership of the elders in the covenant renewal ceremony when the nation entered the Promised Land, for Moses would no longer be around to guide them.

**27:2-4.** The writing of laws on **large stones** coated **with plaster** was common in Egypt. The meaning of the phrase **all the words of this Law** (cf. v. 8) is a little uncertain, but in light of Egyptian custom the reference probably was to the entire Book of Deuteronomy rather than just parts of it.

The significance of this act was twofold. First, it commemorated God's faithfulness in **giving** them **the land** (**just as the LORD, the God of your fathers, promised you**). ("God of your fathers" occurs six times in Deut.; see comments on 1:11.) The **stones** were to be **set up . . . on Mount Ebal** (about 35 miles north of Jerusalem) at the base of which lay the city of Shechem. It was at Shechem that the Lord first "appeared" to Abraham, and there Abraham built his first altar to the Lord (Gen. 12:6-7). The choice of this location emphasized God's faithfulness to the original Abrahamic promises and hinted that the time for their complete fulfillment might be near if only Israel would obey Him. Second, the writing of the Law when they entered the Promised Land symbolized the nation's mission to bring Canaan under the dominance of the Lord's Word.

#### b. The sacrificial offerings (27:5-8)

**27:5-8.** The covenant was to be renewed not only by writing the Law but also with sacrificial offerings. The fact that **the altar** was to be made of uncut **stones** (cf. Ex. 20:25) may mean that the Hebrews (who did not then possess **iron**) were not to develop a dependence on any of the surrounding peoples for iron and thus risk being influenced by them in harmful ways. Or perhaps the uncut stones were meant to suggest that neither the Law nor the sacrificial system was to suffer any human adornment.

The **burnt offerings** (to be totally

consumed on the altar) expressed the people's total dependence on **the LORD.** The **fellowship offerings** (eaten as a communal meal) expressed their thankfulness to Him and their joy in His provision.

The final reminder (Deut. 27:8) to **write** the Law **very clearly** emphasizes the supreme importance of the role of God's Word in the new land.

### c. The challenge to obey the covenant (27:9-10)

**27:9-10.** Though these words were spoken by **Moses and the priests** (cf. Moses and the elders, v. 1) to the Israelites on the plains of Moab (and therefore seem to interrupt the flow of vv. 1-8 and 11-26), they were probably repeated in Shechem as part of the covenant-renewal ceremony. The words **you have now become the people of the LORD your God** do not imply that Israel was not the people of God before that time. They meant that there on the plains of Moab, at that significant turning point in her history, Israel had freshly committed herself again to **the LORD.** Again she was told to **obey** Him and to **follow His commands and decrees.**

### 2. THE BLESSINGS AND CURSES (27:11-26)

### a. The arrangement of the tribes and Levites (27:11-14)

**27:11-14.** This ceremony was **commanded** earlier by **Moses** (11:26-32). After the altar was set up on Mount Ebal (27:1-8) six **tribes** were to assemble **on Mount Gerizim to bless the people** and six were to assemble **on Mount Ebal to pronounce curses.** Actually the people were to stand in front of the mountains (Josh. 8:33). A valley runs between these two mountains in Samaria, with Mount Gerizim to the southwest of Mount Ebal. Shechem is nearby in the valley (see the map "Canaan in the Conquest," near Josh. 3).

The six tribes on Mount Gerizim descended from Jacob's wives, Rachel and Leah. Four of the six tribes stationed on Mount Ebal for the curses were descended from Jacob's concubines, Bilhah and Zilpah. The other two were **Reuben,** Jacob's firstborn, who forfeited his birthright through incest (Gen. 35:22; 49:3-4), and **Zebulun,** Leah's youngest son.

**The Levites** stood between the two

mountains to **recite** the blessings and curses. Actually, only the Levites who were priests attending the ark stood in the middle (Josh. 8:33) and all the other Levites were near Mount Gerizim (Deut. 27:12). In verses 15-26 only the curses have been included and the reason for this is unclear. Other curses are recorded in 28:15-68. Only 12 statements about people who transgressed certain laws were included in 27:15-26.

### b. The curses (27:15-26)

It is difficult to detect a common theme or pattern in these 12 curses, though many of them pertain to actions done by individuals in secret. Eight of the 12 refer to violations of the Ten Commandments: verse 15, the second commandment (5:8-10); 27:16, the fifth commandment (5:16); 27:17, the eighth commandment (5:19); 27:20, 22-23, the seventh commandment (5:18); and 27:24-25, the sixth commandment (5:17).

**27:15.** For the significance of the violation mentioned here (idolatry) see 5:8-9 and the comments there. Even though an offender might manage to keep his self-made **idol . . . in secret** the Lord would see it and the idolater would be **cursed. All the people,** by responding with an **Amen,** were acknowledging that they understood and agreed to the curse's proclamation.

**27:16-18.** On verse 16 see the comments on 5:16 and 21:18-21; and on 27:17 see the comments on 19:14. Though a **blind** person (27:18) would not be able to identify his assailant who was leading him **astray**—a despicable act of unkindness—the Lord would know the offender and bring a curse on him. This curse probably applied to all who mistreated the weak and oppressed members of the community (cf. Lev. 19:14).

**27:19.** It would also have been easy for an Israelite to take advantage of these generally poor classes of people. But God would also defend them (10:18; cf. 24:17, 19-21).

**27:20-23.** These four curses are directed against one who engaged in one of four forbidden sexual relationships. The sixth curse (v. 20) may apply to one who had intercourse with his stepmother or **his father's** concubine while his father was still alive (e.g., Reuben, Gen. 35:22) as well as marriage to a stepmother, or to a concubine of one's father after his death.

The seventh curse (Deut. 27:21) was directed against one who committed bestiality (cf. Ex. 22:19; Lev. 18:23; 20:15-16). Though done in secret, it would be known to the Lord.

The eighth and ninth curses (Deut. 27:22-23) were directed against incest and marriage to (or adultery with) close relatives (cf. Lev. 18:9, 17).

**27:24-25.** The 10th and 11th curses deal with an attempt to violate **secretly** the sixth commandment (against murder; see comments on 5:17).

**27:26.** This last curse demonstrates that the preceding list was representative. Perhaps the 11 examples were chosen, as stated earlier, because most of them could be done in secret and therefore the offender might not be as easily detected as he would when violating other laws. The summary nature of the 12th curse, however, indicates that God desired a wholehearted obedience to the **Law** both in public and in private. Paul used this verse to teach that no one could find eternal life by obeying the Law (Gal. 3:10). Eternal life is received only through God's grace when one places his faith in Jesus Christ as his substitutionary Sacrifice for sin (Rom. 3:24-25; Eph. 2:8-9).

### B. The blessings and the curses (chap. 28)

After Israel entered the Promised Land, Moses commanded her to renew the covenant at Shechem. Then he turned his attention back to Israel's present experience in the plains of Moab. He set before them the blessings and curses of the covenant they were renewing. The curses section (vv. 15-68) is about four times longer than the blessings section (vv. 1-14). This may have been in keeping with the style of the ancient Near Eastern treaties which generally included more curses than blessings. More likely, however, the greater length of the curse section was meant to foreshadow Israel's eventual failure under the covenant.

### 1. THE BLESSINGS (28:1-14)

#### a. Blessings contingent on obedience (28:1-2)

**28:1-2.** God's invitation for Israel to take part in the covenant was a gracious one. However, blessing under this Mosaic Covenant was conditioned on the people's obedience (cf. comments on **obey** in 6:3). For the Mosaic Covenant was made with a people who had already been redeemed by God's gracious deliverance from Egypt. So the covenant was given to Israel that they might enjoy fellowship with **God** and be prepared to receive his **blessings.** One of those blessings would be the exalting of Israel **above all** other **nations** (cf. 26:19).

#### b. The specific blessings (28:3-6)

**28:3-6.** If Israel obeyed the Lord (vv. 1-2), then every aspect of her life would **be blessed.** Both the merchant **in the city** and the farmer **in the country** would be blessed. Israel could expect fertility in both man and animals (v. 4). There would always be food in her homes for daily meals. Since her **kneading trough** would **be blessed** (v. 5) Israel never need experience a famine. In all one's daily work (**when you come in** and **when you go out**) Israelites would enjoy God's blessings. Human happiness comes from obeying the Lord's commands.

#### c. The promises of the Lord (28:7-14)

The preceding section (vv. 3-6) was probably read aloud in covenant-renewal ceremonies in order to state the blessings of covenant obedience. This section (vv. 7-14) was probably Moses' sermonic elaboration of those blessings.

**28:7-14.** Three areas of blessing were singled out. The first area relates to the **nations.** Israel would have supernatural military success (v. 7), and financial prosperity that would cause them to be above other nations (vv. 12b-13), lending to them but never borrowing and always their leader (**the head**) and never their follower (**the tail**). But disobedience would result in the opposite (vv. 43-44).

The second area is agricultural endeavors. Israel would experience **abundant prosperity** in her farming and family life (vv. 8, 11-12a; cf. v. 4). The Canaanites believed that the fertility god Baal sent rain from **the heavens,** but the Hebrews were to know that **the LORD** gives **rain.**

The third area was her reputation. By being God's obedient and **holy people** (cf. 26:19), the Israelites would enjoy such an intimacy with **God** that they would become a testimony to **all the peoples on earth** who would **fear** or stand in awe of Israel (cf. 2:25; 11:25). Israel would experience blessings in all three areas (military and financial success, agriculture, and reputation) if she did **not turn aside from any of the** Lord's **commands** or follow **other gods** (28:14).

### 2. THE CURSES (28:15-68)

#### a. Specific curses (28:15-19)

**28:15-19.** Just as obedience would bring blessings, so disobedience would bring **curses.** (See the chart "The Covenant Chastenings," near Amos 4:6.) No middle ground was possible. The four curses in verses 16-19 are the exact opposite of the four blessings cited in verses 3-6 (though the second and third are reversed, and the words "the young of your livestock," v. 4, are not included in v. 18).

#### b. The Lord's judgments (28:20-68)

This section is Moses' sermonic elaboration of the specific curses in verses 16-19. (Cf. vv. 7-14, which were Moses' elaboration of the blessings in vv. 3-6.) Each individual judgment essentially had one goal: to turn Israel from disobedience.

(1) Horrible destruction. **28:20.** Moses threatened Israel with a painful destruction if she forsook **the Lord. Confusion** was the term for the divine panic that came on Israel's enemies and rendered them helpless in battle or racked them with painful diseases (cf. 1 Sam. 5:9; 14:20). To forsake God is to do **evil.**

(2) Disease. **28:21-22.** The precise identity of the first three **diseases: wasting disease . . . fever . . . inflammation** is unknown. The last two diseases—**blight and mildew**—strike plants. The other two, **scorching heat and drought,** though not diseases, affect both people and vegetation and eventually cause death.

(3) Drought. **28:23-24.** The once-fertile land would be without **rain. The sky** would **be** like **bronze,** that is, the heat of the sun would always be bearing down; no rain clouds would come. Instead of rain there would be **dust** so that nothing could grow (**the ground** would become like **iron**).

(4) Defeat in battle. **28:25-26.** Israel would experience devastating defeats in battle. Instead of her **enemies** fleeing **in seven** directions (cf. v. 7) in panic, *Israel* would **flee** in seven directions. Because of defeat **no one** would be left to bury her corpses.

(5) Physical and mental diseases of Egypt. **28:27-29.** As the **Lord** had once struck **Egypt** with **boils** (Ex. 9:8-12) and sent **confusion** to Pharaoh's army (Ex. 14:23-28) so He would afflict Israel with these things (cf. "diseases" in Ex. 15:26; Deut. 7:15; 28:60; also note 28:35). The physical and mental afflictions would be so great that the Israelites would not have the strength or presence of mind to complete any task (they would **be unsuccessful in everything**), nor could they defend themselves from oppressors.

(6) Oppressed and robbed. **28:30-35.** The afflictions mentioned here result from defeat in battle. The military exemptions mentioned in 20:5-7 would be reversed without God's protection (28:30). Livestock and children would be lost forever (vv. 31-32). Foreign armies would reap the benefit of the farmers' hard work (v. 33). These devastating losses would produce insanity (v. 34) and **painful boils** (v. 35; cf. v. 27).

(7) Exile. **28:36-37.** If Israel refused to serve the living God she would be cast into a strange land to serve lifeless **gods.** Instead of becoming head of the nations (v. 13) she would become the most repulsive **nation** on earth, talked about and ridiculed by her captors.

(8) Crop failure and economic ruin (28:38-44). **28:38-42.** No matter how hard the Israelites would work to produce crops their goal would always be frustrated. **Locusts** and **worms** would obey the sovereign Lord even if Israel would not. So all Israel's crops—grains, **vineyards,** and **olive treees**—would be destroyed. Nor would their children help them overcome the curse **because they** would be lost in **captivity.** This section begins as it ends, with a reference to **locusts** (vv. 38, 42).

**28:43-44.** During the plagues the Lord made a distinction between the Egyptians and Israelites and protected the Israelites from the disasters that fell on Egypt. The reverse would be true in this judgment for **the alien** would profit at Israel's expense, becoming the leader (**head**; cf. v. 13).

(9) Reason for the curses. **28:45-48.**

At this point in the sermon Moses seemed to assume that Israel would definitely receive **all these curses.** It was no longer a matter of "if you disobey," but rather **you did not obey the LORD your God** (v. 45) and **you did not serve the LORD your God** (v. 47). These curses therefore were certain: they **will come upon you** (v. 45). They would have a pedagogical function, however, for as **a sign** they would serve as a warning of God's miraculous intervention in judgments, and as **a wonder** the curses would be so so horrible and comprehensive that they would attract the attention of future Israelites. The curses would also demonstrate the Lord's retributive justice. **Because** Israel refused to serve Him **joyfully . . . in the time of prosperity** she would find herself serving a harsh taskmaster in a time of **dire poverty.** She would again be in slavery, subject to her **enemies** as if she were an ox with **an iron yoke on** its **neck** (cf. Jer. 28:14). Yokes were normally made of wood; an iron yoke would be heavier and more severe.

(10) The horrors of besieged cities (28:49-57). **28:49-52.** The two worst possible curses were saved until the conclusion of the sermon and then specifically illustrated: the **siege** (vv. 49-57) and the exile (vv. 58-68). The foreign **nation** would be swift and powerful (**like an eagle;** in Hab. 1:6, 8 the Babylonians are compared among other things with a sweeping vulture), brutal (**fierce-looking** and **without . . . pity**), destructive (destroying the grain **crops,** vineyards, and olive trees, and killing **young . . . livestock**), and thorough (laying siege **to all the cities throughout** Israel's **land**). No wonder then that Israel would be totally **ruined** (Deut. 28:51).

**28:53-57.** The horrors of **the siege** would come to a climactic manifestation in cannibalism (cf. Lev. 26:27-29; Jer. 19:9). **Even . . . gentle and sensitive** parents would be so starved during the siege they would eat their own **children.** Whereas their enemies would eat or destroy Israel's livestock and crops (Deut. 28:51) the Israelites would devour their own **children,** "the fruit" of their own wombs (v. 4), God's gifts to them. This curse was literally fulfilled when the Arameans besieged Samaria (2 Kings 6:24-29) and when the Babylonians besieged Jerusalem (Lam. 2:20; 4:10). This

was one of the greatest examples of the depth of perversity to which disobedience to God leads.

(11) The destruction of the nation with disease and exile. **28:58-68.** In carrying out the curses on disobedient Israel, **God** would undo all the previous blessings He had lavished on her. Whereas Israel had previously escaped the **fearful plagues** and **diseases of Egypt** (cf. 7:15; 28:27, 35; Ex. 15:26), God would **bring** them on Israel (cf. Amos 4:10). He would also **bring** other kinds **of sickness . . . not recorded in this Book of the Law** (Deut. 28:61).

Whereas God had multiplied her number **as the stars in the sky** (cf. Gen. 15:5; 22:17; 26:4), Israel would be reduced to a **few in number** (Deut. 28:62). And whereas Israel had dwelt securely in **the land,** she would lose her identity by being **uprooted** and scattered **among all nations** (vv. 63-64). Israel had been permitted to serve **the LORD** but now she would be compelled to serve idols (v. 64). Once she lived in security, but now she would **live** in anxiety, despair, and **in constant suspense** and fear for her **life** (vv. 65-66). To escape her misery she will long for **night** to come and then for the daytime. **God** had delivered her from bondage in **Egypt,** but the people would voluntarily return to that misery and in such a humiliated condition that no Egyptian would purchase them as **slaves.**

### C. Conclusion to Moses' third address (29:1)

**29:1.** Some see this verse as an introduction to the fourth address of **Moses** beginning in verse 2, but probably it concludes the covenant renewal ceremony in Moab. This preference is reflected in the Hebrew text which numbers this verse as 28:69 rather than 29:1. The words, **the covenant . . . in Moab, in addition to the covenant He had made with them at Horeb,** have led some to posit the existence of a separate covenant (i.e., a Palestinian Covenant) in addition to the Mosaic Covenant. The wording, however, was not meant to reflect the making of a new covenant, but the renewing of the Mosaic Covenant made at Horeb. Moses' fourth address introduces no new covenantal provisions that were not already made explicit in his other speeches. So Deuteronomy 29:2–30:20 recapitulates the covenant details laid down in the preceding chapters.

## V. The Fourth Address by Moses: A Summary of the Covenant Demands (29:2–30:20)

### A. An appeal for covenantal obedience (29:2-29)

#### 1. HISTORICAL REVIEW OF THE LORD'S FAITHFULNESS (29:2-8)

**29:2-8.** On the significance of this review see the comments on chapters 1–3 and 8:1-5. The new element in this review is Moses' assertion that **to this day the LORD has not given you a mind that understands or eyes that see or ears that hear** (29:4).This does not mean that because Israel was disobedient she could not understand the meaning of the **miraculous** elements of her history. "To this day" suggests that Israel had not *yet* understood these saving events. Her disobedience and rebellion originated from a mindset that could not fully understand the implications of God's saving works. Thus apart from divine enlightening, people always remain insensitive to God's work (cf. Paul's use of this text in Rom. 11:8).

#### 2. THE ESSENCE OF COVENANT RENEWAL (29:9-15)

**29:9-15.** To the extent Israel obeyed **the terms of this covenant** she would **prosper.** In Hebrew, the words **all of you are standing** (v. 10; cf. vv. 12, 15) imply some sort of formal ceremony for renewing the covenant. **Today** occurs three times (vv. 10, 15 [twice]) and **this day** occurs twice (vv. 12-13). So the stress was on the present, which meant that the Israelites were not entering **into a new covenant,** but were committing themselves afresh to the Mosaic Covenant. In this **covenant** renewal the Israelites so committed themselves to obeying **the LORD** that He was able **to confirm** them **as His people** (v. 13) and Himself as their God. This was important because God had promised the patriarchs (**Abraham, Isaac, and Jacob;** cf. 1:8; 6:10; 9:5, 27; 30:20; 34:4) that He would give their descendants that land.

The scope of the **covenant** renewal **also** embraced future generations (**those who are not here today,** 29:15). Therefore the obedience of that present generation

had a great effect on those not yet born.

#### 3. THE CURSES FOR DISOBEDIENCE (29:16-29)

**29:16-18.** Moses reminded the Israelites that they were not naive concerning idolatry. They had seen it **in Egypt** and had fallen into idolatry **on the way** to the Promised Land (Ex. 32; Num. 25). They had seen the pagans' **detestable . . . idols.** They knew how one idolatrous **man . . . woman, clan, or tribe** could defile many with the **bitter poison** of idolatry (cf. Heb. 12:15). "Poison" is literally, "wormwood," a plant known for its bitter pulp and often associated with poison (cf. Amos 5:7; 6:12; Jer. 9:15; 23:15). Therefore they were told to be extremely vigilant against this sin when they entered the land of Canaan and faced new temptations to idolatry.

**29:19-21.** An idolatrous "root" (cf. v. 18) might take hold in Israel through a single **person** who, under the cloak of anonymity, might think he was **safe** from judgment because **the LORD** had said Israel was His people. This idolatrous root, however, would flower into a general apostasy that would bring forth God's judgment. All Israelites would suffer in the judgment (**this will bring disaster on the watered land as well as the dry**). A person who introduced such idolatry into Israel could never escape the consequences of his sin. **All the curses . . . in** Deuteronomy would **fall upon him** and he would have no male heir to carry on **his name,** for it would be blotted **out.** No sin is unknown before the omniscient **LORD** (cf. Heb. 4:13).

**29:22-28.** Judgment would fall, however, not only on the one who introduced idolatry but also on the **whole** nation because they let themselves be swept away by the false worship. The future judgment (**calamities** and **diseases** on the **land;** cf. 28:22b, 59-61) would be so severe that it was compared to the judgment that fell on **Sodom and Gomorrah,** and **Admah and Zeboiim.** These last two cities, near Sodom and Gomorrah, were in a treaty with them (Gen. 14:2). The land would be covered with **salt and sulfur** and therefore be unproductive. This comprehensive judgment must refer to the devastation in the Assyrian and Babylonian invasions.

The devastation would be so complete that **the nations** would **ask why** Israel's God in **anger** had let it happen (Deut. 29:24). **The answer** would **be** that Israel had **abandoned the** Mosaic Covenant by committing idolatry. Even their false worship would prove the truth of God's Word, for **the curses . . . in this book** would come on them just as He had promised. Because they had gone **off** and **bowed down to** false **gods** (cf. 30:17), God in His **anger** would uproot them and take them into exile. Then they would bow to their captors.

**29:29.** **The secret things** of the LORD probably refer to future details that God had not revealed. Yet what He *had* **revealed** (e.g., future judgment for disobedience, future blessing for obdience, His requirements for holiness, etc.) was enough to encourage the Israelites to **follow all the words of** the **Law**.

### B. Promised blessings after Israel's repentance (30:1-10)

1. RESTORATION TO THE PROMISED LAND (30:1-5)

**30:1-2.** Moses had passionately urged the nation to **obey** the LORD and His commands, and had **set the blessings and curses . . . before** them in order to motivate them. Yet he knew his fickle and stubborn people well enough to realize that their apostasy was inevitable and that the worst curses would come upon them—exile and dispersion **among the nations**. However, even in the midst of this curse he foresaw God's blessing. For Israel would come to her senses; she would **take** God's word **to heart**.

**30:3-5.** However, Israel's repentance would be insufficient to reverse the effects of their curses for they would still be under foreign domination. So in response to their repentance, **God** Himself will intervene, and with tender **compassion . . . gather** the nation and **bring** her back to her **land**. He **will restore** Israel's **fortunes**, a theme frequent in the prophets (cf., e.g., Jer. 30:18; 32:44; 33:11, 26; Joel 3:1). The prophets made it clear that this great restoration to **the land** would not take place until the Second Advent of the Messiah just before the beginning of His millennial reign on the earth (e.g., Isa. 59:20–62:12; cf. Jesus' teaching of the regathering in Matt. 24:31; Mark 13:27). This will be a time of spiritual and material prosperity greater

than the nation has ever known (Deut. 30:5).

2. THE PROMISE OF A NEW HEART AND ABUNDANT PROSPERITY (30:6-10)

**30:6.** The promise **that the** LORD **your God will circumcise your hearts** (cf. 10:16) means that God will graciously grant the nation a new will to obey Him in place of their former spiritual insensitivity and stubbornness. After returning to the Promised Land with a new heart they will remain committed to the Lord and therefore will experience abundant blessing (**live**). Loving Him wholeheartedly (cf. 30:16, 20; see comments on 6:5), they would not fall back into apostasy as they had done before. A new heart is an essential feature of the New Covenant (cf. Ezek. 36:24-32), which will not be fulfilled for Israel as a nation until the return of Jesus Christ (cf. Jer. 31:31-34).

**30:7-10.** All the prosperity mentioned here (cf. 28:4) would come on Israel because under the New Covenant the nation will finally be enabled to **obey the** LORD wholeheartedly (cf. **all your heart** and **all your soul** in 30:6; 6:5).

### C. A concluding charge to choose life (30:11-20)

1. THE CLARITY AND ACCESSIBILITY OF THE LAW (30:11-14)

**30:11-14.** The Law was not incomprehensible (**too difficult**) or inaccessible (**beyond your reach**). Though the Law had a heavenly origin God clearly revealed it to Israel so there was no need for anyone to **ascend into heaven to get it** nor did anyone need to travel across an ocean **to get it.** Nor did Israel need a special interpreter of the Law before they could **obey it.** The Law was already written down and Israel had been familiar with its demands in the wilderness. So Moses could say that **the word is very near you.** They could speak it (**it is in your mouth**) and they knew it (it is **in your heart**).

Paul's use of verse 14 in Romans 10:6-8 was based on the fact that Christ fulfilled the Law and is the only Person to have lived perfectly by it (Rom. 10:4-5). Just as the Law was a gracious revelation of God's righteousness, so Christ, who perfectly embodied all that is in the Law, was graciously given by the Father. This word about Christ is therefore at hand ("near you," Rom. 10:8) so no one need bring Christ from heaven or bring Him from the dead for He already has become incarnate and ascended.

2. OBEDIENCE BRINGS LIFE (30:15-20)

**30:15-16.** Moses never taught the Israelites that they were justified by obeying the Law. Early in his first book he stated that Abraham was justified by faith in the Lord (Gen. 15:6). However, in Deuteronomy 30:15-20, Moses was speaking to a believing people about fellowship, not justification. His point was simply that the full enjoyment of **life** would depend on their obeying God's Word. If a believing Israelite sincerely wanted to please **the Lord**—and it was normal for such a person **to love** Him and **walk in His ways**—then he would **live** under God's blessing. So though no one could be justified by the Law, a believer could be blessed under the Law.

**30:17-20.** But if a believer began to embark on a pattern of disregarding the Law he could easily be **drawn away to bow down to other gods** (cf. 29:18) which would bring catastrophic judgment into his life. He would **be destroyed** (killed) and/or taken from **the land** by death or captivity.

So the life of the nation was to consist of her obeying the Lord. This obedience could be passed down from one generation to another since godly parents *usually* produce godly **children.** So parents who choose to obey the Lord were also making a significant choice for their posterity. Since **the Lord is** their **life,** no wonder Moses concluded this message by once again urging the people to **love the Lord** (cf. vv. 6, 16), to **listen to** (i.e., obey) Him, and to **hold fast to Him** (cf. 10:20; 11:22; 13:4).

## VI. The Transition from Moses to Joshua (chaps. 31–34)

Moses provided for the continuity of the covenant during the change in national leadership from himself to Joshua. Certain features of this section were also found in the vassal treaties of the ancient Near East: the depositing of the treaty document in a sacred place (31:24-26), provision for dynastic succession (31:7-8), and provision for future reading of the covenant and other covenant ceremonies (cf. 31:9-13).

### A. The appointment of Joshua and the depositing of the Law (31:1-29)

1. JOSHUA COMMISSIONED BY MOSES (31:1-8)

**31:1-6.** At the time of Moses' death his "eyes were not weak nor his strength gone" (34:7). Yet because of his age (**120 years**) he lacked the strength **to lead** the nation in war. He had also been forbidden by **the Lord** to enter Canaan because of an earlier act of unbelief (Num. 20:1-13). However, God's program for the nation did not depend on any one human leader. It depended only on God's power to fulfill His own covenantal promises. *He* would **destroy** the Canaanite **nations** when Israel attacked under Joshua's leadership. In light of this fact and God's past faithfulness (**what He did to Sihon and Og,** Deut. 31:4), **Moses** charged the nation to be obedient (**do to them all that I have commanded you,** v. 5) and fearless (**be strong and courageous** and **not . . . afraid or terrified,** v. 6; cf. 1:21, 29). They could take comfort in the fact that **the Lord** would always be **with** them.

**31:7-8.** After the charge to the people (vv. 1-6) **Moses** commissioned **Joshua** as the Lord had told him (3:28). Moses had previously reminded the people of God's decision to replace him with Joshua (1:38), but the repetition here **in the presence of all Israel** emphasized both God's and Moses' approval of Joshua. This helped facilitate the transition to the new leadership. Moses then gave Joshua almost the same charge he had just given the people: **Be strong and courageous** (cf. 31:23; Josh. 1:6, 9) and **not . . . afraid** or **discouraged** (cf. Josh. 1:9; 8:1).

2. THE READING OF THE LAW (31:9-13)

**31:9-13.** As the vassal treaties of the ancient Near East contained provisions for their reading in public so did the Mosaic Covenant. **This Law** (v. 9) probably means the entire Book of Deuteronomy, though the translation of the phrase has been debated. The Law and its public reading were trusted **to the priests,** one of whose functions was to teach the **Law** to **the people.** The priests were to read the Law publicly at **the Feast of Tabernacles** (September-October; see comments on 16:13-15) **in the year** of **canceling debts** which came **every seven years** (see comments on 15:1-11). Only the **men** were required to make the pilgrimage to the central sanctuary for the major feasts (cf. 16:16), though family members often went along. But even the **women and children** were to attend this special ceremony every seven years.

This experience was important for two reasons. First, it was rare for an individual to possess a copy of the Scriptures. A person gained a knowledge of the Scriptures through being taught by his parents and the priests and through its public reading at times like this. So the public reading of the **Law** was of great significance.

Second, the experience of the pilgrimage to the central sanctuary—which meant trusting God for their homes left behind and for the journey ahead—reenacted something of the original Exodus from Egypt. It was an ideal time to receive the Word in a spirit of faith so that they might **learn to fear the LORD** (see comments on 4:10) and to **follow carefully all the . . . Law.** "Follow carefully" is an admonition occurring frequently in the latter chapters of this book (16:12; 17:19; 19:9; 24:8; 28:1, 13, 15, 58; 29:9; 31:12). This repetition shows Moses' concern for strict obedience. **Children** too would benefit from this for they also, by hearing it, would learn to fear the **LORD**.

3. THE COMMISSIONING OF JOSHUA BY THE LORD (31:14-23)

**31:14.** The formal commissioning of **Joshua** is mentioned here and also at the end of this section (v. 23), thus providing a framework for the Lord's prediction of Israel's rebellion (vv. 15-22). That in turn served as an extended introduction to the Song of Moses (31:30–32:43). Whereas Moses' commission of Joshua had been public (31:7-8), this one was private with only **Moses and Joshua** appearing before the Lord **at the Tent of Meeting,** the tabernacle.

**31:15-22.** After a life of service to the nation **Moses** heard saddening news from **the LORD . . . these people will soon prostitute themselves to the foreign gods of the land they are entering.** Even though Moses had repeatedly warned them of the dangers of idolatry and of the need to obey the stipulations of the covenant, still the Lord knew they would succumb. In response to their defection God in His anger (cf. 29:20, 24) would withdraw His **face** (presence) **from them.** As

a result, when **disasters** would befall the nation, they would find no relief (31:17-18). However, even in their rebellion they would find the grace of God. In the **song** that Moses would **teach** them they would find the reason for their judgments and the path of repentance (vv. 19-22). The **song** would also serve as a warning of the judgment to come for apostasy. God is fully aware of the tendency of the human heart to stray from Him: **I know what they are disposed to do.**

**31:23.** In spite of this predicted rebellion **the LORD** formally commissioned **Joshua,** giving him a charge (**Be strong and courageous**; cf. v. 7; Josh. 1:6, 8) and assuring him of success with the promise, **I Myself will be with you.**

4. THE LAW TO BE DEPOSITED BESIDE THE ARK (31:24-29)

**31:24-29.** The **book** with **the words of this Law** (v. 24; cf. **this Book of the Law,** v. 26) refers to Deuteronomy. It was to be placed **beside the ark,** not in it. Only the Ten Commandments were placed in the ark (cf. Ex. 25:16 with Ex. 31:18; also note 1 Kings 8:9). Moses' angry words to the people (Deut. 31:27-29) reflected both his righteous indignation and his disappointment in them after hearing God's prediction of their future apostasy (v. 16). Since Moses knew from experience that they were **rebellious and stiff-necked** (cf. 9:6, 13; 10:16), he knew that **after** he was dead they would continue to be **rebellious** and would even **become utterly corrupt** (probably by idol-worship; cf. 4:16, 25; 9:12). As a result God in His **anger** would bring **disaster** on them.

B. *The Song of Moses (31:30–32:43)*

1. THE PROSE INTRODUCTION (31:30)

**31:30.** The **Song** of **Moses** (cf. vv. 19, 21) was to be taught to **Israel** for use in the covenant-renewal ceremony. Thus it is an integral part of Deuteronomy (which dealt with the renewal of the covenant in the plains of Moab), not merely an appendix to Moses' fifth book. Though the song is not prophetic it does have prognostic overtones. Israel's future is depicted in rather gloomy terms for her newly acquired wealth would lead her into apostasy. However, after she underwent severe judgment from the Lord He in compassion would deliver His people and take vengeance on their enemies. So in singing this song the Israelites would be acknowledging two things: (a) their obligation to obey the Lord, and (b) the righteous and certain character of their judgment if they fell into apostasy.

### 2. THE POETIC INTRODUCTION (32:1-3)

**32:1-3.** The appeal to the **heavens** and the **earth** meant that the song had significance for the entire created order. Anyone who followed the **teaching** of Moses in this song and all of Deuteronomy would become fruitful and prosperous in the way **rain** and **dew** refresh the **new grass** and **tender plants.** The content of that teaching was a proclamation of **the name of the LORD,** that is, a description of His character and works. Thus any Israelite who gave serious consideration to the character and work of **God,** thereby evidencing his trust in Him, could expect to enjoy a blessed life.

### 3. A FAITHFUL GOD AND A CORRUPT PEOPLE (32:4-9)

**32:4.** The description of God given in this verse contrasts strongly with the following description of His people (vv. 5-9). **He is the Rock** (cf. vv. 15, 18, 30-31; 2 Sam. 22:2-3; Ps. 18:2; Hab. 1:12). This means that **God** is stable and permanent. So the only stability in life is in clinging to Him, the great Rock. **His works** (actions) **are perfect** (cf. 2 Sam. 22:31) and He is fair **(just)** in **all** His dealings with mankind. Unlike the gods of the ancient Near East whose followers believed they were often immoral and capricious, the Lord can always be counted on. He is **faithful** (cf. Deut. 7:9) and always does what is morally right (He **does no wrong).**

**32:5-9.** In contrast with God's faithfulness and righteousness, His people had become so **warped** that they bore no family resemblance to their **Father.** They could almost always be counted on to do wrong. The depth of the contrast was emphasized by reminding the people that the Lord (Yahweh) was their **Creator** (v. 6), that is, He **formed** the people into a nation at the Exodus (cf. v. 9).

So the **people** were doubly **foolish** in acting so **corruptly** (cf. 31:29). First, they

flouted the grace of their God, and second, they forgot about His power. For if He could make them into a nation, He could also unmake them. If the people doubted that He was their Creator all they had to do was look back into their history (**Remember the days of old,** v. 7). The challenge to remember is given 16 times in Deuteronomy, starting in 4:10 and concluding here.

The **elders** could **explain to** them that God had **set up** the **boundaries . . . of Israel,** making Israel **His people** and **inheritance** (i.e., owning them as His), and that He was absolutely sovereign as **the Most High** over all **nations.**

### 4. THE LORD'S GOODNESS IN CREATING ISRAEL (32:10-14)

**32:10-14.** The description of the Lord as Israel's "Father" and "Creator" (v. 6) is enlarged in these verses. The **desert land** probably refers to Egypt rather than the wilderness. Egypt was **a barren and howling waste** in the nation's experience. Also in comparison with the Promised Land, which flowed with milk and honey, Egypt was like a desert. There in that "desert" Pharaoh tried to slay the firstborn of Israel, but God **shielded . . . and cared for** them. God guarded Israel as a person automatically guards **the apple** (pupil; cf. Ps. 17:8; Prov. 7:2) **of his eye** (cf. Zech. 2:8).

The metaphor of the **eagle** speaks of God's wise and loving parental care. As an eagle must force **its young** out of the **nest** if they are to learn to fly and fend for themselves so **the LORD . . . led** His people into the harsh life of Egyptian bondage and afterward through wilderness wanderings that they might become strong. And like an eagle, the Lord remained ready to "catch them" when necessary. The next two verses became prophetic of the Conquest. Israel rode **on the heights of the land** and enjoyed the prosperity of the Promised Land (Deut. 32:13b-14). **Honey from the rock** and **oil from the flinty crag** suggest that even the most barren places would become fertile. God's goodness was especially seen in His providing varied and rich food and drink, including **curds . . . milk . . . lambs . . . goats . . . rams of Bashan** (a fertile area east of the Sea of Kinnereth, later called the Sea of Galilee), **wheat,** and **wine.**

## 5. ISRAEL'S PROSPERITY LED TO HER APOSTASY (32:15-18)

**32:15.** Many believers learn that prosperity is a more dangerous trial than adversity. In adverse circumstances a believer is reminded of how desperately he needs God's help, but in time of prosperity he may easily forget God. Israel, ironically referred to as **Jeshurun** ("the upright one"; cf. NIV marg. and 33:5, 26), abandoned the Lord, their only hope for salvation, when they became prosperous (**grew fat**). The metaphor of an animal kicking at its owner suggests the mindless nature of Israel's rebellion against **God,** their **Rock** (cf. comments on 32:4).

**32:16-17.** The nation's apostasy took shape in the worship of **idols** (cf. v. 21) which meant they actually **sacrificed to demons** (cf. Ps. 106:37). Demonic control or influence may, in fact, help explain the powerful hold that idolatry exercised over people in the ancient Near East and Israel in particular at different times in her history. The Apostle Paul may have been thinking of Deuteronomy 32:16-17 when he wrote, "The sacrifices of pagans are offered to demons, not to God, and I do not want you to be participants with demons" (1 Cor. 10:20). God was **jealous** (cf. Deut. 4:24; 5:9; 6:15; 32:21) in the sense that He is zealous to protect the honor that belongs to Him alone. He is against sharing His people's affections with other **gods.**

**32:18.** The perversity of Israel's apostasy was underscored by Moses' metaphor; he compared the Lord to a father (**who fathered you**) and a mother (**who gave you birth**). Since only a most perverse person can forget his father's and mother's love, Israel was obviously corrupt.

## 6. THE LORD'S JUDGMENT ON ISRAEL (32:19-27)

**32:19-22.** Israel's apostasy (vv. 15-18) provoked God to great anger (vv. 19-22), which He expressed in judgment on Israel. Yahweh's anger against the apostasy of **His sons and daughters** (v. 19) was not the selfish anger of one who felt slighted by too little attention. Instead it was the righteous indignation of a holy and gracious God toward **children who are unfaithful** and even **perverse** (v. 20), who followed **worthless idols** (v. 21; cf. v. 16).

In His righteous indignation God withdrew His beneficial presence (**I will hide My face from them,** v. 20) and judged Israel by a foreign nation, **those who are not a people** (v. 21). This may mean that **a nation** would conquer Israel which could have never done so if Israel had been following the Lord. Israel had **made** God **jealous** (v. 21; cf. comments on v. 16) and angry, so He would **make them envious** and **angry.**

The metaphor of **a fire** (v. 22) points to the awful consequences and comprehensive nature of God's judgment.

**32:23-27.** Verses 19-22 deal primarily with the Lord's anger and refer to His judgment in only general terms; verses 23-27 set forth the details of His judgment. This devastating judgment would touch every area of life. Israel would experience **famine . . . pestilence and deadly plague . . . wild beasts,** and **vipers** (v. 24), and even severe wars (v. 25) with people of all ages being killed by **the sword** (cf. Ezek. 5:17; 14:21). The devastation from these would be so great that Israel would almost be annihilated (Deut. 32:26). Though the nation deserved to be wiped out, **the Lord** would not allow it, for it would cause her enemies to question His sovereignty and power (v. 27).

## 7. ISRAEL'S LACK OF DISCERNMENT (32:28-33)

**32:28-33.** God's judgment on Israel would reach horrifying depths because she had **no discernment** (v. 28). She was not able to **discern** the catastrophic **end** to which her rebellion was leading (v. 29). Yet the evidence of God's supernatural judgment would be clear (v. 30). A man cannot defeat **1,000** soldiers singlehandedly or **10,000** with a partner unless the Lord, his **Rock** (cf. comments on v. 4), helps him. This judgment could not be attributed to the gods of Israel's **enemies** (v. 31). In fact the enemies who would execute God's judgment on Israel were as evil as **Sodom** and **Gomorrah,** which further underscored the depth of evil and shame into which Israel had fallen (vv. 32-33). So wicked would be Israel's enemies (including the Assyrians and Babylonians) that even **their grapes,** figuratively speaking, would be poisonous and **their wine** like a snake's **venom.**

## 8. GOD'S COMPASSION AND VENGEANCE (32:34-43)

**32:34-35.** Though the Lord would let His enemies execute judgment on Israel,

He would still hold those enemies accountable for their wickedness and **repay** them for their evil (cf. vv. 41, 43). They may think themselves safe from God's judgment since they would have defeated God's people. But God's ways and power are beyond their knowledge; it is as if He kept them **sealed . . . in . . . vaults.**

**32:36-38.** In judging Israel's enemies God would have **compassion on** Israel. The statement **The LORD will judge His people** means that He would judge for them (i.e., vindicate them). However, Israel would not experience His compassion till they relinquished all trust in their own efforts (**when . . . their strength is gone**) and in the false **gods** in whom **they took refuge.** Moses ironically called on Israel to turn for **help** to the false gods, knowing, of course, they would be unable to help Israel.

**32:39-43.** God's goal in judging Israel was not to annihilate her. It was to bring her to the point where she understood that **there is no god besides** the Lord and that He alone has power over **death** and **life** (v. 39). God's lifting His **hand** was the gesture used in taking an oath (cf. Gen. 14:22; Ex. 6:8; Neh. 9:15; Ps. 106:26; Ezek. 20:5). When Israel would come to this realization God would **take vengeance on** His **adversaries** (Deut. 32:41, 43; cf. v. 35). Since another nation would be used by God to defeat Israel's **enemies,** God said their **sword** was *His* **sword** (vv. 41-42). In this act of vengeance God would **make atonement for** (deliver) **His people.**

## C. Preparation for Moses' death (32:44-52)

1. MOSES' LAST CHARGE TO THE NATION (32:44-47)

**32:44-47.** After **reciting all the words of** the **song** (vv. 1-43) **Moses** told **the people** to consider seriously (**take to heart**) **the words** of the song. If they would meditate on the certainty and severity of the judgment that the Lord would send on them for their apostasy, the Song of Moses could serve as a powerful deterrent to future rebellion. The threat of the Lord's retributive justice was given for their spiritual health. A healthy fear of the judgment set forth in the song would also enable them to teach their **children** the need **to obey . . . the**

**words of this Law.** Once again Moses concluded with a reminder that their existence, prosperity, and longevity (cf. 5:16; 6:2; 11:9; 25:15) depended on their obedience to God's commands.

2. GOD'S COMMAND FOR MOSES TO ASCEND MOUNT NEBO (32:48-52)

**32:48-52. Mount Nebo** was one of the more prominent peaks in **the Abarim range** in **Moab**; it overlooked the north end of the Dead Sea. It was here outside the Promised Land that **Moses** would **die,** though God graciously allowed him to **see the land . . . from a distance** (v. 52) before he died. The reason for this discipline is recorded in Numbers 20:1-13. God had commanded Moses to speak to a rock in order to bring forth water for the people who were grumbling against him and Aaron. Moses disobeyed the Lord by hitting the rock twice instead of speaking to it (Num. 20:11), and by arrogantly suggesting that he and **Aaron,** not the Lord, had brought forth the water. For this act of unbelief and failure to give God glory (to **uphold** His **holiness**) before the nation, Moses forfeited his right to lead the people into the Promised **Land.**

## D. The blessing of Moses (chap. 33)

1. THE PROSE INTRODUCTION (33:1)

**33:1. The blessing** of **Moses** given here just **before his death** (34:1-8) is well suited to the context. It was customary for a father to impart a blessing just before his death (cf. Jacob's blessing, Gen. 49). Moses, leader of the Exodus and the mediator of the Sinaitic Covenant, was in a sense Israel's "father." Levi is often omitted in the Old Testament lists of tribes. Here the tribe of Simeon, which later was absorbed by Judah (Josh. 19:1-9), is omitted. Like Moses' preceding song (Deut. 32:1-43) his blessing is given in poetic form. Chapter 33 is difficult in places to interpret because of the use of several rare words, unusual syntactical devices, and various textual problems. The following exposition mainly follows the NIV translation and does not discuss the more technical matters.

2. MOSES' PRAISE OF THE LORD (33:2-5)

**33:2-5.** Moses' praise of God began with a description of the Lord's appearance at **Sinai** when He gave **the Law** to **the people** through **Moses.** This was a major event in Israel's history. To become a nation it was necessary to have a common people (v. 5), a common constitution (the Law, v. 4), and a common land. The sojourn in Egypt molded Jacob's descendants into a common people, and the giving of the Law at Sinai gave them a common constitution.

When God appeared to Moses on Mount Sinai it was as if He had come **from Seir** (Edom) to the northeast and **from Mount Paran** (cf. Hab. 3:3), probably in the wilderness of Paran north of Sinai toward Seir. In the awesome display of His glory on Mount Sinai (Ex. 19:16-19; 24:15-18) angels **(holy ones)** were present. Moses' words in Deuteronomy 33:3-5 seem to reflect the peoples' response in praise. They acknowledged the Lord's love for them, His **people,** and the ministry of the angels ("the holy ones") in mediating the Law (cf. Acts 7:38, 53; Gal. 3:19; Heb. 2:2). The proclamation of the Lord's kingship **over Jeshurun** (a name for Israel; cf. NIV marg. and Deut. 32:15; 33:26) looked back to the nation's deliverance from Egypt and the giving of the Law (**when the leaders** and **the tribes** assembled to receive God's commands). The Lord's position as "king over Jeshurun" may also anticipate His giving them the land of Canaan.

3. MOSES' BLESSINGS ON THE TRIBES (33:6-25)

*a. Reuben (33:6)*

**33:6.** The wish for the tribe of **Reuben** to **live** suggested that it would face some special adversity or had some defect in character that might bring disaster. The latter is probably true in light of the tribe's character as reflected in Judges 5:15-16, and in light of Jacob's pronouncement on Reuben, "You will no longer excel" (Gen. 49:4). The last clause in Deuteronomy 33:6 may be translated "let his men be few" (cf. NIV marg.) or "**nor** let **his men be few.**"

*b. Judah (33:7)*

**33:7.** Since **Judah** marched at the head of the tribes (Num. 2:9) she was first in battle. So this blessing was essentially a prayer for Judah's military success by God's **help.**

*c. Levi (33:8-11)*

**33:8-11.** The **Thummim and Urim** were probably two precious stones used in the casting of lots to receive divine answers in difficult matters (cf. Ex. 28:30 and see comments there; Lev. 8:8; Num. 27:21; 1 Sam. 28:6; Ezra 2:63; Neh. 7:65). They were entrusted to the priestly mediators, priests of the tribe of **Levi.** At first the faithfulness of Levi was praised in its representative Moses, **the man . . . favored** in Levi, who was faithful **at Massah,** also called **Meribah** (cf. Ex. 17:1-7). Then the tribe was praised collectively (Deut. 33:9) for their impartial administration of God's judgment in the matter of the golden calf (Ex. 32:25-29). The priests, of the tribe of Levi, were to teach God's **precepts** and **Law** to **Jacob** (a synonym of the nation **Israel;** cf. Deut. 33:28) and to officiate over the worship in the tabernacle (v. 11). The blessing in verse 11 was a prayer for supernatural enablement for the Levites' success in using their **skills** in God's **work.** The identity of Levi's **foes** is unclear.

*d. Benjamin (33:12)*

**33:12.** Moses' prayer for the security and peace of **Benjamin** as **the beloved of the LORD** shielded by **Him** reflects Benjamin's special status as Jacob's youngest and particularly loved son (Gen. 44:20).

*e. Joseph (33:13-17)*

**33:13-16.** Moses prayed first for Joseph's material prosperity. Crops would grow (**his land** would be blessed) as they received **dew from heaven above** and **waters . . . below.** The **deep** waters may refer to wells or to springs and rivers derived from subterranean waters. **The sun** and **the moon** (lit., lunar "months," i.e., seasons) were also necessary for crop growth. The **gifts of the ancient mountains** and **of the everlasting hills** probably refer to the timber of the forests, used in building houses. The good crops enjoyed by this tribe were called **the best gifts of the earth;** they were given by God, **who dwelt in the burning bush** (Ex. 3).

**33:17.** Moses then prayed for the military success of Joseph, pictured **like a . . . bull** or **ox** goring **the nations.** This tribe was divided into the two tribes of

Manasseh, Joseph's firstborn, and Ephraim, his younger son. They were the largest of the Northern tribes. Though Manasseh was the older son, Jacob gave Ephraim the blessing of the firstborn (Gen. 48:17-20). That was why Moses mentioned Ephraim first and credited ten thousands to him, and just thousands to Manasseh.

### f. Zebulun and Issachar (33:18-19)

33:18-19. Zebulun and Issachar, mentioned together here, were also mentioned together in Jacob's blessing (Gen. 49:13-15) and in the Song of Deborah (Jud. 5:14-15). The phrases, in your going out and in your tents, probably refer to the people's daily lives, that is, they were equivalent to "in your work and in your home." The command to rejoice indicated then that these two tribes could expect God's blessing in their daily lives. The identity of the mountain is uncertain (possibly it was Mount Tabor which lies between the two tribes), but the source of their prosperity was clearly the seas (in Gen. 49:13-15 only Zebulun is associated with the sea). Though neither tribe apparently touched the Mediterranean Sea, Issachar was near the Sea of Kinnereth (Galilee), and Zebulun was only a few miles from the Mediterranean; merchants probably traversed both tribal territories with sea products.

### g. Gad (33:20-21)

33:20-21. The translation of some of these lines is uncertain. But the general sense seems to be that even though Gad had been allotted its territory east of the Jordan, choosing the best land (3:12-17), the tribe still fought valiantly (like a lion) in the conquest of Canaan (cf. Josh. 22:1-6). In this way the Gadites carried out the LORD's . . . will.

### h. Dan (33:22)

33:22. The metaphor of Dan being a lion's cub may imply a potential for great strength. Several modern commentators prefer to translate the Hebrew word rendered Bashan as "serpent." The clause would then read "springing away from the serpent." Though potentially strong, Dan still was timid before a snake. If this is the proper translation the blessing may reflect Jacob's earlier statement, "Dan will be a serpent" (Gen. 49:17).

### i. Naphtali (33:23)

33:23. This blessing described the geographical location of Naphtali as extending southward to the lake, probably the Sea of Kinnereth (Galilee), a fertile area. Like Joseph's sons Ephraim and Manasseh (v. 16), and Asher (v. 24), this tribe would enjoy the favor of God and His blessing.

### j. Asher (33:24-25)

33:24-25. The name Asher means "blessed, happy." To bathe one's feet in oil rather than simply to anoint them would be an extravagant act. Thus the tribe of Asher would experience abundant fertility and prosperity. The bolts of iron and bronze indicate the tribe's military security.

### 4. MOSES' CONCLUDING PRAISE OF THE LORD (33:26-29)

33:26-29. Jeshurun (lit., "the upright one"; cf. v. 5; 32:15) was a name for Israel. The nation's God is incomparable in power as the One who rides on the heavens and the clouds (33:26). No matter what adversity Israel would encounter, the LORD could be there instantly with power to deliver her. Because God is eternal and is a Refuge for His people, His everlasting arms, figuratively speaking, would protect Israel in times of calamity, and would destroy her enemy (v. 27). Having such a wonderful and powerful God the nation could be assured of conquering Canaan and then of living for a while in safety and prosperity (v. 28). If Israel would only serve her incomparable God she would be an incomparable people (O Israel! Who is like you. . . ?) in blessing (saved and shielded by God) and invincible before her enemies (v. 29).

### E. The death of Moses (chap. 34)

### 1. MOSES' VIEWING OF THE PROMISED LAND (34:1-4)

34:1-4. Moses went up on Mount Nebo as the LORD told him to do (3:27; 32:48-50). The top of Pisgah probably refers to a ridge extending from the summit of Mount Nebo. The places Moses viewed start in the north and follow to the south in a counterclockwise direction. Though one could not normally view the western sea (the Mediterranean) from Mount Nebo, perhaps Moses was supernaturally enabled by the Lord to do so (**There the LORD showed him the whole land**). **Zoar** (cf. Gen. 14:2; 19:22-23) may have been at the southern tip of the Dead Sea. God's mention of the **oath** reminded Moses that even though he was not allowed to lead the people into the Promised Land God would still be faithful to His promise to the patriarchs (**Abraham, Isaac, and Jacob**; cf. Deut. 1:8; 6:10; 9:5, 27; 29:13; 30:20) and bring Israel into her new **land**.

### 2. THE DEATH OF MOSES AND SUCCESSION OF JOSHUA (34:5-9)

**34:5-8.** Though **Moses** was being disciplined for his act of unbelief (Num. 20:1-13) by not being allowed to enter the Promised Land, he **died** in faith and as an honored **servant of the LORD**. Additional honor was given to Moses for **the LORD** Himself buried him. It is possible to translate the clause **He buried him** as "he was buried" (meaning that men, not God, buried him; see NIV marg.). But the statement **to this day no one knows where his grave is** indicates that either the Lord alone or through the agency of His angels buried **Moses**. Jude (v. 9) also seems to confirm this interpretation. Moses' burial site, though unknown, was somewhere **in Moab, in the valley opposite Beth Peor**. This was the valley where the Israelites camped while Moses gave them the instructions and blessings recorded in Deuteronomy 5–33 (cf. 3:29; 4:46).

**Moses** was so special that his last moments on earth were spent in intimate fellowship with God who then permitted no human to take part in his burial. Concerning the remark about Moses' health see the comments on 31:2. After the death of **Moses** at the age of **120. . . . the Israelites** mourned for **30 days;** the normal time of mourning a dead loved one was 7 days (cf. Gen. 50:10). Centuries later Moses appeared with Elijah at Christ's transfiguration (Matt. 17:1-3).

**34:9.** Then **Joshua . . . was filled with the spirit of wisdom.** This accompanied Moses' commissioning of him (31:7). "The spirit of wisdom" may refer to the Holy Spirit (cf. Isa. 11:2) or to Joshua's inner spirit. Either way, God gave Joshua supernatural skill for leading **the Israelites.**

### 3. THE EPITAPH OF MOSES (34:10-12)

**34:10-12. Moses** was unique among all the prophets for his intimacy with **the LORD (whom the LORD knew face to face** as a friend; cf. Ex. 33:11; Num. 12:8) and for his **miraculous signs and wonders** and **mighty power** and **awesome deeds** (Deut. 34:11-12). He introduced a new era into the history of God's people, the Age of the Law. The Israelites waited for God to raise up the Prophet **like Moses** (18:15). Thus the book ends on a prophetic note looking forward to the day when "another Moses" would be given to **Israel.** That day finally arrived when the Lord Jesus Christ came as a Servant but also as the very Son of God, surpassing even Moses (cf. Heb. 3:1-6). He offered to take Israel into a new era, the Age of His Grace. The Israelites culminated centuries of rebellion by rejecting that gracious offer. However, the Song of Moses still points forward to the day when that offer will be accepted and God will heal and avenge His people (Deut. 32:36, 43).

# BIBLIOGRAPHY

Craigie, Peter C. *The Book of Deuteronomy.* The New International Commentary on the Old Testament. Grand Rapids: Wm. B. Eerdmans Publishing Co., 1976.

_____. *The Problem of War in the Old Testament.* Grand Rapids: Wm. B. Eerdmans Publishing Co., 1978.

Driver, S.R. *A Critical and Exegetical Commentary on Deuteronomy.* 3rd ed. The International Critical Commentary. 1902. Reprint. Greenwood, S.C.: Attic Press, 1978.

Kitchen, K.A. *Ancient Orient and Old Testament.* Chicago: InterVarsity Press, 1966.

Kline, Meredith G. *Treaty of the Great King.* Grand Rapids: Wm. B. Eerdmans Publishing Co., 1963.

Manley, G.T. *The Book of the Law.* London: Tyndale Press, 1957.

Mayes, A.D.H. *Deuteronomy.* New Century Bible Commentary. Grand Rapids: Wm. B. Eerdmans Publishing Co., 1981.

Reider, Joseph. *Deuteronomy.* Philadelphia: Jewish Publication Society of America, 1937.

# Deuteronomy

Schultz, Samuel J. *Deuteronomy: The Gospel of Love.* Everyman's Bible Commentary. Chicago: Moody Press, 1971.

Thompson, J.A. *Deuteronomy: An Introduction and Commentary.* The Tyndale Old Testament Commentaries. Downers Grove, Ill.: InterVarsity Press, 1974.

von Rad, Gerhard. *Deuteronomy.* Translated by Dorothea Barton. Philadelphia: Westminster Press, 1966.

# JOSHUA

## Donald K. Campbell

## INTRODUCTION

**Title of the Book.** In the Hebrew text the book bears the superscription Y⁺hôšūa‛, the name of its leading figure, Joshua. His name and the title of the book mean "Yahweh saves" or "Yahweh is salvation." The title therefore suitably describes what God used Joshua to do, as recorded in this book, namely, to save His people by conquering Canaan and apportioning it to Israel as their promised homeland.

**Place in the Canon.** In the English Old Testament Joshua appears as the first of the 12 historical books (Josh.–Es.). This follows the Septuagint (the Gr. trans. of the OT) in which the books are grouped into the Pentateuch (Gen.–Deut.), History (Josh.–Es.), Poetry (Job–Song), and Prophecy (Isa.–Mal.). In the Hebrew canon the books are identical, but the groupings are different. They are divided into the Law, the Prophets, and the Writings. The Book of Joshua therefore in this case heads the second division of the Old Testament, the Prophets. The "Prophets" in turn are divided into the "Former Prophets" (Josh.–2 Kings, not including Ruth) and the "Latter Prophets" (Isa.–Mal. without Lam. and Dan.). The "Writings" include (in this order) Psalms, Job, Proverbs, Song of Solomon, Ruth, Ecclesiastes, Lamentations, Esther, Daniel, Ezra, Nehemiah, 1 and 2 Chronicles. Scholars have debated the reason for placing the Book of Joshua among the "Prophets." Some have suggested it was because he held the office of prophet. Others say the historical books, the "Former Prophets," illustrate the principles preached by the prophets.

**Authorship.** The Bible does not identify the author of this book. Many liberal scholars consider it a composite of the documents which supposedly underline the Pentateuch, but a strong case can be made for unity of composition by a single author (e.g., Gleason L. Archer, *A Survey of Old Testament Introduction*. Chicago: Moody Press, 1964, pp. 252-3). Any discussion of authorship should keep the following matters in mind: (1) An eyewitness wrote many parts of the book (cf. the "we" and "us" references in 5:1, 6; and the vivid descriptions of the sending of the spies, the crossing of the Jordan, the capture of Jericho, the battle of Ai, etc.). (2) An early authorship is required by internal evidence (Rahab was alive at the time of writing [6:25]; the Jebusites still inhabited Jerusalem [15:63]; Canaanite cities are mentioned by archaic names, such as Baalah for Kiriath Jearim and Kiriath Arba for Hebron [15:9, 13]; Tyre had not yet conquered Sidon which it did in the 12th century [13:4-6]; the Philistines were not a national menace to Israel as they became after their invasion about 1200 B.C.). (3) Joshua had written parts of the book (cf. 8:32; 24:26). (4) Other parts of the book were clearly written after Joshua's death (cf. 24:29-30—the record of his death; 15:13-14—Caleb's conquest of Hebron [also recorded in Jud. 1:1, 10, 20]; Josh. 15:15-19—Othniel's conquest of Debir [also recorded in Jud. 1:11-15]; Josh. 19:47—the Danites' conquest of Leshem [also recorded in Jud. 17–18]). In light of these factors many evangelical scholars ascribe the book to Joshua himself as the main author with minor additions made by Eleazar the high priest and his son Phinehas.

**Date.** Since an eyewitness wrote much of the book (see the previous section "Authorship"), the date of writing is closely related to the date of the events. Again there is considerable disagreement among scholars on the date of the Conquest of Canaan under Joshua. Some place the Conquest in the 15th century B.C., whereas others date the Conquest in the 13th century B.C. (For more on this subject see the *Introduction* to Ex.) Key verses in deciding the issue are 1 Kings 6:1 and Judges 11:26. According to 1 Kings 6:1 the Israelites left Egypt 480 years before the fourth year of Solomon, that is, before 966 B.C. Adding these figures gives an Exodus date of 1446 B.C. The beginning of the Conquest was 40 years later (after the wilderness wanderings) or 1406 B.C. The evidence from Judges 11:26 confirms this. Jephthah said the period from the Conquest to his time was 300 years (Jud. 11:26). Adding 140 years to cover the period from Jephthah to the fourth year of Solomon gives a total of 480, which agrees with 1 Kings 6:1 (40 years for the wilderness wanderings, plus 300 for the period from Conquest to Jephthah, plus 140 from Jephthah to the fourth year of Solomon equals 480 years). Since the actual Conquest lasted seven years (cf. comments on Josh. 14:10), the land was probably occupied about 1399 B.C. The book, apart from minor additions, could have been completed soon after that.

**Purpose.** The purpose of the Book of Joshua is to give an official account of the historical fulfillment of the Lord's promise to the patriarchs to give Israel the land of Canaan by holy war. A "holy war" was a conflict with religious overtones rather than one with a political motivation of defense or expansion. This can be seen in both the opening charge (1:2-6) and the concluding summary (21:43).

Specifically, the conquest of Canaan under Joshua's leadership was based on the Abrahamic Covenant. God, having dealt with all nations, made Abraham the center of His purposes and determined to reach the lost world through Abraham's seed. The Lord made a contract or covenant with Abraham, promising unconditionally to give a land, a posterity, and spiritual blessing to the patriarch and his descendants (Gen. 12:2-3). Soon thereafter God said He was giving the land to Israel forever (cf. Gen. 13:15). The boundaries of the land were then given to Abraham (Gen. 15:18-21). Later God affirmed that the rightful heirs to the Promised Land were Isaac and his descendants (Gen. 17:19-21). Thus the Book of Joshua records the fulfillment of the patriarchal promise as Israel appropriat-

ed the land pledged to her by her faithful God centuries before. That the nation was later dispossessed reflects not on the character of God but on the fickleness of a people who took divine blessings for granted, fell into the worship of their neighbors' gods, and therefore came under the chastisement God had warned them about (cf. Deut. 28:15-68). But Israel must possess the land forever according to the promise, something that awaits the return of Messiah and the redemption of Israel. According to the Prophet Isaiah, the Messiah will be a "second Joshua," who will "restore the land and . . . reassign its desolate inheritances" (Isa. 49:8).

Paul taught that the events of the Exodus and Conquest are meaningful for Christians in that those events possess significance as types (cf. 1 Cor. 10:1-11). The Greek form of the name "Joshua" ("Yahweh saves" or "Yahweh is salvation") is "Jesus." As Joshua led Israel to victory over her enemies and into possession of the Promised Land, and as he interceded for the nation after it had sinned and been defeated, so does Jesus. He brings the people of God into a promised rest (Heb. 4:8-9); intercedes for His own continually (Rom. 8:34; Heb. 7:25); and enables them to defeat their enemies (Rom. 8:37; Heb. 2:14-15).

# OUTLINE

I. The Invasion of Canaan (1:1–5:12)
   A. The commissioning of Joshua (chap. 1)
      1. Joshua's listening to the Lord (1:1-9)
      2. Joshua's commanding the officers (1:10-15)
      3. Joshua's receiving support from the people (1:16-18)
   B. The spying out of Jericho (chap. 2)
      1. The spies' commission to Jericho (2:1)
      2. The spies' shielding by Rahab (2:2-7)
      3. The spies' intelligence information from Rahab (2:8-11)
      4. The spies' promise to Rahab (2:12-21)
      5. The spies' return to Joshua (2:22-24)

C. The crossing of the Jordan
(chap. 3)
1. Preparation for the crossing
(3:1-4)
2. Consecration for the crossing
(3:5-13)
3. Completion of the crossing
(3:14-17)
D. The erecting of memorials
(chap. 4)
E. The consecration of the Israelites
(5:1-12)
1. The renewal of circumcision
(5:1-9)
2. The celebration of the Passover
(5:10)
3. The appropriation of the land's
produce (5:11-12)
II. The Conquest of Canaan (5:13–12:24)
A. Introduction: The divine
Commander (5:13-15)
B. The central campaign (chaps. 6–8)
1. The conquest of Jericho
(chap. 6)
2. The defeat at Ai (chap. 7)
3. The victory at Ai (chap. 8)
C. The southern campaign
(chaps. 9–10)
1. The alliance with the
Gibeonites (chap. 9)
2. The defense of the Gibeonites
(chap. 10)
D. The northern campaign (11:1-15)
1. The confederation (11:1-5)
2. The conflict (11:6-15)
E. The review of the victories
(11:16–12:24)
1. The conquered areas (11:16-23)
2. The conquered kings
(chap. 12)
III. The Division of Canaan
(chaps. 13–21)
A. The portions for the two and
one-half tribes (chap. 13)
1. The divine command to divide
the land (13:1-7)
2. The special grant to the
Eastern tribes (13:8-33)
B. The portion for Caleb (chap. 14)
1. Introduction (14:1-5)
2. Caleb at Kadesh Barnea
(14:6-9)
3. Caleb during the wilderness
wanderings and the Conquest
(14:10-11)
4. Caleb at Hebron (14:12-15)
C. The portions for the nine and
one-half tribes (15:1–19:48)

1. The allotment for the tribe of
Judah (chap. 15)
2. The allotments for the Joseph
tribes (chaps. 16–17)
3. The allotments for the
remaining tribes (18:1–19:48)
D. The portions for Joshua,
manslayers, and Levites
(19:49–21:45)
1. The special provision for
Joshua (19:49-51)
2. The assignment of cities of
refuge (chap. 20)
3. The appointment of Levitical
cities (21:1-42)
4. Summary of the Conquest and
distribution (21:43-45)
IV. Conclusion (chaps. 22–24)
A. A border dispute (chap. 22)
1. The admonition of Joshua
(22:1-8)
2. The symbolic action of the
Eastern tribes (22:9-11)
3. The threat of war (22:12-20)
4. The defense of the Eastern
tribes (22:21-29)
5. The reconciliation of the tribes
(22:30-34)
B. The last days of Joshua
(23:1–24:28)
1. Joshua's final challenge to the
leaders (chap. 23)
2. Joshua's final charge to the
people (24:1-28)
C. The appendix (24:29-33)

# COMMENTARY

## I. The Invasion of Canaan (1:1–5:12)

### A. The commissioning of Joshua (chap. 1)

1. JOSHUA'S LISTENING TO THE LORD (1:1-9)

**1:1** The words, **After the death of Moses**, link this book with Deuteronomy (cf. Deut. 34:1-9). Before Moses' death **Joshua** was designated his successor (cf. Num. 27:15-23; Deut. 3:21-22; 31:1-8). Joshua had been **Moses'** young **aide** for a number of years (Ex. 24:13; 33:11; Num. 11:28). Joshua was from the tribe of Ephraim (Num. 13:8), and lived 110 years (Josh. 24:29).

Joshua may have felt a sense of loneliness, and waited expectantly near the Jordan River to hear the voice of God. He was not disappointed. When God's servants take time to listen, He always communicates. In the present Age He usually speaks through His written Word. But in the Old Testament He spoke in dreams by night, in visions by day, through the high priest, and occasionally in an audible voice.

**1:2.** In whatever way God communicated with Joshua, the message came through clearly. **Moses** God's **servant was dead.** (Interestingly Moses is called "the servant of the LORD" 3 times in Josh. 1 [vv. 1, 13, 15; cf. Ex. 14:31], and 13 times elsewhere in the Book of Josh. And at the end of Joshua's life he too was called "the servant of the LORD" [Josh. 24:29].) But though Moses was dead, God's purpose was quite alive, and Joshua was now the key figure to fulfill God's program. His instructions were explicit. Joshua was to assume immediate command of **all** the **people** and lead them across **the Jordan River into the land** God was **about to give to them.** No one can question God's right to give Canaan **to the Israelites** for He owns all the earth. As a psalmist later affirmed, "The earth is the LORD's, and everything in it, the world, and all who live in it" (Ps. 24:1).

**1:3-4.** Though the land was God's gift to Israel, it could be won only by hard fighting. The Lord gave them title to the **territory** but they had to possess it by marching on **every** part. The boundaries established by God and **promised** to Abraham (Gen. 15:18-21) and **Moses** (Deut. 1:6-8) were to extend from the wilderness on the south to the **Lebanon** mountain range on the north, and from **the Euphrates** River on the east **to the Great Sea,** the Mediterranean, **on the west.** The added expression, **all the Hittite country,** probably refers not to the extensive empire of that name north of Canaan but to the fact that in ancient times the whole population of Canaan or any part of it was sometimes called "Hittite" (cf. Gen. 15:20). "Pockets" of Hittite peoples existed here and there in Canaan.

Thirty-eight years earlier Joshua had explored this good and fruitful land as 1 of the 12 spies (Num. 13:1-16; there [Num. 13:8] he is called "Hoshea," a variant spelling of his name). The memory of its beauty and fertility had not dimmed. Now he was to lead the armies of Israel to conquer that territory.

What is the extent of these boundaries? The territory actually conquered and possessed in the time of Joshua was much less than what was promised in Genesis 15:18-21. Even in the time of David and Solomon, when the land reached its greatest extent, the outlying districts were only within Israel's sphere of influence.

When will the nation of Israel fully possess the land? The prophets have declared that at the time of Christ's return to earth He will regather the Jews and reign in the land over a converted and redeemed Israel. Full and complete possession of the land awaits that day (cf. Jer. 16:14-16; Amos 9:11-15; Zech. 8:4-8).

**1:5.** As Joshua faced the tremendous task of conquering Canaan, he needed a fresh word of encouragement. From personal observation Joshua knew that the Canaanites and others were vigorous people who lived in strongly fortified cities (cf. Num. 13:28-29). Frequent battles kept their warriors in trim fighting condition. And for the most part the land was mountainous, a fact that would make war maneuvers most difficult. But when God gives a command He often accompanies it with a promise, so He assured Joshua a lifetime of continuous victory over his enemies, based on His unfailing presence and help. The words **I will never leave you** (cf. Josh. 1:9) may be rendered, "I will not drop or abandon you." God never walks out on His promises.

**1:6.** Flowing from this strong affirmation that God would never let Joshua down was God's threefold call to courage. First, Joshua was commanded to **be strong and courageous** (cf. vv. 7, 9, 18) **because** of God's promise of the land. Strength and fortitude would be required for the strenuous military campaign just ahead, but Joshua was to keep uppermost in his mind the fact that he would succeed in causing Israel **to inherit the land** because it had been promised **to their forefathers,** that is, to Abraham (Gen. 13:14-17; 15:18-21; 17:7-8; 22:16-18), Isaac (Gen. 26:3-5), Jacob (Gen. 28:13; 35:12), and the entire nation, the seed of Abraham (Ex. 6:8), as an eternal possession. And Joshua now at last was to **lead** the children of Israel into possession of this Promised Land. What a strategic role he was to play at this crucial time in his nation's history!

While in any given generation the fulfillment of this great and significant promise depends on Israel's obedience to God, there can be no question that the Bible affirms her right to the land. By divine contract the title is hers even though she will not possess it totally and enjoy it fully until she is right with God.

**1:7-8.** Second, Joshua was again commanded to **be strong and very courageous,** being **careful to obey all the Law** of **Moses.** This command is based on *God's power* through His Word. This is a stronger exhortation, indicating that greater strength of character would be required to obey God's Word faithfully and fully than to win military battles! The emphasis in these verses is clearly on a written body of truth. Many critics argue that the Scriptures did not appear in written form until several centuries later but here is a clear reference to an authoritative **Book of the Law.**

To enjoy prosperity and **be . . . successful** in the Conquest of Canaan Joshua was to do three things with regard to the Scriptures: (a) The Law was not to **depart from** his **mouth;** he was to talk about it (cf. Deut. 6:7); (b) He was to **meditate on it day and night,** to think about it (cf. Ps. 1:2; 119:97); (c) He was to **do everything written in it,** to obey its commands fully and to act by it (cf. Ezra 7:10; James 1:22-25).

Joshua's life demonstrates that in a practical way he lived according to the teachings of the Law of Moses, the only portion of the Word of God then in written form. This alone explains the victories he achieved in battle and the success that marked his entire career. In one of his farewell addresses to the nation just before he died he urged the people to live in submission to the Scriptures (Josh. 23:6). Tragically they heeded this charge for only a short time. In succeeding generations the people of Israel refused to be guided by God's authoritative revelation, and they all did what they chose (Jud. 21:25). Rejecting an objective standard of righteousness, they chose a subjective one characterized by moral and spiritual relativism. This in turn plunged the nation into centuries of religious apostasy and moral anarchy.

**1:9.** The third call to courage addressed to Joshua was based on the promise of *God's presence.* This did not minimize the task Joshua faced. He would encounter giants and fortified cities, but God's presence would make all the difference.

Joshua probably had times when he felt weak, inadequate, and frightened. Perhaps he considered resigning before the Conquest even began. But God knew all about his feelings of personal weakness and fear and told Joshua three times, **Be strong and courageous** (vv. 6-7, 9; cf. v. 18). God also urged him **not** to **be** afraid or **discouraged** (cf. Deut. 1:21; 31:8; Josh. 8:1). These charges with their accompanying assurances (God's promise, God's power, and God's presence) were sufficient to last a lifetime. Believers in all ages can be uplifted by the same three assurances.

## 2. JOSHUA'S COMMANDING THE OFFICERS (1:10-15)

The Lord had spoken to Joshua. Now Joshua was to speak to the people, which he did without delay. Joshua's commands had a ring of certainty. The new leader had taken charge with confidence. The situation Joshua and the people faced was not easy. In fact his situation closely paralleled the dilemma Moses and the Israelites encountered at the Red Sea (Ex. 14). In both cases the obstacle occurred at the beginning of the leaders' ministries. Both were impossible to overcome by natural means. Both demanded implicit trust in and absolute dependence on God's miracle-working power.

**1:10-11.** Two matters demanded attention. First, provisions had to be gathered, for even though the daily manna had not yet ceased **the people** were to gather some of the fruit and grain from the plains of Moab for themselves and their cattle. The order to "prepare" was given by **Joshua** to **the officers** (lit., "scribes"), who like present-day adjutants or staff officers relayed their commanding officer's orders to the people. In **three days** (cf. 2:22) the Conquest would begin.

**1:12-15.** Joshua's second item of business was to remind the tribes of Reuben, Gad, and **the half-tribe of Manasseh** that though they had received their inheritance **east of the Jordan,** they were committed to fight with their **brothers**

and assist in conquering **the land** west of Jordan (Num. 32:16-32; Deut. 3:12-20). The key word here is **remember,** and their response (Josh. 1:16-18) shows they had not forgotten their promise and were ready to stand by it. In fact they were to serve as shock troops in leading the attack on Canaan (v. 14, **cross over ahead of your brothers).**

3. JOSHUA'S RECEIVING SUPPORT FROM THE PEOPLE (1:16-18)

**1:16-18.** The response of the two and one-half Transjordanian tribes was enthusiastic and wholehearted. It must certainly have reflected the attitude of all the tribes at this crucial time of preparation for the invasion. What an encouragement this was to the new leader to be sure that the people were united in supporting him. Their pledge of loyalty and obedience (**we will go. . . . we will obey you**) included the solemn declaration that anyone guilty of disobedience would be executed. The tribes even encouraged Joshua to **be strong and courageous!** (cf. vv. 6-7, 9)

But there was one condition: they were willing to follow **Joshua** if he showed clear evidence that he was being led by **God** (v. 17). This was a wise precaution and one to be carefully followed lest Israel's leaders turn out to be false prophets or "blind leaders of the blind."

## B. The spying out of Jericho (chap. 2)

Joshua had been 1 of the 12 spies who had explored the land (Num. 13–14). Now as he faced westward and viewed the land God promised across the turbulent Jordan, it was natural for him to secure information necessary for a successful battle. That battle was the first in a long, difficult war.

1. THE SPIES' COMMISSION TO JERICHO (2:1)

**2:1.** Looming in the middle of the path the invaders must take was the walled city of **Jericho,** the key citadel of the Jordan Valley which commanded the passes into the central highlands. But before attacking it Joshua needed complete information about this fortress—its gates, fortified towers, military force, and the morale of its people. So two secret agents were chosen and sent on a carefully concealed mission. Not even the Israelites were to know of it lest an unfavorable

report dishearten them as it had their fathers at Kadesh Barnea (Num. 13:1–14:4).

Taking their lives in their hands the **two spies** left **Shittim,** seven miles east of the Jordan, and probably traveled north, swimming across the flooded river (cf. 3:15) at some fords. Turning south they approached Jericho from the west side and soon were moving along its streets, mingling with the people.

How the spies chose **the house of a prostitute named Rahab** is not revealed. While some suggest they saw her walking the streets and followed her, it seems better to believe that in the providence of God the men were led **there.** God's purpose for the visit of the spies to Jericho included more than securing military information. A sinful woman was there whom God in His grace purposed to spare from the judgment soon to fall on the city. So the Lord, moving in a mysterious way, brought together two secret agents of the army of Israel and a harlot of Canaan who would become a proselyte to the God of Israel.

Some, from the time of Josephus to the present, have attempted to soften the situation by arguing that Rahab was only an innkeeper, but the New Testament references to her (Heb. 11:31; James 2:25) indicate that she was an immoral woman. This in no way impugns the righteousness of God who used such a person in the fulfillment of His purposes. Instead this incident serves to bring His mercy and grace into bold relief (cf. Matt. 21:32; Luke 15:1; 19:10).

2. THE SPIES' SHIELDING BY RAHAB (2:2-7)

**2:2-3.** The disguise of the spies was not adequate. The entire city was on alert, knowing about the camp of Israel opposite them across the Jordan. Someone detected the agents, followed them to Rahab's **house,** and quickly returned to report to **the king. The king,** responding with alacrity, sent messengers who demanded of **Rahab** that the spies be surrendered. In keeping with oriental custom the privacy of even a woman such as Rahab was respected and the king's men refrained from bursting into her house and searching it.

**2:4-6.** But apparently Rahab also had suspicions about the identity of the **two** visitors. When she saw the soldiers approaching her house she took the spies and hid then beneath **the stalks of flax** which had been placed on her flat **roof** for drying. After flax stalks were pulled up at harvesttime, they were soaked in water for three or four weeks to separate the fibers. Then, after drying in the sun, the flax was made into linen cloth.

Hastening down to open her front door to the king's messengers, she freely admitted that two strangers had come to her house, but how could she know their identity and mission? "They **left** here **at dusk,** just about the time **the city gate** is closed," she lied. "But if you hurry **you** can probably **catch . . . them.**"

**2:7.** The soldiers took Rahab at her word, made no search of her property, but quickly **set out** on a wild-goose chase due east **to the fords of the Jordan,** the most likely escape route.

Was Rahab wrong to lie since her falsehood protected **the spies?** Are there some situations in which a lie is acceptable?

After all, some say, this was a cultural matter, for Rahab was born and raised among the depraved Canaanites among whom lying was universally practiced. She probably saw no evil in her act. Further, if she had told the truth the spies would have been killed by the king of Jericho.

But such arguments are not convincing. To argue that the spies would certainly have perished if Rahab had been truthful is to ignore the option that God could have protected the spies in some other way. To excuse Rahab for indulging in a common practice is to condone what God condemns. Paul quoted a prophet of Crete who said that Cretans' were inveterate liars, and then added, "This testimony is true. Therefore, rebuke them sharply, so that they will be sound in the faith" (Titus 1:13). The lie of Rahab was recorded but not approved. The Bible approved her faith demonstrated by good works (Heb. 11:31), but not her falsehood. (However, some explain Rahab's lying by saying that deception is allowable in war.)

3. THE SPIES' INTELLIGENCE INFORMATION FROM RAHAB (2:8-11)

**2:8-11.** A most remarkable conversation then took place. The king's messengers were gone and Rahab climbed to **the** roof of her home where she talked with **the** two **spies** in the darkness. One is hardly prepared for her declaration of faith which follows. First, she disclosed that she believed that **the LORD,** the God of Israel, had **given** them the **land** of Canaan. Though the army of Israel had not yet crossed the Jordan River, Rahab stated in effect, "the Conquest is as good as over." Second, she revealed to the spies the priceless information that the inhabitants of Jericho as well as the rest of Canaan were utterly demoralized: **All who live in this country are melting in fear because of you.** (Cf. v. 24, and v. 11, **our hearts sank and everyone's courage failed.**) This is as God had said it would be (Ex. 23:27; Deut. 2:25). Since a major objective of the spy mission was to assess the morale of the enemy, this word was indeed "music to their ears." But why the terror? Because of the power of Israel's God which parted **the Red Sea** for the Hebrew slaves 40 years before, and more recently gave them victories over **Sihon and Og,** the mighty **kings of the Amorites east of the Jordan** (Num. 21:21-35). Now that same God was closing in on them and they knew they could not win.

Then Rahab declared her faith in Israel's God: **For the LORD your God is God in heaven above and on the earth below.** Responding to the word she had received about the mighty working of God, Rahab believed, trusting in His power and mercy. And that faith saved her. But how could Rahab have such a remarkable faith and still be a harlot, and so glibly tell lies? The answer would seem to be that as she responded in belief to the message she heard about God's works, she later responded to further messages concerning God's standards of life and obeyed. After all, spiritual maturity is gradual, not instantaneous. Even John Newton, who wrote the gospel song "Amazing Grace," continued for some time after his conversion in the slave trade before he was convicted about this base and degrading practice and gave it up.

4. THE SPIES' PROMISE TO RAHAB (2:12-21)

**2:12-13.** Rahab demonstrated her faith not only by protecting the spies (Heb. 11:31; James 2:25) but also by showing concern for her family's safety.

Admittedly she sought her family's physical deliverance, but she must have desired also that they too become a part of God's people, serving the one true God of Israel instead of being enslaved to the Canaanites' vile and degrading idolatry.

She pursued this urgent matter delicately but persistently, pressing the spies to make a pact with her because of her cooperation with them.

When Rahab asked for **kindness** (*ḥeseḏ*) to be shown to her **family** she used a significant and meaningful word. Found about 250 times in the Old Testament, *ḥeseḏ* means loyal, steadfast, or faithful love based on a promise, agreement, or covenant. Sometimes the word is used of God's covenant-love for His people and sometimes, as here, of relationships on the human level. Rahab's request was that the spies make a *ḥeseḏ* agreement with her and her father's family, just as she had made a *ḥeseḏ* agreement with them by sparing their **lives.**

**2:14.** The response of the spies was immediate and decisive. "**When the LORD gives us the land,** that is, Jericho, we will keep the *ḥeseḏ* agreement. **If you don't** report our mission we will protect you and your family or forfeit **our** own **lives**" (author's paraphrase).

**2:15-20.** As the spies prepared to go they again confirmed the pact by repeating and enlarging the conditions Rahab must abide by. First, her **house** must be marked by a **scarlet cord** hung from **the window.** Because of the position of the house on **the city wall** (see comments on v. 21 about the house on the wall) the cord would be clearly seen by the Israelite soldiers again and again as they would march around the walls (6:12-15). Her home would be clearly marked out and no soldier, however fierce and eager he might be in the work of destruction, would dare violate the oath and kill anyone in that **house.**

Second, Rahab and her **family** were to remain **in the house** during the attack on Jericho. If anybody would wander out and was killed the guilt for his death would be **his own,** not the invaders'. Finally, the spies again emphasized that they would be free of this **oath** of protection if Rahab exposed their mission.

**2:21.** To these conditions Rahab **agreed,** and after the spies left she **tied the scarlet cord in the window.** She probably also hurried and told her family to gather in her house. The door of her house was a door to safety from the judgment soon to fall on Jericho (cf. Gen. 7:16; Ex. 12:23; John 10:9).

Their mission completed, the spies and Rahab exchanged parting instructions concerning their escape (cf. Josh. 2:15-16). Jericho at this time was surrounded by two walls about 15 feet apart. Planks of wood spanned the gap and then houses were built on this foundation. Probably due to the pressure of space in the small city, Rahab's house was one of those built "on the wall." In this way it was "part of the city wall" (v. 15).

5. THE SPIES' RETURN TO JOSHUA (2:22-24)

**2:22-24.** The spies were carefully lowered by a rope through a window of Rahab's house (v. 15). Their escape would have been more difficult, if not impossible, had it been necessary for them to go out the city gate. Scarcely a half-mile west of Jericho are limestone cliffs about 1,500 feet high, honeycombed with caves. Here the spies hid (in **the hills**) for **three days** (cf. 1:11) **until the** soldiers of Jericho gave up the hunt. Then under cover of darkness the spies swam back across the Jordan, made their way quickly to the camp at Shittim (cf. 2:1), and reported **to Joshua** about their strange and stirring adventure and the alarm and utter despondency of the Canaanites. Their conclusion was, **The LORD has surely given the whole land into our hands** for **all the people are melting in fear** (cf. v. 9; Ex. 23:27; Deut. 2:25). How different from the report of the majority of the spies at Kadesh Barnea who said, "We can't attack those people; they are stronger than we are" (Num. 13:31).

## C. The crossing of the Jordan (chap. 3)

1. PREPARATION FOR THE CROSSING (3:1-4)

**3:1.** **Joshua** was a man of action. The spies having reported in, Israel's leader began immediate preparations to cross the Jordan and invade Canaan. As yet Joshua had no knowledge of how this massive group of people was to cross the swollen river (cf. v. 15). But believing that God would somehow make it possible, he moved them all, bag and baggage, the seven miles **from Shittim . . .**

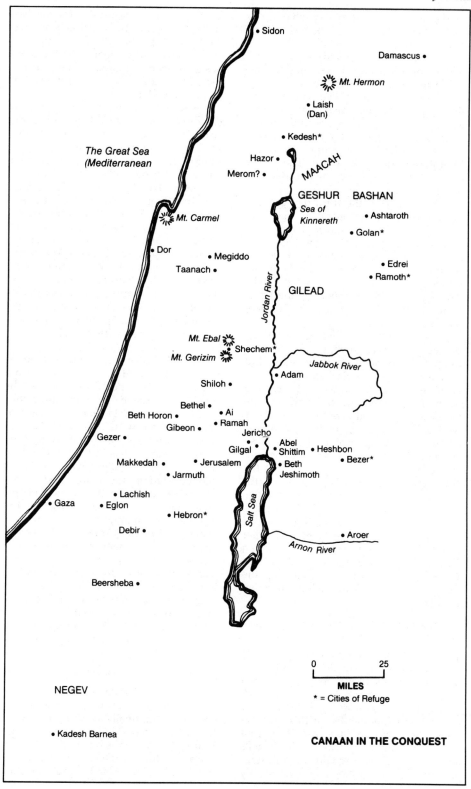

**CANAAN IN THE CONQUEST**

* = Cities of Refuge

0        25

**MILES**

to the Jordan. (Shittim is probably the same as Abel Shittim, mentioned in Num. 33:49.)

**3:2-3.** Having arrived at the river they stopped for **three days.** Time was no doubt needed for the leaders to organize the crossing and pass instructions on to the people. The delay also gave everyone an opportunity to get close and see the river, now a strong and rapid current due to the melting of the winter snows of Mount Hermon in the north. They must have faltered at the seeming impossibility of the crossing.

At the end of the third day of waiting **the people** were given instructions. The pillar of cloud would no longer lead them but they were instead to follow **the ark of the covenant.** No army scouts would advance first into the land but rather **priests** bearing the ark (cf. v. 11). And since the ark symbolized **the LORD** Himself, it was Yahweh who led His people into Canaan.

**3:4.** With the ark going ahead the people were to fall in behind, or possibly to spread around it on three sides. But they were to **keep** their **distance** by some 3,000 feet. Why? Probably to remind them of the sacredness of **the ark** and the holiness of the God it represented. They were to have no casual or careless intimacy with God but a profound spirit of respect and reverence. God was to be considered not "the Man upstairs" but the sovereign and holy God of all the earth.

The distance was also essential so that the largest possible number of this great population could see the ark. God was about to lead them over unfamiliar ground, over a **way** they had not taken **before.** It was new territory so without the Lord's guidance and leadership the people would not know which direction to take.

### 2. CONSECRATION FOR THE CROSSING (3:5-13)

**3:5.** As the day for the crossing approached **Joshua** commanded **the people** to sanctify or **consecrate** themselves. It would be easier to understand if he had said, "Sharpen your swords and check your shields!" But spiritual not military preparation was needed at this time because God was about to reveal Himself by performing a great miracle in Israel's midst. As a person would prepare scrupulously to meet someone of earthly

fame so it was appropriate for the Israelites to prepare for a manifestation of the God of all the earth. The same command was heard at Sinai when the previous generation prepared itself for the majestic revelation of the Lord in the giving of the Law (Ex. 19:10-13).

But that was not all. The people of Israel were to *expect* God to work a miracle. They were to be eager, gripped by a sense of wonder. Israel was not to lose sight of their God who can do the incredible and the humanly impossible.

**3:6-8.** The LORD then told **Joshua** how they would make the crossing, and explained to Joshua that this miracle would magnify or **exalt** him as the leader **of the people.** It was time to establish Joshua's credentials as God's representative to guide **Israel.** What better way to accomplish this than for Joshua to direct their passage through a miraculously parted **river?** After the crossing the people did in fact revere Joshua (4:14), knowing that God was **with** him (3:7; cf. 1:5, 9).

**3:9-13.** But when **Joshua** passed on **the words** of **God** to the people he did not disclose the special promise that he would be exalted by this miraculous event. Rather he told them that this miracle would certify that the living God, in contrast with the dead idols worshiped by the heathen, was in their midst. Further, besides opening a way across the flooded **Jordan,** the living God would also **drive out** the seven groups of people inhabiting the land. The promise, **the living God is among you,** became the watchword of the Conquest, the key to victory over the enemies in the land. It is a promise that appears on almost every page of this book: "I will be with you!" It is a promise that still sustains the Lord's people—the assurance of His presence. Since God is **the Lord** ('ăḏôn, "master") **of all the earth** (cf. Ps. 97:5), He was certainly capable of getting His people across a river.

### 3. COMPLETION OF THE CROSSING (3:14-17)

**3:14-15a.** The day of the crossing of **the Jordan,** the day when Israel was to enter Canaan, finally arrived. The people folded their tents and followed the ark-bearing **priests** to the brink of **the Jordan.** It was the time of the barley **harvest,** the month of Nisan (March-April), the first month of their year (4:19). The river was **at flood stage**—a foreboding sight to the priests and people and a severe test of their faith. Would they hesitate in fear or would they advance in faith, believing that what God had promised (about the water stopping, 3:13) would actually happen?

**3:15b-17.** Dramatic things happened the moment **the priests** carrying **the ark** of the covenant stepped into the muddy, swirling waters. **The water from upstream stopped flowing** (cf. v. 13). Piling up **at a town called Adam,** waters from other streams were **completely cut off** so as not to enter the Jordan. **So the people crossed over opposite Jericho.** This is reminiscent of the Red (Reed) Sea crossing (cf. Ex. 15:8; Ps. 78:13).

Though the place named "Adam" is found only here it is usually identified with Tell ed-Damiyeh, about 16 miles north of the ford opposite Jericho. A wide stretch of riverbed therefore was dried up, allowing the people with their animals and baggage to hurry across (cf. Josh. 4:10).

How could this sensational event occur? Many insist that this was no miracle since the event can be explained as a natural phenomenon. They point out that on December 8, 1267 an earthquake caused the high banks of the Jordan to collapse near Tell ed-Damiyeh, damming the river for about 10 hours. On July 11, 1927 another earthquake near the same location blocked the river for 21 hours. Of course these stoppages did not occur during flood season. Admittedly God could have employed natural causes such as an earthquake and a landslide and the timing would have still made it a miraculous intervention. But does the biblical text allow for such an interpretation of this event?

Considering all the factors involved it seems best to view this occurrence as a special act of God brought about in a way unknown to man. Many supernatural elements were brought together: (1) The event came to pass as predicted (3:13, 15). (2) The timing was exact (v. 15). (3) The event took place when the river was at flood stage (v. 15). (4) The wall of water was held in place for many hours, possibly an entire day (v. 16). (5) The soft, wet river bottom became **dry** at once (v. 17). (6) The water returned immedi-

ately as soon as the people had crossed over and **the priests** came up out of the river (4:18). Centuries later the Prophets Elijah and Elisha crossed the same river on dry ground to the east (2 Kings 2:8). Soon thereafter Elisha crossed back over the river on dry ground. If a natural phenomenon is necessary to explain the Israelites' crossing under Joshua, then one would have to conclude that two earthquakes occurred in quick sequence for Elijah and Elisha, which seems a bit presumptuous.

By this great miracle, the crossing of **the Jordan** River at flood stage by a nation of about 2 million people, God was glorified, Joshua was exalted, **Israel** was encouraged, and the Canaanites were terrorized.

For Israel the crossing of the Jordan meant they were irrevocably committed to a struggle against armies, chariots, and fortified cities. They were also committed to walk by faith in the living God and to turn from walking according to the flesh as they had often done in the wilderness.

For believers today, crossing the Jordan represents passing from one level of the Christian life to another. (It is not a picture of a believer dying and entering heaven. For the Israelites Canaan was hardly heaven!) It is a picture of entering into spiritual warfare to claim what God has promised. This should mean the end of a life lived by human effort and the beginning of a life of faith and obedience.

### D. The erecting of memorials (chap. 4)

**4:1-3.** It was important that Israel never forget this great miracle. So that the Israelites would remember how God acted on their behalf on this historic day God had them erect a 12-stone memorial. This memorial celebrated the crossing of the Israelite multitudes over the dry riverbed of **the Jordan.**

**The Lord** told **Joshua** to direct **12 men,** previously chosen (cf. 3:12), to carry **12 stones from the** bed of the river to the place of the first night's encampment.

**4:4-8.** Calling **the 12 tribal represen-tatives together** Joshua instructed them. They were to return to **the middle of the** riverbed and **each** one was to bring back one **stone.** These stones would be a vivid reminder (**a memorial**) of God's work of deliverance (cf. v. 24) and an effective means for the Israelites to teach their young (vv. 6-7; cf. vv. 21-24).

The response of the 12 **men** was immediate and unquestioning. They could well have feared reentering the Jordan. After all, how long would it stay dry? Whatever fears they may have had were put aside and they unhesitatingly obeyed God's instructions.

**4:9.** Joshua joined these men on their strange mission, and while they were wrenching up great stones from the bed of the river, he **set** another pile of **12 stones** (NIV marg.) in the riverbed itself to mark the precise **spot where the priests stood with the ark of the covenant.** This was apparently done on Joshua's own initiative and expressed his desire to have a personal reminder of God's faithfulness at the very beginning of the Conquest of Canaan.

**4:10-18.** All was now accomplished that **the LORD . . . commanded.** In anticipation of **the Jordan** flowing again the details of the crossing were reviewed. (1) **The priests** and **the ark remained** in the riverbed while **the people hurried** across (v. 10; cf. 3:17). (2) The **armed** men of the Transjordanian tribes, not hampered with families and goods, led the crossing (4:12-13). (3) As soon as all the people had crossed and the special mission for the memorials was completed, **the priests** left the riverbed—they were the first ones in and the last ones out—and resumed their position at the head of the people (vv. 11, 15-17). (4) Immediately **the Jordan** resumed its flow (v. 18).

Thus all the tribes participated in the crossing, though **Reuben, Gad, and the half-tribe of Manasseh** sent only representative armies. The rest of those two and one-half tribes remained on the east side to protect their homes and cities (cf. v. 13). The population of males in those tribes 20 years of age or older totaled 136,930 (Num. 26:7, 18, 34). The **40,000** soldiers (Josh. 4:13) were 29 percent of that adult male population—less than one of every three adult males.

Alexander Maclaren wrote, "The one point made prominent is the instantaneous rush back to the impatient torrent as soon as the curb was taken off. Like some horse rejoicing to be free, the tawny flood pours down, and soon everything looks 'as aforetime' except for the new rock, piled by human hands, round which the water chafed" (*Exposi-*

*tions of Holy Scripture.* London: Hodder & Stoughton, 1908, 3:119).

One can imagine what it must have been like for the Israelites to stand on the riverbank, watching the hurrying torrent covering up their path, and then lifting their eyes to look at the opposite side where they had stood that morning. There was no returning now. A new and exciting chapter in their history had begun.

**4:19-20.** But this was no time for reflection. **Joshua** led **the people** to **Gilgal,** their first encampment in Canaan, about two miles from **Jericho.** There **the 12 stones . . . taken out of the Jordan** were **set up,** perhaps in a small circle. The name Gilgal means "circle," and may have been taken from an ancient circle of stones of pagan significance. If so, the more recent circle commemorating Yahweh's great work would serve to counteract the idolatrous association of the site.

**4:21-23.** The purpose of the stones was clearly pedagogical: to remind Israel for generations to come that it was **God** who brought them through **the Jordan** (cf. vv. 6-7) just as He had taken their fathers through **the Red Sea.**

But how were the **future** generations to know what the stones meant? The answer is clear. Parents were to teach God's ways and works to their children (cf. Deut. 6:4-7). A Jewish father was not to send his inquisitive child to a Levite for answers to his questions. The father was to answer them himself.

**4:24.** However, besides serving as a visual aid for parental instruction of children, the memorial stones had a broader purpose: **that all the peoples of the earth might know that the hand of the LORD is powerful.** As the families of Israel spent their first night in the land, their hearts may well have been filled with uncertainty and fear. The mountains rising steeply to the west looked foreboding. But then the people looked at the 12 stones taken out of the Jordan and were reminded that God had done something great for them that day. Surely they could trust Him for the days ahead.

*E. The consecration of the Israelites (5:1-12)*

Under Joshua's leadership and by miraculous intervention some 2 million soldiers and civilians crossed the Jordan.

A beachhead was quickly established at Gilgal, and from every human point of view it was time to strike immediately at the strongholds of Canaan. After all, the morale of the people of Canaan had utterly collapsed in the face of one old and two recent news items that had spread through the land: (a) that the God of Israel had dried up the Red (Reed) Sea (2:10); (b) that the Israelites had defeated the powerful kings of the Amorites in Transjordan (2:10); (c) that Yahweh had also dried up the waters of the Jordan River so that the Israelites could cross over into Canaan (5:1; cf. 4:24).

As this news spread, so did fear. What better time to strike a paralyzing blow? Certainly the military leaders of Israel must have favored an immediate all-out offensive.

But this was not God's plan. He is never in a hurry though His children often are. From God's point of view Israel was not yet ready to fight on Canaan's soil. There was some unfinished business—and it was spiritual in character. It was time for renewal. Consecration must precede conquest. Before God would lead Israel to victory, He would lead them through three experiences: (a) the renewal of circumcision (5:1-9), (b) the celebration of the Passover (v. 10), and (c) the appropriation of the land's produce (vv. 11-12).

1. THE RENEWAL OF CIRCUMCISION (5:1-9)

**5:1-3.** When the nations of the land were filled with terror (cf. 4:24) **the LORD** commanded **Joshua** to **circumcise** the sons of Israel. He obeyed, even though it must have been difficult for him as a military commander to incapacitate his entire army in that hostile environment.

**5:4-7.** An explanation is given. Though **all the men** of Israel **had been circumcised** before they left **Egypt,** they **died** in the wilderness because of their disobedience at Kadesh Barnea (Num. 20:1-13; cf. Num. 27:14; Deut. 32:51). **Their sons** born during the wilderness wanderings were not **circumcised,** which was further evidence of their parents' spiritual indifference. This sacred rite therefore needed to be performed on this new generation.

**5:8-9.** After all the males were **circumcised . . . the LORD** acknowledged the completed task by declaring, **Today I**

**have rolled away the reproach of Egypt from you.** Since the Israelites were slaves in Egypt, they did not practice circumcision until they were about to leave. No doubt the Egyptians prohibited the practice since it was reserved for their own priests and upper-class citizens. "The reproach of Egypt" may refer to the Egyptians' mocking the Israelites for not having possessed the land of Canaan.

Another indication of this event's importance is the fact that a new significance was attached to the name **Gilgal** (NIV marg.). Not only was the meaning "circle" to remind Israel of the memorial stones (see comments on 4:19-20), but now the related idea of "rolling" would commemorate Israel's act of obedience at the same site.

But why was circumcision so important? The Bible's answer is clear. Stephen, in his dynamic speech before the Sanhedrin, declared that God "gave Abraham the covenant of circumcision" (Acts 7:8). Circumcision, then, was no ordinary religious rite; it was rooted in the Abrahamic Covenant, a contract guaranteeing the everlasting continuation of Abraham's seed and their everlasting possession of the land (Gen. 17:7-8). In this connection God adopted circumcision as the "sign" or symbol of that contract (Gen. 17:11). God instructed Abraham that every male in his household as well as every male descendant of his was to be circumcised. And Abraham immediately obeyed (Gen. 17:23-27).

But why did God choose circumcision as the symbol of His covenant with Abraham and his seed? Why not some other sign or work? The act of circumcision itself symbolized a complete separation from the widely prevalent sins of the flesh: adultery, fornication, and sodomy. Further, the rite had spiritual overtones not only in relation to sexual conduct but in every phase of life. "Circumcise your hearts, therefore, and do not be stiff-necked any longer" (Deut. 10:16; cf. Deut. 30:6; Jer. 4:4; Rom. 2:28-29).

So Israel was to understand that circumcision was not simply a cutting of flesh; also their lives were to be holy. This is why at Gilgal God said, in effect, "Before I fight your battles in Canaan you must have this mark of the covenant in your flesh." **Joshua** understood the cruciality of this divine requirement and led all males in unhesitating obedience.

Paul affirmed that a Christian has been "circumcised" in Christ (Col. 2:11). This circumcision is spiritual not physical, relating not to an external organ but to one's inward being, the heart. This circumcision takes place at the time of salvation when the Holy Spirit joins a believer to Christ. At that time one's sinful nature is judged (Col. 2:13). A Christian is to recognize that fact (Rom. 6:1-2) even though his carnal nature remains a part of him during this life. He is to treat his carnal nature as a judged and condemned (though not yet executed) enemy.

2. THE CELEBRATION OF THE PASSOVER (5:10)

**5:10.** Israel, **camped at Gilgal,** now kept **the Passover.** Without circumcision they would have been unqualified to participate in this important event (Ex. 12:43-44, 48). Interestingly the nation arrived across the Jordan just in time to celebrate the Passover on **the 14th day of the month** (Ex. 12:2, 6). God's timing is always precise!

This was only the third Passover the nation had observed. The first was observed in Egypt the night before their deliverance from bondage and oppression (Ex. 12:1-28). The second was observed at Mount Sinai just before the people broke camp and moved toward Canaan (Num. 9:1-5).

Apparently the Passover was not observed during the wilderness wanderings, but now at Gilgal in Canaan the feast was again observed. The recent Jordan crossing was so similar to the crossing of the Red (Reed) Sea that vivid memories were brought back to those who had been in Egypt (persons under 20 at the time of the Exodus were not excluded from Canaan). No doubt many an Israelite remembered how his father killed a lamb and sprinkled its blood on the doorpost and lintel. Those now in Canaan could still hear the awful death cries of the Egyptians' firstborn. Then there was the excitement of the midnight departure, the terror of the Egyptian pursuit, and the thrill of walking between walls of water to escape Egypt.

Now they were reliving it again. As the lambs were slain they were assured that as the Red Sea crossing was followed by the destruction of the Egyptians, so

the crossing of the Jordan would be followed by the defeat of the Canaanites. So remembering the past was an excellent preparation for the tests of the future.

3. THE APPROPRIATION OF THE LAND'S PRODUCE (5:11-12)

**5:11. The** morning **after** Israel had eaten **the Passover** and were prepared for battle **they ate some of the produce of the land.** Since they gave evidence of wanting to be fully obedient to the Law of God it is probable that they first brought the wave-offering of a sheaf of grain, prescribed in Leviticus 23:10-14. Then the people ate freely of the harvest, including **unleavened** cakes and parched corn. **Roasted** ears of **grain** are still considered a delicacy in the Middle East and are eaten as a substitute for bread.

God had promised to bring Israel into a land of abundance, "a land with wheat and barley, vines and fig trees, pomegranates, olive oil, and honey" (Deut. 8:8). Now at last they had tasted the fruit of the land and realized it was a foretaste of blessings to come.

**5:12.** The next day **the manna stopped.** For 40 long years it had continued (cf. Ex. 16:4-5), but now it ceased as suddenly as it had begun, demonstrating that its provision was not a matter of chance but of special providence.

It is noteworthy that God did not discontinue the **manna** when Israel despised it (Num. 11:6), or even when the unbelieving generation turned away from Kadesh Barnea and wandered in the trackless wilderness. At least for the sake of their children He continued to give it, till they grew and entered the land of promise. Then God stopped performing this miracle since natural **food** was available.

## II. The Conquest of Canaan (5:13–12:24)

### A. Introduction: The divine Commander (5:13-15)

God had just brought the Israelites through three events: the rite of circumcision, the celebration of the Passover, and eating the produce of Canaan. All of these were for Israel's edification. Next came an experience for Joshua alone. It too was extremely meaningful and would shortly be shared with the people.

**5:13.** It seemed obvious that the next

step would be the capture of **Jericho**. But since no divine message of instruction had yet come to **Joshua** (as before the crossing of the Jordan), he went out to reconnoiter the seemingly impregnable city. Was Joshua perplexed as he viewed the secure walls of Jericho? The spies reported at Kadesh Barnea that the cities of Canaan were "large, with walls up to the sky" (Deut. 1:28). Despite Joshua's long military experience he had never led an attack on a fortified city that was prepared for a long siege. In fact, of all the walled cities in Palestine, Jericho was probably the most invincible. There was also the question of armaments. Israel's army had no siege engines, no battering rams, no catapults, and no moving towers. Their only weapons were slings, arrows, and spears—which were like straws against the walls of Jericho. Joshua knew the battle of Jericho must be won because, now that they had crossed the Jordan, Israel's troops had no place to which they could retreat. Further, they could not bypass the city because that would leave their women, children, goods, and cattle at Gilgal exposed to certain destruction.

Pondering these heavy thoughts, Joshua was startled when something came across his sphere of vision. **He** lifted **up** his eyes to see a Soldier brandishing His **sword**. Instinctively he challenged the Stranger, saying in effect, "Who goes there—friend or foe?" If He were a friend, an Israelite, He was off limits and had some explaining to do. Especially was this true since Joshua had given no command for anyone to draw a sword! If the Stranger were an enemy, **Joshua** was ready to fight!

**5:14.** The response was startling and revealing. Something occurred that convinced Joshua this was no mortal soldier. As with Abraham under the oak at Mamre, Jacob at Peniel, Moses at the burning bush, and the two disciples at Emmaus, there was a flash of revelation and Joshua knew he was in the presence of God. It seems clear that Joshua was indeed talking to the Angel of the Lord, another appearance in Old Testament times of the Lord Jesus Christ Himself (cf. 6:2).

The **Commander of the army of the LORD** stood **with a drawn** sword, indicating that He would fight with and for Israel. But the sword also shows that God's long-suffering delay of judgment was over and the iniquity of the Amorites was now full (cf. Gen. 15:16). The Israelites were to be the instruments by whom judicial punishment would fall.

What kind of a military force did this divine Commander lead? The "army of the LORD" was surely not limited to the army of Israel though it may have been included. More specifically, it referred to the angelic host, the same "army" of heaven that later surrounded Dothan when Elisha and his servant appeared to be greatly outnumbered by the Aramean army (2 Kings 6:8-17). In the Garden of Gethsemane at the time of His arrest, Jesus referred to this heavenly army when He said that 12 legions of angels were ready to defend Him (Matt. 26:53). In Hebrews 1:14 they are described as "ministering spirits sent to serve those who will inherit salvation." Though invisible, they serve and care for God's children in times of great need.

**Joshua,** recognizing his heavenly visitor with the drawn sword, **fell** on his face and worshiped, saying, in effect, "Speak, Lord, for Your servant is listening."

**5:15.** The reply of the Lord to Joshua was brief but urgent. Remove **your sandals, for the place where you are standing is holy.** The presence of the holy God sanctified this spot in a strange and defiled land (cf. a similar command to Moses, Ex. 3:5).

This was a deeply significant experience for Joshua. He had anticipated a battle between two opposing armies, Israelite and Canaanite. He had thought this was to be his war and that he was to be the general-in-charge. But then he confronted the divine Commander and learned that the battle was the Lord's. The top general **of the LORD's army** had not come to be an idle Spectator of the conflict, or even an ally. He was in complete charge and would shortly reveal His plans for capturing the citadel of Jericho.

How comforting all this was for **Joshua**. He did not need to bear the heavy burden and responsibility of leadership alone. By removing his sandals he gladly acknowledged that this battle and the entire conquest of Canaan was God's conflict and that he was merely God's servant.

## B. The central campaign (chaps. 6–8)

The pattern of divine strategy for the conquest of Canaan was based on geographic factors. From their camp at Gilgal near the Jordan River the Israelites could see steep hills to the west. Jericho controlled the way of ascent into these mountains, and Ai, another fortress, stood at the head of the ascent. If the Israelites were to capture the hill country they must certainly take Jericho and Ai. This would put them on top of the hill country and in control of the central ridge, having driven a wedge between the northern and southern sections of Canaan. Israel could then engage the armies of the south in battle followed by the more remote enemy in the north. But first, Jericho must fall—and it would if Joshua and the people followed the Lord's plan of action.

### 1. THE CONQUEST OF JERICHO (CHAP. 6)

#### a. The strategy of the conquest of Jericho (6:1-7)

**6:1. Jericho** was a beleaguered city. Orders had been given to close all the gates, and no traffic was permitted **in** or **out.** As Rahab had disclosed to the spies (2:11) the residents of Jericho were filled with terror because of **the** advancing **Israelites** (cf. 5:1).

**6:2.** But there this impressive fortress stood, in full view of Joshua whose conversation with the Commander of the Lord's army continued. This Commander, **the LORD** Himself, promised victory to **Joshua** and announced that He had given **Jericho into** his **hands.** The city, **its king,** and its army would all fall to Israel. The tense of the Hebrew verb is prophetic perfect (**I have delivered**), describing a future action as if it were already accomplished. Since God had declared it, the victory was assured.

**6:3-5.** The battle plan Joshua was to use was most unusual. Ordinary weapons of war such as battering rams and scaling ladders were not to be employed. Rather Joshua and his **armed men** were to **march around the city once** a day **for six** successive **days** with **seven priests** blowing **trumpets** preceding **the ark** of the covenant. **On the seventh day** they were to circle Jericho **seven times** and then **the wall** of Jericho would **collapse** and the city would be taken.

In the Bible the number seven often symbolizes completeness or perfection. There were seven priests, seven trumpets, seven days, seven circuits of the wall on the seventh day. Though God's plan of action may have seemed foolish to men it was the perfect scheme for this battle.

What was the significance of the blaring **trumpets?** These instruments were "jubilee trumpets" (lit. Heb.) used in connection with Israel's solemn feasts to proclaim the presence of God (Num. 10:10). The conquest of Jericho was not therefore exclusively a military undertaking but also a religious one, and the trumpets declared that the Lord of heaven and earth was weaving His invisible way around this doomed city. God Himself, in effect, was saying in the long blasts of these priestly trumpets, "Lift up your heads, O you gates; be lifted up, you ancient doors, that the King of glory may come in" (Ps. 24:7). When Christ returns, He, the King of glory, will enter cities in triumph. The conquest of Jericho was a similar kind of triumphant victory.

**6:6-7.** No battle strategy appeared more unreasonable than this one. What was to prevent the army of Jericho from raining arrows and spears down on the defenseless Israelites pursuing their silent march? Or who could stop the enemy from rushing out of the city gates to break up Israel's line, separating and then slaughtering them? **Joshua** was an experienced military leader. Certainly these and similar objections to the divine strategy flashed into his mind. But unlike Moses at the burning bush who argued with lengthy eloquence against the Lord's plan (cf. Ex. 3:11–4:17) Joshua responded with an unquestioning obedience. He lost no time in calling together **the priests** and soldiers, passing on to them the directions he had received from his Commander-in-chief.

#### b. The sequence of the conquest of Jericho (6:8-21)

**6:8-9.** It was perhaps a little after dawn when a long procession began to unwind out of the camp of Israel. First came **the armed guard** marching under tribal banners, then **seven priests** with **trumpets;** next **the ark** of God, and last **the rear guard.** The army thus had prominent places in the procession but Jericho would fall not through their prowess but because of the power of God.

**6:10-11.** Preserving absolute silence (except for the seven priests blowing their trumpets) this strange parade made its way toward Jericho and then **around the city** like a serpent. Jericho then covered about eight or nine acres and required less than 30 minutes to march around. When the circuit was completed, to the amazement of the Canaanites who probably anticipated an immediate attack, the Israelites **returned** quietly **to camp.**

**6:12-14.** The same procedure was followed **for six days.** No fortress had ever been conquered in this fashion. This strange strategy was probably given to test the faith of **Joshua.** He did not question; he trusted and obeyed. This procedure was also designed to test Israel's obedience to God's will. And that was not easy in this case. Every day they were exposing themselves to ridicule and danger. A Jericho soldier may have looked down from the wall on the army of Israel and asked, "Do they think they can frighten us into surrender by the sound of their rams' horns?" And the rest may have joined in a loud chorus of raucous laughter.

Probably the Israelites received their orders on a daily basis so that their obedience was not a once-for-all matter but a new challenge every morning. That is the way God often deals with His children. They are required to do their "daily march" with little or no knowledge of tomorrow (Prov. 27:1; James 4:14; cf. Matt. 6:34).

The faith of the Israelites triumphed over their fear that the enemy would attack. They also triumphed over any expectation of ridicule and scorn. Never before and seldom after this historic event did the thermometer of faith rise this high in Israel.

**6:15-20a.** On that fateful **seventh day** the procession made the circuit of the walls **seven times.** This parade—consisting of the armed guard, the seven **trumpet**-blowing **priests,** the priests carrying the ark of the covenant, and the rear guard—may have taken about three hours. (On the word **devoted** in vv. 17-18 see comments on v. 21.) (As Joshua recorded, Israel experienced disastrous consequences because of an immediate violation of God's instruction in vv. 18-

19.) At the end of the seventh circuit the clear voice of **Joshua** rang out, **Shout! For the Lord has given you the city!** Also he told them to spare **Rahab** and her family (cf. 2:8-13). So when the priests blasted on **the trumpets . . . the people gave a loud shout.** That shout reverberated through the hills around, startling wild animals and terrorizing the dwellers of Jericho in their homes. At that moment **the wall** of Jericho, obeying the summons of God, **collapsed** (lit., "fell in its place").

**6:20b-21.** The men of Israel clambered over the debris. Finding the inhabitants paralyzed with terror and unable to resist, the soldiers utterly destroyed all human and animal life in Jericho, except for Rahab and her household (cf. v. 17). Though critics have charged that this destruction is a blemish on the Old Testament, it is clear that Israel was acting on divine command. The responsibility for this destruction rests therefore with God and not the Israelites.

The city of Jericho and everything in it was "to be devoted (*ḥērem*) to the Lord" (v. 17). The NASB renders those words "shall be under the ban," a more literal translation. Verse 21 includes a verb form of that noun *ḥērem*: **They devoted** (*wayyaḥărîmû,* from *ḥāram*) **the city to the Lord.** The idea is that the city's contents were to be given over to the Lord by totally destroying them. To convey this, the NIV adds **and destroyed.** (The verb *ḥāram* is trans. "totally destroyed" in 10:28, 35, 37, 39-40; 11:11-12, 21 and "destroy them totally" in 11:20; cf. 1 Sam. 15:3, 8-9, 15, 18, 20. The noun *ḥērem* is trans. "devoted" or "devoted things" in Josh. 6:17-18; 7:1, 11-12, 15; 1 Sam. 15:21; "devoted to destruction" in Lev. 27:29; "set apart for destruction" in Deut. 7:26. Sometimes, however, the idea of destruction is not in the word; cf., e.g., Lev. 27:21, 28.)

The contents of Jericho were to be given "to the Lord" as the firstfruits of the land. Just as the firstfruits of a crop, given to the Lord, pointed to more crops to come, so the conquest of Jericho signified that Israel would receive all of Canaan from Him. No loot from Jericho was to be taken by the people. In carrying out the *ḥērem*, people and animals were to be killed (Josh. 6:17, 21), and other things were either to be destroyed or set apart, as in this case, for the purposes of the sanctuary. These items included "silver and gold and the articles of bronze and iron" (v. 19). All was "devoted" either to destruction or to the Lord's "treasury"; all was to be forfeited by the people.

Furthermore, God has the right to visit judgment on individuals and nations in sin. Is there evidence that the iniquity of the Canaanites was full? Few would question that the idolatrous worship and licentious lifestyle attested by archeological discoveries (e.g., the Ras Shamra tablets) justified the divine judgment on Jericho.

Finally, God's purpose was to bless the nation of Israel in the land and to use her as a channel of blessing to the world. But this would be greatly hindered if they were infected by the degenerate religion of the Canaanites. Gleason Archer declares, "In view of the corrupting influence of the Canaanite religion, especially with its religious prostitution . . . and infant sacrifice, it was impossible for pure faith and worship to be maintained in Israel except by the complete elimination of the Canaanites themselves" (*A Survey of Old Testament Introduction*. Chicago: Moody Press, 1964, p. 261).

Sin is desperately contagious. To compromise with evil is dangerous and invites spiritual disaster.

Various suggestions have been made as to why the walls of Jericho fell at the precise moment when the people shouted: (1) An earthquake caused the destruction. (2) Israelite soldiers undermined the walls while the others marched. (3) Vibrations set up by the trumpet blasts and soldiers' shouts caused the collapse. (4) Shock waves caused by the marching feet of the Israelites were responsible. However, it was a supernatural event. This is clear from the fact that all the wall was destroyed except the portion by the house of Rahab. Actually it is unnecessary to determine the exact means God employed in this or any other miracle. A New Testament writer, reviewing this event centuries later, was content to write, "By faith the walls of Jericho fell, after the people had marched around them for seven days" (Heb. 11:30).

Archeological evidence for the collapse of Jericho's walls in Joshua's day is not as clear as was once supposed. This can be explained by the fact that further excavations have determined that in its long history Jericho has had some 34 walls. (Jericho is one of the oldest cities in the world. Many archeologists hold that it was inhabited as early as 7000 B.C.) The many earthquakes in the area, the thoroughness of Joshua's destruction of the city, and the process of erosion over five centuries until it was refortified in Ahab's time (1 Kings 16:34) also contributed to the meager remains and the extreme difficulty of relating these remains to the time of Joshua's attack. The most significant evidence seems to be extensive pottery remains found on the mound and in the tombs of the area. These findings point to an occupancy of Jericho until about 1400 B.C. Under the pottery is a thick burned layer of ash representing a major destruction. This no doubt points to Joshua's destruction and burning (Josh. 6:24) of the city. (For a thorough discussion of the archeology of Old Testament Jericho, see Leon Wood, *A Survey of Israel's History*. Grand Rapids: Zondervan Publishing House, 1970, pp. 94-9.)

*c. The sequel to the conquest of Jericho (6:22-27)*

As the story of this great Old Testament event moves quickly to its end, two matters are briefly mentioned: the rescue of Rahab and the burning, sacking, and curse on the city.

**6:22-25.** Like an oasis in this doleful account of Canaanite extermination is the story of Rahab's deliverance. Before the city was **burned** (v. 24), **Rahab** was spared. **Joshua** kept the promise made to Rahab by the two spies (cf. 2:12-21) and sent those same **young men** to the **house** where the scarlet cord hung from the window. She and **her entire family** followed them without hesitation to the appointed **place outside** the doomed city. Rahab and her family, being Gentiles, had to be ceremonially cleansed; the men were no doubt circumcised before they could be identified with the people of Israel. Rahab's history is an example of the grace of God operating in the lives of an individual and **her family.** Regardless of her past life she was saved by faith in the living God and even became a part of the messianic line (Matt. 1:5). In keeping with the biblical pattern, Rahab and her family were spared from divine judgment (cf. Gen. 7:1; 1 Thes. 5:9) because of their faith.

**6:26.** Devoting **Jericho** to destruction (cf. comments on v. 21) included the pronouncing of a curse on anyone who would dare to refortify the **city** by rebuilding **its foundations** or **its gates.** Though the site was later occupied for brief periods (18:21; Jud. 3:13; 2 Sam. 10:5) the prohibition against the rebuilding was not violated until the days of King Ahab, 500 years later. Then, as an indication of the apostasy of that period, Hiel the Bethelite attempted to rebuild Jericho's walls, but it cost him the lives of his two sons Abiram and Segub (1 Kings 16:34).

**6:27.** But the chapter recording the spectacular victory in Israel's first battle in Canaan does not end on a minor note. The final words take the reader back to the triumph and its effects: **So the Lord was with Joshua** (cf. 1:5, 9; 3:7), **and his fame spread throughout the land.** The secret to success at Jericho was not Joshua's military genius or his army's skill in warfare. Victory came because he and the people fully trusted God and obeyed His commands (1:6-9).

2. THE DEFEAT AT AI (CHAP. 7)

Unexpectedly Israel next tasted defeat. Up to this point in the Conquest the army Joshua led had experienced only victory. The possibility of a military defeat was the remotest thing from the Israelites' minds, particularly after the triumph over Jericho. Yet God's people are never more vulnerable, never in greater danger, than right after they have won a great victory.

Ai was the next objective on Israel's path of conquest. It was smaller than Jericho but was at a strategic junction of two natural routes ascending from Jericho to the hill country around Bethel. Defeating Ai would also lead to the ultimate control of the main "ridge route" running from north to south along the central highlands.

Many archeologists have identified Ai with the site et-Tell ("the ruin"). Excavations at et-Tell, however, have not yet produced evidence of a settlement there in the time of Joshua. The geography of the area fits perfectly with the details found in Joshua 8. So perhaps the king of Ai was the leader of forces mobilizing for

the battle which occurred at a place that was *already* a ruin rather than a city. Some archeologists, however, are looking for alternative locations of Ai and excavations are underway at the nearby site of Khirbet Nisya.

Though there may still be some question regarding the location of Ai, the importance of the happenings there can be seen from the amount of biblical material given over to a discussion of Israel's defeat (chap. 7) and her victory at that site (chap. 8).

*a. Disobedience (7:1)*

**7:1.** The chapter opens with the ominous word **But.** The gladness of victory was soon replaced by the gloom of defeat. And all this was because of the disobedience of one man. Jericho was placed under God's ḥērem ("ban for destruction"; 6:18-19), meaning that everything living was to be put to death and valuable objects were to be dedicated to the Lord's treasury. No Israelite soldier was to help himself to the booty—but that temptation was too strong for one man.

Though one might wish to give credit to the discipline of Joshua's forces because only one of his soldiers gave in to temptation, even this one did not escape God's notice. God saw Achan's sin in taking **some** of **the devoted things,** and because of it God's wrath **burned against** the entire nation. He considered them collectively responsible and withheld His blessing until the matter was made right. In fact it is apparent that Israel's history would have ended here if God's anger had not been turned away.

*b. Defeat (7:2-5)*

**7:2.** Unaware of Achan's disobedience and eager to take advantage of the first victory, **Joshua** made preparations for the next battle by sending spies 10 miles northwest of **Jericho to Ai,** which was **east of Bethel.** This seems to have been his regular practice (cf. 2:1). (**Beth Aven** ["house of evil"] later was a nickname [Hosea 10:5] for Bethel ["house of God"]. But here it seems to be another place about three miles north of **Ai.**)

**7:3.** When the spies **returned** they spoke with great confidence. They said that **Ai** could easily be conquered with only **two or three thousand men.** The city had **only a few men,** they said. But the spies were wrong. Actually Ai had 12,000 men and women, or about 6,000 men (8:25). Later, when God gave the orders to **Joshua,** He told him, "Take the whole army" (8:1). Though smaller than Jericho, Ai was well fortified and her soldiers well entrenched. Israel was guilty of underestimating the strength of her enemy and of overestimating her own strength. On this occasion there is no mention of prayer and no evidence of dependence on God.

It is a deadly error to underrate the enemy's power. Christians often fail to realize that their enemies are powerful (Eph. 6:12; 1 Peter 5:8). So believers suffer the consequences in ignominious spiritual defeat.

The calamity that befell Israel was due, at least in part, to minimizing the enemy and to assuming that one victory guaranteed another. But life simply does not work that way. Yesterday's victory does not make a believer immune from defeat today. He must continually depend on the Lord for strength. Speaking of a Christian's conflict with evil Paul wrote, "Be strong in the Lord and in His mighty power" (Eph. 6:10).

**7:4-5.** But Joshua sent only **3,000 men** to **Ai,** where sadly they did not conquer but **were routed.** They rushed in terror down the steep pass which they had so confidently climbed in the morning, till the pursuers caught them at some **stone quarries,** where 36 Israelite soldiers were slain. The rest escaped and returned to camp.

As the report of the defeat spread rapidly through the camp the people were utterly demoralized. **The hearts of the people melted, and became like water.** Even though this was Israel's only defeat in the seven-year Conquest of Canaan, the significant matter was not the loss itself or even the deaths of the 36 soldiers. Israel was suddenly filled with terrible misgivings that the Lord's help had been withdrawn. They knew of no reason why it should have been. Had God changed His mind?

*c. Dismay (7:6-9)*

**7:6-9.** Joshua also was stunned by the defeat. In keeping with ancient rites of mourning the leader and the elders **tore** their **clothes** and **the** elders put **dust**

on their heads (cf. Job 1:20; 2:12). They **fell** on their faces **before the ark of the** LORD . . . **till evening.** Then Joshua's perplexity was verbalized as he asked the Lord three questions: (1) **Why did You . . . bring** us here—**to destroy us?** (2) **What can I say, now that Israel has been** defeated? (3) **What then will You do** to protect **Your** reputation?

Joshua seemed to blame God for the defeat and did not even consider that the cause might have been elsewhere. In his first question he even adopted the thinking of the spies against whom he had so vehemently protested at Kadesh (cf. Num. 14:2-3). Joshua's greatest concern was that the news of this defeat might somehow reduce the respect of the heathen for God's **own great name.** Consequently their **name** would be wiped out, that is, they would be destroyed and never remembered.

*d. Directions (7:10-15)*

**7:10-11.** The Lord's reply **to Joshua** was brusque. **Stand up! What are you doing down on your face?** God then explained the cause of the defeat and the need for action. The cause of the disaster was with Israel, not God—**Israel** had **sinned.** In His indictment God angrily used an accumulation of verbs. Advancing from the general to the particular He charged Israel with sinning, violating the **covenant,** appropriating **some of the devoted things** (*haḥērem,* "things devoted for or designated for destruction"; cf. 6:18-19 and comments on 6:21), stealing, lying, and concealing the **stolen** goods. (The goods are named in 7:21.) Till these transgressions were repudiated and expiation made for them, the sin of one person was considered the sin of the nation.

**7:12.** After the fall of Jericho it was recorded, "So the LORD was with Joshua" (6:27). But now the grim announcement came from God, **I will not be with you anymore unless** this sin is judged and the **devoted** things are destroyed.

**7:13-15.** The LORD then revealed the steps to be followed in the purging process. First, **the people** were to **consecrate** themselves. No victory over **their enemies** was possible till this problem was dealt with. Second, they were to gather on the next day to identify the offender, presumably by casting lots (cf. comments on vv. 16-18), exposing first the guilty **tribe,** then **the clan,** then **the family,** and finally the individual. Third, the culprit and all his possessions (not merely the stolen goods) were then to be burned. This sin was considered by God **a disgraceful thing.** Achan's sin was in deliberate disobedience to God's instruction (6:18), and it made the entire nation liable to destruction. If the Israelites did not destroy the Canaanites' goods, God might destroy the Israelites!

### e. Discovery (7:16-21)

**7:16-18.** Joshua rose **early** on the fateful day. All **Israel** was assembled for the ritual of determining the offender. This was probably done by drawing lots, perhaps by taking inscribed potsherds out of a jar. But since God knew who was guilty, why did He not simply reveal his identity to Joshua? The answer is that this dramatic method would impress on the nation of Israel the seriousness of disobeying God's commands. Since the method took time it would also give the guilty person an opportunity to repent and confess his sin. If Achan had responded in this way and thrown himself on the mercy of God no doubt he would have been pardoned as was the guilty David centuries later (Pss. 32:1-5; 51:1-12).

There was a grim silence as the process narrowed from the selection of the tribe of **Judah** to **the clan of the Zerahites,** to the family of **Zimri,** and finally to the trespasser himself, **Achan.** This was no quirk of fate; it was the direction of God's providence. Solomon described the process well: "The lot is cast into the lap, but its every decision is from the Lord" (Prov. 16:33).

**7:19-21.** Strangely, **Achan** had remained silent throughout the entire procedure, though surely fear gripped him and his heart may have pounded furiously as each step brought his discovery nearer. At length **Joshua** addressed **Achan** tenderly but firmly, for though Joshua hated the sin he did not despise the sinner. A public confession confirming the supernatural exposure of the guilty person was necessary.

Achan's response was straightforward and complete. He confessed his sin and gave no excuses. But neither did he express sorrow for disobeying God's order, betraying his nation for booty, and causing the defeat of Israel's troops and the death of 36 men. Any remorse he may have felt was probably only because he got caught.

The three crucial steps in Achan's sin are familiar: he **saw;** he **coveted;** he **took.** Eve took the same tragic steps in the Garden of Eden (Gen. 3:6), as did David with Bathsheba (2 Sam. 11:2-4).

The objects Achan took from Jericho and hid **in the ground inside** his **tent** included (a) **a beautiful robe from Babylonia,** perhaps acquired by someone in Jericho who traded with a Babylonian, (b) **200 shekels of silver,** weighing about 5 pounds, and (c) a 50-shekel (1¼-pound) **wedge of gold.** Achan may well have reasoned, "After all, I have been deprived of the good things of life these many years in the wilderness. Here is a beautiful new and stylish garment and some silver and gold. How could God want to withhold these things from me? They will never be missed, and I am entitled to some pleasure and prosperity." But there was a specific command against taking any of Jericho's booty. (Joshua had told the people that all the silver and gold were to be put in the Lord's treasury, Josh. 6:19.) God's Word can never be rationalized away without penalty.

### f. Death (7:22-26)

**7:22-25.** Achan's confession was quickly verified; the stolen objects were found where he said they were. They were then **spread . . . out before the Lord** to whom they belonged. Then the wretched man was led out **to the Valley of Achor** with the spoil, all his family, his animals, and all his other belongings. The fatal stones felled Achan and his children, and fire consumed their bodies and belongings. Having stolen "devoted" objects Achan himself became contaminated and under the doom of destruction. Since children were not to be executed for their father's sins (Deut. 24:16) it is assumed that Achan's family (except for his wife, who was not mentioned) were accomplices in the crime (cf. comments on Num. 16:28-35).

**7:26.** The final stroke was accomplished by the raising of a historical marker, **a large pile of rocks,** over the body of **Achan.** This seems to have been a common method of burial for infamous individuals (cf. 8:29). It served in this case that good purpose of warning Israel against the sin of disobeying God's express commands.

The Hebrew words for Achan and Achor are probably related. Thus Achan, which possibly means "troubler," was buried in **the Valley of Achor,** the Valley of "Trouble." But because Israel was willing to deal with the sin problem in her midst, God's burning **anger** (7:1) was **turned** away and He was ready to lead them again to victory.

3. THE VICTORY AT AI (CHAP. 8)

a. *The setting of the battle (8:1-2)*

**8:1.** The momentum Israel had achieved by the miraculous crossing of the Jordan and the supernatural victory over Jericho was stopped by the defeat at Ai. Gloom and despair permeated not only all those in the camp but also the heart of Joshua.

But with Achan's crime judged, God's favor toward Israel was restored and He reassured **Joshua** that He had not forsaken him or the people. When Joshua heard God's words of encouragement his heart quickened, for these were the same words Moses spoke in Kadesh Barnea when he sent out the 12 spies (Deut. 1:21). They were also the words Moses said to Joshua 40 years later when he was turning the reins of leadership over to the younger man (Deut. 31:8). And Joshua heard them again when God spoke to him just after the death of Moses (Josh. 1:9). Now at this crucial time in Joshua's life it was good to be reminded and reassured that God was ready to lead if Joshua were ready to listen to *His* plan, which he was.

God's plan involved using all the fighting men of Israel. Though the primary cause of the defeat at Ai was Achan's sin, a secondary cause was underrating the enemy (cf. 7:3-4). That error would now be rectified. God said for Joshua to **go up and attack Ai** and He promised to turn the place of defeat into a place of victory.

**8:2.** Before the actual plan of battle was revealed to Joshua he was told that the spoil of **Ai** and also its **livestock** could be taken by Israel. Jericho had been placed under the ban but Ai was not.

What an irony! If only Achan had

suppressed his greedy and selfish desires and obeyed God's word at Jericho he would later have had all his heart desired and God's blessing too. The path of obedience and faith is always best.

b. *The sequence of the battle (8:3-29)*

The order of events at Ai differed entirely from that at Jericho. The Israelites did not march around the walls of Ai seven times. The city's walls did not fall miraculously. Israel had to conquer the city through a normal combat operation. God is not limited to any one method of working. He is not and will not be stereotyped in His operations.

**8:3-9.** The strategy for the capture of Ai was ingenious. It involved placing **an ambush behind** (west of) **the city.** God Himself had told **Joshua** to do this (vv. 2, 8). The outworking of this plan involved three contingents of soldiers. The first was a group of valiant warriors who were sent by **night** to hide just **west** of the city of **Ai.** Their assignment was to rush into the city and burn it after its defenders had deserted it to **pursue** Joshua and his army. This unit numbered **30,000,** and while this seems like an excessively large number of soldiers to hide near the city, the presence of large rocks in the region made it possible for all these men to remain hidden.

**8:10-11.** The second contingent was the main army which walked the 15 miles from Gilgal **early the next morning** and camped in plain view on the **north** side **of Ai.** No doubt this **entire force** included many thousands of soldiers. Led by **Joshua,** this army was a diversionary force to decoy the defenders of Ai out of **the city.**

**8:12-13.** The third contingent was another **ambush** numbering **5,000 men** who were positioned **between Bethel and Ai** to cut off the possibility of reinforcements from Bethel aiding the men of Ai. **Joshua** was in **the valley** north of Ai, a deep ravine in the hills.

**8:14-22.** The plan worked to perfection. **When the king of Ai saw** Israel's army he took the bait. Pursuing the Israelites who pretended defeat, **the city** of Ai was left unguarded. At Joshua's signal the other troops **quickly** entered and **set** the city **on fire.** The consternation of **the men of Ai** was complete as they witnessed the billows of flame and **smoke**

rising into the sky. Before they could gather their wits they were **caught in** a pincer movement of Israelite soldiers and were destroyed.

**8:23-29.** After **killing all** Ai's soldiers, Israel's army reentered the city **and killed** all its inhabitants. The dead soldiers and citizens totaled **12,000. Plunder** was taken from the city by Israel's soldiers as God had said they could do (v. 2). The city was made a **heap of ruins.** Ai's **king,** previously spared, was hanged **on a tree** till **evening** and then was buried beneath a **pile** of stones (cf. Achan's similar burial, 7:26). The king's **body** was taken off **the tree** at **sunset** because of God's command (Deut. 21:22-23; cf. Josh. 10:27).

Thus Israel, restored to God's favor, won a great victory. After failure came a second chance. One defeat or failure does not signal the end of a believer's usefulness for God.

### c. The sequel to the battle (8:30-35)

**8:30-31.** After the victory of Ai **Joshua** did a strange and militarily foolish thing. Instead of securing the central sector of the land with further victories he led the Israelites on a spiritual pilgrimage. Why? Simply because **Moses . . . had commanded** it (Deut. 27:1-8).

Without delay Joshua led the men, women, children, and cattle from their camp at Gilgal northward up the Jordan Valley to the place specified, the mountains of **Ebal** (Josh. 8:30) and Gerizim (v. 33) which are at Shechem. The march of about 30 miles was not difficult or dangerous since they passed through a sparsely populated area. But how did the Israelites avoid a confrontation with the men of the city of Shechem, a fortress which guarded the entrance to the valley between the mountains?

The Bible does not record every battle of the Conquest and the record of the capture of Shechem may have been omitted. Or the city at that time may have been in friendly hands or it may simply have surrendered without resistance. But why was this location chosen? These mountains are located in the geographic center of the land and from either peak much of the Promised Land can be seen. Here then, in a place that represented all the land, both at the time of entrance into Canaan and also when his leadership

was ending (cf. 24:1), Joshua challenged the people to renew their covenant vows to the Lord.

The solemn and significant religious ceremonies at this location involved three things. First, **an altar of uncut stones** was erected on **Mount** Ebal and sacrifices (consisting of **burnt offerings** and **fellowship offerings;** cf. Lev. 1; 3) were **offered to the** Lord. Jericho and Ai, in which false gods of the Canaanites were worshiped, had fallen. Israel now publicly worshiped and proclaimed her faith in the one true God.

**8:32.** Second, **Joshua** set up some large **stones.** On their surfaces he wrote a copy of **the Law of Moses.** How much of the Law was inscribed is not stated. Some suggest only the Ten Commandments were written, while others think the stone inscription included the contents of at least Deuteronomy 5–26. Archeologists have discovered similar inscribed pillars or stelae six to eight feet long in the Middle East. And the Behistun Inscription in Iran is three times the length of Deuteronomy.

**8:33-35.** Third, **Joshua read . . . the Law** to the people. **Half of the people** were positioned on the slopes **of Mount Gerizim** to the south, the other **half** were on the slopes **of Mount Ebal** to the north, and **the ark of the covenant** surrounded by **priests** was in the valley between. As **the curses** of the Law were **read** one by one, the tribes on Mount Ebal responded, "Amen!" As **the blessings** were likewise read the tribes on Mount Gerizim responded "Amen!" (Deut. 11:29; 27:12-26) The huge natural amphitheater which still exists there made it possible for the people to hear every word and with all sincerity Israel affirmed that the Law of the Lord was indeed to be the Law of the land.

From this point on the history of the Jews depended on their attitude toward the Law which had been read in their hearing that day. When they were obedient there was blessing; when they were disobedient there was judgment (cf. Deut. 28). It is tragic that the affirmations of this momentous hour faded so quickly.

### C. The southern campaign (chaps. 9–10)

Israel's failure to consult the Lord was a major factor in her defeat at Ai and the prayerlessness of her leaders was about to precipitate another crisis.

It all came about when it was least expected. The people had just returned to camp at Gilgal after hearing the Law of God read to them at Mounts Ebal and Gerizim. Much of the Law was inscribed on stones as Israel affirmed her willingness to obey God's Word. It was a time of spiritual victory; it was also a time for a subtle attack from Satan. When God's people think they "have it made" they are most vulnerable to the enemy's assault.

This story unfolds in the next two chapters of the Book of Joshua—the alliance with the Gibeonites (chap. 9) and the defense of the Gibeonites (chap. 10).

### 1. THE ALLIANCE WITH THE GIBEONITES (CHAP. 9)

*a. The deception of the Gibeonites (9:1-15)*

**9:1-2.** Israel's victories over Jericho and Ai aroused the whole country to concerted action. These verses prepare the reader for the southern and northern campaigns of the Conquest, described in chapters 10 and 11.

The frightened **kings** are grouped according to three geographical areas: those from **the hill country** of central Palestine, **the western foothills** (valleys or lowlands), and the coastal plain stretching north to **Lebanon.** That they were not able to unite as planned into one fighting force is a tribute to the success of Joshua's strategy in driving a wedge through the backbone of Canaan.

But powerful confederations did form in both the north and the south. Truces were declared in tribal wars and deadly enemies were ready to make common cause against the invasion force of God's people.

**9:3.** Not all Israel's enemies wanted to fight. The Gibeonites were convinced they could never defeat Israel in war so they pursued peace. Located in the hill country only six miles northwest of Jerusalem and about the same distance southwest of Ai, **Gibeon** was known as "an important city" (10:2) and was head of a small confederation including three neighboring towns (cf. 9:17).

**9:4-6.** After consultation they adopted an ingenious plan to send emissaries to **Joshua** disguised as weary and worn travelers who had been on a long journey. One morning **in the** Israelite **camp at Gilgal** this strange deputation arrived, their **wineskins** old and patched, their **sandals** worn thin, their **clothes** dirty and torn, and their bread **dry and moldy.** As the visitors passed through the bystanders to seek out Joshua, the Israelites no doubt wondered who the strangers were, where they came from, and why they were there.

Untruthful answers were given as soon as the Gibeonites found Joshua. They told him, **We have come from a distant country; make a treaty with us.** But why the emphasis on being from a far country and the deceptive performance to "prove" it? Apparently the Gibeonites had become aware of the provisions in the Mosaic Law permitting Israel to make peace with cities that were at a considerable distance, but requiring them to wipe out completely the cities of the seven nearby Canaanite nations (Deut. 20:10-18; 7:1-2).

**9:7.** At first Joshua and his staff were hesitant and not altogether convinced. They said **But perhaps you live near us.** It was well for them to be on their guard for things are not always what they seem to be. Evil men often try to take advantage of the righteous.

The travelers from Gibeon were called **Hivites** (cf. 11:19); they were descendants of Canaan, a son of Ham (Gen. 10:17). Possibly the Hivites were also the Horites (in Gen. 36:2 Zibeon was called a Hivite, but in Gen. 36:20 he was called a Horite).

**9:8-13.** **Joshua** probed with questions and the wily Gibeonites told their tale. They insisted that they came from a great distance to show respect to the powerful **God** of the Israelites, to be allowed to live at peace as Israel's **servants.** Word had reached them of what God had done for the Israelites **in Egypt** (probably the plagues and the crossing of the Red [Reed] Sea) and of God's victories over **Sihon** and **Og** (Num. 21:21-25; Deut. 2:26–3:11). Interestingly, however, they made no mention of Israel's recent victories over Jericho and Ai because if they had come from a far country they would not have heard of these recent battles. Pursuing this clever ruse they presented their credentials—moldy **bread,** patched **wineskins,** ragged **clothes,** and worn-out **sandals**—and the suspicion of Joshua and the leaders dissipated.

**9:14-15.** Caught off guard by the cunning strategy of the Gibeonites, **the leaders of** the Israelites concluded a formal **treaty with them.** But **Joshua** and the Israelites made at least two mistakes. First, in sampling **their provisions** they accepted as evidence things that were highly questionable. If the visitors were true ambassadors with power to conclude a treaty with another nation they should have had more substantial credentials. It was foolish of Joshua not to demand them.

The second and primary reason for Israel's failure is stated in verse 14: the leaders **did not** seek direction from God. Did Joshua think the evidence to be so beyond question that they needed no advice from Yahweh? Did he think the matter too routine or unimportant to "bother" God with it? Whatever the cause it was a mistake to trust their own judgment and make their own plans. This holds true for believers in all ages (James 4:13-15).

### b. The discovery of the ruse (9:16-17)

**9:16-17.** In **three days** Israel learned that they had been "taken" because the **Gibeonites** lived only about 25 miles from Gilgal, in Canaan proper and not in some far country. An exploratory force confirmed the fraud by discovering the nearby location of **Gibeon** and its three dependent **cities.** "A lying tongue lasts only a moment" (Prov. 12:19). Sooner or later trickery and deceit are exposed. Truth will win out.

### c. The decision of the leaders (9:18-27)

**9:18-19.** How provoked **the Israelites** were when they discovered they had been duped! The people in fact wanted to disregard the treaty and destroy the Gibeonites, but Joshua and his staff said that the enemies' deception did not nullify the treaty. The agreement was sacred because it had been ratified **by an oath** in the name of **the LORD, the God of Israel** (cf. v. 15). To break it would bring down the wrath of God on Israel, a tragedy that later came to pass during David's reign because Saul disregarded this oath (cf. 2 Sam. 21:1-6).

**9:20-27.** Joshua and the princes were men of integrity, men who stood by their word. Though humiliated by what had transpired they did not want to bring disgrace on God and His people by breaking a sacred treaty. Yet, though Israel would not go back on their pledge the deceivers must be punished. **Joshua** therefore addressed **the Gibeonites,** rebuking them for their dishonesty, and announced that they were cursed to perpetual slavery. This slavery would take the form of their being **woodcutters and water carriers for** the Israelites. In order to keep the Gibeonites' idolatry from defiling the religion of Israel their work would be carried out in connection with the tabernacle where they would be exposed to the worship of the one true God.

So the very thing the Gibeonites hoped to attain they lost. They desperately wanted to remain free men; in the end they became slaves. But the curse became a blessing. It was on behalf of the Gibeonites that God worked a great miracle (cf. 10:10-14). Later the tabernacle was pitched at Gibeon (2 Chron. 1:3); still later some Gibeonites helped Nehemiah rebuild Jerusalem's wall (Neh. 3:7). Such is the grace of God. He is still able to turn a curse into a blessing. Though it is usually true that the natural consequences of sin must run their course, the grace of God can not only forgive but also overrule mistakes and often bring blessings out of sins and failures.

### 2. THE DEFENSE OF THE GIBEONITES (CHAP. 10)

### a. The cause of the conflict (10:1-5)

**10:1-2.** Attention shifted suddenly from Gibeon to **Jerusalem,** five miles south. Near panic had seized **Adoni-Zedek** its **king** and for good reason. The treacherous surrender of the Gibeonite cities completed an arc beginning at Gilgal and extending through **Jericho** and **Ai** to a point just a few miles northwest of Jerusalem. The handwriting was on the wall. Jerusalem's security was being severely threatened. If the advances of Israel's armies continued without challenge Jerusalem would soon be surrounded and captured.

**10:3-4.** So the **king of Jerusalem** sent an urgent message to four other kings of southern Canaan stressing the fact that **Gibeon** had **made peace** with Israel, a traitorous and punishable act.

This might pave the way for other cities to surrender in like manner. It was a signal for war. Immediate action had to be taken against Gibeon.

**10:5.** There was a quick response. Little time elapsed before the united force of a **five**-king southern confederacy was laying siege **against Gibeon.** The **kings** were **of the Amorites,** that is, of Canaan's hill country (cf. comments on Gen. 14:13-16).

*b. The course of the conflict (10:6-15)*

**10:6.** Faced with certain slaughter, **the Gibeonites** sent a runner to **Joshua in . . . Gilgal** with an insistent appeal for **help** against the overwhelming force that pressed on them.

But why should Joshua respond to this cry for help from the very people who had deceived him? Why not just sit back and let the Canaanites fight among themselves? The Israelites would then be rid of evidence of an embarrassing failure.

**10:7-8.** That this was not an option for Joshua is made clear by his immediate reaction. Some suggest that this is evidence that the covenant between Israel and the Gibeonites' league was a mutual defense pact. But the scriptural record does not state that. And it seems preposterous that Israel would obligate herself in a treaty to go to the rescue of a "distant" nation which Israel assumed about the Gibeonites when the treaty was adopted.

The reason for Joshua's response lies in the area of military strategy. Up to this time Israel's army attacked one fortified city at a time, at best a long and drawn-out offensive procedure for conquering the entire land of Canaan. But now Joshua sensed he had the strategic break he needed. The combined Amorite armies of southern Canaan were camped together in an open field outside Gibeon. An Israelite victory would break the backs of the enemy forces of the entire region. Furthermore God assured **Joshua** that he need **not be afraid of them** (cf. 1:9; 8:1) for God would give him victory.

Gathering his forces, **Joshua** and his men **marched** the 25 miles **from Gilgal** to Gibeon under cover of darkness. It was a tiresome journey with an ascent of 4,000 feet up steep and difficult terrain. There was no opportunity to rest. The army was fatigued and faced a powerful foe. Clearly God must intervene or all would be lost.

**10:9-10.** Motivated by God's promise of victory, **Joshua** led a **surprise** attack on the Amorite armies of the south, possibly while it was still dark. Panic seized the enemy and after a short stand in which many were killed they broke and fled in wild **confusion** toward the west. Their escape route was through a narrow pass and down the Valley of Aijalon with the Israelites in hot pursuit. This was not the only time that the highroad which led down from the central hill country has been the scene of a rout; in A.D. 66 the Roman general Cestius Gallus fled down this descent before the Jews.

**10:11.** The Amorites however were not able to escape. Using the forces of nature to fight for Israel **the LORD** caused **large hailstones** to fall on the enemy with deadly precision so that **more** were killed in this way than by **swords.**

This entire passage provides a striking illustration of the interplay between the human and divine factors in achieving victory. Verses 7-11 alternate between Joshua (and Israel) and the Lord. They all played important parts in the conflict. The soldiers had to fight but God gave the victory.

**10:12.** But **the day** of the battle of Beth Horon was wearing on and **Joshua** knew that the pursuit of the enemy would be long and arduous. At the most the military leader had 12 hours of daylight ahead of him. He clearly needed more time if he were to realize the fulfillment of God's promise (v. 8) and see the total annihilation of his foes. Joshua therefore took to **the LORD** an unusual request: **O sun, stand still over Gibeon, O moon, over the Valley of Aijalon.**

**10:13-15.** It was noon and the hot **sun** was directly overhead when Joshua uttered this prayer. **The moon** was on the horizon to the west. The petition was quickly answered by the Lord. Joshua prayed in faith, and a great miracle resulted. But the record of this miracle has been called the most striking example of conflict between Scripture and science because, as is well known, the sun does not move around the earth causing day and night. Instead, light and darkness come because the earth rotates on its axis around the sun. Why then did Joshua address the sun rather than the earth? Simply because he was using the language of observation; he was speaking from the perspective and appearance of things on earth. People still do the same thing, even in the scientific community. Almanacs and journals record the hours of sunrise and sunset, yet no one accuses them of scientific error.

The "long day" of Joshua 10, however, must be explained. What *did* actually happen on that strange day? The answers are numerous (an eclipse, clouds over the sun, refraction of the sun's rays, etc.). But the best explanation seems to be the view that in answer to Joshua's prayer God caused the rotation of the earth to slow down so that it made one full rotation in 48 hours rather than in 24. It seems apparent that this view is supported both by the poem in verses 12b-13a and the prose in verse 13b. (**The Book of Jashar** is a Heb. literary collection of songs written in poetic style to honor the accomplishments of Israel's leaders; cf. David's "lament of the bow" in 2 Sam. 1:17-27.)

God stopped the cataclysmic effects that would have naturally occurred, such as monstrous tidal waves and objects flying around. Evidence that the earth's rotation simply slowed down is found in the closing words of Joshua 10:13: **The sun . . . delayed going down about a full day.** The sun was thus abnormally slow or tardy in getting to sunset, that is, its progression from noon to dusk was markedly lethargic, giving Joshua and his soldiers sufficient time to complete their victorious battle.

An important fact that should not be overlooked is that the sun and moon were principal deities among the Canaanites. At the prayer of Israel's leader Canaan's gods were compelled to obey. This disturbance to their gods must have been terribly upsetting and frightening to the Canaanites. The secret of Israel's triumph over the coalition of Canaanites is found in the words, **Surely the LORD was fighting for Israel!** In answer to prayer **Israel** experienced the dramatic intervention of God on their behalf and victory was assured.

*c. The culmination of the conflict (10:16-43)*

**10:16-24.** Taking every advantage of the extended day **Joshua** continued in

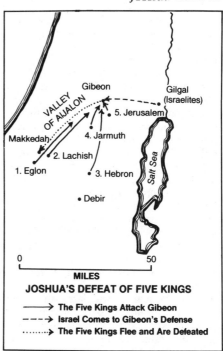

**JOSHUA'S DEFEAT OF FIVE KINGS**

———▶ The Five Kings Attack Gibeon
- - - ▶ Israel Comes to Gibeon's Defense
········▶ The Five Kings Flee and Are Defeated

hot pursuit of the enemy. **The five** strong **kings** and their armies had left their fortified cities to fight Israel in the open. Now Joshua was determined to prevent their retreating back to **their** walled **cities.** When word came that **the five kings** had **hidden in** a **cave** Joshua himself did not stop to deal with them but vigorously pursued the Amorite soldiers, killing all but a **few** who escaped to **their fortified cities.** Then returning to the guarded **cave** he brought out the captured **kings** and executed them. But first, following an eastern custom of conquerors, often pictured on Egyptian and Assyrian monuments, **Joshua** instructed his field **commanders** to **put** their **feet** on the kings' **necks.** This was a symbol of the complete subjugation of the defeated enemy.

**10:25-27.** Then, using words identical to those God had given him, **Joshua** urged his soldiers **not to be afraid** or **discouraged** (cf. 1:9; 8:1) but to **be strong and courageous** (cf. 1:6-7, 9). The victory over the Amorite kings was a sample of Israel's future victories in Canaan, for Joshua said, **This is what the LORD will do to all the enemies you are going to fight. Joshua . . . killed the kings** and their bodies were exposed by **hanging** till sundown (cf. 8:29). Then they were thrown **into the cave** which was blocked by great **rocks,** as had been done earlier (10:18). These rocks became another memorial of Israel's victorious march through Canaan.

**10:28-39.** The defeat of the five kings and their armies sealed the doom of southern Canaan. In a series of quick raids **Joshua** attacked the key military centers themselves to destroy any further military capability. First he **took Makkedah** (v. 28), **Libnah** (v. 29), **Lachish** (v. 31), and **Eglon** (v. 34). These cities, ranging roughly from north to south, guarded the approaches to the southern highlands. Centuries later both Sennacherib and Nebuchadnezzar followed the same strategy in their attacks on Judah.

**Joshua** next drove into the heart of the southern region and defeated its two chief walled cities, **Hebron** (v. 36) and **Debir** (v. 38).

But Jerusalem and Jarmuth, two of the five confederates (v. 5), were bypassed. No explanation is given as to why the defeat of the city of Jarmuth is not mentioned. As for Jerusalem, no doubt Israel's troops were too weary to undertake this difficult task as they returned to camp at Gilgal. At any rate this pagan "island" in the land was to be troublesome to the tribes of Judah and Benjamin until it was conquered by David (2 Sam. 5:7).

**10:40-43.** The extent of Israel's campaign in the south is summarized in verses 40-41 (cf. 11:16). The **region of Goshen,** *not* the Goshen in Egypt (Gen. 45:10; 46:34; 47:1, 4, 6), was probably the area around Debir in southern Canaan. A town named Goshen was 1 of 11 towns "in the hill country" which included Debir (Josh. 15:48-51). Perhaps the area was named for the town. The impressive sweep of victories recorded in Joshua 10 is given credibility by the concluding statement, **All these kings and their lands Joshua conquered in one campaign because the LORD, the God of Israel, fought for Israel.**

With such confidence, **Joshua** and his tired army **returned** to **Gilgal** to make preparations for completing their task.

## D. The northern campaign (11:1-15)

After the exhausting military campaign in the south, Joshua was not to enjoy any prolonged period of recuperation before facing an even greater challenge, a massive coalition of forces in the north. But he was equal to the task.

Israel's leader was both a military genius and a spiritual giant. Militarily, his tactics were skillful: (1) His battles were all offensive. When he learned that an attack was impending, he preceded it by an attack of his own. (2) He used the element of surprise (e.g., against the five Amorite kings besieging Gibeon, 10:9; against the many kings at the Waters of Merom, 11:7; and against Ai when he staged a decoy-rout, 8:14-19). (3) He sent his soldiers to harry the retreating enemy, to prevent them from reaching their cities (10:19-20).

Spiritually, Joshua served as an example to the people: he stood by the promise his spies made to Rahab; he kept faith with the deceptive Gibeonites; he could have used his position for personal gain but he did not.

With such a leader at the helm of affairs in Israel, the Conquest entered its final phase.

### 1. THE CONFEDERATION (11:1-5)

**11:1-3.** The alarm of **the northern** Canaanite **kings** was aroused by Joshua's crushing victories in the south. **Jabin, king of Hazor,** organized a desperate attempt to stop the conquest of the land by the army of Israel. No doubt his attempt would have had a better chance of success if he had joined the coalition of Adoni-Zedek (10:1-3), marching in force from the north to merge with the southern armies to crush Israel at Gibeon. But God restrained Jabin from that move and now he reacted to the crisis with dispatch and near panic.

Messengers fanned out rapidly to the north, south, east, and west, with an urgent call to arms. This may have been quite similar to the summons Saul issued later to Israel to follow him to Jabesh Gilead, killing a yoke of oxen and sending pieces of the animals by couriers who cried, "This is what will be done to the oxen of anyone who does not follow Saul and Samuel" (1 Sam. 11:7). **Kinnereth** (Josh. 11:2; cf. 13:27; 19:35; Num. 34:11; Deut. 3:17; 1 Kings 15:20) is an early name for the Sea of Galilee and also the name of a town on the coast of the lake. "Kinnereth," meaning harp, may refer to the lake's harp-like shape. The New Testament sometimes refers to the Sea of Galilee as the Lake of Gennesaret, a Greek spelling for the Hebrew Kinnereth (e.g., Luke 5:1).

**11:4-5.** Though there was no love lost among those **kings** of the north, the threat of annihilation forced them into an alliance and they rendezvoused a few miles northwest of the Sea of Galilee in a plain near **the Waters of Merom.**

The combined army was impressive. Not only did it include soldiers **as numerous as the sand on the seashore,** but in addition they had **horses and chariots** in great numbers. Josephus, a Jewish historian of the first century A.D., speculated that this northern confederacy included 300,000 infantry soldiers, 10,000 cavalry troops, and 20,000 chariots.

The odds against the Israelites seemed overwhelming. How could Joshua hope to win this battle?

### 2. THE CONFLICT (11:6-15)

The vast host of Canaanites were pitched at the Waters of Merom (v. 5). It was probably their plan, after organizing their detachments and adopting a strategy, to sweep down the Jordan Valley and attack Joshua at Gilgal. But Joshua did not wait for the battle to come to him; he was in fact already marching toward Merom, a five-day trek from his home base. And as he marched he had a lot of time to think about the immense array awaiting him. No doubt he trembled at the prospect of the battle that loomed before him.

**11:6.** Then God spoke. The promise He gave **Joshua** was unmistakably clear: **Do not be afraid of them** (cf. 1:9; 8:1) **because by this time tomorrow I will hand all of them over to Israel, slain.** This was just what Joshua needed and Israel's leader took God's promise at face value, believing that He would give them the victory over their formidable foe. God even told Joshua specifically **to hamstring** (cripple by cutting the leg tendons) **their horses and** to **burn their chariots** (cf. comments on 11:9).

**11:7-9.** The battle took place in two phases. The next day **Joshua** surprised the enemy, attacking them **at the Waters of Merom** and chasing **them** westward to the coast (**to Greater Sidon** and **to Misrephoth Maim**), **and** eastward **to the Valley of Mizpah.** Following God's di-

rection (v. 6) to the letter Joshua killed all of the enemy, **burned their chariots,** and lamed **their horses.**

But why did God command such drastic action, burning the chariots and hamstringing the horses? Because the Canaanites used horses in their pagan worship (and so later did Judah; cf. 2 Kings 23:11). Also there was danger that Israel might trust in these new weapons of war rather than in the Lord. The Psalmist David declared, "Some trust in chariots and some in horses, but we trust in the name of the LORD our God" (Ps. 20:7).

**11:10-14.** In the second phase of the conflict in northern Canaan **Joshua** returned after routing the enemy army and **captured** all the cities of the defeated kings. **Hazor,** however, was singled out for special treatment, probably because it was by far the largest city of ancient Palestine (200 acres in size, compared with Megiddo at 14 and Jericho at 8). Occupying a position of immense strategic importance **Hazor** dominated several branches of an ancient highway which led from Egypt to Syria and on to Assyria and Babylon. This location on the trade routes contributed to the city's wealth. **Hazor** alone among the northern cities was both seized and **burned.** Though **Joshua** may have decided to save the other captured **cities** for later Israelite use, he determined to make an example of **Hazor,** capital **of all these kingdoms** (city states) and the convener of their armies. If great Hazor could not escape, the Canaanites would be forced to acknowledge that any city could be burned if Joshua so decreed.

**11:15.** Thus a decisive victory was won in the north. And the key was obedience to God. **Joshua . . . left nothing undone of all that the LORD commanded Moses.**

### E. The review of the victories (11:16–12:24)

Victory in the north brought the formal end of the Conquest. But before giving the record of how the land was apportioned among the tribes, the author paused to review and summarize the scope of Israel's triumphs in Canaan. He included a description of the conquered geographic areas (11:16-23) and a list of the defeated kings (chap. 12).

## 1. THE CONQUERED AREAS (11:16-23)

**11:16-17.** The battles fought by **Joshua** and his troops ranged over lands that stretched from border to border, from south to north, and from east to west. **The hill country,** the **Negev,** the **Goshen** area, **the western foothills, the Arabah, and the mountains** refer to the central and southern portions of the land (cf. 10:40). "The Negev" is the desert area southwest of the Dead Sea and "the Arabah" is the depression of the Jordan Valley north and south of the Dead Sea. **Mount Halak** is in the southern desert region; **Baal Gad** (exact location unknown) was in the far north, **in the Valley of Lebanon** perhaps 30-40 miles north of the Sea of Galilee.

**11:18:20.** The period of the Conquest lasted **a long time.** Victory did not come easily or quickly; it rarely does. Yet in all the military confrontations only one city, **Gibeon,** sought **peace.** The rest were taken **in battle,** God having **hardened their hearts** (cf. comments on Ex. 4:21; 8:15) to fight **Israel** so that they might be destroyed. The Canaanites' day of grace was gone. They had sinned against the light of God's revelation in nature (Ps. 19:1; Rom. 1:18-20), in conscience (Rom. 2:14-16), and in His recent miraculous works at the Red (Reed) Sea, the Jordan River, and Jericho. Now the sovereign God confirmed the hearts of these unrepentant people in their stubborn unbelief before judging them.

**11:21-22.** Special mention is made of **the Anakites,** the giants who had terrified the spies 45 years before (Num. 13:33; cf. comments on Josh. 14:10), of whom it was asked, "Who can stand up against the Anakites?" (Deut. 9:2) But under **Joshua** those supposedly invincible foes were utterly **destroyed. Only** a few remained, in the remote cities of **Gaza, Gath, and Ashdod**—which later proved to be an unfortunate oversight on Joshua's part because in David's time Goliath came from Gath to defy Israel and her God (1 Sam. 17).

**11:23.** The section concludes with a declaration that summarizes the Book of Joshua as a whole. **So Joshua took the entire land** (cf. v. 16). This looks back and condenses the history of the Conquest in chapters 1–11. **And he gave it as an inheritance to Israel according to their tribal divisions.** These words look forward and summarize the distribution of the land in chapters 13–22.

But how is the statement, "Joshua took the entire land," to be understood when later it was written that "there are still very large areas of land to be taken over"? (13:1) To the Hebrew mind the part stands for the whole. It thus only needs to be demonstrated that Joshua took key centers in all parts of the land to validate the statement that he had conquered the whole land.

A.J. Mattill, Jr. has meticulously analyzed the conquest of Canaan by surveying the geographical divisions of the land and the representative parts of it subdued by Joshua ("Representative Universalism and the Conquest of Canaan," *Concordia Theological Monthly* 35. January 1964:8-17). Included are conquered sites on the coastal plain, the Shephelah (foothills), the central plateau, the Jordan Valley, and the Transjordan plateau. No area was totally bypassed. Joshua did indeed take the entire land, just as God promised he would if he followed the divine Word rather than human wisdom (cf. 1:8). Also see comments on 21:43-45. On the concluding statement **Then the land had rest from war** (11:23), see comments on these words in 14:15.

## 2. THE CONQUERED KINGS (CHAP. 12)

Chapter 12, in concluding the story begun in chapter 1, gives a detailed catalog of the kings defeated by Israel. The preceding chapters obviously then list only the major battles. Only here is the complete list of conquered kings found. It is not claimed that Israel occupied all these cities. Certainly Joshua did not have sufficient manpower to leave a controlling garrison in each place. Joshua no doubt expected the respective tribes to occupy those towns.

**12:1-6.** First were recorded the victories under **Moses** on the **east** side of **the Jordan.** These were important victories over **Sihon** and **Og.** Sihon had ruled over a stretch of land about 90 miles south to north from **the Arnon Gorge** at about the midpoint of **the Sea of the Arabah** (also called **the Salt Sea** and the Dead Sea) up to **the Sea of Kinnereth** (cf. comments on 11:2). Og ruled over a stretch of land extending north from Sihon's northern boundary for about 60 miles (cf. Num. 21:21-35; Deut. 2:24—

3:17). This territory was assigned to the tribes of Reuben and Gad and the half tribe of Manasseh (Num. 32; cf. Josh. 13:8-13). (On **Geshur** and **Maacah** see comments on 13:13.)

**12:7-24.** In this section 16 **kings** of southern Canaan are enumerated first (vv. 9-16) and then 15 kings of northern Canaan (vv. 17-24).

It is surprising to find recorded **31 kings** in a land approximately 150 miles from north to south and 50 miles from east to west. But it must be remembered that these kings reigned over city-states and had only local authority. Apart from the confederations formed by the kings **of Jerusalem** (10:1-5) and **Hazor** (11:1-5), the lack of a central government in Canaan made the Israelites' task easier than it would have been otherwise.

As to the meaning of Joshua's victories one writer stated, "There has never been a greater war for a greater cause. The battle of Waterloo decided the fate of Europe, but this series of contests in far-off Canaan decided the fate of the world" (Henry T. Sell, *Bible Study by Periods*. Chicago: Fleming H. Revell Co., 1899, p. 83).

## III. The Division of Canaan (chaps. 13–21)

### A. The portions for the two and one-half tribes (chap. 13)

Having successfully removed the major military threats to Israel's survival in Canaan, Joshua the aged soldier now became an administrator. The land conquered by bloody warfare had to be assigned to the various tribes and Joshua would oversee this important transaction. It would be a service less exhausting and more suited to his advancing years.

To many people this section of the Book of Joshua, with its detailed lists of boundaries and cities, seems tedious. Someone has said, "Most of this long section reads like a real estate deed." And that is precisely what is found in these lengthy narrations—legal descriptions (after the manner of that ancient day) of the areas allocated to the 12 tribes. Title deeds are important documents so these should not be regarded as insignificant or superfluous.

This was a climactic moment in the life of the young nation. After centuries in Egyptian bondage, decades in the barren wilderness, years of hard fighting in Canaan, the hour had arrived when the Israelites could at last settle down to build homes, cultivate the soil, raise families, and live in peace in their own land. The days of land allotment were a happy time for Israel.

1. THE DIVINE COMMAND TO DIVIDE THE LAND (13:1-7)

**13:1a.** God directed **Joshua** to divide the land west of the Jordan at this time because he was **very old.** Since Joshua died at the age of 110 (24:29), he probably was at least 100 at this time. God's commission to Joshua had included not only conquering the land but also distributing it among the tribes (cf. 1:6). He must therefore move on quickly to this new assignment.

**13:1b-7.** **The land that** remained **to be taken over** is described from south to north and included Philistia (vv. 2-3; see comments on the Philistines at Gen. 21:32); Phoenicia (Josh. 13:4), called here **the land of the Canaanites** but designating the inhabitants of the Syro-Palestinian coastland; and **Lebanon** (vv. 5-6). All this land was now to be allotted to the **nine** and one-half **tribes** since God promised to **drive . . . out** all the enemy (v. 6).

2. THE SPECIAL GRANT TO THE EASTERN TRIBES (13:8-33)

**13:8-13.** Joshua was next called on to recognize and confirm what had already been done by **Moses** on the **east** side **of the Jordan.** The tribes of Reuben, Gad, and the half-tribe of Manasseh, possessing large herds of cattle, were anxious to settle in the rich grazing lands of the Transjordan. But only after their men agreed to fight alongside their brothers to win Canaan proper did Moses agree to give them their land (Num. 32). A survey of the area of Transjordan is given in these verses (Josh. 13:9-12; cf. 12:1-5). **Geshur and Maacah** (already mentioned in 12:5) were not defeated by **the Israelites,** and the reason for this is not given. These countries were located east and northeast of the Sea of Kinnereth (Sea of Galilee).

**13:14.** **The tribe of Levi** received no specific territory of land as did the other tribes (cf. v. 33; 14:3-4; 18:7). Instead the Levites received 48 towns with pastureland for their flocks and herds (14:4;

21:41) as Moses had specified (Num. 35:1-5).

**13:15-32. Reuben** (vv. 15-23) received **the territory** previously occupied by Moab, east of the Dead Sea. **The tribe of Gad** inherited the portion in the center of the region, in the original land **of Gilead** (vv. 24-28).

The allotment to **the half-tribe of Manasseh** (vv. 29-31) was the rich tableland **of Bashan** east of the Sea of Kinnereth.

Centuries before the land was divided Jacob, when dying, had uttered prophecies regarding his sons. His prophecy about his firstborn Reuben was foreboding (cf. Gen. 49:3-4; 35:22). Though Reuben was the firstborn and entitled to a double portion (Deut. 21:17), neither he nor his tribe received it. Now after more than four centuries the punishment for Reuben's sinful deed was passed on to his descendants; the right of the firstborn passed over to his brother Joseph who received two portions, one for Ephraim and the other for Manasseh (Gen. 48:12-20).

Was the request of the two and one-half tribes to settle in Transjordan a wise one? History would seem to answer no. Their territories had no natural boundaries to the east and were therefore constantly exposed to invasion by the Moabites, Canaanites, Arameans, Midianites, Amalekites, and others. And when the king of Assyria looked covetously toward Canaan, Reuben, Gad and the half-tribe of Manasseh were the first to be carried into captivity by the Assyrian armies (1 Chron. 5:26).

**13:33.** By contrast with the rich though dangerous inheritance of these tribes, it is twice emphasized in this chapter (vv. 14, 33) and twice later (14:3-4; 18:7) that **the tribe of Levi received no inheritance** from **Moses.** At first this may seem puzzling, but closer examination reveals that in lieu of territorial possessions the tribe of Levi was allotted the sacrifices or offerings (13:14), the priesthood (18:7), and **the Lord** Himself (13:33). Who could have dreamed of a greater inheritance?

The two and one-half tribes chose, as Lot did, on the basis of appearance (cf. Gen. 13:10-11), and their inheritance was ultimately lost to them. On the other hand the Levites, requesting no portion, were given an **inheritance** of abiding spiritual significance.

## B. The portion for Caleb (chap. 14)

### 1. INTRODUCTION (14:1-5)

**14:1-5.** With the recording of the allotments by **Moses** in Transjordan completed, the account turns to the distribution of the land in **Canaan** proper to the remaining **nine-and-a-half tribes.** The explanation is repeated regarding the dealings with the Reubenites, the Gadites, and the half-tribe of Manasseh; and the arrangements for the tribe of Levi (cf. 13:14, 33; 18:7). Also the method by which the allocations in Canaan were to be made was specified: the land was to be **assigned by lot** (14:2; 18:8; 19:51). **The Lord had** instructed **Moses** that each tribe was to receive territory proportionate to its population with the casting of lots to determine its location (Num. 26:54-56). According to Jewish tradition the name of a tribe was drawn from one urn and simultaneously the boundary lines of a territory from another. This method designated each tribal inheritance. But blind chance did not decide the tribal location, for God was superintending the whole procedure (cf. Prov. 16:33). The inequities of assignments that existed and that caused some tensions and jealousies among the tribes should have been accepted as a part of God's purpose, not as something that was arbitrary and unfair.

### 2. CALEB AT KADESH BARNEA (14:6-9)

**14:6-9.** The time for casting lots arrived and the tribe **of Judah,** receiving the first portion, assembled **at Gilgal.** Before the lots were cast **Caleb,** a "grand old man of Israel," stepped forward to remind **Joshua** of a promise the Lord had made to him 45 years earlier: "I will give him and his descendants the land he set his feet on, because he followed the Lord wholeheartedly" (Deut. 1:36). Caleb's life was ebbing away and he must make a choice. What did he still want most of all? In a remarkable address to Joshua he reviewed the highlights of his life and made his request. His brief autobiography highlighted events **at Kadesh Barnea,** during the wilderness wanderings, and the Conquest.

Caleb is introduced in this passage as the **son of Jephunneh the Kenizzite.**

According to Genesis 15:19 the Kenizzites were a tribe of Canaan in Abraham's day. Caleb's family then was originally outside the covenant and commonwealth of Israel as were Heber the Kenite (Jud. 4:17), Ruth the Moabitess (Ruth 1:1-5), Uriah the Hittite (2 Sam. 11:3, 6, 24), and others. It is apparent that the Kenizzites in part at least joined the tribe of Judah before the Exodus. So their faith was not hereditary but was the fruit of conviction. And Caleb displayed that faith throughout his long lifetime.

Standing before General Joshua, his old friend and fellow spy (Num. 14:6), 85-year-old Caleb (Josh. 14:10) told the story of that never-to-be forgotten day, 45 years before (v. 10), when the 2 of them stood alone against the other 10 spies and the cowardly mob. For Moses had sent 12 spies into Canaan (Num. 13:2); 2 of them were Caleb and Joshua (Num. 13:6, 8). When the spies returned 10 of them praised the land itself but fearfully concluded Israel could not conquer it (Num. 13:27-29, 31-33). Caleb, **however,** dared to disagree (Num. 13:30), and when the fears of the people threatened to bring national rebellion Joshua joined his colleague in urging the people to trust God for victory (Num. 14:6-9). For Caleb's leadership against the unbelieving spies and people, **God** singled him out for blessing and promised him a special reward (Num. 14:24; Deut. 1:36).

Caleb's testimony (Josh. 14:6-12) was simple. He had spoken on that memorable day **according to** his **convictions.** He did not minimize the problems—the giants and the fortified cities—but he magnified God. To him, God was greater than the biggest problem. Caleb had faith in *the power of God.* Not so the other spies. They magnified the problems and thereby minimized God. But Caleb would not follow the crowd. He did not once consider sacrificing his own convictions in order to make the majority report unanimous. Instead he **followed the Lord** his **God wholeheartedly** (cf. v. 14).

### 3. CALEB DURING THE WILDERNESS WANDERINGS AND THE CONQUEST (14:10-11)

**14:10.** The autobiographical story continued as Caleb reminisced about God's faithfulness to him over many years. First he affirmed that God had

kept him **alive** the past **45 years** as **He** had promised. Actually Caleb was the recipient of two divine promises: one, that his life would be prolonged, and the other, that he would someday inherit the territory he had bravely explored near Hebron. But 45 years is a long time to wait for the fulfillment of a pledge, a long time for faith to live on a promise. Yet Caleb did wait through the weary years of the wilderness wanderings and the demanding years of the Conquest. Caleb had strong faith in *the promises of God.* They sustained him in his difficult times.

Caleb's remarks provide information for determining the length of the conquest of Canaan by the Israelites. Caleb stated (v. 7) that he was 40 years old when he went to spy out the land. The wilderness wanderings lasted 38 years, thus bringing Caleb's age to 78 at the beginning of the Conquest. Caleb then said he was **85** at the end of the Conquest. So the Conquest lasted 7 years. This is confirmed by Caleb's reference (v. 10) to God's sustaining grace for 45 years since Kadesh Barnea (38 years of the wanderings plus 7 years of the Conquest).

**14:11.** Interestingly as an octogenarian, Caleb said he felt **as strong** and **vigorous** at 85 as he had at 40!

### 4. CALEB AT HEBRON (14:12-15)

**14:12-14.** Caleb concluded his speech to **Joshua** with an astounding request. At age 85, when he might have asked for a quiet place to spend his last days raising some vegetables or flowers, he instead requested that he be given the same section of land that had struck fear into the hearts of the 10 spies. This was the **inheritance** he desired in fulfillment of God's earlier promise. Though most older people are more apt to talk about old conflicts than to take on new ones, **Caleb** was ready for one more good battle. He was eager to fight **the Anakites** at **Hebron** and take that city for his possession. Caleb chose a large and foreboding task. Not that he was filled with pride in his own ability. Rather he believed God would be with him. Caleb had faith in *the presence of God.*

With flashing eyes and a strong voice he concluded, **The Lord helping me, I will drive them out just as He said.** And drive them out he did, as Joshua

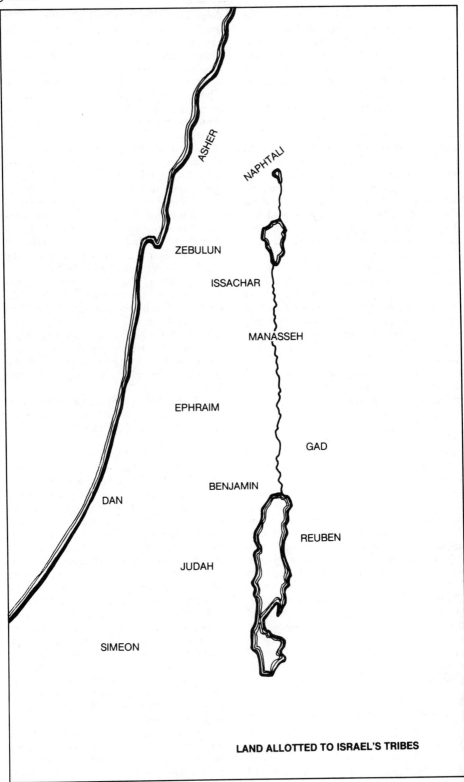

**LAND ALLOTTED TO ISRAEL'S TRIBES**

(15:13-19) recorded. Joshua's response to Caleb's request was twofold: (a) he **blessed Caleb,** that is, he set him apart for God's enablement so he would be enriched and successful in his task, and (b) Joshua **gave him Hebron,** a statement which emphasizes that this land grant was a legal transaction.

**14:15.** A historical note explaining the previous name of **Hebron** as **Kiriath Arba** ends the story. **Arba** was a giant **among the Anakites,** a nation of giants, a fact that causes the heroic faith of Caleb to stand out even more vividly. The concluding words, **Then the land had rest from war** (cf. 11:23 for the same expression at the end of the Conquest proper), show what faith in the Lord can accomplish with respect to land yet to be possessed.

### C. The portions for the nine and one-half tribes (15:1–19:48)

1. THE ALLOTMENT FOR THE TRIBE OF JUDAH (CHAP. 15)

**15:1-12.** Caleb's request having been granted, Joshua returned to the business of dividing the land west of the Jordan among the nine and one-half tribes (see the map). **Judah** was the first to receive an inheritance and as the largest tribe her portion exceeded that of any of the others. Jacob's prophecy regarding Judah and his seed was remarkably fulfilled in her land allotment after the Conquest. First, Judah was surrounded by enemies (Gen. 49:8-9). The Moabites were on the east, Edomites on the south, Amalekites to the southwest, and Philistines to the west. Thus hemmed in by fierce foes, Judah would need strong rulers such as David to survive. Second, the land allotted to Judah was ideally suited to the planting of vineyards (Gen. 49:11-12). It was from a Judean valley (the Valley of Eshcol) that the spies cut down the gigantic cluster of grapes (Num. 13:24). Third, Judah was the tribe from which the Messiah would come (Gen. 49:10; Matt. 1:1, 3; Luke 3:23, 33).

Judah's **southern boundary** (Josh. 15:2-4) extended from the south end of the Dead **Sea** westward to the river **of Egypt** (**Wadi** el-Arish). The **northern** border extended from the northern tip of the Dead Sea westward to **the Great Sea,** the Mediterranean (vv. 5-12). These two bodies of water were the eastern and western limits. Composed mainly of the territory conquered by Joshua in his southern campaign (chap. 10), the area included some fertile tracts, but large parts were mountainous and barren.

**15:13-19.** Included in Judah's portion was **Hebron** (**Kiriath Arba;** cf. 14:15) which had been granted **to Caleb.** The record describes how that courageous warrior claimed and enlarged this inheritance (after Joshua's death), aided by a brave nephew **Othniel** who became his son-in-law (cf. Jud. 1:1, 10-15, 20) and later a judge (Jud. 3:9-11).

**15:20-63.** The **towns** of **Judah** are next listed according to their locations in the four main geographic regions of the tribe: **29 towns** plus **their villages** in the south or **Negev** (vv. 21-32); **42 towns** plus **villages** in **the western foothills** or Shephelah (vv. 33-47); **38 towns** plus **villages** in the central **hill country** (vv. 48-60); **6 towns** plus **villages** in the sparsely populated wilderness of Judah which slopes down toward the Dead Sea (vv. 61-62). The number of towns in the Negev is said to be 29 (v. 32), but 36 are listed (vv. 21-32). This is explained by the fact that seven of these were later given to Simeon's tribe: Moladah, Hazar Shual, Beersheba, Ezem, Eltolad, Hormah, and Ziklag (19:1-7). **Judah** inherited well over 100 cities and seems to have occupied them with little or no difficulty with the significant exception of Jerusalem. **Judah could not** dislodge **the Jebusites, who were living in Jerusalem** (15:63). Was it that the men of Judah "could not" or that they "would not"? Was the failure because of lack of strength or a lack of faith? The account of Judah's inheritance ends on an ominous and foreboding note.

2. THE ALLOTMENTS FOR THE JOSEPH TRIBES (CHAPS. 16–17)

#### a. The territory of Ephraim (chap. 16)

**16:1-3.** The powerful house of **Joseph** made up of the tribes of Ephraim and Manasseh, inherited the rich territory of central Canaan. Because Joseph kept the whole family alive during the famine in Egypt, the patriarch Jacob ordained that Joseph's two sons, Ephraim and Manasseh, should be made founders and heads of tribes with their uncles (cf. Gen. 48:5). Their territory in Canaan was in many respects the most beautiful and fertile.

**16:4-10.** Located immediately north of the **territory** to be assigned to Dan and Benjamin, the allotment of **Ephraim** stretched from **the Jordan** to the Mediterranean and included the sites of some of Joshua's battles as well as **Shiloh** where the tabernacle would remain for about 300 years. To encourage unity some of Ephraim's **towns** were located in the territory of Manasseh (v. 9).

But the men of Ephraim, like those of Judah, **did not** completely drive out **the Canaanites** from their region. Motivated by a materialistic attitude, they chose to put the Canaanites in **Gezer** under tribute to gain additional wealth. That proved to be a fatal mistake for in later centuries, in the time of the Judges, the arrangement was reversed as the Canaanites rose up and enslaved the Israelites. In addition to the historical lesson there is a spiritual principle here. It is all too easy for a believer to tolerate and excuse some pet sin only to wake up some day to the grim realization that it has risen up to possess and drive him to spiritual defeat. It pays to deal with sin decisively and harshly.

*b. The territory of Manasseh (17:1-13)*

**17:1-2, 7-10.** The descendants of **Makir, Manasseh's firstborn,** settled in Transjordan (vv. 1-2). The remaining heirs settled in Canaan proper and were given the territory north of Ephraim extending also from the Jordan River to the Mediterranean Sea (vv. 7-10).

**17:3-6.** Special note is taken of the five **daughters** of **Zelophehad,** a great-great grandson of Manasseh. Because their father died without **sons** they, as **the Lord** had declared in this and other such cases, should receive the **inheritance** (cf. Num. 27:1-11). They now went to the high priest **Eleazar** (Aaron's son, Josh. 24:33) who with **Joshua** and the tribal **leaders** oversaw the allotments to the tribes (cf. 19:51). These five women claimed and received their portion within the territory of **Manasseh.** This incident is significant, for it shows a concern for the rights of women at a time when most societies regarded them as mere chattel.

**17:11-13.** Several cities located in the tribes of **Issachar and Asher** were given to **Manasseh.** These were the Canaanite fortresses of **Beth Shan, Ibleam . . . Dor, Endor, Taanach, and Megiddo.** (Dor, the

third in the list, was also known as **Naphoth.**) Apparently it was considered necessary for military purposes that these cities be held by a strong tribe. The decision, however, was in vain for the sons of Manasseh, like the Ephraimites, chose tribute over triumph.

*c. The complaint of Ephraim and Manasseh (17:14-18)*

**17:14-15.** The descendants of **Joseph** registered a belligerent complaint with **Joshua,** claiming that their **allotment** was too small in light of their large population. With tact and firmness **Joshua** challenged them first to **clear** the trees and settle in the forested **hill country** (v. 15). He suggested that they combine their energies to drive out the Canaanites (v. 18).

**17:16-18.** But this was not what they wanted to hear. They insisted that **the hill country** was **not** sufficient **for** them **and** that **the Canaanites** in the region possessed **iron chariots,** probably chariots of wood covered with iron. Again **Joshua** reminded his fellow tribesmen that they were **numerous and very powerful** and fully capable of expanding their territory by clearing the **hill country** and driving out the enemy **Canaanites.** While there is some similarity between this section and the one recording Caleb's request (14:6-15), their outlooks were opposite. Caleb's request was motivated by faith, whereas that of the Josephites stemmed from fear. The purpose, however, of this episode may well be to alert the Israelites to the fact that the tribes had to act in courageous faith if they were to possess the Promised Land fully.

3. THE ALLOTMENTS FOR THE REMAINING TRIBES (18:1–19:48)

*a. Introduction (18:1-10)*

**18:1-3.** Before the final divisions of the land were made the Israelites moved en masse from Gilgal to **Shiloh,** about 20 miles northwest, from the Jordan Valley to the hill country. Why? Probably because Shiloh, located in the center of the land, was a convenient location where the tabernacle (**the Tent of Meeting**) could remind the people that the key to prosperity and blessing in the land was worshiping and serving Yahweh. The dissatisfaction of the sons of Joseph with their allotment (17:14-18) was an ominous foreshadowing of the future disintegration of the nation because of self-interest. To counteract this tendency the tabernacle was **set up** in Shiloh to promote a sense of national unity.

Further, when the Israelites were thus assembled for erecting the tabernacle and celebrating the new worship center Joshua sensed that a feeling of war-weariness had overtaken them. They were exhausted in the struggle for the conquest of Canaan, so they stopped in the middle of the task of allocating the **tribes. Seven** were still without homes, apparently content to continue a nomadic and purposeless existence such as they had experienced in the wilderness. Their listlessness provoked **Joshua** who took steps to prod them into action. He reproached them sharply: **How long will you wait before you begin to take possession of the land that the LORD, the God of your fathers, has given you?** Apparently the tribes were to initiate matters relating to territorial allocations. Joshua probably viewed every passing day as a day lost in the program of completely occupying the land, a day in which the enemy could return or become more firmly entrenched.

**18:4-7.** Joshua was for action but not before careful preparations were made. Directing the appointment of a commission of 21 men, **3** from **each** of the seven unassigned tribes, he sent them to **make a** topographical **survey of the** remaining **land.** How long this complex task took is not stated, but it was obviously a job that required time and skill. Josephus wrote that these men were experts in geometry. Probably their parents had mastered the science of land surveying in Egypt. Who among them dreamed that their children would ever put that knowledge to use so strategically in their land of promise?

**18:8-10.** Writing their expert observations **on a scroll,** the surveyors then **returned** to **Shiloh** where **Joshua** proceeded to **cast lots** (see comments on 14:1-5; cf. 19:51) to determine the portions of territory to be allotted to the remaining **seven** tribes.

### b. The territory of Benjamin (18:11-28)

**18:11-28. Benjamin** was assigned the land that lay between **Judah and Joseph,** a reference to Ephraim, thus minimizing the incipient rivalry between these leading tribes. Though their area was covered by mountains and ravines, extending only 25 miles from east to west and 15 miles at its widest point from north to south, it included many cities that were important in biblical history— **Jericho . . . Bethel . . . Gibeon, Ramah . . . Mizpah,** and **the Jebusite city . . . Jerusalem** (vv. 21-28). So the site of the future temple in Jerusalem was in the tribe of Benjamin, a fulfillment of Moses' prophecy (Deut. 33:12).

### c. The territory of Simeon (19:1-9)

**19:1-9.** Because **Judah** had **more** territory than it **needed** (v. 9), and in fulfillment of Jacob's prophecy (cf. Gen. 49:5-7), **Simeon** was given land in the southern section of Judah's **territory** with 17 **towns and their villages.** But it was not long before Simeon was to lose her individuality as a tribe, for her territory was incorporated eventually into that of Judah and many of her citizens migrated north to Ephraim and Manasseh (cf. 2 Chron. 15:9; 34:6). This explains why after the division of the kingdom following Solomon there were 10 tribes in the north and only 2 in the south (Judah and Benjamin).

### d. The territory of Zebulun (19:10-16)

**19:10-16.** According to Jacob's prophecy **Zebulun** would "live by the seashore and become a haven for ships" (Gen. 49:13). She was assigned a portion in lower Galilee which many consider to have been landlocked. However, it is possible to understand that a strip of land extended to the Mediterranean Sea forming an enclave in Issachar's territory. Strangely omitted is the city of Nazareth which was within the borders of Zebulun's allotment. (The **Bethlehem** mentioned in Josh. 19:15 is not the Bethlehem village in Judah [Micah 5:2] where Jesus was born.)

### e. The territory of Issachar (19:17-23)

**19:17-23.** Lying east of Zebulun and south of the Sea of Galilee **Issachar** was to occupy the fertile and beautiful valley of **Jezreel,** also a noted battlefield. Until the time of David, however, its people remained in the mountainous district at the eastern end of the valley.

*f. The territory of Asher (19:24-31)*

**19:24-31.** **Asher** was assigned the Mediterranean coastal lands from Mount **Carmel** north to **Sidon** and **Tyre.** By virtue of her vital position she was to protect Israel from northern coastal enemies such as the Phoenicians. By David's time Asher had faded into insignificance though her tribal identity was not lost. Anna the prophetess, who along with Simeon gave thanks for the birth of Jesus, was from the tribe of Asher (cf. Luke 2:36-38).

*g. The territory of Naphtali (19:32-39)*

**19:32-39.** Adjacent to Asher on the east, **Naphtali** had **the Jordan** River and the Sea of Galilee as its eastern boundary. While not highly significant as a region in the Old Testament period, Naphtali occupied lands that were important in New Testament history because the Galilean ministry of Jesus Christ was centered there. Isaiah the prophet contrasted Naphtali's early gloom (due to Assyrian invasion) with its glory when Christ would be there (cf. Isa. 9:1-2; Matt. 4:13-17).

*h. The territory of Dan (19:40-48)*

**19:40-48.** The least desirable portion fell to **Dan.** Surrounded by Ephraim and Benjamin on the north and east and by Judah on the south, her boundaries coincided with theirs so Dan's borders are not described. Only towns are included, which numbered 17. Not only was their original location too small but after part of the territory of Dan was lost to the Amorites (Jud. 1:34) most of the tribe migrated to the far north, and **attacked** and **settled in** the city of **Leshem** (Laish) opposite the northern sector of Naphtali **and named it Dan** (cf. Jud. 18; Gen. 49:17).

So God provided for the needs of each tribe, though in some cases parts of their inheritances were still in the hands of the enemy. The Israelites were to possess the land by faith, trusting God to enable them to defeat their foes. Centuries later Jeremiah purchased a field held by the invading Babylonian army (Jer. 32). And centuries after that a Roman citizen arranged to buy some ground on which the attackers of Rome were camped. Similarly Israel was to claim her tribal inheritances by faith. Failure to do so would be to live in poverty and weakness, conditions which God did not desire for His people.

*D. The portions for Joshua, manslayers, and Levites (19:49–21:45)*

1. THE SPECIAL PROVISION FOR JOSHUA (19:49-51)

**19:49.** Whereas Caleb's **inheritance** was determined first (14:6-15), Joshua's was last. Only after all the tribes had received their allotments did **Joshua** ask for his. What a selfless spirit he possessed, and how his behavior contrasts with many political leaders who use their positions and influence to enrich themselves and their families.

**19:50-51.** Joshua's choice of land further reveals his humility. He asked for **Timnath Serah,** a city in the rugged, infertile, mountainous district of his own tribe (**Ephraim**), when he could have appropriated land in the fairest and most productive area of Canaan. With deep appreciation for his godly leadership the sons of Israel granted Joshua his modest request, **and he built up the town and settled there.** In one of the final pictures of this stalwart leader, Joshua is seen as a builder (in addition to his being a general and an administrator). The combination is rare among God's servants.

All the tribes received their **territories . . . by lot** (see comments on 14:1-5).

2. THE ASSIGNMENT OF CITIES OF REFUGE (CHAP. 20)

One of the first ordinances after the announcement of the Ten Commandments provided for the future establishment of cities of refuge (Ex. 21:12-13). These cities, providing havens for unintentional manslayers, are discussed in detail in Numbers 35:6-34 and Deuteronomy 19:1-14. The present chapter discusses their appointment after the Conquest (see their locations on the map "Canaan in the Conquest" near Josh. 3).

The fact that these cities are discussed in four books of the Old Testament marks them as being of great importance. It is apparent that God wished to impress on Israel the sanctity of human life. To put an end to a person's life, even if done unintentionally, is a serious thing, and the cities of refuge underscored this emphatically.

In the ancient world blood revenge was widely practiced. The moment a person was killed, his nearest relative took responsibility for vengeance. This ancient rite of vendetta was often handed down from one generation to another so that increasingly larger numbers of innocent people died violently. The need in ancient Israel for the refuge that these special cities provided is evident.

**20:1-3.** A clear distinction is made in the Old Testament between premeditated murder and accidental manslaughter (cf. Num. 35:9-15 with Num. 35:16-21). In the case of murder the nearest kinsman became **the avenger of blood,** killing the guilty party. But if a **person** killed another **accidentally** he was provided a place of asylum in one of six **cities of refuge.** However, he had to hurry to the nearest shelter without delay. According to Jewish tradition the roads leading to these cities were kept in excellent condition and the crossroads were well marked with signposts reading, "Refuge! Refuge!" Runners were also stationed along the way to guide the fugitives.

**20:4-6.** Having arrived at the **gate** of a refuge city, the manslayer was to present **his case** (breathlessly!) to **the elders of that city** who formed an ancient court of law (cf. Job 29:7; Deut. 21:19; 22:15). A provisional decision would then be made to grant him asylum till a **trial** could be held in the presence of **the assembly.** If acquitted of premeditated murder he was returned to the city of refuge where he lived till **the high priest** died, after which the manslayer was free to return to his **home.** That could be many years later. Involuntary manslaughter was therefore something to be carefully avoided. Many have puzzled over the meaning of the high priest's **death** in relation to the change in the status of the manslayer. The best explanation may be that the change in priestly administration served as a statute of limitations ending the fugitive's exile in the **city** of refuge.

**20:7-9.** The six designated cities were located on both sides of the Jordan River. On the west side were **Kedesh in Galilee . . . of Naphtali, Shechem in . . . Ephraim,** and **Hebron in . . . Judah.** The cities **on the east side** were **Bezer** in the south in **Reuben, Ramoth in** the region of **Gilead in the tribe of Gad,** and

**Golan in** the northern territory of **Bashan** in Manasseh's **tribe.**

But why is there no record in the Old Testament of a single instance in which this merciful provision of deliverance was utilized? Some critics suggest that these cities were not part of the Mosaic legislation but that this provision was instituted after the Exile. Yet the postexilic books likewise do not refer to their use, so other critics have suggested that the cities were not occupied till the time of Christ. In the face of such shifting arguments it is better to recognize the historicity of these accounts and to explain the silence of the record by the obvious fact that the scriptural authors were selective about what they recorded. Once the provision was made, it was apparently not important to document specific cases of its use.

Israel's benefit of sanctuary reminds believers of Psalm 46:1, "God is our refuge and strength, an ever present help in trouble," and of Romans 8:1, "Therefore, there is now no condemnation for those who are in Christ Jesus." The writer of the Epistle to the Hebrews may have had the Old Testament cities of refuge in mind when he wrote that believers may have great encouragement because they "have fled to take hold of the hope offered to" them (Heb. 6:18). The cities of refuge, then, seem to typify Christ to whom sinners, pursued by the avenging Law which decrees judgment and death, may flee for refuge. Paul's frequent expression "in Christ" speaks of the safety and security possessed by every believer.

3. THE APPOINTMENT OF LEVITICAL CITIES (21:1-42)

**21:1-3.** The last and crowning act of distribution was now described. The leaders of the tribe of Levi stepped forward and laid claim to the **towns** which had been promised to them by **Moses** (cf. Num. 35:1-8). These 48 towns **with pasturelands,** including the 6 towns of refuge, were now assigned to **the Levites.**

**21:4-7.** The distribution is described according to the three main branches of the tribe of Levi corresponding to Levi's three sons—**Kohath . . . Gershon,** and **Merari** (see the chart "Moses' Ancestry from Abraham," near Ex. 6:18).

**21:8-19. Thirteen** towns for the Kohathites were listed first. **Nine** were in the tribes of **Judah** and **Simeon,** including **Hebron (a city of refuge)** and **four** in the **tribe of Benjamin.** These 13 were **for the priests,** Aaron's **descendants.**

**21:20-26.** **Ten** more cities, including **Shechem (a city of refuge),** were assigned the other branches of the Kohathites in **Ephraim . . . Dan,** and western **Manasseh.** Thus the priestly cities fell ultimately within the Southern Kingdom of Judah where the temple would be built in its capital city, Jerusalem.

**21:27-33.** The 13 **Levite** cities **of the Gershonites** were located in eastern **Manasseh . . . Issachar . . . Asher,** and **Naphtali.** Two cities of refuge were included here, **Golan in Bashan** and **Kedesh in Galilee.**

**21:34-40.** The **Merarite** descendants of Levi received **12** cities in **Zebulun** and in the Transjordanian tribes of **Reuben** and **Gad,** including **Ramoth,** a city of refuge **in Gilead.** So 10 of the 48 Levite cities were east of the Jordan—2 in the half-tribe of Manasseh (v. 27), and 4 each in Reuben (vv. 36-37) and Gad (vv. 38-39).

This scattering of the tribe of Levi among the other tribes fulfilled Jacob's curse on Levi as well as Simeon (Gen. 49:5, 7) for their senseless murder of the Shechemites (Gen. 34). In the case of Levi's descendants God overruled to preserve their tribal identity and make them a blessing to all Israel. He did this because the Levites stood with Moses at a time of acute crisis (Ex. 32:26) and because Phinehas (a Levite and Eleazar's son) vindicated God's righteous name in the plains of Moab (Num. 25).

**21:41-42.** But at the time of the assignment many of the Levites' **towns** were under Canaanite control and had to be conquered. Apparently the **Levites** did not always succeed and the other tribes did not offer to help. This would appear to be the simplest explanation for the lack of complete correlation between the list of Levitical cities here and the list in 1 Chronicles 6:54-81. (See the chart on Levite towns on p. 599.)

The potential for good in the dispersion of Levites among the other tribes was almost unlimited. Moses, in his final blessing of the tribes, said of Levi, "He teaches Your precepts to Jacob and Your Law to Israel" (Deut. 33:10). The solemn responsibility and high privilege of the Levites was to instruct Israel in the Law of the Lord, to maintain the knowledge of His Word among the people. Especially in the north and east the Levites ought to have been barriers against the idolatry of Tyre and Sidon, as well as against the heathen practices of the desert tribes.

Someone has estimated that no one in Israel lived more than 10 miles from 1 of the 48 Levite towns. Thus every Israelite had nearby a man well-versed in the Law of Moses who could give advice and counsel on the many problems of religious, family, and political life. And it was essential that Israel obey the Word of God in all areas of life because without this their prosperity would cease and their privileges would be forfeited. But the final word is a sad one. The Levites did not live up to their potential; they did not fulfill their mission. If they had, idolatry and its corrupting influence might never have spread over the land of Israel.

4. SUMMARY OF THE CONQUEST AND DISTRIBUTION (21:43-45)

**21:43-45.** Here the long section describing the allocation of territories and towns ends. The historian looked back to the beginning and summarized the Conquest and division of the land with emphasis on the faithfulness of God. God had kept His promise to give Israel **the land. . . . rest on every side,** and victory over **their enemies.** In fact the Lord faithfully performed every part of His obligation; **not one of** His **promises . . . failed.** This did not mean that every corner of the land was in Israel's possession, for God Himself had told Israel they would conquer the land gradually (Deut. 7:22). Neither do these concluding statements ignore the tragedies that would develop during the period of the Judges, but those would be Israel's fault, not God's. Yet the unfaithfulness of Israel in no way impugned the faithfulness of God. Paul affirmed this fact in his words to Timothy, "If we are faithless, He will remain faithful, for He cannot disown Himself" (2 Tim. 2:13).

Some theologians have insisted that the statement in Joshua 21:43 means that the land promise of the Abrahamic Covenant was fulfilled then. But this cannot be true because later the Bible gives additional predictions about Israel possessing the land after the time of Joshua (e.g.,

Amos 9:14-15). Joshua 21:43, therefore, refers to the extent of the land as outlined in Numbers 34 and not to the ultimate extent as it will be in the messianic kingdom (Gen. 15:18-21). Also though Israel possessed the land at this time it was later dispossessed, whereas the Abrahamic Covenant promised Israel that she would possess the land forever (Gen. 17:8).

## IV. Conclusion (chaps. 22–24)

### A. A border dispute (chap. 22)

A rash and impetuous judgment when the Eastern tribes returned to their own inheritances threatened to bring the newly settled communities into a disastrous civil war. It was a dangerous and potentially explosive situation. The enemy lurked nearby, no doubt eagerly hoping that just such a divisive conflict would take place so they could regain their lost territories. But in God's providence the tragedy was averted and Israel learned some valuable and important lessons.

1. THE ADMONITION OF JOSHUA (22:1-8)

**22:1-4.** The Eastern tribes of Reuben, Gad, and **the half-tribe of Manasseh** had performed well. Called before their general, they were commended for keeping their word to God, **Moses,** and Joshua, by fighting alongside their **brothers** in all the struggles of the conquest of Canaan (cf. Num. 32; Josh. 1:16-18; 4:12-14). For seven long years these men were separated from their wives and families but now the battles were over, the land was divided, and it was time to go home. So Joshua dismissed those soldiers with honor.

**22:5-8.** As the weary but happy soldiers left, they took with them a substantial portion of spoils from the enemy, with instructions from Joshua to share **the plunder** with their **brothers** who had remained at home (v. 8). Extensive **wealth** was acquired by the soldiers, including **herds,** metals, and **clothing.** But why should those who had not endured any of the pain and peril of the conflict enjoy any of the spoils? Possibly many of the men who remained behind would have preferred to go to war, but who then would have raised the crops and protected the women and children? The principle was firmly established that hon-

ors and rewards do not go only to those who carry arms but also to those who stay home to perform the commonplace duties (1 Sam. 30:24).

The returning soldiers also left with six solemn exhortations by Joshua ringing in their ears: (a) **be very careful to keep the commandment and the Law,** (b) **love the LORD your God,** (c) **walk in all His ways,** (d) **obey His commands,** (e) **hold fast to Him, and** (f) **serve Him with all your heart and all your soul.** This charge, short but passionate, called for obedience, love, fellowship, and service. Their military obligations were fulfilled, but Joshua reminded them of their abiding spiritual commitments which were conditions for God's continued blessing. Like an anxious parent who sees a son or daughter leave home for a place where the young person would be separated from spiritual influences, Joshua delivered his earnest charge to the departing warriors. He was perhaps fearful that their separation from the rest of the tribes might cause them to drift away from worshiping the Lord and to embrace idolatry.

2. THE SYMBOLIC ACTION OF THE EASTERN TRIBES (22:9-11)

**22:9-11.** Leaving **Shiloh,** the armies of the Eastern tribes headed excitedly for home. As they approached the **Jordan** River their minds were probably flooded with memories of the miraculous crossing seven years before, of the remarkable victory over nearby Jericho, and of the other triumphs shared with their brothers from whom they had so recently separated. A sense of isolation from the other tribes began to sweep over them. But this was not simply because an ordinary river would separate the Eastern from the Western tribes, for the Jordan is not an ordinary river. Mountains on each side rise to heights above 2,000 feet and the Jordan Valley nestled in between is in effect a great trench 5 to 13 miles wide. During a part of the year the intense heat greatly discourages travelers. This then was a very pronounced river boundary and may have contributed to the fear of these tribesmen that they and their brethren would permanently drift apart. After all, "out of sight" is often "out of mind." What then could be done to keep alive the ties of comradeship forged by those long years of united struggles? What could be done to symbolize the unity between the people on both sides of the river, to remind everyone that they were all the children of the promise?

The answer suggesting itself to the minds of those soldiers was that they should build a huge **altar,** one that could be seen from a great distance, **an imposing altar** that would witness their right to the original altar at the tabernacle. So they erected such an altar **on the Israelite (western) side** of the Jordan River. Why did they not build some other kind of monument? Because they knew that the true basis of their unity was their common worship centered in the sacrifices at the altar.

3. THE THREAT OF WAR (22:12-20)

**22:12.** But the symbol of unity was misconstrued as a symbol of apostasy. When word reached the other tribes they **gathered at Shiloh,** the site of the one true altar (1 Sam. 4:3), prepared **to go to war against** the armies of the Eastern tribes. On the basis of what they had heard (Josh. 22:11) the Israelites concluded that this was rebellion against God, that the others had set up a second altar of sacrifice contrary to the Mosaic Law (Lev. 17:8-9).

"They thought the holiness of God was being threatened. So these men, who were sick of war said, 'The holiness of God demands no compromise.' I would to God that the church of the 20th century would learn this lesson. The holiness of the God who exists demands that there be no compromise in the area of truth" (Francis A. Schaeffer, *Joshua and the Flow of Biblical History,* p. 175).

**22:13-14.** Faced with apparent compromise and disobedience of God's commands the Israelites called for a war of judgment against their brothers. And though one must admire their zeal for truth and their jealousy for purity of worship, it is good that wisdom prevailed over rashness. A decision was made to begin by vigorously remonstrating with the two and one-half tribes in the hope that they would abandon their project. War could thereby be avoided. Eleazar's son **Phinehas,** noted for his righteous zeal for the Lord (Num. 25:6-18), headed a deputation of **10** tribal rulers whose responsibility was to confront the others.

**22:15-20.** Arriving at the scene of the new altar the appointed group charged the Eastern tribesmen with turning **away from the LORD** (vv. 16, 18) and being **in rebellion against Him** (v. 16; cf. vv. 18-19). They reminded the easterners that **the sin of Peor** brought God's judgment on the whole nation (Num. 25), as did the sin of **Achan** (Josh. 22:20; cf. chap. 7). Now the entire congregation was in jeopardy again because of their daring act of rebellion. Such a sin would bring God's anger on the entire nation (22:18; cf. v. 20). Finally it was magnanimously suggested that if those in the two and one-half tribes felt the **land** east of Jordan was **defiled,** that is, not hallowed by God's presence, the Western tribes would make room for them on their side of Jordan. This was a generous, loving offer potentially involving great cost.

4. THE DEFENSE OF THE EASTERN TRIBES (22:21-29)

The Israelite delegation was about to learn how false her rash judgments and stern denunciations had been. The facts behind erecting the great altar by Jordan now came to light.

**22:21-23.** Instead of responding to the fierce reproof in anger, the Eastern tribes in candor and sincerity solemnly repudiated the charge that the altar they erected was in rebellion against God. Invoking **God** as a witness they swore twice by His three names—El, Elohim, Yahweh (**the Mighty One, God, the LORD**), affirming that **if** their act was **in rebellion** against God and His commands concerning worship they deserved His judgment.

**22:24-25.** Why then was the second altar built? They earnestly explained that it was occasioned by the geographic separation of their people and the effect this might have on future generations.

**22:26-29.** The Eastern tribesmen made it clear that they were fully aware of God's laws governing Israel's **worship;** their recently erected **altar** was **not** intended as a place **for burnt offerings and sacrifices** (cf. v. 23) **but as a witness** to all **generations** that the Transjordanian tribes had a right to cross the Jordan and worship at Shiloh. This **altar** was only a copy of the true worship center and an evidence of their right to frequent that one. While their concern for the spiritual welfare of future generations was admirable, it would appear that the action of the two and one-half tribes was unnecessary. God had ordained in the Law that all Israelite males were to appear at the sanctuary three times a year (Ex. 23:17). This, if heeded, would preserve the unity of all the tribes both spiritually and politically. Furthermore, the building of another altar was also a dangerous precedent. John J. Davis comments, "The unifying factor in ancient Israel was not her culture, architecture, economy, or even military objectives. The long-range unifying factor was her worship of Jehovah. When the central sanctuary was abandoned as the true place of worship, the tribes then developed independent sanctuaries, thus alienating themselves from other tribes and weakening their military potential. The effects of this trend are fully seen in the period of the Judges" (Conquest and Crisis, p. 87).

5. THE RECONCILIATION OF THE TRIBES (22:30-34)

**22:30-34.** There was a happy ending to this grave crisis. The explanation of the representatives of the Eastern tribes was fully accepted by **Phinehas** and his delegation as well as by the other tribes when report was made to them. In fact the nine and one-half tribes on the west of the Jordan **were glad . . . and praised God.** In concluding the whole matter **Phinehas** expressed deep gratitude that no sin had been committed and that the wrath of God was not incurred.

In a book describing the occupation and distribution of the Promised Land why should this single incident be treated in such detail? Simply because it illustrates certain principles that were vital to Israel living together in the land harmoniously and under God's full blessing. The same principles apply to those in God's family today:

1. It is commendable for believers to be zealous for the purity of the faith. Compromise of truth is always costly.

2. It is wrong to judge people's motives on the basis of circumstantial evidence. It is important to get all the facts, remembering that there are always two sides to every dispute.

3. Frank and open discussion will often clear the air and lead to reconciliation. But such a confrontation should be approached in a spirit of gentleness, not arrogance (Gal. 6:1).

4. A person who is wrongly accused does well to remember the wise counsel of Solomon, "A gentle answer turns away wrath, but a harsh word stirs up anger" (Prov. 15:11).

## B. The last days of Joshua (23:1–24:28)

The Book of Joshua ends with the old soldier saying farewell. His parting addresses were tinged with sadness, as are nearly everyone's last words. They expressed the deep concern of Joshua who observed a growing complacency on the part of Israel toward the remnants of the Canaanites, an easy acceptance of joint occupancy of the land which was to have been exclusively theirs. With Israel's enemies practically vanquished, Joshua knew well the danger of the people's "letting down." Before his departure from active leadership he felt compelled to warn them that continued obedience to God's commands was essential to continued enjoyment of His blessing. Though some have suggested that these final chapters contain two reports of the same event, it seems better to view chapter 23 as Joshua's challenge to Israel's leaders, and chapter 24 as his charge to the people.

1. JOSHUA'S FINAL CHALLENGE TO THE LEADERS (CHAP. 23)

a. The first round (23:1-8)

**23:1-2.** Some 10 or 20 years after the end of the Conquest and distribution of the land **Joshua . . . summoned** Israel's **leaders,** probably to Shiloh where the tabernacle was located, to warn them earnestly of the dangers of departing from Yahweh. It was a solemn meeting. No doubt Caleb was there, along with Eleazer the priest, and the soldiers of the Conquest who had exchanged their swords for plowshares and were now heads of families, **elders,** and **judges.**

They had come without hesitation in response to Joshua's call to hear the last words of their great chief. And the **old** veteran spoke on one theme—God's unfailing faithfulness to **Israel** and their corresponding responsibility to be faithful to Him. Three times he repeated his central message (vv. 3-8, 9-13, 14-16). Three times, fearful they would not hear and heed, he emphasized the faithfulness of

God and the responsibility of **Israel.**

**23:3-5.** Avoiding any temptation to elevate himself Joshua reminded the leaders of Israel that their enemies had been defeated solely because **the LORD their God** had **fought for** them. The battles were the Lord's, not his. A psalmist reiterated this affirmation (Ps. 44:3). As for the Canaanites, who still lingered about the country, **the LORD . . . God** would **push them out** also so that Israel could **take possession of** the **land** they partially occupied.

**23:6-8.** Turning to impress the Israelites with their responsibility, Joshua passed on the very words Yahweh had armed him with when He instructed him to cross the Jordan: **Be . . . strong; be careful to obey** (cf. 1:6-9). Courage and obedience were the graces that led to the successful Conquest of Canaan and they were no less essential now (cf. 22:5). Specifically Joshua dreaded Israel's conformity to the heathen **nations** around them so he forbade all contact and fraternization, knowing that his people would backslide step by step till in the course of their decline they would prostrate themselves before the shrines of the pagan deities (cf. 23:16). Instead he exhorted them **to hold fast to the LORD** (cf. 22:5).

*b. The second round (23:9-13)*

**23:9-13.** Returning to his theme Joshua again affirmed God's past faithfulness to Israel. Yahweh fought their battles for them (cf. v. 3), and though some of the Canaanites still remained in the land, wherever an enemy had been encountered he had been overcome.

Israel was then solemnly exhorted, on the basis of divine interventions on their behalf, **to love . . . God** (cf. 22:5). This would require diligence and watchfulness because of the near presence of their corrupt neighbors. The temptation would be strong to forsake Yahweh and cleave to the people of Canaan, even intermarrying **with them,** a fateful decision and one fraught with peril to Israel. This danger was graphically described by Joshua in terms of the dire results that would follow. First, **God** would **no longer drive out these nations** but they would remain to mar Israel's inheritance. Second, the Canaanites among them would be like **snares and traps** to entangle

them, **whips** to lash them, and **thorns** that fly back into their faces stabbing their **eyes.** Third, miseries and troubles would increase for Israel until they would be dispossessed of their **good land** (cf. 23:15-16.).

Joshua did not contemplate any possibility of neutrality as he posed the choice to be made. They would either go with Israel's God or the people of Canaan. So it is today. There is no middle course. "No one can serve two masters" (Matt. 6:24; cf. Matt. 12:30).

*c. The third round (23:14-16)*

**23:14-16.** Like a masterful preacher, Joshua restated his discourse, this time emphasizing that he was a dying man, hoping that this would make his words sink more deeply into their hearts. Once more he spoke of God's punctilious faithfulness to every promise (cf. **good promises** in 21:45); once more he warned of the doom caused by disobedience. Joshua's deep anxiety was about the nations that were left in the land. As the old soldier looked into the future he foresaw Israel's sinful compromise with them and the tragic fate that would inevitably overtake the people of God. God's **anger** would **burn against** them, and they would **perish from the** land (cf. **good land** in 23:13, 15-16).

The terrible climax of this message to the nation's leaders emphasized the fact that Israel's greatest danger was not military—it was moral and spiritual. If Joshua were alive today the strong likelihood is that he would say the same thing to this nation.

2. JOSHUA'S FINAL CHARGE TO THE PEOPLE (24:1-28)

Joshua's last meeting with the people took place at Shechem. Whether this second gathering occurred soon after the previous one, whether it was held on an anniversary of the earlier, or whether it was after a long interval cannot be determined.

The geographical setting is of interest. Shechem, a few miles northwest of Shiloh, was where Abraham first received the promise that God would give his seed the land of Canaan. Abraham responded by building an altar to demonstrate his faith in the one true God (Gen. 12:6-7). Jacob too stopped at Shechem on his return from Paddan Aram and buried there the idols his family had brought with them (Gen. 35:4). After the Israelites completed the first phase of the conquest of Canaan they journeyed to Shechem where Joshua built an altar to Yahweh, inscribed the Law of God on stone pillars, and reviewed these laws for all the people (Josh. 8:30-35). Joshua had good reason, therefore, to convene the Israelites at this location. Certainly the stones on which the Law had been written were still standing, vivid reminders of that significant event. From this moment on, that beautiful valley between Mount Ebal and Mount Gerizim would be associated with this poignant farewell scene as their honored leader spoke to them for the last time.

The literary form of this discourse has occasioned much interest and comment. It is now rather well known that the rulers of the Hittite Empire in this period (ca. 1450–1200 B.C.) established international agreements with their vassal states obligating them to serve the Hittite kings in faithfulness and obedience. These suzerainty (overlordship) treaties followed a regular pattern and required periodic renewal. Joshua 24 contains, in the standard suzerainty treaty form of that time, a covenant-renewal document in which the people of Israel were called on to confirm their covenant relationship with God (cf. "Structure" in *Introduction to Deut.*). The parts of the covenant renewal, like a suzerainty treaty, included a preamble (vv. 1-2a), a historical prologue (vv. 2b-13), the stipulations for the vassals with the consequences of disobedience (vv. 14-24), and the writing of the agreement (vv. 25-28). The Mosaic Covenant established at Sinai was not an everlasting covenant; hence it needed to be renewed in every generation. That renewal was now transacted in a formal and impressive ceremony.

### a. Reviewing their blessings (24:1-13)

**24:1-13.** God was identified as the Author of the covenant and **Israel** as **the people** (vv. 1-2a). Following this preamble is the historical prologue (vv. 2b-13) in which Yahweh reviewed His past blessings on His subjects. He brought them out of Ur of the Chaldees (vv. 2b-4), **out of Egypt** (vv. 5-7), and into Canaan (vv. 8-13). Some have said **the hornet** (v.

12; Ex. 23:28; Deut. 7:20) refers to Egyptian armies that may have attacked Canaan before the Conquest. Others say the hornet refers figuratively to the panic experienced by the people of Canaan on hearing of what God had done for Israel (cf. Deut. 2:25; Josh. 2:10, 24; 5:1). Still others suggest that this referred to literal hornets.

It was God who spoke in this recapitulation of Israel's history; 18 times the personal pronoun "I" is used: **I took . . . I gave . . . I assigned . . . I sent . . . I afflicted . . . I brought . . . I delivered,** etc. Like a Hittite king reviewing the benevolent acts he had performed for his vassal subjects, God reviewed the marvelous deeds He had performed for Israel's benefit. Any greatness Israel achieved was not by her effort but through God's grace and enablement. From first to last Israel's conquests, deliverances, and prosperity were because of God's good mercies and were not of their own making.

### b. Rehearsing their responsibilities (24:14-24)

**24:14-15.** The stipulations of the covenant renewal were then stated: Israel must **fear the LORD and serve Him.** In the Hittite treaties all other foreign alliances were to be rejected; so in this covenant Israel was to reject alliances with all foreign gods. Joshua boldly challenged them to **choose** between **the gods** of Ur their ancestors **worshiped** (cf. v. 2) **beyond the River** (i.e., the Euphrates), **the gods of the Amorites** in Canaan, and Yahweh. Then, adding example to exhortation, Israel's venerated leader assured them that whatever their choice his mind was made up, his course clear: **as for me and my household, we will serve the LORD.**

**24:16-18.** **The people** responded with alacrity, moved by the force of Joshua's arguments and the magnetism of his example. They despised the very thought of forsaking the **God** who had delivered them **out of Egypt . . . that land of slavery . . . protected** them in the wilderness, and brought them into the land of promise. "Perish the thought that we should ever be guilty of such ingratitude," was their instant reply. They promised that they too would **serve the LORD.**

**24:19-21.** Joshua spoke again. He

was not at all satisfied with their burst of enthusiasm. Did he detect some traces of insincerity? Had he hoped that the people would bring forth their idols for destruction as Jacob's family had done here some centuries before? (Gen. 35:4; Josh. 24:14, 23) There was no such response so Joshua bluntly declared, **You are not able to serve the LORD. He is a holy God; He is a jealous God. He will not forgive your rebellion and your sins.** Of course Joshua did not mean that God was not a God of forgiveness. He meant that God was not to be worshiped or served lightly, and that to **forsake** Him deliberately to **serve** idols would be a presumptuous, willful, high-handed sin for which there was no forgiveness under the Law (Num. 15:30). Such sin would result in **disaster.** Once more **the people** responded to Joshua's probing words, earnestly reaffirming their purpose to **serve** Yahweh.

**24:22-24.** Joshua spoke a third time, pointedly challenging them to serve as **witnesses against** themselves if they did turn aside from God. And the people immediately replied **Yes, we are witnesses.**

Joshua then spoke a fourth and final time, coming again to the point he had mentioned at the beginning. **Now then . . . throw away the foreign gods that are among you** (cf. v. 14). He had heard the pledge on their lips; now he challenged them to prove their sincerity by their works. Knowing that many of them were secretly practicing idolatry Joshua forthrightly demanded that they remove their foreign gods. Without the slightest hesitation the people shouted, **We will serve the LORD our God and obey Him.** They said they would be obedient servants of God, not slaves of Egypt or of other gods. (The words "serve," "served," and "serving" occur 13 times in vv. 14-24.)

There could be no mixing of allegiance to God with idol-worship. A firm choice had to be made then as in every generation. People must choose between expediency and principle, between this world and eternity, between God and idols (cf. 1 Thes. 1:9).

### c. The reminders of their pledge (24:25-28)

**24:25-26a.** Realizing that further words would be fruitless, and semi-satisfied with the genuineness and sincerity of the people's consecration, **Joshua** solemnly renewed the **covenant.** He wrote down their agreement **in the Book of the Law of God,** which was probably placed beside the ark of the covenant (cf. Deut. 31:24-27). Among the Hittites likewise the suzerainty treaty was placed in the sanctuary of the vassal state.

**24:26b-27.** As a final reminder Joshua also apparently inscribed the statutes of the covenant on **a large stone** slab which was **set up** beneath **the oak** at this sacred location. Archeologists excavating the site of Shechem have uncovered a great limestone pillar which may be identified with the memorial referred to here. Joshua **said** this **stone** was **a witness,** as if it had **heard all the** transactions of the covenant.

**24:28.** Thus leading **the people** of Israel in a sacred ritual of covenant renewal by which they pledged to fear and follow the Lord God, **Joshua** completed his last public act. With the memories of this solemn occasion indelibly impressed on their minds the Israelites returned to their homes in possession of their **inheritance.**

### C. The appendix (24:29-33)

**24:29-31.** Three burials—each of them in Ephraim—mark the close of the Book of Joshua. First it is recorded that **Joshua . . . died at the** advanced **age of 110** years **and** was **buried** in **his** own town (cf. 19:50). No greater tribute could be paid to him than the fact that he was called simply **the servant of the LORD.** He aspired to no greater rank than this.

**24:32.** The burial of **Joseph's bones** is also recorded. His dying request was that he be buried in the Promised Land (Gen. 50:25). Moses, knowing of this request, took Joseph's bones with him in the Exodus (Ex. 13:19). Now after the long years of the wanderings and the Conquest, Joseph's remains, which had been embalmed in Egypt (Gen. 50:26) more than 400 years earlier, were now laid to rest in **Shechem** (cf. Gen. 33:18-20).

**24:33.** The third burial mentioned is that of the high priest **Eleazar, son** and successor **of Aaron.** It was his privilege to be associated with Joshua in the distribution of the land (Num. 34:17; Josh. 14:1; 19:51) and to direct the ministry of tabernacle worship in the crucial years of the Conquest and settlement of Canaan.

Recording three burials is a strange way to end a book like Joshua! But these three peaceful graves testify to the faithfulness of God, for Joshua, Joseph, and Eleazar once lived in a foreign nation where they received God's promise to take His people back to Canaan. Now all three were at rest within the Promised Land. God kept His word to Joshua, Joseph, and Eleazar—and to all Israel. And this encourages God's children today to count on God's unfailing faithfulness.

# BIBLIOGRAPHY

Blaikie, William G. *The Book of Joshua*. The Expositor's Bible. New York: Hodder & Stoughton, n.d. Reprint. Minneapolis: Klock & Klock Christian Publishers, 1978.

Bush, George. *Notes on Joshua*. New York: Newman & Ivison, 1852. Reprint. Minneapolis: James & Klock Publishing Co., 1976.

Campbell, Donald K. *No Time for Neutrality*. Wheaton, Ill.: Scripture Press Publications, Victor Books, 1981.

Cohen, A. *Joshua and Judges*. London: Soncino Press, 1950.

Davis, John J. *Conquest and Crisis*. Grand Rapids: Baker Book House, 1969.

Garstang, John. *Joshua–Judges*. London: Constable & Co., 1931. Reprint. Grand Rapids: Kregel Publications, 1978.

Jensen, Irving L. *Joshua: Rest-Land Won*. Everyman's Bible Commentary. Chicago: Moody Press, 1966.

Kaufmann, Yehezkel. *The Biblical Account of the Conquest of Palestine*. Jerusalem: Magnes Press, 1953.

Miller, J. Maxwell, and Tucker, Gene M. *The Book of Joshua*. The Cambridge Bible Commentary. Cambridge: Cambridge University Press, 1974.

Pink, Arthur W. *Gleanings in Joshua*. Chicago: Moody Press, 1964.

Redpath, Alan. *Victorious Christian Living*. Westwood, N.J.: Fleming H. Revell Co., 1955.

Schaeffer, Francis A. *Joshua and the Flow of Biblical History*. Downers Grove, Ill.: Inter-Varsity Press, 1975.

Woudstra, Martin H. *The Book of Joshua*. The New International Commentary on the Old Testament. Grand Rapids: Wm. B. Eerdmans Publishing Co., 1981.

# JUDGES

## F. Duane Lindsey

## INTRODUCTION

**Title and Place in the Canon.** The English title "The Book of Judges" can be traced back through the Latin (*Liber Judicum*) and the Greek Septuagint (*Kritai*, "Judges") to the Hebrew *šōp̄eṭîm* ("judges"). The title is appropriate as long as the English concept of legal arbitration is expanded to general administrative authority including military deliverance from Israel's enemies.

In the English Bible the Book of Judges is found in those books popularly classified as "the historical books." In the Hebrew Bible it is placed in the division of "the Prophets" (preceded by "the Law" and followed by "the Writings"), specifically "the former Prophets" containing Joshua, Judges, Samuel, and Kings.

**Authorship and Date of Writing.** Internal evidence in the Book of Judges suggests that it was written during the early days of the monarchy—after the coronation of Saul (1051 B.C.) but before the conquest of Jerusalem by David (1004 B.C.). The following three facts support this suggestion: (1) The stylistic motto—"in those days Israel had no king"—repeated toward the end of the book (17:6; 18:1; 19:1; 21:25) looks backward from a period when Israel did have a king. (2) The statement about Jerusalem that "to this day the Jebusites live there" (1:21) is most clearly explained as written before David's conquest of the city (cf. 2 Sam. 5:6-7). (3) The reference to Canaanites in Gezer suggests a date before the time the Egyptians gave that city to Solomon's Egyptian wife as a wedding present (cf. 1 Kings 9:16).

Though there is no internal evidence identifying the author of Judges, the Talmud (Tractate *Baba Bathra* 14b) ascribes to Samuel the Books of Judges, Ruth, and Samuel. Though difficult to substantiate, identifying Samuel as the author of Judges harmonizes with the internal evidence mentioned above and the known fact that Samuel was a writer (1 Sam. 10:25). Judges thus appears to have been written between about 1040 and 1020 B.C. Earlier sources, both written and oral, were no doubt used by the inspired author who chronicled this theologically selective history of Israel from the death of Joshua to the rise of the monarchy.

**Chronology of the Period of the Judges.** Scholars agree that the period of the Judges began with the death of Joshua and ended with the coronation of Saul and the beginning of the monarchy. But scholars differ on how much time elapsed between these two events. Since most scholars agree that the monarchy began under Saul in 1051 B.C., the debate centers on the date of Joshua's death. The problem concerns particularly the date of the Exodus under Moses which many conservative scholars place at 1446 B.C. while most liberal scholars maintain a later date (ca. 1280/60 B.C.). The conservative argument rests on the literal use of the numbers recorded in 1 Kings 6:1 and Judges 11:26. (See the *Introduction* to the Book of Ex. for a discussion of the date of the Exodus.) Scholars who follow the later date of the Exodus consequently date the period of the Judges from about 1220 to 1050 B.C., whereas many who accept the early date of the Exodus say the period of the Judges began about 1390–1350 B.C. and ended about 1050 B.C.

The evidence for beginning the period of the Judges about 1350 B.C. is strong (cf. Eugene H. Merrill, "Paul's Use of 'About 450 Years' in Acts 13:20," *Bibliotheca Sacra* 138. July-September 1981:249-50). The elders who outlived Joshua (Josh. 24:31; Jud. 2:7) would have been no more than 20 years of age in 1444 B.C. when the spies entered the land (Num. 13:2; 14:29), two years after the

Exodus. If they lived to about the age of 110 (Joshua's age at his death; Josh. 24:29), the oldest of them would have died about 1354 B.C. (Having been born in 1464 B.C. or later, and living no more than 110 years of age would date their deaths at 1354 B.C.) The idolatry leading to the first oppression (that by Cushan-Rishathaim, Jud. 3:8) seems to have begun *after* these elders died (2:7).

The next datable event recorded in Judges was the occupation of Gilead by the Ammonites. Jephthah said this took place 300 years (11:26) after the Israelite occupation of Transjordan (ca. 1406 B.C.). Thus 1106 B.C. marked either the beginning of Jephthah's judgeship (probably) or the beginning of the Ammonite invasion 18 years earlier (possibly). The dates of the judgeship of Samson (ca. 1105–1085 B.C.) and the leadership of Eli (ca. 1144–1104 B.C.), and Samuel (ca. 1104–1020 B.C.), can be reconstructed fairly accurately (with Samson's and Samuel's years overlapping) from the rather certain dates of Saul's reign (Merrill, pp. 250-2).

Insufficient evidence is available to support clearly any of the conflicting proposals regarding the *exact* dates for most of the other judges. Contrast, for example, the dates set forth by J. Barton Payne, "Chronology of the Old Testament," *Zondervan Pictorial Encyclopedia of the Bible*. Grand Rapids: Wm. B. Eerdmans Publishing Co., 1975, 1:829-45; Merrill F. Unger, *Archaelogy and the Old Testament*. Grand Rapids: Zondervan Publishing House, 1954, pp. 158-87; John C. Whitcomb, Jr., "Chart of Old Testament Patriarchs and Judges," Study-Graph, 3rd rev. ed. Chicago: Moody Press, 1968; and Leon J. Wood, *Distressing Days of the Judges*, pp. 10-21, 303-4, 341-2, 409-11.

Adding the length of the rule of each judge with its preceding oppression comes to 410 years (if the Philistine oppression and the judging by Samson are reckoned independently), a period too extended to fit the time between Joshua and Saul. Therefore scholars agree that the periods of some oppressions and judgeships overlapped. Such an overlapping of judges is to be expected since many (if not all) of the judges probably ruled in geographically limited portions of Israel.

**Historical and Theological Setting.** *Historically* the Book of Judges is the sequel to the Book of Joshua. The two books are linked together by the repeated record of Joshua's death (Jud. 2:6-9; cf. Josh. 24:29-31). Joshua's military achievements "broke the back" of the Canaanite military coalition throughout the land (Josh. 11:16-23) but left large areas yet to be possessed by the individual tribes (Josh. 13:1; Jud. 1:2-36). Canaanite enclaves raised their heads time and again during the period of the Judges (4:2). The book not only looks back to Joshua's victories but also looks forward to the establishment of the monarchy in Israel (cf. 17:6; 18:1; 19:1; 21:25; also cf. 8:23 with 1 Sam. 8:7; 12:12).

*Theologically* the period of the Judges formed a transition between Yahweh's mediatorial activity through Moses and Joshua and His mediatorial rule through the anointed kings of the monarchy. During the period of the Judges, Yahweh raised up His chosen deliverers whom He anointed with His Spirit to rescue His people Israel from their enemies. It seems ironic that Yahweh had previously given His people into the hands of these enemies as punishment for their sins (cf. comments on Jud. 3:1-6).

**The Function of the Judges.** The Hebrew word *šōpēṭ* ("judge, deliverer") has a wider connotation than the English word "judge." It was a general term for leadership combining the executive (including military) and judicial aspects of governing. Thus the judges of Israel were primarily military and civil leaders, with strictly judicial functions included as appropriate (cf. 4:5).

**Purpose and Theme.** The purpose of the Book of Judges was to demonstrate divine judgment on Israel's apostasy. More particularly the book recorded Israel's disobedience to Yahweh's kingship as mediated through her sovereignly appointed and Spirit-empowered leaders, and the subsequent need for a centralized hereditary kingship as the means through which Yahweh would continue to exercise His kingship over the nation Israel. Israel's disobedience to Yahweh and her worship of Canaanite gods resulted in her failure to experience divine blessing and the full conquest of her ene-

## The Judges of Israel

| Oppressors | Years of Oppression | Judges | Years of Judging | References |
|---|---|---|---|---|
| Arameans | 8 | 1. Othniel | 40 | Judges 3:7-11 |
| Moabites | 18 | 2. Ehud | 80 | Judges 3:12-30 |
| Philistines | ? | 3. Shamgar | ? | Judges 3:31 |
| Canaanites | 20 | 4. Deborah | 40 | Judges 4–5 |
| Midianites | 7 | 5. Gideon* | 40 | Judges 6–8 |
| ? | ? | 6. Tola | 23 | Judges 10:1-2 |
| ? | ? | 7. Jair | 22 | Judges 10:3-5 |
| Ammonites | 18 | 8. Jephthah | 6 | Judges 10:6–12:7 |
| ? | ? | 9. Ibzan | 7 | Judges 12:8-10 |
| ? | ? | 10. Elon | 10 | Judges 12:11-12 |
| ? | ? | 11. Abdon | 8 | Judges 12:13-15 |
| Philistines | 40 | 12. Samson | 20 | Judges 13–16 |

*Abimelech, Gideon's son (Jud. 9), though often considered a judge, is not included here because he usurped authority over Shechem and God did not appoint him as judge.

mies (cf. 3:1-6). The Canaanite influence in moral and social areas led to Israelite apostasy and anarchy, demonstrating the need for a centralized hereditary monarchy in Israel.

# OUTLINE

I. Prologue: Causes Introducing the Days of the Judges (1:1–2:5)
  A. The political-military background—the partial conquest of Canaan by Israel (chap. 1)
    1. The success of Judah and Simeon in conquering southern Canaan (1:1-20)
    2. The failure of Benjamin to displace the Jebusites (1:21)
    3. The partial success of the house of Joseph in occupying central Canaan (1:22-29)
    4. The failure of Israelite tribes in northern Canaan (1:30-33)
    5. The confinement of Dan to the hill country by the Amorites (1:34-36)
  B. The religious-spiritual background—the covenant of the Lord broken by Israel (2:1-5)
    1. The pronouncement by the Angel of the Lord (2:1-3)
    2. The response by the people of Israel (2:4-5)
II. Documentary: Cases Exhibiting the Deeds of the Judges (2:6–16:31)
  A. The introduction to the history of the judges (2:6–3:6)
    1. A summary of the passing of Joshua (2:6-10)
    2. The pattern of the period of the Judges (2:11-19)
    3. The results of the broken covenant (2:20-23)
    4. The identification of the remaining nations (3:1-6)
  B. The description of the oppressions and deliverances (3:7–16:31)
    1. The deliverance by Othniel from the oppression of Cushan-Rishathaim (3:7-11)
    2. The deliverance by Ehud from the oppression of Eglon (3:12-30)
    3. The deliverance by Shamgar from the oppression of the Philistines (3:31)
    4. The deliverance by Deborah and Barak from the oppression of the Canaanites (chaps. 4–5)

5. The deliverance by Gideon from the oppression of the Midianites (6:1–8:32)
6. The judgeships of Tola and Jair following the usurpation of Abimelech (8:33–10:5)
7. The deliverance by Jephthah from the oppression of the Ammonites (10:6–12:7)
8. The judgeships of Ibzan, Elon, and Abdon (12:8-15)
9. The deliverance by Samson from the oppression of the Philistines (chaps. 13–16)

III. Epilogue: Conditions Illustrating the Days of the Judges (chaps. 17–21)
A. Religious apostasy: The idolatry of Micah and the migration of the Danites (chaps. 17–18)
1. The idolatry of Micah the Ephraimite (chap. 17)
2. The migration of the Danites to the north (chap. 18)
B. Moral degradation: The atrocity of Gibeah and the war with the Benjamites (chaps. 19–21)
1. The atrocity against the concubine of the Levite (chap. 19)
2. The war against the tribe of Benjamin (chap. 20)
3. The preservation of the tribe of Benjamin (21:1-24)
4. The characteristics of the period of the Judges (21:25)

# COMMENTARY

## I. Prologue: Causes Introducing the Days of the Judges (1:1–2:5)

The actual account of the heroic deeds of the judges is preceded by what amounts to two introductory sections (1:1–2:5 and 2:6–3:6). The second of these two sections, forming a theological analysis of the era of the Judges, is more properly the literary introduction to the rest of the book. However, it is preceded by a background introduction which treats both political-military features (the partial conquest of Canaan by Israel) and religious-spiritual factors (the broken covenant with Yahweh by Israel).

A major problem of interpretation which arises in this background section (1:1–2:5) is that of its chronological relationship to the death of Joshua. This

great leader's death (previously recorded in Josh. 24:29-31) is again narrated in summary fashion in Judges 2:6-10, especially verses 8-9. Judges 2:10 and following obviously refer to events experienced by the new generation which came to maturity after the death of Joshua. But how do the events of Judges 1:1–2:5 relate to Joshua's death? The book opens with the apparently unambiguous statement, "After the death of Joshua" (1:1), followed by a seeming sequence of events concerning the tribal occupation of Canaan. But if these events followed Joshua's death, why is Joshua's death narrated in 2:8?

Three answers are given to these questions. Some scholars regard all the events of 1:1–2:5 as taking place after Joshua's death, with the second introduction which begins in 2:6 providing a further recapitulation of his death. According to this view apparent parallels between Judges 1 and the Book of Joshua actually refer to two different series of events—the initial military achievements by the army of Israel under the leadership of Joshua, and the subsequent tribal possession of individual areas allotted by Joshua for actual occupation. This view faces many problems including the fact that when all the tribes of Israel were assembled by Joshua (Josh. 24:1), the tribes gathered from their allocated inheritances (Josh. 24:28), thus indicating that at least a significant degree of tribal occupation had already occurred (Josh. 15:13-19).

A second view regards at least Judges 1:11-15 (events associated with the conquest of Debir by Othniel) as parallel with Joshua 15:16-19. According to this view, the narrative in Judges 1 begins after the death of Joshua but changes (perhaps at v. 10) to the pluperfect tense (the tense distinction is a contextual decision in Heb.), and should read, for example, "they had advanced" (v. 10). Though this view is possible, it seems to disrupt the apparent sequence noted throughout the chapter.

A third view recognizes the opening phrase of the book ("After the death of Joshua") as a heading for the Book of Judges as a whole, with the actual events following Joshua's death not being narrated till after the record of that death in 2:8. This view poses fewer chronological

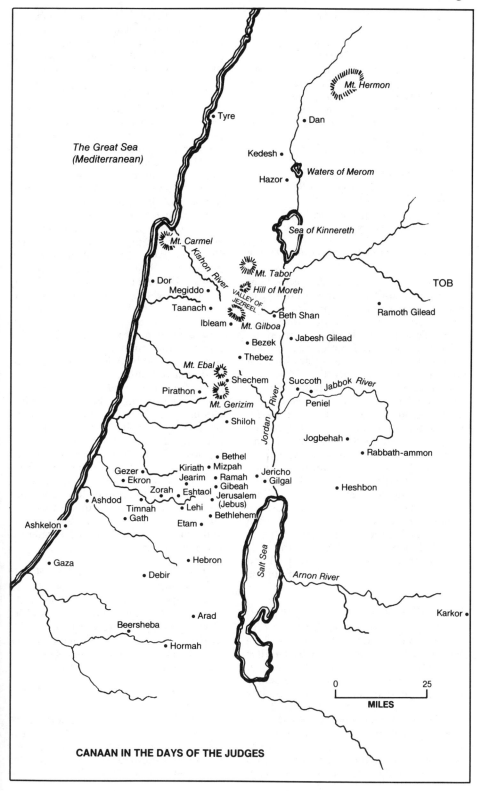

The Great Sea
(Mediterranean)

Tyre

Mt. Hermon

Dan

Kedesh

Hazor

Waters of Merom

Sea of Kinnereth

Mt. Carmel

Kishon River

Mt. Tabor

Dor

Hill of Moreh

Megiddo

VALLEY OF
JEZREEL

TOB

Taanach

Beth Shan

Ramoth Gilead

Ibleam

Mt. Gilboa

Jabesh Gilead

Bezek

Thebez

Mt. Ebal

Shechem

Succoth

Jabbok River

Pirathon

Peniel

Mt. Gerizim

Jordan River

Shiloh

Jogbehah

Rabbath-ammon

Bethel

Kiriath    Mizpah

Gezer

Jearim    Ramah

Jericho

Ekron

Gibeah

Gilgal

Zorah

Eshtaol

Jerusalem

Heshbon

Ashdod

Timnah

Lehi

(Jebus)

Gath

Etam

Bethlehem

Ashkelon

Salt Sea

Gaza

Hebron

Debir

Arnon River

Arad

Karkor

Beersheba

Hormah

0        25

MILES

**CANAAN IN THE DAYS OF THE JUDGES**

problems, and it does justice to the flow of thought in chapter 1.

Whichever view is taken, it is clear that the tribal wars of occupation (chap. 1) occurred after the national wars of conquest under Joshua and his allotment of the tribal territories. Tribal possession of these territories surely began before Joshua's death, whether the record of Judges 1 refers to this phase of occupation or to a later phase of occupation after his death.

## A. The political-military background— the partial conquest of Canaan by Israel (chap. 1)

1. THE SUCCESS OF JUDAH AND SIMEON IN CONQUERING SOUTHERN CANAAN (1:1-20)

### a. The divine affirmation of Judah's primacy (1:1-2)

**1:1-2.** The Israelites' desire to **fight . . . the Canaanites** was in harmony with Joshua's command for them to occupy their allotted tribal territories (Josh. 18:3; 23:5). Though **the land** was given by God, and conquered under and divided by **Joshua,** it was still necessary for each tribe to fight to displace the Canaanites yet remaining. The method whereby they **asked** and **the LORD answered** is not specified, but probably involved the ministry of the high priest at the tabernacle, whether by use of the Urim and Thummim (cf. Ex. 28:30; Num. 27:21; 1 Sam. 14:37-43) or by a verbal form of divine guidance. God's selection of **Judah** (the names of the sons of Jacob throughout this chapter refer to tribal entities) for military preeminence corresponds with Judah's divine elevation in Jacob's patriarchal blessing (Gen. 49:8). On the location of the 12 tribes see the map "Land Allotted to Israel's Tribes" near Joshua 14.

### b. The Judean agreement with Simeon (1:3)

**1:3.** The tribal military alliance of **Judah** and Simeon was a logical one since the **allotted** inheritance of **the Simeonites** was within the southern boundaries of the tribe of Judah (Josh. 19:1-9). Also Judah and Simeon had a natural bond as offspring of Jacob and Leah (Gen. 29:33-35). Their common enemy was **the Canaanites,** probably used here as a generic term for all the inhabitants of Canaan in the area west of the Jordan River. In a more restricted sense, the term "Canaan-

ites" sometimes refers to the inhabitants of the coastal plain and the valleys, whereas the inhabitants of the hill country are sometimes designated as Amorites (Num. 13:29; cf. Jud. 1:34-36; 3:5).

### c. The God-given victory at Bezek (1:4-7)

**1:4-7.** The LORD **gave** victory to **Judah** as they fought **the Canaanites and Perizzites.** The latter group may have been an indigenous people distinct from the Canaanites. Or the term may be social rather than ethnic, referring to "villagers." Judah defeated **10,000 men at Bezek,** probably the same Bezek (modern Khirbet Ibziq) in Manasseh south of Mount Gilboa where Saul mustered his army to attack the Ammonites at Jabesh Gilead (1 Sam. 11:8-11). **Adoni-Bezek** is probably a title meaning "prince of Bezek." However, some scholars identify the name with Adoni-Zedek, a king of Jerusalem (Josh. 10:1, 3). The barbarous act by which the Israelites **cut off his thumbs and big toes** was neither commanded nor commended by God; yet it was recognized by **Adoni-Bezek** as an act of divine retribution since he had done the same thing to **70 kings** (apparently over a long period of time). Though barbarous by modern standards, this act was pragmatic since the loss of the thumbs made it difficult to hold a weapon, and the loss of the big toes hindered one's footing in combat. Since the major function of a king was to lead in battle (cf. 2 Sam. 11:1), this mutilation apparently disqualified him from further royal office. His own people took him to the important Canaanite city-state of **Jerusalem** to live out his days.

### d. The successful attack on Jerusalem (1:8)

**1:8.** Judah's initial success in destroying **Jerusalem** may refer only to the unfortified southwest hill (modern Mount Zion). In any case, **Judah** failed to displace the Jebusites permanently (cf. Josh. 15:63), and the Benjamites were not any more successful (Jud. 1:21).

### e. The Judean conquest in the South and the West (1:9-20)

(1) A summary of the conquest. **1:9.** The region of Canaan south of Jerusalem, corresponding with the tribal allotment of **Judah** (including Simeon), is divided geographically into **the hill country** (the

central mountain range straddling the ridge route from Jerusalem to Hebron), **the Negev** (the semiarid transitional region running east and west from Beersheba), **and the western foothills** (lit., "the Shephelah"), lying between the hill country and the coastal plain (which is not mentioned till vv. 18-19).

(2) The conquest of Hebron. **1:10.** The former name of **Hebron** (meaning "confederacy") was **Kiriath Arba** (meaning "city of four," possibly suggesting an early confederacy of four cities), though some have identified it with Arba, the father of Anak, who may have founded the city (cf. Josh. 14:15; 15:13; 21:11; Jud. 1:20). Hebron is located about 19 miles south by southwest of Jerusalem in a valley lying about 2,800 feet above sea level. Hebron was well known to Abraham (Gen. 13:18) and would later become the Judean capital for the first seven and one-half years of David's reign (2 Sam. 5:5). The populous clans of **Sheshai, Ahiman, and Talmai,** who were descended from Anak (cf. Jud. 1:20; Josh. 15:14) and were indigenous to the south hill country (Num. 13:22, 28; Josh. 11:21-22), were **defeated** by the men of Judah in or near Hebron. Either on this or a previous occasion, Caleb was the leader in defeating Hebron (Jud. 1:20; cf. Josh. 15:14).

(3) The conquest of Debir. **1:11-15.** The strategic royal Canaanite city of **Debir** (cf. Josh. 10:38; 12:13) was at one time identified by scholars with Tell Beit Mirsim, about 11 miles west by southwest of Hebron, but has been more recently identified as Khirbet Rabud, eight miles southwest of Hebron. It is not known why its former name was **Kiriath Sepher** (meaning "city of writing"). **Caleb** had been promised Hebron by Moses because he was one of the two faithful spies who came back from Canaan (Num. 14:24; Josh. 14:6-15; Jud. 1:20). Debir seems also to have been allotted to Caleb, but after conquering Hebron, he enlisted other leaders for the attack on Debir. He did this by offering his **daughter Acsah in marriage to the man who** would undertake the capture of Debir. **Othniel,** Caleb's **younger brother** (or "nephew" if "younger brother" refers to **Kenaz**), captured the city and hopefully the heart of Acsah.

If Kenaz was the personal name of

Othniel's father, he may have had the same mother as Caleb, whose father was "Jephunneh the Kenizzite" (Num. 32:12). Or "son of Kenaz" may mean "Kenizzite" (an Edomite clan associated with the tribe of Judah; cf. Gen. 36:11). Caleb and Othniel would still have been natural Judahites if their mother was of the tribe of Judah. Othniel's reward was the waiver of the customary gift to the bride's family. **Acsah** urged **Othniel** to seek **a field** from **Caleb,** and she herself requested **springs of water** as a bridal blessing (**special favor**) from her father. His abundant response was the gift of **the upper and lower springs.** It is noteworthy that the water supply system at Khirbet Rabud depended solely in the dry season on the upper and lower wells of 'Alaqa about two miles north of the site.

(4) The dwelling place of the Kenites. **1:16.** The Kenites were a nomadic people associated with the Amalekites (cf. 1 Sam. 15:6) and Midianites (cf. Ex. 18:1 with Jud. 1:16). **Moses' father-in-law,** Jethro, was a priest of Midian (Ex. 18:1). **The City of Palms** was the Jericho oasis (Deut. 34:3; Jud. 3:13). **The people of the Desert of Judah** may have been Amalekites. **Arad** (cf. Num. 21:1-3) is Tell Arad, 16 miles south of Hebron though some scholars identify the ancient Canaanite Arad with Tel el-Milḥ, another eight miles to the southwest.

(5) The conquest of Hormah. **1:17.** The Judahites joined **the Simeonites** (cf. v. 3) in attacking one of their allotted cities, **Zephath** (cf. Josh. 19:4), believed to be Tel Masos/Khirbet el-Meshash, about seven miles east of Beersheba. It had been taken earlier (Num. 21:2-3) but now **they totally destroyed the city.** "Totally destroyed" translates the Hebrew *ḥāram,* indicating a holy war in which a city and its occupants were totally "devoted" to destruction (cf. comments on Josh. 6:21). This was reflected in the name given the city—**Hormah** (meaning "devotion or "destruction").

(6) The victory over coastal cities. **1:18.** The cities of **Gaza, Ashkelon, and Ekron** (later associated with Ashdod and Gath in the Philistine pentapolis) were located on the coastal plain. That **Judah . . . took** these cities is contradicted by the Septuagint's "did not take," a translation perhaps influenced by the state-

ment in verse 19 that "they were unable to drive the people from the plains." But this does not negate Judah's initial victory over the cities; it only means that the **men of** Judah were unable to displace the inhabitants and occupy the cities.

(7) The restricted occupation of conquered cities. **1:19.** As **Judah . . . took possession of the hill country,** the LORD **was with** them (cf. v. 22). The stated reason for their inability to **drive the people from the plains** was not the Lord's absence but the enemies' **iron chariots,** introduced by the Philistines about 1200 B.C. But the author later records God's rebuke (2:2-3) which linked nondisplacement of the land's peoples to Israel's disobeying the Mosaic Covenant.

(8) The allotment of Hebron to Caleb. **1:20.** This summary statement relates the defeat of **Hebron** (v. 10) to the occupation of that city by **Caleb,** as **promised** by **Moses** (cf. Num. 14:24; Deut. 1:36; Josh. 14:9; 15:13). Caleb was apparently the leader of the men of Judah in the defeat of the three families **of Anak** (Jud. 1:10, 20).

2. THE FAILURE OF BENJAMIN TO DISPLACE THE JEBUSITES (1:21)

**1:21. Jerusalem** was located on the boundary between Judah and Benjamin. Following Judah's partial and/or temporary victory at Jerusalem (v. 8), **the Jebusites,** who could not be dislodged by **the Benjamites,** continued to dwell on the fortified southeast hill until the time of David (2 Sam. 5:6-9). **The Jebusites** were the Canaanite inhabitants of the city also known as Jebus (Jud. 19:10-11).

3. THE PARTIAL SUCCESS OF THE HOUSE OF JOSEPH IN OCCUPYING CENTRAL CANAAN (1:22-29)

*a. The success of the whole house of Joseph in conquering Bethel (1:22-26)*

**1:22-26.** The key to the victory of **the house of Joseph** (i.e., Ephraim and Manasseh; cf. Gen. 48) over the city of Bethel was that **the LORD was with them** (cf. Jud. 1:19). Their faith in Yahweh and obedience to His covenant stipulations for occupying Canaan brought victory from Him. Yet their failure to displace the Canaanites from other cities mentioned in verses 27-29 demonstrated a growing condition of disobedience and a lack of faith (cf. 2:1-5). **Bethel** ("house of

God"), a city rich in Israelite history (e.g., Gen. 12:8; 28:10-22; 35:1-15), was situated on the border between Ephraim and Benjamin in the central highlands 10 or 12 miles north of Jerusalem. It was strategically located on the north-south trade route, and was a junction for traffic from the Mediterranean seacoast on the west and from the Jordan Valley via Jericho on the east. Bethel has commonly been identified with modern Beitin about 12 miles north of Jerusalem, though some evidence favors el-Bireh 2 miles farther south (cf. David Livingston, "Location of Biblical Bethel and Ai Reconsidered," *Westminster Theological Journal* 33. November 1970:20-44; and "Traditional Site of Bethel Questioned," *Westminster Theological Journal* 34. November 1971:39-50).

When **the spies** who were sent to reconnoiter Bethel were unable to discover any hidden entrance to **the city,** they promised safety to an occupant who revealed the needed access. After the defeat of the city, this man took his family to northern Syria (i.e., **the land of the Hittites;** cf. Josh. 1:4), perhaps his ancestral home, where he established **a city** called **Luz,** named after the ancient name of Bethel (Jud. 1:23).

*b. The failure of Manasseh in occupying southern Jezreel (1:27-28)*

**1:27-28.** The determination of **the Canaanites** to remain in key cities guarding the Jezreel Valley was stronger than the faith of the tribe of **Manasseh** to displace them. Israel's eventual compromise to put the Canaanites to **forced labor** (cf. vv. 30, 33, 35) demonstrated the incomplete obedience that was characteristic of several tribes, as stated in the remainder of chapter 1. The cities are not listed in exact geographical sequence, which would be (from east to west) **Beth Shan,** strategically located east of the Harod Valley; **Ibleam . . . Taanach,** and **Megiddo,** guarding key entrances into the Jezreel Valley; and **Dor,** located on the coast south of Mount Carmel.

*c. The failure of Ephraim in displacing the Canaanites from Gezer (1:29)*

**1:29. Gezer** was strategically located on Ephraim's southwest border at the entrance to the Aijalon Valley. It guarded the crossroads of the eastern branch of the coastal highway and the major west-to-east route through the Aijalon Valley to Jerusalem or Bethel. Like Manasseh farther north, **Ephraim** allowed **the Canaanites . . . to live there among them** (cf. vv. 27-28).

4. THE FAILURE OF ISRAELITE TRIBES IN NORTHERN CANAAN (1:30-33)

*a. Zebulun's failure to displace the Canaanites (1:30)*

**1:30.** The incomplete obedience of **Zebulun** resembled that of Manasseh and Ephraim for they merely subjected **the Canaanites** of **Kitron** and **Nahalol to forced labor.** These unidentified cities may have been located on the northwestern edge of the Valley of Jezreel.

*b. Asher's failure to displace the Canaanites (1:31-32)*

**1:31-32.** The greater disobedience of **Asher** is evident in that **the people of Asher lived among the Canaanite inhabitants of the land** rather than merely putting to forced labor those whom they allowed to live among them, as Manasseh and Zebulun had done (cf. vv. 28, 30). The Canaanite cities listed in verse 31 were located in the area later known as Phoenicia.

*c. Naphtali's failure to displace the Canaanites (1:33)*

**1:33.** The tribe of **Naphtali** likewise **lived among the Canaanite inhabitants of the land,** though they did make **forced laborers** (cf. vv. 29-30, 35) of **those living in Beth Shemesh** and **Beth Anath.** Sites in both Upper and Lower Galilee have been suggested for these cities.

5. THE CONFINEMENT OF DAN TO THE HILL COUNTRY BY THE AMORITES (1:34-36)

**1:34-36. The Amorites** (cf. comments on v. 3) did not allow **the Danites . . . to come down into the plain** even though the Danites eventually put them to **forced labor** in the cities of the Shephelah. That the Amorites basically confined the Danites **to the hill country** eventually led to the migration of the Danites to Laish north of the Sea of Galilee (cf. chap. 18), for the reduced territory of Dan extended little more than four miles from **Aijalon** on the west, at the entrance to the hill country, to Dan's border with Benjamin on the east.

*B. The religious-spiritual background— the covenant of the Lord broken by Israel (2:1-5)*

1. THE PRONOUNCEMENT BY THE ANGEL OF THE LORD (2:1-3)

**2:1a. The Angel of the LORD** (Heb., *Yahweh*) **went up from Gilgal to Bokim.** The Angel of the Lord was not merely "an angel"; He was a theophany—an appearance of the second Person of the Trinity in visible and bodily form before the Incarnation. Prominent during the time of Moses (Ex. 3:2-15; Num. 22:22-35) and Joshua (Josh. 5:13-15), this divine manifestation also appeared during the period of the Judges to Gideon (Jud. 6:11-24) and to the parents of Samson (13:3-21). The Angel of the Lord was Deity for He was called Yahweh (e.g., Josh. 5:13-15; Jud. 6:11-24; Zech. 3) and God (e.g., Gen. 32:24-32; Ex. 3:4), and had divine attributes and prerogatives (cf. Gen. 16:13; 18:25; 48:16). Yet this Messenger of the Lord was also distinct from Yahweh, thus indicating a plurality of Persons within the Godhead (cf. Num. 20:16; Zech. 1:12-13). New Testament allusions suggest that the Angel of the Lord in the Old Testament was Jesus Christ (cf. John 12:41; 1 Cor. 10:4; John 8:56; Heb. 11:26).

"Gilgal" was where the Israelites first camped after they crossed the Jordan. There they were circumcised and dedicated to covenant faith and obedience (Josh. 5:2-12). Gilgal was near Jericho, and perhaps should be identified with Khirbet al-Mafjar about one and one-half miles northeast of Old Testament Jericho. The "oak of weeping" near Bethel (Gen. 35:8, NIV marg.) has been suggested as a possible site for "Bokim" ("weepers"), but that location remains uncertain.

**2:1b-2.** The Angel of the Lord obviously spoke as Yahweh Himself, for He used the covenantal formula to refer to His redemptive mercies in the Exodus and the gracious establishment of the Mosaic **Covenant** (cf. Ex. 19:4; 20:2; Josh. 24:2-13). He rehearsed the divine prohibition to the Israelites regarding Canaanite alliances (**you shall not make a covenant with the people of this land**) and idolatry (**you shall break down their altars;** cf. Ex. 23:32-33; 34:12-16; Num. 33:55; Deut. 7:2, 5, 16; 12:3). Then the Angel, speaking as Yahweh, affirmed the fact of Israel's disobedience (cf. the covenant with the Gibeonites, Josh. 9; and the continuance of the Canaanites in forced labor, Jud. 1:28, 30, 33, 35). God emphasized Israel's disobedience with a question designed to stir their consciences: **Why have you done this?** (cf. NEB, "Look what you have done!")

**2:3.** As a result of Israel's disobedience, the divine aid by which Israel would have driven out the Canaanites was withheld (cf. 2:20–3:6). Intermarriage with the Canaanites led to tolerance of and even participation in their idolatry. The form of their disobedience which incurred divine wrath became in turn the form of the punishment placed on them. The **snare** of Canaanite idolatry anticipated the cycles in the days of the Judges.

2. THE RESPONSE BY THE PEOPLE OF ISRAEL (2:4-5)

**2:4-5.** The weeping of the **Israelites** left little more than the place name (**Bokim,** "weeping") for it apparently did not express true repentance since the people did not turn permanently from their disobedience. The **sacrifices** offered **to the LORD** at Bokim seem to have been only an external ritual rather than an expression of true faith.

## II. Documentary: Cases Exhibiting the Deeds of the Judges (2:6–16:31)

A. *The introduction to the history of the judges (2:6–3:6)*

This section further answers the question, Why were some Gentile nations left in the land? Whereas 1:1–2:5 forms a historical introduction to the book, this section is a literary introduction to the judges' deeds, telling the repeating cycles of history that formed the pattern during the rules of the Judges.

1. A SUMMARY OF THE PASSING OF JOSHUA (2:6-10)

Judges 2:6-9 corresponds with Joshua 24:29-31, thus linking together the close of the book of Conquest under Joshua and the book which records the deeds of the judges.

a. *Israel's obedient years before and after Joshua's death (2:6-7)*

**2:6-7.** Joshua's dismissing of Israel (cf. Josh. 24:28) apparently followed the covenant renewal ceremony at Shechem, described in Joshua 24:1-27. From Shechem each tribe was to return to its **own inheritance** to complete the occupation of the land, to eliminate the local inhabitants, and to destroy the pagan altars. In general this was accomplished as **the people served the LORD** for the period of time embracing **the lifetime of Joshua and of the elders who outlived him** (cf. Josh. 24:31). This service was a faithful response to **all the great things the LORD had done for Israel** in the Exodus from Egypt, the wilderness wanderings, and the initial Conquest of the land.

b. *Joshua's obituary (2:8-9)*

**2:8-9.** In contrast with Moses (cf. Josh. 1:1-9; Num. 27:12-23), **Joshua** died without appointing a successor, thus setting the stage for the period of the Judges. Joshua's epitaph, identifying him as **the servant of the LORD,** linked him with other theocratic servant-rulers (Moses, Josh. 1:1; the kings, 2 Sam. 3:18; 2 Chron. 32:16; and the promised Messiah, Isa. 52:13; 53:11). **At the age of 110,** Joshua **died** and was **buried** at **Timnath Heres** (also known as Timnath Serah, Josh. 19:50; 24:30), traditionally identified with Tibneh about 18 miles north by northwest of Jerusalem.

c. *The rise of a new faithless generation (2:10)*

**2:10.** The new **generation** of Israelites that **grew up** after their faithful fathers died was distinguished by its faithlessness toward the Lord. That they **knew neither the LORD nor what He had done for Israel** could imply a failure of the older generation to communicate God's acts to them (cf. Deut. 6:7). But the word "knew" probably has the sense of "acknowledge" (cf. Prov. 3:6, where "know" is trans. "acknowledge"), thus indicating unbelief rather than ignorance. They rejected both the Lord's grace toward them and their responsibilities toward Him. This led to the idolatrous practices cited in the verses that follow.

2. THE PATTERN OF THE PERIOD OF THE JUDGES (2:11-19)

A history of over three centuries is synthesized in these verses. The author directs attention to a recurring sequence of events in the period of the Judges (illustrated most clearly in the narrative about Othniel in 3:7-11): (a) the *sin* or rebellion of Israel through idolatry or apostasy (2:11-13, 17; 3:7, 12; 4:1; 6:1; 10:6; 13:1), (b) the *servitude* of Israel to foreign peoples due to retribution from the Lord (2:14-15; 3:8), (c) the *supplication* or repentance of Israel (3:9a; cf. 2:18), (d) the *salvation* (military deliverance) and restoration to favor by the Lord through a Spirit-empowered deliverer (judge, vv. 16-18; 3:9b-10), and (e) a period of *silence* when the people and the land had rest, that is, cessation of war (3:11). Before long, however, the pattern was repeated. Yet this was more than just a cycle; it was also a descending spiral (cf. 2:19).

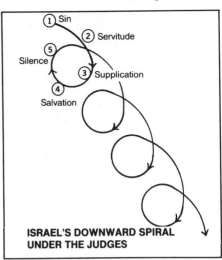

**ISRAEL'S DOWNWARD SPIRAL UNDER THE JUDGES**

*a. The sin or defection of the Israelites (2:11-13)*

**2:11-13.** Israel's sin is highlighted in terms of her forsaking **the Lord . . . who had brought them out of Egypt** and serving or worshiping the **various gods of the peoples around them** (v. 12), identified as **the Baals** (v. 11) or **Baal and the Ashtoreths** (v. 13). The word "baal," which can mean "lord" or "husband," corresponds with the analogy of idolatry as spiritual adultery (cf. v. 17). "Baal" was the Canaanite name for the Syrian god Hadad, god of storms and wars. The plural "Baals" (*bᵉʿālîm*) suggests the many local varieties of the worship of Baal (cf. Baal Peor, Num. 25:3; Baal Gad, Josh. 11:17; Baal-Berith, Jud. 9:4; Baal-Zebub, 2 Kings 1:2). In Canaan the goddess Ashtoreth was the consort of Baal, known in Syria as ʿAthtart and in Babylonia as Ishtar. (Cf. comments on a different goddess, Asherah, mentioned in Jud. 3:7.) Ashtoreth was the goddess of fertility. Baal worship involved the most debasing immorality imaginable.

*b. The defeat and distress of the Israelites (2:14-15)*

**2:14-15.** The Lord's (cf. v. 12) **anger** was His righteous response to Israel's sin and spiritual adultery. The vivid imagery of a slave dealer (**He sold them to their enemies**) indicates the severity of the divine displeasure the Lord manifested in chastening His people. These enemies were located **all around** Israel, as illustrated by the various **raiders who plun-** **dered them** during the days of the Judges. Israel's defeat at the hands of her enemies (v. 15; cf. Lev. 26:17; Deut. 28:25, 48) was the result of **the hand of the Lord** and in response to the previous warning which **He had sworn to them.** Psalm 106:34-42 is a poetic paraphrase of Judges 2:11-15. Because of her defeats in battle, Israel was **in great distress.**

*c. The deliverance by the judges (2:16-19)*

This introductory summary of Israel's "pattern" in the days of the Judges does not specifically mention the supplication of Israel by which "they cried out to the Lord" but this is a recurring part of the pattern in 3:9, 15; 4:3; 6:6-7; 10:10. The supplication may be implied in 2:18 in that "they groaned under those who oppressed and afflicted them."

**2:16.** This summary statement of deliverance attributes it to **judges** whom **the Lord raised up** to save Israel **out of the hands of these raiders.**

**2:17.** It is not clear whether verse 17 refers to continued idolatry even during the period of rest in each judge's lifetime, or whether it views the period of the Judges as a whole, referring to the renewed spiral of disobedience after each judge's demise. In either case, Israel's sin is evident—they **prostituted themselves to other gods** and **turned from the way . . . of obedience to the Lord's commands.** Since the practices of those who worshiped the Canaanite fertility gods involved sexual prostitution, the phrase "prostituted themselves" was literal as well as figurative.

**2:18-19.** Once God had **raised up a judge,** the deliverance from the enemy was effective during the rest of that judge's lifetime because **the LORD had compassion on** His people. **But when the judge died,** Israel reactivated her downward spiral of progressive deterioration by following **ways even more corrupt than** the immediately preceding corrupt generation. (The "fathers" of v. 17 seems to refer to the obedient generation of Joshua's day, while the **fathers** of v. 19 refers to the preceding generation.)

### 3. THE RESULTS OF THE BROKEN COVENANT (2:20-23)

**2:20-23.** This paragraph, along with the next one (which identifies the remaining enemy nations still in the land, 3:1-6), concludes the theological analysis of the period of the Judges. Whereas the pattern identified in 2:11-19 related to surrounding nations that came in and plundered various tribes of Israel, 2:20–3:6 refers to Canaanite peoples already in the land which Israel failed to displace because of lack of faith and obedience.

The LORD allowed the Canaanite nations **to remain** in the land for four reasons: (1) He chose to punish Israel for her apostasy in turning to idolatry (2:2, 20-21; cf. Josh. 23:1-13). In identifying themselves with the peoples of the land through marriage and subsequent idolatry (cf. Jud. 3:6), the Israelites **violated the covenant** that the Lord gave **their forefathers** (cf. Josh. 23:16). Therefore, as God had promised (Josh. 23:4, 13), He would **no longer drive out before them any of the nations Joshua left when he died.** (2) The Lord left the Canaanites in the land **to test** Israel's faithfulness to Himself (Jud. 2:22; 3:4). This provided each generation with an opportunity to **keep the way of the LORD** (cf. "the way of obedience," 2:17) or to continue in the rebellion of their immediate ancestors. (3) The Lord left the Canaanites in the land to give Israel experience in warfare (see comments on 3:2). (4) Another reason is stated in Deuteronomy 7:20-24—to prevent the land from becoming a wilderness before Israel's population increased sufficiently to occupy the whole land.

### 4. THE IDENTIFICATION OF THE REMAINING NATIONS (3:1-6)

**3:1-2.** The list of remaining **nations** is prefaced with two of the reasons the Lord allowed them to remain in the land—**to test** the **Israelites** (previously indicated in 2:22; cf. 3:4), and **to teach warfare to the descendants of the Israelites who had not had previous battle experience,** that is, experience in the kind of "holy warfare" conducted during Joshua's conquest of the land. Thus "warfare" is probably not just "how to fight" but how to fight successfully, depending on the Lord to give the victory.

**3:3.** This list and the list in verse 5 both mention the Canaanites and the Hivites. **The Canaanites** are those peoples mentioned in 1:27-33. **The Hivites** are thought to be the Horites who were previously associated with the Upper Mesopotamian kingdom of Mittanni. The Horites who were best known in Joshua's time were the Gibeonites, the occupants of a confederacy of city-states including Gibeon (Josh. 9:7, 17). The Hivite people listed here lived **in the Lebanon mountains from Mount Baal Hermon to Lebo Hamath** (probably modern Lebweh in the Beqaa Valley 14 miles northeast of Baalbek). **The Philistines,** organized as a pentapolis (a confederacy of five cities), inhabited the southern coastal cities of Ashdod, Ashkelon, Ekron, Gath, and Gaza. Because of the prominence of the city of Sidon at this time, the Canaanite people known as the Phoenicians were also called **the Sidonians.**

**3:4.** This is the third time the Lord's purpose, **to test the Israelites,** is mentioned (cf. 2:22; 3:1).

**3:5-6. The Israelites** descended three steps in their cultural accommodation to paganism: (a) they **lived among the Canaanites,** (b) they intermarried with them, and (c) they **served their gods.** Each step is a natural one leading on to the next. The resulting departure from the Lord has already been described several times in connection with their oppression by foreign raiders (2:11-19). (On the Canaanites and **Hivites,** see comments on 3:3; on the **Hittites,** see comments on 1:26; on the **Amorites,** see comments on 1:3; on the **Perizzites,** see comments on 1:4; and on the **Jebusites,** see comments on 1:21.)

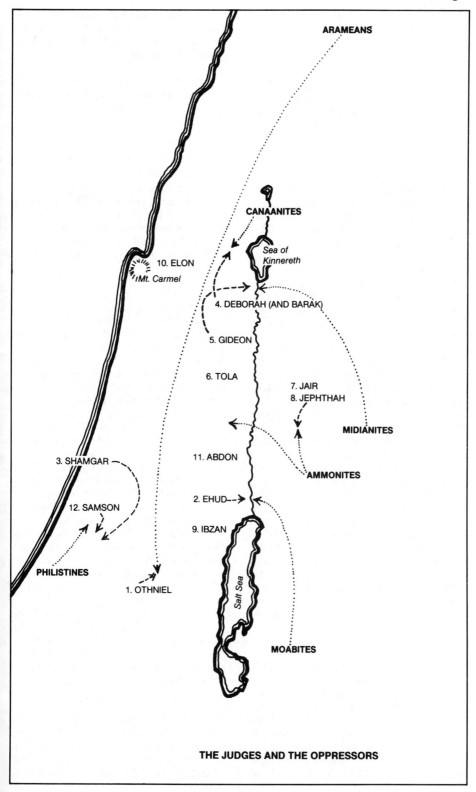

ARAMEANS

CANAANITES

Sea of
Kinnereth

10. ELON
!Mt. Carmel

4. DEBORAH (AND BARAK)

5. GIDEON

6. TOLA

7. JAIR
8. JEPHTHAH

MIDIANITES

3. SHAMGAR

11. ABDON

AMMONITES

12. SAMSON

2. EHUD

9. IBZAN

Salt Sea

PHILISTINES

1. OTHNIEL

MOABITES

**THE JUDGES AND THE OPPRESSORS**

## B. The description of the oppressions and deliverances (3:7–16:31)

### 1. THE DELIVERANCE BY OTHNIEL FROM THE OPPRESSION OF CUSHAN-RISHATHAIM (3:7-11)

This cameo description of Othniel's judgeship maximizes the literary structure and historical pattern of the heroic deeds of the judges while it minimizes the historical detail of this particular deliverance.

### a. The defection of Israel (3:7)

**3:7.** The episode begins with mention of Israel's idolatry. This was a deliberate act of putting Yahweh out of mind and choosing to serve **the Baals** (cf. 2:11) **and the Asherahs** (wooden pillars or images used as objects of idolatrous worship; cf. Ex. 34:13; Deut. 16:21; Jud. 6:25). Asherah was the goddess of the sea in Ugaritic literature in Syria; she was the consort of El. Asherah should not be confused with Ashtoreth, the consort of Baal, in 2:13.

### b. The distress under the Arameans (3:8)

**3:8. Cushan-Rishathaim** is a name meaning "Cushan of Double Wickedness." **Aram Naharaim** is literally "Syria of the Two Rivers," referring to Upper Mesopotamia. Since it seems strange for such a distant nation to plunder Israel, especially in the area of Judah where Othniel lived, some scholars have regarded "Aram" as an alteration of "Edom" (a slight difference in one Hebrew letter), which was located appropriately close to Judah in the south. However, it would not have been unusual for an ambitious **king** in Mesopotamia to invade Canaanite territory, especially at a time when Egypt to the southwest (which had nominal control over Canaan) was weak. In this case, Cushan subjected **the Israelites . . . for eight years.**

### c. The deliverance by Othniel (3:9-10)

**3:9-10.** In response to Israel's supplication (**they cried out to the LORD**), Yahweh **raised up . . . Othniel** as **a deliverer** who, when **the Spirit of the LORD came upon him** (cf. 6:34; 11:29; 13:25; 14:6, 19; 15:14), **became Israel's judge and went to war.** Othniel had already been introduced (1:11-15) as **Caleb's younger brother** (cf. Josh. 15:13-19). As the Lord

sold the Israelites "into the hands of" the oppressing Arameans (Jud. 3:8), so also He gave the enemy **king . . . into the hands of Othniel.**

### d. The duration of peace (3:11)

**3:11.** Thus **peace** was secured **for 40 years,** the remainder of the life of **Othniel.**

### 2. THE DELIVERANCE BY EHUD FROM THE OPPRESSION OF EGLON (3:12-30)

### a. The defection of Israel (3:12a)

**3:12a.** The downward spiral began as **once again the Israelites did evil in the eyes of the LORD** (cf. v. 7). This evil was obviously their disobedience to the Mosaic Covenant, forsaking Yahweh to worship other gods (cf. 2:17, 19).

### b. The distress under the Moabites (3:12b-14)

**3:12b-14.** Once again the sovereign control of God over human affairs is noted in that He **gave Eglon king of Moab power over Israel.** The Moabites were descendants of Lot by his older daughter's incestuous relationship with him (Gen. 19:30-38). They lived in the land east of the Dead Sea between the Arnon and Zered Rivers. They occupied the territory of Reuben to about 25 miles north of the Arnon, and then followed Joshua's route of entrance into the land and captured the Jericho oasis (**the City of Palms**). Israelites had apparently reoccupied Jericho but without refortifying it with city walls because of the curse on whoever did this (cf. Josh. 6:26).

The Moabites were aided in this conflict by **the Ammonites and Amalekites.** The Ammonites were the northeastern neighbors of the Moabites and were related to them as the descendants of Lot by his younger daughter (Gen. 19:38). The Amalekites were bitter enemies of Israel (cf. Ex. 17:8-13; Deut. 25:17-19) who lived a nomadic life in the land south of Beersheba. **The Israelites** (i.e., the Benjamites and perhaps some Ephraimites) **were subject to Eglon** for **18 years.**

### c. The deliverance by Ehud (3:15-29)

**3:15a.** Following the Israelites' supplication, **the LORD . . . gave them a deliverer—Ehud, a left-handed man.** The term "left-handed" is literally "one bound in the right hand." Left-handed-ness does not seem to have handicapped the Benjamites. In fact, they had 700 lefties who were excellent at slinging stones (cf. 20:16). In Ehud's case, being left-handed would provide an opportunity for a daring deed.

**3:15b-19a.** Since **the Israelites sent** Ehud **with** the **tribute** (probably consisting of domestic animals as well as gold or silver and other precious commodities), he was probably a recognized leader in Benjamin. He had personally **made a double-edged sword** (probably a dagger without a hilt) which was short enough (about 18 inches long) to be **strapped to his right thigh under** his long outer garment. After presenting the **tribute to Eglon . . . who was a very fat man** (cf. v. 22), **Ehud** dismissed his attendants who **carried** the heavy tribute, but immediately **turned back** at Gilgal to seek further audience with **King** Eglon. **The idols near Gilgal** were a well-known landmark, whether "idols" means "sculptured stones" (RSV) or "graven images" (ASV marg.). Possibly the reference is to the memorial of 12 stones which Joshua's men had taken from the Jordan River (Josh. 4:1-7).

**3:19b-22.** Ehud intrigued **the king** with the offer of **a secret message,** and so gained private access to Eglon in **the upper room of his summer palace.** Stating **I have a message from God for you,** Ehud plunged his hitherto concealed dagger **into the king's belly** so deeply that **the fat closed in over it.** The concealment of the dagger was accomplished by its unexpected location on Ehud's **right thigh,** from which he deftly grabbed it **with his left hand.**

**3:23-26.** Ehud's escape was well planned. To gain time he **locked** the **doors** of the king's **upper room,** and left undetected, or at least unhindered. His necessary time for escape was gained because the king's **servants** delayed outside his locked door, figuring that the king was **relieving himself** (lit., "covering his feet," a euphemism for body elimination; cf. 1 Sam. 24:3). When they realized they must be mistaken, they finally **unlocked** the **doors** and discovered their slain king. Meanwhile **Ehud** again **passed** the landmark (**idols;** cf. Jud. 3:19) at Gilgal **and escaped to Seirah** (an unidentified place in Ephraim).

**3:27-29.** By means of **a trumpet** blast, Ehud summoned Israelite men whom he led into battle against the disarrayed Moabites. He made no claims for himself but affirmed to the Israelites, **The LORD has given Moab, your enemy, into your hands.** His battle strategy was to seize **the fords of the Jordan** where the fleeing Moabites had to cross to return to their country. The Israelites **struck down about 10,000 Moabites** without allowing any to escape across the Jordan River.

*d. The duration of peace (3:30)*

**3:30.** The defeat of the Moabites was so decisive that they became **subject to Israel.** As a result of the deliverance through Ehud, **the land had peace** for an unprecedented **80 years,** the longest period of rest during the time of the Judges.

3. THE DELIVERANCE BY SHAMGAR FROM THE OPPRESSION OF THE PHILISTINES (3:31)

**3:31.** Shamgar's judgeship appears to have transpired after Ehud's deliverance but before his death (the historical notice in 4:1 continues after Ehud's death rather than after Shamgar's). The name **Shamgar** is Hurrian, but this may infer no more than Hurrian influence on his parents, not that he was a non-Israelite. That he **saved Israel** marks him out as a judge though the only item recorded is that he **struck down 600 Philistines with an oxgoad.** Whether this tally was a lifetime total or the number in a single episode is not indicated. His weapon was a sharp metal-tipped stick about 8 or 10 feet long used to direct animals. The other end usually had a chisel-like blade for cleaning a plow.

4. THE DELIVERANCE BY DEBORAH AND BARAK FROM THE OPPRESSION OF THE CANAANITES (CHAPS. 4–5)

The focus of attention switches to the Northern tribes (cf. 4:6; 5:14-15, 18) who were oppressed by a coalition of Canaanites united under Jabin of Hazor (4:2), apparently a descendant of King Hazor who was conquered by Joshua (Josh. 11:1-13). Unlike the preceding oppressions by foreign invaders, this one was instigated at the hands of the Canaanite population of the land, some of the same people that the Israelites had failed to drive out of northern Canaan (cf. Jud. 1:30-33).

*a. The defection of Israel*
*(4:1)*

**4:1.** That **the Israelites once again did evil** indicated their continuing tailspin into the idolatrous practices of the Canaanites (cf. 2:19; 3:7, 12). This defection seems to have reappeared only **after Ehud died,** indicating his positive influence in leading the people as judge. The dating of this chapter with the judgeship of Ehud suggests that Shamgar's deliverance of Israel (3:31) occurred during rather than after Ehud's period of leadership.

*b. The distress under the Canaanites*
*(4:2-3)*

**4:2-3.** About 200 years earlier **the LORD** had freed Israel from slavery in Egypt. Now, in contrast, He **sold them into the hands of** the Canaanites as punishment for their sins (cf. 2:14; 3:8; 1 Sam. 12:9). **Jabin** was probably a hereditary title (cf. a different Jabin in Josh. 11:1-13). **Hazor** (Tell el-Qedah) was the most important northern Canaanite stronghold in northern Galilee about 8½ miles north of the Sea of Kinnereth (Galilee). Neither Hazor nor its king Jabin play an active role in the narrative in Judges 4–5, for attention is centered on **Sisera,** the Canaanite **commander** from **Harosheth Haggoyim** (cf. 4:13, 16) sometimes identified with Tell el-ʻAmar (located by a narrow gorge where the Kishon River enters the Plain of Acre about 10 miles northwest of Megiddo). The Canaanite oppression was severe because of their superior military force, spearheaded by **900 iron chariots** (cf. v. 13). The oppression lasted **for 20 years,** so that **the Israelites** again **cried to the LORD** for help.

*c. The deliverance by Deborah and Barak*
*(4:4–5:31a)*

(1) The leadership of Deborah. **4:4-5.** **Deborah** (whose name means "honeybee") was both **a prophetess** and a judge (she **was leading Israel**). She first functioned as a judge in deciding **disputes** at her **court,** located about 8 or 10 miles north of Jerusalem **between Ramah and Bethel in the hill country of Ephraim.** She was apparently an Ephraimite though some have linked her with the tribe of Issachar (cf. 5:15). Nothing else is known about her husband **Lappidoth** (meaning "torch," not to be identified

with Barak, meaning "lightning").

(2) The commissioning of Barak (4:6-9). **4:6-7.** Deborah summoned **Barak** who was from the town of **Kedesh in Naphtali,** a city of refuge (Josh. 20:7), usually identified as Tel Qedesh, five miles west by northwest of Lake Huleh, close to the Canaanite oppressors in Galilee. An alternate site, Khirbet el-Kidish on the eastern edge of the Jabneel Valley, about a mile from the southwest shore of the Sea of Galilee, is more closely located to Mount Tabor where the army of Israel was mustered by Barak. Deborah, speaking as the Lord's prophetess, commanded Barak to muster **10,000 men** from the tribes **of Naphtali and Zebulun and lead** them **to Mount Tabor.** Conical Mount Tabor rises to 1,300 feet and was strategically located at the juncture of the tribes of Naphtali, Zebulun, and Issachar in the northeast part of the Jezreel Valley. (Issachar, not mentioned in this chapter, is mentioned in Jud. 5:15.) Mount Tabor was a place of relative safety from the Canaanite **chariots** and a launching ground from which to attack the enemy below. The message from God informed Barak that He would be in sovereign control of the battle (**I will lure Sisera . . . and give him into your hands**).

**4:8-9.** Regardless of his motivation, Barak's conditional reply to Deborah (**if you don't go with me, I won't go**) was an unfitting response to a command from God. Perhaps **Barak** simply wanted to be assured of the divine presence in battle, represented by His prophetess-judge **Deborah.** It is noteworthy that Barak is listed among the heroes of faith (Heb. 11:32). **Deborah** agreed to go but said that Barak's conditional response to the divine command (**the way you are going about this**) was the basis for withholding the honor of victory over Sisera from **Barak** (the LORD **will hand Sisera over to a woman**). Barak no doubt thought she meant herself, but the statement was prophetic, anticipating the role of Jael (Jud. 4:21).

(3) The gathering of the troops. **4:10-13.** Accompanied by **Deborah,** Barak led **10,000 men** from the tribes of **Zebulun and Naphtali . . . to Mount Tabor.** Parenthetically (in anticipation of vv. 17-22), an explanation is given that the nomad, **Heber the Kenite,** had left his clan in

southern Judah (cf. 1:16) **and pitched his tent . . . near Kedesh.** On **Hobab** as Moses' **brother-in-law** (or father-in-law, NIV marg.), see comments on Numbers 10:29. When **Sisera** heard of Barak's action, he positioned his army with its **900 iron chariots** (cf. Jud. 4:3) near the **Kishon River,** probably in the vicinity of Megiddo or Taanach (cf. 5:19) in the Jezreel Valley.

(4) The defeat of the Canaanites. **4:14-16.** At Deborah's command (**Go!**) and encouragement (**the LORD has given Sisera into your hands**), **Barak** led his men **down Mount Tabor** against the much stronger forces of Sisera. As promised by **Deborah . . . the LORD routed Sisera and all his chariots and army.** The means used by God were both human (**by the sword**) and divine (bringing an unseasonable and violent storm that mired the chariots in the floodwaters of the Kishon; cf. 5:20-22). **Sisera abandoned his chariot and fled on foot,** apparently in a northeastern direction past Mount Tabor, while Barak's forces **pursued** the grounded Canaanites till **not a man was left.**

(5) The flight and death of Sisera. **4:17-22. Sisera . . . fled on foot** in the direction of Kedesh (a city of refuge) or perhaps Hazor, and ran toward the tents of **Heber the Kenite** who had **friendly relations** (šālôm, "peace") with **Jabin king of Hazor. Jael, the wife of Heber,** offered Sisera all the expected Near-Eastern hospitality, for she **covered him** either with a fly-net or with a rug for concealment, **gave him a drink** of **milk,** probably yogurt (cf. 5:25), and stood at **the tent** door to divert intruders as he slept. However, **Jael** apparently did not share her husband's allegiance to King Jabin, for as soon as Sisera was **fast asleep,** she took **a tent peg** and with **a hammer . . . drove** it **through his temple into the ground** (cf. 5:26), an unusual breach of Near-Eastern hospitality! Since Bedouin women had the task of pitching the tents, she was an expert with the implements she used. **Jael** then attracted the attention of **Barak** who was going **by in pursuit of Sisera,** and showed him the corpse. Thus Deborah's prophecy (cf. 4:9) was fulfilled, for two women received honor for the defeat of Sisera— Deborah who started it and Jael who finished it.

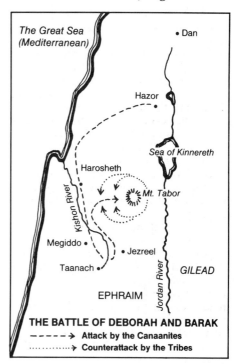

THE BATTLE OF DEBORAH AND BARAK
----→ Attack by the Canaanites
..........→ Counterattack by the Tribes

(6) The destruction of Jabin. **4:23-24.** The defeat of Jabin's army initiated a period of constant decline in Galilee until **Canaanite** forces were no longer a threat to Israel.

(7) The hymn of victory (5:1-31a). **5:1.** This ancient poem, which may have been initially preserved in a collection such as "the Book of the Wars of the LORD" (Num. 21:14) or "the Book of Jashar" (Josh. 10:13), is literally a victory hymn (well known in examples from the 15th to 12th centuries B.C. in Egypt and Assyria). This hymn was no doubt written by **Deborah** herself (cf. Jud. 5:7-9) though **Barak** joined with her in voicing its theme (v. 1). With profound simplicity the hymn ascribes to Yahweh, the covenant God of Israel, victory over Sisera and the Canaanites. It also fills in a few incidental gaps in the narrative not given in chapter 4. It is noteworthy that the theme of blessing and cursing is prominent throughout. The victory hymn has five parts: (a) the heading of the hymn (5:1), (b) the praise by Deborah (vv. 2-11), (c) the muster of the tribes (vv. 12-18), (d) the defeat of the Canaanites (vv. 19-30), and (e) the concluding prayer of cursing and blessing (v. 31a).

**5:2-5.** The opening call to praise the LORD is related to the rise of the volunteer spirit in Israel among both **princes** and **people** (v. 2). A typical proclamation of praise (v. 3) is followed by a historical recital of the Lord's previous saving deeds (vv. 4-5). Yahweh is identified as **the One of Sinai** (cf. Ps. 68:8) and associated with events prior to the crossing of the Jordan under Joshua. The mention of **Seir** (cf. Deut. 33:2) and **Edom** (cf. Hab. 3:3, which mentions Teman, an Edomite town) has led some scholars to locate Mount Sinai just east of the Arabah Valley (south of the Dead Sea), but this is unlikely.

**5:6-8. Deborah** next described the contemporary situation of distress that gripped the Northern tribes of **Israel** (cf. 3:31; 4:2-3) till she **arose a mother in Israel.** Outside the fortified (walled) cities, Israelite **life** in the villages and on the roadways came to a standstill because of the oppression by the Canaanites, which came right up **to the city gates.** This distress was rooted in Israel's idolatry—**they chose new gods.**

**5:9-11.** Deborah praised God because of faithful leaders and **volunteers among the people** who responded in the time of crisis. She called on rich (**who ride on white donkeys**) and poor (**who walk along the road**) alike to hear the song of victory. The **righteous acts of the** LORD were those by which He had intervened to bring salvation and victory to His **people.**

**5:12-18.** The **song** of victory itself begins with a call for **Deborah** and **Barak** to initiate the action. Blessing is pronounced on those tribes that responded freely to the muster for battle—**Ephraim . . . Benjamin. . . . Makir** (a division of the tribe of Manasseh, usually the portion east of the Jordan but here perhaps the combined tribe or just the division west of the Jordan; cf. Num. 26:29; 27:1), **Zebulun,** and **Issachar** (Jud. 5:14-15). The explanation about Ephraim's **roots** being in **Amalek** (v. 14) apparently indicates that the Ephraimites lived in the central hill country previously occupied by the Amalekites. A series of taunts implying curses (cf. the curse on the Israelite city of Meroz in v. 23 for failing to render aid during the battle) is directed against the tribes of **Reuben. . . . Gilead** (apparently Gad and perhaps part of Manasseh),

**Dan,** and **Asher** (vv. 15-17). The tribes of **Zebulun** (cf. v. 14) and **Naphtali,** however, are praised for their parts in the battle (v. 18; cf. 4:6, 10).

**5:19-22. The kings of Canaan** were from the confederacy of Canaanite city-states under Jabin of Hazor whose army was commanded by Sisera. The battle zone included **Taanach** (located five miles southeast **of Megiddo**). The highly poetic language—**from the heavens the stars fought . . . against Sisera**—does not imply a belief that the stars caused rain, but simply affirms divine intervention in the battle. As implied in verse 21, God's intervention took the form of an unseasonable rain (the Canaanites would never have risked taking their chariots into marshy territory in the rainy season) which turned the dry riverbed of the **Kishon** into a raging torrent (cf. 1 Kings 18:40).

**5:23-27.** A **curse** was pronounced on **Meroz** (perhaps located on the route of Sisera's flight) for failure to aid in the battle, but a blessing was pronounced on **Jael** for her act of slaying Sisera (cf. 4:21-22), an act apparently regarded as expressing faithfulness to the covenant people of Israel with whom her clan had been identified through Moses. The vivid picture of Sisera's death (5:26-27) was not intended to narrate the steps of the physical action, but to describe metaphorically and in slow motion, so to speak, the fall of a leader.

**5:28-30.** The pathos of the fallen general is amplified by an ironic description of **Sisera's mother** awaiting the unrealizable return of her son from battle. Her anxiety—**Why is his chariot so long in coming?**—and the hopeful excuses of his delay made by one of her maidens and herself contrast vividly with the real situation.

**5:31a.** It is appropriate for a hymn describing Yahweh's victory over idolatrous enemies to conclude with a curse on evil **enemies** and a blessing on those who are faithful to Yahweh. To be **like the sun when it rises** means to have a life full of blessing.

*d. The duration of peace (5:31b)*

**5:31b.** The deliverance of Israel from Canaanite power under the judgeship of Deborah brought **peace** to **the land** for **40 years.**

5. THE DELIVERANCE BY GIDEON FROM THE OPPRESSION OF THE MIDIANITES (6:1–8:32)

*a. The defection of Israel (6:1a)*

**6:1a.** The downward cycles (see the sketch near 2:11-15) of apostasy (**again the Israelites did evil in the eyes of the Lord;** cf. 3:7, 12; 4:1) and deliverance continued in the case of Gideon whose judgeship receives the most extensive narration in the Book of Judges (100 verses comprising three chapters). The story of Samson is comparable, consisting of 96 verses in four chapters.

*b. The distress under the Midianites (6:1b-6)*

**6:1b-6.** The **seven years** of oppression under **the hands of Midianites** was divine chastening for Israel's idolatry and evil practices. This relatively brief period of oppression was sandwiched in between two 40-year periods of peace (5:31; 8:28). The Midianites were descendants of Abraham and Keturah (Gen. 25:1-2) and were defeated by Israel during the wilderness wanderings (Num. 22:4; 25:16-18). They were a nomadic people who came from near the Gulf of Aqabah and ranged throughout the Arabah and Transjordania, apparently at this time subduing the Edomites, Moabites, and Ammonites as they crossed the Jordan into Canaan as far north as the Jezreel Valley (Jud. 6:33), and as far south and east as **Gaza** (v. 4), perhaps moving westward across the Jezreel Valley and southward along the coastal plain.

The strength of Midianite oppression forced **the Israelites** to hide **themselves** and their produce **in mountain clefts, caves, and strongholds.** However, this was not a continual occupation (like the preceding one of the Canaanites) but a seasonal invasion at harvesttime, **whenever the Israelites planted their crops.** The Midianites' major goal was the appropriation of **the crops** for themselves and their animals. But the cumulative effect of these invasions on Israelite agriculture and food cycles was devastating. Midianite allies included the **Amalekites** (from south of Judah; cf. 3:13) **and other eastern peoples,** a general term for the nomads of the Syrian desert, possibly including some Ammonites and Edomites. On these annual predatory invasions, in typical nomadic style, the oppressors **camped on the land** in such numbers and with such devastation that

they were compared to **swarms of locusts** (cf. 7:12). The Midianites and their allies traveled on innumerable **camels** (cf. 7:12) whose range of distance and speed (as high as 100 miles per day) made them a formidable long-range military threat. This is the first reference to an organized raid using camels (cf. Gen. 24:10-11). The impoverishment that came to Israel drove her to cry **out to the Lord for help.** This cry does not seem to have been an indication of repentance for sin because they apparently were not aware of the moral cause behind the enemy's oppression until the Lord sent a prophet to point this out (cf. Jud. 6:7-10).

*c. The deliverance by Gideon (6:7–8:27)*

(1) The censure of Israel by a prophet. **6:7-10. The Lord . . . sent** an unnamed **prophet** (the only prophet mentioned in the book besides the Prophetess Deborah) to remind Israel of her covenant obligations to **the Lord,** who had delivered them from **Egypt** (cf. Ex. 34:10-16; Deut. 7; Jud. 3:5-6), **not to worship the gods of the Amorites.** The prophet rebuked them for their continued disobedience (**But you have not listened to Me** [God]). This message is similar to that from the Angel of the Lord at Bokim (cf. 2:1-3).

(2) The call of Gideon by the Angel of the Lord (6:11-24). **6:11-12a.** The story of Gideon is introduced not by an affirmation that "God raised up a deliverer named Gideon," but rather by a narration of *how* God raised him up. Gideon's call or commission resulted from a confrontation with **the Angel of the Lord** (who is "the Lord," v. 14; cf. comments on 2:1), who appeared to him as a sojourning stranger and **sat down under the oak in Ophrah.** Since Gideon's father **Joash** was an **Abiezrite** (a clan of Manasseh, Josh. 17:2), this Ophrah was not the place located in Benjamin but rather a northern site possibly near the border of Manasseh in the Jezreel Valley. Possible site identifications are el-Affula (six miles east of Megiddo) or et-Taiyiba (Hapharaim, eight miles northwest of Beth Shan). Gideon's act of **threshing wheat in a winepress** reflected both his fear of discovery by **the Midianites** and the smallness of his harvest. Normally wheat was threshed (the grain separated from the wheat stalks) in an open area on

a threshing floor (cf. 1 Chron. 21:20-23) by oxen pulling threshing sledges over the stalks.

**6:12b-13.** The Angel's introductory remark affirmed the Lord's presence with **Gideon** (**you** is sing.) and described Gideon as a **mighty warrior** ("mighty man of valor," KJV; the words *gibbôr ḥāyil* are also applied to Jephthah, 11:1; and to Boaz, Ruth 2:1). Though this description may have been spoken in satire (at this point Gideon was anything but a mighty warrior!), it probably reflected Gideon's potentiality through divine enablement, as well as expressing his notable rank in the community.

Gideon's initial response ignored the singular pronoun "you" (Jud. 6:12), for he replied, **If the Lord is with us** (pl. pronoun). Gideon questioned the divine promise in view of his people's present circumstances. He correctly concluded, however, that **the Lord** had **put** them **into the hand of Midian.**

**6:14.** "The Angel of the Lord" (vv. 11-12) now spoke as **the Lord** and commissioned Gideon to **Go . . . and save Israel out of Midian's hand.** The words **the strength you have** perhaps assumed the divine presence previously mentioned (v. 12).

**6:15.** **But,** Gideon objected, **My clan is the weakest . . . and I am the least.** This objection might have stemmed from typical Near-Eastern humility, but perhaps it also reflected a good amount of reality.

**6:16.** God's reassurance reaffirmed His presence with Gideon (**I will be with you**) and the ease with which he would accomplish victory over **the Midianites (as if they were but one man).**

**6:17-21.** **Gideon** requested **a sign** to confirm the Lord's promise. This request was granted (cf. v. 21). Meanwhile Gideon's uncertainty regarding the exact identity of his supernatural Visitor prompted him to offer typical Near-Eastern hospitality. The word for **offering** or gift (*minḥâh*), which he proposed to **set . . . before** the Visitor, could refer to a freewill offering in Israel's sacrificial system, or it could refer to tribute offered as a present to a king or other superior (cf. 3:15). The large amount of food prepared by Gideon—goat's **meat** and **broth,** and **bread** made **from an ephah** (one-half bushel) **of flour**—reflected both

his wealth in a destitute time and the typical excessiveness of Near-Eastern hospitality. He no doubt planned to take the leftovers home for his family! But **the Angel of the Lord touched** the food offering **with the tip of** His **staff** and consumed it by **fire,** thus providing the sign Gideon had requested (6:17; cf. Lev. 9:24; 1 Kings 18:38). Then **the Angel . . . disappeared.**

**6:22-24.** Gideon's consternation probably reflected his fear of impending death because of seeing the divine presence (cf. Ex. 33:20). When **the Lord** assured **Gideon** he was **not going to die . . . Gideon built an altar** and named it **the Lord is Peace.**

(3) The destruction of Baal's altar by Gideon (6:25-32). **6:25-26.** **The Lord** gave Gideon a test of obedience. If Gideon was to deliver Israel from the Midianites, he must not only achieve military victory over the enemy but also must remove the cause of idolatry which initially led the Lord to give His people over to the Midianites (cf. v. 1). Therefore God commanded Gideon to destroy his **father's altar to Baal** with its accompanying **Asherah pole** (a cult object probably representing Asherah, Ugaritic goddess of the sea; cf. comments on 3:7). Gideon was then to construct **a proper kind of altar to the Lord,** kindle a fire with **the wood of the Asherah pole,** and offer one of his father's bulls (probably intended originally as a sacrificial animal for Baal) **as a burnt offering** to the Lord.

**6:27.** Gideon's obedience to God's command should not be minimized by his use of **10 . . . servants** (dismantling a Canaanite altar was a massive task), or by the fact that **he did it at night** (the Baal-worshipers would obviously have prevented it if he had tried to do this during the day).

**6:28-32.** The resultant hostility of the community against Gideon was defused by his father's sage advice. Their investigation of the overnight vandalism quickly implicated **Gideon,** whose execution they demanded. **But Joash,** perhaps repentant and inspired by his son's remarkable actions, wisely proclaimed, **If Baal really is a god, he can defend himself.** Perhaps this implied that the people should not overstep Baal's prerogative of self-defense (cf. Elijah's irony about **Baal,** 1 Kings 18:27). This wise advice appealed to the people who then **called Gideon** by the name of **Jerub-Baal**, meaning **Let Baal contend**. Though they apparently applied the name derogatively, it might have later assumed an honorable signification as a witness against Baal's inability to defend himself (cf. Jud. 7:1; 8:29; and comments on Jerub-Baal in 9:1).

(4) The preparation of Gideon for battle. **6:33-35.** Gideon's commission by the Lord seems to have preceded the next (and final) annual invasion of **the Midianites** and their allies. They **crossed . . . the Jordan** River not far south of the Sea of Kinnereth **and camped** in typical Bedouin fashion in the rich agricultural area of the Jezreel Valley. The Lord's deliverance of His people through Gideon began as **the Spirit of the Lord came upon Gideon** (cf. 3:10; 11:29; 13:25; 14:6, 19; 15:14), providing divine enablement through the Holy Spirit's personal presence. Gideon immediately began to muster men, summoning his Abiezrite clan (cf. 6:11, 24) with **a trumpet** and the rest of the tribe of **Manasseh** along with the tribes of **Asher, Zebulun, and Naphtali** by means of **messengers**.

(5) The signs concerning the fleece of Gideon. **6:36-40.** Gideon's apparent lack of faith in seeking a miraculous sign from **God** (cf. Matt. 12:38; 1 Cor. 1:22-23) seems strange for a man who is listed among the heroes of faith (Heb. 11:32). In fact **Gideon** already had a sign from God at the time of his commission (Jud. 6:17, 21). It is noteworthy, however, that Gideon was not using the **fleece** to discover God's will, for he already knew from divine revelation what God wanted him to do (v. 14). The sign related to a confirmation or assurance of God's presence or empowerment for the task at hand. **God** condescended to Gideon's weak faith and saturated the **wool fleece** with **dew**, so much so that Gideon **wrung out . . . a bowlful of water**. Perhaps **Gideon** had second thoughts about the uniqueness of this event since the surrounding **threshing floor** might naturally dry before the fleece. So he requested the opposite— **This time make the fleece dry and the ground covered with dew**. God patiently **did so**, and Gideon was reassured to continue his assignment.

(6) The reduction of the army of Gideon (7:1-8a). **7:1-2. Gideon . . . camped at the spring of Harod** (probably En

Harod at the foot of Mount Gilboa, a spring that winds eastward to the Jordan River through the Harod Valley) with all his men, who numbered 32,000 (v. 3). The Midianite force of 135,000 (cf. 8:10) was camped three or four miles **north of them** at the foot of **the hill of Moreh**, the prominent hill rising like a sentinel to guard the eastern entrance to the Jezreel Valley. God, whose **strength** does not depend on numbers (cf. Ps. 33:16), purposed to **deliver Midian** to Israel through a few men so Israel would **not boast** that they had won the battle themselves. **Gideon** was no doubt perplexed by God's words, **You have too many men**.

**7:3-6.** The means by which the size of Gideon's force was reduced was twofold: (a) **22,000** fearful recruits were summarily dismissed (in harmony with Deut. 20:8) and allowed to return to their homes; and (b) 9,700 apparently lesswatchful men who failed a simple test were also discharged (Jud. 7:4-8; or at least were granted a leave of absence; cf. v. 23).

The permission to **leave Mount Gilead** is puzzling since Gilead was across the Jordan River to the east. Some scholars view "Gilead" as an early copyist's error for "Gilboa," the mount near Gideon's army. Or another Mount Gilead may have been nearby, since some of Gilead's descendants lived on the western side of Jordan. Though the test given to the 9,700 seems simple enough, the words describing it are somewhat ambiguous. As **the men** drank from the spring, **Gideon** was to **separate those who lap the water with their tongues like a dog from those who kneel down to drink**. But how does one "lap . . . like a dog" without "kneel[ing] down" to place his face near the water? Some writers have suggested that a "non-kneeler" scooped the water up in one hand (holding his weapon in the other) from which he **lapped** the water with his tongue. Others have suggested that each used his hand to bring the water to his mouth much as a dog uses his tongue to bring water to his mouth. Whatever the explanation, the test probably identified those who were watchful, though some think it was strictly an arbitrary test for reducing the number of men. Historian Josephus even believed the **300 men** who passed the test were less watchful, which resulted in a greater recognition of God's power.

**7:7-8a.** Now with just a few fighters, **Gideon** was again reassured by a divine promise: **With the 300 men . . . I will save you and give the Midianites into your hands** (cf. 6:14). Gideon's 300 men acquired **the provisions and trumpets of** those who returned **to their tents.**

(7) The encouragement of Gideon concerning victory (7:8b-15). **7:8b-11a.** In spite of all the encouragement and assurance previously given **Gideon,** the Lord knew that he was **afraid to attack,** so God provided two further means of encouragement: (a) a direct divine word (**go down against the camp, because I am going to give it into your hands;** cf. vv. 7, 14-15), and (b) a providentially planned dream narrated by a Midianite and overheard by Gideon (vv. 13-14).

**7:11b-15.** Gideon **and Purah his servant** stalked the outskirts of the Midianite **camp** with its innumerable tents spread out **in the valley** like locusts (cf. 6:5), tents which were outnumbered only by the myriads of **camels** (cf. 6:5). A beautiful demonstration of God's providence was exhibited: **Gideon arrived just as a man was telling a friend his dream** about **a round loaf of barley bread** which **came tumbling into the Midianite camp** and **overturned** a **tent** which it struck. The other Midianite **responded,** perhaps in jest, that **this** must refer to **the sword of Gideon . . . the Israelite** into whose hands **God has given** us **Midianites.** However, the divinely intended symbolism is clear (barley bread aptly described the poverty-stricken Israelites, and the tent referred to the nomadic Midianites). **Gideon** correctly understood it as an encouragement from the Lord that **Israel** would be victorious over Midian. Spontaneously worshiping **God** after this message, Gideon **returned to the** Israelite **camp** and proceeded immediately to marshal his forces, passing on to them the same assurance God had given him— **The LORD has given the Midianite camp into your hands** (cf. 7:7, 9, 14).

(8) The victory over the Midianites by Gideon. **7:16-22.** Gideon divided his small band **into three companies** of men, whose strategic but strange weapons were **trumpets and empty jars . . . with torches inside.** They arrived at the edge of the Midianite **camp** at the providential time of **the beginning of the middle**

**watch** (10:00 P.M.), **just after they had changed the guard** (when the retiring guards would still be milling about their tents). In Gideon's day the first watch was from 6 P.M. to 10 P.M.; the middle watch was from 10 P.M. to 2 A.M.; and the morning watch started at 2 A.M. and went to 6 A.M.

At this critical moment the Israelites **blew their trumpets and broke the jars** (both making a terrible noise and revealing the glowing torches), and **shouted** loudly, **A sword for the LORD and for Gideon!** This battle cry indicated their confidence in the Lord to give them victory and also identified them to the Midianites and aroused fear in them. The word for **trumpets** is šôp̄ārôṯ, "made from animal horns"; they gave a sharp, shrill sound. The jars were pitchers probably made of clay. The confusion in the Midianite camp was unbelievable as they imagined a much larger Israelite force attacking them and as they perhaps mistook their own retiring guards for Israelites. This divinely planned confusion caused the Midianites **to turn on each other with their swords** while the Israelites apparently watched in safety **around the camp.** The Midianite **army fled to** the southeast to **Beth Shittah** (an immediate field site) and **Abel Meholah** toward the Jordan River. Abel Meholah was perhaps Tell Abu Sus, about 24 miles south of the Sea of Kinnereth (Galilee). (Abel Meholah was where Elisha was living when Elijah called him to be his protégé, 1 Kings 19:16.) The army apparently fled in that direction in order to cross the Jordan to reach **Zererah** (possibly Zarethan or Tell es-Saidiya) and **Tabbath** (Ras Abu Ṭalbat).

(9) The summons of Gideon for reinforcements. **7:23-24a.** Gideon summoned reinforcements **from Naphtali, Asher, and all Manasseh** to pursue the fleeing **Midianites.** Those who responded probably included the earlier contingents of Gideon's men who had been dismissed. Gideon also requested aid of the Ephraimites, who were well situated, to cut off **the Midianites** at strategic locations, preventing them from fording **the Jordan** River.

(10) The capture of Oreb and Zeeb by the Ephraimites. **7:24b-25.** The men of Ephraim quickly secured the fords of **the Jordan** (the site of **Beth Barah** is cur-

rently unknown) and **also captured two of the Midianite leaders, Oreb** (meaning "raven") **and Zeeb** (meaning "wolf"), whose **heads** they brought **to Gideon** according to typical Near-Eastern military practice.

(11) The diplomacy of Gideon toward the Ephraimites. **8:1-3.** However, **the Ephraimites . . . criticized** Gideon **sharply** for not inviting them to participate in the initial conflict near the Hill of Moreh (7:1). The "gentle answer" of **Gideon** (cf. Prov. 15:1) demonstrated his tactful diplomacy in the face of Ephraimite jealousy and averted intertribal warfare (cf. Jud. 12:1-6 where Jephthah reacted adversely to Ephraimite jealousy). In Gideon's parable **the full grape harvest of Abiezer** seems to refer to the initial victory in the camp of Midian (Gideon was an Abiezrite, 6:11) and **the gleanings of Ephraim's grapes** (affirmed as a greater victory) then refers to the "mopping up" operations which included slaying the two **Midianite** leaders.

(12) The pursuit of the Midianites into Transjordan (8:4-21). **8:4-9.** Though the Israelite reinforcements destroyed many of the fleeing Midianites, a sizable group, including two Midianite kings, **Zebah and Zalmunna,** escaped beyond **the Jordan** in a southeasterly direction. They were rapidly pursued by **Gideon and his 300 men** who sought food from **the men of Succoth** (v. 5) and **the men of Peniel** (vv. 8-9), two Israelite cities in the Transjordan territory of Gad (cf. Gen. 32:22, 30; Josh. 13:27). Both communities refused aid to **Gideon,** perhaps through fear of reprisal by the Midianites. However, this was tantamount to allying themselves with the Midianites against the Lord and His chosen deliverer. Therefore similar to the earlier curse on the city of Meroz in Deborah's time (cf. Jud. 5:23), Gideon threatened to punish them in retribution for their virtual hostility. To the people of **Succoth** he said, **I will tear** (lit., "thresh") **your flesh with desert thorns and briers** (cf. 8:16). This may mean he would drag them over thorns like a threshing sledge over grain, or "thresh" them by drawing threshing sledges over them. Whatever the exact meaning, death seemed the inevitable result. To the people of **Peniel** he gave the threat, **I will tear down this tower** (cf. v. 17). The tower was possibly a fortress

where people went for safety, like the tower of Shechem (9:46-49) or the tower of Thebez (9:50-51).

**8:10-12.** The two Midianite kings (**Zebah and Zalmunna**) arrived with a surviving force of only **15,000 men** at **Karkor,** an unidentified site thought to be near the Wadi Sirhan well east of the Dead Sea. The 15,000 was a mere 11 percent of the total Midianite force of 135,000. **Gideon** followed a caravan **route . . . east of Nobah** (perhaps Quanawat in eastern Bashan) **and Jogbehah** (modern el-Jubeihat 15 miles southeast of Peniel) and launched a surprise attack on the Midianites, **captured** the two kings, and routed their **army.**

**8:13-17.** Returning northwest to **the Pass** ("ascent") **of Heres** (an unidentified site) **Gideon** forced **a young man of Succoth** to write down **the names of the** city's **77 officials. Gideon** then carried out his previous threat to punish **the elders** of the city (cf. v. 7). **He also** fulfilled his threat to punish the city **of Peniel** (cf. v. 9).

**8:18-21.** With the two Midianite kings in hand, Gideon interrogated them regarding an otherwise unrecorded incident—the slaying of several **brothers** of his **at Tabor,** the conical small mountain just north of the Hill of Moreh. It is not stated whether this took place in the current invasion or on a previous Midianite invasion of the Jezreel Valley. Since Gideon felt obligated by the duty of blood revenge (cf. Deut. 19:6, 12), probably his brothers were murdered in their homes or fields, not in battle. Gideon asked **Jether his oldest son** to **kill them.** This was an honor that the **boy** was not prepared to undertake, though it would have been a fitting insult to the kings to be slain by an untried opponent. They bravely invited Gideon to fulfill the revenge himself, considering it an honor to be slain by the courageous Gideon. **Gideon** obliged them and **took the ornaments** (probably moon-shaped) **off their camels' necks** (cf. Jud. 8:26) as the spoils of war.

(13) The refusal of kingship by Gideon. **8:22-23.** Following this significant victory, **the Israelites** turned **to Gideon** with the request that he **rule** as king over them, that is, establish a ruling dynasty (**you, your son, and your grandson**). **Gideon** declined both the **rule** and the dynasty (but one of his sons, Abimelech,

would later speak for himself; cf. 9:1-6). Probably Gideon spoke words more significant than he realized when he affirmed the theocratic kingship of Yahweh—**The LORD will rule over you.**

(14) The snare of the ephod of Gideon (8:24-27). **8:24-26.** Though he rejected kingship, Gideon did take occasion to indulge in a form of virtual taxation by requesting a **share of the plunder** in the form of **gold earrings,** the total weight coming to about 43 pounds. The term **Ishmaelites** originally referred to another nomadic tribe descended from Hagar (Gen. 16:15) but the term apparently took on a broader usage so that it is here applied to the Midianites.

**8:27. Gideon** took the **gold** he received and made **an ephod, which he placed in Ophrah, his town.** Whatever Gideon's intentions were in this act, the people worshiped this ephod, and **it became a snare to Gideon and his family.** The nature of this ephod is not clear. It may have been patterned after the short outer garment worn by the high priest (Ex. 28:6-30; 39:1-21; Lev. 8:7-8). But rather than being worn as a garment, Gideon's golden ephod was apparently erected and became an idol. In some sense he may have usurped the function of the priest and/or established a rival worship center to the tabernacle. In the end Gideon seems to have returned to the syncretistic society out of which God had called him to deliver Israel.

*d. The duration of peace (8:28)*

**8:28.** As a result of **Gideon's** rout of the Midianites **the land enjoyed peace 40 years.** This is the last period of peace recorded in the Book of Judges. The subsequent activities of Jephthah and Samson did not seem to produce an interim of peace or delay the nation's decline.

*e. The death of Gideon (8:29-32)*

**8:29-32.** Though **Jerub-Baal** (i.e., Gideon; cf. 6:32; 7:1) declined the kingship, he generally lived like a king (**he had many wives** who bore him **70 sons**). He also had a **concubine . . . in Shechem** (who characteristically lived with her parents' family) who **bore him a son . . . named Abimelech.** This set the stage for the next downward spiral in Israel's history of apostasy, a spiral which began in earnest after the death of **Gideon.**

6. THE JUDGESHIPS OF TOLA AND JAIR FOLLOWING THE USURPATION OF ABIMELECH (8:33–10:5)

It may be significant that none of the judgeships recorded in the rest of the Book of Judges resulted in a designated period of peace (contrast 3:11, 30; 5:31; 8:28). This seems to fit the general pattern of progressive political and social decline and moral degeneration in the book. The event that launched the declining phase of the period of the Judges was the abortive kingship of Abimelech. Abimelech, a son of Gideon by a concubine, was not called a judge. In fact his rule included some elements of oppression which were eliminated only by his death and by the subsequent positive judgeship of Tola (who lived in the same general area of the central highlands).

*a. The defection of Israel (8:33-35)*

**8:33-35.** As though they had been waiting for it with expectancy, Gideon's death triggered Israel's immediate return to idolatry (cf. 2:19). Instead of worshiping Yahweh with thanksgiving for all His deliverances, **they set up Baal-Berith as their god,** who had a central shrine at Shechem (9:3-4) where he was also worshiped as El-Berith (9:46). Their accompanying failure **to show gratitude to the family of Jerub-Baal (that is, Gideon;** cf. 6:32; 7:1; 8:29) may have accounted for the apparent ease with which his sons were soon slain by Abimelech (9:5).

*b. The distress under Abimelech (chap. 9)*

(1) The conspiracy of Abimelech at Shechem (9:1-6). **9:1.** (Interestingly in chap. 9 Gideon is always called **Jerub-Baal,** and never Gideon. Cf. comments on "Jerub-Baal" in 6:32.) **Abimelech** was a **son** of Gideon by a concubine (8:31), a secondary wife who might live with her own family and be visited occasionally by her husband. In this social environment, Abimelech was no doubt shunned by his half-brothers (cf. his retaliation, 9:5) but he was accepted by **his mother's** family who lived **in Shechem.**

The city of Shechem had been a significant religious center since the time of Abraham (Gen. 12:6-7). It was located in the narrow valley between the prominent hills of Gerizim and Ebal, the site of the recitation under Joshua of the blessings and cursings of the Law (Josh. 8:30-35) and of the further covenant renewal ceremony before Joshua's death (Josh. 24:1-28). Shechem was situated on a strategic crossroads of the latitudinal route ascending from the coastal highway in the west and descending to Adam, on the Jordan River, and the longitudinal route along the central ridge from Jerusalem in the south to the northern accesses to the Jezreel Valley.

**9:2-5.** Abimelech appealed to his Shechemite heritage in offering himself to **the citizens of Shechem** in place of a corporate rule by **Jerub-Baal's sons,** who may have had neither the desire nor the following to be kings anyway. Some **silver** from the public **temple of Baal-Berith** was donated to **Abimelech . . . to hire reckless adventurers** as his personal cadre. Their first assignment was to murder Abimelech's **70 brothers** on **one stone,** implying a mass public execution. Significantly **Jotham,** Gideon's **youngest son . . . escaped.**

**9:6.** Following the successful removal of potential contenders for power (or was Abimelech's real motive personal vengeance?), **Abimelech** was crowned **king** by the ordinary **citizens of Shechem** and by the upper class who lived in the section of the city called **Beth Millo** ("house of the fortress"). The coronation took place beside **the great tree** (perhaps a well-known sacred tree; cf. Gen. 12:6; 35:4) **at the pillar** (cf. Josh. 24:26). It is doubtful that Abimelech's authority extended much beyond several cities in the vicinity of Shechem.

(2) The response of Jotham to the Shechemites (9:7-21). **9:7.** Gideon's youngest son **Jotham,** who had escaped the massacre by Abimelech (v. 5), courageously **climbed up on the top of Mount Gerizim** southwest of the city, **and shouted** out to the **citizens of Shechem.** He probably spoke from a triangular rock ledge on the side of Gerizim which forms a natural pulpit from which one can be heard as far away as Mount Ebal across the valley. Jotham's speech is noteworthy for its form and content as the first of one of the Bible's few fables (a short story in which animals or inanimate objects, like trees, are personified). Its purpose was to call the Shechemites to account before God (**Listen to me . . . so that God may listen to you**) for accepting as a leader the worthless· murderer Abimelech.

**9:8-15.** The major point of Jotham's parable was that only worthless people seek to lord it over others, for worthy individuals are too busy in useful tasks to seek such places of authority. The features of the parable are clear. **The trees** were seeking a **king,** but were turned down, in turn, by (a) **the olive tree** (v. 8), the most ancient of trees which is busy producing **oil** to be used to honor **both gods and men** (v. 9); (b) **the fig tree** (v. 10), the most common of trees in Israel whose **fruit** is a staple food (v. 11); and (c) **the vine** (v. 12), whose vintage produces **wine which cheers both gods** (i.e., in libations) **and men** (v. 13). In desperation the trees invited **the thornbush** (the buckthorn or bramblebush was used to kindle cooking fires in the wilderness areas of Palestine) to **be** their **king** (v. 14). The qualified acceptance by the thornbush was conditioned on the trees taking **refuge in** its **shade** (v. 15). Jotham employed extreme irony in this statement, for the puny **thornbush** at the foot of other trees scarcely casts a shadow. The threat of **fire** coming **out of the thornbush,** however, was real for farmers feared the wildfires that could spread quickly through the dried tinder of thornbushes.

**9:16-20.** Jotham then applied the parable, which stressed the worthless "bramble king" Abimelech, to rebuke the Shechemites for accepting such a worthless leader. This rebuke actually took the form of a curse (v. 20; cf. v. 57). Jotham began the rebuke with three conditional clauses (v. 16). After a parenthesis (vv. 17-18) describing the good deeds of Gideon and the bad deeds of **Abimelech,** Jotham restated the rebuke: **If then you have acted honorably and in good faith toward Jerub-Baal** (i.e., Gideon), "then may you and **Abimelech** enjoy your relationship!" (v. 19) **But if** the opposite was true (which was Jotham's obvious assumption), **let fire . . . consume** both Shechemites and **Abimelech.** This appropriate statement is specifically designated as a "curse" in verse 57.

**9:21.** It is evident that the Shechemites responded negatively to Jotham's rebuke for he **fled . . . to Beer** ("well"), which is such a common place name in Israel that to try to identify it is only guesswork.

(3) The revolt of the Shechemites un-

der Gaal (9:22-29). **9:22-25. Three years** of life under the leadership of **Abimelech** set the stage for a Shechemite revolt. **An evil** (demonic) **spirit** was **sent** by **God** to fulfill Jotham's curse by arousing distrust or jealousy in the Shechemites, who **set men on the hilltops to ambush and rob** the caravans and other travelers on the strategic trade routes through **Shechem.** Such action would reduce travel and deprive **Abimelech** of tributes and tolls from travelers. That God would send an evil spirit, a demon, shows that He sovereignly rules over all the universe. Even Satan could not attack Job without God's permission (Job. 1:12; 2:6).

**9:26-29.** The undisciplined populace of **Shechem** found a new leader in **Gaal son of Ebed,** who **moved** into Shechem **with his brothers** (perhaps his personal army of brigands). At the time of grape harvest (June-July) the Shechemites held a pagan religious **festival** comparable to but earlier than the Israelite Feast of Ingathering or Tabernacles, which was in September-October (cf. Deut. 16:13-15). At this time of festivity, **they cursed Abimelech** and **put their confidence in** Gaal, who ridiculed both **Abimelech** and **Zebul his deputy,** who was Shechem's governor (Jud. 9:30). Gaal exhorted them to **serve the men of Hamor,** the ancestor of their clan (Gen. 34:26) rather than the half-breed Abimelech. This suggests that a large portion of the Shechemite populace were native Canaanites. Gaal boldly challenged the absent Abimelech, **Call out your whole army!**

(4) The retaliation of Abimelech against Gaal (9:30-49). **9:30-33.** Zebul (cf. v. 28), **the governor of the city,** was angered by the rebel **Gaal.** So Zebul warned **Abimelech,** who lived in nearby Arumah (v. 41), perhaps Khirbet el-Urma between Shechem and Shiloh, to bring his troops **during the night** and **advance against the city** at sunrise to kill **Gaal.**

**9:34-41.** Abimelech went to **Shechem,** concealed **his troops** in **four companies,** and began to move on the city at sunrise. **When Gaal** mentioned their early morning movement, **Zebul** claimed they were only **shadows of the mountains.** But Gaal persisted in recognizing them as **people . . . coming down from the center of the land** (lit., "the navel of the land," apparently a reference to Gerizim located centrally in the central high-

lands). **The soothsayers' tree** may have been the oak of Moreh (Gen. 12:6). When he could deceive **Gaal** no longer, **Zebul** goaded him into leading his forces outside the protective walls of the city to **fight** against Abimelech's troops. After all his bragging, **Gaal** had no other choice but to engage in the encounter, and his Shechemite followers were soundly defeated by **Abimelech.** Then Abimelech returned to **Arumah** while those Shechemites faithful to **Zebul drove Gaal and his brothers out of Shechem.**

**9:42-45.** However, Abimelech's anger had not receded and his fear of further Shechemite revolt led him to **ambush the people** while they worked **in the fields. Two companies** carried out the slaughter while Abimelech secured **the city gate** with a third company. By evening he had **captured the city** and **destroyed** it, having **killed** its inhabitants. He then **scattered salt over it,** symbolic of a sentence of infertility so it might remain barren forever (cf. Deut. 29:23; Jer. 17:6). Archeology has confirmed this 12th-century destruction of Shechem, which remained a ruin till rebuilt by Jeroboam I as his capital (1 Kings 12:25).

**9:46-49.** These verses probably explain an incident within the city, included in the destruction previously recorded in verse 45, rather than a subsequent event outside the destroyed city. **On hearing** of either the slaughter in the fields (vv. 43-44) or the capture of the city gate (v. 44), the Shechemites who had retreated into **the tower of Shechem** (probably the same as the Beth Millo of v. 6), secured themselves in **the stronghold of the temple of El-Berith** (an alternate title for Baal-Berith, v. 4), probably a part of the tower of Shechem. **Abimelech** and his troops **cut . . . branches** from **Mount Zalmon** (perhaps either Mount Gerizim or Mount Ebal) and **set** them **on fire over** the stronghold, so that **about 1,000 men and women . . . died.**

(5) The ignoble death of Abimelech at Thebez. **9:50-55. Abimelech** next **besieged . . . and captured** Thebez, probably to be identified with modern Tubas about 10 miles northeast of Shechem on the road to Beth Shan. This city apparently was a dependency of Shechem which, under Abimelech's control, had

joined in the revolt. Attempting a repeat performance of Shechem, **Abimelech** sought to **set . . . fire to the tower** (within the city) where **the people** had **fled.** However, **a woman dropped an upper millstone on his head and cracked his skull.** The "upper millstone" was either a cylinder-shaped stone from a handmill (about 8 or 10 inches in length and several inches thick) or the large upper stone of a regular mill (about 12 to 18 inches in diameter with a hole in the middle and several inches thick). As he was dying Abimelech (like Saul, 1 Sam. 31:4) commanded **his armor-bearer** to **kill** him. Abimelech did not want it said that **a woman** had killed him. The followers of **Abimelech** (here identified as **Israelites**) **went home** when they **saw** that he **was dead.**

(6) The fulfillment of the curse of Jotham. **9:56-57.** The sacred historian recorded the divine providence behind the destruction of Shechem and the death of Abimelech: **God repaid the wickedness that Abimelech had done** to Gideon and his family; **God also made the men of Shechem pay for all their wickedness.** Thus **the curse of Jotham,** Gideon's **son,** was fulfilled (cf. v. 20).

### c. The deliverances under Tola and Jair (10:1-5)

Tola and Jair were among the so-called "minor judges" but they were no less significant in delivering Israel during the period before the monarchy. The judgeship of Tola in particular was a temporary counteraction to the decay under Abimelech. The judgeship of Jair in Gilead anticipated the judgeship of the next major judge, Jephthah, in the same geographical area.

**10:1-2.** Since **Tola** was a deliverer **in the hill country of Ephraim,** but was **a man of Issachar,** his judgeship may have affected the adjacent tribe of Manasseh where Abimelech's petty kingdom had been established. Since no foreign oppressors are mentioned, his acts of deliverance (he **rose to save Israel**) may have related to internal strife and the sad state of affairs (including Abimelech's rule) which followed the positive influence of Gideon. Tola judged **Israel 23 years** before his death. The site of **Shamir,** his place of residence and burial, has not been identified.

**10:3-5.** After Tola's judgeship, **Jair . . . led Israel 22 years** in **Gilead,** in the Transjordanian area of Manasseh. His noble status is evidenced by his large progeny of **30 sons,** who each had a donkey as his status symbol (cf. 12:14). The "tent villages of Jair" (**Havvoth Jair**) were a group of towns in Bashan named by an earlier Jair (Num. 32:39-42; Deut. 3:14) which were relatively permanent since they were still there in the days of the author of the Book of Judges. Jair's burial place, **Kamon,** may be modern Qamm in Gilead.

### 7. THE DELIVERANCE BY JEPHTHAH FROM THE OPPRESSION OF THE AMMONITES (10:6–12:7)

Judges 10:6-16 seems to be an expanded theological introduction to the judgeships of both Jephthah (10:17–12:7) and Samson (chaps. 13–16) since the oppressors introduced in 10:7 are simultaneously the Ammonites (in the east) and the Philistines (in the west).

### a. The defection of Israel (10:6)

**10:6.** Noteworthy is the numerical correspondence between the seven groups of pagan gods (v. 6) and the seven nations which oppressed Israel (v. 11). **The Baals and the Ashtoreths,** as noted earlier, were the gods of the Canaanites (cf. 2:13). **The gods of Aram** included Hadad or Rimmon (2 Kings 5:18), while **the gods of Sidon** were the Phoenician Baal and Asherah (cf. 1 Kings 16:31-33; 18:19). Moab's chief god was Chemosh (cf. 1 Kings 11:5, 33; 2 Kings 23:13), Ammon's was Milcom or Molech (1 Kings 11:33; Zeph. 1:5), and the Philistines' was Dagon (Jud. 16:23). Amazingly **the Israelites** worshiped these gods of surrounding nations and at the same time **forsook the LORD and no longer served Him.**

### b. The distress under the Ammonites (10:7-9)

**10:7-9.** The Lord again chastened His straying people by foreign oppressors—**the Philistines** in the west (anticipating the narrative of Samson, chaps. 13–16) and **the Ammonites** in the **east,** who oppressed Israel **for 18 years.** Ammon was a Transjordanian kingdom northeast of Moab which was allied with Eglon of Moab in the time of Ehud (3:13). The Ammonites oppressed **Gilead,** the

## Some of the Pagan Gods and Goddesses Worshiped in Nations Surrounding Israel

| Names | Nations |
|---|---|
| 1. Baal | Aram, Phoenicia, Canaan |
| 2. Asherah | Aram, Phoenicia, Canaan |
| 3. Ashtoreth | Aram, Phoenicia, Canaan |
| Other name: 'Athtart (sometimes called Astarte; also known in Babylonia as Ishtar) | Aram |
| 4. Hadad = Rimmon (the Arameans' name for Baal) | Aram |
| 5. Adad = Hadad | Mesopotamia |
| 6. Chemosh | Moab |
| 7. Milcom = Molech | Ammon |
| 8. Dagon | Philistia |
| 9. Resheph | Aram |

Transjordanian area occupied in the south by the tribe of Gad and in the north by the half-tribe of Manasseh. **The Ammonites also crossed the Jordan,** probably on periodic raids **against Judah, Benjamin, and the house of Ephraim** (the area of the central highlands).

c. *The repentance of Israel (10:10-16)*

**10:10-16.** In previous times of distress Israel's calling on **the LORD** was not an evidence of repentance for her sin (cf. 3:9, 15; 4:3). At the time of the Midianite invasions, the Lord sent a prophet to point out her need for repentance (6:7-10). However, on this occasion **the Israelites** demonstrated genuine repentance, first confessing their sins (**We have sinned against You**) and then, after **the LORD** rebuked them (let **the gods you have chosen. . . . save you**), they remained steadfast in their confession of sin and took action to get **rid of the foreign gods** and serve **the LORD**. His mercy toward **Israel's misery** led Him to raise up Jephthah as a deliverer. **The Maonites** (10:12) may refer to the Midianites (cf. v. 12, LXX) or to a clan descended from someone with the Canaanite name of Maon.

d. *The deliverance by Jephthah (10:17–12:6)*

(1) The selection of Jephthah by the elders of Gilead (10:17–11:11). **10:17–11:6.** In response to the Ammonite invasion of **Gilead, the Israelites assembled and camped at Mizpah** (probably Ramath Mizpeh [Khirbet Jalad, about 14 miles northeast of Rabbath-ammon, i.e., modern Amman] or Ramoth Gilead [Tel Ramith, about 40 miles north of Rabbath Ammon]). The first task of Israel was to search for a military **commander.** Their search led them to seek **Jephthah** (11:4-6), a notorious leader of men whose earlier family history is summarized in 11:1-3. Like Abimelech (cf. chap. 9), Jephthah was probably a half-Canaanite (**his mother was a prostitute**). He was driven from home by his half brothers (11:2). **In the land of Tob** (probably north of Ammon and east of Manasseh) he **gathered around** himself **a group of adventurers** (v. 3, probably meaning "a band of brigands").

**11:7-11.** The elders of Gilead persisted in the face of Jephthah's rebuke (v. 8). They cemented their promise that Jephthah would be their civil leader **over . . . Gilead** after he won a military victory by making a formal and solemn oath with **the LORD** as **witness** (v. 10).

This was followed by a formal swearing-in ceremony at **Mizpah.** In contrast with the judgeship of Gideon, who was initially called by the Lord, Jephthah was initially called by other men. However, **the Lord** was called to witness their selection (vv. 10-11) and He placed His Spirit on Jephthah to achieve victory (v. 29).

(2) The diplomacy of Jephthah with the Ammonite king (11:12-28). **11:12-13.** Surprisingly Jephthah's first step as commander of Gilead was to seek a non-military settlement to the conflict. Through **messengers** he asked **the Ammonite king** why he had **attacked** Gilead. The king's reply came in the form of an accusation—**When Israel came up out of Egypt, they took away my land**—which Jephthah proceeded to demonstrate was untrue (vv. 14-27). Yet the Ammonite **king** offered peace to Jephthah for the return of the land. **The Arnon** and **the Jabbok** are rivers that formed the southern and northern boundaries of Ammon. South of the Arnon was Moab. The Arnon flows into the Dead Sea and the Jabbok into the Jordan River.

**11:14-22. Jephthah** applied his knowledge of Israel's history (learned either from written or oral sources) to refute **the Ammonite** king's claim. In passing, **Jephthah** indicated that **Israel** had acquiesced to the refusal **of Edom** (cf. Num. 20:14-21) and **Moab** to permit passage through their lands (Jud. 11:17-18). However, when Israel circled the borders of Edom and Moab, **and camped on the other side of the Arnon** (the more usual northern **border of Moab**), **Sihon king of the Amorites** also refused **Israel** passage northwest to the Jordan River, **and fought** against **Israel. The Lord** gave Israel the victory and **Israel took over all the land of the Amorites . . . from the Arnon to the Jabbok**—the land now under dispute between the Ammonites and the Gileadites (cf. v. 13). This area was really southern Gilead (the rest of Gilead was north of the Jabbok River), and its southern portion (from the Arnon to a line extending eastward from the north end of the Dead Sea) was periodically in Moabite hands.

**11:23-24.** Jephthah thus argued that **the Lord** had given this land to **Israel.** He concluded this point of his argument by indicating that Ammon should be sat-isfied with the land that their **god Chemosh** had given them and should not contest the land **the Lord** had **given** Israel. Historically Chemosh was the god of the Moabites, and Milcam (or Molech) was god of the Ammonites. However, Jephthah seemed to be referring to the god of that portion of the land which had previously belonged to the Moabites before Sihon had pushed Moab south of the Arnon. Another explanation is that the Moabites were in alliance with the Ammonites in this attack on Gilead, so that Jephthah was really addressing the Moabites at this point in his argument. A third possibility is that the Ammonites had adopted the worship of Chemosh by this time.

**11:25-27.** Jephthah also argued that **Balak . . . king of Moab,** to whom part of the area in question used to belong, had consented to Israel's right to this area. In fact, Jephthah claimed, the land at the time of the Ammonite invasion had been Israel's **for 300 years** without any surrounding nations contesting it. Thus Jephthah denied any wrongdoing on Israel's part against Ammon. Ammon was in the **wrong** by warring **against** Israel.

**11:28.** Jephthah's attempt at diplomacy failed since **the king of Ammon . . . paid no attention to** his **message.**

(3) The empowerment of Jephthah by the Lord. **11:29.** The purpose of **the Spirit of the Lord** coming on **Jephthah** was to provide divine enablement in his military leadership against the pagan oppressors whom the Lord had been using to chasten His people (cf. 3:10; 6:34; 13:25; 15:14). The presence of the Holy Spirit with Old Testament leaders was primarily for the purpose of accomplishing services for God, not specifically for holy living. Thus the presence of the Spirit with Jephthah was not necessarily related to his vow or its fulfillment, recorded in the following verses. Jephthah's trip through **Gilead and Manasseh** was apparently to recruit his army.

(4) The vow of Jephthah to the Lord. **11:30-31.** That **Jephthah made a vow to the Lord** was not unusual in the Mosaic dispensation. Jephthah may have made the vow in anticipation of thanksgiving for divinely provided victory over **the Ammonites.** While the vow showed

Jephthah's zeal and earnestness, many have thought it was also characterized by rashness. Some scholars have sought to protect Jephthah from this charge by translating verse 31, "it will be the LORD's *or* I will offer it up as a burnt offering." However, the NIV more likely reflects Jephthah's intention—**I will sacrifice it as a burnt offering.**

(5) The victory of Jephthah over Ammon. **11:32-33.** God fulfilled Jephthah's request and **gave** the Ammonites **into his hands.** Jephthah **devastated 20** Ammonite-occupied **towns** in Gilead, and so **subdued Ammon.** Aroer (Khirbet Arair) was located about 14 miles east of the Dead Sea near the intersection of the Arnon River or the southern boundary of Reuben and the "King's Highway," on the main north-south trade route.

**Abel Keramim** may be identified with Naur about eight miles southwest of Rabbath Ammon (modern Amman). The site of **Minnith** is not known but was probably near Abel Keramim.

(6) The action of Jephthah concerning his daughter. **11:34-40.** Victorious **Jephthah** was met at the door of his house by **his** rejoicing **daughter,** who was jubilantly celebrating her father's victory over Ammon. Emphasis is placed on the fact that **she was an only child.** Anticipating the fulfillment of his vow, Jephthah expressed his great chagrin and sorrow in typical Near-Eastern fashion by tearing **his clothes** (cf., e.g., Gen. 37:29, 34; 44:13; Josh. 7:6; Es. 4:1; Job 1:20; 2:12). His statement, **I have made a vow to the LORD that I cannot break,** may reflect his ignorance of the legal option to redeem (with silver) persons who were thus dedicated (cf. Lev. 27:1-8). Also the Mosaic Law expressly prohibited human sacrifices (cf. Lev. 18:21; 20:2-5; Deut. 12:31; 18:10). Therefore many scholars conclude that when Jephthah **did to her as he had vowed** (Jud. 11:39), he commuted his daughter's fate from being a burnt sacrifice to being a lifelong **virgin** in service at Israel's central sanctuary. Other scholars believe Jephthah's semi-pagan culture led him to sacrifice her as a burnt offering. Strong arguments have been advanced for both views (cf. Wood, *Distressing Days of the Judges,* pp. 288-95; Merrill F. Unger, *Unger's Commentary on the Old Testament,* 2 vols. Chicago: Moody Press, 1981, 1:331).

Most of the arguments for or against Jephthah's offering his daughter as a human sacrifice can be used to defend either position and therefore are not conclusive. For example, the grief of both Jephthah and his daughter readily fits either her death or her perpetual virginity. In either case she would die childless (whether sooner or later) and Jephthah would lack descendants. Her asking for **two months to roam . . . and weep . . . because** she would **never marry** may be one of the stronger arguments for the virginity view. But this could also mean she was wailing in anticipation of her death which of course would render her childless. Though Jephthah made his rash vow, he probably knew something about the prohibitions of the Mosaic Law against human sacrifice. Yet his half-pagan background, combined with the general lawless spirit dominating the period of the Judges (cf. 17:6; 21:25), could readily account for his fulfilling this vow. The record of the local annual custom that arose to remember Jephthah's daughter (11:39-40) lacks sufficient detail to support either viewpoint strongly.

Even the existence of a group of young women serving at the tabernacle is not demonstrably evident from the passages used to support this (Ex. 38:8; 1 Sam. 2:22). Nor does the appeal to the law of options for vows (Lev. 27) apply directly to this situation. Nothing is said there about substitutionary service to God for the sacrifice—only the substitution of monetary payment. Therefore in the absence of any clear evidence indicating the girl's dedication to tabernacle service as a perpetual virgin, the more natural interpretation of the euphemism that Jephthah "did to her as he had vowed" seems to be that he offered his daughter as a human sacrifice.

Whichever position is taken, the attitude of Jephthah's daughter is worth noting. Whether by death or by perpetual sanctuary service, she was to bear no children. This was a cause of great sorrow in ancient Israel. Yet she submitted herself to her father's vow: **You have given your word to the LORD. Do to me just as you promised.** An Israelite custom, though probably somewhat localized, developed from the incident. **Each year the young women of Israel** went **out for four days to commemorate the daughter of**

**Jephthah the Gileadite.**

(7) The conflict of Jephthah with Ephraim. **12:1-6.** The Ephraimites had been attacked by **the Ammonites** (cf. 10:9) but the former's land had apparently not been occupied by the Ammonites as was true of Jephthah's Gileadites. Nevertheless the Ephraimites reacted against **Jephthah** because he had not invited their aid in defeating Ammon. In contrast with Gideon's tactful handling of a similar situation (cf. 8:1-3), **Jephthah** asserted that they had not responded to his call (though the record is silent concerning such an invitation), so he gained **victory over** Ammon without their help. Insults by **the Ephraimites** then led to their destruction by **the Gileadites. The Gileadites** even killed straggling survivors who tried to ford **the Jordan** River to return to **Ephraim.** The Ephraimites were easily identified by their colloquial pronunciation of the Hebrew sound *sh* which they pronounced as an *s.* This civil conflict in Israel cost the Ephraimites **42,000** lives, a high price for jealousy!

*e. The death of Jephthah (12:7)*

**12:7.** Following the victory over the Ammonites, **Jephthah led** (i.e., judged) **Israel six years** until his death.

8. THE JUDGESHIPS OF IBZAN, ELON, AND ABDON (12:8-15)

Three minor judges followed Jephthah, in various areas of Israel.

**12:8-10. Ibzan . . . led Israel** as judge, apparently from his hometown **of Bethlehem.** It is not indicated whether this was Bethlehem in Judah or Bethlehem in Zebulun (cf. Josh. 19:10, 15). Ibzan's community status is evidenced by his large family of **30 sons and 30 daughters,** and his political alliances are suggested by his seeking marriages both for **his sons** and **daughters . . . outside his clan.** He judged **Israel seven years** before he **died.**

**12:11-12. Elon the Zebulunite led Israel 10 years.** Nothing is recorded about him except his place of burial— **Aijalon** (an unidentified city) **in the land of Zebulun.**

**12:13-15. Abdon,** who was from **Pirathon in Ephraim** (located seven miles west by southwest of Shechem), **had 40 sons and 30 grandsons,** each with his own donkey, the status symbol of nobility (cf. the judge Jair, whose 30 sons each rode a donkey; 10:4). Abdon's **eight-**year judgeship may have involved some conflict with **the Amalekites.**

9. THE DELIVERANCE BY SAMSON FROM THE OPPRESSION OF THE PHILISTINES (CHAPS. 13–16)

*a. The defection of Israel (13:1a)*

**13:1a.** Israel's monotonous downward spiral climaxed with the seventh recorded apostasy in the Book of Judges (cf. 3:5-7, 12-14; 4:1-3; 6:1-2; 8:33-35; 10:6-9). This apostasy appears to have been a phase of the idolatrous worship previously described in 10:6 (which included "the gods of the Philistines"), because a resulting oppression by the Philistines (in the west) is mentioned in 10:7 to complement that by the Ammonites (in the east).

*b. The distress under the Philistines (13:1b)*

**13:1b.** The depths of Israelite apostasy and the greatness of Philistine strength were causes for the unprecedented length of oppression—**40 years**—though **the Philistines** continued as a threat until the early years of David's reign (cf. 2 Sam. 5:17-25). Though earlier Philistine settlements had been present in Palestine (cf. Gen. 21:32-34; 26:1-18; Jud. 1:18-19), the Philistines arrived in large numbers during the invasion of the Sea Peoples about 1200 B.C. They organized a pentapolis or confederation of five cities—Gaza, Ashkelon, and Ashdod on the strategic coastal highway, and Gath and Ekron on the edge of the Shephelah or Judean foothills (cf. Josh. 13:3).

When the Philistine aggression moved eastward into the land of Benjamin and Judah, the Israelites accepted that domination without resistance (cf. 14:4; 15:11) till the time of Samuel (cf. 1 Sam. 7:10-14).

How was it that Samson's parents, who were Danites, were still living in the Sorek Valley when much earlier the tribe of Dan had migrated north? (Jud. 18) Apparently a few of the Danite clans stayed behind and did not move northward.

*c. The deliverance by Samson (13:2–16:31)*

Unless the repentance mentioned in 10:10-16 includes the western Israelites who were being oppressed by the Philistines (cf. 10:7)—which is unlikely in view of their apparent acceptance of the Philistine domination (cf. 15:11)—there is no mention of Israel's cry to God before He raised up Samson as a deliverer (contrast 3:9, 15; 4:3; 6:7; 10:10). Since Samson judged Israel 20 years (15:20; 16:31), beginning apparently at about age 20, his entire life span must have approximated the 40-year Philistine oppression which began before his birth (cf. 13:5). He was thus a contemporary of Samuel who with God's help subdued the Philistines after Samson's death (cf. 1 Sam. 7:10-14).

(1) The birth of Samson (13:2-24). **13:2-5.** Samson's parents were **from the clan of the Danites,** perhaps implying that the bulk of the tribe of Dan had already made the move northward to the Huleh Valley (cf. chap. 18), so that only a clan or two remained in their original tribal inheritance. The childless **wife** of **Manoah** of **Zorah** was visited by **the Angel of the LORD.** Zorah, the highest point in the Shephelah, was on a high ridge north of the Sorek Valley and about 14 miles west of Jerusalem. Originally Zorah was a city of Judah (Josh. 15:20, 33), but later it was allotted to the tribe of Dan (Josh. 19:40-41). In this theophany (cf. comments on Jud. 2:1-2) the Lord foretold the **birth** of her **son,** Samson, and said that he was to **be a Nazirite.** A Nazirite (meaning "devoted" or "consecrated") was a person whose vow of separation **to God** included abstaining from **fermented drink,** refraining from cutting his hair, and avoiding contact with dead bodies (Num. 6:2-6). Nazirite vows were normally for a limited period of time but Samson was to be a Nazirite of God all his life (Jud. 13:7). His mother was to share for a time in part of the Nazirite vow (vv. 4, 7, 14). Besides being set apart as a Nazirite, Samson was chosen by God to **begin the deliverance of Israel from the hands of the Philistines.** The completion of this task would be left to Samuel (1 Sam. 7:10-14) and David (2 Sam. 5:17-25).

**13:6-8.** When Manoah's wife reported to him her encounter with this One whom she described as **a Man of God,** who **looked like an Angel . . . Manoah prayed** for His reappearance to **teach** them **how to bring up the boy.**

**13:9-18.** In response to Manoah's

prayer **the Angel of God** (another title for the Angel of the Lord) reappeared, first to his wife and then to **Manoah,** but He merely repeated His previous instructions (vv. 13-14). Not fully realizing the divine character of his Guest (v. 16b), **Manoah** invited the Messenger to stay for a meal. **The Angel** indicated that any provisions should be offered **to the LORD** as **a burnt offering.** On asking the Angel's **name,** Manoah was informed, **It is beyond understanding.**

**13:19-23.** Then **Manoah** sacrificed **a young goat** (cf. v. 15) with a **grain offering** (cf. Lev. 2) **on a rock to the LORD.** He and his wife were amazed as **the Angel of the LORD ascended in the flame** that blazed up from **the altar.** Realizing the identity of the divine Messenger, **Manoah** expressed fear of impending death because of their having **seen God** (cf. Gideon's similar response, Jud. 6:22-23). Manoah's **wife** more practically pointed out that God's acceptance of the sacrifice and the promise of a son indicated that immediate death was not God's plan for them.

**13:24.** In fulfillment of the words of the divine Messenger, Manoah's wife **gave birth to . . . Samson** (a name related to the word for "sun"), who **grew** up under the blessing of **the LORD.**

(2) The moving of Samson by the Holy Spirit. **13:25.** One day **the Spirit of the LORD began to stir** Samson, that is, to empower him to begin to deliver Israel. This happened at **Mahaneh Dan** ("Camp of Dan"; cf. 18:11-12 for the origin of the name) **between Zorah** (Samson's home; cf. 13:2) **and Eshtaol** (a town about one and one-half miles east by northeast of Zorah). Samson was later buried between these two towns (16:31; also cf. 18:2, 8, 11). Samson's leadership as judge or deliverer did not take the form of leading an army against the Philistines. Rather it consisted of his being a lone champion for the cause of his people. His exploits, the record of which begins in chapter 14, distracted the Philistines from more serious invasions into the tribal areas of Benjamin and Judah.

(3) The marriage of Samson to a Philistine woman (chap. 14). **14:1-4.** Samson's exploits with the Philistines began with his desire for **a young Philistine woman** who lived in **Timnah** (probably modern Tell el-Batashi, four miles north-

west down the Sorek Valley from Beth Shemesh). Since marriages were contracted by the parents (cf. Gen. 21:21), **Samson** insisted that his parents **get her for** him **as** his **wife.** Since marriage with a non-Israelite was expressly forbidden by the Mosaic Law (Ex. 34:16; Deut. 7:3), his parents objected to his marrying a Philistine (cf. Jud. 14:3). Other peoples around Israel, whether Egyptians or Semites, practiced circumcision, but the Philistines did not. By citing this fact Samson's parents were deriding the Philistines.

Though Samson's parents objected to his marrying a Philistine, they allowed Samson's wishes to prevail. They **did not know that this was from the** Lord, **who was seeking an occasion to confront the Philistines.** This does not mean that breaking the Law was desired by God but that Samson's decision was overruled by God for His own purpose and glory.

**14:5-7. Samson** took his parents **down to Timnah** to arrange the wedding. He apparently turned aside into **the vineyards of Timnah,** perhaps to obtain grapes, where he was attacked by **a young lion.** Under the empowerment of **the Spirit of the** Lord (cf. 14:19; 15:14) **he tore the lion apart with his bare hands,** probably in the manner Near-Easterners rend a young goat, pulling it in half by the hind legs. That he did not tell **his father** or **mother** about this implies that they had proceeded on to Timnah to complete the betrothal arrangement. When Samson arrived in Timnah, he could then actually talk to **the woman,** perhaps for the first time (before he had only "seen" her, 14:2), and **he liked her.**

**14:8-9.** Some time later, **when** the betrothal period was completed, he was on his way to the wedding. Again **he turned aside** into the vineyards, this time **to look at the lion's carcass** in which he discovered **a swarm of bees and some honey.** He **scooped out** the honey to eat it, and shared it with **his parents** without informing them of its source. While the Nazirite law strictly prohibited contact with a dead person, the purpose of this was to avoid ceremonial uncleanness (Num. 6:7). Since touching the carcass of even a clean animal made a person (with the obvious exception of an officiating priest) ceremonially unclean (Lev. 11:39-40), probably Samson's scooping the honey from the lion's carcass was a viola-

tion of his Nazirite vow. His participation in the wedding feast (Jud. 14:10) may also have violated his vow to abstain from fermented drink. However, only one Nazirite qualification was specifically indicated before his birth—"No razor may be used on his head" (13:5). Later a violation of this specific practice would lead to the removal of the power of God's Spirit from him (16:17-20).

**14:10-14.** At the **seven**-day wedding ceremony, **Samson** conducted the customary **feast** (lit., "drinking party") and was accompanied by **30 companions** (typical "friends of the bridegroom," apparently provided by the Philistine family). **Samson** told his companions **a riddle,** the meaning of which he made more challenging with a wager of **30 linen garments** (large rectangular sheets often used as undergarments) **and 30 sets of clothes** (festal garments, often embroidered). Solving Samson's poetically phrased riddle—**Out of the eater, something to eat; out of the strong, something sweet**—would require a knowledge of his having taken honey from the lion's carcass.

**14:15-18.** Unable to solve the riddle after three days, the companions threatened **Samson's** bride and her family with **death** if she would not obtain the answer for them. They implied that she might have been involved in a scheme with Samson to **rob** them by means of the wager. Samson withstood bridal tears till **the seventh day** of **the feast** when the time to solve the riddle would expire (cf. v. 12). Then Samson's weakness to give in to the tears or pleadings of a woman (cf. 16:16) was expressed. **He finally told her** and **she in turn explained the riddle** to the 30 Philistines. When they informed Samson of the solution which, like the riddle, they phrased in poetic parallelism, Samson retorted concerning his bride with a scornful but picturesque figure of speech: **If you had not plowed with my heifer, you would not have solved my riddle.** In calling her a "heifer" he was ridiculing her for her untamed and stubborn spirit (cf. Jer. 50:11; Hosea 4:16).

**14:19-20.** To fulfill his obligation in the wager (cf. v. 12) Samson attacked **30** Philistines in **Ashkelon** (23 miles southwestward on the Mediterranean coast— far enough away not to be associated with Samson in Timnah) and took **their clothes** to the Philistines **who had explained the riddle.** God overruled Samson's foolishness by the enabling power of **the Spirit of the LORD** (cf. v. 6; 15:14) to accomplish His purpose of disrupting the Philistine status quo of easy dominance over Israel (cf. 14:4). Still angry, Samson **went up to his father's house** in Zorah without returning to his wife on the seventh night of the wedding to consummate the marriage. The bride's father, to avoid the disgrace of what he perceived as an annulment (cf. 15:2), gave her to the best man.

(4) The conflicts of Samson with the Philistines (15:1–16:3). **15:1-5. Samson** later (in **the wheat harvest,** i.e., May) returned to Timnah with a present of **a young goat** (cf. 13:15, 19) for **his wife.** Samson's marriage was apparently the *ṣadīqa* type in which the bride remained with her parents and was visited periodically by her husband (cf. 8:31). Thus Samson's present was probably not a reconciliation gift for his previous behavior, but merely the expected gift on a husband's periodic visit. However, **Samson** soon discovered that his bride had been given to another by **her father** who thought Samson **hated her** (the word is used in a divorce context in Deut. 24:3).

Unimpressed with the offer of marriage to **her younger sister,** Samson again vented his anger on **the Philistines,** this time by burning their **grain** (wheat, Jud. 15:1) fields. He did this by fastening **torches** to the **tied . . . tails** of pairs of **300 foxes** (the Heb. word can also mean jackals which run in packs and are more easily caught). The fiery destruction included the dry **shocks** of grain already harvested along with the dry **standing grain** yet to be harvested and spread also to **the vineyards and olive groves** (thus destroying the land's three main crops; cf. Deut. 7:13; Hag. 1:11).

**15:6-8. When the Philistines** learned that **Samson** caused the destruction, they retaliated by burning **his wife . . . and her father to death** (apparently destroying the entire Timnite household). Motivated again by personal **revenge,** Samson **viciously . . . slaughtered many of** the **Philistines** and then walked to **a cave in the rock of Etam.** The term "viciously" is literally "leg on thigh," a wrestling metaphor for a ferocious attack. Though there

is a town named Etam about 2 miles southwest of Bethlehem in Judah (about 17 miles from Timnah), another possibility is to identify the site with a cleft above the Wadi Isma'in about 2½ miles southeast of Zorah.

**15:9-14.** Pursuing Samson, **the Philistines . . . camped in Judah . . . near Lehi** (lit., "jawbone"; perhaps modern Khirbet es-Siyyaj). When the Judeans learned the reason for the Philistine show of force, they sought **Samson** with **3,000 men** to turn him **over to the Philistines.** Apparently satisfied with the status quo, they asked **Samson, Don't you realize that the Philistines are rulers over us?** When the Judeans **agreed** not to kill him themselves, **Samson** (not wanting to shed Israelite blood) let them surrender him to **the Philistines. They bound him with two new ropes,** but these **became like charred flax and . . . dropped from his hands** when he came near the jubilant Philistines. Again special strength was given him by **the Spirit of the LORD** (cf. 14:6, 19).

**15:15-17.** Grabbing **a fresh jawbone of a donkey** (an old one would have been too brittle), **Samson** slaughtered **1,000** Philistines. His words of triumph included a play on the Hebrew *ḥămôr* which can mean either "donkey" or "heap." Thus the phrase translated **I have made donkeys of them** is often translated "heaps upon heaps" (NASB) and interpreted to mean something like, "I have piled them in heaps." **The place** where this happened was **Ramath Lehi,** which probably means "the hill (height) of the jawbone."

**15:18-19.** The next incident in Samson's life was God's provision of water for him. Samson was extremely **thirsty** after his difficult effort in the hot, dry climate. His cry **to the LORD** was miraculously answered as **God opened up the hollow place** (*maktēš,* lit., "mortar," i.e., basin) **and water came out.** This place where Samson's strength was restored **was** still **called En Hakkore** ("spring of the caller") when the Book of Judges was completed (**it is still there**).

**15:20.** Samson's leadership over **Israel,** summarized at this point, is also noted in 16:31. The **20 years** (about 1069–1049 B.C.) would cover Samson's adult life until his death in Gaza (cf. 16:30-31).

**16:1-3.** The incident of Samson's removing the doors of Gaza showed that his physical strength was unmatched except by his moral weakness. No reason is given why **Samson went to Gaza,** perhaps the most important Philistine city, which was near the coast about 35 miles southwest of his home in Zorah. Whatever the reason, his sensual inclinations overcame him and he spent **the night** with **a prostitute.** Aware of Samson's presence in the city, the Philistines **of Gaza . . . lay in wait for him all night at the city gate,** planning to **kill him** when he left **at dawn.** However, **Samson** arose in **the middle of the night,** apparently catching them by such surprise that he escaped even though he pulled away **the doors of the city gate, together with the two posts . . . bar and all.** In fact, he **carried** the doors **to the top of the hill that faces Hebron.** Whether this is a hill outside of Gaza that has a view eastward toward Hebron, or whether Samson carried the doors uphill 37 miles to a hill outside of Hebron, is not clear from the text. Local tradition identifies the hill as El Montar just east of Gaza. There seems to be no reason why Samson would carry the doors farther, since he had already insulted the people of the city by removing its gate of security.

(5) The downfall of Samson at the hands of Delilah (16:4-22). **16:4-14.** Samson **fell in love with a woman** named **Delilah** (though she was probably a Philistine, she had a Semitic name meaning "devotee" so she may have been a temple prostitute). She was at least the third woman with whom Samson had been involved (cf. 14:1-2; 16:1). The town where Delilah lived **in the Valley of Sorek** (where Samson spent most of his life) is not named, whether Har-heres (Beth Shemesh), or Timnah, or some other town.

The Philistine **rulers** devised a plot to capture Samson. The Bible does not say how many rulers were involved, but probably the number was five, one for each of the major Philistine cities. They hired Delilah to learn **the secret of his great strength and how** to **overpower . . . and subdue him.** The rulers each promised to give her the exorbitant amount of **1,100 shekels of silver,** equal to many thousands of dollars. **Delilah** made three fruitless attempts to gain Samson's confidence and **secret.** Each time he teased her by inventing a means

whereby he would **become as weak** as **any other man** and could be captured: (a) if he were **tied** up with **seven fresh thongs** (i.e., bowstrings prepared from animal viscera); (b) if he were **tied** up with **new ropes that have never been used** (but the effectiveness of this had already been disproven; 15:13); and (c) if his hair (getting closer to the truth) was woven **into the fabric on the loom. Delilah** futilely tried each method, apparently while **Samson** slept (as in 16:13), and seemed to tease him by crying out, **Samson, the Philistines are upon you!** (vv. 9, 12, 14) when in reality she was testing the success or failure of each method before the Philistines, **hidden in the room** (vv. 9, 12), dared show themselves.

**16:15-17.** Samson finally revealed the source of his strength, which was not a magical secret, as the Philistines had supposed, but a supernatural enablement from the Spirit of **God** (cf. 13:25; 14:6, 19; 15:14). This enablement was associated with Samson's special separation to the Lord through his **Nazirite** status, which was especially symbolized by his uncut hair (13:5). Samson explained his Nazirite status to Delilah when he could no longer bear her nagging him for his secret. He said that if his **head were shaved,** he **would become as weak as any other man.** This was not because his strength was in his hair but because cutting it would manifest his disobedience to the Lord, a disobedience that had already begun by his revealing the truth to Delilah whom he had no reason to trust.

**16:18-22.** Samson's indiscretion led to his imprisonment by **the Philistines.** This time **Delilah** sensed that **Samson had told her everything,** so she set the trap again and had **his hair** shaved while he slept **on her lap.** As a fruit of his foolish disobedience to the Lord, Samson's **strength left him.** Apparently Samson was also bound since, when Delilah cried out **The Philistines are upon you!** he attempted to **shake** himself **free.** The tragic fact was that **he did not know that the LORD had left him.** The departure of the Spirit of the Lord was tantamount to discharging him from his role as judge.

The powerless Samson was then **seized** by the Philistines who blinded him **and took him down to Gaza,** a just retribution they no doubt thought for his stealing its city gate (vv. 1-3). They bound **him with bronze shackles** and **set him to grinding** meal between millstones **in the prison,** a woman's work. This may have been a handmill with a saddle-quern (cf. comments on 9:53), since it is not certain that large animal-turned mills were used that early. As time passed while Samson was in prison, his **hair** (the symbol of his Nazirite dedication, 13:5) **began to grow again.** Since the physical growth of his hair would be expected, the point of this observation must have been the anticipation of Samson's renewed strength for one last act of revenge against the Philistines (cf. 16:28-30).

(6) The revenge of Samson on the Philistines. **16:23-30.** The time came for the Philistine **rulers . . . to offer a great sacrifice to Dagon their god.** Dagon was a West Semitic grain deity (cf. 1 Sam. 5:2-7; 1 Chron.10:10) adopted by the Philistines from the Amorites. Since they believed that their **god** had **delivered Samson . . . into** their **hands. . . . they called Samson out of the prison** to **entertain** them (apparently expecting to see some acts of strength, or perhaps just to mock their now-powerless opponent). A Philistine temple was typically a long inner chamber with two major **pillars** supporting the roof. A large group of Philistines (including some **3,000** people **on the roof**) watched **Samson perform,** apparently in an outer court. What his "performing" included is not known. Afterward blind **Samson** had **the servant who** was guiding him take him to **the pillars that support the temple,** on the pretext of resting **against them.** However, he then **prayed to the** Lord for one final feat of strength to obtain **revenge on the Philistines. Samson . . . bracing himself against** the pillars (whether between them pushing outward, or adjacent to them leaning forward), **said, Let me die with the Philistines!** and **pushed with all his might.** God granted his final prayer and **the temple** was demolished, killing **more** people in Samson's death than he had slain **while he lived.** Previously he had killed at least 1,030 Philistines (30 in Ashkelon, 14:19; and 1,000 at Ramath Lehi, 15:14-17).

(7) The burial of Samson by his relatives. **16:31.** Samson's **whole family** (his **brothers**) who had not been mentioned till this incident (**went down** to Gaza and

brought Samson's body back for burial **between Zorah** (his birthplace, 13:2) **and Eshtaol** (cf. 13:25; 18:2, 8, 11) in Manoah's **tomb.** Thus ended Samson's **20 years** of judgeship over **Israel** (cf. 15:20). Though Samson had great ability and was endowed with physical power by the Holy Spirit, he gave in to temptation several times and suffered the consequences. His life is a stern warning to others who are prone to follow the path of sensuality.

### III. Epilogue: Conditions Illustrating the Days of the Judges (chaps. 17–21)

Theologically chapters 17–21 constitute an epilogue giving illustrations of the religious apostasy and social degradation that characterized the period of the Judges. Those conditions were viewed by the author (probably early in the monarchy) as indicative of the anarchy which prevailed when "Israel had no king" (17:6; 18:1; 19:1; 21:25). Historically the events recorded in these chapters form an appendix to the book, having transpired fairly early in the preceding history. An early date is indicated by the presence of the grandsons of both Moses (18:30) and Aaron (20:28) and by reference to the ark at Bethel (20:27-28). Possibly the events in chapters 17–18 took place in the days of Othniel, the first judge.

The epilogue consists of two major sections: (1) Chapters 17–18 interweave stories of the household idolatry of Micah the Ephraimite who hired the Levite Jonathan, Moses' grandson (18:30), as his personal priest, and the migration and tribal idolatry of the Danites. (2) Chapters 19–21 narrate an atrocity perpetrated on another Levite's concubine at Gibeah, and the ensuing civil war against the recalcitrant tribe of Benjamin, leading to its near annihilation.

### A. Religious apostasy: The idolatry of Micah and the migration of the Danites (chaps. 17–18)

1. THE IDOLATRY OF MICAH THE EPHRAIMITE (CHAP. 17)

### a. The acquisition of an image by Micah (17:1-5)

**17:1-5.** It is ironic that **a man named Micah** (meaning "Who is like Yahweh?")

should establish an apostate shrine with an unlawful priesthood. Such a situation came about, in part, when he heard his mother . . . utter a curse against the thief who had stolen her 1,100 shekels of silver, and then confessed, I took it. (These 1,100 silver shekels are not to be confused with the 1,100 silver shekels that each of the Philistine rulers gave Delilah, 16:5, 18.) As a reward for such "honesty," his mother sought to neutralize her curse with a blessing (The LORD bless you, my son!). Her subsequent consecration of the silver to the LORD . . . to make a carved image was in disobedience to the command in Exodus 20:4, and reflects the idolatrous Canaanite influence on the Israelites during this period.

The phrase a carved image and a cast idol suggests two objects of false worship, an image carved out of stone or wood, and a cast idol made out of melted metal poured into a mold. But some scholars think the phrase is a hendiadys (referring to only one molded image), perhaps a wooden idol overlaid with silver which Micah's mother had made and placed in the house. However, in Judges 18:18 the objects are clearly distinct. Micah's mother paid a silversmith 200 silver shekels—equal to several thousand dollars—to make those objects of worship. These were not the only idols in Micah's aberrant shrine (lit., "house of god[s]"), for he had an ephod (possibly as an object of worship; cf. 8:24-27; or for a priest to wear) and some idols (t⁽ᵉ⁾rāpîm; cf. Gen. 31:17-50). He then installed one of his sons as his priest to conduct worship in this shrine (later Micah installed another priest, Jud. 17:12).

b. *The characteristics of the period of the Judges (17:6)*

17:6. The author, writing from the viewpoint of the early monarchy, explained Micah's religious lawlessness as a characteristic of a period without the centralized authority of a king (cf. 18:1; 19:1; 21:25).

c. *The acquisition of a Levitical priest by Micah (17:7-13)*

17:7-13. A young Bethlehem Levite (Moses' grandson, Jonathan son of Gershom; cf. 18:30) moved to the hill country of Ephraim where he was employed by Micah to be his father (a term of honor; cf. Gen. 45:8; 2 Kings 6:21; 13:14) and priest. Micah took care of him like one of his sons. So Micah installed the Levite (cf. Jud. 18:4) as his priest (in addition to Micah's own son, who was made a priest, 17:5). Micah rejoiced because of his superstitious notion that having a Levite (a young man; cf. 18:3) for his priest would bring blessings from the LORD, when in fact it was forbidden in the Law (cf. Num. 3:10). The Levite, of course, was as much (or more) to blame for having accepted the position. These acts of disobedience to God's Law were typical of the Israelites in the time of the Judges.

2. THE MIGRATION OF THE DANITES TO THE NORTH (CHAP. 18)

a. *The problem of the Danites (18:1)*

18:1. This chapter repeats the refrain of the epilogue that Israel had no king (17:6; 19:1; 21:25). This lack of a central authority to muster an Israelite army no doubt aggravated the problem faced by the tribe of Dan, namely, Dan's inability (or lack of faith) to come into an inheritance. The Danites were being pushed by the Amorites (1:34-35; cf. Josh. 19:47) and later the Philistines (with the rest of Israel; cf. Jud. 13:1; 14:4; 15:11). Dan was forced more and more eastward into the territory of Benjamin and Ephraim. Because of Dan's cramped living conditions its people decided to seek a new territory.

b. *The mission of the spies (18:2-10)*

18:2-6. The clans of the Danites sent five warriors from Zorah and Eshtaol (cf. 13:25; 16:31) to explore the land. Early in their journey they lodged for the night in the house of Micah in the hill country of Ephraim (cf. 17:1). There they recognized the voice (probably the Judean accent) of Micah's priest (the young Levite Jonathan; cf. 17:12) and inquired concerning his presence and activities in Ephraim. When they learned that he was functioning as a priest, they superstitiously sought some word of God's blessing on their mission. One wonders about the source of the priest's confident answer: Your journey has the LORD's approval. The outward success of their mission did not correspond with the Lord's revealed plan for the tribe of Dan, and eventuated in the establishing of a major center of idolatry (cf. 18:30-31; 1 Kings 12:28-30).

**18:7.** As **the five** spies continued to explore the land they eventually **came to Laish** (Leshem in Josh. 19:47; modern Tell el-Qadi) about 25 miles north of the Sea of Kinnereth and 27 miles east of Tyre. Located on the north edge of the fertile Huleh Basin, the **land lacked nothing** and **the people . . . were prosperous.** Their town was also isolated from **the Sidonians** by the Lebanon range of mountains, and from Syria by Mount Hermon and the Anti-Lebanon range, so that they were without close military allies. Possibly Hazor had already been destroyed (Jud. 4:2, 23-24), though this may raise some chronological problems concerning the Levite as Moses' grandson (cf. 18:30).

**18:8-10.** Returning home, the five spies reported **an unsuspecting people and a spacious land . . . that lacks nothing whatever.** They encouraged the Danites to **attack** Laish without hesitation. They felt that **God** had given it to them. Though their theological affirmation is debatable, their anticipated victory seemed inevitable.

*c. The expedition against Laish (18:11-28a)*

**18:11-13. The Danites** armed **600 men . . . for battle** who first camped **near Kiriath Jearim** (about six miles east of the Zorah-Eshtaol area). Their campsite, **Mahaneh Dan** ("Camp of Dan"), was where Samson later first sensed the work of God's Spirit in his life (13:25). The Danites then **went on** to **Ephraim** where Micah (cf. 17:1; 18:2) lived.

**18:14-21. The five** spies then informed their fellow warriors about the house and shrine of Micah (cf. 17:5). While the fighters waited outside, the five men **greeted** Micah's **priest,** and then proceeded to steal Micah's **image, ephod,** and idols. When **the priest** challenged them, they told him, **Be quiet!** and invited him to become their tribal **priest** rather than just a **household** priest. He gladly accepted the offer and **went with** them carrying Micah's **ephod, the other household gods, and the carved image** (cf. 17:4-5). Anticipating

that Micah might pursue them, the Danites sent their families and **possessions** on ahead of them and formed a rear guard.

**18:22-26. Micah** soon discovered his loss, and accompanied by his friends and neighbors he pursued **the Danites.** Micah accused them of appropriating his **gods** and **priests.** But when they intimidated him with threats of violence he reluctantly but wisely **turned around and went back home.** His pathetic question concerning his idols—**What else do I have?**—reflects the emptiness of idolatry.

**18:27-28a.** The **peaceful and unsuspecting people** of Laish (cf. v. 7) were no match for the determined Danites who defeated them **and burned down their city.** The people of Laish were 27 miles **from Sidon** (cf. v. 7) **and had no** allies to come to their rescue.

*d. The establishment of idolatry at Dan (18:28b-31)*

**18:28b-31. The Danites rebuilt the city** and **named it Dan after their** tribal **forefather.** More significantly (and sadly), they established a tribal center of idolatrous worship under the priesthood of **Jonathan son of Gershom** (cf. Ex. 2:22) which extended through his descendants **until the time of the captivity of the land.** Many scholars refer this to either the Assyrian captivity of Israel in 722 B.C. (2 Kings 17:6) or the captivity of the Galilean population under Tiglath-Pileser III in 733–732 B.C. (2 Kings 15:29). However, an early monarchial date of the authorship of Judges suggests that the statement refers to an earlier unknown captivity (some have suggested the Philistine capture of the ark; cf. 1 Sam. 4:11). For **Moses** the Hebrew text has inserted a superlinear $n$ into the name of Moses ($m\bar{o}šeh$) to make it read "Manasseh" ($m^e naššeh$). This was apparently a pious scribe's attempt to relieve Moses' grandson, Jonathan, of involvement with idolatry. The reference to **the house of God . . . in Shiloh** (modern Seilun 19 miles north of Jerusalem) implies that the worship at the Danite shrine opposed the true worship of the Lord at Shiloh (cf. Josh. 18:1). This false worship in Dan was a forerunner of that of Jeroboam I who later established a Northern Kingdom shrine at **Dan** (cf. 1 Kings 12:28-31).

## B. Moral degradation: The atrocity of Gibeah and the war with the Benjamites (chaps. 19–21)

### 1. THE ATROCITY AGAINST THE CONCUBINE OF THE LEVITE (CHAP. 19)

#### a. The reconciliation of the Levite with his concubine (19:1-9)

**19:1a.** This chapter opens with the slogan, **In those days Israel had no king** (cf. 17:6; 18:1; 21:25). This indicates that chapters 19–21 illustrate the *anarchy and injustice* that prevailed when the Israelites did not have the centralized authority of a king. Chapters 17–18 illustrate the *idolatry* that characterized the nation.

**19:1b-9.** The **Levite** mentioned in this chapter is not Micah's Levite (chaps. 17–18) though both had connections with **Bethlehem in Judah** and both lived **in the hill country of Ephraim.** The **remote area** (lit., "backside of") was off the main north-south ridge route. This Levite's **concubine** (a second-status wife, a practice that was never divinely approved; cf. 8:31) **was unfaithful to him** (lit., "played the harlot"), after which she returned **to her father's house in Bethlehem.** Four months later the Levite traveled to Bethlehem where he initiated a reconciliation with his concubine. He was **gladly welcomed** by his **father-in-law** who, with typical Near-Eastern hospitality, entertained him for four days and part of a fifth before the Levite decided he could **stay** no longer.

#### b. The arrival of the Levite's entourage at Gibeah (19:10-15)

**19:10-15.** The Levite took his servant, **his two . . . donkeys** (cf. v. 3), **and his concubine,** and traveled northward six miles to pass by **Jebus** (a name for Jerusalem used only here in vv. 10-11 and 1 Chron. 11:4-5, so named for the Amorite group of Jebusites who lived there). He declined his servant's suggestion to **spend the night** in Jebus because it was **an alien city, whose people** were **not Israelites.** The Levite determined to move on to more friendly territory (an ironic and unfortunate decision in view of the following events). So they pressed four miles farther north **to Gibeah** (modern Tell el-Ful) where **they stopped to spend the night.** However, though they **sat in the city square,** the hospitality of

the Benjamites was not forthcoming.

#### c. The hospitality of the old man from Ephraim (19:16-21)

**19:16-21.** At the last minute they were saved from a night of danger **in the city square** by **an old man from the hill country of Ephraim** who invited them to **spend the night** at **his house** in Gibeah.

#### d. The assault by the wicked men of Gibeah (19:22-26)

**19:22-26.** Reminiscent of the wicked Sodomites in the time of Lot (cf. Gen. 19:1-11), **the wicked men** (or "worthless men"; lit., "sons of Belial"; cf. 1 Sam. 1:16; 2:12) **of** Gibeah **surrounded the house** and demanded that the old man send out the Levite to satisfy their homosexual desires. Considering the laws of hospitality more important than chivalry toward the opposite sex, **the old man** offered them instead his **virgin daughter** and the Levite's **concubine.** The men either did not hear or refused his offer, but when the Levite thrust **his concubine . . . outside to them,** they took her and sexually **abused her throughout the night. At daybreak** she was released to return; she fell **at the door** of the house where she died.

#### e. The call of the Levite for tribal vengeance (19:27-30)

**19:27-30. When** the Levite **stepped out** of the door **to continue on his way** (not to look for his concubine!), he discovered her corpse **in the doorway,** and **put her on his donkey and set out for home.** The Levite next performed an almost unbelievable cruelty, cutting **up his concubine limb by limb** (lit., "according to her bones," like a priest preparing a sacrifice) **into 12 parts** (apparently one for each tribe) to be sent **. . . into all the areas of Israel** (cf. 1 Sam. 11:7; 1 Kings 11:30). While this is difficult for modern readers to understand (as well as for the Levite's contemporaries; Jud. 19:30; cf. Hosea 9:9), he meant to arouse the nation to action by calling for a national judicial hearing. Perhaps he was charging them with the responsibility of removing the bloodguiltiness that rested on the entire nation for his concubine's death. The people who **saw** a part of her were appalled and bewildered as to what to do.

### 2. THE WAR AGAINST THE TRIBE OF BENJAMIN (CHAP. 20)

The Benjamite war narrated in this chapter resulted from the inquiry into the death of the Levite's concubine (cf. chap. 19). It describes an unusually dark hour in Israel's history.

#### a. The assembly of Israel at Mizpah (20:1-11)

**20:1-7.** In response to the Levite's call for an inquest, **all the Israelites from Dan to Beersheba** (i.e., from the northern to southern boundaries of Israel; this is a stereotyped expression written from the perspective of the early monarchial author) **and from the land of Gilead** (here referring to all the Transjordanian tribes) **assembled.** They gathered **before the LORD in Mizpah** (Tell en-Nasba, eight miles north of Jerusalem and only four miles north of Gibeah; not the Mizpah in Gilead; cf. 10:17; 11:29). The reference to **400,000 soldiers** need not be understood as 400 contingents or 400 family units, as some scholars have suggested.

**The Benjamites** were not officially represented at **Mizpah** since the men who raped the concubine were from Gibeah in Benjamin. Apparently, however, the tribe of Benjamin received 1 of the 12 parts of the concubine (cf. 19:29; 20:6). On request, **the Levite** explained the circumstances of his concubine's rape and death, and called for Israel's **verdict.**

**20:8-11.** The verdict was unanimous: **All the people rose as one man** against the town of **Gibeah** to **give them what they deserve** by launching an attack. One-tenth of the Israelites' troops collected supplies for those who did the fighting.

#### b. The rejection of the verdict by the Benjamites (20:12-13)

**20:12-13.** The **Benjamites** rejected the request of the other tribes **to surrender those wicked men of Gibeah** for execution in order to **purge the evil** (of bloodguiltiness) **from Israel.** Therefore **Israel** took the final step and attacked Gibeah.

#### c. The mustering of the troops for battle (20:14-18)

**20:14-16.** Having rejected the request of their fellow **Israelites** (cf. v. 13), **the Benjamites** mobilized **26,000 swordsmen** plus **700 . . . left-handed** men from

**Gibeah** who were all experts with slings.

**20:17-18.** As noted previously (v. 2), the 11 tribes had the advantage of a much larger army—**400,000** men. They **went up to Bethel** (meaning "house of God") to inquire of the Lord (probably through the high priest's Urim and Thummim; cf. Lev. 8:8; Num. 27:21; Deut. 33:8) concerning which tribe should lead the attack **against the Benjamites.** The Lord's answer was, **Judah shall go first.** Since the tabernacle (or similar central sanctuary where the high priest could be consulted) was located in Shiloh both before (cf. Josh. 18:1) and after (cf. 1 Sam. 1:9) this incident, some scholars refer "Bethel" here not to the city but to "the house of God" which was at Shiloh (cf. Jud. 18:31, "the house of God was in Shiloh"). However, in 18:31 and elsewhere when the sanctuary is called "the house of God" the Hebrew phrase is *bêt-hā'ĕlōhîm*, not just *bêt-'ēl* (as in 20:18, 26). Possibly the central sanctuary was moved back and forth between Shiloh and Bethel, perhaps more than once. So it is preferable to regard Bethel in verses 18 and 26 as the city on the central ridge route 10 or 12 miles north of Jerusalem.

#### d. The victories of Benjamin over Israel (20:19-28)

**20:19-23.** The location and topography of **Gibeah** made it easy to defend. **The Benjamites came out of Gibeah,** attacked the Israelite **battle positions,** and slayed **22,000 Israelites.** The Israelites **encouraged one another** and regrouped at the same battle **positions** for another day's fighting. In view of their defeat they also **went up** to Bethel **and wept before the LORD,** inquiring this time whether they should continue **to battle against the Benjamites.** The Lord's answer was affirmative: **Go up against them.**

**20:24-28.** The strategy and events of the previous day were repeated on **the second day,** but **this time** Israel lost "only" **18,000** men. This second defeat motivated **the Israelites** to return **to Bethel** where they wept **before the LORD and fasted . . . and presented burnt offerings and fellowship offerings to the LORD** (cf. 21:4). Perhaps one reason the Lord permitted their initial defeats was to bring them back in a spirit of repentance to the neglected sacrificial worship. This time their inquiry about whether they should continue the battle not only received a positive reply (**Go**) but also included a promise of victory (**tomorrow I will give them into your hands**). The mention of **Phinehas son of Eleazar** (i.e., Aaron's grandson) implies that he was instrumental in procuring the oracle from the Lord. It also indicates that this event occurred not much later than the death of Joshua (cf. 18:30).

*e. The defeat of the Benjamites by Israel (20:29-46)*

A general account of the battle (vv. 29-36a) is followed by a detailed and supplementary account (vv. 36b-46).

**20:29-36a.** God's promise of victory (v. 28) did not lead to presumption on Israel's part, for they reviewed and improved their battle strategy by setting **an ambush around Gibeah.** This was accomplished as follows: The Israelites **took up** the same battle **positions** as **before** and then deliberately fled as **the Benjamites** launched their attack, so that **the Benjamites** were **drawn away from the city.** Joshua had used a similar ambush strategy against Ai (Josh. 8:1-29). **Then 10,000 of Israel's finest men** attacked **Gibeah** frontally, and **the Lord** gave them victory in battle. The **Benjamites** lost **25,100** soldiers—almost their entire force of 26,700 (Jud. 20:15).

**20:36b-46.** These verses supplement the previous account by detailing the ambush and the aftermath of the major battle. As the Benjamites were drawn away from the city (cf. vv. 31-32), the Israelites who were waiting **in ambush** dashed **into Gibeah,** slaying the population and setting the city on fire. **The smoke of the whole city going up into the sky** was a prearranged signal for the retreating **Israelites** to turn on the **terrified** Benjamites who **fled** toward **the desert** (eastward; cf. v. 43). Before 600 Benjamites finally escaped to **the rock of Rimmon** (v. 45; cf. v. 47), they suffered a total loss of approximately **25,000 Benjamite swordsmen** (the more exact figure of 25,100 is given in v. 35). The narrative groups their deaths in stages of the battle—**18,000** (v. 44), **5,000 . . . along the roads,** and **2,000** (v. 45).

*f. The aftermath of the defeat of Benjamin (20:47-48)*

**20:47-48.** **Six hundred** Benjamite warriors were able to reach the defensible

stronghold of **the rock of Rimmon** (modern Rammun, four miles east of Bethel), **where they stayed four months** (until they received terms of peace from the Israelites; cf. 21:13-14). They were the only survivors from the entire tribe of Benjamin since the Israelite soldiers destroyed and burned **all the towns** of the Benjamites. Since the destruction included **the animals and everything else they found,** apparently they had placed the Benjamite towns "under the ban" as in holy war (cf. comments on 1:17).

3. THE PRESERVATION OF THE TRIBE OF BENJAMIN (21:1-24)

*a. The national concern for the completeness of Israel (21:1-7)*

**21:1-7.** The atrocity of Gibeah (19:25-26) had been punished and bloodguiltiness had been removed from Israel by the deaths of the Benjamites (20:35). However, with the war and destruction behind them, the Israelites became aware of another painful problem—1 of the 12 tribes of Israel had been nearly exterminated and since only 600 males remained alive, Benjamin was in danger of extinction. The problem was complicated by the fact that the Israelites **had taken an oath at Mizpah** not to **give** their **daughters in marriage** to a Benjamite (cf. 21:7, 18). Of course it was contrary to the Mosaic Law for the remaining 600 Benjamites to marry non-Israelites (cf. Ex. 34:16; Deut. 7:3). A secondary matter faced by the Israelites was the fulfillment of another **solemn oath** to **put to death** any **Israelites** who had **failed to assemble** at **Mizpah.** The primary matter of Benjamite extinction resulted in another period at Bethel when the Israelites **sat before God until evening, raising their voices and weeping bitterly.** The content of their lament was, **Why should one tribe be missing from Israel today?** They also participated in sacrificial worship, giving **burnt offerings and fellowship offerings** (cf. Jud. 20:26).

*b. The expedition of Israel against Jabesh Gilead (21:8-12)*

**21:8-12.** In researching their secondary problem (cf. v. 5), the Israelites **discovered that no one from** the town of **Jabesh Gilead** (located about nine miles southeast of Beth Shan and two miles east of the Jordan River) had responded to the call to Mizpah. So they fulfilled their vow by having **12,000** soldiers exterminate the people of **Jabesh Gilead,** except that they spared the **400** virgins of the city as a step toward solving the primary problem of Benjamite extinction.

*c. The reconciliation of Israel with Benjamin (21:13-18)*

**21:13-18.** The assembly of Israelites next **sent** to the 600 surviving **Benjamites** a formal **offer of peace** (*šālôm,* implying restoration to covenantal participation). They accepted the peace offer and were granted the 400 virgins **of Jabesh Gilead.** Israelite grief continued, however, because 200 Benjamites were still without **wives.**

*d. The provision of the maidens from Shiloh (21:19-24)*

**21:19.** The Israelites conceived a plan, based on a loophole in their oath, which they suggested to the Benjamites. The oath said the Israelites could not "give" (vv. 1, 7, 18) their daughters to the Benjamites, but it said nothing about their daughters being "taken." Conveniently the girls of nearby **Shiloh** (about 13 miles north by northeast of Mizpah) would soon be participating in a local harvest feast where they would dance in the fields near the vineyards. **Lebonah** (modern el-Lubbān) was about 3 miles north of Shiloh.

**21:20-24.** The 200 **Benjamites** were to **hide in the vineyards** until the festivities were in progress, and then each was to **rush from the vineyards and . . . seize a wife . . . and go to the land of Benjamin.** The Israelites would then explain the situation to the men of Shiloh, that they were **innocent** (of breaking the oath of Mizpah; v. 1) since they **did not give** their **daughters** to the Benjamites. So the extinction of the tribe of Benjamin was averted, **the Benjamites. . . . rebuilt the towns and settled in them,** and **the Israelites . . . went home.** Though the people were guilty of scheming to get around their oath, the tribe of Benjamin was saved from extinction.

4. THE CHARACTERISTICS OF THE PERIOD OF THE JUDGES (21:25)

**21:25.** The Book of Judges concludes with a final restatement of human failure concerning the moral and social anarchy

of this period which preceded the monarchy. As stated three times before, **Israel had no king** (cf. 17:6; 18:1; 19:1). The fact that **everyone did as he** wished is a sad commentary on the deplorable spiritual condition of the nation in those days. Though Israel suffered under the oppression of many enemies, God's grace was repeatedly evident when the people turned to Him in repentance. The Book of Judges illustrates both God's justice and His grace—justice in punishing sin and grace in forgiving sin.

# BIBLIOGRAPHY

Armerding, Carl Edwin. "Judges." In *The New Layman's Bible Commentary.* Grand Rapids: Zondervan Publishing House, 1979.

Boling, Robert G. *Judges: Introduction, Translation, and Commentary.* The Anchor Bible. Garden City, N.Y.: Doubleday & Co., 1975.

Bruce, F.F. "Judges." In *The New Bible Commentary.* 3rd ed. Grand Rapids: Zondervan Publishing House, 1970.

Cundall, Arthur E., and Morris, Leon. *Judges; Ruth.* The Tyndale Old Testament Commentaries. Chicago: InterVarsity Press, 1968.

Davis, John J., and Whitcomb, John C. *A History of Israel: From Conquest to Exile.* Grand Rapids: Baker Book House, 1980.

Enns, Paul P. *Judges.* Bible Study Commentary. Grand Rapids: Zondervan Publishing House, 1982.

Garstang, John. *Joshua–Judges.* Grand Rapids: Kregel Publications, 1978.

Gray, John. *Joshua, Judges, and Ruth.* Greenwood, S.C.: Attic Press, 1967.

Inrig, Gary. *Hearts of Iron, Feet of Clay.* Chicago: Moody Press, 1979.

Keil, C.F., and Delitzsch, F. In *Commentary on the Old Testament in Ten Volumes.* Vol. 2. Reprint (25 vols. in 10). Grand Rapids: Wm. B. Eerdmans Publishing Co., 1982.

Soggin, J. Alberto. *Judges: A Commentary.* Old Testament Library. Philadelphia: Westminster Press, 1981.

Wood, Leon. *Distressing Days of the Judges.* Grand Rapids: Zondervan Publishing House, 1975.

# RUTH

## John W. Reed

## INTRODUCTION

**Title and Authorship.** The Book of Ruth is named for a Moabitess who had married a Hebrew man living in Moab. After the death of her husband, Ruth migrated with Naomi, her widowed Hebrew mother-in-law, to Bethlehem in Israel. There God providentially provided for her and led her to marry Boaz, a prosperous Hebrew farmer. Ruth became the great-grandmother of King David. She is listed in the genealogy of Christ in Matthew 1:5.

Ruth and Esther are the only two books in the Bible named for women. Esther was a Hebrew woman who married a Gentile king. God used Esther in a strategic time in the history of Israel to help preserve the nation from destruction. Ruth, on the other hand, was a Gentile woman who married a Hebrew man. God used Ruth to perpetuate the line of the Messiah, the Lord Jesus Christ.

The Book of Ruth is read annually by orthodox Jews on the Feast of Pentecost. This feast commemorates the giving of the Law on Mount Sinai and occurs at the time of the beginning of the offering called the Firstfruits of the Harvest (Ex. 23:16). Ruth's betrothal took place during this festive harvest season, when barley was being winnowed (Ruth 3:2; cf. 1:22).

No one knows for sure who wrote the Book of Ruth. Jewish tradition has attributed the book to Samuel. If he was the author, the book would have been written near the time when David was anointed king of Israel. One of the reasons, then, for Samuel's writing the Book of Ruth could have been to justify David's claim to the throne (through Ruth and Boaz, his great-grandparents).

Most conservative scholars place the date of the writing of Ruth in the Monarchy, either in the time of David or Solomon. Since Solomon is not mentioned in the genealogy at the end of the book (4:18-21), one might deduce that the book was written in David's time. On the other hand an old custom that had ceased to be practiced—the exchanging of the sandal—was explained (4:7). This has caused some to think that the Solomonic period was more likely since additional time would have passed for the custom to have fallen into disuse. Hals has discussed the matter of authorship in further detail (*The Theology of the Book of Ruth*, pp. 65-75).

**Historical and Literary Features.** The Book of Ruth gleams like a beautiful pearl against a jet-black background. The action recorded in the narrative took place during the period of the Book of Judges (Ruth 1:1). Those days were the dark ages of Israel's history. The victories of Joshua had been followed by periods of spiritual declension with but brief periods of revival. As the time of the Judges wore on, the apostasy deepened till the book ended in corruption and bloody civil strife.

The period of the Judges was marked by weak faith and irresponsible conduct. Even Gideon, who exhibited great faith against overwhelming odds during the destruction of the invading Midianites, Amalekites, and eastern desert tribes (Jud. 7:12, 17-21), later failed to seek God's advice in the everyday affairs of his judgeship (Jud. 8:16-17, 21, 27). Gideon had many wives and concubines, who bore him 70 sons (Jud. 8:29-32).

After Gideon's death Abimelech, a son by his concubine in Shechem, killed all the other sons except one and established himself as a godless and bloody king (Jud. 9).

Since Ruth was the great-grandmother of David (Ruth 4:17), who began his rule at Hebron in 1010 B.C., the experiences in the Book of Ruth occurred in the last half of the 12th century. This means that Ruth may have been a contemporary of Gideon (see the chart "The Judges of Israel" in the *Introduction* to Jud.).

The sensual activities of the judge Samson became an archetype of a hero who is mighty in physical strength but weak in spiritual and moral character.

Against this background of national irresponsibility and weak character Ruth, a Moabitess, and Boaz, a Hebrew landowner, shone as bright examples of purity, faith, and responsible living. The Ruth narrative provided a gratifying reminder that even in the darkest times God was at work in the hearts of His faithful remnant.

The degree of permissiveness in Israel was a theme repeated often in the Book of Judges and restated in the book's last verse: "In those days Israel had no king; everyone did as he saw fit" (Jud. 21:25). By contrast the Book of Ruth provides a view of people who acted responsibly, rather than permissively, and with faith in God's sovereign, superintending control.

Ruth also stood in stark relief against the dark background of her own Moabite ancestry. Moses detailed the somber story of the nation of Moab's origin (Gen. 19:30-38). Lot's two daughters despaired of any future after the destruction of Sodom and Gomorrah. In faithless irresponsibility they got their father drunk enough that he would have sex with them in the cave where they lived. The fruits of their incest were Moab and Ben-Ammi. These sons became the founders of the Moabites and the Ammonites, respectively, nations that often warred against Israel.

Ruth the Moabitess broke the tradition of her idolatrous people and her irresponsible ancestor, Lot's older daughter. Ruth became a believer in the God of the Hebrews. She sought her fulfillment as a mother through the righteous requirements of the Mosaic Law. She proved herself to be worthy of being named with the finest women of Israel.

The practice of levirate marriage (the requirement that a man marry the widow of his deceased brother, Deut. 25:5-6) and the activity of the kinsman-redeemer provided an additional backdrop for the narrative. Ruth 4:9-17 discloses the specific aspects of this practice as Boaz took the kinsman-redeemer responsibility and married the widowed Ruth. In this account is a strong overtone of grace since Boaz was not within the immediate circle of levirate responsibility. In other words he was not a brother of the deceased Mahlon. His willing acceptance of this responsibility showed the genuine quality of his character, as well as his love for Ruth.

This willing action of Boaz placed him in contrast with his ancestor, Judah, 1 of Jacob's 12 sons. Judah had not acted responsibly in the case of his daughter-in-law, Tamar. Judah had three sons by his Canaanite wife. Judah's eldest son married Tamar, also a Canaanite. This son, Er, was wicked and God took his life (Gen. 38:7). Judah gave his second son, Onan, to Tamar to perform the levirate responsibility of raising up a son for his dead brother.

Onan "knew that the offspring would not be his" (Gen. 38:9), for children born to him and Tamar would perpetuate not his name but the name of his brother Er. So Onan, though he enjoyed sexual relations with Tamar, spilled his sperm on the ground. Because his refusal to fulfill the levirate responsibility displeased God, Onan also died (Gen. 38:10).

After Onan's death Judah did not give his third son, Shelah, to Tamar. It appeared that the family line would cease. But after Judah became a widower, Tamar posed as a harlot and seduced Judah. She conceived and bore twins, Perez and Zerah. Judah, in spite of Tamar's actions, declared that she was more righteous than he because he had refused to fulfill his responsibility and give his third son to her (Gen. 38:11-30).

When the elders at the gate of Bethlehem witnessed the levirate transaction between Boaz and Ruth, they blessed their union with mention of Perez, whom Tamar bore to Judah (Ruth 4:9-12). Ruth stood in contrast with Tamar in that she gained her levirate fulfillment honorably according to the Mosaic Law, whereas Tamar used a disguise and seduction. Without the births of Perez (to Tamar) and Obed (to Ruth and Boaz) the line from Judah to David would have been broken.

The grace of God was evident in that

He included several non-Israelites in the line of David. Since this was the line through which Christ came, it foreshadowed God's inclusion of Gentiles in the work of David's greater Son, the Lord Jesus Christ. Four non-Israelite women are mentioned in Christ's genealogy in Matthew 1—Tamar (Matt. 1:3), Rahab (Matt. 1:5), Ruth (Matt. 1:5), and Uriah's wife, who was Bathsheba (Matt. 1:6). Tamar was a Canaanite, who became the mother of Judah's children, Perez and Zerah. Rahab was a Canaanite harlot in Jericho who became an ancestress of Boaz (cf. comments on Ruth 4:21). Ruth was a Moabitess who became the mother of Obed. Since Bathsheba, the mother of Solomon by David, had been the wife of Uriah, the Hittite, it was probable that she too was a Hittite.

The Book of Ruth is beautifully written with a symmetrical design. It is a "romantic quest" that began in tragic circumstances and ended in joyous fulfillment. It is a book of seeking. Ruth sought a home, provision, a husband, and ultimately a son. Though she was widowed and without offspring, God gave her a husband and a son.

Naomi lost her husband and her two sons in Moab. In her depression she failed to realize the value of her Moabitess daughter-in-law, Ruth. But the book ends with Naomi's depression turned to joy. Her neighbors reminded her that Ruth was more valuable to her than seven sons. Naomi held in her arms Obed, her grandson. But her neighbors called Obed Naomi's "son" (4:17) because the levirate obligation had been willingly undertaken by the godly Boaz.

Mother-in-law jokes are today part of the stock repartee of comedians. This may have been the case in Naomi's insensitive day as well. But Ruth's love and care for her aging mother-in-law stands as a model for all generations. The fact that Boaz was careful to provide for Naomi along with Ruth indicated that his spirit was in tune with Ruth's in this regard. This is the best of all mother-in-law stories and should be told repeatedly.

**Theological Emphasis.** The writer of Ruth stressed several theological truths. Several names of God were used profusely in the book. "LORD" (*Yahweh*) was used 17 times, "God" (*'ĕlōhîm*) 3 times (1:16 [twice]; 2:12), and "Almighty" (*šadday*) twice (1:20-21). Yahweh was the name that spoke of God's essential nature as a present active force in the lives of His covenant people.

On two occasions the author spoke directly of God's sovereign, superintending grace on behalf of the main characters in the Book of Ruth: (1) Naomi learned "in Moab that the LORD had come to the aid of His people by providing food for them" (1:6). (2) Ruth had been barren for several years in Moab before her husband Mahlon died. Later, as the wife of Boaz, "the LORD enabled her to conceive, and she gave birth to a son" (4:13).

Eight times the characters in the book spoke of God's activity (1:13, 20-21 [four times]; 2:20; 4:12, 14). The Lord was regularly petitioned to answer prayers on their behalf (1:8-9; 2:12; 4:11-12). Five times blessing from the Lord was invoked on behalf of faithful people (2:4 [twice], 19-20; 3:10). Ruth and Boaz committed themselves to carry out their responsibilities in light of God's fidelity (1:17; 3:13). Boaz commended Ruth for seeking refuge under the wings of Israel's God (2:12).

Clearly God would always act responsibly and carry out His plan. The question was whether the people in the Book of Ruth would respond in a responsible manner. Elimelech seemed irresponsible in leaving Bethlehem and going to Moab (1:2). But Naomi acted responsibly in returning (1:7). Orpah returned to her home and her Moabite gods; in contrast Ruth chose to follow Naomi's God and to care for Naomi (1:14-17). Though the nearest kinsman refused to redeem, faithful Boaz acted responsibly in providing redemption (3:12; 4:1-10). Various forms of the Hebrew words "redeem," "redeemer," "redemption," and "kinsman-redeemer" are used 20 times in the book, thus making redemption one of the book's key words.

Another key word is *ḥesed*, which speaks of loyalty borne out of love and kindness toward those to whom a person is responsible. Naomi asked that the Lord would show His *ḥesed* to her daughters-in-law (1:8). Naomi also spoke of the Lord's *ḥesed* to her ("the living") because of what Boaz had done for Ruth (2:20). Boaz affirmed the *ḥesed* of Ruth when she asked him to marry her instead of seeking a younger man. This kindness, Boaz said, was even greater than her earlier kindness to Naomi (3:10). Boaz performed an act of *ḥeseḏ* when he went beyond the bounds of what was required of him in marrying Ruth.

**Message.** The book's message may have been an affirmation of King David's rights to the throne of Israel. The display of God's providence in bringing this to pass can challenge all Christians to believe that God is at work in their lives as well.

The truth of the book for all ages might be stated as follows: The Lord is faithful in His business of loving, superintending, and providentially caring for His people. God's people should also be about His business in the ordinary activities of daily living. Since God's people are recipients of His grace they, like Ruth and Boaz, should respond in faithful obedience to Him and in gracious acts toward other people.

During a period of great irresponsibility in Israel's history the Book of Ruth was a clear call to responsible living. Clearly this message is needed today as well.

Boaz is an illustration of the greater One who came from his family, the Lord Jesus Christ. Boaz acted in grace to redeem Ruth; Christ acted in grace by giving Himself as the Redeemer to provide redemption for all mankind.

# OUTLINE

# COMMENTARY

## I. Introduction (1:1-5)

The narrative begins with the necessary mention of the time, names, places, and events. The mood was somber and foreboding. A famine forced a family in Bethlehem to move to a foreign land. This situation became an opportunity for God to demonstrate His grace. The unfolding of the story revealed how God providentially worked to meet needs.

### A. A tragic sojourn (1:1-2)

**1:1.** The events recorded in the Book of Ruth occurred in the period of **the Judges,** probably during the administration of the judge Gideon (see "Historical and Literary Features" under *Introduction*). The **famine in the land** was probably God's acting in judgment on His sinning people. Many years later in Elijah's day God sent another famine as judgment on Israel for worshiping Baal (1 Kings 16:30–17:1; 18:21, 37; 19:10).

Divine control of the crops was a major factor in the development of events in the Book of Ruth. During the period of the Judges, worship of the Canaanite god Baal was common among the Israelites (Jud. 2:11; 3:7; 8:33; 10:6, 10). Baal was believed to be owner of the land and to control its fertility. Baal's female counterpart was Ashtoreth. Sexual intercourse between these two gods was believed to regulate fertility of the earth and its creatures.

God had commanded the Israelites under Joshua's leadership to purge the land of the Canaanites and their idols (Deut. 7:16; 12:2-3; 20:17). The failure of the Israelites to do so (Josh. 16:10; Jud. 1:27-33) left them open to the temptation to look to the idols rather than to God for agricultural blessing. Perhaps the cultic prostitution and sexual practices used in the worship of Baal also enticed the Hebrew people. Interestingly Gideon's father had built an altar to Baal, but Gideon had destroyed it (Jud. 6:25-34). The Ruth narrative shows the wisdom of trusting in God and His providence rather than in Canaanite gods.

Bethlehem was about five miles south of Jerusalem. Later Obed, son of Ruth and Boaz, was born in Bethlehem and Obed's grandson David was born in Bethlehem (Ruth 4:18-21; 1 Sam. 17:58). Bethlehem, of course, would also be the birthplace of David's greater Son, the Lord Jesus Christ (Luke 2:4-7).

**A man from Bethlehem** decided to take his family to **Moab,** about 50 miles east on the other side of the Dead Sea. He intended to live there for a short period. Nothing is said about why he chose Moab. Probably he had heard that there was no famine there. However, the unfolding events indicate that it was an unwise choice, and that Bethlehem, not Moab, was the place where God would bless him. The inhabitants of Moab were excluded from the congregation of the Lord (Deut. 23:3-6). (On the origin of the Moabites see "Historical and Literary Features" under *Introduction*; cf. Gen. 19:30-38.) They were worshipers of the god Chemosh, a deity whose worship was similar to that of Baal.

**1:2. The man's name was Elimelech,** his wife was **Naomi,** and their **two sons were Mahlon and Kilion.** Some Bible students make much of the fact that the name Elimelech means "My God is king," but he may or may not have lived up to his name. (See comments on vv. 20-21 for a wordplay on Naomi's name.) The term **Ephrathites** was a designation for the inhabitants of Ephrath (also spelled Ephratah and Ephratha), another name for Bethlehem (cf. 4:11; Gen. 35:19; 48:7; Micah 5:2).

### B. A depressing emptiness (1:3-5)

**1:3.** Naomi faced the distressing problem of her husband's death. How long they had lived in Moab before Elimelech's death is not known. But Naomi, though widowed, sorrowing, and in a foreign land, had hope while **her two sons** were still alive. Naomi now became the central figure in the narrative.

**1:4.** Naomi's two sons **married Moabite women . . . Orpah** and **Ruth.** These marriages were not condemned.

Though the Mosaic Law prohibited Israelites from marrying the Canaanites (Deut. 7:3), the Law did not say Israelites could not marry Moabites. However, Solomon's experience later showed that the greatest problem in such a marriage is the temptation to serve the gods of one's foreign wife (1 Kings 11:1-6; cf. Mal. 2:11). No doubt orthodox Israelites would have thought that marrying Moabite women was unwise. The Book of Ruth does not record the length of these marriages but they were childless. Not till Ruth 4:10 does the reader learn which son (Mahlon) married Ruth. **They . . . lived** in Moab **about 10 years** which was probably longer than the family intended to stay (cf. "for a while," 1:1).

**1:5.** Then Naomi's two sons **died.** Jewish tradition has regarded the death of these three males (Elimelech, **Mahlon, and Kilion**) as God's punishment for their leaving Bethlehem. Though that is possible, the text does not indicate it. **Naomi** had now accumulated a great load of personal grief. **Her husband** and her only **sons** had died before their time. She was a stranger in a foreign land. If the family name were to carry on, there had to be an heir. But having no sons, Naomi **was left without** hope. Her Moabitess daughters-in-law offered her no apparent means to an heir.

## II. Seeking a Home by Faith (1:6-22)

The main narrative portion now begins. Dialogue was the primary device used by the author. Fifty-nine of the 84 verses in the book contain dialogue, beginning in verse 8. Naomi resolved to return home, and in so doing she believed that she had to leave her daughters-in-law in Moab because she thought that would be best for them. She received a surprise when Ruth resolved to return with her.

### A. A loving choice (1:6-18)

**1:6-7. Naomi** learned that rain had come to her homeland. The famine was ended and God provided **food** (crops from the field and fruit from the trees). It was **the LORD** who had stopped the famine and given rain; it was not Baal, who the Canaanites believed was the god who sent rain. **Return** is a key word in Ruth. Hebrew forms of this word are used several times in this first chapter. Here is an apt illustration of repentance. Naomi reversed the direction she and her husband had taken. She turned away from **Moab** and the errors of the past. She turned her back on the tragic graves of her loved ones and headed **back** to **Judah,** her homeland.

**1:8 Naomi,** sensing that the prospects of her daughters-in-law for remarriage in Israel would be slight, urged them to stay in Moab. Her telling each of them to return to her **mother's home** was unusual in a male-dominated society. Since Naomi was thinking of their remarriages, she may have referred to their mothers because her daughters-in-law would have discussed their wedding plans with their mothers.

The word **kindness** is the Hebrew word *ḥeseḏ*. It is an important word in the Book of Ruth (cf. 2:20; 3:10) and throughout the Old Testament. It speaks of God's covenant loyalty to His people. It involves grace in that it was extended even when it was not deserved. Here divine will and human action went hand in hand. Both God and humans were doers of *ḥeseḏ*. The basis of Naomi's blessing was the gracious actions of Ruth and Orpah to their husbands and to Naomi. Both young women were worthy in the eyes of their mother-in-law, so she wanted God to be good to them. Though they were foreigners, they had married Israelite men and thus were under God's covenant.

**1:9-10.** Naomi then asked that God would give **each of** them a place of **rest** with **another husband.** This became a key issue in the book. Marriage meant security for a woman. And yet ironically Ruth seemed to be giving up this possibility by leaving Moab. Naomi's kisses were intended as farewells, but both women stated their desire to return with Naomi. Possibly a custom in that day required this.

**1:11.** Three times **Naomi** insisted that they **return** to Moab (vv. 11-12, 15). They needed to be sure to remarry. In the ancient Near East a woman without a husband was in a serious situation because she lacked security. And widows were especially needy. Naomi referred to the levirate custom in Israel in which a brother was responsible to marry his deceased brother's wife in order to conceive a son and perpetuate his brother's name

and inheritance (Deut. 25:5-10). Naomi pointed out that this would not be possible in their case since she had no **more sons.**

**1:12-13.** Naomi said that she was past the age of childbearing. Even if she did acquire a new **husband** and have **sons** it was ridiculous to think that Orpah and Ruth would **wait** for them to grow **up.**

Naomi seemed a bit insensitive to the grief of her daughters-in-law. She thought that her case was **more bitter** than theirs because they still had potential for childbearing. She regarded her plight as a result of God's affliction (cf. vv. 20-21). Naomi was apparently in a stage of grief that caused her to speak in anger against God. And yet she was still a woman of faith. She had no doubt that God was actively involved in their lives (cf. vv. 8-9; 2:20). She saw God as sovereign and the ultimate cause of life's issues.

**1:14. Orpah** should not be unduly criticized for returning to Moab. She was obeying the wishes of **her mother-in-law.** Nothing more is said in the Book of Ruth about Orpah. Presumably she remarried in Moab.

Ruth, however, did the unexpected. Though Orpah chose to seek a husband, **Ruth clung to** Naomi, apparently choosing to follow and serve her widowed mother-in-law rather than seek a husband. In Ruth's mind the decision probably meant that she would never have a husband or children. James would have considered her concern for her widowed mother-in-law a profoundly religious act (James 1:27).

**1:15. Naomi** again urged Ruth to return to her home. She cited the example of Orpah's obedience to her request. Naomi was aware that the decision to return meant the continuing influence of the Moabite **gods** including Chemosh the chief god (Num. 21:29; 1 Kings 11:7), but the importance of Ruth's having a husband seemed to outweigh this concern. Naomi did not make it easy for Ruth to come to faith in the God of Israel.

**1:16. Ruth** had endured three entreaties of her mother-in-law to return home to Moab (vv. 11-12, 15). But she chose life with Naomi over her family, her national identity, and her religious idolatry. In one of the most beautiful expressions of commitment in all the world's literature she laced her future to that of Naomi. She confessed allegiance to the **people** of Israel (**your people**) and to the **God** of Israel (**your God**). Here was a stirring example of a complete break with the past. Like Abraham Ruth decided to leave her ancestors' idolatrous land to go to the land of promise. And Ruth did it without the encouragement of a promise. In fact she made her decision despite Naomi's strenuous encouragement to do otherwise.

**1:17.** Ruth's decision was so strong that it included reference to death and burial. She would stay with Naomi to death and beyond. To seal the quality of her decision, Ruth invoked judgment from Israel's God if she were to break her commitment of loyalty to her mother-in-law. Ruth's conversion was complete. The events that followed show that her life matched her confession.

**1:18. Naomi** then **stopped urging** Ruth to go back to Moab. Since Ruth had invoked God's name in her commitment (v. 17), Naomi acquiesced. Nothing more could be said. The Book of Ruth says nothing about Naomi welcoming her daughter-in-law to the fold of those who trusted in Israel's God. **Ruth** had leaped by faith the barriers that had been thrown up before her.

### B. A bittersweet return (1:19-22)

**1:19.** The **two women** made the arduous journey **to Bethlehem.** The exclusively female character of this portion of chapter 1 continued, for **the whole town** of Bethlehem spoke through its **women.** Their question, **Can this be Naomi?** suggests that they remembered Naomi and that she had experienced an observable change, obviously for the worse.

**1:20.** Naomi's grief and depression, that had expressed itself toward God (v. 13), continued. She stated that her name **Naomi,** which means "sweetness or pleasantness," was improper for her in her condition. She said she should be called **Mara,** which means "bitter." Her reason was that **the Almighty** (šadday) had **made** her **life very bitter.** By speaking of God as "the Almighty" she emphasized His great power (or "provisions"; cf. comments on Gen. 17:1). This great God could not be resisted. The disaster He sent could not be averted. Na-

omi had such faith in God and His personal involvement in her life that she knew the bitter things she experienced were from Him. Her grief was real; obviously she took God seriously.

**1:21.** Naomi's complaint became specific. Years before she **went away** to Moab **full,** with a husband and two sons, but now she came **back empty.** Her grief and depression did not enable her to recognize her Moabitess daughter-in-law as of any significant worth. Later, however, she experienced great benefit through Ruth (4:15). **Naomi** was sure her problem was all God's fault. Her return home had only intensified the depth of her grief. She saw nothing ahead but the loneliness, abandonment, and helplessness of widowhood. Her complaint began and ended with a reference to **the Almighty,** the name of the all-powerful God. But in the face of her deep tragedy God would soon proceed to act in gracious mercy.

**1:22.** This verse provides a transition toward hope for **Naomi,** as well as Ruth. God was not really her antagonist but would through His sovereign, superintending providence act with favor toward both widows.

Naomi had left Bethlehem because of a food famine. She **returned** with a famine in her soul. **The barley harvest** in **Bethlehem,** however, must have been a welcome sight. But Naomi in her depression might not have been impressed. (The barley harvest was in the month of Nisan [March-April]. See the chart "Calendar in Israel," near Ex. 12.)

Naomi thought she was returning empty-handed, but she had **Ruth the Moabitess** with her. And the harvest was ripe; there was hope.

### III. Seeking Provisions Responsibly (chap. 2)

Ruth was now a believer (cf. v. 12). She was in the land of Israel. How would she act? Since Moabites were excluded from the congregation of Israel (Deut. 23:3), she was there by grace. The events in Ruth 2 show how she was received. In this chapter another person, Boaz, a wealthy farmer, is introduced. Would he be a responsible member of the godly congregation of Israel? Naomi was home. Would her grief assuage and her depression heal? By their words and their actions these three persons revealed their true characters.

## A. A God-guided happening (2:1-3)

**2:1.** The female dominance in the story now was modified by reference to an important male. **Boaz** was a near **relative** of **Elimelech,** Naomi's deceased husband (1:2-3; cf. 2:3). Boaz was a man of outstanding qualities. The Hebrew words 'îš gibbôr ḥayil, translated **man of standing,** are literally, "a mighty man of valor." These same words are used of Gideon and Jephthah, each of whom was called a "mighty warrior" (Jud. 6:12; 11:1). They were men of valor—capable, efficient, and worthy in battle. Boaz was a mighty man of valor, capable in his community, and lived an exemplary lifestyle (cf. ḥayil, used of Ruth, in Ruth 3:11).

**2:2.** The author again reminded the readers that **Ruth** was a **Moabitess** (cf. 1:22), perhaps to highlight the favorable treatment she was to receive from Boaz. Ruth understood the rights of the poor in Israel to gather grain in a field after the harvesters had passed through. The corners of the field were to be left for the poor to reap (Lev. 19:9-10; 23:22). Some generous landowners were known to have left as much as one-fourth of their crop for the needy and aliens. Ruth did not wait for **Naomi** to serve her; she took the initiative. **Naomi** encouraged Ruth to **go.**

**2:3.** Because **Boaz** was already introduced into the plot (v. 1), it is clear that Ruth was not in Boaz's **field** by mere chance. She had moved forward in obedience to her rights in the Law of God and was guided by grace into the place God provided. The same providence that later led the Magi to Bethlehem (Matt. 2:1-8) directed Ruth to the appropriate Bethlehem field. Again the author stated that Boaz **was from the clan of Elimelech** (cf. Ruth 2:1). This fact is important to the unfolding of events.

## B. A well-deserved kindness (2:4-17)

**2:4.** The spiritual tone of **Boaz** and his workers was warm and vigorous. When he **greeted** them with the blessing, **The Lord be with you,** they responded similarly, **The Lord bless you.** Faith in the Lord was active in their lives. Boaz spoke the language of faith. Would his

actions also fit his words?

**2:5-6.** When **Boaz** noted a new **young woman** in his field among the gleaners, his interest was stirred. When he asked who she was, **the foreman** identified the new gleaner as **the Moabitess who** had returned **from Moab with Naomi.** Some have felt that the foreman's reference to Moab was intended as a derogatory statement, but the text does not indicate this.

**2:7.** The foreman added that Ruth had asked permission to **glean . . . among the sheaves** (i.e., bundles of barley grain). He said she had **worked steadily from** the time she came in the **morning . . . except for a short rest in the shelter** that apparently was provided for the workers. He noticed that she was a diligent worker.

**2:8-9.** **Boaz** addressed **Ruth** as **my daughter** (cf. 3:10-11) in reference to the age difference between them. He was closer to the age of Naomi (cf. "younger men," 3:10). Boaz not only spoke of his faith in the Lord (2:4); his life corresponded with his words. When he told Ruth to continue gleaning in his field, he apparently meant that she should glean there throughout the several weeks of harvesting (cf. v. 23) barley (March-April) and wheat (June-July). Normally the gleaners would move in after the harvesters had left an area. But Ruth was invited to **follow along** with the **servant girls** as they worked in the reaping. Boaz assured Ruth that she would be protected from any remarks or other embarrassing incidents that might have come from the male workers (cf. v. 15). When she got **thirsty,** she need not be concerned about drawing water. She could **drink from** that provided for the workers. In these several ways Boaz was providing for Ruth beyond what was required by the Law (cf. v. 16).

**2:10.** Ruth responded with utter humility. **She bowed down with her face to the ground,** a gesture common in the ancient Near East, mentioned frequently in the Bible (cf., e.g., Gen. 19:1; 42:6; 43:26; 48:12; Josh. 5:14; 2 Sam. 1:2). She was surprised by the **favor** (cf. Ruth 2:2, 13) she received from this important man. The word "favor" (ḥēn, "grace, favor, acceptance") is used often in the Old Testament (e.g., Gen. 6:8; 18:3; 30:27; Ps. 84:11; Prov. 3:4, 34 ["grace"]). Ruth had expected the opposite of the treatment she received. She was a recipient of grace and was grateful. Yet she was eager to find out **why** she had been singled out for such unusual treatment since she was **a foreigner** and a stranger.

**2:11.** Boaz knew much **about** Ruth. News about her had traveled rapidly throughout the small town. Boaz, deeply moved by what Ruth had **done for** Naomi, spoke to Ruth in words of high affirmation. His words about her leaving her parents and her **homeland . . . to live with a people** she had not met are reminiscent of God's words when He called Abram (Gen. 12:1).

**2:12.** Boaz prayed that God would reward Ruth as repayment for the kindness she had displayed to her mother-in-law. He strengthened his request by asking that she be **richly rewarded by . . . the God** she had **come to** trust. He used a figure of speech known as a zoomorphism, comparing part of God to some aspect of an animal. He said she had taken **refuge** under God's **wings,** like a chick under the wings of its mother hen (cf. Pss. 17:8; 36:7; 57:1; 61:4; 63:7; 91:4; Matt. 23:37). She was trusting in God's protection. Soon Boaz would be used by God to answer his own prayer.

**2:13.** Though Boaz's words could have stirred her to pride, Ruth continued to respond in humility. Naomi had given no words of encouragement to Ruth, but this man spoke comforting words that warmed her soul. She mentioned her gratitude for his **favor** (cf. vv. 2, 10), **comfort,** and kind words, and hoped they would **continue.** She felt she was less important than Boaz's **servant girls.**

**2:14.** Boaz continued his kindness to Ruth. He invited her to eat the good food provided for himself and his **harvesters.** She was not left to fend for herself as gleaners usually were. He provided for her more than she could eat, either to show his genuine concern for and interest in her, or to allow her to have some to take home to her mother-in-law (cf. v. 18). The **wine vinegar** was apparently a delicacy that enhanced the meal. **Roasted grain** was a staple food in that day. It consisted of barley roasted on an iron plate over an open fire.

**2:15-16.** Ruth did not linger at the meal. After she returned to gleaning, **Boaz** ordered his workers to do more

than let her glean among them. In addition they were deliberately to drop handfuls of **stalks** of barley in her path so that she would have abundant provision. This too was beyond what Boaz was required by the Law to do (cf. v. 9). Nor were his men to **rebuke her** or hinder her in any way.

**2:17.** After working hard all day **Ruth . . . threshed the barley,** beat out the grain from the stalks, and had **an ephah.** This was about half a bushel, an unusually generous amount for one day of gleaning. It weighed about 30 pounds and was enough food for many days.

### C. An expression of joy (2:18-23)

Ruth's return home to Naomi ended Naomi's emptiness and filled the older woman with anticipation, thankfulness, and hope.

**2:18.** When Ruth brought home the ephah of barley grain, the results of her toil, Naomi **saw** the large amount. Also **Ruth** gave Naomi the extra portion **she had** saved from her lunch (cf. v. 14). Here was a widow who was not overlooked in the daily supply of food (cf. Acts 6:1). Naomi would be cared for by Ruth.

**2:19.** Naomi requested the name of Ruth's benefactor and prayed a blessing on him before Ruth answered her question. **Ruth** disclosed that she had **worked** in the field of **Boaz.**

**2:20. Naomi** repeated her blessing, now knowing to whom it should be applied (cf. v. 19a). Her night of sorrow with its fog of depression had broken into the dawning of a new day of joy. As God was the source of her sorrow (1:20-21), He was now the source of her joy. God's **kindness** (ḥeṣed; cf. 3:10 and comments on 1:8) again rested on **the living,** Ruth and herself.

Naomi's mind immediately perceived the significance of the situation. Even **the dead** might soon be blessed, in that the name of Elimelech, her dead husband, could live on through her faithful daughter-in-law, Ruth. Boaz was a **close relative,** but more than that, he was a **kinsman-**redeemer. He could act as a redeemer of property and persons. He could act as a *levir,* a Latin term for brother-in-law. Boaz could redeem by fulfilling the levirate law, which required a brother of a deceased man to marry his widow and raise up a son to his name (Deut. 25:5-10). Though Boaz was not a brother to Mahlon, Ruth's deceased husband (Ruth 4:10), he was a close relative to the family and could act as a *levir* if he so desired. Naomi sensed the willingness of Boaz. No explanation is given as to why Naomi did not mention the nearer kinsman-redeemer (cf. 3:12).

**2:21-22. Ruth** had more good news. Boaz had invited her to remain in his field throughout the harvest (cf. vv. 8, 23). Naturally Naomi encouraged Ruth to accept Boaz's generosity. Perhaps to emphasize her need to stay there, **Naomi** reminded **Ruth** of the danger that might lurk in another **field.** This was a reminder of the especially low morals in the days of the Judges and Ruth.

**2:23.** Ruth's loyalty was revealed in her obedience to Naomi's words. She gleaned with Boaz's **servant girls** (cf. v. 8) for the several weeks of **the barley and wheat harvests,** and **lived with** Naomi during that time. However, the tension in the plot continued, for the harvest would soon come to an end. What would happen to the widows after the harvest was over?

## IV. Seeking Redeeming Love (chap. 3)

Naomi was no longer depressed. She became a matchmaker and prepared Ruth to seek the love of her willing kinsman-redeemer, Boaz. The turning point in the narrative is at hand.

### A. A plan for redemption (3:1-5)

During the weeks of the barley and wheat harvests (cf. 2:23), Naomi had time to put her plan together. When the time was right she acted.

**3:1. Naomi** was a persistent person (cf. 1:8-15). She was now resolved to seek rest and security for her daughter-in-law through marriage. Ruth had given up the possibility of remarriage in order to care for the aging Naomi, but now marriage suddenly again became a possibility. It was customary for Hebrew parents to arrange marriages for their children (Jud. 14:1-10). **To find a home** is literally to "find rest" (cf. Ruth 1:9), to be settled and secure in a home with a husband.

**3:2.** Naomi pointed out that since **Boaz** was a relative of theirs, he could be a **kinsman**-redeemer for Ruth. He had an

open and willing heart. So Naomi suggested Ruth go to **the threshing floor** that evening. The people of Bethlehem took turns using the threshing floor. The floor was a flat hard area on a slightly raised platform or hill. In threshing, the grain was beaten out from the stalks with flails (cf. 2:17) or was trodden over by oxen. Then in **winnowing** the grain was thrown in the air and the wind carried the chaff away. The grain was then removed from the threshing floor and placed in heaps to be sold or stored in granaries.

Threshing and winnowing were a time of great festivity and rejoicing. Naomi knew that Boaz was threshing his grain on the day that she had chosen for her plan. She also knew that Boaz would be sleeping near his grain that night, to protect it.

**3:3.** Ruth was to prepare herself by washing and perfuming herself. The words **best clothes** may be rendered "a large outer garment." This was to keep her identity from being detected. She was to observe Boaz **eating and drinking** but was not to **let him know** of her presence.

**3:4.** After Boaz finished eating and drinking, Ruth was to observe **the place where** he retired for the night. Under cover of darkness Ruth was to **go** to Boaz, **uncover his feet, and lie down** there. (On the meaning of the uncovering of the feet, see the comments on v. 7.) Boaz, Naomi said, would then **tell** Ruth what she was **to do.** The implication was clear that Ruth should do whatever he requested.

**3:5. Ruth** stated that she would act in full and unquestioned obedience to the directions of her mother-in-law (cf. 2:22-23).

### B. A claim for redemption (3:6-9)

The preparation for the redemption experience had been carefully made. Now the plan had to be carried out.

**3:6.** Ruth **went** to **the threshing floor** and carried out the plan in exact detail as matchmaker Naomi had laid it out.

**3:7.** Some commentators suggest that what **Ruth** did presented an opportunity for immorality. But nothing in the passage supports this. Her mother-in-law had complete confidence in the integrity of the kinsman-redeemer. **Boaz** could be trusted to act responsibly. And Ruth was recognized by everyone as "a woman of noble character" (v. 11). The uncovering of the **feet** was a ceremonial act that was completely proper. Probably the scene took place in the dark so that Boaz had the opportunity to reject the proposal without the whole town knowing about it.

**3:8-9. Something startled** Boaz **in the middle of the night. He turned** to discover that **a woman** was **lying at his feet.** Boaz asked for the identity of his unusual guest (cf. 2:5). Ruth responded in humility (cf. 2:10): **I am your servant Ruth.** She had put herself under the wings of Yahweh (2:12), and now she asked to be put under the wings of Boaz. In the phrase **the corner of your garment** the word "corner" is *kānāp*, which is translated "wing" in 2:12. She used a poetic image that had its source in the blessing that Boaz had given her. A Moabitess widow was calling the attention of a noted Hebrew to his responsibility. He could now follow through on his benediction (2:12) by becoming Ruth's **kinsman-redeemer** and providing her with the security of marriage.

## C. A pledge of redemption (3:10-15)

Boaz joyfully received Ruth's proposal. The tension of the plot continued, however, because another kinsman had a prior claim on her.

**3:10.** Boaz gave no hint that Ruth had embarrassed him by her actions or that she had done something that was not within her rights or against the customs of the day. Rather than thinking suggestive thoughts as some might have done in such a setting, he immediately blessed Ruth: **The Lord bless you.** He again used the phrase **my daughter,** a reminder of their age difference (cf. 2:8; 3:11). He commended Ruth for her act of **kindness** ("loyalty," *ḥesed*; cf. comments on 1:8) that was **greater than** her decision to serve her mother-in-law. Boaz also commended her for not going **after** a **younger** man. He seemed to believe Ruth could have readily found such a match. He praised her for being willing to marry an older man in order to fulfill her commitment to her first husband, Mahlon (cf. 4:10), and the family name of Elimelech.

**3:11.** Boaz then relieved any imme-

diate fears Ruth might have had by saying that he would **do** as she requested. He might have sensed that she was apprehensive over how he might interpret her bold proposal. Boaz told her that **all** his **fellow townsmen** (lit., the "people of the gate," probably referring to the elders of Bethlehem) considered her a person of the highest reputation. **Noble character** translates *ḥayil* ("valor, worth, ability"), the same word used of the worthiness of Boaz (2:1; cf. Prov. 12:4; 31:10, 29 ["noble"]). They were truly a good match!

**3:12.** The narrative, however, was not nearing the end. Still another complication had to be unraveled. Boaz had already looked into the legal aspects of the proposed marriage; perhaps he had anticipated her request. He knew that Ruth by her marriage into Elimelech's family had a relative who was more closely related to her than he was. But Boaz would do all he could to see that the outcome would be one that satisfied Ruth's request.

**3:13.** Boaz acted responsibly in two ways: (1) He did not send her home in the middle of **the night.** He would protect her and he would touch her only if she could be rightfully his. (2) Also he protected the rights of her nearer kinsman. If the other relative wanted **to redeem,** that was his right. But if the nearer kinsman was **not willing,** Boaz would **surely** do so. He covered his pledge with a **vow.** There was no doubt about how Boaz wanted the matter to eventuate.

**3:14. Ruth lay at his feet until** early **morning.** She arose before daylight. Boaz did not want her life complicated by village gossips, so he urged her not to **let it be known** she had been at **the threshing floor.** Nothing had happened that was improper but gossipers are not careful about facts.

**3:15.** Into Ruth's **shawl** Boaz put **six measures of barley** for her and Naomi. Naomi was entering more and more into the fullness of her wise decision to return to Bethlehem. The "measure" was probably the seah (one-third of an ephah or about 10 pounds). Thus six seahs would equal about 60 pounds. Ruth was a strong woman to be able to carry such a heavy load. Probably Boaz placed the burden **on her** head.

Some Hebrew manuscripts read,

**Then he went back to town,** but others have "she" in place of "he." Since Ruth returned to Bethlehem at that time and Boaz a bit later that morning (4:1), both renderings ("she" and "he") fit the facts.

### D. An anticipation of redemption (3:16-18)

Naomi eagerly sought to know the outcome of Ruth's adventure and predicted that Boaz would quickly resolve the issues that day. Whatever the outcome as to who the redeemer would be, it would be Ruth's day of redemption.

**3:16-17. Naomi** sought to know how it had gone with **Ruth.** As before, she called Ruth **my daughter** (v. 1; 2:2; cf. 1:11-13; 3:18). Ruth gave her a full report and added that **Boaz had** given her the **barley** so that Naomi could share in Ruth's future fulfillment. Naomi had done her matchmaking well and had earned a reward. The aged widow could then rest assured that she would not be forgotten in the future.

**3:18.** Naomi and Ruth had done all they could. The initiative now rested with Boaz. Boaz would **not rest** till he had **settled the matter** that day.

## V. Receiving Redemption's Loving Rewards (4:1-13)

With the action having turned in his direction, Boaz now took the initiative. Would the nearer kinsman take what had been offered to Boaz?

### A. A refusal of redemption (4:1-8)

**4:1. Boaz went up to the town gate** of Bethlehem. The town gate was where personal business and civic affairs of the people were transacted. The threshing floor was below the level of the city itself, and for that reason Boaz went "up" to the gate. The area was quite hilly. **The kinsman-redeemer** closer to Elimelech (3:12) **came** by the gate and **Boaz** asked him to **sit down.** The fact that the man's name was not given may have been poetic justice since he refused to become the redeemer. The words **my friend** became a catch phrase in Israel. Rabbinic writings used the designation for an unknown "John Doe."

**4:2. Boaz** called together **10** of Bethlehem's **elders,** and they also sat down. They would serve as witnesses of the legal transaction (vv. 4, 9-11). Why he

chose 10 is not stated. (Centuries later 10 became the number necessary for a Jewish marriage benediction or a quorum for a synagogue meeting.) This was now a man's world where a public decision was to be made on an important matter that profoundly affected the women who had brought it to this point.

**4:3.** Boaz had a carefully planned strategy. He unfolded the elements in the case step by step. First, he explained that **Naomi** (and Ruth; cf. v. 5) had a field for sale **that belonged to** Naomi's late husband. No information is given as to how she came to possess it. Her poverty apparently required that she sell it. But if possible the land should remain in the family (cf. Jer. 32:6-12).

**4:4.** The nearer kinsman had the first right to the property and Boaz was **next** after him. If Ruth's closer relative would not **redeem** (purchase) it, Boaz was prepared to do so. The man then agreed to **redeem** the piece of land.

**4:5.** But then **Boaz** explained that when the nearer kinsman redeemed **the land,** he must also acquire **Ruth the Moabitess.** Apparently at the death of Elimelech the property had passed to Mahlon so Mahlon's **widow** Ruth was included in the redemption responsibility. A son, to whom the property would belong, should be raised up to perpetuate the family **name.**

**4:6.** When the nearer **kinsman** heard this stipulation about marriage, he refused his right of purchase. He feared that his **own estate** might be endangered. So he gave the right of redemption to Boaz. Why did he change his mind? (Cf. "I will redeem it," v. 4b, with "I cannot redeem it," v. 6.) Perhaps he was too poor to sustain the land and a wife. Or, as some have suggested, perhaps he feared to marry a Moabitess lest the fate of Mahlon, Ruth's first husband (v. 10), befall him. Perhaps the best view is that when he learned from Boaz that Ruth owned the property along with Naomi (v. 5), he knew that if Ruth bore him a son, that son would eventually inherit not only the redeemed property but probably part of his own estate too. In that sense the nearer redeemer would "endanger" his estate. However, if only Naomi were the widow (not Naomi *and* Ruth), then no son from the levirate marriage would inherit part of the redeemer's estate because Naomi was past childbearing.

**4:7-8.** A legal transaction was finalized not by signing a paper but by a dramatic symbolic act that others would witness and remember. The passing of the **sandal** symbolized Boaz's right to walk on the land as his **property** (cf. Deut. 1:36; 11:24; Josh. 1:3; 14:9). After giving his **sandal** to **Boaz,** the unknown **kinsman** moved from the scene and into anonymity. But the name of Boaz has been remembered in all succeeding generations (cf. Ruth 4:14).

### B. An accomplished redemption (4:9-12)

Boaz moved quickly to complete the transaction. He claimed and received the right of redemption, both for Elimelech's land and for Ruth, who was the only widow left capable of giving birth to a son who would perpetuate the family name.

**4:9-10.** Boaz called **the elders** to witness the transaction as he took possession of Naomi's **property** and **acquired Ruth the Moabitess** (cf. 1:22; 2:2, 21; 4:5). Boaz evidenced no reluctance to call Ruth a Moabitess. He respected her as a worthy person. He would raise a son to continue the name of Elimelech and of Elimelech's son, Mahlon. In verses 9-10 all the family members were mentioned again except Orpah. She had also faded into anonymity with the nameless nearer kinsman. Though not stated, it may be assumed that with Ruth, Boaz also took responsibility for **Naomi.** This logically followed from the commitment Ruth had made to her mother-in-law. This was later confirmed by the Bethlehem women (v. 15). Boaz is a beautiful illustration of the Lord Jesus Christ who became mankind's Kinsman-Redeemer and who makes things right before God the Father for those who trust in Him.

**4:11.** The elders gave willing witness to this redemption transaction. They blessed Boaz with the desire that the Lord make Ruth a fertile mother. Their mentioning **Rachel and Leah** has significance. Rachel, named first, had been barren for many years before she bore children. Similarly Ruth had been barren in Moab.

The elders prayed that Boaz would **have standing** (*ḥayil*) **in Ephratah.** This word *ḥayil* ("valor, worth, ability") is used of Boaz (2:1) and of Ruth (3:11). Ephratah (also spelled Ephrath and Ephrathah) was another name for **Bethlehem** (cf. Gen. 35:19; 48:7; Micah 5:2). The elders prayed that Boaz would be **famous** in Bethlehem. God abundantly answered their prayers as many have witnessed.

**4:12.** The elders also prayed for numerous and distinguished progeny for Boaz. Their prayer acknowledged that children are a gift from God (**offspring the LORD gives you**; cf. Ps. 127:3). Little did they realize that from this union would issue Israel's greatest kings including David and the Eternal King, the Lord Jesus Christ. **Perez** may have been named here: (a) because of the levirate connection with **Tamar** (see the *Introduction*), (b) because Perez's descendants had settled in Bethlehem (1 Chron. 2:5, 18, 50-54; note "Ephrathah" and "Bethlehem" in 1 Chron. 2:50-51), and (c) because Perez was an ancestor of Boaz (Ruth 4:18-21).

### C. A rewarded redemption (4:13)

**4:13.** This climax to the narrative is brief but full of meaning. Marriage, God-given conception, and the longed-for heir were all mentioned in a few words.

**Ruth** had been barren in Moab for the entire period of her marriage to Mahlon (1:4-5). Now her faithful obedience was rewarded as God gave her conception. In a sense this foreshadowed the miraculous birth of the Son of God that would take place in Bethlehem when the fullness of time had come (Luke 1:26-38; 2:1-7; Gal. 4:4). The sojourn in Moab lasted at least 10 years (Ruth 1:4). By contrast, within a few short weeks of their return to Bethlehem, Naomi and Ruth had experienced blessing that was rich and full.

## VI. Conclusion (4:14-21)

This conclusion of the narrative contrasts beautifully with its introduction (1:1-5). Deep sorrow turned to radiant joy; emptiness gave way to fullness.

### A. A joyful filling (4:14-17)

**4:14.** Naomi again moved to the center of the scene. **The women** of Bethlehem who had witnessed Naomi's emptiness when she returned (1:19) now praised God that she had received **a kinsman-redeemer.** Had Naomi not been past the time of childbearing (1:12; 4:15) she might have been the one at the feet of Boaz that night on the threshing floor (3:7). The women knew this and they spoke of Boaz as the kinsman-redeemer of Naomi as surely as if she had gone there. They blessed Boaz with a blessing similar to that of the elders (cf. 4:11). They asked that Boaz be **famous in Israel,** a request that God granted. The Book of Ruth is filled with benedictions and blessings of Israel's people (1:8-9; 2:4, 12, 20; 3:10; 4:11-12, 14-15).

**4:15.** The women predicted that Boaz would care for Naomi by renewing her **life** and giving her security for her **old age.** Ruth, whom Naomi had not thought worth mentioning when she came to Bethlehem, was declared by the women to be of more worth **than seven sons.** Seven sons symbolized the supreme blessing that could come to a Hebrew family (cf. 1 Sam. 2:5; Job 1:2). Ruth's worth was related to the occasion of the **birth** of her son.

**4:16-17. Naomi** became the nurse for **Obed.** This may have been a formal act of adoption. The women of Bethlehem named the boy Obed which means "worshiper." Naomi accepted the name. She, the empty one, was now full. The bitter one was now blessed. Naomi had **a son** (actually a grandson but "son" in Heb. often means "descendant"). In time God's providential purpose became clear. The child became the grandfather of King **David.**

### B. A surprising genealogy (4:18-21)

Perez's family line provided documentation for God's providential care. The seemingly ordinary events in the Book of Ruth (e.g., travels, marriages, deaths, harvesting, eating, sleeping, purchasing land) revealed the guiding activity of the sovereign God.

**4:18-20. Perez** was the son of Judah through Tamar (Gen. 38:12-30; Ruth 4:12). **Hezron** was among the family of Jacob that went to Egypt (Gen. 46:12). **Ram** is mentioned in 1 Chronicles 2:9. **Amminadab** was the father-in-law of Aaron (Ex. 6:23). **Nahshon** was head of the house of Judah (Num. 1:7; 7:12; 10:14).

**4:21. Salmon** was **the father of Boaz.** According to Matthew 1:5, Boaz's mother was Rahab, the Canaanite harlot

from Jericho. However, Rahab lived in Joshua's time, about 250-300 years earlier. Probably, then, Rahab was Boaz's "mother" in the sense that she was his ancestress (cf. "our father Abraham," Rom. 4:12, which means "our ancestor Abraham").

**Obed,** Boaz and Ruth's son, became **the father of Jesse,** who became **the father of David** (1 Sam. 17:12). (See the chart "David's Ancestry from Abraham," near 1 Sam. 16:1-13.) Jesus Christ's lineage, through Mary, is traced to David (Matt. 1:1-16; cf. Rom. 1:3; 2 Tim. 2:8; Rev. 22:16). Christ is therefore called "the Son of David" (Matt. 15:22; 20:30-31; 21:9, 15; 22:42). Christ will someday return to earth and will sit on the throne of David as the millennial King (2 Sam. 7:12-16; Rev. 20:4-6).

In spite of all appearances to the contrary, the faithful God had been about His business on Ruth's behalf. Believers should also be about His business. The rewards of responsible living are always the sweet fruit of God's grace.

# BIBLIOGRAPHY

Atkinson, David. *The Message of Ruth: The Wings of Refuge.* Downers Grove, Ill.: InterVarsity Press, 1983.

Barber, Cyril J., *Ruth: An Expositional Commentary.* Chicago: Moody Press, 1983.

Campbell, Edward F., Jr. *Ruth.* The Anchor Bible. Garden City, N.Y.: Doubleday & Co., 1975.

Cundall, Arthur E., and Morris, Leon. *Judges and Ruth.* The Tyndale Old Testament Commentaries. Downers Grove, Ill.: InterVarsity Press, 1968.

Enns, Paul P. *Ruth.* Bible Study Commentary. Grand Rapids: Zondervan Publishing House, 1982.

Gray, John. *Joshua, Judges and Ruth.* Greensboro, S.C.: Attic Press, 1967.

Hals, Ronald M. *The Theology of the Book of Ruth.* Philadelphia: Fortress Press, 1969.

Leggett, Donald A. *The Levirate and Goel Institutions in the Old Testament with Special Attention to the Book of Ruth.* Cherry Hill, N.J.: Mack Publishing Co., 1974.

Lewis, Arthur. *Judges/Ruth.* Everyman's Bible Commentary. Chicago: Moody Press, 1979.

McGee, J. Vernon. *Ruth: The Romance of Redemption.* Pasadena, Calif.: Thru the Bible Books, n.d.

Trible, Phyllis. "A Human Comedy: The Book of Ruth." In *Literary Interpretations of Biblical Narratives.* Vol. 2. Nashville: Abingdon Press, 1982.

Wood, Leon. *Distressing Days of the Judges.* Grand Rapids: Zondervan Publishing House, 1975.

# 1 SAMUEL

### Eugene H. Merrill

## INTRODUCTION

**Names.** The Books of 1 and 2 Samuel take their names from the Prophet Samuel, who is the first important character in the first book. The earliest Hebrew manuscripts made no division between the two books. They simply entitled the whole collection "Samuel." The Septuagint was the first version to divide the material into two parts. That division has persisted to the present day in all translations and versions, including Hebrew-printed Bibles.

**Author.** The authorship of 1 and 2 Samuel is anonymous, though one can hardly doubt that Samuel himself may have written or supplied information for 1 Samuel 1:1–25:1, all of which describes his life and career up to and including his death. It is impossible, however, to say anything with certainty about the authorship of the remainder of 1 Samuel and of 2 Samuel.

**Date.** The date of the composition of the books cannot be determined with any degree of precision. There is no hint that the author(s) knew anything about the fall of Samaria in 722 B.C., and yet he (or one of the authors) clearly lived in the post-Solomonic era, after the division of the kingdom between Israel and Judah (931 B.C.). This is indicated by the reference to Ziklag, a Philistine city which, the narrator wrote, "has belonged to the kings of Judah to this day" (1 Sam. 27:6, NASB), and by references to Israel and Judah (11:8; 17:52; 18:16; 2 Sam. 5:5; 11:11; 12:8; 19:42-43; 24:1, 9).

**Historical Setting.** The events described in 1 and 2 Samuel center about the lives of three important figures—Samuel, Saul, and David. First Samuel opens with the narrative of Samuel's birth, an event which occurred toward the end of the 12th century, about 1120 B.C. Second Samuel concludes with a story of royal succession in which David on his deathbed made provision for his son Solomon to follow him on the throne. This must be dated at 971 B.C. The entire period, then, consists of about 150 years.

The 300 or so years of the history of Israel under the Judges were marked by political, moral, and spiritual anarchy and deterioration. The situation was so pervasive that even the sons of Eli, the high priest at the end of the 12th century, had completely apostatized and had used their priestly office for their own gain and licentious pursuits. Just when it seemed that the nation would cave in on its own rottenness, God intervened and in response to godly Hannah's prayers gave young Samuel to her and the nation. Samuel's strong leadership as judge, prophet, and priest provided respite to the people from both internal and external threat. Unfortunately, however, when he became old and a successor was needed, it was evident to all that his own sons were unfit to take his place. This factor, coupled with the encroachments of the Ammonites on the east side of the Jordan River, prompted Israel to demand of Samuel that he give them a king "like all the other nations" (1 Sam. 8:5, 20). Though disturbed by this request, which implied the rejection of Yahweh as their King, Samuel granted it and selected Saul to be king, a selection determined and sanctioned by Yahweh Himself. Thus the monarchy was established in Israel. The circumstances and timing of its creation were improper, to be sure, but the concept of human royalty was part of the plan of God as revealed as early as the time of the patriarchs (Gen. 17:6, 16; 35:11; Deut. 17:14-20). Finally, with the selection and anointing of David, Israel's second king, Samuel lived to see the inauguration of the dynastic kingship which God had promised as part of His messianic, redemptive plan (Gen. 49:10; Num. 24:17). The Books of Samuel, then, embrace that critical period of Israel's history from judgeship to monarchy, from loose tribal affiliation to strong central government.

**Purpose.** The Books of Samuel provide an account of the history of Israel from the end of the 12th through the beginning of the 10th centuries before Christ. But, as is always true of biblical history, these books should be viewed theologically and not as mere recountings of events divorced from the purposes and plan of God. Since it might be argued that the major theme of biblical theology concerns the establishment of the sovereignty of God over all things, the specific purpose of 1 and 2 Samuel is to show how that sovereignty was delegated to the nation Israel, especially through its line of divinely elected Davidic kings. David and his dynasty demonstrate what it means to rule under God. Also through David's royal house his greater Son, Jesus Christ, eventually became incarnate. Christ perfectly exercised kingship in His own life, and provided in His death and resurrection the basis on which all people who believe can reign with and through Him (2 Sam. 7:12-16; Ps. 89:36-37; Isa. 9:7).

# OUTLINE

I. The Preparations for the Monarchy (chaps. 1–9)
  A. Samuel's birth and childhood (chap. 1)
    1. Samuel's family (1:1-3)
    2. Hannah's problem (1:4-8)
    3. Hannah's prayer (1:9-18)
    4. Samuel's birth (1:19-23)
    5. Samuel's presentation to God (1:24-28)
  B. Hannah's song (2:1-10)
    1. Hannah's exulting in the Lord (2:1)
    2. Hannah's extolling of the Lord (2:2-8)
    3. Hannah's expectation from the Lord (2:9-10)
  C. The situation at Shiloh (2:11-36)
    1. Samuel's progress (2:11, 26)
    2. The sins of the priesthood (2:12-17, 22-25)

  3. The blessing of Samuel's family (2:18-21)
  4. The rejection of the priesthood (2:27-36)
  D. Samuel's call (chap. 3)
    1. The divine voice (3:1-10)
    2. The divine message (3:11-14)
    3. Samuel's vindication (3:15-21)
  E. The ark (chaps. 4–7)
    1. The capture of the ark (chap. 4)
    2. The power of the ark (chap. 5)
    3. The return of the ark (6:1–7:1)
    4. The restoration of the ark (7:2-17)
  F. Selection of a king (chaps. 8–9)
    1. The demand for a king (8:1-9)
    2. The nature of the king (8:10-18)
    3. The introduction of the king (8:19–9:14)
    4. The choice of the king (9:15-27)
II. The Period of Saul (1 Sam. 10–31)
  A. Saul's ascendancy (chaps. 10–14)
    1. Saul's choice by Israel (chap. 10)
    2. Saul's first victory (chap. 11)
    3. The address by Samuel (chap. 12)
    4. Saul's first rebuke (chap. 13)
    5. Jonathan's peril (chap. 14)
  B. Saul's rejection (chap. 15)
  C. Saul and David (chaps. 16–26)
    1. On friendly terms (chaps. 16–17)
    2. On unfriendly terms (chaps. 18–26)
  D. Saul's death (chaps. 27–31)
    1. David at Ziklag (chap. 27)
    2. Saul at Endor (chap. 28)
    3. David's return to Ziklag (chaps. 29–30)
    4. The battle of Gilboa (chap. 31)

# COMMENTARY

## I. The Preparations for the Monarchy (chaps. 1–9)

### A. Samuel's birth and childhood (chap. 1)

1. SAMUEL'S FAMILY (1:1-3)

**1:1-3.** Samuel was the son of **Elkanah . . . an Ephraimite** from **Ramathaim** Zophim. This area, otherwise known simply as Ramah ("the height"), was in the hill country about 15 miles north of Jerusalem. Perhaps, according to Eusebius, it is to be identified with Arimathea, the home of Joseph of Arimathea of New Testament times. (Ramah was Samuel's birthplace [vv. 19-20], residence [7:17], and burial place [25:1].) Elkanah's description as an Ephraimite appears troublesome since Samuel served as a priest, an office reserved exclusively for Levites. However, Elkanah was a direct descendant of Levi (1 Chron. 6:33-38) and was therefore qualified to function in a priestly capacity. He was a Levite by lineage but an Ephraimite by residence. One indication of how lawless were the times in which Samuel was born is his father's bigamous marriages. Often in those days (though it was never sanctioned by God), a man whose wife was infertile would take a second wife by whom he could bear **children** (Gen. 16:1-3; 30:3-4, 9-10; etc.). This explains why Elkanah **had two wives** and why **Hannah,** the beloved but barren one, so fervently desired a son.

### 2. HANNAH'S PROBLEM (1:4-8)

**1:4-8.** Because a Hebrew man's posterity was bound up in his having a son to perpetuate his name, his wife's inability to conceive a son was regarded as a curse from God. (According to Deut. 7:13-14 having children was a sign of God's blessing. Conversely the Israelites considered the inability to bear children as a curse.) But Hannah's barrenness did not diminish Elkanah's love for **her.** In fact he gave her twice what he gave **Peninnah,** his second wife, when they took their offerings to the LORD at **Shiloh,** the place some 15 miles north of Ramah where Joshua had located the tabernacle (Josh. 18:1). This antagonized Peninnah, so she belittled **her rival** Hannah (1 Sam. 1:6-7). One thinks of the jealousy which Jacob's bigamy wrought in Rachel's heart (Gen. 30:1). None of Elkanah's assurances of devotion had any beneficial effect upon Hannah and her sorrow (1 Sam. 1:8). Her only resort was to cast herself entirely on the mercies of God.

### 3. HANNAH'S PRAYER (1:9-18)

**1:9-18.** The Law required all adult Hebrew males to appear at the tabernacle or temple of **the LORD** for the three major religious festivals of the year (Ex. 23:14-17). At this period of history the tabernacle was at **Shiloh** about 15 miles north of

Ramah. Elkanah regularly attended the festivals with his wives, and **Hannah** there poured out her soul to God in petition for **a son.** On one such occasion Hannah **made a vow** that if God would grant her request she would **give** her son **to the LORD for** as long as he lived. This dedication of her son was a commitment to the Nazirite vow, described in Numbers 6:1-8. It was the same vow undertaken by the parents of Samson whom they dedicated to **the LORD** under nearly identical circumstances (Jud. 13:2-5). So intense was Hannah's silent prayer that **Eli,** the high **priest** who was seated nearby, noted the movement of **her lips** and assumed **she was** intoxicated. When the priest learned about her true plight, he assured her that **God** would answer her prayer.

### 4. SAMUEL'S BIRTH (1:19-23)

**1:19-20.** Shortly after Hannah's return to **Ramah,** she **conceived** and in due **course** bore **a son** whom she **named** . . . **Samuel.** Though the name technically means "his name is God" or something similar, **Hannah** may, by assonance, have understood the name to mean "asked of God." She had "asked" (šā'al) God for a son, and He had "heard" (šāma') her. "Samuel," then, would be associated with šămūa' 'ēl, "heard of God," because **she** had **asked the LORD for him.**

**1:21-23.** At the next **annual** festival **Elkanah** went to Shiloh to offer **sacrifice to the LORD** (cf. v. 3), but this time he also paid **his vow** to the Lord. This payment of the vow must have consisted of the offering of Samuel himself whom Elkanah (and Hannah) had promised to give if the Lord would answer their prayers for a son (cf. Lev. 27:1-8; Num. 30:1-8).

**Hannah** and Samuel **did not** accompany Elkanah, for Samuel was not yet **weaned** and was therefore totally dependent on his mother. **Elkanah** saw the wisdom in this and agreed that Hannah and Samuel might remain at home. However, he was perhaps fearful that the temporary withholding of Samuel from the service of the Lord might jeopardize the Lord's favor (in giving them a son who would survive and mature) and so Elkanah prayed that **the Lord** might **make good His word.**

5. SAMUEL'S PRESENTATION TO GOD (1:24-28)

**1:24-28.** After Hannah had **weaned** her son, she fulfilled her pledge and **took** him to **Shiloh** to offer **him to the Lord** as a lifelong Nazirite. Since it was customary for a child to be nursed until he was about three years of age (see the apocryphal 2 Maccabees 7:27), the lad Samuel would be no unusual burden for **Eli** and the priestly staff at Shiloh. Also Samuel would be old enough to learn the rudiments of tabernacle service.

## B. Hannah's song (2:1-10)

This is one of the earliest and most stirring poems in the Old Testament. So messianic in character is it that Mary, the mother of Jesus, incorporated it into her own song of triumph, the Magnificat, in which she praised God for having selected her to be the human mother of Jesus, the Messiah (Luke 1:46-55).

1. HANNAH'S EXULTING IN THE LORD (2:1)

**2:1.** **Hannah,** with clear reference to her rival Peninnah, spoke of her joy **in the Lord** who had helped her achieve satisfaction at last. Horns, used by animals for defense and attack, symbolized strength. Thus Hannah spoke of her **horn** in describing the strength that had come to her because God had answered her prayer.

2. HANNAH'S EXTOLLING OF THE LORD (2:2-8)

**2:2-8.** Through His attributes such as holiness, strength (a **Rock**), knowledge, and discernment (vv. 2-3), and in view of His actions toward both the ungodly and the godly (vv. 4-8), the Lord demonstrates His awesome sovereignty in human affairs. Especially pointed is Hannah's reference (v. 5) to herself and Peninnah respectively: **She who was barren has borne seven children, but she who has had many sons pines away.** Hannah eventually had five other children (v. 21), but the expression "seven children" here symbolizes the full granting of her desire for a son. The breaking of **the bows** (v. 4), satisfying of the **hungry** (v. 5), raising of the dead (v. 6), and elevating of **the poor** (vv. 7-8) refer to the principle that the final disposition of all things is in the hand of **the Lord.** He who created the world (v. 8) was able to cause Hannah to triumph.

3. HANNAH'S EXPECTATION FROM THE LORD (2:9-10)

**2:9-10.** In addition to stating that **the Lord** blesses **His saints but** brings **the wicked** to destruction (v. 9), Hannah closed her poem with the prophetic announcement that the Lord **will give strength to His king and exalt the horn of His anointed.** The reference to a king here in this premonarchial passage has led many critics to maintain that the poem is a redaction from a later period which was placed in Hannah's mouth. This is unnecessary, of course, if one accepts the possibility of predictive prophecy. In addition, the notion of a coming human king was in no way foreign to Israel's expectation since **the Lord** had clearly intimated this as early as the time of Abraham (see *Introduction*). The word parallel to "king" (v. 10) is "anointed," a translation of *māšîaḥ* ("Messiah"). This is the first Old Testament reference to an individual's being "the Anointed One." Though it may be unwarranted to make a direct connection between Hannah's prophecy and Jesus the Messiah, it is evident that the juxtaposition of "king" and "anointed one" points to the royal nature of the anointed one(s) whom God would raise up (see Ps. 89:20-24).

## C. The situation at Shiloh (2:11-36)

1. SAMUEL'S PROGRESS (2:11, 26)

**2:11, 26.** Immediately after the return of his parents to their **home** young **Samuel** began his training **under Eli** (v. 11), a training which was characterized by his development physically, but especially morally and spiritually (v. 26). He grew **in stature and in favor with the Lord and with men,** an appropriate description of a son who, like Mary's, had come as a blessing of God to the world (Luke 2:52).

2. THE SINS OF THE PRIESTHOOD (2:12-17, 22-25)

**2:12-17, 22-25.** The human reason for the birth of Samuel had been recounted. He came in response to a godly mother's prayer. Now it was important to see the divine reason. The Book of Judges asserts, "In those days Israel had no king; everyone did as he saw fit" (Jud. 21:25). This was also true of the priests. **Eli,** though apparently a moral man himself, had lost control of his priestly **sons** who went so far as to appropriate for themselves the choice **meat** of the sacrificial animals which rightfully belonged to **the Lord** as His **offering** (1 Sam. 2:12-17). Moreover, they engaged in ritual fornication in the very precincts of the tabernacle at Shiloh in accord with Canaanite cultic practice (vv. 22-25).

### 3. THE BLESSING OF SAMUEL'S FAMILY (2:18-21)

**2:18-21.** As though to show the contrast between the ungodly and the godly about which Hannah had sung, the narration now contrasts the family of **Samuel** with that of Eli. Though Samuel's **mother** had given **Samuel** to **the Lord**, she retained her maternal love and responsibility. She came yearly to Shiloh to attend to the needs of her son. Nor did **the Lord** forget **Hannah**. As is so often the case, He gave her not only what **she** had **prayed** for but much more—in her case **three sons and two daughters** (cf. the example of Rachel, Gen. 30:22-24; 35:16-18).

### 4. THE REJECTION OF THE PRIESTHOOD (2:27-36)

**2:27-36.** It is no wonder that God rejected the priesthood of Eli and his **sons.** After reviewing the circumstances of the selection of Eli's ancestors to be priests of **the Lord** over **Israel** (vv. 27-28), an unnamed **man of God** announced **to Eli** that his priesthood would end because it had violated the conditions for its ongoing existence (vv. 29-33). Yet **the Lord** would not terminate the office of priest altogether for He would **raise up . . . a faithful priest** (v. 35) whose line of succession (**house**) would be **firmly** established and who would **minister before** His **anointed one** (i.e., the king) forever. In human terms this was fulfilled when the priesthood was taken from Abiathar, descendant of Aaron's son Ithamar, and given to Zadok, descendant of Aaron's son Eleazar (1 Kings 2:27, 35). But in the ultimate sense the "faithful Priest" and "Anointed One" are One and the same, the Lord Jesus Christ. He is both Priest and King (Ps. 110; Heb. 5:6; Rev. 19:16).

## D. Samuel's call (chap. 3)

For centuries God had rarely visited His people with revelation (v. 1). Now He had one to whom He could entrust His message. He called the young lad Samuel.

### 1. THE DIVINE VOICE (3:1-10)

**3:1-10.** Though Samuel had been dedicated to the Levitical ministry at Shiloh and had undergone training in the things of **the Lord,** he **had not yet been** addressed by the direct revelation of God (v. 7). At last the time came for **the Lord** to fulfill His promise to remove Eli's priesthood and establish another, so the divine silence was broken. While **Samuel** was reclining **in the** tabernacle (the meaning of the Heb. *hêkāl*, **temple,** v. 3) attending to the burning **lamp,** he heard the voice of **the Lord,** which he mistakenly took to be that of **Eli.** Finally **Eli** discerned that the lad was being addressed by **the Lord** so he advised him to submit himself to whatever **the Lord** would have him do.

### 2. THE DIVINE MESSAGE (3:11-14)

**3:11-14.** The message consisted of the announcement that the promised removal of Eli's family from the priesthood was about to occur. It was an announcement so shocking that it would cause the **ears** of the people to ring like hammer blows on a bell. The reason is explicitly stated—Eli's **sons** were wicked, and though **he knew** it **he failed to restrain them.** Though the message was given right then to Eli through Samuel, Eli himself lived for a short time thereafter, and indeed the priesthood continued in his family for three more generations. This is clear from 14:3—Ahijah served as priest to King Saul. He is identified as the great-grandson of Eli through Phinehas and Ahitub. The prophecy to Samuel came to pass fully when Abiathar, son of Ahijah (the same as Ahimelech of 22:9-12), was apparently replaced by King David with Zadok after Abiathar sided with Adonijah against Solomon (1 Kings 1:7-8; 2:27, 35). Thus the time between prophecy and fulfillment was more than 130 years. Yet it did come to pass and the priesthood switched to Zadok, a descendant of Aaron's son Eleazar, and it remained with his offspring throughout Israel's subsequent history.

### 3. SAMUEL'S VINDICATION (3:15-21)

**3:15-21.** This first act of **Samuel** as a prophet was recognized by **Eli** as having come from **God.** This was only the beginning of a public ministry as prophet, which would last through a lifetime and be recognized by all the people as a divine calling. The **word** of **the Lord** had been rare in those days (v. 1). Now, however, it would be common, for God had found a man to whom He could entrust it. The sign that **Samuel** was a spokesman for God was the fact that God **let none of his words fall to the ground** (v. 19), that is, everything he prophesied came to pass. **All Israel from Dan to Beersheba** (the northernmost and southernmost towns in Israel—a distance of about 150 miles) **recognized that Samuel was . . . a prophet of the Lord.** There was no clearer indication that a man was called to be a prophet than the fact that his predictive word invariably was fulfilled (Deut. 18:21-22). When it was understood that Samuel's credentials as a prophet were established, a new era was under way. Revelation through priest and ephod was passing away, and revelation through prophets was beginning.

*E. The ark (chaps. 4–7)*

1. THE CAPTURE OF THE ARK (CHAP. 4)

The Philistines, Israel's principal enemy during the period of the last of the Judges (Jud. 10:6-8; 13–16), were a non-Semitic people whose origins were most likely in Crete or in some other part of the Aegean Sea area (Gen. 10:14; see Jer. 47:4; Deut. 2:23; Amos 9:7). They came to Canaan in two different migrations, one as early as Abraham's time (2000 B.C.) and the other about 1200 B.C. They lived in five main towns on the southern Canaan coast—Gaza, Ashkelon, Ekron, Gath, and Ashdod. They were technologically advanced, pioneering in the use of iron and in other skills (1 Sam. 13:19-20). The primary god of their pantheon was Dagon, a deity worshiped also in upper Mesopotamia as a grain god. Some scholars suggest that the Philistine Dagon was represented as having a human torso and upper body and a fish's tail. It may well be that the originally seafaring Philistines brought their fish god with them to Canaan and then adapted him to the Semitic god Dagon (or Dagan, as it is known outside the Bible), because of their need to become a grain-producing people (Jud. 15:3-5).

**4:1-11.** When Samuel was yet a youth, Israel was attacked by **the Philistines at Aphek,** a site about 25 miles west of Shiloh. When it was clear that the Philistines would win, the Israelites **sent men to Shiloh** to bring the **ark of the covenant** to the battlefield, superstitiously supposing that its presence, like a good-luck charm, would turn the tide. The ark *did* represent the presence of **the Lord** in battle (Num. 10:35; Josh. 6:6) but only when the people carried it in faith and by divine leading. Even **the Philistines** were terrified when they knew the **ark** was in **the camp** of Israel, for they had heard about its association with Israel's **mighty gods** who had brought that people out of Egypt more than 300 years before (1 Sam. 4:6-8). Nonetheless, summoning their courage, they **fought** on and **defeated** Israel. In the process **the ark . . . was captured** and the **sons** of Eli, its keepers, were slain (v. 11).

**4:12-22.** When **Eli,** back at **Shiloh,** learned that **the ark** had been taken by **the** pagan **Philistines** and that his **sons** were **dead,** he **fell backward off his** seat, broke **his neck,** and **died.** Shortly thereafter **his daughter-in-law,** Phinehas' **wife,** died as she **gave birth . . . to a son** whom **she named,** appropriately enough, **Ichabod,** "there is no **glory"** (*'î kābôd*). Since the presence of **the ark** represented the presence **of God** in Israel, its capture suggested that not only was **the ark** gone but **God** Himself and all His **glory** were now in enemy hands. To the pagans it was conceivable that gods could be taken into exile (Isa. 46:1-2), but the Israelites should have known that their omnipresent God could not be taken away from them. How heathen Israel's perception of God had become!

2. THE POWER OF THE ARK (CHAP. 5)

**5:1-5.** That the Lord of Israel was not only omnipresent but also omnipotent was a fact that **the Philistines** were about to learn. Bearing **the ark** like a trophy of conquest, they took it first to the **temple of Dagon** at Ashdod, some 50 miles southwest of Shiloh. There they laid it at Dagon's feet (or tail) as though to say that **Dagon** was victor and **the Lord** his prisoner. But **the next** morning **Dagon** lay prostrate **before the ark.** Restored to his pedestal once again, **Dagon,** on **the following** day, again lay in submission before **the Lord,** this time shattered and broken. **Only his** torso **remained** intact. **Head and hands** were **broken off** and lay scattered across **the threshold** or podium. The word translated "threshold" (*miptān*) may also and perhaps ought to be understood as the pedestal on which the idol stood. So embarrassed were the Philistines over this misfortune of their god that they forever after refused to set foot on the scene of his calamity.

**5:6-12.** The Philistine **people** were affected as well, for the Lord sent a plague on the inhabitants **of Ashdod** which was evidently carried by mice ("rats," NIV; 6:4-5) and caused large **tumors** to erupt on their bodies (5:6). The nature of the plague is unclear but seemed to consist of growths particularly in the rectal area as the Hebrew *'ōpel* indicates. Perhaps it was a hemorrhoid-like condition, as suggested in many versions.

In complete despair over this turn of events, the Ashdodites decided to send **the ark** on **to Gath,** some 12 miles southeast and toward Israel. The same disaster befell the Gathites, however (v. 9); so finally **the ark** was moved **to Ekron** where its deadly reputation had already preceded it. The citizens of Ekron fared no better than the others and at once determined to send **the ark** (the chest which, in their view, contained **the God of Israel**) **back to its own** land. This seems naive to modern readers, but people in all times have attempted to box God in and manipulate Him to their own convenience.

3. THE RETURN OF THE ARK (6:1–7:1)

**6:1-12.** After suffering the humiliation of their god Dagon and the painful and fatal consequences of God's **plague,** the **Philistine** lords decided to **return** the **ark of the LORD** to Israel. In accordance with their superstitious techniques they consulted their **priests** and **diviners** who advised them to **send** the **ark back** accompanied with tokens of tribute in the form of **five gold tumors and five gold rats,** representing the five Philistine cities (vv. 17-18). These offerings to **Israel's God** would indicate their acknowledgment of His superiority (v. 5). Furthermore **the ark** should be sent on a **new** driverless **cart,** as a further test of the source of their troubles. If the animals (**two cows** still nursing their young and

not previously **yoked,** v. 7) pulled **the cart** directly back to Israel it would be clear that Israel's God had indeed caused their affliction. **But if** they wandered aimlessly about, the Philistines could attribute their misfortune to mere **chance.**

Though not much is known about divination from the Old Testament, since it was forbidden to Israel, divination texts abound from the ancient Near Eastern world. They indicate both the techniques employed to discover the intent of the gods and those used to avert portended evil. Frequently, as in the present story, it would take a binary form, that is a given test would be applied to which a yes or no response would be possible. Perhaps Gideon's use of the fleece reflects such a divinatory practice, though stripped of pagan overtones. The casting of lots would be similar. In any event, the deepest suspicions of the Philistines were confirmed when the animals made their way **straight** back to Israel. It was obvious that **the LORD** had been at the root of all their troubles.

**6:13–7:1.** The Israelites were so overjoyed to see **the ark** after seven months (6:1) that they offered a sacrifice of **the cows to the LORD** at **Beth Shemesh,** the border town where the ark had been directed, about 15 miles west of Jerusalem (see the map "The Wanderings of the Ark of the Covenant"). Unfortunately **the people of Beth Shemesh** not only **rejoiced** at the return of **the ark** (6:13) and **offered . . . sacrifices** in worship (6:14-15), but they desecrated it by opening it and looking inside (6:19) perhaps to see if the stone tablets of the Law were still there. This violated the Mosaic statute that only **Levites** could handle **the ark** and not even they could touch it directly, to say nothing of looking within it (Num. 4:5, 15, 20). Disobedience in this respect would bring death. The sin of the people of Beth Shemesh was a deliberate, "high-handed" violation of the clear will of God (1 Sam. 6:19; cf. 2 Sam. 6:6-7). (According to the NIV and a few Heb. mss., **70** people were put **to death.** Most Heb. mss., however, have 50,070. This seems an unusually large number, but it may be accounted for in some yet-unknown way.) The point, of course, is that not only unbelievers (the Philistines) suffer when the Law of **the LORD** is disre-

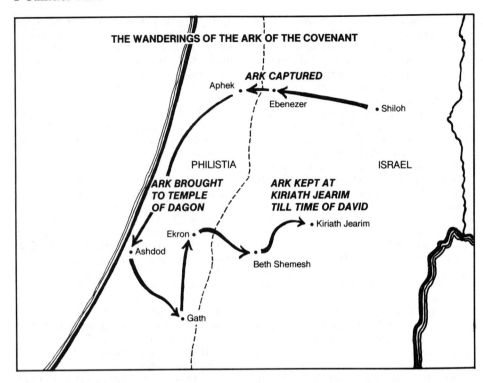

THE WANDERINGS OF THE ARK OF THE COVENANT

garded; believers (the Israelites) also suffer when they do not conform to His strict requirements. After this disaster at Beth Shemesh **the ark** was moved again (1 Sam. 6:21), this time to **Kiriath Jearim** (modern Abu Ghosh, about 10 miles northwest of Jerusalem). No doubt **the ark** was taken there rather than to Shiloh, because the latter was destroyed by the Philistines, perhaps after the battle of Aphek (chap. 4; cf. Jer. 26:9). The ark remained in the custody of the family of Abinadab (1 Sam. 7:1) for about 100 years.

4. THE RESTORATION OF THE ARK (7:2-17)

The return of the ark to Kiriath Jearim seemed to be a tangible sign that God was once again among His people to bless them and deliver them from all their oppressors. The mere presence of the ark did not guarantee God's favor, however, as Israel had learned at the battle of Aphek. Rather, it was submission to the God of the ark that was essential (v. 4).

**7:2.** After **the ark** was at **Kiriath Jearim** for **20 years** Samuel addressed the Israelites (v. 3). In other words, the ark was in Kiriath Jearim for 20 years before Samuel undertook his first recorded public ministry. In actual fact the ark remained at Kiriath Jearim for about 100 years. It was taken there just after the battle of Aphek (1104 B.C.) and remained until David brought it from there to Jerusalem in his first year as king over *all* Israel (1003 B.C.; see 2 Sam. 5:5; 6:1-11).

**7:3-4.** After these 20 long years with the ark at Kiriath Jearim, **Samuel** challenged the people **of Israel** to prove their loyalty to **the LORD** by abandoning their **foreign gods** and turning to **the LORD . . . only.** The plural **Baals** and **Ashtoreths** describe the many local shrines of those Canaanite nature deities. Baal, variously identified as son of El (chief of the Canaanite pantheon) or as son of Dagan (the Mesopotamian deity), was particularly recognized as the god of thunder and rain whose task was to make the earth fertile annually. Ashtoreth (or Astarte) was goddess of both love and war, as were her Babylonian and Greek counterparts Ishtar and Aphrodite respectively. She apparently functioned with Baal as a fertility deity and by their sexual union in some magical way the earth and all its life supposedly experienced annual rejuvenation and fruitfulness. (See the chart "Some of the Pagan Gods and Goddesses Worshiped in Nations Surrounding Israel," near Jud. 10:6.)

**7:5-9. Samuel** next summoned the people to **Mizpah,** some seven miles north of Jerusalem, and there prayed for them and **offered** sacrifice to **the LORD** on their **behalf** (v. 9). This was a common place of assembly for Israel. In the time of the Judges the elders of the tribes gathered there to decide Benjamin's fate following the murder of a Levite's concubine (Jud. 19:1–20:1, 3; 21:1, 5, 8). Later, Saul was presented to Israel as king at Mizpah (1 Sam. 10:17). It was even the capital of Judah after the destruction of Jerusalem by the Babylonians (2 Kings 25:23, 25). The town of Mizpah should probably be identified with modern Tell en-Nasbeh.

**7:10-17.** When **the Philistines** learned of the assembly, they attacked **Israel** at **Mizpah** but **the LORD,** in a mighty demonstration of power (by **thunder**), defeated them. In commemoration of this great triumph **Samuel** erected on the site **between Mizpah and Shen** (whose location is unknown), a monument which he called **Ebenezer,** literally, the "stone of [God's] help." This apparently ended Philistine occupation of **Israelite** soil though **the Philistines** came later time and time again to harass Israel (13:5; etc.). **Amorites** (7:14) refers to the hill-dwellers of southern Canaan (see Num. 13:29; Josh. 10:5). Thereafter **Samuel continued** to **judge . . . Israel** in a **circuit** (approx. 50 miles in circumference) including **Bethel . . . Gilgal . . . Mizpah,** and his hometown, **Ramah** (see the map "The Cities of Samuel").

## F. Selection of a king (chaps. 8–9)

After the battle of Ebenezer (7:12), about 1084 B.C. (see comments on 7:2), the nation of Israel was content to follow Samuel's leadership for the next 30 years or so. Israel had made abortive attempts to establish a human monarchy during the days of the Judges (see Jud. 8:22-23; 9), actions contrary to the theocratic ideal of the kingship of the Lord Himself. But when Samuel had grown old and it appeared he would not live much longer, the people again expressed the desire for a king. God had such a king in mind, one who would be raised up and identified in His own good time (Deut. 17:14-15), but

that time had not yet come. Thus the stage was set for an encounter between Samuel and the people.

### 1. THE DEMAND FOR A KING (8:1-9)

**8:1-6.** Shortly before 1051 B.C., the year Saul became king (**when Samuel** was 65-70 years **old**), the people of **Israel,** aware of Samuel's advanced age and of the wickedness of **his sons** (vv. 3, 5) demanded of the prophet that he select **a king** to rule over them. Samuel's sons, who had been serving as judges **at Beersheba** in Judah, no doubt reminded Israel of the sons of Eli (2:12, 22). Probably the people were afraid that they might return to the wicked days the nation had known before Samuel had been raised up by the Lord. Samuel's sons, **Joel** and **Abijah** were **dishonest** judges, accepting **bribes** and perverting, rather than upholding, **justice. Samuel,** of course, was grieved that they should seek **a king,** for God, who had redeemed them from Egypt to be His people, was their King.

**8:7-9.** But **the LORD told** Samuel that **the people** were rejecting **not** him **but** God. Furthermore God would permit them to have a **king,** but they would live to regret their hasty impulse.

The request for a human king was not in itself improper, for God had promised such a leader (see *Introduction*). But the refusal to wait for God's timing was clearly displeasing to the Lord and to His prophet. In the face of impending conflict with the Ammonites (see 12:12-13) the people wanted a king "such as all the other nations have" (8:5). Even after witnessing the leadership of the Lord in stunning victory over the Philistines at Ebenezer, Israel demanded a fallible, human leader.

### 2. THE NATURE OF THE KING (8:10-18)

**8:10-18.** At last **Samuel** relented. He told **the people** God would give them what they wanted, but **the king** would be a despot, a demanding dictator who would enrich himself at the people's expense. He would press them into his military and domestic enterprises (vv. 11-13, 16, 17). He would appropriate their properties to his own use (vv. 14, 16) and would inflict heavy taxes on them (vv. 15, 17). And **when** all this happened it would be too late to complain, for the people would have reaped the conse-

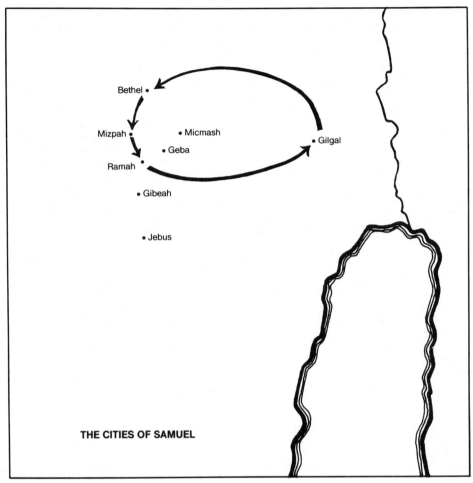

**THE CITIES OF SAMUEL**

quences of their own fleshly desires (v. 18). Shortly after Saul ascended the throne many of these predictions came to pass (14:52) and continued to mark the long history of the monarchy in both Israel and Judah (2 Sam. 15:1; 1 Kings 12:12-15; 21:7).

3. THE INTRODUCTION OF THE KING (8:19–9:14)

**8:19–9:2.** After **the Lord** had agreed to let **the people** have **a king . . . like all the other nations,** Saul was introduced in the story. He was a tall and striking **Benjamite** (9:1) who appeared quite naive and unkingly in many ways. He hailed from the town of Gibeah (10:26), where the concubine of a Levite who had sought hospitality was raped and killed (Jud. 19). Excavations at Tel el-Ful, just three miles north of Jerusalem, have established it as the site of ancient Gibeah. Though **a son** of **Kish,** a man of some

influence (1 Sam. 9:1), Saul had little to commend him to the high position of **king** except his physical impressiveness (9:2). God had to convince both Saul and **the people** that he was the proper candidate.

**9:3-11.** On a mission to find some lost **donkeys** belonging to his **father Kish,** Saul approached the region **of Zuph** (in **the hill country of Ephraim;** cf. 1:1, the home of Samuel). It occurred to Saul's **servant** that since Samuel was a **seer** he could help **find** the animals. In Saul's day a **prophet** was known primarily as **a seer** (*rō'eh*) undoubtedly because the major thrust of his ministry was associated with receiving divine revelation, even in matters as mundane as finding **lost** animals. Later prophets served more as proclaimers of revelation, spokesmen for God (*nābî'*), though of course all prophets were both seers and proclaimers. Samuel, for example, was expressly described by both terms (9:11; 3:20).

**9:12-14.** When Saul and his servant arrived in Samuel's **town,** they found that the prophet was on his way to a nearby **high place** (a place of worhip on a hill) to offer **a sacrifice.** Undaunted, they continued on until they located him.

4. THE CHOICE OF THE KING (9:15-27)

**9:15-27.** Meanwhile **the Lord had revealed . . . to Samuel** that Saul was on his way and that he was the divine choice for king (vv. 15-17). This does not mean that Saul satisfied God's ultimate requirements but only that He was graciously letting the **people** have their own way. When the two met (by God's providential control), **Samuel** not only put Saul's mind at ease concerning the **lost** beasts but also told him that he was God's choice for king (v. 20). Astounded, **Saul** could only reply that he was unworthy of this high honor (v. 21). The transparency and humility of Saul are evident at this stage of his career. **Samuel** then invited **Saul** to sit with him as guest of honor at the sacrificial feast (vv. 22-24) and then to spend the night in his home in **the town** below. Next morning **Samuel** detained him so that he might communicate with him alone (with Saul's **servant** going **on ahead**) the revelation of **God** about his selection as king (vv. 25-27).

## II. The Period of Saul (chaps. 10–31)

*A. Saul's ascendancy (chaps. 10–14)*

1. SAUL'S CHOICE BY ISRAEL (CHAP. 10)

**10:1-8.** As **Samuel** prepared to reveal God's purposes to Saul, he first anointed him with **oil.** In the Old Testament anointing with oil symbolized the setting apart of a person or even an object for divine service (Ex. 30:23-33). It was also accompanied by the presence and power of the Holy Spirit (1 Sam. 10:6, 10; 16:13). When Samuel **poured** oil **on Saul's head,** that act represented God's approval of Saul as **leader** of His people. In confirmation to both Saul and the people of his divine call and commission, Saul was told that he would experience three signs: (a) he would **meet two men near Rachel's tomb at Zelzah on the border of Benjamin** and Ephraim, who would tell him of the whereabouts of the lost **donkeys**; (b) he would meet **three**

**men** at the (oak) **tree of Tabor,** somewhere between Zelzah and Gibeah, who would give him **two loaves of bread**; and (c) he would **meet a procession of prophets** descending **from the high place** at **Gibeah.** Remarkably, he would join in with the prophets in their **prophesying** as **the Spirit** of God enabled him and he would **be changed into a different person.** This is frequently taken to mean that Saul was converted or spiritually regenerated. However, such language for spiritual renewal is foreign to the Old Testament, and Saul's subsequent attitudes and behavior do not bear out that this was his experience (16:14; 18:12; 28:15-16). Actually the Spirit made the inexperienced and unlettered Saul able to assume kingly responsibilities in much the same way as the judges before him were blessed (Jud. 6:34; 11:29; 13:25; 14:6, 19; 15:14).

**10:9-13.** After **Saul** left **Samuel,** the promised **signs** came to pass. So amazed were the witnesses to Saul's dramatic and powerful change of character that they created a proverb which thereafter was quoted to describe a totally unexpected and unexplainable phenomenon: **Is Saul also among the prophets?** This does not suggest, of course, that Saul became part of the prophetic ministry led by Samuel, but only that he was able to exercise a prophetic gift, at least on this occasion, though never having received prophetic training. This was a remarkable and convincing sign of God's presence and power in Saul's life.

Further evidence that Saul did not actually become a prophet lies in the stem of the Hebrew verb here. **He joined in their prophesying** means literally, "He acted like a prophet among them," that is, to all outward appearances he was a prophet because he was able to enter into their activities.

**10:14-16.** **Saul** told **his uncle** about finding **the donkeys** with Samuel's help, **but** Saul **said** nothing **about the kingship.**

**10:17-27.** Sometime later **Samuel** gathered the leaders **of Israel** together at **Mizpah,** a favorite place for assembly in Samuel's day (cf. 7:5-6). After reminding them of their foolish insistence on having **a king** apart from the directive will of **God,** he set about to demonstrate God's selection of Saul by a process of elimination (10:18-19). By lot or some similar means the choice was made of **tribe,** that **of Benjamin . . . clan,** that of Matri; and family, that **of Kish** (vv. 20-21). But when **Saul** was **chosen,** he was nowhere **to be found.** Indicative of his unassuming humility were his initial attempts to avoid the glare of publicity (v. 22) and his refusal to be vindictive against those who ridiculed his selection as king (v. 27). But the masses were convinced of his eminent suitability for the high office and in jubilation cried out, **Long live the king!**

However, in the eyes of the Lord, Saul was disqualified. The prophetic word of Jacob was that the scepter (of kingship) would not depart from Judah (Gen. 49:10). The promised dynasty of kings which would eventually produce the Messiah must originate in Judah. Saul as a Benjamite could not, then, meet the basic prerequisite of lineage. Nonetheless the people had made their demand, and **the Lord** had acquiesced. All that **Samuel** could do was invest Saul with his authority and responsibility as outlined in **a scroll** prepared for this occasion of coronation (1 Sam. 10:25). Undoubtedly the scroll included the Mosaic regulations for kingship found in Deuteronomy 17:14-17. Interestingly **valiant men** were immediately attracted to Saul **in Gibeah** (see comments on 1 Sam. 9:1).

### 2. SAUL'S FIRST VICTORY (CHAP. 11)

**11:1-6.** No sooner had Saul begun his rule than a distant but important part of his kingdom was attacked by the Ammonites. This was the city of **Jabesh Gilead,** about 25 miles south of the Sea of Galilee, east of the Jordan River. Saul's special concern for this community may well lie in possible ancestral ties which he had there. Judges 19–21 records the story of the civil war between Benjamin and the other tribes, which resulted in the annihilation of all but 600 men of Benjamin. With no wives and children it is apparent that the tribe would become extinct. To prevent this the leaders of Israel proposed that the virgin women of any town which had not sent troops to combat Benjamin should be seized and given to these survivors as wives. When it was discovered that Jabesh Gilead had failed in this respect, the 400 virgins of the city were captured and given to the Benjamites. Since Saul was a Benjamite, it is entirely possible that his ancestry sprang in part from Jabesh Gilead.

When **Saul** learned of the plight of Jabesh Gilead, a city so hopelessly besieged by the Ammonites that defeat was inevitable, he became enraged (1 Sam. 11:6) and set about to raise an army capable of delivering the place. So confident was **Nahash,** king of Ammon, that he made **a treaty** with Jabesh Gilead to the effect that if they surrendered he would pluck out every **right eye.** If they resisted, Nahash would probably kill them. The **Jabesh** elders asked for **seven days** of grace in which to find help. Nahash agreed, to spare the expense of a long and costly siege, assuming that Saul, who did not even have an army, would be powerless to intervene.

**11:7-15.** Saul, hearing of the people's plight, **cut up two oxen and sent the pieces . . . throughout Israel,** saying that **anyone who** would **not follow Saul and Samuel** would have their **oxen** similarly dissected. This method of getting the attention of the tribes is remarkably similar to that of the Levite of Ephraim who dissected his concubine's corpse and sent the parts to the various tribes, a part of the story from Judges 19–21 (see comments on Jud. 19:27-30). After assembling 330,000 soldiers **at Bezek,** 12 miles west of **Jabesh Gilead,** Saul marched all night and early in the morning (**the last watch** was the last third of the night) engaged **the Ammonites** in battle, **and slaughtered them.** The distinction between **Israel** and **Judah** (cf. 1 Sam. 15:4; 17:52; 18:16) indicates that 1 Samuel was written after the nation was divided in 931 b.c. into the Northern and Southern Kingdoms. After this decisive victory **Saul** was hailed as a hero and became firmly entrenched in his monarchical role. And he gave **the Lord** all the glory. This achievement convinced even **Samuel** that God had His hand on Saul, so the prophet convened another assembly at **Gilgal** so that the people could **reaffirm the kingship.** Though the evidence is somewhat meager the occasion described is likely a covenant-renewal ceremony, perhaps on the occasion of Saul's first anniversary as king. The presence of **the Lord,** the **king,** and **the people** would suggest this, particularly in light of the sacrificial festival which highlighted the event (1 Sam. 11:15).

## 3. THE ADDRESS BY SAMUEL (CHAP. 12)

**12:1-5.** As **Samuel** had spoken to them earlier about his age and the imminence of his death, so now again he addressed the assembly of **Israel,** this time after Saul had become **king** and had distinguished himself. As though now to reestablish his credibility among them, Samuel asked whether or not the people had ever detected any moral or spiritual flaw in his life. (By contrast, flaws had certainly been evident in his **sons,** 8:3.) The answer, of course, was no. Samuel's intent was to show that just as he could be trusted in the past so his word for the present and the future could also be accepted with confidence.

**12:6-25.** A critical point had been reached in Israel's history. **The people** had demanded and had been given **a king,** contrary to the precise purposes and will of **God.** And that king had led them to a glorious victory in his very first campaign! Now the question was, Would Israel see this victory as evidence of God's blessing and give Him the glory, or would they interpret it as a human achievement devoid of divine enablement? Samuel anticipated that question and sought to direct the people to a fresh recognition of the sovereignty of God and to the need to worship and praise Him as the Source of all their blessing. He did this first by reminding them of how God had redeemed them from **Egypt** and brought them into Canaan (vv. 6-8). He then recounted their disobedience under the Judges (vv. 9-11). (**Jerub-Baal,** v. 11, was another name for "Gideon," Jud. 6:32. **Barak** in the NIV is lit., in the Heb., "Bedon" [see NIV marg.]. Bedon was either another name for Barak or another judge mentioned only here in the OT.) Next Samuel pointed out that the Ammonite menace had prompted them to request a human **king,** a request to which **the LORD** had graciously acceded (1 Sam. 12:12-15). Finally **Samuel** appealed to **the LORD** to send a sign from heaven both to authenticate his own warnings of judgment and to cause the people to revere the God who had called them and who desired to bless and use them (vv. 16-18). The Lord reminded them that their insistent demand **for a king,** though He would grant it, was still

an evil request because it was premature and wrongly motivated.

When **the people** witnessed the display of **thunder and rain,** a phenomenon unheard of in early summer, the time of **wheat harvest** (v. 17), they turned **to Samuel** in earnest penitence and asked the prophet to **pray** that **God** might forgive their hastiness in seeking **a king** (v. 19). In a marvelous manifestation of the grace of God, **Samuel** related to **the people** that God would bless them in spite of their wrong choice if they would only be steadfast in their obedience from this point on. The past could not be undone but their future was untainted and could be devoted to the Lord (vv. 20-22). And Samuel also, as a true mediator, pledged to keep praying for the people. (Centuries later Jeremiah spoke of Samuel as a great man of prayer, Jer. 15:1.) Failure to do so, Samuel said, would be **sin against** God! (1 Sam. 12:23) If the people would respond affirmatively, they could expect God's continued blessing on their nation. But if they did not, they could expect the judgment of God on them (vv. 24-25).

## 4. SAUL'S FIRST REBUKE (CHAP. 13)

**13:1.** If the setting of the reaffirmation of Saul's kingship and Samuel's address on that occasion is the first anniversary of his coronation, it may be that the events of this chapter occurred after his second anniversary. This is a possible interpretation of the textually difficult passage translated by the NIV as **Saul was 30 years old when he became king, and he reigned over Israel 42 years.** The Hebrew is literally, "Saul was years old when he began to reign and he reigned two years over Israel." Obviously a figure has dropped out of the first part of the statement, and the second part cannot mean that he reigned for a total of only two years. Old Testament chronology implies—and Paul in his address at Pisidian Antioch (Acts 13:21) distinctly teaches—that Saul reigned for 40 years, no doubt a round number but close to the actual figure. There is no reason to think that the number "two" is suspect, however, for all manuscripts and versions retain it. It is only the desire to see 1 Samuel 13:1 as a regular formula for kingship (as in 2 Sam. 2:10; 5:4; 1 Kings 14:21; 22:42; etc.) that leads many scholars to postulate that "40" or some other figure

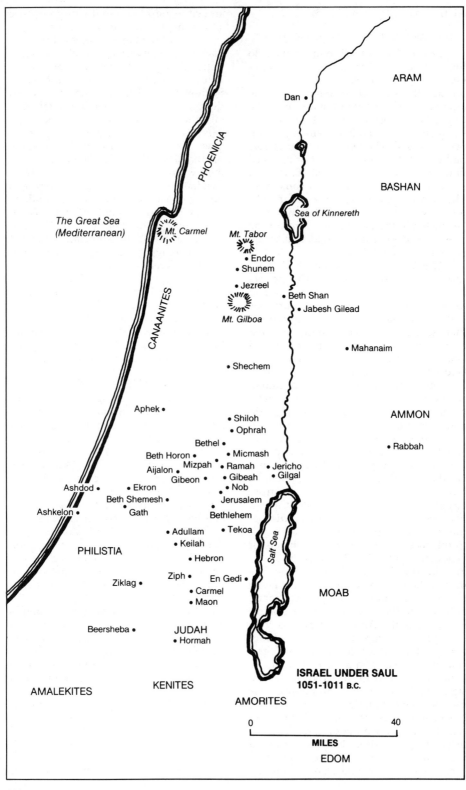

ARAM

Dan •

PHOENICIA

BASHAN

*The Great Sea
(Mediterranean)*

Mt. Carmel

*Sea of Kinnereth*

*Mt. Tabor*

• Endor
• Shunem

CANAANITES

• Jezreel

*Mt. Gilboa*

• Beth Shan
• Jabesh Gilead

• Mahanaim

• Shechem

Aphek •

AMMON

• Shiloh
• Ophrah

Bethel •

• Rabbah

Beth Horon •    • Micmash

Aijalon •   Mizpah   • Ramah   • Jericho
   Gibeon •   • Gibeah   • Gilgal

Ashdod •   • Ekron   • Nob
   Beth Shemesh •
Ashkelon •   Gath •   Jerusalem

   Bethlehem •

PHILISTIA   • Adullam   • Tekoa
   • Keilah

   • Hebron

Ziklag •   Ziph •   En Gedi •
   • Carmel
   • Maon

Beersheba •   JUDAH
   • Hormah

*Salt Sea*

MOAB

AMALEKITES   KENITES

AMORITES

**ISRAEL UNDER SAUL
1051-1011 B.C.**

0                    40

**MILES**

EDOM

is missing. In the context, however, the historian is not introducing a kingship formula (why do so here, well into Saul's reign?), but is probably indicating that the Ammonite threat had come in Saul's first year and now, in his second, the Philistines must be encountered.

A problem remains with the first part of the Hebrew statement, "Saul was years old. . . ." Many scholars, following Origen (ca. A.D. 185–254), postulate "30" (so NIV). Since Jonathan, Saul's son, was already grown then and served as a military commander, Saul would have been older than 30. It is more likely that the figure to be supplied is "40" though this too is difficult to reconcile with the description (1 Sam. 9:2) that Saul was, at the time of his anointing, "an impressive young man." Of course "young" in this latter passage may not be a good translation for the Hebrew *bāḥûr*, a word that could be rendered "choice."

The best translation of 13:1 would seem to be, "Saul was [40] years old when he began to reign, and he reigned over Israel for two years." This is further supported by the next verse which begins with a verb in the preterite tense, a construction indicating a close connection with the previous clause. "Saul chose . . . " (v. 2) implies that after he had reigned for two years Saul began to select and train a regular army, not the larger militia he had used previously.

**13:2-15.** Having learned from his recent experience with the Ammonites, **Saul** set about to create a standing army of **3,000** trained troops—2,000 under his direct control and **1,000** under his son **Jonathan.** These he stationed at **Micmash** and **Gibeah** respectively, in order to avert Philistine attacks. After a preliminary encounter **at Geba,** halfway between Micmash and Gibeah, **the Philistines** (with **3,000 chariots, 6,000 charioteers** and innumerable foot **soldiers**) pushed the Israelite troops eastward all the way to **Gilgal** (vv. 3-7). This is the first of Israel's three major battles with the Philistines in Saul's reign (cf. 17:1-54; 31:1-6). (Though the Heb. reads "30,000 chariots," this is problematic because this would mean 5 chariots for every charioteer. The Heb. words for "30,000" and for "3,000" look almost alike. The one could easily be mistaken for the other when the text was being copied. Perhaps this suggests that the text of 1 Sam. has suffered a bit in transmission.)

There **Saul** waited for **Samuel** to come and offer sacrifice (13:8) as he had been told to do two years earlier (10:8; see comments on 13:1-2). But on the seventh day, the day **Samuel** was to arrive, **Saul** could wait no longer and unlawfully took on himself the priestly task of **offering** community sacrifice. Then **Samuel** came and when he knew that **Saul** had taken liberties by offering the sacrifice, he rebuked him with the words, **You acted foolishly.** Because of this deed, Samuel said, Saul's dynasty would come to an end (**Your kingdom will not endure**), and that of another man would take its place, **a man after** God's **own heart.** The severity of God's judgment on Saul must be seen in the light of God's holiness. As in the instance of the people's careless handling of the ark at Beth Shemesh, so Saul had now violated the holy standards of the Lord by disobeying the Law of Moses (Lev. 6:8-13) and the word of His Prophet Samuel (1 Sam. 10:8). That there was the possibility of the eternal duration of Saul's dynasty is clear from 1 Samuel 13:13, but this in no way teaches that the rise of David's dynasty was contingent on the fall of Saul's. All Samuel said was that Saul's kingship would end and someone else's would begin.

**13:16-18.** Having taken **Geba** from the Philistines (v. 3), **Saul and . . . Jonathan,** after the incident with Samuel at Gilgal, were once again attacked by **the Philistines** from **Micmash.** The latter divided themselves into **three** companies of **raiding parties,** one of which **turned** north of Micmash **toward Ophrah,** the second southwest **toward Beth Horon, and the third** east **toward . . . Zeboim** (the Jordan Valley). The rest of the overconfident Philistine army remained at Micmash.

**13:19-23.** This parenthetical note explains that the Israelites were at a big disadvantage because they were not skilled in the manufacture and use of iron; **the Philistines** had kept them from metallurgy for fear the Israelites would **make swords** and **spears. The Philistines** had apparently learned sophisticated metallurgy from the Hittites or other Anatolian peoples with whom they had come in contact as part of the Sea People's migration from the Aegean Sea area to Canaan around 1200 B.C. Israel had to depend on the Philistines for iron weapons and tools (v. 20). In wartime such services were not available, so **only Saul and . . . Jonathan had** iron weapons (v. 22).

### 5. JONATHAN'S PERIL (CHAP. 14)

**14:1-14.** With the resumption of the skirmish against the Philistines, **Saul** camped near the capital **Gibeah** (v. 2), with **about 600 men.** But **Jonathan** undertook a secret mission into the enemy camp itself near Micmash. On the way Jonathan and his **armor-bearer** passed between two cliffs named **Bozez** and **Seneh** (v. 4). As they came through the narrow crevice they were spotted by **the Philistines,** who challenged them to a contest (v. 12). Having undertaken his mission with confidence in **the LORD** (vv. 6, 10), **Jonathan** knew that he and his servant would prevail. Together they **killed some 20** of the enemy in a small field.

**14:15-23.** Jonathan's heroic encounter shocked and frightened the Philistines. **Saul's lookout** could see the enemy in flight. Knowing that this must have come about because of some Israelite involvement, the king checked to determine who among his troops had undertaken this independent action. **Jonathan and his armor-bearer** were missing.

Meanwhile **Ahijah** the priest (cf. v. 3) came bearing **the ark of** the Lord (vv. 18-19). **It was** still housed at Kiriath Jearim (7:1) but as a symbol of the presence of the Lord, it was summoned by Saul to the battle. When **Saul** saw that the Philistines were in total disarray, he ordered Ahijah to **withdraw** his **hand** (i.e., from the sacred lots, the Urim and Thummim, 14:19; cf. Ex. 28:29-30; 1 Sam. 14:40-42). The will of God was now clear so **Saul,** with Israelite defectors and refugees, achieved a great triumph (vv. 20-23).

**14:24-48.** Prior to this **Saul had** commanded all his men to fast until they had defeated the Philistines. As hungry as they were in the battle, they refused to eat anything, even some **honey** in the forest, for **they feared** the curse that attended their vow to fast. **Jonathan had not** known of the vow, **so** when **he** came

across the honey he ate it and was immediately refreshed (**his eyes brightened;** cf. v. 29). The rest of Saul's army was so famished that after the victory they took the Philistine animals, slaughtered them, and ate them without proper draining of **the blood** (vv. 32-33; cf. Lev. 17:10-14). This so alarmed **Saul** that he hastily built **an altar** on which to offer a propitiatory sacrifice to the Lord (1 Sam. 14:35).

**Saul** then determined to pursue and **plunder** the **Philistines** further but could not get an **answer** from the Lord (v. 37). This meant to **Saul** that someone had violated the fast, and by means of the **lot** (i.e., the Urim and Thummim, vv. 41-42; cf. v. 19) he discovered it was his own **son Jonathan.** Only the interposition of Saul's **men** prevented Jonathan's execution (v. 45).

The major campaigns of **Saul** are listed in verses 47-48 and include victories over **Moab,** Ammon, **Edom . . . Zobah** (the Arameans), **the Philistines,** and even **the Amalekites,** though his success over the latter was tempered by his lack of complete obedience to God (cf. 15:20-23).

**14:49-52.** The royal family consisted of Saul; his wife **Ahinoam;** his three **sons . . . Jonathan, Ishvi** (not the same as Ish-Bosheth or Esh-Baal; cf. 1 Chron. 10:2 where Ishvi is the same person as Abinadab), **and Malki-Shua;** his daughters **Merab** and **Michal** (David's first wife; cf. 1 Sam. 18:27); and **Abner,** who served as Saul's **commander** of the **army.**

Ishvi is probably not the same as Ish-bosheth because Ish-bosheth was apparently Saul's youngest son born after Saul began to reign. For that reason he is not listed in 1 Samuel 14:49 but is listed in the total list of Saul's sons in 1 Chronicles 8:33 (cf. comments on 2 Sam. 2:8).

According to 1 Chronicles 8:33 and 9:39 **Ner** was Saul's grandfather (Ner's son was **Kish** and Kish's **son** was **Saul**), but in 1 Samuel 14:50 Ner appears to be Saul's uncle and Abner his cousin. In 1 Chronicles Abner, though not mentioned, would be Saul's *uncle,* for Abner was Ner's son (1 Sam. 14:50). This seeming contradiction is eliminated by the Hebrew of 1 Samuel 14:50b, which says literally, "Abner son of Ner, uncle of Saul," with the understanding that the ambiguous "uncle of Saul" refers not to Ner but to Abner. Charted, this relationship was as follows:

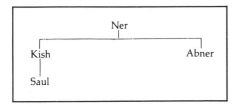

## B. Saul's rejection (chap. 15)

**15:1-8.** Long before the time of Saul, in the days of the wilderness wandering, Israel had been savagely attacked from the rear by **the Amalekites,** a deed the Lord had promised to avenge someday (Ex. 17:8-16). The time had now come, so **Samuel** commanded Saul to **destroy** the Amalekites **totally,** that is, to "place them under the ban (*ḥērem*) of holy war" (1 Sam. 15:3; cf. vv. 8-9, 15, 18, 20-21; Deut. 20:16-18; see comments on Josh. 6:21). However, **Saul** was to spare **the Kenites** since they had **shown kindness** to Israel in the wilderness wandering (1 Sam. 15:6; cf. Ex. 18:9-10 [Jethro was a Kenite, Jud. 1:16]). **Saul** proceeded to do the bidding of Samuel (1 Sam. 15:7-8) but not entirely.

**15:9-35.** When **Saul** saw the fatness of the Amalekite **sheep and cattle** and when he considered the enhancement of his own glory and prestige in bringing back **Agag, king of** Amalek, as prisoner, he could not resist returning them as public exhibits of his leadership (v. 9). That this was Saul's intent is clear from verse 12, which speaks of Saul's erecting **a monument** to **his own honor** at **Carmel** (in Judah, not the Carmel on the upper Mediterranean coast). When accosted by **Samuel** (v. 14), **Saul** tried to justify his disobedience by claiming that the animals were brought as **sacrifice to the LORD** (vv. 13, 15), and were brought because of the insistence of **the soldiers** (vv. 20-21). But **Samuel** responded with a statement of principle that is timeless in its application: **To obey is better than sacrifice, and to heed is better than the fat of rams** (v. 22). In addition to disobeying, Saul was guilty of **rebellion . . . arrogance,** and rejecting God's **word** (v. 23).

The result for **Saul** was the Lord's rejection of him **as king** (v. 26), symbolized by Saul's tearing of Samuel's **robe** (vv. 27-28). This repudiation of Saul and selection of a replacement (David) did not mean that God had misled Samuel or even changed **His mind** (v. 29). Rather, God had from the beginning chosen another, one who would be "after His own heart" (cf. 13:14; 16:1). Though still recognized by the people as their king for about 15 more years, **Saul** was deposed by **the LORD** right then (cf. 16:14), and **Samuel** executed **Agag** (15:32-33). The finality of it all was not missed by **Samuel** for from that day Samuel never visited the **king** again (v. 35). The estrangement between **Samuel** and **Saul** represents that which now existed in permanent form between the Lord Himself and the disobedient king. Though God had permitted Saul to reign in response to the demand of the people, that very concession now **grieved** the heart of **the LORD** (v. 35).

## C. Saul and David (chaps. 16–26)

### 1. ON FRIENDLY TERMS (CHAPS. 16–17)

### a. The choice and anointing of David (16:1-13)

**16:1-13.** After Saul's further rebellion against the Lord and his subsequent rejection by **the LORD,** Samuel was commissioned to seek out the **one** who would succeed Saul on the throne of **Israel.** This one had already been identified as "a man after [God's] own heart" (13:14) and "one of [Saul's] neighbors" who was "better than" he (15:28). David had been chosen from eternity past to be ruler of Israel. The rejection of Saul did not force **the LORD** to a new course of action. Rather, God's action followed His omniscient plan in such a way as to use Saul's disobedience as the human occasion for implementing His higher plan. God had permitted the people to have the **king** of their choice. Now that that king and their mistake in choosing him had been clearly manifested, God proved the superiority of His own wisdom in raising up a king who would come in fulfillment of His perfect will.

After an undetermined length of time in which **Samuel** lamented the rejection of **Saul,** the Lord commanded the prophet to go to **Bethlehem** to select a son of **Jesse . . . to be king** (16:1-3). Jesse was the grandson of Ruth and Boaz (Ruth 4:18-21), and so was in the line of promise (see the chart "David's Ancestry from Abraham"). As the wives of Jacob gave birth to a royal house (Gen. 35:11; 49:10), so Ruth would produce the Davidic dynasty (Ruth 4:11). God did not tell Samuel to be deceptive, but rather to combine the anointing with the business of sacrificing (1 Sam 16:2). **The elders** in **Bethlehem** may have wondered if **Samuel** had come for judgment (v. 4).

After the **seven** older **sons** of **Jesse** were disqualified one by one (vv. 5-10), **David** was singled out by **the Lord** and **anointed** by **Samuel** (vv. 11-13). The anointing, as in the experience of Saul, was accompanied by the coming of **the Spirit** of God mightily on the young lad (v. 13). This was the supernatural authentication of God's will. Later David was anointed king over Judah (2 Sam. 2:4) and then over Israel (2 Sam. 5:3).

### b. David as Saul's musician (16:14-23)

**16:14-23.** As David was invested by the Spirit, that same **Spirit** left **Saul**. This is evidence of the fact that the presence or absence of the Holy Spirit in the Old Testament says nothing about salvation but only that His power worked in those whom God selected for service (cf. Jud. 3:10; 6:34; 13:25; 14:6; 1 Sam. 10:10; 16:13).

With the departure of the Spirit of God, Saul became **tormented** by **an evil spirit** which **God** permitted to come (v. 14; cf. vv. 15-16; 18:10; 19:9). Whether this spirit had sinful or only harmful characteristics, it is quite certain that it was a demonic, satanic instrument (cf. Job 1:12; 2:6; 1 Kings 22:19-22). In his troubled state Saul could find relief only in music, so he commanded that a musician be found (1 Sam. 16:15-17). In His providence God arranged that **David** be the one, so the shepherd boy was introduced to the palace of the king (vv. 18-21). The Holy Spirit empowered **David** to drive away **the evil spirit** that overwhelmed **Saul** (v. 23). Harps had already been mentioned in connection with prophesying (10:5). Later Elisha, when seeking a revelation from the Lord, also requested that a harp be played (2 Kings 3:15). Also Asaph, Heman, and Jeduthun prophesied with harps, lyres, and cymbals (1 Chron. 25:1).

### c. David's triumph over Goliath (chap. 17)

**17:1-51.** Sometime after David commenced his role of court musician, Israel was again in peril at the hands of **the Philistines.** The armies were drawn up on opposite sides of **the Valley of Elah,** a few miles southwest of Jerusalem (vv. 2-3). Apparently intimidated by each other, they decided that the outcome should be determined by a contest of champions who would engage each other in combat. **The Philistines** offered **Goliath,** a giant (about 9'9" tall!), but Israel could find no one worthy, not even **Saul** (vv. 4-11). Goliath **wore a bronze helmet** and **a coat of scale armor** weighing **5,000 shekels,** that is, about 125 pounds, and **bronze greaves.** He was armed with **a bronze javelin,** and a long **spear** with a 15-pound **iron** tip! (v. 7) At last **David** heard of the dilemma and, having been sent to the **camp** of **Israel** with provisions for his **brothers** (vv. 12-22), begged **Saul** to let him take on **the Philistine** (vv. 23-32). Reluctantly **Saul** agreed and **David,** armed only with his confidence in God, a **sling,** and **five smooth stones,** slew Goliath and brought back his severed **head** in triumph (vv. 33-51).

**17:52-58.** When the conflict was over, **Saul** inquired as to the identity of the young warrior and learned that he was David, **son** of Jesse (vv. 55, 58). Why could not Saul recognize David, who had already served him for some time as musician and armor-bearer? One answer is that Saul was not asking who David was but for the first time was curious about David's family connections: **Whose son is that young man?** (v. 55; cf. v. 25) When David himself was interrogated he did not say, "I am David," but only, **I am the son of your servant Jesse of Bethlehem** (v. 58). Another and perhaps better solution is that David's previous service had been brief and intermittent and now several years had passed since Saul had last seen him. If, for example, David had been only 12 years old when he came as Saul's musician and had stayed off and on for only a year or so, he might have been 17 or 18 by the time of the Philistine episode and no longer recognizable to Saul. This view is strengthened by the fact that after David joined himself to Saul this time, the king "did not let him return to his father's house" (v. 15; 18:2). This implies that David's previous tenure

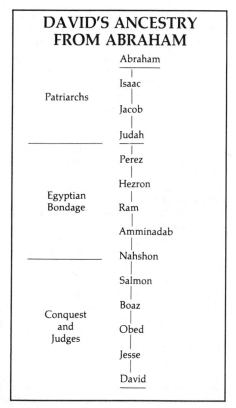

## DAVID'S ANCESTRY FROM ABRAHAM

| | |
|---|---|
| **Patriarchs** | Abraham |
| | Isaac |
| | Jacob |
| | Judah |
| **Egyptian Bondage** | Perez |
| | Hezron |
| | Ram |
| | Amminadab |
| | Nahshon |
| **Conquest and Judges** | Salmon |
| | Boaz |
| | Obed |
| | Jesse |
| | David |

had not been permanent. In any event, one need not posit two sources for chapters 16 and 17 or view the accounts as irreconcilable.

2. ON UNFRIENDLY TERMS (CHAPS. 18–26)

*a. David's flight from Saul (chaps. 18–20)*

(1) David's popularity. **18:1-7.** **David,** as has been seen, was not only chosen from eternity to be the founder of the messianic dynasty of kings, but he was also providentially prepared by the Lord to undertake his royal responsibilities. David had served as a shepherd in the fields and had the loving, protective heart of a shepherd, a fitting attribute of a king. He had learned responsibility and courage by confronting and slaying wild beasts that threatened his flock (17:34-36). He had learned to play the harp, a skill that would make him sensitive to the aesthetic side of life and that would help him compose the stirring psalms which extol the Lord and celebrate His mighty exploits. David had been brought into the palace of the king as musician and warrior so that he might acquire the experience of statecraft. Though an un-

initiated novice at the time of his anointing, he was eminently equipped to be king of Israel at his coronation some 15 years later. But his education was not always pleasant. With his rising popularity among the people came a deterioration of his relationship with **Saul,** for the king became insanely jealous of Israel's new hero.

After David's dramatic victory over Goliath, Saul brought him into his palace once again, this time as a commander of his **army** (18:5). David's favored position in the court was further strengthened by the personal affection felt for him by **Jonathan,** Saul's oldest son (vv. 1, 3). So close did this friendship become that **Jonathan,** though heir apparent to the throne of Israel (cf. 20:31), stripped himself of his own royal regalia and placed it on **David** in recognition of David's divine election to be king (18:4; cf. 23:17). More than once the covenant of friendship between the two men would work to David's advantage. Meanwhile David became so effective militarily that his exploits were celebrated in song: **Saul has slain his thousands, and David his tens of thousands.**

(2) Saul's jealousy (18:8–20:42). **18:8-16.** So enraged was **Saul** at the diminishing of his glory that he, inspired by the demonic **spirit** (v. 10; cf. 16:14-16; 19:9), tried to **spear** David (18:10-11; 19:9-10). But God delivered **David** and gave him even greater popularity (18:12-16).

**18:17-30.** When **Saul** then saw that he could not destroy **David** personally, he determined to let **the Philistines** kill him. This he arranged by proposing that **David** marry his oldest **daughter, Merab.** Saul had already reneged on one marital promise to David (17:25). **David** protested, however, that he was a commoner and had no sufficient bridal **price** (18:25, *mōhar*, not "dowry" as in KJV and others). Before anything further could develop, **Merab . . . was given** to another man (v. 19). Again **Saul** offered his second daughter, **Michal,** who at that time loved **David** (v. 20; cf. 2 Sam. 6:16). But again **David** argued that he was unsuitable to be a **son-in-law** of the king because of his low status (1 Sam. 18:23). In an act of apparent generosity **Saul** waived the usual bridal payment and demanded only that David kill **100** Philistines and bring back their **foreskins** (v. 25), a requirement he more than met by slaying 200 (v. 27). **Saul** had been hoping, of course, that the exploit would cost **David** his life (v. 25). As a result, Saul was again **afraid of** David (v. 29; cf. vv. 12, 15). But David became Saul's **son-in-law** by marrying **Michal** (v. 27), and his military **success** and his popularity increased (v. 30).

**Chapter 19.** After an initial and successful attempt by **Jonathan** to soothe his father's feelings toward **David** (vv. 1-7), **Saul** set in motion further steps to destroy David. First he tried to slay him once more with his own hand (vv. 9-10); then he hired conspirators to murder him **in his bed,** a plot foiled by **Michal** (vv. 11-17). Next Saul **sent men** to **Naioth at Ramah** where **David** had taken refuge with **Samuel** (vv. 18-24). (**Ramah** was Samuel's hometown.) Their efforts were also unsuccessful for they, and later **Saul,** were overwhelmed by **the Spirit of God** who **came** on them and caused them to "act like prophets" (NIV, **prophesied,** vv. 20-21, 23-24). This means that they fell into a trance or an ecstatic state, a condition which immobilized them and made them incapable of accomplishing their evil intentions.

**20:1-23.** Having become persuaded of the irremedial nature of Saul's hostility toward him, **David** sought to learn its source and to determine if there might be a means of reconciliation. The test would be Saul's response to David's absence from the **New Moon** feast (v. 5), held on the first day of every month (Num. 28:11-15). If Saul became upset about David's absence, then David would know that there was no hope of patching up their differences. If, however, the king was amenable, then all was not lost (1 Sam. 20:6-8). **Jonathan** would approach his **father** on the matter and communicate the results to **David** by signaling with **arrows** (vv. 18-23).

**20:24-42.** At first **Saul . . . thought** David was absent because he was **ceremonially unclean** (v. 26). But then Saul's response was what David feared. After David's absence on **the second day,** Saul was filled with rage toward **David** and also toward **Jonathan** (vv. 30, 33). **As long as** David lived, Saul said, there was no hope that his own dynasty would continue (v. 31).

With heavy heart **Jonathan** signaled to **David** the next **morning** by his words

to a **boy** and with **arrows** (vv. 34-40). **Jonathan** and **David** met **and wept together** (v. 41). It was obvious that friendship with Saul was impossible. But **Jonathan** said that his own bond of loyalty with **David** would never be broken (v. 42). Jonathan was giving up a kingdom for the love of a friend.

*b. David's life in exile (chaps. 21–26)*

As far as can be determined, David was a young man of no more than 20 when he was forced to leave Saul's palace and his own home because of Saul's relentless determination to destroy him. Driven to the wilderness area of Judah, the logical place because of his familiarity with it from childhood, David lived out a "Robin Hood" existence for nearly 10 years. This period of time is reckoned from the fact that David was 30 when he began to rule over Judah at Hebron (2 Sam. 5:4), his accession occurring immediately after Saul's death (2 Sam. 2:10-11). David had spent a year and four months among the Philistines just before that (1 Sam. 27:7) and, as just suggested, was only about 20 when exiled from Saul. The events of chapters 21–26 must then represent only a fraction of David's activity during this period. But God was teaching David many things in those days, lessons David still shares with all who read his psalms which find their setting in this turbulent period of his life (see, e.g., Pss. 18; 34; 52; 54; 56–57). All these things were surely working together to prepare David to be the kind of leader who would glorify God and inspire His people.

(1) David at Nob and Gath (chap. 21). **21:1-6.** It is difficult to trace the history of the tabernacle after the capture of the ark in 1104 B.C. The ark itself rested at Kiriath Jearim since then (7:2; 2 Sam. 6:3-4), but the tabernacle is not mentioned or even hinted at till 1 Samuel 21, when it was presumed to be at Nob, the "city of priests," where **David** fled after he made his final break with Saul. Just as David had earlier sought sanctuary with Samuel at Ramah (19:18), so now he went to find sanctuary with **Ahimelech** (also known as Ahijah), **the priest** at **Nob** (21:1), halfway between Jerusalem and Gibeah. Hungry from his flight, David asked the priest for **bread** (v. 3). There was no **ordinary bread,** the **priest** replied (v. 4), but

only the holy showbread (Ex. 25:30, KJV) which had been desacralized by being replaced with fresh bread (1 Sam. 21:6; cf. Lev. 24:5-9). This could be eaten, as Jesus suggested later on (Matt. 12:3-4), but ordinarily only by the priests and certainly only by those who were ceremonially pure (1 Sam. 21:4-5; Lev. 15:18). David's eating illustrated a concession that the Law permitted—life is more holy than bread (Matt. 12:7-8).

**21:7-15.** While **David** was at Nob, he was spotted by a spy of Saul, **Doeg the Edomite,** who informed Saul of David's whereabouts (v. 7; 22:9). Taking Goliath's **sword** which had been kept by the priests at Nob (21:8-9), **David** immediately **fled** for his life and, throwing all caution to the winds, fled to **Gath,** hometown of the dead Philistine hero Goliath (v. 10). Recognized by **Achish,** the lord **of Gath,** David pretended to be insane and so escaped Philistine reprisal (vv. 11-13). This is in line with the practice of the ancient world to regard the **insane** as being in some sense an evil portent and so exempt from harm lest the gods be provoked.

(2) David at Adullam. **Chapter 22.** **David** next moved to **Adullam,** about 20 miles southwest of Jerusalem and 10 miles northeast of **Gath** (v. 1). There he took residence in **the cave** along with **400** other **men** who, for various reasons, were refugees (v. 2). Meantime, sensing a threat to his own family, **David** took them to **Moab** (vv. 3-4), perhaps to live among the kinfolk of his own great-grandmother Ruth. **David** then **went to the forest of Hereth,** east of Adullam, in **Judah** (v. 5), no doubt to be among his own people over whom God had anointed him to reign.

As soon as **Saul** found out about David's return to Judah, he began to blast his followers for their failure to communicate all they knew about David's activities, particularly his close relationship with Jonathan (vv. 6-8). To soothe Saul **Doeg,** who had seen David at Nob, told the king how the priest at **Nob** had assisted David in his need. In his paranoia **Saul** concluded that **Ahimelech** and the other **priests** were conspirators **against** him, and after calling for them and listening to their self-defense he ordered them slain (vv. 11-16). Only **Doeg** was willing to undertake the grue-

some assignment. He **killed** the **85** priests of **Nob** together with their families and livestock (vv. 17-19).

**David** then was joined by **Abiathar** (vv. 20-23), **son of** the priest **Ahimelech,** who **fled to** David after Saul exterminated the whole priestly community. This marked the beginning of David's priestly staff which would later lead the tabernacle worship in Jerusalem.

(3) David in the wilderness (chaps. 23–24). **23:1-18.** While in flight from Saul, **David** did more than remain in hiding. He also fought on behalf of his beleaguered people against the ever-menacing **Philistines.** First, having consulted the LORD by means of the ephod's sacred lots (v. 2; cf. v. 6), he delivered the town **of Keilah,** near the Philistine border, 15 miles southwest of Bethlehem (vv. 1-5). But the people "repaid" his kindness by betraying him to **Saul** (vv. 7-12). So he withdrew with **600** men, who remained faithful to him (v. 13; cf. 27:2; 30:9; 2 Sam. 15:18), **to the Desert of Ziph** (1 Sam. 23:14), a desolate hilly and wooded area between Hebron and the Dead Sea. He was joined there (**at Horesh in the desert**) briefly by **Jonathan,** who again confirmed the legitimacy of David's kingship (vv. 16-18).

**23:19-29. The Ziphites** also betrayed **David** to Saul (vv. 19-23). **David** became aware of this (vv. 22-25), so he escaped to **the Desert of Maon,** 10 miles southeast of Hebron. **Saul** pursued him there, but was temporarily called back to defend Israel against another Philistine raid (vv. 27-28). That gave David opportunity to go to **En Gedi** (v. 29), an oasis 10 miles north of Masada on the Dead Sea.

**Chapter 24. Saul** caught up with **David** at En Gedi and nearly found him. The LORD had other plans, however, and Saul's life was in David's hands as the king went **to relieve himself** (lit., "cover his feet," a euphemism, v. 3) in the same **cave** where **David** was hiding. So close was **David** that he **cut off a** piece of the king's **robe** as evidence of his opportunity to kill him. But even this act convicted **David,** who would not think of harming Saul bodily (vv. 5-7). **David** would not hurt the king, for he regarded **Saul** as the LORD's **anointed** (vv. 6, 10; cf. 26:9, 11, 23). Yet, as **David** said, **the king** had no just cause for hunting him down (24:14-15). In repentance, **Saul** acknowledged

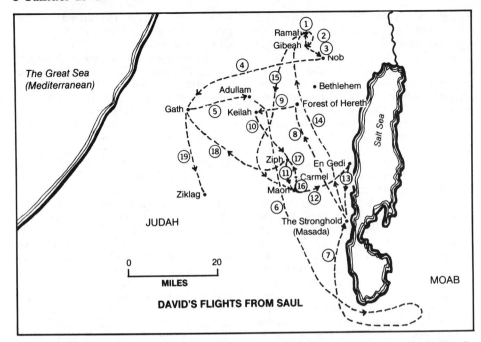

**DAVID'S FLIGHTS FROM SAUL**

David's righteousness (vv. 17-19) and the fact that David would indeed **be king** (v. 20).

(4) David and Nabal. **Chapter 25.** The chapter opens with the death and burial of **Samuel** at **Ramah.** Then **David moved** to **the Desert of Maon** (v. 1; cf. 23:24). There in dire circumstances David thought of **a certain man** named **Nabal,** who **had 1,000 goats and 3,000 sheep,** indicative of his great wealth (25:2-3). Appealing to his past protective attitude toward Nabal (v. 7; cf. vv. 15-16, 21), **David** asked him for provisions to sustain him and his men in the wilderness.

**Nabal,** however, with utter contempt, refused to comply (vv. 4-11). This so angered **David** that he took **about 400 men** with him to take forcibly from Nabal what he wanted. Were it not for the intervention of **Abigail** Nabal's wife, Nabal surely would have been slain. She learned about **Nabal's** foolish reply from **one of the servants.** To avert **disaster** she **took** with her food supplies in sufficient abundance to meet David's requirements (vv. 14-19). When **she met him,** she begged him not to punish her husband for, she said, **He is just like his name**—a **fool** (*nābāl*, "foolish"). Instead, she continued, God would bless David and would eventually make him king (v. 28). For him to kill the senseless **Nabal** would

only burden **his conscience** needlessly (v. 31). Impressed by her wisdom, **David** followed her advice and gratefully **accepted** the food **she had brought** (vv. 32-35).

Abigail's judgment was vindicated shortly thereafter when **Nabal,** after a drunken night, found out how narrow an escape he had had from **David.** The news so shocked him that he had a **heart attack** and died in **about 10 days** (vv. 36-38). **David** saw in this turn of events a sign from God. Obviously struck by the beauty and character of **Abigail,** he proposed marriage to her, a proposal she gladly accepted. Thus David added another wife to **Ahinoam** and **Michal,** whom he had previously **married,** though in his absence from Gibeah, **Saul had given** the latter **to Paltiel** (vv. 43-44; cf. 2 Sam. 3:15-16).

(5) Saul's final pursuit of David. **Chapter 26.** Once again **Saul** learned from **the Ziphites** about David's place of **hiding,** so the king and **3,000 chosen men** went to **the hill of Hakilah** (cf. 23:19) in **the Desert of Ziph** to **search** for **David.** Again the Lord miraculously delivered His chosen one who this time came—with **Abishai,** a skilled and faithful soldier and **Joab's brother** (26:6; cf. 2 Sam. 2:24; 10:14; 18:12; 21:17; 23:18)—so close to the sleeping king that **David**

stole both his **spear and water jug** (1 Sam. 26:5-12). Again **David** dared not harm **the LORD's anointed** (vv. 9, 11, 23; cf. 24:6, 10).

After crossing the ravine opposite Saul, **David** shouted **to Abner,** who supposedly guarded Saul, and tauntingly chided him for his carelessness in allowing **the king's spear and water jug** to be taken (26:13-16). **Saul** then awoke and once more heard David's plea that he be left alone. If God were leading Saul in the pursuit, then David would repent (v. 19). **If, however, men** were responsible, they should **be cursed** by God because they had intervened in God's purposes by driving David **from** both his home (**inheritance,** v. 19) and his public worship of God (**Go, serve other gods,** v. 19).

So evident to **Saul** was God's protection of his young rival that he could only confess his own wickedness (v. 21) and recognize fully and finally that **David** was destined to be the shepherd of Israel (v. 25). So far as can be determined **Saul** became resigned to his fate and never again tried to interfere with the will of God for the kingdom and its next anointed leader (cf. 27:4).

## D. Saul's death (chaps. 27–31)

### 1. DAVID AT ZIKLAG (CHAP. 27)

**Chapter 27.** Though **Saul** at long last had decided that further pursuit of **David** was fruitless because the Lord had ordained him for the throne, **David** did not know this. **So** he reluctantly **left** Judah to find refuge among **the Philistines** (v. 1). This move accomplished two important objectives: (a) it delivered him from any possible danger from Saul, and (b) it ingratiated him with the Philistines so he had no further need to fear them. No less important, this 16-month (v. 7) respite (from the time of his Philistine sojourn until the death of **Saul**) gave him opportunity to develop even further his combat and leadership skills. He needed this time to stabilize himself in view of what he knew must be the soon end of Saul's dynasty and the beginning of his own.

So after many years of running from Saul, **David** finally led his immediate **family (his two wives,** v. 3, **Ahinoam of Jezreel** [cf. 25:43] **and Abigail of Carmel** [cf. 25:42]) and **600** followers (27:2; cf. 23:13; 30:9; 2 Sam. 15:18) to **Gath** and threw himself on the mercy of **Achish,** a Philistine ruler. **David** had tried this before (1 Sam. 21:10-15), but that was early in the period of his estrangement from Saul. At that time **David** was feared by **Achish** and barely escaped with his life. But now it was clear to all that **David** was Saul's mortal enemy and that David could even be useful to the Philistines in their ongoing struggle with Israel. A relationship of lord and vassal was undertaken then between **Achish** and **David** (27:5-6). According to the terms of the covenant they made, David pledged loyalty to Achish in return for a fiefdom. This **Achish** granted in the town of **Ziklag,** a small settlement on the southern frontier of Philistia between Gaza and Beersheba.

This remained David's headquarters for over **a year,** until the death of Saul and David's subsequent move to Hebron (v. 7; 2 Sam. 1:1-2). From there he carried out pillaging raids against various desert peoples, including **the Geshurites** (a tribe bordering the Philistines on the south, Josh. 13:2), **the Girzites** (an otherwise unknown people living between the Philistines and Egypt), **and the Amalekites** (1 Sam. 27:8), killing the people and looting all their livestock and other goods (v. 9). These raids were in the region of the modern Gaza strip, toward the Desert of **Shur,** east of the present Suez Canal (v. 8). But **David** reported to **Achish** that his attacks were against his own tribe **Judah,** or **Jerahmeel,** or **the Kenites,** fabrications which endeared him all the more to the Philistines and persuaded them that he was a true and loyal subject (v. 12).

### 2. SAUL AT ENDOR (CHAP. 28)

**28:1-2.** A day came when **the Philistines** resolved to make another massive assault **against Israel.** Whether they were encouraged to do so because of the obvious instability of the now-aged king Saul and his nation, or because of David's apparent shift of allegiance, or for some other reason, is not clear. But they felt that the time was then propitious. The result, of course, was that **David** found himself in a most compromising position, for he would now be called on to demonstrate his loyalty to his new lord by fighting against his own people!

**28:3-6.** Meanwhile **Saul** also found himself in a desperate situation. **Samuel was dead** (cf. 25:1), and **the Philistines** were camped **at Shunem** (in the Valley of

Jezreel). **Saul, who was at Gilboa,** five miles northwest of Mount Gilboa, **was afraid.** He had purged out **the mediums** (*'ōḇōṯ,* "necromancers," those who communicate with the dead) **and spiritists** (*yiddᵉ'ōnîm,* "soothsayers," those who contact the spirits, v. 3). And **the LORD** refused to **answer** Saul's inquiry for help.

**28:7-14.** Saul at last resorted to a celebrated **medium** at nearby **Endor** who had somehow survived the purge. Disguising **himself . . . Saul** made his way **at night** to Endor, in the Valley of Jezreel just north of Mount Moreh. After putting her at ease, **Saul** asked the medium to contact **Samuel.** Drawing on the demonic powers of necromancy (Deut. 18:10-11), she called up the apparition of **Samuel.** So startled was she by Samuel's appearance that she immediately realized that the work was of God and not herself and that her disguised nocturnal visitor was King **Saul.** This implies that she did not really expect to raise up Samuel but only a satanic imitation. After she described the vision as **a spirit** (*'ĕlōhîm,* "mighty one") and as **an old man** clad in **a robe . . . Saul knew it was Samuel.** That Samuel's appearance, even in visionary form, was not the expected result clearly teaches that necromancers or mediums have no real power over the deceased, especially the righteous, but can only produce counterfeits. Samuel's appearance here is explained by the intervention of the Lord who graciously permitted Saul one last encounter with the prophet whom he had first sought so long ago in pursuit of his father's lost donkeys (1 Sam. 9:6-9).

**28:15-25.** But **Samuel** did not have good news this time. He rebuked **Saul** for his impiety and informed him that **the kingdom** was **torn . . . out of** his **hands and given . . . to David.** Also just as **the LORD** had rejected him as king because of his sin in the Amalekite affair (15:7-26), so He would deliver him **to the Philistines** and bring about his death and that of his **sons.** After reluctantly accepting refreshment (a butchered **calf** and freshly **baked bread without yeast**) from the medium, **Saul** arose and dejectedly walked off into the **night.**

3. DAVID'S RETURN TO ZIKLAG (CHAPS. 29–30)

*a. David's dilemma (chap. 29)*

**Chapter 29.** On the eve of the battle **the Philistines** had rendezvoused **at Aphek,** precisely where they had defeated Israel and captured the ark about 90 years earlier (4:10-11). **Israel** took up positions **by the spring in Jezreel,** on the flank of Mount Gilboa, some 40 miles northeast of Aphek. Among the troops of **Achish,** lord of Gath, were **David and his men.** Though **Achish** had implicit confidence in **David** (29:3) and argued with the other leaders that he should be allowed to fight against **Saul,** he was outvoted (vv. 6-7, 9). Understandably the other **commanders** feared that in the heat of **battle** David would defect to Israel (v. 4). **David,** offering a feeble protest (v. 8) but obviously greatly relieved, was discharged and returned to Ziklag.

*b. David's diplomacy (chap. 30)*

**30:1-7.** In David's absence from **Ziklag,** Amalekite raiding parties had **burned** the town and **carried . . . off** his family and everyone else as prisoners. After great lament (v. 4) and his men's threat to stone him, **David inquired of the LORD** through **Abiathar the priest** concerning His will in the matter. The inquiry was made by means of **the ephod,** the high priest's apronlike garment which contained the Urim and Thummim, the sacred stones used to discern the will of God (cf. Ex. 28:30).

**30:8-31.** Assured of victory (v. 8), **David** and his **men** pursued the Amalekites **to the Besor Ravine** (the Wadi el-Arish, some 20 miles south of Ziklag). When they finally **found** them (with the help of **an Egyptian . . . slave of an Amalekite** [vv. 11-15]), David's **400 men** who were rugged enough to stand the rigorous march (vv. 9-10) defeated the **Amalekites (except** for **400 young** Amalekites who escaped on camelback, v. 17) and retrieved all their families and property intact (vv. 17-20). **The 200** who had remained behind by **the Besor Ravine** (vv. 10, 21) wanted a share of the Amalekite booty. (On David's 600 men, see 23:13; 27:2; 2 Sam. 15:18.) So reasonable did their request sound to **David** that he established a principle **that day** that would thereafter prevail: **The share of the man who stayed with the supplies is to be the same as that of him who went down to the battle** (1 Sam. 30:24). But David's diplomatic masterstroke was his return of the properties stolen by the

Amalekites from the cities and towns **of Judah** (vv. 26-31). Never would they forget his concern for them, and when the time came for him to declare his kingship at **Hebron** he no doubt enjoyed their enthusiastic support.

4. THE BATTLE OF GILBOA (CHAP. 31)

**31:1-6.** Just as Samuel had prophesied (28:19), **the Philistines** quickly and easily defeated **Israel** in the broad plains of the Valley of Jezreel where they, with their chariots (2 Sam. 1:6), had an overwhelming tactical advantage (cf. Josh. 17:16; Jud. 4:3, 13, for the use of iron chariots by the Canaanites in this same area). **Saul,** with **three of his** four **sons**— all but Ish-Bosheth (see 2 Sam. 2:8)—**fled** from **Mount Gilboa. Saul** was overtaken, however, and mortally **wounded** after **his sons** had been slain. Fearing that he might be found by the Philistines and tortured to death (1 Sam. 31:4), he asked **his armor-bearer** to kill him, an order his attendant refused to obey. **Saul** then, in violation of an Israelite taboo, committed suicide (v. 5), an act rarely known among Israelites in the Old Testament (cf. Abimelech [Jud. 9:54], Samson [Jud. 16:30], Ahithophel [2 Sam. 17:23], and Zimri [1 Kings 16:18]). His death by his own hand climaxed a life which had been led in independence of God.

**31:7-10. When the Israelites** learned that their king was dead, **they abandoned their** cities and took to the wilderness. **The Philistines** eventually came on the bodies of **Saul and his three sons,** decapitated the king, displayed **his armor in the temple of** the goddess Ashtoreth (cf. comments on 7:3-4), and impaled **his body** on the city **wall of Beth Shan,** a prominent town on the eastern slopes of Mount Gilboa overlooking the Jordan Valley.

**31:11-13.** So horrified were **the people of Jabesh Gilead** when they became aware of this desecration that they removed **the bodies of Saul and his sons** under cover of **night** and brought **them** to their own city, just 10 miles across the Jordan. Probably to hide their mutilation **they burned** the corpses and **buried** the **bones.** This last act of respect was a tribute of a grateful people to the fact that Saul's first public deed was the rescue of this same city from the Ammonites 40 years before (11:1-11). And one cannot forget that Saul's own tribe, Benjamin, found much of its more recent historical origins in Jabesh Gilead (Jud. 21:8-12). For whatever reasons, the courageous actions of the people of Jabesh Gilead would not be forgotten by David when he at last came to power (2 Sam. 2:4-7). Later David had Saul's and Jonathan's bones exhumed and reburied in Benjamin (2 Sam. 21:11-14).

# BIBLIOGRAPHY

Ackroyd, Peter R. *The First Book of Samuel.* Cambridge: Cambridge University Press, 1971.

Carlson, R.A. *David, the Chosen King.* Stockholm: Almquist and Wiksell, 1964.

Crockett, William Day. *A Harmony of the Books of Samuel, Kings, and Chronicles.* Grand Rapids: Baker Book House, 1951.

Davis, John J. *The Birth of a Kingdom: Studies in 1 and 2 Samuel and 1 Kings 1–11.* Winona Lake, Ind.: BMH Books, n.d.

Hertzberg, H.W. *1 and 2 Samuel: A Commentary.* Philadelphia: Westminster Press, 1964.

Jorden, Paul J., and Streeter, Carole S. *A Man's Man Called by God.* Wheaton, Ill.: Scripture Press Publications, Victor Books, 1980.

Keil, C.F., and Delitzsch, F. "The Books of Samuel." In *Commentary on the Old Testament in Ten Volumes.* Vol. 2. Reprint (25 vols. in 10). Grand Rapids: Wm. B. Eerdmans Publishing Co., 1982.

Kirkpatrick, A.F. *The First Book of Samuel.* Cambridge: Cambridge University Press, 1891.

Laney, J. Carl. *First and Second Samuel.* Everyman's Bible Commentary. Chicago: Moody Press, 1982.

McKane, William. *1 and 2 Samuel.* Torch Bible Commentaries. London: SCM Press, 1963.

Meyer, F.B. *Samuel.* Chicago: Fleming H. Revell Co., n.d. Reprint. Fort Washington, Penn.: Christian Literature Crusade, 1978.

Vos, Howard F. *1, 2 Samuel.* Grand Rapids: Zondervan Publishing House, 1983.

Whybray, R.N. *The Succession Narrative.* Naperville, Ill.: Alec R. Allenson, 1968.

Wood, Leon J. *Israel's United Monarchy.* Grand Rapids: Baker Book House, 1979.

# 2 SAMUEL

### Eugene H. Merrill

## INTRODUCTION

See the *Introduction* to 1 Samuel.

## OUTLINE

## COMMENTARY

### I. David at Hebron (chaps. 1–4)

#### A. Lament for Saul and Jonathan (chap. 1)

**1:1-10.** Shortly after **David returned** to **Ziklag** (cf. 1 Sam. 27:6) from his successful punitive raid against **the Amalekites** (2 Sam. 1:1), he was met by a runner who had returned from Gilboa with the news of **the death of Saul** and his sons (vv. 2-4). When pressed for details, the messenger claimed that he had come on the wounded **Saul** (vv. 5-6), identified himself as **an Amalekite** (vv. 7-8), and when urged to do so by the king had mercifully put him to death (vv. 9-10). This man's report, differing from the account in 1 Samuel 31:3-6, was fabricated. Perhaps he called himself an Amalekite to protect Saul from the charge that he asked a fellow Israelite to do the unthinkable—to kill his own king, the Lord's anointed (cf. 2 Sam. 1:14, 16).

**1:11-16.** So enraged was **David,** after his grief was somewhat assuaged at the end of the day (vv. 11-12), that he commanded the alleged **Amalekite** to be executed (vv. 13-15). His false testimony, far from ingratiating him with David, had sealed his doom. It is ironic that Saul lost his kingdom because he failed to annihilate the Amalekites, and now one who said he was an Amalekite died because he claimed to have destroyed Saul.

**1:17-27.** David's public expression of grief over the deaths of Saul and Jonathan has been preserved in a poem, "The Song of **the Bow**" (vv. 19-27). This in turn is part of a now-lost longer composition referred to by the historian as **the Book of Jashar** (cf. Josh. 10:13). The same epic contained the short quatrain sung by Joshua on the occasion of the defeat of the Amorite league (Josh. 10:12-13).

In David's song, which opens and closes with the refrain, **How the mighty have fallen!** (2 Sam. 1:19, 27; cf. 1:25) **David** warned against telling of the tragedy in Philistia lest the Philistine maidens **rejoice** (v. 20) just as the Israelite maidens had sung of the triumphs of Saul and David years before (1 Sam. 18:7). David then cursed the **mountains of Gilboa** for having been the stage of **Saul** and Jonathan's heroic but fruitless defense against the enemy (2 Sam. 1:21-22). The undying loyalty of **Jonathan** comes in for special praise as David viewed father and son knit together **in life . . . and in death** (v. 23). Even though **Saul** had oppressed the people at times, he had also, David said, brought them luxury and bounty (v. 24). But it was **Jonathan** whom David celebrated with special pathos. All the years of their unbroken friendship are captured in his stirring tribute, **Your love for me was wonderful, more wonderful than that of women.**

## B. Battle between David and Abner (chap. 2)

**2:1-4a.** **David** had looked back and lamented the past, but with the death of Saul came the future to which he had looked since the day of his anointing by Samuel more than 15 years before (1 Sam. 16:13). There was a power vacuum, particularly in **Judah,** now that Saul and three of his sons by his wife Ahinoam were gone. (Saul had two other sons by his concubine Rizpah, 2 Sam. 21:8, 11.) **David,** therefore, sought the mind of God and was told to go **to Hebron** where, at last, he was formally installed by oil-anointing as **king over . . . Judah.** (Later he was anointed a third time, as king of the entire nation, 5:3.) This was a decisive and important move for it immediately alienated him from the Philistines with whom he had taken refuge and made an alliance; it signified the quasi-independence of Judah from Israel, an attitude which would find complete expression at the division of the kingdom after Solomon's death (1 Kings 12:16); and it asserted David's reign as being in rivalry with that of Saul's son, Ish-Bosheth, who succeeded his father in the North.

**2:4b-11. David** at once began to demonstrate his diplomatic skills. He first gained the friendship of the people **of Jabesh Gilead** by commending them for their treatment of Saul's remains (cf. 1 Sam. 31:11-13). David reminded them that now that **Saul** was **dead** he was their sovereign.

Next David began to deal with the problem of succession to **Saul. Abner . . . commander** of Israel's **army** now became the effective power behind the throne. **He** placed **Ish-Bosheth** (known otherwise and certainly originally as Esh-Baal; 1 Chron. 8:33; 9:39), apparently Saul's youngest and least effective **son,** in authority. The name Esh-Baal means "fire of Baal," so to avoid the pagan overtones the name was changed to Ish-Bosheth ("man of shame"). His age of **40 years** (2 Sam. 2:10) when his father died is an important chronological fact. Since he is not listed as one of the sons of **Saul** at the beginning of Saul's reign (1 Sam. 14:49) but is included in the total list of sons (1 Chron. 8:33), he must have been born after Saul became king, thus indicating at least a 40-year reign for Saul (see Acts 13:21; also see comments on 1 Sam. 13:1).

Reigning from **Mahanaim,** in the east-central part of the Transjordan, **Ish-Bosheth** had a brief tenure of only **two years.** The fact that **David** reigned for **seven** and one-half **years** at **Hebron** before he made Jerusalem his capital (2 Sam. 5:5) need not imply that Ish-Bosheth also reigned for seven and one-half years at Mahanaim. This would contradict 2:10. There may well have been an interregnum of some length between Saul and Ish-Bosheth, and clearly **David** reigned for some time over **Judah** from **Hebron** after Ish-Bosheth's death.

**2:12-32.** From the beginning of **David's** reign his real rival in the North was not **Ish-Bosheth** but Abner. As though to clear the air and settle the question of royal succession, **Abner** and David's military leader **Joab** appointed elite troops, **12 men** on a side, to engage in **hand-to-hand** combat at **Gibeon.** The winners would decide the issue. The nature of the contest is unclear. Perhaps it took the form of a wrestling match which ended up in swordplay. The irregular use of daggers is suggested by naming the **place** of the contest **Helkath Hazzurim** ("field of daggers").

The result was a victory for **David's men,** but they were not satisfied to end the contest there. Instead they made hot pursuit of **Abner** and his friends, a chase that resulted in the seasoned warrior **Abner** taking the life of **Asahel,** younger brother of David's leader **Joab** (v. 23). **Joab** and a surviving brother **Abishai** vowed to take revenge (v. 24) but when faced by immensely unfavorable odds gave up the chase (vv. 25-28). **Abner** then made his way home **to Mahanaim** (by way of **the Arabah,** i.e., the Jordan Valley, and **the whole Bithron,** a deep ravine leading to Mahanaim, v. 29), while **Joab returned** by **night** to **Hebron** (v. 32). David lost 20 soldiers, but **Abner** lost 360 (vv. 30-31). The battle was over but not the war.

### C. Conflict between Joab and Abner (chap. 3)

**3:1-11.** The struggle was not limited to individuals but included dynasties. This is evident in verse 1: **The war between the house of Saul and the house of David lasted a long time** (cf. v. 6). The supporters of Saul's family were determined to resist David's designs and to limit him to Judah. But those of David's dynasty were convinced that it was time for "the man after God's own heart" to become ruler of the whole nation. The historian described these power plays by recounting the marriages of **David** to six wives (vv. 2-5; see the chart "David's Family"), especially **Maacah, daughter of Talmai, king of Geshur,** a state northeast of the Sea of Kinnereth (see 15:8). In the North, **Abner** took **Rizpah,** a **concubine** of **Saul,** as one of his own, a common practice in the ancient Near East when one wished to indicate his succession to a king. **Ish-Bosheth** understood the meaning of the act and rebuked **Abner** (3:7). In anger **Abner** responded that he would

now work to deliver **the kingdom** of **Saul** over to **David** (vv. 9-10). Abner would help **establish David's throne over Israel and Judah from Dan to Beersheba.** This ruptured the relationship between **Abner** and **Ish-Bosheth** (v. 11).

**3:12-21.** **Abner** then proposed **to David** that they **make an agreement** (a covenant) and that he would help David secure **Israel. David** demanded that Abner restore, as a sign of his good faith, his long-separated wife **Michal** to him (vv. 13-14; cf. 1 Sam. 18:20-27; 25:44). After this was accomplished (2 Sam. 3:15-16), **Abner** met with Israel's **elders,** especially those from **Benjamin,** Saul's own tribe, and persuaded them that the rule of **David** over them was in their best interest. This, of course, elevated **Abner** considerably in David's estimation, which greatly displeased David's loyal men.

**3:22-39.** Particularly incensed was **Joab.** When he found out that **David** had entertained **Abner** at a feast (v. 20) and made overtures of friendship to him (v. 22), he chided **the king,** saying that Abner's purpose was to spy on David (vv. 24-25). **Joab** then took measures to have **Abner** return to Hebron **from the well of Sirah** (site unknown). Pretending to whisper something of importance to **Abner . . . Joab** drew **him aside** and viciously assassinated him (**stabbed him in the stomach,** v. 27; cf. 4:5-6). This was in revenge for Abner's murder of Joab's **brother Asahel** (3:27, 30; 2:23). **When David** discovered what had happened, he did not rejoice but rather uttered a curse on **Joab** and his progeny (3:29). Joab's murder of Abner took place in Hebron, a city of refuge (Josh. 21:13), where such revenge was not permitted (Num. 35:22-25). **David** then proclaimed a public mourning (2 Sam. 3:31), **buried Abner in** honor at **Hebron** (v. 32), and composed a lamentation (vv. 33-34) in which he spoke of the shameful way in which **Abner** had died. David's compassion and forgiving spirit are evident here, qualities which separated him from ordinary men.

As a sign of his sincerity, **David took** a vow to fast. He also said that he was **weak** compared with Abner. Though he knew that the **sons of Zeruiah** (Joab and his brothers) must be punished, he did not know how to undertake it (vv. 35-39). Zeruiah was David's half sister (1 Chron.

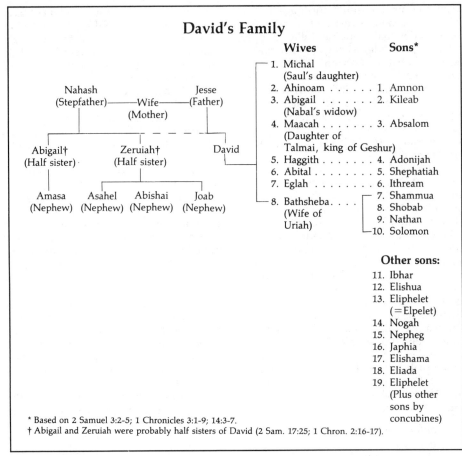

**David's Family**

| | | Wives | Sons* |
|---|---|---|---|
| | | 1. Michal (Saul's daughter) | |
| Nahash (Stepfather)——Wife——Jesse (Father) (Mother) | | 2. Ahinoam . . . . . . | 1. Amnon |
| | | 3. Abigail . . . . . . (Nabal's widow) | 2. Kileab |
| | | 4. Maacah . . . . . . . (Daughter of Talmai, king of Geshur) | 3. Absalom |
| Abigail† (Half sister) · | Zeruiah† (Half sister) | David | |
| | | 5. Haggith . . . . . . . | 4. Adonijah |
| | | 6. Abital . . . . . . . . | 5. Shephatiah |
| | | 7. Eglah . . . . . . . . | 6. Ithream |
| Amasa (Nephew) | Asahel Abishai (Nephew) (Nephew) | Joab (Nephew) | 8. Bathsheba. . . . (Wife of Uriah) |
| | | | 7. Shammua |
| | | | 8. Shobab |
| | | | 9. Nathan |
| | | | 10. Solomon |

Other sons:

11. Ibhar
12. Elishua
13. Eliphelet (=Elpelet)
14. Nogah
15. Nepheg
16. Japhia
17. Elishama
18. Eliada
19. Eliphelet (Plus other sons by concubines)

\* Based on 2 Samuel 3:2-5; 1 Chronicles 3:1-9; 14:3-7.
† Abigail and Zeruiah were probably half sisters of David (2 Sam. 17:25; 1 Chron. 2:16-17).

2:16; cf. 2 Sam. 2:18 and see the chart "David's Family").

## D. Death of Ish-Bosheth (chap. 4)

**4:1-8.** News about Abner's death did not encourage **Ish-Bosheth** to reassert his own authority over **Israel**; on the contrary, it only increased his instability and brought a sense of panic to the nation (v. 1). Sensing that Ish-Bosheth was powerless, two Benjamite assassins—**Baanah** and **Recab** (vv. 2-3)—gained access to Ish-Bosheth's **house** at Mahanaim at midday and slew him in his **bed** (**stabbed him in the stomach,** v. 6; cf. the identical means of assassination of Abner by Joab, 3:27), beheaded him (4:7), and carried **his head** to **David at Hebron** (v. 8).

Within the narrative is a reference (v. 4) to Jonathan's son, **Mephibosheth** (otherwise and originally Merib-Baal, 1 Chron. 8:34). The name change is similar to that of Esh-Baal to Ish-Bosheth, but here the change was from "Baal contends" to "from the mouth of shamefulness." His lameness occurred when **his nurse,** who was carrying the young **five**-year-old lad out of danger after Jonathan's death, dropped him and injured him. Mephibosheth reappears later in the story as one in special need of protection (2 Sam. 9). Hence this parenthetical note prepares readers for what follows.

**4:9-12.** David's response to this deed, which was done obviously to gain his favor, was identical to his reaction when he learned of Saul's death (vv. 9-11; cf. 1:11-16). He ordered the two to be executed, their **hands and feet** to be **cut off,** and their corpses to be hanged publicly at **the pool** of Hebron (4:12). **David** regarded their act as an unjustified assault on a defenseless **man** (v. 11). No doubt David's stern measures of retribution also reflected his genuine love for Saul and his family, even though they had opposed him.

## II. David's Prosperity (chaps. 5–10)

### A. The capital at Jerusalem (chap. 5)

**5:1-3.** With Ish-Bosheth, Saul's son, now dead, the way was clear for **David** to assert his sovereignty over **the North-ern tribes of Israel** as well as **over Judah.** There was a general recognition in the North that this should be done, so a dele-gation from all the tribes went to **Hebron** to encourage David's rule over them. They pointed out that they were his kins-men, his **own flesh and blood,** that is, all were descendants of Jacob. They stated that he had distinguished himself as a hero of **Israel.** But furthermore they were conscious of the calling and anointing of **the LORD** in bringing **David** to power to shepherd them.

With no further hesitation they in-stalled him as **king over** the entire na-tion. David reciprocated by entering into covenant **with them.** Samuel's earlier oil-anointing of David (1 Sam. 16:13) demon-strated God's choice of David. This third oil-anointing, like his second anointing in **Hebron** over Judah (2 Sam. 2:4), was the people's confirmation of that choice and a public installation. David's covenant probably involved an oath in which he pledged to follow the Mosaic require-ments for kingship (Deut. 17:14-20).

**5:4-5.** David began his reign at age **30,** the age at which priests began to serve (Num. 4:3; 1 Chron. 23:3). After **seven** and one-half **years** at **Hebron,** Da-vid decided to relocate the capital. His reason was almost certainly political for he decided on **Jerusalem,** a city on the border between **Judah** and the Northern tribes. The distinction between **Israel and Judah** (2 Sam. 11:11; 12:8; 19:42-43; 24:1, 9) indicates that 2 Samuel was written after the nation was divided in 931 B.C. into the Northern and Southern Kingdoms.

**5:6-9.** Since **Jerusalem** had remained in Jebusite control ever since the days of Joshua (Josh. 15:63) it was considered neutral, so David's **residence** there would demonstrate tribal impartiality. But the very fact that Jerusalem had re-mained Jebusite indicated its security and defensibility. This is seen clearly in the taunting response of its citizens to Da-vid's siege of the city. **Even the blind and the lame can ward you off,** they said. Taking up a position on Mount **Zion, the City of David,** which lay just south of

the Jebusite city (Mount Ophel; see the map "Jerusalem in the Time of the Kings" near 1 Kings 9:15), David prom-ised his men that whoever could discover a means of access to the city would be promoted to commander-in-chief (1 Chron. 11:6). The account in 1 Chroni-cles relates that Joab was able to do so, apparently by passing through the water tunnel which connected Jerusalem's wa-ter supply to its interior reservoirs (2 Sam. 5:8). The Hebrew word for **water shaft** (*ṣinnôr*) may refer instead to a sort of grappling hook (cf. NIV marg.). In any case, the city was entered and incorporat-ed into the capital.

So galling to **David** was the Jebusite sarcasm about "the blind and lame," however, that it became proverbial to speak of his enemies in general as **the blind and lame.** After the city was cap-tured, Mount Zion and Mount Ophel were consolidated into one entity de-scribed here and elsewhere as **the City of David** (5:7, 9; 6:12; 1 Kings 2:10). **The supporting terraces** (2 Sam. 5:9) were lit-erally "the Millo" (NIV marg.). This He-brew word means "filling"; thus this may have been the area between the hills which was filled in to level the whole city. It may also refer to embankments erected to protect the city from the North (1 Kings 9:15, 24).

**5:10-12.** David's capture, expansion, and occupation of Jerusalem made it clear to all Israel and to surrounding peoples as well that **God . . . was with him** and that he was not a renegade tribal chief-tain but a political power with whom they must reckon. This is seen in the attention he received from **Hiram, king of** the Phoenician city-state of **Tyre,** who provided materials and men to build Da-vid **a palace** (cf. 1 Kings 5:1-11). Recogni-tion by a person of such stature con-vinced **David** that God indeed **had established him** and **exalted his kingdom.**

**5:13-16.** One sign of such elevation in the ancient Near Eastern world was the acquisition of a large harem. Though David's action in this respect cannot be defended and eventually brought him untold sorrow, he nonetheless followed the prevailing custom.

**5:17-25. The Philistines** took special note of David's prosperity. Perhaps all through his years at Hebron they had

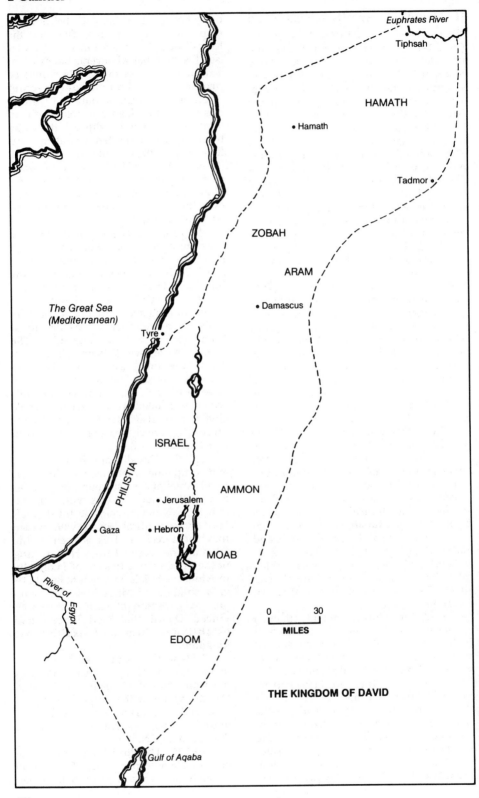

THE KINGDOM OF DAVID

regarded him as a loyal vassal (1 Sam. 27:5-7; 29:3, 6-9). Now, however, they knew beyond question that David, as Saul's successor, was their implacable foe. After securing the promise of God's blessing (2 Sam. 5:19), **David** marched against **the Philistines** who had gathered for battle **in the Valley of Rephaim,** only three or four miles southwest of Jerusalem, and there he administered to them a resounding defeat. The result was that the **place** became known as **Baal Perazim,** "the Lord [here Israel's God] who breaks out." Ironically **the Philistines abandoned their idols** to the Israelites as Israel, in Samuel's early days, had surrendered the ark of the covenant, the token of God's presence, to the Philistines (1 Sam. 4:11).

But **the Philistines came up** to **Rephaim** again (2 Sam. 5:22). This time the divine strategy was different. Israel circled **behind** the Philistines and when they heard a **marching**-like rustle in **the balsam trees** they attacked and drove the Philistines **from Gibeon** (cf. 1 Chron. 14:16) **to Gezer,** a distance of 15 miles. Thus friend and foe could see the evidence of God's protection and power on **David** and his kingdom.

## B. The return of the ark (chap. 6)

**6:1-5.** For 100 long years **the ark** of the covenant had been separated from the tabernacle and other places of worship. After its capture by the Philistines at Aphek (1 Sam. 4:11) it remained in Philistia for seven months, then briefly at Beth Shemesh, and the rest of the time at Kiriath Jearim. Now **David** had taken Jerusalem, a neutral place, and made it the political capital of the kingdom. All that remained was to retrieve **the ark,** place it in the tabernacle he would erect on Mount Zion, and declare Jerusalem the religious center of the nation as well.

David first went with **30,000** men to **Baalah of Judah** (the same as Kiriath Jearim; Josh. 15:9) to bring the ark **from the house of Abinadab,** its custodian. Described as that which bore **the name of** God Himself, **the ark** represented the presence of God who dwelled among His people in a special way (cf. Ex. 25:22). As such, it was to be handled with reverence, even in its transportation from place to place. The Law specified that it be carried by Levites who would bear it

on their shoulders by means of poles passed through gold rings attached to the ark (Ex. 25:14; cf. Num. 4:15, 20). Even the Levites could not touch **the ark** or even look in it because of its holiness. Why David overlooked these requirements it is impossible to know, but he and **Uzzah and Ahio,** two descendants **of Abinadab,** placed the ark on a **cart** and proceeded, with great musical celebration, toward Jerusalem. The use of musical instruments (2 Sam. 6:5) was common in Israel's worship as may be seen, for example, in Psalm 150 where most of the same instruments are listed.

**6:6-11.** Along the way they passed over a rough outcropping of stone, a **threshing** place belonging to **Nacon** (or Kidon; 1 Chron. 13:9), and **the oxen stumbled,** threatening to throw **the ark** from the cart. Instinctively **Uzzah,** one of the attendants, laid **hold of the ark** to prevent its fall, an act of irreverence that cost him his life. The harshness of **the LORD's** discipline must be seen in the light of His absolute holiness which requires that sacred tasks be done in a sacred manner (cf. comments on 1 Sam. 6:19–7:2). Since God **had broken out** ($p\bar{a}$-$ra\d{s}$) in **wrath** on **Uzzah,** David named that place **Perez** ("outbreak against") **Uzzah.** David learned his lesson. He would not move **the ark** again until the Lord gave him instruction. It **remained,** therefore, **in the house of Obed-Edom the Gittite** (a native of Gath) **for three months.**

**6:12-15.** At last the procession began again, this time according to divine requirement. As **the ark** was carried along, **David** offered sacrifice, dressed in priestly attire (**a linen ephod**), and dancing and shouting for joy with the Israelites. Here **trumpets** were played (cf. other instruments in v. 5). David was not a descendant of Aaron, and could not therefore ordinarily qualify to be a priest. He was, however, the anointed of the Lord, the founder of that messianic line that would be fulfilled in the King who would also embrace the offices of priest and prophet (7:12-16; 1 Sam. 2:35; Deut. 18:15-19). Some other Davidic kings functioned religiously as well, though not always properly (1 Kings 3:4; 8:62-63; 2 Chron. 26:16-19).

**6:16-23.** At length the procession made its way into Jerusalem itself. **Mi-**

chal, David's first wife and Saul's **daughter,** saw the **king . . . dancing** excitedly **before the** LORD and, chagrined and embarrassed by his celebrating, later rebuked him for it (v. 20). **David** defended his actions, affirming that he had done nothing wrong (vv. 21-22). **David** apparently separated from her and she never **had any children.** Michal had impugned his holy zeal to be nothing but exhibitionism, a charge which hurt him deeply. (See comments on 21:8.) **The ark** had been placed in a tabernacle which **David had** prepared (6:17). There the king continued his **burnt offerings and fellowship offerings** to **the** LORD and climaxed the festivities with food gifts, **a loaf of bread, a cake of dates, and a cake of raisins to each person in the** assembled **crowd.**

## C. The Davidic Covenant (chap. 7)

**7:1-2. After** David had become well **settled** in Jerusalem and was enjoying a period of peace, his thoughts turned to the idea of building a more permanent structure in which the Lord could reside among His people. The **tent,** he felt, was no longer suitable, especially in comparison with his own elaborate **palace of cedar** (cf. 5:11).

**7:3-17.** Having communicated his desires to the Prophet **Nathan,** whose initial response was favorable, **David** soon learned that his intentions were premature. Since the Exodus **the** LORD had resided among the people in a temporary structure. There was no need now for anything different. In fact it was not God's will for **David** to **build** Him **a house;** instead God would build **a house** for David! (v. 11) God had called **David** from inauspicious beginnings **to be** a shepherd of God's **people** (v. 8). Likewise, God had gathered **Israel** to Himself and would **plant them** securely in their own land. The house to be built for David would be a royal house, a dynasty of kings. It would originate with him but would never end (v. 16). The **kingdom** and its **throne** would be permanent, a realm over which the Son of David would reign **forever** (cf. 23:5).

The promise that David and his seed would be kings fulfilled the even more ancient Abrahamic Covenant blessing that the patriarchs would be the fathers of kings (Gen. 17:6, 16; 35:11). To Judah,

great-grandson of Abraham, was given the explicit pledge that a promised ruler would come from Judah (Gen. 49:10). Samuel anointed this one from Judah, David himself, of whom the Lord said, "He is the one" (1 Sam. 16:12). David was aware of his election by God and of the theological significance of that election as part of the messianic line that would result in a divine Descendant and King (Pss. 2:6-7; 110; cf. Ethan's words in Ps. 89:3-4). The prophets also attested to the Davidic Messiah, the One who would rule over all and forever on His throne (Isa. 9:1-7; 11:1-5; Jer. 30:4-11; Ezek. 34:23-24; 37:24-25; Amos 9:11-15).

The promise that the people of the Lord, David's kingdom Israel, would have an enduring land of their own was also based on earlier commitments of the Lord. The seed of Abraham, God said, would be given Canaan as a home forever (Gen. 13:15; 15:18; 17:8; Deut. 34:4).

As for a temple, David would not be allowed to **build** it, but his son after him would have the honor of doing so (2 Sam. 7:12-13). That this refers to a literal house and not a dynasty is clear from the context, which speaks of the results that would follow if the **son** would be disobedient to the Lord (vv. 14-15). This could not be true of the King who is spoken of as the climactic figure of the Davidic dynastic line. These verses, then, are a good example of an Old Testament passage in which some elements find fulfillment in the immediate future (Solomon and other strictly human descendants of David), while other elements will be realized only in the more distant future (Jesus Christ, the Son of David; cf. Luke 1:31-33).

**7:18-29.** David's response to this magnificent revelation concerning the nature of his kingship was to acknowledge the Lord's goodness in bestowing it (vv. 18-21) and to extol God's incomparable sovereignty **(How great You are. . . ! There is no one like You,** v. 22). This, David said, was seen especially in God's selection of **Israel** and His redemptive grace on her behalf (vv. 23-24). Finally he prayed that **the promise** God had made might indeed find fulfillment to the glory of His own holy name—**so that** His **name** would **be great forever** (vv. 25-29). Interestingly David addressed God 7 times as **O Sovereign** LORD (vv. 18-20, 22, 28-29), words that translate the Hebrew *'ădōnāy* (lit., "Lord") *Yahweh*. David expressed his humility before God by referring to himself as **Your servant** 10 times (vv. 19-21, 25-29).

## D. David's campaigns (chap. 8)

**8:1-2.** God had promised as part of His covenant with **David** that He would give Israel rest from all her enemies (7:11). He now began to do that very thing. First, **the Philistines,** Israel's perennial enemies for more than 125 years, were attacked and **defeated** at **Metheg Ammah,** a town otherwise unknown. Next **David** attacked **the Moabites,** putting **two** out of every three prisoners **to death.** The survivors he put in bondage to Israel, which implies that Moab became a vassal state **to David** as the great king. The reason for this harsh treatment is baffling since David had ancestral roots in Moab and relationships up until then appear to have been amicable (1 Sam. 22:3-4).

**8:3-8. The Arameans** then became David's objective. Consisting of a loose federation of city-states, the Arameans rose to prominence the same time Israel's monarchy rose under Saul and David. David first made an assault on **Hadadezer** (or Hadarezer), **king of Zobah,** an area just north of Damascus. Hadadezer had gone on a campaign to **the Euphrates River** to recover some territory, and in his absence **David** struck. His victory over these Arameans gained him prisoners (**7,000 charioteers and 20,000 foot soldiers**), 1,000 **chariots,** and **100 of the chariot horses,** the latter used for the first time to field a chariot corps in Israel. (Though the Heb. in v. 4 reads "1,700 charioteers," 1 Chron. 18:4, probably a better-preserved text, reads, as the NIV has it, "1,000 of his chariots [and] 7,000 charioteers.") Before David could return, he and his men were attacked by the Aramean troops **of Damascus.** Again **David** prevailed, and after slaying **22,000** of the enemy, he established an occupation force in **Damascus,** thus making Damascus another client state to Israel, required to pay **tribute.** Finally he returned **to Jerusalem** triumphantly, bringing **gold shields** and much **bronze** as trophies of conquest.

**8:9-12.** Having witnessed David's remarkable military successes, **Tou** (Heb.

*Toi*) **king of** the Aramean city-state of **Hamath,** decided to capitulate without struggle and become a vassal of Israel. To symbolize this move **he sent his son Joram** (or Hadoram, 1 Chron. 18:10) to **David** laden with precious **articles of silver and gold and bronze.** These **David** added to all the other spoils he had gained in previous campaigns (2 Sam. 8:11-12): **Edom** (cf. v. 14); **Moab** (cf. v. 2); **Ammonites** (cf. chap. 10); **Philistines** (cf. 8:1); **and Amalek** (David's conquest of Amalek is not narrated in the OT). All these spoils he **dedicated** to the service of the LORD (cf. 1 Kings 7:51).

**8:13-14.** Finally **David** gained far-flung fame by defeating an Aramean army of **18,000** in **the Valley of Salt,** a marshy plain south of the Dead Sea. Though "Aram" (i.e., "Arameans") is in most Hebrew manuscripts, the Septuagint and some other versions have "Edom," a reading that is also supported by a few Hebrew manuscripts and by 1 Chronicles 18:12. The difference in the original language is in only one letter: *d* (as in Edom) and *r* (as in Aram), easily confused in Hebrew. If "Aramean," it may be that the Edomites had solicited Aramean help against Israel. In any event, David again prevailed and brought Edom also under his hegemony. **The LORD gave David victory everywhere he went.**

**8:15-18.** The creation of an empire, though still small in comparison with the great powers of today, required the creation of a bureaucracy to administer its affairs. The principal officers were **Joab,** military commander; **Jehoshaphat,** record keeper; **Zadok** and **Ahimelech** chief **priests; Seraiah . . . secretary; Benaiah** (cf. 23:2-23), leader of the elite Kerethite and Pelethite troops (also mentioned in 1 Sam. 30:14; 2 Sam. 15:18; 20:7, 23; 1 Kings 1:38, 44; 1 Chron. 18:17; Ezek. 25:16; Zeph. 2:5, and possibly related to the Philistines in some way); **and David's** own **sons were royal advisers** (*kōhănîm*). This Hebrew word, usually rendered "priests," is explained in 1 Chronicles 18:17 as "chief officials" (cf. 2 Sam. 20:26). This no doubt is the better meaning since David's sons, as Judeans, were ineligible to serve as priests. The mention of Zadok and Ahimelech together (8:17) indicates the transition that was occurring in the office of priest. Ahimelech,

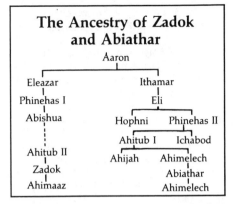

## The Ancestry of Zadok and Abiathar

Aaron

- Eleazar
  - Phinehas I
    - Abishua
      - Ahitub II
        - Zadok
          - Ahimaaz
- Ithamar
  - Eli
    - Hophni
    - Phinehas II
      - Ahitub I
        - Ahijah
      - Ichabod
        - Ahimelech
          - Abiathar
            - Ahimelech

son of Abiathar, was a descendant of Eli (see the chart "The Ancestry of Zadok and Abiathar"), whose priestly line Samuel had said would come to an end (1 Sam. 3:10-14). Zadok was a descendant of Aaron through Eleazar (1 Chron. 6:4-8). Through Zadok the line of priests eventually continued through the remainder of Old Testament times.

### E. David's kindness to Saul's family (chap. 9)

This chapter introduces what is sometimes called the "Succession Narrative," a literary piece which includes chapters 9–20. Its purpose is to show the steps David undertook to succeed Saul and to establish the permanence of his own dynasty. David's first step was to solicit the support of the Northern tribes by extending favor to the surviving members of Saul's household.

**9:1-8.** David had pledged to Jonathan that he would never forget the covenant of friendship that had bound them together (1 Sam. 20:14-17). He therefore called **Ziba,** a **servant** of Saul, and **asked** him if some member of Saul's family had special need (2 Sam. 9:2-3; cf. 1 Sam. 20:42). **Ziba** replied that **Mephibosheth,** the lame **son of Jonathan** (2 Sam. 4:4), was still alive and living at **Lo Debar** (just east of the Jordan, five miles south of the Wadi Yarmuk; cf. 17:27). **David** immediately sent for **him,** restored Saul's personal estate to him, and supported him on a royal pension (9:7). In humility **Mephibosheth** referred to himself as David's **servant** (v. 6) and as **a dead dog** (v. 8), that is, worthless (cf. 16:9).

**9:9:13.** David instructed **Ziba** and his **15 sons and 20 servants** to **farm** Mephibosheth's **land** and to treat him as

David's own son (9:9-11). David's provision for **Mephibosheth** and his letting him eat **at the king's table** (vv. 7, 10-11, 13) again demonstrated David's magnanimous heart. In all this David showed **kindness** (ḥeseḏ, "loyal love") **for Jonathan's sake** (v. 1; cf. v. 7).

### F. David's ambassadors to Ammon abused (chap. 10)

**10:1-5.** Another aspect of David's succession was his international relationships. **David** had brought many of the surrounding nations under tribute to Israel (8:12). Included in these nations was Ammon, a kingdom directly east of the Jordan River. Since Saul's early years Ammon had been ruled by **Nahash.** In fact it was he who had attacked Jabesh Gilead in the beginning of Saul's tenure and was defeated by Saul (1 Sam. 1:1-11).

At last Nahash **died** and was succeeded by **his son Hanun.** Because Nahash had shown **David** some unspecified **kindness, David** sent an envoy to Ammon **to express his sympathy to Hanun** regarding **his father.** This, **David** no doubt hoped, would enable him to have a friendly ally on his eastern flank. But Hanun's advisers, perhaps recalling Saul's victory over Ammon 50 years before, counseled Hanun not to accept David's overtures but rather to view the Israelites as espionage agents. **David's** messengers were not only turned back but their beards were **half** shaved **off** and **their garments** cut away to an immodest length which, to those sensitive Semites, was an unbearable ignominy (cf. Isa. 15:2; 20:4).

**10:6-14.** Recognizing that his insult to David was, in effect, a declaration of war, Hanun engaged 33,000 mercenary troops from the three Aramean kingdoms of **Beth Rehob** (in northern Galilee), **Zobah** (see comment on 8:3), and **Maacah** (east of upper Galilee), and **from Tob,** a small kingdom on the western fringes of the Syro-Arabian desert. **David sent** his forces, led by **Joab** and **Abishai,** to encounter Hanun's own **army** and his mercenaries at Medeba (1 Chron. 19:7), 12 miles due east of the northern end of the Dead Sea. **Joab** directed his attention to the Aramean divisions and Abishai's troops to **the Ammonites,** with the understanding that one would help the other as circumstances required. The result was a smashing victory for Israel.

**10:15-19.** Though the Ammonites apparently learned their lesson, **the Arameans** determined to avenge the disaster of Medeba by recalling their occupation forces from **beyond the Euphrates River** and employing them against **Israel.** Under the command of **Shobach,** general of the **army** of Hadadezer of Zobah, they took up positions at **Helam,** a desert place 40 miles straight east of the Sea of Kinnereth. There **David** met them, and again the Lord gave **Israel** victory. David's men **killed 700 . . . charioteers and 40,000 . . . foot soldiers** and **struck down Shobach.** (Though the Heb. has 700 charioteers, the parallel passage in 1 Chron. 19:18 indicates that 7,000 charioteers were slain. The larger number is preferable since the Chron. account on the whole seems fuller and more comprehensive.) This broke the back of Aramean resistance and brought the Aramean confederates under Israel's domination. Never again did they side with Ammon against the people of Israel.

This is the second account of a subjugation of Hadadezer by David (cf. 2 Sam. 8:3-8). Apparently chapter 8 records an initial reduction of **the Arameans** of Zobah to Israelite vassaldom, while chapter 10 assumes an Aramean rebellion against David's overlordship, a rebellion which was squashed and which resulted in continued Aramean submission.

## III. David's Sin and Domestic Problems (chaps. 11–21)

### A. David's adultery (chap. 11)

**11:1.** Though the Arameans no longer came to their aid, **the Ammonites** stubbornly maintained their hostile posture toward Israel. In the context of David's ongoing problems with these inveterate foes occurred the turning point of his reign.

**In the spring,** after the latter rains were over and it was customary to resume military activity, **David** ordered **Joab** to launch an invasion of **Rabbah,** the capital of Ammon. Though **kings** usually led their armies personally, **David,** for reasons not related, **remained in Jerusalem.**

**11:2-3.** **One evening,** restless on his

bed . . . **David** arose, went to a rooftop **of the palace,** and from there happened to observe **Bathsheba . . . the wife of** his neighbor **Uriah.** She was **bathing** out in the open. One may not fault **David** for perhaps seeking the cooler breezes of the late afternoon, but Bathsheba, knowing the proximity of her courtyard to the palace, probably harbored ulterior designs toward the king. Yet David's submission to her charms is inexcusable, for the deliberate steps he followed to bring her to the palace required more than enough time for him to resist the initial, impulsive temptation (cf. James 1:14-15).

**11:4-5.** Having discovered her identity, he **sent** for **her** at once and, assured of her ritual purity (cf. Lev. 12:2-5; 15:19-28), had intercourse with her. The bathing itself may have been for the purpose of ritual purification and would therefore not only advertise Bathsheba's charms but would serve as a notice to the king that she was available to him. In due time she found that she was **pregnant** by the king and, undoubtedly in great distress, informed him of her condition.

**11:6-13.** The crisis brought by the pregnancy required some kind of suitable resolution, so **David** determined to "legitimize" the impending birth by bringing **Uriah** back from the Ammonite campaign, thus making it possible for him to enjoy the intimacies of marriage. But the subterfuge did not work, for though **David** resorted to two schemes (vv. 8, 13) to induce **Uriah** to **go home** and be with his **wife,** the noble **Hittite** refused. (Though the Hittite Empire had ended by 1200 B.C., pockets of ethnic Hittites continued to exist in Syria and even Israel. **Uriah** was from one of these.) Why should he, he argued, be allowed the comforts of home and a conjugal visit while his friends in combat were deprived of them? Even after **David** plied him with wine, Uriah's sense of loyalty to his comrades prevailed over his desire for his wife.

**11:14-21.** In utter frustration **David** wrote a memo **to Joab** commanding that **Uriah,** when he returned to **the front line,** be abandoned to the enemy by an unexpected Israelite withdrawal. Ironically **Uriah** was the bearer of his own tidings of doom. This plan succeeded; **Uriah** was surrounded and slain. Ordinarily **David** would have been upset by the news of casualties. He would have wondered at Israel's indiscretion in fighting under Rabbah's **wall,** a blunder which had cost **Abimelech, son of** Gideon, his life long ago (Jud. 9:50-54). So **Joab** instructed the courier who bore the news to inform the king specifically that **Uriah** also had died. This he knew would mollify David's anguish.

**11:22-27.** David's response to the news was predictable. He **told the messenger** to tell **Joab** that in circumstances such as war, life and death were matters of blind chance. His instruction back to **Joab** was only that the siege of Rabbah be even more aggressive. Bathsheba soon learned of her husband's tragic death. **After the** customary **time of mourning,** she moved into the king's palace in time to bear their **son.** The LORD was **displeased,** however, and set events in motion that would trouble **David** till his death.

### B. Nathan's rebuke and David's punishment (chap. 12)

**12:1-6.** Sometime after the birth of Bathsheba's son, **Nathan** the prophet told David a story of a **rich man** who, in spite of having everything, stole a **poor** neighbor's only **ewe** (i.e., female) **lamb** to provide a feast for a guest.

Enraged, **David** pronounced that **the man who** would do such a despicable thing ought **to die.** Though the Law contained no such penalty for the theft of property, kidnapping was a capital offense and it may be that David viewed the taking of a pet lamb in this light (Ex. 21:16). In addition, he said, **the** rich **man** must restore **four** lambs for the one stolen for not even the rich man's death could compensate the poor man's property loss (Ex. 22:1).

**12:7-14.** Nathan's reply to all this was a bombshell: **You are the man! The** LORD, he said, had given **David** everything, but he had taken, as it were, the pet lamb of a poor neighbor (v. 9). **David** now would suffer **the sword** as had **Uriah** and David's **wives** would be taken from him as Bathsheba had been stolen from **the Hittite.** This was fulfilled by Absalom (David's own son!) when he lay with David's concubines (16:22). But David's shame would be even greater because, in contrast with David's sin **in secret,** all these things would happen in the

glare of the public eye, **in broad daylight.**

One may wonder, perhaps, why David was not punished with death as he had so sternly advocated for the guilty man. Adultery and murder both were sufficient cause for the execution of even a king (Ex. 21:12; Lev. 20:10). The answer surely lies in the genuine and contrite repentance which David expressed, not only in the presence of Nathan but more fully in Psalm 51. David's **sin** was heinous, but the grace of God was more than sufficient to forgive and restore him, as **Nathan** could testify. And yet, though David could be restored to fellowship with his God, the impact of his sin remained and would continue to work its sorrow in the nation as well as in the king's life.

**12:15-23.** Shortly **after** the interview with **Nathan . . . the child** became terminally **ill.** Despite David's intense fasting and prayer the baby **died** within a week. Only then did **David** cease his mourning, wash, worship, and eat, contrary to custom and much to the amazement of **his** servants. David's response is classic: **While the child was still alive, I fasted and wept. . . . But now that he is dead, why should I fast? Can I bring him back again?** David attested to the irrevocability of death—its finality renders further petition absurd. **I will go to him,** David said, **but he will not return to me.** This reflects his conviction that the dead cannot return to life as it was. Rather it is the living who go to the dead.

**12:24-25.** Eventually another **son** was born to David and Bathsheba, one who bore a double name. Called **Solomon** ("peace") by them, **the** LORD **. . . through Nathan** named **him Jedidiah** ("loved by the LORD").

**12:26-31.** In the meantime, the Ammonite war went well for **Joab.** He had all but captured the Ammonite capital, **Rabbah,** having taken **the royal citadel** and the city's **water supply.** And now, in order that **David** might gain the credit for its fall, **Joab** urged the king to lead the final assault himself. This **David** did. He sacked the city of its wealth, including the 75-pound (**a talent**) golden **crown** of the Ammonite **king** (*malkām,* which could also be a reference to "Molech," the Ammonite god). David also put the survivors to slave labor (using **saws**

... iron **picks, and axes** and working **at brickmaking**) and **returned** in triumph **to Jerusalem.**

## C. Sin and murder of Amnon (chap. 13)

Because of his affair with Bathsheba David had been told by Nathan the prophet that the sword would never depart from his house (12:10). It was not long before he began to experience the heartbreaks of rape and murder within his own family.

**13:1-6. Absalom, son of David** by his wife Maacah (3:3), had a **beautiful sister** named **Tamar. Amnon,** David's firstborn by Ahinoam (3:2), **fell in love with Tamar. Frustrated** in his attempts to win her favor, **Amnon** sought the counsel of his **shrewd** cousin **Jonadab.** Jonadab advised Amnon to **pretend to be ill** and then to plead with his **father** to have **Tamar** bake him **bread** and bring it to him.

**13:7-14.** After **she** had prepared **the bread** before him, **Amnon** told her to dismiss all the servants. Then, despite her urgent pleading, **he grabbed her** and **raped her.** Such loss of a maiden's virginity was an unbearable curse **in Israel** (Deut. 22:13-21). Moreover, such relationships between half brothers and sisters were strictly forbidden in the Law. Those guilty of such things were to be cut off from the covenant community (Lev. 20:17). In this case, of course, **Tamar** was innocent since she had been assaulted (Deut. 22:25-29).

**13:15-19.** In revulsion at what he had done, **Amnon** now **hated** Tamar **more than he had** previously **loved her.** This indicates, of course, that his original feelings had not been love but only lust. To add insult to injury and in further violation of the Law, **Amnon** sent Tamar away. This suggests not only his desire to have her gone from his immediate presence but also his repudiation of her as a bride. He had humbled a **virgin** and the Law demanded that he marry her (Deut. 22:29). Tamar's reaction to all this—putting **ashes on her head** and tearing her royal robe (cf. 2 Sam. 13:31; Job 2:12)—shows the intensity of her sorrow at losing her purity and perhaps any further opportunity for marriage.

**13:20-22.** When **Tamar** got to the house of **her brother Absalom,** he suspected at once what had happened. No doubt he knew full well the propensities of **Amnon.** With plans for vengeance already developing in his own mind he counseled his **sister** to remain silent about the matter and to stay in his **house. David** somehow **heard** what had happened, and though **he was furious** he did not invoke the penalty prescribed by the Law. Perhaps this was because **Amnon** was his oldest son. But **Absalom . . . hated Amnon.**

**13:23-29. Two** long **years** passed before **Absalom** effected his plan for retaliation. He hosted a festival to celebrate the time of sheepshearing, a custom observed in Israel from earliest times (Gen. 38:12-13; 1 Sam. 25:2, 8). **He invited** and **urged** his father David to **join** him at **Baal Hazor** (ca. six miles south of Shiloh), the scene of the festivities, but David declined. **Absalom** then requested that **Amnon** attend in David's place, a request **the king** reluctantly granted. In the midst of the merriment the servants of **Absalom,** on a prearranged signal, attacked and murdered the unsuspecting **Amnon.** Thus a murder avenged a rape.

**13:30-39.** Having heard that **Absalom** had slain **all** of his other **sons . . . David** fell into inconsolable anguish. Even when he later knew that the report was unfounded and that **only Amnon** was **dead** he could not be comforted (v. 36). **Absalom** meanwhile **fled** from Baal Hazor and sought and found refuge with **Talmai,** his maternal grandfather, at **Geshur,** east of the Sea of Kinnereth. There **Absalom** remained for **three years** though his father, finally consoled, **longed to** have him return again.

## D. Absalom's estrangement from David (chap. 14)

**14:1-3.** It was evident to all that David sorely missed his exiled son but no one knew how to achieve Absalom's return and a reconciliation. Finally **Joab,** always a tactician, convinced or commanded a clever **woman** from **Tekoa** (later the home of the Prophet Amos [Amos 1:1]; seven miles south of Bethlehem) to disguise herself as a mourner and **go to the king** with a story which he himself concocted and put **in her mouth.**

**14:4-7.** Having gained access **to the king,** the **woman** related to him that she had **had two sons,** one of whom had murdered **the other.** This meant that the surviving son was liable to blood vengeance at the hands of relatives. Since she was **a widow,** this would mean the elimination of her own source of support (expressed by the figure of speech, **They would put out the only burning coal I have left**). Perhaps even more important, she would have no **heir** to carry on the name and memory of her dead **husband.**

**14:8-11.** Obviously touched by her story, David told **the woman** to return **home** in peace. He would **issue an order** to resolve the matter. She was not convinced that she had fully made her point, however, and pressed her case even further. In the event of any miscarriage of justice, she said, she and her family would bear the responsibility. That is, if the circumstances really did require vengeance (Num. 35:9-21), she wanted **the king** to know that he would not be legally or morally culpable if he did not stop it from being carried out. Patiently David heard her out and again assured her that if anyone tried to prosecute the case he would have to answer to **the king.** Relentlessly she continued, however, till she elicited from David a formal oath that her accused **son** would suffer not even the slightest harm: **As surely as the LORD lives** (cf. comments on 1 Kings 1:29) **not one hair of your son's head will fall to the ground.**

**14:12-14.** Satisfied at last, **the woman** boldly accosted **the king** with the meaning of her parable. In granting amnesty to an unknown murderer it was now incumbent on him that he do the same for his own **son** Absalom. There are circumstances, she said, under which the death penalty need not be applied, particularly where premeditation was not involved (Num. 35:15). Though that was not relevant here, as Absalom had plotted Amnon's death long in advance, there was still the principle of mercy: **God does not take away life; instead, He devises ways so that a banished person may not remain estranged from Him.**

**14:15-20.** Then, to make David think that her remarks about Absalom were only incidental to her real purpose, **the woman** reminded **the king** of the fear that prompted her to come in the first place. She coupled this reminder with effusive flattery of the king's wisdom (**My lord the king is like an angel of God in discerning good and evil,** v. 17; cf. v. 20). But David discerned that "the woman doth protest too much" and asked if **Joab** had something to do with **all this.** Found out in her treachery she had to admit it was true. David's recognition of **Joab** as the instigator lies no doubt not only in the general's recognized craftiness but in the fact that David was surely aware of Joab's interest in Absalom's return.

**14:21-24.** David had no alternative but to act on the sentiment he had expressed to the woman concerning forgiveness, even though he had been conned into doing so. He sent **Joab** to bring his alienated son **back.** But when **Absalom** returned David refused to meet him personally or to let him visit the palace. Perhaps David felt that too ready a reconciliation would lead the people to believe that he did not view Absalom's crime with sufficient seriousness.

**14:25-27.** In order to emphasize Absalom's attributes, features that should have made him attractive to David and which later proved irresistible to the people, the historian described **Absalom** as **handsome** in every way. The reference to his long **hair** (weighing **200 shekels,** i.e., about five pounds, when **he** infrequently **cut** it) is especially made to prepare for Absalom's peculiar undoing—later he was caught by his head (perhaps his hair) in the branches of an oak tree (18:9). His profound love for his violated sister **Tamar** also testifies to his attractiveness; he named his own **daughter** after her.

**14:28-33.** After **two** more **years** of estrangement from his father, **Absalom** twice sought Joab's aid in bringing about a final resolution of their differences. Rebuffed each time, **Absalom** resorted to dramatic action—he set **Joab's** barley **field on fire,** which did get the general's attention. **Joab** then intervened with **the king** and at last made it possible for **Absalom** to be reunited with his father. The meeting was at least superficially cordial, but as subsequent events demonstrated, David's long-delayed acceptance of his son came too late. **Absalom** was embittered and resolved to do whatever was necessary to make David pay for his intransigence.

**E.** *Absolom's revolution (chaps. 15–18)*

1. ABSALOM'S CAPTURE OF THE KINGDOM (CHAP. 15)

**15:1-6.** Absalom's first move to achieve his purposes of revenge was to make himself conveniently available (**by the side of the road leading to the city gate,** with his **chariot** and **50 men**) to hear the complaints of the citizens. Cleverly he insinuated that **the king** was too busy to hear them and that David had not even provided lesser judges to adjudicate their cases. **If only** he were chief **judge . . . Absalom** said, he would listen to one and all and deal impartially in every matter. **Absalom** showed the people great affection by kissing them when they came **to bow . . . before him.** Thus he gradually gained the support of the masses.

**15:7-12.** One day, feeling that his popular support was overwhelming, **Absalom** requested and received permission from **the king** to **go to Hebron,** allegedly to pay **a vow . . . to the LORD** which he had **made** while in exile in **Geshur** (cf. 13:37). For **4 years Absalom** had been weaning the people away from David. (The "4 years" appears in the Lucian recension of the LXX and the Syriac version [Peshitta], but the Heb. has "40 years," a figure which might refer to an event early in David's life, perhaps to his own anointing at Bethlehem, 1 Sam. 16:13.) Now the time was ripe for revolution. When **Absalom** reached **Hebron,** the very center of the Davidic dynasty, where David had begun his reign (2 Sam. 3:2-3), Absalom announced his usurpation of power (15:10). The **200 men** who **accompanied** him **from Jerusalem** were ignorant of his plans. Apparently they were won over as was **Ahithophel . . . David's** own chief **counselor.**

**15:13-23.** News quickly reached the capital that **Absalom** had effected a coup and that all was lost. **David,** convinced of the hopelessness of his cause and anxious to spare **the city** from destruction, made his plans to depart and head east for the Transjordan. He left behind **10** housekeeping **concubines. The people,** including **600 Gittites** (faithful men who had followed him from Gath in Philistia when he was pursued by Saul; 1 Sam. 23:13; 27:2; 30:9), fled with David. He tried to persuade his Philistine mercenary officer, **Ittai** of Gath, to remain behind since he had nothing to fear from **Absalom. But** to his credit **Ittai** refused, preferring to honor his commitment of loyalty by joining **the king** in banishment.

**15:24-29. Zadok and Abiathar,** the two chief priests, were sent **back to Jerusalem** by David. He knew that if it was God's will for him to return as king, he would do so. Hence there was no need to keep **the ark** away from the sanctuary. After all, it was David and not the Lord who was going into exile. Besides, the priests' two sons (**Ahimaaz,** Zadok's **son,** and **Jonathan,** Abiathar's **son;** see the chart "The Ancestry of Zadok and Abiathar," near 8:15-18) could carry to David any revelations which God might give their fathers.

**15:30-37. David** and his loyal supporters in the meantime made their way east across the Kidron Valley and **up the Mount of Olives.** His **covered** head and unshod feet indicated his depth of despair. To make matters worse **David** discovered that his trusted adviser **Ahithophel** had joined Absalom's cause. To contravene **Ahithophel's** effectiveness David recruited **Hushai,** a friend who asked to accompany the king on his way, and persuaded him to **return to** Jerusalem and attach himself to Absalom's court as a counselor. His mission would be to contradict the **advice** of Ahithophel and to communicate Absalom's plans to **Zadok and Abiathar** whose **sons** (cf. v. 27) in turn would relay them to David (cf. 17:21; 18:19). David then continued in his flight, but **Absalom** took firm control of **Jerusalem.**

2. ABSALOM'S SOLIDIFICATION OF POWER (CHAP. 16)

David's forced flight from Jerusalem not only put his own kingship in jeopardy, but it also opened the door to further contention for the throne between the dynasties of Saul and David. Absalom was apparently in the process of seizing power in Jerusalem but this by no means implied that he could also gain control over the Northern tribes. In fact the shakeup in David's own family began to revive hope among the Saulites that they might be able to recover the kingdom for themselves.

**16:1-4.** This is first evident in the reaction of Saul's grandson **Mephibosheth**

to David's withdrawal. While **the king** was heading east across the Judean hills, he was met by Mephibosheth's servant **Ziba** who, out of gratitude to David for his past kindness toward him (chap. 9), now provided the fugitive king **donkeys** and provisions for the journey. But **Ziba** also brought **David** the sad news that **Mephibosheth** had turned against the king, hoping that in the midst of the turmoil occasioned by the revolution he might be able to retrieve Saul's old throne (16:3; but cf. 19:24-30). David then stripped from Mephibosheth the generous pension he had given him earlier and bequeathed it all to **Ziba** (cf. 9:7, 13).

**16:5-14.** David next encountered **Shimei,** another relative of Saul, who greeted the fleeing monarch and his officials at **Bahurim** (east of the Mount of Olives) with curses and physical abuse, pelting them **with stones.** He taunted **David** with the observation that since he was **a man of blood** God was now avenging the death **of Saul** and his family by driving David from power. This was untrue, of course, for David had not raised his hand against Saul, whom he regarded as the anointed of the Lord, but had taken every measure to deal graciously with Saul's survivors. Shimei's real complaint, as is evident from his own admission, was that David sat on the throne of Saul (Saul, **in whose place you have reigned**).

**Abishai,** David's bodyguard and nephew, begged the king to let him decapitate Shimei (whom Abishai called a **dead dog,** i.e., worthless and despised; cf. 9:8). But **David** forbade him to do so, observing that it might well be that Shimei cursed as an instrument of God Himself. If Absalom, David's own **son,** was **trying to** kill him, why should the cursing of Shimei be of concern? God would someday vindicate, but for now there must be no recompense for Shimei's evil conduct. **Shimei** continued his **cursing,** stone-throwing, and dirt-tossing as David **continued** on **the road** to his **destination.**

**16:15-23.** Meanwhile Absalom arrived in **Jerusalem** and was immediately met by **Hushai,** a friend of David who was pretending to be loyal to Absalom. His mission as contradictor to the counsel of **Ahithophel,** Absalom's chief adviser, would be implemented later. When **Absalom** asked **Ahithophel** what he

should **do,** his adviser told him to **lie with** his **father's concubines,** an evidence of his succession (cf. 3:6-7), advice which **Absalom** quickly followed. The words of counsel which **Ahithophel** gave were given credence as though they came directly from **God,** so highly regarded was his wisdom. Hushai's assignment would be difficult indeed.

3. ABSALOM'S PURSUIT OF DAVID (CHAP. 17)

**17:1-14.** The second bit of advice which **Ahithophel** gave **Absalom** was that he, Ahithophel, should be delegated to pursue **David** in order to kill him and **return** everyone else. With their king dead his followers would certainly capitulate and return to Jerusalem peacefully.

Eager for a second opinion, **Absalom** called for **Hushai** and asked him if Ahithophel's counsel was wise. **Hushai** told **Absalom** that David and his men, far from being exhausted, would be more courageous and fearsome than ever. Like **a wild bear** whose **cubs** have been stolen, the king, Hushai said, would be enraged over the loss of his kingdom. To move against him now would be foolish. Initial casualties, which were certain to occur, would cause Absalom's men to despair of victory and thus his cause would be defeated. It would be far better, Hushai continued, for Absalom to wait until he could amass a huge army and then **attack.** David and his host could then be destroyed even if it meant dragging their place of refuge into **the Valley. Absalom** was at once struck with Hushai's sagacity and decided to follow his instruction and reject **that of Ahithophel.** Obviously this was the Lord's doing, to **frustrate** Ahithophel's **advice** and **bring disaster on Absalom.**

**17:15-23.** Hushai immediately communicated Ahithophel's advice and his own to **Zadok and Abiathar,** who then sent their sons **Jonathan and Ahimaaz** from **En Rogel** (south of Jerusalem; see the map "Jerusalem in the Time of the Kings," near 1 Kings 9:15) to **David** with the message that he must hasten his flight. But the young men were spotted and their errand was reported to **Absalom.** Thanks to the boldness and kindness of a **woman** in the village of **Bahurim** east of the Mount of Olives (cf. 16:5), they escaped detection by hiding in a dry **well.** Then they made their way to

David, who by now was at **the Jordan.** Without delay **David** and his followers **crossed the** river where they sought refuge at Mahanaim. Back at Jerusalem, **Ahithophel,** crushed because his counsel to Absalom had been spurned, committed suicide **in his hometown** by hanging himself.

**17:24-29.** Probably **David** chose to go **to Mahanaim** because it was fortified and also had served as the capital of Israel under Ish-Bosheth (2:8). There could well have been a residue of good feeling there toward **David** because of David's past favors to Saul's family, especially to Mephibosheth (9:10-13). While he was there, his meager provisions of food and supplies were augmented by **Shobi son of Nahash** (and brother of Hanun, 10:1), **Makir** of **Lo Debar** (see comments on 9:4), and **Barzillai** of **Rogelim,** 25 miles north of Mahanaim. They brought such items as **bedding . . . bowls . . . pottery,** and extensive food supplies including **wheat and barley, flour and roasted grain, beans and lentils, honey, curds, and sheep, and cheese.** These three men were chieftains tributary to **David,** bound to him by ties of loyalty and obligation. (Barzillai was old and wealthy, 19:32.) Besides, they may have preferred to cast their lot with David, a known quantity, as opposed to Absalom, an unknown.

4. ABSALOM'S DEFEAT AND DEATH (CHAP. 18)

**18:1-5.** **David,** now in security and with his supplies replenished, quickly took measures to reorganize his **troops** and prepare them for the inevitable encounter with Absalom. **A third** of his troops he assigned to **Joab; a third** to **Abishai,** Joab's brother; **and a third** to **Ittai.** David determined that he would lead the attack personally, **but** his comrades dissuaded him. He was **worth 10,000 of** them, they said. **If half** of them died all would go on. But if he died the whole cause would be lost. Reluctantly David agreed to remain behind but commanded his officers that they not harm **Absalom** in the battle.

**18:6-18.** The encounter soon followed **in the forest of Ephraim,** a deserted place in the vicinity of Mahanaim (cf. 17:24, 27) but otherwise unknown. As terrible as Absalom's losses were by the swords of **David's** heroes (18:7), they

were even greater from the elements of that inhospitable terrain (v. 8). **Absalom** himself, in a frantic attempt to escape on **his mule,** rode beneath **a large oak** tree and became tangled in its **branches. He was** suspended **in midair.** A soldier of David found him in this predicament but because David had ordered his men not to hurt **Absalom,** the soldier refused to harm him further. Bloodthirsty **Joab** was not so reluctant, however, and thrust **Absalom** in the **heart** with **three javelins.** Immediately **10** of his attendants **struck** Absalom to make sure he died. Absalom had already erected a memorial (**a pillar** called **Absalom's Monument**) to his own name **in the King's Valley** (traditionally the Kidron Valley immediately east of Jerusalem) because he had **no son** to carry on his name. Joab buried him in a **pit in the forest and piled** over it a memorial cairn.

**18:19-23.** When **Ahimaaz,** David's courier (cf. 15:36; 17:17), announced that he would set out to bear word to David of the army's victory **Joab** forbade him to do so, ostensibly to spare the king unnecessarily early grief over his son's death. Joab may also have been concerned for the well-being of the young messenger for the bearer of such bad news might not be well received. Instead **Joab** dispatched an unnamed **Cushite** (an Ethiopian) who was obviously known to David. He was either considered more knowledgeable as to what had happened to Absalom (see 18:29) or was more expendable. **Ahimaaz** was not to be denied, however, and finally received permission **to go.** Taking a shortcut, he **outran the Cushite.**

**18:24-33.** Both runners were seen from a distance, and when **David** understood that the nearer was **Ahimaaz** he assumed that the message he was conveying was **good** because Ahimaaz himself was **good.** The assumption was unfounded, however, for when **Ahimaaz** finally was able to deliver his message all he could do was speak in general terms of the victory over **Absalom.** The details were left to **the Cushite** who presently **arrived** and shared with **the king** the grisly news that **Absalom** and his confederates were dead. Overwhelmed, **the king** retired to an upper **room** where he privately poured out his heart before God in unremitting grief. The depths of his love for his rebel son are couched in his lament, **If only I had died instead of you.** Two of David's sons, Amnon (13:28-29) and Absalom (18:15), died violent deaths as a consequence of David's sin (12:10).

### F. David's return to power (chaps. 19–20)

1. THE PREPARATIONS FOR RETURN (CHAP. 19)

**19:1-3.** What should have been a day of triumphant joy became to David a day of profound grief. His elation at having regained the kingdom was undercut by his despair at having lost a **son.** So chagrined were David's soldiers that they slipped out of Mahanaim as though they were losers instead of winners.

**19:4-8a. Joab,** who had known before the frustration of doing what he felt was right only to have **the king** turn it against him (cf. 3:27-39; 14:28-33), confronted David and rebuked him for his insensitivity toward his officers and people. It appeared, **Joab** said, that David would have been more satisfied **if Absalom** had lived **and all of** them had died. In order to salvage what little morale was left, Joab urged David to appear before the troops and assure them that he appreciated their selfless service to him.

**19:8b-13.** The remnants of Absalom's army had made their way home and together with the rest of **Israel** found themselves in a quandary. They had rallied behind **Absalom,** but now he was dead. Moreover, David had provided effective leadership in the past. **So why** were **the elders** not **bringing the king back?** Sensing the local officials' indecision, **David sent . . . Zadok and Abiathar, the priests,** to them to **ask** why they were so reluctant to restore David when it was clear that the people were willing and ready to do so. No doubt to shore up his support from Judah especially, David told the priests to promise **Amasa,** his nephew (cf. 17:25; 1 Chron. 2:17), that he would succeed **Joab** as **commander of** the **army** (2 Sam. 19:13). Joab, also David's nephew through another half sister (1 Chron. 2:16), had by now become completely discredited in David's eyes because of his open disagreements with David's policies.

**19:14-23.** The mission of Zadok and Abiathar was successful. With one accord (**as though they were one man**) the people **of Judah** not only invited David to return to rule over them but they also sent a delegation to **the Jordan** River to meet him and help him cross over the river. Included in the delegation were **Shimei** (v. 16), who had cursed David on his way into exile (16:5-8), and **Ziba** (19:17), Mephibosheth's servant who had refreshed David along the way (16:1-4). **Shimei,** realizing the peril in which he now found himself because of David's restoration, prostrated himself **before the king** and sought his forgiveness, a favor David temporarily granted over the objections of **Abishai** (19:21-23; but cf. David's last instruction to Solomon, 1 Kings 2:8-9). The large number of **Benjamites** who accompanied **Shimei** (2 Sam. 19:17) and who were identified by him (v. 20) as elements of **the whole house of Joseph** (i.e., Israel) indicates the first steps taken by the tribe of Benjamin to link itself with Judah.

**19:24-30.** Next came **Mephibosheth** who protested to David that **Ziba** had lied about Mephibosheth's motive for remaining in **Jerusalem** when **the king** was forced to leave. Saul's grandson said he had not tried to use the occasion as an opportunity to bring his grandfather's dynasty back into control as **Ziba** had reported (see 16:3). Whether this was true or not cannot be determined, but David at least was somewhat convinced by Mephibosheth and agreed to return at least half of the estate he had threatened to withdraw from him (19:29; cf. 16:4).

**19:31-38.** Then **Barzillai the Gileadite,** who had provided David with supplies when he had crossed into Transjordan (17:27-29), presented himself to **the king.** Grateful to the 80-year-old for all his goodness, David urged him to move to **Jerusalem** and live out his days on government sustenance. **Barzillai** protested that he was too old to make such a move and preferred to die in his own land. He asked, however, that **Kimham,** perhaps his son, go in his place and be similarly rewarded. This David was more than happy to do.

**19:39-43.** At length David and his entourage **crossed the Jordan** and arrived at **Gilgal** where they were met by a throng of citizens from both **Judah** and **Israel.** The latter were upset that the Judeans claimed **David** as one of their own to the exclusion of the other tribes (v. 41). When the Judeans replied that David was part of their own flesh (v. 42), the Israelite counter-response was that there were 10 tribes of them and therefore their claim was much more weighty. **Besides,** they said, they had been **the first** to insist that David return to rule over the nation (v. 43), a claim for which, incidentally, there is an apparent basis in the preserved narrative (vv. 9-10). The argument reveals the fickleness of the people who had first acquiesced in, if not actively supported, the rebellion of Absalom and now clamored to be first to welcome David **back.** But it also indicates the depth of the schism which was developing between **Israel** and **Judah,** a rift which eventually produced two separate kingdoms.

## 2. THE REESTABLISHMENT OF AUTHORITY (CHAP. 20)

**20:1-3.** The contention between the Israelite and Judean delegations at Gilgal became so heated that **a Benjamite** by the name of **Sheba** announced a revolutionary movement against **David** and led the Israelites to desert the king. David and the Judeans then continued their homeward journey **to Jerusalem** alone. Once there, **David** reasserted his monarchical claims by, among other things, regathering his harem (cf. 15:16). **He provided for them, but** remained sexually aloof because they had been appropriated by his son Absalom (16:21-22).

**20:4-10.** The first matter of state was urgent. It was clear to **David** that he must overcome the rump movement that had been initiated by **Sheba** at Gilgal. So he ordered **Amasa,** his new commander (19:13), to reorganize the army **of Judah . . . within three days** so that Sheba might be brought to heel. **When Amasa** was unable to do so in the allotted **time . . . Abishai,** at David's command, took his own personal elite troops (cf. 18:2) and set out for the North (20:7). On the way they met **Amasa** at **Gibeon,** about five miles north of Jerusalem. **Joab,** though having been demoted and replaced by **Amasa,** was present. Pretending to greet **Amasa** warmly, **Joab** killed him with his **dagger.** Thus **Joab** gained revenge for his loss of rank. What is particularly heinous is the fact that **Joab** and **Amasa** were cousins, sons of two of David's half sisters (1 Chron. 2:16-17). Again, then, the prophecy of Nathan came to pass: "The sword will never depart from your house" (2 Sam. 12:10).

**20:11-22. Joab** at once took command as though nothing had happened. **The troops** were stopping in **the road** to look at Amasa's corpse. So heartless Joab **dragged** Amasa's body to **a field and threw a garment over him,** without bothering to bury him. Summoning reinforcements, **Joab** marched as far north as **Abel Beth Maacah** (four miles west of Dan and north of the Sea of Kinnereth) through the territory **of the Berites** (site unknown). There he found **Sheba** safely ensconced behind **the city** wall, apparently prepared to face a long **siege.** While attempting to batter down **the walls** Joab was contacted by **a wise woman** from **the city** who yelled over the wall that she wanted to talk with him. She told **Joab** of her own fame as a purveyor of wisdom (v. 18) and then asked why he was destroying her **city** which had always been loyal to Israel. The city, as **a mother in Israel,** was a prominent one.

To this **Joab replied** that he was not attacking **the city** itself but only wanted **Sheba,** the rebel who had presumed to lead Israel away from its **king.** If she would assist in delivering Sheba **over** to him, he would end his siege. Soon **the head of Sheba** was thrown over the wall **to Joab.** Successful in his mission, Joab stopped the siege and returned to **Jerusalem.**

**20:23-26.** Apparently David tolerated Joab's assassination of Amasa for **Joab** appears in this list of **David's** royal administrators. Joab **was over Israel's entire army. Benaiah son of Jehoiada was** leader of David's special troops, **the Kerethites and Pelethites** (see comments on 8:15-18). Benaiah eventually replaced Joab at the beginning of Solomon's reign (1 Kings 2:35; 4:4). **Adoniram** (Heb. "*Adoram*") **was in charge of** conscripted **labor** gangs, a position he retained in the government of Solomon. (In 1 Kings 4:6 and 5:14 the Heb. has "*Adoniram*," a longer form of his name.) **Jehoshaphat . . . was** the **recorder** (or chronicler). **Sheva was** official scribe, evidently having succeeded Seraiah (2 Sam. 8:17). **Zadok and Abiathar** remained as chief **priests.** Finally **Ira the Jairite** was David's special minister, having succeeded the king's own sons in that capacity (see comments on 8:18 for the meaning of *kōhēn* in 20:26, usually rendered "priest").

### G. Slaughter and burial of Saul's sons (chap. 21)

**21:1-8.** At some point in David's **reign,** probably toward the end, Israel was afflicted by a **three**-year drought. When he inquired of **the LORD** as to its cause, **the LORD** revealed that it came as punishment for Saul's violation of the covenant made with **the Gibeonites** back in the days of Joshua (Josh. 9:15-21). At that time Israel, under Joshua's leadership, had just destroyed Jericho and Ai and was about to attack the Amorite federation of the Canaanite hill country. The people of Gibeon, who were in the direct line of Joshua's conquest, pretended to be faraway aliens and so escaped annihilation. Moreover, they tricked Joshua into making a covenant with them whereby they would forever serve Israel in menial tasks but could never be harmed. Though the covenant was made deceitfully, its binding nature was recognized by both the Israelites and the Gibeonites.

Saul, in an action not recorded in the biblical account, had slain some Gibeonites during his tenure (2 Sam. 21:1). When David learned that the **famine** had come on Israel as punishment for that covenant violation, he asked the Gibeonite leaders **what** he should **do for** them. They responded by denying any interest in **silver or gold.** Nor, they said, could they, as Israel's vassals, take vengeance into their own hands. Instead they asked that **seven . . . male descendants** of **Saul** be **given over to** them so that they could practice the age-old tradition of *lex talionis*—eye for eye, tooth for tooth, and life for life (Ex. 21:23-25).

David recognized the propriety of their demand, but he also had to balance against it the pledge he had made to **Jonathan** that he would forever preserve his seed (1 Sam. 20:15-16). So David spared **Mephibosheth,** Jonathan's **son,** but singled out others of Saul's offspring for execution. These included **Armoni and** another **Mephibosheth,** sons of Saul's concubine **Rizpah** (cf. 2 Sam. 3:7). The other **five** were all **sons of Merab, daughter** of Saul, by her husband **Adriel**

(cf. 1 Sam. 18:19). (As stated in the NIV marg., many Heb. mss. have "Michal," but that reading makes 2 Sam: 21:8 contradict the statement in 6:23 that Michal died childless. Probably then, the NIV is correct in following the two Heb. mss. and a few other mss. that have "Merab.")

**21:9-10.** These **seven** sons and grandsons of Saul were publicly executed by **the Gibeonites** at the **beginning** of **barley harvest,** early in the spring (see the chart "Calendar in Israel," near Ex. 12:1). As their bodies hung suspended from their places of exposure, **Rizpah,** mother of the first two (v. 8), refused to take them down and bury them. In great grief she lamented for them on a rocky ledge until the coming of the drought-breaking rains. The reason for her action is not entirely clear unless she viewed the vengeance of the Gibeonites as being at the same time the vengeance of God against the land for Saul's sake. The fact that the bodies remained where they were until it rained suggests that God's curse had been on the land and now rested on the executed sons of Saul for "anyone who is hung on a tree is under God's curse" (Deut. 21:23). The coming of **the rain** meant that the curse was ended and the corpses could be taken down and buried. Though the Law stated that a body hung from a tree must be removed by sundown (Deut. 21:23), it implied punishment of an individual for his personal crime. This case had nothing to do with any personal act of murder but rather with violation of a covenant, the results of which brought God's displeasure on the whole nation and required vengeance of a public and extended nature.

**21:11-14.** When **David** saw the devotion of **Rizpah** in protecting the bodies of her sons from the carnivorous birds and beasts, he was reminded of the shameful exposure of the bodies of **Saul and his son Jonathan** on the walls of **Beth Shan where the Philistines had** displayed **them** after the battle of **Gilboa** (1 Sam. 31:11-13). Though the people of **Jabesh Gilead** had brought the bodies away for burial, the remains were interred far from Gibeah, Saul's family home. David resolved to bring their **bones** back from Jabesh Gilead and bury them in the sepulcher of **Saul's father Kish, at Zela in Benjamin. After** this was done **God** again **answered prayer** on behalf of the nation.

**21:15-22.** The chapter concludes with a final word about David's hostility toward **the Philistines.** No longer the robust young warrior of former days, **David** now was old and weak. A Philistine giant, **Ishbi-Benob,** advanced on **David** with a spear (with a **spearhead** weighing **300 shekels** or about seven and one-half pounds) and **a new sword** (the Heb. in v. 16 is lit., "armed with a new thing," without specifying the weapon), threatening to **kill** him. Just in time **Abishai . . . came to David's** aid **and killed** the giant. **David's** warriors advised him **never again** to take to the field of **battle.** His death would mean the end of his leadership, a tragedy synonymous with the snuffing out of Israel's illumination (**the lamp of Israel**) for in and through David were God's covenant blessings to be accomplished (1 Kings 11:36; 15:4; 2 Kings 8:19).

Other Philistine encounters, **at Gob** and **Gath,** followed the one just recorded. At Gob (Gezer in 1 Chron. 20:4), **Sibbecai,** a heroic Israelite, slew **Saph** (Sippai in 1 Chron. 20:4), another Philistine giant (**Rapha** is from "Rephaim," a race of giants; cf. 2 Sam. 21:16).

Again **at Gob, Elhanan** felled a giant, **Goliath.** Because Elhanan was from Bethlehem, some scholars believe that he was David and that the present passage recapitulates David's former exploit. Against this is the lack of evidence to equate Elhanan with David and the fact that the accounts in both verses 18-22 and 1 Chronicles 20:4-8 follow that of David's conquest of Goliath by many years. The chronicler in fact stated that the giant killed by Elhanan was Goliath's brother Lahmi (1 Chron. 20:5). The resolution of the problem might well be that two Philistines were named Goliath, one killed by David and the other by Elhanan. Perhaps the Chronicles version is an attempt to clear up the confusion of two giants with the same name.

A conflict **at Gath** involved a giant (**descended from Rapha;** cf. 2 Sam. 21:16, 18) **with six** digits **on each hand** and **foot.** The genetic strains which produced gigantism must also have caused this malformity. He was slain by **David's** nephew **Jonathan,** named, of course, for David's dear friend. With this giant's death the terror caused by the Philistine giants came to an end.

## IV. David's Final Years (chaps. 22–24)

### A. David's song (chap. 22)

1. EXTOLLING OF THE LORD (22:1-4)

**22:1.** This composition, set between the account of David's Philistine wars (21:15-22) and his list of heroes (23:8-39), is a poem celebrating the providence of God in delivering him from **all his enemies** (cf. v. 4). It is found again in almost identical wording in Psalm 18, a piece that is generally classified from a literary standpoint as a royal hymn of thanksgiving.

**22:2-4.** In a manner characteristic of this literary form, the Psalmist David first acknowledged the greatness and glory of **the LORD** in a series of designations— **Rock . . . Fortress . . . Deliverer . . . Shield . . . Horn of . . . Salvation** (see comments on 1 Sam. 2:1), **Stronghold** (*miśgoḇ*; see comments on Ps. 9:9), **Refuge,** and **Savior.** All God's exploits in the past and promises for the future are predicated on who He is. These descriptions of **the LORD** are especially appropriate in light of the setting of the song, that of flight, conflict, and victory.

2. EXPLOITS OF THE LORD (22:5-20)

**22:5-20.** David was quite conscious of history and of God's providential arrangement of its particulars. He saw this in respect to his own peculiar circumstances (vv. 5-7) which he described hyperbolically as being akin to **death.** So desperate had been his peril that death was imminent. It was only the mercy of **God** in response to his prayer which brought David salvation from heaven (**His temple**).

From David, as a center of God's saving purposes, the exploits of the Lord ranged almost concentrically to the arena of **the** whole **earth** (vv. 8-9). With reference, perhaps, to prevailing pagan myths about Creation, David showed that it is the Lord who controls the earth. In His anger He **shook** the whole cosmos as an expression of His concern for David.

But the sovereignty of God goes even further. He is Lord also of **the heavens** (vv. 10-16). Though Baal, the Canaanite god, was known to his worship-

# David's Mighty Men

| 2 Samuel 23 | 1 Chronicles 11 |
|---|---|
| *"The Three"* | |
| † 1. Josheb-Basshebeth, a Tahkemonite (23:8) | Jashobeam, a Hacmonite (11:11) |
| 2. Eleazar son of Dodai the Ahohite (23:9) | (11:12) |
| 3. Shammah son of Agee the Hararite (23:11) | (*Not mentioned in 1 Chron. 11*, but implied in 11:15-19) |
| *Other honored men* | |
| 4. Abishai the brother of Joab son of Zeruiah (23:18) | (11:20) |
| 5. Benaiah son of Jehoiada (23:20) | (11:22) |
| The *"Thirty"** | |
| 6. Asahel the brother of Joab (23:24) | (11:26) |
| 7. Elhanan son of Dodo (23:24) | (11:26) |
| †8. Shammah the Harodite (23:25) | Shammoth the Harorite (11:27) |
| 9. Elika the Harodite (23:25) | (*Not mentioned in 1 Chron. 11*) |
| †10. Helez the Paltite (23:26) | Helez the Pelonite (11:27) |
| 11. Ira son of Ikkesh (23:26) | (11:28) |
| 12. Abiezer from Anathoth (23:27) | (11:28) |
| †13. Mebunnai the Hushathite (23:27) | Sibbecai the Hushathite (11:29) |
| †14. Zalmon the Ahohite (23:28) | Ilai the Ahohite (11:29) |
| 15. Maharai the Netophathite (23:28) | (11:30) |
| 16. Heled (or Heleb; cf. NIV marg.), son of Baanah (23:29) | (11:30) |
| 17. Ithai son of Ribai (23:29) | (11:31) |
| 18. Benaiah the Pirathonite (23:30) | (11:31) |
| †19. Hiddai from . . . Gaash (23:30) | Hurai from . . . Gaash (11:32) |
| †20. Abi-Albon the Arbathite (23:31) | Abiel the Arbathite (11:32) |
| †21. Azmaveth the Barhumite (23:31) | Azmaveth the Baharumite (11:33) |
| 22. Eliahba the Shaalbonite (23:32) | (11:33) |
| †23. The sons of Jashen (23:32) (These words could be trans. Bene-Jashen, the proper name of one soldier.) | The sons of Hashem (11:34) (These words could be trans. Bene-Hashem, the proper name of one soldier.) |
| †24, 25. Jonathan son of Shammah the Hararite (23:32-33) (The Heb. could refer to two men, Jonathan, and Shammah; cf. NIV marg.) | Jonathan son of Shagee the Hararite (11:34) |
| †26. Ahiam son of Sharar the Hararite (23:33) | Ahiam son of Sacar the Hararite (11:35) |
| †27. Eliphelet son of Ahasbai (23:34) | Eliphal son of Ur (11:35)<br>Hepher the Mekerathite (11:36)<br>Ahijah the Pelonite (11:36) |
| 28. Eliam son of Ahithophel (23:34) | (*Not mentioned in 1 Chron. 11*) |
| 29. Hezro the Carmelite (23:35) | (11:37) |
| †30. Paarai the Arbite (23:35) | Naarai the son of Ezbai (11:37) |
| †31. Igal son of Nathan (23:36) | (*Not mentioned in 1 Chron. 11*)<br>Joel the brother of Nathan (11:38) |
| †32. The son of Hagri (23:36) (The Heb. could be trans. Bani the Gadite.) | Mibhar son of Hagri (11:38) |
| 33. Zelek the Ammonite (23:37) | (11:39) |

| | |
|---|---|
| 34. Naharai the Beerothite (23:37) | (11:39) |
| 35. Ira the Ithrite (23:38) | (11:40) |
| 36. Gareb the Ithrite (23:38) | (11:40) |
| 37. Uriah the Hittite (23:39) "There were 37 in all" (23:39).* | (11:41) |

Zabad son of Ahlai (11:41)

Adina son of Shiza (11:42)

Hanan son of Maacah (11:43)

Joshaphat the Mithnite (11:43)

Uzzia the Ashterathite (11:44)

Shama the son of Hotham (11:44)

Jeiel the son of Hotham (11:44)

Jediael son of Shimri (11:45)

Joha the Tizite (11:45)

Eliel the Mahavite (11:46)

Jeribai son of Elnaam (11:46)

Joshaviah son of Elnaam (11:46)

Ithmah the Moabite (11:46)

Eliel (11:47)

Obed (11:47)

Jaasiel the Mezobaite (11:47)

*The word "30" was either a technical term for David's select soldiers of approximately 30 men (here 32—nos. 6-37). Or the word "30" means exactly 30 men, with some men replacing others as they were killed in battle (e.g., Uriah, no. 37). This could account for the Chronicles list having several more men than the Samuel list.

†These soldiers' names and/or the words identifying their fathers or places of residence differ in the accounts in 2 Samuel and 1 Chronicles. (When the names are the same in both accounts, only the references are given in the right-hand column.) However, most of the changes are slight variations in spelling, an occasional practice in Hebrew. Some names may refer to different individuals (e.g., no. 13, Mebunnai and Sibbecai; and no. 14, Zalmon and Ilai). Perhaps Mebunnai died in battle and was replaced by Sibbecai, a fellow Hushathite.

ers as "the rider of the **clouds**," it is Yahweh who is enthroned in the heavens and who reduces all Creation to His service. With **lightning** and a **voice** like thunder He cried out against His (and David's) **enemies,** terrifying them. The God of Creation rearranged Creation, as it were, on David's behalf.

That David refers to God's mighty works (vv. 8-16) as an expression not of His role of Creator as such, but as One **powerful** to save is clear from the conclusion of the passage (vv. 17-20): God had delivered him from his enemies because he was the object of God's mercy and grace. God's deliverance is expressed in several verbs: (a) **reached down,** (b) **took hold,** (c) **drew . . . out,** (d) **rescued** (vv. 18, 20), (e) **brought out.**

### 3. EQUITY OF THE LORD (22:21-30)

**22:21-30.** God's deliverance of David was followed by His blessings, divine rewards commensurate with David's own **righteousness.** David did not suggest that works are necessary for salvation, which is not the issue here. He was saying, however, that the benefits of God are often obtained in this life by faithful perseverance in godliness. He **kept** God's **ways** (v. 22), **law** (v. 23), and **decrees** (v. 23), and refrained from iniquity (v. 24; cf. vv. 21, 25). God therefore **rewarded** him (v. 25) and showed mercy to him as He does to all who are upright (**faithful . . . blameless . . . pure . . . humble;** vv. 26-28). The wicked, on the other hand, because of their pride cannot expect His favor (v. 28b). With God, who gives **light** as a **lamp** (v. 29), a righteous person is invincible. He can break through barricades (not **a troop**) or **scale** the highest walls (v. 30).

### 4. EXCELLENCE OF THE LORD (22:31-51)

**22:31-51.** In the final section of the psalm David turned once more to the attributes of **the LORD,** but he connected them now to specific ways in which **God** had worked and would work on his behalf. God was described first as a Strengthener (vv. 31-35), One who is **a Shield,** a **Rock,** a **Strength** (lit., "strong Refuge" or "Fortress"), One who gives speed and power to His own servants. He is also a **Shield** (v. 36), and He protects against slipping and falling (vv. 36-37). Again, He is a Subduer of **enemies**

(vv. 38-41). Through **the LORD,** David was able to pursue and destroy his **enemies** so that they could not rise again.

The Lord also is a Support (vv. 42-46). David's enemies called out to God **but** He would not answer them (v. 42). Instead He let David crush them (v. 43), and rule over them as well as over his own people (vv. 44-46).

Finally, David said that the Lord was his **Savior** (vv. 47-51). Though his enemies surrounded him and were about to destroy him, the Lord brought him through triumphantly. As a result David praised Him (v. 50) and acknowledged that all God's benefits of the past were tokens of His promised blessings on both **David and his descendants,** blessings which will endure **forever.**

## B. David's heroes (chap. 23)

**23:1-7.** The list of David's mighty men is preceded by a short poem (vv. 1b-7) titled **the last words of David.** In the first stanza (v. 1) he identified himself as **son of Jesse . . . the man exalted by the Most High, the man anointed by the God of Jacob,** and **Israel's singer of songs.** There is a noticeable progress from the humble son of a Bethlehemite commoner to the poetically gifted king of Israel, a development which David attributed to his having been chosen and anointed by the Lord.

His consciousness of being God's instrument is clear from the second stanza (vv. 2-4), in which he acknowledged that God had spoken **to** him (v. 3) and **through him** (v. 2) to the nation, enabling him to rule righteously **in the** reverential **fear of God.** A king who rules as an agent of God is, he said, like the brilliance of the sun **on a cloudless morning** and like a clear day **after rain.**

In the third stanza (vv. 5-7) David centered on the Davidic **Covenant,** by which **God** chose and blessed him. God had made **an everlasting** commitment with him and his dynasty (**my house**), a covenant that guaranteed his ultimate well-being (cf. 7:8-16). In contrast, **evil men,** like so many **thorns,** will be cast aside to be consumed by the judgment of God (cf. Matt. 13:30, 41).

**23:8-39.** David's gallery of heroes consisted of **37** men (v. 39) who distinguished themselves by mighty exploits of service to God and Israel and who evidently made up his elite troops. These consisted of three **chief men** (vv. 8-17), two others of a second rank (vv. 18-23), and 32 in the longest list (vv. 24-39). (See the chart "David's Mighty Men.") Significant by its omission is any reference to **Joab.** Two of his brothers—**Abishai** and **Asahel**—are listed (vv. 8, 24). Neither the author of Samuel nor that of the Chronicles felt it necessary, perhaps, to list Joab since he was the commander of the whole army throughout most of David's reign (20:23).

Though the spellings of several of the names differ in the corresponding list in 1 Chronicles 11:11-47, the names can usually be equated. The chronicler does, however, add names beyond the 37 in 2 Samuel. Perhaps they were men of lower ranks than those listed in Samuel or perhaps they replaced others (already listed) who had fallen in battle.

The first **three** were (a) **Josheb-Basshebeth, a Tahkemonite,** who slew **800 men . . . in one encounter** (2 Sam. 23:8; on the "300" in 1 Chron. 11:11 see comments there); (b) **Eleazar, son of Dodai the Ahohite,** who **struck down the Philistines** (2 Sam. 23:9-10) **at Pas Dammim** (1 Chron. 11:13; cf. Ephes Dammim in 1 Sam. 17:1); and (c) **Shammah son of Agee the Hararite,** who brought **great victory** over **the Philistines** (2 Sam. 23:11-12).

These **three** also displayed their courage by obtaining **water** from **Bethlehem** for **David** while he was besieged in the summer (**harvesttime**) by **the Philistines** at **Adullam** (vv. 13-15; cf. 1 Sam. 22:1). So touched was **David** by their valor that he refused to **drink** the **water** but **poured it out** as an offering to **the LORD** (2 Sam. 23:16-17). Most scholars deny that the three involved are those just named since the word "three" has no definite article in the Hebrew text in verse 13. On the other hand verse 17 implies that all the foregoing had been done by these three and this time the definite article is used.

Included in the second rank were **Abishai . . . son of Zeruiah** (and nephew of David, 1 Chron. 2:15-16) who **was chief of the** second 3 (or "30," NIV marg.) but not as exalted as the first 3 previously listed (2 Sam. 23:18-19; cf. 1 Sam. 26:6-11; 2 Sam. 10:14; 21:16-17), and **Benaiah,** who achieved notable victories over both

men and **a lion** (23:20-23; cf. 8:18; 1 Kings 1:32, 36, 38; 2:35; 4:4).

The longest list consists of 32 men. Such a group normally consisted of 30 men but might have a few more or less and still be known as "the 30," a technical term for a small military contingent known in Hebrew as *haššᵉlošîm* ("the 30"). Or perhaps two had died in battle (including **Uriah the Hittite,** 2 Sam. 11:14-17) and were replaced.

### C. David's sin in taking the census (chap. 24)

**24:1-3.** It is impossible to determine the date of this episode from 2 Samuel alone, but the parallel version in 1 Chronicles 21 places it just prior to David's instructions to Solomon about building the temple (1 Chron. 21:28–22:19). The census must have come late in David's reign, and may have been part of the plan of dynastic succession in anticipation of Solomon's coming to power.

For reasons not stated, **the LORD** was angry **against Israel** (the **again** of 2 Sam. 24:1 may refer to 21:1), and **He** led **David** to command that a census be taken. In 1 Chronicles 21:1 this motivation is attributed to (lit.) "a Satan" (or adversary). This is no contradiction for the Lord had simply allowed Satan to prompt David to an improper course of action in order that Israel might be punished and that David might be instructed. This is similar to the Lord's permitting Satan to trouble Job (Job 1:12; 2:6) and His allowing an evil spirit to torment Saul (1 Sam. 16:14; see comments there). In any case, the Lord Himself did not incite David to do evil for "God cannot be tempted by evil, nor does He tempt anyone" (James 1:13).

The reasons for David's desire for a census are not clear either, though the fact that he only had military **men** counted (2 Sam. 24:2, 9) suggests that he was interested in determining his military strength. And herein lay the sin—he probably did this so he could boast in human might. This may be implied in Joab's query as to **why** the census was to be undertaken. God was able, **Joab** said, to **multiply** their **troops** as much as necessary, so why did David feel the need to assess his strength?

**24:4-9.** David prevailed, however, and sent census takers throughout the realm. Beginning in the Transjordan they

**went** counterclockwise north **to Dan Jaan** (a variation of Dan), then west and southwest of **Sidon** and **Tyre,** throughout the plains and valleys of Canaanite and Hivite (Horites or Hurrians) population, and south **to Beersheba.** Finally, after **nine months and 20 days,** the report was given; there were **800,000** eligible fighting **men** in **Israel** and **500,000** in **Judah** (v. 9). The figures in 1 Chronicles are 1,100,000 men in Israel and 470,000 in Judah, but the chronicler wrote that the Levites and Benjamites were not included (1 Chron. 21:5-6). The reconciliation of the data may lie in the possibility that 1,100,000 describes the grand total for Israel including the standing army which consisted of 12 units of 24,000 men each (288,000, 1 Chron. 27:1-15) plus 12,000 especially attached to Jerusalem and the chariot cities (2 Chron. 1:14). These 300,000 subtracted from 1,100,000 would yield the 800,000 figure in 2 Samuel 24:9. Also the chronicler may not have included the 30,000-man standing army of Judah (6:1) whereas they were included in chapter 24. This would raise the 470,000 total of Chronicles to the 500,000 of Samuel. This is only one solution, but with so little information available as to how the sums were obtained nothing further can be said with certainty.

**24:10-25.** After **David** received the report, he realized his sin of pride and self-sufficiency and confessed this sin (which he called **a very foolish thing) to the Lord** (1 Chron. 21:7 points out that the Lord punished Israel, thus indicating the evil of the census). The Lord then sent **Gad,** a **prophet,** to **David** with a list of **three** calamities from which he could **choose** and by which the Lord would register His displeasure and purge out the evil. The choices were **three years of famine . . . three months of** enemy pursuit, and **three days of** pestilence (2 Sam. 24:13). (Though the Heb. reads "seven" years of famine, 1 Chron. 21:12, probably a better-preserved text, reads "three," as the NIV has it.) **David** chose the third option, throwing himself on the **mercy** of God (2 Sam. 24:14).

The result was a **plague** which took the lives of **70,000** people. When **Jerusalem** itself was threatened, **the Lord** intervened and commanded His angelic destroyer to desist. **David** then confessed his own personal sin and urged **the Lord**

to spare His innocent people. Then, in order to make proper restitution and atonement, **David** arranged to construct **an altar to the Lord. Gad** told him that it must be built **on the threshing floor of Araunah,** a citizen of Jerusalem, since it was there that **the angel** had been commanded to cease his destruction of the city (v. 16).

According to well-founded tradition, this **threshing floor,** a wide, smooth, ledge-like surface, was on Mount Moriah, just outside the northern wall of David's Jerusalem. But David had no right to it because it was owned by a citizen. When **Araunah** learned of David's desire (v. 21), however, he was willing not only to give the threshing floor **to the king** but also to provide the **wood** and sacrifices needed (v. 22). To this gracious offer David could only give a negative response. How could he **sacrifice to the Lord** what **cost** him **nothing?** That would be a denial of the very meaning of sacrifice. **Araunah** therefore sold him the **threshing floor** and **oxen** for **50 shekels of silver** (the 600 shekels of gold in 1 Chron. 21:25 includes, however, "the site," more than just the threshing floor). Fifty shekels was about 1¼ pounds of silver. The silver David paid was only for the oxen and the threshing floor, and the 600 shekels (15 pounds of gold) mentioned in 1 Chronicles 21:25 was for the lot of land surrounding the threshing floor.

Having obtained the site, **David** **built** the **altar,** offered the sacrifices, and interceded on behalf of his people. God heard and **answered,** and **the land** was healed of **the plague.** This was where Abraham had offered Isaac (Gen. 22:2). And on this same spot Solomon later constructed his magnificent temple (1 Chron. 22:1; 2 Chron. 3:1).

# BIBLIOGRAPHY

See the 14 entries in the *Bibliography* on 1 Samuel, in additon to these 3:

Ackroyd, Peter R. *The Second Book of Samuel.* New York: Cambridge University Press, 1977.

Kirkpatrick, A.F. *The Second Book of Samuel.* Cambridge: Cambridge University Press, 1886.

Moriarty, Fredrick. *The Second Book of Samuel.* New York: Paulist Press, 1971.

# 1 KINGS

## Thomas L. Constable

## INTRODUCTION

**Title.** The Books of 1 and 2 Kings were so named because they record and interpret the reigns of all the kings of Israel and Judah except Saul. (David's last days are mentioned [1 Kings 1:1–2:12] but the events in most of his reign are recorded in 2 Sam. 2–24 and 1 Chron. 11–29.) In the Hebrew Old Testament 1 and 2 Kings were one book and were regarded as a continuation of the historical narrative begun in 1 and 2 Samuel. The Septuagint, the Greek translation of the Old Testament, divided Kings into the two parts that constitute 1 and 2 Kings in English Bibles, though the Septuagint calls those two books "3 and 4 Kingdoms" (and calls 1 and 2 Sam. "1 and 2 Kingdoms"). The title "Kings" came from Jerome's Latin translation (the Vulgate) which was made about six centuries after the Septuagint; Jerome called the two books "The Book of the Kings."

**Scope.** First and 2 Kings provide a record of Israel's history from the beginning of the movement to place Solomon on David's throne through the end of the reign of Zedekiah, Judah's last king. Zedekiah ruled until the surviving Southern Kingdom was taken captive and Babylonian governors were placed in charge of affairs in Palestine.

Three major periods of Israel's history can be distinguished in Kings: (a) the united monarchy (during which time Israel and Judah remained united under Solomon as they had been under Saul and David); (b) the divided monarchy (from the rebellion of Israel against the rulership of Judean kings until Israel was carried off into captivity by the Assyrians); and (c) the surviving kingdom (the record of Judah's affairs from the deportation of Israel to Judah's own defeat and exile by the Babylonians).

First and 2 Kings were not divided as they are because a natural break occurs in the narrative, but because the large scroll of 1 and 2 Kings needed to be divided into two smaller, more easily manageable units. The result was two books which are almost equal in length.

**Date.** The release of Jehoiachin from prison is the last event recorded in 2 Kings. This took place in the 37th year of his imprisonment (560 B.C.). Therefore 1 and 2 Kings could not have been written before that event. It seems unlikely that the return of the Jews from the Babylonian Captivity in 538 B.C. had taken place when 1 and 2 Kings were written; had it occurred, the author would probably have referred to it. Probably 1 and 2 Kings were completed in their final form between 560 and 538 B.C.

**Author.** Though it is obvious that the author utilized various source materials in writing 1 and 2 Kings, the book bears the marks of single rather than multiple authorship. Some of those indicators are the choice of materials recorded (e.g., the records of the deeds and evaluations of the kings, and the ministries of several prophets), the emphases which run throughout the books (e.g., the ministries of the prophets and the evaluation of the kings in relation to the Mosaic Law, and the primacy of the Davidic dynasty), the method of expressing the beginnings and endings of the kings' reigns (e.g., 1 Kings 14:31; 15:1-3, 23-26), and phrases and terms that recur from beginning to end (e.g., "now the rest of the acts of . . . are they not written . . . " "evil in the sight of the Lord"; "he reigned . . . years and his mother's name was . . . " "As surely as the LORD lives").

The identity of the author is unknown, but he may have been an exile who lived in Babylon. Some commentators have pointed to his recording

Jehoiachin's release from captivity in Babylon in support of this conclusion since this event seems to them to have been specially significant for the Jews in captivity. This line of reasoning has led students of 1 and 2 Kings to suggest such notable exilic Jews as Ezra and Ezekiel as the author. Jeremiah has also been suggested. He of course was not a Babylonian exile; he died in Egypt. Ancient scholarship and tradition favor one of these three men above others who have been considered.

**Purpose.** The Books of 1 and 2 Kings were written to record history but, more importantly, to teach the *lessons* of history.

The author's chief historical concern was to preserve a record of the kings of both Israel and Judah. The emphasis in this record is on the royal actions and also on the actions of selected prophets that bear on the period in which they ministered.

More importantly the author sought to evaluate the monarchy by the standard of the Mosaic Law. Besides tracing the decline of the Northern and Southern Kingdoms, he pointed out the reasons for their decline in general and the fate of each king in particular. He may have intended to teach the exiles in Babylon the reasons for their plight so that they would learn from their past. In particular God's faithfulness to His covenant (blessing the obedient and punishing the disobedient) and the evils of idolatry receive strong emphasis.

Second Chronicles, of course, records the history of almost the same period as 1 and 2 Kings. (First Chron. includes the genealogies leading up to David [chaps. 1–9], Saul's death [chap. 10], and David's reign and death [chaps. 11–29].) The purposes and emphases of these two histories differ significantly. The kings of Judah were of more interest to the author of Chronicles whereas both the Israelite and Judean monarchs occupied the interest of the author of 1 and 2 Kings. The Books of 1 and 2 Chronicles emphasize especially the priestly elements in the nation's history, such as the temple and worship, while 1 and 2 Kings give attention to the royal and prophetic elements. In 2 Chronicles the kings of Judah after David are evaluated in refer-

ence to David and the worship of Yahweh; in 1 and 2 Kings the rulers of both kingdoms are evaluated in reference to the Mosiac Law. (For more on the purpose and emphases of 1 and 2 Chron. see the *Introduction* to 1 Chron.)

**Historical Background.** When Solomon came to the throne in 971 B.C. Israel had no strong military threat among its neighbors; Egypt and Assyria were both weak. Assyria grew stronger, however, and in 722 B.C. attacked and took Samaria, the capital of the Northern Kingdom of Israel. Assyria attacked Judah some time later and though it was able to take several southern cities, Jerusalem, the capital of the Southern Kingdom of Judah, did not fall. Assyria exerted control over Egypt too. In 609 B.C. Pharaoh Neco took his army north of Israel to Haran in Aram to assist Assyria in its threat from the Neo-Babylonian Empire. In 605 Babylon, under Nebuchadnezzar, defeated Egypt at Carchemish, moved south into Judah, and after three attacks (in 605, 597, and 586) completely destroyed Jerusalem, carrying all but the poorest Jews into captivity in 586 B.C.

**Chronology.** The major problem facing students of 1 and 2 Kings is the chronology of the rulers, especially those of Judah. In some cases the answer can be found in a coregency or vice-regency, periods during which two kings ruled. In other cases the problem can be solved after one establishes when a king began counting the years of his reign. Judah and Israel used two different methods to determine when a king's reign began, and each nation switched methods at least once during the period of history recorded in 1 and 2 Kings.

A third factor complicates the chronological problems further. Judah and Israel began their calendar years at different times. Space prohibits further explanation of the chronological problems in 1 and 2 Kings. (Some of the books listed in the *Bibliography* give more information.) Though exact dates are a problem, several different chronologies, worked out by conservative scholars, harmonize the narratives. In most cases these systems vary from each other by only one or two years.

The major dates for this period are as

follows: 931 B.C.—the division of the kingdom; 722 B.C.—the fall of Israel; 586 B.C.—the fall of Judah. (See the chart "An Overview of Old Testament History," p. 13. Also see the chart "Kings of Judah and Israel and the Preexilic Prophets," near 1 Kings 12:25.)

**Theology.** The Books of 1 and 2 Kings, like the other historical books of the Old Testament, were written not simply to record facts of historical significance, but to reveal and preserve spiritual lessons which have timeless value. This is evident in 1 and 2 Kings, for example, in the writer's interest in the prophets as well as the kings. God revealed Himself and His message by communicating to and through His servants the prophets. God also revealed Himself through events of history. People's decisions, made in faith and obedience or in unbelief and disobedience, led to inevitable consequences.

God intended that the nation Israel demonstrate to all people how glorious it can be to live under the government of God (Ex. 19:4-6). God chose Abraham to be the father of a family that would become a nation and be a blessing to the whole world (Gen. 12:1-3). This blessing would come to all mankind as Israel would allow the light of God's presence to dwell within her, transform her, and shine out from her as a light to the nations (Isa. 42:6).

The covenant God made with Abraham (Gen. 15:12-21) guaranteed him a land, descendants, and blessing. The promises of this covenant were repeated to his descendants at various times, but on certain significant occasions God amplified and elaborated one of these promises. As Israel prepared to enter the Promised Land God repeated His promise that the Israelites would possess a perpetual lease on the land from God, but that they would occupy this territory to the extent that they were faithful to God, its Owner (Deut. 28–30). In David's day God promised that Abraham's seed who descended through David would be blessed in a special way (2 Sam. 7:11-16). In particular, the king of the Israelites would always be one of one of David's descendants (2 Sam. 7:16). Later God promised Jeremiah that He would bless Israel in a specific way through the New Covenant (Jer. 31:31-34).

The Books of 1 and 2 Kings show that God is faithful to His promised word regarding Israel. Within this large purpose the writer showed how certain human activities affected God's dealings with His people and also how God accomplished His purposes in spite of the opposition of His enemies and the failures of His people.

Whereas Israel in 1 and 2 Kings functioned as a monarchy, it was more a theocracy. The kings of Israel were vice-regents under Yahweh, Israel's true Sovereign. To the extent that Israel's earthly kings faithfully led the nation under her heavenly King's direction, as revealed by God through the Mosaic Law and the prophets, the nation prospered as God intended. But when the earthly kings proved unfaithful, Israel inevitably failed to experience all God's good pleasure for her.

So 1 and 2 Kings reveal God's faithfulness to His Word, His ultimate sovereignty over His own and all other peoples, and His patience. These books also testify to the unbelief and disobedience of all people, even the beneficiaries of God's election and blessing. These books demonstrate that God has not cast off His disobedient people Israel whom He chose to enjoy a privileged relationship with Himself.

# OUTLINE

# COMMENTARY

## I. The Reign of Solomon (chaps. 1–11)

First Kings continues the history of Israel's monarchy where 2 Samuel ends.

### A. The preparations for a new king (1:1–2:12)

This section records the final events of David's rule that led to Solomon's becoming the next king.

1. DAVID'S OLD AGE (1:1-4)

**1:1-2. King David** died at or near the age of 70 (2 Sam. 5:4). From what is said of him in 1 Kings 1:1-4 it is obvious that he was in poor health and quite weak shortly before he died. His inability to retain body heat led his attendants to search for a way to keep David **warm.** Their decision to provide **a young** woman who could keep him warm by lying next to him in bed and also serve as his nurse was in harmony with medical customs of that day. Josephus (A.D. 37–ca. 100), a Jewish historian, and Galen (ca. A.D. 130–200), a Greek physician, refer to this therapeutic practice which continued into the Middle Ages.

The **covers** that David's **servants** placed **over him** to keep him warm were like sheets and blankets, not articles of clothing. That a **virgin** should be sought was reasonable since an unmarried young woman would likely be in vigorous health, free from domestic responsibilities, and able to wait on David continually as his needs might demand.

**1:3.** Since David was **the king** a woman who combined beauty with the other qualities needed in a nurse was sought. An attractive young woman was **found** in the town of Shunem, seven miles northwest of Nazareth, near the foot of Mount Tabor in the tribal territory of Issachar. Abishag's beauty is attested to by the attraction of Adonijah, David's son, to her (2:17). And if Abishag were the Shulammite (an alternate spelling of **Shunammite**) who captivated Solomon's heart (Song 6:13) her beauty apparently attracted many men. However, there is no definite way to link **Abishag** with the Shulammite of the Song of Songs.

**1:4.** The fact that David **had no intimate** (i.e., sexual) **relations with** his nurse Abishag shows that this was not her function and that David was very weak. The king's inability to withstand sexual temptation while in good health resulted in his committing adultery with Bathsheba. He also had had a harem. But now, due to poor health and advanced age, his vigor was gone.

Another reason Abishag is introduced by name in the narrative (v. 3) is because she figured significantly in Adonijah's attempt to capture the throne.

## 2. ADONIJAH'S PLOT (1:5-53)

David's domestic troubles followed him to his deathbed. In his hour of weakness another of his sons (Absalom; cf. 2 Sam. 15) rose up to snatch the kingdom from his grasp.

### a. Adonijah's preparations (1:5-10)

**1:5-6.** **Adonijah** was the fourth son of David (2 Sam. 3:4) and probably the eldest of his brothers living at that time (see the chart "David's Family," near 2 Sam. 3:2-5). The description of Adonijah's decision to seek the throne strongly suggests a selfish motive: he **put himself forward and said** determinedly, **I will be king.**

Adonijah's preparation of **chariots** . . . **horses,** and **50 men to run ahead of him** was probably intended to give him prestige in the people's eyes. It also helped ready his coup d'etat against his father.

The author threw more light on Adonijah by recording that he was a spoiled, undisciplined young man who had apparently received much admiration for his good looks (**he was . . . very handsome)** more than for the quality of his character. Evidently Adonijah expected that his plot would succeed more because he was a popluar figure than because he was a capable person championing a worthy cause.

**1:7.** Among David's staff **Joab** and **Abiathar** forsook the king and sided with Adonijah. Joab was David's nephew, a **son of** his half sister, **Zeruiah** (1 Chron. 2:16). (See the chart "David's Family," near 2 Sam. 3:2-5.) He had served the king faithfully for many years—since David was pursued by Saul. David made Joab the commander-in-chief of his army, a position in which Joab distinguished himself as a brave warrior and intelligent strategist. However, Joab was brutal and used his position to murder at least two important men: Abner (2 Sam. 3:22-30), Saul's commander-in-chief, and Amasa (2 Sam. 20:8-10), who had slain Joab's brother fairly in battle. Joab had not remained completely loyal to David. When Absalom led a coup against David, Joab executed Absalom contrary to the king's orders (2 Sam. 18:5-15).

Abiathar **the priest** had joined David after Saul had Doeg kill all the other priests at Nob (1 Sam. 22:18-20). Because of his commitment to David, Abiathar became an adviser and friend of the king. This incident with Adonijah was Abiathar's first recorded act of disloyalty.

**1:8.** **Zadok the priest** had joined David after Saul was killed in battle (1 Chron. 12:28). He had supported David and had served as his spy during Absalom's rebellion. **Benaiah** (cf. 1 Kings 1:10) was one of David's mightiest warriors and commanders (2 Sam. 8:18; 20:23; 23:20-23). **Nathan the prophet** (cf. 1 Kings 1:10) brought the word of the Lord to the king on at least two occasions (2 Sam. 7:4-17; 12:1-14). If **Shimei** is the same man who cursed David (2 Sam. 16:5-13) and was later forgiven by David (2 Sam. 19:16-23), then Shimei's loyalty now to the king is understandable. However, he may have had his own sinister plot in mind (cf. comments on 1 Kings 2:36-38). Or this may have been another Shimei.

**1:9-10.** **Adonijah** held a feast for his supporters and tried to persuade others to join his cause. His sacrifice was evidently a feast rather than a religious offering. **The Stone of Zoheleth** has been identified on the steep rocky corner that overlooks the plain where the Valley of Hinnom joins the Kidron Valley just south of Mount Zion where the City of David was situated. **En Rogel** is one of the two main springs in the Kidron Valley that supplied water for Jerusalem (see the map "Jerusalem in the Time of the Kings," near 9:15).

Adonijah **invited** to his feast **all** the important people in the government who were not firmly allied with his father **or his brother Solomon,** who was David's and God's chosen prince. Adonijah's actions have been duplicated by aspiring politicians for centuries. In that culture, if Nathan and David's other supporters had been invited and eaten with Adonijah, he would have been bound to protect them, having extended them the fellowship of such a meal.

*b. Nathan's plan (1:11-14)*

**1:11-12.** The fact that **Nathan** took the initiative in countering Adonijah's rebellion suggests that God may have moved His prophet to this action as He had done previously (2 Sam. 12:1). **Bathsheba** enjoyed David's favor from the first moment he saw her on to the end of his life. **Adonijah** had **become king** in the sense that for all practical purposes he was the popular choice, though he had not been anointed or crowned. Nathan's choice of words seems designed to shock Bathsheba into realizing the seriousness of the situation. Apparently David was ignorant of the plot until now (cf. 1 Kings 1:18). Nathan was probably not overstating the danger to Bathsheba and **Solomon** by telling her that she needed to take steps to **save** her **own life and** Solomon's. Adonijah's not inviting them to share food at his feast freed him from the duty of an oriental host to protect their lives.

**1:13-14.** David's promise to Bathsheba that he would make **Solomon** . . .

king after him, to which Nathan referred, is not recorded in Scripture. But in view of what Nathan told Bathsheba to say here, obviously David had made such a promise (cf. 1 Chron. 22:8-10).

Nathan made sure that David's promise would be heard by two witnesses, Bathsheba and himself. Under Mosaic Law at least two witnesses were required to make a charge stick. If **David** was becoming forgetful in his old age a second witness (in this case Nathan) would also confirm that **the king** had indeed made such a pledge.

*c. Bathsheba's report (1:15-21)*

**1:15-16.** Evidently David was confined to his bed (vv. 15, 47). **Bathsheba** treated David like **the king** he was by bowing and kneeling **before** him. She intended to call on him to act as he must in view of the situation. David invited her to explain what she wanted.

**1:17-21.** Bathsheba stated the facts about Adonijah's uprising without exaggeration or embellishment. She called on David to announce publicly who his successor would be by appealing to his sense of duty (v. 20), and his love for her and **Solomon** (v. 21). She pointed out that she and **Solomon** would **be treated as** political **criminals** by **Adonijah.** Customarily in the ancient Near East a new monarch would purge his political enemies when he came to power, as Solomon did later (2:13-46).

*d. Nathan's report (1:22-27)*

**1:22-26.** **Nathan** sought an audience with **the king** while Bathsheba was talking with David. He was admitted and reported the same facts Bathsheba had announced, with a bit more detail as would have been appropriate for a man in his position. Nathan's statement that Adonijah's feast was taking place at that very moment would have encouraged David to act at once. Nathan knew David had promised Bathsheba that Solomon would succeed him (v. 13), but apparently the prophet had learned this from others, not from David.

**1:27.** Rather than reminding David of his promise regarding Solomon which might have annoyed **the king** who may not have wanted many people to know of his choice, Nathan diplomatically asked David if he had planned the present circumstances. The prophet left the initiative with David rather than putting him on the defensive.

### e. David's promise (1:28-31)

**1:28.** **Bathsheba** had evidently left the room when Nathan entered as was customary in that culture. **David** called her to return, which she did.

**1:29-30.** **The king** invoked the sacred name of Yahweh, the living God **who** had **delivered** him from **every** one of his troubles. **As surely as the** LORD **lives** meant that David's intended action was as certain to take place as God's very existence. Those words occur frequently in the Old Testament including 14 times in 1 and 2 Kings (1 Kings 1:29; 2:24; 17:1, 12; 18:10, 15; 22:14; 2 Kings 2:2, 4, 6; 3:14; 4:30; 5:16, 20). David could not more forcefully have guaranteed that he would indeed do what he now said he would do. The God who had delivered David would now, through David, "deliver" Bathsheba and her son. David repeated his promise that **Solomon,** Bathsheba's son, would succeed him as **king** and **sit on** the **throne** that God had promised to bless.

**1:31.** With gratitude for his granting her request **Bathsheba bowed** before her **king.** The expression, **May my lord** the **king . . . live forever** (cf. v. 34), is a common expression found often in Scripture signifying a desire that God would bless a monarch by granting him long life. It is a complimentary wish; God had promised to bless the righteous with length of days. These words therefore implied that the king had acted righteously and was worthy of God's blessing.

### f. David's instructions (1:32-37)

**1:32.** David's plans skillfully defused the rebellion which was building just south of Jerusalem at the spring of En Rogel (cf. v. 9). **Zadok . . . Nathan,** and **Benaiah** were the ranking priest, prophet, and soldier respectively (cf. v. 8), who had remained unallied with Adonijah. Their leadership in the events to follow would demonstrate to the general population that they were acting as the king's representatives.

**1:33. Your lord's servants** were the Kerethites and the Pelethites (v. 38; cf. 2 Sam. 8:18), David's special military guards under Benaiah (2 Sam. 23:22-23).

They were responsible to protect **the king,** his family, and his city. David told them to place **Solomon** on a **mule** and lead **him** through Jerusalem to the place of anointing. Kings rode on mules in the ancient Near East, symbolizing their role as the people's servants. The people would understand that Solomon's riding on a mule implied his kingship. The mule specified by David was to be his **own** personal animal. Perhaps the people would have recognized that mule by its trappings and concluded that David had given Solomon permission to ride it as his designated successor.

The officials were to lead Solomon **down** to the spring of **Gihon.** Two springs provided most of the water for Jerusalem: the En Rogel spring southeast of Jerusalem not far from the city wall where Adonijah was feasting his guests (cf. v. 9), and the Gihon spring about one-half mile north and directly east of Jerusalem also outside the city wall. On that day two processions, one by rebels and one by the king's men, were going to two neighboring springs.

**1:34-35.** At the Gihon spring both **Zadok the priest and Nathan the prophet** were to **anoint** Solomon. There was no prophet in Adonijah's camp. Nathan's presence symbolized the divine choice of Solomon as **king** in a way that Zadok's presence alone could not. Blowing **the trumpet** signaled the official nature of the anointing. Every king of Israel was anointed. The ceremony symbolized the coming of the Spirit of God on His chosen leader through pouring oil on his head.

The **shout, Long live King Solomon!** expressed the people's desire and prayer that the new king's reign would be long and prosperous. The leaders had been instructed to return **up** Mount Zion to the city of David and place Solomon **on** David's **throne.** This would be the ultimate proof of his election. Solomon was to commence his rule at that moment; the official seating on the throne was to be perceived not as simply a symbolic act. David clearly explained that he himself by the authority of his kingly office had **appointed** Solomon **ruler over Israel and Judah** effective immediately. Israel and Judah were distinguished (cf. 4:20, 25) because 1 Kings was written after the kingdom was divided in 931 B.C. and/or because a rift was already evident between the northern and southern parts of the kingdom (cf. 2 Sam. 19:41–20:2).

**1:36-37.** As military commander and the man responsible to execute these orders **Benaiah** responded to his commander in chief. His response, **Amen! May the LORD . . . so declare it,** means, "May what the king has said be what Yahweh has declared." Benaiah then requested that **God** would **be with Solomon** and bless his reign **even** more than He had blessed David's reign.

### g. Solomon's anointing (1:38-40)

**1:38-40. The Kerethites and the Pelethites** were the royal bodyguard troops under Benaiah's personal, veteran command (cf. the "lord's [David's] servants," v. 33; 2 Sam. 8:18). **Gihon,** located east of the City of David in the Valley of Kidron just outside the city wall, was the main source of water for Jerusalem at this time (cf. comments on "Gihon," 1 Kings 1:33). **Zadok . . . took the horn** (perhaps an animal's horn used as a container) **of oil** that was used to anoint kings and priests **from the sacred tent** in Jerusalem and carried it to Gihon. Perhaps this tent, set up by David (1 Chron. 15:1), was similar to the Mosaic tabernacle. The olive oil symbolized the presence and power of God. A great throng of **people** followed the procession and witnessed the anointing. This was a glorious day in the history of Israel and the people celebrated enthusiastically, so much **so that the ground shook.**

### h. The report of Solomon's anointing (1:41-48)

**1:41-48.** Adonijah's party was feasting only a half mile south of Gihon. They **heard** the celebration easily. But it was the blowing **of the trumpet,** the sign that an official function was taking place, that roused **Joab** to inquire about **all the noise in the city.**

Abiathar's son **Jonathan** had been in the city, and arriving at the feast just then, reported what was going on. Adonijah's optimism and complete ignorance of the plot to undercut his rebellion can be seen in his greeting of **Jonathan** (v. 42). Along with relaying the other events already recorded (vv. 43-46) Jonathan added that **the royal officials** had gone **to congratulate . . . David** and

wish God's blessing on **Solomon** (v. 47). Evidently David was confined to **his bed** and did not personally witness the anointing of Solomon.

Jonathan had apparently penetrated the palace or at least obtained information from within it since he reported to Adonijah what David had said in his bedroom (v. 48). Characteristically David praised **God** for one more blessing: allowing him to live long enough to **see** his **successor on** his **throne.**

### i. Adonijah's fear (1:49-53)

**1:49-51.** Adonijah's **guests** scattered as far from the traitor and as fast as they could so they would not be linked with him and dealt with as they felt surely he would be. In the ancient Near East traitors could expect to be purged by a new king. Terror at this prospect drove **Adonijah** to the tabernacle where he claimed refuge by grasping **the horns** on **the** brazen **altar** in the tabernacle courtyard. Such a practice was common in Israel and in other neighboring nations (cf., e.g., Ex. 21:13-14). The symbolism of taking hold of the altar's horns seems to have meant that as God had been gracious to man, as seen in accepting man's offerings to atone for his sins, so one man should be gracious to another man who had offended him.

**1:52-53. Solomon** could have had Adonijah removed from the tabernacle and executed, but instead showed mercy. Solomon followed this pattern of graciousness throughout his reign. The new **king** simply asked for a promise from his half brother that he would not rebel again but would show **himself to be a worthy,** loyal subject. **Adonijah** promised and Solomon sent him **home.** But soon Adonijah conspired again and lost his life as a result (2:13-25).

### 3. DAVID'S CHARGE TO SOLOMON (2:1-9)

The amount of time that elapsed between the events of chapter 1 and this incident is not revealed, but in light of David's poor health and old age (1:1-4, 15, 47) his charge probably was given shortly after Solomon's anointing.

### a. Solomon's relationship to God (2:1-4)

**2:1-4.** The first part of David's **charge** to **his son** concerned what was of primary importance.

**To go the way of all the earth** is a picturesque description of death. **David** was a realist; he knew he would soon **die** so he made plans which included counseling his successor. His charge is reminiscent of Moses' charge to Joshua (Deut. 31:23).

Solomon was encouraged to **be strong** to keep the Word of the Lord. He should **show** himself to be **a man** by being brave to stand for the right and against the wrong. He should **observe what the LORD . . . requires** in the sense of obeying Yahweh. What the Lord requires is to **walk in His ways,** namely, to **keep His decrees** (ordinances), **commands . . . laws, and requirements** (testimonies). These four words (decrees, commands, laws, requirements) refer to the different kinds of precepts in the Mosaic **Law.** Obedience to the propositional revelation of God would guarantee success, David said. God's blessing depended on His people's obedience to the Law **of Moses.** Solomon's personal obedience would result in God's fulfilling **His promise** that David's **descendants** would forever occupy **the throne of Israel** (2 Sam. 7:12-16).

*b. Solomon's dealings with men (2:5-9)*

**2:5-6.** David's instruction to put **Joab** to death did not manifest a vindictive spirit or a cowardly refusal to execute his commander himself. Joab had murdered **two commanders . . . Abner** and **Amasa** (cf. comments on 1:7). David described the **blood** of these two innocent victims as permanently staining Joab's **belt** and **sandals;** the blood clung to him to demonstrate his guilt. In mercy David had not executed the punishment that Joab's actions deserved, probably because Joab had shown David much loyalty and had served him well. But justice had to be done and Solomon had to do it. Joab had been living on borrowed time; soon he had to pay for his crimes.

**2:7. Barzillai of Gilead** (east of the Jordan River) had sustained David and his men **when** they were fleeing **from . . . Absalom** (2 Sam. 19:31-39). David charged Solomon to sustain Barzillai's **sons** at his **table** as Barzillai and his sons had provided sustenance for David in the wilderness. David wanted Barzillai's sons to reap what their father had sown.

**2:8-9. Shimei** a **Benjamite** had not only cursed David but, more seriously, had **threatened** David's life (2 Sam. 16:11). Evidently David had reason to believe that Shimei would again strike at his life. Solomon extended grace to Shimei, but later the Benjamite proved faithless and, like Adonijah, sealed his own doom (1 Kings 2:36-46).

### 4. DAVID'S DEATH (2:10-12)

**2:10.** The picturesque phrase **rested with his fathers** beautifully describes David's death and suggests that his activity did not cease forever. Indeed, the bodies of all believers who die simply "rest" until they are resurrected to live with God and serve Him eternally. **The City of David** (cf. 3:1; 8:1; 9:24; 11:27; 15:8, 24; 22:50) is Jerusalem which **David** captured from the Jebusites and made his capital. In his day Jerusalem was quite small and occupied a peninsula of high ground bounded on the east, south, and west by valleys. Solomon enlarged the city to the north later and other kings expanded it even farther.

**2:11-12.** David **reigned 40 years over Israel** (1011–971 B.C.). For **7 years** his capital was **Hebron** until he moved to **Jerusalem** from which he ruled for 33 years. He was about 70 years old when he died (2 Sam. 5:4). David is remarkable in many respects: he was a warrior, poet, musician, military genius, administrator, and man of God. He experienced outstanding success and crushing failure. He extended the borders and influence of his nation greatly.

He was greatly loved and greatly hated during his lifetime. But perhaps his most significant characteristic was his heart for God. His son **Solomon** succeeded him and enjoyed a reign of peace.

### B. The earlier years of Solomon's reign (2:13–4:34)

The wisdom for which Solomon became famous can be seen clearly in this section of Scripture. Solomon's wise decisions at the beginning of his reign resulted in 40 years (971–931) of peace and prosperity for Israel.

### 1. SOLOMON'S PURGES (2:13-46)

To lay a firm foundation for his reign Solomon had to deal with his and his father's enemies.

### a. Adonijah's execution (2:13-25)

**2:13-14.** **Adonijah** had not abandoned his hope of becoming king (cf. 1:5). But to take the throne he would have to dispose of Solomon. The plot that he conceived was clever. He began his maneuvering by approaching **Bathsheba,** the queen **mother** (but not his own mother, who was **Haggith**; cf. 2 Sam. 3:4), through whom he hoped to receive a favorable decision from Solomon. In view of Adonijah's previous plotting **Bathsheba** initially expressed caution. But he convinced her that his intentions were peaceful; superficially they were, but ultimately they were not. He persuaded Bathsheba to listen to what he had **to say.**

**2:15-16.** Adonijah may have honestly believed that **all Israel looked to** him **as their king,** but this hardly seems to have been the case; Adonijah's wishful dreaming had convinced him of this. The throne had never been his. His saying that the present state of events had **come . . . from the LORD** seems to have been a pious ploy designed to convince Bathsheba that he had accepted Solomon's anointing as God's will and had submitted to it. There is no evidence that Adonijah was ever sincerely interested in what the Lord wanted. But there is much evidence that he was interested in what *Adonijah* wanted! His pious profession along with his apparent acquiescence to Solomon's anointing persuaded Bathsheba that Adonijah had no lingering aspirations to become king. So she gave him permission to proceed with his proposal.

**2:17-18.** Bathsheba apparently interpreted Adonijah's request for **Abishag** (cf. 1:3-4) as simply the desire of a handsome young man for the hand of a beautiful young woman. Bathsheba's excitement for this seemingly innocent love affair moved her to agree to present his request to **the king.** She probably relished the thought of having a part as a matchmaker.

**2:19-21.** **Solomon** respectfully greeted his mother by standing **up to meet her** and bowing **to her** when she entered the **throne** room. He gave her the seat of honor **at his right hand** so she could converse comfortably with him. She had only **one small request;** at least she perceived it as small. Assuming it was a small request, Solo-

mon agreed to grant it.

**2:22-25.** However, he knew immediately that her proposal had far-reaching consequences that would threaten his throne. So he refused to agree to it. **Abishag** had become a member of King David's harem. Even though David never had sexual relations with her, Abishag's presence in the harem entitled her to part of David's inheritance. In the people's eyes she had been David's concubine. "Among the Israelites, just as with the ancient Persians (Herod. iii. 68), taking possession of the harem of a deceased king was equivalent to an establishment of the claim to the throne" (C.F. Keil, "The Books of the Kings," in *Commentary on the Old Testament in Ten Volumes,* 3:32).

Bathsheba may have thought that because Abishag was not really one of David's concubines this would be no problem. But **Solomon** in his wisdom realized that the people would regard Abishag as a concubine and therefore would interpret Adonijah's marriage to her as a claim to the throne. Also since **Adonijah** was **older** (v. 22) than Solomon (cf. 2 Sam. 3:4 with 2 Sam. 5:13-14) the people would assume that he had more right to be **king** than **Solomon.** The people generally did not recognize that God's purposes in election frequently violated the natural order of primogeniture. (For example, God chose the younger brother in His selection of Abraham, Isaac, Jacob, Joseph, and many others.) Solomon's perception of Adonijah's wicked intent led him to reply with much indignation to **his mother.** He had not executed his brother for his attempted coup before David died; **Solomon** had shown him mercy (1 Kings 1:52-53). But **Adonijah** was still plotting against the Lord and His anointed. Solomon was not only just in having **Adonijah . . . put to death,** but he also acted as a good steward of the kingdom that had been committed to him by God (**as He promised**). (On the words **As surely as the LORD lives** see comments on 1:29.) **Benaiah,** the captain of the guard, carried out the king's order immediately.

### b. Abiathar's dismissal (2:26-27)

**2:26-27.** **Abiathar, the priest** who sided with Adonijah, could have been justly executed by Solomon for conspiracy. But because Abiathar was a priest of Yahweh who had **carried the ark** (served as high priest) during David's lifetime and because he had faithfully **shared all** of David's **hardships,** Solomon merely **removed** him from his office and restricted him to his hometown of **Anathoth** three miles northeast of Jerusalem. (Centuries later Jeremiah was born in Anathoth, Jer. 1:1.)

The author of 1 and 2 Kings noted that this act of Solomon fulfilled God's prophecy that Eli's line of priests, of which **Abiathar** was a member (see the chart "The Ancestry of Zadok and Abiathar," near 2 Sam. 8:15-18), would be cut off (1 Sam. 2:30-35). In this brief statement one of the 1 and 2 Kings' author's purposes can be seen clearly: to demonstrate the faithfulness of God to His **Word.**

*c. Joab's execution (2:28-35)*

**2:28-30. The news** that **reached Joab** was evidently what had befallen **Adonijah** and Abiathar (vv. 23-27), his fellow conspirators. Joab had been head of the army under David (2 Sam. 8:16). Now Joab, like Adonijah, sought the protection **of the horns of the** brazen **altar** in the courtyard of **the tent** (tabernacle) in Jerusalem (cf. 1 Kings 1:50). This was a place of refuge for those whose lives were in danger. The Mosaic Law provided refuge there for all but murderers (Ex. 21:13-14).

Why did Joab seek refuge there since he was a murderer? Perhaps he thought that Solomon was after him only because of his part in Adonijah's attempted coup and that **the king** did not know of or care about his murdering Abner and Amasa. But it was for all these sins that **Solomon** sought Joab. Solomon probably did not want to defile the tabernacle by shedding human blood there so he told Benaiah to order **Joab** to **come out.** But the commander refused. Joab would not let go of the altar's horns. **Solomon ordered** that he be treated like the murderer he was and struck **down** on the spot.

**2:31-33.** For his murders Joab was executed without mercy. As long as **Joab** remained alive, David's **house** (dynasty) bore some responsibility for Joab's action since he had murdered **Abner** and **Amasa** (cf. 2 Sam. 3:22-30; 20:8-10) in connection with his official duties. Solo-

mon (like David before him, 1 Kings 2:5-6) wanted to remove any obstacle to God's blessing on his reign and to identify Joab's **guilt** with **his** own **house** alone.

**2:34-35. Benaiah,** head of the royal bodyguard, returned to the tabernacle and carried out the king's order. **Joab** did not die in total disgrace, however, for **he was buried on his own land in the desert.** This was possibly the wilderness of Judea east of Bethlehem. To be buried in one's own land was an honor bestowed on Joab for his long service to David.

Solomon replaced Joab with **Benaiah,** promoting him to head of **the army.** **Zadok the priest** filled the place left by **Abiathar** (cf. v. 27).

*d. Shimei's execution (2:36-46)*

**2:36-38. Shimei** must have been a dangerous man. He was treated as such by both David and Solomon, though what is recorded of him here seems on the surface to be of minor importance. When David fled Jerusalem, being pursued by Absalom, Shimei verbally and physically attacked David and his officials. David's men recognized the danger Shimei posed for the king and asked David's permission to kill him then and there (2 Sam. 16:5-13).

But David did not allow this. He did not pardon Shimei's traitorous actions, but postponed Shimei's execution probably because of all that he was facing at the moment in view of Absalom's rebellion. Shimei was from the same clan as Saul's family (2 Sam. 16:5).

Solomon summoned **Shimei** and passed judgment on him: he was restricted to living **in Jerusalem**; the city would be his prison. In particular Shimei was not to **cross the Kidron Valley** just east of Jerusalem. If Shimei crossed the Kidron he would probably head home to stir up insurrection among the Benjamites. Solomon told Shimei that he would be executed if he disobeyed Solomon's orders. **Shimei** understood his sentence, agreed to abide by it, and did so **for a long time** (three years, 1 Kings 2:39).

**2:39-40.** After **three years . . . two of Shimei's slaves ran off** to **Gath** in Philistia, about 30 miles southwest of Jerusalem. Shimei's decision to leave Jerusalem to pursue **his slaves** revealed his low view of Solomon's authority.

**2:41-46.** **Solomon** then recognized that Shimei's attitude had not changed. Because Shimei had violated the terms of his sentence Solomon had every right to execute the punishment he had graciously postponed. Like Adonijah, **Shimei** had not changed. Solomon reviewed the terms of Shimei's sentence with him to justify his action (vv. 42-43). Solomon's chief concern was the security of **David's throne** (v. 45); this apparently had been David's concern too with respect to Shimei.

As David had commanded (vv. 8-9), **Solomon** put **Shimei** to death. But Solomon's prior mercy in dealing with Shimei (vv. 36-37) absolved **the king** from any charge of being vindictive or unfair.

In all Solomon's dealings with his political enemies—men who conspired against the will of God during David's reign—the young king's mercy and wisdom stand out. Because of his wise handling of these threats to the throne **the kingdom was** then **firmly established in Solomon's hands.**

2. SOLOMON'S PERSONAL WISDOM (CHAP. 3)

The wisdom of Solomon, already evident in the record of his dealings with his political enemies, is reeemphasized in chapter 3.

*a. Solomon's attitudes (3:1-3)*

The king's attitudes toward his office and his God are set forth and account for God's blessing.

**3:1.** This note by the author may be out of chronological sequence with the other events of Solomon's life. It is added here as an important historical fact and a portent of things to come. **Solomon made** a peace treaty **with Pharaoh king of Egypt** (probably Siamon of the 21st dynasty) and sealed it by marrying **his daughter.** The motivation for this marriage was obviously political. Solomon was not as careful about marrying non-Israelites as he should have been. But this union did result in peace with Israel's neighbor to the southwest who was weak during Solomon's reign. Solomon housed this bride in **Jerusalem.** After he **finished** several building projects including **his palace . . . the temple,** and other buildings (cf. 7:2-7), he prepared a special house (a palace) for her (cf. 7:8).

**3:2-3.** During the period of the Judges the Israelites adopted the Canaanite custom of offering sacrifices **at . . . high places.** These were on hilltops and other elevations. The pagan Canaanites felt that the closer they got to heaven the more likely was the possibility that their prayers and offerings would reach their gods. Offering sacrifices at places other than the tabernacle was prohibited in the Law (Lev. 17:3-4). Nevertheless this practice was commonly observed in Israel at this time, even by Solomon. The **temple** refers to Solomon's temple, not the tabernacle. In general, **Solomon** was careful to follow in David's godly footsteps thus demonstrating his love for Yahweh.

*b. Solomon's prayer for wisdom (3:4-15)*

**3:4-5.** The **most important** (popular or largest) **high place** was at **Gibeon** about five miles north of Jerusalem in the territory of Benjamin. There **Solomon** made a great sacrifice to the Lord. Evidently that very night **the LORD** revealed Himself to **the king. . . . in a dream.** Such revelations were not uncommon in ancient Israel (cf. Gen. 28:10-15; 37:5-7; etc.). **God** invited Solomon to **ask for whatever** he wanted. There seems to be a cause-and-effect relationship between Solomon's loving generosity in making his offering to the Lord and God's loving generosity in making him this offer.

**3:6-9.** **Solomon** recognized that God's **kindness** to **David** was due to his father's faithfulness to God which manifested itself in **righteous** actions and **upright** attitudes of **heart.** The king also acknowledged his own immaturity and need for God's wisdom. Solomon was about 20 years old when he took the throne.

In calling himself a **child,** he was admitting his inexperience (cf. 1 Chron. 22:5; 29:1). Solomon was concerned that he would be able to function effectively as the vice-regent of Yahweh. His responsibility as the leader and judge of God's **people** weighed heavily on him. So he requested a **discerning heart** (lit., "a hearing heart") tuned to the voice of **God** so he could lead Israel as God would want the nation to be led. He acknowledged his dependence on God by referring to himself as God's **servant** (1 Kings 3:7-8).

**3:10-14.** **Solomon** placed the good of God's people above his personal peace or prosperity and above any desire to become a powerful and popular king. His values were in the right place from God's perspective. Therefore **God** promised to give him what he requested. He would possess **a wise . . . heart** (v. 12) and be able to discern and render fair judgments (v. 11). Since Solomon sought what was most important God also promised to give him what was of secondary importance, **riches and honor,** to further enable him to govern God's people effectively. Solomon was to be the richest and most honored king of his day. **If** Solomon remained faithful to pursue the will of God, obeying the Law of Moses, God promised he would also live a **long life.**

**3:15.** As is often the case, a blessing from God drew the person blessed into a closer relationship with Himself. Inspired by this revelation **Solomon** turned from the high place and proceeded to the divinely appointed place of worship, the tabernacle. He did not enter the most holy place; only the high priest could enter there once a year (Lev. 16). But the king **stood before the ark of the LORD's covenant,** outside the tabernacle facing toward the ark. **Burnt offerings** expressed the complete dedication of oneself to God and **fellowship offerings** symbolized the fellowship people can enjoy with God and with others through God's grace. Solomon's **feast** expressed his joy and gratitude to the members of **his court.**

### c. Solomon's demonstration of wisdom (3:16-28)

This incident was undoubtedly included at this point to show that God had indeed given Solomon the wisdom He promised (cf. v. 12). Significantly the essence of wisdom is revealed in Solomon's handling of this difficult case. The king had insight into basic human nature (in this case, maternal instincts) that enabled him to understand why people behave as they do and how they will respond in various situations. The opposite of this ability is seen in simply judging people's superficial words and actions.

**3:16-23.** **Two prostitutes** living **in the same house** each had **a baby** three days apart. One of the boy babies **died** during **the night** and his mother exchanged the dead child for the living child. In the **morning** when the other woman discov-

ered that the **dead** son was not hers, the guilty mother refused to admit her wrongdoing. Unable to settle their dispute they appeared before **the king,** each one claiming **the living** infant was hers.

**3:24-27.** Solomon ordered that the baby be **cut . . . in two.** As he had anticipated, the child's mother, not wanting it killed, volunteered to let the other woman have the **baby,** rather than have it killed. When **the other** woman argued that the baby should be **cut . . . in two,** it was evident that she, having no compassion for the child, was not the **living** son's **mother.**

**3:28.** Solomon's **wisdom** in this case became known throughout his kingdom so that he was admired as a wise administrator of **justice.**

### 3. SOLOMON'S POLITICAL ADMINISTRATION (CHAP. 4)

This chapter reflects the wisdom God gave Solomon (cf. 3:12) as manifested in his administrative leadership of Israel.

### a. Solomon's chief officials (4:1-6)

**4:1-3.** Delegation of authority is a mark of wisdom. **Solomon** appointed 11 **chief officials** over his government. Three men are called priests: **Azariah** (v. 2), Zadok, and Abiathar (v. 4). Azariah, a **son of Zadok,** was Zadok's grandson (cf. 1 Chron. 6:8-9). "Son" often means descendant. **Elihoreph and Ahijah** were **secretaries** or scribes. This was an important office; the scribes prepared royal edicts affecting trade, commerce, and military alliances and kept official records. **Jehoshaphat** was the **recorder** who maintained the records of all important daily affairs in the kingdom. Jehoshaphat had also served in this capacity under David (2 Sam. 8:16; 20:24).

**4:4.** **Benaiah** was **commander in chief** of the whole army. **Zadok** and **Abiathar** had served as co-high **priests** under David (2 Sam. 15:35). But Abiathar had sided with Adonijah in the attempted coup so the priest was dismissed by Solomon (1 Kings 2:20-27). Zadok continued as high priest (2:35). Abiathar is listed here as one of Solomon's officials because even though he was fired from being high priest he retained the title and honor after he was deposed. Perhaps Azariah (4:2) and Zadok (v. 4) then

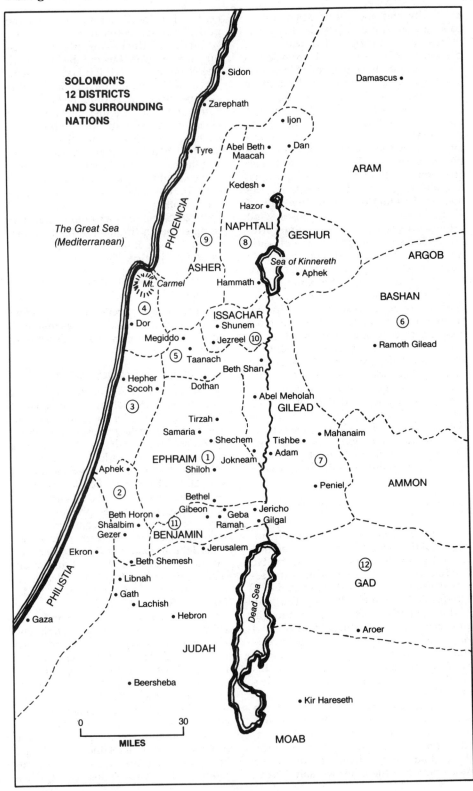

SOLOMON'S
12 DISTRICTS
AND SURROUNDING
NATIONS

• Sidon

Damascus •

• Zarephath

• Ijon

Abel Beth
Maacah

• Dan

• Tyre

ARAM

• Kedesh

PHOENICIA

Hazor •

*The Great Sea
(Mediterranean)*

NAPHTALI

GESHUR

⑨ ⑧

ARGOB

ASHER

*Sea of Kinnereth*

• Aphek

BASHAN

Mt. Carmel

Hammath •

④

ISSACHAR

⑥

• Dor

• Shunem

• Ramoth Gilead

Megiddo •

Jezreel • ⑩

⑤ • Taanach

• Hepher
Socoh •

• Dothan

Beth Shan

③

• Abel Meholah

GILEAD

• Tirzah

Samaria •

Mahanaim •

• Shechem

Tishbe •

• Adam

EPHRAIM ①

Jokneam

⑦

Aphek •

Shiloh •

② • Peniel

• Bethel

AMMON

Beth Horon •
Shaalbim •
Gezer •

Gibeon •
⑪

• Geba

• Jericho

Ramah •

Gilgal •

BENJAMIN

• Ekron

• Jerusalem

• Beth Shemesh

• Libnah

⑫

• Gath

GAD

• Gaza

• Lachish

• Hebron

Dead Sea

PHILISTIA

JUDAH

• Aroer

0        30

• Beersheba

• Kir Hareseth

MILES

MOAB

served together as Abiathar and Zadok had done previously.

**4:5-6.** Two men are listed as sons of **Nathan.** They may have been the sons of one man or the sons of different Nathans. **Azariah** (not the Azariah in v. 2) was in charge of the 12 district officers named in verses 8-19. **Zabud** was of the priestly line and served as the king's **personal adviser. Ahishar** was in charge of the palace, perhaps overseeing the servants and other workers there, and **Adoniram** (cf. 5:14) supervised the **forced labor,** non-Israelites living in Israel who were conscripted to work for **the king** (cf. 5:13-14; 9:15, 21; 2 Chron. 2:2; 8:8).

### b. Solomon's district governors (4:7-19)

**4:7-19. Solomon** made each of his **12 district governors** responsible to supply **provisions** for **the royal household** (and for his thousands of horses, v. 28), one governor for each **month.** These provisions were huge (cf. vv. 22-28). This work doubtless kept these men busy. Interestingly two of the governors were sons-in-law of Solomon (vv. 11, 15). All 12 of them are mentioned only here in the Bible except for **Ahimaaz,** who possibly was a son of Zadok the priest (cf. 2 Sam. 15:27). On the boundaries of the districts see the map "Solomon's 12 Districts and Surrounding Nations." Judah, not included, was perhaps exempted by Solomon from the levy requirement.

### c. Solomon's prosperity (4:20-28)

**4:20.** Solomon's kingdom was unified, secure, strong, and prosperous, with a large population. (On **Judah and Israel** see comments on 1:35.) The people became **as numerous as the sand on the seashore.**

The Israelites had enough to eat and drink, **and they were happy,** enjoying the basic comforts of life (cf. 4:25).

**4:21.** Solomon's domain stretched from **the** Euphrates **River** (cf. v. 24) on the east and north **to the land of the Philistines** on the west and **Egypt** to the southwest. This does not mean that the Abrahamic Covenant was fulfilled in Solomon's day (Gen. 15:18-20), for not all this territory was incorporated into the geographic boundaries of Israel; many of the subjected kingdoms retained their identity and territory but paid taxes (**tribute**) to Solomon. Israel's own geographic

limits were "from Dan to Beersheba" (1 Kings 4:25).

**4:22-25.** The ability of the nation to provide **Solomon's daily provisions** (cf. v. 7) testifies to its prosperity (vv. 22-23). Those provisions included **30 cors** (ca. 185 bushels; cf. NIV marg.) **of fine flour . . . 60 cors** (ca. 375 bushels; cf. NIV marg.) **of meal,** 30 **head** of **cattle . . . 100 sheep and goats,** and wild meat (**deer, gazelles, roebucks**) and **fowl.** These provisions were made possible by the great geographical extent of the kingdom— from the town of **Tiphsah** in the north (on the bank of the Euphrates) **to Gaza** in the south (cf. v. 21). **Each man** living **under his own vine and fig tree** (v. 25) is a figurative expression for peace and prosperity (cf. Micah 4:4; Zech. 3:10). The vine and fig tree were both symbols of the nation Israel and pictured the Promised Land's agricultural abundance.

**4:26-28.** Solomon's numerous **horses** (**12,000;** cf. 2 Chron. 1:14) and many chariots (1,400 according to 2 Chron. 1:14) were kept in several locations (called "chariot cities" in 2 Chron. 9:25; cf. 1 Kings 9:19). Though the Hebrew here has 40,000 **stalls** (cf. NIV marg.), this was probably the error of a copyist in transcribing the text which read **4,000,** the number in 2 Chronicles 9:25. The **horses** and chariots, used for national defense, served as a strong deterrent to potential foreign aggressors. **Barley and straw** for all Solomon's **horses** was supplied daily by **the district** governors.

### d. Solomon's skill (4:29-34)

**4:29.** This additional information about Solomon's wisdom demonstrates God's faithfulness in blessing the king as He had promised (cf. 3:12; 5:12). **Wisdom** is the ability to live life successfully. While Solomon possessed this ability he did not always apply it to his own life. Thus the wisest man who ever lived (i.e., with the greatest wisdom) did not live as wisely as many others who preceded and followed him. Having insight into life does not guarantee that one will choose to do what is right. Solomon's **great insight** was his ability to see the core of issues (e.g., 3:16-27). His **understanding** was vast; today he would be described as a man of encyclopedic knowledge.

**4:30-31.** His **wisdom** exceeded that **of all the men of the East** (cf. Job 1:3) and **all the wisdom of** people in **Egypt,** both areas known for their wisdom. He was also superior to other men renowned for their wisdom, including **Ethan the Ezrahite** (whose name appears in the title to Ps. 89, which suggests that he wrote that psalm), **Heman** (both Ethan and Heman were musicians; cf. 1 Chron. 15:19), **Calcol, and Darda.** The last three of these four were **the sons of Mahol,** but in 1 Chronicles 2:6 they, along with Ethan and Zimri, are said to be "sons [descendants] of Zerah." Apparently Mahol was the father of the four (Ethan, Heman, Calcol, and Darda) and Zimri (whose father was Zerah) was an ancestor several generations earlier (cf. comments on 1 Chron. 2:6).

**4:32-34.** Several hundred of Solomon's **3,000 proverbs** have been preserved in the Book of Proverbs as well as a few in Ecclesiastes. One of his **1,005** songs is the Song of Songs. Solomon's literary output was extremely prolific. He became an authority in botany and zoology too. The statement in verse 34 is a hyperbole (an overstatement to make a point); obviously not every nation on earth **sent** a representative to visit Solomon. The point is that many important visitors from faraway places visited Solomon who received them openly at his court. He was recognized as the wisest man of his day as God had promised he would be.

## C. Solomon's temple and palace (chaps. 5–8)

The author of 1 and 2 Kings was as interested in Solomon's temple as he was in Solomon himself. The provisions the king made for the spiritual strength of his nation were his outstanding contribution to Israel.

1. BUILDING PREPARATIONS (CHAP. 5)

*a. Solomon's request of Hiram (5:1-6)*

**5:1.** Tyre was an important port city on the Mediterranean Sea north of Israel. It was one of the chief cities of Phoenicia, one of Israel's friendly neighboring kingdoms. **Hiram, king of Tyre,** had been an ally and friend of King **David** and had supplied materials and laborers to build David's palace (2 Sam. 5:11). Hiram **sent his envoys to Solomon** to pay his respects to the new **king,** the son of his friend.

**5:2-5.** David had shared with his friend Hiram his desires to build a temple. But **because of the wars . . . David** had to fight, he was not allowed to construct it. **Now . . . peace** prevailed (cf. 4:24-25) and construction could begin. Solomon's assurance of peace would have encouraged Hiram to cooperate with his plans. His intention was **to build** the **temple** God Himself had approved.

**5:6.** Solomon called on Hiram to **give orders** that his subjects provide materials and craftsmen for the project. This may have been done with the authority of a superior but, more likely, Solomon made his words the request of a friend. **Cedars of Lebanon** grew profusely on the western slopes of the Lebanon Mountains east of Tyre, though few remain today. They were very old trees with hard, beautiful wood that was excellent for construction since it was not readily subject to decay or insect infestation. Solomon offered to supply workers to assist Hiram's men in felling the trees and to **pay** the Sidonian laborers **whatever** Hiram considered a fair wage. **The Sidonians** were indeed highly **skilled in felling timber;** doubtless Solomon's recognition of this ability impressed Hiram favorably. Sidon, another Phoenician city, was north of Tyre. Apparently Hiram hired workers from there.

*b. Hiram's treaty with Solomon (5:7-12)*

**5:7-9. Solomon's** suggestion met with an enthusiastic response. **Hiram** had regard for Yahweh, perhaps as a result of his contacts with **David.** Hiram perceived Solomon's wisdom at once. Apparently Solomon's total message to Hiram (vv. 3-6) was not recorded by the author of 1 and 2 Kings since Hiram agreed to provide **pine** as well as **cedar . . . logs.** Hiram suggested that the logs be transported to Solomon on **rafts** and offered to be responsible for this. However, Hiram wanted something in return: **food for** his **royal household.**

**5:10-12.** Solomon agreed to the arrangement and each year **gave** him **20,000 cors** (ca. 125,000 bushels; cf. NIV marg.) **of wheat** and **20,000 baths** (ca. 115,000 gallons) **of . . . olive oil.** Barley and wine were also included (2 Chron. 2:10). Obviously **Hiram** had a large household, which no doubt included his courtiers as well as family members. Apparently wheat and olive oil were not plentifully available in or near Tyre. Due to Solomon's wise initiative (**the LORD gave Solomon wisdom**; cf. 1 Kings 3:12, 28; 4:29) this **treaty** arrangement continued for many years and contributed to **peaceful relations between** the **two** kings.

### c. Solomon's conscription of laborers (5:13-18)

**5:13-18.** Solomon's conscription touched the lives of many non-Israelite (cf. 2 Chron. 8:7-8) males in Israel (183,300 are referred to here). The **king** drafted them for temporary government service which they worked into their schedules along with their private responsibilities. This method of conscripting **forced labor** eventually proved exceedingly distasteful to the Israelites, perhaps because of the way it was administered (cf. 1 Kings 12:18). The **3,300 foremen** plus an additional 550 (9:23) equal 3,850 (cf. the 3,600 foremen in 2 Chron. 2:18 plus 250 in 2 Chron. 8:10).

Working under **Adoniram** (cf. 1 Kings 4:6), the **carriers** transported materials from place to place and the **stonecutters** cut massive limestone blocks out of **the quarry** in **the hills** north of Jerusalem. **The men of Gebal** (modern Byblos, 13 miles north of Beirut, and 60 miles north of Tyre) made a significant contribution by preparing **timber and stone** along with Solomon's and Hiram's **craftsmen.**

### 2. TEMPLE CONSTRUCTION (CHAP. 6)

### a. The dimensions of the structure (6:1-10)

**6:1.** This verse is one of the most important in the Old Testament chronologically because it enables one to fix certain dates in Israel's history. The dates of Solomon's reign have been quite definitely established through references in ancient writings. They were 971–931 B.C. According to this verse, **in the fourth year of** his **reign** Solomon **began to build the temple.** That was in 966 B.C. The Exodus took place **480 years** earlier (1446 B.C.). The month **Ziv** is April-May (see the chart "Calendar in Israel," near Ex. 12:2). Interestingly the rebuilding of the temple, 430 years later under Zerubbabel (536), also began in the second month (Ezra 3:8).

**6:2-3.** A cubit was about 18 inches. So **the temple** was 90 feet **long,** 30 feet **wide,** and 45 feet **high.** It was not large; it had only 2,700 square feet of floor space. But it was strikingly beautiful in appearance because of its white limestone, cedar, and gold exterior. It had a large open front porch (**portico**) that added 15 more feet to its length.

**6:4-6.** The **narrow clerestory windows** were evidently high on the walls above the three stories of **side rooms** that surrounded **the temple** on two or three sides. The temple's **main hall and** the **inner sanctuary** were the holy place and the most holy place, respectively. The **structure around the building** was built against the outer sides and perhaps the back of the temple. This structure was probably about 25-30 feet high and was divided into three stories of side rooms each of which was 7½ feet high on the inside. These rooms were used by the priests for storage and service. The rooms were smallest (7½' wide) on the first floor which also contained hallways and stairways (cf. v. 8), larger on the second floor (9' wide) with some space also given to halls and stairs, and largest on the third floor (10½' wide). The **offset ledges** were apparently the supports for the upper floor which were built into the walls of this surrounding structure. The measurements are probably inside dimensions.

**6:7.** Apparently Solomon felt that the noise of construction was not appropriate for this **temple** in view of its purpose. So he had all the building parts cut and fitted **at the quarry** so that they could be assembled quietly on the **site.**

**6:8-10.** The temple faced east, but the entrance to the surrounding structure (v. 5) was **on the south. The side rooms** on all floors were connected by internal staircases and passageways. Though no **beams** of this side structure were "inserted into the temple walls" (v. 6), the inner walls of the side rooms **were attached to the temple by** cedar **beams** (v. 10).

### b. The Lord's promise to bless Solomon's obedience (6:11-13)

**6:11-13.** During the **temple** construction God reaffirmed **to Solomon . . . the promise** He had previously made **to David.** "The promise" given David to which God referred (v. 12) was that He would

PLAN OF SOLOMON'S TEMPLE

Note: The exact positions and size of the lampstands and golden tables for the bread of the Presence in the holy place are uncertain.

"establish the throne of [David's] kingdom forever" (2 Sam. 7:13). God would do this through Solomon if Solomon would **obey** Him (1 Kings 6:12). Later Solomon's disobedience resulted in God's removing part of the nation from the control of his son Rehoboam. God also promised that if Solomon obeyed the Lord his nation would enjoy God's fellowship and protection. Israel experienced this only partially because of Solomon's later apostasy.

### c. The completion of construction (6:14-36)

**6:14-18.** The entire **interior** of **the temple** was covered **with cedar boards** (on the **walls**) and with **pine** boards (on **the floor**), all overlaid with gold (vv. 22, 30). **The main hall** (cf. v. 5) in front of the **inner sanctuary** (**the most holy place**) was the holy place. The main hall was 60 feet long, twice the length of the most holy place. (See the sketch "Plan of Solomon's Temple.") The interior was decorated with carved **gourds** and **flowers**.

**6:19-22.** Inside the most holy place (a 30-foot cube, all **overlaid . . . with . . . gold**) was **the ark of the covenant. The altar of cedar** was the altar of incense located in the holy place. Solomon's incense altar was made of cedar and **overlaid with gold**; it was also called "the golden altar" (7:48). **Gold chains** were hung in the holy place across the doors that led into the most holy place. First Kings 6:22a recapitulates part of what was stated in verses 14-21. **The altar** (v. 22) is the incense altar located in the holy place.

**6:23-28.** The **cherubim** were sculptured angels, carved from **olive wood. Their wings** were **spread out** so that side by side they extended 30 feet (from the north to the south walls of the most holy place; cf. 2 Chron. 3:13). **Gold** covered **the cherubim** too.

**6:29-35. The walls of the inner and outer rooms,** the most holy place and the holy place, respectively, were decorated with **carved cherubim, palm trees, and open flowers.** The olive wood **doors** leading from the holy place were framed **with five-sided jambs** (frames). Some commentators believe they were sliding doors. The **doors** leading from the porch into **the main hall** (the holy place) were made of **pine** (v. 34). They hung on **four-sided jambs** and were bifold (**each hav-**ing **two leaves** hinged together that folded open against each other and **turned** on **sockets** or pivot points). All the doors were decorated like the walls (vv. 32, 35; cf. v. 29).

**6:36. The inner courtyard** was an open plaza surrounding the temple. There was also an outer courtyard not mentioned here (cf. 2 Chron. 4:9), which was somewhat lower in elevation than the inner courtyard (cf. "upper courtyard" in Jer. 36:10). This inner courtyard (also called the "courtyard of the priests," 2 Chron. 4:9) was separated from the outer (great) court by the wall described here. This wall consisted of **three courses** (rows) **of dressed** (cut) **stone** (limestone) **and one course** (row) of **cedar beams.** (The outer courtyard was also surrounded by a wall.) The size of the inner courtyard is not given, but if the dimensions of the courtyards of the temple are proportionate to those of the tabernacle courtyard, as the dimensions of the temple and tabernacle structures are, the inner courtyard was about 150 feet wide and 400 feet long.

### d. The time spent in construction (6:37-38)

**6:37-38. Seven years** were **spent** building **the temple,** from **the 4th year** of Solomon's reign (966 B.C.; cf. comments on 6:1) to his **11th year** (959 B.C.). More precisely, this was seven and one-half years. **Ziv** is April-May and **Bul,** the eighth month, is October-November.

### 3. SOLOMON'S PALACE (7:1-12)

**7:1-6.** The description of Solomon's **palace** in verses 1-12 raises a question as to whether one building or several were constructed. Probably one palace complex was built that contained several separate but interconnected buildings. The arrangement harmonizes with the style of other large oriental mansions and palaces.

The palace **took** longer to build than the temple (**13 years** compared with 7½; cf. 6:37-38) because it was larger. **The Palace of the Forest of Lebanon** (cf. 10:17, 21; Isa. 22:8) was probably given its name because of the extensive use of Lebanese **cedar** throughout (cf. 1 Kings 7:2-3); it was located not in Lebanon but in Jerusalem. It measured 150 feet by 75 feet and was 45 feet high. The floor space was 11,250 square feet, more than four times the 2,700 square feet of the temple floor (cf. 6:2).

The palace evidently served as an armory (10:17; cf. Isa. 22:8). Apparently next to it was a pillared **colonnade** (a covered walkway surrounding a patio) that had a front **portico** (porch) with a **roof** and supporting **pillars**.

**7:7-11.** Solomon's **throne hall, the Hall of Justice,** was attached to the Palace of the Forest of Lebanon, as were his own residence (v. 8a) and a separate residence **(palace) for Pharaoh's daughter, whom he had married** (v. 8b), all of harmonious **design.** A **great courtyard** (v. 9) united all these buildings into one palace complex. The **structures** were all built of **stone** (except the roofs) and they rested on stone **foundations.** Each stone was **cut to size . . . with a saw.** Palestinian limestone can be cut with a saw when freshly quarried, but hardens when exposed to the elements.

**7:12.** The great palace **courtyard** was protected **by a wall** similar in design to that around **the inner courtyard of the temple** (cf. 6:36). The palace was probably built close to (perhaps south of) the temple, though none of its remains have been found by archeologists.

4. THE TEMPLE FURNISHINGS (7:13-51)

*a. The work of Huram (7:13-47)*

**7:13-14. Huram** (a variant spelling of the Heb. Hiram) should not be confused with Hiram, the king of Tyre (5:1). Huram was a **skilled** craftsman, also from **Tyre . . . whose mother was** an Israelite **widow from . . . Naphtali, and whose father was a** Phoenician **of Tyre.** According to 2 Chronicles 2:14 Huram's mother was from Dan. Perhaps Dan was the tribe into which she was born and Naphtali was her residence, or vice versa. Huram's special talent was working with **bronze** (a copper alloy).

**7:15-22.** Huram **cast two** huge **bronze pillars, each** 27 feet high and 18 feet in circumference. With their **capitals** the pillars were over 34 feet high. (On the alleged discrepancy between verse 15 and 2 Chron. 3:15, see comments there.) Much detail is given in 1 Kings 7:17-20, 22 (cf. comments on 2 Chron. 3:16) to demonstrate the beauty and intricacy of these free-standing monuments.

The **pillars** were **erected** on either side of the temple **portico** (the roofless front porch). **Jakin,** the name of the **south** pillar, means "He [Yahweh] establishes," and **Boaz,** the name of the **north** pillar, means "In Him [Yahweh] is strength." These stood as a testimony to God's security and strength available to the nation as she obeyed Him.

**7:23-26. The Sea** corresponded to the laver of the tabernacle. It too was gigantic in size: 15 feet across its circular rim and 7½ feet high. On the three-to-one ratio of the circumference (45') to the diameter (15') compared with the geometric $\pi$ *(pi),* see comments on 2 Chronicles 4:2. The "Sea" looked like a huge basin resting on the backs of the **12** sculptured **bulls** that supported it, and it could contain **2,000 baths** (ca. 11,500 gallons; cf. NIV marg.) of water. This basin served as a reservoir for the temple courtyard. Second Chronicles 4:5 includes the statement that the laver "held 3,000 baths" (ca. 17,500 gallons). Perhaps this was its total capacity but it actually contained 2,000 baths.

**7:27-40a.** The **10** bronze **movable stands** were evidently used for butchering sacrificial animals. Each was six feet square and five and one-half feet high at its highest point. On the surface of each stand was a **basin** (v. 38) that held about 230 gallons (**40 baths**) of water. Apparently another **basin** (v. 30) drained into a **circular frame** (perhaps a tank) below through an **opening. Each stand had** decorated **panels** on each side, and **four bronze wheels.** These **10 . . . identical** work tables could be wheeled around the inner courtyard (though with difficulty) as needed. **Five** were stationed **on the south side of the temple and five on the north.**

**7:40b-47.** This summary of Huram's handiwork excludes the bronze altar which he also fashioned (2 Chron. 4:1). Recording the crafting of these furnishings in so much detail emphasizes the magnificent beauty, symmetry, and glory of **the temple.** The **bronze** objects were **cast in clay molds in the . . . Jordan** Valley **between Succoth and Zarethan,** about 35 miles north of the Dead Sea and east of the Jordan River. **Bronze** was so abundant that it was **not** even weighed.

*b. The furniture and accessories (7:48-50)*

**7:48-50.** Bronze was used for the furnishings outside the **temple** (vv. 40-45), but the furniture on the inside was made of **gold.** The **golden altar** was the altar of incense. The **table** for **the bread of the Presence** ("showbread," KJV) was possibly one larger table with nine others with it, which, though not mentioned here, are mentioned in 2 Chronicles 4:8 ("10 tables") and 2 Chronicles 4:19 ("tables"). Whereas the tabernacle had one lampstand, the temple had 10 **lampstands** in the holy place (**the main hall**). Other items were all of **gold** as well, including even the door **sockets.**

*c. The furnishings dedicated by David (7:51)*

**7:51.** To all these items were added **the furnishings** King **David** had prepared and dedicated for **temple** service (2 Sam. 8:11; 1 Chron. 22:14; 29:1-9). The **treasuries of the LORD's temple** were probably the rooms of the temple in the surrounding "structure" (1 Kings 6:5-6).

5. THE TEMPLE DEDICATION (CHAP. 8)

*a. The placing of the ark (8:1-11)*

**8:1-2.** After all the new furnishings, utensils, and accessories had been made and placed in position (chap. 6; 7:13-51), **Solomon summoned** the people for the installation of **the ark** and the dedication of the temple. **All the heads of . . . tribes and . . . families** in **Israel** received special invitations. The ceremony was scheduled for the **festival in the month of Ethanim** (the Feast of Tabernacles in September-October [Lev. 23:33-36]; see the chart "Calendar in Israel," near Ex. 12:1). Formerly the ark had rested in the tabernacle David pitched (2 Sam. 6:17) on Mount **Zion,** the southeast portion of Jerusalem called **the City of David** (cf. 2 Sam. 5:7). (See the map "Jerusalem in the Time of the Kings," near 1 Kings 9:15.)

**8:3-5.** As God had prescribed, **the ark** was carried by **the priests** by means of long poles that passed through rings on its sides. It must have been a great day when the ark and the other **furnishings** of David's tabernacle were **carried** through the crowded streets of Jerusalem to their new home. Apparently the tabernacle and its utensils were set aside. The only piece of furniture installed in the temple that was not new was **the ark.** The temple courtyard buzzed with busy priests **sacrificing** more animals than **could** be **counted** as the people joyfully worshiped **the LORD.**

**8:6-9.** The **priests** put **the ark** in **its place** under the outstretched **wings of** the golden **cherubim** in **the most holy place.** As God had commanded they left the **carrying poles** in the rings (Ex. 25:15). When the doors into the most holy place were open the **poles . . . could be seen from the holy place . . . but not from outside.** The statement that the poles **are still there today** suggests that this part of 1 Kings was written before the temple was destroyed in 586 B.C. **The two stone tablets** of the Law **placed** in the ark by **Moses** were still there. They served to remind Israel that the nation was still under the blessings and responsibilities of the Mosaic Covenant. The pot of manna and Aaron's rod that budded, which had been preserved in the ark (Heb. 9:4) for many years, were no longer there. They may have been removed by the Philistines or some other enemy. Or perhaps the objects, being in front of the tabernacle, not in the ark (cf. Ex. 16:33-34; Num. 17:10), were added to the ark sometime later than Solomon and then eventually were lost.

**8:10-11.** The **cloud** that **filled the temple** was a visible representation of the Lord's **glory.** A similar manifestation took place when the tabernacle was dedicated (Ex. 40:34-35).

*b. Solomon's address to the people (8:12-21)*

**8:12-14. Solomon** explained to the people that God had **said . . . He would dwell in** the **cloud** over the temple. A cloud often symbolized God's presence (cf. Ex. 19:9; 34:5; Lev. 16:2; Deut. 4:11; 31:15). It was Solomon's intention that God should abide in the **temple** he had built as God had dwelt within the tabernacle. Solomon had sought to reflect the magnificence of Yahweh in the temple. **Forever** should be interpreted to mean "as long as possible." Turning from addressing **the LORD,** Solomon spoke to the people **standing** reverently before him.

**8:15-21. With His own hand** means Himself (cf. v. 24). The promise Solomon referred to was that God would place His **Name** in Jerusalem (cf. comments on 2 Chron. 6:6). "Name" occurs in Solomon's prayer 14 times (1 Kings 8:16-20, 29, 33, 35, 41-44 [twice in v. 43], 48). The **temple** was not to be a "container" for God (v. 27) but a place for his **Name** to dwell (vv. 16-17, 19-20), that is, a place where His presence and character would be evident.

Solomon gave **David** the credit due him for purposing to build the **temple** (vv. 17-18). Solomon explained that **God** had promised David that his **son** would **build the temple** (cf. 2 Sam. 7:12-13). God had been faithful, and Solomon glorified Him for it. The temple was primarily **a place . . . for the ark,** the throne of God on earth and the repository of God's covenant promises to His redeemed people. In this address Solomon demonstrated humility and thankfulness.

*c. Solomon's prayer of dedication (8:22-53)*

**8:22-24. Solomon stood** and then kneeled (v. 54) on a special bronze platform that had been built in the temple courtyard for the dedication service (2 Chron. 6:13). Solomon began his prayer with worship and praise to God for His uniqueness and His faithfulness in keeping His promises. **Love** translates *ḥesed*, meaning loyal love (cf. 1 Kings 10:9).

The king then proceeded to petition God and to intercede for His people. Nine requests may be noted in this prayer:

(1) God's presence and protection. **8:25-30.** Solomon called on God to continue to be faithful to His **promises** to **David** (vv. 25-26; cf. 2:4) and to continue to **hear** the prayers of His **people** (8:28-30; **hear** occurs five times in these three verses). Of course no temple or even **the heavens** could **contain** the omnipresent God (v. 27). **Heaven** itself is His **dwelling place** (cf. vv. 39, 49; Ps. 11:4; Hab. 2:20). Yet in His majesty He is interested in His people's prayers.

(2) Forgiveness of trespasses. **8:31-32.** Solomon asked God to **judge** righteously in interpersonal disputes among the Israelites.

(3) Forgiveness of sins that had caused defeat in battle. **8:33-34.** The king asked the Lord to **forgive** His **people** when they confessed their sins that caused defeat in combat.

(4) Forgiveness of sins that had brought on drought. **8:35-36.** Solomon also asked God to **forgive** His **people** if they confessed sins that resulted in **rain** being withheld (cf. Lev. 26:18-19; Deut. 11:16-17; 28:23-24).

(5) Forgiveness of sins that had re-

sulted in other calamities. **8:37-40. Famine . . . plague . . . blight . . . mildew, locusts . . . grasshoppers,** enemies, **disaster,** and **disease** were all instruments God used to chasten His sinning people. (See the chart "The Covenant Chastenings," near Amos 4:6.) Again the king asked God to **forgive** those who repented of sin that led to these calamities. Solomon affirmed God's knowledge of people's motives (**hearts**).

(6) Mercy for God-fearing foreigners. **8:41-43.** Solomon interceded on behalf of non-Israelites who would trust Yahweh and pray to Him. By hearing them, God's fame would spread worldwide.

(7) Victory in battle. **8:44-45.** Solomon asked God to **uphold** His **people** when they prayed to Him in times of physical distress in combat.

(8) Restoration after captivity. **8:46-51.** The king seemed to have prophetic insight into the fate of God's people. They did indeed go into captivity because of their sins against God; they called on Him for forgiveness, and they experienced restoration to their land. Centuries later Daniel prayed **toward the land** when he was in Babylon (Dan. 6:10).

(9) Attention to every prayer. **8:52-53.** Solomon summarized his petitions by calling on God to hear His people **whenever they cry out** in prayer. These calamities were all listed in Deuteronomy as curses on Israel for her breaking the covenant (Deut. 28:22, 25, 38, 42, 59; 31:17, 29; 32:24).

In this whole prayer (1 Kings 8:23-53) Solomon called on God, who had been faithful to His promises in the past, to continue to be faithful and to show mercy to His people (His chosen **inheritance,** vv. 36, 51, 53) in the future. Confession and forsaking of sin would result in God's hearing His people's prayers ("hear" occurs 13 times in this prayer, and in the first eight of the nine petitions) and God's forgiving them ("forgive" occurs 6 times).

*d. Solomon's blessing of the people (8:54-61)*

**8:54-55. Solomon . . . had been kneeling** in prayer **with his hands spread out toward heaven** in a posture of supplication. Then he arose to pronounce a benediction on the people.

**8:56-61.** God had **given rest** (peace)

to His people and had kept **all the good promises He** Had given **through . . . Moses.** Solomon reminded the people of this. Then he expressed his desire for three things: That **the LORD** would **be with** Solomon's generation **as He** had been **with** his forefathers, that God would give His people the will to **walk in all His ways,** and that the requests Solomon had made in his prayer would remain close to the heart of **God day** by day. Solomon ultimately desired that **all the peoples of the earth** (cf. v. 43) might **know that** Yahweh **is** the only true **God** (cf. 18:39). In order for all this to take place Solomon reminded the people that they **must be fully committed to the LORD** and obedient to **His** Word. Solomon himself eventually failed to do this.

As the king finished speaking, "fire came down from heaven and consumed the burnt offering and the sacrifices, and the glory of the LORD filled the temple" (2 Chron. 7:1) as it had earlier filled the tabernacle (Ex. 40:34-35; Lev. 9:23-24).

### e. Solomon's sacrifices (8:62-66)

**8:62-63.** The number of animals sacrificed (**22,000 cattle and 120,000 sheep and goats**) seems incredibly large. But records of other sacrifices that involved thousands of animals are extant. One must remember that thousands of priests sacrificed on many auxiliary altars, and the celebration lasted for two weeks.

**8:64-66.** The **same day** Solomon dedicated the temple he also **consecrated . . . the courtyard in front of the temple** with his **offerings.** This dedication took place at the beginning of **the festival** of Tabernacles which normally lasted one week, but was extended to two weeks on this special occasion. The Feast of Tabernacles commemorated Israel's years of wandering in the wilderness (Lev. 23:33, 41-43). It was fitting that the temple should be dedicated at this feast since that permanent sanctuary now symbolized the end of Israel's wanderings. People from as far away as **Lebo Hamath** in northern Israel toward the Euphrates River and **the Wadi of Egypt** (modern Wadi el-Arish) far to the south attended the festivities; all Israel participated. The **people** returned **home** at the end of the feast **joyful** and thankful to God for His goodness to them.

## D. The later years of Solomon's reign (chaps. 9–11)

### 1. GOD'S COVENANT WITH SOLOMON (9:1-9)

**9:1-3.** As God had revealed Himself to **Solomon . . . at Gibeon** (3:4-5), so He did again, probably in Jerusalem. First, **the LORD** assured Solomon that He had **heard** his **prayer** of dedication and that He would **always** abide in the **temple** in a special sense. His people could always count on His **eyes** resting on them and His **heart** compassionately responding to their needs as Solomon had requested.

**9:4-9.** But **the LORD** also warned the king. **If** he would **walk before** God, manifesting attitudes and actions that expressed obedience to the Lord's Word, God would provide an unceasing line of descendants for Solomon who would always rule **over Israel. But if** Solomon or any of his descendants did not follow **the LORD** faithfully, but instead turned aside to **worship** and **serve other gods,** then **the LORD** would do two things: remove **Israel from** her **land** and abandon the temple. The Davidic dynasty, though interrupted for centuries starting with the Babylonian Captivity, will be restored by the Messiah when He sits on David's throne in the Millennium (Ps. 89:30-37). This judgment would cause other peoples to marvel at and **ridicule** Israel. **Scoff** (1 Kings 9:8) literally means "whistle in amazement." People would know that Israel fell because of her idolatry. Not only did later kings lead Israel away from Yahweh to false gods, but also Solomon himself did (11:4-8), and the nation was on the path toward exile (2 Kings 25:1-21).

### 2. SOLOMON'S ACHIEVEMENTS (9:10-28)

### a. His gifts to Hiram (9:10-14)

**9:10-14.** Near the mid-point of Solomon's reign (after **20** of his **40 years**), after he had finished building **the temple** (7 years, 6:38) and his **palace** complex (13 years, 7:1), **Solomon gave 20** villages **in Galilee to** his old friend King **Hiram . . . of Tyre. Hiram** had previously given Solomon **cedar and pine** (cf. 5:10) and much **gold** as well. The amount of **gold** was **120 talents** (9:14; ca. 9,000 pounds). **But when Hiram** visited **the 20 towns . . . he was** disappointed; they were apparently located near unproductive land. Hiram **called them the Land of Cabul**

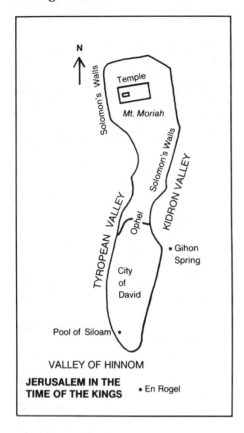

**N**

Temple

Mt. Moriah

Solomon's Walls

Solomon's Walls

Ophel

KIDRON VALLEY

TYROPEAN VALLEY

• Gihon
Spring

City
of
David

Pool of Siloam •

VALLEY OF HINNOM

**JERUSALEM IN THE
TIME OF THE KINGS**  • En Rogel

("Cabul" sounds like the Heb. for "good-for-nothing").

### b. His public works (9:15-19)

**9:15.** In addition to the **temple** (chap. 6) and his **palace** (7:1-12) **Solomon** built **supporting terraces** (probably large level areas between hills made by filling in land), and **the wall of Jerusalem** which he extended farther to the north, more than doubling the size of the city. His wall surrounded the temple and probably the palace which were built to the north of the old City of David (see the map "Jerusalem in the Time of the Kings"). **Hazor, Meggido, and Gezer** were fortress cities. Hazor, north of the Sea of Kinnereth, guarded the northern part of the kingdom. Meggido protected the Valley of Jezreel that stretched from west to east in the central sector of Israel. And Gezer served as a site of defense in western Judah where it discouraged potential southern and western aggressors from attacking Israel. Israel was stronger and wealthier under Solomon than under

any of its other kings.

**9:16-19.** **Gezer** had previously been **captured** and burned by Egypt's **king,** its residents had been executed, and the town had been given by **Pharaoh** as a part of his dowry for **his daughter** who had married Solomon. **Solomon** then **rebuilt** and fortified **Gezer. Lower Beth Horon** (as well as Upper Beth Horon) and Gezer were important defense towns for protection against attacks from Israel's southwest. **Baalath** stood near Gezer. **Tadmor** (later named Palmyra) was located on a caravan route between Damascus and the Euphrates River to Israel's northeast.

Solomon's **store cities,** scattered throughout Israel, were fortified towns in which surplus food was stockpiled. **The towns** where he kept **his chariots and . . . horses** were ready to defend Israel against any invader. Solomon also built up other towns throughout his kingdom for various other purposes.

### c. His labor force (9:20-23)

**9:20-23.** **Solomon** used **slave labor** for his building projects. The **descendants** of the conquered native tribes did the hardest manual labor. (On the various population elements not conquered in the Conquest see comments on 2 Chron. 8:7.) **The Israelites** served as soldiers and supervisors. The labor force was obviously very large. (On the **550** supervisors along with the 3,300 foremen mentioned in 1 Kings 5:16, see comments there.)

### d. His house for Pharaoh's daughter (9:24)

**9:24.** Solomon also built **terraces** by filling in land near the residence he had built for **Pharaoh's daughter** in his **palace** complex (cf. 7:8). She moved there from her other residence in the **City of David** after the palace was completed.

### e. His annual offerings (9:25)

**9:25.** All the offerings mentioned were for worship (on the **burnt offerings** cf. Lev. 1, and on the **fellowship offerings** cf. Lev. 3). The **three** annual occasions were perhaps the Feast of Unleavened Bread, the Feast of Harvest (also called Weeks and Pentecost), and the Feast of Tabernacles (also called Ingathering) since these were the major feasts of Israel (cf. Ex. 23:14-16).

### f. His navy (9:26-28)

**9:26-28.** Archeologists have discovered the remains of **Ezion Geber** at the northern tip of the Gulf of Aqaba. This site, on the east arm of **the Red Sea,** gave Israel access to the east and south by water. Hiram's Phoenician **sailors,** who joined **Solomon's,** were some of the most skillful of their day. **Ophir** was probably in southwestern Arabia (cf. 10:11; Job 22:24; 28:16). The vast amounts **of gold** brought in from expeditions to these lands helped finance and decorate Solomon's vast building projects. While 1 Kings 9:28 has **420 talents** (ca. 16 tons, or 32,000 pounds), 2 Chronicles 8:18 has 450 (see comments on that verse).

### 3. SOLOMON'S GLORY (CHAP. 10)

### a. The queen of Sheba's visit (10:1-13)

This incident seems to have been included here to support the statements made previously that Solomon's reign was so glorious that rulers from all over the world came to see his kingdom and observe his wisdom (4:34). Its function is similar to the story of the two prostitutes (3:16-28) which also illustrated Solomon's wisdom. Interestingly both stories pertain to women, though of different social strata.

**10:1-5. Sheba** is modern Yemen (not Ethiopia), in Arabia, about 1,200 miles from Jerusalem. Sheba may be the land of the Sabeans (cf. Job 1:15; Ezek. 23:42; Joel 3:8). Solomon's expeditions to the east by sea (cf. 1 Kings 9:26-28) would have brought him news of this prosperous and important Arabian kingdom. The queen's primary purpose in visiting **Solomon** seems to have been to see if he was really as wise and wealthy as she had heard (**she came to test him**). Such testing was a sport among ancient Near Eastern monarchs. Probably **the queen** was interested in discussing trade and perhaps defense arrangements as well. Her **very great caravan** reflected her own prestige and also carried her money and expensive gifts for **Solomon.** Visiting heads of state still commonly bring costly gifts to their hosts. **The queen** was especially impressed with Solomon's **wisdom . . . palace . . . food . . . officials . . . servants,** and **burnt offerings** to Yahweh.

**10:6-9.** Originally skeptical, the queen admitted that Solomon's **wisdom and wealth . . . far exceeded** what she had been told. Though probably a pagan, she was willing to credit **the LORD** with giving Israel a wise **king** in whom He **delighted.**

**10:10.** The queen was quite wealthy herself. **She gave** Solomon **120 talents of gold** (ca. 4½ tons), great **quantities of spices, and precious stones** (cf. v. 2).

**10:11-12.** These verses, which seem out of place here, may reflect a trade arrangement that resulted from the queen's visit. **Ophir** may have been close to or a part of the queen's kingdom of Sheba (cf. 9:28). **Almugwood** is strong, beautiful (black outside, ruby red inside), and long-lasting. Solomon used it in the **temple** steps (cf. 2 Chron. 9:11) as well as for the other purposes mentioned here.

**10:13. Solomon gave the queen** gifts, **all she desired and asked for** from him. She **then** began the long trip back home **to her** people.

### b. Solomon's riches (10:14-29)

This section summarizes Solomon's wealth.

**10:14-15.** The revenue of **gold** recorded as being **received** annually (almost 25 tons, or 50,000 pounds) did not include what must have been vast quantities required from trading with **all the Arabian kings** and taxes brought in by **the governors** of Israel. God had told His kings not to multiply gold (Deut. 17:17), but Solomon disobeyed.

**10:16-17. The Palace of the Forest of Lebanon** (cf. 7:2-5; 10:21) must have served as an armory among other things. Each **large . . . shield** was made of **600 bekas** (7½ pounds) **of gold** and each **small . . . shield** had **three minas** (3¾ pounds) **of gold.** (In 2 Chron. 9:16 the small shields are said to be made of 300 bekas of gold. But that is the same amount expressed in a different unit of measure.) Evidently these 500 shields were intended for parade use rather than for battle as **gold** is a soft metal.

**10:18-22.** Solomon's **throne . . . overlaid with gold** reflected the king's glory. The **12 lions,** one on each end of **the six steps** to the throne, may have been intended to represent the 12 tribes of Israel. The wealth of Solomon's kingdom could be seen in the abundance of **gold** which made **silver of** comparatively **little value** even though it was a precious metal. Solomon's **fleet** of traders brought riches from distant lands. The **apes and baboons** may have been pets in vogue at the time.

**10:23-25.** God's promise to make **Solomon** the richest and wisest king of his time was fulfilled. His wealth continued to increase as people (**the whole world** is a hyperbole) who came **to hear** his **wisdom** brought him **gold** and silver **articles . . . spices,** and animals.

**10:26-29.** **Chariots** were the most effective and dreaded military machines of that day. Their mobility and versatility gave Israel a great military advantage and discouraged enemies from invading the wealthy nation. Solomon's **chariot cities,** some have suggested, were Gezer, Hazor, and Megiddo. He purchased **horses . . . from Egypt** (or perhaps Muṣri, in Asia Minor) **and from Kue** (probably Cilicia in modern-day Turkey). He bought **a chariot** for **600** silver **shekels** (ca. 15 pounds) and **a horse** cost **150** silver shekels (ca. 3¾ pounds). In exporting some of them to **the Hittites** and **the Arameans** he presumably made a profit on them.

Though Solomon's wealth enabled him to purchase large quantities of **horses** and **chariots,** this practice was specifically prohibited in the Mosaic Law (Deut. 17:16). The reason for this prohibition was that the Lord wanted His people to depend on Him for their protection. The presence of strong physical defenses in Israel turned the hearts of Solomon and the people away from the Lord with a false sense of security. As is often the case, an abundance of material benefits leads people to think they have no needs when in reality their need for God never diminishes.

4. SOLOMON'S APOSTASY (CHAP. 11)

The internal weaknesses of Solomon's reign which have been only hinted at so far come into full view in this chapter.

*a. His foreign wives (11:1-8)*

**11:1-8.** Besides a **king** being forbidden by God to increase the number of his horses (Deut. 17:16; cf. comments on 1 Kings 10:26-29), a king was also forbidden by God to marry **many** wives "or his heart will be led astray" (Deut. 17:17). This is precisely what happened to **Solo-**

**mon.** His palace apparently included a harem; **He had 700 wives** and **300 concubines.** Solomon's pagan **wives** led him into idolatry just as God had warned (Ex. 23:31-33; 34:15-16; Deut. 7:1-4). **Solomon** did not abandon Yahweh but he worshiped other gods as well. **His heart was not fully devoted to the LORD;** he compromised his affections. Apparently he concluded that since he was a great king he should live like the other great kings of the world even though it meant disobeying God's Word.

**As Solomon grew** older he got farther away from God (cf. 1 Kings 11:33). **Ashtoreth** was a **goddess of** sex and fertility whose worship involved licentious rites and worship of the stars. She was a vile goddess (cf. 2 Kings 23:13). **Molech** worship involved human sacrifices, especially children, which was strictly prohibited by the Law (Lev. 18:21; 20:1-5). **Chemosh** worship was equally cruel and licentious. The **hill east of Jerusalem** on which **Solomon built . . . high** places may have been the Mount of Olives (cf. 2 Kings 23:13).

*b. His sentence from God (11:9-13)*

**11:9-13.** The reason for God's judgment of Solomon is clear: **his heart had turned away from the LORD** (cf. v. 4). Solomon's great sin was a change in his **attitude** toward **God** (v. 11). This happened despite the two times God had revealed Himself to Solomon, making promises to him (3:5; 9:2). His decision to pursue **other gods** led to his disobeying (11:10) God's specific command against idolatry (9:6-7).

**One of** Solomon's **subordinates** (11:11) was Jeroboam, who tore **the kingdom . . . from** Solomon's **son.** The **one tribe** (v. 13) that God left in Rehoboam's hand was Judah. Actually two tribes were left (Judah and Benjamin) but Benjamin was small and the two became known as the Southern Kingdom of Judah. The tribe of Simeon had been given territory south of Judah but later at least part of Simeon moved north (see comments on Josh. 19:1-9). It was **for** David's **sake** that God tempered His judgment with mercy, and did not allow the split in Solomon's day. Whereas David had sinned against God deliberately, his heart remained devoted to the Lord. That is why his sin was not so serious as Solo-

## Kings of Aram in 1 and 2 Kings

| Kings | Dates | Scripture References |
|---|---|---|
| Rezon (=Hezion) | ca. 940–915 | 1 Kings 11:23, 25; 15:18 |
| Tabrimmon | ca. 915–900 | 1 Kings 15:18 |
| Ben-Hadad I | ca. 900–860 | 1 Kings 15:18, 20 |
| Ben-Hadad II | ca. 860–841 | 1 Kings 20;<br>2 Kings 6:24; 8:7, 9, 14 |
| Hazael | 841–801 | 1 Kings 19:15, 17<br>2 Kings 8; 9:14-15;<br>10:32; 12:17-18;<br>13:3, 22, 24-25 |
| Ben-Hadad III | ca. 801–? | 2 Kings 13:3, 24-25 |
| Rezin | ?–732 | 2 Kings 15:37; 16:5-6, 9<br>(cf. Isa. 7:1, 4, 8; 8:6; 9:11) |

mon's. The greatest commandment is to love God with all one's heart (Deut. 6:5).

*c. His external adversaries (11:14-25)*

**11:14-22.** **Hadad** was a prince of **Edom,** Israel's ancient enemy to the southeast. **When David was** at war **with Edom,** Hadad, then **a boy,** escaped **to Egypt.** On the way he went **from Midian,** a kingdom south of Edom and east of the modern-day Gulf of Aqaba, **to Paran,** an area in the Sinai Peninsula between Midian and **Egypt. Pharaoh** took him in and even **gave him a** sister-in-law **in marriage.**

The ancient hostility of the Edomites toward the Israelites must have been aggravated in Hadad's mind by David's slaughter of the Edomites, and **Hadad** lived for the day he could take revenge. Hearing **that David** had died (in 971 B.C.) and that **Joab** was also dead **Hadad** asked **Pharaoh** for permission to go back to Edom. Apparently he caused trouble for Solomon militarily (cf. v. 25).

**11:23-25.** Another enemy of **Solomon** was the rebel **Rezon** (see the chart "Kings of Aram in 1 and 2 Kings"). He was from **Zobah,** a kingdom just south of Damascus (cf. 2 Sam. 8:3-6). Rezon went with some other **rebels** to **Damascus,** the capital of Aram, and **took control** there.

*d. His internal adversary (11:26-40)*

**11:26-28. Jeroboam** was from Ephra-im, the leading tribe of Israel's Northern Kingdom. Apparently he had worked for **Solomon** when the king **built the supporting terraces and . . . filled in the gap in the wall of the City of David.** As a result of his good work **Solomon** promoted him over **the whole** forced **labor force** of the tribes of Ephraim and Manasseh (the house of Joseph).

**11:29-33. Ahijah the prophet** (who was sought out later by Jeroboam, 14:1-18) graphically demonstrated to **Jeroboam** the division of **the kingdom** by tearing his own **new cloak** in **12 pieces** and giving **10** to **Jeroboam.** This must have impressed Jeroboam greatly. The **one tribe** (11:32) to be left with Solomon was Judah (cf. comments on v. 13). Actually two were left—Judah and Benjamin—which were often regarded as one tribe and referred to as Judah. This portrayal by **Ahijah** demonstrated what God had said earlier to Solomon (vv. 11-13). Not only Solomon but also the people of Israel (**they,** v. 33) had **forsaken** Yahweh by worshiping idols (cf. comments on **Ashtoreth . . . Chemosh,** and **Molech** in vv. 5-7).

**11:34-39.** Solomon's **son** (v. 35) was Rehoboam to whom would be given **one tribe** (cf. vv. 13, 32). Like a **lamp** kept burning perpetually in a tent or home, Judah would be a perpetual testimony to God's choice of **David,** who was of the tribe of Judah (cf. 15:4; 2 Sam. 21:17;

2 Kings 8:19).

Jeroboam was told that he would **rule over all that** his **heart** desired (1 Kings 11:37) in **Israel,** that is, he would have freedom to rule as he saw fit. It is remarkable that God's conditional promise to establish Jeroboam's line (v. 38) was similar to His unconditional promise to establish David's line (v. 38). Unfortunately Jeroboam did not value this promise but forfeited it. God prophesied that He would **humble David's descendants . . . but not forever.** This ending of the humbling was fulfilled in the birth of Jesus Christ, David's greatest Son (i.e., Descendant). All that Ahijah prophesied came to pass.

**11:40.** The reason **Solomon tried to kill Jeroboam** is not stated. Perhaps **Jeroboam** tried to take matters into his own hands and seize the kingdom. Or he may have done something else that made it necessary for him to flee **to Shishak the king** (Pharaoh) of **Egypt** (cf. Hadad's escape to Egypt, vv. 14-22). Shishak (945–924), also known as Sheshonk I, later invaded Judah (2 Chron. 12:2-4) and Jerusalem (1 Kings 14:25-26) in Rehoboam's reign.

*e. His death (11:41-43)*

**11:41-43.** The writer of 1 and 2 Kings was led by the Spirit of God to record no more **events of Solomon's reign** though others were preserved in **the book of the annals of Solomon,** which is not extant today (cf. comments on 14:19). This is the first of several such sources mentioned in 1 Kings (cf. 14:19, 29) and 2 Chronicles (cf. 2 Chron. 9:29; 12:15; 26:22; 32:32). **Solomon reigned** for **40 years** (971–931 B.C.). After he died he was given an honorable burial **in the City of David** (cf. comments on 1 Kings 2:10).

Solomon's life ended in tragedy. Solomon was greatly blessed by God but he allowed God's gifts to dominate his affections. The fault lay not with God for giving Solomon so much, but with Solomon who, though he had the wisdom to deal with such temptations, chose to set his affections on the gifts and not on the Giver. The man best qualified to live life successfully chose not to do so. Success in life in the eyes of God does not come automatically with the possession of wisdom but with the applicaton of wisdom to one's life. Spiritual success depends not only on insight but also on choices.

## II. The Earlier History of the Divided Kingdom (chaps. 12–22)

The fatal division of the kingdom of Israel into two nations resulted from a foolish decision by Solomon's son, Rehoboam. However, the tribes that separated had a long history of antagonism that had threatened for many years to split Israel. Judah, the largest tribe in population, enjoyed prominence as the leader of the other tribes in the wilderness march. Judah received the largest area in the Promised Land because of its large population. But Ephraim was the preferred son of Joseph, and though that tribe was not large, it demonstrated a feeling of superiority on occasion (cf. Jud. 9:1-3 [Shechem was in Ephraim]; 12:1-6). The Northern tribes led by Ephraim separated from their brethren to the south briefly during David's reign (2 Sam. 19:41–20:22). So a fault line had developed between these two groups of tribes that opened up and split the monarchy at this stressful time in its history.

### A. The division of the kingdom (12:1-24)

The date when Israel passed from a united to a divided monarchy was 931 B.C.

#### 1. REHOBOAM'S DILEMMA (12:1-5)

**12:1. Shechem** afforded a fitting site for the coronation of a **king** of Israel. At Shechem Yahweh first appeared to Abraham in the land and promised to give him all of Canaan (Gen. 12:6-7). Jacob later settled there (Gen. 33:18-20) and Joseph was buried there (Josh. 24:32). After they had entered the Promised Land the Israelites, at Shechem in the valley between Mount Ebal and Mount Gerizim, dedicated themselves to keep the Mosaic Law (Josh. 24:1-27). This sacred spot now reminded **the Israelites** of their divinely revealed destiny as a nation and of God's faithfulness.

**12:2-5.** Evidently the heads of the Northern tribes under the leadership of the Ephraimites **sent for Jeroboam,** who apparently had just returned from exile in **Egypt** after Solomon's death (cf. 11:40). They wanted him to present their plea for lower taxes **to Rehoboam.** They did this sometime during the coronation festivities. Perhaps **Jeroboam** served as their spokesman. Jeroboam had, of course, been told by the Prophet Ahijah that the kingdom would be divided and that he would rule 10 of the tribes (11:31-39). But he seems to have decided to let events take their course rather than initiating an unprovoked revolution. By reducing the tax load and by lightening the **labor** conscription requirements on his people, King **Rehoboam** could have won the support of his petitioners. But he said that he wanted **three days** to think about their suggestion.

### 2. REHOBOAM'S COUNSELORS (12:6-11)

**12:6-7.** The king asked two groups of counselors for their advice. **The elders** were probably about the same age as **his father Solomon,** having **served** as the former king's official advisers; they were elders both by reason of years and by their office in the government. This group's counsel was wise—to lighten the tax and work load, as the people asked. If taken, this advice would have resulted in peace, at least for a time.

**12:8-11.** Perhaps to appear in control **Rehoboam rejected** this good **advice** and turned to his contemporaries for their opinions. The younger men's counsel was the opposite from what **the elders** had given, but just what Rehoboam wanted to hear. The king was no child at this time; he was 41 years old (14:21). Nor was his decision made on the spur of the moment; he had three days to think it over (12:5). It was a deliberate choice possibly based on what he believed was needed most in the nation at that time.

The wording of Rehoboam's reply to his petitioners, as suggested by his younger advisers, seems almost designed to provoke hostility: he would be far more harsh than his **father,** for his **little finger** was **thicker than** his **father's waist** (an obvious hyperbole intended to express his greater power) and he would **scourge . . . with scorpions** not with his father's **whips.** Perhaps the king and his counselors thought intimidation would send the potential rebels scurrying for cover and would drive any ideas of insurrection far from their minds. "Scorpions" refers to a particularly cruel kind of whip used in that day, with sharp pieces of metal.

### 3. REHOBOAM'S DECISION (12:12-15)

**12:12-15. The king** followed through with his decision and delivered his insulting threat to his petitioners (vv. 13-14; cf. vv. 10-11). Rather than listening **to the people** Rehoboam put his own interests first. **This turn of events,** the writer noted, **was from the LORD** (v. 15) in fulfillment of His prophecy through Ahijah (11:31-39). God's judgment because of Solomon's apostasy was being carried out (11:11-13).

### 4. ISRAEL'S REBELLION (12:16-20)

**12:16-17.** Rehoboam's insensitivity to the Israelites' hardships extinguished any hope they may have entertained of economic recovery. His dictatorial threat alienated his suffering subjects. Then and there they seceded and broke the union of the 12 tribes. Only Rehoboam's closest countrymen from **Judah** did not abandon him. The reply of the Israelites (v. 16) evidently had become a battle cry; it was used years earlier by Sheba who rebelled against David (2 Sam. 20:1).

**12:18-19.** What could have motivated **Rehoboam** to send **Adoniram** (a variant spelling of the Heb. Adoram; cf. NIV marg.), the personification of oppression, (the foreman **of forced labor**), to meet with the rebels at that crucial moment? Perhaps Adoniram was the best-qualified ambassador. Whatever the reason, Rehoboam's "wisdom" proved foolish again. Adoniram died as the target of the rebels' wrath. And **Rehoboam** barely escaped with his own life. What should have been a glorious national celebration (v. 1) turned into a humiliating rout for Judah's new king who fled his own coronation to **escape** assassination by his infuriated subjects. The writer noted that the Israelites were really rebelling **against the house of David,** God's appointed dynasty, which they did **to this day** (i.e., the time this section of the book was written).

**12:20.** Rehoboam's coronation turned into Jeroboam's coronation. The people brought **Jeroboam** forward and **made him king** then and there. This action suggests that plotting had been involved in the rebellion. **Only . . . Judah** (and Benjamin, v. 21) **remained loyal to the** ruler from David's **house** (dynasty).

### 5. REHOBOAM'S REPRISAL (12:21-24)

**12:21.** Having failed to preserve unity through diplomacy **Rehoboam** sought to restore it by force. **The tribe of Benjamin** was Judah's immediate neighbor to the north. The capital city of **Jerusalem** lay almost on the Judah-Benjamin border. Probably for the sake of their close neighbors and the capital, the Benjamites sided with **Judah.** Together these tribes called up **180,000** soldiers to fight their brothers in the 10 tribes to the north.

**12:22-24.** Rehoboam's battle plans were interrupted by a prophet of Yahweh, **Shemaiah. The man of God** made a public announcement that civil war was definitely not God's will and he convinced **Rehoboam** and **the people** to **go** back **home.** To his credit Rehoboam **obeyed the word of the** LORD and did not proceed into battle. Again the writer pointed out the overruling hand of **God** in these affairs (**as the** LORD **had ordered,** v. 24; cf. v. 15).

## B. Jeroboam's evil reign in Israel (12:25–14:20)

Jeroboam could have been an instrument of blessing for Israel. He was divinely chosen and given promises that his dynasty would continue and prosper if he obeyed the Lord (11:38-39). But Jeroboam did not trust or obey the Lord; he committed many serious sins that resulted in the Israelites turning *from* God rather than *to* Him. He planted seeds that bore bitter fruit for Israel as long as it continued as a nation. Twenty kings ruled the Northern Kingdom and not one of them turned the people back to the Lord. Instead of one stable dynasty, Israel experienced several dynasties (see the chart "Kings of Judah and Israel and the Preexilic Prophets").

### 1. JEROBOAM'S IDOLATRY (12:25-33)

**12:25. Jeroboam** chose **Shechem** (where Rehoboam had been crowned, v. 1) as his capital and began at once to fortify it as his stronghold. During its history the Northern Kingdom had three capitals: Shechem, Tirzah (14:17; 15:33), and Samaria (16:23-24). (See the map "Solomon's 12 Districts and Surrounding Nations," near 4:17-19.) Jeroboam also **built up Peniel** (see the map) as a fortress east of the Jordan River, probably to protect Israel from invasion from the east by the Gileadites, who had been consistently loyal to David.

**12:26-27.** Jeroboam's musings reveal an evil heart of unbelief. Rather than believing God's promise to establish his dynasty (cf. 11:31, 37-38), the king sought security by turning the people away from God. His fears that the **people** might **revert to the house** (dynasty) **of David,** that is, to **Rehoboam,** were understandable, but God had told him that He would keep Israel for the house of **Jeroboam.** Fear for his personal safety crept in when he stopped trusting God.

**12:28.** The king's "reforms" all involved religious apostasy. This is why he was such an evil influence in **Israel.** His changes struck at the heart of Israel's strength, her relationship with God. They polluted Israel for generations. Jeroboam researched his ideas; he sought **advice** about how to maintain the secession effectively.

The first change involved new religious symbols. To prevent the Israelites from returning to their magnificent temple and the ark in **Jerusalem** (cf. v. 27) Jeroboam offered substitute objects: **two golden calves** or bulls. Perhaps he actually intended the people to turn from worshiping Yahweh to worshiping his golden idols. His words, **Here are your gods . . . who** delivered **you** from **Egypt,** suggest this.

It is probable, however, that the king may have set up these calves as aids to the worship of Yahweh (W.F. Albright, *From the Stone Age to Christianity.* Rev. ed. Baltimore: Johns Hopkins University Press, 1957, p. 299). This suggestion has the support of ancient Near Eastern tradition which conceived of an image as a support or pedestal for one's god. Jeroboam's decision may have been influenced by what he had seen in Egypt where a bull was commonly used to represent or support a god. Or perhaps more likely, his action was influenced by the Canaanites' similar practice regarding Baal. He seems to have been poorly informed concerning Israel's history, however, since a former golden calf had brought God's wrath down on the Israelites in the wilderness (Ex. 32). Whatever their original purpose these calves became the objects of Israel's worship (cf. Hosea 8:5-6; 13:2-3).

**12:29-30.** New sanctuaries were also

# Kings of Judah and Israel and the Preexilic Prophets

## JUDAH

| Kings* | | Dates | Years |
|---|---|---|---|
| Rehoboam | | 931–913 | 17 |
| Abijah | | 913–911 | 3 |
| Asa | | 911–870 | 41 |
| Coregency† with Jehoshaphat | | 873–870 | (3) |
| Jehoshaphat | | 873–848 | 25 |
| Coregency with Jehoram | | 853–848 | (5) |
| Jehoram | OBADIAH** | 848–841 | 8 |
| Ahaziah‡ | | 841 | 1 |
| Queen Athaliah‡ | | 841–835 | 6 |
| Joash‡ | JOEL** | 835–796 | 40 |
| Amaziah‡ | | 796–767 | 29 |
| Azariah's vice-regency under Amaziah | | 790–767 | (23) |
| Azariah (Uzziah) | | 790–739 | 52 |
| Coregency with Jotham | | 750–739 | (11) |
| Jotham | | 750–735 | 16 |
| Ahaz's vice-regency under Jotham | | 744–735 | (9) |
| Coregency of Jotham with Ahaz | | 735–732 | 4 |
| Ahaz | | 732–715 | 16 |
| Hezekiah's vice-regency under Ahaz | | 729–715 | (14) |
| Hezekiah | | 715–686 | 29 |
| Manasseh's vice-regency under Hezekiah | | 697–686 | (11) |
| Manasseh | NAHUM | 697–642 | 55 |
| Amon‡ | | 642–640 | 2 |
| Josiah | ZEPHANIAH | 640–609 | 31 |
| Jehoahaz | | 609 | 1/4 |
| Jehoiakim | HABAKKUK | 609–598 | 11 |
| Jehoiachin | | 598–597 | 1/4 |
| Zedekiah | | 597–586 | 11 |

(Prophets bracketed along the Judah column: MICAH and ISAIAH span from Jotham through Manasseh; JEREMIAH spans from Josiah through Zedekiah.)

## ISRAEL

| Dynasty§ | Kings | Dates | Years |
|---|---|---|---|
| 1st Dynasty | Jeroboam I | 931–910 | 22 |
| " | Nadab‡ | 910–909 | 2 |
| 2nd Dynasty | Baasha | 909–886 | 24 |
| " | Elah‡ | 886–885 | 2 |
| 3rd Dynasty | Zimri | 885 | 7 days |
| — | Tibni | 885–880 | 6 |
|  | Overlapping reign† with Omri | 885–880 | (6) |
| 4th Dynasty | Omri | 885–874 | 12 |
| " | Ahab | 874–853 | 22 |
| " | Ahaziah | 853–852 | 2 |
| " | Jehoram (Joram)‡ | 852–841 | 12 |
| 5th Dynasty | Jehu | 841–814 | 28 |
| " | Jehoahaz | 814–798 | 17 |
| " | Jehoash (Joash) | 798–782 | 16 |
| " | Coregency with Jeroboam II | 793–782 | (11) |
| " | Jeroboam II — JONAH / AMOS | 793–753 | 41 |
| " | Zechariah‡ | 753–752 | 1/2 |
| 6th Dynasty | Shallum‡ | 752 | 1/12 |
| 7th Dynasty | Menahem | 752–742 | 10 |
|  | Overlapping reign with Pekah | 752–742 | (10) |
| " | Pekahiah‡ | 742–742 | (2) |
|  | Overlapping reign with Pekah | 742–740 | (2) |
| 8th Dynasty | Pekah‡ | 752–732 | 20 |
| 9th Dynasty | Hoshea | 732–722 | 9 |

(Prophets bracketed along the Israel column: ELIJAH spans from Ahab through Jehoram; ELISHA spans from Jehoram through Jeroboam II; HOSEA spans from Jeroboam II through Hoshea.)

*Includes one queen (Athaliah).

†In a coregency the kings ruled together; in overlapping reigns they reigned separately; in a vice-regency a son ruled with his father in a subordinate position.

‡These kings and one queen were assassinated.

§A dynasty is a succession of rulers who are members of the same family or a single ruler of a family different from those before and after him. (The kings of Judah were all of one dynasty because they were all descendants of David.)

**Evangelical scholars differ on the dates of Obadiah and Joel. Some place them at later dates (see the *Introductions* to Joel and Obad.).

Note: In some kings' reigns the dates (e.g., Rehoboam, 931–913), when subtracted, may vary from the number in the "Years" column for that king. This is because the beginning and ending dates for a given king may include only portions of those years in the Gregorian calendar.

The dates of the kings are adapted from Edwin R. Thiele, *The Mysterious Numbers of the Hebrew Kings.* 3rd ed. Grand Rapids: Zondervan Publishing House, 1983.

built to house these calves to replace the temple that contained the ark with its golden cherubim. These were located in the towns of **Dan** in far northern Israel and **Bethel** just north of the Judean border in southern Israel (see the map "Solomon's 12 Districts and Surrounding Nations," near 4:17-19). **The people** were told to conduct pilgrimages to these places rather than traveling to Jerusalem. Thus the Israelites could find a sense of fulfillment in going through similar forms of **worship** (rituals) though they were being disobedient to God.

**12:31.** New **priests** were **appointed . . . from all sorts of people. . . . not** from the **Levites** as God had directed. Jeroboam dismissed the Levitical priests who then migrated to Judah (2 Chron. 11:14). The new priests conducted religious rites for the people at **shrines** Jeroboam **built** at various **high places** convenient to them. This accommodation again gave the people a feeling that they could worship as much as they pleased so they felt less longing for their former ways of worship.

**12:32-33.** Jeroboam **instituted a** new **festival . . . like the festival held in Judah,** a carefully designed counterfeit of the Day of Atonement. Israel's festival was held **in Bethel** and in **the eighth month** (October-November) exactly one month later than Judah's, **a month of** Jeroboam's **own choosing. Priests . . . sacrifices,** and an **altar** were all provided to make Israel's festival just as good as if not "better" than Judah's. But Israel's feast was designed by Jeroboam whereas Judah's feasts had been decreed by God. Jeroboam set the example for his people; he personally **went up to the altar** at Bethel **to make offerings.**

### 2. THE MAN OF GOD FROM JUDAH (13:1-32)

Jeroboam's idolatrous system of worship (12:28-33) was soon condemned by a prophet of the Lord. This man's experiences point out the evil of what Jeroboam did and how deceptive it was. Then the prophet himself fell into a trap.

### a. His prophecy (13:1-10)

**13:1-3.** The mission of this anonymous **man of God** had its origin in **the word of the LORD** (vv. 1-2, 9); this was a prophecy of judgment fully authorized by God. The prophet was sent **from** the Southern Kingdom of **Judah to Bethel**; he lived under the authority of God's Davidic ruler rather than under the influence of the apostate Jeroboam. He uttered his prophecy publicly at the altar **as Jeroboam was standing** near it **offering** a sacrifice.

This man's prophecy is one of the most remarkable in Scripture because it predicted the name and actions of a king who would not appear on the scene for 290 years. **Josiah,** who reigned from 640 to 609 B.C., fulfilled this prophecy just as the man of God predicted (2 Kings 23:15-20). Josiah demolished the Bethel **altar** built by Jeroboam and slaughtered the false **priests** there. **A sign** was often given in prophecies of this kind when the fulfillment would take place many years later. The man of God predicted that **the sign,** a miracle to verify the prophecy, would be performed then. The sign, he said, was that **the altar** would **split apart** that very **day** (cf. 1 Kings 13:5).

**13:4-6.** Jeroboam's reaction to the prophecy was to order the arrest of the prophet. When the king's outstretched **hand,** symbolizing his authority, withered, this illustrated that God's authority was greater than Jeroboam's. **God** could paralyze Jeroboam's might and render it completely useless. The sign (**the altar** splitting **apart**; cf. v. 3) also left no doubt in the minds of those present that the prophecy came from the **God** who controlled Jeroboam and who would judge his wickedness.

**The king** acknowledged God's power and asked **the man of God** to ask **God** to restore his **hand,** which God graciously did. Jeroboam referred to Yahweh as **your God,** not "my God," thereby testifying to his own idolatry.

**13:7-10.** Receiving an immediate cure for his hand's paralysis (cf. v. 6), **the king** extended a great favor and privilege to the prophet. He offered the shelter of his royal palace, a meal, and **a gift.** In the ancient Near East hospitality was a sacred custom. **To eat** a meal with an invited guest under one's roof was to give him a promise of continuing personal protection. **But the man of God** wanted no treaty with wicked Jeroboam. He had been instructed by God not to accept even a meal, which would have placed him in Jeroboam's debt.

Returning home by a different route

would have further illustrated the official nature of the prophet's visit; this was not a pleasure trip, but he was in **Bethel** on business for God. The prophet had obeyed God faithfully up to this point.

### b. His seduction (13:11-19)

This somewhat confusing story may appear at first to contribute nothing to the advancement of the narrative or the writer's purpose. But careful study clarifies its value.

**13:11-14.** A second **prophet** was living in Bethel and was **old**. These are important clues. Old age sometimes tends to make one lazy and complacent. This man's complacency is further suggested by his willingness not only to live in the territory of the apostate king but at the very center of the king's false system of worship.

Why the old prophet **rode after** the prophet **from Judah** is not stated. Perhaps he simply wanted to visit with a younger, more faithful servant of the Lord. Or his motive from the beginning could have been jealousy and his intent could have been to destroy the younger prophet's ministry.

**13:15-19.** In response to the faithful prophet's refusal, **the old** man claimed direct revelation from God through **an angel** who had told him, he said, that the young man should forget his former instructions from **the LORD**. So the prophet of Judah, not suspecting that the old prophet **was lying to him . . . returned** to Bethel and ate **with him.** The apostasy of Jeroboam had infected even a prophet who seems to have had the same selfish motives and practiced the same brazen disobedience as the king. The spirit of apostasy was spreading quickly and was already reaping a grim harvest in Israel.

### c. His death and burial (13:20-32)

**13:20-22.** Even though **the old prophet** had sinned, **the word of the LORD came to** him again, as it did to many other prophets of the Lord who sinned (e.g., Jonah, Elijah). The old man announced the fate of his brother prophet then and there. The younger prophet, because he had disobeyed the Lord's **command,** would not be given an honorable burial. The severity of God's judgment on this man, compared with His dealings with the older prophet who was

also disobedient, seems unfair. But the severity of God's judgment was proportionate to the importance of the younger man's mission. All Israel would have heard about his prophecy of God's judgment on Jeroboam for his disobedience to the word of the Lord through Moses. If God had not judged His own prophet for *his* disobedience to the word given him by God and which he had announced publicly, doubt would have been cast on his prophecy and on God's credibility. By comparison the older prophet's sins were private and were judged privately by God.

**13:23-32.** Lions **on the road** were not common in Israel, but neither were they unknown. Wild animals roamed the land (cf. Jud. 14:5) and occasionally **killed** people. That this beast was divinely sent to judge the younger prophet is clear in that after the **lion** killed the man he stood **beside** the **body** and **neither** ate the corpse nor **mauled the donkey** (1 Kings 13:28). The death of the prophet became public knowledge (v. 25). Out of reverence for **the man of God** the **old prophet . . . picked up** his **body,** mourned **for him, and** buried **him** (v. 29) **in his own tomb** (v. 30). The old prophet undoubtedly suffered the pains of a guilty conscience for having had a part in the man of God's death. He was convinced the prophecy about Josiah would come to pass (v. 32; cf. v. 2).

This story clarifies the importance of consistent and complete obedience to the Word of God, the lesson God was seeking to impress on Jeroboam and His people at that time. It also illustrates that added privilege brings increased responsibility; God dealt with the prophet who had the greater responsibility more severely than he did with the man who had less. The effects of spiritual apostasy even on God's servants can be seen too, especially in the behavior of the older prophet.

### 3. JEROBOAM'S PERSISTENT APOSTASY (13:33-34)

**13:33-34.** That the preceding incident was intended to teach Jeroboam and the Israelites the danger of disregarding the word of the Lord seems clear from this brief passage. The king's sins had been recounted (12:25-33), then he was warned (13:1-32), but still **Jeroboam did**

**not change his evil ways.** Though the appointing of just **anyone** to the priestly office is singled out (v. 33; cf. 12:31) and was perhaps the most serious aspect of his apostasy, it was his total disregard for the will of God as expressed in the Law of Moses that resulted in Jeroboam's **downfall** and **destruction. This was the sin** (i.e., apostasy) from which many others grew. Though God used political situations and social conditions to bring about His ends, this sin by **Jeroboam** was the root cause of Israel's fall.

4. AHIJAH'S PROPHECY AGAINST JEROBOAM (14:1-18)

Whereas the prophecy of the man of God (13:2) dealt primarily with the destruction of Jeroboam's religious system, Ahijah's prophecy addressed Jeroboam's house (dynasty).

*a. The sickness of Jeroboam's son (14:1-5)*

**14:1-5. At that time** probably refers to a time shortly after the incident recorded in chapter 13. Jeroboam's son, **Abijah,** should not be confused with Rehoboam's son of the same name (15:1). Jeroboam's **son** was just a **boy** at this time (14:3, 12, 17). It is not possible to determine what ailed the lad, nor is this information essential to the narrative.

**Jeroboam** obviously did not believe that Yahweh could or would reveal his wife's identity to the prophet. Perhaps the **king** asked her to **disguise** herself because he did not want other people to observe her visiting a prophet of **the Lord. Ahijah the prophet** was living at **Shiloh,** the former site of the tabernacle in Israel. Jeroboam's allusion to Ahijah's prediction of his coronation (cf. 11:29-39) suggests that perhaps the king hoped to receive another welcome prophecy, this time that his son would recover. The gifts of food sent to **Ahijah** may have been simply customary, but in light of Jeroboam's other actions they seem designed to win a positive word from the prophet. **Ahijah** was old and blind, but God gave him a message and insight into the king's plan.

*b. The fate of Jeroboam's dynasty (14:6-18)*

**14:6-7a.** Jeroboam's **wife** hoped to hear a message of deliverance for her boy, but instead she heard a message of doom for her husband, herself, and her

son. The prophet quickly unmasked the actress (**Why this pretense?**). The king's wife thought she had been sent to **Ahijah,** but the prophet said he had **been sent to** her. **The Lord** is **the God of Israel,** not the idols **Jeroboam** had set up. The message he had for her came from Him.

**14:7b-9.** God reminded the king through the prophet that it was He who had **made** him **a leader over** His **people.** But Jeroboam had not followed in David's footsteps as he should have done. In fact God said Jeroboam had **done more evil than all who lived before** him. Whether Jeroboam intended his golden calves to be idols or aids in the worship of Yahweh, God called them **other gods** and **idols.** They were only pieces **of metal.** The king's idolatry had angered the Lord who regarded it as a rejection of Himself.

**14:10-11.** Because **Jeroboam** had led God's people away from God his **house** (dynasty) would be **cut off.** No **male** would be able to perpetuate his line which God compared to **dung.** Jeroboam's family would not be buried but would be eaten by **dogs** and **birds,** a terrible disgrace in the minds of Semites. (This would also be true of Baasha's family, 16:4, and Ahab's family, 21:24.)

**14:12-13.** The **only** male descendant of **Jeroboam** to **be buried** would be Abijah, who would die very soon. His death on the return of the queen to her **home** would signify the sure fulfillment of the more distant aspects of Ahijah's prophecy.

**14:14-15.** Ahijah the prophet said **a king** would be raised up **who** would **cut off** Jeroboam's **family.** This was Baasha (15:27-29). The last part of 14:14, which is subject to several interpretations, probably means that this would surely come to pass. Moreover, the whole nation would experience instability and waver like **a reed. Jeroboam** had planted Israel not in the solid soil of God's Word but in the unsubstantial waters of idolatry, like Egyptian rushes or papyrus reeds. God promised to **uproot** the nation **from the good land that He gave to their forefathers** and to **scatter them beyond the River** Euphrates, which He did in 722 b.c. by the hands of the Assyrians. The Israelites' idolatry was the reason for this judgment. **Asherah poles** (cf. v. 23; 15:13;

16:33) were wooden shafts carved to encourage worship of the Canaanite goddess Asherah.

**14:16.** God's giving **Israel up** must be understood in a limited sense. He promised Abraham that his descendants would be blessed forever (Gen. 12:2-3; 18:17-18; 22:17-18). Later God brought Israel back from captivity but still has not fulfilled all His promises of blessing which they will yet experience (Isa. 62). God did give them up to judgment in captivity, however, which is the forsaking that is in view here.

**14:17-18.** These verses record the exact fulfillment of Ahijah's prophecy of the death of Prince Abijah. The queen must have traveled from Shiloh (v. 2) back to her home in **Tirzah** with a heavy heart. Jeroboam had moved to Tirzah from Shechem (cf. 12:25).

As the Lord's word came to pass immediately in the death of the prince, His long-range prophecies also began to take shape in Jeroboam's reign. One may safely assume that all the territory Solomon ruled except Judah came under Jeroboam's control. Much of this was lost during his reign. This lost area included the land around Damascus to the north which became an independent Aramean state. In the southwest the Philistines repossessed some of their former territory and grew stronger (cf. 15:27). On the east Moab was apparently lost. Ironically Jeroboam's protector in Egypt (11:40), Shishak (Sheshonk I), invaded Judah (14:25) during Jeroboam's reign. This resulted in heavy damage and widespread destruction. Jeroboam was also defeated by King Abijah of Judah (2 Chron. 13:13-20). Israel suffered both in military strength and in territorial holdings during Jeroboam's reign.

5. JEROBOAM'S DEATH (14:19-20)

**14:19-20.** Starting with Jeroboam the events of the reigns of 18 of the 20 kings of the Northern Kingdom are said in 1 and 2 Kings to have been recorded in **the book of the annals of the kings of Israel** (all except Tibni, 1 Kings 16:21-22, and Hoshea, 2 Kings 17:1-6). Similarly the events of the reigns of 14 of the 19 kings of the Southern Kingdom are said in 1 and 2 Kings to be recorded in "the book of the annals of the kings of Judah" (starting with Rehoboam, 1 Kings 14:29).

These books were historical documents, perhaps kept in the royal archives. They are no longer extant. (Also cf. 1 Chron. 27:24, "the book of the annals of King David," and 1 Kings 11:41, "the book of the annals of Solomon," and see "Authorship" in the *Introduction* to 1 Chron.) The writer of 1 Kings selected his material under the inspiration of the Holy Spirit to emphasize the unspiritual aspects of Jeroboam's **22**-year rule over Israel. **Nadab his son succeeded him** on the throne.

Jeroboam must have been a powerful man to have separated Israel from Judah and ruled it for so long a time. But he lacked the commitment to the Lord that would have made him a great and successful king.

### C. Rehoboam's evil reign in Judah (14:21-31)

The scene shifts now to the southern monarchy of Judah.

1. REHOBOAM'S WICKEDNESS (14:21-24)

**14:21. Rehoboam . . . reigned 17 years** (931–913 B.C.). He and all succeeding kings of Judah reigned **in Jerusalem.** Perhaps to contrast this city with the capitals of the Northern Kingdom (Shechem, Tirzah, and Samaria; cf. comments on 12:25) the writer described it as **the city the LORD had chosen,** not like the northern capitals that were chosen by men. The king's mother **Naamah** was one of Solomon's foreign wives. As **an Ammonite** she worshiped the detestable idol-god Molech (cf. 11:5, 33). Probably she was partially responsible for the revival of Canaanite paganism that took place during Rehoboam's reign.

**14:22-24.** Rehoboam turned from the Lord after he had become established on the throne and was strong (2 Chron. 12:1, 14). This revival of idolatry reintroduced conditions that had prevailed in the days of the Judges before David turned the nation to **the LORD.** The Lord's **jealous anger** was directed at those responsible for the sins that destroyed His beloved people. The **high places** were sometimes places where Yahweh was worshiped but not as He had commanded. The **sacred stones** or pillars **and Asherah poles** (cf. 1 Kings 14:15) were aids to the worship of male and female Canaanite idols. The **high**

hills and **spreading** trees were favorite locations for these cultic shrines. **Male shrine prostitutes** (sodomites) were used in pagan worship. The same practices that moved God to purge the land of the moral cancer that plagued it in Joshua's day were those to which the Israelites returned under Rehoboam's leadership.

2. SHISHAK'S INVASION (14:25-28)

**14:25-28. Shishak** (cf. 11:40), **king (pharaoh) of Egypt** (945–924 B.C.), also known as Sheshonk I, was the founder of her 22nd dynasty. He had given asylum to Jeroboam earlier (cf. 11:40). In Rehoboam's **fifth year** Shishak tried to establish Egyptian supremacy over Palestine. His military campaign into Judah, Israel, Edom, and Philistia netted him control of 156 cities. The record of his campaigns is inscribed on the exterior of the Amon temple's south wall at Karnak in Egypt. Shishak captured cities in Judah and threatened to besiege **Jerusalem.** This resulted in **Rehoboam** and the leaders humbling themselves before the Lord and God spared Jerusalem from destruction (2 Chron. 12:2-12). Rehoboam bought Shishak off by giving him many of the **treasures of the temple** and **of the . . . palace** (1 Kings 14:26). These included the 500 **gold shields** made by **Solomon** (cf. 10:16-17). These were replaced by less expensive **bronze shields** which were kept locked up and used mainly in escorting **the king** to the **temple.** Shishak's invasion was the first serious attack against Judah by any foreign power since Saul's days. The Egyptian king was not able to subdue Palestine as he had hoped.

3. REHOBOAM'S DEATH (14:29-31)

**14:29-30.** In addition to **the book of the annals of the kings of Judah** the chronicler noted other contemporary sources where more of Rehoboam's deeds were recorded (2 Chron. 12:13-16). The **continual warfare** mentioned here (1 Kings 14:30) is mentioned briefly again (15:6; cf. 2 Chron. 12:15) but is not explained. In view of Rehoboam's initial plan to regain Israel by force (1 Kings 12:21; which he abandoned after the Prophet Shemaiah reported God's prohibition of civil war, 2 Chron. 11:1-4), these constant wars probably involved border disputes in the territory of Benjamin. It

appears that **Rehoboam** was more successful in these border disputes since he won both the hearts and the land of the Benjamites. The exact border probably changed many times in these early years of the divided monarchy.

The 15 cities Rehoboam fortified were located in Judah and Benjamin, south and west of Jerusalem (see the map "Fifteen Judean Cities Fortified by Rehoboam," near 2 Chron. 11:5-10). Probably after Shishak's invasion they were strengthened to defend Judah against future attacks from Egypt and Philistia.

**14:31. Rehoboam** died **and was buried** in the old **City of David** (cf. comments on 2:10) in Jerusalem. **His mother's name** is given again (cf. 14:21) as part of the regular summary of the kings' reigns. His son **Abijah . . . succeeded him.**

## D. Abijah's evil reign in Judah (15:1-8)

1. ABIJAH'S WICKEDNESS (15:1-6)

**15:1-2.** Abijah's **three-**year reign in **Judah** (913–911 B.C.) was within Jeroboam's **reign** in Israel (931–910 B.C.). **Abijah** was a son of Rehoboam and **Maacah,** a **daughter of** Absalom (**Abishalom** is a variant spelling), David's son. "Daughter" or son does not always mean a descendant in the very next generation; it is often used of a descendant two or more generations removed.

**15:3-6. All the sins** of Rehoboam refer to the same kinds of idolatrous offenses (cf. 14:23-24). The importance of one's affections is emphasized by the reference to Abijah's **heart;** one's affections often determine his actions. God's patience with Abijah was because of His promises to **David** more than to Abijah's own character. (**Him,** v. 4, refers to **David,** not Abijah.) **A lamp** is a picturesque way of describing a successor or successors who would dispel all kinds of darkness; the figure refers to the whole of David's dynasty (cf. comments on 11:36; also see 2 Sam. 21:17; 2 Kings 8:19).

The **war between Rehoboam and Jeroboam** (cf. 1 Kings 14:30) continued **throughout Abijah's lifetime.** One episode is recorded in 2 Chronicles 13:2-20 where Abijah's trust in God resulted in victory in spite of his being outnumbered. Abijah did not abandon the Lord even though he tolerated idolatry.

## 2. ABIJAH'S DEATH (15:7-8)

**15:7-8.** On **the book of the annals of the kings of Judah** see comments on 14:29. The second reference to **war** with **Jeroboam** (cf. 15:6) suggests that the antagonism between Israel and Judah at this time was intense. **Rested with his fathers** is a euphemism for death.

## E. Asa's good reign in Judah (15:9-24)

Eight of the 19 kings of Judah were good. That is, their whole reign was evaluated by God as good even though some of their recorded deeds were evil. Four of these good kings led Judah in religious reforms designed to restore the nation to a purer form of worship and to return the people to obeying the Mosaic Law. Asa was the first good king of Judah (v. 11) and the first reformer.

## 1. ASA'S GOODNESS (15:9-15)

**15:9-10.** Asa **became king** just shortly before Jeroboam's reign in Israel ended in 910 B.C. Asa **reigned . . . 41 years** (911-870 B.C.). **Maacah** was his grandmother (not "mother" as in some versions; cf. v. 2).

**15:11-13.** The divine assessment of Asa's rule was that he **did what was right in the eyes of the LORD,** generally speaking. **David,** of course, was Asa's ancestor, not his immediate **father.**

The writer of 2 Chronicles gave much more information about Asa's reign than is found in 1 Kings. Asa's reign began with 10 years of peace (2 Chron. 14:1). It was probably during this period that he instituted his first series of religious reforms (2 Chron. 14:2-5). At that time he also fortified Judah's defenses (2 Chron. 14:6-8). The peace was broken by an invasion by Zerah the Ethiopian, a commander of the Egyptian King Osarkon I. But Asa defeated the Egyptians, though Judah was greatly outnumbered, by relying on the Lord (2 Chron. 14:9-15). The Prophet Azariah warned Asa to continue to trust in God and not to think that his own power had saved him (2 Chron. 15:1-7). More years of peace followed (2 Chron. 15:19).

Encouraged by God's prophet, Asa embarked on a second period of reformation (1 Kings 15:12-15; 2 Chron. 15:8-18). The expulsion of the sodomites and the destruction of **idols** introduced by Rehoboam and Abijah were part of this re-form, as was Asa's deposing of **his grandmother Maacah** from the official position of **queen mother because** of her **repulsive Asherah pole,** which he **burned . . . in the Kidron Valley** east of Jerusalem.

**15:14-15.** Asa removed some of **the high places** (2 Chron. 14:3) but not all of them (1 Kings 15:14). Nevertheless his **heart was fully committed to the LORD all his life.** In view of **Asa's** self-reliance later in his life this statement probably means that he did not tolerate idolatry but worshiped only the true God. **The silver . . . gold,** and **articles that he and his father had dedicated** probably refer to the booty that Abijah had taken in his war with Jeroboam (2 Chron. 13:16-17) and what Asa had acquired in defeating the Egyptians (2 Chron. 14:12-13). Second Chronicles adds other details of Asa's reform including an account of the formal renewal of the Mosaic Covenant (2 Chron. 15:9-17).

## 2. ASA'S VICTORY OVER BAASHA (15:16-22)

**15:16-17. Baasha king of Israel** (909-886 B.C.) was a perennial enemy of **Asa. Baasha . . . fortified Ramah,** on the Judah-Israel border just four miles north of Jerusalem, so he could maintain control of the traffic between Israel and **Judah.**

**15:18-21.** Asa's plan to divert **Baasha** from strengthening **Ramah** included emptying his treasuries to buy **a treaty** with **Ben-Hadad** I, **the king of Aram . . . in Damascus** (see the chart "Kings of Aram in 1 and 2 Kings," near 1 Kings 11:23-25). **Asa** tried to induce Ben-Hadad to **break** his **treaty with Baasha,** and Asa's plan succeeded. **Ben-Hadad** invaded **Israel** and took some towns near the Sea of **Kinnereth** (later known as the Sea of Galilee), forcing Baasha to move his forces from Ramah to the north. Baasha himself went **to Tirzah,** the capital of Israel at that time (cf. 14:17).

**15:22.** Asa then proceeded to confiscate the building materials (**stones and timber**) Baasha left behind to fortify **Ramah** and used them to strengthen his own defense cities of **Geba** and **Mizpah** near Israel's border. Asa's plan was clever and successful, but it demonstrated lack of trust in God. For getting help from Aram's king, the Prophet Hanani rebuked Asa (2 Chron. 16:7-9). **Asa** resented the rebuke and put Hanani in prison (2 Chron. 16:10). Perhaps Asa's successes against Egypt and Israel made him think too highly of himself.

### 3. ASA'S DEATH (15:23-24)

**15:23-24.** Asa's achievements were recorded in **the book of the annals of the kings of Judah** (cf. 14:29; 15:7). At the end of his life Asa again failed to seek the Lord. When **his feet became diseased** he did not ask for the Lord's help but relied only on the physicians (2 Chron. 16:12). Though Asa's faith was not what it might have been, all in all his relationship with God was characterized by fidelity and blessing during his long reign. Perhaps because of Asa's poor health his son **Jehoshaphat** reigned as coregent with him during the last years of his life (873–870 B.C.). When Asa died, Ahab (874–853 B.C.) was reigning in Israel.

## F. Nadab's evil reign in Israel (15:25-32)

The scene reverts to the Northern Kingdom and shifts back in time to the early years of Asa's reign over Judah.

### 1. NADAB'S ACHIEVEMENTS (15:25-28)

**15:25-26. Nadab** was the brother of Abijah who had died in childhood (14:17). Whether Nadab was older or younger than Abijah is not known. He was the second ruler of the **Jeroboam** dynasty, and **reigned** for **two years** (910–909 B.C.). Nadab continued the policies begun by **his father** which **the LORD** regarded as **evil.** The seriousness of Jeroboam's sins can be seen in that **he had caused Israel to commit** sin as well as sinning himself.

**15:27-28. Baasha killed Nadab** at **Gibbethon, a** strong **Philistine town** southwest of Israel, between Ekron and Gezer. Evidently **Israel** did not capture this town (cf. 16:15-17). Perhaps the siege ended when **Nadab** was killed. His assassin **Baasha** then became **king** of Israel (15:33–16:7).

### 2. THE END OF ISRAEL'S FIRST DYNASTY (15:29-32)

**15:29-32.** Baasha's destruction of the house of **Jeroboam** was intended to secure his own throne. It fulfilled Ahijah's prophecy of the destruction of **Jeroboam's** dynasty (14:14). The reason for this severe judgment is reiterated by the writer here (15:30). Specifically the worship at

the golden-calf shrines is in view. This worship was continued by all of Jeroboam's successors and was frequently condemned by the writer of 1 and 2 Kings (cf. 1 Kings 15:34; 16:19, 26, 31; 22:52; etc.). The reference to the continual warfare in Baasha's day (15:32; cf. vv. 16-22) forms a bridge to the next section.

## G. Baasha's evil reign in Israel (15:33–16:7)

### 1. BAASHA'S ASSESSMENT (15:33-34)

**15:33-34. Baasha** took the throne of Israel **in the third year of Asa** and **reigned** in **Tirzah** the capital (cf. 14:17; 15:21) for **24 years** (909–886 B.C.). His was the third-longest reign of the Israelite kings. However, the brevity of his history as recorded here suggests that his reign was comparatively insignificant. He continued the religious policies begun by **Jeroboam.**

### 2. JEHU'S PROPHECY (16:1-4)

**16:1-4. Jehu** the prophet must be distinguished from Jehu the king of Israel (841–814 B.C.). This prophet was the **son of Hanani.** This Hanani may or may not have been the prophet who warned King Asa of Judah (2 Chron. 16:7-9). God said He had **lifted** Baasha **up from the dust and made** him **leader of** the Israelites. This implies that **Baasha** had a lowly origin. Almost the same words used to describe Baasha's future judgment (1 Kings 16:4) had been given to Jeroboam by the Prophet Ahijah (cf. 14:7, 10-11) and were given later by Elijah to Ahab (21:24). The fact that **Baasha** did not turn to the Lord in spite of his being God's instrument of judgment on the house of Jeroboam suggests his complete blindness to the importance of spiritual matters in his own life and in that of his nation. **Baasha** committed the same sins himself. This indicates that the level of his apostasy was deep.

### 3. BAASHA'S DEATH (16:5-7)

**16:5-7.** The writer followed his regular recording of the facts surrounding the king's death (vv. 5-6) with an additional reemphasis on the reasons for Baasha's judgment by God (v. 7). Baasha's destruction of Jeroboam's **house** (family or dynasty) was one reason. Even though God determined that Jeroboam's dynasty would be destroyed and announced this beforehand through Ahijah, God held Baasha responsible for killing Jeroboam's descendants. In doing so Baasha had not acted under God's direction, but only to gain his own ends.

### H. Elah's evil reign in Israel (16:8-14)

**16:8-10.** Elah assumed the throne **of Israel and . . . reigned in Tirzah,** the capital, for **two years** (886–885 B.C.). He continued the wicked policies of his predecessors (v. 13). No specific accomplishments are recorded for him. He is infamous as the king who was murdered while **getting drunk** (v. 10). As commander **of half** of Elah's **chariots . . . Zimri** was a powerful military officer.

**16:11-14.** Zimri completely **destroyed** Israel's second ruling **family** plus friends of the family in order to avoid retaliation against his coup d'etat. Thus Jehu's prophecy (cf. v. 3) was fulfilled. Again the writer identified the spiritual root of the judgment (v. 13).

### I. Zimri's evil reign in Israel (16:15-20)

**16:15-20.** Zimri's **seven**-day reign (885 B.C.) proved to be the shortest of any Israelite **king. Gibbethon** in Philistia was again under siege by Israel's **army** (cf. 15:27). It probably took a runner two days to reach the army at Gibbethon after the assassination of Elah. The troops immediately heralded **Omri, the commander of the army** (16:16), as the new **king** even though **Zimri** had declared himself king **in Tirzah.** Zimri was not an acceptable candidate for the throne in the minds of **Omri** and his men as they marched back to the capital. They appeared at the city walls (probably after marching about four or five days) and took control of **the city.** Zimri apparently knew he could not retain his throne or save his life, so he did as much damage to **the palace** as he could while taking his life. His death resulted ultimately from his **sins** (v. 19).

### J. Omri's evil reign in Israel (16:21-28)

**16:21-24.** The death of Zimri (vv. 17-18) did not automatically place the kingdom in Omri's hands. **Half** the population including the army sided with him, but the other half preferred **Tibni.** Tibni's strength can be seen in that he was able to oppose Omri successfully for six years (885–880 B.C.). During this time civil war ravaged **Israel** and threatened to **split** the Northern Kingdom **into two** parts. But eventually **Omri** overpowered **Tibni** and became the sole ruler (880–874 B.C.). Omri's army support apparently proved decisive and **Tibni died** (v. 22), probably by being executed.

For the first **six** years of his reign (885–880 B.C.) **Omri** ruled in the old capital of **Tirzah** (cf. 14:17; 15:21, 33; 16:6, 8-9, 15, 17). But then he moved into his brand new capital, **Samaria.** He **built** this **city on a hill,** well situated for defense, seven miles west of Tirzah. Omri paid **Shemer . . . two talents** (ca. 150 pounds) **of silver** for **the hill.** (Samaria was named after Shemer; cf. v. 24.) Archeologists have unearthed evidence that Samaria was built by skillful craftsmen. The site dominated the north-south trade routes. Samaria proved to be almost impregnable as a stronghold against alien attacks because of its elevated position.

**Omri** was probably the strongest leader of the Northern Kingdom up to that time. Assyrian records dating from over a century later refer to Israel as "the land of Omri." During Omri's reign Ben-Hadad I, king of the Arameans in Damascus (see the chart "Kings of Aram in 1 and 2 Kings," near 1 Kings 11:23-25), continued to add to his holdings to the north of Israel. Omri's son, Ahab, had difficulty containing these Aramean aggressors. Also the Assyrian Empire was growing stronger and farther to the northeast under Ashurnaṣirpal II (883–859; see the chart "Kings of Assyria in the Middle and New Assyrian Kingdoms," near Jonah 1:2) and proceeded to expand its territory as far west as the Mediterranean Sea. Faced by these threats on his north, Omri was able to protect Israel well enough to attack and defeat Moab to the southeast at the same time. This victory is referred to on the famous Moabite Stone. Another of Omri's significant achievements was his alliance with the Phoenicians which was sealed with the marriage of his son Ahab to Jezebel, a daughter of the Phoenician king, Ethbaal (cf. 1 Kings 16:31).

**16:25-28.** Though **Omri** is passed over quickly in 1 Kings, he was a powerful and politically effective king. But the major concern of the writer of 1 Kings was Omri's spiritual condition. In this he was the worst Israelite king so far (vv. 25-26). Omri's 12-year reign ended with his death and burial in his new capital city. His rule passed to his son, **Ahab. Omri** was the founder of the fourth dynasty of Israelite kings.

### K. Ahab's evil reign in Israel (16:29–22:40)

1. AHAB'S WICKEDNESS (16:29-34)

**16:29-31.** Ahab ruled Israel from **Samaria** for **22 years** (874–853 B.C.). He was the most wicked king Israel had experienced, even worse than his father Omri who was worse than all before him (v. 25). Ahab's wickedness consisted of perpetuating all **the sins of Jeroboam;** he even **considered** them **trivial.** In addition Ahab **married** a pagan princess, **Jezebel,** who zealously tried to promote her depraved cult as the exclusive religion of Israel. Jezebel's father, **Ethbaal,** was **king of the Sidonians** (Phoenicians), with his capital in Tyre. **Baal** (meaning "lord") is a name used generally in the Old Testament for the male deity the native Canaanite tribes worshiped under various other titles. The Tyrians called him Baal Melqart, but their religion was only a cultic variation of the standard Baal worship common throughout Palestine. Evidently **Ahab** was not forced to marry Jezebel; his choice to marry her is something for which the writer held him responsible.

**16:32-33.** Ahab **built** a temple for **Baal** in the capital of Israel and constructed an **altar for Baal** in it. **Asherah** poles (cf. 14:15, 23; 15:13) were idols carved to stimulate worship of Baal's female counterpart. The writer repeated the seriousness of Ahab's sins for emphasis (16:33; cf. v. 30).

**16:34.** The refortification of **Jericho** was specifically forbidden by **Joshua** after God supernaturally destroyed it (Josh. 6:26). Though the city had been occupied since Joshua's day, Hiel's reconstruction seems to have been the first serious attempt to restore it to its former condition. Joshua's prophecy was fulfilled literally when two of Hiel's sons perished. Perhaps this reference, which seems unrelated to Ahab's accomplishments, was included to show that as God's word was fulfilled in this instance so it would be in Ahab's case. Ahab was setting up a system of worship that God said He would judge, as Hiel had tried to **set up** a city that God had said He would judge.

2. AHAB'S PUNISHMENT (CHAPS. 17–18)

Because of his wickedness Ahab was disciplined by God, who used the Prophet Elijah in a remarkable way to bring Israel back to Himself.

### a. Elijah's announcement of drought (17:1-6)

**17:1. Elijah** had been and was being prepared by the Lord to demonstrate to all Israel that Yahweh, not Baal, is still the only true God. Even Elijah's name, which means "Yahweh is my God," conveyed that fact! Elijah lived **in Gilead** east of the Jordan River near a community called **Tishbe.** Perhaps as Elijah heard reports of Jezebel's increasing maneuverings to replace the worship of the Lord with Baal worship his godly heart was stirred up. God gave him a mission. Armed with God's promise he walked westward to Samaria. Bursting into the palace, he hurled his ultimatum at King **Ahab.** He claimed that **the LORD** is **the God of Israel,** that He is alive (cf. v. 12; 18:10), and that he, Elijah, was God's servant. (On the words "As the LORD . . . **lives**" see comments on 1:29.) Elijah could confidently declare that there would be neither **dew nor rain** because God had promised to withhold these from the land if His people turned from Him to other gods (Lev. 26:18-19; Deut. 11:16-17; 28:23-24). God had apparently revealed to Elijah that He would honor that promise in Elijah's day. This would have struck at the heart of Baalism, for Baal-worshipers believed that their god was the god of rain! The drought, brought on by the true God, showed that He, not Baal, controls the weather. This was a remarkable demonstration of God's superiority and of the total inadequacy and falsehood of Baal worship.

**17:2-4.** Having made his dramatic announcement, **Elijah** was told by **the LORD** to **leave** Samaria, return **eastward, and hide in** a ravine by the wadi **Kerith, east of the Jordan** River. Elijah had to hide because he would soon be hunted by the king (cf. 18:10). The exact location of this seasonal **brook** is not known; it was one of many streams that flowed during the rainy season but dried up when the weather turned hot. God promised to provide food and **drink** for His servant at this unlikely spot.

**17:5-6.** Elijah obeyed **the LORD,** who

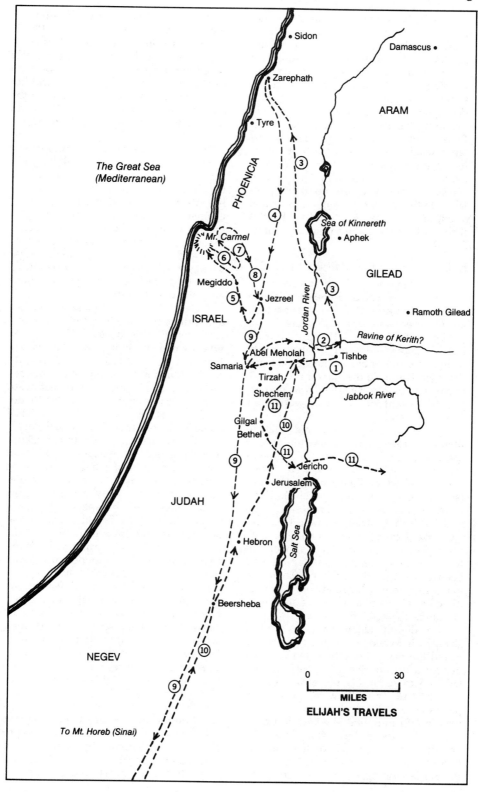

**ELIJAH'S TRAVELS**

miraculously provided for him as He had promised. God directed **ravens,** birds that normally neglect their own young (cf. Job. 38:41), to bring **bread and meat** faithfully to Elijah every **morning** and **evening.** And **he drank** water **from the brook.** The Hebrew word for "bread" (*leḥem*) means food in general, possibly including berries, fruit, nuts, eggs, etc. Perhaps they were brought from a distance where the drought had not yet affected the vegetation. Through this unusual manner of nourishing His prophet physically, God was also nourishing Elijah's faith for later feats of spiritual strength (see the list "God's Miracles through Elijah and Elisha," near 2 Kings 2:13-14).

*b. Elijah's ministry at Zarephath (17:7-24)*

**17:7.** How long Elijah stayed at **the brook** is not revealed. **Some time later** it **dried up** because of the drought which lasted three and one-half years in all (Luke 4:25; James 5:17). Elijah had learned that God would miraculously provide for him, but now he would learn that God could do the same for others—even Gentiles—as well. God was preparing His servant for a great showdown on Mount Carmel.

**17:8-11.** Elijah was directed to **Zarephath,** a town on the Mediterranean coast between Tyre and **Sidon** in Phoenicia, the homeland of Jezebel (cf. 16:31) and the heart of Baal-Melqart territory (see the map "Elijah's Travels"). Zarephath was 80-90 miles from Kerith. God told Elijah that **a widow** would feed him (cf. Luke 4:25-26). Widows were usually poor people; normally they ran out of food first in a famine. This famine had been created by the drought. Therefore going to a widow for food was a strange directive. God was again using an unusual source to feed His prophet.

Obediently Elijah made his way **to Zarephath.** When he entered **the town** he tested the first **widow** he saw by asking her for **a drink.** Her favorable response led him to request **a piece of bread.**

**17:12-16.** The widow recognized **Elijah** as an Israelite and appealed to Yahweh in affirming that she had no **bread;** she had **only a** little **flour** and **oil,** enough for a last **meal for** her **son** and herself. Here was a Gentile woman in Phoenicia who believed in the Lord; she

said she believed He is alive (**As surely as the LORD your God lives;** cf. v. 1; 18:10).

**Elijah** calmed her fears of himself, her hunger, and her imminent death. He asked her to feed him **first . . . and then** use what was left to feed herself and her **son.** Then he gave her a promise on the authority of the word of **God:** she would have **food** until the drought ended.

Her obedient response demonstrated her faith in **the word of the LORD.** The Lord honored her faith by fulfilling His promise miraculously. This miracle of God's continually supplying **flour** and olive **oil** was another polemic (protest) against Baal, just as was the drought. Baal-worshipers believed he was a fertility god, giving rain to make crops grow. But he could not overcome the drought to make wheat and olive trees grow. Only the true God could provide flour and oil in a drought!

**17:17-18. Some time later** (cf. v. 7)— again the exact time is not given—tragedy befell Elijah's hostess. **The woman who owned the house** was the widow. Her young **son** fell **ill** and **finally stopped breathing.** Some Bible critics say the boy was only unconscious, not dead, and that his restoration was therefore not a miracle. However, verses 18, 20, 22-23 make it clear that he had actually died.

The woman had a guilty conscience and immediately concluded that **God** was punishing her for her **sin** by killing her **son.** This is a common reaction among many people who do not know God's ways well when personal tragedy enters their lives (cf. John 9:2-3). What sin she was referring to is not stated.

**17:19-21.** The boy was small enough to be carried in his mother's **arms.** Many homes in Palestine at that time had guest rooms built on their roofs. It was in one such **upper room** that Elijah **was staying.** Elijah's first prayer (v. 20) simply expressed his compassion for the woman who, in addition to the trials of the famine, now **also** had to bear this tragedy. Implicit in the prayer was the desire that **God** relieve her of this added burden. Often in cases of miraculous restoration and healing, God's servant placed his hand on the afflicted one to indicate that the power of God in him was passing to the needy individual (e.g., Matt. 8:3). In this instance **Elijah** out of heartfelt concern **stretched himself out** placing the whole body of the lad in contact with his own. **Three times** Elijah did this, praying each time that **God** would restore the **boy's life.** Persistence in prayer is a fundamental requisite for obtaining one's petitions (cf. Matt. 7:7-8; Luke 11:5-13). It proved effective in this case.

**17:22-24.** God miraculously restored **the boy's life.** This is the first recorded instance in Scripture of restoration to life of one who had died. **Elijah . . . carried** the lad downstairs (the boy was apparently weak) and presented **him to his mother.** This miracle proved to the woman that Elijah was indeed **a man of God** and that **the word of the LORD** that Elijah claimed to speak was indeed **the truth.**

This incident showed the widow and others that the power of the Lord as the true God contrasted greatly with the impotency of Baal.

*c. Obadiah's search (18:1-15)*

**18:1-6. In the third** and last **year of** the famine God directed **Elijah to present** himself **to** King **Ahab.** Elijah had God's word that He would soon end the drought.

The **famine** in the land was particularly **severe in** the capital, **Samaria.** (Cf. the famine[s] in Elisha's days, 2 Kings 4:38; 6:25; 7:4; 8:1.) God was directing this calamity especially at the guilty parties, Ahab and Jezebel. This situation prompted **Ahab** and his trusted servant, **Obadiah,** to go in different directions, looking for **some grass** in the **valleys** or near **the springs** where the most necessary **animals** (**horses and mules**) might graze. **Obadiah** had great responsibility in Ahab's court (**in charge of** Ahab's **palace**). **Obadiah was** also **a devout believer in the LORD** (but not the writer of the Bible book of that name). Whether **Jezebel** knew of Obadiah's commitment to the Lord is not clear, but undoubtedly he and the queen were not close friends. Jezebel's aim was to replace the worship of Yahweh with Baal-Melqart worship. Her plan included **killing off the LORD's prophets** (1 Kings 18:4). **Obadiah,** aware of her strategy, had hidden **100 prophets** of the Lord in **caves** and was supplying **them with food and water**—a difficult task in days of extreme famine and drought. Obviously there were many in Israel (cf. 19:18) and probably also in Judah at that time who believed in the

Lord, though Israel as a whole had apostatized.

**18:7-12a. Obadiah recognized** Elijah when they met somewhere outside Samaria; **Elijah** was a "wanted" man in Israel. Out of respect for the prophet, Obadiah **bowed down to the ground.** He could hardly believe he had found **Elijah.** Elijah, wanting to talk with Ahab (vv. 1-2), asked Obadiah to announce him to his **master. Obadiah,** however, was afraid that **Elijah** would disappear again. **Obadiah** explained to the prophet how **Ahab** had searched for him at home and abroad (v. 10) to no avail. Obadiah affirmed that fact by the familiar words, **As surely as the LORD your God lives** (cf. 17:1, 12). If he reported to his king that **Elijah** had been found, and then could not produce him (**the Spirit of the LORD may carry you** away; cf. 2 Kings 2:16), **Ahab** would regard Obadiah's words as a mocking trick and would probably execute him.

**18:12b-15.** To convince Elijah that his concern was sincere, Obadiah related proof that he was a devout believer in **the LORD** (cf. v. 3) **since** his **youth.** Obadiah seemed to think **Elijah** would have **heard** about his hiding and feeding **the prophets of the LORD.** Perhaps this was known among many of the faithful in Israel, especially the prophets, though of course not by **Jezebel** or her sympathizers. **Elijah** assured Obadiah that he would not disappear but would indeed stand before **Ahab** that same day. Elijah's description of God as **the LORD** (Yahweh) **Almighty** who **lives** and whom Elijah served (cf. 17:1; 18:36) indicates that he was confident in God's ability to handle the physical and spiritual situation in Israel, an assurance that had grown as a result of his experiences at Kerith and Zarephath.

*d. Elijah's vindication of the Lord on Mount Carmel (18:16-46)*

This popular story of Elijah's contest with the prophets of Baal is both exciting and extremely significant in the history of Israel. The first part of this narrative (vv. 16-24) clarifies the reason for the dramatic encounter.

(1) The issue at stake. **18:16-18.** When **Ahab** heard Obadiah's message the king **went to meet** the prophet; **Elijah** maintained the initiative as the spokesman of God to whom the king must sub-

mit. In Ahab's eyes **Elijah** was the **troubler of Israel. Elijah** set the record straight and instructed the king who did not perceive or was not willing to admit that *he* and his **father's** (Omri's) **family** (cf. 16:25-26) were the real reason for Israel's troubles. **Ahab** had **abandoned the LORD's commands** in His Law **and** had instead **followed the Baals.** The plural "Baals" refers to local idols of Baal (cf. Jud. 2:11) sometimes with differing names (e.g., Baal-Berith, Jud. 8:33; Baal-Zebub, 2 Kings 1:2-3, 6, 16). This was the real issue and the root cause of all the trouble in Israel, spiritual as well as physical.

(2) The proposed test (18:19-24). **18:19.** In view of Elijah's directive that Ahab **summon the people from all over Israel,** it is likely that hundreds, if not thousands, congregated **on Mount Carmel.** The Carmel range of mountains, 1,742 feet in elevation at its highest point, extends about 30 miles to the southeast of modern-day Haifa from the shores of the Mediterranean Sea. It is a beautiful series of rounded peaks and valleys from which the sea can easily be seen. It is not known exactly where along this ridge Elijah staged this test; any of several sites is possible; Muḥraka is suggested by many as one of the more probable sites.

The extent of **Baal** worship in Israel can be estimated by the number of priests Jezebel regularly fed: **450 prophets** of the male god and **400 . . . of** the female goddess **Asherah,** Baal's consort.

**18:20-21. Mount Carmel** was agreed on by **Ahab.** It would be a fitting site since it lay between Israel and Phoenicia, the lands of the deities in question. Also Mount Carmel was regarded by the Phoenicians as the sacred dwelling place of Baal. No doubt Ahab was highly pleased with this suggested site for the contest because it would have given the Baal prophets a definite advantage; but this did not worry Elijah. It was also a geographically prominent location and thus a fit setting for Elijah's contest.

When **all** the **people** had **assembled. . . . Elijah** stood before them and challenged them to end their double-mindedness, wavering **between two opinions.** It was not good to try to "walk the fence" worshiping two gods. Apparently the Israelites thought that if Yahweh let them down they could turn to

Baal, and vice versa. Elijah was saying that if One is the true God and the other false they should follow the true One wholeheartedly and forget about the impotent impostor. **The people** could not argue with this statement, so they **said nothing.**

**18:22-24.** Elijah then pointed out that in this contest the odds would be **450 prophets** to 1—a humanly impossible situation in which to win! Elijah knew there were other prophets of Yahweh besides himself (cf. v. 13), but as far as this contest was concerned he was **the only one of the LORD's prophets left.**

Of the **two bulls** required, Elijah let his adversaries select their favorite. Each side would prepare to sacrifice its **bull** as a burnt offering to its god. **Then** they would each **call on** their **god** and **the god who** answered **by fire** would be shown to be the true **God.** Baal was supposedly a fertility god, the one who sent rain, caused the crops to grow, and provided food for his people. He was the one who supposedly sent fire (lightning) from heaven. The three-and-one-half-year drought and famine had been a great embarrassment to the worshipers of Baal. It seemed as if Elijah and his God rather than Baal were in control of the fertility of Israel. So Elijah's test to Baal's followers seemed like a good opportunity to vindicate their god and they readily agreed to it. When the preparations were completed, the test began.

(3) The false prophets' failure. **18:25-29.** All **morning** Baal's **prophets . . . called on** their god and **danced around** his **altar** to arouse him to action. **At noon Elijah began to taunt them,** mocking their ineffectiveness. Sarcastically he suggested that Baal was thinking about other things, or **busy** (lit., relieving himself), away on a trip (the Phoenician sailors believed Baal traveled with them on the Mediterranean Sea and elsewhere), or even **sleeping!** Surprisingly Baal's prophets responded by increasing the fervor of their appeals, working themselves into a frenzy. To propitiate their god they mutilated their own bodies as the **custom** of pagan worshipers has been for centuries. This continued for three hours (**the time for the** Israelites' **evening sacrifice;** cf. v. 36, was 3 P.M.), **but** still **there was no response. No one answered** or **paid attention;** that is, Baal did not respond to

their six-hour chanting for lightning, though rain and lightning often come readily to the Carmel mountain range near the Mediterranean Sea.

(4) Elijah's success (18:30-39). **18:30-32.** When it was obvious to all that the prophets of Baal had failed, **Elijah** invited **all the people** to draw near and observe what he would do. An **altar to the LORD** had been built on the site long before but it was in disrepair. **Elijah** selected **12 stones, one for each of the tribes.** Though the tribes had been divided into two nations they were still one people in God's purposes—with a single Lord, a single covenant, and a single destiny. **With these stones he built an altar . . . and . . . dug a trench around it . . . to hold** about one-third of a bushel **of seed (two seahs** equaled about 13 quarts; cf. NIV marg., and a bushel has 32 quarts). Perhaps the trench on each side of the altar could hold that much seed.

**18:33-35.** After **the bull** had been slain and **laid . . . on the wood,** Elijah gave another strange directive. He called for the whole sacrifice and its **wood** to be soaked with **water** three separate times. The excess **water . . . even filled the trench.** The water—**four large jars** filled three times each!—probably was collected from a spring on the mountain or in the Kishon Valley below (v. 40), or from the Mediterranean Sea. The purpose of this soaking, of course, was to show everyone present that the burning of the sacrifice that was to take place was not a natural phenomenon or a trick but was a miracle. Also the time involved in securing the water would have added to the tension of the hour.

**18:36-39. At the time of the** Israelites' evening **sacrifice** (3 P.M.; cf. v. 29), **Elijah stepped forward and prayed.** Without any of the theatrics of his adversaries Elijah simply addressed **God** as one addresses another living person. His words were designed to demonstrate to the onlookers that all he had done as God's **servant** (cf. 17:1; 18:15) had been in obedience to God's **command** and not on the prophet's own initiative. Elijah simply asked God to show the **people** that He is the true **God** and to turn the **hearts** of the people **back** to Himself.

Instantly **fire . . . fell** from heaven (lightning), consuming **the sacrifice . . . wood,** altar, and even the surrounding **soil** and **water.** Spontaneously the crowd **cried** out in amazement. Since **the LORD** (Yahweh) had answered by fire (cf. v. 24); they acknowledged that **He is** the true **God.**

(5) The consequences (18:40-46). **18:40-42. The Kishon Valley** ran parallel to the Carmel range on its north side. There the people **slaughtered** the false **prophets** in obedience to the command of God through Moses (Deut. 13:12-15) and **Elijah.** Previously **Elijah** had predicted the drought **to Ahab** (1 Kings 17:1); now the prophet told the king there would be **a heavy rain. Ahab** rode off down the mountain to celebrate the end of the drought by eating and drinking, **but Elijah** walked back up the mountain to pray for rain. His posture as he prayed reflected the earnestness of his petition, again for the glory of the Lord.

**18:43-46.** Rains normally came from the west off the Mediterannean **Sea,** so Elijah instructed **his servant to look** in that direction. God answered Elijah's petition as he persevered in prayer. At first the rain **cloud** was **small** (like **a man's hand**), but soon **the** whole **sky grew black** and **heavy rain** descended. The torrent evidently overtook **Ahab** as he **rode** in his **chariot . . . to Jezreel,** his winter capital about midway between Mount Carmel and Samaria. **Elijah** overtook him, running the approximate 25 miles with divinely given energy. **Tucking his cloak into his belt** enabled him to run without tripping over the long garment (cf. comments on "Brace yourself like a man" in Job 38:3; 40:7).

Because of Mount Carmel Elijah had discredited Baal and his worshipers, but he had also humiliated vindictive Queen Jezebel.

### 3. AHAB'S WICKED WIFE (CHAP. 19)

#### a. Elijah's flight (19:1-8)

**19:1-5a.** Jezebel had not been present on Mount Carmel; her husband reported to her what had taken place. Infuriated by Elijah's treatment of her **prophets . . . Jezebel sent a** message to him. He was evidently still in the city of Jezreel as she was (cf. 18:46) when he received her warning. She threatened to take his **life** in 24 hours in retaliation for his slaughtering the 450 Baal prophets.

It is remarkable that her threat terrified **Elijah** as it did. Ironically by contrast he had told the widow in Zarephath not to be afraid (17:13). He had just demonstrated that **the gods** to whom she now appealed in her curse had no power at all. (Her statement that she was willing to be dealt with **severely** by the gods [cf. 2:23; 20:10; 2 Kings 6:31] points up the seriousness of her threat. She was so certain she would kill Elijah that she willingly put her own welfare "on the line.") Evidently Elijah's fear sprang from the power Jezebel possessed. Rather than resting in God for His protection as he had for the past three and one-half years, Elijah **ran for his life.** He ran all the way through the kingdom of Judah to the southernmost town in the land, **Beersheba.**

Still fearful he might be discovered by Jezebel's spies he told **his servant** to stay behind and he traveled alone one more **day's journey** (about 15 miles) **into the** Negev **desert.** Finally **he sat down** under **a broom tree** (a desert bush that grows to a height of 12 feet and provides some, though not much, shade) and rested. He was so discouraged he **prayed that he might die.** Elijah had forgotten the lessons God had been teaching him at Kerith, Zarephath, and Carmel. His eyes were on his circumstances rather than on the LORD. His statement that he was **no better than** his **ancestors** (19:4) suggests that he was no more successful than his forefathers in ousting Baal-worship from Israel. Exhausted and discouraged, Elijah **lay down . . . and fell asleep.**

**19:5b-8.** Elijah woke at the touch of a divinely sent messenger. This **angel** had prepared freshly baked **bread,** still warm, and plenty **of water,** which he invited Elijah to consume. The prophet did so and then returned to his rest. **The angel** probably appeared as a human being as was common in the Old Testament.

Again the angel woke Elijah, perhaps after he had slept for some time, and urged him to **eat** more food since **the journey** before him would require **much** energy. Moses and the Israelites had traveled in that wilderness for 40 years, sustained by the manna God had provided for them and learned lessons of His faithful care and provision. Now Elijah would traverse the same desert for **40 days and . . . nights,** sustained by the bread God provided and would learn the same lessons. A direct trip from Beersheba to Mount **Horeb** (the ancient name for Mount Sinai; cf. Ex. 3:1; 17:6; 33:6; Deut. 5:2; 1 Kings 8:9; Ps. 106:19; Mal. 4:4) would have taken Elijah only about 14 days on foot (a distance of ca. 200 miles). God was reminding him and teaching him during those 40 days and nights. Finally He went to **the mountain of God,** the very place where God had revealed Himself to Moses and the Israelites and where He had entered into a covenant with His Chosen People.

*b. Elijah's revelation (19:9-18)*

**19:9-10.** Arriving at one of the mountains in the Sinai range Elijah found **a cave** and took refuge in it. There he received a revelation from God. **The LORD** began this lesson with the question, **What are you doing here, Elijah?** (cf. v. 13; Gen. 3:9) God had not sent him here as He had directed him to other places (cf. 1 Kings 17:3, 9; 18:1). Elijah had run out because of fear (19:3). Elijah's response revealed that he felt he was standing completely alone and defenseless against the ungodly forces that threatened to overpower him (cf. v. 14). Of course he knew that he was not **the only one left** of all the faithful remnant (cf. 18:13), but he felt all alone. Interestingly Elijah spoke only of the Lord's **prophets** being killed (cf. 18:13a); he made no mention of Baal's 450 prophets who were killed. Fear and discouragement caused him to see only the dark side. He sensed failure in spite of his being **zealous.** Mercifully God did not lecture Elijah or chasten His chafed prophet. God simply gave him a demonstration of His ways.

**19:11-14.** Standing on the mountainside outside his cave (cf. v. 9) Elijah witnessed what Moses had seen in those mountains centuries before (Ex. 19:16-18) and what he himself had seen on Mount Carmel only a few days earlier (1 Kings 18:38, 45), namely, a spectacular demonstration of the power of God, this time in **wind,** an **earthquake,** and **fire.** But on this occasion **the LORD was not in** any of these, that is, they were not His instruments of self-revelation.

Evidently some time later when Elijah was back in his cave (19:13) he **heard** the sound of **a gentle whisper.** Recognizing this as a revelation of God **he pulled** his cloak over part of his face, walked out to the mouth of the cave, and stood there waiting for God to act. God asked the same question He asked earlier (cf. v. 9): **What are you doing here, Elijah?** The prophet's response was identical to his first reply (cf. v. 10), suggesting that even though he may have understood the point of God's display of natural forces for his benefit he still felt the same way about himself.

The message God seems to have intended for Elijah is that whereas He had revealed Himself in spectacular demonstrations of His power in the past at Kerith, Zarephath, and Carmel, He would now use Elijah in gentler, less dramatic ways. These ways God proceeded to explain to His servant (vv. 15-18). God would deal with Elijah's personal feelings about himself later in a gentle way too.

**19:15-17.** The LORD told Elijah to leave there, to **go back the way** he **came** (i.e., through Israel) to **Damascus.** (Cf. God's commands "leave" and "go" to Elijah in 17:3, 9; 18:1; 21:18; 2 Kings 1:3, 15.) The Lord then gave him three assignments: to **anoint Hazael king** of the Arameans in Damascus (see the chart "Kings of Aram in 1 and 2 Kings," near 1 Kings 11:23-25), to **anoint Jehu . . . king** of **Israel,** and to **anoint Elisha . . . from Abel Meholah** (cf. Jud. 7:22) as his own successor. Through these three men God would complete the purge of Baal worship that Elijah had begun. Actually Elijah did only the last of these three directly, but he did the other two indirectly through Elisha, his protegé. Elisha was involved, though strangely, in Hazael's becoming Aram's king (2 Kings 8:7-14) and one of Elisha's associates anointed Jehu (2 Kings 9:1-3).

**19:18.** God then revealed to Elijah that He had preserved **7,000** faithful followers **in Israel** who had **not bowed** before or **kissed** the emblems of idolatry in worship. Such news undoubtedly cheered Elijah. Were it not for the insight into his feelings of fear and discouragement given in this chapter, one might not believe that Elijah was indeed "a man just like us" (James 5:17).

*c. Elijah's successor (19:19-21)*

**19:19-20.** Elijah returned from the Sinai peninsula to find **Elisha** (whose name

means "My God is salvation") near his hometown of Abel Meholah (v. 16) in the Jordan Valley about halfway between the Dead Sea and the Sea of Kinnereth in the Northern Kingdom of Israel. Elisha evidently came from a family that owned lots of land (as implied by the **12** yoke of oxen). **He** himself **was plowing** when Elijah **found** him. Throwing a prophet's **cloak around** a person symbolized the passing of the power and authority of the office to that individual. That **Elisha** realized the meaning of this act is obvious from his reaction. Immediately he started to abandon his former occupation and follow **Elijah.** Elijah gave him permission to say farewell to his family. The unusual reply, **What have I done to you?** is an idiom meaning, "Do as you please" or "What have I done to stop you?"

**19:21.** Elisha sealed his decision by slaughtering **his yoke of oxen** and burning his **plowing** implements. He evidently hosted a farewell banquet, serving his sacrificed animals to his guests for supper. **Then he set out to** accompany **Elijah** as **his attendant.**

4. AHAB'S ARAMEAN ADVERSARY (CHAP. 20)

In this chapter the focus is again on Ahab rather than on Elijah.

*a. The battle over Samaria (20:1-25)*

This was the first of three battles recorded in 1 Kings (cf. 20:26-43; 22:1-38) between Ahab and Ben-Hadad II, king of Aram, Israel's northern neighbor.

(1) Ben-Hadad's attack (20:1-12). **20:1-4.** Ben-Hadad II was evidently the son of Ben-Hadad I whom Asa had hired to attack Baasha some years earlier (cf. 15:18, 20; 20:34). Allied with Ben-Hadad II were **32 kings,** probably rulers of neighboring city-states. Together they **went up** the hill of **Samaria and attacked it,** placing it under siege. Ben-Hadad then **sent messengers . . . to Ahab** with his demands for withdrawal. He demanded Ahab's **silver . . . gold . . . wives, and children.** Greatly outnumbered, Ahab submitted to these terms.

**20:5-9.** Evidently **Ben-Hadad** regretted that he had demanded such "easy" terms after Ahab had accepted them. He felt he could get much more than that. So he sent his **messengers** back with a new demand, namely, that Ben-Hadad's men be allowed to enter the **palace** and the officials' **houses** and plunder them. Ahab assembled **the elders of the land** and pointed out that Ben-Hadad was **looking for trouble. The king** had **not** refused Ben-Hadad's **demands** for his own most valued possessions, but now the Aramean enemy wanted everything of value he could lay his hands on. **The elders and the people** who had also become aware of these demands counseled resistance. Ahab sent his decision back to Ben-Hadad through the **messengers:** he would hold to his **first** promise but not to **this demand.**

**20:10-12.** Shortly thereafter Ahab received a third **message** from his adversary. The Arameans now threatened to destroy **Samaria** totally. Like Jezebel with Elijah, **Ben-Hadad** risked his life in an oath (cf. 19:2; also note 2:23). Ahab replied that Ben-Hadad should not **boast** of victory till he had obtained it. Ben-Hadad's greed and boasting seem to have been heightened since he and his kings were under the influence of strong drink. Since negotiations had broken down **Ben-Hadad . . . prepared to attack** Samaria.

(2) Ben-Hadad's defeat (20:13-25). **20:13. Meanwhile,** as Ben-Hadad was preparing to attack, **a prophet,** whose name is not given, went **to Ahab** with a message from **the LORD.** God, he said, was going to deliver the huge Aramean army into Ahab's **hand** so Ahab would **know** that He is **the LORD.** God's goodness on this occasion obviously was prompted not by Ahab's godliness but by God's own grace. This was another step in His seeking to get His people to acknowledge that He **is the LORD.**

**20:14-16.** Ahab asked **the prophet** what strategy should be employed. He responded that **the LORD** would use **the young officers of the provincial commanders** of the army. The king himself was to lead them into **battle.** Ahab prepared the troops as instructed and **at noon,** when **Ben-Hadad and** his **32 kings** were resting and **getting drunk,** he launched his surprise attack. Even today little is done in the middle of the day in the Near East because the weather is usually so hot.

**20:17-21.** Evidently it was not clear to **Ben-Hadad** if the 232 **men** (cf. v. 15) approaching him were coming to talk **peace** or whether they were intending to fight.

This probably resulted in his being unprepared for their attack. The Israelite **army** (of 7,000; cf. v. 15) followed along **behind** the **young officers** and proceeded to rout **the Arameans. Ben-Hadad** was able to escape **on horseback,** but Ahab **overpowered** his cavalry troops and the **chariots,** inflicting **heavy losses on the** surprised **Arameans.**

**20:22-25.** After Ahab had returned to Samaria **the prophet** went to him again. He warned **the king,** undoubtedly by the word of the Lord, that he should expect Ben-Hadad to **attack . . . again** in the **spring,** the most popular time of the year for kings to wage war (cf. 2 Sam. 11:1). In view of this Ahab was warned to build up his defenses.

In the camp of the Arameans, Ben-Hadad was also receiving advice. His counselors concluded that they had lost the battle because Israel's **gods** were **gods of the hills.** If they would **fight** Israel **on the plains** these gods would not help them and the Arameans would win. They also advised the king to **replace** the 32 allied kings with regular **army** commanders and to build up his forces to their former numbers. Ben-Hadad followed this advice and prepared to return to Samaria the following spring.

*b. The battle of Aphek (20:26-43)*

(1) Ahab's victory (20:26-34). **20:26-27.** As the Lord had revealed (v. 22), **the next spring** (856 B.C.) **Ben-Hadad** assembled his troops and proceeded **to Aphek.** Several towns in **Israel** bore this name (meaning "a fortress"). This one may have been located on the tablelands east of the Sea of Kinnereth between Samaria and Damascus. Ben-Hadad chose a flat battleground this time as his counselors had advised. Ahab led the Israelite army **to meet them.** In comparison with the vast host of the Arameans the Israelite forces looked like **two small flocks of goats.** That Israel was arranged in two groups may indicate that Ahab had in mind a certain battle strategy.

**20:28-30a. The man of God,** evidently the same prophet (vv. 13, 22), informed Ahab that **Israel** would win this battle. Again he said that the Lord's purpose was to prove to Ahab (as well as, perhaps, **the Arameans** and the Israelites) that He is **the LORD** (cf. v. 13).

**Seven days** passed before **the battle**

began. On the very first **day** of combat **the Israelites inflicted 100,000 casualties on the . . . foot soldiers** of the enemy. **The rest of** their troops took refuge within **the city** walls **of Aphek.** But God killed an additional **27,000** by causing **the** city **wall** to collapse on **them.**

**20:30b-34.** While **Ben-Hadad** was hiding **in an inner room** of a city building, his officials advised him to give himself up and plead for mercy. **The kings of . . . Israel** were indeed **merciful** compared with other ancient Near Eastern kings. **Sackcloth** and **ropes** were signs of penitential submission.

Ben-Hadad's agents waited on Ahab and pleaded for Ben-Hadad's life. They called him Ahab's **servant,** indicating the position he was willing to take if he could **live.** Ahab seemed surprised that the Aramean king was **still alive.** Ahab said he was willing to receive **Ben-Hadad** as his **brother,** not as a servant. He was, of course, not his real brother; Ahab had in mind a treaty for defense against Assyria in which he and Ben-Hadad would join as brothers.

**Quick to pick up** this ray of hope, Ben-Hadad's ambassadors affirmed that Ahab's **brother** was alive. They escorted the defeated king to **Ahab** as they had been ordered, and as a gesture of friendship **Ahab** invited Ben-Hadad **up into his chariot,** a position of favor. Quick to placate his enemy, **Ben-Hadad** pledged to **return the cities** his **father** Ben-Hadad I had taken from Ahab's **father** (predecessor) Baasha (cf. 15:20). In addition, the Aramean king offered trade privileges to Ahab **in Damascus** which Ben-Hadad's **father** had enjoyed **in Samaria.** The two kings formalized the **treaty** and with this promise of nonaggression Ahab let Ben-Hadad **go** back home.

Three years later (853 B.C.) Ahab and Ben-Hadad faced their mutual foe, Assyria, led by mighty King Shalmaneser III (859–824 B.C.) and repelled him at Qarqar on the Orontes River in Aram. Ahab supplied 10,000 troops and 2,000 chariots for this coalition. This battle is not referred to in Scripture but a record of it written by Shalmaneser has survived. It is now in the British Museum. (See James B. Pritchard, ed., *Ancient Near Eastern Texts Relating to the Old Testament.* Princeton, N.J.: Princeton University Press, 1955, pp. 278-9.)

**(2) Ahab's disobedience (20:35-43).**
**20:35-36. The sons of the prophets** were students in the schools of the prophets, well-established institutions in Israel designed to perpetuate the Law of Moses and the Word of the Lord. **One of** these young men received an assignment from the Lord. His unusual request that **his companion** injure him with a **weapon** was **by the word of the** Lord. The friend's refusal, though understandable, was an act of disobedient rebellion against the Lord. It was for this reason and the importance of the man of God's mission that the compassionate companion suffered death. Again **the** Lord used **a lion** to execute his will (cf. 13:24).

**20:37-40a. The prophet** then **found** a more willing accomplice who did wound **him.** Playing the part of a wounded soldier **the prophet** waited by the roadside for **King** Ahab to pass on his way back to Samaria. The prophet **disguised himself** using a **headband over his eyes.** Without this the king would have recognized him immediately as a prophet (cf. 20:41). Interestingly this is the second time in 1 Kings when a person disguised himself (cf. 14:2). Later Ahab disguised himself in battle (22:30).

Apparently Ahab thought he had met this man before. **The prophet** told the king that he, the prophet, was told in combat to **guard** a prisoner who got away. The prophet added that either his own **life** was to have been taken **or** he had to **pay a talent** (ca. 75 pounds) **of silver.**

**20:40b-43.** Ahab quickly assessed the storyteller's guilt; this was an obvious case of negligence. As in Nathan's story to David (2 Sam. 12:1-7) the king responded to the prophet in words that judged himself. **The prophet,** immediately revealing his identity, told **the king** he had been negligent in his responsibility to obey the order received from God to execute Ben-Hadad. Though this order is not recorded in the biblical text it is clear that Ahab had received it. Rather than obeying the Lord which probably would have resulted in a final end of the conflict with the vexing Aramean army, Ahab chose to follow his own plan. He believed Ben-Hadad's help against Assyria would be more valuable to Israel than Ben-Hadad's death.

Therefore Ahab would forfeit his

own **life** in exchange for Ben-Hadad's (cf. 1 Kings 22:37). Also Ahab's **people,** the Israelites, would die in place of Ben-Hadad's **people.** Ahab returned to **Samaria** sullen because of this prophecy and angry (cf. 21:4) at himself as well as at God's prophet.

5. AHAB'S CRIMES AGAINST NABOTH (CHAP. 21)

*a. Ahab's proposal (21:1-4)*

**21:1-2.** A period of peace followed the battle of Aphek (20:26-34). **Some time** after the battle the events recorded in chapter 21 took place. This **incident** further illustrates the evil characters of **Ahab** and Jezebel and enables readers to understand God's dealings with them. It also shows God's faithfulness in fulfilling the prophecies given by Elijah (21:20-24).

**Naboth** was Ahab's near neighbor **in Jezreel;** they apparently owned adjoining property. **Ahab** offered to buy Naboth's **vineyard** because it was a suitable piece of ground **for a vegetable garden** he wished to plant. Ahab offered to **pay** for it with **a better vineyard** elsewhere or with cash, whichever Naboth might prefer.

**21:3-4.** Naboth was a God-fearing Israelite. In obedience to the Mosaic Law he refused to sell his paternal **inheritance** (cf. Lev. 25:23-28; Num. 36:7). Evidently Ahab wanted this to be a permanent transaction. Again **Ahab** returned **home sullen and angry** (cf. 1 Kings 20:43). Ahab behaved in a childish manner. Rather than accepting Naboth's decision, Ahab **lay on his bed sulking and** even **refused to eat.**

*b. Jezebel's plot (21:5-10)*

**21:5-7.** When **his wife** asked Ahab why he was behaving strangely, he told her about Naboth's refusal. She had grown up in a culture where the rights of individuals were not honored as they were in **Israel.** It seemed incredible to her that Ahab would not just take what he wanted. That was how a **king** should **act,** according to her way of thinking. If he would not do what was necessary *she* would do so and without hesitation.

**21:8-10.** Knowing how to use the laws of Israel to gain her ends, Jezebel sent **letters** to leaders in **Naboth's** town, asking them to declare a fast and to have **two scoundrels** accuse **Naboth** of cursing

**God and** Ahab so that the people would **stone** Naboth. At least two witnesses were required to condemn a person in Israel (Deut. 17:6-7). Cursing God was a crime punishable by stoning (Lev. 24:16). Cursing the king was not punishable in that way. Jezebel may have added that part of her orders because she may have thought it was also punishable by death.

*c. Naboth's murder (21:11-16)*

**21:11-14.** The leading men of Jezreel obviously feared **Jezebel** more than they feared the Lord because they carried out her orders exactly. When **Naboth** (and his sons; cf. 2 Kings 9:26) were **dead** the **scoundrels** dutifully reported that the job was done.

**21:15-16.** Jezebel then announced **to Ahab** that he could **take possession** of Naboth's **vineyard** because its former owner was now **dead.** The king **got up** from his bed **and went down to take possession of** this property he coveted.

*d. Elijah's prophecies (21:17-26)*

**21:17-19.** Again God chose **Elijah** to bear a message of judgment to **Ahab,** who was then **in Naboth's vineyard.** God told Elijah just what to say (cf. v. 19). Jezebel was directly responsible for Naboth's death but Ahab was ultimately responsible since Jezebel's letter to the elders ordering Naboth's murder had been sent out over Ahab's name (v. 8). Elijah said Ahab had committed the crime of seizing **property** not his own as well as killing Naboth. **The place where dogs licked up Naboth's blood** was in Jezreel. Dogs licking up one's blood was a disgraceful death, especially for a king whose body would normally be carefully guarded and buried with great respect. Elijah left no doubt in Ahab's mind concerning whose **blood** he referred to: **yes, yours!**

**21:20-22.** When **Elijah** approached **Ahab** in the stolen vineyard, the king greeted him with the words, **So you have found me, my enemy.** This suggests that Ahab may have concluded that it would be only a matter of time till Elijah or some other man of God hunted him down. Elijah was not now the "troubler of Israel" (18:17), but the king's "enemy." Ahab had made himself the enemy of the Lord and His people by doing **evil in the eyes of the LORD** (cf. 21:25). When Elijah said the king had **sold** himself, he meant the king had sacrificed his principles to obtain what he wanted, which included a comparatively worthless vineyard. God promised **to bring disaster on** Ahab personally and to **consume** his **descendants,** cutting **off from** him **every . . . male in Israel.** He would have to stand alone without allies (cf. 14:10; 16:3). Ahab's dynasty would be cut off as Jeroboam's and Baasha's had been (cf. 2 Kings 9:9).

**21:23-24.** As for **Jezebel . . . dogs** would eat her **by the wall of Jezreel,** hardly a fitting end for a powerful queen (cf. 2 Kings 9:10, 36-37). Wild dogs lived off the garbage in cities such as Jezreel. Ahab's descendants would not receive honorable burials either but would be consumed by **dogs** and **birds** (cf. 1 Kings 14:11; 16:4).

**21:25-26.** The writer at this point inserted his own evaluation of **Ahab** and **Jezebel** into the narrative of Elijah and Ahab's conversation. Ahab was unique in his wickedness. He **sold himself to do evil in the** Lord's **eyes** (cf. v. 20). **Jezebel,** being void of any spiritual sensitivity and conscience, **urged** him **on** in evil. In pursuing idolatry Ahab **behaved in the vilest manner** by following the sinful ways of **the Amorites** whom God had driven **out** of Palestine when the Israelites entered the land in Joshua's day (Josh. 10:12-13).

*e. Ahab's repentance (21:27-29)*

**21:27-29.** Elijah's predicted judgment crushed **Ahab.** In sincere repentance he **humbled himself** before the Lord. Tearing one's **clothes** (Es. 4:1; Job 1:20), wearing **sackcloth** (Gen. 37:34; 1 Kings 20:31-32; Es. 4:1; Neh. 9:1; Dan. 9:3), and fasting (Neh. 9:1; Dan. 9:3) all manifested a spirit of grief and contrition. God noticed Ahab's change of mind and behavior. Ahab's life was deep-dyed with sin, but in response to his self-humbling, God showed him some mercy. The destruction to come on Ahab's **house** would not be carried out in his own **days** but **in** those **of his son** Joram (2 Kings 9:24-26; 10:17). Jezebel, however, did not repent. She suffered all that God promised she would without mercy (2 Kings 9:30-37).

6. AHAB'S DEATH (22:1-40)

*a. Ahab's alliance with Jehoshaphat (22:1-4)*

**22:1-4. For three years** after the battle of Aphek (cf. 1 Kings 20:26-34) **there was**

**no war between** the Israelites and the Arameans. However, **in the third year** (853 B.C.), shortly after Ahab and Ben-Hadad had fought Shalmaneser at the Battle of Qarqar, Ahab decided that he needed to **retake** the important city of **Ramoth** in **Gilead** from the Arameans who had taken it from Israel earlier. Ramoth was one of the chief cities of the tribe of Gad, 28 miles east of the Jordan and 15 miles south of the Sea of Kinnereth, almost directly east of Jezreel. To field an army large enough to defeat the Arameans Ahab asked **Jehoshaphat** the **king of Judah** to ally with him against Ben-Hadad II. **Jehoshaphat** agreed for political reasons though he should not have done so for spiritual reasons; he was a godly king, faithful to the Lord.

*b. Ahab's prophets' counsel (22:5-12)*

**22:5-7. Jehoshaphat** wanted divine counsel from **the** Lord before he and Ahab embarked on their mission. Ahab apparently could not have cared less. But to satisfy Jehoshaphat, Ahab called for **the prophets, about 400** of them. These were evidently prophets of the Lord; Baal prophets would have been unacceptable to Jehoshaphat. But they were apostate prophets. They had no concern about obtaining and relating the true word of the Lord. Their desire was to give their king the kind of advice they thought he wanted to hear. This would please him and he would favor them. Their answer to Ahab's question somehow led **Jehoshaphat** to believe that they did not have the mind of the Lord. So he requested **a prophet** true to **the** Lord of whom they could **inquire** (cf. 2 Kings 3:11).

**22:8-12.** Ahab replied that there was **one man** of God remaining whom they could contact. However, that one always prophesied evil for Ahab and for that reason Ahab said he hated **him.** Obviously Ahab was more concerned about feeling good than he was about knowing the truth. **Micaiah,** like Elijah, was one of the comparatively few faithful prophets in Israel in that day. Urged on by Jehoshaphat's continuing interest in hearing from **Micaiah,** Ahab sent for him.

Perhaps Micaiah lived in or near **Samaria** where this conversation took place. **The threshing floor** was usually an elevated area; it would have been a good place for Ahab and **Jehoshaphat** to prepare themselves for battle. **The gate of** the city was the most popular place to assemble, so a large crowd was gathered including the 400 **prophets.** One of these prophets, **Zedekiah** (cf. v. 24), had even fashioned some **horns** out of **iron** and claimed blasphemously that God had told him that the two allied kings with the horns would **gore the Arameans** to destruction. With this prediction **all the other prophets** agreed, adding their own optimistic promises of victory.

### c. Micaiah's prophecy (22:13-28)

**22:13-14.** The messenger who was sent to get **Micaiah** urged him to **agree with** the other prophets in giving an optimistic prediction. But Micaiah told him that he would utter whatever words **the Lord** gave him regardless of what **others** might say. Like Elijah, Micaiah was prepared to stand alone.

**22:15-16. The king,** probably Ahab the host, **asked . . . Micaiah** the same question he had asked the other prophets (v. 6). Micaiah seems to have been familiar with this procedure; he had probably been through it several times before. His reply was sarcastic, though probably not delivered in a sarcastic tone which would have been inappropriate for a man of his character. Ahab recognized at once what **Micaiah** was doing. His own reply was equally sarcastic. He had probably never told Micaiah to **swear to tell** him **nothing but the truth** before, as he did not need to. But Ahab's saying that probably sounded good.

**22:17-18.** The time for sarcasm was over. **Micaiah** related the burden of the Lord in all its devastating simplicity and force. Micaiah said he had seen, perhaps in a vision, **all Israel scattered** over **the hills** of Gilead **like sheep without a shepherd,** wandering and in need of leadership. The **Lord** had told the prophet that **these** sheep had **no master,** obviously a reference to Ahab. After the shepherd would be killed in battle the sheep would return **home** without being pursued by the enemy, Aram. Ahab reacted to this sober warning offhandedly (v. 18; cf. v. 8), unwilling to consider it seriously.

**22:19-23. Micaiah** proceeded to explain the rest of what God had shown him, not about the battle but about the advice both kings had been receiving from the 400 prophets. He called on the two kings to **hear the word of the Lord.** Micaiah **saw . . . the host of heaven,** the angelic armies of God, assembled **around** God's heavenly **throne.** Whether the conversation Micaiah then described (vv. 20-23) actually took place in heaven or whether it was a revelation given in anthropomorphic terms to help Micaiah and his audience visualize what was taking place on the threshing floor before them, the point was clear to all: The 400 **prophets** spoke with **a lying spirit** (vv. 22-23) to deceive, and to lead Ahab to **disaster** in battle and **to his death** (v. 20). Micaiah, however, spoke the truth. The Lord had apparently permitted a "lying spirit" (i.e., a demon) to speak through the 400 prophets as a means of bringing **Ahab** to his death.

**22:24-25. Zedekiah** (cf. v. 11) certainly understood Micaiah's message as did everyone else. A slap **in the face** was a great insult (cf. Job 16:10; Lam. 3:30; Micah 5:1), greater then than it is today. The false prophet brazenly or innocently claimed that he had not invented his prophecy himself but that it had been given to him by the Lord.

Micaiah did not need to argue about whose prophecy had come **from the Lord** and whose had come from the lying spirit; time would tell. He was not trying to scare people when there was no real cause for fear. Zedekiah would **find out** who had the true word from the Lord when he fled **to hide in an inner room** (i.e., after Ahab had been killed the false prophets would flee in terror).

**22:26-28.** Ahab's reaction evidences the blindness and folly that overtakes those who disregard the Word of the Lord. Rather than repenting, as he had done previously (21:27), now hardened in sin to the point of insensibility, Ahab ordered that **Micaiah** be given to **Amon, the city** mayor, **and to Joash, the king's son.** "King's son" is apparently a title of a royal official and is not to be taken as the literal son of Ahab (cf. 2 Chron. 28:7; Jer. 36:26; 38:6). Ahab told Amon and Joash to **put** the prophet who had warned him of impending doom **in prison.** **Micaiah** had the final word, however, and it was another gracious but strong warning for Ahab, indicating that the king would not **return** from battle **safely.** The prophet also called on **all**

present to remember his **words** for they would prove that **the LORD** had **spoken through** him when his prophecy came to pass.

### d. The battle of Ramoth Gilead (22:29-40)

**22:29-33.** Despite Micaiah's warning Ahab, **the king of Israel, and Jehoshaphat,** his ally, **went up to Ramoth Gilead** to face Ben-Hadad II, **the king of Aram.** Perhaps Ahab suggested his plan to **enter the battle . . . disguised** (probably as a regular soldier or officer) out of fear for his life in view of what Micaiah had said.

Jehoshaphat did not realize that this tactic would put him in greater danger until the battle began. He may not have been aware of Ben-Hadad's anger against Ahab that led the king of Aram to concentrate his attack on **the king of Israel.** Ben-Hadad may have wanted to kill Ahab alone because he knew that without their king the soldiers of Israel would not fight effectively. Probably the fact that Ahab was now breaking his treaty with Ben-Hadad (cf. 20:34) angered the Aramean king too. Dressed in his royal attire **Jehoshaphat** became the target of the whole Aramean army. Under attack he **cried out** something that told the Arameans **he was not** the man they sought. Perhaps he cried out to God as well as to the soldiers since he trusted in and prayed to the Lord.

**22:34-36.** The manner in which Ahab was fatally wounded is one of many examples in Scripture of God using an incident that would have been regarded as accidental to accomplish His purpose. Ahab was injured by an arrow shot **at random.** The man who shot the arrow did not knowingly aim it at the chink in the king's **armor,** but God directed him and guided the fatal missile to its mark. The king's **chariot** was large enough to accommodate Ahab as he sat **propped up in** it to watch the battle until sunset.

The reference to Ahab's **blood** running down **onto the floor of** his **chariot** sets the stage for the later word about the fulfillment of the prophecy of Ahab's death (v. 38). The battle broke up when Ahab died; Ben-Hadad had achieved his objective as the Israelites could not take Ramoth Gilead.

**22:37-38.** The body of Ahab was returned **to Samaria** where he was **buried.** Had he not repented earlier (21:27) Ahab would not have been buried at all (21:28-29). Ahab's **chariot** was then driven around to an out-of-the-way **pool** where it was **washed.** Ahab was despised by God for his wickedness. The story of Ahab concludes with his **blood** being desecrated in the company of Samaria's despised **prostitutes** and **dogs.** Ahab died as God had predicted he would (20:42; 21:19, 21).

**22:39-40.** In excavating Samaria archeologists discovered more than 200 **ivory** figures, panels, and plaques in one storeroom. Ahab used large quantities of ivory to beautify his **palace** in various ways. He also **fortified** several **cities** in **Israel.**

In addition to the projects just mentioned, Ahab ruled capably in spite of the gross spiritual apostasy that characterized his administration. He was generally successful militarily because of his own native ability and God's mercy on Israel. His alliance with Judah under Jehoshaphat began the first real period of peace between the Northern and Southern Kingdoms since the monarchy had split and it lasted about 30 years until the reign of Jehu began in 841. But in spite of Ahab's other accomplishments his building a Baal altar and temple and encouraging Baal worship (16:32-33) weakened Israel as never before.

### L. Jehoshaphat's good reign in Judah (22:41-50)

**22:41-43a.** Asa's son, **Jehoshaphat,** began his reign in Judah in 873 B.C. as coregent with his father. This coregency existed because of Asa's poor health (15:23) and it continued for three years until Asa's death in 870 B.C. when Jehoshaphat became sole ruler. This was the first instance of coregency since Solomon had ruled jointly with David for a brief time. **Jehoshaphat** was **king** for **25 years** altogether (873–848 B.C.). He was one of Judah's eight good kings and one of its four reformers like **his father Asa.**

**22:43b-44.** According to 2 Chronicles 17:6 Jehoshaphat removed **the high places,** but 1 Kings 22:43 and 2 Chronicles 20:33 indicate that he did not remove them. Apparently he did, but when the people restored them he did not again obliterate the restored high places. Other kings of Judah who did not remove the high places were Joash (2 Kings 12:3),

Amaziah (2 Kings 14:4), Azariah (2 Kings 15:4), and Jotham (2 Kings 15:35). Ahaz sacrificed at the high places (2 Kings 16:4), perhaps ones he restored. Those were then removed by Hezekiah (2 Kings 18:4), rebuilt by Manasseh (2 Kings 21:3), and demolished again by Josiah (2 Kings 23:8, 13, 15, 19).

As mentioned previously (cf. comments on 1 Kings 22:39-40), Jehoshaphat and Ahab united in a treaty which resulted in **peace** between Judah and **Israel** during his reign. Unfortunately this treaty involved the marriage of Jehoshaphat's son Jehoram to Ahab's daughter Athaliah who followed Jezebel's example and caused Judah problems later (cf. 2 Kings 11).

**22:45-47. Jehoshaphat's** achievements and attitudes are more fully expounded in 2 Chronicles 17-20. These included ordering the teaching of the Law of Moses throughout Judah. God miraculously delivered Judah from the united armies of Moab, Ammon, and **Edom** in response to the king's prayers and his obedience to the Lord. He was a strong ruler whose favor Philistia and Arabia courted. Jehoshaphat instituted many judicial reforms in Judah also. The writer of Kings noted his purge of the remaining **male shrine prostitutes** (cf. 1 Kings 14:24; 15:12) in particular.

**22:48-50.** As a result of the unstable political situation in Edom in his day (cf. v. 47) **Jehoshaphat** was able to build **a fleet of trading ships . . . at Ezion Geber** on the northern tip of the Gulf of Aqaba with Israel's king **Ahaziah,** Ahab's eldest **son** (cf. 2 Chron. 20:36). The plan was to bring back **gold** from **Ophir,** in southwestern Arabia (cf. 1 Kings 9:28; 10:11) as Solomon had done. But in some way the fleet was **wrecked** and never fulfilled its mission. **Jehoshaphat** had **refused** to let Ahaziah's **men sail with** his own. This venture resulted in failure and frustration for Jehoshaphat as did all his other joint efforts with Israel.

Jehoshaphat's son **Jehoram** began reigning as coregent with his father in 853 B.C. When Jehoshaphat died in 848 B.C., Jehoram continued to reign till 841.

## M. The beginning of Ahaziah's evil reign in Israel (22:51-53)

**22:51-53.** A short summary of Ahaziah's reign concludes 1 Kings, but the events of his rule follow in 2 Kings.

**Ahaziah . . . of Israel** began his reign of **two** official **years** (one actual year) in 853 B.C. and he ruled until 852, during Jehoshaphat's reign in Judah. Ahaziah was the elder **son of Ahab.** Since Ahaziah had no son his brother Joram (also called Jehoram) succeeded him when he died. His **mother** was Jezebel. Ahaziah followed his parents' evil **ways** and those **of Jeroboam. Baal** worship continued in Israel under his protection and encouragement.

# BIBLIOGRAPHY

Davis, John J., and Whitcomb, John C., Jr. *A History of Israel.* Grand Rapids: Baker Book House, 1980.

Finegan, Jack. *Light from the Ancient Past.* 2nd ed. Princeton, N.J.: Princeton University Press, 1959.

Gray, John. *I & II Kings: A Commentary.* 2nd ed. Philadelphia: Westminster Press, 1970.

Jamieson, Robert. "I and II Kings." In *A Commentary, Critical, Experimental and Practical on the Old and New Testaments.* 3rd ed. Grand Rapids: Zondervan Publishing House, 1983.

Keil, C.F. "The Books of Kings." In *Commentary on the Old Testament in Ten Volumes.* Vol. 3. Reprint (25 vols. in 10). Grand Rapids: Wm. B. Eerdmans Publishing Co., 1982.

McNeely, Richard I. *First and Second Kings.* Chicago: Moody Press, 1978.

Montgomery, James A. *A Critical and Exegetical Commentary on the Books of Kings.* The International Critical Commentary. Edinburgh: T. & T. Clark, 1951.

Thiele, Edwin R. *A Chronology of the Hebrew Kings.* Grand Rapids: Zondervan Publishing House, 1977.

_____. *The Mysterious Numbers of the Hebrew Kings.* Rev. ed. Chicago: University of Chicago Press, 1983.

Wood, Leon J. *A Survey of Israel's History.* Grand Rapids: Zondervan Publishing House, 1970.

# 2 KINGS

### Thomas L. Constable

## INTRODUCTION

See the *Introduction* to 1 Kings.

## OUTLINE

## COMMENTARY

## I. The Later History of the Divided Kingdom (chaps. 1–17)

This section of 2 Kings continues the history of Israel and Judah begun in 1 Kings 12. It ends with the Assyrian Captivity of the Northern Kingdom in 722 B.C.

### A. The remainder of Ahaziah's evil reign in Israel (chap. 1)

The account of the rule of Ahab's elder son Ahaziah continues from 1 Kings 22:51-53.

#### 1. AHAZIAH'S INQUIRY (1:1-2)

**1:1. Moab,** under Mesha its king, **rebelled against Israel** after Ahab died. The death of the Israelite king encouraged Mesha to throw off the burden of taxation that Omri (Ahaziah's grandfather) had imposed when he had brought Moab under Israel's control (cf. comments on 1 Kings 16:21-24). This rebellion was not effective at first but the fact that it began in Ahaziah's reign may suggest that Mesha considered Ahaziah a weaker king than Ahab.

**1:2.** This verse begins a new incident

in Ahaziah's life which occupies the remainder of chapter 1. The king had suffered an injury from falling **through the lattice** covering of a window in **his upper** story **room,** probably to the ground below. His serious injury later proved fatal. The king's veneration of Baal can be seen in his sending **messengers** to **Ekron,** a Philistine city about 40 miles away (see the map "Elijah's Travels," near 1 Kings 17:8-11), to inquire of a pagan idol whether he would recover. **Baal-Zebub** was one of the many local male fertility gods which bore some form of the name Baal (meaning "lord"). Baal-Zebub means "Lord of the flies," but the original spelling in Philistia was probably Baal-Zebul, which means "Exalted lord." He was credited with healing powers. Ahaziah sought some prophetic word of encouragement from the oracle of Baal-Zebub. His failure to inquire of Yahweh, the God of Israel, reveals the depth of his apostasy.

2. ELIJAH'S PROPHECY (1:3-8)

**1:3-4. The Angel of the LORD** (the preincarnate Christ; cf. comments on Gen. 16:9) appeared **to Elijah** as He had appeared to many other Old Testament leaders in the past (e.g., Abraham, Moses, Gideon). His appearances always identified an important revelation. The angel gave Elijah a prophecy to pass on to the king through the royal **messengers** whom Elijah intercepted as they traveled south from Samaria to **Ekron.** Though Ahaziah sought a message from **Baal-Zebub,** he got an answer from the true and living **God.** Perhaps Ahaziah, like his father Ahab, did not want to inquire of a faithful prophet of the Lord since those prophets were consistently opposing rather than supporting **the king** because of his wickedness. God's punishment for consulting a pagan idol rather than Himself was that Ahaziah would fail to recover from his injuries (cf. 2 Kings 1:6, 16).

**1:5-8. The messengers returned to** Ahaziah and reported their meeting with Elijah and his prophecy. Ahaziah knew who Elijah was, of course, since Elijah had consistently opposed his parents, Ahab and Jezebel, for their **Baal** worship. The hairy **garment** (probably made from goats' dark **hair**) and large **leather belt** were part of the dress of prophets at that

time. Cloth woven from hair, as rough as burlap, was sometimes called sackcloth. Since sackcloth symbolized distress or self-affliction (cf. 6:30; Gen. 37:34; 2 Sam. 3:31), Elijah's garb probably visualized the repentance to which the prophets called the people (cf. penitence and sackcloth in Neh. 9:1; Jer. 6:26). Ahaziah recognized his messengers' description of **Elijah** immediately.

3. THE CAPTAINS AND THEIR 50S (1:9-16)

**1:9.** To many readers this story seems like an unnecessarily cruel demonstration of God's power. However, the issues at stake justified severe action. Ahaziah showed complete contempt for **Elijah** and the God he represented by sending a band of soldiers to arrest the prophet like an outlaw and drag him before the throne. Perhaps Elijah's position **on the top of a hill** should have reminded **the captain** of Elijah's victory over the prophets of Baal on Mount Carmel (1 Kings 18:20-40) and of his great God-given power. Either the captain did not make this connection or decided to disregard it. He acknowledged that **Elijah** was a **man of God** (cf. 2 Kings 1:11), but ordered him to **come down** to him in Ahaziah's name.

In 1 and 2 Kings the term "man of God" is a synonym for a prophet. It is used of Shemaiah (1 Kings 12:22), of Elijah seven times (1 Kings 17:18, 24; 2 Kings 1:9, 10-13), of Elisha more than two dozen times in 2 Kings (the first occurrence is in 4:7 and the last is in 13:19), and of two other anonymous prophets (one is mentioned frequently in 1 Kings 13 and in 2 Kings 23:16-17; the other is referred to in 1 Kings 20:28).

**1:10.** Elijah's repetition of the fact that he was indeed a **man of God** (cf. v. 12) shows that this was an important issue; God's reputation was at stake. Was Ahaziah in charge, able to command God's servants to obey *him?* Or was God in charge, able to command Ahaziah's servants to obey *Him?* By sending **fire . . . from heaven** (cf. v. 12) to **consume** the soldiers of the king, God was reminding Ahaziah that He was Israel's Ruler and that the king should submit to His sovereignty. In a play on similar-sounding Hebrew words **Elijah** said that because he was a man ('*îš*) of God, **fire** ('*ēš*) would consume them.

**1:11-12.** Ahaziah disregarded this tragedy and tried again to force **Elijah** to submit to him. This time **the captain** ordered the prophet, **Come down** (cf. v. 9) **at once!** Again **Elijah** reminded the **captain,** undoubtedly for the benefit of those looking on who would report the incident as well as for the officer, that he was indeed God's **man.** The **fire** of judgment **fell** again (cf. v. 10), proving that the first miracle was not just an accident but was the hand **of God** at work in judgment.

**1:13-14.** Still Ahaziah hardened his heart. The **third captain** he sent had more respect for Yahweh and His representative than Ahaziah did. Rather than demanding surrender from a position of assumed superiority this man submitted to Elijah's authority, falling to **his knees before** him. He too recognized **Elijah** as a **man of God,** but unlike the first two captains (cf. vv. 9, 11) he pleaded for mercy. He acknowledged that the **fire** that had **fallen** had come **from heaven** (i.e., was caused by God).

**1:15-16.** The Angel of the LORD directed **Elijah** to **go down with him . . . to the king** and **not be afraid of him**; God had superior power and would control the situation. (This was the sixth time God told **Elijah** to "go" or "leave"; cf. 1 Kings 17:3, 9; 18:1; 21:18; 2 Kings 1:3.) This whole incident, like the contest on Mount Carmel, was designed to demonstrate God's sovereignty to the king and the people of Israel.

Standing before **the king,** Elijah fearlessly delivered the message **God** had given him. Because of Ahaziah's failure **to consult** Israel's God (cf. v. 2) and his determination to lead independently, God would depose him. This is the same message Elijah had given earlier to the king's **messengers** on their way to **Ekron** (vv. 3-4).

### 4. AHAZIAH'S DEATH (1:17-18)

**1:17-18.** Just as **Elijah** had announced (vv. 4, 16), Ahaziah never recovered from his injuries and **died** shortly thereafter. Since **Ahaziah had no son** his brother **Joram** (a variant of the Heb. "Jehoram"; cf. NIV marg.) **succeeded him as king** of Israel. This accession took place **in the second year of Jehoram . . . king of Judah** (i.e., the second year of his coregency with his father **Jehoshaphat,** viz., 852 B.C.). The kings of Israel

and Judah at this time had the same name. (The NIV keeps the two kings distinct by spelling the king of Israel's name "Joram" and the king of Judah's "Jehoram.")

### B. Joram's evil reign in Israel (2:1–8:15)

Much space is devoted to the years when Joram reigned because of Elisha's important ministry which took place then. As always the interest of the writer of 1 and 2 Kings was primarily spiritual rather than political.

### 1. ELISHA'S INAUGURATION (CHAP. 2)

This chapter records the transition that took place in the spiritual leadership of Israel with the assumption of Elijah into heaven. Elisha's miracles here have to do mainly with his inauguration as Elijah's spiritual successor.

#### a. Elijah's assumption into heaven (2:1-12)

**2:1-3.** Departing **from Gilgal** in Israel **Elijah** and his younger fellow prophet **Elisha** headed for **Bethel** on a mission from God. This Gilgal may be modern Jiljiliah (seven miles northwest of Bethel), different from the Gilgal near the Jordan River (see the map "Elijah's Travels," near 1 Kings 17:8-11). **Elisha** had learned somehow (perhaps from **Elijah** himself) that this would be Elijah's last day on earth. Determined to be with his father in the faith till the very end **Elisha** refused Elijah's suggestion that he remain comfortably in Gilgal. A dying person often pronounced blessings on others (cf. Gen. 49) and **Elisha** did not want to miss out on this opportunity to receive God's blessings on his life and ministry.

Some **prophets** of the LORD living at **Bethel** also knew of Elijah's departure and told **Elisha.** These groups or schools of the prophets had been established to teach the Israelites the revealed Word of God. Elijah was Elisha's **master** in the sense of his being the younger prophet's mentor. Elisha's response, **Do not speak of it,** means, "Do not add to my sorrow at this prospect by reminding me of it."

**2:4-5.** Testing Elisha's commitment again, **Elijah** suggested that **Elisha** stay in Bethel rather than accompanying him to his next stop, **Jericho.** Elisha showed his zeal by refusing to leave Elijah. **So they** continued on **to Jericho. The company of the prophets** at Jericho repeated what their brethren in Bethel had said. **Elisha** gave them the same reply (cf. v. 3).

**2:6-8.** Elijah tested **Elisha** a third time, and Elisha again refused to put his own comfort ahead of the possibility of receiving a special blessing from God. So they went toward **the Jordan** River. As the day wore on **50 . . . of the** young **prophets** from Jericho, realizing that Elijah's departure was imminent, followed **at a distance** to observe what would happen to him. At the bank of **the Jordan** River Elijah **. . . rolled** up **his cloak** and, using it as a symbol of God's power, **struck the water with it** (cf. Ex. 14:16, 21-22). A prophet's cloak symbolized his authority under God (cf. 1 Kings 19:19) with which God clothed and empowered him. Miraculously **the water divided** and the riverbed dried up so that **the two** men **crossed over** as the Israelites had crossed the Red Sea and the Jordan River hundreds of years earlier. (This is one of many similarities between the ministries of Moses and Elijah.) Elisha was reminded that the same God with the same power was still alive and active in Israel.

**2:9-10.** Elijah then invited **Elisha** to ask what he wanted from him **before** he would be **taken** away. **Elisha** requested the blessing of the firstborn, **a double portion.** But Elisha wanted spiritual rather than material blessing. He was not asking to be twice as popular as Elijah or to perform twice as many miracles. Elisha was asking to be the successor of Elijah and to be privileged to carry on his ministry under God (cf. "double share of," Deut. 21:17).

However, this was not Elijah's to give; for that reason it was **a difficult thing.** Elijah did not know if God would grant Elisha's request. The sign that He would grant it would be Elisha's actually seeing Elijah being **taken from** him. This was not a condition for Elisha to receive the double portion but the evidence that he would.

**2:11-12.** Suddenly a fast-approaching **chariot . . . and horses of fire . . . separated** Elijah from Elisha. These did not bear **Elijah** into **heaven;** a **whirlwind** did that. The fiery horses and chariot were symbols of God's power in battle. Horses and chariots were the mightiest means of warfare in that day. God was saying in this event that His power was far greater than any military might. It was this power that Elijah had demonstrated and which **Elisha** in his wisdom valued so highly (cf. Ex. 14:9, 17; 1 Kings 10:29; Ps. 104:3-4; Isa. 31:1). The whirlwind was actually a storm with lightning and thunder. Like the pillar of cloud that led the Israelites in the wilderness (Ex. 13:21), it represented God's presence.

God swept Elijah off the face of the earth into His very presence. And **Elisha** did see the event. Elijah had been Elisha's spiritual **father,** his predecessor in the ministry of calling people back to God. Elisha's reference to **the chariots and horsemen of Israel** shows that he regarded Elijah as a powerful instrument whom God had used to wage war against the idolatry in Israel. He would be greatly missed. Elisha **tore** his **own clothes** as an act of mourning (cf. Gen. 37:29, 34; 44:13; Josh. 7:6; Es. 4:1; Job 1:20; 2:12) over the loss of this great spiritual warrior. From then on Elisha would wear Elijah's cloak and would serve with the authority and power it symbolized.

### b. The parting of the Jordan (2:13-14)

**2:13-14.** Elijah's **cloak . . . had fallen from** him as he was taken up into heaven. Using it as **Elijah** had done, Elisha **struck the water** of the Jordan and the river parted again (cf. v. 8). Obviously then he possessed the power of Elijah. His words, **Where now is the LORD, the God of Elijah?** were a call to God to demonstrate His power through him as He had done through Elijah.

### c. The search for Elijah (2:15-18)

**2:15-18.** The 50 **prophets from Jericho** (cf. v. 7), observing the whirlwind and the parting of the Jordan both times, concluded that Elijah's spiritual gifts had been passed **on** to **Elisha.** Out of respect for his special calling they **bowed . . . before him.**

They did not realize as **Elisha** did that **Elijah** had been taken into the presence of God and had not returned to the earth. So they requested permission to send out search parties to locate Elijah. They, like Obadiah, thought he might have been transported by **the Spirit of the LORD** (cf. 1 Kings 18:12), perhaps to **some** remote **mountain or . . . valley.** Knowing their search would be futile, **Elisha** tried to dissuade them. But they

## God's Miracles through Elijah and Elisha

| ELIJAH | | ELISHA | |
|---|---|---|---|
| Miracle | Some of the Elements Involved* | Miracle | Some of the Elements Involved* |
| 1. Elijah fed by ravens | Water and food | 1. Jordan River parted | Water |
| 2. Widow's food multiplied | Flour and oil | 2. Jericho spring water purified | Water |
| 3. Widow's dead son raised to life | Life | 3. Widow's oil multiplied | Oil |
| 4. Elijah's altar and sacrifice consumed | Water and fire | 4. Shunammite's dead son raised to life | Life |
| 5. Ahaziah's 102 soldiers consumed | Fire | 5. Poisonous stew purified | Flour |
| 6. Jordan River parted | Water | 6. Prophets' food multiplied | Bread and grain |
| 7. Elijah's transport to heaven | Fire and wind | 7. Naaman healed of leprosy | Water |
| | | 8. Gehazi's leprosy | — |
| | | 9. Axhead floated | Water |
| | | 10. Horses and chariots surrounded the city of Dothan | Fire |
| | | 11. Aramean soldiers blinded | — |

*Many of these elements—water, flour, oil, fire, and wind—were polemics against Baal, the god of rain, lightning (fire), and vegetation. Even the restoration of two boys back to life (one by Elijah and one by Elisha) was a polemic against the practice of child sacrifice and against the myth that Baal was dead six months each year and then was raised annually. Baal's restoration to life was only mythical; the boys' restoration to life was real.

insisted and in order to avoid appearing heartless Elisha finally gave them permission. They returned **three days** later without Elijah as Elisha had predicted. Elisha's word was thereafter more readily accepted and respected by them.

### d. The purifying of the waters (2:19-22)

**2:19.** The incident recorded in verses 19-22 evidently followed soon after the one in verses 15-18. **Elisha** was still in Jericho. Apparently word about him had spread for now all **the** citizens **of the city** knew of Elisha's power. The leading **men** came to him with a practical problem that gave him opportunity to demonstrate the Lord's desire and ability to bless the people. Jericho had many natural advantages since it was located in a fertile area of the Jordan Valley. **But the water** from a major spring had turned **bad,** perhaps brackish, and when used for irrigation it killed the crops rather than nourishing them. The parallelism between this physical situation and the spiritually polluting influences of Baal worship in Israel is obvious.

**2:20-22.** Elisha's solution, given by **the LORD,** was designed to teach the peo-

ple as well as to relieve their immediate distress. The **new bowl** represented himself, the new instrument in God's hand. **Salt** was known by the Israelites to preserve and purify; it was used in each of their daily grain offerings to the Lord (cf. Lev. 2:13). But adding salt to water normally makes water worse, not better. When **the salt** was put into **the** Jericho **water** the situation miraculously improved. This miracle showed the people of Jericho that the Lord, not Baal, the so-called god of fertility, could heal their barrenness. God's permanent work on the spring would serve as a perpetual reminder of His ability to bring fruitfulness and blessing out of the barrenness and sterility caused by idolatry.

### e. The cursing young men (2:23-25)

**2:23.** As **Elisha** was traveling from Jericho **to Bethel** several dozen **youths** (young men, not children) confronted him. Perhaps they were young false prophets of Baal. Their jeering, recorded in the slang of their day, implied that if Elisha were a great prophet of the Lord, as Elijah was, he should **go on up** into heaven as Elijah reportedly had done.

The epithet **baldhead** may allude to lepers who had to shave their heads and were considered detestable outcasts. Or it may simply have been a form of scorn, for baldness was undesirable (cf. Isa. 3:17, 24). Since it was customary for men to cover their heads, the young men probably could not tell if Elisha was bald or not. They regarded God's prophet with contempt.

**2:24.** Elisha then **called down a curse on** the villains. This cursing stemmed not from Elisha's pride but from their disrespect for **the LORD** as reflected in their treatment of His spokesman (cf. 1:9-14). Again God used wild animals to execute His judgment (cf., e.g., 1 Kings 13:24). That **42** men were **mauled** by the **two bears** suggests that a mass demonstration had been organized against God and Elisha.

**2:25.** Elisha journeyed on from Bethel **to Mount Carmel.** There among other activities he undoubtedly reviewed God's mighty vindication of Himself through Elijah (1 Kings 18:19-46). Elisha's ministry would continue what Elijah had begun (1 Kings 19:16).

From Mount Carmel Elisha **returned to Samaria.** This city, capital of the Northern Kingdom of Israel, was to be the site of many of Elisha's mighty deeds.

These early miracles in Elisha's ministry identified him as a unique spokesman for God with the authority and power of Elijah, one worthy of the greatest respect as a representative of the living God.

### 2. JORAM'S WICKEDNESS (3:1-3)

**3:1-3. Joram** was the second **son of Ahab** to rule **Israel. In the 18th year** after **Jehoshaphat** began reigning as sole **king of Judah,** Joram **became king** over Israel **and . . . reigned 12 years** (852–841 B.C.). Though wicked, he was less **evil** than his **father** Ahab and his **mother** Jezebel. **The sacred stone of Baal . . . made** by Ahab, was evidently an image of that god. Though Joram did get **rid of** this idol he remained sympathetic to and supportive of Baal worship in **Israel** (cf. 10:19-28). For some reason he removed this important image, but continued the religious policies of his parents and his predecessor **Jeroboam** (cf. 1 Kings 12:26-33; 13:33).

### 3. ELISHA'S MINISTRY (3:4–8:15)

The great ministry of Elisha, already begun and revealed in part, is recorded in this large section of stories.

#### a. The battle against Moab (3:4-27)

**3:4-8.** The Moabites **raised** many **sheep.** When Omri subjugated **Moab** he imposed a tribute of **lambs and . . . wool** which the Moabites grudgingly provided for many years. When **Ahab died** in battle, **Mesha** the Moabite **king . . . rebelled against . . . King** Ahaziah (1:1). This rebellion seems to have been ineffective since Mesha also rebelled against Ahaziah's successor, Joram (3:4-27). Eager to suppress this uprising **Joram . . . mobilized all . . . Israel.** Seeking permission to march through Judah to fight Moab from the south, Joram asked **Jehoshaphat** of **Judah** to join him as an ally in battle. Jehoshaphat agreed and pledged his support to Joram. Joram suggested attacking from the south **through the Desert of Edom** rather than from the north, the more normal though heavily defended frontier, and Jehoshaphat agreed.

**3:9-12. Edom** at this time was under Judah's authority and joined the alliance. After marching through Judah down the southwestern coast of the Dead Sea, around the southern end, and into Edom, **the army** ran out of **water.** Joram's expression of dismay (v. 10) indicates that he considered **the LORD** responsible for their predicament. As on an earlier occasion (1 Kings 22:7) **Jehoshaphat** suggested they find a **prophet of the LORD** who could obtain instructions for them. One of Joram's officers volunteered that **Elisha** was nearby. Probably the Lord had directed him there to be ready for this mission; it is unlikely that he was traveling with the army. Pouring **water on the hands** of another for washing was a servant's work; Elisha had been Elijah's minister (cf. 1 Kings 19:21). Evidently the officer thought Joram did not know Elisha, which may have been the case. Whether Joram knew of Elisha or not, **Jehoshaphat** did. Humbling themselves before the prophet, the three kings paid him a visit.

**3:13-19.** Elisha's question, **What do we have to do with each other?** is probably an idiom meaning "Why should I obey you?" The prophet's suggestion that Joram go to his parents' **prophets** implies that since the king promoted Baal worship he should seek his own god. This barb forced Joram to face up to the impotency of Baal. Joram's rejoinder placed the blame for the army's predicament on **the LORD.** He had come to Elisha because now it was up to Yahweh to get them out of their trouble.

**Elisha** was not intimidated by Joram's charge. He knew God had not directed Israel into its difficulty but that the army was there on the king's initiative. Nevertheless for Jehoshaphat's sake **Elisha** consented to seek a word from the Lord. (His words **As surely as the LORD Almighty lives, whom I serve** are strikingly similar to Elijah's words to Joram's father Ahab (1 Kings 17:1; cf. 2 Kings 5:16). Harp music helped put **Elisha** into a frame of mind in which he could readily discern the Lord's direction. (David's harp-playing also helped soothe Saul, 1 Sam. 16:23.)

Elisha received a direct revelation and proceeded to explain God's plan. The **valley** was probably the valley of the Zered on Moab's southern boundary. God would provide **water** enough in an unnatural way so that everyone would know that it was He who had provided. This would be **an easy thing in the** Lord's **eyes.** Ultimate victory would be theirs. Cutting **down** all the **good** trees would make it difficult for the Moabites to have fruit to eat and would mean they would have little shade. Stopping **up all the springs** would limit the Moabites' water supply, and putting large **stones** in the fields would retard cultivation and lessen their productivity.

**3:20-25.** Evidently God caused the **water** from rains in **Edom** to flow down into the valley and fill the trenches that had been dug. This **water** was an expression of God's love for His people. The fact that it had not rained locally probably caused **the Moabites** to think that having water in the valley was impossible. The **morning . . . sacrifice** included a lamb and a grain and drink offering (Ex. 29:38-43).

**The border** where **the Moabites** were stationed **early in the morning** was the boundary between Moab and Edom east and south of the Dead Sea. Not expecting water, the Moabites assumed that **the water** shining in the sunlight

was **blood.** So the Moabite army erroneously concluded that the Israelites, Judahites, and Edomites had had a falling out and had **slaughtered each other—** not an unrealistic possiblity. Rather than advancing with weapons drawn for battle they ran to **plunder** the "dead" soldiers' armor and weaponry. **But** instead, they ran into the waiting ranks of their enemies. Defenseless, **the Moabites . . . fled** before **the Israelites. The Israelites,** and presumably their allies with them, **invaded** Moab, **slaughtered** the people, **destroyed** many **towns,** and did to the fields, **springs,** and trees what God had instructed (cf. 2 Kings 3:19). But **Kir Hareseth,** the major city, could not be taken. It was situated at the end of a valley and successfully resisted the attacks of the stone slingers surrounding it.

**3:26-27.** The city of Kir Hareseth (v. 25) was King Mesha's refuge. Courageously he assembled **700 swordsmen,** broke out of the city, and attacked **the king of Edom,** whom he apparently concluded was the weakest link in the three-nation alliance. He was not successful, however, and was forced back behind the walls. Defeat in battle was regarded by pagan Near Eastern warriors as a sign that their gods were angry with them. To propitiate his god, Chemosh (1 Kings 11:7, 33; 2 Kings 23:13), Mesha offered **his firstborn son,** the heir to his throne, **as a** human **sacrifice on** top of **the city wall.** He was fighting with all his might. It was not Israel's intent to annihilate the Moabites; they only wanted to keep their neighbors from rebelling against their sovereignty to keep them under their control. So offensive to the allies was Mesha's act of sacrificing his son that **they withdrew and returned** home. Israel had won the battle even though they had not destroyed Kir Hareseth or captured Mesha.

Some say **the fury against Israel,** which **was great,** may refer to God's anger. More likely it refers to Judah's anger against Israel for invading Moab in a battle that resulted in their seeing such a repulsive act.

A remarkable archeological discovery, the Moabite Stone, contains Mesha's own record of this battle and other battles with Israel. On this stone the Moabite king claimed to have been delivered from the Israelites by his god

Chemosh on this day. Though it is true that he was not captured at Kir Hareseth and the Israelites withdrew, Israel and her allies were the real victors in this campaign.

The account of this battle provides further proof of the sovereignty of Yahweh and of the complete vanity of idols and idolatry. But even with so many proofs Israel continued to spurn the Lord and foolishly worshiped pagan deities.

### b. The oil for the prophet's widow (4:1-7)

**4:1.** The place where this incident took place is not stated but probably the widow lived in one of the cities where the schools of the prophets were situated, perhaps Bethel, Gilgal, or Jericho. Since the prophet had a **wife** it is clear that **the company of the prophets** was not a monastic settlement (or settlements) of celibates. This widow turned **to Elisha** for help in her hour of need. She appealed to him on the basis that her **husband** had been faithful to the Lord (**he revered the LORD**). The taking of **boys as . . . slaves** in payment for debts was not uncommon in the ancient Near East.

**4:2-7.** Elisha was eager to **help** the widow. His miracles, as contrasted with Elijah's, frequently involved meeting the needs of individuals. Her **little** bit of **oil** was olive oil used for food and fuel. **Elisha** told her to collect **empty jars**; they would be **filled** with oil God would provide. The widow's faith can be "measured" by the number of **jars** she collected in response to the prophet's instructions. Shutting **the door** provided privacy for the task of pouring the **oil**. Not everyone was to see the miracle take place; only the widow **and her sons,** the direct beneficiaries of God's grace, should see it. But later she probably told all her friends about God's miraculous provision. God provided oil enough to fill **all the jars** the woman had collected, all she felt she needed. She returned to Elisha with a report of the miracle and he told her to **sell the oil and pay** her **debts.** There was enough money **left** over for her to **live on** after all her financial obligations had been met. Elisha is called a **man of God,** a term used of several prophets in 1 and 2 Kings (cf. comments on 1:9).

This story demonstrates God's care for His faithful ones who lived in apostate Israel at this time. Widows were always vulnerable and the widow of a prophet would have been even more needy. Yet God miraculously cared for this faithful, dependent believer.

### c. The Shunammite woman (4:8-37)

God's concern for women and their special needs can be seen clearly in both the preceding and this incident. Whereas women were regarded as inferior to men in most ancient Near Eastern societies, God showed His concern for them here as well as in many other portions of Scripture.

(1) The Lord's gift (4:8-16). **4:8-10.** In contrast with the poor widow in the previous story this **woman** in **Shunem** (near Jezreel) was **well-to-do** and had a **husband. Elisha** evidently **stopped** at her house regularly at her invitation as he traveled between Samaria, Jezreel, and other cities. The woman's faith in Yahweh is seen in her desire to be a blessing to the **man of God.** Apparently she was more spiritually sensitive and outgoing then her husband (cf. comments on v. 23). He did, however, consent to his wife's proposal to build a guest **room on the** typically flat **roof** of their house and to furnish it for Elisha's comfort.

**4:11-13.** After **Elisha** had enjoyed this couple's hospitality for some time he desired to do something for them in return. He asked **his servant Gehazi** to express his offer to the woman. Perhaps this was to make the woman feel more inclined to ask for something than she would have if the prophet addressed her. God's grace to His faithful ones can be seen in Elisha's offer (v. 13; cf. v. 2). Elisha obviously enjoyed a position of some influence in the palace even though he opposed Joram's religious policies. The woman's reply (**I have a home among my own people**) expressed contentment with her lot in life; she was at peace and felt no special needs.

**4:14-16.** Determined to return her favors, **Elisha** discussed with **Gehazi** after she left his room what he might do **for her.** Gehazi observed that **she** had **no son** and probably never would have one since **her husband** was old. **Elisha** called **her** back and told **her** that she would have **a son** in **about a year.** This miraculous birth would be God's gift to her for her goodness to His servant. The woman's response to this announcement does not mean that she did not want a son; every Israelite woman did. To be childless was regarded in Israel as a great personal tragedy. Her reply indicates that she felt having a son was impossible. She urged Elisha not to build up her hopes only to disappoint her later.

(2) The child's birth and death. 4:17-23. Like Sarah (cf. Gen. 18:12-13; 21:2) the Shunammite did bear **a son** as God promised. However, one morning while **the child,** evidently still quite young, was out in the fields with **his father** in the heat of harvesttime a violent headache overtook him. He was carried back **to his mother** but failed to improve and **died** shortly thereafter, perhaps from sunstroke. Clearly the lad was dead, not just sick (cf. 2 Kings 4:32), and his mother knew it. Her thoughts turned immediately to Elisha and she prepared to seek his help. Perhaps she did not tell **her husband** that her son had died because she feared he would not let her go if he knew the boy was dead. When she told him she wanted to see Elisha (**the man of God;** cf. vv. 9, 16, 21, 25 [twice], 27 [twice]), he questioned the need since it was **not the New Moon or the Sabbath,** occasions for religious festivals. The husband's spiritual concerns seem to have been superficial and ritualistic. Her words, **It's all right** (v. 23), were designed to avoid further explanation and delay.

(3) The mother's plea (4:24-31). **4:24-26.** Quickly the woman rode her **donkey,** while **her servant** led. Elisha was only a few miles away **at Mount Carmel.** Interestingly she knew where to find him. **When** the prophet **saw her** coming he sent **Gehazi** to intercept her. But she would not be delayed with explanations; she hurried on to Elisha. Her confidence lay in Elisha's ability as a **man of God,** not in **his servant.**

**4:27-28.** Arriving where Elisha was, **she** grasped **his feet,** a gesture indicating extreme humility, need, and desperation. **Gehazi** felt that her behavior was improper, but Elisha recognized it as the expression of deepest grief. **The LORD** sometimes informed his prophets beforehand of situations they would face (e.g., 1 Kings 14:5), but this time He did not.

As is common under extreme stress the woman's first words to Elisha did not tell him why she had come but how she felt about what had happened. She referred to the fact that having **a son** who died was a loss of her **hopes,** much like never having a son at all. She was so heartbroken at her son's death that at the moment she felt it would have been better if he had never been born.

**4:29-31. Elisha** probably understood that the lad had died; he probably would not have done anything without first learning what had happened. He sent **Gehazi** with his **staff,** the symbol of his authority as a prophet of the Lord, and instructed him to **lay** it **on the boy's face.** Either Elisha believed God would honor this method or he wanted to teach a lesson. Gehazi was to go immediately to Shunem; he was **not** to **greet** anyone he met on the way or return their greetings. (People in the East lost much time giving and returning prolonged greetings.) The **mother** told Elisha that she would **not leave** him. (Cf. comments on words similar to **As surely as the LORD lives,** in 1 Kings 17:1. That same and similar phrases occur seven times in 1 Kings and seven in 2 Kings.)

So Elisha **got up** and **followed her** back to Shunem. **Gehazi went on ahead** of Elisha who apparently followed his servant at a slower pace. Gehazi followed Elisha's instructions but **the boy** did not awaken to life. **So Gehazi** returned to his master and reported what had happened.

(4) The prophet's miracle (4:32-37). **4:32-35.** That **the boy** was indeed **dead** is stated again (cf. v. 20). **Elisha. . . . shut the door** of the room so that he could concentrate in prayer on the object of his petition, while Gehazi and the woman stayed outside the room. The earnestness of Elisha's entreaty **to the LORD** is reflected in his prone posture. **The boy's body grew warm** from contact with Elisha; God was beginning to answer the prophet's prayer.

**Elisha** then paced **back and forth in the room,** apparently continuing to pour out his soul in fervent, persistent prayer. He returned to prostrate himself on the body of the lad **once** again. These actions were not some kind of magic; they were the natural physical expressions of a man engaged in earnest prayer. God restored the lad's life, air returned to his lungs, he **sneezed seven times** (seven indicating a work of God; cf. 5:14), **and opened his eyes.** These were the first signs that God had restored his life.

**4:36-37.** Then the prophet told **Gehazi** to **call the Shunammite,** who also was probably praying in some private place. **When she** entered the room and saw her son alive she first **fell at** Elisha's **feet** out of respect and gratitude (cf. v. 27), **and bowed to the ground** before the Lord in worship. **Then she took her son,** probably in her arms, and left the room full of joy and gratitude for what God had done for her.

Throughout this story evidences of the woman's faith keep shining through (cf. vv. 8-10, 16, 21-22, 24-25, 27, 30, 37). God rewarded her trust with a miraculous birth and a miraculous restoration to life. Gehazi's failure to restore the boy to life by using Elisha's staff shows that the living God works in response to the requests of trusting people rather than magically through a fetish (Elisha's staff). Baal, a god of fertility, undoubtedly suffered ignominy as this story of Yahweh's provision of life circulated in Israel (cf. 1 Kings 17:21-22).

### d. The deadly stew (4:38-41)

**4:38-41.** On one of Elisha's trips to **the company of the prophets** located at **Gilgal** a situation developed that provided an object lesson of what **Elisha** was teaching. The fact that this incident took place in a time of **famine** is important to a correct understanding of the story. This famine may have been the same one(s) referred to later (6:25; 7:4; 8:1) or a different one (cf. the famine in Elijah's days, 1 Kings 18:2). (These stories of Elisha's ministry are evidently not in strict chronological order but were arranged by the writer in sequence for a variety of reasons: similar subject matter, related lessons, geographical connections, etc.) Though there was a famine Elisha prepared to feed the prophets with whatever could be collected. He asked **his servant** (Gehazi or another person) to prepare the **stew** pot for a meal.

**One of** the prophets **went out . . . to gather** whatever he could find growing wild to put in the stew. Finding **a wild vine, he gathered some of its gourds. . . . cut them up,** and put them **into the pot.** The unknown gourds had a horrible taste and may have caused some violent physical reactions in those who tasted **the stew.** The prophets concluded that the gourds had poisoned the stew. **Elisha** added some **flour** to the stew. Not much of it could have been available in a famine. But with this additive the stew became quite palatable and the prophets ate it without harm.

In Elisha's day a spiritual famine had resulted from the people's turning from God and His Law. The people were hungry spiritually. In an effort to satisfy their need they had imbibed a false religion called Baalism. It looked harmless enough but proved disgusting and deadly. God's prophets helped counteract the deadly effects of Baalism in Israel.

### e. The multiplication of bread (4:42-44)

**4:42-44. Baal Shalishah** was a town close to Gilgal so this incident may have taken place about the same time as the preceding one. Evidently the famine still persisted. The **man** who brought the **bread** and **grain** to **the man of God** (Elisha; cf. v. 21) was apparently a believer in the Lord, taking these items as the firstfruits offering of his harvest to God (cf. Num. 18:13; Deut. 18:4). When **Elisha** suggested to **his servant** (Gehazi) that the food be given to feed the **100 men** assembled (probably the company of the prophets; cf. 2 Kings 4:38), the servant's response indicated that it was far too little. Nevertheless **Elisha** ordered him to distribute it and assured him that **the LORD** had promised there would be plenty and **some** would be **left over.** The servant obeyed and God multiplied the food as He had promised.

This miracle instructed all who heard of it that God could multiply the limited resources (cf. 1 Kings 17:7-16) that were dedicated to Him and with them nourish and sustain a large multitude. Baal, a god of fertility known as "the lord of the earth," had no such power.

### f. Naaman the Aramean (chap. 5)

Elisha's ministry expanded beyond the borders of Israel as recorded in this story of another miracle he performed.

(1) Naaman's disease (5:1-6). **5:1. Naaman was commander of the army of the king of Aram,** Ben-Hadad II (860–841

B.C.; see the chart "Kings of Aram in 1 and 2 Kings," near 1 Kings 11:23-25). Naaman was a successful and courageous warrior, **highly regarded because** of the victories God **had given** the Arameans under his leadership. However, **he had leprosy** (perhaps this was not leprosy as it is known today; cf. NIV marg.). This dreaded disease degenerated its victims and eventually proved fatal. No cure for it was known. In Israel lepers were normally isolated from nonlepers, but this was not always the custom in other nations including Aram. Naaman was able to carry on his duties as long as the disease permitted him to do so.

**5:2-3.** In the course of their occasional battles with **Israel,** Naaman's forces had captured some Israelites whom they made slaves. One of these was **a young girl** whom Naaman had given to his **wife** as a servant. Evidently Naaman and his wife were kind to this girl because she sought **Naaman's** welfare. **She told her mistress,** who told her husband, that a **prophet** living **in Samaria** could **cure . . . leprosy.** This was Elisha; he lived in a house in the capital city (6:24, 32). Probably the girl had heard of Elisha before she was carried off as a slave. Apparently she assumed he could cleanse leprosy in view of his supernatural power. No leper in Israel, though, was healed in Elisha's day (Luke 4:27). Later the slave girl's faith in the Lord may have been an indirect rebuke to Israel's King Joram who had no faith in God.

**5:4-6.** The Aramean **king** was anxious for his valuable commander to be cleansed, not only because he was a trusted friend but because the dreaded disease would eventually rob the king of his top military commander. **Naaman** set out to visit **King** Joram who he assumed would order the prophet to cure him. **With him** the commander took gifts of **10 talents** (ca. 750 pounds) **of silver, 600 shekels** (ca. 150 pounds) **of gold, and 10 sets of clothing,** all prized gifts in the Near East. He also carried a **letter** from his king to Joram requesting in matter-of-fact terms that **Naaman** be cured.

(2) Naaman's cure (5:7-14). **5:7.** Joram was dismayed when he **read the letter** from Ben-Hadad II. Tearing one's **robes** indicated great anxiety and distress (cf. 2:12; 6:30; 11:14). Israel and Aram had

been at peace, but it appeared to Joram that Ben-Hadad was trying to **pick a** fight again as he had done with Joram's father Ahab (cf. 1 Kings 20:1-3). Joram did not realize that Naaman did not expect *him* to cure the leprosy. Elisha did not even enter Joram's mind. The Israelite king had no use for that prophet who constantly opposed him. Joram wanted as little contact with him as possible.

**5:8-10. When Elisha** learned of Joram's anxiety over Ben-Hadad's letter he sent the king a **message** not to worry. If Joram would send Naaman to him the prophet would cure him. Naaman would learn, even if Joram had not, **that there** was a true **prophet in Israel.** Before long **Naaman** and his whole retinue arrived at **Elisha's** door.

Not at all awed by the great general, **Elisha** did not even go out to meet him; instead he **sent a messenger to** convey his simple "prescription." Naaman was told to dip **seven times in the Jordan** River and he would be free of his disease. The cure lay not in the water of the Jordan but in obedient faith in God's promise through His prophet.

**5:11-14. Naaman** turned from Elisha's house **angry** for two reasons: (1) His pride had been offended by Elisha's offhanded treatment of him; he had expected a cleansing ceremony in keeping with his own dignity. (2) He resented having been told to wash in a muddy river that he considered inferior to the **Abana and Pharpar . . . rivers** in his hometown; the water of the Jordan, he thought, could not possibly do him any good.

The commander's **servants,** however, had not been personally put down as their master had, and could view the situation more objectively. Approaching him tenderly they appealed to him as a **father** to be reasonable. They pointed out that it was not as though Elisha had requested something difficult (**some great thing**). What harm would there be in giving his remedy a try? Undoubtedly feeling rather ashamed Naaman humbled himself and obeyed the word of the Lord. As he obeyed in faith he was **cleansed.** God did even more for him and **restored** his flesh to its soft boyhood texture. God had prescribed that he wash **seven times** (cf. 4:35) to indicate that the healing was completely a work of God, "for seven is the stamp of the works of God" (C.F. Keil, "1 & 2 Kings," in *Commentary on the Old Testament in Ten Volumes*, 3:319). The fact that in Elisha's day an Aramean leper was healed whereas no Israelite leper was (Luke 4:27) points up Israel's apostasy.

(3) Naaman's gratitude (5:15-18). **5:15-16. Naaman** returned from the Jordan to Elisha's house in Samaria (about 25 miles) with a heart full of gratitude and hands full of gifts. Rather than expecting Elisha to come to him he willingly **stood before** the prophet and testified to his belief that Israel's **God** is the only true God. (Unfortunately many in Israel, including her king, had not come to the same realization.) This was the highest purpose of Naaman's healing from God's point of view. Elisha agreed that **the LORD** whom he served **lives** (cf. comments on 1 Kings 17:1; 2 Kings 4:30). But the prophet **refused** to accept any reward for his ministry. Naaman's urging did not budge Elisha. The man of God had not performed his miracle for reward but at the word of the Lord and he did not want anyone to think otherwise. The false prophets could easily be bought, but not Elisha.

**5:17-18.** Since Elisha would not take anything, **Naaman** asked him to give **as much earth as** he could carry back to Damascus on two **mules**. He intended to use this in making an altar to the Lord. Many polytheists believed that no god could be worshiped except in its own land or on an altar built with the dirt of that land.

Naaman proposed to worship only Yahweh Himself (**the LORD**), but superstition shaped his thinking. In the course of his official duties, however, he would have to give token respect to the god of his **master** the king. The god of Damascus was Hadad-Rimmon, a god of rain and thunder, here shortened to **Rimmon**. It was Naaman's duty to participate in this official worship with the king and probably other officials of state. The commander was not prepared to risk his life, as Daniel's three friends would (Dan. 3:12), by refusing to bow before an idol. But one must remember that Naaman was not an Israelite with the advantage of knowledge of the revealed Word of God. Perhaps his responsibility therefore was not as great as an Israelite's would

have been. **Leaning on my arm** (cf. 2 Kings 7:2) is a figurative expression for relying on an assistant for help.

(4) Gehazi's greed (5:19-27). **5:19-21.** Elisha's departing benediction (**Go in peace**) probably was a blessing on the journey ahead of **Naaman** rather than on the compromising behavior the general had outlined (vv. 17-18), which the prophet neither approved nor disapproved verbally.

**Gehazi** became greedy of what Naaman had offered to give Elisha. Evidently he justified his greed by reasoning that since **Naaman** was an **Aramean,** a natural enemy of Israel, he should at least be taken advantage of. So **Gehazi** pursued **Naaman** to **get something from him.** Gehazi was able to overtake the large slow-moving caravan on foot. Naaman **got down from** his **chariot** (cf. 4:26) and **asked** if **everything** was **all right.**

**5:22-24.** Gehazi said **everything** was **all right** but then lied to the commander. He said his **master** had received unexpected guests (**two . . . prophets**) and wanted to give them some **silver** and a change **of clothing** each. Gehazi put this lie in Elisha's mouth and made the request sound very unselfish. **Naaman** was happy to oblige and urged Gehazi to accept twice as much **silver** as well as the clothing. He even provided **two . . . servants** to carry these gifts back to Elisha. **Gehazi** followed **the servants** and when they arrived at **the hill** (on which Samaria was built) **he took the** gifts **from** them **and put them . . . in** his **house.**

**5:25-27.** Shortly thereafter **Gehazi** returned to **Elisha.** He did not realize that God had revealed his whereabouts to **his master.** So to cover one lie he told another. Elisha then explained that he was aware of everything **Gehazi** had done. **Elisha** added that true servants of the Lord should not **take** personal rewards from people, especially influential non-Israelites, in return for blessings that God, not His servant, had given them. False prophets were selfishly lining their own pockets and bringing contempt on the prophetic office; true prophets should avoid conduct that might be misunderstood as self-seeking.

**Naaman's leprosy** had been removed from him for his trust in and obedience to God. Now, ironically, leprosy would **cling to** Gehazi for his lack of trust in and obedience to God. The servant had brought dishonor to Yahweh's name. A bad case of leprosy turned one's skin and hair **white as snow.** Gehazi's judgment was serious because his sin had far-reaching consequences; this story was probably told all over Aram and Israel. As a servant of God Gehazi had more privilege than most people and therefore more responsibility than most people.

This story contains many lessons. Naaman's healing was another great proof of the Lord's power to restore health, power which only Baal supposedly possessed. This incident also helped spread the fame of Yahweh to another part of the ancient world. The contrasting behaviors of Elisha and Gehazi also model positive and negative attitudes and actions for God's servants of all ages.

*g. The floating axhead (6:1-7)*

**6:1-4a.** Another incident involving **the company of the prophets** follows. At one of their schools their accommodations had become inadequate because of the growing number of young men, a tribute to the effectiveness of Elisha's ministry. This may have been the school at Jericho since the young men went to the nearby **Jordan** River for their wood. They intended to **build** new facilities at a new site **there.** Elisha gave his permission for this project and agreed to accompany the workmen.

**6:4b-7.** In the process of cutting **down trees** an **iron axhead** flew off its handle and **fell into the** river. The man wielding the ax **cried out** to his **lord** (i.e., to Elisha) in dismay because his tool had been **borrowed.** Ascertaining **where** the axhead had fallen into the water **Elisha** threw **a stick** into the river. Miraculously **the iron** implement floated to the surface. The workman was able to retrieve it easily.

Certainly this miracle encouraged the group of faithful followers of the Lord that their God really is alive and that He would supernaturally provide for their needs even though many Israelites in that day had turned from the true God to Baal.

*h. The blinding of the Aramean army (6:8-23)*

**6:8-10.** As mentioned previously the Arameans were sometimes **at war** and sometimes at peace **with Israel** during the years of Elisha's ministry. At the time of this particular incident **the Arameans** were making profitable surprise raids into Israel. **The king of Aram** (cf. 5:1) was probably Ben-Hadad II. (Of the major persons in this narrative only Elisha is mentioned by name. This may suggest that readers should focus on the Lord and His prophet.) In preparation for another raid Ben-Hadad planned to pitch his **camp** on the border of Israel from which he could strike unexpectedly. However, **God** informed **Elisha** of the place and the prophet passed his information on **to the king of Israel** (Joram) with a warning to **beware.** Joram **checked** Elisha's information, found it to be correct, prepared for the encounter, and frustrated Ben-Hadad's secret attack. This happened several times.

**6:11-14.** **Enraged** by his continual failure to surprise the Israelites Ben-Hadad concluded that one of his men was tipping off the enemy. An officer assured **the king** that there were no traitors in his camp but that it was **Elisha** who had supernatural knowledge of all his plans. **The very words you speak in your bedroom** mean even his most private conversations were known to the prophet. Obviously this officer had somehow learned of Elisha and his powers.

As long as Elisha remained free the army of Aram would be unsuccessful, so Ben-Hadad ordered that he be located and captured. He stealthily sent a strong contingent of soldiers with **horses and chariots. . . . by night** and completely surrounded **Dothan** (12 miles north of Samaria), where Elisha was staying. The fact that Ben-Hadad would try to take Elisha by surprise even after the prophet had repeatedly anticipated the Arameans' moves indicates the king's lack of faith in the supernatural origin of Elisha's ability. Therefore he needed to be convinced that Yahweh is the living and true God.

**6:15-17.** Since Gehazi had been dismissed as a disobedient servant and "leper" (5:27), the Naaman story must follow this one if Elisha's **servant** here is Gehazi. Or this servant may be someone who replaced Gehazi. **Early the next morning** the servant was terrified to see that **the whole city** was under the Arameans' control, or so he thought. He returned in a frenzy to Elisha and nervously asked, **What shall we do?** The servant's anxiety reflected his lack of understanding and trust in the Lord which, one would think, Elisha's previous revelations would have changed.

Elisha was not at all disturbed by the present situation. He encouraged his aide to stop fearing, and assured him that they had behind them a force superior to that of the enemy. **Elisha** then asked the Lord to enable his servant to see this host and the Lord did so. He gave the servant the ability to **see** the normally unseen world of invisible spirits (angels) that are constantly ready to do God's bidding (cf. Gen. 28:12). The **hills** around Dothan were filled with superior **horses and chariots.** These appeared as fiery agents of God suggesting to the servant their superterrestrial origin (cf. 2 Kings 2:11). **The Lord** had surrounded the armies of Aram and was in control.

**6:18-20.** Proceeding with a divinely revealed strategy **Elisha** called on God to blind the Arameans as they began to converge on Dothan, and God did so.

Elisha said, **This is not the road and this is not the city** for that road and **city** were not where God intended them to go. They unknowingly followed Elisha **inside** the walls of **Samaria,** the capital of Israel. What the Israelite army might not have been able to do except with much fighting and loss of life, God did peacefully through one man. In response to Elisha's prayer God opened **the eyes of** the Arameans and they discovered that they were surrounded and helpless captives at the mercy of the king of Israel.

**6:21-23.** Joram, realizing that **Elisha** was in control, and almost hysterical because of his good fortune, **asked** the prophet, whom he respectfully addressed as his **father** (cf. 5:13), if he should **kill** his prisoners. Elisha said no. Joram probably would not have killed soldiers captured in battle and furthermore God's purpose was not to destroy the Arameans' lives but to save the Israelites' lives. The king then assured them of this in an unusual way. By setting **a great feast** before the soldiers he was expressing confidence in God's ability to control the enemy; Israel had absolutely nothing to fear and could even treat these soldiers as friends because God had

them in His sovereign power. In the ancient Near East eating together under one's roof constituted making a covenant of peace (J. Herbert Livingston, *The Pentateuch in Its Cultural Environment.* Grand Rapids: Baker Book House, 1974, p. 157). The Arameans were now bound by social custom not to attack the friend who had extended his gift of hospitality and protection. For these reasons the Arameans **stopped raiding Israel's territory** for a time.

The reference to the soldiers returning **to their master** suggests that King Ben-Hadad II was not part of the force that had been sent to capture Elisha (cf. 6:13). Evidently this was just part of the total Aramean army.

This incident demonstrates Yahweh is His people's defense. So to depart from Him was the height of folly. Israel's victory by means of God's prophet rather than by warriors undoubtedly encouraged many in Israel and Aram to fear the Almighty God.

*i. The famine in Samaria (6:24–7:20)*

Joram and the nation of Israel failed to turn back to the Lord as a result of the previous incident. Consequently God sent a more severe situation to draw them back to Himself.

(1) The desperate condition (6:24-31). **6:24-25. Some time** after the events narrated in verses 1-23 **Ben-Hadad** II tried again to defeat Israel. This time instead of sending raiding parties (cf. "bands" in v. 23), he **mobilized his entire army** and besieged **Samaria.** Since no one could leave or enter the capital, **a great famine** resulted. It was so severe that one **donkey's head,** one of the least nourishing and most repulsive parts of this animal, unclean to the Israelites, became a highly valued commodity selling **for 80 shekels** (ca. two pounds) **of silver.** Approximately a half pint **of seed pods,** normally considered animal fodder, cost **5 shekels** (ca. two ounces) of silver.

**6:26-27.** Joram's reply (**Where can I get help for you?**) to **a woman** who called **to him** revealed his frustration. He was angry with **the Lord** for permitting this situation (cf. v. 33). God had promised that such conditions would discipline His people if they turned from Him (Lev. 26:29; Deut. 28:53, 57). Joram sarcastically told the woman that he could not provide bread **from the** grain on the **thresh-ing floor** or wine **from the** grapes in the **winepress;** he was not greater than God was supposed to be.

**6:28-31.** Having vented his frustration with these words the king then invited the woman to explain her problem. She said that a friend had persuaded her to cook her **son** but **the next day,** when the friend was to cook **her . . . son . . . she had hidden him.** Learning the desperate extent to which the siege had driven his people, **the king** angrily **tore his robes,** an expression of deep distress and sorrow (cf. 2:12; 5:7; 11:14). **Sack-cloth,** coarse material made from black goat's hair, was worn as a symbol of repentance and self-affliction. But Joram's repentance seems to have been rather shallow in view of his attitude toward God's servant **Elisha.** Rather than dealing with the real cause of God's discipline, his own apostasy, Joram blamed Elisha who had perhaps only explained the reason for Israel's condition. In oath (**May God deal with me, be it ever so severely;** cf. 1 Kings 2:23; 20:10) the king swore to put the prophet to death that very day (cf. Elijah's experience, 1 Kings 19:2).

(2) The prophecies of deliverance (6:32–7:2). **6:32. The elders** who **were sitting with** Elisha **in his house** (cf. 5:9) were the officials of the land. Perhaps they were meeting with the prophet to discuss what should be done. Warned by God, **Elisha** announced that the king was **sending someone to** have him beheaded. Joram did not realize that Elisha was the solution to his problems rather than their source. The prophet's instruction to **the elders** to bar **the door** against the executioner was evidently intended to postpone any violence until Joram himself would arrive. (**Is not the sound of his master's footsteps behind him?**) The instruction would also give Elisha opportunity to announce God's message of imminent deliverance.

**6:33.** When Joram did arrive he asked Elisha why he should **wait . . . any longer** for God to act. Apparently Elisha had told Joram that God had said he should not surrender to Ben-Hadad but should wait for divine deliverance. Since that help was not forthcoming Joram had decided to take matters into his own hands. As he had done many times be-

fore he was disobeying the orders of his Lord through Elisha, acting as an unfaithful administrator (cf. 1 Sam. 15:11). Since, as Joram stated, the **disaster** (the siege and the famine) was **from the Lord,** the king should have obeyed Him.

**7:1-2. Elisha** then announced a prophecy. Within 24 hours the siege would be over and there would be plenty to eat. **A seah** (ca. seven quarts) **of flour** would **sell for a shekel** (about two-fifths of an ounce) **and two seahs** (ca. 13-14 quarts) **of barley** (for cattle to eat) would sell for the same price (cf. v. 16) **at the gate of** the city where business of this sort was normally transacted. These prices were not unusually low but compared with what the people had been paying during the famine (cf. 6:25) they were great bargains.

**The officer** assisting Joram (cf. 7:17 and the comments on 5:8) found this prophecy incredible. His retort expressed his utter disbelief that **God** would or could do this. **Elisha** replied that the officer would **see** the miracle **with his own eyes;** it would indeed take place. But because of his unbelief he would not experience the blessing (cf. 7:17).

(3) The lepers' discovery (7:3-9). **7:3-4.** The **four** lepers may have been housed in huts just outside **the city gate;** they were isolated from contact with non-lepers in Israel. Of their three options, they correctly concluded that their best choice lay in giving themselves up to **the Arameans.** They might be killed but, they reasoned, that would be better than dying gradually of starvation.

**7:5-7.** Entering **the camp of the Arameans** (apparently at night; cf. **dusk,** v. 7, "daylight," v. 9, and "night," v. 12) the lepers found that the enemy soldiers had **fled.** The writer explained the reason for the soldiers' departure. **The Lord had caused** them **to hear** noises from the north and the south that made them think the armies of the Hittites (who earlier had lived in the area now called Turkey but were now living in enclaves in Aram) and the Egyptians were descending on them. They supposed these were reinforcements **hired** by the Israelites. So at **dusk** they retreated eastward toward their homeland. So great was their haste that **they left** many of their animals and supplies behind.

**7:8-9.** At first the lepers filled their

own stomachs and pockets and even **hid** some of their treasure so that they could retrieve it later. But gradually their sense of duty to their fellow Samaritans convicted them. Also they reasoned that if they failed to **report** the situation, others would discover in the morning that the enemy had fled and they would be punished for not announcing the situation to the starving population. Rather than suffer as criminals they preferred to be treated as heroes. So they decided to return to Samaria and proclaim their **good news.**

(4) The cautious investigation (7:10-15). **7:10-12.** The lepers returned to Samaria and told **the city gatekeepers** their story. The news spread like wildfire through the city during **the night** (cf. vv. 9, 11). But **the king** suspected a trap. He calculated that since **the Arameans** had not been able to break into Samaria they had planned this apparent retreat to draw the Samaritans **out,** leaving **the city** open to invasion.

**7:13-15.** One of Joram's **officers** proposed sending only **five** horsemen out to scout **the Aramean** camp. If these soldiers were caught their deaths would **only be** hastened; he thought death was inescapable for all the people in Samaria. Joram liked this plan. So he ordered **two chariots with their horses,** risking four horses (not five as had been suggested) to follow the supposedly fleeing Aramean **army.** The chariot **drivers** followed a trail of discarded **clothing and equipment** all the way to **the Jordan** River, about 25 miles from Samaria. Israel's enemy then had crossed the Jordan and was far away. The drivers **returned** to Samaria and announced the good news **to the king.**

(5) The fulfillment of Elisha's predictions. **7:16-20.** The king apparently threw the gates open before the excited multitudes who streamed out to find food and booty. Those who found the food first were able to sell it to their neighbors for the same prices **the LORD had** predicted through Elisha (cf. v. 1). So heavy was the traffic through the **gate** that **the officer** who assisted the king (cf. v. 2 and the comment on 5:18) and who had been stationed there to insure an orderly departure was **trampled** to death. This man had ridiculed God's ability to do what He said He would do (cf. v. 2). The fate that Elisha had predicted overtook him.

Yahweh, not Baal, provides food; in fact God even foretold exactly when He would provide it. The remarkable way in which God kept the Samaritans safe and sustained them should have turned them and **the king** back to Him. God's future discipline of the Israelites can be understood better in the light of their rejection of His many gracious and miraculous provisions for them.

*j. The preservation of the Shunammite woman (8:1-6)*

This story illustrates God's marvelous care of those who trust in Him even in times of popular apostasy.

**8:1-3.** These verses relate background information. **Elisha** had directed his benefactress and her **family** (cf. 4:8-37) to leave Israel temporarily. **The LORD** had revealed to His prophet that He would bring a **seven**-year **famine** on the **land** (cf. 4:38; 6:25; 7:4). This was a punishment for apostasy (cf. Deut. 11:16-17; 28:38-40; 1 Kings 18:2). Trusting in the word of the **man of God. . . . she and her family** left their home and lived in Philistia for **seven years.** Returning to Israel, the woman appeared before **King** Joram **to beg for her** former property which has been taken over by someone else in her absence. She may not have been asking that her property be given to her but that she be permitted to buy it back since it was apparently her paternal inheritance, guaranteed to each Israelite family by the Law of Moses.

**8:4-5.** Since **King** Joram **was talking to Gehazi** (Elisha's **servant**) when **the woman** called on the king, this incident must have taken place before **Gehazi** became a leper (5:27). Joram's interest in **Elisha** seems to have been motivated by curiosity rather than conviction; there is no evidence that Joram ever abandoned his apostate ways and became a faithful follower of the Lord. Elisha's resuscitation of the Shunammite's **son** (4:32-37) was a great event to recount. Amazingly Gehazi's **telling** of it was interrupted by **the woman** herself who had come to present her request to **the king.**

**8:6.** The woman and her son's timely appearance so impressed Joram that he **asked the woman** to fill in some details of Gehazi's story, which she did. Besides permitting her to return to her former homestead, **the king** even ordered that the proceeds **from** the **land,** since she had **left** it, be paid to her.

The perfect timing of God's actions stands out in this brief narrative. God preserved His faithful Shunammite believer by removing her from the famine before it began and by bringing her before the king at a uniquely propitious moment. Joram had been uniquely prepared by Gehazi to help her. In view of the woman's faith in the Lord, it was remarkable that Joram showed her any favor at all.

*k. Hazael's murder of Ben-Hadad II (8:7-15)*

**8:7-8.** Elisha visited **Damascus,** the capital of **Aram,** and **Ben-Hadad,** as the old enemy of Israel **was ill.** (He died in 841 B.C.) Elisha was well known to the king for the prophet had performed many miracles that affected the Arameans. It was unusual for Elisha to go **all the way up** to Damascus from Israel. The king instructed his official **Hazael** to greet Elisha by taking him **a gift.** Having respect for **the LORD** Ben-Hadad asked Hazael to **ask** God's prophet if he would **recover from** his **illness** (cf. King Ahaziah's similar request, in Elijah's day, which the king planned to ask of the false god Baal-Zebub, 1:2).

**8:9.** The **40-camel** caravan may not have carried as much wealth as one might suppose. It was customary in the ancient Near East to make a great show of giving gifts and it was fairly common to have one camel carry only one gift. Referring to **Ben-Hadad** as Elisha's **son,** Hazael was courteously deferring to **Elisha** (cf. "father" in 5:13; 6:21). Elisha was evidently staying at some house or inn in **Damascus.**

**8:10-11.** In response to Ben-Hadad's question, **Elisha** told Hazael to tell the king that he would **certainly recover** (as he would have if Hazael would not have interfered). Elisha then told Hazael that his master would **in fact die.** Elisha evidently knew that Hazael would murder his master though he did not tell Hazael this. **With a fixed gaze** Elisha **stared** at **Hazael** perhaps hoping to embarrass him out of the deed. Hazael, secretly glad at the news of Ben-Hadad's fate, could not help feeling **ashamed** because Elisha seemed to read his mind. God's revelation to His prophet of what Hazael would do to Israel brought tears to Elisha's eyes and he **began to weep.**

**8:12-13.** In response to Hazael's inquiry Elisha told him he knew the destruction Hazael would cause in Israel. **Hazael** pretended to be offended at the very suggestion of such cruelty. He feigned humility by calling himself **a mere dog,** incapable of **such a feat. Elisha** then explained that **Hazael** would **become king of Aram**; God had revealed this to the prophet.

**8:14-15. Hazael . . . returned** to **Ben-Hadad** and reported the encouraging prediction of his recovery. Rather than waiting for the Lord to arrange his accession to the throne through natural processes, as David had done, Hazael decided to seize the crown. So **the next day** he suffocated his master in a manner that made it look as if Ben-Hadad had **died** of natural causes. As Elisha had predicted **Hazael** was elevated to the throne (cf. v. 13).

Elijah may have previously anointed **Hazael . . . as king** (1 Kings 19:15) or the event just reported may have constituted that act with Elisha carrying out Elijah's assignment. Hazael's cruel domination of Israel was part of God's discipline of His people for their idolatry. Hazael did not come from noble stock; on one Assyrian record Shalmaneser III called him "the son of a nobody" (David Luckenbill, *Ancient Records of Assyria and Babylonia.* 2 vols. Chicago: University of Chicago Press, 1926–1927, 1:246). Hazael reigned as king of Aram from 841 to 801 B.C. during the reigns of Joram, Jehu, and Jehoahaz in Israel, and Ahaziah, Athaliah, and Joash in Judah.

## C. Jehoram's evil reign in Judah (8:16-24)

The scene shifts once again to the Southern Kingdom of Judah as the writer continued his narrative with Jehoshaphat's son Jehoram.

### 1. JEHORAM'S WICKEDNESS (8:16-19)

**8:16-19. Jehoshaphat** appointed **Jehoram** his coregent the year he went off to battle with Ahab at Ramoth Gilead (853 B.C.). He may have thought he would be involved in wars out of the country for many months. Jehoram evidently remained in Jerusalem to run the nation. The 18th year of Jehoshaphat's sole reign in Judah (852) when Ahab's son Joram began to rule in **Israel** (3:1) was the second year of Jehoram's coregency with Jehoshaphat (1:17). **The fifth year of Joram** of Israel was the year Jehoram **began his reign** in Judah alone (848 B.C.). The length of Jehoram's reign, including his coregency was 13 years (853–841) while his sole reign was **8 years** (848–841).

Unfortunately Jehoram's godly father had less of an influence on him than his ungodly wife did. The **daughter of Ahab,** whom Jehoram **married** as part of Jehoshaphat's treaty with Ahab, was Athaliah. Jehoram was one of Judah's **evil** kings. But because of God's covenant with **David** (2 Sam. 7) He did not cut off the Davidic dynasty or **destroy** the Judean nation. (On a Davidic king as a **lamp,** see comments on 1 Kings 11:36; also cf. 2 Sam. 21:17; 1 Kings 15:4.)

2. THE REVOLTS OF EDOM AND LIBNAH (8:20-24)

The writer of 2 Kings mentioned only two of the unfortunate events that marked the reign of Jehoram. One not included was his slaughter of six of his brothers, all sons of Jehoshaphat (2 Chron. 21:2-4). This purge seems to have been Athaliah's idea since no other Judean king practiced such a thing, but Athaliah herself did when she ruled (2 Kings 11:1).

**8:20-22.** Edom had come under Judah's control when Jehoshaphat had defeated a coalition of kingdoms that included Edom (2 Chron. 20:1-29). At that time an Edomite deputy may have been placed on the throne in place of an Edomite king (1 Kings 22:47). Edom had helped Israel and Judah in their campaign against King Mesha of Moab (2 Kings 3:4-27). But in Jehoram's day **Edom rebelled . . . and set up its own king. Jehoram** took his army **to Zair** (probably Seir, another name for Edom) to put down the **rebellion,** but he was unsuccessful and barely escaped with his life. His army retreated **back home.**

**Libnah** was located southwest of Jerusalem near the border of Philistia. Its rebellion seems to have been precipitated by Philistine influence (cf. 2 Chron. 21:16). The Philistines invaded Judah in Jehoram's day and Judah suffered heavy losses at their hands (2 Chron. 21:16-17). The Arabians also rebelled. Both Phi-

listia and Arabia had feared and paid tribute to Jehoram's father (2 Chron. 17:11). Obviously **Judah** was weaker under **Jehoram,** partly because of his wickedness.

**8:23-24. Jehoram** died of a painful disease of the intestines (2 Chron. 21:18-19). Jehoram had been warned by Elijah early in his reign because of his wickedness (2 Chron. 21:12-15), but he did not change his ways and died as Elijah had prophesied. On **the book of the annals of the kings of Judah** see comments on 1 Kings 14:29, and on **the City of David** see comments on 1 Kings 2:10.

*D. Ahaziah's evil reign in Judah (8:25–9:29)*

Most of what is recorded about Ahaziah's brief reign in Judah concerned the activities of Jehu.

1. AHAZIAH'S WICKEDNESS (8:25-29)

**8:25-27.** Ahaziah of Israel should not be confused with Ahaziah of Judah; they were two different kings. Each ruled only one year and their reigns did not coincide. **Ahaziah . . . of Judah** reigned during the last **year of Joram** (Jehoram) **king of** Israel (841 B.C.). His reign commenced while he **was 22 years old** when his father **Jehoram** died. **His** mother **was Athaliah,** the daughter of Ahab and **granddaughter of Omri.** Influenced by his evil mother (2 Chron. 22:3) he followed the wicked **ways** of his ancestors in the Northern Kingdom.

**8:28-29.** Israel and Judah were still allied in Ahaziah's day. That is why he joined his uncle **Joram** in battle **against Hazael king of Aram at Ramoth Gilead.** (This was not the battle at Ramoth Gilead in which Ahab was fatally wounded; 1 Kings 22:29-40. That battle took place 12 years earlier.) **Joram** was **wounded** in this battle and **returned to Jezreel** (cf. 1 Kings 21:1), probably where his winter palace was located, **to recover** (cf. 2 Kings 9:14-15). **Ahaziah . . . went down** from Jerusalem to visit him there. While he was there Jehu attacked and killed Joram (9:14-26) and **Ahaziah** fled to Megiddo (9:27).

2. JEHU'S RISE (9:1-29)

Elijah and Elisha were God's instruments to warn Ahab and many of his relatives of the consequences of apostasy. Jehu was God's instrument to judge that dynasty when the kings failed to repent.

### a. Jehu's anointing (9:1-10)

**9:1-3.** Elijah had been commissioned by God to anoint Jehu king over Israel (1 Kings 19:16). This assignment fell to his successor **Elisha** who delegated it to one of the young **prophets** under his tutelage. Tucking one's long **cloak into** his **belt** (cf. 2 Kings 4:29) enabled a person to move swiftly. The **flask** held the **oil** the young **man** would use to anoint **Jehu** who was still in **Ramoth Gilead** on the east side of the Jordan after the battle there (cf. 8:28-29). Jehu was the commander of Joram's army (9:5). The anointing was to be done privately, as was normal. Pouring the olive **oil** on the **head** was a symbolic way of illustrating the coming of the Spirit of God on a man to enable him to function as king (cf. 1 Sam. 16:13). An announcement of God's will for the king accompanied the ritual. The words are related briefly here (2 Kings 9:3) but more fully later (vv. 6-10).

**9:4-10.** The **young . . . prophet. . . . found** Jehu outdoors in the company of his fellow **officers.** He explained that he had a private **message for** the **commander** who then led the prophet **into** a building where they could talk confidentially. **The prophet** anointed **Jehu** and explained the purpose for which **God** had chosen him. Jehu was **to destroy** Ahab's dynasty. This would **avenge the blood of** the **Lord's prophets and . . . servants** which had been **shed** as a result of Jezebel's influence. God would thoroughly annihilate Ahab's line as Elijah had prophesied (1 Kings 21:21-22, 29), and **Jezebel** would also die as Elijah had foretold (1 Kings 21:23). Jeroboam's dynasty and Baasha's dynasty had ended violently (cf. 1 Kings 15:25, 28-29; 16:3-4) and so would Ahab's.

**Jezebel,** the young prophet said, would be eaten by **dogs,** and not be buried; both facts were ignominious to Semites. The young prophet's mission completed, he **ran** away from **Jehu** and friends as Elisha had told him to do (2 Kings 9:3). Perhaps this was in view of the coup that would soon begin and the accompanying recriminations that often trap innocent victims.

### b. The announcement of Jehu's anointing (9:11-13)

**9:11-13.** The officer's calling the prophet a **madman** probably refers to the prophet's behavior in running away so quickly (v. 10). **Jehu** tried to change the subject when his friends asked him what the prophet had said. He implied that his companions knew the prophet was a little odd. Perhaps the young man's clothing identified him as a prophet. Jehu's friends would not be put off, however. Sensing that the prophet's mission was important, they wanted to know what had happened. So **Jehu** explained that the prophet had anointed him **king over Israel.** Immediately the **officers** arranged a little ceremony (cf. 1 Kings 16:16). They **spread** their **cloaks . . . under him on the bare steps. . . . blew the trumpet, and shouted, Jehu is king!** These were customary rituals for announcing a king (cf. 2 Sam. 15:10; 1 Kings 1:34, 39; Matt. 21:7-9).

### c. Jehu's conspiracy against Joram (9:14-16)

**9:14-16.** Jehu's father **Jehoshaphat** was not the king of Judah by the same name. **Jehu** proceeded with plans to carry out God's will against the house of Ahab. **Israel** had regained **Ramoth in Gilead** from **the Arameans** since Ahab had been defeated there by Ben-Hadad II (1 Kings 22:29-40). While **defending** it from Aramean aggressors under Hazael's command, **King Joram** had been wounded. He **had returned to Jezreel** to recuperate. Jehu probably made his statement (2 Kings 9:15) in the context of his being proclaimed king (v. 13). He wanted to arrive **in** Jezreel and execute **Joram** before the king had heard of Jehu's being hailed as king by his men and before Joram could prepare to defend himself.

### d. Jehu's ride to Jezreel (9:17-20)

**9:17-20.** A **lookout** spotted **Jehu's troops . . . coming** long before he could identify them as Jehu's. He probably saw a cloud of dust on the horizon and concluded that many horsemen were approaching. Fearful that these might be Arameans or bad news from Ramoth, **Joram ordered** a **horseman** to go intercept the convoy and find out who they were. **The horseman** met **Jehu** and posed his question. Jehu's reply was conciliatory. **What do you have to do with**

peace? means "Do not worry about the situation." **Jehu** told the messenger to follow him to Jezreel.

**The king sent out a second** messenger when the first did not speed back to Jezreel with news. His message and Jehu's response were the same as with the first **horseman.** As the troops drew closer to Jezreel **the lookout** observed that the officer leading the convoy was **driving** his chariot very fast, **like a madman** (cf. "madman" in v. 11). This was Jehu's characteristic style and it identified him to the scout on the tower. Jehu was the descendant but not the direct **son of Nimshi** (cf. v. 14).

*e. Jehu's execution of Joram (9:21-26)*

**9:21-23.** Thinking that Jehu brought bad news of the fighting at Ramoth Gilead (the messengers would have hurried back to Jezreel if their news had been good), **Joram** prepared to ride out **to meet Jehu** and get the news himself as quickly as possible. He suspected no rebellion but was so concerned about the war that he did this in spite of his injuries. **Ahaziah,** his guest, joined his uncle **in his own chariot. They met** Jehu **at the plot of ground that had belonged to Naboth** (1 Kings 21).

Joram's question (**Have you come in peace, Jehu?**) meant, "Is there peace at Ramoth?" As yet the king had no inkling of Jehu's plans. Jehu's reply, however, revealed that he was returning to Jezreel as Joram's adversary. He gave a different meaning to the word **peace.** It was Jezebel's **idolatry and witchcraft** that had ruined Israel's peace with God and for which Jehu was setting himself against her son (cf. Ex. 22:18; Deut. 18:10-12). As **Joram** wheeled his chariot around to flee he shouted a warning **to Ahaziah.** "Witchcraft' translates *kᵉšāpîm* (lit., "sorceries"), which is used in the Old Testament only here and in Isaiah 47:9, 12; Micah 5:12; Nahum 3:4. It suggests seeking information from demonic forces. No wonder Jezebel's influence in Israel was so devastating!

**9:24-26.** Jehu took **Joram** completely by surprise; apparently the king was not wearing his armor. Jehu easily **shot** him fatally with an **arrow. Jehu** reminded **Bidkar, his chariot officer,** of the **prophecy** they both had heard Elijah make (cf. 1 Kings 21:17-19). They were fulfilling

that prediction. Jehu's free quotation added a fact not revealed previously: Jezebel had also had Naboth's **sons** killed. Jehu was careful to obey and to fulfill the Lord's word, thus ending Israel's fourth royal dynasty.

*f. Jehu's execution of Ahaziah (9:27-29)*

**9:27-29.** The two accounts of Ahaziah's fate (2 Kings 9:27-29; 2 Chron. 22:9) seem contradictory, but they can be harmonized. Evidently **Ahaziah . . . fled** from Jezreel south by way of **Beth Haggan.** Jehu and his men pursued **him** and **wounded him . . . near Ibleam.** Apparently Ahaziah reached Samaria where he hid for some time (2 Chron. 22:9). Jehu's men sought him, found him, and brought him to Jehu probably in Jezreel. Jehu may have wounded him again there. Then Ahaziah **escaped** and fled west **to Megiddo** where he **died** (2 Kings 9:27). **His servants took** his body back **to Jerusalem** where he was **buried** in the royal cemetery. **The 11th year of Joram** was 841 B.C.

*E. Jehu's evil reign in Israel (9:30–10:36)*

Since Jehu's coronation before the whole nation is not recorded, his reign may be regarded as beginning when Joram died (in 841 B.C.).

1. JEHU'S EXECUTION OF JEZEBEL (9:30-37)

**9:30-31.** By the time **Jehu** returned to **Jezreel. . . . Jezebel** had learned of her son's death. Hearing of Jehu's return **she painted her eyes** and **arranged her hair.** Evidently she anticipated her fate, and wanted to present an imposing appearance to Jehu and to die as a queen. She called out to **Jehu** and he **entered the** city **gate** beneath her window. Her words were sarcastic; she was arrogant to the end of her life. Perhaps she sought to shame Jehu by asking if he came **in peace** (cf. vv. 18-19). Obviously he had not. **Zimri,** of course, also rebelled against his master, Elah (1 Kings 16:9), and he himself died only seven days later by the influence of Omri, the founder of Ahab's dynasty (1 Kings 16:18-19). Jezebel implied that Jehu's rebellion would destroy him as Zimri's had. This implication is clearer in another translation of Jezebel's words: "Did Zimri have peace, who murdered his master?" (Cf. NIV marg.)

**9:32-33.** Jezebel's household was not loyal to her. Several **eunuchs** who waited on the queen were willing to help **Jehu** and pitched their mistress out her **window** at Jehu's command. Probably the window was on a second story or higher. When Jezebel hit the ground **her blood splattered the wall** (evidently the city wall; cf. 1 Kings 21:23) and Jehu's **horses.**

**9:34-37.** After **Jehu** drove his horses and chariot over her corpse, he then went farther into the city where he obtained a meal. He was so satisfied with his accomplishments that his gory act did not affect his appetite. Evidently at first Jehu did not remember Elijah's prophecy about Jezebel's fate. He later ordered that she be buried since **she was a king's daughter** (1 Kings 16:31) though she was also a **cursed woman**—cursed by God for her wickedness. By the time Jehu's gravediggers arrived on the scene, the wild **dogs** had already torn her corpse apart and had carried off all but the **skull . . . feet, and . . . hands.** When they reported this to **Jehu** he remembered Elijah's prophecy (1 Kings 21:23). Ironically she who had caused Naboth and his sons to die undeservedly now died an ignominious death—deservedly—on the ground that had been Naboth's vineyard. This was part of the same plot of ground where Bidkar had thrown the corpse of her son Joram (2 Kings 9:25-26).

Jehu's commentary on the prophecy (v. 37) is in harmony with Elijah's words. The king's complete lack of respect for Jezebel in her death reflects how he and God, as well as the godly in Israel, viewed this callous sinner who had been directly and indirectly responsible for so much apostasy and wickedness among God's people.

2. JEHU'S EXECUTION OF AHAB'S RELATIVES AND FRIENDS (10:1-11)

**10:1-3.** **Seventy sons** (i.e., descendants) **of Ahab** and his ancestors lived **in Samaria,** the capital of Israel. **Jehu,** planning to execute every relative who could possibly succeed Ahab, **wrote letters** to the chief administrators of Israel who were not Ahab's relatives. These included **the officials of Jezreel** (possibly those responsible for the winter palace in Jezreel; cf. 1 Kings 21:1; 2 Kings 8:29), **elders** of Samaria, and others who had been

assigned by Ahab to guard the young male members of the royal family and to rear them properly (cf. 10:6). Jehu proposed that these leaders, whom he assumed would remain loyal to Ahab's dynasty and oppose himself, select a new king from Ahab's **sons.** Jehu challenged them to have this new king and his city **fight** him. Rather than fielding large armies, ancient Near Eastern leaders sometimes proposed that only two individuals join battle and so decide which family would rule (cf. 1 Sam. 17:8-9; 2 Sam. 2:9). This may have been what Jehu was suggesting, or he may have intended to go to war against the whole **house** of Ahab and the city of Samaria.

**10:4-8.** In either case the officials, elders, and guardians **were terrified.** They knew Jehu would win such a contest; he was a powerful and successful army commander who had already killed **two kings,** Joram (9:24-26) and Ahaziah (9:27). Being state officials with no personal connections to the Omride dynasty, they decided to transfer their allegiance **to Jehu.** They said they would **do anything** he told them to do.

**Jehu** sent directions immediately. He commanded them to execute each of Ahab's **70 heirs** and to bring their **heads** to him **in Jezreel** within the next day. The officials did exactly as Jehu had commanded. When the **heads** of **the royal princes** had been collected Jehu had them **put . . . in two piles at the entrance of the . . . gate** of Jezreel where they remained overnight. In the ancient Near East the practice of piling the heads of conquered subjects at the city gate was an effective way of demonstrating subjugation.

**10:9-11.** In the **morning Jehu** assembled **the people** of Jezreel at the city gate. He relieved them of any responsibility for the death of King Joram (**my master**) by admitting that he alone was responsible. This statement would have given Jehu a psychological advantage with the people; he was confessing to them and was not implicating them in his act.

This was all a part of Jehu's strategy which then became clear. He claimed innocence of and implied ignorance of the execution of Ahab's sons. This had been done by Ahab's chief officials but Jehu did not tell the people it had been done at *his* command. Since he had been honest with the people about his own responsibility in killing Joram, the people assumed he was being honest with them about his innocence in this mass murder. Jehu further ingratiated himself with the people by identifying himself with God and His prophet, claiming (rightly so) to be the fulfiller of Elijah's prophecy that Ahab's **house** (dynasty) would be destroyed. In this way Jehu gained popular support for his plot to massacre the officials of Samaria who had murdered Ahab's sons (cf. 2 Sam. 1:14-15). **Jehu wiped out Ahab's heirs in Samaria and Jezreel,** which God approved. But he also executed **all** Ahab's **chief men** (officials, v. 1), **close friends,** and **priests,** which God did not approve and for which God judged Jehu's own dynasty later (cf. Hosea 1:4). Jehu got carried away in his zeal and killed many innocent people who could have helped him be a more effective king than he proved to be.

3. JEHU'S EXECUTION OF AHAZIAH'S RELATIVES (10:12-14)

**10:12-14.** Traveling south from Jezreel **toward Samaria** Jehu and his men **met** a party of **42 men** on the road. He learned that they were **relatives of Ahaziah, king of Judah** who were going from Jerusalem to visit other relatives of **the king** including **the queen mother,** Jezebel. Obviously they had not heard of Jehu's coup. **Jehu** seized them at once since they were part of the house of Ahab and executed them near a **well,** leaving **no survivor.** Not all 42 travelers were necessarily blood relatives of Ahab; some may have been related by marriage. But that would not have mattered to Jehu (cf. v. 11). In 2 Chronicles 22:8 they are called "princes of Judah" and "the sons of Ahaziah's relatives, who had been attending Ahaziah."

4. JEHU'S EXECUTION OF THE REST OF AHAB'S RELATIVES (10:15-17)

**10:15-17.** Continuing his journey, Jehu met **Jehonadab son of Recab.** This man was a faithful follower of the Lord and a strict observer of the Mosaic Law (cf. Jer. 35:6-7, where his name is spelled Jonadab). He **was on his way to meet** Jehu. Meeting Jehonadab, **Jehu** learned that he was a supporter of his policy to purge the land of Ahab's apostate influ-

ence. Joining hands and sharing a **chariot** were signs of agreement and mutual commitment. The new king invited his ally to accompany him to Samaria to witness his **zeal for the LORD.** After they arrived Jehu proceeded to kill all the remaining members of **Ahab's family** in fulfillment of Elijah's prophecy (cf. 1 Kings 21:21).

5. JEHU'S EXECUTION OF THE BAAL PROPHETS (10:18-28)

**10:18-23.** **Jehu** called a special convocation of **the people** of Israel under the pretense that he would **sacrifice** to **and honor . . . Baal.** It was to take place at the central **temple of Baal** that **Ahab** had built in Samaria (1 Kings 16:32). Every leader of the **Baal** cult was required to attend. Obviously Jehu's true religious preferences had not yet become known in Israel. **Jehonadab** (cf. 2 Kings 10:15) accompanied **Jehu** and observed his preparations. **Jehu** carefully guarded against the possibility of any worshipers **of the LORD** being present and slain. He also made sure that none of the **Baal** worshipers would escape.

**10:24-28.** Presumably **Jehu** did not personally participate in the **sacrifices and burnt offerings** of the priests **of Baal;** to have done so would have undermined his attempts to win the support of the faithful in Israel. However, he did offer a **burnt offering,** perhaps to set a trap for the priests **of Baal. Jehu** then **ordered** his **guards and officers** (80 of them) to enter **the temple** and slaughter all Baal ministers. Then **they brought** out **the sacred stone . . . burned it,** probably to dishonor it, and then **demolished** it. However, perhaps two stones were involved, because two different Hebrew words are used for the stones in verses 26 and 27. If the first "stone" was actually a wooden idol, then the second "stone" was the main image **of Baal,** probably a conical stone dedicated to **Baal.**

Jehu's massacre completed the destruction of **Baal worship in Israel** which Elijah had begun. The king was God's instrument of judgment.

6. JEHU'S ASSESSMENT (10:29-31)

**10:29-31.** Though **Jehu** killed the Baal priests, he did not completely obey the Lord. He continued the idolatrous policies **of Jeroboam** with **worship of the**

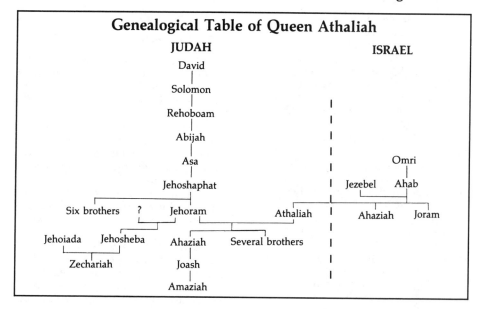

## Genealogical Table of Queen Athaliah

**JUDAH** — David — Solomon — Rehoboam — Abijah — Asa — Jehoshaphat — Jehoram — Ahaziah — Joash — Amaziah; Six brothers; ? ; Jehoiada — Jehosheba — Zechariah; Several brothers

**ISRAEL** — Omri — Ahab; Jezebel; Athaliah — Ahaziah — Joram

**golden calves at Bethel and Dan.**

Because he obeyed the Lord in the matter of judging Ahab's dynasty, **God** promised **Jehu** that four generations of his **descendants** would reign as kings over **Israel.** These were Jehoahaz, Jehoash (Joash), Jeroboam II, and Zechariah. No doubt God's blessing would have been greater if Jehu's **heart** had been more completely devoted to Him. But he did become the head of Israel's fifth royal dynasty.

7. JEHU'S LOSSES (10:32-36)

**10:32-36.** God's discipline on Israel for Jehu's incomplete devotion (cf. v. 31) came in the form of territorial losses. Jehu's reign was characterized by turmoil and unrest. He was not a strong ruler. Social and economic abuses marked his administration. Both the Arameans and the Assyrians humiliated Israel during his leadership. **Hazael,** king of Aram, seized all of Transjordan from **Israel** and later even made inroads into Israel's territory west **of the Jordan** (cf. 12:17-18; 13:7). Before Hazael's attacks, Assyria under Shalmaneser III had forced Jehu to bow before him and pay tribute. A bas relief on Shalmaneser's so-called "Black Obelisk" shows Jehu doing this. This is the only picture of an Israelite king that has been found so far.

Jehu could have used the experience of the seasoned officials he unnecessarily

slew (cf. 10:11). His ruthlessness and deception probably made even his closest allies suspicious of him. The alliance that had united and provided some strength for both Judah and Israel was broken when Jehu killed Judah's king Ahaziah. Israel's treaty with Phoenicia also ended when Jehu killed Joram, Jezebel, and the prophets of Baal. This is how God **began to reduce the size of Israel** in Jehu's reign. In all Jehu **reigned . . . 28 years** (841–814 B.C.).

### F. Athaliah's evil reign in Judah (11:1-20)

Athaliah usurped the throne of Judah. She was Judah's only reigning queen and the strongest Baal advocate among Judah's rulers.

1. JOASH'S PRESERVATION (11:1-3)

**11:1. Athaliah** was **the mother** of the Judean king **Ahaziah,** whom Jehu had slain (9:27-29; 2 Chron. 22:9) in 841 B.C. Athaliah was a daughter of Ahab and Jezebel, and a sister of Ahaziah and Joram who had reigned successively in Israel after Ahab's death. She was the wife of King Jehoram of Judah who had died of an intestinal illness (2 Chron. 21:18-19). Her other sons had all been killed by the raiding Philistines and Arabians ( 2 Chron. 21:17). Now she saw the opportunity to seize the throne for herself. So she proceeded to have all her grandsons killed in total disregard for God's will that the descendants of David should rule over Judah forever (2 Sam. 7:16).

**11:2-3.** **Jehosheba,** a daughter of Athaliah's husband **King Jehoram** (though perhaps not Athaliah's own daughter), was a **sister of** King **Ahaziah** of Judah. She took one of Ahaziah's sons, **Joash,** and hid him so that he was not put to death with the other children. During Athaliah's **six**-year reign (841–835 B.C.) this aunt kept the prince safe by hiding him in **the temple of the LORD** where her husband, Jehoiada, served as high priest (2 Chron. 22:11). (See the chart "Genealogical Table of Queen Athaliah.") Joash was a one-year-old when he was taken by Jehosheba because he was hidden for six years and then was made king at the age of seven (cf. 2 Kings 11:21).

### 2. JEHOIADA'S PLANS (11:4-8)

**11:4-8.** As Athaliah began **the seventh year** of her reign, **Jehoiada** the high priest assembled the military **commanders** at a certain level of authority (those commanding **100** soldiers each), **the Carites** (also called Kerethites [see comments on 2 Sam. 8:18] and possibly Phoenician mercenaries who guarded the city), **and the guards** (lit., "runners," probably royal bodyguards) secretly in Solomon's **temple.** These were all loyalists who did not support the queen. **He showed them** little Joash, then seven years old (cf. 2 Kings 11:21), to assure them that there was indeed a living legitimate heir to the throne. He then outlined his plan to crown Joash as **the king.** The guards (consisting of priests and Levites, 2 Chron. 23:4) were to divide into **three** groups **on the Sabbath,** one group at the **palace,** another at **the Sur Gate** near the temple, and another group **at the gate behind the guard** through which opposition might come. The others, who were going **off . . . duty,** were to **guard the temple.** A ceremony would take place at the changing of the guard on the Sabbath when the temple area would be busy, perhaps on a feast day. The boy was to be fenced off by the soldiers and **anyone who** came near their **ranks** was to be killed. The soldiers were to guard Joash with their lives as he was conducted from the temple to his place of coronation in the temple courtyard.

### 3. JOASH'S CORONATION (11:9-12)

**11:9-11.** On the appointed day **the commanders** did as they had been instructed. **Jehoiada** gave them the special **spears and shields** that were kept **in the temple** and used for state occasions. Their use would have helped the people recognize that the coronation was official as well as important. Since the temple faced east **the guards** evidently made a semicircular arc in front of the building from its northeast to its southeast corners, creating a shielded area in **the temple** courtyard where the anointing would take place.

**11:12.** **Jehoiada** then **brought Joash out** of the temple where he had been living into this protected area of the courtyard, placed the royal **crown on** his young head, **presented him with a copy of the covenant** (the Mosaic Law or a part of it; cf. Deut. 17:18-19), **and proclaimed him king.** At some time in the ceremony, probably near the beginning, the high priest also **anointed** Joash with oil, symbolizing enduement with divine power (cf. 2 Kings 9:6). Undoubtedly Jehoiada had scheduled this coronation for a time when as many people as possible would witness it. When the king had been crowned **the people** raised a roar of approval, **clapped . . . and shouted, Long live the king!**

### 4. ATHALIAH'S EXECUTION (11:13-16)

**11:13-14.** The first that **Athaliah** knew of Jehoiada's plan was when she **heard the noise** of the celebration. **She went** from her palace to **the temple** to find out what was happening. To her amazement, she saw little Joash (**the king**) with the royal crown on his head **standing by the pillar** at the eastern gate of the inner courtyard of the temple, the place the king customarily occupied when he addressed the people in the temple area (cf. 2 Chron. 23:13). An elevated platform was provided for the king to stand on when he visited the temple on festive occasions (cf. 2 Kings 23:3; 2 Chron. 6:13). This is where Joash stood. The queen immediately understood what was taking place, **tore her robes** signifying her great distress (cf. 2 Kings 2:12; 5:7; 6:30), and cried, **Treason! Treason!**

**11:15-16.** What Jehoiada had done

was not treasonous because Joash was a legitimate heir to the throne. Athaliah was not a legitimate heir since she was not a blood descendant of David. *She* was the one guilty of treason. For this reason **Jehoiada the priest ordered the commanders** to arrest her, to lead her out of **the temple** area under guard, and to kill anyone who tried to help her. It was not appropriate to execute anyone in the temple area since it was a place of worship (cf. 2 Chron. 24:20-22). Athaliah **was put to death** with the sword at the place **where the horses** entered **the palace grounds** (the Horse Gate; cf. 2 Chron. 23:15, not the Horse Gate into the city). So ended the life of one of the most wicked women in Scripture, a true daughter of Jezebel.

5. JEHOIADA'S PURGE OF BAALISM (11:17-20)

**11:17. Jehoiada** led the **people** in a rededication of themselves to **the LORD** and His **covenant** given through Moses (cf. Deut. 4:20; 27:9-10) from which they had departed since the days of Jehoshaphat. **He also made a** new **covenant between the king and the people** that the king would lead the people according to the Mosaic Law and the people would obey the king (cf. 2 Sam. 5:3).

**11:18-20. The people** then **tore . . . down** the **temple of Baal** that had been built in Jerusalem and used by Athaliah to promote Baal worship in Judah. They also destroyed **the altars and idols** which this temple contained, **and killed Mattan the** chief **priest of Baal in front of the altars.** This showed deliberate disrespect for the pagan worshipers' false belief that the temple area was a sacred place of sanctuary.

To avoid recriminations by the devotees of Baal, **Jehoiada . . . posted guards at** Solomon's **temple.** At the end of the coronation ceremonies the people led by Jehoiada and his guards conducted **the** new **king** to his **palace** where he sat down **on** his **throne.** The people of Judah as a whole **rejoiced** greatly that once again a descendant of David ruled and that the worship of Yahweh was again made official. The turmoil that had existed in Jerusalem during Athaliah's reign subsided and **the city was quiet** once again. (For more details on the reign of Athaliah, see 2 Chron. 22:10–23:15.)

As Jezebel had promoted Baalism in Israel, her daughter **Athaliah** had encouraged it in Judah. During Athaliah's reign as queen, Baalism gained its strongest foothold in the Southern Kingdom. However, it was never as influential in Judah as it was in Israel, because of the stronger commitment of some kings of Judah to the Lord.

### G. Joash's good reign in Judah (11:21–12:21)

The beginning of Joash's reign marks the commencement of over 100 years of consecutive rule by four men who were all judged as good kings. None of these four—Joash, Amaziah, Azariah (Uzziah), and Jotham—was as good for Judah as Jehoshaphat, Hezekiah, or Josiah, but together they did provide the longest continuous span of God-approved leadership in Judah's history.

1. JOASH'S GOODNESS (11:21–12:3)

**11:21–12:3. Joash** was the youngest king to mount the throne of Judah; he **was seven years old.** His **reign** began in 835 B.C. and ended in 796 B.C., **40 years** later. He was the son of King Ahaziah and a woman named **Zibiah** from **Beersheba** in southern Judah.

**Joash did** the Lord's will as long as his mentor **Jehoiada the priest** lived. But after Jehoiada died Joash turned away from following the Lord. During his years of faithfulness Joash ruled well, but he did **not** remove **the high places** (as was true of most kings of Judah; see comments on 1 Kings 22:43), where **the people** made **sacrifices** and burned **incense** contrary to the Mosaic Law (cf. Deut. 12:2-7, 13-14). These high places may have been regarded by Joash as relatively unimportant as they apparently were considered by his predecessors.

2. JOASH'S TEMPLE RESTORATION (12:4-16)

**12:4-8. Joash** purposed to restore Solomon's **temple** which had fallen into disrepair and had suffered major damage during Athaliah's reign (cf. 2 Chron. 24:7). This was the first temple restoration project recorded in 1 or 2 Kings. The king planned to use the money **brought** by the people in regular **census** offerings (Ex. 30:11-16), vow offerings (Lev. 27; Num. 30), and free-will offerings. But this plan did not work. Apparently revenue from these regular sources was insufficient to support the priests and Levites and also to pay for the temple repairs.

Joash's impatience with **the priests who were responsible for collecting the money** (1 Kings 12:7; 2 Chron. 24:5) suggests that they may not have wanted to divert any funds from their own support. They had been using the money given them by the priestly **treasurers** for the regular expenses of temple service, which was probably legitimate. So **Joash** told them to stop taking **money** from the offerings for this purpose since he was instituting a new procedure. Instead they were to **hand . . . over** what would be collected in a new way to other men who would be responsible to supervise the renovations. **The priests agreed** to separate this project from the regular **temple** service and to let other men be responsible for it.

**12:9-16.** At Joash's instructions **Jehoiada . . . bored a hole** in the top of a large wooden **chest** and **placed it** on the north **side** of **the altar** of burnt offering in **the temple** courtyard. **The priests** then **put into the chest all the money** the people **brought** for **the temple** renovation project. **Whenever . . . the chest** filled up **the royal secretary and the high priest . . . counted the money . . . and put it into bags** where it was stored until needed to pay for materials, labor, and other expenses connected with the project.

This **money** was **not** used for **temple** furnishings at first (v. 13), but later the excess money received was used for that purpose (2 Chron. 24:14). The paymasters, serving **with complete honesty,** were trusted to **pay** out all **the money** due to **the workers.** (Integrity had returned to Judah with her rededication to the Lord.) **The money** received **from** the people as part of their **guilt . . . and sin offerings was** used for the support of **the priests,** not for **the temple** building project. (See 2 Chron. 24:4-14 for the parallel passage.)

Several events transpired during the reign of Joash that are not recorded in 2 Kings but do appear in 2 Chronicles. Jehoiada the high priest died at the uncommonly advanced age of 130 years (2 Chron. 24:15-16). After Jehoiada's voice was silenced Joash followed the counsel of certain Judean officials who advised him to do things that resulted in his turning from the Lord. When the king did this God sent prophets to warn the nation (2 Chron. 24:17-19). Jehoiada's son, Zechariah, who had replaced his father as high priest, also sounded a prophetic warning. But Joash had him stoned to death for his rebuke (2 Chron. 24:20-22).

### 3. JOASH'S RANSOM TO HAZAEL (12:17-18)

**12:17-18. Hazael king of Aram** had defeated Israel during the reigns of Israel's kings Jehu and Jehoahaz (13:3, 22) and then pressed south along the coast into Judah. He captured **Gath,** the Philistine city that had been taken by Judah (cf. 2 Chron. 11:8). **Then he** sent a contingent of soldiers against **Jerusalem.** This unit destroyed "all the leaders of the people" (2 Chron. 24:3). To buy Hazael off, **Joash** gave him **all the sacred objects** and **gifts** that his forefathers and **he . . . had dedicated** to the Lord as well as **all the gold** in the temple and the palace **treasuries** (cf. 2 Chron. 24:23). This ransom caused **Hazael** to withdraw his troops. The whole incident illustrates the weakness of Judah at this time which resulted from Joash's apostasy.

### 4. JOASH'S DEATH (12:19-21)

**12:19-21.** The Arameans had severely wounded **Joash** (2 Chron. 24:25). Evidently he went for recovery to **Beth Millo,** a town **on the road down to Silla.** (The locations of these towns are now unknown.) Several of **his officials,** conspiring against him because he had slain the high priest Zechariah (2 Chron. 24:20-22), **murdered** Joash in his bed. The assassins were **Jozabad** and **Jehozabad,** whose mothers, according to 2 Chronicles 24:26 (see comments there), were an Ammonitess and a Moabitess, respectively. Joash **was buried** in the royal **city** (Jerusalem) but not in the royal tombs (cf. 2 Chron. 24:25) because he was not as respected as some of his ancestors. His son **Amaziah . . . succeeded him as king.**

## H. Jehoahaz's evil reign in Israel (13:1-9)

The scene shifts once again to the Northern Kingdom.

**13:1-3. Jehoahaz** began reigning **in the 23rd year** of Joash's reign in **Judah** and **reigned** for **17 years** (814–798 B.C.).

(The 23rd year of Joash would seemingly mean Joash began reigning in 837. Actually he began in 835 [see the chart "Kings of Judah and Israel and the Preexilic Prophets," near 1 Kings 12:25-33]; different systems of dating began to be used in both Judah and Israel, thus making for a two-year deviation in the dating system.) Jehoahaz was Jehu's **son** and his capital was **Samaria.** Jehoahaz followed **the sins of Jeroboam** throughout his career (cf. Jehu, 2 Kings 10:29). As discipline against Israel for her disobedience to the Mosaic Law, God allowed the Arameans to dominate her. Jehoahaz reigned during the last years of Hazael's administration and early years of his son **Ben-Hadad** III's reign.

**13:4-6.** Because of Aram's distressing oppression King **Jehoahaz sought the LORD's** help. Out of compassion for His people and in spite of the king's idolatry **the LORD provided a deliverer.** This deliverer probably was King Adad-nirāri III of Assyria (811–783 B.C.; see the chart "Kings of Assyria in the Middle and New Assyrian Kingdoms," near Jonah 1:2) who fought against Damascus (as well as against Tyre, Sidon, Media, Edom, and Egypt) and defeated it in 803 B.C. The Arameans consequently turned their attention from attacking **Israel** to defending themselves against the Assyrians. Thus Israel **escaped** Aram's **power** and the people were able to return to **their . . . homes** and live in peace. Israel had to pay tribute to Assyria, but the nation was free from Aram's attacks. This answer to prayer did **not** result in the people repenting of their idolatry, however. Even **the Asherah pole,** a symbol of the pagan goddess Asherah, Baal's consort, **remained** conspicuously **in Samaria.**

**13:7-9.** Jehoahaz's **army** had been decimated by his wars with the Arameans, though some of the Israelite army was lost during the reign of Jehu (cf. comments on 10:32-36). **Dust at threshing time** was blown away and never seen again.

When **Jehoahaz** died he **was buried in Samaria,** and his son **Jehoash** followed him to the throne.

## I. Jehoash's evil reign in Israel (13:10-25)

Jehoash was the third king of Jehu's dynasty to rule over Israel.

### 1. JEHOASH'S ASSESSMENT (13:10-13)

**13:10-11.** When **Jehoash** (a variant of the Heb. Joash; cf. NIV marg.) took the reins of power in **Israel** a king by the name of **Joash** ruled in **Judah.** (The NIV translators have rendered the name of Israel's king Jehoash and that of Judah's king Joash consistently so these men are not so easily confused.) Jehoash began reigning in Israel in 798 B.C. and served for a total of **16 years** until 782 B.C. However, after five years (in 793 B.C.) Jehoash's son Jeroboam II began to reign as coregent with him. The king continued the religious policies of his predecessors and **did evil in the eyes of the LORD.**

**13:12-13.** The statement that normally concludes the writer's history of a particular king occurs here early in the story of Jehoash. These words about Jehoash are repeated almost verbatim in the history of Amaziah of Judah (14:15-16). Jehoash's **war against Amaziah** is described by the writer as a part of the Judean king's reign (14:8-14). **Jeroboam** II **succeeded. . . . Jehoash,** but the son actually began reigning as coregent 11 years before his father's death.

### 2. ELISHA'S PROPHECY (13:14-21)

**13:14.** Elisha the prophet now re-enters the narrative. He was **suffering from** a terminal **illness.** Out of respect for this man of God, King **Jehoash** paid him a visit. The fact that the king **wept over him** reveals that though Jehoash followed in the ways of Jeroboam I (v. 11) he also revered Yahweh. He anticipated the great loss that the death of this servant of God would be to Israel. He regarded Elisha as superior to himself, calling him **my father** in true humility. By the phrase **the chariots and horsemen of Israel,** he showed that he recognized in Elisha, and behind him in the Lord, the real defense and power of Israel against all her adversaries. Elisha had used the same expressions himself when Elijah's ministry was terminated by God (2:12).

**13:15-17.** In view of Jehoash's evidence of faith **Elisha** blessed him with a promise of victory. The **bow and . . . arrows** were symbols of strength and victory that God was going to give Jehoash. By taking **the bow in** his **hands** the **king** was symbolically becoming the agent of God's power. **Elisha put his** own **hands on** Jehoash's **hands** to symbolize that the power the king would exert came from the Lord through His prophet.

Jehoash was to **open** an **east window,** which faced toward the enemy Aramean hosts at Aphek, so that he could **shoot.** Obeying the prophet, the king **shot** an arrow out the window toward Aram. By actually shooting the arrow the king was appropriating the victory symbolized by the arrow. As the king shot, **Elisha** said that **the arrow** represented **victory over Aram. . . . at Aphek** (cf. 1 Kings 20:30) in the Transjordan.

**13:18-19.** Elisha then instructed **the king** to **take the arrows** that remained and to shoot them at the ground. (The Heb. which is trans. **Strike the ground** probably means that the king was to shoot these arrows as he had shot the first one rather than to grasp them together in his hand and strike the ground with them.) The king fired off **three** more arrows **and** then **stopped.** Elisha **was angry with him** for stopping because the king was manifesting failure to trust God to give him as many victories as there were arrows. Jehoash understood what shooting the first arrow symbolized; Elisha had explained it. By letting the king shoot more arrows God was inviting him through Elisha to claim as many victories as he had arrows. God assured him that he would have victory by divine enablement. But perhaps Jehoash felt that God could not or would not do as much for him as Elisha implied. This unbelief explains why Elisha became angry. Jehoash had failed to trust God even though he knew what God had promised. The prophet told the king that had he shot more arrows God would have honored his faith and given him additional victories resulting in Aram's complete destruction. As it was he would now win **only three** victories (v. 25).

**13:20-21.** Shortly thereafter **Elisha died.** Elisha's ministry spanned at least 56 years (including his years of serving as Elijah's servant) since he was called by Elijah during Ahab's reign (which ended in 853 B.C.) and Elisha died in Jehoash's reign (which began in 798 B.C.). The prophet was probably **buried** as most of the early Israelites were in a cave or tomb (v. 21) hewn out of a rock, after his body was wrapped in linen cloths.

Some time later some men were lay-

ing another **man's body** to rest near Elisha's tomb. They were surprised by a group of **Moabite raiders** who were apparently going to rob whomever they met. To flee quickly, the Israelite pallbearers removed the stone in front of **Elisha's** tomb, **threw** the corpse of their friend in the **tomb,** and retreated. **When the** new corpse **touched Elisha's** he **came to life and stood up on his feet.** Evidently the men who placed the body in Elisha's tomb observed this. Doubtless they told their story far and wide, and it probably reached the ears of Jehoash for whom this miracle seems to have been intended primarily. Such a sign of the power of God working even through His prophet's corpse may have both encouraged the king as he anticipated his battles with the Arameans and rebuked him for his lack of faith (cf. comments on vv. 18-19).

3. JEHOASH'S VICTORIES (13:22-25)

**13:22-23.** Even though **Hazael** had his hands full combating his Assyrian foe he kept his foot on Israel's neck too, during **the reign** of Jehoash's **father Jehoahaz. But** because of the Lord's **covenant with** the patriarchs He graciously and compassionately cared for the Israelites, refusing **to destroy them or** cast **them** out of **His presence.** It was God's promise, not the Israelites' goodness, that moved God to be merciful as the writer notes, **to this day,** that is, right to the time 1 and 2 Kings were written.

**13:24-25.** After **Hazael . . . died** (801 B.C.) **Jehoash** engaged the new Aramean king, **Ben-Hadad** III in battle and **defeated** him **three times,** as prophesied by Elisha (v. 19). The battle of Aphek (v. 17), though not mentioned here, may have been one of the three battles. **Jehoash . . . recaptured** the Israelite **towns . . . Jehoahaz** had lost in battle to Hazael in these three encounters (cf. v. 3).

*J. Amaziah's good reign in Judah (14:1-22)*

1. AMAZIAH'S POLICIES (14:1-6)

**14:1-6.** Amaziah . . . **began to reign in Judah** about a year after **Jehoash** had become **king of Israel.** Amaziah was fairly young, **25 years old, when he became king,** and ruled a long time, **29 years** (796–767 B.C.). Much of this time his son Azariah's reign overlapped with his own

(790–767 B.C.). The king **followed** his **father** Joash's **example**; he upheld the worship of **the LORD** but did **not** remove **the high places** (cf. comments on 1 Kings 22:43), where the people worshiped God in disobedience to the Mosaic Law (Deut. 12:2-7, 13-14). Compared with **David**, the founder of his dynasty and Judah's greatest king, Amaziah fell short.

In obedience to God's **Law** (Deut. 24:16) Amaziah did not execute the **children** of his father's **assassins** as was customarily done by Near Eastern monarchs. He trusted God to control these potential rebels.

### 2. AMAZIAH'S WAR WITH EDOM (14:7)

**14:7.** This war with Edom is described more fully in 2 Chronicles 25:5-16. Edom had revolted from Judean control during the reign of Jehoram. Amaziah wanted to regain control of this neighbor because Edom gave Judah access to southern trade routes. The **battle** took place **in the Valley of Salt,** a marshy plain at the south end of the Dead Sea (cf. 2 Sam. 8:13). **Sela,** renamed **Joktheel** by Amaziah, was later named Petra, the stronghold city of Edom carved out of sheer mountain walls.

### 3. AMAZIAH'S WAR WITH ISRAEL (14:8-14)

**14:8-10.** Riding high after his victory over Edom, **Amaziah** decided to challenge **Israel** which had recently suffered defeats by Hazael (13:22). Amaziah's invitation **to Jehoash** constituted a declaration of war.

The Israelite **king** responded to this challenge by sending a warning **to Amaziah** in the form of a parable. Thistles and cedars were common **in Lebanon.** Amaziah was the thistle and Jehoash the cedar. As **a wild beast** could easily squash **a thistle,** so anyone could easily defeat Judah. Jehoash's advice that Amaziah **stay at home** was good, but Amaziah's pride had been hurt by the story. So he committed himself even more strongly to war. His decision was of the Lord who intended that he should suffer defeat because after conquering the Edomites, Amaziah had brought Edomite idols into Judah and had worshiped them (cf. 2 Chron. 25:14, 20).

**14:11-14.** Jehoash seized the initiative and **attacked** Judah. **He** faced **Amaziah** in battle **at Beth Shemesh,** about 15 miles west of Jerusalem. **Judah was** defeated, its troops retreated, and **Amaziah** was **captured.** Jehoash then proceeded **to Jerusalem** where he **broke down . . . 600 feet** of the city **wall. He took** the remaining **gold . . . silver, and** other **articles** of value from **the temple** and **palace,** as well as **hostages, and returned to Samaria.** Apparently when Amaziah was taken prisoner his son Azariah began to reign as Judah's king in Jerusalem (790 B.C.).

### 4. JEHOASH'S DEATH (14:15-16)

**14:15-16.** This second mention of Jehoash's death (cf. 13:12-13) seems to be added here because of the unusual situation that existed with **Amaziah** being held prisoner in Israel. When **Jehoash** died (782 B.C.) Amaziah was released and returned to Judah. Jehoash's successor was his son **Jeroboam** II.

### 5. AMAZIAH'S DEATH (14:17-22)

**14:17-20.** Amaziah (who died in 767) outlived **Jehoash** (who died in 782) by at least **15 years.** After Amaziah returned to Judah he made his son Azariah his vice-regent. They shared the throne (790–767) until Amaziah's death.

The people who **conspired against** Amaziah are not identified but may have been some of his own officials. The king **fled to Lachish,** a former royal city on the southern border of Judah, from which he could have fled the country if his enemies had not caught up with him first. He received a royal burial in the ancient **City of David** section of **Jerusalem.**

**14:21-22.** In 790 B.C. **Azariah** had begun to reign at the age of **16** when **his father Amaziah** was taken prisoner to Israel. Then when his father died in 767, Azariah began his sole reign. His restoration of **Elath** on the coast of the Gulf of Aqaba was probably mentioned here because it was one of Azariah's most significant accomplishments. More information about Azariah is given in 15:1-7.

### K. Jeroboam II's evil reign in Israel (14:23-29)

**14:23-24.** Jeroboam II had served as coregent with his father Jehoash from 793 to 782 B.C. **The 15th year of Amaziah . . . king of Judah** marked the beginning of his sole reign (782 B.C.). In all, **he reigned 41 years** (793–753 B.C.), longer than any other **king of Israel** before him.

Spiritually Jeroboam II followed in the footsteps of his predecessors in Israel. However, politically he was Israel's strongest king. Only a few of Jeroboam II's accomplishments are recorded; these were of lesser importance in view of the writer's emphasis on the spiritually significant aspects of Israel's history.

**14:25-27.** Jeroboam II **restored** Israel's **boundaries** to approximately their extent in Solomon's time (excluding of course the Southern Kingdom's territory belonging to Judah and Benjamin). **Lebo Hamath** (cf. 1 Kings 8:65) was over 150 miles northeast of the Sea of Kinnereth. **The Sea of the Arabah** was the Dead Sea. This territorial extension had been prophesied by **Jonah,** who ministered in Jeroboam II's reign (see the chart "Kings of Judah and Israel and the Preexilic Prophets," near 1 Kings 12:25-33). This prophecy of Jonah is not recorded elsewhere in Scripture. This is the same Jonah who traveled to Nineveh with God's message of repentance for the Assyrians (cf. Jonah 1:1). His hometown, **Gath Hepher,** was located a few miles north of Nazareth in Israel.

The **suffering** of the Israelites came as a result of the oppressive influence of Hazael of Damascus. Out of compassion for His people **the Lord** began to relieve their distress under Jehoash (cf. 2 Kings 13:22-25) and continued to do so under **Jeroboam** II.

**14:28-29.** How God granted the Israelites relief is not explained. Only a few particulars are revealed in these verses. Jeroboam II took **Damascus,** the Aramean capital, **and Hamath.** These cities (and their surrounding territory) **had belonged to Yaudi** (Judah) in the days of David and Solomon but not since that time. By controlling this area Jeroboam II undoubtedly also recovered all of Israel's Transjordanian territory which Hazael had seized (cf. 10:32-33), thus making Israel the largest country on the eastern Mediterranean coast.

Jeroboam II's victories were accomplished because Damascus had been weakened by attacks from the Assyrians to their northeast under Adad-nirāri III (cf. 13:5). Also Assyria herself was weak at this time, suffering from the threat of attack from the Urartu people on their northern frontier, internal dissension,

and a series of weak rulers. Jehoash had been a successful military strategist (cf. 14:11-14), and his son Jeroboam II evidently inherited his father's abilities and even surpassed him.

During Jeroboam II's reign the Prophets Amos and Hosea ministered in Israel (Amos 1:1; Hosea 1:1). Their prophecies give additional insights into life in Israel during Jeroboam's reign. **Jeroboam** II died in 753 B.C. and his son **Zechariah . . . succeeded him** (cf. 2 Kings 15:8-12).

### L. Azariah's good reign in Judah (15:1-7)

**15:1-4.** **Azariah** ("Yahweh has helped") is also called Uzziah ("Yahweh is my strength") in the Old Testament (cf. vv. 13, 30, 32, 34; 2 Chron. 26; Isa. 1:1; Hosea 1:1; Amos 1:1; Zech. 14:5; etc.). **The 27th year of Jeroboam** II's coregency with Jehoash was 767 B.C. In that year Azariah **began to reign** over **Judah** as sole ruler. He had previously served as **king** in his father's place while Amaziah was imprisoned in Israel and as coregent with him after Amaziah returned to Judah. Azariah **was 16 years old when he** began his coregency (in 790 B.C.) **and he reigned** a total of **52 years** (790–739 B.C.) **in Jerusalem.** Up to that time this was the longest reign of any king of Judah or Israel. Azariah was a good king like **his father** (cf. 2 Chron. 26:4-5), but he too failed to remove **the high places** (cf. comments on 1 Kings 22:43) where the people worshiped Yahweh in disobedience to the Mosaic Law (cf. Deut. 12:2-7, 13-14).

**15:5.** The writer of 2 Chronicles gave a fuller explanation of the sin that led to Azariah's becoming a leper (2 Chron. 26:16-21). When Azariah became a leper (in 750 B.C.) he shared the throne with his son **Jotham** as coregent until **he died** in 739. Azariah **lived** a life of limited seclusion as required of lepers in Israel, but still played a part in leading the nation, with his son Jotham serving as executor of **the palace.**

**15:6-7.** In addition to **Azariah's** history being recorded in the book of the **annals of the kings of Judah,** the chronicler added that Isaiah wrote his story (2 Chron. 26:22). Perhaps Isaiah wrote the annals of some of Judah's kings, or there may have been two separate documents.

When the king died he **was buried . . . in the City of David,** undoubtedly in the royal tombs, **and Jotham his son** continued reigning in his place.

**Azariah** was one of Judah's most effective and influential kings. He expanded Judah's territories southward to Elath (2 Kings 14:22), eastward so that the Ammonites paid him tribute (2 Chron. 26:8), and westward by defeating the Philistines (2 Chron. 26:6-7). He fortified Jerusalem and other parts of Judah (2 Chron. 26:9-10, 15), and reorganized the army (2 Chron. 26:11-14). The combined territories of Azariah and Jeroboam II approximated those of David and Solomon. After Jeroboam II's death Azariah became even more powerful and was looked to for leadership by his neighbors who formed a coalition with him to resist the threat of Assyria. Unfortunately he became proud, intruded into the priest's office, and was tragically humbled by God (2 Chron. 26:16-21).

### M. Zechariah's evil reign in Israel (15:8-12)

**15:8-12.** **Zechariah** succeeded **Jeroboam** II in Azariah's **38th year** (753 B.C.), but **he reigned** only **six months.** Like all his predecessors in Israel, he continued the worship of the golden calves at Dan and Bethel that **Jeroboam** I had begun. He was **assassinated** publicly by **Shallum.** The fact that Shallum was allowed to assume the throne suggests that Zechariah did not enjoy strong public support. Zechariah's death fulfilled God's **word** to **Jehu** that four generations would succeed him on Israel's **throne** (10:30). Thus Israel's fifth dynasty came to an end.

### N. Shallum's evil reign in Israel (15:13-16)

**15:13-16.** Shallum's **one-month** reign in 752 B.C. was the second shortest in Israel's history (after Zimri's seven-day reign, 1 Kings 16:15-20). **Menahem** was the commander in chief of Jeroboam II's army (Josephus *The Antiquities of the Jews* 9. 11. 1). He was stationed in **Tirzah,** the former capital of Israel (cf. 1 Kings 15:21, 33; 16:6, 8-9, 15, 17, 23). Menahem, who regarded Shallum as a usurper to the throne, believed that he as commander of the army should succeed Zechariah. Menahem apparently **attacked Tiphsah,**

perhaps near Tirzah and Samaria, **because** its inhabitants, who **refused to** acknowledge him as king, shut **their gates** against him. His violent destruction of the city, even down to murdering **all the pregnant women,** was probably intended to intimidate other Israelite towns into supporting him.

### O. Menahem's evil reign in Israel (15:17-22)

**15:17-18.** **Menahem** began ruling **in the 39th year of Azariah** and **reigned . . . 10 years** (752-742 B.C.). Menahem instituted Israel's seventh dynasty. His apostasy was as bad as that of many of his predecessors.

**15:19-22.** **Pul** has been identified from Assyrian inscriptions as Tiglath-Pileser III (745-727 B.C.; cf. v. 29; 16:7, 10; 1 Chron. 5:26). This is the first mention of **Assyria** in 2 Kings. Pul was one of Assyria's strongest rulers. This invasion of **Israel** took place in 743 B.C. and resulted in Menahem's paying tribute to Pul. In return for the **1,000 talents** (ca. 37 tons) **of silver** Menahem raised from the **wealthy** men of Israel, the Assyrian **king** gave Menahem **his support** and helped him retain his crown.

After **Menahem** died, he was **succeeded** by his son **Pekahiah.**

### P. Pekahiah's evil reign in Israel (15:23-26)

**15:23-26.** **Pekahiah . . . reigned two years** in **Samaria** (742-740 B.C.). He too followed Jeroboam's apostate ways. His reign ended when **one of his** military **officers, Pekah,** led **50 men,** under his command from **Gilead** in Transjordan, to Samaria and there **assassinated** the king. **Argob and Arieh,** possibly princes, were also **killed.** This took place **in the citadel,** the most secure part of the **palace,** in **Samaria. Pekah** then assumed the throne of Israel.

### Q. Pekah's evil reign in Israel (15:27-31)

**15:27-28.** The **52nd year of Azariah** was 740 B.C. (His 52nd year, his last, extended into part of 739.) At this time **Pekah** began to rule over **Israel** from **Samaria.** However, he had apparently never accepted Menahem's claim to the throne and had set up a rival government east of the Jordan River in Gilead. There Pekah lived as a military officer under the Samarian government, till the time was right for him to assert himself. His 20-year reign means that he began ruling in Gilead at the same time Menahem took the throne in Samaria (752 B.C.). His reign overlapped Menahem's and Pekahiah's (752–740 B.C.). In 740 B.C. he assassinated Pekahiah and started ruling in Samaria where he remained until he was overthrown in 732 B.C.

Pekah continued in the sinful ways of his predecessors on the throne of **Israel.**

**15:29.** Part of Pekah's reason for opposing Menahem and his son Pekahiah seems to have been a different conviction regarding Israel's foreign policy toward **Assyria.** Menahem was conciliatory and willing to submit to Assyrian control (cf. vv. 19-20). **Pekah** apparently favored a harder line of resistance. Popular reaction against Menahem's taxing of the people may have encouraged Pekah to make his move. When Pekah had taken power in Samaria he made a treaty with Rezin, king of Damascus, against Assyria. This resulted in **Tiglath-Pileser** III (Pul) leading a campaign into Philistia, Israel, and later Aram in 734–732 B.C. (cf. 2 Chron. 28:5-8). In these battles he **took Ijon,** a town in Naphtali, **Abel Beth Maacah,** just south of Ijon, **Janoah,** another neighboring village, **Kedesh,** just west and north of Lake Huleh, **and Hazor,** south of Kedesh. He **took** all of **Gilead** east of the Jordan River and **Galilee,** the northern portion of Israel, including the territory **of Naphtali,** and he **deported the people to Assyria.** This first deportation of the Israelites probably took place in 733 B.C. A second deportation followed 11 years later in 722 B.C.

**15:30-31.** As a result of Israel's defeat **Hoshea . . . conspired against Pekah . . . assassinated him, and . . . succeeded him as king** of Israel in 732 B.C. On one of the Assyrian inscriptions Tiglath-Pileser III claims to have had a hand in establishing Hoshea on the throne (James B. Pritchard, ed., *Ancient Near Eastern Texts Relating to the Old Testament.* 3rd ed. Princeton, N.J.: Princeton University Press, 1969, p. 284). Evidently Hoshea submitted to being a pawn of Assyria as Menahem and Pekahiah had done.

### R. Jotham's good reign in Judah (15:32-38)

**15:32-35.** The **second year of Pekah** was 750 B.C. when **Jotham . . . began to reign** as coregent with his father Azariah (**Uzziah**). Jotham's **16**-year reign was from 750 to 735 B.C. Actually Jotham continued as coregent with his son Ahaz until 732 B.C., but during this time Ahaz was regarded as the official king.

Jotham was a good king, but he did not remove **the high places** (cf. comments on 1 Kings 22:43).

Only one of Jotham's accomplishments is recorded in 2 Kings. He **rebuilt the Upper** (north) **Gate of the temple,** perhaps to encourage the worship of Yahweh. Jotham's other building projects and his subjection of the Ammonites are recorded in 2 Chronicles 27:3-5. The reason he became a powerful king is that "he walked steadfastly before the LORD his God" (2 Chron. 27:6).

**15:36-38. Rezin, king of Aram, and Pekah,** king of Israel, united **against Judah** to force Jotham and Ahaz to join with them in taking a hard line of resistance against the Assyrian threat. **In those days** refers specifically to the time when Jotham and Ahaz were coregents (735–732; see comments on 16:1). This pressure was from the Lord and proved to be a test of faith for the Judean king (cf. 16:5-8; Isa. 7:1-17). **His father** (2 Kings 15:38) may refer to Jotham's father Azariah who had controlled Jerusalem for 52 years, or to his ancestor David.

### S. Ahaz's evil reign in Judah (chap. 16)

#### 1. AHAZ'S ASSESSMENT (16:1-4)

**16:1-2a.** The **17th year of Pekah** was 735 B.C. It was not until 732, however, that **Ahaz . . . began** his 16-year reign, which continued to 715. As shown on the chart "Kings of Judah and Israel and the Preexilic Prophets," near 1 Kings 12:25-33, the reign of Ahaz's father Jotham was 16 years (2 Chron. 27:1), 750–735. But Jotham did not die until 732. Apparently, then, in the four years from 735 to 732 neither Jotham nor Ahaz was credited with independent rule; they were coregents. In another sense Ahaz's rule began in 744 (see 2 Kings 17:1 and comments there). Therefore he may have been a vice-regent under his father

Jotham from 744 to 735.

**16:2b-4.** Unlike his ancestor **David,** with whom many of the Judean kings were compared, Ahaz **did not do** the will of God. Instead he followed the examples of the wicked **kings of** the Northern Kingdom. He went so far as to sacrifice **his son** (obviously not Hezekiah who succeeded him as king) as a burnt offering to an idol. This heinous sin (cf. 17:17) was a common practice of the Ammonites and the other native pagan Canaanite nations that Israel under Joshua **had** partially **driven out** of the land. Ahaz also promoted worship **at the high places** (cf. comments on 1 Kings 22:43), on **hilltops and under** large trees. These places of worship were so numerous that the writer said hyperbolically that they could be found **under every spreading tree** (cf. 2 Kings 17:10).

2. AHAZ'S ENEMIES (16:5-9)

**16:5-6. Rezin . . . and Pekah** had formed an alliance to resist Assyrian aggression and they wanted Ahaz to join them. Ahaz, however, did not feel Assyria's threat as keenly as did his neighbors who were situated between Judah and Assyria. Ahaz preferred a conciliatory policy with Assyria. Consequently Rezin and Pekah attacked **Ahaz** hoping to force him to join them. **But they** were unsuccessful in this attempt for reasons stated in verses 7-9.

The writer inserted parenthetically here (v. 6) that **Rezin** was successful in taking **Elath** at the northern tip of the Gulf of Aqaba which Azariah had recently made a Judean city (14:22). This important port town thus passed into Aramean control. Judah never was able to recapture it. It later fell to the **Edomites.**

**16:7-9.** Rather than joining Rezin and Pekah **Ahaz** appealed for help **to Tiglath-Pileser** III. Ahaz voluntarily submitted as a **vassal** to Assyrian control and sent a gift of **silver and gold** from **the temple** and **palace** in Jerusalem to encourage Tiglath-Pileser to get his harassing neighbors away from his walls. Tiglath-Pileser obliged **by attacking** and **capturing** Rezin's capital **Damascus.**

This diverted the Arameans from besieging Jerusalem; they had to return home to defend their own territory. Damascus fell to Assyria, **Rezin** was executed, and many of the Arameans were

**deported . . . to Kir,** an area of Assyria, in keeping with the Assyrians' policy of relocating conquered peoples (cf. 15:29; 17:23). Ahaz's decision to appeal to Assyria for help was a foolish one (cf. Isa. 7). Besides losing many of his people to Pekah in the siege (2 Chron. 28:5-8), Ahaz encouraged further Assyrian advancement into Palestine. The chronicler also recorded successful invasions of Judah by the Edomites and the Philistines at that time (2 Chron. 28:17-19). All these losses resulted ultimately from Ahaz's apostasy (2 Chron. 28:19).

3. AHAZ'S APOSTASY (16:10-18)

**16:10-14. Ahaz** traveled **to Damascus to meet Tiglath-Pileser** III. There **he saw an altar** (a large one; cf. v. 15) which was Aramean or, more likely, Assyrian. Ahaz sent **Uriah the high priest** in Jerusalem **a sketch of** this **altar** with instructions to have one **built** just like it. The apostasy of the priesthood at that time can be seen in Uriah's speedy acquiescence. When **Ahaz returned** home he had **the** Lord's **bronze altar** of burnt offering moved aside to give a prominent place to **the new altar.** On it he offered the traditional **offerings** of Judah.

**16:15-18. Ahaz then** commanded that all regular **offerings** be made **on the . . . new altar.** He would **use the bronze altar** only **for seeking guidance** probably from the Lord. **Uriah** cooperated with the king's wishes.

**Ahaz** also **took** the **basins from the** 10 bronze **movable stands** (cf. 1 Kings 7:27-40), **removed the** massive **bronze . . . base** from under **the Sea** (cf. 1 Kings 7:23-26) and substituted **a stone** stand. He also **took** down **the Sabbath canopy** (evidently a covering erected in the courtyard to shade the king and his retinue when they visited the temple), **and removed the royal entryway outside the temple** (a special ramp or stairway that only the king used to enter the temple). What Ahaz did with the pieces of furniture he removed is not explained. It is clear, however, that he willingly disobeyed God who had approved the use and arrangement of the bronze altar and the other furnishings and deferred to Tiglath-Pileser III in order not to offend or anger the Assyrian ruler. Ahaz's other acts of idolatry are recorded in 2 Chronicles 28:2-3, 22-25.

### 4. AHAZ'S DEATH (16:19-20)

**16:19-20. Ahaz . . . was buried** in Jerusalem, but not laid in the royal sepulchres with the other godly kings of Judah (2 Chron. 28:27). This shows that there were influential people in Judah who did not approve of Ahaz's policies.

### T. Hoshea's evil reign in Israel (17:1-6)

**17:1-2. Hoshea** became **king** in 732 B.C., **the 12th year of Ahaz.** Ahaz's reign, which began in 744, included 9 years as vice-regent (744–735), 4 years as coregent with his father Jotham (735–732), and 16 years as principal king (732–715). (Cf. comments on 16:1-2a.) Hoshea began his reign of **9 years** in the 20th year of Jotham (15:30), which was 732 B.C. Jotham's 20 years (750–732) included his 16-year reign (750–735) and 4 years as coregent with Ahaz (735–732). Jotham's reign from 750 to 732 appears to be 18 or 19 years, but it was considered 20 years because he reigned 18 full years and parts of two other years (see note at the bottom of the chart "Kings of Judah and Israel and the Preexilic Prophets," near 1 Kings 12:25-33).

The sins of Jeroboam I are not mentioned in connection with Hoshea. He was a wicked king but perhaps as a result of the tumultuous times in which he lived he did not promote the policies of Jeroboam. According to some Jewish tradition he allowed the Israelites to go to Jerusalem to worship the Lord.

**17:3-6. Shalmaneser** V (727–722 B.C.; see the chart "Kings of Assyria in the Middle and New Assyrian Kingdoms," near Jonah 1:2) had succeeded his father Tiglath-Pileser III on the throne **of Assyria.** He attacked Samaria because **Hoshea** had failed to pay the yearly **tribute** he owed as a **vassal.** Instead of paying his taxes **Hoshea** tried to make a treaty with **So** (Osorkon IV, ca. 727–716 B.C.) **king of Egypt.** This was a foolish mistake because Egypt did not and apparently could not help **Hoshea. Shalmaneser** discovered Hoshea's plan to revolt, **marched** on Israel, and took Hoshea prisoner. Shalmaneser then subdued the remaining territory of the Northern Kingdom: Galilee and Transjordan (the northern and western portions of Israel) had already fallen to Tiglath-Pileser (cf. 2 Kings 15:29). It took Shalmaneser **three years** to capture **Samaria.** He took it in Hoshea's **ninth year** (722 B.C.) **and deported** many of the people to Assyria (cf. 18:9-11). **The Israelites** were sent to various parts of the Assyrian Empire: the town of **Halah** in the area of **Gozan on the Habor** (modern Khabur) **River** that flows into the Euphrates, and various **towns of the Medes** northeast of Nineveh.

### U. Israel's Captivity (17:7-41)

After just over two centuries the Northern Kingdom of Israel ceased to exist as a nation (931–722 B.C.). Seven of her 20 kings were assassinated. All were judged to be evil by God.

### 1. REASONS FOR THE CAPTIVITY (17:7-23)

**17:7-13.** The defeat and deportation of Israel **took place because the Israelites . . . sinned against** God. In view of His miraculous liberating redemption of the nation from Egyptian bondage, their sin was even more serious. How ironic that the last king Hoshea had sought help from Egypt (v. 4) when 724 years earlier (1446 B.C.) Israel had finally escaped from **Egypt.**

Israel did not forsake **the LORD** completely but **worshiped other gods** (idols; cf. v. 12) also (cf. Ex. 20:3). They compromised with their pagan neighbors **and followed the practices** of the very **nations** God dispossessed because of their wickedness. They followed the apostate **practices which** their own **kings,** especially Jeroboam I, **had introduced** into their national life. Though many of their sins were practiced **secretly** they were open to **the LORD.**

Throughout the land the people **built . . . high places** of worship **in all their towns** rather than worship God where and as He had specified for their own good (cf. Deut. 12:2-7, 13-14). They erected **stones** that they regarded as **sacred** (cf. 2 Kings 18:4) **and** wooden **Asherah poles** representing the pagan goddess Asherah at virtually **every** site (cf. 16:4) regarded by the pagans as having special power. Israel also **burned incense** on the heights hoping to placate the gods as their pagan predecessors, whom God **had driven out** of the land for their idolatry, **had done.** Their worship involved **wicked** behavior that angered **the LORD** (cf. 13:3; 17:17). Their idolatry involved disobeying a plainly revealed prohibition by God. **The LORD had sent prophets and seers** with special warnings in addition to those contained in the Mosaic **Law.** These messengers (God's **servants**) had warned (cf. 17:23) both kingdoms to repent and observe God's commandments in the Law.

**17:14-15.** The Israelites, however, refused to **listen** to the prophets (cf. vv. 13-14) **and were as** obstinate as their forefathers who lived before the divided kingdom came into existence. This rebellion manifested lack of confidence **in** Yahweh **their God.** The Israelites deliberately **rejected . . . the covenant** God **had made with their** ancestors as well as **His decrees** (cf. v. 13). They also disregarded **the warnings** God **had given** their forefathers. Choosing instead to follow vain **idols** (cf. v. 12), **they became** vain and **worthless** themselves. They took on the characteristics of the idols, which they put first in their lives. **They imitated the** godless **nations around them** in spite of God's order **not** to follow their example. **They** practiced **the things** God had told them not to do.

**17:16-17.** Forsaking all God's **commands,** they fashioned **two . . . calves** out of metal and worshiped them at Dan and Bethel (cf. 1 Kings 12:28-29; Deut. 4:15-18). In Samaria, their capital city, Israel set up a **pole** that symbolized the Canaanite fertility goddess **Asherah** (2 Kings 13:6). They worshiped the planets and stellar constellations (cf. 21:5; 23:4-5) with their neighbors and practiced astrology (cf. Deut. 4:19). **They** also **worshiped Baal,** the male fertility god of the Near East. They even followed the brutal practice of offering their children as human sacrifices to placate the gods (cf. 2 Kings 16:3; Deut. 18:10). **They practiced divination** (witchcraft) **and sorcery** (consulted evil spirits; cf. Deut. 18:10-11). In doing all these things the Israelites **sold themselves** to sin, thereby provoking the **LORD . . . to anger** (cf. 2 Kings 13:3; 17:11). In all these things the Israelites were disobeying specific commands in the Mosaic Covenant.

**17:18-20.** Because they were so rebellious, God in anger at their attitude disciplined His people by deporting **them from His presence** (i.e., out of the land; cf. v. 23, where He had promised to dwell with them). Exile was one of the curses (judgments) God said He would

bring on the nation if the people disobeyed Him (Deut. 28:45-48). **Only the tribe of Judah** remained. Though Benjamin was part of the Southern Kingdom, it often was not mentioned with Judah because of its small size. **Even** the Southern Kingdom disobeyed **the LORD.** Many Judahites imitated the Israelites and adopted **the practices** their brethren **had introduced.** Because of this God punished the Southern Kingdom too. He sent Judah affliction and let **the people** suffer at the hands of other nations that plundered them till they too were led captive out of their land. (These statements in vv. 18b-20 are editorial comments inserted by the writer of 2 Kings after Judah had been taken into captivity.)

**17:21-23.** God **tore Israel away from** Judah (**the house** or dynasty **of David**) in Rehoboam's day because of the sins of Solomon (1 Kings 11:9-13). The Israelites then **made Jeroboam . . . their king.** He **enticed** the nation **away from** God **and caused them to** worship two golden calves (cf. 2 Kings 17:16). The Israelites followed this form of worship consistently **until** they were **removed . . . from His presence** (i.e., from the land) through captivity in spite of the persistent warnings of **the prophets,** God's **servants** (cf. v. 13). For these reasons—flagrant idolatry, obstinate disobedience, starworship, child sacrifices, and occult practices—the Israelites were removed **from** the land God had given them as their home **into exile in Assyria. They** were **still there** when the writer penned these words.

**2. RESULTS OF THE CAPTIVITY (17:24-41)**

*a. Immediate results (17:24-33)*

**17:24. The king of Assyria** was probably Sargon II (722–705 B.C.). Shalmaneser V died either during or shortly after the siege of Samaria. The policy of Assyria toward conquered lands was to deport many of the most influential inhabitants and then import many leading Assyrians to take their places. Sargon **brought people from Babylon, Cuthah** (a city northeast of Babylon), **Avva** (between Anah and the Habor River; cf. v. 6, on the Euphrates River), **Hamath** (a city in Aram on the Orontes River), and **Sepharvaim** (people from Sippar on the Euphrates above Babylon) **and settled them in the**

towns of Israel, **now** called the Assyrian province of **Samaria.** These Assyrians **took** the leadership in the province and settled down **in** various **towns.**

**17:25-28.** Because the people **did not worship the LORD . . . He sent lions among them.** The lions already in Israel may have multiplied more quickly because of the reduced human population. God sometimes used these wild animals as His agents of judgment (cf. 1 Kings 13:23-26; 20:36); they **killed some of the people.** The Assyrians interpreted this as a punishment from **the God** of Israel whom they viewed as a deity who needed to be placated. Since they did not know how to appease Him they reported the situation to Sargon.

**The king** responded by sending an Israelite priest **back to** Samaria from **Assyria.** He was to **teach the people** about Yahweh and **how to worship** Him. The priest moved to **Bethel.** If this had been his former dwelling place he was probably one of the priests involved in worshiping the golden calf there.

**17:29-33. Each national group** of Assyrian immigrants **set . . . up . . . shrines** for the worship of their **own** pagan **gods** wherever **they settled,** using **the high places** the Israelites had frequented. The national groups (cf. v. 24) and their idols are listed (vv. 30-31) along with some of their pagan practices. **Nergal** was the Babylonian god of the underworld; the exact identity of the other gods is uncertain. As polytheists the foreigners did not hesitate to add Yahweh to their pantheon of gods. They had no priestly caste but **appointed all sorts of their own people** to serve **as priests.** For emphasis the writer wrote twice that these people **worshiped the LORD** and **also . . . their gods.** This syncretism was forbidden by the Lord (Ex. 20:3).

Second Kings 17:24-33 shows how the Samaritan people came into being. The Samaritans, racially a mixture of Israelites and various other ancient Near Eastern peoples, were despised by full-blooded Jews (cf. John 4:9). Possibly, however, the Samaritans were the pure descendants of the Israelites who remained in the land.

b. *Continuing results (17:34-41)*

**17:34-41. To** the **day** of the writing of 2 Kings (and long after, as just noted)

these Samaritans maintained their ways. They did **not worship** God. Though in verses 32-33 they are said to worship the Lord, verse 34 is not contradictory because they did not worship God from the heart and in the ways He specified. **Nor** did the people keep **the laws** He **gave** to Jacob's **descendants.** God had changed Jacob's name to **Israel** to show that he and his descendants were to become a distinct people in the world. This distinctiveness was being broken down by the Samaritans. This distinctiveness is further highlighted by a loose quotation in verses 35-39 of several commands from the Mosaic Law (Ex. 6:6; 20:4-5, 23; Deut. 4:23, 34; 5:6, 15, 32; 6:12; 7:11, 25; etc.). All this again underscored the Israelites' disobedience to their gracious God. God's people **would not listen** to Him **but persisted in their former** sinful ways (2 Kings 17:40). Syncretistic worship continued for generations, to the days of the writer.

## II. The History of the Surviving Kingdom of Judah (chaps. 18–25)

The rest of the Book of 2 Kings records the reigns of the remaining kings of Judah as well as events in Judah immediately after the Babylonian Captivity which started in 586 B.C.

### A. Hezekiah's good reign (chaps. 18–20)

The writer of 1 and 2 Kings devoted more space and gave more commendation to Hezekiah for his accomplishments than to any king except Solomon.

#### 1. HEZEKIAH'S GOODNESS (18:1-8)

**18:1-2.** Evidently **Hezekiah** reigned as coregent with his father **Ahaz** for 14 years (729–715 B.C.) **The third year of Hoshea** was the year in which Hezekiah is said to have begun reigning (as coregent with Ahaz), namely, 729 B.C. He **reigned** alone for 18 years (715–697) and then as coregent with his son Manasseh for 11 years (697–686). Together these two reigns were **29 years** (715–686 B.C.). (See the chart, "Kings of Judah and Israel and the Preexilic Prophets," near 1 Kings 12:25-33.)

**18:3-4.** The commendation that Hezekiah **did . . . right** as **David had done** is made of only three other kings of Judah: Asa (1 Kings 15:11), Jehoshaphat

(2 Chron. 17:3), and Josiah (2 Kings 22:2). Like Jehoshaphat before him Hezekiah **removed the high places** (2 Chron. 17:6) where the Lord was worshiped contrary to the Mosaic Law (cf. Deut. 12:2-7, 13-14). (Later, however, Jehoshaphat did not remove the high places, 1 Kings 22:43; 2 Chron. 20:33. Apparently the people rebuilt them and Jehoshaphat did not remove them again.)

Josiah also destroyed the idols used to aid in the worship of Baal and **Asherah** (2 Chron. 31:1). **The bronze snake** that **Moses . . . made** in the wilderness (Num. 21:5-9) had been preserved and had become a religious fetish. Hezekiah **broke** it up since it was a spiritually unclean thing; it had become a stumbling block to the Israelites. (**Nehushtan** was the name of the snake, a word that sounded like the Heb. for "bronze," "snake," and "unclean thing"; cf. NIV marg.)

**18:5-7a.** Hezekiah's best quality was that he **trusted in the LORD.** He was the greatest of **all the kings of** the Southern Kingdom in this respect. Unlike some of the other kings he did **not apostasize later in life but kept** the Mosaic Covenant faithfully. As a result **the LORD was with him** and blessed him with success **in** all **he undertook.** Whereas the writer of 2 Kings gave only a brief record of Hezekiah's spiritual reforms and activities the chronicler recorded many more, including his cleansing and reconsecration of the temple (2 Chron. 29:3-36), his celebration of the Passover and other feast days (2 Chron. 30), and other religious reforms (2 Chron. 31:2-21).

**18:7b.** Hezekiah's rebellion **against** Sennacherib (705–681 B.C.), **king of Assyria,** precipitated the Assyrian invasion recorded later (18:13–19:36). Hezekiah was anti-Assyrian in contrast with his father Ahaz. But so long as Sargon II remained on the throne Hezekiah wisely did not antagonize the Assyrians. With the accession of Sennacherib, Sargon's son, Hezekiah judged that Assyria was not so strong. He decided to join an alliance with neighboring nations to oppose the northern foe and began making preparations for Assyria's anticipated retaliation.

**18:8.** Hezekiah was successful in defeating **the Philistines** who had taken several cities from Judah during Ahaz's

reign (2 Chron. 28:18). **Gaza** was the southernmost city in Philistia. **From watchtower to fortified city** means wherever he turned.

2. SAMARIA'S CAPTURE (18:9-12)

**18:9-12.** This second account of the fall of **Samaria** (cf. 17:3-6) was added as a historical reference point in view of its great importance in the life of Judah as well as Israel. **Hezekiah's fourth year,** beginning with his vice-regency, was 725 B.C. **At the end of three years** (in 722) Shalmaneser V captured Israel's capital. The places to which the Israelites were deported for resettlement are the same as those mentioned in 17:6. The summary statement in 18:12 states why Israel fell: she was disobedient to the Mosaic Law (cf. 17:7-23).

3. JERUSALEM'S SIEGE BY ASSYRIA (18:13–19:37)

The following section is recorded also in the Book of Isaiah (chaps. 36–37) with only a few changes.

*a. Sennacherib's campaigns (18:13-16)*

**18:13.** Sennacherib's predecessor Sargon II had continued to expand Assyrian territory and to strengthen her hold on conquered peoples. He put down a revolt headed by Hamath (a city north of Damascus; cf. 14:28), fought successfully in Asia Minor, squelched a revolution at Carchemish north of Hamath and deported its population, broke the power of Assyria's hated northern neighboring kingdom Urartu, and moved down into Philistia where he crushed a rebellion led by the city of Ashdod, then the leading city in Philistia.

Sennacherib was a less capable ruler than his father. During Sennacherib's first four years on the throne he was occupied with controlling Babylon. During this time an alliance had formed in which cities of Phoenicia and Philistia as well as Egypt (under Shaboka) and Judah (under Hezekiah) joined together to resist **Assyria.** Certain that Sennacherib would try to put down this uprising, as Sargon had done, Hezekiah prepared for an Assyrian invasion by fortifying Jerusalem (cf. 2 Chron. 32:1-8).

**Sennacherib** led his armies into Judah as expected. This was in 701 B.C., **the 14th year of . . . Hezekiah's** sole **reign** which began in 715 B.C. On their way to

Judah the Assyrians defeated the rebels in Phoenicia, which caused several other members of the alliance to withdraw. Then Sennacherib marched his armies down the coast into Philistia where he brought the Philistine cities into line. Next he **attacked all the fortified cities of Judah** except Jerusalem **and captured** the people. Sennacherib's inscriptions refer to his conquest of 46 strong cities of Hezekiah plus many villages.

**18:14-16.** The Assyrian **king** then set up his headquarters at Lachish, a well-fortified city near the Philistine border in central Judah, in preparation for his siege of Jerusalem.

Understandably **Hezekiah** did not want to fight Sennacherib, whose armies had been consistently successful against other members of the now severely weakened alliance. So Hezekiah **sent** a **message to** Sennacherib **at Lachish.** Judah's king admitted that he had **done wrong** in allying with the other nations against **Assyria.** He offered to **pay whatever** the Assyrian king demanded if he would **withdraw** and not attack Jerusalem. Sennacherib asked for **300 talents** (ca. 11 tons) **of silver and 30 talents** (ca. 1 ton) **of gold. Hezekiah** paid **him all the silver** in **the treasuries** of **the temple** and **palace.** To gather all the gold the king had to strip **off** all **the gold** plating on the temple **doors and** door frames.

*b. Sennacherib's threat (18:17-37)*

The ransom did not satisfy Sennacherib, however, so he sent messengers to demand a complete surrender. At first they presented their claims only to Hezekiah's representatives (vv. 17-27) but then to all the people of Jerusalem (vv. 28-37).

**18:17-18.** The three officers **sent** by Sennacherib were his top men. They went **with a large army** to intimidate **Hezekiah** so he would capitulate without resistance. They advanced by way of **the road to the Washerman's Field** to **the aqueduct of the Upper Pool** that extended from the spring of Gihon to the field where the people washed their clothes. This was within earshot of the wall of **Jerusalem** (cf. v. 26) and was a busy location. The messengers wanted to speak to **the king,** but Hezekiah sent three of his deputies—**Eliakim . . . Shebna,** and **Joah**—to negotiate with Sennacherib's three representatives.

**18:19-22.** Sennacherib's **field commander** spoke for his side and repeated his king's message to **Hezekiah.** What he said was designed to impress Hezekiah with Sennacherib's power and glory, and to intimidate him into surrendering. He asked the basis of Hezekiah's **confidence** that he could possibly withstand the **great king . . . of Assyria.**

Assuming Judah was depending on **strategy** and force, the commander pointed out the weakness of both these resources. **Egypt** was the only member of the alliance yet remaining, and she would splinter like a weak **reed** if any weight of confidence were placed on her. Rather than helping Judah, **Egypt** would hurt her by both failing and frustrating Hezekiah. The commander was correct; Egypt was not strong at that time and could not be counted on for help. If the Judahites' strategy was to rely **on the LORD,** the commander said they should remember that **Hezekiah** had incurred His wrath (he supposed) by removing the **high places and altars** (cf. v. 4) where the Lord had been worshiped throughout the land. The Assyrians obviously had information about what had been going on in **Judah,** but they did not understand that Hezekiah's actions had been carried out in obedience to God's commands, not out of disrespect for Him.

**18:23-24.** The commander called on Hezekiah to strike **a bargain** and surrender. This, the commander reasoned, would be wise. The Judahites had few horses; this was part of the help Hezekiah had hoped to get from Egypt. Even if Sennacherib were to **give** Judah **2,000 horses** Hezekiah could not **put** trained cavalrymen **on them.** Judah's army was probably not really that small, but it was small in comparison with Assyria's. From the commander's viewpoint even 2,000 Judean horsemen were no match for **one** Assyrian **officer.** In other words Judah's army was inferior in both quantity and quality.

**18:25.** The commander's final appeal was a strong one. He claimed that **the LORD** had commanded his master **to attack and destroy** Jerusalem. Though this is improbable it is not impossible (cf. Isa. 45:1-6). The people of Judah had seen Israel fall to Assyria. Might not God's plan be the same for Judah?

**18:26-27.** Hezekiah's three representatives realized that these arguments could make the people lose heart. Since many Jews were perched **on the** city **wall** and were overhearing what was being said the three Judean ambassadors asked the Assyrians to **speak** only **in** the **Aramaic** language which only the educated leaders of Israel understood.

**The commander** refused; he realized the importance of destroying the people's confidence in their ability to succeed in any military encounter against the Assyrian army. The commander replied that he had been **sent** with this message to all the people, not just the leaders of Judah. After all, it was the common people who would suffer most from a long siege and the resulting famine. They would be reduced to eating **their own** excrement and drinking **their own urine.** Nothing could be more repulsive to the residents of Jerusalem than this possibility. The commander wanted the people to conclude that surrender would be better than resistance.

**18:28-31.** Now the Assyrian top officer **called out** to the common people standing around, listening in, and peering over the wall. His words were designed to undermine their confidence in their king and to encourage them to oppose Hezekiah's decision to resist. He claimed **Hezekiah** did not have the power or ability to **deliver** the **city** and that **the** LORD would not **deliver** it either.

It would be better for the people, **the commander** promised, if they surrendered. Rather than siege and starvation there would be peace and plenty to **eat** and **drink.** Each person having his **own vine and fig tree** is a figure of speech for enjoying peace and prosperity (cf. 1 Kings 4:25; Micah 4:4; Zech. 3:10).

When under a siege one of the first needs people faced was **water.** Hezekiah had provided for this need by cutting a tunnel from the spring of Gihon under the wall of the city to the Pool of Siloam (cf. 2 Kings 20:20) but the Assyrians did not know about this or chose to ignore it.

**18:32-35.** In time, the commander said, the Assyrians would transport them to other cities. The people had heard that this was Assyrian policy. But he assured them that they would be sent **to a land like** their **own** where they would have plenty of their favorite foods and drink. The commander punctuated his eloquent and attractive appeal with a call to **choose** surrender and **life** rather than resistance **and** certain **death.** He next focused on Hezekiah's promise to the people that the LORD would **deliver** them if they trusted in Him. His ideas reflect a polytheistic and pagan concept of God but his words could not help but raise questions in his hearers' minds. No other **gods** had been able to deliver their worshipers from the might **of Assyria.** The places mentioned (v. 34) were probably known to the Judahites. **Arpad** was 13 miles north of Aleppo in Aram. **Hena and Ivvah** were north of the Euphrates River east **of Hamath.** (On Hamath and **Sepharvaim** see 17:24.) The commander's reference to the inability of the gods of **Samaria** to deliver the Israelites would have been especially effective since Israel's God was also Judah's God.

**18:36-37.** The Assyrian commander's six rhetorical questions (vv. 33-35) needed no answer and **the people** gave him none; they **remained silent.** Hezekiah had previously instructed the people not to reply to the cunning general's statements. Undoubtedly those forceful arguments aroused much heated discussion among the common people after the Assyrian messengers departed.

The summit conference broke up and Hezekiah's three representatives (cf. v. 18) returned to **the king.** He could see that they had **torn** their **clothes** out of great distress (cf. Gen. 37:29, 34; Josh. 7:6; 2 Kings 5:7; 6:30; 11:14; 22:11; Es. 4:1; Job 1:20; 2:12); they faced a most serious situation. Then they **told him what the** Assyrians **had said.**

*c. The Lord's promise (19:1-7)*

**19:1-2. When** the **king** had **heard** the report of his messengers **he** too **tore his clothes.** He **put on sackcloth,** coarse goats'-hair clothing that symbolized self-affliction and despair (cf. Gen. 37:34; 1 Kings 21:27; Neh. 9:1; Es. 4:1-4; Dan. 9:3). He then **went into the temple** to seek God's face in prayer. **He** also **sent Eliakim** and **Shebna** (cf. 18:18) **and the leading priests,** who were also mourning in **sackcloth, to the Prophet Isaiah** who lived in Jerusalem. Isaiah and Hezekiah knew and respected each other.

**19:3-4.** The king's representatives

conveyed Hezekiah's message that this was indeed a black day in Judah's history. They were distressed, rebuked by God for their sins, and disgraced before their enemies. A crisis had come to a head but now there was not adequate strength to resist the Assyrian invasion. It was like a pregnant woman who finally goes into labor but cannot deliver her child for lack of strength. It seemed as if the whole nation would die. Hezekiah's hope was that God, having been ridiculed by the Assyrians, would act on behalf of His people and prove that He was the true and living God by granting a miraculous deliverance to His people. The king called on the prophet to pray for the small remnant of people left in Jerusalem and Judah.

**19:5-7.** Isaiah responded to the king's request with a message of hope from the Lord. The Lord encouraged the king not to fear the blasphemous words of Sennacherib's underlings. God would cause Sennacherib to decide to return home when he heard a report (of something God had arranged), and there the Assyrian king would die a violent death.

### d. The Lord's diversion (19:8-13)

**19:8.** Evidently Sennacherib's field commander pitched his tents near Jerusalem and waited for Hezekiah to send him a message of surrender. While the commander was there, word reached him that Sennacherib had left Lachish (cf. 18:14). He withdrew from Jerusalem and located his master near Libnah where he was engaged in battle. Libnah was just a few miles north of Lachish. This is why the field commander removed his large army (18:17) from the walls of Jerusalem.

**19:9-13.** Evidently while Sennacherib was at Libnah (or perhaps Lachish) he received a report (cf. v. 7) that Tirhakah, the king of Egypt, who was from Cush (modern-day southern Egypt, Sudan, and northern Ethiopia), and an ally of Hezekiah, was marching up to fight Sennacherib. There is insufficient evidence to support the contention by some scholars that Tirhakah was only a boy at this time, incapable of leading such an attack and that this whole campaign of ⸜Sennacherib's (18:17–19:36) therefore must have taken place in 686 B.C. rather than in 701 B.C.

Somehow Sennacherib knew that the **king of Judah** had been told (by Isaiah) that Yahweh would deliver Jerusalem from the Assyrians. He sent a message **to Hezekiah** not to believe this prophecy even though it looked as if the Assyrians were withdrawing. He boasted of previous victories in **all the** surrounding **countries.** His armies had destroyed many of **them completely.** Surely Jerusalem would not be spared, he claimed.

None of **the gods of the** defeated peoples had been able to deliver them, had they? Sennacherib obviously granted the Lord no greater respect than the idols of the nations. To reinforce his warning the Assyrian king mentioned 10 cities and nations, 5 of which had not been referred to previously. **Gozan** was located on the Habur River east of **Haran,** the town where Abraham lived for some time. **Rezeph** was probably Rusafah (or Risafe) northeast of Palmyra and south of Haran. **Eden** was a small kingdom in the Euphrates basin west of the Balikh River, and **Tel Assar** was one of the cities in this area. The 5 other sites were mentioned in 18:11, 34.

### e. Hezekiah's prayer (19:14-19)

**19:14-16.** When the king had **received . . . and read** Sennacherib's message which had been carried to him by **messengers** (cf. v. 9) he returned **to the temple** to pray again (cf. v. 1). His prayer included a recognition of God's sovereignty (v. 15), mention of the defiance of the Assyrians (vv. 16-18), and a request for deliverance (v. 19). Spreading **the letter. . . . before the Lord,** Hezekiah addressed Him as Israel's **God,** whose throne was the atonement cover ("mercy seat," KJV) on the ark of the covenant **between the cherubim.** God had said He would dwell between the cherubim in a unique sense (1 Sam. 4:4; 2 Sam. 6:2; 1 Chron. 13:6). The king recognized that God is a Spirit, not a piece of wood or stone (cf. 2 Kings 19:18). He **alone** (cf. v. 19) was the real Ruler of Judah, the Sovereign **over all the kingdoms of the earth** including Assyria, and the all-powerful Creator of **heaven and earth.** Hezekiah besought God to listen carefully to what he would say and to view closely what was happening. He then reported Sennacherib's blasphemous insults.

**19:17-19.** Hezekiah could easily understand why Assyria had successfully defeated her foes; the **gods** in which those nations trusted for protection were mere pieces of **wood and stone.** They were created objects, not the Creator (cf. v. 15). So they had no power and were easily **destroyed.** But Hezekiah appealed to the living God to **deliver** His people **from** Sennacherib's **hand.** Hezekiah believed He could; this was a prayer of faith. And the objective of the king's petition was God's glory, not primarily his own survivial. He asked God to vindicate Himself and to demonstrate that He was not just an impotent idol **so that** the whole world would acknowledge Him.

Hezekiah's petition is one of the finest prayers in Scripture.

### f. The Lord's answer (19:20-34)

**19:20.** The Lord's answer to Hezekiah's request (vv. 15-19) came through **Isaiah,** and was delivered to the king by a messenger. God assured **Hezekiah** that his **prayer** had been **heard.** God then announced a message of judgment against **Sennacherib** for his blasphemy.

**19:21-24.** The first part of God's answer (vv. 20-28) gave the reason for His judgment on Sennacherib. The figurative, poetic language was probably used to stress the importance and divine source of the answer.

**The Virgin Daughter of Zion** suggests that Jerusalem had never been conquered since it had passed into Israelite control. Jerusalem would despise and mock Sennacherib, shaking **her head as** the Assyrian king fled from her. Sennacherib had **raised** his insulting **voice** in blasphemy and **pride,** not against the city but **against** her God, **the Holy One of Israel** (see comments on this title under "Internal Evidence" in the section on "Unity" in the *Introduction* to Isa.). This was his great sin and his undoing. He and his **messengers** had insulted **the Lord** by claiming their victories were a result of their own might.

Though Sennacherib may have literally cut down the trees **of Lebanon** the description (v. 23) probably represents his destruction of various nations' leaders. "Lebanon" probably refers especially to the Northern Kingdom of Israel. Its **choicest** trees were its leaders. Assyria had dominated Israel and had killed many of its best citizens. Sennacherib boasted that he had **dug** up many for-

eign **lands** and had taken for himself what satisfied him at their expense. He had done this to the Southern Kingdom of Judah, here referred to figuratively as **Egypt.** (Or perhaps Egypt refers to his defeat of an Egyptian army at the Judean town of Eltekeh.) He boasted that his siege had kept her life-giving resources from flowing.

**19:25-26.** Addressing Sennacherib in this prophecy, God said that king was not responsible for Assyria's success. Instead God had **ordained . . . planned,** and **brought . . . to pass** all that had happened (cf. Isa. 10:5). The **fortified cities** were those the Assyrians had destroyed. The conquered **people** had no **power** to resist and in fact could not even attain normal full strength, like the shallow-rooted **grass** that grew **on the housetops** but died prematurely. This had been God's doing.

**19:27-28.** The Lord knew all about Sennacherib and his proud raging in rebellion **against** Himself. Because the Assyrian monarch hated God and had spoken insolently against Him, God would take the king captive as Sennacherib had taken so many other people captive.

The **hook** and the **bit,** which portray catching a fish and controlling a horse, are uniquely appropriate. On some ancient monuments the Assyrian conquerors pictured themselves as leading their captives with a line that passed through rings that had been placed in the victims' noses. God promised to do to them as they had done to others. He would lead them back from where they had come and reduce them to their former humble state.

**19:29-31.** Through Isaiah God then promised **Hezekiah** a **sign** that these predictions (vv. 26, 28) would indeed come to pass. The sign was a near-future miracle that would confirm the fulfillment of the more distant aspects of the prophecy.

For two years the people of Jerusalem would be able to **eat** the produce of their land. It would not be stolen by the Assyrians who would have lived off the land if they had returned to besiege the capital. The Judeans had not been able to plant crops outside the city walls because of the Assyrians' presence. But God promised that He would feed them for two years by causing the seed that had been sown naturally to grow up into an adequate crop. **The third year** people could return to their normal cycle of sowing and reaping.

This provision of multiplied food was further designed to illustrate God's plan to multiply miraculously the people of Judah who had been reduced to small numbers. Sennacherib claimed to have taken 200,150 prisoners from Judah. However, though Judah seemingly might cease to be a nation through attrition, God promised to revive it. Like the crops, **a remnant** of people would **take root . . . and bear fruit,** that is, be established and prosperous. God's **zeal** on behalf of His people would perform this (cf. Isa. 9:7).

**19:32-34.** Sennacherib's fate was then revealed. He would **not** forcefully take Jerusalem, besiege it, **or** even **shoot an arrow** against it. Instead **he** would **return** to his own homeland without even entering Jerusalem. God promised to **defend** Jerusalem **and save it** from Sennacherib's wrath. God would do this **for the sake of** His own reputation (cf. v. 19) and because of His promise to His servant **David** (cf. 1 Kings 11:13).

*g. Sennacherib's departure (19:35-36)*

**19:35-36.** **That** very **night** while **the Assyrian** army lay sprawled across the Judean countryside **the Angel of the Lord** (cf. comments on Gen. 16:9) executed **185,000** of their soldiers. **When the** Jerusalemites arose in **the . . . morning** they discovered the extent of the catastrophe. **Sennacherib** probably recognized this as a supernatural event. In any case he concluded he should return to **Nineveh** where he **stayed** for some time.

*h. Sennacherib's death (19:37)*

**19:37.** Years later (in 681 B.C.) Sennacherib **was worshiping in the temple of his god Nisroch.** This Assyrian deity was represented as being part eagle and part human. The temple was probably in Nineveh, Assyria's capital. There the king fell prey to the plot of assassins, two of **his** own **sons.** Ironically his god was not able to deliver him even in its temple. The murdering sons fled **to the land of Ararat** (Armenia), about 300 miles north of Nineveh. Armenia is now divided between Russia, Turkey, and Iran. Another son, **Esarhaddon** (681–669 B.C.), **succeeded** Sennacherib **as king.** Thus the word

of the Lord (v. 7) came to pass.

4. HEZEKIAH'S ILLNESS (20:1-11)

*a. Hezekiah's petition (20:1-7)*

**20:1. In those days** refers to days of the invasion of Jerusalem by Sennacherib, recorded in 18:13–19:36. God added 15 years to Hezekiah's life in response to his petition for mercy (20:6). Hezekiah died in 686 B.C. which would place this incident in 701 B.C., the year of Sennacherib's invasion (cf. Isa. 38).

Hezekiah's serious illness (with some kind of boil, v. 7) may or may not have been directly connected with the invasion by Sennacherib. God sent **Isaiah** to announce to **Hezekiah** that he would **die.** The prophet instructed him to prepare for this by setting his **house** (affairs) **in order.**

**20:2-3. Hezekiah** responded to this bad news by praying earnestly **to the Lord.** The king reminded God of his faithfulness to Him, his **wholehearted devotion,** and his **good** behavior as God's vice-regent. He **wept bitterly** perhaps because he felt his death would give Sennacherib something to boast about, perhaps because his heir, Manasseh, was still very young, and perhaps because he wanted to continue living and reigning.

**20:4-6.** The king's appeal in prayer was effective with **God. Before Isaiah had left** the palace on his way home **the Lord** gave him a second message: to return to the king with word announcing a postponement of his death. **Hezekiah** had behaved like a true son of **David** in the way he reacted to God's first message. Hezekiah's **prayer** (what he said) **and** his **tears** (how he felt about what he said) moved God to **heal** him. Isaiah announced that in three days the king would be well enough to worship God in **the temple.** God promised to **add 15 years** to Hezekiah's **life** (from 701 to 686). The Lord also promised to **deliver** Hezekiah and Jerusalem from Sennacherib's siege and to defend Jerusalem for His own **sake and for** David's **sake** (cf. 19:34).

**20:7. Isaiah** then gave Hezekiah a treatment for his illness. The **poultice of figs** was well known in the ancient world as a means of helping to heal boils and ulcers, but Hezekiah's physicians had not prescribed it. Some think the remedy was designed to demonstrate God's supernatural power at work in granting the king's recovery.

### b. Hezekiah's sign (20:8-11)

**20:8.** Requesting a **sign** that God would indeed do what He had promised was common among the Israelites (cf. Jud. 6:17, 36-40; 1 Cor. 1:22). God did not object to such a request if the sign were requested to strengthen the faith of the person seeking it. Signs were miracles that signified that what God had said He would indeed do. Perhaps the imminent danger that Hezekiah faced from Sennacherib led him to ask for this sign.

**20:9-11.** God let the king choose whether **the shadow** would **go forward,** as it normally would, or backward. Ahaz's **stairway** (v. 11) was evidently a stairway King **Ahaz** had built. It may have been constructed as a sundial to measure the time of day or it may have simply been a regular staircase used by God on this occasion to provide the sign Hezekiah had requested.

By offering to advance **the shadow** God undoubtedly intended to advance it faster than was normal since the usual rate would have been no sign at all. **Hezekiah** requested the most obvious and dramatic alternative: that the sun's shadow be reversed **10 steps.** It is not necessary to insist that God reversed the rotation of the earth to effect this miracle. Some similar miracles were evidently limited in their scope, being local rather than universal (cf. Ex. 10:21-23; Josh. 10:12-13).

### 5. HEZEKIAH'S VISITORS (20:12-19)

This incident evidently took place shortly after Hezekiah recovered from his illness (cf. Isa. 39:1-2).

### a. Hezekiah's reception (20:12-15)

**20:12-13.** **Merodach-Baladan** reigned as **king of Babylon** for two periods of time, 721–710 and 703–702 B.C. In 702 B.C. he fled to the country of Elam where he continued his efforts to resist Assyrian control as a refugee. It was probably during this period that he sought the support of Judah as an ally by sending this embassy. (See comments on Isa. 39:1 on the sequence of these events: Hezekiah's illness, Merodach-Baladan's visit, and Sennacherib's attack.) He courted **Hezekiah's** favor by sending a **gift** when he

heard that **Hezekiah** had become sick. Merodach-Baladan also wanted to ask about the miracle that had occurred in the land (2 Chron. 32:31).

**Hezekiah . . . showed** his Babylonian visitors the full extent of his wealth and armaments partly because he concluded his ally should know how much Judah would be able to contribute to their joint anti-Assyrian effort.

**20:14-15. Hezekiah** made no attempt to hide what he had done from **Isaiah** who had been sent by God to inquire about the visitors. The king of Judah likely did not think that his desire to form an alliance with **Babylon** was either an expression of lack of confidence in God or a foolish move politically.

### b. Hezekiah's judgment (20:16-19)

**20:16-18.** Because Hezekiah's heart was proud (2 Chron. 32:25), God announced through **Isaiah** that the Babylonians would carry away **all** that **Hezekiah** had shown them. **Some of** the royal family who had not yet been **born** would also **be taken** captive and be made **eunuchs in the palace** in Babylon. Eunuchs were often high-ranking officials (*sārîs*; see comments on Dan. 1:3).

**20:19. Hezekiah** repented of his pride (2 Chron. 32:26) and humbly accepted the fact that God's judgment would come on the nation (**the word of the LORD . . . is good**). He was also grateful for the **peace and security** Judah would enjoy by God's mercy in his **lifetime.**

### 6. HEZEKIAH'S DEATH (20:20-21)

**20:20-21.** The building of **the tunnel** from the Gihon spring to **the Pool** of Siloam was singled out by the writer as one of **Hezekiah's** more important achievements (cf. 2 Chron. 32:30). Hezekiah had this 1,777-foot tunnel dug from the oldest source of **water,** just outside the wall of Jerusalem, under the wall to a reservoir inside **the city.** He then covered up the spring so the Assyrian invaders would not discover it and cut off Jerusalem's water supply. This tunnel, dug from both ends to the middle, was a remarkable engineering feat which still can be seen today.

Years before **Hezekiah** died he made his son **Manasseh** vice-regent in 697 B.C. The father and **son** ruled together until

Hezekiah died in 686 B.C. Then Manasseh **succeeded** Hezekiah and ruled **as sole king.**

## B. Manasseh's evil reign (21:1-18)

Though Manasseh reigned longer than any other king of Judah or Israel, the record of his reign is brief.

### 1. MANASSEH'S WICKEDNESS (21:1-9)

**21:1-6.** When **Manasseh was 12 years old . . . he** began ruling as vice-regent with his father Hezekiah (697 B.C.). In all **he reigned . . . 55 years.**

Rather than continuing the God-honoring policies of his father, Manasseh reverted to those of his grandfather Ahaz and reestablished **the detestable practices of the** native Canaanite peoples. **He** also **rebuilt the high places** which had been so common in the nation (cf. comments on 1 Kings 22:43; also note 1 Kings 3:2-3) until **Hezekiah** had purged the land of them (2 Kings 18:4). Manasseh reerected **altars to Baal and made** a **pole** to represent **Asherah** (cf. 21:7) as Ahab had done in Samaria (1 Kings 16:33). Manasseh defiantly **built altars** to idols right **in the temple** and its courtyards which God had said were to be reserved for worship of the true and living God (1 Kings 8:29). Manasseh also opened the doors of the nation to Assyrian astral worship again (2 Kings 17:16; 23:4-5).

Manasseh also practiced human sacrifice and offered one of **his own** sons to the Ammonite god Molech in the Valley of Hinnom (cf. 1 Kings 11:7, 33; 2 Kings 23:10, 13). **Sorcery . . . divination . . . mediums, and spiritists** were all part of Manasseh's religious system even though these were prohibited in the Mosaic Law (cf. comments on 17:17). The king believed that all forms of worship were better for the people than the exclusive worship of Yahweh prescribed in the Law. His policies provoked **the LORD . . . to anger** (cf. 21:15; 22:13, 17; 23:19, 26; 24:20) and were **evil** (cf. 21:2) **in** His **eyes.**

**21:7-9.** Manasseh further desecrated **the temple** by placing in it **the carved Asherah pole he had made** (cf. v. 3). By so doing he gave an idol the place that God alone deserved (cf. v. 4 and comments on God's **name** in 1 Kings 8:16-20; 2 Chron. 6:6). This act showed no respect for God's promises to the king's **forefa-**thers or His faithfulness to His promises. Manasseh treated the **Law** of **Moses** with contempt and **led** the **people** of God away from His commandments. Amazingly the people under Manasseh practiced **more evil** (cf. 2 Kings 21:15-16) **than** the Canaanites before them.

### 2. JERUSALEM'S FATE (21:10-15)

**21:10-13.** God's judgment against Manasseh and **Judah** came **through . . . the prophets** (probably Isaiah and perhaps others). **The Amorites** were one of the most wicked people of Palestine in Joshua's day. Besides practicing idolatry himself Manasseh compounded his wickedness by leading the Judeans **into sin** with him. Therefore God promised that the news of **Jerusalem** and Judah's **disaster** would shock all who heard it. He said He would **stretch** the straight **plumb line** (symbolizing destruction) against **Jerusalem** and Manasseh as He had done to **Samaria** and **the house** (family or dynasty) **of Ahab.** God would cleanse Judah of all her corruption as a dishwasher scours a **dish.**

**21:14-15.** God also said He would **forsake** what remained of His **inheritance** (i.e., Judah) **and** cause **their enemies** to discipline them. The Judeans would be robbed and spoiled **by their** enemies. This judgment would come on them for all their **evil** (cf. vv. 9, 16) since their birth as a nation when God led them **out of Egypt.** Though Judah had undergone other judgments, this one would be the most severe.

### 3. MANASSEH'S DEATH (21:16-18)

**21:16-17.** The **innocent blood** Manasseh **shed** included that of his own son (v. 6) and the sons and daughters of those who followed his examples of worship. According to Jewish tradition Isaiah was put to death by Manasseh by being sawed in two (Heb. 11:37 may refer to Isaiah).

The chronicler reported that Manasseh for his sins was taken captive to Babylon (2 Chron. 33:11) by the king of Assyria, probably Ashurbanipal (669–626 B.C.). There Manasseh repented of his sins and God in His grace allowed Manasseh to return to Jerusalem after a period of captivity (2 Chron. 33:12-13; cf. 2 Chron. 33:18-19). After his restoration the king cleaned up much of the idolatry in Judah (2 Chron. 33:15-17). Manasseh's sins had stained Judah deeply, however, and even later reforms under Josiah could not avert God's judgment (2 Kings 23:26).

**21:18.** When **Manasseh** died he was not **buried** in the royal tombs with the good kings of Judah but was laid to rest **in his palace garden** instead. His son **Amon . . . succeeded him.**

### C. Amon's evil reign (21:19-26)

**21:19-22. Amon** began ruling when he **was 22 years old,** but he lived only **two** more **years** (642–640 B.C.). Amon did not continue the policies of his father's later rule but reverted to the syncretistic, idolatrous worship that had characterized Manasseh's earlier reign (cf. vv. 2-7). Amon abandoned **the Lord** completely.

**21:23-26.** Fearing a continuation of the havoc that **Amon's** policies were sure to bring, some of the king's **officials . . . assassinated** him. A popular uprising followed, however, in which Amon's murderers were brought to justice and executed.

On Amon's death his son **Josiah** was placed on the throne. Amon was buried with his father **in the** palace **garden** (cf. v. 18).

### D. Josiah's good reign (22:1–23:30)

1. JOSIAH'S GOODNESS (22:1-2)

**22:1. Josiah** was one of Judah's best kings. Peace, prosperity, and reform characterized his reign. Josiah was only a lad of **eight . . . when he** was crowned **king,** and **reigned** over Judah **31 years** (640–609 B.C.). During his reign world power passed from Assyrian to Babylonian leadership. Nineveh, the capital of Assyria, was destroyed in 612 B.C., and the Assyrian Empire fell in 609.

**22:2.** Like Asa and Hezekiah before him Josiah **did what was right in the** sight **of the Lord and** followed the good **ways of his** ancestor **David.** He did not deviate from this course at any time during his reign.

The chronicler added that Josiah began to seek after the Lord when he was 16 and he began his religious reforms when he was 20 (2 Chron. 34:3-7).

2. JOSIAH'S REFORMATION (22:3–23:25)

Josiah was the fourth and final reformer among Judah's kings, following

Asa, Jehoshaphat, and Hezekiah. But Josiah's reforms were more extensive than those of any of his predecessors.

*a. Josiah's repairs (22:3-7)*

**22:3-7. The temple** had fallen into disrepair and had been desecrated by Manasseh who had built pagan altars and images in it (cf. 21:4-5, 7, 21). In Josiah's **18th year** as king, at age 26, he began to **repair the temple** and restore it to its former condition. He **sent the secretary, Shaphan** (perhaps like a secretary of state) along with other high government officials (cf. 2 Chron. 34:8) to begin **the temple** renovations. (On Shaphan's immediate descendants see the chart "The Line of Shaphan," near Jer. 26:24.) For some time **money** had been **collected** for this purpose. Now enough was in hand to begin the work. The procedure was similar to that followed by Joash (cf. 2 Kings 12:10). As then, the supervisors proved trustworthy. (See 2 Chron. 34:8-13 for more details of this aspect of Josiah's reform.)

*b. Hilkiah's discovery (22:8-13)*

**22:8-10.** In the process of renovating **the temple** a copy of **the Book of the Law** (either the Book of Deut. or, more likely, the entire Pentateuch, the first five books of the Bible) was **found.** Evidently Manasseh or Amon had destroyed other copies so that the discovery of this one constituted an important find. **Hilkiah the high priest** shared his discovery with **Shaphan who** also **read it.** After reporting progress on the restoration to Josiah, **Shaphan . . . informed the king** of this important discovery and **read from it** to him.

**22:11-13.** In distress Josiah **tore his robes** (cf. Gen. 37:29, 34; Josh. 7:6; 2 Kings 5:7; 6:30; 11:14; 19:1; Es. 4:1; Job 1:20; 2:12) and wept (2 Kings 22:19) on hearing what God required of His people as he compared that with how far they had departed from His will. He then sent five of his top officials to **inquire of the Lord** what should be done. Josiah feared the **anger** of the Lord and wanted to turn it away from all **the people** of **Judah,** not just himself. The shock expressed by **the king** at the contents of **the Law** reveals that Judah had not consulted the Law for a long time.

### c. Huldah's prophecy (22:14-20)

**22:14.** The fact that the king's five officers (cf. v. 12) sought out **the Prophetess Huldah** suggests that she was highly regarded for her prophetic gift. Other prophets also lived in and around Jerusalem at this time including Jeremiah (Jer. 1:2), and Zephaniah (Zeph. 1:1), and perhaps Nahum and Habakkuk. But the five consulted Huldah for reasons unexplained. This woman **was the wife of Shallum** who was responsible for the royal or priestly **wardrobe. She lived in . . . the Second District of Jerusalem** which was the part of the city lower in elevation than the rest.

**22:15-18.** After consulting **the Lord** Huldah sent His message back to **the king.** God would surely send **disaster on** Jerusalem and the **people** of **Judah** as He had warned in the Law of Moses. This judgment would come **because they** had **forsaken** Him and made **idols** and **burned incense to** them. God's **anger** burned **against** His people (cf. v. 13) basically because they had forsaken His appointed way whereby they could experience blessing, enjoy life, and demonstrate to all other peoples how glorious it was to live under the Lord's leadership.

**22:19-20.** Josiah would experience God's mercy personally, however, because he had responded to God's Word and had **humbled** himself **before the Lord when** he **heard** the Law of Moses. God said that the king would die and **be buried** before judgment would descend on Judah. His death in 609 was four years before Nebuchadnezzar's first attack on Jerusalem in 605.

### d. The reading of the Law (23:1-3)

**23:1-2.** The king did not wait for the temple renovation to be completed before he **called** the assembly described here; this convocation took place soon after the Law was discovered. To this important **temple** ceremony he summoned **all the elders . . . the priests,** and **prophets** (no doubt including Jeremiah and Zephaniah) and **all the people from the least to the greatest.** The king **read . . . all the words of the Book.** Perhaps this was the whole Pentateuch but more likely it was the sections promising blessing for obedience and discipline for disobedience (Deut. 27:15–28:68).

**23:3.** Standing **by the pillar** (cf. 11:14) in the temple courtyard **the king** led the people in a rededication of themselves to **the Lord** and His Word. He first pledged himself **to follow the Lord** faithfully and to carry out the words **written in** the Law of Moses (cf. 1 Kings 2:3). **Then all the people** promised to do the same (cf. Ex. 19:8; Josh. 24:21-24).

### e. Josiah's reforms (23:4-14)

**23:4-7.** Josiah then removed everything connected with the worship of false gods that his ancestors had set up in Judah and Jerusalem. **The doorkeepers** were Levites responsible for controlling who entered **the temple.** This house of worship was cleansed of all the paraphernalia that had been brought inside to be used in the worship of **Baal . . . Asherah,** and the astrological deities (cf. 21:3-5). Josiah had these **burned** (cf. Deut. 7:25) **in the . . . Kidron Valley** (cf. 2 Kings 23:6, 12) just east of **Jerusalem.** To desecrate the very center of pagan worship he **took the ashes** of these relics **to Bethel.** He also drove **away the pagan priests** who had led the people in various forms of idolatry. The Hebrew word rendered "pagan priests" is $k^e m\bar{a}r\hat{i}m$, used elsewhere only in Hosea 10:5 and Zephaniah 1:4. It refers to idol-priests, priests who prostrated themselves before idols. The king then removed **the Asherah pole from the temple** (cf. 2 Kings 21:7), **burned it** in the **Kidron Valley** (cf. 23:4), and scattered its ashes (cf. v. 4) **over the graves of the** idolatrous **common people. Male shrine prostitutes,** who served as part of the pagan worship, had set up tents in **the temple** courtyard. These Josiah **tore down** as he did the shelters that had been erected there where female idolaters wove materials used in some way in the worship of **Asherah.**

**23:8-9.** Josiah reassembled **all the Le**vitical **priests** and proceeded to desecrate **the high places** (cf. comments on 1 Kings 22:43) where the Lord had been worshiped contrary to the Law of Moses (Deut. 12:2-7, 13-14). Hezekiah had demolished them also (2 Kings 18:4), but Manasseh rebuilt them (21:3). Josiah destroyed those pagan places of worship **from Geba** on Judah's northern frontier **to Beersheba** on its southern border. He also destroyed **the shrines** (high places) located **at the gates** near the residency **of Joshua,** the **governor** of Jerusalem, and at the other gates of **the city.** These altars had been placed **to the left** of the gate as people entered the city. **The** Levitical **priests** who had offered sacrifices on the **high places** were **not** allowed to **serve at the** rededicated **altar** in the temple, but Josiah did permit them to eat the **unleavened bread** brought to the temple (cf. Lev. 6:9-10, 16).

**23:10-11. Topheth** was the place where worshipers of **Molech,** the god of Ammon (cf. v. 13), burned their children as sacrifices. This was **in the Valley of Ben Hinnom** at the south side of Mount Zion (cf. Josh. 15:8). Josiah **desecrated** this site so that no idolater would worship there again. He also **removed the** sacred **horses** that were used in formal processions honoring **the sun.** These animals had been **dedicated** by **the kings of Judah** (probably Ahaz, Manasseh, and Amon) and were stabled in the temple courtyard. Josiah also **burned** up the ceremonial **chariots** used in these idolatrous processions.

**23:12-14. Ahaz** had evidently built an **upper room** on one of the buildings at the gate of the temple. **On the roof near** that structure Ahaz had built **altars,** probably to the stars and planets (cf. Zeph. 1:5; Jer. 19:13; 32:29). Hezekiah undoubtedly destroyed these altars but apparently Manasseh or Amon had rebuilt them.

**Manasseh** also **had built** altars in **the temple** courtyards (2 Kings 21:5). All these Josiah destroyed and tossed **into the Kidron Valley** (cf. 23:6). He **also desecrated the** altars that had been erected on the southern hill of the Mount of Olives which became known as **the Hill of Corruption.** These altars dated back to Solomon's reign (1 Kings 11:5, 7). Josiah removed all **the** pagan **sacred stones** and **Asherah poles** (cf. 2 Kings 23:6, 15) at that site also. **Human bones** rendered those sites unclean and unsuitable as places of worship thereafter.

*f. Jeroboam's altar (23:15-20)*

**23:15-16.** The ancient **altar** that **Jeroboam** I had erected (cf. 1 Kings 12:28-29) **at Bethel** (ca. 931 B.C.) also toppled in Josiah's purge. To desecrate (cf. 2 Kings 23:10, 13) the site forever Josiah removed **the bones** of the people who had been

buried in **the tombs** cut out of a hillside nearby **and burned** them **on the altar** (obviously before the altar was demolished). These bones probably belonged to the priests (cf. 1 Kings 12:31-32) who out of reverence for the altar had been buried near it. This act by the king fulfilled the prophecy of **the man of God** from Judah who had predicted it in the days of Jeroboam, even calling Josiah by name (1 Kings 13:2-3).

**23:17-18.** Learning that a certain **tombstone** marked the grave of **the man of God** from **Judah** who had predicted Josiah's action (cf. comments on v. 16), **the king** ordered that his grave not be disturbed out of respect for him. The bones of the old prophet **from** Bethel (in **Samaria,** the Northern Kingdom, not the city of Samaria which had not yet been built) who had been buried next to the younger prophet (1 Kings 13:31-32) were left undisturbed too.

**23:19-20. Josiah** even extended his purge into the territory of the old Northern Kingdom. His ability to do so reflects the weakness of the Assyrian Empire which controlled **Israel** at this time. Some of the Israelites who remained in their land after the fall of **Samaria** still worshiped at the **high places** that Josiah now destroyed. **The priests** whom **Josiah** executed in Israel were probably not Levites but idolatrous priests like those Jeroboam had appointed (cf. 1 Kings 12:31).

*g. Josiah's Passover (23:21-23)*

**23:21-23.** Josiah did more than simply eliminate idolatry. He also reestablished the divinely ordained **Passover** feast. This important feast commemorated God's redemption of His people from their bondage in Egypt. It was also Israel's oldest feast. (On **this Book of the Covenant,** cf. v. 2.) This observance by Josiah was conducted with more careful attention to the Law than any Passover **since the days of the Judges.** It also was unusual because **people** from both the kingdom of **Judah** and the old kingdom of **Israel** participated together (2 Chron. 35:18). The observance of this feast is described in detail in 2 Chronicles 35:1-19. It took place in Josiah's **18th year of** reign. Apparently all the reforms just described (2 Kings 22:3–23:20) took place that same year (cf. 22:3).

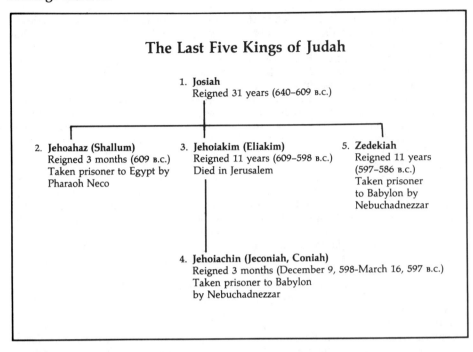

# The Last Five Kings of Judah

**1. Josiah**
Reigned 31 years (640–609 B.C.)

**2. Jehoahaz (Shallum)**
Reigned 3 months (609 B.C.)
Taken prisoner to Egypt by
Pharaoh Neco

**3. Jehoiakim (Eliakim)**
Reigned 11 years (609–598 B.C.)
Died in Jerusalem

**5. Zedekiah**
Reigned 11 years
(597–586 B.C.)
Taken prisoner
to Babylon by
Nebuchadnezzar

**4. Jehoiachin (Jeconiah, Coniah)**
Reigned 3 months (December 9, 598-March 16, 597 B.C.)
Taken prisoner to Babylon
by Nebuchadnezzar

### h. Josiah's greatness (23:24-25)

**23:24-25.** Josiah's purge weeded out even the informal practitioners (**mediums and spiritists**; cf. 21:6) of rites God had condemned (Lev. 20:27; Deut. 18:9-12). **Household gods** were worshiped as sources of prosperity and as oracles. These were destroyed as well as all other **idols** throughout **Judah and Jerusalem.** Josiah **did** all this in direct obedience to the Mosaic **Law.** There was not a king **before** or **after** him who so conscientiously observed the Word of **the LORD** (cf. Deut. 6:5; Jer. 22:15-16).

### 3. JUDAH'S JUDGMENT (23:26-27)

**23:26-27.** Even Josiah's reformation, as great as it was, could not dispel the accumulated wrath of God **against Judah** for her years of rebellion, especially under Manasseh's leadership (cf. 22:16-17). The Lord's words in 23:27 may be a direct quotation of a prophecy given through an unnamed prophet at that time, or a free quotation taken from God's previous words of warning. God would reject His people, their **city,** and His **temple** in the sense of handing them over to their enemies for discipline. To be removed **from** His **presence** (cf. 24:3, 20) meant being **removed** from the land (cf. 17:18, 20, 23).

### 4. JOSIAH'S DEATH (23:28-30)

**23:28-30. Other events of Josiah's reign** were recorded in the source noted by the writer.

Josiah's death is explained more fully in 2 Chronicles 35:20-27. Josiah seems to have been motivated to fight **Pharaoh Neco** II (610–595 B.C.) **of Egypt** in the desire to frustrate any hope **Assyria** or Egypt might have had of regaining strength and attacking Judah. Egypt and Assyria were allies and were trying to stop Babylonia from becoming the new world leader. Josiah evidently regarded Babylonia as a lesser threat than Assyria or Egypt. As Pharaoh Neco marched his troops up the Mediterranean coastline in 609 B.C., **Josiah** headed northwest with his army, determined to stop Neco **at Megiddo,** a well-fortified stronghold in old Israel. Unfortunately for Judah, Josiah died in the ensuing battle. **His body** was returned **to Jerusalem** where it was given a royal burial. The officials of Judah placed his son **Jehoahaz** on the throne.

Josiah was a strong influence for righteousness in his day and also a most capable ruler. The success of his sweeping reforms indicates that he had the ability to overcome strong popular opinion which undoubtedly opposed his convictions. His influence even extended into the territory of the fallen Northern Kingdom. Tragically his reign ended prematurely.

### E. Jehoahaz's evil reign (23:31-35)

**23:31-32.** Josiah had four sons, three of whom ruled over Judah after their father's death (1 Chron. 3:15; see the chart "The Last Five Kings of Judah"). **Jehoahaz** was the middle son agewise and was chosen by the people to succeed Josiah. He **was 23 years old when he** acceded, but he **reigned** only **three months** (in 609 B.C.). His grandfather **Jeremiah** was not the prophet of the same name since that prophet was not permitted by God to marry (Jer. 16:2). In the brief time Jehoahaz ruled he determined to revert to the ways of his idolatrous ancestors rather than follow his father's good example.

**23:33.** When **Pharaoh Neco** defeated Josiah at Megiddo (cf. v. 29) Judah fell under Egyptian control. Neco summoned the newly appointed king of Judah to **Riblah** on the Orontes River about 65 miles north of Damascus. The Egyptian king later continued marching northward toward his encounter with Nabopolassar the Babylonian at Haran even farther north. Evidently Neco judged Jehoahaz to be an uncooperative vassal so he imprisoned him and sent him to Egypt (v. 34) where Jehoahaz eventually died (cf. Jer. 22:10-12). Neco also **imposed** a heavy tax **on Judah . . . of 100 talents** (ca. 3¾ tons) **of silver and a talent** (ca. 75 pounds) **of gold.**

**23:34-35.** **Neco** then placed Jehoahaz's older brother **Eliakim** on the throne of Judah and **changed** his **name to Jehoiakim** (from "God has established" to "Yahweh has established"). The naming of a person was regarded in the ancient Near East as a sovereign prerogative; by doing this Neco was demonstrating that he controlled Judah. **Jehoiakim** submitted to Neco's lordship and provided the tribute of **silver and gold** the Egyptian king required by taxing **the people** of Judah.

### F. Jehoiakim's evil reign (23:36—24:7)

#### 1. JEHOIAKIM'S WICKEDNESS (23:36-37)

**23:36-37.** **Jehoiakim** was two years older than his brother Jehoahaz (cf. Jehoiakim's age of **25** with Jehoahaz's age of 23, in 609 B.C.). Jehoiakim **reigned . . . 11 years** (609–598 B.C.) as a puppet

king. **His mother's** hometown **Rumah** was near Shechem (cf. Jud. 9:41). Jehoiakim too failed to follow his father's good example but chose the path of idolatry and self-reliance. Jehoiakim was a weak ruler. This can be deduced by the fact that even though he was the eldest son of Josiah he was not chosen by the people of Judah to succeed his father. Also Neco sensed that Jehoiakim would be easier to control than his brother Jehoahaz.

#### 2. JUDAH'S ENEMIES (24:1-7)

**24:1-4.** **Nebuchadnezzar** had succeeded his father Nabopolassar as king of Babylon in 605 B.C. Earlier that year **Nebuchadnezzar** had led his father's army against the Egyptians under Pharaoh Neco and had defeated them at Carchemish on the Euphrates River in northern Aramea. This battle established Babylonia as the strongest nation in the Near East. Egypt and its vassals, including Judah, passed under Babylonian control with this victory.

Nebuchadnezzar **invaded the land** of Judah later the same year (605 B.C.) in order to bring Judah securely under his rule. At that time he took some captives to Babylon including Daniel and others (cf. Dan. 1:1-3). **Jehoiakim** submitted to Nebuchadnezzar **for three years,** but then Jehoiakim revolted and unsuccessfully appealed to Egypt for help. He was eventually taken prisoner to Babylon (2 Chron. 36:6), but apparently was released or escaped because he died in Jerusalem (Jer. 22:19; cf. comments on 2 Kings 24:10-11). **Judah** was plagued by raiding bands from Babylonia, Aramea, Moab, and Ammon, who took advantage of Judah's weakened condition later in Jehoiakim's reign. God **sent** these enemies against **Judah** to punish her for her sins according to the words of **the Prophets** Isaiah, Micah, Jeremiah, Habakkuk, and others. God was removing the people **from His presence** (cf. 17:18, 20, 23; 23:27) **because of the sins of Manasseh** (cf. 21:1-16).

**24:5-7.** Jeremiah the prophet despised **Jehoiakim** for his wickedness (cf. Jer. 22:18-19; 26:20-23; 36). When Jehoiakim died in 598 B.C. in Jerusalem his son **Jehoiachin . . . succeeded him** on the throne of Judah. Jehoiakim did not receive a royal burial (Jer. 22:19).

Pharaoh Neco **did not** again assert

himself to regain the territory he had lost to Nebuchadnezzar between **the Wadi of Egypt** (Wadi el-Arish) in the south **to the Euphrates River** in the north which included all of Palestine. This too was part of God's sovereign plan to discipline His people and illustrates the strength of Babylonia at this time.

### G. Jehoiachin's evil reign (24:8-17)

1. JEHOIACHIN'S WICKEDNESS (24:8-9)

**24:8-9. Jehoiachin** began reigning when his father Jehoiakim died. He ruled Judah only **three months** while he **was 18 years old** and, like Jehoiakim, **he did evil in the** sight **of the LORD.**

2. THE SECOND DEPORTATION (24:10-17)

**24:10-12. Nebuchadnezzar** had sent troops against **Jerusalem** late in Jehoiakim's reign because the Judean king continued to resist Babylonian control and to look to Egypt for help in throwing off the Babylonian yoke. Jehoiakim may have died in the **siege** of Jerusalem, or he may have been killed by raiders from some other country that harassed Judah (v. 2). **Nebuchadnezzar himself** decided to go up against Jerusalem but by the time he arrived (in 597 B.C.) Jehoiakim had died and Jehoiachin had replaced him as king. **Jehoiachin . . . surrendered to** Nebuchadnezzar along with the queen **mother** and all his **attendants . . . nobles,** and **officials.** Nebuchadnezzar then **took** the king **prisoner** to Babylon.

**24:13-16. Nebuchadnezzar** also took **all the treasures** of **the temple** and **palace** including **the gold articles** that remained from Solomon's days. This invasion took place in fulfillment of God's Word (1 Kings 9:6-9). Nebuchadnezzaar also took captive virtually **all the officers** and **7,000** soldiers (2 Kings 24:16) as well as **1,000 craftsmen** and **artisans.** In all, **10,000** people were taken captive including the Prophet Ezekiel (Ezek. 1:1-3). **Only the** most poor **people** remained in Judah. This was the second time Judahites had been deported to Babylon; the first deportation followed Nebuchadnezzar's victory in 605.

**24:17.** None of Jehoiachin's sons sat on Judah's throne, as Jeremiah had predicted (Jer. 22:30). The Babylonian king set up **Jehoiachin's** uncle **Mattaniah** as **king.** This man was the third son of Josiah to rule Judah (see the chart "The Last Five Kings of Judah," near 2 Kings 23:31-32); he was the younger brother of Jehoahaz and Jehoiakim. Nebuchadnezzar exercised his sovereign prerogative and **changed** Mattaniah's **name to Zedekiah** (see comments on 23:34).

### H. Zedekiah's evil reign (24:18–25:7)

Though Zedekiah was king of the Southern Kingdom the people of Judah apparently did not recognize him as such at the time. This may have been due in part to his being placed on the throne by a foreign king (2 Chron. 36:10-13). This explains why inscriptions from the time refer to Jehoiachin as Judah's last king (Pritchard, ed., *Ancient Near Eastern Texts Relating to the Old Testament,* p. 308).

1. ZEDEKIAH'S WICKEDNESS (24:18-20)

**24:18-20. Zedekiah was 21 years old when he** began his rule, **and he reigned . . . 11 years** (597–586 B.C.). **He did evil** as his brother **Jehoiakim had done.** Jehoiakim is mentioned probably because he reigned 11 years whereas Zedekiah's immediate predecessor Jehoiachin reigned only three months. Again the reason for Judah's troubles is said to be **the LORD's anger** with His people for their apostasy (cf. 21:6, 15; 22:13, 17; 23:19, 26). Therefore He cast them **from His presence** (i.e., out of the land; cf. 17:18, 20, 23; 23:27; 24:3).

For several years **Zedekiah** submitted obediently to his master in Babylon. But finally under continuing pressure from nationalists at home (cf. Jer. 37–38) the king foolishly **rebelled.** He made an alliance with Pharaoh Hophra (589–570 B.C.) who was anti-Babylonian and aggressive.

2. JERUSALEM'S FINAL SIEGE (25:1-7)

**25:1-3.** In January 588 B.C. (in **the 10th month of Zedekiah's** ninth **year) Nebuchadnezzar** again **marched against** and besieged **Jerusalem.** The **siege** was lifted briefly when Egypt attacked Nebuchadnezzar (Jer. 37:5) but the Babylonians defeated Judah's ally easily and resumed the **siege.** The Jerusalemites suffered the consequences of this extended siege: **famine** and fear.

**25:4-7.** Finally the Babylonians broke **through the wall** of Jerusalem. This was on July 16, 586 B.C., the fourth month of Zedekiah's 11th year (vv. 2-3). The few remaining soldiers (cf. 24:16) **fled by night through** a gate in a section of the wall where it was double. They headed east **toward the Arabah** (the Jordan Valley) but were overtaken and captured near **Jericho.** Zedekiah fled the city with the soldiers (Jer. 39:4) and **was** also **captured.** He was taken to Nebuchadnezzar's field headquarters **at Riblah** (cf. 2 Kings 23:33) on the Orontes River north of Damascus. (Nebuchadnezzar was also conducting campaigns against Tyre and other Judean cities according to the Lachish Letters [D. Winton Thomas, ed., *Documents from Old Testament Times.* New York: Harper and Brothers, 1958, pp. 212-7].) There Nebuchadnezzar **killed** Zedekiah's **sons** (to cut off the heirs to the throne) **before his eyes,** blinded **Zedekiah** (to make further rebellion virtually impossible; cf. Ezek. 12:3), placed **him in shackles,** and transported **him to Babylon** (cf. Jer. 32:4; 34:1-3; 39).

## I. Judah under Babylonian government (25:8-30)

### 1. JERUSALEM'S BURNING (25:8-12)

**25:8-12.** About four weeks after the breakthrough into the city (cf. vv. 3, 8) **Nebuchadnezzar** sent **Nebuzaradan, commander of his imperial guard,** to burn **Jerusalem.** This was **on the 7th day of the fifth month** of Nebuchadnezzar's **19th year** (August 14, 586 B.C.). However, Jeremiah 52:12 reads "the 10th day" (cf. comments there). This officer led his troops in burning down **every important building** in Jerusalem including **the temple and the royal palace** which had stood for almost four centuries. Then **the whole . . . army** proceeded to break **down** vast sections of the city wall so that the remaining inhabitants could not defend themselves against their Babylonian conquerors. **Nebuzaradan** also removed all but **the poorest people,** carrying the majority off to **Babylon.** Some of these captives had surrendered to the Babylonians but others had not. The remaining farmers were intended by Nebuchadnezzar to keep **the land** from growing completely wild.

### 2. THE TEMPLE'S DESTRUCTION (25:13-17)

**25:13-17. The Babylonians broke . . . the** large **bronze pillars** and pieces of furniture in **the temple** area to make **the bronze** easier to transport. The smaller

furnishings of **bronze . . . gold,** and **silver** were simply packed up and carted off **to Babylon.**

**The two pillars** on the temple porch were so huge that the amount of **bronze** in them **could** not **be weighed** (cf. 1 Kings 7:15-22; Jer. 52:20-23).

### 3. THE LEADER'S EXECUTION (25:18-21)

**25:18-21. Seraiah,** an ancestor of Ezra (Ezra 7:1), and other priests were taken captive to preclude their leading another revolt. For the same reason the **chief** officer and **advisers** were arrested. Nebuchadnezzar **executed** all 72 of these leaders **at Riblah,** his field headquarters (cf. 2 Kings 25:6).

### 4. GEDALIAH'S MURDER (25:22-26)

**25:22-24. Gedaliah** was a descendant of **Shaphan,** Josiah's secretary of state who had implemented that king's reforms (22:3). **Gedaliah** was a friend of Jeremiah (Jer. 39:14) who followed that prophet's counsel to cooperate with the Babylonians. Since **Gedaliah** assumed a pro-Babylonian stance Nebuchadnezzar **appointed** him **governor** of **Judah. Gedaliah** set up his headquarters **at Mizpah** (about eight miles north of Jerusalem) since Jerusalem lay in ruins. In Mizpah a party of pro-Egyptian leaders and their followers who had escaped execution by the Babylonians called on him. The governor tried to convince these men to remain **in the land** and **serve** Nebuchadnezzar for their own good.

**25:25-26.** Some time later, however, **Ishmael . . . who was of royal** descent and apparently wanted to govern **Judah,** conspired against **Gedaliah** and slew him (cf. Jer. 41:2). Gedaliah had been warned of this possibility but had refused to take it seriously (Jer. 40:13-16). Gedaliah's associates were **also** slain. Fearing reprisals from Nebuchadnezzar, **all the** Judahites including **the army officers** who had failed to prevent this assassination **fled to Egypt** for safety, forcing Jeremiah to go with them (Jer. 41:1–43:7).

### 5. JEHOIACHIN'S BLESSING (25:27-30)

**25:27-30.** The 12th month of **the 37th year** of Jehoiachin's captivity in **Babylon** was March 560 B.C. (he was taken captive in 597; cf. 24:15). Earlier, in 562, a new king, **Evil-Merodach,** had become ruler **of Babylon.** (Evil-Merodach's rule was from 562 to 560; see the chart "Kings of the Neo-Babylonian Empire," in the *Introduction* to Dan.) He changed the former policy of treating the Judean king like a criminal and gave him privileges because he was a king. **Jehoiachin** was treated with greater respect **than** the **other** conquered **kings who were** also prisoners **in Babylon.** This treatment may have been a result of Jehoiachin's repentance before the Lord, though such a change of heart is not mentioned in the text. **For the rest of his life** Jehoiachin lived in minimum security **prison** conditions and **ate regularly** the food Evil-Merodach provided for him (cf. Jer. 52:31-34).

The positive note on which 2 Kings ends reveals again the Lord's mercy, which stands out repeatedly in 1 and 2 Kings. This notation also points to the continuation of the Davidic dynasty which God had promised would lead His people forever (2 Sam. 7:16). Evil-Merodach's attitude toward Jehoiachin was followed by policies that allowed the Israelites more freedom. When Cyrus overthrew Babylonia he allowed the Jews to return to their land (Ezra 1:1-4).

## BIBLIOGRAPHY

See *Bibliography* on 1 Kings.

# 1 CHRONICLES

## Eugene H. Merrill

## INTRODUCTION

In the early Hebrew manuscripts 1 and 2 Chronicles were one scroll. The earliest evidence of the division of the book into two is the Septuagint, the Greek version of the Old Testament, of about 200 B.C. Since the original material presented the historical record in one unbroken account, one should read and study 1 and 2 Chronicles together in order to appreciate the unity and progressive development of the argument of the books.

**Authorship.** The author of 1 and 2 Chronicles is not mentioned in the Old Testament but Jewish tradition has suggested that it was Ezra. However, there is no way to be certain in the matter. So it has become customary to refer to the author as "the chronicler," a term which may not be entirely satisfactory but which is accurate enough in the absence of more precise information. Scholars generally agree that the work's uniformity of style, flavor, and viewpoint necessitate a single author. Yet 1 and 2 Chronicles, more than any other Old Testament books, testify to their dependence on several earlier written sources. More than half of 1 and 2 Chronicles has parallels in 1 and 2 Samuel and 1 and 2 Kings, for example. This does not mean that the chronicler used these books as direct sources, however. Most scholars agree that there is little or no evidence that 1 and 2 Chronicles has any quotations from them. On the other hand there are references to "the book of the annals of King David" (1 Chron. 27:24), "the book of the kings of Israel and Judah" (2 Chron. 27:7; 35:27; 36:8), "the book of the kings of Judah and Israel" (2 Chron. 16:11; 25:26; 28:26; 32:32), "the book of the kings of Israel" (1 Chron. 9:1; 2 Chron. 20:34), "the annals of the kings of Israel" (2 Chron. 33:18), "the records

of Samuel the seer" (1 Chron. 29:29), "the records of Nathan the prophet" (29:29; 2 Chron. 9:29), "the records of Gad the seer" (1 Chron. 29:29), and others (see, e.g., 2 Chron. 9:29). Whoever the author was, he was a meticulous historian who carefully utilized official and unofficial documents.

**Date.** Nearly all biblical scholars agree that 1 and 2 Chronicles could not have been written later than the end of the fifth century B.C., perhaps around 400. Liberal critics maintained at one time that a date around 300–250 B.C. was more suitable because of allegedly late characteristics such as references to the highly developed organization of priests and Levites, the use of vocal and instrumental music in worship, the anti-Samaritan polemic, the midrashic type of scriptural interpretation (narratives setting forth or illustrating religious teachings), and the mention of the Persian word *daric* (1 Chron. 29:7). All these features are now known to have been used as early as the fifth century; in addition such factors as the character of the Hebrew language in 1 and 2 Chronicles argue for an earlier rather than later date. The latest person named in 1 and 2 Chronicles is Anani, of the eighth generation from Jehoiachin (1 Chron. 3:24). Jehoiachin was taken captive by the Babylonians in 598 B.C. If 25 years are allotted for each generation, Anani would have been born between 425 and 400 B.C. If David's posterity was so important to the chronicler, a point that cannot be denied, it is incredible that he did not list any descendants after about 400 if the book were written later than that time. This genealogical datum is also helpful in determining the *earliest* possible time of composition as well, since eight generations could not lie between 598 B.C. and any time much earlier than 400 B.C. That is, the book could not have been written before 400 B.C.

# 1 Chronicles

**Purpose and Structure.** These two elements will be considered together since the one explains the other. In Hebrew, the name of the one scroll for 1 and 2 Chronicles was known as $dib^e r\bar{e}$ $hayy\bar{a}m\hat{i}m$, "the words concerning the days." This is a historical account of the "days" of the Davidic kings of Israel and Judah. The Greek title *Paraleipomena* ("Things omitted") in the Septuagint wrongly implies that the only purpose of 1 and 2 Chronicles is to preserve information not given in Samuel or Kings.

It is obvious that 1 and 2 Chronicles take the form of a history commencing with Adam (1 Chron. 1:1) and ending with the decree of Cyrus of Persia (2 Chron. 36:23) in 538 B.C. This view must be tempered by the fact that the period from Adam through the death of Saul is related only in genealogical registers interspersed with fragmentary narrative sections that especially emphasize the lineage of David and the priestly and Levitical orders. In His elective purposes God chose Israel—and her supreme king, David—from among all the nations on the earth. So David and Judah are the focal points of 1 and 2 Chronicles.

The emphasis on the Davidic and political history and the priestly and Levitical religious institutions intimated in the genealogical section (1 Chron. 1–9) finds confirmation in the remainder of 1 and 2 Chronicles. The reign of Saul is described in only one chapter (1 Chron. 10) and this is merely a record of his death. The purpose of this narration of Saul's death is to prepare for David's succession. David's reign is then the subject of the last 19 chapters of 1 Chronicles (chaps. 11–29). The reign of Solomon is described in 2 Chronicles 1–9 and the rest of the dynastic history is given in chapters 10–36. Though there are sporadic references to Israel, the Northern Kingdom, the whole thrust of 2 Chronicles 11–36 is centered in the Southern Kingdom. The history of the divided kingdom is always viewed in that light. David and the Davidic descent is the great theme.

The subsidiary but significant strand of the book—its preoccupation with religious matters—also is incipient in the genealogical section (1 Chron. 1–9). The priestly and Levitical lines of origin and descent prepare the way for the unusual attention to the temple and temple worship, evident from the time of David onward. Since Chronicles was composed in the postexilic period long after the monarchy had ceased as a viable institution, political as well as religious power became more and more the priesthood's responsibility. This could well account for the emphasis on the priests and their associates. More important, however, was the need to prepare the people for a heightened understanding of the messianic implications of the priesthood. David's intense interest and involvement in worship was not without design. As king, he was a type of the messianic King (cf. Pss. 2; 110; etc.), and as a priest (1 Chron. 15:25-28; cf. 2 Sam. 6:12-15), David was also a type of Christ, the messianic Priest. The twin emphases of 1 and 2 Chronicles—on David as king and on the priesthood as a royal function with messianic implications—are central to a theological understanding of these books.

Some writers believe that the chronicler is guilty of biased historiography. He failed, they say, to report David's adulterous affair with Bathsheba, for example, but was careful to detail the repentance of the evil King Manasseh, a feature missing in 2 Kings. While these examples, along with many others, could be cited as instances of supposedly "slanted" history writing, one must not make the mistake of interpreting them as errors of fact. It is incorrect to charge the chronicler with prejudicial reporting.

One cannot deny that as a whole David and the monarchy appear in a better light in Chronicles than in Samuel and in Kings. But this has been generally overstated. Though David's adultery is omitted in 1 Chronicles, other episodes that are recorded certainly place him in less than a favorable light. A few examples are his mishandling of the ark (1 Chron. 13:9-14), his polygamy (14:3-7), and his premature request to build a temple for the Lord (chap. 17). Furthermore since all scholars admit that the account of David's adultery in 2 Samuel 11 was well known and written long before 1 and 2 Chronicles were composed, there was no need to repeat it.

The best resolution of the charge of bias seems to be that the elements in 1 and 2 Samuel and 1 and 2 Kings which do not directly and positively contribute to the purpose of 1 and 2 Chronicles were not included since they would have been extraneous. The purpose of 1 and 2 Chronicles is to show God's elective and preserving grace in His covenant people through David, the messianic king and priest. The purposes of 1 and 2 Kings are different. These books explain the fall and destruction of Samaria and Jerusalem as evidence of divine judgment of God's people who had forsaken His covenant requirements. The Books of 1 and 2 Chronicles, though not avoiding this theme, show that the gracious God of all the earth and all the ages has a better plan by which He will achieve redemptive reconciliation. That plan does not do away with David; on the contrary, it eventuates in a greater "David" (the Messiah) who is both King and Priest.

The chronicler's emphasis on David, the priesthood, and the temple would have been a source of great encouragement to postexilic Judah. The nation had fallen into captivity, a comparatively small remnant had returned, and the restored temple was meager compared with its former splendor (cf. Hag. 2:3). But God's promises will not fail. In His time the temple will be filled with His own glory. And the Davidic line once more will be established and the Messiah will rule on David's throne in the kingdom. The religious and political sides of the covenant sovereignty of the Lord will be reestablished. This assurance would have instilled fervent joy and anticipation in the hearts of the remnant of God's people who otherwise saw all about them only a vague reminiscence of the glory their fathers had known in former years.

# OUTLINE

# COMMENTARY

## I. Genealogies (chaps. 1–9)

As suggested under "Purpose and Structure" in the *Introduction*, the emphasis in 1 and 2 Chronicles is on the Davidic dynasty in Judah and the Levitical line. The genealogies are given to show how David and Judah were chosen by God. That divine selection is traced back to patriarchal and even prepatriarchal times.

### A. Patriarchal genealogies (chap. 1)

Careful comparison of this passage with the genealogical lists in Genesis reveals little difference in substance. The author either cited Genesis directly (though not always in the form of the Heb. text) or used sources which in turn

depended on Genesis. His purposes, however, precluded a mere copying of the Genesis texts. Rather he used those texts selectively to include nations, tribes, and individuals that were relevant to his overall design.

#### 1. GENEALOGY OF ADAM (1:1-4)

**1:1-4.** The names here, based on Genesis 5:3-32, trace the ancestry of the human race from the first man, **Adam**, through **Noah** and his three **sons.** This enabled the chronicler not only to root the Chosen People in Israel and the Davidic line but also to show how they derived from only one of the three sons of Noah, that one through whom redemptive blessing would come, namely, **Shem** (cf. Gen. 9:26-27).

#### 2. GENEALOGY OF JAPHETH (1:5-7)

**1:5-7.** In the reverse order in which the names of Noah's sons are usually given, **Japheth** is mentioned here first. For the identification of these names and the others as ethnic or geographic names, see the comments on Genesis 10:2-4.

#### 3. GENEALOGY OF HAM (1:8-16)

**1:8-16.** This list is almost identical to Genesis 10:6-8, 13-18. There is even an abbreviated narrative concerning **Nimrod** (1 Chron. 1:10; cf. Gen. 10:8-12), a fact that points decidedly to the view that the chronicler had the Genesis genealogies before him.

#### 4. GENEALOGY OF SHEM (1:17-27)

**1:17-23.** The tracing of the line of **Shem** follows that of Japheth's and Ham's lines because it is most important theologically. The Shemites (i.e., Semites) are the Noahic line from which Abraham, Israel, and hence David originated. The basis for this first part of the list is Genesis 10:22-29.

**1:24-27.** This genealogy of Shem has the added feature of a brief summation of names in which the first five names (**Shem** through **Peleg**), which are central to the line of descent, are repeated (cf. vv. 17-19). In addition five other names are given (**Reu** through **Abram**; cf. Gen. 11:18-26). Striking by omission are the names of Abram's brothers, Nahor and Haran (which are found in Gen. 11:26). (The **Nahor** in 1 Chron. 1:26 is Abraham's grandfather, not his brother.)

Abraham's brothers were left out by the chronicler because they were not in the line from Adam to David.

### 5. GENEALOGY OF ABRAHAM (1:28-34)

**1:28-31.** This section is arranged around the descendants **of Abraham** according to their mothers. First, the descent of **Ishmael,** son of Hagar, appears (cf. Gen. 25:12-16). As founder of the various Ishmaelite and, ultimately, Arabic tribes he was important to the chronicler's own historical situation (cf. 1 Chron. 27:30; 2 Chron. 17:11; 21:16; 22:1; 26:7; also cf. Neh. 2:19; 4:7; 6:1).

**1:32-33.** This second section lists the offspring of **Keturah, Abraham's concubine,** all of whom are listed in Genesis 25:2-4. Of interest is the chronicler's omission of the descendants of **Dedan** (who *are* given in Gen. 25:3b), probably because of the geographic distance of the "Dedanites" from Judah (cf. Jer. 25:23).

**1:34.** This third section merely introduces Abraham's line through Sarah, his wife, and **Isaac,** son of Sarah. It mentions Isaac's two **sons** . . . **Esau and Israel** (Jacob), whose own genealogies then follow in verses 35-54 (Esau's line) and chapters 2–7 (Jacob's line).

### 6. GENEALOGY OF ESAU (1:35-54)

**1:35-42.** The descendants of Esau, who settled in the land of Edom, east and south of the Dead Sea (cf. Gen. 36:8), are listed in two divisions here, as they are in Genesis. First are **the sons of Esau** (1 Chron. 1:35-37) and then "the kings who reigned in Edom" (vv. 43-54). Some Bible versions read as if **Timna** (v. 36) was a son of **Eliphaz.** But in Hebrew the name Timna is feminine, and in Genesis 36:12 she is said to be a concubine of Eliphaz (son of Esau), and mother of **Amalek.** Having mentioned Timna, the chronicler then identified her as a native "Seirite" (1 Chron. 1:38-39; she was a daughter of **Seir**), a pre-Edomite. Then the chronicler spoke of her family connections (vv. 38-42). This corresponds to the order in Genesis 36:20-29 except that in most Hebrew manuscripts there are minor spelling variations in four names (cf. NIV marg. for the names **Alvan,** 1 Chron. 1:40, **Hemdan,** v. 41, **Akan,** v. 42, and **Dishan,** v. 42). Moreover, the wives of Esau are mentioned in Genesis 36 but are not listed in 1 Chronicles 1.

Why this was done is not known.

**1:43-54.** The lists of Edomite **kings,** apart from minor spelling differences are identical here with Genesis 36:31-43. These Edomite kings are not otherwise known but the relationship of the Edomites to Israel and Judah was so close and of such long duration that the chronicler's interest in them is not surprising.

## B. Genealogy of Judah (chap. 2)

### 1. SONS OF JUDAH (2:1-4)

**2:1-2.** At last the author arrived at the people who were the focus of interest in his theological history. David and the Davidic dynasty were Judeans so it is fitting that Judah's genealogy is traced first (2:3–4:23) after listing Israel's 12 **sons** (2:1-2).

**2:3-4.** The details of the sordid story (Gen. 38) of Judah's sons, two of whom (**Er and Onan**) were slain by the Lord and the third (**Shelah**) withheld from **Tamar,** are not discussed here. The chronicler wanted to introduce the two sons of **Judah** (**Perez and Zerah**) in order to follow the line through Perez to the Davidic family.

### 2. GENEALOGIES OF PEREZ AND ZERAH (2:5-8)

**2:5-8.** These verses mention only selective and representative descendants (**sons** often means descendants of later generations) of **Perez** and **Zerah** as is clear from the fact that **Achar** (or Achan) is here noted as **the son of Carmi** (v. 7) and Carmi's father is not mentioned at all. Perhaps **Zimri** (v. 6) is a variant spelling of Zabdi because in the story of Achan's sin (Josh. 7) Achan was a son of Carmi, who was a son of Zabdi (Josh. 7:1, marg.), son of Zerah. Even so, the period from Zerah (born ca. 1877 B.C.) to Achan (an adult in 1406, Josh. 7) was almost 500 years, much too long for four generations. The chronicler's reference to Zerah, then, is primarily to introduce **Ethan, Heman, Calcol, and Darda** (Dara in most Heb. mss.; cf. marg.), all actually the sons of Mahol, whose ancestor was Zerah (cf. comments on 1 Kings 4:31), and celebrated sages to whom Solomon was compared (1 Kings 4:31; Ps. 89, title).

### 3. GENEALOGY OF HEZRON (2:9-41)

**2:9-20.** The chosen line now continues through **Hezron,** son of Perez, Judah's son. In line with Ruth 4:18-21, the descent goes on to **David** (1 Chron. 2:9-15; see the chart "David's Ancestry from Abraham" near 1 Sam. 16:1-13). The lineage also includes David's immediate family and half sisters (1 Chron. 2:16-17; see the chart "David's Family" near 2 Sam. 3:2-5). **Caleb,** another son of Hezron, was not the Caleb who was Joshua's associate. (In 1 Chron. 2:9 the Heb. has "Kelubai"; cf. marg., a variant spelling of **Caleb;** cf. v. 42.) His lineage follows in verses 18-20 and is expanded later in verses 42-55.

**2:21-24. Segub,** another son of **Hezron,** was born of **the daughter of Makir,** a son of Manasseh (Gen. 50:23) and **father of Gilead** (Num. 26:29). The name of Gilead was given to the upper Transjordan district. The incident of the taking of **60** Gilead **towns** by **Geshur and Aram** (areas northeast of Gilead) is otherwise unknown in the Old Testament. Another son, born posthumously to **Hezron** by his wife **Abijah,** was **Ashhur.**

**2:25-41.** The oldest son of **Hezron, Jerahmeel** (cf. v. 9), is mentioned last. His family descent appears only here, though Jerahmeelites were viewed as a clan closely related to Judah in David's time (1 Sam. 27:10).

4. GENEALOGY OF CALEB (2:42-55)

**2:42-55.** The line of **Caleb,** Hezron's third son (cf. v. 9), introduced briefly in verses 18-20, is expanded here. Many of these names appear elsewhere as place-names (e.g., **Ziph,** Josh. 15:24; **Mareshah,** Josh. 15:44; **Hebron,** Josh. 15:54; **Tappuah,** Josh. 15:34; **Rekem,** Josh. 18:27; **Shema,** Josh. 15:26; etc.). This does not prove a connection, but since most of these places lay in Judah they were probably founded by the various Calebites listed here.

Of particular interest are the references to **Bethlehem** (1 Chron. 2:51, 54), birthplace of both David and Jesus. The town was founded by or named after the great-grandson of Caleb through Caleb's wife **Ephrathah** (v. 50, spelled Ephrath in v. 19). The combination of Bethlehem and Ephrath(ah) appears also in the story of Rachel's death in childbirth (Gen. 35:19), where it is used anachronistically; in Ruth 4:11 in reference to blessing on Ruth; and in Micah 5:2 with respect to the birth of the Messiah.

## C. Genealogy of David (chap. 3)

Almost like an interruption in the grand sweep of the genealogy of Judah, the line of David appears. This is in order to make clear that he succeeded in the Perez-Hezron line and that his own descent could be traced to the very end of Judah's history (from the chronicler's historical vantage point).

1. SONS OF DAVID (3:1-9)

**3:1-9.** Though Solomon was the son in the promised line of succession from David (22:9-10), for completeness David's other sons were included (3:1-9). This list should be compared to 2 Samuel 3:2-5, where one notes correspondence except in the name of the **second** son by Abigail (see the chart "David's Family" near 2 Sam. 3:2-5). The chronicler calls him **Daniel,** while he is Kileab in 2 Samuel 3:3. Though he may have had two names it is obvious that the chronicler is not, here at least, slavishly following 2 Samuel. The names of the **six** sons born in **Hebron** (1 Chron. 3:1-4a) are followed by those of David's **nine** sons born **in Jerusalem** (vv. 4b-8; cf. the corresponding list in 2 Sam. 5:14-16). Four of these were sons by **Bathsheba** (the Heb. has Bathshua, a variant spelling; cf. NIV marg.). This is the only place she is mentioned in Chronicles. (For comments on this see the *Introduction*.) Also **Eliphelet** (the one in 1 Chron. 3:6) and **Nogah** (v. 7) are not included in 2 Samuel but are mentioned again in 1 Chronicles 14:4-7 (see comments there). Perhaps the occurrence of two Eliphelets (3:6, 8) means that one died and another, born later, took his name. Perhaps Nogah also had died and 2 Samuel preserves only the names of surviving sons.

2. DESCENDANTS OF SOLOMON (3:10-24)

**3:10-24.** This list of **Solomon's** descendants is in effect a list of Judah's kings from Solomon through **Zedekiah** (vv. 10-16) and their exilic and postexilic continuation (vv. 17-24). Athaliah, the queen who ruled between **Ahaziah** and **Joash,** is not mentioned (v. 11). That is because she was only a political usurper and was not in the true dynastic succession (cf. 2 Kings 11). Of the sons of **Josiah, Johanan** (1 Chron. 3:15) is otherwise unknown. He cannot be Jehoahaz (2 Kings 23:31) because Jehoahaz was younger than **Jehoiakim** (cf. 2 Kings 23:36). This means that **Shallum** (1 Chron. 3:15) is identical to Jehoahaz who, though the next-to-youngest son of Josiah, preceded his brothers on the throne (cf. Jer. 22:11-12).

The remainder of the succession followed by the chronicler is Jeconiah (Heb.; cf. NIV marg. of 1 Chron. 3:16; also known as **Jehoiachin**; cf. v. 17 and 2 Kings 24:8, and Coniah, Jer. 22:24, marg.). Then came **Pedaiah** (1 Chron. 3:18), **Zerubbabel** (v. 19), **Hananiah** (v. 19), **Shecaniah** (v. 21), **Shemaiah** (v. 22), **Elioenai** (v. 23), and **Hodaviah** (v. 24).

Three difficulties here must be addressed. First, Zerubbabel (v. 19) is elsewhere called the son of **Shealtiel,** not the son of Pedaiah (Ezra 3:2, 8; 5:2; Neh. 12:1; Hag. 1:12, 14; 2:2, 23; Matt. 1:12; Luke 3:27). Since Shealtiel and Pedaiah were brothers (1 Chron. 3:17-18) the best solution seems to be that Shealtiel died early on and his role of dynastic succession was assumed by his younger brother Pedaiah. The second problem concerns Luke's account of the genealogy in which he identifies Shealtiel as the son of Neri, whose descent is not from Solomon but from David's son Nathan (Luke 3:27-31). The answer may lie in the possibility that since Jeconiah had no male heir to sit on the throne (cf. Jer. 22:30), a daughter of Jeconiah married Neri, son of Melki (Luke 3:27-28; not the Melki of Luke 3:24), of the line of Nathan. Legally Shealtiel, as grandson of Jeconiah, would continue the Davidic dynasty through Solomon, a viewpoint espoused by Matthew (Matt. 1:6-12).

The third conflict appears in Zerubbabel's line. The chronicler lists Zerubbabel's seven sons and one daughter (1 Chron. 3:19b-20). But none of them is mentioned in the genealogies of either Matthew or Luke. Matthew, who traces Jesus' descent from David through Solomon, wrote that the son of Zerubbabel was Abiud (Matt. 1:13). Luke, viewing it through Nathan, said Rhesa was that son (Luke 3:27). It is entirely possible, of course, that the Shealtiel and Zerubbabel of Luke are not the same as those of 1 Chronicles and that Luke preserves a genealogy of Mary straight from David through Nathan, a line of succession that has no other connection with the chronicler's genealogy (cf. comments on Luke

3:27). This would preclude the suggested solution to the second problem previously mentioned (and would, in fact, eliminate the problem altogether). This still leaves the variance between 1 Chronicles 3:19b-20 and Matthew 1:13. One may conjecture that Abiud is another name for one of the seven sons of Zerubbabel listed in Chronicles or that his name is missing from that list to begin with. That such a thing is possible may be seen in 1 Chronicles 3:22 where the historian wrote that **Shemaiah** had **six** sons but listed only five names.

### D. Genealogy of Judah (4:1-23)

Having traced the Davidic line specifically and in detail (chap. 3), the chronicler returned to that of Judah generally. His intent here was: (a) to provide genealogical and geographical information and (b) to show the preeminence of the role of the Davidic tribe of Judah among the tribes by dealing with Judah first and by appealing to the antiquity of her residence in her allotted area (4:22b).

**4:1-7.** Verse 1 is a heading for the whole list, a matter that is clear from observing that the five named **descendants of Judah** are, in fact, sequential generations (cf. chap. 2). **Reaiah** (4:2) was no doubt identical to Haroeh (2:52) and was founder of **the Zorathites,** better known as the family from which Samson came (Jud. 13:2). The Hurites (**descendants of Hur,** 1 Chron. 4:3-4; cf. 2:19-20, 50-51) were distinguished as the family of the Bethlehemites. The Ashhurites (4:5-7) were the clan which produced **Tekoa,** the village of a wise woman (2 Sam. 14:2) and of Amos the prophet (Amos 1:1).

**4:8-15.** **Jabez** (vv. 8-10; cf. 2:55), whose ancestral roots are not delineated, prayed for God's blessing and received it. The village named after him was celebrated as the home of scribes. The Recahites (**men of Recah,** 4:11-12) are not otherwise identified. The Kenazites (vv. 13-15), however, were the prominent clan from which came both **Caleb,** Joshua's colleague, and his son-in-law, **Othniel,** Israel's first judge. Caleb was called a Kenizzite in the Conquest story (Josh. 14:6) and Othniel was called the "son of **Kenaz,** Caleb's younger brother" (Jud. 1:13), obviously a different **Kenaz** from the founder of the clan and to be distinguished also from Caleb's grandson of that name (1 Chron. 4:15).

**4:16-20.** The descendants of **Jehallelel** (v. 16) of **Ezrah** (vv. 17-18), of Hodiah (v. 19), and of **Shimon** (v. 20) are mentioned in the Bible only here. Verse 18 contains the interesting information that **Mered,** a son of Ezrah (v. 17) had married a **daughter** of an Egyptian Pharaoh. This would date the origins of this clan well before Moses' time, when Israel was still in favor with Egypt (cf. Ex. 1:8).

**4:21-23.** The genealogy of Judah closes with a brief summation of the family **of Shelah** (vv. 21-23), the youngest son **of Judah** by Bathshua (2:3). Shelah had been promised as husband to Tamar (cf. Gen. 38:5, 11, 14). His descendants were busy in **linen** manufacture (1 Chron. 4:21) and ceramics (v. 23) and also **ruled** over **Moab** in **ancient times.**

## E. Genealogy of Simeon (4:24-43)

**4:24.** **Simeon** is listed after Judah because it received no tribal allotment of its own and was eventually assimilated into Judah (cf. Josh. 19:1-9). The list of sons in 1 Chronicles 4:24 differs somewhat from the list in Genesis 46:10 where there are six names (Ohad being added) and there are variations in spelling. The names in Exodus 6:15 agree perfectly with those in Genesis 46:10. The list in Numbers 26:12-13, on the other hand, is almost identical to the chronicler's rendition, with only Jakin for **Jarib** as the third son being different.

**4:25-43.** The remainder of Simeon's genealogy has no Old Testament parallels. Of interest is the note that the Simeonites did not increase much in population (v. 27) but were limited to certain restricted areas of **Judah,** primarily in the south-central Negev (vv. 28-33). Eventually they prospered, however, particularly by means of the **rich** pasturelands they had appropriated from the original Hamitic settlers (vv. 39-40). If **Gedor** (v. 39) should be read Gerar (Gerara in the LXX) this locates them in the west part of the upper Negev, not far from modern Gaza. This would explain why the **Hamites** (v. 40), people of Egypt, were there, for Egypt was not many miles away. The chronicler indicates that a violent removal of the Hamites occurred **in the** time **of Hezekiah** (715–686 B.C.) and involved the **Meunites** as well (v. 41). These people are mentioned again in reference to

Uzziah's exploits in the Negev (2 Chron. 26:7) but cannot be further identified.

In Hezekiah's day **500 . . . Simeonites** spread to the east, to **the hill country of Seir** (the same as Edom), where they displaced a remnant of the **Amalekites** who had **lived there,** possibly from the time of David (1 Chron. 4:42-43; cf. 1 Sam. 30:16-20).

## F. Genealogies of the Transjordan tribes (chap. 5)

The rationale for the order in which the remaining tribal genealogies appear is somewhat elusive but possibly Reuben is introduced next because that tribe was named after the eldest son of Israel. Gad (vv. 11-22) and the eastern half of Manasseh (vv. 23-26) are listed after Reuben because all were located east of the Jordan River.

### 1. REUBEN (5:1-10)

**5:1-2.** The lineage of **Reuben** is introduced by an explanation of that tribe's fall from divine favor and replacement by **Judah.** As Jacob's **firstborn,** Reuben would ordinarily expect to be the son through whom the leadership and covenant blessing would be transmitted. But Reuben committed adultery with his father's concubine Bilhah (Gen. 35:22), and so forfeited his privileges. The right of primogeniture then fell to **Joseph** (i.e., Joseph's **sons,** Ephraim and Manasseh, Gen. 48:15-22), **though** through Judah came **a** ruler (David), and through him *the* Ruler, Jesus Christ (cf. comments on Gen. 49:8-12).

**5:3-10.** The genealogy of **Reuben** includes his four **sons** (cf. Num. 26:5-11) and selected generations thereafter. From a certain **Joel** (1 Chron. 5:4) eventually came **Beerah** (v. 6) **whom Tiglath-Pileser** III (745–727 B.C.) **took** captive when he conquered Samaria. By that time **the Reubenites** occupied all the Transjordan, including not only the area from the Arnon River (**Aroer** was on that river) **to Nebo** in the north but also **Gilead** (east of the Jordan River) and on north and northeast **to the Euphrates River.** On the **war** with **the Hagrites** see comments on verses 18-22.

### 2. GAD (5:11-17)

**5:11-17. The Gadites** settled in **Bashan,** south and east of the Sea of

Kinnereth and north of the Yarmuk River. There was no clearly defined border between **Gilead** and **Bashan** (v. 16) so no doubt the Eastern tribes mingled rather freely. The descendants of Gad listed here appear nowhere else, the names evidently having been compiled from documents of the period of **Jeroboam II of Israel** (793–753 B.C.) and **Jotham . . . of Judah** (750–735 B.C.).

3. EXPLOITS OF THE EASTERN TRIBES (5:18-22)

**5:18-22.** The chronicler interrupted the genealogies to comment on military matters common to the Eastern tribes. He recounted their **war** with **the Hagrites** (cf. v. 10) and their allies. The Transjordanian tribes, with their **44,760** soldiers, achieved a signal triumph by God's help in answer to **their prayers.** The number of captured **livestock** was huge (v. 21), revealing that that land area was fertile for **sheep** grazing. This occurred in the days of Saul (v. 10), perhaps in connection with Saul's Ammonite wars (cf. 1 Sam. 11:1-11). **The Hagrites,** known now from Assyrian inscriptions, were replaced by the victorious Israelites **until the Exile** (1 Chron. 5:22), perhaps the Assyrian Captivity of some Israelites led by Tiglath-Pileser III in 734 B.C. (not to be confused with the final Assyrian Captivity of Israel in 722 B.C.).

4. THE HALF-TRIBE OF MANASSEH (5:23-26)

**5:23-26.** The **half-tribe** mentioned here had been allocated a territory east of the Jordan, from Gad in the south to **Mount Hermon** in the north (cf. Num. 32:39-42; Deut. 3:12-17; Josh. 13:29-31). Though their leaders were celebrated for military exploits, they led the people into idolatry. As a result they were deported along with **the Reubenites** and **Gadites,** by **Pul (Tiglath-Pileser** III) of Assyria. For the places where they were sent, see comments on 2 Kings 17:6. The site of **Hara,** not mentioned in 2 Kings, has not yet been identified.

### G. Genealogy of Levi (chap. 6)

1. DESCENDANTS OF LEVI (6:1-15)

**6:1-3a.** Levi's genealogy begins by referring to the line of which **Moses** and **Aaron** were a part because of their obvious importance. After the reference to the three **sons of Levi,** the chronicler concentrated on **Kohath** and his off-

spring through **Amram.** The length of time between Levi's death and Moses' birth (ca. 1800–1526 B.C.) requires that the sequence (Levi—Kohath—Amram—Moses) represents a much longer list of names (see comments on Num. 26:58-59). The names here probably refer to tribe, clan, family, and individual respectively (cf. Josh. 7:16-18). Moses is mentioned no further here because the purpose of this list is to trace the high priestly line.

**6:3b-15. Aaron** was the first high priest (Ex. 28:1) and his descendants followed after in their respective generations. The list here agrees with that in Ezra 7:1-5 except for minor spelling variations and Ezra's omission of six names, from **Meraioth** to **Azariah** (1 Chron. 6:7-10). Also the chronicler indicated that **Jehozadak** was the son of **Seraiah** who was captured by Nebuchadnezzar (vv. 14-15). Ezra identified *himself* as a son of Seraiah, however (Ezra 7:1). Since Ezra could not have been born much before 500 B.C. and the Babylonian Captivity was in 586 B.C., he must have meant that he was not the son of Seraiah in the strict sense but a more distant descendant. The additions and omissions in these parallel lists should caution Bible students not to assume that genealogical lists are always complete. The compilers always had their special reasons for including some names and not others. The chronicler's theological view of Israel reveals itself in his comment that the last of the Aaronic priests **was deported when the LORD sent Judah and Jerusalem into exile by the hand of Nebuchadnezzar** (1 Chron. 6:15; cf. the Exile of the Northern Kingdom, 5:22, 26).

2. OTHER DESCENDANTS OF LEVI (6:16-30)

**6:16-21.** The historian next recapitulated the tribal descent of Levi by listing **the sons** and grandsons **of Levi** (vv. 16-19) and their subsequent generations of prominent persons (vv. 20-30). He began with **Gershon** whose line he traced for seven generations (vv. 20-21). (The Heb. here has Gershom, a variant spelling; cf. marg., though the name is usually Gershon; cf. Ex. 6:16.)

**6:22-30.** Next is **Kohath,** Levi's son who was not only an ancestor of Aaron (vv. 2-3) but also an ancestor of the prophet-priest **Samuel.** Kohath's son

Amminadab (v. 22) is otherwise known as Izhar (cf. vv. 2, 18, 38). Whereas Aaron, then, was a Kohathite and founder of the priestly line, Samuel, though a Kohathite, could not function as a high priest. Samuel could (and did), however, officiate at the tabernacle and performed other ministries which evidently included sacrifice (Num. 3:27-32; cf. 1 Sam. 1:21; 2:11; 9:11-14; etc.). Finally, **the descendants of Merari,** Levi's third **son,** are noted, especially the descent through **Mahli** (1 Chron. 6:29-30).

### 3. LEVITICAL MUSICIANS (6:31-48)

**6:31-38.** This section contains the names of **the tabernacle** musicians whom **David** appointed from the three Levitical families (vv. 31-32). The Kohathite list (vv. 33-38) begins with **Heman** (not the Heman in 2:6), **son of Joel** and grandson **of Samuel** (6:33). Samuel's ancestry is then retraced (cf. vv. 27-28; and cf. 1 Sam. 1:1, where the same names appear back to **Zuph**; cf. 1 Chron. 6:35, with slight spelling variations: Elihu for **Eliel,** and Tohu [called Nahath in v. 26] for **Toah**). Though this version of the Kohathite lineage agrees essentially with that in verses 22-28, the differences are significant enough to suggest that the chronicler may have used two different sources in his own compilations. Two people (Assir and **Elkanah,** vv. 22-23) between **Korah** and **Ebiasaph** are not listed in verse 37. And spelling variations (or different individuals) occur in six instances; Eliel (v. 34) for Eliab (v. 27), Toah (v. 34) for Nahath (v. 26), **Zuph** (v. 35) for Zophai (v. 26), **Joel** (v. 36) for Shaul (v. 24), **Azariah** (v. 36) for Uzziah (v. 24), and **Zephaniah** (v. 36) for Uriel (v. 24). Interestingly four Elkanahs are in this genealogy (vv. 23, 25 [the same as the one in v. 36], 34-35).

**6:39-43.** The Gershonite order begins with **Asaph,** famous as a singer and psalmist (cf. titles of Pss. 50; 73–83). The remainder of the list contains many names not found in the preceding section (1 Chron. 6:20-21).

**6:44-48.** The Merarite singers begin with **Ethan** (called Jeduthun in 9:16) and are traced back to **Merari** through **Mushi** (6:47). This list is not a repetition of the earlier list (vv. 29-30) because the names simply do not match. Mahli, son of Merari (v. 29), is not the same as **Mahli,**

son of Mushi (v. 47). Merari had two sons, Mahli and Mushi (v. 19); Mahli's succession appears in verses 29-30 and Mushi's in verses 47-48. The purpose of this entire section (vv. 31-47) is to justify the ministry of David's chief musicians— Heman, Asaph, and Ethan—by describing their pure Levitical lineage.

### 4. AARONIC PRIESTS (6:49-53)

**6:49-53.** In distinction from the ministry of music carried out by the Levitical orders (vv. 31-48) was that of the sacrifices for **atonement** carried out by **the descendants of Aaron.** To emphasize the propriety of David's Zadokite priesthood, the chronicler again (cf. vv. 3-8) traced the Aaronic lineage from **Aaron** to **Ahimaaz,** son of **Zadok.**

### 5. SETTLEMENTS OF THE LEVITES (6:54-81)

**6:54-81.** The places where the Levites settled are described by **clans** with Kohath again appearing first. (See the chart "Levite Towns Listed in Joshua 21 and 1 Chronicles 6.") Some of the towns were for Kohathites who were priests (vv. 57-60) and others were for Kohathites in nonpriestly roles (vv. 61, 64-70). One of the towns in **Benjamin** was **Anathoth** (v. 60). The Prophet Jeremiah was a son of a priest from Anathoth and hence must have been a Kohathite (Jer. 1:1).

**The Gershonites** settled in **13 towns** in **Issachar, Asher, Naphtali,** and eastern **Manasseh** (1 Chron. 6:62). These towns are named in verses 71-76 and include the important city **Kedesh** of **Naphtali** (v. 76), as well as a **Kedesh** in the **Issachar** tribe (v. 72).

To **the Merarites** fell cities in **Zebulun . . . Reuben,** and **Gad** (vv. 77-81). In all, 48 cities were designed for the use of Levi (cf. Josh. 21:41) since that tribe had been assigned no tribal allotment (cf. Num. 35:1-8).

## H. Genealogies of six Northern tribes (chap. 7)

### 1. ISSACHAR (7:1-5)

**7:1-5.** The descent of this tribe is not traced fully. In agreement with Genesis 46:13 and Numbers 26:23-25 there were four **sons of Issachar,** but the chronicler went on to feature the line **of Tola.** For some reason he also gave population figures: **22,600** military **men in** David's era

# Levite Towns Listed in Joshua 21 and 1 Chronicles 6

| *Towns for Kohathites Who Were Priests* | *Joshua 21:9-42* | *1 Chronicles 6:54-81* |
|---|---|---|
| In Judah and Simeon | 1. Hebron | 1. Hebron |
| | 2. Libnah | 2. Libnah |
| | 3. Jattir | 3. Jattir |
| | 4. Eshtemoa | 4. Eshtemoa |
| | 5. *Holon** | 5. *Hilen** |
| | 6. Debir | 6. Debir |
| | 7. *Ain** | 7. *Ashan** |
| | 8. Juttah | (Juttah)† |
| | 9. Beth Shemesh | 8. Beth Shemesh |
| In Benjamin | 10. Gibeon | (Gibeon)† |
| | 11. Geba | 9. Geba |
| | 12. Anathoth | 10. *Alemeth** |
| | 13. *Almon** | 11. Anathoth |
| *Towns for Kohathites Who Were Not Priests* | | |
| In Ephraim | 14. Shechem | 12. Shechem |
| | 15. Gezer | 13. Gezer |
| | 16. *Kibzaim‡* | 14. *Jokmeam‡* |
| | 17. Beth Horon | 15. Beth Horon |
| In Dan | 18. Eltekeh | — |
| | 19. Gibbethon | — |
| | 20. Aijalon | 16. Aijalon |
| | 21. Gath Rimmon | 17. Gath Rimmon |
| In western Manasseh | 22. *Taanach‡* | 18. *Aner‡* |
| | 23. *Gath Rimmon‡* | 19. *Bileam‡* |
| *Towns for Gershonites* | | |
| In eastern Manasseh | 24. Golan | 20. Golan |
| | 25. *Be Eshtarah** | 21. *Ashtaroth** |
| In Issachar | 26. *Kishion‡* | 22. *Kedesh‡* |
| | 27. Daberath | 23. Daberath |
| | 28. *Jarmuth** | 24. *Ramoth** |
| | 29. *En Gannim** | 25. *Anem** |
| In Asher | 30. *Mishal** | 26. *Mashal** |
| | 31. Abdon | 27. Abdon |
| | 32. *Helkath** | 28. *Hukok** |
| | 33. Rehob | 29. Rehob |
| In Naphtali | 34. Kedesh | 30. Kedesh |
| | 35. *Hammoth Dor** | 31. *Hammon** |
| | 36. *Kartan** | 32. *Kiriathaim** |
| *Towns for Merarites* | | |
| In Zebulun | 37. Jokneam | (Jokneam)† |
| | 38. Kartah | (Kartah)† |
| | 39. *Dimnah** | 33. *Rimmono** |
| | 40. *Nahalal‡* | 34. *Tabor‡* |
| In Reuben | 41. Bezer | 35. Bezer |
| | 42. *Jahaz** | 36. *Jahzah** |
| | 43. Kedemoth | 37. Kedemoth |
| | 44. Mephaath | 38. Mephaath |
| In Gad | 45. Ramoth | 39. Ramoth |
| | 46. Mahanaim | 40. Mahanaim |
| | 47. Heshbon | 41. Heshbon |
| | 48. Jazer | 42. Jazer |

\* The two cities in each of these 12 pairs have only minor spelling variations.
† These four cities are not included in the Hebrew manuscripts of 1 Chronicles (see NIV margs.).
   Perhaps these cities, though assigned by Joshua, were not conquered by the Israelites.
‡ The two cities in each of these five pairs differ in name. The cities originally assigned by Joshua (ca. 1399 B.C.) may
   have changed names by the chronicler's time (ca. 400 B.C., after the exiles' return), almost 1000 years later. Or five
   of the cities assigned may have never been conquered by the Israelites.

(1 Chron. 7:2; cf. 2 Sam. 24:1-9) who descended from Tola, **36,000** who came from **Uzzi** (1 Chron. 7:4), and a total of **87,000** (v. 5), which included 28,400 others from unnamed families.

## 2. BENJAMIN (7:6-12)

**7:6-12.** This genealogy is greatly expanded in chapter 8 as a climax to the pre-Davidic history, but appears here in a succinct form characteristic of the other Northern tribes. Though Genesis 46:21 lists 10 **sons of Benjamin,** Numbers 26:38-41 names 5 and the chronicler names **3** (1 Chron. 7:6-7) and 5 (8:1-2). (See comments on 8:1-5 for an explanation that Benjamin's 10 "sons" [Gen. 46:21] probably included some grandsons.) The first 2, **Bela** and **Beker,** are mentioned in Genesis 46:21, but **Jediael** is mentioned nowhere else unless he was the same as Ashbel (Gen. 46:21; Num. 26:38; 1 Chron. 8:1). The truncated nature of this list in 1 Chronicles 7:6-12 is also clear in that Bela here had **5** sons whereas in 8:3-5 he had 9. On the other hand Beker had 9 sons (7:8) but is not mentioned at all in chapter 8. Similarly, Jediael's son **Bilhan** (7:10) does not appear in chapter 8. The reason Bela's descent was traced in chapter 8 to the exclusion of the others is clear, of course: Saul was in his succession (8:33).

The **Shuppites and Huppites** descended from **Ir** (7:12), a son of Bela (v. 7, assuming Ir = Iri). The **Hushites** descended from **Aher,** son of Benjamin (if Aher = Ahiram = Aharah, Num. 26:38; 1 Chron. 8:1, and if Ahiram/Aharah is a son of Benjamin).

The census figures were **22,034** for **the sons of Bela** (7:7), **20,200** for **the sons of Beker** (v. 9), and **17,200** for **the sons of Jediael** (v. 11). This grand total of 59,434 fighting men is thought by many scholars to be far too many for David's time since the tribe of Benjamin had been decimated by civil war and reduced to 600 men in the time of the Judges (Jud. 20:44-48). However, since that event was early in the era of the Judges, probably 400 years before David's census (cf. 1 Chron. 21:1-7), the 600 families could easily have multiplied to that extent.

## 3. NAPHTALI (7:13)

**7:13.** The names of the four **sons of Naphtali** listed here correspond with those in Genesis 46:24 and Numbers 26:48-49 (except that **Jahziel** in 1 Chron. 7:13 is spelled Jahzeel in Num. 26:48).

## 4. MANASSEH (7:14-19)

**7:14-15a.** The genealogy **of Manasseh** does not appear in Genesis since Manasseh was at that time part of Joseph. Manasseh and **his Aramean concubine** had a son **Makir** (cf v. 17b; Num. 26:29; Josh. 17:1), who was Gilead's **father** (cf. Num 26:29; 36:1). **Asriel,** descended from Manasseh, is not mentioned in Numbers 26:29. The dual reference to **Maacah** (1 Chron. 7:15-16) is best explained by the coincidence that this was the name of Makir's sister as well as his **wife.**

**7:15b-19.** A second prominent **descendant** of Manasseh through Makir was **Zelophehad,** who was distinguished because he had no sons (cf. Num. 36:1-9; his five **daughters** are named in Josh. 17:3). Though this genealogy centers in Makir and his offspring (inhabitants of the Manasseh territory in the Transjordan), the Manasseh elements west of the Jordan were represented by **Hammoleketh,** Makir's **sister,** the four **sons of Shemida** (1 Chron. 7:18-19); Zelophehad and his daughters; and perhaps Asriel (v. 14; cf. Josh. 17:2-6).

## 5. EPHRAIM (7:20-29)

**7:20-24.** The descent **of Ephraim,** second son of Joseph, culminates here in Joshua (v. 27), Moses' illustrious successor. Ephraim's first son, **Shuthelah,** produced a line which several generations later included a second **Shuthelah** (vv. 20-21). Two other sons of Ephraim, **Ezer and Elead,** were slain by the early (pre-1200 B.C.) Philistines of Gath, a tragedy that caused **their father** much sorrow (vv. 21-22). Since **Ephraim** himself was born in Egypt before the famine (cf. Gen. 41:50-52), this episode may have occurred in Egypt (in which case the **men of Gath** went down to Egypt to kill Ephraim's sons). Or, more likely, some Israelites, though living in Egypt, continued to have access to Canaan, even maintaining agricultural pursuits there. In support of this is the statement that Ephraim had a **daughter . . . Sheerah,** who founded two settlements in Canaan, **Beth Horon** and **Uzzen Sheerah.** Again, this could only have been in the period of Egyptian sojourn.

**7:25-29.** Through Ephraim's son **Rephah** eventually came **Joshua**. The fact that eight generations lay between Ephraim and Joshua would also argue for the Egyptian sojourn setting for the previous two incidents concerning Ephraim's sons and daughter (vv. 21-24). The post-Conquest **settlements** of Ephraim follow in verses 28-29. The territory is roughly from **Bethel** on northward to the Valley of Jezreel and from the Jordan River to the Mediterranean Sea.

### 6. ASHER (7:30-40)

**7:30-40.** The first part of this list is paralleled by Genesis 46:17 and Numbers 26:44-46, but the names from **Birzaith** (1 Chron. 7:31) through **Rizia** (v. 39) appear only here. The **men** of war (**26,000**, v. 40) were descendants from **Asher** (v. 30). (Helem in v. 35 may be the same person as **Hotham** in v. 32.)

## I. Genealogy of Benjamin (chap. 8)

**8:1-5. Benjamin** and his descendants were briefly introduced earlier (7:6-12) but now a full genealogy is given. Its purpose was obviously to trace the lineage of Saul and his immediate family. As noted, not all the names of Benjamin's **sons** listed here are the same as those in 7:6 (see comments there). There are five here, of whom only two, **Bela** and **Ashbel** (perhaps the same as Jediael) are mentioned in 7:6. On the other hand Genesis 46:21 lists Bela, Beker, and Ashbel, and also lists as sons (Gera, Naaman, and Ard) those whom the chronicler viewed as Benjamin's grandsons. (Ard of Gen. 46:21 is possibly the same as Addar of 1 Chron. 8:3; cf. Num. 26:40.) Similarly Numbers 26:38-39 counts Shupham and Hupham as Benjamin's sons while the chronicler (1 Chron. 8:5) calls them grandsons (**Shephuphan** is a variant spelling of Shupham and **Huram** a variation of Hupham). However, Numbers agrees with the chronicler that Ard and Naaman were grandsons of Benjamin (Num. 26:40). What all this suggests is that "son" frequently means grandson or even a more remote descendant and that not every list is complete. Since 1 Chronicles 8 is longer and more comprehensive than the other lists (Gen. 46:21; Num. 26:38-40), one may assume that Benjamin had five sons (1 Chron.

8:1-2) and that the other lists were editorially selective.

**8:6-28. Ehud** had already been identified as a grandson of Jediael (7:10), probably otherwise known as Ashbel. Ehud's family (8:6) engaged in hostility against other Benjamites (**Naaman, Ahijah, and Gera,** v. 7a) events otherwise unattested. **Shaharaim** (v. 8) is probably the same as Ahishahar (7:10), a son of Bilhan, so the line is still traced through Ashbel (= Jediael), Bilan, and others. Shaharaim lived for a time in **Moab,** where he **divorced his wives Hushim and Baara.** Through a third **wife Hodesh** (8:9) he had seven other **sons,** but the chronicler's interest was in the descent through **Hushim** (v. 11a). It passed from Shaharaim through **Elpaal** (v. 11b) **and Beriah** (v. 13). This list concludes with **sons of Shimei** (vv. 19-21), **of Shashak** (vv. 22-25), and **of Jeroham** (vv. 26-27), none of whom can be otherwise identified. **All these** descendants of Benjamin, the chronicler wrote, **lived in Jerusalem** (v. 28), which was possible, of course, only after Jerusalem was taken by David and made Israel's capital (cf. 2 Sam. 5:1-10).

**8:29-40.** In the second major city of Benjamin, namely, **Gibeon,** lived a line of Benjamites to which **Saul** was related. It is impossible to discover the linkage between this line and any of those of the previous section because this line begins only with Saul's great-grandfather **Jeiel,** a period much later than that presupposed by most of verses 1-28.

The descent appears to be: (a) Jeiel (v. 29), (b) **Ner** (v. 30; cf. 9:36), (c) **Kish** (8:33), and (d) **Saul** (v. 33). (Cf. comments on Ner, Kish, and Saul in 1 Sam. 14:50-51.) Next are the sons of Saul: **Jonathan, Malki-Shua, Abinadab** (= Ishvi; cf. comments on 1 Sam. 14:49), **and Esh-Baal** (= Ish-Bosheth; cf. 1 Sam. 14:49; 2 Sam. 2:8). A grandson of Saul, **Merib-Baal** (1 Chron. 8:34), also known as Mephibosheth (2 Sam. 4:4), is prominent in the annals of history as are his father **Jonathan,** his uncle Ish-Bosheth, and his grandfather Saul. Following Mephibosheth's (Merib-Baal's) son **Micah** (1 Chron. 8:34; cf. 2 Sam. 9:12), however, are names (1 Chron. 8:35-40) which do not appear elsewhere in the Bible except in another genealogy of Saul (9:41-44).

## J. Citizens of Jerusalem (9:1-34)

### 1. POLITICAL LEADERS (9:1-9)

**9:1.** No doubt verse 1a is a summary statement concerning **the genealogies** of **all Israel** which also includes **Judah** before the Babylonian deportation. The purpose of the remainder of chapter 9 is to identify **the people** who settled in Jerusalem and Gibeon after their return from the Exile.

**9:2-9.** After a brief mention of the return of the various groups in general (v. 2), the chronicler went into some detail with each group. By **Israelites** he meant the people of **Judah . . . Benjamin . . . Ephraim, and Manasseh** who settled **in Jerusalem** (v. 3). The descendants of Judah represent all three lines—that of his sons **Perez** (v. 4), Shelah **(the Shilonites,** v. 5; cf. Gen. 38:5), and Zerah (1 Chron. 9:6; cf. Gen. 38:30).

Benjamin's descendants were traced through four lines—**Hassenuah** (1 Chron. 9:7), **Jeroham** (v. 8), **Micri** (v. 8), and **Ibnijah** (v. 8)—none of whom was an immediate son of Benjamin.

The list of settlers here should be compared with the list in Nehemiah 11:4-9, the structure of which is essentially the same as the chronicler's. The names of the lineage of **Judah,** however, do not correspond unless **Uthai** (1 Chron. 9:4) is Athaiah (Neh. 11:4) and **Asaiah** (1 Chron. 9:5) is Maaseiah (Neh. 11:5). If so, one must assume a different selection of ancestors from these men back to Judah. Also Nehemiah does not mention the line through Zerah. This no doubt explains the different census figures—**690** in 1 Chronicles 9:6 and 468 in Nehemiah 11:6. The Benjamite lists agree more closely, at least at the beginning, where **Sallu** is **son of Meshullam,** in both cases (1 Chron. 9:7; Neh. 11:7). However, the chronicler named four lines of descent and Nehemiah only one, that of Sallu back to Jeshaiah (Neh. 11:7). Chronicles has a total of **956** Benjamite men (1 Chron. 9:9) while Nehemiah (11:8) has 928. Since there is no way of knowing the basis for these respective figures, one cannot account for their differences.

### 2. PRIESTS (9:10-13)

**9:10-13.** The six priestly families here—**Jedaiah, Jehoiarib, Jakin, Azariah . . . Adaiah,** and **Maasai**—correspond (with some spelling variations)

to the six in Nehemiah 11:10-14 except that (in Neh. 11:10) Jedaiah is the son of Joiarib ( = Jehoiarib). Moreover, Nehemiah's list is evidently more comprehensive since it includes more names. Finally, the chronicler's total of **1,760** persons (1 Chron. 9:13) differs from Nehemiah's total of 1,192. Since there is no hint of the basis for these figures, it is impossible to know what accounts for their differences.

### 3. LEVITES (9:14-16)

**9:14-16.** The seven families of **Levites** who lived in Jerusalem (v. 34; cf. "the Holy City," Neh. 11:18) and vicinity (Netophah; cf. 1 Chron. 9:16, was a suburb of Jerusalem) are the same as those of Nehemiah 11:15-18, though there is considerable variation in the spelling of some names and additions and omissions of still others. The reasons for these differences are unclear.

### 4. GATEKEEPERS AND OTHERS (9:17-34)

**9:17-27.** The tasks of the Levites in the preceding list (vv. 14-16) are not spelled out, so it may be assumed that they were primarily of a sacrificial nature. But the Levites of this section (vv. 17-27) were responsible to open and close the temple **gates** at the appropriate times and to **guard** them against improper intrusion. The names here are paralleled in Nehemiah to some extent (Neh. 11:19-23), though Nehemiah's account is shorter. Strangely **Shallum,** described by the chronicler as the **chief** gatekeeper (1 Chron. 9:17), was not mentioned by Nehemiah. (On Shallum's grandfather's name **Ebiasaph,** v. 19, see comments on 26:1.) Shallum's position was especially important as he was in charge of **the King's Gate,** which led to the main, eastern entrance to the temple (cf. Ezek. 46:1-2). That had been his ancestors' role even back to the time of the tabernacle when **Phinehas son of Eleazar** had been their supervisor (1 Chron. 9:19-20; cf. Num. 3:32). The enigmatic reference to **Zechariah** (1 Chron. 9:21; cf. 26:2) suggests that in Davidic times the role of the ancestors of Shallum was shared by another Levitical family whose responsibility was the gate of **the Tent of Meeting** (the tabernacle) proper.

In all, the chronicler wrote, the Levite **gatekeepers** in Jerusalem and the surrounding **villages** totaled **212.** (In

Neh. 11:19 the gatekeepers totaled 172, but that verse implies that only the families of Akkub and Talmon were counted while 1 Chron. 9:17 adds the names Shallum and Ahiman.) This evidently was the pool from which the manpower was drawn since 22 were needed each day (26:17-18). They each served for a **seven-day** period (9:25) at which time they were relieved for an indeterminate period of time.

**9:28-34.** Besides the gatekeepers **some** Levites were responsible for **the articles** and foodstuffs **in the temple service.** This included **the furnishings,** vessels, **flour. . . wine. . . oil, incense . . . spices,** and **bread** (vv. 28-32; cf. Lev. 24:5-9). Other Levites **were musicians** who were free from all other duties and for convenience were assigned living quarters in **the temple** complex itself.

### K. Genealogy of Saul (9:35-44)

**9:35-44.** This genealogical record is almost identical to that of 8:29-40 (which adds the family of Eshek, brother of Azel, 8:39). But because the chronicler was about to narrate the death of **Saul** (chap. 10) and the succession of David (11:1-3) he repeated Saul's genealogy (9:35-44).

## II. The Reign of David (chaps. 10–29)

### A. Death of Saul (chap. 10)

**Chapter 10.** As pointed out in the *Introduction*, the major objective of 1 and 2 Chronicles is to enhance the reign of David and his dynasty by showing it to be divinely ordained and directed. One effective way of achieving this was to set the beginnings of that reign against the tragic end of Saul's reign (cf. Saul's 40 years [1051–1011 B.C.] with David's dynasty of 425 years [1011–586]). The chronicler assumed, of course, that the life and tenure of **Saul** were well known to his readers, having occupied most of 1 Samuel. So he turned immediately to the point at issue—the **death** of **Saul** as an act of God's judgment.

The narrative of the Philistines' conquest of **Israel** at **Mount Gilboa** (1 Chron. 10:1-12) is practically identical to 1 Samuel 31 (see comments there). For some reason Chronicles adds the item that the Philistines **hung** Saul's **head in the temple of Dagon** (1 Chron. 10:10) but

omits the fact that they hung his body on the wall of Beth Shan (1 Sam. 31:10).

In 1 Samuel 31 there is no moral or theological observation about the death of **Saul** and the transference of his **kingdom** to **David.** The chronicler, however, pointed out (1 Chron. 10:13-14) that God's judgment fell because of Saul's disobedience to His **word** (cf. 1 Sam. 13:13-14; 15:23). Another reason was Saul's recourse to demonic spirits (1 Sam. 28:7).

### B. David's heroes (chaps. 11–12)

**11:1-3.** The story of David's reign from **Hebron** and the steps taken by him and others to gain control over **all Israel** is briefly recounted in 1 Chronicles. The reason, again, is that the details were well known from 2 Samuel. Only those nuances necessary to the chronicler's special emphases need be repeated. On the other hand those men God used to help establish David's kingdom play a significant role in Chronicles. The chronicler did not refer to any factors (such as Abner's machinations, 2 Sam. 2:8-32) that might tend to overemphasize the human element, giving Saul's family a hand in David's success. The narration opens, then, with an appeal **to David** by the men of **Israel** that he be **their ruler.** They recognized that his kingship was a matter of divine appointment (1 Chron. 11:2).

David responded by making a covenant (**compact**) with **the elders,** a pact that probably consisted of an oath in which he pledged his loyalty to the requirements of the Law of Moses for human kingship (cf. Deut. 17:14-20).

**11:4-9.** David next **marched to Jerusalem, that is, Jebus** (cf. Josh. 18:16, 28; Jud. 19:10-11), centrally and neutrally located between Israel and Judah, which he proceeded to conquer and occupy. This was possible because **Joab** breached the walls of the Jebusite fortress, possibly by locating the water tunnel and gaining entrance thereby (cf. 2 Sam. 5:8). **The fortress of Zion** was evidently a hill overlooking the Jebusite **city** which **David** added to the original settlement. He himself **took up residence** on Zion (1 Chron. 11:5, 7) and extended the whole city north to the terraces, encompassing the entirety with walls. This **was called the City of David** (cf. 2 Sam. 5:7, 9; 6:12; 1 Kings 2:10). **The supporting terraces** (1 Chron. 11:8) is literally, "the Millo"

(NIV marg.). This Hebrew word means "filling," so this may have been the area between the two hills (Jebus and Zion) which was filled in to level the whole city. The chronicler's account of the capture of Jerusalem singles out **Joab** as the hero, a point not made in 2 Samuel. This assured Joab the position of **commander-in-chief** (1 Chron. 11:6).

**11:10-14.** The narrator then introduced the rest **of David's mighty men.** First, Joab and three others—**Jashobeam . . . Eleazar** (vv. 11-12), and Shammah (2 Sam. 23:11)—comprised the inner circle of the commander and three mighty men. Joab was David's nephew, son of his half sister Zeruiah (cf. 1 Chron. 2:16; also cf. 18:15; 26:28; 27:24). Jashobeam, **chief of the officers** (or "chief of 30" [or "of 3"], LXX; cf. NIV marg.) was famous for slaying **300** at once (11:11). Second Samuel 23:8 has 800. The difference may be due to a scribal error in copying Chronicles for the Hebrew numerical symbols 300 and 800 look much alike. Eleazar distinguished himself by defending **Pas Dammim,** with David, against **the Philistines** (1 Chron. 11:12-14). The third great hero, Shammah, is not included in this list; his exploits are recounted in 2 Samuel 23:11-12.

**11:15-25.** A second group of **three** mighty men is introduced by the story of their risking **their lives** to get **David . . . water** from **Bethlehem** when he was hiding from the **Philistines** at **Adullam. David** was so moved by their self-sacrifice that **he refused to drink** the water; **instead, he poured it out** on the ground as a sacrificial offering. This event, paralleled in 2 Samuel 23:13-17, may have occurred at the time of David's first encounter with the Philistines (2 Sam. 5:17-21) after his capture of Jerusalem.

**Abishai . . . brother of Joab** (cf. 1 Chron. 2:16) is named among this second group of **three.** Because of his courage in slaying **300** of the enemy he was counted as head of this second group of **three** (11:20-21). Yet he was not promoted to the level of the first **three.**

**Benaiah** became known because of his slaughter of the **two** mighty Moabites, **a lion in a pit,** and **an Egyptian . . . seven and a half feet tall. Benaiah** was put **in charge of** David's **bodyguard** (vv. 22-25). Later Solomon advanced him to Joab's place as commander-in-chief (cf.

1 Kings 2:35).

**11:26-47.** The list of remaining heroes is nearly identical to the list in 2 Samuel 23:24-39 except for spelling variations and other minor differences. The Chronicles list does, however, include (in 1 Chron. 11:41-47) 16 names after **Uriah the Hittite** which are not in 2 Samuel. If the five named members of the two groups of three (1 Chron. 11:10-14 and vv. 15-25; cf. comments on 2 Chron. 11:10-21) are not counted, the Chronicles list (1 Chron. 11:26-41a) has 30 heroes from **Asahel** (v. 26) through Uriah the Hittite (v. 41a), not counting **the sons of Hashem** (v. 34). "The sons of Hashem" could refer to (a) an undesignated number of unnamed soldiers, (b) the previously listed two or three men (vv. 32b-33), or (c) perhaps to an individual ("the sons of Hashem" could be trans. "Bene-Hashem"). The extra 16 after Uriah, then, are an addendum to the original list. (According to 2 Sam. 23:39 there were 37 men in all. For an explanation of this total, see the comments on 2 Sam. 23:8-39 and the chart "David's Mighty Men" near that passage.)

**12:1-7.** Most of the mighty men of David listed in 11:26-47 were his fellow tribesmen of Judah. In addition to these, defectors went **to David** from many other tribes. While he was in exile from **Saul** at **Ziklag** (cf. 1 Sam. 27:1-7), David was joined by several of Saul's own kin **from . . . Benjamin.** These 23 **men** are listed in 1 Chronicles 12:3-7.

**12:8-18.** The next group of men to join David were 11 **Gadites** (vv. 8-15) who lived on the east side of the Jordan (v. 15). They came to David's aid in **his stronghold, in the desert,** apparently during his years of pursuit by Saul. They **crossed the Jordan in the first month,** probably April-May, **when** the river **was overflowing** (cf. Josh. 3:15; 4:19). They were fierce, capable **warriors (their faces were the faces of lions),** and amazingly quick-footed **(swift as gazelles).**

With the Gadites came many others from Benjamin and **Judah** (1 Chron. 12:16-17). As their leader **Amasai** said, they knew that **God** was with **David** and would **help** him, so they wished to associate themselves with him (v. 18).

**12:19-22.** When **David . . . went with the Philistines to** engage Israel in battle at Gilboa (cf. 1 Sam. 28:1-4) some

**men of Manasseh** came to his aid. But along with David they were dismissed from the battlefield lest they would defect to **Saul** (1 Chron. 12:19). **When David** returned **to Ziklag** the seven **Manasseh** men accompanied him, and even **helped** him pursue and defeat the Amalekites who had pillaged his town in his absence (cf. 1 Sam. 30).

**12:23-40.** The chronicler also enumerated the **soldiers** (many of them **brave** and **experienced**) who made up the delegations seeking to encourage David to expand his rule beyond **Hebron.** They came from **Judah . . . Simeon . . . Levi . . . Benjamin . . . Ephraim,** western **Manasseh . . . Issachar . . . Zebulun . . . Naphtali . . . Dan . . . Asher . . . Reuben, Gad,** and eastern **Manasseh**—a total of well over 300,000 men of war (vv. 23-37). All the tribes were named in order to show that David's support was broad-based, a point not made in 2 Samuel. This point is also made by describing their meeting with **David at Hebron** as a time of great festivity and **joy** (1 Chron. 12:38-40).

## C. Transporting the ark (chap. 13)

**13:1-6.** After **David** had taken Jerusalem from the Jebusites and made it the capital of the then-united **Israel** and Judah, he was eager to make it the religious center as well. This could not be done, however, till **the ark** of the covenant was returned to a permanent resting place in Jerusalem. The Philistines had captured the ark at Shiloh (1 Sam. 4:4, 11), exhibited it for several months in Philistia (1 Sam. 6:1), and then returned it to Israel (1 Sam. 6:2-12) where it was housed at Beth Shemesh (1 Sam. 6:13-15) and Kiriath Jearim for about 100 years, from about 1104 to 1003 B.C. (see comments on 1 Sam. 7:2).

Early in David's reign at Jerusalem he commissioned **priests and Levites** from **throughout** the land **(from the Shihor River,** Josh. 13:3; Isa. 23:3; Jer. 2:18, a stream at Israel's southern border at **Egypt, to Lebo Hamath;** cf. 2 Chron. 7:8, Israel's northern boundary) **to bring the ark** back **from Kiriath Jearim** (also called **Baalah**) to Jerusalem (1 Chron. 13:1-6, see the map "The Wanderings of the Ark of the Covenant" near 1 Sam. 6). The ark was referred to as **the ark that is called by the name.** This identification of

God's presence with His name was common in later portions of the Old Testament, especially in Chronicles, but was also known in Moses' time (cf. Deut. 12:5, 11, 21; 14:23-24; 16:2, 6, 11; 26:2).

**13:7-14.** With great pageantry the procession with **the ark** made its way (vv. 7-8) till it hit a rough place in the road and the **cart** on which the ark was riding began to jostle and tip. Instinctively **Uzzah reached out** to keep **the ark** from falling, and for his sacrilege he was **struck** dead (vv. 9-10). The reason, of course, was not only the intrinsic holiness of the ark but the fact that it was being transported improperly. The Law of Moses stipulated that the ark was to be carried by the Levites using poles inserted through its corner rings (Ex. 25:13-14; cf. 1 Chron. 15:2, 13, 15).

The impropriety of David's action and its subsequent punishment by the **Lord** resulted in a delay of **three months** in the movement of **the ark,** a time when it was sheltered in **the house of** a certain **Obed-Edom** (13:13). Because of its presence God **blessed** Obed-Edom and his family (v. 14). A proper attitude toward the things of God brings blessing while a cavalier spirit brings divine displeasure.

## D. David's establishment in Jerusalem (chaps. 14–16)

### 1. HIS PALACE (14:1-2)

**14:1-2.** At about the time **David** was arranging for the arrival of the ark (chap. 13) he was also undertaking several building projects (15:1). Chief among these was the construction of his own royal **palace,** a task that was considered essential in the ancient Near East in order to authenticate the reign of a new king. Having entered into a friendly alliance with the Phoenician King **Hiram,** David engaged him and his artisans in the project of providing **cedar logs** and doing the work of construction, using skills for which the Phoenicians were famous (cf. 2 Chron. 2:8-9). **David** recognized that he had been elevated by **the Lord** to great prominence.

### 2. HIS FAMILY (14:3-7)

**14:3-7.** Another symbol of oriental regal splendor was the accumulation of a large harem of **wives** and concubines. Though the Lord forbade polygamy (cf. Deut. 17:17), David succumbed to the custom of the day. The list of 13 sons here, those born **in Jerusalem,** differs from the list in 2 Samuel 5:14-16 by adding **Elpelet** (spelled Eliphelet in 1 Chron. 3:6) and **Nogah** (14:5-6). These two—Elpelet (alias Eliphelet) and Nogah—are also in the genealogy in 3:5-9 (cf. comments there). In another spelling variation, **Beeliada** in 14:7 is Eliada in 3:8. (Cf. the chart "David's Family" near 2 Sam. 3:2-5.)

3. HIS VICTORIES OVER THE PHILISTINES (14:8-17)

**14:8-12.** Another evidence of David's newly found power and grandeur was his successful encounter with Israel's perennial enemies, **the Philistines.** When they saw **that David** was no longer a trusted ally or perhaps even a vassal (see comments on 2 Sam. 5:17-25), **the Philistines** attacked Israel in **the Valley of Rephaim,** a few miles southwest of Jerusalem. **God** gave Israel victory by breaking **out against** the enemy (cf. NIV marg.) like a flood so the battle site became known as **Baal Perazim.** Ironically, more than a century earlier **the Philistines** had captured the ark of the Lord (1 Sam. 4:11), but now in panic they left **their** own idols.

**14:13-17.** After **the Philistines** were defeated by **David** they did not lose heart altogether; they returned again to Rephaim. This time the Lord instructed David to set an ambush. When Israel would **hear** a **sound of marching in the . . . balsam trees** (i.e., a loud rustling of the leaves) this would be their signal that the Lord was already leading their army into **battle** and they should follow. **David** had such a victory (pursuing the enemy **from Gibeon to Gezer,** about 15 miles) that **all** other **nations** heard of it and feared **him.**

4. ARRIVAL OF THE ARK (CHAP. 15)

**15:1-13.** At last **David . . . prepared** once more to relocate and house **the ark** of the covenant **in Jerusalem.** Though he planned to place the ark in a substantial temple (17:1-4), for the present he set up **a tent** (15:1), perhaps similar to the Mosaic tabernacle. Then, careful to observe proper protocol (vv. 2, 13, 15), he gathered **the priests** and **Levites** and commanded them to transport **the ark** from the house of Obed-Edom (cf. 13:14) to its new shrine in Jerusalem. The priests

were **Zadok and Abiathar** (15:11; see the chart "The Ancestry of Zadok and Abiathar" near 2 Sam. 8:15-18) and **the Levites** came from the three Levitical families of **Kohath . . . Merari,** and **Gershon** (1 Chron. 15:5-7). They were **Uriel** (vv. 5, 11; cf. 6:24), **Asaiah** (15:6, 11; cf. 6:30), and **Joel** (15:7, 11; cf. Joah, 6:21).

In addition, there were three other **Levites,** all from the family of Kohath. **Shemaiah** was of the clan of **Elizaphan** (15:8, 11; cf. Ex. 6:22), **Eliel** of the clan of **Hebron** (1 Chron. 15:9, 11; cf. Ex. 6:18), and **Amminadab** of the clan of **Uzziel** (1 Chron. 15:10-11; cf. Ex. 6:18). There were thus four Levites of Kohath and one each of the other two branches, plus 862 assistants.

**15:14-24.** After the prescribed consecration (Num. 8:5-13) all these set about the task of transporting **the ark** (1 Chron. 15:14-15). This included more than merely moving the object, however. It was accompanied by great religious celebration. So **David** ordered the Levitical leaders to **appoint** musicians who would join in the great procession (v. 16). The chief of these were **Heman, son of Joel** (and grandson of Samuel, 6:33), **Asaph,** and **Ethan** (15:17), who sounded **the bronze cymbals.** Eight other musicians (v. 20) played **lyres according to** *alamoth* (probably a musical term; cf. NIV marg. and the title to Ps. 46). Six others (1 Chron. 15:21) played **harps** set to *sheminith* (also a musical term; cf. NIV marg. and title to Ps. 6). **Kenaniah, the head Levite, was in charge of the** vocal music since he had special expertise in that area (1 Chron. 15:22). Four others **were to** protect **the ark,** probably two in front of it (v. 23) and two behind it (v. 24b); between them was a contingent of seven trumpeters (v. 24).

**15:25-29.** Somewhere in the procession, perhaps at its head, **David** danced (v. 29), **clothed in** the garments of a priest (a **robe of fine linen** and **a linen ephod,** v. 27). **Michal,** his wife, watching **from a window . . . despised him** for she mistook his holy zeal for exhibitionism (cf. comments on 2 Sam. 6:20).

5. APPOINTMENT OF RELIGIOUS PERSONNEL (CHAP. 16)

**16:1-6.** Having **brought the ark** into **the tent . . . pitched for it** and having completed the sacrifices of **burnt offer-**

**ings and fellowship offerings,** David **blessed the people** of Israel and distributed **bread** and cakes **of dates** and **raisins to each** one (vv. 1-3). He then **appointed . . . Asaph** to be in charge of **the ark** in its new surroundings (vv. 4-5; cf. v. 37) and to offer prayers and praises to **the LORD** (v. 5). With Asaph were certain other **Levites,** all mentioned in 15:17-18, who were to accompany the praises with musical instruments. A model of such praise, a piece undoubtedly composed by **David** for this occasion, follows (16:8-36).

**16:7-36.** This hymn of thanksgiving is actually a compilation of passages from other psalms, a fact which suggests the priority of those psalms. David then must have excerpted parts from his earlier poetry and woven them together into this beautiful piece. The parallels are as follows:

| 1 Chronicles | Psalms |
|---|---|
| 16:8-22 | 105:1-15 |
| 16:23-33 | 96:1b-13a |
| 16:34-36 | 106:1b-c, 47-48 |

For an explanation of the contents of this hymn in 1 Chronicles see the comments on the respective psalms.

**16:37-38.** Others who served with Asaph included two Obed-Edoms. One (v. 38a) was a musician and minister of the ark (15:21, 24; 16:5), who may be the same man who looked after the ark in his own home (13:14). The other **Obed-Edom** was a gatekeeper identified as a **son of Jeduthun** (16:38b); he is also mentioned in 26:4, 8, 15. This Jeduthun should not be confused with the chief musician Jeduthun (16:41-42; 25:1, 3; 2 Chron. 5:12) who was also known as Ethan (1 Chron. 6:44; 15:17) and was a descendant of Merari. The Jeduthun in 16:38, whose son was Obed-Edom, was a descendant of Korah (26:1, 4), a grandson of Kohath.

**16:39-43.** The reference to **Zadok** as **priest** of **the tabernacle** at **Gibeon** reveals the reason for the retention of two high priests. Zadok, of the Aaronic line of Eleazar (6:4-8), was in charge of the Gibeon sanctuary, while Abiathar, of the line of Ithamar (24:6), officiated at the new tent-shrine in Jerusalem. The origin of Gibeon as the site of a tabernacle is not known but it must not have been deemed illicit since David appointed Zadok as priest there and later on Solomon

offered sacrifices there with God's approval (cf. 1 Kings 3:4-10). In fact it appears that sometime after the ark was taken from Shiloh the tabernacle was moved also, eventually ending up at Gibeon (1 Chron. 21:29). Zadok thus was ministering at the original Mosaic house of worship. While Asaph was with Abiathar in David's tabernacle which housed the ark, **Heman and Jeduthun** (also called Ethan; cf. 6:44; 15:17) functioned with Zadok at the original Mosaic tabernacle of Gibeon.

### E. David's desire for a temple (chap. 17)

**17:1-15.** After David's **palace** was completed and he was living comfortably in it, he was struck by the disparity of his sturdy surroundings and the relatively flimsy temporality of the **tent** for **the ark.** Expressing a desire to provide the Lord with a temple (suggested by the word **house,** v. 4), **David** found **Nathan the prophet** to be encouraging at first (v. 2). But after the Lord appeared **to Nathan** in a dream and forbade such a project, David learned that God would **build a house for** David instead! (v. 10; cf. vv. 25, 27) "House" here means dynasty.

The divine message to David through Nathan is almost identical here in its wording to 2 Samuel 7:1-17 (see comments there). Whereas 2 Samuel 7:15 refers to Saul by name, the chronicler simply called him David's **predecessor** (1 Chron. 17:13). This may reflect a certain abhorrence toward Saul on the chronicler's part. (For the content of Nathan's message, vv. 4-14, see comments on 2 Sam. 7:4-17.)

**17:16-27.** David's prayer of response to the covenant promise is also virtually the same in Chronicles and Samuel (cf. 2 Sam. 7:18-29). Notable in Chronicles is an emphasis on David's **exalted** position (1 Chron. 17:17), a theme which is in keeping with the general tenor of the book. (For the content of David's prayer, vv. 16-27, see comments on 2 Sam. 7:18-29.)

### F. David's foreign affairs (18:1–20:8)

1. THE PHILISTINES AND MOABITES (18:1-2)

**18:1-2.** The chronicler, like the author of Samuel (2 Sam. 8:1), put **the Philistines** at the head of his list of peoples conquered by **David.** The reference to **Gath** may indicate the limit of David's conquest, and perhaps suggests that the enigmatic "Metheg Ammah" in 2 Samuel 8:1 is another name for Gath.

The description of Moab's defeat is much milder in tone than that in 2 Samuel 8:2. The chronicler merely mentioned that Moab became a vassal state, whereas Samuel spoke of David's systematic slaughter of two thirds of the population. The reason may be the chronicler's overall purpose to extol the Davidic dynasty, the roots of which are at least partially found in Moab with his great-grandmother Ruth (Ruth 4:13, 21).

### 2. THE ARAMEANS (18:3-11)

**18:3-11.** The chronicler's narrative of David's dealings with **the Arameans** of **Zobah** (vv. 3-4), **Damascus** (vv. 5-8), and **Hamath** (vv. 9-11) is in all essentials the same as that in 2 Samuel 8:3-12. (See comments on 2 Sam. 8:4 for an explanation of the differences in numbers in that verse and those in 1 Chron. 18:4.) The cities belonging to **Hadadezer** ("Hadarezer" in Heb.) were called **Tebah** ("Betah" in Heb., a variant spelling; cf. NIV marg.) and Berothai. Apparently then David took bronze from three cities: Tebah (also known as Tibhath), **Cun,** and Berothai. Tou's **son Hadoram** is spelled Joram in 2 Samuel 8:10. David **dedicated . . . to the LORD** (for the temple construction) the wealth acquired from the **nations** he conquered (cf. 2 Sam. 8:7-13; 1 Chron. 22:14; 26:26; 29:2-5).

### 3. THE EDOMITES (18:12-13)

**18:12-13.** In his recounting of the Edomite conquest, the chronicler gave credit for its success to David's nephew **Abishai (Zeruiah** was a half sister of David, 2:16), who killed 18,000 Edomites, rather than to David himself (cf. 2 Sam. 8:13). This is unusual in that the chronicler generally promoted **David** rather than his underlings. **The Valley of Salt** is evidently in **Edom,** near the Dead Sea.

The superscription to Psalm 60 states, on the other hand, that *Joab,* Abishai's brother, killed *12,000* Edomites in the Valley of Salt. Perhaps this difference is explainable by noting that the entire campaign was under Abishai's direct command, and that Joab was responsible (with the soldiers in his contingency) for killing two thirds of the Edomites.

### 4. THE ROYAL ADMINISTRATION (18:14-17)

**18:14-17.** Possibly Abishai (rather than David) was mentioned in verse 12 because the chronicler was about to list other figures prominent in David's administration. **Shavsa** (v. 16) is spelled Seraiah in 2 Samuel 8:17. **David's sons,** his **chief officials** (*ri'šōnîm,* "chief ones"), are called royal advisers in 2 Samuel 8:18 (see comments there).

### 5. THE AMMONITES (19:1-20:3)

**19:1-5.** The war with **the Ammonites** was introduced by the chronicler the same way it was introduced in 2 Samuel—the **king** of Ammon had **died** and **David** had **sent a delegation** to comfort the king's **son** and successor, **Hanun** (1 Chron. 19:1-2; cf. 2 Sam. 10:1-2). But David's messengers were humiliated by the Ammonites, with the result that they returned to Israel in embarrassing ignominy (1 Chron. 19:3-5).

**19:6-7.** The ensuing account of the preparations for war and the battle itself differs in several ways from the details of wording and fact in 2 Samuel 10. The chronicler mentioned that **Hanun** hired the Arameans of Mesopotamia (**Aram Naharaim**), **Aram Maacah, and Zobah** for **1,000 talents of silver** (ca. 37 tons; cf. NIV marg.), while 2 Samuel 10:6-7 lists Arameans of Beth Rehob, Zobah, Maacah, and Tob. There is no contradiction here; the two historians merely mentioned those Arameans of special interest to them, for whatever reason. Likewise, the Samuel report omits the information about the price paid to the mercenaries. The chronicler also pointed out that the total Aramean chariot force consisted of **32,000** units (1 Chron. 19:7), but the author of 2 Samuel gave the number of infantrymen ("foot soldiers"), which was 33,000 (2 Sam. 10:6).

**19:8-19.** The account of the strategy for preparation is practically the same in 2 Samuel and 1 Chronicles. **The Ammonites** guarded the gate of **their** capital **city** (Rabbah; cf. 20:1) and the Arameans took to the surrounding fields (**the open country**). This meant that **Joab,** David's commander, would have to defeat the Arameans on the outer perimeter before he could even get close to the Ammonites themselves. In order to effect this, **Joab** divided his **troops** into two units, one of which he led **against the**

Arameans and the other he entrusted to his brother **Abishai** to engage **the Ammonites** (19:10-11). After agreeing to come to each other's aid if need be (v. 12), Joab and Abishai undertook the campaign. Confident in **the LORD** (v. 13), they achieved success. **The Arameans** were routed, and **the Ammonites** retreated to the security of the fortifications of their **city,** Rabbah (vv. 14-16).

Meantime **the Arameans** called for reinforcements **from** across the Euphrates **(the River)** and **with Shophach** (spelled Shobach in 2 Sam. 10:15) as their leader engaged David's troops at Helam (2 Sam. 10:16-17) in the Transjordan. Again **David** was victorious, killing **7,000 . . . charioteers** (cf. comments on 2 Sam. 10:18), **40,000** infantrymen, and **Shopach** himself (1 Chron. 19:16-18). This squelched any further desire of **the Arameans** to confront **David;** in fact the Arameans made themselves **vassals** to Israel (v. 19).

**20:1-3. The Ammonites** remained in **Rabbah** until the next **spring** when **Joab** once again took up the siege of the city. The chronicler wrote that **David remained in Jerusalem** and in line with his overall design wrote nothing of David's adulterous and murderous activities (cf. 2 Sam. 11:2–12:25). Reasons for the omission of the stories of Bathsheba and Uriah are discussed in the *Introduction*. Chronicles also omitted the report of how **David,** who **took** the great **crown** of **gold** (weighing ca. 75 pounds) from the Ammonite king, happened to be at Rabbah. (The words **their king** could also be trans. "of Milcom," the name of the Ammonite god; cf. NIV marg.) According to 2 Samuel 12:26-29, after Joab had taken the city's water supply, he invited David to come and personally lead the attack on the citadel or inner fortification. Having captured the city, David reduced its population to slave **labor** involving **saws . . . picks . . . axes,** and brickmaking (cf. 2 Sam. 12:31). Thus the Ammonites also came under David's authority.

### 6. THE PHILISTINES (20:4-8)

The chronicler's record of David's conquests begins and ends with references to wars against the Philistines (18:1; 20:4-8). Israel had no more inveterate and persistent foe than the Philistines and Israel was never able to dominate

them completely.

The author of 2 Samuel also recounted the series of Philistine wars (2 Sam. 21:15-22) but placed his record several chapters after the Ammonite wars narrative (2 Sam. 10–12). He had at least two reasons for this: (1) He first discussed in detail the involved stories of David's personal and family tragedies which befell him because of his affair with Bathsheba (2 Sam. 13:1–21:14), none of which occupied the interest of the chronicler. (2) In 2 Samuel 22–23 are David's hymn of praise and his catalog of heroes, many of whom were prominent in the Philistine hostilities. It may well be then that the Philistine war annals (2 Sam. 21:15-22) were placed immediately before 2 Samuel 22–23 because they dealt with a common theme. Also Chronicles treats the Philistine campaigns more briefly than 2 Samuel. For example, the latter refers to David's hand-to-hand fight with the giant Ishbi-Benob (2 Sam. 21:15-17), in which David nearly lost his life and was then advised by Abishai not to take part in further combat. But the chronicler passed over that episode. Perhaps he did so because of his interest in emphasizing the positive aspects of David's reign, a pervasive theme in his writings.

**20:4-5.** Chronicles includes three instances paralleled in 2 Samuel 21:18-22, though with some differences. First was the battle of **Gezer** (Gob in 2 Sam. 21:18), 20 miles northwest of Jerusalem, in which **Sibbecai** (cf. 1 Chron. 11:29) slew **Sippai,** a Philistine giant. Next **Elhanan son of Jair** slew **Lahmi,** Goliath's **brother** (20:5). In 2 Samuel 21:19 Elhanan is identified as the son of Jaare-Oregim of Bethlehem. This is no problem, however, because Jair may be identified with Jaare-Oregim; the latter name may actually be translated "Jair the weaver" (cf. NIV marg.; 2 Sam. 21:19). But in 2 Samuel 21:19 Elhanan is said to have slain Goliath, not Lahmi. A further complication is introduced by the reference in 1 Chronicles 11:26 to a certain "Elhanan son of Dodo from Bethlehem." Since nothing more is known of this Elhanan one may assume he is different from Elhanan son of Jaare-Oregim.

The major problem of harmonization between 2 Samuel 21:19 and 1 Chronicles 20:5 has to do with who was slain. Was Lahmi slain or was it his brother Goliath?

It is common knowledge that David himself killed Goliath (1 Sam. 17), so some scholars suggest that Elhanan was none other than David. According to this view, David killed *both* Goliath (2 Sam. 21:19) and the brother of Goliath (1 Chron. 20:5). However, there is no evidence that David was also known as Elhanan or is it possible to equate Jesse, David's father, with Jair or Jaare-Oregim. Much more likely is the probability that the original manuscript of 2 Samuel 21:19 read "the brother of Goliath" and that in scribal transmission the words "the brother of" were somehow omitted.

**20:6-8.** The third Philistine war narrative reveals that a mutant Philistine giant met death at the hands of **David's** nephew **Jonathan** (cf. 2 Sam. 21:20-21). There follows a succinct summary of the defeat of the Philistines, epitomized in the deaths of **descendants of Rapha** (1 Chron. 20:8). Rapha was the ancestral father of a race of giants, known as Rephaites, who coexisted with the early Philistines and perhaps even intermarried with them (cf. Gen. 14:5; Deut. 2:11, 20; 3:11; 1 Chron. 20:4).

### G. David's census and the Lord's punishment (21:1–22:1)

**21:1-7.** The chronicler did not state David's motivation for taking **a census of Israel** except to say **Satan . . . incited** him to do so and David wanted to **know how many . . . fighting men** there were. In 2 Samuel 24:1, however, the historian revealed that the Lord was angry with His people and used David's census as an occasion to punish him and them. No contradiction is here for the Lord simply let Satan tempt David to undertake the census, much as He permitted Satan to attack Job (cf. Job 1:12 and comments on 2 Sam. 24:1-3). In His sovereignty God's ultimate authority extends even to the workings of Satan. David's immediate purpose was to assess his military strength (1 Chron. 21:5). This incurred divine displeasure because it suggested that he was relying more on military capabilities than on God's power. Probably that is why David admitted that his action was sin (v. 8).

**Joab,** despite his objections to David's edict (v. 3), had to undertake the census (v. 4) and reported the totals of **1,100,000 men** of Israel and **470,000** of **Judah** (v. 5). **Joab did not** count the Levites or Benjamites, however, since **Levi** could not participate militarily (cf. Num. 1:47-49) and the attempt to complete the census was frustrated apparently before **Benjamin** could be counted (cf. 1 Chron. 27:24). Also David's command was repulsive to Joab (21:6). The Samuel account indicates that 800,000 combat troops were available in Israel and 500,000 in Judah (2 Sam. 24:9). The NIV suggests that the 1,100,000 (**in all Israel**) *included* the 470,000 of Judah (1 Chron. 21:5), thus giving a total of 630,000 for Israel proper. The 800,000 of 2 Samuel 24:9 might then include an *estimate* of 170,000 Levites plus 630,000 other Israelites, though such a large number of Levites is difficult to imagine. The 500,000 Judeans of 2 Samuel could also include an *estimated* 30,000 Benjamites who were not counted by the chronicler.

Another possible solution (cf. comments on 2 Sam. 24:9) is that the chronicler's grand total of 1,100,000 included a standing army of 300,000, thus reducing the total to 800,000 given in 2 Samuel. Also the 500,000 Judeans (in the 2 Sam. account) may have included the 470,000 of 1 Chronicles along with a standing army of 30,000 (2 Sam. 6:1).

**21:8-15a.** At some point **David** realized the evil of his project and sought the Lord's forgiveness. This no doubt was granted but the purposes of **the Lord** had to be served—**Israel** had to be chastened. So the message came **to David** through the Prophet **Gad** that David was to **choose one of** three judgments **God** would bring on the people. There could be **three years of famine,** or **three months of** pursuit by the enemy, or **three days of** direct divine retribution by a **plague** (vv. 11-12).

Rather than choosing one of the three options, **David** placed himself in God's **hands,** who then destroyed **70,000 men** by a plague. Satisfied, **the Lord** turned from His judgment.

**21:15b-25.** The Angel of the **Lord,** elsewhere identified with God Himself, was probably the preincarnate Christ (cf. Gen. 16:13; 18:1-2; 22:11-12; 48:16; Jud. 6:16, 22; 13:22-23; Zech. 3:1; cf. comments on Gen. 16:7). He appeared to David near **the threshing floor of Araunah** (cf. 2 Sam. 24:16; the Heb. in 1 Chron. 21:15

has the variant spelling Ornan; cf. NIV marg.) **with a . . . sword in His hand.** David and the elders repented publicly and **David** pleaded that the rest of the **people** might be spared and that further punishment be meted only to him and his **family.**

The Angel then commanded **Gad to tell David to . . . build an altar . . . on the threshing floor** so he might offer appropriate propitiatory sacrifices. To do this it was necessary to acquire the threshing floor from **Araunah,** a Jebusite who lived just north of Jerusalem. Meanwhile **Araunah** had seen **the Angel** (v. 20) so when **David approached** him **Araunah . . . bowed down** and offered to **give** the **threshing floor** to David without price (vv. 21, 23). **David** refused his kind offer, however, and insisted that he could not offer anything to **the LORD** that had cost him **nothing** (vv. 22, 24). So the king **paid Araunah 600 shekels of gold** (ca. 15 pounds). However, according to 2 Samuel 24:24 David paid a much smaller amount (50 shekels of silver, ca. 1¼ pounds). This problem is explained by noting that the silver paid for the threshing floor and oxen (2 Sam. 24:24) and that the gold paid **for the site,** a large plot of ground apparently adjacent to the threshing floor.

**21:26–22:1.** After David **built** the **altar** he **offered** up **burnt offerings and fellowship offerings,** the former to plead God's forgiveness of his sin and the latter to speak of the renewal of unbroken covenant relationship which would follow. God's response was favorable as indicated by His answering **with fire from heaven.**

It was too late to save the 70,000 who had perished (21:14) but Jerusalem itself was spared by David's intercession (v. 27; cf. v. 16).

The chronicler noted that **David** took this response from **the LORD** as a sign that that place was now one of special significance. As a result he began to worship there regularly instead of going to **Gibeon** where the Mosaic **tabernacle** was located (cf. 16:39). **David** did not go to Gibeon, the historian says, **because he was afraid of the sword of the Angel of the LORD** (21:30). This probably means that David, as a result of this whole experience, now knew that Araunah's threshing floor, not Gibeon, was God's choice

for the location of central worship. This is confirmed by the next verse (22:1): **David** solemnly proclaimed that this new site would now be **the house of the LORD.** When Solomon later built the temple it was on this same piece of land (cf. 2 Chron. 3:1), a place hallowed also because it was the Mount Moriah on which Abraham offered to sacrifice his son (Gen. 22).

### H. David's plans for a temple (22:2-19)

The plan and purpose of the chronicler are both clear in this passage. He had preceded his narrative on David's intention to build a temple by telling the story of the acquisition of its site (21:1–22:1). Now the chronicler stressed David's importance in connection with the temple by elaborating on the king's desire to build a temple and establish a systematic program of worship. Samuel's version mentioned only David's wish to build a temple (2 Sam. 7:2, 5) and left the matter once David's request had been denied. Even 1 Kings is silent about any further steps David might have taken to prepare Solomon for the construction of a temple. But the chronicler, while not denying the fact that God said David was not to build the temple (1 Chron. 17:4-12), was aware that David was permitted to prepare plans and materials for the project. There follows then a description of these steps.

**22:2-5.** David first selected **stone-cutters** from among **the aliens** of the land to quarry and prepare stones for the temple (**the house of God**). These aliens may have included Phoenicians as they were particularly adept at masonry. In addition, **iron-** and **bronze-**workers undertook the manufacture of **nails** and other metal **fittings.** Also David secured a countless number of **cedar logs** from Lebanon. He made all these **preparations,** he said, because his **son Solomon** was so **young** (cf. 29:1) he did not have the expertise necessary to provide a temple suitable for the great God of Israel.

**22:6-10.** When all was ready David **called . . . his son** and told him that it had been his own desire **to build** the **house** of the LORD but **the LORD** had forbidden it because David was a man of war. In the eyes of God the shedding of **blood** in war was incompatible with building a place of worship. It was therefore to be left to **Solomon, a man of peace**

(whose name is related to the word for "peace"), to oversee the actual building. Remarkably the Lord, through David, said that Solomon would be His **son** and that Solomon's dynasty (i.e., his **kingdom**) would last **forever** (cf. 28:7). The kings of the Davidic dynasty, as sons of God in a special sense is an important theme in the Bible. Psalm 2, for example, refers to the king ("His anointed," Ps. 2:2) as God's son (Ps. 2:7). And the author of Hebrews, citing Psalm 2, applied it to Jesus Christ (Heb. 1:5; 5:5). The Davidic kings were not only physical ancestors of Christ but also their role as "sons of God" prepared the way for the concept of Jesus' divine sonship.

**22:11-16.** David then charged Solomon to obey in the matter of the temple and to **keep the Law of the LORD** in every way. To do so would bring blessing (**success,** v. 13). Finally David pointed out to Solomon the extent of David's preparation. The king had accumulated **100,000 talents of gold** (3,750 tons) and **1 million talents of silver** (37,500 tons)—together, 41,250 tons (or 82½ million pounds)—a staggering amount of weight and value! Probably this accumulation was largely plunder from conquering surrounding nations (2 Sam. 8:7-13; 1 Chron. 18:11). David had also gathered tradesmen skilled in **every** necessary **kind of work.** All that was needed was for Solomon to **begin the work.**

**22:17-19.** Turning to **the leaders of** the nation, **David** instructed them to seek **the LORD** and also to assist Solomon in every way **to build** the temple (**the sanctuary of the LORD**) and place within it the holy **ark** which symbolized the presence of **God.**

## I. David's theocratic organization (chaps. 23–27)

### 1. THE LEVITES IN GENERAL (CHAPS. 23–24)

**23:1-6.** At the end of David's life, after he had already effectively turned the reins of government over to **Solomon** (v. 1), he undertook the task of organizing and ensuring the perpetuation of a religious and political structure that would best meet the nation's needs. David took a count of **the Levites** from **30 years** of age (the legal age for their ministry; cf. Num. 4:3) upward. The total of **38,000** was then divided into **24,000** for **the work of the temple . . . 6,000** as offi-

cials and judges . . . **4,000** as **gatekeepers,** and **4,000** musicians (1 Chron. 23:3-5). Each of these was in turn **divided . . . into groups** according to their familial descent from **Levi** (v. 6).

**23:7-11.** The list of **Gershonites** begins with the sons of Gershon, **Ladan** ("Libni" in 6:17) **and Shimei.** The names that follow were not immediate descendants but were men in David's time who sprang from these two branches and became leaders of the various Levitical groups. The **Shimei** in 23:9 is not the same as the Shimei in verses 7 and 10. The summary statement in verse 9b makes this clear (vv. 8-9 list the descendants of **Ladan,** not Ladan's brother). The line of Ladan, then, produced a total of six leaders. Three were traced directly to Ladan (v. 8) and three others were through a Ladanite descendant, Shimei (v. 9).

**Shimei,** son of Gershon (v. 7), gave rise to **four** leaders (v. 10), but since the second two (**Jeush and Beriah**) had small families they combined to make **one** group (v. 11).

**23:12-20.** One of Kohath's descendants (**Amram**) fathered **Aaron and Moses** (see comments on Num. 27:57-65). **Aaron,** of course, **was set apart** for priestly service (v. 13) but Moses' descendants were limited to lesser Levitical duties (v. 14). Through Moses' two sons **Gershom and Eliezer** arose leaders such as **Shubael** (v. 16) and **Rehabiah** (v. 17).

A second son of Kohath, **Izhar,** was the source of the line which produced **Shelomith** (v. 18). A third son, **Hebron,** sired four Levitical leaders (v. 19). Kohath's last son, **Uzziel,** fathered the line of **Micah** and **Isshiah** (v. 20).

**23:21-32.** As for Levi's third son, **Merari,** his two sons, **Mahli and Mushi,** gave rise, respectively, to **Eleazar and Kish** on the one hand (vv. 21-22) and to **Mahli, Eder, and Jeremoth** on the other (v. 23). The chronicler concluded the lists by reiterating David's purposes in allocating the Levites' assignments. Since these purposes presupposed a much larger ecclesiastical burden, David lowered the age of Levitical service to **20** from the previously designated 30 (vv. 24, 27; cf. v. 3). This would permit many more men to function.

The Levites' principal tasks were to assist the priests (**Aaron's descendants**) in the **temple** precincts (v. 28), to prepare the **bread** of the Presence and **grain offerings** (v. 29), and **to thank and praise** God at the times of **burnt** offerings (vv. 30-31).

**24:1-3.** To implement the foregoing plan, David enlisted **Zadok** and **Ahimelech,** the two chief **priests,** to help him divide first the priests and then the Levites **into** the **divisions** in which they would serve. As the chronicler pointed out, Zadok was **a descendant of** Aaron's son **Eleazar** and Ahimelech (son of Abiathar; cf. v. 6) descended from Aaron's son **Ithamar** (v. 3). (On the death of **Nadab and Abihu** see Lev. 10.) Though it is impossible elsewhere to establish Ahimelech's descent from Ithamar, it is interesting to note that Ahimelech was a direct successor of Eli, the high priest during Samuel's childhood. (According to 1 Sam. 22:9, 11, 20 Ahimelech was son of Ahitub, son of Phinehas, son of Eli.)

**24:4-5.** Since there were more **descendants** of **Eleazar** than of **Ithamar,** the result of the apportionment was **16** divisions of the former and **8** of the latter. By having 24 divisions, each would serve about two weeks a year. Gradually then, their service would move around the calendar. The phrase **officials of the sanctuary and officials of God** can be rendered "officials of the sanctuary, that is, officials of God," to distinguish them from civil officials.

**24:6-19.** The priests' and Levites' **names** were recorded by **the scribe Shemaiah . . . in the presence of** David and the kingdom rulers. **Zadok** and **Ahimelech** were listed first and then their **family** members, descendants of **Eleazar** and of **Ithamar,** were listed (vv. 7-18) in an apparently alternating fashion (v. 6b). These are names of individuals, but they also became attached to the divisions which they founded. For example, **Jehoiarib** and **Jedaiah** (v. 7) are also listed among those who returned from the Babylonian Exile (9:10; cf. Neh. 7:39). Zechariah, father of John the Baptist, was from the division of **Abijah** (1 Chron. 24:10; cf. Luke 1:5). Most of the remaining names are nowhere else attested as priests.

**24:20-31.** The Levites who were not priests were divided into ministering groups. Their roster begins with **Amram** and his descendant **Shubael** (v. 20), and

Shubael's descendant **Jehdeiah.** The second Amramite was **Rehabiah** and his son **Isshiah** (v. 21; cf. 23:16-20). The **sons of** Izhar were listed next (24:22; cf. 23:18), then those **of Hebron** (24:23; cf. 23:19), and of **Uzziel** (24:24-25; cf. 23:20). These were all Kohathites (cf. 23:12).

The chronicler next listed the line **of Merari,** third son of Levi (24:26-30). The names are the same as those in 23:21-23 except for the addition of **Jerahmeel** to **Kish** (24:29) and an entirely new line— that of **Jaaziah** (vv. 26-27). For some unknown reason the Gershonite line is omitted though it was given in 23:7-11. By means of **lots** the various divisions undertook their service (24:31; cf. v. 5; Luke 1:9) so that all were **treated** alike in the kinds of service they rendered (cf. 1 Chron. 23:28-32).

### 2. THE LEVITICAL MUSICIANS (CHAP. 25)

**25:1.** The temple ministry of vocal and instrumental music had previously been assigned to **Asaph, Heman, and Jeduthun** (also known as Ethan; cf. 15:17, 19), but chapter 25 lists the names of their kin who performed this ministry with them and those who succeeded them. It is called a **ministry of prophesying** (25:1) which no doubt meant a sort of musical proclamation of divine revelation and expressions of hymnic praise and worship (cf. 1 Sam. 10:5; 2 Kings 3:15). Their appointment by **David** and the military **commanders** perhaps suggests a close connection between the religious and military establishments. This may suggest overtones of the ancient concept of holy war in which music and the ark of the Lord accompanied His armies in battle (cf. Josh. 6:1-11).

**25:2-31. The sons of Asaph** are listed in verses 2, 9a, 10-11, 14 (**Jesarelah,** v. 14, is another spelling for **Asarelah,** v. 2; cf. NIV marg. for v. 14). With their **sons and relatives** they made up 4 of the 24 divisions of musicians. The **sons** of **Jeduthun** (v. 3) with their **sons and relatives,** constituted 6 divisions (vv. 9b, 11 [**Izri** is spelled **Zeri** in v. 3; cf. NIV marg. for v. 11], 15, 17, 19, 21). The **sons** of **Heman** (v. 4) consisted of 14 divisions in all, each of whom is named in the list of lots (vv. 13, 16, 18 [**Azarel** is a variant of **Uzziel** in v. 4; cf. NIV marg. for v. 18], 20, 22-31). The 24 divisions, each with 12 men, totaled **288** men (v. 7). The appointments of specific responsibilities by **lots** guaranteed that there would be no favoritism in assigning **their duties** (v. 8).

### 3. THE LEVITICAL GATEKEEPERS (26:1-19)

**26:1-3.** The **gatekeepers** were evidently closely related to the musicians in function since they too were affiliated with **Asaph.** The first major division was that of **Meshelemiah** (vv. 1-3), whose seven sons are said to be **Korahites,** that is, descendants of Korah, son of Izhar, son of Kohath, son of Levi (cf. Ex. 6:16, 18, 21). Meshelemiah himself was a **son of Kore, one of** Asaph's **sons.** On the other hand since Asaph is elsewhere (1 Chron. 6:39-43) listed as a descendant of Gershon (Kohath's brother), it may be better to understand Asaph here as a shorter form of Ebiasaph, the spelling given in 9:19 (and spelled Abiasaph in Ex. 6:24).

**26:4-5.** The second division was that of the family of **Obed-Edom.** The statement that **God had blessed Obed-Edom** seems to identify him with the Obed-Edom who had sheltered the ark in his house and was blessed by God for so doing (13:14). However, as suggested earlier (see comments on 16:38), the Obed-Edom who protected the ark went on to be a minister before the ark in the temple. Obed-Edom the gatekeeper of this present passage must be the Obed-Edom of 16:38 who is identified as a son of Jeduthun.

The observation that Jeduthun (also called Ethan) was a descendant of Merari (6:44-47) and the fact that Obed-Edom here (26:4) was of the line of Kohath raises no difficulty if Obed-Edom the gatekeeper was the son of a different Jeduthun. There were, then, Obed-Edom the musician and minister of the ark (13:14; 15:21; 16:38a) and Obed-Edom the regular gatekeeper (16:38b; 26:4, 8, 15). Apparently the first Obed-Edom was also an occasional gatekeeper (15:18) or doorkeeper (15:24; cf. 16:4-5).

**26:6-11.** The third division of gatekeepers consisted of a subdivision of the family of Obed-Edom headed by **Shemaiah.** All three divisions of the Kohathite branch of Levites totaled 80 persons (vv. 8-9). **The Merarite** branch was represented by **Hosah** and his family which provided **13** men. In all, therefore, there were three Kohathite divisions (vv. 2-3,

9, 4-5, 6-8) and one of Merari (vv. 10-11).

**26:12-19.** All these **gatekeepers** were assigned their stations by **lots** (v. 13) as were the musicians and other priests and Levites (24:5, 31; 25:8). **The East Gate** became the responsibility of the family of **Shelemiah** (the same as Meshelemiah, 26:1). **His son Zechariah** manned the **North Gate** (v. 14). **The South Gate** and **storehouse** fell by lot to **Obed-Edom** and **his sons** (v. 15). Finally **the West Gate** and **Shalleketh Gate** (otherwise unknown) were presided over by **Shuppim and Hosah** (v. 16). The meaning of Shuppim is unclear since, as a personal name, it appears only here and in 7:12 ("Shuppites," clearly not relevant to 26:16). There were to be 22 gatekeepers in all at any one time (vv. 17-18), though certainly this means leaders only (cf. v. 12) for there were 4,000 gatekeepers altogether (cf. 23:5).

### 4. THE LEVITICAL TREASURERS (26:20-28)

**26:20-25.** As noted in the NIV margin, the words **Their fellow Levites were** come from the Septuagint. The Hebrew reads, "As for the Levites, Ahijah was." This makes good sense and should be followed here. Admittedly the name Ahijah does not occur elsewhere in chapters 23–26 and he is not otherwise identified, but this is insufficient grounds for rejecting the Hebrew text in favor of the Septuagint. Ahijah, then, was **in charge of** all **the treasuries of the** temple. The treasuries consisted of the revenues from tithes, offerings, and other sources which were presented to the Lord by His people (cf. Ezra 2:69).

The management **of the treasuries** was the responsibility of (a) Levites descended from Gershon, son of Levi, through the line **of Ladan** (also spelled Libni; cf. Ex. 6:17; 1 Chron. 6:17) and headed by the family of **Jehieli** (26:21-22), and (b) Levites descended from Kohath (the clans of which are listed in v. 23; cf. 23:12) through the line **of Moses** and headed by **Shubael** and his descendants (26:24-25; cf. 23:16).

**26:26-28.** The portion of the treasury which had accumulated through military **plunder** (v. 27) and the other special dedicatory offerings of **David** (v. 26), **Samuel . . . Saul . . . Abner,** and **Joab** (v. 28) was under the jurisdiction **of Shelomith,** a descendant of Moses' second son

Eliezer (v. 25; cf. 23:17 [the Shelomith in 23:18 was not the Shelomith of 26:25]).

## 5. THE LEVITICAL ADMINISTRATORS (26:29-32)

**26:29-32.** The Amramites were over the treasury, as verses 23-28 indicate, but their brethren **the Izharites** provided external leadership; that is, they were charged with duties in outlying areas **away from the temple** (v. 29). Descendants of Hebron, the third son of Kohath, were also assigned to such work throughout the kingdom: **1,700** of their number, under **Hashabiah,** served in the Western tribes (v. 30) while **2,700** more, under **Jerijah,** were in Transjordania (vv. 31-32). The implementation of this arrangement took place in David's **40th** (and last) **year.** The 6,000 officials and judges of 23:4 may be the 1,700 and 2,700 "external" Levites (26:30, 32) plus the Levites in charge of the temple treasuries (vv. 20-22).

## 6. THE MILITARY AND POLITICAL STRUCTURE (CHAP. 27)

**27:1-15.** David's organization of the army of Israel consisted of 12 **divisions** of **24,000 men** each, each division serving on active **duty** one **month** each **year.** It is impossible to determine the geographic entities involved but perhaps the monthly musters corresponded roughly to tribal patterns (cf. 1 Kings 4:7-19). Most of the names of David's divisional commanders appear in the lists of his heroes. The prowess of **Jashobeam** (1 Chron. 27:2), a Judean (**descendant of Perez,** v. 3), was described in 11:11 (cf. 2 Sam. 23:8, NIV marg.). **Dodai** was father of Eleazar, a mighty man (1 Chron. 11:12). Dodai's assistant was **Mikloth** (1 Chron. 27:4). **Benaiah,** assisted by his son **Ammizabad** (27:5-6), was a famous warrior of the "second three" (11:22-25) and **was over the Thirty.** Asahel, of course, was David's own nephew and Joab's **brother** (27:7; cf. 11:26). **Shamhuth** (spelled Shammoth in 11:27) was in charge on **the fifth month.** Ira (27:9) of Tekoa also was listed in 11:28.

**Helez . . . an Ephraimite** (27:10), was listed only as a **Pelonite** earlier (11:27). **Sibbecai** (27:11) was also a Judean (Zerah, cf. v. 13, was a son of Judah; cf. 2:4) and is on the hero list (11:29). **Abiezer** (27:12), **a Benjamite** of the village of Anathoth (cf. Jer. 1:1), is also

mentioned in 1 Chronicles 11:28. **Maharai** (27:13), another Judean descended from Zerah (cf. v. 11), is in 11:30. **Benaiah the Pirathonite** (27:14), not to be confused with the Benaiah of verse 5, is listed in 11:31. Finally, **Heled,** a descendant of Israel's first judge **Othniel** (27:15), was commander of **the 12th** division. His connection with Othniel is not mentioned in the hero lists (11:30; cf. 2 Sam. 23:29, where his name is spelled Heldai).

**27:16-24.** The officials **over the tribes** may have been of a quasi-military nature. Most of these leaders are mentioned only here, though **Zadok** (v. 17) and **Elihu** (v. 18; called Eliab in 1 Sam. 16:6) are well known elsewhere. Conspicuous by their omission are the tribes of Gad and Asher. The ideal total of 12 tribes survives, however, by the inclusion of **Levi** (1 Chron. 27:17) and two parts **of Manasseh,** east and west (vv. 20-21). Having given the roster of tribal **officers** the chronicler again mentioned David's ill-conceived census, a tabulation that remained incomplete because of the Lord's obvious displeasure (vv. 23-24; cf. 21:2-5). Having counted only **the men** of military age, **David** left off and once again trusted in the hand of God to bring deliverance. (On **the book of the annals of King David,** see comments on 1 Kings 14:19.)

**27:25-34.** This final list records the names of supervisors over various aspects of David's bureaucracy. **Azmaveth** was over the king's **storehouses** in Jerusalem while **Jonathan** oversaw royal assets elsewhere (v. 25). **Ezri** was in charge of farm labor (v. 26), **Shimei** of **the vineyards** (v. 27), **Zabdi** of the vintage (v. 27), Baal-Hanan of **the olive and sycamore-fig trees,** and **Joash** of the **olive oil** supplies (v. 28). **Shitrai** was over the **herds . . . in Sharon** (v. 29; Sharon was west of the central hill country along the Mediterranean), **Shaphat** over the valley **herds** (v. 29), **Obil** over **the camels** (v. 30), **Jehdeiah** over **the donkeys** (v. 30), and **Jaziz** over **the flocks** (v. 31). **Jonathan, David's uncle** (perhaps nephew is the meaning of the word here; cf. 2 Sam. 21:21), was **a counselor** and **Jehiel** was the tutor(?) of David's **sons** (1 Chron. 27:32). **Ahithophel was** another **counselor** (cf. 2 Sam. 15:12) and **Hushai** a close confidant (1 Chron. 27:33). Though the chronicler did not relate the story of

Ahithophel's disloyalty to David in Absalom's rebellion (2 Sam. 15:31), he did mention Ahithophel's succession **by Jehoiada** and **Abiathar** (2 Sam. 15:35). The list ends with **Joab . . . the commander of the royal army** (1 Chron. 27:34).

## J. David's farewell address (28:1–29:22a)

### 1. DAVID'S INSTRUCTIONS CONCERNING THE TEMPLE (28:1-10)

**28:1-10. David** had already communicated to Israel's leaders (who are all enumerated in chap. 27) his desire to construct a temple for **the LORD.** In fact he had already started collecting the building materials (chap. 22). Now, with the end of his life imminent, he summoned all the leaders again to encourage them to recognize Solomon's leadership and to follow him in this magnificent enterprise. In the temple, David said, would be placed **the ark of the covenant,** a holy object which symbolized the earthly throne of the heavenly King.

**David** then reviewed the history of his own attempts to build the temple, attempts that did not come to fruition because God had ordained that **Solomon** (a man of peace, 22:9) would be its builder (28:2-7). **Solomon** was qualified because he was the **chosen** son of David, who was himself chosen from the elect tribe of **Judah** (v. 4). Solomon was said to be the "son of God" (**My son,** v. 6) in a peculiar way (cf. 17:13 and comments on 22:10). If Solomon remained true to **the LORD** his **kingdom** would endure (28:6-7; cf. 22:10).

David concluded his instructions with a **charge** both to the people (28:8) and **Solomon** (vv. 9-10) to keep the divine covenant and to trust God to bring the temple project to a happy conclusion. David told Solomon to **serve** God completely (cf. v. 9) and willingly, aware that **the LORD** knows every person's **thoughts** and motives.

### 2. DAVID'S PLANS FOR THE TEMPLE (28:11-21)

**28:11-21.** In a most remarkable declaration **David** shared with **Solomon the plans** and specifications for **the temple** and its furnishings which **the Spirit** of God had revealed to him (vv. 11-12, 19). The construction would be done by human hands but **the plan** and significance of **the temple** were from **God.** This also included the ministry of **the priests and Levites** (v. 13) and **the weight of** the **gold** and **silver** from which the sacred temple furnishings were to be made (vv. 14-18). Not wanting to leave anything to chance, **David** wrote down every detail of the heavenly revelation (v. 19). He encouraged Solomon to **be strong** for the task (cf. v. 10), **courageous,** and not fearful because **God** was **with** him (v. 20) and the workers would willingly assist him (v. 21).

### 3. DAVID'S APPEAL FOR OFFERINGS (29:1-9)

**29:1-5a.** Turning to the assembled crowd **David** again stressed the inexperience of young **Solomon** (cf. 22:5) and the importance of realizing that they were about to build not a palace for a mere human king but **the temple** of the Almighty **God.** Therefore the **task** was **great** and required an extensive amount of materials. Then, by way of example, he pointed out that he had already made official contributions of **gold . . . silver . . . bronze . . . iron . . . wood,** precious stones, and other materials necessary for **the temple** (28:2). **Besides** this he pledged to give of his own **personal** resources **3,000 talents of gold** (ca. 110 tons) from **Ophir** (cf. 1 Kings 9:28; 10:11; 22:48; 2 Chron. 8:18; 9:10; Isa. 13:12) on the east African coast or the western coast of Arabia, and **7,000 talents of . . . silver** (ca. 260 tons). These amounts were **over and above** the large amounts he had already given (see comments on 1 Chron. 22:14).

**29:5b-9.** On the basis of his own commitment (vv. 2-5) David then urged the other **leaders** to participate in the giving, an invitation they gladly accepted. They **willingly** (cf. v. 9) contributed in all **5,000 talents** of gold (ca. 190 tons), **10,000 darics of gold** (ca. 185 pounds), **10,000 talents of silver** (ca. 375 tons), **18,000 talents of bronze** (ca. 675 tons), and **100,000 talents of iron** (ca. 3,750 tons). In addition they gave **precious stones** as they were able. The result was great joy on the part of the masses and **David** himself. The gold, silver, and bronze David and the leaders gave (22:14; 29:4, 7) weighed a massive total of more than 46,610 tons (or 93.22 million pounds), not counting the other metals, stones, and lumber!

4. DAVID'S PRAYER AND SACRIFICES OF DEDICATION (29:10-22a)

**29:10-20.** After the almost spontaneous reaction of generosity by the people, **David** turned to **the LORD** in worship. He first extolled Him as the **God of . . . Israel** (v. 10) and spoke of God's attributes of eternality, omnipotence, **glory,** and sovereignty (vv. 10b-11). David then acknowledged Him as the One able to provide people's needs (v. 12b). Next he offered thanksgiving and **praise** (v. 13) with a confession that even the gifts which had just been presented were possible because the Lord was their original Giver (cf. James 1:17) of all things **from His hand** (1 Chron. 29:14-16). Moreover, David prayed, the gifts were of no avail if given insincerely, so he said that he and the others, had **given** from purest motives (v. 17; cf. 28:9).

Finally, referring to **God** as the One who had made a covenant in the past with the nation's ancestors **Abraham, Isaac, and Israel,** he prayed that the Lord would **keep** the people willing and **loyal** (29:18) and would continue His blessing, especially in enabling **Solomon** to have complete **devotion** to God and to the building of the temple (v. 19; cf. 28:9). After his prayer, **David** asked the **assembly** to **praise the LORD** (29:20).

**29:21-22a.** **Next day** the prayers of dedication were confirmed by the offering of an enormous number of sacrificial animals (3,000 in all), the giving of which brought the people **great joy** before the LORD.

### K. David's successor to the throne (29:22b-30)

**29:22b-23.** The last recorded act of **David** was his acceptance of the co-regency of **Solomon . . . as king** (cf. 1 Kings 1:38-40; 2:1). How long they ruled together cannot be known but it must have been only briefly. **Zadok** also was anointed (again).

**29:24-25.** With Solomon's succession came the recognition by the people that he now was the king in **David's** stead.

Divine confirmation of this was apparent in the Lord's great blessing on **Solomon.** God **exalted** him, gave him unprecedented **royal splendor** (v. 25; cf. v. 23, "he prospered").

**29:26-30.** These last verses summarize David's reign from his accession at **Hebron** (2 Sam. 5:1-5) till his death. A complete record of his reign, the chronicler wrote, could be found **in the records of Samuel** (perhaps referring to 1 Sam. 1-24), **Nathan,** and **Gad** (perhaps 1 Sam. 25-2 Sam. 24 is the record of Nathan and Gad). To these accounts the chronicler added his own record (1 Chron.) with his particular purposes in view.

# BIBLIOGRAPHY

Ackroyd, Peter R. *I and II Chronicles, Ezra, Nehemiah*. Torch Bible Commentaries. London: SCM Press, 1973.

Coggins, R.J. *The First and Second Book of the Chronicles*. New York: Cambridge University Press, 1976.

Curtis, Edward Lewis, and Madsen, Albert Alonzo. *A Critical and Exegetical Commentary on the Books of Chronicles*. The International Critical Commentary. Edinburgh: T. & T. Clark, 1910.

Keil, C.F. "The Books of the Chronicles." In *Commentary on the Old Testament in Ten Volumes*. Vol. 3. Reprint (25 vols. in 10). Grand Rapids: Wm. B. Eerdmans Publishing Co., 1982.

Myers, Jacob M. *I Chronicles*. The Anchor Bible. Garden City, N.Y.: Doubleday & Co., 1965.

Sailhamer, John. *First and Second Chronicles*. Chicago: Moody Press, 1983.

Slotki, I.W. *Chronicles: Hebrew Text and English Translation with an Introduction and Commentary*. London: Soncino Press, 1952.

Zöckler, Otto. "The Books of the Chronicles." In *Commentary on the Holy Scriptures, Critical, Doctrinal, and Homiletical*. Vol. 4. Reprint (24 vols. in 12). Grand Rapids: Zondervan Publishing House, 1960.

# 2 CHRONICLES

**Eugene H. Merrill**

## INTRODUCTION

See the *Introduction* to 1 Chronicles.

## OUTLINE

I. The Reign of Solomon (chaps. 1–9)
   A. Solomon's wisdom and prosperity (chap. 1)
   B. Building of the temple (2:1–5:1)
      1. The preparations (chap. 2)
      2. The temple proper (chap. 3)
      3. The temple furnishings (4:1–5:1)
   C. Dedication of the temple (5:2–7:10)
      1. Housing of the ark (5:2-14)
      2. Solomon's blessing and prayer (chap. 6)
      3. Solomon's sacrifices (7:1-10)
   D. God's blessings and curses (7:11-22)
   E. Solomon's successes (chaps. 8–9)
      1. Political success (8:1-11)
      2. Religious success (8:12-16)
      3. Economic success (8:17–9:31)
II. The Reign of the Davidic Dynasty (chaps. 10–36)
   A. Rehoboam (chaps. 10–12)
      1. Division of the nation into Israel and Judah (chap. 10)
      2. Rehoboam's fortifications and family (chap. 11)
      3. Egypt's attack on Jerusalem (chap. 12)
   B. Abijah (chap. 13)
   C. Asa (chaps. 14–16)
      1. Asa's obedience to the Lord (chap. 14)
      2. Asa's reforms (chap. 15)
      3. Asa's treaty with Aram (chap. 16)
   D. Jehoshaphat (chaps. 17–20)
      1. Jehoshaphat's powerful kingdom (chap. 17)
      2. Jehoshaphat's alliance with Ahab (18:1–19:3)
      3. Jehoshaphat's appointment of judges (19:4-11)
      4. Jehoshaphat's defeat of a foreign alliance (20:1-30)
      5. Jehoshaphat's last days (20:31-37)
   E. Jehoram (chap. 21)
   F. Ahaziah (22:1-9)
   G. Athaliah (22:10–23:21)
   H. Joash (chap. 24)
      1. Joash's temple restoration (24:1-16)
      2. Joash's wickedness and assassination (24:17-27)
   I. Amaziah (chap. 25)
   J. Uzziah (chap. 26)
   K. Jotham (chap. 27)
   L. Ahaz (chap. 28)
   M. Hezekiah (chaps. 29–32)
      1. Cleansing of the temple (chap. 29)
      2. Hezekiah's great Passover (30:1–31:1)
      3. Reestablishment of proper worship (31:2-21)
      4. Sennacherib's invasion (32:1-23)
      5. Hezekiah's sickness and prosperity (32:24-33)
   N. Manasseh (33:1-20)
   O. Amon (33:21-25)
   P. Josiah (chaps. 34–35)
      1. Josiah's reformation (chap. 34)
      2. Josiah's great Passover (35:1-19)
      3. Josiah's fatal encounter with Neco (35:20-27)
   Q. Jehoahaz (36:1-4)
   R. Jehoiakim (36:5-8)
   S. Jehoiachin (36:9-10)
   T. Zedekiah (36:11-16)
   U. The Babylonian Conquest and Exile (36:17-21)
   V. The decree of Cyrus (36:22-23)

# COMMENTARY

## I. The Reign of Solomon (chaps. 1–9)

### A. Solomon's wisdom and prosperity (chap. 1)

**1:1-6.** From the beginning of his reign **Solomon** established firm control **over his kingdom.** This was made possible by God's presence and blessing (v. 1).

**Solomon** and Israel's **leaders** made a pilgrimage to the tabernacle (the **Tent of Meeting**) **at Gibeon** to offer sacrifices on the great **bronze altar (made** by **Bezalel;** cf. Ex. 31:11, under Moses' direction, Ex. 38:17) that was still located **there** (cf. 1 Chron. 16:39-40; Ex. 38:1-7). **The ark,** however, was still **in Jerusalem** (2 Chron. 1:4; cf. 1 Chron. 15:1), where it had been brought **from Kiriath Jearim** by **David** (see the map "The Wanderings of the Ark of the Covenant" near 1 Sam. 6). Along with the other national leaders Solomon expressed his devotion to **the** LORD by offering **1,000 burnt offerings** on that one occasion (2 Chron. 1:6).

**1:7-13.** **That night** the Lord responded to Solomon's expression of worship by appearing to him (in a dream; cf. 1 Kings 3:5) and inviting him to request **whatever** he wanted. Because **Solomon** was young and inexperienced (1 Chron. 22:5; 29:1) he was apprehensive about his ability to rule the great nation (**as numerous as the dust of the earth**; cf. Gen. 13:16) **over** which **God** had placed him. So he requested that he might receive **wisdom and knowledge** to lead the people (2 Chron. 1:8-10). "Wisdom" (*ḥokmâh*) refers to discernment and judgment while "knowledge" (*maddāʿ*) means practical know-how in everyday affairs.

The unselfish character of Solomon's choice prompted the Lord to grant not only what **Solomon . . . asked for** but also more. God said He would **also give** Solomon **wealth, riches, and honor** unlike any other **king** of Israel (vv. 11-12; cf. 1 Chron. 29:25).

**1:14-17.** To show God's faithfulness to His promise, the chronicler itemized the material blessings that came to **Solomon.** The king acquired **1,400 chariots and 12,000 horses** (or charioteers; cf. NIV marg.; the Heb. word *pārāšîm* can mean either horses or charioteers), which he stationed in **chariot cities** (cf. 1 Kings 9:19) and **in Jerusalem.** It is not possible to identify the chariot cities today though some have suggested Gezer, Hazor, and Megiddo, based on 1 Kings 9:15.

**Silver and gold,** the chronicler wrote in hyperbole, became **as common** as the ubiquitous **stones** of Israel, and **cedar** was like the common **sycamore-fig trees** of **the** western **foothills.**

Also Solomon **imported** (by trade) **horses** and chariots with great profit. He brought them **from Egypt** (or perhaps Muṣri, in Asia Minor) **and . . . Kue** (*qᵉwēʾ*; not "in droves" as in KJV), probably Cilicia in the south portion of modern-day Turkey (cf. NIV marg.). No doubt Solomon kept some and **exported** the rest, especially to **the Hittites and . . . Arameans.** A chariot cost **600 shekels of silver** (ca. 15 pounds) and **a horse** cost **150** silver shekels (3¾ pounds). Presumably Solomon realized a handsome profit on each one as he traded them. Yet he should not have **accumulated** such great numbers of **horses** and amassed so much silver and gold (Deut. 17:16-17) because of the temptation to trust in those material things rather than in God.

### B. Building of the temple (2:1–5:1)

1. THE PREPARATIONS (CHAP. 2)

God had denied David the opportunity to build the temple. However, David had received detailed instructions about its erection and furnishings and had purchased the site and gathered together materials and workmen to bring it to pass (1 Chron. 21:18–22:19; 28–29). It now fell to his son and successor Solomon to bring the dream to reality.

**2:1-6.** **Solomon** first drafted aliens to provide the labor. They consisted of **70,000 . . . carriers** and **80,000** stonemasons, and **3,600 . . . foremen** (v. 2; cf. v. 18). **Solomon** then notified **Hiram** (the Heb. here has Huram, a variant spelling; cf. NIV marg.), **king of** the Phoenician city-state of **Tyre,** that he was ready to begin the **temple** about which his **father David** had probably informed Hiram (cf. 1 Kings 5:3). This **temple** would be the **place** for offering **sacrifices,** and it would be grand and glorious to befit the **God** who is above **all other gods** (2 Chron. 2:5). Solomon's reference to other gods does not imply that he believed in their existence. It was a way of setting forth to Hiram, a polytheistic pagan king, the uniqueness and incomparability of the Lord God of Israel (cf. Isa. 40:18-26; 46:3-7). Of course such a God cannot be housed in a mere earthly **temple,** Solomon confessed, since **even the highest heavens cannot contain Him.**

**2:7-10.** Nonetheless the temple was to be as appropriate as human creativity could make it. Since the Phoenicians were famous the world over for their architectural and building skills, Solomon solicited Hiram to send . . . **a man** of requisite abilities **to work** with his own **craftsmen** (v. 7). Hiram should also provide **timber** (on **algum** and its uses see comments on 9:10-11), the hewers of which would receive **20,000 cors** (ca. 125,000 bushels) **of ground wheat, 20,000 cors of barley, 20,000 baths** (ca. 115,000 gallons) **of wine, and 20,000 baths of olive oil** (2:8-10).

**2:11-12.** This appeal was readily received by **Hiram,** who recognized the legitimacy and divine origin of Solomon's succession as **king,** so he proceeded to comply. Hiram's acknowledgment of the **LORD** (*Yahweh*), **the God of Israel,** as the Creator of **heaven and earth** (v. 12) was just a formal courtesy and tells nothing of his own personal faith.

**2:13-16.** The man whom Hiram chose to send to Solomon was **Huram-Abi,** a half-Israelite **whose mother was from** the tribe of **Dan.** According to 1 Kings 7:14, his "mother was a widow from the tribe of Naphtali." This difference may be explained by understanding Dan to be her tribe by birth and Naphtali her residence, or vice versa. The terms and conditions Solomon set were acceptable to Hiram in every way. He would immediately **cut** and ship the timber **by sea** to the Israelite port of **Joppa** (cf. Jonah 1:3; Acts 9:36-43; 10:32; 11:5) from where it would be transported overland **to Jerusalem.**

**2:17-18.** With the arrangements now complete, **Solomon** gathered his work gangs, drawing them not from Israelites but from resident **aliens** (v. 17; cf. 1 Chron. 22:2). This presupposes class structures in which non-Israelites were sometimes forced into public service projects such as this project of temple building (cf. Josh. 9:22-27). The numbers in 2 Chronicles 2:18 correspond with those given in verse 2 (cf. comments on 8:10).

### 2. THE TEMPLE PROPER (CHAP. 3)

**3:1.** At last the work **began** at **Mount Moriah,** just north of the old Jebusite city of Ophel, on the spot marked by **the threshing floor of Araunah** (Heb., Ornan; cf. NIV marg.). This was **the place** designated by the **LORD** and purchased **by David** as a site for sacrifice at the time of David's illicit census (cf. 1 Chron. 21) and as a site for the temple (1 Chron. 22:1). Also the place was holy to Israel as the place where Abraham started to offer Isaac to the Lord in obedience to God's command (cf. Gen. 22). Known today as the Temple Mount, it is occupied by a Moslem mosque called the Dome of the Rock. Recent excavations, however, suggest that the site of **the temple** (and thus that of Araunah's threshing floor) may have been immediately north of the Dome of the Rock (see Asher S. Kaufman, "Where the Ancient Temple of Jerusalem Stood," *Biblical Archaeology Review* 9. March-April 1983: 40-59).

**3:2.** The construction commenced **on the second day of the second month** of Solomon's **fourth year.** According to the best chronological calculations this would be 966 B.C. The author of 1 and 2 Kings added the interesting fact that this was 480 years after the Exodus, an event which would then be dated at 1446 B.C. (1 Kings 6:1).

**3:3-4.** The main **temple** structure rested on a **foundation** of **60 x 20 cubits,** or 90 x 30 feet, on the basis of 18-inch **cubits. The portico** (porch) on **the front** was **20 cubits** (30 feet) **long,** thus extending **across the** entire **width of the** main **building.** According to 1 Kings 6:3, the portico was 10 cubits (15 feet) wide. The entire edifice, then, was 105 feet long and 30 feet wide.

The height of the temple was 30 cubits (1 Kings 6:2) but the portico was **20 cubits** (30 feet) **high.** (See the sketch "Plan of Solomon's Temple" near 1 Kings 6:1-10.) The entire interior of the portico was gilded with **gold.**

**3:5-7. The main hall,** the room known in the tabernacle as "the holy place" (cf. Ex. 26:33), was **paneled** with **pine** (or perhaps the Heb. word means cypress) and **covered** with **gold** decorations. This consisted of engraved **designs** of **palm** trees and chains. The meaning of this symbolism is not clear though the palm may represent the tree of life (cf. Gen. 2:9; 3:20, 22; Rev. 2:7; 22:2, 19) or something similar. **Precious stones** were inset here and there. **The gold** was from **Parvaim.** Though this land cannot yet be identified, it must have been a source of unusually **fine gold.** With this **gold** the artisans veneered every surface of **the temple** interior. They then engraved figures of **cherubim** in the gold of **the walls.** These creatures symbolized the awesome presence and glory of God. The angelic beings which these carvings represented had their wings outspread ("covering ones," as the Heb. word *kerûbîm* may suggest). The Lord was said to dwell between the cherubim (cf. Num. 7:89; 2 Kings 19:15; Pss. 80:1; 99:1).

**3:8-14.** The smaller chamber, **the most holy place,** was **20 x 20 cubits** (30 x 30 feet). Its interior was also plated **with gold—600 talents** (ca. 23 tons; cf. NIV marg.) of it—fastened with **gold nails** which **weighed 50 shekels** (1¼ pounds; cf. NIV marg.).

Within this room was the ark of the covenant (1 Kings 6:19) which apparently, as in the tabernacle, was placed in the most holy place between the two **cherubim** (cf. Ex. 25:10-22). The ark represented or symbolized the Lord's dwelling among His people. The **cherubim** evidently faced **the main hall** (2 Chron. 3:13), from within the **most holy place,** each with a total wingspan of 10 cubits (15 feet). From one wingtip to another they thus stretched from one side **wall** of the **temple** to the other (vv. 11-12).

Just before the two **cherubim** and hiding them and the most holy place from the main hall was the veil or **curtain** with its various colors (**blue, purple, and crimson**) and fabrics (**yarn and . . . linen**) with representations of **cherubim** woven **into it** (v. 14). Thus the temple proper had two rooms, the main hall (the holy place) and the most holy place, the former being exactly twice the size of the latter. The curtain served as a partition between them.

**3:15. In front of the temple** were **two** free-standing **pillars . . . 35 cubits** (52½ feet) tall including a 5-cubit (7½ feet) **capital.** But according to 1 Kings 7:15 these pillars, made of bronze, stood 18 cubits (27 feet) high. One explanation of this alleged discrepancy is suggested by the NIV which supplies the word

**together** in 2 Chronicles 3:15. The thought is that when the heights of the two pillars are added together they total 35 cubits. This is a close (though not exact) harmonization because two pillars of 18 cubits each total 36, not 35. Perhaps a better solution is to recognize that the Hebrew figures for 18 and 35 are so similar that a scribe copying verse 15 could easily have read 35 when the text actually said 18. Architecturally it seems more reasonable that the pillars would be in line with or less than the height of the temple, not towering far above it. The temple height was 30 cubits (45 feet, 1 Kings 6:2), so each pillar was probably 18 cubits (27 feet) not 35 cubits (52½ feet).

**3:16.** The Hebrew word rendered **interwoven** is translated "in the inner sanctuary" in the NASB (cf. NIV marg.). In copying the text, scribes probably transposed some Hebrew letters so that the original *brbd* ("interwoven") became *bdbr* ("in the inner sanctuary"). The reading "interwoven" is supported by 1 Kings 7:17 which speaks of interwoven **chains.**

Above the band of **chains** at the **top** of each pillar was a band of **100** engraved **pomegranates.** Actually 200 pomegranates were on each pillar (2 Chron. 4:13), thus suggesting that there were two bands or rows (1 Kings 7:18) of 100 each. The pomegranates on each pillar were interwoven among the chainlike lattice, with seven chains on each pillar (1 Kings 7:17). Since the capitals on top of the pillars were five cubits high (2 Chron. 3:15) and since each capital's top portion, shaped like lilies, was four cubits high (1 Kings 7:19) that left one cubit for the chains and pomegranates.

**3:17. The pillars** stood before the **temple,** which faced east. So **one** pillar was on **the south** side and **one** on **the north.** The pillar on **the south** was **named Jakin** ("He establishes"; cf. NIV marg.) and the other was **Boaz** ("in Him is strength"; cf. NIV marg.). So the pillars symbolized the fact that the Lord had established His house and would maintain it forever (cf. 7:16).

3. THE TEMPLE FURNISHINGS (4:1–5:1)

**4:1.** Along with or after the temple's construction Solomon commissioned the manufacture of the furnishings of the temple and its precincts. The first article listed is the great **bronze altar** which measured **20 cubits long, 20 cubits wide, and 10 cubits high** (30 feet x 30 feet x 15 feet). Though the steps are not mentioned here, they must have led to the top of the altar (cf. the altar in the millennial temple, Ezek. 43:17). The bronze altar stood in the courtyard directly in front of the temple (cf. Ex. 40:6; 2 Kings 16:14).

**4:2-6, 10. The Sea of cast metal** was a huge round basin **10 cubits** (15 feet) in diameter and **5 cubits** (7½ feet) in depth. Its circumference of **30 cubits** (45 feet) comports well with its 10-cubit diameter according to the formula of C (circumference) = $\pi$ (3.14159) x D (diameter), a discovery of much later geometricians. The slight difference between 30 cubits and 31.4159 cubits (3.14159 x 10 cubits diameter) can be explained by noting the common practice of giving approximate figures. Even today people speak of a circle's circumference being three times its diameter. Another explanation is that the *inside* circumference of the basin may have been exactly 30 cubits and the outer circumference 31.4159 cubits.

Under the basin's **rim** was a frieze consisting of **two rows** of engraved **bulls, 10** bulls **per cubit** (18 inches). These engravings were obviously highly stylized since the Hebrew here says literally, "bull-like forms," whereas 1 Kings 7:24 has "gourd-like forms" as though there were room for interpretation.

The basin rested on the back of **12** manufactured **bulls, 3 facing** each of four directions. These probably represented Israel's 12 tribes and their arrangement in the wilderness camps (cf. Num. 2). The capacity of the Sea was **3,000 baths** (ca. 17,500 gallons; cf. NIV marg.), though 1 Kings 7:26 says 2,000 baths. Many scholars suggest that this difference may be explained by the view that the chronicler considered the basin as cylindrical and the author of Kings as hemispherical. This explanation, however, presumes that the respective authors could not agree on the actual shape of the vessel, an unlikely possibility. Perhaps the best reconciliation is that the Sea had a capacity of 3,000 baths but actually contained only 2,000.

The basin was **placed** east of the temple, **south** of the bronze altar (2 Chron. 4:10), and served as a wash basin for **the priests** as they underwent their ceremonial cleansings (v. 6b). There were also **10** wash **basins . . . 5** on each **side** of the temple in which the items **used for . . . burnt offerings** were washed (v. 6; cf. 1 Kings 7:38).

**4:7-8.** Inside the main hall of **the temple** were **10 gold lampstands . . . 5 on the south** wall **and 5 on the north.** (The former tabernacle had only one lampstand.) In the same locations were **10 tables** (possibly for the "bread of the Presence"; cf. comments on v. 19) and in unspecified places **100** golden basins.

**4:9, 11a. The courtyard of the priests** was probably "the inner courtyard" mentioned in 1 Kings 6:36, and **the large court** was, of course, "the great courtyard" of 1 Kings 7:12. The first of these was no doubt the area immediately around the temple and the other was in the vicinity of the temple complex. The **bronze** doors of the large court must have been gates in the walls surrounding the entire temple area.

Listed last are the various utensils used in conjunction with the bronze altar: **the pots and shovels** to remove ashes and the **sprinkling bowls** to contain the blood (2 Chron. 4:11a).

**4:11b-18.** The work of **Huram** (called Huram-Abi in 2:13), described in detail in 3:3–4:11a, is summarized in 4:11b-16a. To this summation is added the information that these **bronze** objects (v. 16) were **cast** by use of **clay molds** in **the Jordan** Valley **between Succoth and Zarethan** (v. 17). Recent exploration has revealed the probable location of this industry, about 35 miles north of the Dead Sea and east of the Jordan River, just north of the Jabbok River. So abundant was **the bronze** used that it was **not** even weighed (v. 18). Much if not all of the bronze came from David's conquest of the Arameans (1 Chron. 18:3-8).

**4:19-22.** These verses describe the remaining **furnishings** and utensils, some of which were mentioned already. These are **the golden altar,** on which incense was burned (cf. the tabernacle's gold-covered altar of incense, Ex. 37:25-29); **the tables** for **the bread of the Presence** ("showbread," KJV), probably the 10 tables mentioned in 2 Chronicles 4:8; **the** 10 gold **lampstands** (cf. v. 7); the various parts and attachments of the lampstands such as the **lamps and tongs** of **solid gold**

(v. 21); and miscellaneous items such as **gold wick trimmers, sprinkling bowls** (cf. v. 8), **ladles** (or spoons), **and censers** (for burning incense).

The emphasis here is not merely on the articles, since there is some obvious repetition with previous verses, but on the fact that they were made of **pure gold.** So extensive was its use that the **doors** both to **the main hall** (the holy place) and **the most holy place** were made of **gold** (v. 22). According to 1 Kings 7:50 even the door sockets were made of gold. All this points up the richness and lavishness of the **temple** as a fitting tribute to the God who manifested Himself there.

**5:1. When all . . . the temple** was completed (a construction project that lasted seven years; cf. 1 Kings 6:38), **Solomon** directed that **the furnishings** be brought into the **temple** and also that the offerings **David had** previously gathered (cf. 1 Chron. 22:14; 29:1-9) be **placed** within the temple **treasuries.** So great were David's and the leaders' contributions that Solomon's craftsmen had not used all those metals.

## C. Dedication of the temple (5:2–7:10)

### 1. HOUSING OF THE ARK (5:2-14)

**5:2-6.** The only object which had not been put in the temple, but which was indispensable to its true function, was **the ark.** It had remained in a tabernacle **David** had built on Mount Zion (1 Chron. 15:1) but all was ready now for its removal to Solomon's temple. The time chosen for this momentous event was **the festival in the seventh month,** the Feast of Tabernacles in September-October (Lev. 23:33-36). This was in 959 B.C. With great fanfare the tribal leaders gathered to witness the procession **from Zion** (here the southeast portion of Jerusalem; cf. 2 Sam. 5:7, just south of Moriah where the temple was built). Apparently **the ark** had been temporarily removed from Moriah while the temple was under construction there. **The priests who were Levites,** bore not only **the ark** but also David's tabernacle and all its **furnishings** (2 Chron. 5:2-5). Like David before him, **Solomon** celebrated the transporting of the ark by **sacrificing** innumerable animals (v. 6).

**5:7-10.** When **the ark** arrived at the temple, **the priests,** the only persons authorized to do so, took it into **the most holy place** and placed it **beneath the** overarching **cherubim** (vv. 7-8). When the doors to the most holy place were open the **poles . . . could be seen** from **the holy place, but not from** the **outside.** The only contents in **the ark** were the **two** stone **tablets** of the Law (v. 10). The author of Hebrews wrote that the ark also contained Aaron's rod and a pot of manna (Heb. 9:4). This is nowhere attested in the Old Testament (Ex. 16:33-34 and Num. 17:10 state that the rod and manna were placed in front of the tabernacle, not in the ark). But these extra objects may have been added to the original contents sometime later than Solomon. Or perhaps they had been lost by Solomon's time.

**5:11-14.** After **the priests . . . withdrew from** the temple, they were joined by other priests and Levitical **musicians** who **stood** to **the east . . . of the** great altar (i.e., in front of it) and lifted up their voices and instruments (**120 . . . trumpets,** plus **cymbals and other instruments**) in loud and joyous **praise to** God. On this special occasion all 24 priestly and Levitical **divisions** (v. 11) were represented. They did not follow the prescribed order of ministry (cf. 1 Chron. 24:1-19) because of the unique significance of this celebration. In their praise the musicians sang of the Lord's goodness and **love** (ḥeseḏ, "loyal love"; cf. 2 Chron. 6:14; 7:3, 6; 20:21). The LORD showed His approval by filling **the temple** with the **cloud of glory,** which represented His presence in **the temple** (cf. Ex. 40:34-35; Ezek. 10:3-4).

### 2. SOLOMON'S BLESSING AND PRAYER (CHAP. 6)

**6:1-11.** The appearance of the glory of God in the cloud (5:13-14) reminded **Solomon** that God had made His presence known to Moses in the same way though in a much more modest tent, or tabernacle. Now, however, **the LORD . . . would dwell** in a more permanent magnificence (vv. 1-2). Solomon addressed the people in a blessing (vv. 4-11). First he praised **God** for having **fulfilled** His promises **to . . . David** by choosing him and his dynasty, selecting **Jerusalem** as the divine "residence," and permitting the erection of **a temple** (vv. 4-6). The term **name,** which occurs 14 times in this chapter and 14 times elsewhere in 2 Chronicles, refers to God's attributes or presence (cf. 1 Chron. 13:6). **David** had not been allowed to build **the temple** but God in His infinite grace had ordained that Solomon, David's **son,** do so and now that **promise** had come to pass (2 Chron. 6:7-11).

**6:12-21.** After blessing the people, **Solomon** offered a dedicatory prayer (vv. 14-42). Kneeling on a specially constructed **bronze platform . . . in the center of the outer court** (vv. 12-13), he extolled **the Lord** for His **covenant**-keeping faithfulness (vv. 14-15). **Love** translates *ḥesed,* meaning God's loyal love (cf. 5:13; 7:3, 6; 20:21). The king then implored the **Lord** to continue His favor on David's dynasty as the people continued to serve Him **according to** the Law (6:16-17). In one of the finest statements of divine transcendence found in the Scriptures, Solomon acknowledged the insufficiency of a mere **temple,** no matter how grand and commodious, to **contain** the Lord of **the heavens** (v. 18). Yet Solomon was persuaded of God's interest in human affairs. He besought the **Lord** to recognize the **temple** as a focal point of His communion with **Israel** (**hear** occurs five times in vv. 19-21) and to respond **from heaven** (cf. vv. 23, 25, 27, 30, 33, 35, 39), His true **dwelling place** (cf. vv. 30, 33, 39; 30:27). Because Solomon spoke of the Israelites praying **toward this place** (6:21; cf. vv. 34, 38), centuries later Daniel faced Jerusalem as he prayed (Dan. 6:10).

**6:22-31.** Solomon also prayed that the **temple** might be the place where God would adjudicate **wrongs** between individuals (vv. 22-23), where He would forgive the nation when it was **defeated** in battle because of **sin** (vv. 24-25), and where He would hear their prayers of repentance when drought (vv. 26-27) and other disasters would befall them as a result of divine judgment (vv. 28-31).

**6:32-39.** In a spirit of magnanimity, Solomon also entreated the Lord to **hear** the prayers of foreigners who might go to the **temple** to seek His face (vv. 32-33). Solomon prayed that in times of **war** the Lord would bless His people in battle (vv. 34-35). If, however, they sinned and were taken **captive to** a foreign **land** and there repented, Solomon prayed

that they would be forgiven (vv. 36-39).

**6:40-42.** In a closing hymnic refrain, Solomon interceded for the temple (God's **resting place**), the **priests,** the people (**saints**), and himself as the **anointed** successor to David (cf. Ps. 132:8-11). God should do these things, Solomon suggested, because of His **kindnesses** (pl. of *ḥesed,* "loyal love"; cf. 2 Chron. 5:13; 6:14; 7:3, 6; 20:21), which He had **promised to David** and to his dynasty.

3. SOLOMON'S SACRIFICES (7:1-10)

**7:1-3.** As though to dramatize His answer to Solomon's prayer visually, **the Lord** sent down **fire** to consume **the sacrifices** that had been prepared (cf. Lev. 9:24; 1 Chron. 21:26), and the cloud of His **glory . . . filled the temple** once again (cf. 2 Chron. 5:13-14). So overwhelmed were the people by God's theophanic presence that they fell to **their faces** and acclaimed His covenant faithfulness (**love,** *ḥesed,* "loyal love"; cf. 5:13, 6:14; 7:6; 20:21).

**7:4-7.** Then the assembled worshipers **offered** more **sacrifices**—with **Solomon** alone offering **22,000 . . . cattle** and **120,000 sheep and goats.** In praise **the priests** and **Levites** played their **musical instruments** (v. 6). So numerous were the sacrifices that Solomon instructed that they be made in a specially constructed and dedicated area in **the courtyard** before **the temple.**

**7:8-10. For seven days** the festivities went on with the **people** of **the Lord** gathered **from Lebo Hamath** (Israel's northern boundary toward the Euphrates River) **to the Wadi of Egypt** (modern Wadi el-Arish, south of Gaza). Finally, **on the eighth day,** which followed the seven-day Feast of Tabernacles (Lev. 23:36), the people assembled once **more** just before returning **to their homes.** In all, the temple celebration lasted 15 days, for having begun in the seventh month (2 Chron. 5:3) and probably on the 15th day (cf. Lev. 23:39), the Feast of Tabernacles extended through the 22nd day. The **festival** mentioned in 2 Chronicles 7:9b is certainly the Tabernacles feast, so **the dedication of the altar** (v. 9a), which also lasted **seven days,** preceded the Tabernacles festival and began on the eighth day of that **month.**

## D. God's blessings and curses (7:11-22)

**7:11-12.** Included in every covenant text in the ancient Near East as well as in many of those in the Old Testament was a section containing blessings and curses. The blessings would become effective if the subservient party would stay loyal to the great king while the curses would be expected to fall on the disobedient (cf. Deut. 27–28). In line with God's covenant with David and Solomon such a section now follows. **The LORD appeared to** Solomon and assured him that his work on **the temple** and its dedication pleased Him (2 Chron. 7:11-12). (Interestingly, chap. 7 has only a passing reference to Solomon's building of **the royal palace,** no doubt because of the chronicler's planned emphasis on the **temple** [see the *Introduction* to 1 Chron.]. In 1 Kings 7:1-12 details are given on Solomon's **palace** construction.)

**7:13-22.** God then encouraged Solomon by the promise that if His judgment (by drought, **locusts,** or a **plague**) should fall on the nation for **their sin,** they need only **turn** to the Lord in earnest humility and repentance and they would find forgiveness and restoration (vv. 13-15). This promise, in answer to Solomon's prayer (6:26-31), was given because God's presence among His people Israel is eternal, focused particularly on the **temple** (7:16). The covenant theme comes through clearly in the Lord's declaration that if Solomon would obey Him (v. 17) he could be assured of God's reciprocal blessing in the perpetuation of his dynastic **rule** (v. 18; cf. 1 Chron. 17:11-14). Conversely, if Solomon and the nation should fall **away** from the Lord and **serve other gods** they would be exiled and their magnificent **temple** destroyed (2 Chron. 7:19-20). This does not suggest that the Davidic Covenant is conditional from God's standpoint. He had said it would be forever (2 Sam. 7:13, 15-16). But Solomon's (or any king's) enjoyment of it would depend on his obedience to **God.**

Later Solomon did worship **other gods** (1 Kings 11:4-8), as did many of his successors, so the nation was exiled (2 Chron. 6:36; 36:17-18, 20) to Babylon and the temple destroyed (36:19). Everyone who would witness the desolation of the **land** and the **temple** would know that it was a mark of God's judgment on His people because of their sin (7:21-22).

## E. Solomon's successes (chaps. 8–9)

### 1. POLITICAL SUCCESS (8:1-11)

**8:1-2.** Within **20 years** of his accession (i.e., by 951 B.C.) **Solomon** had completed **the temple . . . and his own palace** and had **rebuilt** certain **villages that Hiram** had ceded to Israel. According to 1 Kings 9:10-14, these towns, 20 in all, had originally been given by Solomon to Hiram but Hiram was displeased with them. The chronicler was possibly referring to the return of these rejected towns to Solomon who then restored them.

**8:3-6.** At that time **Solomon** began his conquest of foreign states, commencing with the Aramean city of **Hamath Zobah,** almost 300 miles north of Jerusalem. He then refortified **Tadmor** (later known as Palmyra), a **desert** oasis trading center on the main highway from Mesopotamia, about 150 miles northeast of Damascus. He did the same with the newly acquired **cities** around **Hamath.** In Israel proper **he rebuilt Upper . . . and Lower Beth Horon** to make them strong fortresses, and undertook similar projects at **Baalath** and other storage **cities** and military centers. **Beth Horon** was about 10 miles northwest of Jerusalem on the border between Judah and the Northern tribes (Josh. 18:13). Baalath was in the territory of Dan (Josh. 19:44). The other unnamed cities probably include Hazor, Megiddo, and Gezer (cf. 1 Kings 9:15).

**8:7-10.** **Solomon conscripted** his forced **labor** from among non-Israelite population groups still living **in the land.** These included **Hittites** (originally from central Anatolia, in modern-day Turkey), **Amorites** (early hill-dwellers in Canaan), **Perizzites** (a Canaanite subtribe), **Hivites** (perhaps the same as the Indo-Aryan Hurrians), **and Jebusites** (the original Canaanite inhabitants of Jerusalem)—peoples not fully subjugated by Israel in the Conquest (Jud. 3:1-6). **The Israelites** were exempted from such drudgery, serving instead in the army and as labor foremen. The **250** supervisors were only Israelites whereas the 550 officials in 1 Kings 9:23 probably included Canaanite foremen as well. In addition to the 250 Solomon had 3,600 other foremen (2 Chron. 2:18), a total of 3,850 (which equals 3,300, 1 Kings 5:16, plus 550, 1 Kings 9:23).

**8:11.** A final political achievement

by **Solomon** was his relocation of his wife, the **daughter** of the Pharaoh of Egypt, **from** David's old **palace** on Mount Zion (**the City of David**; cf. 5:2; 1 Kings 3:1; 1 Chron. 11:5) **to** her new **palace** on the temple mount (cf. 1 Kings 7:8; 9:24). The reason given is that she, an Egyptian, would profane David's palace which at one time had had such close connection with **the ark** of the covenant. Though the chronicler did not relate how the daughter of the Egyptian king (Pharaoh Siamun of Dynasty 21?) had become Solomon's **wife,** the fact that she had implies the political strength and status of Israel's king for he must have been regarded by Pharaoh as at least his equal.

2. RELIGIOUS SUCCESS (8:12-16)

**8:12-16.** Solomon's spiritual devotion, evidenced by the many sacrifices he gave at the dedication of the temple (7:5), was typical of his religious commitment, in the view of the chronicler. True, 2 Chronicles does not mention Solomon's introduction of pagan shrines and worship, a point stressed in 1 Kings 11:1-13. But the chronicler, though he surely knew those things, did narrate what must have been Solomon's general practice of fulfilling Mosaic sacrificial requirements (2 Chron. 8:12-13). **Solomon** also maintained the priestly and Levitical **divisions** established by **his father** (vv. 14-15). Last but not least, Solomon had begun and had completed **the temple,** his highest religious achievement.

3. ECONOMIC SUCCESS (8:17–9:31)

**8:17-18.** Much of Solomon's prosperity was due to his maritime industry, an enterprise he was able to undertake with Phoenician help. Operating out of **Ezion Geber and Elath,** seaports on the eastern arm of the Red Sea (known today as the Gulf of Aqaba or Gulf of Eilat), his and Hiram's sailors **sailed to** distant points such as the land of **Ophir** (cf. comments on 1 Chron. 29:4) whence they imported **450 talents of gold** (ca. 17 tons, or 34,000 pounds), apparently on one voyage. (First Kings 9:28 has 420 talents, ca. 16 tons. One of the two figures may be due to a copyist confusing the two similar-looking Heb. letters for 450 and 420.)

**9:1-8.** Another source of revenue **came to Solomon** from **the queen of She-** ba, possibly the land of the Sabeans (cf. Job 1:15; Ezek. 23:42; Joel 3:8) in southwestern Arabia. Having **heard of** his **wisdom** (cf. 1 Kings 10:1-13), she traveled over 1,200 miles **to test him.** In her camel **caravan** she brought **spices . . . gold, and precious stones** as tokens of her friendship. So impressed was she with Solomon's **wisdom** and prosperity **she was overwhelmed. She** said that what she saw **far exceeded the report** she had **heard.** Surely, she said, Solomon's workmen must be **happy,** and the **God** who could bless in all these ways was to be praised. Like Hiram's words of **praise** (2 Chron. 2:12), hers too were probably a formal courtesy, not an indication of her conversion to Yahweh.

**9:9-12. Then** the queen of Sheba bestowed her gifts, the **gold** alone amounting to **120 talents** (4½ tons, or 9,000 pounds), **spices, and precious stones.** The **spices** exceeded in quality (and quantity?) anything ever seen before in Israel. The land of **Ophir** (cf. comments on 1 Chron. 29:4) yielded not only **gold** but also **algumwood** (cf. algum in 2 Chron. 2:8; perhaps a name for sandalwood) **and precious stones.** The **algumwood** was employed in the **steps of the temple** and **the royal palace** and as frames for **harps and lyres. Solomon** also **gave** gifts **to the queen.**

**9:13-16.** Other evidences of Solomon's prosperity follow. His annual income in **gold** was **666 talents** (25 tons, or 50,000 pounds). This did not include profits through taxation or tolls on caravans and other **merchants.** The source of this massive wealth of **gold and silver** was both external (from **all the kings of Arabia**) and internal (**governors of the land**). With the **gold** he **made 200 large shields,** each containing **600 bekas** (7½ pounds) of **gold,** and **300 small shields . . . each** with half that amount (**300 bekas**) of **gold.** (In 1 Kings 10:17 the amount of gold in each of the small shields is said to be three minas each. That is the same amount, expressed in a different unit of measure.)

These shields were only ornamental for they were placed in **the Palace of the Forest of Lebanon,** one of Solomon's public buildings in Jerusalem, probably built mostly of cedar (cf. 1 Kings 7:2; Lebanon was the major source of cedar). The royal palace was a separate building (cf. 1 Kings 7:2 with 1 Kings 7:8).

**9:17-24.** Solomon's **throne** was decorated **with ivory and overlaid with . . . gold.** With great detail the chronicler described its **six steps,** gold **footstool,** arms, and **12** guardian **lions,** one on each **end of each step.** His drinking vessels and other table service were of **gold** only, for **silver** was thought, by comparison, to be of insufficient **value. Every three years** the king sent out merchant **ships** in order to acquire exotica such as **gold, silver . . . ivory . . . apes, and baboons!** As a result he was regarded as the wealthiest monarch of his day. And his wealth increased as visitors came regularly **to hear** his God-given **wisdom,** bringing, of course, their extravagant tokens of appreciation, including **articles of silver and gold . . . robes,** weaponry, **spices . . . horses, and mules.**

**9:25-28.** In summation, the historian wrote of Solomon's military (v. 25) and political (v. 26) power (his rule extended **from the** Euphrates **River to** Egypt's **border;** cf. 1 Kings 4:21, 24) as well as his incalculable wealth, produced largely through his trading expertise (2 Chron. 9:27-28). (Vv. 25, 27-28 are similar to 1:14-16.) The extent of Solomon's kingdom did not fulfill the Abrahamic Covenant (Gen. 15:18) because many countries in that territory only paid tribute to Solomon (1 Kings 4:21) and were not assimilated into the nation Israel.

**9:29-31.** Then the chronicler appended the note that information on **other** affairs of **Solomon's reign** could be found in the writings of the Prophets **Nathan** (cf. 1 Kings 1:11-13), **Ahijah** (cf. 1 Kings 11:29), and **Iddo** (cf. 2 Chron. 12:15; 13:22). **Solomon reigned . . . 40 years** (971–931 B.C.) and was **succeeded** by his son **Rehoboam.**

## II. The Reign of the Davidic Dynasty (chaps. 10–36)

### A. Rehoboam (chaps. 10–12)

1. DIVISION OF THE NATION INTO ISRAEL AND JUDAH (CHAP. 10)

**10:1.** Strangely, though Solomon must have had many sons, none is mentioned except **Rehoboam** whom he begot by Naamah the Ammonitess (cf. 1 Kings 14:21). Having no doubt sensed the increasing spirit of alienation on the part of **Israelites** in the northern part of the kingdom against his father, Rehoboam **went to Shechem** to be formally coronated. This city had held an important part in Israel's life since the time of Abraham. Joshua had reaffirmed the Mosaic Covenant there and from that time Shechem had been more or less the unofficial capital of the north (cf. Josh. 24:1-28).

**10:2-11. Jeroboam** was formerly the foreman of labor in Ephraim, in which Shechem was located. When he **heard** that Solomon had died, **he returned from Egypt** where **he had fled** from **Solomon** sometime previously (v. 2; cf. 1 Kings 11:26-28, 40). By popular demand **Jeroboam** headed a delegation which appealed **to Rehoboam** to **lighten** their load of **labor** and taxation (2 Chron. 10:3-4). Asking for **three days** to consider the matter, **Rehoboam consulted** with the old advisers of **his father,** who counseled him to listen to the Israelites. Then he turned to his own **young** peers who urged him not to relent but rather to make the people's **yoke** all the **heavier** (vv. 5-11). Rehoboam's young advisers said his heavier burden would be like his **little finger** being **thicker than** his **father's waist** and like **scorpions** (a cruel kind of whip with sharp pieces of metal) compared with his father's **whips.**

**10:12-16.** When **Rehoboam** again confronted **Jeroboam** and the people, he repeated the policy advocated by his **young** cohorts (vv. 12-14). This, the chronicler wrote (v. 15), **was** of **God,** however, for He had already promised **Jeroboam** that he would rule over the Northern tribes (cf. 1 Kings 11:29-39). Surely enough, when the assembly heard the words of Rehoboam they disassociated themselves from the house of **David** (**To your tents, O Israel!** cf. 2 Sam. 20:1) and, in effect, declared their independence of Judah (2 Chron. 10:16).

**10:17-19.** This left only **Judah** to **Rehoboam.** So serious was the cleavage that **Adoniram** (Heb. has Hadoram, a variant spelling), perhaps the new work manager over Ephraim (cf. 1 Kings 4:6), was **stoned . . . to death** by **the Israelites** when **Rehoboam sent** him to them to arbitrate their differences. Finally realizing the hopelessness of gaining unified control, **Rehoboam** fled for his life **to Jerusalem.**

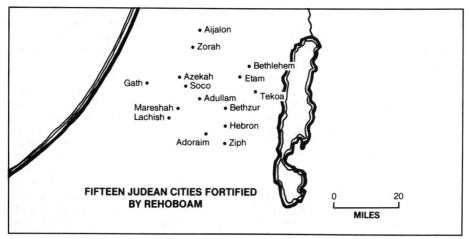

**FIFTEEN JUDEAN CITIES FORTIFIED
BY REHOBOAM**

0        20
MILES

## 2. REHOBOAM'S FORTIFICATIONS AND FAMILY (CHAP. 11)

**11:1-12.** When Rehoboam arrived in Jerusalem he amassed an army of **180,000 . . . men** from **Judah and Benjamin** (Benjamin had become part of Judah politically) and made plans to launch an attack on the rebel tribes. His plans were interrupted, however, by **the word of the LORD** through **Shemaiah** the prophet (cf. 12:5, 15) who proclaimed that the rupture of the kingdom was in the plan **of God** (11:2-4). **Rehoboam** nonetheless **built** defensive outposts in a number of places throughout **Judah and Benjamin,** the 15 cities listed here forming pretty much a circular defense all around **Judah** (vv. 5-12; see the map "Fifteen Judean Cities Fortified by Rehoboam").

**11:13-17.** Meantime **the priests and Levites** of the North came south to join Rehoboam **because Jeroboam** (as the 1 Kings 12:25–14:16 account relates in detail) had removed them from office and replaced them with an illegitimate priesthood (2 Chron. 11:13-15). The devout populace of the North also recognized the impropriety of the new Jeroboam cult and for at least **three years** made their pilgrimages **to Jerusalem to offer** worship **to the LORD** (vv. 16-17).

**11:18-23.** In keeping with the chronicler's purpose to magnify the Davidic dynasty, it is interesting that he, unlike the author of 1 and 2 Kings, related that Rehoboam's wife was a descendant of David from two sides (2 Chron. 11:18-19). Her father **Jerimoth** is otherwise unknown but here is identified as a **son of** David. Her mother was **Abihail, daugh**ter of David's brother **Eliab.** (So Jerimoth married his cousin Abihail.)

Rehoboam's second wife, **Maacah,** was a **daughter of Absalom** (v. 20). This may not be David's son Absalom, however, for he apparently left no children who achieved adulthood except a daughter Tamar (cf. 2 Sam. 14:27; 18:18). Moreover, Maacah's father is otherwise named Abishalom (1 Kings 15:10) and Uriel (2 Chron. 13:2).

By this second wife of Rehoboam, **Abijah** was born. **Rehoboam loved** his second wife **more than any** other **of his. . . . 18 wives and 60 concubines** (11:20-21). Like his father Solomon and his grandfather David he was guilty of polygamy (cf. Deut. 17:16-17). **Abijah** was his father's choice to succeed him as **king** so **Rehoboam** made him crown **prince** (cf. 2 Chron. 13:1). To palliate the other **sons,** however, Rehoboam gave them political appointments, with handsome remunerations (11:23).

## 3. EGYPT'S ATTACK ON JERUSALEM (CHAP. 12)

**12:1-4. Rehoboam** had not been ruling long when it became apparent that his border fortifications were inadequate to guard **Judah** against the invasion of the Egyptian army under King **Shishak** I (who ruled ca. 935–914 B.C.). Shishak had earlier given asylum to Jeroboam (cf. 1 Kings 11:40). Shishak, also known as Sheshonk, was the founder of Egypt's 22nd dynasty. On the walls of the temple of Amon at Karnak, Egypt he carved the names of Israelite cities he conquered.

In Rehoboam's **fifth year** (926 B.C.) the Lord brought Shishak as a punishment for Rehoboam's sin of abandoning the Law of the LORD (cf. 1 Kings 14:22-24). **With 1,200 chariots and 60,000** cavalry and aided by his Libyan, Sukkite (Egyptian foreign mercenaries), and Cushite allies, the Egyptian king had no difficulty in overrunning the fortresses and was ready to attack **Jerusalem** itself.

**12:5-8.** At that point **the Prophet Shemaiah** (cf. 11:2; 12:15) told **Rehoboam** that the Egyptian invasion was a divine retribution for Judah's sin and that only sincere repentance would turn it aside. Recognizing the justice of their punishment **the leaders** humbly turned to **the LORD** who therefore promised to deliver them from destruction but would allow them to become vassals of the king of Egypt. In this way they would come to appreciate the merciful rule of the Lord in contrast with the cruel ways of human **kings.** How long this relationship lasted is unknown though it surely did not outlast the reign of Rehoboam.

**12:9-11.** Before **Shishak** withdrew from **Jerusalem,** he plundered **the temple** and **the royal palace** of all their **gold.** The gold supply was so diminished that **Rehoboam** had **to replace** the golden ornamental **shields** (cf. 9:15-16) with **bronze.** To protect the new **shields** from theft, **guards** carried them from the **guardroom** to the **temple** and back, **whenever** Rehoboam went to the temple.

**12:12-16.** In later years **Rehoboam** regained his power and wealth, at least to some degree. He died at age 58 **and was buried in** Jerusalem (**the city of David**) with his kingly ancestors. His **reign,** characterized by an **evil heart toward the LORD** and incessant war with **Jeroboam,** was chronicled, the historian said, in the annals of the Prophets **Shemaiah** (cf. 11:2; 12:5) and **Iddo** (cf. 9:29; 13:22).

### B. Abijah (chap. 13)

**13:1-2a.** By a different chronological system at use in **Judah** from that in Israel, **Abijah** began his reign **in the 18th year . . .** of Jeroboam of Israel but only in the 17th year of his father Rehoboam, though both began to rule at the same time. Thus Abijah came to power in 913 B.C. and reigned until 911 (see comments on his mother **Maacah** at 11:20-21).

**13:2b-12.** **Abijah** took up the hostilities with **Jeroboam** which had prevailed in the days of Abijah's father. So massive

had the strife between them become that Judah fielded **400,000 . . . men** and Israel **800,000** during some point of their antagonism at least (vv. 2b-3). Hoping to forestall a bloody encounter, **Abijah** addressed his Israelite brothers from **Mount Zemaraim,** perhaps a short distance east of Bethel (cf. Josh. 18:22). He reminded them that the true **kingship** lay with David's dynasty, not with Jeroboam. God had made with **David . . . a covenant of salt,** suggesting durability (cf. comments on Lev. 2:13; Num. 18:19). In fact Jeroboam's rebellious action was possible only because **Rehoboam . . . young** (i.e., relatively so, for he began reigning at age 41; cf. 2 Chron. 12:13) and naive as he was, had been duped by his counselors (13:7).

The Israelites **indeed** had **a vast army,** Abijah said, but since they had exiled the true **priests** and **Levites** (cf. 11:14b-15) and chosen other **gods** (**golden calves;** cf. goat- and calf-idols, 11:15) they could have no hope of victory for the Lord God was on the side of Judah. **God is with us; He is our Leader,** Abijah affirmed (13:8-12). (However, cf. Abijah's sins, 13:21; 1 Kings 15:3.) Abijah referred to only 1 **lampstand,** though Solomon's temple had 10 (2 Chron. 4:7). Perhaps this 1 was the original lampstand Moses made for the tabernacle.

**13:13-18.** While Abijah's warning was being sounded, **Jeroboam** set up an **ambush . . . behind** the troops of **Judah.** Then Israel attacked from **both front and rear.** But Judah **cried out to the LORD. . . . the priests blew their trumpets** (cf. Num. 10:9), and the soldiers **raised** their **battle cry. God** then **delivered** Israel **into** Judah's **hands** (2 Chron. 13:16). **Judah** was **victorious because** of her reliance **on the LORD** (v. 18). Altogether Israel suffered **500,000 casualties** (v. 17) out of **800,000** men (cf. v. 3).

**13:19-22.** Thus defeated, Israel retreated and left Judah to occupy (a) **Bethel,** where **Jeroboam** had set up a golden calf for worship (1 Kings 12:26-29, 33), (b) **Jeshanah** (now Burj el-Isaneh, four miles south of Shiloh), and (c) **Ephron** (four miles northeast of Bethel). **Jeroboam** never recovered from this blow and **died** at about the same time as Abijah (910 B.C.). **Abijah,** like his father and grandfather, was strong politically. Like them he too was involved in polygamy (cf. 2 Chron. 11:21), having **14 wives**

and 38 children. Other details on Abijah, the chronicler noted, were **written** by **the Prophet Iddo** (cf. 9:29; 12:15).

## C. Asa (chaps. 14–16)

As has been stressed repeatedly, one of the chronicler's major purposes was to provide a comprehensive and systematic account of the divine selection of David and his dynasty and its historical development. This is why the kings of Judah dominate the record and those of Israel appear only when they relate to affairs in the Southern Kingdom. This is contrary to the approach in 1 and 2 Kings where, if anything, the rulers of Israel are pivotal and those of Judah, at least till the fall of Samaria, are almost incidental. So it is not surprising that little is said of Jeroboam in 2 Chronicles 10–13. This neglect of Israel's kings continues to be the rule in the remainder of 2 Chronicles. So the chronicler proceeded to discuss the reign of Asa (chaps. 14–16), Judah's next king, with no mention of Jeroboam's successor in Israel.

### 1. ASA'S OBEDIENCE TO THE LORD (CHAP. 14)

**14:1-5. Asa,** son of **Abijah,** occupied the Davidic throne for 41 years (911–870 B.C.; cf. 16:13). His **10 years** of **peace** (cf. 14:6) preceded the attack by Zerah (vv. 9-15). **Asa** was assessed as a generally **good** ruler who destroyed pagan objects of worship and urged compliance with the covenant of **the LORD.** The **sacred stones and . . . Asherah poles** (v. 3) were Canaanite fertility symbols which played an important role in the people's depraved nature religion. (On **the high places** see comments on Num. 33:52.) The Asherah poles were probably images of Asherah, Baal's mother and El's consort, and may have served as incense stands in Baal worship.

**14:6-10.** Militarily Asa refortified Judah's defensive posts (vv. 6-7), apparently the ones his grandfather Rehoboam had **fortified** (11:5-12) and which Shishak had captured (12:2-4). **Asa** raised **an army . . . from Judah** and **Benjamin** of 580,000 **brave** spearmen and bowmen (14:8). This he did perhaps in anticipation of the invasion by **Zerah the Cushite** (from Cush, modern-day southern Egypt, Sudan, and northern Ethiopia), apparently the mercenary general under Osorkon I of Egypt (914–874 B.C.), suc-

cessor to Shishak. With a vast army (see NIV marg.) **and 300 chariots,** Zerah met **Asa** at **Mareshah** (ca. 25 miles southwest of Jerusalem; cf. 11:8; Micah 1:15). **Zephathah** is mentioned only here in the Bible. Libyans were included in Zerah's army (cf. 2 Chron. 16:8). Whereas Shishak had been successful in his invasion of Judah (12:2, 4, 9), Zerah was not. Shishak's success was probably because of Rehoboam's sins (11:21; 12:1-2) whereas Zerah's defeat was because of Asa's faithfulness (cf. 14:2).

**14:11-15.** Asa turned to **the LORD** in urgent prayer and was granted a smashing victory. Falling in uncounted numbers, **the Cushites fled** to Gerar (ca. 20 miles farther southwest of Mareshah), to an area that may have already been in Egyptian hands. When **Asa** got there he plundered **Gerar** and the surrounding **villages** and **returned to Jerusalem** in triumph, with **plunder** that included many animals as well as other material goods. Judah had no more war with Egypt till Josiah and Neco met in battle in 609 B.C. (35:20-24).

### 2. ASA'S REFORMS (CHAP. 15)

**15:1-7.** In due course **Azariah son of Oded,** a prophet of **the LORD** mentioned only here, **went . . . to . . . Asa** and challenged him to remain true to **the LORD** so that he could continue to enjoy God's blessing. He was told not to lead the people into lawlessness (**without the true God** means without His presence and blessing, **and without the Law,** v. 3, probably means without knowledge of or obedience to it) and anarchy (**great turmoil,** v. 5, and **distress,** v. 6) such as they had experienced in the past, probably in the time of the Judges. Instead Azariah told Asa to **be strong.**

**15:8-15.** Asa responded to this message from **the prophet** by intensifying his destruction of **idols** (cf. 14:3-5) and repairing the great bronze **altar** of **the LORD's temple** which, for some unspecified reason, had suffered damage. **Then he assembled . . . the people** of his kingdom, including defectors **from Ephraim, Manasseh, and Simeon. . . . in the third month** (May-June) **of** his **15th year** (896 B.C.). (Apparently some Simeonites, who had not been assimilated into the tribe of Judah, had migrated north.) Asa's purpose was to renew the **covenant** made between the LORD and their fathers under Moses (15:12). Using some of the livestock they had seized from the villages around Gerar (cf. 14:15), the priests offered up a sacrifice of **700 . . . cattle and 7,000 sheep and goats** (15:11). Those refusing to renew the covenant **were to be put to death** for by their refusal they indicated their enmity to **the LORD** and acceptance of other gods (v. 13; cf. Deut. 13:6-9). The people **wholeheartedly** pledged their continued faithfulness (2 Chron. 15:14-15).

**15:16-19.** Perhaps the most striking evidence of Asa's reformation was his removal of **his** own **grandmother Maacah from** being **queen mother.** (The Heb. *'ēm* can mean either mother, NASB, or "grandmother," NIV.) As "queen mother" she may have been Asa's mother; if so it is coincidental that his grandmother was also named Maacah (cf. 11:20). **She had made** an **Asherah pole,** a Canaanite fertility symbol (cf. comments on 14:3), which **Asa** destroyed **and burned . . . in the Kidron Valley** (cf. 29:16; 30:14), just east of Jerusalem. So Asa eradicated foreign worship from Judah, except for some **high places** that remained (cf. 14:3)—usually sites of pagan altars.

He also enriched **the temple** with **silver and gold** given by Abijah and himself, presumably to help replace some of what Shishak had plundered in Asa's grandfather's day (12:9). Finally, God gave **Asa** a period of peace **until** his **35th year** (876 B.C.; but see comments on 16:1).

3. ASA'S TREATY WITH ARAM (CHAP. 16)

**16:1.** In Asa's **36th year** he was confronted by **Baasha, king of Israel,** who built a fortress at the Israel-Judah border at **Ramah,** about six miles north of Jerusalem. Baasha's purpose was to prevent further movement of Israelites south to **Judah.** A problem surfaces here in that the dates of Baasha (909–886 B.C.; cf. 1 Kings 15:33) necessitate his death 10 years before the 36th year of Asa. This has led some scholars to conclude that the 35th year (2 Chron. 15:19) refers to the 35th year of the kingdom of Judah since its division from Israel in 931 B.C. This would be 896 B.C. But this is unlikely for the 35th year of the kingdom would hardly be called "the 35th year of Asa's reign." More likely is the suggestion that the numbers may rest on a copyist's mis-

reading of Hebrew figures whereby 35th (15:19) and 36th (16:1) may have been misread for 15th and 16th. This would push the date of the events of chapter 16 back to 895, within Baasha's reign.

**16:2-6. Asa** felt so threatened by this turn of events that he bribed **Ben-Hadad** the Aramean **king** of **Damascus** to make a defense **treaty** with him and to **break** his (Ben-Hadad's) **treaty with Baasha. Ben-Hadad** did so and invaded northern **Israel,** taking several important **towns. Dan** and **Abel Maim** (or Abel Bethmaacah, 1 Kings 15:20) were about 10 miles north of Lake Huleh, and **Ijon** (modern Merj Ayyun) was just north of Abel Maim. This diverted **Baasha** from barricading **Ramah** so that **Asa** dismantled Baasha's work there and used the materials (**stones and timber**) to build his own defenses at **Geba and Mizpah,** both on the border of Judah and Israel. Geba is probably Gibeah (the city of Saul); Mizpah may be modern Nebi Samwil.

**16:7-10.** Asa's reliance on Ben-Hadad brought the rebuke of **Hanani the seer** (i.e., prophet) who chided the **king** for having forgotten that it was **the LORD,** not mere soldiers, who had given victory over the **Cushites** (14:12) **and Libyans.** As a result of this foolish action, **Asa** would experience **war** to the end of his days. This so angered **Asa** that he cast the prophet into **prison** and took out his frustrations on **the people.**

**16:11-14. The book of the kings of Judah and Israel** (not 1 and 2 Kings) recorded more details on **Asa's reign.** Later, when **Asa** suffered a foot **disease** in his **39th year** of rule (872 B.C.) he refused to **seek** God's **help** but **only** turned to **the physicians.** Two years later (870) he **died** and was **buried** with an impressive state funeral. The **fire** was not a cremation.

Though **Asa** was generally an upright king, his reign was marred by his reliance on the ungodly Ben-Hadad and his failure to trust the Lord in his illness. The dates of Jehoshaphat, Asa's son (873–848), reveal a coregency of some three years. This may reflect the period of Asa's incapacity.

*D. Jehoshaphat (chaps. 17–20)*

1. JEHOSHAPHAT'S POWERFUL KINGDOM (CHAP. 17)

**17:1-9.** Asa was **succeeded** by **Jehoshaphat his son,** a man whose reign was generally complimented by the chronicler. The **king** built up Judah's defenses **against Israel** (including **towns** in **Ephraim . . . his father Asa had captured**; cf. 15:8); he **followed** the LORD, removing heathen worship and its accoutrements (17:3-4, 6; on the **Baals** [pl.] see comments on Jud. 2:11, and on **the Asherah poles** see comments on 2 Chron. 14:3); he received **gifts** which brought him **wealth and honor** (17:5); and he **sent** out teachers (**officials. . . . Levites,** and **priests**) all over **Judah** to instruct **the people** in the **Law** (vv. 7-9). This last act he did in his **third year** (v. 7), perhaps after the death of Asa.

**17:10-19.** Jehoshaphat also enjoyed the respect of **surrounding** nations, so much so that they left him in peace and **some** (including **Philistines** and **the Arabs**) even **brought** him **tribute** as a sign of his sovereignty over them. The reason for this respect was the vast military might which **Jehoshaphat** amassed. He fortified and supplied defense emplacements **in Judah** (vv. 12-13) and enrolled an army of 780,000 men of **Judah** and 380,000 of **Benjamin** (vv. 14-18). This did not include those **stationed in the** fortifications (v. 19). These numbers seem unusually large. His father Asa had 300,000 from Judah and 280,000 from Benjamin (14:8). Some suggest that Jehoshaphat's troops consisted of military units whose composition is now unclear (e.g., the Heb. word for "thousands" might be, it is suggested, a technical term for a unit of perhaps no more than 100 men, so Judah would have had 780 such units). However, since David, more than 100 years earlier, had 500,000 Judean soldiers (2 Sam. 24:9), Jehoshaphat's roster of 780,000 may not be excessive.

### 2. JEHOSHAPHAT'S ALLIANCE WITH AHAB (18:1–19:3)

**18:1-3a.** One result of Jehoshaphat's formidable strength was his attractiveness to **Ahab, king of Israel,** who both feared him and wished to use him as an ally. **Ahab** was the second king of the Omride dynasty of Israel, the most illustrious family in the Northern Kingdom's history. He had come to power at about the same time as **Jehoshaphat** (Ahab reigned from 874 to 853 B.C.) and was related to Jehoshaphat **by a marriage** alliance (Jehoshaphat's son Jehoram had married Athaliah, Ahab and Jezebel's daughter, 21:6; 22:2b). Toward the end of Ahab's life (in 853) he was engaged in bitter hostilities with the Arameans in the Transjordan (cf. 1 Kings 22:1-4). **Jehoshaphat** went to **Samaria,** Israel's capital, to see **Ahab.** After flattering Jehoshaphat with an elaborate banquet **Ahab** urged him to go to **Ramoth Gilead** to join him in war against the Arameans.

**18:3b-7.** Jehoshaphat agreed to go to **war** with Ahab on condition that **the** LORD give His approval. Ahab then gathered his **400** false and mercenary **prophets** (perhaps prophets of Asherah; cf. 1 Kings 18:19b) who gave their blessing to his plans. **Jehoshaphat,** however, knew the prophets were charlatans so he asked for a true **prophet of the** LORD. The only **one** available was **Micaiah son of Imlah,** but Ahab hated **him because** he would not compromise his integrity and give Ahab any **good** words (cf. 2 Chron. 18:17).

**18:8-11.** While **Micaiah** was being summoned, **the** other **prophets** continued to predict victory. **Zedekiah** was especially dramatic in his approach, holding in his hands some **iron horns** which he said symbolized Ahab's ability to thrust through the enemy.

**18:12-17.** Then **Micaiah** arrived, having been instructed to tell King Ahab what he wanted to hear. Micaiah declined to do so. But when he was first asked the outcome of the campaign he pretended to give assurance of victory (v. 14b). But he soon gave the true message of **the** LORD, predicting a defeat for **Israel.** He compared **Israel** to **sheep** whose **shepherd** (Ahab) is taken away.

**18:18-27.** Then **Micaiah** related a vision in which he **saw** God commission a demonic **spirit** to inspire the **prophets** of **Ahab** to lie to him (vv. 18-22). On hearing that, **Zedekiah** (cf. v. 10) **slapped Micaiah,** who then predicted that Zedekiah would suffer calamity in the day of Israel's defeat (vv. 23-24). Ahab then returned **Micaiah** to **Amon,** the mayor of Samaria, **and to Joash the king's son** (v. 25). "King's son" is apparently a title of a royal official, not a literal son of Ahab (cf. Jer. 36:26; 38:6; 2 Chron. 28:7). Ahab also commanded that **Micaiah** be imprisoned, but as Ahab left, the man of God once more promised that **the king** would not **return** whole (18:25-27).

The vision of Micaiah is troublesome to some as it seems to suggest that God is the author of deceit (vv. 18-21). However, it is clearly just one of many examples of the sovereignty of God who does not initiate evil but sometimes allows it to occur for His own purposes (cf. 1 Sam. 16:14; Job 1:12; 2:5-6; 2 Cor. 12:7).

**18:28–19:3.** Having disregarded Micaiah (18:25), Ahab **and Jehoshaphat** went forth to **battle.** Despite being **in disguise,** Ahab was struck mortally by an enemy arrow and **died** at the close of the **day. Jehoshaphat** was spared by the goodness of **God** and managed to escape unscathed. When he got back to **Jerusalem,** however, he was met by the Prophet **Jehu** (cf. 20:34) **the son of Hanani** (cf. Hanani and Asa in 16:7) who rebuked him for his ungodly alliance with Ahab (19:1-2). The prophet did praise him, though, for his removal of paganism in Judah (cf. 17:6) and his love for **the LORD** (19:3).

3. JEHOSHAPHAT'S APPOINTMENT OF JUDGES (19:4-11)

**19:4-11.** Part of Jehoshaphat's program of reform was his personally traveling through **Judah** to encourage **people** to turn **back to the LORD.** He also **appointed** godly **judges** throughout **the land,** arbiters whose task it was to judge without **partiality or bribery** (cf. Deut. 16:18-20). He did the same **in Jerusalem** with a kind of supreme court charged with hearing the matters referred to them from outlying districts. **Over** this court he selected **Amariah the chief priest** to oversee religious cases and **Zebadiah** (not the same Zebadiah as in 2 Chron. 17:8, who was a Levite) to be **over** civil cases. **The Levites** would **serve** as officers to implement the work of the judges as a whole.

4. JEHOSHAPHAT'S DEFEAT OF A FOREIGN ALLIANCE (20:1-30)

**20:1-2.** Shortly after the disastrous adventure at Ramoth Gilead (chap. 18), **Moabites . . . Ammonites,** and **Meunites** launched an attack **on Jehoshaphat** from across the Jordan. The Meunites (cf. 1 Chron. 4:41; 2 Chron. 26:7) were an Arabian tribe living in Edom and elsewhere east and south of the Dead Sea. The **army** mentioned in 20:2, then, was from Edom (cf. Mount Seir [Edom] in vv. 10, 22-23), not from Aram (Heb.; cf. NIV

marg., v. 2). **Jehoshaphat** learned that this great host was **already** at **Hazazon Tamar (En Gedi;** cf. 1 Sam. 23:29), on the west shore of the Dead Sea, and would soon head for Jerusalem.

**20:3-12.** This situation prompted the king to proclaim a national **fast** (perhaps to show the people's sincerity; cf. 1 Sam. 7:6) and to **seek** God. He then addressed the LORD in prayer before **the temple . . . courtyard** (cf. 2 Chron. 4:9). **Jehoshaphat** first extolled **God** for His sovereign **power** (20:6) and then recalled God's grace in giving them, Abraham's **descendants,** the **land** (v. 7; cf. Gen. 15:18-21) and temple (**sanctuary,** 2 Chron. 20:8). (**Abraham** was also called God's **friend** in Isa. 41:8 and James 2:23.)

Next Jehoshaphat reminded the Lord of His promise to deliver them if they would only seek Him before His **temple** (2 Chron. 20:9; cf. 6:28-31). The prayer closed by referring to the immediate need—Judah was being assaulted by the same nations they had spared en route to Canaan **from Egypt.** They now needed the Lord's help (**we have no power to face this vast army** and **we do not know what to do**) to deliver them from their ungrateful attackers (20:10-12).

**20:13-19.** After Jehoshaphat's moving prayer, **the Spirit of the LORD came** on the Levite **Jahaziel** and empowered him to address **the assembly.** His message was one of comfort. (Twice he said, **Do not be afraid or discouraged,** vv. 15, 17.) **The battle,** he said, was **not** theirs **but God's.** David had spoken similar words when facing Goliath (1 Sam. 17:47). The next day they should depart and meet the enemy in the narrow mountain **pass** called **Ziz,** somewhere in the wilderness of Judah southeast of Jerusalem. But when the enemy was in sight they need only **stand** and watch what God would do. The assembly then **fell down in worship** to the **LORD,** and some Levites gave **loud** praise to Him.

**20:20-26.** Next day **Jehoshaphat** and the singers led the way to the conflict in **the Desert of Tekoa.** (Tekoa, Amos' hometown, Amos 1:1, was ca. 12 miles south of Jerusalem.) The singers inspired **the people** with their words of encouragement to trust **the LORD.** Then, at the moment of encounter, **the LORD** caused such confusion among the enemy troops that they turned on **one another.** The

Ammonites and the Moabites fought against the Meunites until the latter were annihilated, and after that the Ammonites fought against the Moabites. The slaughter was so great that **the men of Judah** could not **carry** away all the **plunder.** With thanksgiving to God they gathered **in the Valley of Beracah** ("praise") and offered their praise to God for His enduring **love** (2 Chron. 20:21; *ḥeseḏ*, "loyal love"; cf. 5:13; 6:14; 7:3, 6).

**20:27-30.** The soldiers then **returned** home to praise **God** at **the temple** with musical instruments. So obvious was God's hand on His people that **all** other nations feared Him. From then on **Jehoshaphat** enjoyed **peace.**

5. JEHOSHAPHAT'S LAST DAYS (20:31-37)

**20:31-33.** The chronicler concluded the annals of **Jehoshaphat** by mentioning his age **(35)** at accession, his length of reign **(25 years),** and the **name** of his mother **(Azubah).** His final assessment of the king was positive for the most part—**he walked in the ways of . . . the LORD** as had **his father.** Yet Jehoshaphat had allowed **the high places** to remain and had not brought his **people** to a steadfast commitment to the Lord. Earlier he had removed the practice of pagan worship at the high places (17:6), but apparently some people had restored them and the king did nothing about it.

**20:34-37.** Besides the details of **Jehoshaphat's reign** preserved in the records of the Prophet **Jehu** (cf. 19:2; also note comments on 33:18; 1 Kings 14:19; and comments under "Authorship" in the *Introduction* to 1 Chron.), the chronicler added a note about the king's ill-fated venture **with Ahaziah,** son of Ahab (cf. 1 Kings 22:49), the two of whom attempted **to construct** merchant **ships** at **Ezion Geber** (cf. comments on 2 Chron. 8:17). The plan was frustrated by **the LORD** because, as the Prophet **Eliezer** (from **Mareshah,** where the Cushites were defeated by Asa, 14:9-15) announced, **Jehoshaphat** had sinned by his temporary ungodly **alliance** (cf. chap. 19) **with** the Omride dynasty. Somehow **the ships were wrecked** before they ever sailed.

## E. *Jehoram (chap. 21)*

**21:1-3. Jehoshaphat** was succeeded by his son **Jehoram,** the oldest of his seven sons. **Jehoshaphat** gave to each of the others properties and goods.

**21:4-7. When Jehoram** came to power, however, he killed **his brothers** along with others of the royal family, perhaps because of his close ties with the wicked rulers of Israel (vv. 4, 6). He too would suffer a cruel death after a brief reign of only **eight years** (v. 5, 848–841 B.C.). Like his father, **Jehoram** had a close tie with the Omrides, going so far as to marry Athaliah, **daughter of Ahab** (v. 6; cf. 22:2). Despite Jehoram's personal **evil,** however, **the LORD** did not **destroy** the nation, for he remembered his everlasting **covenant** with **David** (21:7; cf. 1 Chron. 17:4-14). Like **a lamp** that was kept burning in one's tent or house, so David's line would continue (cf. 2 Sam. 21:17; 1 Kings 11:36; 15:4; 2 Kings 8:19).

**21:8-11.** Since the time of David and Solomon, Israel and **Judah** had held certain foreign provinces, including **Edom.** Moab had finally revolted from Israel's King Joram, in the last years of Jehoshaphat and, in an action not recounted by the chronicler, the two kings had attempted, apparently unsuccessfully, to regain their tribute state (cf. 2 Kings 3). Now **Edom** revolted from **Judah,** an action which called forth a futile response from **Jehoram** (2 Chron. 21:8-10a). **Libnah** also **revolted** (v. 10b), probably as a result of renewed Philistine pressure against the lowlands region where Libnah was located (cf. v. 16). All these setbacks occurred, the narrator wrote, **because Jehoram had** led **the people** away from **the LORD** and into pagan practices (vv. 10b-11).

**21:12-15.** In a final word of condemnation the Prophet **Elijah** sent **a letter** to **Jehoram** in which he charged the king with behaving like an Israelite and not like his godly fathers (vv. 12-13). **Now the LORD** would **strike** the nation and Jehoram's family **with a heavy blow** and would afflict him with an incurable **disease of the bowels** (vv. 14-15).

This letter from Elijah is of more than passing interest because it is the only known written message from the great prophet. Some scholars allege that it could not be authentic since, they say, Elijah was translated to heaven before Jehoram began to reign. But Elijah was still living on earth in the days of Joram, son of Ahab, who succeeded his brother Ahaziah in 852 B.C. (cf. 2 Kings 1:17).

This event, the author of 2 Kings wrote, occurred "in the second year of Jehoram . . . king of Judah." Though Jehoram's sole regency in Judah began in the year of Jehoshaphat's death (848), he co-reigned with his father from 853 to 848. It is still true, of course, that Jehoram could not have murdered his brothers until after 848 so the matter of Elijah's knowledge of this fact still remains. Since there is no certain way to date Elijah's translation perhaps it did not take place until 848 or even later.

**21:16-20. The prophecies of Elijah came to pass.** Judah was invaded by **the Philistines** and South Arabians **who lived near the Cushites** (of the Cush that was in southern Arabia, not the Cush in northeastern Africa). They looted the royal **palace** and **carried off** the **king's** family except **the youngest** son. **Jehoram** was **afflicted** by the promised **disease** (cf. v. 15), diagnosis of which is impossible in view of the scant information in verses 15, 18-19. His burial was without fanfare (**no** funeral **fire** was burned **in his honor** as was done for Asa, 16:14). Jehoram's death was **to no one's regret** because he had brought such misery on the nation. Like several other Judean kings he **was buried** in Jerusalem **but not in the tombs of the kings** (cf. 24:25; 26:23; 28:27).

### F. Ahaziah (22:1-9)

**22:1-5a. Ahaziah** was **Jehoram's youngest** and only surviving **son** (cf. 21:17). **He became king** and **reigned for one year** (841 B.C.). He **was 22 years old** at the time. The Hebrew has "42" (cf. NIV marg.) but that is probably a copyist's error for 22 (cf. 2 Kings 8:26). Since his father was dead and **his mother** was **Athaliah,** daughter **of Ahab** (and **granddaughter of Omri**), it is little wonder that Ahaziah's brief tenure was **evil.** He followed his father's **advisers** in every respect including **their counsel** that he go **to war** with **Hazael king of Aram** in league with **Joram,** Ahab's **son** and **king of Israel.** Ahab had died **at Ramoth Gilead** (2 Chron. 18:34), and now **Hazael,** having murdered Ben-Hadad, was **king of Aram** (2 Kings 8:14-15).

**22:5b-9. Joram,** Israel's king, was **wounded** in the battle near Ramoth Gilead and **returned to** his secondary resi-dence at **Jezreel to recover. Ahaziah** then went to **visit . . . Joram,** probably because of their close family ties (Joram was Athaliah's brother and thus Ahaziah's uncle). While both were at Jezreel, **Jehu son of Nimshi,** an Israelite military officer whom **the LORD had** chosen to be Israel's next king (cf. 2 Kings 9:1-13), met them. After **Jehu** killed Joram (2 Kings 9:24), he pursued **Ahaziah** (who had fled to **Samaria,** about 20 miles south) and **brought** him back to Jezreel.

The chronicler seems to have implied that **Ahaziah** died at Jezreel (2 Chron. 22:9) while the author of Kings wrote that Ahaziah died at Megiddo (2 Kings 9:27). Probably the two accounts are supplementary. Ahaziah fled to Samaria and was **captured** there by Jehu's **men,** who brought him back **to Jehu.** Meanwhile Jehu left Jezreel and met Ahaziah as he was being returned. Jehu's men wounded him and Ahaziah escaped to Megiddo where he died (2 Kings 9:27).

The king's servants **buried him** in Jerusalem (2 Kings 9:28). In addition to murdering the two kings, **Jehu** almost annihilated the royal families of both Israel and **Judah** (2 Chron. 22:8; cf. 2 Kings 10:1-14). This left Jehu in power in the north; and **there was no** male survivor in the Davidic dynasty except Joash, an infant son **of Ahaziah** back in Jerusalem (cf. 2 Chron. 22:11).

### G. Athaliah (22:10–23:21)

**22:10-12.** The empty throne of Judah was left by default to **Athaliah,** Ahaziah's wicked Israelite **mother,** who finished the bloody massacre begun by Jehu and destroyed all remaining members of the Judean **royal family** she could find. This meant, of course, that she put to the sword many of her own flesh and blood since she was the queen mother! Thanks to **Jehosheba,** sister of **Ahaziah,** the infant **Joash,** her nephew, was spared and placed under close security during the **six years** of Athaliah's reign (841–835 B.C.).

**23:1-3.** In the **year** 835 **Jehoiada** the priest (and husband of Jehosheba, 22:11) made his move. Eager to restore the Davidic family, and specifically Joash, to the throne, he engineered a plot with five army officers to assemble **the Levites** and leaders of **Judah** in **Jerusalem** and persuaded them to support the young **king** in a formal **covenant** ceremony.

**23:4-7.** Jehoiada then divided the **priests and Levites** up by thirds and stationed them at **the temple,** the **palace,** and **the Foundation Gate** (the Sur Gate in 2 Kings 11:6 is perhaps just another name for the same gate). The lay leaders were stationed in **the** temple **courtyards.** Since only **the priests and Levites** who were then **on duty** were authorized to **enter the temple,** the others were to remain outside to protect **the king.**

**23:8-15.** All the assembly then took up **spears** and **shields** from **the temple** storerooms and awaited the appearance of young Joash. When all was ready **Jehoiada . . . presented him** to the crowd, crowned him, gave him **a copy of the covenant** (i.e., the Law) as protocol required (cf. Deut. 17:18-20), **anointed him,** and led the acclamation, **Long live the king!**

**When Athaliah heard** the clamor **she** rushed out to **the temple** and saw in a moment that she had been the victim of a coup. In grief over her loss she **tore her robes** (cf. Gen. 37:29, 34; Josh. 7:6; Job 1:20; 2:12) **and shouted, Treason!** This was not a bloodless coup, for **Jehoiada** ordered Athaliah and her followers dragged from the temple area and had her executed at **the Horse Gate** of **the palace** complex.

**23:16-21.** Jehoiada then led the whole populace in **a covenant** oath that **he . . . the people,** and the king would be loyal to **the LORD.** In keeping with this vow they **went to the temple of Baal** and destroyed **it** and its **altars and idols** and slew **Mattan the priest of Baal** (in compliance with the Law, Deut. 13:5-10). **Jehoiada** then restored the regular priestly and Levitical assignments just as **David** had prescribed they be carried out. Finally, he took **the king** with all the entourage of leaders to **the palace and seated** him **on the throne** officially. At last Judah knew peace once more.

## H. Joash (chap. 24)

### 1. JOASH'S TEMPLE RESTORATION
(24:1-16)

**24:1-3.** Joash, apparently the only surviving son of Ahaziah, began to reign at the age of **seven** and held the kingship for **40 years** (835–796). He was under the tutelage of **Jehoiada the priest** for the first several **years** and Joash remained

righteous before **the LORD** all that time. **Jehoiada** even selected **two wives** for **Joash.**

**24:4-7.** Eventually (perhaps as much as 20 years later; cf. 2 Kings 12:6) the young monarch **decided to restore the temple** which had deteriorated during the apostate days of Athaliah. To do so required the raising of funds, so he ordered **the priests and Levites** to go throughout the land and **collect** the temple taxes required by the Law of Moses (cf. Ex. 30:12-16). Presumably these had not been gathered for many years. When **the Levites** were slow to **act,** Joash rebuked **Jehoiada** for not having seen the task to completion (2 Chron. 24:4-6). Part of the reason for the need of temple restoration was the fact that God's house had been looted and its contents used for the worship of **the Baals.**

**24:8-16.** Having given up on the Levites, Joash **issued** a formal **proclamation** that **all the people** of the kingdom must **bring** their taxes to **the temple** and put them in a specially prepared **chest** near the temple **gate** (vv. 8-9). The response was so generous that the **chest** was filled and had to be emptied over and over again (vv. 10-11). The money was then used to pay the workmen commissioned to do **the temple** restoration (v. 12). They did **the work** quickly, carefully, and well within the budget for when the job was **finished** the workers had **money** left over with which to provide furnishings and utensils for the **temple** worship (vv. 13-14). Unfortunately, however, **Jehoiada . . . died** and with him died the spirit of reformation (vv. 15-16).

### 2. JOASH'S WICKEDNESS AND ASSASSINATION
(24:17-27)

**24:17-20.** Joash seemingly was as easily influenced to do evil **after the** priest's **death** as he was to do good before. He began to listen to **officials** who pandered to him and he allowed **the temple** worship to decline and be replaced by Canaanite fertility rites (vv. 17-18a). This naturally displeased **the LORD** so **He sent prophets** to protest this evil but to no avail (vv. 18b-19). Finally **God** sent **Zechariah,** Jehoiada's **son,** to tell **the people** that because they had **forsaken** God **He** had **forsaken** them (v. 20).

**24:21-22.** This so infuriated the mob that they **stoned** Zechariah **to death in,** of all places, the temple **courtyard!** Even **Joash,** forgetting **the kindness** of **Jehoiada** to him, took part in the murder of Zechariah. Perhaps this was the Zechariah Jesus referred to in Matthew 23:34-35. If so, Zechariah may have been the son of Berekiah and also the "son" (i.e., grandson) of Jehoiada (cf. comments on Matt. 23:35). However, Jesus may have been referring not to this Zechariah in 2 Chronicles but to the Zechariah who wrote the Old Testament book that bears his name, for he *was* the son of Berekiah. As Zechariah expired he pronounced a divine curse on the **king.**

**24:23-27.** Soon the prophet was vindicated. The very next **year** (in the spring) the Arameans **invaded Judah . . . killed** her **leaders,** and took away great **plunder.** (Other battles between Judah and the Arameans occurred in the reigns of Ahaziah, 22:5, and Ahaz, 28:5.) The Arameans did this even though they were greatly outnumbered. It was clear that this was God's **judgment . . . on Joash.**

After **the Arameans withdrew,** leaving the king **wounded,** Joash's confidants **killed him** because of what he had done to Zechariah. No doubt they thought this would allay the divine wrath. Even in death Joash was dishonored for he, like several other Judean kings, was **not** buried in the royal **tombs** with his ancestors (cf. 21:20; 26:23; 28:27) and Jehoiada the righteous priest (24:16). The names of the two assassins are also given in 2 Kings 12:21, but the chronicler added that they were **an Ammonite** and **a Moabite.** Apparently this was his way of blaming foreigners for this deed against an anointed son of David. **The book of the kings** may be the Old Testament Books of 1 and 2 Kings.

*I. Amaziah (chap. 25)*

**25:1-4.** Joash was succeeded by his son **Amaziah,** who enjoyed a reign of **29 years** (796–767 B.C.). The chronicler's summary of his character is that he pleased **the LORD, but not wholeheartedly.** One of his first official acts was the avenging of his father's murder (cf. 24:25-26) but his heart for God is seen by his sparing the assassins' **sons** in accord with Moses' principle that **children** must not be punished for the **sins** of **their fathers** (cf. Deut. 24:16).

**25:5-10.** Amaziah's interest in military affairs was manifested by his conscripting an army of **300,000 men.** He even went so far as to hire **100,000** Israelites for **100 talents of silver** (ca. 3¾ tons; cf. NIV marg.). However, this was tantamount to making an ungodly alliance, which was made pointedly clear to him by **a man of God** (whose name is unknown), who reminded the **king** that **the LORD** was **not with Israel,** so He would not be with Judah **in battle** if Israel went along. **Amaziah** was convinced of the correctness of this advice but wondered how he would get back the silver he had already **paid.** To this the prophet responded that **God** could **more than** make it up to Amaziah. **So Amaziah** sent the Israelites **home,** but they became angry (**furious** and **in a great rage**) that they were prevented from participation. No doubt they felt gypped out of their plunder.

**25:11-16.** Judah then marched against the **men of Seir** (Edomites; cf. Gen. 36:9; 2 Chron. 20:2 with 20:22) in **the Valley of Salt** (probably the salt plains south of the Dead Sea) and **killed 10,000** of them. (For other battles fought there see Gen. 14:3; 1 Chron. 18:12.) With unusual brutality the Judeans took an additional **10,000 men** as prisoners and **threw them** over **a cliff** to their deaths. (High cliffs were in that area; cf. Obad. 1, 3.)

**Meanwhile** the frustrated Israelite troops (cf. 2 Chron. 25:6, 10) **raided** Judean outposts in central and southern Israel (see comments about **Beth Horon** in 8:5), **killed 3,000** persons, and took **great** amounts of their possessions.

**When Amaziah returned from** his victory over **the Edomites,** he **brought** as a part of the spoils the idols of that land. He went so far as to **set them up** and worship them, a blasphemous act that prompted **the LORD** to send **a prophet** (also anonymous; cf. 25:7) to rebuke **him. Why,** the man of God asked, should **Amaziah** worship gods which could **not** even **save their own people? The king** was cut to the quick and threatened to kill the man of God on the spot if he would not desist. In his last words to the king **the prophet** announced that Amaziah would come to know God's punishment because of his idolatry and rejection of the prophet's **counsel.**

**25:17-19. Amaziah** then turned his attention to the Israelite raids on his outposts. He in effect challenged **Jehoash . . . king of Israel** (grandson **of Jehu**) to wage war. **But Jehoash** answered in the form of a parable or fable. It concerned **a thistle** (Amaziah) who demanded of **a cedar** (Jehoash) that the cedar **give** his **daughter** as a wife for the thistle's **son.** The thistle was rewarded for his presumptuousness by being overrun by **a wild beast** (Israel's army). Jehoash interpreted his own story by comparing Amaziah to a mere bush who, because he **defeated** the minor power of **Edom,** thought he was equal to a mighty tree. He ought to know better and refrain from conflict.

**25:20-24. Amaziah** paid no heed, **however,** to Jehoash's belligerent refusal, **for God** had determined to use **Jehoash** as His punishing rod for Amaziah's idolatry. As a result **Israel attacked** Judah, achieved a smashing victory, and **captured Amaziah** himself **at Beth Shemesh** (ca. 15 miles southwest of Jerusalem). From there they **brought** the humiliated king **to Jerusalem** itself, **broke down** a long **section** (**600 feet**) of its walls **from the Ephraim Gate** (cf. Neh. 8:16; 12:39) on the north **to the** northwest **Corner Gate** (cf. Jer. 31:38, Zech. 14:10; see the map "Jerusalem in the Time of Nehemiah," near Neh. 2), and **took all** the temple **articles** that were under **the care of** the family of **Obed-Edom** (cf. 1 Chron. 26:4-8) and the **palace treasures** and prisoners back **to Samaria.**

**25:25-28. Amaziah** either remained alive at Jerusalem or was returned there later for he outlived **Jehoash** by **15 years.** He had become unpopular with his own people **in Jerusalem,** however, and was forced finally to go into exile at **Lachish** (ca. 30 miles southwest of Jerusalem). He was not safe even there, for a band of assassins found him, **killed him,** and **brought** his body **back** for burial. His father Joash had been assassinated too (cf. 24:25-26).

## J. Uzziah (chap. 26)

**26:1. Amaziah** apparently had made no plans for his succession, for after his untimely death **the people** took his young son **Uzziah** (Azariah in 2 Kings 14:21 is a variant spelling) and elevated him to kingship. Only **16 years old** at the time, Uzziah reigned for the extraordinarily long period of 52 years (cf. 2 Chron. 26:3; 790–739 B.C.). A serious chronological problem emerges here. Amaziah reigned from 796 to 767, so if Uzziah commenced his reign in 790 he co-reigned with his father for 23 years. Yet the chronicler (and the author of 2 Kings as well) seemed to indicate that Uzziah's tenure *followed* that of Amaziah and that Uzziah was only 16 years old at the time. How then could his coregency be for 23 years?

The chronological data for both kings are very well established on grounds too complicated to be considered here. (For a full discussion see Edwin R. Thiele, *The Mysterious Numbers of the Hebrew Kings.* Rev. ed. Grand Rapids: Wm. B. Eerdmans Publishing Co., 1983, pp. 113-23.) The narratives can be viewed in a way that legitimately comports with the dates mentioned earlier. The best solution appears to be that the leadership of Judah, fearing early in Amaziah's reign that he was unstable and incompetent, made his young son Uzziah viceregent. In other words after Amaziah had reigned only six years (796–790) Uzziah, *then* (in 790) 16 years old, was appointed second to the king. From then until Amaziah's death (767) they reigned together for 23 years (790–767). Then Uzziah reigned alone for 29 years until his own death.

This would require, of course, that the chronicler meant that the people of Judah had made Uzziah vice-regent at the age of 16 (2 Chron. 26:1). In support of this reconstruction is the fact that Uzziah received religious instruction from Zechariah (v. 5). Zechariah, however, was stoned to death by some Judeans before the death of Amaziah's predecessor Joash (24:21-22), who died in 796. Uzziah, then, obviously was of a teachable age before 796 (by 796 he would have been 10 years old). His major independent accomplishments could not have come about until his sole regency began in 767 so these are the ones with which the historian is particularly concerned.

**26:2.** Uzziah recovered **Elath** from Edom and **rebuilt** it. (On Elath's location see comments on 8:17.) Apparently Edom repossessed Elath when Edom rebelled from **Judah** in the reign of Jehoram

(21:8-10), Uzziah's great-great-grand-father. Later in the reign of Ahaz, Uzziah's grandson, Edom regained Elath (2 Kings 16:6).

**26:3-8.** God rewarded Uzziah's godliness with **success** in several areas, including military adventures. 'He destroyed the Philistine towns of **Gath, Jabneh, and Ashdod** and **rebuilt** others in the region. He was successful also in campaigns **against the Arabs** of **Gur Baal** (site now unknown) and **the Meunites** (cf. 1 Chron. 4:41). **The Ammonites** recognized his sovereignty over them and **his fame** (cf. 2 Chron. 26:15) **spread** to Egypt's borders.

**26:9-15.** Internally **Uzziah** masterminded the construction of fortress **towers in Jerusalem** at various points on the walls, perhaps including the portion of wall Jehoash had destroyed (cf. 25:23). (On **the Corner Gate** see comments on 25:23; on **the Valley Gate,** probably on Jerusalem's western wall, see Neh. 2:13, 15; 3:13; and on **the angle of the wall** see Neh. 3:19-20, 24-25.) He also undertook massive agricultural projects **in the desert** as well as **the foothills** and plains. He reorganized **an army of 307,500** men (similar in size to Amaziah's army, 2 Chron. 25:5) into **well-trained** and well-equipped **divisions** under **2,600** leaders. He pioneered the use of certain advanced weapons such as catapults to hurl **arrows** and **large stones** a great distance. All this enhanced his reputation (cf. 26:8) and increased his strength.

**26:16-20.** Uzziah's great power led to **pride,** which proved to be **his downfall** (cf. Prov. 16:18; 18:12). Apparently he began to depend on men and weapons rather than on **the Lord.** He even presumed to offer **incense in the temple,** a sacrilege for which **Azariah the priest** and **80 other . . . priests** roundly condemned him. He was **unfaithful** to the Law (2 Chron. 26:16-18), which limited this function to the priest (Ex. 30:7-8). Uzziah responded in rage but the propriety of the priests' rebuke was immediately evident when the king's **forehead** broke out with **leprosy.** This rendered the king ceremonially unclean so that he had to **leave** the **temple** at once (2 Chron. 26:19-20; cf. Lev. 13).

**26:21-23.** Until the day of his death **Uzziah** was **leprous** to such an extent that he had to be quarantined and had to

yield the reins of government to **Jotham his son.** Even in death he was ostracized because of his disease and was buried **near** his **fathers** (ancestors), not *with* them (cf. 21:20; 24:25; 28:27). Other information on **Uzziah** may be found, the chronicler indicated, in the writings of **the Prophet Isaiah** (cf. Isa. 1:1; 6:1).

### K. Jotham (chap. 27)

**27:1.** The reign of Uzziah's son **Jotham** began in 750 b.c. and hence overlapped Uzziah's by about 11 years (till Uzziah died in 739). This fact is understandable in light of Uzziah's incapacity in the last years of his life (26:21). But Jotham also co-reigned with his son for four years (735–731) so that the reference to his length of reign as **16 years** (cf. 27:8) does not include that period. His dates as principal ruler were the 16-year period of 750–735.

**27:2-4.** His record was nearly blameless (cf. v. 6) but **the people** were still unfaithful to **the Lord** (cf. 2 Kings 15:35). His building projects included repairing **the Upper Gate** (cf. 2 Chron. 23:20) **of the temple** (i.e., the north side of the outer court) and reconstructing the **Ophel** wall which encompassed the old city of Jerusalem (cf. 33:14). Jotham also followed up Uzziah's projects in the **hills** and forest **areas.**

**27:5-9.** Evidently **the Ammonites** had slacked off in their payment of tribute (cf. 26:8) so **Jotham** brought them to heel by conquering **them.** They now were required to pay **100 talents of silver** (3¾ tons), **10,000 cors of wheat** (62,000 bushels), **and 10,000 cors of barley.** This they did for three successive **years,** after which perhaps the burden was lessened. The rest of **Jotham's** affairs could be found in the records of **the kings of Israel and Judah,** perhaps some of which are preserved in the Books of 1 and 2 Kings (cf. 2 Kings 15:32-38).

### L. Ahaz (chap. 28)

**28:1-4.** **Ahaz** co-reigned for four years with Jotham (cf. comments on 27:1). So, as the historian noted, Ahaz **reigned** (alone) for **16 years** (731–715). **Unlike David his father** (i.e., ancestor), Ahaz was evil, walking in the pattern **of the kings of Israel** (those in the Northern Kingdom, all of whom were wicked). He **made** Baal **idols,** offered **sacrifices in the**

**Valley of Ben Hinnom** (cf. 33:6), which included human victims (even **his** own **sons**!); and practiced the Canaanite cult on **the high places** (cf. comments on 14:3) and in the sacred groves (cf. other comments about his sins in 28:19, 22-25).

Human sacrifice was particularly associated with the Ammonite god Molech and was vehemently condemned in the Law (cf. Lev. 18:21; 20:2-5; Deut. 12:31). It was practiced especially in the Hinnom Valley, just south and west of Jerusalem, a place later known as Gehenna (from *gê*, "valley," and the proper name *Hinnom*). Because of the fires which burned there both in these sacrificial orgies and to consume garbage, Gehenna became a term for hell (cf. comments on Matt. 5:22).

**28:5-8.** Because of Ahaz's gross sins against God, he fell into the hands of **the Arameans** (whose **king** was Rezin, 2 Kings 16:5), who **took many** Judeans as **prisoners . . . to Damascus.** This was the third time the Arameans fought Judah (cf. 22:5; 24:23). Ahaz also suffered defeat by the armies **of Israel** under their King **Pekah,** who killed **120,000** Judean **soldiers** in **one day.** These included several casualties within Ahaz's own family and court. Also Israel **took . . . 200,000 wives, sons, and daughters** of Judah off **to Samaria.**

**28:9-15.** As 2 Kings 16:5 indicates, Ahaz was not totally overcome but he clearly was in great jeopardy. Meanwhile **Oded,** a **prophet** in **Samaria,** persuaded the leaders of Israel that **God** was displeased (**angry**) with Israel's taking these prisoners **of Judah** to make them **slaves. The leaders** (four of them are named in 2 Chron. 28:12) therefore ordered the returning army **not** to **bring** the **prisoners** to Samaria. So the leaders gave the prisoners **food** and clothing and led the **prisoners** to **Jericho** where they could be repatriated to their own country. Ironically Israel listened to the Lord whereas **Judah** did not.

**28:16-18.** Not satisfied that Israel's kind overtures were signals of a new and friendly era, **Ahaz** entered into negotiations with **the king of Assyria,** who at that time was Tiglath-Pileser III (745–727 B.C.). Isaiah had tried to prevent Ahaz from turning to Assyria (cf. Isa. 7:4-9). This move was necessary, Ahaz thought, because of intensifying pressure from **the Edomites** (cf. comments on 2 Chron.

26:2) to the east and **the Philistines** to the west (**the foothills**) and south (**the Negev,** the desert south of **Judah**). In addition, of course, was the continuing threat from the Arameans and Israelites (cf. 28:5-8), a factor mentioned in 2 Kings 16:5-9 and Isaiah 7:1-17.

**28:19-27. Tiglath-Pileser** proved to be a curse rather than a blessing for despite receiving a generous bribe from **Ahaz . . . from the temple** and the **palace,** the Assyrian king gave no **help.** The author of Kings wrote that Tiglath-Pileser heeded Ahaz and went on to attack and defeat Damascus, the Aramean capital (2 Kings 16:9). But this does not contradict the chronicler, who was more concerned with spiritual than military repercussions. Ahaz's entanglements with the Assyrians led eventually to disaster. This may be seen in his adoption of Aramean **gods,** whom he sought to placate because the Arameans had defeated Judah (2 Chron. 28:5).

This Aramean victory signified to **Ahaz** that these **gods** must be superior to Israel's God (*Yahweh*). What Ahaz failed to note was that these same Arameans (and their gods) had been vanquished by the Assyrians. Logically, then, should not Ahaz have embraced the Assyrian gods? In any case, Ahaz abandoned **the Lord** and robbed and barred **the temple.** In their place he established pagan worship centers throughout **Jerusalem** and the entire land (cf. vv. 2-4). As a final indictment of this evil king the author remarked that on his death he was buried **in . . . Jerusalem but . . . not . . . in the tombs of the kings** (cf. 21:20; 24:25; 26:23). Repeatedly the chronicler noted that Judah's troubles were God's judgment (in **anger**) on Ahaz's and Judah's sins (28:9, 19, 25b).

## M. Hezekiah (chaps. 29–32)

### 1. CLEANSING OF THE TEMPLE (CHAP. 29)

**29:1-9. Hezekiah,** whose independent reign lasted **29** years (715–686 B.C.), also apparently co-reigned with his father Ahaz for 14 years (729–715). The account of his life in 2 Chronicles covers his 29-year period after 715. Israel, the Northern Kingdom, had already fallen to the Assyrians in 722 B.C. and its people had been deported in large numbers (cf. 2 Kings 17:1-6).

Hezekiah was one of Judah's greatest kings (2 Kings 18:5). **In the very first month** of **his** sole **reign** (in 715) **he opened** the temple **doors** to repair **them** and restore the Lord's house, since Ahaz, his wicked father, had barred **the temple** (2 Chron. 28:24). Hezekiah gathered **the priests and the Levites** before the temple **(on the east side)** and commanded them to **consecrate** themselves to the work of purifying and repairing **the temple,** which, in the years of Ahaz especially, had fallen into a sorry state of deterioration. **The LORD** in His **anger** (cf. 28:9, 25) had therefore sent judgment on the nation, so much so that some of them had gone into **captivity** to the Arameans, Israelites, and Edomites (cf. 28:5-8, 17).

**29:10-14.** Hezekiah now intended to renew the ancient Mosaic **Covenant with the LORD** so that He might once again bless the nation. To this call the **Levites** assented and by their allotted divisions began to do the **work. The Gershonites** and **Merarites** evidently made up the smaller groups (v. 12) while **the Kohathites** were further subdivided by the clans of **Elizaphan** (v. 13; cf. 1 Chron. 15:8) and **Heman** (2 Chron. 29:14; cf. 1 Chron. 15:17). **Asaph,** however, was a Gershonite and **Jeduthun** was a Merarite (2 Chron. 29:13-14). Of the 14 Levites in all, 6 were descended from Kohath and 4 each were of Gershon and Merari.

**29:15-19.** They, with their comrades, began to remove **to the Kidron Valley** (cf. 15:16; 30:14) **everything** impure from **the temple.** In this action **Hezekiah** was **following the word of the LORD,** as given in Deuteronomy 12:2-4. Then for eight **days,** they reconsecrated everything outside **the temple** and **for eight more** everything inside. When the Levites had finished, they **reported** to Hezekiah that they had not only reconsecrated **the temple** and all its contents but had retrieved **all the** objects **Ahaz** had carried away to use in his pagan services (2 Chron. 29:18-19; cf. 28:24).

**29:20-30. The next** day **Hezekiah** led the people in a great festival of sacrifice (including 28 animals **as a sin offering;** cf. Lev. 4:1–5:13) to make atonement for their sins (2 Chron. 29:20-24). With the musicians in their prescribed places, the sacrifices, including also a **burnt offering** (cf. Lev. 1), began to the accompaniment of vocal and instrumental music (2 Chron. 29:25-28). **The Levites** played

**cymbals, harps, and lyres,** as **David** had **prescribed** when he moved the ark to Jerusalem (cf. 1 Chron. 15:16, 19; 16:4-5). Why **Gad** and **Nathan** are mentioned here is not clear. Also **the priests** played **trumpets,** as was done when Solomon took the ark to the temple (2 Chron. 5:12-13). Then **the king** and the people prostrated themselves before **the LORD** while psalms of **David** and **Asaph** were sung (29:29-30).

**29:31-36.** Since the **offerings** just made were for the kingdom, **the temple,** and the collective covenant community (v. 21), **Hezekiah** now gave individuals an opportunity to participate. The people **brought. . . . 70 bulls, 100 rams, and 200 male lambs** as **burnt offerings** (v. 32). The people also brought **600 bulls, and 3,000 sheep and goats** as **sacrifices** (v. 33) for burnt offerings and **thank offerings** (v. 31). The thank offerings were called **fellowship offerings** in Leviticus 3; 7:11-21. These burnt and thank offerings were expressions of personal piety above and beyond those offered on behalf of the nation as a whole. **Drink offerings** were included for they were part of the daily **burnt offerings** (Ex. 29:38-41). Because of a shortage of **priests . . . the Levites** assisted in slaughtering the animals. Thus in his first month **Hezekiah** had reestablished proper **temple** worship, an accomplishment that **brought** great rejoicing (2 Chron. 29:35b-36).

**2. HEZEKIAH'S GREAT PASSOVER (30:1–31:1)**

**30:1-5.** In anticipation of what must have been the first **Passover** of his reign, **Hezekiah sent** out invitations throughout all **Israel and Judah** including even **Ephraim and Manasseh** to encourage the faithful to attend. Some of the people in those two Northern tribes had apparently not been taken captive by Assyria. This feast was usually held in the first month (of the religious calendar; cf. Ex. 12:1-2), but Hezekiah had not been able to recruit sufficient priestly personnel that early (cf. 2 Chron. 29:34) nor had the **people** been able to arrive from distant points (30:3). So it was decided to hold it **in the second month,** that is, April-May (cf. Num. 9:10-11).

**The plan** was acceptable to **the king** and **the people,** so an announcement was sent out **from Beersheba to Dan** (the southernmost and northernmost cities in

Judah and Israel) with the expectation of great attendance (cf. 2 Chron. 30:13).

**30:6-14.** Hezekiah's proclamation (vv. 6-9) was to the effect that those Israelites who had **escaped** Assyrian deportation should repent of their sins and turn **to the LORD . . . submit to** Him, and **serve** Him. They should express the genuineness of their contrition by assembling at the temple in **Jerusalem (come to the sanctuary)** to celebrate the Passover. This was one of the three annual festivals which every adult male was supposed to attend in Jerusalem (Deut. 16:16). By assembling for the Passover, they would bring God's forgiveness and could even expect the return of their captured loved ones. Their repentance would divert God's **fierce anger,** for He **is gracious and compassionate.**

Alas, the message was spurned except for a few who came from **Asher, Manasseh . . . Zebulun** (2 Chron. 30:10-11), **Ephraim,** and Issachar (v. 18). In addition, of course, **the people** of Judah came with united purpose and commitment (v. 12) **to celebrate the Feast of Unleavened Bread** (v. 13). This seven-day festival followed immediately after the Passover (cf. Ex. 12:11-20; Lev. 23:4-8; and comments on Mark 14:1a). Indicative of the people's dedication was their disavowal once more of heathen **altars** (2 Chron. 30:14), discarding **them** into **the Kidron Valley** (cf. 15:16; 29:16).

**30:15-20.** When **the priests and the Levites** saw the dedication of the throngs of people they were chagrined and quickly **consecrated themselves** (by **burnt offerings**) for the service of **Passover** (vv. 15-16). Ordinarily the laity could offer their own **Passover lambs** in sacrifice (cf. Ex. 12:3). But because of the laxity of many of the Israelites in those apostate days, especially in the Northern Kingdom, they were **ceremonially** unclean and thus **could not** slaughter their own Passover lambs. Nonetheless they did eat of **the Passover** even though they were ritually disqualified (2 Chron. 30:17-18a). When **Hezekiah** realized this, he **prayed** on their behalf that **God** might be more impressed with the sincerity of their hearts and motives than with matters of mere ceremonialism (vv. 18b-19). The essence of God's grace is seen in His favorable response to the king's prayer (v. 20).

**30:21-27.** During the seven-day **Feast of Unleavened Bread,** which followed the Passover, the people praised **the LORD** with joy. **The Levites** also faithfully discharged their office (singing **praise,** eating the **assigned portion** of the sacrifices, and offering **fellowship offerings;** cf. Lev. 3; 7:11-21), which **Hezekiah** encouraged them to do. In fact all the people were so caught up in their devotion to and **joy** in the Lord that they decided to extend the festivities for another week.

This impressed the **king** and his officials, so he **provided** at his own expense **1,000 bulls and 7,000 sheep and goats for** sacrifice by the people, and **the officials provided . . . 1,000 bulls and 10,000 sheep and goats. Since the days of Solomon,** the chronicler related, **there had** never **been** anything **like this. God heard** from **heaven, His . . . dwelling place** (cf. 2 Chron. 6:21, 30, 33, 39; Ps. 11:4; Hab. 2:20), and blessed their outpouring of praise and consecration.

**31:1.** The most reasonable follow-up of the great 15-day festival ensued. **The Israelites** (and probably the Judeans) **went** through **Judah and Benjamin** destroying **all** remaining remnants of Baal's sacred **places** (cf. comments on 14:3). They then did the same **in Ephraim and Manasseh,** and **returned to their** homes.

3. REESTABLISHMENT OF PROPER WORSHIP (31:2-21)

**31:2-4.** Based on the requirements and guidelines of the Law, **Hezekiah** next proceeded to reestablish proper temple worship. He gave instruction concerning the service of **the priests and Levites** (v. 2), assigning them their 24 **divisions** (1 Chron. 24); he **contributed** animals for **the burnt offerings** for daily, weekly, monthly, and annual sacrifices (2 Chron. 31:3; cf. Num. 28–29; 1 Chron. 23:30-31); and he directed **the people** to support **the priests and Levites** (2 Chron. 31:4).

**31:5-13.** The citizens of Jerusalem and the surrounding towns and cities complied by presenting **the firstfruits** (cf. Ex. 23:19a; Num. 18:12) and tithes (cf. Lev. 27:30-33; Num. 18:21-24) of their produce of field crops and livestock and all other goods (2 Chron. 31:5-6). For four months they continued bringing their gifts to the temple (v. 7). **The third month** was May-June, the beginning of grain harvesting, and **the seventh month**

was September-October, the time of vine and fruit harvesting (see the chart "Calendar in Israel" near Ex. 12).

The people's gifts were **piled** in great **heaps** (2 Chron. 31:8). In fact **Azariah the chief priest** said that the quantities **Hezekiah** saw represented a surplus beyond what **the priests and Levites** needed. So the king ordered that **storerooms** be prepared **in the temple** to accommodate the excess (vv. 9-11). **Conaniah** with **his brother Shimei** were placed over 10 **supervisors** whose ministry was to oversee the collection and distribution of all these **gifts** (vv. 12-13).

**31:14-21.** As for the **gifts** made **to the** Lord Himself—a way of describing **freewill** (voluntary) **offerings** (cf. Lev. 7:11-21), these were the responsibility of **Kore** and his six associates. It was their duty to distribute them to **the priests** who lived in 13 towns outside Jerusalem (2 Chron. 31:14-15; cf. Josh. 21:13-19). Even the priests' young boys **three years old** and above received freewill offerings for they would someday serve as priests (2 Chron. 31:16). **The Levites,** on the other hand, received their portions only if they were at least **20 years old** (cf. 1 Chron. 23:24). Obviously there were many more **Levites** than **priests.** The **families** of both the priests and the Levites were, of course, supported similarly (2 Chron. 31:17-18) since the Law of Moses forbade the clergy from engaging in secular work to provide for themselves (cf. Num. 18:21-24). Finally, any **priests** or **Levites** who did not live in either Jerusalem or a designated priestly town were not to be overlooked (2 Chron. 31:19). All these things, the chronicler wrote, **Hezekiah** did **wholeheartedly** (a word used by the chronicler six times: 1 Chron. 29:9; 2 Chron.6:14; 15:15; 19:9; 25:2; 31:21) and in strict compliance with the Lord's **commands** (31:20-21).

4. SENNACHERIB'S INVASION (32:1-23)

**32:1-8.** Shortly **after . . . Hezekiah** began his independent reign he broke the treaty which had existed between his father Ahaz and the Assyrians (2 Kings 16:7) and rebelled against Assyria (2 Kings 18:7). This probably occurred at the time Sargon II (722–705 B.C.) of **Assyria** was preoccupied with rebellions in his Babylonian provinces and so could not punish Hezekiah. Sargon's successor

Sennacherib (705–681) did decide to bring **Judah** into line, however, so he led a campaign against **Hezekiah** in that king's 14th year (2 Kings 18:13), 701 B.C. At first the Assyrians **laid siege** to the various military towns, but then moved **on Jerusalem** (2 Chron. 32:1-2).

Hoping to prevent Jerusalem's capture, Hezekiah took measures to conceal the city's **outside** water supplies (vv. 3-4). **The stream** was probably the Gihon spring (v. 30). **Then he** repaired breaches in **the wall** and built **towers on it.** He even constructed an outer **wall,** greatly strengthened the **terraces** (the meaning of the Heb. word *millô*) below the walls of the city (v. 5; cf. 1 Kings 9:24), and added to the nation's weaponry. Next he mobilized **the people** under army **officers** and **encouraged them. . . . not** to fear but to trust **the** Lord, a **Power** far superior to Assyria. Hezekiah's reassurance that **God** was **with** them **to help** them (cf. 2 Chron. 14:11; 20:4; 25:8) helped build the people's **confidence** in the Lord in the face of the awesome Assyrians (cf. comments about the Assyrians in the Book of Nahum). Not mentioned in 2 Chronicles is the fact that Hezekiah tried to stave off Sennacherib by giving him huge amounts of gold and silver (2 Kings 18:14-16).

**32:9-15.** Before **Sennacherib** arrived in person he sent an embassy from **Lachish** (a key city 30 miles southwest of **Jerusalem**), bearing terms of surrender **for Hezekiah** to accept (vv. 10-15). In his message he boasted that **no** other **god** had **been able** to protect **his people from** the Assyrians. (Some of those nations and cities are listed in 2 Kings 19:12-13.) How then could Israel expect the Lord to do so since He was just another **god?** In fact Israel, Sennacherib said, had no god since **Hezekiah** had removed His **high places and altars.** (Assyria of course worshiped many **gods.**)

**32:16-23.** Sennacherib's taunt was followed by still other addresses and **letters** bearing the same theme—**the** Lord is just another impotent **god** unable to save **His people.** The Assyrian delegation even spoke **in Hebrew** to the Judeans **on the wall,** to make sure that even the common people would hear and understand every word and so become demoralized (vv. 16-19).

Desperate, **Hezekiah** turned to **the**

LORD with **the Prophet Isaiah** and together they sought divine deliverance. God gave the **king** a reassuring answer through the prophet (2 Kings 19:20-34) and then **sent an angel** who destroyed the Assyrian host, forcing Sennacherib to retreat in humility (2 Chron. 32:20-21a). The author of 2 Kings elaborated by stating that 185,000 Assyrians were slaughtered (2 Kings 19:35). Sometime after Sennacherib's return (though the chronicler did not seem to suggest a passing of time), the Assyrian king was murdered by two **of his sons** (identified in 2 Kings 19:37) in **the temple of his god** Nisroch (cf. Isa. 37:38) in Nineveh. According to Assyrian historical annals this assassination occurred in 681 B.C., 20 years after the aborted campaign against Jerusalem in 701. As a result of this miraculous deliverance of **Jerusalem** and similar experiences, Judah's God and king were given **gifts** and recognition from **all the** surrounding **nations** (2 Chron. 32:22-23).

5. HEZEKIAH'S SICKNESS AND PROSPERITY (32:24-33)

**32:24-30.** The story of **Hezekiah's** illness and miraculous healing (on the **sign** see 2 Kings 20:11) and extension of life is greatly abbreviated by the chronicler (2 Chron. 32:24; cf. 2 Kings 20:1-11; Isa. 38:1-8) perhaps because his intent here was to emphasize **the pride** of the king and not his piety (2 Chron. 32:25-26). The reasons for such pride could well be the accomplishments which the historian cataloged in verses 27-31. He had wealth **and honor**; he **built** storage facilities, agricultural settlements, and **villages**; he rerouted the city's **water** supply from **the Gihon spring** (in the Kidron Valley on the east) **to the west side,** and **succeeded** in these and many other undertakings. The tunnel of Hezekiah was dug through solid rock from the Gihon spring to the Pool of Siloam, a distance of 1,777 feet with workmen digging from each end and meeting in the middle.

**32:31-33.** However, Hezekiah foolishly and proudly displayed all the wealth of the temple and his palace to the Babylonian envoys of Merodach-Baladan (2 Kings 20:12-19; Isa. 39). The chronicler without details simply recorded that **God** allowed all this **to test him and to know everything that was in his heart.** That is, God wanted to show Hezekiah himself

the consequences of pride. After Hezekiah died he **was buried** with honor among **his fathers** (royal ancestors). His **other** deeds, the historian said, were found in the records of **Isaiah** (cf. Isa. 36–39) and **of the kings of Israel and Judah.**

*N. Manesseh (33:1-20)*

**33:1-9.** In complete contrast with his godly father was **Manasseh,** an **evil** king of Judah who **reigned** for **55 years** (697– 642). Though he reigned with Hezekiah for some 11 years, the young king either learned nothing from his father or quickly repudiated it, for he set about to rebuild **the high places . . . altars,** and sacred **poles** dedicated **to the Baals** and **Asherah,** the female fertility goddess of the Canaanites (cf. comments on 14:3). Manasseh also **worshiped** the gods of the heavens, represented in the pagan mind by **the starry hosts** (i.e., the sun, moon, stars, and planets) in violation of Deuteronomy 4:19. In fact he even placed pagan shrines (**altars**) of the stellar gods within **the temple of the** LORD itself. Like his grandfather Ahaz, he also offered **his** own **sons** as human sacrifices **in the Valley of Ben Hinnom** (cf. 2 Chron. 28:3 and comments there). Manasseh also **practiced sorcery** (seeking to gain power from evil spirits), **divination** (seeking to interpret the future by omens), **and witchcraft** (seeking to control others through communication with evil spirits), all of which were commonly employed in other nations of the ancient Near East to discern the planned activities of the gods.

Manasseh **consulted mediums and spiritists,** diviners whose specialty was to seek to consult the dead. Perhaps most serious of all, he set up the **image** (of Asherah; cf. 2 Kings 21:7) within the **temple,** which was to be reserved exclusively for the Lord (2 Chron. 33:7-8; cf. 7:16). The king also caused innocent people to die (2 Kings 21:16). So **Manasseh led** his nation away from God (2 Chron. 33:9).

**33:10-13.** Because **Manasseh and his people** ignored **the** LORD, His punishment was swift and sure. **Assyria,** the instrument of the Lord, came down **against** Judah. With great ruthlessness they bound **Manasseh . . . put a hook in his nose** as though he were a wild bull, and **took him** off **to Babylon,** Assyria's southern province. After a time Manasseh repented before **the** LORD and soon was allowed to return to his own land and people. The chronicler included this fact about Manasseh's restoration (not given in 2 Kings) to emphasize, no doubt, the fact that even the most wicked scions in David's dynasty could and did receive forgiveness if they met the Lord's conditions. This would give hope to the exilic and postexilic community of Jews.

**33:14-17.** When Manasseh returned **he rebuilt the outer wall** on the east side of Jerusalem from **the Gihon spring** (cf. 32:30) northwesterly to **the Fish Gate** (see the map "Jerusalem in the Time of Nehemiah," near Neh. 2) and from Gihon south to encircle **Ophel,** the original old city. He also regarrisoned the fortress **cities** throughout **Judah,** probably in anticipation of another Assyrian onslaught (2 Chron. 33:14). He then removed all the pagan idols and other accoutrements for which he had been responsible (v. 15; cf. vv. 3-5) and **restored** the proper worship of **the Lord** (v. 16). But **the people** had become used to worshiping **at the high places,** and so continued there though they only worshiped **the Lord** (v. 17).

**33:18-20.** Manasseh's **other** activities and achievements were recorded **in the annals of the kings of Israel** (v. 18) and the documents **of the seers** (v. 19). "Israel" here, as in 20:34, probably stands for Judah, since only the Southern Kingdom was in the land (cf. comments on "the annals" in 1 Kings 14:19 and under "Authorship" in the *Introduction* to 1 Chron.). Because of his general wickedness he was not **buried** in the tombs of the kings but **in his** own **palace** (2 Chron. 33:20).

### O. Amon (33:21-25)

**33:21-25.** Amon, in his brief **two-**year reign (642–640 B.C.), imitated the wickedness of **Manasseh.** But **unlike his father, he did not** repent. So **Amon's** top leaders **assassinated him.** As it turned out this was an unpopular move for the assassins themselves were disposed of and **Josiah,** Amon's **son,** was put in power by the masses.

### P. Josiah (chaps. 34–35)

1. JOSIAH'S REFORMATION (CHAP. 34)

*a. Preparations for temple repairs (34:1-13)*

**34:1-7.** **Josiah,** son of Amon, who was only **eight years old when** his father

died, ruled over Judah for **31 years** (640–609 B.C.) Much like his great-grandfather Hezekiah, Josiah loved **the Lord** and **began to** demonstrate this actively by the time he was 16 years old. **In his 12th year** as king (age 20) he initiated a campaign to rid the land of all vestiges of Canaanite religion. Apparently Manasseh's purge (33:15) related only to the **idols** and pagan **altars** in the temple, not to those throughout the land (33:3).

Josiah went so far as to scatter the **smashed . . . idols** and other paraphernalia **over the graves of** their worshipers and to burn **the bones of the** pagan **priests on their** very **altars.** And this purge was not limited to Judah. In Israel all the way up to **Naphtali** in the north the work of extirpation of idolatry went on.

**34:8-13.** Then, in Josiah's **18th year** (age 26) he commissioned **Shaphan . . . Maaseiah,** and **Joah** to **repair** and refurbish **the temple.** (This was one of several times that kings of Judah restored the temple.) These men took **money** which had been collected for that purpose from all over Israel and Judah and gave it **to Hilkiah the high priest** to enable him to hire workmen and **to purchase** materials for the task ordered by the king. The supervisors were **Levites,** two of the **Merari** branch and two of the Kohath branch. Those four were skillful musicians, a statement that probably attests to their artistry and sensitivity in all things pertaining to the temple and worship. It was their task to oversee the workmen at every point. **Levites** with other skills and assignments served as foremen.

*b. Discovery of the Book of the Law (34:14-33)*

**34:14-21.** In the course of paying **out** some of the temple **money** one day, Hilkiah the **high priest** (cf. v. 9) **found** a copy of **the Book of the Law of the Lord.** Because of certain higher critical assumptions, many scholars limit this document to Deuteronomy. There is no reason to do so, however, even though Deuteronomy may be in mind in certain places in the present narrative. The "book" may well have included the entire Pentateuch (Gen.–Deut.).

When **Shaphan** (cf. v. 8) **the secre-**tary took the scroll to Josiah and **reported** on the progress of the work, **Shaphan** began to **read** a few passages **from it** to **the king.** Realizing the significance of the message, **the king . . . tore his robes** (as an expression of grief; cf. comments on 23:13) and issued a command **to Hilkiah** and the others that the entire text be studied and that the mind of **the LORD** in relation to it be ascertained. He was concerned that his ancestors had incurred God's **anger** by not obeying God's **Word.** Josiah's personal display of grief may have been in reaction to statements in Deuteronomy concerning the role and responsibility of the king as covenant leader, a role he probably felt he had not fulfilled (cf. Deut. 17:18-20).

**34:22-28.** Strange as it may seem, the Books of Moses had apparently been destroyed except for this one copy preserved in the temple. How or when this happened is a mystery but the most likely occasion was the almost complete eradication of the worship of the Lord in the days of Manasseh and Amon (chap. 33). To find out what needed to be done **Hilkiah** and his colleagues **went to . . . the Prophetess Huldah,** who resided in a suburb (**the Second District**) of **Jerusalem.** Her husband **Shallum** was the overseer **of the wardrobe** for either the king or the priests. **She** related to them that **God** was **going to bring** His judgment on the land—all according to **the curses written in the** newly found scroll (cf. Deut. 28:15-68; Lev. 26:14-39). Though the wrath of God was sure because of the nation's apostasy and idolatry, Josiah himself would be spared because of his wholehearted devotion to **the LORD.** The impending doom would be postponed until after Josiah's death.

**34:29-33.** When Josiah heard Huldah's message, he gathered **all the elders** and **all the people** to **the temple** and read to them **the Book of the Covenant which had been found.** This may be the section known by that phrase in Exodus 20:1–23:33, or it may be all of Deuteronomy. Then, as **king** and representative of **the people,** Josiah **stood** and affirmed his intent to renew his **covenant** vows and keep all the statutes prescribed by **the covenant.** He **then** had all **the people** of the kingdom do the same. In summation, he **removed** idolatry from the land and in its place established faithful worship of **the LORD** and adherence to His covenant demands.

## 2. JOSIAH'S GREAT PASSOVER (35:1-19)

### a. Preparation for the Passover (35:1-9)

**35:1-4.** In Josiah's 18th year (v. 19, age 26), the same year in which the temple was repaired (34:8), he **celebrated the Passover** (cf. Hezekiah's Passover celebration, chap. 30). Having charged the **priests** and **the Levites** to fulfill their designated responsibilities for the occasion, he instructed that the **ark** be left **in the temple** and **not . . . carried** in procession as had been done in the wilderness before there was a permanent place for it. They were free now to do other things. First, they were to divide up by their stated **divisions** as **David** had instructed (cf. 1 Chron. 24), and **Solomon** reaffirmed (2 Chron. 8:14). In the court of the temple they were to perform their ministry on behalf of the people according to clans.

**35:5-9.** Next the priests and **Levites** were to **slaughter the Passover lambs** and **prepare** them for consumption by the people (cf. 30:16-17). Out of the royal flocks and herds the king **provided** for the **people . . . 30,000 sheep and goats** and **3,000 cattle.** (Hezekiah, for the Passover celebration in his day, had given 7,000 sheep and 1,000 bulls, 30:24.) Josiah's leading **officials also** gave generously. Finally, the chief priests **gave** their fellow **priests 2,600 Passover offerings** (i.e., sheep and goats) **and 300 cattle** while the heads of **the Levites** gave their Levitical colleagues **5,000 Passover offerings** (sheep and goats) **and 500 cattle.**

### b. Celebration of the Passover (35:10-19)

**35:10-14.** When all was ready the festival began with the slaughter of the **lambs** by **the Levites** who then handed over **the blood** to **the priests** for sprinkling on the great altar. **The burnt offerings,** those sheep and goats not intended for use in the Passover, were distributed along with the **cattle** to **the people. The Passover** sacrifices were then **roasted** and **boiled** as the Law required (cf. Ex. 12:7-9; Deut. 16:7). **After** that the Levites prepared **the burnt offerings** for their own and the priests' consumption since the priests were so busy with the Passover service. Since only lambs and goats were sacrificed as Passover victims and for evening and morning offerings (cf. Ex. 29:38-45) the cattle were used for thank or fellowship offerings (cf. Lev. 3:1-5).

**35:15-19.** In addition to the **Levites** involved in sacrifice were **the** Levite **musicians** and **gatekeepers,** all of whom could remain at **their posts because their** comrades attended to their sacrificial meals. The festivities of **the Passover** continued on through the whole **seven**-day period of **the Feast of Unleavened Bread.** Not since . . . **Samuel,** the chronicler reported, had **such a Passover** been **celebrated.**

3. JOSIAH'S FATAL ENCOUNTER WITH NECO (35:20-27)

**35:20.** By the year 609 B.C. Assyria had become so weak that she had lost practically all her empire, especially to the Babylonians (or Chaldeans). Nineveh had fallen in 612 so the Assyrians had concentrated their forces around Haran and Carchemish on the upper Euphrates River. The Babylonians decided to advance against them there to destroy them once for all, but **Egypt,** more fearful of Babylonia than Assyria, launched an attack through Palestine with the idea of coming to Assyria's assistance at Carchemish. **Josiah** in the meantime favored the Babylonians and therefore set out to intercept the Egyptians under Pharaoh **Neco** (609–595 B.C.) and prevent them from getting to **Carchemish.**

**35:21-27.** **Neco** tried his best to dissuade **Josiah** from this course of action, arguing that **God** was **with** him (Neco) in his mission and would **destroy** Josiah if he did not back off. Neco had indeed received such instructions from the Lord God, but **Josiah** intervened anyway and despite disguising **himself** (like Ahab; cf. 18:29) was fatally **wounded** on the battlefield at **Megiddo.** For centuries the flat plains of Megiddo have been the scene of many battles. Armageddon (lit., the mountain of Megiddo) will be the scene of Christ's battle at His second coming (Rev. 16:16; cf. Rev. 19).

Though Josiah survived till he reached **Jerusalem . . . he died** there and **was buried** with **his fathers.** So shocking was the good king's death that **Jeremiah** the prophet **composed laments** for the occasion which, the chronicler wrote, were sung to his very **day. The Laments** are probably not the Book of Lamentations. **Other** incidents **of** Josiah's life were recorded **in the book of the kings of Israel and Judah.**

## Q. Jehoahaz (36:1-4)

**36:1-4.** **Josiah** had at least four sons (cf. 1 Chron. 3:15), three of whom became kings of Judah (see the chart "The Last Five Kings of Judah," near 2 Kings 23:31-35). The first of these (though not the oldest; cf. 2 Chron. 36:5) was **Jehoahaz,** an appointee by **the people** after Josiah's tragic death. He remained in power for only **three months** because for reasons not given, Neco **dethroned him,** levied on **Judah** a tax of **100 talents of silver** (3¾ tons) **and a talent of gold** (75 pounds).

Then Neco replaced Jehoahaz with his brother **Eliakim** whom Neco renamed **Jehoiakim.** The act of renaming showed Neco's superiority and control over the new king. **Jehoahaz** was then taken prisoner **to Egypt.** All this presupposes Egyptian control of Judah, a situation which prevailed from 609 to 605 B.C.

## R. Jehoiakim (36:5-8)

**36:5-8.** **Jehoiakim,** a wicked king, reigned **in Jerusalem 11 years** (609–598 B.C.), part of the time under Neco and the Egyptians and part of the time under **Nebuchadnezzar** and the Babylonians. Because of his wickedness (cf. Jer. 26:21-24) **the LORD** allowed him to fall to **Nebuchadnezzar** who had driven the Egyptians out of Palestine by 605 B.C. In that year Daniel and his friends were taken captive to Babylon (cf. comments on Dan. 1:1). Jehoiakim had at first been loyal to Nebuchadnezzar but after three years (in 602) he rebelled (cf. 2 Kings 24:1). The chronicler (but not the author of 2 Kings) reported that Jehoiakim was then **bound . . . with bronze shackles** and taken **to Babylon** along with sacred objects **from the temple.** This was Nebuchadnezzar's first of three attacks on Jerusalem—in 605, 597, and 586 B.C. Apparently Jehoiakim was released or escaped from Babylon because he was given a dishonorable burial outside the gates of Jerusalem (Jer. 22:18-19). His wicked reign was also recorded **in the book of the kings of Israel and Judah.**

## S. Jehoiachin (36:9-10)

**36:9-10.** **Jehoiachin,** son of Jehoiakim, **was 18 when he** succeeded his father (most Heb. mss. have 8; cf. NIV marg., which seems unlikely since he had wives; cf. 2 Kings 24:15). **He reigned**

only **three months and 10 days** (598–597 B.C.). He too was **evil** so when **Nebuchadnezzar** undertook his next western campaign in the spring (NIV marg.) he took the young king and his family into captivity (along with 10,000 Jews, 2 Kings 24:13-14) and set **Zedekiah** on Judah's throne. In 2 Kings 25:27-30 is the additional information that Jehoiachin was released from Babylonian imprisonment in the 37th year of his captivity (560 B.C.) and was placed on a royal pension in Babylon for the rest of his life. This is now confirmed in the Neo-Babylonian texts (James B. Pritchard, ed., *Ancient Near Eastern Texts Relating to the Old Testament*, 3rd ed. Princeton, N.J.: Princeton University Press, 1969, p. 308). This was two years after Nebuchadnezzar died and may have been because of Daniel's influence.

### T. Zedekiah (36:11-16)

**36:11-16.** Having removed Jehoiachin, Nebuchadnezzar replaced him with his uncle (cf. v. 10) **Zedekiah,** Judah's last king in Old Testament times. His **11-year reign** (597–586 B.C.) was **evil,** a situation well documented by the Prophet **Jeremiah** (cf. Jer. 21:3-7; 32:1-5). Zedekiah **rebelled against King Nebuchadnezzar** in his ninth year (588 B.C.; cf. 2 Kings 25:1), and despite the increasing peril of his predicament he **would not turn to the LORD** nor would any of the other **leaders** or the general population. Yet **the LORD** in His mercy (**pity**) continued to send warnings through the prophets (**His messengers**) but the people **despised** the word of the Lord and **mocked** His prophets. Thus **there was no remedy** (cf. Jer. 5:10-13; 7:12-15).

### U. The Babylonian Conquest and Exile (36:17-21)

**36:17-20.** At last Nebuchadnezzar's army came (under God's leading) and delivered a smashing blow that brought Judah's independence to an end. **Young** and **old** alike were **killed** and many of the others taken as prisoners. The valuable treasures of **the temple** were looted and the building itself burned and reduced to rubble, along with **the palaces.** Also the city's **wall** was broken down. Those who **escaped** death were taken **to Babylon** where they existed as slaves till Babylon's fall to **Persia** in 539 B.C.

**36:21.** The historian then observed that **the land** of Judah at last **enjoyed its Sabbath rests,** a period of **70 years** prophesied **by Jeremiah** (cf. Jer. 29:10). This probably refers to the approximately 70-year period from the first deportation under Nebuchadnezzar (605 B.C.) to the rebuilding of the temple foundation by the returning exiles in 536 (cf. Dan. 9:2; Ezra 1:1). Since Israel and Judah had failed to keep the sabbatical years (every seventh year the land was supposed to lie fallow, Lev. 25:1-7) throughout her history, the Lord would enforce on the land a 70-year "sabbath" (cf. Lev. 26:34-35).

### V. The Decree of Cyrus (36:22-23)

**36:22-23.** The chronicler closed his historical narrative on an optimistic note. God had brought His people into the judgment of exile but He also eventually delivered them, a chastened and repentant people who would form the nucleus of a continuing Davidic dynasty. To accomplish this the Lord raised up the mighty **Cyrus king of Persia** (559–530 B.C.). In his **first year** over Babylon (538) he issued a decree which allowed the **people** of **Judah** to return to their land and rebuild their **temple.** This proclamation—identical to Ezra 1:2-3a (see comments there) and confirmed by the discovery of a Babylonian inscription—was prompted by **the LORD . . . God** as fulfillment of Jeremiah's prophetic word (Jer. 25:12; 29:10; cf. Daniel's prayer in Dan. 9:4-19). Most of the kings of Israel and Judah had failed to obey the Lord and to lead the people in godliness. Ironically God stirred up the spirit of a pagan king to make possible the historical events which will eventually lead to the second coming of Jesus Christ, the incarnate God and King of Israel.

## BIBLIOGRAPHY

Ackroyd, Peter R. *I and II Chronicles, Ezra, Nehemiah.* Torch Bible Commentaries. London: SCM Press, 1973.

Coggins, R.J. *The First and Second Books of the Chronicles.* New York: Cambridge University Press, 1976.

Curtis, Edward Lewis, and Madsen, Albert Alonzo. *A Critical and Exegetical Commen-*

tary on the Books of Chronicles. The International Critical Commentary. Edinburgh: T. & T. Clark, 1910.

Keil, C.F. "The Books of the Chronicles." In Commentary on the Old Testament in Ten Volumes. Vol. 3. Reprint (25 vols. in 10). Grand Rapids: Wm. B. Eerdmans Publishing Co., 1982.

Myers, Jacob M. II Chronicles. The Anchor Bible. Garden City, N.Y.: Doubleday & Co., 1965.

Sailhamer, John. First and Second Chronicles. Chicago: Moody Press, 1983.

Slotki, I.W. Chronicles: Hebrew Text and English Translation with an Introduction and Commentary. London: Soncino Press, 1952.

Williamson, H.G.M. 1 and 2 Chronicles. The New Century Bible Commentary. Grand Rapids: Wm. B. Eerdmans Publishing Co., 1982.

Zöckler, Otto. "The Books of the Chronicles." In Commentary on the Holy Scriptures, Critical, Doctrinal, and Homiletical. Vol. 4. Reprint (24 vols. in 12). Grand Rapids: Zondervan Publishing House, 1960.

# EZRA

## John A. Martin

## INTRODUCTION

**Name.** Josephus (*Against Apion* 1. 8), Jerome (*Preface to the Commentary on Galatians*), and the Talmud (*Baba Bathra* 15a) considered the Books of Ezra and Nehemiah as one. Also the Hebrew Bible has the books together as a single work. However, there is evidence that the two books were originally separate. The lists in Ezra 2 and Nehemiah 7 are basically the same. This would militate against the idea that the two books were originally one, for it would seem strange to repeat the same list in one volume. The name Ezra for the title of the first work comes from the major person in the second half of the book, who also appears in chapters 8 and 12 of the Book of Nehemiah.

The name of the Book of Ezra is complicated by the way the Septuagint named some of its books. In the Septuagint the name Esdras (Ezra) refers to a number of books. First Esdras (also called Esdras A) is an apocryphal book. Second Esdras (Esdras B) contains the canonical Books of Ezra and Nehemiah. However, sometimes Nehemiah is called Esdras C (or G if one accurately reflects the third Heb. letter, which is *gimel*). The Apocrypha has still another Esdras, alternately called II Esdras or IV Esdras.

**Canonicity.** The Book of Ezra has been accepted as canonical since before the time of the Septuagint (ca. 200 B.C.), which may have been only about 250 years after the book was written. Few scholars in modern times have therefore questioned the canonicity of the Book of Ezra.

**Author.** Though Ezra is not referred to in the book as having written it, he has long been supposed to be the book's author. Internal evidence points to this fact for in 7:27–9:15 the author refers to himself in the first person. Hebrew tradition also has considered Ezra the author. He was a priest and a scribe of the Law (7:21). Undoubtedly Ezra had documents at his disposal for the historical sections in chapters 1–6. Many Bible students have noted similarities between the style of Ezra and the style of 1 and 2 Chronicles. Therefore some suppose that Ezra was the author of all three. (See comments in *Introduction to 1 Chron.*)

**Date.** The Book of Ezra covers two distinct time periods. Chapters 1–6 cover the 23 years from the edict of Cyrus to the rebuilding of the temple in Jerusalem (538–515 B.C.). Chapters 7–10 deal with the events after Ezra returned from Babylon (458 B.C.). The two exceptions are 4:6, which refers to an event in the reign of Xerxes (485–465) and verses 7-23, which parenthetically include a letter written later during the reign of Artaxerxes (464–424). The time of writing of the completed book could not have been earlier than about 450 B.C. (when the events recorded in 10:17-44 took place). Ezra was a contemporary of Nehemiah (Neh. 8:1-9; 12:36).

**Historical Setting.** The setting of the book is the postexilic era when the faithful Israelites were returning from Babylon to Judah so that they could reestablish their temple worship. In all the books written during the postexilic period the temple and temple worship are vital subjects. (These include 1 and 2 Chron.; Ezra; Neh.; Hag.; Zech.; and Mal.—all except Es. in which the people were unfaithful to the command of the Lord given through Isaiah and Jeremiah to return to the land after the Captivity.) The people who returned to the land of promise were publicly acknowledging that they believed God would reestablish the nation and usher in a time of kingdom blessing.

There were three returns from Bab-

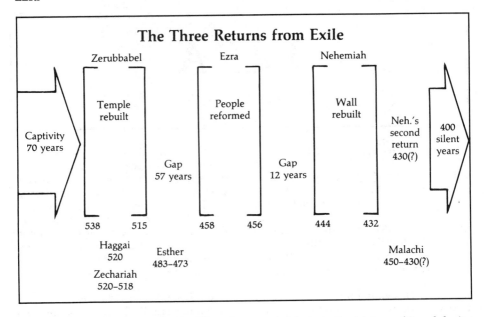

## The Three Returns from Exile

Zerubbabel — Temple rebuilt

Ezra — People reformed

Nehemiah — Wall rebuilt

Captivity 70 years

Gap 57 years

Gap 12 years

Neh.'s second return 430(?)

400 silent years

538    515    458    456    444    432

Haggai 520

Esther 483–473

Zechariah 520–518

Malachi 450–430(?)

ylon to the land of Israel (in 538, 458, and 444 B.C.), just as there had been three deportations from the land to Babylon (605, 597, and 586 B.C.). The first return was led by Zerubbabel (Ezra 1–6; Hag.; Zech.) in 538 B.C. The rebuilding of the temple was of vital importance for this group. The second return was under Ezra (Ezra 7–10) in 458 B.C. The people needed reforming; they needed to return to their covenant obligations. The third return was led by Nehemiah in 444 B.C. Nehemiah's concerns were to rebuild the walls of Jerusalem and, as in Ezra's time, to lead the people back to obedience to the Lord. The Book of Malachi was probably written in Nehemiah's time. The events in the Book of Esther occurred between the events recorded in Ezra 6 and Ezra 7. (See the chart "The Three Returns from Exile." Also see the chart "Chronology of the Postexilic Period" near Ezra 1:1.)

**The Text.** Nearly a fourth of the Book of Ezra was written in Aramaic; the rest was written in Hebrew. The Aramaic sections (67 of 280 verses) are 4:8–6:18 and 7:12-26. The material in these verses was mainly copied from official correspondence for which Aramaic was the standard language (*lingua franca*) of the day.

**Purpose.** The Book of Ezra was written not simply to record miscellaneous his-

torical facts in the history of Israel during the Jews' return to the land. This book, like all books in the Bible, had a theological purpose. The purpose of Ezra's book can be seen by reflecting on the audience for which it was written. As stated earlier, the book may have been written around 450 B.C. Thus the original readers were exiles who had returned under Zerubbabel and Ezra, but who were then wavering in their relationship to God. Ezra wrote to encourage the remnant to be involved in true temple worship and to remind them to fulfill their covenantal obligations because of God's mercy. The highlight of the book is in chapters 9–10, which tells of the people's proper response after sin was found in their midst. Ezra wanted his readers to emulate that same attitude of dependence on God, which believers of all times should have.

## OUTLINE

I. The First Return and Rebuilding under Zerubbabel (chaps. 1–6)
   A. The proclamation of Cyrus (1:1-4)
   B. The reaction of the Israelites (1:5-11)
   C. The list of people who returned (chap. 2)
      1. The list recorded (2:1-63)

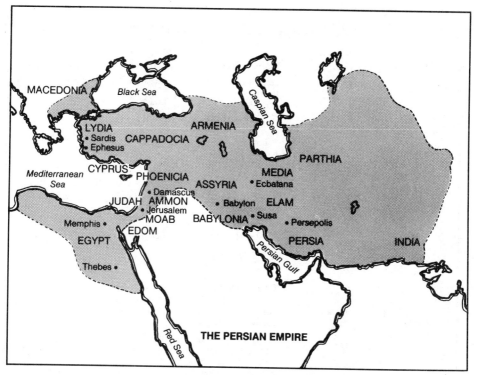

THE PERSIAN EMPIRE

2. The total numbers given (2:64-67)
3. The restoration begun (2:68-70)
D. The rebuilding of the temple (3:1–6:15)
   1. The altar and foundation rebuilt (chap. 3)
   2. The rebuilding opposed (4:1–6:12)
   3. The temple completed (6:13-15)
E. The dedication of the temple and the celebration of the Passover (6:16-22)
   1. The temple dedicated (6:16-18)
   2. The Passover celebrated (6:19-22)
II. The Second Return and Reform under Ezra (chaps. 7–10)
A. The return to the land (chaps. 7–8)
   1. The introduction of Ezra (7:1-10)
   2. The circumstances prompting the return (7:11-28)
   3. The list of the returnees (8:1-14)
   4. The details of the journey and arrival (8:15-36)
B. The reform in the land (chaps. 9–10)
   1. The people's sin of

intermarriage reported (9:1-4)
2. Ezra's prayer to God (9:5-15)
3. The people's confession of sin (chap. 10)

# COMMENTARY

## I. The First Return and Rebuilding under Zerubbabel (chaps. 1–6)

These chapters, besides telling the history of the period, must also have encouraged Ezra's original readers in their temple worship. As they read about the rebuilding process they would have been made aware of the great personal sacrifices the Jews had made in constructing the temple. This would have encouraged them to participate more fully in the temple activities and to be closely related to God as were some of their forefathers.

### A. The proclamation of Cyrus (1:1-4)

**1:1. Cyrus,** the **king of** the extensive Persian **realm** (see the map "The Persian Empire"), drafted **a proclamation** that allowed the Israelites to return to their land and rebuild their temple. **Cyrus** made the proclamation in his **first year** (538 B.C.). This was the first year of his reign over

## Chronology of the Postexilic Period

| Persian Kings | Dates of Their Reigns | Biblical Events | Scripture References | Dates |
|---|---|---|---|---|
| Cyrus | 559–530 B.C. | Edict of Cyrus for the return | Ezra 1:1-4 | 538 B.C. |
| | | First return of 49,897 exiles, under Zerubbabel (to build the temple) | Ezra 2 | 538 |
| | | The altar and temple foundation built | Ezra 3:1–4:5 | 536 |
| Cambyses | 530–522 | | | |
| Smerdis | 522 | | | |
| Darius I | 521–486 | Haggai prophesied | Book of Haggai | 520 |
| | | Zechariah prophesied | Book of Zechariah | 520–518 |
| | | The temple completed | Ezra 5–6 | 515 |
| Xerxes (Ahasuerus) | 485–465 | Accusation against Judah | Ezra 4:6 | 486 |
| | | Esther became queen | Esther 2:17 | 479 |
| Artaxerxes I (Artashasta) | 464–424 | Artaxerxes stopped the rebuilding of Jerusalem | Ezra 4:7-23 | ca. 464–458 |
| | | Second return of 4,000-5,000 exiles, under Ezra (to beautify the temple and reform the people) | Ezra 7–10 | 458 |
| | | Third return of exiles, under Nehemiah (to build the walls of Jerusalem) | Book of Nehemiah | 444 |
| | | Nehemiah's second return | Nehemiah 13:6 | ca. 430 |
| | | Malachi prophesied | Book of Malachi | 450–430 (?) |

Babylon, but he had been king over other territories for more than 20 years. He had been in power since 559 when he became the king of Anshan. Then he became **king of** Medo-**Persia** about 550 B.C. He conquered Babylon in October 539, and became the king of Babylon, a title of honor denoting the highest position in the civilized world. (See the chart "Chronology of the Postexilic Period.")

As is evidenced from Cyrus' attitude concerning the God of Israel (whom he did not worship) he was not a true believer in Yahweh. Cyrus' concern was to establish strong buffer states around his empire which would be loyal to him. Also by having his subject peoples resettled in their own countries he hoped to have the gods in various parts of his empire praying for him to his gods Bel and Nebo. The famous Cyrus Cylinder (538 B.C.), which records his capture of Babylon and his program of repatriating his subject peoples in their homelands, includes this statement: "May all the gods whom I have resettled in their sacred cities daily ask Bel and Nebo for a long life for me."

The fulfilling of Jeremiah's words (Jer. 29:10; cf. Jer. 25:11-12) was totally God's doing. Seventy years of Jewish captivity in Babylon were about to end. The first deportation of Jews to Babylon was in 605 B.C. Cyrus' decree in 538 was 67 years later. By the time the people returned and built the altar in 536, 70 years were almost up.

The edict came about because **the LORD moved the heart of Cyrus.** The Hebrew words translated "moved the heart" (also trans. "stirred [up] the spirit") were a favorite expression of biblical writers in the postexilic period (Ezra 1:5; 1 Chron. 5:26; 2 Chron. 21:16, "aroused"; 36:22; Jer. 51:11; Hag. 1:14). This shows the sovereign hand of God behind the events of history.

**1:2-3. Cyrus** said that Yahweh, **the God of heaven,** had **appointed** him **to build a temple . . . at Jerusalem.** Part of this decree is recorded in 2 Chronicles 36:23. Also the decree was filed in Ecbatana, where Darius I found it about 520–518 B.C. (Ezra 6:1-5). God had promised the Jewish remnant that He would raise up Cyrus as His servant to restore the fortunes of His people (Isa. 44:28; 45:1, 13). Under the Holy Spirit's guidance, the Prophet Isaiah referred to Cyrus by name about 150 years before the king made his decree. Josephus wrote that Cyrus was shown the prophecy in Isaiah 44:28 and wanted to fulfill it (*The Antiquities of the Jews* 11. 1. 1).

"The God of heaven" is a title of God used 9 times in Ezra (1:2; 5:11-12; 6:9-10; 7:12, 21, 23 [twice]—more than in any other Bible book—and 10 times in other exilic and postexilic books (2 Chron. 36:23; Neh. 1:4-5; 2:4, 20; Dan. 2:18-19, 28, 37, 44). Elsewhere in the Old Testament that phrase occurs only four times (Gen. 24:3, 7; Ps. 136:26; Jonah 1:9). It points to God's sovereignty. He is the One who made heaven (Gen. 14:19, 22; 2 Chron. 2:12; Ps. 115:15), who is in heaven (Deut. 4:39; 1 Kings 8:30, 39, 43, 49; Ecc. 5:2), and who reigns from His throne in heaven (Isa. 66:1). Though Cyrus was a monarch over an extensive empire, Yahweh is far greater for He rules from heaven.

The emphasis in Ezra 1:2-3 on **the temple** sets the tone for this and other postexilic books. The temple was of utmost importance in the life of the people of Israel. Without the temple there could be no sacrificial system, which was the nation's lifeblood in its relationship to God. "The God of heaven" (v. 2) is also **the God of Israel** who Cyrus said was **in Jerusalem.**

**1:4.** Cyrus' edict also instructed the returnees' neighbors in Persia to give them the equivalent of money (**silver and gold**), material **goods . . . livestock,** and **freewill offerings** (cf. v. 6). The freewill offerings were **for the temple** and the other gifts were for the people themselves. This is reminiscent of the Exodus

from Egypt when God miraculously took the nation out of bondage and had the Egyptians aid them with gifts of silver, gold, and clothing (Ex. 3:22; 11:2; 12:35). Now God was effecting a new "Exodus," again bringing His people who had been in bondage back into the land of promise, much as He had done under Moses and Joshua. The people had been in bondage to Babylon because of their failure to keep their covenantal obligations, which Moses had given them during the first Exodus. Once more God was miraculously working in the life of the nation.

### B. The reaction of the Israelites (1:5-11)

**1:5-11.** The religious leaders (**priests and Levites**) along with the **heads** of the two tribes (**Judah and Benjamin**) that had been taken into exile by the Babylonians spearheaded the return to Israel to rebuild the temple, **the house of the LORD.** The Jews who returned totaled 49,897 (2:64-65). The **neighbors** of the returnees obeyed the king's decree by contributing to the effort (1:6). Even **Cyrus** contributed to the return by giving back **the articles belonging to the temple of the LORD.** These were the **dishes . . . pans . . . bowls,** and **other articles** (vv. 9-10) **Nebuchadnezzar had** taken **from** the **Jerusalem** temple in 605 B.C. (Dan. 1:2), in 597 B.C. (2 Kings 24:13), and in 586 B.C. (2 Kings 25:14-15; Jer. 27:16; 52:18-19; cf. Ezra 5:14; 6:5; Dan. 5:2-3) and placed in a **temple** in Babylon, perhaps the Esagila temple built in honor of the god Marduk. **Mithredath** is a Persian name, and the word for **treasurer** (*gizbār*) is also Persian.

In Ezra 1:9-10 the **articles** total 2,499 but in verse 11 the total number of **gold** and **silver** items was **5,400.** Why the difference? Surely Ezra would not be so foolish as to make a major mistake such as that when he so carefully wrote the rest of the book under the Holy Spirit's inspiration. Even if one were to assume (as do many critics) that a redactor brought together in verses 9-11 two variant traditions, it would seem likely that Ezra would try to reconcile them in some way. It seems better to suppose Ezra first listed some of the items, perhaps the bigger and more valuable ones (vv. 9-10), then referred to the total number of items both the larger and more valuable and the smaller and less significant (v. 11).

Another problem pertains to **Sheshbazzar** (v. 11), who was called **the prince of Judah** (v. 8). Three views about his identity are suggested: (1) Some feel that **Sheshbazzar** was a Persian name for Zerubbabel. Both are said to have laid the foundation of the temple (3:8-10; 5:16). Zerubbabel, which means "begotten in Babel," was a grandson of Jehoiachin (1 Chron. 3:17-19), who had been deported to Babylon but had been released from confinement (2 Kings 25:27-30). Zerubbabel's relationship to Jehoiachin would explain the title "the prince of Judah." However, it would seem strange that Zerubbabel would have a second pagan name rather than having one name that reflected Yahweh worship (Sheshbazzar being a pagan deity). If Zerubbabel and Sheshbazzar were two names of the same person, it is strange that he was never again referred to by the name Sheshbazzar except in Ezra 5:15-16.

(2) A second view is that this man was a Jew who was appointed governor by Cyrus but who died shortly after arriving in Palestine and was replaced by Zerubbabel. Though plausible, no solid evidence exists for this view.

(3) A third view is that Sheshbazzar was the Shenazzar in 1 Chronicles 3:17, and therefore was Zerubbabel's uncle.

(4) A fourth view is that Sheshbazzar was a Persian official who was sent to oversee the use of the king's money and to make sure the king's wishes were carried out. It has been suggested that because Sheshbazzar was a Persian official the returnees later referred to him (Ezra 5:15-16) to support their claim of legitimacy for their building project. (See comments on 5:13-16.)

## C. The list of people who returned (chap. 2)

### 1. THE LIST RECORDED (2:1-63)

**2:1-63.** The list is divided into several parts. All of **the people of the province** (i.e., of **Judah**) returned to their hometowns (v. 1). Ezra first recorded the 11 civil and religious leaders who were prominent (v. 2). **Jeshua** was the high priest (3:2); his name is spelled Joshua in the Books of Haggai and Zechariah. He was a grandson of Seraiah (cf. 1 Chron. 6:14 with Hag. 1:1), a priest whom **Nebuchadnezzar** killed at Riblah (2 Kings 25:18-21). The **Nehemiah** in Ezra 2:2 was

not the Nehemiah who returned to Jerusalem more than 90 years later, 444 B.C. Nor was the **Mordecai** here Esther's cousin (Es. 2:5-7), who lived in Susa about 60 years after the Jews' first return.

Nehemiah 7:7 records 12 names rather than 11 (cf. Ezra 2:2). (Three names have different spellings. In verse 2 **Seraiah, Reelaiah,** and **Rehum** are probably the same persons as Azariah, Raamiah, and Nehum, respectively, in Neh. 7:7.) Nahamani's name, not in Ezra's list, may have been dropped out by an early scribal error in the copying of the original manuscripts. It is likely that 12 men would have originally been listed as symbolic heads of the 12-tribe nation (cf. 12 male goats offered for the 12 tribes of Israel, Ezra 6:17).

Then Ezra listed people by their 18 families and clans, totaling 15,604 (2:3-20). Next came a listing of inhabitants (totaling 8,540) from 21 towns and villages (vv. 21-35; see the map "Postexilic Samaria and Judah"). Then **the priests** (4,289 of them) were listed (vv. 36-39), followed by 341 **Levites** which included **singers** and **gatekeepers** (vv. 40-42). **The temple servants** (vv. 43-54) and **descendants of** the royal **servants** (vv. 55-58) totaled **392.** The **652** returnees who **could not** clearly trace their ancestry (vv. 59-63) were listed last. **The priests** who could not delineate their genealogies were not allowed by **the governor** (*tiršāṯā'*, a Persian term, possibly a reference to Sheshbazzar [cf. comments on 1:8] or to Zerubbabel) **to eat . . . the most sacred food** till **a priest** was **ministering with the Urim and Thummim.** The Urim and Thummim were parts of the high priest's breastplate, probably two stones used in some way in determining God's will (cf. Ex. 28:30; Lev. 8:8; Num. 27:21; Deut. 33:8; 1 Sam. 28:6; Neh. 7:65).

Though such a list of names and locations seems unnecessary to some modern readers, it would have been of great encouragement to the original readers as they saw their own families and towns represented.

### 2. THE TOTAL NUMBERS GIVEN (2:64-67)

**2:64-67.** When added together the numbers in verses 2-42, 58, and 60 which list the returnees come to 29,829 (including the 11 prominent men listed in v. 2). However, the total in verses 64-65—**the**

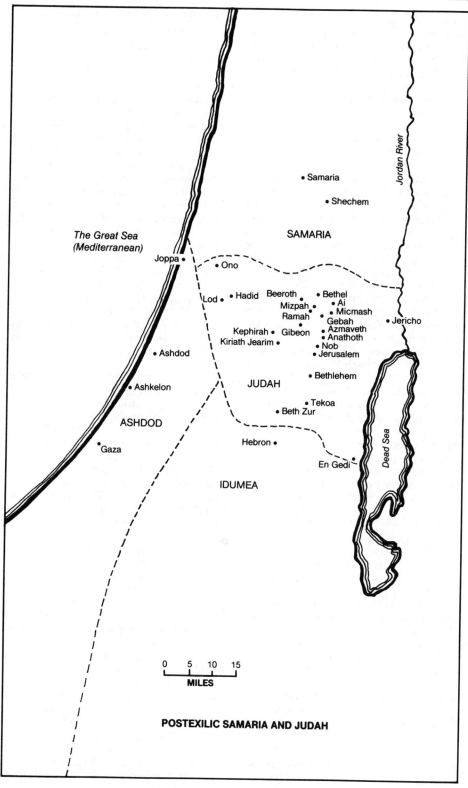

**POSTEXILIC SAMARIA AND JUDAH**

**whole company**—is 49,897. The larger number may include women and children. It may also include Jews from the 10 Northern tribes who might have joined the remnant of the two Southern tribes of Judah and Benjamin (cf. 1:5). It may also have included the priests who could not delineate their genealogies (2:61-62).

Ezra's grand total of 49,897 is very close to Nehemiah's total of 49,942 (Neh. 7:66-67). Nehemiah's extra 45 people are in the singers (Ezra had 200 but Nehemiah referred to 245). This may have been a scribal error, an error not in the original manuscripts but in the numerous copyings of the text in its transmission. A scribe, in copying Nehemiah 7:67, may have inadvertently picked up the 245 in verse 68, in reference to mules, and inserted that number for the 200 singers. This kind of error may also account for several variations in the other numbers in these lists. (For further discussion see the comments on Neh. 7. Also see the chart "The Lists of Exile Returnees in Ezra 2 and Nehemiah 7," near Neh. 7:8-62.)

Even the animals were counted—a total of 8,136, most of them **donkeys,** commonly used for riding (Ezra 2:66-67).

The journey from Babylon to Israel was about 900 miles and took about four months (cf. 7:8-9), but Ezra did not state how long the return trip took. His focus was not on the people's hardships but on their task of rebuilding the temple.

3. THE RESTORATION BEGUN (2:68-70)

**2:68-69.** When the returnees **arrived** back in Palestine **at the house of the Lord** (i.e., at its location site) they **gave** of their possessions **according to their ability.** They gave large amounts of money and material to begin the temple-building project. The list of precious metals and materials differs from the corresponding list in Nehemiah 7:70-72. Ezra's **61,000 drachmas of gold** are 41,000 in Nehemiah. Ezra recorded **5,000 minas of silver** while Nehemiah referred to 4,200. Ezra mentioned **100 priestly garments** whereas Nehemiah recorded 597. These differences were probably early scribal errors.

**2:70.** The people then **settled in** their ancestors' **towns** and villages (see the map "Postexilic Samaria and Judah").

## D. The rebuilding of the temple (3:1–6:15)

1. THE ALTAR AND THE FOUNDATION REBUILT (CHAP. 3)

**3:1-2.** The first task facing the people was the rebuilding of **the altar** of **burnt** offering, directly east of where the temple building itself would be located. This was essential for reestablishing the sacrificial system which set these people apart as a nation and which was used by God as a means for atoning for their sins. **The seventh month** may refer to the seventh month after the people left Babylon or to the seventh month after they arrived in **Jerusalem.** This was in September-October (see the chart "Calendar in Israel" near Ex. 12). In years past, the seventh month had been a great month religiously for Israel. Three religious festivals were held in the seventh month: the Feast of Trumpets on the 1st day (Lev. 23:23-25), the Day of Atonement on the 10th day (Lev. 23:26-32), and the Feast of Tabernacles on days 15-21 (Lev. 23:33-36, 39-43; Num. 29:12-39; cf. Ezra 3:4).

The words, **The people assembled as one man,** suggest they all agreed that the building project must begin. The men who headed up the constructing of the altar were **Jeshua,** the religious leader (a descendant of Aaron), **and Zerubbabel,** the civil leader (a descendant of David), along with **fellow priests** (other descendants of Aaron) and **associates** (other descendants of David). They built the altar so that they could offer sacrifices **in accordance with what** was **written in the Law of Moses.** It was imperative that the returnees would come back to the Mosaic Covenant. Because their forefathers had left the covenant, the nation had been driven into Captivity. The former exiles did not want to make that same mistake.

**3:3-6.** Even though the returnees had **fear of the peoples around them,** foreigners who had been deported by the Assyrian Empire into Palestine, **they built the altar,** and offered **burnt offerings on it** (cf. Lev. 1; 6:8-13), starting **on the first day of the . . . month** (Ezra 3:6). These were the first sacrifices made there in 50 years—since 586 B.C. when the temple was torn down. Other **sacrifices** were offered in connection with **all the appointed feasts,** including, for example, **the Feast of Tabernacles** on days 15-21 of that seventh month (cf. Lev. 23:33-36, 39-43; Num. 29:12-39). The **sacrifices** showed that the people wanted to be responsive to the Law of God.

**3:7-9.** There was a period of preparation for building the temple foundation for **the work** did not begin till **the second month of the second year after their arrival** (May-June 536, exactly 70 years after the first deportation in 605). Why this delay of seven months after the altar was built? Because they had to get organized and secure the building materials. The wood (**cedar logs**) came **from Lebanon,** shipped along the coast **to Joppa** and then carried overland to **Jerusalem** (see the map "The Persian Empire" near 1:1). Lebanon was well known for its cedar forests and its fine woodworkers. For the first temple, 430 years earlier (in 966 B.C.), Solomon had received much of his building materials (cedar, pine, and algum logs) and craftsmen from Lebanon (1 Kings 5:1-10, 18; 2 Chron. 2:1-16). Solomon began his project in the second month (May-June; 1 Kings 6:1), the same month this rebuilding began under Zerubbabel. Since **Tyre** and **Sidon** in Lebanon were under the Persian Empire, **Cyrus** had to authorize this transaction (cf. Ezra 6:3-4), in which the logs, as in Solomon's time, were paid for by **money . . . food . . . drink, and oil.**

**Zerubbabel** appointed **the Levites** as supervisors of the construction project. Centuries earlier Levites were involved in the tabernacle construction (Ex. 38:21) and in caring for and transporting it (Num. 1:50-51; 3:21-37). Now they were involved in the temple construction. Three Levite groups of supervisors were mentioned (Ezra 3:9)—**Jeshua** and his family, **Kadmiel** (cf. 2:40) and his family, and the family **of Henadad.**

**3:10-11.** Nothing is mentioned about the actual process of laying the temple **foundation** or the length of time involved. This is because the focus was on the results of this project on that community of people who had braved the rugged conditions. They were following the command of Cyrus but, more importantly, they were following the command of their God with whom they were in covenant. As **the foundation . . . was laid** the **people** were careful to follow in the traditions of their forefathers who had been rightly related to God under the Mosaic Covenant. As **the priests . . . and the Levites** led the dedication service for the temple's foundations, they did the things that were **prescribed by David.** The order followed was the same as when David brought the ark to Jerusalem. At that time priests blew trumpets and Asaph sounded cymbals (1 Chron. 16:5-6). Here the priests blew **trumpets** and **sons** (descendants) of Asaph played the **cymbals.** The order was also similar to the time when the ark was brought to the temple in Solomon's day (2 Chron. 5:12-13), when Asaph and others played cymbals, harps, and lyres; and the priests blew trumpets. In this rebuilding service the priests and Levites sang, **He is good; His love to Israel endures forever,** words almost identical to the song of praise in 2 Chronicles 5:13 (cf. Ps. 136:1). This song of praise is highly significant for by it the religious leaders were acknowledging that Yahweh had again established His loving protection over the nation. The word "love" (ḥeseḏ) is God's covenantal loyal love which exists forever with His people Israel. Now that the temple worship was being reestablished, the people again recognized the commitment of God's unending covenantal love.

**3:12-13.** In contrast with the joy many people experienced on that occasion, a few of **the older priests and Levites and family heads, who had seen the former temple** (destroyed 50 years earlier in 586 B.C.) were discouraged. Perhaps they contrasted the roughness of the current project with the grandeur of the Solomonic temple. Sixteen years later (in 520 B.C.) the same emotion of discouragement again hit the builders of the **temple** (Hag. 2:1-9). The two sounds, the **joy** and the **weeping** (from sadness), mingled together and were so loud that they were **heard far away.**

2. THE REBUILDING OPPOSED (4:1–6:12)

Ezra did not record all the events in those 21 years (from 536) till the temple was finished (in 515). That is because he was making a theological point that the temple of the Lord was completed despite opposition that might have stopped any other project. The temple was the basis for the postexilic community's fellowship with God. Not till the temple was built could the people really live in accord with the covenant. Ezra's account of this interim period differs in tone from Haggai's account of opposition (from 520 to 518). Ezra did not dwell on the sinful condition of the people as they lived in the land as did Haggai (Hag. 1). Ezra's account focused on external pressures from the surrounding peoples, whereas Haggai focused on the internal attitudes of the people who valued material possessions above spiritual things (Hag. 1:4-6).

### a. Attempts of enemies to stop the building (4:1-5)

**4:1-2.** The enemies used two methods of opposition to try to keep the **temple** from being built. First they offered to **help** in the construction process, thereby hoping to infiltrate the ranks and sidetrack the building project. When that did not work, they frightened the builders (perhaps with threats on their lives) and even hired counselors to frustrate them (vv. 4-5). **The enemies of Judah and Benjamin** refer to the people living in Palestine since the time of the fall of the Northern Kingdom in 722 B.C. The Assyrian Empire, which conquered the 10 Northern tribes, deported some of the people away to Assyria and brought in other peoples to intermarry (2 Kings 17:23-24). This tactic prevented strong nationalistic uprisings in the conquered lands.

The "enemies" (called "the peoples around them," Ezra 4:4) were the descendants of these mixed peoples and the forefathers of the New Testament Samaritans. These people in Ezra's day claimed that they worshiped the same **God,** that is, Yahweh, the God of Israel. But they had a syncretistic form of worship; they worshiped both Yahweh and others (2 Kings 17:29, 32-34, 41). Therefore their statement (Ezra 4:2) was not fully accurate and was apparently made to mislead the leadership of the returned band. **Esarhaddon, king of Assyria, who brought us here,** was the Assyrian monarch who aggressively pursued the policy of partial deportation and to whose reign these enemies could trace their ancestry in Palestine. Esarhaddon, a son of Sennacherib, ruled from 681 to 669 B.C. Some people, however, had been displaced into Samaria earlier by the Assyrian kings Sargon II (722–705) and Sennacherib (705–681). Judah and Benjamin's enemies

were also appealing on the basis of the fact that they, like the Jews, were a "displaced people," having been brought in from the outside. In a sense they were downplaying the nation of Israel's "roots" in the land.

**4:3-5.** The response by the governmental side (**Zerubbabel**) and the religious side (**Jeshua**) was decisive and immediate. They had two reasons for not wanting to be sidetracked by this offer of help. First, the temple was for **the LORD the God of Israel,** who was not the god these people worshiped. Second, they had been commissioned by **King Cyrus** himself to undertake the **building** project and therefore had every right to carry it out on their own. This rebuff brought on the second form of opposition. As already stated, the enemies tried **to discourage** the workers **and make them afraid.** This policy of harassment continued on till **the reign of Darius, king of Persia,** who ruled from 521 to 486. It was during his reign, in 515, that the temple was completed. The account of the building program under Darius is resumed in Ezra 4:24 after a parenthesis in verses 6-23.

### b. Parenthetical letters (4:6-23)

These letters to and from Artaxerxes are out of place chronologically, but they follow here logically to show that the opposition Ezra had begun to describe (vv. 1-5) continued on for many years—to 485 B.C., the year Xerxes began to reign (v. 6) and on into the days of Artaxerxes (464–424). Artaxerxes was the king who was reigning during the events recorded in chapters 7–10. For the names and dates of the Persian kings in the postexilic period, see the chart "Chronology of the Postexilic Period" near 1:1. Thus the letters may have been written at the time of Ezra's return (458 B.C.). Therefore the letters were written nearly 80 years later than the account into which they were placed. Ezra was not being deceptive by placing the letters here in his book since he clearly dated them by the ruler under which they were written. Anyone familiar with the history of that part of the world at that time (as were the inhabitants of Israel when the Book of Ezra was written) would have clearly seen what Ezra was logically doing.

**4:6.** Opposition continued during

the time of **Xerxes.** Xerxes, also known as Ahasuerus in the Book of Esther, ruled from 485 to 465. Ezra recorded nothing of the nature or results of the **accusation** except that it apparently kept the Israelites from working on building projects. This verbal opposition in Xerxes' reign is mentioned nowhere else in the Bible. This verse sets the stage for the following letter which was written in the reign of Persia's next king.

**4:7.** Opposition against the Jews was strong during the time of **Artaxerxes.** The focus of the narrative is on two letters written during his reign (464-424). Because the enemies' **letter** and the king's reply brought the work on the city walls and foundations to a halt, it seems logical that **the letter was written** before the return of Nehemiah, for under Nehemiah the building projects resumed and were completed. Though the letter was composed by people who spoke a northwest Semitic dialect (like Hebrew) it was written **in the Aramaic language** (the trade language of the day). It was in square **Aramaic script** rather than in the slanted Hebrew type of script or in cuneiform signs. Ezra 4:8–6:18 and 7:12-26 are in Aramaic. Perhaps **Bishlam, Mithredath,** and **Tabeel** were men from Samaria.

**4:8-10. Rehum the commanding officer and Shimshai the secretary** were probably Persians who were persuaded to write the letter. In their introduction Rehum and Shimshai tried to point out to King **Artaxerxes** that the participants in this opposition were from various parts of the world. Their complaint was not merely from a single isolated group. **Judges and officials** from various parts of the Persian Empire (see the map "The Persian Empire" near 1:1) and people who had been deported to **Samaria** under the reign of the Assyrian King **Ashurbanipal** 200 years earlier were opposed to the work. Ashurbanipal (669–626) continued the deporting done by his father Esarhaddon (4:2).

**4:11-16.** The writers **of the letter** (cf. **This is a copy** of the letter, v. 23; 5:6; 7:11) identified with the Persian king by noting that they were his **servants.** The letter itself is recorded in 4:12-16. The opponents noted that **the Jews** were **restoring the walls and repairing the foundations.** Their opposition was obviously

not against the rebuilding of the temple, for it had been completed in 515 B.C. The opposition was against an attempt to begin rebuilding the **walls** of **Jerusalem** which the opponents called **that rebellious and wicked city** (cf. vv. 15, 19). The apparent reason for the complaint was that if the city was allowed to be fortified, then Jerusalem and the territory which Jerusalem would control would no longer pay **taxes** or **tribute** money to the crown. This would dishonor **the king.** Therefore the complainers felt it was their patriotic duty to tell **the king** what was happening so that he could **search** the **records** and see that Jerusalem was **a rebellious city,** which is **why** it **was destroyed.** The letter added that if the city of Jerusalem was fortified then the Jews would take back all the territory they had previously occupied and the Persian **king** would have no territory left **in Trans-Euphrates.** They claimed he would lose a huge portion of his empire.

**4:17-23.** In his **reply** the **king** actually strengthened the position of the Israelites by leaving open the possibility that their work might resume later by his permission. This, of course, did happen under the leadership of Nehemiah. The king did **search** the archives and **found** that **Jerusalem** had been **powerful** at one time. What an encouragement this must have been to Ezra's original readers to recall the years of David and Solomon and to know that even a pagan king acknowledged the sovereignty of their empire centered at Jerusalem. The **king** commanded that the building projects **stop . . . until I so order.** This was the same king who later (444 B.C.) changed this edict and allowed Nehemiah to return and rebuild the walls of Jerusalem (Neh. 2:1-9). However, the immediate result was a forced cessation of the building activity because the enemies used **force** to back up a legal document from the Persian king.

*c. The result of the opposition (4:24)*

**4:24.** The narrative now picks up where it left off after verse 5 (vv. 6-23 are a lengthy parenthesis). The result of the opposition during Cyrus' reign was that **work** on the temple was suspended **until the second year of . . . Darius** (520 B.C.), some 18 years after the people had returned to the land for the purpose of rebuilding **the house of God.**

### d. The continuation of the work (5:1–6:12)

This section informs the readers of certain historical events under the reign of Darius, and also helps its readers understand that the temple rebuilding was sovereignly ordained by God and carried out through pagan rulers, this time Darius I (521–486).

**5:1-2.** The work on the temple had been stopped (4:1-5, 24), from 535 to 520 B.C. Now under the influence of two important prophets, **Haggai** and **Zechariah,** it was resumed. The preaching of these two men is recorded in the biblical books bearing their respective names. Haggai prophesied from August to December 520 B.C., and Zechariah prophesied for two years beginning in October-November 520. They were **helping** by exhorting and encouraging (cf. 6:14; Hag. 1:8; 2:4; Zech. 4:7-9). They were vitally concerned with the building of the temple because they realized that their nation could never fulfill the obligations of the Mosaic Covenant till the temple worship was reinstated. Both of these **prophets** placed the blame for the hard times the nation experienced during this period on the people's lack of obedience in not rebuilding the temple. However, Ezra did not deal with that question in his book. He stressed the outside opposition which was also a factor in slowing the work. The building process itself was spearheaded by **Zerubbabel** and **Jeshua,** the civil and religious leaders, respectively.

**5:3-5.** But as soon as the work was resumed, another effort (cf. 4:1-5) was made to stop it. Israel's leaders came into direct conflict with the duly established local authorities who were responsible to the Persian crown. In a Babylonian record dated 502 B.C. the name **Tattenai** and his office as **governor of Trans-Euphrates** are mentioned. Syria-Palestine was under him, an area including but much larger than Israel. **Shethar-Bozenai** was probably an assistant to Tattenai. It would have been Tattenai's responsibility, on hearing of this building activity in his territory, to investigate it. Major political unrest was seething at the beginning of Darius' reign. Possibly Tattenai thought the temple-**building** project in Jerusalem would grow into a full-scale rebellion against the empire.

The group of officials **asked** Zerubbabel and Jeshua **who authorized** the project (the word **structure** is lit., "wooden structure"), and asked for **the names of** the people responsible for it (cf. 5:9-10). But despite this challenge, the work did not stop because **the eye of their God was watching over** them (cf. "God . . . was over them," v. 1). Occurring frequently in Ezra and Nehemiah are the words "the *hand* of the LORD was on him" and similar expressions (Ezra 7:6, 9, 28; 8:18, 22, 31; Neh. 2:8, 18). God was providentially caring for them (by His "eye") and blessing them (by His "hand"). Clearly God was at work in spite of this opposition because through it the project was eventually given help.

**5:6-10.** Ezra recorded **the letter** (cf. **This is a copy** of the letter; 4:11, 23; 7:11) **Tattenai . . . sent to King Darius** about the building activity going on in Jerusalem (5:7-16). Tattenai began his letter by noting that **work** was being done on **the temple of the great God** in Jerusalem. This does not mean that Tattenai believed Yahweh of Israel was the supreme God. Most likely he meant that the God to whom the Jews were building the **temple** was the major God of the area. In the ancient Near East there was a highly developed belief in local deities. Tattenai noted that **large stones** and **timbers** (cf. 6:4; 1 Kings 6:36) were being used in the work and that the Jews were working **with diligence** and were **making rapid progress.** He added that he had asked **who authorized** the work (cf. Ezra 5:3) and that he had asked for **the names** of those who were leading the building program (cf. v. 4).

**5:11-12.** Tattenai's letter then included the Jews' answers to his questions (vv. 11-16). Zerubbabel and Jeshua called themselves **servants of the God of heaven and earth,** not servants of Persia! For comments on the title "the God of heaven" see 1:2. The true God, Yahweh, was superior to Darius' god, Ahura Mazda, whom Darius called "the god of heaven." **Years** earlier **Israel** had **a great king,** Solomon, and had had a beautiful **temple.** It was a prominent structure in the ancient world. **But because** of sin (**our fathers angered the God of heaven**), God **handed them over to Nebuchadnezzar.** The Jews knew why the **temple** was **destroyed** and the people **deported.** In

God's promise/threat (Deut. 28) He said that the people would be taken into captivity if they did not live according to the covenant He instituted with them as they were ready to enter the land of promise. Not only was Nebuchadnezzar involved in the fall of Jerusalem; God Himself was responsible! Nebuchadnezzar was merely an agent of God's anger on His people (cf. "My servant Nebuchadnezzar" in Jer. 25:9; 27:6; 43:10)—an anger which was designed to purify the nation so that some would return to the land as a believing remnant. The Exile did not mean that Yahweh was defeated by Nebuchadnezzar's gods.

**5:13-17.** In response to Tattenai Zerubbabel and Jeshua stated that **Cyrus** had allowed a remnant to return to **Jerusalem** to **rebuild** the temple and even gave them **articles** which had been taken from Solomon's **temple** (cf. 1:2-4, 7-11). The letter-writers also recounted the fact that **Cyrus** gave **Sheshbazzar** the task of carrying out the king's command—to return the **articles** and to build another **temple** in the city. Sheshbazzar was mentioned to show Tattenai that the building program was legal. Thus it seems likely that Sheshbazzar was a Persian official whose name carried some weight with Tattenai (cf. comments on 1:8 on several views of Sheshbazzar's identity). Are **Sheshbazzar** and Zerubbabel the same person? Many think so because Sheshbazzar **laid the** temple **foundations,** and so did Zerubbabel (3:8-10). However, this is not absolute proof that the two men were identical. Sheshbazzar could have been responsible, as the king's representative, to see that the work was begun, and Zerubbabel the Jewish leader who completed the task. Tattenai and the officials asked that the king research the records in Babylon (cf. 6:1-2) to find out if what the Jews had said about **a decree** from **Cyrus** was true. That such records were carefully kept is attested by archeology.

**6:1-5.** Tattenai had requested that Babylon's **archives** be **searched** for the document (5:17) but it was not found there. Instead the **scroll** (of papyrus or leather) **was found in . . . Ecbatana** (modern Hamadan), 300 miles northeast of Babylon and capital **of Media** (6:1-2). The scroll was in Ecbatana, because that is where **Cyrus** had spent the summer of

538, when he issued the **decree.** This Ecbatana record was an official "minute" with three details that the verbal and written proclamation (1:1-4) apparently did not contain: (1) **The temple** was **to be 90 feet high and 90 feet wide, with three courses of large stones and one of timbers** (cf. 5:8; 1 Kings 6:36). (2) The project was to be financed by funds from **the royal treasury.** This shows the earnestness of Cyrus' repatriation program. (3) The returned **gold and silver articles** were to be put in **their places in the temple.**

**6:6-12.** King **Darius** then gave three instructions to **Tattenai** and his associates: (1) He told them to leave the Jews alone and **not interfere** with the building of the **temple** (vv. 6-7). The words **stay away from there** were a common Aramaic legal statement. This was to be in accord with the edict of the great King Cyrus. (2) Tax money was to be used to help finance the project and animals were to be supplied **daily** so that **sacrifices** could be made at the altar of the new temple along with food items for the **offerings** (vv. 8-10). Flour (from **wheat**), **salt,** and **oil** were to be used in the grain offerings (Lev. 2:1-2, 7, 13), and **wine** for drink offerings (Lev. 23:13) on feast days. (3) **Anyone** who disobeyed the edict was to suffer a horrible fate (Ezra 6:11-12). He was to be **impaled on** a **beam** taken from **his** own **house,** and **his house** was to be demolished. Execution by impaling was practiced in the Assyrian and Persian Empires. Darius wanted no disturbance in this part of his vast kingdom. The pagan king acknowledged that **God** had **caused His name to dwell** at **Jerusalem.** Darius probably thought of Yahweh as a local deity (cf. comments on 5:6-10), whereas Ezra, in recording that statement, knew of the covenantal significance in Yahweh's name dwelling in Jerusalem.

So Tattenai's inquiry backfired. Instead of stopping the temple work, he had to let it proceed and even had to help pay for it out of his **revenues!** Darius' curse on anyone who would **destroy** the **temple** was fulfilled in: (a) Antiochus Epiphanes, who desecrated it in 167 B.C., and died insane three years later; (b) Herod the Great (37–4 B.C.), who added extensively to the temple to glorify himself, and who had domestic trouble and died

663

of disease; and (c) the Romans, who destroyed the temple in A.D. 70, and later had their empire destroyed.

### 3. THE TEMPLE COMPLETED (6:13-15)

**6:13-15. Tattenai,** to his credit, **carried . . . out** the instructions of **Darius,** and did so **with diligence** (cf. "with diligence" in 5:8; 6:12; 7:21, 23). The work was done by **the** Jewish **elders** who were encouraged by **the preaching of** the Prophets **Haggai** and **Zechariah** (cf. 5:1). Ezra noted that the ultimate decree for the building of **the temple** was from **God** Himself. God worked through the commands of the pagan Persian kings, **Cyrus, Darius, and Artaxerxes.** Workers, prophets, **kings,** and God were all involved. Artaxerxes had nothing to do with building the temple; apparently his name was added to round out the account, for he had decreed the building of Jerusalem's walls (Neh. 2:1, 8). He also helped provide for sacrifices at the temple (Ezra 7:12-17). Some have suggested that Artaxerxes' name may have been added by an early scribe but there is no textual evidence of that. Actually in the Hebrew the words "the temple" are not in 6:14. It reads literally, **They finished** their **building,** thus speaking in general terms of the total reconstruction of Jerusalem under the decrees of the three kings. But verse 15 specifically mentions **the temple.**

The temple was completed in Adar (February-March) of 515—21 years after the work started in 536, and 4½ years after Haggai began his prophesying. This was 70½ years after the temple had been destroyed on August 12, 586.

### E. The dedication of the temple and the celebration of the Passover (6:16-22)

### 1. THE TEMPLE DEDICATED (6:16-18)

**6:16-18.** After the temple was finished, it was then dedicated. The comparatively small number of animals sacrificed (**100 bulls, 200 rams, 400 male lambs,** and **12 male goats**) contrasted sharply with the tremendous amount sacrificed by Solomon at the dedication of the first temple (22,000 cattle and 120,000 sheep and goats; 1 Kings 8:63). This points up the comparative poverty of the postexilic community. The 12 goats for the **sin offering** show that the postexilic community still envisioned a unified Israel consisting of all 12 **tribes** even though only 2 had survived with any strength.

The leaders of the sacrificial system—**the priests** and **the Levites**—were **installed . . . according to . . . the Book of Moses,** that is, according to that portion of the Law in which the legal system is described—in parts of Leviticus and Numbers (Lev. 8; Num. 3:5-10; 8:5-14). One of the motifs of Ezra, Nehemiah, and 1 and 2 Chronicles is that the postexilic community was under the leadership of godly men who were steeped in the Scriptures and attempted to do everything according to the Law. This shows that they had learned from the Exile that God's people suffer if they do not live up to their covenantal obligations.

### 2. THE PASSOVER CELEBRATED (6:19-22)

**6:19-21.** Beginning with verse 19 the text is again in Hebrew (4:8–6:18 are in Aramaic). **On the 14th day of the first month** (April 515 B.C.) **the Passover** was **celebrated.** The temple had been completed in the 12th month (Adar; v. 15) and fittingly, in the very next month, **the Passover** was reinaugurated. This was the first time in 70 years that the people partook of this feast which commemorated their forefathers' release from Egyptian bondage (cf. Ex. 12:1-14; Lev. 23:5).

The Israelite returnees **ate** the Passover **with all who had separated themselves from the unclean practices of their Gentile neighbors.** This second group might have been: (a) Gentiles living in Judah (cf. Num. 9:14), or more likely (b) Jews who had remained in the land and had defiled themselves by practices that went against the Law, and then repented of those sins, thereby "separating" themselves.

**6:22.** The **seven-**day **Feast of Unleavened Bread** was on days 15-21 of the first month, immediately after the Passover (cf. Lev. 23:6-8). The reference to Darius as **the king of Assyria** is not an anachronism (though the Assyrian Empire had ended in 609 B.C.) for the Persian Empire included what was once Assyria. Perhaps this title was a grim reminder that Assyria's harsh tactics were now ended. She was the first to deport Israelites from their land; but now a contingent of Jews was settled back in their land.

This eight-day celebration (the Pass-

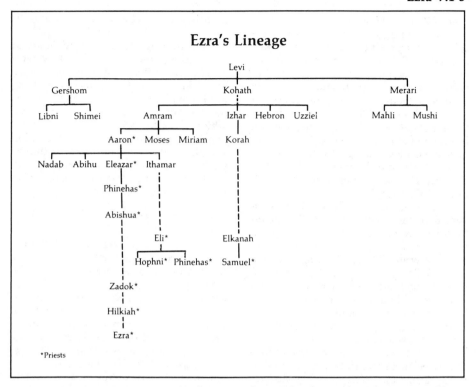

## Ezra's Lineage

Levi

Gershom     Kohath     Merari

Libni   Shimei     Amram     Izhar   Hebron   Uzziel     Mahli   Mushi

Aaron*   Moses   Miriam     Korah

Nadab   Abihu   Eleazar*   Ithamar

Phinehas*

Abishua*

Eli*     Elkanah

Hophni*   Phinehas*   Samuel*

Zadok*

Hilkiah*

Ezra*

*Priests

over, Ezra 6:19, and the seven-day Feast of Unleavened Bread, v. 22), 900 years after the first Passover, signaled the end of the Exile for a remnant of the nation was once again back in fellowship with Yahweh. Since the temple worship was restored, it was important for people who wanted to be in fellowship with God and live according to the covenantal obligations to be in the place where the sacrificial system was being practiced. The people had seen firsthand that God works through history, for He had caused pagan kings to issue decrees which let them return to the land of promise (much as He had caused Egypt's Pharaoh to release Israel). The original readers of Ezra's book would rejoice in that fact and would be encouraged to participate fully in the temple worship, which had been reestablished at such great cost.

## II. The Second Return and Reform under Ezra (chaps. 7–10)

These chapters describe a second return of exiles from Babylon, this time under Ezra in 458 B.C. (7:7). Here Ezra often wrote in the first person ("I" and "we"). Ezra, a priest who knew the

Scriptures, knew the importance of having the people back where the sacrificial system was being practiced.

### A. The return to the land (chaps. 7–8)

The emphasis in these chapters is on the character of Ezra, which sets the scene for chapters 9 and 10 where sin is uncovered in the postexilic community. Ezra is presented as a man who was strongly motivated by the Law of God.

### 1. THE INTRODUCTION OF EZRA (7:1-10)

The events which transpire in this section of the narrative occurred during the reign of Artaxerxes who was introduced earlier in the book (4:8-23; 6:14). The return occurred in the king's seventh year, which was 458 B.C.

**7:1-5. After these things** points to a gap of 57 years since the events at the end of chapter 6. The temple was completed in 515 B.C. in the reign of Darius I. After Darius' death in 486 his son Xerxes ruled for 20 years (485–465). Since Xerxes was the Ahasuerus mentioned in the Book of Esther, the events of that book occurred between Ezra 6 and 7. Then Xerxes' son Artaxerxes ruled from 464 to 424. From 515 to 458 (Artaxerxes' seventh year, 7:7) was 57 years.

Ezra's lineage is traced back to **Aaron**, the first **priest** (see the chart "Ezra's Lineage"). This list is abbreviated, for it does not name every generation. Between **Azariah** and **Meraioth** (v. 3) six names appear in the genealogy in 1 Chronicles 6:7-10 (cf. comments there). Since **Seraiah** was the high priest when Jerusalem fell in 586 (2 Kings 25:18), Ezra may have been his great-grandson. Because of his priestly ancestry, Ezra, like the priests, had authority to teach (cf. Lev. 10:11; Ezra 7:10).

**7:6. Ezra . . . was a teacher well-versed in the Law of Moses.** The word "teacher" translates *sōpēr*, a broad word that means, a "recorder, scribe, secretary, or writer" (e.g., 2 Sam. 8:17; Es. 3:12; 8:9; Ps. 45:1). The word also referred to a learned man who could read and write (e.g., Jehudi in Jer. 36:23) and a learned man who could teach what he read in God's Law. Ezra was called a "teacher" (*sōpēr*) four times (Ezra 7:6, 11-12, 21; cf. v. 25). And he was called "Ezra the scribe" six times in Nehemiah (8:1, 4, 9, 13; 12:26, 36). "Well versed" translates *māhîr*, which is rendered "skillful" in Psalm 45:1.

Ezra had the blessing of the pagan King Artaxerxes as well as the blessing of the covenant **God of Israel.** A few years later Nehemiah had an official position before **the king** (Neh. 1:11), but Ezra held no such position. It is enough for the author to note that he was a teacher who was well versed in the Law. That was to be his major function in life. Because of the king's favor Ezra was promised that he could have whatever he wanted. Rather than ask for something personal, Ezra used the monarch's favor to advance the cause of **God** and His people.

For the first of eight times in the Books of Ezra and Nehemiah, mention is made of God's **hand** being **on** Ezra and Nehemiah (Ezra 7:6, 9, 28; 8:18, 22, 31; Neh. 2:8, 18).

**7:7-10.** Not much is said here about the trip **from Babylon** to **Jerusalem** or the preparations for it. These few verses are a summary of the journey that is detailed in the rest of chapter 7 and in chapter 8. Returning with **Ezra** were groups of people corresponding to the groups in Zerubbabel's return (chap. 2). The trip back to the land took exactly four

months, from **the first** to **the fifth** months, from Nisan 1 (March-April) to Ab 1 (July-August). **The good hand of . . . God was on** Ezra because he **devoted himself to the study and observance of the Law of the LORD, and to teaching** it. "Devoted himself" is literally, "set his heart firmly" (cf. 2 Chron. 19:3; 30:19), which gives the idea that Ezra was inwardly determined. His determination was directed toward doing three things: studying God's Law, obeying it, and teaching it to others—an inviolable order for a successful ministry!

2. THE CIRCUMSTANCES PROMPTING THE RETURN (7:11-28)

**7:11-12. Artaxerxes** wrote a letter (cf. **This is a copy of the letter;** 4:11, 23; 5:6) **to Ezra** that allowed Ezra and others to return to Israel. (On Ezra as **a teacher** see comments on 7:6.) No reason for the decree was given. It can be surmised that Ezra had asked for permission to take a group back and that this decree was the official granting of his request. The decree was sent **to Ezra** personally.

**7:13-26. Artaxerxes** listed certain freedoms the people were to have as they journeyed to and lived in **Israel.** He gave them permission **to go to Jerusalem** (v. 13). He gave them **silver and gold** to take with them and he allowed them to get more in **Babylon** (vv. 15-16, 20). He said that they could offer sacrifices **on the altar** at **the temple** (v. 17). They were also given freedom to make their own decisions (v. 18). They could take back the utensils of **worship** for **the temple** (vv. 19-20). (Apparently not all of them had been carried back with Zerubbabel; cf. 1:7-11.) They could have **whatever** else they needed for the temple **up to** a certain limit (7:21-22). The wheat, oil, and salt were for use in the **grain offerings** (cf. 6:9; Lev. 2:1-2, 7, 13), and the wine was for **drink offerings** (cf. Ezra 6:9; Lev. 12:13). As noted in the NIV margin, the amounts were enormous: **100 talents** (3¾ tons) **of silver, 100 cors** (600 bushels) **of wheat, 100 baths** (600 gallons) **of wine, 100 baths of olive oil, and salt without limit. The priests** and **Levites** were not to be taxed (Ezra 7:24).

In return for granting these privileges the king was to receive some benefits from the expedition. He wanted to avoid uprisings or feelings of anger against him (v. 23) and to have order in that part of his empire (vv. 25-26). **Ezra was responsible to administer justice to all the people** of the area, that is, to **all who** knew **the laws of** his **God**—the Jewish people. Ezra also was to administer the judicial system by handing out punishment to any who would **not obey** (v. 26).

**7:27-28.** Ezra's response to the king's decree shows what kind of man he was. He praised **the LORD** for what was being done under him. By calling Yahweh **the God of our fathers** he linked himself with the godly line that had been concerned with proper sacrificial worship. He also noted that God had given this idea to the king (**put it into the king's heart**). Ezra added that the purpose of all this was **to bring honor to the house of the LORD.** The privileges granted by Artaxerxes were for God's glory, not Ezra's.

Ezra also said that God's **good favor** was shown to him in front of all the king's pagan **advisers** and **officials.** "Good favor" translates ḥeseḏ, God's covenantal love for His people. (That Heb. word is rendered "love" in 3:11, in each verse in Ps. 136, and elsewhere.) It refers to more than love; it means covenantal love, love borne out of loyalty to a commitment. Because Ezra saw that God was working through him (**the hand of the LORD my God was on me**; cf. Ezra 7:6, 9; 8:18, 22, 31), he began the task of selecting people to make the difficult trip. This probably was difficult and must have involved much personal contact and persuasion. But he was successful in enlisting **leading men . . . to go** with him.

3. THE LIST OF THE RETURNEES (8:1-14)

**8:1-14.** This list consists of the major men (**family heads**) who returned as well as the numbers of those who accompanied them. Most of the people listed were related to the families who had returned previously under Zerubbabel (537 B.C.) 79 years earlier (chap. 2). Many of the family names in 8:3c-14 are mentioned in 2:3-15. **Gershom was a descendant of Phinehas,** son of Aaron's third son Eleazar (Ex. 6:25), and **Daniel** was descended from **Ithamar,** Aaron's fourth son (Ex. 6:23). The total number of men who returned was 1,514 including 18 heads of families and 1,496 other men.

With the 258 Levites assembled later (Ezra 8:15-20) the number came to 1,772. With women and children, the group may have totaled between 4,000 and 5,000. Even so, this group was much smaller than the near-50,000 on the first return (2:64-65).

4. THE DETAILS OF THE JOURNEY AND ARRIVAL (8:15-36)

*a. Levites recruited for the journey (8:15-20)*

**8:15.** Levites were to function as teachers of the Law (cf. Lev. 10:11; Deut. 33:10). Therefore they were to have an extremely important role in the reestablished community. **The people** desperately needed to understand the importance of the Law as they faced their situation as returnees from exile. The **Levites** would have a difficult time in the new land for they were to be involved in the disciplined ministry of temple service. Perhaps that is why none were present when Ezra and his group were ready to depart from **the canal** of **Ahava** (cf. Ezra 8:21, 31), whose location is unknown. This canal may have been a tributary of the Euphrates River. Even Zerubbabel had comparatively few Levites on his return (733 [2:40-58], less than 1.5% of the 49,897 [2:64-65]).

**8:16-17.** Therefore Ezra **sent** 9 **leaders** and 2 **men of learning** to secure some Levites and **temple servants** from the man **Iddo.** Ezra **told** the messengers **what to say,** which seems to indicate that this was a delicate task which needed to have some weight behind the message. The 11 messengers were sent to **Casiphia,** whose location is no longer known.

**8:18-20.** The men were able to secure 38 Levites from two families—18 from **Sherebiah's** family and 20 from Jeshaiah's relatives—as well as **220 . . . temple servants.** Only then was Ezra ready to start on the important journey. Without the Levite teachers of the Law and people to serve at the temple all would be lost and the trip futile.

*b. Preparations made for the journey (8:21-30)*

**8:21-23.** First, spiritual preparation was made for the journey. Ezra was concerned with matters pertaining to God's people. So Ezra **proclaimed a fast** in preparation for the journey. He wanted the assembled group thereby to **humble themselves before . . . God** in order to **ask Him for a safe journey** for themselves, their **children,** and their **possessions.** Being humble before God shows one's spiritual dependence, his acknowledgment that God is in total control. Ezra did not want **to ask** for military protection (**soldiers and horsemen**) because he had already publicly announced that **God** would take care of the people as they returned. In contrast, Nehemiah readily accepted a military escort on his way back to the land (Neh. 2:9).

**8:24-27.** Next, physical preparation was made for the journey. Ezra divided the **silver . . . gold,** and **articles** among 24 of the key men in the group. These items were gifts for the temple, given by Persian officials and by nonreturning Israelites. They included 25 tons **of silver, silver articles** weighing 3¾ tons, 3¾ tons **of gold, 20 bowls of gold** that weighed about 19 pounds, and **two** expensive **bronze** objects. All this would be valued at many millions of dollars today. No wonder Ezra was concerned about the people's safety (v. 21).

**8:28-30.** Ezra charged these key men with the responsibility of getting the precious metals and valuables back to **Jerusalem** safely. In his charge he said that these material possessions were **consecrated to the LORD** and that **the silver and gold** were freely given by God's people. He emphasized the need for guarding the money and articles carefully by noting that they would all be **weighed** on arrival to be sure none had disappeared. **The priests and Levites** accepted the responsibility of taking the metals and utensils to **Jerusalem.**

*c. The people journeyed and arrived (8:31-36)*

**8:31-34.** Only a few statements were made about the journey and the arrival. The group left Babylon on the 1st day of the first month (7:9) and they left **the Ahava Canal** on **the 12th** of the same month. Since they were at the canal three days (8:15), the site of their canal encampment was about nine days' travel from Babylon, perhaps 100-130 miles away.

The total journey was about 900 miles and must have been difficult for a group without a military escort. However, Ezra was content merely to relate that

**the hand of our God was on us** (cf. 7:6, 9, 28; 8:18, 22) and that the Lord granted the returnees protection. On arriving in **Jerusalem,** after a **three-**day rest, **everything** was turned over to the priests and **Levites** and **weighed** (vv. 33-34). Several of these temple officials are also mentioned in the Book of Nehemiah: **Meremoth** (Neh. 3:4, 21), **Jozabad** (Neh. 11:16), and **Binnui** (Neh. 3:24).

**8:35-36. Then the exiles** offered sacrifices to **God.** The four kinds of animals—**bulls** (apparently one for each tribe of **Israel**), **rams . . . lambs,** and **goats**—were the same as those offered at the temple dedication (6:17), but now the number was smaller. A copy of **the king's** edict was given to the surrounding officials (**royal satraps** and **governors**), who were to carry out his wishes under Ezra's leadership. This caused the surrounding peoples to assist the Jewish postexilic community. The section ends in an interesting climax—God's good hand was so evident on His people that even surrounding peoples helped them in the sacrificial system, the means of fellowship with **God.**

## B. The reform in the land (chaps. 9–10)

In contrast with the highpoint of God's blessing on the people at the end of the previous section (8:36), this section opens with a statement about the severe sin into which the people of the postexilic community had fallen. The reason the people were back in the land was so that they would be able to worship God according to the ways of their forefathers under the Law. However, when the people returned to the land they still had a tendency to wander away from the words of God that had been written by Moses.

1. THE PEOPLE'S SIN OF INTERMARRIAGE REPORTED (9:1-4)

**9:1-2.** Ezra's return had a profound effect on the people of Israel. The man who was devoted to the accurate teaching of the Law became the focal point of a major reform. This occurred less than five months after his arrival (cf. 7:9 with 10:9). **The leaders came to me** suggests that these were men who had previously returned to the land under Zerubbabel and had established themselves as leaders and had looked into the problem.

Ezra's return may have pricked their consciences as they reflected on the Law of God. They realized that something had to be done about the situation if the nation was to enjoy fellowship with the Lord. Outward sacrifice was fine, but only if it was accompanied by an inward conformity to the Word of God (Hosea 6:6; Micah 6:6-8).

The Jewish leaders reported to Ezra that some Israelites had been involved with their pagan neighbors' **detestable practices** (cf. Ezra 9:11, 14) which meant they had married Gentiles. One of God's major prohibitions was that His people were not to marry outside the community of believers (Ex. 34:11-16; Deut. 7:1-4). This was not because of racial difference, for the peoples of the surrounding areas were of the same Semitic race. The reason was strictly religious. If God's people married outside Israel they would be tempted (as was Solomon; 1 Kings 11:3-5) to get caught up in pagan idolatrous worship. Intermarrying with people who did not worship Yahweh was symptomatic of the way the people forsook other aspects of God's Law. If they would break this aspect of the Law in the most intimate of human relationships then they would probably also break the Law in other less intimate human relationships. The peoples listed in Ezra 9:1 were many of those God had warned about centuries before (Deut. 7:1), as well as the surrounding nations of Ammon, Moab, and Egypt. Unfortunately some religious and civil **leaders** had been in the forefront of this evil practice.

**9:3-4.** Ezra's response was typical of the response of godly people in the Old Testament when they found out about sin. Tearing his **tunic and cloak** was a sign of mourning (cf. Num. 14:6; Josh. 7:6; Es. 4:1; Job 1:20), and pulling **hair from** his **head and beard** was a sign of unusual grief or of intense anger (Isa. 22:12). He was **appalled** because of the people's sin (Ezra 9:3; cf. v. 4). Ezra knew that it was for just this sort of sin that his nation had gone into captivity (cf. v. 7). Perhaps he was afraid they would go into captivity again (cf. v. 8).

2. EZRA'S PRAYER TO GOD (9:5-15)

Ezra's prayer reveals much about him. He identified with the nation in their sin even though he himself was in-

nocent of the offense (cf. Dan. 9:5-6, 8-11, 13, 15-16). Ezra understood that the nation stood together under the covenant and that this breach of responsibility, especially since it had been led by leaders of the nation, could jeopardize the entire nation before God.

**9:5. The evening sacrifice** was around 3 P.M. Ezra's physical position (**on** his **knees with** his **hands spread out to the LORD**) showed that he was throwing himself on the mercy of **God.** Ezra knew that the nation was guilty (vv. 6-7; cf. vv. 13, 15) so he assumed a position of begging before the Lord. There was no excuse for the people's actions. Ezra's prayer was made at the temple with weeping (10:1).

**9:6-7.** Ezra confessed the continuing problem of sin among the people of the nation. He reacted to the sin with embarrassment, using terms such as **ashamed and disgraced.** He felt embarrassed because it was for **guilt** like this that the nation had gone into **captivity** in the first place **at the hand of foreign kings** (viz., Sargon II and Nebuchadnezzar). The Captivity was to be a method of purifying the people and reestablishing a close relationship between them and God. Apparently the Exile had not accomplished its purpose because of the people's tendency to stray from their covenantal obligations. Like a flood their **sins,** Ezra said, had engulfed them for their sins were **higher than** their **heads.**

**9:8-9.** Ezra acknowledged the grace of **God** in allowing the people to return to the land. He reminded God and himself that it was the Lord's graciousness that allowed **the kings of Persia** to grant the Jews freedom to return to the land of promise **to rebuild** the temple. But now they were back in **bondage**—bondage to sin.

**9:10-12.** Ezra then confessed the men's present sin of intermarriage. Ezra asked, **What can we say after this?** By this question he was acknowledging that the nation had no excuse before God (cf. v. 6). No explanation was given for the leaders' disobedience. They had broken God's **commands** to remain pure before Him, and to separate from the **corruption** and **detestable practices** (cf. vv. 1, 14) in **the land.** They had directly disobeyed the clear Word of God. Foreign marriages contaminated Israel, fostered the foreigners' **prosperity,** weakened Israel spiritually, and decreased her opportunity to enjoy the land's crops.

**9:13-14.** The conclusion Ezra reached was that **God** would be totally just in destroying them in His anger so that **no remnant** would be left (cf. "remnant" in vv. 8, 13, 15). They deserved even greater punishment than God was giving them (cf. v. 6). In a nutshell, Ezra was describing the position of all mankind before God. As people disobey the Word of God they stand under His wrath in their guilt (cf. "guilt" in vv. 6-7, 13, 15; cf. John 16:8; James 2:10).

**9:15.** Ezra's prayer included no specific request; he simply threw himself on God's mercy. By this he concluded his prayer in the same way he began. He acknowledged that no one in the entire community was worthy to **stand** before the **righteous** God. In his prayer Ezra affirmed several attributes of **God:** grace (v. 8), kindness (v. 9), anger (v. 14), and righteousness (v. 15). Ezra was asking God to be merciful on the basis of His loyal love for the nation.

## 3. THE PEOPLE'S CONFESSION OF SIN (CHAP. 10)

As already noted, the leaders were sensitive to the fact that there was a problem (9:1-2). Now other concerned Israelites joined Ezra in his grief.

### a. The people acknowledged their sin (10:1-4)

**10:1-4.** Many people acknowledged that something had to be done about the situation. Apparently this sin had gone on and had been tolerated for some time. Children were born to some of those who had intermarried (vv. 3, 44). No doubt some devout Jews were grieved because of this sin in the community. Perhaps they were afraid to speak up or had tried and were rebuffed. In any case, now that some of the leaders were joining Ezra in bemoaning the sin, these righteous people joined in the mourning and began to demand that something be done. **A large crowd of Israelites** gathered with **Ezra** and **wept bitterly.**

One man, **Shecaniah,** spoke for all the people who were weeping. He acknowledged the unfaithfulness of the nation but he felt that **there** was **still hope for Israel.** He suggested that the people **covenant before . . . God** to divorce the

foreign **women** and **send** them **away** along with the **children** they had borne. This was to be done **according to the Law.** Shecaniah promised Ezra that the people would stand behind him in such a decision. Shecaniah was calling on the nation to do something distasteful and difficult, something that could cause bitter division between family members and friends. However, he appealed on the basis of the Law of God which was supposed to be the people's rule of life. The Law also was a safeguard for this situation, for an Israelite could marry a woman from outside the nation if she had become Jewish in faith. Perhaps that is why each marriage was investigated thoroughly (vv. 16-19)—to see if any women had become Jewish proselytes.

Though divorce was not the norm, it may have been preferable in this situation because the mixed marriages, if continued, would lead the nation away from true worship of Yahweh. Eventually they would destroy the nation. On the other hand some Bible students believe this plan was not in accord with God's desires (cf. Mal. 2:16). Do two "wrongs" make one "right"? Perhaps Ezra wrongly followed Shecaniah's advice in requiring these divorces. However, no specific support for this view is indicated in Ezra 10.

### b. The people took an oath (10:5-8)

**10:5-8.** The people's sincerity in their confession and repentance was shown by the fact that they **took** an **oath** before **God.** Taking an oath was not a light matter; it bound the oath-taker to do what he had promised. If he did not, he would be punished.

**Ezra withdrew** to fast and mourn by himself. **Jehohanan** was the same as Johanan (Neh. 12:23). He was the grandson of Eliashab (Neh. 12:10-11), who was the high priest (Neh. 13:28). Hence, **son of Eliashab** (Ezra 10:6) means "grandson of Eliashab" ("son" in Heb. often means a grandson or even a later descendant). **A proclamation** was sent out to **all the exiles to assemble in Jerusalem. Anyone who** did not come would lose **his property** and would **be expelled from the assembly of the exiles.** In effect such a person would no longer have any legal rights. Ezra had this authority to send out a proclamation with threat of punishment, because of the edict of the king (cf. 7:26).

### c. The people gathered at the temple (10:9-15)

**10:9-11.** **The square** to the east of the temple could accommodate thousands of people. The temple area was always the center of action in the Book of Ezra. On the appointed day (**three days** after the proclamation, in November-December 457) as the people were gathering, a rainstorm was in progress. This was the rainy season (v. 13). However, because of the oath (v. 5) and because of the threat of punishment the meeting went on as scheduled. The people were **distressed** out of fear of God's wrath and over concern about their families being separated. As **Ezra** addressed the group, he cited their sin of unfaithfulness, pronounced their **guilt,** and challenged them to acknowledge their sin and do something about it by becoming **separate** from their **foreign wives.**

**10:12-15.** The people **responded** that they agreed, but that the matter would take some time because of the large number of people involved and because of the rain. (In fact, it took three months, vv. 16-17.) Someone suggested that each man who had **married a foreign woman** should make an appointment **with the elders and judges** of his hometown so that the matter could be settled locally. This was a good suggestion because the elders and judges of each town would know the individuals involved. They would know whether the women involved were worshipers of the Lord or were still involved in pagan worship. Four leaders **opposed** the plan, though it is not clear why. Perhaps they wanted to take care of the matter right away; or perhaps they did not want to take care of it at all. At least one of them, **Meshullam,** was guilty (v. 29).

### d. The marriages examined (10:16-17)

**10:16-17.** In just 11 days the examining began (cf. vv. 9, 16). It took three months for all the marriages to be examined, from **the first day of the 10th month** (December-January 457) to the **first day of the 1st month** of the next year (March-April 456). Obviously the problem was widespread and could not be settled in a day (v. 13). Each case was judged individually so that justice would

be done. By this action the community was not saying that divorce was good. It was a matter of following God's Law about the need for religious purity in the nation (Ex. 34:11-16; Deut. 7:1-4). **Ezra** wrote nothing about what happened to these **foreign women** or their children. Presumably they returned to their pagan countries.

### e. The offenders listed (10:18-44)

**10:18-44.** Ezra concluded his account by listing the offenders in the **foreign** marriages. Involved in this serious sin were 17 **priests** (vv. 18-22) and 10 **Levites** including a singer and 3 **gatekeepers** (vv. 23-24), and 84 others from around the nation (vv. 25-43). As the leaders had said (9:1), some priests and Levites were guilty. The guilty priests each offered **a ram . . . as a guilt offering** in accord with Leviticus 5:14-15. The family names in Ezra 10:25-43 correspond closely to those in 2:3-20. **Some of** these **had children by these** marriages (10:44). This was a grievous separation from God's covenant. Unfortunately the people would again slip into the same kind of sin only one generation later (Neh. 13:23-28).

The narrative ends abruptly at this point. The message of the book is complete. In order for the people to be back in fellowship with the Lord it was absolutely necessary for them to have proper temple worship (Ezra 1–6) and to live according to God's Word (chaps. 7–10).

# BIBLIOGRAPHY

Ackroyd, Peter R. *I and II Chronicles, Ezra and Nehemiah.* London: SCM Press, 1973.

Batten, Loring. *The Books of Ezra and Nehemiah.* The International Critical Commentary. Edinburgh: T. & T. Clark, 1913.

Coggins, R.J. *The Books of Ezra and Nehemiah.* The Cambridge Bible Commentary on the New English Bible. Cambridge: University Press, 1976.

Fensham, F. Charles. *The Books of Ezra and Nehemiah.* The New International Commentary on the Old Testament. Grand Rapids: Wm. B. Eerdmans Publishing Co., 1982.

Ironside, H.A. *Notes on Ezra, Nehemiah, and Esther.* Neptune, N.J.: Loizeaux Brothers, 1972.

Keil, C.F. "Ezra." In *Commentary on the Old Testament in Ten Volumes*. Vol. 3. Reprint (25 vols. in 10). Grand Rapids: Wm. B. Eerdmans Publishing Co., 1982.

Kidner, Derek. *Ezra and Nehemiah*. The Tyndale Old Testament Commentaries. Downers Grove, Ill.: InterVarsity Press, 1979.

Laney, J. Carl. *Ezra and Nehemiah*. Every-man's Bible Commentary. Chicago: Moody Press, 1982.

Myers, Jacob M. *Ezra, Nehemiah*. The Anchor Bible. Garden City, N.Y.: Doubleday & Co., 1965.

Ryle, H.E. *The Books of Ezra and Nehemiah*. Cambridge: University Press, 1917.

Slotki, Judah J. *Daniel, Ezra, Nehemiah*. London: Soncino Press, 1951.

# NEHEMIAH

## Gene A. Getz

## INTRODUCTION

**Historical Background.** God had promised Israel that if they obeyed Him, He would bless them as a nation. If they did not, then He would judge them and cause them to be taken into captivity (Deut. 28). That promise was repeated to Solomon with a specific application to his own life. If he, as king of Israel, obeyed the Lord he would experience God's continual blessing. If Solomon did not obey Him, God would take away his power and position as king of Israel (1 Kings 9:1-9).

As happened so frequently among many of Israel's leaders, a good beginning had an unfortunate ending. Solomon sinned against God, particularly by marrying many foreign wives and worshiping their false gods (1 Kings 11:1-5). So the kingdom was split in 931 B.C. The 10 Northern tribes were initially ruled by Jeroboam, and the Southern tribes (Judah and Benjamin) were ruled at first by Rehoboam.

Both kingdoms, however, continued to be characterized by idolatry and immorality. And as God had forewarned, His hand of judgment fell on all Israel because of their sin. The Northern Kingdom fell first and the people were taken into captivity by the Assyrians in 722 B.C. The Babylonians brought about the fall of the Southern Kingdom in 586 B.C.

The Israelites of the Northern Kingdom were absorbed into Assyria and eventually into other cultures. However, the people of the Southern Kingdom remained intact in Babylon, and after the power of Babylon was broken by the Medes and Persians in 539 B.C., many Jews returned to their homeland.

In 538 B.C. the first group returned to Judah under the leadership of Zerubbabel (Ezra 1:1–2:2). Over a period of years and tremendous opposition from the Samaritans, the returnees eventually succeeded in rebuilding the temple in 515 B.C. (See the chart "The Three Returns from Exile," in the *Introduction* to Ezra.)

A number of years later—in 458 B.C.—a second group of Jews returned, led by Ezra (Ezra 7:1-10). Arriving on the scene, they found the Jews in Israel in a state of spiritual and moral degradation. They had intermarried with the unbelieving peoples of the surrounding nations and were participating in their pagan practices. However, through Ezra's faithful teaching ministry, the majority of these people turned from their sins and once again followed God's will for their lives.

In 444 B.C., 14 years after Ezra's return to Jerusalem, Nehemiah also returned and God used him to guide Judah in rebuilding the city's walls and in reordering the people's social and economic lives. What he accomplished in a brief period of time was an incredible feat. How he accomplished this goal is one of the major emphases in the book that bears his name.

**Name.** On the name of the Book of Nehemiah in relation to the Book of Ezra see "Name" in the *Introduction* to Ezra.

**Author.** Most Bible expositors agree that Nehemiah authored the book that bears his name. Much of the book is a first-person account of the circumstances surrounding his return to Jerusalem (chaps. 1–7; 12:31–13:31).

Nothing is known about Nehemiah's childhood, youth, or family background, except that his father's name was Hacaliah (1:1) and he had a brother named Hanani (1:2). Possibly Nehemiah's great-grandparents were taken into captivity when Jerusalem fell to the Babylonians. Nehemiah was probably born in Persia sometime during or soon after Zerubbabel's ministry in Jerusalem.

Nehemiah had risen to a position of prominence in his pagan environment. He was serving King Artaxerxes as his personal cupbearer (1:11; cf. 2:1).

This important position in the king's court gives insight into Nehemiah's life and character. A mighty monarch such as the king of Persia would select for that position a man who was wise and discreet, and consistently honest and trustworthy. Nehemiah's position alone reveals much about his intellectual capabilities, his emotional maturity, and his spiritual status.

Nehemiah probably wrote the book that bears his name soon after all its events were completed. This means the book was written about 430 B.C. or shortly thereafter.

# OUTLINE

# COMMENTARY

## I. The Rebuilding of the Walls (chaps. 1–6)

### A. Nehemiah's prayer voiced (chap. 1)

1. THE REPORT FROM JERUSALEM (1:1-3)

**1:1-3.** While serving at the Persian winter palace in **Susa** (cf. Es. 1:2; Dan. 8:1; also see the map "The Persian Empire," in the *Introduction* to Ezra), **Nehemiah** one day received a report from several **men** who had come **from Judah.** One of them was his own brother, **Hanani;** later Nehemiah appointed him to a high position in Jerusalem (7:2). This report came **in the month of Kislev,** that is, November-December (see the chart "Calendar in Israel," near Ex. 12:1) **in the 20th year** of Artaxerxes the king (cf. Neh. 2:1). Artaxerxes, Persia's sixth king, began reigning in 464 B.C., so this year was 444.

The report instantly depressed Nehemiah. It pertained to his people and their land. The Jews in Judah (a **province** of Persia) were greatly troubled and disgraced, and Jerusalem's **wall** was **broken down and its gates** had **been burned.** (Six gates were later repaired, 3:1, 3, 6, 13-15.) This left the city defenseless against enemy attacks. The people had been rebuilding the walls (Ezra 4:12) but were stopped by Artaxerxes who was pressured by some Samaritans and Rehum, the commanding officer, who may have been a Persian responsible to Artaxerxes (Ezra 4:17-23).

Because of Nehemiah's position in the king's court, he must have been aware of Rehum's initial letter and Artaxerxes' subsequent response. However, he had probably not received word as to the results of the letter, though no doubt he feared for his brothers in **Jerusalem.** It is with this prior knowledge that he received the disappointing report from Jerusalem with a sense of deep regret and despair.

2. THE RESPONSE OF NEHEMIAH (1:4)

**1:4.** On receiving this dismal report, Nehemiah **sat down and wept** (cf. Ezra 10:1). For a number of **days** he **mourned . . . fasted, and prayed** to **the God of heaven** (cf. Neh. 1:5; 2:4, 20; see comments on Ezra 1:2). His praying was continual ("day and night," Neh. 1:6). Fasting, though not a requirement of the Law except on the annual Day of Atonement, often evidenced one's distraught condition (cf. 2 Sam. 12:16; 1 Kings 21:27; Ezra 8:23).

### 3. THE CONTENTS OF THE CUPBEARER'S PRAYER (1:5-11)

*a. Nehemiah's acknowledgment of God's greatness (1:5)*

**1:5.** Nehemiah faced a situation he knew he could not solve by himself. But he also knew that with God all things are possible (cf. Jer. 32:17). Nehemiah began his prayer by acknowledging that fact: **O LORD, God of heaven** (cf. Neh. 1:4), **the great and awesome God** (cf. 4:14; 9:32). "LORD" (Yahweh) speaks of His covenant relationship to Israel, "God of heaven" refers to His sovereignty, and the words "great and awesome" are mindful of His power and majesty. Surely such a God could answer Nehemiah's prayer. As the "LORD" He **keeps His covenant of love** (ḥesed, "loyal love") **with those who love . . . and obey** Him.

*b. Nehemiah's confession of Israel's sins (1:6-7)*

**1:6-7.** In this **prayer** of confession of **the sins of the people of Israel**, Nehemiah included himself. As the Prophet Daniel had prayed almost 100 years before (Dan. 9:4-6) and as Ezra had prayed (Ezra 9:6-15), Nehemiah acknowledged that he shared the responsibility for Israel's disobedience to God's laws. He said **I confess** and three times he said **we.**

He placed himself and Israel in a submissive attitude under the Lord by calling himself God's **servant** (cf. Neh. 1:10-11) and by calling them His **servants** (cf. vv. 10-11; also note **Your servant Moses,** vv. 7-8).

*c. Nehemiah's request for God's help (1:8-11)*

**1:8-11.** Nehemiah reminded God—to lead Him to act, not to recall for Him something forgotten—that He had told **Moses** that if the nation Israel was **unfaithful** He would disperse them from their homeland (Lev. 26:27-28, 33; Deut. 28:64), **but** that if they obeyed Him then those who were exiled would be regathered to Jerusalem (Deut. 30:1-5). On Jerusalem as a place where God would cause His **name** to dwell, see comments on

Deuteronomy 12:5; 2 Chronicles 6:6. Since the Jews belonged to God (**Your servants and Your people;** cf. Deut. 9:29) and He had **redeemed** them, it was reasonable that God should respond to Nehemiah's **prayer** on their behalf, keeping His "covenant of love" (Neh. 1:5). Speaking for fellow Jews who revered God's **name** (i.e., honored His revealed character), Nehemiah asked that He hear their **prayer** (v. 11; cf. v. 6).

Humanly speaking only one person could make it possible for Nehemiah to help the Jews in Jerusalem—the king he served. Years earlier, Artaxerxes had issued a decree to stop the construction work in Jerusalem (Ezra 4:21; see comments on Neh. 1:1-3), and he was the only one who could reverse that order. That is why Nehemiah prayed specifically, **Give Your servant** (cf. v. 6) **success today by granting him favor** (lit., "compassion") **in the presence of this man.** Nehemiah was referring of course to King Artaxerxes (cf. 2:1). A favorable relationship with the king could open the door for his petition.

As the king's **cupbearer,** Nehemiah was responsible for tasting the wine before serving it to the king to be sure it was not poisoned. Nehemiah therefore had frequent access **to the king.**

### B. Nehemiah's prayer answered (2:1-8)

#### 1. NEHEMIAH'S OPPORTUNITY AND RESPONSE (2:1-4A)

**2:1-4a.** Four months went by before Nehemiah's opportunity came—from Kislev (1:1, November-December) to **Nisan** (March-April). Nisan was still in Artaxerxes' **20th year** (cf. 1:1) because the regnal year started in Tishri (September-October). As Nehemiah was going about his usual duties **the king** noticed something different about Nehemiah's countenance. He was **sad. The king** was immediately curious about Nehemiah's state of depression, since this was the first time he had seen his cupbearer dejected. **The king asked** a pointed question, **Why does your face look so sad when you are not ill?**

Nehemiah was careful in replying. In fact he was even **afraid.** A servant was never to let his negative emotions show before the king, for it might suggest dissatisfaction with the king. To do so might jeopardize his position or even his life.

Also Nehemiah knew that his request was a bold one. As already stated, a few years earlier this king had stopped the rebuilding of Jerusalem and now Nehemiah was going to ask that the order be reversed. The cupbearer was risking his life! But his response was wise, no doubt reflecting the fact that he had been thinking about this opportunity, should it come, for a number of months.

In Nehemiah's response he avoided naming Jerusalem, perhaps so that he would not touch a sensitive "political nerve" in **the king.** He appealed to the king's sense of respect—his sense of "rightness" regarding proper respect for the dead. Nehemiah said **the city where** his ancestors were **buried** was **in ruins** and the **gates** had been burned (cf. 1:3). This was a sad state of affairs for the Jewish city. Seventy-one years before (in 515 B.C.), the temple had been rebuilt. The year was now 444; yet the city itself still needed much rebuilding.

Artaxerxes' heart responded to Nehemiah's statements. So he asked Nehemiah what **the king** might do about the situation. With Judea being a Persian province, the cupbearer may have reasoned that perhaps the king would now be sensitive to Jerusalem's condition.

2. NEHEMIAH'S REQUEST TO THE KING (2:4B-8A)

**2:4b-6.** Obviously Nehemiah had prepared for this moment he had **prayed** for. Besides seeking God's help in prayer, he utilized all the human resources available, including his intellectual capabilities, his past experiences, his accumulated wisdom, his role and position in life, and people with whom he came in contact (in this instance, the king of Persia).

Between the king's question (v. 4a) and Nehemiah's answer (v. 5), the cupbearer "breathed" a brief prayer **to the God of heaven** (cf. 1:4-5). This short prayer—whatever its unvoiced words— was built on his praying for four months. No doubt he asked for wisdom in stating his request properly and for a favorable reply from **the king.**

Speaking with courtesy (**If it pleases the king**; cf. 2:7; this appears elsewhere only in Es. 1:19; 3:9; 5:4, 8; 7:3; 8:5; 9:13) and humility (**your servant**), Nehemiah asked the king to **send** him **to the city in**

**Judah where** his ancestors were **buried so that** he might **rebuild** the city. Again the cupbearer avoided mentioning Jerusalem specifically (see comments on "the city" in Neh. 2:3). The fact that **the queen** was seated there suggests this was a private gathering, since it was not customary for queens to appear at formal banquets.

**The king** then **asked** Nehemiah when he would return. This question indicated that the king would give him permission. Nehemiah responded immediately with a specific **time** frame, again indicating forethought on his part.

**2:7-8a.** Nehemiah then asked for the biggest favor yet. Knowing he would face opposition from his enemies, he requested **letters** of permission from **the king** to allow him to pass through the various provinces in the **Trans-Euphrates,** the large area west of the Euphrates River. Nehemiah also asked that the king write **a letter to Asaph,** the man in charge **of the king's forest.** Nehemiah knew he would need access to **timber** for rebuilding **the gates** and the **wall** and other parts of **the city. The citadel** (cf. 7:2) was a fortification to protect **the temple.** The fact that Nehemiah knew the name of the man in charge of the king's forest near Jerusalem may indicate that he had done some careful research.

Artaxerxes' permission to rebuild the city of Jerusalem is the decree Daniel had prophesied 95 years earlier in 539 B.C. This decree was issued on March 5, 444 B.C. (see comments on Dan. 9:25).

3. NEHEMIAH'S TRIBUTE TO GOD (2:8B)

**2:8b.** Though Nehemiah had worked diligently to prepare himself for the time when he would have opportunity to share his burden with the king, and though he demonstrated unusual wisdom in responding to the king's questions, he knew that ultimately his success depended on God's help. So he wrote that the king's granting of his **requests** was **because** God's **gracious hand . . . was upon** him (cf. v. 18; Ezra 7:6, 9, 28; 8:18, 22, 31).

*C. Nehemiah's preparation for the work (2:9-20)*

1. HIS ARRIVAL IN JERUSALEM (2:9-10)

**2:9-10.** The journey to Jerusalem, even though Nehemiah probably took the shortest route possible, would have taken at least two months (see comments on 6:15). Ezra's trip, 14 years earlier, took four to five months (Ezra 7:8-9). On the way Nehemiah showed **the governors** of the provinces **the king's letters** of authorization. **Also** the **king** even provided a military escort for him! But as soon as Nehemiah arrived, he began to face opposition. **When Sanballat the Horonite** (perhaps meaning he was from Beth-Horon about 15 miles northeast of Jerusalem) and his associate **Tobiah,** from Ammon, **heard** that Nehemiah had arrived on the scene to help Israel, they were **very** displeased. Immediately they began to plan how to stop Nehemiah from achieving his goal. Perhaps they were hoping to gain control of Judah. In fact in the Elephantine papyri written in 407 B.C., 37 years after this event, Sanballat was called "governor of Samaria." But Nehemiah's motivation remained undaunted. He knew that God had brought him to this moment in Israel's history and he was about to tackle a project that others, for almost 100 years before him, had been unable to complete.

### 2. HIS SURVEY OF THE WALLS (2:11-16)

**2:11-16.** Nehemiah knew there was no way he could share with the people in **Jerusalem** what **God** led him to accomplish without first doing some research and planning. After taking time (**three days**), presumably to think, pray, and get acquainted with some people there, he took **a few men** into his confidence, men he could trust.

Then he made a careful survey of **the walls** to analyze the problem he faced. He did so at **night,** apparently to avoid letting others know his plans before they were firmly fixed in his mind. During these night hours he gained perspective and, as outlined in chapter 3, developed an effective plan to accomplish the task he had come to **Jerusalem** to perform. In his nighttime inspection he rode his horse or mule (**mount,** 2:14) from the **Valley Gate** in the southwest wall east to **the Jackal Well,** the site of which is unknown, **and** to **the Dung Gate** in the southeast part of the city. Possibly this is the same as the Potsherd Gate (Jer. 19:2). **The Fountain Gate** was north of the Dung Gate on the eastern wall. **The King's Pool** may be the same as the Pool of Siloam which was near the King's Garden (Neh. 3:15), or the King's Pool may have been south of the Pool of Siloam. Apparently the rubble there kept him from proceeding on his mount **so he went up the valley** (probably the Kidron Valley east of the city). Either he went all round the entire wall or, more likely, he retraced his steps from the eastern wall. He went back into the city at his starting place, **the Valley Gate.** (See the map "Jerusalem in the Time of Nehemiah," near 3:1.)

### 3. HIS CHALLENGE TO THE PEOPLE (2:17-20)

**2:17-18.** After Nehemiah had completed his secret survey and was satisfied that he had developed a workable plan, the time had come to reveal to the Jews why he was **in Jerusalem. Them** refers to the people mentioned in verse 16: "Jews [i.e., common people], priests . . . nobles . . . officials." First he challenged them to notice their deplorable circumstances, which had brought them **trouble** and **disgrace** (cf. 1:3). Then he challenged them to **rebuild the wall of Jerusalem,** and followed his challenge with a personal testimony as to how God's **gracious hand** (cf. 2:8) had granted him favor before **King** Artaxerxes.

When Nehemiah gave his challenge, the people's negative feelings became positive. Despair turned to hope. They responded and began the **rebuilding** process.

**2:19-20.** Apparently word spread quickly regarding the Jews' response to Nehemiah's challenge. As soon as their enemies heard the news they stepped up their efforts to hinder the process. They used every demoralizing technique they knew, beginning with ridicule (*bûz* means "to despise or regard with contempt") and the suggestion that they were rebels. Joining **Sanballat** and **Tobiah** (cf. v. 10) was **Geshem** (cf. 6:1-2, 6) **the Arab.**

But Nehemiah was ready for their insidious attack. He affirmed that **the God of heaven** (cf. 1:4-5; 2:4) would enable them to succeed. The Jews, God's **servants,** would rebuild, but the three opponents had **no share** or **claim** (present) **or historic right** (past) to the city.

Once again Nehemiah brought the task—both in the eyes of Judah and his enemies—into clear focus. Their dependence was not to be on their abilities, human resources, or personal genius. Their hope was in the God of heaven!

Nehemiah exhibited many characteristics necessary for effective leadership. Donald K. Campbell lists 21 such factors (*Nehemiah: Man in Charge*, p. 23):

1. He established a reasonable and attainable goal.

2. He had a sense of mission.

3. He was willing to get involved.

4. He rearranged his priorities in order to accomplish his goal.

5. He patiently waited for God's timing.

6. He showed respect to his superior.

7. He prayed at crucial times.

8. He made his request with tact and graciousness.

9. He was well prepared and thought of his needs in advance.

10. He went through proper channels.

11. He took time (three days) to rest, pray, and plan.

12. He investigated the situation firsthand.

13. He informed others only after he knew the size of the problem.

14. He identified himself as one with the people.

15. He set before them a reasonable and attainable goal.

16. He assured them God was in the project.

17. He displayed self-confidence in facing obstacles.

18. He displayed God's confidence in facing obstacles.

19. He did not argue with opponents.

20. He was not discouraged by opposition.

21. He courageously used the authority of his position.

## D. Nehemiah's delegation of the work (chap. 3)

A task so enormous as rebuilding the walls of Jerusalem, especially under adverse conditions, called for unusual organizational effort. The uniqueness of Nehemiah's plan is evident in this chapter. Several aspects of his delegation of the work are evident.

He assigned everyone a specific place to work. This coordination stands out in the phrases "next to him," "next to them," "next to that," "the next section," "beside him," and "beyond

them," which occur 28 times in this chapter.

Assignments were made near people's houses (vv. 21, 23-24, 26, 28-30). Reasons for this plan are obvious. First, people who were assigned to sections of the wall near their homes would be more personally involved and consequently more highly motivated. Second, they would not have to travel to another part of the city to do the job, wasting valuable time. Third, in case of attack they would not be tempted to leave their posts, but would stay and protect their families. Fourth, the whole task would be a family effort, utilizing all available talent.

Commuters also had a part. Men whose homes were outside of Jerusalem—in Jericho (v. 2), Tekoa (vv. 5, 27), Gibeon (v. 7), and Mizpah (v. 7)—were assigned to sections of the wall where there were few homes. Those workers were asked to complete tasks that would not be as conveniently handled by the permanent residents in Jerusalem.

Assignments were also made by vocation. For example, the high priest and his fellow priests were assigned to rebuild the Sheep Gate (v. 1). This was of particular interest to them, because animals were brought through that gate to the temple for sacrifice. Other priests are mentioned in verses 22, 28. Other workers whose vocations are listed include goldsmiths (vv. 8, 31-32), perfume-makers (v. 8), district and half-district rulers (vv. 9-12, 14-19), Levites (v. 17), and merchants (vv. 31-32). Even one man's daughters were involved (v. 12).

### 1. WORKERS ON THE NORTH WALL (3:1-5)

The map "Jerusalem in the Time of Nehemiah" shows the 10 gates and four towers mentioned in this chapter. Of the 10 gates, 6 were repaired (vv. 1, 3, 6, 13-15).

**3:1-2.** Nehemiah's account of the repairs begins with **the Sheep Gate** at the northeast of the wall, and proceeds counterclockwise. The Sheep Gate is known to have been in that location because it was near the Pool of Bethesda (John 5:2), which archeologists have located in that area.

**Eliashib the high priest** (cf. Neh. 13:4) was a grandson of Jeshua (12:10), the high priest in Zerubbabel's day (Ezra 3:2). Eliashib and other **priests** (cf. Neh.

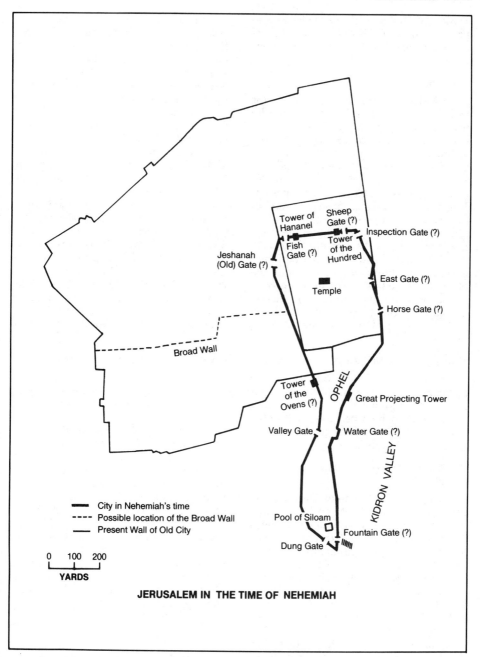

Tower of Hananel

Sheep Gate (?)

Inspection Gate (?)

Fish Gate (?)

Tower of the Hundred

Jeshanah (Old) Gate (?)

East Gate (?)

Temple

Horse Gate (?)

Broad Wall

Tower of the Ovens (?)

OPHEL

Great Projecting Tower

Valley Gate

Water Gate (?)

KIDRON VALLEY

City in Nehemiah's time
Possible location of the Broad Wall
Present Wall of Old City

Pool of Siloam

Fountain Gate (?)

Dung Gate

0   100   200
YARDS

**JERUSALEM IN THE TIME OF NEHEMIAH**

3:22) repaired and **dedicated** the Sheep Gate and then repaired the walls to **the Tower of the Hundred** and **the Tower of Hananel** (also mentioned in 12:39; Jer. 31:38; Zech. 14:10). The exact locations of these two towers are not known, but they were between the Sheep Gate and the Fish Gate.

**3:3-5. The Fish Gate** may have been

the gate through which the people of Tyre brought fish they sold (13:16). **Meremoth,** a priest's **son** (cf. Ezra 8:33), also worked on a second **section** (Neh. 3:21), as did **Meshullam** (v. 30), whose daughter was married to Tobiah's son (6:18). **The men of Tekoa,** Amos' hometown (Amos 1:1) about 12 miles south of Jerusalem, **repaired** a **section.** Though the nobles of Tekoa did **not** help in the project, others from Tekoa took on another section, on the east wall (Neh. 3:27).

### 2. WORKERS ON THE WEST WALL (3:6-12)

**3:6-12.** Between **the Jeshanah** (or "Old"; cf. NIV marg.) **Gate** (v. 6) and **the Broad Wall** (v. 8) was the Gate of Ephraim (cf. 12:39). **Gibeon and Mizpah** were a few miles northwest of Jerusalem. (Meronoth's site is unknown.) Somewhat surprisingly, those towns were **under . . . the governor of Trans-Euphrates** (cf. 2:9). The exact sites of those gates and of **the Tower of the Ovens** (3:11) is not known, but the tower may have been near the ovens in the street of the bakers (Jer. 37:21). A goldsmith and a perfume-maker (Neh. 3:8) took on a different line of work when they went into construction labor. Even rulers of Jerusalem's districts and half-districts (vv. 9, 12; cf. vv. 14-15) took up tools for the building project.

### 3. WORKERS ON THE SOUTH WALL (3:13-14)

**3:13-14.** The **Valley Gate** was where Nehemiah's nighttime inspection tour began and ended (2:13, 15). **The Dung Gate** was so named because it led to the Hinnom Valley south of the city where refuse was dumped.

### 4. WORKERS ON THE SOUTHEAST WALL (3:15-27)

**3:15-16.** The **Fountain Gate** was on the east wall, north of the Dung Gate. **The Pool of Siloam** was near **the King's Garden,** near which Zedekiah, Judah's last king, had gone in his attempt to escape from Jerusalem while the Babylonians were conquering the city (Jer. 39:4). **The tombs of David** refer to those of David and his descendants, the kings of Judah. David was buried in this area, "the city of David" (1 Kings 2:10). **The artificial pool** may be the King's Pool (Neh. 2:14) or perhaps the "lower pool" (Isa. 22:9). **The House of the Heroes** may have been the barracks of David's select soldiers, or "mighty men" (2 Sam. 23:8).

**3:17-27.** Binnui (v. 18) also **repaired another section** (v. 24). **The armory** (v. 19) is another point near the eastern wall. **The angle** was apparently some turn in the wall. Another **angle** is mentioned in verses 24-25.

Private houses were some of the points of reference: **the house of Eliashib the high priest** (vv. 20-21; cf. v. 1), **Benjamin** and Hasshub's **house** (v. 23), and **Azariah's house** (vv. 23-24). Other houses were mentioned later including the priests' houses (v. 28), Zadok's house (v. 29), Meshullam's house (v. 30), and "the house of the temple servants and the merchants" (v. 31).

**Meremoth** (v. 21) **repaired** two sections (cf. v. 4), as did the Tekoites (vv. 5, 27). **Priests** (v. 22; cf. v. 1) and **Levites** (v. 17) were involved in the repair work, closer to the temple than to other parts of the wall. The **tower** (v. 25) was near the **palace,** presumably the palace built by Solomon (1 Kings 7:1-8). **The court of the guard** may have been part of Solomon's great courtyard near his palace (1 Kings 7:9-12). **The hill of Ophel** (Neh. 3:26) was the area between the city of David and the temple mount. Understandably **the temple servants** lived near the temple area.

### 5. WORKERS ON THE NORTHEAST WALL (3:28-32)

**3:28-32.** The **Horse Gate** (v. 28) on the east wall may have been where horses entered the palace area. **The East Gate** (v. 29) was directly east of the temple area. **Malkijah** (v. 31) is the third man by this name in this chapter (see vv. 11, 14). His wall **repairs** extended south to the **house of the temple servants,** who are mentioned in verse 26 as living on the hill of Ophel. **Merchants** also lived in that area near the temple servants. **The Inspection Gate** was at the northeast corner of the wall (cf. **the corner** in v. 24). **The room above the corner** was a room on the wall whose purpose is not known. **The Sheep Gate** brings the reader back to the starting point (cf. v. 1).

### E. Nehemiah's reactions to opposition (chap. 4)

Chapter 3 might give the impression that once Nehemiah had carefully assigned everyone to a particular section of the wall, from that time on everything progressed smoothly. Not so! God's work seldom goes forward without opposition. In fact, as seen in the chart "Nehemiah's Problems and His Responses," this new leader in Judah faced many problems.

# Nehemiah's Problems and His Responses

| Problems | Responses |
|---|---|
| 1. Walls broken and gates burned (1:2-3) | 1. Grief and *prayer* (1:4), and motivation of the people to rebuild (2:17-18) |
| 2. False accusation of the workers (2:19) | 2. Confidence that God would give them success (2:20) |
| 3. Ridicule of the workers (4:1-3) | 3. *Prayer* (4:4-5) and action (greater diligence in the work, 4:6) |
| 4. Plot to attack the workers (4:7-8) | 4. *Prayer* and action (posting of a guard, 4:9) |
| 5. Physical exhaustion and threat of murder (4:10-12) | 5. Positioning of people by families with weapons (4:13, 16-18) and encouragement of the people (4:14, 20) |
| 6. Economic crisis and greed (5:1-5) | 6. Anger (5:6), reflection, rebuke (5:7), and action (having the people return the debtors' interest, 5:7b-11) |
| 7. Plot to assassinate (or at least harm) Nehemiah (6:1-2) | 7. Refusal to cooperate (6:3) |
| 8. Slander against Nehemiah (6:5-7) | 8. Denial (6:8) and *prayer* (6:9) |
| 9. Plot to discredit Nehemiah (6:13) | 9. Refusal to cooperate (6:11-13) and *prayer* (6:14) |
| 10. Tobiah moved into a temple storeroom (13:4-7) | 10. Tossing out Tobiah's furniture (13:8) |
| 11. Neglect of temple tithes and offerings (13:10) | 11. Rebuke (13:11a), stationing the Levites at their posts (13:11b), and *prayer* (13:14) |
| 12. Violation of the Sabbath by business activities (13:15-16) | 12. Rebuke (13:17-18), posting of guards (13:19), and *prayer* (13:22) |
| 13. Mixed marriages (13:23-24) | 13. Rebuke (13:25-27), removal of a guilty priest (13:28), and *prayer* (13:29) |

## 1. SANBALLAT'S PSYCHOLOGICAL WARFARE (4:1-3)

**4:1-3.** As noted earlier (2:10) **Sanballat** was displeased when he **heard** that Nehemiah had returned to Jerusalem to help the Jews. Sanballat, however, did not know of God's interest in His people. Sanballat's displeasure turned to intense anger (4:1; cf. v. 7). So with **his associates,** including Tobiah (2:19; 4:3; also cf. v. 7; 6:1, 12, 14) and Geshem (2:19), and **in the presence of** Samaritan soldiers, Sanballat **ridiculed the Jews.** He accused them of rebelling against King Artaxerxes (2:19) and by a series of questions he suggested they were incapable of completing the project (4:2). Calling them **feeble** he asked if they would **offer sacrifices.** That is, could they possibly complete the walls so that they could then give sacrifices of thanksgiving? The question about finishing **in a day** suggests that the Jews did not know what they were undertaking. And how, Sanballat asked, could they use **burned,** weakened bricks from the **heaps of** debris? **Tobiah the Ammonite** (cf. 2:19), standing nearby, also tried to discourage the Jews. Ridiculing them, he said they were so inept in their work that **a fox,** weighing only a few pounds, **would break** it down by merely climbing **up on it.**

## 2. NEHEMIAH'S SPIRITUAL RESPONSE (4:4-6)

**4:4-5.** Prayer was a distinct and consistent part of Nehemiah's approach to problem-solving. When faced with Sanballat's demoralizing attack, he immediately asked God for help: **Hear us, O our God, for we are despised.**

Like some of the imprecatory prayers in which the psalmists invoked God's condemnation on His enemies, Nehemiah's prayer in this instance was severe and condemning. He prayed that Sanballat and his cohorts would be taken captive and that they would be judged for **their sins.**

How should a Christian interpret this kind of praying, especially in view of what Jesus Christ said about praying for one's enemies? (Matt. 5:44; cf. Rom. 12:14, 20) Several facts need to be noted. First, in opposing the Jews, Sanballat "and company" were actually opposing God. Second, God had already pronounced judgment on Israel's enemies. Nehemiah was praying according to God's will—that God would deliver Jerusalem from her enemies (Josh. 1:5). Third, Nehemiah was praying that God would bring about what He had promised Abraham regarding those who curse His people (Gen. 12:3). Fourth, vengeance belongs to God, not to Nehemiah or other believers (cf. Deut. 32:35; Rom. 12:19). Also see comments on the imprecatory psalms in the *Introduction* to the Book of Psalms.

**4:6.** After praying, Nehemiah and the Jews continued with the work. Some Christians pray and then wait for things to happen, but not Nehemiah! As in all his efforts, he blended the divine perspective with the human. He faced Sanballat's opposition with *both* prayer and hard work. Once he committed the problem to the Lord, he trusted God to help them achieve their goal. And while praying and trusting, they **rebuilt the wall** to **half its height.** At this juncture their task was half completed. Sanballat and Tobiah's efforts at demoralizing the Jews failed. The Jews rose above their enemies' attempts at discouragement. Because **the people worked** so diligently and enthusiastically (**with all their heart**), they were able to complete half the job in a surprisingly short period of time. Nehemiah wrote later (6:15) that the entire task was completed in 52 days (about eight weeks of 6 days each), so possibly this halfway point took about four weeks.

3. SANBALLAT'S CONSPIRACY (4:7-12)

**4:7-9.** The Jewish workers' rapid progress naturally increased the threat to their enemies, who became **very angry** (cf. v. 1). So they decided to take more overt and corporate action. Joining **Sanballat** and the Samaritans from the north, **Tobiah** and **the Ammonites** from the east, Geshem (cf. 2:19) and **the Arabs** from the south, were **men** from **Ashdod,** a Philistine city, from the west. **They all plotted together to** attack **Jerusalem,** apparently from all sides.

The corporate strategy of Judah's enemies was met by a corporate response. Again the people (**we**) **prayed** for help, and then added action to their prayers by posting **a guard** round the clock **to meet this threat.**

**4:10-12.** However, the problem was not automatically solved. In fact the builders faced some new problems. They were physically and psychologically exhausted and the work seemed endless (v. 10). Furthermore they faced the threat of a secret attack (v. 11) which Nehemiah knew was not idle talk (v. 12).

4. NEHEMIAH'S STRATEGY (4:13-15)

**4:13-15.** Nehemiah established a new strategy to meet the threat of enemy infiltration. He positioned **some of the people behind the lowest points of the wall** with **swords, spears, and bows.**

This must have been a difficult decision for Nehemiah. To place *whole* families together—including women and children—put tremendous pressure on fathers particularly. In case of outright attack, they would have no choice but to stay and fight for and with their family members. But Nehemiah knew it was the only decision he could make if they were to survive and succeed in rebuilding the walls.

Obviously fear gripped these people. So Nehemiah gathered them together and charged them to face the situation courageously (**don't be afraid**) and to **remember** the **great and awesome** Lord (cf. 1:5) who was on their side, and to **fight** to save their families. **When** their **enemies heard** that **their plot** had been discovered, they did not attack and the people resumed their construction **work.**

5. THE COMPLETION OF THE WALLS (4:16-23)

**4:16-18a.** As the Jews continued their work they were more cautious. Nehemiah had **half the men . . . work while the other half** guarded them **with spears,**

shields, bows, and armor. Perhaps they were divided around the wall: a few workers, next to them a few guards, a few more workers, more guards next to them, and so on. The officers in Jerusalem, who apparently had not yet been given responsibilities in the project, were enlisted to stand guard behind the workers. As some workers carried materials, presumably bricks and mortar, they each did so with one hand, while holding a weapon (probably a spear or sword) in the other. Each of the wall-workers (masons) worked with both hands but had his sword at his side. Though this arrangement meant fewer bricklayers were on the job, the work was well defended!

4:18b-20. In addition Nehemiah stationed a trumpeter next to him—a man who would follow Nehemiah everywhere he went as he supervised the work. In case of an attack, the trumpet blast would rally the people to the place of attack. Again Nehemiah encouraged the people (cf. 2:20; 4:14), this time stating that their God would fight for them.

4:21-23. The people worked diligently, from early morning till nighttime. Those living outside the city did not even return to their homes. Venturing outside Jerusalem at night would have been a dangerous risk. Through each night some workers stood guard, knowing the city was vulnerable to attack even then. They did not even take off their clothes to clean up after work; they kept a diligent watch at all times.

## F. Nehemiah's handling of internal problems (5:1-13)

Some say the events in this chapter happened after the wall was completed. It is argued (a) that calling a large assembly (v. 7) would have endangered the city, leaving it almost defenseless, and (b) that Nehemiah would not have been appointed governor till after the wall was completed. However, verse 16 suggests that the "wall work" was continuing.

### 1. THE PROBLEMS AND NEHEMIAH'S INITIAL RESPONSE (5:1-7A)

5:1-5. Up to this point Nehemiah's challenges as a spiritual leader focused primarily on those outside of Judah. But before the walls were finally rebuilt, he encountered the most difficult and intense kind of problem almost every spiri-

tual leader has to face sometime—problems within. For Nehemiah, those problems centered not on Sanballat, Tobiah, or Geshem but on his own people, the Jews. There were four such difficulties. First, the people face a food shortage. They said they needed to get grain for food to keep themselves and their families alive (v. 2). The work on the wall hindered their tending their crops. And this crop failure was called a famine. Second, others had grain (buying it from others), but to get it they had to mortgage their fields . . . vineyards, and homes (v. 3). Third, others, not wanting to mortgage their property, had to borrow money from their Jewish brothers to pay property taxes to King Artaxerxes (v. 4). This problem was compounded by the fact that they were charged exorbitant interest rates by their own Jewish brothers.

This led to a fourth problem. To repay their creditors they had to sell their children into slavery (v. 5; cf. Ex. 21:2-11; Deut. 15:12-18). This of course left them in a hopeless state.

All these difficulties created an internal crisis in Judah. And they meant "double trouble" for Nehemiah. Not only were their enemies a constant threat to their security and state of well-being, but now many Jews were actually taking advantage of other Jews. Morale, which was already low (Neh. 4:10-12) because of external pressures, physical exhaustion, and fear, now took another plunge because of these internal problems.

5:6-7a. Nehemiah's initial response to all this was deep anger. His intense emotion was directed at certain people's selfishness, greed, and insensitivity. Some people were hurting and suffering, and those who should have been the most compassionate (the nobles and officials) were most guilty of exploitation.

Though Nehemiah's anger was certainly righteous indignation, he did not take immediate action. Spending time reflecting on the problem enabled him to cool down, to see the facts in proper perspective, and to decide on a course of action (v. 7a).

### 2. NEHEMIAH'S ACTION (5:7B-11)

5:7b-9. After regaining his emotional equilibrium, Nehemiah confronted the situation head on. First, he rebuked those who were violating God's command not to charge their own people interest (cf. Ex. 22:25; Lev. 25:35-38; Deut. 23:19-20). Money could be loaned (Deut. 15:7-8) but not to gain interest from another person's distresses. Second, calling **a large meeting,** Nehemiah pointed out the inconsistencies of their behavior compared with what he and others in exile had done personally to help their **brothers.** He and others had already purchased (redeemed) some indentured Jews who were sold to foreigners (cf. Lev. 25:47-55). But now the opposite was happening; Jews were **selling** their fellow Jews *into* slavery.

Also God's reputation was at stake. This immoral and unethical behavior was bringing reproach on the One who had delivered their country from both Egyptian bondage and Babylonian Captivity. So he exhorted them to live **in the fear of . . . God** (i.e., to trust, obey, and serve Him) and thus avoid **the reproach of** their **Gentile enemies.**

**5:10-11.** Nehemiah's final action was intensely personal. He referred to his own example and that of others who were already helping those in need by **lending** them **money and grain.** He was already doing something about the problem. So he was not asking the people to do something he was not exemplifying in his own life.

Some Bible translations and commentaries suggest that Nehemiah was admitting his own guilt of charging interest on his loans. This, however, seems inconsistent with his high leadership qualities and his charge to the nobles and officials about their guilt (v. 7).

Nehemiah then asked those guilty of exploitation to return what they had taken from others. Mortgaged **fields, vineyards, olive groves** (the groves are mentioned here for the first time; they were not referred to in vv. 3-5), **and houses** were to be returned (perhaps with the income made from the **grain, new wine, and oil** from those fields), charging interest (**usury**) was to stop, and the interest received from the loans was to be returned. The interest was a **100th part,** that is, one percent a month. He emphasized the urgency of this exhortation by asking them to act **immediately.**

### 3. THE PEOPLE'S RESPONSE (5:12-13)

**5:12-13.** No doubt Nehemiah was pleased when the people responded to his exhortations. But knowing that words are cheap and easy to say on the spur of the moment under public pressure, he **made the** guilty leaders (**nobles and officials;** cf. v. 7) take another step—to **take an oath** affirming that they would **do what they had** said. **The priests** witnessed the oath-taking. Nehemiah visualized for them the grave consequences that would come if they lied to God. Shaking **out the folds of** his **robe** (cf. Paul's action in Acts 18:6), which served as pockets, he asked that **God** similarly **shake out of His house . . . every** person who failed to keep his oath. This gesture indicated rejection, something like shaking the dust off one's feet (Matt. 10:14; Acts 13:51).

### G. Nehemiah's service as governor (5:14-19)

Presumably sometime while the city wall was being rebuilt, Nehemiah was appointed governor of Judah. This was the highest position of leadership in the nation at that time.

Later, as Nehemiah wrote this historical account of his years in Jerusalem, he evidently inserted these observations (vv. 14-19) about his perspective on that leadership position. Apparently he included these verses here in the narrative because of their relationship to the events described in verses 1-13.

### 1. HIS REFUSAL TO USE HIS PRIVILEGES (5:14-15, 17-18)

**5:14-15.** Nehemiah served as Judah's **governor** for **12 years,** from Artaxerxes' **20th year** (444 B.C.) to **his 32nd year** (432 B.C.) This Hebrew word for governor is *peḥâh* derived from the Akkadian word *pāḥatu.* (The word for governor in 7:65, 70; 8:9; 10:1 is a Persian word.) One of the "fringe benefits" of being **governor** was a **food** allowance, granted him by the Persian officials, perhaps for official entertaining of guests. However, Nehemiah did not take advantage of what was rightfully his. In providing food for many Jews and in entertaining dignitaries from other nations (v. 17), he served food and wine out of his personal resources. This practice contrasted with the former **governors,** who charged **the** Jewish **peo-**

ple . . . **40 shekels** (about one pound; cf. NIV marg.) **of silver** besides the food allowance of **food and wine.** Even those governors' **assistants** took advantage of their position and oppressed **the people,** demanding their payments. Nehemiah's **reverence for God** kept him from placing a heartless burden on his fellow Jews. This is still another evidence of his sterling leadership qualities: compassion for those under him and refusal to use his privileges at the expense of others.

**5:17-18.** Exactly who all the **150 Jews** were for whom Nehemiah provided food is not known, though some of them were **officials.** The cost to supply **one ox, six . . . sheep, and some poultry** daily was no doubt great. Even so, Nehemiah willingly bore the cost "out of his own pocket" rather than place **heavy** demands **on** the **people.**

2. HIS INNOCENCE OF CONFLICT OF INTEREST (5:16, 19)

**5:16.** As governor, Nehemiah could have loaned people money to pay their taxes, having them use their land as collateral. And then, when they could not pay back what they had borrowed, he could have applied the world's standard and taken their land. He, along with other leaders in Judah, could have exploited the poor. But he did **not acquire any land** in this way, or by outright purchases. He was careful not to abuse his position as governor in any way, thereby jeopardizing the people's respect for him. In fact he continued working right along with the people in the construction project. He did not hesitate to "get his hands dirty" in this important building program, and was never sidetracked by other interests. His motives were pure, and he never lost sight of God's calling in his life. He was in Jerusalem to help the people, not exploit them. He was there to exemplify God's Law, not violate it. He was there to rebuild the **wall,** not a personal empire.

**5:19.** As a man of prayer, Nehemiah was in touch with God. He prayed that **God** would **remember** him (i.e., not fail to act on his behalf) because of his concern **for** the **people.** Seven times in his prayers recorded in this book Nehemiah asked God to remember (v. 19; 6:14 [twice]; 13:14, 22, 29, 31). Remember **me with favor** is the same prayer he voiced

at the end of the book (13:31).

## H. Nehemiah's response to opposition against him personally (6:1-14)

1. THE FIRST SCHEME: ASSASSINATION PLOT (6:1-4)

**6:1-3.** When . . . **Sanballat, Tobiah, Geshem** (cf. 2:19), and other **enemies** heard that **the wall** was completed and that the only thing remaining was to **set the doors in the gates,** those "wall opponents" again attempted to halt the work. This time they were more subtle; their sole object of attack was Nehemiah himself. By removing him from the scene or by at least destroying his credibility with the Jews, they reasoned that they might be able to defeat the work. Each of their three attacks on him was different, but each was designed to take his life or discredit his effectiveness as a leader.

This first attack was more subtle than the others. **Sanballat and Geshem** invited Nehemiah to **meet** with them **in one of the villages on the plain of Ono.** The plain of Ono was named after the town of that name (cf. 1 Chron. 8:12; Ezra 2:33; Neh. 7:37; 11:35). It was near Lod about 25 miles northwest of Jerusalem, about 6 miles southeast of Joppa. As seen on the map "Postexilic Samaria and Judah," near Ezra 2, Ono was near the border of Samaria, Sanballat's home province. On the surface it appeared that Sanballat and his cohorts wanted to have a peace conference, but their hidden motive was to harm Nehemiah.

Nehemiah suspected foul play. Why would they want him a day's journey away from Jerusalem? Then he could not oversee the **work,** and by outnumbering him they might do him **harm.** Though he could not prove his enemies' motives at the moment, he chose a method that would eventually demonstrate whether they were sincere. He simply **sent messengers to** tell **them** he was involved in **a great** (important) **project** and could not leave it unsupervised. By responding in this way Nehemiah was not openly questioning their motives. In fact he was giving them an opportunity to prove their motives were sincere, if they had really wanted to make peace.

**6:4.** Sanballat and Geshem's response tipped their hand. Rather than countering with an offer to meet with Nehemiah in Jerusalem, **four times they**

sent . . . **the same message** and Nehemiah responded four times with his **same** refusal.

Nehemiah could have impatiently attacked their motives on their third or fourth request. But he patiently waited it out till *they* revealed their motives. And this they did with their fifth response, which involved their second scheme.

2. THE SECOND SCHEME: SLANDER (6:5-9)

**6:5-7.** When Nehemiah's enemies realized he would not leave Jerusalem and meet with them, they tried another tactic. They put pressure on him, trying to force him to meet with them in the plain of Ono. **Sanballat sent his** servant **to** Nehemiah **with an unsealed letter.** The letter reported an alleged rumor that Nehemiah was trying to set himself up as the **king** of **the Jews,** which in turn would be a threat to Artaxerxes (**the king**).

This letter was insidious in several ways. First, the letter made it seem as if they had Nehemiah's welfare at heart. The letter implied that their reason for conferring with him was to protect him.

Second, and more basic to their motive, they were attempting to get Nehemiah to respond out of fear. Third, the letter may have contained an element of truth. Possibly some well-meaning religious leader in Judah had interpreted Nehemiah's presence as a fulfillment of Old Testament prophecies regarding the coming Messiah-**King.**

**6:8-9.** Nehemiah's bold response demonstrated his trust in God. He outrightly denied the accusation. He told his fellow workers that the letter was designed **to frighten** them into **thinking** their wall-building would bring Artaxerxes' wrath down on them. Then, as Nehemiah regularly did, he **prayed,** this time asking God for strength.

3. THE THIRD SCHEME: TREACHERY (6:10-14)

**6:10.** Persisting in their evil planning, Nehemiah's enemies then tried to destroy his credibility by luring him into **the temple.** They hired **Shemaiah,** a man "on the inside," to propose a solution to Nehemiah. Claiming to be a prophet, he purposely locked himself in his house, supposedly from some debility or ritual defilement, and sent word for Nehemiah to visit him. Perhaps Shemaiah devised

an urgent situation that would arouse Nehemiah's curiosity.

Shemaiah must have been a man Nehemiah trusted, for it would have been illogical for him to meet secretly with someone he did not trust. When Nehemiah arrived, Shemaiah suggested they **meet** in **the temple** behind closed **doors.** He pretended to be protecting Nehemiah from would-be nighttime assassins.

**6:11-14.** Nehemiah discerned two flaws in Shemaiah's so-called prophecy. First, God would hardly ask Nehemiah to **run** when the project on the walls was nearing completion. Second, no true prophet would ask someone to violate God's Law. Only priests were allowed in the sanctuary (Num. 3:10; 18:7). If Nehemiah, not being a priest, entered the temple, he would have desecrated it and brought himself under God's judgment. He would **not** disobey God to try to gain safety from his enemies. Nehemiah was convinced that Shemaiah was a false prophet, employed by **Tobiah and Sanballat** to trick him. If the governor had entered the temple and lived, his people would know he disregarded God's commands. Once again Nehemiah prayed, this time that God would **remember** (see comments on Neh. 5:19) his enemies and judge them for their evil scheming. In this imprecation he also included **the Prophetess Noadiah,** mentioned only here, who with other false **prophets** was seeking **to intimidate** him.

*I. Nehemiah's completion of the project (6:15-19)*

**6:15-19.** The walls were **completed . . . in 52 days,** on **the 25th** day of **Elul,** which was about September 20. The project began in the last few days of July and continued through August and into September. The previous November-December (Kislev) was when Nehemiah first heard about the problem (1:1), and in March-April (Nisan) he presented his plan to the king (2:1). As stated earlier, the trip to Jerusalem took two or three months (April or May to June or July), as long as or longer than the building program itself.

The enemies' **self-confidence** dissipated as they saw that the **work** was **done with** God's **help.** Opposing Him, they were fighting a losing battle! One reason **Tobiah** the Ammonite (cf. 2:10,

19) was able to make some inroads into Judah was that he was related to the Jews in two ways (also cf. 13:4). His father-in-law was **Shecaniah son of Arah** (cf. Ezra 2:5), and his daughter-in-law was **the daughter of Meshullam son of Berekiah,** who worked on two sections of the wall (Neh. 3:4, 30). **Many** Jews were therefore loyalists to **Tobiah,** perhaps having trading contracts with him, and they **kept** telling Nehemiah **good** things about Tobiah. Yet **Tobiah** tried **to intimidate** the governor-builder with threatening **letters.**

## II. The Restoration of the People (chaps. 7–13)

### A. The security of the city (7:1-3)

**7:1-3.** Besides repairing the walls, the builders repaired the gates. The last part of the project was setting **the doors in** the gates (cf. 6:1). **Hanani** was Nehemiah's **brother** who had reported the Jerusalem problems to the cupbearer (1:2). **Hananiah . . . a man of integrity,** had deep spiritual convictions. Nehemiah, knowing that his enemies were still around, ordered that security measures be maintained: **the** city **gates** were **to be opened** only a few hours each day; and citizens, probably many of whom had been wall-repairers, were to serve **as guards.**

### B. The census of the returnees (7:4-73a)

**7:4-7a.** Comparatively **few people** were residing in **Jerusalem** (v. 4) so Nehemiah wanted to populate it with people of pure Jewish descent (cf. 11:1-24). To register the present population Nehemiah began with the **record of those who had. . . . returned** with **Zerubbabel** and others (7:5-7). The list of names in verse 7 is almost identical with the list in Ezra 2:2, except that Nehemiah included **Azariah** and **Nahamani.**

**7:7b-65.** Some scholars suggest that the list in Ezra 2 is that of the returnees before they departed from Babylon and that Nehemiah 7 gives **the list of** those who actually arrived in Jerusalem or the list of the community sometime after their arrival. The two chapters, however, give no indication of those differences. The variations in the lists are seen in the chart "The Lists of Exile Returnees in Ezra 2 and Nehemiah 7." The list included people by 18 families and clans (vv. 8-

25) and a listing of inhabitants from 20 towns and villages (vv. 26-38; see the map "Postexilic Samaria and Judah," near Ezra 2). Then **the priests** (4,289 of them) were listed (Neh. 7:39-42), followed by mention of 360 **Levites** which included **singers** and **gatekeepers** (vv. 43-45). **The temple servants** (vv. 46-56) and **descendants of** Solomon's **servants** (vv. 57-59) totaled **392** (v. 60). These were followed by reference to **642** returnees who could **not** trace their ancestries (vv. 61-62). Some of **the priests** could **not** clearly trace their genealogies so they were not allowed by **the governor** (*tiršāṯā'*, a Persian term, possibly a reference to Sheshbazzar—see comments on Ezra 1:8—or to Zerubbabel) **to eat the sacred food** till **a priest** was **ministering with the Urim and Thummim** (see comments on Ezra 2:63).

The groups enumerated in Nehemiah 7:8-62 total 31,089, whereas the groups enumerated in Ezra 2:3-60 total 29,818. The difference of 1,281 is seen in 19 of the 41 items. These variations may be copyists' errors or Ezra and Nehemiah may have had reasons for the different figures which were unstated and therefore unknown today.

**7:66-69.** Nehemiah's grand total of 49,942 people is very close to Ezra's total of 49,897 (Ezra 2:64-65). The extra 45 in Nehemiah's total are the **singers** (Nehemiah **had 245** whereas Ezra referred to 200). A scribe, in copying Nehemiah 7:67, might have inadvertently picked up the 245 in verse 68, in reference to mules, and inserted that number for the 200 singers. He then might have mistakenly omitted verse 68 (cf. NIV marg.). The total then was probably as Ezra recorded it— 49,897.

But how does one account for the difference between the enumerated 31,089 and the 49,897—a difference of 18,808? The larger number may include women and children. Or it may include Jews from the Northern tribes who might have joined the remnant in Judah and Benjamin. It may also include the priests who could not delineate their genealogies (vv. 63-64).

Nehemiah's enumeration even included the animals—a total of 8,136, most of them **donkeys,** used for riding. There was about one donkey available for every seven people.

## The Lists of Exile Returnees in Ezra 2 and Nehemiah 7

| Family Clans | Ezra 2:3-60 | Nehemiah 7:8-62 | Difference |
|---|---|---|---|
| Parosh | 2,172 | 2,172 | |
| Shephatiah | 372 | 372 | |
| Arah | 775 | 652 | − 123 |
| Pahath-Moab | 2,812 | 2,818 | + 6 |
| Elam | 1,254 | 1,254 | |
| Zattu | 945 | 845 | − 100 |
| Zaccai | 760 | 760 | |
| Bani (Binnui)* | 642 | 648 | + 6 |
| Bebai | 623 | 628 | + 5 |
| Azgad | 1,222 | 2,322 | +1,100 |
| Adonikam | 666 | 667 | + 1 |
| Bigvai | 2,056 | 2,067 | + 11 |
| Adin | 454 | 655 | +201 |
| Ater | 98 | 98 | |
| Bezai | 323 | 324 | + 1 |
| Jorah (Hariph)* | 112 | 112 | |
| Hashum | 223 | 328 | +105 |
| Gibbar (Gibeon)* | 95 | 95 | |
| *Inhabitants from Towns* | | | |
| Bethlehem and Netophah | 179 | 188 | + 9 |
| Anathoth | 128 | 128 | |
| Azmaveth (Beth Azmaveth)* | 42 | 42 | |
| Kiriath Jearim, Kephirah, and Beeroth | 743 | 743 | |
| Ramah and Geba | 621 | 621 | |
| Micmash | 122 | 122 | |
| Bethel and Ai | 223 | 123 | − 100 |
| Nebo | 52 | 52 | |
| Magbish† | 156 | — | − 156 |
| The other Elam | 1,254 | 1,254 | |
| Harim | 320 | 320 | |
| Lod, Hadid, and Ono | 725 | 721 | − 4 |
| Jericho | 345 | 345 | |
| Senaah | 3,630 | 3,930 | +300 |
| *Priests* | | | |
| Jedaiah | 973 | 973 | |
| Immer | 1,052 | 1,052 | |
| Pashhur | 1,247 | 1,247 | |
| Harim | 1,017 | 1,017 | |
| *Levites* | 74 | 74 | |
| *Asaph singers* | 128 | 148 | + 20 |
| *Gatekeepers* | 139 | 138 | − 1 |
| *Temple servants* | 392 | 392 | |
| *Descendants of Delaiah, Tobiah, and Nekoda* | 652 | 642 | − 10 |
| Totals | 29,818 | 31,089 | +1,271 |

*The names in parentheses are the variant spellings in the Book of Nehemiah.
† This name and number may have been omitted from Nehemiah's list by a copyist's oversight.

**7:70-72. Heads of the families** and even **the governor** (see comments on v. 65) and **the people** gave large amounts of money and materials to begin the work of the temple. Nehemiah's 41,000 **drachmas of gold** are 61,000 in Ezra 2:69. Nehemiah referred to 4,200 **minas of silver** (totaling more than 2½ tons; cf. NIV marg.) whereas Ezra refers to 5,000 silver minas. The 597 priests' **garments** mentioned by Nehemiah are 100 in Ezra. Again these differences are probably caused by scribal errors in copying the manuscripts.

**7:73a.** The people **settled in their** ancestors' **towns** and villages.

### C. The ministry of Ezra (7:73b–10:39)

1. THE ISRAELITES' OBEDIENCE TO THE LAW (7:73B–8:18)

The pattern in 7:73b–10:39 reflects the suzerainty-vassal treaties of the ancient Near East (see comments on 9:5b-31). The covenant was to be read at regular intervals (chap. 8), sin was confessed (chap. 9), and obedience was promised (chap. 10).

**7:73b–8:9. When the seventh month** arrived **the Israelites** were **settled in their towns** (cf. 7:73a). The seventh month was September-October (see the chart "Calendar in Israel," near Ex. 12:1). Then **the people** met near **the Water Gate** or the east wall (cf. Neh. 3:26, and see the map "Jerusalem in the Time of Nehemiah," near 3:1) to hear **Ezra,** a **scribe** (cf. 8:4, 9, 13; 12:26, 36) and also a **priest** (8:2, 9; 12:26), **read** and teach **the Law of Moses** (the five books of Moses).

Ezra had returned to Jerusalem in 458 B.C., 14 years before Nehemiah, also with the blessing of King Artaxerxes (Ezra 7). His primary purpose in going to his homeland was to teach the Jews God's Law.

In Ezra 7:6, 11-12, 21 he was called a teacher. Of course Ezra and Nehemiah were contemporaries (cf. Neh. 12:33, 36). Ezra's descent from Eleazar, Aaron's third son, is seen in the chart "Ezra's Lineage," near Ezra 7:1-5.

When Ezra first arrived in Jerusalem, the moral and spiritual condition of the people was deplorable (Ezra 9:1-4; 10:2, 10). But as he prayerfully taught them God's Word, they began to respond to and to obey the laws of God. A few years later Nehemiah arrived in Jerusalem and challenged them to trust God to help them rebuild the walls.

The effectiveness of Ezra's ministry is also reflected in the people's behavior after the walls were completed. The two-month building program was an interlude in Ezra's teaching, but apparently it helped motivate the people to want to know more of God's Law. They themselves asked Ezra to continue his teaching ministry among them (Neh. 8:1). This was **the first day of the seventh month,** the day which was to be the Feast of Trumpets (Lev. 23:24; Num. 29:1). Adults and children **who were** old enough **to understand** (Neh. 8:2-3) listened attentively all morning as Ezra **faced** west by **the Water Gate** (cf. v. 1).

Standing **on a . . . platform** (not a podium as in the NASB or a pulpit as in the KJV) above the people **Ezra** read from the Law, while 13 men, perhaps priests (cf. v. 7), **stood** on the platform **beside him.** As he read, **the people . . . stood** (v. 5). He then **praised the LORD, the great God** (cf. 1:5; 4:14).

The people's response to the reading of the Scriptures and to Ezra's praises must have been an emotional experience for this scribe and priest. Lifting **their hands** toward heaven they shouted **Amen! Amen!** in an expression of agreement with God's Word. **Then they** fell on their knees and **bowed** low as they **worshiped the LORD** (8:6).

Nehemiah did not explain exactly how Ezra and the Levites read and explained God's **Law** to this large crowd that may have numbered between 30,000 and 50,000 people (7:66-67). Possibly Ezra read sections of the Law in the presence of **all the people** (8:3), and then at certain times **the Levites** circulated among them and made **it clear** (pāraš, "to make distinct or interpret," possibly means here "to translate" from Heb. to Aram.) and explained (gave **the meaning** of) what Ezra had read as the people stood in groups (vv. 7-8).

The most gratifying thing that happened, of course, is that the people obeyed God's Word. What they heard touched their emotions, for they wept as they heard **the Law** (v. 9). Apparently they were remorseful over their past disobedience to the Law and contrite over their sins.

**8:10-18. Nehemiah** then encouraged

the people to consider the **day . . . sacred** and **to eat,** give to others in need, and rejoice in **the LORD,** their source of **strength.** Holiness and **joy** were to go together!

The next **day** the spiritual leaders— **heads of . . . families** (i.e., heads of clans), **priests and . . . Levites—gathered** to hear more of God's Word from **Ezra.** Another response of the people was their celebrating the Feast of Tabernacles. The sequence in chapter 8 is striking: intellectual response to the Word (vv. 1-8), emotional response to the Word (vv. 9-12), and volitional response to the Word (vv. 13-18).

The spiritual leaders discovered this instruction about **the feast** in Leviticus 23:37-43. This was celebrated from the 15th to the 22nd of **the seventh month** (Tishri). Since they discovered these instructions on the second day of the seventh month (Neh. 8:2, 13), the timing was perfect. They had exactly two weeks to prepare for it. So they had **the people** get **branches from** various kinds of **trees** (v. 15) and build **booths** (temporary shelters) in various places, including **the square . . . by the Gate of Ephraim** (see the map "Jerusalem in the Time of Nehemiah," near 3:1). This recalled their days of wandering in the wilderness (Lev. 23:43). Their celebration of the Feast of Tabernacles was unmatched since **the days of Joshua.** When the altar was completed in 536 B.C. the people then celebrated the Feast of Tabernacles (Ezra 3:4), but here the **joy** and involvement was much greater. **Ezra read** the **Law** during the Feast of Tabernacles, because Moses had indicated that this was to be done every seven years (Deut. 31:10-13).

2. THE ISRAELITES' CONFESSION OF SIN (9:1-37)

"The Word of God had a tremendous impact on the Restoration community. It pointed the people to their sin (8:9), led them to worship (8:12, 14), and gave them great joy (8:17)" (J. Carl Laney, *Ezra/Nehemiah,* p. 104). Now the Word led to their confession of sin.

**9:1-5a.** The Feast of Tabernacles concluded on the 22nd day of the month (see comments on 8:14). After one day's interval, the 23rd, the people assembled **on the 24th.** They **separated** from **foreigners** (cf. 10:28). Then they confessed their sins, evidenced by **fasting** (cf. comments

on 1:4), **wearing sackcloth** (cf. Gen. 37:24; Es. 4:1-4; Pss. 30:11; 35:13; 69:11; Isa. 22:12; 32:11; 37:1-2; Lam. 2:10; Dan. 9:3), a dark coarse cloth made from goats' hair, **and having dust on their heads** (cf. Josh. 7:6; 1 Sam. 4:12; 2 Sam. 1:2; 15:32; Job 2:12; Lam 2:10; Ezek. 27:30). These were signs of mourning and grief.

For about three hours the people again **stood** (cf. Neh. 8:7) while **the Law** was **read.** Then for another three hours they **confessed their sins** and worshiped **the LORD.** Several **Levites,** some of whom were mentioned in 8:7, were involved in leading the people in their **praise** of the eternal **God.** Five of the eight Levites in 9:4 are listed in the group of eight in verse 5 (**Pethahiah** is also mentioned in 11:24). These five may have been the same or different men. One group was involved in petition (v. 4) and the other in praise (v. 5). **The stairs** (lit., "ascent") may have led to some part of the temple complex or they may refer to the platform mentioned in 8:4.

**9:5b-31.** The material in 9:5b–10:39 follows the normal covenant form used in the ancient Near East: preamble (9:5b-6), historical prologue (9:7-37), acceptance of the covenant (9:38–10:29), and the stipulations (10:30-39). The prayer in 9:5b-31 was voiced by the Levites on the people's behalf. It rehearses major events in Israel's history, first stating God's glory (v. 5b), uniqueness (v. 6a), and Creation of the universe (v. 6b). The Levites then spoke of God's work with **Abram—** calling him from **Ur** (Gen. 12:1) and making **a covenant with him** (Gen. 15:4-21). Then they recounted God's deliverance of Israel from **Egypt** (Neh. 9:9-12; cf. Ex. 1–15), and the giving of the Law (Neh. 9:13-14) and of manna (**bread from heaven**) and **water** (v. 15; cf. Ex. 16–17). On God's swearing an oath by His **uplifted hand,** see comments on Exodus 6:8.

**But** the Israelites' ancestors became disobedient and rebellious against God even to the point of worshiping a **calf-idol** (Neh. 9:16-18; cf. Ex. 32). However, God was still **gracious and compassionate, slow to anger and abounding in love** (cf. Ex. 34:6; Num. 14:18; Pss. 86:15; 103:8; 145:8; Joel 2:13; Jonah 4:2). God continued to **guide them . . . instruct them,** and provide for them (Neh. 9:19-21). He helped them conquer their enemies **Sihon** and **Og** (v. 22; cf. Num.

21:21-35), and brought them into **the Promised Land** under Joshua (Neh. 9:23-25). In all this they enjoyed God's **great goodness** (cf. v. 35).

Again the people **rebelled** (v. 26; cf. v. 17) so God gave them over to oppressors. But because of His **great compassion** He raised up **deliverers**, the Judges, who freed them (vv. 27-28). Through the centuries of Israel's sin (v. 29) God continued to be **patient** and to admonish them **by** the Holy **Spirit . . . through** the **prophets** (v. 30). But as a result of their ongoing sinning they were taken into exile (vv. 30-31).

**9:32-37.** In this concluding part of the Levites' prayer, they asked for relief, again acknowledging God's power, majesty (cf. 1:5; 4:14), and loyalty. Throughout Israel's history she experienced **hardship** because of her disobedience. **Assyria** was the first great power after Egypt that menaced Israel and Judah, beginning in the ninth century, over 400 years before Nehemiah's time. Even while the Israelites were **enjoying** God's blessings (from His **great goodness**; cf. 9:25) in the **land**, they were still sinful.

Now they were **slaves** in their own land! (v. 36) Being slaves meant that they had to pay taxes to Persia, and Judah's governmental leaders had to give the Persian **kings** tribute from the produce of the land. Nehemiah's prayer ended with a plaintive admission of their **great distress.**

**3. THE ISRAELITES' PROMISE TO OBEY (9:38–10:39)**

*a. The signatories (9:38–10:27)*

**9:38–10:27.** The civil **leaders,** religious leaders (**Levites and . . . priests**), and all the people agreed to put **their seals** to a written **agreement** that they would obey the stipulations of the Mosaic Law (cf. v. 29). The list begins with **Nehemiah,** who again set an excellent example for the people. Many of the 24 names in 10:1-8 are listed in 12:12-21, names of heads of families. **These were . . . priests** (10:8). Ezra is not listed, but he was a descendant of **Seraiah** (v. 1). After the priests, 17 **Levites** were listed, 6 of whom were involved in reading the Law (8:7). The other group of signers of the agreement were 44 **leaders,** that is, heads of families. Some of them are listed in 7:8-25.

*b. The stipulations (10:28-39)*

**10:28-29. The rest of the people** did not place their seals to the written agreement, but they did **join** in binding **themselves . . . to follow** God's **Law.** Gatekeepers, singers, and temple servants were listed in 7:44-60. All others are included under the rubric **all who separated themselves from** foreign **peoples** (cf. 9:2). Their commitment, though not indicated by seals, was evidenced by **a curse** (that called down calamity if they failed to carry through on their agreement) **and an oath.** The curse may refer to the cursings God stated in the Deuteronomic Covenant (Deut. 28:15-68).

**10:30-39.** The stipulations they spelled out in the agreement include (a) avoidance of intermarriages (v. 30; cf. Ex. 34:16; Deut. 7:3-4), (b) keeping **the Sabbath** and the sabbatical **year** (Neh. 10:31; cf. Ex. 20:8-11; 23:11-12; 31:15-17; Lev. 25:2-7; Deut. 15:1-3), and (c) supporting the temple **service** by giving a **third of a shekel** (about one-eighth of an ounce) annually (Neh. 10:32-33). According to Exodus 30:11-16 the temple gift was to be one-half a shekel annually, but here it was valued lightly. These temple **offerings** gave the **priests** and **Levites** money for maintaining the bread on the table of the Presence (Ex. 35:13; 39:36; Num. 4:7), for making various **offerings,** for celebrating monthly and annual **festivals,** and carrying out other **duties.** (See comments on Neh. 13:10-11 regarding the people's failure to keep this commitment.)

Other responsibilities to which the leaders and people pledged themselves were (d) contributing **wood** for the fire on **the altar** of burnt offering, which was to burn continually (Lev. 6:12-13), (e) giving **the firstfruits of** their **crops** (Ex. 23:19; Deut. 26:1-3) and their **firstborn . . . sons** and animals (Num. 18:15-17; Deut. 12:6) to the Lord, and (f) paying annual **tithes** (Lev. 27:30; Num. 18:21-24). **The Levites** were to tithe **the tithes** they received (Neh. 10:38-39; cf. Num. 18:26) to help provide for the priests' needs.

The final statement of the agreement, **We will not neglect the house of our God** (Neh. 10:39), summarizes obligations (c) through (f). Under Ezra's and Nehemiah's leadership the people had been led to place a higher priority on spiritual things, including the care of the restored temple. This was even more important than restoring the city's walls.

## D. The list of Judean residents (11:1–12:26)

Comparatively few people lived in Jerusalem because of the rubble in the city (7:4). Now that the walls and gates were repaired, the city was ready to be occupied by more people.

### 1. OCCUPANTS IN JERUSALEM (11:1-24)

**11:1-4a.** Along with **the leaders,** one-tenth of the Israelites were to reside **in Jerusalem,** here called **the Holy City** (cf. v. 18; Isa. 52:1; Dan. 9:24; Rev. 11:2). They were chosen by **lots** (cf. Prov. 16:33). Those **who volunteered** (Neh. 11:2) were either the ones chosen by lots who gladly moved to the city, or were additional **men.** Some **priests** and **Levites** including **temple servants . . . lived in** surrounding **towns** and villages and "commuted" to **Jerusalem** when they served in the temple. Others who were not civil or religious leaders took up residence **in Jerusalem.** They were of the tribes of **Judah** and **Benjamin.**

**11:4b-19.** The descendants of various family heads who moved into Jerusalem included **468** laymen of the tribe **of Judah** (vv. 4b-6), **928** laymen of the tribe **of Benjamin** (vv. 7-9), 1,192 **priests** (vv. 10-14), 284 **Levites** (vv. 15-18), and 172 **gatekeepers** (v. 19)—3,044 men in all. According to 1 Chronicles 9:3 descendants of Ephraim and Manasseh also lived in Jerusalem. The total of "provincial leaders" (Neh. 11:3) from Judah included **Athaiah . . . a descendant of Perez, and Maaseiah . . . a descendant of Shelah** (vv. 4-5). Perez and Shelah were sons of Judah (cf. Gen. 38:2-5, 26-29). Another son of Judah, Zerah, mentioned in Genesis 38:30 and 1 Chronicles 9:6, is not referred to in Nehemiah 11:4-6. This explains why 1 Chronicles 9:6 has 690 and Nehemiah 11:6 has 468 in the census. In the Benjamite list Nehemiah named one line of descendants (v. 7) but the chronicler included four lines of descent. This may or may not account for Nehemiah's figure of 928 Benjamites (v. 8) being slightly lower than the Chronicles figure of 956 (1 Chron. 9:9).

The priests were from six family heads (Neh. 11:10-14): **Jedaiah; the son of Joiarib; Jakin; Seraiah . . . Adaiah;** and **Amashsai.** In 1 Chronicles 9:10-13, the names refer to the same individuals, with a few spelling variations. The son of Joiarib is Jehoiarib, Seraiah is Azariah, and Amashsai is Maasai. It is difficult to know why the 1,192 priests differ from the total of 1,760 in 1 Chronicles 9:13.

The list of Levite family heads in Nehemiah 11:15-18 and the list in 1 Chronicles 9:14-16 have several variations in spelling and additions or omissions (e.g., **Bakbukiah** may be the same as Bakkakkar, and **Abda** may be Obadiah; cf. Neh. 12:25). The chronicler listed Heresh, Galal, and Berekiah whereas Nehemiah does not, and Nehemiah lists **Shabbethai** and **Jozabad,** who did **outside work** on the temple (11:16) whereas 1 Chronicles does not.

The gatekeepers' family heads were two, whereas 1 Chronicles 9:17 names four. This may account for the difference in the total gatekeepers: **172** in Nehemiah 11:19 and 212 in 1 Chronicles 9:22.

**11:20-24. The rest of the Israelites . . . were in** Judean **towns** (v. 20) except for **temple servants** in Ophel (cf. 3:26), the hill in the city that led north to the temple. **Uzzi was** over **the Levites** (11:22). **The singers were under the . . . orders** of the king (v. 23), presumably Artaxerxes. **Pethahiah** (v. 24; cf. 9:5) was the **agent** who represented the Jews' affairs to Artaxerxes and informed them of **the king's** wishes and directives.

### 2. OCCUPANTS IN VILLAGES OF JUDAH AND BENJAMIN (11:25-36)

**11:25-30.** In the postexilic period under Nehemiah **some of the people of Judah** settled in 17 towns and their surrounding villages as far south as **Beersheba** (vv. 27, 30), about 32 miles south of Jerusalem, **to the Valley of Hinnom,** immediately south of Jerusalem (cf. Josh. 15:8). **Kiriath Arba** was an older name for Hebron (Josh. 14:15).

**11:31-35.** The 15 places where **the descendants of** Benjamin lived were north of Judah. **The Valley of the Craftsmen** may have been near **Lod and Ono.** (See the locations of many of the cities in vv. 25-35 on the map "Postexilic Samaria and Judah," near Ezra 2.)

**11:36.** Some of the **. . . Levites** who were living in **Judah** moved north to **Benjamin.**

### 3. LIST OF PRIESTS AND LEVITES (12:1-26)

**12:1-7.** David had appointed 24 priestly divisions to serve in the temple (1 Chron. 24:7-19) when it would be built. Now Nehemiah listed the 22 **leaders of the priests** who had **returned** from Babylon **with Zerubbabel** and **Jeshua,** almost 100 years earlier, in 538 B.C. Perhaps two names were dropped from the list in copying or perhaps it was not possible to fill the roster of 24.

**12:8-9.** The names of 8 of the Levites who returned with Zerubbabel are listed here. **Their associates** brought the number to 74 (Ezra 2:40), or to 202 if the Levite singers (Ezra 2:41) are included. Of the 8 names, Ezra listed only 2, **Jeshua** and **Kadmiel** (Ezra 2:40). **Mattaniah** and **Bakbukiah** (Neh. 12:8-9) in Zerubbabel's day (v. 1) should not be confused with men by the same names in Nehemiah's day (11:17) though their work of leading **songs of thanksgiving** (cf. 12:24) was similar.

**12:10-11.** The many generations of high priests extended from Aaron to Jehozadak, who was taken into exile to Babylon (1 Chron. 6:3-15). Then **Jeshua** the high priest returned from Babylon with Zerubbabel (Ezra 2:1-2; Neh. 11:1). Jeshua's descendant **Eliashib** (12:10) was the high priest in Nehemiah's day (3:1; 13:4, 7, 28). Some scholars suggest that the reference to Eliashib's line to **Jaddua,** three generations later, was added by someone after Nehemiah's time. However, it was certainly possible that Eliashib's great-grandson was born while Nehemiah was still living. **Jonathan** is probably the same as Johanan in 12:22.

**12:12-21.** These verses list **the heads of the priestly families** in **the days of Joiakim,** the son of Jeshua the high priest (cf. v. 10). Twenty names are listed here, corresponding roughly to the 22 names in verses 1-7. Hattush in verse 2 and Maadiah in verse 5 are not in the list in verses 12-21. Harim (v. 15; cf. 10:5) is spelled Rehum in 12:3. Minjamin in verse 17 is spelled Mijamin in verse 5.

**12:22-26.** **Darius** is probably Darius II who ruled Persia from 423 to 404 B.C. According to the Elephantine papyri **Johanan** was high priest in 408 B.C. Possibly Nehemiah lived to see Johanan's son **Jaddua** become high priest sometime between 408 and 404.

**The book of the annals** was an official record book of the Levite **family heads. . . . up to the** days of **Johanan. The Levites** mentioned in verses 24-25 **served in the days of** the high priest **Joiakim** (cf. vv. 10, 12), **and in the days of Nehemiah** and **Ezra.** Hashabiah may be the man mentioned in 3:17; **Sherebiah** and **Jeshua** are mentioned in 12:8 as being involved in leading songs of thanksgiving, sung antiphonally. Possibly Jeshua **son of Kadmiel** should read "Jeshua, Binnui, Kadmiel," as in verse 8.

**Mattaniah** and **Bakbukiah** (cf. 11:17) were associated with music in 12:8 but here (v. 25) they were gatekeepers. **Obadiah** was probably the same as Abda (11:17). Possibly they served in both capacities. **Meshullam** (also mentioned in 3:4, 30) may be a variant spelling for Shallum, who along with **Talmon and Akkub were gatekeepers** (cf. 1 Chron. 9:17).

## E. The dedication of the wall (12:27-47)

### 1. THE PREPARATION FOR THE DEDICATION (12:27-30)

**12:27-30.** Nehemiah had **the Levites,** who had settled in various towns around **Jerusalem** (cf. 11:3, 20) join the others in the holy city for the ceremonies to dedicate the rebuilt **wall.** It was to be a time of singing **songs of thanksgiving** (cf. 12:8) to God with musical instruments (cf. 1 Chron. 25:1). **Singers,** who were Levites, assembled from south of **Jerusalem** (**the villages of** Netophah), the east (assuming **Beth Gilgal** is the same as Gilgal), and the north (the Benjamite towns of **Geba and Azmaveth**). The preparations also included ceremonial cleansing of all **the people** and of **the gates and the wall.** This was done no doubt by sprinkling the blood of sacrificed animals.

### 2. THE PROCESSION OF THE TWO CHOIRS (12:31-42A)

**12:31-42a.** Nehemiah assembled **two** great **choirs to** sing **thanks** (cf. vv. 8, 27); the number in each choir is not indicated. The choirs probably began near the Valley Gate, which interestingly is the place where Nehemiah began and ended his nighttime inspection of the ruined walls months earlier (2:13-15). The first procession moved counterclockwise on the southern and eastern wall **toward the Dung Gate** (12:31) and past **the Fountain Gate** up **to the Water Gate.** Because both **choirs** entered the temple (v. 40), the first one may have proceeded on the wall up to the East Gate (see the map "Jerusalem in the Time of Nehemiah," near 3:1). The procession included the following: **Ezra,** who **led the** group (12:36), the choir, **Hoshaiah . . . half the leaders of Judah** (v. 32), **priests** (seven of them named and **some** with **trumpets**), and **Zechariah** and his eight **associates . . . with musical instruments.**

**The second choir** moved clockwise, presumably starting at the Valley Gate and going past various gates and towers (see comments on chap. 3) till they arrived at **the Gate of the Guard.** This group included the choir, Nehemiah, **half the officials** (12:40), **priests** (seven of them named and with **trumpets**), and eight others who apparently were singers. The parallel arrangement of the two processions is striking.

Their walking **on top of the wall** (vv. 31, 38) visually demonstrated that the walls were strong, a rejoinder to Tobiah's earlier mocking claim that the wall would be so weak that even a fox on top of it would break it down (4:3). Perhaps Nehemiah wanted Tobiah to see that with God's help the project was completed in spite of his and others' opposition. Since the people now carried no spears, swords, or bows (cf. 4:16, 18), the enemies had no doubt withdrawn. Seeing the two large processions marching on the walls must have been an impressive sight.

3. THE PARTICIPATION IN WORSHIP (12:42B-43)

**12:42b-43.** In the temple ("the house of God," v. 40) the choir leader **Jezrahiah** led the two large **choirs. Sacrifices** were made and the people **rejoiced** so loudly that they **could be heard far away.**

4. THE PROVISION OF CONTRIBUTIONS (12:44-47)

**12:44-47.** Nehemiah took advantage of this celebration to provide for ongoing worship. **The storerooms** to which the people were to bring their **contributions, firstfruits, and tithes** that were **required by the Law** were side rooms on the temple (cf. 1 Kings 6:5; 1 Chron. 28:11; 2 Chron. 31:11; Neh. 10:37-39; 12:25; 13:4, 12-13). Nehemiah had **the ministering priests and Levites** follow the order of responsibilities outlined more than 500 years earlier by **David** (1 Chron. 22–26)

and presumably established by **Solomon.** Music had been an important part of David's preparations for the temple, under the leadership of the musician **Asaph** (1 Chron. 15:19; 16:4-5,,37). Besides being an effective administrator Nehemiah was also a man of worship. He was concerned with praise by music and praise by gifts.

The people had made a binding agreement to provide for the priests and Levites (see comments on Neh. 10:37-39).

## F. The reforms under Nehemiah (chap. 13)

For 12 years Nehemiah served as governor of Judah, from Artaxerxes' 20th year to his 32nd year (5:14; cf. 13:6), that is, from 444 B.C. to 432 B.C. Other than his rebuilding and dedicating the wall, getting the people to agree to keep the Law, and organizing the work of the priests and Levites in the temple, little is known about Nehemiah's 12-year rule. Undoubtedly that was a successful period of time in his life.

When the 12 years were up Nehemiah returned to Persia (perhaps to the city of Susa; cf. 1:1; or to the capital, Persepolis), evidently once again to serve King Artaxerxes (cf. 2:6). How long he remained in this position is not known. Perhaps it was two years or so. While he was gone some rather startling changes took place in Judah, changes involving serious violations of the Mosaic Law. When Nehemiah once again returned to Judah (perhaps around 430 or later), he faced a task that in some respects must have been even more difficult than rebuilding the wall.

1. ISRAEL'S EXCLUSION OF FOREIGNERS (13:1-3)

**13:1-3. On that day** refers not to 12:44 but to the time after Nehemiah returned to Jerusalem to be governor again, as indicated in 13:4-7. The portion of the Law (**the Book of Moses**) that **was read** is Deuteronomy 23:3-5. The Ammonites and Moabites had resisted Israel's march to Canaan, and the Moabites **had hired Balaam** to **curse** Israel but **God . . . turned** that attempted **curse into a blessing** (Num. 22–25). Therefore Ammonites and Moabites were to have no part in Israel's temple worship. Being reminded of this **the people** in Nehemiah's day eliminated those foreigners (as stated in

Neh. 13:4-9, 23-28). Interestingly once again the reading of God's Word had an effect on **the people** (cf. 8:1-6, 13-17; 9:3).

2. NEHEMIAH'S ENCOUNTER WITH TOBIAH (13:4-9)

**13:4-5.** When Nehemiah returned to Jerusalem he was shocked to find that **Eliashib, the** high **priest** in Judah (cf. 3:1, 20; 13:28), had prepared **a large** room in the temple for **Tobiah.** Eliashib and Tobiah were **closely associated,** which may mean family ties (cf. Tobiah's relationships by marriage with several Jews, 6:17-18). Tobiah had been an enemy of Nehemiah, opposing the wall-building (2:10-19; 4:3, 7; 6:1, 12, 17, 19); but now that Nehemiah was gone (13:6) Tobiah the Ammonite (cf. comments on vv. 1-3) moved into the **temple!** The room he occupied had been one of the temple storerooms (v. 4; see comments on 12:44), a side room for storing **grain offerings** (13:4-5). There Tobiah could oppose God's work while posing to assist it!

**13:6-9.** Artaxerxes is called the **king of Babylon** because his rule over the Persian Empire included Babylon. Nehemiah's return to Artaxerxes (at either Persepolis, the capital, or Susa) was in 432. **Some time later** (perhaps two years or more) Nehemiah asked to return **to Jerusalem.** How long he stayed this second time is not stated. Malachi may have ministered about that same time (see the chart "Chronology of the Postexilic Period," near Ezra 1:1).

Hearing what the high priest **had done** for **Tobiah** (Nehemiah called it an **evil thing**; cf. Neh. 13:17), Nehemiah was deeply distressed. **Eliashib** had been involved in restoring the walls (3:1), but now inconsistently he had allowed an opponent to reside inside the temple complex! Understandably Nehemiah was so angry that he went into the temple room and tossed out **all Tobiah's household goods.** He then had the **rooms** (apparently Tobiah had also occupied some rooms adjacent to the large chamber) purified, either ceremonially or by fumigation or both, and restored the temple articles and **offerings** that belonged there.

3. NEHEMIAH'S ENCOUNTER WITH THE OFFICIALS IN JUDAH (13:10-14)

**13:10.** Nehemiah's next task pertains to why Tobiah was able to occupy one of the temple storerooms. They were empty because the people had failed in their commitment to bring their tithes and offerings **to the Levites.** As a result **the Levites** and others who were to live off these offerings as they performed spiritual services for the people had to work in the **fields** caring for **their** livestock (cf. Num. 35:1-5). This meant they had less time to work in the temple.

**13:11-14.** Nehemiah reprimanded **the** Jewish **officials** for neglecting this aspect of the work of the temple (**the house of God**; cf. vv. 4, 7, 9, 14). Malachi addressed this problem too (Mal. 3:8-10). The officials had failed to make sure the people of Judah obeyed the Lord in these matters. What made this problem even more distressing for Nehemiah, and difficult to believe, is that these leaders had previously signed a document promising before the Lord and the people that they would never again let this happen (Neh. 9:38; 10:14-29, 35, 37, 39). They had even said specifically, "We will not neglect the house of our God" (10:39b).

Besides rebuking the leaders for their neglect, Nehemiah took action to correct the problem (cf. 13:17-19). He **stationed** the Levites **at their posts** in the temple and appointed four men—a **priest,** a **scribe,** a **Levite,** and an **assistant,** all **trustworthy** (v. 13)—to oversee the distribution of the peoples' **tithes** (**grain, new wine, and oil,** v. 12; cf. v. 5; 10:39). Also Nehemiah, as he so often did, prayed for God's help in the matter (13:14). **Remember** was a plea for help, not merely a request that **God . . . not** forget something (cf. "remember" in vv. 22, 29, 31; 5:19; 6:14 [twice]). Judah's leader did not want his efforts of reform to be undone by the people's neglect.

4. NEHEMIAH'S ENCOUNTER WITH THOSE WHO WERE PROFANING THE SABBATH (13:15-22)

**13:15-16.** Another commitment Israel had made in writing was to keep God's laws regarding **the Sabbath** (10:31). But when Nehemiah returned to Jerusalem he found that the people had also violated this promise. They were working on **the Sabbath** as they did on the other days of the week. They were **treading** grapes in the **winepresses,** and transporting the **wine,** along with **grain . . . grapes, figs,** and **other** merchandise, **into**

Jerusalem to sell it. They also were buying **fish** and other items from people of **Tyre** who resided **in Jerusalem.**

**13:17-22.** Again Nehemiah met the problem with a rebuke and action (cf. vv. 11-13). In rebuking their **Sabbath** desecration (calling it a **wicked thing;** cf. v. 7), he referred to a similar sin in Jeremiah's day (cf. Jer. 17:19-27) which God punished by the Exile (**calamity**). Nehemiah had the city **doors . . . shut** on **the Sabbath,** beginning on Friday evening, with guards posted to see that merchandise was not **brought in.** Even so, some **merchants** stayed all **night outside** the walls, perhaps hoping people would slip outside in the darkness to purchase their goods. When Nehemiah heard of this, he threatened to use force against them. Then he told **the Levites** (cf. Neh. 13:30) to help **guard the gates** (cf. 7:1; 11:19). Again (cf. 13:14) he asked **God** to help in this problem, showing **mercy** to him out of His **great love** (ḥeseḏ, "loyal love").

5. NEHEMIAH'S ENCOUNTER WITH THOSE WHO VIOLATED THEIR MARRIAGE COMMITMENTS (13:23-31)

**13:23-24.** The people **of Judah** had also promised in writing that they would not intermarry with pagan people (10:30). Yet when Nehemiah arrived back in Jerusalem, he found that many of the **men** had violated this commitment also (cf. Ezra 9:1-4; 10:44; Mal. 2:10-11) by marrying **women from** the Philistine city of **Ashdod,** and Ammonite and Moabite (cf. comments on Ezra 10:1-3) women. This too had been forbidden in the Mosaic Law (Ex. 34:12-16; Deut. 7:1-5). These mixed marriages even meant that **their children** were speaking their mothers' **language,** not Hebrew (**the language of Judah**).

**13:25-27.** Again Nehemiah responded with a rebuke (cf. vv. 11, 17). Also he asked God to judge them (**called curses down on them**) and even struck some of them physically, pulling **out their hair,** probably from their beards. To lose one's beard was a disgrace (2 Sam. 10:4; also see Isa. 50:6). He **made them** swear before **God** that they would not continue to commit this violation of God's Law. He reminded them of Solomon's **sin** in marrying **foreign women** (cf. 1 Kings 11:1-8). This was **wickedness,** an act of unfaithfulness.

Nehemiah's pulling out the men's hair may seem to be violent and inappropriate for a man of God. However, Nehemiah was concerned that God's judgment not fall again on Judah. He knew **God** would not tolerate this sin.

**13:28-29.** Even the priesthood was contaminated by this sin! A grandson of **the high priest** Eliashib (cf. 3:1, 20; 13:4) had married Sanballat's daughter. **Sanballat,** perhaps governor of Samaria, had vigorously opposed Nehemiah's work (cf. 2:10, 19; 4:1, 7; 6:1-2, 5, 12, 14), and now he, like Tobiah (cf. 6:17-18; 13:4), had apparently planned through this family relationship to destroy God's work. Nehemiah had thrown Tobiah's furniture out of the storeroom (v. 8); now he chased the guilty husband **away.**

Nehemiah prayed that **God** would judge the high priest's grandson. Who else is included in his word **them** is not specified, but probably Sanballat was in mind. Mixed marriages **defiled** the priesthood for a priest was to marry "only a virgin from his own people" (Lev. 21:14).

**13:30-31.** This problem, like the others reported in this chapter (cf. vv. 9, 22), called for ceremonial purifying. Again **the priests and the Levites** were **assigned** their **duties.** (Nehemiah was great at getting people to work!) He **also made** sure the people brought their **contributions** and **firstfruits** to the temple (cf. comments on vv. 10-13).

For the fourth time in this chapter this great leader prayed that **God** would **remember** him (see comments on v. 14), that is, that God would bestow His blessings on him in return for his diligence.

This book underscores the importance of physical protection for God's people in Jerusalem but, more importantly, it stresses the need for His people to obey His Word, not giving in to sin through neglect, compromise, or outright disobedience.

# BIBLIOGRAPHY

Ackroyd, Peter R. *I and II Chronicles, Ezra, Nehemiah.* Torch Bible Commentaries. New York: Harper & Row, 1973.

Barber, Cyril J. *Nehemiah and the Dynamics of Effective Leadership.* Neptune, N.J.: Loizeaux Brothers, 1976.

Brockington, L.H. *Ezra, Nehemiah, and Esther.* New Century Bible. Greenwood, S.C.: Attic Press, 1969.

Campbell, Donald K. *Nehemiah: Man in Charge.* Wheaton, Ill.: SP Publications, Victor Books, 1979.

Fensham, F. Charles. *The Books of Ezra and Nehemiah.* The New International Commentary on the Old Testament. Grand Rapids: Wm. B. Eerdmans Publishing Co., 1982.

Getz, Gene A. *Nehemiah: A Man of Prayer and Persistence.* Ventura, Calif.: G/L Publications, Regal Books, 1981.

Ironside, H.A. *Notes on Ezra, Nehemiah, Esther.* Neptune, N.J.: Loizeaux Brothers, 1972.

Jamieson, Robert. "The Book of Nehemiah." In *A Commentary Critical, Experimental and Practical on the Old and New Testaments.* Vol. 2. Grand Rapids: Wm. B. Eerdmans Publishing Co., 1945.

Keil, C.F. "Nehemiah." In *Commentary on the Old Testament in Ten Volumes.* Vol. 3. Reprint (25 vols. in 10). Grand Rapids: Wm. B. Eerdmans Publishing Co., 1982.

Kidner, Derek. *Ezra and Nehemiah: An Introduction and Commentary.* The Tyndale Old Testament Commentaries. Downers Grove, Ill.: InterVarsity Press, 1979.

Laney, J. Carl. *Ezra/Nehemiah.* Everyman's Bible Commentary. Chicago: Moody Press, 1982.

Myers, Jacob M. *Ezra, Nehemiah.* The Anchor Bible. Garden City, N.Y.: Doubleday & Co., 1965.

Swindoll, Charles R. *Hand Me Another Brick.* Nashville: Thomas Nelson Publishers, 1978.

# ESTHER

## John A. Martin

## INTRODUCTION

**Historical Setting.** The Book of Esther is unique in several ways. For one thing it is a book with several historical problems. The book contains interesting and informative eyewitness accounts about the Persian Empire which were true to life in that period of history but which are difficult to verify from outside sources (see comments under "Historicity").

The book takes place in the Persian period (539–331 B.C.) after many Israelites had returned from the Exile to the land of Palestine to rebuild the temple and set up the sacrificial system. Most Israelite captives, however, chose not to return to their homeland. They should have done so for Isaiah and Jeremiah had urged the yet-to-be-exiled nation to come out of Babylon (Isa. 48:20; Jer. 50:8; 51:6) after 70 years (Jer. 29:10) and return to the place where the Lord could bless them under the covenantal promises (Deut. 28). Esther and Mordecai had not returned to the land and did not seem interested in complying with the prophetic command to return. The Persian monarch mentioned in the Book of Esther is Xerxes (485–465), known from other sources as Ahasuerus (see NIV marg.), a strong, effective ruler. The events in this book occurred between those recorded in Ezra 6 and Ezra 7 (see the chart "Chronology of the Postexilic Period" near Ezra 1:1). The events in the Book of Esther extend over a decade—from 483 B.C. (Xerxes' 3rd year, Es. 1:3) to 473 (the end of Xerxes' 12th year, 3:7).

**Characteristics.** Esther is the only book of the Bible in which the name of God is not mentioned. The New Testament does not quote from the Book of Esther, nor have copies of it been found among the Dead Sea Scrolls. The Law is never mentioned in the book nor are sacrifices or offerings referred to. This fits the view that the Jewish people residing in the Persian Empire were not following God's will. They were shunning their responsibility to return to Palestine and to become involved in temple worship.

Prayer is never mentioned in the book, though fasting is. In other postexilic books prayer is important to the main characters (both the books of Ezra and Neh. are good examples), but in the Book of Esther nothing is said about Mordecai or Esther praying. Both Esther and Mordecai seem to have lacked spiritual awareness except in their assurance that God would protect His people.

**Recipients.** Knowing who the original recipients of a Bible book were helps in interpreting that book. The Book of Esther includes a number of dates which tie the account to a particular time in the Persian Empire, but no hint is given when the book was written nor is there any explicit evidence about its original readers.

Some scholars suggest that the book was composed in the Persian Empire and then transported back to Palestine and added to the collection of biblical books (OT mss. considered canonical). More likely, however, is the view that the author lived in Palestine and wrote this account of events transpiring in the Persian Empire for the benefit of his fellow returnees to the land. It is unlikely that the book was written for Persian readers. No doubt it was composed to encourage Israelites that God was working on their behalf, even through some people who had refused to come back to the land.

At the time of the writing of the book (see comments under "Author and Date") the Jews in Palestine were going through difficult times in their struggle to rebuild their nation and to reestablish temple worship. It had taken the nation 21 years to complete the building of the temple (536–515) and, as is evident from the last half of the Book of Ezra, the people were not in good spiritual condition during the reign of Artaxerxes (464–424). Of course both Ezra and Nehemiah noted the reason for the nation's lowly condition: the people had not been following the Deuteronomic Covenant and therefore were under God's curse rather than under His promise of blessing. The Book of Esther, then, would have been a great encouragement to these struggling Jews. It would have helped them realize that the surrounding peoples which seemed so awesome could never conquer the unique people of God. Israel was protected by God even though a large number of them were outside the land. The Book of Esther would also encourage them to worship the God of Israel, though He is not mentioned by name in it.

**Author and Date.** The book gives no hint of who wrote it. But whoever it was knew the Persian culture well. The account has all the marks of a person who was there for he described the events as an eyewitness. And he was probably a Jew. Some have suggested that Ezra or Nehemiah wrote the account but no specific evidence supports that view. Many critics of the Book of Esther claim that it was written at a much later date because of its language and style, but recent investigations have shown this idea to be unfounded. The document as it stands could have been written sometime between 470 and 465, during the latter years of Xerxes' reign (cf. 10:2-3), or in the reign of his son Artaxerxes (464–424). There is no need to suppose that a well-known person was the author.

**Historicity.** Objections to the historicity of the events in the Book of Esther are usually along three lines:

1. One of the purposes of the Book of Esther (see under "Purpose") is to describe the origin of the religious Feast of Purim. Though scholars debate what the word "Purim" means and what it signifies, the Book of Esther explains that the feast is a celebration of God's miraculous deliverance of His people from Haman. What appeared to be an event of "chance" was, of course, the sovereign intervention of God. Many critics, however, argue that this is too simple an explanation and that the story of the Feast of Purim arose as a folktale. However, no evidence whatever contradicts the Esther account as a reliable explanation of how the Feast of Purim began. It cannot be shown to have derived from another source.

2. Many doubt that the account is historical because they say no outside records mention any of the characters in the book. But outside records do refer to Xerxes; however, they make no reference to a queen named Esther or to Mordecai or Haman. In response, it must be admitted that there is no mention of Esther outside this book. (Mordecai, though, is referred to; cf. comments on 2:5-7.) But the fact that Esther is not mentioned in other sources does not prove that she did not exist. Herodotus and Ctesias recorded that a woman named Amestris was Xerxes' queen. She was the mother of the next ruler, Artaxerxes. However, Herodotus discussed Amestris not in connection with the reign of Xerxes, but with the reign of her son many years later. If Amestris is identified with the biblical woman named Vashti who was deposed in 482 (Artaxerxes was born in 483) and then is not mentioned again until her son assumed the throne in 464, there would be time for Esther to have assumed the throne as queen all the way up to the death of Xerxes or at least till the time when the Book of Esther ends. Even if Vashti were deposed before the book was written, the author might have included that fact because it would have fit the book's purpose. The idea that Esther could not have existed because no extant historical record mentions her by name is an argument from silence. Her existence actually fits nicely into the chronology of the Persian period.

3. Some critics presume that the account of King Xerxes seems improbable. Why would the king pick a new queen in such an irrational manner? In response, it must be repeated that no evidence whatever exists which shows that the biblical account is unreliable. In fact the irrationality of Xerxes and the large harem he acquired in Susa have been referred to in other sources.

Much evidence does support the historicity of the facts in this book. Xerxes was a real king in Persia. His drinking parties were well known. Xerxes did have an irrational temper, occasionally exhibiting fits of rage (1:12; 7:10). He did have a palace in Susa and a large harem there. Various features of the court can also be substantiated from other sources.

**Purpose.** As noted earlier, the Book of Esther was written to encourage the returned Jewish exiles by reminding them of the faithfulness of God who would keep His promises to the nation. The author was describing God's unfailing preservation of His people (even "disobedient people" such as Esther and Mordecai—those not back in the land). The author was also explaining how the Feast of Purim began. That feast, each time it was celebrated, would encourage the remnant.

## OUTLINE

## COMMENTARY

### I. Esther Placed in a Position of Prominence (1:1–2:20)

This first major section of the book describes the need for God's deliverance of His people, and the background of that deliverance. Undoubtedly many of the original readers, like readers today, would be helped by knowing the background of the story. The author described in some detail the setting of the Persian banquet and the reasons Esther came into a prominent position. Besides carefully conveying historical facts, the author was also a good narrator.

*A. Vashti deposed by Xerxes (chap. 1)*

1. THE KING'S 187-DAY CELEBRATION (1:1-9)

**1:1.** The account opens with the mention of **Xerxes who ruled over 127 provinces . . . from India to Cush** (cf. 8:9). Xerxes, called Ahasuerus throughout the Hebrew text of Esther (cf. NIV marg.), ruled the Persian Empire for 21 years from 485 to 465 B.C. He is mentioned elsewhere in the Bible only in Ezra 4:6 and Daniel 9:1. The vast extent of his empire has been confirmed by several outside sources which state the size of that empire in similar words (see the map "The Persian Empire" near Ezra 1:1). Judah was one of the provinces over which the king ruled (cf. Neh. 1:2). "India" corresponds to present-day West Pakistan; "Cush" was a term for the upper Nile region which included present-day southern Egypt, all of Sudan, and northern Ethiopia.

**1:2. King Xerxes** had an elaborate palace in Persepolis as well as a winter **citadel** (palace) in **Susa** (cf. Neh. 1:1). Persepolis and Ecbatana (Ezra 6:2) were other major cities in the Persian Empire (see the map "The Persian Empire," near Ezra 1:1). An inscription from the time of Xerxes' son Artaxerxes noted that the palace was destroyed by fire sometime in Artaxerxes' reign. Reference in Esther 1:2 to this citadel has been confirmed by archeological work at Susa. An author from a later period probably would not have known about the palace so it can be inferred that the author of this book was someone who was close to the events chronologically.

**1:3-4. In the third year of his reign** (483 B.C.) Xerxes **gave a banquet** to which he invited **his nobles and officials** as well as **military leaders . . . princes,** and **nobles of the provinces.** Mention of these leaders fits the known fact that the Persian Empire had a large administrative system. Though not stated, this banquet probably corresponds to the great feast Xerxes gave when he was planning to invade Greece. According to Herodotus it took Xerxes four years to get ready for the invasion he launched in 481. (Herodotus' four years would extend from the beginning of Xerxes' reign in 485.) No doubt the **180 days** involved planning sessions in which all the provinces' leaders were being prepared for the war effort, as well as being impressed with Xerxes' **wealth** and **splendor.** The campaign was to be a costly affair.

The Book of Esther says nothing about Xerxes' invasion of Greece, but other sources state that he wanted to avenge his father's defeat at Marathon near Athens. Xerxes' immense fleet defeated the Greeks at Thermopylae but was defeated at the famous Battle of Salamis in 480 B.C. and the Battle of Plataea in 479. He had to retreat home. Esther gained the favor of the king in 479 B.C., the seventh year of his reign (2:16). This would have been after his defeat by Greece. Thus these events recorded in Esther fit the facts known from secular sources.

**1:5-9.** At the end of the 180 days Xerxes gave another **banquet;** this one lasted **seven days** for **people** in **Susa.** Both great and small were invited. The descriptions of the decor of the king's palace **garden** (vv. 6-7) add to the feeling that the writer had firsthand knowledge of the setting and the occasion. Perhaps Mordecai was among the guests at the seven-day banquet. **Linen . . . silver,** and **marble,** and **other costly stones** are known to have been used in Persia, and Persian **couches** (cf. 7:8) **of gold and silver** were referred to by Herodotus. **Blue** and **white** were the royal colors (cf. 8:15). Drinking vessels (**goblets**) of expensive material were a Persian luxury. The feast was livened by the fact that any **guest** could **drink in his own way,** that is, he could drink as much or as little as he desired. In other words the king was liberal with the **wine.** Meanwhile **Queen Vashti** was giving a separate **banquet for the women.** Separate banquets were not unusual in that culture.

2. VASHTI DEPOSED (1:10-22)

**1:10-12.** Xerxes told his **seven eunuchs** (cf. 6:14) **to bring . . . Vashti** into his banquet hall so that **her beauty** could be admired by the male guests. **But** she **refused to come.** One of the eunuchs named here is referred to later (**Harbona** in 7:9). This order was given **on the seventh day,** that is, the last day of the feast which had turned into a drunken party. The mention of "seven eunuchs" serving the king fits the era in which the account took place. It was a well-known practice then for young men who served the **king** to be castrated so they would have no illusions of starting their own dynasties.

Vashti's refusal is not explained by the author. There is no implication that the king wanted her to do anything immoral or to expose herself. Perhaps she simply did not wish to be in mixed company at that time. It has been suggested that if this queen was Amestris, perhaps she refused to go to the banquet because she was pregnant with Artaxerxes, who was born in 483. Regardless of the reason for her refusal, her action was a breach of etiquette. **The king** was used to getting whatever he desired whenever he desired it. Therefore her response made him **furious** (cf. 7:7).

**1:13-15. The king** consulted **wise**

men about what he should do. These **seven** men **had special access to the king** and were the ones who knew the **law** well. Herodotus has confirmed the fact that this use of wise men was a feature of ancient Near Eastern courts. Throughout the ancient Near East wise men played important roles in governments (e.g., Daniel's position in the Babylonian and Persian Empires). The crime the **queen** had committed was that she disobeyed a **command** of the king. Obviously **the king** and queen did not share an emotionally intimate relationship. This was true of **Xerxes** and the women in his harem. This is again apparent later when Esther noted to Mordecai that she had not even seen the king for a month and was afraid to ask to see him (4:11).

**1:16-22.** **Memucan,** one of Xerxes' wise men, suggested that he have the **queen** deposed (v. 19) so that other noble **women** (v. 18) of the empire (and in fact **all the women,** v. 20) would not follow Vashti's example and **despise their husbands** (v. 17) and the empire be filled with female **disrespect and** marital **discord** (v. 18). It is difficult to see how this punishment would cause the women of the empire to **respect their husbands** but that was the idea behind the decree. This is partially explained by the fact that the men had been drinking heavily (v. 10). (The words "if it pleases the king" occur nine times in the OT, seven of them in the Book of Es.: Neh. 2:5, 7; Es. 1:19; 3:9; 5:4, 8; 7:3 ["your majesty" is lit., "the king"] 8:5; 9:13.)

The idea **pleased** the **king and his nobles** so an edict was sent throughout the empire in various languages (cf. 3:12), stating **that every man should be ruler over his own household.** A vast relay communications system, something like an ancient pony express, made it possible to spread news throughout the empire quickly (cf. 3:13; 8:10). This bit of information helps set the stage for the rise of Esther.

## B. Esther elevated to queen (2:1-20)

Esther, a Jewess, was placed in a position in which she could help the nation Israel. Her being elevated to queen happened even before Israel needed help. The original readers would realize that this was another instance of God protecting His covenant people.

### 1. SOLUTION PROPOSED FOR A NEW QUEEN (2:1-4)

**2:1-4.** After **the anger** of the king **subsided,** apparently sometime later, he realized that he had been foolish in his actions. Throughout the book it is evident that **the king** was led along by his officials. It appears that he was somewhat provincial in his outlook. Like all men of power he had to rely on others to be his eyes and ears on the outside, and did not always receive the best information.

In this case it was suggested to **the king** that **beautiful young virgins** (unmarried women) be brought to **Susa,** placed under **Hegai** (the **eunuch . . . in charge of the** harem) and given **beauty treatments** (cf. v. 9), and that **the king** be allowed to pick from them a woman to replace **Vashti.** His **personal attendants** (probably "the wise men who understood the laws . . . seven nobles," 1:13-14) had suggested that Vashti be deposed. So now they certainly did not want Xerxes to reinstate her for fear that she would turn against them. The suggestion **appealed to the king and he followed it.** The fact that he had a harem in Susa is known from other sources. New women were constantly being brought into the Persian harem to replace the older women.

### 2. ESTHER TAKEN INTO THE HAREM (2:5-11)

**2:5-7.** **Mordecai** is a Babylonian name taken from the god Marduk. The name *mrdk* is attested in fifth-century Aramaic documents. Mordecai was **a Jew of the tribe of Benjamin.** He had tried to hide the fact that he and his cousin were Jews (vv. 10, 20). Verse 6 may mean that Mordecai was deported by **Nebuchadnezzar** along with **Jehoiachin** (597 B.C.). But this would mean that Mordecai would have been about 115 years old by the time of Xerxes' third year and Esther would have been 80. It is better to understand that **Kish,** Mordecai's great-grandfather, was the one who was carried away in the 597 deportation.

Mordecai's **cousin,** Esther, also a Benjamite, had been raised by him, apparently because her parents died when she was young. Her father was Abihail (v. 15; 9:29). The name **Esther** ("star") is Persian. Her Hebrew name, **Hadassah,** means myrtle. She was beautiful, **lovely** in form and features.

**2:8-11.** **Esther** was taken into Xerxes' harem to await **the king's** choice, along with **many** other young women of the kingdom who were summoned to **Susa.** Esther immediately pleased **Hegai,** the eunuch (cf. v. 3) and as a result was given a favorable position **in the harem.** He saw that she had **beauty treatments** (cf. v. 3) **and special food,** apparently food of a better-than-ordinary quality. Esther was even given **seven maids** to serve her. The wait in the harem was at least 12 months (v. 12) so Esther must have appreciated her favored position.

**Esther** kept her Jewish nationality a secret (cf. v. 20), not telling Hegai, her maids, or anyone else **because Mordecai had** told **her** not to. From this and other statements in the book it is clear the author was making the point that God protected and used Esther and Mordecai *in spite of* the fact that they were not living according to the Law commanded by God to the people of Israel. By Law Esther was not to marry a pagan (Deut. 7:1-4) or have sexual relations with a man who was not her husband (Ex. 20:14), and yet this was the purpose of her being included in the harem. **Esther** could be contrasted with Daniel who refused to eat the things from the king's table (Dan. 1:5) because the food would include items considered unclean by the Jewish Law. Apparently Esther had no qualms about the food she ate (Es. 2:9). She certainly did not set herself apart as Daniel had done.

3. ESTHER CHOSEN TO BE QUEEN (2:12-20)

**2:12-15.** Esther became extremely popular during her year of preparation for her night with the king. Each girl's **beauty treatments** were designed to enhance her attractiveness. **Myrrh,** a gum from a small tree, gives a fragrant smell.

**Esther** was not in a beauty contest simply to win the king's affections; the women were being prepared to have sexual relations with **the king.** This is suggested by the words **in the evening she would go there and in the morning return.** After that they would be transferred to another harem, under **Shaashgaz,** which consisted of **the concubines.** Most of the women were relegated to living the rest of their lives in the harem of the concubines, many probably never

again seeing **the king.** When **Esther** went to **the king** she followed the instructions of **Hegai** the **eunuch.**

**2:16-20.** Esther **was taken to King Xerxes** in 479 B.C., his **seventh year, the 10th month (Tebeth** was the Babylonian name for December-January). **The king was attracted to Esther** and therefore **made her queen** in place **of Vashti.** Then a big **banquet** was prepared and **he proclaimed a holiday** and gave away many **gifts.** Throughout all this, Esther had still not revealed that she belonged to the Jewish nation (cf. v. 10). Apparently there was a gathering of another harem of **virgins** during the time **Mordecai was . . . at the king's gate** (cf. v. 21; 3:2). His being at the king's gate probably meant that Mordecai held an official position in the empire's judicial system. His position thus helped set the stage for the following events. This fact about Mordecai shows how he could have uncovered an assassination plot and how a feud started that threatened the entire Jewish nation.

## II. The Jews Marked for Extermination (2:21–4:3)

Many have noted that the Book of Esther is a great short story. Like Ruth, another little book in the Bible about a woman, Esther has all the earmarks of great literature, including a conflict, an antagonist, tension, and irony. The antagonist, Haman, is introduced here and his conflict with Mordecai began.

### A. A feud and Haman's hatred of the Jews (2:21–3:6)

1. KING SAVED BY MORDECAI (2:21-23)

**2:21-23.** Again a reference to Mordecai's position **at the king's gate** (cf. v. 19) as a judiciary official points to God's sovereign control over these events. Learning about a plot by **Bigthana and Teresh,** royal guards, **to assassinate** the **king,** Mordecai **told Queen Esther,** who **reported** this **to the king.** She gave **credit to Mordecai** for uncovering the scheme. **The two** men involved in the plot **were hanged on a gallows** (or "post," NIV marg.; cf. 5:14). Rather than being hanged by the neck on a modern-type gallows, the men were probably impaled on a stake or post (cf. Ezra 6:11). This was not an unusual method of execution in the Persian Empire. Darius, Xerxes' father, was known to have once impaled 3,000 men. A record of this assassination attempt was written in **the annals,** the official royal record (cf. Es. 6:1-2).

## 2. HAMAN PROMOTED (3:1-6)

**3:1. Haman** was promoted to the highest position by **Xerxes.** This occurred **after these events** (i.e., after Mordecai saved the king from the assassination and the two men were executed). It is reasonable to suppose that Mordecai expected a reward for his work on behalf of the king. But no reward was given then, possibly because of some bureaucratic bungle. Later this neglect appalled and surprised the king (cf. 6:1-3).

Because Haman was an **Agagite,** some have supposed that he was descended from Agag, king of the Amalekites (1 Sam. 15:8). However, it seems unlikely that a high-ranking Persian official would be related to a west Semite who lived 600 years earlier. Archeologists have uncovered an inscription which indicates that Agag was also the name of a province in the Persian Empire. This probably explains why Haman was called an Agagite.

**3:2-4.** Haman's promotion meant that the other nobles had to kneel **down** to him, that is, they had to pay him special respect. This was not an act of worship, such as that commanded of the three Hebrew young men in Daniel 3:8-15. Since the **officials at the king's gate** had to kneel before **Haman,** the people probably also had to bow before the king himself. **Mordecai** said he would not bow to **Haman** (cf. Es. 5:9) because **he** (Mordecai) **was a Jew.** Probably this persistent (**day after day**) refusal stemmed more from pride than from religious scruples. For several years **Mordecai** had not let Esther tell the king she was a Jewess (2:10, 20), but now Mordecai was using their national heritage as an excuse for not giving honor to a high Persian official.

**3:5-6. Haman . . . enraged** by Mordecai's refusal (cf. 5:9), set out to find **a way to** kill **all . . . the Jews,** not just **Mordecai.** This was an early case of anti-Semitism. In this literary plot, a climax is now reached in the tension. (Later a second climax was reached when Haman was revealed to be the plotter against the Jews; 7:6.) If the Jews were killed

throughout the whole kingdom of Xerxes, this would include those in the land of Palestine. These latter Jews were faithful to the Lord, worshiping in the rebuilt temple and living according to the stipulations of the Law (cf. comments on Ezra 1–6). A massive execution of thousands of Jews would thwart God's program. However, God cannot be thwarted (Job 42:2). He can overturn man's diabolical efforts, sometimes by miraculous acts, and sometimes through seeming acts of happenstance as in the following sequence. God is always working on behalf of His people.

## B. King persuaded by Haman to destroy the Jews (3:7-15)

### 1. LOT CAST BY HAMAN (3:7-9)

**3:7.** The author included a seemingly obscure part of the account by recording that Haman used a *pur,* a Babylonian word for **the lot,** to decide when the Jews should be killed. The original readers of this book would have understood that God was working to protect His people even in the timing of events. As things worked out, the Jews had almost a year in which to prepare themselves for the conflict with their enemies.

A little more than four years had gone by since Esther had become queen, in 478 B.C. (2:16). On the first day of the year, in **Nisan** (April-May) 474 B.C., at the beginning of Xerxes' **12th year,** the *pur* was cast **to select a day and month.** *Pur* is the basis of the name of the Feast of Purim (9:26). Presumably the day selected was when the execution of the Jews was to begin. **Haman,** along with many people in the Persian Empire, was extremely superstitious (cf. 6:13). The Persian religious system stressed fate and chance. Haman was allowing fate, by the casting of the lot, to dictate his move against the Jewish nation. Little did he then realize that the God who created all things and controls all events was in control of that situation, the lot-casting (Prov. 16:33; cf. comments on Acts 1:26). God had already prepared a means of delivering His people from Haman's plot. The month chosen by the lot was **the 12th month** (February-March)—almost a year later. The day, stated later (Es. 3:13), was the 13th of the month (cf. 8:12; 9:1).

**3:8-9. Haman** went in to the **king** to

present his plan. Falsely accusing all Jews of refusing to **obey the king's laws,** he suggested that **the king** would be better off if the Jews, **scattered** throughout the empire, were exterminated. Haman said he himself was willing to bear the costs involved in carrying out this **decree.** Haman must have been a man of immense wealth. As the highest official he undoubtedly had many opportunities to add to his personal fortune. **Ten thousand talents of silver** weighed about 750,000 pounds, an enormous amount worth millions of dollars in present-day currency. That was the staggering sum which Haman was willing to pay. Possibly this huge sum made the king suspicious of Haman. Surely he could not have acquired so much money without being crooked. (Interestingly, however, the king did not make him pay the money; v. 11.) At that time Persia used silver as its monetary standard.

### 2. KING'S PERMISSION GIVEN (3:10-11)

**3:10-11.** Xerxes, as before, was easily influenced by his officials (cf. 1:16-22; 2:2-4). He accepted Haman's advice and acquiesced. By giving his **signet ring** to **Haman,** Xerxes was allowing **the enemy of the Jews,** as Haman was now called, to send out a proclamation to the empire in the king's name. Five times in the Book of Esther, **Haman** is called the Jews' enemy (cf. 7:6; 8:1; 9:10, 24). The signet ring, when impressed on clay, made a special imprint, which, like a signature, represented the king's authority (cf. 3:12; 8:2, 8; Gen. 41:42; Dan 6:17; Hag. 2:23). The king noted that Haman could **do with the people as** he pleased. Little did **the king** realize that his queen, Esther, was a Jewess and would be included in this hideous plan.

### 3. PROCLAMATIONS SENT OUT (3:12-15)

**3:12-15.** **Haman's** proclamation, sent out under **the king's** name to all the **provinces** and in various languages (cf. 1:22), called for the death of **all** Jewish people including **women and little children.** Haman intended to rid the world of God's covenant people. Also the executioners were ordered to confiscate property owned by **Jews.** The day the decree was dispatched was in March 474 B.C. (On the quick dispatching of this edict see comments on 1:22.)

**The edict . . . bewildered** the people in **the city of Susa** (cf. 8:15). Apparently such a decree had never before come from the royal court. Haman's bloodthirstiness, along with Xerxes' seeming indifference to such atrocities, was incredible even to a sophisticated society which was used to cruel behavior. Perhaps other minority populations wondered if they would be the next to be annihilated.

### C. Mordecai mourned (4:1-3)

**4:1-3.** Whatever had been Mordecai's reasons for not bowing to Haman, he was now in great mourning. His feud with Haman, whether legitimate or not, had caused a great crisis for his whole nation. He feared that God's Chosen People would be destroyed and God's program thwarted. He knew the amount of money Haman had agreed to spend on this vast project as he had a copy of the edict (vv. 7-8). Wearing **sackcloth and ashes** and crying publicly signified **mourning** (cf. Gen. 37:34; Jer. 49:3; Dan. 9:3; Joel 1:13; Jonah 3:6). **Mordecai** was identifying himself to the public as one in great distress. Perhaps he was remorseful for having revealed his nationality (Es. 3:4) and thus having endangered the lives of thousands of his people. Everywhere **Jews** heard of the edict, and they had the same response. Certainly many Jewish people must have prayed fervently, though the Book of Esther does not mention it. Meanwhile God was working behind the scenes to deliver His people.

### III. Calamity Averted by Esther (4:4–9:19)

Nothing has been said so far in the Book of Esther to suggest Esther and Mordecai were people of great faith in Yahweh. But here it is revealed that they at least believed that God was concerned for the welfare of His Chosen People. In this climactic section the interworkings of various events reveal God's sovereignty in working on behalf of His own. Though God's name is not mentioned, the abundance of "happenstances" surely point to God's control.

### A. Communications between Esther and Mordecai (4:4-17)

**4:4-8.** The action in this section centers around **Hathach, one of the king's**

eunuchs assigned to Esther. Though Esther had not been in the presence of the king for a month (v. 11), this did not mean that she had fallen from his favor. As his queen she had many luxuries and was waited on by maids and eunuchs, who told her about Mordecai's mourning. She assigned Hathach . . . to find out why Mordecai was carrying on that way in public places. Esther may have been embarrassed about him. Or perhaps she was concerned for his welfare since she sent out new clothes for him to wear so he would not be seen in sackcloth and ashes. Esther's unique position in the harem apparently shut her off from normal lines of communication. She did not seem to be aware of the edict about the execution of the Jews.

In response to Hathach's inquiry to Mordecai in the open square, Mordecai gave him a copy of the edict to show to Esther. He also told Hathach to tell her all the details of how the edict came about and to urge her to go to the king on behalf of her people to beg for their lives. The words "her people" revealed to the eunuch Hathach, if he did not know it before, that Esther was a Jewess. Without some reprieve from the king, Esther and Mordecai and all their people would die.

4:9-11. Esther's response to Mordecai was not encouraging. Persian monarchs (like those in most ancient nations) were protected against unwanted visitors. Esther reminded Mordecai that she could not simply enter the king's inner chambers unannounced or she might be put to death. The king had the power to execute anyone who disturbed him without an appointment. For the king to extend the golden scepter to someone showed that he approved of the visit and that the person was welcome and not in danger of death (cf. 5:2). Since Esther had not been summoned by him for a month she did not know whether his attitude toward her would be favorable.

4:12-14. Mordecai's response to Esther has often been taken as a great confession of faith. Actually, though, Mordecai apparently was expecting help from the Persian monarch. However, Mordecai did believe God in some way would protect His people: deliverance would arise from another place if Esther would not approach Xerxes about the Jews' plight. Though Mordecai is not pictured as a pious man who was righteous in his dealings before God, he at least had a sense of the covenantal relationship between God and Israel. He was aware that the promises to Abraham, Moses, and David would not be fulfilled if the entire nation was wiped out. Therefore he was confident that God would act on their behalf. He hoped that God would work through Esther because of her unique position.

Mordecai reminded Esther that if she did not attempt to avert this terrible calamity she would surely die, even though she was a member of the royal household. Whether Haman's power was great enough to reach to the palace and execute the queen is not stated. Mordecai simply planted the idea in Esther's mind that she would die if she did not act. Therefore death by order of the king for entering into his presence would be no worse than waiting and meeting death at the hands of Haman.

4:15-17. Esther understood the situation well. In concluding her reply to Mordecai she noted, If I perish, I perish. She resolved to carry out the wishes of Mordecai and go to the king even if it meant her death. In this section, as elsewhere in the book, Esther and Mordecai are seen as great patriots on behalf of the Jewish nation, but are not presented as righteous people, like others in the Old Testament who fully trusted the Lord. Nothing is said about Esther praying (though many commentators say that her fasting meant she also prayed). She simply instructed Mordecai to fast. . . . for three days (with the Jews . . . in Susa) as she and her maids would also do.

B. Plot exposed by Esther (chaps. 5–7)

These chapters mark the climax of the book. Here the tables are turned and evil is overcome by good. God's people are preserved through an unlikely set of circumstances. It is obvious to readers who trust the Lord that He was sovereignly at work, accomplishing His purposes. The original readers in postexilic Palestine would also be reminded that God would protect them against anything that might come their way. Even the forgetfulness of a pagan king could be used by God to preserve and protect His people.

### 1. BANQUET PREPARED (5:1-4)

**5:1-4.** After the three days of fasting in which **Esther** participated (cf. 4:16) she was ready to go to **the king** with her request. Actually she went **on the third day** because part of a day was counted as a whole day (cf. comments on Matt. 12:40). Even though she had not been with the king in over a month (Es. 4:11), **he was pleased** that she came (though she had been apprehensive) and **he held out . . . the gold scepter** toward **her** (cf. 4:11; 8:4). He sensed that she had come to request something so he asked her for her **request.** And he even offered to give her whatever she wanted **even up to half the kingdom** (cf. 5:6; 7:2; Mark 6:23). This apparently was an idiom to express the point that **Esther** could request whatever she desired and that her wish would be fulfilled. Esther's request was simple: she asked that Xerxes and **Haman come . . . to a banquet** she had **prepared.**

### 2. SECOND BANQUET PREPARED (5:5-8)

**5:5-8. The banquet** was readied and **Haman** was told to come as **Esther** had requested. It was an unusual honor to be invited to a banquet with the queen, for Persian officials were protective of their wives. When **the king** asked what she wanted and again promised to fulfill her wish (cf. v. 3; 7:2), **Esther replied** that she would tell him the next day at a second **banquet.** Why **Esther** did not relate Haman's plot at the first banquet is not stated. Perhaps **Esther** was afraid to voice her complaint to **the king.** Perhaps she had second thoughts about telling him at all. Or perhaps she sensed that he was not in the right frame of mind for her to tell him on that day. From a literary standpoint, this delay raises the tension level as the story moves to its climax. A person reading Esther for the first time would be in a high state of agitation as the tension increased. Xerxes' response to Esther's suggestion is not given here, but Haman's later boasting (5:12) shows that **the king** was in obvious agreement with the idea.

### 3. HAMAN GLOATED, AND BUILT GALLOWS (5:9-14)

**5:9-14. Haman** was euphoric (**happy and in high spirits**) about his sudden good fortune with **the king** and the queen (v. 12) but, in contrast, he was enraged about **Mordecai, the Jew,** who still refused to bow down to him (cf. 3:2, 5). Haman was so overwrought about Mordecai that he could not enjoy his good position. On this occasion, to relieve himself of his rage and anxiety about **Mordecai,** he gathered his family and **friends** and spent time boasting about the **wealth** he had amassed and the family he had raised (he had 10 **sons;** 9:7-10, 12). As a social braggart (cf. 6:6) he also reminded them of his promotions in rank in the government, capping it off by telling them that on two successive days he was to be the guest of honor at a private **banquet** with only **the king** and **queen** present. However, he admitted that all his money and fame did not satisfy him because of **Mordecai.**

Haman's **wife, Zeresh, and all his friends** were no better than he was. They suggested that Haman **have a gallows built** that would be **75 feet high** and that he **have Mordecai hanged on it** before the banquet so he would have nothing bothering him when he went to the feast. **The gallows** probably was an impaling stake, a common method of execution in the ancient world (cf. comments on 2:23). The purpose in suggesting such a tall stake was so it would be a lesson to all who saw it. The person on the stake would be visible from all directions, since he would be higher than all the trees. This spectacle would solemnly emphasize that Haman was in control (cf. 3:1) and that no one should try to stand in his way.

**Haman** undoubtedly felt that with Mordecai gone there would be no organized opposition from the Jewish camp. He would be freed from his enemy forever. Here the tension in the Haman-Mordecai conflict reached its peak. From this point on it was relieved little by little through circumstances that had already been set in motion. As the events unfold, the reader is reminded of seemingly insignificant or forgotten events that the skillful narrator had previously mentioned but had not highlighted. God was sovereignly at work behind even such a hateful act as building a gallows (cf. Acts 2:23; 4:27-28).

### 4. MORDECAI HONORED BY XERXES (CHAP. 6)

The tension which had been building throughout the account now began to dissipate. Previously understated facts take on new meanings. Almost incredible circumstances point to God's hand guiding the course of events. The entire course of history for the Jewish nation was changed because a pagan king, hundreds of miles from the center of God's activities in Jerusalem, could not sleep. Jewish people all over the Persian Empire, and especially in Palestine itself, were unaware of God's dealings till long after the fact. But read in the light of God's covenants to Abraham, Moses, and David, the readers could well appreciate the sovereign action of God.

**6:1-3.** During the **night** before Esther's second banquet, **Xerxes** was unable to **sleep** (cf. Dan. 6:18). The author had not written why Esther asked for a delay before telling the king her request (Es. 5:7), but the reason was now made clear. God was going to elevate **Mordecai,** to prepare **the king** to react unfavorably to Haman. Because of the king's sleeplessness he asked for some **of the chronicles** (court annals; cf. 2:23) to be **read to him.** Sometimes, as is known by many people with insomnia, reading can help put a person to sleep! Through Xerxes' insomnia God caused him to learn about Mordecai's deed. Of all the texts that could have been selected by the librarian (from the records of Xerxes' 12 years of rule up to that time), the one that contained the account of Mordecai's uncovering the assassination plot (2:21-23) was read to **the king.** Extrabiblical sources confirm that the Persian kings maintained an elaborate recording system (cf. Ezra 6:1-2). Herodotus noted that the king kept especially clear records of those who served him well. Once again God's sovereignty is evident. When Xerxes asked **what honor** Mordecai had been given for saving the king's life (about five years before; cf. Es. 2:16 with 3:7), the king found that he had not been rewarded. Undoubtedly a bureaucratic oversight had occurred. However, if Mordecai had been immediately rewarded for his saving the king there would have been no need for the elaborate plan which would soon be carried out by the king through the mouth of Haman (6:6-10). Once again unusual circumstances worked to preserve God's people.

**6:4-6.** In the morning (cf. 5:14) **Haman . . . entered the** palace **outer court**

to ask that **Mordecai** be hanged. **The king** asked **who** was **in the court** and **Haman** "just happened" to be there. Obviously the tables were being turned. Everything that was meant for evil against the Jews was turning out for good for them. What a comfort this must have been to the original Jewish readers in postexilic Palestine as they observed their tenuous position among the nations. They could rejoice in the fact that God cared about them and that He would continue to preserve them as He had under Xerxes.

When **Haman** was ushered into the king's presence, he must have felt honored. And when **the king asked . . . What should be done for the man the king delights to honor?** the egotistical **Haman** was beside **himself** with joy and enthusiasm. He thought that **the king** was speaking about him.

**6:7-9.** Haman responded to **the king** by mentioning several things that should be done for the person **the king** wished **to honor:** (1) Haman recommended that such a man should have the appearance of royalty, by wearing a kingly **robe** and riding **a royal** steed, one **the king** had already **ridden.** Some have suggested that the Bible is in error when it speaks of a horse wearing **a royal crest . . . on its head.** They think that the man, not the horse, should have worn the crown. However, a relief actually shows a horse with a crown on its head, signifying that it was a royal horse. (2) Haman said that the honored man should be served by one of the **most noble princes.** (3) The princes were to take the man **through the city** on this **horse,** clearing the way before him and pointing out to all who watched that this **man** was honored by **the king** (cf. Gen. 41:42-43). Haman did not need money (cf. Es. 3:9). He craved respect from his peers and from the population at large (cf. 5:11). Even though he was fabulously wealthy and had more power than anyone outside the royal family (3:1), he wanted even more respect from the people of the city. Haman's lust for respect (from Mordecai) is what got him into trouble in the first place (cf. 3:2, 5; 5:9, 13).

**6:10-13.** Haman's ideas apparently appealed to **the king;** he **commanded Haman** to carry them out **for Mordecai the Jew.** This is the first of five times Mordecai is called "the Jew" (cf. 8:7; 9:29, 31; 10:3), apparently to highlight the fact that a Jew, though opposed by **Haman,** was given a prominent position in Susa in the Persian Empire. What a turn of events; what irony for Haman! **Mordecai,** whom he hated, had to be honored by **Haman.** He who wanted respect *from* Mordecai had to give respect *to* Mordecai. Haman had to carry out the king's order even though it embarrassed and angered him greatly. **Afterward** he **rushed home,** had **his head covered in grief,** and **told Zeresh his wife** and **friends** the reversal of his fortunes.

Earlier Mordecai had publicly grieved over his people (4:1); now Haman privately grieved over his own humiliation. When Haman had left his wife in the morning he had been elated. Now the bottom had fallen out from under him. To make matters worse, **his advisers and his wife** all saw nothing but trouble for him in the future. They noted that Mordecai's **Jewish origin** meant that Haman was doomed. Exactly what they meant by that statement is difficult to determine. It is known that in the Persian religions much was made of omens and signs. Fate, chance, and luck were considered important in everyday life. The Book of Esther stands as a polemic against such a fatalistic view of the world. To many who are not of the covenant community, Israel, the world's events appear to be fatalistic and to happen by chance. But those who are the people of God's covenant know that God overrules fate. He moves events and circumstances for His good pleasure. Pagan advisers and the pagan wife of an evil man unknowingly stated the central thrust of this book: neither Haman nor any other human can possibly **stand against** God's Chosen People, the Jewish nation (many of whom were then back in the Promised Land with a rebuilt temple, offering sacrifices to God at Jerusalem).

**6:14.** Now, with his world crashing down around his head, **Haman** was hustled off to Esther's second **banquet,** which once he desired but now dreaded. He may have well wondered what the king would say to him at the banquet.

Haman stands as a prototype of all anti-God activists who oppose God's people. Like authors of many short stories, God led the author of the Book of

Esther to make his historical figures into symbols of much larger proportions. As the regathered nation read this account, they could have looked back over their history and noted other times when men had tried to set aside God's promises to their nation and had failed. They could therefore rest assured that in the future God would do the same. Even though God's people often disobeyed Him, even though they were often not spiritually or even physically where God wanted them to be, deliverance would come. God would so work in history that He would be vindicated and His people delivered.

5. XERXES TOLD OF PLOT, HAMAN HANGED (CHAP. 7)

**7:1-4.** What **Haman** knew about **Esther** is not stated. If he knew of the connection between Mordecai and Esther he may have been even more terrified at the prospect of attending this second banquet given by Esther. This was the fifth banquet mentioned in the Book of Esther: two were given by **the king** (1:3, 5), one by Queen Vashti (1:9), and two by **Queen Esther** (5:4, 8). During the banquet **the king** again asked Esther her **request,** and again he promised that he would grant it to her (cf. 5:3, 6). This time Esther got right to the point and gave her **petition** and **request . . . life** for her and her **people.** It was now clear to Xerxes what her nationality was (cf. 2:10, 20). She explained that all her **people** had been **sold** (i.e., the king was offered a bribe by Haman; cf. 3:9; 4:7) into extinction (cf. 3:13). Showing her subservient position to the king, she added that if they had merely been **sold** into slavery she certainly would not have bothered **the king.** Esther's statement not only shows the unbelievable power of the king, but also the condition to which she was reduced. **Esther** may have been apprehensive, not knowing if the king would grant her request. It was quite possible that he would fly into a rage, as he had done with Vashti (1:12).

**7:5-6.** However, this time **the king** did not become furious. He requested more information about who was doing **such a thing** to **Esther** and her people. Undoubtedly a look of terror was on Haman's face as he realized that he was about to be exposed before the most powerful man on the face of the earth.

Haman must have known that his execution was assured now that "fate" was working against him. **Esther** revealed that **vile Haman** was the **enemy** (cf. 3:10; 8:1; 9:10, 24).

**7:7-8.** *Now* **the king** was filled with **rage** (cf. 1:12 and cf. Haman's anger on two occasions, 3:5; 5:9). The reason why the king left the palace to go outside to his **palace garden** is not given. It has been suggested that he went out to control his anger, but that is unlikely in view of his other behavior. Others have suggested that he was thinking up a way to execute Haman legally, but that is unlikely because any word of the king was law. Others have said that Xerxes was trying to figure out a way to spare Esther and her nation. Whatever the reason, Esther and **Haman** were left together in the banquet hall.

While begging **Esther** to spare **his life**—though he realized **that the king had already decided his fate**—Haman fell **on the couch** (cf. 1:6) on which **Esther was reclining.** Persians (and later Greeks, Romans, and Jews) reclined on couches when they ate. At just that moment (another so-called "happenstance" in the sovereignty of God) **the king** returned and accused **Haman** of assaulting **the queen.** However, Haman was not assaulting her but **was** merely **falling** on her couch. It is highly unlikely that Haman and Esther were alone in that banquet hall. No doubt people who were serving the meal and the guards were also present. The word **they** (7:8) suggests that several people were there. What is meant by their covering **Haman's face** is uncertain. Probably they did this because Haman was now a doomed man, condemned to death.

**7:9-10.** **Harbona, one of the** king's seven **eunuchs** (cf. 1:10), told **the king** about the **gallows** which Haman had built during the previous night to kill **Mordecai** (5:14). Possibly Haman was hated by many people in the city of Susa, especially in government circles. Many might have been glad to see Haman killed. Harbona obviously knew of Haman's plot to kill Mordecai. At the king's orders, **Haman** was taken and **hanged . . . on** his own **gallows** (i.e., impaled; cf. comments on 2:23). The tables had now been turned, but the Jews were still left with a major problem. **The king's** edict to

eradicate them was still in effect. Per a Persian decree there would still be a great slaughter of many innocent people because of the wicked actions of a now-dead man.

### C. Jews delivered, and took revenge (8:1–9:19)

God had sovereignly worked in various circumstances so that the Jews could be delivered. Now it was the Jews' turn. They would have to fight to retain what was theirs. They had to take part actively in their own deliverance. The Jewish people back in the land would also be encouraged to work hard and carry out their responsibilities before God in His sovereign plan.

#### 1. MORDECAI RECEIVED ROYAL POSITION (8:1-2)

**8:1-2.** Apparently **Haman** was considered a criminal, for his property was confiscated. The king's **signet ring,** which had been given **Haman** to authorize the edict against the Jews (3:10), was now given to **Mordecai.** Again the tables turned against Haman, even after his death. For one thing **Mordecai** now had the power that Haman previously had. For another, Haman, who had hoped to confiscate the Jews' property (3:13), now had his own property removed and given to, of all people, **Esther,** who in turn **appointed** Mordecai to oversee it.

#### 2. SECOND PROCLAMATION SENT OUT (8:3-14)

**8:3-6.** Since the edict to exterminate the Jews (3:13) was still in effect, something had to be done. So **Esther** appeared before **the king** a second time without an invitation (cf. 5:1-2). This time **she begged him to put an end to the evil plan** which was in effect because of **Haman. The king** was favorable toward her and once again held out **the gold scepter to** her (cf. 4:11; 5:2).

Esther's request was simple. She wanted a second decree written and sent out which would override the first decree. Again she was willing to be known as a Jewess for she spoke of **my people** and **my family** (cf. 7:3).

**8:7-8.** The **king** noted that **Esther** and **Mordecai** now had the power and resources that previously belonged to **Haman** and therefore they should use that power to their advantage. Though

Haman's decree could not be revoked, a second one could supersede it. Xerxes even gave Mordecai authority to **write** the **decree** any way he wished and to stamp it with **the king's** authority by using his **signet ring** (cf. 3:10, 12; 8:2).

**8:9-14.** The decree Mordecai wrote was **sent** out in **the third month . . . Sivan** (June-July) 474. Since this was a little over two months after Haman's decree (3:12) the Jews had about nine months to prepare themselves for the conflict (up to the 13th day of the 12th month, the date Haman had chosen by lot; cf. 3:7, 13; 9:1). As was the case with the previous decree (cf. 3:12), this one too was dispatched (cf. 1:22; 3:15) by horsemen throughout the whole empire **from India to Cush** (cf. 1:1) and was **written in the** appropriate languages for **each province.** The edict gave **the Jews . . . the right** to **protect themselves** and the right to **annihilate** (cf. 3:13; 7:4) and **plunder** any group that fought against them. **The Jews** could take away the property of **their enemies** as Mordecai had "taken away" the property of Haman.

### 3. JEWS REJOICED (8:15-17)

**8:15-17. Mordecai** wore clothes which told of his royal position—**royal garments . . . a large crown,** and a **purple** linen **robe. Blue and white** were the Persian royal colors (cf. 1:6). He now held the position and status Haman had held (3:1). Previously under Haman's edict the city of Susa had been "bewildered" (3:15). Now under the edict of Mordecai **the city of Susa held a joyous celebration.** And obviously **the Jews** were elated. Their rise to power caused **many** Gentiles to become Jewish proselytes. God's good hand was then becoming obvious to the world at large. No longer were these events being viewed simply as happenstance; now people were beginning to realize that the God of **the Jews** was protecting them.

### 4. JEWS TOOK REVENGE (9:1-19)

**9:1-4.** When the appointed **day** of the battle came, **the tables were turned** on **the enemies of the Jews.** As **the Jews assembled** in various **cities** to face their attackers, the Gentiles became **afraid of them.** In fact even the government authorities **helped the Jews.** The people who attacked the Jews may have seen

this as an opportunity to get rich at someone else's expense. However, since they had no backing from others they were in a cause which they could not win.

Only by God's sovereign intervention was **Mordecai** now in a position of authority. **He became more . . . powerful** and enjoyed a good **reputation.**

**9:5-15.** On the day of the battle (13th day of the 12th month, i.e., in March 473) **in the citadel of Susa the Jews killed . . . 500 men** plus Haman's **10 sons.** When **the king** asked **Esther** what she wanted, she requested that **the Jews in Susa** be given one more day to carry out the task of rooting out the ones who were trying to destroy them and that **Haman's 10** slain **sons be hanged on gallows** (i.e., impaled; cf. 2:23; 7:10). On the second day the Jews killed an additional **300 men. The Jews** were not doing this for money, as Haman had hoped to do (cf. 3:13), for three times it is stated that the Jews **did not lay their hands on the plunder** (9:10, 15-16). Many have questioned why the Jews wanted to impale the already dead bodies of Haman's 10 sons. This was not an unusual practice in the ancient Near East. It was a visual warning that others better not commit the same crime as the punished ones.

**9:16-19.** In the outlying **provinces . . .** 75,000 individuals were **killed** by the **Jews** in one day, but there, as well as in Susa, **they did not** take any **plunder** from the victims. Only in Susa did the fighting last for two days. For that reason **Jews in Susa** celebrated **on the 15th** day of the 12th month (after the slaughters on **the 13th and 14th**), whereas Jews in the villages celebrated **on the 14th** (after the slaughter on **the 13th**).

## IV. Feast of Purim Established (9:20-32)

**9:20-22.** The Feast of Purim was not established by the Mosaic Law. It was commanded by **Mordecai** (vv. 20-28) and by Esther (vv. 29-32). The two-day feast was for remembering the goodness of God working through a number of circumstances to protect His people from extinction. Mordecai wrote a proclamation that **the Jews** were to **celebrate** the event **annually** with eating, rejoicing (cf. 8:17), **giving . . . food,** and sharing with **the poor.**

**9:23-32.** The feast was **called Purim**

(v. 26) **because of** Haman's use of **the** *pur* . . . **the lot** to determine the time of the execution (3:7). **The** *pur* became a symbol of God's using circumstances to deliver His own.

**Esther . . . along with Mordecai,** wrote a **second letter** confirming that **the Jews** were to celebrate the feast (9:29-32). Unlike Haman's decree her **words,** sent to the Jews (her "people") throughout the vast empire, were for **good will and assurance.** A copy of her letter was also included in the royal archives (cf. 2:23; 6:1; 10:2).

## V. Greatness of Mordecai Described (chap. 10)

**10:1-3.** The book closes by speaking of **King** Xerxes' power; but more importantly the closing verses extol **Mordecai,** once a hated Jew in the Persian **Empire.** He was promoted by **Xerxes** and revered by **the Jews.** He was their great patriot **because he worked** hard for them **and spoke up** on their behalf to Xerxes. However, it is noteworthy that the Book of Esther nowhere states that Mordecai was a righteous individual or that he was careful to follow the Law. Many have doubted that a Jew could have such a high rank in the Persian Empire. However, it is known that many foreign people were fully assimilated into the mainstream of life in the empire (e.g., Daniel; Dan. 5:29; 6:1-2, 28).

As the original Jewish readers read this account they would have been struck by the way God was sovereignly protecting them, often when they did not even know it. Many things in the Book of Esther happened that were beyond anyone's control except that of God, who oversees history. And the Book of Esther is filled with irony, with ways in which events turned out unexpectedly and in favor of God's people. Queen Vashti, a Persian, was deposed so that Esther, a Jewess, could become queen and save her people. Haman, once exalted, was brought low, and **Mordecai and the Jews,** once hated, were exalted and hon-

ored. A decree that would have wiped out the Jews was overruled by one which led to the destruction of nearly 76,000 enemies of the Jews. No wonder Purim was celebrated yearly with such rejoicing: to help the Jews remember that God is in control and that people should faithfully worship and serve their great God.

# BIBLIOGRAPHY

Baldwin, Joyce G. *Esther.* The Tyndale Old Testament Commentaries. Downers Grove Ill.: InterVarsity Press, 1984.

Berg, Sandra Beth. *The Book of Esther: Motifs, Themes and Structure.* Missoula, Mont.: Scholars Press, 1979.

Cohen, A. "Esther." In *The Five Megilloth.* London: Soncino Press, 1946.

Hess, Margaret. *Esther: Courage in Crisis.* Wheaton, Ill.: Scripture Press Publications, Victor Books, 1980.

Ironside, H.A. *Notes on Ezra, Nehemiah, Esther.* Neptune, N.J.: Loizeaux Brothers, 1972.

Keil, C.F. "Esther." In *Commentary on the Old Testament in Ten Volumes.* Vol. 3. Reprint (25 vols. in 10). Grand Rapids: Wm. B. Eerdmans Publishing Co., 1982.

Knight, G.A.F. *Esther, Song of Songs, Lamentations.* London: SCM Press, 1955.

McGee, J. Vernon. *Esther: The Romance of Providence.* Pasadena, Calif.: Thru the Bible Books, n.d.

Moore, Carey A. *Esther.* The Anchor Bible. Garden City, N.Y.: Doubleday & Co., 1971.

_____. *Studies in the Book of Esther.* New York: KTAV Publishing House, 1982.

Strean, A.W. *The Book of Esther.* The Cambridge Bible for Schools and Colleges. Cambridge: University Press, 1907.

Whitcomb, John C. *Esther: Triumph of God's Sovereignty.* Everyman's Bible Commentary. Chicago: Moody Press, 1979.

# JOB

### Roy B. Zuck

## INTRODUCTION

**Job and the Problem of Suffering.** One of the best-known examples of undeserved suffering is recorded in the Book of Job. In a matter of minutes Job, a prominently wealthy and godly man, lost all his material possessions, all his children, and his health. His wife gave him no support, for she suggested he end his misery by cursing God. Then, adding anguish upon anguish, his friends condemned him rather than consoled him. Furthermore God seemed to be ignoring Job, refusing for a long time to answer him and rise to his cause.

Job's intense suffering was financial, emotional, physical, and spiritual. Everyone was against him including, it seemed, even God, whom he had served faithfully. Yet Job was a spiritually and morally upright man (1:1, 8; 2:3). Could any suffering be *more* undeserved? Should not such a righteous person be blessed, not badgered, by God? The fact that Job, an outstanding citizen and upright person, had so much and then lost so much makes him a supreme example of affliction that defies human explanation.

Many individuals can identify with Job, whose distresses were agonizingly prolonged and so seemingly unfair. Many people wonder why they should undergo affliction, why *they* should experience tragedy, heartache, and adversity. For *anyone*, suffering is hard to comprehend, but especially so when it strikes the undeserving. When pain does not seem to be punishment for wrongdoing, it is puzzling. The Book of Job addresses the mystery of unmerited misery, showing that in adversity God may have other purposes besides retribution for wrongdoing.

This book also addresses the problem of attitudes in affliction. Job's experience demonstrates that a believer, while undergoing intense agony, need not renounce God. Question Him, yes; but not deny Him. Like Job, he may long for an explanation of his experience; but being unable to comprehend the cause of his calamity, he need not curse God. Though Job came close to doing so, he did not actually denounce God as Satan had predicted.

The Book of Job also teaches that to ask why, as Job did (3:11-12, 16, 20), is not wrong. But to demand that God answer why, as Job also did (13:22; 19:7; 31:15), *is* wrong. To insist that God explain one's adversities is inappropriate for it places man above God and challenges God's sovereignty.

**Literary Style.** The Book of Job has been heralded as a masterpiece unequaled in all literature. Thomas Carlyle's often-quoted statement about Job bears repeating: "There is nothing written, I think, in the Bible or out of it, of equal literary merit" ("The Hero as a Prophet," *Our Heroes, Hero-Worship, and the Heroic in History.* Boston: Ginn, 1901, p. 56).

The Book of Job has a unique structure. It is a mixture of prose and poetry, and of monologue and dialogue. The prologue (chaps. 1–2) and the epilogue (42:7-17) are narrative prose; the lengthy material in between is poetry (except the opening verse in each chapter that introduces a new speech, and 32:1-6a). This prose-poetry-prose pattern, though seen in other compositions of the ancient Near East, is unique among the books of the Bible. Another way of viewing the structure of the book is seen in the chart "Parallels in the Structure of the Book of Job."

Irony is used throughout the book; some of the numerous examples are mentioned in the commentary (also see Gregory W. Parsons, "Literary Features of the Book of Job," *Bibliotheca Sacra* 138. July-September 1981:215-8; and Edwin M. Good, *Irony in the Old Testament.* Phil-

## Parallels in the Structure of the Book of Job

- *a.* Opening narrative (chaps. 1–2)
  - *b.* Job's opening soliloquy (chap. 3)
    - *c.* The friends' disputation with Job (chaps. 4–28)
  - *b¹.* Job's closing soliloquy (chaps. 29–31)
    - *c¹.* Elihu's disputation with Job (chaps. 32–37)
    - *c².* God's disputation with Job (38:1–42:6)
- *a¹.* Closing narrative (42:7-17)

adelphia: Westminster Press, 1965, pp. 196-240).

The literary form of the Book of Job is probably a composite of a lawsuit (several legal terms are frequently used by Job, his friends, and God), a controversy dialogue or wisdom disputation, and a lament. Job voiced many laments against himself, God, and his enemies (see the chart "Job's Laments," adapted from Claus Westermann, *The Structure of the Book of Job: A Form-Critical Analysis*).

Job is an outstanding literary production also because of its rich vocabulary. Dozens of words in this book occur nowhere else in the Old Testament.

Five different words are used for lions (4:10-11), six synonyms are used for traps (18:8-10), and six for darkness (3:4-6; 10:21-22). The vocabulary of the Book of Job reveals influences from several languages besides Hebrew, including Akkadian, Arabic, Aramaic, Sumerian, and Ugaritic (cf. R. Laird Harris, "The Book of Job and Its Doctrine of God," *Grace Journal* 13. Fall 1976:10-4).

The book abounds with similes and metaphors, many of them from nature. The book touches on many subjects including astronomy, geography, hunting, mining, travel, weather, zoology, and the terminology of law courts.

No wonder Alfred Tennyson labeled the book "the greatest poem of ancient or modern times" (cited by Victor E. Reichert, *Job*, p. xiii).

**Author.** No one knows who wrote the Book of Job, when it was written, when its events occurred, or where Job lived. These facts, shrouded in mystery, add to the book's appeal and charm.

Suggestions on who may have authored the book include Job himself, Elihu (the fourth friend, who spoke toward the end of the book, chaps. 32–37), Moses, Solomon, Hezekiah, Isaiah, someone after the Babylonian Exile such as Ezra, and an anonymous author 200 years before Christ. Jewish tradition says that Moses wrote the book. Others argue for Solomon as the author because of his interest in poetic literature (e.g., Prov., Ecc., and Song) and a few similarities between Job and Proverbs (e.g., Job 28 and Prov. 8).

The details of the lengthy conversations recorded in the Book of Job give the impression that it was written by an eyewitness. Job would recall as well as other eyewitnesses what was said. In the 140 years he lived after being restored to health, he would have had ample time to compile the work. This view seems more plausible than the view that an author hundreds of years later compiled what had been handed down by oral tradition over many centuries.

In Old Testament times a person sometimes recorded events about himself in the third person. Of course, someone else may have written the last two verses (Job 42:16-17), which tell of Job's age and death. That too was not uncommon (e.g., Deut. 1–33 was written by Moses, but Deut. 34, on Moses' death, was added by someone else).

Some scholars suggest that the Book of Job was compiled over many years by several authors and editors, each of whom added small portions to the initial work. However, numerous features point to a single author (cf., e.g., Marvin H. Pope, *Job*, p. xli), and many cross-references within the book point to its unity.

**Date.** Views on the time when Job lived range all the way from the Patriarchal Age (Abraham, Isaac, and Jacob—ap-

## Job's Laments

| | Self-laments | Laments against God | Laments against "Enemies" |
|---|---|---|---|
| Job's opening soliloquy (chap. 3) | 3:11-19, 24-26 | 3:20-23 | 3:3-10 |
| Job's first speech (chaps. 6–7) | 6:1-12 7:1-10 | 7:12-21 | 6:13-20 |
| Job's second speech (chaps. 9–10) | 9:25-31 | 9:17-23; 10:8-17 | |
| Job's third speech (chaps. 12–14) | 14:1-6, 7-15 | 13:3, 14-16, 23-27 | |
| Job's fourth speech (chaps. 16–17) | 17:4-10 | 16:9-14 | |
| Job's fifth speech (chap. 19) | | 19:7-12 | 19:13-19 |
| Job's sixth speech (chap. 21) | | | |
| Job's seventh speech (chaps. 23–24) | 23:3-12 | | |
| Job's eighth speech (chaps. 26–31) | 29:2-6, 12-20; 30:16-19, 24-31 | 30:20-23 | 30:1-15 |

proximately 2100 to 1900 B.C.) to the sixth century B.C. Several factors point to the time of the patriarchs:

1. Job lived 140 years after his calamities (42:16) so he may have lived to about 210. This corresponds roughly to the length of the patriarchs' lives. Terah, Abraham's father, died at the age of 205; Abraham lived to be 175; Isaac lived 180 years; and Jacob died at the age of 147.

2. Job's wealth was reckoned in livestock (1:3; 42:12), which was also true of Abraham (Gen. 12:16; 13:2), and Jacob (Gen. 30:43; 32:5).

3. The Sabeans and Chaldeans (Job 1:15, 17) were nomads in Abraham's time, but in later years they were not nomadic.

4. The Hebrew word $q^e\acute{s}\hat{\imath}t\hat{a}h$, translated "piece of silver" (42:11), is used elsewhere only twice (Gen. 33:19; Josh. 24:32), both times in reference to Jacob.

5. Job's daughters were heirs of his estate along with their brothers (Job 42:15). This, however, was not possible later under the Mosaic Law if a daughter's brothers were still living (Num. 27:8).

6. Literary works similar in some ways to the Book of Job were written in Egypt and Mesopotamia around the time of the patriarchs.

7. The Book of Job includes no references to the Mosaic institutions (priesthood, laws, tabernacle, special religious days and feasts).

8. The name *šadday* is used of God 31 times in Job (compared with only 17 times elsewhere in the OT) and was a name familiar to the patriarchs (see comments on Gen. 17:1; also cf. Ex. 6:3).

9. Several personal and place names in the book were also associated with the patriarchal period. Examples include (a) Sheba, a grandson of Abraham (Gen. 25:3), and the Sabeans from Sheba (Job 1:15; 6:19); (b) Tema, another grandson of Abraham (Gen. 25:15), and Tema, a location in Arabia (Job 6:19); (c) Eliphaz, a son of Esau (Gen. 36:4), and Eliphaz, one of Job's companions (Job 2:11; these two Eliphazes, however, are not necessarily the same person); (d) Uz, a nephew of Abraham (Gen. 22:21), and Uz, where Job lived (Job 1:1). Though it cannot be stated with certainty, possibly Job lived in Jacob's time or shortly thereafter.

Job was a common West Semitic name in the second millennium B.C. Job was also the name of a 19th-century-B.C. prince in the Egyptian Execration texts. Other occurrences of the name are found in the Tell el-Amarna letters (ca. 1400 B.C.) and in Ugaritic texts.

# OUTLINE

# COMMENTARY

## I. Prologue (chaps. 1–2)

In this prose prologue, Job's spiritual character, his family and possessions, Satan's accusations and attacks on Job, Job's reactions, and the arrival of his friends—all are set before the reader in rapid fashion. By contrast, the pace in the following dialogue (3:1–42:6) is slow. The rapid narrative style in the prologue gets the reader quickly into Job's agonizing confrontations with his friends and God.

### A. Job's character (1:1-5)

#### 1. JOB'S PLACE AND PIETY (1:1)

**1:1.** The location of **the land of Uz,** where Job **lived,** is uncertain. Though often identified with Edom, southeast of the Dead Sea, Uz was distinguished from it in Jeremiah's time, if not before (Jer. 25:20-21). Uz was then a "daughter" of Edom, that is, a possession or neighbor of Edom (Lam. 4:21). Some scholars suggest that Uz was in Bashan, south of Damascus; others say Uz lay east of Edom, in northern Arabia. The customs, vocabulary, and references to geography and natural history relate to northern Arabia. Whatever Uz's location, it was near a desert (Job 1:19), it was fertile for agriculture and livestock-raising (1:3, 14;

42:12), and it was probably outside Palestine.

**Job** was **blameless** ("without moral blemish," or "morally whole") **and upright** ("straight" in the sense of not deviating from God's standards). Also **he feared God,** that is, he was aware of, revered, and submitted to God's majesty. And he **shunned evil,** rejecting the opposite of God's character. That assessment, repeated by God to Satan (1:8; 2:3), shows that Job's friends were totally wrong in accusing him of being a willful sinner.

### 2. JOB'S PROSPERITY (1:2-3)

**1:2-3.** Job had **seven sons,** often considered evidence of divine blessing (cf. Ruth 4:15; 1 Sam. 2:5) **and three daughters.** This family size was common in those times. He was remarkably wealthy. His **7,000 sheep** provided clothing and food. The **3,000 camels** provided transportation and milk. The 1,000 **oxen (500 yoke)** provided food and milk, and the power for plowing. The **500 donkeys** also provided transportation. Such a huge livestock estate required much land and many **servants.**

As **the greatest man among all the people of the East,** Job was the wealthiest of an apparently prosperous group of people in northern Arabia. The "people of the East" are identified with Kedar, in northern Arabia (Jer. 49:28). Job was also unusually wise, for the men of the East were noted for their great wisdom, expressed in proverbs, songs, and stories.

Additional biographical facts about this patriarch are given elsewhere in the Book of Job. He was highly respected (Job 29:7-11), a fair and honest judge (29:7, 12-17), a wise counselor (29:21-24), an honest employer (31:13-15, 38-39), hospitable and generous (31:16-21, 32), and a farmer of crops (31:38-40).

### 3. JOB'S POSTERITY (1:4-5)

**1:4-5.** Each time **his** seven **sons** held a feast (possibly a birthday party) in one of **their homes** along with **their . . . sisters** (cf. v. 13) **Job would** purify (sanctify) them by 10 **burnt** offerings, one **for each** child. He was concerned that they receive forgiveness of any sins committed knowingly or unknowingly. His concern that they might have inwardly **cursed**

God anticipates, ironically, Satan's insinuation that Job would curse God (2:5).

Job was an exemplary person. His sterling qualities made his upcoming adversities, by contrast, all the more severe. No one deserved suffering less than he did, and few if any have suffered more.

### B. Job's calamities (1:6–2:10)

#### 1. JOB'S FIRST TEST (1:6-22)

Job was subjected to two tests, one on his possessions and offspring (vv. 6-22) and one on his health (2:1-10). In each test are two scenes, one in heaven and one on earth. Each scene in heaven includes an accusation by Satan against Job, and each scene on earth includes an assault by Satan against Job and Job's reaction.

#### a. Satan's first accusation (1:6-12)

**1:6-8.** When **the angels** (lit., "sons of God"; unfallen angels are God's "sons" in the sense that they are His creation; cf. 38:7) **came to present** (lit., "stationed") **themselves before** God to report on their activities, **Satan** (lit., "the accuser") was **with them.** He had and still has access to heaven (cf. Rev. 12:10). He said he was **roaming through** and walking **back and forth** on **the earth,** apparently looking for those whom he could accuse and dominate (1 Peter 5:8). Satan's **going** on the earth may also suggest his exercising dominion over it and its people. To walk on land often symbolized dominion over it (cf. Deut. 1:36; 11:24; Josh 1:3; 14:9). Satan, of course, is "the god of this Age" (2 Cor. 4:4; cf. Eph. 2:2) and "the whole world is under the control of the evil one" (1 John 5:19).

The Lord spoke of **Job** by the honorable title **My servant** (cf. Job 2:3; 42:7-8 [three times in v. 8]) and referred to him as a supreme example of piety: **There is no one on earth like him.** Satan had and has dominion over much of the world, but **God** pointed out that Satan could not dominate Job!

**1:9-12.** Satan responded by attacking Job's motives: **Does Job fear God for nothing?** "For nothing" (*ḥinnām*) is rendered "without any reason" in 2:3 (see comments there). Because Satan could not deny God's assessment of Job's godliness, he questioned *why* Job was pious. The accuser suggested that Job was serving God not out of love but only because of what he got from God in return. If Job's rewards were removed, out would go his reverence.

Satan's subtle suggestion that worship is basically selfish hits at the heart of man's relationship to God. The Book of Job does more than raise the question of the suffering of the righteous. It also, through Satan's words, deals with the motives for godly living. Will anyone serve the LORD if he enjoys no personal gain from it? Is worship a coin that buys a heavenly reward? Is piety part of a contract by which to gain wealth and ward off trouble?

Satan suggested that if God removed His protecting **hedge around** Job and removed **everything he** owned, then Job would **curse** God. Job, Satan claimed, would no longer insert his coins of worship if nothing came out of the machine. Job, in other words, was worshiping for selfish reasons. This accusation also attacked the integrity of God, for it suggested that the only way He can get people to worship Him is to promise them wealth. Perhaps this indictment against His character is one of the reasons God let Satan buffet Job. Surely God knew Job's heart, but He used Job as a demonstration to silence **Satan**. In addition, God wanted to deepen Job's spiritual insight.

*b. Satan's first assault (1:13-19)*

**1:13-15.** Satan began his assaults on Job when his 10 children **were feasting** in the eldest **brother's house** (vv. 13, 18; cf. v. 4). The assaults were alternately caused by human and "natural" forces: a Sabean attack (v. 15), "the fire of God" (v. 16), a Chaldean raid (v. 17), a great desert wind (v. 19). God permitted Satan to move both kinds of causes to accomplish his purposes—and to do so in rapid, precise timing. Job, while reeling in shock from the news of one loss, was stunned by another.

**The Sabeans,** who stole the 1,000 **oxen** and 500 **donkeys** and slaughtered **the servants,** may have been from the region of Sheba in southwest Arabia, or from a town called Sheba, near Dedan, in upper Arabia (Gen. 10:7; 25:3).

**1:16-17.** **The fire of God,** which **fell from the sky and burned up the** 7,000 **sheep and the servants,** was probably started by lightning (cf. "the fire of the

LORD" in 1 Kings 18:38).

**The Chaldeans** attacked in companies from **three** sides and stole the 3,000 **camels** and slaughtered **the servants.** At that time the Chaldeans were fierce, marauding inhabitants of Mesopotamia. They possibly came from the north, unlike the Sabeans who had come from the south. Apparently the raids by those two groups were surprise attacks.

**1:18-19.** The **mighty** desert **wind** that **struck the four corners of the house** suggests a tornado or whirling wind, building in momentum as it whipped across the desert. The wind toppled the house, causing it to fall on Job's 10 children.

All Job's livestock had been stolen; all his servants had been murdered (except perhaps four messengers who had **escaped to** report; they were either Job's servants or others who had witnessed the tragedies); and all his children had been killed. In a few minutes, Job had plummeted from wealth and prosperity to grief and pauperism. Would he also plummet from loyalty to God to disloyalty?

*c. Job's response to the first test (1:20-22)*

**1:20-22.** In response to the fierceness of Satan's rapid fourfold assault, **Job . . . tore his robe,** symbolizing inner turmoil and shock (cf. 2:12; Gen. 37:29, 34; 44:13; Jud. 11:35), **and shaved his head** (cf. Isa. 15:2; Jer. 48:37; Ezek. 7:18), depicting the loss of his personal glory. Falling **to the ground,** not in despair, but in obeisance to God, Job worshiped.

Job recognized that his loss resembled his birth and his death: he had been **naked** at birth, and he would be naked at death. Similarly, now he was figuratively naked. The words **naked I will depart** (lit., "return there") suggest that he would return to his mother's womb. But how could that be? Speaking of the womb of one's mother was sometimes a poetic way of referring to the earth (cf. Ps. 139:15; Ecc. 5:15; 12:7). The connection is obvious; for man, formed in the womb, is also made "from dust from the ground" (Gen. 2:7; cf. Gen. 3:19; Job 10:9; 34:15; Ps. 103:14), and the earth, when it yields crops, "living" things, is something like a mother giving birth to a baby.

Recognizing God's sovereign rights **(The LORD gave and the LORD has taken** away), Job **praised** the LORD. It is truly remarkable that **Job** followed adversity with adoration, woe with worship. Unlike so many people, he did not give in to bitterness; he refused to blame **God** for **wrongdoing** (cf. Job 2:10).

Job's amazing response showed Satan was utterly wrong in predicting that Job would curse God. Devotion *is* possible without dollars received in return; people *can* be godly apart from material gain. Job's saintly worship at the moment of extreme loss and intense grief verified God's words about Job's godly character.

### 2. JOB'S SECOND TEST (2:1-10)

#### a. Satan's second accusation (2:1-6)

**2:1-4.** In Satan's second test he again indicted God's words and impugned Job's motives and character (cf. 1:6-8). The Hebrew for **without any reason is** *ḥinnām*, the same word **Satan** had used in 1:9. Though **Satan** accused **Job** of having an ulterior motive in his worship, **God** threw this back at the accuser, saying that Satan had *no* reason to incite God against the patriarch. In this third scene, back in heaven, **Satan** implied that Job was still worshiping God because he had not yet given up his life. **Skin for skin! A man will give all he has**—possessions and children—**for his own life.** "Skin for skin" was a proverbial saying, possibly about bartering or trading animal skins. Satan insinuated that Job had willingly traded the skins (lives) of his own children because in return God had given him his own skin (life). This again implied that Job was selfish.

**2:5-6.** **Satan** suggested that if Job were made to suffer physically, he would **curse** God to His **face** (cf. 1:11) for Job would have no reason for worship. He would see that God was against him. Surprisingly **the LORD** permitted Satan to afflict Job but not to kill him. God knew that Job would not deny Him.

#### b. Satan's second assault (2:7)

**2:7.** The first test involved Job's wealth, children, and nearly all his servants; the second one involved his health. **Satan** immediately caused **Job** to have **painful sores** over all his body.

The two Hebrew words translated "painful sores" were used of the plagues of "festering boils" in Egypt (Ex. 9:8-11; Deut. 28:27) and of Hezekiah's illness

(2 Kings 20:7, "boil"). Some scholars say the disease may have been smallpox; others say it was elephantiasis. It was apparently some skin condition with scabs or scales, such as pemphigus foliaceus (cf. Rupert Hallam, "Pemphigus Foliaceus," in *The British Encyclopaedia of Medical Practice.* 2nd ed. 12 vols. London: Butterworth, 1950-52, 9:490-2).

This disease, as attested by physicians today, matches the symptoms of Job's afflictions—inflamed, ulcerous sores (Job 2:7), itching (v. 8), degenerative changes in facial skin (vv. 7, 12), loss of appetite (3:24), depression (3:24-25), loss of strength (6:11), worms in the boils (7:5), running sores (7:5), difficulty in breathing (9:18), darkness under the eyes (16:16), foul breath (19:17), loss of weight (19:20; 33:21), continual pain (30:17), restlessness (30:27), blackened skin (30:30), peeling skin (30:30), and fever (30:30).

#### c. Job's reaction to the second test (2:8-10)

**2:8. Job . . . sat among the ashes,** on or near a pile of dung ashes and garbage outside the city. Missionaries in primitive cultures have reported that pemphigus foliaceus patients have soothed their sores with ashes. How humiliating for Job! He who had sat at the city gate as a local judge (29:7) was now outside the city with beggars, scraping his itching, running sores with **a piece of broken pottery.**

**2:9-10a.** When Job's **wife** urged **him** to forget his **integrity** (related to the word "blameless" in 1:1), **curse God and** (as a result) **die, he** called her a **foolish** (*nāḇāl*, "spiritually ignorant or nondiscerning") **woman.** Unknown to her, this advice that he curse God was exactly what Satan had twice predicted Job would do (1:11; 2:5). When Job needed comfort from her, he received another terrible blow—evidence of her bitterness toward God. In calm confidence in God's ways Job pointed out that **trouble** (*rā'*, "evil, calamity") as well as **good** comes **from God** (cf. Ecc. 7:14; Lam. 3:38). This contrasts starkly with most peoples' view that trouble means God's very existence is questionable! Later Job affirmed to his friends that he would retain his integrity till death (Job 27:5).

**2:10b.** The affirmation, **In all this, Job did not sin in what he said,** proved wrong Satan's predictions that Job would curse God, and it vindicated God's words (cf. 1:22).

## C. Job's comforters (2:11-13)

**2:11.** Hearing about Job's perils, **three** of his **friends—Eliphaz . . . Bildad,** and **Zophar,** apparently prominent men—**met together** and visited Job. "Eliphaz" is an Edomite name (Gen. 36:4), and as a **Temanite** he was from either Teman in Edom, known for its wisdom (Jer. 49:7; Obad. 8), or Tema in Arabia. "Bildad" is not used elsewhere in the Bible, and **Shuhite** may suggest a relationship to Shuah, Abraham's youngest son by Keturah (Gen. 25:2). The name "Zophar" is used only in Job, and his lineage as a **Naamathite** is unknown, though some have suggested that Naamah, a Canaanite town inherited by Judah (Josh. 15:41), was his hometown. Elihu, was also present though he is not mentioned till later (Job 32).

Eliphaz was probably the eldest of the three, for he is listed first (2:11; 42:9), he spoke first in each of the three rounds of speeches (chaps. 4–5; 15; 22), his speeches were longer and more mature in content, and God addressed him as the representative of the others (42:7).

The purpose of the three comforters was to **sympathize with** Job **and comfort him.** But their speeches soon became anything but comforting!

**2:12-13.** Job was so disfigured by the disease that **they . . . hardly recognized him** (cf. 6:21). Then they expressed their grief and despair in three ways; **they** wept **aloud** (in emotional shock and sorrow), **tore their robes** (in brokenheartedness; cf. 1:20), and threw **dust on their heads** (in deep grief; cf. 1 Sam. 4:12; 2 Sam. 1:2; Neh. 9:1).

Sitting down in silence with him for a week may have been their way of mourning over his deathlike condition, or it may have been an act of sympathy and comfort, or a reaction of horror. Whatever the reason, in the custom of that day they allowed the grieving person to express himself first.

## II. Dialogue (3:1–42:6)

### A. Job's death wish (chap. 3)

The silence of Job and his friends was broken when Job bemoaned that he had ever been born and expressed his longing to die. Perhaps this week of ago-

ny impressed on him his sense of loss and reinforced the relentless pain of his disease. Perhaps too he reflected on the injustice of his condition.

In his sad soliloquy of a death wish, Job did not curse God, as Satan had predicted (1:11; 2:5), nor did Job contemplate suicide. But he did regret his birth (3:1-10), wished he had been born dead (vv. 11-19), and longed to die (vv. 20-26).

1. JOB'S WISH THAT HE HAD NOT BEEN BORN (3:1-10)

**3:1-3.** Job . . . **cursed the day of his birth** (lit., "his day") but interestingly he did not curse God. He wanted his birthday to be wiped from the calendar (cf. v. 6). Job then referred to **the night** which, personified, **said, A boy is born** (lit., "conceived").

In the following verses he elaborated on his day of birth (vv. 4-5), and his night of conception (vv. 6-7a). Then he concluded this poetic unit (vv. 3-10) by mentioning the reason he longed for the removal of his birthday (v. 10).

**3:4-6.** That **day—may it turn to darkness** is an interesting reversal of God's first-day creative act: "Let there be light" (Gen. 1:3). By praying **May God above not care about it** (lit., "seek it or look for it"), Job hoped that God, by not noticing that day, would therefore not notice him.

In Job 3:4-6 Job referred to darkness five times, using four different words. He longed that the day would be (a) "darkness" (ḥōšek, v. 4), and he asked that **darkness** (ḥōšek) **and** (b) **deep shadow** (ṣalmāwet, v. 5, used only in Job; cf. 10:21; 24:17; 28:3; 34:22; 38:17) and (c) **blackness** (kimrîr) would **overwhelm its light** (lit., "terrify it," v. 5). That word for "blackness," used only here in the Old Testament, means the blackness accompanying an eclipse, tornado, or heavy storm clouds. Then Job longed that (d) **thick darkness** would **seize the night** of his conception. The Hebrew word for thick darkness ('ōpel) is used five times in Job (v. 6; 10:22 [twice]; 23:17; 28:3).

**3:7.** Continuing his personification of the night, Job wished that the **night** had been **barren** (lit., "stony"), meaning, of course, that his mother would have been barren (as unproductive as stony ground). Emotional Near Easterners customarily shouted when a boy was born, but Job said, **May no shout of joy be heard in** (lit., "pierce") **it** (the night).

**3:8.** Job's words, **May those who curse days curse that day, those who are ready to rouse Leviathan,** refers to a custom of enchanters who claimed to make a day unfortunate (to curse it) by raising Leviathan (cf. 41:1; Pss. 74:14; 104:26; Isa. 27:1), a seven-headed sea monster of ancient Near Eastern mythology. When aroused, the dragon would cause an eclipse by swallowing the sun or moon. So if the daytime or nighttime luminary were gone, Job's birthday would, in a sense, be missing. Job was not saying he believed in this mythology. He was probably doing nothing more than utilizing for poetic purposes a common notion his hearers would understand. (See comments on the Leviathan in Job 41.)

**3:9-10.** The sufferer's wish that **its** (his conceptual night's) **morning stars** would **become dark** refers to the planets Venus and Mercury, easily seen at dawn because of their brilliance (cf. 38:7). **The first rays of dawn** are literally, "eyelids of the morning," a metaphor in which the morning rays of sunlight coming over the horizon at dawn are likened to the opening eyelids of a person waking up. The same figure is used later (41:18).

By longing for his conceptual night to be shrouded in darkness (3:6), be barren (v. 7), and never to turn to day (v. 9), Job was saying he wished he had never been conceived in his mother's womb. Unfortunately, he said, **the doors** of his mother's **womb** were **not shut;** he was conceived. If her womb had been shut, he would not have seen **trouble** in this life. "Trouble" ('āmāl, "sorrow, labor") is also used in 4:8; 5:6-7; 7:3; 11:16; 15:35; 16:2 (lit., "comforters of trouble").

### 2. JOB'S WISH THAT HE HAD DIED AT BIRTH (3:11-19)

Because Job's desire to blot out his night of conception and the day of his birth could not be fulfilled, he longed to have been stillborn. That, he said, would have been better than his present condition. After cursing his birthday, he subsided into a quieter reflection on the trouble-free condition he would have enjoyed if he had been born dead.

**3:11-12.** A stillbirth or miscarriage (vv. 11-12) would have resulted in rest in death (vv. 13-15). He repeated that same

idea: a stillbirth (v. 16) would have resulted in death (vv. 17-19).

Job asked two questions (vv. 11-12). First he wondered why he could not have died as he **came** out of **the womb.** Job voiced the same complaint again (10:18-19; cf. his death wishes in 3:20-23; 6:8-9; 7:15; 14:13). Having been born dead would have been better than his present existence of turmoil. In the second question, the receiving of the **knees** refers either to his mother's taking him in her lap soon after birth, or to the patriarchs' custom of placing a newborn child on the knees of a paternal ancestor as a symbol that the child was acknowledged as in his line (cf. Gen. 50:23). Had Job's mother not **nursed** him from her **breasts,** he would have died.

**3:13-15.** Death at birth would have been so much better. In death he would have **peace** and **rest** (cf. vv. 17-18), whereas in life he had turmoil. In fact he would be in an enviable position with exalted personalities, including **kings . . . counselors,** and rich **rulers.**

**3:16-19.** Longing to have been a miscarried, **hidden** ("buried") fetus and so be **like an infant who never saw the light of day** (cf. vv. 6-7, 9), Job again referred to the restful condition he could have had in death. **There the wicked,** Job thought, no longer are in **turmoil** ("agitation, raging"; the same Heb. word rōgez is used in v. 26; 14:1, "trouble"; and 37:2, "roar") in their restless sin and rebellion; **the weary . . . rest;** prisoners are at **ease** (no longer hearing their taskmasters shouting at them to work harder); **the small and the great are** together; **and the slave is freed.** Job, weary with agony, would rest at death; he would no longer be a captive to his disease; he would be free from his slavery to trouble. This picturesque language expresses the experience of rest which a dead person seemingly has, in contrast with the restless condition of the living, who suffer. All who suffer intensely as Job did can appreciate his longing for release through death.

### 3. JOB'S WISH THAT HE COULD DIE THEN (3:20-26)

**3:20-22.** For the fourth of five times in this soliloquy, Job asked, "Why?" (cf. vv. 11-12, 16, 23; also cf. 7:20; 13:24) Since he had been conceived and born, and since he was not a stillbirth, he longed to die then as an adult. That would end his suffering. And yet death did not come. Referring once again to the subject of light and darkness as indicative of life and death (cf. 3:3-9; Ecc. 11:7-8; 12:2), he asked, **Why is light given to those in misery, and life** (cf. Job 3:23) **to the bitter of soul?** To Job it seemed incongruous that people like himself who are physically miserable and inwardly bitter are "given" life (cf. v. 23) when they really don't want it. The Hebrew word for "misery" is related to the noun for "trouble" (v. 10). Neither those who wait quietly (**long for death**) nor those who **search for it** find it. **Death . . . does not come.** Like buried **treasure,** it is not found. When sufferers finally do **reach the grave,** Job said, they are glad **and rejoice** because death releases them from pain.

**3:23-24.** Job again asked **why** (the fifth "why" in this chapter; cf. vv. 11-12, 16, 20) **life** should be **given** (cf. v. 20) to someone who does not want it. Job's **way** ("path") was **hidden** (cf. "hidden treasure," v. 21) so that he could not see where he was going. In fact Job said **God** had **hedged** him **in.** Here for the first time Job asserted that God was the cause of his affliction. Satan had used the word "hedge" to refer to God's protection of Job (1:10). Now Job used the word to refer to God's restrictions on him. His suffering limited his freedom of movement. Therefore Job was **sighing** rather than eating; his illness had made him lose his appetite. And his groaning was unending **like** the **water** of a waterfall. The word for **groans** is used of the roaring of a lion (4:10; cf. Ps. 32:3).

**3:25-26.** At the beginning of Job's trials, when he heard of the loss of one blessing, he **feared** the loss of another. And hearing of the second one, he feared yet another, and so on. His restless, turbulent condition is summarized in the conclusion of this soliloquy. Though he longed for **peace** with **quietness** and **rest** (cf. vv. 13, 17-18), he experienced **only turmoil** (lit., "agitation"; cf. v. 17).

Job's desire for death, his craving for the grave, emphatically underscores the extremities of his financial, physical, intellectual, emotional, and spiritual pain. Only those godly people who have relished release from life's woes through the gate of death can fully appreciate

Job's mournful wail. Job here voiced not the injustice of his plight but the intensity of it. Later, as his agony wore on, he spoke of its injustice.

## B. The first round of speeches (chaps. 4–14)

After Job broke the week-long silence (2:13) with his outcry of anguish, his three companions—Eliphaz, Bildad, and Zophar (2:11)—felt compelled to speak. Shocked at his death desire, they took on themselves the responsibility of correcting Job for his brash remarks.

Each friend spoke and was in turn answered by Job. The cycle occurs three times, with one variation in the third round: the third friend did not speak a third time.

Throughout their speeches, the friends remained adamant in their theological position. Their view was that the righteous are rewarded and the unrighteous punished (cf., e.g., 4:7-8); so Job, having willfully sinned, was in need of repentance. Their syllogistic reasoning was as follows: (a) all suffering is punishment for sin; (b) Job is suffering; (c) therefore Job is a sinner. But this contradicted what God said of Job (1:1, 8; 2:3).

The friends became more vitriolic and specific as their speeches progressed. In the first round (chaps. 4–14), the three hinted at Job's sin, urging him to repent. "But if it were I, I would appeal to God" (Eliphaz, 5:8); "if you are pure and upright" (Bildad, 8:6); "if you put away the sin that is in your hand" (Zophar, 11:14).

The second round moved from suggestion to insinuation. Eliphaz said that the wicked are endangered (chap. 15), Bildad asserted that they are ensnared and forgotten (chap. 18), and Zophar affirmed that they are short-lived and lose their wealth (chap. 20). They all hoped Job would get the point and know that they were talking about him. Yet in the second cycle they said nothing about repentance.

The third round included open accusation. Eliphaz cited several sins of which he said Job was guilty (22:5-9), and Bildad announced outrightly that man is a worm (25:5-6). Only Eliphaz repeated that Job needed to repent (22:21-23).

And yet in all this, Job affirmed his innocence (6:10; 9:21; 16:17; 27:6) while also arguing that God had afflicted him (6:4; 9:17; 13:27; 16:12; 19:11). How else could Job explain his agony? But why God was doing it was beyond his comprehension (two times in these speeches he asked God "why," 7:20; 13:24; also cf. "why" in his opening soliloquy, 3:11-12, 16, 20, 23).

Job felt that if he could get God to appear in court with him, Job could prove that God was doing him wrong (13:3; 16:21; 19:23; 23:4; 31:35).

### 1. ELIPHAZ'S FIRST SPEECH (CHAPS. 4–5)

#### a. His rebuke of Job (4:1-6)

**4:1-2.** Aware that Job's solo tirade (chap. 3) had been an impatient outburst against his troubles, **Eliphaz,** probably the eldest of the three (cf. comments on 2:11), feared that any words he could speak might be met by Job with a similar or stronger impetuosity. So he asked, **If someone ventures a word with you, will you be impatient?** Eliphaz felt he had to take the risk and speak. He could not let Job get by with such an affront to the Almighty.

**4:3-5.** Eliphaz commended Job for having **instructed . . . strengthened,** and **supported** others emotionally and spiritually by his **words** of counsel. But that compliment contained a rebuke, for Eliphaz suggested that Job was unable to take his own medicine. He had advised others to be patient under trial, **but now trouble** had come to him and he was **discouraged.** In fact calamity struck (the same word Satan used in 1:11 and 2:5) and Job was **dismayed** (lit., "terrified, in panic"; also used in 21:6; 22:10; 23:15-16). Job had been a great encourager, but he could not encourage himself. Eliphaz failed to realize that one who is suffering cannot easily encourage himself; Eliphaz should have been the one to encourage Job!

**4:6.** Eliphaz then asked, **Should not your piety** (related to the word "feared," 1:1) **be your confidence, and your blameless ways** (lit., "the integrity [cf. 'blameless,' 1:1] of your ways," NASB) **your hope?** Perhaps this was a tongue-in-cheek rebuke of Job for his lack of confidence because he was no longer fearing God. Or possibly it was a reminder that because Job had had reverence for God in the past he could also trust Him now. Later, however, Eliphaz questioned Job's

"piety" (reverence, 15:4).

#### b. His reasoning about suffering (4:7-11)

**4:7-9.** Eliphaz then presented his theory on suffering: the **innocent** never perish (cf. "perished," "perishes," and "perish" in vv. 7, 11, 20); the **upright** (cf. 1:1, 8; 2:3) are not **destroyed;** but **those who plow evil and . . . sow trouble** (ʿāmāl; cf. 3:10) will also harvest trouble (cf. Prov. 22:8; Hosea 8:7; 10:13), and the wicked **perish** under God's **anger.** Such a theory, however, simply does not fit all the facts. Many times the innocent *do* suffer (e.g., Luke 13:4-5; John 9:1-3; 1 Peter 2:19-20), and often the wicked seemingly have no problems. This was Job's point throughout the book; Eliphaz's view of an airtight doctrine of retribution does not jibe with reality.

Eliphaz's authority for his theory was what he himself had seen in his lifetime (**as I have observed,** Job 4:8; cf. 5:3; 15:17). Inherent in this authority base, however, is a flaw: his observations, though undoubtedly extensive, were not universal. Bildad's authority was history ("Ask the former generations," 8:8), supposedly a broader base than the observations of one man. Zophar, blunt, discourteous, and dogmatic, merely assumed that what he said was true, without trying to back his statements up with some other authority.

**4:10-11.** Eliphaz added that though **lions** are strong, their **teeth** can be **broken,** they can perish **for lack of** food, and their **cubs** can be **scattered** by a hunter. Similarly, this senior spokesman hinted, Job, who used to be strong (cf. vv. 3-4), was broken and his children lost. **Lions** (five different Heb. words are used for "lion" in vv. 10-11) deserve to suffer because they bring problems to people; so Job also deserved to suffer.

#### c. His report of a vision (4:12-21)

**4:12-16.** Eliphaz sought to add authority to his theological viewpoint by relating his experience as if it had occurred in **dreams.** Though some might challenge his limited observations, who could prove his dreams wrong? **A word was secretly** spoken in **a whisper** (cf. v. 16) to him in his dreams. In his fright his **bones** shook and his **hair . . . stood** straight up. The **spirit** (v. 15), an indistinct **form** (v. 16), must have been unusually disturbing as he saw it pass by, then stop, remain quiet, and whisper.

**4:17-21.** Apparently the words Eliphaz claimed he heard in his dream are given in these verses. For three reasons it is doubtful that the words were a revelation from God: (a) "a word" (v. 12), not "a word of the LORD," came to Eliphaz; (b) the word came "secretly" (i.e., in an elusive manner, v. 12); and (c) the message seemed to picture God as unconcerned about man (vv. 17-21).

**Can a mortal be more righteous than God?** "Mortal" renders 'ĕnôš, "weak, mortal, man"; this word is used 30 times in Job. **Can a man** (geḇer, "strong man") **be more pure than his Maker?** ("Maker" also is used in 9:9; 32:22; 35:10; 36:3; 40:19.) Scholars differ on how to translate the Hebrew word "from" in the literal phrases "from God" and "from his Maker." One rendering makes it comparative (as in the KJV and NIV): "more righteous than God," "more pure than his Maker." Another is suggested by the NASB: "before God," "before his Maker." Either way, Eliphaz implied a negative answer: Man cannot be righteous and clean before God (and certainly not more so than God). God does not **trust . . . His servants** (angels) and **He charges His angels** (i.e., fallen angels and Satan) **with error.** Therefore man certainly cannot be trusted.

Eliphaz pictured people's mortality in several ways: They **live in** mere perishable **houses** made **of clay,** built on **dust;** they are **crushed more** easily **than a moth;** they are **broken to pieces like** a vessel and their **tent** cords are **pulled up.** People perish, dying **unnoticed** and **without wisdom** (to die without ever finding wisdom was the ultimate disaster for someone in the East). These words from the friend-turned-antagonist are a not-so-subtle attack on Job. His houses were not secure; he was scattered (materially) like a moth easily crushed between one's fingers; his life was disrupted and unsettled (like a tent toppling over with no tent cord to hold it up; cf. 5:24; 8:22; 15:34). Job obviously was not a wise person, according to Eliphaz. This dream-report was given to support his theory of suffering: Job was suffering because he was a sinner. What Eliphaz apparently failed to consider is the fact that if all people, being unjust and impure,

suffer, he would be included too!

### d. His recommendation to Job (5:1-16)

**5:1-7.** Eliphaz denied any possibility of angels (**holy ones**) intervening on Job's behalf because the angels cannot be trusted (4:18). Eliphaz interpreted Job's lament (chap. 3) as the **resentment** of **a fool** and as a simpleton's **envy** which would kill, not heal. "Resentment" renders the word ka'aś, which suggests "vexation" (as in NASB) or "provocation to the point of anger or grief." In Job this word is used three other times; 6:2, "anguish"; 10:17, "anger"; and 17:7, "grief." Eliphaz mercilessly spoke of Job as **a fool** who had begun to prosper (**taking root**) but was **suddenly . . . cursed** (cf. 4:9, 19) by God and therefore lost **his children** and **his wealth**—a grim, cruel reminder of Job's calamities. According to Eliphaz, the source of those afflictions was not **the soil** or **the ground**; rather, they came from within man. **Man is born** for **trouble** ('āmāl; probably an allusion to Job's words in 3:10) as certainly **as sparks** from an open fire **fly upward.** "Sparks" is literally "sons of Rešep," perhaps a poetic allusion to the Ugaritic god of lightning, pestilence, and flames.

**5:8-16.** In light of his cause-and-effect view of sin, Eliphaz advised Job to **appeal to God** because He is majestic, powerful (v. 9), and benevolent, sending **rain** for crops (v. 10); He encourages and helps the downcast and sorrowing (v. 11), frustrates **the crafty** (vv. 12-14), and delivers the needy and **the poor** (vv. 15-16). To save **the needy from the sword in their mouth** means to deliver them from slander (cf. v. 21). Though that advice was not wrong in itself, Eliphaz wrongly assumed that Job had sinned deliberately.

### e. His reminder of God's blessings (5:17-27)

**5:17-27.** Eliphaz said Job's problems were disciplinary: **God** was correcting him, so Job should welcome His discipline, **not despise** it. If Job would have the right attitude God would bless him. Though God punishes (**wounds** and **injures**), **He also** restores (**binds up**) and heals. He delivers **from six calamities** and even **seven** (following one number with the next highest expresses thoroughness or emphasizes the final item; cf. Prov. 30:15, 18, 21, 29; Amos 1:3, 6, 9,

11, 13; 2:1, 4, 6). Eliphaz then mentioned **famine,** war, slander, **destruction,** and wild **beasts.** He would have good crops (**a covenant with the stones** means the stones would not hinder his farming); security (regarding the **tent,** cf. Job 4:21; 8:22; 15:34), numerous **descendants,** health, and a long life. Going **to the grave in full vigor like** stacked **sheaves** of grain beautifully pictures a life lived to the full and ready to be ended (cf. 42:17).

Eliphaz smugly concluded his first speech by reminding Job of the authority of his observations (**we have examined** them) and urged Job to heed them.

### 2. JOB'S FIRST REPLY TO ELIPHAZ (CHAPS. 6–7)

*a. Job's defense of his complaining (6:1-7)*

**6:1-3.** The patriarchal sufferer said that the reason he was complaining was that his **anguish** or irritation (*ka'aś*; cf. 5:2, "resentment"; 10:17, "anger"; 17:7, "grief") was heavy. But if his complaining were compared **on the scales** with his **misery,** his misery would be heavier, in fact, heavier than wet **sand.** His **words** (chap. 3), seemingly **impetuous,** were nothing compared with his suffering.

**6:4-7.** God was shooting poisoned **arrows** at him (cf. 7:20; 16:12-13; Lam. 3:12-13). As **a wild donkey** does not bray and **an ox** does not **bellow** when they have food, so Job would not have complained if his situation were more normal.

**Food** tastes better with **salt;** the two go together. And **the white of an egg** needs some flavoring; otherwise Job refused **to touch it.** So Job's trouble and his wailing went together, and his complaining, he said, should be excused.

*b. Job's despair in his suffering (6:8-13)*

**6:8-10.** Job hoped for death; he wanted **God** to **grant** his **request** that he die (voiced in 3:20-23 and also in 7:15; 10:18-19; 14:13). His misery would end if **God would . . . crush** (cf. 4:19) him, **loose His hand** from sustaining Job's life, and **cut** him **off.** The Hebrew verb translated "loose" carries the idea of setting prisoners free (e.g., Ps. 105:20) and the Hebrew verb rendered "cut off" pictures a weaver cutting thread. The one **consolation** and **joy** in Job's pain was that he was innocent of defying God. This is the first of several of Job's affirmations of his innocence (cf. Job 9:21; 16:17; 27:6).

**6:11-13.** Job had no need to **be patient** (cf. 4:2) because he had nothing to **hope** for (cf. 7:6; 14:19; 17:15). His **strength** was gone. Did Eliphaz think that Job had **the strength of stone** or that he was as insensitive as **bronze?** Job's next question (6:13) should be taken as a negative statement, introduced by a strong affirmative particle meaning "indeed." Thus Job stated that he had no **help** in himself and no resources.

*c. Job's disappointment in his friends (6:14-23)*

**6:14-17.** When a **man** is in despair (cf. v. 26) **his friends,** Job felt, ought to be loyal. Job in his pain had not turned from fearing God (cf. **the Almighty** in 5:17), but even if he had, he would still need companionship.

His friends had been like a riverbed. In the rainy season, a wadi is filled with rushing, raging water from **melting snow,** but in the summer when it is most needed it dries up. So his friends, when most needed, disappointed him (cf. v. 21).

**6:18-23.** Travelers in **caravans** from **Tema,** in northern Arabia, and **merchants** from **Sheba,** in southwestern Arabia, both known for their trading, had gotten lost looking **for water** in the riverbeds. So they were **distressed.** Similarly Job was **disappointed,** expecting **help** from his three fellows (**you** is pl.) but getting none. In fact seeing Job's **dreadful** condition (cf. 2:12) they were **afraid.** Perhaps he meant they were afraid of being punished by God if they sympathized too deeply with one who had supposedly offended God. Job had never asked for their help before, but why wouldn't they help him now when he needed their aid?

This expression of disappointment in his friends is the first of several themes Job repeatedly came back to in his speeches (see the chart "Repeated Themes in Job's Responses").

*d. Job's plea to the three (6:24-30)*

**6:24-27.** Having voiced his keen disappointment in his friends' lack of help, Job then pleaded with them to tell him **where** he had gone **wrong.** "Where's the evidence for your idea that I have sinned?" He could benefit from **honest**

## Repeated Themes in Job's Responses

### First round of speeches

| | First speech | Second speech | Third speech |
|---|---|---|---|
| 1. Disappointment in his friends | 6:14-30 | — | 12:1-3; 13:1-12 |
| 2. Declaration of God's greatness | — | 9:1-12 | 12:7-25 |
| 3. Disillusionment with God's ways | 7:11-19 | 9:13–10:17 | 12:4-6 |
| 4. Despair with life (or desire for death) | 6:8-13; 7:1-10 | 10:18-22 | chapter 14 |
| 5. Desire for vindication with God | 7:20-21 | — | 13:13-19 |

### Second round of speeches

| | First speech | Second speech | Third speech |
|---|---|---|---|
| 1. Disappointment in his friends | 16:1-5; 17:3-5 | 19:1-4 | 21:1-6 |
| 2. Declaration of God's greatness | — | 19:28-29 | 21:19-22 |
| 3. Disillusionment with God's ways | 16:6-17 | 19:5-22 | 21:7-18, 23-34 |
| 4. Despair with life (or desire for death) | 17:6-16 | — | — |
| 5. Desire for vindication with God | 16:18–17:2 | 19:23-27 | — |

### Third round of speeches

| | First speech | Second speech |
|---|---|---|
| 1. Disappointment in his friends | — | 26:1-4 |
| 2. Declaration of God's greatness | 23:8-17 | 26:5–27:12; chapter 28 |
| 3. Disillusionment with God's ways | 24:1-17 | — |
| 4. Despair with life (or desire for death) | (24:18-25)* | (27:13-23)*; chapters 29–30 |
| 5. Desire for vindication with God | 23:1-7 | chapter 31 |

*The wicked die.

**words** even though they might be **painful,** but how did *their* words help? Not only were their words of no help; they even treated *his* **words** like **wind.** The three friends seemed as opposed to him as if they were taking undue advantage of an orphan or even selling a **friend!** (**Cast lots for** can be rendered "overwhelm" or it can mean "cause [a net] to fall on.")

**6:28-30.** Perhaps his friends could not bear to look on his disfigured **face,** for Job asked them **to look** at him. He wanted them to note his honesty (**Would I lie?**), and to turn from making **unjust** and false accusations. He was not speaking wickedly, but he could easily **discern** (lit., "taste") **malice** on their part.

*e. Job's pattern of misery (7:1-5)*

**7:1-5.** Job said that **man** (*'ĕnôš,* "weak, mortal man"; cf. comments on 4:17) is like: (a) a soldier (**hard service** translates *ṣābā',* "military service"; cf. 14:14; Isa. 40:2) fulfilling his time of enlistment with its toils; (b) **a hired** hand, destined to hard labor; (c) **a slave** who works in the hot sun and longs for the end of the day; and (d) **a hired** worker **waiting** to be paid. But Job's condition was worse. For he had **months,** not just days, **of futility** (lit., "emptiness"). Instead of being able to rest in the shade at the end of the day, his **nights** were miserable. (**Misery** translates *'āmāl,* "trouble"; cf. Job 3:10; 4:8; 5:6-7.) His nights were long as he tossed and turned in pain. Who could possibly sleep with his **body** covered **with worms** (probably eating his dead flesh) and dirty **scabs**? (lit., "clods of dust") The scabs on his **skin** hardened and cracked; his sores were festered with pus.

*f. Job's prayer to God (7:6-21)*

**7:6-10.** As Job turned to God, he first

spoke of the brevity of life (cf. 9:25-26; 10:20; 14:1-2, 5; 17:1). His life was passing by more rapidly **than a weaver's shuttle** (7:6), it was as short as **a breath** (v. 7), and it was vanishing like **a cloud** (v. 9). His days were ending **without hope** (cf. 6:11; 14:19; 17:11, 15). Job sensed he would **never** again **see happiness** (in contrast with the happiness Eliphaz held out for him, 5:17-26). In fact God would no longer **see** him (cf. 7:17-19, 21; he would be **gone,** in **the grave** never to **return** (cf. v. 21).

**7:11-12.** After asking God to remember the brevity of his life, Job spoke without restraint in bitter complaint to Him. **Am I the sea, or the monster of the deep, that You put me under guard?** Job complained that God was watching and harassing him. This monster was an allusion either to Ugaritic mythology in which the sea god Yam was defeated by Baal or to the Babylonian myth in which Marduk overcame the sea monster Tiamat and set a guard over her. Of course Job was not giving credence to those myths (cf. comments on 3:8), but was using known stories to depict his condition. Like the sea or sea monster dominated and confined by a false god, so Job felt as if he were in a subhuman condition in which the true God was guarding him like a defeated enemy.

**7:13-15.** Job then accused God of frightening him **with dreams** so that he could not even escape from his problems by sleep. Job again expressed his desire to end his misery by **death** (cf. 3:20-23; 6:8-9; 10:18-19; 14:13).

**7:16-19.** Because he **would not live forever** in his present body, Job longed for God to leave him **alone.** Why should God hound, harass, and haunt him when his life was drawing to a close and his **days** had **no meaning** (lit., "were futile," *hebel*; cf. Ecc. 1:2). Job 7:17-18 are similar to Psalm 8:4, except that the words in the psalm express awe at God's concern, whereas Job expressed remorse that he was haunted continually by God— examined **every morning** and tested **every moment.** In frustration, Job felt that God gazed at him (cf. Job. 10:14; 13:27; 31:4) continually and would not **let** him **alone even for an instant** (lit., "until I swallow my saliva!" an idiom still used in Arabic).

**7:20-21.** Job then asked God to tell him how he had **sinned** (earlier he had asked his friends a similar question, 6:24). Why should God, the **Watcher of men,** continue to stare at Job and to hit him like a **target** (cf. 6:4). If Job were a sinner, **why** didn't God **forgive** him and be done with it? (Here again is another "why" question by Job; cf. 3:11-12, 16, 20, 23.) The time would come when God would no longer toy with and tantalize His enemy, Job. Job would **soon** be dead (cf. 7:6-10); so if God wanted to grant him forgiveness, He should do so at once. To **lie down in the dust** meant to be dead (cf. 10:9; 17:16; 20:11; 34:15).

This prayer to God (7:6-21) was a cry of bitter despair. In Job's life, which was quickly passing away, Job thought God was constantly tormenting and terrifying him. Sadly, no relief was in sight.

### 3. BILDAD'S FIRST SPEECH (CHAP. 8)

Bildad accused Job of impugning the justice of God (v. 3) whereas Eliphaz had accused Job of resenting God's discipline (5:17). Both of these self-appointed consultants held the view that a man's calamities are the consequences of his crimes (8:11-13; cf. 4:7-8). Bildad, like Eliphaz, invited Job to repent as the way to recovery (8:5-7; cf. 5:8).

#### a. Bildad's defense of God's justice (8:1-7)

**8:1-2.** Beginning abruptly and bluntly, **Bildad** asked two questions, one pertaining to Job's windy **words** and the other pertaining to God's upright management of the moral universe (v. 3). Accusing Job's words of being **a blustering wind,** Bildad probably was picking up on Job's own reference to wind (6:26). The Hebrew word translated "blustering" is unusual; it means strong and abundant; thus Job's words, to Bildad, were like a forceful, continuous windstorm. Perhaps Bildad also was hinting that Job's rash, wild words were destructive, like the windstorm that killed his 10 children (1:19).

**8:3-4.** Bildad argued that to complain against **God** meant that Job was accusing Him of injustice (cf. comments on *mišpot* in 9:19). Since God never does **pervert** ("distort," used twice in 8:3) **justice,** He certainly would not be punishing Job for nothing. If Job had *not* sinned, then his suffering would mean that God had perverted His ways. And to Bildad that was unthinkable! Obviously, then, Job had sinned.

Anyone who has **sinned against** God suffers the consequences, Bildad said. Job's **children** illustrated that fact. They died because they sinned, and now Job was dying because he sinned. Why else would Job be suffering? Bildad and his cohorts were blinded to other purposes in suffering besides retribution. Surely this cruel, heartless remark hurt Job deeply. After all, he had offered sacrifices to cover his children's sins (1:5).

**8:5-7.** If Job were as **pure and upright** as he claimed to be, all he needed to do was **look to God and plead with** (lit., "implore the grace of") Him (cf. 5:8). "Look" translates *šāḥar* ("to seek or search"), the same word Job had used in 7:2d. Bildad was saying Job should seek God, not expect God to search for him. Such a simple step, Bildad claimed, would result in God's restoring Job to a **place** of blessing that would make his former estate seem like nothing! However, since Job had *already* pleaded with God (7:20-21) and nothing happened, Bildad's counsel was inappropriate.

*b. Bildad's proof from history (8:8-10)*

**8:8-10.** Eliphaz had supported his viewpoints by appealing to his own experiences (4:8). Bildad tried to upstage him by introducing a supposedly greater authority, the observations made by people in past **generations.** Since Job's and his compatriots' knowledge was limited (**we . . . know nothing**) and their lives were short (**shadow** may refer back to Job's words about life's brevity, 7:6-7, 9), they could learn from their ancestors. Their **words** came **from their understanding,** and were not words merely from their mouths, as were Job's words. How could Job dare suggest that the accumulated wisdom of many others was wrong? Bildad believed that if the dead could speak they too would testify that people suffer because of their sin.

*c. Bildad's illustrations from nature (8:11-19)*

**8:11-19.** To depict this cause-and-effect principle, Job's antagonist number two gave three illustrations—two from plant life and one from the insect world. Just as **papyrus** wilts **without** the **water**

of a **marsh** even **more quickly than grass,** so a person who opposes **God . . . the godless** (*ḥānēp*, used eight times in Job, meaning "profane" or "irreligious") will perish. Anything such a person may depend on for hope—such as Job's alleged innocence—is as useless and inadequate as leaning on **a spider's web.**

Job's wasting away, Bildad asserted, might be likened to **a well-watered plant** (with extensive **shoots** above the ground and entwining **roots** below the ground among **rocks** and **stones**) which is then pulled up (**torn**). It is then forgotten (**that place disowns it**) and **other plants grow** in its place. The words **its life withers away** are literally, "this is the joy of its way" (cf. NIV marg.), that is, the only joy such a plant could experience is knowing that something else will replace it. Again, such virulent talk must have only compounded Job's emotional wounds. Certainly Job was not forgetting God, nor was he a godless person (cf. 1:1, 8; 2:3) relying on perishable material things.

*d. Bildad's slim offer of hope (8:20-22)*

**8:20-22.** Once again affirming God's justice (cf. v. 3), Bildad said, **Surely** (cf. v. 19) **God does not reject a blameless** (cf. 1:1, 8; 2:3) person, **or strengthen** the wicked. If Job were blameless (cf. 8:6) he would not be treated this way by God. Job, then, could experience **laughter** and **joy** once again, and any who opposed him would be shamed (ironically Job's friends became his **enemies** and were later shamed; cf. 42:7-9). Besides blessing the blameless, God punishes the unrighteous (cf. 8:4, 13) by removing their **tents** (cf. 4:21), their places of security and protection. Bildad's speech ended with the words, **no more,** the same words with which Job concluded his speech in 7:21.

Bildad's harsh words included another heartless hint at Job's losses. The antagonist's attempt to defend God's justice only intensified Job's frustration about the Lord's apparent injustice. Since the sufferer had not sinned, the counselor's words were wasted.

**4. JOB'S FIRST REPLY TO BILDAD (CHAPS. 9–10)**

How could a man plead with God, the majestic Sovereign? (9:1-13) Job would be overwhelmed by Him if he dared confront Him (9:14-20) because, said Job, God destroys people whether they are innocent or not (9:21-24). Even though Job's case was hopeless (9:25-35), he would speak up anyway (10:1-2) and challenge God for treating His creature cruelly (10:3-17). Job would ask God to give him a little relief before he died (10:18-22).

### a. God's awesome power (9:1-13)

**9:1-13. Job** was aware of what Bildad had said (**I know that this is true**); he knew that the wicked perish (8:13). But that only compounded Job's problem. Why then was *he* suffering?

In Eliphaz's dream, the voice had asked, "Can a mortal (*'ĕnôš*, 'weak, mortal man'; cf. comments on 4:17) be more righteous than (or 'be righteous before') God?" Job responded to that by asking, with almost the same Hebrew words, **how can a mortal** (*'ĕnôš*, "weak, mortal man") **be righteous before God? To dispute with** God (*rîḇ* "bring a court litigation against Him"—one of the many legal terms in the book), as Eliphaz had suggested (5:8), would be impossible. Ironically, though Job did try to subpoena God (cf. 10:2; 13:22; 14:15; 31:35-37), he found that when God finally did speak, Job **could not answer Him!** (cf. 40:3-5)

The reason Job sensed his inadequacy to present his case to God is that God, he said, is awesome in **wisdom** and **power** (cf. 12:13). Again ironically, God displayed those same two attributes when later He spoke to Job (38:1–40:2; 40:6–41:34). It would be too risky to resist God, Job knew. God can move **mountains** (9:5), cause earthquakes (v. 6), and cloud over **the sun** and **stars** (v. 7). (God, not Leviathan, eclipses the sun; cf. 3:8.) He stretched **out the heavens** (9:8; cf. Isa. 40:22) like a tent over the earth, and He **treads on the waves,** that is, His power is evident in sea storms. In His creative power He made the starry **constellations** (Job 9:9). Also He does miraculous works (v. 10, an ironic quotation of Eliphaz's words in 5:9). Furthermore Job cowered under God's invisible nature (9:11; cf. Col. 1:15; 1 Tim. 1:17; Heb. 11:27), irreversible power (Job 9:12), and irresistible **anger** (v. 13; cf. v. 5). The reference to God's passing by (v. 11) may be Job's upstaging of Eliphaz's dream of a spirit passing by his face (4:15). **Even the cohorts of Rahab** (cf. 26:12; Isa. 51:9) submit to God. This refers to the Babylonian

creation myth in which Marduk defeated Tiamat (another name for Rahab, and for Leviathan; cf. Job 7:12) and then captured her helpers. Later Rahab became a nickname for Egypt (Pss. 87:4; 89:10; Isa. 30:7).

Since God in His anger conquers all the forces of evil, both real and mythical, how could Job hope to contend with Him? Job sensed his situation was helpless and hopeless.

### b. God's arbitrary power (9:14-24)

**9:14-20.** Since God is so great (vv. 4-13), Job again wondered **how** (cf. "how" in v. 2) he could possibly plead his cause (**dispute with** is lit., "answer"; cf. "answer" in v. 15) and win. Since he would be speechless in God's presence, all he could hope for from such a **Judge** would be **mercy.** He thought he probably would not even get **a hearing,** that God **would crush** and **overwhelm** him. In both **strength** (cf. vv. 13-19a) and **justice** (cf. vv. 19b-24) God is supreme, thus leaving Job with no hope. ("Justice" translates *mišpoṭ,* a juridical term used frequently in Job and meaning justice or legal equity, 8:3; 9:19; 19:7; 27:2; 31:13; 34:5, 12; 37:23; 40:8, litigation, 9:32; 14:3, legal charges, 22:4, or a court case, 13:3, 18; 23:4.) In fact Job was afraid he would become confused and witness in court against himself (**my mouth would condemn me**; cf. 15:6 and comments on 40:8).

**9:21-24.** For the sake of argument Job had said, "*If* I were innocent" and "blameless" (v. 20). Now he affirmed, **I am blameless** (cf. "blameless" in 1:1, 8; 2:3; 4:6; 8:20; 9:22; 12:4; 22:3; 31:6). Several times Job avowed his innocence (cf. 6:10; 10:7; 16:17; 27:6). But even so, Job concluded, what difference does it make? Whether **blameless** or **wicked,** God would arbitrarily destroy him. Such an indiscriminate action—like **a scourge** bringing **death** to **the innocent,** and **wicked . . . judges** ruling over a nation—enraged Job. Here, for the first of several times, Job accused God of unfairness. As Job viewed life's injustices—his and others—he protested the notion of his contenders that God never perverts justice (4:7; 8:3).

### c. Job's despair (9:25-35)

Job sensed that his case was useless because (a) his days were fleeting (vv. 25-

26), (b) God held him guilty no matter what he did (vv. 27-31), and (c) no one could mediate his case (vv. 32-35).

**9:25-26.** Bemoaning the brevity of life (cf. 7:6-9; 10:20; 14:1-2, 5; 17:1), Job said his days were fleeting like **a runner . . . like boats of papyrus,** the Egyptian speedboats of that day, and **like eagles.** The word for "eagles" is *nešer* (also used in 39:27), a word that may include both eagles and vultures. Perhaps here Job had in mind the peregrine falcon that can speed up to 120 miles per hour as it swoops **down on** its **prey.** These three (runner, boats, and a falcon) depict speed on land, sea, and air.

**9:27-31.** Job's plight was great for even if he tried to **forget** his problem and **smile** (cf. his lack of joy, v. 25), he would still be **guilty** before God. So **why** even try? Even if he were to clean himself up (outwardly as a sign of inward purity) he thought God was so against him that He would toss him into a cesspool!

**9:32-35.** Again the idea of debating his situation **in court** seemed useless (cf. vv. 3, 14). After all, God **is** divine and **not a man.** Furthermore no arbiter could possibly stand above both God and man (who could be greater than God?), listen impartially to both sides (**lay his hand upon us both**), and **remove God's rod** of affliction and **His terror** (cf. 13:21; 18:11). *If* such were possible, Job would confront God fearlessly; **but,** he said in despair, **I cannot.**

### d. Job's desperation (chap. 10)

(1) Job's challenge to God. **10:1-7.** Since no mediator could arbitrate Job's case, he decided to become his own defense attorney. Risk was involved. He was taking his life in his hands (**I loathe my very life;** cf. 9:21). But he would vent his **complaint** in his **bitterness** even if it killed him. Rehearsing his speech, he would give **God** an order (**Do not condemn me;** cf. 9:20; 15:6; and comments on 40:8) and would insist that God list **His charges . . . against** him. In this sudden burst of self-confidence (contrast 9:3, 14, 32), Job said he would confront God with several questions: (1) Does God get some kind of sadistic pleasure out of abusing Job, whom He had made with His very **hands?** (cf. 10:8-12; 14:15) (2) Does God have **eyes** like a man and have to investigate Job? (3) Are God's **days**

short so that He has to **probe after** Job's sins? Surely God is not like that. And yet, knowing of Job's innocence, God still seemed to oppress him.

(2) Job's reminder to God. **10:8-12.** In destroying Job with His hand (cf. v. 7), God was being inconsistent because He had previously created Job in his mother's womb by His **hands.** Like a potter, God had **molded** Job, so why should he so soon be discarded to the **dust** from which he had been made? (cf. 7:21; 34:14-15; Ps. 104:29-30; Ecc. 3:20; 12:7) Job said his intricate embryonic development was like the curdling of **milk** into **cheese,** a process in which he was given **skin and flesh and knit . . . together** (cf. Ps. 139:13, 15) **with bones and sinews.** After giving him **life** (cf. Job 12:10; 27:3; 34:14-15) and watching **over** his **spirit** (cf. 29:2; 36:7), why should God turn against him? Again Job thought God was being inconsistent (cf. 10:3).

(3) Job's blaming of God. **10:13-17.** Maybe, Job opined, God had in **mind** this affliction all along. God was **watching** him (cf. 7:19-20; 13:27; 31:4) ready to chalk up every **offense.** Yet even in his innocence Job had no boldness before God (in contrast with his spurt of confidence recorded in 10:2-7). For God was stalking him **like a lion** (cf. 16:9), ready to pounce on him with His **awesome** strength (cf. 9:4-13) and summon **witnesses against** him. (**Anger** is *ka'aś,* "an angered irritation or resentment"; cf. 5:2; 6:2, "anguish.") Job's innocence, he sensed, meant nothing to God, since the Sovereign was against him, no matter what (cf. 9:15-20).

(4) Job's request to God. **10:18-22.** Once more the complainant asked for death (cf. 3:20-23; 6:8-9; 7:15; 10:18-19; 14:13), wishing he had never been born (cf. 3:17). Had he gone, like a stillborn, directly from **the womb** to the tomb, he would have bypassed all this misery. But since he was about to die (cf. 7:6-9; 9:25-26; 14:1-2, 5; 17:1) he asked God to give him at least a brief reprieve with **a moment's joy** (cf. "joy" in 9:25). Death would be final (**no return**) and gloomy. Four Hebrew words for darkness were amassed to depict the darkness of the grave (**gloom,** *ḥōšek;* cf. 3:4, "darkness"; **deep shadow,** *ṣalmāweṯ;* cf. 3:5; **deepest night,** *'êpâh,* used only here and in Amos 4:13, "darkness"; and **darkness,** *'ōp̄el;* cf.

Job 3:6; 23:17; 28:3). This speech, like some others of Job's ended on a doleful note about death (cf. 3:21-22; 7:21; 14:21-22).

### 5. ZOPHAR'S FIRST SPEECH (CHAP. 11)

Zophar retorted viciously to Job for claiming to be innocent and for accusing God of malpractice in the universe. This third friend hardly lived up to the name "friend"; he was rude, insensitive, and brash.

#### a. His rebuke of Job's words (11:1-6)

**11:1-6.** Zophar was furious because of Job's many **idle** words (vv. 2-3), his mocking of God (v. 3), and his boast that he was blameless (v. 4). In stinging sarcasm, Zophar said he wished **God** *would* answer Job (cf. 9:3, 16) and give him insight into **true wisdom,** which is difficult to penetrate (**has two sides** is lit., "double, folded over"). Zophar said God was letting Job off easy, giving him less punishment than he deserved! This certainly was a heartless jab.

#### b. His praise of God's wisdom (11:7-12)

**11:7-10.** Zophar's laud of God's wisdom may have been a rejoinder to Job's comments about His wisdom (9:4). Zophar pointed out that the Lord's mysterious, plummetless, unknowable wisdom exceeds the height of **the heavens . . . the depths of the grave,** the length of **the earth,** and the breadth of **the sea.** How, then, could Job possibly **oppose** God in **court?** (cf. 10:2)

**11:11-12.** Since God is so wise, Zophar reasoned, certainly He knows the difference between **deceitful** and honest people, though Job did not seem to think so (cf. 9:22). Zophar called Job a nitwit (**a witless man,** lit., "a man who is hollowed out," i.e., empty in the head). The chances of Job's becoming **wise** were no greater than the possibility of **a wild** donkey, considered the most stupid animal, giving birth to **a man**! This was another insensitive barb.

#### c. His plea for Job's repentance (11:13-20)

**11:13-20.** Like Eliphaz and Bildad, Zophar recommended that Job repent (vv. 13-14) and receive restoration. God would **then** remove his **shame** (cf. 10:15) and give him security and confidence. Job would be able to **forget** his **trouble**

('āmāl; cf. comments on 3:10) and he would have joy (11:17; cf. 9:25; 10:20), security, **hope,** and **rest** (11:18). Fear would be gone and people would again look to him for leadership. If Job continued in his wickedness, however, he would die (his **eyes** would **fail**), he would be trapped by his sin (cf. 18:8-10), and his **hope** would die with him.

These first speeches by Job's compatriots offered no comfort. Though their generalities about God's goodness, justice, and wisdom were true, their cruel charge that Job repent of some hidden sin missed the mark. They failed to see that God sometimes has other reasons for human suffering.

### 6. JOB'S FIRST REPLY TO ZOPHAR (CHAPS. 12-14)

The arguments of the committee of three hardly silenced Job. In fact this speech is the longest so far. Job castigated his self-selected jurors and their view of God (12:1–13:19), and again turned to God with his case (13:20–14:22).

#### a. Job's repudiation of his friends (12:1–13:19)

(1) Job's retort to the three (12:1-12). **12:1-3. Job** jeered their alleged wisdom. He sarcastically responded to Zophar's snidely calling him a stupid donkey (11:12) by saying that they thought they were so smart that when they would **die** all **wisdom** would be gone! Though Job was in pain, he could still think. He was **not inferior to** them (a point he repeated in 13:2); in fact what they said about God was only common knowledge.

**12:4-6.** God used to respond to Job's prayers but now, even though he was still **blameless** (cf. 1:1, 8; 2:3; 9:21-22), **God** had let Job **become a laughingstock.** It seemed so unfair, Job observed, for **men at ease** (like the three advisers!) to have such an attitude toward his **misfortune** while **the tents of** the wicked were **secure,** despite what Eliphaz and Bildad had said (4:21; 8:22). To **carry their god in their hands** speaks of those who make and carry idols. Why should idolaters prosper while Job, a man of true piety, suffered?

**12:7-12.** Again Job responded to Zophar's comment about the son of a donkey (11:12) by telling him (**you** in 12:7-8 is sing.) he needed to learn from animals . . . **birds,** even **the earth,** and **fish.** Job said that all of them were smarter than Zophar, knowing that calamities come from God's **hand** (cf. 2:10), not necessarily from one's sin. They also knew that their very **breath** (like that of man; cf. 10:12; 27:3; 34:14-15) comes from God's **hand.** Job said he could see through the friends' faulty arguments just **as** his **tongue** tasted **food** (cf. 6:30). He said he was surprised that the three were not displaying **wisdom** which normally accompanies older people (cf. Elihu's similar words in 32:7). This refuted Bildad's assertion that wisdom comes from age (8:8-10). So in 12:1-12 Job gave responses to all three of his friends.

The word **LORD** (*Yahweh,* v. 9) occurs only here in the poetic discourses. Elsewhere in Job it occurs only in chapters 1–2; 38; 40; 42. Therefore some scholars say this occurrence in 12:9 is a later insertion. However, the name Lord is intentionally conspicuous here by its rare occurrence within the debates. In the Book of Job, this name for God is spoken only by Job (1:21; 12:9). All other instances are in prose narrative portions (in statements such as "The LORD said to Satan," 1:7). In 1:21 Job acknowledged that calamities came from the Lord and in 12:9 he affirmed that same truth.

(2) Job's recounting of God's wisdom and power (12:13-25). **12:13-16.** Job was saying, in effect, "You say God is wise and powerful (5:9-12; 11:7-10), but I know more about that than you do." **God** can reverse the fortunes of leaders and even entire nations. In His **wisdom and power** (cf. 9:4) God can control nature, tearing down what man had built, imprisoning **man** (cf. 37:6-7), and bringing **drought** and flood.

**12:17-21.** Also all people are under God's control. He humbles **counselors** (was Job referring to his three friends?), **judges. . . . kings. . . . priests,** well-**established** officials, **advisers . . . elders. . . . nobles,** and **the mighty.** By stripping away their wisdom and power, God reveals His superior wisdom and power.

**12:22-25.** God in His wisdom can bring to **light** things that are difficult to comprehend (in mental **darkness**), things that leaders (vv. 17-21) are supposed to do. God is sovereign over **nations,** setting them up and putting them down. He can also darken **leaders** by depriving

them **of their reason** and sending them into an intellectual **waste** (the same Heb. word is rendered "formless" in Gen. 1:2), causing them to **grope** and **stagger.**

While one would normally expect leaders to be powerful and elders to be wise (cf. Job 12:12), God sometimes reverses that; for Job's advisers, older than he, were not as wise.

(3) Job's requests to the three (13:1-19). **13:1-4.** Job had **seen** and **heard** what they were saying about God; and he was **not inferior to** them (cf. 12:3; **you** in 13:2, 4-6 in Heb. is pl.). But they were not the ones he wanted to debate. He wanted **to argue** (*yākaḥ,* "dispute, debate in court") his **case with God.** Why waste time arguing with this terrible triad who were smearing the facts **with lies** about his being a sinner and who were **worthless** medical doctors with no prescription to alleviate his pain?

**13:5-12.** Their words, Job complained, revealed their folly; hence their silence would show their **wisdom.** Repeatedly in this chapter he pleaded for their listening, attentive ears, not their ignorant words (cf. vv. 6, 13, 17, 19). He wanted them to **listen** to his **argument** (this Heb. noun is related to the verb "argue" in v. 3) and his **plea** to God. It would do them no good to be deceitful in accusing him of sin, for the impartial **God** would not benefit from their **partiality.** Certainly they could not be God's defense attorneys (**argue the case for** translates *rîb,* a legal term, "to bring a court litigation"). In fact if God scrutinized their lives, they could not possibly **deceive Him. He would . . . rebuke** (from *yākaḥ,* the word for "argue" in v. 3 and related to "argument" in v. 6) them and **terrify** (*bāʿaṯ;* also in 7:14; 9:34; 13:21) them. Later they actually were reproved by God, when He convicted them of the errors of their views (42:7-9).

These men were incompetent to counsel, for their words were **proverbs of ashes,** a fitting description in view of the pile of ashes where Job was sitting (2:8). Their arguments, behind which they hid like fortresses made **of** weak **clay,** failed to help Job.

**13:13-19.** Fearlessly Job was ready to speak out to God and to take the consequences (**let come . . . what may**) even though it meant risking his **life.** The NIV marginal reading, "He will surely slay me," is preferable to the better-known rendering, **Though He slay me.** Anticipating the **jeopardy** (cf. v. 14) involved in his presenting his case to God, he was determined to **defend** (*yākaḥ*; cf. v. 3) his case even though it might kill him! But he was willing to risk it because of the remote possibility that God would exonerate him. Verses 14-16 show that Job was confused in his thinking. Perhaps God would kill him, but maybe not if Job's defense was well delivered. Job's willingness to dare to confront God showed he was not **godless.** Again Job asked these self-hired attorneys, these lawless lawyers, to **listen** to his **case** (cf. vv. 5-6, 13; in vv. 6, 13, 17 in Heb. the verbs and the word **your** are pl.), for his case was **prepared** (*'ārak*, "his arguments were marshaled") and he was certain God would acquit him. Later Elihu used that same verb in telling Job that man cannot marshal or "draw up" arguments against God (37:19). This contrasts with his earlier words of despair that God would *not* acquit him (9:28); his emotions were fluctuating. If **anyone** could possibly **bring charges against** him, only then could he **be silent and die.** His own silence, then, would replace the silence he requested from his protagonists.

### b. Job's presentation of his case to God (13:20-28)

**13:20-28.** Having stated his readiness to present his own self-defense at the risk of God's striking him dead, Job then turned to **God** with his argumentation. But first he requested that God not intimidate him (cf. **terror[s]** in 9:34; 18:11), the defendant, in court. It was only right that he be given a fair trial (cf. 9:16-19). **Then** Job offered to meet God as either defendant or plaintiff. But when he asked God to enumerate his **sins** (cf. 6:24), God did not appear in court. Job asked God why He remained silent and considered Job His **enemy** (cf. 19:11; 33:10). **To torment a . . . leaf** or **chase after . . . chaff** was to molest the worthless, to hit a frail, helpless person who was down. Why, Job wondered, should God conjure up past **sins** of his adolescence and punish him for them? There was no sin at the present that deserved such terrible affliction. Why would God treat him like a prisoner, watching him closely (cf. 7:19-20; 10:14; 31:4) and marking his **feet** so He could trace Job's steps?

After this sudden dash of daring, Job quickly subsided into a feeling of despair, continuing to pine away like a **rotten** moth-eaten **garment.**

### c. Job's despair of hope (chap. 14)

In a sudden shift of mood, Job turned from confidence that he could win his court case against God to a melancholy lament about life's futility and death's certainty.

(1) The brevity of life (14:1-6). **14:1-4.** Man's **few days** are troublesome (the Heb. for **trouble**—the same word *rōgez* rendered "turmoil" in 3:17, 26—means agitation), and brief (cf. 7:6, 9; 9:25-26; 10:20; 14:5; 17:1) **like a** withering **flower** and fading **shadow** (cf. 8:9; Ecc. 6:12), constantly under God's scrutiny (cf. Job 7:20), and basically **impure** (cf. 9:30-31; 25:4).

**14:5-6.** Not only is **man's** life short; his **days** and **months** are **determined** by God, with time **limits** beyond which **he cannot** go. Since man is so hemmed in and his days so ephemeral, the least God could do would be to turn **away from** gazing on man (cf. 7:19; 10:20) and not harass him.

(2) The futility of death (14:7-17). **14:7-12.** When **a tree** is chopped **down it will** spring up **again.** Personifying a tree as if it had a human nose, Job spoke of a tree scenting **water** and then growing. In contrast with the world of botany man has no such hope. When he **dies and is laid low** (*hālaš*, "to be disabled or prostrate"), he is gone. (The Heb. word for **man,** v. 10, is *geber*, "strong man"; cf. v. 14. Even strong men die! **He** in v. 10b is *'ādām*, the generic term for "mankind," and **man** in v. 12 is *'îš*, "male.")

This does not teach annihilation (cf. comments on v. 14). It simply means that a person cannot relive his entire life on earth in the same physical body. Though in the ground, he is not like a tree **stump** which, with its **roots . . . in the soil,** can spring up again. But a person *is* like **water** that evaporates; when it is gone, it cannot be retrieved. Death is final. At this point Job, in his way of seeing things, denied the possibility of physical resurrection. Death, he stated, is not a **sleep** from which people can be awakened. Soon, however, Job wondered if resurrection might be possible (v. 14).

**14:13-14.** Even though a buried corpse cannot normally be revived (some exceptions are recorded in the Bible, of course; cf. 1 Kings 17:17-23; 2 Kings 4:18-37; John 11:43-44; Matt. 27:52-53; 28:5-7), being **in the grave** would be, for Job, a hiding place from God's **anger** (cf. God's anger in Job 16:9; 19:11). Job could endure that **time** if God would limit it and not forget to resurrect him. But is resurrection possible? Pondering that faint possibility—**If a man dies, will he live again?** —Job said he was willing to **wait** out his **hard service**—(ṣābā', "military service," also trans. "hard service" in 7:1; Isa. 40:2) in this life, anticipating his "release" (NIV marg.; the Heb. for **renewal** is used of one group of soldiers relieving another group). Death, with its release from the burdens of this life, would be like an honorary discharge or a changing of the guard. A person continues to exist after death, for he is transferred from one condition to another.

**14:15-17.** Returning to the subject of legal court proceedings, Job affirmed his certainty that God would summon him to court, for He would be longing (cf. 7:21) to see Job, His "handwork" (cf. **hands** in 10:3, 8). Job said that when God spoke, he would **answer** Him. And yet when God *did* speak, Job could not answer even one of His questions (40:4-5). Though counting his **steps** (cf. 31:4) God would no longer record his **sin**, for his **offenses** would be hidden (**sealed up in a bag**). For Job such a prospect was wonderful. But in 14:18-22 he plummeted back into despondency.

(3) The absence of hope (14:18-22). **14:18-20.** Though Job anticipated that *death* would release him from life's woes (v. 14), still he had no hope for reprieve *before* the grave. Like a crumbling **mountain,** like **stones** worn down by **water,** and like **soil** washed **away** by rainstorms, **so the hope** of man ('ĕnôš, "weak, mortal man"; cf. comments on 4:17) wears away. At death God forcibly overcomes him, changes **his countenance** (i.e., a person's face, once flush with life, becomes pallid at death), and sends **him away** from all he knew and possessed in this life.

**14:21-22.** In death a parent cannot see **his sons . . . honored** nor can he sympathize with their problems. In his postdeath life Job thought man's **pain** is

physical (as **his** cold **body,** lit., "flesh," is devoured by worms) and mental (he **mourns** in the sadness of his loneliness and separation). Fittingly Job ended this first bout in a morose tone, for he certainly was in pain and without hope.

## C. The second round of speeches (chaps. 15–21)

In this second duel of desert discourses, Eliphaz, Bildad, and Zophar persisted in their theory that suffering always stems from sin. Here they became more vicious than in the first round. Missing from these speeches is a call to repent. Added is a more hostile, hardened attitude. Underscoring the fate of the wicked, these arguers at the ash pile stressed the dangers facing the wicked (Eliphaz, chap. 15), the traps awaiting the wicked (Bildad, chap. 18), and the short-lived wealth of the wicked (Zophar, chap. 20).

### 1. ELIPHAZ'S SECOND SPEECH (CHAP. 15)

In his first speech Eliphaz approached Job with a degree of decorum and courtesy, but not so this time. Now he lambasted the bereaved, dejected sufferer with the notion that he was a hardened sinner, disrespectful of his elders and defiant toward God.

### a. A reprimand of Job's perverse attitude (15:1-16)

**15:1-3.** Perturbed by Job's irreverent talk (vv. 1-6) and assumed wisdom (vv. 7-16), **Eliphaz** accused the protagonist of **empty notions.** Like **the hot east wind,** the dreaded desert sirocco, Job's **words** blew hard but were useless (cf. 8:2). "Useless" translates sākan ("to benefit or serve," plus the negative particle lō'; cf. 22:2). Job later returned the accusation by calling Eliphaz's spiels windy (16:3).

**15:4-6.** According to Eliphaz, Job (**you** is emphatic in Heb.) hindered the cause of reverence (cf. 6:14) before **God.** Job's words stemmed from **sin** within, and therefore were the basis of his being condemned. Job's present attempt at self-defense (apart from his past sins Eliphaz said Job was guilty of) was sufficient cause for God's prosecuting him. **Your own mouth condemns you** is a response to Job's words in 9:20 ("my mouth would condemn me") and 10:2 ("Do not condemn me"; cf. comments on 40:8).

**15:7-10.** Eliphaz became Job's prosecutor, not his consoler. He lambasted Job for claiming to be the wisest person alive, as if he were the oldest and had some kind of inside track to **God's council** chambers. But Job had only claimed his knowledge was equal, not superior, to theirs (cf. 12:3; 13:2). Eliphaz lashed out that Job knew nothing they did **not know** (cf. 13:2). *They* were **older**—and therefore, they implied, wiser—than Job. To contest their theology was to show disrespect for the elderly, an unthinkable insult in those days.

**15:11-13.** Job ought to be content, Eliphaz felt, with the assurance that God was actually consoling him through Eliphaz. His **consolations** were **spoken** of **gently** by Eliphaz (5:17-27). He said that Job, in his emotional eruptions, became irrational, venting his **rage against God.** Such an attitude, resulting in venomous **words** against man and God, could hardly go unpunished. Eliphaz probably had in mind Job's audacious words in such verses as 6:4; 7:15-20; 10:2-3, 16-17; 13:20-27.

**15:14-16.** No **man** (*'ĕnôš,* "weak, mortal man"; cf. comments on 4:17), **born of woman** (a pickup of Job's phrase in 14:1; cf. 25:4), can **be pure** or **righteous** before **God.** So how could Job claim innocence (9:21; 12:4) when not even angels (**holy ones**) and **the heavens** are pure? This repeats what Eliphaz argued earlier (4:17). Surely *Job* **is vile** (i.e., repulsive) **and corrupt** (sour like milk; cf. Pss. 14:3; 53:3) and guzzles sin as if it were **water.**

*b. A reminder of the fate of the wicked (15:17-35)*

**15:17-20.** To his own observations (**what I have seen;** cf. 4:8) Eliphaz added the authority of the ancients (as Bildad had done; 8:8). The sages of the ages, **wise men** from times before their **land** had become infested with **alien** philosophies (perhaps suggesting that Job's thinking had been thereby corrupted), could inform Job that **the wicked man suffers torment.** "Suffers torment" translates the Hebrew word *ḥôl,* which means "to writhe or whirl." Here in its intensive form it speaks of writhing or tossing about in pain or anxiety (cf. "swirling" in Jer. 23:19 and "in great distress" in Es. 4:4). **Ruthless** means "terror-striking,"

giving the idea that Job was a tyrant who struck fear into other people.

**15:21-26.** Eliphaz enumerated (in vv. 21-35) 17 terrible troubles that befall a sinner. This friend-turned-enemy hoped to force Job to repent of his terrible ways. (1) **Terrifying sounds** are heard by a tyrant who terrifies others (cf. "ruthless," v. 20). Job had certainly heard some terrifying news (1:14-19). (2) **Marauders attack him,** which is exactly what the Sabeans and Chaldeans had done to Job's livestock and servants (1:15, 17; cf. Job's words about marauders in 12:6). (3) **Darkness** (*ḥōšek,* also used by Eliphaz in 15:23, 30; cf. 3:4; 10:21) haunts him, possibly a reference to the darkness of death. (4) **He is marked for the sword,** that is, destined to be a victim of violence, possibly because he himself was violent against others. (5) Without food and desperate, **he wanders** aimlessly, trying to escape his attackers, sensing that any day he might be killed (he would enter **the day of darkness;** cf. vv. 22, 30). (6) **Distress and anguish** hound him **like a king** ready **to attack** (cf. Job's words about **terror** in 9:34; 13:21; also cf. 18:11; 20:25). Job had said God overpowers man (14:20), but Eliphaz pointed out that a person's own anguish, not God, destroys him.

Why such misfortunes? The reason, this verbal pugilist said, is that a sinner is defiant (**shakes his fist**) and arrogant against **God (vaunts himself),** attacking God head-on. This contradicted Job's words that God was attacking *him* (7:20; 13:24; cf. 19:11; 33:10).

**15:27-35.** The first six calamities befalling the wicked (vv. 21-24) are followed by an explanation of the reasons for such punishment (vv. 25-26). Now the order is reversed; Eliphaz first gave a reason (v. 27) for the disasters he then mentioned (vv. 28-35). Self-indulgence (a fattened **face** and bulging midline) was the reason. A chubby person represented self-absorbed luxury and spiritual insensitivity (cf. Ps. 73:7, NIV marg.; Jer. 5:28).

Eliphaz proceeded with his list: (7) The wealthy wicked will come to ruin, forced to live in ghost **towns,** abandoned **houses,** and **crumbling** residences. (8) The transgressor will lose his **wealth,** a cruel recall of Job's privation (Job 1:13-17; cf. 20:12-26). (9) **Darkness** (cf. 15:22-23) overtakes him. (10) Fire will blight his crops. (11) He will vanish, being blown **away** by the hot anger of God's **breath.** (12) A wicked person who trusts in **worthless** possessions will actually gain **nothing.** This supported Eliphaz's contention that Job was trusting in his opulence, an accusation Job later firmly denied (31:24-25). (13) Though gaining nothing materially (15:31), the rebel *will* **be paid** (i.e., he will receive from God the deserved punishment for his sin). (14) Like a **vine** without **grapes,** and a dying **olive tree,** a reprobate dies prematurely, thus losing his hoped-for affluence and security. (15) Nor, said Eliphaz, will **the godless** (cf. 8:12-13) have children. (16) And an unjust person who accepts **bribes,** thereby favoring some and mistreating others, will have his **tents** burned (cf. the burning of Job's possessions by "the fire of God," 1:16; also cf. the trio's references to tents, 4:21; 8:22; 18:15; 20:26). (17) Using the figure of conception and childbirth, he said that wicked people are characterized by **trouble** ('āmāl; cf. comments on 3:10; 16:2), **evil** ('āwen, used before by Eliphaz in 4:8 and 5:6, "hardship"; and later in 22:15), and **deceit.**

By affirming that all these mishaps come to wicked people in this life, Eliphaz did not have all the facts. His attempt to jolt Job into repentance failed.

2. JOB'S SECOND REPLY TO ELIPHAZ (CHAPS. 16–17)

a. *Job's disgust (16:1-5)*

**16:1-5.** What disappointing consolers these so-called friends turned out to be! They told **Job** nothing new (cf. 9:2), and they were **miserable comforters** (lit., "comforters of trouble," 'āmāl, the same word Eliphaz had just used, 15:35). They compounded rather than eased his trouble. Furthermore they babbled with **long-winded speeches** and arguments (cf. "blustering wind," 8:2; and "hot east wind," 15:2), unlike good counselors who console and listen. Apparently Job was surprised that Eliphaz came back at him a second time as if something **ails** him (**you** in 16:4-5 is pl., but in v. 3b it is sing).

If they could change places, Job could fire verbal bullets at them and deride them (to **shake** one's **head** was to mock; cf. 2 Kings 19:21; Ps. 22:7). But he would not do that. Instead he would give

encouragement and **comfort** (as he had done in the past for others; Job 4:4; 29:21-23) in order to provide some **relief** to their problems. He would condole, not condemn.

b. *Job's distress (16:6-17)*

**16:6-8.** Once again Job turned to bemoan his torment at the hands of God. Whether he spoke up or not, his **pain** lingered on. **God** had **worn** him down and weakened him with all his agony; he was distressed because for one thing his offspring and servants (**household**) were killed, and for another he was physically emaciated, as his **gauntness** clearly showed (cf. 17:7).

**16:9-14.** Like a savage beast **God,** in His hostility, Job sensed, attacked him, tore at him **in . . . anger** (cf. 14:13; 19:11), and snarled and glared at him. Besides that, people made fun of him (cf. 30:1, 9-10), struck him, and in their opposition amassed themselves **against** him like soldiers. **God** had left him in the hands of **evil men** and **the wicked,** an obvious contradiction of Eliphaz's hints that Job was wicked (15:12-35).

Job accused God of shattering him (cf. 16:7) and, again like a beast (cf. v. 9), grabbing him **by the neck** and crushing him (cf. 9:17). Besides being like a fierce beast, God was like an archer, using Job for **target** practice (cf. 6:4; 7:20), wounding him, and causing his **gall** to spill out. Job also likened God to **a warrior** attacking him. In all this, Job was again wrong in attributing hostility to God. Yet he could see no other explanation.

**16:15-17.** Because of God's attacks, Job wore **sackcloth** (like burlap) as a symbol of grief (cf. Gen. 37:34; 2 Kings 19:1; Neh. 9:1; Es. 4:1; Lam. 2:10; Dan. 9:3; Joel 1:8, 13), thrust his **brow** (lit., "animal horn"), **in the dust,** the figure of a defeated animal. His tears made his **face . . . red,** and his anguish put **shadows** under his eyelids. Yet Job was **free of violence,** not ruthless as Eliphaz had suggested (15:20), and his praying was from **pure** motives, not selfish ones. So his ordeal was unexplainable. Why should he be in such torment when he was not a terrible person?

c. *Job's desire (16:18–17:5)*

**16:18-21.** Job pleaded with the **earth** that it not **cover** his **blood,** that is, that his injustice be vindicated (cf. Gen. 4:10) and that his cry for justice not be buried and forgotten.

Turning from earth to **heaven** Job was confident that there he had a **witness,** or an **advocate** (*śāhēḏ*, an Aram. word, used only here in the OT), one who is an **intercessor** (*mēlîṣ*, "an interpreter or ambassador"; cf. Job 33:23, "mediator"; Gen. 42:23, "interpreter"; Isa. 43:27, "spokesman"). This **friend,** Job hoped, would plead (*yāḵaḥ*, "argue, debate in court") **with God** on his behalf. Since no mediator could rise *above* both God and man (Job 9:33), Job wanted a spokesman, a kind of heavenly defense attorney who could speak on God's level. Job's companions had not spoken on his behalf, so he needed someone who would.

**16:22–17:2.** Since Job thought his life was drawing to a close (**only a few years. . . . my days are cut short**; cf. 7:6, 9; 9:25-26; 10:20; 14:1-2, 5; 17:11), with death being final (**no return**; cf. 7:9; 10:21; 14:12), he needed an intercessor's help right away. He was depressed (**my spirit is broken**), for all he could see around him with his tear-filled **eyes** (cf. 16:16, 20; 17:7) were his friends (whom he called **mockers!**) with **their hostility.**

**17:3-5.** Though God was against him (cf. 16:7-9, 11-14), only **God** could provide a **pledge** for him in court, a bond given to the defendant as a guarantee that no advantage would be taken against him. To **put up security** is literally, "to strike hands," a practice by which an agreement was ratified (cf. Prov. 6:1; 11:15; 17:18; 22:26). This arrangement with God was necessary since Job's cohorts were mindless of his innocence and even denounced him, hoping to gain some **reward** for supposedly defending God. Such faithless friendship meant that instead of a reward, judgment might come on their **children** in the form of blindness.

### d. Job's dilemma (17:6-16)

**17:6-9.** Job's wish for a court spokesman and for bail from God was followed by another expression of hope and then a note of pathos. People sneered at him, speaking of him in **a byword** (lit., "a proverb"; cf. 30:9), and they spat (cf. 30:10) on his **face,** a most insulting, abhorrent act. So intense was his **grief**

(*ka'aś*, "agitation"; cf. 5:2, "resentment"; 6:2, "anguish"; 10:17, "anger") that even his eyesight was dimmed, possibly by tears (cf. **eyes** in 16:16, 20; 17:2, 5), and he was emaciated (a **shadow;** cf. 16:8).

Anyone who was **upright** and **innocent** would be **appalled at** (cf. 18:20) such outlandish treatment of Job. By this Job implied that his disputants were *not* upright. Even so, he would **hold to** and even grow in his convictions, certain of his **righteous** position before God.

**17:10-16.** Job sarcastically challenged the trio to **try again** to find some wrongdoing in him, but he knew they could not, partly because they were **not . . . wise** (cf. 12:2). His life was fading and his **plans** and **desires** were unfulfilled, even though the friends had held out hope to him (by appealing for his repentance). However, such hope of restoration, saying **light** was coming (cf. Zophar's words in 11:17-18) was unrealistic. Job thought his only **hope** was **the grave** where there is **darkness** (cf. 10:21-22) and **corruption** by **the worm** (cf. 21:26; 24:20) which would be closer to him in the tomb than his dearest relatives. As Job had said three times before (6:11; 7:6; 14:19), he had no **hope** of ever recovering. The hope they held out to him would vanish with him in the grave.

### 3. BILDAD'S SECOND SPEECH (CHAP. 18)

Bildad repeated many themes his senior had spoken (chap. 15; see Roy B. Zuck, *Job,* pp. 81-2 for details). In describing the wicked's fate Bildad emphasized their being trapped (18:8-10). Also he spoke of their experiencing calamity (vv. 11-12); being diseased (v. 13); and losing serenity (v. 11), possessions (vv. 14-16), and fame (vv. 17-18). Such a fate, Bildad implied, awaited Job.

### a. His denunciation of Job (18:1-4)

**18:1-4.** Indignant at Job's insolent words, **Bildad** berated him. Job had expressed surprise that Eliphaz attacked him a second time (16:3), but Bildad wondered when Job would stop talking. The first line of 18:2 is literally, "How long (cf. 'How long' in 8:2) will you hunt for words?" (cf. 18:2, NASB) Later Job came back with the same, "How long?" (19:2) Job had said Bildad and the others were not wise (17:10), but Bildad replied that *Job* was the one who was not **sensible.**

Job had said **stupid** animals had more know-how than his advisers (12:7-9), but Bildad resented such strong language. Job had said God tore at him in His anger (16:9), but Bildad responded that Job was tearing *himself* by *his* **anger.** How could Job expect God to alter reality for *his* sake? Would everything give way to him, as if he were the only man on **earth?** Would God bend His ways just for Job, removing even firm things such as **rocks?** (Cf. Job's words in 14:18 about a rock.)

### b. His description of the fate of the wicked (18:5-21)

**18:5-12.** Bildad, with Job in mind, gave a ruthless account of the misfortunes that come on **the wicked.** His **lamp,** burning in his house and symbolizing life and prosperity (cf. 21:17; Prov. 13:9; 20:20), goes **out,** plunging him into total darkness and confusion. He is **weakened** physically, defeated by his boomeranging **schemes.** In fact dangers await him like **a net** (for catching birds; cf. Prov. 1:17) and **its mesh** (the covering over a pit), a **trap,** a **snare . . . a noose . . . on the ground,** and **a trap . . . in his path.** Here Bildad used six Hebrew words for traps, more synonyms for these objects than in any other Old Testament passage. Whatever Job would do, Bildad affirmed, would ultimately ensnare him. So Job would be terrified wherever he turned (cf. **terror[s]** in Job 9:34; 13:21), with **calamity** and **disaster . . . ready** to pounce on him **when he** fell.

**18:13-21.** Bildad's reference to a sinner's **skin** being eaten **away** obviously alludes to Job's skin problem. Diseases are **death's** children for they serve death; so death's **firstborn** meant the worst of those diseases. **Torn from . . . his tent,** as Job was (cf. "tent[s]" in 4:21; 8:22; 15:34; 21:28), the reprobate is **marched off to the king of terrors,** that is, death. The houses of the wicked are burned and their security is gone. (Bildad's references to **roots** and **branches** recall his comments on botany in 8:11-19; cf. Job's words in 14:8 and Eliphaz's in 15:32.) No one remembers a wicked person who is in **darkness** (cf. 12:25; 15:30; 18:5-6), **banished,** and with no **descendants** to carry on his name, a terrible fate in the Middle East.

Job had said upright people would be appalled at his condition (17:8), but Bildad retorted that people everywhere **are appalled** not so much by the grief of the wicked as by their troubles and horrible end. With a note of finality, Bildad punctuated his point: **An evil man** (*'awāl,* "an unrighteous person," used later by Job three times: 27:7; 29:17; 31:3) will get what is coming to him. Amazingly Bildad insinuated that Job did not even know **God.** Since Job refused to repent, how could he possibly be righteous?

### 4. JOB'S SECOND REPLY TO BILDAD (CHAP. 19)

This chapter records one of Job's lowest points, emotionally and spiritually, and also one of his highest. After bemoaning the animosity of his accusers (vv. 1-6), of God (vv. 7-12), and of his relatives and friends (vv. 13-22), Job rose to a new level of spiritual confidence, certain that he would see God and be vindicated by Him (vv. 23-29).

### a. The animosity of his three friends (19:1-6)

**19:1-6.** Nettled by the trio's wordy assaults, with which they were tormenting, crushing, and reproaching him **10 times** (a Heb. idiom meaning "often"; cf. Gen. 31:7, 41; Num. 14:22; Dan. 1:20), **Job** threw back at Bildad his words, **How long?** (cf. 8:2; 18:2, "When . . . ?") Then Job maintained that **if** he had sinned, it was his problem, not theirs. **If** they were going to act superior to him, they should realize that *he* had not sinned and trapped himself as Bildad had said (18:8-10); *God* had trapped him. He said **God** had **wronged** him, perverting justice in his case (this Heb. word for "wronged" is trans. "pervert" in 8:3). Again Job placed the blame squarely on God (cf. 3:23; 6:4; 7:17-21; 9:13, 22, 31, 34; 10:2-3; 13:24-27; 16:7-14; 17:6). How else could he account for his plight?

### b. The animosity of God (19:7-12)

**19:7-12.** In his outcry (cf. 30:28) against God's violence (**I've been wronged** paraphrases the one Heb. word *hāmās,* "violence"), Job was further frustrated by God's silence (cf. 30:20) and seeming indifference to **justice.** In eight hostile actions, God had flouted Job: (a) **He** obstructed Job's path (cf. 3:23) and (b) darkened it (cf. 12:25); (c) He **removed** Job's **crown** (i.e., his place of esteem in the community; cf. 29:7-11; 30:1, 9-10); (d)

He demolished Job like a building; (e) **He uproooted Job's hope like a tree** (cf. 14:7). Besides all that, (f) God was angry with Job (cf. 14:13; 16:9), (g) considered Job His enemy (cf. 13:24; 33:10; certainly Job was wrong here for Satan, God's chief enemy, was also Job's enemy). Also (h) God assaulted Job like an army building **a siege ramp against** a beleaguered city wall and encamping **around** his **tent.** Bildad had enumerated many disasters encountered by the wicked (18:5-21), but Job responded that such catastrophes had come to *him* from, of all people, God Himself. Why God should buffet one of His own is always one of the most baffling questions a believer faces.

*c. The animosity of his relatives and others (19:13-22)*

**19:13-17.** The sufferer's plaint was also nurtured by loneliness. **Brothers** (perhaps comrades, not blood relatives), **acquaintances. . . . kinsmen . . . friends,** and **guests** abhorred and forsook Job—including even the three men who, though with him physically, abandoned him emotionally. Speaking of his household, Job then listed **maidservants,** his own personal **servant,** and even his **wife** and **brothers** among those who rejected him. His personal attendant refused to respond to him and his wife (this is the only mention of her apart from 2:9-10) stayed away because of his disease-caused halitosis.

**19:18-20.** Youngsters made fun of Job instead of showing the customary respect due to elders (cf. 30:1, 9-10). Job then lumped with the children those who had been his **intimate friends**—probably meaning "Eliphaz and Company"—and **those** he loved. Job lacked even the solace that normally comes from friends and loved ones in times of affliction.

Besides all that, his physical pain did not subside. He continued to lose weight (he was only **skin and bones;** cf. 18:13), and he had barely eluded death (**escaped with only the skin of** his **teeth**). If, as some suggest, "the skin of my teeth" meant his gums (NIV marg.) then he was saying his body was so run down that even his teeth had fallen out and only his gums were unaffected. However, the more common interpretation seems preferable.

**19:21-22.** In a poignant plea Job then begged his **friends,** probably sarcastically, to **pity** him. It was enough for **God** to have **struck** him (on God's **hand;** cf. 1:11; 2:5; 6:9; 12:9; 13:21); **why** did they need to be ruthless too, like animals after his **flesh?**

*d. The certainty of seeing God (19:23-29)*

Just after Job was at his lowest ebb, he rose to his highest peak. Forlorn, wracked by pain, and maligned by both God and people, he then mounted in spirited confidence to a future vindication of his cause. This was a "magnificent burst of faith" (W.B. MacLeod, *The Afflictions of the Righteous.* London: Hodder & Stoughton, n.d., p. 173).

**19:23-24.** Job expressed his desire for a permanent written record of his **words** of innocence and protest, either **on a scroll** or **engraved in rock** in letters filled with **lead.** Then present and future generations could know of his guilelessness.

**19:25.** In his jubilation of faith Job affirmed his certainty that God his **Redeemer lives.** Though Job believed God was against him, he knew that only God could vindicate his innocence. Job would die, but God lives on as his Defender, Protector, or Vindicator (*gōʾēl,* "a person who defended or avenged the cause of another, or who provided protection or legal aid for a close relative who could not do so for himself"; cf. Lev. 25:23-25, 47-55; Num. 35:19-27; Prov. 23:10-11; Jer. 50:34). Job knew **that in the end** God would **stand upon the earth** and, like a witness for the defendant at a court trial, would testify that Job was innocent. In that way all would not only read of his uprightness (Job 19:23-24) but also all would hear of it—from God Himself!

**19:26. After my skin has been destroyed** may be rendered, "After my skin has been flayed" (or "stripped off"), that is, after he had died from the constant peeling away of his skin (another symptom of pemphigus foliaceus; cf. comments on 2:7 and see 30:30) or after worms (cf. 17:14; 24:20) in his grave had eaten away his skin (though "worms," supplied in the KJV, is not in the Heb. text).

After he was dead, Job then would **see God.** He would continue in a conscious existence; he would not be annihilated or sink into soul sleep. But how could he say he would see the Lord **in his flesh** after he had just said he would die? Either he meant he would receive a resurrection body (in which case the Heb. preposition *min*, here trans. "in," would be trans. "from the vantage point of"; in 36:25 *min* is used in that sense) or he meant he would see God "apart from" any physical flesh at all (*min* normally means "without"; cf. 11:15b), that is, in his conscious existence after death but before the resurrection. Favoring the first view is the point that whereas *min* normally means "without," it takes on the meaning of "from the vantage point of" when it occurs with the verb "to see" (*hāzâh*). Favoring the second view is the fact that since 19:26a speaks of his condition in death, one would expect that verse 26b in Hebrew parallelism would also refer to death rather than to an after-death resurrected condition.

**19:27.** So certain was Job of his seeing God that he repeated this point. The Hebrew word for **see** (*hāzâh*) is the same in verses 26 and 27a. Also Job twice emphasized the word **I** (vv. 25, 27)—literally, "I, even I, know," and "I, even I, will see" **Him.** This gazing on God for all eternity will be **with** his **own eyes** (either the eyes of his resurrected body, or figuratively the eyes of his soul). Job would no longer be like a stranger to God, for God would be on his side.

This thought so overwhelmed Job that he exclaimed, **My heart yearns** (lit., "my kidneys," considered the seat of the emotions, "waste away") **within me!** He was emotionally drained by the very thought of meeting God and having Him once and for all vindicate rather than vitiate his cause.

**19:28-29.** If Job's friends continued to **hound** (the same word is trans. "pursue" in v. 22) him—to get him to accept their view that sin had precipitated his suffering, and that **the trouble** lay within **him**—God would eventually strike them down by **the sword** (perhaps a retort to Eliphaz's word about the sword in 15:22). *Then* they would see that God punished the sin of the wicked. Rather than God punishing *Job* for being wicked, *they* would be the recipients of God's **wrath** for they had repeatedly harassed an innocent victim. Confident that they were wrong about his spiritual state and that he was right, Job was able to look beyond

death to his being acquitted by God and fellowshiping with Him.

### 5. ZOPHAR'S SECOND SPEECH (CHAP. 20)

This sixth speech by Job's companions is the most stinging of all the diatribes. Infuriated and insulted, Zophar blasted Job, seeking to convince him that his wealth had vanished because that is what happens to those who deprive the poor.

#### a. The anger of Zophar (20:1-3)

**20:1-3.** Like his two partners before him, **Zophar** could not remain silent; he too had to speak another time. **Troubled** and **disturbed** at Job's rude words, Zophar felt he must respond. Job had said the three had insulted him numerous times (19:3), but now Zophar volleyed the notion that Job had insulted *him.* Some comforter he turned out to be!

Job had said God "closed their minds to understanding" (17:4), but Zophar retorted that his **understanding** forced him to **reply.** He had to share his insights!

#### b. The brief prosperity of the wicked (20:4-11)

**20:4-11.** Since Job claimed to **know** so much (a false accusation, for Job did not claim that), he should be aware, Zophar argued, that from the beginning of human history any **joy** experienced by a sinner **is brief** and for **a moment.** Job may be arrogant, Zophar arrogantly affirmed (!), but he will be brought low and die. Though high as **the heavens** he will, in contrast, be brought low like **dung.** People will not know where he is, for he will have vanished **like a dream** (four men in the Book of Job spoke of dreams: Eliphaz, 4:13; Job, 7:14; Zophar, 20:8; Elihu, 33:15). He will be unseen (20:9, a retort to Job's words in 7:8), **his children** will have to pay his obligations **to the poor** (since he had oppressed them, 20:19), and he will lose all his ill-gotten **wealth.** Repeatedly in this oration, Zophar mentioned wealth (vv. 10, 15, 18, 20-22, 26) and its transience, an expansion of Eliphaz's earlier statement along that line (15:29). All this suggested that Job acquired his riches dishonestly. A wealthy man, if wicked, will find that his energy will be buried with him. Zophar here may have been responding to Job's mention of **vigor** in 18:7 (cf. 21:23 and "dust" in 10:9).

### c. The impoverishment of the wicked (20:12-19)

**20:12-16.** A sinner may enjoy sin-gained wealth like some **sweet** delicacy that he relishes **in his mouth,** but like **sour** food he will lose it. Wealth becomes like poisonous snake **venom** (cf. v. 16) with its bitter consequences.

**Riches** gained by godless means are not retained, Zophar argued. In fact they are vomited **up** and they **kill** the wicked like the deadly **poison of serpents** (cf. v. 14) or the venom of an adder's **fangs.**

**20:17-19. Streams** with their drinking water, and **honey and cream,** symbols of prosperity, cannot be enjoyed by sinners. "Cream" may be curdled milk or a kind of yogurt, a delicacy in the Middle East. As a transgressor dies, he must **give back** (cf. v. 10) the results of his toil and profits from his business without having enjoyed them. The reason for all this is that he took advantage of **the poor,** even taking their **houses,** in order to enrich himself. Of course Zophar had Job in mind, but later the suffering saint, here badgered again by verbal blows, denied such accusations (29:12, 15; 31:16-22).

### d. The anger of God against the wicked (20:20-29)

**20:20-23.** Though always **craving** for more wealth (another unfair charge by Zophar), a wicked person will find that it **cannot save** him for it **will not endure.** Troubles will come **upon him** (**misery,** 'āmāl, was a response to the same Heb. word used by Job in 3:10, 20; 7:3; 16:2; see comments on 3:10), and just when he is enjoying his prosperity (with **his belly;** cf. 20:14, full), **God will** lash out at him in His **anger** (cf. v. 28). The one who was angry, it seemed, was Zophar, not God! Zophar's vinegar-mouthed diatribe falsely and viciously incriminated Job as a selfish profiteer, heartlessly tyrannizing the poor. Such an arraignment was totally unfounded.

**20:24-29.** If Job tried to escape from God's anger, one **weapon** would down him if another did not. Pulling out the **arrow** (cf. 6:4) to try to save himself would do no good (cf. 16:13). He would experience **terrors** and **darkness** (cf. 15:30; 18:18), and **fire** (cf. 18:15; 22:20) would enshroud and **devour** his wealth.

God will not let a wicked person escape, Zophar averred. **The heavens** and **the earth** would witness **against him,** an obvious rejoinder to Job's desire that the earth not hide God's injustice to him (16:18) and his longing that his witness and intercessor in heaven act on his behalf (16:19-21).

His theft of the houses of the poor (20:19) will be requited by **his** own **house** being carried off by **a flood** (cf. 22:16) in **God's wrath** (cf. 20:23). **Such is the fate,** Zophar summarized, of **the wicked.** This is what **God** has **appointed for them** as their **heritage** (cf. 27:13). How then, as Zophar saw it, could Job think that his situation was any different? Since he had lost his wealth so suddenly, how else could such a calamity be explained except that he was wicked?

Zophar, of course, in his philosophical shortsightedness, made no allowance for a person being afflicted for any reason other than retribution for sin. In his stubborn invective, he flared at Job with venomous words, like the poisonous snake he spoke about.

### 6. JOB'S SECOND REPLY TO ZOPHAR (CHAP. 21)

In this speech Job responded to the view of the three arguers ("you" in vv. 2, 27-29, 34 is pl., and the verbs in vv. 2-3a, 5, 29, 34 are pl.) about the destruction of the wicked. Unlike his other talks, here he said nothing directly to God. Many of his remarks in verses 7-33 are direct refutations of Zophar's words in chapter 20 (see Zuck, *Job,* p. 98, for a list of these contrasts).

### a. Request for silence (21:1-6)

**21:1-3.** If his troublesome counselors would only **listen** to what **Job** was saying, then they would console him (**consolation** renders the same Heb. word Eliphaz used in 15:11; in both verses the Heb. is pl.). This is an important reminder that sufferers want a listening ear, not a condemning mouth. Then, he added sarcastically, Zophar could **mock on** (this verb is sing., whereas as stated earlier, the verbs in 21:2-3a are pl.).

**21:4-6.** Since Job was complaining to God, not to them, why did he **not** have the right to **be impatient?** (cf. 4:2; 6:2-3) They ought to be amazed at his terrible appearance (he wanted them to **look at** him as well as listen) as they were at first

(2:12). According to Bildad, people everywhere were horrified at what happens to a wicked person (18:20), so why could they not show at least a little concern about *his* situation, since they thought he was such a sinner? In fact they should be silent, putting their hands on their mouths (cf. 29:9; 40:4). Even Job's thinking about his own deplorable situation disturbed him emotionally (he felt **terrified**; cf. 4:5, "dismayed"; 22:10; 23:15-16) and physically (his **body** trembled).

*b. The prosperity of the wicked (21:7-16)*

**21:7-16.** How could the contenders' viewpoint, especially Zophar's, be right about the brevity of the wicked's enjoyment of life (15:29, 32-34; 18:5; 20:5, 8, 22) when Job knew that **the wicked live on** into ripe **old** age (cf. 20:10), **their children** with **them, their** houses secure (cf. 20:28), seemingly with no judgment from God? (cf. 20:23, 28-29) The livestock of many sinners prospers, the wicked enjoy **music,** and even die easily. Besides, they cynically flaunt **God,** even wondering what they **would . . . gain by praying to Him.** This is strongly redolent of Satan's accusation that Job was seeking personal gain by worshiping God (1:9-11), but of course Job knew nothing of Satan's affront. Job, however, knew that **their prosperity** did not come, ultimately, from **their own hands**; it was provided by God, whom they scorned! Therefore Job was not about to walk in the way of **the wicked** (cf. comments on 22:16-18).

Justice then is not always meted out in this life. Often the godless prosper and the godly perish. "Stern judgment in the life to come is the only possible corrective for this apparent triumph of wickedness. Postmortem retribution is clearly taught in both Testaments—compare Psalm 9:17; Isaiah 5:14-15; 30:33; Ezekiel 32:22-25; Matthew 7:13; 2 Thessalonians 1:8-9—although more clearly in later times than in the age of Job" (Gleason L. Archer, Jr., *The Book of Job: God's Answer to the Problem of Underserved Suffering,* p. 77).

*c. The death of the wicked (21:17-26)*

**21:17-21.** To Bildad's claim that "the lamp of the wicked is snuffed out" (18:5) in death and that calamity and disaster are ready to overtake him (18:12), Job asked, **how often** (asked three times in 21:17-18) do these things really happen?

This so-called **fate** allotted by God's **anger** (cf. 20:28; 21:30) to **the wicked,** as Zophar asserted (20:23, 29), hardly fits the facts. Sinners are seldom blown away suddenly and easily **like straw** or **chaff.**

Suppose his associates were to respond to Job that punishment for people he mentioned will come on their *children.* Job objected to that attempted way out by stating that a wicked person ought to suffer for his **own** sins under God's **wrath** for once he is dead, he could not **care** about any judgment on his **family** (cf. 20:10).

**21:22-26.** God's judging of the wicked does not follow the limited theology of Job's friends. God does not, as they suggested, often cut off the wicked (20:5) and judge their children instead. In His inscrutable ways He may allow **one man** to live on in prosperity and good health (Job's references to **vigor,** 21:23, and **bones,** v. 24, respond to Zophar's words in 20:11) and He may allow another man to be deprived and thus bitter. And yet in death they are alike, **in the dust** consumed by **worms** (cf. 17:14; 24:20; also cf. Ecc. 9:2-3). Wealth or health are not ways by which to judge a person's character. One may be wicked, and die either young or old; or he may be godly, and die either young or old. These facts obviously conform more to reality than did the rigid view of Job's three prattling prosecutors.

*d. The death of the wicked in prosperity (21:27-34)*

**21:27-33.** Job said he was aware of how they might try to answer him. They would ask Job to point out **where . . . wicked** wealthy people were living (cf. 8:22; 18:21; 20:28). Job answered this anticipated question with another question: Had the three contestants **never questioned** travelers? Many people who travel have money and yet many of them, though **evil,** do not face **calamity** or **wrath.** No one dares denounce or confront wicked, influential people or requite them. Such a popular person lives on, and even has an honorable burial, with people guarding **his tomb** after a crowd follows his casket in the funeral procession.

**21:34.** Their consoling (cf. v. 2), Job evaluated, was only **nonsense** (*hebel,* "empty, futile, useless"; cf. "no meaning" in 7:16 and comments on Ecc. 1:2) and were evidence of their being faithless (*mā'al*, "unfaithful, treacherous"). Job simply could not buy their explanation of suffering; in fact their viewpoint meant they were unfaithful to him, their long-time friend.

## D. The third round of speeches (chaps. 22–31)

In cycle one Job's visitors implied that he was a sinner and appealed to him to repent. In the second foray they insinuated that he was guilty and stressed the terrible fate of the wicked, but voiced no challenge for repentance. In the third verbal battle they attacked him by accusing him of specific sins, and only Eliphaz again gave a call for Job to turn back to God. Job stood his ground in response during all three rounds of attack. He denied (a) the premise of their implications, (b) their assertion that the wicked always suffer, and (c) that he himself was a deliberate transgressor.

### 1. ELIPHAZ'S THIRD SPEECH (CHAP. 22)

Eliphaz opened this speech abruptly without even mentioning Job's wordiness. He seemed determined to bring Job to his knees, to force him to repent for his wrongdoing.

#### a. God's uninterest in Job (22:1-5)

**22:1-3.** Man's goodness is of no **benefit to God**; He would **gain** nothing if Job **were righteous** or **blameless,** as Job so vociferously affirmed. Since God is not affected by whether one person is prosperous and another poor (cf. 21:23-26), they must be that way because of their righteousness or lack of it. How else could one explain such seeming indiscriminate conditions? **Eliphaz** simply could not accept the idea that God would be responsible for any deviations from justice.

**22:4-5.** Therefore it was totally unreasonable, Eliphaz said, for Job to think that God would rebuke him for being righteous. Why would God bring **charges against** someone who was not guilty?

#### b. Job's social sins (22:6-11)

**22:6-9.** With no evidence, Eliphaz indicted Job for several social evils: (1) Job took **security** from others (**brothers** here, as in 19:13, means countrymen),

**leaving them naked.** If a debtor gave his outer garment to a creditor as a pledge of payment, the garment was to be returned at night to protect the debtor from the cold (Ex. 22:26-27; Deut. 24:10-13). Failing to return such a garment was a sin. Later Job answered this false charge specifically (Job 31:19-22).

(2) Job refused to give **water** and **food** to people in need, even **though** he was **powerful** and **honored** and could obviously afford to give occasional meals to **hungry** travelers. Job also answered this false arraignment (31:16, 22).

(3) Abuse of **widows** and orphans, an atrocious felony (Ex. 22:22; Deut. 27:19; Jer. 7:6; 22:3; Zech. 7:10), was another indictment from Eliphaz. Again Job responded to this accusation (Job 31:16, 21-22). Certainly Eliphaz's theology was wrong when he lied in order to back up his position about Job's conduct.

**22:10-11. Snares,** terrifying **peril,** darkness, and **a flood** result from mistreating others, according to Eliphaz. Such a wicked person's life is hindered ("snares" is trans. "trap" in 18:9), he is frightened (cf. 18:11; 20:25; also cf. 4:5; 21:6; 23:15-16), in darkness he is confused and frustrated (cf. 15:30; 18:18; 20:26), and he faces devastating catastrophes such as a flood (cf. 20:28). Job, of course, was experiencing all these problems, but not, as Eliphaz presumed, as consequences of sin.

#### c. Job's spiritual defiance (22:12-20)

**22:12-14.** Once again Eliphaz stressed God's distance above man (cf. 4:17-19; 5:9; 15:14-16). Since **God** is so majestic, in **heaven** beyond the distant **stars,** how could Job be so insolent with **God,** questioning His knowledge and awareness of man and His ability to **judge** since He is separated from man by the **clouds?** But Eliphaz twisted what Job had said (21:22), thus again revealing the bankruptcy of his own airtight theological system. Job had said God *does* know, and that was the very thing that frustrated Job. Job had not said God cannot see man; in fact he affirmed just the opposite (7:17-20; 14:6).

**22:15-18.** The senior accuser then maligned Job for being a malicious sinner following the **path** (cf. 23:11) of **evil men** who **were carried off . . . by a flood,** possibly the flood in Noah's day. They defied **God,** telling Him to **leave** them **alone** (even though He blessed them), which was now what Job was wanting. This sneering quotation of what Job had just said (21:14-16) reveals Eliphaz's hateful haughtiness. He then added, **I stand aloof from the counsel of the wicked,** an exact quotation of Job's words (21:16), mockingly belittling Job for rejecting the wicked. Eliphaz wanted it known that *he* was rejecting the ideas of the wicked, but that he was doing so by **not** agreeing with wicked Job!

**22:19-20.** When sinners come to **their ruin,** then **righteous** people—Eliphaz and others—**rejoice** that justice is done. Job had said they could mock him (21:3), so now Eliphaz said he would gladly **mock** sinners (including Job!). Eliphaz, at first courteous (4:2), had now become unbelievably vicious. He even sounded like Bildad and Zophar, both of whom had spoken of the wicked person's possessions being burned up (18:15; 20:26).

*d. Eliphaz's appeal for repentance (22:21-30)*

**22:21-30.** Having conjured up home-made lies about Job and having twisted Job's statements into falsehoods, Eliphaz again pleaded with Job to repent.

Eliphaz set forth what Job needed to do: (a) **Submit to God,** rather than questioning and accusing Him; (b) **be at (make) peace with Him;** (c) **accept** God's teachings (as if Job were not willing to do that!); (d) assimilate and live out **His words;** (e) **return to the Almighty;** (f) get rid of **wickedness** (again assuming that Job was a secret sinner); and (g) quit trusting in wealth (**assign your nuggets to the dust, your gold of Ophir,** 28:16; Isa. 13:12; on the southwestern Arabian coast, **to the rocks in the ravines**). This last point was another false insinuation. How could Eliphaz prove that Job trusted in his material things? In fact he now had no gold in which to trust!

If Job would meet those conditions, Eliphaz proposed, God would then restore him and give him these blessings: (a) **prosperity** (Job 22:21), (b) restoration (v. 23) to fellowship with God, (c) trust in God (v. 25, **the Almighty will be your gold** and **silver**), (d) **delight in the Almighty** (the fifth time Eliphaz referred to God by that title in this chapter: vv. 3, 17, 23, 25-26), (e) fellowship with **God**

(v. 26), (f) answered prayers (v. 27), (g) desire to **fulfill** his **vows** (v. 27), (h) success (v. 28), (i) help to other people who were **low** and discouraged (v. 29), (j) deliverance of others through his intercessory prayers offered from a clean life (v. 30).

Eliphaz's point seemed to be that though Job's piety would not affect God one way or the other, it would affect Job.

2. JOB'S THIRD REPLY TO ELIPHAZ (CHAPS. 23–24)

Ignoring Eliphaz's allegations till later (chap. 31), Job reflected on two problems: injustices he experienced and injustices others experienced. Job wanted to present his case to God (23:1-7), but God remained inaccessible and unfair (23:8-17), and was also strangely silent about the vices of others (chap. 24). Such inequities, accompanied by divine silence, baffled Job.

*a. Job's desire to find God (23:1-9)*

**23:1-7.** In his bitterness (the fourth of five times he spoke of it; cf. 3:20; 7:11; 10:1; 27:2) and groaning Job still sensed that God's **hand** of affliction was weighing him down (cf. 13:21; 33:7). (**Heavy in spite of my groaning** should read, as in the NIV marg., "heavy on me in my groaning.") Job certainly wanted to turn to God (as each debater had advised, 5:8; 8:5; 11:13; 22:23), but he could not **find Him** (cf. 13:24). **If** God could be found then Job would present his **case** (23:4, *mišpōt*, another court term used frequently in the Book of Job), arguing persuasively (cf. 10:2) and weighing God's reply (23:5). Faced with the facts of Job's innocence, God would no longer **oppose** Job with His awesome **power** or **press charges** (*rîb*, lit., "contend, or bring a court litigation") **against** him. Earlier Job had stated that it would be pointless to present his case before God (9:14-16), but now he was certain that **an upright man,** meaning himself, **could present his case** (*yākaḥ*, "argue, debate in court") and the **Judge** (cf. 9:15) would acquit him and his troubles would terminate.

**23:8-9.** If a judge does not appear in court, cases cannot be presented to him. Because of that problem, Job searched in all directions for God, but in vain. God continued to be silent, to elude Job.

### b. Job's declaration of innocence (23:10-12)

**23:10-12.** Job felt that God was evading him, because if He did show up, He, knowing **the way** of godliness Job followed, would have to declare him not guilty. Yet the sufferer perceived that when God finished with him in court, he would **come forth** (or, in view of Ugaritic and Akk. parallels, "shine" [H.H. Rowley, *Job*, p. 202]) like **gold**. Finishing with Job's trial in court may be the meaning of verse 10, rather than the more common view that God was putting him through a test so that he would be more pure than before. Job could lay claim to gold-like purity all along—before and during the trial—because he had **followed** the Lord closely, keeping to **His way** (in contrast with Eliphaz's accusation that Job followed "the old path" of "evil men," 22:15) **without** deviating and while obeying Him (cf. 22:22) and relishing every word of **His**. This is another of Job's many affirmations of his nonguilty status.

### c. Job's exacerbation with God's sovereignty (23:13-17)

**23:13-14.** Again Job recoiled from the idea of confronting God in a court hearing. How could he dare counter God (cf. 9:3, 14, 17) who is unique (**He stands alone** is lit., "He is in one," i.e., He is in a class by Himself) and **does** what **He** wishes (cf. Ps. 115:3), including what He had in mind for Job (cf. Job 10:13).

**23:15-17.** Since God was so elusive (vv. 3, 8-9) and sovereign (vv. 13-14), Job was **terrified** (*bāhal*, "disturbed, dismayed," 4:5; 21:6; 22:10; 23:15-16) and weakened (**faint**). Terror came not because of his sinful nature, as Eliphaz suggested (22:10), but because of the Lord's awesome nature. Even so, Job would **not be silenced by the darkness** (*ḥōšek*; cf. 3:4) or **thick darkness** (*'ōpel*; cf. 3:6) of trouble that weighed him down.

### d. Job's concern over God's indifference (24:1-17)

(1) God's indifference toward judging overt sinners (24:1-12). **24:1-8.** If God would post on a universal bulletin board His schedule for judging, people would be less frustrated over His seeming lackadaisical attitude toward sin. People steal land (by moving **boundary stones** to take in part of a neighbor's field) and **flocks,**

orphans' and widows' animals (a patent reply to Eliphaz's charge that Job mistreated the needy, 22:9), and **force . . . the poor** off the road so they cannot even beg. So the victimized hide for fear and wander about **in the desert,** gleaning what little they can in **fields** and **vineyards,** while going about unclothed (cf. 24:10), **cold,** and wet.

**24:9-12.** Oppressors even yanked young babies from their widowed mothers to pay off debts. Again Job said **the poor** were unclothed and **hungry,** and were forced to **carry the sheaves** of grain from the fields, to **crush olives** (**among the terraces** may mean between the rows of olive trees), and **tread** grapes in **the winepresses** while thirsty. Even in cities, people were **wounded** and **dying . . . but God** seemed oblivious to it all. This disturbed Job because he was suffering for no specific **wrongdoing,** while others, who sinned openly and deliberately, went off scot-free.

(2) God's indifference toward judging secret sinners. **24:13-17.** Murderers, burglars, and adulterers work at **night,** thinking their crimes will go undetected. They refuse to operate in **the light** (cf. John 3:19-20); they love the **deep darkness** (*ṣalmāwet*; cf. comments on Job 3:5, "deep shadow"). God seems to be apathetic toward them too.

### e. Job's certainty over the wicked's eventual punishment (24:18-25)

These verses seem to contradict what Job had just said (vv. 1-17), for here he stated that God *does* punish the wicked. Therefore some scholars assign these words (vv. 18-24) to Zophar, others to Bildad, and still others to Job in quotation marks as if he were quoting one of the three in order to rebut them (v. 25). However, these could just as well be Job's words, in which he affirmed his confidence that though the wicked live on and get away with sin, *eventually* they are punished. This would oppose Zophar's view that the wicked die young (20:5) and would confirm Job's previously stated position that "the wicked live on" (21:7). Job's position was that *both* the righteous and the wicked *suffer* and *both* prosper. This differs drastically from the insistence of the three disputers that only the wicked suffer and only the righteous prosper.

**24:18-25.** Oppressors, Job argued, are unstable like **foam on . . . water.** Their **land is** under a curse and therefore unproductive (**so that no one goes to the vineyards** to glean grapes; cf. Lev. 19:9-10; 23:22). When they die, even their mothers (their wombs) forget them, worms eat their bodies (cf. Job 17:14; 21:26), and they **are broken like a tree.** People who mistreat widows (cf. 24:3) will be judged by **God** in **His power.** Such sinners may **become** settled, but God is fully aware (cf. 34:21) of their **feeling of security.**

Though they are in high positions for some time, God eventually debases them and they join **others** in the grave. Once prosperous, like **heads of** full-grown **grain** of barley or wheat, **they are cut off** just as sheaves are cut. They are not destroyed immediately, as the three maintained, but eventually. Why they should even prosper at all, while nonchalantly going about their sins, was Job's enigma. But he remained unmoved in his viewpoint, for it fit the facts, whereas the opinion of his colleagues did not.

3. BILDAD'S THIRD SPEECH (CHAP. 25)

Bildad's brief lecture shows he was running out of arguments with which to answer Job. Like Eliphaz in his third speech (chap. 22) and unlike his own previous speeches (chaps. 8; 18), Bildad said nothing about Job's windy words. The majesty of God, in contrast with the insignificance and iniquity of *all* men, not just of Job and the wicked, is the theme of this speech. Possibly this was a last-ditch effort to get Job to see how useless it is for an impure human to try to schedule a court hearing with the majestic God.

**25:1-3.** Since **God** rules (has **dominion**) He should be respected (**awe**), and Job, **Bildad** may have hinted, was not doing that. In His greatness God **establishes order** or harmony in **heaven** (so He is just; cf. 8:3). He rules over count-less **forces,** probably referring to angels (so He is omnipotent). Also **His light** (the light of the sun) pervades everything, picturing His omniscience.

**25:4-6.** Here Bildad, rather than responding to Job's concerns about injustice (chaps. 23–24), simply repeated Eliphaz's twice-trumped-up theme (4:17-

18; 15:14-16) that **man** (*'ĕnôš*, "weak, mortal man"; cf. 25:6 with comments on 4:17) cannot possibly be **righteous** or **pure.** (In using the phrase **one born of woman** as a synonym for weak man, Bildad intentionally picked up Job's wording in 14:1; cf. 15:4.) As Eliphaz had said (15:15), "Even the heavens" in all their brilliance "are not pure." **The moon** only reflects light, **and the stars** (cf. 22:12) lack purity before God because, in comparison with His glory, they are dim. How then could puny **man** (*'ĕnôš*; cf. 25:4) or **a son of man,** suggesting man's creation from mere dust, hope to stand before God? Man is so much smaller than the starry universe and is only **a maggot** and **a worm.** This disgusting suggestion may have intentionally harked back to Job's words about his many sores being covered with worms (7:5).

Bildad sought to humiliate Job, to awaken him to his own unworthiness. But this unkind speech accomplished nothing because Job had already admitted the facts of God's majesty and of universal sin.

A review of the speeches of Job's associates shows that they were poor counselors. They failed in several ways: (1) They did not express any sympathy for Job in their speeches. (2) They did not pray for him. (3) They seemingly ignored Job's expressions of emotional and physical agony. (4) They talked too much and did not seem to listen adequately to their advisee. (5) They became defensive and argumentative. (6) They belittled rather than encouraged Job. (7) They assumed they knew the cause of Job's problems. (8) They stubbornly persisted in their views of Job's problem, even when their ideas contradicted the facts. (9) They suggested an inappropriate solution to his problem. (10) They blamed Job and condemned him for expressing grief and frustration. Counselors today do well to be sure they do not fail in similar ways.

4. JOB'S THIRD REPLY TO BILDAD
(CHAPS. 26–31)

In contrast with the shortest speech in the book (chap. 25) chapters 26–31 comprise the longest. Job replied first to Bildad ("you" in 26:2-4 is sing.) but later (in chaps. 27–31) to all three ("you" in 27:5, e.g., is pl.).

*a. Job's description of God's majesty in nature (chap. 26)*

Here Job sought to show Bildad that he, Job, knew more about God's majesty than his pugilist did. But first he sarcastically rebuked Bildad, hinting that Bildad, not Job, was the puny one.

**26:1-4.** In stunning irony, **Job** mocked Bildad's futile attempt to help him. Bildad had treated Job as if he were **powerless . . . feeble** (cf. 18:7), and **without wisdom** (cf. 18:2). But Bildad, Job asserted, had not supported him, or strengthened him, or given him any helpful **advice** or **insight** at all. About all Bildad could think about was what happens to the wicked (8:8-19; 18:5-21) and about man's debased condition (25:4-6). No one **helped** Bildad with his **words,** which obviously were of no value. He and his cohorts were "worthless physicians" (13:4) and "miserable comforters" (16:2).

**26:5-6.** Some commentators ascribe verses 5-14 to Bildad, to make his third speech longer, or to Zophar to give him a third verbal assault. However, it was typical of Job to outdo his disputers in statements about God's transcendence. Did Bildad think he knew something of the majesty of the Almighty? (25:2-3) Then he ought to listen to what Job knew of the Lord's supremacy!

**God** is over **death** (26:5-6), outer space and the earth (v. 7), the clouds (vv. 8-9), light and darkness (v. 10), things on the earth (mountains and the sea, vv. 11-12), and the sky (v. 13).

Before God **the dead** are lying in **anguish** (an indication of conscious torment; cf. Luke 16:24) **beneath the waters,** where the dead were envisioned to be, and in *šeʾôl* ("sheol") or **Destruction** ("Abaddon," a synonym of sheol; cf. Job 28:22; 31:12).

The word "dead" ("departed spirits," NASB) translates the Hebrew word *reṗāʾîm*, which sometimes is used of a people known as the "Rephaites" and sometimes is used to refer to the dead. The Rephaites were tall like the Anakim (Deut. 2:20-21). At least four giant Rephaites are mentioned by name in the Old Testament: Og (Deut. 3:11; cf. Josh. 12:4; 13:12); Ishbi-Benob (a descendant of Rapha; 2 Sam. 21:16); Saph (2 Sam. 21:18; spelled Sippai in 1 Chron. 20:4); and Goliath (2 Sam. 21:19). Second Samuel 21:20

refers to another tall Rephaite, who is unnamed. Rephaites are mentioned in Genesis 14:5; 15:20; Deuteronomy 2:11; 3:13; and Joshua 17:15.

In Ugaritic, Rephaites were the chief gods or aristocratic warriors, apparently called that because both groups were seemingly giant-like in their power. When *reṗāʾîm* in Ugaritic was used of the dead it seemed to suggest "the elite among the dead." In Hebrew it may suggest the elite among the dead (cf. Isa. 14:9, "those who were leaders in the world") or it may simply be a synonym of other common words for the dead. *Reṗāʾîm* occurs in Psalm 88:10b, "those who are dead"; Proverbs 2:18, "the spirits of the dead"; 9:18, "the dead"; 21:16, "the dead"; Isaiah 14:9, "the spirits of the departed"; 26:14, "departed spirits"; 26:19c, "dead." Job's point in Job 26:5 seems to be that even the elite dead are in anguish because God knows and sees them.

**26:7-10.** God sustains the **skies** (cf. v. 13) **over empty space** and supports **the earth** on **nothing**—statements amazingly in accord with facts not known or agreed on by scientists till a few hundred years ago. In the **clouds** in the sky God gathers up water (evaporation), and He can cover **the . . . moon** with **clouds.** At the **horizon . . . light and darkness** seem to separate. The horizon is circular, for the verb **marks out** translates the word *ḥûq*, "to draw a circle," and suggests the curvature of the earth. This too accords with the facts known by scientists only in recent times.

**26:11-14.** Not only is God awesome in His control over space and the earth in space. He also is majestic on the earth. He causes earthquakes and **sea** storms, which He then calms. **The pillars of the heavens** figuratively refer to mountains that seem to support the sky (cf. 9:6). The raging sea is pictured as a sea god named **Rahab** (cf. comments on 9:13), whom God defeated. **The gliding serpent** may be another description of this sea god, also known as Leviathan (Isa. 27:1). God is over the sea, and He is also superior to all mythological representations of evil.

By the wind, God's **breath,** He clears the sky of clouds after a storm. This reveals **His power** and **wisdom** (cf. Job 9:4).

All these evidences of God's power

over nature (of things below, above, and on the earth) are only meager indications (**the outer fringe**) of what He does. People are so distant from God that they **hear** only a **whisper** (cf. 4:12) and obviously then cannot possibly fully comprehend all God's activities in His **power.**

### b. Job's description of the fate of the wicked (chap. 27)

**27:1-6.** Before addressing the plight of the wicked (vv. 7-23) **Job** again affirmed his innocence (vv. 1-6) perhaps in an effort to show that he was not one of the godless. Repeatedly Job had accused **God** of injustice (6:4; 7:20; 10:2-3; 13:24; 16:12-13; 19:7; 23:14) and of giving him inner **bitterness** (3:20; 7:11; 10:1; 23:2). Even so, Job again affirmed his innocence as he had done before in responses to Eliphaz (6:10, 29-30; 16:17; 23:10-12), Bildad (9:21-22; 10:7), and Zophar (12:4; 13:18-19). He said that **as long as** he lived (27:3, 6), with God's **breath** in him (cf. 10:12; 12:10; 34:14-15), he would not **admit** to wrongdoing; he simply could not accept his friends' (**you** is pl. in 27:5, 11-12) viewpoint, or **deny** (cf. **denied** in v. 2) his **integrity** which his wife had urged him to do (2:9). Even with all his friends' badgering, Job was confident that he would retain his **righteousness** and that his **conscience** would **not reproach** (ḥārap̱, "speak sharp, accusing things against") him.

**27:7-12.** Imprecating his **enemies** (did Job have in mind his fellows at the ash pile?), he then asked four questions that pointed to the hopeless condition of **the godless** person ('awāl, "an unrighteous person"; cf. 18:21; 29:17; 31:3). When dying (**when God takes away his life;** cf. God as the source of life, 10:12), he will call on **God,** but since he prays only when in **distress** God will not answer him.

Job said he, in contrast with the wicked, could even instruct his compatriots about God's **ways** (thus reversing what Eliphaz said in 22:22). Since they had **seen** evidences of God's works, they were wrong to continue their false and empty (**meaningless,** heḇel, 7:16; 9:29, "in vain"; 21:34, "nonsense"; 35:16, "empty") accusations, claiming **God** was punishing an innocent person.

**27:13-23.** Many scholars assign these words to Zophar because this would give

him a third speech and because the words seem more consistent with him than with Job. However, Job had already spoken of the fate of the wicked (24:18-24). He never denied the ultimate punishment of God's enemies, but he *did* deny their immediate judgment, contrary to Zophar's claim (20:5; 21:7). If Zophar could speak of **the fate** of **the wicked** and their **heritage** (20:29), so could Job. A vile person's family members are subject to death by warfare (**the sword**), starvation, or **the plague.** He will also lose his possessions. Though he may be "filthy rich," with vast amounts of **silver** and many **clothes,** they will pass into the hands of others. His **house** will be as empty as a deserted **cocoon,** as unstable as a temporary shelter **made by a** farmer for guarding his crops. His wealth will be **gone** suddenly, and will quickly be carried off by a storm, the strong sirocco **east wind.** It will make fun of him (clap **its hands** and hiss) while he tries to escape its merciless **power.**

### c. Job's discussion of God's wisdom (chap. 28)

In this chapter Job affirmed people's inability to ascertain God's wisdom fully, in contrast with the triad of antagonists who claimed they knew what God was doing in Job's life. Though seemingly an isolated chapter (which some say was spoken by one of the three, by God, or by an unnamed spokesman), this discourse does agree with Job's earlier words about man's inability to know God's wisdom and with Job's words about God's sovereignty over death and nature (cf. 28:24-27 with 26:5-13).

**28:1-11.** Men search for numerous metals underground (vv. 1-2—**silver . . . gold. . . . iron . . . copper**—and precious gems such as **sapphires** (v. 6; cf. v. 16). (Though the Iron Age began ca. 1200 B.C., when tools were commonly manufactured from iron, iron was known long before that; cf., e.g., Gen. 4:22.) Miners dig shafts in **the darkness** underground and dangle from ropes to reach remote areas. Beneath its surface **the earth,** overturned by miners at work, is in rubble as if it had been burned.

Birds with keen sight and stealthy animals cannot see or walk on the underground treasure troves. In his mining operations, man hammers away at the rocks, digs **tunnels,** and even finds where **rivers** begin which he must dam up (NIV marg.). As a result he is able to bring **hidden** underground **things to light.** These verses are arranged in an interesting structure (as suggested by David J. Clark, "In Search of Wisdom: Notes on Job 28," *The Bible Translator* 33. October 1982:401-5):

a. Getting valuable metals from the earth (Job 28:1-2)
   b. Going underground (v. 3)
      c. Remoteness of the mines (unseen by people, v. 4)
a¹. Getting valuable metals and gems from the earth (vv. 5-6)
      c¹. Remoteness of the mines (unseen by birds and animals, vv. 7-8)
   b¹. Going underground (v. 9)
a². Getting valuable metals from the earth (vv. 10-11).

**28:12-19.** In spite of man's technological skills, he cannot find, unaided, the greatest treasure of all, **wisdom.** Its value is not fully known by **man** (*ĕnôš,* "weak, mortal man"; cf. comments on 4:17). He can discover other hidden treasures under the earth's surface (28:4, 10), but he **cannot** discover wisdom in the inhabited earth (**the land of the living**) or in any ocean. Nor can wisdom be purchased in a market with other precious metals and jewels man has uncovered (**gold . . . silver. . . . onyx . . . sapphires. . . . crystal. . . . coral . . . jasper . . . rubies,** or **topaz**), for **wisdom** far exceeds their value (cf. Prov. 3:13-15; 8:11; 16:16).

**28:20-27.** After repeating the two questions Job asked before (v. 20; cf. v. 12), he affirmed that no animal, person, or bird can see **wisdom** (just as one cannot see mountain-hidden metals, vv. 4, 7-8). And just as the sea does not know where wisdom is obtainable (v. 14), neither do **Destruction** ("Abaddon," NIV marg; cf. 26:6) nor **Death** know. The only One who knows is **God,** for **He** is omnipresent (He **sees** what animals, people, and birds are unable to see, 28:7, 21). In creating the universe, God determined the elements; **the force** (lit., "weight") **of the wind,** the amount of water, the **decree** (i.e., limit) **for the rain,** and where each **thunderstorm** would occur. In His creative genius, **He** saw and valued **wisdom** (cf. Prov. 8:27-30), in contrast

with man's inability to do so (cf. Job 28:12-13).

Verses 12-27 have an interesting arrangement:

a. Inaccessibility of wisdom (vv. 12-14)
   b. Wisdom's value beyond [gold, silver] jewels (vv. 15-19)
a¹. Inaccessibility of wisdom (vv. 20-22)
   b¹. Wisdom's value known by God (vv. 23-27).

**28:28.** God told **man** (*ādām,* "mankind") that the essence of **wisdom** is to **fear** ("venerate and submit to") **the LORD,** even when man cannot understand His ways, and **to reject evil,** living in accord with God's standards of holiness. Honoring God (the positive) involves hating sin (the negative; Prov. 8:13). Job's accusers had insisted that he was not fearing God or eschewing sin and that therefore he was not wise. In Job 28 he argued the opposite: *he* was fearing God and hating evil (as God Himself had already said of Job, 1:1, 8; 2:3), but *they* were not! Therefore wisdom and **understanding** were his, not theirs.

This closing verse also links these words of Job with chapter 29, in which he cited evidences that he revered the Lord, and with chapter 31, in which he enumerated evidences that he was not involved in sin.

*d. Job's concluding soliloquy (chaps. 29–31)*

As Job spoke to God alone in these closing chapters, he was like an attorney summarizing his arguments before a jury. He discussed his past pre-affliction glory (chap. 29), delineated his present gloom (chap. 30), and delivered his final oath of innocence (chap. 31).

(1) Job's past glory (chap. 29). This chapter expands Job's earlier words, "All was well with me" (16:12). **29:1-6.** In previous **months** (thus suggesting that his disease extended over at least several months' time; cf. 7:3) **God** had **watched over** him (cf. 10:12) and **blessed** him. To have God's **lamp** over him, like a lamp suspended in a tent (cf. 18:6; Ecc. 12:6, "bowl" means "lamp") meant to be under His favor. Also God guided him **through** the **darkness** of difficulties, befriended him, and was **with** him. Job had a happy home (his **children were** with him, in contrast with their now being dead), and he was prosperous (**cream** and **olive oil** were symbols of plenty).

**29:7-11.** The suffering saint also enjoyed social prestige as a judge (elders held court sessions at the city **gate**; cf. Deut. 21:19; 22:15; Josh. 20:4, which may partially account for Job's use of legal terms). He was respected not only by those younger than he but, contrary to normal customs, also by older persons. The silence of his elders at the city gate, where they waited for his words of wisdom (cf. Job 29:21-23), was missing from his three gabby associates! Others had put **their hands** on **their mouths** (to gesture their silence), but not these three! (21:5; cf. 40:4) Job was then **well** spoken **of** (29:11), not maligned as his present company was doing to him (19:2-3).

**29:12-17.** Why was Job so highly respected? One reason is that he helped the needy (vv. 12-13, contrary to Eliphaz's charges, 22:6-7, 9), including **the poor,** orphans, the **dying,** and bereaving widows. Another reason is that he administered **justice** (29:14-17), championing the causes of and assisting **the blind,** the **lame,** the **needy,** and **the stranger,** and overturning their oppressors (**the fangs of the wicked,** *'awāl,* "an unrighteous person"; cf. 18:21; 27:7; 31:3). Ironically Job's associates failed to help *him* now that *he* was down.

**29:18-20.** Job had fully expected God's blessings to continue, with his living a long life (**days** like the **sand**) of stability (**roots**), prosperity (**dew**), an honorable reputation (**glory**), with perennial strength (pictured by a new **bow;** cf. 30:11).

**29:21-25.** Besides being blessed (vv. 2-6), helping others (vv. 7-17), and expecting his health and vigor to continue (vv. 18-20), Job's **counsel** was welcomed —contrary to the attitude of his three uninvited guests! People had eagerly welcomed his opinions, like the soil drinking in **the spring rain.** In his counseling he even encouraged others by his smile; in contrast one wonders if the three friends ever uplifted Job with warm smiles. Job's counselees had taken his advice (**I chose the way for them**), and respected him (cf. v. 11) as if he were a **chief** or **king.** Besides, he also comforted those who grieved, another area in which his assailants failed.

(2) Job's present gloom (chap. 30). **30:1-8.** Job bewailed his present misery, which contrasted so starkly with his pre-disease days. He now was disrespected socially (vv. 1-15), in pain physically (vv. 16-19), abandoned spiritually (vv. 20-23), opposed socially (vv. 24-26), and exhausted physically and emotionally (vv. 27-31).

Young people, rather than respecting Job, mocked him (cf. vv. 9-10; 12:4; 16:10; 19:18), an unthinkable discourtesy in the ancient Near East. Having enjoyed "the respect of the most respectable" he now suffered "the contempt of the most contemptible" (Francis I. Andersen, *Job: An Introduction and Commentary,* p. 235). They were urchins of no **use** to him whatever, with no physical stamina (30:2), thin, hungry, and wandering about the desert (v. 3), rummaging for **food** (v. 4, **broom tree** roots tasted bitter), chased from normal society (v. 5), living in wadis, **among the rocks . . . in holes** (v. 6), sounding like braying wild donkeys, and hiding under **bushes** (v. 7). This scum of society—a **brood** without even names—considered *Job* scum!

**30:9-15.** In their attitude toward the poor, afflicted sufferer, these urchins mocked (cf. 16:10) and detested him and even **spit in** his **face** (cf. 17:6). In his God-induced affliction (cf. 16:9) Job was as weak (cf. 16:7) as an **unstrung . . . bow** (cf. 29:20). Even so, they unrestrainedly attacked him like an army (cf. 16:13-14), making it impossible for him to do anything (**they** broke **up** his **road**). No wonder Job spoke again of being overwhelmed by **terrors** (cf. "terrors" in 6:4; 13:21; 24:17; 27:20 and "terrified" in 21:6; 23:15-16). No longer did Job feel respected or safe.

**30:16-19.** Job then spoke of his physical agony. As his life was vanishing, nighttime was miserable, like a sword piercing to his **bones** (cf. 33:19), causing unending **pains.** Again, for the eighth time, he mentioned God's **great power** (cf. 9:4; 10:16; 12:13; 24:22; 26:12, 14; 27:11). He felt **God** had grabbed him by his clothes (NIV marg., if this is the meaning of this difficult Heb. sentence) and thrown him **into the mud.** To be like **dust and ashes** means: (a) that he looked haggard and emaciated, ashen in color, or (b) that he actually had ashes on his sores (cf. comments on 2:8), or (c) that he felt inwardly dejected. Ironically this anticipates Job's later words about repenting in dust and ashes (42:6).

**30:20-23.** Added to his social rejection (vv. 1-15) and physical pain (vv. 16-19), was his feeling of being neglected by God (vv. 20-23). His **cry** to **God** was ignored (cf. 19:7; 31:35) even though God saw him (cf. 7:19-20; 10:14; 13:27; 31:4). In fact God even turned against him, Job felt, attacking him (cf. 16:12) and tossing him **about** as in a violent windstorm (as Job had said God does to the wicked, 27:21).

**30:24-31.** His three peers had done to Job what no one else would think of doing: they opposed him when he was **broken** and **in . . . distress.** Yet Job had sympathized and **grieved** with people in *their* **trouble.** Hoping to get some help (**good** and **light**) from his friends Job got the opposite. Certainly their antagonism was undeserved!

Then Job again elaborated on his physical and emotional pain: inner **churning** or turmoil, **days of suffering** (cf. v. 16), **blackened** skin (from his disease; cf. v. 30), crying for relief, wailing like **jackals** with their doleful howls, and like screeching **owls** (or, perhaps better, "ostriches," as in the NASB, with their weird groans; cf. Isa. 13:21; 34:13; Micah 1:8), blackened and peeling **skin** (cf. Job 19:26), and intense **fever.** Consequently his joy (harps and flutes often played joyful tunes) became grief; he was **mourning and . . . wailing** like someone in a funeral dirge. His emotional pain is expressed in 30:24-26, 29, 31; verses 27-28, 30 relate to his physical pain.

Such manifold misery, as Job voiced in this chapter, had led him down a path of great depression.

(3) *Job's oath of innocence* (chap. 31). This solemn oath is Job's final effort to compel God to do something about his plight. The negative form of confession, in which the accused wished on himself a curse if he were in fact guilty of the charges, is a strong form of denial. Job used the "if guilty" oath repeatedly ("if" occurs 19 times in vv. 5, 7 [3 times], 9 [twice], 13, 16-17, 19, 21, 24-26, 29, 31, 33, 38-39), sometimes followed by the imprecation "let" or "then may." Besides denying Eliphaz's charges against him (22:6-9) and other sinful actions, Job also denied infractions of attitudes and motives.

**31:1-4.** First, Job denied being guilty of **lustfully** desiring someone of the opposite sex. Job knew that the **heritage** God gives sinners is **ruin** (**wicked** translates *'awāl,* "an unrighteous person"; cf. 18:21; 27:7; 29:17) and **disaster,** as both Zophar and Job had spoken of the "heritage" (20:29; 27:13). Job therefore did not **look** on female beauty in lust because God *looked* on him, seeing all he did (cf. 7:19-20; 10:14; 13:27) and followed his **every step** (cf. 14:16).

**31:5-8.** Job then denied he had dealt dishonestly with others (cf. **deceit** in 27:4). If he had cheated in weighing out goods for others then he was willing for **God** to use **scales** in an **honest** way to judge him. Confident that he was aboveboard in business, Job knew that God would admit he was **blameless. If** he were guilty of deviation in his conduct (**steps** and **hands**) or inner motives, he was willing to starve as a result of his **crops** being ruined (cf. 31:12).

**31:9-12.** The third sin the defendant denied was adultery (v. 1 pertained to lustful viewing; this pertains to sexually immoral actions). **If** it could be proved that he was guilty of such a heinous crime, Job asked that his **wife** be demeaned (grinding **grain** was a menial task, Ex. 11:5) and degraded sexually by **men** (pl.). Such **a sin,** he acknowledged, is **shameful** and deserves punishment. Furthermore, like **a fire** it destroys a person's life, leading **to Destruction** ("Abaddon," a synonym of sheol; cf. Job 26:6; 28:22).

**31:13-15.** Job also affirmed his fair treatment of his servants. **If** he were unjust with them when they had some complaint, then he would be unable to face **God** now that *he* was complaining to Him. In two parallel questions, that may have startled Job's onlookers, he admitted their equality with him as objects of God's creative work **in the womb** (cf. 10:8-11).

**31:16-23.** In answer to Eliphaz's false allegations (22:7-9), Job **denied** oppressing **the poor** and **needy.** He was not selfish (31:17), for he shared his food with orphans and even took them in under his roof. He encouraged widows (v. 16) and counseled them against oppressing creditors (v. 18), and he gave **clothing** and even **fleece** to those who lacked it even if they were unappreciative (vv. 19-20). He never mistreated orphans **in court** (lit., "in the gate," the place of court proceedings; cf. 29:7); **if** he had, he asked that his **arm** would **fall . . . off** (cf. **hand,** 31:21). He was unusually considerate of the needy, for he feared God's punishment. He knew that his money and rank would not forestall judgment **from God.**

Job's self-defense in verses 13, 16-22 (and in 29:12-17, 25) implied that he had done a better job than the Lord in carrying out justice.

**31:24-28.** Materialism and idolatry were two other sins Job denounced. Eliphaz had implied that Job was trusting in his riches (22:24), but the patriarch affirmed that he never did so and was not proud of his **wealth.** Besides his heart not being **enticed** toward women (31:9), his **heart** was not even inclined to worship the sky's luminaries, a common practice in the ancient Near East. Such worship of creation would be punished by the Creator (**God on high;** cf. v. 2).

**31:29-34.** Other sins Job said he was not guilty of were being glad over **the trouble** of an enemy (an inner attitude) or calling on God to judge (**curse**) him (an outer action). People in his family and his workmen always had plenty to eat, and even travelers enjoyed his hospitality. Nor did he hide his **sin as men do** (or, perhaps better, "as Adam did," NIV marg.). Had he been hypocritical, the public would have found it out sooner or later and would have scorned him.

**31:35-37.** Job longed that **someone** would **hear** him, for his committee of accusers was not really listening to his views (cf. 13:6, 17; 21:2). So, like a defendant in court, he signed (figuratively) his statement of **defense,** ready for God to **answer** him. He was so confident of his innocence that he would proudly **wear** God's written indictments, knowing they could easily be proved false. He called God his **Accuser** (lit., "Man of my indictment"). This was a daring move, for accused people usually do not want their plaintiff's indictments, whether true or false, to be publicized. Job would refute all God's incriminations, doing so in confidence **like a prince.**

**31:38-40.** As a wealthy landowner, Job could have mistreated his employees, but he denied any fraud or injustice. If hired farmers had been overworked in the fields or underpaid, his **land** would have cried **out** (a personification) and their **tears** in the **furrows** (spoken in a hyperbole) would have testified **against** him. In one final denial and imprecation, Job stated that if he withheld **payment** from his tenant farmers or had disheartened them by unreasonable demands or difficult working conditions, he wished his **wheat** fields would grow thornbushes and his **barley** fields weeds. This would mean a loss of much income in retaliation for his withholding his farmers' income.

With this oath of innocence, in which **Job** denied almost a dozen sins of action or attitude, he rested his case. Ending his arguments against the belligerent team of tyrants, he hoped to *force* God to move. He apparently felt that such an ultimatum would make God break His silence. If Job were innocent, then God would be required, according to legal practice, to speak up and affirm it. If Job were guilty, then God would be expected to bring down the imprecations on him. But, as Job found out, God *still* remained silent. The sovereign God cannot be pushed into a corner, or pressured into action by anyone's demand.

## E. Elihu's four speeches (chaps. 32–37)

Job had persisted in his claim to innocence and had repeatedly rejected the view of his comrades-turned-critics that suffering is only retributive. Since the three could not get him to budge, they finally gave up (32:1).

And yet, though Job silenced his babblers, he could not induce God to speak. Job hoped to coerce God to admit to unfairness and therefore to relieve him from his agony.

Since the debates stalemated and since God said nothing, a fifth person then entered the ring. Elihu, a young bystander, angered at both sides of the debate, took advantage of the silence and rose to defend God's justice and sovereignty. Elihu's sensitivity to Job's need contrasts with the harsh words of the three. His views reflect greater insight into Job's situation than the three antagonists possessed. For this reason it is wrong to call Elihu a brash, heartless, young fool, as do some commentators.

Many commentators think Elihu's four speeches (chaps. 32–37) were added to the book by an editor years (even centuries!) after the original version was written. Four arguments are used to defend that idea: (1) Elihu is mentioned nowhere else in the book. (2) Elihu's style and language differ from the rest of the book. (3) Elihu's views add nothing to the argument of the book. (4) Job did not answer Elihu.

These arguments are answerable, however: (1) Elihu need not have been mentioned earlier in the book since he was a silent onlooker not yet involved in the disputation. And Elihu was not condemned by God in 42:7-8 along with Eliphaz and his two companions probably because Elihu was closer to the truth than were the three.

(2) Admittedly Elihu's style differed from that of the other four debaters. He used 'ēl for God more than did the others (his 19 uses of 'ēl compare with Job's 17, Eliphaz's 8, Bildad's 6, and Zophar's 2; see Samuel Rolles Driver and George Buchanan Gray, *A Critical and Exegetical Commentary on the Book of Job,* pp. xlii-iii). Elihu also used a number of Aramaic words more than the three counselors did (ibid., pp. xlvi-vii). These differences, however, simply point up his distinctive character (Édouard Dhorme, *A Commentary on the Book of Job,* p. ciii).

(3) Elihu's view of suffering differed from that of the three. They had claimed that Job was suffering because he had sinned, but Elihu said that Job was sinning (in an attitude of pride) because he was suffering. Elihu pointed out that God can use suffering to benefit people (33:17, 28, 30; 36:16). Elihu put his finger on Job's wrong attitude of complaining against God (33:13; 34:17) and suggested that Job humble himself before God (33:27; 36:21; 37:24).

(4) True, Job did not answer Elihu. But this may be because Elihu's words silenced him. Perhaps Elihu's suggestions hit home, causing Job to reflect on his sin of questioning God's ways. Furthermore, Elihu's orations provided a bridge from Job's insistence for vindication (chap. 31) to God's speeches. If the Elihu portion is not original, then God responded immediately to Job's demand, an action which is inconsistent with God. Also the Elihu speeches create an added element of suspense, as the reader awaits God's answer.

---

## Addressees in Elihu's Speeches

**First speech**
> To all four (32:6-9)
> To the three (32:10-14)
> To Job (32:15–33:33)

**Second speech**
> To the three (34:1-15)
> To Job (34:16-37)

**Third speech**
> To Job (chap. 35)

**Fourth speech**
> To Job (36:1–37:1)
> To the three (37:2-13)
> To Job (37:14-24)

---

1. ELIHU'S FIRST SPEECH (CHAPS. 32–33)

After Elihu is introduced in the prose section (32:1-5), he gave four speeches; (a) 32:6–33:33, (b) chapter 34, (c) chapter 35, and (d) chapters 36–37.

*a. Introduction to Elihu (32:1-5)*

**32:1-3.** Job's **three** opponents gave up the battle because they could not persuade him to deny his innocence and confess to having led a wicked life. Sensing that all four debaters were talked out (cf. vv. 5, 15-16), **Elihu** then pitched in. Elihu's father **Barakel** was a **Buzite,** probably a descendant of Abraham's nephew Buz (Gen. 22:20-21). Interestingly Uz, the older brother of Buz (!), was possibly the person after whom "the land of Uz" (Job 1:1) was named.

Elihu was **angry** (cf. 32:5) with both sides of the debate. He was incensed **with Job** because he defended **himself** against all wrongdoing while accusing **God** of doing wrong (cf. 40:2). Job was more willing to cast aspersions on God's character than to admit to any sin. Also Elihu was inflamed **with the three . . . because they** pronounced **Job** guilty but without adequate evidence (cf. 32:12). Anger seemed to characterize much of these verbal bouts. The three pugilists were mad at Job; he was mad at them and at God; and he sensed that God was angry with him. And now Elihu was infuriated too!

**32:4-5. Elihu,** however, had been patient during the lengthy controversy, deferring to their age as was the custom in the ancient Near East (cf. 29:8a, 21; 32:6-

7, 11-12a). Seeing that **the three men had** run out of ways to play their one string, Elihu was irritated (cf. vv. 1-2). Perhaps **his anger was aroused** because he felt they should have done more than merely pounce on Job repeatedly as if he were an inveterate sinner who needed to repent.

### b. Elihu's introduction of himself (32:6-22)

Before Elihu actually began his argument against Job (starting in 33:1) he first took a number of sentences to justify his right to speak. Rather than these words being a sign of braggadocio, as some writers suggest, they seem to be necessary as a way for Elihu to be accepted and to gain a hearing. For him, a silent listener, to barge in without defending why he should be allowed to enter the debate, would have been obtrusive. A pushy attitude might mean he would have been turned off with no one listening. Yet Elihu was confident he had insight into Job's situation (32:10, 17; 33:33; 36:2-4).

(1) Elihu's defense of his wisdom. **32:6-9.** Admitting his younger age, **Elihu** said he dared not interrupt and give his views (he mentioned **what I know** four times: vv. 6, 10, 17; 33:3), because **wisdom,** as was acknowledged in those days, supposedly resided with the elderly (cf. 12:12). One's **advanced years** gave him more experience and hence more insight. However, Elihu reasoned that younger persons are not necessarily without wisdom because it comes from God, not from **years. The spirit in a man** may refer to the Spirit of God (cf. NIV marg.), who is often associated with wisdom (Gen. 41:38-39; Ex. 31:3; Num.

27:18-21; Isa. 11:2; Dan. 5:11-12) as its source. **Understanding,** Elihu dared suggest, is not limited to **the aged. (The old,** Job 32:9, is lit., "many," possibly meaning those who have lived many years.)

(2) Elihu's disappointment with the three (32:10-14). **32:10.** Elihu now asked that they **listen to** him since he had listened for so long to them. Eight times he voiced his request that the three and/or Job listen to him (v. 10; 33:1, 31, 33; 34:2, 10, 16; 37:14), apparently expressing his apprehension that they might not hear him out because of his youth. But yet Elihu believed he had some knowledge on the issue at hand that had not yet been aired (**what I know**; cf. 32:6, 17; 33:3).

**32:11-13.** He had been patiently silent **while** they spoke and he heard their **reasoning.** (Their **searching for words** might possibly suggest that some time [hours or even days] may have lapsed between some of the speeches.) With their **arguments** they had **not . . . proved Job wrong** in his claim to an upright life. Therefore they should not claim to be wise or claim that if they could not **refute** him, **God** would. The second line of verse 13 could be understood, however, as Elihu's own suggestion, rather than as part of his quotation of the three. If so, then his point was that they should let *God* defeat Job's arguments, since man could not do it.

**32:14.** Elihu then stated that his approach would be different. He had no need to defend himself **against** verbal attacks by **Job,** as the three had felt it necessary to do, and Elihu would **not** re-

---

## Overview of Elihu's Speeches

| Job's Complaints | Elihu's Answers |
|---|---|
| 1. God is silent; He does not respond to me (13:22; cf. 33:13). | *First speech:* God *does* speak—through dreams and pain (chap. 33). |
| 2. God is unjust; He does not relieve me of my suffering (19:6-7; 27:2; cf. 34:5-6). | *Second speech:* God is just (chap. 34). |
| 3. God is unconcerned; He does not reward me for my innocence (10:7; cf. 35:3). | *Third speech:* God is sovereign (chap. 35). |

spond to Job **with** their **arguments.**

(3) Elihu's desire to speak out (32:15-22). **32:15-19.** Since the three had run out of **words** (cf. vv. 1, 5), Elihu felt his time to speak had come. He would **tell what** he knew (cf. vv. 6, 10; 33:3), **for** he was **full of words.** And verbose he was! The verses of his speeches (32:6–37:24, excluding 34:1; 35:1; 36:1) total 157, about the same as Job's final speech (chaps. 26–31, excluding 26:1; 27:1; 29:1) of 158 verses, and longer than the combined speeches of any of the three alleged friends (cf. Eliphaz's 110 verses, Bildad's 46, and Zophar's 47).

**The spirit within me** may refer to Elihu's inner spirit, not the Spirit of God, in view of the following two verses. **Wineskins** (animal skins used to hold wine) expand and **burst** if they have no hole for venting the fermenting gases from the wine. Elihu said he felt that way, about to burst from being filled with ideas and not having the opportunity till then to voice them.

**32:20-22.** Elihu felt compelled to **speak,** to reply to the three and to Job. Yet in his responses he would not take sides (he disagreed with both sides) nor would he **flatter** either party in an effort to win its favor. He said that to be guilty of **flattery,** an unfair tactic, would mean God, who gave him life (**my Maker;** cf. 4:17; 9:9; 35:10; 36:3; 40:19), would **take** it **away.**

*c. Elihu's first answer to Job (chap. 33)*

As seen in the chart "Overview of Elihu's Speeches," this young theologue was responding to three of Job's complaints. First Elihu replied to Job's charge that God is silent.

(1) Elihu's request that Job listen (33:1-7). **33:1-4.** Three times Elihu addressed **Job** by name (vv. 1, 31; 37:14), and seven other times mentioned Job's name (32:12, 14; 34:5, 7, 35-36; 36:16). In contrast, the three older speakers never once mentioned Job's name either directly or indirectly.

Job had asked his three friends to **listen** to him (13:6, 17; 21:2); now Elihu turned that around and asked that Job hear *him* (cf. comments on 32:10). The young debater had paid attention to the three (33:12); now he asked that Job give him *his* full **attention.** Elihu's **words,** which he was **about to** speak (they were

on the tip of his **tongue),** were sincere (**from an upright heart**) and would reveal insights into Job's situation (cf. **what I know,** 32:6, 10, 17). Elihu viewed himself as an equal with Job for both, he said, were created by God. Elihu said he was **made** by **God** (the Holy **Spirit** is involved in creating man) and given **life** (cf. Gen. 2:7) by **the breath of the Almighty** (cf. Job 12:10; 27:3; 34:14-15); Job had also said he was made by God (31:15).

**33:5.** The youthful speaker, after hearing Job out, challenged him to respond **if** he possibly could (cf. v. 32). Job, he said, should **prepare** his response and be ready to **confront** Elihu as in verbal combat. The word *'ārak,* translated "prepare," means to arrange in order, often in the sense of marshaling military forces or weapons in battle order (cf. 1 Sam. 17:8, "line up for battle," and Job 6:4, "marshaled"), and so figuratively to arrange one's words or legal case (cf. 32:14, "marshaled"; 37:19, "draw up"; 13:18, "prepared"; 23:4, "state"). The word *yāṣab,* here rendered "confront," means to take one's stand or position, sometimes in the sense of readiness for battle (1 Sam. 17:16; Jer. 46:4, 14; Job 41:10). Elihu was ready for a skirmish! Of course Job had already set forth his arguments; perhaps his numerous forays with his other so-called friends had left him battle-weary.

**33:6-7.** Though ready to take on Job and to show him the danger of criticizing **God,** Elihu did not intend to lord it over the sufferer, as the three disputants had done. He admitted to equality with Job because they were both frail human beings, made **from clay** (cf. Job's similar words in 10:9 and cf. comments on 33:4). Therefore Job need not **fear** Elihu for he would treat Job kindly. He would not terrify him as Job had said God had done (7:14; 9:34; 13:21; 23:15-16). Elihu promised that in this debating he would not pressure Job (his **hand** would not **be heavy** on him), as Job had said God had done (23:2, "His hand is heavy"; cf. 13:21, "withdraw Your hand").

Though verbose, Elihu was less arrogant and presumptuous than the other spokesmen.

(2) Elihu's summary of Job's charges against God. **33:8-11.** The junior attorney had listened carefully to Job, as evidenced by his quoting Job's **very words.**

---

# Elihu's Quotations of Job

**In Elihu's First Speech**

| | |
|---|---|
| 33:9a | "I am pure" (cf. 6:10; 9:21; 10:7; 12:4; 16:17; 31:6). |
| 33:9b | "Without sin" (cf. 13:23; 23:11). |
| 33:9c | "I am clean and free from guilt" (cf. 9:20-21; 10:7; 27:6). |
| 33:10a | "God has found fault with me" (cf. 10:6). |
| 33:10b | "He considers me His enemy" (cf. 13:24; 19:11). |
| 33:11a | "He fastens my feet in shackles" (cf. 13:27). |
| 33:11b | "He keeps close watch on all my paths" (cf. 7:17-20; 10:14; 13:27). |

**In Elihu's Second Speech**

| | |
|---|---|
| 34:5a | "I am innocent [righteous]" (cf. 9:15, 20; 27:6). |
| 34:5b | "God denies me justice" (cf. 19:6-7; 27:2). |
| 34:6a | "I am right" (cf. 27:5-6). |
| 34:6b | "I am guiltless" (cf. 10:7; chap. 31). |
| 34:6d | "His arrow inflicts an incurable wound" (cf. 6:4; 16:13). |
| 34:9 | "It profits a man nothing when he tries to please God" (cf. 21:15). |

**In Elihu's Third Speech**

| | |
|---|---|
| 35:2 | "I will be cleared by God" (cf. 13:18; 23:7). |
| 35:3 | "What profit is it to me, and what do I gain by not sinning?" (cf. 21:15) |

**In Elihu's Fourth Speech**

| | |
|---|---|
| 36:23 | "You [God] have done wrong" (cf. 19:6-7). |

---

Elihu reviewed Job's position by stating that Job had criticized **God** for unfair treatment, even though Job was not guilty. Many of the words in Elihu's review accurately reflect what the sufferer had said (see the chart "Elihu's Quotations of Job").

(3) Elihu's refutation of Job's claim that God was silent (33:12-33). **33:12-13.** Elihu directly confronted Job, telling him, **in this you are not right.** "This" probably refers to Job's accusing God of injustice (vv. 10-11). The reason Job should not charge God with wrongdoing is that **God is greater than man.** Because of His sov-

ereign majesty (which Job recognized) he ought not criticize God. God, in other words, has purposes in His doings that may be beyond man's comprehension and, as God, He has the right to do as He wishes. To **complain to** God that He does not answer **man's words** is wrong, Elihu contended. The word "complain" is from *rîb*, a legal verb meaning "to present or debate an indictment in court," used by Job five times (9:3, "dispute"; 10:2, "condemn"; 13:8, "argue"; 13:19, "bring charges"; 23:6, "press charges") and by God once (40:2, "contends"). Four times Job used the noun *rîb* (13:6, "argument";

29:16, "case"; 31:13, "grievance"; 31:35, "my Accuser," lit., "man of my indictment"). Job had felt God was pressing charges against him in court (10:2) **but,** Elihu said, Job should not respond by pressing charges against God!

**33:14-18. God** *does* **speak,** Elihu maintained. God does so in various ways—**now one way, now another.** One means is through dreams (vv. 14-18) and another is through illness and pain (vv. 19-22). The problem is that often **man** does not sense that God is communicating.

When people **dream,** Elihu said, God **may speak in their ears** (lit., "opens or uncovers the ears of men" [*ĕnôš,* "weak, mortal man"; cf. comments on 4:17]). To open one's ears meant to reveal something to him. The words **terrify them with warnings** is one possible translation of the Hebrew. Another possible rendering is "seals their instruction" (NASB; cf. KJV) and another is "seals their discipline." If the NIV rendering is correct, Elihu's point is that dreams can terrify a person (cf. Eliphaz's similar response, 4:12-17), to warn him. If the second or third suggested rendering is right then Elihu's idea may be that God makes certain that the dreams will lead one to a more informed or disciplined life.

Such dreams, whether of a warning, instructional, or disciplinary nature, are designed to **turn** people **from wrongdoing** or **pride** (the sin Elihu believed Job was guilty of; cf. 36:9) and **to preserve** them alive (**pit,** referring to the grave, is used five times in chapter 33; vv. 18, 22, 24, 28, 30). Yet Job had said that when God terrified him with dreams (7:14), he wanted to die (7:15). Whereas in Old Testament times God often spoke in dreams as well as through other media (Heb. 1:1), He now communicates to people through Christ, the Living Word (Heb. 1:2), and the Bible, the written Word (2 Tim. 3:16).

**33:19-22.** Another way God gets people's attention, Elihu suggested, is by causing them **pain.** A serious illness (with **distress in** one's **bones,** i.e., intense inner pain; cf. 30:17) can steal one's appetite and cause him to lose weight (cf. Job's appetite loss and emaciation, 3:24; 6:7; 19:20) so that his **bones** protrude. Such a sickness can bring a man close to death (**the pit**; cf. comments on 33:18).

**The messengers of death** may refer to angels who bring (or announce) death (cf. Ps. 78:49).

**33:23-24.** In sickness God may send **an angel** (*malʾāk*) as a mediator (*mēlîṣ*) to: (a) remind a person of the proper conduct and attitudes he should maintain in his life (**what is right**) and to (b) intercede with God to keep him from dying (**going down to the pit**). Elihu disagreed with Eliphaz, who had said that no angels could assist Job (5:1). Elihu was also disagreeing with Job, who felt he had no intercessor to arbitrate his case (9:33). By the words **one out of a thousand** (cf. Job's use of that phrase in 9:3) Elihu meant that such intervening angels are plentiful, or, perhaps better, that they are rare (cf. Ecc. 7:28). The angel's interceding work (in contrast with angelic "messengers of death," Job 33:22) was based on his providing **a ransom for** the sick person. The "ransom," while not specified, means something that can be regarded as a consideration or reason for the sufferer to be relieved from his illness.

**33:25-28.** As a result of the angelic intercessor, the sufferer **is restored** to health and enjoys spiritual strength as well, including prayerful communion with **God,** acceptance by God, fellowship with God, **joy** in God's presence (cf. Eliphaz's similar words in 22:26 and Bildad's in 8:21), and restoration **to his** former **righteous state** (cf. Bildad's words in 8:6). In addition he tells others: (a) that he **sinned** but that his punishment of illness was less than his sin called for (cf. 11:6), and (b) that God diverted him from death (**the pit**; cf. comments on 33:18) and restored him to life (**to enjoy the light,** i.e., of the sun, which means to enjoy life; cf. v. 30; Ecc. 11:7). Thus out of his affliction comes a deeper walk with God and a ready witness before others.

**33:29-30.** According to Elihu, **God** often brings dreams and illness (both bad experiences) to **man.** The idiom **twice, even three times** means often (or perhaps, as some suggest, it refers to the three means Elihu had discussed: dreams, illness, an angel). Again Elihu stated why: negatively, to divert people from death (**the pit**; cf. comments on v. 18) and positively, to help them enjoy **life** more than before (cf. v. 28). Though illness may seem to be leading to death

(vv. 21-22), God can use it to deter a person *from* death (vv. 24, 28, 30) and to give him a more fruitful life.

**33:31-33.** Again the new spokesman asked **Job** to bear with him, by hearing him out. Then if Job had something **to say,** he could **speak up . . . but if not,** Elihu would continue. **Listen** and **be silent** (v. 31) are repeated in verse 33.

For Elihu, suffering, though related to sin (v. 27), was more protective than punitive. The first three speakers said God afflicts in order to punish; Elihu said God afflicts in order to teach. He emphasized that suffering can help divert one from sin and resultant death, whereas the three older men felt that unrequited sin would surely lead to death.

All four counselors were wrong about Job's case, however, for all assumed a sin-results-in-suffering viewpoint. When God spoke (chaps. 38–41), He did so directly, not through an angel. And Job's experience *did* result in his enjoying a deeper relationship with God (42:2, 5-6, 9) and he *did* enjoy a long and full life (42:10, 12, 16).

2. ELIHU'S SECOND SPEECH (CHAP. 34)

Since Job remained silent (cf. 33:32), Elihu continued. His second speech was a defense of God's justice, an answer to Job's allegation that God was unfair. The young protagonist spoke first to the three older visitors (34:1-15), as indicated by the plural "you" and "men" (vv. 2, 10) and "us" in verse 4, and then to Job (vv. 16-37) as indicated by the singular "you" (vv. 16-17, 33).

*a. Elihu's desire that his elders hear him out (34:1-4)*

**34:1-4.** Elihu again asked his elders, whom he respected (**you wise men . . . you men of learning;** cf. vv. 10, 34), to **listen to** him (cf. his uses of "listen" in 32:10; 33:1, 31, 33; 34:10, 16; 37:14). Again Elihu picked up Job's words (cf. 12:11) when he referred to the need for the debaters to test the accuracy of his **words as the tongue** can discern the quality of the **food** it **tastes.** They would need to decide the **right** thing about Job's case.

*b. Elihu's denunciation of Job's claim that God was unjust (34:5-9)*

**34:5-9.** Again Elihu quoted several of Job's statements (see the chart "Elihu's

Quotations of Job," near 33:9-11). Then siding with the three, Elihu accused **Job** of being a deliberate sinner, associating with ungodly people, and claiming that **man** gains **nothing** by worshiping **God** (cf. 9:30-31; 35:2). Drinking **scorn like water** is redolent of Eliphaz's words in 15:16. Though Elihu was certainly wrong in saying Job associated with the **wicked,** he was correct in condemning Job for pouncing on **God** in a scornful, rebellious way. To say that a person is no better off for having served God is a complaint Elihu answered later (chap. 35).

*c. Elihu's defense of God's justice and impartiality (34:10-20)*

**34:10-15.** Sounding like Bildad, Elihu rose to the defense of God's justice, affirming that **God** cannot **do evil** or **do wrong** (cf. v. 12; 8:3, "Does God pervert justice?"). Though Job had complained that God had denied him justice (27:2), Elihu cited several evidences in support of His unflinching justice. (1) God gives **man what he deserves,** meting out punishment for sin (34:11). (2) For **God** to **do wrong** (v. 10) or **pervert justice** (cf. 8:3) would be inconsistent with His character and therefore **unthinkable** (34:12). (3) Having independent authority as the world's Sovereign, no one could influence **Him** away from justice (v. 13). (4) As the Sustainer of human life God, if He wished, could withdraw **His spirit** (or "Spirit," NIV marg.) **and breath** instantly and everyone **would perish** at once (cf. 12:10; 27:3; 33:4), but in His goodness to mankind He does not do that.

**34:16-20.** For the third time in this speech, Elihu requested that his audience of four hear him out (**hear . . . listen;** cf. vv. 2, 10). He then continued citing evidences that God is fair in His dealings. (5) If God were unjust, how could He **govern** the world? (v. 17) To accuse the **just . . . One** of injustice is obviously wrong. (6) God does not hesitate to judge incapable and wicked **kings . . . nobles . . . princes,** and the rich. Partiality on God's part is out of the question because He is not influenced by men's power or money. **All** are equal under Him as **the work of His hands.** In fact God can quickly, even by surprise at midnight (cf. v. 25), bring the wicked to death and remove **the mighty** (cf. v. 24). How, then, could Job say God is unfair?

### d. Elihu's discussion of the punishment of the wicked (34:21-30)

**34:21-30.** Elihu may have been responding here to Job's concern about God's delay in executing justice (24:1-21). As further evidences of God's justice (see comments on 34:10-20), Elihu pointed up these facts: (7) God has all the facts in every case, for in His omniscience **He sees** everything everyone does (v. 21; cf. 24:23) so sinners cannot escape His judging by hiding in the darkness. Unlike human judges, God **has no need** to investigate cases (34:23; cf. Zophar's words in 11:11). God can put down **the mighty** (cf. 34:20) and set **up others in their place,** overthrowing and crushing **them in the night** (cf. v. 20). (8) God is fair for He does not overlook **wickedness. His eyes are on the ways of men** (v. 21) recalls Job's similar words in 24:23. God punishes those who reject and disregard Him and who mistreat **the poor** and **the needy** (34:26-28). (9) God's justice is seen in that, even though He may choose for a while to do nothing about sin and to remain **silent** to Job's and others' pleas for speedy justice, **yet** He as the Sovereign Ruler **over man and nation alike** will see that **a godless man** (ḥānēp, "irreligious person"; cf. 8:13) does not continue indefinitely and triumph endlessly (34:29-30). Job might not see God when He chose to remain silent (cf. Job's complaint along that line, 23:8-9) but that did not give him the right to **condemn** God (cf. 19:7; 30:20).

### e. Elihu's arraignment of Job's nonrepentance and rebellion (34:31-37)

**34:31-33.** Elihu was stunned that Job would have the audacity to speak **to God** the way he did. Job had affirmed his innocence repeatedly. But then, as if to put God on the spot, Job said that if God would show him where he had gone **wrong,** he would then stop sinning (cf. 6:24; 7:20-21; 10:2; 13:23). But Elihu felt, and rightly so, that such talk was uncalled for, that it was seeking to tell **God** what to do. Since God is sovereign, He will not stoop to man's **terms,** especially in the face of a nonrepentant attitude. Elihu then said that Job would have to **decide** whether God would **reward** him when he was unrepentant.

**34:34-37.** Any person who is **wise** knows that Job's speeches (in which he criticized God for injustice) lacked **knowledge** (cf. 35:16; 38:2) and **insight.** Therefore **Job** ought to **be tested to the utmost for** speaking like the **wicked.** This statement sounds much like Zophar's words (11:5). Elihu sensed in **Job** a rebellious attitude, for Job (by the derisive gesture of clapping **his hands** to silence others) scorned others for defending God's justice.

Elihu was correct in chiding Job for rebelliously (a) questioning God's justice (34:17), and (b) demanding that God answer Him (v. 29) and show him where he had sinned (v. 32). But Elihu seemed to share something of the heartless attitude of the three elder counselors by wishing that Job would be **tested** "to the utmost," and by assuming that Job's many words (cf. 35:16) meant he was **against God.**

### 3. ELIHU'S THIRD SPEECH (CHAP. 35)

In this speech Elihu defended God's sovereignty in answer to Job's charge that God did not reward him for his innocence. Elihu's answer was twofold: (a) Since God is supreme, He is not affected one way or the other by man's innocence or sin, and (b) God was not answering Job's cries because of his pride.

### a. Job's inconsistency (35:1-3)

**35:1-3.** How could Job ever hope to be vindicated **by God** (cf. 13:18) as being innocent while at the same time he insisted that his innocence was of no value before God? Such a position was inconsistent, **Elihu** argued. Elihu had earlier quoted Job as having asked **what profit** or **gain** he would receive for serving God (34:9; cf. 21:15).

### b. Man's inability to affect God because of God's greatness (35:4-8)

**35:4-8.** Replying to both Job and to the three (**your friends with you** probably refers to the three, not to Job's supposed wicked companions), Elihu pointed out that since **the heavens** and **the clouds** are higher than man, certainly God is higher than man. Therefore God is not affected adversely by man's **sins** or benefited by man's **righteous** condition. (Cf. Eliphaz's similar words about the stars, 22:12, and God's indifference to man, 22:2-3.) A person's **wickedness** or

**righteousness** affects only man, not God. When God shows mercy it is not because man has persuaded Him to do so, and if He inflicts judgment it is not because man has injured Him. God is sovereign and therefore self-determining. He is not bribed by man; His standards for judging people are firm, impartial, and uninfluenced. But since a person's moral conduct does affect himself, it *does* make a difference for *him* whether he sins or not (cf. 35:3).

### c. Man's inability to influence God because of man's pride (35:9-16)

**35:9-11.** When people are in trouble (**under . . . oppression**) they often turn to **God** for a way out, but they do not turn to Him as their **Maker** (cf. 4:17; 9:9; 32:22; 36:3; 40:19), the One who can give joy *in* times of trouble (**songs in the night**). Nor do they express gratitude to Him for giving them more intelligence than **beasts** and **birds** possess.

**35:12-15.** Therefore God **does not** respond to people's **empty** (insincere) cries for help, for such prayers stem from pride (**arrogance**; cf. 36:9). If such proud prayers are not answered, certainly Job's cries of arrogance and impatience would not be heard. Job claimed that he could **not see** or find God (9:11; 23:8-9; cf. 34:29); yet he had placed his **case** in God's hands (13:18; 23:7). But Elihu sensed another inconsistency in Job (cf. comments on 35:2-3): the sufferer was willing to **wait for** God in His justice to clear him, and yet Job felt, according to Elihu, that God did nothing about sin (24:1-12). Elihu here misconstrued Job, for the patriarch did not say God *never* punishes the wicked; though not punished in this life, they *will* receive judgment from God at death.

**35:16.** For **Job** to talk out of both sides of his **mouth** (wanting God to clear him, and yet being concerned that God does nothing to put down sin) was to make **empty** (*hebel*; cf. comments on this word in Ecc. 1:2) **talk,** speaking many **words** (cf. Job 34:37) without wisdom (cf. 34:35).

Elihu felt that Job could not be cleared by God (35:2) as long as he questioned the value of serving Him (v. 3) and prayed from a heart of pride (v. 12), while thinking that God does nothing about wickedness (v. 15).

### 4. ELIHU'S FOURTH SPEECH (CHAPS. 36–37)

In his second speech (chap. 34) Elihu had defended God's justice, and in his third speech (chap. 35) he championed God's sovereignty. Now in his final speech he spoke again of both of those attributes—first, of God's justice (and power) in His dealings with man (36:1-26) and then, of His sovereignty (and benevolence) in His dealings with nature (36:27-37:24). In this way Elihu sought to answer both Job (32:2; 33:10-12) and his three elders (32:3, 12).

### a. Elihu's defense of God's justice and power in His dealings with man (36:1-26)

(1) Elihu's confidence in his own insights. **36:1-4.** As the youthful counselor began his fourth oration (suggested by the words **Elihu continued**; cf. "Then Elihu said" in 34:1 and 35:1, which introduced his second and third speeches), he was so full of ideas to share (32:18-20) that he asked Job not to become impatient (**Bear with me**). He still had more to say in defense of God. In self-confidence Elihu said his **knowledge** (cf. 36:4) was **from afar,** that is, he had a wide range of insights, in contrast with Job who, Elihu twice said, was "without knowledge" (34:35; 35:16). Elihu's first concern, as before (34:10-12, 17) was to extol God's **justice.** Again he referred to God as **my Maker** (cf. 4:17; 9:9; 32:22; 35:10; 40:19). Not lacking self-confidence, Elihu affirmed that his words were correct and that he was **perfect in knowledge.** However, the words "one perfect in knowledge" may refer to God, as they certainly do in 37:16. This view is supported by the recently discovered Ebla tablets (Mitchell Dahood, "Are the Ebla Tablets Relevant to Biblical Research?" *Biblical Archaeology Review* 6. September-October 1980:58).

(2) God's just dealings with the wicked and the righteous. **36:5-7.** Though not translated in the NIV, the Hebrew word for "Behold" introduces four statements by Elihu about God's power (vv. 5, 22, 26, 30). Though **God** is just (vv. 6-7) He **is** also **mighty;** and though He is mighty He does not lack mercy (He **does not despise men**). Again Elihu sided with the three worn-out debaters by maintaining that God does not allow **the wicked** to live (cf. v. 14; 15:27-35; 20:5-29) in contrast with Job's insistence that many sinners do live on in prosperity to a ripe old age (21:7,

27-33). Elihu affirmed, on the other hand, that God restores **afflicted** righteous people, giving them deserved blessings, watching over them in care (though Job felt this was no longer true of him, 29:2; 10:12), and even honoring **them with kings** and exalting them. This sounds much like the arguments of the three, that God always rewards people *in this life* in accord with their conduct. Job, as seen in 27:13-23, did not question God's general practice of justice. But Job did challenge the views that God always metes out justice *before* death and that God was being just with *him.*

(3) God's design in suffering—to lead people to repent of pride (36:8-12). **36:8-10.** Sometimes righteous people (**men** is lit., "they" and probably refers to the righteous mentioned in v. 7) undergo trials (**are bound in chains**) and are subjected to **affliction** (such as being chained, **held fast by cords,** to a bed of pain). "Affliction" (*'ānî,* "being weak or poor") is also used in verse 21. "Affliction" in verse 15 translates a different Hebrew word (see comments there). When God afflicts the godly, He does not forsake them. By it, He calls to their attention their wrong conduct (**what they have done**), their transgression (**have sinned** means "have transgressed"), and their arrogance (**arrogantly** is lit., "they show themselves to be strong," a form of the verb *gāḇar,* "to be strong"). For a person to show himself strong before God means he vaunts himself against God (this form of the verb is rendered "vaunts himself" in 15:25). Removal of pride, as Elihu had said before (33:17), is one of God's purposes in afflicting His own. By pain God gets people's attention and teaches them (**makes them listen** is lit., "opens their ears," as in 33:16 and 36:15).

**36:11-12.** A godly sufferer, Elihu suggested, who will listen to God and will once again **obey and serve Him** will then prosper and enjoy **contentment.** Learning from suffering and turning from pride was Elihu's point earlier (33:23-28). This sounds like the theology of the three, but they stressed that Job was guilty of sinful *actions* whereas Elihu was concerned more with Job's sinful *attitude* of pride. But believers who in pride refuse to learn from their God-induced inflictions (**they do not listen** to His cor-

rective instruction; cf. 36:10) **will perish by the sword** (cf. 33:18) **and die without the knowledge** (cf. 34:35; 35:16) God wanted them to have. Job should not think of his calamities as proof that he was essentially ungodly (the view of the three agitators ) or as evidence that God had forsaken him (as Job maintained). Instead he should see his afflictions as a means of helping him become humble before God.

(4) The reactions of people to suffering. **36:13-15.** True sinners, **the godless** (*ḥānēp,* "irreligious"; cf. 8:13) **in heart** resent problems by which God may bind them (cf. 36:8). They refuse to **cry for help** or if they do, it is not in sincere repentance (27:8-9). As a result **they die** at a young age, as Zophar had asserted (20:5, 11), and are treated in judgment like hardened sinners, **male prostitutes** in pagan **shrines.** ("Male prostitutes of the shrines" translates one Heb. word *qᵉḏēšîm,* which is lit., "consecrated ones," i.e., individuals [males or females] given over to depraved rites, probably in idolatrous worship; cf. Deut. 23:18; 1 Kings 15:12.)

On the other hand God delivers those who are afflicted (the word for **those who suffer** is *'ānî,* "poor, afflicted," and suggests those who are righteous; cf. comments on "affliction," Job 36:8). "He opens their ears" (a lit. trans. for **He speaks to them**) and apparently they listen and obey (cf. v. 11). **Affliction** (v. 15) translates *laḥaṣ,* "oppression or distress," from the verb *lāḥaṣ,* "to squeeze, press, or oppress." (A different Heb. word is trans. "affliction" in vv. 8, 21.) God, Elihu maintained, brings a repentant believer out of the dire straits or situations which squeeze him in. Elihu used an interesting wordplay in verse 15 in that "delivers" is the word *ḥālaṣ* and "affliction" is the word *laḥaṣ.*

The result—whether death and deliverance—all depends on one's heart and his response to difficulties. If Job did not admit to pride, Elihu implied, he would be showing that he was godless. But if he turned from shaking his fist in God's face, he would demonstrate that he was one of God's own.

(5) The reactions of Job to suffering (36:16-26). **36:16-19.** God was seeking to free Job from **distress** (*ṣar,* "straits, a cramped situation"; also used in v. 19),

and take him into **a spacious place** (cf. Pss. 18:19; 31:8), a picture of prosperity with no obstructions, and give him rich and abundant **food**. Therefore Job should not be preoccupied with God's seeming failure to exercise **justice**. He was full (*mālēʾ*, **laden**) with that problem (Job 36:17), whereas he could have his **table** full of (*mālēʾ*, **laden** with) delightful edibles (v. 16).

Elihu's advice, then, to Job was that he be sure his longing for his former condition of prosperity did not **turn** him **aside** (cf. v. 21) from God's path. (**Bribe** may be rendered "ransom or recompense," as in 33:24. Perhaps it means here "the large price Job is paying by his suffering.") As many people have learned, money and accomplishments cannot buy a person *out of* **distress** (*ṣar*, "straits, a cramped situation"; cf. 36:16) or sustain him with peace *in* distress.

**36:20-21.** Nor should Job be so concerned about **the night** when **people** are involved in sin (cf. 24:13-17). Elihu's words in 36:20 are difficult in the Hebrew. Another possible meaning is that Job should not long for the night of death (KJV; cf. 3:20-23), that is, he should not anticipate death as a release from his suffering (3:13, 17). Instead he should repent of his pride. Job ought to be careful that he not turn to sin, by complaining, **which** he seemed **to prefer to** bearing his **affliction** (*ʿānî*; cf. comments on 36:8) without complaint. To find fault with God would not bring Job relief from his trials.

**36:22-26.** Elihu then turned Job's attention to **God** and spoke of **His power** (cf. v. 5; 37:23), instructional ability (cf. 36:9-10), independence (no one can tell God what to do by prescribing **His ways**), justice (no one can prove, as Job had tried to do, that God has ever **done wrong**; cf. 19:6-7), incomprehensible greatness (36:26), and eternality (v. 26). God's **years** are innumerable and unending in contrast with man's few years (9:25; 14:1-2, 5; 16:22). So in view of God's perfections, Job ought to refrain from the sin of reproving God and ought to praise **His** great **work**, as other godly people have done, even **in song**. Everyone (**mankind** rightly translates, *ʾāḏām*) is aware of God's majestic work even when **men** (*ʾĕnôš*, "weak, mortal man"; cf. comments on 4:17) view His awesome creation (e.g., the stars) **from** a distance. Job had frequently spoken of God's greatness (9:4-13; 10:16; 12:13; 21:22; 23:13; 24:22; 26:14; 27:11), but Elihu was seeking to point out that being aware of God's majesty and criticizing Him are inconsistent.

### b. Elihu's defense of God's sovereignty and benevolence in His dealings with nature (36:27-37:24)

Having referred to God's "ways" and "work" (36:23-24), which man sees (36:25), Elihu then elaborated on God's doings in nature in the autumn storm (36:27-33), the winter (37:1-13), and the summer (37:14-18).

In his third speech (chap. 35) Elihu had spoken of God's sovereignty. Now he returned to that subject but with an added emphasis that God's control over nature involves His benevolence toward the earth, animals, and people.

(1) God's sovereignty in the autumn storm (36:27-33). **36:27-31.** God manages various aspects of nature: evaporation (v. 27a), **rain** (vv. 27b-28), **clouds** (v. 29a), thunder (v. 29b; cf. v. 33; **His pavilion** is a picturesque description of the sky), **lightning** (vv. 30, 32), and the ocean. **Bathing the depths of the sea** (v. 30) should not be understood as describing the lightning; it should be translated "and covers the depths of the ocean," meaning that God so floods the bottom of the oceans with water that people on land cannot see it.

God uses evaporation, precipitation, thunder, and lightning both to judge people (possibly a trans. to be preferred to **governs the nations**) and to bless them by giving them **food** (v. 31; cf. Acts 14:17). Sometimes God uses rain to bring calamity on individuals (cf. 37:13) besides rain's more normal purpose of nourishing the soil.

**36:32-33.** Referring again to the **lightning**, Elihu said God **fills His hands with** it in the sense of, speaking figuratively, shooting lightning bolts like arrows. **Thunder** precedes the storm and even **cattle** sense **its approach**. "Thunder" was mentioned in verse 29 but here it is literally, "noise." **The coming storm** is the NIV's probably correct attempt to make specific the Hebrew word "it." The difficult Hebrew in the second line of verse 33 has been rendered in many ways (cf. NIV marg.; also see H.H. Rowley, *Job*, p. 301).

(2) God's sovereignty in the winter (37:1-13). **37:1-5.** People have always been fascinated by the awesome spectacle of lightning and thunder, God's "light and sound program," and Elihu was no exception. His **heart** pounded and palpitated. Perhaps an actual storm was approaching for he urged his debating audience to **listen** ("listen" is pl.) **to the roar** (*rōgez*, "agitation," rendered "turmoil" in 3:17, 26) **of His voice.** Thunder is often referred to as God's mighty voice (37:2, 4-5). Five times Elihu mentioned the **lightning** (36:30, 32; 37:3, 11, 15), which is sent by God. How God accomplishes these awesome **things** is **beyond** human comprehension (v. 5; cf. 36:26, 29), a truth that Eliphaz had affirmed once (5:9) and that Job had spoken of twice (9:10; 26:14).

**37:6-13.** Many people have experienced the restraining effect of a snowfall or a heavy **downpour**—events in nature that point people to God and **His work** (cf. 36:24; Rom. 1:20). He **stops** man's activities and **animals** run for shelter and hibernate when **the tempest** (windstorm) **comes . . . from its chamber,** picturesquely describing a storm being stored in a room (cf. Job 38:22) till **God** releases it. **Cold . . . winds** blow, **ice** is formed (by God's merely breathing, as it were), and lakes and rivers freeze over. Storm **clouds,** with **lightning** (cf. 36:30, 32; 37:3, 15) throughout them, **swirl around . . . the . . . earth.** Following God's **commands,** they bring judgment on some people by ruining their crops, flooding their possessions, and drowning them (cf. comments on 36:31a). Other times the storm clouds **water** the soil and thus demonstrate **His love** (cf. 36:31b; Acts 14:17)—evidence that His power is balanced with His benevolence.

(3) God's sovereignty in the summer. **37:14-18.** Elihu then challenged **Job** to contemplate what he had been saying about **God's wonders** (cf. v. 16). In a series of questions, Elihu pointed up Job's ignorance about God's power in nature. Man does not **know how God** can possibly guide **the clouds,** cause **lightning** (cf. comments on v. 3), or even **hang** the clouds in the sky. Man is ignorant, but God **is perfect in knowledge.** Nor is man capable of doing what God does, such as **spreading out** a clear, blue,

summer sky, which seems **hard** like **a mirror of . . . bronze** (cf. Deut. 28.23), causing people to perspire in the still, hot weather.

(4) Job's inability to understand God's ways (37:19-24). **37:19-21.** If Job could not comprehend the observable actions of God in nature, how could he possibly dare **draw up** (*'ārak*, "prepare, arrange, marshal"; cf. 13:18) his **case** for a legal battle with God, as Job had said he wanted to do? Job could not succeed against God because man is in **darkness,** that is, ignorant, about God (cf. 38:2). To ask **to speak** in God's presence, as Job wanted to do (10:2; 13:3, 22), to accuse Him of wrongdoing would be like asking **to be swallowed up** or destroyed by God! Puny man cannot even **look at the sun** in its brightness without being blinded. How than could he hope to endure in God's presence?

**37:22-24.** Perhaps sensing God's approach in a windstorm (38:1), Elihu said that **God** was coming. In Ugaritic myths Baal was said to have left his golden palace in the northern mountains. But here the true God **comes** from **the north . . . in golden splendor,** a picture of His **awesome majesty.** As Job had said, God is **beyond** the **reach** of man's mental powers (26:14; cf. Elihu's similar words, 36:26, 29; 37:5). Then Elihu summarized the two attributes he had been defending repeatedly: God's **power** (cf. 36:22) or sovereignty, and **His justice** (cf. 34:12, 17). Elihu was sure that God's dealings with Job were **not** to **oppress** or oppose him, though Job, before Elihu spoke, could see no other explanation.

Elihu's final word was a recommendation that Job **revere** (or "fear"; cf. comments on 1:1) God, which would mean doing away with self-conceit or pride (thinking of oneself as **wise in heart**; see NIV marg.). Fearing God involves recognizing God's supremacy and man's inferiority because of his finiteness. Once again Elihu put his finger on Job's problem—pride before God (cf. 33:17; 36:9).

Job said nothing after Elihu's speeches, possibly because he saw some truth in what Elihu was saying. According to this youthful informant, God's justice should not be questioned or His sovereignty challenged, because His ways are beyond human understanding. According to Elihu, calamities can serve to remove pride and to protect people from more grave difficulties. God, then, is to be worshiped, not criticized; He is to be extolled, not examined.

Elihu fittingly prepared the way for God to speak. He did so: (a) by defending God; (b) by sensitizing Job to his need for humility; (c) by describing God's wonders in natural revelation, which God elaborated on; (d) by probing Job with thought-provoking questions (33:13; 34:17-19, 33; 35:2, 6-7; 36:19, 22-23, 29; 37:15-18, 20), a tactic that God continued; and (e) by targeting on Job's basic problem—justifying himself and condemning God—which God Himself later mentioned (cf. 32:2 with 40:8).

### F. God's two speeches and Job's replies (38:1–42:6)

At last Job's plea that God answer him was granted. Repeatedly Job had knocked on heaven's door, longing for God to answer (13:22; 31:35). Or he wished that an arbiter (9:33) or an advocate or intercessor (16:19-20) would speak on his behalf.

But God's response was nothing like Job had anticipated. Job wanted a legal hearing, an opportunity to prove the illegality of God's onslaughts against him, the patriarchal plaintiff. But instead of answering Job's charges about the Sovereign's injustices, God asked Job questions! Instead of answering Job's subpoena, He issued a subpoena to Job! Rather than explaining the theory of evil or the role of suffering, God rebuked Job for presuming to challenge His ways.

In more than 70 questions—none of which Job could answer—God interrogated Job regarding numerous aspects of inanimate and animate nature. These two science examinations ranged in subject matter from the constellations to the clods, from the beasts to the birds. The wonders of God's creation are dazzlingly displayed in outer space, in the sky, and on the earth. Though Job was dumbfounded by this barrage of questions, flunking both lengthy quizzes, he *did* meet God face to face. This reassured the complainer that God had not abandoned him after all.

What was the purpose of God's rebuking response? By displaying His power and wisdom, God showed Job his ignorance and impatience. How could Job

comprehend or control God's ways with man, when he could not comprehend or control God's government in nature? Since Job could not answer God on these matters how could he hope to debate with God? Since God has His own ways and designs in the sky and with animals, does He not also have His own purposes in His dealings with people? Though people cannot understand God's doings, they can trust Him. Worship should stem from an appreciation of God Himself, not a comprehension of all God's ways. Though puzzled, people should still praise.

God did not explain His ways to Job; He exhibited them, thus showing that the sovereign Creator and Sustainer of the universe does not owe puny man an explanation. Man is to report to Him, not vice versa. Yet, though God did not explain His design in man's difficulties, His purpose in pain, He *did* reveal Himself.

This divine confrontation—the Bible's longest recorded oration by God Himself—is in two parts (38:1–40:2 and 40:6–41:34) with Job's response of humility (40:3-5) following the first part, and his response of repentance (42:1-6) after the second part.

This divine discourse "reaches dazzling heights of poetic splendor" (Victor E. Reichert, *Job*, p. 195). Its exuberant exaltation of God's wonders in nature exceeds all other exclamations of His creative power. No wonder Job was silenced, humbled, and repentant!

#### 1. GOD'S FIRST SPEECH (38:1–40:2)

##### a. God's opening rebuke and challenge to Job (38:1-3)

**38:1.** God's appearance was accompanied by a **storm,** possibly the storm Elihu may have sensed was approaching (37:22). "Storm" translates $s^e\bar{a}r\hat{a}h$, "a tempest or storm accompanied by violent wind" (also used, e.g., in 2 Kings 2:1, 11; Isa. 40:24, "whirlwind"; Ps. 107:25; Isa. 29:6, "tempest"; Ezek. 1:4, "windstorm"). Ironically "a mighty wind" caused the death of Job's 10 sons and daughters. Now a violent storm accompanied God's communication. Whereas the one was the occasion of ruin resulting in personal sorrow, this one was the occasion of revelation resulting in personal submission. Sometimes God used storms to dramatize awesome occasions (cf. Ex.

19:16-17; 1 Kings 19:11-13).

**38:2-3.** Opening with a rebuke, God accused Job (by means of a question) of darkening **counsel,** of beclouding God's design for the universe. Job's questioning confused rather than clarified the issues (cf. Elihu's comment about man's darkness, 37:19). For Job to suggest that God had become his enemy would only confuse others about God rather than shed light on His ways. Because of this Job, though he sometimes extolled God, did not really know whereof he spoke when he blamed God for being unfair. Job's **words** were **without knowledge** (as Elihu had twice said; 34:35; 35:16).

Then God told Job to get ready for His questions. (**Brace yourself like a man;** cf. 40:7, is lit., "gird up your loins like a man," geḇer, "strong man," that is, tuck your outer robe-like garment into your sash-belt as a man does before taking on a strenuous task such as running or fighting in a battle, Ex. 12:11; 1 Kings 18:46.) Job was to be alert so he could **answer** God intelligently. This is a striking reversal of Job's words to God, "Let the Almighty answer me" (31:35). Job the plaintiff had now become the defendant!

*b. God's questioning of Job regarding inanimate nature (38:4-38)*

In a series of questions on cosmology, oceanography, meteorology, and astronomy, God challenged Job's competence to judge His control of the world. God used irony to point up Job's ignorance (e.g., "Tell Me," vv. 4, 18; "Surely you know!" vv. 5, 21).

(1) Questions about the earth (38:4-21). **38:4-7.** Job was immediately confronted with his insignificance, for he was not present **when** God created the earth. Since he did not observe what had taken place then, he could not **understand** it. How could he hope to advise God now? Creating the earth is depicted like constructing a building with a **foundation. . . . dimensions. . . . a measuring line. . . . footings,** and a **cornerstone.** When God put the earth into orbit, it was similar to placing parts of a building in place.

Job was absent when **the morning stars** (possibly Venus and Mercury; "morning stars" were mentioned by Job in 3:9) **sang** and **the angels** (lit., "the sons of God"; cf. 1:6; 2:1) **shouted** with **joy**

over God's Creation of the earth. The stars' singing is a poetic personification, not a reference to the noise made by stars as detected by radio astronomy. In Psalm 148:2-3 angels and stars are together commanded to praise the Lord.

**38:8-11.** The origin of the earth was depicted as being like the construction of a building (vv. 4-7); the origin of the oceans was described like childbirth. Job was not in God's obstetric delivery room when He created the oceans, seas, and lakes, which were like a baby coming **from** a **womb** (cf. v. 29). God confined the waters, His newborn, by means of shorelines (**shut . . . behind doors . . . fixed limits for it and set its doors and bars** [as on a city gate] **in place**). The waters could no longer cover the entire globe as they had done (cf. Gen. 1:2, 9; Ps. 104:9). God separated the waters on the globe from the land; also above the earth's waters He placed **the clouds** (cf. Gen. 1:6) which like a baby's **garment** (cf. Job 38:14), shroud the earth's waters at night **in thick darkness.** In limiting the waters' **proud waves,** pounding at the shore, God may have subtly hinted at His control of Job in his proud allegations. God obviously had these cosmological elements under control.

**38:12-15.** God's control of the earth also includes the daily sequence of **dawn** and darkness. The dawn causes the **wicked,** who are active at night (cf. 24:14-17; John 3:19), to hide. It is as if **the morning** light were shaking them out of a blanket (Job 38:13), causing them to be **broken** in their power (**upraised arm,** v. 15; cf. 40:9). As the sun comes up the earth's contours become evident and **the wicked** no longer have darkness, which they call **their light,** in which to work. Since Job had nothing to do with establishing or controlling this aspect of Creation how could he question God's doings now?

**38:16-18.** God also put Job in his place by asking if he had ever explored such unseen realms as: (a) **the springs of the sea** (the Heb. word for "springs," nēḇek, occurring only here in the OT, probably refers to springs of water pouring into oceans from the ocean floors), (b) **the recesses of the deep** (the depths of the oceans), (c) **death,** pictured as having **gates** which open for its entrants (cf. Pss. 9:13; 107:18; Isa. 38:10) and pictured as being in darkness (cf. NIV marg.), and (d) the extensive regions **of the earth.**

**38:19-21.** God personified **light** and **darkness** as living in houses. By rhetorical questions the Lord pointed up to the complainant that he, a mere human, had no way of following the light, at sunset, to see where it goes, or of pursuing the darkness, at sunrise, to see **where** it resides. Their **places** and **dwellings** are inaccessible in the sense that Job could not explain how God moves the earth around the sun. **Surely you know** (cf. v. 5), **for you were already born!** was God's ironic way of affirming that Job did *not* know since he was *not* around when God set the earth's rotation in motion. Job's years were few compared with God's eternity (cf. 36:26).

(2) Questions about the sky (38:22-30). **38:22-24.** Job had no idea how God makes **snow** or **hail,** pictured as if they were kept in **storehouses** (cf. Pss. 33:7; 135:7; Jer. 10:31) and released by God when He chooses. Causing hail in battle (cf. Josh. 10:11) is an example of what Elihu had said about God's using elements of weather to stop people from working (Job 37:6-7), or to punish people (37:13). Job could not predict where God would dispense **lightning** flashes (cf. Elihu's words along this line in 36:30, 32; 37:3, 11, 15; cf. 38:35) or where the **winds** would blow.

**38:25-30.** Nor can God's ways with the **rain** and **ice** (cf. Elihu's comments about them in 36:27-28; 37:6, 10) be comprehended by man. Only God **cuts a channel** (an imaginary path) in the sky through which rain and **the thunderstorm** (cf. 28:26) come. **Man** does not even see where God often makes rain to fall—in **a desert** and a **wasteland.**

Again using the figure of childbirth (cf. 38:8) God asked Job if he knew whether **the rain** and **dew** have **a father** and **the ice** and **frost** have a mother. This may possibly be an allusion to and a polemic against the Canaanite myth that viewed rain as the semen of the gods, by which "mother earth" supposedly bears her "children," the crops. Certainly no one knows completely how the earth's Master sends rain and formulates elements of cold weather, including dew, ice, frost, and **frozen** lakes and rivers.

(3) Questions about stars and clouds (38:31-38). **38:31-33.** Job knew that God

made the **Pleiades . . . Orion,** and **Bear** constellations (9:9), but here God pointed out that Job had nothing to do with holding together the cluster of stars known as the Pleiades, nor could he alter the configuration of stars in the Orion **constellation,** nor cause the Bear (perhaps the Big Dipper) to appear at night. And since Job knew nothing of **the laws of the heavens,** the principles by which God regulates the stars, planets, and moon, how could he begin to criticize God's laws in His dealings with mankind? **Dominion over the earth** is **God's,** not Job's.

**38:34-38.** God also belittled Job by pointing to his inability to call down rain at will or to send down **lightning bolts** (cf. v. 24). In verse 36, difficult to translate, the word **heart** could perhaps be rendered "cloud layers" and the word **mind,** "celestial phenomenon" (see Rowley, *Job,* pp. 315-6). If those translations are accepted, they fit God's practice in this chapter of personifying inanimate nature. The clouds and lightning bolts seem to operate as if they have minds of their own. Or if the NIV rendering of verse 36 is correct then the thought is that God gives man wisdom; yet man in all his wisdom cannot tabulate the number of **clouds** nor can he time the "tilting" of the clouds (like animal skins that hold **water)** to moisten **the dust** and **the clods.**

*c. God's questioning of Job regarding animate nature (38:39–39:30)*

The 12 animals described here—six beasts, five birds, and an insect—all exhibit the creative genius and providential care of God. Fittingly the list begins with the lion, the king of the beasts, and ends with the word for eagle, the king of the birds (perhaps, however, the word for eagle refers to the griffon-vulture; see comments on 39:27). Job's incompetence and ignorance are seen in that he could not provide food for the first two animals (38:39-41), did not know of the birth of their offspring (the next two, 39:1-4), did not set them free or tame them (the two in 39:5-12), did not give them their odd ways (the two in 39:13-25), or provide them with their ability of flight (the last two, 39:26-30). One might think that animals, being under man, could be controlled and cared for by man. But God showed Job that he was in some ways inferior to even the animal kingdom.

(1) Lions and ravens. **38:39-41.** For his own safety, Job stayed clear of **lions,** not hunting their **prey** for them. Nor could he even provide **food for** black ravens, whose **young** are often forgotten by their parents. Job could not be the nourisher of the world's wild kingdom. Therefore since **God** cares for them (Jesus said ravens are fed by God, Luke 12:24), who are of less value than humans, would He neglect His care of people?

(2) Goats and deer. **39:1-4.** Job did not even **know when** certain animals **give birth** to their young or did he know their gestation periods. Totally apart from man's help or knowledge, but obviously under God's supervision, **mountain goats** and deer **bring forth their young,** who soon **grow** up, **leave** their parents, and fend for themselves (cf. references to the "young" in 38:41; 39:30). This mountain goat may be the Nubian Ibex, a goat in the wilds of the Middle East that hides when it bears its young. Even now relatively few people have ever seen these goats when they are bearing their offspring (Avinoam Danin, "Do You Know When the Ibexes Give Birth?" *Biblical Archaeology Review* 5. November-December 1979:50-1).

(3) Wild donkeys and wild oxen (39:5-12). **39:5-8.** Even the mere act of releasing **wild** donkeys out in the desert where they roamed **the wasteland,** lived in **the salt flats** (perhaps around the Dead Sea), rejected the noise of civilization, and ranged **the hills,** was beyond Job's abililty. Only God can help such animals survive.

**39:9-12.** In contrast with setting wild donkeys free, Job could not *tame* a **wild ox.** This animal, perhaps the auroch, resisted domestication. It would not serve Job or stay in his barn overnight, like a domesticated cow. Nor would it submit to plowing. Though unusually strong, it would not do **heavy work** for man. Nor would it pull a cart with **grain** from a field to a **threshing floor.** If Job could not tame even this one wild animal, how could he hope to challenge God's ways with man?

(4) Ostriches, storks, war horses, and locusts (39:13-25). **39:13-18. The ostrich,** a bizarre bird, is odd-featured, weighing up to 300 pounds and reaching a height of seven or eight feet. It flaps its

**wings** but it cannot fly. Unlike birds that fly, such as the **stork,** an ostrich **lays** its **eggs** in a nest **on the ground.** In fact several ostrich hens lay their eggs in one nest, but if there is no more room in the nest they deposit their eggs outside the nest **in the sand.** There other brooding hens, in the confusion of getting in and out of the nest, often crush these eggs. Ostriches' seeming unconcern for or even cruel treatment of their **young** (v. 16; cf. Lam. 4:3) evidences their lack of **wisdom** and **good sense.** Hens may desert the nest if they are overfed, or if impatient they may leave the nest before all the chicks are hatched. If a human disturbs a nest, an ostrich may trample the eggs. Or a hen may sit on eggs in another nest, forgetting her own. (For these and other examples of ostrich stupidity see George F. Howe, "Job and the Ostrich: A Case Study in Biblical Accuracy," *Journal of the American Scientific Affiliation* 15. December 1963:107-10.) Yet in spite of its stupidity, an ostrich can run 40 miles an hour, faster than a **horse.** Would Job even *think* of making such a peculiar bird?

**39:19-25.** Nor did Job have anything to do with creating the war **horse,** with its **strength** and its **mane,** ability to leap **like a locust** while **snorting,** pawing, and eagerly and fearlessly entering a battle. His rider's weapons on **his side,** he prances **the ground** as if eating it up, while waiting for **the trumpet . . . blast** to signal the charge. Snorting, he smells **the scent of battle** from a distance, and hears **the battle** commands. The spirited nature of the poetry in these verses matches the horse's vitality. Since Job was inferior to the strength of this horse, certainly he was inferior to the horse's Creator.

(5) Hawks and eagles. **39:26-30.** The hawk's annual migration **toward the south** occurred without Job's **wisdom.** On the other hand **the eagle** soars and builds its **nest** at **high** altitudes, **on a cliff** or **rocky crag,** where with keen vision he (cf. 28:7) spies **food** at great distances below. Devouring carcasses and sucking **blood** may suggest that this bird is the griffon-vulture rather than the eagle (George Cansdale, *Animals of Bible Lands.* London: Paternoster Press, 1970, p. 144). The Hebrew *nešer* may include both eagles and vultures (cf. 9:26).

This view of a few of the world's fauna demonstrates that Job, unable to contend with creation, hardly qualified to condemn the Creator. At the same time these words point up God's delight in His creation. His stars and angels sang and shouted when He made the earth (38:7), and He apparently enjoys His animal world. Also, God *uses* creation to limit the wicked (38:15), to aid man (38:23), to water the earth (38:26, 37-38); He *controls* and *limits* creation (38:8-9, 11); He *regulates* creation (38:12, 25, 31-33). And in the animal world God *provides* for animals (38:39-41; 39:29-30), *helps* them (vv. 1-4, 26-28), *frees* them (vv. 5-12), and *strengthens* them (vv. 13-25). In contrast Job could do none of these. Obviously God's orderly creation is provided for and well cared for; yet Job thought God's cosmic plan was arbitrary and that He lacked control, provision, and care.

### d. God's closing rebuke and challenge to Job (40:1-2)

**40:1-2.** God's first speech, which began with a rebuke and a challenge (cf. 38:2-3), also concluded with a rebuke and a challenge. The rebuke is in the form of a question. **The one who contends** refers to **Job.** Twice (10:2; 23:6) Job considered God's (10:1) contending with him (*rîḇ*, bringing a court case against him), but now ironically, God turned the accusation around. (Cf. Elihu's words, "Why do you complain [*rîḇ*] to Him?" [33:13]) How could Job now dare indict God? Since Job had accused **God** he should **answer** these questions (cf. "answer Me" in 38:3; 40:7).

### 2. JOB'S FIRST REPLY TO GOD (40:3-5)

**40:3-5.** Seeing that man is not the world's master, and that God controls and cares for His creation, Job acknowledged (a) his insignificance (**unworthy** comes from the verb *qālal*, "to be silent, trifling, small, insignificant") and (b) his inability to defend himself further. His former self-confidence ("I will say to God, Do not condemn me," 10:2; "Then summon me, and I will answer," 13:22; "You will call and I will answer You," 14:15) now was changed to humble submission ("**how can I reply to You?**"). Never again would Job approach God like a stately prince (31:37). Job admitted that he could not respond to God, as God

had challenged him to do (38:3; 40:2). His only response was silence—**I put my hand over my mouth**—a gesture he had suggested for his disputants ("clap your hand over your mouth," 21:5).

Job had spoken his piece, repeating himself before God (**I spoke once even twice**), but now he felt he should **say no more.** However, this response of the former plaintiff included no note of repentance. He was humbled, but not yet repentant. So God summoned him to answer more questions.

### 3. GOD'S SECOND SPEECH (40:6–41:34)

Like God's first speech, this one included a challenge (40:6-7), a rebuke (40:8-14), and questions about nature (40:15–41:34). God's first speech pointed to inanimate and animate creation; this oration called Job's attention to only two animals. Unlike the first speech this one did not end with a closing rebuke and challenge (cf. 40:2).

### a. God's challenge and rebuke to Job (40:6-14)

**40:6-8.** Again speaking **out of the storm** (cf. comments on 38:1) God repeated verbatim His previous challenge (38:3) that Job **brace** himself **like a man** and that he **answer** God's questions. God then rebuked Job with a **question** (cf. the questions in 38:2; 40:2): **Would you discredit My justice?** Only here did God refer directly to Job's accusation of the Sovereign's supposed unfairness.

In the next question **Would you condemn Me to justify yourself?** the word "condemn" is the verb *rāšaʿ*, "to act wickedly or to condemn as wicked." This is an amazing reprimand by God, for this verb has occurred several times already in the Book of Job. Job had said he would unwittingly condemn himself if God confronted him (9:20a). Then he said he would tell God not to condemn him (10:2). Eliphaz told Job that the sufferer was condemning himself by his words (15:6), and Elihu believed that the three had condemned Job (32:3) Now God said the One who was really being condemned was God Himself! Job's self-justification that *he* was not acting wickedly resulted in his saying that *God* was acting wickedly.

**40:9-14.** To contend with God suggests an assumed equality with God. And yet no mortal possesses that. Job did not have God's strength (**arm** symbolizes strength; cf. 38:15; Ps. 89:13; Isa. 40:10; and cf. **hand** in Job 40:14), or the ability to terrify by his **voice.** Without these resources to rule the world and rectify its wrongs how could Job rightfully criticize?

If his libels against the sovereign Lord were to be accepted as true, then Job would first have to prove his ability to govern the universe. Defaming God, as Job had done, was in essence a usurping of divine authority, an attempt to put himself in **God's** place. So, as God reasoned, if Job wanted the job of world Ruler, then he would need to prove he was qualified. Job would need to dress the part, putting on God's **glory and splendor,** His **honor and majesty.** Of course, he would be disqualified in even that. His assignment, God said, was to **unleash** his **wrath,** humiliating the godless and **proud** merely by looking at them (cf. the Leviathan's ability to look down on the haughty, 41:34), and then crushing and burying **them.** Since Job had accused God of neglecting to punish **the wicked** (21:29-31; 24:1-17), God ironically suggested He turn over the responsibility to Job to see if he could fulfill it. Only if Job could carry out such an awesome task, would God **admit to** the complainer's independence and self-sufficiency and the validity of his criticisms.

*b. God's questioning about two animals (40:15–41:34)*

God's first speech displayed a panorama of nature including 12 animals, but in His second speech His zoom lens focused on only 2 animals. God thereby impressed Job with his mere puniness and with God's majestic power.

Scholars differ in their views as to who these creatures were. Against the view that the behemoth (40:15-24) and Leviathan (chap. 41) are mythological, as some suggest, are these facts: (1) God told Job to "look at" the behemoth, (40:15). (2) God said He "made" the behemoth, as He had made Job (40:15). (3) The detailed descriptions of both animals' anatomies befits real not mythological beasts. (4) Animals in myths were based on real creatures, but were given exaggerated features. (5) The 12 animals in 38:39–39:30 were real, which would cause one to expect these 2 to be real also. (6) Though sometimes elsewhere in

Scripture the Leviathan may be mythological (e.g., 3:8; Ps. 74:14; Isa. 27:1), it is also spoken of elsewhere as a created being (Ps. 104:24, 26). And the plural Hebrew word for behemoth is used in Joel 1:20, where it is rendered "wild animals."

However, though these are apparently actual animals, they may *also* represent proud, wicked elements in the world. In the ancient Near East these beasts, in their brute force (Job 40:16-18; 41:12, 22, 26-29) and agitation of the waters (41:31-32), symbolized the chaotic effect of evil. (This helps explain how the crocodile then became the basis for the idea of a mythological dragon, a creature that causes extreme chaos in the waters.) In Egypt the Pharaoh, in preparation for his enthronement, ritually harpooned (with the help of others) a male hippopotamus and occasionally a crocodile, to dramatize his ability to dispel chaos and maintain order. The king could carry out this difficult harpooning task only because of his supposed superhuman, godlike strength. But God was showing Job that he did not have that ability. Since he could not conquer the animalistic symbols of evil, how could he subdue evil people?

The association of both animals with the water (40:21-23; 41:31-32) ties this speech to the first divine discourse (38:8-11, 16).

(1) The behemoth. **40:15-24.** God mentioned several things about the behemoth: its position with Job as a fellow creature (v. 15), its diet (v. 15), its physical strength (vv. 16-19), its habitat (vv. 20-23), and its fierceness (v. 24). The word **behemoth** is the plural of "beast." Since one animal is described in verses 15-24, the plural probably points up the animal's greatness. Suggestions as to the identity of this animal include an elephant, a rhinoceros, a plant-eating brontosaurus (dinosaur), a water buffalo, and a hippopotamus. The common view that this huge creature is the hippopotamus is supported by several observations: (1) The hippo is herbivorous (it **feeds on grass like an ox,** v. 15). Therefore **wild animals** do not fear being attacked by it (v. 20). (2) It has massive **strength** in its **loins,** stomach **muscles . . . tail . . . thighs,** metallike **bones** and limbs (vv. 16-18). Unlike the elephant, a hippopota-

mus' stomach muscles are particularly strong and thick. The rendering that his tail **sways like a cedar** (possibly meaning a cedar branch, not a cedar trunk) suggests to some that "tail" means the trunk of an elephant. However, Ugaritic parallels indicate that the verb "sways" (which occurs only here in the OT) means "stiffens." In that case the hippopotamus' tail, though small, was referred to. The tail stiffens when the animal is frightened or is running. (3) The hippopotamus was the largest of the animals known in the ancient Near East (**he ranks first among the works of God,** v. 19). The adult hippo of today weighs up to 8,000 pounds. "There may have been an especially gigantic variety that flourished in the Jordan in those days, and as such he may have outclassed even the elephant . . . " (Gleason L. Archer, Jr., *The Book of Job,* p. 107). (4) The hippo is difficult if not impossible to kill with a mere hand sword. The words **His Maker can approach him with His sword** (v. 19) suggest that *only* God dare approach the beast for hand combat. Nor can he be captured or harpooned when only his **eyes** or **nose** show above the water (v. 24). (5) As a hippopotamus **lies hidden . . . in the marsh. . . . the stream,** and **the river** (vv. 21-23), its sustenance (perhaps vegetation) floats down from **the hills** (v. 20). This huge creature is undistrubed by river turbulence for the rivers are his habitat (v. 23). An elephant or brontosaurus would hardly be described this way. A surging river would hardly reach the depth of a brontosaurus' mouth.

(2) The leviathan (chap. 41). The discussion of the leviathan is longer than God's comments on any of the other animals. That fact, coupled with the vicious nature of the leviathan, an animal that even attacks man (v. 8), makes chapter 41 climactic. This beast has been variously interpreted as the seven-headed sea monster Lotan of Ugaritic mythology, the whale, the dolphin, a marine dinosaur that survived the Flood, and, most likely, the crocodile. Archer suggests it was a giant crocodile of the Jordan River, not the Egyptian crocodile (*The Book of Job,* p. 107). Man's attempt to capture this animal and the detailed description of the monster's anatomy suggest that it was an actual creature. Calling the behemoth

and the leviathan dinosaurs wrongly dates Job's lifetime within only a few hundred years of the Flood. The crocodile fits God's description of the leviathan's back (vv. 13, 15-17, 23), teeth (v. 14), chest and undersides (vv. 24, 30), and its churning of the waters (vv. 31-32). (See comments on vv. 18-21 for answers to suggestions that this is a dragon.) The behemoth and leviathan have many similarities (see Roy B. Zuck, *Job,* p. 180), so if one is an actual animal, then the other probably is also.

As discussed earlier, in the ancient Near East both animals were symbols of chaotic evil.

God spoke of this creature's inability to be captured by fishing equipment and tamed by man (vv. 1-11), its awesome anatomy (vv. 12-25), and the leviathan's inability to be captured by hunting equipment (vv. 26-34).

**41:1-11. A fishhook . . . a rope. . . . a cord,** and **a hook** are inadequate to capture so fierce an animal (vv. 1-2). It is not so easily tamed that it would, personified like a human, plead to be released or agree to being tamed and used as **a pet** (vv. 3-5). **Merchants** cannot sell it, since it is seldom captured (v. 6). Larger fishing equipment, such as **harpoons** and **spears** (v. 7), and even **hand** combat (v. 8) are useless. Since people are afraid at even the sight of a crocodile, **no one** would dare wake it up (vv. 9-10). God then used this fierce amphibian to illustrate man's inability to oppose God (**to stand against** Him) or to **claim** He owes them something (since **everything** is His). If Job panicked at seeing a crocodile, how did he dare confront the crocodile's Maker, telling Him He had done wrong? If the beast's power exceeded Job's strength, certainly Job would be impotent before God.

**41:12-17.** God then reminded Job of the crocodile's anatomy (vv. 12-25). It is difficult to catch a crocodile because of its **strength** (v. 12), the protective armor of its tough hide (v. 13), jaws (**the doors of his mouth**) that man cannot pry open by hand (v. 14), sharp **teeth** that terrify (v. 14), and its **back . . . rows of shields** that weapons **cannot** penetrate (vv. 15-17).

**41:18-21.** The movements of a crocodile's nose, eyes, and mouth also put people in panic. A crocodile can stay completely submerged underwater for about five minutes. When it comes up for air and sneezes the water out **from** its **nostrils,** the spray looks like **flashes of light** in the sun. When this reptile emerges from the water, its small **eyes,** with slits for pupils like a cat's eyes, are seen first, **like** the dawn's **rays.** Interestingly in Egyptian hieroglyphs, the crocodile's eye represents the dawn (Victor E. Reichert, *Job,* p. 216).

Do the **firebrands** from its **mouth** and the **smoke** and **flames** from its nostrils (vv. 19-21) mean this is a mythical dragon, after all? No. These may be explained as the way God spoke of the crocodile's breath and water, which when emitted from its mouth, look in the sunlight like a stream of fire. This poetic language, probably spoken in hyperbole, accentuates this beast's frightful nature. This language also is the basis for the concept of a dragon in mythology. (See comments under "b. God's questioning about two animals [40:15–41:34].")

**41:22-25.** With a strong **neck,** tight (cf. v. 15) and **firm** flesh, and unusually **hard** chest, this creature causes **dismay** in people. No wonder, **when he rises up** out of the water, even **the mighty** tremble and run. The Hebrew word rendered "When he rises up" is actually a noun, "from his proud lifting up." Job had said *God's* "proud lifting up" (or "uprising" or "loftiness"; "splendor" in 31:23) had terrified him and would terrify the three controversialists (13:11). How inconsistent then for Job, terrified by God's loftiness, to suppose he could confront God.

**41:26-34.** Strong hunters (cf. v. 25) in those days seldom confronted fierce crocodiles because their normal weaponry—the **sword . . . spear . . . dart,** and **javelin**—had **no effect** on that animal's tough hide (vv. 15-17, 23). Instruments of **iron** or **bronze** were easily broken by this beast. Objects propelled through the air, such as **arrows** or **slingstones** bounced harmlessly off its hide. Nor could a crocodile be felled with **a club** or a **lance.**

The hide of this animal's **undersides** is so **jagged** that when he walks in **the mud** he leaves marks that look **like a threshing sledge** (with its sharp points) has been pulled through the mud. Swimming in a river, a crocodile so stirs the water that it looks as if it were **boiling.** Saying that his agitating the water is **like**

**a pot of ointment** means that it looks like foam caused by an apothecary when he boils ointment.

Another terrifying aspect of the leviathan is its speed. It moves through the water so fast that it leaves a shiny **wake,** whitecaps of waves that appear like **white hair.**

**Nothing** equals this **creature;** he is afraid of nothing, yet everyone is terrified of him. Even a **haughty** man crouches in fear before a crocodile. This unconquerable animal is therefore **king** over **proud** beasts and man. Whereas Job could not humble the haughty merely by looking down on them (40:11-14), the leviathan, a mere animal, could do so. God's concluding statements that the crocodile **looks down on** the "haughty" and is supreme **over** the "proud" would have reminded Job that his pride before *God,* the crocodile's Fashioner, was both precarious and dangerous.

In this second lecture (40:6–41:34) God was therefore challenging Job to subdue these monsters—a task he obviously could not do—if he wanted to maintain order in God's universe. Job had been concerned that God had not dealt with evil; so God was showing Job that he was unqualified to take over God's job of controlling and conquering evil for he could not even conquer the animal *symbols* of evil. In fact God had *made* these animals, which suggests that evil forces are not beyond God's control. He permits evil and chaos to rule for a time just as he had given Satan permission to test Job (1:12; 2:6).

Man cannot subdue singlehandedly a hippopotamus or a crocodile, his fellow creatures (40:15). Nor can man conquer evil in the world, which they symbolize. Only God can do that. Therefore Job's defiant impugning of God's ways in the moral universe—as if God were incompetent or even evil—was totally absurd and uncalled for.

### 4. JOB'S SECOND REPLY TO GOD (42:1-6)

**42:1-2.** In Job's first response (40:3-5) he admitted his finiteness in the face of God's display of numerous wonders of nature above, on, and under the earth. But he did not admit to God's sovereignty or to his own sin of pride. **Job** now confessed those two things in his second reply. Overwhelmed by the strength and fierceness of the behemoth and the leviathan, Job sensed his own inadequacy to conquer and control evil, which they represented. He therefore saw anew the greatness of God's power and sovereignty. Job's words **I know that You can do all things** point up the folly of his questioning God's ability to govern the universe. Job's efforts to thwart (lit., "cut off") God's **plan** were now seen as futile.

**42:3.** Job quoted God's question **Who is this that obscures My counsel without knowledge?** to infer that God was right. Job had spoken without knowledge (as Elihu had said, 34:35; 35:16); he talked about things beyond his comprehension, things **too wonderful** (cf. "wonders" in 37:14) or awesome in creation **for** him **to know.** Job now discarded his complaints about God's inability to rule the world with justice. The idea that he could boldly refute any of God's trumped-up charges (23:4-7; 31:35-36) was now abandoned.

**42:4-5.** Again Job quoted the Lord, this time citing God's challenge at the beginning of each of His two speeches (38:3; 40:7): **I will question you, and you shall answer Me.** This quotation implied an admission that Job was unable to answer any of the Sovereign's barrage of rhetorical questions. Job admitted to flunking God's biology examinations.

Job had only **heard of** God's doings. The complainer was not an eyewitness of the act of Creation, a fact God called to his attention near the beginning of His first speech (38:4-11). Nor could Job even view firsthand many aspects of natural Creation (38:16-24; 39:1-4). His perspective of God's total workings was therefore limited and secondhand.

But now that Job was addressed directly by God, this experience exceeded his previous knowledge, like seeing (**now my eyes have seen You**) compared with hearing. This thrilling view of God, probably spiritual insight, not physical vision, deepened his perspective and appreciation of God. What Job now knew of God was incomparable to his former ideas, which were really ignorant. This personal confrontation with God silenced his arguing and deepened his awe.

**42:6.** Having gained insight (v. 5) into God's ways and character—His creative power and genius, His sovereign

control, and His providential care and love—Job confessed his own unworthiness and repented. **I despise myself** means he rejected his former accusations of God spoken in pride. God had already rebuked Job for indicting, faulting, and discrediting Him (40:2). Job then repented **in dust and ashes,** a way of expressing his self-deprecation (cf. Gen. 18:27). Throwing dust in the air so that it came down on one's head (cf. Job 2:12) and sitting in or near ashes or with ashes on one's body (cf. 2:8; Isa. 58:5; Dan. 9:3) were signs of a humbled condition. Having grieved over his losses, Job now grieved over his sin.

Obviously he did not repent of the sins which his three friends had conjured up. He stuck persistently to his position that his suffering was not merited by precalamity sins (Job 27:2-6). But, as Elihu had pointed out, bitterness and pride had followed his loss of wealth, family, and health (32:2; 33:17; 35:12-13; 36:9; 37:24). At first, however, Job's response was proper (1:21-22; 2:10). Job now saw, as God had challenged him (40:10), that no one can stand accusingly against Him. Realizing that God is not obligated to man, Job's questions vanished and his resentment left. He was now satisfied, for God had communicated with him about His own person, not about Job's problems. Now Job was willing to trust the Sovereign, whose ways are perfect (Ps. 18:30), even when he could not understand. Undoubtedly God forgave him of his former sin of pride.

## III. Epilogue (42:7-17)

This section, like the opening (chaps. 1–2), is written in prose. God now turned to the three critics, before He restored Job's prosperity and family.

### A. God's condemning of Job's friends (42:7-9)

**42:7.** God spoke **to Eliphaz,** probably the eldest of the three, and said He was **angry with** him and his **two** companions (similar to Elihu's reaction to the three, 32:3) for they had **not spoken of Me what is right, as My servant Job has.** They who had assumed a position of defending God were now on the defensive themselves. As Job had predicted (13:7-9) matters did not turn out well for them. They thought they knew God's ways but they did not expect this! The words, **My servant Job,** spoken by God four times in 42:7-8, point up his restored position as a trusting and obedient servant of the Lord (cf. 1:8; 2:3).

By insisting that suffering is always retributive, the three rhetoricians were limiting God's sovereign ability to use suffering for other purposes. As a result, they cruelly indicted innocent Job.

How then did Job speak "what is right"? Had he not repeatedly and proudly challenged God, accusing Him of injustice and unwarranted silence? Yes, but he had now repented of his proud accusations (42:6) and therefore he was accepted by God. Furthermore, he never cursed God, as Satan had predicted and his wife had urged (1:11; 2:5, 9), though he came close to it. Though Job continued to contend with God, he never renounced Him. Also his view of God's power and wisdom exceeded that of the three.

**42:8-9.** To the utter surprise and chagrin of the three critics, God told them to offer **a burnt offering** of **seven bulls and seven rams,** a large **sacrifice.** And they were to have **Job pray for** them as their mediator (cf. his earlier work as a priest, 1:5). Never once had they prayed for *him.* But now Job, whom they had condemned and badgered, and who had rejected their counsel, was to intercede for them. What an amazing irony!

They had defended God's justice in striking **Job** down. But now they saw that God is concerned with more than justice; He is also known for love and grace. Repentance, which they had recommended for Job, was now what *they* had to do. They too were silenced—and corrected—by God's direct communication. Elihu was excluded from this act of repentance because he, though not having all the truth on Job's situation, was nearer the truth than the other three.

Job had longed for a mediator between himself and God (16:19-21) since his three countrymen were not interceding for him; but ironically he himself became a mediator for *them,* even though they did *not* ask for one.

## B. God's restoring of Job's prosperity and family (42:10-17)

**42:10-11.** Job's vision of God's transcendence and his ensuing repentance paved the way for his forgiveness of and intercessory praying for his three friends. Then his forgiving spirit toward them paved the way for God to bless him. His painful disease was cured either at this time or immediately after his repentance (v. 6).

**All his brothers . . . sisters, and** acquaintances (probably including the forgiven three!), who had forsaken him (19:13-14), heard of his restoration. They now dined **with him in his house. They comforted . . . him** regarding his **trouble** (*rā'âh,* "calamity"), though this was probably less consoling than if they had done so earlier. This woe, as **Job** himself had acknowledged (1:21; 2:10), was **brought** on by **the LORD** (through the instrumentality of Satan). Then, to show their kindness, they **each . . . gave him a piece of silver** (*qᵉśîṭâh,* a word used only here and in Gen. 33:19 and Josh. 24:32), **and a gold ring** (*nezem*), referring either to a nose ring (Gen. 24:22) or an earring (Gen. 35:4).

**42:12.** God restored to Job twice the number of livestock he had before (v. 10; cf. 1:3) so that his later years were **more** prosperous **than the first.** Perhaps he used the silver and gold received from his siblings and countrymen to purchase fresh livestock, from which the number probably grew by breeding over a period of time.

Did this outpouring of material blessing from God mean that the theory of the three self-appointed jurors was correct, after all? (They had predicted that prosperity follows repentance, 5:8, 17-26; 8:5-7, 21; 11:13-19.) No, the restoration of wealth was a token of God's grace, not an obligation of His justice. Since Job had (unknowingly) silenced Satan by not cursing God, and since he had repented of his pride, his suffering did not need to continue. The restoring of his estate demonstrated to his friends that God had restored him. Furthermore the Book of Job does not deny the general biblical principle that God blesses the righteous. Instead the Scriptures show that the principle is not invariable and airtight. God in His sovereignty can give—or hold back—blessings in accord with His purposes.

**42:13-15.** Job's grief over the loss of his 10 children was relieved somewhat, though probably not fully, by the birth of

10 others. The names of the **three** youngest **daughters** are given, whereas the names of Job's other 17 children are unknown. **Jemimah** means "dove," **Keziah** means "cinnamon perfume" (cassia, from $q^e\dot{s}i\hat{a}h$, is a cinnamon bark from which perfume is made), and **Keren-Happuch** means "horn of eyepaint" (i.e., an animal-horn bottle for holding a dye used to make eyelashes, eyelids, and eyebrows more attractive). These names speak of the girls' striking beauty, for which they were well known. Another interesting fact about the **daughters** is that they shared **with their brothers** in receiving from Job **an inheritance**—an unusual occurrence in those days. In later years a daughter received her father's inheritance only if she had no brothers (Num. 27:8).

**42:16-17.** Following his terrible ordeal, **Job lived 140 years.** If he was about 70 when the calamities struck, he lived to be about 210. According to Jewish tradition, his latter years (140) were exactly twice the number of his former ones (70). Job **saw his** descendants **to the fourth generation,** that is, he lived to see his great-great-grandchildren. His death came, not when he was in intense agony from his losses (as he had prayed, 3:20-26; 10:18-22), but later when he was **full of years.**

This book, probably the oldest in the Bible, deals with mankind's most pressing problems: the question of suffering and man's relationship with God. Job's experience billboards the truth that man's worship of God does not stem from a businesslike contract, whereby he earns material rewards from God. Man's relationship to God is not a juridical arrangement in which He is obligated to reward man for every good act. Instead, man is to trust Him, worship Him regardless of his circumstances, and rely on the perfections of His character even when God's ways are not fully understood.

Misfortune does not mean God has forsaken His own. It does mean He has plans that the sufferer may know nothing of. A believer's unmerited tragedy may never be fully understood. Yet he can realize that God is in charge, that God still loves him and cares for him. This is what Job learned. His three denouncers said suffering's purpose is always *discipline* (punishment for wrongdoing); Job felt it was for *destruction* (thinking God was determined to destroy him); Elihu stressed that the aim is *direction* (to keep him from death). But God had two purposes: *demonstration* (that Satan's allegations were false) and *development* (of Job's spiritual insight). Therefore to attack God, to malign Him, challenge Him, accuse Him, bait Him, or try to corner Him—all of which Job did—are out of the question for a believer. To criticize God's wisdom only shows one's own ignorance. The chasm between God and man leaves no place for pride and self-sufficiency.

Job did not receive explanations regarding his problems; but he did come to a much deeper sense of the majesty and loving care of God. Thus he came to trust Him more fully, knowing that His ways should not be challenged. Though often inexplicable and mysterious, God's plans are benevolent and beneficial.

# BIBLIOGRAPHY

Andersen, Francis I. *Job: An Introduction and Commentary.* The Tyndale Old Testament Commentaries. Downers Grove, Ill.: InterVarsity Press, 1976.

Archer, Gleason L., Jr. *The Book of Job: God's Answer to the Problem of Undeserved Suffering.* Grand Rapids: Baker Book House, 1982.

Baker, Wesley C. *More Than a Man Can Take: A Study of Job.* Philadelphia: Westminster Press, 1966.

Barnes, Albert. *Notes, Critical, Illustrative, and Practical, on the Book of Job.* 2 vols. Glasgow: Blackie & Son, 1847. Reprint. Grand Rapids: Baker Book House, 1950.

Davidson, A.B. *The Book of Job.* Cambridge: Cambridge University Press, 1903.

Dhorme, Édouard. *A Commentary on the Book of Job.* Translated by Harold Knight. New York: Thomas Nelson Publishers, 1967.

Driver, Samuel Rolles, and Gray, George Buchanan. *A Critical and Exegetical Commentary on the Book of Job.* The International Critical Commentary. Edinburgh: T. & T. Clark, 1921.

Ellison, H.L. *A Study of Job: From Tragedy to Triumph.* Grand Rapids: Zondervan Publishing House, 1971.

Gordis, Robert. *The Book of God and Man: A Study of Job.* Chicago: University of Chicago Press, 1965.

_____. *The Book of Job: Commentary, New Translation, and Special Studies.* New York: Jewish Theological Seminary of America, 1978.

Green, William Henry. *The Argument of the Book of Job Unfolded.* 1874. Reprint. Minneapolis: James & Klock Christian Publishers, 1977.

Howard, David M. *How Come, God?* Philadelphia: A.J. Holman Co., 1972.

Johnson, L.D. *Israel's Wisdom: Learn and Live.* Nashville: Broadman Press, 1975.

_____. *Out of the Whirlwind: The Major Message of the Book of Job.* Nashville: Broadman Press, 1971.

Pope, Marvin H. *Job.* 3rd ed. The Anchor Bible. Garden City, N.Y.: Doubleday & Co., 1973.

Reichert, Victor E. *Job.* London: Soncino Press, 1946.

Rowley, H.H. *Job.* The Century Bible. Greenwood, S.C.: Attic Press, 1970.

Schaper, Robert N. *Why Me, God?* Glendale, Calif.: Regal Books, 1974.

Stedman, Ray C. *Expository Studies in Job: Behind Suffering.* Waco, Tex.: Waco Books, 1981.

Thomas, David. *Book of Job: Expository and Homiletical Commentary.* 1878. Reprint. Grand Rapids: Kregel Publications, 1982.

Westermann, Claus. *The Structure of the Book of Job: A Form-Critical Analysis.* Philadelphia: Fortress Press, 1981.

Zuck, Roy B. *Job.* Everyman's Bible Commentary. Chicago: Moody Press, 1978.

# PSALMS

## Allen P. Ross

## INTRODUCTION

Of all the books in the Old Testament the Book of Psalms most vividly represents the faith of individuals in the Lord. The Psalms are the inspired responses of human hearts to God's revelation of Himself in law, history, and prophecy. Saints of all ages have appropriated this collection of prayers and praises in their public worship and private meditations.

**Title of the Psalms.** The English title "Psalms" (or "Psalter") is derived from the Greek translation of the Old Testament. In the Codex Vaticanus (fourth century A.D.) the title *Psalmoi* and the subtitle *Biblos psalmôn* ("Book of Psalms") are used; in the Codex Alexandrinus (fifth century) the name *Psalterion* appears. The Greek word *psalmos,* which translates the Hebrew *mizmôr,* signifies music accompanied by stringed instruments. Under the influence of the Septuagint and of Christianity, the word *psalmos* came to designate a "song of praise" without an emphasis on accompaniment by stringed instruments (Christoph Barth, *Introduction to the Psalms.* N.Y.: Scribners and Sons, 1966, p. 1). Because *mizmôr* is used in the titles of 57 of the psalms, the Greek translators used the translation of that word for the title of the entire collection.

In the Hebrew Bible the title of the book is *sēper tᵉhillîm,* "Book of Praises," referring to their content rather than form. This title is fitting for the collection of hymns used in Israel's worship, because most of the psalms contain an element of praise. Claus Westermann, in his study of the individual lament psalms, concludes that he found no psalms that do not progress beyond petition and lament to the praise of God (*The Praise of God in the Psalms,* p. 74). In the titles *tᵉhillâh* ("praise") is found only once (Ps. 145), but it is used some 28 times in the book. *Tᵉhillîm* may be a technical term for the book, because the normal plural of *tᵉhillâh* is *tᵉhillôt.*

**Place in the Canon.** In the Hebrew Bible the Book of Psalms belongs to the third part, the Writings (after the Law and the Prophets). In the Hebrew manuscripts Psalms usually appears first in the Writings.

This arrangement of the biblical canon is not followed by the English versions, where the order is based on the Greek and Latin versions. Here the arrangement of the Prophets and the Writings seems to be topical and chronological.

### Nature of the Psalms

*1. Religious lyric poetry.* The Psalms are the largest collection of ancient lyrical poetry in existence. Lyric poetry directly expresses the individual emotions of the poet. As part of the Old Testament, this poetry is also necessarily religious. Religious lyric poety is the expression of these emotions and feelings as they are stirred by the thought of God and directed to Him (A.F. Kirkpatrick, *The Book of Psalms,* p. x).

Many psalms address God directly with their poetic expressions of petition and praise. They reveal all the religious feelings of the faithful—fears, doubts, and tragedies, as well as triumphs, joys, and hopes. The psalmists frequently drew on their experiences for examples of people's needs and God's goodness and mercy. Singing of past deliverances in easily remembered didactic poetry provided support and comfort for believers in their hours of trial, as well as warning them against unbelief and disobedience. In this regard the psalmists rejoiced over the Law of God as their guide for conduct and direction for prosperity. Several psalms also incorporate Israel's "wisdom" or philosophy of life. These hymns reflect the moral teachings of Proverbs and other pieces of Wisdom literature.

Because the Psalms formed the "hymnal" of the temple, they often celebrate the ordinances of the sanctuary and exult in the privilege of drawing near to God in His holy mountain. This aspect of the psalms, combined with their display of personal religious feelings, makes them the most powerful and complete expression of the worship of ancient Israel. Set in the form of lyric poetry, they became unforgettable.

The Psalms reveal that the Israelites were an intensely religious people, worshipers of God with a strong sense of right and wrong. Regarding themselves as God's covenant people, they opposed wickedness and unbelief. Their daily activities, their national celebrations, and their military activities were carried out with religious commitment. The fact that the songs reflect this commitment makes them all the more serviceable for the edification of the entire household of faith.

*2. Evocative language.* Lyric poetry differs from other literary forms in that it is a more concentrated form of discourse with more consciously artistic elements. Concentration is achieved through the use of images, symbols, figures, emotive vocabulary, and multiple meanings. The imagery used in the Psalms is earthy, for the Israelites were largely a nation of farmers and shepherds living in the countryside close to nature. It was also militaristic, because they were often involved in wars to conquer the land, and defensive wars against the ravages of empires which at times were part of God's discipline. To understand fully the poetic expressions they used, one must sense the people's cultural experiences.

Evocative language used in poetic discourse enabled the psalmists to convey several things at the same time. Because the truth was presented in word pictures, it evoked in the reader the feelings that the poet had when he wrote the lines; it excited in the reader the emotional significance of the words as well as their intellectual meanings. For example, the poet could picture the vitality and stability of a godly person through the image of a tree planted by water, or the fear of the fainthearted through the im-

age of melting wax, or the verbal attacks of the wicked through the imagery of swords and arrows. So an exposition of the Psalms must be sensitive to such images in order to appreciate both the intellectual and the emotional meanings of the poetry. In a word, the Psalms must be treated as religious lyrical poetry.

Several headings are used to designate the types of psalms in the book. *Mizmôr*, translated "psalms," heads 57 psalms. The term signified a song accompanied by stringed instruments. "Song" translates *šîr*; it is used of 32 songs. A *maśkîl* is probably "a contemplative poem." Thirteen psalms are labeled with this heading. The designation *miḵtām* is found with 6 psalms. Later it was understood to mean "epigram" or "inscribed poem," but this is disputed. Five psalms are labeled "prayers" (*tᵉpillâh*), and 1 is called a "praise" (*tᵉhillâh*, Ps. 145).

*3. Meter.* The fact that the psalms are artistic means that they display in fuller measure and with greater frequency the components of artistic form, including patterns, design, unity, balance, harmony, and variation. The psalmists were imaginative and creative; they regarded their artistry as crucial to the meaning of its content.

Basic to the pattern of poetry is meter. Hebrew poetry certainly has meter and rhythm, but it is not possible as yet to identify and determine that meter with any degree of certainty. Most commentators are satisfied to count the number of accented Hebrew words or word units in a line as the basis of their poetical analysis. Because only a few psalms consistently follow a metrical pattern of accented words, attempts to reconstruct the text according to preconceived or novel ideas of meter are unconvincing.

*4. Parallelism.* The predominant feature of Hebrew poetic structure is the repetition of meaning in parallel expressions—the so-called poetic parallelism. The biblical verse of poetry normally has two or more of these parallel units. The relationship between the parallel units must be studied to determine the emphasis of a verse as a whole. The following categories of parallelism have become standard, and may be used to articulate the relationships of the units (also see

A.A. Anderson, *The Book of Psalms*, 1:40-2; and James L. Kugel, *The Idea of Biblical Poetry: Parallelism and Its History*. New Haven, Conn.: Yale University Press, 1981).

*Synonymous parallelism* describes the closest similarity between each of the two consecutive lines. A term or unit of thought in one part is paralleled by an equivalent term or unit of thought in the other. In the following examples parallel elements have been divided in accord with the accented words in the Hebrew verse:

"Then Israel / entered / Egypt;//
Jacob / sojourned / in the land of Ham" (Ps. 105:23, author's trans.).

*Antithetical parallelism* balances the parallel elements through the opposition or contrast of thoughts:

"In the morning / it flourishes / and is renewed;//
in the evening / it fades / and it withers" (90:6, author's trans.).

*Emblematic parallelism* occurs when one of the parallel units is a metaphorical illumination of the other:

"As a father / pities / his children,//
so the Lord / pities / those who fear Him" (103:13, author's trans.).

The word order need not be the same in the parallel expressions in the verse. In fact sometimes the word order in the second part is inverted to form a chiasm in the poetry. Moreover, the parallelism is frequently *incomplete*. Two types may be distinguished:

*Incomplete parallelism with compensation* refers to a verse when only some of the terms are parallel, even though each part has the same number of terms:

"You will destroy / their offspring / from the earth,//
and their children / from among the / sons of men" (21:10, author's trans.).

This type may also appear with repeated expressions in a step-parallelism known as *climactic parallelism*:

"Ascribe / to the LORD / O heavenly beings,//
Ascribe / to the LORD / glory and strength,//
Ascribe / to the LORD / the glory of His name;//
Worship / the LORD / in holy array" (29:1-2, author's trans.).

*Incomplete parallelism without compensation* refers to a verse in which one of the lines has fewer terms:

"O LORD, / do not rebuke / me in Your anger,//
or discipline me / in Your wrath" (6:1).

When the second parallel expression is all compensation (i.e., when it simply continues the thought of the first), the parallelism is designated as *formal* (and thus not really parallelism at all):

"I have installed / My King//
on Zion / My holy hill" (2:6).

Some still find it helpful to use Lowth's general category of "synthetic parallelism" instead of "incomplete parallelism." In synthetic parallelism the second line develops the idea of the first.

Parallelism describes the relationship of expressions within verses (*internal parallelism*); at times it also reflects the relationships between verses (*external parallelism*).

*5. Stylistic arrangements.* Apart from a few psalms, the arrangement of lines of poetry into stanzas or strophes is not common. Psalm 119 is perhaps best known for this, for it is divided into 22 strophes of eight verses each. A few psalms have a refrain to mark out their strophic arrangements (e.g., 42:5, 11; 43:5; 57:5, 11; 80:3, 7, 19).

Certain psalms are alphabetically arranged as acrostics, that is, each verse begins with a different letter of the Hebrew alphabet in consecutive order (Pss. 9–10 [together these two psalms are one acrostic poem]; 25; 34; 37; 111–112; 145). This style is also used in Psalm 119 where each of the eight verses in each of the 22 sections begins with the same letter. Among other purposes, this structuring would have been an aid to memory.

*6. Music and melody.* In the praises of Israel mention is made of music and musical instruments. Cymbals, timbrels, wind instruments, and stringed instruments of various types are named, showing that musical accompaniment must have been on a grand scale.

Also many notices in the headings of the psalms indicate musical activities. Foremost is "to the choirmaster" (*lamnaṣṣēaḥ*, "for the director of music," NIV) occurring in 55 psalms. Though there are many speculations about this heading, it probably referred to the chief musician in charge of temple music. The psalms so designated may have at one time comprised a collection of songs delivered to the temple for service.

The "sons of Korah," found with Psalms 42; 44–49; 84–85; 87–88, probably refers to musical performers from this family. Otherwise multiple authorship is required, and dual authorship would be required for Psalm 88. Yᵉdûtûn ("Jeduthun," Pss. 39; 62; 77) may also refer to a guild of musicians, for Jeduthun was one of David's chief musicians (1 Chron. 16:41).

Other headings also serve as musical indicators. Nᵉgînôt (Pss. 4; 6; 54–55; 67; 76) means "with stringed instruments." Psalm 61 has nᵉgînat (sing.), "with a stringed instrument," though the NIV also renders this plural. Šᵉmînît (Pss. 6; 12) probably means "with an eight-stringed lute." Neḥîlôt (Ps. 5) is obscure, but may refer to flutes used in expressing lamentation. Gittît (Pss. 8; 81; 84) is also difficult; it may mean "wine song" or "instrument from Gath." 'Ălāmôt (Ps. 46) probably means "maidens"; it may refer to a song sung by female voices.

Selâh, found within many psalms but not in their headings, may indicate when the worshipers were to "lift up" their voices (perhaps selâh is related to sālal, "to lift up or elevate"). It is used 71 times in the psalms. Selâh was not originally in the psalms; it was added later. Even so, it is quite ancient.

Several psalms also include melody indicators. "To the [tune of the] lily (lilies)" is found with Psalms 45, 60, 69, and 80. "To the doe of the morning" (lit. Heb.) occurs with Psalm 22. "To the silent dove of the distances" (lit. Heb.) is the heading of Psalm 56. "Do not destroy" occurs with Psalms 57–59, and 75. The meaning of 'al-mût labbēn with Psalm 9 (rendered "To the tune of 'The Death of the Son' " in the NIV), of 'al-māhălat with Psalm 53, and of 'al-māhălat lᵉ'annôt with Psalm 88 is disputed and uncertain. These notes in the superscriptions of the Hebrew psalms could refer to melodies used, or to some liturgical idea.

**Authorship and Historical Notices.** Commentators have long debated the translation of the lāmed preposition

which traditionally has been taken to designate the authorship of the psalms (e.g., lᵉdāwid, "of David"). Modern scholars have been skeptical of these notices on the basis of a number of historical, grammatical, and theological reasons. Many believe that David may have written a number of the psalms, but it is not possible to tell which ones, if any.

Scripture does attest that David was a singer of songs and the primary organizer of the musical guilds for the sanctuary (1 Chron. 15:3-28; 16:4-43; 23:1-5; 25; 2 Sam. 6:5; also cf. 1 Chron. 13:8). The traditions of Israel remember David as a writer of sacred poetry.

Moreover, the grammatical construction of the lāmed preposition with the name "David" (lᵉdāwid) certainly may represent authorship. The preposition can be translated "to," "for," or "of," or a number of other ways. Its use to distinguish authorship has been well attested in the Northwest Semitic inscriptions, other Semitic dialects such as Arabic, and other biblical passages such as Habakkuk 3:1 ("of Habakkuk"). Though a translator could interpret the preposition otherwise, sufficient evidence supports its usage in designating authorship.

However, each psalm must be taken individually, and headings that use the lāmed preposition must be translated in accord with the internal evidence of the psalms, since the preposition is used in a variety of ways. The overly negative reaction to these headings as marks of authorship is part of the general skepticism of the antiquity of the Psalms themselves. Though many critical scholars have posited dates in the postexilic and Maccabean periods for many of the psalms, evidence from the Ugaritic tablets of Ras Shamra has proved the antiquity of this kind of poetic expression. Expositors of the Psalms should therefore investigate the evidence thoroughly concerning the superscriptions that seem to indicate authorship. It must also be remembered that Christ and His apostles considered them as witnesses to the individual psalms' authorship.

If the notices of authorship stand, the following tabulation would be instructive for the study of the 90 psalms so designated: Psalm 90 is attributed to Moses; 73 of the psalms are credited to David; Psalms 50, 73–83 came from Asaph;

Heman the Ezrahite wrote Psalm 88; Ethan the Ezrahite (cf. 1 Kings 4:31) wrote Psalm 89; and Solomon is attested to be the author of Psalms 72 and 127. (Asaph, Heman, and Ethan were Levite musicians, 1 Chron. 15:17, 19; cf. 1 Chron. 6:39; 2 Chron. 5:12.)

The writing of the Psalms, then, spanned a period from Moses through the return from the Captivity, for some of the psalms, as indicated by their content, are clearly postexilic.

In addition to the *lāmed* preposition with a name to indicate the author, several psalms have short bits of information about the life of David. It is difficult to tell when these superscriptions were written, but there is no reason to doubt their antiquity. Fourteen psalms have historical notations:

Psalm 59 is connected with 1 Samuel 19:11.

Psalm 56 is connected with 1 Samuel 21:10-15.

Psalm 34 is connected with 1 Samuel 21:10–22:2.

Psalm 52 is connected with 1 Samuel 22:9.

Psalm 54 is connected with 1 Samuel 23:15-23.

Psalm 7 may be related to 1 Samuel 23:24-29 (but this is problematic).

Psalm 57 is related to the incident at Adullam (1 Sam. 22:1-2) or at En Gedi (1 Sam. 24).

Psalm 142, another passage that reports David's being in a cave, could refer to either of the above references as well.

Psalm 60 is from 2 Samuel 8:8, 13; and 1 Chronicles 18:9-12.

Psalm 18 is almost identical to 2 Samuel 22.

Psalm 51 is based on the incident of David's sin recorded in 2 Samuel 11–12.

Psalm 3 seems to be connected with 2 Samuel 15–18.

Psalm 63 may be related to 2 Samuel 15:23.

Psalm 30 may be connected with 1 Chronicles 21:1–22:1. (The contents of Ps. 30 suggest that David wrote it for the dedication of the temple after he sinned in numbering the people and he purchased the plot of ground for the temple.)

So the superscriptions attest that many of the psalms were written by David himself, and that several were connected with events while he was young.

**Formation of the Psalter.** Since the writing of the Psalms ranged over such an extended period, there must have been various stages in its collection. David's organization of the music for worship in the temple has already been mentioned. Psalm 72:20 has the note, "This concludes the prayers of David son of Jesse." Several psalms before Psalm 72 are not credited to David, and 17 psalms after it are. So this notice probably refers to an earlier collection of psalms.

Other kings in their reforms also reorganized the musical guilds and temple musicians. Solomon organized temple singing (2 Chron. 5:11-14; 7:6; 9:11; Ecc. 2:8). Jehoshaphat did also (2 Chron. 20:21-22) and so did Jehoiada (2 Chron. 23:18). Under Hezekiah's reform the musical guilds were reestablished (2 Chron. 29:25-28, 30; 30:21; 31:2). Hezekiah instructed the Levites to sing praises with the words of David and of Asaph (2 Chron. 29:30), suggesting that two collections of the Psalms existed. Later, Josiah reinstituted temple music and musical guilds (2 Chron. 35:15, 25).

The development of the Psalter would have been gradual, then, with frequent revisions and organizations. The first stage would have been the writing of individual psalms, some of which were collected for worship. Not all ancient Hebrew psalms found their way into this hymnbook. The songs of Moses (Ex. 15:1-18; Deut. 32:1-43), Miriam (Ex. 15:21), Deborah (Jud. 5), Jonah (Jonah 2), and even some of David's hymns (2 Sam. 1) were not included. In David's time Levites also prepared psalms for temple services (1 Chron. 16:4).

The collection of the psalms would have been the next stage. Possibly some songs of David were collected, as well as Asaph's. Other collections such as the songs "of ascents," or pilgrim songs (Pss. 120–134) may also have been gathered.

These smaller collections would then have been included in the books that now exist. Book I is made up of Psalms 1–41; Book II comprises Psalms 42–72; Book III is Psalms 73–89; Book IV is Psalms 90–106; and Book V includes Psalms 107–150. Each section concludes with a doxology, and the entire Psalter concludes with Psalm 150, a grand doxology. The earliest evidence for this fivefold division comes from the Qumran scrolls (found near the Dead Sea) copied soon after the beginning of the Christian era.

The final stage of the formation of the Psalter would then have come with the work of the final editor. The present order shows the impress of one individual's influence. Yet the collection does not seem to have one developing argument running throughout.

So by the close of the Old Testament canon the collections of songs and psalms had been united into their present form.

**The Text of the Psalms.** At least three text types are present in the manuscripts of the Psalms. The Hebrew Bible, that is, the Masoretic text (MT), certainly represents the superior text. The manuscripts of this family preserved the best readings, even though they were at times archaic, rare, or difficult. Such preservation demonstrates the high regard the scribes had for the text they received. Nevertheless translators and commentators have occasionally taken liberties in emending the text in an effort to resolve some of the difficulties. The changes suggested need to be evaluated carefully.

In the Greek Septuagint (LXX) text the Psalms are based on a different and inferior textual tradition than the Masoretic text. Where the Hebrew is particularly rare or difficult, and the Greek translators had some difficulty, they often smoothed out the text in their renderings. Jerome and the translators of many English Bibles depended rather heavily on the Greek.

The numbering of the Psalms in the Greek text differs from the Hebrew. This is important to remember when consulting Roman Catholic commentaries, or the Latin or Greek texts themselves. The following illustrates this:

| MT | LXX |
|----|-----|
| Psalms 1–8 | Psalms 1–8 |
| 9–10 | 9 |
| 11–113 | 10–112 |
| 114–115 | 113 |
| 116:1-9 | 114 |
| 116:10-19 | 115 |
| 117–146 | 116–145 |
| 147:1-11 | 146 |
| 147:12-20 | 147 |
| 148–150 | 148–150 |

Moreover, the Greek and English versions do not include the superscriptions as part of the numbering of the verses as the Hebrew does. Frequently, then, the verse numbers in the Hebrew text (and references in books that refer to the Heb. text) will be one or more verses higher.

A third text type is attested in the Dead Sea Scrolls' Psalms scroll. This text is also inferior to the Masoretic text.

**Trends in Studying the Psalms.** Over the centuries there have been prevailing approaches to the study of this collection. Most conservatives probably rely on the old but serviceable historical commentaries, some of which come from the last century. Commentaries by J.A. Alexander, Franz Delitzsch, Alexander Maclaren, and J.J.S. Perowne provide historical and grammatical interpretations of the text. Sometimes, however, they go beyond the clear evidence in their reconstructions of the occasions of the Psalms.

The literary-analytical method of studying Scripture can be seen in the commentary by C.A. Briggs. On the basis of the Psalms' theological ideas, poetic structure, and philology, he believed that most of the psalms were written in the Maccabean period (ca. 150 B.C.).

A more profitable series of studies came from the form-critical approach to the Psalms. Hermann Gunkel pioneered this approach in his *Einleitung in die Psalmen* (Introduction to the Psalms, trans. by Thomas Horner. Philadelphia: Fortress Press, 1967). This method considered that the Psalms were to be sung with ritual acts in Israel's worship. First Samuel 1:24–2:10 and 1 Chronicles 16:1-37 provided evidence for this approach to psalmody. The task, then, was to determine the setting out of which each psalm grew.

Form critics also determined that the psalms which came from the same ritual activities in the temple would share common features such as vocabulary, ideas and moods, and forms of expressions. By comparing these similar features, one could then collect the different types of psalms.

From this approach, categories for the types of psalms were recognized. They include individual laments, national laments, thanksgivings by individuals, and hymns. There are also minor types such as royal psalms, pilgrim psalms, victory psalms, songs of Zion, songs of enthronement, *tôrâh* (Law) psalms, and wisdom psalms.

Many form critics assumed that they could trace the development of these types. As a result, most of the psalms were relegated to priestly compositions for liturgical purposes, not to poems of individual saints who wrote of their experiences with God. This endeavor of form criticism has caused many expositors to reject the entire approach. This is unfortunate because many helpful things have come from this method.

The following classifications of kinds of psalms have been used to great benefit in understanding the Psalms.

*1. Individual laments.* These psalms correspond roughly to prayers for help out of distress. They have the following parts:

a. Introductory cry to God. The psalmist turned to God immediately and poured out his heart in a short address (frequently a summary of the direction of the psalm).

b. Lament. The psalmist then gave full expression to his lamentable state. In describing his difficulty, he stated what his enemies had done, what straits he was in, and what God had or had not done.

c. Confession of trust. Turning from his complaint, the psalmist declared his full confidence in the Lord. Some of these sections are expanded into complete psalms of trust or confidence.

d. Petition. The psalmist then requested that God intervene on his behalf and rescue him.

e. Vow of praise or expression of praise. The psalmist concluded his lament with a full expression of his praise to God for answering his prayer. Because this section is part of the prayer out of distress, it has been described as a vow—it is what he would say in the midst of the congregation when the Lord answered his prayer. Being sure that the Lord would answer, he began the praising in the praying. Claus Westermann suggests that in the midst of the psalmist's praying God heard and inclined Himself to the psalmist (*The Praise of God in the Psalms*, p. 79). The sudden assur-

ance of this response led the psalmist into a full expression of praise.

*2. National laments.* These psalms follow the same pattern as the laments of individuals, but they are usually shorter. They include an introductory address and petition, a lament, a confession of trust, a petition, and a vow of praise. In each of these psalms the nation faced some difficulty, and together the people approached God with their lament.

*3. Thanksgiving psalms.* These psalms, also called psalms of declarative praise, take a different form. They include these five elements:

a. Proclamation to praise God. The psalmist normally began with an expression such as, "I will praise," because the psalm was a means by which he told others what God had done for him.

b. Introductory summary. The psalmist frequently offered a brief statement of what God had done.

c. Report of the deliverance. The psalmist then detailed his deliverance. He normally explained that he cried out to the Lord, the Lord heard, and the Lord delivered him.

d. Renewed vow of praise. The psalmist here actually gave God the praise he promised to give.

e. Praise or instruction. The psalm ended with direct praise of God, or it incorporated an extended section of instruction for others.

Samples of thanksgiving or declarative praise psalms are 21, 30, 32, 34, 40, and 66.

*4. Descriptive praise psalms (hymns).* These do not tell primarily of some personal deliverance; rather they offer direct praise to God. These psalms follow a slightly different arrangement.

a. Call to praise. The psalmist invited others to praise the Lord.

b. Cause for praise. The psalmist gave the reasons for the praise. This section normally included a summary and then a full development of the reason for praise. The cause was usually the greatness of God and His grace, amplified by specific illustrations.

c. Conclusion. The psalmist closed the song with a new exhortation to praise the Lord.

Samples of descriptive praise psalms are 33, 36, 105, 111, 113, 117, and 135.

Other types of psalms will be discussed in the *Commentary*. The most important of these are the wisdom psalms, pilgrim psalms, royal psalms, and enthronement psalms. The wisdom psalms are closely related in their motifs to the Wisdom literature of the Old Testament (e.g., Prov.). Among the features that may be present in them are the "better" sayings (Ps. 119:72), numerical sayings (62:11-12a), admonitions to "sons" (34:11), blessing formulas (1:1), emphasis on the Law (119), and contrasts between the righteous and the wicked (1:6; 49).

Psalms 120–134 have been called pilgrim songs. These all have the heading, "A song of ascents." Though this designation in the superscription has been given a variety of interpretations, it most likely refers to Israel's "goings up" to Jerusalem for the three festivals (cf. 1 Sam. 1:3; Ps. 122:4; Isa. 30:29; also see Ex. 23:17; Ps. 42:4). The contents of many of these psalms appear to be well suited to a visit up to Jerusalem.

Psalms in which the anointed king is in the foreground are called royal psalms. The text refers to some high point in the career of the monarch, such as his coronation (Ps. 2), his wedding (Ps. 45), or his going forth into battle (Pss. 20; 144). The Davidic Covenant is set to poetry in Psalm 89. Psalm 110 anticipates the king's coming in conquest, and Psalm 72 envisions his glorious reign. On the relationship of these psalms to *the* King, the Messiah, see the comments on those psalms.

The enthronement psalms are characterized by the expression "the Lord reigns" (Pss. 93; 96–97; 99) the Lord is "the great King" (Pss. 47; 95), or the Lord "comes to judge" (Ps. 98). Commentators interpret these expressions differently. Some say these psalms refer to an annual festival that celebrated the Lord's reign over the earth. However, there is no conclusive evidence that such an "enthronement festival" was ever held. Others have understood the phrase to refer to the Lord's reign over Israel. This would fit Psalm 99, but does not do justice to the contents of the others. It has also been taken to refer to God's universal reign (Alva J. McClain, *The Greatness of the Kingdom*. Grand Rapids: Zondervan

Publishing House, 1959, p. 22). Psalm 93 could be taken in this way, but again the ideas of the enthronement psalms anticipate something more dramatic.

Though something may be said for the enthronement psalms signifying characteristics of the reign of God at various stages (i.e., great acts of salvation by which His sovereignty is displayed), the fullest meaning of the terminology used pertains to the messianic kingdom. The language these psalms employ, language reminiscent of the epiphany at Sinai, harmonizes well with the prophetic oracles of the expected messianic kingdom. In fact the expression "God reigns" is found in Isaiah 52:7, which refers to the future reign of the Suffering Servant.

The study of the enthronement psalms has led many modern scholars to take a "cultic" approach to the Psalms. This approach is a development of the form-critical method; it argues that the annual autumnal festival was the center of the worship or "cult" of Israel. One proponent of this view is Sigmund Mowinckel (*The Psalms of Israel's Worship*). He argues that every fall Israel held a festival in which the Lord was enthroned in the temple, thereby ensuring God's reign over the universe for another year. Mowinckel's evidence is gathered from the biblical references to the Lord's reign or judging (Pss. 47; 93; 95–99), to the Lord's victory over nature, and to people at a festival rejoicing at the prospect of the Lord's reign. The material is sketchy, so he supports the idea from similar festivals of the surrounding nations of the ancient Near East, notably Babylon with its *Akitu* festival.

Others have interpreted the festival differently. Artur Weiser (*The Psalms: A Commentary*) agrees that a fall festival was central to the use of the enthronement psalms, but suggests that it was a covenant renewal rather than an actual enthronement of the Lord. He points up similarities with Joshua 24.

Hans-Joachim Kraus (*Worship in Israel*. Richmond, Va.: John Knox Press, 1966) sees a more complex picture of the fall festival. He views the festival as a remembrance of the Exodus and the wilderness wanderings, a covenant renewal celebration, and a tradition of Canaanite concepts of kingship emerging in the reigns of David and Solomon.

If such a fall festival actually existed and formed the key to the entire Psalter, it is surprising such is not mentioned anywhere in Scripture. Probably some of the psalms were used in connection with the fall festivals. But it is unlikely that the majority of the psalms were part of a festival patterned after pagan mythological ideas. This approach has also been criticized on the basis of the evidence from the ancient Near Eastern festivals (see Kenneth A. Kitchen, *Ancient Orient and Old Testament*. Downers Grove, Ill.: Intervarsity Press, 1966, p. 102).

This approach to the study of the Psalms, however, has provided a needed emphasis. Many of the psalms were probably connected with ritual and worship in David's tabernacle and/or Solomon's temple. Too often conservative commentators are oblivious to the worship setting of the tabernacle and the temple.

Besides the numerous references to worship and the temple ritual within the Psalms, liturgical indicators are given in some of the superscriptions. Psalm 30 is "For the dedication of the temple," Psalm 92 is designated "For the Sabbath Day,"and Psalm 100 is a psalm to be used at the offering of the thanksgiving sacrifice (Lev. 7). "A petition" (lit., "to bring to remembrance") is the superscription of Psalms 38 and 70, apparently intended to remind the Lord of the one making the petition. The meaning of *šiggāyôn* in Psalm 7 is obscure. To these the title "A song of ascents" (Pss. 120–134) may be added. These songs were sung en route to or at the great festivals in Jerusalem.

Israel's religious calendar (see the chart "Calendar in Israel," near Ex. 12) is important in understanding the background of some of the psalms. The three great annual festivals are discussed in Exodus 23:14-19 and Leviticus 23:4-44. At Passover and Unleavened Bread in the spring, at Weeks or Pentecost (also called Firstfruits) in the early summer, and at Atonement and Tabernacles in the fall, the people were to go to Jerusalem and celebrate God's bounty in the harvests. At those gatherings the people would be involved in the ritual of the temple and in using the Psalms in praise.

The Psalms frequently refer to musical instruments, singing, and clapping in the religious activities. Psalm 5:7 speaks of entering God's house to worship. (Ps. 68:24-27 refers to the procession to the sanctuary accompanied by singers; cf. 42:4.) And Psalm 122:1 tells of the joy involved in a pilgrimage to the temple.

On many occasions Israel worshiped at the temple. Sabbath days, New Moons, Sabbath years, and Jubilees all provided occasions for praising God in the sanctuary.

Worshipers could come spontaneously as well. Freewill offerings could be brought to express thanks (*tôḏâh*; cf. Lev. 7:12-18; Ps. 50:14-15), for answers to prayer (1 Sam. 2:1-10), purification from ritual uncleanness or disease (Lev. 13–15), vindication in legal conflicts, atonement for sins (Ps. 51:13-17), or as special vows. On such occasions the worshiper brought his offering to be shared by those in attendance, and made his praise known (probably in the form of a declarative praise psalm) for the enrichment of the congregation.

No doubt the prayers in the Psalter also found widespread use by those who came to pray for forgiveness, healing, protection, deliverance, and comfort, as they have throughout the history of the church.

So individually or communally, the Psalms no doubt were frequently sung or said near the sanctuary. Their messages and how they were used are instructive for believers today, as the following exposition seeks to show. The prayers of the psalmists exhibit great confidence in the Lord, so great that many times they turned to praise before the answers actually came. A close study of the Psalms shows how such confidence was developed. In addition the praises of the psalmists show a genuine and spontaneous enjoyment of God's benefits. To receive from God and not praise Him was sin. The declaration of God's benefits was the final part of the process. It was also part of the enjoyment of God, for one naturally tells of the things he enjoys most (C.S. Lewis, *Reflections in the Psalms*. New York: Harcourt, Brace and World, 1958). Thus when the Scriptures call believers to praise God, they are calling them to enjoy God and His benefits. And when God blesses someone, that fact is to be shared in the congregation so that all may enter into the praise and enjoy God and His benefits.

In Israel this normally involved sharing the sacrifical meal of the worshiper who came to praise God. His sacrifice, a token of the bounty, would accompany his praise. God thus was enjoyed by His people who were thereby inspired to pray to and praise Him more.

**Theology of the Psalms.** Because the Psalms record such a vast range of religious ideas and impressions, it is difficult to discover a specific theology for the collection. Indeed, almost all the theological ideas of the Old Testament surface here. Yet one predominant emphasis does recur throughout. The psalmists assumed or expressed the belief that the Lord, who sovereignly rules the universe, will establish His just rule on the earth in and through His people. When faced with opposition from the wicked or from physical difficulties, they prayed for its realization in their lives, confident that the Judge of all the earth would bring vindication. When righteousness triumphed, they praised God for the triumph of His righteous cause among people.

The psalmists' participation in the worship and appreciation of the Law demonstrated their confidence in God's theocracy. At times they looked beyond their experiences to the Lord's actual reign of righteousness on earth at the Messiah's coming. How clear an understanding they had of the details of God's revelation is impossible to say. It is clear, however, that they confidently expected God to set things right.

The psalmists did not hesitate to avow their loyalty to God and His covenant. In their zeal to champion righteousness, their words frequently contain imprecations or curses. They prayed that God would break the arms of the wicked (Ps. 10:15), smash their teeth (58:6), and turn His wrath on them (69:22-28). It must be remembered that the psalmists were filled with zeal for God's theocracy. Thus these expressions were not indications of personal vendetta. The psalmists, in fact, protested that their kindness to such people had been betrayed by treachery (109:4-5). Their prayers represent their longing that God's cause be vindicated on earth, that sin would be judged—which God would do eventually.

Of course the New Testament believer has a different prayer life because of his understanding of the full revelation of God. Yet to pray for God's will to be done or for Christ to come quickly, is also to pray for the vindication of the righteous and the judgment of the wicked.

The psalmists also abhorred pagan ideas and customs, which they knew threatened the faith of the nation. Many aspects of foreign polytheistic beliefs are attacked in a subtle manner (less subtle than the prophetic oracles). These polemics may at times be a passing reference (such as the description of the Lord as the One "who rides on the clouds," 68:4, rather than the Canaanite Baal who is likewise described). At other times the polemics form the substance of the entire psalm (such as Ps. 29 which attributes a storm in Canaanite territory to the Lord rather than Canaan's storm god Baal).

Many scholars say these references are mythological borrowings from the Semitic world. However, though the Israelites shared a common vocabulary and imagery with their neighbors, these polemical portions show a spiritual parting of the ways. The fact that many Israelites ran after other gods made these polemics even more urgent. If the truth was to be secured and perpetuated from generation to generation, false and corrupting beliefs had to be destroyed. Therefore students of the Psalms must be aware of the polytheistic threats to Israel's faith as well as the historical struggle they brought to the righteous.

The conflict with forces of evil, whether pagan beliefs or apostate Israelites, forced genuine believers to contend for the faith vigorously, to avow their integrity and loyalty openly, and to hope for deliverance from God. The psalmists looked for that deliverance in this life. One would have expected that the psalmists, with all their persecution, suffering, and distress, would have despaired of this life and looked for contentment in the life to come. But this is not the case. They sensed that death would end their service and praise of God (though other Scripture passages, written later, indicate that this is not so). It was in this life that God's loyal love, faithfulness, and righteousness could be experienced (Pss. 6:5; 30:9; 88:4-5, 10-12; 115:17).

Nowhere in the Psalms is there a clear, unambiguous expression of hope in the resurrection, the kind of statement made in the Prophets (Isa. 26:19; Ezek. 37:1-14; Dan. 12:2). However, some passages in the Psalms do seem to break through to express a hope of continued fellowship with God after this life (Pss. 16–17; 49; 73). Yet the expressions used in such passages are used elsewhere for temporal, earthly experiences. For example the psalmists used the Hebrew $š^{e}\hat{o}l$ (sheol) to designate the realm of departed spirits, but also the grave and (figuratively) extreme danger. Psalm 49:15 expresses the hope of deliverance from sheol and of entrance into the presence of God. To the psalmist this may have meant a "hope of glory," but it may also have signified temporal deliverance and continuance in service, for Psalm 30:3 also mentions a deliverance from sheol that David experienced.

A.F. Kirkpatrick notes how easily these passages adapt themselves to a hope in the future life, as indicated by later biblical revelation. "Unquestionably these psalms (Pss. 16–17; 49; 73) do contain the germ and principle of the doctrine of eternal life. It was present to the mind of the Spirit who inspired their authors. The intimate fellowship with God of which they speak as man's highest good and truest happiness could not, in view of the nature and destiny of man and his relation to God, continue to be regarded as limited to this life and liable to sudden and final interruption. It required but a step forward to realize the truth of its permanence, but whether the psalmists took this step is doubtful" (*The Book of Psalms*, pp. xxv-xxvi). If they did take such a step, it was by faith.

The same ambiguity applies to the messianic psalms. With the knowledge of full revelation in Jesus Christ, one can look back to the Psalms, in fact to the entire Old Testament, and see that they often speak of Christ (cf. Luke 24:27). Yet to Old Testament believers, the full meanings of these passages were not often evident. On the one hand a psalmist described his own suffering or triumph, and on the other hand those expressions, which may have seemed extravagant for the psalmist's actual experience, later became true of Jesus Christ. Looking back one can say, with Delitzsch, "For as God

the Father molds the history of Jesus Christ in accordance with His own counsel, so His Spirit molds even the utterances of David concerning himself, the type of the Future One, with a view to that history" ("Psalms," in *Commentary on the Old Testament in Ten Volumes*, 5:307).

Typology is thus a form of prophetic statement. It differs from prophecy in that it may be discerned as typological only after its fulfillment is known. Once this antitype is revealed, one may look back and see that certain expressions and images have meanings besides the historical experience. The New Testament writers drew heavily on the Psalms to express many aspects of the person and work of Jesus, the Messiah. As the anointed Davidic King par excellence, Jesus is the great Antitype of the messianic psalms, those psalms that have the king in the foreground. Expositors must exercise caution, however; they must recognize that not *all* the contents of messianic psalms apply to Christ (i.e., not all the parts are typological). Therefore one must remember that these psalms had a primary meaning in the experience of the authors. The analysis of the historical, contextual, and grammatical meaning of the text should precede the analysis of the New Testament application to Jesus.

Many commentators have made some use of Delitzsch's five types of messianic psalms ("Psalms," pp. 68-71).

*1. Purely prophetic psalms.* This category probably applies to Psalm 110 which refers to a future Davidic King who would be the Lord. The New Testament (Matt. 22:44) identifies this King as Jesus Christ, not any other Davidic king.

*2. Eschatological psalms.* Psalms 96–99, the so-called enthronement psalms, among others, describe the coming of the Lord and the consummation of His kingdom. Though they do not refer to a Davidic king, Scripture intimates that they will be fulfilled in the second coming of Christ.

*3. Typological-prophetic psalms.* In these psalms the writer describes his own experience with language that goes beyond that experience and becomes historically true in Jesus (e.g., Ps. 22).

*4. Indirectly messianic psalms.* These psalms were written for a contemporary king or for royal activities in general. But their ultimate fulfillment is in Jesus Christ (Pss. 2; 45; 72).

*5. Typically messianic psalms.* These psalms are less obviously messianic. The psalmist in some way is a type of Christ (cf. 34:20), but other aspects of the passage do not apply. Perhaps, in this case Jesus and the apostles were applying familiar psalmic expressions to their experiences (e.g., 109:8 in Acts 1:20).

Certainly the language of the Psalms expresses the hopes and the truths of the faith in a most memorable way, not only as they point to Christ but also as they reflect the struggles of the faithful. The Psalms have served God's people down through the ages as the inspiration for and often the instrument of praise to God. But they have also brought comfort and hope to individual souls in their times of greatest needs, teaching them how to pray, and giving them the confidence of answered prayers and a renewed trust in their Lord. Often the Psalms change dramatically from the pouring out of a lament to a description of the answer, as if it had already happened. This expressed the psalmists' confidence that God would answer their prayers. So sure were they of God's answers that they praised the Lord in detail in anticipation of the victories. Only through genuine faith can a believer find assurance of answered prayer while praying. The psalmists had such assurance, for their praising accompanied their praying.

# OUTLINE

I. Book I (Pss. 1–41)
II. Book II (Pss. 42–72)
III. Book III (Pss. 73–89)
IV. Book IV (Pss. 90–106)
V. Book V (Pss. 107–150)

# COMMENTARY

## I. Book I (Pss. 1–41)

### Psalm 1

Psalm 1 is a fitting introduction for the Psalter in that it summarizes the two ways open to mankind, the way of the righteous and the way of the wicked. It may be classified as a wisdom psalm because of its emphasis on these two ways of life, the use of the similes, the announcement of blessing, and the centrality of the Law for fulfillment in life. The motifs in this psalm recur again and again throughout the collection.

The psalm describes the blessed man who leads an untarnished and prosperous life in accord with the Word of the Lord, and contrasts him with the ungodly who shall perish.

### A. The blessed man (1:1-3)

**1:1.** With three trilogies of expressions the psalmist described the life of the **blessed** man: he **does not walk . . . stand** or **sit** in the **counsel . . . way** or **seat** of **the wicked** (ungodly), **sinners,** or **mockers** (scorners). With each parallel unit the expression becomes more intense. This signifies a progression from a casual influence of ungodly people to collusion with them in their scorn against the righteous. One who is **not** characterized by this evil influence is "blessed," that is, he is right with God and enjoys the spiritual peace and joy that results from that relationship.

**1:2.** A godly person is influenced not by unrighteous people but by his meditation on the Word of God. Such meditation necessarily involves study and retention. This is possible only if he has a desire to do so, here referred to as a **delight.** The psalmists found direction, not drudgery, from **the Law of** God.

**1:3.** For all who take their delight in living by God's Word, there is prosperity. Under the image of a fruitful **tree,** the psalmist declared that **whatever** the righteous do will prosper (cf. 92:12-14). Two qualifications need to be noted. First, the **fruit,** that is, the prosperity, is produced **in its season** and not necessarily immediately after planting. Second, what the godly person does will be controlled by the Law of God (1:2). So if a person meditates on God's Word, his actions will be godly, and his God-controlled activities will prosper, that is, come to their divinely directed fulfillment.

### B. The wicked (1:4)

**1:4.** In strong contrast with a blessed person (v. 1) is an ungodly person. The

Hebrew word *rāšā'* is often translated **wicked** (cf. vv. 1, 5-6) but that may connote gross evil. People described by *rāšā'* are not in covenant relationship with God; they live according to their passions. They are not godly. They may do kind and charitable deeds, but God's evaluation of them is that they are without eternal merit.

The psalmist compared them to **chaff,** the worthless husks of the grain blown **away** by **the wind** in the process of winnowing. Such is the contrast with the fruitful (cf. v. 3), valuable, righteous person.

### C. The judgment (1:5-6)

**1:5.** On the basis of the contrast between the godly and **the wicked,** the psalmist wrote that God will separate **the righteous** from the wicked **in the judgment.** The righteous are those who are related by covenant with the Lord, who live by His Word, who produce things of eternal value. God will divide the righteous and sinners as a man separates wheat from tares.

**1:6.** The basis for this judgment is the Lord's knowledge. The first half of the verse, **The Lord watches over** (lit., "knows") **the way of the righteous,** is best understood by the antithetical parallelism, **the way of the wicked will perish.** Salvation in the day of judgment is equated with being known by the Lord (cf. Matt. 7:23). In Psalm 1:6 "the way of the righteous" is contrasted with "the way of the wicked." "The way" means one's whole manner of life including what directs it and what it produces. The worthless life of the ungodly will not endure.

## Psalm 2

This psalm is familiar to students of the New Testament by virtue of its relevance for Christ. However, the passage was a royal psalm in the Old Testament and therefore was used by the Davidic kings. (Other royal psalms are 18, 20–21, 45, 72, 89, 101, 110, 132, 144.) Its contents describe a celebration at the coronation despite opposition by rebellious people in surrounding territories. In a word, the psalmist exhorted the pagan nations to abandon their rebellious plans against the Lord and His anointed king and to submit to the authority of the Son whom

God has ordained to rule the nations with a rod of iron. (As indicated in Acts 4:25, Ps. 2 was written by David.)

### A. The rebellion of the nations (2:1-3)

**2:1-3.** The first three verses express the psalmist's amazement at the plans of **the nations** to overthrow the Lord and **His Anointed One** (*māšîaḥ,* "Messiah," which in Gr. is *christos,* the Christ). Every king anointed by a prophet was a "messiah," an anointed one. If he obeyed God his rule had the authenticity of God's election and the support of God's power. This often made the plans of other nations futile.

Verse 1 expresses the psalmist's amazement in the form of a rhetorical question. He cannot believe "the nations" would **plot** something destined to fail. These earthly **kings** actually were taking a **stand . . . against the Lord** (v. 2) when they stood against His Anointed One.

Verse 3 records the nations' resolution: they wished to be free of the political control of this king. Their expression describes their bondage to this king as if they were tied down. This they could not tolerate.

### B. The resolution of the Lord (2:4-6)

**2:4.** The psalmist turned from his description of the nations (vv. 1-3) to portray the Lord's response to their plan. In a bold description he envisioned God laughing at it. **The Lord** sits **enthroned** (cf. 9:11; 22:3; 29:10; 55:19; 102:12; 113:5; Isa. 6:1) high **in heaven** and discerns how foolish is their plan to oppose Him. The description is anthropomorphic; God's reaction is stated in human terms.

**2:5-6.** Based on His contempt for their evil plan God will speak in **His** burning **wrath** against them. Probably verse 6 summarizes what He says, for His resolution to install His **king** in Jerusalem will be the end of their rebellion. **Zion,** referred to 40 times in the Book of Psalms, was originally a Canaanite city conquered by David (2 Sam. 5:7). Later Zion referred to the temple area and then to the entire city of Jerusalem (cf. comments on Lam. 1:4; Zech. 8:3). **Holy hill** is a synonym for the temple mount (cf. Pss. 3:4; 15:1; 24:3; 78:54; Dan. 9:16, 20; Obad. 16; Zeph. 3:11).

When God establishes His king, He

also subjugates those who oppose His king. It was true with David; it will also be true at the end of the age with David's greater Descendant, Jesus Christ.

### C. The declaration of the king (2:7-9)

**2:7.** The psalmist now spoke of God's affirmation of the king to show by what right the king rules. **The decree** refers to the Davidic Covenant in which God declared that He would be **Father** to the king, and the king would be His son. So when David became king, God described their affiliation as a Father-son relationship. So the expression "son" took on the meaning of a messianic title.

**You are My son** (cf. NIV marg.), quoted from the Davidic Covenant (2 Sam. 7:14), is appropriated here by the king to show his legitimate right to rule. **Today** then refers to the coronation day, and the expression "I have begotten you" (NIV marg.) refers not to physical birth but is an extended metaphor describing his becoming God's "son."

**2:8.** The significance of this adoption of the king as God's anointed son is seen in his **inheritance.** As a son inherits from his father, so the king inherits the kingdom from his "Father." The verse continues the quotation from the Lord's decree, extending an invitation to the king to **ask** for his inheritance, which someday will encompass **the ends of the earth.** People living in these **nations,** including the rebellious nations (v. 1), will be subjugated by the Lord's anointed.

**2:9.** This subjugation is expressed in harsh terms: he will smash (**dash . . . to pieces**) all rebellious people as he establishes his reign. The imagery is probably drawn from Egyptian execration customs in which the Pharaoh used his **scepter** to smash votive jars (**pottery**) that represented rebellious cities or nations. The Hebrew verbs in the verse—*ra'a'* ("break," NIV marg.) and *nāpaṣ* ("dash to pieces, shatter")—describe a crushing blow for the rebels. The NIV's and LXX's **rule** is similar to "break," but "rule" does not do justice to "shatter" or to the context. The verse describes the beginning of the rule, putting down rebellion.

### D. The exhortation of the psalmist (2:10-12)

**2:10-11.** In view of all that the Lord had determined for His "son," the psalmist exhorted the foolish nations to submit to the king before his wrath was kindled. Many times in the Psalms God is referred to as **King** (v. 6; 10:16; 24:7-8, 10; 29:10; 44:4; 47:2, 6-7; 48:2; 68:24; 84:3; 95:3; 98:6; 99:4; 145:1; 149:2). The psalmist instructed the earthly **kings** to use wisdom and abandon their foolish rebellion (cf. 2:1). They would **be wise** to **serve the LORD with fear and rejoice with trembling.** "Serve," "rejoice," "fear," and "trembling" describe the religious responses of the righteous in worship. They are to lead lives of submission, not rebellion; lives characterized by fear and trembling, not arrogance; lives filled with exultation, not the gloom of oppression.

**2:12.** The image here is that of submission to a sovereign: **Kiss the son!** Unusual in the verse is the apparent use of *bar,* an Aramaic word for son. Therefore the versions translate it differently. Jerome rendered it, "Give pure (*bar* is a Heb. word for pure) worship," or "Worship in purity," rather than translating the word as "son." However, in an address to the nations an Aramaic term was not out of place. Moreover, "kiss" pictures homage (cf. 1 Kings 19:18; Hosea 13:2). At any rate it is clear that the psalmist is telling the earth's kings to submit to the Lord and to His anointed son, Israel's king.

The urgency of their submission is expressed by the suddenness of **his wrath.** It is not immediately clear whether this wrath is the Lord's or the king's. The nearest antecedent is the king (the son) who will smash opposition (Ps. 2:9). However, in the psalm the two persons are inseparable; a person serves the *Lord* (v. 11) by submitting to his *son* (v. 12). If the nations' kings do not submit, the king will destroy them, because the Lord in **angry** opposition to their plans has decreed that His son will have the throne.

The final note of the psalm expresses blessing for those **who take refuge in Him.** (The thought of taking refuge in God occurs many times in the Pss.) Again, to submit to the son is to take refuge in the Lord's anointed, and therefore in the Lord as well. Only in the son is there safety from the wrath of God.

The psalm is rich in New Testament application. Reflecting on how the leaders of Israel crucified Jesus, the Messiah,

Peter was quick to identify those Jewish leaders with the pagan kings of Psalm 2 (Acts 4:25-26).

The typological significance of the "son" is seen fulfilled in Hebrews 1:5. This coronation psalm is quoted here in referring to the exaltation of Christ at His resurrection (cf. Acts 13:33) and Ascension. By this He is "declared . . . to be the Son of God" (Rom. 1:4), a messianic title. When the Father instructs His Son to ask for His inheritance, then He will bring His Son again into the world (Heb. 1:6). The Second Coming will mean wrath to all who rebel against God and His anointed King, but great joy and refuge for all who by faith submit to God's plan to rule the world through David's greater Son, Jesus Christ. So the title of "son" from the Davidic Covenant (2 Sam. 7:14) ultimately becomes the designation of Jesus Christ as King.

## Psalm 3

The superscription of this psalm identifies it as written by David. In Book One (Pss. 1–41) 37 of the 41 psalms (all except 1–2; 10; 33) are ascribed to David. Psalm 3 is said to have been written when he fled from his son Absalom (cf. 2 Sam. 15–18). It is a confident prayer of the king who had fled from the palace and was surrounded by enemies. In spite of innumerable adversaries who were convinced that he had no hope, God's elect, David, found God's safety and protection through the night and thereby had confidence in His ultimate deliverance.

### A. Surrounded by enemies (3:1-2)

**3:1-2.** The psalm begins with David's lament: **many . . . foes** were surrounding him. In fact forces of the opposition had driven him from the palace and were then surrounding him. Their taunt was that he had no hope of being delivered by **God.** This arrogant remark was designed to say that God had abandoned David.

### B. Sustained by God (3:3-6)

**3:3.** In the face of such antagonism, David found comfort in God's character. Using the metaphor of **a shield,** he said that God was the true Source of his protection (in spite of their taunts). The psalmists often spoke of God as a shield

to depict His protection (7:10; 18:2, 30; 28:7; 33:20; 59:11; 84:11; 115:9-11; 119:114; 144:2). David was confident that God would restore him to his throne. The words **lifts up my head** express restoration to dignity and position (see the same idiom in Gen. 40:13, 20; 2 Kings 25:27, KJV).

**3:4-5.** The reason for David's burst of confidence (v. 3) is expressed in verses 4-5. God had sustained him through the night in the midst of his enemies, and that protection was a token of the complete deliverance he expected. The Hebrew tenses in these verses are difficult to translate. Though they may be rendered by the English present tense, it is probably better to translate them as past tenses: I cried **to the LORD** and **He** answered **me.** He would have said this the morning after he prayed. (On **His holy hill** see comments on 2:6.) The answer to his prayer was then explained (again in the past tense): **I lay down, and** I slept; **I awoke, because the LORD** sustained **me.**

**3:6.** On the basis of this deliverance, the psalmist expressed his absence of **fear** over the **thousands** who took their stand **against** him **on every side.**

### C. Saved by God (3:7-8)

**3:7-8.** These verses record David's confident petition for complete deliverance from his enemies. Perhaps David was saying in verse 7b that **God** had always destroyed his **enemies** and therefore he prayed that God would do it again. However, it may be better to understand the verbs as expressions of his confidence—he was so sure that God would destroy them that he wrote as if it had already happened.

The imagery of the destruction is bold. David used terms referring to crushing blows to state that God would utterly destroy his enemies.

His conclusion is didactic. **Deliverance** comes **from the LORD.** God's **people** should pray to Him under similar circumstances, so that they may share this blessing. So the psalm instructs those who are in the midst of danger to trust in the Lord for protection while they sleep (v. 5).

## Psalm 4

Bible students have widely recognized that this psalm is closely connected with Psalm 3. The two psalms, based on the similarities in their expression and structure, may have stemmed from the same crisis. If so, then David may have written Psalm 4 after he spent the night in the midst of danger (cf. 3:1, 5-6). The connection between the two psalms is not certain. However, the message of Psalm 4 is as follows: having cried out to God for help, the psalmist warned his enemies not to sin against God by wronging him, because God had set him apart in protective care, a fact that caused him to rejoice in the face of opposition. (On the superscriptions or headings to this psalm and many others, see the comments under "Authorship and Historical Notices" in the *Introduction*.)

### A. Call to God (4:1)

**4:1.** The psalm begins with an introductory cry for **God** to **hear** his prayer. **Give me relief** (an imperative in the NIV) is actually in the perfect tense. God had set the psalmist at large, that is, He had given him relief in the midst of his **distress.** To this God he directed his **prayer.**

### B. Warning for the enemies (4:2-5)

**4:2.** In contrast with the righteous God (v. 1), David's rebels were mere mortals (**men** is lit., "sons of men"). He asked **how long** they would **turn** his **glory into shame** with their rebellion and lies ("lies" [NIV marg.] is preferable to **false gods**). The intrigue of Absalom, if this was in David's mind here, was partly an attempt to tarnish David's reputation (2 Sam. 15:3). The verbs **love** and **seek,** however, point to the desired end and not to the means.

**4:3.** This verse is the basis for the psalmist's amazement (v. 2) and his advice (v. 4). Because **the LORD** had **set apart** the psalmist in love, He would answer his prayer. David described himself as one of **the godly** (*ḥāsîd*), an object of God's covenantal loyal love. In the care of God, David was safe and God would **hear** and respond to his prayers.

**4:4-5.** The only recourse, then, for the wicked was to abandon their sinful plans and become worshipers of the Lord. Diligent souls searching for the Lord would be led to act properly toward David. They would desist from their opposition, that is, they would **be silent.**

**Trust in the LORD** would result in

**right** (proper) **sacrifices,** offered with a right spirit (cf. Deut. 33:19; Ps. 51:19). If Absalom was in David's mind, then David was referring here to the empty sacrifices by which Absalom and his cohorts sought to enhance their cause (2 Sam. 15:12). A man of faith would yield in obedience to the Lord.

### C. Joyous peace in God (4:6-8)

In the face of opposition, David joyfully expressed his peace and security in God.

**4:6.** This verse probably refers to the **many** discontented people following David. They would follow anyone who could **show** them **good** prospects. David's answer to their question was a prayer for blessing (cf. Num. 6:24-26); that God would cause His **face** to **shine** on them (i.e., bestow His favor; cf. Pss. 31:16; 44:3; 67:1; 80:3, 7, 19; 119:135). God would satisfy their complaint, as He had done so often in Israel's history.

**4:7-8.** The **joy** and contentment David experienced in trusting in the LORD was **greater** than the mirth of the harvest festivities. Even in distress and away from the visible evidence of God's goodness, he enjoyed **peace** and **safety** in his God (on **sleep;** cf. 3:5). True joy and peace depend not on circumstances but on God's protection and provisions (cf. Gal. 5:22; Rom. 14:17).

### Psalm 5

This psalm is a prayer of David when he was exposed to danger by unscrupulous enemies. It has been argued that because verse 7 mentions the temple (which Solomon built), David could not have written the psalm. But the Hebrew word used here for temple (*hêkāl*) is also used of the tabernacle (cf. 1 Sam. 1:9; 3:3). Furthermore the word "house" in Psalm 5:7 can refer to the tabernacle (cf. "house of the LORD" in 23:6; Josh. 6:24; 1 Sam. 1:24) as well as the temple.

In entreating God to hear his morning prayer, David expressed his confidence in drawing near to God (who hates iniquity) and prayed for divine leadership and blessing for the righteous, and destruction for the wicked.

### A. Morning prayer (5:1-3)

**5:1-3.** The psalmist pleaded with God to **hear** (**Give ear. . . . Listen**) his lament as he prayed **morning by morning** (lit., "in the morning") with full **expectation.** "In the morning" is repeated in verse 3 for emphasis. It stresses that his first thoughts each day were prayer.

### B. Confidence in God (5:4-7)

**5:4-6.** The psalmist expressed his confidence in approaching a **God** who hates iniquity (**evil**). An evil person **cannot dwell** with such a God. People who are presumptuous and boastful, who do not shrink from murder or deceit, God hates and will **destroy.** They are totally detestable to Him.

**5:7.** In contrast with such wickedness David did not extol his own virtues. Rather he stressed God's **mercy** (*ḥeseḏ*, "loyal love") toward him. **By** this he could approach the tabernacle (cf. comments on **house** and **temple** in the first paragraph under Ps. 5) to worship the Lord **in reverence.** The Hebrew word for **bow down** (often trans. "worshiped," e.g., Ex. 34:8) signifies prostrating oneself, a posture that represents the proper inner attitude toward God in worship. The wicked are arrogant; a worshiper is humble before God.

### C. Prayer for guidance (5:8-12)

**5:8.** David's prayer for guidance is the central idea of verses 8-12. This prayer is for guidance **in . . . righteousness.** Because God is righteous, and because the enemies are wicked (vv. 4-6), David's desire was to follow the path of right conduct (**make straight Your way before me**) and not be numbered among those God hates. The word for **enemies** comes from the verb "to lie in wait."

**5:9-10.** In view of this present danger, David's prayer turned to a more urgent plea for God to judge his foes. He then cataloged their sins. They were untrustworthy in their words, deceitful in their flattery. They planned **destruction.** What they said (**their throat** is substituted by metonymy for "their words") brought death (**is an open grave**). Apparently their speech was flattering on the surface but vile in its intent (**they speak deceit**; cf. v. 6). For this, David called on **God** to hold **them guilty.**

**5:11-12.** The psalm closes with a note of encouragement (**be glad . . . sing for joy. . . . rejoice**) that God blesses and

protects **those who love** Him. Singing is a natural way to praise the Lord; this is the first of more than 70 references to singing in the Psalms. **The righteous** are those who love His **name.** The Lord's "name" (mentioned more than 100 times in the Pss.) refers to His character and attributes revealed to mankind. Here the manifestation of His name means **protection** and **favor as with a shield** (cf. 3:3).

### Psalm 6

The servant of the Lord, being reproved by the chastening rod, petitioned God for deliverance. Finding assurance that his prayer had been heard, he warned his persecutors to depart for they were about to be put to shame.

This is one of the penitential psalms. David had been suffering from some illness that brought him near death. However, it is difficult to associate this psalm with any known event in his life.

### A. Prayer for relief from suffering (6:1-3)

**6:1.** In his introductory cry David pleaded that God would stop chastening him in His anger. In Hebrew the words **not . . . in Your anger** precede the words **rebuke me,** and "not" in **Your wrath** comes first in the second line. The forward position of these words emphasizes the manner of the chastening. If God's wrath against David were to continue, he could not survive.

**6:2.** David's prayer was then expressed positively. He wanted the LORD to relieve him of his sufferings (**be merciful . . . heal me**) because he was in extreme pain. Bones denotes one's whole physical structure, the person himself. To say that one's **bones are in agony** is to say emphatically that his body is wracked with pain. This is often mentioned in the Psalms (31:10; 32:3; 38:3; 42:10; 102:3, 5).

**6:3.** The words in this verse are highly emotional. The question **how long?** is unfinished because of his intense frustration. (Cf. "How long?" in 13:1-2; 35:17; 74:10; 79:5; 80:4; 82:2; 89:46; 94:3; 119:84.) He longed for God's healing.

### B. Prayer for deliverance (6:4-5)

**6:4.** In his earnest prayer for deliverance, David gave two reasons why God should answer. One is that the LORD should rescue him **because of** His **unfail-**

ing love. God had shown Himself again and again to be abundant in loyal love (ḥeseḏ), so David pleaded for deliverance on the basis of God's character.

**6:5.** David said the second reason the Lord should turn to him is because of the absence of **praises** (tôḏâh) in **the grave.** If he died because of his illness, he then could not praise God for delivering him from it. So David reasoned that if God desired someone to stand in the sanctuary and proclaim that God delivered him, then God would have to do so.

### C. Lament over illness (6:6-7)

**6:6-7.** David offered his lament proper. Using hyperbolic language he called attention to the severity of his suffering. Throughout the **night** he suffered in agony. His health was wasting away and he was in **sorrow,** apparently **because of** his enemies. If God did not deliver him, he would die; then people would know that his **foes** were God's chastening rod.

### D. Assurance of restoration (6:8-10)

**6:8-10.** Turning to his adversaries David exhorted them to depart **from** him, for he was confident that God had **heard** his prayer and would deliver him. His final prayer was that all those who persisted as his **enemies** be put to shame. He wanted the dismay and **disgrace** he felt at their hands to be turned **back** on them (cf. 40:14; 7:2).

Through the agony of suffering, the righteous can be confident that God will hear their **weeping** and answer their prayers for deliverance.

## Psalm 7

In praying for deliverance from his slanderous enemies, the psalmist solemnly affirmed his innocence and appealed to the righteous Judge of the earth to vindicate him by judging the wicked.

The superscription refers to David's experience with "Cush, a Benjamite," referred to only here in the Bible. The song comes from a time David was hunted by Saul's men (1 Sam. 22:8; 24:9; 26:19). Šiggāyôn ("**shiggaion**") may mean a poem written with intense feeling.

### A. Prayer for intervention (7:1-2)

**7:1-2.** David confidently prayed for deliverance **from** his enemies who were about to **tear** him to pieces **like a lion** (cf.

10:9; 17:12; 22:13, 21; 35:17; 57:4; 58:6). He knew that if God did not **rescue** him, **no one** could. Psalm 7:2 has the first of many occurrences in the Psalms of the word "rescue."

### B. Protestation of innocence (7:3-5)

**7:3-5.** David solemnly affirmed that there was no iniquity in his **hands.** These verses are framed in the expressions of an oath. **If I have done this . . . if I have done evil . . . then let my enemy pursue and overtake me.** In view of his prayer for deliverance, this must be taken as a solemn assertion of his integrity.

Verse 4 seems to express his enemy's slanderous charge that he had "done evil to" one **who** was at **peace with** him, robbing him **without cause.**

So David invoked death by his enemy's hand if he were guilty as they charged. To **sleep in the dust** means to be dead and buried (cf. Dan. 12:2). It does not mean unconscious existence in death. It simply suggests that a dead person appears to be asleep (cf. 1 Thes. 4:13).

### C. Appeal for vindication (7:6-9)

**7:6-7.** David appealed to God, the righteous Judge of all the earth, to vindicate his cause. The words **arise . . . rise up,** and **awake** are meant to prompt **God** to act in **justice** before **the assembled** congregation.

**7:8-9.** In verse 8 the verb **judge** means "vindicate," for David pleaded for judgment that would reveal his own **righteousness** and **integrity.** He also pleaded that the omniscient **righteous** Judge would **end the violence of the wicked and make the righteous secure.** Understandably the prayer of the righteous often is for God to set things right on earth. **Most High** is the first of 23 occurrences of this title of God in the Psalms; it occurs 3 times in this psalm (vv. 8, 10, 17), though the Hebrew words differ slightly. "Most High" speaks of God's exalted, sovereign position in heaven.

### D. Description of God's justice (7:10-17)

**7:10-11.** David described how **God,** his **Shield** (cf. comments on 3:3), in saving **the upright in heart,** brings direct judgment on the wicked. Because **God is**

a righteous Judge (cf. 9:8), He is angry every day. Obedient believers can be comforted in the fact that people's wickedness does not go unnoticed. But they can also be advised that vengeance belongs to the Lord; He will repay (cf. Deut. 32:35; Rom. 12:19; Heb. 10:30).

7:12-13. Like a warrior God prepares His deadly weapons for the wicked. Swords, bows (v. 12), and arrows (v. 13) often provide the imagery for God's decree of judgment that will destroy the wicked.

7:14-16. Next David stated how God traps the wicked with their own plans. If someone conceives trouble, it will not produce its intended results. Rather the evil scheme will be turned back on the plotter (cf. pit in 9:15; 35:8; 57:6; Prov. 26:27). This is retribution from God, for the punishment fits the crime (an eye for an eye, a tooth for a tooth, etc., Ex. 21:24-25). Jesus said that they "who draw the sword will die by the sword" (Matt. 26:52).

7:17. The psalm ends with David's vowing to thank and praise God for His righteousness, a righteousness yet to be manifested in the psalmist's experience. So even though he was slandered and attacked, David wholeheartedly trusted in his righteous LORD (the Most High; cf. comments on v. 8) for vindication and equity.

## Psalm 8

In this psalm David marveled that the glorious Lord of heaven, whose name is excellent, should graciously use people in the earth's dominion. The passage considers the dignity of mankind as God's representative on earth, without noting the Fall's consequence of chaos and rebellion.

### A. The Lord's majesty (8:1)

8:1. The beginning and ending of the psalm (vv. 1, 9) give the same exclamation of God's majestic . . . name. The name, that is, the revealed character of God, is exalted above all Creation. The word majestic suggests splendor and magnificence. It is a fitting note of praise for the Lord of Creation.

The vocative O LORD, our Lord is important in this idea. Addressing God by His personal name Yahweh ("LORD"), David then identified Him as "our Lord"

('ăḏōnay), the Sovereign or Master. "Lord" stresses God's dominion over His Creation.

The Hebrew of the last part of verse 1 is difficult. Though the text has an imperative verb, most translations (including the NIV) apparently take it as an infinitive and render it as a statement about God's majesty: You have set. It describes His exaltation (glory) as being high above the heavens.

### B. The Lord's strength (8:2)

8:2. David marveled that God uses strength (cf. NIV marg.) from children to silence His enemies (and the foe and the avenger). (The NIV translates 'ōz, "strength" by the word praise because "strength" here may indicate "praise for [God's] strength"; cf. Matt. 21:15-16.) The idea is that the Lord has ordained that the weakest shall confound the strong (cf. 1 Cor. 1:27). Mankind, even weak children and infants, represents the strength of God in the earth.

### C. The Lord's Creation (8:3-8)

David now examined the marvelous theme that God should graciously entrust his dominion to man.

8:3-4. The psalmist first observed the great work of Creation (including the heavens . . . the moon, and the stars) as God's finger work, and then was amazed that finite man (the Heb. for man here is 'ĕnôš, "mortal, weak man") should have such a responsibility over it. The rhetorical questions in verse 4 emphasize that man is an insignificant creature in the universe (cf. 144:3). Yet God cares for him immensely. It amazed David that the Lord of the universe even thinks about man.

8:5. God's creation of man is described as one of power and dignity, for he was made . . . a little lower than God ('ĕlōhîm; cf. NIV marg.). The KJV followed the Septuagint in translating this word "angels." The NIV has chosen heavenly beings, which follows the same interpretation. Though in some cases 'ĕlōhîm may refer to angels, this is not its main meaning. Man was created as God's own representative on earth, over the Creation, but lower than God. David was amazed that God should exalt finite man to such a place of honor.

Hebrews 2:6-8 quotes this psalm to

contrast man's failure with his exalted destiny. Jesus Christ, the Son of Man, is the last Adam (1 Cor. 15:45, 47); all things will be subjected to Him when He comes to fulfill God the Father's intended plans for the Creation.

**8:6-8.** David reflected on man's position as God's representative in His Creation. After God made Adam and Eve, He commanded them to have dominion over all the earth (Gen. 1:28). All living creatures were to be **under** them. But because of sin that dominion has never been fully realized. In fact it was through a subordinate, the serpent, that man rebelled against God's order.

### D. The Lord's majesty (8:9)

**8:9.** The psalm closes with the same expression of praise for God's **majestic . . . name** with which it began (cf. v. 1). God's majesty has been displayed in His care and design for finite man.

## Psalm 9

Psalms 9 and 10 may have originally been one psalm, as they are in the Septuagint. They are connected by their form in the Hebrew, for nearly each stanza (approximately every other verse) begins with a successive letter of the Hebrew alphabet. Also the two psalms have similar wording. For example, "in times of trouble" is found in 9:9 and 10:18, and in only two other passages in the Psalms. Also each of the two psalms closes with an emphasis on mortal men (9:20; 10:18). Finally each psalm mentions "the nations" (9:5, 15, 17, 19-20; 10:16).

Yet there is warrant for the two psalms being separate. Psalm 9 is a triumphant song of thanksgiving, while Psalm 10 is a complaint and prayer over godless men in the nation. Because Psalm 9 is complete in itself, it is better to regard Psalm 10 as a related psalm.

Psalm 9 is a song of thanksgiving for vindication. Ascribed to David, this psalm is set "to the tune of 'The Death of the Son.' " What that means is unknown. In the psalm David praised the Lord for manifesting His righteousness in judging wicked nations, and for being a true and eternal Judge in whom the afflicted may trust. He then prayed that God would give him further cause for praise by seeing his affliction and removing it from him.

### A. Praise: Manifestation of righteousness (9:1-12)

**9:1-2.** The first portion of the psalm (vv. 1-12) speaks of God as the true Judge and the Hope of the afflicted. In view of this, David resolved to **praise** Him wholeheartedly, to **tell of** His **wonders,** to be joyful in God, and to **sing** to Him. "Wonders" (*niplā'ôt*, "things extraordinary or surpassing") is used frequently of God's works in the Psalms.

**9:3-6.** The cause for David's praise is recorded in these verses. The Lord manifested His righteousness (v. 4) by vindicating David's cause. His **enemies** were turned **back** (v. 3), **rebuked,** and **destroyed** (v. 5). Even the **name** of **the nations** (also mentioned in vv. 15, 17, 19-20) was **blotted out.** Such a description vividly portrayed their defeat—not even their name would be perpetuated. **Memory of them** was destroyed after **their cities** were demolished (v. 6).

All of this, David wrote, was evidence that God **upheld** his **cause,** and rules **righteously** from His **throne** (v. 4).

**9:7-10.** On the basis of the deliverance spoken of in verses 3-6, David declared that **the LORD** is a true and eternal Judge and a Fortress for the afflicted. The psalmist's praise at first was directed to **the LORD** and His eternal reign over the earth (vv. 7-8). Then David applied that truth to people's needs. The afflicted and **the oppressed,** those who are most frequently ignored or abused by human judgment, are championed by the righteous Judge. The Lord God is their **Refuge** and **Stronghold in times of trouble.** The word *miśgōb,* used twice in verse 9 and translated both "refuge" and "stronghold," suggests security and protection in a high, safe place of retreat. *Miśgōb,* one of several words used in the Psalms to speak of security and safety in God, is translated "stronghold" in Psalms 18:2; 144:2, and "fortress" in 46:7, 11; 48:3; 59:9, 16-17; 62:2, 6; 94:22. Another Hebrew word translated "refuge" in the Psalms is *maḥseh,* "shelter from danger." It is used in 14:6; 46:1; 61:3; 62:7-8; 71:7; 73:28; 91:2, 9. Still another word translated "refuge" in the Psalms in the NIV is *mānôs* ("a place to flee to," 59:16; 142:5). Knowing of God's security and protection, His own can **trust** Him.

**9:11-12.** This praise section (vv. 1-12) closes with the psalmist's exhortation to the people, especially **the afflicted** whom God **does not ignore** (v. 12), to **sing praises to the LORD** (cf. v. 2) and tell **what He has done** (v. 11).

### B. Prayer: Aid for the afflicted (9:13-20)

**9:13-14.** In view of God's past deliverances, David now called on God to respond to his affliction and give him reason to praise. The psalmist asked the LORD to notice **how** his **enemies persecute** him. In danger of dying, he called on God to rescue him **from the gates of death** (cf. Job 38:17; Ps. 107:18; Isa. 38:10). If delivered, he would then praise the Lord **in the gates of the Daughter of Zion** (i.e., the tabernacle in Jerusalem).

**9:15-16.** David's prayer was supported by his confident trust in **the LORD.** In verses 15-18 David rehearsed the reputation God has for destroying the wicked who afflict the needy. Verse 15 may have been written in anticipation of the enemy's destruction as is done in the "confidence" sections in various psalms. If so, David foresaw how the wicked would fall **into** their own **pit** (cf. 7:15) and **net** (cf. 35:8; 57:6). Nevertheless the Lord's **justice** is well **known,** for the evil that **the wicked** devise returns on them.

**9:17-18.** The destiny of **the wicked,** who **return to the grave** (šᵉ'ôl, sheol), is contrasted with **the needy** and **afflicted** (cf. vv. 9, 12), who **will** see their **hope** fulfilled. The expression **forget God** is sometimes contrasted in the Psalms with the word "remember," a term that signifies faith and prayer. Those who reject and ignore the Lord have no hope.

**9:19-20.** The psalm closes with the prayer that the LORD would **arise** and put mortal **man** ('ĕnôš; cf. comments on 8:4) to fear in a terrifying judgment. Such a destruction would make the wicked realize that **they are but** human ('ĕnôš) and that they cannot oppress those who trust in the LORD.

## Psalm 10

The idea of praise for righteous vindication, clearly evident in Psalm 9, is less pronounced in Psalm 10. This is a prayer for God not to delay His help for the afflicted. The psalmist described the awesome power of the wicked in their impiety toward God and their lurking against the helpless. Then he pleaded

with God to arise and avenge the oppressed by breaking the wicked.

### A. Description of the wicked (10:1-11)

**10:1.** The first part of the psalm is a forceful description of the wicked's vicious power. But at the beginning the writer turned his complaint to the Lord, who seemed to be uninterested in the plight of the oppressed. The fact that the wicked may triumph caused the psalmist to ask **why** the LORD was hiding Himself from the **trouble** (cf. "why" twice in v. 13). The question is a bold expression of the true feelings of oppressed people who cry out for help.

**10:2-7.** In these verses David delineated the character of the oppressor. Full of pride (**arrogance,** v. 2, and **boasts,** v. 3) **the wicked man** afflicts **the weak** and speaks abusively of **the LORD** (cf. v. 13). The wicked person is confident (**pride,** v. 4, **haughty,** v. 5), and has **no room for God** or God's **laws.** Such a person is convinced that he cannot be moved from his wicked ways. He thinks he can continue undisturbed in his prosperity (v. 5) and happiness (v. 6; cf. 73:3). His words are deceitful and destructive (10:7). The clause **trouble and evil are under his tongue** means that the words he speaks will cause calamity.

**10:8-11.** Here the psalmist described the wicked as lurking (**lies in wait** occurs three times in vv. 8-9) **in secret** places **like a lion** (cf. comments on 7:2) to attack **his** helpless (cf. 10:12) victims, and to drag **them off** as a fisherman does with **his net.** This imagery of a lion and a fisherman suggests cunning men waiting to attack. The afflicted (i.e., the righteous) **are crushed** by the wicked. Since God may not immediately rescue them, the wicked person is convinced that **God** does not care for or see the righteous.

### B. Appeal for vengeance (10:12-18)

**10:12-15.** Making an earnest cry for vengeance, the psalmist called on **God** to **arise** (cf. 9:19) and help **the helpless** (cf. 10:9). One reason for this request is that **the wicked** should not be allowed to despise **God** (cf. v. 3) and to think he can get away with his actions (cf. **why** in v. 1). The Lord should be motivated to respond because the afflicted trust **God** who sees **trouble and grief** and is their **Helper** (v. 14). The psalmist's specific request was that God would punish **the wicked** (v. 15). Here the imagery is again graphic: to **break** one's **arm** means to destroy his power. If God so judges the wicked by such a destruction, then they would be called **to account for** their deeds. The psalmist would then no longer be able to say that God does not see his deeds (cf. v. 13) or care for the afflicted.

**10:16-18.** The psalm closes with an expression of confidence that the writer's prayer has been heard. Here as well as in Psalm 9 the psalmist declared that **the LORD is** sovereign (cf. 9:7) and that those in **the nations** (cf. 9:5, 15, 17, 19-20) who oppose Him **will perish** (cf. 9:3, 5, 15). The psalmist was sure that the LORD hears the **cry** of **the afflicted** and defends their cause, so that the wicked—who are mere mortals (*'ĕnôš*; cf. 9:20 and comments on 8:4)—will not **terrify** them anymore.

Faith that God defends the afflicted and the needy against the tyranny of the wicked was a comfort to the psalmist and the basis for his prayer.

## Psalm 11

The historical setting of this psalm is unknown; apparently David was in desperate straits with his life in danger. The temptation to run from danger challenged his confidence in God. The psalm's message is as follows: faced with the temptation to flee at a time when lawful authority was being destroyed, the psalmist held fast to his faith in the Lord, who will ultimately destroy the wicked whom He hates and deliver the righteous whom He loves.

### A. Temptation to flee (11:1-3)

**11:1.** The psalm begins with the psalmist's repudiation of the temptation to **flee** from danger. David marveled at this suggestion from the fainthearted because it defied his faith in the Lord. His initial declaration, **In the LORD I take** (or have taken) **refuge,** counteracts their suggestion.

The fainthearted advised David to flee **like a bird to** a **mountain** where he would be safe. But instead he fled to the Lord for safety.

**11:2.** This temptation came because **the wicked** were out to destroy the righteous, including David. The wicked **bend** their bows to fasten **the strings** on them, and then place **their arrows** on the strings **to shoot** in secrecy (cf. 10:8-9) **at the upright.** It may be that a literal attack is in view, but more likely the bows and arrows denote slanderous words that destroy, as is often true in the Psalms.

**11:3.** If **the foundations** of society are overthrown, **what can the righteous do?** These foundations refer to the Law and the order of society based on the Lord's rule. The temptation from the fainthearted, then, was based on a fear that the nation might crumble. Their view was experiential and earthward. David's view was higher.

### B. Confidence in the Lord (11:4-7)

**11:4.** David contrasted the problem on earth with the exalted position of **the LORD** in heaven. "What can the righteous do?" the fainthearted had asked (v. 3). David responded that the righteous can trust in the real Source of secure government—**the LORD,** whose **throne** is exalted in the heavens, **His holy temple,** far from the dissimulation of the wicked. Because the Lord is sovereignly ruling over the earth, He sees and thoroughly investigates the activities of **the sons of men** (cf. 33:13-14). **He observes** is literally, "His eyes see," and **His eyes** is literally, "His eyelids." Eyelids normally contract when examining closely. This bold anthropomorphism stresses the precise omniscience of God.

**11:5.** God **examines** (tests, refines) **the righteous, but** He hates **the wicked and** people **who love violence.** God is opposed to all who choose wickedness and violence in opposition to His will.

**11:6.** The psalmist then looked to a sudden and swift judgment **on the wicked. He will rain** could also be translated, "May He rain." **Burning sulfur** is reminiscent of God's judgment on Sodom and Gomorrah (Gen. 19:24). **Fiery coals** may possibly be translated "snares." If so, the psalmist was anticipating a fitting judgment for the wicked—they would be trapped. At any rate **scorching** judgment is their destiny.

**11:7.** In contrast with God's judgment on the wicked (v. 6), **the LORD,** who **is righteous . . . loves justice** (lit., "righteousness"). The **upright**—those who by faith trust Him and seek to follow His ways—**will see His face.** This means that the righteous are admitted to His presence and enjoy His blessings.

## Psalm 12

This psalm expresses David's confidence in the untarnished words of God that assure him He will deliver those who seek His salvation. This expression of confidence comes in the midst of a culture that oppressed the weak with deception. The setting of the psalm is unknown, but many incidents in the life of David could have prompted such a psalm (cf. 1 Sam. 23:11, 19; 26:19). But the language of the psalm is general enough to fit several situations.

### A. Prayer for deliverance (12:1-4)

The psalmist cried out to God (vv. 1-4) for deliverance from the midst of a lying and arrogant people.

**12:1-2.** His introductory cry laments the fact that **the godly** were apparently extinct. People who showed **faithful** covenant loyalty had disappeared from the land. (The word for "faithful" is ḥasîd, related to ḥeseḏ, "loyal love or covenant loyalty.") In their place were those who lied and deceived. Their words were dishonest and therefore untrustworthy. The society had become altogether corrupt. There seemed to be no trustworthy, honest people on whom the psalmist could depend.

**12:3-4.** So the psalmist prayed that **the LORD** would **cut off . . . flattering,** lying **lips.** These people were filled with pride (they were **boastful**), assuming that through propaganda, flattery, and deception they could achieve their goals. Saying, **we will triumph with our tongues,** they assumed they could do as they pleased: **Who is our master?** David wanted God to destroy them and end their arrogant boasting.

### B. Assurance of deliverance (12:5)

**12:5.** The psalmist received assurance that **the LORD** would **arise** and free **the weak and . . . the needy** from **oppression.** God promised to deliver those who trusted in Him **from those who** were maligning **them.**

### C. Confidence in God's Word (12:6-8)

**12:6.** Because of assurance from God that the afflicted would be delivered (v. 5) the psalmist expressed confidence in the untarnished words of God, even though he knew the wicked were all around him.

In contrast with the wicked's words, the Lord's words are pure (**purified**) and true. Their untarnished nature is compared to the process of refining **silver**; it is as if **the words of the LORD** had been **refined . . . seven times,** the number of completeness and perfection. What God says is true (**flawless;** cf. 18:30) and reliable. His words are not tainted with deceit and false flattery (in contrast with the wicked's words, 12:2-3) but are fully dependable.

**12:7-8.** Therefore the psalmist trusted in God's word that He would **keep** them **safe** in the midst of proud **people** who **strut about** in smug self-confidence, placing a premium on things that are **vile** (zūllûṯ, a word used only here in the OT, means something squandered or worthless). Verse 8 pictures worthless and ruthless **men** who exercise authority and power through deceptive words. Yet God's words, which are true, affirm that such people will be destroyed.

## Psalm 13

This psalm records the cry of the afflicted and therefore harmonizes with several of the preceding psalms. Here David rested confidently on the loyal love of the Lord (v. 5), even though he found no immediate deliverance from the oppression of the adversary, God's enemy.

### A. Lament over distress (13:1-2)

**13:1-2.** In a series of rhetorical questions designed to motivate God to answer his prayer, David asked God **how long** (four times in these two verses; cf. comments on 6:3) He would wait before answering. David felt ignored by God and forgotten. Would this continue indefinitely? Wrestling inwardly (**with my thoughts** is lit., "in my soul"), David lamented that he spent **every day** in this distressing situation, that his **heart** was filled with struggles and **sorrow.** As a result of his apparently being forsaken by God, his enemies triumphed **over** him.

### B. Petition for deliverance (13:3-4)

**13:3-4.** David called on the Lord to **look . . . answer,** and rescue him from his situation. **Give light to my eyes** was

David's way of requesting divine wisdom or perspective on his need. He earnestly prayed this lest he **sleep in death** (cf. comments on 7:5; **fall** is lit., "die"), thus bringing triumphant joy to his **enemy.**

### C. Confidence in the Lord (13:5a)

**13:5a.** David expressed his **trust in** the Lord's **unfailing love** (*ḥeseḏ*), the loyal love the Lord has for those who trust in Him. The enemies of David were challenging the faithfulness of God's love to one of his covenant believers.

### D. Praise for salvation (13:5b-6)

**13:5b-6.** The psalmist, assured that his prayer had been heard, resolved to rejoice and **sing to the LORD** for giving him **salvation** and for dealing bountifully with him. (This is the first of several dozen references in the Pss. to God's being **good.**) He fully anticipated the end of his long wait.

## Psalm 14

Knowing that the human race is foolish and corrupt, and that the Lord will destroy such people for their actions, the psalmist longed for the establishment of the Lord's kingdom on earth. (See comments on Ps. 53, which is almost identical to Ps. 14.)

### A. Appraisal of the human race (14:1-3)

**14:1.** David affirmed God's indictment on the human race: they are fools. Verse 1 gives a summary description of **the fool** (*nāḇāl*, one who is morally insensitive and impious). A fool believes that **there is no God,** and leads a **corrupt** life. These two statements are related. As a practical atheist (i.e., living his life as if there were no God) he is separated from the wisdom revealed in God's Word. As a result he is corrupt, spoiling whatever he does. His actions **are vile,** that is, he does abominable things that the Lord hates. Without faith **no one** can please God, so **there** are none **who** do **good.**

**14:2.** The psalmist's evaluation of the human race was based on the Lord's looking **down** to examine people (**the sons of men**). Examples of the Lord's seeing how wicked the race was include Babel (Gen. 11:1-9) and Sodom (Gen. 18:21). The psalmist pictured **the LORD** looking **to see if** anyone had understanding, that is, if **any** were seeking **God.** The

beginning of wisdom is fear of the Lord (Prov. 1:7). Since the fool refuses to accept this fact, he has no understanding.

**14:3.** In searching for prudent people, God saw that the entire human race had **turned aside** and **become corrupt** (lit., "sour" like milk). This word *'ālaḥ,* which occurs only here and in Job 15:16 and Psalm 53:3, is used in a moral sense. (This word for corrupt differs from the word for corrupt in 14:1.) Consequently God said that not **one** solitary person **does good.** The only hope for the race, the Scriptures teach, is for individuals to turn to the Lord for salvation.

### B. Punishment of the wicked (14:4-6)

**14:4-6.** David revealed the outcome of the struggle between these workers of iniquity and the righteous. He was amazed at the ignorance of **evildoers** who think they can freely **devour** God's **people.** Their wickedness is most pronounced in their vicious attack on His people. They are oblivious to the fact that God will overwhelm them, because in attacking the people of God they are attacking **God.** He is **present in the** midst of His people. So the psalmist foresaw that the wicked will be in great **dread** when the Lord judges them for persecuting His own. They may **frustrate** the lives of God's people (**the poor**) for a time, but those people will be vindicated because they trust in **the LORD . . . their Refuge** (*maḥseh,* "shelter from danger," a word used of the Lord nine times in the Pss: 14:6; 46:1; 61:3; 62:7-8; 71:7; 73:28; 91:2, 9).

### C. Longing for the kingdom (14:7)

**14:7.** David yearned for the establishment of the Lord's kingdom (cf. Matt. 6:10). **The LORD,** when He delivers His nation **Israel** from the presence of the wicked (cf. Rom. 11:26-27), will bring great joy to **His people** (cf. Zeph. 3:14-16). The psalmist was clearly longing for the establishment of God's righteous rule from **Zion** (cf. comments on Ps. 2:6) and for the destruction of the wicked who persist in ungodliness.

## Psalm 15

This psalm explains who is worthy to be a "guest" of the Lord. The psalmist delineated the flawless character of one who is fit to worship in the Lord's sanctuary.

## A. The question: Who may abide? (15:1)

**15:1.** David pondered the matter of **who may dwell in** the Lord's **sanctuary** (the tabernacle), located on the **holy hill,** that is, Zion, the City of David (cf. 2 Sam. 6:10-12, 17 and comments on Ps. 2:6). The question is concerned with who was eligible to be a "guest" of the Lord and **live** in the place where His presence rested. It was a spiritual question: who can draw near to God and worship in His dwelling place?

## B. The answer: The righteous may abide (15:2-5)

**15:2a-b.** The question in verse 1 is answered in summary fashion first (v. 2a-b) with two descriptions, and then delineated (vv. 2c-5) with an additional eight. The acceptable person is one **whose walk is** (a) **blameless.** Also his actions are (b) **righteous.** The metaphor of the "walk" is used throughout the Bible for one's pattern of life and conduct (cf. 1:1). "Blameless" (*tāmîm*) means complete, sincere, or perfect. A blameless person lives in obedience to God and maintains a life of integrity.

His activities are in harmony with God's standards, that is, they are righteous. David thus declared that if someone were to go into the presence of the Lord in Zion, he must be an obedient and righteous servant. The wicked and the hypocritical did not belong in the sanctuary.

**15:2c-5a.** After the general statement in the first two lines of verse 2, David spelled out what such a flawless person's character is like.

(1) The first characteristic of the righteous is that he **speaks . . . truth** sincerely. He is not like double-minded flatterers (cf. 12:2). (2) A righteous person does not **slander** maliciously. (3) Nor does he harm or (4) discredit **his neighbor.** A neighbor (or friend) is anyone with whom he comes in contact. A blameless individual's remarks do not harm or destroy any neighbor.

(5) Also a righteous person **despises . . . vile** people and **honors** believers **who fear the Lord.** A person who is "vile" (from *mā'as,* and therefore not the same word for vile in 14:1) is a reprobate, one who is worthless. But one who fears the Lord is living a life of faith and obedience.

(6) A righteous person also **keeps his oath even when it hurts.** Even if he took an oath rashly (Lev. 5:4), he would conscientiously keep his word.

(7) He does not lend **his money** for usury (lit., "he does not put the bite on them"). He does not take advantage of one who must borrow. Taking interest from fellow Israelites was forbidden as unbrotherly (Ex. 22:25; Lev. 25:36).

(8) A righteous person **does not** take bribes **against the innocent.** The Law of course forbade this (Deut. 27:25). Instead a righteous person champions the cause of the innocent and the needy.

**15:5b.** David concluded that one who follows this pattern of life **will never be shaken** (cf. 16:8; 21:7; 30:6; 62:2, 6; 112:6). Not only will he enjoy fellowship in the Lord's presence, but also he will experience divine blessing and security.

The fact that there are 10 descriptions of one who qualifies to abide with the Lord (sincere, righteous, honest, without slander, without doing wrong, without reproaching, distinguishes between good and evil, keeps his oath, does not take interest, does not accept bribes) suggests a comparison with the Ten Commandments (though the two lists do not correspond in every item). Obedience to God's revealed will is the requirement for full participation in the sanctuary.

## Psalm 16

This psalm is a celebration of the joy of fellowship that David realized comes from faith in the Lord. The psalm may have been written when he faced great danger in the wilderness or opposition in his reign. Whatever its occasion, David was convinced that because he had come to know and trust the Lord as his Portion in life, he could trust Him in the face of death.

## A. The Lord is his Portion in life (16:1-8)

**16:1.** In verses 1-8 David reviewed how he had come to know and trust in the Lord. Verse 1 seems to summarize the entire psalm: **Keep me safe, O God, for in You I take refuge.** Then David developed the idea of his having taken refuge in the Lord.

**16:2.** David announced his exclusive trust in **the Lord.** His statement of faith was, **You are my Lord; apart from You I have no good thing** (cf. 34:10; 84:11).

**16:3-4.** Based on his commitment to the Lord, the psalmist described the society of friends with whom he was identified. He delighted in godly people **(saints) in the land,** whom he considered to be the noble **(glorious) ones.** God had called His people to be a holy nation (Ex. 19:6), and God's servant recognized that such were his company. They were the faithful who served the Lord. The others, **those . . . who run after other gods,** will face **sorrows** and difficulties. David would not endorse their actions, or help them with their vain worship, or even mention the **names** of their gods. His loyalty was with righteous believers.

**16:5-6.** In direct address to the Lord, the psalmist extolled His blessings. David compared the **Lord** to a **portion** (cf. 73:26; 119:57; 142:5) allotted to him by inheritance. The Lord was all he needed to satisfy his heart in life. Besides his portion **and** his **cup,** the Lord had **assigned** him **a delightful inheritance. The boundary lines . . . in pleasant places** speak of portions of land measured by line and distributed by **lot.** In other words he compared God's blessings to the best inheritance a person could receive. The Lord had given him a wonderfully full life.

**16:7-8.** As a result of all this bounty, David praised **the Lord** because He counseled him **at night** (as well as in the daytime) and because He guided him safely. (**Praise** is lit., "bless," which means "to speak well of." This is the first of about two dozen times in the Pss. where the Lord is said to be "blessed," usually trans. "praised" in the NIV.) Because of this David knew that he would **not be shaken** (cf. comments on 15:5b) from his walk of integrity and enjoyment of the blessings he had in the Lord.

### B. The Lord will preserve him (16:9-11)

**16:9-11.** David was assured that the Lord would preserve his life in the face of death. He rejoiced because God enabled his **body** to **rest** securely even when confronted with death. The reason he could rest is that God would **not abandon** him **to the grave, nor . . . let** His **holy one see decay.** This verse refers to David, who describes himself as God's "holy one," that is, one of God's saints (cf. v. 3). He

took comfort in the fact that God would not, at that time, allow his body to die and decay in the grave. In fact God had caused him to know **the path of life** so he anticipated experiencing further **joy in** God's **presence** (v. 11).

Verses 8-11 were cited by Peter on the day of Pentecost (Acts 2:25-28) and Psalm 16:10b was quoted by Paul at Antioch (Acts 13:35-37) in reference to Christ's resurrection. So the words of David are also typological; they transcended his own experience and became historically true in Christ. Preservation from the decaying grave is the idea behind both David's and Jesus' experiences, but with David it came through a *deliverance* from death, whereas with Jesus it came through a *resurrection* from death.

Death posed no threat to David because he enjoyed great blessing and fellowship with the Lord. God would not permit death and the grave to interrupt that marvelous fellowship. So in a fuller sense this is true of believers today, who having the full revelation about the doctrine of resurrection, can say that even when they die, God will not let death destroy that full fellowship they enjoy with the Lord (2 Cor. 5:8; Phil. 1:23). This expression of faith is possible because Christ conquered death (Luke 24:6) and rose to become the firstfruits of all who sleep (1 Cor. 15:20).

## Psalm 17

In this psalm David was conscious of his own integrity while he was surrounded by enemies whose portion was in this life only. He prayed to be kept from the evil world that oppressed him as he looked to a glorious future in the Lord's presence.

The psalm is similar in many ways to Psalm 16, but there is a major difference. In Psalm 16 David was aware of danger in the background, but his faith encouraged him not to fear. In Psalm 17, however, the danger was pressing in on him, so help from the Lord was urgently needed.

### A. The prayer of a righteous man (17:1-5)

**17:1-2.** David asked God to **hear** his **righteous plea,** to **listen to** him, to **give ear to** his **prayer.** This threefold request to God strikes a note of urgency.

This prayer did not come from someone who was unrighteous or hypocritical (one with **deceitful lips**). David avowed his integrity before God, so that God could **see** that he was **right** and would vindicate him.

**17:3.** In his integrity (vv. 3-5), David maintained that if he were examined (**probe . . . examine . . . test**) by God, he would be found pure. That is because he **resolved . . . not** to **sin**. To live righteously before God, one must resolve in his heart to serve and obey Him.

**17:4-5.** Moreover, David had **kept** himself separate **from the ways of** those who destroy. His life had been patterned after God's **Word**. He had **held to** God's **paths,** that is, he had followed the way God wished him to live. He had **not slipped** from this path.

## B. Prayer for protection from the world (17:6-12)

David prayed to be kept from evil people in the world because they are full of vicious pride.

**17:6-7.** His prayer was based on God's loyal **love** for him. The Lord's **great** love is revealed by the fact that He saves **those who take refuge in** Him. David, at this point, was taking refuge, so he desired to be shown that great love.

**17:8.** David prayed that he would be kept in the center of God's watchful care. His two figures of speech in this verse have been most helpful to believers of all ages. **The apple of** the **eye** seems to refer to an eye's pupil, symbolizing one's sight. In other words the psalmist prayed for God's direct and careful attention.

The other figure, **the shadow of Your wings,** is also mentioned in 36:7; 57:1; 61:4, "shelter"; 63:7; 91:4 (cf. Ruth 2:12; Matt. 23:37). This image comes from the animal world, comparing God's protective care to that of a bird with its young. So David was praying for care and protection from the Lord.

**17:9-12.** The reason for the prayer's urgency is the nature of **the wicked,** which David delineated in an effort to motivate God to action. They tried to destroy David (v. 9); they spoke with callous indifference and pride (v. 10); and they relentlessly pursued him **like a lion** after its **prey** (vv. 11-12; cf. comments on 7:2).

## C. The prospect of a glorious future (17:13-15)

**17:13-14a.** In contrast with David's present persecution by worldly men (vv. 6-12) he looked to the prospects of the future. His urgent prayer for the LORD to **rise up** and deliver him from these wicked people **whose reward** (portion) **is in this life** (v. 14) was a reminder of his present dilemma. Because they did not follow the LORD . . . **this life** was their only hope of enjoyment. They persecuted the righteous in a number of ways, physically and verbally.

In David's prayer he called on God's **sword** to **rescue** him. This may refer to the fact that God at times uses human armies, even of **the wicked,** to punish nations (cf. Isa. 10:5).

**17:14b-15.** In contrast with these who live for this life and face God's "sword," David anticipated a far greater blessing for himself and others, including satisfied appetites and **wealth for their children. In righteousness,** he wrote, he would **see** God's **face** (cf. 11:7); **when** he awakened, he would **be satisfied with seeing** God's **likeness.** The psalmist was not anticipating death, or an awakening in resurrection from death. Rather he was contrasting the destruction of the wicked, who live their lives without God, with his life, which was lived in God's grace.

Nevertheless the words are appropriate as a description of his enjoyment of God's presence. Though David may have thought of spiritual blessing and God's presence, the words lend themselves nicely to believers today, who with full New Testament revelation can anticipate a far more glorious prospect than they experience in this life.

## Psalm 18

The superscription of this psalm credits the words to David after the Lord delivered him from the hand of all his enemies including "Saul." After reviewing all that the Lord was to him David then recorded his deliverance by the Lord and rejoiced in the mercies shown him. This psalm is a song of gratitude for victory by the warrior-king who at last was at peace. The psalm is also recorded in 2 Samuel 22 with slight variations. Perhaps some of the wording in 2 Samuel 22 was changed in this psalm for use in public worship, but this cannot be proved.

## A. Description of the character of God (18:1-3)

**18:1-3.** In his vow to praise God, David multiplied metaphor after metaphor to describe all that the Lord was and had been to him. He expressed his **love** for **the LORD** who had shown mercy to him throughout his many struggles.

David described **the LORD** as a **Rock** (cf. vv. 31, 46) because He provided stability and security for him. About 20 times in the Psalms the Lord is said to be a Rock. David also compared God to a **fortress** (the same Heb. word [*mᵉṣûḏâh*] is used of God in 31:3; 71:3; 91:2; 144:2). "Rock" and "fortress" picture a high place of refuge and defense to which one might flee for protection. To **take refuge** in the **LORD** is far better than hiding in a man-made fortress or behind a huge rock.

David also compared God to a **shield** (cf. 18:30 and comments on 3:3) and a **stronghold** (*miśgōḇ*; cf. comments on 9:9), both military terms suggesting protection and deliverance from enemies. As the **Horn of** his **salvation** God gave him strength. Animal horns were symbols of strength. They later symbolized rulers (cf. 148:14; Dan. 7:8, 11, 20-21, 24; 8:21-22; Rev. 17:12).

Because the Lord had defended and delivered David from all his **enemies,** He was **worthy of** David's **praise.**

## B. Report of the deliverance by God (18:4-29)

In an extended section of praise, David reiterated his sufferings and perils, and also the Lord's great supernatural deliverance.

**18:4-5.** In verses 4-19 David reported how God supernaturally delivered him. Being in **the cords of death** means that he was in such difficult distress that without divine intervention he would have died. **Destruction overwhelmed** him like a flood (**torrents**). The trappings **of death** were before him, and he was without human resources to save him.

**18:6-15.** When David **cried to** the **LORD,** God intervened **from His temple** to **help** him. (God's help is mentioned frequently in the Pss.) David then described this intervention as a tremendous

epiphany, or appearance of the Lord. David said that **the earth trembled and quaked . . . because** of God's anger against His and David's enemies (v. 7); **smoke** and **fire came from His nostrils** and **mouth** (v. 8); **He . . . came down** with **clouds** (v. 9); **He soared on the wings of the wind** (v. 10); **dark rain clouds** accompanied Him (v. 11); **clouds,** hail, and **lightning** were with Him (v. 12); thunder (the Lord's **voice;** cf. Job 37:2, 4-5) **resounded** (Ps. 18:13); **lightning** bolts (cf. Job 36:30, 32; 37:3, 11; 38:24, 35) like **arrows . . . scattered the enemies** (Ps. 18:14); and the basins **of the sea . . . and the** earth's **foundations** were exposed at His coming (v. 15). This poetic description of God's divine intervention in battle portrays a tremendous storm in which God used many of the awesome phenomena of nature. Such terrible events were understood as expressions of God's judicial wrath (cf. v. 7).

**18:16-19.** In these verses David explained that by such an intervention the Lord **rescued** him. It was as if David were drowning in the midst of his **strong** enemies, and the Lord **drew** him **out. . . . because He delighted in** him (vv. 16, 19).

Such a dramatic portrayal of divine intervention suggests similarities with the giving of the Law (Ex. 19:16-18). Similar events are recorded in Joshua 10:11; Judges 5:20; and 1 Samuel 7:10. Descriptions like this are also frequent in prophetic visions of divine intervention (e.g., Isa. 29:6; 30:27; 64:1; Hab. 3:3-4).

**18:20-24.** After describing his deliverance by the Lord, David explained it in terms of his faith in **the LORD** his God. By faith David had kept his integrity (**righteousness,** vv. 20, 24) before God. This deliverance was because God was rewarding David for **the cleanness** (vv. 20, 24) **of** his **hands** (i.e., his life). David attested that he had not turned **from . . . God,** that he had walked in God's **ways,** obeyed **His laws** and **decrees,** and **kept** himself **from sin.** God honored His obedient servant with tremendous victories.

**18:25-29.** By faith, David also understood the nature of the **LORD** and how He revealed Himself to mankind. God rewards people according to their inner character: faithfulness **to the faithful** (*ḥāsîḏ,* related to *ḥeseḏ*), blamelessness **to**

the blameless, purity to the pure, but shrewdness to the crooked (*'iqqēš*, "twisted, perverse," a word also used in 101:4; Prov. 2:15; 8:8; 11:20; 17:20; 19:1; 22:5, "wicked"; 28:6). His dealings are always just.

Moreover, God saves the humble (lit., "the poor or afflicted") but defeats the arrogant (eyes that are haughty means a proud look; cf. Ps. 101:5; Prov. 6:17; 30:13). God sets right the affairs of man. For David, this meant that the Lord preserved him alive (kept his lamp burning; cf. Job 18:5-6; 21:17; Prov. 13:9; 20:20; 24:20) from the enemy. With God's help David could advance against and defeat any enemies.

### C. Rejoicing in God's blessings (18:30-50)

**18:30-31.** In the first part (vv. 30-45) of this section of praise David rejoiced over God's character and His benefits to him. God's **way,** the psalmist said, **is perfect** and His **Word . . . flawless** (cf. 12:6; Prov. 30:5). Again (cf. Ps. 18:2) he said God was his **Shield** (cf. comments on 3:3), **Refuge,** and **Rock** (cf. 18:46). God can be trusted for safety and salvation.

**18:32-45.** Here David described how **God** prepared him **for battle,** giving him **strength,** agility, and efficiency (vv. 32-34); how God gave him **victory** over his **enemies,** pursuing, crushing, and destroying them (vv. 35-42), and how God gave him rule over other **nations** (vv. 43-45; cf. 2 Sam. 8). Because God is perfect (Ps. 18:30) He could make David's **way perfect** (v. 32). The predominant thought throughout these verses is that David attributed every ability and victory of his **to the Lord.** Everything he had done and everything he now enjoyed was due to the Lord's enabling.

**18:46-50.** Consequently David acknowledged the living **God** (v. 46) and promised to **praise** Him (v. 49). Proof that **the Lord** is alive is that He had rescued David **from** his **enemies.** As his **Rock** (v. 46; cf. vv. 2, 31) God was his source of safety and security. The **Lord** had given **His king great victories** and had shown His loyal love (*ḥesed,* **unfailing kindness**) **to His anointed** servant, **David.** And God would also give victories to David's **descendants.**

Psalm 18 is a victor's song of gratitude to God for all that had been accomplished.

### Psalm 19

David was moved by observing that the heavens, under the dominating influence of the sun, declare the splendor of God's handiwork. By comparison, he then described the dominating influence of the Law of the Lord which enlightened him. Then he prayed for complete cleansing so that his life would be acceptable to God. The psalm, therefore, surveys both God's natural revelation and His specific revelation, which prompts a response of self-examination.

The Old Testament frequently joins the description of the Lord as Law-Giver and Creator. Accordingly in the first part of this psalm, *'ēl* ("God") is used (v. 1) to denote His power as the Creator, and in the second part, *Yahweh* ("the Lord") is used (vv. 7-9, 14), the personal name by which He made Himself known as Israel's covenant God.

The psalm may also be polemical against pagan belief. In polytheistic centers, the sun god was the god of justice. In this psalm, the Lord God is the Creator of the heavens, including the sun that pagans worship, and He is the Law-Giver, establishing justice in the earth.

### A. Natural revelation of God's glory (19:1-6)

**19:1-4b.** David announced that **the heavens declare the glory** (splendor) **of** God's handiwork. Verse 1 is a summary statement: the majestic Creation is evidence of the even more majestic Creator-God.

The heavens continually (**day after day . . . night after night**) **display** the fact that there is a Creator (v. 2). Even though Creation does not speak audibly in words (cf. niv marg.) its message (**voice**) **goes out** to the ends of **the earth.** The message from nature about the glory of God reaches all nations, and is equally intelligible to them all (cf. Rom. 1:18-20).

**19:4c-6.** Dominant **in the heavens** is **the sun. Like a bridegroom** who excitedly leaves his house on his wedding day, the sun **rises;** and **like a champion** runner racing on **his course,** the sun **makes its circuit.** These verses do more than speak of nature as a witness to God's glory; they also undermine pagan beliefs, for the same imagery was used of the sun god in ancient Near Eastern literature.

### B. Specific revelation from God's Law (19:7-11)

**19:7.** In verses 7-9 David described the efficacious nature of the Law of the Lord. Just as the sun is the dominant feature of God's natural revelation (vv. 4c-6), so **the Law** was the dominant element in God's specific revelation in the Old Testament.

The **perfect** Law of God (cf. "flawless" in 12:6; 18:30; Prov. 30:5) can change people. It revives **the soul** and the Law's **statutes** can be trusted to make one **wise**.

**19:8.** The Law's **precepts** give **joy to the heart** and its **commands** enlighten one's **eyes**, that is, brighten his life and guide him. The statutes (v. 7), precepts, commands (v. 8), and ordinances (v. 9) are all specific instructions within the Law. Joy and guidance fill the soul of one who meditates on and follows God's commands.

**19:9. Fear** is here a synonym for the Law, for its purpose was to put fear into human hearts (Deut. 4:10, KJV). The Law is **pure. . . . sure,** and **righteous.** It was designed to cause believers to obey God and lead **righteous** lives.

**19:10-11.** David next disclosed his personal reaction to God's perfect Law. He found the statutes desirable and enjoyable. In extolling their value to him, he compared them to gold and honey— **they are more precious than gold**, the most valuable commodity in the ancient Near East, and **sweeter than honey**, the sweetest substance known in the ancient Near East. The Law was not a burden to believers who were trying to please God with their lives. For David, **keeping** God's statutes, which **warned** him of the dangers of folly and sin, brought **reward.**

### C. Prayer for cleansing (19:12-14)

**19:12-14.** Contemplation of the holy Law led David to pray for complete cleansing so that he could live an upright (**blameless**) and acceptable life before God, his **Rock** (cf. 18:2, 31, 46) and **Redeemer.** (On the psalmist's request that his **meditation** be **pleasing** to God; cf. 104:34.) He prayed that he would be forgiven for **hidden faults** and preserved from sinning willfully. For sins commit-

ted in ignorance, the Law provided atonement; but for **willful sins,** sins committed with a high hand, there was no ceremonial prescription, though forgiveness was still available if the person repented and confessed (cf. Ps. 51). Therefore he needed the perfect Law and God's enabling to restrain him from such sins.

## Psalm 20

This brief chapter is a royal psalm; the king was about to go to war, but before he did he stopped to pray in the sanctuary, where he was joined by the congregation who interceded for him. Having rehearsed the intercessory prayer of the people for their monarch who was praying for victory, the king expressed the assurance he had received from the Lord for an overwhelming victory.

### A. The intercession of the people (20:1-5)

**20:1-4.** In intercessory prayer the congregation prayed in unison that God would **answer** their king's request for victory and protection (v. 1), and **send** him **help from the sanctuary** (the tabernacle), the dwelling place of God (v. 2). They prayed that his **sacrifices** which accompanied his prayer would be acceptable (v. 3), and that his heart's **desire** would be fulfilled (cf. 21:2) and his **plans** would be successful (20:4).

**20:5.** The assembled worshipers then voiced their confidence that **God** would answer their king's prayers. They anticipated shouting **for joy** over their triumph. Then they repeated their intercession in support of his prayers: **May the LORD grant all your requests.**

### B. The assurance of the king (20:6-8)

**20:6.** The psalmist, who was the king, expressed the assurance he had received: because he trusted in **the LORD** he knew he would have an overwhelming victory.

On the basis of his faith he was convinced that the Lord would answer and save him, God's **anointed.** The Hebrew verb **saves** may be translated "saved." In the Psalms strong confidence is often expressed by the past tense, as if something had already happened. He was certain God would save him.

The deliverance David expected

would be majestic. It would be a triumphant victory by **the saving power of** God's **right hand**—the symbol of power (cf. Ex. 15:6, 12; Pss. 45:4; 60:5; 63:8; 89:13; 108:6).

**20:7.** In contrast with those who **trust in** military equipment (or in horses, 33:17), David trusted in the Lord. The verb for **trust** is actually "keep in memory or ponder" (*zākar*). Contemplation of the Lord builds confidence in Him.

The object of his faith was **the name of the LORD.** God's "name" is His nature, His reputation and character. David's faith came from meditating and pondering on the known reputation of **God.**

**20:8.** Because of God's character David envisioned a great defeat of the enemy. He foresaw the certainty of his army's victory.

### C. Repeated intercession (20:9)

**20:9.** The assembled worshipers responded in unison with a prayer for the LORD to demonstrate that assured deliverance by saving **the king** in battle. The request that the Lord would **answer** is at the beginning and ending of the psalm (vv. 1, 9).

## Psalm 21

Psalm 21 is closely related to Psalm 20 in its structure and contents. It may be the thanksgiving psalm after the battle for which the prayer in Psalm 20 was made. In Psalm 21 Psalmist David rejoiced in the strength of the Lord who had responded to his faith with an overwhelming victory. David also was encouraged by the faithful who anticipated future victory by the power of God.

### A. Rejoicing in the strength of the Lord (21:1-7)

**21:1-6.** The royal psalmist praised the LORD who displayed His **strength** in battle. Referring to himself in the third person David expressed **his joy in the victories.** He praised God for giving **him the desire of his heart** (cf. 20:4); for giving him good things (cf. 21:6), including **a crown of pure gold** (possibly the crown of an Ammonite king, 2 Sam. 12:30); for answering his prayer **for life;** for **the victories** God had **granted him** along with abundant **blessings** (cf. Ps. 21:5) and **joy.**

**21:7.** The reason for this great deliverance in answer to prayer is that **the king** trusted in **the unfailing love** (*ḥeseḏ*) **of** the Lord **Most High.** Therefore he knew he was secure (he would **not be shaken;** cf. comments on 15:5).

### B. Anticipation of further blessing (21:8-12)

**21:8-10.** The king was now addressed by the congregation. Because he trusted in **the LORD,** they knew he would defeat his **enemies** convincingly. (On God's **wrath** being like **fire** see 79:5; 89:46; 97:3.) David would inflict a tremendous defeat on his **foes,** the objects of God's "wrath," thus ending **their** hopes of having any **posterity.**

**21:11-12.** Even **though they** schemed to overthrow the king, they would **turn** in fear from before him. Thus the king, who trusted in the Lord, was assured of future victories.

### C. Vow to praise (21:13)

**21:13.** The congregation vowed to **sing and praise** the **might** and power of the **LORD,** who alone is to **be exalted.**

## Psalm 22

The psalmist apparently felt forsaken by God, as he was surrounded by his enemies' scornful persecution. He lamented his tremendous suffering and his desperate struggle with death, pleading with God to deliver him from such a horrible end. Apparently his prayer was answered, for he was able to declare to the elect and to the world that the Lord answered his prayer.

No known incident in the life of David fits the details of this psalm. The expressions describe an execution, not an illness; yet that execution is more appropriate to Jesus' crucifixion than David's experience. The Gospel writers also saw connections between some of the words in this psalm (vv. 8, 16, 18) and other events in Christ's Passion. Also Hebrews 2:12 quotes Psalm 22:22. Thus the church has understood this psalm to be typological of the death of Jesus Christ. This means that David used many poetic expressions to portray his immense sufferings, but these poetic words became literally true of the suffering of Jesus Christ at His enemies' hands. The interesting feature of this psalm is that it does not include one word of confession of sin, and no imprecation against enemies. It is primarily the account of a righteous man who was being put to death by wicked men.

### A. Fervent prayer of one who is forsaken (22:1-10)

David, apparently feeling forsaken by God and scoffed at by his enemies, was confident that God would not fully abandon him. Verses 1-10 form the psalmist's general introductory cry out of distress; they include two cycles, one of lament (vv. 1-5) and one of confidence (vv. 6-10).

1. CYCLE ONE (22:1-5)

**22:1-2.** Though sensing that God had forsaken him (v. 1), the psalmist drew renewed confidence from the fact that God had answered his ancestors' prayers (v. 4). David's initial cry, **My God, my God, why have You forsaken me?** is an expression appropriated by Christ on the cross (Matt. 27:46; Mark 15:34). God, whom David was addressing as "my God," had seemingly forsaken him. David prayed constantly (**by day** and **by night**) but there was no **answer.**

**22:3.** The confidence he mustered was from the knowledge that God answers prayer. God is **holy,** distinct from all the false gods of the pagans in that He is alive and acts. In fact God is **enthroned** (cf. comments on 2:4) and therefore received **praise** from the Israelites for answered prayer.

**22:4-5.** David's ancestors, putting **their trust** in the Lord, prayed in their distress and were **delivered** by Him. So David was encouraged to keep on praying.

2. CYCLE TWO (22:6-10)

**22:6-8.** The psalmist, though **scorned by men,** was convinced that the God of his youth would not abandon him forever. David lamented the fact that men **despised** him. He felt like **a worm,** worthless, defenseless, and treated with utter contempt. **They** hurled **insults** at him (cf. Matt. 27:39, 44), mocking his faith since **the LORD** was not rescuing **him.** The expressions used in Psalm 22:8 were adapted by those who mocked at Jesus' cross (Mat. 27:42-43), not realizing that they were fulfilling this prophecy and that He was the suffering Messiah.

**22:9-10.** The psalmist's confidence was drawn from his training as a child. From the very beginning he was trained to trust in the Lord, who had **brought** him **out of the womb.** All his life the Lord had **been** his **God.**

### B. Lament of the suffering king (22:11-18)

**22:11.** David lamented his desperate struggle with death at the hands of inhuman enemies. He summarized his lament with a quick plea that the Lord **not . . . be far** off, since **trouble** was **near** and he was helpless.

1. CYCLE ONE (22:12-15)

Again in two cycles (vv. 12-15 and 16-18; cf. the cycles in vv. 1-5 and 6-10) David described his enemies and his sufferings.

**22:12-13.** David compared his enemies to cruel and insensitive beasts (**bulls** and **lions**) who would destroy him and then described his agony. **Bulls of Bashan** were well-fed cattle (cf. comments on cows of Bashan in Amos 4:1) east of the Sea of Kinnereth (Galilee). Several other times David spoke of his enemies as lions (cf. Ps. 7:2; 10:9; 17:12; 22:21; 35:17; 57:4; 58:6).

**22:14-15.** Because of his enemies' attacks, David's strength was sapped **like** poured-out **water,** and his joints were racked. Moreover, like melted **wax** his courage (**heart**) was gone—he had lost his desire to resist. His **strength** was gone and his **mouth** was dry. In his weakness he was at the brink **of death.**

2. CYCLE TWO (22:16-18)

**22:16.** David again (cf. vv. 12-15) described his enemies and his agony. His enemies tortured him and watched him insensitively. He compared them to **dogs** (cf. v. 20), who in the ancient world were scavengers. Like dogs, his foes (**evil men**) **surrounded** him, waiting till he was dead so they could tear at his limbs. To compare his enemies to dogs was to say that he was almost dead. The words **they have pierced my hands and my feet** figuratively describe such a tearing as if by animals. Of course in the New Testament, these words in reference to Jesus Christ have greater significance (cf. Luke 24:39-40).

**22:17-18.** After speaking of his enemies (v. 16) the psalmist again described his agony. He was weak and emaciated. His enemies stared at him, considering him as good as dead, so they divided up his **garments,** his last possession (cf. Matt. 27:35).

### C. Petition for deliverance from death (22:19-21)

**22:19-21.** David prayed that the LORD (his **Strength**; cf. 28:7-8; 46:1; 59:9, 17; 81:1; 118:14) would **help** him by saving his life **from the power of** his wicked enemies, who were like **dogs** (cf. v. 16), **lions** (cf. v. 13 and comments on 7:2), and **wild oxen** (cf. bulls, 22:12-13). In his prayer, he became confident that he had been heard. In the Hebrew the last part of verse 21 breaks off in the middle of the prayer and states, "You have heard" (cf. NIV marg.). The psalmist may have received an oracle of salvation, for in the rest of the psalm he said he would praise God for His deliverance.

### D. Praise and encouragement for prayer (22:22-31)

**22:22.** David addressed **the congregation** of the people with his vow to **praise** the Lord. Verse 22 is quoted almost verbatim in Hebrews 2:12 as Jesus' praise for deliverance. Of course Jesus' prayer to be delivered from death (Heb. 5:7) was answered in a different way— He was raised from the dead. The psalmist was apparently rescued so that he did not die.

**22:23-26.** Then the psalmist called on the congregation to **praise** the LORD with him because He did **not** despise **the afflicted one** (the suffering psalmist) but **listened to his cry for help** (cf. vv. 1-2) and answered his prayer. On the basis of this **praise** David said he would **fulfill** his **vows** and he encouraged the congregation to **praise** the Lord with him. Moreover, he encouraged them to keep on praying (**may your hearts live forever** means "do not give up"; cf. "heart" in v. 14).

**22:27-31.** The psalmist then turned his attention to the world at large. He anticipated that the world would **turn to** and worship (**bow down before**) **the LORD** (v. 27) because He is the sovereign King, the One who **rules over the nations** (v. 28), including **the rich** and the dying. From generation to generation the

people of the earth **will be told** that **the** LORD answered his prayer and rescued him, so therefore the Lord can be trusted. Of course applied to Jesus Christ, these words became more significant. When people would hear how God answered His prayer by raising Him from the dead (Heb. 5:7), many would turn to Him in trust and worship.

## Psalm 23

Using the images of a shepherd and a gracious host, David reflected on the many benefits the Lord gave him in the dangers of life, and concluded that God's persistent, loving protection would restore him to full communion.

### A. The Lord as Leader (23:1-4)

**23:1.** The psalmist employed the figure of a **shepherd** to recall the blessings he enjoyed from **the LORD** (cf. God as Shepherd in 28:9; 80:1). The metaphor was a natural one for David, the shepherd-king. It was also a common metaphor in the ancient Near East, as many kings compared themselves to shepherds in their leadership capacity. The prophecy of the coming Messiah incorporated the same (Isa. 40:11), and Jesus identified Himself as that expected "Good Shepherd" (John 10:14). He is also called the "Great Shepherd" (Heb. 13:20) and "the Chief Shepherd" (1 Peter 5:4). Because the Lord was David's Shepherd, his needs were met.

**23:2a.** The first blessing David experienced was spiritual nourishment. As a shepherd leads sheep to fresh grass for feeding, so the Lord leads His people. One who follows the Lord does not lack any spiritual nourishment. Under-shepherds (cf. Acts 20:28; 1 Peter 5:2) are expected to feed the flock (Ezek. 34:1-10; John 21:15-17) as well. Food for the soul is the Word of God (Heb. 5:12-14; 1 Peter 2:2).

**23:2b-3a.** A second blessing that comes from the Lord's leading is spiritual restoration. As a shepherd leads his sheep to placid **waters** for rest and cleansing, so the Lord **restores** or refreshes the **soul.** Here the spiritual lesson is clear: the Lord provides forgiveness and peace for those who follow Him.

**23:3b.** The third blessing that comes from the Lord's leading is guidance **in** the right way (**paths of righteousness**). A good shepherd knows the right paths on which to bring the sheep home safely. So too the Lord loses none of His sheep, but guides them in the right way. He does so partly because of His reputation (**for His name's sake**).

**23:4.** The fourth blessing from the Lord's leading is protection. If one finds himself in a **valley of** deep darkness (or **shadow of death**), he need not **fear.** The Lord is **with** him and will protect him. The **rod** and **staff** are the shepherd's equipment to protect the sheep in such situations. David was comforted by the Lord's presence and protection. Believers are never in situations the Lord is not aware of, for He never leaves or forsakes His people (cf. Heb. 13:5).

### B. The Lord as Provider (23:5)

**23:5.** In this verse the scene changes to a banquet hall where a gracious host provides lavish hospitality. Under this imagery the psalmist rejoiced in the Lord's provision. What was comforting to David was that this was **in the presence of** his **enemies.** Despite impending danger, the Lord spread out **a table** for him, that is, God provided for him.

The image of anointing the **head with oil,** which was refreshing and soothing, harmonizes with the concept of a gracious host welcoming someone into his home. In view of the table and the oil David knew that his lot in life (his **cup**) was abundant blessing from the Lord.

### C. The response of faith (23:6)

**23:6.** David realized that the Lord's good loyal **love** (*ḥeseḏ*) would go with him everywhere through **all** his **life.** God's blessings on His people remain with them no matter what their circumstance may be. (Cf. God's **goodness** in 27:13; 31:19; 69:16; 86:17; 109:21; 116:12; 142:7; 145:7.) So he concluded **I will dwell in the house of the LORD forever.** The house of the Lord referred to the sanctuary (tabernacle). For the rest of his life (lit., "length of days") he would enjoy full communion with the Lord. In fact the Hebrew verb translated "I will dwell" conveys the idea of returning; the same verb is translated "He restores" in 23:3. Perhaps the psalmist was in some way separated from the sanctuary and full enjoyment of its spiritual benefits. His meditation on the Lord's leading and provi-

sions prompted him to recall his communion with the Lord in His presence, in the sanctuary.

## Psalm 24

In preparation for the entry of the great King of glory, the psalmist stated that those with clean hands and pure hearts may ascend to His holy place.

Many think this psalm was written for the occasion of David's taking the ark of the covenant to Jerusalem (2 Sam. 6), though this cannot be proved. If such were true, then the "ancient doors" (Ps. 24:7) refer to the old fortress that then received the ark, the symbol of the Lord's presence. Or perhaps the psalm speaks of some other return to Jerusalem after a victory in battle.

### A. Ascent to the holy place (24:1-6)

**24:1-2.** David praised the Lord because **everything in . . . the world** belongs to Him who created it. This is a general acknowledgment of God's sovereignty over all things.

**24:3-4.** David then pondered **who** could go into the presence of such a sovereign Lord (i.e., to the tabernacle on **the hill** [cf. comments on "holy hill" in 2:6] **of the LORD** and its **holy place**). The answer, perhaps given by priests at the sanctuary, is that one whose conduct is pure and whose worship is faithful may do so (cf. Ps. 15). **Clean hands** refers to right actions, and **a pure heart** refers to a right attitude and will. Only those who do not worship an **idol** can be true worshipers, and can walk by faith in integrity.

**24:5-6.** The lesson is followed by the affirmation that **those who seek** after **God** will be blessed with righteousness. This may refer to worshipers seeking entry into the sanctuary.

### B. Entry of the King of glory (24:7-10)

**24:7.** The psalmist offered an exhortation (v. 7) and then an explanation (v. 8). If **lift up your heads, O you gates** refers to the city of Jerusalem then he was calling for the ancient gates to open wide for the triumphant entry. This was a poetic way of displaying the superiority of the one entering. They should lift up their heads because **the King of glory** is about to **come in.**

**24:8-10.** David then gave an explanation. By question and answer he stated that **this King of glory** is the **LORD**, who is **mighty in battle.** The **LORD** had shown Himself **strong** by giving them great victories; so He is the glorious King who will enter the city. One can visualize a procession of triumphant Israelites carrrying the ark, the symbol of the Lord's presence, going up to the sanctuary to praise Him. The ideas in the exhortation (v. 7) and the explanation (v. 8) were repeated in verses 9-10. The repetition stressed the point: **The LORD** is a glorious **King** who is coming **in.** Only pure worshipers can enjoy His presence.

## Psalm 25

David confidently turned to the Lord for divine instruction and forgiveness from his iniquity because of His mercies for Israel. This psalm is a meditation on the character of God that prompts the humble to respond with confession and prayer. The psalm is an acrostic, as each verse begins with a successive letter of the Hebrew alphabet.

### A. Prayer for guidance and pardon (25:1-7)

The psalmist was not ashamed to turn to the Lord for instruction and forgiveness for the sins of his youth (v. 7).

**25:1-3.** David stressed his confidence in turning to the **LORD.** He lifted **up** his **soul** to the Lord without **shame,** for none who **trust** and **hope** (cf. vv. 5, 21) in the Lord **will . . . be put to shame** (cf. v. 20), that is, they will have their prayers answered and their needs met. This contrasts with their **enemies** and the **treacherous.**

**25:4-7.** David prayed first for instruction (vv. 4-5; cf. vv. 9, 12) and guidance (v. 5; cf. v. 9). He desired that God would **show** him His **ways,** including **truth,** and **teach** him His **paths.** Then he prayed for pardon (vv. 6-7). Based on God's **mercy and love,** which had been known for ages, he prayed that **the sins of** his **youth** not be held against him. (Three times he prayed **remember.**)

### B. Reiteration of the prayer (25:8-22)

The psalmist reiterated his prayer for instruction in the true way (cf. vv. 4-5) and pardon (cf. vv. 6-7) for his afflicted soul, but now his prayer was grounded on the revealed character of the Lord.

**25:8-10.** David extolled the nature of God: He is **good and upright** and **loving and faithful.** On the basis of these attributes He teaches **sinners** and **guides the humble.** Sinful humans need the gracious guidance of **the LORD.**

**25:11.** The psalmist prayed for pardon for his great **iniquity—for the sake of** the Lord's **name** (His revealed character).

**25:12-14.** Here David described a person who **fears the LORD:** he is one in whom the **LORD confides** by revealing **His covenant** to him (v. 14) and instructing him (v. 12b; cf. vv. 4-5, 8-9). These statements remind the reader of the Wisdom literature, especially Proverbs. A person who fears the Lord (Prov. 1:7; 9:10; 15:33; 31:30) is instructed by the Lord's Word.

**25:15-22.** The psalm concludes with a prayer for the Lord's **gracious** deliverance. Beginning with his own affirmation that he trusts **the LORD** for deliverance (v. 15), the psalmist called on God to forgive (v. 18; cf. vv. 6-7, 11) his **afflicted** soul and deliver him from the **distress** caused by his cruel **enemies** (v. 18). Again he asked that in being rescued he **not be put to shame** (cf. v. 20), and he affirmed his **hope** in God (v. 21; cf. vv. 3, 5; hope in the Lord is mentioned more than two dozen times in the Pss.). The last request was for deliverance of **Israel . . . from** her **troubles** (v. 22).

The psalm strongly links the prayer for deliverance and guidance to confession of sin. The way of the Lord requires this.

## Psalm 26

Psalm 26 is a strong affirmation of integrity and a prayer that God would recognize it. No time in the life of David clearly presents itself as an occasion for this passage. The psalm is similar in many ways to Psalm 25, but Psalm 26 does not include a prayer for pardon. The psalmist here declared that he kept separate from sinners, and identified himself with the worship of the Lord. On the basis of this, he prayed with confidence that the Lord would spare him from a fate like that of sinners.

### A. Assertion of integrity (26:1-3)

**26:1-3.** David offered a twofold introductory petition: **the LORD** (a) should act justly toward him (v. 1) and (b) should **examine** his claim (v. 2; cf. 139:23). The LORD could discern that he had been consistent in his faith (26:1a) and in obedience to the Lord and His **truth** (v. 3).

### B. Proof of integrity (26:4-8)

**26:4-5.** David proved his integrity by his separation from sinners (vv. 4-5) and his identification with worshipers (vv. 6-8). He in no way identified with **the wicked** and the **deceitful.** He did **not sit** (vv. 4a, 5b) with them or consult them (cf. 1:1). In fact he hated their assemblies.

**26:6-8.** The setting of these verses is the sanctuary (cf. **altar,** v. 6, and **house,** v. 8). David's worship was with integrity (he washed his **hands;** cf. 24:4, **in innocence**) and sincerity (he praised the Lord and told of His **deeds**). In contrast with his reaction to the assemblies of the wicked (26:5) David loved the sanctuary, where the **glory** of the LORD . . . **dwells.**

### C. Prayer for the reward of integrity (26:9-12)

**26:9-12.** David petitioned the Lord to spare him from a common fate **with sinners** with whom he did not associate (cf. vv. 4-5). David was probably referring to premature death (**soul** in Heb. refers to one's life).

If swift judgment took the **wicked** away, it should not touch one who remained separate from them.

In expectation of the Lord's delivering him from such a fate, David said he would **praise the LORD** in the congregation (cf. vv. 7-8). Many times in the Psalms the writers prayed to be redeemed (v. 11) from trouble (*pādâh,* "to ransom, redeem," is used in 31:5; 44:26; 49:7; 55:18; 69:18; 78:42; 119:134). That Hebrew word was often used when referring to Israel's deliverance from Egypt (cf. Deut. 7:8; 9:26; 13:5; 15:15; 24:18; 2 Sam. 7:23; Micah 6:4).

## Psalm 27

David at first expressed jubilant confidence in the Lord in spite of a host of enemies who threatened his life. But suddenly his mood changed: he anxiously prayed that the Lord would not forsake him, but would help and comfort him in his time of need. Because the Lord was his Source of comfort and hope, he strengthened himself to wait for the Lord. The psalm is one of courageous trust.

### A. Confidence that dispels fear (27:1-3)

**27:1.** David expressed great confidence in **the LORD:** because **the LORD** was his **Light . . . Salvation,** and **Stronghold** (*mā'ôz,* "a strong fortified place"; cf. 37:39; 43:2; 52:7), nobody could harm him. Light signifies understanding, joy, and life (cf. 18:28) and the stronghold (cf. 18:2) signifies defense. With these provisions from the Lord, **whom shall** a believer **fear?** (cf. 27:3) Obviously the answer is no one.

**27:2-3.** In response to this question David spoke of the **enemies** who came **against** him. Even if they broke in on him, he would remain **confident** in the Lord, without **fear** (cf. v. 1).

### B. Communion that brings security (27:4-6)

**27:4.** David further expressed his confidence in **the LORD** by his longing to dwell in His **house.** He would love to abide there **all** his **life,** to enjoy His **beauty** and **to seek Him** there in the **temple.** (*Hêkāl* does not refer here to Solomon's temple since it was not yet built. The Heb. word means a magnificent structure, such as the tabernacle; cf. vv. 5-6; 5:7; 1 Sam. 1:9; 3:3; the temple, 2 Kings 24:13; or a palace, Pss. 45:15; 144:12; Dan. 1:4.)

**27:5-6.** To dwell in the presence of the Lord would add to David's security. The Lord would keep him safe **in the day of trouble** and establish him securely in danger. Consequently he would triumph (his **head** would **be exalted**) over his **enemies** and joyfully **sing** praises **to the LORD.** Perhaps the idea of safety in the sanctuary, where his enemies could not reach him, caused David here to meditate on the Lord's protection. The word for **shelter** (*sēter*) is also used in 32:7 ("hiding place"); 91:1; 109:114 ("refuge") to speak of God's protection. David certainly knew the true Source of security.

### C. Earnest prayer in faith (27:7-14)

**27:7-10.** Apparently the Lord was not granting David protection promptly, for he prayed earnestly and with some anxiety for help. He asked the Lord **not** to **forsake** him since he was in great need. God had instructed the righteous to pray (to **seek His face**), and that is what David was doing. Therefore God ought not refuse to help him (to **hide His face**; cf. 102:2; 143:7). Moreover, David affirmed that he was the **servant** of the LORD, and that the Lord had **been** his **Helper.** On the basis of this motivation, he begged the Lord **not** to **reject** him. His prayer was strengthened by the knowledge that the Lord would not **forsake** him, even if his parents did (which of course was unlikely).

**27:11-12.** David asked God to **teach** him the **way** to go (cf. 25:4-5) **because** his enemies were lying in wait for him. He asked **not** to be turned **over to** his **foes,** who were **false witnesses** sworn to destroy him.

**27:13-14.** In the end, however, the psalmist's confidence surfaced again; he rejoiced in the prospect of waiting **for the LORD.** David was **confident** that he would survive and remain alive (**in the land of the living**) to **see** God's blessing. Therefore he strengthened himself to **wait for the** Lord's deliverance.

## Psalm 28

The psalmist was convinced that the Lord would distinguish him from the wicked when He overthrows them and would preserve him from his distress. Therefore he prayed that the Lord would save and shepherd His people. This psalm is a companion to Psalm 26, but here the danger was imminent.

### A. Petition to the Lord (28:1-4)

**28:1.** Addressing the LORD, the psalmist prayed to be kept separate from the wicked when they are overthrown. This was an urgent plea. If God would not respond, he would die (**pit,** *bôr,* is a synonym for grave; cf. 30:3).

**28:2-4.** David then asked (a) that the Lord would favor him as he cried for **mercy** and **help** (v. 2), (b) that the Lord would not **drag** him off with hypocritical sinners (v. 3), and (c) that the Lord would justly punish the wicked (v. 4).

### B. Confident praise to the Lord (28:5-8)

**28:5-8.** In addressing the congregation, the psalmist confidently expressed his anticipation that **the LORD** would answer his prayer: the wicked will be overthrown permanently. Because the wick-

ed disregard **the works of the LORD,** they will be destroyed. This prompted words of **praise . . . to the LORD:** (a) because **He . . . heard** David's prayer (v. 6; cf. v. 2); (b) because He was David's **Strength** (cf. v. 8; 22:19; 46:1; 59:9, 17; 81:1; 118:14) **and Shield** (cf. comments on 3:3) in that **the LORD** enabled him to escape the schemes of the wicked so that he could rejoice in the Lord (v. 7); and (c) because the Lord saves **His people** (cf. 18:2) and like **a fortress** defends His king (**His anointed one,** 28:8). The fact that the Lord showed Himself to be His people's Savior prompted praise from them.

### C. Prayer for deliverance and guidance (28:9)

**28:9.** The psalmist returned to his prayer (v. 9) after expressing his confident anticipation of the outcome (vv. 5-8). He asked for salvation for the nation Israel (God's **inheritance;** cf. 33:12; 78:62, 71; 79:1; 94:14; Deut. 4:20; 9:26, 29; Joel 2:17; 3:2; Micah 7:14, 18) and guidance from **their Shepherd** (cf. Pss. 23:1; 80:1) **forever.** This prayer that the Lord would bear them up was a request that He sustain them through all their trials and tribulations.

## Psalm 29

David witnessed an awesome thunderstorm moving across the land of the Canaanites, and attributed it to the power of the Lord. He called on the angels to glorify Him who sits as King forever over nature. Psalm 29 is a polemic against pagan beliefs in false gods who were credited with being responsible for storms.

### A. Call to praise (29:1-2)

**29:1-2.** The psalmist called on the angels to glorify **the LORD. O mighty ones** is literally, "sons of the mighty," that is, God's angelic beings. The poetry here is climactic, repeating the expression **ascribe to the LORD** three times (with slight changes each time in the words that follow) and expanding the idea until the final line calls for **worship** in **holiness.** The angels were invoked to give God the credit for His **glory** and power (**strength**). Such praise should be accompanied by holiness (NIV marg.), using the imagery from Israel's solemn assemblies, for **the LORD** is holy.

### B. Cause for praise (29:3-9)

The psalmist described the Lord's omnipotent control of nature in a terrifying storm.

**29:3-4.** David attributed the rise of the storm **over the** mighty **waters** (the Mediterranean Sea) to **the voice of the LORD.** Though **voice** may be a poetic designation of thunder (cf. 18:13), it probably also was meant to convey that He who created by His word (cf. Gen. 1:3, 6, 9, 14, 20, 24) also controls nature by His word so that a thunderstorm evidences His power.

**29:5-7.** As David witnessed **the voice of the LORD** at the height of the storm, he said it moved inland and destroyed **the great cedars of Lebanon,** rumbled the great mountains with earthquakes (v. 6), and scattered forked **lightning** in the skies (v. 7). **Lebanon** (v. 6) and **Sirion** are mountains in the Anti-Lebanon range.

All this was by the decree of the Lord. In fact seven times **the voice of the LORD** is mentioned in verses 3-9: the storm evidenced His complete majesty.

**29:8-9.** The storm (**the voice of the LORD**) shook not only the mountains (v. 6) but also **the Desert of Kadesh.** This Kadesh was a town about 75 miles north of Damascus, not Kadesh in the south. As the storm moved on, it shook the fauna and flora in the eastern wilderness. The storm made the hinds calve (as most versions translate the Heb.; cf. KJV, NASB, NIV marg.) prematurely due to fear, and stripped the leaves from the trees in **the forests.** As a result all creatures **in His temple,** perhaps angels again (cf. v. 1), shouted praises of **glory** to His power.

### C. Conclusion (29:10-11)

**29:10.** The psalmist concluded that **the LORD** rules **as King forever** and is able to bless His people. Since **the flood** probably refers to the universal inundation in Noah's day, **sits enthroned** should be translated "sat enthroned" (cf. NIV marg.). Perhaps David recalled this incident to support his contention that the present storm was the Lord's work. If there was any doubt that the Lord controlled nature, that would settle it. He is **the LORD** of Creation.

**29:11.** This demonstration of power was an encouragement **to His people,** for He shares His power (**strength**) with them. The strength available to His people (v. 11) is His own strength (v. 1). The same Hebrew word ('ōz) is used in both verses. The power that can raise a storm is available to benefit those who trust in Him. Just as God can cause a storm to be still, so too can He bring **peace** to **His people.** Jesus' miracles over nature, especially calming the storm on the Sea of Galilee (Mark 4:37-39), demonstrate that all power was given to Him.

## Psalm 30

The superscription says that this is "a psalm . . . for the dedication of the temple," written by David. This title may refer to David's dedication of the site of the temple (1 Chron. 21:26; 22:1) after the numbering of the people. (The Heb. word trans. "temple" is lit., "house," and could refer to the tabernacle [tent] in which David placed the ark, 2 Sam. 6:17.) A problem with this view is that the psalm mentions God's discipline of David (cf. Ps. 30:7) perhaps by some physical illness (v. 3) for his pride (v. 6). It may be that the illness was figurative, not literal, and referred to David's inner remorse (1 Chron. 21:13) for having through pride caused a plague which killed 70,000 Israelites (1 Chron. 21:2, 8, 14). Others take the title to be a liturgical designation for its use in dedicating buildings constructed later (e.g., Ezra 6:16; Neh. 12:27).

From his experience of deliverance from God's chastening for his sin, David praised the Lord because His anger is temporary, but His favor is permanent.

### A. Deliverance from chastening (30:1-5)

David acknowledged the Lord's deliverance and called the congregation to praise Him.

**30:1.** He vowed to praise the **LORD** because he was **lifted** up from his distress. **The depths** (or the depths of the earth) speaks of nearness of death (cf. 71:20; 130:1). The rescue removed any opportunity for his **enemies** to **gloat.**

**30:2-3.** Here David described his answer to prayer **for help:** God **healed** him and **spared** his life. This is stated figuratively as well: God **brought** him **up from the grave** ("sheol"; cf. NIV marg.). He was about to die, perhaps because of a physical illness, but the LORD healed him. God's deliverance prevented death.

**30:4-5.** Because of God's deliverance

the psalmist called on the people to **sing to** and **praise** the LORD. The reason for the praise is the temporary nature of God's **anger** to him; it was but for a **moment,** only **for the night. In the morning** came deliverance and joy.

## B. Chastening for independence (30:6-10)

**30:6-7.** David recorded his prayer for deliverance from his sin of independence of the LORD. In pride he **felt secure,** thinking he would **never be shaken** (cf. comments on 15:5). The word "secure" (*šelew*) implies a careless ease. Apparently he had forgotten his need to trust in the Lord and boasted in self-confidence.

As a result, God disciplined him (30:7). Previously when God had **favored** him, He made him secure (**mountain** is a figure for the strength of his position); **but when** God disciplined him, He **hid** His **face,** an expression that signifies the removal of blessing and protection.

**30:8-10.** When God brought the plague, because of David's pride (2 Sam. 24:15) David **cried** out to Him, pleading that there would be no benefit **in** his **destruction** and death (on **pit;** cf. Ps. 30:3 and comments on 28:1). If God wanted **praise** from the psalmist, then He would have to preserve him from the grave (cf. Isa. 38:18). This was the reasoning behind David's prayer for mercy and **help** (cf. Ps. 30:2).

## C. Deliverance from discipline (30:11-12)

**30:11-12.** Using terminology from festive occasions (**dancing** and **joy**) David rehearsed how God delivered him from his lamentable state (on **sackcloth**; cf. 35:13 and comments on Gen. 37:34). As a result of this answer to prayer David sang praises to the Lord. Thus he vowed to acknowledge and thank the LORD his **God** (cf. Ps. 30:2) **forever.** Every deliverance a believer experiences should likewise prompt a full expression of praise.

## Psalm 31

Psalm 31 is another "psalm of David" in a time of great need, a prayer from one who was despised, defamed, and persecuted. So much of David's life was spent in this condition that the Book of Psalms includes many of his prayers that grew out of such situations. In this passage he exhorted the afflicted to love the Lord and to be strong because the Lord would protect them from men's evil plans. David explained that he learned this truth as he committed his life into the hands of the Lord when his foes plotted to kill him.

## A. Cry to be rescued (31:1-2)

**31:1-2.** These verses record David's introductory cry to the LORD, his **Refuge** (cf. vv. 2, 4). He prayed for the Lord to **come quickly to** his **rescue** (cf. 69:17; 70:1, 5; 71:12; 79:8; 102:2; 141:1; 143:7) and be his **Rock** and **Fortress** (cf. 31:3 and comments on 18:2). His only protection and safety were in the Lord.

## B. Confidence in His love (31:3-8)

David confidently committed his life into the hands of the Lord, his Rock, knowing that he would rejoice in God's love (cf. vv. 16, 21).

**31:3-4.** The psalmist's confidence is stated strongly in these verses. The Lord his **Rock . . . Fortress** (cf. v. 2), and **Refuge** (cf. vv. 1-2; 18:2) would **lead** him out of danger.

**31:5.** With confidence in the Lord (vv. 3-4) he committed his **spirit** into the hands of the LORD, praying that **the God of truth** (cf. Isa. 65:16) would **redeem** him (see comments on Ps. 26:11). The same confident resting in God during the onslaught of the wicked was expressed by the Savior (Luke 23:46). A sufferer who has faith in God may pray to Him and leave the problem in His hands (1 Peter 4:19).

**31:6-8.** In addition to his trust, David asserted that he despised **those who cling to worthless idols. The LORD** is faithful, worthy of all **trust.** Therefore David confidently anticipated praising His loyal **love.** He wrote (v. 8) as if the deliverance had already been granted. With such genuine faith, believers can sing of triumph in anticipation of God's delivering them.

## C. Lament over the danger (31:9-13)

**31:9-13.** The psalmist pleaded for grace from the LORD because his life was in danger (**distress**). In **sorrow . . . grief,** and **anguish** he was at the point of perishing (vv. 9-10). (On **bones** see comments on 6:2). **Because of** his **enemies** he was rejected and **forgotten** by **friends**

(31:11-12). Because **many** plotted against his **life** he faced **terror on every side** (cf. Jer. 20:10).

### D. Prayer for deliverance (31:14-18)

**31:14-18.** Emphasizing that he trusted God and had placed himself in the Lord's **hands** (vv. 14-15a; cf. v. 5) the psalmist prayed that **God** would **save** him (vv. 15b-16) and silence his arrogant enemies (vv. 17-18). (On God's **face** shining, see comments on 4:6.) They with **their lying lips** should **be silenced** rather than he, with his praises.

### E. Praise and exhortation (31:19-24)

**31:19-24.** David praised **the LORD** (**How great is Your goodness**) for His protection of the faithful in general (vv. 19-20), and for delivering him by His **love** (v. 21; cf. vv. 7, 16) in spite of David's unbelief (v. 22). On the basis of what he had learned about the Lord's deliverance of **the faithful,** he encouraged the **saints** to **be strong** in their faith and **hope in the LORD** (vv. 23-24).

## Psalm 32

David, having experienced divine chastening and forgiveness (possibly for the sin of adultery and murder recorded in 2 Sam. 11), encouraged others to seek the Lord who deals graciously with sinners. If they refuse submission they will endure chastening.

This psalm may be a companion to Psalm 51, referring to David's sin with Bathsheba. At that time David refused for a year to acknowledge his sin. Psalm 51 was his prayer for pardon; Psalm 32 would then follow it, stressing God's forgiveness and the lesson David learned.

### A. The blessing of forgiveness (32:1-2)

**32:1-2.** The psalmist, having received God's forgiveness for his **sins,** expressed his joy over that fact. **Blessed** is used in 1:1 of a person who leads an untarnished life. Here it is used of one who has forgiveness. God forgives fully, for He **does not count** a truly penitent person's **sin . . . against him.**

### B. The chastening of the unrepentant (32:3-5)

**32:3-5.** The psalmist experienced forgiveness when he acknowledged his sin, but it came only after divine chastening.

**When** he was **silent** and did not confess his sin, he was weakened physically (on **bones** see comments on 6:2) and grieved inwardly. The **hand** (or power) of the Lord **was heavy** on him (32:4), that is, God dealt severely with him. The result was that his vitality (**strength**) was **sapped** (or dried up) **as in the** summer **heat.** This expression may refer to physical illness with burning fever, or it may describe in poetic language his remorse of conscience.

Therefore he confessed his **sin to** God. This is the way of restoration, for God **forgave** him.

### C. The advice of the forgiven (32:6-11)

**32:6-7.** David encouraged others to seek the Lord because He deals graciously with sinners. The time to **pray** is when the Lord **may be found.** If this is done, calamities (spoken of as **mighty waters**) **will not** overwhelm. On the basis of this note of comfort, David turned to praise the Lord as his **Hiding Place** (*sēṭer*, also used in 27:5, "shelter"; 91:1, "shelter"; 119:114, "refuge"). God protects **from trouble** those who trust Him, and He gives them occasion to praise.

**32:8.** David also counseled others not to refuse to submit to the Lord until He forces it, but to make their confessions willingly. Some take the speaker in verse 8 to be God rather than David because of the words **watch over you** (cf. 25:8, 12; 73:24). But David seems to have assumed here the role of a teacher (cf. 34:11; 51:13).

**32:9-11.** The psalmist advised his readers to submit to **the LORD** rather than resist stubbornly **like** a **horse or . . . mule** that has to be **controlled.** Those who trust Him will experience His faithful loyal **love** (*ḥeseḏ*) and will be able to **sing** praises to Him.

## Psalm 33

The psalmist called on the righteous to praise the Lord because His Word is dependable and His work righteous. Those who trust in Him are assured that He will fulfill His promises to them and consummate His work of salvation.

This psalm is a hymn of praise. It may have resulted from a national victory, but there is no evidence to specify which victory. The Hebrew has no superscription; the Septuagint, however, ascribes the psalm to David.

## A. It is fitting to praise the Lord (33:1-3)

**33:1-3.** These verses include the psalmist's call to praise, in which he summoned the **righteous** to rejoice in **the LORD** because **it is fitting.** Praise is the natural response of God's people for receiving His benefits. But their praise should be spontaneous and fresh—new mercies demand new songs (cf. **a new song** in 40:3; 96:1; 98:1; 144:9; 149:1). It should also be done well or **skillfully.** The best talent that a person has should be offered in praising Him.

## B. The Lord is dependable and righteous (33:4-19)

**33:4-5.** The reason for praise, detailed throughout this psalm, is summarized in these verses. The Lord's **Word** and work (**all He does**) are dependable, and **the LORD** is righteous and loyal (*ḥesed,* **unfailing love;** cf. vv. 18, 22).

**33:6-11.** These verses develop the thought in verse 4 that His Word and work are reliable. First the psalmist spoke of the power of **the word of the LORD** in Creation (vv. 6-9). Because God **spoke,** Creation **came** into existence. What God decrees, happens. Therefore **all** peoples **of the world** should worship **Him.**

Then the psalmist spoke of the power of **the LORD** in history (vv. 10-11). God's plans foil **the plans of the** wicked **nations** (cf. 2:1-6). His purposes are sustained, no matter what people endeavor to do. Surely a God with such powerful words and works should be praised.

**33:12-19.** These verses develop the idea that **the LORD** is righteous, just (cf. v. 4a), and loyal (cf. v. 5b). Verse 12 expresses the psalmist's joy over being part of God's elect **people,** recipients of His loyal love. (On Israel as God's **inheritance,** see comments on 28:9.) The psalmist then stated that God **sees all** people **from** His exalted position in **heaven** (**His dwelling place;** cf. 2 Chron. 6:21, 30, 33, 39; 30:27). He sees even their inner thoughts (Ps. 33:13-15). God does not save the self-confident (vv. 6-17). Those who look to a **king,** or human **strength,** or **a horse** cannot find **deliverance** (cf. 20:7). Rather **the LORD** saves and preserves those who trust and **hope** in Him (33:18-19; cf. "hope" in vv. 20, 22 and

**unfailing love** in vv. 5, 22). This is the lot of Israel, the **blessed . . . nation** (v. 12).

## C. God's people trust in Him (33:20-22)

**33:20-22.** The conclusion of the psalm is a reassertion of faith in **the LORD.** God's people demonstrate their faith in three ways. First, they **wait in hope** (cf. 25:5, 21; 39:7; 62:5; 71:5) **for** deliverance from the Lord as their **Help** (cf. 30:10; 40:17; 46:1; 54:4; 63:7; 70:5; 115:9-11; 146:5) and **Shield** (cf. comments on 3:3). Second, they **rejoice** in **Him** whom they **trust** (33:21). Third, they pray for His **unfailing love** (*ḥesed;* cf. vv. 5, 18) to **rest** on them. So they are confident (**hope**) He will consummate His program of salvation.

## Psalm 34

This song of praise is attributed to David when he escaped from Abimelech by feigning insanity (1 Sam. 21:11). In the psalm David called on the congregation to praise the Lord for their salvation. And after affirming that God is good to those who trust Him, he instructed the people on how to live a long life.

## A. God is good to His people (34:1-10)

**34:1-3.** Verses 1-10 are filled with David's praise. In verses 1-3 David called the people to **praise** the LORD with him. He resolved to praise God continually so that **the afflicted** would **rejoice.** But here he called for all the people to **exalt** the LORD **with** him.

**34:4-6.** David here recorded the report of his deliverance. Because he cried and was **delivered** (cf. "delivers" in vv. 7, 17, 19), he was convinced that God's people **are never** put to **shame.** Instead they **are radiant** because God hears them (cf. vv. 15, 17) and rescues them from their **troubles** (cf. vv. 17, 19).

**34:7-10.** David declared that **the Angel of the LORD** (possibly the Lord Himself; cf. comments on Gen. 16:9) **camps around those who fear** (cf. Ps. 34:9, 11) the Lord. In military imagery David envisioned divine protection (cf. Gen. 32:2; 2 Kings 6:16).

Those who trust in **the LORD** experience genuine happiness—if they **taste and see.** All who **fear the LORD,** that is, all who are genuine worshipers, will **lack nothing** (cf. Ps. 23:1), or **no good thing** (cf. 16:2; 84:11).

## B. God blesses the righteous with life (34:11-22)

**34:11-14.** Verses 11-22 include David's instructions to the people on how to achieve a full life in the Lord. He exhorted them to **listen** to his instruction concerning **the fear of the LORD.** The instruction was essentially that of a righteous, peaceful **life** (v. 12), shunning **evil** and treachery (v. 13), and doing **good** (v. 14). This is wisdom teaching about the way of the righteous, which produces a life of quality with God's blessing.

**34:15-21.** For those who live righteously in **the LORD** (cf. **righteous** in vv. 15, 17, 19, 21), several assurances are given. First, **the LORD** looks favorably **on the righteous,** a sign of protection (v. 15), but He **is against** the wicked and will **cut off** their **memory . . . from** the living (v. 16; cf. Prov. 10:7b). Second, **the LORD hears** (cf. Ps. 34:6, 15) the prayers of **the righteous** who are broken **in spirit** and are not arrogant and stubborn (vv. 17-18). Third, **the LORD . . . delivers** (cf. vv. 4, 7, 17) **the righteous** from his **troubles** (cf. v. 6) so that not one of **his bones** is **broken.** This is an expression of complete protection from cruel oppression. Verse 20, as well as Exodus 12:46b, was used by God in referring to the Savior in John 19:36.

**34:22.** In summary, the psalmist asserted that **the LORD redeems His servants** (cf. comments on "redeems" in 26:11); **no one who** trusts **in Him will be** lost. That this verse represents a summation of the reason for praise can be seen by the arrangement in the Hebrew text. This psalm is an acrostic: each verse begins with a different letter of the Hebrew alphabet in order, but one letter in the Hebrew alphabet is omitted (between vv. 5-6), thereby finishing the acrostic with verse 21. The last verse, then, breaks the sequence and calls attention to itself.

## Psalm 35

This psalm is a combination of three laments over the opposition of David's enemies. Each lament develops the unified cry for deliverance from enemies who hated him without a cause.

## A. Prayer for deliverance from destroyers (35:1-10)

The psalmist petitioned the Lord to deliver him from his enemies who wished to kill him, who hated him for no good reason.

**35:1-6.** David's prayer began with a plea for the **LORD** to act as his Champion (vv. 1-3) and to rout his enemies (vv. 4-6). Like worthless **chaff** (v. 5) blown away by **the wind** in threshing, so he wished his worthless enemies would be cast aside. His prayer, that **the Angel of the LORD** would drive **them away,** was a prayer for retributive justice, that the Lord would render to them what they had planned for him.

**35:7-10.** They had sought to take his life unaware as a hunter hides his **net** and digs **a pit** to catch an unwary animal. David prayed that their traps for others would ensnare **them** (cf. 7:15; 9:15; 57:6) **by surprise** and bring about **their ruin** (cf. 35:4; 38:12; 40:14; 70:2). **Then,** David said, he would praise **the LORD** with joy, wholeheartedly (**my whole being**) for rescuing those (**the poor and needy**) who are at the mercy of the mighty.

## B. Lament over unjust hatred (35:11-18)

With an emphasis on the lament, the psalmist petitioned the Lord for help from those who unjustly hated him.

**35:11-18.** Here David described his lamentable state. Essentially he had been repaid **evil for good** (vv. 11-12). He had fasted and prayed for his enemies **when they were ill,** putting **on sackcloth** (cf. 30:11 and comments on Gen. 37:34), and **when** his **prayers** were not answered, he mourned and wept for them (Ps. 35:13-14). However, **when** he was in difficulty, they gleefully **mocked** (vv. 15-16). Because of this injustice he pleaded for help from **the LORD,** who up till then had not responded (v. 17). (On **how long?** see comments on 6:3, and on his enemies as **lions,** see comments on 7:2.) But when the Lord would answer, David said he would **praise** Him **in the . . . assembly** (35:18).

## C. Petition for justice (35:19-28)

Here the psalmist petitioned the Lord for deliverance from the wicked by asking that He render justice against those who stir up trouble by their accusations against peaceful people. Here again the theme of the wicked's unjust treatment of the righteous forms the lamentable reason for his petition.

**35:19-21.** David prayed that the Lord

would not let the wicked triumph because their vicious words stirred up strife. Again he stressed that they were his **enemies without cause** (cf. v. 7). They winked at each other (cf. Prov. 6:13; 10:10; 16:30), revealing their malicious intentions. They devised **false accusations against those who** wished to **live quietly,** slanderously claiming to **have seen** them in some wrongdoing.

**35:22-26.** Though David's enemies falsely claimed to have seen him in sin and were vocal about it, David knew that the LORD had **seen** *them* in *their* wrongdoing. So he asked **God** to end His silence (i.e., not be inactive) and **rise to** the psalmist's **defense.** By vindicating David, the LORD would rightly **put to shame and confusion** all the foes' gloating (cf. v. 19).

**35:27-28.** David's final prayer was that the people **who** looked for his **vindication** would have occasion to be joyful and praise **the** LORD for it. Because his enemies hated him without a cause (cf. vv. 7, 19) he was convinced that the Lord would vindicate him, so that he could exalt and praise Him continually (**all day long**).

## Psalm 36

In this psalm David received an oracle concerning the philosophy and lifestyle of unbelievers as they plotted their wicked schemes. David found relief in his experiential knowledge of the glorious nature of the Lord, who brings abundant blessings to believers. As a result, he prayed that the Lord would continue His loyal love and righteousness so that the wicked would not destroy his integrity.

### A. An oracle concerning the wicked (36:1-4)

**36:1.** David received **an oracle** from the Lord **concerning the sinfulness** (*pešaʿ,* "transgression") **of the wicked.** So he recorded what he learned. The philosophy of the wicked is based on their absence of the **fear** (*paḥad,* "dread"—not the usual word *yirʾâh,* "fear") **of God.** They have **no** dread of the Lord; they sense no terror because of their actions, so they proceed in their wickedness.

**36:2-4.** Having no dread of the Lord, a wicked person commits evil continually. He soothes his own conscience (**flatters himself**) to hide his iniquity, because

if he saw it from God's viewpoint he would **hate** it. His speech is licentious and deceptive. His life has long **ceased** to be worthwhile, for as **he commits himself to a sinful course** of action, he has no inclination to **reject** evil. He even **plots evil** (cf. Hosea 7:15; Nahum 1:11) at night while going to sleep.

### B. The appreciation of God's portion (36:5-9)

**36:5-6.** In contrast with the wickedness that surrounded him (vv. 1-4), David found relief by meditating on the glorious attributes of the LORD, and the abundant blessings that come to believers. His philosophy of life was based on an experiential knowledge of the Lord's loyal **love** (*ḥesed;* cf. vv. 7, 10), **faithfulness . . . righteousness,** and **justice.** These attributes are inexhaustible resources for believers. Through them the LORD preserves **man and beast** throughout life.

**36:7-9.** The result of this philosophy is blessing for believers (cf. the results of a wicked person's philosophy, vv. 2-4). God's loyal **love** (cf. vv. 5, 10) is precious, because humans can take **refuge** in the Lord like chicks taking refuge under their mother hen's **wings** (v. 7; cf. 17:8; 57:1; 61:4; 63:7; 91:4). The psalmist then used the imagery of the temple to say that believers enjoy the provisions of God's **house** (36:8). Moreover, Eden and Creation are suggested in the next blessings—**drink from** the **river of delights** ("delights" is "Eden" in Heb.), and **life** and **light** (i.e., understanding, joy, and life) come from God, their Source. So in contrast with the corruptions of the wicked, an obedient believer's life is characterized by security in the Lord, abundant provisions, life, and understanding in God's presence.

### C. Preservation of integrity (36:10-12)

**36:10-12.** David prayed that the Lord would **continue** His protective **love** (cf. vv. 5, 7) so that his integrity would be preserved from the influence of **the proud** and **wicked** who would be destroyed.

## Psalm 37

This psalm of David seems to build on the previous one. Here he instructed the righteous not to be disturbed over the prosperity of the wicked who reject God, for divine justice will yet be granted. Using a series of proverbial expressions, the psalmist exhorted the righteous to trust in the Lord continually and not fret about evil people who are about to be cast down. The message is similar to that in Psalms 49 and 73, as well as the Book of Job.

### A. Trust and fret not (37:1-8)

**37:1-8.** In this first section of the psalm David called for trust despite the presence **of evil men.** One should not be **envious of** sinful people and their prosperity (cf. vv. 7-8; cf. Prov. 23:17; 24:1) because they will wither **like the grass** (cf. Pss. 90:5; 102:4, 11; 103:15-16; Isa. 40:6-8; 1 Peter 1:24) and **will soon die** (Ps. 37:1-2). Rather one should **trust in the LORD** who can answer prayers of the heart (vv. 3-4). The promise, **He will give you the desires of your heart,** is based on the condition, **delight yourself in the LORD.** One who delights in Him will have righteous desires. If a person trusts in **the LORD** (cf. v. 3) God will gloriously vindicate him (vv. 5-6).

Therefore the righteous should **not** envy or **fret** (cf. v. 1; Prov. 24:19) **when** the wicked **succeed.** Fretting **leads only to evil,** including **anger** (Ps. 37:7-8).

### B. The wicked will be justly punished (37:9-22)

**37:9-11.** David described (a) the impending judgment on **the wicked**—they **will** shortly **be cut off** (vv. 9a, 10)—and (b) the contrasting truth that **the meek will inherit the land** (vv. 9b, 11). This promise of inheriting the land (cf. vv. 22, 29, 34) was reiterated and broadened by Jesus (see comments on Matt. 5:5).

**37:12-22.** Five contrasts form the basis of the affirmations in verses 9-11: (1) **The wicked** devise evil **against the righteous . . . but the Lord laughs at** them (vv. 12-13). (2) **The wicked** attack the meek, **but** their own violence will destroy them (vv. 14-15). (**Poor** and **needy** occur together here for the first of six times in the Pss.: v. 14; 40:17; 70:5; 74:21; 86:1; 109:22.) (3) It is **better** to have **little** than to be **wicked** with much, for their **wealth** will be lost (vv. 16-17). (4) **The LORD** knows and protects the way of the upright, **but the wicked will perish** (cf. 1:6) like grass (cf. 37:2) and

**smoke** (vv. 18-20). (5) Because **the wicked** selfishly keep what they **borrow** but the righteous are generous (cf. v. 26), **the LORD** will repay with justice (vv. 21-22), including **the righteous** inheriting **the land** (cf. vv. 9, 11, 29, 34).

### C. The Lord loves and blesses the just (37:23-31)

**37:23-31.** In contrast with the retribution for the wicked, the psalmist delineated the blessings of the Lord for **the righteous:** (1) **The LORD** establishes and protects the ways of the righteous (vv. 23-24). (2) The Lord provides food for them (vv. 25-26). (3) He **loves** and protects **the just** who **do good** (cf. v. 3), giving them security in **the land** (vv. 27-29; cf. vv. 9, 11, 22, 34). (4) **The righteous** person speaks **wisdom** because **the Law of . . . God is in his heart** (vv. 30-31).

### D. The conflict of good and evil (37:32-40)

**37:32-38.** The psalmist concluded his meditation by describing the struggle between the wicked and the righteous. His solution to the problem of wicked people was to contrast their evil plot to destroy the righteous with God's **power** to preserve. **The wicked lie in wait** to destroy, **but the LORD will not** forsake His own (vv. 32-33). One who waits on **the LORD** will enjoy security (v. 34; cf. vv. 9, 11, 22) and **the upright . . . man of peace** will have **a future** (or, perhaps better, will see his "posterity"; cf. NIV marg.). By contrast the **wicked** will flourish (v. 35; cf. v. 7b) **but** they **will be cut off** (vv. 36, 38; cf. v. 34).

**37:39-40.** David concluded that in a world with wicked people on every hand, **the LORD** is **the Salvation** and **Stronghold** (*mā'ôz,* "a strong fortified place"; cf. 27:1; 43:2; 52:7) for those who **take refuge in Him** from **the wicked.**

## Psalm 38

Psalm 38 is a song of sorrow. It is titled "a petition" (lit., "to bring to remembrance"; cf. comments on the title to Ps. 70). The psalmist was severely chastened by the Lord for personal sin, and grievously plagued by his enemies. In his extreme plight he pleaded that the Lord in compassion would deliver him. His hope was in the Lord to whom he confessed his iniquity.

## A. The Lord's discipline (38:1-12)

**38:1-2.** David pleaded that the LORD stop chastening him in His **wrath** (cf. 6:1). This **discipline** was apparently painful and harsh, as the figures of the **arrows** and the **hand** reflect.

**38:3-8.** David lamented his sufferings for the chastening of his sin. **Because of** his sin he had lost his **health** (cf. v. 7) and his fitness (**soundness;** on **bones,** see comments on 6:2). He had been made to **bear** his **guilt,** which had **overwhelmed** him (38:4). His illness was a festering, painful, debilitating one **brought** on by **sinful** foolishness (vv. 5-6). He was crushed in **body** (cf. v. 3) and spirit (he was **feeble . . . crushed,** and **in anguish**).

**38:9-12.** David then described the effect of his suffering on others. First, his pitiable state lay **open before** the LORD (vv. 9-10). God knew that he sighed at the point of death. Second, his **friends** avoided him (v. 11). Third, his enemies spoke evil of him and planned ways to deceive him and **ruin** him (v. 12; cf. 35:4, 8; 40:14; 70:2).

## B. The sufferer's hope (38:13-22)

The second portion of the psalm expresses David's confidence that the Lord would have compassion on him and rescue him.

**38:13-16.** His hope was in the LORD alone. Negatively, **like a deaf . . . mute** he made no reply (vv. 13-14) to the wicked who plotted his destruction (cf. v. 12). Rather he waited **for** the LORD to **answer** his prayer and end their triumphant gloating.

**38:17-20.** David's need was great and his situation desperate. His **pain** (cf. v. 7) was constant. Moreover, he confessed his sin, recognizing that **sin** was the cause of his suffering (cf. vv. 3-4). But his **enemies** were **vigorous** and **numerous,** and thrived on **evil** and **slander.** The sufferer sensed that God must rescue him soon.

**38:21-22.** David's petition was urgent. He entreated the LORD . . . **not** to **forsake** him but **to help** him because He was his **God** and **Savior.**

## Psalm 39

David acknowledged that God had made man's life brief. So he cast himself on the Lord as his only hope, praying that God would stop chastening him so he could enjoy his remaining days.

The psalm continues the theme of Psalm 38, but his enemies' onslaught had subsided. He seems to have suffered a prolonged illness that brought him near death.

## A. Acknowledgment of life's brevity (39:1-6)

**39:1-3.** David submitted to the knowledge that his life was brief (vv. 1-6). First, he resolved not to **sin** by his words. He kept **silent** in the presence of his enemies, but suppressing his feelings only aggravated his suffering.

**39:4-6.** Second, he sought relief from his frustration by submitting to the Lord's determination of his life. He prayed that the LORD would help him know the brevity of **life** (cf. 90:10, 12). This prayer was prompted by the awareness that **life** is brief in duration—like a **handbreadth** and **a breath** (cf. Job 7:7; Pss. 39:11; 62:9; 144:4). All one's labors in which he **heaps up** his possessions are **vain,** for life is short.

## B. Confidence in life's only hope (39:7-13)

**39:7.** Realizing that his afflictions were due to his sins, David cast himself wholly on the LORD to make his brief sojourn in life enjoyable. He expressed his commitment to the Lord in the words **My hope is in You** (cf. 25:5, 21; 33:20; 62:5; 71:5).

**39:8-11.** David petitioned the Lord to stop chastening him (vv. 8-9). God rebukes people for **sin** and consumes **their wealth like a moth** eating a garment (v. 11; cf. Job 13:28; Isa. 50:9; 51:8; Hosea 5:12; James 5:2). Because the psalmist was **overcome,** he prayed for God to **remove** His **scourge** (Ps. 39:10).

**39:12-13.** The psalmist's final prayer in this psalm was that God would hear his plea and treat him not as **a stranger** but with favor, by making his remaining days enjoyable.

## Psalm 40

This psalm includes thanksgiving (vv. 1-10) and petition (vv. 11-17). In the first part David gladly offered himself as a sacrifice to God because of the great salvation granted him. In the second part he lamented the distress that had come on him and prayed for deliverance.

### A. Sacrificial dedication to God (40:1-10)

**40:1-4.** The psalm begins with David's joyful report to the congregation about his deliverance and an encouragement to them to trust the Lord. **God** did something wonderful for him after a long period of prayerful, patient waiting. Using figurative language to describe his distress and release, he affirmed that **the Lord** saved him from his dilemma (like being in a **slimy pit** with **mud and mire**) and established him firmly **on a rock.** This deliverance gave him **a new song** for rejoicing (cf. 33:3; 96:1; 98:1; 144:9; 149:1).

On the basis of this deliverance he declared the blessedness of one who trusts in **the Lord** alone, without looking to the wicked (**the proud** and idol-worshipers).

**40:5.** David expressed appreciation for the Lord's innumerable and wonderful acts of deliverance (**wonders**). If he tried to **speak** of all the things God had **planned for** His own, **they would be too** numerous to tell.

**40:6.** Recognizing his rich benefits from God prompted the psalmist to dedicate himself. He recalled that God preferred his body to his sacrifices. Some have suggested that the words **my ears You have pierced** refer to the custom of boring a slave's ear (Ex. 21:6), meaning, "You have bound me as a slave to Yourself." However, it is more likely that this statement is a recognition that God had given him the ability to hear and obey the Word of the Lord (cf. NIV marg., "opened"). The Septuagint translated it much more generally, "a body You have prepared for me" (cf. NIV marg.), which captured the idea of the context.

**40:7-8.** David responded to the truth in verse 6 by yielding his life to do God's will. He presented himself willingly to the Lord, received direction from the book (**the scroll**), and expressed his **desire** to **do** the **will** of **God.** These verses present a marvelous example of what is involved in dedicating oneself to God's will in accordance with His Word.

Verses 6-8 take on a greater significance when cited in Hebrews 10:5-7 where the writer contrasted Christ's perfect obedience with the insufficiency of the Mosaic sacrifices. The words are ap-

plied to Christ's Incarnation to fulfill God's purpose for Him as prescribed in the book.

**40:9-10.** Part of the will of the Lord, according to David's compliance with it, is praise. So in these verses he announced that he willingly spoke to the congregation of many of the Lord's attributes, including His **righteousness . . . faithfulness . . . salvation. . . . love,** and **truth.**

### B. Supplication to God for deliverance (40:11-17)

**40:11-12.** The tone of the psalm changes dramatically here to one of urgent prayer. David began his supplication by petitioning the Lord to continue His **mercy** (lit., "compassion"), loyal **love,** and **truth** because of the many **troubles** and **sins** that surrounded him. The troubles he was experiencing were directly related to his many sins (cf. 25:17-18; 38:2-14).

**40:13-16.** His prayer became more specific as he asked for a quick deliverance (**come quickly;** cf. v. 17) from his troubles. He believed that the Lord, in rescuing him, should confound all those who sought to **take** his **life** and bring him **ruin** (vv. 14-15; cf. 35:4, 8; 70:2). By His turning **back** David's enemies **in disgrace** (cf. 6:10; 70:2), the righteous would be encouraged to **rejoice** and praise the Lord. These would be the effects of God's answer to his prayer.

**40:17.** Then the psalmist, being **poor and needy** (see comments on 37:14), repeated his prayer that **the Lord. . . . not delay** (cf. 40:13) in helping him (see comments on 30:10).

## Psalm 41

In this psalm David instructed the congregation that those who aided the needy would themselves obtain deliverance. In relation to this he recalled his prayer for revenge on those who did not have mercy on him but took advantage of his illness. Psalm 41 is a lesson based on a prayer for help against treachery.

### A. The merciful obtain mercy (41:1-3)

**41:1.** The psalm begins with the general principle that **the Lord** will show mercy to one **who has regard for the weak.** This spirit wins divine approval and a corresponding reward.

**41:2-3.** Specific blessings given the merciful include protection and security **in the land** (cf. 37:9, 11, 22, 29). Also **the LORD** will **not** give **him** over **to . . . his** enemies, and **will sustain him** in **illness.**

### B. The vengeance for treachery (41:4-10)

Still addressing the congregation, the psalmist pointed out that the Lord will justly punish those who take advantage of the afflicted. David developed this idea by reiterating his prayer in his experience.

**41:4-10.** His prayer had been one for healing after confessing his sin (v. 4). However, he lamented the fact that his **enemies** took advantage of his condition. Wanting him to **die** (v. 5), they feigned friendship while slandering him (v. 6), **saying** that he would **never** survive (vv. 7-8). **Even** his trusted **friend** betrayed **(lifted up his heel against)** him (v. 9). These words, of course, were quoted by Jesus concerning Judas (John 13:18). But here David had in mind the treachery of his friend Ahithophel, who betrayed him, and then hanged himself (2 Sam. 16:20–17:3, 23).

David's prayer had been motivated partly by his desire to **repay** his foes for their treachery (Ps. 41:10).

### C. Deliverance for integrity (41:11-13)

**41:11-12.** Addressing God directly, David noted that God delivered him (cf. v. 1) from his enemies because he had **integrity.**

**41:13.** This doxology (cf. 106:48) concludes the first major section (Book I) of the Book of Psalms.

## II. Book II (Pss. 42–72)

In Book II 7 psalms (Pss. 42; 44–49) have the headings, "of the Sons of Korah." This is probably not a designation of the authors, but a reference to the fact that these psalms were delivered to them to be performed. One psalm in Book II is by Asaph (Ps. 50), 20 are by David (Pss. 51–70), 3 are anonymous (Pss. 43; 67; 71), and 1 is by Solomon (Ps. 72).

## Psalm 42

Apparently Psalms 42 and 43 belonged together at one time, many Hebrew manuscripts having them as one psalm. This is evident from the fact that the refrain is repeated twice in Psalm 42

(vv. 5, 11) and at the end of Psalm 43 (v. 5). Psalm 42 was the expression of the psalmist's yearning for God, and Psalm 43 was his praise at the prospect of full communion with God.

### A. Longing for the living God (42:1-5)

In the first stanza, the psalmist wrote that he longed for the living God as he was taunted by his enemies, but was confident that he would yet praise Him.

**42:1-2.** The psalmist compared his yearning **for the living God** to the longing of a **deer** for **water.** The animal's need for water to sustain its life forms a fitting simile for a soul's need of the living **God** (cf. 143:6), the Source of spiritual life.

**42:3-4.** The writer explained that he had been yearning in **tears** while his enemies had been taunting him. They continually (**all day long;** cf. v. 10; 38:12) taunted his faith with the question, **Where is your God?** (cf. 42:10) while he was separated from the formal place of worship. He could only recall his joyful participation in the festal processions in Jerusalem.

**42:5.** In this refrain (cf. v. 11; 43:5) the psalmist in a rhetorical question encouraged himself, though downhearted (42:6), to **hope in God,** for he was confident that he would **yet** be able to **praise Him** as before.

### B. Overwhelmed by his enemies (42:6-11)

In this second stanza, the psalmist lamented that his enemies had stormed over him like great billows, but again he had hope that he would yet praise the Lord.

**42:6.** The psalmist lamented his deep depression. Because his **soul** was **downcast** (cf. v. 5) he prayed to the Lord. The mountainous region in the tribe of Dan refers to the place from which he prayed. He was apparently miles north of the Sea of Kinnereth (Galilee). Yet he longed to be not on **Mount Mizar** (a peak in the Mount **Hermon** range) but on Mount Zion (cf. 43:3).

**42:7.** His distress is figuratively portrayed by billows and **waves.** Trouble had come **over** him like one wave after another, personified as if they were calling to each other to come down in the **waterfalls.** He had been overwhelmed as if by a flood.

**42:8.** Then the psalmist confidently called on **the LORD** to deliver him. He mustered confidence in the Lord—confidence that **His love** and **His song** would be **with** him continually (**by day** and by **night**). His **prayer** refers to his praise.

**42:9-11.** In his prayer (v. 8) he asked God **why** he had to continue suffering physically (on **bones,** see comments on 6:2) and emotionally (going **about mourning**) under oppression (cf. 43:2). He reminded the Lord that his enemies taunted his faith continually (cf. 42:3). In this way he hoped to motivate the Lord to answer.

In verse 11 he repeated his refrain (cf. v. 5; 43:5).

## Psalm 43

This psalm completes the song begun in Psalm 42. Though Psalms 42 and 43 are one psalm in many Hebrew manuscripts, Psalm 43 is also an independent song of praise. In it the psalmist asked the Lord to lead him back to Jerusalem where he longed to serve and praise.

### A. Vindication from his enemies (43:1-3)

**43:1.** In his petition to be brought back to Jerusalem the psalmist prayed for vindication from his enemies, who were **ungodly . . . deceitful, and wicked.** He asked God to **plead** his **cause** in their presence.

**43:2.** His prayer is based on the confidence that **God** was his Safety. However, since God was indeed His **Stronghold** (*māʿôz,* "a strong fortified place"; cf. 27:1; 37:39; 52:7), he was troubled by his distress at the hands of his **enemy** (cf. 42:9). God had seemingly **rejected** him.

**43:3.** Vindication from his foes' taunting him would come through the psalmist's being brought safely to Jerusalem to worship. So he prayed that God's **light and . . . truth** would **guide** Him to God's dwelling place, the **holy mountain** (cf. 48:1; 87:1; 99:9). This refers to Jerusalem where David's tabernacle and later Solomon's temple were erected. "Light" represented understanding and life, and "truth" represented God's faithful Word by which the psalm-writer would find guidance. He awaited God's manifestations for direction.

### B. Resolution to praise (43:4)

**43:4.** The psalmist expressed his vow to **praise . . . God** for his deliverance when he returned to **the altar** in Jerusalem. Arriving there, the longing of his soul would be satisfied with **God,** his **joy and** his **delight.**

### C. Encouragement for the soul (43:5)

**43:5.** The refrain from Psalm 42:5, 11 is repeated here. The psalmist found encouragement for his **downcast** and **disturbed** soul in the **hope** (confidence) that he would **yet praise** the Lord.

## Psalm 44

Psalm 44 is a lament of the nation in a time of unequaled disaster. Because of God's deliverance of the nation's ancestors, and because of the people's present faith, they prayed earnestly that God would give them victory. Their prayer was prompted by the fact that they were experiencing defeats which they did not understand. The psalm is unique as an assertion of national fidelity (contrast Lam. 3).

### A. The historic faith of the nation (44:1-8)

The people asserted their confidence in the Lord, based on His past dealings with the nation and her present faith.

**44:1-3.** After stating that Israel knew of God's marvelous works in the past (v. 1), they recalled specifically that the Lord gave them the land under Joshua (v. 2). This was recognized as a miraculous work of God, by His **hand . . . arm,** favor (**face** shining; cf. comments on 4:6), and love, not by their own strength.

**44:4-8.** As a result of hearing what **God** had done, the nation trusted in Him as her **King.** Sometimes the psalmist wrote as if one person were involved (e.g., "my King"), but usually he wrote as if the entire nation were speaking (e.g., **our enemies**), indicating that the singular pronouns may be collective. The people experienced similar great **victories. . . . through** God in their lifetime, and were confident (**in God** each made his **boast**) regarding the future.

### B. The humiliating defeat of the nation (44:9-16)

**44:9-12.** In spite of past victories (cf. vv. 3-4, 7) the nation had been subjected to a humiliating defeat. First the defeat is described literally, attributing it to the fact that the Lord **no longer** fought for them (vv. 9-10). Then the defeat was vividly described in figurative language (vv. 11-12): they were **scattered** like **sheep** (cf. v. 22) and were **sold** as slaves for trifling amounts which suggested their small worth.

**44:13-16.** As a result, the nation had been **made . . . a reproach.** Israel's enemies mockingly derided them, causing them inward feelings of ignominy (**disgrace**) and **shame.**

### C. The protection of innocence (44:17-22)

**44:17-22.** Because this defeat was undeserved, the nation was perplexed. After affirming her integrity (v. 17), the nation affirmed her **covenant** loyalty to God. She had **not** gone astray after other gods and therefore did not deserve this crushing defeat (vv. 18-19). In fact **God** had not accused the nation of idolatry (vv. 20-21). Had they been involved in it, He in His omniscience certainly would have known it. **Yet for** His **sake** they faced **death** continually (**all day long**). That is, because they fought a holy war for Him, they were experiencing this disaster and were treated like **sheep to be slaughtered** (cf. v. 11).

### D. The prayer for victory (44:23-26)

**44:23-26.** The nation asked God for help (**rouse Yourself!**) for she saw no reason why He should ignore her **misery.** Moreover, the nation felt that God must rescue her (**rise up and help us**) because she was at her lowest (**brought down to the dust;** i.e., about to die). Though the nation was seemingly rejected by God and had apparently lost a battle (even though she had been faithful), she wholeheartedly trusted in the LORD to **redeem** (cf. comments on 26:11) her. This is the proper age-old response of the genuine believer to suffering (cf. Job 13:15, "Though He slay me, yet will I hope in Him").

## Psalm 45

This is a royal psalm celebrating the wedding of the mighty king. The psalm begins with lavish praise to the royal groom for all his splendor, majesty, and righteousness. This is followed by a re-port of the counsel given to the bride before she was brought to the king's palace in all her glory. Then the psalmist predicted universal and eternal remembrance of the king's name through his progeny.

The psalm has a lengthy superscription and an extended introduction concerning its nature. The song is set "to the tune of 'Lilies' " and is called "a wedding song" (lit., "a song of loves").

### A. Praise for the royal bridegroom (45:1-9)

**45:1.** The psalmist explained that this hymn is inspirational. His **heart** was **stirred** (lit., "boiling over") with this **noble theme.** What he would pour forth in hymnic praise was so inspired, he said, that it was like a finely written and edited work. It was not possible for him to contain himself as he wrote **for** his majesty **the king.**

**45:2.** The writer said the king was transcendent and **excellent** in his person. Of all humans he was the fairest. For example, his words were gracious—evidence that **God** had **blessed** him.

**45:3-5.** Since the king was a **mighty** man of valor, the hymnist called on him to demonstrate his valor by riding **forth** to champion **truth, humility, and** justice. Because the king was just, he prospered. As **nations** fell before him, his victories would be magnificent.

**45:6-7.** The king was righteous in his administration. In a surprising extravagance of language, the psalmist addressed the king as **God** ('ĕlōhîm). This is not entirely unique; judges in Moses' day were designated in this way as God's just representatives (cf. Ex. 21:6; 22:8-9; Ps. 82:1). As God's representative, this king would have an everlasting **throne** and a righteous reign (**a scepter of justice**). Because he loved **righteousness** and hated **wickedness,** God had blessed him with abundant **joy.**

Psalm 45:6-7 undoubtedly refers to the promise of an eternal throne for the house of David (cf. 2 Sam. 7:16) which will be fulfilled in Jesus Christ when He returns to reign forever. Hebrews 1:8-9 quotes this passage in reference to the exaltation and dominion of Christ. Whether the psalmist used the word 'ĕlōhîm to mean God or His human representative, the writer of Hebrews demonstrated that it points up the essential difference between the Son and the angels (cf. Heb. 1:5, 7).

**45:8-9.** The king was joyfully blessed on his wedding day. His **robes** (royal garb) were perfumed with several fragrances. **Myrrh** is a fragrant gum from trees in Arabia (cf. its use as a perfume in Prov. 7:17; Song 1:13). **Aloes** may come from a scented wood (cf. Num. 24:6; Prov. 7:17; Song 4:14). **Cassia** may be from the fragrant roots of a plant. **Ivory** beautified the **palaces,** joyful stringed **music** was played (probably on lyres and harps), and **daughters of kings** were **honored.** With him was his **bride** adorned in **gold** jewelry from **Ophir,** a prominent source of gold, probably in western Arabia (cf. 1 Kings 9:28; 10:11; 22:48; Job 22:24; 28:16; Isa. 13:12).

### B. Advice for the bride of the king (45:10-15)

**45:10-11.** The psalmist gave his charge to the bride before she was conducted into the king's presence. He instructed her to do homage to her **lord** the king, forsaking her **people.** He explained that because **the king** desired (the Heb. means more than was **enthralled by**) her **beauty,** she should **honor him.**

**45:12.** Following his advice, he said that she would have blessing if she obeyed his instruction. She would receive **a gift** from **Tyre** and wealthy people would **seek** her **favor** perhaps by giving her expensive gifts.

**45:13-15.** The scene then shifted to the court where the bride was ushered into the king's presence. She was beautiful **(glorious)** in her **gold** (cf. v. 9) and **embroidered** gown, as the joyful procession of bridesmaids **led** her **to the king.**

### C. The benediction on the wedding (45:16-17)

**45:16-17.** The writer predicted the prosperity of the marriage—their **sons** would become the **princes** of **the land.** So the king would be remembered and honored **throughout** the **nations.**

There can be little doubt that this psalm was in the mind of John as he wrote Revelation 19:6-21. As he looked forward to the marriage of Christ, the Lamb, in heaven, he recalled how the bride clothed herself with acts of righteousness in preparation for Him (Rev.

19:6-8). Then John described the royal groom going forth to battle in righteousness (Rev. 19:11-21). Psalm 45, then, is typological of the greater Davidic King, Jesus Christ.

## Psalm 46

The psalmist magnified God as the saints' sure Defense at all times. He explained that God's presence makes Zion secure from all her enemies. Thus the psalm is incorporated in the Songs of Zion, because of the centrality of Jerusalem in its message.

### A. God is the Defense of His saints (46:1-3)

**46:1-3.** The psalmist declared that **God** is the **Refuge** (*maḥseh,* "shelter from danger"; cf. comments on 14:6) **and Strength** (cf. comments on 18:1) of believers. In other words they find safety and courage by trusting in Him, who is always **present** to **help** them (see comments on 30:10) in their troubles. So the saints need **not fear,** even if many perils come against them. The language is hyperbolic, to describe how great the perils may be that could come. No matter what happens, those trusting in Him are safe.

### B. God is present in Zion (46:4-7)

**46:4-5.** The psalmist observed that the peace of Jerusalem—**the city of God** with **the holy place where** God dwelt (i.e., made His presence known)—was secured by **God.** The Lord's presence was like a peaceful flowing **river** (in contrast with perilous torrents, v. 3). (Cf. Isa. 8:6; 33:21, where the Lord is compared to a river encircling His city.) Because **God** was **within her,** the city would **not fall.** (Years later, however, the city *did* fall. Because of extensive idolatry in the temple, Ezek. 8, God's presence left, Ezek. 10. Without His protective presence, Jerusalem fell to the Babylonians.)

**46:6-7.** The psalmist then described God's mighty power: by His powerful word God **melts** the **nations** that roar against Him (cf. 2:5). Though **kingdoms** would **fall,** Jerusalem was safe.

Thus **the LORD Almighty** is like a **fortress** (*miśgob,* "a high safe place," trans. "fortress" in 46:11; 48:3; 59:9, 16-17; 62:2, 6; 94:22, and "stronghold" in 9:9; 18:2; 144:2) to His people (cf. 46:11).

They find safety when they trust in Him.

### C. God will be exalted in the earth (46:8-11)

**46:8-11.** The psalmist exhorted the saints to observe the saving mighty deeds of God. These deeds portray how **God** brings peace to His people, destroying weapons throughout the earth. God Himself calls for the people to trust in Him and **know that** He is **God,** for He **will be exalted** throughout **the earth.** Verses 8-10 no doubt greatly encouraged the people of Jerusalem, as the final verse (v. 11) reiterates (cf. v. 7). Also to saints of all ages, the call for a silent trust in God's saving power, in anticipation of universal peace, has been a source of comfort and strength.

## Psalm 47

This psalm is a song about the Lord, the great King (cf. vv. 2, 6-7). It has been classified as an enthronement psalm, celebrating His universal reign. Other enthronement psalms are 93, 95–99. It should be understood as prophetically portraying the coming kingdom of God, manifestations of which were enjoyed by Israel. In Psalm 47 the psalmist called on all peoples of the earth to pay homage to Israel's holy Monarch—the Lord—as He assumes His kingship over them all.

### A. Homage to the sovereign King (47:1-4)

**47:1-2.** The psalmist called on **all the nations** (cf. vv. 3, 8-9) to rejoice in homage to **the Lord Most High,** who is **the great King** (cf. vv. 6-7) **over all the earth** (cf. v. 7). Such shouts **of joy** (cf. v. 5) could come only from willing subjects of this King.

**47:3-4.** The reason for giving homage to Him is expressed in verses 3-4. As stated generally in verse 2, He is the great King over the earth. Specifically, this was demonstrated by His subduing the **nations** when He **chose** Israel as His **inheritance.** This subjugation of foreign nations was experienced in a small measure in Israel's history, but will be especially true in the coming Millennial Age.

### B. The reigning of the sovereign King (47:5-9)

**47:5-6.** The psalmist, picturing God's ascending His throne **amid shouts of** ac-clamation and the playing **of trumpets,** called for the peoples to praise their **King** (note the fourfold occurrence of **sing praises** in v. 6).

**47:7-9.** The psalmist called for **praise** because the Lord **reigns** (cf. 93:1; 96:10; 99:1; 146:10) **over the nations** (cf. 47:1, 3, 9). This expression, common to this type of psalm, most likely is a prophetic statement of future certainty. So the psalmist anticipated the sure rule of God in which all **nobles** and **kings** will gather before Him as their Sovereign. In His **exalted** position the Lord will someday reign over all the earth and every knee shall bow before Him (Phil. 2:9-11). To those who believe in Him, the confidence that the truths of this psalm will be fulfilled brings comfort and encouragement during distressing times.

## Psalm 48

Psalm 48 is a song about Zion, the city of God, the great King. In praising God who loves Jerusalem, the psalmist sang of the city's glory and security because the Lord delivered it from the enemy. On the basis of this, he offered praise to God.

### A. Zion is the city of our God (48:1-3)

**48:1.** The psalm begins with a summary of the theme: **God,** whose **holy mountain** (cf. 43:3; 87:1; 99:9; note comments in 2:6 on the "holy hill"), **the city** of Jerusalem, is greatly to be praised.

**48:2-3.** The psalmist then described this holy city. Its lofty beauty (cf. 50:2) is **the joy of the whole earth.** It is **like the . . . heights of Zaphon,** probably a sacred mountain some miles north of Jerusalem. But the greatest feature of **Zion** (cf. comments on 2:6) is that **God is in her citadels** (cf. 48:13). Jerusalem's strength and safety ("fortress" translates *miśgōb;* cf. comments on 9:9; 46:7) are because of His presence (cf. 46:5).

### B. God makes Zion secure (48:4-8)

**48:4-7.** The psalmist now described the defeat of Zion's enemies. **Kings** were assembled against her, but they were terrified **when . . . they saw** Zion. They were **seized** with **terror** and **trembling** like **a woman in** child **labor.** God **destroyed them** swiftly, **like ships of Tarshish** (possibly large seagoing merchant ships on the Mediterranean) **shattered by**

**an east wind.** Many have taken this passage as a tribute to God's deliverance of Jerusalem from the invading Assyrian armies (cf. Isa. 10:8; 33:3, 14).

**48:8.** The psalmist confirmed the report that **the LORD Almighty** (lit., "the Lord of armies") had made Zion **secure.** This title of the Lord is frequently used in passages referring to military battles. His armies are both terrestrial (Israel's soldiers) and celestial (angels).

### C. Zion rejoices in her God (48:9-14)

**48:9-10.** The psalmist offered praise to God for His **unfailing love** (ḥeṣeḏ, "loyal love") and **righteousness. Praise** of God fills **the earth,** for God's power demonstrates His faithfulness.

**48:11-14.** The psalmist then invited the congregation in **Zion** and all **Judah** to rejoice in **God** by observing the strength of the city (her unharmed **towers . . . ramparts,** and **citadels;** cf. v. 3) which He had preserved. **This God** who had made them secure **will be** the **Guide** for believers **forever.**

### Psalm 49

This psalm is a wisdom poem, dealing with the age-old problem of the prosperity of the wicked (cf. Ps. 73). The poet called his work a dark saying (riddle, 49:4) that is worth analyzing. He had observed that the wicked are prosperous and rich, and filled with pride and a sense of security. But the wise psalmist stated that they are no better than the beasts of the field. In the final analysis, the hope of the righteous is better than the false security of the wicked.

### A. Announcement of the dark saying (49:1-4)

**49:1-4.** The psalmist called the **world** to **listen** to his saying. **All** people, **rich and poor alike** (the subject of the psalm), should **hear** his **wisdom.** He explained that his **words,** though wise, would be dark, that is, they would be like a **riddle** in that discernment and **understanding** are necessary for perception. Indeed, many of life's difficulties require spiritual perception to forestall despair.

### B. Observation of the prosperity of the wicked (49:5-12)

**49:5.** In verses 5-12 the wise poet reported his observation that the pros-

perous have a false security. He introduced his theme in verse 5 by stating that he marveled that he ever feared **evil** times brought on by the **wicked.** Their glory is only temporary.

**49:6-9.** He developed this idea by noting that the proud and arrogant cannot **redeem** (cf. comments on 26:11) **another** person's **life.** Life is too costly for a man to **ransom,** even by **great riches.** Wealth cannot prevent death.

**49:10-12.** The truth stated in verses 6-9 is known even among the wealthy. They—as well as **the foolish—die** (cf. Ecc. 2:15-16) and **leave their wealth to** their heirs (cf. Ecc. 2:19-21). Their new places of residence will be the grave, even though their earthly dwellings or **lands** may bear their names. Man's body, like the bodies of animals, dies (cf. Ecc. 3:19-20).

### C. Encouragement in the abiding hope (49:13-20)

**49:13-14.** The wise psalmist concluded that the doom of the proud is sure, but the hope of the righteous is eternal. He introduced this contrast by marveling at the folly of proud people's lives. Death **is the fate** of the self-righteous and **of those** who follow them. They are turned into **the grave** (sheol) where **death will feed on them.** Their glory will be consumed in the grave. The psalmist was not concerned at this point with God's judgment on the wicked, other than the departure of their earthly glory.

**49:15.** As for the righteous, **God will redeem** them **from the grave.** Again the terminology contrasts with the ruin of the wicked, and includes in germ form the hope of the resurrection.

**49:16-20.** The writer said that it is foolish to be jealous of unbelieving wealthy people for their doom is sure. Though they enjoy great **splendor** and **prosper** in this life, they pass away into darkness, **taking nothing with** them (cf. Ecc. 5:15). The advice is clear: **do not be overawed when a man grows rich.** A proper perspective is necessary for spiritual discernment of **life.** The destiny of the righteous is far better than the fleeting glory of the wicked.

### Psalm 50

This didactic psalm, written by Asaph, a leading Levite musician

(1 Chron. 16:4-5) who also wrote Psalms 73–83, deals with man's worship of God and duty to his neighbor, which are in the two portions of the Decalogue (Ten Commandments). Asaph described a scene in the heavenly courtroom in which the Lord will examine His people. Asaph then declared that the Lord had indictments against two sins of His people: formalism in worship and hypocrisy in living. To please God His people must bring sacrifices of thanksgiving from obedient, trusting hearts.

## A. The Lord's appearance to judge (50:1-6)

**50:1-3.** Asaph described a courtroom scene in which **the Mighty One, God, the LORD**—three designations for the Lord—came to judge. Everyone on **the earth,** from east to west, was summoned before Him. **From** beautiful **Zion** (cf. comments on 2:6; also see 48:2, 11-12), the place of the temple, **God shines forth.** As He **comes** to judge, His presence is accompanied by devouring **fire** and a raging **tempest.** These phenomena, frequently accompanying theophanies, signify His consuming judgment.

**50:4-6.** Asaph then visualized the participants in the case. The inhabitants of the universe will be the witnesses (**the heavens** and **the earth** standing for the inhabitants of each). When He judges **His people,** all the universe will witness it. The defendants in the case will be the saints, **who** have **made a covenant with** Him. And **God** is the righteous **Judge.** With this scene envisioned, Asaph then reported the Lord's two charges against His people (vv. 7-15 and 16-23).

## B. The Lord's indictment against formalism (50:7-15)

**50:7-13.** Asaph, announcing the Lord's first of two charges **against** His **people,** described their formalism in worship. The charge was given as a word from **God,** their **God,** so they would take heed. God did **not** reprove them, however, for their meticulous keeping of the letter of the Law in offering the prescribed **sacrifices.** But Israel failed to realize that God did not need their bulls or **goats** (v. 9; cf. v. 13), for He is the Lord of all Creation. He already owns **every animal** and knows **every bird.** He instituted the sacrifices not because He needed the animals but because the people desperately needed Him. He is not like the gods of the pagans who supposedly thrived on food sacrifices. The Lord does not depend on man's worship for survival.

**50:14-15.** Israel should offer their sacrifices of thanksgiving from a genuine trust in the Lord. The solution to formalism is to worship in genuine faith, which is why Asaph called on the people to **sacrifice thank offerings.** The Hebrew word for thank offerings is *tôdâh*, from the verb *yādâh*, "to acknowledge, thank." Such an offering could not be given unless the offerer had experienced God's work on his behalf. If he was in distress and called on **God,** the Lord would answer. Then the offerer would praise the Lord as a spontaneous expression of his enjoyment of God's benefits. If the people had been praising they would have enjoyed His benefits, not worshiping in an empty ritualistic form.

## C. The Lord's indictment against hypocrisy (50:16-23)

**50:16-17.** Asaph, announcing God's second charge, decried the nation's hypocritical living. He first rebuked **the wicked** for reciting His **laws** and speaking of His **covenant** as their profession of faith, for they actually hated God's **instruction.** Though these wicked people assembled with those who loved the Lord, **God** knew their hearts.

**50:18-21.** The psalmist then selected several examples of their wickedness. While appearing righteous, they tolerated and took part in theft (cf. Ex. 20:15), adultery (cf. Ex. 20:14), and **slander** (cf. Ex. 20:16). He warned them not to confuse God's patience with His approval. God's silence did not mean that He agreed with their actions. Instead the Lord would **rebuke** them directly (**to your face**).

**50:22-23.** Asaph instructed the hypocrites to **consider** their ways before it was too late. Again he called on them to sacrifice **thank offerings** (cf. comments on v. 14) from hearts that are right with God.

So the psalm indicts God's people for formalism and hypocrisy in worship. Jesus' advice to "worship in spirit and in truth" (John 4:24) provides the proper correctives for these faults.

## Psalm 51

Few psalms have found as much use as this one among the saints of all ages, a fact which bears witness to the spiritual needs of God's people. Psalm 51 stands as a paradigm of prayers for forgiveness of sins. Its superscription ascribes the occasion to David's sin of adultery with Bathsheba (2 Sam. 11), an incident in which David broke several of the Ten Commandments. Believers have been comforted by the fact that since David's sins were forgiven theirs can be too.

Poetry often develops the intensity of a moment. Such a moment with David came when he, having been confronted with his sin, confessed it (2 Sam. 12:13a). Because this psalm deals only with confession and has no word of the forgiveness (which did follow immediately in the historical narrative, 2 Sam. 12:13b), this psalm must be understood as a full meditation on the importance of confession. After a believer sins, he must obtain forgiveness if he is to enjoy full participation in the service of the Lord.

The message of this psalm is that the vilest offender among God's people can appeal to God for forgiveness, for moral restoration, and for the resumption of a joyful life of fellowship and service, if he comes with a broken spirit and bases his appeal on God's compassion and grace.

### A. Introductory prayer (51:1-2)

David appealed to God's love and compassion as he petitioned the Lord to forgive him by grace and cleanse him from sin.

**51:1a.** God's attributes of **unfailing love** (ḥeseḏ) for His servant and His **compassion** for the helpless, were the basis for David's appeal for mercy. Even the verb **have mercy** was a prayer for **God** to act in accord with His nature. It is also a recognition that David did not deserve forgiveness. God's forgiveness is by His grace alone.

**51:1b-2.** The three verbs David employed here are figurative. **Blot out** implies a comparison with human records that can be erased; **wash away** (kāḇas) compares forgiveness with washing clothing (often viewed as an extension of a person), **and cleanse** is drawn from the liturgical ceremonial law in which one might be purified for temple participation. These requests (cf. vv. 7, 9) stressed

David's desire for God's total forgiveness of his **transgressions . . . iniquity,** and **sin.**

### B. Confession (51:3-6)

David confessed that he had sinned against the Lord (vv. 3-4), and then lamented his moral impotence (vv. 5-6).

**51:3-4.** When he said that his **sin** was constantly **before** him, it must be remembered that his confession came about a year after he had sinned (the young child died a week after the confession; cf. 2 Sam. 12:13-18). Perhaps David had so rationalized his actions that he did not sense his guilt until Nathan approached him. At any rate, he confessed that he had **sinned** against the Lord. And he submitted to the Lord's will, acknowledging that anything God decided about him would be just.

**51:5-6.** David then acknowledged that he was morally impotent. He was born **a sinner,** that is, at no time in his life was he without sin. This ran contrary to God's moral demands on his life. From his early days he faced **inner** tension, knowing that God desires **truth** and **wisdom,** that is, reliable and productive living.

### C. Petition (51:7-12)

In connection with his confession, David petitioned God first for forgiveness (vv. 7-9), then for inner renewal (vv. 10-12).

**51:7-9.** In his prayer for forgiveness the psalmist made the same requests as before (cf. vv. 1b-2) but in reverse order: **cleanse . . . wash,** and **blot out.** When David spoke of God's cleansing him **with hyssop,** he was alluding to the use of hyssop at the religious ceremonies to sprinkle sacrificial blood on the altar. This represented the removal of sin through the shedding of blood (cf. Heb. 9:22). David then asked God to let him once again **rejoice** in the knowledge of being right with God. (On the association of **bones** with emotional anguish, see comments on Ps. 6:2.) The king asked God to remove his **sins** judicially.

**51:10-12.** As a corrective for his sinful nature, David petitioned **God** for inward renewal of his **heart** attitude (v. 10), preservation in service (v. 11), and restoration of **joy** (v. 12). He was aware that he had become indifferent in his attitudes so he needed renovation. He was also aware that Saul was removed from the kingship for his sin (signified in the OT by the departure of the **Holy Spirit**), so David asked that God not **take** away His Spirit and depose him too. In the New Testament the Spirit does not leave believers; at the moment of salvation He indwells them (cf. John 14:16; Rom. 8:9). But a Christian may be cast aside from service because of sin (cf. 1 Cor. 9:27). David was also aware that in order to experience the joy he once had in his **salvation,** he needed God's inner spiritual renewal.

### D. Vow of praise (51:13-17)

David promised God that if He forgave him he would participate fully in His service. The requests in these verses are for things that result from forgiveness, and so they form indirect requests for forgiveness.

**51:13.** First, David said that if God forgave him, he would **teach . . . sinners** God's **ways** (i.e., how He deals with penitent sinners). Naturally, to be able to teach this he himself must first experience forgiveness.

**51:14-15.** Second, David said if God forgave him, he would **sing** and **praise** God. Only when delivered from his bloodguiltiness could he join in praising **God.**

**51:16-17.** Third, David promised that if **God** forgave his sins he would sacrifice to God. He knew that God did not desire simply an animal **sacrifice** from him (cf. 40:6). He needed to find forgiveness before he could sacrifice a peace offering to God. The sacrifice he had to bring was **a broken and contrite** (crushed) **heart**—a humbled **spirit** fully penitent for sin. That is what God desires and will receive.

In the Old Testament, anyone who sinned as David did had to receive a word from a priest or prophet indicating he was forgiven. Only then could the penitent person again take part in worship and make a peace offering. In the New Testament the word of forgiveness is forever written in God's Word—the blood of Jesus Christ cleanses from sin (1 John 1:7). Yet even in the New Testament a believer must have a spirit broken of all self-assertion; he must acknowledge his need before God to find spiritual renewal and cleansing (1 John 1:9).

### E. Prayer for prosperity (51:18-19)

**51:18-19.** These verses have often been considered a later addition to the psalm because they do not readily relate to the psalm's theme. However, the anticipation of right **sacrifices** (v. 19) is closely related to verses 16-17. The prayer for the building **up** of **the walls of Jerusalem** could be a prayer for general prosperity of the city's defenses; but it could also be figurative, requesting the strengthening of the moral defenses of the nation (i.e., edifying the king). **Righteous** worship is compatible with moral prosperity.

### Psalm 52

This psalm ascribed to David pertains to the occasion of Doeg's treachery (1 Sam. 21–22). The character described in this psalm portrays just such a man. David, who trusted in the Lord, contrasted his faith with the treacherous man who followed a course of iniquity.

### A. The destruction of the man of treachery (52:1-7)

**52:1.** Addressing the evil **man** directly, David chided his treachery (vv. 1-5). David was amazed that the man could actually **boast** in his **evil** in view of the fact he was **a disgrace** to **God.**

**52:2-4.** The treacherous man, Doeg (see the superscription), had a **deceitful tongue** as sharp as a **razor** (cf. "swords" in 55:21), for what he said destroyed others (cf. James 3:6, 8). He thrived on a wicked and false way of life, loving words that devour.

**52:5.** Because of such wickedness, David predicted that **God** would pluck the wicked man out of **the land of the living,** that is, death would swiftly remove him forever.

**52:6-7.** David then anticipated the joy that this would bring to **the righteous.** They would **see** what happens to a person who trusts not in the Lord but in his own ill-gotten riches for strength. (**Stronghold** translates *mā'ôz,* "a strong fortified place"; cf. 27:1; 37:39; 43:2.)

### B. The destiny of the man of faith (52:8-9)

**52:8-9.** In striking contrast with Doeg, the treacherous man (vv. 1-7), David portrayed his own blessed state in the Lord. He compared himself to a green **olive tree,** a figure of prosperity in God's presence (cf. Hosea 14:6). This contrasts with the wicked who will be rooted up (Ps. 52:5). The metaphor of a **flourishing** tree was used in Psalm 1:3.

David's flourishing was because of **God's unfailing love,** in which he said he trusted **forever.** So he vowed to go on praising God **for what** He had **done.** David would wait (**hope**) in God's **name** (which signified His attributes and actions; cf. Ex. 34:5-7) and then he would **praise** Him among the **saints.**

So the righteous, unlike people of treachery, place their confidence in God's love, for there abide justice and blessing.

## Psalm 53

This passage is another version of Psalm 14, adapted for Book II (*'ĕlōhîm,* "God," is substituted for Yahweh, LORD). The psalm is David's, set to *māhălaṯ,* possibly a well-known tune. The psalm reports that the entire human race is evil and that God will overthrow sinners. Therefore the psalmist longs for the establishment of God's kingdom.

### A. Revelation of the human race (53:1-3)

**53:1.** David received a revelation of God's view of the human race: **they are** all fools. His summary description is in this verse: **the fool** believes **there is no God;** thus his life is **corrupt** and **vile** (i.e., abominable to God). In fact **no one . . . does good.**

**53:2-3.** He then reported the details of this revelation. God investigates the human race to see if there is **one** prudent person, but the search is fruitless. The entire human race has **become corrupt** (*'ālaḥ,* "soured" like milk, used only here and in 14:3; Job 15:16). This word for corrupt differs from the word for corrupt in Psalm 53:1. **Not . . . one** single person is without sin (cf. Rom. 3:10-12).

### B. Anticipation of the destruction of the wicked (53:4-5)

**53:4-5.** David expressed his amazement at the ignorance of those who persecute the righteous. He foresaw that the wicked will be in great terror and **shame** when **God** destroys them. This judgment is so certain that the psalmist envisioned it as already accomplished.

### C. Longing for God's kingdom (53:6)

**53:6.** David expressed a yearning for the establishment of God's kingdom when He **restores** the captives. Thus a time is coming when the wicked presence of unbelievers will end and God's people, **Israel,** will **rejoice.**

## Psalm 54

This is a confident prayer of David when he, being pursued by Saul, was betrayed by "the Ziphites" (cf. 1 Sam. 23:19). Though David was being hotly pursued by ungodly men who sought his life, he confidently trusted in the Lord's abilities for complete deliverance.

### A. Save me by Your name (54:1-3)

**54:1-2.** The first part of the psalm (vv. 1-3) records David's urgent **prayer** for deliverance. He based his petition on the **name** of God. His "name" (cf. v. 6) represents who He is and what He has done (cf. Ex. 34:5-7). David had come to know the mighty power of **God** who is able to **save.**

**54:3.** The reason for the appeal was that violent **men** were trying to destroy him. These **men** had no **regard for God.**

### B. God is my Help (54:4-7)

**54:4-5.** The second portion of the psalm (vv. 4-7) records David's confident assertion of his trust in God. He declared that **God is** his Helper (see comments on 30:10) and Sustainer. This led him to pray that God would requite **evil . . . on those who** slandered him. He asked that God demonstrate His **faithfulness** to him.

**54:6-7.** In full confidence that God had heard his prayer and would deliver him **from all** the **troubles** brought on by his **foes,** David promised to **praise** God with **a freewill offering.** This refers to the fellowship offerings (Lev. 3; 7) that accompanied and expressed praises for deliverance. They were offered voluntarily by devout believers. David again (cf. Ps. 52:9) spoke of the Lord's **name** (cf. 54:1) as **good.**

## Psalm 55

This psalm records David's experience of persecution through the betrayal of an intimate friend. Commentators speculate that the occasion was Ahithophel's treachery (2 Sam. 15:31), but this is far from certain.

In the psalm David called on God to enable him to escape from his terrible plight. He lamented the oppression that had come through being betrayed by his close friend. Yet David expressed his personal confidence in God who redeems.

## A. David's terrifying oppression (55:1-8)

**55:1-8.** This first section records his **prayer** to be delivered from his terrible oppression. He cried out to **God,** pleading that God **hear** his restless complaint (vv. 1-2a). His **enemy** was staring at him and angrily reviling him, reducing him to **fear . . . trembling,** and **horror** (vv. 2b-5). So he longed to escape from the hostility (vv. 6-8), like **a dove** flying **away** to a place of refuge **in the desert,** to a **shelter** (*miplāṭ,* "a place of escape," used only here in the OT) **from** the **storm.**

## B. David's painful betrayal (55:9-15)

**55:9-11.** The psalmist asked God to **confuse the wicked** who oppressed him. The basis of this imprecatory prayer is that **the city** (perhaps Jerusalem) was filled with **violence and strife** and **malice and abuse,** which in turn were caused by **threats and lies** by the wicked.

**55:12-14.** The painful part of his exposure to this destructive violence was that it came through the betrayal of a faithful **companion.** David said he could have borne the oppression of **an enemy** or could have hidden from **a foe** but far worse was the fact that he was betrayed by a **close friend.** David addressed the traitor (**it is you**), recalling how they worshiped the Lord together with the congregation (**throng**).

**55:15.** Thus the psalmist wished God's swift destruction (by **death**) on all his **enemies** (cf. v. 23).

## C. David's personal confidence (55:16-23)

**55:16-21.** Expressing his confidence in the Lord, David said **the LORD saves me.** Knowing this, he would continue to call out to Him in his **distress,** for the Lord, who redeems (*pādâh;* cf. comments on 26:11) him in **battle,** would hear him. God, the sovereign Ruler, hears the prayers of His own; He also hears and knows about the violence of the wicked. Having **no fear of God,** they are defeated by the Lord. Included among those who

do not fear God was David's **companion,** who broke **his covenant** and became deceitfully destructive. This "friend's" talk was **smooth** and **soothing** but animosity was **in his heart.** Four times David spoke of his enemies' **words** being sharp and destructive like **swords** (cf. 57:4; 59:7; 64:3).

**55:22-23.** David's confidence found expression in his words to the saints to entrust (**cast**) their burdens (**cares**) onto **the LORD** (cf. 1 Peter 5:7). God will **never** forsake **the righteous** (cf. Deut. 31:6; Heb. 13:5). But He will destroy (cf. Ps. 55:15) **bloodthirsty and deceitful men** who afflict the righteous.

## Psalm 56

Psalm 56 is a song of trust ascribed to the time of David's visit to Gath (see 1 Sam. 21:10; Ps. 34). The psalm is set "to the tune of 'A Dove on Distant Oaks.' " David asserted that even though his enemies waited to destroy him, he trusted confidently in the Lord who knew his sufferings. His confidence led him to anticipate praising God for deliverance from this danger.

## A. Enemies conspired against David (56:1-7)

David prayed that the Lord would destroy those who conspired to kill him.

**56:1-2.** These verses include his introductory cry (**Be merciful to me, O God**) in his great peril. Proud **slanderers** hotly pursued (cf. 57:3) him **all day long** (cf. 56:5).

**56:3-7.** But because his confidence was **in God, whose word** he praised, he realized that he need **not** fear mere humans (**mortal man** translates *bāśār,* "flesh"; cf. "man" in v. 11). So again the psalmist laid his problem before the Lord and prayed that God would destroy his enemies (vv. 5-7). The problem is that his enemies were continually twisting his **words . . . plotting to** destroy him, and dogging his **steps.** He had no rest from their pursuit.

## B. But God was for him (56:8-13)

David reiterated his confidence that the Lord knew about his suffering and would protect him.

**56:8-9.** He was confident because God knew him intimately, even recording his **tears.** The image of his tears being collected in a wineskin (NIV marg.) means that God did not forget his suffering. Because of that fact, he could say in full confidence, **God is for me.**

**56:10-11.** Here the psalmist reworded the refrain of verse 4 (see comments there). Trusting in God's **word,** he knew that mortal **man** (*'ādām*; a different word for man is used in v. 4) is powerless to thwart **God.**

**56:12-13.** David's confidence led him to anticipate that **God** would deliver him from danger so that he might live (**walk . . . in the light of life**) obediently **before** Him. As in other psalms, David was so confident **God** would deliver him that he wrote in the past tense (**You have delivered me**). So he vowed to praise God for this with **thank offerings.**

## Psalm 57

Psalm 57 resembles the preceding psalm in its message and structure, except that its mood is more triumphant. The superscription attributes the writing to David's experience of hiding from Saul in a cave (cf. the superscription to Ps. 142), but which cave is not known (cf. 1 Sam. 22; 24). The psalm consists of two sections, each ending with a refrain (Ps. 57:5, 11), in which David expressed his desire that God be exalted. David prayed for deliverance from his destructive enemies, and then sang a song of triumph for God's faithful love in expectation that the wicked would be caught in their own devices.

### A. The need for divine intervention (57:1-5)

**57:1-3.** The first stanza (vv. 1-5) is the psalmist's cry that **God** would rescue him. He cried for **mercy** (cf. 56:1) from **God** as he took **refuge in the shadow of** God's **wings** (cf. 17:8; 36:7; 61:4; 63:7; 91:4) **until the disaster** had **passed.** He had no one else to turn to for safety. His trust was well founded, however, for it was God who sent **from heaven . . . His love** (*ḥeseḏ*, "loyal love") **and . . . faithfulness** (cf. 57:10). Because of God's attributes David knew He would deliver him from the hot pursuit (cf. 56:1-2) of the wicked.

**57:4.** David's confident cry to God was followed by a lament about his predicament. He compared his enemies to **lions** (cf. comments on 7:2) and other

ravenous beasts that wanted to devour him. Their **teeth** and **tongues** were like military weapons as they slandered and blasphemed him. (On the tongue being like **swords**; cf. 55:21; 59:7; 64:3.) He deplored being surrounded by taunting, bloodthirsty men.

**57:5.** In this refrain (cf. v. 11) David expressed his desire that God **be exalted . . . above the heavens** and **the earth.** This will happen, of course, when God defeats His enemies and vindicates His righteousness.

### B. The occasion for the song of triumph (57:6-11)

This second stanza is the psalmist's song to God for His loyal love and faithfulness in anticipation of victory.

**57:6.** David spoke again of his predicament but added that he expected his foes' destruction. **They spread a net. . . . they dug a pit . . . but they** had **fallen into it.** This is the fourth time David had written along that line (cf. "pit" in 7:15; and "pit" and "net" in 9:15; 35:8). Of course the language of nets and pits depicted the attempts of the wicked to catch him.

**57:7-11.** These verses are almost identical to 108:1-5. In light of the certain destruction of the wicked, David vowed to **sing** a song of victory. With his faith established in the LORD, he could **praise** Him early in the morning in anticipation of what **God** would do. David said he would praise the Lord's **love** (*ḥeseḏ*, "loyal love") and **faithfulness** (cf. 57:3) where others would hear him.

In the refrain in verse 11 (cf. v. 5), David again expressed his desire that God **be exalted . . . above the heavens** and **the earth.**

## Psalm 58

David denounced unrighteous judges who were wickedly destructive in their work. He called on God to destroy them swiftly and irrevocably. Then the righteous would be strengthened in their cause.

### A. Rebuke of unjust judges (58:1-5)

By means of questions and answers, David decried the effect of the land's unjust judges.

**58:1.** David questioned the leaders' integrity: **Do you rulers . . . speak just-**

ly? **Do you judge uprightly?** Because the rulers and judges were unrighteous, justice in the nation was perverted.

**58:2-5.** *No* is the answer to the question in verse 1. They did not do justice; they planned **injustice** and **violence.** Later Micah wrote along the same lines about the leaders in his day (cf. Micah 3:1-3, 9-11; 6:12). These **wicked** judges went **astray** from **birth,** speaking **lies.** They were like serpents that poison without concern for **the charmer.** In other words they were deliberately destructive and deaf to remonstrance. They would not listen to correction.

### B. Swift judgment on the judges (58:6-9)

**58:6-8.** David called on God to wipe out the wicked judges. He boldly asked God to **break** their **teeth,** that is, to keep them from communicating their injustice. They were ferocious as **lions** (cf. comments on 7:2), whose teeth, like **fangs,** needed to be torn out. David also prayed that the judges would meet a sudden end, by (a) vanishing as **water** evaporates, so that **their arrows** (i.e., their words) would be ineffectual; (b) melting away as a snail perishes in a drought; and (c) dying suddenly like **a stillborn** who does **not see the sun.**

**58:9.** The destruction of **the wicked** will be swift. A fire that burns **thorns** or brambles dies quickly (cf. comments on Ecc. 7:6). **Before . . . pots can** be placed on the fire, it goes out. God will sweep the wicked **away** before their malicious evil, like a fire, can finish its work.

### C. Encouragement for the just (58:10-11)

**58:10-11.** David anticipated the joy of those who will see God's justice carried out on the unjust judges. Again the language is metaphorical and hyperbolic; **the righteous** bathing **their feet in the blood of the wicked** suggests a military victory.

David also anticipated that this victory would be recognized as proof that **God** will reward righteousness and judge **the earth.** People will not be left to the decisions of unjust judges forever.

## Psalm 59

This is a prayer by David for defense from bloodthirsty men. It has the familiar motif of unshaken trust in God. David prayed that the Lord would make him safe and secure from his enemies, and humiliate them so that all would recognize God's sovereignty.

The setting of the psalm is identified as Saul's siege of "David's house" (1 Sam. 19:8-11a). Michal, however, helped David escape through a window (1 Sam. 19:11b-14).

### A. Conspiracy against the innocent (59:1-5)

**59:1-5.** Again David prayed for deliverance from a desperate situation. He asked to be saved **from evildoers . . . bloodthirsty men** who lay **in wait** to kill him, who conspired **against** him, even though he had **done** nothing **wrong. God,** David said, should **punish all** who act so treacherously.

### B. Triumph over treachery (59:6-10)

**59:6-7.** David compared his enemies to **snarling . . . dogs** that **prowl about** at night (cf. v. 14). By their words and deeds they showed themselves to be arrogant, thinking that not even God heard them. Their words were sharp and offensive like **swords** (cf. 55:21; 57:4; 64:3).

**59:8-10. But** the psalmist was confident that his enemies would not succeed. He knew that **God** mocks the pagans (cf. 2:1, 4). Therefore he would **watch for** God, His **Strength** (cf. 59:17 and comments on 18:1) and **Fortress** (*miśgōb*; cf. 59:16-17 and comments on 46:7), to rescue him and enable him to see the downfall of the wicked who slandered him.

### C. Demonstration of justice (59:11-13)

**59:11.** David prayed that the LORD, his **Shield** (cf. comments on 3:3), would punish the wicked in a way that people would learn that He is sovereign. The wicked should **not** simply perish, because they would be forgotten. Rather, they should be made to **wander** in humiliation as outcasts and fugitives.

**59:12-13.** David also prayed that their proud **curses and lies** be exposed, that they be **caught in** the act and consumed so others would know **that God rules** in justice.

### D. Anticipation of praise (59:14-17)

**59:14-17.** David was confident that despite the presence of his enemies (whom he again compared to **snarling . . . dogs**; cf. v. 6) he would praise God for **strength** (cf. v. 9), **love,** and security (as his **Fortress**; cf. v. 9 and comments on 46:7, and his **Refuge,** *mānôs,* also used in 142:5).

## Psalm 60

Psalm 60 is a didactic psalm ("for teaching") based on David's experiences in military victories. It is a prayer for victory, for when David was waging war in the north against the Arameans, Edom invaded Judah. The psalm may have been written when or soon after David, Joab, and Abishai crushed Edom (2 Sam. 8:13; 1 Kings 11:15-16; 1 Chron. 18:12). (See comments on 1 Chron. 18:12 where the number of Edomites said to have been killed was 18,000, whereas this psalm's superscription has "12,000.")

Because David knew that both victory and defeat come from the Lord, he prayed for divine aid for victory over Israel's enemies. He was assured that God would help him triumph.

### A. Prayer for deliverance (60:1-5)

**60:1-3.** The psalmist turned to the Lord to ask for restoration from Israel's disastrous predicament—a disaster brought on by God's anger. The Lord had **torn . . . open** the **land** and staggered David's troops. Because the disaster of defeat was brought by the Lord, He was the only One who could bring them victory.

**60:4-5.** The meaning of verse 4 is difficult to determine, but it seems to be reproachfully sarcastic: God had mustered His people to war (**raised a banner**) but then He led them to defeat (fleeing before the enemy's **bow**). Israel was championing God's cause, but God was letting them get defeated.

Therefore David asked God to deliver by His power (His **right hand**; cf. Ex. 15:6, 12; Pss. 20:6; 45:4; 89:13; 108:6) **those** He loves. Psalm 60:5-12 is identical to 108:6-13.

### B. Assurance of triumph (60:6-8)

**60:6-8.** The psalmist quoted the words of the Lord that assured them victory. God had declared that because all tribes and lands are His, He would deliver His people and subjugate their enemies. He would **parcel out Shechem**

**and . . . the Valley of Succoth,** that is, He would give the land to His people. Twenty miles east of Shechem, in the tribe of Ephraim, is Succoth, a city in the tribe of Gad, near the Jordan River. **Ephraim,** a centrally located and large tribe in Israel, was strong. Like a **helmet** she was a defense for the nation. **Judah** was the **scepter** of the Lord, that is, David (from Judah) was God's ruler even though he was threatened. Israel's enemies would be reduced to menial labor. **Gilead,** east of the Jordan River, and **Manasseh,** a tribe on both sides of the river, belonged to Him. **Moab** would be like a **washbasin** brought to the conqueror. **Edom** would be like a slave to whom God, like a warrior, would throw his shoe. **Philistia** would hear God's triumphant **shout** after David's victory.

### C. Confidence in God (60:9-12)

**60:9-12.** Through three rhetorical questions the psalmist acknowledged that the Lord, the One who had rejected them in the battle (cf. vv. 1-4), would **lead** them to victory. But because human effort is futile, David prayed that **God** would **give** them **aid against the enemy,** confident that **with God . . . victory** was theirs.

Thus it is clear that victory or defeat belongs to God. When disaster comes, one's only hope is God.

## Psalm 61

David, feeling faint and inadequate, found assurance in the strength of his Rock and encouragement in God's enduring promises. Many have suggested that this psalm describes one of David's narrow escapes in the rocky wilderness, but no historical setting is given.

### A. Lead me to the rock (61:1-2)

**61:1-2.** The psalmist petitioned the Lord for strength and security because his **heart** was overwhelmed. He asked that God **lead** him **to the rock that is higher than** he was. "Rock" denotes a place of safety; but David wanted to be led to a rock he could not reach by himself. If **God** did this, he would be safe.

### B. I long to dwell in Your tent (61:3-7)

David expressed his confidence in the Lord who had promised strength and security.

**61:3-4.** David found comfort in the character of the Lord. As his **Refuge** (*maḥseh*, "shelter from danger"; cf. comments on 14:6) and high **Tower** God had defended him against his foes. Now, however, the psalmist longed **to dwell** in God's presence (**in His tent** and under His **wings**; cf. 17:8; 36:7; 57:1; 63:7; 91:4, like a bird protected by its mother). This is the most secure place of **refuge**.

**61:5-7.** Then on the basis of God's promise to him, David prayed for protection in God's presence. **God** had **heard** him and had **given** him **the heritage of those who fear** His **name**; true Israelites who feared the Lord remained loyal to David's kingship and did not rebel. Thus he prayed that God would extend **the king's** (his own) **life** and that God would continue to **protect him** by His **love** (*ḥesed*, "loyal love") **and faithfulness,** or His faithful love.

## C. Then I will sing praise (61:8)

**61:8.** The king vowed to **sing** to and **praise** the Lord for His protection over him. Once delivered, he would **fulfill** his **vows** (cf. v. 5), praising the Lord daily.

# Psalm 62

This psalm reflects David's confident trust in the Lord in spite of opposition. In silence he waited for God, his Strength and Security, to deliver him from his deceitful enemies. The psalm contrasts the security of trusting God with the insecurity of relying on human devices. The psalm falls into three stanzas of four verses each.

## A. Rest in God when enemies assault (62:1-4)

**62:1-2.** The theme of this psalm is stressed in verse 1 when David wrote that he waited in silence for God. **My soul finds rest in God alone** (cf. v. 5) is literally, "Only to God is my soul silence." Only to God did he look with complete calmness. He knew that since God was his **Rock** (cf. comments on 18:2), **Salvation,** and **Fortress** (cf. comments on 46:7), he could not **be shaken** (cf. 62:6 and comments on 15:5). As warriors used to feel at ease in an impregnable fortress, so David rested in the Lord.

**62:3-4.** This confidence led David to marvel at the attempt of some people to thrust **him down.** The image of a **tottering fence** suggests weakness and susceptibility. As men try to **topple** a city wall or fence, the wicked attempted to overthrow David whom they thought was vulnerable. They hoped to accomplish this through **lies.** They blessed David **with their** words, **but in their hearts they** cursed him.

## B. Trust in God at all times (62:5-8)

**62:5-8.** Repeating that he waited in silence for the Lord, David confessed that his only **hope** was **in God** (cf. 25:5, 21; 33:20; 39:7; 71:5). Again he affirmed that God was His Source of safety (**Rock**), deliverance (**Salvation**), and security (**Fortress;** cf. 62:2) and that therefore he was secure (he would **not be shaken;** cf. comments on 15:5). God was his **Salvation** and his Glory (**Honor**). Without God's innumerable deliverances, David would have been crushed by his foes.

Therefore the psalmist instructed the saints to **pour out** their **hearts** before Him in continual **trust,** realizing He is their **Refuge** (*maḥseh*, "shelter from danger"; cf. 14:6; 46:1; 61:3; 71:7; 73:28; 91:2, 9).

## C. God will reward each person (62:9-12)

**62:9-10.** The psalmist warned that it is foolish to trust in humans. He described how transitory life is, whether a person is of low or high position. People **are nothing** but **a breath** (*hebel*, "a vapor"; cf. 39:5, 11; 144:4 and comments on Ecc. 1:2). They are so insignificant that, if weighed, the scales would not even move. Their might is powerless against God. Therefore one should not trust in the powerful advances of the wicked. **Riches** are not to be trusted either (cf. Prov. 11:28; 23:5; 27:24).

**62:11-12.** The psalmist contrasted this with the fact that **God** has declared that the power is His. David **heard** God say two things: that He is **strong** and **loving.** So justice will be meted out to everybody. How much better then to find rest in the powerful **God** than in human devices.

# Psalm 63

The faith expressed in Psalms 61 and 62 reaches a climax in this marvelous hymn of David, written in the wilderness. It refers to a time when David, as king, was separated from the ark, the formal place of worship (2 Sam. 15:25). The psalmist satisfied the longing of his soul for worship by praising God for His loyal love even in his distress. As a result, he confidently anticipated a time of joy when his enemies would be stopped.

## A. Thirsting for God (63:1-2)

**63:1.** David's experience in the **dry,** waterless wilderness prompted him to think of the thirst of his **soul** for **God.** Because his soul thirsted for and longed for his **God,** he wrote, **Earnestly I seek You.** This may also be translated, "Early will I seek You." This has prompted many believers to read this psalm in the mornings. To seek someone early suggests doing so earnestly.

**63:2.** David's longing for God came because of his vision of God's **power** (strength) **and . . . glory.** This awareness of God came before his enemies had driven him into the wilderness. The ark was the symbol of the Lord's glory and strength (cf. 1 Sam. 4:21). David had had the joy of seeing the evidence of God's presence **in the sanctuary,** the tabernacle in Jerusalem.

## B. Satisfying the soul with praise (63:3-8)

**63:3-4.** In spite of his separation from the sanctuary, David found satisfaction in praising God, for it brought joy and comfort to his heart. He praised God for his loyal **love,** which **is better than life.** This was the **praise** of one who, when in a dry desert (v. 1), thought more of God than of life-sustaining water.

**63:5-6.** Moreover, praising God would satisfy his **soul** as much as **the richest of foods** would satisfy his body. **Praise** to Him gave vitality to his spiritual life. Praising God is the natural expression of a heart that meditates on God, a heart that thinks of Him **through . . . the night.**

**63:7-8.** The immediate cause of the psalmist's meditation and praise was the safety and support he found in God. **Because** God was his **Help** (see comments on 30:10) and Strength (His **right hand** upheld him), David stayed **close to** Him **in the shadow of** His **wings** (cf. 17:8; 36:7; 57:1; 61:4; 91:4) and continued to praise Him by singing.

## C. Rejoicing in victory (63:9-11)

**63:9-11.** David turned from his thoughts on praise as the food of the soul to his present situation. But in view of what he knew of God, he fully anticipated that his enemies would **be destroyed** and suffer ignominious deaths. For this deliverance he, **the king,** would **rejoice in God,** as **all** who are loyal to Him have occasion to do. **Praise,** then, is essential for one's spiritual life. It should stem spontaneously from God's intervention on behalf of a believer. Praise, in other words, is an evidence that God is at work, meeting His people's needs.

## Psalm 64

This is another of David's prayers for God's judgment on the enemies of the righteous. David prayed for protection from those who conspired against him. He then delineated their malicious plans against the righteous. He was convinced that God would turn these schemes on the wicked themselves.

## A. The prayer for protection (64:1-2)

**64:1-2.** David introduced this psalm with a cry of **complaint** to **God.** Lamenting that a **crowd of evildoers** had conspired against him, he told God he needed His protection.

## B. The problem of malicious schemes (64:3-6)

**64:3-4.** David described how the wicked prepare their attack on **the innocent.** He compared their speech to **swords** (cf. 55:21; 57:4; 59:7) and **arrows**—weapons that pierce and destroy. Their slanderous attacks came **suddenly** like an **ambush.** They were confident in what they did; they attacked others **without fear.**

**64:5-6.** Moreover, the wicked encouraged **each other in** their **plans** to do injustice. They thought they had a **perfect** crime, assuming they could sin without being discovered. This, David concluded, shows how **cunning** (cf. 83:3) a human **heart** can be.

## C. The prophecy of divine judgment (64:7-10)

**64:7-8a.** David predicted that God would intervene and strike them. They might be cunning (v. 6) **but God will shoot them with arrows.** This is justice in which the punishment fits the crime. Their **tongues,** like arrows against others (v. 3), will be turned **against them** by God, and their slanderous plans (cf. vv. 5-6) will actually **bring** themselves **to ruin.**

**64:8b-10.** Everyone **who** would **see them** would **scorn** them for their evil plans. Moreover, seeing the destruction of the wicked, people would **fear** (cf. "fear" in v. 4) **the LORD** and tell of His **works.** God's judgment would have a lasting effect on people. As for **the righteous,** they will have reason to **rejoice,** to renew their trust in Him as their **Refuge,** and to **praise Him.**

## Psalm 65

David may have written this psalm to be sung annually when the first grain of the year's barley harvest was brought to the Lord and waved by the priest as a dedication offering (see Lev. 23:9-14 and comments there). It is a song of harvest blessing in celebration of God's goodness to His people. In this "song" David declared that God, who hears prayers, atones for sin, a provision that results in God's bounty. David also announced that God uses His supernatural power to aid His people. Based on these displays of God's good pleasure, the songwriter anticipated God's blessing on the land, which would bring the people prosperity.

### A. Blessing in God's courts (65:1-4)

**65:1-4.** The psalmist expressed his conviction that when **God** atones for sin He blesses abundantly. The psalm begins with a mention of mankind's preparation to **praise** God because He hears **prayer** (vv. 1-2). The occasion for the prayer was apparently their overwhelming **sins,** but God **atoned for** their **transgressions** (v. 3). One who thereby is brought **near to** the presence of the Lord will experience happiness (he is **blessed;** cf. 1:1) and satisfaction (**with . . . good things,** 65:4). Atonement for sin made possible the praise of the people and their entrance on festival days into the **courts** of the tabernacle (the word for **temple** is *hêkāl,* a magnificent house; cf. comments on 5:7).

### B. Awesome deeds of God's power (65:5-8)

**65:5-8.** The psalmist was confident that **God** answers prayer; He is **the hope** of people in the farthest regions **of the earth.**

God's answers to prayer often come by **awesome deeds;** this is natural for God. He demonstrated His **power** and **strength** by forming **the mountains** and soothing **the seas** and **their waves.** God's **wonders** bring **fear** to people and **songs of joy** throughout the world (**where morning dawns and evening fades**).

### C. Abundant provision of harvest (65:9-13)

**65:9-13.** The psalmist was convinced that Israel would have an abundantly good year when **God** poured out His blessings on the land. Verse 9a summarizes God's **care for the land,** and verses 9b-13a develop the theme of God's blessings on the land. God's control of the **water** produces the **grain** (v. 9b); God's rain **showers** prepare the land for produce (v. 10); God's blessing produces an abundant harvest (v. 11); God causes uncultivated areas to be enriched with grass (v. 12). In a word, the **flocks** and **grain** flourish under His blessing (v. 13a).

The psalmist concluded that all of nature shouts **for joy** (v. 13b), that is, abundant fruitfulness testifies to God's blessing.

## Psalm 66

This is another psalm of thanksgiving to the Lord. It too, like Psalm 65, may have been written to celebrate a festive occasion, but the precise occasion is unknown. In the first section (vv. 1-12) the psalmist (not specified as David) wrote in the first person plural ("us," "our"), and in the second section (vv. 13-20) he wrote in the first person singular ("I," "me," "my"). In the psalm the nation acknowledged God's deliverance and called on the nations to join her in praising the Lord.

### A. The nation praised God (66:1-12)

Verses 1-9 are addressed to the nations, and verses 10-12 are addressed to God. The psalmist called on nations everywhere to praise the Lord for His great deliverance of Israel.

**66:1-4. All the earth,** that is, everyone on it, was urged to **praise** the Lord by shouting (v. 1), singing (vv. 2, 4), and speaking (vv. 3-4). They were encouraged to be jubilant because of His **awe-**

some works (cf. v. 5), which resulted in His **enemies** cringing **before** His **great . . . power.**

**66:5-7.** The psalmist then called on the nations to **see** that God's **awesome . . . works** (cf. v. 3) on **behalf** of man demonstrate His sovereignty. Israel's crossing the Red Sea and the Jordan River were notable acts of God's power of deliverance. Therefore people should realize that **He rules forever by His power,** putting down rebels and delivering His people.

**66:8-9.** Israel then called on the **peoples** of the earth to bless **God** because by these and other awesome deeds **He** had **preserved** them.

**66:10-12.** Here the nation acknowledged that **God** had **tested** them with all kinds of burdens and oppressions, but finally **brought** them **to** the **place of** abundant blessing. This acknowledged that it was God who led them all the way and delivered them.

### B. The psalmist led their praise (66:13-20)

The psalmist, the leader of the congregation, offered animal sacrifices and declarative praise to God.

**66:13-15.** In these verses he addressed God and in verses 16-20 he addressed the congregation. The psalmist said he would go **to** God's **temple** and offer **burnt offerings.** This would **fulfill** a vow he made **when** he cried out of distress (**trouble**).

**66:16-20.** Here he addressed the congregation in praise to **God** (a declarative praise). He told them that God responded to his prayer (**I cried out to Him**) and **God** delivered him. However, it **would not have** happened that way if he had clung to **sin** (cf. Prov. 28:9; Isa. 59:2). But **God** *did* listen and answer his **prayer.** The point is clear: God's people, when in need, should purify their hearts and pray to Him. Then He will answer and not withhold **His** loyal **love,** and other believers may praise and exalt Him.

### Psalm 67

Having prayed for God's mercy and blessing so that His saving ways may be known (Ps. 66), the psalmist now called on the people to praise God for His righteous judgments so that they might enjoy His bounty.

### A. May God be gracious (67:1-2)

**67:1-2.** The writer asked for God's merciful dealings by using part of the priestly blessing (v. 1; see Num. 6:24-26). God's making **His face shine** on them refers to divine favor and approval (cf. comments on Ps. 4:6). The purpose of this prayer is that God's saving **ways** would **be known** throughout the world. For if God saved them, others would hear of it.

### B. May the people praise Him (67:3-7)

**67:3-7.** In verses 3-4 the psalmist called on people to **praise . . . God** with **joy** because He rules **justly.** In verses 5-7 he called on them to **praise . . . God** so that He in turn would **bless** them by giving them a bountiful **harvest.** Recognizing God's blessings encourages people to **fear** and worship **Him.**

### Psalm 68

This is "a song" celebrating God's triumphal ascent to Mount Zion. If the superscription of Davidic authorship is correct, then the occasion may have been David's conquering the city (2 Sam. 5:6-8), or moving the ark to Zion (2 Sam. 6), or some triumphal procession after a victory, or his victories in general. Some scholars disregard the superscription, and relate the psalm to some other occasion such as the Jews' return from the Exile, though there are no clear historical references to this in the poem. Its figurative language makes the psalm adaptable to several occasions. No doubt the psalm, if written by David, would have been used at subsequent victories. The greatest triumph to which the psalm is related is Christ's Ascension, for Psalm 68:18 was paraphrased and applied to Him by Paul (Eph. 4:8).

The psalmist reviewed the history of Israel from the wilderness wanderings to the occupation and conquest of the land. He emphasized God's choice of Zion, which resulted in Israel's taking many Canaanites as captives and the Israelites receiving gifts or spoils from the captives. This is the reason he sang praises: God was marching triumphantly on behalf of the oppressed. David called on others to join him in praising their strong Lord.

## A. Fear and praise over God's triumph (68:1-6)

**68:1-3.** David prayed that **God** would show His awesome power. The words in verse 1 are almost the same as the words Moses said whenever the Israelites set out on their march in the wilderness (Num. 10:35). When **God** arises in power **the wicked perish** like **smoke . . . blown away by the wind** and as **wax melts before the fire. The righteous,** safe from the wicked, **rejoice** greatly (cf. Prov. 28:12; 29:2).

**68:4-6.** David invited the people to **praise** in song the One **who rides on the clouds** (cf. v. 33; 104:3; Isa. 19:1), a poetic description of God's exalted majesty, chosen as a polemic against a similar epithet for Baal. **God** is worthy of praise because of His triumphant work: He delivers and comforts the downtrodden (**fatherless** and **widows**) and oppressed (**prisoners**), while leaving **the rebellious** desolate in the desert.

## B. Remembrance of God's triumphant conquest (68:7-18)

The psalmist now traced the development of the Lord's "movement" from the wilderness to His occupation of Zion.

**68:7-10.** When **God** led His **people . . . through the** wilderness **wasteland,** earthquakes and **rain** occurred (cf. 77:16-19). Weary in the desert, His people (called His **inheritance;** cf. comments on Deut. 4:20) were **refreshed** by the rainfall. And God graciously **provided for the poor.**

**68:11-14.** The psalmist then rehearsed the victorious occupation of **the land** of Canaan from which **kings** (vv. 12, 14) were driven out. Verse 13, though difficult to understand precisely, seems to refer to Judges 5:16 which speaks of reproval of some Israelites who were remiss in supporting the Conquest. While some Israelites were sleeping at night in the open air, refusing to engage in battle, God blessed His **dove** (i.e., Israel; cf. Ps. 74:19). Their prosperity (probably spoils taken from defeated enemies) was like **silver** and **gold** on the **wings** and **feathers** of a dove. The **snow . . . on Zalmon** may refer to a snowfall on a mountain near Shechem (cf. Jud. 9:48) which helped Israel rout the enemy. Or it may suggest that God's victory was as refreshing as freshly fallen snow.

**68:15-18.** These verses speak of the Lord's choosing Zion above other **mountains** and of His triumphant entry into it like a conqueror. The great **mountains of** the land **of Bashan** refer to the Hermon mountain range, only a few miles north of Bashan. Choosing Zion for His dwelling place, God entered the city with a vast company (**thousands of thousands**) of angelic hosts, pictured here as riding in chariots. Thus the Lord went all the way **from Sinai** (cf. v. 8) to **His sanctuary** in Zion. His entrance into Jerusalem (when David conquered it, 2 Sam. 5:6-8, or when David moved the ark to Jerusalem, 2 Sam. 6) was like a mighty conqueror ascending **on high** with **captives,** receiving tribute **from** the vanquished, **the rebellious.**

Psalm 68:18 was referred to by Paul in Ephesians 4:8 (cf. comments there). However, rather than quoting the Hebrew, Paul apparently followed the Jewish interpretation of the day (the Targum), which paraphrased this verse as follows: "You did ascend to the firmament, O Prophet Moses! You led captivity captive; you taught the words of the Law; you gave [not 'received,' as in the Heb.] gifts to the sons of men." (This interpretation saw Moses as God's representative.) Paul followed this Jewish exegesis because it explained that the conqueror *distributed* the gifts to His loyal subjects. The apostle applied that idea to Christ's victory over the forces of evil and His granting spiritual gifts (cf. Eph. 4:11) to those on His side. By this analogy (based more on the Jewish interpretation of the psalm than on the exact Heb. wording) Paul emphasized the greatness of believers' spiritual victory in Christ.

## C. The effect of God's victory (68:19-31)

**68:19-23.** David praised **the Lord . . . God** who **bears** believers' **burdens** and **saves** them **from death.** David was convinced that God's entrance into Zion on behalf of His people would result in the complete destruction of His and her **enemies.** He would **bring** Israel **from** dangers (as those experienced in **Bashan** when she conquered Og, Num. 21:33-35) and from other awesome experiences (as when she crossed the Red Sea, suggested by the words **the depths of the sea;** cf. Isa. 51:10). God would cause Israel to be victorious over her enemies, pictured as putting her **feet in** their **blood** while **dogs** licked the blood (cf. 1 Kings 22:38).

**68:24-27.** God's triumphal entrance **into** Zion and **the sanctuary** is again described here, pictured like a victory parade with **singers** and other **musicians.** All who saw God's victorious entrance should **praise** Him. The tribes of **Benjamin** and Judah, one small and one large, represent the southern portion of the kingdom and **Zebulun** and **Naphtali** represent the northern portion. Perhaps the last two are mentioned because of the praise bestowed on them in Deborah and Barak's song (Jud. 5:18).

**68:28-31.** The writer then asked **God** to demonstrate His **power** again. Seeing His **strength** and His **temple,** pagan **kings** would pay tribute in submission to Him. **The beast among the reeds** (v. 30) is a symbolic representation of the enemy, perhaps **Egypt** (v. 31). **Bulls** suggests Egypt's strength. But **envoys** from this people and from **Cush,** her neighbor to the south, eventually would be **humbled** and scattered, and would **submit . . . to God.**

### D. Call to praise (68:32-35)

**68:32-35.** The psalmist called the nations to **sing praise** to the Rider of **the . . . skies** (cf. v. 4), in recognition of His **power** and **majesty** displayed in **Israel** and **in the skies** and given **to His people.**

## Psalm 69

David pleaded with God to rescue him from destruction because he bore reproach and rejection by his brethren for the Lord's sake. Praying that God would requite the inhumanity of his oppressors, he looked forward to universal praise and restoration.

### A. David's enemies hated him without a cause (69:1-4)

**69:1-4.** In his troubles the psalmist turned to the Lord. He used the imagery of drowning to describe his being at the brink of death, and would have died if **God** had not rescued him. His problem was brought on by numberless **enemies** who sought **to destroy** him. They hated him for no **reason** (cf. 35:19) and **forced** him to give up his possessions (which he **did not steal**).

### B. He was zealous for God's house (69:5-12)

**69:5-12.** David sought to motivate **God** to act on his behalf, for he was suffering because of his zeal for the Lord. Even though he was a sinner (v. 5) that was not the cause of his problem this time. Rather he was suffering **for** the Lord's **sake** (v. 7). His own relatives hated him even though he had **zeal** for the Lord (vv. 8-9). Their **insults** against God were directed to him. When he was in grief, he fasted (a sign of mourning; cf. Jud. 20:26; 1 Sam. 31:13; 2 Sam. 12:16; 1 Kings 21:27; Neh. 1:4) and wore **sackcloth** (another sign of mourning; cf. Gen. 37:34; 1 Kings 21:27; Neh. 9:1; Es. 4:1-4; Pss. 30:11; 35:13; Lam. 2:10; Dan. 9:3). Even then his enemies (including judges, those **who** sat **at the gate**) and **drunkards** sang derisively about him.

### C. He prayed to the Lord (69:13-28)

**69:13-18.** The psalmist petitioned the **LORD** to save him from imminent death. In God's timing (**the time of Your favor**) and out of His **love** (*ḥeseḏ*, vv. 13, 16) and **mercy** He should **quickly** (cf. comments on 31:2) **rescue** (69:14, 18) and **redeem** (*pāḏâh*; cf. comments on 26:11) him from his misery and **trouble.** Again he used the image of miry **waters** that would drown him (cf. 69:2).

**69:19-21.** David found confidence in the knowledge that God knew of their reproach (cf. **scorn** in v. 10) and mistreatment of him (giving him gall [*rō'š,* possibly a poisonous plant] to eat and **vinegar** to drink). The word for **food** (*bārût*) means a meal given "to a mourner by sympathetic friends. Its use emphasizes the hypocrisy of their conduct" (A. Cohen, *The Psalms,* p. 219).

**69:22-28.** In his imprecation against his enemies, David prayed that their own food would cause their downfall, that **their eyes** would **be darkened so they** could not **see,** and that **their backs** would **be bent** in grief. He asked that they would be overtaken by God's **wrath** and their residences made desolate because of their deaths. These punishments were just, because **they** persecuted God's people (v. 26).

David then prayed that God would find them guilty and blot them **out of the book of life** (cf. Rev. 20:15). In the Bible the opening of books speaks of judgment (cf. Dan. 7:10; Rev. 20:12). It is as if God "listed" the names of the righteous. But of course in His omniscience God does not need written records. The point is that the wicked have no share in God's eternal blessings.

### D. The Lord hears the needy (69:29-36)

**69:29-33.** David again prayed in his distress that the LORD would be His salvation (cf. v. 13) and would protect him. Confident that God would deliver, he vowed to praise the Lord. David knew that thanksgiving was more pleasing to God than offering an ox or a bull. Horns were a sign that the animal was mature; only animals with split hoofs could be sacrificed (Lev. 11:3). The poor and the needy (cf. Ps. 70:5) would see God's rescue of David and be glad and encouraged. They would be assured that the Lord would hear their cry too since He does not despise His own.

**69:34-36.** David called for universal praise to God in anticipation of His delivering the nation, and the people's settling in the land.

In this psalm the prevailing tone is prayer for deliverance from suffering for the Lord's sake. Parts of the psalm were applied to the life of Christ: hatred against Him (v. 4; cf. John 15:25), His zeal (Ps. 69:9; cf. John 2:17), and vinegar given to Him on the cross (Ps. 69:21; cf. Matt. 27:48). So this psalm is partly typological of Christ. He is the epitome of the righteous who are persecuted for their zeal in doing God's will.

## Psalm 70

This short psalm records a prayer by David for a quick rescue from his present evil plight. It also anticipates the rejoicing that will follow. The heading says it is "a petition" (lit., "to bring to remembrance"; cf. the title to Ps. 38). Perhaps this was a note that the psalm was to be used in connection with the offerings (cf. 1 Chron. 16:4), which would help "remind" the Lord of the petitioner's request.

### A. Hasten to help me (70:1-3)

**70:1-3.** The psalmist cried out to God to help him quickly (cf. v. 5 and comments on 31:2). Enemies tried to bring him to ruin (cf. 35:4, 8; 38:12). So his plea was urgent. He prayed that those who

had shamed and disgraced him (69:19) would themselves be in shame (70:2-3; 71:13) and turned back in disgrace (cf. 6:10; 40:14), no longer able to scorn him (Aha!).

### B. Let God be exalted (70:4-5)

**70:4-5.** The psalmist then prayed that all who seek the LORD and love His salvation would be glad and would say, Let God be exalted! Calling himself poor and needy (cf. 40:17; see comments on 37:14), he prayed for hasty deliverance (cf. 70:1). God was His only source of help (cf. comments on 30:10).

## Psalm 71

Psalm 71 combines elements from other psalms (22; 31; 35; 40). Yet it is a unit in itself expressing the faith of an older person throughout most of his lifetime. In response to his prayer the psalmist, who is not identified, anticipated the same marvelous response the Lord had given him all his life. So, vowing to praise God as he had always done, he confidently asked to be delivered from those who sought his harm and derided him for his faith.

### A. Prayer for help from the Lord (71:1-4)

**71:1-4.** The psalmist turned to the LORD, praying for deliverance from the wicked. This request is filled with expressions of his confidence in the Lord's ability to save: God was his Refuge (v. 1), Rock of refuge (v. 3; cf. 31:2), and Fortress (the same Heb. word is used in 18:2; 31:4; 91:2). The psalmist wanted continued safety and security (71:3) along with rescue from wicked people (v. 4).

### B. Prayer from a lifelong trust (71:5-13)

**71:5-8.** The psalmist reaffirmed his confidence in the LORD in spite of his afflictions. God was his Hope (cf. 25:5, 21; 33:20; 39:7; 62:5), the One in whom he trusted from his youth up (cf. 71:17). Though many wondered at him (he was to them like a portent), he would continue to trust in the Lord, his strong Refuge and to praise Him (vv. 6, 8) and His splendor (cf. comments on 29:2). (The Heb. word for "refuge" here is *maḥseh*, "shelter from danger," also used in 14:6; 46:1; 61:3; 62:7-8; 73:28; 91:2, 9. It differs from the verb in 71:1 trans. "I have taken refuge" [*ḥāsâh,* related to the noun *maḥseh*] and from the word rendered "refuge" in v. 3 [*mā'ôn,* "dwelling"; cf. 90:1; 91:9].)

**71:9-13.** The psalmist then prayed for continued care (**do not forsake me;** cf. v. 18) in his **old** age, for many sought to harm him. They thought **God** had **forsaken him**—a rather strange presumption!—and supposed they could **seize him** and kill him. So the psalmist asked that God **quickly** (cf. comments on 31:2) help him and put them to **shame** (cf. 71:24), **scorn, and disgrace** (cf. 70:2-3).

### C. Continuation of a life of praise (71:14-24)

Because the aging psalmist had trusted the Lord all his life, he vowed to continue to praise God for future deliverances.

**71:14-18.** The writer expressed his determination to **hope** in and **praise** God for His **righteousness,** fathomless **salvation,** and **mighty** saving **acts** (cf. v. 24).

His life, from his **youth** up (cf. v. 5) had been filled with praise for God's **marvelous deeds.** Now **when** he was **old** (cf. v. 9) he still desired to praise Him, but **God** must not **forsake** him (cf. v. 9) if he was to **declare** God's **power.**

**71:19-21.** The psalmist rehearsed some of the great things God had done for him. In **righteousness** (cf. vv. 2, 15) God had **done** many **great things** (v. 19). Therefore He is incomparable. The rhetorical question, **Who, O God, is like You?** is asked several times in the Psalms, with slight variations in wording (cf. 35:10; 77:13; 89:6; 113:5; also note Ex. 15:11; Micah 7:18).

God had shown the aging psalmist that He, being able to deliver from **troubles,** would **restore** his **life again,** bringing him up **from the depths of the earth,** that is, from the point of death (cf. Pss. 30:1; 130:1). Therefore he was confident that God would **honor** and **comfort** him **once again.**

**71:22-24.** In these closing verses the psalmist vowed to **praise . . . God,** by singing, by playing musical instruments (**the harp** and **the lyre**—apparently both were stringed instruments—each mentioned a number of times in Pss.), by shouting, and by telling (cf. v. 15) of God's **acts** (cf. vv. 16-17). The title **Holy One of Israel,** used frequently in the

Book of Isaiah, occurs only three times in the Book of Psalms (71:22; 78:41; 89:18). This **praise** would last **all day long** because God would put all his enemies to **shame** (cf. 71:13).

### Psalm 72

Two psalms (72; 127) are attributed to "Solomon." If Psalm 72 is his, it may describe his reign. Also it speaks of the millennial reign of the Messiah. The psalm describes the blessings that flow from the righteousness of God's theocratic ruler. The psalmist fully expected that the king would reign in righteousness and peace on behalf of the oppressed, and that his dominion would extend over many kings, from sea to sea. The psalmist prayed for the blessing of peace and prosperity, basing his appeal on the fact that the king is a savior of the oppressed and is therefore worthy of honor, power, and dominion.

### A. Prayer for righteous judgments (72:1-7)

**72:1-4.** The psalm opens with a prayer that God would give **the king** divine ability to **judge** righteously (vv. 1-2). The psalmist anticipated that the king, ruling **in righteousness** (vv. 1-3 each include the word **righteousness**), would **bring prosperity** (cf. v. 7) and peace. Also he would judge on behalf of **the afflicted** (cf. v. 12) and **the needy** (cf. vv. 12-13) and punish those who exploit the poor.

**72:5-7.** Preferable to the words **He will endure** (from the LXX) is the translation, "You will be feared" (from the Heb.; cf. NIV marg.). Taken that way, the verse refers not to the human king but to God who endures **through all generations.** Or if the NIV rendering is accepted, then the thought may be that the king's name or reputation endures for generations (cf. v. 17). When a king's reign is righteous, his rule is refreshing to the people. **Like rain** on soil, an upright ruler enables **the righteous** to **flourish** and **prosperity** to **abound.**

### B. Anticipation of his dominion (72:8-11)

**72:8-11.** The psalmist anticipated that his kingdom would extend **from sea to sea** and **from** the Euphrates **River** around the world. People who live in the wilderness would **bow before him, and his enemies** would be humiliated in subjection (**lick the dust**). **Kings** on **distant shores** would **bring tribute to him** and **bow** before **him.** These **kings** would come from faraway places, including **Tarshish** (possibly Tartessus in southwest Spain), **Sheba** (cf. v. 15; present-day Yemen in southwestern Arabia), **and Seba** (in upper Egypt; cf. Gen. 10:7).

### C. Justification for dominion (72:12-14)

**72:12-14.** The psalmist explained that the king was worthy of such dominion (v. 8) and the honor given him (vv. 9-11) because he was a savior for the oppressed. **He will deliver the needy** (**needy** occurs three times in vv. 12-13) and the destitute (cf. v. 4) **who cry** to him. **He will take pity on the weak** and **rescue them,** considering **their blood** (i.e., their lives) **precious** to him.

### D. Ascription of praise (72:15-20)

**72:15-17.** Because of his magnificent and righteous reign, people would respond with gifts for **him** (e.g., **gold from Sheba;** cf. the massive amount of gold brought to Solomon by the queen of Sheba, 1 Kings 10:10), with prayers on his behalf, and with blessings on **him.** The people would pray for agricultural prosperity (cf. Ps. 72:3, 6-7), with **grain** and **fruit** in abundance. **Lebanon,** with its cedar forests, was a picture of a flourishing land. The blessings of such a king's rule are reciprocal; he blesses the **nations** (perhaps through trade and peaceful alliances) and they in turn speak well of **him.**

**72:18-20.** Verses 18-19 record the second doxology in the book, thus ending Book II (Pss. 41–72). They include words of **praise . . . to the LORD God . . . of Israel** and the request that **His glory** be evident everywhere. Verse 20 states that **this** ends **the prayers of David.** However, this probably refers to an earlier collection of psalms, because 18 other psalms after this one are attributed in their superscriptions to David (Pss. 86; 101; 103; 108–110; 122; 124; 131; 133; 138–145).

## III. Book III (Pss. 73–89)

Eleven of the 17 psalms in this section are attributed to Asaph (Pss. 73–83),

one to David (Ps. 86), three to the sons of Korah (Pss. 84–85; 87), one to Heman (Ps. 88), and another to Ethan (Ps. 89). Asaph, Heman, and Ethan were Levite musicians in David's day (1 Chron. 15:17, 19).

## Psalm 73

This psalm strikes the same theme as Psalm 49, and thus may be classified as a wisdom psalm or at least may be studied for its wisdom motifs. In it "Asaph" told of the doubts which nearly overwhelmed him when he compared the life of a worldly man with his own. But then he confessed the sinfulness of his thoughts and explained that the contrast in their destinies enabled him to keep a proper perspective.

### A. Prosperity of the wicked (73:1-14)

**73:1-3.** Asaph began this psalm by affirming that though **God is good to** those in **Israel** who trust Him and **are pure in heart** (cf. v. 13), he himself nearly **slipped** (cf. 94:18) in his confidence in the Lord. The psalmist emphasized his own situation by beginning four verses with the Hebrew expression translated **But as for me** (73:2, 22-23, 28). His offense was that he was envious of **the prosperity of the wicked.** Why should the people who *oppose* God be better off than those who trust Him? This problem was so overwhelming he **almost** lost faith in God's goodness.

**73:4-12.** Asaph explained the prosperity that troubled him. He observed that the wicked do not seem to suffer trouble as other people do (vv. 4-5). They cover **themselves** with **pride** and **violence** (v. 6). Their **evil** devices are unbounded (v. 7). Their speech is scornful, malicious, and arrogant, as if they owned **the earth** (vv. 8-9). Many **people** are carried away by their evil (they **turn to them,** v. 10) and presumptuous self-confidence, thinking **God** does not **know** of their sin (v. 11; cf. 94:7). With no cares in the world (cf. 73:4-5, 12) **wicked,** arrogant people continue to prosper.

**73:13-14.** Asaph said he was confused over the value of his salvation. He felt that he had cleansed himself **in vain** (cf. **pure** in v. 1) because since trusting the Lord he had been **plagued** and chastened. Like many saints before and after him, Asaph was puzzled that God seemed to prosper the wicked and punish the righteous.

## B. Destiny of the wicked and the righteous (73:15-28)

**73:15-20.** Asaph overcame his doubts by considering the **destiny** of the wicked. First, he acknowledged the impiety of his former conclusion in view of this consideration. His words are like a confession, for he knew the treachery his words could have been to the congregation (v. 15). The entire conflict was painful (**oppressive**) to him, **till** in **the sanctuary** he **understood** what will happen to the wicked. God will set **them** in dangerous (**slippery**; cf. "slipped" in v. 2) places where they will stumble and fall, be **cast . . . down** in **ruin,** and **suddenly** be **destroyed.**

When God finally sets things right, the wicked will be like **fantasies** (**a dream**), counterfeits of reality. This was the negative aspect of the solution to Asaph's problem.

**73:21-26.** The positive aspect of the solution was Asaph's conviction of his own glorious destiny. He confessed that his perspective had been dulled by brutish ignorance. If he had not been so **ignorant,** he admitted, his **heart** would not have been so bitter (vv. 21-22). (**Grieved** is lit., "grew sour"; **embittered** is lit., "felt stinging pains.") His true position was in stark contrast with the wicked, for he knew God was **always with** him (v. 23) and would **guide** him wisely (**with** His **counsel**) and receive him **into glory** (v. 24). "Into glory" could also be translated "with glory," meaning that God would guide him through his troubles so that he would enjoy honor (and not shame; cf. 4:2) in this life. Since "glory" for individuals in the Old Testament seldom meant heavenly glory the psalmist was probably looking for deliverance in his lifetime. This would demonstrate that he was in God's favor. Of course believers today know from the New Testament that God's punishment of the wicked and blessing of the righteous extend beyond death.

In addition, Asaph affirmed that God was his only possession **in heaven** or **on the earth.** Though Asaph was overwhelmed, **God** was his **Strength** (cf. 18:1) and His **Portion** (cf. 16:5; 119:57; 142:5). Some wicked people prosper materially but only the spiritual "possessions" of the righteous will last.

**73:27-28.** Asaph concluded that **those who are far from** God and **are unfaithful** will be destroyed, but that those who are **near God** find joy and safety. Though he had nearly slipped in his confidence in God (cf. v. 2) he now was reassured that God was keeping him secure. God was his **Refuge** (*maḥseh*, "shelter from danger"; cf. 14:6; 46:1; 61:3; 62:7-8; 71:7; 91:2, 9). Nearness to God always helps believers maintain a balanced perspective on material things and on the wicked.

## Psalm 74

Asaph asked God to remember His people because their enemy had devastated the sanctuary. He prayed that God, who had helped destroy their enemies in the past, would not permit their reproach.

## A. Prayer for remembrance (74:1-2)

**74:1-2.** The psalmist asked **God** not to continue His hot **anger . . . against the sheep of** His **pasture** (i.e., God's people; cf. 79:13; 95:7; 100:3). God should **remember** (and have regard for) those He has redeemed (cf. Ex. 15:13) to be His **inheritance** (cf. comments on Deut. 4:20), and He should remember His dwelling place on **Zion.** (**The tribe** stands for the nation, as seen in Jer. 10:16.)

## B. Lament over the destruction (74:3-9)

**74:3.** Asaph prayed that God would take note of and rescue His people for **the enemy** had ruined **the sanctuary** and jeopardized the nation. The word **ruins** and the statements in verses 4-8 suggest a complete devastation of the sanctuary (cf. Ps. 79). The historical event to which this refers is uncertain. The only occasion that matches this devastation is the invasion by the Babylonians in 586 B.C., but that is too late, if the Asaph of David's time is the author. Perhaps this Asaph is a later member of the Asaph musical guild.

**74:4-8.** According to this psalm, the enemy had **roared in** and demolished **the place. The carved** work was **smashed** by **axes and hatchets,** the **sanctuary** (**the dwelling place**; cf. 76:2; 84:1; 132:5, 7; **of** God's **name,** i.e., the place where God revealed His character; cf. "name" in

74:10, 18, 21) was **burned,** and all the assembly places in the land were also **burned.**

**74:9.** What troubled the psalmist was that there was **no** prophet to give spiritual counsel to the people or to explain **how long this** problem would last.

### C. Appeal for help (74:10-17)

**74:10-17.** Since no prophet was available (v. 9) the psalmist himself appealed to **God** for help, asking **how long** (cf. v. 9 and see comments on 6:3) **the enemy** would continue to **mock** (cf. 74:22) and **revile** God (cf. v. 18). Asaph suggested that God no longer remain inactive but rather show His **right hand,** a symbol of His power, **and destroy them** (v. 11). Asaph sought to motivate **God** by reminding Him of His past help: God is the sovereign **King** and Savior (v. 12), God delivered Israel through **the sea** (the Red Sea, v. 13), He **crushed . . . Leviathan,** a seven-headed mythological monster symbolic here of Egypt's power (v. 14), and He has complete power over nature (vv. 15-17), including **rivers. . . . day** and **night,** the **sun and moon,** and the seasons. Because of what God had done in the past, Asaph wanted Him to act now.

### D. Regard for the covenant (74:18-23)

**74:18-23.** The psalmist appealed to God not to forget the awful mocking by **the enemy** (cf. vv. 10, 22) and to protect His **dove,** a defenseless bird (i.e., Israel; cf. 68:13), and look on His **covenant** so that His people—**oppressed . . . poor, and needy** (see comments on 37:14)— would not suffer the **disgrace** of defeat. **God** should note, he said, that the enemies are blasphemers who **mock** Him (74:22; cf. vv. 10, 18). Therefore He should not forsake His people, but should **defend** His **cause** and defeat His loud, boisterous **enemies.**

### Psalm 75

This psalm celebrates anticipated victory. The psalmist recognized that God will establish judgment at the appointed time, and that the judgment will destroy the wicked and exalt the righteous. On the basis of this he warned the wicked to submit to God who alone can deliver.

### A. God appoints judgment (75:1-3)

**75:1-3.** On behalf of the people, Asaph praised **God** for His nearness and His wondrous works (v. 1). Notable among God's deeds is His judging (v. 2; cf. v. 7; 94:2); and even though His judging causes **the earth** to **quake,** He sustains it (75:3).

### B. God is the Judge (75:4-8)

**75:4-6.** God warns the wicked to change their heart attitude toward Him. They should not arrogantly defy God. Lifting **up . . . horns,** a metaphor from the animal world, signifies a defiant, strutting, self-confidence. Moreover, the wicked should not speak with a stiff **neck,** that is, in stubborn rebellion against God. The wicked should realize that when He judges, no help comes from any earthly direction.

**75:7-8.** The psalmist warned the wicked that because **God** is the Judge (cf. v. 2) they will experience His full wrath. This is pictured as being made to drink **a cup . . . of foaming wine** (cf. Job 21:20; Isa. 51:17; Jer. 25:15). **All the wicked** will be forced to undergo a staggering judgment from God, as they **drink it** to the last **dregs.**

### C. God's judgment is praiseworthy (75:9-10)

**75:9-10.** Asaph vowed to **sing praise to . . . God** because of the triumph of the righteous. In verse 10 God may be speaking, declaring that His cutting **off** the defiance **of all the wicked** and exalting **the righteous** will be cause for praise.

### Psalm 76

This is a song of praise for the power of the God of Jacob. The psalmist declared that God made Himself known in Jerusalem by executing judgment. Describing how God destroyed the wicked and delivered the righteous led Asaph to exhort the leaders to pledge their allegiance to God.

### A. God's judgment is known (76:1-3)

**76:1-3. God** made Himself **known** by destroying Israel's enemies. He devastated **the weapons** of those who made war against Jerusalem, or **Salem** (used elsewhere only in Gen. 14:18; Heb. 7:1-2) and **Zion.** (On God's **dwelling place** being in Jerusalem see Pss. 74:7; 84:1; 132:5, 7.)

## B. God's judgment is just (76:4-10)

**76:4-6.** Asaph praised the Lord as the God of **light,** the One who is glorious and illuminating. His majesty exceeds even the **mountains rich with** wild **game.** This phrase, literally, "mountain of prey," may mean that **God** is more majestic than the strongholds of the enemy. The soldiers of these enemies are swiftly destroyed (v. 5) by God's **rebuke** (v. 6).

**76:7-10.** The psalmist then explained that **God** in wrath accomplishes His sovereign purposes over His foes. No one **can stand** in the sight of this fearsome (cf. vv. 11-12) God. When God's **judgment** issued **from heaven** to deliver the righteous (**the afflicted**), the earth stood in silence and awe. God's **wrath against** wicked **men** results in believers praising Him and deters those who are not destroyed from giving full vent to their sins.

## C. God's judgment is fearful (76:11-12)

**76:11-12.** Believers should **fulfill** their **vows to . . . God,** bringing **to the One to be feared** (cf. v. 7) what is due Him. By their allegiance to God people can escape His fearful judgment on world **rulers.** He can cause those who arrogantly rebel against Him to fear Him.

# Psalm 77

The Psalmist Asaph cried earnestly in the night from his troubled spirit, searching his soul for an answer to his distress. He found comfort in meditating on God's mighty deliverance at the Exodus. This meditation bolstered the psalmist's courage and led him to try to get God to show His mighty power again.

## A. The problem (77:1-9)

**77:1-3.** Asaph related that he **cried** earnestly all **night** for **God to hear** him, but was disquieted and confused when he **remembered . . . God** (cf. vv. 6-7). Apparently his effort to find comfort from prayer failed.

**77:4-6.** Then the psalmist told how he searched his **spirit** for comfort. As God **troubled** him by keeping him awake, he **thought about the former days** when he could sing **in the night** about God's deliverances. But now he was perplexed (**mused;** cf. v. 3) because he had no occasion for praise.

**77:7-9.** Asaph was perplexed because he seemed to be abandoned by **the LORD.** He wondered if God had cast Israel off, by discontinuing **His favor. . . . love** (*hesed,* "loyal love"), and **promise** and by withholding His mercy and **compassion** because of His **anger.**

Apparently, then, the nation was in distress. God had not answered their prayers, which greatly troubled the psalmist's soul.

## B. The solution (77:10-20)

The psalmist's comfort and hope came from his musing on God's great deliverance of Israel at the Exodus.

**77:10-15.** Asaph decided to recall (**remember . . . meditate . . . consider,** vv. 11-12) God's **miracles** (v. 11) performed in the past by His **right hand** (v. 10, i.e., in power; cf. "arm," v. 15). Asaph based his **appeal** on those **works** and **deeds.** His immediate reflection led him to praise the incomparably **holy** and **great . . . God** as Redeemer (vv. 13-15). God is incomparable because he **performs** miraculous, **mighty** deeds, such as the redemption (deliverance) of His people from Egypt by His **arm** (i.e., strength). The question, **What god is so great as our God?** does not imply that other gods live. It indicates that God far exceeds every false god people worship (cf. similar questions in 35:10; 71:19; 89:6; 113:5; Ex. 15:11; Micah 7:18).

**77:16-18.** Asaph vividly described the phenomena that accompanied the display of power when God redeemed His people from Egypt. **Waters** responded to Him (at the crossing of the Red Sea), and **clouds . . . thunder . . . lightning (Your arrows),** and earthquakes revealed His power (cf. 68:7-9; 97:2-5).

**77:19-20.** God used **Moses and Aaron** to lead His people miraculously out of danger **through the** Red **Sea** as if they were **a flock** of sheep (cf. 78:52; 79:13; 100:3).

So the implication of this praise-filled meditation is that God will again miraculously rescue His **people,** people whom He has redeemed to Himself.

# Psalm 78

Psalm 78 continues the tradition of passing on the record of God's marvelous works of old from one generation to another. Psalmist Asaph implored his generation to keep the Law and not forget God's works and rebel. They should not do as their ancestors in the wilderness did, who were slain by the Lord's anger, or as a later generation did when Shiloh was plundered before the Lord chose David. The poem is a sad recounting of how their ancestors forgot God's works, but it also recounts how the Lord graciously delivered them.

### A. The tradition of instruction (78:1-8)

**78:1-8.** Asaph called the **people** to **hear** his instruction (v. 1) about the Lord's **deeds . . . power, and . . . wonders** (v. 4) that He would make **known** to his **generation**. These had been handed down from earlier generations as God had commanded. **The Lord** planned this so that the nation might **trust** Him and obey the Law (v. 7), not stumbling in unbelief and rebellion **like their** unfaithful **forefathers** (v. 8).

### B. The disobedience of Ephraim (78:9-11)

**78:9-11.** It is difficult to know for sure which event these verses refer to. Ephraim's failure in **battle** and her disobedience to God, whenever they occurred, may have resulted in Judah's being made preeminent over Ephraim (cf. vv. 67-68).

### C. The marvelous deeds that men forget (78:12-72)

In the rest of the psalm Asaph reviewed God's intervention in Israel's history. In verses 12-39 the writer recounted the marvelous things God did for Israel's ancestors at the Exodus and in the desert and their failure to obey Him. In verses 40-72 Asaph recounted the marvelous things God did for the nation from the time of the plagues to His giving them David as their king, and also the people's disobedience.

**78:12-20.** Asaph described God's wonders in the plagues (cf. vv. 43-51; Ex. 7–11) in **Zoan,** capital city of **the land of** Goshen **in** northeast **Egypt** (Ps. 78:12), at the crossing of **the** Red **Sea** (v. 13; cf. Ex. 14:21-22), and in the wilderness (Ps. 78:14-16; cf. Ex. 13:21; 17:6). **But** the people murmured and rebelled **against Him** (Ps. 78:17-20). Doubting God's ability (cf. v. 22), they put Him **to the test** (cf. vv. 41, 56) expecting Him to do miracles for

them when they were out of His will.

**78:21-33.** Asaph told how **the Lord** met the Israelites' murmuring first with **anger** in sending **fire** (vv. 21-22; cf. Num. 11:1-3), then by showering them with **manna** (Ps. 78:23-25; cf. Ex. 16:14-31), called **the bread of angels** because it was sent by God (cf. Ex. 16:4), then with the **meat** (Ps. 78:27-29) of quails (cf. Ex. 16:13) driven in by southeast winds (cf. Num. 11:31). Asaph also recalled that **God's anger** (cf. Ps. 78:21) destroyed those who **craved** (vv. 30-33; cf. Num. 11:33).

**78:34-39.** Asaph added that **whenever** the Lord punished His people, they **turned to Him** as **their Rock** and **Redeemer,** even though **their hearts were not** right. But God forgave them, repeatedly restraining **His anger,** because **He remembered . . . they were** mere humans with fleeting lives (vv. 38-39).

**78:40-55.** Asaph lamented **how often** the people **rebelled . . . in the desert,** forgetting the mighty works that demonstrated God's **power** (vv. 40-42). So, having briefly referred to the plagues in **Egypt** (v. 12), he now described some of them in greater detail (vv. 43-51; cf. 105:28-38). **Sycamore**-fig trees were common **in Egypt.** He also wrote about God's great deliverance of the people through the wilderness as **He led** them **like a flock** (78:52-54; cf. 79:13), and about the Conquest of the **land** (78:55).

**78:56-64.** Then Asaph sadly recalled how the people tested **God** (see comments on v. 18), **rebelled against** Him, and turned to false gods (vv. 56-58). Because of this the Lord was **angry** and had **Shiloh** plundered so that **the ark** was captured (vv. 59-61; cf. 1 Sam. 4:4-11). Many **people** were killed at that time (Ps. 78:62-64), including the **priests** Hophni and Phinehas.

**78:65-72.** Asaph then reminded the people how **the Lord awoke,** figuratively speaking, like a mighty **man** and saved His people from their **enemies. But then He rejected the tents of Joseph,** Manasseh and **Ephraim** (see comments on vv. 9-11), representing the Northern tribes, and **chose** Judah's **Zion** for the location of **His sanctuary,** and **David His servant** to be His king. The disbelief and disobedience that brought disaster at the Battle of Aphek (1 Sam. 4:1-11) marked the turning point to a new priesthood and a new sanctuary, and a king to lead the people, God's **inheritance** (cf. Pss. 78:62; 79:1; see comments on Deut. 4:20).

## Psalm 79

Complaining that Jerusalem had been devastated, the saints slaughtered, and their enemies encouraged to scoff, the psalmist pleaded with the Lord not to remember their sins but to deliver them for His name's sake. This psalm is similar in several ways to Psalm 74.

### A. Lament over the destruction of Jerusalem (79:1-4)

**79:1-4.** The writer lamented that **the nations** had **invaded** the land of God's people (His **inheritance**; cf. comments on Deut. 4:20), **defiled** the **temple,** and plundered the holy city. Moreover, they had slaughtered many of God's servants, leaving them unburied for predators to devour. All this had made Israel an object of **scorn** and **reproach.**

### B. Plea for deliverance (79:5-12)

**79:5-9.** The psalmist then pleaded with the LORD not to remember their sins but to help them in their **need.** He wanted to know **how long** (cf. comments on 6:3) the Lord would **be angry** with their **sins,** with His **jealousy** burning **like fire** (cf. 89:46). God was asked to destroy their enemies and deliver His own **quickly** (cf. comments on 31:2) **for** His **glory** and **for** His **name's sake,** that is, because of His reputation.

**79:10-12.** Seeking to motivate the LORD to answer his plea for deliverance, the psalmist desired that He would keep the Israelite **prisoners** alive and end the nations' mockery of God's people (**Where is their God?** cf. 42:3, 10; 115:2) by turning on them **seven times** (i.e., thoroughly; cf. 12:6) and ending the nations' **reproach** against God's supposed inability to help His own.

### C. Promise of praise (79:13)

**79:13.** After the Lord would release His **people** from bondage, the psalmist promised that then they, **the sheep of** His **pasture** (cf. 74:1; 95:7; 100:3), would be eternally grateful and would **praise** Him **forever.**

## Psalm 80

In his prayer that the Lord would restore and save Israel, the psalmist la-

mented the awful calamity brought on them by their enemies. He described the blessing and cursing of the nation as a vine that flourished and was then destroyed. He repeated the refrain (vv. 3, 7, 19) that God should turn and save them.

### A. Appeal to Israel's Shepherd (80:1-3)

**80:1-2.** The psalmist appealed to the Lord, the **Shepherd** (cf. 23:1; 28:9) of His people, the sheep, to help the tribes in their distress. The Lord is pictured sitting **enthroned** in the temple above the gold-covered **cherubim** (cf. 99:1; 1 Kings 6:23-28) over the ark of the covenant. **Joseph,** representing the Northern Kingdom, and **Benjamin,** representing the Southern Kingdom, were Rachel's two sons; **Ephraim** and **Manasseh,** Joseph's sons, were her grandsons.

**80:3.** The psalmist then prayed that **God** would **restore** and save His people by His grace. This refrain recurs in verses 7, 19. The concept of divine favor is expressed by the image of one's **face** shining on another, like a beaming countenance of approval (cf. Num. 6:25; and comments on Ps. 4:6).

### B. Discipline from God (80:4-7)

**80:4-7.** The psalmist lamented the fierce discipline **God** had brought on His **people.** He cried out to God, asking **how long** (cf. comments on 6:3) His **anger** would be directed against them. The situation was as if **God** (like a Shepherd) had been feeding His people **tears.** He had brought painful calamity on them so that they wept uncontrollably (expressed in hyperbole that their tears were drunk **by the bowlful**). But the most painful aspect of God's chastening was that Israel's **enemies** mocked them (cf. 79:10).

Again the refrain expressed the desire that God would **restore** His people by His favor (cf. 80:3, 19).

### C. Removal of blessing (80:8-14b)

**80:8-11.** The psalmist pictured Israel as **a vine** that God brought from **Egypt** and **planted** in the land. It flourished so that it spread to the **mountains** in the south, to the **cedars** of Lebanon in the north, to **the Sea** (the Mediterranean to the west) and to **the River** (the Euphrates) on the east.

**80:12-14b.** However, this prosperity had withered. By a rhetorical question the writer lamented that God had **broken down** the **walls** of the nation to enable others to plunder her. The Hebrew word for "walls" (also used in 89:40; Isa. 5:5) does not mean city walls but walls around vineyards. The enemies who plundered Israel are here described as **boars** and beasts.

The figure of Israel as a vine may have been prompted by Genesis 49:22. It is used also in Isaiah 5:1-7; 27:2-6; Jeremiah 2:21; 12:10; Hosea 10:1. Jesus spoke of Himself as a Vine (John 15:1, 5) for He, being the promised Seed, represented and fulfilled God's purposes for Israel. Where she failed, He succeeded.

The first two lines of Psalm 80:14 are a refrain similar (but different in wording) to verses 3, 7, 19.

### D. Promise of obedience (80:14c-19)

**80:14c-16.** Asaph continued to speak of the **vine,** lamenting that **the root** that had been **planted** and **the son** who had grown had been destroyed (**cut down**). "Son," a literal rendering of the Hebrew, refers to the nation that sprang from "the root." So "son" could be rendered "branch" (cf. NIV marg.). Again (cf. comments on v. 12) this imagery may come from Genesis 49:22. The Hebrew term "son" is also used for the nation in Exodus 4:22 and Hosea 11:1. Again the New Testament (Matt. 2:15) applied a prophet's words (Hosea 11:1) to Christ the Seed as the Representative of Israel.

**80:17-19.** The psalmist prayed that God's **hand** would restore them. **The man at Your right hand** may allude to Benjamin, which means "son of the right hand." **The son of man** refers to Israel (again as a son). Asaph said that if **God** would bless His own, the people would be faithful to Him.

Once more the psalm includes the refrain which requests that God would restore His people by His favor (cf. vv. 3, 7).

## Psalm 81

This song is a festive celebration in memory of the Lord's deliverance. It has been traditionally identified with the Feast of Tabernacles (Lev. 23:33-36, 39-43; Deut. 16:13-15). Some have argued, on the basis of Psalm 81:5, that the Passover was the occasion for Asaph's writing Psalm 81, since the Passover was inaugu-rated in Egypt. But the jubilation in the psalm fits the Tabernacles festival better. In the psalm Asaph summoned the people to the festival which God had ordained as a memorial to His great deliverance of them from bondage in Egypt. Using the witness of history, the writer declared that the Lord would turn their affliction away if they would obey Him.

### A. Summons to the celebration (81:1-5)

**81:1-2.** The psalmist called the congregation to **sing** aloud to the Lord their **Strength** (cf. 22:19; 28:7-8; 46:1; 59:9, 17; 118:14), and to praise Him with musical accompaniment.

**81:3-5.** Then the psalmist exhorted them to appear at the festival because it was a statute for the nation to keep. The Law stipulated that adult males were to make pilgrimages three times a year to Jerusalem to celebrate the Feasts of Passover (in association with the **Feast** of Unleavened Bread), Weeks, and Tabernacles (Deut. 16:16). The Feast of Tabernacles began on the 15th day of the seventh month (Lev. 23:33) when the moon was full. The seventh month was September-October (see "Calendar in Israel," near Ex. 12:1). **Israel** began to hear God's commandments in **Egypt** (in His instructions to her regarding the Passover). It was like a voice they had never heard before (NIV marg.).

### B. Report of God's revelation (81:6-16)

These verses record God's communication to Israel as if He spoke directly to the nation.

**81:6-7.** First, the psalmist wrote that God said that by the Exodus He relieved the Israelites of their **burden** (in the Egyptian bondage when they had to carry bricks in baskets), and in the wilderness He **tested** them at . . . . **Meribah** (Ex. 17:7; Num. 20:13; Pss. 95:8; 106:32). The Feast of Tabernacles reminded Israel of the wanderings.

**81:8-10.** The psalmist then recalled God's revelation of Himself and His Law to His **people.** He had promised if they would hold their allegiance to Him (v. 9; cf. Ex. 20:3-6), He would provide their needs bountifully since He had **brought** them **up out of Egypt** (cf. Ex. 20:2). They should not turn to any **foreign god** because only He could satisfy them abundantly.

**81:11-12.** Asaph then reported God's words about their disobedience. Because they did **not submit to** Him, He let them run to their own destruction.

**81:13-16.** The psalmist recorded God's promise that if they would obey Him He would **subdue their enemies** and give them prosperity (**wheat** and **honey**; cf. Deut. 32:13-14). The words in Psalm 81:6, 11-15 address **Israel** in the third person (**their**) whereas the words in verses 7-10, 16 are in the second person (**you**). The abrupt change in verse 16 introduces the blessings that come to God's people who obey Him (v. 13).

## Psalm 82

Declaring that God judges His human judges, Asaph called for Him to act on His justice. Asaph warned that judges without understanding, who ignore God's appointment of them, will perish.

### A. God judges human judges (82:1)

**82:1.** The psalmist envisioned **God** presiding over an **assembly** of judges. The word **gods** ('ĕlōhîm) is used here for authorities in Israel (cf. 45:6; Ex. 21:6; 22:8-9). Some have thought this refers to angels (e.g., the Syriac trans.) in God's heavenly court. However, the remainder of the psalm clarifies that these are God's representatives who are in authority on earth.

### B. God's indictment of judges (82:2-7)

Using God's words, the psalmist warned these magistrates to do their jobs right.

**82:2-5.** The indictment (v. 2), given in the form of a rhetorical question, is that His people were **unjust** and partial. (On the words **how long,** see comments on 6:3.) Instead they should judge fairly and champion the cause of the **oppressed** (including **the weak . . . fatherless . . . poor,** and **needy**). This is the essence of righteous judging.

However, the human judges under God's indictment roam the earth without spiritual or intellectual understanding and in moral **darkness** so that **the foundations of the earth are shaken,** that is, law and order are undermined (cf. 11:3).

**82:6-7.** God warned the wicked judges that they will perish. He had appointed them as "**gods**" (cf. v. 1) and as **sons of the Most High,** His representa-

tives on earth. But despite their exalted position, they were held accountable by God. Jesus appealed to verse 6 when He was accused of blasphemy (John 10:34). Since Israel's judges were, in a sense, "sons" of God, Jesus said He was not blaspheming to call Himself the Son of God.

### C. Call for judgment (82:8)

**82:8.** Asaph called on **God** to arise and **judge the earth,** that is, all its inhabitants, **for all** are His and therefore are responsible to Him.

## Psalm 83

The psalmist lamented the great danger from the many enemies that hemmed in Judah to crush her. He prayed that God would muster His power to destroy them, as He had done in former victories.

### A. Danger of destruction (83:1-8)

**83:1-8.** These verses record Asaph's lament over Judah's grave situation. As in many other lament psalms, the writer turned immediately to **God,** asking Him to respond (v. 1).

The psalmist delineated how Judah's enemies had taken counsel to destroy her (vv. 2-5). As God's **enemies** they plotted cunningly (cf. 64:6) **against** God's **people** (83:3) and **against** God Himself (v. 5). They conspired to **destroy** the **nation** and wipe out any remembrance of her. These foes included numerous surrounding nations: **Edom . . . Ishmaelites** (also called the **descendants of Hagar**), **Moab . . . Gebal** (Byblos), **Ammon . . . Amalek . . . Philistia** and the city of **Tyre.** Mighty **Assyria** also supported this coalition which included **the descendants of Lot,** the Moabites and Ammonites (Gen. 19:36-38).

### B. Powerful deliverance (83:9-18)

Verses 9-18 of the psalm record Asaph's prayer that God would use His power to overthrow Judah's enemies.

**83:9-12.** The psalmist's prayer at the outset alluded to past victories over the Midianites through Gideon (Jud. 7–8) and against **Sisera** through Deborah and Barak (Jud. 4–5). **Endor** is near Taanach, mentioned in Judges 5:19. Asaph spoke again of Gideon's victory, **Oreb and Zeeb** being the leaders of the Midianite warriors (Jud. 7:25) and **Zebah and Zalmun-na** the Midianite kings (Jud. 8:5-6, 12, 18).

**83:13-16.** The psalmist asked that God would **make them like** windblown **tumbleweed** and **chaff** (cf. 1:4), insecure and pursued, and that He would hotly pursue them **as fire consumes** a **forest** on a mountain. Asaph wanted God's wrath to be like a stormy **tempest** from which they could not escape. This defeat would **shame** them and cause many to turn to the LORD.

**83:17-18.** The psalm closes with a re-iteration of the prayer that the wicked **be ashamed** (cf. v. 16) and disgraced. By trifling with people God cherishes, they would learn the hard way that God **alone** is the sovereign LORD.

## Psalm 84

This passage is a companion to Psalms 42 and 43, because it expresses the same yearning for the formal place of worship. Technically it is a pilgrimage song, though it is not in the collection of pilgrim psalms (Pss. 120–134). In Psalm 84 the pilgrim declared the blessedness of a believer who in faith journeys to the temple to pray to the Lord. The author is unknown; it was to be sung by the Korahites.

### A. The soul's longing for the Lord (84:1-4)

**84:1-2.** The psalm breaks out with praise for the **dwelling place** (cf. 74:7; 76:2; 132:5, 7) of the LORD **Almighty** (cf. 84:3, 8, 12; lit., "Yahweh of hosts," i.e., armies). For this place (the temple with its **courts**; cf. v. 10) the psalmist's **heart and . . . flesh** (body) longed. To yearn for the temple meant to long **for the living God** Himself (cf. 42:2). In that day people could approach God through the temple priests. The psalmist's faith was thus in the living, powerful Lord God.

**84:3-4.** The psalmist conveyed his intense yearning for **God** and His temple by noting the enviable position of those in the temple—nesting birds and ministering servants (priests **who dwell in** the temple rooms).

### B. The pilgrimage to the temple (84:5-7)

**84:5-7.** The psalmist declared the blessedness (cf. v. 12; i.e., the joyous privileges and great benefits) of **those** who demonstrate their faith by going **on pilgrimage** (cf. Deut. 16:16) to appear in Jerusalem (**Zion**) **before** the Lord.

On their pilgrimage they were strengthened by God's blessings. **The Valley of Baca** ("balsam tree") was apparently a waterless place that became **a place of springs**. The **rains** would **cover** the arid valley **with pools** of water, a vivid picture of God's blessings on the faithful pilgrims.

### C. The prayer of the pilgrim (84:8-12)

**84:8-9.** The pilgrim, once he arrived in God's dwelling place in Zion, prayed for the king, who was like a **shield** protecting the people, and was God's **anointed one** (cf. 2:2). As the LORD **God Almighty** (lit., "Yahweh, God of hosts") and the **God of Jacob,** He is able to intervene on behalf of His people and deliver them.

**84:10-12.** The pilgrim-psalmist stated why he longed to go to Zion: he was confident that God would answer his prayer. Reaffirming his intense love for the temple and its **courts** (cf. v. 2), he said that **one day** there was **better . . . than a thousand elsewhere**; to be a servant there was better than living in the lavish **tents of the wicked.** The reason, of course, was that God was at the temple and would bless and protect (be **a Sun and Shield**; cf. comments on 3:3) and bestow **favor** and **good** things (cf. 16:2; 34:10) on those who would **walk** blamelessly. Another prerequisite for receiving God's blessings is trust.

## Psalm 85

The psalmist acknowledged the goodness of God in restoring His people and forgiving their sins. He then prayed that the Lord would remove His wrath from His people. The psalmist's confidence in the Lord came from God's promise of salvation.

### A. Prayer to God (85:1-7)

**85:1-3.** The song begins with praise to God for restoring the nation. This restoration evidenced the fact that God had forgiven and **covered all their sins,** and had **set aside** His **wrath** and anger.

Some scholars say this psalm was written in the early days of the exiles' return from the Babylonian Captivity; this is hard to prove. Their view, however, does stress that the forgiveness of the nations' sins ended God's wrath and prompted His people's return.

**85:4-7.** The psalmist prayed that the Lord would again turn His wrath away and deliver them. He wanted the Lord to **put away** His **displeasure,** and not continue to **be angry.** Apparently the past restoration referred to in verses 1-3 inspired this prayer for another restoration. Revived, they would again be able to **rejoice** and experience His **unfailing love** (*ḥeseḏ*).

### B. Promise from God (85:8-9)

**85:8-9.** The psalmist said he would **listen** for word from **the LORD** who **promises peace** (*šālôm,* "welfare"; cf. v. 10; Es. 10:3) **to His . . . saints.** He gives **salvation so that His glory may** be evident **in the land.** "Glory" means the manifestation of His presence (cf. Isa. 60:1-2; Zech. 2:5).

These ideas expressed in God's revelation to Israel find their ultimate fulfillment in Christ. This promise of peace and salvation through the glory of the One who dwells among men may have been in John's mind when he wrote John 1:14.

### C. Faith of the psalmist (85:10-13)

**85:10-13.** The writer was confident that **the LORD** would cause His attributes (**love** [*ḥeseḏ*], **faithfulness,** and **righteousness**) to work together to provide **peace** (welfare; cf. v. 8), **righteousness,** and prosperity (cf. 84:11).

## Psalm 86

Because God is good and forgiving, and because He is incomparably able to do great things, the psalmist petitioned Him to show His strength in the face of opposition from the proud.

The psalm is ascribed to David. It seems to be a mosaic of expressions from the other psalms. Nevertheless it has a unique emphasis in the Book of Psalms.

### A. Prayer for protection (86:1-5)

**86:1-5.** In his prayer David earnestly requested that God **hear . . . answer. . . . guard. . . . save. . . . have mercy on,** and **bring joy to** him because of his **poor and needy** condition (see comments on 37:14). Essentially in these requests he desired that God preserve him (cf. 25:20)

by His mercy. David called himself a **servant who trusts in** the Lord, one who lifts **up** his **soul** to God (cf. 25:1).

This prayer was based on the fact that God is **kind,** ready to forgive, and **abounding in love** (cf. 86:15; Ex. 34:6).

### B. Praise for power (86:6-13)

**86:6-10.** David repeated his call for the LORD to **hear** him. His confidence that **in** his **trouble** God would **answer** him was strengthened by his knowledge that the Lord is incomparable (**there is none like You;** cf. Ex. 15:11), fully able to do what he asked (**no deeds can compare with Yours**). People from **all . . . nations** will serve Him, and He **alone** is the **great . . . God.** This theme of God's incomparable greatness is also reflected in the psalm's sevenfold use of the word **Lord** (*'ăḏōnay*), which stresses His lordship and sovereignty (Ps. 86:3-5, 8-9, 12, 15).

**86:11-13.** The psalmist prayed for instruction so that he might be even more faithful to **God** in His greatness. He desired to know God's **way** so that he could dedicate himself to it with **undivided** loyalty. In addition he vowed to **praise** God's greatness wholeheartedly (cf. **heart,** v. 11). Because of God's love He **delivered** David from death.

### C. Petition for strength (86:14-17)

**86:14-17.** Because the proud had risen against David, he asked **God** for **strength.** His **enemies** were ruthless men with no **regard for** the Lord. But by contrast the Lord is **compassionate** (cf. 111:4), **gracious . . . slow to anger,** loving, and faithful (cf. Ex. 34:6; Neh. 9:17; Pss. 103:8; 145:8; Joel 2:13; Jonah 4:2). David's prayer for "strength" in the face of his peril was based on the greatness of **God.** He also asked for **a sign of** God's **goodness,** that is, deliverance so that others would **see** and know it was God at work.

## Psalm 87

This psalm expands on the idea in Psalm 86:9, that nations will someday worship the Lord. Psalm 87 is a song about the glorious things said about Zion, the city of God. After depicting Zion as God's glorious city, the psalmist described how the nations will gather to her as children, and how joyful are those who dwell there.

## A. The glorious city of God (87:1-3)

**87:1-3.** The first verse stands as a single-line summary of the psalm's theme: God **has set His foundation on the holy mountain** (cf. 43:3; 48:1; 99:9), that is, **He** has chosen **Zion** as His dwelling place above **all** others.

Besides Zion being loved by the Lord, **glorious things** were **said** about it. Some of those things are mentioned in the rest of the psalm (cf. Isa. 11:10).

## B. The nations gathered to Zion (87:4-6)

**87:4.** The psalmist listed some of the nations that will be gathered to Zion. They will be like children who were **born** there (vv. 4-6). God's purpose is to reconcile people to Himself, and these statements anticipate that five nations—**Rahab . . . Babylon . . . Philistia,** Phoenicia (represented by **Tyre**), and **Cush** (present-day southern Egypt, Sudan, and northern Ethiopia)—will be **among** the peoples **who acknowledge** Him. "Rahab," representing Egypt (cf. Isa. 30:7), was probably the name of a powerful demonic force thought to be behind that nation.

**87:5-6. Zion** will be enriched in that day by this acquisition of new citizens. All nations in that day will look to Zion as the "mother city." God's writing their names in a **register** figuratively describes His ensuring them a place **in Zion.**

## C. Joy in Zion (87:7)

**87:7.** This verse is a brief glimpse of the rejoicing that the other believing nations will bring to Zion. The second line of the verse states the substance of their musical praise: **All my fountains are in You.** "Fountains" signifies that Zion will be the source of all blessing and pleasure, because of the Lord's presence there.

## Psalm 88

Psalm 88, written by Heman (cf. 1 Chron. 15:19; 16:41-42; 25:1, 6) the Ezrahite (a wise person, 1 Kings 4:31), has been called one of the saddest psalms in the Psalter. It voices the diligent prayer of one who suffered constantly. The psalmist lamented the terrible and fierce affliction that had brought him to the point of death. Yet he steadfastly prayed to the Lord night and day, basing his appeal on the fact that he would be useless to the Lord in the grave.

## A. His terrible affliction (88:1-9a)

**88:1-2.** The introduction is given in these verses: the psalmist prayed (cf. v. 13) constantly (**day and night**) to **God** for deliverance.

**88:3-9a.** In describing his affliction, Heman first compared himself to those who are forgotten in **the grave.** His troubled **life** was near death (v. 3), he was considered dead (v. 4, **pit** is a synonym for grave; cf. v. 6; 28:1; 30:3, 9; 69:15; 143:7). He was like **the dead,** without God's **care** (88:5).

Then in direct address Heman declared that God had brought this trouble on him. God laid him **in the lowest pit** (cf. v. 4), God's **wrath . . . overwhelmed** him like **waves,** and God had separated him **from** his **friends** by his **grief.**

## B. His earnest prayer (88:9b-12)

**88:9b-12.** The psalmist stated that he continued to pray earnestly to the LORD. He reasoned that a **dead** person cannot **praise** God's works and attributes **in the grave.** (He wrote this from a human, physical perspective, but it does not contradict other verses that speak of conscious existence after death.) He said the Lord should deliver him so that he could declare His glory. True believers want to praise the Lord, and to Heman death seemed to be the end of that opportunity.

## C. His steadfast faith (88:13-18)

**88:13-18.** For the third time the psalmist affirmed his faith by his **cry to** God **for help** (v. 13; cf. vv. 1-2). Then, questioning why the LORD had apparently rejected him (v. 14), he again stated that his affliction was terrible (vv. 15-18). Like Job in some ways, this psalmist **suffered** under what appeared to be God's **wrath,** separated from his friends **and loved ones,** and was almost in despair (**darkness**). Yet, knowing that God was his only Source of hope, he continued to pray.

## Psalm 89

This royal psalm is a prayer that God would honor the Davidic Covenant (2 Sam. 7:5-16). The psalm is attributed to "Ethan" (a Levite, 1 Chron. 15:17-18, and a wise person, 1 Kings 4:31) but the exact occasion of its writing is unknown. Various military defeats, such as the invasion of Judah by Shishak of Egypt (1 Kings 14:25) and the Babylonian Exile, have been suggested.

Faced with the perplexing problem of the affliction and defeat of the anointed Davidic king, the psalmist implored the Lord to remember His oath and end this disaster. Ethan sought to motivate the Lord to answer his prayer by rehearsing the covenant promises and the divine attributes on which they rest. So the psalm is a study in the age-old apparent conflict between the promises of a faithful, loving God, and the catastrophes that often occur.

Several key words used repeatedly show something of the psalm's emphasis: "love" (ḥeṣeḏ, vv. 1-2, 14, 24, 28, 33, 49), "faithfulness" (vv. 1-2, 5, 8, 33, 49), "throne" (of David; vv. 4, 14, 29, 36, 44), "David My servant" (vv. 3, 20; cf. v. 50), "anointed" (vv. 20, 38, 51), "covenant" (vv. 3, 28, 34, 39).

This psalm, because of its several references to the Davidic Covenant (vv. 3-4, 27-29, 35-37, 49), affirms that the Messiah, a descendant of David, will sit on David's throne and rule over Israel. This, taken literally, supports the position that Christ is not *now* sitting on David's throne in heaven but *will* rule on his throne on the earth (cf. comments on 2 Sam. 7:5-16).

### A. The faithfulness of God (89:1-4)

**89:1-4.** The psalmist vowed to praise the Lord for His **love** and **faithfulness** (repeated in vv. 1-2; cf. v. 49; 92:2). Ethan's wholehearted belief that God is faithful was the basis for his appealing to the Lord in his dilemma. Since God made **covenant** promises **to David** (cf. 2 Sam. 7:5-16), should not He, the faithful God, keep His promises?

### B. The nature of the covenant God (89:5-18)

**89:5-14.** The psalmist praised **the LORD** for His remarkable attributes (vv. 5-8) and marvelous works (vv. 9-14). God, he said, is faithful (vv. 5, 8), incomparable (v. 6), fearful, and **mighty.** (On the question, **Who is like the LORD?** cf. 35:10; 71:19; 77:13; 89:6; 113:5; Ex. 15:11; Micah 7:18.) His great works include his ruling over the **sea,** crushing **Rahab** (see comments on Ps. 87:4) with His power (**strong arm**), creating **the heavens** and

**the earth,** and working with strength (His **arm . . . hand,** and **right hand**; cf. "right hand" in 17:7; 18:35; 20:6; 45:4; 60:5; 63:8; 108:6) and **righteousness.** Even the mountains (including **Tabor and Hermon**) were personified as if they rejoiced in the Lord's creative **power.**

**89:15-18.** In view of God's attributes (vv. 5-8) and works (vv. 9-14) the psalmist spoke of the blessings of those who trust and fellowship with this marvelous God. They enjoy the benefits of His **righteousness. . . . strength,** and protection (**shield**). Being exalted like an animal's **horn** (cf. v. 24) speaks of being favored and blessed with strength (cf. 92:10; 112:9).

### C. The promises of the covenant (89:19-37)

**89:19-20.** The psalmist reminded the Lord that He had chosen **David,** a young **warrior,** to be His **anointed** servant.

**89:21-25.** Then the psalmist reminded God that He had promised to **strengthen** and protect the king from all his enemies by His strength (**hand . . . arm**; cf. v. 13), to **love** him, and to extend his influence **over the** Mediterranean **Sea** and **the rivers.**

**89:26-29.** Then the psalmist spoke of the special relationship the Davidic king had with **God.** It was like a **Father-**son relationship (cf. 2 Sam. 7:14). Moreover, God in His unfailing covenant had promised that David's **line** (dynasty) and **throne** would last **forever** (cf. Ps. 89:35-37; 2 Sam. 7:12-13, 16).

**89:30-37.** The Lord had sworn not to break His covenant even if the people disobeyed. If they disobeyed, **the rod** would be brought on them (i.e., God would punish them), but He would not remove His **love** or **faithfulness** by ending the **covenant.** His promises, including those in the Davidic Covenant (cf. vv. 27-29), stand **forever.**

### D. The prayer for the Lord to remember His oath (89:38-52)

**89:38-45.** The psalmist now lamented the fact that the king had been afflicted and defeated in spite of God's covenantal promises. Ethan wrote that God had cast off His **servant** (vv. 38-39), **broken** his vineyard **walls** (cf. comments on 80:12) and defenses (89:40), made him weak in battle (v. 41), strengthened (**exalted the**

right hand of) his enemies (vv. 42-43), and cast down his throne in shame (vv. 44-45).

**89:46-52.** The psalmist petitioned the LORD (on the question **How long. . . ?** cf. comments on 6:3) to **remember** His oath and come to his aid, for his **life** was **fleeting.** He was near **death** and was bearing the reproach of his **enemies.** So the psalmist's only hope in the disaster was to pray that God in His **love** and **faithfulness** (cf. 89:1-2) would honor His word.

The doxology in verse 52 ends Book III (Pss. 73–89).

## IV. Book IV (Pss. 90–106)

In this section of 17 psalms all but 3 are anonymous. Psalm 90 was written by Moses and Psalms 101 and 103 were composed by David.

## Psalm 90

Contrasting God's eternity with human transitoriness, and confessing that man's days pass away in God's wrath, the psalmist prayed that the compassionate God would give His people success for their labors and joy for their sorrows.

According to the superscription the psalm is "a prayer of Moses, the man of God" (cf. Deut. 33:1). There are no compelling reasons to reject this view, though many commentators do. If it was written by Moses, the occasion of his writing it is unknown. However, the period of the wilderness wanderings, when a generation of Israelites perished in the desert, readily suggests itself as the background for the psalm. If Moses was the author this is the oldest of the 150 psalms.

### A. Man's transitoriness (90:1-12)

This portion of the psalm contrasts God and man, and gives the response which that contrast prompts.

**90:1-6.** These verses discuss the disparity between the everlasting **God** and finite humans. In humility the psalmist acknowledged that God is the saints' eternal **dwelling place** (i.e., protecting shelter) because He is **from everlasting to everlasting** (vv. 1-2). In **all generations** people have taken refuge in Him. (The Heb. word for **world,** _tēbēl_, v. 2, a poetic synonym for **earth,** means the productive part of the earth. This word is used fre-

quently in the Book of Pss.) But the Lord, who is above the limitations of time (vv. 3-4), turns mortals (**men** translates _'ĕnôš_, "weak man" to destruction. The word for **dust** (_dakkā'_, from _dākā'_, "to crush"), used only here in the Old Testament, means something pulverized like dust.

**A watch in the night** (cf. 63:6) was approximately four hours (Jud. 7:19 refers to a middle watch, suggesting three periods). Such a portion of the night, when man sleeps, is brief.

Man is like the **grass** that withers (cf. Pss. 37:2; 102:4, 11; 103:15-16; Isa. 40:6-8) in the heat of the day—God sweeps them **away** to **death** (Ps. 90:5-6). Human life is thus frail and brief, in comparison with the everlasting God.

**90:7-12.** Man's life is transitory because of God's wrath against sin. The psalmist said that man is **consumed by** God's **anger,** for He sees man's sins; even so-called **secret sins** are open to Him. Since man is a sinner, all his life is spent **under** God's **wrath,** and his life is greatly limited—to **70 years** (or a few more years, for some people)—and life flies **away** in death like a fleeting bird (cf. Job 20:8). No one can understand God's powerful wrath (Ps. 90:11).

Because life is so brief, and because it is spent under God's wrath on sin, the psalmist, representing God's people, implored God for **wisdom** in numbering their **days** (cf. 39:4), that is, realizing how few they are (cf. 39:5-6). (**Our days** occurs in 90:9-10, 12, 14 and "days" in v. 15.)

### B. God's compassion (90:13-17)

**90:13-15.** The psalmist pleaded with the Lord to **have compassion on** His **servants** (cf. v. 16). This was their only hope.

In showing compassion the Lord was asked to turn their sorrow (cf. v. 10) into **joy.** If God satisfied them with His loyal **love** (_ḥesed_), they could then rejoice **all** their **days.** The psalmist asked God to let them rejoice for as long as He had given them over to **trouble.** Verses 14-15 seem to suggest that the nation was undergoing a particularly severe period of chastening for sin, a "night" of trouble as it were. **The morning** suggests a new era of joy for God's people.

**90:16-17.** The psalmist also asked that **God** would display His **splendor** (cf. comments on 29:2) to His **servants** (cf.

90:13) and extend His **favor** to them rather than consume them in His wrath. Then they would enjoy success in their labors, even though life is short.

When God rebukes one for his sin, he feels most frail and transitory. But when he is blessed by God's favor he feels most worthwhile; he shares in **the work** of the everlasting God. Weakened by God's discipline, one is keenly aware of his mortality; abiding in God's love and compassion, he is aware of being crowned with glory and honor (cf. 8:5-8).

## Psalm 91

Because the psalmist was convinced that there is security in trusting in the Most High God, he encouraged himself that he would be delivered from the various frightening attacks of the wicked. He knew that the Lord had appointed His angels over him to protect him.

This psalm is a beautiful testimony about security in life. Several terms link Psalms 90–92, thus suggesting they are a unit. "Dwelling" occurs in 90:1 and 91:9; "grass" in 90:5 and 92:7; "spring(s) up" in 90:6 and 92:7; "make . . . glad" in 90:15 and 92:4; "Your deeds" in 90:16 and 92:4; "Most High" in 91:1, 9 and 92:1. Also the judgment of the wicked is mentioned in 91:8 and 92:11.

### A. Security in God (91:1-2)

**91:1-2.** The psalmist expressed his great confidence in the fact that whoever trusts in the Most High finds security and protection. The titles of God in verse 1 (**Most High** and **the Almighty**) are significant, for they stress His power as the sovereign Ruler of the world. (On the meaning of "Almighty," *šadday*, see comments on Gen. 17:1.)

The images of **the shelter** and **the shadow** vividly portray divine protection. "Shelter" (*sēṯer*) is a hiding place (also used in Pss. 27:5; 32:7; 119:114, "refuge"). The shadow, perhaps the shadow of a bird's wing (cf. 91:4), also pictures shelter and protection as well as comfort. **God** is also the believer's **Refuge** (*maḥseh*, "shelter from danger"; cf. v. 9 and comments on 14:6) **and . . . Fortress** (*mᵉṣûḏâh*, "strong protection"; used in 18:3; 31:3; 71:3; 144:2). Psalm 91:1-2 admirably expresses the fact that safety is in **the Lord.**

### B. Deliverance by angels (91:3-13)

The psalmist, encouraging himself, expanded on the theme of the Lord's protection from danger.

**91:3-8.** He enumerated how God delivers a believer from various frightening attacks: (1) God delivers **from the fowler's snare** (v. 3a; cf. 124:7), a figure for insidious attempts against his life. (2) God delivers **from . . . deadly pestilence** (91:3b). (3) God covers him with **His wings** (v. 4a), a figure of safety and comfort (cf. 17:8; 36:7; 57:1; 61:4; 63:7). (4) God protects with **His faithfulness** (91:4b), explained here by the metaphor of a **shield and rampart.**

As a result of God's help in these ways one who trusts in the Lord **will not fear . . . terror** at **night,** attack **by day . . . pestilence** or **plague** (vv. 5-6). Destruction that might lay thousands in defeat will not affect a trusting believer; rather, he will **see . . . the wicked** destroyed (vv. 7-8).

**91:9-13.** The psalmist explained that **no harm** or **disaster** can **befall** those who have made **the Lord** their **refuge** (*maḥseh*, "shelter from danger"; cf. v. 2 and comments on 14:6) because He has commissioned **angels** to care for them. Angels protect from physical harm and give believers strength to overcome difficulties, pictured here as wild lions and dangerous snakes. Satan, in tempting Christ, quoted 91:11-12 (Matt. 4:6), which shows that even God's most marvelous promises can be foolishly applied.

### C. God's promise of protection (91:14-16)

**91:14-16.** The psalmist wrote as if God Himself spoke to confirm the psalmist's faith. In return for the psalmist's love, **the Lord** promised to **rescue him** from danger, **protect him** from harm, **be with him in trouble . . . honor him,** and **satisfy him.** All the kinds of danger mentioned in this song are ineffective against one who rests in the shadow of the Almighty.

## Psalm 92

### A. It is good to praise the Most High (92:1-7)

**92:1-3.** The psalm begins with the declaration that **it is good to praise the . . . Most High** (cf. 91:1, 9) with **music . . . to proclaim** His **love** and faithfulness (cf. 89:1-2) daily. By "good" the psalmist meant that it is fitting because of the great, praiseworthy things God has done.

**92:4-7.** Here the psalmist elaborated on God's praiseworthy actions. The writer sang because of the Lord's **deeds . . . great works,** and **profound . . . thoughts.** Specifically he was thinking of God's vindication of the righteous by His destroying **senseless . . . evildoers** who sprout **like grass** (cf. 90:5) and **flourish** for a short time (cf. Pss. 49; 73).

### B. The Lord is exalted forever (92:8-15)

**92:8-9.** Verse 8 forms a wonderful link between verses 1-7 and 9-15. In contrast with the wicked who flourish briefly (v. 7) the LORD reigns with absolute supremacy **forever.** Because of this His **enemies will perish.**

**92:10-11.** In verses 10-14 the psalmist anticipated what the truth in verses 8-9 meant for himself. God would surely exalt his **horn** and anoint him. Here again he wrote with such confidence that he described God's work as if it had already happened. An animal horn pictures strength (cf. 89:17, 24; 112:9), and the "oil" represents festivity and restoration of vitality. So because God is **exalted** (cf. 92:8), He will likewise bless His people. Moreover, the righteous will see the complete destruction of the **wicked** (v. 11; cf. v. 7).

**92:12-15.** The wicked may flourish but like grass their prosperity is short-lived (v. 7). On the other hand **the righteous will flourish like . . . palm** trees and cedars **of Lebanon.** These trees picture fruitfulness and vitality (v. 14) under God's good hand (cf. 1:3). Those who are so blessed will proclaim the righteousness of **the LORD,** their **Rock** (cf. comments on 18:2).

## Psalm 93

This is one of the "enthronement psalms" (or "theocratic psalms" as they are sometimes called), which celebrate the Lord's reigning on the earth. Other enthronement psalms are 47, 95–99. No doubt they were used in Israel's worship to praise God's sovereignty; but they are also prophetic pictures of the consummation of the ages when the Lord will establish His righteous millennial rule on earth through the Messiah.

In Psalm 93 the psalmist exulted over the reign of the Lord, who has established His throne on high above the oceans and dwells in His holy temple.

### A. The Lord establishes His reign (93:1-2)

**93:1-2.** The psalmist foresaw **the** LORD reigning (cf. 47:8; 96:10; 97:1; 99:1; 146:10) majestically on the earth, **armed with strength.** Clothing in the Old Testament was considered an extension of a person; so the expression **robed in majesty** (cf. 104:1) describes the Lord as majestic and powerful in His reign.

Also by His rule the **whole world** will be **firmly established** (cf. 96:10). This means that all the moral and legal orders of life will be solidified under His dominion. Since His **throne was established** in **eternity** past, His reign on earth is solidly insured.

### B. The Lord is mighty (93:3-4)

**93:3-4.** The psalmist praised the might of the LORD, which is greater than **the seas** with their raging **waves** and roaring noise. In the Old Testament the sea is sometimes an emblem of hostility (cf. Isa. 17:12-13). In pagan Canaanite mythology Baal attained a position of power (and a house that was corrupt) through struggling with and overcoming Prince Yamm, the sea (in Heb. *yām* means "sea"). But these two verses, a polemic against Baalism, show that **the** LORD, not Baal, is **mightier than the . . . sea.** The sea is not mythological; it is a force of nature under God's power (e.g., the Red Sea, Pss. 106:9; 114:3, 5).

### C. The Lord's house is holy (93:5)

**93:5.** Because the **house** of the LORD is filled with **holiness** (in contrast with Baal's corrupt place; cf. comments on vv. 3-4) the Lord's commands are sure. Holiness is the quality that sets the Lord apart from all others. It is made known by His power. This psalm has praised God's power, the evidence that He is alive and active, unlike pagan gods. Because He rules in power and holiness, everyone is to follow His statutes.

## Psalm 94

This psalm recognizes the fact that vengeance belongs to the Lord. The psalmist called on the Lord to wreak vengeance on proud people who insolently oppress the righteous. The writer was confident that the Lord will not forsake His people but will deliver them, for the wicked have no place in the Lord's reign.

## A. Prayer for vengeance (94:1-7)

**94:1-3.** Verses 1-7 record a prayer that **God** would avenge the **jubilant** wicked. In verses 1-3 the psalmist affirmed that vengeance belongs to the Lord. Because God is the **Judge of the earth,** it is He who must repay **the wicked.** Here again a psalmist asked **How long?** (cf. comments on 6:3) The continuing joy of the **wicked** seems out of place since they oppose **God** (cf. 73:3-12).

**94:4-7.** To justify his request, the psalmist lamented the oppression that the proud insolently inflict on the righteous. The speech of the wicked is **arrogant.** They oppress God's **people,** His **inheritance** (cf. v. 14 and comments on 28:9; Deut. 4:20). The wicked destroy the needy and oppressed (the very ones righteous leaders must help; cf. Ps. 72:4, 12-14). The wicked do all this because they are convinced that **the Lord . . . pays no attention to them** (cf. 73:11).

## B. Warning about judgment (94:8-15)

**94:8-11.** The psalmist called on the wicked to consider their ways. He was amazed that the wicked had not **become wise**—God knows their **futile** plans and efforts to oppress the righteous. The logic here is simple but forceful: **He who** created the human **ear** surely can **hear; He who formed the eye** surely can **see;** etc.

**94:12-15.** Here the psalmist expressed his confidence in the Lord. A person God may **discipline** is **blessed** because he is taught **from** the **Law.** Even though a believer is oppressed by wicked people, he can take comfort that God can use such oppression to **teach** him and that God will give him rest from adversity when **the wicked** are destroyed. The psalmist was sure that God **will not** forsake **His people . . . His inheritance** (cf. v. 5 and comments on 28:9; Deut. 4:20), but will reestablish justice.

## C. Consolation from the Lord (94:16-23)

**94:16-19.** The psalmist's only consolation was in the Lord. After asking **who** would **stand** on behalf of his cause **against** sinners, the writer acknowledged that his security was from **the Lord.** When he was almost defeated by despair (**when** his **foot** was **slipping;** cf. 73:2), God's **consolation** quieted his anxious heart and gave him **joy.**

**94:20-23.** Then the psalmist anticipated God's retribution on the wicked. The **corrupt throne** (lit., "throne of wickedness") refers to villainous rulers whose legislation would seek to destroy **the righteous.** These have no part with God. So the psalmist trusted in **the Lord,** his **Fortress** (*miśgob;* cf. comments on 9:9; 46:7), **Rock,** and **Refuge** (cf. comments on 18:1), knowing that the Lord **will repay them for their sins** by destroying **them.**

## Psalm 95

This "enthronement psalm" calls for the people to acknowledge that the Lord is a great King above the gods. (Other enthronement psalms are 47; 93; 96–99.) But having exhorted the congregation to worship their Creator, the psalmist warned them against unbelief as in the days of the wilderness wanderings when God's rest was not experienced.

## A. Praise for the Lord's sovereignty (95:1-7a)

This first section of the psalm is a typical praise song.

**95:1-2.** The psalmist called the congregation to **sing** (cf. comments on 5:11) praises **to the Lord.** He is designated here as **the Rock of our salvation,** a figure of God's provision of security by delivering His people. Apparently the congregation had experienced some such deliverance, for which they were to give **thanksgiving.**

**95:3-5.** **God** is worthy of the joyful praise mentioned in verses 1-2 because of His majesty. He is **the great King** (cf. 98:6; 99:4; and comments on 5:2) over **all gods.** Mentioning these gods (idols) does not acknowledge their reality. It is a statement of God's sovereignty and superiority over every force, real and imagined. Everything in Creation—including things the pagans venerated as gods— the Lord **made,** and therefore He has power over it all.

**95:6-7a.** In these verses, which conclude the praise section of the psalm, the psalmist exhorted the congregation to **worship . . . the Lord . . . for He is**

their **God,** and they are His sheep (cf. 74:1; 79:13; 100:3). The title of **Maker** may refer to His formation of the nation (cf. Deut. 32:6). **The flock** suggests again that the Lord, the Shepherd of His **people** Israel, leads and provides for them.

### B. Warning against unbelief (95:7b-11)

**95:7b-11.** In this didactic section the psalmist warned the nation not to repeat the folly of unbelief that cost their ancestors the promised **rest** in the land. This warning was prompted by the mention of the Lord's care for His people (v. 7a); in the history of the nation too often that care was reciprocated by disobedience. The incident referred to here is the people's murmuring at Rephidim (Ex. 17; Num. 20:1-13). The names given to the place reflect the incident. **Meribah** (cf. Pss. 81:7; 106:32) means "strife" and **Massah** means "testing," for the people strove with the Lord and **tested** Him. So God swore that they could not **enter** the land, but must perish in the wilderness. The younger generation would enter the Promised Land.

In exhorting his audience the psalmist began with the word **Today,** a rhetorical device to stress the immediacy of the opportunity. They must not resist God's **voice** calling them to trust and obey. In the Bible the word **hearts** often means people's wills. To **harden** one's heart meant to refuse to obey. If this psalm's hearers also disobeyed through unbelief, God would keep them from attaining rest in the land.

This passage is quoted in Hebrews 3:7-11 as a warning for Christians who through unbelief (Heb. 3:12) were in danger of not receiving the promised rest (cf. comments on Heb. 3:7-12). In its fullest sense, that rest signifies the Lord's coming kingdom on earth, when believers will experience spiritual and temporal rest in the Lord. Believers, of course, enter that rest positionally when they cease from their works and trust Him.

The warning in Psalm 95 anticipates this because it is part of a song that celebrates the Lord's kingship (v. 3), a kingship that can only be served by true worshipers.

### Psalm 96

In this psalm about the reign of the Lord, the psalmist called on people ev-erywhere and all the elements of nature to praise God because He is greater than all pagan gods and because He will reign in righteousness and truth.

### A. The earth is to praise His majesty (96:1-6)

**96:1-3.** The psalmist invited **all the earth** (i.e., people everywhere; cf. 97:1; 98:4; 100:1) to praise **the Lord.** They were to **sing** (cf. comments on 5:11) **a new song** to Him (cf. 33:3; 40:3; 98:1; 144:9; 149:1). Singing a new song suggests that new mercies had been received. The people were told to announce **His salvation** and His **deeds** throughout the world, which would bring Him **glory** (cf. "glory" in 96:6-8).

**96:4-6.** The **Lord** is **worthy of** the **praise** called for in verses 1-3 because He is greater than **all gods** (cf. comments on 95:3; also note 97:9). Those **gods,** worshiped among **the nations, are** only **idols. He** is the One who **made** everything and is therefore superior. Moreover, His temple (the **sanctuary**) is characterized by **splendor** (cf. 96:9 and comments on 29:2; also called **majesty** and **glory**) and **strength** (cf. 96:7). In other words He is glorious and strong in the midst of His people.

### B. The nations must recognize His reign (96:7-10)

**96:7-9.** The psalmist called for the **families** (lit., "tribes") of the earth to **ascribe . . . glory and strength** (cf. v. 6) to God and **worship** Him. Someday every knee must bow (Phil. 2:10) before this sovereign **Lord,** whose **holiness** is awesome.

**96:10.** People everywhere should praise Him because He **reigns** (cf. 47:8; 93:1; 97:1; 99:1; 146:10). When the Lord returns to **judge** and reign on earth His reign will at last be **established** (cf. 92:1) with righteousness.

### C. All nature should rejoice (96:11-13)

**96:11-13.** The psalmist called on nature to **rejoice** because the Lord will come to **judge the world in righteousness** (cf. 97:2; 98:9) **and . . . truth.** These bold personifications (of **the heavens . . . the earth . . . the sea . . . the fields,** and **the trees**) may indicate that all Creation will flourish when righteousness reigns on earth, when the curse is replaced by blessing. Then earth will no longer groan, waiting for the day of redemption as it is doing now (Rom. 8:20-22). Then nature will sing.

Psalms such as this must have been uplifting for the psalmists as they have been for believers of all ages. Many psalms express a longing for the Lord to destroy wickedness and establish righteousness on the earth. The laments of the psalmists will no more be uttered when the Lord reigns in righteousness and truth.

## Psalm 97

This is a didactic psalm based on a vision of the Lord. The psalmist envisioned the magnificent coming of the Lord in all His splendor. Depicting the Lord coming to reign and to judge His adversaries in righteousness, the psalmist exhorted the saints to hate evil and rejoice in the Lord (cf. 2 Peter 3:10-11, 14).

### A. Announcement of the Lord's reign (97:1)

**97:1.** The psalmist introduced the record of his vision of the Lord by calling on **the earth** (i.e., people in it; cf. 96:1; 98:4; 100:1) to **rejoice** over the establishment of the Lord's kingdom. **The Lord reigns** is also stated in 47:8; 93:1; 96:10; 99:1; 146:10.

### B. The epiphany of the Lord (97:2-9)

**97:2-5.** The psalmist described the Lord's magnificent reigning appearance. In her worship Israel no doubt understood that these verses spoke figuratively of the presence of the Lord's glory. In their fullest meaning, however, they describe the coming of the Lord to reign over the earth.

The Lord's coming is accompanied with **clouds and thick darkness,** often a picture of awesome judgment (cf. Deut. 4:11; 5:22-23; Ps. 18:9, 11; Jer. 13:16; Ezek. 30:3, 18; 32:7-8; 34:12; Joel 2:2; Amos 5:18-20; Zeph. 1:15). God's rule is based on **righteousness** (cf. Ps. 96:13). A consuming **fire** is also a manifestation of His appearance, for by it He in His wrath destroys **His foes** (cf. 21:9; 50:3; 79:5; 89:46; Heb. 12:29; Rev. 20:9). **Lightning** flashes terrify the world. **Mountains melt like wax** (cf. Micah 1:4). The elements of nature that men fear, and the parts of

Creation considered the most solid, all announce the coming of **the Lord of all the earth** (cf. Micah 4:13; Zech. 4:14). Often in Scripture such phenomena accompany the appearance of **the Lord.**

**97:6-9.** The psalmist described the effects of this epiphany. **The heavens** declare **His righteousness** and **glory.** In other words His appearance to establish righteousness on earth will be announced to the world.

Pagan idol-worshipers will be **put to shame** for they will know instantly that they have been wrong. This thought prompted the psalmist to call even the **idols** to **worship** the Lord! So the people of God rejoice because of the triumphant exaltation of their righteous **Lord.** Since He is **over all the earth** (cf. v. 5), He is higher than all false **gods** (cf. 96:4-5), and deserves people's praise.

### C. Call to righteousness (97:10-12)

**97:10.** On the basis of this prospect, the psalmist instructed **those who love the Lord** to despise **evil** (cf. Prov. 8:13), that is, to live in faithful obedience to His righteous standards. By being **faithful** they will be delivered from **the wicked.**

**97:11-12. The righteous** are called on to acknowledge and **praise** the righteous **Lord** with gladness because of their blessings of **joy** and spiritual prosperity (spoken of as **light;** cf. 27:1; 36:9).

## Psalm 98

In this psalm the writer exhorted all the earth to sing and praise the Lord who reigns, because He had done marvelous things in saving Israel by His power and will judge the world in righteousness.

### A. God has made His salvation known (98:1-3)

**98:1-3.** The psalmist invited his readers to **sing to the Lord a new song** (cf. 33:3; 40:3; 96:1; 144:9; 149:1) because in His strength (**right hand** and **arm** are symbols of power) He has provided **salvation** and **revealed His righteousness.** God's great **salvation** is possible because of His loyal **love** (ḥeseḏ) and **faithfulness** (these may be trans. "faithful, loyal love"). Remembering His covenant with His people Israel, **the Lord** delivered and saved them.

## B. God will judge the world in righteousness (98:4-9)

**98:4-8.** Anticipating the Lord's final salvation of His people prompted the psalmist to call **the earth** (inhabitants in it; cf. 96:1; 97:1; 100:1) to rejoice before Him. Everyone should **shout for joy** (98:4a, 6b) and **sing** with various musical instruments **before the LORD, the King** (cf. 95:3; 99:4; and comments on 5:2). Even nature (including **the sea**. . . . **rivers,** and **mountains**; cf. 96:11-13) is called to resound and rejoice **together.**

**98:9.** Why should people praise **the LORD?** Because He **comes to judge the. . . . world in righteousness** (cf. 96:13). The psalmist was again envisioning the Lord's coming and its purpose. He will bring salvation (98:3) and justice.

## Psalm 99

The psalmist encouraged everyone to exalt the Lord with praise for two reasons: because He is holy and because He mercifully answers His people's prayers.

## A. The Lord who reigns is holy (99:1-5)

**99:1-3.** The psalmist offered praise to the holy **LORD** who reigns. The common theocratic expression again begins this psalm: **The LORD reigns** (cf. 47:8; 93:1; 96:10; 97:1; 146:10). Therefore everyone should **tremble.**

God is described as sitting **enthroned between the** gold-covered **cherubim** (cf. 80:1) over the ark of the covenant (cf. 1 Kings 6:23-28). So He is **great** in **Zion,** where the temple was located. People everywhere should **praise** this **great** Sovereign. His dwelling in Zion and His righteous reign speak of His greatness and His holiness, which are the predominant reasons for praise mentioned in this psalm.

**99:4-5.** The power and righteousness of **the King** (cf. 95:3; 98:6; and comments on 5:2) manifest His holiness, so the psalmist praised Him for these.

Verse 5 is a refrain (cf. v. 9) in which everyone is invited to **exalt the LORD . . . and worship at His footstool** (i.e., before the temple with its ark located inside).

## B. The Lord who reigns is merciful (99:6-9)

**99:6-9.** The psalmist spoke of the Lord's merciful dealings with his ancestors in spite of Israel's iniquities. **Moses . . . Aaron,** and **Samuel** prayed and were **answered.** God **spoke to them** (i.e., Israel) **from the pillar of cloud** (cf. Ex. 13:21) and they obeyed. Even after **Israel** sinned and was **punished,** the **LORD . . . answered** their prayers and forgave them. So praise is due this Monarch not only because of His holiness (Ps. 99:3, 5) but also because of His merciful dealings with His people. God's mercy prevents His own from being consumed by His righteous judgment.

Verse 9 is a refrain (cf. v. 5 with its similar wording) in which God's people are told to **exalt the LORD** with praise and **worship at His holy mountain** (cf. 43:3; 48:1; 87:1), Zion.

## Psalm 100

The superscription states that this psalm (or song) is "for giving thanks." It was used in the temple with the sacrifices of praise. The expressions in this psalm reflect the preceding enthronement psalms (Pss. 47; 93; 95-99) that celebrate the Lord's rule.

The psalmist exhorted the congregation to serve the Lord with gladness because He is the Creator, and to enter His temple with much thanksgiving because He is good and faithful.

## A. Serve the Lord with gladness (100:1-3)

**100:1-2.** Verses 1-3 include a call for praise and joyful service. People everywhere (**all the earth;** cf. 96:1; 97:1; 98:4) should **shout . . . to the LORD;** they are not to be subdued in their praise of Him. Moreover, they are to **serve** Him **with gladness.** This service, **with joyful songs,** may mean worship.

**100:3.** **The LORD** should be praised and worshiped joyfully because He is sovereign. He is the Creator, and those who trust Him **are His** possession. They follow Him, for they are **the sheep of His pasture** (cf. 74:1; 79:13; 95:7; also note 23:1; 80:1).

## B. Enter His courts with thanksgiving (100:4-5)

**100:4-5.** This second part of the psalm is a call to the saints to **enter** Jerusalem (God's **gates**) and to go to the temple (**His courts**) to offer their **thanksgiving** sacrifices for His blessings to them.

The people should **praise** the Lord for His goodness, love, and **faithfulness.** These benefits endure from generation to generation. So every generation that experiences God's goodness, love, and faithfulness can join in praising Him with "The Old One-Hundredth."

## Psalm 101

Speaking to the Lord, King David said he was determined to maintain purity in his empire by removing wickedness from himself, his court, and his capital. When justice prevailed, the Lord would be pleased to dwell in their midst. So in a sense this psalm is a charter by which David ruled under God.

### A. God's loyal love and justice (101:1)

**101:1.** The psalmist sang of the Lord's qualities of **love** (ḥesed) **and justice.** These are characteristics of the divine rule (cf. 89:14), foundational to His effective reign.

### B. David's personal integrity (101:2)

**101:2.** David said he resolved to live **a blameless life,** with a **blameless heart** before God. His lifestyle of integrity would begin in the privacy of his own **house.** This contrasted sharply with the corrupt lives of most kings of the ancient Near East.

### C. David's purity in the palace (101:3-8)

David elaborated on the path of purity he had said he would follow (v. 2). That pure life would begin with him and extend to those who served him. This was a requirement if he was to enjoy the Lord's blessing on his reign.

**101:3-4.** David said he would keep himself pure by not tolerating **evil.** He would not allow **vile . . . faithless,** and **perverse** people and their activities to be around him. "Vile thing" is literally, "things of Belial" (worthless and wicked). "Perverse" ('iqqēš) means "crooked, twisted" (cf. comments on 18:26).

**101:5-6.** The king also wrote that he would surround himself with faithful servants. He would **silence** (cf. v. 8) slanderers and not tolerate the arrogant. **Haughty eyes** (cf. 18:27; Prov. 6:17; 30:13) refers to **a proud** look. David would look for **faithful** people to serve him, those whose lives were **blameless** (in integrity)

as his own was at that point (cf. Ps. 101:2).

**101:7-8.** David also indicated he would purge the wicked from throughout the nation, not just from the palace. As he administrated justice daily (cf. Jer. 21:12), he would **cut off** deceptive people and **the wicked.** "Cut off" often implies capital punishment, but it may also mean removal from service and fellowship.

## Psalm 102

The unique superscription to this psalm points to a private, meditative use for suffering saints. The ideas recall those in Psalms 22, 69, 79. Psalm 102 also has similarities to some statements in Isaiah 40–66.

Hoping that God would speedily answer him, the psalmist lamented that he was overwhelmed and was in desolate straits because of the enemy's reproach. But he found comfort in the fact that the Lord abides, and would not forsake him—a truth that has led many generations of saints to praise God.

### A. Answer me quickly (102:1-2)

**102:1-2.** The psalmist prayed earnestly that God would **hear** him and **not hide** His **face** (cf. 27:9; 143:7). **In** his **distress** he urged the Lord to **answer** him **quickly** (cf. comments on 31:2).

### B. I wither away (102:3-11)

**102:3-7.** The psalmist described his lamentable condition to the Lord. His **days** were being consumed away **like smoke,** his **bones** (cf. comments on 6:2) were burning (i.e., he felt inwardly exhausted), his **heart** was withering **like grass** (cf. 102:11; 37:2; 103:15-16; Isa. 40:6-8). Having no appetite, he was **groaning** in physical agony. Emaciated (cf. Job 19:20), he felt desolate, **like** a mournful-looking **owl** or **a bird** sitting **alone.** His strength was gone, he was inwardly depressed, and he had lost his will to live.

**102:8-9.** The psalmist's dilemma was intensified when he heard that his **enemies** mocked his plight. To **eat ashes** (cf. Isa. 44:20) means to have ashes on one's head as a symbol of mourning. Mourning and weeping (**tears;** cf. Ps. 80:5) were so continuous that they were like his daily diet.

**102:10-11.** Moreover, he was convinced that God's **wrath** had consumed him. **Because** God had allowed this to happen, he felt his life was about over, **like the evening shadow** that indicates a day is almost gone (cf. 144:4) and like the withering **grass** (cf. 102:4).

### C. He will not despise the destitute (102:12-22)

**102:12-13.** The complaints of the psalmist (vv. 3-11) were followed by his confidence that the LORD would answer his prayers. **You** in Hebrew is emphatic, stressing the contrast between the psalmist and the LORD. The transition to praise was sudden: the Lord sits **enthroned** (cf. comments on 2:4) **forever** and He would respond, for it was **time to show favor to** His people in Jerusalem.

**102:14-17.** He was confident that the Lord, who had established His reign in Zion, would not forsake those who love Him. The Lord's **servants** loved even Zion's **stones** and **dust** (a figure of the servants' intense concern for the city in its calamity) partly because it was His dwelling place. Others too—**the nations** and their **kings . . . will revere. . . . the LORD** for He **will rebuild Zion.** This indicates that the psalmist had widened his thoughts from his own weakness to reflect on the Lord's sovereignty, which guaranteed that the city would be restored. Perhaps the psalm was occasioned by a calamity in the capital city. Even so the psalmist was convinced that the Lord would answer the people's **prayer.**

**102:18-20.** Praise for deliverance was then anticipated. **Future** generations would **praise the LORD** when they heard how He **looked down from . . . heaven** (**His sanctuary on high**) and heard **the groans of** His people in their destitute condition. The omniscient God's taking a close look at His people is mentioned often in the psalms; it shows His great concern. The Lord sometimes intervened to deliver those about to die.

**102:21-22.** As a result of this deliverance, **the name of the LORD** would be praised when everyone gathered **to worship** Him **in Zion.**

### D. Your years will never end (102:23-28)

**102:23-28.** Here the psalmist returned to his personal complaint. The Lord had weakened him (cf. vv. 4-10),

seemingly about to cut his **life . . . short** (cf. vv. 3, 11). So he appealed for an extension of his life, asking that he not die prematurely: **Do not take me away . . . in the midst of my days.** Since God's **years go on** (v. 24; cf. v. 27), speaking figuratively of His eternality, the writer wanted his own life to continue for at least a while longer.

Speaking of God's eternality in contrast with His Creation was an expression of the psalmist's confidence in the Lord. **The earth and the heavens. . . . will perish** (cf. 2 Peter 3:10; Rev. 21:1), wearing **out like** old clothes. By contrast God is unchanging (Mal. 3:6; Heb. 13:8) and eternal (His **years will never end**; cf. Ps. 102:27). Therefore He will be faithful to all generations (to the saints' **children** and to **their descendants**).

Verses 25-27 are applied to Christ in Hebrews 1:10-12. The psalmist was addressing the eternal Lord, and the writer of Hebrews identified Jesus Christ as the eternal One, the Creator and Sustainer of the world. This is a strong affirmation of the deity of Jesus Christ.

## Psalm 103

After reviewing the mercies of God toward him, David found hope in his people's covenant relationship with the Lord, though they were sinful and frail. In this confidence the psalmist called on all creation to bless their Lord.

This psalm, a celebration of deliverance, seems to speak of the answer to the prayer in Psalm 102.

### A. The mercies of God (103:1-5)

**103:1-2.** David told himself (**O my soul**) to **praise the LORD** with **all his being,** that is, to put his whole heart in his **praise** of God's **holy name** (cf. 33:21). This was certainly warranted in view of the Lord's many **benefits.**

**103:3-5.** David praised the Lord for His many mercies, including forgiveness of **sins** (v. 3a), healing of sicknesses (v. 3b), deliverance from death (v. 4a; **pit** is a synonym for the grave), enrichment of his life with loyal **love** (cf. vv. 8, 11, 17) and tender **compassion** (cf. vv. 8, 13; 116:5; 119:156), satisfaction (**with good things;** cf. 104:28; 107:9), and renewal. Crowning suggests bestowing blessing (as in 8:5). Like an eagle that remains strong throughout its long life, the psalmist was spiritually vigorous under God's hand (cf. Isa. 40:31).

### B. The compassion of God (103:6-18)

Alluding to certain facts in Israel's history, David meditated on the covenant loyalty the Lord maintained with frail sinners.

**103:6-8.** First, David recalled the Lord's covenant with Moses. After a word of praise for the Lord's **righteousness,** David said that God revealed Himself **to Moses** and Moses' **people** as a **compassionate** (cf. vv. 4, 13; 86:15; 111:4; 145:8) **and gracious** God, who is therefore **slow to anger** and abounds in covenant loyalty (**love,** ḥesed; cf. 103:4, 11, 17). Verse 8 is based on God's words to Moses on Mount Sinai (Ex. 34:6; cf. Neh. 9:17; Pss. 86:15; 145:8; Joel 2:13; Jonah 4:2). Because of these attributes God is faithful to His people and will deliver them from oppression.

**103:9-12.** David then explained that the Lord mercifully forgives sins. Because God is slow to **anger** (cf. v. 8) **He** does **not always accuse** (rîb, "bring a court case against") a man of sin **nor** deal with him **according to** his **sins.** And because of His **great . . . love** (cf. vv. 4, 8, 17) He completely separates sins from the sinners by forgiving them.

**103:13-18.** In these verses David wrote that though man's life is transitory, he is established by the Lord's **covenant. The Lord has compassion** (cf. vv. 4, 8) on His frail people (v. 13) **for He knows how** frail the nature of **man** is (vv. 14-16). Man is made of insignificant **dust** (cf. Gen. 2:7) and his life is brief **like** the **grass** (cf. Pss. 37:2; 90:5; 102:4, 11; Isa. 40:6-8) and wild flowers. Nevertheless **from everlasting to everlasting the Lord's** covenant **love** (cf. Ps. 103:4, 8, 11) **is with those who** obey **Him.** Here again (cf. 102:24-27) the eternality of the Lord is seen as a comfort for frail human beings. Man's hope is not in other fragile creatures, but in the eternal God.

### C. The praise of God (103:19-22)

**103:19-22.** David declared that the Lord's dominion is **over all** the earth. Therefore all **angels,** God's **heavenly hosts,** who are His **servants,** and all His Creation (**His works**) **everywhere** should **praise the Lord.** David closed his psalm in the way he began: by exhorting himself (**O my soul**) to **praise the Lord.**

### Psalm 104

Psalm 104 begins the same way Psalm 103 begins—with the words, "Praise the Lord, O my soul." Psalm 104 is a glorious psalm in praise of God's marvelous Creation and of His sustaining of that Creation. Whereas Psalm 103 praises the Lord's compassion with His people in history, this psalm portrays the Lord's power, wisdom, and goodness to all Creation. The psalmist spoke of God's stretching out the heavens in light, His sovereign control of the deep, His adorning the earth as a dwelling place for man, His arranging night and day for life, and His preparing the sea for its life. He then praised God who gloriously reigns over Creation and renews it by His Spirit. In view of this the psalmist prayed that God would purge sinners, who are out of harmony with Creation.

### A. Prologue (104:1a)

**104:1a.** The psalmist encouraged himself to **praise the Lord** (cf. v. 35; 103:1, 22).

### B. Praise for the Creator (104:1b-23)

**104:1b-4.** In verses 1b-23 the psalmist praised the majesty of the Lord (**You are very great** and **clothed with splendor**; cf. comments on 29:2; **and majesty**; cf. 45:3) as is seen in His works. The writer began with a poetic description of the heavens. **Light,** created on the first day (Gen. 1:3-5), is appropriate to the nature of the Lord. To be clothed "in light" means to be characterized by it. In Creation the Lord spread out **the heavens like a tent** (cf. Gen. 1:6-8; Isa. 40:22), that is, the skies cover the earth as a tent covers tent dwellers. God's dwelling place is pictured figuratively as being in **upper chambers on** the **waters.** He was like a builder making a private room by laying the foundation **beams** above the waters of the sky.

Also the Lord formed all the heavenly elements including **clouds . . . wind,** and **fire.** (On His riding the clouds, see comments on Ps. 68:4.) Psalm 104:4 suggests that God arrays His angels (**messengers**) with physical phenomena, similar to ways He often manifested Himself.

**104:5-9.** The psalmist reiterated how God founded **the earth** and **covered it**

with **the waters.** In poetic imagery the earth is seen as firmly established **on . . . foundations,** and "covered" with water (**the deep**) **as with a garment.** The psalmist vividly portrayed the Lord's gathering **the waters** into rivers and oceans with **a boundary** (i.e., with shorelines beyond which **they cannot** go; cf. Job 38:9-10; Jer. 5:22). God's rebuking the waters suggests they were a chaotic force to be calmed and "conquered." Some of the wording in Psalm 104:7-9 sounds like the Flood account, but the psalmist was referring to Creation.

**104:10-18.** In adorning the earth as a place for living, God placed **springs** in the valleys to **give water** for animals (vv. 10-12), and He **makes** things **grow** that give **food** for animals and **man,** and **oil** (from olive trees) to smooth man's **face** (vv. 13-15). Also God provides dwelling places for animals and birds (vv. 16-18). In His wisdom God made the earth amazingly well suited for all forms of life.

**104:19-23.** The Lord made **the moon** and **the sun** to rule the times when various creatures on earth are active.

### C. Praise for the Lord's dominion (104:24-32)

**104:24-30.** The psalmist broke forth with praise to the LORD for all of His Creation, made in His great **wisdom.** The earth's many living forms (**creatures**) are under His dominion.

Ocean **creatures** of various sizes— including the **large. . . . leviathan** (here a real animal, not a mythological creature; cf. comments on Job 41)—wait for **food** and other **good things** (cf. Pss. 103:5; 107:9) from God (cf. 104:21). But if He hides from them **they are** troubled, as He controls life and death in the oceans. He takes **away their breath** and **they die;** He sends His **Spirit** and others are born.

Water is a predominant theme in this psalm (vv. 3, 6-16, 25-26). In the minds of ancient sages, water was a powerful force. This psalm portrays the Lord's sovereignty over it.

**104:31-32.** The psalmist called for **the glory of the LORD** to continue since He has such powerful control over Creation.

### D. Prayer for harmony in Creation (104:33-35a)

**104:33-35a.** The psalmist responded to the greatness of God's Creation by

doing two things. First, he vowed to **praise . . . God** with song and pleasing **meditation** (cf. 19:14). This is the proper response of a worshiper who remembers his Creator. Second, he prayed that **sinners** would **vanish from the earth** because they are out of harmony with God's Creation.

### E. Epilogue (104:35b)

**104:35b.** The psalmist again encouraged himself (**O my soul**) to **praise the LORD** (cf. v. 1; 103:1, 22). The final "Praise the LORD" translates the Hebrew *halₑlû-yāh* (whence the Eng. "hallelujah"), which occurs here for the first of 23 times in the Psalms (104:35; 105:45; 106:1, 48; 112:1; 113:1, 9; 115:18; 116:19; 117:2; 135:1, 3, 21; 146:1, 10; 147:1, 20; 148:1, 14; 149:1, 9; 150:1, 6).

## Psalm 105

By tracing some aspects of the history of Israel (from Abraham to the wilderness wanderings)—as the Lord moved His people miraculously in fulfillment of His covenant promises—the psalmist praised the greatness of the Lord's love for His own.

### A. Praise for the Lord's greatness (105:1-6)

**105:1-6.** The psalmist began with a call (to Israel, v. 6) to **praise** and **rejoice** because of the Lord's many **wonderful acts** and **His holy name.** His name means His attributes that are revealed to man. Israel should depend on **the LORD** (**look** and **seek His face**), remembering His miraculous works.

### B. Praise for the Lord's faithfulness (105:7-41)

**105:7-11.** The psalmist turned to offer praise for the Lord's remembrance of His promises to the nation. The nation should remember Him (v. 5) because **He remembers** them! (v. 8; cf. v. 42) **The LORD . . . God,** who exercises universal rule (**His judgments are in all the earth**), remembered (i.e., fulfills) **His covenant** and His oath. His covenant **made with Abraham** (Gen. 12:1-3; 15:18-21) was confirmed in Isaac's presence (Gen. 22:15-18) and also given **to Jacob** (Gen. 28:13-15; 32:12). **Israel,** God said, would be a great nation and would possess **the land** He promised.

**105:12-41.** The psalmist then traced something of the history of Israel in which the Lord fulfilled His promise to make **Israel** a great nation. First, the writer stated that the Lord protected them while they sojourned in other lands (vv. 12-15). Perhaps this refers to Abraham's journey from Ur in Chaldea to Haran (Gen. 11:31), Canaan (Gen. 12:4-5), Egypt (Gen. 12:10-20), and his living in the Negev (Gen. 20:1). Second, **the LORD** sovereignly led Israelites into Egypt and exalted **Joseph** (Ps. 105:16-22; cf. Gen. 37; 39-41). Third, in **Egypt** the **LORD made His people very fruitful** even though they were oppressed (Ps. 105:23-25; cf. Ex. 1:6-14). Fourth, through **Moses . . . and Aaron** the Lord worked **wonders in** Egypt (**the land of Ham;** cf. Ps. 105:23). These wonders were the plagues on Egypt (vv. 26-36) that oppressed the Egyptians (cf. Ex. 7–11; Ps. 78:44-51). God rescued His people with great booty (105:37). In fact **Egypt was** relieved **when they left** (v. 38). Fifth, the Lord led the Israelites through the wilderness and provided **quail,** manna (**bread of heaven**), and **water** from **the rock** (vv. 39-41). So even during Israel's wanderings He was faithful to them.

### C. Praise for the Lord's deliverance (105:42-45)

**105:42-45.** The psalmist spoke again of how the Lord **remembered His** word (v. 42; cf. v. 8) and **brought . . . His people** out of Egypt and led them to the Promised Land (vv. 43-44). They were redeemed from bondage so **that they might** obey His word (v. 45).

This psalm expresses joy over God's faithfulness to His word in redeeming **His Chosen** People. So those who receive His benefits should remember His works and respond with obedience. On the words **Praise the LORD** (*hal<sup>e</sup>lû-yāh*), see comments on 104:35.

## Psalm 106

In spite of God's faithfulness to Israel (Ps. 105) her history was filled with faithlessness and ingratitude. Psalm 106, a confessional psalm, traces some of the Israelite's rebellious activities and God's judgments on them. The psalmist then prayed that the Lord would deliver His people from their captivity. A similar confession is found in Nehemiah 9. In addition, this psalm has similarities with Isaiah 63 and Ezekiel 20.

### A. Praise for God's goodness (106:1-5)

**106:1-5.** The psalmist praised God for His incomparable goodness, loyal **love,** and power (vv. 1-2). On the words **Praise the LORD** (*hal<sup>e</sup>lû-yāh*), see comments on 104:35. Since all who **do what is right** are **blessed** by **the LORD** (106:3), the psalmist prayed that when God blesses His **people** He would remember him too. That way he could **enjoy . . . prosperity** and **joy,** and give God **praise.**

### B. Confession of sin (106:6-46)

**106:6.** The psalmist introduced the theme of confession with a general statement that they, the Israelites in the psalmist's day, had **sinned** as their **fathers** (i.e., ancestors) had done. This prompted him to relate their ancestors' sins.

**106:7-12.** The psalmist then recounted the sins of the people in the wilderness. First, he wrote of their sin at the crossing of **the Red Sea** (vv. 7-12; cf. Ex. 14:11-12). **Yet** the Lord **saved them** (cf. Ex. 14:26-30) to show **His mighty power,** and **they believed** (cf. Ex. 14:31) and **sang** praises to Him (cf. Ex. 15:1-21).

**106:13-33.** Then the psalmist spoke of the people's sins as they traveled to the Promised Land. **They soon forgot** God's **miracles** (cf. vv. 21-22) and began to crave (cf. Num. 11:4) and **God. . . . sent** a plague (**a wasting disease**) on **them** (cf. Num. 11:33). They also murmured out of envy over **Moses and . . . Aaron,** so God destroyed **Dathan** and his **company** (Ps. 106:16-18; cf. Num. 16; 26:8-9). **At Horeb,** the ancient name for Mount Sinai (cf. Deut. 5:2; Mal. 4:4), **they made a** golden **calf** in violation of the Law. **God. . . . would** have destroyed **them** if Moses had **not** interceded (Ps. 106:19-23; cf. Ex. 32).

They murmured again (**grumbled**) so God **swore . . . with uplifted hand** (cf. comments on Ex. 6:8) **that** they would die in the wilderness (Ps. 106:24-27; cf. Num. 14:26-35). They **despised the pleasant land** by disbelieving **the LORD.**

At **Peor** they sinned again (this time in idolatry with the Moabites), and **Phinehas . . . intervened** to stop **the plague** (Ps. 106:28-31; cf. Num. 25).

At **Meribah . . . Moses** lost patience

with them when **they rebelled against . . . God** (Ps. 106:32-33; cf. 81:7; 95:8; Ex. 17:7; Num. 20:2-13). As a result of his impatience Moses also lost the privilege of entering the land of promise (Num. 20:12).

**106:34-46.** The psalmist then reminded the people of their failure to **destroy** the inhabitants of the land, **as the LORD had commanded them** to do (Deut. 7:1-2). Instead of obeying the Lord's command to demolish the Canaanites' **idols** (Deut. 7:5, 16, 25-26), Israel **worshiped** them (cf. Jud. 2:11-12) and even **sacrificed their sons and . . . daughters to demons** (Ps. 106:37; cf. Deut 32:17) associated with **the idols** (Ps. 106:38).

Because Israel sinned so grievously, **the LORD was angry** (cf. Jud. 2:14, 20) **with His people** and gave **them over to the** oppression of **enemies.**

**Many times,** however, God **delivered them** (Ps. 106:43-46). This refers to His raising up judges to deliver Israel from her oppressors (cf. Jud. 2:16) because of **His covenant** and **His** faithful **love** (*ḥeseḏ*). Thus the Lord constantly brought judgment on His disobedient people, but He also constantly responded to their cries.

### C. Prayer for deliverance (106:47-48)

**106:47-48.** After retracing the nation's sin and God's punishment, the psalmist prayed that they would be again delivered (**gather us from the nations** apparently suggests the nation was dispersed) so that they might **praise** Him.

The doxology in verse 48 closes Book IV of the Psalter. This verse is similar to the doxology that concludes Book I (see 41:13). On the words **Praise the LORD** (*halᵉlû-yāh*), see comments on 104:35.

## V. Book V (Pss. 107–150)

Of these 44 psalms, 15 are by David (108–110; 122; 124; 131; 133; 138–145), 1 is by Solomon (Ps. 127), and the other 28 are anonymous.

## Psalm 107

This psalm is a call to praise addressed to the redeemed of the Lord. The psalmist motivated them to praise Him by portraying how He delivered His people out of the wilderness, broke the bonds of prisoners, restored the sick, showed His power to mariners in the sea, and providentially governs nature and human affairs.

### A. Call for the redeemed to praise (107:1-3)

**107:1-3.** God should be thanked for His enduring loyal **love** (cf. v. 43), especially by **the redeemed** who benefit from it. The psalm may have been written during the Babylonian Exile because of the words in verses 2b-3.

### B. Cause for praise: Deliverance (107:4-32)

In these verses the psalmist cited four examples of the Lord's deliverances of His people. In each case the people pleaded for the Lord to help them out of their distress and He did so (vv. 6, 13, 19, 28). Also in each case the psalmist urged the people to thank God for His unfailing love and wonderful deeds (vv. 8, 15, 21, 31).

**107:4-9.** First, He delivered **some** from wandering in the wilderness. Unable to find their way, **hungry . . . thirsty,** and dying, they **cried . . . to the** LORD and **He led them** to safety. So people should praise **the** LORD because He satisfied **with good things** (v. 9; cf. 104:28) those who were **thirsty** and **hungry** in the wilderness.

**107:10-16.** Second, the Lord released **prisoners** from bondage. Those who were chained in dark prisons because **they had rebelled against . . . God. . . . cried** out and were freed from the **darkness** and **chains.** The Jewish Targum suggests this refers to King Zedekiah and the nobles of Judah in exile in Babylon. So people should praise **the** LORD because He delivers from bondage.

**107:17-22.** Third, **the** LORD delivered the sick from death. When rebellious sinners were afflicted and **near the gates of death** (cf. Job. 38:17; Ps. 9:13; Isa. 38:10), **they cried** out **to** Him **and He** restored **them,** healing them by **His word.** So people should praise **the** LORD and **sacrifice thank offerings** (i.e., praise offerings) because of their restored health.

**107:23-32.** Fourth, God delivers sailors in trouble at **sea.** Mariners see His **works** as He calls up a storm (**tempest**). **Their courage** melts, and being **at their wits' end** (lit., "all their wisdom was swallowed up"), they call on Him. He calms **the storm** and delivers them from their danger, guiding them safely to their destination. So people should praise **the Lord. . . . in the assembly.**

### C. Cause for praise: Dominion (107:33-43)

The psalmist spoke of the Lord's providential governing of the world as a second major reason for praise (cf. vv. 4-32).

**107:33-38.** The Lord has great power over nature. (The past-tense verbs in the NIV in these verses may be rendered in the pres. tense.) He can turn **a desert** into a watered area (v. 33) or conversely He can make a **fruitful land** become a wasteland (cf. Deut. 29:23). He does this **because of the wickedness of** the people in the land (cf. Deut. 29:24-28).

On the other hand God made the barren land become habitable (**a city where they could settle;** cf. Ps. 107:4, 7) and **fruitful** (vv. 35-38). This He did for the benefit of the poor and needy, so that **their numbers greatly** flourished.

**107:39-43.** The Lord also has power over people's experiences. He humbles and brings down the proud, but He lifts up the poor and **needy.** So the redeemed praise **the Lord** (**the upright see and rejoice) but . . . the wicked** are silenced.

A **wise** person will **consider** these meditations carefully, noting the Lord's **great love** (ḥeseḏ; cf. vv. 1, 8, 15, 21, 31).

### Psalm 108

This is a song of triumph in praise of the Lord's loyal love, given with the full expectation that all His enemies will be destroyed in their own devices. Because David was convinced that God will exult in the subjugation of the nations, he prayed for divine leadership. Verses 1-5 are almost the same as 57:7-11, and 108:6-13 are identical with 60:5-12. No doubt the parts were joined for some liturgical purpose.

### A. Song of triumph (108:1-6)

**108:1-6.** David sang this song of triumph in praise of God's **great . . . love** and remarkable **faithfulness** (v. 4; cf. 115:1; 117:2; 138:2). The psalmist expressed his desire that God **be exalted . . . over all the earth** so that His saints might **be delivered.** His **right hand** suggests His power (cf. Ex. 15:6, 12; Pss. 20:6; 45:4; 60:5; 89:7-13).

### B. Confidence of victory (108:7-13)

**108:7-13.** David was convinced that the Lord will subjugate the tribes of the earth to **Judah** (vv. 7-9; see comments on the identical verses in 60:6-8). Realizing his need for God's leadership, he prayed for help **against** his **enemies** in full confidence that **God** would destroy them (108:10-13; see comments on the identical verses in 60:9-12).

### Psalm 109

The psalmist prayed that the Lord would take vengeance on his enemies who opposed him with evil devices. The psalmist also heaped curses on the wicked. The superscription attributes the psalm to David, but it is not clear whether the references in the psalm are to his time as king or before. The psalm is filled with imprecations (see "Theology of the Psalms" in the Introduction). These are the zealous prayers of the righteous who stand for God's cause on earth. Their sentiment is harsh, but the threat of the wicked against the righteous was severe.

### A. Lament over deceptive enemies (109:1-5)

**109:1-5.** David cried out to **God, whom** he praised, **not** to be **silent** but to deliver him from the danger of **wicked . . . men.** They were **deceitful** (v. 2) and hateful (v. 3), and rewarded his **friendship** with false accusations, reciprocating his good with **evil** and **hatred.**

### B. Imprecations on the wicked (109:6-20)

In an extended section of imprecations, David wished that in retribution the wicked would be made desolate and dispossessed.

**109:6-15.** David prayed that his enemy would be opposed (v. 6), be **found guilty** (v. 7), die (so that **his wife** would become **a widow** and **his children** vagabonds, vv. 8-10), be made poor by an extortioner and plunderers (v. 11), and be pitied by **no one** (v. 12). David also prayed that his enemy's posterity would **be cut off** (v. 13) and that the sins of his enemy's ancestors would **be remembered** by the **Lord** (vv. 14-15). These were the longings of David's zealous heart for retribution. On the psalmists' imprecations see "Theology of the Psalms" in the Introduction.

**109:16-20.** Reasons for the imprecations in verses 6-15 are given here. This wicked man took advantage of **the poor . . . the needy** (cf. v. 22), **and the brokenhearted** (v. 16). **He loved to** heap curses on other people (v. 17); it was a part of him like the clothing he wore and the **water** he drank (v. 18). Therefore *he* should be cursed (v. 17); cursing should envelop and confine him (v. 19). This would be God's way of paying back (cf. v. 5) **those who** accused and slandered David (v. 20).

## C. Prayer for help (109:21-31)

**109:21-25.** David turned to his **sovereign LORD** for help and deliverance because he was in great need. He was apparently weak (**poor and needy**; cf. vv. 16, 31 and see comments on 37:14) and perishing (he was fading **away** and thin **from fasting**) under the oppression of those wicked men. Besides being in danger, they scornfully mocked him.

**109:26-31.** David's prayer for **help** was based on his desire that the wicked would understand that the LORD would vindicate him (vv. 26-27), and that he might **rejoice** when they were **put to shame** and **disgrace** (vv. 28-29). David vowed he would testify of (**extol**) the LORD for delivering him (**the needy one**; cf. v. 22) **from** the oppressor.

# Psalm 110

The words of this psalm are addressed to the psalmist's "LORD." The expressions are those of a prophet who had received a revelation from God. The king was also a priest, a fact that looks beyond the order of Aaron, which was not a royal order. This is one reason the psalm has been classified as a prophetic psalm. Jesus quoted Psalm 110:1 in Mark 12:36 (cf. Matt. 22:44; Luke 20:42) to demonstrate that He the Messiah was to be David's Lord, not merely David's Descendant (Mark 12:35, 37). By Jesus' use of the passage one also notes that David wrote Psalm 110, that it was inspired by the Holy Spirit, and that it refers to the Messiah. Psalm 110:1 is also quoted in Acts 2:34-35 and Hebrews 1:13. Attempts to date Psalm 110 in the Maccabean times, when some priests held temporal power, are therefore futile. Those leaders were priests first and also had civil power but in Psalm 110 the King is a Priest.

The union of the offices of priest and king in the Messiah was prophesied in other passages (e.g., Zech. 6:12-13). If Psalm 110 related to some incident in David's life, it is difficult to articulate. Perhaps it was written about the time David knew that the Anointed One was to have a righteous kingdom (2 Sam. 23:2-4). At the end of his life David knew that he was not that one, but that a greater One was coming who would have dominion, power, and glory forever.

In Psalm 110, David received an oracle about the exaltation of his Lord. He then described the holy army of this King-Priest-Messiah and His defeating all nations.

## A. The oracle of exaltation (110:1-2)

**110:1-2.** David heard a heavenly conversation between **the LORD** (*Yahweh*) and David's **Lord** (*'ădōnay*), that is, between God the Father and the Messiah. The verb **says** is *nᵉ'um*, a word often used to depict an oracle or a revelation. In this oracle Yahweh said that David's Lord, the Messiah, is seated at Yahweh's **right hand** (cf. v. 5), the place of authority, until the consummation of the ages (cf. 2:8-9). At that time **the LORD** will send David's Lord, the Messiah, to make his **enemies** subject to Him. **A footstool** pictures complete subjugation. With His **scepter** the Messiah **will . . . rule** over His **enemies.**

## B. The dominion of the Messiah (110:3-4)

**110:3.** Others will accompany the Messiah, willingly offering themselves to take part in His **battle.** But this will be no ordinary battle. This will be righteous judgment poured out on the wicked. Hence holiness is the required adornment. As the Israelites of old had to consecrate themselves to the Lord before going into battle, so at the consummation of the ages must believers be **holy** (cf. 2 Peter 3:10-11, 14).

The youthful **warriors** are compared to **the dew** (NIV marg.) **of** the morning. This suggests several ideas, including their freshness, their sudden appearance, their glittering numbers, and even the time of their appearance: in the early morning (**the womb of the dawn**). Therefore Messiah's servants will have made freewill offerings to Him, will be adorned in holiness, and will appear suddenly with youthful vigor.

**110:4.** The LORD (Yahweh) has affirmed by oath that the Messiah will be **a Priest forever, in the order of Melchizedek.** The people of the Messiah will have an eternal High Priest. Melchizedek was the king of Salem (Jerusalem) and priest of the Most High God (Gen. 14:18; Heb. 7:1). Years after he ruled in Jerusalem, David and his descendants ruled there.

That ancient unity of priest and king in one person will be reunited in the Messiah, a fact which necessitates the end of the line of Aaron's priesthood. This is precisely the point of the writer to the Hebrews, who four times said Melchizedek is a type of Christ (Heb. 5:6; 6:20; 7:17, 21). As a Priest Jesus sacrificed Himself by His death on the cross (Heb. 7:27-28; 10:10). Not in Aaron's line (cf. Heb. 7:11-18), He is the eternal High Priest (cf. Heb. 7:21-26, 28) of the New Covenant (cf. Heb. 8:13; 9:15). Because He is also the promised Davidic King, both offices are united in one Person.

### C. The victory of the Messiah (110:5-7)

**110:5-7.** David anticipated the glorious victory of the Messiah. David's **Lord** (the Messiah; cf. v. 1) is seated at God the Father's **right hand** (cf. Heb. 8:1; 10:12), the place of authority. When the Messiah-Priest comes He will defeat (**crush**) **kings** (cf. Rev. 16:16; 19:13-15) and **judge . . . nations** (cf. Joel 3:2, 11-14). His refreshing Himself with a **drink** along **the way** figuratively pictures His renewed vigor, and His lifting **up His head** speaks of His being exalted.

According to the New Testament Christ, accompanied by His saints, will return to judge the world and establish His kingdom on earth.

### Psalm 111

The psalmist vowed to praise the Lord in the assembly for His great and marvelous works of redemption that lead people to fear Him. This psalm is similar to Psalm 112 in its structure and message. Psalm 111 praises the righteousness of the Lord; Psalm 112 extols the blessings of a person who comes to fear Him. Both draw on expressions found elsewhere in the Psalms and in Proverbs. In addition, both are alphabetical songs, or acrostics. Some ancient versions suggest that Psalm 111 was written in the time of Haggai and Zechariah.

### A. Praise in the assembly (111:1-3)

**111:1-3.** The psalmist vowed to **extol the LORD** wholeheartedly **in the council of the . . . assembly** of the saints. He said he would **praise the LORD** for His marvelous **works** and **deeds** that are remembered by those who enjoy (**delight in**; cf. 112:1) **them** and the benefits they bring.

### B. Praise for God's marvelous works (111:4-9)

**111:4-9.** The psalmist now enumerated the marvels of God's work. The theme is announced in verse 4: **the LORD** has made His works memorable; He **is gracious and compassionate** (86:15; 103:8; 145:8). In His grace the Lord has helped mankind and is therefore **remembered** in praise.

Examples of His works are cited in 111:5-6. He gives **food** (cf. 132:15; 136:25; 145:15; 146:7) to **those who fear Him; He remembers His covenant,** that is, He faithfully keeps His promises: in the Conquest He gave His people the **lands** He promised.

God's **works . . . are faithful** and His word is dependable (111:7). All His works are firmly established by His covenant so that He faithfully performs them (v. 8). So **He provided redemption for His people** by **His covenant** (v. 9).

Because the Lord is faithful, **His name** is therefore **holy and awesome.** This means He is holy in a way that prompts people to fear Him.

### C. Fear of the awesome Lord (111:10)

**111:10.** The psalmist concluded that **the fear of the LORD** (cf. 112:1) **is the beginning of wisdom** (cf. Prov. 1:7). People who **follow** Him and His standards **have good understanding.** Worship and obedience will then be accompanied by **praise** that **belongs** to Him.

### Psalm 112

This psalm enumerates some of the blessings enjoyed by a person who fears the Lord. Then it anticipates the exaltation of the righteous and the grievous destruction of the wicked.

## A. The blessing of the one who fears the Lord (112:1)

**112:1.** Building on the end of the previous psalm, this verse says that one who **fears the Lord** and delights **in His** Law is **blessed** (cf. 1:1-2). On **praise the Lord** (*hal‌ᵉlû-yāh*), see comments on 104:35.

## B. The blessings of the righteous (112:2-9)

**112:2-9.** Five blessings that come to one who fears God are enumerated: (1) He is **blessed** with physical and material prosperity because He is **righteous** (vv. 2-3). (2) **Light** is given **even in darkness . . . for the upright** (v. 4). This could refer to prosperity (in place of disaster) or to discernment. (3) He receives goodness in return for being **generous** (cf. v. 9) and just (v. 5). (4) He will be firmly established in his faith, unshakable (cf. comments on 15:5), with **no fear** of what man might do to him (112:6-8). (5) Because he gives **to the poor** (cf. v. 5) **his horn** (cf. 89:17, 24; 92:10) **will be lifted** up, that is, he will be made strong and honorable by **the Lord.**

## C. The anxiety of the wicked (112:10)

**112:10.** In contrast with the blessings of God-fearers, **the wicked** will be filled with anxiety over God's goodness to the righteous. **The wicked,** who are about to perish (**waste away**), will be powerless over the righteous.

# Psalm 113

The psalmist called on all the Lord's servants everywhere to praise God because even though He is exalted on high He lowers Himself to exalt the oppressed. J.J. Stewart Perowne (*The Book of Psalms,* 2:322) rightly observes that this psalm is a connecting link between the song of Hannah (1 Sam. 2:1-10) and The Magnificat of Mary (Luke 1:46-55). The psalm also describes the nature of the Lord in a way that anticipates the *kenōsis,* Jesus' emptying Himself of glory when He came to earth (Phil. 2:7).

Psalms 113–118 form the *Hallel,* a collection of songs sung at the great festivals of Israel—Passover, Pentecost, and Tabernacles—as well as on other holy days. At Passover, for example, Psalms 113–114 were sung before the meal, and 115–118 after it.

## A. Call to praise (113:1-3)

**113:1-3.** The psalm begins and ends with the words **Praise the Lord** (*hal‌ᵉlû-yāh;* cf. v. 9; the endings of Pss. 115–117; and comments on 104:35). The psalmist summoned the **servants of the Lord** to **praise** His **name,** for it is worthy of **praise** at all times. **The name of the Lord** (His revealed attributes) deserves praise in all the world—from east to west.

## B. Cause for praise (113:4-9)

Believers should praise the Lord (cf. vv. 1-3) because of His greatness (vv. 4-5) and His grace (vv. 6-9).

**113:4-5.** He is incomparable—no one is **like** Him (cf. 35:10; 71:19; 77:13; 89:6; Ex. 15:11; 2 Sam. 7:22) for He **sits enthroned** (cf. comments on Ps. 2:4) **on high.**

**113:6-9.** God's greatness (vv. 4-5) is not something He clings to; rather, He comes **down to** see what is in **the heavens and** on **the earth.** He condescends to intervene graciously in human affairs.

Two examples of God's gracious dealings are given, one in verses 7-8 and the other in verse 9. God exalts—thus sharing His nature with man—the miserable and **the poor** to places of prominence and prosperity. The poor hover near the refuse **heap** outside the city for warmth from the perpetual burning and for food from the garbage. But God exalts them, the lowest of society, to an equal portion with the highest (**with princes**). God does not do this with *every* poor person, but when He does it for some His gracious dealings are evident. In the New Testament the truth takes on a spiritual significance, for those who trust in the Lord are given an inheritance in the heavenlies, through the grace of God.

The other example is that of **the barren woman** who becomes **a happy mother.** In Israel's history several barren women were given children (e.g., Sarah, Rachel, Hannah). To the Israelites, this was a mark of God's gracious blessing.

The point of the psalm is that God by His grace does marvelous and mighty deeds for those in need and distress. That is why He is worthy of praise. The psalm concludes with the admonition to worship, **Praise the Lord** (*hal‌ᵉlû-yāh;* cf. v. 1).

## Psalm 114

This psalm celebrates the deliverance of God's people at the Exodus—a fitting song to be sung at Passover which was instituted at that time (Ex. 12). The psalmist recalled how the sea fled and the mountains trembled when Israel escaped from Egypt. In a bold poetic stroke, he interrogated the mountains and the sea concerning their reaction, and then called on the earth to tremble at the presence of the Lord who brought water from the rock.

### A. The fleeing of the sea and trembling of the mountains (114:1-6)

**114:1-4.** The psalmist recalled the mighty power of God that was displayed in Israel's past history. He announced that **when** God brought them **out of Egypt . . . Judah became** His **sanctuary,** which meant that Judah became the tribe in which He placed the temple. When He brought them out of Egypt and into Canaan, **the** Red **Sea** and **the Jordan** River **turned back** and **the mountains skipped like rams** and **lambs,** that is, they quaked.

**114:5-6.** The psalmist interrogated the **sea** and the **mountains,** challenging them to explain why they reacted to the Lord as they did (cf. vv. 3-4). This bold personification was designed to say that all Creation recognized and obeyed the Creator's will. The Lord's presence in the Old and New Testaments is frequently evidenced by His display of power.

### B. The call for the earth to tremble (114:7-8)

**114:7-8.** The psalmist, instead of answering his question in verses 5-6, instructed the **earth** to continue to **tremble** before **the Lord.** The reason is that the Lord had **turned the rock,** a dry solid, **into . . . water,** beneficial to His people. Fear and trembling should always be the response to God's **presence** and awesome power.

## Psalm 115

The psalmist called on the Lord to vindicate His honor among the nations. After demonstrating God's sovereignty and voicing contempt against pagan idols, he invited all to trust in the Lord for He would bless them abundantly.

This psalm may have been written at a time when the nation was humiliated by idolaters. The psalm instructs people to trust in the Lord, not in worthless idols.

### A. Call for vindication (115:1-2)

**115:1-2.** Acknowledging the unworthiness of the people in contrast with God's **glory . . . love, and faithfulness** (cf. 108:4; 117:2; 138:2), the psalmist asked the LORD to vindicate the worthiness of His great **name.** There was no reason that the idolaters of **the nations** should taunt believers with their question, **Where is their God?** (cf. 79:10)

### B. Declaration of God's sovereignty (115:3-8)

**115:3-8.** In verse 3 the psalmist declared his theme: **God** is sovereign. He alone **is in heaven,** and **He does whatever** He desires (cf. 135:6; Job 23:13). The significance of this is seen in contrast with the pagans' **idols. Made** of metal, they are only the works of men's **hands** (Ps. 115:4) so they are totally impotent. Though idols have **mouths . . . eyes . . . ears . . . noses . . . hands . . . feet,** and **throats,** they **cannot speak . . . see . . . hear . . . smell . . . feel . . . walk,** or talk (cf. 135:15-18). People who construct idols and those who **trust in them** become **like them**—powerless before the Lord God.

### C. Call to faith (115:9-11)

**115:9-11.** The psalmist exhorted **Israel** to **trust in the LORD,** not in idols, for only He can protect them—as **their Help** (cf. comments on 30:10) **and Shield** (cf. comments on 3:3). Everyone in Israel—including priests (**house of Aaron**) and other worshipers (those **who fear Him;** cf. 115:12-13; 118:2-4)—should **trust in** Him.

### D. Promise of blessing (115:12-18)

**115:12-15.** God's people are encouraged to trust the living God because He will **bless** them all (vv. 12-13) including priests and other worshipers (cf. vv. 10-11). The psalmist then prayed for blessings on the people and their **children** by God. The title **Maker of heaven and earth** points to His sovereign work in Creation (this title is also used of God in Job 4:17; 32:22; 35:10; Pss. 121:2; 124:8; 134:3; 146:6; Ecc. 11:5; Jer. 10:16).

**115:16-18.** The psalmist concluded this psalm by extolling the LORD. Unlike the idols He owns the highest heavens and has given the earth . . . to man. Since the dead do not . . . praise, the psalmist and his fellow believers praised Him. He was confident that God would deliver them from their idolatrous enemies, so that they could continue to praise Him then and forevermore. The psalm ends with Praise the LORD (hal‍°lû-yāh; cf. comments on 104:35).

## Psalm 116

The psalmist recalled how the Lord delivered him from certain death and enabled him to have a prolonged life of service. Because of this he vowed to acknowledge the Lord in the temple. If Psalm 115 is a congregational song, Psalm 116 is a personal song of thanksgiving for deliverance from imminent death.

### A. Proclamation to praise (116:1-2)

**116:1-2.** The beginning of this psalm is a unique expression of love for the LORD, an expression that came from someone delivered by Him. Because of this, the psalmist resolved to call on Him as long as he lived.

### B. Report of the deliverance (116:3-11)

**116:3.** As a means of instructing others, the psalmist testified to his deliverance by the Lord (vv. 3-11). He recalled how he was in peril of death (v. 3). His words dramatically depict that he was hunted by death and the grave. He had almost died.

**116:4-6.** Then the psalmist cried to the LORD to save him. The deliverance he experienced prompted him to instruct the congregation about the LORD. God is gracious and compassionate, protecting and saving those in great need, including the psalmist.

**116:7-11.** He then drew lessons from his experience for others to follow. First, believers can return and rest because God delivers from death (vv. 7-8). The psalmist's suffering and anxiety had been removed so that he could lead a peaceful and tranquil life of service.

Second, God delivers those in need so that they may live obediently before Him (v. 9).

Third, God is the only One who is

completely trustworthy (vv. 10-11). The words I believed refer to verse 9b, that is, he believed that he would live. This was his confidence, even though he was greatly afflicted, and felt that he had been deceived by all (who apparently had said he would not be delivered). Faced with certain death, he knew that God was trustworthy, so he cried out to Him.

### C. Vow of praise (116:12-19)

**116:12-14.** The writer, asking what he could give the LORD in repayment for His goodness (cf. v. 7; 13:6; 142:7), vowed to praise Him in the congregation. It has been suggested that the cup refers to the part of the sacrifice he would give for having been given salvation (deliverance). This is probably correct; otherwise, the expression would be completely figurative, that is, he would praise (lift up) God for his lot (his "cup") which was "salvation." In either case he would praise God, which was a paying of vows (cf. 116:18). Others would hear him and be edified, which is one of the purposes of public praise.

**116:15-19.** The psalmist, knowing that the LORD cares intensely about the death of His saints, acknowledged that he was a servant (vv. 15-16) of the LORD and would praise Him publicly (vv. 17-19). The death of a saint is not something the LORD considers as cheap; He does not let His people die for no reason. Here the deliverance of a saint from the brink of death (vv. 3, 8) resounded to God's praise and the edification of saints for ages to come. The psalm ends with Praise the LORD (hal‍°lû-yāh; cf. comments on 104:35).

## Psalm 117

Psalm 117 is an invitation to people everywhere to praise the Lord for His loyal love and faithfulness.

### A. Call to praise (117:1)

**117:1.** The psalmist called on the nations to praise the LORD, and on peoples everywhere to laud Him.

### B. Cause for praise (117:2)

**117:2.** The attributes of the LORD are the cause for praise. His love (ḥeseḏ) is His covenant loyalty for His people, which is great.

This word *ḥeseḏ* is often accompanied by the word *'emeṯ*, "truth" or **faithfulness** (cf. 108:4; 115:1; 138:2). Because the Lord's word is reliable, He is faithful. This term strengthens the concept of His covenant loyalty.

The psalm ends with the familiar words **Praise the Lord** (*halᵉlû-yāh*; cf. comments on 104:35).

## Psalm 118

This psalm completes the group of *Hallel* songs (Pss. 113–118). Possibly Psalm 118 was written for the Feast of Tabernacles, perhaps even the first celebration of that Feast when the people returned from the Exile. The contents certainly suggest that God, in reestablishing His nation, triumphed over the nations and their plans. At least it can be said that the contents describe a festal procession to the sanctuary to sacrifice to and praise the Lord. Because the song was sung at the festivals, expressions in the psalm were on the lips of the people at Jesus' entry into Jerusalem at the beginning of the Passion Week (118:25-26; Matt. 21:9). Also this psalm may have been sung in the Upper Room after the Lord's Supper (Matt. 26:30).

This psalm in its Old Testament setting, however, was a song for praising the Lord's loyal love. The psalmist recounted how the Lord triumphed over all the nations surrounding Israel. Then he exulted in the fact that their salvation was God's marvelous work and that the stone which the builders rejected had become the prominent part of God's work.

### A. Praise for God's loyal love (118:1-4)

**118:1-4.** In response to the call to acknowledge the Lord's goodness (v. 1; cf. v. 29) the nation **Israel,** the priests **(the house of Aaron),** and all the worshipers **(those who fear the Lord;** cf. 115:9-13) declared that **His** loyal **love** is everlasting. Psalm 118:2-4 suggests that the words were spoken antiphonally, in which the psalmist called for praise, and the people answered with it.

### B. Acknowledgment of triumph (118:5-21)

**118:5-9.** In summary fashion the psalmist announced that **the Lord** delivered him from distress (v. 5). On the basis of this he reminded the people (vv. 6-9), that since **the Lord** was **with** him, he need not fear what others might **do to** him (cf. Heb. 13:6). And because **the Lord** was his **Helper** (cf. Ps. 27:9) he could be sure of **triumph.** Therefore the people too could be sure that **it is better to** turn **to the Lord than to trust in** human resources.

**118:10-13.** The psalmist then delineated how **the Lord** gave him confidence in the midst of his enemies. **Surrounded** by enemies who tried to destroy him, he was able to triumph. The threefold refrain (vv. 10-12)—**in the name of the Lord I cut them off** (lit., "circumcised them")—refers to his victory over **the nations.** They were **cut off** suddenly like dry **thorns** that burn quickly (cf. Isa. 9:18). In it all **the Lord helped** him (cf. Ps. 118:7).

**118:14-21.** These verses speak of the effect of the psalmist's triumph. He joyfully praised **the Lord** as his **Strength** (cf. 22:19; 28:7-8; 46:1; 59:9, 17; 81:1), **Song** (i.e., his Source of joy), and his **Salvation** (cf. 118:21). God's **right hand** speaks of His strength. Because of this the psalmist declared that he would **live** and would enter **the gates of righteousness** and **give thanks** (vv. 19, 21; cf. v. 28) to God. The references to the gates and to praising suggest that the psalmist was anticipating joining the congregation in the sanctuary to praise **the Lord** for His great **salvation** (deliverance).

### C. Significance of the triumph (118:22-29)

**118:22-24.** The psalmist explained that **the Lord** had taken **the stone** that **the builders rejected** and had marvelously made it **the capstone** of the nation. Therefore the people should **rejoice.** In those days great empires easily set up and removed kings. Perhaps those great nations discounted Israel as a nation. Yet the Lord took that "stone" and made it "the capstone" of His rule on earth. The image of the stone may have suggested itself from the temple construction work going on in the postexilic community.

The psalmist, perhaps the congregation's leader, may have thought of his king as the stone, for in Israel kings often represented the nation. Certainly in Jesus' Parable of the Landowner and the Tenants (Matt. 21:33-44) He applied the psalm in that way. Jesus is the Stone and the Jewish leaders, the builders of the nation, had rejected Him. But God made Him the Capstone. Thus the kingdom would be taken from them and given to others (Matt. 21:43). The fact that this psalm was probably popular at the Passover festival made Jesus' use of it all the more forceful.

**118:25-29.** The psalmist prayed then for his people's salvation and prosperity. The words **save us** (v. 25) and **Blessed is He who comes in the name of the LORD** (v. 26) were proclaimed at Jesus' Triumphal Entry (Matt. 21:9; "Hosanna" translates the Heb. for "save"). The people believed that Jesus was the Coming Savior. In fact the phrase **with boughs in hand** (Ps. 118:27) may have prompted their putting the branches down for Jesus (Matt. 21:8). The second half of Psalm 118:27, though difficult in the Hebrew, probably refers to the custom at the Feast of Tabernacles of waving branches before the Lord. Then later, when the psalm was used in all the feasts, this part of verse 27 became simply an expression in the hymn without boughs literally being in people's hands.

But the people in Jesus' day knew that He claimed to be the Messiah, and that this psalm spoke of the Coming One. So they appropriated its message for the occasion. Fittingly Jesus identified Himself as the Stone who would bring salvation to those who prayed to Him, "Save us."

Because the psalm is typically prophetic of the Messiah, the earlier references to "cut off" (vv. 10-12) may also have a higher significance in relation to the work of Christ. In the Old Testament, circumcision was the means by which a male Israelite was identified with the covenant, but circumcision came to signify "inner circumcision" (cf. Deut. 30:6), belief that set one apart to God. Paul wrote that a true Jew is one whose heart is circumcised (Rom. 2:29).

Perhaps Psalm 118 anticipated the time when the Stone, Jesus, would turn to the nations who would receive Him (cf. John 1:12). If so, His triumph is in a sense different from its meaning when it was historically recorded in Israel. For the psalmist, Psalm 118:25-29 spoke of the procession coming to the temple to worship, and the one coming "in the

name of the LORD" was the worshiper. At the altar the worshiper would **give . . . thanks** (cf. vv. 19, 21) and acknowledge **the LORD** God for His goodness and loyal **love.** In Jesus' Triumphal Entry this psalm, sung by the people as they moved in the procession to the temple, was most appropriate as He entered Jerusalem to begin His work of salvation for those who would believe.

## Psalm 119

The psalmist was persecuted by men of rank and authority, who ridiculed his beliefs, seeking to put him to shame and make him give up his faith. But he strengthened himself by meditating on the Word of the Lord, which to him was his comfort, his prized possession, his rule of life, and his resource for strength—all of which drove him to desire it even more.

This psalm is written in an acrostic (alphabetical) arrangement. In each paragraph (strophe) of eight verses each line begins with the same letter of the Hebrew alphabet. (The 22 strophes correspond to the 22 letters of the alphabet.) So verses 1-8 each begin with the first Hebrew letter, verses 9-16 each begin with the second letter, and so on.

The psalm is largely a collection of prayers and meditations on the Word of God, referred to by 10 synonyms.

"Law" (*tôrâh*), occurring 25 times in the psalm, denotes direction or instruction. More often the word refers to a body of teaching, probably Deuteronomy and Leviticus, if not the whole Pentateuch. In fact in John 10:34 the corresponding Greek word for "Law" seems to include the entire Old Testament.

"Word" (*dābār*) occurs 20 times in the psalm. It is a general term for God's revelation, but the "Ten Commandments" are called "Ten Words" (literal Heb., Deut. 4:13).

"Saying" (*'imrâh*, often trans. "promise" in the NIV) occurs 19 times. It is often a poetical synonym for *dābār*.

"Commandment" (*miṣwâh*) occurs (in the Heb.) 21 times in the plural (usually trans. "commands" in the NIV) and once in the singular collectively. It signifies a definite, authoritative command. It is frequently joined with the next two words.

"Statutes" (*ḥūqqîm*) occurs 21 times.

In the Psalms it is always in the plural. Literally it means "things inscribed." So it refers to enacted Laws (and is trans. "decrees" in the NIV).

"Judgment" (*mišpoṭ*) occurs 19 times in the plural (often trans. "laws" in NIV), and 4 times in the singular. It represents a judicial decision that constitutes a precedence, a binding law. In the Pentateuch it referred to the laws after the Ten Commandments. The word can also mean God's judgmental acts on the wicked.

"Precepts" (*piqqûdîm*) occurs 21 times. It is a poetical word for injunctions, found only in the Psalter (always in the pl.).

"Testimony" (*'ēḏâh*) occurs 22 times in the plural and once in the singular. It is a solemn attestation, a declaration of the will of God. It is a general word for ordinances that became God's standard of conduct. It is usually rendered "statutes" in the NIV.

"Way" (*derek*), used five times in the plural and six times in the singular, is a metaphorical term describing the pattern of life marked out by God's Law.

"Path" (*'ōraḥ*), used five times in Psalms, is parallel to "way."

The psalmist often spoke of several responses he had toward God and His Word: "delight" (Ps. 119:16, 24, 35, 47, 70, 77, 92, 143, 174), "love" (vv. 47-48, 97, 113, 119, 127, 132, 159, 163, 165, 167), "obey" (vv. 8, 17, 34, 44, 56-57, 60, 67, 88, 100-101, 129, 134, 145, 158, 167-168; cf. "obeyed" in vv. 4, 136 and "obeying" in v. 5), "meditate" (vv. 15, 23, 27, 48, 78, 97, 99, 148), and "rejoice" (vv. 14, 74, 162). He also wrote that he wanted God and His Word to "renew" him (vv. 25, 37, 40, 107, 149, 154, 156; cf. vv. 50, 93) and "preserve" him (vv. 88, 159). Twelve times the psalmist referred to himself as God's servant (vv. 17, 23, 38, 49, 65, 76, 84, 124-125, 135, 140, 176).

### A. Blessings of obedience (119:1-8)

**119:1-8.** The psalmist delighted in the fact that those **who walk** in wholehearted obedience **to the Law** are **blessed** (vv. 1-3). This prompted him to wish that he were more obedient in view of God's **commands** to follow His laws (vv. 4-6). So the psalmist vowed to give thanks **as** he learned more about God's **statutes** (vv. 7-8).

### B. Cleansing by God's Word (119:9-16)

**119:9-16.** The psalmist declared that a person cleanses **his way** (conduct) **by** obeying God's **Word** (v. 9). The psalmist testified that he had internalized and rejoiced in God's **Word** so that he might be morally pure (vv. 10-14). He continually meditated in the Law (vv. 15-16).

### C. Appreciation of God's Word (119:17-24)

**119:17-24.** The psalmist asked God to **open** his **eyes** so that he could **see** the marvelous blessings of God in the **Word** (vv. 17-18). He hungered for the Word (vv. 19-20). Because God curses the wicked who disobey Him, he prayed that the Lord would **remove** those who reproached him. In contrast with them, he meditated on and delighted in God's **Law** (vv. 21-24). Frequently in this psalm he referred to the wicked and those who oppressed him (vv. 23, 53, 61, 69-70, 78, 85-87, 95, 110, 115, 119, 122, 134, 155, 157-158, 161).

### D. Prayer for understanding (119:25-32)

**119:25-32.** The psalmist prayed for quickening since he was **laid low** (v. 25). He then asked God for understanding, strengthening, and keeping (vv. 26-29). When God gave him understanding, he would comply because he treasured the **Law** (vv. 20-32).

### E. Loyalty to God's Word (119:33-40)

**119:33-40.** The psalmist declared his loyalty to the Word, which he observed with his whole **heart** (vv. 33-35). He prayed that the Lord would **turn** him away from covetousness and vanity (vv. 36-37). He desired God to confirm His ordinances to him (vv. 38-40).

### F. Salvation through God's Word (119:41-48)

**119:41-48.** The psalmist called on God to deliver him through His **love** and His **Word** (promise, v. 41). **Then** he would have an **answer** for his enemy (v. 42). He prayed (and affirmed) that **the Word** would continue to be his pattern of life (vv. 43-46). He delighted in God's **commandments** and loved them (vv. 47-48).

## G. Hope from God's Word (119:49-56)

**119:49-56.** Declaring his **hope** in the **Word** (v. 49), which **renews . . . life** (v. 50), he decried the proud (**arrogant**; cf. vv. 69, 78, 85) who scorned his faith and hated the **Law** (vv. 51-53). He sang about and meditated on the Word (vv. 54-56).

## H. Obedience to God's Word (119:57-64)

**119:57-64.** Because God was the psalmist's **Portion** (cf. 16:5; 73:26; 142:5), he called on God for mercy (119:57-58). He had lived in accordance with the Word (vv. 58-60), and continued his devotion while he was surrounded by enemies (vv. 61-62). His companions were also believers (vv. 63-64).

## I. Trust in God's Word (119:65-72)

**119:65-72.** The psalmist trusted that the LORD would deal with him **according to** His **Word** (v. 65). He then asked for further instruction to prevent his going **astray** (vv. 66-68). He declared his trust in the midst of slander (vv. 69-70; cf. vv. 51, 53), and admitted that through affliction he realized more of the value of **the Law** (vv. 71-72; cf. v. 127).

## J. Hope in God's Word (119:73-80)

**119:73-80.** The psalmist believed that God created him and had given him **hope in** the **Word** (vv. 73-74; cf. v. 81). Knowing that **in faithfulness** God had **afflicted** him (cf. vv. 67, 71), he asked God to **comfort** him and put **the arrogant** (cf. vv. 51, 69, 85-122) **to shame** (vv. 75-78). He then prayed that **those who fear** the LORD would likewise **turn to** Him in accord with His Word and that he would be kept **blameless** (vv. 79-80).

## K. God's Word is faithful (119:81-88)

**119:81-88.** The psalmist admitted that his **soul** almost fainted while waiting for God's **Word** (vv. 81-82). He was weakened much as **a wineskin in the smoke** becomes shriveled. So he asked **how long** (cf. comments on 6:3) it would be until he was vindicated (119:83-86). He asserted that though his enemies almost consumed him, he had **not forsaken** God's **Law** (vv. 87-88).

## L. God's Word is sure (119:89-96)

**119:89-96.** God's **Word** is settled in heaven and is attested by His **faithful-**ness (vv. 89-91). The psalmist's **delight** (cf. 1:2; 119:174) in the established **Law** had enabled him to win the victory (vv. 92-95). He concluded that God's Word is **boundless** (v. 96) in its values.

## M. God's Word is sweet (119:97-104)

**119:97-104.** The psalmist declared his **love** and devotion to the **Law,** which gave him more **understanding** and wisdom than his **enemies . . . teachers,** and **elders** (vv. 97-100). By God's **Word** he had **kept** himself pure (vv. 101-102; cf. vv. 9, 104). He extolled the **promises** of God as **sweet** (v. 103). **Understanding** and purity (v. 104) summarize the points made in verses 98-101.

## N. God's Word is a light (119:105-112)

**119:105-112.** Recognizing that God's **Word** was his **light** to direct him (cf. v. 130; Prov. 6:23) the psalmist vowed to **follow** it (Ps. 119:105-106). In his distress (vv. 107-110) he called for help and affirmed that he would joyfully follow God's **statutes** and **decrees** (vv. 111-112).

## O. God's Word is awe-inspiring (119:113-120)

**119:113-120.** The psalmist stated that he hated double-mindedness, and that he loved and hoped in God's **Word** because God was his **Refuge** (sēter, "hiding place"; cf. comments on 27:5) and his **Shield** (cf. comments on 3:3). The writer then addressed the wicked, demanding that they leave him (119:115), and asked God to **sustain** and deliver him (vv. 116-117) because of His judgment against the **wicked** (vv. 118-119). The psalmist then said he trembled **in awe** at the judgments of God (v. 120; cf. v. 161).

## P. Vindication from God (119:121-128)

**119:121-128.** The psalmist asked God to protect him from **arrogant** (cf. vv. 51, 69, 78, 85) **oppressors** and to **deal with** him in justice and **love** (vv. 121-124). He sought to motivate God to respond by explaining his loyalty as God's **servant** (vv. 125-126; cf. vv. 122, 124). He added that he loved the Lord's laws (valuing them **more than gold**; cf. v. 72) and hated false ways (vv. 127-128; cf. vv. 101, 104).

## Q. God's Word is wonderful (119:129-136)

**119:129-136.** The psalmist declared

his delight for God's **wonderful** Word which **gives light** (vv. 129-131; cf. v. 105). He then prayed that the Lord would **turn to** him and establish him by directing, redeeming, blessing, and teaching him (vv. 132-135). (On God making His **face shine,** see comments on 4:6.) He expressed concern over those who hate God's **Law** (119:136).

### R. God's Word is righteous (119:137-144)

**119:137-144.** The psalmist declared that because the LORD is **righteous** His Word is **righteous** (vv. 137-138). He testified of his own **zeal** for the Word, which was **pure** (vv. 139-142). He found comfort in God's righteous **laws** when he was in affliction (vv. 143-144; cf. v. 92).

### S. God's Word is true (119:145-152)

**119:145-152.** The psalmist called on the LORD to deliver him because he obeyed, hoped **in,** and meditated on His **Word** (vv. 145-149). His enemies, though **near** him, were **far** removed **from** God's **Law** (v. 150). God, however, was also **near** him and His words were reliable (vv. 151-152).

### T. Love for God's Word (119:153-160)

**119:153-160.** The psalmist called on God to **deliver** him because he had **not forgotten** His **Law** (vv. 153-154). Knowing that **salvation is** not available to **the wicked** (v. 155), the psalmist affirmed that God's **compassion** (lit., "compassions") was **great** toward him (v. 156). He lamented that he had **many** enemies who did **not obey** God's **Word** (vv. 157-158). In contrast, however, the psalmist loved God's Word, which is **true,** and therefore asked to be preserved (cf. v. 88) from his enemies (vv. 159-160).

### U. Rejoicing in God's Word (119:161-168)

**119:161-168.** The psalmist affirmed that though princes hated him **without** a **cause** he trembled in awe **at** God's **Word** (cf. v. 120). He rejoiced **in** the worth of the **Law,** loved it, and praised God repeatedly for it (vv. 162-164). Those like himself who **love** God's Word and hope in Him for **salvation** enjoy **great peace** (šālôm, "well-being," vv. 165-166). The writer then said he had observed the Law out of **love** for it (vv. 167-168; cf. v. 163).

### V. Deliverance by God's Word (119:169-176)

**119:169-176.** The psalmist called on God to hear his **supplication** and **deliver** him (vv. 169-170). He desired to **praise** God for His **Word** (vv. 171-172). He asked God to enable him to **live** since he delighted in His **Law** (vv. 173-175; cf. v. 92). The psalmist concluded this lengthy but rich psalm by confessing that he had gone astray **like a lost sheep** and by asking God to rescue him by His Word (v. 176).

## Psalm 120

The title "song of ascents" identifies each of Psalms 120–134 as a pilgrim song to be sung when the Israelites "ascended" (went up) to Jerusalem for the annual feasts. Four of these 15 psalms are ascribed to David (Pss. 122; 124; 131; 133), 1 to Solomon (Ps. 127), and the other 10 are anonymous.

In Psalm 120, the psalmist prayed for deliverance from treacherous people who wanted war while he was for peace.

### A. Deliverance from liars (120:1-2)

**120:1-2.** The pilgrim prayed for deliverance from liars who would destroy him. He was sure that God would answer him.

### B. Destruction of the wicked (120:3-4)

**120:3-4.** The pilgrim, by directing a question to the wicked, affirmed that the Lord would destroy them. **The broom tree** was used for firewood because it burned longer than many other woods. The imagery of **sharp arrows** and **coals** of fire speaks of retribution against people with **deceitful** tongues.

### C. Declaration for peace (120:5-7)

**120:5-7.** The pilgrim lamented his having to **dwell in** the midst of **those who hate peace** (vv. 5-6). **Meshech** (Gen. 10:2) and its barbarous people lived in the far north. **Kedar** (in northern Arabia) was where some nomadic Ishmaelites lived (cf. Gen. 25:13). The psalmist was saying that these two names represented the enemies that surrounded him.

He declared that he, in contrast, was **a man of peace** (Ps. 120:7). For that reason he knew the Lord would vindicate his cause.

# Psalm 121

The pilgrim, contemplating his journey through the hills to Jerusalem, found assurance that the Lord, the Keeper of Israel, would keep him at all times on his journey.

## A. Contemplation of the journey (121:1-2)

**121:1-2.** The pilgrim-psalmist, as he contemplated his journey through the hills to Jerusalem, asked **where** his **help** came **from.** He found the answer to his question in the affirmation of his faith that **the Lord,** who created **heaven and earth**—with those **hills**—was his only Source of **help.** On the title "**Maker** of heaven and earth" see comments on 115:15.

## B. Assurance of God's protection (121:3-8)

In verses 3-8 the person changes from "I" and "my" (vv. 1-2) to "you" and "your." Verses 3-8 are therefore the words of someone, perhaps a priest, accompanying the pilgrim.

**121:3-4.** The person speaking assured the pilgrim that he would have divine protection. God, **who watches over** (cf. vv. 5, 7-8) His own, will not **slumber** or **sleep, that is,** He will not be indifferent to or disregard them. The Lord will be alert in protecting His own.

**121:5-6.** The assurance was then given that **the Lord** would protect the pilgrim at all times. The Keeper of Israel (cf. v. 4) was the pilgrim's Keeper as well, protecting him as a **shade** protects one from the blazing sun. **The sun** and **the moon** stand for dangers that occur in the **day** and in the **night.**

**121:7-8.** The psalm closes with the psalmist's renewed affirmation that **the Lord will keep** and **watch over** (cf. vv. 3-5; i.e., protect) the pilgrim **from all harm** at all times (vv. 7-8).

# Psalm 122

The pilgrim-psalmist, designated in the superscription as David, recalled his delight in going up to Jerusalem, which was the nation's spiritual and civic center. He then called for everyone to pray for the peace and security of Jerusalem for the sake of the godly and for the sake of God Himself.

## A. Delight at the pilgrimage (122:1-2)

**122:1-2.** The psalmist recalled how he delighted at the prospect of the pilgrimage to **Jerusalem.** Then he relished the experience of actually **standing** within the city's **gates.**

## B. Acclaim of the city (122:3-5)

**122:3-5.** The psalmist acclaimed the **city** of **Jerusalem** for its physical splendor, with its full population **closely compacted together.** He then lauded it as the spiritual center to which the nation's **tribes** went on their annual pilgrimages. He also cited it as the seat of justice (cf. Jer. 21:11-12).

## C. Prayer for peace (122:6-9)

**122:6-9.** The psalmist asked the people to **pray for the peace** and **security** of the city and its inhabitants (vv. 6-7; cf. 125:5; 128:6). He himself then prayed for **peace. . . . for the sake of** his **brothers,** the righteous pilgrims (122:8), and for **prosperity** for **the sake of the** sanctuary, God's dwelling place (v. 9).

# Psalm 123

Lifting up his eyes to God in heaven, the slave-pilgrim called for mercy because the people were filled with contempt from the scoffing of the proud.

## A. Trust in the Lord (123:1-2)

**123:1-2.** The psalmist affirmed his trust in **the Lord** of **heaven. I lift up my eyes** means that he looked to the Lord in prayer for deliverance. He compared his trust to that of a slave waiting for a word from a **master** or a mistress. On behalf of the people, the psalmist continued to **look to . . . God** for help.

## B. Relief from contempt (123:3-4)

**123:3-4.** The psalmist asked God for **mercy** because the people were filled with **contempt,** that is, they had **endured much ridicule from the . . . arrogant.** Despite this taunting of their faith, they would pray for God's **mercy** until He answered.

# Psalm 124

Realizing that if the Lord had not been on their side the nations would have swallowed them up, the pilgrim blessed the Lord, who allowed them to escape.

### A. Protection by the Lord (124:1-5)

**124:1-5.** In this part of the psalm the writer attested to the Lord's protection. He called for the nation to realize that her victory was due to the Lord's being **on their side** (vv. 1-2). Then he explained what would have happened **if the LORD had not been on** their **side**: the nations in **their anger** would have destroyed them (vv. 3-5). Here he used the imagery of swallowing (cf. Num. 16:30; Jer. 51:34), and the imagery of floodwaters (cf. Lam. 3:54). **The raging waters** (lit., "proud waters") suitably suggests the arrogance (cf. Ps. 123:4) of the enemies. This could apply to various times in Israel's history, but it may affirm the Lord's deliverance from the Babylonian Captivity. If the return from the Exile is in view, then David was not the author as the superscription, added later, states. Rather, "David" in this case would indicate a later Davidic "king" (i.e., a potential occupant of the Davidic throne).

### B. Help in the name of the Lord (124:6-8)

**124:6-8.** The psalmist turned to **praise . . . the LORD, who** had **not** abandoned them (v. 6) but had enabled them to escape (v. 7). The enemies' devices were compared both to **teeth** and the **snare** of a fowler (cf. 9:13).

The people's escape was by **the LORD, the Maker of heaven and earth** (cf. comments on 115:15). The faith attested here is reminiscent of that expressed in Psalm 121.

## Psalm 125

Righteous believers are secure in the Lord, who will not let them be tested to the point of being shaken from their integrity. However, those who turn aside in unbelief will be banished from His blessings along with the wicked.

### A. Affirmation of security (125:1-3)

**125:1-3.** Verse 1 summarizes the psalmist's theme that believers are secure and unshakable. He compared them to **Mount Zion,** which **endures forever.**

This imagery is continued in verse 2. Observing how **the mountains surround Jerusalem,** he declared that **the LORD surrounds His people,** protecting them on all sides.

The reason for these affirmations is made clear in verse 3. Apparently foreign domination was a burden on the nation. The psalmist said that God would not permit this **scepter** (lit., "rod") of wickedness to rest on the lot of **the righteous** to the extent it would drive them into wickedness. In other words the test would be limited to what they could endure so they should not abandon their trust in **the LORD.**

### B. Prayer for prosperity (125:4)

**125:4.** The pilgrim-psalmist prayed that the **LORD** would bless **those who are good** and **upright in heart.**

### C. Warning of insecurity (125:5)

**125:5.** Those who did **turn** aside to crookedness at that time would suffer the same fate as the wicked (they would be banished). So God's people should be loyal in their faith and should continue to pray for **peace** for the nation (cf. 122:6-8; 128:6).

## Psalm 126

This pilgrim psalm seems to reflect the struggle of the returned exiles. The psalmist was joyful because the Lord had restored them to their land, but he prayed for a full restoration of the captives. He found comfort in the principle of sowing and reaping.

### A. Praise for the restoration (126:1-3)

**126:1-3.** The psalmist, speaking for the returned exiles, recalled the joy that they experienced **when the LORD brought** them **back.** They were greatly comforted and **filled with laughter** and **joy.** Comfort is suggested by the words "men restored to health" (NIV marg.; these words fit the situation better than **men who dreamed**; cf. Isa. 38:16, and are well supported by various versions and the Dead Sea Scrolls). Also **the nations** realized that **the LORD** had **done** marvelous **things** for His people. It was a time of jubilation after a time of great sadness (cf. Ps. 137).

### B. Petition for full restoration (126:4)

**126:4.** The psalmist, however, prayed that the **LORD** would complete the restoration. He compared the returning exiles to **streams in the Negev** (the desert south of Judah), which in the dry season have little or no water but which in the rainy season overflow their banks. Under God's "showers of blessings" the highways from the east would be full of returning captives.

## C. Confidence in God's blessing (126:5-6)

**126:5-6.** The psalmist found encouragement in the principle of sowing and reaping. These verses are connected to verses 2-3 by their references to great **joy.** Also verse 4 is the connecting link because of its use of the verb "restore" (also used in the Heb. in v. 1) and because of the comparisons with nature (cf. vv. 5-6).

The setting in verses 5-6 is agricultural. After the land had been neglected for so long, it was almost impossible to work it. The planting would be difficult, but persistence would doubtless bring a harvest. The sowing with **tears** (i.e., agonizing over the work) would signify anything someone did to help advance God's theocracy (e.g., encouraging people to respond to the Lord and return to the land). The joyful harvesting (**reap**) would then refer to other people who returned to the land in faith. The psalmist was convinced that continued labor, no matter how agonizingly difficult and frustrating, would result in more people returning to the land of Israel.

The metaphors of sowing and harvesting have been widely used by believers (cf. Gal. 6:7). Jesus spoke of sowing as spreading the message of the kingdom, and spoke of the harvest as people who received Him by faith (Matt. 13:1-8, 18, 23).

## Psalm 127

This pilgrim psalm is ascribed to Solomon. It records the blessing of the Lord in domestic life. The psalmist recognized that dependence on the providence of the Lord assures valuable domestic enterprises and safeguards. The writer then epitomized that bounty in the reward of children, who in those days helped defend a family.

## A. Labor is vain without God's providence (127:1-2)

**127:1-2.** In words that reflect Ecclesiastes (a fitting relationship if Solomon was the psalmist), the author said that it is vain to attempt things without the

Lord. **Builders** work on a **house . . . in vain** unless **the** LORD **builds it, watchmen . . . guard in vain** unless **the** LORD **watches,** and being anxious over one's labor **for food** and working long hours is **in vain** (cf. 128:2). The point is that work done independently of God will be futile. But a person who trusts in the Lord will find rest. Without the Lord, all domestic work is in vain.

The **toiling** (127:2) should not be taken to mean that people need not be diligent, for the Scriptures elsewhere say they should. Rather, that verse stresses that to work long days without divine providence and support is futile. The thought continues from verse 1.

## B. Children are evidence of God's providence (127:3-5)

**127:3-5. Children,** the psalmist wrote, are some of the Lord's providential blessings (see **blessed,** v. 5). They are **a reward from** the LORD. **Sons** help defend the family for they are **like** weapons (**arrows**) **in the hands of a** mighty man. Sons are capable of defending the family in civil cases (at **the gate** civil cases were discussed and decided).

The imagery of arrows and of defense "in the gate" was natural for a nation endangered from without and within.

## Psalm 128

After declaring the blessedness of those who fear the Lord, the psalmist enumerated some of the blessings of the good life and voiced his prayer for greater blessings.

## A. Statement of blessing (128:1)

**128:1.** The psalmist announced the heavenly bliss of people **who fear the** LORD (cf. v. 4) and obey Him (cf. 1:1-3).

## B. Enumeration of blessings (128:2-4)

**128:2.** A righteous person will find **prosperity** as a result of his work. Laboring in anxious independence of God is vain (127:2), but working under God and in obedience to His ways is fruitful (cf. 1:3).

**128:3-4.** Speaking again of fruitfulness (cf. v. 2), the psalmist referred to children obtained through his **wife.** The imagery of plants (**a vine**) and trees (**olive shoots**) naturally suggested growth and fruitfulness. The person **who fears the Lord** is blessed in this way (cf. v. 1).

At the religious festivals whole families gathered in Jerusalem. So it is no surprise to see an emphasis in some of the pilgrim psalms on God's blessings in the domestic area of life.

### C. Prayer for blessings (128:5-6)

**128:5-6.** The pilgrim prayed for further blessings from God on people who fear Him (cf. v. 1). Those blessings include seeing **Jerusalem** prosper and living long enough **to see** one's grandchildren. Then the psalmist prayed for **peace** on the nation (cf. 122:6-7; 125:5).

## Psalm 129

Speaking for Israel, the psalmist declared that the Lord delivered her from the ravages of the wicked. He then prayed that the Lord would put to shame those who hate Zion.

### A. Declaration of deliverance (129:1-4)

**129:1-2.** The psalmist encouraged Israel to testify (**let Israel say**; cf. 124:1) that the wicked who had continued to oppress them from the beginning had **not** been victorious.

**129:3-4.** The imagery of plowing **furrows** describes the extreme suffering that the enemies inflicted on Israel (v. 3). It is as if they had **plowed . . . long** furrows down their backs.

Deliverance from such suffering is attributed to the righteous **Lord** (v. 4). He had **cut** them loose. Perhaps the figure from verse 3 is continued here: God may have broken the plower's harness so the plowing could not continue. Or the word **cords** in verse 4 may simply refer to subjugation (cf. 2:3).

### B. Prayer for punishment (129:5-8)

**129:5-8.** The psalmist prayed that **all** his enemies **who** hated **Zion,** the city of the Lord, would be put to **shame** (v. 5). He prayed that they would wither up so they could not be found (vv. 6-7). **Grass on the housetops** suggests that grass seeds blown by the wind sometimes fell on flat roofs and then began to grow but withered because of no depth of soil.

In greeting someone, it was normal to wish God's **blessing** on him (cf. Ruth 2:4). But the psalmist asked that people

**not** do this for the wicked (Ps. 129:8). They do not deserve the Lord's blessing.

## Psalm 130

Psalm 130 is an earnest cry for the Lord to show His people mercy. The psalmist, sure that God forgives sins, exhorted the nation to join him in waiting in hope for the time when the Lord would redeem them from all their iniquities.

### A. Prayer for mercy (130:1-2)

**130:1-2.** The psalmist cried **out of the depths** (cf. 30:1; 71:20), a figure of speech suggesting his insurmountable difficulty, even to the point of death. He prayed that the **Lord** would answer his **cry for mercy.** The exact problem is not specified, but it seems to be suggested in 130:8. The nation may have been in trouble because of divine punishment for her iniquities.

### B. Confidence of forgiveness (130:3-4)

**130:3-4.** The psalmist recognized that no one could **stand** if God dealt with sinners according to what they deserved. To "mark" (keep **a record of**) **sins** means to hold one accountable for his sins.

The comfort is that **with God there is forgiveness** (selîḥâh, "pardon," also used in Neh. 9:17; Dan. 9:9 [NIV, "forgiving"]). This is the reason for the Lord's not keeping records of sins; He forgives. Believers throughout all ages have rejoiced over this fact, for apart from this, none could endure His judgment!

God forgives so that the forgiven will fear Him. This general word for fear often includes the ideas of worship and obedience. The Scriptures state that many results come from fearing the **Lord**; the most notable is that the person keeps himself from sin. The forgiveness of God cannot be treated lightly. It turns sinners into saints, people who follow Him in obedience.

### C. Hope in the Lord (130:5-8)

**130:5-6.** The psalmist testified that he was patiently waiting **for the Lord.** He compared his **wait** to that of a city's **watchmen** looking for the first rays of dawn, for then they would be relieved of their duties by other guards. He eagerly looked for God's new merciful dealings with the nation.

**130:7-8.** The people were encouraged to **put** their **hope in the LORD.** The reason is that **with** Him **is** loyal love (*ḥeseḏ*) and **full** pardon. Because of His loyalty to **Israel** God would **redeem** her **from all** her **sins.** This was the psalmist's hope and prayer. Apparently "the depths" (v. 1) refer to the nation's spiritual calamity. Only when God forgave the people's sins and pardoned them would they be delivered. Because they believed this, they looked for that day of redemption.

People today who have come to know Him as the God of forgiveness also look for full redemption.

## Psalm 131

Asserting that he had not been proud or followed lofty endeavors, pilgrim David spoke of his childlike trust, his hope in the Lord.

### A. Humility (131:1-2)

**131:1.** David affirmed that he had not been arrogant. Pride is essentially independence from and disobedience to God. The psalmist knew that he depended on the LORD. **Proud** ambition (**haughty** eyes; cf. 18:27; 101:5; Prov. 6:17; 30:13) and selfishly ambitious endeavors (**great matters**) had not been his pursuits.

**131:2.** David then testified to his humility. His **soul** was not disturbed by selfish ambition and passion. He had **stilled** and silenced his soul. **Like a weaned child,** no longer wanting his mother's milk, he was content without that which used to seem indispensable. A mature believer leaves the clamor of proud ambition and rests in the Lord.

### B. Hope (131:3)

**131:3.** David called for **Israel** to **hope in the LORD** forever. To trust in Him is the antithesis of pride.

## Psalm 132

This psalm is a prayer of the congregation that the Lord would remember David's vow concerning the dwelling place for the ark. The congregation found the answer to this prayer when they resolved to worship at the temple. They were reminded of God's promises that David's line would continue, that Zion would be His dwelling place, and that the Messiah would appear.

It is difficult to know the setting of the psalm. Perhaps it was a prayer by the returned exiles who wondered about the fulfillment of God's promises to David, primarily the promises of eternal dominion to David's family and of worship in righteousness in Zion.

### A. Remember David (132:1-5)

**132:1.** The theme of the psalm is expressed in the opening cry to the **LORD** to **remember David.** David's life and work were keenly felt at the time of the restoration from Babylon, as he was the king who had centralized the nation's worship in Zion.

**132:2-5.** The specific aspect of this prayer was David's **oath . . . not** to rest **till** he found **a place for the LORD** to dwell. This probably refers to David's desire to build the temple (2 Sam. 7). That desire evidenced his great devotion, for which **the LORD** made a covenant with him. The Davidic Covenant was to the later community under Ezra and Nehemiah what the Abrahamic Covenant had been to Moses. This prayer in Psalm 132 calls for God to honor His promises at a time when they seemed jeopardized.

### B. Let us worship (132:6-10)

Here the tone of the psalm changes, for the congregation began to feel confident that their prayer would be answered.

**132:6-8.** The congregation recalled Israel's hearing that the ark (v. 8) of the covenant was **in Ephrathah** and finding it. It had rested for 20 years in **Jaar** (i.e., Kiriath Jearim, 1 Sam. 7:1-2) until David moved it to Zion (2 Sam. 6). (Ephrathah, also called Ephrath, Gen. 35:16, 19; 48:7, was an older name for Bethlehem or the name of the area around Bethlehem.)

The people resolved to **worship** in the place David had designated for the ark (the **dwelling place;** cf. Pss. 74:7; 76:2; 84:1; 132:5, 13, and **footstool** of the Lord). It was God's dwelling place in the sense that it was **His** earthly throne. It was called **the ark** of God's **might** because in battle it symbolized God's strength and victory.

**132:9-10.** The people's prayer for the Lord to visit them was accompanied by their prayer that the **priests be clothed**

with **righteousness** (cf. v. 16; Zech. 3:1-7), that the **saints sing for joy,** and that the Lord not **reject** David, His **anointed** king. These verses were all a part of the people's prayer when **David** established Zion as the center of God's kingdom. The psalmist here appropriated the prayer for the returnees from the Exile so that God would honor His promises to David's descendants as well. As the earlier community had followed the ark to its resting place and there prayed for blessing on the priests and David, so this community prayed for the priests in their day, descendants of the covenant's earlier ministers.

## C. The Lord swore an oath (132:11-18)

**132:11-18.** These verses record a revelation from **the LORD** confirming His earlier promises to David. The Lord reiterated His **oath to David** that **descendants** of his would sit on David's **throne forever** (vv. 11-12; cf. 89:3-4, 27-29, 35-37). **The LORD** then affirmed His choice of Mount **Zion** (132:13-14) which He would **bless . . . with abundant provisions,** including **food** (cf. 111:5; 136:25; 145:15; 146:7) for the **poor . . . salvation** for the **priests** (cf. 132:9), and **joy** for the **saints.** God also promised the appearance and crowning of His **Anointed One,** the Messiah (vv. 17-18).

The burning **lamp** is a figure from the furnishings of the tabernacle. Here it signifies the continuation of the Davidic dynasty (cf. 2 Sam. 21:17; 1 Kings 11:36). The "Anointed One," first David, then his descendants, and eventually the Messiah (Christ) will be triumphant over His enemies.

An animal **horn** symbolized strength and vigor. Appropriately it sometimes was used of powerful rulers (cf. Dan. 7:24). This horn will **grow** (ṣāmaḥ, lit., "sprout"). Zechariah may have had this passage in mind in his prayer (Luke 1:69). Related to this verb is the noun ṣemaḥ ("Branch"), a messianic title (Jer. 23:5; 33:15; Zech. 3:8; 6:12). The expression then signifies the messianic King, who is David's Descendant. The "Branch" is the Coming One who will unite the offices of priest and king.

Thus Psalm 132 is an encouraging confirmation that no matter what the circumstances, God's promises will be fulfilled.

## Psalm 133

Here the Psalmist David described the beauty of unity that exists among brethren.

### A. The goodness of unity (133:1)

**133:1.** In this short pilgrim psalm David exclaimed how wonderful it is for believers to dwell **together in unity.** This thought was appropriate for the religious festivals when Israelite families came together to worship their Lord.

### B. The description of unity (133:2-3)

**133:2.** David compared the unity mentioned in verse 1 to the **oil** that consecrated Aaron (cf. Lev. 8:12). This imagery from the priesthood was appropriate because of the pilgrims being in Jerusalem. The oil poured **on Aaron's** head flowed **down** on his **beard** and shoulders, and onto the breastplate with the names of all 12 tribes. The oil thus symbolized the unity of the nation in worship under their consecrated priest. As the oil consecrated Aaron, so the unity of the worshipers in Jerusalem would consecrate the nation under God.

**133:3.** David then compared the unity mentioned in verse 1 to **the dew** that covers the mountains. The picture of oil running down (v. 2) no doubt suggested dew coming down from Mount **Hermon** in the north onto **Mount Zion.** The dew of Hermon was heavy; it symbolized what was freshening and invigorating. The refreshing influence of the worshiping community on the nation was similar to the dew on vegetation. This was a fitting symbol of the Lord's **blessing** on His people.

## Psalm 134

Addressing the priests and the Levites who kept watch at the temple, the pilgrim asked that heavenly blessings be given them from Zion.

### A. Call to praise (134:1-2)

**134:1-2.** The pilgrim called on the priests, the Lord's **servants** who ministered in the temple (**the house of the LORD**), to **praise** Him with uplifted **hands.**

### B. Prayer for blessing (134:3)

**134:3.** The pilgrim then prayed that the Creator (**the Maker of heaven and**

earth; see comments on 115:15) would **bless** them. The passage forms a fitting benediction to the pilgrim psalms (Pss. 120–134).

## Psalm 135

This song of praise is a mosaic of the Law, the Prophets, and the Psalms. In it the psalmist called on the priests to praise the Lord, so it builds on Psalm 134. It is a song of praising the Lord's greatness and faithfulness to His people.

### A. Call to praise (135:1-3)

**135:1-3.** Following the introductory **Praise the Lord** (*halᵉlû-yāh*; cf. vv. 3, 21 and comments on 104:35), the psalmist called the priests, the **servants of the Lord** in the temple, to praise Him (cf. 134:1). The preliminary reasons are that God **is good** and **praise . . . is pleasant.**

### B. Cause for praise (135:4-18)

**135:4-7.** The reasons for praise given in verses 4-18 all stress God's sovereignty. First, He chose **Israel** as **His treasured possession** (cf. Deut. 7:6). Second, He is **greater than all** the pagan **gods.** So He is sovereign, doing **whatever pleases Him** (cf. Ps. 115:3), **in the heavens and on the earth** (cf. Jer. 10:13), including control over **clouds . . . lightning,** and **wind.** (On **storehouses** see comments on Job 38:22.)

**135:8-12.** This theme is now expanded in relationship to Israel's history. In the Exodus (vv. 8-9) God defeated **Egypt,** smiting their **firstborn** (the 10th plague; cf. 136:10) after sending other **signs and wonders** (plagues 1-9).

God destroyed **nations** and **kings** to give Israel her land (135:10-11; cf. 136:17-18). **Sihon** and **Og** were two powerful **kings** the Lord helped **Israel** destroy just before they entered the land (cf. 136:19-20; Num. 21), which was their inheritance (cf. Ps. 136:21-22).

**135:13-14.** The sovereignty of God is then mentioned in reference to Israel's future history. **The Lord,** who is eternal, **will vindicate His people** because of His **compassion on** them.

**135:15-18.** If verses 8-12 correspond with verse 4, then verses 15-18 correspond with verse 5. The psalmist gave specific illustrations of the Lord's sovereignty over pagan gods (cf. 115:4-8). They were, he declared created **by . . .**

men (135:15). Idols **cannot speak . . . see . . . hear** or breathe (perhaps v. 17b means they cannot smell). Most importantly, they cannot save (v. 18).

### C. Conclusion (135:19-21)

**135:19-21.** The psalmist reiterated his call for **Israel** and her priests (**house of Aaron**) and Levites (**house of Levi**) to **praise** God **from Zion.** The psalm closes with the same words with which it began (**Praise the Lord**; cf. vv. 1, 3 and comments on 104:35).

## Psalm 136

This psalm is similar to Psalm 135, except that it has a refrain which stresses the theme. The theme is "praise the Lord who performed great wonders," and the refrain is "because of His enduring loyal love." The structure of Psalm 136 suggests that it was used antiphonally in worship, with one part of the congregation making a statement or phrase and the other part responding with the refrain (cf. Ezra 3:11; 2 Chron. 7:3, 6).

The Lord's loyal love (*ḥeseḏ*), mentioned in each of the 26 refrains, is His covenant faithfulness to His Chosen People whom He loves. The celebration of God's love in this liturgical psalm gave Israel a favorite song for festivals. This psalm is often referred to as "the Great Hallel" (cf. Pss. 111–113; 115–117).

### A. Call to praise (136:1-3)

**136:1-3.** The psalmist called the congregation to thank (cf. v. 26) **the Lord,** who is **the God of gods** and **the Lord of lords** (cf. Deut. 10:17). Between each expression here and throughout the psalm the reason for the praise is expressed: **His** loyal **love endures forever.**

### B. Cause for praise (136:4-25)

**136:4-9.** Verse 4 provides the introductory summary of the cause for praise: the marvelous acts (**wonders**) that issued from God's loyal **love.** The first example of His wonders for man is Creation (vv. 5-9). He **made the heavens,** stretched **out the earth,** and **made the great lights (the sun. . . . the moon,** and the **stars**).

**136:10-25.** The second example of God's marvelous works was **His** aid to Israel. The psalmist related that the Lord: (a) triumphed over **Egypt** in the 10th plague (v. 10; cf. 135:8) and in bringing

**Israel.** . . . **with a mighty hand and out-stretched arm** (cf. comments on Deut. 4:34) across **the Red Sea** (Ps. 136:11-15); (b) **led His people through the** wilderness (v. 16); and (c) triumphed over the **kings** of the land (including **Sihon** and **Og,** vv. 17-20; cf. 135:10-12) to establish His people in the **land** safely (136:21-22; cf. 135:12). In all this God worked on behalf of **His** people who had been enslaved, freeing them **from** their **enemies** (136:23-24).

The third demonstration of His enduring **love** was feeding **every creature** (v. 25; cf. 111:5; 132:15; 145:15; 146:7).

### C. Conclusion (136:26)

**136:26.** As the psalmist concluded this psalm, he again called for **thanks** (cf. vv. 1-3) to be given **to the God of heaven** because of **His** enduring **love.** This is the only place in the Book of Psalms where this title of God is used (cf. comments on Ezra 1:2).

## Psalm 137

In pathetic but beautiful language the exiled psalmist mourned the plight of those who wept in a strange land and could not sing their songs of Zion. Opposite to his intense love for Zion was his hatred for the destroyers of Zion; so he turned to voice imprecations against Edom and Babylon who had destroyed the city of God.

Reflecting the exilic period, this psalm may have been written toward the end of the Babylonian Captivity. Perhaps the psalmist felt that the Persians' kind treatment of the Babylonians was an insufficient judgment on those who devastated Israel.

### A. Mourning for Zion (137:1-4)

**137:1.** The psalmist recalled that the exiles in **Babylon** . . . **sat** down **and wept** over the destruction of **Zion** (Jerusalem). **The rivers** refer to the Euphrates and the canals and waterways stemming from it.

**137:2-4.** So great was the exiles' grief that even the singers were silent. The exiles **hung** their **harps** on poplar trees (v. 2) for they could not **sing** their **songs** about their homeland when their oppressors taunted them to **sing** of glorious **Zion** (v. 3), as the Israelites were **in a** hostile **foreign** land (v. 4).

### B. Faithfully remembering Jerusalem (137:5-6)

**137:5-6.** The psalmist vowed to retain **Jerusalem** in his memory. He wished that his **right hand** would **forget its skill** and that he would become mute if he failed to **remember . . . Jerusalem,** his **highest joy.** The people's intense grief over the destruction of their city (where the tribes gathered to praise the Lord) is contrasted here with their greatest joy.

### C. Imprecating Zion's destroyers (137:7-9)

The last part of this psalm must be understood in the light of the great mourning of the Jews in exile. As an imprecation (cf. comments under "Theology of the Psalms" in the *Introduction*), it is a prayer for God to exact vengeance on their captors and those who aided them.

**137:7.** This is a plea for God to **remember . . . the Edomites** (cf. the psalmist's remembering, v. 6) who had rejoiced while the city of **Jerusalem** was being destroyed and encouraged the destroyers (cf. Ezek. 25:12; Joel 3:19). So the psalmist wanted God to bring retribution on Edom.

**137:8-9.** The psalmist addressed his curse to **Babylon** directly. The Babylonians should note that the Lord would destroy them measure for measure, that is, their little ones would be dashed **against the rocks** (cf. Isa. 13:16) for the Babylonians apparently had done this to the Jerusalemites. This is perhaps the most painful imprecation in the Book of Psalms. To the exiled psalmist, those who had ravaged the Holy Land deserved no better. Great sadness and bitterness filled the hearts of the Israelites who were in captivity (cf. Lam. 1–2).

## Psalm 138

David vowed to praise the Lord's loyal love and goodness for answering his prayer. He made known his wish that all kings would acknowledge the Lord's favor to the lowly, and then expressed his confidence that the Lord would also deliver him by His loyal love.

### A. Praise from the psalmist (138:1-3)

**138:1-3.** David vowed to **praise** the LORD wholeheartedly **before the "gods,"** and to worship Him in the **temple** for His loyal **love . . . faithfulness** (cf. 108:4;

115:1; 117:2), **name,** and **Word.** "Gods" could refer to the pagan gods, in which case David was praising the true God in spite of their supposed presence. Or "gods" may refer to human leaders (as judges or kings), though pagan gods seems preferable here.

The reason David would praise the Lord is that God had **answered** his prayer, thus strengthening his faith.

### B. Praise from all kings (138:4-5)

**138:4-5.** David prayed that **all the kings** would acknowledge and **praise** God **when they** heard of His Word and His great **glory.**

### C. Deliverance by the Lord (138:6-8)

**138:6-8.** David explained that **the LORD** should be praised (vv. 4-5) because He does not judge by human standards. Though He **is on high** (i.e., exalted; cf. 113:4), **He looks** to **the lowly** (cf. 113:7-9), not to **the proud.**

David expressed confidence that the **LORD** would deliver him from his **foes** by His **right hand** (His power) and according to His loyal **love.** Even though David was confident in **the LORD,** he asked that God not let him down.

## Psalm 139

God's omniscience, omnipresence, and omnipotence are the subjects of David's meditations in this beautiful psalm. In this psalm David asked God to examine him thoroughly to affirm his innocence. The psalm has four strophes of six verses each. The message progresses significantly from one subject to another. His first meditation is on God's knowledge, that every aspect of his life was searched out and controlled by what the Lord knew. He then realized it was impossible to escape from such omniscient control, no matter how far or fast he might go, for God is everywhere. David then stated that God has such control over him because in His power He created Him secretly and planned his life with great care. On the basis of these meditations, David then affirmed his loyalty to God and prayed for God to prove him by examining him.

### A. The omniscience of the Lord (139:1-6)

**139:1.** The theme of verses 1-6 is announced in the opening verse: the **LORD** knew David penetratingly. David said God's knowledge came as if He had scoured every detail of David's life and thus knew him intimately.

**139:2-4.** Samples of how well God knew David are stated here. The Lord (**You** is emphatic in Heb.; cf. v. 13) knew every move he made; the two opposites of sitting and rising represent all his actions (this is a figure of speech known as a merism; cf. vv. 3, 8). God knew not only David's actions; He also knew his motivations (**thoughts;** cf. v. 17). **Afar** evidently refers not to space but to time.

The daily activities of the psalmist were also thoroughly **familiar** to the Lord. The opposites of **going out** in the morning and **lying down** at night represent the whole day's activities (another merism; cf. vv. 2, 8).

But the one sample that epitomizes God's omniscience is in verse 4. Before the psalmist could frame **a word on** his **tongue,** the **LORD** was thoroughly familiar with what he was about to say. (The Heb. for "word" is *millâh* and the similar-sounding word for **completely** is *kūllâh.*)

**139:5-6.** David's initial response to this staggering knowledge was that he was troubled. Like many who respond to the fact of God's omniscience, he thought it was confining, that God had besieged him and cupped His **hand** over him.

Moreover, this kind of **knowledge** was out of David's control—it was **too wonderful for** him. The word "wonderful" is in the emphatic position, at the beginning of the sentence. On the meaning of "wonderful" as "extraordinary or surpassing," see comments on 9:1. In other words divine omniscience is **too** high for humans to comprehend (also cf. comments on 139:14).

### B. The omnipresence of the Lord (139:7-12)

**139:7.** The thought of such confining knowledge (vv. 1-6) may have prompted David's desire to escape, as verses 7-12 suggest. This is indicated in verse 7 by two rhetorical questions: there is absolutely no place where he could escape from the **presence** of the Lord (cf. Jer. 23:24).

**139:8-10.** Hypothetical examples of where David might try to escape are given here. He first asserted that the Lord is present in **the heavens** above and in sheol (NIV marg.) below. These opposites signify that all areas in between (a third merism in this psalm; cf. vv. 2-3) are also in the Lord's presence.

Moreover, if he could fly at the speed of light (**the wings of the dawn**) from the east across the sky to the west (**far side of the** Mediterranean **Sea**) he could not escape from the Lord.

God's presence then began to take on a new meaning for the psalmist, as if the light were dawning on him. Now, he stated, the **hand** of the Lord would lead and comfort him.

**139:11-12.** David developed the theme of **light** a little further. **The darkness** might bruise him (probably referring to the oppressive nature of darkness). (**Hide** is an interpretive rendering of šûp̱, "to crush or bruise"; cf. "crush" in Gen. 3:15; Job 9:17, its only other uses in the OT.) But David could not be concealed from God, for **darkness** and **light** are the same to Him because of His omniscience and omnipresence.

### C. The omnipotence of the Lord (139:13-18)

The thought that darkness cannot conceal anyone from the Lord (vv. 11-12) brought to David's mind this meditation in verses 13-18: God knew all about him when He created him in his mother's womb. Verse 13 begins with "For," indicating that this strophe (vv. 13-18) explains the preceding two strophes (vv. 1-6, 7-12): since God can create a person, He certainly knows him intimately and is with him everywhere.

**139:13-14.** The theme of verses 13-18 is announced here: the Lord (**You** is emphatic in Heb.; cf. v. 2) **created** him **in** his **mother's womb.** The language is figurative in that creating and knitting describe God's sovereign superintendence over the natural process of reproduction (on knitting; cf. Job. 10:11).

This fact prompted the psalmist to break forth in **praise** over the thought of how marvelously he had been **made.** Even David's rudimentary knowledge of the marvels of the human body led him to be in awe and wonder. The words **wonderfully** and **wonderful** are mindful of God's marvelous knowledge (Ps. 139:6).

**139:15-16.** Then David stressed certain features of God's superintendence

over him. In the womb he **was woven together** (lit., "embroidered"; cf. "knit," v. 13, suggesting his veins and arteries). When he was being formed in the womb he was as remote to the human eye as the lower part **of the earth** (cf. comments on Job 1:21). But God **saw** every detail. David's **frame** means his skeleton and his **unformed body** is his embryo. Moreover, God prerecorded **all the days** of the psalmist before he was even born. This statement may mean that God determined how long he would live, but in view of verses 1-4, it more likely refers to everyday details. God marvelously planned out his life.

**139:17-18.** This thought led David to conclude that the Lord's plans (**thoughts;** cf. v. 2) for His people are most **precious** and in fact are innumerable. They are also most relevant, for each morning when he awakened, God was **still with** him, extending His thoughts toward him.

### D. The loyalty of David (139:19-24)

The psalmist's attention then turned to the trouble he was in. So he asserted his loyalty to the Lord and took comfort from his knowledge of the Lord's presence.

**139:19-22.** The psalmist petitioned **God** to **slay the wicked** men who were trying to kill him. These enemies apparently were taking the **name** of the LORD in vain (cf. Ex. 20:7), using it for an **evil** purpose. Because they were God's enemies, David affirmed that they were *his* **enemies** too and that he would **have nothing** to do with them. To **hate** them meant to reject them (cf. comments on Mal. 1:3), to disavow any association with them.

**139:23-24.** David concluded this psalm with a prayer for **God** to **search** and **test** him (cf. 26:2) in order to prove his loyalty, thus showing that he was not like the wicked mentioned in 139:19-22. The verb "to search," is also used in verse 1 in a statement about God. David asked God to **test** him as a refiner tests metal. Since God knows everything (cf. vv. 1-6) He would also know David's **anxious thoughts** (the same Heb. word is rendered "anxiety" in 94:19). God would also know if the psalmist had **any offensive way** (lit., "way of pain," i.e., pain caused by being afflicted for wrongdoing). Such an examination David was convinced, would yield evidence of his loyalty. The Lord in His leading would then preserve his life (**everlasting, '***ôlām***,** probably means prolonged life) here as he followed the Lord.

All believers who come to understand the attributes of God discussed in this psalm find them a great source of comfort, and a great prompting to obey Him.

## Psalm 140

The psalmist uttered harsh imprecations on the wicked who sought to poison and ensnare him with their vicious devices. He spoke these imprecations in full confidence that the Lord would secure justice for the afflicted against their attacks. This is the substance of his opening prayer.

### A. Petition (140:1-8)

**140:1-5.** David called on **the Lord** to deliver him from the wicked who planned to destroy him. Verses 1-2 include his introductory cry and verses 3-5 give his lament. He wanted God to **rescue** and **protect** (cf. v. 4) him **from men of violence** (cf. vv. 4, 11), from people who think up and carry out **evil plans** (cf. v. 8) **every day.** The imagery in the lament shows that these foes were vicious. Their speech was **sharp** and destructive, like **a serpent's** venom (v. 3). **The wicked** planned **to trip** him in his actions, so he needed God's help (v. 4). Like hunters laying snares, they had **set traps for** him (v. 5; cf. 141:9-10; 142:3). His enemies, besides being dangerous and deadly (140:3), were deliberately trying to kill him (vv. 4-5).

**140:6-8.** David reiterated his opening **cry for** help, praying that **the wicked** would not have their way in carrying out **their** evil **plans** (cf. v. 2) and being **proud** of their success. In his prayer the psalmist described the Lord as his strong **Deliverer who shields** his **head in . . . battle.** This military figure stresses divine protection from the wicked.

### B. Imprecations (140:9-11)

**140:9-11.** David voiced several harsh imprecations on the wicked, which were designed to match their wickedness. He hoped that their nasty words (cf. v. 3) would bring them **trouble.** He also

hoped that **burning coals** would **fall** on **them** (cf. 11:6) reminiscent of God's judgment on Sodom and Gomorrah (cf. Gen. 19:24). And he hoped that **disaster** would overtake the **slanderers** (cf. their "poison," Ps. 140:3). Again he called his enemies **men of violence** (cf. vv. 1, 4).

### C. Confidence (140:12-13)

**140:12-13.** David was convinced **that the Lord** would maintain his **cause** as one who was **poor** and **needy** (cf. 40:17; 70:5; 86:1; 109:22) and that **praise** would be given by **the righteous** to the Lord, who champions their cause. They would dwell in His presence in peace (cf. 102:28).

## Psalm 141

The superscriptions to Psalms 141–145 attribute them to David. Psalm 141 is an evening prayer for sanctification and protection. David asked that he not speak against the Lord, or fall into alluring temptations of the wicked, but that he would be kept from the devices of the wicked who would hear his song of testimony.

### A. The evening prayer (141:1-2)

**141:1-2.** David, comparing his prayer to the evening oblation at the sanctuary, called on the Lord to answer him **quickly** (cf. comments on 31:2). He wanted his **prayer** to be a sweet aroma to the Lord, similar to the **incense** in **the evening sacrifice** (around 3 P.M.) which would ascend and please the Lord. In the Book of Revelation incense appropriately pictured prayer (Rev. 5:8; 8:3-4). **Lifting up** his **hands** as a gesture in prayer is also mentioned in Psalms 28:2; 63:4; 134:2.

### B. The prayer for sanctification (141:3-7)

**141:3-4.** The substance of David's evening prayer was that the Lord would direct his words and his actions aright. He wanted God to **set a guard** at his **lips** to prevent wrong speech. Moreover, he desired that God preserve his **heart** (i.e., his willful desires) from **wicked** allurements. **Their delicacies** refers to sensual luxuries procured by wicked activities (cf. Prov. 4:17).

**141:5-7.** David would not resist the rebukes of the **righteous**—they in fact were like anointing **oil,** helpful and refreshing (cf. Prov. 9:8b; 15:31; 17:10; 19:25; 25:12). But his **prayer** was **against . . . the wicked**; he anticipated they would be utterly destroyed after they learned that his **words** were correct.

## C. The prayer for protection (141:8-10)

**141:8-10.** Along with David's prayer to be preserved from the allurements of the wicked (vv. 3-7) is his request for protection. He asserted his confidence in the Lord His **Refuge** (cf. comments on 2:12) and asked that he **not** be given **over to death.** This meant, he prayed further, that God should deliver him from **the wicked** by letting their **snares . . . traps,** and **nets** (cf. 140:5; 142:3) catch them.

## Psalm 142

This psalm, also attributed to David, was written "when he was in the cave," fleeing from Saul (cf. the superscription to Ps. 57). The psalmist cried to the Lord for help, for God was the only One he could depend on. David was utterly helpless before his enemies and no one seemed to care for his life.

## A. Cry to the Lord (142:1-2)

**142:1-2.** David, possibly addressing others with him, exclaimed that he cried out **to the Lord** (cf. v. 5) **for mercy,** voicing his **complaint** and his **trouble.**

## B. Lament (142:3-4)

**142:3-4.** Addressing the Lord, David stated that God knew his **way** (cf. 139:2-3) **when** his **spirit** weakened (cf. 77:3; 143:4, 7). Apparently under pressure he had lost his fight for his resistance was weakened. The trouble arose from a trap (**snare**) laid for him by an enemy (cf. 140:5; 141:9-10).

He then called on God to **look to** his **right** (where normally someone would be standing to guard him) because he was without **refuge** and support—**no one** cared **for** his **life!** His only hope was the Lord to whom he prayed.

## C. Petition (142:5-7)

**142:5.** When David cried to God (cf. v. 1) he affirmed his confidence in Him: God was his safety (**Refuge;** cf. 141:8) and his life. God was his **Portion,** his allotment, all he had (cf. 16:5; 73:26; 119:57).

**142:6-7.** In his **desperate** situation (cf. 79:8), likened to a **prison,** he petitioned the Lord to **rescue** him **from** his **strong** enemies (cf. 18:17) so he could then **praise** God's **name** (His revealed attributes) for what He had done. Also **the righteous** could **then** joyfully **gather about** him (lit., "crown themselves," i.e., rejoice in triumph) **because of** the Lord's **goodness** (cf. 13:6; 116:12) in answering his prayer.

## Psalm 143

In this psalm the thought of David's spirit fainting (vv. 4, 7) is developed from the previous psalm (142:3). Psalm 143 is a prayer for deliverance and guidance. When the psalmist prayed for merciful relief from the wicked who oppressed him, he acknowledged that no living man is righteous. He desired deliverance and guidance and found encouragement from remembering God's ways.

## A. Complaint (143:1-6)

**143:1-4.** David called on the Lord for **mercy** and **relief,** based on God's **faithfulness and righteousness** (cf. v. 11). In contrast **no** human **is righteous** (cf. Ecc. 7:20). David was acknowledging that his sufferings were partly punishment for sins, for he desired that God **not** judge him.

His complaint is expressed in Psalm 143:3-4 specifically. **The enemy** had attacked David and driven him out, so that he was in **darkness** (cf. 88:6, i.e., in gloom emotionally) and might as well have been **dead.** His **spirit** grew weak (cf. 142:3; 143:7) from this oppression.

**143:5-6.** Yet David mustered confidence when he remembered the former **days.** His faith was rekindled and his spirit strengthened when he recalled the mighty **works** of the Lord in the past. So he prayed eagerly for the Lord to meet the needs of his hungry, thirsty (cf. 42:2) heart. The image of **parched land** portrays his soul's great spiritual need at that moment, that God would come to his rescue.

## B. Petition (143:7-12)

**143:7.** His confidence (v. 5) led to his petition for deliverance; he prayed for quick (cf. comments on 31:2) deliverance lest he in his weak **spirit** (cf. 142:3; 143:4) **go down to the pit** (a synonym for grave). Asking God **not** to **hide** His **face** (cf. 27:9; 102:2) meant he did not want God to overlook him.

**143:8-12.** The prayer in verse 7 is detailed in verses 8-12. First, he desired that the loyal **love** (*ḥesed*; cf. v. 11) of the LORD lead him in **the way** he **should go** (v. 8). Second, he wanted to be rescued **from** his **enemies** (v. 9; cf. 140:1; 142:6). Third, he wanted to be taught by the **Spirit** of **God** (143:10). And fourth, David wanted to be preserved alive by God's **righteousness** (cf. v. 1) and **love** (cf. v. 8) from his **enemies** (vv. 11-12). Each of these prayers was based solidly on his trust in the LORD. As God's **servant,** David trusted in Him. Even though he had sinned and was now in trouble, he was confident God would guide him to safety.

## Psalm 144

After blessing God for glorious deliverances in past battles, and marvelling that God took note of perishing people, King David prayed for divine intervention in combat. He expressed confidence that because the Lord gives victory the nation would experience peace and prosperity.

### A. Blessing for past victories (144:1-2)

**144:1-2.** David praised **the** LORD for having subdued people under him. In this **praise** he used several expressions to portray the fact that the Lord enabled him to win victories. The Lord had taught him how to fight, and God was his **Rock** (cf. 18:46; also note 18:2), his **Fortress** (*meṣûdâh*; cf. 18:3; 31:3; 71:3; 91:2), his **Stronghold** (*miśgoḇ*; cf. comments on 9:9), his **Deliverer** (cf. 18:2; 40:17; 70:5; 140:7), and his **Shield** (cf. comments on 3:3). These all stress the protection and deliverance given David while God was solidifying the empire under him.

### B. Prayer for divine intervention (144:3-11)

**144:3-4.** Having praised the nature of God, David then voiced his petition for victory in battle (vv. 3-11). The thought that God would subdue anyone under him caused him to marvel at the possibility of God's intervention on man's behalf (cf. comments on 8:4). Since **man is like a vapor** (*heḇel*; cf. 39:5, 11; 62:9; and comments on Ecc. 1:2) that vanishes away

and a **shadow** that is soon gone (cf. Job 8:9; Ps. 102:11) why would God stoop to help him?

**144:5-8.** But since God did care for him, he prayed for divine intervention in the war. He desired that the LORD would descend in glorious power. Even God's touching **the mountains** would cause them to **smoke** (cf. 104:32) from the fires of burning trees. David asked the Lord to use **lightning** (His **arrows;** cf. 18:14) to **scatter the enemies.** By this gracious intervention he hoped to be delivered from his enemies who were as strong as **mighty waters** and who were **deceitful** (cf. 144:11).

**144:9-11.** David immediately broke out in a declaration of his confidence. He vowed to praise the Lord with **a new song** (cf. 33:3; 40:3; 96:1; 98:1; 149:1) for delivering **him from the deadly sword.** Then he repeated his prayer for deliverance from his enemies, whom he described in words nearly identical to those in 144:7b-8.

### C. Prospect of peace and prosperity (144:12-15)

**144:12-14.** Because the Lord would rescue His servant the king, the land would enjoy great benefits. First, the subjects of the king would greatly prosper, **like** growing **plants** and exquisitely **carved** palace **pillars** (v. 12). Second, the nation would prosper economically—with **barns** full of crops and with numerous **sheep** and **oxen** (v. 13). Third, the people would be blessed with peace (v. 14).

**144:15.** So David concluded that any **people whose God is the** LORD will be **blessed.** This royal psalm shows that divine intervention in a holy war on behalf of the Lord's anointed brings peace and prosperity.

## Psalm 145

This psalm of David is titled "A psalm of praise"—the only one in the Psalter with that title. Here begins the grand doxology of the entire collection, for praise plays a greater part of Psalms 145–150 than in most of the others. The word "praise" occurs 46 times in these six psalms.

In Psalm 145 David praised the Lord for His mighty acts which are told from one generation to another, for His gracious provision of an everlasting kingdom, and for the manner in which He responds to those who love Him.

### A. Praise for God's mighty acts (145:1-7)

**145:1-3.** David vowed to **praise** the Lord His **King** (cf. 149:2) and His **name** (His revealed attributes) **every day** because He is **great.** The greatness of **the LORD** is unfathomable; **no one** has plumbed its depths.

**145:4-7.** David told how great God's **acts** have been, which will be declared from **generation** to generation. Believers tell of the **splendor** (cf. v. 12 and comments on 29:2) **of** His **majesty . . . speak of** His **works . . . meditate on** them, **sing of** them, and **celebrate** them and His **goodness.**

### B. Praise for God's everlasting kingdom (145:8-16)

**145:8-10.** David then wrote of the marvelous nature of God, affirming that He **is gracious and compassionate** (cf. 111:4), **slow to anger, and** full of loyal **love** (the identical statement, in Heb., is given in Ex. 34:6; Neh. 9:17; Pss. 86:15; 103:8; Joel 2:13; Jonah 4:2). Because God **is good** and compassionate **to all,** all His works and His **saints** praise Him.

**145:11-13a.** The saints' praise (v. 10) would include their gratitude for His **kingdom.** From generation to generation people **will tell of** God's **kingdom . . . might . . . mighty acts,** and how His **kingdom . . . endures through all generations** (cf. Dan. 4:3, 34).

**145:13b-16.** David then instructed the congregation on the Lord's grace and mercy to man. He **is faithful to all His promises,** He uplifts **those who fall,** He provides **food** for all (cf. 111:5; 132:15; 136:25; 146:7), and He satisfies their **desires** (cf. 145:19). These are the characteristics of the One whose dominion is everlasting (v. 13), which is why He is called faithful.

### C. Praise for God's acts of deliverance (145:17-21)

**145:17-21.** David extolled **the LORD** for being **righteous** and **loving.** (On **all He has made;** cf. vv. 9-10, 13.) Therefore God answers the prayers of the needy— **those who fear Him** and love **Him**— when they **call** to **Him.** Therefore all

should **praise His . . . name** (v. 21; cf. v. 1). Once again God's greatness and grace are reasons for praise.

### Psalm 146

Praise for the greatness and the grace of God is the subject of this psalm as well as of Psalm 145 and others. Here the psalmist vowed to praise God all his life because the One who made the heavens and the earth is faithful and just to the oppressed of the earth.

### A. Lifelong praise (146:1-4)

**146:1-2.** After the initial **Praise the LORD** (*halˁlû-yāh*; cf. v. 10 and comments on 104:35), whichs begins and ends each of Psalms 146–150, the psalmist vowed to **praise the LORD all** his **life.**

**146:3-4.** The psalmist instructed the congregation to **put** their **trust** in the One who is infinitely more powerful than **mortal** man, **who cannot save.** A person's **plans** die with him. At death the **spirit** of man **departs** and the body returns to dust (cf. 104:29; Ecc. 3:20). So one who trusts in man will have no reason for praising.

### B. Praise for the Creator (146:5-6)

**146:5-6.** In contrast with the warning not to trust in man (v. 3) the psalmist **blessed** anyone who trusts in the sovereign **LORD . . . God,** his **help** (cf. comments on 30:10) and **hope.** This One, he explained, is **the Maker of heaven and earth** (cf. comments on 115:15); because He is **the LORD** of Creation He **remains faithful.**

### C. Praise for the gracious Lord (146:7-10)

**146:7-9.** The idea of God's faithfulness (v. 6) suggested to the psalmist many ways in which the Lord is gracious and righteous to people. He helps **the oppressed . . . gives food to the hungry** (cf. 111:5; 132:15; 136:25; 145:15), releases **prisoners . . . gives sight to . . . blind** people, raises **up** the defeated, **loves the righteous,** protects the sojourner, and leads the orphan and **widow** to security. **But,** because He is just, He also leads **the wicked** away into frustration.

**146:10.** The psalmist concluded that **the LORD reigns** (cf. 9:7; 47:8; 93:1; 96:10; 97:1; 99:1) **forever.** As the eternal Ruler, He is sovereign (146:6), gracious (vv. 7-

9b), and just (v. 9c). So He merits the closing **Praise the Lord** (*hal^elû-yāh*; cf. v. 1).

## Psalm 147

The psalmist praised the Lord God for His greatness in sustaining all Creation, and for His grace in healing afflicted believers and giving them His Word. He called the congregation to join him in praise for they too received His many benefits. God is to be praised for His grace (vv. 2-3, 6, 10-14, 19-20) and His greatness (vv. 4-5, 8-9, 15-18).

### A. God heals the brokenhearted (147:1-6)

This psalm has three rounds of praise (vv. 1-6, 7-11, 12-20).

**147:1.** After exclaiming *hal^elû-yāh* (**Praise the Lord**; cf. v. 20 and comments on 104:35) the psalmist stated **how good it is to . . . praise** the One who is most praiseworthy. It is **pleasant** (cf. 135:3) **and fitting** (cf. 33:1).

**147:2-3.** In His grace **the Lord** built **up Jerusalem** again after the Exile. This rebuilding shows that He is the God who **heals the brokenhearted.** Those who repent and turn to Him are healed and restored.

**147:4-6.** God's greatness is seen in His sustaining power in the universe He created (cf. vv. 8-9, 15-18). He knows **each** of the myriads of **stars** (cf. Isa. 40:26). Yet the One who has so much power and **understanding** (cf. Isa. 40:28) **sustains the humble** in the face of opposition. This too displays His grace.

### B. God delights in those who fear Him (147:7-11)

**147:7-9.** In a second cycle of praise, the psalmist told everyone to praise God musically. He should be praised because of His greatness in Creation (cf. vv. 4-5, 15-18). With **rain** and **food** He sustains plant and animal life (on **ravens,** see comments on Job 38:41).

**147:10-11.** God should be praised because even though He is so great, He **delights** not in the mighty but in anyone who trusts **Him.** This is more evidence of His grace (cf. vv. 3, 6, 12-14, 19-20).

### C. God gave His Word (147:12-20)

**147:12-14.** In a third round of praise (vv. 12-20) the psalmist called on **Jerusa-** lem to **praise** the One who gave them security, **peace,** and **the finest of wheat,** all further evidences of His grace.

**147:15-20.** In His greatness **His word** operates in **the earth** (v. 15) and by **His word** He controls nature, including sending **snow . . . frost. . . . hail. . . . icy** winds, and **breezes** (vv. 16-18). The greatest display of grace from this great and powerful God **to Israel,** however, was that He gave **His Word,** His revelation, to her and to **no other nation.**

So the writer summoned praise for the gracious and great Lord of Creation who heals and reveals. The psalm closes with *hal^elû-yāh* (**Praise the Lord;** cf. v. 1).

## Psalm 148

The psalmist called all of heaven and its hosts to praise the Lord because He has established them by decree. And he called the earth to praise His glorious name because He had exalted Israel.

### A. Praise for the Creator (148:1-6)

**148:1-4.** After he exclaimed **Praise the Lord** (*hal^elû-yāh*; cf. v. 14 and comments on 104:35; 146:1) the psalmist summoned all creation above the earth to **praise the Lord. The heavens**—the **sun . . . moon . . . stars,** and elements of nature in the heavens (**waters above the skies**)—were all personified as capable of worshiping the Lord. The **angels** in the heavens were also called on to praise Him (cf. 103:20).

**148:5-6.** All Creation should **praise . . . the Lord** because He **created** it all by His command and has established it all by His **decree.** His word is powerful and is sure and abiding.

### B. Praise for Israel's God (148:7-14)

**148:7-12.** The psalmist summoned all earthly hosts to **praise the Lord. Sea creatures,** elements of nature (cf. 147:15-17) **mountains . . . hills . . . trees,** animal life, **rulers,** and peoples of various ages should praise the Lord.

**148:13-14.** One reason they should **praise** is that **His name** is glorious. As Creator, **His** own **splendor** (cf. comments on 29:2) is greater than that of all His Creation. Also He had **raised up . . . a horn** (a strong one, i.e., a king; cf. 89:17; 132:17) for His beloved **Israel.**

So again the psalmist summoned the people's **praise** (*hal^elû-yāh*; cf. v. 1) for

God's word and His work in Israel.

## Psalm 149

The psalmist invited Israel to sing praises to the Lord who gives salvation to the meek and enabled His people to execute vengeance on the nations.

### A. Call to praise (149:1-3)

**149:1-3.** After exclaiming **Praise the Lord** (*hal⁰lû-yāh*; cf. v. 9 and comments on 104:35; 146:1), the psalmist called Israel to praise **the Lord** by singing **a new song** (cf. 33:3; 40:3; 96:1; 98:1; 144:9; 149:1) **in the assembly.** Rejoicing in Him, **their Maker** (cf. 95:6) and **King** (cf. 145:1), they should **praise** Him with song, **dancing** (cf. 150:4), and musical instruments. Their whole beings should enter into the praise.

### B. Cause for praise (149:4-5)

**149:4-5.** The Lord's **people** should praise Him because He **takes** pleasure in them and gives them **salvation.** For this they should **rejoice** and **sing** even when resting.

### C. Conclusion (149:6-9)

**149:6-9.** The psalmist then called on Israel to take **the praise of God . . . in their mouths** and a **sword in their hands** to execute God's justice on the wicked. Israel was being encouraged to put down evil antagonism against the Lord and His anointed. Then **praise** was again summoned to **the Lord** (*hal⁰lû-yāh*; cf. v. 1).

## Psalm 150

Because of God's mighty excellence in His works, the psalmist called for praise to be rendered in the sanctuary with all kinds of musical instruments.

### A. Call for praise (150:1)

**150:1.** After again exclaiming *hal⁰lû-yāh* (**Praise the Lord**; cf. v. 6 and comments on 104:35; 146:1), the psalmist called for **praise** to be given **in the sanctuary** (lit., "holy place," probably referring here to heaven, God's dwelling place; cf. 11:4, 102:19) and in God's **heavens.**

### B. Cause for praise (150:2)

**150:2.** This **praise** (v. 1) is called for because of His **mighty excellence** in the things He does.

### C. Renewed call for praise (150:3-5)

**150:3-5.** Praise is to be given with musical instruments (including trumpets, harps, lyres, tambourines, stringed instruments, flutes, and **cymbals**), and with **dancing** (cf. 149:3).

### D. Concluding call for praise (150:6)

**150:6.** Appropriately the last verse of the Psalter includes a call for every living thing **that has breath** to praise the **Lord.** Then the Book of Psalms closes with a final *hal⁰lû-yāh* (**Praise the Lord**; cf. v. 1).

# BIBLIOGRAPHY

**Introductory Works**

Anderson, Bernhard W. *Out of the Depths: The Psalms Speak for Us Today.* Philadelphia: Westminster Press, 1974.

Bullinger, E.W. *Figures of Speech Used in the Bible.* 1898. Reprint. Grand Rapids: Baker Book House, 1968.

Drijvers, Pius. *The Psalms: Their Structure and Meaning.* New York: Herder and Herder, 1965.

Gunkel, Hermann. *The Psalms: A Form-Critical Introduction.* Translated by Thomas M. Horner. Philadelphia: Fortress Press, 1967.

Keel, Othmar. *The Symbolism of the Biblical World: Ancient Near Eastern Iconography and the Book of Psalms.* Translated by Timothy J. Hallett. New York: Seabury Press, 1978.

Mowinckel, Sigmund. *The Psalms in Israel's Worship.* Translated by D.R. Ap-Thomas. Nashville: Abingdon Press, 1962.

Sabourin, Leopold. *The Psalms: Their Origin and Meaning.* New York: Alba House, 1974.

Westermann, Claus. *The Praise of God in the Psalms.* Translated by Keith R. Crim. Richmond, Va.: John Knox Press, 1965.

_____. *The Psalms: Structure, Content & Message.* Translated by Ralph D. Gehrke. Minneapolis: Augsburg Publishing House, 1980.

**Commentaries**

Allen, Leslie C. *Psalms 101–150.* Word Biblical Commentary. Vol. 21. Waco, Tex.: Word Books, 1983.

Anderson, A.A. *The Book of Psalms.* 2 vols. New Century Bible. Grand Rapids: Wm. B. Eerdmans Publishing Co., 1981.

Barnes, Albert. *Psalms*. 3 vols. In *Notes on the Old Testament, Explanatory and Practical*. Vols. 19-21. 1868. Reprint. Grand Rapids: Baker Book House, 1950.

Cohen, A. *The Psalms*. London: Soncino Press, 1945.

Craigie, Peter C. *Psalms 1–50*. Word Biblical Commentary. Vol. 19. Waco, Tex.: Word Books, 1983.

Delitzsch, Franz. "Psalms." In *Commentary on the Old Testament in Ten Volumes*. Vol. 5. Reprint (25 vols. in 10). Grand Rapids: Wm. B. Eerdmans Publishing Co., 1982.

Goldingay, John. *Songs from a Strange Land: Psalms 42–51*. Downers Grove, Ill.: InterVarsity Press, 1978.

Kidner, Derek. *Psalms 1–72*. London: InterVarsity Press, 1973.

_____. *Psalms 73–150*. London: InterVarsity Press, 1975.

Kirkpatrick, A.F. *The Book of Psalms*. Cambridge: University Press, 1902. Reprint. Grand Rapids: Baker Book House, 1982.

Perowne, J.J. Stewart. *The Book of Psalms*. 2 vols. 4th ed. London: George Bell and Sons, 1878. Reprint (2 vols. in 1). Grand Rapids: Zondervan Publishing House, 1976.

Rogerson, J.W., and McKay, J.W. *Psalms 1–50*. New York: Cambridge University Press, 1977.

_____. *Psalms 51–100*. New York: Cambridge University Press, 1977.

_____. *Psalms 101–150*. New York: Cambridge University Press, 1977.

Weiser, Artur. *The Psalms: A Commentary*. Philadelphia: Westminster Press, 1962.

Wiersbe, Warren W. *Meet Yourself in the Psalms*. Wheaton, Ill.: SP Publications, Victor Books, 1983.

# PROVERBS

## Sid S. Buzzell

## INTRODUCTION

The Book of Proverbs is a book of moral and ethical instructions, dealing with many aspects of life. The teachings in this book guide its readers in how to lead wise, godly lives and how to avoid the pitfalls of unwise, ungodly conduct.

It has a broad, timeless appeal because of its great variety of subjects and their relevance to everyday life. Proper and improper attitudes, conduct, and characteristics are referred to repeatedly and in succinct, penetrating ways. Proverbs is God's book on "how to wise up and live." It is His treasure book of wisdom.

If the Israelites would follow God's decrees and laws, they would be considered a people of wisdom and understanding (Deut. 4:5-6). This is true for all believers because "the statutes of the LORD" make "wise the simple" (Ps. 19:7). The Book of Proverbs showed the Israelites how their faith in the Lord and His Word should affect their daily lives. And it shows how believers in all ages can be wise in God's and others' eyes.

The Book of Proverbs rounds out the Old Testament by adding an important emphasis. The Israelites were to keep the Law and to hear and obey the Prophets, but the people were also to apply the truths of the Law and the Prophets to every aspect of living. Even if an Israelite broke no commandments in the Mosaic Law and offended no prophet he still might not be leading a full life. Proverbs warns against the illegal and the immoral, but it also focuses on leading an aggressively dynamic life.

**Authorship and Date.** The authorship and date of Proverbs cannot be considered apart from understanding the book's structure. The book is comprised of eight sections (see the *Outline*) written at various times and including several authors or editors. The heading "The Proverbs of Solomon" in 1:1 introduces chapters 1–9 (sections I and II). Since Solomon reigned from 971 to 931, the Proverbs he wrote may be dated in the 10th century. According to 10:1, Section III (10:1–22:16) is also the work of Solomon.

Section IV (22:17–24:34) is called the "sayings of the wise" (22:17; 24:23). The identity of these wise men is uncertain so the date of their sayings is also uncertain. Perhaps they lived before Solomon's time and he compiled their sayings, adding them to his repertoire. Or they may have lived in Solomon's day and their sayings were added by an anonymous editor.

The proverbs in Section V (chaps. 25–29) were written by Solomon but were compiled by men of Hezekiah (25:1). Since Hezekiah reigned from 729 to 686 those chapters were recorded sometime in those years.

Sections VI (chap. 30) and VII (31:1-9), were written by Agur and King Lemuel, respectively. Those men were non-Israelites, perhaps Arabians; their identities and origins are obscure.

Section VIII (31:10-31) may be a continuation of the words ascribed to Lemuel (31:1) but its construction as a separate acrostic poem and its stylistic distinction from 31:1-9 mark it off as an independent piece. If it is, its authorship is not known.

The book took its final form at least as late as Hezekiah's time (because of 25:1). Whether his men compiled the entire book is uncertain. The final date of compilation is generally considered to be around 700 B.C., assuming Agur and Lemuel wrote before then. Of course the writing and compiling were done under the superintending work of the Holy Spirit, the divine Author of all Scripture (2 Tim. 3:16).

It is appropriate that Solomon authored most of the book since he, the wisest person in his day (1 Kings 4:29-31,

34), authored 3,000 proverbs (1 Kings 4:32; cf. Ecc. 12:9). The Holy Spirit guided him to select only several hundred of them for inclusion in the Scriptures.

Presumably Solomon wrote Song of Songs in his early adult years, Proverbs in his middle years, and Ecclesiastes near the end of his life as he reflected on his experiences.

**Purpose.** The fivefold purpose of Proverbs is given in the introduction to the book (Prov. 1:2-4, 6): (a) "for attaining wisdom and discipline," (b) "for understanding words of insight," (c) "for acquiring a disciplined and prudent life," (d) "for giving prudence to the simple," (e) "for understanding proverbs and parables, the sayings and riddles of the wise." These purposes focus on helping readers live wisely and skillfully.

Proverbs were employed by parents and teachers to impart wisdom in a manner that made learning an adventure, a challenge. The purpose in using a proverb was to help the young acquire mental skills that promote wise living. Both the content and the structure of the sayings contributed to the hearers' development. The process was a challenge and the product a reward.

Of the several words for wisdom and related synonyms used in Proverbs, the primary and most frequent one is *ḥokmâh*. It occurs 45 times in Proverbs. In the Old Testament *ḥokmâh* is used of the skill of craftsmen, sailors, singers, mourners, administrators, and counselors. These workers and others, being knowledgeable, experienced, and efficient in their areas of expertise, were considered skillful; they were therefore "wise." Similarly in the spiritual realm a person who possesses *ḥokmâh* in reference to God is one who is both knowledgeable and experienced in following God's way. So in the Bible's Wisdom literature being wise means being skilled in godly living. Having God's wisdom means having the ability to cope with life in a God-honoring way. Crawford H. Toy wrote that "wisdom is the . . . knowledge of right living in the highest sense" (*A Critical and Exegetical Commentary on the Book of Proverbs*, p. 5).

Many ancient cultures in the Near East had wisdom writings (see the section "Relationship of Proverbs to Other Ancient Wisdom Literature"). Though the Book of Proverbs is somewhat similar to that literature, the wisdom promoted in Proverbs contains an element not found in those works. Wisdom in Proverbs includes practical sagacity, mental acumen, and functional skill, but it also includes moral, upright living which stems from a right relationship to the Lord. The statement "The fear of the LORD is the beginning of wisdom" (9:10) makes the Hebrew concept of wisdom unique. (Cf. 14:16, "A wise man fears the LORD." Also note 1:7; 15:33; Job 28:28; Ps. 111:10.) To be wise in the biblical sense one must begin with a proper relationship to God. To fear the Lord means to respect Him for who He is and to respond to Him in trust, worship, obedience, and service. If God is not honored and His Word not followed, then wisdom, as the Hebrew sages defined it, can never be attained.

The purpose of the Book of Proverbs then, is to develop in others, especially the young, a wise, skillful approach to living, which begins with being properly related to the Lord.

**Addressees.** The frequent occurrence of the address "my son" and "my sons" in this book has raised some question about the relationship between Solomon and his "audience." The words "my son" were written by Solomon 15 times in chapters 1–7 and twice elsewhere (19:27; 27:11). They are used 5 times in the sayings of the wise men (23:15, 19; 23:26; 24:13, 21) and once by Lemuel's mother (31:2). "My sons" occurs 4 times (4:1; 5:7; 7:24; 8:32), all by Solomon. Originally these verses with "my son(s)" were addressed orally either to students of Solomon and to students of others in the royal court, or by Solomon and others to their sons in their homes. Favoring the school environment is the fact that learners were sometimes called "sons" of their teachers. Favoring the home environment is the fact that instruction was given by mothers (1:8; 6:20; also note 23:19, 22-26) as well as by fathers. Also Lemuel's mother taught her son an oracle (31:1-2). In its written form the Book of Proverbs is useful for parents in instructing their sons and daughters, as well as helpful, obviously, for personal Bible study. The fact that the book is a collection of sayings suggests that the proverbs were brought together from various situations with various intended audiences in mind. At any rate the book was—and is—an excellent primer for the young (and adults too, for that matter) on wise, godly living.

## Literary Style

*1. Meaning of the word "proverb."* "Proverb" translates *māšāl*, which probably comes from a verb meaning "to be like, to be compared with." A proverb, then, is a statement that makes a comparison or summarizes a common experience (i.e., the sentence is "like" or is compared to reality). Each of the pithy sayings in much of the Book of Proverbs is a *māšāl* (cf. 1:1; 10:1; 25:1), but brief proverbial sayings are also found elsewhere in the Old Testament (e.g., Gen. 10:9; 1 Sam. 10:12; 24:13; 1 Kings 20:11; Jer. 31:29; Ezek. 12:22; 16:44; 18:2).

*Māšāl* also means a "byword" (e.g., Deut. 28:37, "an object of scorn"; 1 Kings 9:7; 2 Chron. 7:20; Jer. 24:9; Ezek. 14:8). The sense seems to be that the person or nation called a byword becomes an object lesson for others. *Māšāl* may also be used of a prophetic oracle (Num. 23:7, 18; 24:3, 15, 20-21, 23) or a taunt (Isa. 14:4) of several verses in length. Perhaps the idea here is that the statements point to what the speaker wished the people were like. Job's "discourse" (Job 29–31) is a *māšāl* in the sense that it summarizes what his experience was like. "Parable" is another way of rendering *māšāl* (Ezek. 20:49); here it suggests that the parabolic story resembles some life incident. This is similar to the translation *māšāl* as "allegory" (Ezek. 17:2). Proverbs are also associated with riddles (Ps. 49:4; Prov. 1:6).

The Book of Proverbs includes a few longer discourses (e.g., 6:12-14, 16-19; 7:6-23; 30:11-14, 18-19, 21-23; 31:4-5) along with its single-verse maxims.

*2. Parallelism.* Proverbs is written entirely in poetic style. The predominant structural feature of Hebrew poetry is so-called poetic parallelism. Usually the two poetic lines in a verse have a parallel relationship.

In *synonymous parallelism* the terms or units of thought in one line are paralleled by similar terms or units of thought in the second line. Sometimes every unit in one line is matched in the next line (e.g., 1:2; 2:11). This is called complete synonymous parallelism. Other times only some of the units in one line are matched in the next line (e.g., in 1:9 the words "They will be" are not matched in the second line). This is called incomplete synonymous parallelism.

In *antithetical parallelism* one line is the opposite of or contrasts with the other line (e.g., 10:1; 11:1). Most of the verses in chapters 10–15 are antithetical.

In *emblematic parallelism* one line illumines the other by a simile or a metaphor (e.g., 10:26; 25:12, 23).

In *synthetic parallelism* the second line simply continues the thought of the first line. Sometimes the second line gives a result of the first line (3:6; 16:3) and other times the second line describes something in the first line (6:12; 15:3). Sometimes one line gives a preference over what is referred to in the other line. There are 19 such "better . . . than" verses (12:9; 15:16-17; 16:8, 16, 19, 32; 17:1, 12; 19:1, 22; 21:9, 19; 22:1; 25:7, 24; 27:5, 10; 28:6). "How much worse" or "how much more" is another kind of synthetic parallelism (11:31; 15:11; 17:7; 19:7, 10; 21:27). Most of the verses in 16:1–22:16 have either synonymous or synthetic parallelism.

Not all verses in Proverbs have two lines. Some have three (e.g., 1:27; 6:13, 17; 27:22; 30:20, 32-33; 31:4), a few have four (e.g., 30:9, 14-15, 17, 19), and one verse has even six lines (30:4). In the three-line verses, usually the first and second lines are related in some way and the second and third lines are parallel in some way (e.g., in 27:27 the second line is in synthetic parallelism to the first line, completing its thought, and the third line is in synonymous parallelism with the second line). However, the three lines in 1:27 are all in synonymous parallelism. The book *Walking in Wisdom: Studying the Proverbs of Solomon,* by William E. Mouser, Jr., is a helpful discussion of how to analyze the points being made in various kinds of parallelism in the Book of Proverbs.

Usually, though not always, the second line in a two-line parallelism does more than merely repeat the words or thought of the first line. The second line may expand the first, or complete it, define it, emphasize it, be more significant than it, enlarge on it, be the opposite of it, an alternative to it, or a counterpart of it. This pattern in which the second line is underscored is what James L. Kugel calls "A, and what's more, B" (*The Idea of Biblical Poetry: Parallelism and Its History.* New Haven, Conn.: Yale University Press, 1981, pp. 7-27, esp. p. 13).

As brief maxims, the verses in Proverbs are distilled, to-the-point sentences about life. They boil down, crystallize, and condense the experiences and observations of the writers. The brief but concentrated nature of the maxims cause their readers to reflect on their meanings. They tell what life is like and how life should be lived. In a terse, no-words-wasted fashion, some statements in Proverbs *relate* what is commonly observed in life; others *recommend* or exhort how life should be lived. And when advice is given, a reason for the counsel usually follows.

Many of the proverbial maxims should be recognized as guidelines, not absolute observations; they are not iron-clad promises. What is stated is generally and usually true, but exceptions are occasionally noted (e.g., cf. Prov. 10:27 with Ps. 73:12).

**Subject Matter.** The Book of Proverbs focuses on human character and conduct. The book's observations and admonitions about life are addressed to individuals, not to the nation Israel as such. As already stated under "Purpose," the Book of Proverbs stresses wise living. This is synonymous with godly living, for one who is godly or righteous is wise in God's eyes. By contrast a wicked or unrighteous person is foolish. The characteristics and consequences of these two paths of living are referred to repeatedly in Proverbs. They are summarized in Psalm 1:6: "For the LORD watches over the way of the righteous, but the way of the wicked will perish."

Many human emotions, attitudes, and relationships are spoken of in Proverbs, and often they are set in contrast. Some of these many topics are listed in the chart, "Positive and Negative Topics and Other Subjects in Proverbs." One common method of studying Proverbs is to compile the verses dealing with a topic and to analyze all that is said on that topic. For example, see the chart "Words

and Speaking in Proverbs," near 6:16-17. Various verses in Proverbs deal with rural life and urban life; with business ethics, social contacts, and civil justice; with family relationships, moral standards, and inner attitudes and motives. No wonder the book has such universal appeal!

Little is said in Proverbs about the afterlife. The stress is on life now. Rewards for godly living are said to be given in the present, and ungodly living results in problems in this life (cf. comments on Ecc. 2:24-26; 11:9). Life's choices, as Proverbs stresses, are clear-cut.

The Book of Proverbs also focuses on God: His character (sovereign, faithful, holy, omniscient, omnipotent, just, etc.), His works, and His blessings. The name Yahweh ("LORD") occurs 87 times in Proverbs.

Man's relationship to the Lord is also stressed in the book. A person can lead a godly, wise life only as he fears and trusts the Lord. Proverbs stresses being rightly related to God and then being rightly related to others.

**Relationship of Proverbs to Other Ancient Wisdom Literature.** Though Solomon's wisdom exceeded that of all others (1 Kings 4:30-31), he was not the only wise man. Egypt had wise men (Gen. 41:8; Ex. 7:11; 1 Kings 4:30; Isa. 19:11-12) and Edom was known for its wisdom (Jer. 49:7; Obad. 8). Babylon too had its wise men (Isa. 47:1, 10; Jer. 50:35; 51:57; Dan. 1:4, 20; 2:13-14; 5:8).

In Egypt's and Babylon's wisdom literature several works are collections of proverbs or include at least some proverbial sayings. Examples from Egypt are *The Instruction of the Vizier Ptah-Hotep* (ca. 2450 B.C.), with advice on how to be a successful state official; *The Instruction of Amen-em-Het* (ca. 2000 B.C.), a father's words to his son about how people he had favored disappointed him; *The Instruction of Amen-em-Ope* (ca. 1300–900 B.C.), a king's teachings to his son about life, using some words similar to those in Proverbs (e.g., "Listen, my son," "path of life," "the way"). The fact that some sayings in *The Instruction of Amen-em-Ope* parallel parts of Proverbs (e.g., Prov. 22:17–24:22) has raised the question of whether Proverbs borrowed from this

# Positive and Negative Topics
## and Other Subjects in Proverbs

### Positive (Righteous/Wise)

Wisdom, wise
Righteous
Life
Knowledge
Work, diligence
Orderliness
Success
Self-control
Faithfulness
Obedience
Honesty, integrity
Justice, fairness, equity
Truth
Honor
Commendation
Humility
Purity
Encouragement
Peace
Love
Mercy, kindness
Generosity
Joy
Hope
Good company
Friendliness
Wealth
Virtue
Soberness
Friendliness
Trust
Pleasure
Quietness
Contentment
Teachableness

### Negative (Wicked/Foolish)

Folly, fool
Wicked
Death
Ignorance
Laziness
Disorderliness
Failure
Anger
Unfaithfulness
Rebellion
Cheating, deceit
Injustice, unfairness, inequity
Lying, deception
Dishonor
Criticism
Pride
Impurity
Slander
Strife, jealousy
Hatred
Cruelty
Greed
Sadness
Anxiety
Bad company
Animosity, enmity
Poverty
Shame
Drunkenness
Unfriendliness
Worry
Misery
Talkativeness
Envy
Unteachableness

### Other Subjects

Fear of the Lord
Husbands
Wives
Fathers
Mothers
Children
Kings, rulers
Masters
Slaves
Prostitutes
Orphans and the needy
Business dealings
Hypocrisy
Stealing
Rebuke
Gluttony, food

Egyptian writing, or the Egyptian writer borrowed from Proverbs, or whether both wrote independently about common concerns. On this question see the comments on 22:17–24:22.

Samples of Babylonian wisdom literature that include proverbs are *Counsels of Wisdom* (ca. 1500–1000 B.C.), *Akkadian Proverbs* (ca. 1800–1600 B.C.), and *The Words of Ahiqar* (700–400 B.C.).

The fact that some maxims in the Book of Proverbs are similar to these Egyptian and Mesopotamian writings does not undo the divine inspiration of the Scriptures. God guided the writers of the Book of Proverbs so that their writings, inspired by the Holy Spirit, recorded exactly what God wanted included in the biblical canon. Furthermore, most of these nonbiblical writings are more secular than the Book of Proverbs and sometimes are even rather crass in their moral tone. Proverbs' emphasis on fearing God is obviously missing from these other works. In spite of certain similarities in style and content to other works, the Book of Proverbs stands unique as part of God's written revelation.

# OUTLINE

# COMMENTARY

## I. The Preface (1:1-7)

In these verses the author introduced himself and his literary form (v. 1), gave an extended statement of why the proverbs were recorded (vv. 2-6), and stated a theological reason why his readers should become the kind of people he wanted them to be (v. 7).

## A. The author and the literary form (1:1)

**1:1.** Scholars differ on whether this reference to **the proverbs of Solomon** includes the entire book or just the first section (1:2–9:18). Since various authors and editors are named in other sections, this phrase probably covers chapters 1–9, with the same phrase in 10:1 introducing 10:1–22:16. (See "Authorship and Date" in the *Introduction*.)

The word "proverbs" gives not only the title of the book but also designates the type of literature in the book. On the meaning of *māšāl* ("proverb") see "Literary Style" in the *Introduction*. As discussed there, though *māšāl* usually means a brief, pithy saying, it can also refer to longer discourses. The word "proverb" then refers to various forms of wise, insightful pronouncements.

## B. The purpose of the book (1:2-6)

### 1. SUMMARY STATEMENT (1:2)

**1:2.** The Proverbs were written to encourage others: (a) to acquire a disciplined skill in right living (**for attaining wisdom and discipline**) and (b) to gain mental acumen (**for understanding words of insight**). The first of these is elaborated in verses 3-5 and the second in verse 6. As stated in the *Introduction* under "Purpose," this word *ḥokmâh* ("wisdom") in the Old Testament often refers to the mental and physical skills of craftsmen, sailors, singers, mourners, administrators, counselors, and others; but other times, as in Proverbs, it focuses on the application of moral and ethical principles that result in skillful, godly living. A person with this wisdom has "expertise" in godly living. Such wise, skillful living is a life of "discipline" (cf. v. 3) and order. Discipline translates *mûsār*, "moral discipline or correction." In Hebrew the word "understanding," also used in verses 5 ("discerning") and 6 ("understanding"), means insight, or the ability to see "between" issues.

### 2. EXPANDED STATEMENT (1:3-6)

**1:3-5.** These verses elaborate on the qualities of life that must be acquired for leading a wise life. **A disciplined** (cf. v. 2) **and prudent** (cf. v. 4) **life** is one with high moral standards, a life in which one does what is **right . . . just, and fair** (cf.

2:9). An immoral or unjust person can hardly be called wise in God's sight!

**The simple** (*peṭî*, 1:4) refers to a person who is naive and untaught. He is not an imbecile, one who cannot comprehend, or a fool who despises wisdom. Instead, he is one whose exposure to life and wisdom has been limited. Because of inexperience he is gullible and easily influenced. Therefore he needs **prudence** (cf. 1:3), that is, cleverness or sensibleness (*'ormâh*, used elsewhere only in 8:5, 12; Ex. 21:14 ["schemes"; NASB, "craftily"]; Josh. 9:4 ["a ruse"; NASB, "craftily"]). The word *peṭî* ("simple") is used 14 times in Proverbs (Prov. 1:4, 22, 32; 7:7; 8:5; 9:4, 6, 16; 14:15, 18; 19:25; 21:11; 22:3; 27:12). On words for "fool" in Proverbs see comments on 1:7.

"The simple" and **the young** need wisdom: "prudence," **knowledge, and discretion** (*mᵉzimmâh*, "wise planning"; also used in 2:11; 3:21, "discernment"; 5:2; 8:12). In 12:2 and 14:17 *mᵉzimmâh* is used in a negative sense to mean crafty or wicked planning. Also the experienced (**the wise,** *ḥākom*, and **the discerning,** 1:5; cf. v. 2) are reminded of their need to grow in wisdom (in **learning** and **guidance**). "Guidance" (*taḥbūlôṯ*), literally, "steerings" (like the tackle for directing a ship), suggests moving one's life in the right direction. This Hebrew word is used elsewhere only in Job 37:12 ("direction"); Proverbs 11:14; 12:5 ("plans"); 20:18; 24:6.

**1:6.** A person who understands "words of insight" (v. 2) understands the meaning of **proverbs . . . parables,** and **the sayings and riddles of the wise.** The word for "riddle" (*ḥîḏâh*) means an indirect, oblique, or enigmatic statement (like a figure of speech) which needs interpretation. It is used of Samson's riddle (Jud. 14:12-19) and of the "hard questions" the Queen of Sheba asked of Solomon (1 Kings 10:1; 2 Chron. 9:1).

## C. The theme of the book (1:7)

**1:7.** Fearing the Lord, Solomon wrote, **is the beginning of knowledge. The fear of the LORD** occurs 11 times in Proverbs (and "fear the LORD" occurs 4 times). "Beginning" is the Hebrew *rēʾšîṯ* which means "the start." One cannot gain knowledge of spiritual things if he begins at the wrong point, refusing to fear the Lord (i.e., to recognize God's character and respond by revering, trusting, worshiping, obeying, and serving Him). *Rē'šît* also means the capstone or essence. The essence of true knowledge is fearing God. Apart from Him a person is ignorant of spiritual things (Rom. 1:22; Eph. 4:18; 1 Peter 1:14). The words of Proverbs 1:7a are repeated in 9:10 near the end of the first section (also cf. Job 28:28; Ps. 111:10).

In contrast with those who fear God and have knowledge, **fools despise wisdom and discipline.** "Despise" translates the Hebrew *bûz,* "to hold in contempt, to belittle, to ridicule" (cf. Num. 15:31; Neh. 2:19). *Bûz* is also used seven other times in Proverbs: 6:30; 11:12; 13:13; 14:21; 23:9, 22; 30:17. Three Hebrew words are translated "fool" in Proverbs. One kind of fool (*kᵉsîl*) is characterized by a dull and closed mind. He is thickheaded and stubborn. This word occurs more frequently in Proverbs than the other two words; it is used 49 times in this book. By his laziness and shortsightedness, this kind of fool rejects information from others (cf. 15:14). Another word for fool is *nābāl.* It is used only three times in Proverbs (17:7, 21; 30:22) and refers to one who lacks spiritual perception. A third kind of fool (*'ĕwîl*) is arrogant and flippant as well as mentally dull. He is coarse and hardened in his ways. This word is used 19 times in Proverbs and only 7 times elsewhere. The "fools" in 1:7 are those who in their arrogant, coarse ways reject God and wisdom (cf. v. 29). Two kinds of people are contrasted in this verse: those who humbly fear God and thus acquire true knowledge, and the arrogant fools who by their refusal to fear God demonstrate that they hold wisdom and discipline in contempt (cf. "wisdom and discipline" in v. 2). These two kinds of people are contrasted throughout much of the book.

## II. The Words of Solomon on Wisdom's Values (1:8–9:18)

This lengthy section is an introduction to the collection of terse sayings contained in the remaining chapters of the book. The purpose of this section (1:8–9:18) is to whet the appetite of the reader(s) ("my son[s]") so he will apply his heart to his parents' wise sayings. Solomon piles statement on statement to demonstrate the superiority of wisdom

over any other way of life. Besides the warnings against crime and adultery, his statements focus on a productive and meaningful existence. The material may be divided into 16 subpoints.

### A. The value of wisdom in giving honor (1:8-9)

**1:8.** The words **my son** (and "my sons") are used frequently in the first nine chapters and four times in 22:17–24:34. They probably refer to Solomon's own son(s), not to students of a sage, because of the reference to their mother in 1:8. (For more information on this matter see "Addressees" in the *Introduction.*) **Listen** is commanded several times (4:1, 10, 20; 5:1, 7; 7:24; 8:32; 19:20; 22:17; 23:19, 22). **Teaching** renders the Hebrew word *tôrâh,* usually translated "Law." When used, as here, with a specific person (e.g., mother) it is translated "teaching" (cf. 3:1; 4:2; 6:20; 13:14). Since parents in ideal Jewish homes taught their children God's Law (cf. Deut. 6:4-7), the same word (*tôrâh*) was used both for the Law and for instruction in it.

**1:9.** If children heeded their parents' teachings, they were promised **a garland** (some kind of **head** ornament; cf. 4:9) and a neck **chain** (cf. 3:3, 22). That is, heeding parental instruction would give them an attractiveness of life and position. They would be honored. The implied contrast is that disobedience and rebellion lead to dishonor.

### B. The value of wisdom in preserving from disaster (1:10-33)

1. THE DISASTER THAT ACCOMPANIES THE PURSUIT OF WICKEDNESS (1:10-19)

The appeal of the wicked, so attractive initially, is presented in its full scope. A foolish person is dazzled by the prospects of acquiring wealth easily and being gratified quickly by the immediate (vv. 10-14), but a wise person views the consequence of such sin and folly.

**1:10-14.** The pressure of peers can be strong, especially on young people. Therefore they need to avoid the invitations by the wrong kind of people (**sinners**) who invite them to take part in murder and theft. To **give in** to such influence is a downward step (cf. v. 15). **Let's lie in wait for someone's blood** (cf. 12:6) clearly spells out their murderous intentions. (Cf. comments on "lie in wait," 1:18.) These sinners are ready to take people's lives in order to take their money, to **swallow them** just as **the grave** (šᵉʾôl, not the afterlife here) or **the pit** (a synonym of grave) "swallow" the dead. In their greed for gaining possessions (v. 13) they urge the young (here the father's **son**) to join them (v. 14), promising to divide the booty.

**1:15-19.** Again Solomon urged his **son . . . not** to get involved with such people (cf. v. 10). To **set foot on their paths** (cf. 4:14) is to be involved in an almost irreversible course of action that quickly involves them in **sin** and bloodshed (cf. 1:11). **Birds** are smart enough to avoid **a net** they see **spread** out to catch them. But these gangsters, more stupid than birds, not only see the trap; they even set it for themselves! They lie **in wait** to shed others' **blood,** but they **themselves** are caught in their own trap (cf. v. 32; 26:27; 28:10). The humor of this boomeranging result is evident, that **ill-gotten gain** (1:19; cf. 10:2; 28:16) cannot be enjoyed. Thieves steal money but then **it takes** their **lives!** In other words crime does not pay.

2. THE DISASTER THAT ACCOMPANIES THE NEGLECT OF WISDOM (1:20-33)

Wisdom, personified like a woman, appeals to everyone (vv. 20-23), but a fool ignores her appeal (vv. 24-28) at his own risk (vv. 29-33). Wisdom is also personified as a woman in 3:16-18; 4:3-6; 8:1-21, 32-36; 9:1-6; 14:33.

**1:20-23.** Whereas the sinners in verses 10-19 were probably secretive about their appeal to the young man, here **wisdom** shouts **in the street,** and other **public** places in **the city.** In two rhetorical questions she invites three groups to forsake their ways. They are those who would be more likely to refuse her appeal. They are the **simple ones** (peṭî; see comments on v. 4), the **mockers** (cf. Ps. 1:1), **and fools** (kᵉsîl; cf. comments on Prov. 1:7). By responding to wisdom's **rebuke** a foolish person can become wise (v. 23). Rebuke is mentioned frequently in Proverbs as a helpful kind of verbal correction (vv. 23, 25, 30; 3:11; 9:8 [twice]; 13:1; 15:31; 17:10; 19:25; 25:12; 27:5; 30:6).

**1:24-28.** To reject and ignore wisdom and not learn from its **rebuke** (cf. vv. 23, 30) has serious consequences. When **troubles** come, as they inevitably do to

everyone, wisdom mockingly refuses to help sinners. Wisdom's laughing at **disaster** and **calamity** seems cruel. But this simply means that spurned advice will haunt its rejecter when calamity comes. She had called them and they had refused. Now this would be reversed with the same results; **they** would **call . . . but** she would **not answer.** When a fool who has earlier rejected wisdom attempts to start over and follow the wise path, his efforts are of no avail. Wisdom rejected cannot be reclaimed after she has withdrawn her invitation.

**1:29-33.** To reject "Lady Wisdom's" call is to hate **knowledge** (cf. v. 22) and to refuse to **fear the LORD** (cf. v. 7 and comments there). So fools will suffer the consequences **of their** actions (v. 31). They reap what they sow (cf. Gal. 6:7). As illustrated in Proverbs 1:19, folly (**the simple,** peṭî, and **fools,** kᵉsîl, v. 32) ultimately results in death. By contrast, heeding the way of wisdom gives **safety** (3:23) and peace.

These contrasts between the consequences of folly (1:32) and of wisdom (v. 33) set the tone for the rest of the book.

## C. The moral values of wisdom (chap. 2)

In this chapter the father instructed his son ("my son"; cf. 1:8) on the efforts needed for attaining wisdom (2:1-6), the moral benefits of wisdom's attainment (vv. 7-10), and the protection of wisdom from immoral people (vv. 11-22).

1. THE PURSUIT OF WISDOM (2:1-6)

**2:1-4.** Eight verbs are used in these verses: **accept . . . store up** (v. 1), **turning . . . applying . . . call . . . cry** (v. 3), **look . . . search** (v. 4). The objects of these activities are the teacher's **words** and **commands** (v. 1; cf. "commands" in 7:1), **wisdom** and **understanding** (2:2), and **insight** and **understanding** (v. 3; cf. "understanding," meaning discernment, in vv. 6, 11). Effort must be expended for one to become wise. Getting wisdom involves openness, retention, hearing (with the **ear**), applying (with the **heart;** cf. v. 10), requesting, and diligent searching.

**2:5-6.** The three "ifs" in verses 1, 3-4 are followed by **then,** which introduces the result. Seeking and valuing wisdom lead to a person's understanding (discerning) **the fear of the LORD** and **know-**

ing **God.** This is the same truth stated in 1:7. **The LORD** is the source of that **wisdom** (cf. James 1:5). As a person fears the Lord, he gains wisdom, **knowledge** (cf. Prov. 1:4; 2:10), **and understanding** (cf. vv. 2-3, 11).

2. THE MORAL BENEFITS OF WISDOM (2:7-10)

**2:7-10.** Wisdom gives positive, health-inducing moral benefits. It keeps one from evil and contributes to holiness. Wisdom is a matter of the heart, and of moral conduct, not just of intellectual attainment. This is made clear by the words **upright** and **blameless** (cf. v. 21), **the just,** and **faithful ones** (from ḥeseḏ, those who are loyal to God). Elsewhere in Proverbs the word for **victory** is translated "sound judgment" (3:21; 8:14; 18:1). In 2:7 it means success, the *result* of sound judgment. Like **a shield** (cf. Ps. 3:3) God protects those who by His wisdom are morally upright, those who are His (cf. Prov. 1:33). Moral living enables a person to be equitable with others, to do what is **right and just and fair** (cf. 1:3). "Fair" translates the same word rendered "upright" in 2:7. One's conduct is suggested by the synonyms **walk . . . course . . . way,** and **path** (vv. 7-9; cf. vv. 12-13, 15, 18-20).

A person who strives for **wisdom** (vv. 1-4) will find that it **will enter** his **heart** (v. 10). Obtaining wisdom requires diligence on man's part in pursuing God's will; yet wisdom is a gift from God (cf. v. 6). Having such **knowledge** from God gives inner joy or pleasure.

3. THE PROTECTION OF WISDOM FROM IMMORAL PEOPLE (2:11-22)

Wisdom is valuable; therefore it should be sought after (vv. 1-4). For one thing it guards from wicked men (vv. 12-15) and wicked women (vv. 16-19) and keeps one going in the right paths (vv. 20-22).

**2:11-15.** A general statement about wisdom's protection (v. 11) links verses 7-8 with verses 12-15. God protects (v. 8), and the **discretion** He gives also protects (v. 11; cf. 4:6; 13:6). Verses 12-15 take on added meaning when they are related to the warning in 1:10-19. **The ways** and **words** of the **wicked . . . are perverse** (2:12). "Perverse" and **perverseness** (v. 14) are the same word in Hebrew. Coming from the verb "to turn, turn from,

overturn," they suggest something that is "turned away" from the normal. This Hebrew word occurs eight times in Proverbs (2:12, 14; 6:14, "deceit"; 10:31-32; 16:28, 30; 23:33, "confusing") and only once elewhere (Deut. 32:20, "perversity"). Such people turn away from **the straight** (lit., "upright"; cf. Prov. 2:7) **paths** to **dark** (i.e., evil) **ways.** They even enjoy their perversity, their **crooked . . . ways.** "Crooked" translates 'iqqēš ("twisted") which is also used in 6:12 ("corrupt"); it is rendered "perverse" in 11:20; 17:20; 19:1; 28:6 and "wicked" in 22:5. Their deeds are distortions of morality. **Ways** (2:12-13, 15) and **paths** (vv. 13, 15) help relate this passage to other parts of chapter 2 (cf. "way" in v. 8, "ways" in v. 20, "path" in v. 9, and "paths" in vv. 18-20; also cf. 4:19; 7:25; 8:20).

**2:16-19.** Wisdom **(it)** also protects from **(will save you . . . from;** cf. v. 12) immoral women (cf. 7:4-5). **The adulteress** ('iššâh zārâh) and **the wayward wife** (noḵrîyâh) are synonymous terms.

The first term can mean a non-Israelite (as Ruth in Ruth 2:10) or (as in Prov. 2:16; 5:3, 20; 7:5; 22:14; 23:27) a woman who because of her immorality was outside the circle of her proper relations. In Proverbs noḵrîyâh is used in 2:16; 5:20; 6:24; 7:5; 23:27. Whereas wicked men use perverse words (2:12) the adulteress uses **seductive words** (cf. 5:3; 6:24; 7:5, 21). **The partner of her youth** refers to her husband (cf. "the wife of your youth," 5:18), and **the covenant** which she **ignored** is her marriage vows. Forgetting her commitment to her husband, she became promiscuous. To be involved with such a person (in **her house) leads** to **death;** adultery puts a person on an irretrievable path that eventually results in physical death (cf. 5:5; 7:27). It is fatal. **The spirits of the dead** translates rᵉp̄ā'îm, which occurs also in 9:18; 21:16 (see comments on Job 26:5). On **paths** (Prov. 2:18-19) see comments on verses 13, 15 (cf. 5:6).

**2:20-22.** A person who pursues wisdom (vv. 1-4) avoids the wrong kind of people (vv. 11-19) and can have the right kind of companions (**good men** and **the righteous**). Merely escaping immorality is insufficient for a man of wisdom; he must also progressively pursue the good. As a result God blesses him. For the Israelites, residing **in the land** (of Canaan) was a sign of God's favor (cf. Ex. 20:12; Ps. 37:3, 9, 11, 29). The contrast between **the upright** and **the blameless** (cf. Prov. 2:7), who will enjoy God's agricultural prosperity, and **the wicked** and **the unfaithful,** who will no longer be in **the land** because of either exile or death, recalls the contrast in Psalm 1:6 (cf. Prov. 10:30).

### D. The blessings of wisdom (3:1-12)

After another strong encouragement to pursue his teaching (vv. 1-4) the father-teacher gave four commands (vv. 5-12). Each deals with a danger of misusing a gift of God. The son is told (a) to trust in God and not lean on his own understanding (vv. 5-6), (b) to fear God and not be wise in his own eyes (vv. 7-8), (c) to honor God and not fail to give to Him (vv. 9-10), and (d) to appreciate God and not misunderstand His discipline and its value (vv. 11-12). These verses follow an alternating pattern of commands and rewards: commands (v. 1), reward (v. 2), commands (v. 3), reward (v. 4), commands (vv. 5-6a), reward (v. 6b), commands (v. 7), reward (v. 8), command (v. 9), reward (v. 10), commands (v. 11), reward (v. 12). The rewards include longevity and prosperity (v. 2), favor with God and people (v. 4), fewer problems (v. 6), health (v. 8), prosperity (v. 10), and awareness of God's love (v. 12).

1. THE APPEAL TO FOLLOW THE FATHER'S TEACHING (3:1-4)

**3:1-2.** Again the **son** (cf. 1:8, 15; 2:1; 3:11, 21) is urged—both negatively (**do not forget**) and positively (**keep**)—to heed what he was being taught. As in 1:8; 4:2; and 6:20, 23 **teaching** translates *tôrâh* (see comments on 1:8). (On **commands**; cf. 2:1; 4:4; 6:20.) If these instructions are part of one's inner **life,** two benefits will be realized: longevity (cf. 3:16; 4:10; 9:11; 10:27; 14:27; 15:24), a sign of God's blessing (cf. Ex. 20:12), and **prosperity.** The word for prosperity, *šālôm,* is often translated "peace." Though it includes peace and prosperity, it is broader in meaning. It also suggests wholeness, health, and harmony.

**3:3-4. Love** translates *hesed,* loyalty to one's covenant or commitment. That quality along with dependability (cf. "love and faithfulness" in 14:22; 16:6; 20:28) should grace one's life like a **neck** chain (cf. 3:22; 1:9; 6:21) and should be written, figuratively, on one's **heart** (cf. 6:21; 7:3). These statements were not intended to encourage the use of phylacteries (see comments on Deut. 6:8-9), but to encourage strong association with and adherence to the parents' teachings. The results of such adherence are **favor and a good name** (good reputation). "Favor" translates *hen,* from the verb *hānan,* "to be gracious or to show favor." The noun is translated "grace" in Proverbs 3:34; "kindhearted" in 11:16; "favor" in 3:4; 13:15; 28:23; and "charm" in 31:30. "Good name" is rendered "good understanding" in 13:15. The Hebrew *śēkel ṭôb* includes the idea of competence and effectiveness, and therefore a reputation for prudence.

2. THE COMMAND TO TRUST IN THE LORD AND NOT LEAN ON ONE'S OWN UNDERSTANDING (3:5-6)

**3:5-6.** To **trust in the LORD** wholeheartedly means one should **not** rely (**lean**) **on** his **understanding,** for human insights are never enough. God's ways are incomprehensible (Isa. 55:8-9; Rom. 11:33-34); yet He is trustworthy. All the wisdom a person may acquire can never replace the need for full trust in God's superior ways. **Heart** in Hebrew refers to one's emotions (Prov. 12:25; 13:12; 14:10, 13) but more often to his intellect (such as understanding, 10:8; discernment, 15:14; reflection, 15:28); or will (5:12).

As a person trusts in the Lord and acknowledges Him (this is not a nod of recognition but an intimate knowledge of God) **in all** his **ways** (cf. **all your** heart, 3:5), he finds that God makes his **paths straight.** This means more than guidance; it means God removes the obstacles, making a smooth path or way of life, or perhaps better, bringing one to the appointed goal. (On ways and paths, cf. v. 17 and see comments on 2:13, 15.) Proverbs teaches that those who follow wisdom have an easier, less problematic life (e.g., 3:10, 16, 24-25).

3. THE COMMAND TO FEAR THE LORD AND NOT ADMIRE ONE'S WISDOM (3:7-8)

**3:7-8.** Young people who acquire wisdom need to remember that they did **not** become **wise** by themselves; wisdom comes from God (2:6). This reminder is similar to 3:5b. A heart awareness of and proper response to God (**fear the LORD;** cf. comments on 1:7) help prevent the **evil** of pride (cf. Rom. 12:16). (On shunning evil; cf. Prov. 8:13; 14:16; 16:6; Ps. 97:10.) As a result God gives **health** and vigor (cf. Prov. 4:22). Health in one's **bones,** mentioned several times in Proverbs (3:8; 12:4; 14:30; 15:30; 16:24; 17:22), suggests, as is well known today, that spiritual and physical health are related.

4. HONOR THE LORD AND DO NOT WITHHOLD ONE'S OFFERING (3:9-10)

**3:9-10.** In Israel, honoring **the LORD with . . . the firstfruits of all** one's **crops** was a way of expressing gratitude to Him for His provisions (Deut. 26:1-3, 9-11). It was a way of acknowledging God and His help (Prov. 3:6). In return, God **then** (cf. v. 4) promised to fill the **barns** (with grain) and the **vats . . . with new wine** (*tîrôš,* "freshly squeezed grape juice"). *In general* it is true that godliness results in gain, that piety brings prosperity (cf. v. 2; Deut. 28:1-14; Matt. 6:33). But this kind of generalization, common in Proverbs, does not disallow God from making exceptions. Otherwise God is invested in, rather than honored. Proverbs 3:10 is well balanced by verses 11-12, as Derek Kidner appropriately observes (*The Proverbs: An Introduction and Commentary,* p. 64).

5. APPRECIATE THE LORD AND DO NOT MISUNDERSTAND HIS DISCIPLINE (3:11-12)

**3:11-12.** The God who can be trusted to smooth out obstacles and bring one to his appointed goal (vv. 5-6) and to supply one's material needs (vv. 9-10) demonstrates His love by **discipline.** The warning to the **son** (cf. vv. 1, 21) is twofold: **do not despise** ("reject or take lightly") the Lord's discipline, and **do not resent** ("loathe or abhor") **His rebuke** (see comments on 1:23 and cf. Job 5:17; Heb. 12:5-6). Physical punishment and verbal correction are hard to accept but they demonstrate God's loving concern. The same is true of a parent's discipline of his children (cf. Deut. 8:15). Loathing such discipline—thinking that God **disciplines** because He enjoys causing pain—overlooks the benefits that come from such correction.

E. *The high value of wisdom (3:13-20)*

**3:13-15.** Because **wisdom** brings happiness (**blessed;** cf. v. 18 and see comments on Ps. 1:1) and because wealth often does not bring genuine happiness (Ecc. 5:10-12), wisdom's value far exceeds the worth of precious metals such as **silver . . . gold,** and also **rubies** (cf. Prov. 8:10-11, 19). The words **profitable** and **yields better returns** (lit., "brings a higher yield") are the language of a trader or investor. What wisdom returns to her possessor is of greater value than anything gold or silver can purchase.

**3:16-18.** Wisdom, personified as a woman, gives with both hands, that is, generously. **Her right hand** gives longevity (cf. v. 2) and from **her left hand** she gives **riches** (what silver and gold can purchase) **and** more (viz., **honor;** cf. v. 4; 4:8; 8:18; 21:21; 22:4). Besides giving a **long life** (3:16; see comments on v. 2), wisdom also provides a quality life: pleasantness and **peace** (*šālôm;* see comments on v. 2). Long life with no thought for its quality could be a curse rather than a blessing. (On **ways** and **paths;** cf. v. 6 and see comments on 2:13, 15.)

A quality kind of life is often mentioned in Proverbs: 3:22; 4:13, 22; 6:23; 8:35; 10:11, 16-17; 11:19, 30; 12:28; 13:14; 14:27; 16:22; 19:23; 21:21; 22:4. A long and fruitful life is expressed in the figure of a tree (3:18). Much as the **tree of life** was a source of life (Gen. 2:9), so wisdom is a source of life. (Prov. also refers to a tree of life in 11:30; 13:12; 15:4.)

**3:19-20.** When God created the world, He used **wisdom . . . understanding,** and **knowledge.** If *God* needed these, then certainly people need them. The relationship between God and wisdom in His Creation is discussed in more detail in 8:22-31.

F. *The value of wisdom in building relationships with others (3:21-35)*

**3:21.** The familiar **my son** (cf. vv. 1, 11) introduces a plea that the son embrace valued qualities. **Sound judgment** translates the Hebrew word that is rendered "victory" in 2:7 (see comments there). **Discernment** (*mᵉzimmâh*) is translated "discretion" in 1:4. The last part of 3:21 is like the first part of 4:21.

**3:22-26.** These verses mention a number of benefits that come to those who heed the exhortation in verse 21. These benefits include **life** (v. 22; cf. comments on v. 18), **safety** (v. 23; cf. 1:33; 2:7-

8), avoidance of troubles (cf. 3:6), peaceful **sleep** (v. 24), **confidence** in the future (vv. 25-26a), and avoidance of traps set by the wicked (cf. 1:15-18). The long life referred to in 3:22 may be partially attributed to the peace of mind so graphically pictured in verses 23-26.

**3:27-35.** These verses include five sample maxims about relationships with others, with verses 27-31 each beginning with the words **Do not.** These are examples of what it means to be wise. They may be grouped into three relationships (vv. 27-28, 29-30, 32-32): (1) The command **Do not withhold good from those who deserve it** (v. 27) is literally, "Do not withhold good from its owners." The idea is, fulfill an obligation such as paying wages to a hired laborer (Lev. 19:13b; Deut. 24:15). Proverbs 3:28 seems to reinforce the point of verse 27, but it may expand the idea to being generous to the poor. This is "right and just and fair" (1:3). (2) To **harm . . . a neighbor** (3:29) violates his trust, and to **accuse** him falsely (v. 30) violates the ninth commandment (Ex. 20:16). To **plot** translates *ḥāraš,* "to plow," from which comes the idea of plans being thought up or devised as furrows in a field are plowed. The word is also used in Proverbs 6:14, 18 ("devises"); 12:20; 14:22 (twice: "plot" and "plan"). (3) Some people **envy a violent man** (3:31; cf. 23:17; 24:1, 19) because they see the money he has or the pleasures he supposedly enjoys. But God gives four reasons why such envy is uncalled for: (1) **The LORD** hates such **a perverse** (from *lûz,* "to be devious"; cf. 14:2) person, whereas **the upright** in contrast enjoys fellowship with God (3:32). (2) The Lord curses **the wicked but . . . blesses . . . the righteous** (v. 33). (3) God **mocks** arrogant **mockers** (cf. comments on 1:22), causing their actions to boomerang on them, whereas **the humble** receive His **grace** (cf. James. 4:6; 1 Peter 5:5). (4) **The wise** are honored (cf. Prov. 3:16) **but fools** (*kᵉsîl;* see comments on 1:7) are shamed. These verses show that the words "upright," "righteous," "the humble," and "the wise" are basically synonymous in the Book of Proverbs.

## G. An exhortation to acquire wisdom (4:1-9)

This appeal to acquire wisdom is similar to several other passages in chapters 1–9 (1:8-9; 2:1-6; 3:1-2, 21-26; 4:10, 20-22; 5:1-2; 6:20-22; 7:1-3, 24; 8:32-36). Wisdom gives life (4:4), protection (v. 6), and honor (vv. 8-9). This instruction is valid because of its enduring quality, and it is valuable because of the honor it brings.

**4:1-2.** The father's exhortation begins with the command to **listen** (cf. 1:8; 4:10, 20; 5:1, 7; 7:24). Usually the words were addressed to "my son," but here and in 5:7; 7:24; 8:32 it is plural, **my sons. Pay attention** is also repeated in 4:20; 5:1; 7:24; 22:17. As in 1:8; 3:1; 6:20; 13:14, *tôrâh,* normally translated "Law," is here properly translated **teaching** (see comments on 1:8).

**4:3-6.** Solomon spoke of his boyhood when his parents David and Bathsheba **taught** him. He was then their **only child** though later he had three brothers (1 Chron. 3:5). Proverbs 4:4b-9 quote from Solomon's father David. By quoting these words Solomon was passing the instruction on to his sons. The three generations involved here illustrate Deuteronomy 6:2. David had urged young Solomon to obey his **words** wholeheartedly (**with all your heart**; cf. Prov. 3:5) so that he would live (cf. 3:1-2). **Keep my commands and you will live** is repeated in 7:2a.

Perhaps David's encouragement to Solomon to **get wisdom** helped influence Solomon to ask God for it (1 Kings 3:5-14). Wisdom was to be pursued (three times Solomon said "get"; Prov. 4:5 [twice], 7) and valued (**love her**; cf. 8:17, 21) because **she** (wisdom is again personified as a woman) protects (cf. 2:7-8, 11; 3:21-23) and guards.

**4:7-9.** As stated in 3:13-15 "nothing" can compare with **wisdom.** Therefore it **is supreme,** well worth all the effort and cost involved in acquiring it. As **wisdom** is valued and loved (cf. 4:6), she gives **honor** (3:16), and an attractive life, pictured as a beautiful wreath (1:9) and **a crown of splendor** (used in 16:31 of gray hair, or age). The opposite is also implied: a foolish, unwise life is dishonorable, unattractive, and shameful. Solomon experienced both wisdom and folly and therefore both kinds of results.

## H. The value of wisdom in preserving from trouble (4:10-19)

The ways of wisdom (vv. 10-13) and of wickedness (vv. 14-17) are described and the son-learner is again urged to pursue the former and avoid the latter. The lesson is summarized in verses 18-19 by picturing the destinations of both paths.

**4:10-13.** Once more Solomon addressed one of his sons (**my son**; cf. v. 20), urging him to **listen** (cf. vv. 1, 20 and see comments on 1:8) because heeding his father's words would give him a longer **life** (cf. 3:2, 16; 9:11; 10:27; 14:27; 15:24). **Straight paths** (4:11) are unrestricted paths (cf. 3:6), which are easier to walk in. This thought is amplified in 4:12: one's **steps** are **not . . . hampered** (lit., "narrowed or cramped," that is, he is not in distress). The crooked, devious path of sin is the way of problems and hardships (cf. "path" and "way" in vv. 14, 18-19 and see comments on 2:12-15).

Again an eager acquiring of **wisdom** is encouraged (4:13; cf. vv. 5-7) because it gives **life** (cf. v. 10).

**4:14-17.** In verses 14-15 six urgent commands are given to steer clear of the path of the wicked, and verses 16-17 state the reason for the urgency in verses 14-15. **Wicked** people are so taken up with **evil** that they are unable to **sleep till they** hurt someone (cf. 1:15-16). Sin is so much a part of them that it is like their food (**bread** and **wine**).

**4:18-19.** The **path of the righteous,** which is "the way of wisdom" (v. 11), **is like the first** rays of light in the morning, which gradually increase to **the full light of** noonday. With light on his path a believer can follow "straight paths" (v. 11) and "not be hampered" or "stumble" (v. 12). By contrast the way or path of **the wicked** (cf. v. 14) is characterized by **deep darkness** ('ăpēlâh, intense blackness in the middle of the night; cf. 7:9; Ex. 10:22) which causes him to **stumble.**

## I. The value of wisdom in producing health (4:20-27)

**4:20-22.** Another exhortation to hear and **pay attention to** instruction (cf. v. 1; 5:1) opens this section. The author's words (cf. 4:4; 2:1) were to be in his son's view (cf. 3:21) and in his **heart.** The major incentive was the offer of **life** (cf. 4:10, 13, 23) **and health** (cf. 3:8).

**4:23.** The **heart** (cf. comments on 3:5) should be guarded for out of it (a **wellspring**) come one's actions (cf. Luke 6:45). Here the word "heart" means more than mental or emotional capacity; it also

encompasses one's values (cf. Matt. 6:21).

**4:24-27.** These verses apply the command to guard one's heart (v. 23), including what one says (v. 24), sees (v. 25), and does (vv. 26-27). (See comments on 6:17-18.) The mention in 4:24 of **mouth** and **lips** is similar to Christ's teaching on the relationship between one's heart and his speech (Luke 6:45c). **Perversity** comes from 'iqqēš, "crooked" (cf. Prov. 2:15). **Corrupt** or foul **talk** (cf. 6:12) should never be on the lips of one who trusts the Lord (cf. Eph. 4:29).

Each believer should focus his **eyes** (Prov. 4:25) on the wise path (cf. v. 11), concentrating on it and not being distracted. And his conduct should be upright, as he stays on **level paths** (cf. v. 11b) and does not turn aside to **evil** (cf. v. 15; 1:15). Again paths and **ways** (4:26) are used to refer to one's conduct (cf. 2:13, 15, 20; 3:6, 17; 7:25; and cf. "path" and "way" in 4:18-19; also note 8:20). "Proverbs provides both a goal and route. The goal is successful living and the route is the way of wisdom" (Robert L. Alden, *Proverbs: A Commentary on an Ancient Book of Timeless Advice,* p. 48). Though wisdom keeps one on the right path (cf., e.g., 2:12) here the encouragement is to keep oneself on the **straight** way.

## J. The value of wisdom in preserving from adultery (chap. 5)

Specific instruction is given concerning the dangers of the adulteress (vv. 1-6), the final price of infidelity (vv. 7-14), and the delights of married love (vv. 15-20). Then a reminder is given that sin is ultimately an issue with the Lord (vv. 21-23). As in 1:14-19, chapter 5 portrays against the immediate pleasure of sin its long-range consequences. If a person is wise, he sees this long-range view.

**5:1-6.** This chapter, like other portions in Proverbs, begins with the exhortation that the **son pay attention** and **listen** (cf. 4:1, 10, 20; 5:7; 7:24) to his father's **words,** for doing so gives **discretion** (cf. 1:4) and **knowledge.** Speaking (**lips,** 5:2) **wisdom** helps the son ignore the words (**lips,** v. 3) **of an adulteress** (zārâh; see comments on 2:16). Her deceptive, seductive words are persuasive, sweet like **honey,** the sweetest substance in ancient Israel, and **smoother than** (cf. 6:24; 7:21) olive **oil,** the smoothest substance in ancient Israel. **But** what seems attractive at first becomes **bitter** and **sharp** later. Involvement in adultery is like tasting **gall,** the bitterest substance known (from a plant), or like being cut by **a double-edged sword.** The adulteress leads men **to death** (cf. 2:18; 7:27; 9:18). Her sin makes her unaware that her ways **are crooked** (lit., "staggering or unstable"), in contrast with the "straight paths" of 4:11.

**5:7-8.** Again Solomon urged his **sons** (cf. comments on 4:1) to **listen** (cf. 4:1, 10, 20; 5:1; 7:24) and adhere to **what** he said. He urged them **not to turn** . . . **from** his teachings, but to turn from the adulteress. They were **not** even to **go near** . . . **her house** (cf. 2:18) because of the danger of succumbing to her temptations.

**5:9-14.** Failure to keep away from the adulteress can result in many losses: loss of **strength** (which may mean losing one's health, self-respect, or both), loss of a long life (v. 9), loss of money (cf. 6:26; 29:3b)—by paying the adulteress, paying her husband, or paying child support—and loss of health (5:11). Falling prey to lust also brings remorse when a person recognizes too late that he did not heed his parents' (here called **teachers**) instructions which inevitably leads to **ruin** and disgrace before others.

**5:15-18.** The rewards of chastity are a further encouragement to moral purity. A **cistern** . . . **well** . . . **springs** . . . **streams,** and **fountain** control water, keeping it from being dissipated **in the streets.** Similarly marital love with one's **wife** (v. 18) is pictured as enjoying one's cistern or fountain (cf. Song 4:12, 15). Sexual desires should be controlled and channeled in one's marriage, not wasted as described in Proverbs 5:7-14. Some commentators say the word **them** (v. 17) refers to children; others say it continues the metaphor of streams picturing one's sexual desires. As a person would not get water from his neighbor's cistern because he had his own (2 Kings 18:31), so a man should have his physical needs met by his own wife, not someone else's.

**5:19-20.** The **breasts** of a man's wife are soft to the touch and **graceful** in appearance like a **deer** (cf. Song 4:5; 7:3). Therefore a husband should be **captivated** (cf. Prov. 5:20; the verb *šāgâh* means "go astray," cf. v. 21; but it may also

suggest the idea of being captured) **by her love,** not the affections of an adulteress. By two rhetorical questions (v. 20) the author pointed up the folly of being **captivated** (cf. v. 19) **by an** immoral woman and loving someone else's **wife.**

**5:21-23.** The dire consequences of adultery (vv. 7-14) should motivate a person to avoid it. But four even higher motivations are given in verses 21-23: (1) Since God sees **man's ways** (cf. 15:3; Job 31:1, 4; Heb. 4:13), adultery committed in secret is known by **the LORD.** (2) Also God **examines** man's conduct (on ways and **paths** see comments on Prov. 4:26). Man cannot escape God's scrutinizing. (3) Sin ensnares (cf. 1:17-18), and ties a person down like ropes (5:22). Though people like to talk about being "free" to sin as they wish, **sin** actually takes away freedom. (4) Being undisciplined (cf. v. 12) in one's moral life results in death (cf. vv. 5, 11). Such living is foolish because it leads one **astray** from God's standards. "Led astray" is from the same word *šāgâh* rendered "captivated" in verses 19-20. **Folly** appears 21 times in Proverbs. To yield to sexual lust is folly.

## K. The value of wisdom in preserving from poverty (6:1-11)

Solomon warned against two practices that lead to poverty: foolish financial entanglements (vv. 1-5) and laziness (vv. 6-11). In a sense both pertain to finances because the former guards against unnecessary loss of what one has earned and the latter against the inability to earn any money at all.

### 1. WARNING AGAINST FOOLISH FINANCIAL ENTANGLEMENTS (6:1-5)

**6:1. My son** occurs in verses 1, 3, 20 in chapter 6. **If** a person cosigned a note involving high interest rates for someone else's loan, that cosigner was urged to get out of the obligation as soon as possible ("free yourself," vv. 3, 5). In Israel lending was intended as a means of helping a fellow Israelite, not as a money-making transaction as it is today. No interest was to be charged a fellow Israelite (Ex. 22:25; Lev. 25:35-37). Interest could be applied to a loan to non-Israelites, but even then usury (unreasonably high interest rates) was illegal. Exorbitant interest often resulted in injustice (cf. 2 Kings 4:1; Neh. 5:1-11) which the Law sought to prevent. The warning in Proverbs 6:1 is not against borrowing or lending but against being held accountable for another person's high-interest loan. Putting **up security** is referred to frequently in Proverbs (11:15; 17:18; 20:16; 22:26-27; 27:13).

Some say the word **neighbor** here means "stranger," and that cosigning is acceptable for one's relatives but not for strangers. The parallel word **another** suggests, however, that cosigning is advised against altogether ("neighbor" probably means "anybody"). Does this exhortation, then, speak against guaranteeing payments on a loan for one's own relatives? No. The restriction seems to be against loans with exorbitant rates of interest.

Striking **hands in pledge** was a gesture something like shaking hands. It was like "signing on the dotted line."

**6:2.** The words **trapped** and **ensnared** (cf. v. 5) indicate that by accepting responsibility for someone's high-interest debt, the son would be placing himself in a financial situation over which he had no control (cf. v. 3). Agreeing by word of **mouth** to cosign such a debt could lead to serious trouble.

**6:3-5.** In intense language Solomon urged that a person who has agreed to be security for another's loan should seek to get out of that trap. To fall **into your neighbor's hands** means that the outcome of the situation is in the neighbor's control. **Humble** is a strong word meaning "to crush or tread oneself down, to demean" and **press your plea** suggests being boisterous. One should free himself from a debt agreement, even if so doing demands great humiliation and obnoxious pleading. This urgency is stressed in verses 4-5. Nothing should stand in the way; not even one night was to pass before the situation should be taken care of. Just as **a gazelle** or **a bird,** if trapped, would immediately begin struggling for its life, so a person snared by a foolish debt agreement should frantically fight to be **free** of it (cf. v. 3).

### 2. WARNING AGAINST LAZINESS (6:6-11)

**6:6-8.** A person can become financially destitute by laziness as well as by foolish dealings. Solomon was probably not calling his son a **sluggard;** he was speaking rhetorically to anyone who might hear or read the message. The He-

brew word for sluggard ('*āṣēl*) occurs 14 times in Proverbs and nowhere else in the Old Testament. It refers to more than laziness. In 15:19 a sluggard is contrasted with the "upright," and in 21:25-26 a sluggard is contrasted with the "righteous." A sluggard is associated in 19:15 with the "shiftless." A lazy, irresponsible person is challenged to learn from **the ant** (also mentioned in 30:25) **and be wise.** Ants, known for being industrious, are commended here for their initiative. Apparently ants have no leader—**no commander** to direct them, **no overseer** to inspect their work, no **ruler** to prod them on. **Yet** they work better than many people under a leader! Ants also work in anticipation of future needs, storing and gathering while it is warm, before winter comes. The virtue of wisdom is not in being busy but in having a proper view of forthcoming needs that motivate one to action (cf. 10:5). Those who act only when commanded do not possess wisdom.

**6:9-11.** By two questions (v. 9) Solomon urged the **sluggard** to **get** out of bed and start working. Verses 10-11, repeated later in 24:33-34, point up the danger of a person continuing to nap when he ought to be working: **poverty will come on** him suddenly in the same way a robber or **an armed man** (a soldier) quickly attacks an unsuspecting victim. Poverty is mentioned frequently in Proverbs (6:11; 10:15; 11:24; 13:18; 14:23; 21:5; 22:16; 24:34; 28:19, 22; 30:8; 31:7). With his time squandered the lazy person cannot rectify his situation and has little or no money to meet his needs. Obviously such a person is unwise.

### L. The value of wisdom in preserving from dissension (6:12-19)

By describing a person who deceives and stirs up strife (vv. 12-15) and the activities such a person engages in (vv. 16-19), Solomon urged his son to avoid disaster (v. 15) and God's hatred (v. 16).

**6:12.** The **scoundrel and villain** refer to one person, as evidenced by the use of singular verbs in verses 12-15. "Scoundrel" (cf. 16:27; 2 Sam.16:7; 1 Kings 21:10) is literally, "man of belial," someone who is worthless and wicked. Later the word belial came to be used of the devil, the most worthless, wicked person of all (2 Cor. 6:15). A scoundrel is known by his **corrupt** (lit., "twisted"; see comments on Prov. 2:15) **mouth** (cf. 4:24), his false and deceptive words.

**6:13-14.** By sinister body language the scoundrel's actions contradict what he says. By winking (cf. 10:10; 16:30; Ps. 35:19) and gesturing in some way **with his feet** and **fingers** he signals certain messages to his fellow conspirators. He plans (see comments on Prov. 3:29) **evil** actions (cf. 1:11-14) from a deceitful **heart** so that people are not aware of his intentions until it is too late. Though he feigns sincerity, underneath he is perverted and causes **dissension,** drawing others into discord or strife. Dissension (cf. 6:19) is caused by hatred (10:12), and uncontrolled temper (15:18), perversity (16:28), greed (28:25), and anger (29:22). (Also see these additional verses on strife: 17:1; 18:6; 20:3; 22:10; 23:29; 26:21; 30:33.)

**6:15.** Besides causing discord among people by his deceptive words and his sinister gestures, a scoundrel brings **disaster** on himself. It comes unexpectedly and quickly (**in an instant** and **suddenly**) with no way to offset it (**without remedy**). Whether natural consequences or more direct divine intervention is in view is not clear. But his downfall is quick, complete, and certain.

**6:16.** The Lord's hatred of the scoundrel's activities (vv. 12-14) is described in verses 16-19. These two sections are linked by the words "stirs up dissension" (vv. 14, 19).

The **six . . . seven** pattern is also used in Job 5:19, and a similar pattern of other numbers plus one is used in Proverbs 30:15-16, 18-19, 21-31. The purpose of this kind of numerical pattern (x and x + 1) is not to give a complete list. Instead it is to stress the final (x + 1) item, as the culmination or product of its preceding items.

**6:17-19.** A person with **haughty eyes** (i.e., a proud look; cf. 8:13; 30:13; Pss. 18:27; 101:5), **a lying tongue** (cf. Prov. 12:19; 21:6; 26:28), **hands that** murder (**shed innocent blood;** cf. 1:11), **a heart that** plots (see comments on 3:29) **wicked** actions (cf. 4:16; 6:14), **feet that** move quickly **into** sin (cf. 1:16), and one who **lies** against someone when witnessing in court (cf. 12:17; 14:5, 25; 19:5, 9; 21:28; 25:18) is a person who causes discord (see comments on 6:14) **among** friends. Apparently by his lies he causes friends

to be suspicious of each other. Lying, referred to twice in this list of things God hates (vv. 17, 19), is one of the many wrong uses of words that are condemned in Proverbs. (The chart "Words and Speaking in Proverbs," which lists the many wrong and right uses of one's words referred to in Prov., arranges these subjects topically. For a list of some of the many other topics in Prov. see the chart "Positive and Negative Topics and Other Subjects in Proverbs," in the *Introduction.*)

The scoundrel (v. 12) uses various parts of his body in violation of the commands in 4:23-26, as seen in these passages: heart, mouth, lips, eyes, feet (4:23-26); mouth, eye, feet, fingers, heart (6:12-14); eyes, tongue, hands, heart, feet (vv. 17-18).

## M. The value of wisdom in preserving from sexual immorality (6:20–7:27)

Five times in chapters 1–9 Solomon spoke to the problem of sexual immorality: 2:16-19; 5:3-23; 6:20-35; chapter 7; 9:13-18. (Though 9:13-18 does not mention adultery or an adulteress, Folly, personified as a woman, may suggest such a person. See comments there.) Proverbs 6:20-35 warns against adultery and chapter 7 illustrates the seductress' ways and the consequences of involvement with her.

### 1. WISDOM PRESERVES FROM ADULTERY (6:20-35)

**6:20-21.** Once again Solomon exhorted his son (cf. comments on **my son** in 1:8) to heed his **father's** and **mother's** instructions (cf. 1:8) and adhere to them inwardly (6:21a; cf. 3:1; 7:3b) and have his life graced by them (6:21b; cf. 3:3, 22; 7:3a).

**6:22-23.** Parental instruction provides guidance, protection (cf. 2:11), and counsel (6:22). That teaching should be given from God's Law, for the parents' **commands,** like the Word of God, should be like **a lamp** and **a light,** giving guidance to one's conduct (Ps. 119:105). **Discipline** (cf. Prov. 1:2, 7), though painful (cf. Heb. 12:11a), helps keep a person on the right path, leading him in **the way of life.**

**6:24.** Wisdom, acquired from God's Word taught by one's parents (vv. 20-23) helps protect **from** adultery (cf. 2:12, 16-

# Words and Speaking in Proverbs

| I. Wrong Uses of Words | II. Right Uses of Words |
|---|---|
| **A. Lying**<br>6:16-17a; 10:18a; 12:19, 22a; 17:4b, 7; 19:5b, 9b, 22b; 21:6; 26:28a | **A. Words that help and encourage**<br>10:11a, 20a, 21a; 12:14a, 18b; 15:4a; 18:4, 20-21 |
| **B. Slandering**<br>10:18b; 30:10 | **B. Words that express wisdom**<br>10:13a, 31a; 14:3b; 15:2a, 7a; 16:10, 21b, 23b; 20:15 |
| **C. Gossiping**<br>11:13; 16:28b; 17:9b; 18:8; 20:19; 26:20, 22 | **C. Words that are few**<br>10:19; 11:12b; 13:3a; 17:27a |
| **D. Constant talking**<br>10:8, 10b, 19; 17:28; 18:2; 20:19b | **D. Words that are fitting (kind, appropriate, pleasant)**<br>10:32a; 12:25; 15:1a, 4a, 23; 16:24; 25:11, 15 |
| **E. False witnessing**<br>12:17b; 14:5b, 25b; 19:5a, 28a; 21:28; 25:18 | **E. Words that are true**<br>12:17a, 19a, 22b; 14:5a, 25a |
| **F. Mocking**<br>13:1b; 14:6a; 15:12; 17:5a; 19:29a; 21:11a; 22:10; 24:9b; 30:17 | **F. Words that are carefully chosen**<br>13:3a; 15:28; 16:23a; 21:23 |
| **G. Harsh talking (perverse, reckless, harsh, evil, sly words)**<br>10:31b-32; 12:18a; 13:3b; 14:3a; 15:1b, 28b; 17:4a; 19:1, 28b | |
| **H. Boasting**<br>17:17a; 20:14; 25:14; 27:1-2 | |
| **I. Quarreling**<br>13:10; 15:18; 17:14, 19; 19:13; 20:3; 21:9; 19; 22:10; 25:24; 26:17, 20-21; 27:15 | |
| **J. Deceiving**<br>7:19-20; 12:2; 15:4b; 25:23 | |
| **K. Flattering**<br>26:28b; 28:23; 29:5 | |
| **L. Ignorant or foolish words**<br>14:7; 15:2b, 7-14; 18:6-7 | |

19). **The immoral woman** (lit., "woman of evil")—perhaps unmarried—may be the prostitute mentioned in 6:26. **The wayward wife** (cf. 2:16; 7:5; 23:27) is a sexually promiscuous married woman (cf. "another man's wife," 6:29). In verse 26 she is called an "adulteress," literally, "a wife of a man." On nokrîyâh ("wayward") see comments on 2:16. Such women have **smooth** tongues; they speak seductively (cf. 2:16; 5:3; 7:5, 21).

**6:25.** This verse gives a warning and verses 26-29, 32-35 speak of the reasons for the warning. Lusting **in** one's **heart** (cf. comments on 3:5; 4:23) after a physically attractive and sexually promiscuous woman, whether married or unmarried, is wrong. Jesus spoke along a similar line (Matt. 5:28). Men who have fallen into the sin of adultery have often begun with lustful looking. If a man looks at such a woman, she may seek to **captivate** him **with her** flirting **eyes.**

**6:26.** Immorality is costly! A **prostitute** (cf. 7:10; 23:27; 29:3) can reduce a man to utter poverty, having only **a loaf of bread,** by spending money for her services (cf. 29:3). And a wayward wife (cf. comments on 6:24) can prey on one's **very life,** that is, bring him to ruin and death (cf. 2:18-19; 5:5, 14; 7:22-23, 26-27).

**6:27-29.** One cost of sexual unfaithfulness is stated in verse 26, and another in verses 27-35. Dire consequences are inevitable (vv. 27-29) and severe (vv. 30-35). As it is impossible to hold **fire** on one's **lap** without burning **his clothes** or to **walk on . . . coals without** burning one's **feet,** so it is impossible to commit adultery **with another man's wife** without being harmed. Illicit sex is like playing with fire! Such a man will be punished, possibly by the woman's husband (cf. v. 34).

**6:30-31.** People may sympathize with (but not approve of) **a thief** if he is attempting to avoid starvation. However, he had to repay **sevenfold** even if it cost him everything (similar to the man being reduced to a loaf of bread, v. 26). The thief's punishment, though difficult, is less severe than the adulterer's. One who "steals" another's wife finds no forgiveness and no leniency.

**6:32-35.** Involvement in **adultery** shows one's stupidity (cf. 7:7; 9:4, 16); he goes ahead in his sin while knowing that severe consequences will follow. He **destroys himself** (cf. 6:26b; Deut. 22:22); adultery is a kind of "suicide." Also he is disgraced and shamed; in contrast with a thief (Prov. 6:30), an adulterer is despised. And the wife's husband, learning about their conduct, becomes jealous, furious (cf. 27:4), and vengeful against the adulterer (apparently blaming the guilty man more than his wife). The anger of such a husband cannot be dispelled by bribery, no matter how **great it is.** Bribery is frequently condemned in Proverbs (6:35; 15:27; 17:8), in the Law (Ex. 23:8; Deut. 16:19; 27:25), and elsewhere (e.g., Job 36:18; Ps. 15:5; Ecc. 7:7; Isa. 33:15).

### 2. WISDOM PRESERVES FROM THE SEDUCTRESS (CHAP. 7)

In 6:20-35 the concerned father gave words of instruction about the tragedy of adultery. In chapter 7 he stated dramatically how a simple, naive youth can be subtly trapped by a seductive woman. Solomon exhorted his son to heed the father's teaching (vv. 1-5), depicted the tactics of the adulteress (vv. 6-23), and concluded with a warning to beware of her trap (vv. 24-27).

#### a. The father's instruction (7:1-5)

**7:1-2.** Chapter 7 begins with Solomon's familiar plea for his son (on **my**

**son** see comments on 1:8) to hear, assimilate, and live by his parents' teaching. This instruction included the father's **words** (cf. 2:1; 4:4-5, 20; 5:1), **commands** (cf. 2:1; 3:1; 4:4; 6:20, 23; 7:2), and **teachings** (cf. the sing. "teaching" in 1:8; 3:1; 4:2; 6:20, 23). Because of their help the son was to **keep** (cf. 3:1; 4:4, 21; 6:20), **store up** (cf. 2:1; 10:14), and **guard** them like a treasure. If he did so he would enjoy a full and meaningful life (cf. 3:18; 4:4c; 8:35). **Apple** ('îšôn) is literally the center of a thing; in 7:9 it denotes the center or middle of the night, that is, intense darkness. The pupil, the center of the **eye** (cf. Deut. 32:10; Ps. 17:8), is the most sensitive and carefully guarded of the human body's exposed organs.

**7:3.** In 3:3 the son was exhorted to bind his father's teachings around his own neck. In 7:3 he was exhorted to **bind them** like rings **on** his **fingers.** Also as in 3:3 he was to **write them on** his **heart** (cf. 6:21).

**7:4-5.** In Old Testament times one's **sister** was considered an intimate relative. Therefore "sister" was sometimes used as a synonym for one's wife (cf. Song 4:9-10, 12; 5:1-2). Similarly a person is to be familiar with **wisdom** as if it were his sister or wife. The same is true of **understanding** ("insight"; cf. Prov. 2:2), which is to be like a **kinsman** (cf. Ruth 3:2). One's closeness to understanding should be like the intimate ties between relatives. Wisdom and understanding, often seen as synonyms in Proverbs, **keep** young men **from the adulteress** and **the wayward wife** (see comments on Prov. 2:16; 6:24), who tempt with **seductive words** (cf. 6:24; 7:21). "Seductive" is related to the word "smoother" in 5:3.

#### b. The victim's naiveté (7:6-9)

Verses 6-23 read like an eyewitness account. The relating of the conversation in verses 14-20 may indicate that Solomon reconstructed the account from his or others' experiences or that he talked with the young man in the account after the event. Probably Solomon did not actually hear the conversation from his vantage point in the window.

**7:6-9.** Looking from his latticed **window** Solomon **saw** some **simple** (peṭî, naive or gullible; see comments on 1:4) **young men,** and **among** them was one **who lacked judgment** (cf. 6:32; 9:4, 16;

10:13). This points up his naiveté, not his foolishness or lust. **Walking** toward **her house** probably does not imply that he was purposely going there. Yet he may well have known she lived there. **He was going** where the temptation was in the evening, **as the day was** concluding and darkness was setting in. **The dark of night** is, literally, "in the center of night, even darkness" ("center" is rendered "apple" in 7:2). As Robert L. Alden wrote, "If you want to avoid the devil, stay away from his neighborhood. If you suspect you might be vulnerable to a particular sin, take steps to avoid it" (*Proverbs: A Commentary on an Ancient Book of Timeless Advice*, p. 63).

### c. The seductress' character (7:10-12)

**7:10-12.** The **woman,** who was married (v. 19), went **out . . . to meet** the young man, sensing that he would be an easy prey. She was (a) brazen in her attire (**dressed** seductively **like a prostitute**), (b) secretive (**crafty intent** is lit., "secretive in heart"), (c) **loud** (cf. 9:13), (d) **defiant** against God's laws and her marriage vows, (e) a gadabout, and (f) furtive (**lurks** in the streets).

### d. The seductress' tactics (7:13-20)

**7:13-14.** Surprising him, **she** suddenly embraced **and kissed him and** then boldly (**with a brazen face**) spoke to him. By referring to her **peace offerings at home** and **vows** she probably was referring to a sacrifice she made (hypocritically, of course) with meat left over (Lev. 7:16-17). Portions of the sacrificial animal were taken home by the offerer. Without refrigeration the meat needed to be consumed; so a feast usually accompanied the sacrifice. Her religious activity, however, was a pretense, an effort to cloud any sense of wrongdoing she may have had.

**7:15-18.** Building his ego up by flattery (v. 15), she then sought to lure him by describing the sensuous nature of her bedroom. The **linens** on the **bed** were imported **from Egypt** (presumably exquisite and expensive) and she had **perfumed** her **bed** with three spices: **myrrh, aloes, and cinnamon** (see comments on these same spices, Song 4:14). In suggesting that all night they **drink deep of love** she was using a figure of speech that likened sexual relations to drinking from

a fountain (cf. Prov. 5:18; Song 4:12, 15).

**7:19-20.** The woman sought to assure the young man that they would not be caught by her **husband** (lit., "the man") for he was away on a business trip and would **not be home till the full moon** (at least several days away), so she was unfaithful to him (cf. 2:16-17).

### e. The victim's response (7:21-23)

**7:21-23.** Unable to resist her **persuasive,** seductive, **smooth talk** (cf. v. 5; 2:16; 5:3), he suddenly (**all at once**) **followed her** to her house and bedroom. He was **like** a dumb animal (**an ox**) being led to **slaughter** while being completely unwary of his plight. He was also **like a deer stepping into a noose.** As noted in the NIV margin, "deer" is from the Syriac, whereas the Hebrew has "fool" (cf. KJV and NASB). This verse, difficult to translate, could be rendered, "like fetters for the correction (or discipline) of a fool." He was captured like a fool whose feet are put in fetters and is taken to a correctional institution. He was suddenly overtaken like an animal shot with **an arrow** or **like a bird** being caught in **a snare.** Oblivious to these dangers, he was trapped with no way to escape. He was taken in before he realized that failure to resist this temptation (as Joseph did; cf. Gen. 39:6-12) would **cost him his life** (cf. Prov. 6:32).

### f. The father's closing exhortation (7:24-27)

**7:24-25.** The words **Now then** introduce the father's exhortation, based on the preceding verses. **My sons** (pl.) are addressed as in 4:1; 5:7 and again Solomon their father urged them to **listen to** him (cf. comments on 1:8) attentively (**pay attention**; cf. 4:1, 20; 5:1; 22:17). He advised them to steer clear of the adulteress, by **not** turning their hearts (see comments on 4:23) **to her** (in their imaginations or fantasies) and by not physically going near her (7:25). The word **turn** is *śāṭâh,* "turn aside," a word used only six times in the Old Testament, including 4:15 (and Num. 5:12, 19-20, 29, where it is rendered "goes [gone] astray"). The word **stray** (*tāʿâh*) means "to wander." Obviously the young man got himself in trouble because he strayed or wandered near the temptress' house (Prov. 7:8).

**7:26-27.** The reason for the exhortation in verses 24-25 is given in verses 26-27. **Many** others had been victimized by this temptation. To be in **her house** (and with her in her bed) is to place oneself on a fast **highway to the grave** and physical **death** (cf. 2:18-19; 5:5; 9:18). A young man involved in illicit sex may die from punishment meted out by an angry husband, or from poverty, or from venereal disease, or from spiritual and emotional anguish.

## N. The value of wisdom demonstrated in her virtues and rewards (8:1-21)

Solomon the teacher, personifying wisdom as a woman, wrote about her invitation (vv. 1-5), her virtues (vv. 6-11), and her rewards (vv. 12-21).

### 1. WISDOM'S CALL (8:1-5)

**8:1.** Wisdom's public invitation begins with two rhetorical questions (v. 1). The adulteress went out in the streets (7:8-12) to seduce the young man. But **wisdom,** like a virtuous woman, is seen in the streets offering her services to all who will receive them (cf. her calling aloud in 1:20-22). The lack of virtue that characterized the adulteress is contrasted with wisdom's sterling attributes. Whereas the seductress' ways are secretive and deceptive, wisdom's ways are open and honest. One who succumbs to the adulteress finds shame and death, but wisdom's followers acquire prudence for wise living.

**8:2-3.** Wisdom's call is made where she can be heard and where people traverse: hilltops, **the way,** intersections, **the gates** (where court cases were heard and business was conducted) and **the entrances.**

**8:4-5.** From verses 4-31 wisdom (I) speaks. She invites **all mankind;** wisdom is available to anyone. But specifically she calls to the **simple** (*peṭî*; see comments on 1:4) and the **foolish** (*keṣîl;* see comments on 1:22)—those most in need of her and more likely to ignore her invitation. Both the adulteress and wisdom appeal to the naive. Wisdom urges the simple to **gain prudence** (*'ormâh;* see comments on 1:4; cf. 8:12), a sensibleness in one's approach to life, cleverness in a good sense. And fools are urged to **gain understanding** (cf. 1:2, 6), insight, or sharp discernment.

### 2. WISDOM'S VIRTUES (8:6-11)

**8:6-9.** In verses 6-11 the straightforwardness and integrity of wisdom are presented. The young men being taught by Solomon should **listen** to wisdom (v. 6, the exhortation) because what she says is right (vv. 7-9, the reason). The young should choose wisdom (v. 10, the exhortation) because of its great value (v. 11, the reason). Wisdom speaks: **lips** (v. 6b), **mouth** (v. 7a), **lips** (v. 7b), and **mouth** (v. 8a) are referred to alternately. And her words are **worthy** (lit., "noble or princely") **things.** This word could also be translated "valid" as in 2 Samuel 15:3 or "right" as in Isaiah 30:10. The idea is that wisdom's words correspond to reality; therefore they are **right** ("upright or straight"; trans. "faultless" in Prov. 8:9), **true,** and **just** (cf. 1:3; 8:15, 20). Therefore **none of** wisdom's words are **crooked** ("twisted") **or perverse** (*'iqqēš;* see comments on 2:15). They also point in the right direction. People with insight (8:9) know that what wisdom offers is **right** "straightforward or honest"), and people "in the know" find wisdom's words **faultless** (lit., "upright or straight"; trans. "right" in v. 6).

**8:10-11.** Wisdom urges people to receive her **instruction** and **knowledge rather** than **silver . . . choice gold** (*ḥārûs,* pure, refined gold; called "fine gold" in v. 19), or **rubies** (cf. 3:13-15). The idea that wisdom's value exceeds material wealth is expounded in 8:18-21, which states that wisdom provides what is needed to gain and appreciate wealth. Also wisdom contributes to a person's integrity and peace, something silver, gold, and rubies cannot do. And in Proverbs those qualities are of greater value than anything one can buy.

### 3. WISDOM'S REWARDS (8:12-21)

The abundance of personal pronouns (I, mine, me, my—16 occurrences in 10 verses) makes wisdom herself the focus and not her rewards.

**8:12-13.** If a person has **wisdom** he also has **prudence** (see comments on 1:4; cf. 8:5), **knowledge, and discretion.** All three of these nouns are in 1:4. Some scholars say 8:13 disrupts the flow of thought between verses 12 and 14. However, verse 13 is a reminder that sensible, discreet living (v. 12) is not associated in any way with the vices mentioned in verse 13. Verse 13 shows that wisdom is moral as well as mental. One who fears **the LORD** (see comments on 1:7) and therefore is wise will **hate** (reject) **evil** (cf. 3:7; 14:16; 16:6, Ps. 97:10), **pride . . . arrogance, evil behavior, and perverse** talk. The word for "perverse" (*tahpūkâh*) is used eight times in Proverbs (cf. comments on 2:12).

**8:14-16.** Wisdom enables people to give wise **counsel and sound judgment,** and to **have understanding** (insight) **and power** (i.e., valor). Wisdom makes a person courageous like a soldier of valor. **Kings . . . rulers . . . princes,** and **nobles who rule** well do so by God's wisdom; they **make laws that are just.** The fact that many of Israel's and Judah's kings and her neighbors did not make fair laws shows that they lacked God's wisdom.

**8:17-18.** Wisdom, available to all, is acquired only by those who **love** her (cf. v. 21; 4:6) and **seek** her (cf. 2:1-4). Those who are wise receive **riches and honor** (cf. 3:16), **enduring wealth** (cf. 8:21; 14:24; 15:6; 22:4), **and prosperity.** "Enduring" is literally "surpassing" or "eminent." The riches that come to the possessor of wisdom are genuine, not artificial substitutes purchased with silver or gold. Being honored in a community is a product of one's walk (conduct) rather than one's wealth by itself. "Prosperity" is literally "righteousness" (cf. v. 20). Godly living is the major benefit from having wisdom.

**8:19-21.** The word **yield** (v. 19) is a term used in the marketplace; the verb focuses attention on wisdom's ability to produce benefits far superior to what **fine gold** (*ḥārûṣ*; cf. v. 10) and **silver** provide. Wisdom goes with **righteousness** and **justice** (cf. v. 8). The form of the Hebrew verb **walk** conveys the idea of walking steadily or continuously. (On the distinction between righteousness and justice see comments on Amos 5:7.) As in many places in Proverbs, **way**(s) and **paths** are used synonymously (see comments on Prov. 2:13). As stated in 8:18, those who love (cf. v. 17) and acquire wisdom gain wealth (cf. 3:16; 14:24; 15:6; 22:4). Like many statements in Proverbs, this one is a generalization to which exceptions should be noted. Material substance is replenishable (keeping one's **treasuries full**) because of the skill a wise person has to maintain it.

## O. The value of wisdom to the Lord in Creation (8:22-36)

Wisdom's many claims (vv. 6-21) are credible because of her association with the Lord in Creation. She existed before the world was created (vv. 22-29) and she participated with the Lord in Creation, sharing His joy at its accomplishments (vv. 30-31). Because of wisdom's unique role she makes a final plea for people to acquire her (vv. 32-36).

### 1. WISDOM'S EXISTENCE BEFORE CREATION (8:22-26)

**8:22.** Wisdom's scope of expertise is broadened from her present ability to enrich individuals (vv. 12-21) to her past involvement in Creation. Wisdom is obviously in view here; **me** clearly refers back to "I, wisdom" (v. 12). Wisdom existed before the Creation of the world (**before** occurs five times in vv. 22-23, 25-26) and therefore was present when God created the universe ("when" occurs seven times, vv. 24, 27-29).

Some Bible students say that wisdom in verses 22-31 refers to Christ. Of course He does reveal God's wisdom to believers (1 Cor. 1:30) and in Him is all wisdom and knowledge (Col. 2:3), but Proverbs 8:22-31 gives no indication that it is Christ who is referred to as wisdom. If that were so, then all other references to wisdom in Proverbs should refer to Christ too, which is unlikely. It is preferable to see wisdom spoken of here figuratively as a *personification of God's attribute of wisdom.*

**8:23-26.** Before creating the universe, God **appointed** (or "installed," as trans. in Ps. 2:6) wisdom. Proverbs 8:23 refers to wisdom existing **before** God created **the world** (cf. Gen. 1:1-5), before the waters were separated, making clouds and **oceans** (on the second day of Creation, Gen. 1:6-8), and before the dry land appeared (on the third day of Creation, Gen. 1:9-10). Wisdom is pictured as having been born (Prov. 8:24-25).

### 2. WISDOM'S WORK IN CREATION (8:27-31)

**8:27-29.** Wisdom, then, was present **when** God **set the heavens in place** (v. 27a; cf. Gen. 1:1-5), when He separated the waters making **clouds** and oceans (Prov. 8:27b-28; on the second day of Creation, Gen. 1:6-8), and when He caused the dry land to appear (Prov. 8:29;

on the third day, Gen. 1:9-10). On the word **deep** (Prov. 8:27) see comments on Genesis 1:2.

**8:30-31.** Wisdom is said to have been a **craftsman** at God's side when He created the world. This attribute of God, personified as an assistant in the Lord's creative work, poetically indicates that God was wise in what He created. Being **at His side** implies intimate association. Saying that God's work is characterized by wisdom does not suggest that wisdom itself was the designer. *God* was the Designer. This is an important distinction. Wisdom's claim to be present before and during Creation and to be involved in it gives an important credibility to her claim to reward man. Wisdom, personified, rejoices **in** God's **presence** and in His created **world,** including **mankind.**

If God involved wisdom in His creative work, then certainly people need wisdom!

### 3. WISDOM'S PLEA AND PROMISES (8:32-36)

**8:32-34.** Here wisdom herself addressed the young men as **my sons,** as the father had already done three times (4:1; 5:7; 7:24). The words **Now then** relate this appeal to wisdom's preceding claims. In verses 32-34 the words **listen** and **blessed** are used alternately (listen, v. 32; blessed, v. 32; listen, v. 33; blessed, v. 34; listens, v. 34). Wisdom's threefold call to young men to **listen** is mindful of Solomon's frequent call to them to listen (see comments on 1:8). By listening to wisdom's instruction and following it, they become **wise** and are "blessed." This blessing comes from following wisdom eagerly (**watching** and **waiting**).

**8:35-36.** Wisdom gives **life** (cf. 3:18; 4:4, 22; 7:2; 9:11; 19:23) and the Lord's **favor** (cf. 12:2; 18:22). The word for "favor," *rāṣôn*, is used 14 times in Proverbs, and means "acceptance, goodwill, or approval." It comes from the verb *rāṣâh*, "to be pleased with." Rejecting wisdom results in harm (cf. 6:32; 7:23; 9:12b) and **death** (cf. 2:18; 5:5; 7:27). Wisdom is the way of life and folly is the way of death. These are people's two choices.

### P. The value of wisdom summarized by contrasting her invitation with folly's invitation (chap. 9)

This chapter summarizes 1:8–8:36 by contrasting the invitations of wisdom

(9:1-6) and of folly (vv. 13-18). Between the two invitations a brief series of tersely stated proverbs contrasts the nature and consequences of those who respond to each invitation (vv. 7-12). Wisdom and its rival folly are portrayed as two women each preparing a feast and inviting young men to their houses. Wisdom is portrayed as a responsible woman of character and wealth preparing a banquet, while folly is portrayed as a harlot inviting young men to a sensual meal of stolen water and food eaten in secret.

### 1. WISDOM'S INVITATION (9:1-6)

In Proverbs wisdom is frequently personified as a dignified lady (1:20-33; 3:16-18; 4:3-6; 8:1-21, 32-36; 9:1-6). In 9:1-6 she is a builder and a homemaker preparing a banquet for those lacking wisdom.

### a. Wisdom's preparation of her banquet (9:1-2)

**9:1.** The common Hebrew word for **wisdom** is *ḥokmâh,* but here it appears to be in the plural form (*ḥokmôt*) with a singular verb **has built** (though some construe *ḥokmôt* also as sing. in keeping with analogous forms in Canaanite dialects). This is also the case in 1:20; 24:7; Psalm 49:3. If the form is plural it may suggest wisdom's fullness. "Lady Wisdom's" activities of building **her house,** including hewing **out** for it **seven pillars,** suggest the industriousness that accompanies wisdom. Bible scholars have offered various suggestions about the meaning of these seven pillars (e.g., the six days of Creation and God's seventh day of rest; or the sun, moon, and the five planets that were known at that time). It seems preferable to say the seven pillars suggest that the house was large and spacious. This is consistent with statements in Proverbs that relate wisdom to a high station in life.

**9:2.** The meal that "Lady Wisdom" prepared included **meat and mixed . . . wine** (cf. v. 5). **Prepared her** meat is literally, "slaughtered her slaughter" (i.e., she butchered animals and cooked their meat). Mixing the wine may refer to diluting it, a custom in ancient Israel (cf. the apocryphal 2 Maccabees 15:39 and *The International Standard Bible Encyclopaedia.* Grand Rapids: Wm. B. Eerdmans Publishing Co., 1939, 5:3087). Undiluted wine was considered distasteful by the

Jews, and the wine for the Passover consisted of three parts water and one part wine. Or perhaps the custom of mixing spices with the wine to enhance its flavor may be in view (cf. Ps. 75:8; also note Isa. 5:22). Or possibly both are intended.

### b. Wisdom's invitation to her banquet (9:3-6)

**9:3.** Having prepared the meal the gracious hostess **sent out her maids** to invite people to attend the banquet (cf. Matt. 22:2-3). **The highest point of the city** (cf. Prov. 8:2) was an elevated spot where many would hear the invitation being called out. "Madam Folly" also called from such a high point (9:14).

**9:4-6.** The words of Wisdom's invitation include at least verses 4-6 (and possibly also vv. 7-12, as indicated by the quotation marks in the NIV). Those invited to Wisdom's fare were the **simple** (*peṭî*, "naive, gullible"; see comments on 1:4; cf. 8:5; 9:16) and **those who lack judgment** (see comments on 6:32). Those most needing her attention were invited to be Wisdom's guests. They were to **come** and **eat** and **drink,** that is, people without wisdom should acquire it and benefit from it. They were to **leave** their **simple ways** (*pᵉṯā'îm,* 9:6, the pl. of "simple" in v. 4). This could mean "simple ones." But the second part of the verse which invites the guests to **walk in the way of understanding** suggests that "simple ways," referring to the habits of the naive, is preferable. As already stated (3:18; 4:4; 7:2) the result of wisdom is life (**you will live;** cf. 9:11; 19:23).

### 2. CONSEQUENCES OF ACCEPTING THE INVITATIONS (9:7-12)

At first these verses seem to interrupt the flow of the passage, coming as they do between Wisdom's invitation (vv. 1-6) and Folly's invitation (vv. 13-18). However, this section's position is appropriate, for it points to the consequences of accepting the two invitations. Those who heed Wisdom respond to and learn from rebuke (v. 8b; see comments on 1:23), add to their knowledge (9:9), and enjoy life (v. 11). But those who heed Folly's call are not open to correction (vv. 7-8a) so they suffer (v. 12b). They are mockers, unwilling to be corrected. Folly's invitation only hardens them in their ways.

**9:7-8a. A mocker** (see comments on 1:22), who is **wicked,** is unteachable. When someone corrects him he responds in an attitude of hatred by lashing out with insulting verbal abuses (9:7-8a). **Abuse** (*mûm*) means a blotch or defect. When corrected, a wicked person hurls back the rebuke by defaming his would-be counselor. Such a mocker is hardened in his ways.

**9:8b-9.** On the other hand **a wise** person appreciates **rebuke** because he learns from it. Rebukes can be helpful to the one who is willing to learn from them (15:31; 17:10; 19:25; 25:12; 27:5-6). By being teachable (cf. 10:8a; 12:15b; 14:6b; 15:32b; 21:11b) one becomes **wiser** (cf. 1:5). As elsewhere in Proverbs a wise person is **a righteous** person. Godly character should underlie one's mental sagacity.

**9:10-11.** The theme of the book (1:7a) is restated in 9:10a, with two variations: the Hebrew word for **beginning** here differs from the word for beginning in 1:7. In 9:10 it means "prerequisite" (see comments on 1:7). And the word **wisdom** is used in 9:10 whereas "knowledge" is used in 1:7a.

Personal **knowledge of** God—called in Proverbs **the Holy One** only here and in 30:3—gives insight into life.

Wisdom (**me,** 9:11) assures a person a long **life** (cf. v. 6; 3:2, 16; 4:10; 10:27; 14:27; 15:24).

**9:12.** As stated frequently in Proverbs in different ways, **wisdom** brings rewards and mocking brings suffering. Some of the rewards are mentioned in verses 8a-11.

### 3. FOLLY'S INVITATION (9:13-18)

**9:13.** Folly's feast is presented in contrast with Wisdom's feast. In similar fashion Madam **Folly** (the fem. form of *kᵉsîl;* see comments on 1:7), portrayed as a harlot, made her wares available. She **is loud** (cf. 7:11), **undisciplined** (lit., "naive or gullible," like her guests; cf. 9:16), and ignorant. She is attractive but unruly. Here, as elsewhere, Folly offers immediate gratification whereas Wisdom offers long-term satisfaction.

**9:14-15.** Unlike Lady Wisdom, who prepared for (vv. 1-2) and searched out her guests (vv. 3-6), Madam Folly merely sat **at the door** and called out. But she, like Wisdom, called from **the highest**

**point of the city** (cf. v. 3). Folly appealed to **those who** passed by (cf. 7:8, 10). Those **who go straight on their way** could refer to those who might otherwise pass on by without stopping or those who were leading upright lives. Perhaps both ideas are involved.

**9:16-17.** Folly called for guests by intentionally using the same words as Lady Wisdom (cf. v. 4 and comments there). Since drinking water from one's own fountain refers to sex in marriage (5:15-16), the **stolen water** may refer to illicit sex (cf. 7:18-19). In this way Madam Folly appealed to her guests' baser desires. **Food eaten in secret** also suggests a clandestine activity.

**9:18.** Though her invitation may seem attractive, the end result is not life (cf. v. 11); it is death (cf. 2:18; 5:5; 7:27). Madam Folly is obviously a wayward woman. This suggests that sexual immorality is the height of folly. The two paths of Wisdom and folly resulting in life or death reach a vivid climax in chapter 9. Almost every verse in the remainder of the book points to one or both of these paths and/or their consequences.

## III. The Proverbs of Solomon (10:1–22:16)

This long portion of the Book of Proverbs contains 375 sayings. The development of thought is limited to the two (or sometimes more) lines of each verse. Chapters 10–15 continue the subject matter so dominant in chapters 1–9 contrasting the righteous (or wise) with the wicked (or foolish). The remainder of the section (16:1–22:16) is more varied in subject matter.

Most of the verses in chapters 10–15 are contrasts (in antithetic parallelism); the second line in most of the verses begins with "but." Only a few of the verses in 16:1–22:16 are contrasts; most of the verses are either comparisions (in synonymous parallelism) or completions (in synthetic parallelism), with the conjunction "and" introducing the second line in many of the verses.

The frequent change of subject from one verse to another may be intentional, to force readers to grapple with and meditate on the thoughts in one verse before moving on to the next. However, occasionally two or more consecutive verses are linked by a common subject or word.

For example 10:4-5 discusses both laziness and diligence, and 10:11-14, 18-21, 31-32 refer to talking. "LORD" is mentioned in each verse in 16:1-7, the key word in each verse in 16:12-15 is "king," 15:16-17 both begin with the word "better," each verse in 12:9-11 discusses domestic scenes, and each verse in 11:9-12 begins with the same Hebrew letter.

### A. Proverbs contrasting righteous and wicked living (chaps. 10–15)

**10:1.** On **the proverbs of Solomon,** see "Authorship and Date" in the *Introduction.* With Solomon having authored chapters 1–9 (see 1:1) and chapters 25–29 (see 25:1), along with 10:1–22:16, he wrote about 84 percent of the book, all of it of course being inspired by the divine Author, the Holy Spirit.

**A wise son** is contrasted here with "a foolish son," in 13:1 with a mocker, and in 15:20 with a foolish man. A son who has become wise, by heeding his parents' teachings (5:1-2), **brings joy to his father,** a fact stated several times in Proverbs (15:20; 23:15, 24; 27:11; 29:3). A **foolish** (*kᵉsîl*; see comments on 1:7) **son,** on the other hand, grieves **his mother.** This does not mean that a foolish son does not grieve his father, as is clearly stated in 17:21, 25; 19:13. Nor does 10:1 mean that a mother's heart is not gladdened by a son's wisdom. The use of "father" in one line and "mother" in the other is typical of proverbial literature. Both parents experience either the joy or the grief, just as both are involved in teaching (1:8; 4:3-4; 6:20).

**10:2.** To say that **treasures** are **of no value** seems like a startling, almost contradictory statement until one remembers that the treasures are **ill-gotten** (cf. 1:19; 28:16; Micah 6:10), gained unjustly (cf. Prov. 16:8) by theft or deceit. An example of this is addressed in 1:11-14, 18-19. Such treasures are no good because they dwindle away (13:11; 21:6) and do not forestall death (11:4). Of course money acquired dishonestly may provide some pleasure and be valuable for a while but in the long run it does not satisfy.

**10:3.** Verses 3-5 discuss diligence and sloth. Satisfaction of one's appetite is related to **the LORD** (v. 3); poverty and wealth result from laziness and diligence, respectively (v. 4); industry characterizes a wise son and sleep characterizes a

925

shameful son (v. 5). **The righteous** is literally, "the soul of the righteous." Since "soul" emphasizes the whole person, God has said here that He meets all one's needs, including the needs of his body for food (cf. Ps. 37:19, 25). **The craving of the wicked** refers to their evil desires to bring about destruction and disaster. God can keep them from carrying out such plans. Like many verses in Proverbs, this verse is a generalization. It is usually true that the godly do not starve and that the wicked do not get all they desire.

**10:4-5.** If a person refuses to work he will be **poor** (a word used often in Prov.), whereas a hard worker eventually is rewarded. (Besides laziness other reasons for poverty are mentioned in Prov. See comments on 14:23.) One example of diligence and therefore of wisdom (**wise** is from the verb *śākal* meaning "to be prudent or to have sound judgment"; cf. 1:3; 16:20) is harvesting **in the summer** while the **crops** are ripe. An example of laziness is a son **who sleeps** rather than works **during harvest** (in contrast with the ants, 6:6-11). In fact such a person brings shame (the meaning of **disgraceful**), probably to his parents.

**10:6.** Whereas a **righteous** person receives **blessings,** it is different with **the wicked. Violence overwhelms** his **mouth.** The same statement is made in verse 11. Since the word for "overwhelms" can be translated "covers" (as it is in v. 12), the idea is either that his mouth conceals or deceptively hides violence (NIV marg.), or that violence characterizes what a person says. As Jesus stated, "The evil man brings evil things out of the evil stored up in his heart" (Luke 6:45).

**10:7.** Speaking of blessings and the righteous (v. 6), even *thinking* about **righteous** people of the past can **be a** source of spiritual **blessing.** By contrast most people want to forget **the wicked.** Like their character, even their names are corrupt, rotting like a corpse.

**10:8-9.** A **wise** person is teachable, willing to become wiser (cf. 1:5; 9:9). **But** a **fool** (*'ĕwîl*, a coarse, hardened fool; see comments on 1:7; cf. 10:21) does not quit **chattering** long enough to learn anything. In Proverbs needless talking is often associated with folly. Such a person **comes to ruin,** a phrase repeated only

two verses later (v. 10; cf. 13:3). "Ruin" is mentioned five times in chapter 10 (vv. 8, 10, 14-15, 29). An honest person (v. 9) is secure (cf. a similar thought in 3:23; 18:10; 28:18) in his walk (his conduct) **but** a person whose **paths** are **crooked** (lit., "twisted"), whose conduct is wicked, in contrast with a person **of integrity,** eventually **will be** discovered for what he truly is.

**10:10.** Verses 10-12 deal with interpersonal relations. Winking **maliciously** with one's cohorts suggests sinful intentions (cf. 6:13; 16:30; Ps. 35:19). No wonder this leads to **grief** on the part of the victims of their evil plans, or the victim's loved ones. Yet a talkative **fool** will himself eventually get into trouble (cf. the same line in Prov. 10:8b).

**10:11.** The words of a **righteous** (and wise) person are like **a fountain of life** (cf. 13:14; 14:27; 16:22; also note 18:4). His words of wisdom are free-flowing and as refreshing as a cool spring to a weary desert traveler. On the second part of 10:11; see comments on verse 6b.

**10:12.** **Hatred** results in **dissension** (cf. 6:14) because people who despise each other can hardly work or live together in peace. **Love** contributes toward peace because it **covers** or forgives the faults of others (cf. 17:9). It does not dwell on those faults (cf. 1 Cor. 13:5; James 5:20; 1 Peter 4:8). "Covers" is *kāsâh,* the same word rendered "overwhelms" in Proverbs 10:6, 11. A wicked one's words are covered *over* with violence, **but** a righteous person covers *up* **wrongs** by forgiving the wrongdoers.

**10:13-14.** These statements contrast the wise and the fool. While **the discerning** person is characterized by his wise statements, one lacking **judgment** (cf. v. 21; 6:32; 7:7; 9:4, 16; 11:12; 12:11; 15:21; 17:18; 24:30; 28:16) experiences trouble. He may be punished by **a rod** on **the back** (cf. 14:3; 26:3). A **wise** person stores **up knowledge**; he holds it in for the right occasion without spouting off his knowledge. What **a fool** says, however, causes him trouble and eventually **ruin** because he foolishly speaks the wrong things and gets himself in trouble (cf. 10:19).

**10:15-16.** These verses are together because they both discuss **wealth.** The first line of verse 15 is repeated in 18:11. Though wealth should not be placed above honor (28:20) and should not be trusted in (11:4; 23:5), it can provide a hedge against some disasters. **Poverty** is a continually suppressive problem to **the poor** (cf. 14:20; 18:23; 19:7; 22:7). The Hebrew word here for poor is *dal*, "feeble, weak, helpless," translated "poor" or "helpless" in 19:4, 17; 21:13; 22:16; 28:3, 8, 11, 15; 29:7, 14. Proverbs also uses several other words for "poor" and "poverty."

**Wages** (10:16) refers not to money but to the natural result or "return" for **righteous** living. That result is a meaningful **life** (cf. 3:18, 21-22; 4:4; 7:2a). But **the wicked** reap trouble (Gal. 6:7).

**10:17.** The word **life** links verses 16 and 17. A person **who** learns from **discipline** is an example to others of **the way to** a meaningful life, whereas those who refuse to learn from discipline cause **others** to go **astray.** One's conduct affects not only himself but others as well, either favorably or unfavorably.

**10:18.** Each of verses 18-21 refers to some aspects of talking. The subject of **hatred** was introduced in verse 12, and in verse 18 another thought is added to the subject. When a person hates someone but tries not to show it he is often forced to lie. And hatred often leads to slandering the other who is despised. The second line in verse 18 begins with **and** rather than "but," to show that the two thoughts of hatred and **slander** are not opposites. Such lying and slandering, born out of hatred, characterize **a fool.**

**10:19.** Constant talking will eventually lead to **sin** and get a person into trouble (cf. "chattering" in vv. 8, 10; also note James 3:2-8). This is obviously folly because the ability to keep silent **is wise** (cf. Prov. 11:12).

**10:20.** In contrast with the degrading talk of the wicked (lying, slandering, and gabbing, vv. 18-19) **the** words **(tongue) of the righteous** are uplifting and therefore are valued like **choice silver.** However, with **the wicked** not even their thoughts **(heart)** have **value,** let alone their words!

**10:21.** The word "tongue" links verses 19 and 20, the word **lips** unites verse 21 with verse 18, and **the righteous** ties verses 20 and 21 together. One of the reasons righteous words are valuable (v. 20) is that they **nourish** or benefit others spiritually. Death comes to those who are **fools** (*'ĕwîl*; cf. v. 8 and see comments on 1:7) because they **lack judgment** (cf. 6:32;

7:7; 9:4, 16; 10:13; 11:12; 12:11; 15:21; 24:30; 28:16). Since the first part of 10:21 refers to talking, the second part probably implies that fools lack judgment in what they say. Their wrong kind of talking does not even nourish themselves; they are left spiritually undernourished and starved.

**10:22.** After the word "LORD" the Hebrew adds the word "it" for emphasis. So the first line reads, **The blessing of the LORD,** *it* **brings wealth.** The second line affirms the idea that wealth given by the Lord (to the righteous and diligent) is not accompanied by **trouble,** the tragedies of ill-gotten gain (cf. v. 2).

**10:23.** Most of verses 23-32 contrast the righteous and the wicked. A **fool** (*kesîl*, a thickheaded person; see comments on 1:7) enjoys sinning, whereas the wise prefer **wisdom.** This contrast between **evil conduct** and wisdom shows that wisdom in the biblical sense is moral in nature.

**10:24-25.** By stressing repeatedly in Proverbs that disaster comes to **the wicked** and various rewards are for the righteous, Solomon sought to convince the uninitiated and naive that the long-range, not the immediate, fruits of wisdom and folly should be kept in view. Many **wicked** people dread calamity and they receive it! And **the righteous** often receive what they want, namely, blessing. God is the ultimate Source of both. A **storm** can come suddenly, bringing disaster to **the wicked** by destroying their lives and property (cf. 1:27; 6:15; 29:1), but **the righteous** are more secure (cf. 10:9, 30; 12:3).

**10:26.** Just **as vinegar** (made from wine) is sour tasting, and as **smoke** irritates **the eyes, so** a **sluggard** (see comments on 6:6-11) aggravates his employers, **those who send him** to do some work or go on an errand. He is aggravating because he fails to carry out his responsibilities.

**10:27-30.** These verses mention several blessings that come to **the righteous**: long **life . . . joy,** safety, and security. Usually **the wicked** have none of these, when seen from the perspective of eternity. Longevity for **the righteous** and the brief lives of **the wicked** are frequent themes in Proverbs (3:2, 16; 4:10; 9:11; 14:27; 15:24). On **the fear of the LORD** see comments on 1:7 (also cf. 2:5; 3:7; 8:13;

9:10; 14:26-27; 15:16, 33; 16:6; 19:23; 22:4; 23:17; 24:21). Joy comes to those who love the Lord, but the desires of the wicked for joy are not fulfilled (cf. 10:24; 11:7). By going in the way of the Lord, that is, by following His standards, the righteous have a refuge of safety (*mā'ôz*; cf. Ps. 31:2, 4; Nahum 1:7). They are secure in the land (cf. Prov. 10:9, 25) but the wicked are not (cf. 2:21-22).

**10:31-32.** These two verses also address the subject of talking (cf. vv. 11-14, 18-21). The righteous speak wise words (cf. v. 11). **Brings forth** is literally, "bears fruit." As a tree naturally brings forth fruit so wise words are a natural result of uprightness (cf. Luke 6:43-45). Thus they are fitting or appropriate (see comments on Prov. 10:14). **Perverse,** used in both verses 31 and 32, means to be turned away from what is normal (cf. 2:12).

**11:1.** The Lord hates **dishonest scales** (lit., "balances of deceit"), **but** is pleased with **accurate weights** (lit., "perfect stones"). Dishonesty in business was condemned and honesty commended (cf. 16:11; 20:10, 23; Lev. 19:35-36; Deut. 25:13-16; Micah 6:10-11; also note Amos 8:5). To increase their profits many merchants used two sets of stone weights when weighing merchandise. Lighter stones were placed on the scales when selling (so that a lesser quantity was sold for the stated price), and heavier ones were used when buying (so that more was obtained for the same price). With the absence of coinage, scales were used in most daily commercial transactions. The reference to "the Lord" puts commercial matters in the spiritual realm.

**11:2.** This verse contains an interesting combination of words. **Pride** leads to **disgrace,** its opposite, while **humility** (this Heb. noun is used only here and its verbal form is used only in Micah 6:8, "walk humbly"), which pictures a submissive, modest spirit before both God and man, leads to or is accompanied by **wisdom.** Proverbs 13:10 also contrasts pride and wisdom. The word for "pride" (*zādôn*, "arrogance"; cf. 13:10) is from the verb *zîd*, "to boil up" (cf. "cooking," Gen. 25:29) and sounds much like the Hebrew word for disgrace (*qālôn*).

**11:3.** Verses 3-8 refer to the value of righteousness in guiding and protecting from hardships. **Integrity** (trans. "blameless" in Job 1:1; Prov. 11:20) refers to

moral wholeness, being without moral blemish. When integrity is a way of life, it **guides** like a shepherd. **Duplicity** is the contrasting characteristic. The noun *selep* is used only here and in 15:4 ("deceitful"); the related verb *sālap* means "to pervert, subvert, or overturn." It is rendered "overthrows" in 13:6 and "frustrates" in 22:12.

**11:4. The day of wrath** (cf. "wrath" in v. 23) probably refers to **death. Wealth** cannot buy long life; only **righteousness** can aid in that (cf. 10:2b). In 10:27 fearing the Lord is said to contribute to longevity.

**11:5.** Righteous living results in **a straight way** (cf. 3:5-6), a life with fewer obstacles and troubles (cf. 11:8), but **wickedness** leads to a person's downfall.

**11:6.** Another benefit of righteous living is deliverance, escape from troubles (see comments on v. 5) or death (v. 4). But even the **evil desires** of an **unfaithful** (lit., "treacherous") person get him in trouble (cf. v. 3). He is **trapped** (1:17-18; 6:2; 7:22-23; 12:13), for his desires lead him to sin.

**11:7.** Death for the **wicked** puts an end to all he hoped to accomplish. Neither his wealth (v. 4) nor his **power** can divert death. Obviously it is futile to forsake righteousness to gain power.

**11:8.** As stated in verses 3, 5-6, **righteous** living helps avert **trouble** (cf. 12:13). As in the Book of Esther, the trouble which wicked Haman planned for Mordecai came on Haman **instead** (Es. 3–7).

**11:9.** Verses 9-15 discuss community relationships: one's **neighbor** (vv. 9, 12), the city (vv. 10-11), a gossip (v. 13), advisers for a nation (v. 14), and a cosigner (v. 15). A **godless** person can defame another merely by what he says (cf. comments on 10:18-19a). The Hebrew word for "godless" is *ḥānēp*, "profane." The verb *ḥānap* is translated "defiled" (Jer. 3:1), "pollute(s)" (Num. 35:33), "desecrated" (Ps. 106:38). Contrasted with a profane person, who is careless in what he says, is **the righteous** person who escapes **through knowledge.** Perhaps this means he escapes the injury of slander either because he knows it is not true or because he knows to stay away from profane people.

**11:10-11.** These verses refer to the beneficial effect that **righteous** people can have on public life. People of **a city** appreciate and take delight in the prosperity of and God's **blessing** on its **upright** citizens because they exalt **the city**. That is, such people help keep a city sound economically and morally (cf. Jer. 22:2-5). Conversely citizens are glad when **the wicked**—who lie, slander, deceive, rob, and murder—die (cf. Prov. 28:12, 28) because then the city is safer. Wicked people's words (**mouth;** cf. 11:9)—not to mention their deeds!—can destroy a city economically and morally.

**11:12-13.** In these community relationships (vv. 9-15), right and wrong talking is mentioned several times: in verses 9, 11-13. Anyone who **derides** (*bûz,* "to despise, belittle, hold in contempt"; cf. comments on *bûz* in 1:7b) **his neighbor** (cf. 14:21) **lacks judgment** (see comments on 6:32; 10:13). It simply makes no sense to slander (cf. 10:18) one who lives or works nearby. Since that makes for friction and dissension, it is wise to keep quiet (hold one's **tongue;** cf. 10:19) even if he does know something unpleasant about his neighbor. Divulging **a secret** by malicious **gossip** is a betrayal of trust (also stated in 20:19). "A gossip" is literally "one who goes about in slander." Gossiping is also condemned in 16:28; 18:8; 26:20, 22.

**11:14. Guidance** (*taḥbūlôt,* also used in 1:5) is a nautical term used of steering a ship. The "steerings" or counsel of **advisers** can be helpful (cf. 15:22; 20:18; 24:6). A wise person is open to others' opinions and counsel. Without such counsel, he may make serious mistakes.

**11:15.** Putting **up security for** someone poses serious problems (see comments on 6:1-5; cf. 17:18; 22:26-27).

**11:16.** Most of the verses in 11:16-31 refer in some way to the rewards of righteous and kind living. Verse 16 contrasts the **respect** or honor acquired by **a kindhearted** (*ḥēn,* "gracious") **woman** (cf. a kind man, v. 17) with the **wealth** attained by **ruthless** men. Women of commendable character are also mentioned in 12:4; 14:1; 19:14; 31:10-31. The word **only** suggests that wealth is much inferior to honor (e.g., the inadequacies of wealth are mentioned in 1:19; 10:2; 11:4). The word for "ruthless" (*'ārîṣ*) means one who strikes terror because of his wickedness. This keeps him from enjoying honor, respect, or even peace of mind.

**11:17.** Verses 17-21 all contrast the outcomes of wicked and righteous living. Both kindness (**kind** translates *ḥesed,* "loyal love") and cruelty are reciprocal: kindness **benefits** its giver (for the kindness is returned by its recipients), and cruelty boomerangs, harming both its recipient and its giver (cf. 13:20).

**11:18.** Even the **wages** a sinful person earns are **deceptive,** that is, he thinks his money will help him get ahead, but he finds that it is ultimately of no benefit (v. 4). On the other hand sowing **righteousness,** leading a righteous life, **reaps** rewards that *are* beneficial and lasting. "Deceptive" in Hebrew is *šāqer* and **reward** is the similar-sounding *śeker,* an intended alliteration and assonance to call attention to those words.

**11:19. Righteous** living is rewarded with **life** (cf. 12:28) and wickedness is rewarded with **death,** a frequent theme in Proverbs. A sinner receives harm (11:17), useless money (v. 18), and eventually death (v. 19).

**11:20.** In Proverbs the **LORD** is said to detest many kinds of sinful attitudes and actions: crooked (**perverse,** *'iqqēš,* means crooked or distorted; see comments on 2:15) living (3:32; 11:20), lying (12:22), hypocrisy (15:8), wicked conduct (15:9), wicked thoughts (15:26), pride (16:5), injustice (17:15), and dishonesty in business (20:10, 23). Also see 6:16-19. On the other hand the Lord takes delight **in those** who are morally whole (**blameless;** cf. 11:3) and are truthful (12:22).

**11:21. Be sure of this** is a translation of the idiomatic phrase "hand to hand" (also in 16:5b). This may refer to clasping hands over an agreement on a transaction, which closed a deal. What is certain is that sinners will be punished and the **righteous will** not be.

**11:22.** Israelite women wore nose rings for ornamental purposes, like earrings and rings on fingers today. How incongruous to suppose a nose **ring** would beautify a pig, a notoriously unclean animal! Similarly it is incongruous to suppose that a woman's physical beauty can excuse her lack of **discretion** (moral perception). This verse has an unusual impact by comparing **a beautiful woman** to an ugly pig. Outward female beauty with indiscreet conduct is valueless and morally ugly. This is the first of many verses in Proverbs that use the word **like** or "as" to make a comparison, in what is called emblematic parallelism.

**11:23.** What **the righteous** long for (cf. 10:24; 13:4) **ends** in (or "is") **good.** Conversely what **the wicked** hope for (cf. 10:28b; 11:7) ends **in** (or "is") **wrath** (cf. 11:4). This means either that God's wrath comes on the wicked and thwarts their desires or that the wicked desire **only** to vent their wrath.

**11:24-26.** These verses encourage generosity. By giving **freely** a person has plenty, a seeming paradox (cf. 2 Cor. 9:6). Conversely a person who is miserly, failing to help **others** in obvious need, will himself always be in need (cf. 28:22). By being **generous** (Prov. 11:25) a person prospers and is in turn helped (cf. v. 17). **Grain** (v. 26) in a farming society was a major medium of exchange; hoarding it could drastically affect prices. But a person who sold his grain and did not hoard it was a **blessing** to others.

**11:27-28.** If a person pursues (**seeks** translates *šāḥar*, "to look early or eagerly for," like looking for the dawn) **good** things in and for others **he** himself in turn receives **goodwill** (*rāṣôn*, "acceptance"; see comments on 8:35, "favor"; cf. 14:9) from others. It is reciprocal, as in 11:17a, 25. If a person **searches** for **evil** (distress or tragedy) to come on others it will come on **him** (cf. 11:17b). To have money is not wrong but to trust in it is (cf. 1 Tim. 6:9-10) because it and its owners are transitory (cf. Ps. 62:10; Prov. 23:5; 27:24; James 1:11). **But the righteous,** trusting in the Lord, flourish **like a green leaf** (cf. the tree in Prov. 11:30 and Pss. 1:3-4; 92:12-15; Jer. 17:7-8).

**11:29.** To bring **trouble on** one's own **family** members means that such a person will be disinherited from the estate; he will receive **only wind,** or nothing. And rather than being wealthy and having servants, such a **fool** becomes a **servant!**

**11:30.** As a result **(fruit) of righteous** living a person becomes **a tree of life** (cf. 3:18; 13:12; 15:4), a source of a meaningful life for others (cf. the leaf in 11:28). This contrasts with a fool who troubles his family (v. 29). **Wins souls** in verse 30 does not mean soul-winning or evangelism. Since "win" is literally "attract or take," the idea may be that a righteous person attracts others to wisdom. This fits the thought in the first part of the

verse of a tree giving life to others by its fruit.

**11:31. If the righteous** must be punished in this life (**on earth**) when they do wrong, then certainly (**how much more**) those who are committed to sin and evil will be punished (cf. v. 21). Or the first part of the verse can mean that the righteous are blessed in this life. "How much more" also occurs in 15:11; 19:7; 21:27 and "how much worse" is in 17:7; 19:10. Verse 31 of chapter 11 is a summary of verses 29-30.

**12:1.** To love (i.e., willingly accept or desire) **discipline** (*mûsār,* "moral discipline or correction"; cf. 1:2, 7; 10:17) shows that a person **loves** (desires) **knowledge.** He wants to be on the right path, to be wise. To hate (reject and despise) **correction** shows that one **is stupid** (*ba'ar,* "to be brutish or dull-minded" like an animal; also used in 30:2, "ignorant"). Similar thoughts are given in 12:15; 13:1, 13, 18; 15:5, 10, 12, 31-32.

**12:2.** Proverbs uses many words to describe the righteous and the wise, such as upright (11:3, 11), blameless (11:5), a man of understanding (11:12), trustworthy (11:13), kind (11:17), generous (11:25), prudent (12:16, 23), truthful (v. 22). In verse 2 **good** is another characteristic. Such a person is blessed with God's **favor** (*rāṣôn,* "acceptance"; see comments on 8:35). But a person who is **crafty** (cf. 14:17) or deceptively shrewd not only is not favored by God; he is also condemned ("declared guilty"; cf. Ex. 22:9) by God.

**12:3.** Being settled and stable in their land was valued by the Israelites. But not everyone experienced it (cf. v. 7; 10:25). A wicked person would be **uprooted** like a plant torn up by the roots, which describes exile and/or death.

**12:4.** A **wife of noble character** (cf. 31:10; Ruth 3:11) is like a **crown** on **her husband's** head, that is, her strength of character (*ḥayil* is lit., "strength") makes her husband proud and honored. She adds dignity to him. Conversely **a disgraceful wife** (one who is not noble or strong morally) decays **his bones** (cf. comments on Prov. 3:8); her shame gives him inner pain.

**12:5.** Verses 5-9 contrast the righteous and the wicked. **The righteous** have **plans** or desires for themselves and others that are fair and honest, but **the**

wicked counsel others in **deceitful** ways, with **advice** that is dishonest and self-serving (and warped, v. 8). One's thoughts and words are usually consistent with his character.

**12:6.** The **wicked** seek to destroy other people by their **words** of advice, as stated in verse 5, which is deceitful. **The upright,** however, try to rescue **them,** the victims attacked by gossipers and slanderers.

**12:7.** When the **wicked** try to overthrow others (v. 6) they themselves **are overthrown** (cf. 1:18) in death. Their trap traps *them.* And they **are no more**; they cease to exist. **But the house** (family) **of a righteous** individual is secure (cf. 12:3; 14:11).

**12:8.** The attitudes people have toward the righteous and the wicked are contrasted: praise is for the wise (**wisdom** here is *śēkel,* "prudence or sound judgment"; cf. 1:3) and hatred is for those **with warped minds.** "Warped" (ʾāwâh) is one of several words in Proverbs for crooked. It means "bent or twisted." Their thinking is distorted.

**12:9.** Verses 9-11 pertain to domestic scenes. A contrast is presented by the words **better** and **than** instead of "but." This is the first of 19 verses in Proverbs that use the "better . . . than" formula: verse 9; 15:16-17; 16:8, 16, 19, 32; 17:1, 12; 19:1, 22; 21:9, 19; 22:1; 25:7, 24; 27:5, 10; 28:6.

It is preferable to be unknown (**be** or pretend **to be a nobody**) and yet be in an honorable position (able to hire **a servant**) than it is to boast that one is **somebody** and yet be starving (cf. 13:7). What good is such a claim if one cannot put food on the table?

**12:10.** A **righteous** person is concerned about more than himself or his family. His kindness extends to his animals (pets and livestock). **Cares for the needs of his animal** is literally, "knows the soul of his beast." He sympathetically understands the life-needs of his animals (cf. 27:23). By contrast **the kindest** thing a sinner does is really **cruel.** He does not know how to treat his livestock properly.

**12:11.** Diligent farming results in plenty of **food** (cf. 28:19a; also note 14:23). **But** chasing (an intensive verbal form meaning to pursue frantically) **fantasies** (things that are empty or worthless), either mentally or physically, does

not get the farming done and so one **lacks** food (cf. 28:19b). To neglect one's work while thinking about other things shows lack of **judgment** (see comments on 6:23; 10:13).

**12:12.** What **wicked** people acquire by devious means is desired by other wicked people. **Plunder,** literally "net," refers to what is caught in the net. In contrast with the temporary nature of what evil men steal (cf. 1:19; 10:2-3; 11:4-5) is **the root of the righteous** which **flourishes.** A righteous person is like a plant whose secure root (cf. 10:30) causes it to be green (cf. 11:28) and to bear fruit (cf. 11:30).

**12:13.** Verses 13-20, 22-23 all refer in one way or another to right and wrong talking (cf. 10:11-14, 18-21, 31-32; 11:9, 11-13). Being **trapped** is a common figure in Proverbs (see comments on 11:6). A **righteous** person, speaking righteously or rightly, is therefore not entangled, as is **an evil** person, by what he says. He **escapes trouble** (cf. 11:8, 21; 12:21).

**12:14. The fruit of** one's **lips** are his words (cf. 13:2). His speaking brings **good things** to **him** (benefits himself; cf. 11:17) as well as to others. Though perhaps less obvious, these benefits are as great as the results of manual labor.

**12:15-16.** Two marks of **a fool** and of **a wise man** are given in these verses: the **fool** (ʾĕwîl, "a hardened, thickheaded fool") thinks his **way** is **right** (cf. 21:2), which explains why he will not receive instruction (cf. 1:7); when he is annoyed (perhaps by an insult) he immediately shows it. A wise (**prudent;** see comments on 12:23) **man,** in contrast, is open **to advice** (cf. 10:17; 11:14; 12:1), and is not annoyed by insults. **Overlooks** means not that he ignores the **insult** but that he controls his response to it or forgives it. The same verb (kāsâh) in 10:12 is translated "covers." "Insult" is rendered "disgrace" in 11:2.

**12:17.** The correct talk of a righteous person is seen in his testifying honestly in court (**gives** is an intensive verb carrying the idea of "bursts forth" or "breaks out"), **but** an unrighteous person deliberately **tells lies** in court (cf. 6:17, 19; 14:5, 25; 19:5, 9; 21:28).

**12:18-19. Reckless words,** which may not be intended to hurt, can in fact be very hurtful, piercing **like a sword.** They are not thought through. Who has not spoken something thoughtlessly only to find that his careless words were harmful? But words spoken from a **wise** heart can do just the opposite; they can heal (cf. 15:4) instead of hurt. The effects of words of kindness (cf. 12:25), encouragement, and truth **endure,** but falsehood and liars will not. **Only a moment** translates an idiom, which is literally, "the blinking of the eyes" (cf. Job 20:5).

**12:20.** As stated so often in Proverbs **deceit** characterizes the wicked (v. 5; 6:14; 11:18; 14:8; 15:4; 26:19, 24, 26) **but joy** comes to people **who** desire and work for others' **peace** (*šālôm,* "well-being"). On the word **plot** see comments on 3:29.

**12:21.** The **righteous** experience not only joy (v. 20) but also protection. **Befalls** may be rendered "shall be allowed to happen to." Conversely, **the wicked** experience **trouble** (cf. 11:8, 21; Ps. 32:10).

**12:22.** Again **lying** is referred to (cf. vv. 17, 19; 21:6; 26:28); **the LORD** hates it because it so directly opposes His standard of truth (cf. Ps. 31:5). (Cf. comments on Prov. 11:20 regarding other things He **detests.**) Truthfulness is commended (cf. 12:17, 19; 14:5, 25) for it promotes justice.

**12:23.** A **prudent man** is not anxious to demonstrate **his knowledge**; he is not like **fools** who blurt **out folly.** "Prudent" translates *'ārûm,* "shrewd" in a good sense, a word used elsewhere only in Job (5:12; 15:5) and Proverbs (12:16, 23; 13:16; 14:8, 15, 18; 22:3; 27:12).

**12:24.** Diligence and laziness are contrasted here and in verse 27, and in 10:4; 13:4 (also cf. 12:11). The idea that a **diligent** person **will rule** may not mean that he becomes an official, but that he is in charge of whatever his situation may be. **Laziness,** on the other hand, may lead a person into slavery or servanthood (cf. 11:29), in which he has to work harder.

**12:25.** As is well known today in the fields of medicine and psychology, anxiety can weigh **a man down** (lit., "causes a man to bow down" or depresses him). An empathetic **kind word,** however, can give an anxious, depressed person support and can cheer **him up** (cf. v. 18).

**12:26.** A **righteous** person does not take on just anybody as a friend; he chooses his friends carefully. **Is cautious** could be translated "searches out" (cf. Deut. 1:33) or "investigates" (cf. Ecc.

7:25). **The wicked,** however, are unconcerned about who becomes their friends. The wicked lead other wicked people **astray** for they are all on the wrong path.

**12:27.** A **lazy** person (cf. v. 24) refuses to **roast his game.** "Roast" (*hārak*), used only here in the Old Testament, is difficult to translate precisely. It may mean the lazy man will not even go after food. Or (as in the NIV) it may mean that he hunts some game, but is too lazy to cook it. Diligence, however, leads a hunter to value what he has acquired. This suggests that a lazy person does not value what he owns.

**12:28.** Righteous conduct (**way**) leads to **life,** which probably here means temporal blessing, not eternal life (see comments on 3:18). The second line of 12:28 is difficult in the Hebrew. The NIV rendering **along that path is immortality** is a commendable translation. Though some scholars object to the idea of immortality in the Old Testament, it is certainly taught in several passages (e.g., Job 19:25-27; Ps. 16:10; Isa. 25:8).

**13:1.** Verses 1-3 each refer to talking. **A wise son** (cf. 10:1) is receptive to parental **instruction** (cf. comments on 12:1). The word **heeds,** though not in the Hebrew, is implied. The opposite of a wise, teachable son is **a mocker** (cf. 14:6; 15:12; 17:5; 19:29; 21:11; 22:10; 24:9; 30:17) who refuses to **listen to** and profit from a **rebuke** (see comments on 1:23).

**13:2.** The first clause in this verse is similar to 12:14a. **The fruit of** one's **lips** is his talk, here referring obviously to a righteous person. By speaking positively and helping others with one's words (cf. 12:18b) he in turn is blessed. What he gives he receives. **The unfaithful** (lit., "treacherous") desire not to help others but to harm them, by violent words and deeds. (Cf. "craves" in 13:4.)

**13:3.** Being careful about what one says helps keep him out of trouble (cf. 14:3; 21:23). But speaking **rashly** (hastily and thoughtlessly; cf. 12:18) brings on trouble (cf. **ruin** in 10:8, 14) to the one who speaks and to others. By his reckless words he makes promises he can't keep, divulges private information, offends, or misrepresents. People learn not to depend on what he says and do not want to be around him. He may also suffer physically or financially.

**13:4.** A lazy person (on **sluggard** see

comments on 6:6) has desires (**craves** refers to a deep-seated physical drive or appetite; cf. "craving" in 13:2), but his desires are not satisfied because he is not willing to work. However, diligence (see comments on 12:24) enables a person to be **satisfied** (cf. 11:23).

**13:5.** As stated in 8:13, fearing the Lord involves hating what God hates. Since He hates falsehood (12:22), so do **the righteous.** Lying degrades and leads to mistrust and injustice. **The wicked,** however, by preferring falsehood, **bring shame** (lit., "cause a stink") **and disgrace** on others and themselves.

**13:6.** Again righteous, wise living **guards** or protects a person (cf. v. 3; 2:11; 4:6; also note 12:21). On **integrity** see comments on 11:3. Wicked, unwise living offers no protection to **the sinner.** He is easily overthrown.

**13:7. Pretends** refers to an adopted lifestyle rather than to playacting. A person may **be rich** in material goods but have **nothing** socially or spiritually. Conversely another person may **be poor** materially but rich spiritually.

**13:8.** The words **riches** and **poor** tie this verse with the previous one. A man of wealth may need to use his money to buy himself out of trouble (**ransom his life**) **but a** poor person is not threatened with kidnapping or theft. Being poor has at least one advantage.

**13:9.** A **light** and a **lamp,** common metaphors (cf. 6:23; 20:20; 21:4; 24:20; Job 18:5-6; Ps. 119:105), refer here to physical life. If a lamp in a Near Eastern tent went **out** at night, the surroundings were pitch dark, mindful of the darkness of death. **The righteous** will have a long life, but **the wicked** will die early.

**13:10. Pride** (*zāḏôn,* from *zîḏ,* "to boil"; cf. 11:2) means an unyielding arrogance. Such an inflated, know-it-all view of oneself leads to quarreling, in contrast with a humble, wise spirit that makes one willing to learn and **take advice** (cf. 12:15; see "quarreling" in the chart "Words and Speaking in Proverbs," near 6:17-19).

**13:11. Dishonest money,** gained illegitimately (cf. "ill-gotten treasures," 10:2), does not last (cf. 10:2; 13:22; 23:5). On the other hand **money** can **grow** by being accumulated honestly **little by little.**

**13:12.** It is good for a person to have hope, but if it is not fulfilled for a long time (**deferred** means "put off or long drawn out") then he experiences disappointment (his **heart** becomes **sick**). But when a hope is **fulfilled** (cf. vv. 4, 19), a person is refreshed. The gratification of hope gives encouragement like a tree that gives life (cf. **tree of life** in 3:18; 11:30; 15:4).

**13:13.** Despising parental or other **instruction** results in a person having to make a "payment" of guilt and punishment. **But** respecting such instruction to the point of following it results in the "reward" of blessing. **Scorns** translates *bûz* ("to despise, hold in contempt, or ridicule"; cf. 14:21 and see comments on 1:7).

**13:14.** Being taught by and heeding **a wise** person is as refreshing and life-sustaining as **a fountain of life** (10:11; 14:27; 16:22). Along with the benefit of wise teaching is another aspect: it protects **from the snares of death** (an identical statement is made in 14:27b). Wisdom may help keep a person from a premature death (cf. 1:32-33; 2:11; 4:20-22; 8:35-36), pictured here as an animal trap that ensnares suddenly. With the second line of 13:14 being a dependent clause, this verse has synthetic parallelism (see "Literary Style" in the *Introduction*) rather than the antithetic parallelism of most of the verses in chapters 10–15.

**13:15. Good understanding** translates *śēkel ṭôḇ* which the NIV renders "good name" in 3:4 (see comments there). In 3:4 and 13:15 these Hebrew words are associated with **favor** (*ḥēn,* "grace or graciousness"). By contrast, the life **of the unfaithful** (lit., "treacherous") **is hard.** The Hebrew for "hard" (*'êṯān*) means "ever-flowing" like a river (Ps. 74:15), "enduring" like a nation (Jer. 5:15), or "long established" like leaders (Job 12:19). Perhaps in Proverbs 13:15 it refers to the calloused, ongoing conduct of the wicked, who are so entrenched in their ways that they are find it difficult to turn from them.

**13:16.** Normally a person's conduct is consistent with his character (cf. 4:23-24). One who has **knowledge** shows prudence (*'ārûm,* "shrewd" in a good sense; see comments on 12:23; cf. 12:16), **but a fool** (*kesîl;* see comments on 1:7) **exposes his folly** (cf. 12:23b) "like a peddler who openly spreads his wares before the gaze of all men" (Crawford H. Toy, *A Critical and Exegetical Commentary on the Book of Proverbs*, p. 273).

**13:17.** Whereas an unreliable **messenger** gets **into trouble** (perhaps by his laziness; cf. 10:26; or his foolish conduct; cf. 26:6) and is therefore disappointing, a reliable messenger **brings healing,** that is, he contributes to the welfare of those for whom he works.

**13:18.** Ignoring **discipline** (*mûsār,* "moral discipline or correction"; cf. 1:2) results in **poverty and shame** because a person without self-discipline is lazy and others are ashamed of him. **But** heeding **correction** (i.e., reasoning or arguing) results in honor. Openness to taking advice is mentioned frequently in Proverbs (e.g., 12:1; 13:1, 13).

**13:19.** The word **fools** unites verses 19 and 20 though the subject matter of these verses differs. Verse 19a, like verse 12b, speaks of the satisfaction and joy that come when a hope or dream is realized. Fools on the other hand continue on in their sin. This implies that their hopes are *not* **fulfilled.**

**13:20.** One way to become **wise** is to associate with **wise** people, including companions and teachers. Conversely to associate with **fools** brings problems. The Hebrew words for **companion** (*rō'eh*) and **suffers harm** (*yērôa'*) sound a bit alike. The influence of good and bad associations is a common theme in Proverbs (1:10-11; 2:12; 4:14-17; 16:29; 22:24-25; 23:20-21; 28:7).

**13:21.** Verses 21-23 refer to poverty and **prosperity.** Trouble comes to **the sinner** like an animal chasing him; he can't escape. One such problem is hunger, mentioned in verse 25. Righteous people, however, who in Proverbs are equated with the wise and the diligent, enjoy good things in life, another frequent theme in Proverbs (3:2; 8:18; 10:6, 22; 21:21; 28:25). These statements in 13:21 are generally true, though exceptions could be cited.

**13:22.** A morally **good man** is so blessed that he can help his grandchildren by including them in his will. **But** any **wealth** a sinner may acquire is lost and eventually passes into the hands of **the righteous.** Perhaps this comes about by the sinner's foolish and unwise handling of his funds.

**13:23.** A **poor** man **may,** by his labor, **produce** enough **food** to feed himself (cf. 12:11a), **but** without protection from **injustice** he may lose it. Verse 22 of chapter 13 speaks of a sinner losing his money; verse 23 speaks of those who suffer at the hands of such sinners.

**13:24.** Verses 24-25 and 14:1-4 speak of various home scenes. A loving parent inflicts temporary discomfort on his children (by spanking with a **rod**) to spare them the long-range disaster of an undisciplined life. Refusal to **discipline** one's child when he needs it shows that a parent's genuine love and concern are questionable. Other verses in Proverbs on child discipline are 19:18; 22:15; 23:13-14; 29:15, 17. God also disciplines His own (cf. 3:11-12; Heb. 12:6).

**13:25.** God supplies the physical needs of **the righteous.**

**14:1. The wise woman** and **the foolish** woman probably refer to individuals rather than to wisdom and folly personified as in 9:1, 13. **Builds** may not refer to constructing a physical **house** but caring for a household and causing it to flourish. Whereas a woman of wisdom builds up her household, a woman of folly lives in such a way that her household is neglected.

**14:2.** A person's attitude toward **the LORD**—either fearing Him (see comments on 1:7) or despising **Him**—shows up in his behavior. His conduct is either **upright** or **devious** (cf. 2:15).

**14:3.** The **talk** of a fool (*'ĕwîl,* one who is arrogant, hardened and thickheaded in his ways) results in his being punished with **a rod** (not the same word for rod in 13:24) on **his back** (cf. 10:13; 26:3). **Wise** words, however, **protect** a person from such punishment (cf. 13:3).

**14:4.** If a farmer has **no oxen** for plowing, **the manger** (animal food trough) in his barn **is empty,** that is, clean. **But** by spending time and money to feed and clean up after oxen, he will have plenty of food, **an abundant harvest,** because of the strong oxen's plowing. Meaningful results of any kind require investing time, money, and work.

**14:5.** The contrast between true and false testimony is also mentioned in 12:17; 14:25. False witnessing in court is denounced in 19:5, 9; 21:28; 24:28; 25:18.

**14:6.** It is unusual to read in Proverbs that a **mocker** (see comments on 13:1) **seeks wisdom,** but this shows that lack of desire is not his problem so much as lack of meeting the primary condition, fearing the Lord (1:7; 9:10). Apparently mockers look for wisdom in the wrong places. **Knowledge** is **easily** acquired by people who have discernment in spiritual things. They know where to look for true knowledge.

**14:7.** Verses 7-9 all include statements about fools. Verse 7 is the first imperative statement in the section beginning with 10:1. Also 14:7 is written in synthetic parallelism for the second line explains the first line. Since one's associations can influence him for good or bad (cf. 13:20), he ought to steer clear of being with the **foolish** (kᵉsîl) for they speak without **knowledge.** They cannot offer the young anything of value.

**14:8.** **The prudent** ('ārûm, "shrewd" in a good sense; cf. v. 18; see comments on 12:23) think things through and therefore are not easily deceived, but **fools** find that their own **folly** (cf. 14:18, 24, 29) trips them up. They think their ways are right (12:15).

**14:9.** When a fool sins, he makes fun of the idea of **making amends for** it. In contrast with **fools** who refuse to change their sinful ways are **the upright** who experience **goodwill,** that is, acceptance (on rāṣôn; see comments on 8:35) by God and man.

**14:10.** One's inner pain (**bitterness**) and **joy** cannot be fully experienced by anyone else. They are individual, private feelings in one's own soul.

**14:11.** Final destinies are the subject of verses 11-14. **The wicked** person's **house** (meaning either his possessions or his family members) **will be** demolished (cf. 15:25) and will not last. On the other hand the upright's **tent** (possessions or family members) **will flourish** (lit., "bud or sprout," like a tree budding with blossoms or sending out shoots). This pictures growth, prosperity, and stability.

**14:12.** This verse is repeated verbatim in 16:25. A path (**way** of life) may seem **right** (level or straight) to some people. **But** because **it leads to death** it is the way of sin and folly (cf. 5:5, 23; 7:27; 9:18; 11:19; 21:25). **Man** cannot get away with sin.

**14:13.** By his **laughter** a person may give the impression that he is enjoying life when actually in his **heart** he is hurting emotionally (cf. v. 10; 15:13b). The words **joy may end in grief** refer either to the fluctuating nature of human emotions or to the idea that joy is seldom pure, untainted by any grief.

**14:14.** Both the wicked and the righteous—**the faithless** (lit., "backslider in heart") **and the good—will be** recompensed in accord with their conduct (cf. 1:31). What they sow they will reap (Gal. 6:7).

**14:15.** Verses 15-18 speak of the way of the fool and begin and end with a reference to the simple and the prudent. The **simple** (peṭî, "naive, gullible"; see comments on 1:4) are easily influenced (see, e.g., 7:7-10, 21-23), **but** the **prudent** ('ārûm; cf. 14:8, 18 and see comments on 12:23) think before they act.

**14:16.** The words **the Lord** are not in the Hebrew in this verse though perhaps they are implied. The verse is literally, **a wise** person **fears . . . and shuns evil** (cf. 3:7; 8:13; 16:6; Ps. 97:10). **A fool,** driven by his impetuous (**hothead**) nature, is wild (**reckless**) with regard to evil.

**14:17.** **Quick-tempered** connects this verse with the preceding one. Such a person **does foolish things** (cf. v. 29; 15:18). "Flying off the handle"—not controlling one's temper—causes a person to do and say ridiculous things, which he may later regret and be unable to undo. Even more difficult to live or work with is a person who is **crafty** (cf. 12:2) or scheming (mᵉzimmâh; see comments on 1:4). A person who schemes and works underhandedly to get his way and to oppose others **is hated** by others because he is untrustworthy. He goes astray (14:22).

**14:18.** Because of his gullibility **the simple** (cf. v. 15 and comments there) person receives **folly,** not wisdom (cf. v. 24). The opposite kind of person—**the prudent** (see comments on v. 8; cf. v. 15)—is blessed with more **knowledge.**

**14:19.** **Evil men will bow down in the presence of . . . good** men. Since this is seldom experienced now—it is usually the other way around—this verse may be speaking of the future when the wicked will be subject to the godly.

**14:20-21.** Verse 20 refers to people shunning their **poor . . . neighbors.** In verse 21 this is called sin. Besides the economic frustrations that come with poverty, poor people suffer socially as people often refuse to associate with them (cf. 19:4, 7). Verse 20 of chapter 14 contrasts this social problem of the poor with the fact that many people want to befriend **the rich.** Verse 21 contrasts showing hatred toward one's poor **neighbor** with giving kindness. The attitude of despising (**despises** translates *bûz*, "to hold in contempt, to belittle, to ridicule"; cf. "scorns," 13:13; see comments on 1:7) is sin, whereas being **kind to the needy** (cf. 14:31; 19:17; 28:27) brings blessing from the Lord.

**14:22.** This verse includes the first question in this section that begins with 10:1. A person who plots **evil** (on the word **plot** see comments on 3:29) errs from the path of upright living. Conversely a person who plans (**plan** is the same word as "plot") **good** actions for others (cf. "kind" in 14:21) is characterized by **love** (*ḥesed*, "loyal love") **and faithfulness** (cf. 3:3; 16:6; 20:28).

**14:23.** **Hard work** pays off (cf. 10:4; 12:11, 24) whereas people who merely **talk** about work become poor (cf. 6:10-11). Other causes of poverty mentioned in Proverbs are stinginess (11:24; 28:22), haste (21:5), hedonism (21:17), oppression (22:16), favoritism (22:16).

**14:24.** **The wise** are crowned, that is, blessed with **wealth** (cf. 3:16; 8:18, 21; 15:6; 22:4) because of their diligence (14:23), **but** foolish conduct results not in blessings but in more **folly** (cf. v. 18).

**14:25.** Telling the truth when giving testimony in court can save **lives** from the death penalty, whereas **false** testimony, which deliberately deceives, may send the innocent to death or prison while wrongly acquitting the guilty. People who **witness** in court cases (cf. v. 5) are in a strategic position; they can have a great influence over other people's lives.

**14:26-27.** These two verses are linked together as both refer to the fear of **the Lord** (see comments on 1:7). In 14:26 fearing Him provides security (cf. v. 32) and protection against a life of ruin for believers **and** also **for** their **children** who are influenced by their godly parents to fear God. In verse 27 fearing **the Lord is a fountain of life** (cf. 10:11; 13:14; 16:22), that is, one's fear of the Lord assures longevity (cf. 3:2, 16; 9:10-11; 10:27; 15:24) for it protects **from the snares of death** (cf. 10:2b; 11:4b; 13:14b).

**14:28.** People are **a king's** greatest resource. **But** having no one over whom

to rule would make his high title and position worthless. A pompous title with no meaningful responsibilities draws little respect.

**14:29.** Being **patient** (cf. 16:32; 19:11) under trying circumstances evidences wisdom, but an impatient person who loses control of his temper (cf. 14:16-17) reveals **folly.** The Hebrew *rûm* (**displays**) means "to exalt or lift up for show." Controlling one's temper is always wise, and losing it is never wise!

**14:30.** A person's emotions affect his physical condition, as it is well known today (cf. 15:13, 30; 17:22; 18:14). **A heart at peace** (or, "a mind of health," i.e., a healthy disposition) helps produce a healthy **body,** but envy, an ardent agitating desire to have or achieve what one sees in others, produces adverse effects physically (on **bones,** see comments on 3:8).

**14:31.** To take advantage of **poor** people is like sinning against God (cf. 17:5) since God is the **Maker** of all people (cf. Job 31:13, 15) and because He defends the cause of the poor (Prov. 22:22-23). The righteous, wise person is **kind to the** poor (14:21; 19:17; 28:27) for this **honors God.**

**14:32.** Problems can be disastrous for **the wicked** (cf. 6:15) because they have no hope in the Lord. When **the righteous,** on the other hand, face **death** they **have a refuge,** namely, in God.

**14:33.** **Wisdom** is everywhere present (in the hearts of the wise **and even among fools**; cf. 1:20-22; 9:1-4) but **she** (again wisdom is personified as a woman; cf. comments on 1:20-33) receives various kinds of responses.

**14:34.** **Righteousness** among a group of **people** has a beneficial effect (**exalts** means "to lift up," used here in a moral sense), **but sin** among them has an adverse effect (it **is a disgrace,** "reproach," a word used only here and in Lev. 20:17). Though people may seem to be getting away with sin, ultimately it catches up with them and shames them.

**14:35.** **A king** is pleased when his servants are prudent (the word **wise** here means "prudent"), **but** if they are not prudent they cause him shame (the meaning of **shameful;** the word is also used in that way in 10:5; 19:26; 29:15) and he becomes angry with them. **Wrath** translates *'eḇrâh,* an outburst of anger.

The same is true of employees today: prudence pays off and lack of it causes employers problems.

**15:1.** Verses 1-2, 4, 7, 14b, 23, and 28b refer to talking, a subject frequently addressed in Proverbs (see the chart "Words and Speaking in Proverbs," near 6:17-19).

A gentle (lit., "soft") **answer** can dispel a potentially tense situation by dissolving a person's **wrath** (ḥēmâh, "rage"). Being conciliatory in such a situation requires forethought, patience, self-control, and kindness, virtues commonly lauded in Proverbs. A harsh (lit., "hurtful") **word,** by contrast, arouses rather than dissolves **anger.**

**15:2.** The **tongue** (words) **of the wise commends** (lit., "does well by") **knowledge** (cf. v. 7). The wise not only possess knowledge but also their use of it makes it attractive and desirable. A **fool,** however, **gushes** (lit., "bubbles forth," also used in v. 28) his **folly.** His many words, bubbling out like water from a spring, show how foolish he is. **The mouth of** a fool also reveals his sin (v. 28) and feeds on folly (v. 14).

**15:3.** In His omniscience God sees and knows what everyone does (cf. 5:21; Heb. 4:13; also note **the eyes of the Lord** in 2 Chron. 16:9), **keeping watch** like a watchman guarding a city. **Wicked** people should be warned and **good** people comforted by this truth. He sees even death and destruction (Prov. 15:11). The second line of verse 3 is a participial clause that completes the thought of the first line, so this verse has synthetic parallelism (see "Literary Style" in the *Introduction*).

**15:4.** Words can encourage or depress an individual. Words that bring **healing,** that contribute to a person's emotional health, are like **a tree of life** (cf. 3:18; 11:30; 13:12), a source of strength and growth. Words that are **deceitful** (selep, "subversive"; used in the OT only here and in 11:3, "duplicity") can crush **the spirit** (cf. 15:13; 17:22; 18:14), or depress one's morale.

**15:5.** If a son refuses to learn from **his father's discipline** (mûsār; see comments on 1:3) he is **a fool** ('ĕwîl, a coarse and hardened fool; see comments on 1:7). Also he is stupid (12:1), a mocker (13:1; 15:12), and self-hating (v. 32). He will die (v. 10). To follow parental **correc-**tion is wise. **Shows prudence** translates the verb 'āram, "to be shrewd" in a good sense (also used in 19:25), similar to the noun 'ormâh (in 1:4; 8:5, 12) and the adjective 'ārûm (12:23; 13:16; 14:8, 15, 18; 22:3; 27:12). Heeding the advice of one's parents brings honor. (Cf. similar concepts in 12:1; 13:1, 13, 18.)

**15:6.** As stated several times in Proverbs, **righteous** (and wise) living generally results in prosperity (cf. 3:16; 8:18, 21; 14:24; 22:4), though there are many exceptions, but money acquired by **the wicked** (and unwise) results in **trouble** (cf. "trouble" in 15:27; note 1:19; 10:2).

**15:7. Wise** people share helpful facts, but **fools** (kᵉsîl) do not. They spread folly (v. 2). Peoples' words (**lips**) reveal what is in their **hearts** (cf. heart and lips in 4:23-24).

**15:8-9.** The Lord detests (cf. 6:16-19) **the sacrifice** and **the way of the wicked,** as well as their very thoughts (15:26). (On other things the Lord detests see comments on 11:20.) God hates sacrifices offered by **wicked** people (cf. 1 Sam. 15:22; Isa. 1:11; Jer. 7:22; Amos 5:22) because those offerings are given hypocritically. Because "the way" (conduct) of the wicked is detestable, so are their sacrifices. However, **the prayer of the upright pleases Him** so He hears them (Prov. 15:29). Offering sacrifices, an external act, is no substitute for a life of **righteousness,** which obviously God **loves.**

**15:10.** In verses 10-12 the second line expands the thought of the first line. When a person **leaves the path** of uprightness and righteousness (cf. vv. 8-9), he will receive **stern discipline** (mûsār, "moral correction"); and if he refuses **correction** (vv. 5, 12; cf. 10:17; 12:1) altogether, he will pay for it (13:13) with poverty, shame (13:18), and death (15:10).

**15:11. Death** (šᵉʾôl) **and destruction** (ʾăḇaddôn, from ʾāḇaḏ, "to perish or die") may be synonyms of the grave and of the dead in it (cf. 27:20; Job 26:6; "destruction" [ʾăḇaddôn] is also used in Job 28:22; 31:12; Ps. 88:11). Since God can see the dead in their graves, surely He can see living people's **hearts** (cf. Prov. 15:3), that is, their motives, thoughts, and desires (cf. Ps. 38:9a). Man's heart deceives him but God knows it (Jer. 17:9-10).

**15:12. Correction** here is not the word usually rendered "correction" in the NIV in Proverbs. Here it is the word for rebuking or reproving (as in 9:7-8; 19:25; 25:12). **A mocker** (cf. 13:1) **resents** (lit., "does not love") such reproof and refuses to learn from **wise** people (note the contrast in 15:31). This shows that mocking is evidence of folly.

**15:13.** Verses 13-15 refer to **a happy heart,** a discerning heart, and a cheerful heart. Inner joy (*śāmaḥ*; see comments on v. 21) shows on a person's **face,** but inner grief (**heartache**; cf. 14:13) depresses a person's morale (**crushes the spirit**; cf. 15:4; 17:22; 18:14). Happiness and depression are issues of the heart. What a person is inwardly has more lasting impact on his emotional state than do his circumstances. Some people hold up under difficult circumstances better than others because of inner strength.

**15:14.** A person who has discernment **seeks** more **knowledge** (cf. 18:15; 19:25; 21:11) and it comes to him easily (14:6). **But . . . a fool feeds on** (*rā'âh,* "grazes" like cattle), and is content with, his **folly,** (cf. 15:2, 21).

**15:15.** In contrast with **the oppressed** (*'ānî,* lit., "those who are bowed down," the humble, afflicted; often trans. "needy" as in 14:21), who are miserable, are those who are **cheerful** (cf. 15:13) and as a result have **a continual feast;** they enjoy life in spite of adverse circumstances. Therefore people ought to encourage the oppressed by helping them.

**15:16.** Verses 16 and 17 are 2 of the 19 "better . . . than" verses in Proverbs (see comments on 12:9). Generally a person would choose **wealth** (abundance) over poverty. But if he has poverty (a **little;** cf. 16:8) and **the fear of the LORD** (see comments on 1:7) that combination (cf. 1 Tim. 6:6) is certainly preferable to wealth if the money brings **with** it turmoil (*meḥûmâh;* cf. Isa. 22:5, "tumult"; Deut. 7:23, "confusion"; 1 Sam. 14:20; Ezek. 7:7, "panic"; Zech. 14:13). The statement in Proverbs 15:16 suggests (a) that the wealth mentioned here is not possessed by one who fears the Lord and (b) that fearing God gives peace, not confusion.

**15:17.** Like verse 16, verse 17 contrasts poverty (having a mere **meal of vegetables**) with prosperity (**a fattened calf**). Normally people would choose luxury over privation, but what is more important **is love.** Many people have found that a home where material possessions

are few but love for each other is present is far better than a house of great opulence where people hate each other (cf. 17:1). Love makes one's difficult circumstances endurable, whereas **hatred** undoes all the enjoyments that good food might otherwise bring.

**15:18. A hot-tempered man** (lit., "a man of rage"; cf. similar expressions in 14:16-17, 29; note 19:19; 22:24) **stirs up dissension** (cf. 6:14, 19; 10:12; 16:28; 28:25; 29:22; see comments on 6:14). This may be one reason for the turmoil and hatred mentioned in 15:16-17. Patience (cf. 14:29; 16:32; 19:11; 25:15), however, can quiet quarrels. **A patient man** is, literally, a man "slow to anger" (cf. James 1:19).

**15:19.** As hatred and anger bring problems (15:17-18) so does laziness. **Thorns in the path** (cf. 22:5; 24:30-31) depict problems that keep a person from getting what he wants; his life has obstructions. **The upright,** however, are diligent and therefore have fewer problems; their lives are more like a smooth **highway** (cf. 4:26).

**15:20.** Verses 20 and 21 speak of the impact of wisdom and folly on one's life. Love in a home brings peace (vv. 16-17), and obedient and **wise** conduct brings joy (*śāmaḥ*) **to** the parents, **but** folly does not. In fact only a fool **despises his mother.** Here rather than stating that folly in a son grieves his mother (as in 10:1) that reaction on her part is implied and the fool's attitude toward her is stated.

**15:21.** Whereas a wise son brings joy (*śāmaḥ*) to his father (v. 20), a foolish person (one **who lacks judgment,** lit., "void of heart"; see comments on 6:32; 10:13) has joy (*śāmaḥ*) in his **folly** (also see comments on *śāmaḥ* in 15:13, 23, 30). A wise person has **a straight course** (cf. clear "highway," v. 19b). The implication is that a foolish person's course is crooked (and obstructed, as in v. 19a).

**15:22.** Four times the Book of Proverbs focuses on the importance of getting advice from others in regard to one's **plans** (11:14; 15:22; 20:18; 24:6).

**15:23.** In verses 23, 30, 33 the second line begins with **and,** pointing up synonymous parallelism (see "Literary Style" in the *Introduction*). Appropriately spoken words (cf. 25:11-12), saying the right thing at the right time, delights (*śāmaḥ*; see comments on 15:20) not only the hearer but also the one who says them. **Timely** words (whether of love, encouragement, rebuke, or peacemaking) are beneficial.

**15:24.** Each of verses 24, 26-33 refers directly or indirectly to a characteristic of the godly: **wise** (v. 24), humble (v. 33), pure (v. 26), honest (v. 27), cautious (v. 28), prayerful (v. 29), joyful (v. 30), teachable (vv. 31-32), and reverent before the Lord (v. 33). Wisdom can **keep** a person from a premature death, a point often made in Proverbs (cf. 3:2, 16; 4:10; 9:11; 10:27; 14:27).

**15:25.** Verses 25 and 26 both refer to the Lord's reactions to man's character. **The proud** (gē'eh, also used in 16:19, from the verb gā'âh, "to rise up or be lifted up") accumulate possessions, including **houses**, but **the LORD tears** them **down** (cf. 14:11), whereas He protects widows.

Land, a precious commodity to the Israelites, was marked by **boundaries** to preserve its original parameters (Deut. 19:14). Land was kept in a family and its boundaries were important (Prov. 22:28; 23:10-11). The vulnerability of widows made them easy prey to thieves who would seek to steal their land, so the Lord Himself promised to keep **widow's** boundaries from being moved.

**15:26.** The LORD detests not only the sacrifices and conduct **of the wicked** (vv. 8-9) **but** also even their **thoughts** (or plans; trans. "schemes" in 6:18). **But the** thoughts **of the pure are** a delight **to Him.** God in His omniscience knows everything.

**15:27.** The Hebrew word for **greedy** (bāṣa', "to cut or break off") suggests making gain unjustly or by violence. (On "a greedy man" see 28:25.) A dishonest father, providing for his **family** by unjust or violent means, will eventually cause his wife and children to suffer (cf. **trouble** in 11:29; 15:6). Accepting or giving **bribes** is a form of dishonesty or greed because they pervert justice (see comments on 6:35). So to reject bribes helps prolong one's life and prevent trouble for one's family.

**15:28.** A **righteous** person **weighs** (carefully muses on or considers) his **answers** before giving them rather than blurting out the first thing that comes to his mind. That way his words are more appropriate and timely (v. 23). A fool, however, **gushes** out (lit., "bubbles

forth," also used in v. 2) **evil** words like water bubbling out of a spring.

**15:29.** Because God detests **the wicked** (vv. 8-9, 26) He distances Himself from them, refusing to hear them. **But He hears** the praying **of the righteous** (cf. Ps. 34:15, 17; 1 Peter 3:12) because their prayers please Him (Prov. 15:8).

**15:30.** A positive person's encouragement, whether nonverbal (by **a cheerful look,** lit., "bright eyes") or verbal (**good news;** cf. 25:25), is helpful and uplifting. **Brings joy** translates śāmaḥ, also in 15:20-21, 23, 31. As in verse 13a, emotional health contributes to physical well-being (**health to the bones;** see comments on 3:8).

**15:31.** Verses 31-33 speak of conditions for entering the ranks of the wise: listening to (and heeding) rebuke (v. 31), heeding correction (v. 32), and fearing the Lord and being humble (v. 33). Heeding a **rebuke** (see comments on 1:23) can be **life-giving** (cf. 1:33) because such a person is impressed by it (17:10), learns from it (19:25), and is considered **wise.**

**15:32.** To ignore **discipline** (mûsār, "moral correction"; cf. vv. 5, 10) results in loss of life and knowledge, which shows that the ignorer actually hates **himself** (cf. "harms himself," 8:36).

**15:33.** **The fear of the LORD** (see comments on 1:7) is not only the beginning of knowledge, but it also **teaches . . . wisdom.** By fearing (reverencing, trusting, obeying, serving, and worshiping) the Lord a person learns wisdom. **Humility,** associated with fearing the Lord, must precede the **honor** (cf. 18:12b; 29:23) that accompanies wisdom. (The fear of the Lord and humility are also connected in 22:4.)

### B. Proverbs exalting righteous living (16:1–22:16)

Most of the 191 verses in this section are either comparisons (in synonymous parallelism) or completions (in synthetic parallelism), and only a few are contrasts (antithetic parallelism). Verses 1-7, 9 of chapter 16 each speak of the Lord; verses 1, 3, 9 refer to man's plans and God's sovereignty over them. Those plans are expressed in what one says ("the tongue," v. 1) and does ("steps," v. 9). Verses 1, 5, and 9 refer to the heart and verse 2 mentions man's motives. Pride (v. 5), evil (v. 6), and injustice (v. 8) are denounced. Though man is strongly encouraged in Proverbs to acquire wisdom, he is not released from dependence on the Lord.

**16:1.** A person may make **plans** (placing things in order, like arranging soldiers in battle lines; cf. Gen. 14:8) in his **heart** (cf. Prov. 19:21) **but** God guides what comes out of the heart in man's words (**the reply of the tongue**). God in His sovereignty prevails over **man** (cf. 16:9). One's heart and his speech are closely related (cf. 4:23-24).

**16:2.** A person may think nothing is wrong with what he does; outwardly it may **seem innocent. But** God knows his heart, whether the **motives** behind his actions are pure or not. The LORD judges people on the basis of *why* they act (cf. 17:3; 21:2) because He sees human hearts (cf. Matt. 6:4, 8, 18).

**16:3.** Committing one's **plans** (vv. 1, 9) **to the LORD** is essential to success. This verse, however, does not offer divine assistance to *all* plans. The fool (1:32) and the sluggard (6:9-11) are said to come to undesirable ends. **Commit** is literally "roll" (cf. Ps. 37:5).

**16:4.** God **works** all things **for His** (or "its") **own ends** (cf. Rom. 8:28), including **the wicked for** destruction. Though this may be difficult to understand and accept, punishment for the unrepentant is in keeping with God's justice and is a truth frequently taught in the Scriptures (including Prov. 16:5).

**16:5.** God **detests** pride, or independence of **the LORD** (for other things He detests see comments on 11:20); therefore He will punish it. **Be sure of this** is literally "hand to hand" (see comments on 11:21).

**16:6.** Though unrepentant sin "will not go unpunished" (v. 5), God in His **love** (*hesed,* "loyal love") **and faithfulness** (cf. 3:3; 14:22; 20:28) has provided a way for **sin** to be **atoned for.** After a person's sins have been atoned for by his trust in the Lord, he is not to continue in sin. He is to avoid **evil** (cf. 16:17) by fearing **the LORD** (see comments on 1:7; cf. 3:7; 8:13).

**16:7. When** a person pleases **the LORD** (by, for one thing, avoiding evil, v. 6) **he** (either that person or the Lord) **makes** that person's **enemies** to be at peace with him.

**16:8.** This **better . . . than** verse (see comments on 12:9) is similar to 15:16 ex-

cept that here **righteousness** is substituted for "the fear of the LORD," **much gain** replaces "great wealth," and **injustice** is used instead of "turmoil." One who amasses revenue (the meaning of the Heb. word for "gain," which is also used in 10:16, "income"; and in 15:16, "great wealth") dishonestly (cf. 10:2, 16; 13:11; 15:27) eventually will be punished. So righteous living—even if it means having **little**—is certainly better.

**16:9.** A man makes **plans** for his actions **but the LORD determines** (or establishes) how he will go (**his steps**). The meaning here is the same as in verse 1 but "steps" are mentioned instead of "tongue."

**16:10.** "King," "kings," and "a king's" are mentioned in verses 10, 12-15. When **a king** of Israel spoke **an oracle,** he did so as God's representative and therefore was to be a just ruler (cf. Deut. 17:18-20).

**16:11.** On **scales** and **weights** see comments on 11:1 (also cf. 20:10, 23). The king established the weights and measures (see "its weight . . . by the royal standard," 2 Sam. 14:26), but here the statement is made that **the LORD** was behind those standards. Therefore they should be honored. To use dishonest weights and measures was to disobey both the king and God.

**16:12-13.** Kings hate **wrongdoing** (v. 12) and value honesty (v. 13); at least they should, for a righteous, honest ruler will establish (make firm or secure) a king's **throne** (cf. 20:28; 25:5; 29:14). Dishonesty and injustice will cause his reign to topple. **Kings** should **value** honesty not only in themselves but in others also.

**16:14.** If someone angers a king he may be executed; only wisdom can **appease** his anger (cf. Ecc. 10:4). **A king's** power is irresistible; one's only recourse is to seek to pacify it.

**16:15.** One way to brighten **a king's face** is given in verse 13, to be honest. **A rain cloud in spring** (the "latter rain" in March or April) was welcomed as rain was needed for a good crop. A king's **favor** signaled much better fortune than his wrath. His favor was also compared to dew (19:12).

**16:16. Wisdom** is more desirable **than gold,** and **understanding . . . than silver** (cf. 3:13-15; 8:10-11, 19).

**16:17. The upright** person seeks to

avoid **evil** (cf. v. 6; 3:7; 8:13). Guarding **his way** (i.e., maintaining upright conduct) is a means of guarding one's **soul** (inner life with its drives, appetites, and desires) from sin.

**16:18-19.** These verses discuss pride, humility, and disaster. **Pride** leads to one's downfall (cf. 18:12; 29:23). Pride is so despicable that a person should avoid it even if it means being economically **oppressed.** One may **share plunder** (acquired through violent or dishonest means) **with the proud** but such dishonesty will not go unpunished (cf. 15:25).

**16:20.** A person who **gives heed to** (lit., "is prudent" with regard to, or "ponders"; trans. "takes note of" in 21:12) **instruction** (*dābār*, "word"; also trans. "instruction" in 13:13), **prospers** (cf. 19:8), that is, has God's blessing of happiness. Such a person is also one **who trusts in the LORD** and therefore is **blessed.**

**16:21.** Verses 21, 23-24 refer to wise and pleasant words. A person who is **wise** is known for his discernment, his ability to see to the heart of issues. The word for **pleasant** (*meteq*, "sweetness") is used in 27:9 ("pleasantness"). A similar word (*mātôq*, "sweet") is used in 16:24; 24:13; 27:7. Sweet (i.e., attractive or helpful) **words promote instruction** in the sense that they make learning (cf. 1:5) desirable. Harsh words do the opposite.

**16:22.** The word for **understanding** in this verse is *śēkel*, "prudence or insight," also used in 13:15 (and in 12:8; 19:11; 23:9, where it is trans. "wisdom"). Prudence is like **a fountain of life** (cf. 10:11; 13:14; 14:27); it is refreshing, life-sustaining, and inexhaustible. **Folly** on the other hand results in **punishment.** Fools do not learn and their foolish conduct requires discipline (*mûsār*).

**16:23.** A **wise** person is careful about what he says (**guides his mouth** is lit., "causes his mouth to be prudent") for he wants to help, not hurt. He does not blurt out whatever comes to his mind (cf. 15:28b). As a result **his lips promote instruction** (see comments on 16:21 on "promote instruction").

**16:24.** **Pleasant** (i.e., "delightful"; this Heb. word differs from the word "pleasant" in v. 21) **words are** as **sweet** (see comments on v. 21 on *mātôq*) and therefore as desirable as honey from **a honeycomb** (cf. Ps. 19:10). Appropriately

spoken words (cf. Prov. 15:23) that encourage, soothe, or commend can be most pleasant and even uplifting to the point of helping a person feel better physically (see comments on **bones** in 3:8).

**16:25.** This statement is identical with 14:12 (see comments there). Apparently this was repeated for the sake of emphasis.

**16:26.** **Hunger** can motivate people, sometimes even lazy people, to work so that with their wages they can buy food. This verse has an interesting wordplay: though a person is working as a laborer for someone else, his **appetite** is "working" for himself. Diligence is encouraged in 10:4-5; 12:24; 14:23; 28:19.

**16:27.** Verses 27-30 refer to troublemakers of various kinds—those who plot evil (v. 27), stir up strife (v. 28), lead others into violence (v. 29), and persist in sin (v. 30). **A scoundrel,** literally, "a man of belial" (cf. 6:12), is worthless and wicked, and lives in deep moral degradation. He **plots evil** (cf. 1:10-14; 6:14; 12:20; 14:22; 24:2, 8). "Plots evil" is literally "digs a calamity," which suggests the effort he puts forth to dig a pit to trap others. One of the main ways in which he does this is by words that burn **like . . . fire** (cf. James 3:5-6).

**16:28.** A **perverse man** (lit., "a man of perversity"; see comments on 2:12) **stirs up dissension** (cf. 6:14, 19; 10:12; 15:18; 28:25; 29:22), causing strife between friends. And by his **gossip** (cf. 11:13; 18:8; 20:19; 26:20, 22) he causes **close friends** (cf. 17:9) to doubt and distrust each other.

**16:29.** A **violent man** (lit., "a man of violence"; vv. 27-29 each begin with "a man of" in Heb.) is not content to sin; he wants to lead others with him in his wicked ways (see, e.g., 1:10-14).

**16:30.** By winking (cf. 6:13; 10:10; Ps. 35:19) and pursing **his lips** an evil person signals to others nonverbal clues (facial gestures) to communicate his intentions to be involved in **perversity** (cf. Prov. 16:28; see comments on 2:12) and **evil** (cf. 16:27).

**16:31.** Young men glory (take pride) in their strength (20:29), but old men may take pride in their **gray hair,** which is like a distinguished **crown** (cf. crown **of splendor** in 4:9). Longevity is a result of **righteous** living (cf. 9:6; 10:27), but not all who are aged have lived righteously.

**16:32.** In this **better . . . than** proverb (see comments on 12:9) having patience and a controlled **temper** is honored above being a soldier. In a land where safety depended on might and skill in warfare, this statement may seem surprising. Yet conquering oneself (cf. 14:17, 29; 25:28; 29:11) is of greater virtue than conquering **a city.**

**16:33.** The results of casting lots (cf. 18:18; see comments on Es. 3:7; Acts 1:26) may seem like mere chance, but God controls even them (cf. man's efforts and God's sovereignty in Prov. 16:1-2, 9).

**17:1.** Each of verses 1-20 relates closely or loosely to strife or peace. As stated in the similar **better . . . than** proverbs of 15:16-17, having a peaceful **and quiet** though spartan meal (**dry crust**) is far better than having a lot to eat (**a house full of feasting,** lit., "sacrifices," i.e., full of meat from animals sacrificed to the Lord; cf. 7:14) in a house where there is **strife.** Harmony in one's relationships is to be desired over a sumptuous supply of food.

**17:2.** Sometimes a **servant,** because he is **wise** ("prudent"; trans. "gives heed to instruction" in 16:20), can inherit an estate or part of it and be placed by his master in a powerful position **over a disgraceful son** (who brings shame to his parents; cf. 19:26). Interestingly Jeroboam rose over Solomon's disgraceful son Rehoboam and became the leader of 10 of the 12 tribes (1 Kings 12).

**17:3.** As **silver and . . . gold** are purified under intense heat (cf. 27:21), so a believer's **heart** is purified by the heat of trials which **the Lord** brings (James 1:2-3; 1 Peter 1:7).

**17:4.** **A wicked** person and **a liar** both feed on what enhances their characteristics. They readily listen to gossip, **evil** talk that plots wicked schemes, lies, and slander. **Malicious** translates *hawwōt,* which means "engulfing ruin, destruction, as accomplished by one person against another." (Cf. "gossip" in 11:13; 16:28; 18:8; 20:19; 26:20, 22.)

**17:5.** One way of engulfing others by malicious talk (v. 4) is to mock those who are **poor.** Since the poor are made in God's image, as all people are, to mock them is to speak against God, **their Maker** (cf. 14:31; 18:23). Equally bad is being glad when other people experience ca-

lamities (cf. 24:17). A person who **gloats over** the misfortunes of others will himself experience misfortune (he will be punished).

**17:6.** **A crown** (cause for joy and dignity) of older people (cf. 16:31) is their grandchildren. Also **children** should be proud of their **parents.** These expressions of joy and **pride** depend, of course, on the family members being properly related to God (Deut. 6:2) and to each other.

**17:7.** Verses 7-9 refer to various forms of injustice: lying, bribing, and gossiping. **Arrogant lips** is literally, "lips of excess," and refers to one who says too much. **Fool** is *nābāl,* used only three times in Proverbs (vv. 7, 21; 30:22). It refers to one who lacks spiritual perception and sensitivity. A *nābāl* should not talk a lot because he seldom knows what he is talking about. Similarly **lying** is totally inappropriate for a **ruler** (*nādîb,* noble or official, 17:26); a ruler should be a man of integrity, honesty, and trustworthiness (cf. "noble," *nādîb,* in Isa. 32:8). A ruler who tells lies is like a fool.

**17:8.** This verse does not encourage bribery, which is condemned in verse 23; 15:27; Exodus 23:8; Deuteronomy 16:19; 27:25 (see comments on Prov. 6:35). Verse 8 of chapter 17 is simply speaking from the giver's perspective; **a bribe** "works like **a charm.**" To say bribes are effective (cf. 18:16; 21:14) is not to approve them; it simply states the way things are.

**17:9.** Covering **over** (see comments on 10:12) **an offense** is an evidence of love and therefore **promotes love. But** repeating or gossiping about others' sins can lead **friends** to be suspicious of each other (cf. 16:28).

**17:10-11.** Verses 10-16 each refer to some form of evil or foolish action. Verse 10 contrasts the receptivity of a discerning person with that of **a fool.** A mere **rebuke** (see comments on 1:23) helps a wise person **more than** the physical punishment of **100 lashes** given to a fool (*kesîl;* cf. 17:12, 16; see comments on 1:7). Since no more than 40 lashes were allowed by Law (Deut. 25:2-3), this reference to 100 lashes is probably hyperbole. The wise are sensitive and learn readily, but a thickheaded fool is unresponsive even after extreme measures of correction. **An evil** person (Prov. 17:11) insists on being rebellious; he refuses to learn from correction or rebuke (v. 10). Eventually he is brought to justice and punished (cf. 11:21; 16:5) by **a merciless official.**

**17:12.** A mother **bear** whose **cubs have been robbed** is angry and therefore dangerous (cf. Hosea 13:8). But a worse danger is meeting **a fool** (*kᵉsîl*; cf. Prov. 17:10, 16; see comments on 1:7). Not all fools are equally dangerous but, as Robert L. Alden suggests, "Consider meeting a fool with a knife, or gun, or even behind the wheel of a car; a mother bear could be less dangerous" (*Proverbs: A Commentary on an Ancient Book of Timeless Advice*, p. 134).

**17:13.** If someone **pays back evil** when he has received **good** he shows that his heart is evil (v. 11) and foolish (v. 12). So he will experience no more "good" (blessings). Instead **evil** (calamity) **will** stay with **his house,** that is, his family.

**17:14. Starting a quarrel** (cf. v. 19) may seem like a minor matter. But it often grows beyond control like a small crack in **a dam** which increases in size until the dam breaks. **So** the answer is to refuse to let an issue fester; it should be dropped **before a dispute** even starts.

**17:15.** Injustice in a court case—whether **acquitting the guilty** or **condemning the innocent** (cf. v. 26)—is hated by **the LORD** (cf. comments on 6:16).

**17:16.** A **fool** (*kᵉsîl*; cf. vv. 10, 12; see comments on 1:7) is so simple he thinks he can buy wisdom. He comes with money in hand, but fails to realize he lacks the one resource necessary for gaining **wisdom**: a genuine, heartfelt **desire** for it.

**17:17.** Some Bible translations make a contrast in this verse between **a friend** and **a brother** by beginning the second line with "but." The NIV's **and** seems preferable; it conveys the idea that both the friend and the brother are valued. However, in 18:24 a friend is extolled above a brother (relative). True friends—and relatives—are faithful in times of **adversity** as well as prosperity.

**17:18.** Being a reliable friend in times of adversity (v. 17) is different from a foolhardy agreement to provide financial security for a high-interest loan (see comments on 6:1-5). On **lacking in judgment** see comments on 6:32; 10:13.

**17:19.** Friendship (v. 17) helps overcome strife, unwise financial obligations may cause strife (v. 18), and quarreling

(v. 19), perverse motives, bad morals, and deceptive words (v. 20) all contribute to strife. Quarreling (cf. v. 14) shows that its initiator **loves sin** because a quarrel inevitably leads to trouble. Building **a high gate** either refers to a literal high door which a wealthy person builds to show off his pride or it refers figuratively to his bragging. Either way pride is present, which results in a fall (11:2; 16:18; 18:12; 29:23).

**17:20. Perverse** (*'iqqēš*) means "twisted or distorted" (see comments on 2:15). A person whose motives and morals (**heart**) are distorted will **not prosper** (be blessed by God; cf. 16:20). From a perverse heart a person speaks deceitfully; he lies. This will result in **trouble** (*rā'āh*, "calamity," trans. "evil" in 17:13).

**17:21.** Parents grieve deeply over a foolish, disappointing **son** (cf. v. 25; 10:1). Two words for **fool** are used in 17:21. The first is *kᵉsîl*, one who is dull and thickheaded. The other is *nābāl*, one who lacks spiritual perception and sensitivity (cf. v. 7; 30:22).

**17:22.** As in 15:13, 15, 30; 18:14, one's inner life affects his physical well-being. **A cheerful heart** translates two Hebrew words that are rendered "a happy heart" in 15:13. The word for **medicine** occurs only here in the Old Testament. **A crushed spirit** refers to being depressed or saddened (cf. 18:14). An example of a crushed spirit is a father's grief over a wayward son (17:21). On **the bones** see comments on 3:8.

**17:23.** Verse 8 referred to the fact that bribes often help people get what they want. Verse 23 affirms the purpose of bribes: **to pervert** ("bend") **justice.** Judges who accept bribes secretly are **wicked** (i.e., guilty). This is ironic because judges should exercise justice, including punishing those who are guilty.

**17:24.** The first line of this verse is literally, "In front of a man of discernment (cf. v. 10) is wisdom." A wise person finds **wisdom** in obvious places whereas **a fool's eyes wander** and never discover it.

**17:25.** This verse, in repeating the thought of verse 21, uses a stronger word for **grief.** The Hebrew *ka'as* means sorrow (Ecc. 1:18; 7:3), provocation (Prov. 27:3), annoyance (12:16), or irritation. **Foolish** children bring **bitterness to** mothers.

**17:26.** This is the first of four proverbs with the words **It is not good** (cf. 18:5; 19:2; 25:27; cf. "is not good" in 24:23; 28:21). Again injustice in the courts is denounced (cf. 17:15). **To punish an innocent** person (cf. 18:5) **or to flog officials** (only kings or judges could order this to be done) who are serving with **integrity** is, like bribery (17:23), perverting the cause of justice.

**17:27-28.** A wise **man** is cautious in what he says; he thinks before he talks (cf. 14:8) and does not gab. This reveals that he **is even-tempered** (lit., "cool of spirit"; cf. the recent phrase "keeping one's cool"). Restraint in talking may **even** cause **a fool** (*ʾĕwîl*, an arrogant, hardened fool; see comments on 1:7) to be considered **wise.**

**18:1.** Some people, out of selfishness, avoid friendly relations with others. Their self-centeredness makes them enemies of **sound judgment** (cf. 3:21; 8:14). **Defies** is *lāʿaḡ*, translated "mock(s)" in 1:26; 17:5; 30:17.

**18:2.** The double trouble of the **fool** is his "closed mind" and "open mouth" (Derek Kidner, *The Proverbs: An Introduction and Commentary*, p. 127). He does not really want to gain knowledge; he only wants to share **his own** views. His mouth "gushes folly" (15:2). Yet if he would keep quiet people would think he is wise (17:28). Results of a fool's talkativeness are mentioned in 18:6-7.

**18:3.** Sinful living is accompanied by **contempt, and with shame comes disgrace.** These words of dishonor contrast with the benefits of upright, wise living, which include honor and dignity (4:7-9). In 18:3 an interesting progression is suggested: "contempt" leads to "shame" which leads to "disgrace" (cf. "disgraceful" in 10:5; 17:2).

**18:4.** Verses 4, 6-8, 20-21 refer to talking. **Words . . . are** like **deep waters,** possibly meaning water in a cistern, in that (as in 20:5) they are "hidden" or "of difficult access." Words spoken out **of wisdom,** however, are fresh and **bubbling** like water from a **fountain.** Unlike the fool who airs his unwise and therefore unhelpful ideas (18:2), a wise person's words are helpful and encouraging (cf. 10:11; 13:14).

**18:5.** Being **partial to the wicked** is an injustice condemned frequently in Proverbs (17:15, 26; 24:23; 28:21). Equally bad is depriving **the innocent of justice**

in the courts (cf. 17:23).

**18:6-7.** A fool finds himself in trouble because he speaks thoughtlessly (cf. v. 2) from a corrupt heart. **Lips** and **mouth** (v. 6) are mentioned in reverse order in verse 7. His words are so out of place that others whip him (cf. "beatings," 19:29). And his talk **is his** downfall; it ensnares him (cf. 5:22).

**18:8.** **Gossip** (cf. 11:13; 16:28; 26:20) is **like choice morsels** (lit., "things greedily devoured," a Heb. word used only here and in 26:22, which is identical with 18:8). Hearing gossip is like eating a delicacy (something not everyone else hears). Therefore, like food being digested, gossiped news is assimilated in one's **inmost parts** (i.e., is retained and remembered).

**18:9.** A person who does **his work** poorly or carelessly **is a brother** (i.e., is similar) **to one who destroys.** A poor or unfinished job differs little from a project that someone demolished; both projects are valueless.

**18:10-11.** Verses 10-12 discuss true and false security. The refuge of **the righteous** is stated in verse 10, and the refuge of **the rich** is mentioned in verse 11. The righteous turn to **the name of the Lᴏʀᴅ,** that is, to His revealed character. By putting their trust in Him they **are** as **safe** (cf. 29:25) as a person hiding from the enemy in **a strong tower.** Though **wealth** is more desirable than poverty and does help keep a person from disaster (cf. 10:15 where the first line is identical with the first line of 18:11), money cannot replace the Lord as a base of security. The wealthy *think* (**imagine**) that their wealth can protect them from harm as a high city **wall** used to protect from enemy troops, but the wealthy are wrong. Money simply cannot shield people from many problems.

**18:12-14.** It is also wrong to trust in oneself. This verse should be read with the two preceding verses. **Is proud** translates *gābāh*, "to be high, exalted, haughty"; it is related to the noun *gōbāh*, "haughtiness," in 16:18. A person who thinks he is superior to others will experience a **downfall** (cf. 11:2; 16:18; 29:23a). **Humility** on the other hand results in strength and can give a person the determination to live; it can help bring him through an illness, as physicians know. But if a person is **crushed** ("stricken or prostrated"; cf. 15:13; 17:22) inwardly, if his inner strength is gone, medicine can hardly sustain him. A physically ill person can be borne along by his **spirit,** but if his **spirit** is down too, if he is depressed, what or **who can** lift him out of his illness?

**18:15.** The **discerning** and **the wise** are eager to increase their **knowledge.** They desire it with their hearts (cf. 15:14) and they listen for it with their **ears** (cf. 23:12). "Knowledge" occurs in the Hebrew in both lines, for emphasis, though the NIV translates it only in the first line and represents knowledge in the second by the word **it.**

**18:16.** Giving **a gift** to buy one's way before influential people is close to bribery (cf. 17:8, 23) though it may be less blatant. Still 18:16 is not approving or encouraging the use of such gifts; it simply states that it is done.

**18:17.** Verses 17-19 discuss the settling of disputes. In dealing with a dispute (a lawsuit) a judge needs to hear both sides of a **case** before answering (cf. v. 13) or making a decision. The same is true of parents when their children argue.

**18:18.** One way of settling **disputes** in Bible times was by **casting the lot** (cf. 16:33; see comments on Es. 3:7; Acts 1:26). The yes-or-no decision given by lots helped avoid an ongoing conflict or litigation between **strong opponents.**

**18:19.** The reason for the caution urged in verses 17-18 is given here. When a **brother** (the word can mean either a friend or a blood relative) is **offended** in a dispute, it may be as difficult to restore his friendship as it would be to conquer a heavily **fortified city.** The estranged relationship is **like . . . barred gates,** hard to remove.

**18:20-21.** A person's words, figuratively called **the fruit of his mouth** (cf. "fruit of his lips," 12:14; 13:2) and **the harvest from his lips,** can benefit himself when his words are positive and uplifting. However, one's words (**tongue**) may bring **death** as well as **life.** A witness in a court, for example, can help determine by his words whether a defendant lives or dies. **Those who love it** (the tongue) refers to people who are talkative (cf. 10:19; 18:2; 20:19); they will suffer the consequences (**eat the fruit;** cf. 18:20) of what they say.

**18:22.** Matrimony is desirable because **a wife** is "a suitable helper" (see Gen. 2:20 and comments there). **The LORD** sanctions marriage for He states that finding a wife is a **good** thing and that God is pleased with marriage (on the noun **favor,** *rāṣôn,* see comments on 8:35; cf. 12:2).

**18:23.** Unfortunately **a poor** person's plea **for mercy** from a **rich** person is often met with harsh words. This does not excuse such a response; it simply states a fact. Arrogant treatment of less fortunate people is wrong. Indirectly this verse warns against characteristics that might lead to poverty such as laziness (6:10-11), stinginess (11:24), unteachableness (13:18), and talkativeness (14:23).

**18:24.** If a person has **many companions,** or numerous friends chosen indiscriminately, he may find himself in trouble (lit., "be broken in pieces"). A wordplay is intended here, for the Hebrew word for companion is *rēʿeh* and the word for break in pieces (**come to ruin**) is *rāʿaʿ.* It is better to have a true friend (lit., "one who loves"; cf. 17:17) than many less reliable companions.

**19:1-2.** The first line of this verse is the same as the first line of 28:6. It is **better** to be **poor** and honest (cf. 19:22b; **blameless** means morally whole; cf. 2:7, 21; 11:5; 28:10, 18; Job 1:1) **than** to be a **fool** (*kᵉsîl,* "dull, thickheaded"; cf. comments on 1:7) who speaks words that **are perverse** (*ʿiqqēš;* "twisted"; see comments on 2:15). The word for "poor" (*rāš*) means destitute or hungry; it is not a dishonorable term suggesting poverty from laziness. A fool may try to get rich by devious means, but honesty is still a better policy, even if it means going hungry.

**Zeal** (*nepeš,* normally trans. "soul") here means inner drive or vitality. It refers not so much to ecstatic exuberance as to ambitious drive which **without** adequate **knowledge** may lead to **hasty** blunders. Such haste (cf. 21:5; 29:20) may result in a person missing **the way,** that is, making mistakes. As the modern-day proverb puts it, "Haste makes waste."

**19:3.** Foolishness **ruins** a person's **life** (lit., "overturns or subverts his way"). Bringing problems on himself, a fool is responsible for his own actions. He should not blame the results of his carelessness on the will of **the LORD,** but he does.

**19:4.** Verses 4-6 speak of false friendships. The first line of verse 4 is developed in verse 6, and the second line of verse 4 is expanded in verse 7. Most wealthy persons have **many friends** (cf. 14:20b); some stay around him in the hope of getting some of his wealth. Poverty, on the other hand, though bad enough in itself, often results in loss of friends. Many people, unfortunately, want to avoid the embarrassment of associating with poor people (cf. 14:20a; 19:7).

**19:5.** One form of false friendship is to be **a false witness** in court (cf. v. 9; 14:25). Perjury, however, will eventually be punished (cf. 12:19; 21:28). **Pours out** is literally "breathes out or spews out" (also used in 6:19; 12:17, "tells"; 14:5).

**19:6. Curry favor** (lit., "stroke the face") refers to blatantly insincere flattery. Flattering **a ruler** is often done to take advantage of other people, sometimes to pervert justice. The rich, with money to buy friends, are subject to many such offers of "friendship."

**19:7.** In contrast with the rich (v. 6), **a poor** person often cannot find **friends** (cf. 14:20). In fact he is a nuisance even to **his relatives.** His efforts to find a friend are often unsuccessful because people **avoid him** (cf. 19:4).

**19:8. Wisdom** translates *lēḇ* (lit., "heart") which here means "sense" (rendered "understanding" in 15:32). Living sensibly shows that a person **loves his . . . soul.** This does not refer to vanity or narcissism but to genuine concern for one's destiny. **Cherishes** is literally, "keeps, guards, or preserves" (cf. 19:16). To keep watch over one's **understanding** results in benefits to one's soul (8:35-36); he **prospers** (cf. 16:20) spiritually and emotionally (as well as materially).

**19:9.** This verse is identical to verse 5, except for the last verb. Apparently this thought is repeated because of the seriousness of lying in court.

**19:10. Luxury** is "inappropriate" (the meaning of **not fitting**) for fools (or is honor appropriate, as stated in 26:1). But even more inappropriate is **a slave** in a position of rulership over those who ought to be ruling (cf. 17:2; Ecc. 10:7). A slave is probably unqualified to lead so his leadership position is inappropriate.

**19:11. Patience,** extolled several times in Proverbs (14:29a; 15:18b; 16:32; 25:15), stems from and is a mark of **wisdom** (*śēḵel,* "prudence," also used in 12:8; 13:15; 16:22, "understanding"; 23:9). In contrast is one who is hotheaded and impatient (14:17, 29b; 15:18a; 19:19; 22:24; 29:22). A prudent, patient man is not easily upset by people who offend him; in fact he overlooks offenses (cf. 12:16), knowing that to harbor resentment or attempt revenge only leads to more trouble. Overlooking them is his **glory,** that is, it is honorable.

**19:12.** A king may be enraged by some people (cf. 16:14; 20:2) but at the same time extend **favor** (*rāṣôn,* "goodwill, pleasure"; see comments on 8:35) to others. The contrast is as great as that between the ominous **roar of a lion** (cf. 28:15) and the refreshing **dew** (cf. rain cloud in 16:15).

**19:13. A foolish son** (cf. 10:1; 15:20; 17:21, 25) brings **ruin** (lit., "chasm") to his father; a foolish son is like an overwhelming catastrophe that sucks a person into a deep pit. Fathers with foolish sons can testify to the engulfing agony that sinks them into depression and despair.

**A quarrelsome wife** is a problem too. This is the first of five references in Proverbs to a quarrelsome wife (lit., "quarreling of a wife"; cf. 21:9, 19; 25:24; 27:15). She **is like a constant dripping** (these two words in Heb. occur only here and in 27:15) as her quarreling continues relentlessly, is irritating, and is difficult to restrain (27:16). Crawford H. Toy summarized an Arab proverb: "Three things make a house intolerable: *tak* (the leaking through of rain), *nak* (a wife's nagging), and *bak* (bugs)" (*A Critical and Exegitical Commentary on the Book of Proverbs,* p. 373). The word for quarrelsome (*māḏôn*) is used more often in Proverbs than in any other Old Testament book. It is also translated "dissension" (6:14, 19; 10:12; 15:18; 28:25; 29:22), "disputes" (18:18-19), "quarrel(s)" (17:14; 22:10; 26:20), and "strife" (23:29).

**19:14.** A young man may receive part or all of his parents' estate by virtue of his having been born into their family. **A prudent wife,** however, is **from the LORD** (cf. 18:22). This is a strong statement in a culture in which fathers often selected wives for their sons. Probably then 19:14b refers to God's providence in guiding fathers who selected their future daughters-in-law. Interestingly a prudent wife is seen in contrast with a quarrelsome wife (v. 13).

**19:15.** The words **deep sleep** refer to a heavy sleep (cf. Job 4:13; 33:15) sometimes induced by God (Gen. 2:21; 15:12; 1 Sam. 26:12). **Laziness** can cause a person to be so inactive that he easily falls into a deep sleep, totally oblivious to the precious time he is losing (cf. Prov. 20:13). A **shiftless man** is literally, "a soul (or person) of laxness" (*r<sup>e</sup>miyyâh* is used four times in Prov. and once elsewhere, Jer. 48:10, "lax"). Laziness leading to hunger is also seen in Proverbs 6:9-11.

**19:16.** The words **obeys** and **guards** are the same in Hebrew, and may be rendered "keeps" (cf. comments on v. 8). To keep, that is, to obey **instructions** (cf. v. 20) is self-preserving; to do the opposite is self-destructive (1:32; 6:32; also see "ruin" in 10:8, 10, 14, 29; 13:3). To be **contemptuous of** (*bāzâh*, "to despise or disregard with contempt") **his ways** refers to either the ways of Solomon the father-teacher, or to God's ways, or to the learner's ways. In view of 19:8 the third option may be preferable.

**19:17.** Being **kind to the poor** (*dal*, "feeble, weak, helpless"; see comments on 10:15) refers to a concern that goes beyond "pity." It refers to giving a helping hand, to meeting their needs. Benevolence to the poor is encouraged in the Law (Deut. 15:7-11) and in Proverbs (Prov. 14:21b, 31b; 22:9; 28:27). Lack of such kindness is condemned (14:31a; 21:13; 22:16; 28:3, 27b). Giving to the poor is like lending **to the LORD** as it is an investment God will **reward**. God blesses people's generosity with His generosity.

**19:18.** This verse is an imperative, unlike most of the verses in Proverbs which are declarative sentences. The command, **discipline your son,** is a strong warning against parental passivity. It is consistent with 13:24; 22:15; 23:13-14. A child guilty of wrongdoings should be chastised in his early years while **there is hope** for him. To neglect such needed discipline may contribute to the child's **death**. Death refers either to capital punishment under the Law (Deut. 21:18-21) or to the danger of natural consequences accompanying the child's foolish behavior, in which he destroys himself. Death is often the lot of the fool (Prov. 1:32), the wicked (10:27), and the sluggard (21:25).

**19:19.** A **hot-tempered** person (cf. 15:18; 22:24; 29:22) repeatedly gets himself in trouble and has to **pay** for it. If a self-controlled person would **rescue him** from his penalty, the hot-tempered person would probably take advantage of that help so that the kindness would **have to** be repeated. A hot-tempered person, in other words, does not learn. Like many undisciplined sons, he is incorrigible.

**19:20.** Listening (see comments on 1:8) to counsel and accepting (cf. 2:1; 4:10; 10:8) **instruction** (*mûsār*, "moral correction and discipline") will make a person **wise. In the end** (cf. 5:4; 14:12) could mean the end of one's life but more likely it refers to some time after the instruction is given.

**19:21.** A person may and should make **plans** (cf. 16:1, 9) **but** God can sovereignly overrule and accomplish His **purpose** through what one seemingly plans on his own.

**19:22.** Loyalty (*ḥesed,* **unfailing love**) is a virtue people desire in others. But lying, an evidence of the absence of loyalty, is so despicable that poverty is preferred to it (cf. v. 1).

**19:23.** One who fears **the LORD** (see comments on 1:7) has **life** (cf. 11:19; 12:28) and is secure and at peace with himself and others (cf. 3:26).

**19:24.** The **sluggard** (cf. 6:6, 9; 10:26; 13:4; 15:19; 20:4; 22:13; 24:30; 26:13-16) is so lazy that, comically, he does not even have the strength to lift **his hand** from his **dish . . . to his mouth** to satisfy his hunger. This idea is repeated in almost the same words in 26:15.

**19:25.** Suffering and mistreating others are the subjects of verses 25-29. When **a mocker** is flogged (cf. v. 29), **the simple** (*peṭî;* see comments on 1:4) **learn prudence** (*'ārûm;* see comments on 15:5). But mockers do not learn (cf. 9:8; 13:1; 21:11). "The simple" are the untaught, uninitiated, open-minded, who here are warned by the public punishment of another. Whereas flogging is needed for mockers, a mere verbal **rebuke** (see comments on 1:23) is enough for **a discerning** person.

**19:26.** A grown **son** who **robs** (assaults or mistreats) **his father** (cf. 28:24) **and drives . . . his mother** off their property, **brings shame and disgrace** to himself and his society. To disregard the instruction of one's parents is bad enough, but to abuse them physically (or to curse them, 20:20) is despicable.

**19:27.** When a person stops **listening to instruction** he is not learning (cf. v. 20). Being wise is not a static state. This is the only place between 7:1 and 23:15 where the words **my son** occur.

**19:28. A corrupt witness** deliberately distorts and **mocks at justice.** The word "corrupt" is literally, *belial*, "worthless and wicked" (see comments on 6:12). A false witness (see comments on 14:5) associates with **the wicked** who gulp **down evil,** that is, pursue sin with an insatiable appetite.

**19:29. Penalties . . . and beatings** (cf. 10:3b; 14:3a; 26:3), designed to correct wayward behavior, do no good for **mockers** and **fools.** This again points up the incorrigible ways of mockers (cf. 19:25).

**20:1. Wine** and **beer** are personified as people of degraded character: **a mocker** (cf. 19:25, 29) and **a brawler.** The idea is that wine mocks the one who drinks it and beer makes him aggressive. *Yayin,* the most common word for wine, usually referred to fermented grape juice but sometimes was unfermented. Beer (*šēḵār,* rendered "strong drink" in the KJV) referred to drinks made from barley, dates, or pomegranates. It was intoxicating (Isa. 28:7) and was forbidden for priests (Lev. 10:9), Nazirites (Num. 6:1-3), and others (Isa. 5:11). Intoxicating drinks can lead people **astray,** causing them to do foolish things. Other passages in Proverbs that condemn drunkenness are 23:20-21, 29-35; 31:4-5.

**20:2.** Kings are mentioned in verses 2, 8, 26. A **king's wrath** (cf. 14:35; 16:14) **is like the roar of a lion** (cf. 19:12; 28:15). It is dangerous to anger a ruler because he has power to take an offender's **life.** In fact making *any* person angry may pose problems.

**20:3.** Avoiding **strife** is honorable, though the way some people are **quick to quarrel** would make one think they thought *quarreling* is honorable. Such people are fools. Arguments can be avoided by overlooking insults (12:16), by dropping issues that are potentially volatile (17:14), and by getting rid of mockers (22:10).

**20:4.** In the Middle East the **season** for plowing and planting is the winter, the rainy season. **A sluggard** avoids the discomfort and work of plowing a muddy field in the cold, **so at harvesttime he looks** for a crop from his field **but he has nothing.** Without effort and advance planning there are few results; lack of work leads to lack of benefits.

**20:5.** A person's plans are like **deep waters** (cf. 18:4) which a wise person can draw **out.** That is, a discerning person can help another bring to the surface his true thoughts, intentions, or motives. Often a wise counselor can help a person examine his true motives—thoughts he may not fully understand otherwise.

**20:6.** Loyalty (*ḥeseḏ,* **unfailing love**) and faithfulness are desirable qualities (cf. 3:3; 19:22), but not everyone who **claims to have** them actually does. In fact faithfulness is usually missing. Keeping one's word and being loyal to one's commitments are important.

**20:7.** Verses 7-11 refer to various kinds of conduct. Usually a **righteous man,** a person who consistently behaves aright and is **blameless** (morally whole; cf. 2:7; 10:9), has **children** who are **blessed.** His children, seeing his example of integrity, are encouraged to be the same kind of people.

**20:8.** Kings often served as chief judges (e.g., Solomon, 1 Kings 3:16-28). By carefully examining (**with his eyes**) a case, a just **king** could detect (winnow or sift **out;** cf. Prov. 20:26) **evil** motives and actions. He could not easily be fooled.

**20:9.** Some people may claim to be perfect and **without sin,** but such a claim is false. What they claim (cf. v. 6) does not match what they are. All have sinned (Rom. 3:9-12, 23; cf. 1 Kings 8:46; Ecc. 7:20).

**20:10.** One evidence of a person's impure motives and depraved actions (v. 9) is his dishonesty in business dealings (cf. v. 23). God hates (see comments on 6:16; 11:20) **differing weights and . . . measures** used in selling or buying merchandise to get more money dishonestly (see comments on 11:1; cf. 16:11).

**20:11-12.** As already indicated (v. 6), what a person says does not always indicate what he is. This is true of children as well. Their **actions** and **conduct** reveal what they are like, whether they are **pure** (cf. v. 9) **and right** (cf. v. 7). One's behavior reflects his character. Therefore it is important not only to listen with one's **ears** to what people say but also to observe with ones **eyes** what people do (v.

12). **Both** senses should be used to see if people are consistent.

**20:13.** Laziness, here spoken of as **sleep** (cf. 6:9-10; 19:15a), leads to poverty (cf. 6:11; 10:4a; 19:15b), but diligence, referred to here as staying **awake,** leads to abundance of **food** (cf. 10:4b). Sleeping when one ought to be working results in lack of food (cf. 10:5).

**20:14.** Sometimes a shrewd **buyer** will downplay to a seller the value of a product in order to get its price lowered. **Then** having bought it, the buyer brags about the "deal" he got. Though merely stated as a fact, the verse implies that this action is wrong and that a person who sells products needs to be on guard against dishonest bargain hunters.

**20:15. Gold** and **rubies,** though rare and valuable (cf. 3:13-15), are **in abundance** compared with the **rare** and valuable ability to **speak knowledge,** to speak wise, appropriate words that fit the occasion.

**20:16.** This verse is repeated verbatim in 27:13. A debtor's outer garment could be taken by a creditor as collateral to guarantee that the debtor would pay (Ex. 22:26). Here a creditor is commanded to **take the garment of** a person who cosigns **for a stranger,** especially if the stranger is **a wayward woman.** Obviously without the garment as a pledge the creditor is taking a big risk that he may never be paid by the debtor *or* the cosigner! Other Proverbs passages that refer to the danger of cosigning for debts are 6:1-5 (see comments there); 11:15; 17:18; 22:26-27.

**20:17.** The taste of **food gained** dishonestly (cf. dishonest dealings in vv. 10, 14) may at first seem **sweet** (cf. "Stolen water is sweet; food eaten in secret is delicious," 9:17) but eventually it is as unpleasant as eating **gravel.** This contrasts the short-range pleasure of sin with its long-range consequences. Sin, usually attractive in its immediate payoff, ultimately turns on its host (cf. 7:14-23).

**20:18.** Getting **advice** from others when making **plans** (cf. 15:22), particularly in warfare (cf. 11:14; 24:6; Luke 14:31), is important.

**20:19.** Since gossiping **betrays a confidence** (also stated in 11:13a), a person ought to be careful with whom he shares secrets. Gossiping is also denounced in 16:28; 18:8; 26:20, 22. So people who talk

**too much** should be avoided because they will probably divulge information that should be kept confidential.

**20:20.** In the Old Testament a person who cursed his parents violated the fifth commandment (Ex. 20:12) and committed a capital offense. Death was the penalty for cursing (and rebelling against) parents (Ex. 21:17; Lev. 20:9). To have one's **lamp . . . snuffed out** was a picturesque way of referring to death (see comments on Prov. 13:9; cf. 24:20; Job 18:5-6; 21:17). **Pitch darkness** is literally, "pupil (of the eye) of darkness," referring to the darkest part of the night (see comments on "apple" in 7:2).

**20:21. An inheritance quickly gained** may refer to getting one's inheritance prematurely by request, as in the Parable of the Prodigal Son (Luke 15:11-20) or by dishonesty (as in Prov. 19:26). Such wealth may be squandered and often squelches initiative and work. As a result, the recipient is **not . . . blessed at the end,** or later.

**20:22.** Verses 22-24 each refer to the Lord's involvement with man's actions. To take vengeance in one's hands is **wrong** (cf. 17:13; 24:29; Deut. 32:35; Rom. 12:19). It is far better to leave the punishment of injustice in the Lord's hands, for in time **He will deliver.**

**20:23.** This verse is similar to verse 10, except that in verse 10 dishonest weights and measures are referred to, whereas here dishonest **weights** and **scales** are mentioned. See the comments on 11:1.

**20:24. The Lord** guides **a man's steps** (cf. David's similar statement in Ps. 37:23), that is, God directs his decisions and conduct (cf. Prov. 16:1, 9; 19:21). Since God has the ultimate "say" in one's life, it is often difficult for a person to **understand** fully **his own way.**

**20:25.** Making rash promises without thinking them through is dangerous (cf. Deut. 23:21-23; Ecc. 5:4-5). Making a vow **rashly** and *then* considering what he did can get a person in as much trouble as if he stepped into an animal **trap.** It is better to think before acting.

**20:26.** Kings are responsible to separate **the wicked** from the righteous and to try to correct the behavior of the wicked by inflicting punishment. The first of these responsibilities is suggested by winnowing (cf. v. 8) and the second by

**threshing.** In farming, grain is threshed before it is winnowed. In threshing, a sledge with spikes is pulled **over** the stalks of grain to separate the grain from the stalks and to free the seeds from the seed coverings (the chaff). In winnowing the farmer tosses up the grain so that the wind can carry away the unwanted chaff. A **king** (or other ruler) should see that the wicked are detected and punished. This is important in maintaining order and justice.

**20:27.** A king ferrets out sinners (v. 26) and **the LORD** ferrets out one's inner heart. Just as a **lamp** shows up what is in the darkness, so God reveals what is in man's **spirit** and **searches out his inmost being** (cf. v. 30).

**20:28.** Love (ḥesed, "loyal love"; cf. v. 6) **and faithfulness** (cf. 3:3; 14:22; 16:6) are necessary requirements for an effective ruler. Loyalty (**love**) keeps him on the **throne** (cf. 16:12); disloyalty and unreliability could cause people to replace him with a different ruler.

**20:29.** In Hebrew culture the **young** and **the old** each had a particular excellence not possessed by the other. The young took pride in **their** physical **strength,** the older in their wisdom, revealed by their **gray hair** (cf. 16:31).

**20:30.** The purpose of corporal punishment (**blows . . . wounds . . . beatings**) is not to inflict pain but to veer one's conduct from sin. Such punishment, however, is not merely to change a person's conduct out of fear of physical pain but to help him mature (to **purge** his **inmost being**; cf. v. 27).

**21:1.** Chapter 21 begins (vv. 1-3) and ends (vv. 30-31) with references to the Lord. Verses 2, 8, 26, 28 of chapter 20 referred to kings. Now again the king is mentioned. The heart of the king is **in** God's **hand** (cf. Ecc. 9:1) as are the plans of all people (cf. Prov. 16:1, 9). A farmer directs water by digging canals. Similarly **the LORD** directs the hearts of kings, as, for example, Pharaoh (Ex. 10:1-2), Tiglath-Pileser (Isa. 10:5-7), Cyrus (Isa. 45:1-6), and Artaxerxes (Ezra 7:21; Neh. 2:1-8). God is sovereign (cf. Prov. 21:30).

**21:2.** Divine involvement in man's heart is not limited to kings (v. 1). This verse is almost the same as 16:2. A person may think nothing is wrong with his **ways** (conduct; cf. 12:15), **but the LORD** knows what is in his **heart.** "Man looks at the outward appearance, but the LORD looks at the heart" (1 Sam. 16:7). The Lord accurately evaluates (**weighs;** cf. Prov. 16:2; 24:12) one's motives and tests them (17:3). God is sovereign (21:1) and also omniscient (v. 2).

**21:3.** God prefers people's obedience—their doing **what is right** (cf. v. 7) **and just**—over their **sacrifice.** In Israel involvement in the sacrificial system was no substitute for the "sacrifice" of righteous living (cf. 1 Sam. 15:22). **The LORD** detested the hypocrisy in a wicked person who brought an animal sacrifice to Him (cf. Prov. 15:8; 21:27).

**21:4.** Eight times in this chapter the wicked are referred to (vv. 4, 7, 10, 12 [twice], 18, 27, 29). Arrogance (cf. **haughty eyes** in 6:17) and pride (cf. 21:24), as well as hypocrisy (v. 3), is what the wicked thrive on. But pride is **sin.** Pride is **the lamp of the wicked,** that is, it is their very life (see comments on 13:9; cf. 20:20; 24:20).

**21:5.** Verses 5 and 6 refer to wealth. A person who diligently and carefully **plans** his work and works his plans contrasts with a careless one who makes hasty decisions and actions without thinking them through. The one results in **profit** and the other in **poverty** (cf. 14:23). As in 10:4, **diligent** work is associated with wealth. Diligence and laziness are contrasted in 12:24, 27; 13:4, and being hasty is also mentioned in 19:2; 29:20.

**21:6.** Verses 6-8 refer to the wicked—their lying, violence, and devious actions. Wealth (**a fortune**) acquired in dishonest ways (by **lying**) will not last (cf. 10:2; 13:11); it will fade quickly like a **vapor** (cf. 23:4-5; 27:24). **And a deadly snare** is the way some Hebrew manuscripts, the Septuagint, and the Vulgate read, but most Hebrew manuscripts read "seekers of death" or "for those who seek death." The thought is either that money gained dishonestly will ensnare rather than bless a person, ultimately bringing him to his death, or that seeking money dishonestly is like seeking or pursuing death.

**21:7.** People who are guilty of **violence** to others will find that it will boomerang (just as evil talk does, 12:13); eventually they themselves will be dragged away like fish caught in a net. In Habakkuk 1:15 the verb gārar (**drag . . . away**) is used of catching and dragging fish in a net. **The wicked** will be punished because even though they know **what is right** they **refuse to do** it.

**21:8. Devious** and **upright** describe the conduct **of the guilty** and **the innocent,** respectively. The Hebrew words for "guilty" and "devious" occur only here in the Old Testament. This verse, in antithetical parallelism, contrasts the crookedness of guilty people with the uprightness (straightforwardness or "rightness") of godly people. In 20:11 "innocent" (*zak*) is translated "pure," and "upright" (*yāšār*) is translated "right." Interestingly in 21:8 the Hebrew for "guilty" is *wāzār* and immediately following it is the similar-sounding Hebrew word for "but . . . the innocent" (*wᵉzak*).

**21:9.** The statement about **a quarrelsome wife** is repeated in 25:24. Similar thoughts are stated in 19:13; 21:19; 27:15-16. Verses 9, 19 of chapter 21 are 2 of the 19 **better . . . than** verses in Proverbs (see comments on 12:9). The point made in 21:9, 19 is the preference of living in cramped quarters (**on a corner of** a flat **roof,** v. 9) or in a desolate area ("a desert," v. 19) where one can at least have peace and quiet rather than in **a** spacious **house with** an argumentative, contentious wife. A wife who causes strife makes a home unpleasant and undesirable.

**21:10. The wicked** person **craves evil** as if he were addicted to it (cf. 4:16). He is mean even to those near him (**his neighbor**).

**21:11.** As stated in 19:25 (a verse almost identical with 22:11) the public punishment of a scoffer may cause **the simple** (*peṭî,* "naive, openminded") to become wise.

**21:12. The Righteous One** refers to God, not man, because only He fully knows what **the wicked** do and can bring them **to ruin** (or, "calamity"). **Brings** is literally "overthrows or subverts" (cf. 13:6; 19:3, "ruins"; 22:12).

**21:13.** A person who heartlessly disregards the needs of **the poor** (*dal,* "feeble, weak, helpless"; see comments on 10:15) is wicked (21:10-12). **He** himself **will** be disregarded when he is in need.

**21:14.** Giving someone **a gift** may help calm his **anger** for the recipient senses that the gift evidences love or at least concern. Even a secret **bribe** works to alleviate **wrath** (cf. 17:8). This does not condone bribery (cf. Ex. 23:8; Deut. 16:19); it simply states a fact.

**21:15.** Verses 15 and 16 refer to punishment of evil. Only **the righteous** can welcome **justice** because **evildoers** are its victims. **Terror** translates *mᵉhittâh* ("dismay, ruin, undoing"), a word used more in Proverbs than in any other Bible book (cf. 10:14-15, 29; 13:3; 14:28; 18:7, "undoing").

**21:16.** Being unwise is pictured as straying **from the path of understanding** (*śākal,* "being prudent"). Deliberately turning one's back on wise, godly living results in death. **The dead** translates *rᵉpā'îm,* as in 2:18; 9:18 (see comments on Job 26:5). An unwise person leaves the company of the wise only to find himself **in the company of** dead people!

**21:17.** Loving **pleasure** (the word rendered "joy" in v. 15) results in poverty. *Maḥsôr* is yet another word for being poor. It means "deficient, destitute, or in need." It is used in Proverbs more often than in any other Old Testament book (6:11; 11:24; 14:23; 21:5, 17; 22:16; 24:34; 28:27). Proverbs 21:17a does not argue for a dismal, stoic life, but against living *only* for pleasure and self. If a person continues to use up his **wine and oil,** he will not become rich.

**21:18.** This verse does not mean that **the wicked** redeem **the righteous.** Instead it may mean that the wicked who have caused the righteous to suffer will themselves suffer and will thereby "set free" (**become a ransom for**) the righteous, for the godly will no longer suffer at the hands of the wicked.

**21:19.** On the **quarrelsome . . . wife** see comments on verse 9 (also cf. 19:13; 25:24; 27:15).

**21:20.** A **wise** person **stores** up **food** like an ant preparing for winter (6:6-8), **but a foolish** person is shortsighted. Caring only for the pleasures of the present time, he does not save for the future; he consumes **all** his food and therefore has nothing to eat between harvests.

**21:21.** Being righteous and loyal (*ḥesed,* **love**) results in **life** (cf. 3:18, 22; 4:13, 22; 8:35), **prosperity** (cf. 3:2, 16; 8:18; 13:21; 15:6; 28:25), **and honor** (3:16, 35; 4:8; 8:18). All three of these blessings are also cited in 22:4 (cf. Matt. 6:33).

**21:22.** A **wise** person is able to conquer **the mighty** (cf. 24:5). One whose strength is his wise, godly character is pictured as conquering another who trusts in physical fortifications. Wisdom gives strength and safety (as well as the blessings mentioned in 21:21).

**21:23.** This verse is similar to 13:3. **Guards** and **keeps** translate the same Hebrew word. Being careful and wise in what one says is a way of keeping out of trouble (cf. 12:13; 14:3).

**21:24.** Three words for pride describe the **mocker** (cf. v. 11; 13:1; 14:6; 19:29; 22:10): **proud . . . arrogant . . . pride.** The first and third words are related (*zēḏ* and *zāḏôn*), and the Hebrew word for "arrogant" is *yāhîr*, used only here and in Habakkuk 2:5. The Hebrew uses even two other words for haughty and proud in Proverbs 21:4. Mocking shows that a person thinks he is superior to others. This attitude is detestable (cf. 16:5) to God and others!

**21:25-26.** Both of these verses speak of a lazy person, a sluggard (see comments on 6:6, 9). He longs for things, but by refusing **to work** he eventually starves. In contrast to the lazy who long for things but do not have them, **the righteous** have and willingly give.

**21:27.** As stated in 15:8 God detests sacrifices brought by **wicked** people, for they are hypocritical. Their hearts do not match their actions. But it is even worse when they intentionally have **evil** motives in bringing sacrifices, perhaps going to the priests with pride or deceit.

**21:28.** Repeatedly Proverbs speaks against perjury, giving **false witness** in court (6:19; 12:17; 14:5, 25; 19:5, 9; 25:18). Both the false witness and the judge or others who follow his line **will be destroyed.** God punishes dishonesty!

**21:29.** In his arrogance and hypocrisy **a wicked** person **puts up a bold front.** He tries to persuade people to believe him, often by deceit and lies. On the other hand a righteous (**upright**; cf. vv. 8, 18) person reflects on his conduct, seeking to be honest, nonhypocritical, and consistent in all he does. His desire to be sure (**gives thought to** is lit., "makes sure or establishes") that his actions are right contrasts sharply with the bullheaded bravado of a wicked person who exercises no caution.

**21:30.** Human wisdom is no match against God's wisdom. **No wisdom** or plans of any person can ultimately thwart

the Lord's plans, for He is sovereign (cf. vv. 1-2; Job 42:2) and all-wise.

**21:31.** Human effort, like human wisdom (v. 30), has its limitations. It is useless to fight against God (v. 30), or without Him (v. 31). Soldiers may use horses in **battle, but** the superiority of a cavalry unit against foot soldiers is no guarantee of **victory.** That comes only from **the LORD,** who can turn battles His way in spite of man's efforts (cf. Pss. 20:7; 33:17).

**22:1.** Having **a good name** (cf. 3:4; Ecc. 7:1), that is, an honorable reputation because of good character, is to be valued far above having much wealth. **Riches** are useless (cf. Prov. 1:19; 10:2, 13:11) if in gaining them one ruins his character.

**22:2.** The **poor** are mentioned several times in this chapter (vv. 2, 7, 9, 16, 22). A person may acquire wealth (v. 1) but that does not completely separate him from the poor, for both are creatures whose **Maker** (cf. 14:31) is **the LORD.** God therefore is concerned about everyone, regardless of their economic status.

**22:3.** This verse is repeated in 27:12, and a similar thought is stated in 14:16. This is another contrast between the **prudent** (*'ārûm*, "shrewd in a good sense"; see comments on 12:23) and **the simple** (*peṯî*, "naive, untaught"). The one is aware of **danger** and wisely avoids it (cf. 22:5); the other may see danger **but** puts forth no effort to avoid it, so he suffers **for it.** This is illustrated in 7:7-23.

**22:4. Humility and the fear of the LORD** go together (cf. 15:33). A person cannot be fearing God (worshiping, trusting, obeying, and serving Him) and be filled with selfish pride at the same time. **Wealth . . . honor, and life** result from fearing God, and as in 21:21 (see comments there) they also come from righteous living. So the fear of the Lord and righteousness are closely related.

**22:5. The wicked** have problems; **thorns** (cf. 15:19) **and snares** (cf. 21:6) are **in** their **paths.** Like thorns, their conduct keeps them from getting ahead, and like snares they are stopped like a trapped animal. A wise person, on the other hand, being aware of those consequences (cf. 22:3) is cautious and avoids the paths of the wicked.

**22:6.** This is perhaps the best-known verse in Proverbs on child training. The other verses on child-rearing (13:24;

19:18; 22:15; 23:13-14; 29:17) are all on discipline. The Hebrew word for **train** (*ḥānak*) means to dedicate. It is used of dedicating a house (Deut. 20:5), the temple (1 Kings 8:63; 2 Chron. 7:5), and an image (Dan. 3:2). The noun *ḥănukkâh* speaks of the dedication of an altar (Num. 7:10; 2 Chron. 7:9) and of the walls of Jerusalem (Neh. 12:27). Only in Proverbs 22:6 is the verb translated "train." *Ḥānak* seems to include the idea of setting aside, narrowing, or hedging in. The word is sometimes used in the sense of "start." Child-training involves "narrowing" a child's conduct away from evil and toward godliness and starting him in the right direction. Gleason L. Archer points out that this Hebrew verb is similar to the Egyptian *ḥ-n-k*, which means "to give to the gods" or "to set up something for divine service." He suggests that in verse 6 this gives "the following range of possible meanings: 'Dedicate the child to God,' 'Prepare the child for his future responsibilities,' 'Exercise or train the child for adulthood' " (*Encyclopedia of Bible Difficulties*. Grand Rapids: Zondervan Publishing House, 1982, p. 252).

**In the way he should go** is literally, "upon the mouth of his way." "Upon the mouth of" is a Hebrew idiom meaning "according to" or "in accord with." A servant would respond "upon the mouth of" or at the command of his superior. But what does "the way" mean? Scholars have interpreted this differently. Does it mean according to the way he *ought* to go (KJV, NASB, NIV) either vocationally or morally? Or does it mean, as others have suggested, according to the demands of his personality, conduct, or stage in life? Since "way" in Proverbs does not mean personality or stage in life, it is preferable to say that "way" means *proper* way, the path of wise, godly living, which is emphasized frequently in Proverbs—basically the way of wisdom. It is from this proper behavior pattern or godly lifestyle that he will not turn **when he is old,** that is, when he is grown (attains adulthood).

Some parents, however, have sought to follow this directive but without this result. Their children have strayed from the godly training the parents gave them. This illustrates the nature of a "proverb." A proverb is a literary device whereby a general truth is brought to bear on a specific situation. Many of the proverbs are not absolute guarantees for they express truths that are necessarily conditioned by prevailing circumstances. For example, verses 3-4, 9, 11, 16, 29 do not express promises that are *always* binding. Though the proverbs are generally and usually true, occasional exceptions may be noted. This may be because of the self-will or deliberate disobedience of an individual who chooses to go his own way—the way of folly instead of the way of wisdom (see v. 15 and comments there). For that he is held responsible. It *is* generally true, however, that most children who are brought up in Christian homes, under the influence of godly parents who teach and live God's standards (cf. Eph. 6:4), follow that training.

**22:7.** Unfortunately a **rich** person may "lord it over" a **poor** person, **and** a **lender** is master of **the borrower.** This suggests that a person should be careful before making a large loan. He may become like a slave, a poor, oppressed person.

**22:8.** A person **who sows** seeds of **wickedness** (*'awlâh*, "injustice") will reap a harvest of **trouble** (*'āwen*, "trouble or sorrow," rendered "harm" in 12:21). Trouble is the inevitable result of sin (cf. Hosea 10:13; Gal. 6:7). **Fury** renders a word that means "overflowing rage." What the wicked achieve through their fury or wrath **will** not last; their manipulative techniques will be exhausted. This thought is encouraging to the oppressed. The trouble the wicked bring on others will come on themselves.

**22:9.** A **generous man** is, literally, "a good eye." (In 23:6 and 28:22 "a stingy man" is, lit., "an evil eye.") Willingness to share **food with the poor** (*dal*, "feeble, weak, helpless") shows that a person is genuine; he looks at others with the desire to help them, not to take advantage of them (cf. generosity to the poor in Deut. 15:10; Prov. 14:21, 31; 28:27).

**22:10.** A **mocker** (cf. 9:7-8, 12; 13:1; 14:6; 15:12; 19:25, 29; 21:11, 24; 24:9) causes **strife** (contention), quarreling, **and insults** (*qālôn*, "disgrace"; used eight times in Prov. and only nine times elsewhere). So by removing a troublemaker, trouble also leaves.

**22:11.** Purity of motives and thought (**a pure heart**) and **gracious** words are appreciated by a **king** (cf. 14:35; 16:13). Naturally he wants to have people like that around him. So purity and graciousness are advantageous; they help give a person a friendship with leaders in high positions.

**22:12.** In His omniscience (cf. **eyes of the LORD** in 15:3) God guards **knowledge.** On the other hand **unfaithful** (lit., "treacherous") **words** will be overturned or subverted (*sālap;* cf. 13:6; 19:3; 21:12). To be wise, then, is to be under God's protection. To be unwise and treacherous, even in what one says, is to be on a path that will end in frustration.

**22:13.** The extreme excuses made by a lazy person to avoid work are ridiculous. (On the word **sluggard,** see comments on 6:6.) Most probably **a lion** (cf. 26:13) would not be roaming the streets of an Israelite town. And if a lazy person actually feared being **murdered** he would *never* go outside!

**22:14.** To listen to the words **of an adulteress** and be seductively led into sin by her (cf. 2:16-22; 5:3-6; 7:10-23) is like falling into a **pit** (cf. 23:27) from which there is no escape. The dire consequences of adultery are part of God's punishment in His **wrath** on sin.

**22:15.** Though **folly** (from *'ĕwîl,* an arrogant, flippant, hardened fool) **is . . . in the heart of a child . . . discipline** can help expel that kind of attitude and replace it with wisdom. "Discipline" (*mûsār*) is moral correction, which includes spankings (**the rod**; cf. 13:24; 23:13-14; 29:15), verbal correction, and other forms of discipline.

**22:16.** Buying influence or favoritism with **gifts** (cf. 17:23) for those who do not need them (**the rich**) while oppressing **the poor** (*dal,* "feeble, weak, helpless"; see comments on 10:15) to gain **wealth** will boomerang. Ironically such actions result *not* in wealth but in poverty!

## IV. The Sayings of the Wise Men (22:17–24:34)

This section falls into two parts. The first part (22:17–24:22) is introduced as "the sayings of the wise" (22:17), and the second part (24:23-34) is introduced by the statement, "These also are the sayings of the wise" (24:23). In style this section includes at least 20 instances in which two verses express a complete thought, rather than one verse as in

10:1–22:16 (see, e.g., 22:17-18, 20-21; 23:1-2). Also seven verses have three lines rather than the normal two lines (22:29; 23:5, 29, 31; 24:14, 27, 31), and two verses each have four lines (23:7; 24:12). "My son" occurs 5 times (23:15, 19, 26; 24:13, 21) whereas it occurs 15 times in chapters 1–9 and only once (19:27) in 10:1–22:16 and twice (27:11; 31:2) in the remainder of the book. "A wise son" occurs once (23:24) in 22:17–24:34 compared with 5 times in 10:1–22:16.

Many of the sayings are warnings, using the words "do not" (see 22:22, 24, 26, 28; 23:3-4, 6, 9-10, 13, 17, 20, 22-23, 31; 24:1, 15, 17, 19, 21, 28-29). Interestingly each of the 30 sayings in 22:22–24:22 includes a reason for the warning or other advice and several of the sayings in 24:23-34 include reasons.

The sayings in 22:17–24:34 were written by wise men other than Solomon, and were compiled either in his lifetime or later. As stated in 22:20, the first portion (22:17–24:22) includes 30 sayings. The outline in the comments on 22:17–24:22 shows how this section may be divided into 30 sayings (e.g., 22:22-23, the first saying; 22:24-25, the second saying).

Many scholars have maintained that these wise men borrowed from the Egyptian work *The Instruction of Amen-em-Ope,* which has 30 sections. However, this seems unlikely for several reasons:

(1) The sayings in the Egyptian work are much longer than those in Proverbs. The 30 chapters in *Amen-em-Ope* range in length from 7 to 26 lines, whereas most of the sayings in Proverbs are 4 lines long with a few being shorter and a few a little longer.

(2) The date of *The Instruction of Amen-em-Ope* is disputed. John A. Wilson writes, "A date anywhere between the 10th and 6th centuries B.C. is possible, with some weight of evidence for the 7th–6th centuries" (*Ancient Near Eastern Texts Relating to the Old Testament,* ed. James B. Pritchard. Princeton, N.J.: Princeton University Press, 1955, p. 421). If this work were written 500 or 600 years before Christ, its date was then much later than Solomon's time (he reigned 971–931 B.C.) but later than Hezekiah's reign (715–686 B.C.). The latest time indication in Proverbs is Hezekiah's day (25:1). Proverbs then could not have copied from the Egyptian work.

(3) An unusually small number of verses in Proverbs 22:22–24:22 are similar to the work from Egypt. Pritchard quotes D.C. Simpson, who suggests the following parallels (*Ancient Near Eastern Texts Relating to the Old Testament*, p. 424, n. 46).

| Proverbs | The Instruction of Amen-em-Ope |
|---|---|
| 1st saying, 22:22-23 | Chapter 2, 4:4-5 |
| 2nd saying, 22:24-25 | Chapter 9, 11:13-14 |
| 3rd saying, 22:26-27 | Chapter 9, 13:8-9 |
| 4th saying, 22:28 | Chapter 6, 7:12-13 |
| 5th saying, 22:29 | Chapter 30, 27:16-17 |
| 6th saying, 23:1-3 | Chapter 23, 23:13-18 |
| 7th saying, 23:4-5 | Chapter 7, 9:14–10:5 |
| 8th saying, 23:6-7 | Chapter 11, 14:5-10 |
| 8th saying, 23:8 | Chapter 11, 14:17-18 |
| 9th saying, 23:9 | Chapter 21, 22:11-12 |
| 10th saying, 23:10-11 | Chapter 6, 7:12-15; 8:9-10 |
| 25th saying, 24:11 | Chapter 8, 11:6-7 |

Only 11 of the 30 Proverbs sayings have similarities to 9 of the *Amen-em-Ope* chapters. This can hardly be considered an extensive borrowing or dependence of Proverbs on the Egyptian work. Either *Amen-em-Ope* borrowed from Proverbs or each was written independently of the other. Using the number 30 may simply have been a common literary device. Any similarities between the secular Egyptian work and the Bible do not annul the Scriptures' verbal inspiration, for God the Holy Spirit guided wise men to write exactly what He wanted written in Proverbs, even if a few of those sayings were similar to proverbial sayings in Egypt.

## A. Thirty sayings of the wise (22:17–24:22)

### 1. INTRODUCTION TO SAYINGS 1-10 (22:17-21)

**22:17-19.** The exhortations in verse 17 to **pay attention** (cf. 4:1, 20; 5:1; 7:24), **listen** (cf. 1:8; 4:1, 10, 20; 5:1, 7; 7:24; 8:32-33), and **apply your heart** (cf. "applying your heart," 2:2) are calls to pursue and obey what is presented in the 30 sayings. Reasons for the exhortation are given in verses 18-19: **it is pleasing** to memorize the sayings (**keep them in your heart**) and to be able to quote and talk about

them (**have . . . them . . . on your lips**) because they encourage people to **trust . . . in the** LORD.

**22:20-21.** On the **30 sayings** see comments under the heading "IV. The Sayings of the Wise Men (22:17–24:34)." The **counsel** in these **sayings** comes from the **knowledge** of the wise men whose **words** were **true.** Again (cf. 22:18-19) a reason is stated: **so that** the learner **can give sound answers.** "Sound" translates "reliable." The same word, *'ĕmet*, is rendered **reliable** in verse 21. The one **who sent you** may be the learner's teacher or employer.

### 2. SAYINGS 1-10 (22:22–23:11)

**22:22-23.** *The 1st saying.* These verses give a strong warning against taking advantage of the **poor** (cf. 14:31). **The poor** (*dal*, "feeble, weak, helpless") and **the needy** are easy prey for wicked people who can get their way **in court** by bribery and false accusations. But the defenseless are defended by **the** LORD who champions their cause and justly takes from those who unjustly take from the needy.

**22:24-25.** *The 2nd saying.* The warning here is against being a friend or even associating **with a hot-tempered man** (lit., "an owner or possessor of anger"; cf. 19:19) or **one easily angered** (lit., "a man of wrath") because such an association leads a person to take on wrathful **ways,** which are foolish (14:17, 29), divisive (15:18), and sinful (29:22), and become **ensnared** (cf. 29:6), caught up in a situation which is hard to get out of.

**22:26-27.** *The 3rd saying.* The high risks in putting **up security for debts** is mentioned several times in Proverbs (6:1-5; see comments there; 11:15; 17:18; 20:16; 27:13). Striking **hands in pledge** means to confirm an agreement, like the gesture of shaking hands (see comments on 6:1). **If** a debtor fails to pay, the creditor will hound the cosigner, and if the cosigner cannot **pay,** then his furniture may be taken as payment. This serious consequence results from becoming foolishly entangled in others' financial problems.

**22:28.** *The 4th saying.* Six times the Bible mentions the sin of moving **boundary** stones (Deut. 19:14; 27:17; Job 24:2; Prov. 22:28; 23:10; Hosea 5:10). A farmer could easily increase the extent of his own land and decrease his neighbor's by moving the stones at the boundary lines.

This form of stealing violated the eighth commandment (Ex. 20:15).

**22:29.** *The 5th saying.* Being diligent and **skilled** (*māhîr* can also mean "quick or prompt") in one's **work** is the best way to influence an employer. Diligence often results in a promotion (serving **before kings** and **not** just **obscure** people). Hearing about a good worker, a king (or other leader) will want to hire him.

**23:1-3.** *The 6th saying.* When invited to a banquet hosted by a prestigious host (e.g., **a ruler**), a person ought to be humble and restrained. He should be aware of **what is** around him, and **if** he is tempted to be gluttonous (cf. "gluttons" in v. 21; 28:7) he should restrain his appetite. Humorously the guest is advised to **put a knife to** his **throat** (rather than to his food)! This does not mean he should commit suicide but that he should cut back on his gorging. **Gluttony,** interestingly, translates the Hebrew *nepeš*, which has a variety of meanings including physical life (13:3, 8), oneself (19:8; 21:23), one's appetite (16:26) or craving (10:3), and the seat of those cravings (21:10 is lit., "the wicked soul craves"). From that stems the idea of gluttony in 23:2.

Foods that are **delicacies** in a royal banquet may be **deceptive.** A ruler-host may *seem* to be friendly by serving a sumptuous meal, but in reality he may be planning to betray his guest or do him an injustice (cf. v. 7). The banquet may be a "buttering-up" occasion.

**23:4-5.** *The 7th saying.* These verses warn against overwork for the sake of gaining **riches.** This speaks not against being industrious but against consuming oneself for money. Wise **restraint** in this area (as well as in what one eats at a banquet, vv. 1-2) is needed, especially in the present day when materialism drives many people to excessive work loads in order to accumulate more money. The reason for this advice is that riches are temporary and unstable (cf. 27:24). The first part of 23:5 is literally, "If you cause your eyes to fly after it" (i.e., wealth). Ironically, flying after wealth results in wealth flying away **like an eagle.**

**23:6-8.** *The 8th saying.* Verses 1-3 advised against greedily eating food served by a generous ruler. Verses 6-8 warn against eating **food** served by **a stingy man** (lit., "an evil eye," which occurs only here and in 28:22 in the OT; cf. comments on "a generous man," lit., "a good eye," in 22:9). Craving **his delicacies** is as wrong and dangerous as craving the delicious foods served by a ruler (23:3). When a guest realizes his host is **thinking** only of **the cost** of the food while hypocritically feigning generosity (**eat and drink**), the guest is repulsed. The guest wants to **vomit up** (or spit up) the food since it was not served honestly and since he finds that his **compliments** were **wasted.**

**23:9.** *The 9th saying.* Trying to teach **a fool** (*kᵉsîl*, "dull, thickheaded, stubborn fool"; see comments on 1:7) is useless. He does **not** welcome what is said by a teacher who speaks prudently (**wisdom** renders *śēkel*, "prudence," also used in 12:8; 13:15; 16:22, "understanding"; 19:11).

**23:10-11.** *The 10th saying.* Verse 10a is identical with 22:28a, and 23:10b-11 is partially similar to 22:22-23. Stealing land from a neighbor by moving his **boundary stone** is bad enough but to take **fields** from children of widows is worse yet! The Lord, in His concern for **the fatherless** (Deut. 10:18; Pss. 10:14, 17-18; 68:5; 82:3; 146:9) opposes all who mistreat and steal from fatherless children. He is **their Defender** (*gō'ēl*, a person responsible for meeting the needs of a troubled or defenseless close relative).

### 3. INTRODUCTION TO SAYINGS 11-30 (23:12)

**23:12.** This verse serves as a break in the long string of sayings and introduces sayings 11-30 much as 22:17-21 introduced sayings 1-10. **Apply your heart** (cf. 22:17b) suggests diligence and desire for **instruction** (*mûsār*, often trans. "discipline," as it is in 23:13). Applying **your ears** is another way of saying "pay attention and listen" (cf. 22:17a).

### 4. SAYINGS 11-30 (23:13–24:22)

**23:13-14.** *The 11th saying.* Children need **discipline** (*mûsār*, "moral correction," both verbal and physical; cf. 1:2, 7). Physical punishment (by **the rod** or a stick; cf. 13:24; 22:15; 29:15) is approved in the Bible though "rod" may also be used figuratively for any form of discipline. The pain caused by spankings may make the parent and the child think the child will **die,** but that is **not** so. The punishment will actually *deliver* him **from**

physical **death** (*šᵉʾôl,* the grave), not *cause* his death.

**23:15-16.** *The 12th saying.* This appeal to **my son** (cf. vv. 19, 26) illustrates that a wise child learns from parental discipline (vv. 13-14). The truth that a **wise** rather than a foolish son gladdens his father's **heart** is also stated in 10:1; 15:20; 23:24; 27:11; 29:3. Wisdom is to be internalized in one's **heart** (cf. 23:17, 19, 26; also note v. 12; 22:17). The father's heart and **inmost being** refer to his inner self, his intellectual and emotional being. A wise heart is revealed by speaking **what is right.**

**23:17-18.** *The 13th saying.* Envying **sinners** (cf. 3:31; 24:1, 19; Ps. 37:1), wanting to do what they do, is senseless because they have no **hope** (24:20) whereas the wise and godly do. The immediate pleasure of sin cannot be compared with the ultimate **hope** associated with **the fear of the Lᴏʀᴅ** (cf. 19:23; 24:21).

**23:19-21.** *The 14th saying.* By listening and heeding his father's instruction and desiring **the right path** (proper conduct), a **son is wise.** One way to stay on "the right path" is to avoid drunkenness (see comments on **wine** in 20:1) and gluttony (cf. 23:2). These two sins cause **drowsiness,** which results in laziness and poverty. Other evils of strong **drink** are discussed in verses 29-35.

**23:22-23.** *The 15th saying.* Verses 22, 24-25 each refer to one's **father** and/or **mother.** Heeding parental instruction and advice is again encouraged. This is repeated often in Proverbs, apparently because of children's tendency to go their own ways. Wise children respect their parents **when** they are **old.** To **despise** (*bûz,* "to hold in contempt," a verb used often in Prov.; see comments on 1:7) them is to disobey the fifth commandment (Ex. 20:12). Buying **the truth** suggests spending whatever energy or financial resources are necessary to acquire truth, along with **wisdom, discipline** (*mûsār,* see comments on Prov. 23:12-13), **and understanding** (cf. 1:2-6).

**23:24-25.** *The 16th saying.* Verse 24 is another evidence that in Proverbs being **wise** (cf. v. 15) in God's view means being godly or **righteous.** Interestingly the words **has great joy** and **rejoice** translate the same Hebrew word *gîl,* and **delights** and **be glad** translate *śāmaḥ.* **The father** is said to have given the **son** life (v. 22) and

the **mother . . . gave** the son **birth.** Wise, godly living, in obedience to the parents' discipline, not only benefits the child; it also benefits the parents.

**23:26-28.** *The 17th saying.* Again the son (**My son;** cf. vv. 15, 19; 24:13, 21) was exhorted to follow his father's teaching. The words **give me your heart** (cf. 23:15, 17, 19) appeal to the son's thoughts and values so that his lifestyle (**ways**) will follow that of his father. The son's **eyes** as well as his lips (22:18) and ears (23:12) are important. What one sees, says, and hears should be pleasing to the Lord. The urgency of the father's appeal is related to the dangers of sexual waywardness (cf. 5:20; 6:24; 7:5; 20:16). Two kinds of immoral women are in view, the unmarried (the **prostitute**) and the married (the **wayward wife**). (On the Heb. words for these terms see the comments on 2:16.) Immoral women are like **a deep pit** (cf. 22:14) or a **well** in that they confine and trap men (cf. 6:27-35; 7:21-27), making it impossible for them to escape the consequences. **Men** need to be on guard against wayward women who seek to seduce them, springing on them suddenly (cf. 7:7-10) **like a bandit,** adding to the number of their victims. Of course the Bible also warns against men seducing women.

**23:29-35.** *The 18th saying.* These verses present the longest and most articulate warning in Proverbs against drunkenness (cf. vv. 20-21; 20:1; 31:4-5). Six questions call attention to emotional problems (**woe** and **sorrow**), social problems (**strife** and **complaints**), and physical problems (**bruises**—from beatings or bumping into things while staggering— and **bloodshot eyes**) that stem from lingering long **over wine** and **mixed wine** (*mimsoḵ,* used only here and in Isa. 65:11). **Wine** seems attractive (Prov. 23:31); **it is red,** sparkling, and smooth— the senses of sight and taste. But eventually (**in the end;** cf. 5:4; 14:12; 16:25; 19:20; 25:8; 28:23; 29:21) it is as devastating and painful as **a snake** bite.

Drunkenness also leads to mental problems (23:33): hallucinations and imagining **confusing** ("perverse or abnormal"; see comments on 2:12) **things.** Physically a drunkard is off balance as he walks. In his stupor he may imagine himself moving like a sailor swaying at the **top** of a ship's **rigging.** Also a drunkard is insensitive to pain when people **hit** him (cf. "bruises," 23:29). Sensing his stupor he still longs to escape by having **another drink.** Alcohol controls him; he is a slave to wine.

**24:1-2.** *The 19th saying.* Three times in these 30 sayings a warning is given against being envious of the **wicked** (cf. 23:17; 24:19; also see 3:31). In 23:17-18 and 24:19-20 the reason for not envying sinners is that their future is bleak. Here the reason is that they plan **violence** (cf. v. 8) and **talk about** the **trouble** they will bring on others (cf. 1:10-19). What is in **their hearts** comes out in **their** talk (**lips**; cf. 4:23-24).

**24:3-4.** *The 20th saying.* Sayings 20-22 pertain to wisdom. Plotting evil is mentioned a number of times in Proverbs (3:29; 6:14; 12:20; 14:22; 16:27, 30; 24:2, 8). The best policy is to stay away from such people. **By wisdom . . . understanding,** and **knowledge** houses are **built . . . established,** and **filled with . . . treasures.** This may refer to constructing literal houses or, perhaps more likely, to the undertaking of any enterprise. Folly and sin do not contribute to security and prosperity, but wisdom does. This fact contrasts with the violence mentioned in verse 2.

**24:5-6.** *The 21st saying.* Besides giving security and prosperity (vv. 3-4) wisdom provides **strength** to accomplish various tasks (cf. 21:22). **A wise** person is not self-reliant; he looks to others for counsel on how to win a battle (cf. 11:14; 20:18; also note 15:22). On the word **guidance** see comments on 1:5.

**24:7.** *The 22nd saying.* **A fool** (*'ĕwîl,* "an arrogant, hardened fool"; see comments on 1:7) cannot appreciate, comprehend, or **say** anything wise. **Wisdom** (here in the pl., as in 1:20; 9:1, for emphasis) is beyond him. Therefore **at the gate,** where legal and judicial decisions were made by wise leaders, he was (or should have been) silent.

**24:8-9.** *The 23rd saying.* A person **who** continually thinks up (cf. v. 2) **evil** schemes becomes **known as a schemer** (lit., "an owner or possessor of evil plans"; cf. "crafty" in 12:2; 14:17). Such scheming is foolish because it is sinful and leads to mockery (see comments on **a mocker** in 13:1), which people **detest** (cf. "detest" in 8:7; 16:12; 29:27).

**24:10.** *The 24th saying.* Giving in to

the pressure of **trouble** (a different word for trouble in v. 2 means "sorrow or mischief ") shows that a person's strength is limited. This may subtly suggest that person is not wise, because, as stated in verse 5, wisdom gives strength. The Hebrew includes a wordplay by placing the word for **small** (*ṣar,* "narrow, tight, restricted") immediately after the word for "trouble" (*ṣārâh*).

**24:11-12.** *The 25th saying.* Verse 10 referred to trouble that comes on a person; verses 11-12 refer to trouble that comes on others. People here who are **being** taken **to death** and **slaughter** probably are victims of unjust oppression rather than guilty people being condemned. Some people may claim they are ignorant of others' plights, but God knows who is guilty of willful ignorance and **He** will judge (**repay**) it (cf. Matt. 25:41-46). **He . . . weighs the heart** (cf. Prov. 21:2), that is, He knows and considers peoples' inner motives and thoughts. God is concerned about the plight of the poor and the helpless (cf. 22:22-23; 23:10-11).

**24:13-14.** *The 26th saying.* Much as **honey,** the sweetest substance known in the ancient Near East, **is good** and tastes **sweet,** so **wisdom is** beneficial and desirable to the soul because it gives a person **future hope** (cf. 23:18). **Honey** is mentioned six times in Proverbs (5:3; 24:13 [twice]; 25:16, 27; 27:7). **My son** occurs in the 30 sayings five times (23:15, 19, 26; 24:13, 21).

**24:15-16.** *The 27th saying.* Sayings 27-29 are warnings (**Do not**) like sayings 1-4, 6-11, 14, 18-19. Verses 15-16 warn that it is futile for **the wicked** to attempt to destroy the **righteous** and his possessions. Because of God's protection the **righteous** person recovers from robberies and attacks but the wicked who instigate such schemes (cf. vv. 2, 8) find that *they* are the ones who suffer (cf. 1:18-19). Examples of this kind of judicial boomeranging are seen in Daniel 3 and 6.

**24:17-18.** *The 28th saying.* God is disgusted with those who **gloat** over someone's failure. Gloating over the disasters experienced by the poor is condemned in 17:5; in 24:17 gloating is not even permitted when an *enemy* has a problem. Gloating may cause God to side with one's enemy and to withdraw **His wrath . . . from** that enemy. God hates gloating because it suggests a superior attitude over others.

**24:19-20.** *The 29th saying.* For the third time in the 30 sayings envy of sinners is condemned (cf. 23:17; 24:1). Fretting over what sinners have and do (cf. Ps. 37:1) and wanting to join them is wrong because they have **no future hope.** They will die (on **the lamp** being **snuffed out** see comments on 13:9). The righteous and wise, on the other hand, do have hope for the future (cf. 23:18; 24:14). **Evil** and **wicked** are used as synonyms in both verses 19 and 20.

**24:21-22.** *The 30th saying.* Fittingly, fearing **the LORD** (cf. comments on 1:7) is referred to in the last of the 30 sayings. The Lord **and the king—those two**—are the agents who punish **the rebellious** (cf. Rom. 13:1-7; 1 Peter 2:13-17). The **calamities they can bring** refer either to troubles the rebellious bring on others or, more likely, to the calamities God and the king can bring on rebels. The Hebrew word for "calamities" (*pîd*) is used only here in Proverbs and four times in Job.

## B. Additional sayings of the wise (24:23-34)

These verses present an additional six sayings of the wise men (see comments on 22:17). These proverbs discuss justice and injustice in the courts, honesty, priorities, false witnessing, revenge, and laziness.

### 1. THE FIRST SAYING (24:23-25)

**24:23-25. Partiality in judging is** condemned in Deuteronomy 1:17; 16:19; Proverbs 17:15; 18:5; 28:21. Letting **the guilty** go free **is not good** either (cf. comments on 17:26); perverting justice results in leaders being cursed and denounced. On the other hand exercising justice against **the guilty** brings judges **rich blessing;** those judges are respected and appreciated.

### 2. THE SECOND SAYING (24:26)

**24:26. An honest answer is** literally, "upright or straight words." This may tie in with verses 24-25. How are honest words and kisses alike? As **a** sincere **kiss** shows affection and is desirable, so an honest (and perhaps straightforward) answer shows a person's concern and therefore is welcomed.

### 3. THE THIRD SAYING (24:27)

**24:27.** Israelites, most of whom farmed land, needed to plow and sow seed (to **get** their **fields ready;** cf. comments on vv. 30-31) before they attended to more immediate creature comforts. Whether **house** should be taken literally (constructing a house) or figuratively (getting married and having a family), the principle is the same: it is important to have one's priorities straight.

### 4. THE FOURTH SAYING (24:28)

**24:28.** Verses 23b-25 spoke of judges; verses 28-29 comment on the witnesses in court. Giving false testimony—and thereby harming someone's reputation or unjustly acquiring things from him, or even taking his life—is frequently forbidden in Proverbs (see comments on 6:19). It is prohibited by the ninth commandment (Ex. 20:16). Being deceptive in what one says in court is wrong (see comments on "deceit" in Prov. 12:20).

### 5. THE FIFTH SAYING (24:29)

**24:29.** If this verse relates to verse 28 (rather than being a separate saying), then it refers specifically to revenge gained through perjury. If it is a separate saying, then it is a more general warning against revenge (cf. Deut. 32:35; Ps. 94:1; Prov. 20:22; Rom. 12:19; Heb. 10:30).

### 6. THE SIXTH SAYING (24:30-34)

Some of these statements about the sluggard are similar to those in 6:6-11 (see comments there). The writer made some observations about laziness (24:30-31), reflected on it (v. 32), and drew some conclusions about its consequences which he addressed to the sluggard (vv. 33-34).

**24:30-31. The sluggard,** a word used 14 times in Proverbs, is here called a person **who lacks judgment** (see comments on 6:32; 10:13). The lazy person did not get his fields ready (cf. 24:27). He so neglected them that **thorns** and **weeds** grew up (cf. 15:19) leaving no room for crops. And **the stone wall** around **the field** had not been repaired.

**24:32-34.** As the writer of these verses reflected on what he **observed,** he **saw** the **lesson:** indolence—staying in bed and resting when it is time to work—leads to **poverty** (see comments on 6:11). With no crops to harvest, a lazy person has nothing to eat and nothing to sell to others for income. Suddenly he awakens to the reality of the plight; poverty comes on him surprisingly **like a bandit** or suddenly like an attacking soldier. Interestingly the 30 sayings begin with a reference to the poor (22:22; *dal*, "feeble, weak, helpless") and the additional 6 sayings end with a reference to poverty (*maḥsōr*; "lacking, being in need").

## V. Proverbs of Solomon Collected by Hezekiah's Men (chaps. 25–29)

**25:1.** Hezekiah's **men,** perhaps royal scribes, **copied** (lit., "removed," i.e., from one book or scroll to another) more than 100 of Solomon's **proverbs.** This was about 250 years after **Solomon** wrote them. Hezekiah's men grouped many of these proverbs in units of similar thoughts.

**25:2.** Verses 2-7 are sayings about the king. Though the king probably was Solomon, these proverbs applied to all kings of Israel and Judah. **God** has chosen not to reveal everything about Himself and His plans (cf. Deut. 29:29). This means that **kings,** to make proper decisions, must investigate matters fully. Whereas God delights in concealing some things, kings delight in being investigative.

**25:3.** This verse is the first of many verses in chapters 25–26 that make comparisons, using the words "like" or **as;** 12 are in chapter 25 (vv. 3, 11-14, 18-20, 23, 25-26, 28) and 13 in chapter 26 (see comments on 26:1).

God hides some of His knowledge from kings, and **kings** hide some of their knowledge from their subjects. Rulers, responsible for knowing what is going on and for investigating issues fully (25:2), need not reveal everything they know. "Search out" in verse 2 and **unsearchable** in verse 3 connect these two verses.

**25:4-5.** Just as undesirable slag is removed **from . . . silver** (cf. 27:21), so **wicked** people are to be removed **from the** king. Getting rid of wicked assistants (cf. 20:8, 26) enables a king to have a righteous reign. The last line of 25:5 is nearly identical to that of 16:12.

**25:6-7.** It is wrong for a person to try to promote himself to a king, claiming to be **great** when he is not. **It is** far **better for** the king to promote him **than for** the king **to humiliate** him in front of a **noble-man** whose position the status seeker is desiring. Christ illustrated this in a parable (Luke 14:7-10).

**25:8.** In Hebrew the words **seen with your eyes** are the last words of verse 7 (cf. KJV, NASB). Some versions (e.g., NIV, RSV) put those words with verse 8. The phrase makes verse 7 long for a proverb and also makes far less sense there than with verse 8.

Verse 8 warns against **hastily** taking another person **to court** (cf. 24:28). The reason is that the plaintiff may lose the case and be ashamed, for what he thought he saw may not have been what actually took place.

**25:9-10.** In providing evidence against a neighbor in a court case a plaintiff may be forced to **betray** a friend's **confidence.** As a result the friend may shame him and the plaintiff may have an irretrievable loss of **reputation.** It is risky business to accuse others publicly in court.

**25:11-12.** An appropriate and properly timed **word** (cf. 15:23; 24:26)—which sometimes may be a **rebuke** (see comments on 1:23)—can be attractive and valuable, like **gold** apples set against a **silver** sculpture or carving, or like a **gold** earring **or** other **ornament.**

**25:13. Snow** in the mountains (not snow falling on the crops in the dry season) is refreshing during the heat of **harvesttime.** Similarly **a trustworthy messenger** is refreshing to one **who** sends **him** (cf. 13:17). An unreliable messenger is referred to in 10:26 and 26:6.

**25:14. Clouds and wind** usually give farmers promise of **rain.** But if no rain comes, the farmers are keenly disappointed. Similarly people who claim they will give presents but never keep their promises are frustrating to the supposed recipients. A person ought not promise something if he knows he cannot follow through.

**25:15. Patience** and a **gentle** (lit., "soft") **tongue** (cf. 15:1) **can be** unusually influential, accomplishing far more than loss of temper and harsh words. A soft tongue breaking **a** hard **bone** is an unusual figure of speech—how can a tongue break a bone? The idea is that softly spoken words can accomplish difficult things. Also persuading **a ruler** to follow some difficult course of action takes patience.

**25:16-17.** Just as eating **too** much **honey** can cause a problem (cf. v. 27; 27:7), so visiting a neighbor **too** often may cause him to **hate** the frequent visitor. Overdoing anything can be a problem. **Seldom** is literally, "make precious," that is, "make it valuable" by its rarity. A person should refrain from frequently visiting his neighbor, to avoid being a nuisance, but he should visit enough so that his visits are valued.

**25:18.** Giving **false testimony** in court **against** a **neighbor** (see comments on 6:19) can crush, divide, or pierce like **a club . . . sword, or . . . arrow.** Lying can wound a person's character and even destroy his life as effectively as weapons.

**25:19. A bad tooth** and **a lame foot** can be problems, especially because a person relies on them to eat and walk. Also relying on a person who turns out to be untrustworthy can be disappointing and troublesome. Job expressed this concern over his friends (Job 6:14-15). An example of an unreliable person is one who lies in court (Prov. 25:18).

**25:20.** Trying to perk up by **songs** a person who is discouraged or depressed (**a heavy heart**) is as cruel as stealing his **garment** in **cold** weather. It is also **like** pouring **vinegar . . . on soda**; it is useless and it causes a violent reaction. Being insensitive and unsympathetic does much harm.

**25:21-22.** Kindness to one's **enemy**—giving **him food** and **water**—is like heaping **burning coals on his head** (quoted by Paul in Rom. 12:20). Sometimes a person's fire went out and he needed to borrow some live coals to restart his fire. Giving a person coals in a pan to carry home "on his head" was a neighborly, kind act; it made friends, not enemies. Also the kindness shown in giving someone food and water makes him ashamed of being an enemy, and brings God's blessing on the benefactor. Compassion, not revenge, should characterize believers (cf. Prov. 24:29). Alternately, light on this passage may come from an Egyptian expiation ritual, in which a person guilty of some wrongdoing would carry a pan of burning coals on his head as a sign of his repentance. Thus treating one's enemy kindly may cause him to repent.

**25:23. As** surely as an Israelite could predict the consequences of **a north wind,** so one can predict the consequences of **a sly tongue** (lit., "a tongue of secrecy," i.e., a slanderous tongue). One **brings rain** and the other **angry looks.** Slander leads to anger. However, in Palestine rain does not normally come from the north. So perhaps this saying originated outside Palestine (Derek Kidner, *The Proverbs: An Introduction and Commentary,* p. 160).

**25:24.** Solitude in cramped quarters with peace is **better . . . than** (cf. comments on 12:9) living in a spacious **house** with a cantakerous, contentious **wife.** This verse is identical to 21:9 (also cf. 21:19).

**25:25.** The impact of receiving **good news** (cf. 15:30) **from a** friend or relative who lives far away is **like** a refreshing drink of **water to a** tired person. In Bible times news traveled slowly; thus long periods of anxious waiting usually followed the departure of a loved one or friend to **a distant land.**

**25:26. A righteous man who** lets his reputation be compromised is **like** pure water being tainted and ruined by mud or other pollutants. The value of a pure **spring** or **well** in an arid country lends force to the statement. Once a spring or well is contaminated it may never be pure again, and disappoints those who come to it for a drink. A righteous person who defects to sin disappoints others who look to him.

**25:27.** Seeking to exalt oneself (seeking **one's own honor;** cf. v. 6; 27:2) is as bad as overeating **honey** (cf. 25:16; 27:7). Both bring problems.

**25:28.** Without walls **a city** was vulnerable to enemy attacks. And an undisciplined person, **who lacks self-control** (cf. 14:17, 29; 16:32; 29:11), is also vulnerable to trouble.

**26:1.** Thirteen verses in this chapter are comparisons, using the words **like** or "as" (cf. comments on 25:3). Each of verses 1, 3-12 refers to a fool or fools. **Snow in summer or rain in harvest** is inappropriate, highly unusual, and potentially damaging to crops. Putting **a fool** in a position of **honor** (cf. 26:8) is inappropriate (cf. 19:10) and may injure others who follow him as a model.

**26:2.** The unpredictable, **fluttering** nature of a bird's flight demonstrates a person's inability to place a **curse** on another who does not deserve it. Balaam experienced that same inability (Num. 23:8).

**26:3.** Just as a **horse** is motivated by **a whip** and a **donkey** is controlled by **a halter** rather than by reason, so a fool needs to be controlled by **a rod** (physical punishment) because he does not respond to appeals to his intellect (cf. 10:13; 14:3; 19:29).

**26:4-5.** These two sayings belong together; they complement each other. Their point is that one should not be drawn down to a fool's level (v. 4) but at times he must use the fool's language to refute the **fool** so he does not become conceited (v. 5; cf. vv. 12, 16). Wisdom is needed to determine when to apply verse 4 and when to apply verse 5. The Jewish Talmud suggests that verse 4 pertains to foolish comments that can be ignored and that verse 5 refers to erroneous ideas that must be corrected. **You** in verse 4 is emphatic and may be translated "you, even you."

**26:6. Sending . . . a message by . . . a fool** is useless and potentially damaging. It is **like cutting off one's feet,** that is, the message does not get delivered; it is as if the sender tried to take it himself by walking the distance without feet. **Drinking violence** is self-damaging, just like relying on an unfaithful messenger.

**26:7. A fool** cannot be trusted with a message (v. 6); also **a proverb** in his **mouth** (cf. v. 9) is as useless as limp **legs** to a **lame** man (cf. 25:19). A fool does not know what to do with a proverb; he does not understand it or apply it. Feet (26:6) and legs (v. 7) tie these two verses together.

**26:8.** It is senseless and possibly harmful to tie **a stone** into **a sling.** The stone might slip out and damage the thrower. So bestowing **honor** on **a fool,** for whom honor is inappropriate (v. 1), is senseless and may damage the reputation of the one giving the honor. His wisdom will be questioned.

**26:9.** As seen in verse 7, **a proverb** spoken by **a fool** is useless. Here it is compared to **a thornbush in** the **hand** of a drunkard. This could mean one of several things: (1) The drunkard may inflict damage on others by waving a thornbush around dangerously. (2) He may be so insensitive to pain that he does not feel a thorn in his hand, much as a fool is insensitive to wisdom. (3) A man who is so

drunk that he cannot pull a thorn out of his hand is like a fool who cannot apply a proverb that he can quote (Robert L. Alden, *Proverbs: A Commentary on an Ancient Book of Timeless Advice,* p. 187). Perhaps the first meaning is to be preferred.

**26:10.** The absurdity of an employer hiring **a fool or any passer-by** is like a berserk **archer** (cf. v. 18) indiscriminately shooting without aiming. Hiring "just anybody" will actually harm the hirer.

**26:11. As a dog** eats **its vomit** (quoted in 2 Peter 2:22), **so a fool** cannot learn from experience. He **returns to** his habits even though they are disgusting.

**26:12.** Concluding the series of statements on the fool (vv. 1, 3-12) is this saying that even **a fool** is better off than one who is **wise in his own eyes** (cf. vv. 5, 16). Self-conceit or pride blinds a person to his sense of need; at least a fool may sense his need for correction.

The last part of verse 12 is repeated in 29:20b. Pride and being proud are addressed frequently in Proverbs (3:34; 8:13; 11:2; 13:10; 15:25; 16:5, 18-19; 21:4, 24; 29:23; cf. 26:5, 12, 16).

**26:13.** Verses 13-16 speak about the sluggard (cf. 6:6-11). **The sluggard** goes to bizarre measures to avoid leaving his house, such as saying **a lion** is **roaming** loose (see comments on 22:13).

**26:14.** The **sluggard,** though tossing in **bed,** seems anchored to it **as a door** is joined to the jamb. He will not even exert the energy needed to get up.

**26:15.** This picture of a **lazy** person starving because he refuses to feed himself is also found in 19:24 (see comments there).

**26:16.** In his self-conceit (cf. vv. 5, 12) **the sluggard** thinks he is smarter **than** anyone (**seven men**). Yet his answers lack discretion (lit., "taste").

**26:17.** Verses 17-28 refer to quarrels (vv. 17, 20-21), deceit (vv. 18-19, 24-26), gossip (vv. 20, 22), and lying (vv. 23, 28). **One who** grabs **a dog by** its **ears** may expect to be bitten. So **is a passer-by,** someone not directly involved, **who meddles in** (lit., "excites himself over") another's **quarrel.** He causes trouble for himself by interfering in a situation he knows little about.

**26:18-19.** The berserk archer is again referred to (cf. v. 10) to picture a troublemaker. After deceiving **his neighbor** he tries to avoid being accused by saying he

**was only joking.** But that is humor in bad taste. His deception, like a deadly arrow, has already done its damage.

**26:20-21. Fire** and strife relate these two verses. **A quarrel dies down** without **gossip** (cf. gossiping in 11:13; 16:28; 18:8; 20:19; 26:22) just as **a fire goes out** when its fuel is removed (v. 20). Conversely quarreling contributes to (**kindling** is lit., "heat up") **strife** (cf. 17:1; 18:6; 20:3; 22:10; 23:29; 30:33) just as **charcoal** and **wood** build up a **fire.**

**26:22.** See comments on 18:8, where the same statement is made. Here gossiping fits with 26:20-21.

**26:23. A coating of glaze** refers to an attractive coating **over** a piece of pottery. This is likened to **fervent** (*dālaq*, "to burn or kindle") **lips** and **an evil heart.** A person who tries to disguise his evil motives and character by zealous speech is like an attractive glazed-over jar. (Note Jesus' reference in Luke 11:39 to the clean outside of the cup and dish; also note Matt. 23:27.)

**26:24.** Verses 24-26 expand the idea in verse 23 (**lips . . . heart,** and "speech" tie verses 23-25 together). **A malicious** person plans **deceit** (cf. v. 19) but seeks to disguise it by his smooth talk ("lips").

**26:25.** This verse warns against being taken in by a malicious person whose words are **charming** (cf. vv. 23-24) but whose **heart** (cf. vv. 23-24) is filled with **seven** (i.e., numerous; cf. "seven men," v. 16) **abominations** (cf. 6:16-19).

**26:26. Malice** (*śin'âh*) is translated "hate" or "hatred" in 10:12, 18; 15:17 (cf. the verb *śānē'*, "hates," in 26:28). Though a scoundrel can hide his feelings temporarily through deceit, they will eventually be known. **The assembly** refers to any group called together for some purpose. Perhaps this group is assembled to administer justice.

**26:27.** Destruction by one's own devices is the subject of this verse and of Psalms 7:15; 9:15; 35:8; 57:6. If Proverbs 26:27 is related to verses 23-26 the point is that attempts to trap or destroy others will eventually turn on the schemer (cf. 1:18-19; 28:10). Many times Proverbs affirms that sin boomerangs.

**26:28.** People who lie are actually hateful (see comments on malice in v. 26); they desire to harm others by slandering their reputations. And people who flatter to help achieve their selfishly

deceptive ends (cf. vv. 23-26) bring **ruin** either to themselves, their victims, or both.

**27:1.** Sixteen of the 27 verses in this chapter deal with relationships with people (vv. 2-6, 9-11, 13-18, 21-22). This warning about tomorrow's uncertainty is repeated in James 4:13-16. The Hebrew word for **boast** is translated "praise" in verses 2 and 21. A person should not praise himself about what he will do the next **day** because he really has no way of knowing for sure **what** will happen.

**27:2.** Praising oneself is evidence of pride and therefore is wrong. Not only should a person refrain from boasting about what he will do (v. 1); he should also refrain from boasting about what he has done.

**27:3.** Verses 3-6 discuss various interpersonal relationships. The burden of being provoked **by a fool** is a **heavy** one indeed. In fact it **is heavier than** a large **stone** and more burdensome than **sand.** So a wise person should not react to a fool even when the fool's actions and words are irritating.

**27:4.** When a person is angry and furious he can be **cruel** toward others. His words and actions may cause others to cower in fear. But jealousy is even worse because it may include **anger** and **fury** and merciless revenge, as illustrated in 6:32-35. **Who can stand before jealousy?** is one of the few rhetorical questions in Proverbs.

**27:5.** If a person's love is genuine, he will not fear to tell his friend about a fault or correct him. Rebuking (see comments on 1:23) is to be preferred to **hidden** (lit., "closed up, withdrawn") **love.** In other words correcting a person's fault is an evidence of love, but failing to correct him shows one's love is withdrawn. This verse is one of 19 "better . . . than" verses in Proverbs (see comments on 12:9).

**27:6. An enemy** (lit., "one who hates") **may** seem to be a friend by his many **kisses,** and a true **friend** (lit., "one who loves") may seem to be an enemy by **the wounds** he inflicts (probably inner hurts that come from being rebuked or criticized; see v. 5). Yet, ironically, the rebukes may actually be more genuine expressions of friendship.

**27:7.** If a person is **full** of food then **honey,** which ordinarily he would crave, is no longer desirable. Conversely, **to a hungry** person **even** something **bitter** may seem **sweet** because it satisfies his need for food. This verse may be teaching that one's attitude toward material possessions is influenced by how much he possesses. Those who have much do not appreciate or value a gift as much as do those who have little.

**27:8.** This verse may speak against a person abandoning his responsibilities at **home** along with its comforts. Just as **a bird** wandering **from its nest** too early or too far brings hardship on itself, so a young person leaving home too soon may find himself unable to care for himself (e.g., the prodigal son, Luke 15:11-32).

**27:9.** A friend's **earnest counsel** is as sweet or pleasant as the fragrance emanating from **perfume and incense.** Genuine advice shows that a person cares.

**27:10.** This proverb is designed more to exalt long-term friendship than to denigrate family ties. Normally in times of adversity, **a brother** (relative) is helpful (17:17). But if the brother lives a great distance **away,** a **neighbor** may be far more helpful (cf. 18:24).

**27:11.** This is the only verse in chapters 25–29 that includes the term **my son** (see comments on 1:8). Again Proverbs affirms the fact that a wise son brings **joy to** his father (cf. 10:1; 15:20; 23:15, 24; 29:3). In fact having a son who is **wise** also means that a father **can answer** critics who may accuse him of being an incompetent father. The son who leads a life of wisdom is evidence of good child-rearing.

**27:12.** This verse is nearly identical to 22:3 (see comments there).

**27:13.** This proverb is the same as the one in 20:16 (see comments there and on 6:1-5).

**27:14.** Blessing (i.e., praising or commending) a **neighbor** is commendable, but not **early in the morning.** Timing and sensitivity to others who are sleeping are important. The wrong time for the right action causes it to be received **as a curse.**

**27:15-16.** **Dripping** water pictures the irritating nature of **a quarrelsome wife** (cf. 19:13 and comments there). Like water dripping **on a rainy day,** she is annoying and never stops quarreling. She is as impossible to restrain as **the wind.** Trying to constrain her contentious spirit is as impossible as trying to pick up a handful of **oil.** She is both unsteady and slippery.

**27:17.** When **iron** is rubbed against another piece of **iron** it shapes and **sharpens** it. Similarly people can help each other improve by their discussions, criticisms, suggestions, and ideas. On the influence of companions, whether good or bad, on one's life see 13:20; 22:24-25. A nagging wife (27:15), however, stimulates a husband toward anger.

**27:18.** Nurturing and cultivating **a fig tree** are necessary if a farmer is to have a good crop of figs (cf. 12:11; 28:19); and a servant who attends to the needs of **his master will be honored.** In other words working well at one's job brings favorable results.

**27:19.** The Hebrew is obscure; literally it reads, "Like water face to face, so is the heart of man to a man." Just **as water,** like a mirror, **reflects a** person's **face, so a** person's **heart** or mind **reflects** what he is really like. Or as water reflects a face, so thoughts (expressed in words) reflect one's personality.

**27:20.** The grave (on **death and destruction** see comments on 15:11) is personified as having an appetite. Seemingly it always wants another live person dead. Likewise **the eyes of man** are **never satisfied.** People constantly want to see new things (cf. Ecc. 1:8) and to own new things.

**27:21.** Heat both tests and refines **silver** (cf. 25:4) and **gold,** showing what the metals are really like. (This first line of 27:21 is identical with 17:3.) **Praise** tests a person in a similar way in that his reaction to it shows what he is really like. If he gloats over it, he shows himself to be arrogant; he "knows" he is good. But if he accepts the praise modestly, he shows his humility.

**27:22.** A **fool** (*ʾĕwîl,* "an arrogant, hardened fool"; see comments on 1:7) and **his folly** are so inseparable that if he is punished repeatedly, like **grinding . . . grain with a pestle,** he still remains foolish.

**27:23-27.** These five verses are a brief treatise on life in an agricultural society. Earlier a cluster of five verses discussed the consequences of laziness (24:30-34). A farmer should care for his **flocks** and **herds** because they are a better investment than many things. Flocks and herds multiply through their offspring, but money when it is spent is gone (cf. 23:5) and being a king (having **a crown**) does not last. **Hay** and **grass** provide food for livestock, which in turn supply people's needs for **clothing** (lambs' wool), money (from selling **goats**), and **milk** and food for one's family and servants. It is important to care for one's resources, to work hard, and to recognize God's provisions through nature.

**28:1.** Like chapters 10–15, chapters 28–29 have a number of antithetical verses, verses of contrast in which the second line is introduced by "but." Eighteen verses of contrast are in chapter 28 (vv. 1-2, 4-5, 7, 10-14, 16, 18-20, 25-28), and 12 are in chapter 29 (vv. 3-4, 6-8, 11, 15-16, 18, 23, 25-26). In these two chapters rulers, kings, and other people in power are mentioned frequently (28:2-3, 12, 15-16, 28; 29:2, 4, 12, 14, 26). Five of the six references in Proverbs to the Law are in these two chapters (28:4 [twice], 7, 9; 29:18; cf. 31:5). Other frequent subjects are the poor and poverty (28:3, 6, 8, 11, 19, 22, 27; 29:7, 13-14), and the wicked (28:1, 4, 12, 15, 28 [twice]; 29:2, 7, 12, 16, 27) and the righteous (28:1, 12, 28; 29:2, 6-7, 16, 27).

The guilty consciences of **the wicked** cause them to run from imagined pursuers (28:1). Knowing they have done wrong, they suspect they are being chased by lawmen. By contrast **the righteous are as bold** (i.e., self-confident; cf. "confidence" in 31:11) **as a** young **lion.** God gives them courage; they have no fear of reprisal from wrongdoing.

**28:2.** Unrest and rebellion in a nation results in turnover of leadership. For example, the Northern Kingdom had **many rulers,** 20 kings in nine dynasties. **Order,** however, is maintained in a nation by good rulers who have insight and **knowledge** about how to govern.

**28:3.** The Hebrew word for **ruler** in this verse differs from the word for "rulers" in verse 2. In fact "ruler" (v. 3) translates two words which are literally, "a strong man" (*geḇer*) who is destitute and hungry (*rāš*; cf. NIV marg.; vv. 6, 27). When a man in need **oppresses the poor** (*dal*, "feeble, helpless, weak"; see comments on 10:15), he opposes people who in some ways are like him, who could be his friends. Such cruelty and perversion of justice are **like a** hard **rain** which de-

stroys rather than nourishes **crops.**

**28:4.** Oppressing the poor (v. 3) is an example of forsaking **the** Mosaic **Law** (cf. "Law" in vv. 7, 9). And when people turn from obeying God's commands, they usually begin to commend (**praise**) and side with **wicked** people. Lawkeepers (cf. v. 7), however, **resist** wicked lawbreakers, seeking to uphold justice (cf. 18:5; 24:25).

**28:5.** When people disobey the Law and the Lord, their sense of uprightness and morality is perverted. They find it difficult even to **understand** ("have insight into") **justice.** On the other hand the righteous, **those who seek the Lord,** have a keen sense of justice.

**28:6.** This verse is almost identical to 19:1, except that there a fool's "lips" (words) are perverse, whereas in 28:6 **a** rich man's **ways are** said to be **perverse** (*'iqqēš*, "twisted"; see comments on 2:15). Perhaps this suggests that a perverse rich man is a fool. It is better to be **poor** (*rāš*, "destitute"; cf. 28:3, 27) and honest (**blameless,** "morally whole"; cf. 2:7, 21; 11:5; 28:10, 18) than to be rich and wicked. This is the last of the 19 **better . . . than** proverbs (see comments on 12:9).

**28:7.** A **son** who obeys **the Law** (cf. v. 4) is wise; he has insight. The Hebrew word for **discerning** is translated "understanding" in verse 2. Associating with **gluttons** is foolish and shows lack of insight, for it can start a person on the path of drunkenness, laziness , and, ironically, even poverty (cf. 23:20-21). Furthermore, a gluttonous son brings disgrace to **his father.** This implies that a discerning son (28:7a) brings joy to his father.

**28:8.** A person who charged **exorbitant interest** of others and thus became rich would eventually lose **his wealth** which would be distributed **to the poor** (*dal*, "feeble, weak, helpless"; cf. vv. 3, 11, and see comments on 10:15). Justice eventually overtakes injustice.

**28:9.** Refusing to obey God's **Law** (cf. vv. 4, 7) has disastrous results. **Prayers** of such a person are hypocritical. Therefore those prayers, hated by God, are not answered (cf. 15:8; Ps. 66:18; Isa. 59:2). If a person does not listen to (obey) the Lord, the Lord will not listen to him.

**28:10.** One who causes the righteous to sin will be trapped by his own devices (cf. 1:18; 26:27). In contrast, **the blameless** (cf. 28:6, 18) will be enriched. The wicked who lead others astray are suddenly trapped and die, but the righteous live on and **receive** their parents' **inheritance.**

**28:11.** The **rich** and the **poor** (*dal,* "feeble, weak, helpless"; see comments on 10:15) are again contrasted (cf. v. 6). A discerning poor person can **see through** the pretentious facade of a conceited rich person who thinks he knows it all (cf. **wise[r] in his own eyes** in 26:5, 12, 16). Having money does not mean a person is wise. **Discernment** ("insight") is translated "understanding" in 28:2 and "discerning" in verse 7.

**28:12.** As in verses 1 and 28, the righteous and the wicked are contrasted. When a **righteous** leader rules a nation, the people are happy (cf. 11:10), for there is order (cf. 28:2) and justice. **But when . . . wicked** leaders are in charge, good people **go into hiding** (also stated in v. 28a) to get away from oppression (cf. vv. 15-16) which causes them to groan (29:2).

**28:13.** After a person **sins** he may try to conceal (trans. "covers over" in 17:9) that fact from God and others. But hiding sin does not pay off. Solomon's father David knew this from experience (Ps. 32:3-4). It is far better to deal with sin by confessing and renouncing it. As David found out, confession results in God's **mercy** and forgiveness (Pss. 34:5; 51:1-12).

**28:14.** The words **the LORD** are added in the NIV as they are not in the Hebrew. The word **fears** translates *pāḥad,* "to be afraid," as in 1:33; 3:24-25. In 1:7; 3:7 the word for "fear" is *yārē',* "to reverence." Probably, then, 28:14 is referring to the fear or dread of the consequences of sin (cf. v. 13). A person who has that kind of dread will be happy (**blessed**; cf. Ps. 1:1) and will not harden **his heart** and fall **into trouble** (cf. Prov. 29:1).

**28:15-16.** The danger of **a wicked man** rising to power, introduced in verse 12, is expanded here. A wicked ruler is cruel and devastating like a **lion** (cf. 19:12; 20:2) **or a bear.** The **helpless** are the weak (*dal,* often trans. "poor," as in 28:3, 8, 11). A **ruler** who tyrannizes **lacks judgment** or good sense (see comments on 6:32; 10:13). In contrast, a person who refuses to abuse his power for personal **gain** (cf. **ill-gotten** treasures in 1:19; 10:2) **will enjoy** the blessing of **a long life.**

This implies that a tyrannical leader will not live long.

**28:17.** A murderer's guilty conscience hounds him, tormenting him and causing him to try to escape punishment. His only escape is **death.** One who tries to console or rescue **him** is out of line; to aid a criminal is wrong. However, rescuing the innocent *is* encouraged (24:11-12).

**28:18.** A **blameless** (see comments on v. 6) life (**walk**) brings safety (cf. 1:33; 3:23; 18:10; 28:26), **but** a person **whose ways are perverse** (from *'āqaš,* "to twist"; cf. the adjective *'iqqēš* in v. 6; 2:15) **will suddenly fall.** Similar statements are given in 10:9; 28:10.

**28:19.** This verse is almost identical to 12:11 (see comments there). A farmer **who works** hard will have plenty to eat (cf. 27:18). In contrast with the diligent, the indolent **who** chase their **fantasies** will not get their work done and **will have** their **fill of poverty,** not food (cf. 14:23).

**28:20.** The way to become **richly blessed** is by being **faithful** ("trustworthy"), not by using get-rich-quick schemes. Being **eager to get rich** often leads to devious, dishonest ways (cf. 13:11; 20:21) resulting in the person being punished either by the courts or by poverty or both (cf. 28:22). Others who **will not go unpunished** are referred to in 6:29; 11:21; 16:5; 17:5; 19:5, 9.

**28:21.** Showing **partiality** (cf. 18:5; 24:23) **is not good.** This is the last of six "not good" sayings in Proverbs (17:26; 18:5; 19:2; 24:23; 25:27; 28:21). In court cases some judges show partiality to those who bribe them even with a small bribe such as **a piece of bread.** It is ironic that justice can be so easily perverted especially when bribery is so firmly denounced (see comments on 6:35).

**28:22.** A **stingy man** is literally, "a man with an evil eye" (see comments on 23:6). Ironically a person who greedily tries **to get rich** quickly (cf. 28:20) will end up in **poverty,** the opposite of his goal (cf. 11:24b).

**28:23.** Giving a needed rebuke rather than overlooking it or **flattering** a person (cf. 29:5) is difficult. But **in the end** (later) a wise person is grateful for it (cf. 27:5; see comments on 1:23). On the word **favor** see comments on 8:35.

**28:24.** A son who heartlessly says nothing is **wrong** in robbing his parents (cf. 19:26) is like a destroyer. Disgracing them (cf. 28:7), **he is** like a person **who destroys.** That is, he has destroyed their honorable reputation and peace of mind.

**28:25. Greedy** is literally, "large of soul" and refers to an uncontrolled, avaricious appetite for material things. Because greed is selfish it results in **dissension** or strife. In this way, greed is a companion to deceit (6:14), hatred (10:12), temper (15:18), perversity (16:28), and anger (29:22). The one **who trusts in the Lord** rather than in riches gained by greed **will prosper** (cf. 11:25).

**28:26.** In contrast with one who trusts in the Lord (v. 25) is a person **who trusts in himself** (cf. 14:12). He **is a fool** (*keṣîl*, "dull, thickheaded"; see comments on 1:7). A person who is wise, not trusting in himself, will be **safe** (cf. 3:5-6; 28:18; 29:25).

**28:27.** Being generous **to the poor** (*rāš*, "destitute, hungry," also used in vv. 3, 6; cf. 29:7) does not mean the giver will then have to "do without." Just the opposite is true; he **will lack nothing.** Generosity is rewarded (cf. 11:24-25; 14:21b, 31b; 19:17; 21:26; 22:9; Deut. 15:10). However, a person who ignores the needs of the poor **receives . . . curses** from them (cf. Prov. 11:24b, 26a).

**28:28.** The first part of this verse is like verse 12b. The second part of verse 28 adds another thought: **When the wicked perish** (cf. 11:10), as they will, **the righteous** can then **thrive** (lit., "become great"; cf. 29:2) without having to be in **hiding.**

**29:1.** A man who is **stiff-necked,** that is, hardened and refusing to repent or submit to repeated correction (**many rebukes;** see comments on 1:30), **will suddenly be destroyed** (cf 1:27; 6:15; 10:25a; 28:18) in death. No longer will a **remedy** be available.

**29:2.** When **righteous** leaders are in control (**thrive,** lit., "become great"; cf. 28:28, which may have this meaning) of a government, **the people** are glad because they are more secure and prosperous. But **when . . . wicked** leaders are ruling, **the people groan** (cf. 28:12) under cruel oppression (cf. 28:15; 29:16).

**29:3.** The **joy** of a wise man's **father** (cf. 10:1; 15:20; 23:15, 24; 27:11) is contrasted with a father's **wealth** being squandered by a son who associates with **prostitutes.** According to 2:12, 16; 5:1-3,

7-11 wisdom keeps one from adultery.

**29:4. Justice** brings a nation **stability** and joy (cf. vv. 2, 7, 14; 14:34; 16:12; 20:8, 26; 21:15; 28:12), whereas a greedy leader contributes to the nation's downfall. **One who is greedy for bribes** is literally, "a man of offerings or contributions." The Hebrew word for "bribes" usually refers to sacred offerings; here it may refer to taxes. Rehoboam illustrated the truth of this proverb (1 Kings 12:1-19), which he might well have heard from his father Solomon.

**29:5. Flatters** is literally, "makes (a person) smooth." In 2:16 and 7:5 the word is rendered "seductive." This flattery in 29:5 is smooth talk that deceives because it intends to harm. A flatterer, however, suffers for it (cf. 26:28). He is caught in the very **net** he set for others (cf. 29:6; 1:18; 28:10).

**29:6. An evil** person is caught in his self-designed trap (cf. comments on v. 5), while the **righteous** live happy, carefree lives. They need not worry that their actions might boomerang on them.

**29:7. Righteous** people want to see **justice** rather than oppression extended to **the poor** (*dal*, "feeble, weak, helpless"; cf. v. 14 and see comments on 10:15). **But the wicked** do not care whether the poor get treated fairly or not. One's relationship to God shows up in his attitude toward the needy.

**29:8.** Verses 8-11 contrast angry fools with honest, wise people. **Mockers** (cf. 1:22) laugh at moral restrictions and **stir up** (lit., "fan or blow on" embers) trouble. Mockers keep things in an uproar. These troublemakers get others angry and incite rebellion. (Cf. "anger" and "angry" in 29:11, 22.) The **wise,** however, help calm **a city** by averting **anger** and its rebellious results.

**29:9.** The word "righteous" connects verses 6 and 7. Here **wise** links verses 8 and 9. Trying to win a **court** case **with a fool** (*'ĕwîl*, "an arrogant, hardened fool") should be avoided because he follows his emotions rather than logic (cf. 27:3) as he keeps things in turmoil (**no peace**) with his angry (cf. 29:11) ranting (raging and scoffing).

**29:10.** Honest people are hated by fools, who would prefer killing the honest so they could not testify against the wicked in court. **Integrity** is often translated "blameless" (e.g., 28:6, 10, 18).

**29:11. A fool** (*kᵉsîl*; see comments on 1:7) readily gives in to **anger** (cf. 15:1; 29:8, 22), **but a wise** person maintains self-control (cf. 14:29; 16:32). **Keeps himself under control** is literally, "calms it back" like stilling a storm. The verb is used only here and in Psalms 65:7; 89:9 where it refers to calming the sea's waves.

**29:12. If a ruler** takes the advice of liars, then he encourages wickedness in the people around him. But if he instead rewards honesty then it will be encouraged and falsehood will be punished (cf. 20:8, 28).

**29:13. The poor man** (*rāš*, "destitute, hungry"; cf. 28:3, 6, 27) **and the oppressor** are opposites morally. One thing poor victims **have . . . in common** with their persecutors is that they both were given **sight** by the LORD (cf. 22:2 and "Maker" in 14:31; 17:5). Each can see the other.

**29:14. Fairness** (cf. v. 7) toward those least able to care for themselves (**the poor**, *dal*, "feeble, weak, helpless"; see comments on 10:15) is a mark of a good **king** (cf. v. 4) whose **throne** is therefore **secure** (cf. 16:12; 20:28). God blesses rulers who are concerned about the poor, and people appreciate such rulers.

**29:15.** In Hebrew **the rod of correction** literally reads "the rod and correction." Either the rod is the instrument of correction (in which case a figure of speech called a hendiadys is used), or both the rod (physical punishment; cf. 13:24; 22:15; 23:13-14) and verbal correction (lit., "rebuke") are to be used. **A child** who is not disciplined and is **left to** himself (allowed to do as he pleases and have whatever he wants) will become an unruly person. He will disgrace (bring shame to; cf. 19:26; 28:7) **his mother.**

**29:16. When . . . wicked** leaders govern a nation (see comments on **thrive** in v. 2), **sin** is encouraged. But as stated many times in Proverbs, the wicked will eventually fall and **the righteous will** live to **see** it and will then rejoice (cf. 28:12, 28).

**29:17.** Disciplining one's **son** results in the parents having **peace** and joy later because their son will behave and grow wiser (cf. 10:1). The verb **discipline** (*yāsar*) is related to the noun "discipline" (*mûsār*; cf. 1:2, which means "moral discipline or correction").

**29:18.** The familiar KJV "where there is no vision" is misleading. The word "vision" is the **revelation** (*ḥāzôn*) a prophet receives. Also the KJV translation "the people perish" does not refer to unsaved **people** dying in sin. The verb *pāra'* means **to cast off restraint.** So the verse is stating that without God's Word people abandon themselves to their own sinful ways. On the other hand keeping (obeying) God's **Law** (cf. 28:4, 7) brings happiness.

**29:19.** This verse, coupled with verse 21, seems to suggest that discipline is needed for one's servants as well as for his sons. Sometimes **words** are not enough; **a servant** may know the words but obstinately refuse to do as he is told. If so, other forms of correction are needed.

**29:20. A man who speaks in haste** is **a fool** because he blurts out thoughtless, insensitive remarks (cf. "gushes" folly and evil, 15:2, 28), sometimes answering before he listens (18:13). In fact he is worse than a fool. Speaking in haste and being conceited are two things for which there is less hope than for being a fool (cf. 26:12). This kind of person brings trouble on himself and others (cf. 17:19-20; 18:6-7).

**29:21.** The importance of disciplining, not pampering, servants is again touched on (cf. v. 19). Failure to discipline a **servant** and to require him to carry out his responsibilities will result in **grief** (a Heb. word used only here in the OT) **in the end** (later) to his master.

**29:22.** The effects of a volatile temperament warn against losing control of oneself. An **angry . . . hot-tempered** (lit., "owner of wrath"; see comments on 22:24) person causes strife (cf. 26:21; 30:33) and **commits many sins,** perhaps including cursing or insulting others, misusing God's name, being rude, lacking kindness, being cruel or oppressive, and being proud.

**29:23.** The reverse effects of **pride** and humility warn against the one and encourage the other. Ironically pride, by which a person seeks to elevate himself, actually results in his being brought **low** (*šāpal*) whereas one who is **of lowly** (*šāpal*) **spirit** is elevated by others to a position of **honor** (cf. 3:34; 15:33; 16:18-19; 18:12). God hates pride (see comments on 6:17) because it influences a person to live independently of Him.

**29:24.** The accomplice of a thief becomes **his own enemy** because his involvement in crime works against him. In court he takes an **oath** but then must either lie or say nothing. If he testifies he will implicate himself, and if he says nothing he is assumed guilty (Lev. 5:1).

**29:25.** To **fear** ("tremble," not the word for reverence before God; e.g., 1:7; 8:13; 9:10) **man** ensnares in the sense that one's actions are controlled or confined by the person who is dreaded. It is far better to trust **in the LORD** because that brings safety (cf. 18:10; 28:18, 26). The words **is kept safe** are from the verb *śāgab*, "to be inaccessibly high or to be exalted." Security in the Lord removes intimidation by man.

**29:26.** People may **seek an audience with a ruler** (cf. 19:6) to curry his favor or influence or to gain justice, but they have no guarantee that justice will be done. The ruler might even "prove to be a snare" (29:25). True **justice** comes **from the LORD**; He will make things right in the end. Therefore trusting Him is more important than any dread of man.

**29:27.** The antagonism existing between **the righteous** and **the wicked** is given in surprisingly graphic terms. **Detest,** in both lines of the verse, is a strong verb that may be translated "to consider abominable or detestable, to abhor." It is used of God's attitude toward idolatry and of the sacrifice of children (Deut. 12:31) and of other abominable and unclean acts. The righteous are so concerned for honesty that they, like God, hate what is dishonest. And the distaste of the wicked for **the upright** reveals their perverse values. All of Proverbs, of course, contrasts the righteous and the wicked. Here they are seen as stark opposites.

## VI. The Words of Agur (chap. 30)
### A. Introduction (30:1)

**30:1.** The identity of **Agur** is unknown. He seems to have been humble (vv. 2-4) and observant and inquisitive (vv. 5-33). **An oracle** translates *maśśā',* which means a weighty message (see comments on Zech. 9:1). Agur's words were addressed **to Ithiel and to Ucal,** whose identities are also unknown.

### B. Knowledge about God (30:2-9)
#### 1. MAN'S IGNORANCE OF GOD (30:2-4)

**30:2-3.** In calling himself **the most ignorant of men,** Agur may have been writing in irony. If so, he was contrasting himself with someone who arrogantly claimed wisdom, a person he challenged to answer (v. 4). Or the statement in verse 2 may be Agur's sincere response to the reflections he recorded in verse 4. "Ignorant" translates the Hebrew word *ba'ar* which means "to be brutish or dull-minded" like an animal (cf. Ps. 73:22; Prov. 12:1, "stupid"). In the second clause in 30:2 Agur wrote that he had less than human intelligence. Agur sensed his lack of **wisdom** because he did not know the infinite God (**the Holy One;** cf. 9:10). Knowing God is the basis of true wisdom (1:7; 15:33).

**30:4.** The only answer to the five questions in this verse is God. Only He can go **up to heaven and come down,** reminding one of Christ, the Son of God. And only God can hold **the wind in . . . His hands** (i.e., control the wind), and figuratively wrap **the waters in His cloak** (perhaps referring to the clouds; cf. Job 26:8), and only He has fixed **the earth** in its place (cf. Job 38:4, 6; Prov. 8:29). The question, **What is His name?** asks what His true character is like. The inquiry, What is **the name of His son?** suggests the question, "Has He imparted His nature or attributes to any other who may in any sense be called His 'Son'?" (T.T. Perowne, *The Proverbs,* p. 180) **Tell me if you know** reflects Agur's desire to know the nature of God.

#### 2. MAN'S KNOWLEDGE OF GOD THROUGH HIS WORD (30:5-6)

**30:5-6.** Verse 4 emphasized man's inability to know by himself the nature of God. Now verses 5-6 show how **God** may be known: through His **Word,** which **is flawless** (lit., "purified" like the smelting of silver; cf. Ps. 12:6). Man can know God only because He has revealed Himself through the written Word, the infallible Scriptures. Those who trust in God have a personal relationship with Him; they are shielded by **Him.** Proverbs 30:5 is almost identical to Psalm 18:30. The warning not to **add to His words** may refer to the danger of adding human speculation to divine revelation. Man should derive his understanding of God (his theology) not from human ideas but from God's Word. God rebukes those who think they can know more of God than what He has revealed about Himself. In fact they are often so far off base that God calls them liars.

### 3. MAN'S PRAYER TO GOD (30:7-9)

**30:7-9.** The words **two things** introduce a series of six numerical sayings in this chapter (vv. 7-9, 15b-16, 18-19, 21-23, 24-28, 29-31). This prayer for "two things" affirms the humility introduced in verses 2-3. Realizing his frailty, the writer asked **the Lord** for specific help in two areas of weakness **before** he died: protection from lying, and provision of **daily** sustenance (**bread**; cf. Matt. 6:11) without the temptations of wealth or **poverty.** Wealth might cause him to **disown** and forget **the Lord** (cf. Deut. 8:12-17) thinking he could care for himself; and poverty might cause him to **steal** and thus **dishonor** God's character.

## C. Observations about life (30:10-33)

### 1. ADVICE (30:10)

**30:10.** This verse is a warning not to meddle in another person's domestic affairs. A **master** may **curse** the person who falsely accuses his **servant.** In contrast with the "undeserved curse" of 26:2, this curse will "hit its target" so to speak, because it is deserved. This saying may stand as a self-contained maxim or, perhaps more likely, it introduces 30:11-14.

### 2. FOUR KINDS OF UNDESIRABLE BEHAVIOR (30:11-14)

Though not introduced as a numerical series (see comments on v. 7) four kinds of people are mentioned: those who are disrespectful, hypocritical, arrogant, and oppressive.

**30:11.** The sin of cursing one's parents (cf. v. 17) is mentioned in 20:20 (see comments there).

**30:12.** People who think they **are pure** (morally clean) before God but who still **are not cleansed** of **their** moral **filth** of sin are hypocrites.

**30:13.** Haughtiness (cf. 6:16-17; 21:4; Pss. 18:27; 101:5; Isa. 10:12), which the Lord despises, contrasts with Agur's attitudes of humility and reverence (Prov. 30:2-3, 7-9). **Eyes** connects verse 13 with verse 12.

**30:14.** People who oppress **the poor** (*'ānî,* "afflicted, humbled") and **needy** (*'ebyôn,* "people needing help"; cf. 31:9, 20) are like voracious beasts whose sharp **teeth** tear their prey (cf. Ps. 14:4).

### 3. FOUR THINGS NEVER SATISFIED (30:15-16)

**30:15-16.** This numerical listing deals with insatiable desires. The **cry** of the **daughters** of a bloodsucking **leech** (**Give! Give!**) introduces the theme. Leeches graphically depict the attitude of greed, with its tenacious insistence on having more of what is desired. On the stylistic feature of **three** followed by **four** (x and x + 1), which is used in verses 15, 18, 21, 29, see comments on 6:16. Four **things** are personified as **never satisfied: the grave** (*šeʾôl*) wants to take in more of the dead (cf. 27:20), **the barren womb** longs to give birth to a child, the **land** always wants **water, and fire** wants to continue to consume. Death and fire are destructive, and the womb and water are life-giving. Greed always wants more.

### 4. WARNING (30:17)

**30:17.** This saying may have been placed here to point to the fact that disrespect for one's parents is as bad as the insatiable greed mentioned in verses 15-16. An arrogant child who **scorns** (*bûz,* "to hold in contempt or ridicule"; see comments on 1:7) his or her parents (cf. v. 11) will die, and his corpse will remain unburied and be food for the birds of prey.

### 5. FOUR AMAZING THINGS (30:18-19)

**30:18-19.** What do the ways **of an eagle in the sky . . . a snake on a rock . . . a ship** in the ocean, and **a man with a** woman have in common? Some writers say the ways of these four are mysterious; others say their ways are nontraceable; others suggest that they each easily master an element that is seemingly difficult. Another suggestion is that they each go where there are no paths. "The way of a man with a **maiden**" refers to a man's affectionate courting of a woman.

### 6. WARNING (30:20)

**30:20. An adulteress** contrasts with the woman in verse 19. Here it is not the man's way with a woman, but an immoral woman's **way** with men (cf. 2:16-19;

5:1-14; 7; 22:14; 23:27-28). She takes a casual approach to her sinful ways, treating them as lightly as eating a meal and asserting that **nothing** is **wrong** (cf. 28:24) with adultery.

### 7. FOUR UNBEARABLE, UNFAIR THINGS (30:21-23)

Verses 21-31 include three lists of people and creatures that pertain to leadership or a perversion of it. The word "king" occurs in each list (vv. 22, 27, 31).

**30:21-23.** The statements that **the earth trembles** and **cannot bear up** are hyperboles. Also by a figure of speech known as metonymy the earth represents the people who are on it. The people tremble because social turmoil follows the sudden elevation of inexperienced, unqualified people to positions of power and success. It is not appropriate (a) for **a servant** to become a **king** (the servant is unprepared), (b) for a **fool** (*nābāl*, "one who lacks spiritual perception and sensitivity"; cf. 17:7, 21) to be **full of food** (he might become bullheaded regarding the needs of others), (c) for **an unloved** (lit., "hated") **woman** to be **married** (she brings grief to the marriage), and (d) for **a maidservant** to become a **mistress** (for she, like the servant in 30:22, does not know how to direct others). Harmony in society is encouraged when people maintain their proper roles and do not assume positions they are incapable of handling.

### 8. FOUR SMALL, WISE THINGS (30:24-28)

These verses build on the thought in 21:22; 24:5, which refers to wisdom triumphing over physical strength.

**30:24-26.** One of the **small** but **wise** creatures are **ants.** Though they have **little strength** they survive because of their foresight (see comments on 6:6-8). **Conies** (or rock badgers; cf. NIV marg.) are about the size of rabbits. Because they are rather ineffective at defending themselves, they wisely live in **crags** (cf. Ps. 104:18) that give them natural safety.

**30:27-28. Locusts have no** apparent leader (**king**) but fly in an amazing order and can devastate miles of crops like an approaching army (cf. Joel 1:4-7). **A lizard,** so small that it **can** easily **be caught** by **hand,** may be seen even **in kings' palaces,** seemingly having the run of the place. Two ideas emerge from these two

insects and two animals: (a) physical limitations may be compensated for in other ways; (b) since God protects and provides for even the humblest and lowest of His creatures, He certainly will provide for His own people.

### 9. FOUR STATELY CREATURES (30:29-31)

**30:29-31.** In contrast with lowly creatures like the four in verses 25-28 are those that appear noble **in their** bearing and walk. These include the **lion,** from whom people and other animals retreat because of its strength, the **strutting rooster** (lit., "girded at the loins"), a male **goat** with its arrogant appearance, **and a king** who may strut with pride as he is seemingly invincible **with his army** in his presence. In God's order of things, some creatures are small and in humble positions and others are more prominent.

### 10. ADVICE (30:32-33)

**30:32-33.** In contrast with creatures who strut in pride (vv. 29-31) is a person who has **played the fool** (the verb *nābal,* "to be spiritually imperceptive and insensitive"; cf. the noun *nābāl* in v. 22; 17:7, 21). By exalting himself and planning **evil** (cf. 6:14) he causes trouble. To **clap** one's **hand over** his **mouth** (cf. Job 21:5; 40:4) was a way of saying he should stop being proud and making trouble. As sure **as churning . . . milk** makes **butter and the twisting** of a **nose** brings **blood, so** the agitation and **stirring up** of **anger produces** trouble. Churning, twisting, and stirring up translate the same Hebrew word *mîṣ,* "squeezing or wringing," which occurs only here in the Old Testament. In an interesting wordplay "nose" (*'ap*) and "anger" (*'appayim*) are similar Hebrew words. Pride and anger work against humility, which is commended and promoted in Proverbs 30.

## VII. The Words of Lemuel (31:1-9)

A mother told her son about the dangers of wayward women (v. 3; cf. 23:26-28) and wine (31:4-7; cf. 23:29-35) and reminded him of his responsibility to champion the cause of justice.

**31:1.** Nothing is known about **Lemuel** except that he was a **king.** The instruction in verses 2-9 was addressed to him by **his mother.** This is unusual for elsewhere in Proverbs a father was addressing his son(s), though twice a mother's teaching is referred to by the father (cf. 1:8; 6:20). On the word **oracle** see comments on 30:1 and Zechariah 9:1.

**31:2-3.** Lemuel's mother addressed her **son,** which is the Aramaic word *bar.* Also **kings** in verse 3 is Aramaic. Her **vows** may mean that she made a vow, as Hannah did, before his conception (1 Sam. 1:11) or afterward. Either way she wanted him to know that he was special to her. She warned him that adultery has a debilitating effect on one's mind and body (cf. Solomon's warnings against adultery in Prov. 2:16-19; 5:1-14; 7; 22:14, and the wise men's warning in 23:27-28).

**31:4-5.** In verses 4-7, Lemuel's mother warned about the dangers of alcoholism. Her advice echoes 20:1; 23:20-21, 29-35. The particular danger of drunkenness to a king lies in its tendency to cloud his memory and judgment, resulting in injustice (18:5) to **the oppressed** (cf. 31:8).

**31:6-7.** **Beer** ("strong drink"; cf. comments on 20:1) and **wine** (mentioned in reverse order from the way they are mentioned in 31:4) may have been acceptable as anesthetics or drugs to deaden physical pain or deep emotional bitterness (and the pain of those who were dying). Or verses 6-7 may be saying that though others may have used drink as an escape, the king was not to do so.

**31:8-9.** This second reference to justice (cf. **rights** in v. 5) in such a short discourse speaks strongly for its importance. A king who defended those who could not defend **themselves** and who were of little threat and made little contribution to him would be noted as a just and gracious man. He was to **judge fairly,** regardless of a person's social status. The word for **destitute** (used only here in the OT) means people who are passing away; they are "on their last legs." **The poor** (*'ānî,* "afflicted, humbled") **and needy** (*'eḇyôn,* "people needing help"; cf. 30:14; 31:20), who were easily oppressed, were also to be defended by the king.

## VIII. The Noble Wife (31:10-31)

This final section of Proverbs is an acrostic poem exalting a noble wife. Each of the 22 verses begins with a consecutive letter of the Hebrew alphabet. These verses were written by Lemuel, Lemuel's mother, Solomon, or someone whose

name is unknown. This last view is probably correct.

**31:10.** The **wife of noble character** (*ḥayil*) is also mentioned in 12:4 (cf. "noble" in 31:29). Ruth was called "a woman of noble character" (Ruth 3:11). The word for noble character is translated "capable" in Exodus 18:21. The question **who can find?** (cf. Prov. 20:6) does not suggest that such women are nonexistent but that they should be admired because they, like noble men, are rare. Also they are **more** valuable **than rubies** (cf. a similar statement about wisdom in 8:11).

**31:11.** The noble wife's **husband** is mentioned three times (vv. 11, 23, 28) and is referred to as "him" in verse 12. His **confidence in her** is complete. He trusts her. Her careful household management enhances their family's wealth. He **lacks nothing of value** by way of household goods.

**31:12.** This kind of woman is an asset, not a liability, to her husband. **Good** comes to **him** that can be directly attributed to her. She supports and encourages him. And she is faithful in helping him **all . . . her life.**

**31:13.** She is involved in weaving and sewing as indicated in verses 13, 19, 22, 24. She uses **wool and flax,** and linen (vv. 22, 24) made from flax. **With eager hands** is literally, "with the delight of her hands," suggesting that she enjoys her work.

**31:14.** The noble wife also does shopping. She is **like . . . merchant ships** that brought unusual and fascinating merchandise **from** other places. She too brought interesting and unusual items home from her shopping.

**31:15.** Though she has household help she herself **gets up** early, before daybreak, to help prepare breakfast and **food for** other meals, and to delegate work (**portions**) to **her** servants.

**31:16.** The wife's considering and buying **a field** have caused some to question the validity of this poem because women, it is argued, were not permitted to do that in those days. However, in this wealthy household she apparently had money to invest. Then **out of her earnings** from various investments (cf. "trading," v. 18, and "sells," v. 24) she plants **a vineyard.** She has a business mind and she works hard.

**31:17.** She works energetically (lit.,

"girds her loins with strength") and with vigor (cf. "works" in v. 13). She has a healthy attitude toward **work.**

**31:18.** Her wise business dealings are again referred to (cf. "earnings," v. 16, and "sells," v. 24). The fact that **her lamp does not go out** speaks of her planning ahead. The five virgins whose lamps did not go out were praised for their fore-sight (Matt. 25:4). The extinguishing of one's lamp pictured calamity (Job 18:6; Prov. 13:9; 20:20; 24:20).

**31:19.** Verses 13, 19, 22, 24 refer to her weaving and sewing. She makes cloth by spinning wool or flax (v. 13) on a **distaff,** using a **spindle.**

**31:20.** The noble wife is also selfless and generous. She sells some things for profit but she also gives **to the poor** and **the needy** (see comments on these words in 30:14; cf. 31:9; also note 11:25; 21:26). Possibly 31:20 refers to her giving cloth she has made (v. 19) to the poor who have none.

**31:21.** Cold weather does not cause this woman to panic **for her household** (cf. v. 25b); she is prepared for it. She has **clothed** them **in scarlet,** that is, she has provided expensive garments. She spares no cost in protecting her family from the cold.

**31:22. She** even **makes** her family's bed **coverings. She** clothes herself **in fine linen and purple.** Linen is made from flax (v. 13) and purple is a dye made from a shellfish. Her own clothes were evidences of her family's well-to-do position.

**31:23.** A noble woman enhances **her** husband's standing among those who transact legal and judicial affairs **at the city gate** (cf. v. 31) **among the elders.** Though she is obviously aggressive and competent, she functions in a way that honors her husband's leadership rather then denigrates it. She respects him and builds him up.

**31:24.** Again her clothing enterprise is mentioned. She makes linen clothes for herself (v. 22) but is such a good seam-stress that she also **makes** enough to sell. **Linen garments** were expensive. Supply-ing **merchants with sashes** (belts) speaks of her productivity.

**31:25.** Clothing is here referred to metaphorically to indicate that her ap-pearance is one of **strength and dignity.** She is no shameful weakling. Also **she**

can **laugh at the** future, that is, face it with confidence (cf. v. 21). Though 27:1 cautions against boasting "about to-morrow," that does not do away with preparing for it (as ants do, 6:6-8; 30:25).

**31:26.** In keeping with the theme of Proverbs, this woman is praised for her **wisdom and faithful instruction.** The in-struction probably refers to her teaching her children and her servant girls.

**31:27.** She is involved in manage-ment (**she watches over . . . affairs of her household**). Yet she is also directly involved in various activities as a house-wife. She is **not** idle (cf. vv. 13, 17).

**31:28-29. Her children . . . call her blessed.** She is positive and optimistic and enjoys her role in life. **Her husband . . . praises her** by telling others she is the greatest of the **noble** women (cf. v. 10).

**31:30.** Her secret is her godly charac-ter. She is physically charming and beau-tiful but those qualities may not last. **But** as **a woman who fears the LORD,** she is **praised** by her husband (v. 28) and oth-ers (v. 31). Appropriately here near the end of Proverbs, the book concludes the way it began, by referring to fearing the Lord (1:7).

**31:31.** The writer urged his readers to recognize and **reward** the faithful dili-gence and kindness of such a woman. She along with her husband (v. 23) should be honored publicly. Honoring a *woman* at the . . . *gate* was not normally done in Israel. But an unusual woman called for unusual recognition.

The virtues of a noble wife are those that are extolled throughout the Book of Proverbs: hard work, wise investments, good use of time, planning ahead, care for others, respect for one's spouse, abili-ty to share godly values with others, wise counsel, and godly fear (worship, trust, service, obedience). As Proverbs has stat-ed repeatedly, these are qualities that lead to honor, praise, success, personal dignity and worth, and enjoyment of life. In the face of the adulteress' tempta-tions mentioned often in Proverbs, it is fitting that the book concludes by extol-ling a virtuous wife. Young men and oth-ers can learn from this noble woman. By fearing God, they can live wisely and righteously. *That* is the message of Proverbs.

# BIBLIOGRAPHY

Alden, Robert L. *Proverbs: A Commentary on an Ancient Book of Timeless Advice.* Grand Rapids: Baker Book House, 1983.

Bullock, C. Hassell. *An Introduction to the Poetic Books of the Old Testament.* Chicago: Moody Press, 1979.

Cohen, A. *Proverbs.* London: Soncino Press, 1946.

Delitzsch, Franz. "Proverbs." In *Commentary on the Old Testament in Ten Volumes.* Vol 6. (25 vols. in 10). Grand Rapids: Wm. B. Eerdmans Publishing Co., 1982.

Draper, James T., Jr. *Proverbs: The Secret of Beautiful Living.* Wheaton, Ill.: Tyndale House Publishers, 1971.

Eims, LeRoy. *Wisdom from Above for Living Here Below.* Wheaton, Ill.: SP Publications, Victor Books, 1978.

Harris, R. Laird. "Proverbs." In *The Wycliffe Bible Commentary.* Chicago: Moody Press, 1962.

Jensen, Irving L. *Proverbs.* Everyman's Bible Commentary. Chicago: Moody Press, 1982.

Jones, W.A. Rees, and Walls, Andrew F.

"The Proverbs." In *The New Bible Commentary.* London: InterVarsity Press, 1953.

Kidner, Derek. *The Proverbs: An Introduction and Commentary.* The Tyndale Old Testament Commentaries. Downers Grove, Ill.: InterVarsity Press, 1964.

Lawson, George. *Exposition of Proverbs.* Reprint. Grand Rapids: Kregel Publications, 1980.

McKane, William. *Proverbs.* Philadelphia: Westminster Press, 1970.

Mouser, William E., Jr. *Walking in Wisdom.* Downers Grove, Ill.: InterVarsity Press, 1983.

Murphy, Roland E. *Wisdom Literature: Job, Proverbs, Ruth, Canticles, Ecclesiastes, Esther.* The Forms of the Old Testament Literature. Vol. 13. Grand Rapids: Wm. B. Eerdmans Publishing Co., 1981.

Oesterly, W.O.E. *The Book of Proverbs.* New York: E.P. Dutton & Co., 1929.

Perowne, T.T. *The Proverbs.* Cambridge: Cambridge University Press, 1916.

Toy, Crawford H. *A Critical and Exegetical Commentary on The Book of Proverbs.* The International Critical Commentary. Edinburgh: T. & T. Clark, 1899. Reprint. Greenwood, S.C.: Attic Press, 1977.

# ECCLESIASTES

**Donald R. Glenn**

## INTRODUCTION

**Authorship and Date.** The author of Ecclesiastes identified himself, in Hebrew, as *Qōhelet* (1:1-2; cf. 1:12; 7:27; 12:8-10). Though this is sometimes treated as a proper name and hence transliterated, the presence of the article on the Hebrew word in 12:8 (and probably also in 7:27) shows that it is a title. The Old Testament uses this title of no other person. Nor is the form of the verb from which the title is derived used elsewhere. Therefore the exact meaning of this term is in doubt. Suggestions for its significance are generally drawn from the related Hebrew noun "assembly." For example, the Septuagint entitles the book *Ekklēsiastēs* ("one who calls an assembly"), whence the English word "Ecclesiastes." Several English versions of the Bible translate *Qōhelet* in relation to the function he supposedly played in the assembly (e.g., "The Teacher," NIV; "The Preacher," KJV; "The Leader of the Assembly," NIV marg.).

The author also identified himself as a "son of David" (1:1), a "king in Jerusalem" (1:1), and "king over Israel in Jerusalem" (1:12). Moreover, in the autobiographical section (1:12–2:26) he said he was wiser "than anyone who [had] ruled over Jerusalem before" him (1:16); that he was a builder of great projects (2:4-6); and that he possessed numerous slaves (2:7), incomparable herds of sheep and cattle (2:7), great wealth (2:8), and a large harem (2:8). In short he claimed to be greater than anyone who lived in Jerusalem before him (2:9). These descriptions have led many Jewish and Christian interpreters to identify the author as Solomon though his name is never explicitly used in the book.

Solomonic authorship of Ecclesiastes was generally accepted until the Age of the Enlightenment (17th century) when the use of literary and historical criticism

and linguistic analysis led to its general abandonment by scholars of all persuasions, including such noted conservative commentators as E.W. Hengstenberg, Franz Delitzsch, Edward J. Young, and H.C. Leupold. The primary reason for this denial of Solomonic authorship has been linguistic. Some scholars have pointed out that the Hebrew of Ecclesiastes differs in vocabulary and syntax from that of the period of Solomon and is much closer to a later stage of Hebrew reflected in the Mishnah (ca. A.D. 200). Also certain Aramaic and Persian words in the book have led scholars to date the book after Solomon. On the basis of those characteristics, Ecclesiastes is generally assigned to the late postexilic period (ca. 350–250 B.C.), though Hengstenberg, Delitzsch, Leupold, and Young all argue for the late Persian period (ca. 450–350 B.C.). The presence of fragments of manuscripts of Ecclesiastes at Qumran from the late second century B.C. and its acknowledged influence on the apocryphal Ecclesiasticus (ca. 190 B.C.) exclude any date later than 250–200 B.C.

Scholars who date the book late and deny Solomonic authorship generally explain the autobiographical references as literary devices to validate the author's arguments. It is said that such a literary device was used by the author of the pseudepigraphical Wisdom of Solomon (ca. 150–50 B.C.). However, some recent studies have shown that some of the features explained as characteristic of Aramaic and/or late Hebrew can also be shown in Canaanite-Phoenician literature of the pre-Solomonic era. Gleason L. Archer, who has summarized some of these features, has further argued that the Hebrew in Ecclesiastes is unique, unlike that of any Hebrew literary work from any preexilic or postexilic period (*Zondervan Pictorial Encyclopedia of the Bible.* Grand Rapids: Zondervan Publishing House,

1975, s.v. "Ecclesiastes," 2:184-7). Thus the linguistic argument against Solomonic authorship is somewhat inconclusive.

Alleged discrepancies between the social and political conditions reflected in the book and those in the time of Solomon—for example, oppression (4:1; 8:9), injustice (5:8), and corrupt government (5:8-9; 10:16-20)—are likewise not compelling arguments against Solomonic authorship. Though they may apply to the condition of the Jews under Persian or Greek domination (as those who deny Solomonic authorship claim), they could also refer to social evils in the latter years of Solomon's reign when his subjects chafed under his harsh rule (cf., e.g., 1 Kings 12:4, 9-11). Alleged discrepancies between the autobiographical allusions in Ecclesiastes 1:12, 16 and the history of Solomon are likewise unproved. Those who argue against Solomon as the author say that the verb "was" in 1:12 means "I . . . was [and am no longer] king." However, the verb could just as well be translated "I . . . have been [and still am] king." The reference to those who "ruled over Jerusalem before me" (1:16) may refer to non-Israelite rulers as well as Israelite rulers. Thus there are no compelling internal inconsistencies in identifying the author as Solomon.

In summary, though many scholars deny Solomonic authorship because of the supposed lateness of the language of Ecclesiastes, recent studies have called into question the validity of their linguistic evidence and reopened the possibility of identifying the unnamed author with Solomon. Since the evidence is inconclusive, the following commentary assumes the traditional view that Solomon was the human author. However, regardless of who wrote it, whether Solomon or a later Jewish sage, the presence of this book in the Bible indicates that it is God's Word.

**Theme and Purpose.** There can be little doubt about the theme of Ecclesiastes; it is announced both at the beginning (1:2) and the end (12:8) of the book and is often echoed throughout (e.g., 1:14; 2:11, 17, 26; etc.). The author ("the Teacher") declared that everything is "meaningless" (NIV) or "vanity" (KJV, RSV, NASB). This includes toil (1:14; 2:11, 17; 4:4, 7-8), wisdom (2:15), righteousness (8:14),

wealth (2:26; 5:10; 6:2), prestige (4:16), pleasure (2:1-2), youth and vigor (11:10), life (6:12; 7:15; 9:9), and even the future after death (11:8). The word *hebel*, translated "meaningless," elsewhere refers concretely to a breath, a wind, or a vapor (e.g., Prov. 21:6; Isa. 57:13). In Ecclesiastes several phrases are used parallel to *hebel*: "chasing after the wind" (Ecc. 1:14; 2:11, 17, 26; 4:4, 16; 6:9), "no advantage" (3:19; cf. 5:11; 6:8), "nothing . . . gained" (2:11; cf. 2:22; 3:9; 5:16; 6:11). Thus metaphorically this Hebrew word means what is unsubstantial or without real value. Occasionally it also refers metaphorically to some other characteristics of wind or vapor: (a) what is fleeting or transitory (cf. 6:12 where it is parallel to "few" [days] and "days he passes through like a shadow," 3:19; 7:15; 9:9; 11:10); (b) what is enigmatic or perplexing (cf. 6:2; 8:10, 14); or (c) what is unseen and obscure (cf. 11:8).

Why did Solomon pass this verdict on man's toil? Because work, he felt, produces nothing of lasting value. Also man's work is often prompted by motives which sow the seeds of their own discontent—for example, rivalry (4:4, 6) and an insatiable desire for added wealth (4:8; 5:10; 6:9). And toil brings no lasting pleasure (2:10-11) no matter how great one's accomplishments (2:4-6) or how much one is rewarded for it (2:7-8). Moreover, one always runs the risk of losing the fruit of his labor. It can be lost through oppression or injustice (5:8-9), through some unpredictable misfortune (5:14), or through the judgment of God (2:26; cf. 5:6). Even if a person manages to retain the fruit of his labor throughout his life, he "can't take it with him" but must leave it to someone else (2:18; 5:15). Moreover, since the beneficiary of the fruit of a man's labors has not toiled for it (2:21) and may even be a fool (2:19), all the results of a man's labor may be squandered and his efforts ultimately go for naught.

Solomon saw a similar deficiency in a man's wisdom and righteousness because they provide no absolute guarantee of success. Wisdom does have a decisive advantage over folly (2:13-14), wealth (7:11-12), and physical strength or military might (9:16, 18; 7:19). And wisdom does make it easier to succeed even in hazardous tasks (10:8-10, esp. v. 10b; cf.

8:1-6, esp. v. 5; 10:2-4, esp. v. 2). However, wisdom's results can be vitiated through a little sin (9:18; cf. 7:7-9), a little folly (10:1), improper timing (10:11), or even a lack of proper appreciation (9:15). Moreover, wisdom is not always rewarded (9:11); a wise man is subject to the same unpredictable misfortunes as a wicked person (9:1-2, 12). Finally, any ultimate advantage in wisdom is obliterated by death; a wise man dies and is forgotten just like a fool (2:14-16).

Righteousness too provides no sure reward. Though Solomon affirmed that righteousness is rewarded and wickedness is punished (8:12-13), he had sometimes seen just the opposite (8:14; cf. 7:15; 8:10), and had observed wickedness practiced even in the courts (3:16) and had seen justice and people's rights denied (5:8). Though some of these inequities could perhaps be explained from the fact that absolute righteousness is impossible (7:20, 28-29), the truth is that the righteous are subject to the same unpredictable misfortunes as the wicked (9:1-2) and ultimately die just as the wicked do (9:3).

These observed inequities in the distribution of justice and the unpredictability of fate make all of life chancy in Solomon's view. Though he believed that God is providentially in control of all things (3:11; 6:10; 7:14; 9:1) and that everything has its appropriate time (3:1-8), there is a certain inscrutability about God's providential dealings even for the wisest people (3:11; 8:17). Thus Solomon repeatedly affirmed the inability of people to predict the future (7:14; 8:7; 9:1; 10:14) and to pick the best courses of action (6:12; 11:6). Moreover, the inscrutability of providence is not confined to this life; even life after death, contrary to the statements of some expositors, held no guarantees for Solomon.

Though he did indeed believe that God would judge people's deeds (3:17; 11:9; 12:14), he nowhere explicitly stated or even implied that this would take place *after* a person dies. Solomon confined his discussion of rewards and opportunities to enjoy God's favor to this life (9:4-7, esp. v. 5, "the dead . . . have no . . . reward," and v. 7, "it is now that God favors what you do"). Thus life after death was obscure to Solomon (11:8) and held no promise of redressing all the inequities and enigmas he had pointed out.

His reluctance to speculate about life after death (cf. 3:19-22) was in keeping with his method of demonstrating his theme, the method of empirical testing (e.g., "I have seen/saw"; 1:14; 3:16; etc.). His purpose for doing this, though nowhere stated, may be inferred from his conclusion (12:13-14) and from other intimations in the book (2:24-26; 3:14; 7:18). He intended to demonstrate empirically to people the insecurity of all human effort to provide any real meaning, value, or significance to their lives "under the sun" and to drive them to trust in God alone.

Even the enjoyment theme (2:24-26; 3:12, 22; 5:18-20; 8:15; 9:7-9; 11:7-10), though often mistakenly interpreted as the Epicurean counsel of despair, is closely tied to this purpose. Thus the enjoyment of life—joy in one's labor, enjoyment of its fruits—comes only as a gift of God (2:24-26, esp. v. 25; 3:13; 5:19-20; cf. 9:7). And it comes only to those who please God (2:26), who fear Him (8:12), and whose enjoyment of life is tempered by the recognition that God will judge their deeds (11:9). Thus the dominant mood of the book is pessimism, but the author, Solomon, was no pessimist, cynic, or skeptic as some critics have claimed. He was a believer who sought to destroy people's confidence in their own efforts, their own abilities, their own righteousness and to direct them to faith in God as the only possible basis for meaning, value, and significance to life "under the sun."

However, Solomon did not say that a person's efforts had no value whatever. One's labor can accomplish great things and gain him some pleasure (2:10). Skill can make it easier to succeed (10:10). Righteousness can give more security than wickedness (8:12-13). But in the light of the Fall (7:29), the inscrutability of providence (6:12), the imminence of death (12:1-7), and the obscurity of life after death (3:19-21; 11:8), labor, skill, and righteousness hold little promise of security or ultimate value.

Though Solomon wrote to combat the growing secularization of religion in his own day, his words provide a valid critique of modern secular humanism. Life is indeed short; it is filled with many enigmas and inequities. Apart from the assurance of future judgment and life after death furnished by the historical facts of Christ's crucifixion and resurrection (cf., e.g., Acts 17:30-31), the future after death is dark and obscure. However, in spite of this, life should not be abandoned or filled with despair. Rather, life should be lived in complete trust in God, be received and enjoyed as a gift from His good hand, and be lived in the light of His future judgment.

**Unity and Structure.** The view that Ecclesiastes consists of a combination of the contradictory views of three men (a skeptic, a writer of wisdom, and a believer)—a view common among critics at the beginning of the 20th century—has been largely abandoned. And the unity of the book, at least its thematic unity, has been generally affirmed. However, there is still no general consensus that the book follows a logical development or argument. Many scholars see the book as a loose collection of wisdom sayings similar to the Book of Proverbs. Other scholars see a connected argument only in the first part of the book (Ecc. 1–6) and a collection of practical exhortations in the second part (chaps. 7–12).

Among the many attempts to demonstrate a detailed argument throughout the book, two have gained some popularity. One method of tracing the argument, long in vogue, sees the repetition of the enjoyment theme at 2:24-26; 5:18-20; 8:15-17; 11:7-10 as concluding the arguments of four major sections.

A second method of tracing the argument, suggested by the methods of rhetorical criticism and involving the repetition of set formulas, is gaining current popularity and forms the basis for the outline in this commentary. Thus the main body of the book may be divided into two sections: (a) 1:12–6:9 emphasizes the limitations of all human effort (it is "meaningless and a chasing after the wind"), and (b) 6:10–11:6 emphasizes the limitations of human wisdom (man does not/cannot know/discover). Of the material that stands outside this structure 1:3-11 is a poem in support of the theme announced in 1:2, the vanity or futility of human endeavor, and 11:7–12:14 contains a poem recommending that people enjoy life as stewards of God (11:7–12:7). This final poem is followed by a reitera-tion of the theme (12:8) and a final conclusion (12:13-14) to "fear God and keep His commandments." As Robert K. Johnston has noted ("Confessions of a Workaholic: A Reappraisal of Qoheleth." *Catholic Biblical Quarterly.* 38 January-March 1976:18), this introductory and concluding material nicely summarizes Solomon's argument: *all human endeavors lack ultimate value; life should be enjoyed in the fear of God, as a gift from His hand.*

# OUTLINE

I. Introduction: The Futility of All Human Endeavor (1:1-11)
  A. Title (1:1)
  B. Theme: The futility of human effort (1:2)
  C. General support: The futility of human effort demonstrated from nature (1:3-11)
    1. Thesis: No ultimate profit in human labor (1:3)
    2. Proof: Ceaseless, wearisome rounds (1:4-11)
II. The Futility of Human Achievement Empirically Demonstrated (1:12–6:9)
  A. Personal observations on the futility of human achievement (1:12–2:17)
    1. Futility of human achievement shown by personal investigation (1:12-15)
    2. Futility of human wisdom shown by personal reflection (1:16-18)
    3. Futility of pleasure-seeking shown by personal experience (2:1-11)
    4. Futility of a wise lifestyle shown by reflection on death (2:12-17)
  B. The futility of human labor empirically demonstrated (2:18–6:9)
    1. Labor's fruits may be squandered by someone else (2:18-26)
    2. Labor cannot alter God's immutable, inscrutable providence (3:1–4:3)
    3. Labor is often motivated by inappropriate incentives (4:4-16)

# COMMENTARY

## I. Introduction: The Futility of All Human Endeavor (1:1-11)

In this introductory section the author identified himself (v. 1), stated his theme (v. 2), and defended it in general terms (vv. 3-11).

### A. Title (1:1)

**1:1.** As with other wisdom literature in the Old Testament (e.g., Prov. 30:1; 31:1; cf. Prov. 1:6; 22:17; 24:23) the author of Ecclesiastes identified this book as his own. Elsewhere (Ecc. 12:11), however, he also claimed divine authority for it. The author identified himself only by his titles: **the Teacher,** a **son of David,** the **king in Jerusalem.** As indicated in the *Introduction* under "Authorship and Date" these titles plus other information in the book (cf. 1:12, 16; 2:4-9) suggest that the author was Solomon.

### B. Theme: The futility of human effort (1:2)

**1:2.** After identifying himself as the author, Solomon declared most emphatically that everything is futile or **meaningless.** Five times in this one verse he used *hebel,* the Hebrew word for "meaningless." Four of those times are in a twofold repetition of a Hebrew superlative construction which the KJV renders "Vanity of vanities" and the NIV renders **Meaningless! Meaningless!** and **Utterly meaningless!** As indicated in the *Introduction's* "Theme and Purpose," he used this metaphorical term throughout the book to refer to what is without real substance, value, permanence, significance, or meaning. Here at the outset he applied this to **everything,** by which he meant all human endeavors, as is obvious from verse 3 and his argument throughout the book.

### C. General support: The futility of human effort demonstrated from nature (1:3-11)

In support of his theme, Solomon argued first in broad general terms that it is impossible for human efforts to have permanent value. He did this in a poem on the ceaseless rounds of generations (v. 4) and of nature (vv. 5-7), introduced by a rhetorical question (v. 3) and followed by a poetic conclusion (vv. 8-11).

## 1. THESIS: NO ULTIMATE PROFIT IN HUMAN LABOR (1:3)

**1:3.** Solomon followed the announcement of his theme (v. 2) with a rhetorical question which demanded a negative answer. By this device, a common feature in his argumentation (2:2; 3:9; 6:8, 11-12; etc.), he denied any profit or **gain** to a person's **labor**. The term "gain" (*yiṭrôn*), unique to the Book Ecclesiastes, occurs seven times (1:3; 2:11 ["gained"], 13 ["is better"]; 3:9; 5:9 ["profits"], 16; 10:10 [not trans. in the NIV]). "Gain" refers literally to what is left over (a gain or a profit) or metaphorically to what is advantageous or of benefit. Though some things have relative advantage over others (e.g., light over darkness and wisdom over folly, 2:13), Solomon affirmed at the outset that people gain no ultimate advantage or profit from all their toil. By the phrase **under the sun** he meant "down here on the earth." He used this phrase repeatedly (29 times) throughout the book, often in connection with man's toil.

## 2. PROOF: CEASELESS, WEARISOME ROUNDS (1:4-11)

Solomon supported his thesis by referring to the ceaseless rounds of generations (v. 4) and of nature (vv. 5-7). From them he concluded that people's labor, like these ceaseless rounds, produces nothing permanent or satisfying (vv. 8-11).

### a. The impermanence of man (1:4)

**1:4.** The first fact Solomon cited in support of his thesis is the impermanence of a person's existence. In contrast with **the earth,** the scene of one's labor, which **remains** (lit., "stands") **forever,** every person is a transitory being, a small part of the coming and going **generations.**

### b. The ceaseless rounds of nature (1:5-7)

**1:5-7.** The second fact Solomon cited in support of his thesis is the ineffectiveness of labor, demonstrated by nature's ceaseless activity. Mere activity in and of itself produces nothing of ultimate value. **The sun** and **the wind** are in constant motion but never arrive at any fixed goal or lasting rest. The **streams** continually **flow** to **the sea, yet the sea is never full.** (NASB's "to the place where the rivers flow, there they flow again" is preferred to NIV's **to the place the streams come from, there they return again.**) Thus all the activity of nature is monotonous (**round and round . . . ever returning**) and wearisome (**hurries** in v. 5 means lit., "pants [from exhaustion]"; cf. Jer. 14:6), without effecting any progress or reaching any fixed goal.

### c. The repetition of human endeavors (1:8-11)

**1:8-11.** Next Solomon argued that what is observable in the rounds of nature is also true of all human endeavor. **Nothing** happens or is done that is really **new** (v. 9). Things are only apparently **new** (v. 10a) because people do not recollect former actions, events, and accomplishments (vv. 10b-11). (NASB's "earlier things . . . later things" is preferred to NIV's **men of old . . . those who are yet to come** because the missing noun or antecedent is to be supplied for the Heb. adjectives "earlier" and "later" from **all things** in v. 8 and **anything** in v. 10.) As several commentators note, Solomon did not intend by this to deny human creativity but to deny the complete newness of people's accomplishments. For example, man's journey to the moon and the discovery of America, though different, were both explorations of distant places, involving adventure and risk. And the invention of dynamite and of the atomic bomb shared the element of discovering an "explosive." Thus what is true in the realm of nature—the constant repetition of previous accomplishments—is in essence true of the activity of people and is included in the observation that all things produce only indescribable weariness and lack of satisfaction (all things **are wearisome,** v. 8).

## II. The Futility of Human Achievement Empirically Demonstrated (1:12–6:9)

This long section is united by the repetition of the phrase "meaningless, a chasing after the wind." Apart from its occurrence at 4:4 where it seems to introduce a new section, this formula stands near the end of each of several sections and announces Solomon's verdict on the value of human achievement (1:12-15), human wisdom (1:16-18; 2:12-17), pleasure-seeking (2:1-11), and toil or labor (2:18–6:9).

## A. Personal observations on the futility of human achievement (1:12–2:17)

The four parts of this section, which contain Solomon's allusions to his own experiences, are clearly tied together in two pairs. Thus the repetition of the wisdom, madness, and folly motif (1:17; 2:12) is not redundant but deals with wisdom's relationship to his personal investigation into the value of human achievements (1:12-15) and to his personal experience of the futility of pleasure-seeking (2:1-11).

### 1. FUTILITY OF HUMAN ACHIEVEMENT SHOWN BY PERSONAL INVESTIGATION (1:12-15)

**1:12-15.** Solomon began his argument on the futility of human achievement by citing his own personal investigation into its value. Alluding to his wide opportunities for observation because of his position as the **King** of **Israel** (v. 12; cf. v. 16; 2:12), he stated that, aided by his surpassing **wisdom** and knowledge (1:13; cf. v. 16; 1 Kings 4:26-34), he had made a thorough (indicated by the use of the synonyms **study** and **explore** in Ecc. 1:13) and comprehensive investigation of all kinds of human activities (i.e., **all that is done under heaven**; cf. "under the sun," v. 14). He concluded that they are all **a heavy burden** (v. 13, 'inyan rā', "a bad or unpleasant task"; trans. "a miserable business" in 4:8 and "some misfortune" in 5:14) and thus futile or **meaningless.** In fact they are as useless as **chasing after the wind,** a graphic picture of effort expended with no results gained since no one can catch the wind by running after it. Solomon used this phrase nine times, all in the first half of the book (1:14, 17; 2:11, 17, 26; 4:4, 6, 16; 6:9).

Solomon based this verdict on his observations which had shown him that human achievements leave much to be desired. Human effort and action cannot remedy all the irregularities or counteract all the deficiencies observable in the nature of **things** (1:14-15; cf. 7:13).

### 2. FUTILITY OF HUMAN WISDOM SHOWN BY PERSONAL REFLECTION (1:16-18)

**1:16-18.** Solomon also argued that when he reflected (v. 17) on his surpassing **wisdom** and vast experience (v. 16) by means of which he had conducted the preceding investigation (cf. v. 13) and

had reached his somber conclusion, he realized that it held little real advantage over **madness and folly** (i.e., foolish ideas and pleasures; cf. 2:2, 13-14). His pursuit of **wisdom** was as frustrating as **chasing after the wind,** and its acquisition, far from alleviating the depression created by his somber verdict, merely increased his mental anguish (**sorrow**) and sadness of heart (**grief**).

### 3. FUTILITY OF PLEASURE-SEEKING SHOWN BY PERSONAL EXPERIENCE (2:1-11)

Turning from the report of his careful investigation into the value of human achievement in general (cf. 1:12-15), Solomon next described an experiment he conducted on the value of pleasure. Emphasizing the objective nature of his experiment under the guiding hand of wisdom (2:3, 9), he announced the goal and conclusion of his experiment (vv. 1-2), described the means by which he sought and found pleasure (vv. 3-10), and related them to the ultimate value of his accomplishments (v. 11).

#### a. The conclusion: Pleasure has little value (2:1-2)

**2:1-2.** Solomon stated that in his quest to find something worthwhile in life (**to find out what is good**; cf. v. 3, "to see what was worthwhile [same Heb. word as the word 'good'] for men to do"), he experimented **with pleasure.** But he concluded that it was futile or **meaningless** because it was foolish and accomplished little or nothing. Solomon's question, **And what does pleasure accomplish?** is again rhetorical, expecting a negative answer (cf. 1:3).

#### b. The experiment: Pleasure-seeking is futile (2:3-11)

**2:3.** In Solomon's quest to find something worthwhile to do, he even experimented—though deliberately and with restraint, not blindly or in uncontrolled excess (**my mind still guiding me with wisdom**; cf. v. 9b)—with sensual indulgence (e.g., **cheering myself with wine**) and with what he would otherwise have characterized as a foolish or frivolous lifestyle (**embracing folly**). He wanted to test the effects of pleasure-seeking and frivolity to **see** if they were really **worthwhile.**

**2:4-10.** In his inquiry into the value

of pleasure he denied himself no avenue through which pleasure might be gained. As the richest and most powerful man who had ever lived **in Jerusalem** (v. 9; cf. 1 Kings 10), he surrounded himself with pleasureful objects such as magnificent buildings and **vineyards** (Ecc. 2:4; cf. 1 Kings 7:1-11), luxuriant **gardens and parks** (Ecc. 2:5) filled with **trees** (vv. 5-6), a great retinue of **slaves** (v. 7; cf. 1 Kings 10:5) who were available to serve him, musicians to meet his aesthetic needs, and a large **harem** (Ecc. 2:8; cf. 1 Kings 11:1-3) to satisfy his physical desires. Moreover, with the wealth from his great **herds and flocks** (Ecc. 2:7) and his great treasures of **silver and gold** (v. 8; cf. 1 Kings 10:14-15, 27) he could buy anything his heart **desired** and indulge in every **pleasure** (Ecc. 2:10).

**2:11.** However, though he could gain some satisfaction from the joy of accomplishment and had indeed experienced pleasure from it all (cf. v. 10), when he reflected on the real value of what he had accomplished, he concluded that it **was meaningless** and **a chasing after the wind** (cf. 1:14, 17; 2:17, 26; 4:4, 6, 16; 6:9). There was no real or ultimate gain (cf. 1:3) from all his accomplishments **under the sun** (cf. comments on "under the sun" in 1:3).

4. FUTILITY OF A WISE LIFESTYLE SHOWN BY REFLECTION ON DEATH (2:12-17)

**2:12-16.** The reason Solomon passed this verdict on the ultimate value of his accomplishments was the sad fact of the universality of death. Pointing out that his experiment with the value of pleasure could perhaps be duplicated but not exceeded ("for what can the man do who comes after the king? Only what he has already done," v. 12b, RSV), Solomon reflected on the relationship between wisdom and folly, namely, that **wisdom** enabled him to enjoy pleasure and the fruits of his labor judiciously (cf. vv. 3, 9) as opposed to riotous hedonism (**madness and folly,** v. 12; cf. 1:17). He concluded that there was indeed some advantage to **wisdom.** (**Better** translates the word *yiṭrôn* rendered "gain" in 1:3 [see comments there]. It refers to something excelling over something else.)

A **wise man** has the foresight to avoid danger while a **fool** gets into trouble as though he stumbles around in the dark (2:14; cf. Prov. 4:18-19 for a similar metaphorical use of light and **darkness**).

However, because **both** the wise man and the fool share **the same fate** (Ecc. 2:14)—they both **die** and are ultimately **forgotten** (v. 16; cf. 9:5)—he concluded that there was no real advantage to being **wise,** that is, to living wisely as opposed to living foolishly (2:15).

**2:17.** This also led Solomon to view life as repugnant or distasteful. He said he **hated life, because the work . . . was grievous to** him. (The word trans. "grievous" [*rā'*] is the antonym for the word trans. "good" or "worthwhile" in vv. 1, 3.) If, he concluded, it does not ultimately make any difference how one lives and if there is nothing ultimately worthwhile to do, then **all** of life and all its accomplishments are futile or **meaningless, a chasing after the wind** (cf. 1:14, 17; 2:11, 17, 26; 4:6, 16; 6:9).

B. *The futility of human labor empirically demonstrated (2:18–6:9)*

Having discussed the futility of human achievements in general (1:12-15) and the futility of his own achievements (2:1-11) in view of death (2:12-17), Solomon then turned to consider the value of the toil he had expended in accomplishing them (2:18-20) and the value of human toil in general (2:21–6:9). He shifted from using "I" and "my" in 2:1-18 to using "he," "a man," and "his" in 2:19-20. Twenty-three of the 34 occurrences of the Hebrew word for "toil" and "labor" in Ecclesiastes appear in this section, which may be divided into four paragraphs (2:18-26; 3:1–4:3; 4:4-16; 5:1–6:9) on the basis of the recurring formula "meaningless, a chasing after the wind."

1. LABOR'S FRUITS MAY BE SQUANDERED BY SOMEONE ELSE (2:18-26)

a. *Labor's fruits may be squandered by one's heir (2:18-21)*

**2:18-21.** Life was not the only thing Solomon found to be ultimately repugnant; he also viewed all his labor with distaste. **I hated all the things I had toiled for** is literally, "I hated all my toil." Thus he viewed his work **under the sun** (vv. 18-20; cf. comments on 1:3) with **despair** (2:20) because there was no permanence to its fruits, to the things he accomplished through it. Though what he accomplished (vv. 4-6) and accumulated (vv. 7-8) might survive him, he would have no **control** over how it would be used after his death (v. 19; cf. Ps. 49:10). A person who inherited it, who had **not** had to work **for it** (Ecc. 2:21), and who consequently had no real appreciation for it, might be a **fool** (v. 19) who would squander it. So Solomon declared toil to be futile or **meaningless** (vv. 19, 21) and the loss of its fruits **a great misfortune** (v. 21).

### b. Thus labor is not worth the effort (2:22-23)

**2:22-23.** Viewed in the light of the impermanence of its fruits Solomon asked whether a man's labor in this life (**under the sun**; cf. comments on 1:3) was really worth it all. In the final analysis, he declared, all that really resulted from it was the expenditure of a lot of painful labor and restless activity which is futile or **meaningless.**

### c. It is best to enjoy labor's fruits as God enables (2:24-26)

**2:24-26.** In view of the impermanence of the fruits of a man's toil, Solomon recommended that a man enjoy its fruits (eating and drinking are only metaphorical for partaking of all its fruits) **and find satisfaction in his work** (cf. 3:13; 5:18; 8:15) as he himself had done (2:10). However, he warned that this was possible only if **God** enabled one to do so: **without Him, who can eat or find enjoyment?** Moreover, he warned that **God** only enables those who please Him to do so. Often sinners amass **wealth** which ultimately is enjoyed by **one who pleases God,** a task he identified as futile or **meaningless, a chasing after the wind** (cf. 1:14, 17; 2:11, 17; 4:4, 6, 16; 6:9).

Two points from 2:24-26 should be noted. First, Solomon stated that God's disposition of wealth and the enjoyment of one's labors and its fruits are based on whether a man is pleasing to God or is a **sinner.** As is clear from the words "the man who pleases" God and "the sinner" elsewhere in Ecclesiastes (7:26; cf. 8:12), this implies that a person will be judged on the basis of his ethical behavior and his trust in **God** or lack of it. Second, Solomon wrote that this judgment would take place in this life (not in a life after death) and would involve temporal not eternal rewards. These two points (en-

joyment of life and judgment), which are brought together only here, are crucial in the development of the book. The enjoyment theme, mentioned at crucial times in the book (3:12-13, 22; 5:18-20; 8:15; 9:7-10), is here specifically related to the theme of judgment (11:9; 12:14), and to the advice to fear God and keep His commandments (12:13).

### 2. LABOR CANNOT ALTER GOD'S IMMUTABLE, INSCRUTABLE PROVIDENCE (3:1–4:3)

The argument in this section revolves around the repetition of the word "time" in 3:1-8, 11, 17 and other repeated phrases such as "I have seen" or "I saw" (3:10, 16; 4:1), "I know" (3:12, 14), and "I thought" (3:17-18). Solomon argued that God has appointed a time for everything (3:11), even for injustice (3:16-17) and oppression (4:1-3). All this is part of the eternal (3:14), immutable (3:14), inscrutable (3:11) providence of God which renders a person's toil profitless (3:9).

### a. Thesis: Everything has its time (3:1-8)

(1) Thesis stated. **3:1.** Solomon said, **There is a time . . . for every activity under heaven** (cf. 8:6). By the word "activity" Solomon meant people's deliberate, willful acts. The Hebrew word for "activity," always used of people, literally means "desire," and then by metonymy "what one desires" (cf. Isa. 58:13). For these willful acts people are held accountable (cf. Ecc. 3:17). Each activity, wrote Solomon, has its proper "time" (point in time) and **season** (duration).

(2) Thesis illustrated (3:2-8). Solomon followed his general statement with a poem on 14 opposites, each of which happens in its time. The fact that Solomon utilized polar opposites in a multiple of seven and began his list with birth and death is highly significant. The number seven suggests the idea of completeness and the use of polar opposites—a well-known poetical device called merism—suggests totality (cf. Ps. 139:2-3). Though the exact meaning of some of these "activities" is uncertain, Solomon intended to affirm that all a person's activities, both constructive and destructive, and all his responses to people, objects, and events happen in their times.

**3:2-3.** The list begins with a reference to the beginning and end of a person's life, two events over which he really has no control. Solomon continued by referring to the deliberate acts of one who begins and ends vegetable life (**a time to plant and a time to uproot**), takes and saves human life, and constructs and destroys buildings. Perhaps all these are suggested by the concept of birth and death.

**3:4.** From the concept of death and destruction, Solomon wrote of the human responses to those events. People experience weeping and mourning, and their opposites, laughing and dancing, two activities by which joy is expressed.

**3:5-6.** How the two opposites in verse 5 are related to each other and to those in verses 2-4 is uncertain. Many interpretations have been suggested for the meaning of the phrases **a time to scatter** (or "cast away," KJV) **stones and a time to gather them.** Perhaps it is best to see them as referring to the gathering and rejecting of building materials. This relates these opposites both to the idea of building (v. 3) and to the thought of keeping and throwing away (v. 6).

Solomon then spoke of the display of affections (v. 5b), probably of a man to a woman and perhaps also of a woman to a man. He then wrote about searching for a thing or giving it up as lost and about keeping a thing or throwing it **away** (v. 6). All the opposites in verses 5-6 seem to involve man's interest in things or affection for persons.

**3:7.** This verse may refer to actions associated with mourning (tearing one's clothes and remaining silent; cf. Job 2:12-13), and its end (sewing one's clothes and speaking out). If so, it would relate to the mourning in Ecclesiastes 3:4.

**3:8.** Solomon closed his list of opposites by referring to life's two basic emotions, **love** and **hate,** and the most hostile expression of the latter, **war,** and its opposite, **peace.** It may be significant that the list closes, somewhat as it began, with a set of opposites (war and peace) over which a person has little control.

*b. Significance: Toil is profitless (3:9)*

**3:9.** Turning from the thesis that every activity has its time, Solomon again raised the question of the value of a person's work, expecting rhetorically the same somber answer as before (cf. 1:3; 2:11), that there is no profit (**gain,** *yiṯrôn;* cf. comments on 1:3) in one's **toil.**

*c. Reason: God's design is inscrutable (3:10-11)*

**3:10-11.** To support the implied negative answer to his question in verse 9, Solomon referred to three observations he had drawn from his reflection on all the human activity represented in the opposites, verses 2-8. This activity is suggested by the word **burden** (*'inyān*), which is translated "task" in the NASB. (1) Solomon observed that **God . . . has made everything beautiful** (or, "appropriate"; the same word is trans. "proper" in 5:18) **in its time,** that is, God in His providential plans and control has an appropriate time for every activity. (2) Solomon observed that God has put **eternity in the hearts of men.** People have a longing or desire to know the extratemporal significance of themselves and their deeds or activities. (3) Solomon added that people **cannot** know the works of **God . . . from beginning to end,** that is, they cannot know the sovereign, eternal plan of God. Human labor is without profit because people are ignorant of God's eternal plan, the basis by which He evaluates the appropriateness and eternal significance of all their activities. Because of this ignorance there is an uncertainty and latent temporality to the value of all one's labor.

*d. Recommendation: Enjoy life as God enables (3:12-13)*

**3:12-13.** Since man in his ignorance of God's plan cannot be sure of the appropriateness or lasting significance of his labor, Solomon again recommended the present enjoyment of life (cf. 2:24), stating that **there is nothing better for men than to be happy** as long as **they live** (cf. 5:18; 8:15). The words **do good** (in the NIV and NASB) should be rendered "enjoy themselves" (RSV). No moral qualification is suggested here as a requirement for receiving God's gift of enjoyment (as there is in 2:26). Most commentators are undoubtedly correct in pointing to the parallel words **find satisfaction** (lit., "see good") in 3:13. There "good" is used in a nonethical sense (cf. 2:24; 5:18 for the same idiom).

Again Solomon indicated that this ability to enjoy life comes as a **gift of God** (cf. 2:25). Christian D. Ginsburg properly renders 3:13 as a conditional sentence: "If any man eats and drinks and finds satisfaction in all his toil, it is a gift of God" (*The Song of Songs and Coheleth,* pp. 311-2).

### e. Purpose: That man may fear God (3:14-15)

**3:14-15.** Anticipating that people who cannot understand God's plan might accuse Him of being arbitrary, Solomon described the nature of God's plan and the response it should elicit. Solomon said the work of God is eternal (**everything God does will endure forever**) and perfect and immutable (**nothing can be added to it and nothing taken from it**; cf. 7:13). In support of this last point Solomon referred as he did in 1:9 to the repetition of natural events: **Whatever is has already been, and what will be has been before.** He added that this is part of God's deliberate plan. **God will call the past to account** may also be rendered "God calls back the past" (NIV marg.) or "God seeks what has passed by" (NASB). Some commentators suggest the paraphrase, "God seeks to repeat what has passed." Franz Delitzsch summarizes the thought of this statement: "The government of God . . . does not change; His creative as well as His moral ordering of the world produces with the same laws the same phenomena. . . . His government remains always, and brings . . . up again that which hath been" ("Ecclesiastes" in *Commentary on the Old Testament in Ten Volumes,* 6:264). The response **God** wants people to have to His immutable, inscrutable plan is one of fear, reverence, and humble submission: **so men will revere Him.**

### f. Application: The place of injustice in God's plan (3:16–4:3)

The most likely exception to the appropriateness of any activity and the perfection of God's plan is the problem of injustice and oppression in the world.

(1) Observation: Injustice in the world. **3:16.** Anticipating a possible objection to the perfection of God's plan (cf. comments on another anticipated problem in vv. 14-15), Solomon stated that he had not ignored the problem of injustice (cf. 4:1; 8:14). He himself had observed in this life (**under the sun;** cf. comments on 1:3) that injustice was often evident in a place where one should least expect it—in the courts, **the place of judgment** and **of justice.** The repetition of the phrase **wickedness was there** emphasizes his surprise and consternation. Moreover, he affirmed in 3:17 that God was not ignoring injustice; He has both a future disposition and a present purpose for it.

(2) Future disposition: God will judge. **3:17.** Solomon affirmed that **God will** judge **both the righteous and the wicked** (cf. 11:9; 12:14) but that this **judgment** will come only in His **time.** The time of this judgment is ambiguous; it is future and in God's time but the verse neither states nor implies that it will be in the afterlife. Solomon undoubtedly believed with the wisdom writers in general that the judgment would take place on earth (cf., e.g., Job 27:13-23; Pss. 37:2, 6, 9, 11, 13, 15, 17-40; 73:18-20, 27; Prov. 22:22-23).

(3) Present manifestation: To demonstrate human finitude (3:18-21). **3:18-20.** The connection of verses 18-21 with the preceding is not well reflected in most English translations. The phrase **as for men** means literally, "for the sake of/because of men" and is generally taken by commentators to refer back to the injustice mentioned in verse 16: "injustice is both for the sake of and because of men." Thus Solomon affirmed a second purpose for injustice, namely, that by it God shows people **that they are like the animals** (lit., "they are animals, they with respect to themselves"). This does not say that people are nothing more than animals, with no immortal souls. It does suggest that people, like **animals,** die (cf. Ps. 49:12, 20). They have a common mortality, as Ecclesiastes 3:19-20 indicates.

Both people and animals **come from** the same **dust** of the earth, are animated by **the same** life **breath** (cf. Job 34:14-15; Ps. 104:29), and **go to the same place,** that is, return **to** the dust (Ecc. 3:20). So Solomon argued that **man has no advantage over** an **animal,** for both are transitory (*hebel* can be rendered "transitory" here rather than **meaningless;** cf. 6:12, and *kōl* can be rendered "both" rather than **everything,** as in 2:14; 7:18).

**3:21.** Moreover, any possible advantage man might claim over an animal was, according to Solomon, beyond empirical demonstration. This is indicated by his rhetorical question, **Who knows if the spirit of man rises upward and if the spirit of the animal goes down into the earth?** No living person can *observe* or demonstrate a difference between people and animals by watching them as they die. Some commentators, it is true, say that Solomon is here affirming a difference in the destinies of men and animals. They see vestiges of a belief in man's immortality expressed here and point to the absence of an "if" in the Hebrew text before spirit (cf. KJV, NASB). However, this conflicts with several things: (a) the context where Solomon is emphasizing the sameness of man's fate with the animals (vv. 19-20); (b) the use of the word "spirit" in this passage which refers to the breath of life which man shares with the animals (v. 19); (c) the rhetorical question in verse 22, "Who can bring him to see what will happen after him?" which denies Solomon's knowledge of an afterlife; and (d) the uniform testimony of many Bible versions which do reflect an interrogative in verse 21. Solomon had earlier argued that death negates all differences between a wise person and a fool (2:14c-16). Here he argued that death negates all differences between people and animals. Though people are endowed with a sense of rationality and a sense of eternity (3:11), injustice demonstrates their finitude, mortality, and ignorance of God's plan.

(4) Recommendation: Enjoy life. **3:22.** Since people are mortal (vv. 19-21), Solomon recommended that **a man . . . enjoy his work** (and probably, by metonymy, the fruits of his work or labor; cf. 2:24; 3:12). This **is** man's **lot** (a word that means lit., "portion, share, or allotment"; NASB translates this wrongly in 5:18-19; 9:9). This was especially pertinent in view of the fact that, as he had shown, people are ignorant of God's plan and cannot know what the future, including life after death, holds for them. He summarized this point in the rhetorical question, **Who can bring him to see what will happen after him?**

(5) Alternative response: Gloomy despair. **4:1-3.** Solomon also supported his advice to enjoy life (cf. 3:22) by describing his further reflections on injustice: **Again I looked** at **all the** acts of **oppression** (cf. 3:16) that occur on the earth (**under the sun;** cf. comments on 1:3). Plaintively Solomon lamented the desperate and hopeless plight of **the oppressed** who cry out for help but find none because of the irresistible **power**

and authority **of their oppressors.** The repetition of the words **they have no comforter** emphasizes their plight. Therefore Solomon stated that a man is better off **dead** or, better still, never having been born than having to witness (and possibly experience—the verb "see" often means "experience," as in 8:16) **the evil** oppression that takes place on earth because of injustice. In other words the only alternative to enjoyment of life as a gift from God's hand is the gloomy despair caused, in part at least, by reflection on unchecked oppression.

3. LABOR IS OFTEN MOTIVATED BY INAPPROPRIATE INCENTIVES (4:4-16)

This section employs the characteristic refrain "meaningless, a chasing after the wind" as a bracketing introductory and concluding formula (vv. 4, 16). This device, called an *inclusio*, is a common rhetorical feature in biblical literature (cf., e.g., Ps. 8:1, 9). Ecclesiastes 4:4-16 is also characterized by the repeated use of the word "meaningless" (vv. 4, 7-8, 16) and the word "better" (vv. 6, 9, 13) by which Solomon characterized certain motivating incentives of labor as futile and inappropriate.

*a. Labor is sometimes motivated by envy (4:4-6)*

**4:4-6.** The first inappropriate incentive Solomon referred to was envy of others. He said that **all labor and all achievement** (undoubtedly hyperboles) **spring from man's envy of his neighbor** and that envy is futile or **meaningless** and **a chasing after the wind** (cf. 1:14, 17; 2:11, 17, 26; 4:6, 16; 6:9). Some uncertainty exists about the meaning of 4:5 because the metaphors **folds his hands** and "eats his meat" (lit. trans. for **ruins himself**) refer elsewhere to sloth and self-destruction (Prov. 6:10-11; 24:33-34; Isa. 49:26). However, the view that Ecclesiastes 4:5 refers to a commendation of contentment with the simple needs of life ("eats his meat"; cf. Ex. 16:8; Deut. 12:20) with a minimum of effort (i.e., folding his hands) fits in better with Solomon's recommendation in Ecclesiastes 4:6 to be content with **one handful** (i.e., a little) accompanied by **tranquillity** ("rest," NASB; "quietness," KJV; the same Heb. word is rendered "rest" in 6:5 and the related Heb. verb is rendered "rested" in

Ex. 20:11) rather than a lot (**two hand-fuls**) accompanied by **toil** and anxious striving, which he characterized as **chasing after the wind** (cf. Ecc. 4:4).

### b. Labor is sometimes motivated by selfish greed (4:7-12)

**4:7-8.** Selfish greed is another inappropriate incentive that Solomon said is futile or **meaningless** (that word, occurring at the beginning of v. 7 and the end of v. 8, points up another *inclusio*; cf. comments under "3. Labor is often motivated by inappropriate incentives [4:4-16])." On the words **under the sun** see comments on 1:3. Greed is the insatiable covetousness characterized by a man's having **no end to his toil, not** being con-**tent with his wealth,** and not sharing with anyone, not even a **son** or **brother** (this refers to sharing in partnership, not to inheritance, as vv. 9-12 make clear). In the end, Solomon stated, such a greedy person would wake up and realize that it was futile or **meaningless** to toil incessantly to gather wealth which he neither shared nor enjoyed. Such a greedy person's questions, asked rhetorically, show his disparaging of his behavior. Solomon added that such futile or meaningless toil was **a miserable business** (*'inyan rā',* "a bad or unpleasant task"; trans. "a heavy burden" in 1:13 and "some misfortune" in 5:14; cf. *'inyan,* "burden," in 3:10).

**4:9-12.** In contrast with the futility of selfish greed, Solomon commended sharing with others by citing several advantages that come from companionship: better profit (**a good return**) from one's labor (v. 9), **help** in time of difficulty (v. 10), comfort in time of need (v. 11; one's body heat can keep another person from freezing), protection in time of danger (v. 12). The last three of these are illustrated by examples from the benefits of two persons traveling together. In the case of the second and third of these (vv. 10b, 11b) Solomon lamented the perils of isolation (characteristic of selfish greed; cf. "a man all alone," v. 8a).

Having set forth the advantages of joint effort and the mutual benefits of sharing one's toil and its fruit with another, Solomon stated climactically that if **two are better than one** (v. 9) then **three** are even better (v. 12). One's efforts and benefits should not be confined to merely two persons.

### c. Labor is sometimes motivated by the desire for advancement and prestige (4:13-16)

**4:13-16.** The emphasis in these verses is on the transitory nature of fame and prestige. However, the precise interpretation and significance of these verses is somewhat unclear because of the ambiguity of the number of individuals involved and their relationship with each other. It is unclear whether there are two young men who in turn succeed to the throne of an old and foolish king or whether there is only one young man. It is also unclear whether the pronouns (in Heb.) in verse 15 refer to the poor yet wise young man (v. 13a) or to the old and foolish king (v. 13b). Though there are several ways to interpret these ambiguities, it seems best to follow the interpretation reflected in general in the NIV. Taken in this way the passage refers to **a poor but wise youth** who had advanced from poverty (**he** was **born in poverty within his** [i.e., the old king's] **kingdom**). The young person also lacked influence (he had **come from prison**; cf. Joseph's situation, Gen. 39:20–41:45). From this lowly position the youth advanced to great popularity and prestige: **all who lived and walked under the sun** (i.e., "on the earth"; cf. comments on "under the sun" in Ecc. 1:3) **followed the youth,** the king's successor. He also had great authority; he became the master of innumerable subjects (4:16; lit., "no end to all the people before whom [at whose head] he was"; cf. Num. 27:17). However, his prestige and authority were short-lived: **those who came later were not pleased with the successor.**

This passage illustrates the moral of Ecclesiastes 4:13: it is better to be poor (and without influence) than to be powerful and influential. Why? Because power, influence, and prestige are all transitory. Though the truth of verse 13 also commends wisdom over folly and commends responsiveness to criticism or counsel over unresponsiveness, these are not directly illustrated in the passage, which is confined to the futility of advancement. The point of the passage seems to be that the desire for prestige and advancement, two incentives which often motivate a person's labor, is, like envy and greed, futile or **meaningless** and **a chasing after the wind** (cf. 1:14, 17; 2:11, 17, 26; 4:4, 6; 6:9).

4. LABOR'S FRUITS MAY SOMETIMES NOT BE ENJOYED (5:1–6:9)

The argument of this passage has often been misunderstood. This is because of three things: (a) the use of the imperative mood in 5:1-7, (b) the absence of formal indications of divisions within 5:1–6:9, and (c) the failure of some commentators to make some connections between verses which Solomon apparently intended. This passsage concludes with the last of nine occurrences of the characteristic formula "meaningless, a chasing after the wind" (6:9).

a. Labor's fruits may be lost to God through a rash vow (5:1-7)

5:1-7. These verses are often wrongly interpreted as an interlude in Solomon's argument. They are assumed to give advice on proper worship, including the proper attitude for worship (v. 1), the proper practice of prayer (vv. 2-3), and the proper payment of vows (vv. 4-7). In reality, however, they are an important part of Solomon's argument, warning against the folly of rash vows which could cause a person to lose the fruits of his labor through God's destroying **the work** of his **hands** (v. 6). Thus Solomon warned against the folly of rash vows which he called **the sacrifice of fools** (v. 1) and **the speech of a fool** (v. 3). He warned against uttering a hasty and ill-considered **vow to** the Lord: **Do not be quick with your mouth; do not be hasty in your heart** (v. 2).

Solomon also warned that it would do no good to try to get out of fulfilling such a **vow** by pleading with the priest that it **was a mistake** (v. 6, something done inadvertently; cf. "error" in 10:5). **The temple messenger** probably refers to the priest as in Malachi 2:7. The basis for this warning was Deuteronomy 23:21-23, where vows were described as voluntary but binding once made, because failure to fulfill them was called sin and would result in God's punishment. Thus Solomon called foolish vows wrongdoing (**they do wrong,** Ecc. 5:1) and warned that a person's **mouth** could **lead** him **into sin** (v. 6), which could result in God's displeasure (v. 4) and anger (v. 6). Such a sin can ultimately lead to the loss of all a person worked for (v. 6).

Since a rash vow might result in the destruction of the fruits of one's labor (and his labor might thus prove futile), Solomon compared rash vows to futile or **meaningless** dreams. This is the thought in verse 7a, which may be translated somewhat literally, "Through many dreams there is futility and also through many words." So Solomon exhorted his readers to fear **God** (v. 7b), being cautious not to make rash vows (vv. 1-2) and to **fulfill** the vows they had made (v. 4).

b. Labor's fruits may be lost to corrupt officials through extortion (5:8-9)

The point of these verses and their connection with Solomon's argument has often been misconstrued because of erroneous interpretations of some enigmatic expressions in verses 8b-9. Though many other interpretations are possible, as is obvious from the diversity in various translations (e.g., KJV, NASB, NIV), these verses probably refer to a hierarchy of corruption. This view, reflected in the NIV, seems to fit Solomon's overall argument in 5:1–6:9 best.

5:8-9. Having shown that the fruits of labor could be lost through a rash vow to God (vv. 1-7), Solomon added that one should **not be surprised** if the result of his labor were lost to the next highest authority, the king and his officials. In terms much briefer than but similar to Samuel's view of some typical evils of kingship (1 Sam. 8:10-18), Solomon described the oppressive exactions of officials at all levels. They were watching not to protect **the poor** and **oppressed** (cf. Ecc. 4:1) but to find ways to squeeze revenue out of the officials under them. At the head of this whole corrupt system was **the king** who **himself** profited **from the fields** of the oppressed. The potential of all a man worked for, **the increase from the land,** could be **taken** or extorted **by all** these corrupt officials.

Many commentators, arguing that Solomon would scarcely have depicted his own government in such poor light, have seen this passage as evidence that he did not write this book. But there is no evidence that Solomon was referring to any specific government. Like the other references in 2:18–6:9 (e.g., the hypothetical case in 4:13-16), Solomon was generalizing. Moreover, Israel's demand that Rehoboam, Solomon's successor (1 Kings 12:1-10), reduce his oppression suggests that the provincial governors under Solomon had made financial demands to support his opulence (1 Kings 4:7, 22-23). Solomon's government could scarcely be excluded from the truth in Ecclesiastes 5:8-9.

### c. Labor's fruits may not be enjoyed because of one's own covetousness (5:10-12)

**5:10-12.** Having shown that the fruits of one's labors might not be enjoyed because they might be lost to God (vv. 1-7) or to governing officials (vv. 8-9), Solomon next argued that a person's own covetousness might keep him from enjoying them. Calling covetousness or the love of **money** futile or **meaningless,** Solomon argued that a covetous person **never** derives enjoyment from his **wealth** (v. 10) because his increased wealth merely brings him increased anxiety (v. 12b). While **a laborer** might rest content with **little or much,** a covetous person cannot sleep (his **abundance permits . . . no sleep,** v. 12). He has to be constantly on guard to protect his riches from the ever-growing number of people who would try to **consume them.** Thus Solomon asked satirically **what benefit** a covetous person gets from increased riches **except to** keep an eye on them (v. 11, lit., "to look at them with his eyes"). In summary, Solomon argued that the only results of increased wealth for a covetous person are increased anxiety and increased vigilance, not increased enjoyment.

### d. Toiling to accumulate the fruits of labor may result in misery (5:13-17)

**5:13-14.** Solomon concluded his treatment of the futility of toil by showing how transitory its fruits really are and how striving to accumulate them brings only misery. Such striving and loss is **a grievous evil** (or, perhaps better, "a depressing misfortune"); the word for "grievous" (ḥōlâh) is literally, "sick"; and the word for "evil" (rāʿâh) is often used for disaster or misfortune. Solomon emphasized this by referring to a person who had carefully treasured up or **hoarded** his **wealth** and then **lost** it all **through some misfortune** (not "bad investment" as in the NASB; this same expression, ʿinyan rāʿ, refers in 1:13 to "a heavy burden" and in 4:8 to "a miserable business"). Such misfortunes would include the examples in 5:1-7, 8-9, experiences

such as those of Job (Job 1:13-19), *and* bad investments. As a result of such loss a man would have **nothing** to leave his **son** (Ecc. 5:14). Hoarding wealth may thus even bring **harm** (i.e., "misery") to **its owner** (v. 13). This is worse than accumulating wealth without knowing who will control it later (2:17-23).

**5:15-17.** Moreover, Solomon argued that even if wealth were not lost but kept throughout life, one could not "take it with him." Everyone enters the world with nothing, and leaves it with **nothing** (cf. Ps. 49:17). Since a person cannot take any fruits of his **labor** with him when he dies, he really gains nothing from his labor (Ecc. 5:16, **what does he gain?** [yitrōn; cf. 1:3] is again rhetorical; cf. 3:9). All his effort is as wasted as if he had toiled **for the wind.** Solomon called **this too . . . a grievous evil** ("a depressing misfortune"; cf. 5:13). He added that the misery that accompanies the windy or empty effort of toiling to accumulate wealth is like gloom (**he eats in darkness;** cf. **frustration, affliction, and anger**). The word "affliction" (ḥōlî, related to the word trans. "grievous" in vv. 13, 16) means literally, "sickness." Here as in verses 13, 16 it refers to psychological illness (cf. comments on v. 13).

### e. Labor's fruits are to be enjoyed as God enables (5:18–6:9)

Having shown in some detail the futility of labor, climaxed graphically by setting forth the misery that often accompanies toiling to accumulate wealth, Solomon again recommended the enjoyment of life (cf. 2:24-26; 3:12-13, 22). But he warned that there are serious obstacles to such enjoyment.

(1) Recommendation: Enjoy labor's fruits as God enables (5:18-20). **5:18.** In contrast with the misery (rāʿâh, "evil, disaster, misfortune") that accompanies toiling to accumulate wealth, Solomon declared that the only **good** (ṭôb, the antonym of rāʿâh and what motivated Solomon's experiment in 2:1, 3) **and proper** (or "fitting" [NASB]; trans. "beautiful" in 3:11) thing is **for a man** to enjoy the fruits of and **to find satisfaction in his** hard **labor. This is** man's **lot** ("portion, share, allotment"; cf. 3:22; 5:19; 9:9).

**5:19-20.** The results of a man's labor (i.e., his **wealth and possessions;** cf. 6:2) and the ability **to enjoy them** and to **be**

**happy** (cf. 8:15) **in his work** are gifts of **God** (cf. 2:24; 3:13). (The NIV trans., "when God gives any man wealth and possessions and enables him to enjoy them," is preferable to the NASB which implies that everyone who is given wealth and possessions is also "empowered" to enjoy them, which is contradicted in 6:2.) However, the NIV phrase **to accept his lot** should be translated "to receive his lot"; it emphasizes enjoyment as a gift. This ability to enjoy life, this **gladness of heart** with which **God** occupies those thus gifted, keeps a person from brooding over life's brevity (**days of his life** in 5:20 refers back to "few days" in v. 18).

(2) Warning: Some people are not able to enjoy the fruits of their labor (6:1-9). **6:1-2.** However, Solomon warned that some men are given great **wealth**—so great that they lack **nothing** they desire—but they are not enabled by **God** to **enjoy** it. Someone else enjoys it **instead.** This problem **weighs heavily on men** (cf. 8:6; not "is prevalent among men," NASB). The fact that Solomon failed to specify the nature of this inability has led to a diversity of interpretations of 6:2 and its relationship to verses 3-6. It is difficult to decide whether verses 3-6 constitute a continuation of verses 1-2 or, as many interpreters suggest, a separate and contrasting case. Two factors speak in favor of seeing no break between verses 2 and 3: (1) No formal indicators of a break are given. (2) The interpretation that there is a break rests too heavily on the inappropriateness of the term **stranger** applying to an heir. (The Heb. word "stranger," which appears only here in Ecc., sometimes indicates only someone other than oneself, as in Prov. 27:2.) It is preferable to interpret the inability to enjoy one's possessions (Ecc. 6:2) as caused either by misfortune robbing a man of the fruits of his labor (5:13-14) or a miserly, lifelong hoarding of its fruits that rob him of the experience of enjoyment (5:15-17). Solomon called both of these **a grievous evil** (5:13, 16), a term similar to that applied in 6:2 to God's not enabling a man to enjoy his wealth. The terms, though translated the same, are similar but not identical. In 5:13, 16 $r\bar{a}'\bar{a}h$ $\d{h}\hat{o}l\bar{a}h$ is lit., "sick evil" or "depressing misfortune"; the term in 6:2 is $\d{h}\hat{o}l\hat{i}$ $r\bar{a}'$ "evil sickness" or "a malignant disease."

**6:3-6.** The futility and grievousness of unenjoyed wealth is worse than the tragedy of being **stillborn.** A rich man is described in hyperbolic terms of extreme blessing: (a) great wealth ("he lacks nothing his heart desires," v. 2), (b) great progeny (**a hundred children**), and (c) a long life (he lives **many years, does not receive proper burial** [lit., "has no burial," i.e., even if he were to live forever; cf. Pss. 49:9; 89:48 for a similar concept], and **lives a thousand years twice over**). The stillborn is described in terms of ultimate futility: (a) **It** has no **meaning** (i.e., it does it no good to be born), (b) it disappears into **darkness,** (c) it is forgotten (**its name is shrouded** in **darkness**), (d) **it never saw the sun** ("the light of day"), and (e) it never **knew** what life is like. A wealthy person and a stillborn share the same fate; they **all** ($k\bar{o}l$ should be trans. "both"; cf. 2:14, 3:19; and comments on 7:18) **go to the same place** (i.e., the grave; cf. 3:20). And yet the lot of a stillborn is better because **it has more rest** (i.e., freedom from toil, anxiety, and misery; 6:5) than a richly blessed person whose soul is never satisfied.

**6:7.** Solomon concluded his description of the tragedy of unenjoyed wealth with a recommendation that one be content with what he has. With a word play on his earlier use of the word "heart" (lit., "soul") in verse 2, Solomon warned that there is always a danger of a man's desire (lit., "soul") outstripping his acquisitions. The soul of a man who "lacks nothing his heart [lit., 'soul'] desires" (v. 2) is not satisfied (cf. v. 3). Similarly though a man must indeed work to meet his basic needs, to fill his stomach (**all man's efforts are** [lit., "work is"] **for his mouth**), his desires (**appetite,** lit., "soul") may **never** be **satisfied.**

**6:8-9.** The **wise** and even the **poor** have no **advantage** over the **fool.** Though a poor person might know **how to** get along in the world (lit., "know how to walk before the living"), he is susceptible to desires that outstrip his acquisitions. So Solomon concluded his lengthy treatment of the futility of toil (2:18–6:9) by recommending that one be content with what he has rather than constantly longing for more. **Better what the eye sees than the roving of the appetite** (lit., "soul"; "heart" in v. 2 and "appetite" in v. 7 are also lit., "soul"). This clause is rendered in the NASB, "What the eyes see is better than what the soul desires." The reason for this wise advice is that constantly longing for more is futile or **meaningless, a chasing after the wind.** This is the last of nine occurrences in Ecclesiastes of the phrase "chasing after the wind" (cf. 1:14, 17; 2:11, 17, 26; 4:4, 6, 16). This phrase fittingly opens and concludes the first half of the book on the futility of human achievement.

## III. The Limitations of Human Wisdom Empirically Demonstrated (6:10–11:6)

As indicated under "Unity and Structure" in the *Introduction*, this section is characterized by the repetition of the phrases "do(es) not/cannot know" (6:12; 9:1, 12; 10:14; 11:2, 6) and "do(es) not/cannot discover" (7:14, 24, 28; 8:17). As many commentators note, this section is characterized by many imperatives, recommendations, and commendations (e.g., "it is good," 7:18; or "X is better than Y"; 7:2, 5; 9:16, 18). This second half of the book thus contains much practical advice on how to live. However, this advice is given in the light of constant reminders of man's ignorance of the providence of God (i.e., "What God has done," 7:13; cf. 8:17) and what the future holds (e.g., 9:1; 10:14; 11:2). This advice is intended to encourage people to fear God (7:18; 8:12; 12:13) and lead lives that please Him (7:26; cf. 2:26).

### A. Introduction: Everything is immutably and inscrutably foreordained (6:10-12)

**6:10-12.** Solomon introduced his discussion on the limitations of human wisdom by reverting to two themes he had used earlier to demonstrate the futility of human toil, namely, the immutability (1:15; 3:14; cf. 1:9) and inscrutability (3:11, 22) of divine providence. Solomon said that the nature and essence of everything that exists, including people, was foreordained long ago: **whatever exists has already been named** ("calling by name" parallels "creating," Isa. 40:26) **and what man is has been known** ("knowing" parallels "setting apart" and "appointing," Jer. 1:5). Furthermore Solomon said it was useless for a person to argue (**no man can contend**) about what is foreordained because God who had done it is

too powerful for man. **The more** man argues with **words** against God, **the less** he accomplishes (cf. Ecc. 10:12-15). Moreover, **man** is ignorant of what is best for him to do and of what the future holds (6:12). The questions are again rhetorical and call for negative answers.

Man is transitory in nature. His **days** are **few,** transitory (rather than **meaningless;** cf. comments on 3:19), and pass **like a shadow** (cf. comments on Job 14:2 for the meaning of this simile). As for man's future, he does not know **what will happen** (lit., "what will be after him") either before (Ecc. 7:14) or after death (3:22). Solomon thus stressed that man is ignorant of his place in God's foreordained plan of all things.

### B. Man cannot fathom the plan of God (chaps. 7–8)

These chapters are characterized by the repetition of the phrase "cannot discover" (7:14; 8:17; in 7:28 the NIV translates the same Heb. verb "finding" and "found"), and "who can discover" (7:24), another rhetorical question. This section deals with human inability to discover or fathom the plan of God, called "what God has done" (7:13), "the scheme of things" (7:25), "all that God has done" (8:17), "what goes on under the sun" (8:17).

1. MAN'S IGNORANCE OF THE SIGNIFICANCE OF ADVERSITY AND PROSPERITY (7:1-14)

The key to this section is found in verse 14a where Solomon declared that God is the author of both adversity and prosperity and that He so mingles them together that man in his finite understanding cannot discover anything about his future. The ramifications of this for Solomon were that adversity might have positive benefits and prosperity might have ill effects. But the effects of either depend on how one responds to them, whether wisely or foolishly. Thus in verses 2-4 Solomon portrayed the positive benefits of the greatest adversity, death, if wisely considered, and in verses 11-12 he portrayed the benefits of prosperity if wisely used. In the verses between (vv. 5-10) he warned that both adversity and prosperity offer many temptations to abandon a wise lifestyle and live like a fool. Interestingly in pointing up preferences, he used the word "better" eight times (vv. 1 [twice], 2-3, 5, 8 [twice], 10).

### a. How one lives matters (7:1)

**7:1.** The connection between the two halves of this verse are not as incidental or insignificant as some commentators claim. By using the Hebrew word for "oil" (**perfume**), which was both a symbol of joy (cf. 9:8) and prosperity (cf. Job 29:6) and a metaphor for reputation (cf. Song 1:3), Solomon combined the ideas of joy, prosperity, and reputation with the ideas of **birth** and **death.** So he suggested that it is **better** to come to the end of life with a good reputation (**good name**) than to have a joyful and auspicious beginning which, because of folly, might result in nothing.

This set the tone for the sayings which followed in which Solomon recommended how people should respond wisely to adversity and prosperity (cf. Ecc. 7:14) and warned them not to respond foolishly. Though Solomon had already demonstrated the limitations that death made on one's reputation (2:16; cf. 9:5) and though he would shortly demonstrate the limitations of wisdom (cf. 7:23-24; 9:11), he certainly did not advocate living foolishly (cf. his own example in 2:3, 9-11). After all, he did say that enjoyment of life was something God gave only to those who please Him (2:26), and he did warn that such enjoyment should be tempered by an awareness that God will judge everyone's deeds (11:9; 12:14).

### b. It is wise to reflect on the brevity of life (7:2-4)

**7:2-4.** Solomon followed his comment about the value of maintaining a good reputation till death with a series of sayings about the wisdom of reflecting on the brevity of life. Reminding his readers that **death is the destiny of every man,** Solomon said that **the living should take this to heart,** or reflect on it. Continuing to comment on the "heart" (the seat of reflection and of moral decision and action; cf. Prov. 4:23), a word that occurs in each of these three verses, Solomon recommended (Ecc. 7:4) that people reflect soberly on the brevity of life (**the heart of the wise is in the house of mourning**) rather than be involved in foolish pleasure (**the heart of fools is in**

**the house of pleasure**). It is in this sense that Solomon said **a house of mourning** should be preferred to **a house of feasting,** that is, sober reflection should be preferred to levity. In the same vein he added that **sorrow is better than laughter.**

Such sober reflection can lead to moral improvement (**a sad face** [reflective of a serious mood; cf. Gen. 40:7] **is good for the heart**). Solomon's advice thus had in view wise moral behavior. This is similar to Psalm 90:12, where Moses, after lamenting the brevity of human life, said, "Teach us to number our days aright, that we may gain a heart of wisdom." Present-day society, which emphasizes self-centered hedonism, desperately needs to heed this reminder.

### c. Foolish pleasure is vain and frivolous (7:5-6)

**7:5-6.** Comparing the frivolous pleasure **of fools**—their songs and their **laughter**—to **the crackling of** quick-burning **thorns under** a **pot** (cf. Ps. 118:12), Solomon said it was **meaningless,** vain, or useless. Thus it is more beneficial to live life wisely in light of the sober warning of life's brevity than to live as if life were one continual banquet (Ecc. 7:2-4). Also **it is better to** give **heed** to the warnings, corrections, and rebukes of the **wise** than to engage in foolish pleasure.

### d. Adversity and prosperity bring temptations (7:7-10)

**7:7.** Having recommended that it was wise to live life in light of its brevity and to heed the warnings of the wise, Solomon then warned his readers that adversity and prosperity offer many temptations to abandon a wise lifestyle and to live like a fool. With a further wordplay on the word "heart" (cf. comments on vv. 3-4), Solomon said that the temptation to prosperity could even corrupt **the heart** of **a wise man;** he might give in to bribery. Moreover, he could succumb to the pressures of adversity. Oppression (the normal meaning of this word rather than **extortion;** cf. 4:1; 5:8) might turn him **into a fool.**

**7:8-10.** While suffering adversity a person might also be tempted in other ways to live like a fool. He might become impatient (v. 8) or be **provoked** to **anger** (v. 9), or complain about his lot, longing for **the** good **old days** (v. 10). Also in the light of an auspicious **beginning** he might become proud or haughty (v. 8). All these actions and attitudes are essentially contrary to the submissive attitude Solomon later implied in view of God's sovereignty (v. 13). Therefore they are foolish (v. 9b) and unwise (v. 10b).

*e. Prosperity is beneficial if used wisely (7:11-12)*

**7:11-12.** When accompanied by wisdom, prosperity can be beneficial. Solomon stated that wisdom is an added boon to prosperity. The translation, "Wisdom along with an inheritance is good" (NASB), is preferable to **Wisdom, like an inheritance, is a good thing** (NIV). The Hebrew preposition *'im* regularly means "with," and Solomon's purpose here was not to compare wisdom to prosperity but to show the value of prosperity *accompanied by* wisdom. **Wisdom,** in addition to providing **shelter** (lit., "shade") or protection (cf. Num. 14:9 for the metaphorical use of this word), **preserves the life of its possessor.** Other things being equal, a person who avoids a foolish lifestyle will live longer (cf. Ecc. 7:17; Prov. 13:14).

*f. God's providence is immutable and inscrutable (7:13-14)*

**7:13-14.** Solomon closed his treatment on the wise response to adversity and prosperity by reminding his readers that **God** sovereignly disposes of both and that His disposition of them is immutable (cf. 3:14) and inscrutable. Though people might find fault with God's ways (**what God has done**), no one can change what He thinks is wrong or unfair (**Who can straighten what He has made crooked?**). Moreover, God so mingles together adversity and prosperity that **man cannot discover anything about his future** (cf. 8:7; 10:14). In view of this, Solomon recommended submission to God's sovereignty, enjoying the **good** times (**be happy**) and remembering (**consider**) in **bad** times that adversity has inscrutable purposes beyond finite human understanding (cf. 8:17).

2. MAN'S IGNORANCE OF THE SIGNIFICANCE OF RIGHTEOUSNESS AND WISDOM (7:15-29)

The argument of this section has generally been misunderstood. This may

be due to a failure to relate it to the preceding section (vv. 1-14) and the failure to recognize that Solomon was seeking to combat a false concept, namely, the rigid application of the doctrine of retribution by some of the wisdom teachers of his day. (Cf. Job 4:7-9; 8:20; 34:11-12; 36:6-7 for examples of overly rigid applications of this doctrine.)

Solomon argued that prosperity (cf. Ecc. 7:11-12) was no sure indication of God's pleasure, nor was adversity (cf. vv. 2-4) a sure sign of His anger. Solomon had seen the wicked prospering and the righteous perishing (v. 15). So a person should not depend on his righteousness as the means of guaranteeing reward (v. 16). Moreover, absolute righteousness is impossible because no one is so righteous that he always avoids sin (v. 20) or so wise that he is always able to avoid the snares of wickedness and folly (vv. 26-28). Besides, Solomon said, no one is wise enough to understand God's scheme of things (v. 24).

*a. Avoid depending on your righteousness and living wickedly (7:15-18)*

These verses contain advice on how to live in the light of God's enigmatic disposition of prosperity and adversity. In the light of the exceptions to the doctrine of retribution which Solomon had observed (v. 15), he advised against depending on one's own righteousness (v. 16). However, he continued to warn against indulging in wickedness because of its potential danger (v. 17).

**7:15.** Solomon said that in his brief or fleeting lifetime (not a **meaningless life** as in NIV; cf. comments on 3:19; 6:12) he had **seen** exceptions to the doctrine that God rewards the righteous and punishes the wicked. He had seen the **righteous . . . perishing** and the **wicked . . . living long.** The word "in" in the phrases **in his righteousness** and **in his wickedness** can here mean "in spite of." These phrases "in his righteousness" and "in his wickedness" argue against the common view that in 7:16 Solomon was warning against legalistic or Pharisaic self-righteousness. Such would have been a sin and would have been so acknowledged by Solomon who was concerned about *true* exceptions to the doctrine of retribution, not supposed ones (cf. 8:10-14 where this doctrine is discussed again).

**7:16-18.** These verses have generally been interpreted as teaching the "golden mean" or a moderate lifestyle, avoiding both overzealous righteousness and overindulgent sinfulness. And righteousness here is generally interpreted as referring to legalistic or Pharisaic self-righteousness. But this interpretation fails to relate these verses adequately to Solomon's argument against the rigid application of the doctrine of retribution in God's distributing adversity and prosperity. Moreover, the meaning of the verb *tiššômēm* (from *šāmēm*) must be correctly interpreted. Though almost universally interpreted in the sense of "to **destroy** or ruin oneself," the verb in this form never means this elsewhere. Instead it means "to be appalled or astounded" (cf. Dan. 8:27, "appalled"; Ps. 143:4, "dismayed"). This fits in nicely with Solomon's argument here. He urged his readers **not** to **be overrighteous** or **overwise** "lest they be confounded or astonished." He meant they should not depend on their righteousness or wisdom to guarantee God's blessing because *they* might be confounded, dismayed, or disappointed like the righteous people whom Solomon had seen perishing in spite of their righteousness (Ecc. 7:15).

Also the fact that God did not punish in some cases (cf. v. 15b) should not be taken as a license to sin (**do not be overwicked**, v. 17); God might judge them and they might die before they had to (**die before your time**; cf. Ps. 55:23). Solomon closed his argument in this section by noting that **it is good to** follow both warnings and by recommending that one who **fears God** (cf. Ecc. 3:14; 5:7; 8:12; 12:13) should **avoid all** (or better, "both") **extremes** (7:18). As in 2:14 and 3:19, the Hebrew word *kōl* can mean either "both" or "all." The two extremes to avoid are (a) depending on one's own righteousness and (b) becoming loose in one's living (being overly wicked).

It should be noted what Solomon *did not* say or imply in 7:16-18. Solomon's advice should not be taken to imply that he believed in halfhearted obedience to God's commands or advocated a little wickedness and a little folly. Though he believed that complete righteousness is unattainable (v. 20) and that some folly is

unavoidable (see comments on vv. 26-29), he never advocated folly or wickedness. Instead he advocated living life in the light of God's judgment (11:9; 12:14). Though he had observed exceptions to the doctrine of retribution (7:15; 8:10-11), he nevertheless believed that God would judge (3:17; 8:12-13). Solomon's only uncertainty about God's judgment was its timing; like everything else, it would be in God's time (3:17; cf. 3:11). So people should avoid folly and wickedness as much as possible and live as wisely and as righteously as possible.

*b. Wisdom though valuable gives inadequate protection (7:19-24)*

Solomon had recognized the inadequacy of righteousness to provide protection because of a seemingly uneven application of the doctrine of retribution (v. 15). Moreover, he added, no person is truly righteous (vv. 20-22). Though he acknowledged wisdom's protective power (v. 19), Solomon also demonstrated from his own experience that complete wisdom is unattainable (vv. 23-24).

**7:19.** Since righteousness cannot always protect from adversity (as demonstrated in vv. 15-16), some other protective power—perhaps that of wisdom—is needed. Solomon affirmed that wisdom does give more protection than military strength: **Wisdom makes one wise man more powerful than 10 rulers in a city.** (See an example of this in 9:13-18; cf. Prov. 21:22.)

**7:20-22.** The need for wisdom is here made explicit by the Hebrew particle *kî* ("for," KJV; "indeed," NASB; not trans. in the NIV). Solomon noted that wisdom is needed "for" (or "because") righteousness is ineffective. No one is truly **righteous; no one continually does . . . right** ("good," NASB) **and never sins.** This absence of true righteousness is easily seen in the practice of one's servants (v. 21) and himself (v. 22); both had **cursed** ("reviled," JB) **others.**

**7:23-24.** However, Solomon immediately added that **wisdom** also has its limitations. Though he himself had applied all his great wisdom (1:16) to understand the enigmas in God's distribution of prosperity and adversity (7:1-18) and though he was **determined to be wise** (v. 23), he acknowledged that true wisdom was far **beyond** him. He also noted that nobody can comprehend or grasp what has happened (v. 24). The rendering, "Whatever has happened lies beyond our grasp, deep down, deeper than man can fathom" (NEB) gives the thought well. The NIV wrongly adds the word **wisdom** to verse 24 (the Heb. phrase *mah šᵉhāyâh* means "what has happened" or "what exists," as in 1:9; 3:15; 6:10).

### c. True righteousness and true wisdom are nonexistent (7:25-29)

This passage is often misinterpreted because of the failure to understand the wisdom concepts being used here. Contrary to the views of many modern commentators the terms in these verses are used with moral and ethical connotations. Of course this is true of the phrases and terms one "who pleases God" (v. 26), "sinner" (v. 26), and "upright" (vv. 28-29). But also, as in Proverbs, the term "folly" is virtually synonymous with "wickedness" (v. 25); "wisdom" (v. 25) is virtually synonymous with "righteousness." Wisdom emphasizes moral skillfulness, while folly emphasizes moral indiscretion (cf. Prov. 1:3; 2:1-3 with Prov. 2:9-11).

Also a proper understanding of this section depends on recognizing that Solomon personified folly somewhat as he did in Proverbs 1–9. The woman who is a snare (Ecc. 7:26) is "Lady Folly," symbolized and epitomized in Proverbs by the adulteress (cf. Prov. 9:13-17 with Prov. 7; also cf. Zech. 5:7-8). Thus Solomon argued in this section that in his search to discover the place of wisdom in the scheme of things (Ecc. 7:25) he found that, though folly was a fate worse than death, only those pleasing to God escape folly's clutches (v. 26). He also discovered in this same search that such people are rare—in fact they are nearly nonexistent (v. 28). However, he noted that such a situation is not of divine but of human origin (v. 29).

**7:25.** The terminology in this verse is similar to Solomon's description of his earlier reflection on the relationship between wisdom and folly (2:12-17). He had already demonstrated the limitations of wisdom from his own experience (7:23-24). Now he reported on an investigation into the value of wisdom in relationship to wickedness and folly that further confirmed wisdom's limitations. The synonyms **to understand, to investigate, and to search** emphasize his diligence in seeking to comprehend **wisdom and the scheme of things.** ("And" should be rendered "in," pointing to "wisdom" and "scheme" as a hendiadys, a figure of speech in which two coordinated nouns form one concept. E.g., in Gen. 3:16 the literal Heb. phrase "pain and childbearing" refers to "pain in childbearing.") By this diligent search Solomon hoped **to understand** how stupid and insane **wickedness** and **folly** really are.

**7:26.** Solomon said that he made several discoveries in his investigation. First he discovered that "lady Folly" is worse (**more bitter**) **than death.** She **is a snare** and **a trap,** whose ways confine a person like **chains** (cf. Prov. 2:18-19; 5:3-6; 7:24-26). Second he discovered that only **the man who pleases God** (cf. Ecc. 2:26) can **escape her.**

**7:27-28.** Solomon also reported that in his continuing quest to **discover the scheme of things** (**still searching** modifies "scheme"), he made a third discovery: hardly anybody is **upright.** That this, however, is the nature of Solomon's third discovery may not be too clear because of (a) the elliptical nature of the wording in verse 28b, (b) the misunderstanding of the parallelism of the verse, and (c) the figures of speech employed in it. When Solomon said that he **found one . . . man among a thousand,** he did not define what he meant by "man." The Hebrew word is *ʾāḏām*, the generic word for man as well as the proper name Adam. Some commentators suggest that Solomon meant that nobody is as good as he was intended to be, that is, like Adam before the Fall. The NIV, on the other hand, adds the word "upright" to verse 28, understanding an ellipsis of this word which appears in verse 29. However, it is probably more in keeping with the argument of verses 26-29 to supply the ellipsis from verse 26, "a man who pleases [or, 'is pleasing to'] God." Using hyperbole, Solomon said that such men are extremely rare, that is, one in a thousand (cf. Job 9:3; 33:23 for the same figure).

Then Solomon added that **not one** such **woman** may be found. This does not mean that one out of every thousand males is pleasing to God and that no women at all please Him. Such a point hardly fits Solomon's argument. Instead, in the last line of Ecclesiastes 7:28 Solomon used (a) a kind of complementary parallelism in which the generic term *'āḏām* ("man") is explained as including also the feminine gender in the sense of "mankind," and (b) a kind of graded numerical sequence in which the second of two terms gives the climax or point (cf. Prov. 30:15, 18, 21). In this parallelism and numerical sequence his purpose was to say that such people—both men and women—are not only scarce but are non-existent; there is "not one" **among them all.** This is also supported by the fact that "men" in Ecclesiastes 7:29 is "they" in Hebrew (i.e., both men and women).

**7:29.** Solomon, however, quickly noted that the reason for man's universal perversion was man's devising, not God's. **God made mankind** (*'āḏām*; cf. v. 28) **upright, but men** (lit., "they," i.e., men and women) **have gone in search of many schemes** (cf. "scheme" in vv. 25, 27 and "schemes" in 8:11). In other words, though people cannot know God's "scheme of things" they do follow their *own* schemes, which causes them to lack true uprightness, true righteousness, and true wisdom, and to fail to please God.

3. MAN'S IGNORANCE OF THE ENIGMA OF DIVINE RETRIBUTION (CHAP. 8)

The key to interpreting this chapter properly is seeing how its two parts are related. The chapter begins with a question and a statement that magnify the value of wisdom (v. 1) and closes with an acknowledgment of wisdom's limitations (v. 17). Wisdom enables a wise man to avoid the king's wrath (vv. 2-9), but not even a wise man can figure out the enigmas in God's distribution of justice (vv. 10-17).

*a. A wise man can avoid the king's wrath (8:1-9)*

The background for this section is the recognition of the absolute authority of the king (cf. Prov. 24:21-22) and the need for proper decorum to avert his wrath (cf. Prov. 14:35; 16:14; 20:2).

(1) A wise man knows the proper decorum. **8:1.** A **wise man** is able to practice proper decorum. In two rhetorical questions Solomon affirmed that only a wise man can size up situations properly and act accordingly. Only he **knows**

**the explanation** (*pēšer*) **of things.** The noun *pēšer* occurs only here in Hebrew. In the Aramaic in Daniel it refers to the interpretation of dreams (cf. Dan. 5:12). Here it is applied to the Hebrew word *dāḇār* ("matter, affair," trans. "things" in the NIV). Because of his wisdom a wise person knows how to act graciously and avoid brash behavior which would lead to his harm (cf. Prov. 14:35). For the two figures of speech (in the last two lines of Ecc. 8:1) where behavior is reflected in one's **face** or **appearance,** see Numbers 6:25 and Proverbs 7:13.

(2) Obedience to the king is of paramount importance. **8:2-4.** Solomon then set forth examples of proper decorum before a king. A king has great authority: he *can* (not **will** as in the NIV) **do whatever he pleases,** his **word is supreme,** and no one **can say to him, What are you doing?** (Cf. Job 9:12; Isa. 45:9 where the same idea is applied to God.) Therefore people should **obey** the king, maintain allegiance to him (**do not be in a hurry to leave** his **presence,** i.e., as suggested by the Heb. to resign from his service; cf. 10:4), and not be rebellious toward him by standing **up for a bad cause.**

(3) Proper decorum averts harm (8:5-9). **8:5-7.** Affirming that obedience to a king's **command** would avert **harm,** Solomon commended the value of wisdom, saying that **the wise** person would **know** the best course of action and when to apply it (**the proper time and procedure,** lit., "time and judgment"). Such wisdom is necessary, according to Solomon, because people (*'āḏām* is generic, referring to people in general) suffer harm (**a man's misery weighs heavily upon him**). The word for "misery" (*rā'âh*) is related to the word for "harm" (*rā'*) in verse 5. This misery comes because people are ignorant of "what will happen" and "when it will happen" (v. 7, NASB; not **what is to come** as in the NIV for the Heb. word means "when," not "what").

**8:8-9.** The reason for such misery is the inescapable consequences of wickedness that arise from such ignorance; just as **no man** can control **the wind** (cf. Prov. 27:16), postpone **the day of his death,** or be **discharged** while in the midst of battle, so **no** man can escape the consequences of his **wickedness.** The first three clauses in Ecclesiastes 8:8 are parallel in Hebrew and are comparative to the last clause. Solomon observed these things as he **applied** his **mind** (cf. 1:17; 8:16) to what was **done under the sun** (cf. comments on 1:3).

The consequences Solomon had in view here resulted from a ruler's anger (the harm a wise man can escape by proper decorum; cf. 8:1) as is clear from verse 9 where Solomon referred to a ruler lording **it over others to** their **hurt**. (The NIV marg., "to their hurt," is preferred to "to his own hurt." The pronoun refers back to "others," which is lit., 'ādām, "men.")

b. Even a wise man cannot understand God's judgment (8:10-17)

This section is often misunderstood because verses 16-17 are often separated from it and placed with 9:1–11:6 (cf., e.g., Christian D. Ginsburg, *The Song of Songs and Coheleth*, p. 406). However, the recurrence of the divider phrase "cannot discover" (8:17; cf. 7:14, 28) argues for the inclusion of verses 16-17 with verses 10-15. This is also supported by the bracketing effects of verse 1 ("the wise man . . . knows") and verse 17 ("man cannot discover" and "a wise man . . . cannot really comprehend"). Verses 16-17 thus refer in particular to the enigma of God's work of divine judgment.

(1) Failure to punish wickedness is a great enigma (8:10-14). **8:10-12a.** Solomon had noted that wickedness is not always punished (cf. 3:16; 4:1). He had seen that **the wicked** have access to **the holy place** (i.e., the temple), die, are **buried,** and even are praised **in the city where they** practiced wickedness. Affirming that such a contradiction of the doctrine of retribution was **meaningless** (hebel; cf. 1:2) or enigmatic, Solomon lamented the fact that **a wicked man** could sin with impunity (i.e., commit **100 crimes and** live **a long time,** 8:12). According to Solomon, man's failure to carry out retribution (e.g., to punish **a crime . . . quickly,** v. 11) often leads to more wrongdoing: then **the hearts of the people are filled with schemes to do wrong** (cf. 7:29).

**8:12b-14.** These verses are one long sentence in the Hebrew. Verse 14 is the main clause of a subordinate clause consisting of verses 12b-13 and introduced by the Hebrew particle gam (meaning "though," not "still" or "yet" as in NASB, KJV; not trans. in NIV) before the words **I**

**know.** Solomon firmly believed in the doctrine of retribution: life is **better** for **God-fearing** people (cf. 3:14; 5:7; 7:18; 12:13) but does **not go well** for **the wicked** whose lives will be shortened (cf. Prov. 2:22; 10:27; 29:1). Yet Solomon had observed contradictions to retribution. He had seen the **righteous . . . get what the wicked deserve and** the **wicked . . . get what the righteous deserve.** Solomon affirmed emphatically that such a contradiction in the distributing of divine justice is enigmatic or **meaningless** (cf. Ecc. 8:10; "meaningless" occurs as a bracket at the beginning and the end of v. 14).

(2) Enjoy the life God gives. **8:15.** Having shown that there are enigmatic contradictions in the doctrine of retribution—righteousness is not always rewarded and wickedness is not always punished, and sometimes the wicked prosper and the righteous meet with disaster—Solomon again recommended **the enjoyment of life.** He said that life's best is to enjoy the fruits of one's labor (i.e., **to eat and drink;** cf. 2:24; 3:13; 5:18) **and** "to rejoice" or **be glad** (cf. 3:12; 5:19). Also he noted that this **joy** would enliven one's labor (i.e., it would **accompany him in his work**). As is obvious from earlier occurrences of this theme (cf. 2:24-26; 3:12, 22; 5:18-20), this is not Epicurean hedonism based on despair but is a note of submission. Man cannot control or predict adversity or prosperity; however, each day's joys should be received as gifts from God's hand and be savored as **God** permits (3:13; 5:19). All this is to be while one is **under the sun** (twice in 8:15; cf. comments on 1:3).

(3) No man can comprehend God's providence. **8:16-17.** Solomon closed his treatment of the enigma of contradictions in divine retribution much as he had concluded his discussions on the significance of adversity and prosperity (7:1-14) and on the significance of righteousness and wisdom (7:15-29), namely, by acknowledging man's ignorance of God's ways (cf. 7:14b, 28a). After searching diligently (**I applied my mind;** cf. 1:17; 8:9) **to** gain **wisdom** and observing **man's** many activities, he concluded that man is ignorant of God's work (the phrases **all that God has done** and **what goes on under the sun** are synonymous). In emphatic terms, repeating the negative three times

(v. 17) and the verb "comprehend" twice —**no one can comprehend . . . man cannot discover . . . he cannot really comprehend**—Solomon said that no one can understand God's ways (3:11; cf. Isa. 55:9; Rom. 11:33) **even if** he expended all his energies or were **wise** and claimed he could.

## C. Man does not know what will happen (9:1–11:6)

This section is characterized by the repetition of the phrase "no man knows" (cf. 9:1, 12; 10:14) and "you do not know" (cf. 11:2, 6). It deals with man's inability to predict what will happen to him, whether good or bad (cf. 9:1), or whether his work will fail or succeed (cf. 9:11-12; 11:2, 6). Contrary to the writings of some, this formula ("no man knows" and "you do not know") serve to *introduce* the subsections, not *conclude* them, as is evident from their occurrences in 9:1 and 11:2.

### 1. NO ONE KNOWS WHAT WILL HAPPEN TO HIM (9:1-10)

#### a. Summary: No one knows what awaits him (9:1)

**9:1.** This verse closely relates verses 2-10 to the preceding section, as indicated in the NIV translation, **So I reflected on all this and concluded that the righteous and the wise and what they do are in God's hands.** The "all this" that Solomon "reflected on" is human ignorance of the significance of righteousness and wickedness in God's sovereign disposition of adversity and prosperity (chaps. 7–8). Solomon "concluded" (lit., "my heart saw") from his prior reflections "on all this" that people are not masters of their own fate; people and "what they do" are subject to God's sovereign will (i.e., they "are in God's hands"; cf. Prov. 21:1 for a similar use of this figure). Since one does not know God's providence, neither does he know whether he will experience prosperity or adversity, or **whether** he will be the object of **love** or **hate** (for a similar use of these two nouns; cf. Mal. 1:2-3).

#### b. All people are subject to the same fate (9:2-3)

**9:2-3.** Solomon supported the statement that nobody knows what awaits him (v. 1) by stating that **all** people **share** the same fate or **common destiny.** However, there is some ambiguity as to the nature of that fate because of a common failure to relate the beginning of verse 2 to the end of verse 1. The same fate or destiny relates to the "love or hate," adversity or prosperity, referred to in verse 1. The Hebrew is literally, "whether it will be love or hate, no man knows"; both (i.e., love and hate—for this use of *kōl*; cf. 2:14; 3:19; 7:18) are before them (i.e., the righteous and the wise, 9:1). Both love and hate are experienced by everyone; there is one fate (or destiny) for **the righteous and the wicked.** This commonality of fate applies to **the good and the bad,** those who are ritually **clean** as well as those who are ritually **unclean, those who offer sacrifices** as well as **those who do not. . . . those who are afraid to take** God's name in **oaths** (cf. Ex. 20:7, "misuse the name of the LORD") as well as **those who** are not afraid to do so. **The same destiny** befalls **all** these. The bad part of all this (i.e., **the evil in everything that happens under the sun**), Solomon wrote, is that this common fate causes people to be rampant in sin (people's **hearts . . . are full of evil and . . . madness;** cf. Ecc. 8:11). Solomon added that not only does everybody (including the righteous and the wise, 9:1) share this same inscrutable distribution of adversity and prosperity *during* life, but they also share the same ultimate fate *after* life; **they** all **join the dead.**

#### c. Life is preferable to death (9:4-6)

**9:4-6.** However, despite the fact that all people, both righteous and wicked, are subject to the same inscrutable distribution of adversity and prosperity and ultimately join one another in death, they should not despair of life. Life has advantages over death. Comparing the lot of **a live dog** with that of **a dead lion,** Solomon affirmed that it is better to be alive and dishonored (cf. 1 Sam. 17:43; the dog was the most despised animal) than to be honored and dead (cf. Prov. 30:30; the lion was the most honored beast). **The living** at least have consciousness and **hope,** things they can look forward to enjoying. But **the dead** have no consciousness (they **know nothing**) or hope of **reward** or enjoyment. Moreover, their passions—**their love, their hate, and their jealousy**—are stilled. As Ginsburg has noted, the concepts of consciousness and unconsciousness here are not in their barest forms as though these verses taught soul sleep. Instead they should be understood in the context of enjoying life (Ecc. 9:7-9) and possessing the capacities for enjoyment; the living have those capabilities but the dead do not (*The Song of Songs and Coheleth,* pp. 414-5). Thus the living have opportunities and capacities for fruitful labor but the dead do not (v. 10). The living have opportunities for reward from that labor, but the dead do not (v. 5; the word trans. "reward" refers to wages or earnings). The living have capacities for enjoyment (vv. 7-9), but the dead do not (v. 6). Solomon was not describing what the state of the dead *is*; he was stating what it is *not*. He did this to emphasize the lost opportunities of this present life, opportunities for serving God and enjoying His gifts (cf. Isa. 38:11, 18-19 for similar ideas). Solomon added that the dead **never again . . . have a part in anything that happens under the sun** (cf. comments on Ecc. 1:3). The word for "part" (*ḥēleq,* "lot, portion, allotment") is the word he used elsewhere of life and its enjoyments (3:22; 5:18-19; 9:9).

Some commentators see a contradiction between 9:4-6 and 4:2-3 ("the dead . . . are happier than the living"). However, no real contradiction is here because Solomon was stating that a person who experiences the pressures of oppression (4:1) may feel that death is preferable. On the other hand in 9:4-6 (and in vv. 7-10) Solomon stressed that when a person is dead opportunities for enjoying life are gone. The two passages view life and death from different perspectives.

### d. Enjoy life as God enables (9:7-9)

**9:7-9.** In view of the uncertainties of what the future may bring, whether adversity or prosperity (vv. 1-3), and in view of the certainty of death with the loss of all opportunity for enjoyment (vv. 4-6), Solomon again recommended enjoying life as God's good gift (cf. 2:24-26; 3:12-13, 22; 5:18-19). Solomon here spelled out in greater detail than elsewhere some of the aspects of life which should be enjoyed: **food** (lit., "bread") and **wine** which sustain life and make it merry (cf. Ps. 104:15), fine clothes and

pleasant lotions (cf. 2 Sam. 12:20 where they are the opposites of mournful grief), enjoyment of **life with** one's **wife** (cf. Prov. 18:22). In short, these include both the basic necessities of life and some luxuries God bestows as His gifts (cf. Ecc. 5:19). Solomon underlined the need to enjoy these gifts by emphasizing life's brevity. He did this by almost repeating a phrase, **all the days of this meaningless life** and **all your meaningless days.** "Meaningless" here (*heḇel*) should be rendered "fleeting" (cf. comments on 3:19; 6:12; 7:15).

Affirming that **this is** one's **lot** (*ḥēleq;* cf. 3:22; 5:18-19 and contrast 9:6 where the same word is trans. "part") **in life** and **labor under the sun** (cf. comments on 1:3), Solomon encouraged his readers to enjoy life because it is God's will for them to do so. He stated, "God has already approved your works" (NASB; preferred over NIV's **God favors what you do**). By this he summarized what he had previously said about the enjoyment of life: (a) wealth and possessions, which stem from one's "labor," ultimately are gifts of God (5:18-19), (b) only God gives the ability to enjoy the fruits of one's labor (cf. 2:24; 3:13; 5:18), and (c) the ability to enjoy those things depends on whether one pleases God (2:26). So the statement "God has already approved your works" means that possessing God's gifts and the ability to enjoy them evidence God's prior approval that one can do so; if God had not so approved the gifts, one could not enjoy them.

### e. Labor diligently while you can (9:10)

**9:10.** Besides encouraging his readers to enjoy life as God enabled them, Solomon also encouraged them to work diligently. The idiom **whatever your hand finds to do** means "whatever you are able to do" (cf. 1 Sam. 10:7). Whatever a person is able to do, he should **do it with all** his **might,** that is, expend all his energies. The reason for this advice is that when death comes all opportunities for work and service will cease. In death a person will have no further energies or abilities to work; there will be **neither working nor planning nor knowledge nor wisdom.** (This does not suggest soul sleep; see comments on Ecc. 9:5.)

2. NO ONE KNOWS WHETHER HIS WISDOM
WILL SUCCEED (9:11–10:11)

The preceding section (9:1-10) began
with a statement that the righteous and
the wise are subject to the same uncertain future as anyone else (9:1). Then in
9:2-10 Solomon discussed this fact with
regard to the *righteous* (in contrast with
the wicked), and now (in 9:11–10:11) he
showed that the wise are also subject to
an uncertain future.

*a. Introduction: Wisdom is subject to the
uncertainty of the future (9:11-12)*

**9:11-12.** The fact that wisdom is subject to the future's uncertainty is introduced by a series of five human abilities,
each of which fails to succeed. The last
three relate to a wise person: **the wise
. . . the brilliant . . . the learned.** As a
**race** is not always won by the swiftest
runner, or a victory in a **battle** always
won by the mightiest soldiers, so also the
wise do not always earn a living (i.e.,
gain **food,** lit., "bread"), get rich, or acquire a great reputation (gain **favor**).

The reason for such failures is that
**all** people are subject to times of misfortune (**time and chance** is another example of a hendiadys; cf. comments on 7:25)
which no man is able to predict (9:12, **no
man knows . . . his hour**; lit., "his
time"). This refers back to times of misfortune (v. 11), not merely to death.
Comparing such times of misfortune to a
**net** and a **snare** by which **birds** and **fish**
are **caught,** Solomon said that such **evil
times** come suddenly and **unexpectedly
upon them,** thus nullifying their abilities.

*b. Wisdom may be unrewarded because of
negligence (9:13-16)*

**9:13-16.** An **example of wisdom** not
being rewarded (v. 11) is a **poor** wise
**man** who had delivered a **small,** poorly
defended **city** from a siege by **a powerful
king.** But the **poor man's wisdom** went
unrewarded because **nobody remembered** him (also in 1 Sam. 25:31
"remember" conveys the idea of "reward"). Solomon said this example **greatly impressed** him, that is, it was significant to him (lit., "it was great to me" in
the light of his previous discussion, Ecc.
9:11-12). Though **wisdom** had proven
**better than strength,** that is, military
might (cf. 7:11-12; 9:18; Prov. 21:22), that
**poor** wise man received no benefit from

his wisdom. His **wisdom** was **despised
and his words** were not **heeded,** and he
remained poor and unremembered (i.e.,
unrewarded with wealth or social esteem; cf. Ecc. 9:11).

*c. Wisdom's value may be nullified by a little
folly (9:17–10:1)*

**9:17–10:1.** After giving the example
of the poor wise man whose wisdom did
not benefit him (9:13-16) Solomon
warned that though wisdom deserves attention, its value can be nullified by a
little folly. Alluding to his previous example, Solomon said **The quiet words of the
wise are more to be heeded than the
shouts of a ruler of fools** because **wisdom is better than weapons of war** (cf.
7:19; 9:16). Playing on the word "good"
or "better"—the same Hebrew word
*ṭôbâh*—and the contrast between "one"
and "much," Solomon said that **one sinner destroys much good.** In other words,
**a little folly** can destroy the great value
of **wisdom,** as **dead flies** in **perfume** ruin
it by giving it **a bad smell.** The use of the
Hebrew words for **outweighs** and **honor**
is another interesting wordplay, for both
words are used for weight or value and
social esteem.

*d. Wisdom's value may be nullified by a
ruler's caprice (10:2-7)*

Speaking of "errors," literally "sin"
(v. 4; cf. "sinner," 9:18), "fool," and
"fools" (10:3, 6; cf. "folly," v. 1), Solomon gave another example of how a little
folly nullifies the great value of wisdom.
Though wisdom suggests ways to maintain one's position at court (vv. 2-4), that
position may be subverted by an error of
some leader.

**10:2-4.** Solomon set forth the value
of wisdom by stating that a **wise** person
has the quality of **heart** and mind that
will protect him from danger (cf. 7:12).
This is stated in the words **inclines to the
right,** which are literally "is at his right
hand" (as in the KJV); as is well known,
the right hand was the place of protection (cf. Pss. 16:8; 110:5; 121:5). Conversely a **fool** lacks such **sense** which is evidenced by his foolish behavior. Using a
common figure for moral behavior—
walking in the way (cf. 1 Sam. 8:3;
2 Kings 21:21)—Solomon said that **even
as he walks along the road, the fool
. . . shows everyone how stupid he is.**

Solomon then gave an example of how wisdom can protect one who possesses it. With a deliberate wordplay on the double sense of the Hebrew verb *nûaḥ*, meaning "to leave or abandon" or "to give rest to," Solomon advised that the wisest course when confronted with a king's **anger** is not to **leave** (*tannaḥ*) one's **post** (i.e., not to resign his office; cf. Ecc. 8:3) because calm and cool composure (cf. Prov. 14:30 for a somewhat similar use of the noun "calmness") could **lay great errors** (lit., "sins"; actually it is the anger caused by such sins, a metonymy of cause for effect) **to rest** (*yannîaḥ*; cf. Prov. 16:14 for a similar idea).

**10:5-7.** Though Solomon affirmed that a wise man's good sense might suggest ways to maintain his position before an angry king (v. 4), he also noted that one's position or job is not always awarded on the basis of merit. The Hebrew word for "errors" in verse 4 means sins, but the word for "error" is verse 5 means an inadvertent mistake, something done without proper consideration (cf. 5:6 where the same word is trans. "mistake"). The word for "ruler" in 10:5 differs from "ruler's" in verse 4. In verse 4 the word for ruler's (*môšēl*) emphasizes one's dominion or reign, whereas in verse 5 the word for ruler (*šallîṭ*) emphasizes one's sovereignty or domineering mastery (the same root is in 8:4 [*šilṭôn*, "supreme"] and 8:9 [*šallaṭ*, "lords it over"]). Solomon stated that he had seen **an evil** *rā'âh*; cf. 5:13, 16; 6:1) **under the sun** (cf. comments on 1:3), **the sort of error that arises from a ruler,** that is, the kind of reversal of roles that results from a ruler's caprice. Solomon had seen **fools** occupying **high positions while the rich** (who were supposedly therefore wise; cf. Prov. 14:24; 19:10) occupied **the low** positions. He also had **seen slaves** riding **on horseback,** a position of honor (cf. Jer. 17:25), **while princes** went **on foot like slaves.** Thus since position was not assigned on the basis of merit but on the basis of a ruler's caprice, the value of wisdom was often nullified.

*e. Wisdom's value may be nullified by improper timing (10:8-11)*

**10:8-9.** Verses 8-11, whose figurative language and proverbial character have occasioned a great variety of interpreta-tions, are carefully related to one another. Thus the repetition of the words **snake** and **bitten** at the beginning (v. 8) and "snake bites" at the end (v. 11) forms a bracketing effect (an *inclusio*). Also Solomon repeated the Hebrew word *yiṭrôn* ("profit"; cf. comments on 1:3) in 10:10-11 (rendered "advantage" in v. 10 by NASB and not rendered at all in NIV). Though wisdom has advantages, that gain can be lost when wisdom is not applied or is applied too late.

Moreover, the reference to "ax" (v. 10) serves as a bridge between verse 9b, the last of four proverbs in verses 8-9, and the two contrasting proverbs in verses 10-11. Solomon strung together four proverbs that set forth the potential dangers inherent in representative daily tasks—digging **a pit,** tearing down **a wall,** quarrying **stones,** splitting **logs**—dangers which could only be averted by applying wisdom or prudence.

**10:10-11.** In log-splitting (v. 9) a man can either use wisdom and sharpen his **ax** or leave it **unsharpened** and exert **more** energy. Applying wisdom to using an ax makes it easier to succeed. "Wisdom has the advantage of giving success" (NASB).

However, in a contrasting proverb (v. 11) Solomon noted that a man's wisdom or skill has **no profit** if it is not applied at the proper time; **if a snake bites before it is charmed,** the **charmer** is in trouble. Thus Solomon showed in this series of proverbs that though wisdom is valuable in dangerous and difficult tasks, its value can be nullified by improper timing.

3. CRITICISM IS RISKY IN VIEW OF ONE'S IGNORANCE OF THE FUTURE (10:12-20)

Because there are few verbal links between the two parts (vv. 12-15 and vv. 16-20) in this section, it is crucial to see the link between Solomon's warning in verse 20 with the proverbial material in verses 12-15 and the link between his warning in verse 20 with the material in verses 16-19. Noting that multiplying words is foolish and self-destructive in view of one's ignorance of the future (vv. 12-15), Solomon warned against criticizing governmental officials (v. 20) even if their profligate leadership deserves such criticism (vv. 16-19). In this way Solomon counseled submission to governmental authority, a theme he had already broached in 8:2-3 and 10:4, which is well documented in other wisdom literature (e.g., Prov. 14:35; 24:21-22).

### a. It is foolish to multiply words (10:12-15)

**10:12-15.** Solomon began this passage by contrasting the words of a wise man with those of a fool; **a wise man's** words **are gracious** (or, better, "win him favor"; Prov. 13:15 ["favor"]; 22:1 ["esteemed"] make similar use of this Heb. word *ḥēn*), **but** a fool's words are self-destructive (i.e., they consume him).

Using a merism, a figure of speech in which polar opposites are chosen to indicate totality (cf. examples in Ecc. 3:2-8), Solomon characterized a fool's speech as foolish and **wicked madness** both **at the beginning** and **at the end** (i.e., from start to finish). Though such is true of a fool's speech, he continues to multiply **words** (cf. 5:3; 6:11), oblivious to the fact that **no one knows** the future, **what is coming** in days ahead and **what will happen after** death. Besides being ignorant of the future, a fool is also ignorant of the most obvious; **he does not know the way to town** (cf. 10:3). This is a proverbial expression for extreme ignorance like the modern proverb, "He doesn't know enough to come in out of the rain." This is why a fool finds his **work** such a chore (it **wearies him**).

### b. Criticism of profligate leadership is risky (10:16-20)

**10:16-17.** Solomon then strung together a series of proverbs describing the erosive effect of profligate leadership on a country and then warned against criticizing such bad leaders. In the first two of these proverbs, Solomon contrasted the sorry state of a nation whose leaders are incompetent and undisciplined (v. 16) with the fortunate (**blessed**) state of a nation whose leaders are competent and disciplined (v. 17). The former kind of leaders are childish (the "king is a child," NIV marg.; cf. Isa. 3:4 and 1 Kings 3:7 for the idea of incompetence and inexperience underlying this description). But the latter kind of leaders are well prepared by **noble birth** and training. Incompetent leaders are intemperate: they **feast in the morning** and are involved in revelry and **drunkenness** (Ecc. 10:17; see Isa. 5:11 and Acts 2:15 for similar ideas). But competent leaders are temperate: they **eat at a proper time—for strength and not for drunkenness.**

**10:18-20.** Solomon added that profligate, incompetent leaders are **lazy,** causing the ruin of the state and the loss of its protection, such as the sagging of **rafters** and the leaking of roofs. In their undisciplined lifestyle, they are involved in raucous feasting and merrymaking, which deplete state funds. The NEB renders this verse, "The table has its pleasures, and wine makes a cheerful life; and money is behind it all." The clause **money is the answer** (*ya'ăneh* from *'ānâh*) **for everything** means that the rulers *think* money can meet all their demands.

However, Solomon warned against criticizing such inadequate leaders. Aware that their hearts were the wellsprings of their thoughts and actions (Prov. 4:23), Solomon warned against reviling **the king even in** one's **thoughts** or cursing a **rich man** (i.e., a man in authority) in one's **bedroom.** The reason for such advice is that a report may get back to the king or rich person; **a bird** may tell them, that is, an unknown source may disclose one's secret criticisms.

### 4. WORK DILIGENTLY DESPITE IGNORANCE OF THE FUTURE (11:1-6)

Solomon closed his discussion on people's ignorance of the future (9:1–11:6) with some practical advice about their activities in view of such ignorance. To emphasize that man is ignorant of the future Solomon said, "You do not know" three times (11:2, 5-6); he also said, "You cannot understand" (v. 5). However, he counseled that ignorance of the future should lead not to inactivity or despair, but to diligent labor.

**11:1-2.** Solomon noted that people are as ignorant of God's providential dealings in human affairs (cf. 3:11; 8:17) as they are of "the path of the wind" and the formation of a baby in its "mother's womb" (11:5). Moreover, people do not know which of their ventures "will succeed" (v. 6) or what calamities might come on the earth (v. 2) and wipe out the results of their work. Even so, people should engage in diligent, active labor. Like the benefits that come from the seafaring trade of foodstuffs, so active involvement in business gives a promise of some return (v. 1; cf. 1 Kings 9:26-28;

10:22; Ps. 107:23 for references to maritime trade). But in view of the possibility of **disaster** a person should make prudent investments in numerous ventures **(to seven, yes to eight)** rather than put all his "eggs in one basket" (Ecc. 11:2; cf. Gen. 32:7-8 for a practical example of this advice). The NEB accurately reflects this interpretation of Ecclesiastes 11:1-2, "Send your grain across the seas, and in time you will get a return. Divide your merchandise among seven ventures, eight maybe, since you do not know what disasters may occur on earth."

**11:3-4.** Switching to an example of sowing seed and reaping a harvest, Solomon urged his readers not to sit around waiting for the most opportune moment to work but to be diligent constantly. The future is as beyond one's control as the acts of God in nature—the falling of **rain,** the uprooting of **a tree** by a gale. So waiting for just the right moment to **plant** (when there is no **wind** to blow away the seed) or to **reap** (when there is no rain in **the clouds** to threaten the ripened harvest) would result in inactivity.

**11:5-6.** In watching for **the wind** a farmer has no idea which **path** (direction) it will take. He is as ignorant of that as he is of something he cannot see such as a baby's **body** being **formed in** its **mother's womb.** Man cannot know the future or **the work of God** who has made and controls **all things** (cf. **Maker,** a title of God, in Job 4:17; 32:22; 35:10; Pss. 115:15; 121:2; Jer. 10:16). Using another merism (cf. Ecc. 10:13)—the polar opposites of **morning** and **evening** (11:6) to indicate total days—Solomon urged his readers to work diligently, sowing their **seed** all day long, because they could **not know which** sowing would **succeed, whether this or that, or whether both** would **do equally well.** Thus in two examples, one from maritime trade (vv. 1-2) and one from farming (vv. 3-4, 6) Solomon urged people toward constant, diligent effort and prudent diversified investment of their energies and resources, recognizing that all is in God's sovereign control.

## IV. Conclusion: Live Joyously and Responsibly in the Fear of God (11:7–12:14)

Solomon has shown that human effort is futile because its results are not permanent and the prospect of enjoying those results is insecure (1:12–6:9). He has also shown that people cannot know which of their efforts will succeed because they are ignorant of God's plan and of what the future holds (6:10–11:6). Now Solomon returned to the theme of the enjoyment of life (cf. 2:24-26; 3:12, 22; 5:18-20; 8:15; 9:7-9) and explicitly related it to the idea of living acceptably before God. This is similar to what he had done at the first mention of this theme (2:24-26). The latter theme, that of living responsibly before God, is found at both the beginning (11:9; 12:1) and the end (12:13-14) of this section. The need for responsible living is further underlined by repeating the theme of the futility of all else (12:8) and by a brief treatment of the book's authority and value (12:9-12).

### A. A call to live joyously and responsibly (11:7–12:7)

The three parts of this section are closely related. In the first part (11:7-8) Solomon called for enjoyment of life in view of the darkness of death. In the second (11:9-10) he urged that this enjoyment begin in one's youth because youth is fleeting; but he added that enjoyment should be tempered by responsible living because everyone is answerable to God. In the last part (12:1-7) Solomon underlined the urgency of this responsible enjoyment in one's youth because old age is a time of increasing gloom and of decay of one's powers, culminating in death.

### 1. ENJOY LIFE BECAUSE THE DARKNESS OF DEATH IS COMING (11:7-8)

**11:7-8.** Solomon wrote metaphorically of light and darkness as figures of life (cf. Job 3:20; 33:30) and death (cf. Ecc. 6:4-5; Job 10:20-22; 18:18). He characterized the future after death as obscure and enigmatic (**everything to come is meaningless**; cf. Ecc. 8:10, 14 for similar uses of the Heb. *hebel* referring to what is "meaningless" in the sense of being enigmatic). Solomon encouraged his readers to **enjoy** life as long as they **live** because life, like the pleasant **light of the sun,** should be enjoyed before the coming of the dark night of death which will last forever. The words, **the days of darkness . . . will be many,** is an intentional understatement (cf. 12:5 where the grave is called one's "eternal home"; also cf. Job 7:9; 14:10-12).

### 2. ENJOY LIFE IN YOUR YOUTH, REMEMBERING THAT GOD WILL JUDGE (11:9-10)

**11:9-10.** Solomon reiterated his advice to enjoy life (cf. v. 8), emphasizing that a person should do so in his **youth.** Elsewhere Solomon had said that enjoying life consists of eating and drinking (2:24; 3:13; 8:15; 9:7), wearing nice clothes and pleasant lotions (9:8), enjoying marital bliss (9:9), and finding satisfaction in one's work (2:24; 3:22; 5:18). Now Solomon encouraged his readers to do whatever their hearts desired ("follow the impulses of your heart and the desires of your eyes," 11:9, NASB). However, those desires should be tempered with an awareness that **God will** judge.

As previously noted (cf. comments on 2:24-26; 3:17; 7:15-18), there is no reason to believe from either explicit or implicit arguments in this book that Solomon believed this judgment would take place in the afterlife. Instead, like other wisdom writers of his era, he emphasized a temporal judgment within a man's lifetime (cf. comments on 2:24-26 and see 7:17). This may even be indicated in 11:10 where Solomon said a person should **banish anxiety from** his **heart** (psychological) and **cast off** the **troubles of** his **body** (physical). These imperatives are obviously the opposite side of the advice to **be happy** (v. 9) and contrast with the psychological gloom and declining physical vigor depicted in 12:2-5. Yet such passages as Proverbs 5:7-14 and Psalm 39 show that a means of avoiding these effects is a wise lifestyle lived in the fear of the Lord.

### 3. LIVE RESPONSIBLY IN YOUR YOUTH FOR OLD AGE AND DEATH ARE COMING (12:1-7)

Solomon underlined the thought of responsible living in one's youth by vividly depicting in a series of word pictures the increasing gloom and declining powers of old age which culminate in death. These word pictures are arranged in three groups, each introduced with "before" (vv. 1-2, 6) and modifying the basic imperative, "Remember your Creator in the days of your youth" (v. 1).

#### a. Live responsibly before the miseries of old age come (12:1)

**12:1.** The command **Remember your Creator** means to revere God, to keep His laws faithfully, to serve Him responsibly,

remembering that because He created people, everyone owes Him his life. This meaning is obvious (a) from the preceding verses (11:9-10) on living joyously but responsibly, (b) from the final advice at the end of the book to "fear God and keep His commandments" (12:13), and (c) from the meaning of the verb "remember" (in Deut. 8:18 and Ps. 119:55 "remember" is parallel to keeping the Law; in Jud. 8:34 it is contrasted with self-reliance and worship of other gods; in Ps. 63:6 it is parallel to meditating on and faithfully following God).

The epithet for God, "your Creator," emphasizes Him as the Author of life, who gives it and takes it away (cf. Ecc. 12:7; and the allusion to Gen. 2:7; 3:19).

Using a wordplay on the word "troubles" in Ecclesiastes 11:10 ("the troubles of your body"), Solomon advised responsible living in one's **youth, before the days of trouble come,** that is, the days of old age whose troubles he figuratively depicted in 12:2-5, **the years** in which he said they would find little or **no pleasure.**

#### b. Live responsibly before gloom and decay set in (12:2-5)

Using various figures to depict the declining joy and waning physical powers of old age, Solomon advised responsible living before old age sets in.

**12:2.** The miseries of old age ("the days of trouble," v. 1) and the approach of death (vv. 6-7) are likened to recurring rainstorms. As **clouds** often block out the light of **the sun,** the **moon, and the stars,** so old age is a period of diminishing joy (**light**) and increasing gloom (**dark**), heralding the approach of the long night of death. This obviously alludes to the earlier figurative use of light and darkness to depict life and death (11:7-8). This allusion would have been obvious to the ancient Hebrews who held a more dynamic view of death than people have today. Any decrease in the vitality of a person, even a young person, was viewed as the onset of death (cf., e.g., Pss. 18:4-5; 88:3-5).

**12:3.** Many diversified attempts have been made to interpret the highly figurative statements in verses 3-5. (For a brief, yet fairly comprehensive treatment of most views, cf. G.A. Barton, *A Critical and Exegetical Commentary on the Book of*

*Ecclesiastes.* Edinburgh: T. & T. Clark, 1908, pp. 186-91.) Though some interpreters have tried to explain this passage under a rigid adherence to one figure—either the decline of an estate or the gloom of a household after the death of its head—it seems that Solomon chose the various pictures to depict the declining physical and psychological powers of old age. Thus he referred to the days of misery (v. 1) and the days of decreasing joy and increasing gloom (v. 2) as a time **when the keepers of the house tremble** (the arms and hands grow weak). Also **the strong men stoop,** that is, the legs grow bent and feeble. **The grinders cease because they are few** refers to the teeth becoming fewer, and **those looking through the windows grow dim** refers to the eyesight beginning to fail.

**12:4.** **The doors to the street are closed** may picture the lips sinking in, due to the loss of teeth. **When men rise up at the sound of birds** suggests that old people get up early because of their inability to sleep. **All their songs grow faint** speaks of hearing that becomes impaired.

**12:5.** Being **afraid of heights and of dangers in the streets** points up lack of vigor and the fear that makes older people afraid to venture out. **The almond tree blossoms** refers to the hair turning gray and white (almond blossoms are white). **The grasshopper drags himself along** speaks of the body being bent and one's walk being slowed; the grasshopper, normally moving about quickly, is an apt figure of the past liveliness of one's childhood and youth. **Desire no longer is stirred** speaks of diminished appetites. The decline of physical powers culminates in death and **man goes to his eternal home** (i.e., the grave; cf. comments on 11:8-9) and people grieve (**mourners go about in the streets**).

### c. Live responsibly before death comes (12:6-7)

**12:6.** Solomon urged people to live responsibly **before** death comes; the idea, **remember Him,** is repeated from verse 1. Solomon then referred to life under the two common figures of light ("golden lamp," JB) and water (cf. Ps. 36:8-9 for a similar use of these two figures of speech). The dissolution of the body is suggested by light being extinguished: **the silver cord** holding a **golden bowl** (in which the light burns) snaps and the bowl **is broken.** Death is also referred to by water being unavailable: **the pitcher** which holds water **is shattered** and **the wheel** by which it is drawn from **the well** is **broken.**

**12:7.** The final description of death, by which Solomon sought to motivate people toward responsible living, was that of the reversal of Creation. **The dust** of the body **returns to the ground it came from** and the breath of life (**spirit** and "breath" are translations of the same Heb. word *rûaḥ*) **to God who gave it.** This obviously alludes to part of the Creation account (Gen. 2:7; man was made from the dust of the ground and was given breath). This makes it evident that Solomon was not referring to the return of individual human spirits to God for judgment. Similar descriptions of death (as a dissolution of the body and the withdrawal of the breath of God) are referred to in Job 34:14-15 and Psalm 104:29-30 (cf. Job 10:9).

Moreover, a comparison of these passages with Ecclesiastes 12:7 makes it clear that the description of the return of the breath of life given here does not contradict 3:20. There Solomon, writing about the common destiny of people and animals, had denied the possibility of demonstrating a difference in the disposition of their life breaths, that is, whether a human's breath went upward to God and whether an animal's went down to the earth. A comparison of 12:7; Job 34:14-15; Psalm 104:29-30; and Genesis 1:30 shows that Solomon would have affirmed the same destiny for life in animals, that is, it also returns to God.

### B. Final advice in view of the futility of all human endeavors (12:8-14)

Solomon closed this book by reiterating his theme of the futility of all human endeavor (v. 8; cf. 1:2) and by recommending that people fear God and keep His commandments (12:13-14). He underlined the validity of this summarization of his book by referring to the sources of its authority (vv. 9-12).

### 1. REITERATION OF THE THEME: THE FUTILITY OF ALL HUMAN ENDEAVOR (12:8)

**12:8.** Having demonstrated the limitations of all human efforts (1:12–6:9) and of all human wisdom (6:10–11:6), Solomon then reiterated the theme with which he opened his book (1:2): **Everything is meaningless** (*hebel*). As was stated in the comments on chapter 1, the immediately following context (1:3-11) shows that this statement applies to all human endeavor. Here (12:8) it applies to all that preceded, the futility of human efforts and human wisdom (1:12–11:6). Obviously, however, not included in this assessment is the advice to enjoy life as God enables, a course which Solomon repeatedly recommended (cf. 2:24-26; 3:12, 22; 5:18-20; 8:15; 9:7-9) and which he had just discussed explicitly in relationship to the fear of God (11:7–12:7). Apart from enjoying one's lot in life in the fear of God, life is indeed **meaningless.**

2. THE PECULIAR AUTHORITY OF THIS BOOK (12:9-12)

**12:9-10.** Solomon underlined the validity of the teaching in this book and the advice he offered in it by referring to its authority and by warning his readers about the futility of seeking answers from different kinds of books. Solomon first referred to his personal qualifications as a wisdom **Teacher**—one of the three kinds of leaders (prophets, priests, teachers) through whom God revealed His will to Israel (cf. Jer. 18:18; Ezek. 7:26). Solomon said he **was . . . wise** and **imparted knowledge to the people.** He took thoughtful care in producing this book; he said **he pondered** (i.e., carefully weighed in his mind) **and searched out and set in order** (i.e., carefully arranged) **many proverbs.**

Also Solomon said that he sought to give his book an aesthetically pleasing form without sacrificing the truth of what he wrote. He "sought to find delightful [or pleasing] words and to write words of truth correctly" (NASB).

**12:11-12.** Solomon related this book to the purpose and goal of other wisdom books (**the words of the wise** and **their collected sayings**) and to the ultimate source of their authority. Like ox **goads** and **firmly** planted **nails,** Solomon's teaching, like the words of other wise people, provides a guide and stimulus to godly living (cf. Acts 26:14 for an illustration of goads) and a secure basis for living (cf. Jer. 10:4 for a usage of nails). Moreover, like some other words of the

wise these words have divine authority; they were **given by one Shepherd.** This refers to God and His care and concern (cf. Gen. 49:24; Ps. 80:1; in Ps. 95:6-7 the concepts of Shepherd and Creator are combined as they are in Ecc. 12:1, 11). Because of the peculiar value and authority of the words of the wise—of which this book was an example—Solomon warned his son (cf. "my son" in Prov. 1:8, 10, 15; 2:1; 3:1, 11, 21; 4:10, 20; 5:1, 20; 6:1, 3, 20; 7:1; 19:27; 23:15, 19; 23:26; 24:13, 21; 27:11) and all his readers not to seek answers beyond those God had given through the wise. If they would keep looking for answers in **many** other **books,** they would wear themselves out.

3. FINAL ADVICE: FEAR GOD AND KEEP HIS COMMANDMENTS (12:13-14)

**12:13.** The book concludes (**here is the conclusion of the matter**) with an explicit recommendation to **fear God and keep His commandments.** These words were not added by someone other than Solomon, as is often claimed, but are the culmination of many other implicit references in Ecclesiastes to fear God and serve Him acceptably (cf. comments on 2:24-26; 7:15-18; 11:9-10; 12:1). Here Solomon said such reverence and service are everyone's duty (NASB's "this applies to every person" is preferred to NIV's **this is the whole duty of man**).

**12:14.** The fact that revering God is every person's responsibility is underlined by the truth that **God will bring every deed** (every human act) **into judgment** (cf. 3:17; 11:9) **including every hidden thing** (cf. Matt. 10:26). Everyone is answerable to God for everything he does, whether obvious or concealed. Though this is often taken as referring to a future judgment after death, a comparison of Psalm 90:7-8 and a proper understanding of Ecclesiastes 2:24-26; 7:15-18; 11:9-10 show that this is doubtful. Though a future judgment after death is indeed the solution to the enigma Solomon had observed in the unequal distribution of justice in human history (cf. 7:15; 8:14), no evidence suggests that Solomon believed in such a judgment. Life after death was as enigmatic to him (cf. 11:8) as the unequal distribution of justice. His emphasis was on *this life* ("under the sun") and its opportunities for service (cf. 9:10; 12:1-7) and enjoyment (cf. 2:24-26; 3:12, 22; 5:18-20; 8:15; 9:7-9; 11:7-10); he thought life after death offered no such opportunities (cf. 9:5-6, 10). Therefore he did not comment on any differences *after* death between the righteous and the wicked, the wise and the fools, man and beast.

Many other Scripture passages, of course, do point up the eternal blessings of the righteous and the eternal punishment of the wicked. Solomon lived on the other side of the Cross and in the comparative darkness of the progress of revelation; nevertheless he affirmed belief in God and in His justice (cf. 3:17; 8:12b-13). He was content to leave judgment, along with everything else, to God's timing (3:17) for "He has made everything appropriate in its time" (3:11, NASB). So Solomon counseled his readers to enjoy life in the fear of God as God enables. Would that people who live on this side of the Cross would be as content as Solomon was to leave the enigmas of life in God's hands, to serve Him acceptably, and to enjoy life as He enables!

# BIBLIOGRAPHY

Delitzsch, Franz. "Ecclesiastes." In *Commentary on the Old Testament in Ten Volumes*. Vol. 6. Reprint (25 vols. in 10). Grand Rapids: Wm. B. Eerdmans Publishing Co., 1982.

Eaton, Michael A. *Ecclesiastes*. The Tyndale Old Testament Commentaries. Downers Grove, Ill.: InterVarsity Press, 1983.

Ginsburg, Christian D. *The Song of Songs and Coheleth*. 1857. Reprint. New York: KTAV Publishing House, 1970.

Goldberg, Louis. *Ecclesiastes*. Bible Study Commentary. Grand Rapids: Zondervan Publishing House, 1983.

Gordis, Robert. *Koheleth—the Man and His World: A Study of Ecclesiastes*. 3rd ed. New York: Schocken Books, 1968.

Johnston, Robert K. "Confessions of a Workaholic: A Reappraisal of Qoheleth." *Catholic Biblical Quarterly* 38. January–March 1976:14-28.

Kaiser, Walter C., Jr. *Ecclesiastes: Total Life*. Everyman's Bible Commentary. Chicago: Moody Press, 1979.

Lange, John Peter, ed. "Ecclesiastes." In *Commentary on the Holy Scriptures*. Vol. 7. Reprint (25 vols. in 12). Grand Rapids: Zondervan Publishing House, 1960.

Laurin, Robert. "Ecclesiastes." In *The Wycliffe Bible Commentary*. Chicago: Moody Press, 1962.

Murphy, Roland E. *Wisdom Literature: Job, Proverbs, Ruth, Canticles, Ecclesiastes, Esther*. The Forms of the Old Testament Literature. Vol. 13. Grand Rapids: Wm. B. Eerdmans Publishing Co., 1981.

Reichert, Victor E., and Cohen, A. "Ecclesiastes." In *The Five Megilloth*. London: Soncino Press, 1946.

Wright, Addison G. "The Riddle of the Sphinx: The Structure of the Book of Qoheleth." *Catholic Biblical Quarterly* 30. October-December 1968:313-34.

Wright, J. Stafford. "The Interpretation of Ecclesiastes." *Evangelical Quarterly* 18. January-March 1946:18-34.

# NG OF SONGS

## Jack S. Deere

**and Purpose.** The Song of the Song of Solomon in ~~some Bible~~ versions, e.g., KJV, NASB) is perhaps the most difficult and mysterious book in the entire Bible. A cursory glance at the Song's history of interpretation reveals a diversity of opinion unequaled in the study of any other biblical work. The Song has been interpreted as: (a) an allegory, (b) an extended type, (c) a drama involving either two or three main characters, (d) a collection of Syrian wedding songs (a view held by E. Renan, J. Wetzstein, Umberto Cassuto, and others) in which the groom played the role of a king and the bride played the role of a queen, (e) a collection of pagan fertility cult liturgies (held by Theophile Meek), and (f) an anthology of disconnected songs extolling human love (held by Robert Gordis).

Viewed as an allegory, the details of the book are intended to convey hidden spiritual meanings, with little or no importance attached to the normal meanings of words. Jewish tradition (the Mishnah, the Talmud, and the Targum) viewed the book as an allegorical picture of the love of God for Israel. Church leaders, including Hyppolytus, Origen, Jerome, Athanasius, Augustine, and Bernard of Clairvaux, have viewed the book as an allegory of Christ's love for His bride, the church. Origen, for example, wrote that the beloved's reference to her being dark (Song 1:5-6) means the church is ugly with sin, but that her loveliness (1:5) refers to spiritual beauty after conversion. Others said the cooing of the doves (2:12) speaks of the preaching of the apostles, and some have suggested that 5:1 refers to the Lord's Supper. These examples show that the allegorical approach is subjective with no way to verify that any of the interpretations are correct. The Song of Songs nowhere gives an interpreter the suggestion that it should be understood as an allegory.

Some scholars view the book as an extended type, with Solomon typifying Christ and the beloved being a type of the church. This differs from the allegorical approach in that the typical view sees Solomon as a historical person and does not seek to discover a mystical meaning for every detail in the book. However, the Scriptures give no indication that various aspects of Solomon's life are divinely intended types of Christ.

Those who see the book as a drama (e.g., Franz Delitzsch, H. Ewald, and S.R. Driver) fail to note that the literary genre of a full-fledged drama was not known among the Israelites. Also the book cannot be analyzed into acts and scenes like a drama.

Scholars differ widely on the structure of the Song, its unity or lack of it, the nature of its metaphors, and the nature of the love extolled by the Song. In short, almost every verse has been the subject of lively debate by the Song's interpreters. Probably no other book of the Bible has such a variegated tapestry of interpretation.

Many evangelical scholars interpret the Song of Songs as a lyric poem which has both unity and logical progression. The major sections of the Song deal with courtship (1:2–3:5), a wedding (3:6–5:1), and maturation in marriage (5:2–8:4). The Song concludes with a climactic statement about the nature of love (8:5-7) and an epilogue explaining how the love of the couple in the Song began (8:8-14).

Some scholars say the book involves three characters, not two. Those three are the beloved, her shepherd-lover, and Solomon who wooed her away from the shepherd. No problem exists, however, with Solomon also being a shepherd (the two-character view) since he owned many flocks (Ecc. 2:7).

The purpose of the book is to extol

human love and marriage. Though at first this seems strange, on reflection it is not surprising for God to have included in the biblical canon a book endorsing the beauty and purity of marital love. God created man and woman (Gen. 1:27; 2:20-23) and established and sanctioned marriage (Gen. 2:24). Since the world views sex so sordidly and perverts and exploits it so persistently and since so many marriages are crumbling because of lack of love, commitment, and devotion, it is advantageous to have a book in the Bible that gives God's endorsement of marital love as wholesome and pure.

**Author and Date.** Song of Songs 1:1 attributes the authorship of this book to Solomon. Six other verses in the book refer to him by name (1:5; 3:7, 9, 11; 8:11-12). He is also referred to as the "king" (1:4, 12; 3:9, 11; 7:5). That a king is the lover referred to in the book is confirmed by references to his expensive carriage (3:7-10) and to the royal chariots (6:12). Solomon was a lover of nature (1 Kings 4:33), and the numerous references in the Song of Songs to flora, fauna, and other aspects of nature are consistent with his being its author. The book, then, was probably written sometime during Solomon's reign, between 971 and 931 B.C. Some wonder how Solomon could be the author of a book that extols faithfulness in marriage when he was so unfaithful, having 700 wives and 300 concubines (1 Kings 11:3). Perhaps the answer is that the "beloved" in the Song whom he married was his first wife. If so, then the book may have been written soon after his marriage, before he fell into the sin of polygamy.

Some interpreters have suggested that the maiden in the book was Pharaoh's daughter (1 Kings 3:1). But the beloved in the Song of Songs is never called a queen. She was probably from Lebanon (Song 4:8), not Egypt.

**Unity.** Many interpreters say that the book is an anthology, a collection of love songs that have no connections and that teach no lessons. However, several arguments speak for the book's unity: (1) The same characters are seen throughout the book (the beloved maiden, the lover, and the daughters of Jerusalem). (2) Similar expressions and figures of speech are used throughout the book. Examples are: love more delightful than wine (1:2; 4:10), fragrant perfumes (1:3, 12; 3:6; 4:10), the beloved's cheeks (1:10; 5:13), her eyes like doves (1:15; 4:1), her teeth like sheep (4:2; 6:6), her charge to the daughters of Jerusalem (2:7; 3:5; 8:4), the lover like a gazelle (2:9, 17; 8:14), Lebanon (3:9; 4:8, 11, 15; 7:4), and numerous references to nature. (3) Hebrew grammatical peculiarities found only in this book suggest a single author. (4) The progression in the subject matter points to a single work, not an anthology. As stated earlier, the book moves logically from the courtship (1:2–3:5) to the wedding night (3:6–5:1) to maturation in marriage (5:2–8:4).

# OUTLINE

2. The attractiveness of the lover (5:9-16)
3. The lover in his garden (6:1-3)
4. The reconciliation: The lover's praise of his beloved (6:4-13)

B. Praise of the beloved and her love (7:1-10)
   1. The beloved's charms (7:1-6)
   2. The lover's desire (7:7-9)
   3. The refrain of mutual possession (7:10)

C. An invitation from the beloved (7:11-13)

D. The beloved's desire for a greater intimacy (8:1-4)

V. The Conclusion: The Nature and Power of Love (8:5-7)

A. A picture of love (8:5)

B. An explanation of love (8:6-7)

VI. The Epilogue: How Love Began (8:8-14)

# COMMENTARY

## I. The Superscription (1:1)

**1:1.** This verse identifies the author of the Song as Solomon. As Israel's third king Solomon ruled from 971 to 931 B.C. Solomon was perhaps more gifted with literary skill than any other king of Israel for he wrote 3,000 proverbs and 1,005 songs (1 Kings 4:32). It is appropriate that a subject as wonderful as romantic love is described in sublime language by a competent human author, writing of course under the Holy Spirit's inspiration. Interestingly, of the more than 1,000 songs Solomon wrote, only this one was designed by God to be included in the biblical canon. Solomon is mentioned by name in six other verses: Song of Songs 1:5; 3:7, 9, 11; 8:11-12.

The title **Song of Songs** offers a clue to the interpretation of the work. It is *one* song out of many songs. The reader therefore is not to view the work as a collection of songs but rather as one unified song. The words "Song of Songs" suggest the superlative, as in "most holy" (Ex. 29:37) which is literally, "holy of holies." As a superlative the title may mean that this is the best of Solomon's 1,005 songs or, more likely, that this is the best of *all* songs. In either case the Song sets before its readers a paradigm

for romantic love in courtship and marriage.

## II. The Courtship (1:2–3:5)

This section contrasts sharply with the other two major sections (3:5–5:1; 5:2–8:4). Though this section (1:2–3:5) abounds with expressions of sexual desire, great sexual restraint is exercised by the lovers. However, after the wedding procession (3:6-11) there is a notable absence of sexual restraint in the Song. So this section points up the fact that in romantic courtship restraint ought to be observed.

### A. Introduction: The expressions of longing, insecurity, and praise (1:2-11)

1. THE THEME OF LONGING (1:2-4)

**1:2-4a.** As indicated in the margins, the NIV has indicated the male speaker as the "Lover" and the female speaker as the "Beloved." Other speakers are identified in the NIV as "Friends" in verse 4b and in 5:2, 9; 6:1, 13; 8:5, 8-9. In some instances the speakers are difficult to determine and are therefore debatable. Suggestions as to the speakers, with a few variations from the NIV margins, are summarized in the chart "Speakers in the Song of Songs."

The Song begins with a soliloquy by the beloved in which she first expressed her strong desire for her lover's (Solomon's) physical affection (**kisses,** 1:2). The rapid interchange between the third person (**him,** v. 2a, and **his,** vv. 2a, 4b) and the second person (**your** and **you,** vv. 2b-4a) is confusing to modern readers, but it was a regular feature of love poetry in the ancient Near East. This stylistic device gave a strong emotional quality to the poetry. When she spoke of his love (v. 2b) she was referring to the physical expressions of his **love** (the Heb. word for "love" is the pl. *dōdîm,* also used in 4:10). The statement **your love is more delightful than wine** means that his physical affections were exhilirating, refreshing, and a great source of joy (cf. 1:4).

The **pleasing** aroma of his **perfumes** made him even more attractive to her. Mention of perfumes led her to compare his **name** to **perfume.** A person's name represented his character or reputation (cf. 2 Sam. 7:9). So comparing Solomon's

## Speakers in the Song of Songs

| The beloved | Friends of the beloved | Solomon (the lover) | God | The beloved's brothers |
|---|---|---|---|---|
| 1:2-4a | 1:4b | | | |
| 1:4c-7 | 1:8* | | | |
| | | 1:9-10 | | |
| | 1:11* | | | |
| 1:12-14 | | 1:15 | | |
| 1:16-2:1* | | 2:2 | | |
| 2:3-13 | | 2:14 | | |
| 2:15-3:11* | | 4:1-15 | | |
| 4:16 | | 5:1a-d | 5:1e* | |
| 5:2-8 | 5:9 | | | |
| 5:10-16 | 6:1 | | | |
| 6:2-3 | | 6:4-9 | | |
| | 6:10* | | | |
| 6:11-12* | 6:13a | 6:13b-7:9a | | |
| 7:9b-8:4 | 8:5a | | | |
| 8:5b-7 | | | | 8:8-9 |
| 8:10-12 | | 8:13 | | |
| 8:14 | | | | |

* In these verses the speakers suggested here differ from those designated in the NIV margins.

name to perfume meant that his *character* was pleasing and attractive to the beloved. For this reason, she said, many were attracted to him.

The statement **the king** (cf. Song 1:12; 3:9, 11; 7:5) **has brought me into his chambers** may be rendered as a request: "May the king bring me into his chambers." In this sense she was expressing her desire for intimacy and marriage with the lover. This matches the first part of 1:4, **Take me away with you.** In summary, this opening soliloquy suggests that physical desire is a characteristic of romantic love and that properly channeled the desire is good, not evil. One ought to be "intoxicated" with love for one's own mate (cf. Prov. 5:18-19), rather than with wine, drugs, or other people. However, the choice of a marriage partner should be based on far more than purely physical considerations. The beloved's speech indicates that the character ("name") of a person is vitally important in the selection of one's spouse.

**1:4b.** The beloved's "friends" (see NIV marg.), elsewhere referred to as the "daughters of Jerusalem" (v. 5; 3:10; 5:8,

16) and "daughters of Zion" (3:11), spoke in 1:4b. Many suggestions have been given concerning the identity of the "daughters of Jerusalem," such as female wedding guests, ladies of the royal court, concubines in the royal harem. Most likely they refer to the female inhabitants of Jerusalem. That city is frequently referred to as the "mother" of its inhabitants (cf. Isa. 51:18; 60:4; Ezek. 19:2, 10; Hosea 2:2, 5).

The chorus is a literary device in the Song whereby the beloved and her lover express their emotions and thoughts more fully. By praising Solomon (**you** is masc. sing.) in Song of Songs 1:4 the "daughters" seemed to be agreeing with one another that the couple had an ideal romance. The last line in verse 4 may be the words of the beloved (see NIV marg.) or, perhaps better, the words of the friends.

### 2. THE THEME OF INSECURITY (1:5-8)

**1:5-6.** The beloved's suntanned appearance (**dark am I**) revealed that she worked in the fields. This made her feel insecure (**do not stare at me**) among the city dwellers and in particular the women of Jerusalem. She compared her dark skin to **the tents of Kedar,** which were made of black goats' hair. The people of Kedar were nomads in northern Arabia who descended from Ishmael (Gen. 25:13). They were known for their archery (Isa. 21:16-17) and flocks (Isa. 60:7; Jer. 49:28-29; Ezek. 27:21; also see Ps. 120:5; Isa. 42:11; Jer. 2:10). Apparently **the tent curtains of Solomon** were also black.

Her explanation for her dark appearance was almost an apology. Because of hard outdoor work in **the vineyards,** required of her by her brothers, she was forced to neglect the cultivation of her **own vineyard,** that is, herself and her appearance (cf. Song 8:12).

**1:7.** The beloved's feelings of insecurity helped arouse in her a desire for her lover's presence. She addressed him as though he were a shepherd (a common epithet for a man in ancient Near Eastern love poetry). The verse is either a soliloquy (assuming the lover is absent) or, if he is present, a request for a meeting later in the day. If she could not be with him she said she would **be like a veiled woman.** This enigmatic expression means either that she would be mistaken for a prostitute (cf. Gen. 38:14-15) or, more likely, that without Solomon she would be as sad as a person in mourning (cf. Ezek. 24:17, 22).

**1:8.** The reply in this verse is usually credited to the lover since he was addressed in the preceding question (v. 7). If Solomon is the speaker then the verse is probably a playful or teasing response. However, the verse seems too cold and distant in tone for Solomon. So it may be a disdainful reply by the friends: **"If you,** of all people, **do not know** where he is, go to the other **shepherds** where you really belong anyway" (**graze your young goats**).

### 3. THE THEME OF PRAISE (1:9-11)

**1:9-11.** The answer to the beloved's feelings of insecurity (vv. 5-6) was the praise of her lover. Frequently he called her his **darling** (vv. 9, 15; 2:2, 10, 13; 4:1, 7; 5:2; 6:4). In ancient Arabic poetry, women were sometimes compared to horses as objects of beauty, but the reference in 1:9 is probably more specific. The words **a mare harnessed to one of the**

**chariots of Pharaoh** is literally, "a mare among the chariots of Pharaoh." Stallions, not mares, were used to pull chariots in antiquity. A mare, therefore, *among* the chariots might well start a chaotic experience. The point of the comparison is that in Solomon's opinion she was as beautiful and sought after as if she were the only woman in a world full of men. When he further stated that she was **beautiful** with jewelry (**earrings** and necklaces, v. 10), the daughters of Jerusalem (**we,** v. 11) were forced to change their attitude of disdain (v. 6) and to agree with royal opinion. They even agreed to make her **earrings.** Verse 10 includes the first of numerous times in the book where he said she is beautiful (cf. v. 15 [twice]; 2:10, 13; 4:1 [twice], 7; 6:4; 7:1, 6). In summary, since the beloved had felt self-conscious about her appearance, the lover praised her physical beauty so that her detractors were forced to agree with him.

### B. The growth of love and its intensity (1:12–3:5)

This section consists of a series of units in the progression of the lovers' courtship. Their longing for and praise of each other expand and intensify, and the insecurity of the beloved is resolved. The first unit (1:12–2:6) records a growing intensity in desire, praise, and security. The refrain (2:7) is an appeal for patience since love cannot be forced. The second unit (2:8-17) records the reward of patience and a growth in intimacy. The third unit (3:1-4) records the most intense longing yet, and after an appropriate refrain, which is an appeal for patience (3:5), the longing is followed by the reward of marriage (3:6–5:1).

### 1. MUTUAL PRAISE (1:12–2:6)

**1:12-14.** The beloved praised **the king** for his pleasing and attractive characteristics which were like **perfume** (cf. comments on v. 3) whose function was to attract rather than repel. He was constantly in her thoughts just as the smell of the **myrrh** (in her **sachet** around her neck) was constantly in her nostrils. Myrrh was a pleasant-smelling gum that exudes from small trees in Arabia. It is mentioned frequently in the Song of Songs (v. 13; 3:6; 4:6, 14; 5:1, 5 [twice], 13). All other men, compared with him, were like the desert. Among them he stood out like a beautiful **cluster of** flowers in a desert oasis. **Henna** (cf. 4:13) **blossoms** were white, and **En Gedi** was an oasis on the west coast of the Dead Sea. Earlier David had fled to En Gedi while running away from Saul (1 Sam. 23:29; 24:1).

**1:15.** The lover returned her praise by commending not only her beauty (**beautiful** occurs twice in this v.) but also her tranquil character. In antiquity **doves** (cf. 2:12, 14; 4:1; 5:2, 12; 6:9) were noted for their cleanliness and tranquility. "According to Rabbinic teaching, a bride who has beautiful **eyes** possesses a beautiful character; they are an index to her character" (S.M. Lehrman, "The Song of Songs," in *The Five Megilloth,* p. 4).

**1:16-17.** Both of these verses may be seen as spoken by the beloved (rather than v. 16 by the beloved and v. 17 by the lover, as in the NIV). Though she recognized his physical good looks (**handsome**) she was more taken by the charm of his personality (**Oh, how charming!**). The word "charming" means "pleasant" or "lovely" and the combination, handsome and pleasant, was as rare then as it is now. This is the first of about two dozen times she referred to him as **my lover. The beams** of **cedars** and the **rafters** made of **firs** probably do not refer to a literal building but figuratively to the pastoral setting in which they first met. This is also suggested by the **verdant** (green) **bed** (couch). The field where they fell in love and sat talking was green.

**2:1.** Here the beloved spoke of herself as **a rose of Sharon,** the fertile coastal region of Israel from Caesarea to Joppa. The Hebrew word for rose is *ḥăḇaṣṣelet.* In Isaiah 35:1, its only other occurrence in the Old Testament, it is translated "crocus," which may be the meaning here. It was a common meadow flower. The **lily** too was a common flower mentioned often in the Song of Songs (2:1-2, 16; 4:5; 5:13; 6:2-3; 7:2). Though in her humility she likened herself to common flowers of the field, her statement (2:1) reflects a significant contrast with her earlier self-consciousness (1:5-6). Her improvement probably was because of her lover's praising her (1:9-10, 15).

**2:2.** The lover echoed his beloved's newfound sense of worth by comparing her to **a lily** and all other women to **thorns.** He agreed that she was a lily (v. 1) but not just any lily! She was as unique among all others as a single lily would be **among** many **thorns.**

**2:3-6.** The beloved's reciprocal praise of her **lover** was also expressed metaphorically. As **an apple tree** would be a delightful surprise in a **forest** so Solomon was a delightful and rare "find" **among** all the other **men.** He was unique, sweet, and fragrant.

The beloved's praise of her lover reveals three aspects of romantic love that are important to women. First, she felt protected by him. Sitting **in his shade** was a metaphor for protection, not only in the Bible but also in the literature of the ancient Near East. She had worked in the sun (1:6) but now she enjoyed resting under his protection. Second, they cultivated the kind of relationship that allowed them to know each other intimately. The word **taste** expressed a knowledge of someone through intimate personal experience (cf. Ps. 34:8, "Taste and see that the LORD is good"). Third, the beloved appreciated the fact that Solomon let others see his love for her. As a **banner** (a military standard) was easily seen by the troops as they marched, so Solomon's **love** for his beloved was easily seen by anyone who observed their relationship. He was not ashamed of her; instead he delighted in her and it was evident to others. One way he showed this was by taking her to his **banquet hall** (cf. "table" in Song 1:12) in the palace.

These three things—protection by her lover, intimacy with him, and obvious displays and expressions of love from him—are crucial factors that enable a woman to develop a sense of security and self-worth and thereby to enjoy a stable marriage.

The beloved had begun to experience these three things with Solomon during their courtship so it is no wonder that she became **faint with love** (2:5; cf. 5:8). The theme of lovesickness was common in ancient Near Eastern love poetry. So she expressed her desire for his strengthening and his embrace. Physically weakened, she needed stimulation from food such as **raisins** and **apples.** Perhaps "raisins" should be translated "raisin cakes," a Near Eastern delicacy (1 Chron. 12:40; Isa. 16:7; Hosea 3:1).

Since Song of Songs 2:5 is a request,

verse 6 should probably be translated as a request also ("May **his left arm** be **under my head, and** may **his right arm** embrace **me**") rather than a declarative statement.

### 2. THE REFRAIN (2:7)

**2:7.** This refrain, spoken by the beloved to the **daughters** (inhabitants; cf. comments on 1:4b) **of Jerusalem,** appears again in 3:5 and part of it in 8:4. In these three verses the refrain serves as a structural indicator to mark the ending of one section and to introduce the next one. The meaning of the refrain is that **love** cannot be forced but must be patiently waited for. In other words the beloved reminded all those desiring a relationship like the one she and Solomon enjoyed to wait patiently for God to bring it into their lives. **Gazelles** (2:17; cf. v. 17; 3:5; 4:5; 7:3; 8:14) and **does** are graceful, agile animals. It was natural for a beloved one, thinking of the fields and forests (2:1, 3), to make an oath by mountain animals.

### 3. A VISIT TO THE COUNTRY (2:8-17)

The preceding sections (1:2–2:7) seem to have a royal setting (1:4; 2:4) though outdoor scenes were mentioned, (e.g., 1:14; 2:1-3). But the setting for 2:8–3:5 is the country, near the beloved's home. She probably lived in Lebanon, north of Israel (cf. 4:8, 15). More importantly, however, the intensity of the couples' longing for each other increased and their sense of intimacy grew.

**2:8-9.** As Solomon approached his beloved's home, she excitedly described him coming as **a gazelle or a young stag** (cf. v. 17; 8:14). This emphasized his attractive appearance, strength, and agility (cf. comments on gazelles in 2:7). He approached the **wall** around her parents' home and then peered **through the lattice.** He was anxious to see her.

**2:10-13.** Solomon, her **lover,** asked his **darling** to go for a walk in the countryside. At the beginning and ending of his invitation he said, **Come with me** (vv. 10, 13; cf. 8:14). The elaborate description of spring was probably meant to do more than simply emphasize the beauty of the setting. It is likely that he was also describing their relationship. In a sense when one falls in love the feeling is like spring for everything seems fresh and new. The world is seen from a different perspective, which is how Solomon felt when he was with his beloved. Several statements refer to the beauty of spring: (1) **The winter is past.** The word for winter ($s^e \underline{t}aw$, used only here in the OT) refers to the cloudy season of March and April with the "latter" **rains.** (2) **Flowers appear** in the spring, adding delightful colors to the landscape, causing people to sing for joy. (3) **Doves** coo, "announcing" spring's arrival. (4) **Fig** trees put forth their **early fruit** (cf. Nahum 3:12). The early figs were either those that had remained unripened on the trees from the previous summer and then ripened at the beginning of spring, or were small edible buds that appeared in March. (5) Grape **vines** blossom, giving off **their fragrance** just before the grapes appear. **Blossoming** translates $s^e m\bar{a}\underline{d}ar$ which occurs only here and in Song of Songs 2:15 ("in bloom"). So spring stimulates the senses of sight, sound, taste, and smell.

**2:14.** Another characteristic of genuine love is the desire to be alone with one's lover. This desire seems to be easily experienced during courtship, but unfortunately it often fades in marriage. Yet if love is to grow a couple must find time to be alone. Doves (cf. v. 12 and see comments on 1:15) hide in **rock** crevices, reluctant to leave. The lover likened his beloved to such a **dove,** hesitant to join him in the countryside. So again (cf. 2:10, 13) he urged her to leave her home and join him so he could enjoy her **sweet-**sounding **voice** and **lovely** face.

**2:15.** The beloved rather than the lover may well be the speaker here. She was probably speaking poetically about their relationship rather than about literal **foxes** and **vineyards. Foxes** were noted for their destructive tendencies in crop fields, so their reference to those animals probably suggested metaphorically some problems in their relationship. The beloved was asking her lover to take the initiative in solving the problems that were potentially harmful to their relationship. "The foxes represent as many obstacles or temptations as have plagued lovers throughout the centuries. Perhaps it is the fox of uncontrolled desire which drives a wedge of guilt between a couple. Perhaps it is the fox of mistrust and jealousy which breaks the bond of love. Or it may be the fox of selfishness and pride which refuses to let one acknowledge his fault to another. Or it may be an unforgiving spirit which will not accept the apology of the other. These foxes have been ruining vineyards for years and the end of their work is not in sight" (S. Craig Glickman, *A Song for Lovers*, pp. 49-50). Even in ideal courtships and marriages most couples encounter some potentially destructive problems. Their willingness to solve them together is an evidence of their maturity.

**2:16-17.** Though they had some problems in their relationship (see comments on v. 15), the beloved knew that her **lover** belonged to her and she belonged to him. They were committed to each other. She could rest in the shepherd-like quality of his love despite the struggles they shared. She said **he browses** (lit., "he pastures" his flock) **among the lilies** (cf. 6:3). Speaking to herself (using the personal pronouns **mine, his,** and **he**) in 2:16, it is likely that verse 17 is also a soliloquy. Her thoughts of their mutual possession of each other naturally led to her desire for physical intimacy. So in her mind she invited him to **turn** (i.e., to her) with the strength and agility of **a gazelle or . . . young stag** (cf. v. 9; 8:14). **Rugged hills** (*hārê bāter*) is literally, "hills or mountains of separation or cleavage." Some say this refers to actual mountains—perhaps "hills of Bether" (NIV marg.), though the location of such a site is unknown. In that case the hills separated the couple, but this seems unlikely since he was already at her wall and lattice (2:9). It seems preferable to take this as a subtle reference to her breasts (cf. 4:6), thus an inner longing that they consummate their marriage. If that is the meaning, then she wanted that intimacy to last during the night till **the day breaks** (lit., "breathes") at dawn and the night **shadows** vanish. When their marriage was consummated they did this (see 4:5-6). As already stated, in expressing their love in their courtship, the beloved and her **lover** used restraint. Yet because of their deep love and commitment to each other they longed for their wedding day to come.

4. THE BELOVED'S FEAR OF LOSING HER LOVER (3:1-4)

**3:1-4.** The king returned to Jerusalem, leaving his beloved at her home in the country. The phrase **All night long on my bed** indicates that the experience she was describing took place in a dream. When a person loves another person deeply, it is natural to fear losing him or her. In her dream she lost her lover and sought to **find him.** The repeated expression **the one my heart loves** (once in each of these four verses) revealed the depth of her love for Solomon.

In her dream she went to a **city** (either a town near her home or Jerusalem) to look **for him,** but she was unsuccessful. She even asked **the watchmen,** men who guarded **the city** at night, if they had **seen** him. Apparently they had not. When she **found** him in her dream, she took him **to** her **mother's house,** the most secure place she knew.

5. THE REFRAIN (3:5)

**3:5.** This refrain marks the end of the section on the courtship (1:2–3:5) and the beginning of the wedding section (3:6–5:1). Perhaps the wedding was to be seen as a reward for patience on the beloved's part. On the meaning of 3:5, see comments on 2:7.

## III. The Wedding (3:6–5:1)

### A. The wedding procession (3:6-11)

Marriages in the ancient Near East were usually sanctioned through civil contracts rather than through religious ceremonies. Except for Proverbs 2:17 and Malachi 2:14 marriage covenants or contracts are not mentioned in the Old Testament. However, examples of Jewish civil marriage contracts have been found in the remains of the Jewish colony at Elephantine, Egypt dating back to the fifth century B.C. The marriage of Ruth and Boaz before a court of elders rather than before priestly officials (cf. Ruth 4:10-11) also illustrates the "civil" rather than religious character of wedding ceremonies. It is not surprising, therefore, to find that weddings took place not in the temple (or later in the synagogue), but rather in the couples' homes.

A central feature of a wedding ceremony was a procession to the bride's home led by the groom, who then escorted her back to their new residence. Next a wedding feast was given which lasted up to a week or even longer. Though the feast was prolonged the couple consummated their marriage on the first night. The wedding feast is not described in the

Song of Songs but both the wedding procession (3:6-11) and the wedding night (4:1–5:1) are presented in some detail. Verse 11 of chapter 3 refers to the "wedding" and to "Solomon," who of course was the groom.

**3:6.** The author spoke as a narrator in this verse, as if he were a spectator watching the approaching wedding procession, which was elaborate. What at first appeared in the distance to be a great **column of smoke** was actually **incense** (lit., "frankincense"; see comments on 4:6) burning in front of the procession. The fact that the incense was **made from all the spices of the merchant** emphasizes the costly nature of this display. The **myrrh** (see comments on 1:13) added another fragrance to the procession.

The pomp and beauty of this procession were wholly appropriate in light of the event's significance. The Scriptures teach that marriage is one of the most important events in a person's life. Therefore it is fitting that the union of a couple be commemorated in a special way. The current practice of couples casually living together apart from the bonds of marriage demonstrates how unfashionable genuine commitment to another person has become in contemporary society. This violates the sanctity of marriage and is contrary to God's standards of purity.

**3:7-8.** The **60 warriors** accompanying **Solomon's carriage** (cf. v. 9) were friends of the groom. It was common for a groom's friends to go with him in the wedding procession. But they were also **the noblest** and most **experienced** soldiers in **Israel,** probably Solomon's royal bodyguard. David had a bodyguard (2 Sam. 23:23) and so possibly did Solomon. Since the caravan may have had to travel some distance (cf. "coming up from the desert," Song 3:6, and note also the mention of Lebanon in 4:8, 15), the king was taking no chances with the safety of his bride. If bandits would appear at **night** and terrorize the bride, the soldiers were ready for them. The lesson is valid today for a would-be husband. He should give proper thought and planning to protect his bride. One form this takes is providing economic security for her.

**3:9-11.** Solomon's **carriage** was **made** of the very best, that is, **wood from Lebanon** (possibly his bride's homeland; cf.

4:8, 15). The carriage was adorned with the most expensive materials, **silver . . . gold,** and **purple** (representing royalty) fabric. Solomon offered his bride the best he had. And his love for her brought out the best in him. Others shared the couple's joy by helping prepare for the procession (**the daughters**—female inhabitants—**of Jerusalem** helped make the interior of the carriage and did so gladly) and by watching it (**look at King Solomon**). In the procession he wore a **crown.** This was not his royal crown, but a **crown . . . his mother** (Bathsheba, 1 Kings 2:13) gave **him**; it probably depicted happiness more than royalty.

## B. The wedding night (4:1–5:1)

### 1. THE BEAUTY OF THE BELOVED (4:1-7)

**4:1.** The first to speak on their wedding night was Solomon and his words praised his bride's beauty. Three times on the wedding night he told her she was **beautiful** (vv. 1 [twice], 7; cf. comments on 1:10). Women in the ancient Near East did not ordinarily wear a veil except at the time of their wedding, and then removed it in the wedding chamber. (This is why Rebekah immediately veiled herself when she learned the identity of Isaac, her husband-to-be, Gen. 24:65. It also explains why Laban was able to deceive Jacob with Leah on their wedding night, Gen. 29:19-25.) So Solomon, seeing her **eyes behind** her **veil** (cf. Song 4:3) said they were **doves.** Doves were known for their tranquility in the ancient world, and since one's eyes are "windows of his soul" reflecting his character, Solomon was praising her calm and innocent character (cf. 1:15).

To say that her **hair** was **like a flock of goats** coming down **Mount Gilead** (cf. 6:5) hardly sounds like a compliment, but it was. Seen from a distance the dark hair of Palestinian goats was beautiful in the sunset as a flock was **descending from the mountains.** The beloved's dark hair had the same beautiful quality. Mount Gilead was a mountain range east of the Jordan River in Gilead, known for its fertile pastures and many flocks (cf. Micah 7:14).

**4:2-3.** Her **teeth** were white (**like a flock of sheep just shorn**) and perfectly matched (**each has its twin**). Her **lips,** being red and thin, were **like a scarlet ribbon.** "Ribbon" is literally "thread," referring to the perfect outline and delicately formed shape of her lips. Her teeth and lips made her **mouth** beautiful. The beloved's **temples,** probably including her cheeks, were reddish and sweet **like pomegranate** fruit.

**4:4. The tower of David** may have been the tower (cf. Neh. 3:25) of the king's palace. This tower may have been built or used by David for military purposes, or it may have been built by Solomon and given David's name. The custom of hanging **shields** on the tower was symbolic of the warriors' allegiance to and valor for a particular king or country (cf. Ezek. 27:10-11). The **warriors** probably referred to David's elite corps of men (2 Sam. 23:8-39). By comparing her **neck** to the tower Solomon was emphasizing not so much her neck's symmetry and beauty as he was making a statement about her person. She had a queenly bearing and appearance as awesome and majestic as King David's tower.

**4:5.** When the groom said his bride's **breasts** were **like . . . fawns** he was comparing their softness, not their color or form. Looking on the soft coat of a little fawn makes a person want to stroke it. Solomon wanted his bride to know that her soft and gentle beauty had kindled his desire for her and he wished to express that desire with his caresses.

**4:6.** At this point Solomon was overcome with desire for his bride and resolved to fulfill her silent request (see comments on 2:17). **The mountain of myrrh** and **the hill of incense** refer to the beloved's breasts. The primary point of comparison was not in the visual area, but rather in the realms of function and value. Myrrh and incense were used to perfume the body as well as the bedroom in order to make a person and the surroundings more attractive (cf. 3:6). They would give their love to each other till the morning. Myrrh (see comments on 1:13) and incense (lit., "frankincense," a balsamic gum that exudes from the wood of shrubs and trees of the genus *Boswellia*) were not native to Palestine. Both were luxury items that had to be imported at considerable cost. A mountain of myrrh or a hill of frankincense would have been greatly valued. To Solomon, therefore, his bride's breasts were attractive and of great value to him.

**4:7.** Solomon summarized his praise

by ascribing perfect beauty to his bride. She had **no flaw,** or physical defect. She was perfect in appearance. (Later she called him "my flawless one," 5:2.) Solomon praised eight parts of his bride's body: her eyes, hair, teeth, lips, mouth, temples, neck, and breasts.

Compared with this lavish praise of the beloved's beauty, some wives today may feel uncomfortable about their own appearance. However, one must remember that initially the daughters of Jerusalem did not seem to regard the beloved as a beautiful woman. Unlike the other royal ladies she was not fair-skinned, a preeminent sign of beauty in the ancient world (see comments on 1:5-6). Yet in her lover's eyes she was **beautiful,** even though she did not meet the objective standards of beauty in her society. In other words, though few people in any age meet their own particular culture's standard of beauty, a woman is beautiful in the eyes of her lover simply because he loves her. Every husband who genuinely loves his wife can say, "To me you are beautiful and there is no flaw in you."

Two features of 4:1-7 call for comment. First, these verses include one reference to the first person ("I" in v. 6). His total attention was focused on his bride and her beauty. The conclusion to be drawn from this is that sex, when enjoyed properly within marriage, draws attention from oneself to one's mate, to his or her needs and pleasures. Second, the metaphors and imagery which Solomon used in praising his beloved were drawn from a pastoral setting: doves, goats, sheep, pomegranates, fawns, gazelles, mountains, hills. Solomon's bride, having been raised in the country, understood and appreciated these images. Praise drawn from this well-known realm would have created a sense of peace and security in her on the anxious night when her new life began in new surroundings. Later (7:1-9) after she became accustomed to "royal" living, Solomon drew on royal imagery (as well as pastoral scenes) in praising her beauty.

2. THE KING'S REQUEST (4:8)

**4:8.** The beloved may have lived in **Lebanon** near the mountains mentioned in this verse. **Amana** is the eastern part of the Anti-Lebanon range facing Damascus, and **Senir** and **Hermon** are two peaks in the Hermon range (though Deut. 3:9 speaks of Senir as a synonym for Hermon). However, it is unlikely that she lived by **lions' dens** or **haunts of . . . leopards.** The lions and leopards may represent fearful places or circumstances. In other words Solomon was asking his bride to leave her thoughts of home and put her fears behind her in order to concentrate completely on him, as he had done for her. The fact that Solomon called her **my bride** five times (vv. 8-12) also confirms that chapter 4 depicts their wedding night.

3. THE KING'S PRAISE OF HIS BRIDE'S LOVE (4:9-11)

Apparently the bride granted Solomon's request (v. 8) to turn all her attention to him, for in this section he praised her physical expression of love and its effect on him.

**4:9.** The words **stolen my heart** mean to be robbed of either one's willpower or his ability to think clearly. The effect of his bride's love was so powerful that even a **glance** from her beautiful **eyes** (cf. v. 1; 1:15) or even seeing an article of jewelry or clothing associated with her was enchanting to Solomon. Five times he called her his **sister** (4:9-10, 12; 5:1-2) because in the ancient Near East "sister" was an affectionate term for one's wife.

**4:10.** The word rendered **love** (*dōḏîm*; cf. 1:2) was used for physical expressions of romantic love. The verse might be more accurately translated, "How delightful are your kisses. How much more pleasing are your caresses than wine." Her physical expressions of love had a more refreshing and intoxicating effect on him **than wine,** just as *his* expressions had earlier affected *her* (cf. 1:2). Even her **perfume** added to the excitement of their love. The senses of sight, touch, smell, and sound were involved in their lovemaking.

**4:11.** The beloved gave herself freely with joy. She was not at all passive in their lovemaking. Her kisses were as desirable as **milk** and as sweet as **honey.** Milk and honey are combined here probably to allude to the fact that Canaan was a land of milk and honey (see comments on Ex. 3:8). Just as the land, rich in agricultural prosperity, was a source of blessing and joy to the people, so her kisses were a source of joy to him. Besides ap-

plying perfume to herself she also applied it to her clothes. **Lebanon,** because of its cedar trees (1 Kings 5:6; Pss. 29:5; 92:12; 104:16; Isa. 2:13; 14:8; Hosea 14:5), was known for its **fragrance** (Hosea 14:6).

4. THE KING'S PRAISE OF HIS BRIDE'S PURITY (4:12-15)

**4:12.** The **garden locked up . . . spring enclosed,** and **sealed fountain** all suggest "inaccessibility." The king was obviously praising his bride's virginity. Gardens were walled to keep out intruders (cf. Isa. 5:5; cf. "wall" in Song 2:9). Springs were sometimes covered, and fountains were sealed on the sides with clay to indicate private ownership. Similarly, she had kept herself "sealed" from all others, thus preserving her purity for her husband.

**4:13-14.** By extending the metaphor of the garden (begun in v. 12) Solomon conveyed to his beloved how much he valued her purity. She was like a rich exotic garden, with rare and valuable plant life. Such a garden was therefore valuable, attractive, and desirable. Included were **fruits,** flowers, plants, trees, and **spices. Pomegranates** (cf. v. 3) were a delicacy in Bible times. **Henna** (see comments on 1:14) is a flower with white blossoms. **Nard** is a fragrant ointment from a plant native to India (cf. Mark 14:3; John 12:3), and **saffron** is a powder from the pistils of a plant in the crocus family (cf. comments on "rose" in Song 2:1). **Calamus** (also mentioned in Isa. 43:24; Jer. 6:20; Ezek. 27:19) is possibly sweet cane. Other perfumes were **cinnamon,** from the bark of a tall tree, **myrrh** (see comments on Song 1:13), **and aloes,** a plant native to an island in the Red (Reed) Sea, whose partially decayed wood gives off a fragrance. These items would make an unusual garden, valuable for its pleasant tastes, sights, and smells. Similarly Solomon valued his bride for her pleasing attractiveness.

**4:15.** This part of the metaphor contrasts with her inaccessibility as a garden and water in verse 12. The water is pure and wholesome, like **flowing water streaming down from Lebanon** (cf. "Lebanon" in vv. 8, 11), and is now accessible to Solomon. When the bride surrendered her virginity to her husband, she was no less pure for doing so. The progression from **a garden fountain** to **a well** to "water streaming down" indicates that his beloved more than quenched Solomon's desire for her and fully satisfied him. As mountain streams are refreshing so she refreshed him.

5. THE CONSUMMATION OF THE MARRIAGE (4:16–5:1)

**4:16.** The beloved's request that the winds **blow on** her **garden,** that is, herself (cf. vv. 12, 15) was a delicate, poetically beautiful invitation to her lover to fully possess her (**come into** her). She wished to be his with her charms as available as fruit on a tree (cf. v. 13).

**5:1.** With exhiliration Solomon declared that their marriage was complete. He had totally enjoyed his **garden** (cf. vv. 12, 15-16), that is, his **bride.** Possessing her was more delightful than gathering **myrrh** in a garden, as sweet as eating **honey,** as enjoyable as drinking the best **wine** and **milk** (cf. 4:11).

The NIV margin attributes the last part of the verse, **Eat, O friends, and drink; drink your fill, O lovers,** to the "friends" of the couple. However, it is unlikely that friends, wedding guests, or any other persons would have been present in the bedroom at the consummation of the couple's marriage. A more plausible suggestion is that the speaker was God Himself. Only their Creator would have been a "guest" on that occasion. Since their love was from Him it was fitting that He approve it. He invited them to enjoy sexual love in marriage as if it were a banquet ("eat . . . and drink"). This clearly indicates God's approval of marriage, which He designed in the Garden of Eden (cf. Gen. 2:24).

## IV. The Maturation of the Marriage (5:2–8:4)

This section of the Song of Songs deals with the growth of the couple's marriage. The intimacy, joy, and physical desire of their wedding night did not fade as is often common in many marriages. They nourished their life together so that the joy of their married life increased rather than decreased. This does not suggest, however, that they did not encounter problems potentially harmful to their relationship. This section opens with the problem of indifference and offers a paradigm for the successful resolution of a serious marital problem.

### A. Indifference and its resolution (5:2–6:13)

The bride's indifference is introduced by her dream (5:2-7). This problem caused the temporary absence of her husband-lover. Asking the daughters of Jerusalem to help her find him (5:8), she described his attractiveness. The conversation between the beloved and the daughters laid the foundation for the reconciliation of the husband and wife (6:4-13).

1. THE PROBLEM: THE WIFE'S INDIFFERENCE AND THE HUSBAND'S ABSENCE (5:2-8)

**5:2.** In a dream (**I slept but my heart was awake**; cf. another recorded dream, 3:1-4) the wife was approached by her husband, who said **Open to me** (cf. 5:6). The fact that the **lover** no longer addressed her as "my bride" indicates there is a time lapse between verse 1 (the wedding night) and verse 2. The couple should no longer be regarded as newlyweds. But he did address her by other affectionate terms: **my sister** (see comments on 4:9), **my darling** (cf. 1:9, 15; 2:2, 10, 13; 4:1, 7; 6:4), **my dove,** and **my flawless one** (cf. 4:7). This is the first record of his using all these terms of endearment. His **head** and **hair** were covered **with dew,** as he had been outside. Dew in Israel was often heavy.

**5:3-4.** She said in her dream that she had already gotten ready for bed. But this trivial excuse for not opening the door revealed her indifference or apathy toward her husband. Somehow she had grown cool toward his advances. But he did not accept her excuse. He tried to open the door but failed and then left. Then her compassion was aroused for him and she decided to open the door. The Hebrew expression translated **my heart began to pound for him** is used elsewhere to express pity or compassion (e.g., Isa. 16:11; Jer. 31:20). It was not used to express sexual arousal as some scholars have maintained.

**5:5-7.** When the beloved in her dream went to the door **to open** it for her husband (**my lover;** used of him six times in vv. 2, 4-6, 8), she found **myrrh** on the door **handles** and got some on her **hands.** Myrrh was sometimes associated with lovemaking (Prov. 7:17; Song 4:6; 5:13). Perhaps the **lover** had put liquid myrrh on the door handles as a token of affection for his beloved. He had wanted more than relief from the discomfort of the night air.

However, the beloved responded too late (vv. 6-7). When she set out to look for him she was **found** and beaten by the city **watchmen.** In her first dream the watchmen helped her look for her lover (3:3), but this time they mistook her for a criminal. In her dream this action by the watchmen may indicate that she was to blame for her separation from her lover. More importantly the dream symbolized the pain of separation brought about through her selfishness and the dream dramatized her need of the **lover** for her well-being and protection.

**5:8.** The beloved sought the daughters' (see comments on 1:5) help in finding her **lover.** The message they were to give him, **I am faint with love,** meant that she now wanted his embrace (cf. 2:5-6). Though she had been indifferent to him (5:2-3), her attitude changed so that now she was anxious for him.

2. THE ATTRACTIVENESS OF THE LOVER (5:9-16)

**5:9.** The daughters (v. 8) asked the beloved what was so special about her lover that they should help look for him. This question gave her an opportunity to praise her husband, which helped rekindle her former feelings of love.

**5:10-16.** In appearance his skin was **ruddy** and in character he was **outstanding.** The metaphors in verses 11-15 were not meant to be taken as visual comparisons for the most part. They indicate her husband's value and attractiveness. For instance, **his head** was not the color of **gold** (v. 11), but was as valuable as gold. (**His hair** was **wavy and black**; cf. his description of her hair, 4:1.) **His eyes** were not shaped **like doves** (5:12), but were peaceful and gentle like doves, reflecting his peaceful and gentle character (cf. his similar description of her eyes, 1:15; 4:1). Gray or black doves **washed in milk** pictured the dark pupils of his eyes set off by the whites of his eyes. **His cheeks** were delightful and desirable like **spice** or perfume. **His lips** were soft and beautiful **like lilies** to which had been applied flowing **myrrh** (5:13; cf. v. 5) to give an additional fragrance. **His arms** (lit., "his hands") were as attractive and valuable as **gold** (like his head, v. 11, and his legs, v. 15). **His body** (lit., "his abdo-

men") was as handsome as **ivory** and **sapphires** (v. 14). **Polished** or smooth ivory may have also referred to the hard muscular shape of his abdomen. **His legs** were strong, handsome, and valuable like **marble** and **gold** (cf. vv. 11, 14). **His** overall **appearance** was breathtaking; he was tall **like** the imposing **cedars** of **Lebanon** (v. 15; cf. Amos 2:9). **His mouth** (speech and kisses) was highly desirable. He was handsome in every way (Song 5:16).

3. THE LOVER IN HIS GARDEN (6:1-3)

**6:1-3.** The cause of the couple's separation (the indifference of the beloved) was overcome, as evidenced by her praise of her **lover** (5:10-16). Yet they were still separated at this point. So the question of the daughters (5:8) concerning his whereabouts (6:1) addressed the problem of their being apart. Having heard of his handsome appearance, the daughters were now anxious to help find him. **Which way did** he go? they wanted to know.

She answered that he was in **his garden** where **spices** and **lilies** were growing (6:2). This indicated that their separation was more in the emotional realm than in the spatial for she apparently had always known his whereabouts. Her statement of mutual possession (**I am my lover's and my lover is mine,** v. 3) is the inverse of her earlier passionate declaration (2:16a; cf. 7:10). This indicates that the emotional distance had been overcome on her part and she was confident that it had also been overcome on his part. All that was needed for a complete reconciliation was a statement of forgiveness or acceptance from the lover. **He browses** is, literally, "he pastures" his flock (cf. 2:16b).

4. THE RECONCILIATION: THE LOVER'S PRAISE OF HIS BELOVED (6:4-13)

**6:4-10.** In their reconciliation the first words of the lover to his beloved were words of praise. She was as **beautiful . . . as Tirzah,** a lovely city which later became the capital of four kings of the Northern Kingdom: Baasha, Elah, Zimri, and Omri (1 Kings 15:21, 33; 16:8, 15, 23). The beloved was also **lovely** like **Jerusalem,** which was called "the perfection of beauty" (Lam. 2:15). The beloved's beauty was so awesome that it "unnerved" him as if he faced an army **with banners.** Her **eyes** were so stunningly beautiful (cf. Song. 1:15; 4:1) that they overwhelmed him. By repeating part of the praise he had given her on their wedding night (4:1-3) he was indirectly telling her that his love for her had not diminished since that first night. (For the meaning of the metaphors on her **hair. . . . teeth,** and **temples** in 6:5-7, see the comments on 4:1-3). In fact his love and appreciation for her had grown since then. He assured her that she was totally **unique** (6:8-9a) as his **dove** (cf. 5:2), an opinion shared by **her mother** (6:9b) and also **the maidens** (lit., "daughters"), **queens, and concubines** (v. 9c). On seeing the husband and wife reconciled, the women were amazed at her beauty. They **praised her** (v. 9), he said, by stating that she was as fair as **the dawn . . . the moon . . . the sun,** and **the stars.**

**6:11-13.** These verses tell the story of the couple's reconciliation from the beloved's point of view. She knew that he had "gone down to his garden" (v. 2). So she **went** there **to see if** their love was still **in bloom** (v. 11). As a person would look in the spring for **new growth,** buds on grape **vines,** and pomegranate blossoms, so she looked for fresh evidence of their love. When she found him there his first words were words of praise (vv. 4-10), indicating that their love was in fact flourishing.

One of the most difficult verses in the Bible to interpret is verse 12 (see NIV marg.). The Hebrew can be translated in several ways. One translation which has much to commend it is this: "I became enraptured, for you placed me on the **chariots** of the **people** of the prince."

When the husband's first words in the garden were words of praise, she "became enraptured"; she was beside herself with joy. He then placed her on his own chariot at the head of his entourage. As they left, the inhabitants begged her to stay (**come back**—stated four times in v. 13) and the lover noted the intensity of their desire to **gaze on** the **Shulammite.** The Hebrew word rendered "Shulammite" is actually the feminine form of the name Solomon. Thus it means the "Solomoness." "How you gaze. . . ?" (v. 13b) is better than **why would you gaze. . . ?** They gazed at her and her beauty, he said, as if they were viewing a

graceful **dance.** In some way the town of **Mahanaim** is associated here with the dance, though the point of the association is not clear. Mahanaim was east of the Jordan River where David fled from Absalom (2 Sam. 17:24).

### B. Praise of the beloved and her love (7:1-10)

This section portrays the maturing of the couple's marriage. The progress in their love is revealed in two ways. First, the imagery in these verses is much bolder and more intimate than the imagery the lover used on the wedding night (4:1-11). Such an increase in sexual freedom is a normal part of a healthy, maturing marriage. Second, the climactic nature of the refrain in 7:10 also speaks of this maturation.

1. THE BELOVED'S CHARMS (7:1-6)

**7:1.** The beloved's **feet,** he said, were **beautiful** and the shape of her **legs** reminded him of the exquisite **work** of a master artisan.

**7:2.** The comparison of the beloved's **navel** to **a rounded goblet** of **wine** would be grotesque if taken as a visual comparison. The lover meant that her body was as desirable and as intoxicating as wine (cf. 4:10). Likewise the comparison of her **waist** to **a mound of wheat** would be absurd if interpreted visually. Wheat was one of the main food sources in ancient Palestine (Deut. 32:14; 2 Sam. 4:6; 17:28). Thus his wife was both his "food" (wheat) and "drink" (wine) in the sense that her physical expressions of love nourished and satisfied him.

**7:3-4.** On the comparison of her **breasts** to **fawns** see the comments on 4:5. Her **neck** was beautiful and valuable **like an ivory tower** (cf. 4:4). Her **eyes** were beautiful and their effect on him was as refreshing as **the pools of Heshbon,** a Moabite city (Num. 21:25) famous for its fertility and water reservoirs. "The soft glance of her eyes reflects the peace and beauty of the Heshbon pools" (Lehrman, "The Song of Songs," p. 26). Those pools were near the city **gate of Bath Rabbim,** whose location is unknown. Possibly Bath Rabbim was the name of the gate. Her well-shaped **nose** was like **the tower of Lebanon . . . toward Damascus.** This strong tower helped protect Damascus so her lovely features reflected her strong character.

**7:5.** By comparing her **head** to **Mount Carmel,** he meant that she had a queenly bearing that was majestic and awesome. (On the majesty of Mount Carmel see Isa. 35:2; Jer. 46:18.) The beloved's **hair** (cf. Song 4:1; 6:5) was so beautiful that the powerful monarch Solomon was **held captive by its** beauty.

**7:6.** The lover concluded his praise of his beloved's charms with a summary statement of her perfect beauty, calling her **O love.**

### 2. THE LOVER'S DESIRE (7:7-9)

**7:7-9a.** In the remainder of the lover's speech he compared his wife's **stature** with the stately **palm** tree and her **breasts** to its **clusters of** dates. He also spoke of his desire for her **breasts,** comparing them to desirable and tasty **clusters** of grapes. He wanted to enjoy the sweet and intoxicating **fruit** of her love. Even her **breath** was sweet-smelling **like apples** and the kisses of her mouth were sweet **like . . . wine** (cf. 4:10).

**7:9b.** The beloved used the same image of wine (cf. v. 9a) to express her desire to satisfy her husband's wish for her. The rapid interchange of speakers (the beloved is not introduced as the speaker in v. 9b) reflected their excitement in giving and receiving kisses and caresses. The intermingling of their **lips** in kisses was stylistically reflected by the poem's intermingling of their voices.

### 3. THE REFRAIN OF MUTUAL POSSESSION (7:10)

**7:10.** The refrain of mutual possession was already given in 2:16 and 6:3. Here, however, the clause **my lover** "is mine" is replaced with **his desire is for me.** This is a more emphatic way of stating possession. How much more could a husband belong to his wife than for him to desire only her? She had so grown in the security of his love that she could now say that his only desire was for her. She had become so taken by his love for her that here she did not even mention her possession of him.

### C. An invitation from the beloved (7:11-13)

**7:11-13.** In the preceding unit (vv. 1-10) the husband took the initiative in their lovemaking; in this unit (vv. 11-13) she took the initiative. This is the first time in the Song where the beloved made a direct unambiguous request for sex. Previously her desire had been expressed in the third person (e.g., 1:2a; 2:6). Now, having grown more secure in the love of her husband, she felt free to initiate the lovemaking. So she asked him to **go to the countryside** where they could **spend the night** together.

Spring is a universal symbol for love. The beloved used the image of spring to ask whether there was still the same freshness and anticipation that had initially characterized their relationship (cf. 2:10-13). The answer, given by herself, was affirmative. Signs of spring were budding **vines** of grapes, blooming **pomegranates,** and fragrant **mandrakes.** Mandrakes, plants similar in size to apples and red in color, were supposedly aphrodisiacs (cf. Gen. 30:14-16).

### D. The beloved's desire for a greater intimacy (8:1-4)

In these verses the beloved revealed a growing desire for greater intimacy with her husband-lover and rejoiced in the multifaceted nature of their relationship.

**8:1.** In the ancient Near East public displays of affection were frowned on except in the case of certain family members. Thus the beloved wished that her husband **were . . . like a brother** to her so that it would be acceptable to display her affection for him at any time.

**8:2-4.** The beloved playfully assumed the role of an older sister (**I would lead you**—the verb *nāhag* is always used of a superior leading an inferior) and even the role of the mother. The lady of the house **would give** special **wine** to the guests. So the beloved shared the characteristics of a sister, an older sister, and a mother in her relationship to her husband. The Song also portrays the lovers as friends (cf. 5:1, 16). Thus the lovers had a multifaceted relationship.

As his wife, she wished for his caresses. The Hebrew of 8:3 may be translated, "May **his left arm** be **under my head and** may **his right arm** embrace **me**" (cf. 2:6). But again she urged the **daughters of Jerusalem** (cf. comments on 1:5) not to force her expressions of **love** on her husband (cf. 2:7; 3:5).

## V. The Conclusion: The Nature and Power of Love (8:5-7)

This section sums up the message of the Song of Songs with an enigmatic picture of love (v. 5) and a following explanation (vv. 6-7).

### A. A picture of love (8:5)

**8:5.** No answer is given to the question **Who is this coming up from the desert leaning on her lover?** because none is needed. (In 3:6 the question was asked of the *groom*, "Who is this coming up from the desert?") A final picture of the Song's couple is presented here. The wilderness or desert had two symbolic associations in the Old Testament. First, the wilderness was associated with Israel's 40-year period of trial. In their love the couple had overcome trials which threatened their relationship (e.g., the insecurity of the beloved, 1:5-6; the foxes, 2:15; and indifference, 5:2-7). Second, the desert or wilderness was used as an image of God's curse (cf. Jer. 22:6; Joel 2:3). The couple's coming up out of the wilderness suggests that in a certain sense they had overcome the curse of disharmony pronounced on Adam and Eve (Gen. 3:16b; see comments there).

The image of the desert in Song of Songs 8:5a gives way to the image of **the apple tree** in verse 5b, in which the beloved speaks. The apple tree was sometimes used as a symbol of love and romance in the ancient world. The image here recalls the beginning of their love. The beloved **roused** (better, "awakened") her lover to love. The "awakening" is a metaphor for new life or rather a new way of perceiving life, which her love had brought to him. Much as he was the product of his parents' love and was brought into the world by physical **birth,** the lover had now received a second "birth" or "awakening" through the love of his beloved.

### B. An explanation of love (8:6-7)

These verses may be divided into three parts: a request by the beloved (v. 6a), an explanation about the power of love (vv. 6b-7a), and a concluding practical application (v. 7b).

**8:6a.** In Old Testament times **a seal** was used to indicate ownership of a person's valued possessions. So the beloved asked to be her lover's most valued possession, a possession that would influence his thoughts (**over your heart**) and his actions (**over your arm**). Such a demanding request required the explanation which she gave in verses 6b-7a.

**8:6b-7a.** These verses sum up the nature and power of the **love** depicted in the Song. It is as universal and irresistible as **death,** exclusive and possessive (in the sense of being genuinely concerned for the one loved) as **the grave,** passionate (as **blazing fire**) and as invincible and persevering as **many waters** and **rivers.** And all this is true because love is supported by the Creator who possesses all power. The words **like a mighty flame** are, literally, "like the very flame of the LORD" (cf. NIV marg.). Thus the Lord is portrayed as the Source of this powerful love.

**8:7b.** The final statement about the **love** depicted in the Song is that it is priceless. **All** one's **wealth** would be totally inadequate to purchase such love. In fact such money **would be . . . scorned,** because love cannot be bought. Any attempt to "buy" love depersonalizes it.

If love is priceless, how then can it be obtained? The answer is that it must be given. And ultimately love is a gift from God. The epilogue explains how the beloved received this priceless gift of love.

## VI. The Epilogue: How Love Began (8:8-14)

Verses 8-12 are a flashback explaining (a) the protection of the beloved by her older brothers when she was young and (b) her subsequent initial meeting with Solomon. The Song concludes in verses 13-14 with statements that show the couple's love has not lost its intensity.

**8:8-9.** The beloved grew up in a home where her older brothers made definite plans to prepare for her marriage (**the day she is spoken for**). If she displayed good character and judgment and resisted temptation (**if she is a wall**) then they would allow her a large measure of freedom and reward her. **Towers of silver** may be translated "a turret (sing.) of silver," referring to a beautiful, much-valued head ornament, or it may simply refer figuratively to their adorning her as people adorned defense towers with silver. But if she were reckless and prone to immorality (**if she is** open to advances like **a door**) then they planned to restrict her freedom (figuratively spoken of as enclosing **her with** cedar **panels,** like barricading a door with planks).

**8:10.** The beloved's own testimony is that she was chaste (**I am a wall**). Therefore she did not need the restrictions her brothers suggested. Having grown up and matured physically, she was then pure for her husband which enabled her to give him (Solomon) **contentment.** The Hebrew word for contentment (*šālôm*) provides an interesting wordplay because it sounds much like Solomon's name (*šᵉlōmōh*).

**8:11-12.** Apparently they first met in **a vineyard** that **Solomon** had leased **out** to her brothers. (The location of **Baal Hamon** is unknown.) **Each** tenant was to grow enough grapes to make **1,000 shekels** (about 25 pounds) **of silver** for the landowner. And each tenant would receive **200 shekels** (about 5 pounds) **of silver** as his wages. As stated near the beginning of the book (1:6), the beloved worked in the vineyard, submitting to her brothers' discipline. While there she met Solomon and he fell in love with her. **My own vineyard** is a metaphor for the beloved's own person (cf. 1:6). Only she could give herself to another (she said her own vineyard was hers **to give**) and she freely chose to give herself to Solomon. Even her possessions (including her income, **1,000 shekels**) were his.

**8:13-14.** These words of the two lovers recall early passionate requests from their courtship days which show that their love had not lost its intensity. He said to her, **let me hear your voice** (cf. 2:14); and she requested that he (whom she again called **my lover**) **be like a gazelle or like a young stag** (cf. 2:17; also see 2:9). In their courtship she had longed for him to take her as his bride (see comments on 2:17). Now in their marriage she longed with the same intensity for his strength and agility. Like the "hills" in 2:17, the **mountains** in 8:14 may refer to her breasts. Being **spice-laden** means they were perfumed (see comments on some of the spices mentioned in 4:13-14).

The Song of Songs is a beautiful picture of God's "endorsement" of physical love between husband and wife. Marriage is to be a monogamous, permanent, self-giving unit, in which the spouses are intensely devoted and committed to each other, and take delight in each other. "For this reason a man will leave his father and mother and be united to his wife, and they will become one flesh" (Gen. 2:24).

The Song of Songs shows that sex in marriage is not "dirty." The physical attractiveness of a man and woman for each other and the fulfillment of those longings in marriage are natural and honorable. But the book does more than extol physical attraction between the sexes. It also honors pleasing qualities in the lovers' personalities. Also moral purity before marriage is praised (e.g., Song 4:12). Premarital sex has no place in God's plans (2:7; 3:5). Faithfulness before and after marriage is expected and is honored (6:3; 7:10; 8:12). Such faithfulness in marital love beautifully pictures God's love for and commitment to His people.

# BIBLIOGRAPHY

Carr, G. Lloyd. *The Song of Solomon: An Introduction and Commentary.* The Tyndale Old Testament Commentaries. Downers Grove, Ill.: InterVarsity Press, 1984.

Dillow, Joseph C. *Solomon on Sex.* Nashville: Thomas Nelson, 1977.

Ginsburg, Christian D. *The Song of Songs and Coheleth.* New York: KTAV Publishing House, 1970.

Glickman, S. Craig. *A Song for Lovers.* Downers Grove, Ill.: InterVarsity Press, 1976.

Gordis, Robert. *The Song of Songs and Lamentations.* Rev. ed. New York: KTAV Publishing House, 1974.

Harper, Andrew. *The Song of Solomon.* Cambridge: Cambridge University Press, 1907.

Lehrman, S.M. "The Song of Songs." In *The Five Megilloth.* London: Soncino Press, 1946.

Pope, Marvin H. *Song of Songs.* The Anchor Bible. Garden City, N.Y.: Doubleday & Co., 1977.

Rowley, H.H. "The Interpretation of the Song of Solomon." In *The Servant of the Lord and Other Essays on the Old Testament.* London: Lutterworth Press, 1952.

# Prophets to Judah, Israel, Edom, and Assyria

| Prophets to Judah | Prophets to Israel | Prophet to Edom | Prophets to Assyria |
|---|---|---|---|
| **Before the Exile—In Judah** | | | |
| Joel | | Obadiah | Jonah |
| Isaiah | Hosea | | |
| Micah | Amos | | |
| Jeremiah | | | Nahum |
| Habakkuk | | | |
| Zephaniah | | | |
| **During the Exile—In Babylon** | | | |
| Ezekiel | | | |
| Daniel | | | |
| **After the Exile—In Jerusalem** | | | |
| Haggai | | | |
| Zechariah | | | |
| Malachi | | | |

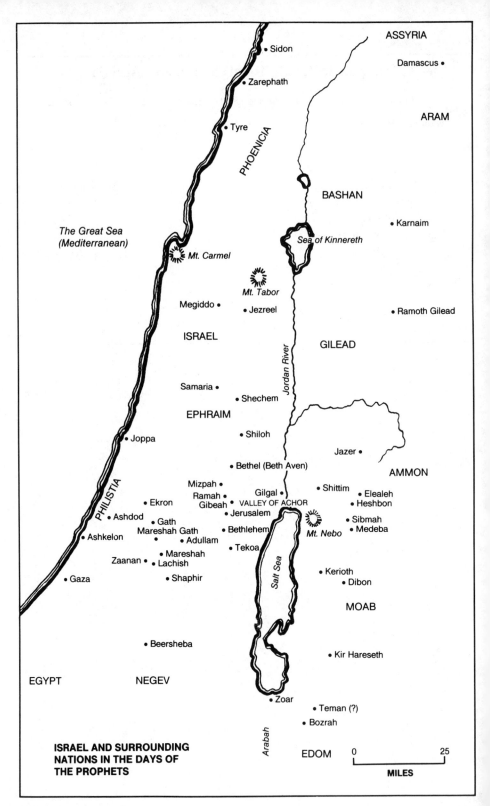

ISRAEL AND SURROUNDING
NATIONS IN THE DAYS OF
THE PROPHETS

# ISAIAH

## John A. Martin

## INTRODUCTION

The Book of Isaiah is one of the most-loved books of the Bible; it is perhaps the best known of the prophetic books. It contains several passages that are well known among Bible students (e.g., 1:18; 7:14; 9:6-7; 26:8; 40:3, 31; 53). It has great literary merit and contains beautiful descriptive terminology.

Isaiah also contains much factual material about the society of Israel around 700 B.C. Besides pointing out the shortcomings of the people the prophet noted that God always has a remnant of believers through whom He works.

Isaiah spoke more than any other prophet of the great kingdom into which Israel would enter at the Second Advent of the Messiah. Isaiah discussed the depths of Israel's sin and the heights of God's glory and His coming kingdom.

**Author and Date.** The author of this book was Isaiah the son of Amoz (Isa. 1:1). The name "Isaiah" means "Yahweh is salvation." Though more is known about Isaiah than most of the other writing prophets, the information on him is still scanty. Probably Isaiah resided in Jerusalem and had access to the royal court. According to tradition he was a cousin of King Uzziah but no firm evidence exists to support this. He did have personal contact with at least two of Judah's kings who were David's descendants (7:3; 38:1; 39:3).

Isaiah was married (8:3). He had two sons, Shear-Jashub (7:3) and Maher-Shalal-Hash-Baz (8:3). Some have supposed from Isaiah's commissioning (chap. 6) that he was a priest, but no evidence in the book supports this.

The year of Isaiah's death is unknown but it was probably after Hezekiah's death in 686 B.C. (and therefore probably in Manasseh's sole reign, 686–642) because Isaiah wrote a biography of King Hezekiah (2 Chron. 32:32). Isaiah's death would have occurred after Sennacherib's death (Isa. 37:38), which was in 681 B.C. Since the prophet's ministry began sometime in Uzziah's reign (790–739 B.C.) Isaiah ministered for at least 58 years (from at least 739, when Uzziah died [6:1], to 681, when Sennacherib died).

According to tradition dating from the second century A.D., Isaiah was martyred by King Manasseh. Justin Martyr (ca. A.D. 100–165) wrote that Isaiah was sawed asunder with a saw (cf. Heb. 11:37).

As is true of all other prophetic books in the Old Testament (except Lam.), the Book of Isaiah bears the name of its author (Isa. 1:1). Many modern scholars divide the book into two or more parts and say that each part had a different author. However, according to strong Jewish and Christian tradition the book had only one author. No doubt was cast on the Isaian authorship until the 18th century when critics began to attack a number of Old Testament books and to question their authorship and internal unity. (See the next section on "Unity.")

Isaiah prophesied in the reigns of Uzziah, Jotham, Ahaz, and Hezekiah, all kings of Judah (1:1). The reigns of these kings (including coregencies) were: Uzziah (790–739), Jotham (750–732), Ahaz (735–715), and Hezekiah (715–686). (See the chart "Kings of Judah and Israel and the Preexilic Prophets," near 1 Kings 12:25-33.)

These years in Israel's history were a time of great struggle both politically and spiritually. The Northern Kingdom of Israel was deteriorating politically, spiritually, and militarily and finally fell to the Assyrian Empire in 722 B.C. The Southern Kingdom of Judah looked as though it too would collapse and fall to Assyria, but it withstood the attack. In this political struggle and spiritual decline Isaiah rose to deliver a message to the people in Judah. His message was that they should trust in the God who had promised them a glorious kingdom through Moses and David. Isaiah urged the nation not to rely on Egypt or any other foreign power to protect them for the Lord was the only protection they would need.

Hosea and Micah were Isaiah's contemporaries. Many have noted several parallels between the messages and vocabularies of Isaiah and Micah (see the *Introduction* to the Book of Micah).

The Book of Isaiah is the first of the 17 Old Testament prophetic books not because it is the oldest but because it is the most comprehensive in content.

**Unity.** Many scholars question the unity of the book, holding that it was originally two books (with chaps. 40–66 written by "Deutero-Isaiah," who supposedly lived during or after the Babylonian Captivity) or even three (chaps. 1–39; 40–55; 56–66 with the last division written by "Trito-Isaiah"). Many conservative scholars have answered liberal scholars' arguments against the unity of the book. The evidence for its unity is both external (evidence outside the Bible and in other books of the Bible) and internal (evidence within the book itself).

*1. External evidence.* As already stated, Jewish tradition has uniformly ascribed the entire book to Isaiah. The Dead Sea Scrolls include a complete copy of the Book of Isaiah, thus pointing to its acceptance as one book by the Qumran community in the second century B.C. The Septuagint, the Greek translation of the Hebrew Old Testament in the second century B.C., gives no indication that the Book of Isaiah was anything other than a single book.

Christian tradition has uniformly assumed that Isaiah was a single work until the 18th century when liberals began to challenge that position.

The New Testament writers assumed that Isaiah was the author of the entire book. In the New Testament all the major sections of Isaiah are quoted under the title Isaiah. For example, John 12:38 ascribes Isaiah 53:1 to Isaiah, and John 12:39-40 ascribes Isaiah 6:10 to Isaiah. Several portions of Isaiah 40–66, which are quoted in the New Testament, are ascribed to Isaiah (Isa. 40:3 in Matt. 3:3; Mark 1:2-3; John 1:23; Isa. 40:3-5 in Luke 3:4-6; Isa. 42:1-4 in Matt. 12:17-21; Isa. 53:1 in Rom. 10:16; Isa. 53:4 in Matt. 8:17; Isa. 53:7-8 in Acts 8:32-33; Isa. 65:1 in Rom. 10:20). Interestingly Isaiah is mentioned by name 22 times in the New Testament, more than any other Old Testament prophet.

Jesus Christ assumed that Isaiah was the author of the whole book. Jesus was given the "scroll of the Prophet Isaiah" (Luke 4:17-19) which He unrolled and from which he read Isaiah 61:1-2.

*2. Internal evidence.* Some of the same terms occur throughout the whole book. For example, "the Holy One of Israel" a title for God, occurs 12 times in chapters 1–39 and 14 times in chapters 40–66. This title is used only 6 times elsewhere in the entire Old Testament (2 Kings 19:22; Pss. 71:22; 78:41; 89:18; Jer. 50:29; 51:5).

The "highway" motif occurs in several parts of the book (Isa. 11:16; 19:23; 35:8; 40:3; 62:10). The "remnant" theme occurs in 10:20-22; 11:11, 16; 28:5; 37:4, 31; 37:32 and also in 46:3 (KJV).

The establishment of justice is a theme in the first division of the book (9:7; 11:4; 16:5; 28:6; 32:16; 33:5) and in the second division (42:1, 3-4; 51:5). And "peace" is mentioned 11 times in chapters 1–39 and 15 times in chapters 40–66. "Joy" occurs 13 times in chapters 1–39 and 19 times in chapters 40–66. Also the Hebrew word *na'ăṣûṣ* ("thornbush") occurs in the Old Testament only in Isaiah 7:19 and 55:13 ("thornbushes" in 33:12 translates a different Heb. word).

Similar passages occur in both parts of the book:

| 1:15 | 59:3, 7 |
|------|---------|
| 1:29 | 57:4-5 |
| 2:3 | 51:4 |
| 10:1-2 | 59:4-9 |
| 28:5 | 62:3 |
| 29:18 | 42:7 |
| 29:23 | 60:21 |
| 30:26 | 60:19 |
| 33:24 | 45:25 |
| 35:6 | 41:18 |

The theological unity of the book argues for a single author. This theological factor is strong evidence for persons who believe that the Bible is the Word of God. Chapters 40–55 emphasize the fact that

God would deliver His people from captivity in Babylon. Through Isaiah God predicted that Cyrus would appear on the scene (44:28–45:1) and deliver Judah from captivity. In chapters 40–55 (esp. 43:5-6, 16, 19) the theological point is made that God was telling His people about the return from the Exile beforehand so that they would believe in Him when that event came to pass. In this way He differed greatly from the surrounding nations' gods. As the sovereign God He can foretell events; this ability proves His uniqueness in contrast with false gods.

However, liberal scholars, denying the predictive element in Old Testament prophecy, say that the references to Cyrus mean that chapters 40–55 must have been written after Cyrus ruled Persia (559–530 B.C.). But if those chapters were written *after* the time of Cyrus this means that the God of Israel did not foretell that event and is no different from the gods of the surrounding nations. Therefore to say that chapters 40–55 were written after Cyrus' time strips those chapters of theological validity and makes them almost meaningless.

**Purpose.** Isaiah's primary purpose was to remind his readers of the special relationship they had with God as members of the nation of Israel, His special covenant community.

Like the other writing prophets, Isaiah knew of the Abrahamic Covenant (Gen. 12:2-3; 15:18-21; 17:3-8, 19) in which God promised that Israel would (a) enjoy a special relationship with Him, (b) possess the land of Canaan, and (c) be a blessing to others.

Isaiah was also aware of the Mosaic Covenant, given Israel at the time of the Exodus from Egypt and repeated by Moses to the generation of Israelites who were about to enter Palestine. Throughout the Book of Deuteronomy God through Moses had promised the people that as members of the covenant community they would be blessed by Him if they lived according to the Mosaic Covenant (e.g., Deut. 28:1-14). But He also warned them that if they did not obey His commands and decrees they would experience the curses (punishments) spelled out in the covenant (Deut. 28:15-68) including exile from the land (see the chart "The Covenant Chastenings," near Amos 4:6).

However, because of the Abrahamic Covenant in which God promised blessing on Israel and the world, Moses could confidently affirm that even after the people had been exiled from the land the Lord would someday bring them back to the land of promise and establish them in His kingdom.

So Isaiah was calling the people of Judah back to a proper covenantal relationship with God. He was reminding his generation of the sinful condition in which they were living and of its consequences. God would judge the nation, but He would also eventually restore them to the land (cf. Deut. 30:1-5) with full kingdom blessings because of His promises to Abraham.

Isaiah was aware (from Deut. 28:49-50, 64-67) that Judah was destined for exile as had recently befallen the Northern Kingdom. His book, then, was directed to two groups of people: (a) those of his generation, who had strayed from the covenantal obligations given them in the Mosaic Law, and (b) those of a future generation who would be in exile. Isaiah was calling the first group back to holiness and obedience, and he was comforting the second group with the assurance that God would restore the nation to their land and would establish His kingdom of peace and prosperity. The theme of "comfort" is dominant in Isaiah 40–66 ("comfort" occurs in 40:1 [twice]; 51:3, 19; 57:18; 61:2; 66:13; "comforted" occurs in 52:9; 54:11; 66:13; and "comforts" is used in 49:13; 51:12; 66:13)—13 times compared with only 1 occurrence of "comforted" (12:1) in chapters 1–39.

**Themes and Theology.** Some difficulty exists in determining a central theme for Isaiah around which all the other material in the book revolves. Some have suggested that the book has two themes, one for chapters 1–39 and another for chapters 40–66. Judgment seems to be the emphasis in the first part, and salvation and comfort are prominent in the second. Since Isaiah followed the theology of Deuteronomy (punishment must come for failure to live according to the Mosaic Covenant before a time of blessing can come), the two parts of Isaiah can be reconciled. Chapters 1–39 point out the nation's problem of sin which must be rectified before a proper relationship with the covenant God can be restored. Judgment, emphasized in chapters 1–39, is the purifying force that leads to the forgiveness and pardoning of sins emphasized in chapters 40–66 (cf. 27:9). Ultimately redemption for Israel must come from the "ideal Servant," the Messiah, who will accomplish what the servant-nation cannot do. This accounts for the so-called "Servant Songs" in the second major division of Isaiah (42:1-9; 49:1-13; 50:4-11; 52:13–53:12).

But chapters 40–66 emphasize more than redemption from sin. Those chapters go beyond that to speak of a change in the cosmos, of the Lord's restoration of His created order. In chapters 1–39 judgment on sin is stressed; in chapters 40–66 atonement for that sin *and* the resulting change in people and the world system are discussed. Judgment, then, must come before blessing can follow.

Isaiah had a lofty view of God. The Lord is seen as the Initiator of events in history. He is apart from and greater than His Creation; yet He is involved in the affairs of that Creation.

In the ancient Near East names were more meaningful than they are today. A person's name was an indication of his or her character. The Book of Isaiah is no exception, for in this book the meanings of God's names play an important role in several prophetic utterances. Isaiah used the name "the LORD" (*Yahweh*) by itself more than 300 times, making it by far the most prominent name for Deity Isaiah used. Since this name is the covenant name for God, it is natural that Isaiah used it often. He also frequently used the name "God" (*'ĕlōhîm*) in both parts of the book. It is noteworthy that "God" occurs six times in chapter 40 (vv. 1, 3, 8-9, 27-28; "God" in v. 18, however, translates the shorter form *'ēl*), which introduces the section on comfort for the covenant people. As the one supreme Deity, God can give comfort to His people. (See earlier comments on the theme of "comfort" in Isa.) *'Ēl* seems to be used as a polemic against the other gods, for a number of its occurrences appear in the section in which the Lord was speaking of His sovereignty over false gods (chaps. 40–48). Four times God affirmed, "I am God (*'ēl*)—43:12; 45:22; 46:9 (twice). "Lord"

(*'ăḏōnāy* or the shortened form *'āḏôn*) suggests God's dominance over His Creation and is used numerous times in Isaiah, many of them in chapters 1–39. "The LORD Almighty" (*Yahweh ṣ²ḇā'ôṯ*; KJV, "the LORD of hosts"), the most common compound name for God in the Book of Isaiah, appears 46 times in chapters 1–39 and 6 times in the remainder of the book. This compound title links the covenant name of God (*Yahweh*) with His sovereignty over all heavenly powers.

God is also called "the Lord, the LORD Almighty" (*'ăḏōnāy Yahweh ṣ²ḇā'ôṯ*) 10 times. He is referred to as "the God of Israel" 12 times, and "the Holy One of Israel" 25 times. "Redeemer" is used of God 13 times, all in chapters 41–63, which stress God's redeeming work for Israel, and only one other time in the rest of the Old Testament. Certainly Isaiah centered his theology and his book on God and the work that He was doing and would continue to do in the world.

# OUTLINE

# COMMENTARY

## I. The Retribution of God (chaps. 1–39)

In this first major division of the book, Isaiah wrote much about the judgment that was to come on Judah because of her failure to follow the Mosaic Covenant. God's punishment would prove to the nation that He fulfills His Word. This section also speaks of judgment which is to come on the whole world (chaps. 13–23). All nations of the earth stand guilty before the Holy One of Israel.

In this section on judgment Isaiah also emphasized blessing which will come to the nation because of her covenantal relationship with the Lord. For example, in the Lord's indictment of Judah (chaps. 1–6) 1:24-31 refers to the nation's restoration, 4:2-6 speaks of a remnant of survivors, and 6:13 refers to a "holy seed" or a remnant. In the prophecies on deliverance (chaps. 7–12) Judah, Isaiah wrote, would be delivered from the Aram-Israel alliance (7:3-9; 8:1-15; 9:7–10:4). But also God's glorious empire, the millennial kingdom (Rev. 20:1-6) will rise (Isa. 11) and the regathered people will sing a song of salvation (chap. 12).

In chapters 13–23, on God's judgment on the nations, the prophet wrote that Israel will be restored to the land and will rule over the peoples who have oppressed her (14:1-2). Moab will go to Israel for protection and the establishment of justice and order (16:1-5). The worship of the true God will signal peace on earth (19:19-25).

In the section on punishment and kingdom blessing (chaps. 24–27) much is said about restoration. God will preserve His people (chap. 25) and will be praised by the restored ones (chap. 26). Evil will be judged (27:1) and the remnant restored (27:2-6). Judgment will have a refining effect (27:7-13).

In the section on the woes (chaps. 28–33) a word of comfort is included at the end of each of three portions of these chapters. Judgment will purge the people (28:23-29), a remnant will glorify the Lord (29:17-24), and the Lord will bless and protect His people (30:23-26; 31:4-9). The King will reign in justice and righteousness (chaps. 32–33).

Even in the vengeance section (chaps. 34–35) Isaiah mentioned that a remnant will be gathered together (34:16-17) and the land will be freed from the curse and the remnant will live in joy (chap. 35).

In beautiful and varied language Isaiah made the point that sin must be rooted out of the nation and the world. Eventually, in the Millennium, righteousness will be enforced and the nation will dwell in prosperity and peace because of her renewed relationship with the Lord.

## A. The Lord's indictment of the nation (chaps. 1–6)

### 1. THE HEADING FOR THE BOOK (1:1)

**1:1.** Isaiah's prophecies focus on **Judah and Jerusalem.** His book is called a **vision,** which suggests that the prophet "saw" (cf. 2:1) mentally and spiritually as well as heard what God communicated to him. This word "vision" also introduces the books of Obadiah, Micah, and Nahum.

**Isaiah** was familiar with the city of Jerusalem and its temple and royal court. By this time the Northern Kingdom (Israel) was in its final years. The Northern Kingdom fell in 722 B.C. to the Assyrians who were seeking to conquer the entire Syro-Palestine area. Isaiah wrote specifically for the Southern Kingdom (Judah),

which would fall to Babylon a little more than 100 years later in 586 B.C.

For comments on Isaiah **son of Amoz** and the time of Isaiah's ministry (in **the reigns of Uzziah, Jotham, Ahaz, and Hezekiah**) see "Author and Date" in the *Introduction.*

### 2. THE LORD'S LAWSUIT AGAINST THE NATION (1:2-31)

These verses are in the form of a covenant lawsuit against Judah. In effect, it is a microcosm of chapters 1–39. The Lord, through His messenger Isaiah, indicted His covenant nation for her breach of the Mosaic Covenant, and offered His complete forgiveness to those who would repent but judgment to those who continued to rebel. In 6:9-13 God pointed out to Isaiah that most of the nation, however, would not repent.

#### a. The Lord's accusation that His people broke the covenant (1:2-9)

**1:2a.** Isaiah, speaking for the Lord, invoked the **heavens** and the **earth** to **hear** the following accusation against the people. Calling on the heavens and the earth was a way of informing the nation that all creation would agree with what God was about to say.

**1:2b-3.** In this type of lawsuit the accuser first established his own innocence in the matter. **The LORD,** like a parent, did this by noting that the people of Judah, His **children** (cf. v. 4), had **rebelled** (cf. "rebels" in v. 28) **against** Him, who was innocent in the matter. The Hebrew word rendered "rebelled" (*pāša‘*) was used in treaties to speak of a vassal state's disobedience to the covenant made with it by the suzerain nation. *Pāša‘* also occurs in 66:24, the final verse in the book.

Even animals know their masters, but the nation Israel did **not know** and did **not understand** God, her **Master.** (Israel, though often referring to the Northern Kingdom, is sometimes, as here, used of the nation of 12 tribes as a whole, and thus includes Judah.) An **ox** is unusually submissive; in Bible times a **donkey** was known for its stupidity. Therefore to say Israel was less knowledgeable than these domestic animals was an amazingly strong affirmation of her stupidity. These animals were more aware of their owners and the source of sustenance (**manger** was a feeding trough for animals) from their owners than were God's people. Israel did not know God or realize that He was her Provider. By being rebellious (1:2b) the nation failed to carry out God's commands, which proved they did not really "understand" God.

**1:4.** In His lawsuit God elaborated on the **sinful** condition of the **nation.** This idea that the nation was sinful (*ḥāṭā'*) occurs a number of times in the book (e.g., cf. "sinned" in 42:24; 43:27 and "continued to sin" in 64:5).

Isaiah spoke of the "sins" (*ḥāṭā'îm*) of the people (1:18) and noted that the Suffering Servant came to remove "the sin (*ḥēṭ'*) of many" in the nation (53:12). Because of their sin, the **people** stood guilty before God (cf. Rom. 3:9, 19, KJV). Because they were evildoers, they were corrupt (cf. Rom. 3:10-18 and the word "corrupt" in Gen. 6:12). Their deliberately defiant attitude against God is indicated by the words **forsaken . . . spurned,** and **turned their backs.**

As stated in the *Introduction*, the words **the Holy One of Israel** are used by Isaiah 25 times. This title appropriately contrasts the people's sin with God's holiness.

Though the people had turned their backs on God, in the future He will turn His back on Israel's sin by forgiving her. After Hezekiah was raised from his sickbed, he praised the Lord for placing his sins behind God's back (Isa. 38:17).

**1:5-7.** When the covenant people turned their backs on God (v. 4) certain consequences followed (cf. Deut. 28:15-68). Isaiah recounted what was happening to them to help them understand that their difficult times had come because of their disobedience. Isaiah first used the figure of a person who had been **beaten** and was bruised over his entire body (Isa. 1:5-6). Though these untreated **wounds . . . welts, and open sores** characterized the nation's spiritual condition, Isaiah was also speaking of her condition militarily. They were beset on all sides by hostile forces and were losing some of their territory to foreign nations (v. 7). They should have realized that these terrible problems had come because of their spiritual condition. Whether Isaiah was describing the soon-coming situation in the Northern Kingdom to be brought

about by the Assyrian invasion (in 722 B.C.) or whether he was speaking prophetically of the coming destruction of Judah (586 B.C.) is open to conjecture though it more likely refers to Judah. His words **desolate . . . burned,** and **stripped** were written as if the devastation had already happened. Thus he emphasized its certainty.

**1:8-9.** Isaiah then pictured Jerusalem's inhabitants (**the Daughter of Zion;** cf. Jer. 4:31; Lam. 1:6; 2:13; Micah 1:13; 4:8; Zech. 9:9; and see comments on Lam. 2:1; Zech. 8:3) as being **like a shelter in a vineyard** or **a hut in a** melon **field.** Those were temporary structures built to shade from the sun persons who guarded the crops against thieves and animals. Such huts were usually "alone" and easily attacked. Judah **would have been like Sodom** and **Gomorrah,** totally devastated, if it had not been for God's grace in leaving **some survivors.** (Centuries later Paul quoted this verse in Rom. 9:29.) In fact Judah *was* like those two wicked cities in her sin. (Cf. the mention of both cities in Isa. 1:10, and of Sodom in 3:9; Ezek. 16:46, 48-49; 55:56.) Isaiah's reference to those two cities no doubt reminded some Judahites of the Lord's reference to them in Deuteronomy 29:23.

*b. The Lord's instructions on how the nation should deal with her guilt (1:10-20)*

**1:10.** Building on his reference to **Sodom** and **Gomorrah** in verse 9, Isaiah likened the **rulers** and **people** of Judah to those evil cities. Both the leaders and the populace—those in all levels of society—were to **hear** (cf. v. 2) God's **word.**

**1:11-15.** The Lord rejected the people's appeal to several aspects of religious ritual—including animal **sacrifices** (v. 11), **incense** (v. 13a), festivals and feasts (vv. 12, 13b-14), and prayers (v. 15)—as compensation for their iniquity.

Some people have mistakenly said (from v. 11) that God had not established the sacrificial system. But this is wrong. Isaiah's point is that the people assumed that merely by offering sacrifices at the altar they would be made ceremonially clean before God. Even multiple sacrifices are **meaningless** (v. 13) and therefore do not please God when the "worshiper" does not bring his life into conformity with God's standards. Also the careful observance of monthly **offerings**

(**New Moons**; cf. Num. 28:11-14) and **Sabbaths** (weekly as well as annual Sabbaths on the Day of Atonement and the Feast of Tabernacles, Lev. 16:31; 23:34, 39) were **meaningless** to God when they were not done with the proper attitude. The same was true of their **assemblies** on the Sabbath (Lev. 23:3), and the **festivals** and **feasts** including the Passover (Lev. 23:4-7), the Feast of Weeks (Lev. 23:15-21), the Feast of Trumpets (Lev. 23:24), the Day of Atonement (Lev. 23:26-27), and the Feast of Tabernacles (Lev. 23:34).

Such observances God called **evil** because they were carried out hypocritically, with sinful hearts (cf. Isa. 1:4). Therefore those national gatherings, rather than pleasing God, were an obnoxious **burden to** Him (v. 14).

In addition, the people's **many prayers** were ineffective because of their guilt (v. 15). The words **spread out your hands** denoted asking for help (cf. 1 Kings 8:22; Lam. 1:17). Those hands, however, were **full of blood** (Isa. 1:15). By treating the needy unfairly (cf. vv. 16-17), the people were like a murderer spreading out his bloodstained hands to God in prayer. This spiritual condition made Judah's religious ritual ludicrous. Obviously God would never **listen** to (i.e., answer) such prayers! (cf. Ps. 66:18) Inward righteousness must accompany outward ritual for that ritual to mean anything to God.

**1:16-20.** The Lord offered complete forgiveness to the repentant, but promised judgment on the rebels who continued to reject Him. The people had the mistaken idea that they could live any way they pleased so long as they made restitution in the sacrificial system. But instead of trusting in religious ritual (vv. 10-15) the people were to obey God and have the right attitudes toward Him and the right actions toward others.

The people needed to be **clean** inwardly (like a murderer washing his bloodstained hands). And they needed to replace their **evil** (cf. v. 13) deeds with right actions. As stipulated in the Mosaic Covenant they needed to evidence their trust in and obedience to the Lord by helping needy people—**the oppressed . . . the fatherless,** and **the widow** (cf. v. 23; 10:1-2; Deut. 24:17, 19-21; 26:12; 27:19).

God then invited the sinful people to come to their senses (Isa. 1:18) and admit they had been wrong in their attitudes and practices. The invitation **Come now, let us reason together** was more than a call for negotiations between the people and God. The word "reason" (*yākaḥ*) is a law term used of arguing, convincing, or deciding a case in court. The people were to be convinced by their argumentation with God that He was right and they were wrong about their condition. (Other court terms in this chapter are **justice . . . defend,** and **plead,** v. 17.) If they acknowledged the depth of their sins—that their iniquities were like blood-colored stains on their souls (**scarlet,** a red dye made from a worm, and **crimson,** red-colored cloth)—then God in His grace would cleanse them, making them spiritually **white** like **snow** or **wool.** Acknowledgment of sin was to precede God's cleansing. And the same is true today.

The **obedient** (v. 19) would **eat the best from the land,** that is, they would have bountiful crops as promised in the Mosaic Covenant (Deut. 28:3-6, 11). By contrast, those who refused to turn to God (rebels; cf. Isa. 1:23, 28) would be defeated by enemies (**devoured by the sword,** v. 20; Deut. 28:45-57). This was certain **for the . . .** Lord **has spoken** (cf. Isa. 40:5; 58:14).

### c. The Lord's lament over Jerusalem (1:21-23)

**1:21.** The contrast between the original condition of Jerusalem under David and the early years of Solomon's reign with the condition of the people in Isaiah's day is detailed. At one time Jerusalem was considered **faithful** like a devoted wife. Now, however, the **city** was **a harlot.** The imagery of prostitution is common in the prophetic books (esp. Jer. and Hosea). This figure is based on the fact that in marriage, as in the relationship between God and Israel, a covenant was made. When a person becomes a prostitute he or she mars the marriage covenant. In the same way when a person left the true God for idols he marred his covenant with the Lord.

Jerusalem had been known for executive **justice** and upholding **righteousness.** "Justice" refers to proper judicial procedures, and "righteousness" is the behavior of those who sought this standard. (Cf. these two in Prov. 8:20; Isa.

5:7; 28:17; Amos 5:7.) **But now** instead of righteousness "living," **murderers** were present. "Murderers" may refer to those who took advantage of the needy (cf. Isa. 1:23 and comments on v. 15).

**1:22-23.** Their **silver** and **wine,** which used to be valuable, had become worthless: **dross** metal and watered-down wine. Dross is the residue left in the smelting process after pure silver is removed. Like worthless dross, the nation would be "thrown away." The people would be exiled if they would not repent and turn to the Lord.

The rebellious **rulers** in the city were leading the people into ruin by theft, bribery, and injustice to the helpless (cf. comments on v. 17). **The fatherless** and **widows** could not even get hearings because they had no money for bribing the rulers. This situation was especially abhorrent to God because His covenant people were bound to Him and therefore to each other. But now they had no concern for each other's property and needs.

### d. The Lord's declaration of the sentence (1:24-31)

God's lawsuit ended with His pronouncing judgment on the guilty nation. In this chapter God is pictured not only as one of the parties in the litigation but also as the Judge who will decide what will happen to the guilty party. Those who were obstinate, refusing to repent, would be judged, but the repentant would be redeemed.

**1:24-26.** God's judging will bring Him **relief from** the displeasure caused by His **foes** (**enemies** within the covenant community). It will be like a purging agent, getting rid of the **dross** (v. 25; cf. v. 22), leaving only the pure silver. Vengeance was not for the purpose of "getting even" with unfaithful people. Its purpose was to turn the nation back to a proper relationship to God. The LORD **will** see that the right kind of **judges** are in office **as in** former times (David's and Solomon's empires), and Jerusalem **will** once again **be called the City of Righteousness** and **the Faithful City** (v. 26). References to "the faithful city" (vv. 21, 26) serve as a literary device called an *inclusio* to tie these two verses together.

**1:27-31.** The contrast between the fate of the remnant and the wicked is detailed in these verses. The remnant will dwell in the new **redeemed** city of Jerusalem (**Zion**; cf. v. 8) where God's **justice** will be present (cf. v. 26). **Rebels** (cf. vv. 20, 23) **will perish,** after being embarrassed that they were ever involved in idol worship near **sacred** oak trees (cf. 57:5) and in **gardens** (cf. 65:3; 66:17). Whereas they once enjoyed worshiping idols (probably including Baal), in those pleasant surroundings they would become like fading **oak** trees and a dry **garden.** Though once strong (like a **mighty man**) in defying God the unrighteous **and his work . . . will burn.** This unquenchable burning probably refers to the destruction by the Babylonian army *as well as* eternal judgment.

### 3. AN AFFIRMATION OF RESTORATION (2:1-5)

Immediately after the stinging indictment (in the form of a lawsuit) of the nation's sinful practices (1:2-31) Isaiah introduced a concept which was to be a hallmark of his prophecy. A time will come when Jerusalem will have the primary position in the world. Micah 4:1-3 is almost identical to Isaiah 2:1-4.

**2:1-2a.** The message recorded in these verses **is what Isaiah . . . saw concerning Judah and Jerusalem** (cf. 1:1). The prophets in Israel had at one time been called "seers" because of their divinely given power to "see" or foretell what would happen (1 Sam. 9:9). Here Isaiah was foretelling the future of Jerusalem and Judah. In the prophecies of restoration which are prominent in Isaiah's book, he was not specific as to the exact time when they would be fulfilled (perhaps he did not know; cf. 1 Peter 1:10-11). Here he simply said **in the last days.** Other Bible passages make it clear that these predictions will be fulfilled in the Millennium, Christ's 1,000-year reign on the earth. Because of God's covenant promises to Abraham, Moses, and David, Isaiah knew that Israel will again be in the land and will again have a superior position among the nations.

**The mountain of the LORD's temple** refers to the mount where the temple was built (and where the millennial temple will be built, Ezek. 40–43). Often in the Scriptures **mountains** denote governmental authorities (Dan. 2:35; Amos 4:1). Here God's rule from the temple will be preeminent (**chief**). The theme of the prominence of the temple mount in Jerusalem is repeated often in Isaiah's prophecies all the way to the end of the book (Isa. 11:9; 25:6-7; 27:13; 30:29; 56:7; 57:13; 65:11, 25; 66:20). Isaiah clearly wanted his readers to be aware that God will protect His covenant nation despite their spiritual insensitivity and even though they would go into captivity.

**2:2b-3.** When these events take place many **nations will** be attracted to Jerusalem (cf. 14:1; 27:13; 66:23; Zech. 8:23; 14:16) and to God's **house** (the temple, Isa. 2:2a). The attraction will be the Lord's **ways . . . paths . . . Law,** and **Word** which will be made known from that place. In fact **the LORD** Himself will give forth the Law (51:4). (**Zion,** referred to dozens of times by Isaiah, more than by any other author of Scripture, is here a synonym of **Jerusalem**; cf. 4:3; 40:9, 52:1; 62:1. See comments on Zech. 8:3.) In the Millennium, people everywhere will realize that God's revelation is foundational to their lives. They will want to know it (**He will teach us**) and to live according to it (**walk in it**).

**2:4.** This is one of the more familiar verses in the Book of Isaiah. God will have a worldwide ministry of judging and settling disputes. **He will** require **nations** and **peoples** everywhere to abstain from warfare. Universal peace, with no military conflict or training, will prevail because the implements of warfare (**swords** and **spears**) will be turned into implements of agriculture (**plowshares** and **hooks**; cf. Joel 3:10). At this time of worldwide peace the nations will go to Jerusalem to learn from God (Isa. 2:2). Peace will come not by human achievement but because of God's presence and work in Jerusalem. At that time Israel will be filled with God's Spirit (Ezek. 36:24-30) and her sins will be forgiven (Jer. 31:31-34).

**2:5.** Isaiah closed this short section with an exhortation for his readers to **walk** (live) **in the light of the LORD.** The prophet called Israel the **house of Jacob,** a reference to Jacob's descendants. Isaiah used this term eight times (vv. 5-6; 8:17; 10:20; 14:1; 29:22; 46:3; 48:1) whereas it is used only nine times by all the other prophets. When great truths about the future are given in the Scriptures, readers are often reminded of how they should live in the present (e.g., 1 Thes. 4:13-18; 5:1-8; 2 Peter 3:10-14;

1 John 3:2-3). In view of the fact that in the Millennium all nations will stream to Jerusalem to learn God's Word, it would be sensible for Israel, already knowing that Law, to follow it (walking in its "light") until the Lord sets up His glorious kingdom.

**4. THE PRESENT CONDITION AND FUTURE CONSEQUENCES (2:6–4:1)**

Judah's present condition (2:6-11) and its consequences (2:12–4:1) contrast with the glorious kingdom Isaiah had just described (2:1-5). As was true throughout much of Israel's history, the people were not obeying the Lord and therefore had to be disciplined by Him.

*a. Judah's likeness to pagan peoples (2:6-11)*

**2:6-9.** God had **abandoned** His **people** (on **the house of Jacob** see comments on v. 5) not because He no longer loved them but because they had become like the **pagans** around them. The people of Judah were as superstitious as the people in **the East,** that is, they were following the practices of the Assyrian Empire, which at that time was encroaching on the entire Syro-Palestinian area. (Or perhaps the people of "the East" were Arameans; cf. 9:12.) At the same time Judahites were engaging in **divination like the Philistines.** The Philistines occupied the southwestern part of Canaan and had sought to control Israel. So Israel was influenced by pagan practices from several sources. That Philistines were involved in divination is evident from 1 Samuel 6:2; 2 Kings 1:2. Divination (from '*ānan*, "to practice sorcery"; cf. Lev. 19:26; Deut. 18:10, 14; 2 Kings 21:6; Micah 5:12, "cast spells") was the attempt to control people or circumstances or to seek to know the future through power given by evil spirits (demons).

Isaiah's irony here is strong, for Judah should have known what her future would be because of the Word of God; yet she was trying to discern the future by pagan means. No wonder Isaiah asked God **not** to **forgive** her (Isa. 2:9). Judah had great material wealth (**silver and gold**) and military strength (**horses** and **chariots,** v. 7) which they no doubt mistakenly thought came to them because of their worshiping **idols.** This probably led to pride and self-confidence because God said they would **be brought**

**low** and **humbled** (v. 9; cf. vv. 11-12, 17). Their sinful condition made judgment a necessity.

**2:10-11.** Ultimately only one Person will be **exalted.** That One will be **the LORD alone** (v. 11; cf. v. 17). When the Lord comes to judge, people will seek to escape His judgment by hiding in caves (cf. vv. 19, 21; Rev. 6:16). They will fear His **splendor** (cf. Isa. 2:19, 21), realizing that their arrogance (v. 11; cf. v. 17) and wealth (vv. 7-8) cannot save them. Throughout this section (2:6–4:1) and many others in the Book of Isaiah, there is an interesting interplay between the judgment which the Lord will inflict on the nation by the Assyrian and Babylonian Captivities and the judgment which will come on Israel and the whole world in the "last days" just before the Millennium. Probably Isaiah and the other prophets had no idea of the lengthy time span that would intervene between those exiles and this later time of judgment. Though many of the predictions in 2:10-21 happened when Assyria and Babylon attacked Israel and Judah, the passage looks ahead to a cataclysmic judgment on the whole world ("when He rises to shake the earth," vv. 19, 21).

### b. The Lord's day of reckoning (2:12-22)

When the Lord comes to establish justice on the earth human values will be reversed. Things that people had considered important will be considered unimportant and some things that people thought were insignificant will be highly valued.

**2:12-18.** God **has a day** (cf. "day" in v. 17) **in store,** a scheduled time of reckoning for sinners. **The LORD Almighty** (*Yahweh ṣᵉbā'ôt*) is an appellation used of God 62 times in Isaiah's book; 52 times alone and 10 times in the title "the Lord (*'ăḏōnāy*), the LORD Almighty." It denotes His military might and strength. When this Almighty One comes nothing will be able to stand in His way. **Proud** people **will be humbled** (cf. vv. 9, 11, 17), and even the great cedar trees in the forests **of Lebanon,** north of Israel, and oak trees (cf. 1:29) in **Bashan** (meaning "fertile plain"), east of the Sea of Kinnereth (later named Galilee), will be no match for the Lord. **Mountains,** perhaps suggesting governmental authorities (cf. comments on 2:3), and their military defenses repre-

sented by towers and **fortified** walls, cannot oppose Him (vv. 14-15). He will also demolish man's trade efforts typified by the merchant ships, the hub of which existed in the city of Tyre, north of Israel (v. 16). Everything that seemed to **man** in his **arrogance** to be permanent and secure will be swept away. **The LORD alone will be exalted** (cf. v. 11) when He demolishes Judah's **idols** (cf. v. 8). This may refer to the time when the Babylonians captured Judah in 586, but the ultimate judgment will be in the future at Christ's Second Advent.

**2:19-22.** When the Lord's vengeance comes, people will try to escape by fleeing into **caves** (cf. vv. 10, 21). They will be terrified because God will **shake the earth** (see comments on Hag. 2:6-7). Carrying their **idols** made with **silver** and **gold** (cf. Isa. 2:7) will hinder their escape, so the people will toss them aside to **rodents and bats** (v. 20). Once again Isaiah's sense of irony is strong: things highly valued will be thrown aside to detestable creatures that people hate. In verse 21 Isaiah again spoke of people hiding in caves away from God's terror (cf. vv. 10, 19a) when **He** will **shake the earth** (cf. v. 19b).

Then the prophet called on Judah to **stop trusting in man** (v. 22; cf. Ps. 118:8-9). Man is merely like a vapor. His **breath** can be snuffed out quickly. Therefore to trust in him is nonsensical, for man is easily removed (Isa. 2:9, 11-12, 17). In view of God's coming judgment Judah should begin to turn to Him in the present. God's glory should cause them to live righteous, holy lives and thus escape His severe judgment.

### c. Judgment on Judah for her actions (3:1-15)

Having affirmed in broad terms (2:9-21) that judgment would come, Isaiah gave examples of present sins in the nation that needed to be judged by God.

**3:1-7.** God would **take** away from . . . **Judah** any semblance of good government and replace it with a sense of futility. Because of her sin **the LORD** would take away all the supplies and people on which she relied: **food** and **water** (v. 1), soldiers (v. 2), civil (**judge**) and religious (**prophet**) leaders (v. 2), wise people (v. 2), military leaders (v. 3a), and skilled workers (v. 3b). The fact that Isaiah included **the soothsayer** (v. 2) and the **clever enchanter** (v. 3) in this list does not mean he was endorsing them. He was merely noting those on whom the nation was depending for survival and security. The Mosiac Covenant prohibited involvement in soothsaying and enchanting (Deut. 18:10-14). Isaiah himself wrote about Babylon trusting in this kind of activity (Isa. 47:12).

In contrast with these people who were considered wise and mighty the Lord would raise up foolish, weak leadership. Inexperienced **boys** and **children** (3:4; cf. Ecc. 10:16, NIV marg.) would be unable to stop oppression and conflict (Isa. 3:5). Anybody who could be grabbed would be placed in charge of the people, his only qualification (v. 6) being that he owned a **cloak. But** the only thing over which he would rule anyway would be a **heap** of **ruins.** The leaders would have no solution to the problem shortages the people would face (v. 7). Isaiah was speaking of the coming devastation of Judah by the Babylonian army.

**3:8-9.** The reason such destruction would come on **Judah** (v. 1) is that everything the nation said and did was **against** her covenant God. The people defied God and were open about **their sin** much **like** the people of **Sodom** (cf. Gen. 18:20; 19:1-11; see comments on Isa. 1:9-10). Therefore the coming **disaster** was **brought** on by **themselves. Woe** (*'ôy*) is an interjection of distress or of a threat voiced in the face of present or coming disaster. Isaiah's book includes 22 occurrences of that word or its companion word *hôy*, more than in any other prophetic book.

**3:10-12.** When God judges, **the righteous** need not fear; they will be justly rewarded for **their deeds. But the wicked will be** recompensed (**paid back**) for . . . **their** deeds (cf. comments on Rom. 3:7-11). God's judgment is always fair. Wicked people often think that sinful living is the way to get ahead in life. Isaiah noted, however, that it is far better for a person to live righteously. The leaders (**guides**) were turning the nation away **from the** proper **path** (Isa. 3:12). **Youths** may refer to minors in age or to adults who were naive like the young. The reference to **women** may mean that wives were influencing their husbands who were rulers, or that the male leaders lacked vigor.

**3:13-15.** Isaiah pictured **the LORD** seated in a courtroom ready to judge **the people** and especially the **leaders.** By stating that **He rises to judge** Isaiah meant that God, having the authority to judge, was about to do so. Two charges were leveled against the leaders. The first is that they had **ruined** God's **vineyard** (v. 14), that is, God's people (5:1, 7; cf. Ps. 80:8-18; Jer. 2:21; 12:10; Ezek. 15:6-8; Hosea 10:1). Like husbandmen caring for a vineyard, the leaders were to care for the people. But they had ruined the **people** by oppressing (**crushing,** Isa. 3:15a) them. The second charge is that they had taken advantage of **the poor** (vv. 14b, 15b) by plundering them (stealing what little they had) and **grinding** their **faces.** This violated the commands in the Book of Deuteronomy not to oppress others, especially widows, orphans, and the poor. Concern for the poor is also encouraged and illustrated in the New Testament (Acts 9:36; 10:4, 31; 24:17; James 1:27; 2:1-9). A materialistic, oppressive spirit was symptomatic of the leaders' self-centeredness. Rather than seeing their leadership positions as service opportunities they saw them as means of making money at the expense of others.

*d. Judah's fall after her pride (3:16—4:1)*

Judah's proud condition was illustrated by Jerusalem's society women. Isaiah contrasted what they looked like then with what they will look like after God's judgment comes on them.

**3:16.** The **haughty** wealthy **women of Zion** (Jerusalem) were trying to attract attention by the way they walked (proudly, **with outstretched necks**), flirted, minced along, and dressed. Isaiah may have implied that the entire nation was proud.

**3:17—4:1.** In contrast with their pride, wealth, and beauty, the **women of Zion** (cf. 3:16) would be in deep distress. They would have **sores on** their **heads** and would be **bald.** This baldness may refer to their shaving their heads, either in mourning or for medical reasons, because of their head sores. Being in deep distress they would not care how they looked. In fact **the LORD** would cause the Babylonian soldiers to take **away** all the women's fine jewelry and wardrobes (vv. 19-23). **Instead of fragrance** they would have an awful odor (v. 24) perhaps from their head sores (v. 17). Taken captive by the Babylonians, the women would be pulled by **a rope** and would wear **sackcloth,** black coarse cloth made from goats' hair and symbolizing mourning (cf. Gen. 37:34; 1 Kings 21:27; Neh. 9:1; Es. 4:1; Isa. 15:3; 22:12; 32:11; 37:1-2; Lam. 2:10; Ezek. 27:31; Dan. 9:3). Their **beauty** would be replaced by painful **branding** by their captors. The women would mourn because their **men** (husbands, brothers, and male friends) would be dying **in battle** (Isa. 3:25). The city would be so **destitute** of men and the women would be so disgraced that they would compete to gain a husband (4:1). Isaiah's picture of the Jerusalem socialites and their plight might be humorous if it were not so pathetic and realistic. Years later Jeremiah wrote that the women resorted to eating their own children during the siege (Lam. 2:20; 4:10; cf. Lev. 26:27-29; Deut. 28:53-57; Jer. 19:9).

### 5. THE HOLY SURVIVORS (4:2-6)

After God's original indictment or "lawsuit" (1:2-31) He gave a promise of restoration (2:1-5). Now at the close of the stinging reiteration of judgment (2:6–4:1) is another section on comfort (4:2-6). In spite of the terrible blow facing the nation because of its sin, some people would survive. Isaiah's initial audience might have thought he was speaking of those who would survive the Exile. However, in the light of Matthew 24:4-30 he was referring to the people who will survive the difficulties in the Great Tribulation just before the Lord Jesus Christ returns to set up His kingdom.

**4:2.** In spite of the coming severe judgment, divine blessing would eventually come. Sometimes the phrase **in that day** refers to the Babylonian attack on Jerusalem (e.g., 3:7, 18; 4:1), but here (see the statements in vv. 2, 5) as in 2:11-12, 17 it means the millennial reign of Christ.

Some interpreters say **the Branch of the Lord,** who is **beautiful and glorious,** refers to the believing remnant. It seems better, however, to take the "Branch" as a reference to the Messiah since this is its meaning in Jeremiah 23:5; 33:15; Zechariah 3:8. The term "Branch" is a fitting figure for the Messiah because He "sprouted" from David's line (Jer. 33:15) and will bear fruit. Just as people delight in fruit from their land so **the survivors**

will delight in the Messiah, **the Fruit of the land.** The Branch is suggestive of Jesus' words that He is the Vine (John 15:1).

**4:3-4.** The mark of distinction for surviving Israel will be holiness, not wealth or prestige. Their sins will be forgiven. Speaking again of **the women of Zion** (cf. 3:16–4:1) Isaiah noted that they, representing the nation, **will** be cleansed **by a spirit of judgment and a spirit of fire,** as the judging will be like fire that will burn **away** the nation's undesirable **filth** (sin). Only the sovereign work of **the Lord,** not human effort, will be able to **cleanse** (cf. 1:25) the nation (cf. Zech. 13:1). John the Baptist said that Jesus would "baptize . . . with fire" (Matt. 3:11), that is, purify the nation by an act of judging (cf. Mal. 3:2-5).

**4:5-6.** In this yet-future time of blessing for redeemed Israel **the glory** of God will be evident in Jerusalem (**Mount Zion**). As God's glory was visible to Israel in the Exodus from Egypt in a **cloud . . . by day** and **fire by night** (Ex. 13:21-22; 40:34-38; cf. 16:10), so also will His glory be visible when the redeemed nation will be in her land of promise. God's glory, like a tent, will provide safety and peace.

### 6. THE WORTHLESS VINEYARD (5:1-7)

In the first stanza (vv. 1-2) of this song which Isaiah composed he sang about God's care for His vineyard and the condition of the vineyard. The second stanza (vv. 3-6) details what God said in view of her condition. In the third stanza (v. 7) the vineyard in the figure is identified. Elsewhere God referred to Israel as a vineyard (3:14; Ps. 80:8-18; Jer. 2:21; 12:10; Ezek. 15:6-8; Hosea 10:1).

**5:1-2.** In his **song** Isaiah pictured his **loved One** (i.e., God), planting **a vineyard on a fertile hillside,** removing the **stones** (of which there are many in Israel!) and planting only the best **vines. He built a watchtower,** a stone structure from which to guard the vineyard (cf. "shelter," 1:8). And He made **a winepress** in anticipation of producing good wine. However, only poor **grapes** grew on His vines.

**5:3-6.** The words in these verses in the song are "spoken" by God. He asked the people **of Judah** to **judge** the situation. They were to tell whether the **bad**

grapes were the fault of the **vineyard** Owner. Though God could have done nothing **more** to make the **vineyard** productive (v. 4) there was one thing He would now **do**: He would let it be destroyed (vv. 5-6). By removing the protective **hedge . . . its wall** (probably of stone) around it, He would allow animals (including foxes, Song 2:15) to enter and destroy it. Without cultivating the vines, thornbushes would **grow** up and smother them. Nor would God let **rain** fall on the **vineyard**. Because of the nation's sinful actions (their bad fruit), destruction would come. Without God's protection Judah would be ruined.

**5:7.** The **vineyard** in this song is identified as **Israel** and **Judah**. As elsewhere in Isaiah, "Israel" is sometimes a synonym for the Southern Kingdom (Neh. 1:6; 13:3). Delighting in His people, God wanted good fruit, that is, **justice** and **righteousness** (cf. comments on Isa. 1:21). Instead He **saw** only **bloodshed** (cf. 1:15) and **heard cries of distress.** Because of its "bad grapes" (injustice) most people would be killed or taken into captivity. Isaiah used two interesting cases of assonance (similarity in word sounds) to stress the contrast between what God expected in His people and what happened to them. "Justice" (*mišpāṭ*) was replaced with "bloodshed" (*miśpoḥ*), and instead of "righteousness" (*ṣᵉḏāqâh*) there was "distress" (*ṣᵉʿāqâh*).

### 7. AN INDICTMENT ON SIN (5:8-30)

Though verses 8-30 are not a part of the song in verses 1-7, they fit into Isaiah's train of thought nicely because their six indictments ("woes") are against the "bad fruit" the nation had been producing. Between the second and third woes God referred to the consequences of Judah's sins (vv. 13-17); after the sixth woe He did a similar thing (vv. 24-30).

#### a. Woe to materialists (5:8-10)

**5:8-10.** Each of the six indictments is introduced by **Woe** (*hôy;* see comments on 3:9). Some people were acquiring much **land** at the expense of their fellow countrymen (cf. Micah 2:1-2). Selling houses permanently in a walled city was allowed under the Law, but selling houses in unwalled cities and fields was allowed only until the Year of Jubilee when the houses would revert back to

their former owners. Because God had given the people the land they were not to get rich at others' expense. Because of this sin the big **houses** and **mansions** the people once enjoyed would be empty, for many people would be killed and, as noted in the Mosaic Covenant (Deut. 28:20-24), their crops would fail. Normally a large **vineyard** would **produce** many gallons of **wine,** but here the amount would be a mere six gallons (**a bath**). And six bushels (**a homer**) **of seed** would normally yield scores of bushels of **grain,** but ironically the grain would be only one-half a bushel (**an ephah**), just 1/12 the amount of seed sown!

#### b. Woe to drunkards (5:11-12)

**5:11-12.** Apparently heavy consumption of wine was prevalent in Isaiah's day for this sin is mentioned in two of the six woes (cf. v. 22). People were so addicted to wine that, unlike most drunkards, they rose **early in the morning** to drink. They also stayed **up late at night.** In their revelry they enjoyed music **at their banquets,** but cared nothing **for the deeds of the LORD.** Their lack of **respect for the work of His hands** meant they abused other people made in the image of God. Caring only for their own pleasures, they had no concern for the Lord or for others.

#### c. Results of Judah's lifestyle (5:13-17)

**5:13-17.** Because of Judah's lifestyle she would experience several results, the worst being **exile.** Included in that experience would be death by **hunger** and **thirst** (v. 13). Many would **die,** both **nobles and masses,** since death has no respect for rank (v. 14). The carousing drunkards (**brawlers and revelers**) of whom Isaiah had just spoken (vv. 11-12) would also die (v. 14). All proud people would be humiliated (cf. 2:11-12, 17) regardless of their previous stations in life (5:15). With the houses of the wealthy ruined (cf. vv. 8-9) and desolate, **lambs** would easily **graze** there (v. 17). This destruction of the nation would lead to a display of God's **justice** and holiness (v. 16). This does not mean that He delights in revenge. Rather, He keeps His word as spoken in the covenant. His discipline of the nation would show that He still loved her and would someday bring her back into a favored position.

### d. Woe to the doubters of God (5:18-19)

**5:18-19.** Perhaps Isaiah referred here to people who were genuinely questioning whether God was in control of the nation. Though attached to **sin** and **wickedness** by **cords** and **ropes** (i.e., deeply involved in sin) they wondered if God could save their nation. Apparently they wanted **God** to deliver them even though they did not want to give up their sinful practices. They wanted to **see** God act (**let Him hasten His work**) without any spiritual change on their part. However, deliverance, both personal and national, does not work that way. A spiritual change must be made before God will save His people from destruction.

### e. Woe to those calling evil good (5:20)

**5:20.** Some people lead others astray by their perverted values. **Evil**—for example, adultery, idolatry, materialism, murder, and many other sins forbidden in the Scriptures—is often held up as being **good.** Those who say such things are under the threat (**woe**) of God's judgment.

### f. Woe to conceited ones (5:21)

**5:21.** Thinking themselves **wise** and **clever,** some people were not relying on God's power to deliver the nation. They thought they could protect themselves.

### g. Woe to the drunken bribe-takers (5:22-23)

**5:22-23.** Rather than being **heroes** and good government authorities, many leaders were known for their heavy **drinking.** They were ready to be bribed, not caring for the people they were ruling. They were more concerned for their own pleasure than for the rights of **the innocent.** Therefore *they* (those leaders) would be judged.

### h. Further results of Judah's lifestyle (5:24-30)

Isaiah had already mentioned a number of the judgments to come on the people because of their sins (vv. 13-17). Now he spoke again of the consequences of disobeying the covenant stipulations.

**5:24-25.** These people Isaiah had been writing about would be burned like **straw** and **dry grass** and their **flowers** blown **away like dust.** This was because they had deliberately disobeyed God's Word (on **the LORD Almighty** see comments on 1:9; on **the Holy One of Israel** see comments on 1:4). Because of **the LORD's anger** many would die **in the streets** of Jerusalem. **His** raised **hand** (cf. 14:27) suggests His executing punishment; **the mountains** shaking from an earthquake speaks of His awesome presence (cf. Ex. 19:18; 1 Kings 19:11; Jer. 4:24; Hab. 3:10).

**5:26-30.** When God's judgment would come on Judah, the **nations** of Egypt and Assyria (7:18), and later Babylon would respond as if God had raised **a banner** as a signal for war. Those nations would seemingly come from **the ends of the earth,** a phrase Isaiah used frequently to suggest people everywhere (5:26; 24:16; 40:28; 41:5, 9; 42:10; 43:6; 45:22; 48:20; 49:6; 52:10; 62:11). The soldiers, responding **speedily,** would be vigorous (5:27) and well armed. Their chariots would be fast (v. 28). Ferocious like **lions** (v. 29) they would completely devastate Judah (v. 30). They would cover Judah like a **sea** and blot out the sun like **the clouds,** a picture of **distress** and gloom.

### 8. ISAIAH'S COMMISSION (CHAP. 6)

Though this is one of the better-known chapters in the Book of Isaiah, at least three problems in it have caused debate among Bible students.

The first problem concerns the chronological relationship of chapter 6, which records God's call of Isaiah, to the preceding five chapters on judgment and deliverance. Did Isaiah minister for a period of time before being commissioned, or is this chapter out of order chronologically but in order logically? Some have argued that since the vision occurred "in the year that King Uzziah died" (v. 1) Isaiah must have had some previous ministry (chaps. 1–5) since he is said to have ministered *during* the reign of Uzziah (1:1). It can be countered, however, that Isaiah saw this vision anytime up to 12 months before the king's death. In that sense then his vision *was* "in" Uzziah's reign.

It is possible, as some suggest, that Isaiah, seeing the sinful condition of the nation (chaps. 1–5), set himself apart from that nation until he saw the vision of God and then realized that he too was part of the sin problem. He also was "a man of unclean lips" (6:5).

On the other hand it is possible that

the vision and commissioning of chapter 6 came *before* he delivered the messages in chapters 1–5 and that he recorded this experience here as a fitting logical climax to the stinging indictment in those chapters. Chapter 6 emphasizes the extreme depravity of the nation, contrasting it with God's holiness. Here Isaiah also emphasized that the people lacked spiritual insight and would not turn from their sinful condition.

A second problem pertains to whom Isaiah saw. Isaiah "saw the LORD" (v. 1), whom he called "the LORD Almighty" (v. 3) and "the King, the LORD Almighty" (v. 5). Because the Apostle John wrote that Isaiah "saw Jesus' glory" (John 12:41), Isaiah may have seen the preincarnate Christ, who because of His deity is the Lord. The prophet did not see the very essence of God for no man can see Him (Ex. 33:18; John 1:18; 1 Tim. 6:16; 1 John 4:12) since He is invisible (1 Tim. 1:17). But there was no problem in Isaiah's seeing God in a vision or a theophany, much as did Ezekiel (Ezek. 1:3-28), Daniel (Dan. 7:2, 9-10), and others.

A third problem is related to the fact that Isaiah's vision was in the temple (Isa. 6:1). Was Isaiah there because he was a priest? Jeremiah was the son of a priest (Jer. 1:1) and Ezekiel was a priest (Ezek. 1:3), but the Book of Isaiah says nothing about Isaiah being of priestly lineage. If he were not carrying out priestly duties he may have been a worshiper there when he saw the heavenly vision. Or perhaps he, like Ezekiel (Ezek. 8:1-4), was not physically in the temple but was transported there in a vision.

*a. Isaiah's vision of the Lord (6:1-4)*

**6:1.** Since Isaiah ministered during **King** Uzziah's reign (1:1) Isaiah's vision of God **in the year . . . Uzziah died** would have occurred within the 12 calendar months before or after the king's death in 739 B.C. If the vision occurred *before* Isaiah began his ministry then obviously the vision was before the king's death. However, if the vision came sometime *after* the prophet's ministry started—see comments earlier under "B. Isaiah's commission (chap. 6)"—then Isaiah could have seen the vision within the calendar year (739 B.C.) either shortly before or shortly after the king died.

This time notation points to a contrast between the human king and the divine King (v. 5), God Himself and to some contrasts between Uzziah and Isaiah. In Uzziah's long (52-year), prosperous reign (2 Chron. 26:1-15) many people were away from the Lord and involved in sin (2 Kings 15:1-4; **Uzziah** is also called Azariah). By contrast, God is holy (Isa. 6:3). In pride, Uzziah disobediently entered the temple (insensitive to the sin involved) and was struck with leprosy which made him ceremonially unclean (2 Chron. 26:16-20). Isaiah, however, was sensitive to sin, for he stated that he and his people were spiritually unclean (Isa. 6:5). Though Uzziah was excluded from the temple (2 Chron. 26:21) Isaiah was not.

Three things struck Isaiah about God: He was **seated on a throne,** He was **high and exalted,** and **the train of His robe filled the temple.** In the most holy place of the temple in Jerusalem, God's glory was evident between the cherubim on the atonement cover over the ark of the covenant. Therefore some Israelites may have erroneously thought that God was fairly small. However, Solomon, in his dedicatory prayer for the new temple, had stated that no temple could contain God and that in fact even the heavens could not contain Him (1 Kings 8:27). Therefore Isaiah did not see God on the ark of the covenant, but on a throne. Almost 150 years later Ezekiel had a similar experience. He envisioned God being borne along on a great chariot throne by living creatures called cherubim (Ezek. 1). To Isaiah, the throne emphasized that **the Lord** is indeed the true King of Israel.

God's being "high and exalted" symbolized His position before the nation. The people were wanting God to work on their behalf (Isa. 5:19) but He *was* doing so, as evidenced by His lofty position among them.

The Lord's long robe speaks of His royalty and majesty. His being in the temple suggests that though He hates mere religiosity (1:11-15) He still wanted the nation to be involved in the temple worship. The temple and the temple sacrifices pictured the righteous dealings of the sovereign God with His covenant people.

**6:2-4. Seraphs,** angelic beings who were **above** the Lord, are referred to in the Scriptures only here. "Seraphs" is from *śārap*, which means "to burn," possibly suggesting that they were ardent in their zeal for the Lord. It is also noteworthy that one of the seraphs took a *burning* coal to Isaiah (v. 6). They had **six wings** (the four living creatures Ezekiel saw each had four wings, Ezek. 1:5, 11). Covering **their faces** with **two wings** indicates their humility before God. Their covering **their feet** with **two** other wings may denote service to God, and their **flying** may speak of their ongoing activity in proclaiming God's holiness and glory.

In **calling to one another** the seraphs, whose number is not given, were proclaiming that **the LORD Almighty** is **holy.** The threefold repetition of the word **holy** suggests supreme or complete holiness. This threefold occurrence does not suggest the Trinity, as some have supposed. The Trinity is supported in other ways (e.g., see comments on Isa. 6:8). Repeating a word three times for emphasis is common in the Old Testament (e.g., Jer. 22:29; Ezek. 21:27). The seraphs also proclaimed that **His glory** fills the **earth** (cf. Num. 14:21) much as His robe filled the temple. By contrast the people of Judah were unholy (cf. Isa. 5; 6:5) though they were supposed to be a holy people (Ex. 22:31; Deut. 7:6).

As the seraphs cried out, Isaiah saw **the temple** shake and then it **was filled with smoke** (Isa. 6:4). The **thresholds** (cf. Amos 9:1) were large foundation stones on which **the doorposts** stood. The shaking (cf. Ex. 19:18) suggested the awesome presence and power of God. The smoke was probably the cloud of glory which Isaiah's ancestors had seen in the wilderness (Ex. 13:21; 16:10) and which the priests in Solomon's day had viewed in the dedicated temple (1 Kings 8:10-13).

### b. Isaiah's response to the vision (6:5)

**6:5.** This vision of God's majesty, holiness, and glory made Isaiah realize that he was a sinner. When Ezekiel saw God's glory he too responded with humility. (Cf. the responses of Job, Job 42:5-6; Peter, Luke 5:8; and the Apostle John, Rev. 1:17.) Isaiah had pronounced woes (threats of judgment) on the nation (Isa. 5:8-23), but now by saying **Woe to me!** (cf. 24:16) he realized *he* was subject to judgment. This was because he was unclean. When seen next to the purity of God's holiness, the impurity of human

sin is all the more evident. The prophet's **unclean lips** probably symbolized his attitudes and actions as well as his words, for a person's words reflect his thinking and relate to his actions. Interestingly Isaiah identified with his people who also were sinful (**a people of unclean lips**).

### c. Isaiah's cleansing and message (6:6-13)

**6:6-7.** Realizing his impurity, Isaiah was cleansed by God, through the intermediary work of **one of the seraphs.** It is fitting that a seraph (perhaps meaning a "burning one") **touched** Isaiah's **lips** with a hot **coal . . . from the altar,** either the altar of burnt offering, on which a fire was always burning (Lev. 6:12), or the altar of incense where incense was burned each morning and evening (Ex. 30:1, 7-8). This symbolic action signified the removal of the prophet's **guilt** and his **sin.** Of course this is what the entire nation needed. The Judahites needed to respond as Isaiah did, acknowledging their need of cleansing from sin. But unlike the prophet, most members of the nation refused to admit they had a spiritual need. Though they, through the priests, burned sacrifices at the temple, their lives needed the purifying action of God's "fire" of cleansing.

**6:8.** The rest of this chapter deals with the message Isaiah was to preach to Judah. Significantly he was not called to service till he had been cleansed. After hearing the seraph's words (vv. 3, 7) he then **heard the** Lord's **voice.**

God asked, **Whom shall I send? And who will go for Us?** The word "Us" in reference to God hints at the Trinity (cf. "Us" in Gen. 1:26; 11:7). This doctrine, though not explicit in the Old Testament, is implicit for God is the same God in both Testaments.

The question "Who will go?" does not mean God did not know or that He only *hoped* someone would respond. He asked the question to give Isaiah, now cleansed, an opportunity for service. The prophet knew that the entire nation needed the same kind of awareness of God and cleansing of sin he had received. So he responded that he would willingly serve **the Lord** (**Here am I**).

**6:9-10.** Probably Isaiah, responding as he did in verse 8, thought that his serving the Lord would result in the nation's cleansing. However, the Lord told him his message would *not* result in much spiritual response. The people had not listened before and they would not listen now. The Lord did not delight in judging His people, but discipline was necessary because of their disobedience. In fact the **people**, on hearing Isaiah's message, would become even more hardened against the Lord. Interestingly six of the seven lines in verse 10 are in a chiasm: **heart . . . ears . . . eyes** are mentioned in lines 1-3, and in lines 4-6 they are reversed: **eyes . . . ears . . . hearts.** This is a common arrangement of material in the Old Testament. Possibly this pattern emphasizes the "eyes," mentioned in the middle. Jesus quoted part of this verse to explain that Israel in His day *could* not believe because they *would* not believe (see comments on John 12:40).

**6:11-13.** Isaiah's response to the message implies that he was ready to speak whatever God wanted him to say. Yet he wondered **how long** he would have to go on delivering a message of judgment to which the people would be callous. The **Lord** answered that Isaiah was to proclaim the message **until** His judgment came, that is, till the Babylonian Exile actually occurred and the people were deported from **the land** (v. 12), thus leaving their ruined **cities** and **fields** (v. 11). Though Isaiah did not live that long, God meant he should keep on preaching even if he did live to see Judah's downfall. The **tenth** that remained **in the land** (v. 13) refers to the poor who were left in Judah by Nebuchadnezzar (2 Kings 24:14). But most of them were laid waste (Jer. 41:10-18; 43:4-7).

Isaiah, perhaps discouraged by such a negative response and terrible results, was then assured by **the Lord** that not all was lost. A remnant would be left. God compared that remnant to **stumps** of **terebinth and oak** trees. From this stump or **holy seed** of a believing remnant would come others who would believe. Though Judah's population would be almost totally wiped out or exiled, God promised to preserve a small number of believers **in the land.**

## B. Prophecies of deliverance (chaps. 7–12)

In these chapters the prophet focused on the deliverance God would bring the nation. Judah's deliverance

from the Aram-Israel alliance (7:1-4) pictures her ultimate deliverance. And the fall of the Assyrian Empire (10:5-19), resulting in "deliverance" for Judah, pictures the fall of all nations who oppose God and His people. Isaiah did not say that these deliverances would bring about the glorious kingdom. But he did indicate that the glorious kingdom, the Millennium, eventually will come (chap. 11). It will be greater than any previous kingdom. In that kingdom "the holy seed" (6:13), the believing remnant (10:20-21), will sing a song of thanksgiving (chap. 12).

### 1. THE BIRTH OF IMMANUEL (CHAP. 7)

Isaiah prophesied about a Child to be born who in some way would relate to the nation's deliverance. The birth of the Baby, to be named Immanuel, has great significance for the line of David.

### a. The historical situation (7:1-2)

**7:1-2. Rezin,** king **of Aram,** northeast of Israel, **and Pekah . . . king of Israel** (752–732) had made an alliance. Rezin may have usurped the throne of Aram, and Pekah was a usurper. Rezin was Aram's last king, and Pekah was Israel's next-to-last king. After Jeroboam II (793–753) of Israel died, the Northern Kingdom became increasingly weak. Rezin convinced Pekah to join him against Pekah's southern neighbor Judah (2 Kings 15:37; 16:5). They threatened to replace Judah's King **Ahaz** with a puppet king, "the son of Tabeel" (Isa. 7:6). Perhaps Tabeel was a district or a person in Aram. The prospect of such formidable enemies as Aram and Israel caused the people of Judah to be afraid. **The house of David** (v. 2) refers to King Ahaz who was of that kingly line. Hearing of the **Aram**-Israel alliance **Ahaz** was terrified. **Ephraim,** Israel's largest tribe, represented the entire nation, as is also the case in the Book of Hosea (see, e.g., Hosea 4:17; 5:3, 5, 9-14). This was in the year 734 B.C. Perhaps Ahaz thought he could call on the Assyrian King Tiglath-Pileser III (745–727) to come to his aid and attack the Aram-Israel confederacy.

### b. The assurance that Judah would not be destroyed (7:3-9)

**7:3.** God told **Isaiah** to go with his **son . . . to meet** King **Ahaz** at the end of the aqueduct of the Upper Pool. This pool was a reservoir that held water from the Gihon Spring near Jerusalem. (Isa. 22:9 refers to a Lower Pool.) Perhaps Ahaz was there to inspect the city's water supply in anticipation of an attack by Aram and Israel. The aqueduct was near the road to the Washerman's Field, just outside Jerusalem's city walls. This was the place where, about 33 years later, Sennacherib's spokesman would hurl his challenge to the Jerusalemites (36:2). The name of Isaiah's son, Shear-Jashub (which means "a remnant will return"; cf. 10:21) illustrated the prophet's message. The nation of Judah would not be destroyed by the Aram-Israel alliance.

7:4-6. Isaiah told Ahaz not to be afraid of Rezin and Pekah, for they were mere smoldering stubs of firewood. Their lives would soon end; like firewood they would be burned up and gone. Both men died two years later in 732 B.C. Aram and Israel threatened to invade Judah, split it between the two conquering nations, and set up a puppet king.

7:7-9. In response to the Aram-Israel threat the Sovereign Lord had an answer: It (the attack) would not take place; it would not happen. The reason was that both of those nations were headed by mere (only, vv. 8-9) men. Ironically Isaiah referred to Pekah by name only once (v. 1). Four other times he called him "the son of Remaliah" or Remaliah's son (vv. 4-5, 9; 8:6). He and Rezin could not thwart God's plans.

In fact Isaiah made the startling prophecy that within 65 years Israel would no longer even be a people because they would be so shattered (7:8). Isaiah gave this prophecy in 734 B.C., so 65 years later was 669. When Assyria conquered Israel in 722, many Israelites were deported to other lands by Assyria and foreigners were brought into Samaria (2 Kings 17:24). However, in 669 many more foreigners were transferred to Samaria by Ashurbanipal (Ezra 4:10), king of Assyria (669–626). This "shattered" Israel, making it impossible for her to unite as a nation ("a people").

The second sentence in Isaiah 7:9 has been translated in various ways. But it challenged Ahaz to believe what Isaiah was telling him. Obviously Ahaz was not alive 65 years later. But he could have faith that God would fulfill both predic-

tions: that Israel would be shattered 65 years later and that in his day the northern confederacy (Aram and Israel) would not overpower Judah. If he did not believe those predictions he too would fall.

### c. Ahaz's rejection of a sign (7:10-12)

7:10-12. As a means of strengthening his faith Ahaz was told to ask the Lord . . . for a sign, an attesting miracle that would confirm God's word. The king could choose any miraculous work he wished, from the deepest depths to the highest heights. This was a figure of speech, a merism, that mentioned two extremes with the intention of including all the areas in between them. With a miracle performed simply for the asking, Ahaz would have visible confirmation that Isaiah's words (vv. 7-9) were truly from the Lord. Ahaz could count on the fact that the northern alliance would not defeat Judah.

But Ahaz refused to request a sign, saying he would not . . . test God (cf. Deut. 6:16). This answer sounded pious but probably the way he said it showed he was not believing Isaiah. Perhaps he did not *want* to believe Isaiah, who had been prophesying about the eventual destruction of Judah if her people did not return to the Lord.

### d. The Lord's response (7:13-25)

7:13. Ahaz, by rejecting the offer of a sign from God's messenger, was in effect rejecting the One who sent the prophet. The house of David (cf. v. 2) refers not to all David's descendants, but to Ahaz and those kings of Judah who would descend from him. Ahaz's answer was impious. He said he did not want to test the Lord, but by refusing to follow God's directive to ask for a confirming miracle, he *was* testing the Lord's patience (as well as man's patience).

7:14-16. Though Ahaz refused to request a sign that would have confirmed the truth of Isaiah's message, the prophet said God would give him one anyway. The sign was to be a boy named Immanuel. Three elements pertain to the sign: (1) The boy would be born of a virgin (v. 14). (2) He would be raised in a time of national calamity (v. 15; on the curds and honey see comments on v. 22). (3) While he was still a youth, the two-king alliance would be broken (v. 16).

"Virgin" translates 'almâh, a word used of an unmarried woman of marriageable age. The word refers to one who is sexually mature. It occurs elsewhere in the Old Testament only in Genesis 24:43 ("maiden"); Exodus 2:8 ("girl"); Psalm 68:25 ("maidens"); Proverbs 30:19 ("maiden"); Song of Songs 1:3 ("maidens"); 6:8 ("virgins"). It also occurs in 1 Chronicles 15:20 (alamoth) and in the title of Psalm 46 (alamoth may be a musical term). The child's name Immanuel means "God (is) with us."

Most Bible scholars hold one of three views on the virgin in Isaiah 7:14-16:

(1) The boy of whom Isaiah wrote was conceived shortly after Isaiah spoke this message. A young woman, a virgin, married and then had a baby. Before he would be old enough to tell the difference between good and evil the northern Aram-Israel alliance would be destroyed. According to this view the woman was a virgin when Isaiah spoke his prophecy but was not when the boy was born because he was conceived by sexual relations with her husband. Some say this child was born to Isaiah (8:3-4). They point out that 8:1-4 corresponds in a number of ways to 7:14-17. But this view must be rejected because (a) Isaiah's wife already had a child (Shear-Jashub, v. 3) and so was not a virgin, and (b) the second child born to Isaiah's wife was not named Immanuel (8:3). In this view Ahaz would have known this woman, and hearing of the child's birth and his name Immanuel he would understand that Isaiah's prophecies were correct.

(2) A second view sees the predicted birth as exclusively messianic and the virgin as Mary, Jesus' mother. It is argued that in Isaiah 7:14 the virgin is said to **be with child** (lit., "the virgin is or will be pregnant"). It is also argued that Matthew, stressing the fact that Joseph and Mary's marriage was not consummated till after Jesus' birth (Matt. 1:18, 25), affirmed that Jesus' birth fulfilled Isaiah's prophecy (Matt. 1:21-23).

Proponents of this view point out that since Isaiah spoke this prophecy to the house of David (Isa. 7:13) and not just to Ahaz himself, the sign was given not just to the king but to the entire kingly line and the entire nation. However, if the fulfillment did not occur until Joseph and Mary's day, how does the prophecy relate to Isaiah's point that the Aram-Israel confederacy would soon be defeated? And how does the birth of the Lord Jesus relate to the eating of curds and honey (v. 15) and to the breaking of the alliance before the boy was old enough to know good and evil? (v. 16) Proponents of this view answer that the time is similar: the two years of Jesus' babyhood (before He would know between right and wrong) point to the same time segment, two years, within which the Aram-Israel threat would be gone.

(3) A third view, a combination of the first two, sees the prophecy as directed primarily to Ahaz regarding the breaking of the alliance. The 'almâh was a virgin when Isaiah spoke his message, but then she would marry and have a baby. When the Aram-Israel alliance was broken the boy would still be young. Centuries later the Holy Spirit led Matthew to quote Isaiah 7:14 as a statement that was also true of a virgin birth (i.e., a birth to a woman who was still a virgin). This is the first of many prophecies about the Messiah given by Isaiah. (See the chart "Messianic Prophecies in the Book of Isaiah.")

The sign must have had some significance for the historical situation in which it was given. The sign involved not only the birth and the boy's name (Immanuel, "God [is] with us," would assure the people of God's presence), but also a designated length of time: **before the boy knows enough to reject the wrong and choose the right, the land of the two kings . . . will be laid waste.**

Within about three years (nine months for the pregnancy and two or three years until the boy would know the difference between good and evil) the alliance would be broken. It was broken in 732 B.C. when Tiglath-Pileser III destroyed Damascus. After Tiglath-Pileser had defeated Aram and put Rezin to death Ahaz went to Damascus to meet the Assyrian monarch (2 Kings 16:7-10). Ahaz liked an altar he saw in Damascus, and had a sketch of it drawn so a similar altar could be set up in Jerusalem. No wonder Isaiah and God were angry with Ahaz. Even after the alliance had been broken by Tiglath-Pileser Judah had no peace. Though Assyria did not defeat Judah, she had to pay Assyria a heavy tribute. Isaiah foretold the consequences of Ahaz's attitude (Isa. 7:17-25).

## Messianic Prophecies in the Book of Isaiah

1. He will be called before His birth to be God's Servant (49:1).

2. He will be born of a virgin (7:14).

3. He will be a Descendant of Jesse and thus in the Davidic line (11:1, 10).

4. He will be empowered by the Holy Spirit (11:2; 42:1).

5. He will be gentle toward the weak (42:3).

6. He will be obedient to the Lord in His mission (50:4-9).

7. He will voluntarily submit to suffering (50:6; 53:7-8).

8. He will be rejected by Israel (49:7; 53:1, 3).

9. He will take on Himself the sins of the world (53:4-6, 10-12).

10. He will triumph over death (53:10).

11. He will be exalted (52:13; 53:12).

12. He will come to comfort Israel and to bring vengeance on the wicked (61:1-3).

13. He will manifest God's glory (49:3).

14. He will restore Israel spiritually to God (49:5) and physically to the land (49:8).

15. He will reign on David's throne (9:7).

16. He will bring joy to Israel (9:2).

17. He will make a New Covenant with Israel (42:6; 49:8-9).

18. He will be a light to the Gentiles (42:6; 49:6).

19. He will restore the nations (11:10).

20. He will be worshiped by Gentiles (49:7, 52:15).

21. He will govern the world (9:6).

22. He will judge in righteousness, justice, and faithfulness (11:3-5; 42:1, 4).

**7:17-19.** God said He would send **the king of Assyria** to **Judah.** These would be the worst enemy attacks **since** the 10 Northern tribes (here called **Ephraim;** see comments on v. 2) **broke . . . from** the 2 Southern tribes in 931 B.C. From Ahaz's day on, Judah was troubled by the Assyrian Empire, to which it had to pay a large tribute. Ahaz called on Tiglath-Pileser to rescue him from Aram and Israel, which the Assyrian king gladly did. However, Tiglath-Pileser gave Ahaz trouble, not help (2 Chron. 28:20-21). Then in Hezekiah's reign Sennacherib, king of Assyria, invaded Judah, who had asked for help from **Egypt** (Isa. 30:1-5), and was about to take it when, in 701 B.C., God miraculously delivered Jerusalem (chaps. 36-37). God's hand was in all this for He would **whistle for flies from** Egypt (i.e., Egyptian soldiers were as numerous and bothersome as flies) **and for bees from . . . Assyria** (i.e., Assyrian soldiers who were vicious as bees).

**7:20-25.** Judah would experience deprivation and humiliation. **Assyria,** like **a razor,** would **shave** Judah's **hair.** In the ancient Near East shaving one's hair and beard was a sign of humiliation or deep distress (cf. Job 1:20; Isa. 15:2; Jer. 47:5; 48:37; Ezek. 7:18; Amos 8:10; Micah 1:16). **The abundance of . . . milk** was a distressful factor, not a good one. With many animals dying, a farmer's **young cow and two goats** would have no young to nurse, and so the milk (and **curds** from it) would be plentiful for the people. **Honey** would also be abundant because wild flowers would grow in the desolate fields and bee swarms would be more plentiful. All this would fulfill the sign given Ahaz by Isaiah (Isa. 7:15): he **will eat curds and honey.** Also the farmers would have no crops because of the ruined farmland. The vineyards would be ruined along with the cultivated **land,** and only **briers and thorns** (mentioned three times in vv. 23-25) would grow.

The land would be good only for grazing by **cattle** and **sheep.**

**In that day** (v. 21) denotes a time of judgment on the nation of Judah. Often this phrase (as in 4:2, e.g.) is used eschatologically to refer to the time of extreme judgment in the Great Tribulation just before the Messiah will return to establish the millennial kingdom. But sometimes as here (7:21) it refers to a judgment to come on the nation soon. The near judgment pictures the extreme judgment to come at the end of the age.

### 2. THE COMING DELIVERER (8:1–9:7)

This section is closely related to the previous chapter. It concerns the same event, namely, the deliverance from the Aram-Israel alliance and the subsequent Assyrian invasion that would eventually extend to Judah. Chapter 7 included several "negatives"—Ahaz's rejection of God's Word through Isaiah, Ahaz's continued unbelief, and the difficult times that would come to Judah. This section focuses on a positive note: the nation would be delivered and this deliverance would picture another Deliverer, who will bring an even greater deliverance.

*a. The coming fall of Israel and Aram (8:1-4)*

Isaiah had already prophesied of the fall of the Aram-Israel alliance (7:4-17). Now he gave another prophecy of the same event. As in chapter 7, this prediction also involves the birth of a baby, this time to Isaiah and his wife, a prophetess. Some have suggested that this birth fulfilled the prediction in 7:14. However, the two accounts have several differences. The child in 8:1-4 was not named Immanuel (cf. 7:14). The child in 8:1-4 was born to Isaiah's wife. She was not a virgin because Isaiah already had at least one child (7:3), unless the wife in 8:3 refers to a second wife of Isaiah. This, however, seems unlikely. This birth probably occurred some time after the prediction in 7:14 because according to 8:4 the fall of the alliance would occur fairly soon—before the child was even able to say "my father" or "my mother." Most children can say those words before or soon after they are one year old. Apparently God graciously allowed this second prediction of the Assyrian destruction of Aram to be given to Judah. This prophecy was witnessed by several important people, to prove to the nation once again that Isaiah was speaking for the Lord and that his words were true.

**8:1.** Isaiah was to use a visual aid to help secure the prophecy in the minds of his audience. On **a large scroll** Isaiah was to record the name of a son to be born to him soon. The son's name was to be announced even before he was conceived, thus pointing to the certainty of the birth. The name **Maher-Shalal-Hash-Baz,** the longest personal name in the Bible, means "quick to the plunder, swift to the spoil." Soldiers would shout these words to their comrades as they defeated and plundered their foes. Isaiah's listeners, remembering his prophecy of the fall of the Aram-Israel alliance (7:4-17), would have understood the significance of his son's name as they continued to listen to his prediction of impending doom for Aram and Israel.

**8:2.** God said He would **call in** two **witnesses** (Num. 35:30; Deut. 17:6; 19:15), who could confirm that His words were true. **Uriah the priest** is mentioned later in an unfavorable light (2 Kings 16:10-16) when he complied with Ahaz's order to change the temple worship after the Aram-Israel alliance had been broken. Apparently he was an influential priest. **Zechariah son of Jeberekiah** is nowhere else mentioned by that full title. He may have been a prophet during the time of Uzziah (2 Chron. 26:5) or a Levite who helped cleanse the temple in Hezekiah's day (2 Chron. 29:12-13).

**8:3-4. The prophetess,** Isaiah's wife, is unnamed. She was called a prophetess either because she was married to a prophet or because she had the God-given ability to prophesy. The latter seems preferable. Isaiah's son, **Maher-Shalal-Hash-Baz,** was a sign of the coming break in the Aram-Israel alliance against Judah. In about a year and nine months (nine months for the pregnancy and one year of the child's life), Assyria would **plunder** both **Damascus** (Aram's capital city) and **Samaria** (Israel's capital). This happened in 732 B.C., which confirms the date of 734 for Isaiah's prophecy. When Damascus and Samaria fell, Judah should have turned to God as Isaiah had told them to. Unfortunately Uriah, one of the two witnesses (v. 2), followed Ahaz's orders after 732 B.C. and changed the temple worship to conform with the pagan worship practiced at Damascus.

### b. The coming Assyrian invasion (8:5-8)

**8:5-6.** **This people** could refer to the Northern Kingdom of Israel since she was the nation that **rejected** Judah in favor of aligning with Aram, under its king **Rezin** (cf. 7:1). **The gently flowing waters of Shiloah,** also called Siloam, then would refer by metonymy to the city of Jerusalem. These waters were a spring that fed a small reservoir within Jerusalem's walls. This gentle pool contrasted with the "mighty floodwaters" (8:7) which would destroy the people. On **the son of Remaliah** see comments on 7:4. Others interpret "this people" to refer to Judah (the house of Ahaz and his people). They had rejected God ("the gentle waters") and therefore the mighty flood (Assyria) would come and engulf them. This of course happened in 701 B.C. when the Assyrians invaded Judah.

**8:7-8.** Because Israel allied with Aram, she would be swept away by **the mighty floodwaters** from **the River,** a normal designation for the Euphrates River, which ran through the Assyrian Empire. **The king of Assyria** (cf. 7:17) would **sweep** down on the Northern Kingdom like a river in flood stage overflowing **its banks.** Amazingly this "floodwater," that is, Assyria, would continue **on into** the land of **Judah** (701 B.C.). Assyria would cover Judah up **to the neck,** meaning that Judah would be almost but not quite drowned.

Isaiah changed figures of speech and pictured Assyria as a giant bird whose **wings** would **cover** the entire **land,** ready to devour it.

This message was given to **Immanuel** ("God [is] with us"). Isaiah had used that word (7:14) when he told Ahaz that a boy, soon to be born, would be a sign that the nation would not perish at the hands of Aram and Israel. Now the Assyrians would try to "drown" the land of Judah. But the word Immanuel assured the hearers that God had not forgotten His covenant people and would be with them (cf. 8:10). The next verses (vv. 9-15) discuss that fact.

### c. The coming victory from God (8:9-15)

Though Judah would be almost defeated by the Assyrian invasion (vv. 1-8), Isaiah noted that Judah should not fear because she would experience victory.

**8:9-10.** The great truth of chapters 7-9 is that God was with Judah. Isaiah uses the same term Immanuel to close verse 10—**God is with us.** Even though the **nations** would **raise** a **war cry** and **prepare for battle** against Judah, they would not succeed. They would **be shattered,** a fact stated three times in verse 9 for emphasis. Even though they would carefully work out a **strategy** and a **plan** for battle they would not succeed because God was with Judah ("Immanuel" in Heb.; cf. 7:14; 8:8). That great truth separated Judah from all other nations of the world. Because God has promised to be with His people they were to have faith in Him no matter how bad their circumstances. He would not desert them. Thus God and Isaiah were proved right, and Ahaz was rebuked for his lack of faith (cf. 7:9).

**8:11-15.** The Lord had promised to be with His people (v. 10), but many in both Israel and Judah refused to believe He would keep His promise. The LORD warned Isaiah **not to** be like many of those **people** (v. 11). Again Isaiah emphasized that the people of Judah should not be afraid of the Aram-Israel alliance or of the Assyrian threat looming on the horizon (v. 12). Rather they were to be afraid of **the LORD Almighty. He is the One** they should **fear** and **dread** (v. 13; cf. **fear** and **dread** in v. 12 and see the comments on "fear" in Deut. 4:10). The Lord **will be a sanctuary,** a place of safety, for those who believe in Him, **but for** those who do not believe Him, He will be the means of destruction (a **stone . . . a rock. . . . a trap, and a snare**). Peter quoted part of Isaiah 8:14 (1 Peter 2:8), referring to those who reject Jesus Christ. Isaiah's message follows an emphasis in the Old Testament. God promised that those who believe in and obey the Lord will be blessed but those who refuse to believe in and obey Him will be disciplined.

### d. The names that confirm God's coming help (8:16-18)

**8:16-18.** Having been warned by God "not to follow the way of this people" (v. 11), Isaiah reaffirmed his dependence on God. By binding **the testimony** and sealing **the Law** (cf. v. 20), Isaiah was in effect inscribing it on the hearts of the

Lord's **disciples.** Because Hebrews 2:13 ascribes Isaiah 8:17c-18a to Christ, some interpreters feel that all of Isaiah 8:16-18 was spoken by the Messiah. Certainly the attitude conveyed in these verses was that of the Lord Jesus Christ. But in the context of Isaiah 7–9 these words should be ascribed to Isaiah (with the writer of Heb. applying them to Christ). This was the prophet's attitude in spite of all the opposition he saw around him. Isaiah's confidence is expressed twice in 8:17. **I will wait for the LORD** and **I will put my trust in Him.** The fact that the Lord was **hiding His face** (withholding His blessings) was no surprise to the people of faith. The Lord's withdrawal was because most of the Judahites failed to follow Him. Even so, Isaiah still had confidence in the Lord, knowing that he and his **children** were **signs and symbols** of the Lord's sovereign rule **on Mount Zion** (Jerusalem; cf. 2:3).

In what way were they signs and symbols? Each one had a name that held significance for the nation's future. Isaiah's name, "Yahweh is salvation," was a reminder that God will ultimately deliver His people. Maher-Shalal-Hash-Baz's name reminded the people that the Aram-Israel alliance would be broken by the Assyrians who would plunder those nations. The name Shear-Jashub kept before the people the truth that a believing remnant would return from captivity (cf. 10:21-22).

### e. The coming deliverance of Judah by God's Word (8:19-22)

**8:19-22.** Isaiah again spoke of the people's sinful bent. Most people want to know the future. Even people in Judah were pulled into the pagan practice of consulting **mediums and spiritists,** who specialized in trying, by whispering and muttering, to contact **the dead** (cf. comments on Deut. 18:10-12). Isaiah questioned the rationality of going to the dead to find out the future instead of inquiring of the living **God.** The place to look was in **the Law and . . . the testimony** (cf. Isa. 8:16), which contained everything the nation needed to know about her future. A person's failure to heed God's **Word** means he has **no** spiritual **light** (cf. John 3:19-20). Spiritists and mediums and those who consult them will eventually be judged by God (Isa. 8:21-22). In

their distress they will look up to **God** and **curse** Him and **look** to **the earth** where they will face **distress** and then **be thrust into . . . darkness** (cf. 2 Peter 2:17). Ironically those who seek to consult the dead will be forced to join them!

### f. The future deliverance of the nation (9:1-7)

In these verses Isaiah spoke of the coming Deliverer who will effect the changes in the nation of which the prophet had been speaking. The Messiah's coming will lead the nation into joy and prosperity, which had been lacking for years. His coming will fulfill the promises to Abraham and David about the prosperous kingdom. The "child" motif again is evident (v. 6; cf. 7:14-16; 8:1-4, 18). The Child will grow up to be the Deliverer (9:7), not a *sign* (8:18) of deliverance but the Deliverer Himself. He will effect the changes necessary for prosperity and spirituality to come to the nation.

**9:1.** A time will come when **gloom** and darkness (8:22) will be a thing of **the past.** The gloom on the northern section of Israel came because of discipline. God **humbled . . . Zebulun and . . . Naphtali** for a while. Though Isaiah was probably using these two tribal names to represent the Northern Kingdom, it is striking that Jesus' upbringing and early ministry was mostly in that very area near the Sea of Galilee. His presence certainly "honored" that area. In 732 B.C. this northern portion of Israel became an Assyrian province under Tiglath-Pileser III, thus humbling the people there and putting them in gloom. Under Gentile domination, that area was called **Galilee of the Gentiles.**

**The way of the sea** describes a major international highway running through this region. This is the only place where the Bible used this phrase, but it appears often in Assyrian and Egyptian records. The invading Assyrian soldiers took that route when they invaded the Northern Kingdom. From that area the Messiah will arise and will wipe away the gloom and darkness brought on by Gentile domination.

**9:2.** With typical Hebrew parallelism the prophet described the effect of the Messiah on this northern part of Israel. **The people** were **in darkness** (cf. 8:22) and in **the shadow of death.** Then they saw **a great light** and **light . . . dawned** on them. Matthew applied this passage to Jesus, who began His preaching and healing ministry in that region (Matt. 4:15-16).

**9:3-5. You** probably refers to God the Father, who will lead the people from spiritual darkness into light (v. 2) by sending the Child (v. 6), the Messiah. The light will increase **their joy** like the joy at harvesttime or the joy of winning a battle and **dividing the plunder.** "Joy" is another emphasis of Isaiah's, mentioned more than two dozen times in the book. This will be a supernatural work of God much like the nation's deliverance when Gideon defeated Midian (Jud. 7:1-24; Isa. 10:26). It will be like taking a burden off one's back (9:4). At that time, after the Child-Messiah will come, the implements of warfare will be destroyed (v. 5) because in His reign of universal peace implements of war will not be needed (cf. 2:4).

**9:6-7.** Here Isaiah recorded five things about the coming Messiah.

1. He was to be born **a Child.** The implication, given in parallel style, is that this Child, **a Son,** was to be born into the nation of Israel (**to us**) as one of the covenant people.

2. He will rule over God's people (cf. Micah 5:2) and the world (Zech. 14:9). **The government will be on His shoulders** figuratively refers to the kingly robe to be worn by the Messiah. As King, He will be responsible to govern the nation. In Isaiah's day Judah's leaders were incompetent in governing the people. But the Messiah will govern properly.

3. He will have four descriptive names that will reveal His character. He will be the nation's **Wonderful** (this could be trans. "exceptional" or "distinguished") **Counselor,** and the people will gladly listen to Him as the authoritative One. In the kingdom many people will be anxious to hear the Messiah teach God's ways (2:3). He is also the **Mighty God** (cf. 10:21). Some have suggested that this simply means "a godlike person" or hero. But Isaiah meant more than that, for he had already spoken of the Messiah doing what no other person had been able to do (e.g., 9:2-5). Isaiah understood that the Messiah was to be God in some sense of the term.

This Deliverer will also be called the **Everlasting Father.** Many people are puzzled by this title because the Messiah, God's Son, is distinguished in the Trinity from God the Father. How can the Son be the Father? Several things must be noted in this regard. First, the Messiah, being the second Person of the Trinity, is in His essence, God. Therefore He has all the attributes of God including eternality. Since God is One (even though He exists in three Persons), the Messiah is God. Second, the title "Everlasting Father" is an idiom used to describe the Messiah's relationship to time, not His relationship to the other Members of the Trinity. He is said to be everlasting, just as God (the Father) is called "the Ancient of Days" (Dan. 7:9). The Messiah will be a "fatherly" Ruler. Third, perhaps Isaiah had in mind the promise to David (2 Sam. 7:16) about the "foreverness" of the kingdom which God promised would come through David's line. The Messiah, a Descendant of David, will fulfill this promise for which the nation had been waiting.

The Messiah is also called the **Prince of Peace,** the One who will bring in and maintain the time of millennial peace when the nation will be properly related to the Lord. Together, these four titles give a beautiful picture of the coming Messiah's character (Isa. 9:6 includes the first of Isaiah's 25 references to peace.)

4. The Messiah, seated **on David's throne** (Luke 1:32-33), will have an eternal rule of **peace** and **justice.** His rule will have **no end**; it will go on **forever** (cf. Dan. 7:14, 27; Micah 4:7; Luke 1:33; Rev. 11:15). Following the kingdom on earth, He will rule for eternity. He will maintain **righteousness** (cf. Jer. 23:5), as His rule will conform to God's holy character and demands.

5. This will all be accomplished by **the zeal of the LORD Almighty.** The coming of the millennial **kingdom** depends on God, not Israel. The Messiah will rule because God promised it and will zealously see that the kingdom comes. Without His sovereign intervention there would be no kingdom for Israel.

Apparently Isaiah assumed that the messianic Child, Jesus Christ, would establish His reign in one Advent, that when the Child grew up He would rule in triumph. Like the other prophets, Isaiah was not aware of the great time gap between Messiah's *two* Advents (cf. 1 Peter 1:10-12; and see comments on Isa. 61:1-2).

### 3. EXILE FOR THE NORTHERN KINGDOM (9:8–10:4)

After giving a glorious description of the coming Messiah, who will usher in the kingdom for the nation and whose reign will last forever, Isaiah focused on the nation in his day. Some have questioned why Isaiah placed these verses here. But, characteristic of this great prophetic writer, he alternated the message of judgment with the message of blessing. In contrast with the Messiah's future reign of justice and righteousness (9:6-7; 11:4; 16:5; 28:6, 17; 32:16; 33:5; 42:1, 3-4; 51:5), the nation in Isaiah's day was ruled by leaders who did not care about the people under them (cf. 5:7).

#### a. Israel judged because of arrogance (9:8-12)

**9:8.** Though Isaiah was writing to the nation of Judah he often used the Northern Kingdom of **Israel** (also called **Jacob**) as an example of the fact that God judges His sinful people. The **message** was one of coming judgment on the North. When these words were written, the Northern Kingdom was already in some disrepair (v. 10a). The coming **fall** of Israel (in 722 B.C.) should have warned Judah that God is active in the affairs of His people. Judah should have realized that she too would be destroyed if she persisted in the activities that characterized the North.

**9:9-12.** The coming judgment on Israel would be widely known, but it would not be enough to turn her back to God. **Ephraim,** one of Israel's largest tribes, often represented the entire Northern Kingdom (cf. 7:2, 17). **Samaria** was the Northern Kingdom's capital city. Apparently Israel's inhabitants felt that they would experience only a temporary setback (**the bricks have fallen**) and in proud confidence thought they could **rebuild.** In fact they felt that they would be able to make their nation better than ever. But this was not to be the case. They were going to be squeezed by **Rezin's foes** (Rezin was the king of Aram, 7:1, an ally of Israel). Those foes were **from the east** (other **Arameans;** Rezin was king of part of Aram) **and Philistines from the west** (cf. 2:6). This was the

Lord's doing. But even this judgment did not appease God's wrath because the people continued to refuse to deal with their sin. So God would continue to chasten them. This section (9:8-12) ends with a refrain which is repeated three more times in the following verses: **Yet for all this His anger is not turned away, His hand is still upraised** (vv. 12, 17, 21; 10:4). This repetition heightens the effect of God's intense anger and underscores the certainty of continued judgment.

#### b. The entire nation judged (9:13-17)

**9:13.** The prophet lamented that even though the Northern Kingdom had suffered at the hand of God, they still had **not returned to Him.** So their continued refusal would lead to more judgment. Israel was like a child who stubbornly refuses to obey his parents and therefore is punished more severely.

**9:14-17.** Israel's refusal to turn to God would result in the most severe judgment imaginable. The whole nation, from rich to poor and from old to young, would be cast aside. **Both head and tail** (v. 14, explained in v. 15) is a merism, a figure which gives opposite extremes to include the whole spectrum. **Elders (the head)** and false **prophets (the tail),** guides **and those who are guided,** and **young men . . . the fatherless . . . widows**—these were all **ungodly and wicked** and therefore would be judged by God. On the refrain in verse 17b see comments on verse 12.

#### c. A description of wickedness (9:18-21)

**9:18-21.** The people's **wickedness** (cf. v. 17) is pictured as burning them up **like a** huge **fire** with a large **column of smoke.** The judgment would come not only from God (v. 11) and from enemies of the nation (v. 12), but also from within. The nation would destroy itself by its own wicked deeds. **People** would oppose each other (v. 19), **devour** each other (v. 20), and even entire tribes will be in conflict (v. 21). On the refrain in verse 21b see comments on verse 12.

#### d. Woe to unjust people (10:1-4)

**10:1-4.** The corrupt leaders in Israel were perverting the cause of justice and righteousness, in contrast with the Messiah's justice and righteousness (9:6-7). So Isaiah pronounced **woe** (see comments on 3:9) on those people. The readers should have realized that this woe would befall them if they followed their leaders' wicked ways. Israel's leaders were guilty of six things: They were (a) making **unjust laws** and (b) issuing **oppressive decrees.** These actions were repulsive because the Israelites were supposed to care for each other as members of God's people redeemed from Egyptian slavery by their God. Also they were (c) depriving **the poor** (*dal,* "feeble, weak, helpless") **of their rights,** (d) taking away **justice,** (e) hurting **widows,** and (f) **robbing the fatherless.** These actions, which involved taking advantage of people who could not defend their rights, violated God's Law (Ex. 22:22; 23:6; Deut. 15:7-8; 24:17-18; cf. Isa. 1:17). Because of this behavior, the nation would go into captivity (10:3-4). In **disaster . . . from afar** (i.e., from Assyria) no one would **help** them, as they had refused to help those in need. In **anger** God's judgment would fall (see comments on 9:12).

### 4. ASSYRIA'S FALL AND THE GREAT KINGDOM'S RISE (10:5–12:6)

In this section Isaiah again contrasted two kingdoms: the Assyrian Empire and God's millennial kingdom. Assyria would fall because it dared to defeat God's people. Even though God used the Assyrian Empire to punish Israel, He did not like the attitude Assyria displayed. (Isaiah picked up that theme again in chaps. 13–23.) God's glorious empire will come after the fall of Assyria though not immediately afterward. Isaiah was merely contrasting the two.

### a. The fall of the Assyrian Empire (10:5-34)

(1) Assyria's fulfilling of God's will (10:5-11). Isaiah described Assyria's mission (vv. 5-6) and her motives (vv. 7-11).

**10:5-6.** God had commissioned Assyria to chasten Israel as **the rod of** His **anger** and **the club of** His **wrath.** Because Israel was **godless** and had angered God with her sin, Assyria would **plunder** her cities and ruthlessly **trample** her people. God often uses unlikely instruments to accomplish His purposes in the world (cf. His using Babylon against Judah, which puzzled Habakkuk, Hab. 1:6-17). Isaiah was not claiming that Assyria was godly or that the empire even knew that God was using it to do His bidding. In His

sovereignty He directed Assyria to be His tool for vengeance.

**10:7-11.** Though Assyria was a tool in God's hands (vv. 5-6) God was **not** pleased with her. She had the wrong attitude in conquering Israel. Discounting the greatness of Israel's God, Assyria assumed that Israel and Judah were like any other nation. Assyria had conquered the Aramean cities of **Calno** (the same as Calneh, Amos 6:2), **Carchemish . . . Hamath . . . Arpad, Damascus,** and Israel's capital **Samaria.** So Assyria thought she could easily take **Jerusalem.** Since these other conquered cities had greater gods, in the minds of the Assyrians, than did Jerusalem, that city could be taken more easily (cf. the Assyrians' similar boasting in Isa. 36:19-20; 37:12). Though God was using Assyria, her motives were purely political and expansionist.

(2) Assyria's punishment (10:12-19). **10:12-14.** After using Assyria to punish **Jerusalem,** God would then **punish Assyria** because of the king's **willful pride** evidenced by his **haughty look** (cf. Pss. 18:27; 101:5; Prov. 6:17; 30:13). The words of the Assyrian **king** in Isaiah 10:13-14 express the empire's haughty pride. The king felt that what had been achieved had been done by his **strength** and **wisdom** (six times he said **I** and three times **my**). He took other nations and their wealth as easily as a person takes **eggs** from a **nest.** No one was able to oppose his military might.

**10:15-19.** Because of Assyria's pride, the Lord said He would judge the king of Assyria and his empire. The instrument (**ax** or **rod** or **club**; cf. vv. 5, 24) is not above the one **who uses it.** Therefore Assyria, though used by God, was not above Him. The LORD said He would destroy the Assyrian army by **disease** and **fire.** God would destroy Assyria's soldiers like trees (cf. v. 33-34) consumed by a forest fire. **The remaining trees** (soldiers) would be so few that even **a child could** count them. In 701 B.C. 185,000 Assyrian soldiers surrounding Jerusalem were killed (37:36-37). Then in 609 B.C. the Assyrian Empire fell to Babylon. The fall of the Assyrian Empire is a prototype of the fall of all who oppose God and His plans for His covenant people.

(3) The remnant of Israel. **10:20-23.** In spite of judgment on **Israel,** a **remnant** will return to the land and trust in

(rely on) the LORD (not on Assyria; cf. Hosea 5:13; 7:11; 8:9). In that day often refers to the last days when the Lord will punish the wicked and set up His righteous kingdom (cf. Isa. 4:2). However, here it seems to refer to the more immediate judgment on the Northern Kingdom by Assyria (cf. 10:27) and the return of a remnant from that empire. Though Israel had many people like . . . sand (cf. Gen. 22:17; 32:12; 2 Sam. 17:11), only a few would return. Destruction, though overwhelming, would be fair (righteous) and would be on the whole land (the Northern Kingdom).

(4) Assyria's yoke to be lifted. 10:24-27. Isaiah then assured his readers that the Assyrian burden would be removed from Judah. They need not be afraid of the Assyrians. After God had used them to accomplish His purpose against Israel, He would turn His anger against Assyria and punish her (cf. 37:36-37). This would be like His destruction of the Midianites by Gideon (Jud. 7:1-24; cf. Isa. 9:4) and the two Midianite leaders at the rock of Oreb (Jud. 7:25). God would destroy Assyria (figuratively called the waters; cf. Isa. 8:7) as He destroyed Egypt. God promised to lift the Assyrian burden and yoke from Judah (cf. 9:4).

(5) Assyria's defeat (10:28-34). 10:28-32. The route the Assyrian invaders would take in trying to defeat Judah in 701 B.C. was from the northern boundary of Judah at Aiath (another name for Ai), about eight miles north of Jerusalem, southward to Nob, about two miles north of Jerusalem. The sites of 8 of the 12 towns are known (all except Gallim . . . Laishah . . . Madmenah, and Gebim).

10:33-34. Assyria would not succeed in its plan to take Jerusalem. The LORD Almighty is the One who cuts down the lofty trees (the Assyrian soldiers and leaders; cf. v. 18). Isaiah had already reminded the people that they need not worry about the Assyrian aggression because He was on their side (vv. 24-27). Even Lebanon, known for its thick forests of cedar trees, would fall before God. Certainly, then, Assyria should not think it could escape.

b. The rise of God's glorious empire (11:1–12:6)

The Assyrian Empire would fall (10:5-34), but another empire would arise. This section about God's empire (11:1–12:6) includes a description of the Messiah, the kingdom itself, and the remnant who will inhabit the kingdom. Besides contrasting this kingdom with the Assyrian kingdom, Isaiah also contrasted it with the sinful actions of Israel in his day.

11:1. The Lord would cut down the forests and the mighty trees (10:33-34), that is, foreign soldiers and leaders, but God's kingdom will arise by a Shoot coming up from the stump of Jesse, David's father (cf. Rev. 22:16). Isaiah undoubtedly was thinking of God's promise to David (2 Sam. 7:16) that a Descendant of David will rule over his kingdom (cf. Isa. 9:7) forever. This Branch, the Messiah (cf. Jer. 23:5), will bear fruit, that is, prosper and benefit others. (He is the Root; cf. Isa. 11:10.) This Hebrew word for branch (nēṣer) differs from the word used for branch in 4:2 (ṣemaḥ). However, the concept is the same. (Yônēq in 53:2 for "tender shoot" is still another word.) He will come directly from the line of David (cf. Matt. 1:1) and will fulfill God's promises in the Davidic Covenant.

11:2-3a. In these verses the character and work of the "Branch" are described. The Spirit of the LORD will rest on Him, that is, the Holy Spirit would empower Him (at Jesus' baptism, Matt. 3:16-17) for His work which would be characterized by wisdom . . . understanding . . . counsel . . . power . . . knowledge, and the fear of the LORD. The attributes of the Holy Spirit would characterize the Messiah. Because of His wisdom, understanding, counsel, and knowledge He is the Wonderful Counselor (Isa. 9:6). Isaiah referred to the Holy Spirit more than did any other Old Testament prophet (11:2 [four times]; 30:1; 32:15; 34:16; 40:13; 42:1; 44:3; 48:16; 59:21; 61:1; 63:10-11, 14).

He is characterized by the fear of the LORD and has delight in it (11:3) just as His people should have. To fear God is to respond to Him in awe, trust, obedience, and worship. (Interestingly all three Persons of the Trinity are suggested in vv. 1-2.) The Messiah constantly seeks to do what God the Father wants Him to do. This contrasted with the religious leaders in Isaiah's day who were unconcerned about following God's Word.

11:3b-5. As world Ruler, the Messiah will judge the world (cf. 2:4). But He will **not** be like an ordinary judge who may be swayed by superficial knowledge. He will **judge** impartially and in **righteousness. The needy** and **the poor** will not be oppressed by Him as they often are by human leaders (10:1-2). The oppressed will be the beneficiaries of His justice, and **the wicked** will be slain. His reign will be characterized by **righteousness** (11:5; cf. 9:7; 16:5) **and faithfulness** as if they were integral parts of His clothing, as a **belt** and **sash.**

**11:6-9.** Isaiah described the righteous kingdom which the Messiah will set up. The curse will be lifted, peace and harmony will be present, and wild animals will again be tame and harmless to domesticated animals and humans. The **wolf . . . leopard . . . lion,** and **bear** are mentioned as examples of wild animals that will dwell safely with farm animals (the **lamb . . . goat . . . calf. . . . cow,** and **ox**). **A little child** will be safe with lions, bears, cobras, and vipers (cf. 65:25). And on the temple mount (God's **holy mountain**; cf. 27:13; 56:7; 57:13; 65:11, 25; 66:20) tranquility will prevail.

Many Bible students interpret these verses nonliterally, because they suppose such changes in the animal world are not possible. However, because the Messiah is "God [is] with us" (7:14) and He will be dwelling with His people, it need not be difficult to envision these changes in nature. Though the curse of sin will be removed to some extent it will not be totally removed until the end of the millennial kingdom when finally death will be abolished (Rev. 20:14).

The reason such tranquility is possible is that all **the earth will be full of the knowledge of the LORD** (Isa. 11:9; cf. Jer. 31:34; Hab. 2:14). This means more than people knowing intellectually about the Lord. The idea is that people everywhere will live according to God's principles and Word. Animals will be affected, as well. This will occur in the Millennium when the Messiah will be reigning (Isa. 9:6-7), Jerusalem will have prominence in the world (2:2), and Judah and Israel will be regathered to the land in belief and will be living according to the New Covenant. The Millennium can hardly be in existence now since these factors do not characterize the present age.

**11:10.** Israel will have a special place

in the kingdom because of the Abrahamic Covenant (Gen. 15:18-21; 17:7-8; 22:17-18), the Davidic Covenant (2 Sam. 7:16), and the New Covenant (Jer. 31:33-34). But people in other nations will also benefit from the kingdom. The Messiah, **the Root of Jesse** (cf. comments on "stump of Jesse," Isa. 11:1), will be a means of rallying for the **nations** (cf. v. 12; Zech. 14:9, 16). Jesus Himself made the same point that many people from outside Israel will have a part in God's kingdom (Luke 13:29). God had promised Abraham that through his line all peoples on the earth would be blessed (Gen. 12:3). The dispensational teaching that Israel has a special place in God's program because of His promises to Abraham does not exclude the Gentiles from also having a special place.

**11:11-12.** In verses 11-16 Isaiah spoke of the Lord's gathering the **people** of Israel and Judah from all over the world. He compared it to a second "Exodus," like the release from Egypt about 700 years earlier. That first Exodus was one of Israel's most significant events for in only three months after that God gave the Mosaic Covenant, thus marking the beginning of Israel as a nation.

The remnant will be drawn by God from the north (**Hamath**), south (**Egypt** and **Cush**), east (**Assyria . . . Elam . . . Babylonia**) and west (**islands of the sea**)—**from the four quarters of the earth.** Both **Israel** and **Judah** will be regathered (v. 12; cf. Jer. 31:31-34). This was important as the Northern Kingdom would go off into captivity, and Judahites in Isaiah's day might have thought it unlikely that both parts of the nation would ever be united.

**11:13-14.** In that day of regathering, **Ephraim** (the Northern Kingdom) **will not be jealous of Judah** (the Southern Kingdom) and the South **will** have no hostilities **toward** the North.

Reunited **they** (Israel and Judah) will occupy the land and defeat their enemies. **Philistia** refers to the southwestern edge of Israel along the Mediterranean Sea. **People to the east** may be those in northern Arabia (see comments on Job 1:3) and beyond (see comments on Isa. 11:11). **Edom . . . Moab, and the Ammonites** were south and east of Israel. In the kingdom period Israel will no longer be bothered by these or other enemies (cf. Obad. 19).

**11:15-16.** When Israel returns to her land at the beginning of the Millennium, God will prepare the way for her. **The Gulf of** Suez will be dried up to enable Israelites to return from Egypt and Cush (cf. v. 11), and **the Euphrates River** will be divided into shallow canals so that the people can return to **Israel** from the east. This drying of the waters will be reminiscent of the first Exodus when Israel crossed the Red Sea (lit., "Sea of Reeds") on dry land (Ex. 14:21-22). The return **from Assyria** (Isa. 11:16), perhaps representative of all places from which the remnant would come, will be like Israel's "exit" **from Egypt.** Isaiah did not know when this new Exodus would take place; he may have thought it would occur soon.

**12:1-3.** Chapter 12 stresses that when the remnant is regathered to the land they will rejoice. The two stanzas in this chapter are each introduced by the words "In that day you will say" (vv. 1, 4).

**In that day** (cf. 10:20; 11:10) refers to the time of deliverance which has been described in 11:1–12:6. When the nation is regathered and the Messiah is reigning the remnant, designated by the word **I,** will utter these words of praise. The remnant is distinguished from the nations, referred to in verse 4. In verses 1-3 God is praised because His **anger has** been **turned away,** Israel has been **comforted** (v. 1), and **the LORD is** (i.e., is the Source of) **strength . . . salvation,** and **song.** ("Salvation" is mentioned at the beginning and end of v. 2.) Israel's "salvation" will be more than spiritual peace of mind and deliverance; it will also include prosperity. To **draw water from the wells of salvation** (v. 3) pictures living according to God's principles and thus participating **with joy** in the blessings He will provide.

**12:4-6.** The remnant will thank **the LORD** and will call on each other to let the world know **what** God **has done,** probably meaning what He will have done for Israel and Judah. God's **name** (His revealed character) is to be **exalted** (vindicated) before the world, so that people everywhere will realize that He fulfills His promises. And people will **sing to** Him because of His **glorious** deeds.

The remnant also will remind them-

selves of the greatness of God, **the Holy One of Israel** (cf. comments on 1:4). Being reassured that God is **among** them, they will be joyful (cf. 12:3). Chapter 12 is a fitting climax to the contrast between the fall of the Assyrian Empire, which was threatening Judah in Isaiah's day, and the rise of God's glorious kingdom, which will certainly come. Eventually all the world will know of God's truth.

## C. Judgment on the nations (chaps. 13–23)

A major break occurs between chapters 12 and 13, but not as major as some interpreters have suggested. Even in chapters 13–23 Isaiah reiterated some of the same themes he voiced earlier: God uses various means to punish sin, and will judge those nations who are arrogant against His covenant people. These messages against nine sinful Gentile nations or cities around Judah were probably not written for *them* to read. The messages were probably to be read by God's covenant people to show that God actually will judge Israel's enemies. This would reassure Judah that God will establish His kingdom.

Isaiah wrote these messages when Assyria was about to attack the Syro-Palestine area. The coming devastation caused by the Assyrians would have a tremendous impact on Israel and also on other nations of the Near East. The culmination of Assyrian attacks came when Sennacherib, king of Assyria, sacked the city of Babylon in 689 B.C., thus showing that Babylon, the greatest city in its day, was not immune to the advancing Assyrians. Many commentators have assumed that Isaiah's message in 13:1–14:27 about the fall of Babylon referred to its fall to Medo-Persia in 539. However, it seems better to see this section as pertaining to the Assyrian attack on Babylon in 689. This ties in better with the Assyrian threat Isaiah had written about in 7:17–8:10, beginning with the attacks under the rule of Tiglath-Pileser III (745–727). (See the chart "Kings of Assyria in the Middle and New Assyrian Kingdoms," near Jonah 1:2.)

Each of the three great writing prophets included prophecies about God's judgment on Gentile nations (Isa. 13–23; Jer. 46–51; Ezek. 25–32). Isaiah and Jeremiah emphasized the destruction of

Babylon (though referring to different destructions) whereas Egypt is singled out for severe judgment in Ezekiel's prophecies.

In his oracles Isaiah moved westward from Babylon to Tyre. These prophecies are some of the most difficult in the entire book and it is not surprising that differing views of interpretation are held. Part of the difficulty is the lack of any extrabiblical written records about the destruction of many of these areas. Isaiah was picturing the final destruction God will bring on all the world (Isa. 13:11; cf. vv. 6, 9). But it seems that he was also picturing the soon-coming destruction from the Assyrians. Assyria's stated purpose was to "destroy . . . many nations" (10:7). The Lord would let the Assyrian Empire do that, but later He would judge it for its pride and haughtiness against Israel and her God (10:12-19).

## 1. BABYLON (13:1–14:27)

### a. Introduction (13:1)

**13:1.** This section (13:1–14:27) is ascribed to **Isaiah son of Amoz** (cf. 1:1). This is significant in view of the fact that it is clearly prophecy spoken *before* the fall of Babylon. This is important for many believe that Isaiah 40–66 could not have been written by Isaiah son of Amoz because he could not have prophesied about something yet future. The passage in 13:1–14:27 shows that Isaiah's writing about events *before* they happened *was* possible.

This section is **an oracle,** sometimes translated "burden," as it comes from the verb meaning "to be lifted or carried." It was a weighty or burdensome kind of message to deliver. It is a common term in the prophetic writings (13:1; 14:28; 15:1; 17:1; 19:1; 21:1, 11, 13; 22:1; 23:1; 30:6; Jer. 23:33-34, 36, 38; Ezek. 12:10; Nahum 1:1; Hab. 1:1; Zech. 9:1 [see comments there]; 12:1; Mal. 1:1). Isaiah's oracle concerns **Babylon.** Babylon deserved God's wrath, for that city had long been a rallying point of anti-God activity. From its very beginning (Gen. 11:1-9) it had been characterized by rebellion against God. Over the centuries, as various dynasties ruled over that city, it was viewed as a place of hatred against the God of Israel. Even in the Tribulation it will be a center of hatred against God (Rev. 17–18).

### b. God's army against Babylon (13:2-18)

(1) The forming of God's army. **13:2-5.** The army referred to in these verses is clearly God's because He said He **summoned** His **warriors to carry out** His **wrath** against Babylon; that is, they would do His bidding. This army was **a great multitude. . . . like** an amassing of entire **nations.** Coming **for war** they would assemble **from faraway lands, from the ends of the heavens.** This is not a specific geographical description as much as a way of saying that his great army would include soldiers from many places. Though Isaiah was writing about the military strife in his day, a similar mustering of vast armies will occur just before the millennial kingdom (Rev. 16:12-16).

(2) The nearness of the day of the Lord. **13:6-13. The day of the LORD** refers to the time of the Lord's judgment on the wicked world and/or deliverance of His people. (See comments on "the day of the LORD" under "Major Interpretive Problems," in the *Introduction* to Joel.) In Isaiah's day that judgment was coming because of the tremendous political turmoil of the next several decades that would culminate with the fall of Babylon to the Assyrians in 689 B.C. That political turmoil was similar to the judgment which will come on the whole world just before God establishes His millennial kingdom on the earth. This judgment **from the Almighty** would cause people to be in extreme distress, in pain **like a** woman's **labor** pains (cf. Isa. 21:3; 26:17; Jer. 4:31; 6:24; 13:21; 22:23; 30:6; 48:41; 49:22, 24; 50:43; Micah 4:9-10). The day of the Lord, expressing His **anger** (Isa. 13:3, 13) against sin, will **destroy . . . sinners** (v. 9) and **punish the world for its evil** and its proud attitude toward God (v. 11; cf. v. 19; 10:6, 12-13). The statements in 13:10 about the heavenly bodies (**stars. . . . sun . . . moon**) no longer functioning may figuratively describe the total turnaround of the political structure of the Near East. The same would be true of **the heavens** trembling **and the earth** shaking (v. 13), figures of speech suggesting all-encompassing destruction. Again, all this is similar to the final judgment to come on the world. On the luminaries not shining, see 34:4; Ezekiel 32:7; Joel 2:10, 30-31; 3:15; Zechariah 14:6-7; Matthew 24:29; and on the final shaking

of the earth see Isaiah 24:18; Joel 2:10; 3:16; Haggai 2:6-7, 21-22. Because so many will die in battle, people will be **scarcer than** the rare and valuable **gold of Ophir,** a town probably located on the southwestern coast of Arabia (cf. Job 22:24; 28:16).

(3) The army's unrelenting attack. **13:14-18.** In the day of the Lord, described in verses 6-13, the army formed by God (vv. 1-5) would attack unrelentingly. The people attacked would be utterly powerless to stop the invasion. They would be like **antelope** and **sheep,** defenseless creatures that are easy prey for hunters. People within the Assyrian Empire from other countries would try to escape the coming destruction (they **will flee to** their **native** lands). Terrible things would happen, including death **by the sword** (v. 15), infanticide, plundering, and rape (v. 16). The destruction would be unrelenting in that the invaders would not be dissuaded by money (v. 17) and they will have **no mercy on** babies (cf. v. 16) or **children** (v. 18).

The statement **I will stir up against them the Medes** (v. 17) has caused much discussion among Bible students. Many interpreters, because of the mention of the fall of Babylon (v. 19), assume that Isaiah was (in vv. 17-18) prophesying Babylon's fall in 539 (cf. Dan. 5:30-31) to the Medes and Persians. However, that view has some difficulties. In the Medo-Persian takeover in 539 there was very little change in the city; it was not destroyed so it continued on much as it had been. But Isaiah 13:19-22 speaks of the *destruction* of Babylon. Also the word "them," against whom the Medes were stirred up (v. 17), were the Assyrians (referred to in vv. 14-16), not the Babylonians. It seems better, then, to understand this section as dealing with events pertaining to the Assyrians' sack of Babylon in December 689 B.C. As Seth Erlandsson has noted, "The histories of the Medes, Elamites, and Babylonians converge around the year 700 in the struggle against the Assyrian world power and . . . Babylon assumes a particularly central position in that great historical drama from the latter years of the 8th century down to the fall of Babylon in 689" (*The Burden of Babylon: A Study of Isaiah 13:2–14:23.* Lund, Sweden: C.W.K. Glerrup, 1970, pp. 91-2).

*c. God's soon-coming destruction of Babylon (13:19-22)*

**13:19-22.** The recipient of this destruction is **Babylon** the city, not the entire empire. Because of her **pride** (cf. v. 11) and godless idolatry Babylon would **be overthrown by God.** The overthrow, as already stated, was done by the Assyrians, God's instrument of wrath under King Sennacherib. Just as God overthrew the wicked cities of **Sodom and Gomorrah** (Gen. 19:24-25), so He would overthrow the wicked city of Babylon. The destruction would be extensive, which was true of Sennacherib's sack of the city. Isaiah's description of the devastation of Babylon—no inhabitants for **generations** and no tents or flocks, but instead **jackals . . . owls . . . wild goats,** and **hyenas**—is typical of the way ancient Near Eastern cultures described the desolate condition of demolished cities (Erlandsson, *The Burden of Babylon,* p. 118). The Hebrew in Isaiah 13:20a can be translated, "She will not be inhabited for a long time and she will not be lived in for generation after generation." A few years after this destruction, Babylon was rebuilt by Sennacherib's son Esarhaddon (681–669 B.C.). All this preceded the rise of the Neo-Babylonian Empire in 626 and its fall to Medo-Persia in 539. Ultimately Babylon will again be rebuilt and then destroyed by God a final time (Rev. 18; cf. comments on Jer. 50:1–51:58). Isaiah was convinced that the destruction he wrote about would come quickly (**her time is at hand**). It came in 689 B.C. (see comments on Isa. 14:3-4a).

*d. God's compassion on Israel (14:1-2)*

**14:1-2.** The fall of Babylon (and of other nations, 14:24–21:17; 23) would assure God's people that He would work on their behalf. In spite of the destruction to come on the nation Israel, God **will** again **have compassion.** This contrasts with 9:17, where Isaiah said God in punishing His nation would *not* have compassion ("pity" translates the same word as "compassion" in 14:1). **Once again He will choose** the nation to be His people, as He had done at Mount Sinai. **Jacob** and **Israel** here probably refer to all 12 tribes, as they do in Exodus 19:3. God's choosing of Israel (and of Judah, Jerusalem, David, and Solomon) is an important Old Testament theme (cf. Deut. 7:6), especially in 1 and 2 Chronicles and the Psalms (1 Chron. 16:13; 28:4-5, 10; 29:1; 2 Chron. 6:6, 34, 38; 7:12; 12:13; 33:7; Pss. 33:12; 47:4; 78:68, 70; 89:3; 105:6, 43; 106:5; 132:13; 135:4). The fact that non-Israelites (**aliens**) will **join** Israel is also a recurring theme in Scripture (Isa. 56:6; 60:10; 61:5). Israel's role will be reversed (14:2): rather than Israel being exiled as **captives** in other **nations**, other nations will serve **Israel.** Israel will be prominent.

*e. A taunt against Babylon (14:3-21)*

(1) The defeat of the tyrant (14:3-8). **14:3-4a.** Verses 3-21 record a song or a **taunt** that will be sung by people freed from the fear of **the king of Babylon.** The song's overall message is that people will be amazed that this great king is cast down like the monarchs of other cities. People will rejoice in his demise for they had lived in fear of him.

Who is this king of Babylon? Many expositors hold the view that he is Satan, the ultimate personification of pride. Tertullian (ca. A.D. 160–230) and Gregory the Great (ca. 540–604) were the first to present this view, now widely accepted. Though verses 12-14 seem to support the view, little else in the chapter does. Though many hold that verses 12-14 refer to the entrance of sin into the cosmos by Satan's fall, that subject seems a bit forced in this chapter. (However, Ezek. 28:12-19 *does* refer to Satan's fall; see comments there.)

It seems more natural to view this proud tyrant as Sennacherib (705–681). There are interesting parallels between the description of the tyrant in Isaiah 14 and the curse against Sennacherib in 37:21-29. But wasn't Sennacherib king of Assyria rather than Babylon? He was king of both because Babylon was a vassal of Assyria from the end of the 10th century B.C. Occasionally the vassal ruler over Babylon revolted against Assyria, but in 728 Tiglath-Pileser III, Assyria's aggressive ruler from 745 to 727, was crowned king of Babylon. Nineveh was Assyria's capital, but Babylon became the center of its cultural life. Because of this assimilation, the worship of Babylon's god Marduk gained popularity in Assyria. Sargon II (722–705) and Sennacherib (705–681), later Assyrian monarchs, also called themselves kings of Babylon. After Sargon II died in 705 there was much

rebellion in the Assyrian Empire. The Elamites put Mushezib-Marduk over Babylon (692–689); he made an alliance with several nations including the Medes. To subdue the rebellion in Babylon, Sennacherib marched there in 689 and destroyed it. He even released over the city's ruins huge volumes of water to attempt to devastate the city (Erlandsson, *The Burden of Babylon,* p. 91). However, a few years later the city was rebuilt by Sennacherib's son and successor Esarhaddon.

Sennacherib's death by assassination (2 Kings 19:37) eight years after he destroyed Babylon would give great joy and comfort to the surrounding nations, especially Judah. (Sennacherib was the king who had failed in his attempt 12 years earlier, 701 B.C., to capture Jerusalem, Isa. 37; 2 Kings 18:13–19:36.)

**14:4b-8.** The one whose **fury** (v. 4; cf. v. 6) would **end** is **the oppressor** who had **struck down peoples** and aggressively **subdued nations.** His death would bring **rest . . . peace** and joy (**singing**) to the entire region. This rest is pictured symbolically by the great cedar trees **of Lebanon** saying that they were then safe. No longer would they be in danger of being **cut . . . down** to provide tribute to Sennacherib.

(2) The death of the tyrant. **14:9-11.** The grave (*šᵉᵓôl*) is pictured as a great throne room where the **leaders** and **kings** of the earth go when they die. **Spirits of the departed** translates *rᵉpāᵓîm,* which is rendered "departed spirits" in 26:14 and "dead" in 26:19; Job 26:5 (see comments on Job 26:5). This tyrant (Sennacherib) is envisioned as having died and as being met by the kings already in the grave. Amazed at the fate of this glorious king, whose splendor had surpassed theirs, they were **all astir.** His coming would even make **them rise from their thrones** (as if they sat on thrones in the grave) to greet him. They would act amazed that he had **become weak** and dead **like** them. Though he had lived in **pomp** with music (**harps**) he would now lie in corruption. **Maggots** and **worms** would decompose his body in the grave.

(3) The arrogance and fate of the tyrant. **14:12-15.** In his military might this great king had **laid low the nations,** including Phoenicia, Philistia, Egypt, Moab, Edom, Cilicia, much of Judah, and

northern Arabia. But he would fall like a **morning star.** The brilliance of a star in the early **dawn** suddenly vanishes when the sun rises. Sennacherib, because of his great power, thought himself godlike, but now by startling contrast he would be in the grave. In the ancient Near East, kings had supreme power; many were deified by their subjects. The people taunting this tyrant pictured him ascribing godlike characteristics to himself. Ascending **to heaven . . . above the stars** and being **enthroned on . . . the sacred mountain** recalls the belief of several Semitic peoples that the gods lived on Mount Zaphon. "Sacred mountain" translates ṣāpôn (lit., "the north"). By ascending the mountain **above . . . the clouds,** he was seeking to make himself **like** God, **the Most High.** (The language used here, of course, is hyperbolical.) Yet he would be **brought** low **to the grave** (**pit** is a synonym for grave). Nothing could save him from death and from decay in the grave.

(4) A lesson to be learned from the defeat of the tyrant. **14:16-21.** One lesson to be learned from the death of this great one is that all kings, no matter how invincible they may seem, will pass from the scene. People would **ponder** Sennacherib's **fate,** finding it hard to believe he was the same one **who** had **made** everyone **tremble** in fear by devastating **cities** and taking so many people **captives** (vv. 16-17). In his death he was not even given a decent burial as are most **kings** who **lie in state** (v. 18). He would be cut off completely, killed **by the sword** and **trampled underfoot** (v. 19). He was assassinated by his sons Adrammelech and Sharezer, who were then unable to rule in his place (**they** would **not rise to inherit the land,** v. 21) because they had to run for their lives (2 Kings 19:37).

*f. Babylon's destruction by Assyria (14:22-23)*

**14:22-23.** After the people's taunt song (vv. 4-21) **the LORD Almighty** affirmed that the people of **Babylon** would be destroyed (v. 22). Ruined by Assyria (689 B.C.) the city of Babylon would be a desolate **place for owls** (cf. 13:20-22). In fact Sennacherib described Babylon in similar words after he destroyed it. Again, this destruction, rather than the takeover by Medo-Persia in 539 B.C., is probably referred to here (see comments on 14:3-4a), because the latter attack did not demolish the city.

*g. Assyria's defeat (14:24-27)*

**14:24-27.** Many interpreters feel that these verses are a separate section. But it seems preferable to see them as part of the oracle beginning in 13:1. Though the Lord was using the Assyrian Empire for his purposes He would eventually judge that empire harshly (10:5-19). Assyria's plan to destroy Jerusalem was thwarted (10:7), but God's plans would be carried out (14:24). He would **crush the Assyrian** in His **land, on** His **mountains** (v. 25). This probably refers to the great slaughter of the Assyrian army when it surrounded Jerusalem (37:36-37). Because of God's sovereign control **over all nations** nothing can thwart His plans by turning back **His hand** (14:27).

2. PHILISTIA (14:28-32)

**14:28-32.** This oracle, though written about Philistia, was for Judah's benefit (cf. v. 32). Isaiah received **this oracle** (cf. comments on 13:1; Zech. 9:1) from God **in the year** in which **King Ahaz died** (cf. Isa. 6:1, "in the year that King Uzziah died"), 715 B.C. God condemned the Philistine cities for thinking they were safe from destruction. They were rejoicing **that the rod that struck** them was **broken.** This probably does not refer to Israel, or to Judah's King Ahaz, but to Assyria. Ashdod, the Philistine city, and Judah revolted against Assyria; but in 711 B.C., only four years after this oracle, Assyria defeated Ashdod and made Philistia an Assyrian province. This happened under Assyria's ruler Sargon II (722–705; cf. 20:1). Therefore Philistia had felt secure (**in safety,** 14:30) but it would suffer defeat **by famine** and the sword. Philistia should **wail** since Assyria was coming like an uncontrollable **cloud of smoke.** However, **Zion** (Jerusalem) need not fear for it would not fall till much later (to Babylon in 586).

3. MOAB (CHAPS. 15–16)

A major question pertaining to this prophecy is when the oracle was written. In the final paragraph (16:13-14) God said that judgment would come on Moab "within three years." For the views as to what this refers to, see the comments on those verses.

For centuries Moab, east of the Dead Sea, had been an enemy of Israel. In Israel's wilderness wanderings, Moabite women seduced Israel's men (Num. 31:15-17). In the time of the Judges Israel was oppressed by Moab for 18 years (Jud. 3:12-14). Saul fought Moab (1 Sam. 14:47) and David defeated Moab (2 Sam. 8:2, 12). Solomon was influenced by his wives to build an altar to Moab's god Chemosh (1 Kings 11:7-8). Mesha, Moab's king, had to pay tribute to Ahab, king of Israel (2 Kings 3:4). After Ahab died (in 853 B.C.) Mesha rebelled against Joram (also called Jehoram) but was defeated (2 Kings 3:5-27). The destruction of Moab described in Isaiah 15–16 caused the Moabites, under Assyrian attack, to flee south to Edom.

### a. The defeat of Moab (chap. 15)

(1) Lament over Moab. 15:1-4. In chapters 15–16 Isaiah mentioned the names of several Moabite cities and towns. Ar and Kir had been destroyed before Isaiah recorded this oracle. These unlocated towns may have been near the southern end of the Dead Sea. Dibon (modern-day Dhiban) was one of Moab's main cities. Nebo, not to be confused with Mount Nebo, is either present-day Khirbet Ayn Musa or Khirbet el Mukkayet. Medeba is modern-day Madaba. Shaving one's head (cf. Job. 1:20; Jer. 47:5; Ezek. 7:18; Amos 8:10; Micah 1:16) and cutting off one's beard were signs of humiliation (Isa. 7:20; Jer. 48:37). Wearing sackcloth, coarse dark cloth, pictured one's dejected inward state of mourning (see comments on Isa. 3:24). Here the Moabites were bewailing the last of their cities. People in Heshbon and Elealeh (cf. 16:9), in northern Moab, wailed. Even Moab's soldiers wailed because of their inability to protect their cities.

(2) Moab's flight from the enemy. 15:5-9. Isaiah's heart was emotionally disturbed by Moab's distress (cf. his similar heart tugs in 21:3-4; 22:4). The Moabites, fleeing the invading Assyrians, went south into Edom. Zoar was the northernmost Edomite city, directly south of the Dead Sea. Eglath Shelishiyah has not been discovered, but it was probably in the desert region. Luhith is unidentified but it is linked in parallel structure to

Horonaim (cf. Jer. 48:34), which was in southern Moab.

The waters of Nimrim (Isa. 15:6) probably refer to the Wadi en-Numeirah, in southern Moab. Since it was dried up, the refugees went farther south to the Ravine of the Poplars, possibly near the Dead Sea's southern tip. The wailing extended to Eglaim and Beer Elim, sites presently unknown, but perhaps near Moab's southern border. Perhaps Dimon (v. 9) is Dibon (cf. NIV marg.). The water supply there was bloody, indicating much death and destruction had occurred there. But the bloodshed was not over. More terror was to come. It was as if the survivors were being chased relentlessly by a lion.

### b. Protection for Israel (16:1-5)

16:1-5. In the midst of the devastation coming on Moab, protection was to be found in Israel. The Moabites had now fled all the way south to strongholds in Edom such as Sela, about 50 miles south of Moab's southern border. If they really wanted to be safe they should have joined themselves to Jerusalem (the Daughter of Zion; cf. 1:8), sending lambs on ahead as tribute. Isaiah could suggest this because he had already prophesied that Jerusalem would be spared from destruction by Assyria (10:24-34). Frustrated like . . . birds . . . the women of Moab were begging for protection and help (16:2-4a). But, as God promised, eventually the destroyer—also called the oppressor and the aggressor—would himself by destroyed (cf. 14:4-5). God in His love (ḥesed, "loyalty") will see that the One from the house of David, the Messiah, will sit on David's throne (2 Sam. 7:16) and judge the world fairly (in justice and righteousness, a frequent topic in Isaiah's book; cf. Isa. 9:7; 11:4; 28:6; 32:16; 33:5; 42:1, 3-4; 51:5). Only through Judah could this be accomplished; the forces of Moab were obviously inadequate.

### c. The pride of Moab (16:6-12)

16:6-12. Isaiah exposed the pride and conceit of Moab (cf. Assyria's pride, 13:11). The people of Moab should have realized their impotence before the Assyrians and turned to God through their neighbor Israel, but they refused to do so. Because of their pride, confident that they did not need God, the fruitfulness and productivity of their land would be stopped (16:7-10). Several words indicated that the fruit to be lost was grapes: **raisin cakes** (a delicacy; cf. 1 Chron. 12:40; Hosea 3:1) **of Kir Hareseth** (cf. Isa. 16:11), another city in Moab, possibly the same as Kir (15:1), **vines of Sibmah** (16:8-9), **choicest vines. . . . vineyards** (vv. 8, 10), **wine . . . presses. Harvests** (v. 9) and **orchards** (v. 10) suggest other fruits too. (On **Heshbon** and **Elealeh** in v. 9 see 15:4.) The invading army and the drought which would accompany it would wipe out Moab's chances for survival. Isaiah felt deeply **for Moab** (16:11; cf. 15:5); his **heart** responded to her calamities as the strings of **a harp** respond when played. Moab's religious ritual of sacrificing **at her high place** and praying at **her shrine** would not help alleviate God's judgment (16:12).

### d. The destruction of Moab (16:13-14)

**16:13-14.** **Moab** had already suffered greatly. Now the prophet announced that there would be further destruction **within three years.** And it would be *precisely* that period of time, just **as a servant . . . would count** the years till his servitude would end. This is similar to chapter 7 in which Isaiah told Ahaz that the Aram-Israel alliance would break up in a few years. Possibly this oracle against Moab was written about the same time, picturing Tiglath-Pileser's coming invasion of Moab in 732 (after he invaded Aram). Or perhaps Isaiah was saying that Moab would be attacked in three years (701) by Sennacherib, in the year he invaded Judah. Isaiah's contemporaries could have watched current events to see if **the LORD** really was prophesying through him. When they saw that his words came true, they could be assured that his message of salvation for Judah (16:5) would also come true.

### 4. DAMASCUS (17:1-11)

**17:1-3.** The **oracle** (cf. comments on 13:1) in 17:1-11 was directed against **Damascus,** the capital city of Aram. The Northern Kingdom of Israel had allied with Aram (7:2) against the Assyrian threat. Here (17:1-11) Isaiah was again noting that Aram and Israel would be defeated by the Assyrians (cf. 8:4). **Damascus** would **become a heap of**

**ruins,** no longer **a city.** Since Aroer was a city in Moab, the words **the cities of Aroer** are difficult to understand. Some Septuagint (Greek) manuscripts read that Damascus and her cities will be "abandoned forever." With the cities around Damascus deserted, animals will make the ruins their home (17:2). Both **Ephraim,** representing Israel, and **Damascus,** representing Aram (cf. 7:8), would be defeated (17:3). Assyria defeated **Aram** in 732 and Israel in 722.

**17:4-6.** This is the first of three sections beginning with the phrase **in that day.** The others are verses 7-8 and verses 9-11. This refers to the time of God's wrath on His enemies followed by His blessings showered on His people. In some passages, it has eschatological implications (referring to the Tribulation and the Millennium), but in others it refers only to the current situation. In verses 4, 7, 9 the phrase "in that day" refers to the situation mentioned repeatedly throughout the first portion of Isaiah—the invasion of Aram and Israel by the Assyrian army. Because of that invasion Israel would face difficulties, compared to **the fat of** one's **body** wasting **away** (v. 4), and to the barren appearance of a field (v. 5) and **an olive tree** (v. 6) after harvest. **The Valley of Rephaim** (cf. Josh. 15:8; 18:16) was a fertile area west of Jerusalem where David had twice defeated the Philistines (2 Sam. 5:18-20, 22-25). As a few **olives** are left on an olive tree's higher **branches,** so a few people would be left, but most of them would be slaughtered.

**17:7-8.** When Israel would be invaded by the Assyrians, God's people would **look to their Maker** to see **the Holy One of Israel** (cf. comments on 1:4). When faced with the terror and distress of warfare they would realize the inadequacy of worshiping idols. **The altars** were those set up to idolatrous gods, not to the true God. **The Asherah poles** were wooden symbols of Asherah, Canaanite fertility goddess and consort of Baal. In the Northern Kingdom of Israel, widely influenced by Baalism, were many Asherah-worshipers. But when under Assyrian attack, Israel would realize that only the Lord could deliver them.

**17:9-11.** As a result of the judgment **in that day** (see comments on v. 4) Damascus and her **strong cities** would be abandoned and **thickets and underbrush** would grow. Because of her unfaithfulness to the true **God** and her having **forgotten** Him, her efforts at planting **vines** and getting a **harvest** (as if she were secure, in a time of peace) would be fruitless. The plants would be diseased and the people would be in **pain.**

5. THE LAND OF WHIRRING WINGS (17:12–18:7)

**17:12-14.** Many interpreters place verses 12-14 with the previous section. However, the fact that **Oh** (*hôy*; see comments on 3:9) is the same Hebrew word translated "woe" in 18:1 may indicate that 17:12-14 goes with chapter 18.

**The raging . . . nations** (17:12; cf. Ps. 2:1) are said to be **like the roar of surging waters.** These **peoples** were the Assyrians, whom God was using to judge His people. Apparently the "nations" (pl.) means the particular nation which was the dominant power in its day, namely, Assyria. When God would punish (rebuke) **them** (the Assyrians), they would become **like chaff** (cf. Isa. 29:5), the light and useless part of grain which, when winnowed, blows away. How appropriate that though Assyria brought **terror** in **the evening,** the enemy would be **gone** before **morning,** for such was the case with the Assyrian army (37:36-37). Though the Assyrian soldiers had plundered many cities of Judah, 185,000 soldiers were slaughtered overnight.

**18:1-2.** The message in chapter 18 is directed against **the land of whirring wings,** the nation of **Cush.** (On the word **woe**; see comments on "Oh" in 17:12 and comments on 3:9.) The whirring wings may refer to locusts. Cush included modern-day southern Egypt, Sudan, and northern Ethiopia. Apparently the Cushites sent **envoys** in swift-moving **papyrus boats** (cf. Job 9:26) to suggest that Israel form an alliance with them against the Assyrians. The Cushites, a people who were **tall,** fearsome, and **aggressive,** spoke a language that would have sounded **strange** to Hebrews because it was non-Semitic. Like Egypt, Cush **is divided by rivers** (cf. Isa. 18:7) that is, by branches of the Nile. Nothing is known elsewhere in the Bible or from extra-biblical sources about any contacts of this nation with Israel in a joint venture against Assyria.

**18:3.** The prophet exhorted the Cushites to go back home and not try to form an alliance because the Lord would defeat the enemy at the proper time. The Cushites represented **all** the **people of the world** who desired to see the Assyrians fall. But the Lord promised through Isaiah that **when** the time would come to fight the Assyrians they would know it and would see the enemy fall.

**18:4-6.** God's plans would linger much **like** the summer **heat** and harvest **dew. The Lord** told Isaiah that He would wait till the proper time to cut off the enemy. Isaiah had already been given the reason for this (10:12, 25, 32). But the Assyrian army first had to complete the task God gave them, to punish the people of Israel by taking them captive. However, once God's purposes had been accomplished He would intervene and **cut** them **off** (18:5) just when they, like grapes, were beginning to ripen, to extend their empire. They would be killed and would **be left** on the mountains as food for wild **birds** in the **summer** and **wild animals** in the **winter.**

**18:7.** After the Assyrian defeat, **the Lord** would cause the people of Cush (cf. vv. 1-2) to take **gifts** to the Lord at **Mount Zion,** where His **name** dwelt (see comments on Deut. 12:5). Whether this occurred after the fall of Assyria is not known. Possibly Isaiah was speaking of the millennial kingdom when peoples from around the world will worship **the Lord** (cf. Zech. 14:16) because of His gracious acts.

6. EGYPT (CHAPS. 19–20)

Chapter 19 focuses on Egypt; chapter 20 concerns both Egypt and Cush (cf. chap. 18). As in the other oracles the historical situation, the impending Assyrian advance throughout the whole region, serves as a backdrop for the prophecies.

*a. Egypt to be punished (19:1-15)*

Some people wanted to look to Egypt for protection against the Assyrian threat. But Isaiah pointed out that Egypt would be no help, because she too would be overwhelmed by God's judgment.

(1) Egypt's internal troubles. **19:1-4.** Judgment was coming against **Egypt** from **the Lord.** God is pictured as riding

**on a swift cloud** (cf. Pss. 68:4, 33; 104:3). In Canaanite mythology this same idea is used of Baal, the god of rain and fertility. However, the Lord, not Baal, is the true Giver of rain (something Egypt would sorely need, Isa. 19:5-10) and fertility. The gods of Egypt—of which there were many (see the chart "The Plagues and the Gods and Goddesses of Egypt," near Ex. 7:14)—would not be able to save their people from coming judgment. Their **idols** would **tremble before Him,** which would cause the people to be disheartened and depressed (Isa. 19:1). The coming judgment would cause internal divisions (v. 2) and despair among the people when they would realize that their gods, only mere **idols,** and their occult practices (cf. **mediums and . . . spiritists,** 8:19; Lev. 19:31; 20:6) could not save them. Now they would be overtaken by **a cruel master and a fierce king,** the Assyrian empire's king. Egypt, who centuries before had been a cruel master over Israel (Ex. 1:11-14), would now be the object of cruelty. This Assyrian king was Esarhaddon, who conquered Egypt in 671 B.C. This judgment would come from **the Lord, the Lord Almighty** (Isa. 19:4), Israel's Master and great covenant-keeping God.

(2) Egypt's lack of fertility. **19:5-10.** To show that the judgment really would be from God, Isaiah said that the destruction would affect nature. A drought would ruin the economy and cause the people whose work depended on **the Nile** to be depressed. **The river** (v. 5) undoubtedly refers to the Nile, Egypt's "lifeblood," the source of the nation's agricultural growth. Without the Nile, Egypt could not have survived. The annual flooding of **the Nile** over the fields enriched the soil. With the drying up of the Nile (brought on by God, not by military conquest), papyrus **reeds . . . plants,** and **every sown field** would wilt (vv. 6-7). **Fishermen** using either **hooks** or **nets** would not be able to pursue their livelihood (v. 8), and those who derived their income from working with **flax** (cf. Ex. 9:31; which depended on water for its growth), or **linen** made from flax, or other **cloth,** would not be able to ply their trade (Isa. 19:9-10). The entire economy depended on **the Nile** River.

(3) Egypt's wisdom unable to help. **19:11-15. Egypt** was well known in the ancient world for its wisdom writings and its **wise men.** But Isaiah warned **Egypt** not to count on her wise men to save the nation from the coming destruction. **The officials of Zoan** (vv. 11, 13; cf. Zoan, a city in Egypt's Delta, in Num. 13:22; Ps. 78:12, 43; Isa. 30:4; Ezek. 30:14), **the wise counselors of Pharaoh** (Isa. 19:11), and **the leaders of Memphis** (v. 13; cf. Jer. 2:16; 44:1; 46:14, 19; Ezek. 30:13, 16; Hosea 9:6) thought their wisdom might save them from their coming judgment. But their wisdom was foolishness compared with the wisdom of **the Lord Almighty** who was planning the onslaught. No one in **Egypt** could do anything to avert the destruction; they were like staggering drunkards before **the Lord.** Neither the leaders (the **head** and the **palm branch**) nor the populace (the **tail** and the **reed;** cf. Isa. 9:15) could hold back God's judgment. At one time **Zoan** was Egypt's capital city (ca. 2050-1800). Memphis, on the Nile about 20 miles north of Cairo, was the first capital of united **Egypt** (ca. 3200 B.C.) and one of the major cities during much of its long history.

### b. Israel to control Egypt (19:16-25)

The phrase "in that day" appears five times in this passage (vv. 16, 18-19, 21, 23). As stated earlier (see comments on 17:4, 7, 9) the phrase often refers to judgment followed by blessing. In 19:16-25 Isaiah emphasized the outcome of the judgment on Egypt; eventually Egypt will fear the Lord, realizing that He is the true God.

(1) Judah's control of Egypt. **19:16-17.** In contrast with Isaiah's day when Judah was thinking about turning to Egypt for help, a time will come when Egypt will recognize **Judah** as the dominant force in the world. **The Egyptians will be like women,** that is, Egypt will be in **terror** of Judah because they will realize that **Judah** is under **the uplifted hand** (strength) of **the Lord Almighty.** This will be a reversal of the situation in the prophet's time.

(2) Egypt's allegiance to the Lord. **19:18.** The **five cities in Egypt** no doubt represented the rest of the nation. To **speak the language of Canaan** apparently does not mean that the Egyptians will stop speaking their own language. Rather, because of their new worship (swear-

ing **allegiance to the LORD Almighty**; cf. vv. 20, 25) in offering sacrifices in Jerusalem, they will have to be fluent enough in Hebrew to get by (cf. vv. 19, 21; Zech. 14:16-19). The meaning of **the City of Destruction** (*heres*) has caused much debate. It seems preferable to follow the reading preserved in the Dead Sea Scrolls and the Vulgate, namely, "the City of the Sun" (*ḥeres*), meaning Heliopolis (cf. NIV marg. and Ezek. 30:17). Heliopolis, one of the major cities in the south end of Egypt's Delta, was dedicated to worship of the sun god. Such a significant change (i.e., worshiping the Lord instead of the sun god) will prove to the world and to Israel that Egypt will be serious in its new worship.

(3) True worship to be instituted. **19:19-22.** In **Egypt an altar** will be built **to the LORD** along with **a monument . . . at** Egypt's **border. Egypt** will openly avow that she is worshiping the God of Israel. This will be national policy (suggested by the monument, which **will be a sign and witness**) and also private worship (suggested by the altar). **Egypt** will be in the same position as Israel, God's covenant people, for when the Egyptians will ask God for help **He will** give it to them (v. 20). They will also be involved in the sacrificial worship system (v. 21; cf. Zech. 14:16-19; Mal. 1:11), and God will **heal them** after they repent and ask for help. This situation was almost unbelievable for the people of Judah in Isaiah's day. But it *will* occur. It will take place after the Messiah has returned and established His millennial kingdom.

(4) Peace to be established on earth. **19:23-25.** The situation described by Isaiah in verses 19-22 will not be limited to Egypt. **Assyria** and the rest of the earth will also be recipients of blessing **in that day,** the Millennium. People will travel on **a highway from Egypt to Assyria,** and people in those two nations—enemies in Isaiah's day!—**will worship together.** In Isaiah's day Judah was hoping that Egypt would save her from the **Assyrians.** But remarkably, in the Millennium these three powers, **Assyria, Egypt,** and **Israel,** will have a harmonious, peaceful relationship under God's hand of blessing. All this, of course, will fulfill part of the promise to Abraham that "all peoples on earth will be blessed through" him (Gen. 12:3).

*c. Egypt's inability to help Israel (chap. 20)*

**20:1.** Isaiah interposed a narrative section here to drive home what had been said in chapter 18 against Cush and in 19:1-17 against Egypt. Some in Judah wanted to form an alliance with these two nations to help stave off the Assyrian threat. Chapter 20 shows the foolishness of such a course of action. In 711 B.C. **Ashdod,** a Philistine city, was captured by the **commander**-in-chief of the Assyrian king **Sargon** II (722–705). The capture of Ashdod was to signal to the Judahites that they could not count on foreign alliances to protect them, for the Assyrians believed their advances could not be stopped.

**20:2-6. For three years** Isaiah did not wear his outer garment of **sackcloth** (also the attire of Elijah, 2 Kings 1:8), or his **sandals.** (He was not completely naked.) This object lesson was to show how the Egyptians and Cushites would be treated by the victorious Assyrian forces. When those nations (**Egypt and Cush**) would fall to the Assyrians (Isa. 20:4), the Judahites who thought an alliance with those countries would help them would **be afraid** and ashamed (v. 5). People would realize that if **Egypt** and **Cush** had fallen to **Assyria,** then they had no chance for **escape** (v. 6). Judah, then, should trust in **the LORD** for protection rather than in the foreign alliance they were contemplating.

7. THE DESERT (21:1-10)

Many interpreters assume that since Elam (v. 2), Media (v. 2), and Babylon (v. 9) are mentioned, Isaiah must have been referring to the fall of Babylon to the Medo-Persian Empire in 539 B.C. However, passages referring to the fall of Babylon in 539 indicate that it was something about which Israel was to rejoice (because it soon resulted in the return of the Jews to their homeland), whereas this fall of Babylon was terrifying, something to be feared. "The Desert by the Sea" (v. 1) most likely refers to the area around the gulf known today as the Persian Gulf, that is, territory near Babylon.

As already mentioned, in Isaiah's previous oracles (chaps. 13–20) he wrote of the Assyrian incursion into other countries in the ancient world and the effects it had on the Syro-Palestine region. In 722 B.C. a Chaldean prince from the Persian Gulf region, named Marduk-apal-iddina (called Merodach-Baladan in 39:1), revolted against Assyria, captured Babylon, and was crowned king of Babylon. Elam, a nation northeast of Babylon, supported his revolt. Not till 710 B.C. was Sargon able to evict Marduk-apal-iddina from Babylon. After the death of Sargon in 705 Marduk-apal-iddina along with Elamite troops revolted against Sennacherib. In 702 Sennacherib finally defeated him (and Elam) and devastated his home area around the Persian Gulf. Undoubtedly Isaiah was prophesying about this situation. Hezekiah, king of Judah, and other members of his royal court felt that Marduk-apal-iddina would be able to break the strength of the Assyrian Empire. But Isaiah was warning them that this would not happen.

**21:1.** In this **oracle** (see comments on 13:1) Isaiah pictured an invasion of **the Desert by the Sea** (i.e., Babylon by the Persian Gulf) as being like an approaching **desert** storm. The **invader** was probably Marduk-apal-iddina (Merodach-Baladan) who arose suddenly from the desert regions to revolt against Assyria.

**21:2.** God gave Isaiah a **vision** about the Babylonian uprising against Assyria. The prophet heard the battle cry for **Elam** and **Media** (north of Elam) to attack Babylon and free it from Assyria. I refers to the invader in the vision (see comments on v. 1); he said he would stop **the groaning . . . caused** by **the traitor,** the Assyrian Empire which had caused most nations in the region to "groan" under the devastation caused by her conquests. Apparently Marduk-apal-iddina felt that he would be able to stop the Assyrian advance and thereby liberate the entire region.

**21:3-5.** Isaiah now contrasted his feelings with the actions of those around him. Because of this prophecy he was about to utter he was in **pain** like that of **a woman in labor,** a simile often used by the prophets (see comments on 13:8 and cf. 26:17). **Bewildered,** he trembled and was in a state of **horror** (cf. 15:5-7; 22:4). By contrast, the people around him were living as if nothing was happening. They continued in a festive attitude (21:5a) not realizing the implications of what was happening. Perhaps Isaiah had in mind

the feasting which would be done when Marduk-apal-iddina's (Merodach-Baladan's) men came to Jerusalem (chap. 39). Isaiah realized that Babylon under Marduk-apal-iddina's control could not change what God had ordained. So rather than eating they should have prepared for battle, implied by the words **oil the shields.** Shields made of animal skins needed to be rubbed with olive oil to prevent their cracking.

**21:6-10a.** God told Isaiah to have someone be on the **lookout** for the battle between Babylon and Assyria. The watchman was to look for anyone who would come his way to **report** on the battle (vv. 6-7). The watchman looked **day after day** till finally someone came with the message that **Babylon** had **fallen** and **its gods** lay **shattered on the ground** (v. 9). The emotional impact of this message on the people of Judah, who were hoping Babylon's revolt would be successful, would be stunning. They had hoped that the alliance Hezekiah made with Bablyon would break the Assyrian domination. But it was not to be. Sennacherib pushed Marduk-apal-iddina out of Babylon and as stated earlier (see comments on chap. 13), the Assyrian king eventually destroyed the city in 689 B.C. Babylon's fall seemed like the last straw. Now no one could stop the Assyrian Empire. So Judah felt **crushed** emotionally like grain **on the threshing floor** (cf. Jer. 51:33).

**21:10b.** Isaiah reiterated that his message was from **God.** He was only telling what he had **heard from the LORD Almighty** (cf. comments on 1:9). Judah must not rely on the Babylonians to save them. This man from the Desert by the Sea (Marduk-apal-iddina) would not be successful.

### 8. EDOM (21:11-12)

**21:11-12.** This brief **oracle** (see comments on 13:1) seems to be against Edom because of the reference to **Seir** (21:11). Seir is an alternate name for Edom because the mountains of Seir were given as a possession to Esau and his descendants (Josh. 24:4). The name **Dumah** may be a wordplay on "Edom" since Dumah means silence or stillness (cf. NIV marg.) and **the watchman** in the oracle saw no activity. More likely, however, Dumah is a transliteration of Udumu or Udumai, the Akkadian designation for Edom. Both Tiglath-Pileser (in 734) and Sargon (in 711) mentioned taking tribute from Udumu. Was there any chance Edom's political situation would change? The answer was no, not immediately. Even though **morning** was **coming,** another **night** would follow. It did not look as if the situation would change soon.

### 9. ARABIA (21:13-17)

**21:13-17.** The Assyrian threat is the background of this **oracle** (see comments on 13:1) too. The **Dedanites** (21:13) were a tribe from southern Arabia. **Tema** (v. 14; cf. Job 6:19; Jer. 25:23) was a well-known oasis in northwestern Arabia, and **Kedar** (Isa. 21:16-17; cf. 42:11) was in northern Arabia. This oracle discusses the difficult times the people of **Arabia** would soon experience at the hands of the Assyrians. **Within one year** Kedar's **pomp** would **end** (Kedar was known for its tents, Ps. 120:5; Song 1:5; also cf. Jer. 49:28-29, which were a beautiful black). **The warriors of Kedar** would experience a great defeat (Isa. 21:16-17). The Arabians would be fugitives, running for their lives from the sword. The oracle would be fulfilled, for **the LORD, the God of Israel,** had **spoken** (v. 17). In 715 Sargon II wrote that he had defeated a number of Arabian tribes and had them deported to Samaria.

### 10. JERUSALEM (CHAP. 22)

Chapters 13–23 are more than a catalog of judgments against various nations. They also discuss the responses of various peoples to the Assyrian threat in the days of Isaiah. Jerusalem, "the Valley of Vision," was also under God's judgment and needed to respond properly to the Assyrian threat. That Isaiah was speaking of Jerusalem is evident in 22:9-10.

#### a. Judgment against Jerusalem (22:1-14)

It is not certain which Assyrian invasion Isaiah was speaking of in these verses. Perhaps it was the invasion of Sennacherib, who surrounded Jerusalem in 701 B.C. (chaps. 36–37). From God's perspective the purpose of that invasion was to encourage Judah to turn to Him and repent of her sinful ways. Unfortunately the people did not respond positively to the invasion and used it as a

time for revelry (22:2) and for shoring up the city's defenses (vv. 8-11).

**22:1-4.** This **oracle** (see comments on 13:1) pertains to **the Valley of Vision** (cf. 22:5). Often Jerusalem is referred to as a mountain (e.g., Mount Zion), but here the city is called a valley. This also fits because a valley—the Kidron—runs between two hills directly east of the city. From this city God was revealing Himself to Isaiah; hence it was called the Valley of Vision. Jerusalem was filled with people (in **commotion** and **tumult**; cf. v. 5) from the surrounding towns and villages in Judah. (Sennacherib wrote that he had captured 46 towns of Judah.) The important people (**leaders**) had escaped but were **captured** (v. 3) by the Assyrians. People still inside the city of Jerusalem went **up on the** flat **housetops** (v. 1) to observe the enemy outside the city walls. Because the Assyrian advance had caused **the destruction of** many of Isaiah's **people** (v. 4), he lamented (cf. his remorse in 15:5-7; 21:3-4).

**22:5-8a.** Jerusalem was being besieged and the people inside the walls could do nothing about it. The people realized that the enemy's advancing to the very walls of Jerusalem was **a day** of judgment brought on by **the Lord, the LORD Almighty** (cf. vv. 12, 14-15, 25). The attack was not happenstance; it had come because of the people's disobedience (cf. vv. 12-14). In the city people were in **tumult** and **terror** as they saw the enemy camped outside waiting for an opportunity to get inside to sack and burn the city (v. 5). The Hebrew words for "tumult," **trampling,** and "terror" sound much alike. They are $m^e h\hat{u}m\hat{a}h$, $m^e b\hat{u}s\hat{a}h$, and $m^e b\hat{u}k\hat{a}h$. Soldiers from **Elam,** east of Assyria with its capital at Susa, and **Kir,** perhaps an Assyrian province (2 Kings 16:9; Amos 1:5; 9:7), joined the Assyrian warriors. Perhaps Isaiah mentioned these two areas of the Assyrian Empire to point out (by a figure of speech known as a merism) that troops from all over the empire were now gathered at Jerusalem's very door. Enemy **chariots** were in the **valleys** around Jerusalem, and **at the city gates** enemy **horsemen** were ready to attack (Isa. 22:7). Since Judah was defenseless, this was certainly a frightening time!

**22:8b-11.** One would think that in such a precarious position the nation would turn back to God and repent. Obviously the city could not deliver itself (v. 8a). However, in their sinful condition the people still tried to do things their own way. Rather than count on God for protection they wanted to depend on their own strength. So they got out **the weapons** from **the Palace of the Forest,** which Solomon had built (1 Kings 7:2; cf. 1 Kings 10:17, 21). It got its name from the huge cedar columns brought to Jerusalem from Lebanon. Apparently armaments were stored in that building in Isaiah's day.

At the time of Sennacherib's threat Hezekiah took several defense measures: (a) he repaired broken parts of the wall (cf. 2 Chron. 32:5) of **the City of David** (cf. 2 Sam. 5:7, 9); (b) he collected **water in the Lower Pool** (cf. 2 Chron. 32:4); (c) he demolished some **houses to** use their material for repairing **the wall;** and (d) he preserved the city's **water** supply in **a reservoir between the two walls.** The exact location of this reservoir and the meaning of the two walls and of **the Old Pool** are not known. Perhaps the reservoir refers to the Pool of Siloam which Hezekiah connected to the Gihon Spring (2 Chron. 32:30) by his now-famous underground water tunnel, which extends 1,777 feet and was carved out of solid rock. This marvelous feat of engineering was successful. But it could not be a means of the nation's deliverance, for the people refused to look for help to God who had given them the water **long ago.**

**22:12-14.** When the people saw the enemy they should have repented, realizing they were helpless before the Assyrians. Pulling **out** their **hair** (cf. Ezra 9:3; Neh. 13:25) and wearing **sackcloth** (cf. comments on Isa. 3:24) were signs of mourning. But instead of mourning (22:12) the Jerusalemites "lived it up" in **revelry** (cf. v. 2), banqueting, and wine-**drinking** in the face of their impending death (**tomorrow we die,** v. 13). They did not believe God was powerful enough to save them and to follow through on His promises. Therefore a pronouncement of woe came to the people through Isaiah: this sin of lack of trust in **the LORD would not be atoned for.** Eventually the curses of the Mosaic Covenant (Lev. 26:14-39; Deut. 27:15-26; 28:15-68) would come on the nation of Judah.

*b. Judgment against Shebna (22:15-25)*

**22:15-19.** The reason for this section on judgment (vv. 15-25) is not explicitly stated. **Shebna** was a high court official, a **steward,** involved in the negotiations with Sennacherib when he besieged Jerusalem (2 Kings 18:18, 26, 37; 19:2; Isa. 36:3, 11, 22; 37:2). Some think that his position as steward (secretary) **of the palace** gave him a position second only to the king. Why he was to be deposed from this important **position** is not stated. Perhaps he opposed Isaiah's message of impending judgment. He apparently shared the attitudes of the Jerusalemites Isaiah had described (22:2, 11-13).

The impiety of Shebna apparently involved his trying to make a permanent name for himself by fashioning **a grave,** as people did in many of the surrounding nations. Perhaps he thought that by being buried in a prominent **grave** site (**on the height**) his name would live on in spite of the current conditions. However, Isaiah prophesied that Shebna, rather than having a permanent resting place, would be demoted and would **die** in **a large** foreign **country,** probably Assyria. There is no record of what happened to him other than the prophecy given here by Isaiah.

**22:20-25. Eliakim,** the palace administrator and a godly man, would fill Shebna's important position (vv. 20-21). Eliakim also was involved in the negotiations with Sennacherib (2 Kings 18:18, 26, 37; Isa. 36:3, 11, 22; 37:2). He would be a respected leader (like **a father** to the Judahites) and a faithful administrator who would make wise decisions (22:22). In contrast with Shebna, who was to be cast away, Eliakim was to be **like a** well-driven **peg** (v. 23a), a firm foundation for the nation. He would be an honorable person (v. 23b), and would cause **his family** name to be well known to humble people (figuratively called **lesser vessels**) and to more influential family members (called **bowls** and **jars**). However, Isaiah warned that eventually even this **peg** would come to an end (v. 25), signifying that eventually the kingdom of Judah would be taken away into captivity.

**11. TYRE (CHAP. 23)**

*a. A prophecy of Tyre's fall (23:1-14)*

As in the other prophecies (chaps. 13-22) this one about Tyre also pertains to the Assyrian aggression at the end of the eighth century B.C. Though Tyre was not destroyed until some 200 years later, the trade of this great city was cut off between about 700 and 630 B.C.

**23:1.** This **oracle** (see comments on 13:1) begins with a call to a fleet of merchant ships to **wail** (cf. 23:14) in distress during their trading voyages on the Mediterranean Sea. On **ships of Tarshish** see comments on Ezekiel 27:25 (cf. Isa. 23:14; 60:9). Those ships were docked at the island of **Cyprus,** about 150 miles northwest of **Tyre,** when the news of Tyre's destruction reached them.

**23:2-5.** Phoenicia, with its chief city ports of **Tyre** (vv. 1, 3, 8, 15, 17) and **Sidon** (vv. 2, 4, 12), depended on seafaring trade for its economy. The Phoenicians greatly benefited by the wares she received in international commerce, and in turn those other countries, including **the island** of Cyprus, were **enriched** by Phoenician trade. **Grain** from Egypt was one of the staples channeled through the Phoenician trading centers of **Tyre** and **Sidon.** Shihor (cf. Josh. 13:3; 1 Chron. 13:5; Jer. 2:18) was in eastern Egypt and may be a branch of the Nile River. **The grain of the Shihor** referred to grain grown in the fertile land watered by that part of the Nile. The wealth of Sidon and Tyre (the **fortress,** *māʿōz,* trans. "stronghold" in Pss. 27:1; 37:39; 43:2; 52:7 and "refuge" in Nahum 1:7) did not come from their own efforts. It came by trading with the Mediterranean nations. Thus **the sea,** personified, could say that it had not gone through the **birth** experience; it had produced quick wealth without going through the pain (Isa. 23:4; cf. 66:7-8). But the demise of Tyre was bad not only for Phoenicia; it was also bad for the places from which the trade came, such as **Egypt** (23:5).

**23:6-9.** People in **Tarshish** were to **wail** too (cf. vv. 1, 5, 14) because of their economic losses. Tarshish was rich in silver (Jer. 10:9), iron, tin, and lead (Ezek. 27:12). Therefore Tarshish was probably in the West Mediterranean where mineral deposits were plentiful. Many scholars identify Tarshish with Tartessus in southwest Spain. The people of that region would be in despair because of the fall of that great trading center, **Tyre,** which was a **city of revelry** (cf. Isa. 23:12) and an ancient **city.** According to He-

rodotus Tyre was founded around 2700 B.C. However, the people of Tarshish needed to realize that their difficulty came directly from the God of Israel. **The LORD Almighty** (v. 9) **planned** the humbling of this great and wealthy city (**the bestower of crowns**), proud of its **glory** and **renowned** for its commercial enterprise.

**23:10-14.** Throughout the entire Mediterranean region—from **Tarshish** in the northwest to the **Nile** River in the southeast, and to Cyprus in the northeast (vv. 10, 12)—people would mourn and weep for the fall of **Phoenicia** (v. 11). The Phoenicians would have no more protection than did **the Babylonians** who were defeated by **the Assyrians** (v. 13; cf. 21:1-10). **Reveling** would end in **Sidon,** probably along with the revelry in Tyre (cf. 23:7). (On the words **Virgin Daughter** see the comments on 47:1.) To escape **to Cyprus** would not help. The trading **ships of Tarshish** were advised by Isaiah to **wail** because the Mediterranean world's great trading center would be gone (v. 14; cf. v. 1).

### b. A prophecy of Tyre's future (23:15-18)

**23:15-18.** The **70 years** mentioned by Isaiah (v. 15) were probably from about 700 to 630 B.C. when Phoenicia's trading was greatly restricted by the Assyrians. In 701 Assyria installed Tubuʿalu (Ethbaal III) over **Tyre.** But around 630 Assyria declined in power, enabling Tyre to regain its autonomy and restore its trade.

This 70-year span is called **the span of a king's life** (cf. Ps. 90:10). **But** after **70 years** . . . **Tyre** would again become a trading center, like a **prostitute** (Isa. 23:15-17) who was **forgotten** but who returned to her illicit practice, singing to attract lovers to her again. Tyre would again **ply her trade with** various nations. But this time the profits from her trading would somehow benefit those who feared **the LORD** (v. 18). It is difficult to know exactly what Isaiah was referring to. Some have suggested that the 70 years referred not to the time from about 700 to 630 but to the coming Babylonian Captivity of Judah (605–536 B.C.) and that at the end of those years materials from Tyre were used in construction of the temple complex in Jerusalem which was built by the postexilic community. But Tyre's trading was not restricted during those years (except for Nebuchadnezzar's 13-year siege of the city from 587 to 574).

## D. Punishment and kingdom blessing (chaps. 24–27)

God's judgment on the nations through the Assyrian invasions (chaps. 13–23) forms a backdrop for the Lord's eventual judgment on the whole world (24:1, 4). Known as "Isaiah's apocalypse," chapters 24–27 describe the earth's devastation and people's intense suffering during the coming Tribulation and the blessings to follow in the millennial kingdom.

### 1. A TIME OF JUDGMENT (CHAP. 24)

**24:1-3.** The coming desolation and ruin of the whole **earth** ("earth" is mentioned 16 times in this chap.) will be by the direct intervention of **the Lord,** and will level all of society. No advantage will come from having a high rather than a low position, for all will come under God's hand of judgment (v. 2). The world will be **laid waste and totally plundered** (v. 3; cf. Rev. 6; 8–9; 15–16). This is certain because **the Lord** said so.

**24:4.** In this worldwide judgment, **the earth** will wither (dry **up**). Even important people (**the exalted**) will **languish.** No one will be spared from this eschatological judgment.

**24:5.** The reason such devastation will come is that the **people,** not living as they should, will have **defiled** the **earth.** In creating the world God said it was "very good" (Gen. 1:31). But people in their sin defiled the good earth, by disobeying God's **laws,** violating His **statutes,** and breaking His **everlasting covenant.** "The everlasting covenant" probably refers not to the Abrahamic or Mosaic Covenants but to the covenant people implicitly had with God to obey His Word. Right from the very beginning mankind refused to live according to God's Word (Gen. 2:16-17; 3:1-6; cf. Hosea 6:7). And throughout history people have refused to obey God's revelation.

**24:6-13.** Because people have "defiled" **the earth** by their sins (v. 5), judgment will come. They must **bear** the consequences of their **guilt.** God's judgment is likened to a burning fire that consumes all but a **few** on the earth (v. 6). In the earth's devastation vineyards will wither

and music (with **tambourines** and harps) and parties (vv. 7-9, 11) will stop. The fruit of the vine is often associated in the Bible with joy (e.g., 16:9; Zech. 10:7). **The . . . city** (Isa. 24:10; cf. 25:2), representative of **the** whole **earth** (24:13), will be in **ruins** with all its houses uninhabited. When God pours out His wrath on the unbelieving world in the Tribulation, all will be **desolate** and gloomy. Little will be left, as after the harvesting of olives (cf. 17:6) or grapes.

**24:14-16a.** The word **they** probably refers to the righteous who will be left after God's judgment on the earth. Though few in number (v. 6) they will delight in the fact that the earth is cleansed from people's sin. They will **raise their voices** and **shout** to proclaim **glory to the Lord . . . the God of Israel.** Everywhere—in **the west** (v. 14), **the east** (v. 15), **the islands of the sea** (v. 15), and **the ends of the earth** (v. 16; cf. comments on 5:26)—the same song is proclaimed: **Glory to** God, **the Righteous One.** The believing remnant will view the earth's desolation as a righteous act by the righteous God. It will not be viewed in the way the Assyrian advance was viewed— as a cruel, unfair punishment.

**24:16b.** In contrast with the future joyful song of glory to the God of Israel (v. 16a), the distress in Isaiah's day caused him to pronounce **woe** on himself (cf. 6:5). All around him were **treacherous,** unfaithful people on whom judgment must fall.

**24:17-20.** Because of the people's treachery (v. 16) and their other sins, they would suffer. They would **fall into a pit** used to capture animals or **be caught** by **a snare** (trap). Trying to escape one danger they will be overcome by another calamity. God's judgment will be like a great rainstorm and earthquake. The earthquake will cause great crevices to open in the earth and swallow up people. In the earthquake **the earth** will reel **like a drunkard** and will sway **like a temporary unsturdy hut** in a field, blowing **in the wind.** (This Heb. word for "hut" is used in the OT only here and in 1:8.) Judgment will come because of **guilt** (cf. 24:6), the guilt of the whole world in rebelling against God.

**24:21-23.** Isaiah again (cf. v. 1) stated that the coming judgment will be God's direct intervention: **the Lord will pun-**

**ish.** Natural disasters will occur only because the Lord will cause them to happen. **The powers in the heavens** may refer to spiritual forces opposed to God (cf. Rev. 19:20; 20:2). **The kings on the earth below** undoubtedly refer to political forces that will be banished. Those powers in the heavens and on the earth will become like cattle when the Lord herds them **together** and places them **like prisoners . . . in a dungeon.** Their punishment **after many days** refers to the great white throne judgment after the Millennium when all the unrighteous will have to stand before God and be judged for their evil deeds and lack of faith in Him (Rev. 20:11-15). When this judgment takes place **the LORD,** the Messiah, will be reigning **on Mount Zion** (Isa. 24:23; see comments on 1:8) **and in Jerusalem.** He will reign **gloriously,** that is, His glory will be manifest (cf. 24:15-16). In the 1,000-year kingdom the Messiah **will reign** as King over the earth (Zech. 14:9) from Jerusalem, God's "centerpiece" (Isa. 2:2-4; Micah 4:1-5). After the Millennium and the great white throne judgment God will reign for eternity from the New Jerusalem (Rev. 21:2, 10), which will be filled with the glory of God and therefore will not need the light of **the moon** or **the sun** (Isa. 24:23; cf. Rev. 21:23).

## 2. A TIME OF BLESSING IN THE KINGDOM (CHAPS. 25–27)

### a. The Lord's preserving of His people (chap. 25)

This chapter is a praise psalm extolling the Lord's deliverance of His people. Soon after God in His judgment will wipe out sinful people (chap. 24) the Messiah's glorious kingdom will begin. In poetry Isaiah described the praise that will be ascribed to the Lord in the Millennium for His marvelous work.

(1) Praise to the Lord for the coming kingdom. **25:1-5.** Speaking in the first person Isaiah described the situation which will exist when the kingdom is established on the earth. The prophet ascribed **praise** to the Lord's **name** (His revealed character) for His **marvelous** acts of judgment (vv. 2-3) and deliverance (vv. 4-5). God's judgment on **the city,** representative of the world (cf. 24:12-13), will cause **peoples** from **ruthless nations** to **honor** and **revere** God.

This will fulfill the promise given Abraham that all the world's nations will be blessed through Israel (Gen. 12:3). The theme of Gentiles knowing and worshiping God in the kingdom is common in the prophets (see, e.g., Isa. 2:3; 11:9; 49:7; 56:6; 66:20-21; Zech. 14:16-19; Mal. 1:11).

When the Lord will establish His kingdom on the earth, a reversal of fortunes will occur (Isa. 25:4-5). **The poor** (*dal,* "feeble, weak, helpless") and **the needy** ('*ebyôn,* "oppressed") will be rescued and **the ruthless** will be **stilled.** God's care for the poor and the needy is mentioned many times in the Old and New Testaments. The reversal of fortunes, in which those who depend on God are helped and those who depend on themselves are judged, is a major theme of Scripture (e.g., 1 Sam. 2:1-10; James 5:1-6). **The ruthless** in their harsh treatment of others are **like a storm** and the oppressive desert **heat.** But God's judgment on them will be like **a cloud** that suddenly covers the sun, thus limiting its heat.

(2) Effects of the coming kingdom (25:6-12). The deliverance that the Lord will bring will include the wiping away of death (vv. 6-8), the rejoicing of His people (v. 9), and judgment on His enemies (vv. 10-12).

**25:6.** God's deliverance of His people in the kingdom is pictured as a banquet **feast** on the **mountain** of the **LORD Almighty.** Mountains are often symbols of governmental authority (e.g., Dan. 2:44-45) but here the mountain probably refers to Jerusalem (Mount Zion) from which the Messiah will rule in the kingdom. **Food** will be provided **for all peoples,** which fact once again stresses the worldwide extent of God's kingdom over those who believe. This does not mean that everyone who lives in the Millennium will be saved (though only redeemed people will enter the Millennium at its beginning); instead it means that people in all areas of the world will be saved. **The best of meats and the finest of wines** picture God's ability to supply the needs of His people during that time. Some Bible interpreters say this refers symbolically to God's care for His people in the present age. However, Isaiah was speaking of a future time when (after God's worldwide judgment) His people in Israel and other nations will feast together in peace and prosperity. This is the 1,000-year reign of Christ.

**25:7-8.** Death, pictured as a **shroud** and a **sheet,** the covering placed over a dead body, will be swallowed up or done away with. This will mean that **tears** of grief caused by the separation of the dead from the living also will be a thing of the past. This removal of death and wiping **away** of **tears** will take place at the end of the 1,000-year reign of Christ (Rev. 21:4), when death, Satan, and hell will be thrown into the lake of fire (Rev. 20:14) and the new heavens and new earth established (Rev. 21:1-3). Since God's future kingdom includes both the Messiah's millennial reign and the eternal state, Isaiah telescoped them together (cf. Isa. 65:17-25). Elsewhere the first and second comings of Christ are seen together (9:6-7; 61:1-3). The certainty of future prosperity and joy and absence of death would encourage Judah in Isaiah's day to trust in the LORD and not lose heart.

**25:9. In that day** (cf. 24:21), the day when the believing remnant will be delivered, **they** (the saved ones) **will** affirm their trust **in** the Lord, who **saved** them. In response they will say **let us rejoice and be glad in** the **salvation** He provided. Meanwhile, in Isaiah's day, believers in Judah were to rejoice in the Lord's salvation.

**25:10-12.** Isaiah referred to Moab as representing those who oppose God and will be judged by Him. Moab was east of Israel across the Dead Sea. Israel and Judah had many altercations with Moab, that was known for her **pride** (v. 11; cf. 16:6). She felt that the works of her **hands** and her **cleverness** would protect her, but it would not. Moab—and all God's enemies—will be totally destroyed, **trampled,** and brought **down . . . low** (cf. 26:5) **to the very dust.** Only God's people, in Israel and in other nations, will enjoy God's time of prosperity and blessing.

*b. The redeemed to praise the Lord (chap. 26)*

The prophet wrote a song that will be sung by the redeemed when the Messiah will establish the millennial kingdom. Isaiah was picturing himself standing in the redeemed land with the remnant listening to the people express

their thanks to and confidence in God.

(1) The humble to be exalted (26:1-6). **26:1. This song,** to **be sung in . . . Judah,** first emphasizes the reversal of fortunes (cf. 25:1-5): the humble will be exalted and the oppressors vanquished. In contrast with "the city" that will be destroyed (24:12-13; 25:2), the redeemed will **have a strong city.** Throughout the world the redeemed will live in cities and towns, but the strong city (Jerusalem) where the Messiah will reign pictures the security of the world's redeemed inhabitants. Because of the Messiah's presence there, that city is figuratively said to have **salvation** for **its walls and ramparts.**

**26:2-4.** This city will be opened for **the righteous nation,** a reference to the remnant of Israel. Other nations will have places in the kingdom, but believers in Israel will have special positions.

People who **trust in the LORD** enjoy **perfect** (i.e., complete, genuine) **peace** (cf. Phil. 4:7), now as well as in the Millennium. This availability of inner tranquility encourages believers to continue trusting **the LORD** (Isa. 26:4) because He is firm like a **Rock** (cf. 17:10; 44:8; see comments on Ps. 18:2) and He is **eternal.**

**26:5-6.** In contrast with the righteous who enter this special city of God, people who try to dwell in **the lofty city** (i.e., who persist in their pride) will be abased (cf. 25:12) because they did not trust in Him (26:3-4). **The oppressed** and **the poor** will **trample** those wicked people (v. 6). This was a reversal of fortunes, an act of God's justice against the proud who had taken advantage of the poor. Isaiah was not implying that some special merit was given the poor. He was reflecting the scriptural principle that God has special concern for the poor who seek Him (see, e.g., 25:4).

(2) Deliverance to come from God (26:7-21). The song continues by expressing the certainty that deliverance has come to the remnant, not because of their own efforts, but because of God's work on their behalf. Therefore they will continue to trust in Him.

**26:7-9.** In a confession of trust the prophet affirmed that it is good for people to live righteously, because God smooths out their **path.** That does not mean righteous people never have any problems. Isaiah was reflecting the truth that certain consequences follow one's actions so that if a person lives according to God's rules he will have favorable consequences, but if he disregards God's Word he will experience dire consequences. The remnant walk according to Scripture (God's **laws,** v. 8a) and yearn for God (vv. 8b-9a). Those who refuse to heed God's ways **learn** of God's **righteousness** when they are eventually judged.

**26:10-11.** Many **wicked** people **do not learn righteousness** when God bestows His **grace** (v. 10); they learn it only when He judges them (cf. v. 9). Living where the righteousness of God is revealed (**in a land of uprightness,** i.e., Judah), many people still did not live righteously. A favorable environment is not enough; there must be a change of heart.

Though chapter 26 is a song of the redeemed, verses 10-11 indicate that Isaiah was writing for the people of his day, many of whom were spiritually insensitive, unconcerned about God's **majesty** and works (His **hand**). Isaiah asked the Lord to **put** them **to shame** (v. 11) and to take vengeance on them. In this way God's character would be vindicated. Isaiah was not asking this for his own sake but for the sake of God who desires that His people lead holy lives.

**26:12-15.** In the kingdom believers will enjoy the **peace** God gives and will recognize God's work on their behalf (v. 12). They will affirm that they remained true to God (**Your name** [character] **alone do we honor**) even though they will have been under the domination of others (v. 13). Those who will seek to dominate the remnant will be **dead,** under God's judgment. **Departed spirits** translates $r^e p\bar{a}'\hat{i}m$, also used in the last line of v. 19 (see comments on 14:9). In contrast the remnant will endure in **the land** God promised the patriarchs and their descendants (26:15).

**26:16-18.** The Lord's discipline on His people will not be easy to bear; it will be a time of great distress, a time when they will **barely whisper a prayer** either because of thirst or because of terror. Isaiah then compared their distress to the painful experience of childbirth (cf. comments on 13:8). Childbirth, once it begins, must continue until it is finished. However, the nation of Israel will seem to give **birth to wind,** that is, her travail

will continue but will avail nothing; it will not result in deliverance. Unbelievers in Israel will be judged and will not enter the Millennium.

**26:19.** Even though Israel's travail will not be efficacious, Isaiah was confident that her believing **dead will** be resurrected. This resurrection of Old Testament saints will occur at Christ's second coming (Dan. 12:2). When they **wake up** (i.e., when **their bodies** are resurrected) they will **shout for joy.** They will be refreshed in the way morning **dew** refreshes the grass (cf. Hosea 14:5), that is, they will experience God's blessings in the Millennium.

**26:20-21.** Isaiah wrote that the future remnant should **hide** during the time of distress (God's **wrath** in the Tribulation), knowing that deliverance from the Lord will come. Eventually the Lord will set matters right by punishing **people . . . for their sins.** All sins will be made known (**the earth will disclose the blood shed upon her**), whether they have been done in secret or in public. These words would have encouraged the remnant in Isaiah's day to remain true to **the LORD,** knowing that He will eventually judge sin. After that judgment is accomplished, believers will be able to sing the song recorded in chapter 26.

### c. Salvation for Israel and Judah (chap. 27)

This chapter may be divided into three sections each beginning with the phrase "in that day" (v. 1, vv. 2-11, vv. 12-13).

(1) The culmination of judgment. **27:1.** This verse, referring to the culmination of God's judgment on the world, ties in with the judgment mentioned in 26:21. With a **sword** the LORD will cut up a great serpent called **Leviathan.** This **gliding . . . coiling serpent** is the many-headed sea dragon mentioned in Psalm 74:13-14. In Ugaritic literature (of Ugarit, a city-state in North Syria) reference is made to a similar seven-headed creature. Isaiah, though not believing this ancient Semitic myth, simply referred to Leviathan to convey his point (cf. Job 3:8). Leviathan, the twisting **monster of the sea,** was viewed in Ugaritic literature as an enemy of order in Creation. But the Lord can stop this chaotic state and establish order on the earth and in people's

hearts. When God's judgment comes **in that day**, when He slays the wicked at the end of the Tribulation, it will be like His slaying the chaotic dragon **Leviathan.**

(2) The song of the vineyard. **27:2-6.** The vineyard symbolizes Israel (see comments on 5:7). In the song of the vineyard in 5:1-7 destruction was emphasized; in the song of the vineyard in 27:2-6 the promise of protection is the major theme. In the first song the vineyard was to be made a wasteland because of the people's sinful condition. In the second song the **vineyard** (Israel) is to be made **fruitful.** After God judges Israel (v. 1), the nation will be spiritually fruitful. This fruitfulness comes because of the Lord's constant protection and care (v. 3). If the vineyard (Israel) does not please **the LORD,** He must judge it (v. 4), but He much prefers that they turn to Him in repentance as their **Refuge** (v. 5). This desire that Israel be in the proper covenant relationship with Him is borne out by the repetition of **let them make peace with Me.** When the Kingdom Age arrives, **Jacob** (a synonym for **Israel**) will be productive again (cf. 35:1-3, 6-7; Amos 9:13-14; Zech. 14:8) and will be the nation through which God will bless the **world** (cf. Gen. 12:3).

(3) The coming judgment (27:7-11). **27:7-8.** Because **the LORD** cares for His people He will judge them and purify them so they can be fruitful. Isaiah foretold that judgment would come on Israel. But He will not treat her the way He treats her enemies (v. 7). He will judge her **by warfare and exile** (v. 8; cf. Deut. 28:64-68). **The east wind,** strong in the Middle East, may refer figuratively to Babylon, east of Israel, which took Judah into captivity. The Exile would help purify Judah so that she would not worship foreign gods and goddesses.

**27:9-11.** The sin of the nation had to **be atoned for.** Of course atonement for all sin is through the death of Jesus Christ. But in view of Israel's covenant relationship with God, she had to be driven out of the land because of her disobedience to the Law (Deut. 28:49-52, 64). Evidence of that atonement would be her pulverizing her **altar stones** dedicated to idolatrous gods, and removing the **Asherah poles,** wooden symbols of the Canaanite pagan goddess of fertility.

Because of Judah's **sin,** her **city** (i.e., Jerusalem) would be destroyed and its **people** removed. Jerusalem was destroyed by the Babylonians in 586 B.C. and was left **desolate.** Isaiah said **calves** would **graze** in Jerusalem's ruins and being hungry would **strip** tree **branches** of their bark. **Women** then would cut off the branches and use them for firewood. In judging His senseless people, God, **their Maker** and **Creator,** temporarily withdrew His **compassion on them.**

(4) The regathering of Israel. **27:12-13.** **The Lord** promised that **in that day** (cf. vv. 1-2) He **will thresh** (i.e., judge) a large area **from the . . . Euphrates to the Wadi of Egypt.** In other words the Lord will judge this large area of land for the purpose of bringing His people back to Jerusalem and its environs. The Wadi of Egypt may be the stream that marks the southwest border of Canaan (Num. 34:4-5; 1 Kings 8:65). Or perhaps it refers to the Nile, since the point of Isaiah 27:13 is that the Lord will regather His people from both Assyria and Egypt, two great enemies of Israel in most of her history up to Assyria's fall in 609 B.C. The people will be regathered to **the holy mountain in Jerusalem,** that is, the temple mount where the Messiah will reign (cf. 24:23). In God's kingdom on earth Israel will dwell in the land of Palestine as believers.

### E. The woes (chaps. 28–33)

Isaiah continued his theme of judgment with a series of "woes" against various groups who were opposing his words. Here he was attacking primarily the rulers of the Northern and Southern Kingdoms for their failure to heed God's Word and for looking to other means for protection. They were trusting in their wealth (chap. 28) and foreign alliances (chaps. 30–31). But neither of these, Isaiah said, could help them. Only the coming Deliverer could save them from the enemies around them (chaps. 32–33). God's plans cannot be thwarted by the obstinate refusal of people to believe in Him. He will sovereignly provide peace and security for the remnant through the messianic Deliverer.

### 1. WOE TO EPHRAIM AND JUDAH (CHAP. 28)

The strong pronouncements in this chapter are directed against the Northern

Kingdom (vv. 1-13) and the Southern Kingdom (vv. 14-29). Before long the Northern Kingdom would fall to the Assyrians (722 B.C.). Writing to the people of the South, Isaiah was encouraging them not to be like their Northern brothers and sisters. God's judgment was designed to bring the people to repentance before Him (vv. 23-29), not to "get even" with them.

### a. Woe to Ephraim (28:1-13)

(1) The state of the Northern Kingdom (28:1-8). **28:1.** In this first **woe** (*hôy,* an interjection suggestive of impending doom or grief; cf. comments on 5:8), Ephraim, a prominent tribe representative of the Northern Kingdom, is likened to a drunkard. The area of the North was **fertile** at that time. Samaria, the capital city built by Omri (1 Kings 16:24), overlooked a fruitful **valley** (cf. Isa. 28:4). Because of Samaria's **beauty** it was called a **wreath** (cf. v. 3). The possibility of material prosperity was great. However, the Northern Kingdom was throwing away the blessings of God as a drunkard throws away his money in the pursuit of **wine.** Apparently drunkenness was a problem in both the Northern and Southern Kingdoms, so the figure of a drunkard is apt.

**28:2-4.** Isaiah predicted that Assyria, **like a** strong **hailstorm and** windstorm, would go against the 10 Northern tribes. Samaria, like an ornamental **wreath** (cf. v. 1), would **be trampled underfoot** by Assyria with no regard for its worth. Samaria, the **beauty** of Israel overlooking **a fertile valley** (cf. v. 1), would become **like a** ripened **fig,** which is eaten by a stranger before it can be harvested. Early figs were considered a delicacy (cf. Hosea 9:10; Micah 7:1). The Northern Kingdom would have no safety; she would be taken into exile.

**28:5-6.** Though Samaria, the capital of Ephraim, has twice been described as a wreath (vv. 1, 3), now **the LORD Almighty** is said to be like **a beautiful wreath.** He, not a prosperous beautiful city, should be honored. **In that day,** when the Lord establishes the Millennium, **the remnant** will be honored by the Lord and will be under the One **who sits in judgment.** Even in the Assyrian siege of Samaria the Lord gave **strength to** the Israelite soldiers, enabling them to hold

off the siege for three years.

**28:7-8.** Returning again to the picture of the Northern Kingdom as a drunkard (cf. v. 1), Isaiah referred to the people and their leaders (**priests and prophets**) being drunk at a banquet where **the tables are covered with vomit.** They were intoxicated even **when** supposedly **seeing visions** (the false prophets) or **when rendering decisions** (the false priests). No wonder the nation was ripe for judgment!

(2) Ephraim's refusal to believe (28:9-13). **28:9-10.** The speakers in verse 9 are probably the priests and prophets mentioned in verses 7-8. They were angry that Isaiah was treating them as if they were young **children.** They felt they were adults who could think for themselves; they had no need for someone to tell them what to do or think. So they mimicked Isaiah as if he were speaking "baby talk" to them (v. 10). **Do and do, do and do, rule on rule, rule on rule** (cf. v. 13) is a series of sounds in Hebrew (*ṣaw lāṣāw, ṣaw lāṣāw, qaw lāqāw, qaw lāqāw*). Mocking Isaiah's messages, the leaders were acting as if he were an adult "lecturing" a little child. **A little here, a little there** was a method used in teaching children, inculcating a little at a time. In other words they were refusing to take Isaiah's words seriously. They wanted nothing to do with his message or his ministry.

**28:11-13.** Following up on the leaders' mimicking, Isaiah said that if they did not want to listen to his "lecturing" then they would be "lectured" by another people who had a difficult and different speech. **Foreign lips** would deliver the message of judgment on them. Isaiah was referring to the Assyrians who were advancing on Israel and would soon conquer it. Though God had offered Israel **rest** and **repose** they refused to **listen** to Him and His messenger. Therefore **the LORD** would turn their mocking back on them and they would **be injured . . . snared, and captured** by a people whose language they did not understand.

### b. Woe to Judah (28:14-29)

The message to Israel of destruction by foreign invaders was also for Judah. Though she would not be completely destroyed, because Jerusalem would not be taken, Judah would face much suffering. The people of the Southern Kingdom had much the same attitude as their Northern brothers. They too were scoffing at God's revelation through Isaiah.

**28:14-22.** The people of Judah should not think they were guiltless before God. The leaders of **Jerusalem**, like their counterparts in the North, were responsible to guide and lead the people toward godliness. But they scoffed, boasting of several things. They said since they had made **a covenant with death**, the **scourge** could not **touch** them, and **a lie** and a **falsehood** were their **hiding place** (vv. 14-15). Why would the rulers of Jerusalem say such a thing? It seems that Isaiah was using imagery rich in the symbolism of Semitic mythology. For example, in the Ugaritic pantheon death was personified as the god of the underworld. The Jerusalem leaders were trusting in other gods to save them from the coming scourge, the Assyrian invasion. However, to trust in false gods was futile. The LORD sets the **stone** and the **sure foundation**, that is, only He is the basis for physical and spiritual salvation (v. 16). Whether Isaiah thought of the **cornerstone** as the Messiah or simply as genuine belief in the Lord is not clear. In other passages the cornerstone refers to Christ (Zech. 10:4; Eph. 2:20; 1 Peter 2:6).

The Lord responded to each of these boasts. Their **covenant with death** would **be annulled** (Isa. 28:18), their **lie** would be swept **away** (v. 17), and they would be defeated by the **scourge** (v. 18) that would continue **day** after day (v. 19). **This message** of judgment would **bring sheer terror** (v. 19) as the people realized its implications. To seek protection from false gods would be as inadequate as lying in a **bed** that **is too short** or trying to cover oneself with a **blanket** that is **too** small. The destruction would sweep down into Judah (**Mount Perazim** and **the Valley of Gibeon,** 1 Chron. 14:11, 16, are near Jerusalem, where David defeated the Philistines). Therefore they should **stop . . . mocking** Isaiah's message given by **the LORD Almighty.**

**28:23-29.** Isaiah then inserted a word of comfort into this message of woe and judgment. The judgment would last for only a short while as it was designed to purge the people. A **farmer** must crush his crops to get the desired results. For example, **caraway** and **cummin,** aromatic herbs, are **beaten out with a rod** or **stick,**

not threshed, because their seeds are so small. **Grain** is **ground** by millstone, after the wheat stalks are threshed. Various crops must be treated differently so no one step (plowing, harrowing, **planting,** or **threshing**) is done continuously.

Similarly God would bring about judgment but not forever. He is the Master "Farmer," who knows how to handle each "crop." Therefore the Southern Kingdom should submit to Him because He is **wonderful in counsel** (cf. 9:6) **and magnificent in wisdom** (cf. 11:2).

### 2. WOE TO JERUSALEM (CHAP. 29)

*a. Judgment coming on Jerusalem (29:1-4)*

**29:1-4.** In this second of five "woes" in chapters 28–33 Isaiah continues with the theme of the last part of the first woe (28:14-29). Judgment was coming on Jerusalem and on Judah, and its purpose was to get the nation to return to God. Unlike the judgment that would sweep away the Northern Kingdom, this judgment on Jerusalem, though very severe, would be averted by the Lord. Jerusalem would not fall into the hands of the Assyrians.

**Ariel** undoubtedly refers to Jerusalem as can be concluded by the parallel phrase **the city where David settled** (cf. 2 Sam. 5:7, 9, 13). Many interpreters say **Ariel** means "lion of God," in which case the city is seen as a strong, lionlike city. Ariel may also be translated "altar hearth," as in Isaiah 29:2; Ezekiel 43:15-16. Jerusalem is the place where the altar of burnt offering was located in the temple.

Though Jerusalem is where **festivals** were celebrated before God (Isa. 29:1), the city would be besieged and fighting and bloodshed would turn it into a virtual **altar hearth.**

Though the Assyrians under Sennacherib surrounded Jerusalem in 701 B.C. it was as if God had done so (**I. . . . I . . . I . . . My,** vv. 2-3). Being humiliated (**brought low**), Jerusalem spoke softly rather than in loud tones. Though Jerusalem would be surrounded it would not be taken at this time. This assurance should have encouraged the people to trust God and to worship Him properly.

*b. Deliverance coming for Jerusalem (29:5-8)*

**29:5-8.** Jerusalem's protection described in these verses refers to her deliverance from Assyria, recorded in chapter 37. It would have seemed impossible to hope that the Assyrians would not take the city. Only by God's sovereign intervention was Jerusalem spared. Though 29:5-8 refers to the Assyrian soldiers becoming **like . . . dust** and **chaff** when they were slaughtered, these verses also seem to have eschatological overtones. At the end of the Tribulation when **nations** (vv. 7-8) will **attack** Jerusalem (Zech. 14:1-3), **the LORD Almighty will come** and destroy each attacking nation. The threat of those **nations** will vanish like **a dream.** When the Assyrian soldiers were destroyed in Isaiah's day, no doubt the people of Jerusalem were delirious with joy. But shortly the difficulty of that situation subsided in their thinking, and life returned to normal. Rather than turning back to God the nation got more deeply involved in sin.

### c. Jerusalem's understanding of God's revelation (29:9-24)

In this section a contrast is drawn between the people's present spiritual insensitivity and their future spiritual understanding.

**29:9-12.** The Jerusalemites' spiritual insensitivity was in itself a judgment from God. The people were told to **blind** themselves (v. 9) but **the LORD** also caused the blindness (v. 10). The fact that **the prophets** and **the seers** did not see and understand clearly was part of God's judgment. They did not understand God's revelation about His judgment on the Assyrians that Isaiah recorded on **a scroll** (vv. 11-12). No one, either people **who** could **read** or those who couldn't, could understand this truth.

**29:13-14.** The **people** of Jerusalem, professing to know God, were formally involved in acts of **worship** but they did not worship God from **their hearts.** They were more concerned with man-made legalistic **rules** than with God's Law, which promotes mercy, justice, and equity. Because of that, God would judge them; their **wisdom** would **vanish.**

**29:15-16.** God pronounced **woe** on those who thought He did not see their actions. They attempted **to hide their plans from** God by doing things at night. They were not thinking clearly, for God can hide things from man (vv. 10-12) but not vice versa. Such thinking twisted the facts and confused **the potter** with **the clay.** A jar, however, cannot deny that the potter made it, or say that **the potter** is ignorant (cf. 45:9; 64:8). Actually the *people* knew **nothing** of what was going on, but *God* always knows everything.

**29:17-21.** However, things in the future will be different. The phrase **in a very short time** refers to the coming millennial kingdom. Some think it refers to the time when the Assyrian army was slaughtered (37:36), but the conditions described in 29:20-21 seem to nullify that interpretation. **Lebanon,** which was then occupied by Assyrian troops, will eventually be productive (**fertile**) again. The second occurrence of the words **fertile field** may refer to Mount Carmel. When the Millennium comes **the deaf** and **the blind . . . will hear** and see (cf. 32:3; 35:5). This contrasts with 29:10-12, which referred to the nation's impaired sight. **The needy will rejoice** in **the LORD** because of what He will do for them, and conversely **the ruthless** who deprived **the innocent of justice** will be punished (vv. 20-21; cf. v. 5).

**29:22-24.** The attitude of the people of Jerusalem and Judah will completely change. They will **no longer . . . be ashamed** (v. 22) or brought low (v. 4) by foreign domination and their own sin (cf. 1:29). As **their children** grow up in safety they will realize that God has protected them and will worship (**stand in awe of**) Him. The Lord's delivering them from Sennacherib was a foretaste of the ultimate deliverance they will experience. People **who are wayward** and **who complain** will change and **will accept instruction.** No longer will blindness prevail; then they will know God's ways (cf. 29:18).

### 3. WOE TO THE OBSTINATE CHILDREN (CHAP. 30)

This oracle (chap. 30) and the next one (chap. 31) center on the folly of attempting to make an alliance with Egypt to ward off the Assyrian threat. At this time Egypt was waning as a world power and could be of no real assistance to Israel and Judah in their fight against the strong Assyrian Empire. But a strong faction in Judah, rather than turning to God for protection, wanted to seek aid from Egypt.

### a. The woe pronounced (30:1-5)

**30:1.** This **woe** (see comments on 3:9) was pronounced against those in Judah who wanted to form **an alliance.** The prophet spoke to those people as if they were children, and **obstinate children** at that. Like children, they did not have the proper perspective to know what was best for them. Floundering in their desire to save themselves and their nation, they were forming **plans** but not God's plans. Actually their plans were sinful because they were not what God wanted them to do.

**30:2-5.** An alliance with **Egypt,** made **without consulting** the Lord, would **put** Judah **to shame** (vv. 3, 5 [twice]). The Jews even sent a delegation to two Egyptian cities—**Zoan** and **Hanes** —to talk about an alliance, but the talks were doomed to fail. The **officials in Zoan** were incapable of helping (see comments on 19:11). The location of Hanes is unknown, but it may have been in the Egyptian Delta near Zoan. The Lord had already said many times through Isaiah that He would use Assyria to wipe out the Northern Kingdom and to punish the Southern Kingdom. So to look to a crumbling empire for help was useless and could only result in **disgrace** (vv. 3, 5).

### b. The oracle about the Negev (30:6-17)

**30:6-7.** As the **envoys** (cf. v. 4) traveled to Egypt they had to pass through **the Negev,** a desolate, dangerous area with wild **animals** (**lions** and **snakes**). The delegation from Judah took expensive gifts to Egypt on the **backs** of donkeys and **camels.** Judah's people were so desperate for help that they were willing to risk **hardship** and go to great expense. But Isaiah called Egypt—a nation unable to **help**—**Rahab the Do-Nothing.** In Ugaritic literature Rahab was the name of a female sea monster associated with Leviathan (see comments on 27:1; cf. Job 9:13; 26:12). Perhaps the hippopotamus, an animal that often sits in the water of the Nile doing nothing, represents that mythical water beast. Understandably Rahab came to be a poetic synonym for Egypt (and also for a demon behind Egypt) when God overpowered the Egyptian soldiers in the sea at the Exodus (cf. Isa. 51:9; Pss. 87:4; 89:10). So **Egypt,** Isaiah wrote, was good for nothing; she could not assist Judah in any way.

**30:8-11.** The people did not want to listen to God's instructions through Isaiah. So God told him to **write** down his message so that they could not claim they had never heard it. In the future, the **scroll** on which the message was written would **witness** against them. They were like **rebellious . . . children** (cf. v. 1), **unwilling to listen to the** Lord, to receive messages from His **prophets.** They did not want to be confronted with the truth from God, **the Holy One of Israel** (cf. v. 12 and see comments on 1:4).

**30:12-17.** Immediately after they said they did not want to be confronted by the Holy One of Israel (v. 11) ironically Isaiah **did** confront them with more words from **the Holy One of Israel** (cf. v. 15). Rejecting Isaiah's **message** (vv. 9-11) and relying **on oppression** (i.e., fraud, or plans to avoid God's counsel) and **deceit** (which Egypt would practice on them), they would undergo judgment.

That judgment would come suddenly—like a cracked **wall** that would collapse on them (v. 13). And it would be severe—like a pot so **shattered** that the **pieces** cannot be used for anything (v. 14). Though the Lord had called for **repentance** and **trust** so that the Judahites might have **salvation** and **strength** (v. 15) they did not want any **of it.** Instead they depended on military might (v. 16). But if they were to rely **on horses** (cf. 31:1), God said they would be forced to **flee** (30:16-17), being easily alarmed by the enemy. They would stand alone **like a banner on a hill** as a warning to others not to count on military strength.

### c. The Lord's graciousness to His people (30:18-33)

**30:18-22.** Though the people had turned from **the LORD,** He longed **to be gracious** and compassionate **to** them (v. 18; cf. v. 19) for they were in a covenant relationship with Him. He is also the **God of justice,** giving blessings to those **who** depend on **Him.** In the Millennium Israel will again be faithful to **the LORD.** And when she calls on Him (not on some other nation) for help, **He will answer.** Though she experienced difficulties (e.g., having only **bread** to eat and **water** to drink in times of calamity), eventually God will bless her. The Israelites will readily listen to their spiritual guides (**teachers**) such as the prophets and priests (in contrast with rejecting them, v. 10); no longer will the teachers need to hide for safety. The people will be sensitive to God's Word, as if He were saying, **This is the way, walk in it.** They will be conscious of God's leading at all times. When they heed His instructions they will then get rid of their **idols** (cf. 31:7; Hosea 14:3b; Micah 5:13-14), things that are defiled and morally dirty.

**30:23-26.** Isaiah then described what times will be like when the people live according to God's Word and are obedient to Him. In the Millennium God will **send . . . rain,** and crops will be **plentiful** (cf. Deut. 28:1-14). Even the animals will have plenty to eat (Isa. 30:23-24). **The day of great slaughter** may refer to the Battle of Armageddon (cf. Rev. 16:16; 19:17-21). After Israel's and God's enemies are defeated, Israel will enjoy great peace and an abundance of **water** in the land (Isa. 30:25).

Also light will be increased, for **the moon will** be **like the sun** and the sun **will be seven times brighter** than normal. Perhaps this is figurative language but it is difficult to know for sure. At that time the Lord will heal His people of **the wounds** (cf. 1:5) **He inflicted,** that is, He will restore them to the place of blessing.

**30:27-33.** Isaiah now spoke again of the present situation, prophesying that the Assyrian army (v. 31), which was surrounding Jerusalem, would be defeated (37:36). This occurred in 701 B.C. God in His **anger** would rush against His enemies. Like **dense clouds . . . a fire,** and a **torrent** (cf. v. 30) His **wrath** would overtake the enemy. **He shakes the nations in** a **sieve,** like a farmer shaking grain to clear it of small pebbles (cf. Amos 9:9). This defeat of Assyria would cause Judah to **rejoice** much as they did in their three annual festivals (Ex. 23:14-17) when they went to the temple on Mount Zion, **the mountain of the Lord** (cf. Isa. 11:9; 27:13; 56:7; 65:25; 66:20), who is the nation's **Rock** (cf. 17:10; 26:4; 44:8; cf. comments on Ps. 18:2), its source of security.

Merely by a command (**voice,** Isa. 30:30-31) of **anger** (cf. vv. 27-28) God would **shatter Assyria with His scepter** and **rod.** This would cause Judah to rejoice (cf. v. 29) with music from **tambourines and harps** (cf. 24:8). The Assyrian army would be destroyed like a pile of **wood** or a sacrifice in **Topheth,** an area in the Valley of Hinnom south of Jerusalem where children were sometimes sacrificed to the false Ammonite god Molech (2 Kings 23:10; Jer. 7:31; cf. Jer. 7:32; 19:6, 11-14). This fire was **for the king,** perhaps Hezekiah, as if he were to use it in destroying his enemy. By God's **breath** (cf. Isa. 30:28) He would figuratively kindle the fire by which He would consume the bodies of the Assyrian soldiers. His breath would be like **sulfur,** which burns with great intensity (cf. Gen. 19:24; Job 18:15; Ps. 11:6; Ezek. 38:22; Rev. 9:17-18). This speaks of the eternal torment of the wicked in "the lake of fire" (KJV; Rev. 19:20; 20:10; 21:8).

### 4. WOE TO THE EGYPTIAN ALLIANCE (CHAPS. 31–32)

Like the previous woe (chap. 30) this one was directed against the Egyptian alliance which some people of Judah wanted to make (chap. 31). But this oracle also speaks about the messianic King who will someday deliver His people (chap. 32).

### a. The woe pronounced (31:1-3)

**31:1-3.** This **woe** (see comments on 3:9) was pronounced on those who went **to Egypt for help** (cf. 30:1-2), and who relied on Egyptian **horses** (cf. 30:16) and **chariots** instead of on God. Both actions —going to Egypt and acquiring horses— violated God's stipulations in the Deuteronomic Covenant (Deut. 17:16). Since God **does not** go **back** on **His words,** He would judge the nation for her disobedience. **The Egyptians** could not help Judah (cf. 30:3, 5, 7) for they were weak **men.** Only **God** could ultimately protect them from their enemies. If Judah persisted in seeking an alliance with Egypt, **both** countries would meet disaster.

### b. The Lord's protection (31:4-9)

**31:4-5.** God assured the people that His greatness would protect them from the terrifying Assyrian threat. **As a lion** meets up with a flock of sheep and is unafraid of a number of **shepherds, so** the Lord was not afraid of the Assyrians. He promised **to do battle on Mount Zion,** and **like birds** flying **overhead** He would **shield Jerusalem** and not let it fall into the enemy's hands.

**31:6-7.** Since Judah would be rescued by God (v. 5), Isaiah called on the nation to turn back **to Him.** Eventually they would throw their **idols** away (cf. 30:22) in favor of the true God. Therefore Judah ought to throw them away now. Their future hope in the kingdom should change their present behavior. The future reality should have an ethical impact on their lives.

**31:8-9.** Isaiah affirmed again (cf. 30:31) that **Assyria** would **fall,** but only because of God's work (by **a sword that is not of man).** The Assyrian **commanders,** seeing Judah's **battle standard** and their soldiers being slaughtered (by the Angel of the Lord; cf. 37:36), would be terrified. The **fire** may refer to the fire of the altar of burnt offering that burned continually, and the **furnace** is literally a baking oven. By protecting Judah, God would see that the fire on the altar continued to burn.

### c. A time of justice and righteousness (32:1-8)

Because the Lord would protect Jerusalem, He will also bring about a time when righteousness will abound.

**32:1-2.** In the Millennium the **King** (cf. comments on 33:17), that is, the Messiah, **will reign in righteousness** (11:1-5; cf. Jer. 23:5), and **rulers** under Him (cf. 2 Tim. 2:2; Rev. 5:10; 20:6; 22:5) **will** be just. In fact every person entering the Millennium will be a believer. **Each** one will be protective of others **like a shelter from the wind** and will refresh others **like . . . water in the desert** and a **rock** that gives shade from the desert heat.

**32:3-8.** In the Kingdom Age, people will **see** and **hear** spiritual things clearly (cf. 29:18; 35:5; 42:7) in contrast with Judah's spiritual insensitivity (29:10-12). People will **understand** God's Word and will speak the truth clearly (32:4). Fools and scoundrels will no longer be **respected.** As in the Book of Proverbs **the fool** (nābāl, "senseless") is one who is **evil** (Isa. 32:6). He teaches falsehood and disregards the needs of others. In contrast with the scoundrel who wickedly plots to take advantage of **the poor** and **the needy. . . . the noble** person **plans** to do good to others. Because he is righteous **he stands**; he will continue to live.

### d. Future judgment and blessing (32:9-20)

**32:9-14.** This message addressed to the **women** is reminiscent of 3:16-26. The women of Judah should not complacently think that God's judgment would not come, for the devastation would begin soon, in **little more than a year.** Probably this refers to Assyria's final push into Judah in 701 B.C., but it cannot be proved. The first evidence of the judgment would be the failing of the **harvest** of grapes and other **fruit,** perhaps because the Assyrians would overrun the fields. Therefore because of the ravaging of **the land** the **women** would mourn. (On **sackcloth** see comments on 3:24.) If **the noisy city** to be **deserted** (32:14) refers to Jerusalem then Isaiah meant that the Assyrian attack was the beginning of the end for Jerusalem, which fell to the Babylonians 115 years later (in 586 B.C.). In that case Isaiah was not saying (v. 10) that the judgment would be completed in about a year but that it would *begin* in about a year. However, perhaps "the noisy city" refers to any one of the 46 Judean cities Sennacherib king of Assyria claimed to have defeated. The desolation (whether by Assyria or Babylon) would come on the land **forever** ('ôlām). This Hebrew word does not always carry the same force as the English word "forever." From verse 15 it is obvious that Isaiah saw a day when the desolation would cease. So it is better to understand 'ôlām here as meaning "for a long indeterminable time."

**32:15a.** After speaking of desolation on Judah (vv. 9-14) Isaiah described a time of future blessing on the land and the people (vv. 15-20). That great time— the Millennium—will come about after **the** Holy **Spirit is poured** out (cf. 44:3) on Israel **(us) from on high.** Other prophets also spoke of this outpouring of the Holy Spirit, including Ezekiel (Ezek. 36:26-27; 37:14), Joel (Joel 2:28-29), and Zechariah (Zech. 12:10, NIV marg.). As the redeemed of Israel enter the millennial kingdom they will have the same benefit of the indwelling presence of the Holy Spirit as do believers in the Church Age today. Therefore they will have an inward compulsion to do the will of God (Ezek. 36:27).

**32:15b-20.** Along with the outpouring of the Spirit will be fertility, justice, and security. Israel's deserts will be **fertile** (cf. 35:1-2), and with **justice** and **righteousness** (cf. 9:7; 11:4; 16:5; 33:5) will come **peace** and **quietness** (32:17) and security for the redeemed (cf. Amos 9:15; Micah 4:4; Zech. 3:10; 14:11). Under the Deuteronomic Covenant if the people obeyed God the land would be productive. Similarly in the kingdom, righteous living will result in fertility. In contrast with the destruction that would come in Isaiah's day (Isa. 32:19), the redeemed nation is assured that they will be **blessed** with agricultural productivity (cf. Ezek. 36:30) and with no rivalry over each other's grazing land.

5. WOE TO THE DESTROYERS (CHAP. 33)

This final woe describes the greatness of God's judgment on those who live unrighteously (vv. 1-12) and the wonder of His blessings on the redeemed in the kingdom (vv. 13-24).

*a. Woe to the enemies of God's people (33:1-12)*

**33:1.** Verses 1-12 discuss the **woe** (see comments on 3:9) of judgment to come on people who live unrighteously, who are traitors to the truth. The **destroyer** was the Assyrian enemy, and the **traitor** probably refers to those within Judah who wanted to form alliances either with Egypt or with other powers to protect them from Assyria. None of them would succeed in their efforts, for the destroyer would **be destroyed** and the traitor **betrayed.**

**33:2-4.** The words in these verses seem to be those of the righteous remnant waiting for the LORD to deliver them. They will long for His grace (cf. 30:18-19) and the Lord Himself. Longing for His **strength** and **salvation** (deliverance) they were confident that He would **scatter** the **nations** who opposed Israel. Then speaking to the nations who will be judged, the remnant will say that the **plunder** which those **nations** had taken from others will be taken from them. That plundering will be as complete and irreversible as **locusts** destroying everything in their path.

**33:5-6.** Speaking now to the remnant, Isaiah said that the **exalted** Lord (cf. 6:1) will eventually **fill Zion with justice and righteousness** (cf. 9:7; 11:4; 16:5; 32:16) when the kingdom is established. But in order to have these things, including **salvation . . . wisdom, and knowledge** they must **fear . . . the LORD** (cf. Prov. 1:7; 15:33). Fearing God does not mean being terrified of Him (except for those who are being or will be judged). It means to recognize and respect Him and His authority and righteous demands, which in turn results in godly living, worshiping, trusting, serving, and obeying Him. Those who fear Him find Him to be their **sure Foundation,** their Source of inner security and peace (cf. "Rock," Isa. 26:4).

**33:7-12.** Those in Judah who thought they could achieve **peace** through an alliance (cf. **envoys** in 30:4, 6) would **weep bitterly.** Assyrian terror would be everywhere and people would be unable to travel **the roads** because of lurking danger. **Lebanon,** north of Israel and well known for its cedar forests, would wither. **Sharon** was the coastal plain south of Mount Carmel extending inland to the hill country of Ephraim. A fertile area, Sharon would become a desert **like the Arabah** (which means "arid" or "dry"), the desolate rift valley extending from the Dead Sea south to the Gulf of Aqabah. **Bashan** ("fertile plain"), east of the Sea of Kinnereth (later named the Sea of Galilee), was productive agriculturally (cf. Jer. 50:19) and known for its oak trees (Isa. 2:13; Ezek. 27:6; Micah 7:14; Zech. 11:2). **Carmel** ("fruitful land") was a mountain range thickly forested and well watered at that time. This destruction would show that the people could not save themselves. When **the LORD** would use the Assyrians against Judah, Judah's plans for peace would come to nothing. It was as if the people gave **birth** like a mother to nothing but **chaff** and **straw,** which can easily **be burned** up.

*b. The deliverance of the righteous (33:13-24)*

In contrast with the destruction of the destroyer and traitor, the righteous will live. Isaiah noted the kind of people who will be saved (vv. 13-16) and then described the land in which they will live (vv. 17-24).

**33:13-16.** God called on people everywhere (**far away** and **near,** v. 13) to **acknowledge** His righteous actions and His **power. Sinners** asked **who** can endure God's awesome judgment (a **consuming fire**), and the prophet responded that those who **can dwell with** God walk **righteously** and speak **what is right** (v.

15). They do not extort or take **bribes.** They refuse to be involved in **plots of murder** and other sins (cf. Ps. 15). These people will be safe and will enjoy God's blessings (Isa. 33:16). Therefore the people should live by God's standards even though the nation as a whole would be judged by Him.

**33:17-24.** The prophet then described the fruitful land in which these redeemed individuals (vv. 15-16) will dwell. This is the kingdom of Israel where righteousness and peace will flourish in the **land. The King** (cf. 32:1; 33:22; 43:15; Micah 2:13; Zeph. 3:15; Zech. 14:9), the Messiah, will be there (Isa. 33:17), and the people **will see** Him. They will think back on their **former** times (vv. 18-19) and realize that those who did not live righteously will be with them no longer. No foreign invader will be among them, including the Assyrians, **those arrogant people,** who spoke an **incomprehensible** language (v. 19; cf. 28:11). **Jerusalem** will be **peaceful** and secure (33:20), and **no** warships will attack the nation Israel (v. 21). Being properly related to **the Lord,** the people will acknowledge Him as their **Judge . . . Lawgiver . . . King** (cf. v. 17), and Savior (v. 22).

Assyria's defeat will be like a shipwreck, after which the many **spoils** on the ship **will be divided** among the Israelites. So much **plunder** will be there that plenty will be left by the time **even . . . lame** people get there. Illness will be wiped away (cf. 57:18-19; 58:8; Jer. 33:6) and **the sins of** the redeemed remnant **will be forgiven** (Isa. 33:24; cf. Jer. 31:34; 33:8; 36:3; 50:20). Peace, prosperity, and salvation will come by God's sovereign work not by foreign alliances or human cunning.

## F. Vengeance and blessing (chaps. 34–35)

These two chapters form a fitting climax to the judgment and salvation motifs which have been spoken of extensively by Isaiah. Chapters 36–39 record the historical fulfillment of many of the prophecies in the first half of the book. Discussion of the judgment on Assyria (30:27-33; 31:8-9; 33:1, 18-19) naturally led to a discussion of God's judgment on the whole world in the Tribulation. God's vengeance on the world will be followed by millennial blessing on His covenant people, Israel.

### 1. THE LORD'S DAY OF VENGEANCE (CHAP. 34)

This chapter includes an invitation to the nations (v. 1), God's coming judgment on the nations (vv. 2-4), and an announcement of judgment on Edom (vv. 5-17), a representative of all nations hostile to Israel.

### a. An invitation to hear (34:1)

**34:1.** The Lord invited all **nations** and **peoples** to **hear** the announcement He was about to make (cf. 1:2).

### b. Judgment on the whole world (34:2-4)

**34:2-4.** In God's judgment of **wrath** against the **armies** of **all nations** the **dead bodies** will rot on the ground. Also **the stars . . . will be dissolved.** Catastrophic events in the **sky** will accompany the Messiah's return to the earth to establish His millennial reign (cf. Joel 2:10, 30-31; 3:15; Zech. 14:6-7; Matt. 24:29). However, Isaiah 34:4 may refer to the judgment of the sixth seal in the Tribulation (Rev. 6:12-13), or to the eternal state, after the Millennium, when the sun will not be needed (Rev. 21:1). Or perhaps Isaiah was speaking figuratively of a change in the whole power structure in the Millennium when human kings will be done away with and God alone will be in control.

### c. Judgment on Edom (34:5-17)

Isaiah used Edom as an example of God's judgment against the world. The Edomites were descendants of Esau, Jacob's older brother. Their father Isaac told Esau he would live in an infertile area (Gen. 27:39-40). Because Edom became a perpetual enemy of Israel (cf. comments on Ezek. 35; 36:5), she was an appropriate example of what the Lord will do to all nations that fight against His people.

**34:5-8.** God's slaughter of **Edom** by His **sword** is pictured as a great **sacrifice in Bozrah** (cf. 63:1), modern-day Buseirah about 25 miles southeast of the Dead Sea, where various animals were slaughtered for sacrifice. God's reason for judging Edom is that He must **uphold Zion's cause** (34:8). (On the **day of vengeance**; see 61:2; 63:4.) Having promised to bless His Chosen People, He must fulfill His promises. Therefore when they are attacked He goes to their aid.

**34:9-17.** As a result of God's sword of judgment on Edom, **her land will** seem to be ablaze (cf. Obad. 18) with **sulfur** (see comments on Isa. 30:33) and burning **pitch,** a tar-like substance seemingly unquenchable. The land **will lie desolate** for many generations (34:10; cf. v. 11). **Edom's** cities and territories will be inhabited by wild birds and animals, which do not normally inhabit populated villages and towns. **Owls** (vv. 11, 13), ravens (v. 11), **jackals** (v. 13), **hyenas . . . wild goats** (v. 14), **falcons** (v. 15), and other **desert creatures** (v. 14) will thrive because no people will be there (v. 12). Edom's defenses will be overgrown with thornbushes (v. 13). The wild creatures will live in Edom **from generation to generation** (v. 17; cf. v. 10) because God's **Spirit will** so direct them (v. 16).

2. THE LORD'S DAY OF BLESSING (CHAP. 35)

The description in this chapter of the land and the people is a highlight of the first half of the book. This is the desired millennial state for which the nation has longed since God first promised it to Abraham. This is the state that mankind constantly longs for—a utopia in which peace and fertility prevail. This condition will not come, however, till after God's judgment on the world (chap. 34). This emphasis in Isaiah rules out postmillennialism, which teaches that the world will get increasingly better thus bringing in the kingdom which will be *followed* by the Messiah's return. The amillennial teaching that there will be no earthly kingdom at all because the Old Testament promises to Israel are being fulfilled in the church today is also foreign to Isaiah's thought. Isaiah taught that the Lord will regather believing Israel, Abraham's physical descendants, and will establish God's long-awaited kingdom on earth. That promised restoration is not being fulfilled in the church today in any sense.

**35:1-2.** In the Millennium **the parched land will** become rich agricultural land (cf. 32:15). The dry areas of the nation will become fertile (figuratively expressed as being **glad**) and will **blossom.** Apparently God will bring about climatic changes that will result in more rain in those areas. **Lebanon . . . Carmel, and**

**Sharon,** which were becoming barren (see 33:9 and comments there), will once again become fruitful areas of agriculture. People in those areas **will see the** Lord's **glory,** that is, they will see the fruitfulness that comes because of righteousness; they will see Him who will be dwelling in their midst as King (cf. comments on 33:17).

**35:3-4.** Isaiah now spoke again to the people in his day. He encouraged the believing remnant to live according to God's covenantal stipulations. They should encourage the depressed (those with **feeble hands**), the terrified (those whose **knees . . . give way**), and the **fearful,** for **God** in **divine retribution will . . . save** (deliver) them.

**35:5-7.** Changes will occur in the people and the land. Because of God's healing power (cf. 33:24) those who are **blind** will see, those who are **deaf** will hear (cf. 32:3; 42:7) those who are **lame** will **leap** (cf. 33:23), and those who cannot talk will **shout.** The Messiah will bring this about.

The land will change from dryness to a well-watered condition (cf. 35:1-2; 41:18; 43:19-20; 44:3-4). **Water will** be plentiful, helping **grass . . . reeds, and papyus . . . grow,** all of which require much water. Though some interpreters take these statements as figurative of spiritual blessings, it seems preferable to take them as literal statements, especially in view of the covenant promises (Deut. 28:1-14). With the Lord living among His people and with righteousness being practiced by them, the Lord will provide physical healing and agricultural fecundity.

**35:8-10.** Righteous pilgrims will once again travel to Jerusalem. They will go on **a highway** known as **the Way of Holiness,** for it will lead to God's city where His ways will be followed. It will **not** be traveled by **the unclean** or **wicked fools.** No **ferocious** animals will hinder the travel of **the redeemed** on that highway. In the millennial kingdom God's people will once again be involved in certain aspects of Old Testament formal worship (Zech. 14:16-19; Ezek. 40–44). Since righteousness and a desire to do the will of God will be esteemed, the people will willingly follow His instructions for worship. Also the redeemed will be indwelt by the Holy Spirit (Ezek.

36:24-28). **The ransomed of the LORD** will have **everlasting joy,** with no **sorrow,** for they will realize what God has done for them. They will rejoice that He will have saved them from destruction and brought them to peace and prosperity, in fulfillment of His promises.

### G. Historical interlude: Judah to be in captivity (chaps. 36–39)

The historical material in these chapters concerns two events which are foundational to a proper understanding of Isaiah's theology and Judah's history. The first event (chaps. 36–37) concerns the Assyrian threat which God miraculously dissipated. This event climaxes Isaiah's argument in chapters 1–35. In those chapters he had argued that God brought the Assyrians into Judah as a punishment for Judah's sins and as a catalyst to turn them back to Him. However, he had prophesied that Jerusalem would not fall to the Assyrians and that God would miraculously destroy the Assyrian army because of their pride.

The second event (chaps. 38–39) concerned Hezekiah's breach of the covenant when he was delivered by God from death but then allowed pride to enter his heart. This event serves as a foundation for chapters 40–66 which speak of the deliverance from the Babylonian Captivity prophesied in 39:5-8.

### 1. GOD'S SUPERIORITY TO ASSYRIA (CHAPS. 36–37)

Probably these chapters were written before the similar accounts in 2 Kings 18–19 and 2 Chronicles 32:1-23. Isaiah wanted to portray Hezekiah as one who believed in God and who was miraculously delivered from the Assyrian threat by a sovereign act of God. The point of these chapters is that God can and does fulfill His Word to His people. He had told them on a number of occasions that the Assyrians would be defeated; now that promise was fulfilled.

### a. Sennacherib's threatening of Jerusalem (36:1–37:4)

The Assyrians were convinced that they were invincible and that the God of Israel was no different from any other gods they had overcome on their westward march. So in 36:1–37:4 Isaiah stressed the pride of the Assyrians, and

that their arrogance would result in God's judging them (cf. 10:15-19).

(1) The setting. **36:1-3.** This attack occurred in 701 B.C. This was **the 14th year of . . . Hezekiah's** sole **reign** (cf. 2 Kings 18:13), which began in 715. Some scholars have proposed that **Sennacherib** (705–681) made several attacks against Jerusalem, but extrabiblical evidence does not seem to support that view. Sennacherib boasted of taking 46 walled villages in **Judah.** He went from the north along the coast defeating (among others) the towns of Aphek, Timnah, Ekron, and **Lachish.** Lachish was then his staging area for attacking a number of other towns. From Lachish he sent **a large army** against **Jerusalem** to surround it and to demand its surrender.

The Assyrian **commander stopped at the aqueduct of the Upper Pool, on the road to the Washerman's Field.** Besides setting the stage geographically, that information has theological significance. Ahaz had faced the Aram-Israel challenge at that same place (Isa. 7:3). Isaiah had told Ahaz that he would not fall to his enemy, that the Lord would deliver him. But Ahaz had refused to believe the man of God. Now **Hezekiah** was also confronted with a message of deliverance from the same man of God. The geographic notation heightened the tension over the question of whether Hezekiah would respond positively to the Word of God. **Eliakim . . . Shebna . . . and Joah** (cf. 22:20; 36:11, 22; 37:2) were chosen to negotiate with the Assyrians. These men, in important positions, were trusted by Hezekiah.

(2) The commander's mockery (36:4-10). **36:4-7. The field commander** was the main Assyrian spokesman. According to 2 Kings 18:17 two other leading officials were with him. (The KJV and NASB translate "field commander" by "Rabshekah," as if the word were a proper name. This, however, is probably not correct.) As a representative of the Assyrian Empire, his words of mockery characterized the whole empire. In speaking for the Assyrian **king** the field commander asked the Jerusalemites **whom** they were **depending** on for victory (Isa. 36:4-5). To depend **on Egypt** would be like leaning on a **splintered reed**—it would do no good and would even be harmful. Amazingly this was

what Isaiah had been saying about Egypt. The odds were overwhelmingly against the people of Jerusalem who had no means of escape for thousands of enemy troops were surrounding them.

The commander then said that it would be foolish to depend on **God** (v. 7). Apparently this commander had heard of Hezekiah's partial reforms (2 Kings 18; 2 Chron. 31) in which he had **removed** the **high places,** sites of worship on hills throughout **Judah.** The commander did not really understand the situation for he may have thought that Hezekiah was no longer depending on God since he had removed many **altars** from the land, leaving only one **altar** in **Jerusalem.**

**36:8-10.** To the commander, Jerusalem's only reasonable action was to surrender. Mockingly he even offered to **give** the Jews **2,000 horses if** they could find **riders** for them to fight against him. But he claimed that even 2,000 could not fight off *one* Assyrian low-ranking **officer.** Finalizing his argument, the commander said that the **Lord** had ordered him to **destroy** Judah. This was meant to terrorize the people by making them think that God had actually turned against them. Of course Isaiah had said that Jerusalem would not fall to the Assyrians, so the commander was wrong.

(3) The commander's challenge (36:11-20). **36:11-12.** Realizing the seriousness of their situation the three Judahite negotiators (cf. v. 3) requested that the negotiations be carried on in **Aramaic** rather than **Hebrew.** Aramaic, a major diplomatic language in that day, is similar to Hebrew. But it is different enough that many of the common people would have had difficulty understanding negotiations spoken in it. The three leaders were concerned that panic would spread throughout the city if **the people** heard the Assyrian's demands in Hebrew. However, the commander refused because he said he was sent to speak to every Jew in earshot, not just to these three. Confident of an Assyrian victory, he said the Jerusalemites would be forced to **eat** and **drink their own** body waste to survive in the siege.

**36:13-20.** Calling **out** to the people **in Hebrew,** the Assyrian **commander** urged them **not** to **let Hezekiah deceive** them into thinking the **Lord** would de-

**liver** them (vv. 13-15). Then the commander told the people that Sennacherib promised them prosperity in another **land** (vv. 16-17). Again the commander exhorted the people not to be deceived by **Hezekiah** (cf. vv. 13-15) for **the gods** of other nations had not been able to deliver them (vv. 18-20).

**Hamath and Arpad** were in Aram. The location of **Sepharvaim** is uncertain but it may be near Hamath and Arpad. Hamath and Sepharvaim were two of the cities from which people were brought to repopulate Samaria after its fall (2 Kings 17:24). The commander also boasted that since **Samaria** was not helped by its god (it had fallen to Assyria 21 years earlier, 722 B.C.), why should the people of **Jerusalem** count on their God to protect them?

(4) The people's response. **36:21-22.** Though no doubt terrified, **the people** followed Hezekiah's instructions not to answer the Assyrian spokesman's taunts. **Eliakim . . . Shebna,** and **Joah** (cf. vv. 3, 11) **told** Hezekiah **what the . . . commander had said.** They had **torn** their **clothes,** a sign of distress and/or mourning (cf. 37:1; Gen. 37:29; Josh. 7:6; 2 Kings 11:14; 19:1; 22:11; Es. 4:1; Job 1:20; 2:12).

(5) Hezekiah's faith (37:1-4). **37:1-2.** Like the envoys, **Hezekiah** in distress **tore his clothes.** He was disturbed because of the Assyrian threat and also because the name of the Lord had been profaned. Putting **on sackcloth** was another act of mourning (see comments on 3:24). In trust and dependence on God Hezekiah **went into the temple of the Lord,** showing symbolically that the nation now could do nothing on their own—their destiny was completely up to God. He also sent his top leaders **Eliakim** and **Shebna** along with **the leading priests . . . to . . . Isaiah.** Why Joah (cf. 36:3, 11, 22) is not mentioned is not known.

**37:3-4.** The men informed Isaiah of the situation, asked for a word from **the Lord** to **rebuke** the Assyrians, and then asked the prophet to **pray** for them. **Hezekiah** was thereby acknowledging that the Lord spoke through Isaiah. This contrasts with Ahaz's attitude (chap. 7) when he was confronted by a national calamity 33 years earlier, 734 B.C. In the leaders' report to Isaiah they picked up his imagery of distress (from 26:17-18) about a woman who is about **to deliver** a baby but has **no strength** and would die in the process.

*b. Isaiah's response from the Lord (37:5-7)*

**37:5-7.** In Isaiah's brief word to the messengers from **the LORD** he first told them **not** to **be afraid** of the Assyrians. God had heard that they had **blasphemed** Him (cf. v. 4). Then the prophet said that the Assyrian **king** would **return** home and would be killed there (the fulfillment of this is recorded in vv. 36-38).

*c. God's defeat of Assyria (37:8-38)*

**37:8-13.** Sennacherib **had left Lachish** and was at **Libnah,** about five miles north of Lachish. Word had come that **Tirhakah** was coming to assist **Judah** in her fight against **Assyria.** Tirhakah was called **the Cushite king of Egypt.** He was from Cush, south of Egypt, and ruled Egypt at that time. In 701 Tirhakah was an army commander; he actually did not become king of Cush until 690; but since he was king when Isaiah wrote this account, Isaiah called him the king.

Again Sennacherib told **Hezekiah** that other nations' **gods** had not been able to help them against the Assyrian advance (cf. 36:18-20). **Gozan,** a city on the Habor River, was conquered about 100 years earlier by the Assyrians. **Haran,** a city in Aram, was at that time an Assyrian stronghold. **Rezeph,** also an Aramean city, was captured about 100 years earlier by the Assyrians. **Eden** was probably in northern Mesopotamia, and may refer to a territory in which **Tel Assar** was a city. (See comments on **Hamath . . . Arpad,** and **Sepharvaim** in 36:19.) The location of **Hena** is not known. The site of **Ivvah** is also unknown but it may have been in the Babylonian region.

**37:14-20.** Receiving the communication (a **letter**) from Sennacherib, **Hezekiah prayed** a great prayer of faith in **the temple** (cf. v. 1). By placing the matter in God's hands (v. 14), he was calling God's attention to it (though of course he believed that God already knew). The king began his prayer with praise (vv. 15-16). Referring to Him as the **God of Israel,** the king recalled the special covenant position Israel had with **the LORD.** God's being **enthroned between the cherubim** refers to His presence in the Jerusalem

temple and thus with His people (1 Kings 8:10-13). (On the cherubim see comments on 1 Kings 6:23.) Besides being the God of Israel, **the LORD** is also **over all the kingdoms of the earth,** including Assyria! Hezekiah also stated that God is the Creator.

Then Hezekiah asked God to intervene for His glory, so that the other nations would know that He, **the LORD** of Israel, is the true **God** (Isa. 37:17-20). Hezekiah requested deliverance from the Assyrians so that nations everywhere would acknowledge God's sovereignty.

**37:21-35.** Responding to Hezekiah's prayer, the Lord **sent a message to** him through **Isaiah** that **Assyria** would be defeated (cf. God's first reply, vv. 6-7). That message included three parts.

First, the Assyrians would be driven back (vv. 21-29). Deliverance would come to **Jerusalem** (**the Virgin Daughter of Zion**; see comments on 1:8; 47:1) for Assyria would flee (cf. 37:7). The tables would be turned and Zion would mock Assyria (v. 22). This would come about as an answer to Hezekiah's prayer (v. 21) and as punishment on the Assyrians for their blasphemy (vv. 23-24; cf. 36:20; 37:4, 17) and pride (**I** and **my** occur seven times in vv. 24-25). Sennacherib claimed to have felled the choicest tall **cedars** and **pines** in **the heights** (mountains and hills) **of Lebanon** (cf. 10:34). This may refer to his overrunning Lebanon or it may be a figurative way of saying he conquered leading nations. He also claimed to have conquered **Egypt** though it is questionable that he ever entered Egypt. However, he did defeat the Egyptians in Philistia. Those successes came only because the Lord allowed them, for He **ordained** them all. The nations Sennacherib conquered were weak and **like grass** on flat **housetops** (cf. Ps. 129:6) readily **scorched** by the sun. But now the Lord, knowing Sennacherib's **rage,** would cause him to go back to his land as if he were being led like an animal (Isa. 37:29), that is, in disgrace. This is fitting because the Assyrians were known for leading their captives by hooks in their noses.

Second, God assured **Hezekiah** that **a remnant** would remain (vv. 30-32) and that life would go on as usual. For the next two years life would be difficult as they sought to get their crops back to normal, **but in the third year** (the normal time it takes for a vineyard to begin producing grapes) there would be a bountiful harvest. **The LORD** would do this because of his **zeal** for Judah.

Third, the message again addressed **the king of Assyria** (vv. 33-35). God told him that he would **not** set foot inside the **city** of Jerusalem or even **build a siege ramp against** its walls. He would have to **return** home because God Himself would **defend** the **city** of **David.**

**37:36-38.** The account of the destruction of the Assyrian army (predicted by Isaiah in 30:27-33; 31:8-9; 33:1, 18-19) is almost anticlimactic, occupying only three verses. The overnight slaughter did not come from the hand of an enemy but by **the Angel of the LORD,** who killed **185,000** soldiers. This angel may have been the preincarnate Christ (see comments on Gen. 16:7) though not all scholars agree on this. **Sennacherib** was assassinated 20 years later (681 B.C.) by two of **his sons.**

### 2. JUDAH'S CAPTIVITY IN BABYLON (CHAPS. 38–39)

These chapters concern an interesting event in Hezekiah's life. Though God miraculously healed the king, his pride led to national calamity. In chapters 36–37, Hezekiah was a man of faith, but here he was a man of pride. This account is also recorded in 2 Kings 20.

#### a. Hezekiah's healing from his illness (38:1-8)

(1) Isaiah's prophecy that Hezekiah would die. **38:1.** From verse 6 it is clear that Hezekiah's illness preceded Sennacherib's surrounding of Jerusalem, recorded in chapters 36–37. Merodach-Baladan, mentioned in 39:1, ruled from 721 to 710 and nine months in 703–702 B.C. (he ruled before Sennacherib's invasion of Judah in 701). Though chapters 38–39 precede chapters 36–37 chronologically they follow them here because Hezekiah's folly led to the prophecy of the Babylonian Captivity, and because chapters 38–39, as stated earlier, prepare the way for chapters 40–66. Hezekiah's illness included a boil (38:21). **Isaiah** told him he would **die.**

(2) Hezekiah's prayer for a longer life. **38:2-3.** Hezekiah's prayer does not explicitly state a request to live longer,

but it is implied. Many have criticized Hezekiah for this request. However, self-preservation characterizes nearly everyone. **Hezekiah** asked **the LORD** to **remember** the **good** things he had done as king (cf. 2 Kings 18:5-8).

(3) God's answer to Hezekiah. **38:4-6.** In response to the king's **prayer** God said through **Isaiah** that He would grant the king **15** more **years.** Since **Hezekiah** died in 686 B.C. this illness would have been in 701 (see the chart "Kings of Judah and Israel and the Preexilic Prophets," near 1 Kings 12:25-33). In addition, God would not allow the Assyrians to take Jerusalem. These facts would have been a great comfort to Hezekiah.

(4) God's sign. **38:7-8.** God confirmed His promise to Hezekiah by a **sign** (cf. comments on v. 22). Apparently a special **stairway** had been built as a time device, a kind of sundial. As **the sun** went down in the west, a **shadow** would move upward on the staircase so that people could ascertain the time of the day. Interestingly **Ahaz** had rejected a sign from **the LORD** (7:10-12) but now on a staircase named for him his son Hezekiah was given a sign. How this miracle of the reversal of the sun's shadow occurred is not known. Perhaps the earth's rotation was reversed or perhaps the sun's rays were somehow refracted.

#### b. Hezekiah's song of thanksgiving (38:9-20)

(1) Hezekiah's statement about his condition. **38:9-15.** After he was healed **Hezekiah** wrote a song to express his thanks to God. His **illness** came, he said, **in the prime** of his **life. Death** was referred to figuratively as having **gates** through which a person entered (cf. Job 38:17; Pss. 9:13; 107:18). His statement that in death he would **not . . . see the LORD** does not mean he had no hope of heaven. It probably means that he would no longer have the benefit of enjoying God's blessings in this life. He would be without friends (Isa. 38:11) as his **house** (his body) was dismantled. By death he would be **cut . . . off** like a cloth being cut from a weaver's **loom.** He had hoped he would get well (v. 13) but he got worse (vv. 13-14). His illness was as if God were **a lion** breaking **all** his **bones,** a figure of speech depicting his deep inner anguish. In some way his cries of pain were like the sound of a bird and his

mourning like the doleful sound of a **dove** (cf. 59:11; Nahum 2:7). Hezekiah realized that this experience should humble him because God had brought on this illness.

(2) Hezekiah's affirmation that God was his strength. **38:16-20.** Hezekiah was grateful that God **restored** him **to health.** After the experience he could see that **it was** really **for** his **benefit** that it happened (v. 17; cf. Rom. 8:28). He sensed for one thing that God's **love** was with him and that God did not punish him in accord with what his **sins** deserved. When he said that those who are dead **cannot praise** the LORD (Isa. 38:18) he was not denying life after death. He was simply noting that in death one's activities on earth are stopped and that one's service on earth for God terminates (Ps. 30:9). However, Hezekiah affirmed that while he was still alive he would proclaim the Lord's **faithfulnesss** (Isa. 38:19). Because **the** LORD healed him, the king said he would sing to the Lord **in the temple.**

### c. Hezekiah's healing (38:21-22)

**38:21-22.** In the parallel account in 2 Kings these two verses in Isaiah precede the giving of the sign (see 2 Kings 20:7-9). **A poultice of** dried **figs,** a common treatment for boils and ulcers in those days, applied **to the boil** (possibly an inflamed ulceration), was used by God medicinally to promote the healing. This is an example of healing occurring because of a combination of prayer, medicine, and God's work. Hezekiah's question, **What will be the sign. . . ?** did not evidence lack of faith. In fact it was the opposite. Believing that he would be healed, he asked God for confirmation of His word.

### d. Isaiah's prophecy of captivity (chap. 39)

**39:1. Merodach-Baladan . . . sent** envoys from Babylon to **Hezekiah** with **letters and a gift.** Seemingly they went to congratulate the king on his **recovery.** But there was probably more to it than that. Merodach-Baladan was Marduk-apal-iddina, the invader (see comments on 21:1-10). Twice he had tried to break away from the Assyrian Empire, and once had succeeded in taking the city of Babylon. After his second reign (of nine

months in 703–702 B.C.) he was deposed by Sennacherib and went to Elam. While there (and while still known as **the king of Babylon)** he actively tried to form an alliance with other nations to throw off the Assyrian yoke. Undoubtedly his friendly visit after Hezekiah's illness was intended to persuade the king of Judah to join the rebel alliance in the fight against Assyria. This made Hezekiah's indiscretion all the worse in view of Isaiah's words that God was using Assyria to punish the whole region (chap. 10). The visit was also God's test of Hezekiah's heart (2 Chron. 32:31). Merodach-Baladan's visit preceded Sennacherib's attack on Jerusalem in 701 (since some of the wealth there had not yet been given to Sennacherib as tribute, 2 Kings 18:16). Therefore it seems as if all three events occurred in 701, in this order: Hezekiah's illness, Merodach-Baladan's visit, Sennacherib's attack.

**39:2.** In pride **Hezekiah . . . showed** the Babylonian **envoys** everything of value **in his storehouses. . . . palace,** and **kingdom.** Apparently Hezekiah was acting as if those riches all belonged to him and not to God. Undoubtedly **Hezekiah** thought he could impress the Babylonian emissaries, but they probably were thinking more of his ability to pay great sums of money to aid in the fight against Assyria.

**39:3-7.** When **Isaiah** heard of the foreigners' visit, he asked **Hezekiah . . . what** they said and **where** they came **from.** The king answered the second question but not the first one. When the prophet learned that **Hezekiah** had shown him all his **treasures. . . . Isaiah** gave him a two-part prophecy of judgment. First, the king's wealth would **be carried off to Babylon.** That was an astounding statement at that time because the great threat then was Assyria, not Babylon. The Babylonian envoys had come from a rebel force that was on the run and that had been defeated repeatedly. Second, **some of** the king's **descendants** would be forced to serve in the royal court of **Babylon.** The beginning of this was fulfilled in 605 B.C. when Daniel and a number of other royal sons were taken into the king's service in Babylon (Dan. 1:1-7). (On **eunuchs,** *sārîs,* see comments on "officials," Dan. 1:3.)

**39:8. Hezekiah** felt glad that **there**

would **be peace and security** during his days.

## II. The Restoration by God (chaps. 40–66)

Whereas the first portion of the book (chaps. 1–39) is filled with messages of judgment, this portion emphasizes restoration and deliverance. This section divides into three parts of nine chapters each (chaps. 40–48; 49–57; 58–66). The first two parts each conclude with the statement, "There is no peace . . . for the wicked" (48:22; 57:21). These prophecies of deliverance center around three events: (1) Deliverance from captivity in Babylon (already prophesied by Isaiah, 39:7). This is the main subject of chapters 40–48 and the chief deliverer is Cyrus, mentioned near the middle of the section (44:28–45:1). (2) The rejection and restoration of the Suffering Servant. This is discussed in 52:13–53:12, near the middle of chapters 49–57. (3) The consummation of God's restoration of Israel and the world. At the heart of this third section (chaps. 58–66) is the coming of the Messiah (chaps. 61–63).

When Isaiah wrote these prophecies of restoration Judah still had over 100 years of difficulty ahead of her before she fell to Babylon, and then she faced 70 years of captivity. Anticipating the future Captivity and God's restoration, Isaiah wrote to encourage the Judahites to live righteously in the present, despite forthcoming difficult circumstances.

For support for the view that all the Book of Isaiah, including chapters 40–66, was written by Isaiah the son of Amoz, see "Unity" in the *Introduction*.

### A. Deliverance of God's people (chaps. 40–48)

In these chapters the prophet reminded the people of their coming deliverance because of the Lord's greatness and their unique relationship with Him. He is majestic (chap. 40), and He protects Israel and not the world's pagan nations (chap. 41). Though Israel had been unworthy (chap. 42) the Lord had promised to regather her (43:1–44:5). Because He, the only God (44:6–45:25), was superior to Babylon He would make Babylon fall (chaps. 46–47). Therefore Isaiah exhorted the Israelites to live righteously and to flee away from Babylon (chap. 48). Ju-

dah's people are viewed as being in Babylon (43:14; 47:1; 48:20) and Jerusalem in ruins (44:26).

1. THE MAJESTY OF GOD (CHAP 40)

### a. Words of comfort: Deliverance is coming (40:1-11)

**40:1-2.** These words of comfort in verses 1-11 begin with **God** saying to His people (through Isaiah) that their time of trial was almost over. The repetition of the word **comfort** is for emphasis. Looking ahead to the Exile, Isaiah wanted the covenant nation (**My people**) to be comforted. As stated in the *Introduction* the words "comfort," "comforted," "comforts" occur 13 times in chapters 40–66.

**Jerusalem** was to be addressed **tenderly** (lit., "to the heart," i.e., in gentle, encouraging words; cf. Hosea 2:14) as a mother would speak to her child. The 70-year Captivity was seen as almost over. **Hard service** translates the Hebrew word for "warfare" and "time of enlistment in war." Judah's captivity was like the hardships of war. That time of trial had come because of **her sin.** But now her sin had **been paid for** so that God's blessings could begin. As stated in the Mosaic Covenant, God would bless His people if they lived according to His Word. However, if they disobeyed Him, He would curse them and eventually cast them out of the land of Israel (Deut. 28:15-68, esp. vv. 49-52, 64). Now that cursing was seen as almost accomplished, Israel could have a new start. To receive **double for all her sins** does not mean to be punished beyond what she deserves but in keeping with what she deserves. The point is that she has now received "full" or "sufficient" punishment for all her sins (cf. "double" in Isa. 51:19; 61:7).

**40:3-5. A voice** (probably Isaiah's, different from the voice in v. 6) called out to the people to **prepare the way for the LORD** (v. 3) and His **glory** (v. 5). True prophets were "voices," for their messages were from God. They were calling the nation to get back into a proper relationship with Him. Each Gospel writer applied Isaiah 40:3 to John the Baptist (Matt. 3:1-4; Mark 1:1-4; Luke 1:76-78; John 1:23). John was a **desert** prophet who prepared the way for Jesus Christ, and who **in the wilderness** made **a high-**

way for Him (cf. Matt. 3:3). However, here in Isaiah the entire nation was in a spiritual wilderness, and each Israelite needed to get ready spiritually for the appearing of the Lord.

Raising the valleys and lowering the mountains refer in hyperbole to workmen leveling or smoothing out the roads on which a dignitary would travel when he came to visit an area. Today an equivalent is, "roll out the red carpet." In Isaiah's day he was calling Israel to be "smoothed out" so that the Lord could come to the nation and rule. This was emphasized by all the prophets—ethically the nation must be righteous. Eventually the nation **will** be "smoothed out" spiritually when **the** glory **of the LORD** is **revealed** (Isa. 40:5). Isaiah was thinking of the millennial kingdom when the Lord will be revealed in His glory, that is, when His unique splendor will be evident everywhere. As Isaiah wrote elsewhere, the Messiah would suffer and would also appear in glory. However, apparently he was not aware of the time interval that would elapse between these two aspects. Though the disciples saw Jesus' glory (John 1:14), **all mankind** has not yet seen it, but they **will see it** in the Millennium. This coming glory is certain **for the . . . LORD has spoken it** (cf. Isa. 1:20; 58:14). The word of the Lord is sure and cannot be broken.

**40:6-8.** A second **voice** (cf. v. 3) spoke. This voice, probably God's, gave the command, probably to Isaiah, to **cry out.** The voice told him to contrast the difference between people and God. People are temporary and they change. They **are like** wild **grass** and **flowers** that come up in the springtime only to fade and fail when the weather gets hot (cf. Pss. 37:2; 102:11; 103:15-16). By contrast, **God** never fails for His **Word** endures **forever.** This fact would greatly comfort and encourage the people in exile who read these words. Because God's Word stands, His prophecy that the people would be restored to their land was sure to be fulfilled.

**40:9-11.** Perhaps the one **who** was to take **good tidings to Jerusalem** was someone who was passing on Isaiah's message. The messenger was to tell loudly **to the towns of Judah** that **God** was coming (v. 9) to Jerusalem, restoring His people from exile. Presumably Isaiah

envisioned the return from exile as leading immediately into the Millennium, though of course Bible passages written later indicate an extensive time gap between the two events. God was described first as **the Sovereign LORD** who is a powerful, conquering King (v. 10). He not only **rules** in power, but He also brings booty (**His reward,** i.e., blessings) **with Him. Arm** suggests strength, a concept Isaiah frequently mentioned (40:10; 51:5 [twice], 9; 52:10; 53:1; 59:1, 16; 60:4; 62:8; 63:5, 12). God was also pictured as a tender **Shepherd** (cf. Pss. 23:1; 80:1; John 10:11, 14; Heb. 13:20; 1 Peter 2:25; 5:4), who carefully **carries** and **leads** the weak and helpless members of **His flock** (cf. Jer. 13:17, 20; Micah 4:8; 5:4; 7:14; Zech. 10:3). These two aspects of the Lord's character are emphasized throughout this second portion of Isaiah's book.

*b. Additional words of comfort: God is majestic (40:12-26)*

The various aspects of God's majesty discussed in these verses are repeated often by Isaiah throughout the next eight chapters. For example, God's knowledge and creative power are stressed in 44:24–45:8, and His uniqueness is emphasized in 44:6-23.

(1) God's incomparable knowledge (40:12-17). **40:12-14.** By five rhetorical questions Isaiah emphasized that God, in creating the universe (v. 12), did not need anyone to assist Him (vv. 13-14). He is such a great Creator that all **the waters** of the globe were held, as it were, in **His hand.** Figuratively, He can measure the vast starry universe **with the breadth of His hand.** Also all the earth's **dust** could be put **in a basket** of His; and **the mountains** and **hills,** though vast, are so small compared with Him that He, figuratively speaking, could weigh them all on small **scales.** Though the immensity of Creation is awe-inspiring, no one on **earth** is God's equal.

In verses 13-14 Isaiah spoke of the infinite knowledge and skill **the LORD** possesses. No one on earth can claim to have **taught** the LORD anything. He did not need to **consult** anyone. Isaiah was probably thinking of the Creation account (Gen. 1) in which God spoke and Creation came into being. In irony God had also pointed out to Job by numerous questions that his knowledge was nothing compared with God's (Job 38:2–39:30).

**40:15-17.** Since God's Creation is so grandiose, the people of **the nations are** as **nothing** before Him (like a mere **drop** of water or **dust** particles on **scales**). All the wood and the animals in fertile, wooded **Lebanon,** north of Israel, would be inadequate for sacrifices that would be significant before the great God. **The nations** who do not know the Lord are **worthless and less than nothing** before Him.

(2) God's uniqueness compared with idols. **40:18-20.** With irony Isaiah wrote about two idols—one made of metal by a **craftsman** and then overlaid **with gold** and decorated with **silver** ornaments, and another selected by a **poor** man from **wood** and fashioned so that it **will not** fall over. (Other passages denouncing idols are 41:7; 44:9-20; 45:16, 20; 46:1-2, 6-7; Pss. 115:4-7; 135:15-18; Jer. 10:8-16; Hab. 2:19.) Both of these idol-makers used materials God created, and skills that God gave them! God, however, is unlike any idol. He is the Creator of **all** things including people. God is unique.

(3) God's sovereign control over the world (40:21-26). **40:21-22.** From His sovereign position in heaven God watches over His created universe. **You** (used four times in v. 21) refers to people in general. The force of the first question, for example, is "Doesn't everyone know this?" (cf. v. 28) The Lord is like a king sitting **enthroned above the circle** (*ḥûg,* "horizon," which is circular; cf. Job 26:10; Prov. 8:27) **of the earth** and over His **people** who by comparison seem **like** mere **grasshoppers. The heavens** (the sky) are pictured as spread **out like a tent** for Him to live in (cf. Ps. 104:2). Isaiah was not presenting a detailed idea of God's abode. He was merely using imagery that his readers would easily understand.

**40:23-24.** In controlling history God establishes **rulers** and removes them (cf. Dan. 2:21). This truth would have been comforting to Isaiah's original readers who were living under the threat of the Assyrian Empire and who heard his prophecy that the Babylonian Empire would take them into captivity.

**40:25-26.** God, who cannot be compared to anyone or anything (cf. v. 18; 46:5) knows everything about His Cre-

ation and sustains it. In His **strength** He created and also controls and sustains millions upon millions of stars, **each** one of which He, amazingly, has named (cf. Ps. 147:4). In Isaiah 40–66, God is frequently referred to as Creator and Maker, probably as a polemic against the lifeless idols of Babylon. He created the heavens, the earth, people, Israel, and darkness, and will create the new heavens and new earth.

*c. Further words of comfort: God watches over His people (40:27-31)*

Isaiah's readers were under the threat of Assyria. Years later Isaiah's readers during the Babylonian Captivity were under the domination of a godless empire. So Isaiah encouraged the people to remember that God never relaxes; He is always watching His people.

**40:27.** God's people should never think He has forgotten them. **Jacob** and **Israel** are synonyms for all 12 tribes. In chapters 40–49, Isaiah used these two words together 16 times (40:27; 41:8, 14; 42:24; 43:1, 22, 28; 44:1, 5, 21, 23; 45:4; 46:3; 48:1; 49:5-6). Though the people of the Northern Kingdom were already exiled to Assyria, **God** was still watching over the few believers who remained true to Him. His covenant people should never think God did not see or remember them.

**40:28-31.** On the question **Do you not know?** see comments on verse 21. Since **God,** who unlike pagan idols is eternal and **the Creator,** never grows **weary** (v. 28) **He** can give **strength to** those who are **weary** or **weak** (vv. 29-31). Among Isaiah's original readers **those who hope in the LORD** were believers who remained faithful to God. They were the ones who would be restored. For his readers in captivity Isaiah was probably speaking of a national refreshing when the captives would be released and would return to their land. Even though in captivity they were **weary** the LORD would help them endure and **soar . . . like eagles,** to be uplifted emotionally and spiritually.

2. A CHALLENGE TO THE NATIONS (CHAP. 41)

This challenge from the Lord to the nations stemmed from His special relationship with Israel. He would sovereignly protect Israel but the other nations would not enjoy that protection.

### a. God's confrontation of the nations (41:1-7)

**41:1.** The Lord confronted **the nations** and the **islands** (the remotest places where humans live) face to face in **judgment.** Of the 15 occurrences of "islands" in the Old Testament, 14 are in Isaiah. Together the islands and nations suggest all the world's peoples. In suggesting that they **meet together,** God was not asking that they negotiate; instead He was asking that they come together and realize the truth of His words.

**41:2-4.** God now told the nations that because He controls history, they in the final analysis really have no control over their future. For example, He **stirred up** a leader **from the east** (cf. v. 25 about God stirring up one from the north). This one from the east who would serve God's purpose was called **in righteousness.** This did not mean that warrior was righteous, but that he would carry out God's righteous plan on the earth. He would fulfill God's will even if he was unaware of it. God would hand **nations over to him** and subdue **kings before him,** that is, the conqueror could not be stopped in his conquests (turning enemies **to dust** and **chaff).**

Who was this conqueror? Because he would follow a **path his feet** had **not traveled before,** he could not be an Assyrian king (Assyria had invaded the west on several occasions). Since Isaiah was writing in advance for people who would be enslaved in Babylon, he must have been referring to that great Persian ruler Cyrus, whom he mentioned by name in 44:28 and 45:1. The Lord had planned this and would carry it out (41:4). In emphatic terms the **LORD** affirmed that **He** is the One who brings events to pass.

**41:5-7.** Mockingly Isaiah noted that alliances between the nations would not help them withstand the advance of Cyrus and the Persians as they carried out God's will. In **fear** the nations everywhere would be driven to help and encourage **each . . . other** (v. 6). (On **islands** see comments on v. 1; and on **the ends of the earth** see comments on 5:26.) Rather than turn to the true God, these idolatrous people would get more and more involved in **idol**-worship (41:7). The idols, which Isaiah had already mocked (see comments on 40:19-20), would not help them offset Cyrus' conquests.

### b. God's protection of Israel (41:8-20)

**41:8-10.** God sovereignly chose **Israel** (also called **Jacob** and Abraham's **descendants**) to be His servants (cf. 43:10) and to do His will. Unfortunately she often failed to be a faithful **servant** so God had to punish her. Taking the nation **from the ends of the earth** (see comments on 5:26) probably refers to God's regathering Israel after the Babylonian Captivity, rather than His leading Abraham from Ur of the Chaldees. Israel's being **chosen** by God is a frequent theme in the second major division of the Book of Isaiah (41:8-9; 42:1; 43:10, 20; 44:1-2; 45:4; 49:7; 65:9, 15, 22). Even though Israel was exiled because of sin and unbelief, she still was **not rejected** by God. Since the covenant the Lord made with Abraham was unconditional (Gen. 15), his descendants need **not fear.** The Lord remains their **God** (cf. Isa. 43:3) so He will continue to be with them (cf. 43:5) and **strengthen** (cf. 40:31), **help** (cf. 41:13-14), and **uphold** them.

**41:11-16.** In contrast with God's choosing and helping **Israel,** He will not protect nations **who oppose** her. They will perish (vv. 11-12). With the Lord's help Israel will defeat the nations as if she were **threshing** and winnowing grain (vv. 15-16). This, however, will not be by her own power because she is a **worm** and is **little** (v. 14). Israel should not **be afraid** (cf. v. 10; 43:5; 44:2, 8; 54:4). God is her **Redeemer,** a title Isaiah used of God 13 times (41:14; 43:14; 44:6, 24; 47:4; 48:17; 49:7, 26; 54:5, 8; 59:20; 60:16; 63:16), 5 of them with the title **the Holy One of Israel** (41:14; 43:14; 48:17; 49:7; 54:5). This help from God will cause Israel to **rejoice in** Him (41:16).

**41:17-20.** In God's care for Israel He will see that extremely thirsty persons will encounter **rivers . . . springs,** and **pools of water in the desert** (vv. 17-18; cf. 35:1-2, 6-7; 43:19-20; 44:3-4). In many places in the Middle East water is scarce, so this figure is most apt. God will also cause trees (seven kinds are mentioned) to grow **in the desert** whereas normally most of those trees grow only in fertile areas. In the Millennium the climate of the land of Israel will be changed so that the land will be well-watered and fertile. **People** will **know** that God, **the Holy One of Israel** (cf. 41:14, 16), **has done this.**

### c. God's knowledge of the future (41:21-29)

**41:21-24.** With the information the nations have received in verses 1-20, they are now challenged to use their **idols** to recall past events and predict the **future**. By doing **something** the nations might then cause others to **fear. But** their inability to tell the future shows that their gods are ineffective and **worthless.** Someone who would choose such a nation would be **detestable.**

**41:25-29.** In contrast with idols (vv. 21-24), which are man-made and unable to help people, God can and does tell the future. God predicted that a strong leader would come **from the north** and **from the east** (**the rising sun**) who would easily destroy many nations. This was Cyrus (see comments on v. 2). He was from the east (Persia was east of Israel) and also from the north as his conquests extended to the north of Israel. Only God could predict such a thing; **no one** else could even hint at it. Only He could **tell Zion** and **Jerusalem** that **a messenger** would give them **good** news about the Jews being released by Cyrus (cf. 40:1-5, 9-11). This proves that the Lord is the true God and **all** idols are **false** gods amounting **to nothing.** Those who believe in such idols have an empty faith; those **images** offer no more help than the **wind** and they confuse people's minds.

### 3. THE INDIVIDUAL SERVANT CONTRASTED WITH THE SERVANT NATION (CHAP. 42)

Verses 1-17 in this chapter are the first of Isaiah's "Servant Songs" referring to the Messiah. Israel is called the servant of the Lord (41:8; 42:19; 43:10; 44:1-2, 21; 45:4; 48:20). And the Messiah, on whom God has placed His Spirit (42:1; cf. 11:2), is also called the Servant (cf. 49:3, 5-7; 50:10; 52:13; 53:11). Which servant Isaiah was referring to in each passage must be determined by the context and the characteristics assigned to the servant. Israel as God's servant was supposed to help bring the world to a knowledge of God, but she failed. So the Messiah, the Lord's

Servant, who epitomizes the nation of Israel, will fulfill God's will.

### a. The Servant and His work (42:1-17)

**42:1-4.** Some Bible students say **My Servant** here refers to Israel, which is clearly the case in verse 19. True, Israel was upheld and **chosen** by the Lord, and was His **delight.** However, the statements in verses 1b-4 suggest that here the Servant is the Messiah. This **One** has the **Spirit** of God **on Him** (cf. 11:2), **and He will bring justice to the nations** (cf. 9:7; 11:3-4; 16:5). He will be gentle (42:2-3a)—most people would break a weak, useless **reed,** but **He will not** do so—and He will be faithful (v. 3b) and **not . . . discouraged** (v. 4). He gave the **Law** in which **the islands** (i.e., people in remote parts; cf. 41:1) **will . . . hope.** Matthew 12:18-21 quotes Isaiah 42:1-4 with some minor variations, relating it to Jesus and His ministry in Israel. As God's Servant, Jesus did what Israel could never do. He perfectly carried out the will of the Father so that people everywhere may believe in the Holy One of Israel.

**42:5-7.** The LORD promised to assist the Servant in His mission, which **God** can do because He is the Creator (cf. 40:12-14, 26). He **created the** immense **heavens** and **the earth** (cf. 44:24; 45:12, 18; 48:13; 51:13, 16) and life in it, including man, giving him **breath.** Speaking to His Servant (42:6-7) God assured Him that He had been **called** to perform the will of God. To be **called . . . in righteousness** (as Cyrus also would be, 41:2), meant to be responsible to do God's righteous will. Of course the Messiah, unlike Cyrus, lived a righteous life (for He is God). Because **the LORD** would **take hold of** the Servant's **hand** the Messiah would have the power to carry out God's will.

Also the Servant was assured that He would **be a covenant for the people** (cf. 49:8). He would fulfill God's covenant promises to Israel, and would also be **a light** (cf. 42:16; Luke 1:79) **for the Gentiles** (cf. Isa. 49:6). Spiritually unredeemed Israel and the Gentiles are **blind,** and they are **captives . . . in darkness.** Though Cyrus would be the servant to release Jewish captives from exile, the Messiah gives spiritual **release** (cf. 61:1; John 8:32; Col. 1:13), sight (cf. John 9:39-41), and light (cf. John 8:12) to those who trust Him. (On **eyes** being opened; cf.

Isa. 32:3; 35:5.) This spiritual salvation to both Jews and Gentiles will eventuate in the glorious messianic kingdom.

**42:8-9.** The LORD, Israel's covenant-keeping God, had given the prophecy recorded in verses 6-7 and He **will not** let **idols** take credit for it (cf. comments on 41:21-24). In view of all that God had already done for Israel (**the former things**) these **new things** (cf. 48:6) of which He had been speaking would certainly happen. No other god can foretell such things. If, as some scholars argue, someone other than Isaiah wrote chapters 40–66 *after* the Jewish captives were released by Cyrus, then Isaiah's point in 42:9 and elsewhere is destroyed. Isaiah was affirming that God, unlike idols, *can* tell the future. And this divine ability adds to His **glory** (v. 8).

**42:10-17.** People everywhere (in **the ends of earth**; cf. 41:5 and see comments on 5:26) should **sing** this **song** of **praise** to **the LORD.** These should include (a) people who make their living by **sea** commerce, (b) those who **live** in the **islands** (cf. 41:1, 5), and (c) those in **the desert** regions and **towns. Kedar** (cf. 21:16-17) is an area in Northern Arabia, and **Sela** was a city in Edom. People everywhere should **sing** and **shout. . . . to the LORD** because of His victory **over His enemies** at the Messiah's second coming.

God, seemingly **silent** for **a long time,** will act in judgment though, humanly speaking, it will be painful for Him (42:14). He will **dry up** the places where people do not revere Him (v. 15). But He will **guide** those who trust in Him, giving them **light** (cf. v. 7) and smoothing their **paths** (v. 16). However, pagans **who trust in idols** will be ashamed (v. 17; cf. 44:9, 11; 45:16).

### b. Israel's current condition (42:18-25)

**42:18-20.** Later when Jews in the Babylonian Exile would read this chapter in Isaiah, they might wonder why they were experiencing such difficulties. Isaiah answered this implied question by pointing out that though **the LORD** said He would lead them they were being punished because spiritually they had been **deaf** and **blind** (cf. v. 16). Now God told them to **hear . . . look,** and **see.** The **blind** and **deaf . . . servant** (v. 19) refers to Israel, not the Messiah. They *should* have been a light to the Gentiles (v. 6),

helping others come to know God. But they failed. Though they saw and heard certain events they disregarded them (cf. 43:8; 48:8).

**42:21-22.** The Mosaic **Law** stipulated that if Israelites lived according to God's righteous standards He would bless them. In that sense the Law was **great and glorious.** Living by it would reveal to others **His righteousness. But** if Israel did not keep His stipulations they would be driven out of the land (Deut. 28:49-53). Their cities would be **looted** (cf. Isa. 42:24) and the people put **in prisons** (in exile). **No one** could **rescue them** except of course the Lord.

**42:23-25.** Why would Israel be plundered? (cf. v. 22) Was it because **the LORD** could not protect them? No, it was because the Lord was punishing them for disobeying the **Law** (cf. v. 21). Though God in His **anger** against their sin would destroy Jerusalem **in flames** and lead them into captivity, they still would be blind to their sin and His ways (cf. vv. 19-20). That is why the Lord would send His Servant to open their eyes.

### 4. A PROMISE TO REGATHER THE UNWORTHY SERVANT (43:1–44:5)

Judah's exile was pictured as drawing to a close (40:2) for the Lord was raising up a leader who would release them (41:2-4, 25). God would also raise up a Servant, the Messiah, to give them spiritual release (42:1-17). However, the nation was still in spiritual captivity (42:18-25). Now the Lord exhorted the nation not to fear (43:1-7) for their condition would show the world that He is truly the only God (43:8-13). He would restore them from Babylon, bringing them back home in a new "Exodus" (43:14-28). Therefore He said again they were not to fear (44:1-5).

### a. Israel exhorted not to fear (43:1-7)

**43:1-2. Jacob** (also called **Israel;** see comments on 40:27) need have no **fear** in her captivity because God had **created** (cf. v. 7) and **formed** her (cf. vv. 7, 21; 44:2, 24) and had **redeemed** her from bondage in Egypt. "Redeemed" translates *gā'al,* "to buy out of slavery" (cf. comments on "Redeemer" in 41:14 and note "redeemed" in 44:22-23; 48:20; 52:9; 63:9). Reference to this Exodus was fitting in view of what Isaiah wrote in

43:14-28 about a new "Exodus" in which God would bring the people back to their homeland from Babylon. To be **called** (cf. 48:12) **by name** points up Israel's special relationship with **the LORD** as His covenant people. This is similar to a shepherd calling his sheep by name in his personal care for them. Because of God's past work in creating, redeeming, and caring for Israel, He would continue to protect her. Therefore in difficult times, pictured as floodwaters and **fire,** Israel should not give up and fear, for God would **be with** her and protect her.

**43:3-4.** A second reason Israel need not fear is that God loves her. This special love is not because of something the nation did or some quality she possesses. It is because of His choosing. As a **ransom** or reward for releasing the Jewish captives, Persia was enabled by God to conquer **Egypt . . . Cush** (modern-day southern Egypt, all of Sudan, and northern Ethiopia), and **Seba,** possibly the same as Sheba in southern Arabia (cf. 60:6; Job 6:19; 1 Kings 10:1-13) where the Sabeans lived (cf. Job 1:15; Isa. 45:14; Ezek. 23:42; Joel 3:8). In contrast with non-Israelites (represented by these three nations), Israel is **precious** and **honored** because of God's **love.**

**43:5-7.** A third reason Israel need not fear (**do not be afraid**; cf. 41:10, 14; 44:2, 8; 54:4) is that God, who was **with** them (cf. 41:10), promised to **bring** them back to their land. Though Isaiah was referring primarily to the restoration from Babylon (2 Chron 36:22-23; Ezra 1:1-4), he was also speaking of a wider regathering. At the second coming of Christ Israel will be regathered to her land (Matt. 24:31) from around the world —**from the east . . . west** (Isa. 43:5), **north,** and **south** (v. 6), and even from **the ends of the earth** (see comments on 5:26). These regathered ones who will be **called by** God's **name** and are those He **created** (cf. 43:1) and **formed** (cf. vv. 1, 21; 44:2, 24) **for His glory** (cf. 44:23); they will display His attributes.

*b. Israel to be a witness to the world (43:8-13)*

**43:8-10.** God invited Israel, still spiritually **blind** and **deaf** (cf. 42:20; 48:8), to be brought before **the nations.** God challenged the nations to **bring . . . witnesses to try to prove** that they could predict the future (cf. 41:21-23). Then He said that the Israelites, as His **witnesses** (cf. 43:12; 44:8) and His chosen servant (cf. 41:8-9), demonstrate that **He** is the only God (43:10). He existed **before** any **god was** made, and He will continue to exist long **after** the last idol perishes.

**43:11-13.** The Lord's deliverance of Israel also shows that He is the true God. He is her only **Savior** and no one can oppose His plans. "Savior" is another title of God that Isaiah used frequently (cf. 17:10; 43:3; 45:15, 21; 49:26; 60:16; 62:11; 63:8). God's revealing His plans and saving His people could not be duplicated by any **foreign god.** Israel's existence **witnesses** to His sovereignty and eternity. No one can **reverse** what **God** puts into action or thwart His plans (cf. Job 42:2).

*c. Israel promised deliverance from Babylon (43:14-21)*

**43:14-15.** Verses 14 and 16 are introduced by the statement, **This is what the LORD says,** a statement used frequently by Isaiah in the second major division of his book (43:14, 16; 44:2, 6, 24; 45:1, 11, 14; 48:17; 49:7-8; 50:1; 52:4; 56:1, 4; 65:8, 13; 66:1, 12) to stress the divine authority behind his words. The Lord calls Himself Israel's **Redeemer** (cf. comments on 41:14), **the Holy One of Israel** (cf. comments on 1:4), **the LORD, the Holy One, Israel's Creator** and King (cf. comments on 33:17). He said He would change **the Babylonians** from conquerors to the conquered. Babylon's **ships** may have been the trading vessels she used on the Euphrates River and the Persian Gulf.

**43:16-21.** God, who in the first Exodus brought Israel out of Egypt and drowned the Egyptian **army,** would do an even greater thing. Therefore forgetting **the past** (v. 18), Israel should realize God would do **a new** work. In this new "Exodus," the return from the Exile, the Jews would be going through desolate **desert** land where God would **provide water** and **streams** in abundance (cf. 35:6-7; 41:18; 44:3-4). Therefore His **Chosen** People (cf. comments on 41:8-9), whom He created (**formed**; cf. 43:21; 44:2, 24), would **praise** Him (cf. 42:10-13). Still a third and more glorious "Exodus" will take place when the Messiah returns to regather His people (cf. 43:5-6) and establish His millennial reign on earth.

### d. Israel's deliverance to be by God's grace (43:22-28)

**43:22-25.** The future "Exodus" from Babylon would not come as the result of Israel's religious acts, including prayers, **offerings . . . sacrifices . . . incense,** or **calamus** (possibly sweet cane; cf. Song 4:14; Jer. 6:20; Ezek. 27:19). They had not bothered (**wearied,** Isa. 43:22) themselves in the sacrificial system, **but** their **sins** had wearied **God!** (cf. Mal. 2:17) Without the Jerusalem temple the exiles were obviously unable to take **sacrifices** to the altar. So with no **offerings their unforgiven sins** piled up! However, God would forgive them because of His grace, **for** His **own sake.**

**43:26-28.** Though the Lord would forgive Israel (v. 25), He still needed to discipline them. Suggesting that they **state** their **case** (v. 26), the Lord then stated *His* case against them. Their **first father**—either Adam (cf. Hosea 6:7) or Abraham (cf. Gen. 12:18)—had sinned as had their **spokesmen,** the prophets and priests. Therefore God would punish Israel with **disgrace . . . destruction,** and **scorn** (Isa. 43:28), which He did in the Babylonian Captivity.

### e. Israel again exhorted not to fear (44:1-5)

**44:1-2.** Again the prophet emphasized God's choosing (see comments on 41:8-9) and forming (cf. 43:1, 7, 21; 44:24) Israel. (On the word **listen,** see comments on 46:3.) Since God promised to **help** her, she need **not be afraid** (cf. 41:10, 14; 43:5; 44:8; 54:4). (On **Jacob** as God's **servant** see comments on 41:8.) **Jeshurun,** meaning "the upright one," is a poetic synonym for Israel, used elsewhere only in Deuteronomy 32:15; 33:5, 26.

**44:3-5.** The Lord will revive Israel physically and spiritually. He will **pour water on the . . . land,** making it well watered (cf. 35:6-7; 41:18; 43:19-20) and He **will pour** His Holy **Spirit** (cf. 32:15) on their **descendants.** This outpouring of the Spirit will occur when the people have returned in belief to the land (cf. Ezek. 36:24, 27; Joel 2:25-29) just after the Messiah's second coming to establish the Millennium. Redeemed **Israel** will prosper numerically **like grass** and **poplar trees,** and they will want to be known as righteous individuals (Isa. 44:5), un-

ashamed of Him and their nation.

### 5. THE LORD'S UNIQUENESS AS THE ONLY GOD (44:6–45:25)

This section emphasizes that the Lord is the only God and that therefore idol-worship is illogical and absurd. His uniqueness and sovereignty are (a) contrasted with the idols (44:6-23), (b) revealed by His prophesying the coming of Cyrus (44:24–45:8), (c) shown by His having created everything (45:9-13), and (d) demonstrated by the fact that eventually Gentiles will proclaim Him to be the Lord (45:14-25). Addressed primarily to Gentiles, 44:6–45:25 would also have encouraged the covenant people, especially those in captivity, as they would read that their captors would someday acknowledge the true God of Israel.

### a. God's sovereignty over nonexistent idols (44:6-23)

(1) The uniqueness of God. **44:6-8.** Several titles stress God's sovereignty: **Israel's King** (cf. 43:15), **Redeemer** (cf. 43:14; see comments on 41:14), **the LORD Almighty** God, and **the First** and **the Last** (i.e., the eternal One; cf. 48:12; Rev. 1:17; 2:8; 22:13). The Lord argued for His uniqueness (**apart from Me there is no God;** cf. Isa. 43:11; 44:6; 46:9) by challenging anyone to tell of the past and the future (44:7; cf. 41:22-23). Since His knowledge of the future (from **long ago**) proves His uniqueness, His people should **not be afraid** (cf. 41:10, 14; 43:5; 44:2; 54:4). They themselves are **witnesses** (cf. 43:10, 12) to His uniqueness, strength, and stability (**Rock;** cf. 17:10; 26:4; 30:29).

(2) The unprofitableness of idols. **44:9.** Idol-worship does **nothing** for those who practice it; it only shows them up as being spiritually **blind** and **ignorant.** Pagans view their worship of idols as meritorious, but it will ultimately bring them **shame** (cf. v. 11; 42:17; 45:16).

(3) The weakness of idol-makers. **44:10-14.** People who make idols **will** experience **shame** (cf. v. 9) and disrepute. The fact that **craftsmen are nothing but men** (cf. 40:19) epitomizes the foolishness of idol-worship. A **blacksmith** who **gets hungry** while making **an idol** from metal, and a **carpenter** who has to **outline** his idol on wood, do not inspire confidence in their idols. The gods themselves have

no life for they are made from metals or from **trees** which ironically the true God **made.**

(4) The material nature of idols. **44:15-20.** From the same piece of **wood** a workman **makes an idol** and **bakes bread.** What folly to bow down to wood, part of which is used to cook one's food and to keep **himself . . . warm!** People who pray that an **idol**—mere wood—would **save** them (v. 17) are ignorant and have no spiritual sight or comprehension (v. 18; cf. 6:10). Having **their eyes . . . plastered over** may refer to a religious rite in which mud was applied to worshipers' eyes. Idolaters do not **think** of the incongruity of using part of a piece of wood **for fuel** for baking and roasting and making an idol (sarcastically called by Isaiah **a detestable thing**) **from what is left.** To worship wood is to feed **on ashes** (cf. Ps. 102:9), that is, to trust in something totally worthless, something that deceives.

(5) The joy of the Lord's redeemed. **44:21-23.** The contrast between **Israel** and deluded people who make and worship idols (vv. 9-20) is striking. Believers in Israel were redeemed but idol-makers were deceived. Israel was to **remember** that God can foretell the future (vv. 6-8) and that idols are really nothing (vv. 9-20). Therefore she should worship the Lord who has forgiven her sins (cf. 43:25) and **redeemed** her. Some, however, think **these things** refer to what follows and that Israel was to remember she had been redeemed. In either case the nation was to **sing.** In fact all nature is personified as being asked to sing (cf. the **mountains** in 49:13) about Him who **redeemed Jacob** and who **displays His glory in Israel** (cf. 43:7). In contrast with the other nations' spiritual darkness, Israel will live in the light of God's glory.

*b. God's prophecies about Cyrus (44:24–45:8)*

The fact that God predicted more than 150 years in advance that a man named Cyrus would release the Jewish exiles points to God's uniqueness. To approach the Bible with an antisupernaturalistic bias and say that the references to Cyrus were added later, *after* he released the captives, causes the passage, as stated earlier, to lose its emphasis on God's uniqueness in predicting the

future. This would mean that God is no different from idols—the very point Isaiah is disproving!

**44:24-28.** The LORD, Israel's **Redeemer** (see comments on 43:14), **who formed** her (cf. 43:1, 7, 21; 44:2), is the Creator of **all things** including **the heavens** and **the earth** (cf. 42:5; 45:12, 18; 48:13; 51:13, 16) and the One who makes **false prophets . . . diviners,** and supposedly **wise** people look foolish. Those who said God could not release His people from Babylon would be proved false when God's **predictions** were fulfilled. Through the prophets, **His messengers,** He said **Jerusalem** would again have people living in it. **Cyrus** would allow the exiles to go back and rebuild their capital city **Jerusalem** (cf. 45:13) and **the temple.** In 586 B.C. Nebuchadnezzar and his forces broke through Jerusalem's walls, burned the houses and the temple, and carried many captives into exile. Cyrus, founder of the Persian Empire, first came to the throne of Anshan in Eastern Elam in 559. In 549 he conquered the Medes and became the ruler of the combined Persian and Median Empire. In 539 he conquered Babylon (Dan. 5:30) and the very next year issued a decree that the Jews could return to Jerusalem and rebuild the temple (2 Chron. 36:22-23; Ezra 1:1-4). In doing this Cyrus was serving God's purposes as if he were God's **shepherd.** Those returnees built the temple, completing it in 515 B.C., and years later (in 444 B.C.) Nehemiah went to Jerusalem to rebuild the city walls (see comments on Neh. 1–2; Dan. 9:25).

**45:1-4.** Besides issuing a decree permitting the captives to return home, **Cyrus** also avenged God's wrath on the **nations.** Amazingly the Lord called Cyrus **His anointed.** The word "anointed" referred to the relationship Israel's first two kings, Saul and David, had with God (1 Sam. 10:1; 16:6). Since Israel in exile had no king, Cyrus functioned in a sense as her king (the anointed one) to bring about blessing. Like the Messiah (lit., "the Anointed One") who would come after him, Cyrus would have a twofold mission: to free the people, and to bring God's judgment on unbelievers.

Cyrus would easily conquer other nations (Isa. 45:1b), with God's help (v. 2), and would receive wealth from the nations he overcame (v. 3). This he did in conquering Lydia and Babylon. All this would be **for the sake of Jacob,** God's **Chosen** People (see comments on 41:8-9). And even though Cyrus would enjoy a special relationship with God (God called him **by name;** cf. 43:1) and was honored by God, he still was not a believer for he did **not acknowledge** the Lord as the true God.

**45:5-7.** Again the uniqueness of **God** is stressed. The fact that **there is no other** is stated in verses 5-6, 14, 18, 21-22 (also see 43:11; 44:6; 46:9). In Cyrus' day the Lord was not universally acknowledged, but eventually He will be (cf. Phil. 2:10-11). People will realize that all that happens—**light** (life), **darkness** (death), **prosperity,** and **disaster** (not "evil" as in the KJV; cf. Amos 3:6)—comes from God. As the sovereign LORD of the universe He can **do** everything.

**45:8.** When the millennial kingdom is established on the earth the **heavens,** figuratively speaking, will **rain down righteousness** (God's standards will be followed). And **salvation,** like a great harvest, will **spring up.** That is, people everywhere will know **the LORD** (cf. v. 6; 11:9; Hab. 2:14).

### c. God's sovereignty in Creation (45:9-13)

**45:9-13.** The Lord can work sovereignly over individuals on **the earth** because He **created** it. When someone who is created voices disapproval of the Creator's work he risks receiving a pronouncement of impending doom (**woe,** vv. 9-10; cf. comments on 3:9) from **the LORD. A potsherd,** a broken, discarded piece of pottery, has no right to question **the potter.** Nor does a child have the right to question why his parents **brought** him into the world. In the same way **Israel** has no right to question God her **Maker** (45:9, 11), the world's Creator (v. 12), in His plans to **raise up Cyrus** (v. 13). Cyrus' task was again stated: to allow freed **exiles** to rebuild God's **city,** Jerusalem (cf. 44:28).

### d. Gentile submission to God (45:14-19)

**45:14-17.** In the Millennium Gentiles will realize that Israel's **God is** the only God. People from **Egypt** and **Cush** and the **Sabeans** (see comments on 43:3) will be subservient to **Israel** and will admit that **there is no other god** (cf. 45:6, 18, 21-22; also note Zech. 14:16-19; Mal. 1:11).

Though at times it seems as if the Lord is hiding, He really is the **Savior of Israel** (see comments on Isa. 43:11). Whereas people who persist in idol-worship will be ashamed (cf. 42:17; 44:9, 11; 45:24) believing Israelites **will never** be ashamed (cf. 54:4; Rom. 9:33; 10:11; 1 Peter 2:6) for they will enjoy God's salvation forever.

**45:18-19.** Again God's creative power (cf. 42:5; 44:24; 45:12; 48:13; 51:13, 16) is proof that what He predicted about Cyrus is true. Another proof is the very nature of God's word. He speaks only what is true. In captivity the Jews could count on the fact that the Lord would deliver them from exile by Cyrus.

### e. The Lord's appeal to the Gentiles (45:20-25)

**45:20-25.** The Lord appealed to the Gentiles to turn from wooden **idols** and **be saved** from coming destruction. They were to note the prophecies **God** had given and to acknowledge His uniqueness as the only **God** (vv. 21-22; cf. vv. 5-6, 14, 18) and to **turn to** Him because eventually everyone will acknowledge His sovereignty (cf. v. 14; Mal. 1:1; Rom. 14:11; Phil. 2:10-11). Even so, some Gentiles will be saved, recognizing that only in Him is **righteousness** available. But many will continue to rage **against Him** (Isa. 45:24). However, **Israel,** God's covenant people, **will be** justified (**found righteous**) **in the LORD,** and in that they **will** rejoice (**exult**).

### 6. THE LORD'S SUPERIORITY OVER BABYLON (CHAPS. 46-47)

Babylon would be used by God to judge Judah, but she in turn would be destroyed by God. Her gods, mere idols, would not be able to save her from defeat (chap. 46), and Babylon would fall in spite of her sorceries and wisdom (chap. 47).

### a. The Lord's superiority over Babylon's gods (chap. 46)

**46:1-2.** The Babylonian gods would not be able to save Babylon from being conquered. **Bel,** not to be confused with the Canaanite Baal, was another name for Marduk (cf. Jer. 50:2), god of the sun. **Nebo,** son of Marduk, was the god of learning, writing, and astronomy. Large **images** of those gods, **carried about** on Babylon's New Year's Day festival, were heavy and **burdensome.** So those idols could not help relieve the Babylonians' **burden.** In striking contrast, the God of Israel sustains and carries His people (Isa. 46:3-4).

**46:3-4.** God's admonition to His people to **listen** to Him is frequent in Isaiah's prophecies (44:1; 46:3, 12; 47:8; 48:1, 12, 14, 16; 51:4; 52:8; 55:2). Besides caring for and carrying His people (see comments on 46:1-2), God also sustains them throughout their lives. From the time of conception (v. 3) to **old age** (v. 4) the Lord watches over His own and rescues them from trouble.

**46:5-7.** Gods of **gold** and silver (cf. 40:19) cannot **be compared** (cf. 40:18, 25) to the true God because such gods are incapable of action. Pagans hired craftsmen **to make** heavy gods out of precious metals and then had to **carry** them to their resting places, from which they could not **move.** This is one of several times Isaiah belittled idols (cf. 40:18-20; 41:7; 44:9-20; 45:16, 20; 46:1-2). Unlike the false gods, the true God can **answer** peoples' prayers and **save** them.

**46:8-11.** The **rebels,** people of Babylon (cf. v. 12), were to **remember** that **God** is the only God; He is unique (v. 9; cf. 43:11; 44:6; 45:5-6, 14, 18, 21-22). Proofs of God's uniqueness include His knowledge and control of the future (cf. 45:21) and His abililty to bring Cyrus **from the east** (cf. 41:2) like a quick **bird of prey** to accomplish His plans.

**46:12-13.** The **stubborn-hearted** and those **far from righteousness** were the Babylonians (cf. rebels, v. 8), who would be defeated by the Persian Empire. God would bring against the unrighteous Babylonians His **righteousness,** that is, Cyrus, who would carry out God's righteous will. This would result in **salvation** for **Zion,** deliverance from exile for Jerusalem, which would mean Israel would again display God's **splendor** or glory (cf. 44:23).

*b. The Lord's assurance of Babylon's fall (chap. 47)*

Isaiah described Babylon's fall to the Persians in 539 B.C., more than 150 years before the event took place. The Babylonians, Judah's captors, would become captives.

**47:1-3.** When conquered, **Babylon** would become a humbled servant, sitting **in the dust,** an act depicting great mourning (cf. Jonah 3:6). The words **Virgin Daughter** personify the people of a city as a young, innocent girl (cf. Isa. 23:12; 37:22), probably meaning that the city's walls had never been breached. The people would **no** longer be **tender** and **delicate** like a virgin because of the hardships they would face. As servants of the conquerors, they would have to **grind** the **flour,** unable to worry about their clothing or modesty. Some of them would have to flee across **streams.** Many of them would be raped and abused (47:3).

**47:4.** This verse records the response of Israel when they would sense the relief coming to them because of Babylon's defeat. Seeing God's vengeance on their captors (v. 3b), they would praise the Lord for they would recognize that release from exile would come from God, not themselves. So they would call God their **Redeemer** (cf. comments on 43:14), **the LORD Almighty,** and **the Holy One of Israel** (cf. comments on 1:4).

**47:5-7.** The Lord had used Babylon to judge Judah, but that ruthless nation, like Assyria (cf. Isa. 10), had abused its power (cf. Hab. 1:6-11). So God's sentence was pronounced on Babylon: **no** longer would she be . . . **queen of kingdoms** (cf. "eternal queen" in Isa. 47:7). Babylon was considered nearly impregnable.

Babylon had been able to conquer Judah, God's **inheritance** (see comments on Deut. 4:20), only because God allowed it (Isa. 47:6). Merciless, **the Babylonians** even treated **the aged** Jewish captives harshly. Therefore God would treat everyone in Babylon harshly (v. 3b). The Babylonians never considered the possibility that they would not be in a position of power **forever** (v. 7). Babylon thought she was **the eternal queen** (cf. v. 5).

**47:8-11.** Babylon thought that she could never be defeated (v. 8). But the Lord said that she would lose her **children** and become **a widow. . . . on a single day,** speaking figuratively of her desolation from defeat (cf. Jerusalem as a widow, Lam. 1:1). Though Babylon thought she was unique—**I am, and there is none besides me** (Isa. 47:8, 10)—she was wrong; *God* is the One who is unique, as Isaiah had stated repeatedly (43:11; 44:6; 45:5-6, 14, 18, 21-22; 46:9).

Babylon prided herself in her sorcerers who supposedly "told the future" and cast **spells** to influence others (cf. 47:12). **Sorceries** (vv. 9, 12) translates *kešāpîm*, a word used in the Old Testament only here and in 2 Kings 9:22; Micah 5:12; Nahum 3:4. It suggests seeking information about the future by means of demonic forces. Such supposed **knowledge**, however, was unreliable, for the sorcerers could not foresee Babylon's forthcoming **calamity** and would not be able to **conjure it away.**

**47:12-15.** The Lord mockingly urged the Babylonians to **keep on** in their **spells** and **sorceries** (cf. v. 9), which the city had been involved in **since childhood** (cf. v. 15), that is, since the nation was founded. In sarcasm He suggested the **astrologers** and **stargazers . . . save** them. Astrology was common in Babylon (cf. Dan. 2:2, 4-5). But their work was worthless, **like** mere **stubble,** the dried stalks of grain that burn quickly. Those religious leaders could not **save** even **themselves,** let alone Babylon. Yet they persisted in their **error.**

### 7. AN EXHORTATION FOR ISRAEL (CHAP. 48)

#### a. An exhortation to remember God's prophecies (48:1-11)

**48:1-5.** The Lord reminded His people—called the **house of Jacob . . . Israel,** and **the line of Judah**—of their hypocrisy. They took **oaths,** invoking God's **name,** but they were **not** righteous. They thought that being **citizens of** Jerusalem (**the holy city;** cf. 52:1), though they were not living there, and claiming to **rely on . . . the Lord,** were adequate. Comfortable in the Babylonian Empire (and later the Persian Empire), they considered it unimportant to go back to Jerusalem. **The Lord** said He had prophesied what would happen (48:3), apparently referring to the coming Captivity. But knowing of the coming Exile, the people were **stubborn** (v. 4), refusing to change their ways. Again one reason God made those predictions was to point up His superiority to **idols.**

**48:6-8.** Israel had disregarded the previous prophecies, so God would give her **new** prophecies (v. 6), predictions that God's wrath would be delayed (cf. v. 9) and that she would be freed from captivity. Those plans were **created now,** not that God had never thought of them before, but that they would be put into effect at that time. From Deuteronomy 30:1-5, Israel knew she would be brought back to the land after captivity, and her dwelling in the land was assured by the Abrahamic Covenant (Gen. 15:18-21). But until Isaiah's prophecies were given she did not know *how* God would deliver her. This was so the people would not feel smug (Isa. 48:7b), thinking their own cunning had set them free. They actually were spiritually insensitive (v. 8; cf. 42:20; 43:8) because they were **treacherous** and rebellious. So their physical and spiritual deliverance would come not from their goodness or their own plans, but from God's grace.

**48:9-11.** The Lord would **delay** His **wrath,** that is, withhold it so His people could return to Judah. This would be for His **sake** primarily (vv. 9, 11; cf. 43:25). The Exile was to refine them so they would return to the land in belief. That refining, however, was **not** with **silver.** This means either that the refining was not accomplished with money, or that the process could not be compared to silver, or that unlike silver which becomes pure, the nation would not. Whatever the meaning, the Captivity was like being in a **furnace,** to test them, not destroy them. If God would go back on His word about the return, His reputation would be **defamed.**

#### b. An exhortation to note God's sovereignty (48:12-19)

**48:12-15.** Urging the nation to **listen to** Him (cf. comments on 46:3), God once again spoke of His unique position as the only God. (On **the First** and **the Last** see comments on 44:6.) Isaiah repeatedly wrote about two proofs of His uniqueness: (a) His creative power (cf. 42:5; 44:24; 45:12, 18; 51:13, 16) and (b) His ability to foretell the future, in this case, the fall of **Babylon** by means of Cyrus, God's **chosen ally** (cf. "shepherd" and "anointed," 44:28; 45:1). God **called him** and would help him **succeed.** No other god could have predicted this.

**48:16.** The Lord, who is speaking, said He had not been secretive about Cyrus' defeat of Babylon. Suggestions on who is speaking in the second part of verse 16, beginning with the words **And now,** include Cyrus, Israel, Isaiah, and the Messiah. Probably the Messiah,

God's Servant, is intended because of His association (as in 42:1; also note 11:1-2) **with the Spirit.** Just as Cyrus would not fail in his mission (48:15), so the Messiah-Servant, sent by God with the Holy Spirit on Him, will not fail in His mission.

**48:17-19.** The LORD, Israel's **Redeemer** (cf. comments on 41:14) and **Holy One,** had constantly been teaching and guiding **Israel** through the Law. But they **had** not **paid attention to** His **commands.** Had they done so, they would have experienced not the Exile but **peace** and **righteousness,** and none of their **children** would have been killed.

### c. An exhortation to flee Babylon (48:20-21)

**48:20-21.** With Cyrus' edict (2 Chron. 36:22-23; Ezra 1:1-4) allowing the Jews to return home, God urged His people to **leave Babylon** quickly **(flee).** Because this return was like being **redeemed** (gā'al, "to buy out of slavery"; cf. 43:1)—this time from Babylon, not Egypt —the people could rejoice. After the Egyptian Exodus God provided water in **the deserts** and **from the rock** (cf. Ex. 17:1-7). Here too, it is implied, God would provide for them in their second "Exodus."

### d. The absence of peace for the wicked (48:22)

**48:22.** In contrast with joy (v. 20) for those who obey the Lord **there is no peace . . . for the wicked,** either in the nation Israel or among Gentile nations. This brief statement is repeated in 57:21.

## B. Restoration by the Suffering Servant (chaps. 49–57)

The previous nine-chapter section (chaps. 40–48) dealt mainly with Cyrus and his mission in the Jews' restoration. These nine chapters (49–57) deal primarily with the Servant-Messiah fulfilling His ministry of restoring the covenant people to the land just before the Millennium will begin. Neither person would fail in his mission. Because of the similarity of their missions, several of the same expressions and figures of speech are used in the two nine-chapter sections.

Chapters 49–57 may be divided into four parts: (1) The Servant, being rejected by His people, will take salvation to the Gentiles (chaps. 49–50). (2) The believing remnant will be exalted (51:1–52:12). (3) The Servant, however, will be abased and then exalted (52:13–53:12). (4) Salvation through the Servant will come to Jews and Gentiles in the Millennium (chaps. 54–57).

### 1. THE SERVANT TO BE REJECTED (CHAPS. 49–50)

#### a. The Servant's mission (49:1-13)

(1) The Servant's ministry to the Gentiles (49:1-6). **49:1-3.** God's **Servant** (vv. 3, 5-6) is the speaker in verses 1-5; God addressed Him in verse 6. Like **the** LORD, He called on the **islands** (see comments on 41:1) and the **nations** to **listen** (see comments on 46:3) to Him because of His special "calling" from the Lord. His **mouth** was **like a sharpened sword,** that is, it was a weapon to destroy the disobedient (cf. 1:20; also note Heb. 4:12; Rev. 1:16; 19:15). He was also likened to a sharp **arrow.** The Servant was to **display** God's **splendor** (Isa. 49:3; cf. 60:21; 61:3).

Why is the Servant here called **Israel?** This cannot refer to the nation because the Servant is to draw that nation back to God. The Messiah is called Israel because He fulfills what Israel should have done. In His person and work He epitomizes the nation.

**49:4.** The Servant saw little visible reward for His service. No change was evident in the nation by which the Servant could claim He had accomplished what He set out to do (cf. John 1:11). However, this did not bother Him for He trusted that in due time **God** would **reward** Him.

**49:5-6. Formed . . . in the womb** as God's Servant (cf. v. 1), the Messiah's commission is to restore **Jacob** and **Israel** (see comments on 40:27) to **the** LORD. With **God** as His **strength,** He would also be **a light for the Gentiles** (cf. 42:6; Luke 1:79) so that **salvation** from the Lord would extend to people in **the ends of the earth** (see comments on Isa. 5:26).

(2) The Lord's promise to the Servant. **49:7. The** LORD assured the Servant—**despised and abhorred by** His people—that He would succeed in His ministry to the Gentiles. **Kings** and **princes** will bow down to Him because He has been **chosen** by the LORD. In His first coming Jesus Christ was rejected by His own people (John 1:10-11), but at His

second coming all will **bow** before Him (Phil. 2:10-11).

(3) Israel's restoration. **49:8-12.** In the Millennium, here called **the time of God's favor** and **the day of salvation,** the Lord will enable the Servant **to be a covenant for the people** (cf. 42:6; i.e., to fulfill God's covenant promises to Israel; see comments on Jer. 31:31-34 on the New Covenant).

When **the land** is restored **the captives** will return to the Promised Land from various places around the world (Isa. 49:9; cf. v. 12). The land will be fertile with **pasture** (v. 9) and **water** (v. 10) and **mountains** and valleys will be changed (v. 11). As in 40:3-4, this may signify a change in the people's lives. The location of **Sinim** is uncertain, but many think it is the Aswan region of Egypt (NIV marg.).

(4) The prophet's response. **49:13.** As the prophet spoke, he called on nature, personified, to **rejoice** (on the **mountains** rejoicing see 44:23). The reason for rejoicing is that **the LORD comforts** and has **compassion** (cf. 49:10) on those who need help, including Gentiles.

*b. Israel assured of the return (49:14-26)*

**49:14-16.** In verses 14-21 the prophet recorded a dialogue between Israel and God. **Zion** (i.e., the people in Jerusalem) felt as if God had **forgotten** her (v. 14). But God replied that He certainly had **not** forgotten Israel. He could not possibly do so because He is like **a mother** to the nation. Furthermore, the nation was inscribed, as it were, on His **palms.** Therefore whenever He, figuratively speaking, lifts up His hands He sees the nation's name which reminds Him of her.

**49:17-21.** Judah's captors will **depart** (v. 17) and **be far away** (v. 19) and Judah's **sons** will begin to return (vv. 17-18). This will brighten up the nation as **a bride** enjoys **ornaments.** This return will be so great that the land (personified by **you** and **your,** vv. 19-21) will not be large enough for all the inhabitants, called its **children.**

But when the people returned from the Babylonian Captivity they were a comparatively small, struggling band. The return mentioned in verses 19-21 seems to be much larger and therefore probably refers to Israel's return at the beginning of the Millennium.

**49:22-26.** When Israel returns to the land in the future **the Gentiles** will worship before **the LORD** and will be friendly toward Israel. In fact the Gentiles will even help transport Israelites to Palestine. Gentile leaders will be subservient to Israel, which will cause her to realize that **the LORD** really is in control of the world (v. 23). It is unusual for **captives** to be **rescued,** but God will see that it is done for Israel. Israel's enemies will be destroyed, which will cause the whole world to acknowledge that **the LORD** is Israel's God and her **Savior** (cf. comments on 42:11), **Redeemer** (cf. comments on 41:14), and **the Mighty One of Jacob** (cf. 60:16).

*c. Israel exhorted to walk by faith (chap. 50)*

The statements about Israel's future were to evoke an ethical response. Israel was rebellious but the prophet pleaded for her to trust in the Lord, not in her own devices.

(1) The Lord's "divorce" of Zion. **50:1-3.** The LORD declared that He was temporarily "divorcing" Zion because she had rejected Him without cause. He explained to Zion's children that He temporarily **sent away** their **mother** because she sinned. In the Mosaic Law a husband could give his wife a divorce certificate detailing her fault(s) and she would be required to leave the home (Deut. 24:1). Israel's captivity was like a wife having to leave her husband **because of . . . sins.** Isaiah also pictured Israel's exile as being like sons **sold** into indentured servitude because of a great debt. Yet Israel's rejection of Him was unreasonable (Isa. 50:2). Did they think God could not **ransom** or **rescue** them? Of course He could. He is the One who can withhold rain and **dry up . . . rivers** (cf. Deut. 28:23-24).

(2) The Servant's growth by experience (50:4-9). **50:4-6.** In verses 4-9 the Servant is speaking, for He addresses God as **the Sovereign LORD** (vv. 4-5, 7, 9). As the Lord taught the Servant daily how to comfort **the weary** (v. 4), the Servant did **not** rebel against that instruction (v. 5). In fact He even gave His body to those who persecuted Him (v. 6). Jesus, before He was crucified, was beaten, mocked, and spit on (Mark 14:65; 15:16-20). In extremely difficult circumstances, more difficult than what Isaiah's original readers were facing, the Servant was obe-

dient and submissive (cf. 1 Peter 2:22-23).

**50:7-9.** The Servant was convinced that He will be vindicated by **the Sovereign Lord who helps** Him (vv. 7, 9). Even if it did not seem as if He were winning a battle, He was convinced that He was doing God's will. The Servant was aware that those who falsely accused Him will eventually **face** Him as their Judge and will come to nothing. Like moth-eaten garments, they will perish (cf. 51:8).

(3) The prophet's exhortation. **50:10-11.** Isaiah exhorted the Servant's followers—those who fear **the Lord** and obey His **Word,** but who are **in the dark** (i.e., living in difficult times when the Servant was rejected, v. 6)—to walk by faith, trusting **in the . . . Lord.** If they insist on walking by their own **light** they will suffer the fate of those who reject Him. They **will lie down in torment** (cf. Luke 16:23, 28; also note Rev. 20:13-15; 21:8). This admonition was directed to those living in Isaiah's day. But all who refuse to **trust** the Lord will suffer eternal damnation.

2. THE REMNANT TO BE EXALTED (51:1–52:12)

a. *The Lord's comfort of the remnant (51:1-16)*

(1) The remnant's origin in the covenant. **51:1-3.** Here **the Lord** is speaking to those **who pursue righteousness** (cf. Matt. 5:6) and **seek** Him. The believing remnant in Israel is to think back on their background. **The rock from which** they **were cut,** figuratively speaking, is explained in verse 2 as **Abraham** and **Sarah,** the "founders" of the nation. God **made him many,** that is, gave the patriarch many descendants as He had promised (Gen. 12:2; 15:5; 17:6; 22:17). For many years Abraham and Sarah had no children, but they believed God (Gen. 15:6). These people too are to believe Him. Though they have not yet seen the fruition of God's promises about Israel being a nation in the land (Gen. 15:18-21) they do have His sure word that God's kingdom will be established on the earth. Because of the Lord's **compassion** (cf. Isa. 49:10, 15) the land will someday be fruitful **like Eden . . . the garden of the Lord.** Because of this, **joy** (cf. 51:11) will abound among the remnant.

(2) The Lord's justice to extend over the world. **51:4-8.** God's **Law** will be known (cf. 2:3) and **justice** and **righteousness** (see comments on 1:21) will be established for **the nations** and **the islands** (see comments on 41:1) by His **arm** (i.e., His power; cf. 51:9 and see comments on 40:10). **The heavens and the earth** will pass away (**vanish like smoke** and **wear out like a garment;** cf. Heb. 1:11), **but** the Lord's work (**salvation**) and standards (**righteousness**) **will** continue forever (Isa. 51:8). Therefore, knowing this fact, the remnant with God's **Law** (v. 4) within them and eternal hope before them, should take courage and not be disheartened by their enemies' **insults** (cf. vv. 12-13; also note the **Suffering** Servant's response in 50:6). Those enemies will perish **like a** moth-eaten **garment,** a metaphor the Servant used earlier (50:9).

(3) The remnant's prayer for another "Exodus." **51:9-11.** These verses could be taken as a prayer of the righteous remnant (though some scholars say they record the prophet's words as he reflected on what would happen to that remnant). The plea is that God in His power (**arm;** cf. v. 5) would rise again (**Awake;** cf. v. 17) and save His people as He did in the Exodus (**as in the days gone by**). The question **Was it not you?** (vv. 9-10) was a way of affirming that the Lord did these things for their forefathers. (On **Rahab,** a mythical sea **monster** representing Egypt, see comments on 30:7.) When Israel escaped from Egypt the Egyptian army was drowned in **the sea.** The Israelites crossed over the Red (Reed) Sea on dry ground (Ex. 14:21-31). In the same way **the Lord** by His strength will allow Israel to **return** in a new "Exodus" to her homeland (**Zion**) with **joy** (cf. Isa. 51:3).

(4) The Lord's promise and power. **51:12-16.** The Lord now spoke to the remnant that was living in **fear** of destruction. He gave comfort reminding them that the ones they feared were only **men** (like **grass;** cf. 40:6-8) and that God is the all-powerful Creator (cf. 42:5; 44:24; 45:12, 18; 48:13; 51:16). The imprisoned remnant would soon be freed to return to the Promised Land in another "Exodus" (v. 14) because **the Lord,** the Creator God (vv. 15-16) is **their** God. He is intimate with them and protects them with His **hand** because they belong to Him in a unique relationship as His people (cf. Hosea 2:1, 23).

### b. The Lord's comfort of Jerusalem (51:17–52:10)

(1) Jerusalem to be freed. (51:17–52:6). **51:17-23.** The remnant (or the prophet) had asked God to awaken (be alert; cf. v. 9) and do something. Now God asked **Jerusalem** to be **awake** (cf. 52:1) because He is doing something—their calamity was coming to an end. In their exile the Jerusalemites had **drunk** (i.e., experienced; cf v. 21) God's wrath fully—all the way to the bottom of **the cup** (cf. v. 22). In the terrible destruction of Jerusalem many young men (**sons**) had died (v. 18). **Ruin . . . destruction, famine, and sword** spoke of the awful plight of the city (v. 19). The destruction was so terrible that the city experienced **double calamities.** Young men, objects of God's **wrath,** had been killed (cf. v. 20) in Jerusalem's streets.

However, the Lord pronounced that the time of judgment was over (v. 22). Now the judgment, again pictured as a **cup** to be **drunk,** would be given to her **tormentors** who had walked on the dead bodies in Jerusalem (v. 23). The Babylonians, who had destroyed Jerusalem, would in turn suffer God's wrath.

**52:1-6.** **Jerusalem** was to **awake** not only because her exile was almost ended (v. 1) but also because she would be freshly adorned with new clothes, that is, she would be rebuilt. Jerusalem's pagan conquerors—**the uncircumcised and defiled**—would never again invade and pollute **the holy city** (cf. 48:2). This no doubt refers to the time when the Messiah will establish God's kingdom on earth, for only then will pagans never again trample the city. To **shake off . . . dust** means to stop mourning (dust on one's head was a sign of mourning, Job 2:12). **Jerusalem** will be freed from her **chains,** never again to be enslaved. She had been **sold** because of her sins (cf. Isa. 50:1) but now she would **be redeemed** (*gā'al,* "to purchase out of slavery"). However, God did not *have* to buy them. He will graciously bring them back to Him and they will pay **nothing.**

Then God briefly reviewed the history of the nation in slavery. They had been slaves in **Egypt** and more recently **Assyria** had conquered the Northern Kingdom and also exacted tribute from Judah (52:4). Now another power, Babylon, would take **away** Judah and **mock** them (v. 5) and blaspheme God. Through all this the Lord's power to bring them back each time should show the people that He is the only unique God. Eventually when they return in belief they will **know** Him.

(2) The Lord to return to Zion. **52:7-8.** The prophet exulted in the **good news** to be proclaimed when the time of blessing (spoken of in 51:17–52:6) will begin. Though Israel experienced great joy at the return from Babylon in 536 B.C., the joy Isaiah wrote about in 52:7-8 will be when Israel's Messiah **returns to Zion** to reign. His reign will be one of **peace.**

(3) The remnant to be joyful. **52:9-10.** When **the LORD** returns, the righteous remnant will sing joyfully because He will have **comforted** and **redeemed** His **people.** This work of grace on their behalf will show **all the nations** His power (**arm;** see comments on 40:10) and **the salvation** He provides. (On **the ends of the earth** see comments on 5:26.)

### c. The Lord's exhortation to return (52:11-12)

**52:11-12.** As in the Exodus out of Egypt and the Exodus away from Babylon, so in Israel's yet-future return, the righteous remnant is exhorted to get away from the evil places where they will be living: **Depart, depart. . . . come out.** However, there will be a difference: they **will not** have to **leave in haste** (cf. 48:20). Since **the LORD** will be with them and will protect them they need have no fear.

### 3. THE SERVANT TO BE EXALTED (52:13–53:12)

This is perhaps the best-known section in the Book of Isaiah. Several parts of this passage are quoted in the New Testament: Isaiah 52:15 in Romans 15:21; Isaiah 53:1 in John 12:38 and Romans 10:16; Isaiah 53:4 in Matthew 8:17; Isaiah 53:7-8 in Acts 8:32-33; Isaiah 53:9 in 1 Peter 2:22; and Isaiah 53:12 in Luke 22:37.

Most of this vivid passage concerns the suffering and rejection of the Servant, but the main point (in Isa. 52:13; 53:11-12) is that His suffering will lead to exaltation and glory. True, the suffering is important, but His glory, which will be revealed, is equally important for it will show that the Servant did the will of God voluntarily.

The Servant was rejected (chaps.

49–50), and then the remnant was exalted (51:1–52:12). Now the Servant is to be exalted (52:13–53:12).

### a. The reaction of the nations (52:13-15)

**52:13.** Two important points are made in this verse: the **Servant will act wisely,** doing what the Lord wants Him to do, and He **will be . . . highly exalted.** His being **lifted up** refers not to the kind of death He died on the cross, but to His being exalted at God's right hand (Phil. 2:9; Col. 3:1; Heb. 1:3; 8:1; 10:12; 12:2; 1 Peter 3:22).

**52:14. Many** will be **appalled** (this could also be trans. "awestruck or astonished") **at** the Servant. But who are the "many"? They are probably the people in "many nations" and their "kings" (v. 15). By human standards Jesus was not attractive when He was on the earth (53:3). But when people see Him at His second coming those who did not consider Him important will be absolutely astounded. They will see Him from a new perspective.

**52:15.** The Servant will **sprinkle** people in **many nations.** "Sprinkle" is associated with cleansing by the priest under the Mosaic Law (Lev. 4:6; 8:11; 14:7). This Servant, whom many have not considered important at all, will actually provide the most important thing for nations and their **kings,** namely, cleansing from sin (cf. John 1:29; Heb. 10:14). That is why they **will shut their mouths.** They will be appalled that they had miscalculated the situation so badly. Realizing their great mistake, they will have nothing to say. Eventually, when they see Him exalted in His Second Advent, **they will** finally **understand** and **see** clearly.

### b. The report of the death of the Servant (53:1-12)

This report on the death of the Servant will be given by enlightened Israel after they realize the significance of His death on their behalf. Like the nations, they badly miscalculated the Servant's importance to them.

(1) Israel's confession regarding her rejection of the Servant (53:1-3). Isaiah wrote that Israel will confess that she did not value the Servant. She would reject Him because He was considered an ordinary person.

**53:1.** The Jewish remnant will lament the fact that so few people will believe their **message** about the Servant, and that so few will acknowledge their message as coming from God and His strength (**arm;** see comments on 40:10).

**53:2.** Though lamenting the fact that few people will believe (v. 1), the remnant will realize that **nothing** about the Servant's **appearance** would automatically attract a large following (cf. v. 3). He **grew . . . before** God as **a tender shoot** (i.e., coming from David's line; cf. 11:1), and as **a root out of dry ground,** that is, from an arid area (spiritually speaking) where one would not expect a large plant to grow. In His appearance He did not look like a royal person (in **beauty** and **majesty**). The remnant was not excusing people for rejecting the Servant; it was merely explaining why the nation rejected Him.

**53:3.** The nation Israel **despised and rejected** the Servant who experienced **sorrows** ($mak^e\bar{o}b$, "anguish or grief," also used in v. 4) **and . . . suffering** ($h\breve{o}l\hat{i}$, see comments on "infirmities" in v. 4). He was the kind of individual people do not normally want to look at; they were repulsed by Him. For these reasons the nation did **not** esteem **Him;** they did not think He was important. Yet He was and is the most important Person in the world, for He is the Servant of the Lord.

(2) Israel's realization about the Servant's substitutionary death (53:4-6). **53:4.** Though not realizing it at the time, the nation *will* realize that the Servant bore the consequences of their sin. His taking **our infirmities and . . .sorrows** ($mak^e\bar{o}b$, see comments on v. 3) speaks of the consequences of sin. The verb **took up,** rendered "bore" in verse 12, translates $n\bar{a}\acute{s}\bar{a}$', "to carry." His bearing "infirmities" ($h\breve{o}l\hat{i}$, lit., "sickness," the same word trans. "suffering" in v. 3) refers to illnesses of the soul. His healing many people's physical illnesses (though not all of them) in His earthly ministry anticipated His greater work on the Cross. Though He does heal physical ailments today (though not all of them) His greater work is healing souls, giving salvation from sin. That this is the subject of Isaiah 53 is clear from the words "transgressions" (v. 5), "iniquities" (vv. 5, 11), "iniquity" (v. 6), "transgressions" (v. 8), "wicked" (v. 9), "transgressors" (v. 12

[twice]), and "sin" (v. 12). The Servant vicariously took on Himself all the sins (and spiritual anguish caused by sin) of the nation (and the whole world) and **carried** (*sābal*, "to carry as a burden"; cf. 46:4, 7) them on Himself (cf. 1 Peter 2:24; 3:18). When Jesus was crucified, Israel thought His hardships (being **stricken . . . smitten,** and **afflicted**; cf. Isa. 53:7) were deserved for His supposedly having blasphemed God. Actually He was bearing the judgment that *their* sin required.

**53:5.** **Pierced . . . crushed . . . punishment . . . wounds** are words that describe what the remnant will note about the Servant's condition on their behalf and because of their **transgressions** (*pešaʿ*, "rebellion"; cf. v. 8; 1:2) and **iniquities.** As a result those who believe in Him have inner **peace** rather than inner anguish or grief (see comments on "infirmities" in 53:4) and **are healed** spiritually. Ironically His wounds, inflicted by the soldiers' scourging and which were followed by His death, are the means of healing believers' spiritual wounds in salvation. Jesus' physical agony in the Crucifixion was great and intense. But His obedience to the Father was what counted (cf. Phil. 2:8). His death satisfied the wrath of God against sin and allows Him to "overlook" the sins of the nation (and of others who believe) because they have been paid for by the Servant's substitutionary death.

**53:6.** The redeemed remnant (and others) will acknowledge that they were guilty and that the Lord made the Servant the object of His wrath in order to take away their guilt. **Sheep** tend to travel together, so if the leading sheep turns aside from the path for grass or some other purpose, usually all the sheep do so. They tend to follow the lead sheep which is often dangerous. Similarly all Israel had turned aside (cf. 1 Peter 2:25) from following the Lord, from keeping His commandments. The essence of sin is going one's **own way,** rather than God's way. That **iniquity** had to be punished, so **the LORD . . . laid** the punishment for that iniquity (cf. Isa. 53:11) not on the "sheep" (Israel and other sinners) that deserved it, but on the Servant who died in their place.

(3) Israel's account about the Servant's death (53:7-9). The Servant died willingly (v. 7) and for others' transgressions (v. 8), even though He is righteous (v. 9).

**53:7.** As noted, the tendency of sheep is to follow others (v. 6), even to their destruction. In verse 7 the quiet, gentle nature of sheep is stressed. Seeing many **sheep** sheared for their wool or killed as sacrifices, Israelites were well aware of the submissive nature of sheep. Jesus, as the **Lamb** of God (John 1:29), quietly submitted to His death. He did not try to stop those who opposed Him; He remained **silent** rather than defend Himself (Matt. 26:63a; 27:14; 1 Peter 2:23). He was willingly **led** to death because He knew it would benefit those who would believe.

**53:8.** After His **oppression** (being arrested and bound, John 18:12, 24) **and judgment** (sentenced to die, John 19:16) Jesus was led to His death. He died not because of any sins of His own (for He, the Son of God, was sinless, 2 Cor. 5:21; Heb. 4:15; 1 John 3:5) but because of **(for)** the sins (**transgression,** *pešaʿ*; cf. Isa. 53:5) of others. To be **taken away** means to be **taken** to death. It is parallel to being **cut off from the land of the living,** an obvious reference to death, and **stricken.** The words **and who can speak of His descendants?** mean He was cut off in the prime of life and left no descendants. Those words, however, could also be translated, "and who of His generation considered" (cf. NIV marg.) meaning that few of those who lived then considered His death important. Some verbs in this verse ("was cut off, was stricken"), like those in verse 4 ("smitten, afflicted") and verse 5 ("was crushed"), indicate by their passive voice that these actions were done to Him by God the Father (cf. v. 10; 2 Cor. 5:21, "God made Him . . . to be sin for us").

**53:9.** The soldiers who crucified Jesus apparently intended to bury Him **with the wicked** like the two criminals (John 19:31). However, He was buried **with the rich,** in the **grave** of a rich man named Joseph (Matt. 27:57-60).

(4) The Lord's promise about the blessing of the Servant (53:10-12). **53:10.** The suffering and death of the Servant was clearly **the LORD's will.** In that sense He was "slain from the Creation of the world" (Rev. 13:8). The statement, **the LORD** made the Servant's **life a**

**guilt offering,** does not mean that Jesus' *life* satisfied the wrath of God but that His life which culminated in His *death* was the sacrifice for sins. As indicated in Isaiah 53:7-8 He had to die to satisfy the righteous demands of God. The word for "guilt offering" is *'āšām,* used in Leviticus 5:15; 6:5; 19:21 and elsewhere of an offering to atone for sin.

His death and burial appeared to end His existence (He was "cut off," Isa. 53:8), but in actuality because of His resurrection Jesus **will see His offspring** (those who by believing in Him become children of God, John 1:12) **and** He will **prolong His days** (live on forever as the Son of God). He will be blessed (**prosper;** cf. Isa. 53:12a) because of His obedience to **the will** (plan) **of the LORD.**

**53:11.** His **suffering,** which included His death, led to **life** (His resurrection). **Satisfied** that His substitutionary work was completed ("It is finished," John 19:30), He now can **justify** (declare righteous those who believe; see comments on Rom. 1:17; 3:24) **many** (cf. Isa. 53:12). **By His knowledge** could be translated "by knowledge of Him" as in the NIV margin. **He** bore the punishment (cf. vv. 4, 6), for **their iniquities** (cf. v. 6), so that many people would not have to die. Because He died, they live.

**53:12.** Having willingly followed God's plan, the Servant is exalted (cf. 52:13). To have **a portion** and **divide the spoils** pictures a general, after winning a battle, sharing goods taken from the enemy (cf. Ps. 68:18; Eph. 4:7-8). Because He **was numbered with the transgressors,** that is, was considered a sinner (cf. Matt. 27:38) and **bore the sin** (cf. Isa. 53:6) **of many,** that is, everyone, He is exalted and allows believers to share in the benefits of that exaltation. And because He is alive (cf. v. 10), He now intercedes (prays; cf. Rom. 8:34; Heb. 7:25) **for . . . transgressors** (related to the word *pešaʻ,* "transgression[s]," in Isa. 53:5, 8).

This great passage gives a tremendously complete picture of what the death of Jesus Christ accomplished on behalf of Israel (John 11:49-51) and the whole world (1 John 2:2). His death satisfied God's righteous demands for judgment against sin, thus opening the way for everyone to come to God in faith for salvation from sin.

### 4. SALVATION TO COME FROM THE SERVANT (CHAPS. 54–57)

These chapters speak of the great salvation which will come to Israel (chap. 54) and proselytes (55:1–56:8) on the basis of the work of the Servant, and of the condemnation which will come on the wicked (56:9–57:21). Ultimately the Servant will establish the millennial kingdom. Unlike Israel, He will not fail in His mission.

### a. Salvation for Israel (chap. 54)

(1) Israel's numerical growth. **54:1-3.** In Israel a **barren woman** was disgraced, for children aided in family chores and helped the parents in their old age. Fertility on every level was a sign of God's blessing. For example, when Hannah was not able to have children she was devastated, but when the Lord allowed her to have a son she sang for joy (1 Sam. 1:1–2:10). Israel was like a woman who had no children and was therefore in a continual state of mourning. But by God's sovereignty and grace He will enable her to have many **children.** So she will break **into song** and **shout for joy.** Jerusalem, once desolate and mourning (Lam. 1:1-5), will be revitalized and teeming with people. Also like a nomad who has so many children he has to **enlarge** his **tent** to accommodate them all, Israel's **descendants will** increase and even **settle in** the **cities** of foreign **nations** because there will not be enough room for them in their homeland.

(2) Israel's regathering. **54:4-8.** The LORD will regather Israel the way a man would take back his **wife.** The nation need have no **fear** (cf. 41:10, 14; 43:5; 44:2, 8) of **disgrace,** for she will no longer be desolate and helpless like a widow. **God,** like a **husband** (cf. Jer. 3:14; 31:32; Hosea 2:16), will take **back** Israel, His **wife.** He is **the LORD Almighty . . . the Holy One of Israel,** her **Redeemer** (cf. Isa. 54:8; see comments on 41:14), and in His uniqueness He is **the God of all the earth,** that is, its Creator and Sustainer. The Lord had **deserted** His people for a short while (**a brief moment**). Though not stated here, Isaiah had given the reason for it several times: because of the nation's sins (cf. 50:1) and God's commitment to His word. But because of His **compassion** (54:7) and **kindness** (*ḥesed,*

"loyal love," v. 8, trans. "unfailing love" in v. 10), He will restore the nation to Himself. The short **moment** during which God **hid** His **face** (i.e., abandoned Israel because of His **anger** against her sin) contrasts with the **everlasting** nature of His covenant loyalty.

(3) Israel's security. **54:9-10.** After the Flood, in which God executed His anger against the world's depravity, He promised **never again** to devastate **the earth** in the same way (Gen. 9:11). Similarly God promised that the day is coming when He will **never . . . rebuke** Israel **again.** Statements like this show that Isaiah was speaking of the millennial kingdom rather than the return from the Babylonian Captivity, for the nation has suffered God's anger many times since the postexilic return. Even if the world could be punished again as in the Flood, God's **love** (ḥeseḏ; cf. v. 8) and **compassion** will never cease. The **covenant of peace** (also mentioned in Ezek. 34:25; 37:26) refers to this promise which God had just made. God will give His people lasting peace (cf. Isa. 9:7; 32:17-18; 54:13; 55:12; 66:12; Jer. 30:10; 33:6, 9; 46:27).

(4) Israel's peaceful future (54:11-17). **54:11-12.** Jerusalem, the **afflicted city,** had been through many troubles, called **storms,** and no one had **comforted** her (cf. Lam. 1:2, 9, 15-17, 21). However, the Lord will **build** up the city **with stones** made of **precious** gems, symbolic of His care and esteem for the value of the city.

**54:13-14.** Israelites always considered the training of their children a high priority. Many wanted them to be true to the Lord and not guided by the pagan world around them. In the Millennium, the children **will be taught by the LORD** Himself and will enjoy His **peace** (cf. comments on v. 10). **Righteousness** will prevail (cf. 33:5; 46:13; 58:8; 62:1-2) and Jerusalemites will no longer **fear** for the Lord will protect her from **tyranny.**

**54:15-17.** In the millennial kingdom no nation will be allowed to defeat Israel because the Lord has so decreed. Nations rise and fall on the basis of His word. In the past He allowed **the destroyer** (Babylon) to overcome His people, but this will never again occur. Peace and safety are **the heritage** of those who trust in **the LORD.**

*b. Salvation for the Gentiles (chap. 55)*

(1) An invitation to come to the Lord. **55:1-2.** God invites people in need to **come** (this word occurs four times in v. 1) to Him. By coming they indicate that they are trusting in and relying on Him for salvation and are agreeing to obey His commandments. The blessings God gives them are available **without cost.** Salvation is a free gift of God, whether it refers to spiritual redemption or physical deliverance. Probably both are intended here. The Lord asked the people how they could be interested in other things besides Himself as He is the only One who can bring genuine satisfaction. Throughout all history people have tried to find satisfaction through many things other than God.

(2) An everlasting covenant. **55:3.** By coming to the Lord people will have life and the benefits of God's **everlasting covenant** with **David** (2 Sam. 7:11b-16) in which the Lord **promised** that David's line would continue forever. **Kindnesses** renders the word ḥeseḏ (here in the pl.), God's covenantal "loyal love," which relates to His loyal covenant with David (see ḥeseḏ, "love," in 2 Sam. 7:15). Some interpreters say the "everlasting covenant" refers to the New Covenant (Jer. 32:40; Heb. 13:20). That is possible but the reference to David points to the Davidic Covenant, which also is said to last forever (2 Sam. 7:16). Just as God promised to keep His good hand on David, so He assured those who come to Him that He will never remove His good hand (His blessings) from them. He will always be with them and consider them His people.

(3) Nations to be under Messiah's leadership. **55:4-5.** The word **Him** refers not to Israel, but to the Messiah (David's "Son"; cf. Matt. 1:1) for He will be the world's **Leader and Commander.** The word **you** (Isa. 55:5) probably refers to Israel, to whom many nations will go to worship **the LORD.** They will recognize the Lord's **splendor** ("glory"; cf. 35:2; 46:13; 49:3; 60:9, 21; 61:3; 62:3).

(4) Salvation available to all (55:6-13). **55:6-7. The wicked** (v. 7) are commanded to **seek** and **call on** the LORD (v. 6), and to do so **while He may be found,** because when His judgment comes it will be too late. Such seeking and calling means that an individual will **turn from**

his former evil **way** and **thoughts.** Turning to the Lord one receives **mercy** and **pardon.** In every dispensation the Lord has required the same thing for salvation: trust in Him. Israelites, though God's covenant people, were saved only by believing in **the LORD.**

**55:8-9.** God's compassion on those who turn to Him (vv. 6-7) comes because His **thoughts** and **ways** are far superior to human **thoughts** and **ways,** which in fact are evil (cf. v. 7). God's plan is something people would have never dreamed of.

**55:10-11.** Having spoken of the future time of blessing (the Millennium) and the salvation which leads to it, the Lord then assured believers that His **Word . . . will accomplish what** He says it will. His word is like **rain** and **snow** that water **the earth** and help give it abundant vegetation. In the Near East dry hard ground can seemingly overnight sprout with vegetation after the first rains of the rainy season. Similarly when God speaks His Word, it brings forth spiritual life, thus accomplishing His **purpose.**

**55:12-13.** Because of salvation the effects of sin will be reversed in the Millennium, including the provision of inner **joy** and **peace** (see comments on 54:10) and changes in the physical creation. After Adam and Eve sinned in the Garden of Eden thorns and thistles began to choke out the good vegetation and Adam's work to grow good crops was increased (Gen. 3:17-19). But in the future even nature will be joyful (Isa. 55:12b). **The trees** personified as clapping with **hands** (branches moving in the wind) suggests the joy people will have because of the changes in nature. Various kinds of trees will grow **instead of the thornbush** and **briers.** Fertility on the earth will be a sign that God is in control. Many interpreters say this imagery (v. 13a) symbolizes what God does in a person's heart at salvation. True, God does change individuals. But the earth will indeed be unusually fertile during the whole Millennium (cf. 35:1-2, 41:18-19; 44:3a).

*c. Gentiles included in Israel's blessings (56:1-8)*

(1) A command to be righteous. **56:1-2.** People are urged to **do what is right** (cf. 1:17) because God's **salvation** (spiritual deliverance and physical protection) will come soon. Again Isaiah linked present behavior with future salvation and blessings. Because the Lord will bring salvation to those who believe, they should act justly in the present.

In Isaiah's day a righteous person (a believer who does what is right, 56:1) lived according to God's Law, an expression of His righteous standards. Keeping **the Sabbath** was important under the Law (Ex. 20:8-11), for a person by not engaging in agricultural or business pursuits on that day thereby acknowledged that he believed God would take care of him and bless him. Since the Sabbath was a sign of Israel's covenant with God, keeping the Sabbath signified that a person believed in the covenant and the Lord. Such a person also turned **from doing . . . evil** (cf. Isa. 55:7).

(2) A promise that believing foreigners will be blessed (56:3-8). **56:3-5.** Gentiles, people outside the covenant community, who followed **the LORD** were not to think they would have no salvation or part in the millennial kingdom. Even foreigners (cf. 14:1) and **eunuchs** who join themselves to the Lord are welcome. This contrasts with the exclusion of eunuchs under the Mosaic Law (Deut. 23:1). Keeping the **Sabbaths** and obeying God's **covenant** stipulations (cf. Isa. 56:6) would demonstrate their loyalty to **the LORD** (cf. vv. 1-2). In fact they will be memorialized forever (v. 5). This is striking because a **eunuch,** unable to sire children, has no way of passing on his name through **sons.**

**56:6-8. Foreigners** who **love . . . the LORD** are acceptable to God and will be regathered along with believing Israelites. Redeemed Gentiles, though not in the covenantal family of Israel, can still receive God's blessings. They show their devotion to **the LORD** by their service, worship, and obedience (keeping **the Sabbath** and God's **covenant** stipulations; cf. v. 4). As God promised Abraham, through him all peoples of the world will be blessed (Gen. 12:3). These Gentiles will be gathered to Zion (His **holy mountain;** see comments on Isa. 11:9) along with **Israel,** where they too will worship the Lord in **prayer** and **offerings.**

## d. Condemnation of the wicked (56:9–57:21)

Throughout most of this second nine-chapter division of Isaiah (chaps. 49–57) the emphasis has been on the future glorious state of the redeemed remnant in the kingdom to be established by the Messiah. Now in 56:9–57:21, which concludes these nine chapters, Isaiah reflected on the spiritual situation in his day. In view of their glorious future, one would suppose that his people would want to obey the Lord in anticipation of that kingdom. But this was not true in Isaiah's time.

(1) The call to Gentiles to destroy Israel. **56:9-12.** The Lord called for the **beasts** (Gentile powers, probably Babylon) to **devour** (punish) Israel because she was spiritually insensitive. The **watchmen** (cf. Jer. 6:17; Ezek. 33:7), priests and religious leaders, were **blind** and ignorant and were like **dogs** who like to **sleep** and eat. Good **shepherds** know the best grazing ground for their flocks. But these leaders were ignorant (cf. Isa. 56:10) shepherds going **their own way** like their sheep! (cf. 53:6) They were more interested in their own gain than in their people's welfare. Concerned only with their own pleasure, they failed to consider that judgment will come (56:12).

(2) The righteous to die. **57:1-2.** The society then was so bad that **the righteous** people in Israel (also called **devout** and **those who walk uprightly**) had to die in order to find **peace.** Observing the **evil** all around apparently frustrated them. They could do nothing to turn the nation back to the Lord. The only way **the righteous** could be spared from such frustration was to die.

(3) Israel's involvement in false religions (57:3-10). **57:3-4.** In contrast with the righteous people mentioned in verses 1-2, the rest of the Israelites were engaged in false religious practices picked up from pagans around them, including sorcery (from *'ānan;* see comments on 2:6) and religious prostitution (cf. Hosea 4:14). In fertility religions "worshipers" engaged in sexual relations with **prostitutes,** supposedly identifying in that way with gods and goddesses to help guarantee fertility in crops, animals, and families. Such people in Israel were **mocking** the righteous while they were involved in shameful deeds. By such actions they

were **rebels** against God.

**57:5-8.** Worship centers were set up on hillsides, probably so that the people could imagine themselves closer to their gods. Often such centers were in lush forest areas to picture the fertility being sought by the worshipers. Thus the people, as Isaiah wrote, would **lust among the oaks** (cf. 1:29). Sometimes the people were also involved in child **sacrifice** in attempts to appease the wrath of various gods (cf. Ezek. 20:31; Hosea 13:2). They were in the habit of giving **offerings** to their **idols** and sacrificing to foreign gods on the **high** hills where they also were involved in adultery (Isa. 57:6-7). Their homes were supposed to be centers of learning about the Lord, but the people had made them places of idol worship and adultery (v. 8). (Cf. the use of pagan symbols with God's command in Deut. 6:9.) **Beds** and **nakedness** may refer to sexual perversity involved in such worship or they may symbolize idolatry (which was sometimes likened to spiritual adultery).

**57:9-10.** The worship of **Molech,** an Ammonite god, was sometimes accompanied by child sacrifice (2 Kings 23:10; Jer. 32:35), but sending representatives to Ammon to worship their god sometimes resulted in death (**you descended to the grave**). Yet in the face of these difficulties the people still refused to give up their sinful **ways.** They simply renewed their **strength** and continued on in sin.

(4) Israel's forgetfulness of God. **57:11-13.** Most of the Israelites had forgotten the true God, apparently because He had seemingly **been silent.** So in irony the Lord said He would **expose** their **righteousness and . . . works.** Their alleged righteous works, when exposed, would be shown for what they really were, and as a result their deeds would be of no help to them before the Lord. When in trouble, God said sarcastically, they should **cry out** to their gods. But they would find that God will **blow . . . away** their **idols.** In contrast those Israelites who trust the Lord **will inherit the land** (cf. Pss. 25:12-13; 37:9, 11, 22, 29; 69:35-36), that is, they will enjoy physical blessings, including the temple mount (God's **holy mountain;** see comments on Isa. 11:9) again belonging to Israel.

(5) The Lord's promise of forgiveness. **57:14-21.** The exhortation to **pre-**

pare a **road** for the **people** of faith recalls 40:3-5 which speaks of a road being prepared for the Lord. Now the faithful are walking to the Lord. Even though He is majestic (**high and lofty;** cf. 6:1), eternal, and **holy** (cf. 6:3), He fellowships (**lives**) with those who are **contrite and lowly in spirit** (cf. 66:2). His accusations and anger do not last **forever,** because of His grace. In the past He had to be harsh with His people because of their **greed** and independence. But when they repent He forgives them, giving healing, guidance, and **comfort.** The forgiven ones enjoy **peace. . . . but the wicked** have no **rest** and **no peace** (cf. 48:22). They are doomed for punishment because they refuse to turn to the Lord.

## C. Restoration realized and completed (chaps. 58–66)

In this final nine-chapter section of the book, Isaiah looked to the present and the future. In his day most of the people were not righteous (chap. 58). Because of their depravity the restoration of the nation must be God's initiative (chap. 59). Eventually peace and prosperity will come to Israel and the whole world (chap. 60). Isaiah wrote of the coming of the Messiah and of the Father (61:1–63:6) and of the nation's prayer and the Lord's response (63:7–65:25). In conclusion the prophet wrote again that God will fulfill His promises to Israel as well as the entire world (chap. 66).

### 1. THE RESTORATION TO COME BY GOD'S INITIATIVE (CHAPS. 58–60)

#### a. Obedience required (chap. 58)

(1) The reminder of the people's sins. **58:1-2.** God called for heralds to go about telling the nation of **their rebellion** (*pešaʿ*, "transgressions," from *pāšaʿ*, "to transgress"; see comments on 1:2; also cf. 1:5; 53:5, 8; 59:13) and **sins.** Like a trumpet used to get people's attention, the heralds were to **shout.** Outwardly the people seemed **eager** to want **to know** God and for **God to** be **near them.**

(2) The concern of the people. **58:3a.** The people voiced their concern that they were in difficulty though they seemed to be doing what the Law required. They **fasted** and **humbled** themselves, but they feared that God had not **seen it** or **noticed.** Apparently they thought that by going through the "motions" of religion (without any inward reality of faith) they would be blessed.

(3) The response of the Lord (58:3b-14). The Lord responded by pointing out that He was more interested in their obedience than their rituals. Unfortunately they, like many people, had confused rituals with relationship, outward acts with true obedience.

**58:3b-5.** Their fasts did not alter their poor relationship with others. They were disregarding other peoples' needs by exploiting their employees (cf. Deut. 24:14-15; James 5:1-6) and by **quarreling** and fighting. Therefore their prayers would not **be heard,** for their kind of **fasting** was not what the Lord accepted. Their hearts, not just their **heads,** needed to bow before **the Lord.**

**58:6-7. Fasting** was to encourage a person to respond positively to God's commands. In the Old Testament only one fast was commanded—the annual Day of Atonement (Lev. 16:29, 31). Only after the fall of Jerusalem were fast days instituted (Zech. 7:3, 5; 8:19). Ironically on the other hand many *specific* commands were *not* being followed. So the Lord reminded the people that they should be just (Isa. 58:6) and openhanded with those in need—**the hungry** (cf. v. 10), **the poor . . . the naked** (v. 7). The Israelites were to consider themselves members of one family who at one time had been slaves in Egypt. Therefore they were not to neglect each other. When someone shared with one in need, it was a reminder that everything he owned belonged to the Lord.

**58:8-12.** If the people had inner **righteousness** (revealed in outward acts of justice and mercy, vv. 6-7), **then . . . the Lord** would bless them (cf. Deut. 28:1-14) with **light** (often a picture of blessing; cf. Isa. 58:10), **healing** (spiritual restoration), righteousness (high standards), protection from trouble, and answered prayer (vv. 8-9a). If they would **do away with . . . oppression** and gossip and would help others in need (cf. v. 7), then the Lord would bless them (give them **light;** cf. v. 8). He would give guidance, satisfaction, strength, fertility (**like a spring**), and physical restoration (rebuilding the **ruins**).

**58:13-14. Sabbath** observance was a barometer of one's faithfulness to the

Mosaic Covenant (cf. comments on 56:4-6). By following the rules for **the Sabbath** a person acknowledged the importance of worshiping God and showed that he depended on God to bless him materially for that time he took off from work. By putting God first and not seeking to do as he wished, a person would have **joy,** not only in spiritual salvation (**ride on the heights**) but also in prosperity (**feast on the inheritance**). All this was certain because **the LORD has spoken** (cf. 1:20; 40:5).

*b. Salvation to come by God's initiative (chap. 59)*

Because of the depravity of the nation, national salvation and prosperity would have to come from God's initiative. In chapter 59 the Lord again spoke of the people's sins and His provision of salvation because of the Abrahamic Covenant.

(1) The Lord's ability to save. **59:1.** The prophet reminded the nation that **the LORD** could **save** them in spite of their difficult circumstances. He is powerful enough—His **arm** (cf. v. 16; see comments on 40:10) **is not . . . short.** And He is caring enough—He is not **dull** of hearing. This implies that Israel simply needed to call out to God and He would come to her rescue.

(2) Israel's spiritual depravity (59:2-15a). **59:2-8.** However, though the Lord could save them, the nation's **sins** had **separated** them **from** the Lord (cf. Ps. 66:18; Prov. 28:9). Though He could **hear** them (Isa. 59:1) He chose **not** to (v. 2). Sin prevents prayer from being answered (cf. Ps. 66:18). Those sins included murder, lying, injustice (cf. Isa. 59:9, 11, 14-15), and planning **evil** (vv. 3-4). Their actions were like those of deadly poisonous snakes (**vipers** and **an adder**), for they were harming each other. Just as people can see through **cobwebs,** which therefore are inappropriate **for clothing** (v. 6), so God could see through the **evil deeds** of these people and judge them. In a hurry to do **evil** things, they were bringing **ruin** to others (v. 7) and were constantly traveling down evil **paths.** As a result they knew no **peace** (cf. 48:22; 57:20-21).

**59:9-15a.** Here the prophet, using first-person plural pronouns (**us. . . . we. . . . our**), identified with the people (cf.

6:5). Israel was so corrupt spiritually, without **justice** (cf. 59:4, 11, 14-15) **and righteousness,** that it was as if they were in **darkness** and were **blind** and **dead.** As a result, the oppressed were angry **like** growling **bears** and moaned **like doves.** They wanted **justice** and help **but** found **none** (v. 11). Isaiah confessed that the people were noted for their **many . . . sins,** deliberate **rebellion** (cf. 1:5; 58:1) **against the LORD,** lying, injustice, and dishonesty (59:12-15a).

(3) The Lord's promise to help Israel (59:15b-21). **59:15b-16a.** Because of her depraved condition (vv. 2-15a), no one but **the LORD** could save the nation. Being **displeased** with her injustice (cf. vv. 4, 9, 11, 14), He realized **there was no one to intercede** on her behalf. Isaiah was not saying that the Lord did not want to get involved, but that Israel was totally incapable of helping herself. Only God could help her. This is true of salvation in any era. No one can save himself. Only God can forgive sin and change a person's heart.

**59:16b-20.** In His power (by **His . . . arm;** cf. v. 1 and comments on 40:10) God provided **salvation,** both spiritual and physical, **for him** (i.e., for Israel personified as a man). Like a warrior God goes forth to fight for His people. **Righteousness** is **His breastplate** and **salvation** is His **helmet** (cf. Paul's use of this imagery in Eph. 6:14, 17). God's other **garments** are **vengeance** and **zeal.** This verse (Isa. 59:17) means that God supplies righteousness and salvation (cf. v. 16) for His people as He zealously executes vengeance on **His enemies** (v. 18). Because of this, people everywhere will acknowledge **His glory,** overpowering majesty, and strength (**like a pent-up flood** let loose). When **the LORD** executes judgment on His enemies (at Christ's second coming), the Messiah **will** go **to Zion.** He will be **the Redeemer** (see comments on 41:14) of **those** Israelites who turn to Him in repentance (59:20). Showing their future hope, the nation was being encouraged to repent.

**59:21.** When the Messiah returns in judgment (v. 18), He will inaugurate His **covenant** (elsewhere called the New Covenant, Jer. 31:31), pouring His **Spirit** on believing Israelites (cf. Ezek. 36:27a; Joel 2:29) and instilling His words within them (Jer. 31:33-34; Ezek. 36:27b).

## c. Peace and prosperity to come (chap. 60)

(1) God's glory to come to Israel. **60:1-3.** Because of the Lord's redeeming work (59:19a, 20-21), **light** (blessing) will fall on Israel, who in turn is to **shine** forth, as a spiritual light to the **nations,** revealing God's Word and **glory** to them. In that way, she will be instrumental in removing the spiritual **darkness** that pervades the world (cf. 29:18; John 12:35; Acts 26:18; Rom. 2:19; Col. 1:13; 1 Peter 2:9). When **the LORD** returns to live among His people (Isa. 60:2) the nations will be attracted to the light of **His glory** (cf. vv. 19-20) and will flock to Israel for the **light** (the blessings of salvation from spiritual darkness). This will occur in the Millennium. Though everyone entering the Millennium will be saved, people will be born during that 1,000-year period of time. Many of them will come to salvation because of God's work on Israel's behalf.

(2) The nations' wealth to come to Israel. **60:4-9.** At the beginning of the Millennium when Israel will be regathered to her land, her **sons** will **come from** great distances (cf. v. 9). Also Israel will rejoice because redeemed people from **the nations** (v. 5; the "sheep" of Matt. 25:31-46) will want to join Israel in her worship in Jerusalem (cf. Zech. 14:16-19). Those people will bring **wealth** to Israel (cf. Isa. 60:11; 61:6; Hag. 2:7-8; Zech. 14:14). Examples of the kinds of wealth to be brought are **gold . . . incense. . . . flocks . . . rams** and **silver** (Isa. 60:6-7, 9). Examples of the nations that will bring those riches are: (a) **Midian,** south of the Dead Sea; (b) **Ephah,** a branch of the Midianites as Midian was Ephah's father (Gen. 25:4; 1 Chron. 1:33); (c) **Sheba,** probably the Sabeans in southwest Arabia (see comments on Seba in Isa. 43:3); (d) **Kedar** in northern Arabia; (e) **Nebaioth,** apparently an Arabian tribe (Nebaioth was Ishmael's eldest son, Gen. 25:13); and (f) **Tarshish** (probably in southwestern Spain; see comments on Isa. 23:1), whose **ships** will bring not only riches but also Israelites. Some of this wealth will be used **as offerings** (60:7; cf. 56:6-7) and some will be used to **adorn** the **temple** (cf. 60:13), undoubtedly the millennial temple (Ezek. 40–43). This wealth, brought in haste (Isa. 60:8), will all be to **honor . . . the LORD,** who

will have manifested His **splendor** (glory) in Israel (cf. v. 21; 35:2; 46:13; 49:3; 55:5; 61:3; 62:3).

(3) The nations to acknowledge Israel. **60:10-14.** Israel will occupy the foremost position in the world's political, economic, religious, and social structures. **Foreigners** and **kings** (cf. vv. 3, 11) will assist in rebuilding Jerusalem's **walls,** evidence of God's **favor** and **compassion** in contrast with His **anger** (cf. 57:16-18). The flow of **wealth** into Jerusalem will be steady (60:11). And any **nation** that might try to rise up against Israel will be defeated by God (v. 12).

Even wood will be brought from **Lebanon** for the temple construction, thus again making it a place of beauty for the Lord (cf. v. 7). God called the temple His **sanctuary** and **the place of** His **feet.** People from the nations that formerly despised Israel will recognize that Jerusalem or **Zion,** is God's chosen **city,** the place where He dwells.

(4) Righteousness to come to Israel (60:15-22). **60:15-16.** During this time of blessing righteousness will be evident throughout the land. In contrast with Israel's having been **forsaken and hated** (cf. v. 14), God **will** cause others to take **pride** in her. Much as a nursing child gets sustenance from its mother, so Israel will be sustained by the wealth of the **nations** (v. 16; cf. vv. 5, 11; 61:6). This blessing will cause Israel to recognize all the more that **the LORD** really is the unique God of the world, her **Savior** (see comments on 43:11), **Redeemer** (see comments on 41:14), and her **Mighty One** (cf. 49:26).

**60:17-22.** Wealth to be brought to Jerusalem (cf. vv. 5-9) will include not only **gold** and **silver** (already mentioned in v. 9), but also **bronze** and **iron.** The city will be peaceful and joyful. Also the Lord will protect her as her **Light** and **Glory** (v. 19; cf. vv. 1-2). Her **people** will **be righteous,** displaying God's **splendor** (v. 21; cf. comments on v. 9), and they will be numerous (v. 22). The Millennium will be a utopia for which many people have longed.

## 2. THE COMING OF THE MESSIAH AND THE COMING OF THE FATHER (61:1–63:6)

### a. The coming of the Messiah (chap. 61)

**61:1-3.** In verse 1 all three Persons of the Trinity are mentioned: the **Spirit . . .**

the Sovereign LORD, and the Messiah. Three factors indicate that **Me** refers to the Messiah: (1) The association of the Holy Spirit with the anointing points to Jesus Christ. After being anointed with oil, Israel's first two kings, Saul and David, were blessed with the Spirit's ministry (1 Sam. 10:1, 10; 16:13). Similarly Christ was anointed by the Holy Spirit (Matt. 3:16-17) to be Israel's King. The Hebrew word for Messiah (*māšîaḥ*) means "the Anointed One," and Christ (*christos,* from *chriō,* "to anoint") is the Greek equivalent of *māšîaḥ.* (2) Part of this passage (Isa. 61:1-2a) was read by Jesus (Luke 4:18-19) in reference to Himself. (3) The mission of this Anointed One was Jesus' ministry: to **preach good news**, to heal and free (Isa. 61:1; cf. 42:7), **to proclaim . . . favor and . . . vengeance** (61:2), and **to comfort** (vv. 2-3). When Jesus read from this passage He stopped in the middle of the sentence, after the word "favor" (Luke 4:18-19). By doing this He was showing that His work would be divided into two advents. In His First Advent He did the things mentioned in Isaiah 61:1-2a; in His Second Advent He will do the things in verses 2b-3. When He returns He will bring judgment on unbelievers (Micah 5:15; Rev. 19:15-20); this will be **the day of** God's "vengeance" (cf. Isa. 34:8; 35:4; 63:4). But the Messiah will also "comfort" Israel, for she will have undergone great persecution, the Great Tribulation, in the preceding years (cf. Dan. 7:21, 24-25; Rev. 12:13-17).

When the Messiah comes He will change believing Israelites' sadness to joy, a truth Isaiah mentioned frequently. In place **of ashes,** put on one's head as a sign of mourning (cf. 2 Sam. 13:19; Es. 4:1; Dan 9:3), they will wear **a crown.** Light olive **oil,** when applied to one's face and hair, would soothe him and brighten his spirits (cf. Pss. 23:5; 45:7; 104:15; Ecc. 9:8; Matt. 6:17; Heb. 1:9), thus dispelling **mourning.** Another sign of joy is a bright **garment** (cf. Ecc. 9:7-8). Israel will be righteous (cf. Isa. 54:14; 58:8; 60:21; 62:1-2) and like stalwart oak trees will **display** God's **splendor** (cf. 35:2; 46:13; 49:3; 55:5; 60:9, 21; 62:3).

**61:4-9.** After the Messiah's Second Advent Israel **will rebuild** her **ruined cities,** even those that had been destroyed many years before. Israel will be so re-

vered that Gentiles (**aliens** and **foreigners**) will join her (cf. 14:1; 60:10) in her farming and shepherding. As a nation of **priests** each one will know **the LORD,** and have access to Him, and mediate on behalf of others, as did the Levitical priests. This was to be one of Israel's functions in the world (Ex. 19:6), but unfortunately she will not fully carry out that responsibility till in the Millennium. **Nations** will bring their **wealth** to Israel (see comments on Isa. 60:5, 11). The **double portion** refers to the inheritance the eldest son in a family would receive from his father's estate (Deut. 21:17). The eldest son was given special honor. Similarly Israel, like the Lord's firstborn (Ex. 4:22), will be honored. Because of these blessings and God's giving Israel **an everlasting covenant** (the New Covenant; cf. Jer. 32:40; Ezek. 16:60; 37:26; Heb. 13:20), people everywhere **will acknowledge that** she is indeed God's special **people.**

**61:10-11.** In these verses the prophet seems to be speaking for the redeemed remnant who will rejoice (cf. comments on 9:3) in response to God's blessings mentioned in 61:1-9. **Salvation** and **righteousness** are pictured as clothes worn by the people (cf. God's "clothes," 59:17). In other words the Israelites are characterized by salvation (God's redeemed people) and righteousness (those who are living by God's standards; cf. 58:8; 60:21). To picture their joy and blessing **a bridegroom** wore a fancy headgear, like a priest's turban, and the **bride** wore costly jewelry. God will cause Israel's **righteousness** to **spring up** in (be known by) other **nations** (cf. 61:11; 62:1-2) much **as the soil** sustains the growth of plants.

*b. Preparation for the coming of the Lord (chap. 62)*

Much of this chapter speaks of preparation being made for the coming of the Lord and for the restoration of His people, thus expanding the thoughts in 40:3-5, 9.

**62:1-5.** Is the speaker in these verses the Messiah, the Lord (God the Father), or the prophet? Since "I" in verse 6 seems to be the Father, verses 1-5 may also be spoken by Him. The Lord announced that He will continue to work on **Jerusalem's** behalf until her **righteousness . . . salvation,** and **glory** are observed by the rest of the world (cf.

61:10-11) and the city is **called by a new name.** That name is not stated here but several names are given later, in 62:4, 12 (cf. 60:14). In the ancient Near East names often signified one's anticipated or present character. So Jerusalem's having a new name means it will have a new righteous character. Like **a crown** or **diadem** (a large metal ring worn on the head) adorning one's head so Jerusalem will be an adornment to **the LORD.** She will display His **splendor** (cf. 35:2; 46:13; 49:3; 55:5; 60:9, 21; 61:3), that is, her inhabitants will manifest His character in their conduct.

The city's new relationship with God is compared to the happiness of a marriage. Rather than being called **Deserted** (cf. 62:12) or **Desolate,** previous characteristics of the city, Jerusalem will be named **Hephzibah** ("My delight is in her") and **Beulah** ("Married one"). The words **so will your sons marry you** (Jerusalem) imply that people again will live in Jerusalem and **God** will be happy about the wonderful state of affairs.

**62:6-9.** In the ancient world **watchmen** were stationed **on** city **walls** (often in towers) to watch for any approaching enemy. While on guard they were never to sleep. Righteous Israelites, like watchmen, were to be alert on Jerusalem's behalf. They were to **give** themselves and God (**Him**) **no rest till He establishes Jerusalem,** that is, they were constantly to ask God that the city become **the praise of the earth,** so blessed by God that people everywhere would extol her (cf. 60:15; 61:11).

The "watchmen" were to hold God to His promises, knowing that is what He desires. God's people should pray for things even when they know God has promised them. Jesus made this clear when He taught His disciples to pray that the kingdom will come (Matt. 6:10). When Jerusalem is restored, it will **never again** fall to its enemies (Isa. 62:8-9). God has assured it by oath (**sworn by His right hand) and by His** power (**arm**; see comments on 40:10).

**62:10-12.** Verses 10-12 were written as if the Lord were on His way, so His people should be ready. The repeated commands, **Pass through, pass through** and **build up, build up,** convey a sense of urgency; quickly **the people** are to **pre-**

pare themselves spiritually for His coming (see comments on 40:3-5, 9). To **raise a banner** was a way of announcing something. **The nations** are to be informed that **the** LORD is coming to Jerusalem. When He arrives word is to be given throughout the world (on **the ends of the earth** see comments on 5:26) that He, Israel's **Savior** (see comments on 43:11), has come to **reward** Jerusalemites with His blessings. Giving the people of the city new names (**The Holy People, The Redeemed of the** LORD, and **Sought After**) speaks of the new character Israel will have. Because of God's redemption the people will be holy (Ex. 19:6; Deut. 7:6), and Gentiles will visit **the city. No longer** will it be **deserted** (Isa. 62:12; cf. v. 4; 60:15; Zech. 14:11).

### c. The coming of the Lord (63:1-6)

**63:1.** When the Lord returns two questions will be asked of Him: **Who is this?** (twice in v. 1) and "Why are Your garments red?" (v. 2) He will be **coming from Edom** (cf. 34:5-9), the wicked nation southeast of Israel that often opposed God's people and therefore is under God's wrath (Mal. 1:4), and **from Bozrah,** a city (modern-day Buseirah) in Edom. Coming from there God's **garments** will be **crimson** (Isa. 63:1) and red (v. 2) because they are **stained** with blood (v. 3) from slaughtering His enemies (the nations, vv. 3, 6) in Edom. **Robed in splendor** signifies His power and glory as He will stride **forward** toward Israel **to save** (deliver) her (cf. Rom. 11:26).

**63:2-6.** The Lord's **garments** spattered with blood will appear **red** as if He had been in a **winepress.** "Red" ('āḏōm is a wordplay on "Edom" ('ĕḏôm). A **winepress** was usually a shallow pit with a hole on the side leading out to a container. As individuals trampled on grapes in the press, the juice flowed through the hole into the container. Obviously some juice would also splatter on the workers' clothes. As the Lord will fight and defeat **the nations** (cf. 34:2) in the Battle of Armageddon (cf. Zech. 14:3; Rev. 16:16; 19:15-19), He will take **vengeance** on them (cf. Isa. 34:8; 35:4; 61:2) in His **anger** and **wrath.** God's **wrath** is also pictured as being like a winepress in Revelation 14:19-20. Though that day will bring doom to the Lord's enemies, it will mean deliverance (**redemption** and **salvation,**

Isa. 63:4-5) for those of His covenant people who turn to Him.

### 3. THE NATION'S PRAYER AND THE LORD'S RESPONSE (63:7–65:25)

This section records a pathetic prayer of the Jewish remnant and the Lord's appropriate response. Isaiah was writing for the exiles in Babylon who would view their situation as somewhat hopeless. They would not be able to sense how God could possibly help them in their distress. However, they would remember the way the Lord had helped His people in bringing them out of bondage in Egypt. This would encourage them to pray for release from *their* bondage. In responding to their prayer, the Lord explained that their sin caused their distress and promised that He would deliver them and bring them into the promised kingdom.

#### a. The prayer of the nation (63:7–64:12)

**63:7-9.** Before stating their two requests—that God be compassionate toward them (vv. 15-19) and that He punish their enemies (64:1-7)—the righteous remnant said it would recite (**tell of**) the Lord's goodness in the past. (The word **I** refers to Isaiah, representing the nation.) Because of their distress, recalling God's past help in the nation's Exodus would reassure them of the Lord's concern. His actions on their behalf (**for us**) would be **kindnesses** (pl. of ḥeseḏ, meaning expressions of His covenantal "loyal love"), extended to **Israel** because of **His compassion** (63:7), **love, and mercy** (v. 9). As His people and His **sons,** they would know God as **their Savior** (see comments on 43:11). Seeing their ancestors in **distress** in Egypt (cf. Ex. 2:23-25; 3:7), God **redeemed** (gāʾal, "to buy out of slavery"; cf. Isa. 43:1) **them. The angel of His presence** is probably the Angel of the Lord, the Lord Himself (cf. Ex. 33:14; see comments on Gen. 16:10).

**63:10.** In spite of all God did for Israel, she **rebelled** against Him. "Rebelled" is not from pāšaʿ, "to revolt or rebel against a covenant stipulation," but mārâh, "to be contentious, to be rebellious" (cf. Ps. 78:8; Jer. 5:23). From almost the beginning of the wilderness experience Israel rebelled against God (Ex. 17:1-7). This **grieved** the **Holy Spirit** (cf. Eph. 4:30), the only place in the Old Testament where this statement is made. (Cf. references to the Spirit in Isa. 63:11, 14; see comments on 11:2.) Because of this rebellion God **fought against them,** bringing troubles, distresses, and enemies to discipline them.

**63:11-14.** At various times in her history Israel, when disciplined by God, would recall how in the great Exodus He used **Moses** like a **shepherd** to bring them out of Egypt by **His . . . arm** (v. 12; see comments on 40:10) **of power,** leading **them through the sea** (63:11; cf. Ex. 14:16), also referred to as **the waters** (Isa. 63:12) and **the depths** (v. 13). Being freed from Egypt was like giving **a horse** free rein **in open country** or like letting **cattle** graze on a wide **plain.** As God gave them **rest** and guidance, His reputation was made known.

**63:15-19.** The remnant would beg God to **look down** on them and remember their plight in the same way He had remembered the distress of their forefathers in Egypt (cf. v. 9). They would long for a display of both His strength and His love. Though they had not been following in the tradition of **Abraham** or **Israel** (i.e., Jacob), God was still their **Father** (cf. 64:8) and **Redeemer** (see comments on 41:14). Penitently the remnant would ask that God sovereignly **return** them, His **servants,** to Him, reminding Him that the temple (**Your sanctuary**) was destroyed (63:17-18). (This is one of many places in chaps. 40–66 which shows that Isaiah, living more than 100 years before the Babylonian Captivity, wrote prophetically to prepare that future generation of exiles for it.) Though the nation had belonged to God for centuries (**from of old**), it had been a long time since the people were in a proper relationship with God and His theocratic rule **over them.**

**64:1-7.** The second plea of the remnant is recorded in these verses (the first is in 63:15-19). Realizing their uncleanness (64:5-7), they would ask God to smite their **enemies** (vv. 1-4). They would pray that the Lord would **rend the heavens** (the sky is pictured as a piece of cloth He would tear), **come down** (vv. 1-2; cf. "look down," 63:15), and execute judgment on **the nations. Fire** and boiling **water** picture judgment (cf. Jer. 1:13-14; Mal 4:1, 5). The **awesome things** (Isa. 64:3) probably refer to the phenomena of fire, darkness (Deut. 4:11-13), and earthquake (Ex. 19:16-19) when God gave the Mosaic Law. This revealing **God**—the only God (Isa. 64:4; cf. 1 Cor. 2:10)—**acts on behalf of those who** believe in Him and who therefore willingly **do** what is **right.** Recalling this, the remnant would ask that God work on *their* behalf. They would confess their **sin** (Isa. 64:5b), spiritual uncleanness (v. 6a), weakness (v. 6b, **like a** shriveled **leaf**), and lack of prayer (v. 7). However, they would not blame God for their dreadful condition; they would know that their wasting **away** was **because of** their **sins.** Therefore they would have to count on God's faithfulness and promises.

**64:8-12.** This final part of this beautiful prayer by the righteous remnant is a confession of trust in the LORD. The remnant would address God as their **Father** (cf. 63:16) and as **the Potter.** Israel was to be like obedient children and as submissive as **clay** (cf. 29:16; 45:9). Therefore the remnant would obediently and submissively ask the Lord to withhold His anger and to **look** on them (cf. 63:15) as His own. The remnant would remind God that Israel's **cities** including Jerusalem had been destroyed and that **even the temple** had **been burned.** The nation would urge God to do something about the situation (64:12), thereby breaking His silence (cf. 62:1; 65:6) and withholding His punishment on her.

*b. The response of the Lord (chap. 65)*

In several ways the Lord's response to the remnant's prayer sums up the message of the entire Book of Isaiah. The Lord said that though He had constantly been presenting His love to Israel, they had rejected Him which made judgment necessary (vv. 1-7). However, in that judgment, a remnant will be preserved (vv. 8-12). The consequences of righteous living differ from those of wicked living (vv. 13-16). The Lord will establish a glorious kingdom in which peace and righteousness will flourish (vv. 17-25). Throughout the chapter, as well as throughout the book, the prophet implicitly pleaded for the people to place their trust in the Lord, their covenant God, and to live righteously.

**65:1-7.** Constantly reaching out to Israel, God **revealed** Himself **to those who did not** even **ask for** that revelation. Only because of His grace did He do so,

even calling out to them, **Here am I.** Yet they did not respond. He was always ready to help them (holding **out** His **hands;** Paul quotes vv. 1-2 in Rom. 10:20-21), but they continued to be stubborn, independent, and evil. They provoked God by (a) worshiping in pagan **gardens** (cf. Isa. 1:29; 66:17); (b) being involved in necromancy (supposedly consulting the dead, while sitting **among the graves,** 65:4; cf. 8:19); (c) disregarding His dietary laws (65:4b; cf. 66:3, 17; Lev. 11:7); and (d) being religiously arrogant till they became as repulsive and irritating to Him as **smoke in** a person's nose. Because of their sins, **the** LORD would judge them. The Assyrian threat (Isa. 1–37) and the Babylonian Exile (chaps. 38–66) were two of the ways the Lord disciplined His people. The consequences of sin had to be faced; God would **pay** them **back** in judgment for their idolatrous worship in high places (cf. 57:7).

**65:8-12.** Though judgment was addressed to the whole nation (vv. 6-7), it will not be total. As a few grapes are left when vineyards are gleaned (Deut. 24:21), so a remnant will be left who will return to the land (**possess My mountains**) and cultivate it, and **pasture** their **flocks** there again. **Sharon,** the coastal plain south of Mount Carmel, is excellent land for agriculture, and **the Valley of Achor** (cf. Hosea 2:15) west of Jericho was known for its sheep-herding.

On the other hand people are destined for **slaughter** if they do not trust **the** LORD, and if they disregard the temple (on God's **holy mountain;** see comments on Isa. 11:9). **Fortune** and **Destiny** were names of gods Israel worshiped in her attempts to know the future. Food and drink were set before those idols to seek to please them. Such people, God said, are doomed to die by **the sword,** for they refused to **listen** to Him and deliberately chose to go on sinning (cf. 66:4).

**65:13-16.** Contrasts between people who are the Lord's **servants** and those who have departed from Him are dramatically presented in these verses. His servants **will eat . . . drink,** and **rejoice,** while the rejectors will be **hungry . . . thirsty,** and shamed. God's servants will **sing** for **joy** whereas the rejectors will **wail,** be cursed, and **put . . . to death.** God's **servants . . . will** receive **another name,** that is, will be given a new character (cf. 62:2), so that they will take oaths honestly (**by the God of truth**; cf. Ps. 31:5). God will forget their previous difficulties and sins because of His grace.

**65:17-25.** In these verses the Lord described the millennial kingdom, which is seemingly identified here with the eternal state (**new heavens and a new earth**). In Revelation, however, the new heavens and new earth (Rev. 21:1) *follow* the Millennium (Rev. 20:4). Most likely Isaiah did not distinguish between these two aspects of God's rule; he saw them together as one. After all, the Millennium, though 1,000 years in duration, will be a mere pinpoint of time compared with the eternal state.

The need for new heavens and a new earth is suggested in Isaiah 51:6. During the Millennium Jerusalem will be a place of **joy** (65:18). Also the Lord Himself **will rejoice over** it, for sorrow will be vanished (v. 19). Though death will still be present, life spans will be extended (v. 20) and people will **enjoy** safety and the produce of their **vineyards** (vv. 21-22). God's blessing will be on their work and families (v. 23) and He will speedily **answer** their prayers (v. 24). Wild animals will lose their ferocity (cf. 11:6-8; Hosea 2:18) and harmony and safety will prevail under God's good hand (Isa. 65:25). (On God's **holy mountain** see comments on 11:9.)

4. THE LORD'S FULFILLMENT OF HIS PROMISES (CHAP. 66)

As the climax to the book, this chapter fittingly describes the Millennium, the time toward which history has been looking, which was promised to Abraham.

*a. The Lord to esteem the humble (66:1-2)*

**66:1-2.** God is pictured figuratively as sitting on a **throne** (cf. 6:1) with **the earth** as His **footstool** (cf. Acts 7:49). Because of His majesty no one can **build** a **house** for Him to dwell in (1 Kings 8:27); *He* is the Creator. Yet what He values above His inanimate Creation are people who are **humble and contrite** (cf. Isa. 57:15) and who follow His **word.** In one way or another, this has been Isaiah's message throughout this book. God wants His people to follow the truth He has revealed to them. For Israel that was primarily the Mosaic Covenant. Pointing

the people back to the Word of God, Isaiah was indicating that they needed to obey it if they were to enjoy His blessings.

*b. The Lord to judge (66:3-6)*

**66:3-6.** The strange comparisons in verse 3 indicate that the people's religious **sacrifices** and offerings were only external ritual. In their hearts the people were murderers, perverters of God's dietary laws (cf. 65:4; Lev. 11:7), and idolaters. In reality they were going **their own ways** (cf. Isa. 53:6) rather than the Lord's way. Therefore **harsh** judgment would come. (The last four lines of 66:4 are almost identical with 65:12; see comments there.) People in Israel who professed to know **the LORD** but **who** actually hated and discriminated against God's people would be shamed by His discipline when **the temple** would be destroyed by the Babylonians.

*c. The Lord to give birth to His nation (66:7-21)*

**66:7-11.** Israel's return to the land will be so remarkably quick that it will be like a woman giving **birth** to **a son** before (v. 7) or as soon as (v. 8) she has any **labor . . . pains**! God does not start something and leave it unfinished. As surely as a woman's **womb** opens, not closes, for **delivery,** so God will do for **Jerusalem** what He has set out to do. This then is cause for rejoicing. The people of Israel will **delight in** Jerusalem as an infant delights in her mother's sustenance.

**66:12-13.** As stated many times in the Book of Isaiah, **peace** will come to **Jerusalem** (cf., e.g., 48:18; 55:12) and the nations' **wealth** will flow to her (cf. 60:5, 11; 61:6). In 66:11-12 Jerusalem is compared to a mother; in verse 13 God is compared to **a mother** who **comforts her child.**

**66:14-18.** When God restores His people to Jerusalem (vv. 10-13) in the Millennium, they **will rejoice** and prosper, but on His and her enemies He will swoop down in judgment like a **fire** (cf. 2 Thes. 1:7-9) and **a whirlwind** to slay them. This **judgment** will be fair because of their abominations: worshiping in idolatrous **gardens** (cf. Isa. 1:29; 65:3) and eating ceremonially unclean animals such as **pigs** (cf. 65:4; 66:3; Lev. 11:7) **and**

rats (cf. Lev. 11:29). When the Messiah returns, His judgment will be on **all nations** (cf. Zech. 14:3; Rev. 19:17-18) and because of that judgment the world will **see** His **glory.**

**66:19-21.** People outside Israel will turn to Him and worship Him. The remnant of believing Israelites will travel as missionaries to other parts of the world, to tell Gentiles about God's **glory.** Those places and peoples will include **Tarshish,** probably in southwestern Spain (cf. 23:1, 6, 10, 14; 60:9), **Libyans** in northern Africa, **Lydians** in western Asia Minor, **Tubal** in northeastern Asia Minor, **Greece,** and **distant islands.** These and other peoples will be converted and will travel to **Jerusalem** to worship in **the temple** (cf. 2:2; Zech. 8:23). **Some of them** will even be selected as **priests and Levites,** thus showing that all the nations will in fact be blessed through Israel (cf. Gen. 12:3).

*d. The Lord to establish new heavens and new earth (66:22-24)*

**66:22-24.** Israel will be as enduring **as the new heavens and the new earth** (see comments on 65:17). **All mankind** (i.e., people from all nations) **will** worship **the LORD,** bowing **down before** Him. As Isaiah had frequently written, these righteous ones will contrast greatly with **those who rebelled** (*pāša'*; see comments on 1:2) **against** the **LORD.** They will suffer eternal torment (cf. Mark 9:48). This awesome way in which the majestic Book of Isaiah concludes points to the need for unrepentant people to turn to the Lord, the only God, the Holy One of Israel.

# BIBLIOGRAPHY

Alexander, Joseph A. *Commentaries on the Prophecies of Isaiah.* 1865. Reprint (2 vols. in 1). Grand Rapids: Zondervan Publishing House, 1980.

Allis, Oswald T. *The Unity of Isaiah: A Study in Prophecy.* Nutley, N.J.: Presbyterian and Reformed Publishing Co., 1952.

Barnes, Albert. *Notes on the Old Testament, Explanatory and Practical: Isaiah.* 2 vols. Reprint. Grand Rapids: Baker Book House, 1950.

Bultema, Harry. *Commentary on Isaiah.* Translated by Cornelius Lambregtse. Grand Rapids: Kregel Publications, 1981.

Delitzsch, Franz. "Isaiah." In *Commentary on the Old Testament in Ten Volumes.* Vol. 7. Reprint (25 vols. in 10). Grand Rapids: Wm. B. Eerdmans Publishing Co., 1982.

Gray, George B. *A Critical and Exegetical Commentary on the Book of Isaiah.* Vol. 1: *Introduction and Commentary on I–XXVII.* The International Critical Commentary. Edinburgh: T. & T. Clark, 1912.

Herbert, A.S. *The Book of the Prophet Isaiah: Chapters I–XXXIX.* Cambridge: Cambridge University Press, 1973.

Jennings, F.C. *Studies in Isaiah.* New York: Loizeaux Brothers, 1935.

Kaiser, Otto. *Isaiah 1–12: A Commentary.* Philadelphia: Westminster Press, 1972.

_____. *Isaiah 13–39: A Commentary.* Philadelphia: Westminster Press, 1974.

Leupold, H.C. *Exposition of Isaiah.* 2 vols. Grand Rapids: Baker Book House, 1968.

MacRae, Allan A. *The Gospel of Isaiah.* Chicago: Moody Press, 1977.

Martin, Alfred. *Isaiah: The Salvation of Jehovah.* Chicago: Moody Press, 1967.

Martin, Alfred, and Martin, John A. *Isaiah: The Glory of the Messiah.* Chicago: Moody Press, 1983.

Mauchline, John. *Isaiah 1–39.* London: S.C.M. Press, 1962.

Orelli, C. von. *The Prophecies of Isaiah.* Translated by J.S. Banks. Edinburgh: T. & T. Clark, 1889.

Westermann, Claus. *Isaiah 40–66: A Commentary.* Philadelphia: Westminster Press, 1969.

Wright, G. Ernest. *The Book of Isaiah.* The Layman's Bible Commentary. Richmond, Va.: John Knox Press, 1964.

Young, Edward. *The Book of Isaiah.* 3 vols. The New International Commentary on the Old Testament. Grand Rapids: Wm. B. Eerdmans Publishing Co., 1965, 1969, 1972.

_____. *Studies in Isaiah.* Grand Rapids: Wm. B. Eerdmans Publishing Co., 1954.

_____. *Who Wrote Isaiah?* Grand Rapids: Wm. B. Eerdmans Publishing Co., 1958.

# JEREMIAH

## Charles H. Dyer

## INTRODUCTION

Jeremiah was the premier prophet of Judah during the dark days leading to her destruction. Though the light of other prophets, such as Habakkuk and Zephaniah, flickered in Judah at that time Jeremiah was the blazing torch who, along with Ezekiel in Babylon, exposed the darkness of Judah's sin with the piercing brightness of God's Word. He was a weeping prophet to a wayward people.

**Authorship and Date.** The author of the book is "Jeremiah son of Hilkiah" (1:1). The exact meaning of Jeremiah's name (*yirmᵉyāhû* or *yirmᵉyâh*) is disputed. Suggested meanings include "Yahweh establishes," "Yahweh exalts," and "Yahweh hurls down." Jeremiah's father, Hilkiah, was a member of the Levitical priesthood and lived in Anathoth, a small village about three miles northeast of Jerusalem (see the map "The World of Jeremiah and Ezekiel"). This city was one of those given to the descendants of Aaron the priest by Joshua (cf. Josh. 21:15-19). Probably this Hilkiah is not the same as his contemporary by the same name who discovered the Law in the temple during the reign of Josiah (cf. 2 Kings 22:3-14). Like Ezekiel (Ezek. 1:3) and Zechariah (Zech. 1:1; cf. Neh. 12:1, 4, 16), Jeremiah was from the priestly line. However, no evidence indicates that he ever entered the priesthood in Jerusalem.

Jeremiah's ministry extended from "the 13th year of the reign of Josiah" (Jer. 1:2) until the Exile of the Jerusalemites (1:3). Thus he prophesied from about 627 B.C. till at least 586 B.C. In fact Jeremiah 40–44 indicates that Jeremiah's ministry continued beyond the fall of Jerusalem to at least 582 B.C. In his book Jeremiah included a large number of chronological references that help date many of his prophecies.

A major difficulty is trying to determine how the various prophecies in the Book of Jeremiah were compiled. Many scholars feel that the book is an anthology of selected sayings from Jeremiah (or his disciples) that were later collected and arranged, often rather haphazardly. Some deny that a purposeful order can be (or should be) determined in the text.

The chart "The Dating of Jeremiah's Prophecies" shows how his prophecies are arranged chronologically. Three observations may be made.

(1) Obviously there is no chronological consistency. Unlike Ezekiel, whose prophecies are arranged in chronological order, Jeremiah often placed prophecies together that are dated years apart.

(2) Jeremiah's messages were given during times of stress, upheaval, and need. Chapters 1–6 and 11–12 correspond roughly to the time of King Josiah's reforms. The next major burst of prophetic activity (chaps. 7–10; 14–20; 22:1-19; 26) came when Nebuchadnezzar rose to power. The rest of Jeremiah's prophecies came at the time of the first deportation to Babylon, the second deportation to Babylon, the secret plot to rebel against Babylon, and the final siege and deportation to Babylon. Chapter 52 was written at a later date.

(3) The book itself gives evidence of multiple stages of growth. That is, Jeremiah, at different stages of his ministry, collected his prophecies and rearranged them in a definite pattern (cf. 25:13; 30:2; 36:2, 32). Jeremiah could have completed the final form of chapters 1–51 after he was taken hostage to Egypt (cf. 51:64). But what about chapter 52? Jeremiah 52, nearly identical to 2 Kings 24:18–25:30, was written sometime after 561 B.C. when King Jehoiachin was released from prison in Babylon (Jer. 52:31). Apparently this last chapter was appended to Jeremiah's prophecies by the same writer who compiled the Book of Kings. The chapter

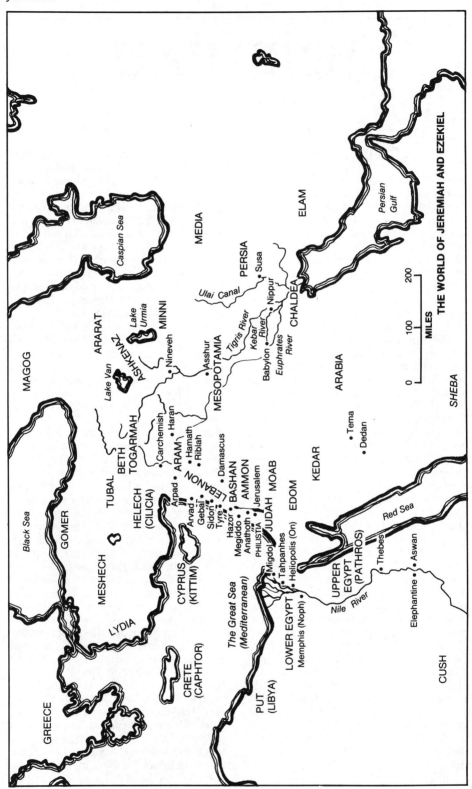

THE WORLD OF JEREMIAH AND EZEKIEL

MILES

0    100    200

GREECE

MESHECH

LYDIA

GOMER

Black Sea

TUBAL

MAGOG

HELECH
(CILICIA)

BETH
TOGARMAH

Caspian Sea

ARARAT

ASHKENAZ

Lake Van

Lake
Urmia

MINNI

MEDIA

Carchemish

Haran

Nineveh

Asshur

MESOPOTAMIA

Tigris River

PERSIA

Susa

Ulai Canal

Nippur

ELAM

Persian
Gulf

Arpad

ARAM

Hamath

Riblah

Damascus

Kebar River

Babylon

Euphrates
River

CHALDEA

CYPRUS
(KITTIM)

Arvad

Gebal

Sidon

Tyre

LEBANON

Hazor

Megiddo

Anathoth

BASHAN

AMMON

Jerusalem

JUDAH

MOAB

PHILISTIA

EDOM

KEDAR

Tema

Dedan

ARABIA

SHEBA

CRETE
(CAPHTOR)

The Great Sea
(Mediterranean)

Migdol

Tahpanhes

Heliopolis (On)

Red Sea

PUT
(LIBYA)

LOWER EGYPT

Memphis (Noph)

UPPER
EGYPT
(PATHROS)

Thebes

Aswan

Nile River

Elephantine

CUSH

was added to show that Jeremiah's words of judgment had been fulfilled and that Jehoiachin's release foreshadowed God's promises of restoration and blessing.

**Historical Background.** Jeremiah's ministry spanned the final five decades of Judah's history. His call to service came in 627 B.C. in the 13th year of King Josiah (cf. 1:2), Judah's last good king. Josiah's reign was the final ray of light before the darkness of idolatry and foreign intrigue settled over the Davidic throne. Josiah came to the throne when he was eight years old, and provided 31 years of relative stability for Judah.

Internally the nation of Judah was gripped by the idolatry that King Manasseh had promoted during his 55-year reign (2 Kings 21:1-9). In 622 B.C. (Josiah's 18th year) Judah experienced her final spiritual renewal (cf. 2 Kings 22:3–23:25). Prompted by the rediscovery of a copy of the Mosaic Law in the temple, Josiah embarked on a diligent effort to rid the nation of idolatry. He succeeded in removing the outward forms, but his efforts did not reach into his subjects' hearts. After Josiah's untimely death, the people returned to their wicked ways.

Internationally the Assyrian Empire, which had dominated the ancient Near East for centuries, was on the brink of collapse. The capital city, Nineveh, had been destroyed in 612 B.C., and in 609 the retreating Assyrian army was defeated at Haran. The beleaguered remains of the once-great Assyrian Empire staggered to Carchemish just across the Euphrates River (see the map "The World of Jeremiah and Ezekiel").

This collapse of Assyria was caused largely by the rise of another power—Babylon. In October 626 the Chaldean prince Nabopolassar had defeated the Assyrian army outside Babylon and claimed the throne in Babylon. The kingdom he founded came to be known as the Neo-Babylonian Empire. He consolidated his empire, and by 616 he was on the march to expand his territory. The combined army of the Babylonians and Medes destroyed Nineveh in 612.

Babylon's rise and Assyria's collapse created a realignment of power throughout the area. Judah, under Josiah, threw off the yoke of Assyrian dominion and

enjoyed a brief period of national independence. This independence was shattered, however, by events in 609 B.C.

Egypt sensed an opportunity for expansion in Assyria's collapse. If a weakened Assyria could be maintained as a buffer state to halt Babylon's westward advances, Egypt would be free to reclaim much of western Palestine (including Judah) which she had lost to Assyria earlier.

Though Egypt had always feared a powerful Assyria, she now feared the prospect of a powerful Babylon even more. So Egypt entered the conflict between Assyria and Babylon on Assyria's side. In 609 Pharaoh Neco II marched with a large Egyptian army toward Haran to support the remaining Assyrian forces in a last attempt to retake their lost territory.

King Josiah knew what the consequences would be for Judah if Egypt were successful. He did not want Egypt to replace Assyria as Judah's taskmaster. So Josiah mobilized his army to stop the Egyptian advance. A battle took place on the plain of Megiddo—and Judah lost. Josiah was killed in battle and the Egyptian army continued on toward Haran (2 Chron. 35:20-24).

Whether Josiah's attack had an effect on the battle's outcome is not known, but possibly he delayed the Egyptian army from arriving in time to provide the assistance Assyria needed. Assyria failed in its bid to recapture the land, and it ceased to be a major force in history.

The city of Carchemish then became the line of demarcation, and the powers facing each other were Egypt and Babylon. After the defeat of Judah, Egypt assumed control of Palestine. Judah had appointed Jehoahaz king in place of his father Josiah; but after a reign of only three months he was deposed by Neco and taken to Egypt. (See the chart "The Last Five Kings of Judah," near 2 Kings 23:31-32.) Neco then plundered the treasuries of Judah and appointed Jehoiakim, another son of Josiah, as his vassal king (2 Kings 23:34-35).

In 605 B.C. another major shift occurred in the balance of power. For four years the Egyptians and Babylonians had faced each other at Carchemish with neither side able to gain the upper hand. Then in 605 crown prince Nebuchadnez-

**Jeremiah**

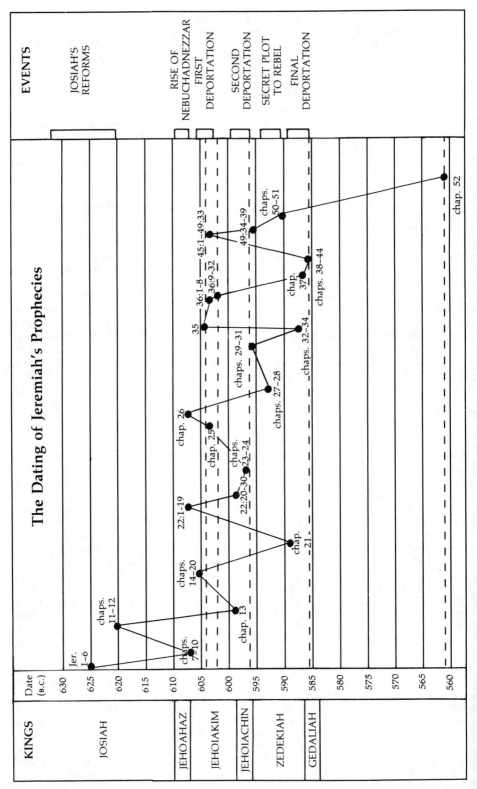

## The Dating of Jeremiah's Prophecies

zar led the Babylonian forces to a decisive victory. The army of Babylonia smashed through the Egyptian defenses at Carchemish and pursued the forces to Egypt.

Two other events in 605 B.C. influenced Judah's history. First, King Jehoiakim switched allegiance to Babylon after the Battle of Carchemish and agreed to serve as a vassal king for Nebuchadnezzar (2 Kings 24:1). Second, on August 15, 605 Nabopolassar, the king of Babylon, died. Nebuchadnezzar returned to Babylon to claim the throne.

Nebuchadnezzar solidified his rule over this territory by appointing kings and taking "hostages" to assure continued loyalty. During this campaign he took Daniel captive (Dan. 1:1-6).

Judah remained a vassal state until late in 601 B.C. At that time Nebuchadnezzar made another advance through Palestine. His objective was Egypt, but his goal was not achieved. The army of Babylon suffered a major defeat and was forced to retreat.

Jehoiakim was a political chameleon. He had switched allegiance from Egypt to Babylon in 605 when Nebuchadnezzar had defeated Egypt. After Babylon's defeat in 601, however, he again changed sides and supported Egypt (cf. 2 Kings 24:1). This was a fatal mistake.

By December 598 Nebuchadnezzar's army was prepared for an attack. His chief objective was to take Jerusalem to teach it (and no doubt other vassal nations too) the awful consequences of rebelling against Babylon. Jehoiakim died during the time of Babylon's attack, and was followed to the throne by his son, Jehoiachin. Jehoiachin saw the folly in opposing Babylon, and Jerusalem surrendered in March 597.

Nebuchadnezzar replaced the new king, looted the city, and removed the chief individuals. Jehoiachin, after a three-month reign, was deported to Babylon, and his uncle, Zedekiah, was installed as Judah's vassal king.

Along with Jehoiachin, Nebuchadnezzar also deported 10,000 of the leaders, skilled laborers, and soldiers of Jerusalem (cf. 2 Kings 24:12-16). This was probably when Ezekiel was taken to Babylon. Five years later he began his prophetic ministry in Babylon.

Because Judah's new king, Zedekiah, was weak and vacillating, Judah

eventually collapsed. His 11-year reign was marred by spiritual decline and political instability. Rather than learning from the mistakes of the past, Zedekiah repeated them.

With the enthronement of another Pharaoh (Hophra) in Egypt in 588, Judah was once again enticed to revolt from Babylon (2 Kings 24:20–25:1; Jer. 52:3-4). A coalition of vassal states (Judah, Tyre, and Ammon) refused to remain under Babylon's control. Nebuchadnezzar's response was swift and harsh. The army of Babylon surrounded Jerusalem and began a long siege. In July-August 586 the city fell and was destroyed.

**Structure and Style.** Four characteristics are evident in the Book of Jeremiah.

*1. Lack of chronological arrangement.* As noted earlier under "Authorship and Date" the book has no chronological progression. Jeremiah compiled his prophecies in stages, but not chronologically. For example, many of Jeremiah's prophecies against the nations were written early in his ministry (cf. 25:1, 13). Yet the content of these prophecies is recorded near the end of the book (cf. 46:1–49:33). Thus one must look for some other reason for the arrangement of the prophecies in their present order.

*2. Autobiographical nature.* Writing an intensely personal book, Jeremiah revealed the nation's response to his ministry and his personal feelings about his messages. He wept over the impending destruction (9:1; 13:17; 14:17) and complained about the ridicule he was forced to endure (20:7-10). He also recorded his self-doubt (1:7-8) and his doubts about God's justice (12:1-2).

*3. Different literary materials.* Three types of literary materials are found in the Book of Jeremiah: poetic discourses, prose discourses, and prose narratives. The arrangement of these materials can provide a key to the underlying structure of Jeremiah. They are in the book as follows:

Chapters 1–25 Mixture of poetic and prose discourse with occasional narrative

Chapters 26–29 Mixture of prose discourse and narrative

Chapters 30–31 Poetic discourse

Chapters 32–33 Prose discourse

Chapters 34–36 Mixture of prose discourse and narrative

Chapters 37–45 Narrative in chronological order

Chapters 46–51 Poetic discourse

Chapter 52 Narrative in chronological order

These literary materials seem to offer major breaks in the content of the book. The significance of these divisions will be discussed next.

*4. Logical arrangement of material.* If Jeremiah did not arrange his book chronologically, how *did* he arrange it? The best answer seems to be that he used a broad logical arrangement of his material to convey an overall message to the people. That is, as Jeremiah compiled his subsequent collections of his prophecies, he rearranged them in a logical pattern. The arrangement developed his theme of God's judgment. Chapters 2–45 focused on God's judgment on Judah and chapters 46–51 focused on God's judgment on the Gentile nations.

The various literary materials provide additional keys for dividing Jeremiah's book. Thus chapters 2–25 (mixture of poetic and prose discourse) contain Jeremiah's 13 messages of judgment on Judah. These were followed by chapters 26–29 (mixture of prose discourse and narrative) which indicated how the people responded to Jeremiah and his message. The Jews' rejection assured this judgment. However, before the judgment began, Jeremiah pointed ahead to Judah's future hope (chaps. 30–31, poetic discourse; and chaps. 32–33, prose discourse). Chapters 34–36 (mixture of prose discourse and narrative) continue the theme of rejection from chapters 26–29. Judah's destruction was inevitable because she had rejected the Word of God. Jeremiah sketched the events that occurred before, during, and after the fall of Jerusalem in chapters 37–45 (narrative in chronological order). God accomplished His judgment on the nation because of her sin. And yet if God's Chosen People were judged for their sin, how could the rest of the world hope to escape? In chapters 46–51 (poetic discourse) Jeremiah turned to these other nations and foretold their judgment. The different literary materials were used by Jeremiah to mold and shape his message.

# OUTLINE

C. Prophecy against Moab
   (chap. 48)
   1. Moab's land to be destroyed
      (48:1-10)
   2. Moab's complacency to be
      shattered (48:11-17)
   3. Moab's cities to experience
      catastrophe (48:18-28)
   4. Moab's pride to cease
      (48:29-39)
   5. Moab's destruction to be
      complete (48:40-47)
D. Prophecy against Ammon
   (49:1-6)
E. Prophecy against Edom (49:7-22)
F. Prophecy against Damascus
   (49:23-27)
G. Prophecy against Kedar and
   Hazor (49:28-33)
H. Prophecy against Elam (49:34-39)
I. Prophecy against Babylon
   (chaps. 50–51)
   1. The announcement of
      judgment (50:1-10)
   2. The fall of Babylon (50:11-16)
   3. The restoration of Israel
      (50:17-20)
   4. The attack on Babylon
      (50:21-40)
   5. The anguish of Babylon
      (50:41-46)
   6. God's vengeance against
      Babylon (51:1-14)
   7. God's sovereignty over
      Babylon (51:15-26)
   8. The summons to the nations
      against Babylon (51:27-33)
   9. God's revenge on Babylon
      (51:34-44)
   10. The warning to the remnant
       in Babylon (51:45-48)
   11. The certainty of Babylon's fall
       (51:49-53)
   12. God's repayment of Babylon
       (51:54-58)
   13. Seraiah's symbolic mission
       (51:59-64)
IV. Conclusion (chap. 52)
   A. The fate of Jerusalem (52:1-23)
      1. The fall of Zedekiah (52:1-11)
      2. The destruction of the city
         (52:12-16)
      3. The destruction of the temple
         (52:17-23)
   B. The fate of certain people
      (52:24-34)
      1. The fate of those in the city
         during its fall (52:24-27)

2. The fate of the exiles (52:28-30)
3. The fate of Jehoiachin
   (52:31-34)

# COMMENTARY

## I. Introduction (chap. 1)

The Book of Jeremiah opens by introducing its readers to the prophet. His
background and call into the prophetic
ministry set the stage for the rest of his
book.

### A. The prophet's background (1:1-3)

**1:1. Jeremiah** gives information on
his family background (v. 1) during the
time he ministered (vv. 2-3). He was **one
of the priests,** descended from the priestly line of Aaron. His father, **Hilkiah,** was
probably not the high priest Hilkiah who
discovered the copy of the Law during
the time of Josiah (2 Kings 22:2-14). The
name "Hilkiah" was evidently a common
name given to several men in the Old
Testament who were priests or Levites
(1 Chron. 6:45-46; 26:10-11; 2 Chron. 34:9-
22; Neh. 12:7; Jer. 1:1).

Jeremiah's hometown was **Anathoth**
which was **in the territory of Benjamin.**
The village of Anathoth was about three
miles northeast of Jerusalem. The territory of Benjamin bordered the territory of
Judah, and the dividing line extended
roughly east to west and passed beside
Jerusalem (cf. Josh. 18:15-16). Anathoth
was a city allocated by Joshua to the
priests (Josh. 21:15-19). Solomon exiled
Abiathar the priest to Anathoth for supporting Adonijah as David's successor
(1 Kings 1:7; 2:26-27).

**1:2-3.** Jeremiah was born a priest, but
began functioning as a prophet when he
received **the word of the LORD.** A prophet was one through whom God spoke
directly to His people. God's call of Jeremiah came **in the 13th year of the reign
of Josiah.** Josiah became king of Judah in
640 B.C., so his 13th year was 627 B.C.
Josiah was the last righteous king of Judah. After his untimely death in 609 B.C.,
every king who ascended Judah's throne
was unworthy of the task. Jeremiah continued as God's spokesman **down to the
fifth month of the 11th year of Zedekiah.**
That date was July-August 586 B.C. Thus
Jeremiah's ministry lasted at least 41
years. However, this verse probably re-

fers to Jeremiah's ministry to the nation of **Judah** until **the people of Jerusalem went into exile** because 39:11–44:30 records events of Jeremiah's ministry that occurred *after* August 586.

## B. The prophet's call (1:4-10)

**1:4-5.** God's call of Jeremiah as a prophet, though brief, contained a message designed to motivate him for his task. God revealed that His selection of Jeremiah as a prophet had occurred **before** he had even been **formed . . . in the womb.** The word **knew** (*yāda'*) means far more than intellectual knowledge. It was used of the intimate relations experienced by a husband and wife ("lay," Gen. 4:1) and conveyed the sense of a close personal relationship ("chosen," Amos 3:2) and protection ("watches over," Ps. 1:6). Before Jeremiah was conceived God had singled him out to be His spokesman to Israel.

Jeremiah had been **set . . . apart** for this ministry. The verb translated "set apart" (*qādaš*) means setting something or someone apart for a specific use. Individuals or objects "set apart" (or sanctified or made holy) for use by God included the Sabbath Day (Ex. 16:23; 20:8), the tabernacle and its furnishings (Ex. 29:44; 40:9), and the priests (Ex. 29:1; 30:30). God had marked Jeremiah from conception and reserved him for a special task. He was appointed to be **a prophet to the nations.** Though Jeremiah proclaimed God's Word to Judah (chaps. 2–45), his ministry as God's spokesman extended beyond Judah to Gentile nations (chaps. 46–51).

**1:6.** Jeremiah responded to God's appointment with a measure of self-doubt. He first objected that he did **not know how to speak.** Jeremiah was not claiming that he was physically unable to talk. He was claiming a lack of eloquence and speaking ability required for such a public ministry.

He also objected that he was **only a child** (*na'ar*). This word was used of infants (Ex. 2:6; 1 Sam. 4:21) and of young men (Gen. 14:24). Jeremiah's age is not given, but possibly he was in his late teens or early 20s at this time. By using the term "child" Jeremiah was emphasizing his lack of experience. He felt ill-prepared to be God's ambassador to the nations.

**1:7-10.** God gave three answers to Jeremiah's objections. First, He stressed the authority under which Jeremiah was to act. Jeremiah should not use inexperience as an excuse for evading his task. He would have no choice in the selection of his audience or his message. Rather, he was to **go to everyone** to whom God sent him and **say whatever** God commanded. Jeremiah did not have to be an eloquent elder statesman—he was simply to be a faithful messenger.

Second, God stressed that He would protect the future prophet. Evidently Jeremiah was afraid for his personal safety. Certainly his fears were based on his awareness of the times because the people did try to get rid of him (cf. 11:18-23; 12:6; 20:1-2; 26:11; 37:15-16; 38:4-6). Yet God told Jeremiah **not** to **be afraid of them,** because He would be on his side. The people would try to kill Jeremiah, but God promised to **rescue** him.

Third, God showed Jeremiah the source of his message. Jeremiah's call must have come in the form of a vision (cf. Ezek. 1:1) because he noted that **the LORD reached out His hand** to touch Jeremiah's **mouth.** This visible manifestation of God was His object lesson to tell Jeremiah that the Lord Himself would **put His words in** Jeremiah's **mouth.** Jeremiah need not worry what to say; God would provide the very words he would speak.

God then summarized the content of Jeremiah's message (Jer. 1:10). It would be a message of both judgment and blessing to **nations and kingdoms.** God used two metaphors to describe Jeremiah's mission (cf. 31:28 for a later use of the same two metaphors). Comparing Jeremiah to a farmer, God said he would **uproot** (announce judgment) **and . . . plant** (announce blessing). Comparing Jeremiah to an architect, God said he would **tear down . . . destroy, and overthrow** (pronounce judgment) and **build** (pronounce blessing).

## C. The prophet's confirming visions (1:11-16)

God confirmed His call to Jeremiah by giving him two visions. The first (vv. 11-12) focused on the nature of the message Jeremiah would deliver and the second (vv. 13-16) pointed out the content of that message.

## 1. THE BLOSSOMING ALMOND BRANCH (1:11-12)

**1:11.** God's first confirming vision caused Jeremiah to **see the branch of an almond tree.** The Hebrew word for "almond tree" is *šāqēd*, from the word "to watch or to wake" (*šāqad*). The almond tree was named the "awake tree" because in Palestine it is the first tree in the year to bud and bear fruit. Its blooms precede its leaves, as the tree bursts into blossom in late January.

**1:12.** The branch represented God who was **watching to see that** His **word is fulfilled.** God used a play on words to associate the almond branch with His activity. The word for "watching" is *šōqēd*, related to the Hebrew noun for "almond tree." Jeremiah's vision of the "awake tree" reminded him that God was awake and watching over His word to make sure it came to pass.

## 2. THE BOILING POT (1:13-16)

**1:13.** God's second confirming vision caused Jeremiah to **see a boiling pot.** The pot was a large kettle that was evidently sitting on a fire because it was "boiling" (lit., "blown upon," *nāpûaḥ*, indicating a wind or draft blowing on the fire to help bring the cauldron's contents to a boil). The pot was **tilting away from the north** indicating that its contents were about to be spilled out toward the south.

**1:14-16.** The tilting pot represented **disaster** that **will be poured out on** those **who live in** Judah. The direction from which the pot was facing represented **the peoples of the northern kingdoms** whom God was summoning to punish the nation **of Judah.** Some scholars feel that God was referring to a Scythian invasion, but it seems better to understand His message as a reference to the coming invasion by Babylon and her allies (cf. 25:8-9). Though Babylon was located to the *east* geographically, the invading armies followed the trade routes along the Euphrates River in their march to Judah. Thus those armies did approach from the *north* (cf. 4:6; 6:1, 22; 10:22; 13:20; 15:12; 16:15; 23:8; 25:9, 26; 31:8; 46:24; 47:2; 50:3, 9, 41). They would **set up their thrones in the entrance of the gates of Jerusalem,** indicating that the city would fall to them. Jeremiah recorded the fulfillment of this prophecy in 39:2-3 after the Babylonians captured Jerusalem.

Judah's fall to Babylon would be God's judgment for her idolatry. **In forsaking** God and **worshiping what their hands** had **made** the people of Judah had violated their covenant with God (cf. Deut. 28). The sin of Judah brought about her downfall.

## D. The prophet's challenge (1:17-19)

**1:17-19.** After explaining the task, God charged Jeremiah to take up the challenge. **Get yourself ready!** is literally, "gird up your loins" (cf. Ex. 12:11; 2 Kings 4:29; 9:1; Luke 12:35; Eph. 6:14; 1 Peter 1:13). God gave him the needed strength to **stand** against the people of Judah. Through God's enablement Jeremiah would be as strong as **a fortified city, an iron pillar, and a bronze wall.** God's strength to withstand attack would be needed because all the people would oppose Jeremiah's message. They would **fight against** Jeremiah, but God assured him that they would **not overcome** him.

## II. Prophecies concerning Judah (chaps. 2–45)

This section begins with Jeremiah recording 13 oracles of divine judgment against the nation of Judah (chaps. 2–25). He then indicated the personal conflicts that ensued as the people rejected his messages (chaps. 26–29). The judgment of Judah was now sealed; but before he chronicled the execution of that judgment, Jeremiah inserted God's message of future comfort for Israel and Judah (chaps. 30–33). Though Judah would go into captivity, God would not abandon His people. After this message of future hope, Jeremiah recorded the fall of Judah to Babylon (chaps. 34–45). Then the word of judgment he had pronounced was fulfilled.

## A. Divine judgment on Judah (chaps. 2–25)

These 13 messages of judgment include nine general prophecies of judgment (chaps. 2–20) and four specific prophecies of judgment (chaps. 21–25).

### 1. JEREMIAH'S NINE GENERAL PROPHECIES OF JUDGMENT (CHAPS. 2–20)

#### a. Jerusalem's faithlessness (2:1–3:5)

**2:1-3.** Jeremiah's first message confronted **Jerusalem** with her waywardness. To emphasize this Jeremiah contrasted Judah's former devotion (vv. 1-3) with her present departure from God (v. 4–3:5). At the time of the Exodus Israel **loved** God and **followed** Him **through the desert**. Israel had her lapses of faith when she murmured against God in the wilderness wanderings, but God in His grace and "forbearance" (Rom. 3:25) passed over her. Yet for the most part she had remained faithful as a nation.

**Israel** had been set apart as **holy to the Lord** (cf. Ex. 19:6; 22:31). Just as **the firstfruits of the harvest** belonged to God (cf. Lev. 23:9-14), so Israel had been chosen as the first nation to worship the Lord. Those **who devoured her** were as guilty as those who ate of the firstfruits dedicated to God, and God would bring **disaster** on them (cf. Gen. 12:3).

**2:4-8.** Israel's faithfulness to God, however, did not last. **Jacob** (a synonym for **Israel,** v. 4) **followed worthless idols** (v. 5; cf. vv. 8, 11; 8:19; 10:8, 14-15; 14:22; 16:19; 18:15; 51:17-18) forgetting that **the Lord** had **led** them **through the** desert (2:6) **into a fertile land.** And the people **defiled** the **land** with their idolatry (v. 7).

Jeremiah singled out the three groups charged with leading the nation and exposed their lack of obedience (v. 8). **The priests** who were to instruct the people in the ways of God **did not know** God, that is, they themselves did not have an intimate relationship with the One about whom they were teaching (see comments on "knew" in 1:5).

**The leaders** (*rō'îm,* lit., "shepherds") were the political and civil leaders appointed by God to guide and protect the nation. In the early history of Israel this function was fulfilled by judges, but later the duty was assigned to kings. Ironically the ones who were to lead Judah were themselves in need of correction. They **rebelled against** the One who had appointed them to their task.

**The prophets** were the third group charged with leading the nation. But instead of declaring God's words of rebuke and correction, they **prophesied by Baal** and urged the people to follow **worthless idols** (cf. comments on 2:5). Baal was a Canaanite god of fertility whose worship was a constant thorn in Israel's side (cf. 1 Kings 18:18-40; 2 Kings 10:18-28; 21:1-3).

**2:9-12.** Having clearly shown the faithlessness of the people, Jeremiah used the image of a court case to focus on the seriousness of Israel's sin. God would **bring charges** (*rîb,* a legal term for filing a court case or lawsuit; cf. Micah 6:1-2). Jeremiah asked the people to go on a "field trip" to observe the faithfulness of the Gentiles. But whether they went **to the coasts of Kittim** (Cyprus) in the west or **to Kedar** (north Arabian desert tribes) in the east, the results would always be the same: no pagan society had **ever changed its gods.** The idolatrous nations surrounding Israel were more faithful to their false gods than Israel had been to the true God of the universe.

**2:13.** Israel had **committed two sins.** The first was one of omission: she had **forsaken** her God. Her second sin was one of commission: she had replaced her true God with false idols. Man's heart, like nature, abhors a vacuum. Using imagery that those residing in Judah would understand, Jeremiah compared the nation's actions to someone abandoning a **spring of living** (running) **water** for **broken cisterns.** The most reliable and refreshing sources of water in Israel were her natural springs. This water was dependable; and its clear, cool consistency was satisfying. In contrast, the most unreliable source of water was cisterns. Cisterns were large pits dug into the rock and covered with plaster. These pits were used to gather rainwater. This water was brackish; and if the rains were below normal, it could run out. Worse yet, if a cistern developed a crack it would not **hold** the **water.** To turn from a dependable, pure stream of running water to a broken, brackish cistern was idiotic. Yet that is what Judah did when she turned from God to idols.

**2:14-16.** Judah's apostasy brought severe repercussions. Her **land** was **laid waste** by foreign invaders (compared to **lions**) and her **towns** were **burned and deserted.** The reference to **Memphis** (cf. Ezek. 30:13, 16) **and Tahpanhes** (cf. Ezek. 30:18), cities in Egypt, could refer to Pharaoh Shishak's invasion of Judah in 925 b.c. (1 Kings 14:25-26) or to Pharaoh Neco's killing King Josiah in 609 (2 Kings 23:29-30). In both instances Egypt triumphed over Judah and **shaved the crown of** Judah's **head.**

**2:17-19.** In addition to **forsaking the Lord** (v. 13) for false gods, Judah had also forsaken **the Lord** for false alliances.

The nation vainly went from **Egypt** to **Assyria** trying to forge treaties that would guarantee her safety (cf. v. 36; Ezek. 23; Hosea 7:11). **Shihor** is a branch of the Nile River (NIV marg.; cf. Josh. 13:3; 1 Chron. 13:5; Isa. 23:3). No alliance could protect Judah from her sin. Only after she received her judgment would she realize how **evil and bitter it** was to **forsake the LORD.**

**2:20.** Judah's spiritual apostasy was matched by her spiritual adultery. By describing Judah as a spiritual nymphomaniac Jeremiah pictured her insatiable lust for false gods. Jeremiah painted four verbal pictures (vv. 20-28) of Judah to describe her wayward state. The first picture was an animal that had broken its yoke. Judah **broke off** her **yoke** that had bound her to the Lord and followed after the gods of her heathen neighbors (cf. 5:5). She set up worship centers **on every high hill** (frequently called "high places") to serve these gods (cf. 3:2; Ezek. 6:1-7, 13). Spiritually Judah was acting like **a prostitute,** though Jeremiah's words could also refer to the sexual perversions that accompanied the worship of Baal (cf. Hosea 4:10-14).

**2:21.** Jeremiah's second picture of Judah is one of **a choice vine** from **reliable stock** that God **had planted** and nurtured. Judah is often pictured as God's vine in the Old Testament (cf. Isa. 5:1-7; Ezek. 15) and in the Gospels (cf. Matt. 21:33-46). God did all He could. for the nation, but in spite of His care she became **a corrupt, wild vine,** incapable of producing any good fruit.

**2:22.** The third picture of Judah was of someone with a **stain** that could not be washed off. Her sin was so ingrained that even **soda** (lye, a strong mineral alkali) and **soap** (a strong vegetable alkali) could not remove the stain.

**2:23-25.** Jeremiah's fourth picture of Judah is of a wild animal in **heat.** Like **a swift** female **camel** Judah vigorously pursued her false gods (on the word **Baals** in the pl., see comments on Jud. 2:11; also cf. Jer. 9:14); like **a wild donkey** she could not be restrained in her lust for those **foreign gods.**

**2:26-28.** Judah's pursuit of false gods caused her to be **disgraced.** Though she was ascribing her very existence to idols of **wood** and **stone,** yet when **trouble** came she had the audacity to ask God to

**come and save** her. Her false **gods** were impotent, yet **Judah** had as **many gods as** she had **towns** (cf. 11:13)—showing the multiplication of her idolatry.

**2:29-30.** Judah had become spiritually irresponsible. In spite of her sin she felt she could **bring charges against** God. This is an ironic reversal of verse 9 where God brought charges against Judah. Judah was charging God with harassment, but God's judgment was deserved because the people had **all rebelled against** Him. God had **punished** the **people,** but His chastisement was intended to bring **correction.** Yet the people refused to **respond,** and even murdered God's messengers, the **prophets.**

**2:31-33.** Judah's irresponsibility showed up most clearly in her forgetfulness of God's past dealings. The **people** thought they were **free,** independent of God. **A bride** would never forget **her wedding ornaments** that identified her as a married woman, but Judah had **forgotten** her God who had adorned her and set her apart from the other nations of the world. And she had done this **days without number.** Jeremiah sarcastically concluded that Judah had become so **skilled** in the art of **pursuing** illicit **love** that even the **worst of women** could learn new secrets of seduction by observing her perverse ways.

**2:34-35.** Another indication of her irresponsibility was her involvement in the shedding of innocent blood. Her clothes were covered with **the lifeblood of the innocent poor.** Had these people been caught **breaking in,** that is, caught in burglary and were killed, then the one responsible for the death was considered guiltless (Ex. 22:2). But those Judah killed were not killed for crimes they had committed; they were "innocent." Yet Judah continued to claim, **I am innocent. . . . I have not sinned.** She would therefore experience God's **judgment.**

**2:36-37.** A fourth indication of Judah's irresponsibility was her fickle foreign policy. She was constantly **changing** her **ways** in her dealings with other nations (cf. v. 18; Ezek. 23). Yet she would find that any new alliance with **Egypt** would be just as disappointing as her past alliance with **Assyria** (cf. 2 Kings 16:7-9; Isa. 7:13-25). **The LORD** had **rejected** these nations so Judah could **not be helped by them.**

**3:1-5.** Jeremiah ended his first message by exposing the spiritual harlotry of Judah. If a couple divorced and the **wife** married **another man,** she was prohibited by Law from ever being reunited with her first husband (Deut. 24:1-4). Yet Judah had separated from her Husband, Yahweh, and had **lived as a prostitute** (cf. Jer. 2:20) **with many lovers.** Such actions were defiling (on **defiled,** cf. 3:2, 9 and see comments on 23:11). There was the possibility that God would not take His people back. Obviously this would be a temporary rejection because Jeremiah later recorded God's promise of Israel's national restoration under a New Covenant (cf. 3:18; 31:31-33).

Israel's spiritual harlotry was obvious. It was hard to find a **place where** she had **not been ravished** in her spiritual union with false gods (cf. 3:9 and comments on 2:20). Her eager wait **by the roadside . . . for lovers** was the type of activity commonly employed by cult prostitutes (cf. Gen. 38:13-14, 20-21). Judah's desire for idolatrous lovers was as keen as a marauding **nomad in the desert** who waited for passing caravans to plunder.

God judged Judah by withholding **showers** and **spring rains** (cf. Deut. 28:23-24; Jer. 14). Yet Judah refused **to blush with shame.** Though she **called** out to God, **My Father, my Friend from my youth,** and asked Him to stop being **angry,** her words were hollow cries designed merely to manipulate God. Her **talk** was of friendship, but her actions never changed. She continued to do **all the evil** she could.

*b. Repentance in light of coming judgment (3:6–6:30)*

Jeremiah's second message is a distinct prophecy that was probably given at a different time from the first message. Yet the content of this prophecy is logically related to 2:1–3:5 and forms a fitting conclusion to the first message. In light of Judah's sin God summoned the nation to repent. The prophecy is dated generally "during the reign of King Josiah." Perhaps it can be placed sometime between the beginning of Jeremiah's ministry in 627 B.C. and the discovery of the Law in 621 B.C. (cf. 11:1-8).

(1) The summons to repentance (3:6–4:4). **3:6-11.** God revealed to Jeremiah the story of two sisters—**Israel** and **Judah** (cf. Ezek. 23). The Northern Kingdom of Israel **committed adultery** on all the **high** places of the land, a reference to her extensive idol worship. God in His patience waited for her to **return to** Him, but **Israel** refused and continued in her idolatry. Moreover, **her unfaithful sister Judah** was watching Israel sin. God's response was to give Israel a **certificate of divorce and** to send **her away** (cf. comments on Hosea 2:2). Jeremiah was referring to the destruction of the Northern Kingdom of Israel by Assyria in 722 B.C. (cf. 2 Kings 17:5-20).

Unfortunately **Judah** did not learn from Israel's fall. Instead she **also . . . committed adultery.** Indeed Judah added hypocrisy to the sin of Israel because Judah committed the same sins while making a **pretense** of returning to **the LORD.** Thus **Israel** in spite of her sin was still **more righteous than unfaithful Judah.**

**3:12-18.** Jeremiah paused in his condemnation of sin to offer a **message** of repentance and hope to the Northern Kingdom. If **Israel** would **return** to her God (cf. 7:3; 26:13), He would **frown on** her **no longer** and extend His mercy. But the people needed to **acknowledge** their **guilt** of rebellion and idolatry.

God promised to gather a remnant (one . . . **from every town and two from every clan) and bring** them up to Jerusalem (**Zion;** see comments on Lam. 1:4 and Zech. 8:3). This remnant would have **shepherds** (leaders; cf. Jer. 10:21; 22:22; 23:1-2, 4) **who** would provide the leadership intended by God, and their **numbers** would increase **greatly**—a sign of God's blessing (Deut. 30:5, 9).

**The ark of the covenant,** which was lost after Babylon destroyed Judah in 586 B.C., would **not be missed,** and another ark would not **be made.** In place of the ark will be **The Throne of the LORD,** a title by which the city of **Jerusalem** will be known. It is significant that Ezekiel (cf. Ezek. 43:7) also pictured the millennial temple as a place where God's throne will be. Evidently Christ will rule from the temple during the millennial period. God's rule from Jerusalem will extend over **all nations** who will go to Jerusalem to worship Him (cf. Zech. 14:16-19).

In addition to spiritual renewal Judah and Israel will also experience physical restoration. **The house of Judah** and **the house of Israel** will reunite as a nation (cf. Jer. 31:31-33; Ezek. 37:15-28). They will return from their captivity **to the land** God had promised to their **fore-fathers as an inheritance.** Israel and Judah divided as a nation in 931 B.C., and have never reunited as a nation under God. The fulfillment of this promise awaits the return of Christ.

**3:19-20.** God's desire was to bless His people. He wanted to **treat** them **like sons** and to restore their **inheritance, but** the nation was **like a woman** who was **unfaithful to her husband.** The road-block to restoration was **Israel,** not God.

**3:21-25.** It is possible that in these verses Jeremiah was painting an idealistic picture for **the people of Israel.** The people mourn for their condition (v. 21), God offers repentance (v. 22a), and the people feel abject and heartfelt remorse for their sin (vv. 22b-25). But the Book of Jeremiah leads one to believe that the **people** did not follow this example. It still awaits the future repentance of the nation when Christ returns as King (Zech. 12:10–13:1).

The section opens with the people **weeping and pleading.** Their cry was prompted because of their transgressions **(they** had **perverted their ways)** and because they had **forgotten . . . their God.** In Jeremiah's ideal picture of repentance the nation finally realized the depth of the pit into which she had fallen. God responded to the nation's cry by offering to help her if she would **return.**

Israel's response is a model of true repentance. She consciously determined to **come to . . . God** because of who He is. Admitting that her **idolatrous commo-tion** which had been rampant in the land was **a deception,** the nation acknowl-edged that only in **God is there salvation for Israel.** The **shame** and **disgrace** of her past actions forced her to admit that she had **sinned against the LORD.**

**4:1-2.** God promised to respond pos-itively if **Israel** and Judah would indeed **return to** Him. However, the repentance had to be genuine. The **detestable idols** had to be removed from God's **sight,** and the people could **no longer go astray** af-ter their false gods. Yet if **the nations** of Israel and Judah did repent, they would **be blessed by** God.

**4:3-4.** Jeremiah then used two meta-phors to show the need for repentance.

The first metaphor pertained to farming. Just as a farmer does not sow his seed on unplowed ground, so God does **not sow** His seed of blessing in unrepentant hearts. **The men of Judah and . . . Jeru-salem** needed to **break up** the **unplowed ground** of their hearts through repen-tance. The second metaphor came from the Jewish practice of circumcision. Cir-cumcision was a sign of being under God's covenant with Israel (cf. Gen. 17:9-14). The men, though circumcised physi-cally, needed to **circumcise** their **hearts** so that their inward condition matched their outward profession (cf. Deut. 10:16; 30:6; Jer. 9:25-26; Rom. 2:28-29).

Unless Judah did exercise true re-pentance—not just outward profession— God's **wrath** would be released and would **burn like fire** against the **people.** And once God's wrath was released **no one** could **quench it.**

(2) The warning of coming judg-ment (4:5-31). **4:5-9.** Lest the people won-der what form God's wrath might take, Jeremiah described the coming judgment as the unleashing of Judah's enemies to the north. The command would go out to **sound the trumpet,** which would **signal** the approach of the enemies' armies (cf. Hosea 5:8; Joel 2:1; Amos 3:6). In re-sponse, those living in the countryside would **flee for safety** to Jerusalem (**Zion**) to escape the **disaster from the north** that was bringing **destruction.**

The approaching army of Babylon in its ferocity was like **a lion** that had **come out of his lair** to attack the **land** of Judah. The invasion would leave the **towns** of Judah **in ruins without inhabitant.** Real-ization of the coming destruction would cause the people to **lament** and to wear **sackcloth,** rough, coarse material, sym-bolizing mourning (cf. Jer. 6:26; 48:37; 49:3; Gen. 37:34; 1 Kings 21:27; Neh. 9:1; Pss. 30:11; 35:13; 69:11; Lam. 2:10; Dan. 9:3) because God's **fierce anger** had **not** been **turned away** (cf. Jer. 4:4).

The day of God's judgment would hold special dread for Judah's leaders. **The king and the officials** along with **the priests** and **the prophets** would be para-lyzed by fear as they watched the annihi-lation of their country. Yet the destruc-tion came in part because of their failure to provide the leadership Judah needed (cf. 2:8).

**4:10.** This verse, Jeremiah's response

to God, is one of the most difficult verses in the book to interpret. The prophet claimed that God had **deceived** the **people** by promising they would **have peace when** in fact God had brought His **sword** of judgment to their **throats.** Had God misled His people by lying to them about their fate? This interpretation must be rejected because it is out of character with the nature of God (cf. Num. 23:19). In fact God's true prophets had been predicting judgment, not peace (cf. Jer. 1:14-16; Micah 3:9-12; Hab. 1:5-11; Zeph. 1:4-13). Only the false prophets had been proclaiming peace (cf. Jer. 6:14; 14:13-14; 23:16-17). Therefore it is better to see Jeremiah complaining that God had allowed these false prophets to proclaim their message.

**4:11-12.** Jeremiah returned to God's announcement of the coming invasion of Judah. God compared the armies to **a scorching wind** that blows in from **the desert.** Wind affected the lives of everyone in Palestine. The refreshing breezes from the Mediterranean Sea helped the farmers in winnowing grain, and also brought the life-sustaining dew which nourished the land during the summer. However, the hot, dry, east **wind,** the sirocco, that blows in from the desert causes serious difficulties. It is **not** used **to winnow** because it is **too strong.** Instead, the sirocco could wither vegetation (Gen. 41:6) and cause extreme discomfort for those who had to endure it (Jonah 4:8). Also Ezekiel compared Babylon's invasion to the coming of the east wind (Ezek. 17:10; 19:12).

**4:13-14.** Using a different illustration, God compared the advance of Babylon's army to an approaching storm. The soldiers were sweeping into Judah **like the clouds,** and their **chariots** swirled along **like a whirlwind.** In light of Judah's certain destruction God again graciously called the people to repentance. If they were to **wash the evil from** their **heart** they would **be saved** (delivered) from their impending doom.

**4:15-18.** The approach of Babylon's soldiers would be signaled by messengers **from Dan** in the extreme north of Israel and **from the hills of Ephraim** 30-40 miles north of **Jerusalem.** The word brought by these heralds was that **a besieging army** was **coming . . . against the cities of Judah.**

God sent this force to punish Judah **because** the nation had **rebelled against** Him. Judah herself was responsible for the calamity. It was her **own conduct and actions** that **brought this . . . punishment** from God.

**4:19-22.** Jeremiah responded to the news of the coming invasion by crying out in **anguish.** His **heart** pounded and he could not **keep silent** as he thought of the approaching **battle** and the **disaster** it would bring Judah. Jeremiah concluded by admitting that the **people** of Judah were **fools** (*'ĕwîl,* a person lacking sense and morally corrupt). They were like **children** and had **no understanding** of the way of righteousness which they should have been following. In an ironic reversal of Proverbs 1:2-3 the people were **skilled** (*ḥăḵāmîm,* "wise") **in doing evil,** but ignorant in knowing **how to do good.**

**4:23-28.** Jeremiah pictured God's coming judgment as a cosmic catastrophe—an undoing of Creation. Using imagery from the Creation account (Gen. 1) Jeremiah indicated that no aspect of life would remain untouched. God would make Judah **formless and empty** (*tōhû wāḇōhû*), a phrase used to describe the chaos that preceded God's works in Creation (cf. Gen. 1:2). The **light** that had pierced into the darkness during Creation (cf. Gen. 1:3-5) **was** now **gone. The mountains** and **hills,** which had been separated from the waters (cf. Gen. 1:9-10), were now **quaking** and **swaying** at the judgment of God. The **people** along with **every bird. . . . and the fruitful land** were again removed. The land became as barren as it had been before the creation of life (Gen. 1:11-13, 20-26).

God's imagery was so awesome that some might have thought He would totally destroy the land of Israel. To guard against this misunderstanding, God qualified His statement (Jer. 4:27). Though **the whole land** would **be ruined** as He judged the people, He still promised that He would **not destroy it completely** (cf. 5:18). Nevertheless **the earth** would **mourn;** judgment would come (4:28).

**4:29-31.** As the armies approached Judah people in **every town** fled to avoid being killed. The people hid in **the thickets** and **among the rocks,** hoping not to be apprehended by the soldiers. By contrast the Jerusalemites tried to **dress** themselves **in scarlet** with **jewels of gold** and **eyes** that were shaded **with paint** (to make them appear larger). They tried to dress like a harlot to allure the Babylonians away from their attack (cf. Ezek. 16:26-29; 23:40-41). But the ruse would not work because Jerusalem's former **lovers** now sought her **life**.

As the Babylonians pressed their attack, Jeremiah pictured **the Daughter of Zion** (Jerusalem) crying out in agony like **a woman in labor** (cf. Isa. 13:8; 21:3; 26:17; Jer. 6:24; 13:21; 22:23; 30:6; 48:41; 49:22, 24; 50:43; Micah 4:9-10). She stretched out **her hands** for assistance which never materialized as her **life** ebbed out before her **murderers**.

(3) The reasons for coming judgment (chap. 5). **5:1-3.** Judah was to be judged because of her corruption. God sent Jeremiah on a divine scavenger hunt in **Jerusalem**. He had to **find** only **one person** who dealt **honestly** with his fellow Israelites or who was actively seeking **the truth**. If he could find just **one,** God would **forgive this city**. Unfortunately Jeremiah's search was less fruitful than the one made at Sodom (cf. Gen. 18:22-23). The people **refused correction** and their **faces** were **harder than stone,** indicating their stubborn refusal **to repent**.

**5:4-6.** Jeremiah assumed that those he encountered were **only the poor**—the uneducated masses who were uninstructed in the **requirements of** the righteous **God**. Surely, he thought, if he went **to the leaders . . . they** would **know the way of the LORD**. But Jeremiah's visit brought only disappointment (cf. 2:8). The leaders had joined the people and **had broken off the yoke** of service to God (cf. 2:20).

So **God** would judge leaders and followers alike for their sin. Jeremiah referred to three wild animals to picture the coming punishment. By breaking away from her Master's yoke, Judah had opened herself up to attack from marauding beasts. The **lion**, the **wolf**, and the **leopard** symbolized the ravages of Babylon's **attack** on Judah.

**5:7-9.** God asked Judah two rhetorical questions. First, He asked **why** He **should . . . forgive** Judah (v. 7). Second, He asked why He **should . . . not punish** Judah for her sin (v. 9). Between the

two questions God described Judah's character in a way that made the answers obvious. He could not forgive Judah because she had **forsaken** Him and **sworn by** false **gods**. Though God had provided for them, the people, acting like **lusty stallions,** went after each others' wives. God would punish Judah for her idolatry and adultery.

**5:10-19.** **Judah,** God's choice vine, had become a wild vine (2:21), so God called His invaders to **go through** Judah's **vineyards** and prune off the dead **branches**. Though the nation would **not** be destroyed **completely,** those individuals who did **not belong to the LORD** would be removed in judgment.

The people refused to believe that God would ever destroy Jerusalem. Instead they announced that **He** would **do nothing. The prophets**—Jeremiah, Ezekiel, and others who were predicting doom—were, the people said, just full of **wind**. God therefore told Jeremiah that His **words** would be **fire** that would consume the **people**. God would bring **a distant nation** (Babylon) **against** Judah—a nation **whose language** the Judeans did **not know**. These **warriors** would **devour** the crops, **herds,** and children of the Judeans; and they would **destroy the** mighty **fortified cities** which Judah trusted for protection.

God again emphasized that He would **not destroy** Judah **completely** (cf. 4:27). He would preserve a remnant. When these captives asked **why** they had been defeated, **God** told Jeremiah to say that they had **forsaken** God to serve **foreign gods** in their **own land**. Therefore God would have them **serve foreigners** (the Babylonians) **in a** foreign **land**. His punishment fit their sin.

**5:20-31.** Judah had become willfully ignorant of God. Though she had **eyes** and **ears,** she did **not see** or **hear** (i.e., comprehend) the true character of God (cf. Ezek. 12:2). She refused to **fear,** or reverence, God (cf. Prov. 1:7). Though even **the sea** remains within its **everlasting barrier** (cf. Job 38:10; Ps. 104:9), the **people** of Judah refused to stay within God's covenant limits. Instead they **turned aside** and went **away**. They refused to see God's gracious hand at work, providing them the **fall and spring rains** which assured the **. . . harvest**.

Jeremiah then specified some of the

people's **sins. Wicked** people, who were **rich and powerful,** were waiting to **snare** the poor. They refused to help the downtrodden (**the fatherless** and **the poor**). **The prophets,** who were to proclaim God's word of truth, were prophesying **lies;** and **the priests,** who were to instruct the people in the ways of God, were instead ruling **by their own authority** (cf. 2:8). Yet these aberrations of righteousness were condoned by the **people** who loved **it** that **way.** All the elements of society preferred wickedness to righteousness.

(4) The certainty of coming judgment (chap. 6). **6:1-3.** Jeremiah again used the symbol of an alarm being sounded to announce an impending invasion (cf. 4:5-6), to signal Babylon's coming attack. The **people of Benjamin** (cf. 1:1), just north of Jerusalem, were to **flee for safety.** But instead of stopping at the capital city, they were to **flee from Jerusalem** and continue heading south. The **trumpet** would be sounded at **Tekoa,** about 11 miles southeast of Jerusalem (cf. Amos 1:1). And the **signal** fires at **Beth Hakkerem,** a vantage point midway between Jerusalem and Bethlehem, would be lit to warn the inhabitants of the land to flee. God threatened to **destroy** Jerusalem so completely that **shepherds** would **pitch their tents** and graze their herds on its site. This extensive destruction is confirmed by Nehemiah (cf. Neh. 1:3; 2:3, 11-17).

**6:4-6a.** As the enemy massed **against Jerusalem** they were eager to attack. They hoped to **attack at noon**; but before the preparations were completed **the shadows of evening** had begun to stretch through the valleys around the city. Most armies would wait till the next day to begin, but the Babylonians decided to begin their **attack** that **night.** God directed the soldiers of Babylon as they built **siege ramps** to breach the city's defenses (cf. Ezek. 4:1-2).

**6:6b-9.** Jerusalem had to be **punished** because of her **oppression.** Her **wickedness** was so profuse it poured forth like **water** from **a well.** Unless she would **take warning** and repent, she would become **desolate.** God would have Babylon **glean** Jerusalem **as thoroughly as** one gleans **a vine** when **gathering grapes.**

**6:10-15.** Jeremiah responded in amazement to Judah's unbelief. But no one would **listen to** him as he tried to warn them of the coming calamity. This is the first of more than three dozen times in Jeremiah where the people did not listen to (i.e., they disobeyed) God's **Word.** Indeed **their ears** were **closed** (lit., "uncircumcised"), and they found God's Word to be offensive. But Jeremiah had to speak God's word of judgment; he could not **hold it in** (cf. 20:9).

God's wrath was to be poured out **on** all elements of society—from the **children** to **the old** (and everyone in between). The people would lose **their houses** along with **their fields and their wives** to the coming invaders. Such action would occur because all sections of society were corrupt. Both the **prophets** and the **priests** practiced **deceit,** and the nation was injured. **The wound** refers to the people's spiritual malady and its spiritual and physical effects (cf. 8:11, 22; 10:19; 14:17; 15:18; 30:12, 15; cf. "wounds" in 19:8; 30:17; 49:17; 50:13). The prophets and priests were proclaiming **peace** (cf. 8:11; 23:17) though God had not given them that message. These charlatans had **no shame** about lying to the people. In fact they were so hardened in their ways that **they** did **not even know how to blush** when their sin was exposed. God promised that these false leaders would **fall** when the city was destroyed (cf. 8:12).

**6:16-21.** Judah was in danger of destruction because she had strayed from **the ancient paths** of God's righteousness. Yet though God urged her to **walk in** the **good way** where she would **find rest,** Judah refused. Prophets were like **watchmen** (men assigned to watch for and warn a city of impending danger), but the nation refused to **listen.**

Judah **rejected** God's **Law,** thinking she could substitute rituals for obedience. God responded by showing His disdain for **incense** that had been imported **from Sheba** in southwest Arabia (cf. 1 Kings 10:1-13; Ezek. 27:22) and for **sweet calamus** (possibly sweet cane, Ex. 30:23; also cf. Song 4:14; Isa. 43:24) **from a distant land.** The elaborate **burnt offerings** and **sacrifices,** divorced from a genuine love for God, did **not please** Him. Instead of accepting this hypocritical worship, God vowed to **put obstacles** in the way of the **people** so they would stumble. The nature of the obstacles is not given, but it is likely that God was again referring to the Babylonians (cf. Jer. 6:22).

**6:22-26.** Jeremiah concluded his second message by again pointing to the foe **from . . . the North** (cf. 1:13-15; 4:5-6; 6:1). The coming army was **cruel** and would **show no mercy** to those it captured, an apt description of the Babylonians (cf. Hab. 1:6-11). As they came **in battle formation** their goal was **to attack** Jerusalem.

The report of Babylon's advance would bring **anguish** to those in Judah, like a woman's labor pains (cf. comments on Jer. 4:31). The people would be afraid of leaving their cities because of **a sword** which would strike them down. Instead they would **put on sackcloth,** a dark, rough cloth worn at times of mourning (Gen. 37:34; 2 Sam. 3:31; 1 Kings 21:27; Es. 4:1-4) and penitence (Neh. 9:1; Dan. 9:3; Matt. 11:21). The sadness experienced by Jerusalem would be similar to that experienced by one who had lost **an only son.**

**6:27-30.** God appointed Jeremiah as **a tester of metals,** or an assayer, and the **people** of Judah were **the ore.** As Jeremiah observed the nation, he concluded **they** were **all hardened rebels.** God tried to refine them through judgment, **but the refining** efforts were useless. The **wicked** had **not** been **purged out** in the refining process so the nation was like **rejected silver.** God's attempts to reform the nation had failed, so judgment was inevitable.

### c. False religion and its punishment (chaps. 7–10)

These chapters, often known as Jeremiah's temple address, focus on God's punishment of the people because of their false religion. The people believed that God's punishment would never extend to Jerusalem or to them (cf. 5:12-13) because of the presence of God's temple and because of their outward display of religion (cf. 6:20). Jeremiah's temple address destroyed this false hope and exposed the festering sore of idolatry that was producing spiritual gangrene in the people. The events described in chapter 26 probably indicate the people's response to this message.

(1) The temple sermon and Judah's false worship (7:1–8:3). **7:1-8.** God summoned Jeremiah to **stand at the** entrance to the temple and announce His **message** to those coming there **to worship.** The message was similar to that just recorded: the people had to **reform** their **ways** (cf. 3:12; 26:13) if they wanted to continue living there.

Jeremiah answered the objection voiced by the people to his message. They believed judgment would not come because in Jerusalem was located **the temple of the Lord** (repeated three times to emphasize their belief in its protecting power). The people of Judah viewed **the temple** as a talisman or good luck charm that could ward off any attack.

But **God** did not value buildings over obedience. God's protection would remain only if the people would **change** their **ways** (7:5; cf. v. 3). Jeremiah listed three examples to illustrate the change God wanted. The first two related to actions toward fellow Israelites, and the third related to actions toward God. (1) The people were **not** to **oppress** the helpless in society—people who could not easily protect themselves if wronged (cf. Deut. 14:29; 16:11; 24:19; Ps. 94:6). (2) They were **not** to **shed innocent blood** (cf. Deut. 19:10-13; 21:1-9). (3) And they were **not** to **follow other gods.** If these evidences of faithfulness to God's covenant were observed, God would allow the nation to **live . . . in the land.** But for the people to trust in **the temple** building rather than in obedience to the covenant for their protection was to put their faith **in deceptive words that** were **worthless.**

**7:9-15.** Judah felt so secure because of the presence of God's temple that she believed it was **safe to do all** kinds of **detestable things.** Her vileness had actually turned the temple into **a den of robbers** (cf. Matt. 21:12-13). What she failed to realize was that God had **been watching** and was aware of her deeds.

Jeremiah pointed to Israel's past to expose the fallacy of believing that the mere presence of God's temple would avert disaster. He asked the crowd to remember **the place in Shiloh** where the tabernacle of God had first dwelt (Josh. 18:1; Jud. 18:31; 1 Sam. 1:3; 4:3-4). They were to observe what God **did to it because** of Israel's **wickedness.** The Bible is silent on the fate of Shiloh; but after the

Philistines captured the ark of the covenant (1 Sam. 4:10-11) the priests evidently fled to Nob (1 Sam. 22:11) and Shiloh was abandoned as Israel's central worship center (cf. Ps. 78:56-61). Archeological studies also indicate that the village of Shiloh was destroyed about 1050 B.C., probably by the Philistines.

The point of Jeremiah's message was that **what** God **did to Shiloh** He would also **do to the . . . temple.** If Judah did not change her ways God would **thrust** her **from** His **presence just as** He had done with the Northern Kingdom (**Ephraim**) in 722 B.C. (2 Kings 17:5-20, esp. v. 20). The temple bore God's **name** (Jer. 7:10, 12, 14; cf. v. 30) in the sense that it was a symbol of God's presence (His "name" refers to His revealed attributes).

**7:16-20.** God prohibited Jeremiah from interceding for Judah because He would **not listen** (cf. 11:14; 14:11-12). The nation's sin had progressed to the point where Jeremiah's pleas were futile. To illustrate how degraded **Judah** had become God highlighted one aspect of her idolatrous worship. Throughout Judah, families were uniting to prepare **cakes of bread** (flat cakes possibly formed into the image of the goddess; cf. 44:19) **for the Queen of Heaven** (probably Ishtar, the Babylonian goddess of love and fertility). The families were also offering **drink offerings** (usually wine) **to other gods.** Yet such idolatrous rituals were only **harming** those who participated in them; their false worship did not damage God. For the people would bear the consequences of their actions when God's **anger** and **wrath** would be **poured out** on all Judah.

**7:21-29.** The people of Judah offered all the correct **sacrifices,** but they failed to realize that God had given another **command** at Sinai. He had called on Israel to **obey** Him and to **walk in all the ways** He established for them. Unfortunately Israel refused to **listen or pay attention** to this command of God. Though God continually **sent** His **prophets** to warn the people, they refused to **pay attention** (cf. 25:4-7).

Jeremiah was not to expect the response of people in his day to be any different from people's response in the past. Indeed God told Jeremiah that the nation would **not listen to** him. So Jeremiah was to **cut off** his **hair,** a sign of deep mourning (cf. Job 1:20; Isa. 15:2-3; Jer. 48:37; Ezek. 7:18), and **take up a lament** ($q\hat{\imath}n\hat{a}h$, "funeral dirge") for the nation. The time of mourning could commence because the destruction of Judah was assured. God had already **abandoned** that **generation to His wrath.**

**7:30-34.** God continued to elaborate on the sin **of Judah** which brought her judgment. **The people** had **set up . . . idols** in the temple itself so that even the **house** of God was **defiled** (cf. Ezek. 8:3-18). Outside the city **they** had **built the high places of Topheth** (cf. Jer. 19:6, 11-14) which were located **in the Valley of Ben Hinnom** (cf. 19:2, 6; 32:35; also called simply the Valley of Hinnom). Here they practiced child sacrifice, burning **their sons and daughters in the fire** (cf. 2 Kings 21:6; 2 Chron. 33:6; Jer. 19:5). The origin of the word "Topheth" ($t\bar{o}pe\underline{t}$) is uncertain, but possibly it came from a word for "cookstove" or "oven." The change in vowels was deliberate; the vowels from the word $b\bar{o}\check{s}e\underline{t}$ ("shame") were transferred to the other word to emphasize the shameful character of the practices there. This "high place of shame" was located in the Valley of Hinnom, immediately south and west of the city. In this valley the refuse from the city was burned. In Greek the Valley of Hinnom (Heb., $g\hat{e}$-$hinn\bar{o}m$) became known as Gehenna ($geenna$) to picture the fiery corruption of hell (cf. Matt. 5:22, 29-30; 2 Peter 2:4). God vowed that the name of this place would be changed to **the Valley of Slaughter** because of the great number of **dead** bodies that would be burned after the destruction of Jerusalem. The prediction about **birds** and **beasts** eating the **carcasses** affirms the Mosaic Covenant because of the people's disobedience (Deut. 28:26). **Joy** will be gone (cf. Jer. 16:9; 25:10) when the city would **become desolate.**

**8:1-3.** Even the dead would not escape God's judgment. **The bones** of all the **officials** who had worshiped false gods but who had died before the fall of Jerusalem would **be removed from their graves** and **exposed** to the elements they had once **worshiped.** They would remain as **refuse . . . on the ground** (cf. 25:33). Those who survived the fall of Jerusalem would be banished, and their lives would be so terrible that they would **prefer death to life.**

(2) God's retribution on the people (8:4–10:25). **8:4-7.** God asked a series of questions to expose Judah's stubborn refusal to turn back to Him. When people **fall down** they try to **get up** again. If someone **turns away** from the right path he tries to **return** as quickly as possible. But though most **people** learn from their mistakes, Judah refused **to return.** Failing to acknowledge any wrongdoing, she pursued her **own** ways with determination **like a horse charging into battle. Even** migratory birds **observe the time of their migration, but** Judah did **not** realize that it was time to return to her God. She had even less wisdom than a bird!

**8:8-13.** Judah felt superior in her wisdom to other nations because she had **the Law of the Lord.** Unfortunately that Law was being **handled . . . falsely** by **the scribes.** Their rejection of God's Law would bring judgment (cf. Deut. 28:30-45). This attitude encompassed all the people **from the least to the greatest.** The leaders were treating the nation's sin lightly—they would **dress** (or bandage) **the wound** (cf. Jer. 8:22 and comments on 6:14), assuming the injury was **not serious** when in fact it was terminal. Jeremiah 8:10b-12 repeats the message the prophet had given in 6:12-15 (cf. comments there). The truth was repeated for emphasis. God would punish the nation by taking **from them** the blessings of the **harvest** that He had earlier **given them.**

**8:14-17.** Jeremiah pictured the panic that would ensue when God's judgment began. The people would **flee to the fortified cities** knowing that **God** had **doomed** them **to perish** there. Their hopes **for peace** were dashed and the **terror** of the Babylonians filled the land. As the sound **of the enemy's horses** echoed southward **from Dan** in the north, the **land** trembled as it waited in dread for the army to **come to devour.** God compared the Babylonians to **venomous snakes** that would **bite** the Judeans.

**8:18–9:2.** Jeremiah responded to Judah's plight by making a heartfelt cry to God. He asked God to **listen to the cry of** the **people** who had been deported to **a land far away.** Those captured by the Babylonians wondered how their city could have fallen since God's temple was there. In anguish they questioned if Judah's **King,** Yahweh, was **no longer there.** God responded by indicating that

Jerusalem's destruction was brought about by their sin, not by His absence. God brought the army of Babylon because Judah had **provoked** Him **to anger with their . . . idols.**

God gave Judah every opportunity to repent, but she continued to rebel. Jeremiah 8:20 recorded the mournful cry of those who learned the consequences of sin too late. **The harvest,** representing God's opportunities to repent, was **past.** By not taking advantage of God's provision for deliverance from judgment when it had been available, the people were now without hope (**we are not saved**).

Jeremiah's reaction to Judah's fate mixed sadness and despair. He so identified with his people that he was **crushed** by the fact of their destruction. In vain he sought for **balm** from **Gilead** to heal **the wound** of his **people** (cf. v. 11 and comments on 6:14). "Balm" was the resin of the storax tree that was used medicinally. Gilead, east of the Jordan River, was famous for its healing balm (cf. Gen. 37:25; Jer. 46:11; 51:8; Ezek. 27:17). The grief caused Jeremiah to wish his **eyes** would become **a fountain of tears** so he could **weep** continually (**day and night**) for those who had been **slain.** This heartfelt empathy with his people's suffering earned Jeremiah the nickname, "the weeping prophet" (cf. Jer. 13:17; 14:17). Yet his empathy for their suffering was balanced by his revulsion at their sin. An isolated **lodging place** in **the desert** was preferable to living with the **unfaithful people** of Judah.

**9:3-6.** A person used his **tongue** as an archer would use **a bow**—it became a weapon **to shoot lies.** Honesty was not being practiced by those living in Judah. One had to watch his **friends,** and no one could **trust** his **brothers.** As the very fabric of society unraveled, **no one** would speak **the truth.** Jeremiah (**you** is sing.) lived in a nation that was full **of deception** and refused **to acknowledge** God.

**9:7-9.** God responded to Judah's deception by seeking to **refine and test** her **because of** her **sin** (cf. 6:28-30; Ezek. 22:18-22). God would place Judah in the crucible of judgment and deal with her **deceit.** God rhetorically asked Jeremiah if He should **not** indeed **avenge** Himself **on** the **nation** because of her sin.

**9:10-16.** Jeremiah began to **weep and wail** over the land of **Judah** because the

Babylonian invasion and deportation made it **desolate and untraveled.** God responded by indicating He would **make Jerusalem a heap of ruins** that would be inhabited only by wild **jackals** (cf. 10:22; 49:33; 51:37). He asked the **wise** men of Judah to explain **why** the **land** was **ruined and laid waste.** Before anyone could answer, God stated the obvious. The destruction came **because** the people had turned from God's **Law** and had **followed the Baals** (cf. 2:23 and see comments on Jud. 2:11). **This** was why God would **scatter them among** the **nations** and why many in Judah would be killed by **the sword** (cf. Ezek. 5:2, 12).

**9:17-24.** Jeremiah listed three separate pronouncements from **the LORD** (vv. 17-21, 22, 23-24) each beginning with a similar phrase. In the first section (vv. 17-21) God called for **the wailing women,** professional mourners, to lament for Jerusalem. These mourners were then to **teach** their **daughters . . . another . . . lament.** This funeral dirge was over the **death** of **the children** and **the young men** who were killed when the Babylonians broke into the city.

In the second section (v. 22) God pictured the severity of the massacre by Babylon. **The dead bodies** would resemble the **cut grain** left **behind the reaper** in a field. But there would be **no one** left **to gather** this gruesome "harvest."

The third pronouncement (vv. 23-24) summarized the response God expected from the people. The people were not to **boast** in their human **wisdom** or **strength** or **riches** for these would not last. Instead a person should **boast** only to the extent **that he understands and knows** God. Again the word "know" (*yāḏa'*) pictured an intimate knowledge of God (see comments on 1:5). God wanted the people to be intimately acquainted with His **kindness, justice, and righteousness.** "Kindness" (*ḥeseḏ*) refers to God's loyal love (cf. 31:3; 33:11; Lam. 3:22). God would stand by His commitment to His people. "Justice" (*mišpoṭ*) is a broad term that pointed to governing justly. God would vindicate the innocent and punish the guilty. "Righteousness" (*ṣeḏāqâh*) conveys the idea of conforming to a standard or norm. God's standards of conduct were supposed to be Israel's norm.

**9:25-26.** If personal achievement or ability would not please God (v. 23), nei-

ther would outward conformity to religious rituals. God would **punish** those **circumcised only in the flesh** whether they were near or far. Judah's faith in her covenant sign was a misplaced faith because people in some other nations also practiced this ritual—and they were not under God's covenant. Judah's actions exposed the fact that the nation was **really uncircumcised . . . in heart** (cf. 4:4).

**10:1-5.** The first 16 verses of chapter 10 are parenthetical. Before continuing his discussion of the coming Exile, Jeremiah focused on the nature of the God who would bring this judgment. God addressed the entire **house of Israel,** which included the Northern Kingdom already in exile, and explained the foolishness of idols. Israel was **not** supposed to **learn the ways of** idolatry practiced by **the nations** around her, nor was she to **be terrified by signs in the sky.** These "signs" were most likely unusual occurrences such as eclipses or comets which were thought to be signs of coming events given by the gods.

Such idolatrous practices were **worthless** (*ḥeḇel*, "breath"; cf. comments on *ḥeḇel* in Ecc. 1:2) because the "gods" being honored were created by their worshipers (cf. Isa. 40:18-20). A person would chop down **a tree,** give the wood to **a craftsman** who fashioned it to the desired shape. This "god" was then covered **with silver and gold** and fastened to a base so that it would **not totter.** Once the god was made by man it had to **be carried** to its destination. It was as lifeless as **a scarecrow in a melon patch.** Certainly such a "god" could not **speak** to impart knowledge to its followers. So God exhorted His people **not** to **fear** those false idols. The idols had **no** power to **harm** those who disregarded them or power to **do any good** for those who followed them.

**10:6-16.** Jeremiah responded to God's description of idols by affirming that the LORD truly is unique. There is **no one . . . like** Him (vv. 6a, 7b; cf. Isa. 40:18, 25). The **worthless wooden idols** (cf. Jer. 10:15 and comments on 2:5), were decorated with **silver . . . from Tarshish and gold from Uphaz.** Tarshish was a city probably in southern Spain, or was a technical term for a "mineral-bearing land." Uphaz is either a location (now unknown), or a textual variant for

Ophir, a land in Arabia known for its gold (cf. 1 Kings 9:28; 10:11; 22:48; Job 22:24; 28:16; Ps. 45:9; Isa. 13:12), or a technical term for "refined gold." Jeremiah described the LORD as the true (genuine) God in contrast with the false idols. He is alive but they were lifeless; and He is eternal whereas they came into existence through the work of craftsmen and were subject to decay.

Jeremiah 10:11 is the only verse in this book written in Aramaic instead of Hebrew. Aramaic was the trade language of the day. Probably this verse is in Aramaic because it was directed to the pagan idolaters surrounding Israel. God spoke in a language they would be sure to understand. His message to these idolaters was that their false gods, who had no part in creating the universe, would themselves ultimately perish from God's universe.

In contrast with the false idols the Lord was responsible for Creation (vv. 12-13). He made the earth and stretched out the heavens. (Vv. 12-16 are virtually the same as 51:15-19.) Only He has the power and wisdom to have accomplished such a feat. This power of the Lord was mirrored in His continuing revelation in nature. By focusing on the awesomeness of a thunderstorm with clouds . . . lightning . . . rain, and wind, Jeremiah illustrated the continuing power of God (on storehouses; cf. comments on Job 38:22; also cf. Pss. 33:7; 135:7; Jer. 51:16).

When God's grandeur would finally be manifested, those who had made worthless idols (cf. 10:8 and comments on 2:5) would be shamed at the objects of mockery they had once worshiped. In contrast God would be known as the Portion of Jacob (cf. 51:19). A "portion" (ḥēleq, "share") usually referred to something allotted to an individual (cf. Gen. 14:24; Lev. 6:17; 1 Sam. 1:5). God, in a real sense, belonged to Israel. But at the same time Israel belonged to God. She was His inheritance (see comments on Deut. 4:20). God is also the Maker of all things (cf. Job 4:17; 32:22; 35:10; Pss. 115:15; 121:2; Ecc. 11:5) in contrast with the lifeless idols who can make nothing! Jeremiah ended this parenthetical portion (Jer. 10:1-16) by identifying this true God who was inseparably bound to His people. His name is the LORD Almighty.

10:17-22. After discussing the superiority of God to idols (vv. 1-16), Jeremiah continued his temple address by describing the coming destruction and Exile. The people of Jerusalem were to gather up their meager belongings to leave the land (cf. Ezek. 12:3-16). God vowed to hurl out those living in the land so they would be captured and carried into captivity.

Jerusalem responded in anguish to the Captivity. The wound she had suffered was incurable (see comments on Jer. 6:14). The city was also pictured as a tent that had collapsed. Her sons were deported, and the shepherds (rō'îm, "leaders"; cf. 2:8) who were to guide the flock had allowed the flock to be scattered (cf. 23:1-2; Ezek. 34:1-10). The attack from . . . the north would decimate Judah so that her towns would be desolate (cf. Jer. 9:11).

10:23-25. Jeremiah concluded his temple address with a prayer to the LORD. The prophet admitted that a person's life cannot be considered his own as though he is free to direct his own steps. God is in control, and only those who let God direct their ways will be truly blessed (cf. Prov. 3:5-6; 16:9; 20:24). Because Judah's judgment was inevitable, Jeremiah pleaded that it might come only with God's justice and not with His anger. That is, Jeremiah was asking for God's patience and leniency in dispersing judgment lest the nation be reduced to nothing. By using the word me Jeremiah was identifying with and representing Judah. Then Jeremiah asked that God's judgment of Judah be accompanied by His judgment on the nations. They refused to call on God's name, and they had devoured and destroyed God's covenant people.

### d. The broken covenant (chaps. 11–12)

Jeremiah's fourth message focused on Judah's broken covenant with her God. Though the message itself is undated, several markers help date the passage to 621 B.C., six years after Jeremiah began his ministry. That year the temple was being repaired as part of King Josiah's reforms, and a copy of the Law was discovered in the renovation (cf. 2 Chron. 34:14-33). Several of Jeremiah's references seem to allude to this discovery of God's Law and the realization of the broken covenant (cf. Jer. 11:3-5). Jeremiah called on the people to heed the words of the covenant that Josiah read to them (11:6; 2 Chron. 34:19-32).

(1) The violation of the covenant (11:1-17). **11:1-5.** God told **Jeremiah to listen to** the stipulations of His **covenant** and to relate those terms **to the people of Judah and . . . Jerusalem.** The specific portion of the covenant God mentioned were **the terms** that regarded obedience and disobedience to His Law (cf. Deut. 28). On Canaan as **a land flowing with milk and honey** see comments on Exodus 3:8.

**11:6-8.** As Jeremiah called out to the people to **follow** the **words** of the **covenant,** he also reminded them of the nation's past failure. Though God had repeatedly **warned** the nation to **obey** Him, they refused to **pay attention.** Because of this God **brought on them all the curses of the covenant.** Israel's history was one of rebellion and correction.

**11:9-13.** Though King Josiah forced an outer conformity to **the covenant,** his reform did not penetrate the hearts of the people in a lasting way. After Josiah died the people returned to their idolatrous ways. **Among the people** was a **conspiracy** to abandon the covenant. Instead of heeding the warning of Jeremiah (vv. 2-8) they **returned to the sins of their** ancestors **to serve** false **gods.** Both the Northern Kingdom (**Israel**) and the Southern Kingdom (**Judah**) followed this wayward path.

Judah's deliberate decision to follow after idols assured her doom. God vowed to send **a disaster** from which the nation could not **escape.** In that hour of distress the people would **cry out to** God, and also to their idols, but neither would **help them at all.** Judah's abundance of **gods** and **altars** (cf. 2:28) would be her downfall, not her deliverance. Though Josiah tried to rid the land of idolatry (2 Chron. 34:33), the number of **incense** altars devoted to the **shameful god Baal** (cf. Jer. 11:17) were still as numerous **as the streets of Jerusalem.**

**11:14-17.** The people's sin was so pervasive that God again commanded Jeremiah **not to pray for** them because He would **not listen** to their prayers for deliverance in **their** coming **time of . . . distress** (cf. 7:16; 14:11). Jeremiah 11:15 has caused much concern for translators.

Apparently the thought is this: the **beloved** were the people of Judah who were in God's **temple** (lit., "house"). Evidently some people came to the temple to offer **consecrated meat** as a sacrifice, believing that this ritual would **avert . . . punishment.** Yet they never ceased to **engage in** their **wickedness.**

God then pictured their judgment like an **olive tree** being **set . . . on fire,** probably by lightning, in **a mighty storm.** God had **planted . . . Judah** as His people, and He would now uproot them because they had **provoked** Him **to anger** by their idolatry.

(2) The consequences of violating the covenant (11:18–12:17). **11:18-23.** The people responded to Jeremiah's rebuke by trying to kill him. This is the first episode in their continuing opposition to his ministry (cf. 1:8, 17-19). However, God **revealed their plot to** Jeremiah. These enemies planned to **cut** Jeremiah **off from the land of the living,** that is, to kill him. His response was to ask God to execute His **vengeance** on these conspirators.

God responded by assuring Jeremiah of His swift judgment. The plot against Jeremiah was formulated by **the men of Anathoth,** Jeremiah's own hometown (1:1), who ordered him **not to prophesy** or he would **die by** their **hands.** God promised to **punish** these rebels with **the sword** and with **famine. Anathoth** would suffer **disaster** because of her opposition to God's message and messenger.

**12:1-6.** Jeremiah responded to God's revelation of the plot against his life by complaining about the prosperity of the wicked. Though admitting that God was **righteous** whenever he brought **a case** (*rîb*; cf. 2:9, 29) **before** Him, still Jeremiah wanted to question God about His **justice.** Specifically he wanted to know **why . . . the way of the wicked** seemed to **prosper** if God was indeed angry with their sin (cf. Job 21:7; Pss. 73:3-5, 12; 94:3). In fact it seemed to Jeremiah as if God Himself had **planted them** because **they** had **taken root** and were bearing **fruit** materially.

Jeremiah asked God to judge the unrighteous (cf. Jer. 11:20). He hoped that God would **drag them off like sheep to be butchered** (cf. their having treated him like "a gentle lamb led to the slaughter," 11:19). Just as Jeremiah was "set apart" by God for his task (1:5) so he wished that God would set . . . apart the wicked for their day of slaughter!

God had judged the nation because of the sins of the wicked, but the righteous also suffered in this judgment. In 12:4 Jeremiah was not contradicting what he had just said about the prosperity of the wicked (v. 1). The thought is probably that even in times of difficulty the wicked seemed to come through better than the righteous. God had sent a drought to judge the nation (cf. 14:1-6; Lev. 26:19-20; Deut. 28:22-24) so that the land was parched and the grass was withered. Yet the people refused to acknowledge God's hand of judgment. They believed that God was indifferent to their sin as they claimed that He would not see what happens to them (cf. Pss. 73:11; 94:7).

God's answer to Jeremiah's question was something of a surprise. God indicated that if Jeremiah found his present circumstances difficult, his future situation would be even worse (Jer. 12:5). God used two metaphors to make this point—a race and a cross-country walk. If Jeremiah had raced with men on foot and was complaining about being worn . . . out, how could he compete later with horses? Or if Jeremiah would stumble (bāṭaḥ, should be trans. "trust"; cf. NIV marg.) in safe country, how could he manage if he were thrust into the thickets by the Jordan? "Thickets" were the dense growth along the Jordan River. The idea of this second question could possibly be paraphrased: If Jeremiah could trust in God only in a time of peace, how would he manage when the going got tough?

God continued His response to Jeremiah by indicating that even his own family had betrayed him. Evidently they had joined the plot against Jeremiah at Anathoth. So God warned Jeremiah not to trust them in spite of their outward words of praise.

**12:7-13.** God continued His pronouncement of judgment that was interrupted in 11:18 by the explanation of the plot against Jeremiah's life. God would forsake and abandon Judah and turn her over to her enemies. By describing the nation as His house, His inheritance (cf. 10:16 and comments on Deut. 4:20), and

the one He loved, God was indicating that the judgment was not coming from the hardened heart of a capricious king. Though He wanted to do just the opposite, God was forced to judge because of the people's sin. The nation had become like a lion who had raised her voice (roars) in opposition to Him.

The nation had changed so much that she had become . . . like a speckled bird of prey. A "speckled" (colored) bird was one whose markings were different from the other birds of prey. Consequently those other birds would surround and attack this strange bird. Judah had become so different that the other nations of the world would attack her.

The devastation coming on Jerusalem was compared to shepherds and their flocks entering a vineyard and ruining it by trampling it down. God's once-productive nation would become a wasteland as the sword of the LORD (i.e., the Babylonians' swords wielded as God's instruments) killed its inhabitants. Those who had sown wheat would reap only thorns (because of the devastation of war) and would be forced to bear the shame of their harvest of judgment.

**12:14-17.** Jeremiah closed his fourth message by giving God's promise/threat to the nations. Those wicked neighbors who had seized Israel's inheritance (cf. vv. 7-9) would themselves be uprooted from their lands (cf. 25:12-14, 27-29; 46–51). In contrast God would later uproot the house of Judah from these Gentile nations where they had been scattered and would restore them to their land (cf. 31:7-11; Ezek. 37:1-14).

Though God will judge these Gentile nations, He will later have compassion on them and restore them to their own lands. This will happen when Christ returns to establish His millennial kingdom on earth. Those nations that learn well the ways of God's people and swear by His name will be blessed and established. However, any nation that rebels will be destroyed (cf. Zech. 14:9, 16-19).

*e. The linen belt and the wineskins (chap. 13)*

The people were not responding to Jeremiah's message, so God had him perform a symbolic act to get their attention (vv. 1-11). Jeremiah also began using parables to gain their interest (vv. 12-14). These unusual means of communication were designed to arouse the curiosity and interest of his unresponsive audience. Later Ezekiel was commanded to use similar techniques in his ministry in Babylon (cf. Ezek. 4:1–5:4).

(1) The illustration of the linen belt (13:1-11). **13:1-7.** God commanded Jeremiah to **buy a linen belt** and wear it **around** his **waist.** He was **not** to **let it touch water.** Some scholars have felt that verses 1-7 describe a vision Jeremiah had. But nothing in the text indicates that the event did not actually occur. In fact verse 2 says that Jeremiah actually carried out the assignment. A **belt** (*'ēzôr*) was a sash or cloth tied around one's **waist** (cf. 2 Kings 1:8; Isa. 5:27). The fact that the belt was made of "linen," the material used for the priestly raiment (cf. Lev. 16:4), would have held some significance for those observing Jeremiah's actions.

After wearing the belt for a time, God told him to **take** it **to Perath and hide it . . . in a crevice in the rocks.** Perath (*perāt*) is usually translated "Euphrates" (cf. Jer. 51:63); many have felt that Jeremiah walked to the Euphrates River, a round-trip journey of about 700 miles, to bury this sash. However, another possibility is that Jeremiah traveled to the village of Parah (*pārâh*) about three miles northeast of Anathoth in the tribe of Benjamin (cf. Josh. 18:21, 23). A deep wadi in this area, known today as 'Ain Farah, fits the description of a place with crevices and rocks. In Hebrew the spelling for "to Parah" and "to Euphrates" are identical (both are *perātāh*; cf. Jer. 13:4-7). By using a location so close to home the people were able to observe Jeremiah's symbolic actions, and the similarity of name would remind the nation of the army from the Euphrates that was coming to destroy them.

**Many days later** God told Jeremiah to retrieve **the belt** he had buried. (Another round-trip walk of 700 miles would have been necessary if Perath is the Euphrates! This adds further support to the view that the place where Jeremiah was sent was the nearby village of Parah.) As he **dug up the** sash he found that its exposure to the elements had made it **completely useless.** The garment had rotted.

**13:8-11.** God interpreted Jeremiah's symbolic actions. The message was one of judgment on the **wicked people** who refused **to listen to** God's **words.** The belt **bound around** Jeremiah's **waist** represented **Israel** and **Judah.** As long as it remained around his waist it occupied a position of **renown and praise and honor.** However, when it was removed from his waist and buried it became **completely useless.** So Israel and Judah had become ruined by departing from their God to serve false gods.

(2) The parable of the wineskins. **13:12-14.** Jeremiah announced what seemed to be a self-evident parable to the people. He declared, **Every wineskin should be filled with wine.** "Wineskin" (*nēbel*) can refer to an animal-skin bottle (1 Sam. 10:3; cf. Luke 5:37) or to an earthen jar or pitcher (Jer. 48:12; Lam. 4:2). Because the containers were to be smashed together (Jer. 13:14), they were probably jars.

The people scoffed at Jeremiah's self-evident proverb. Of course **every** wine jar **should be filled with wine. Then** Jeremiah drove home the point of the parable. The empty jars represented **all who** lived **in the land** including the leaders and the people. God would **fill them with drunkenness**—a symbol of judgment (cf. Isa. 49:26; 63:6; Jer. 25:15-25; 51:7, 39). He would then **smash** the people like jars, **one against the other.** Nothing would prohibit God **from destroying them.**

(3) The message on sin and its results (13:15-27). **13:15-17.** Because of the approaching **darkness** of judgment Jeremiah warned the **arrogant** people of Judah to acknowledge their sin and to **give glory to . . . God.** "Darkness" and dark clouds often picture impending doom (cf. Ezek. 30:3, 18; 32:7-8; 34:12; Joel 2:2; Amos 5:18-20; Zeph. 1:15). If they refused to **listen . . . because of** their **pride** Jeremiah would **weep bitterly** (Jer. 14:17) to himself **because** they would surely be **taken captive.**

**13:18-19.** Jeremiah turned from the multitudes to address **the king and . . . the queen mother.** They are not identified here, but probably the king was Jehoiachin (also known as Jeconiah) and the queen mother was Nehushta—the widow of Jehoiakim (cf. 29:2; 2 Kings 24:8, 12, 15). Jeremiah exhorted them to humble themselves in light of the coming Exile. Since they went into captivity in 597 B.C. after his reign of just three months (2 Kings 24:8) this prophecy must have been penned during that three-month period.

Jeremiah called on the king and queen mother to **come down from** their **thrones** in humility because their **crowns** would soon **fall** off when Nebuchadnezzar removed them from office. Their deportation to Babylon was a foretaste of Judah's judgment because the whole nation would **be carried into exile.**

**13:20-27.** Jeremiah urged the leaders to look at the armies **coming from the north** (1:14; 4:6; 6:1, 22; 10:22) who would remove **the flock** (cf. 10:21; 13:17) that had been **entrusted to** them. Those with whom Judah had once tried to be aligned as her **allies** would become her cruel taskmasters (cf. Isa. 39:1-7; Ezek. 23:14-27). As a result, Judah would be in **pain** like **a woman in labor** (cf. comments on Jer. 4:31).

**If,** when the judgment came, the people asked **why,** God let them know in advance that it was **because of** their **many sins.** Judah was as incapable of reforming herself as a dark-skinned **Ethiopian** was of changing **his skin** pigmentation or as a **leopard** was of removing **its spots.** Her sin was so ingrained that she was **accustomed to doing** only **evil.**

God would **scatter** the people in exile **like chaff** that was blown in every direction **by the desert wind** (cf. 4:11-12). This judgment was not accidental. It was **the portion . . . decreed for** Judah by God **because** of her trust **in false gods.**

Using language to match Judah's lewd conduct God declared that He would **pull up** her **skirts** to expose her to the nations. The nations would see her **adulteries and** her **lustful neighings** (like wild animals; cf. 2:23-24) that characterized her **shameless prostitution.** Her **detestable acts** of idolatry had been **seen** by God, and she would suffer the consequences.

### f. The drought and prayer (chaps. 14–15)

(1) The plight because of the drought (14:1-6). **14:1-4.** One of the covenant curses God threatened to send on the disobedient nation was **drought** (cf. Lev. 26:18-19; Deut. 28:22-24). Jeremiah had already mentioned God's use of drought (Jer. 3:3; 12:4), though it is uncertain whether he was pointing to one major drought or to a series of droughts that came during Judah's final years.

The severity of the drought produced **a cry** of distress **from Jerusalem.** The rainfall had ceased and the stored **water** was running out. Though **nobles** sent **their servants** to **the cisterns** for **water,** they returned **with their jars unfilled.** Those who had rejected the Living Water of life for false cisterns (2:13) now found their physical water supply matching the spiritual water supply to which they had turned. The **ground** began to crack from a lack of **rain,** and **the farmers** became **dismayed** (cf. 14:3) as they watched their crops wither away. Jeremiah recorded that both the people in the city and the farmers in the country would **cover their heads,** a sign of grief or shame (cf. 2 Sam. 15:30).

**14:5-6.** The drought also affected the animals of **the field.** For example, the normally protective **doe** was forced to abandon **her newborn fawn because** of lack of **grass. Wild donkeys** were also **on the barren heights** panting for water (cf. Ps. 42:1) **like jackals.** Their usually good **eyesight** now failed them as they looked in vain for any **pasture** in which to graze.

(2) The pleading because of the drought (14:7–15:4). **14:7-9.** The severity of the drought forced the people to cry to God for deliverance. While admitting their **sins** and their **backsliding,** they asked God to intervene and supply rain. By calling God the **Hope of Israel** (cf. 17:13) and the **Savior,** the people acknowledged God's unique position as the only One who could deliver their nation from its current crisis.

Though God had the power to help, He did not answer the people's pleas for rain. He was acting **like a stranger** or **traveler** who had no real concern for the country through which He was traveling. God's failure to act reminded them of **a man taken by surprise** (one who had been ambushed and overcome before he could offer any resistance) or a **warrior** who was **powerless.** Because of God's lack of action the people pleaded with Him **not** to **forsake** them.

**14:10-12.** At first God's reply seems rather startling. Instead of accepting the people's confession, He upbraided them for their waywardness. God knew that their confession was only superficial. They claimed God as their Lord, but they refused to **restrain their feet** from following evil. Because of their continuing bent toward sin, God said He would **not accept** their superficial confession. Instead He would **punish them for their sins.**

God again told Jeremiah **not to pray for the . . . people** (cf. 7:16; 11:14). Their feeble efforts to manipulate God took several forms. **They** would **fast** and **offer burnt offerings,** hoping to appease **the LORD** and avert His wrath. But God cannot be bought off. He vowed to **destroy** the rebels **with the sword, famine, and plague**—the three hammerblows of divine judgment (cf. Lev. 26:23-26; Jer. 21:6-7, 9; 24:10; 27:8, 13; 29:17-18; 32:24, 36; 34:17; 38:2; Ezek. 5:12; 6:11; 7:15; 12:16; Rev. 6:8; also note Jer. 42:17, 22; 44:13).

**14:13-16.** Jeremiah interrupted God by reminding Him that the false **prophets** were contradicting His message. Instead of the **sword** or **famine,** they were announcing that God would give **lasting peace** to Jerusalem (cf. 5:12-13; 6:13-14; 7:4, 9-10; 27:16; 28:2-4).

God answered Jeremiah by explaining that the messages of these false prophets were **lies** because they had not been **appointed** by Him. Their messages were **delusions of their own minds.** God would judge them for their lies by destroying both the false **prophets** and those who listened to them. They would all **perish by sword and famine** (cf. 14:13, 18).

**14:17-18.** Jeremiah's sorrow burst forth at the thought of Jerusalem's judgment. His **eyes** welled up **with tears** as he cried continually (**night and day**) over Jerusalem's fall (cf. 9:1, 18; 13:17; Lam. 3:48-51). For some reason he pictured the city as a **virgin daughter,** who had **suffered a** mortal **wound** (cf. comments on Jer. 6:14) and Jeremiah was grieving over her loss. In the **country** (the countryside surrounding Jerusalem) lay the corpses of **those slain by the sword.** Those who escaped to **the city** were slowly falling to **the ravages of famine.** Prophets and priests, who should have set the people aright, were deported to Babylon.

**14:19-22.** The people again addressed God and pleaded for His intervention. They were puzzled as to why God would **despise** them and **why** He **afflicted** them (cf. "why" in vv. 8-9). Though they **hoped for peace,** they had experienced **only terror.** This concern prompted them again to **acknowledge** their **wickedness** (cf. v. 7) and **guilt** and to ask God to help them.

Their appeal for God's help was based on His personal character (**for the sake of Your name;** cf. v. 7), His temple (His **glorious throne;** cf. 3:17; 17:12), and His **covenant** (cf. 11:2-5). The people were quick to remind God of His obligations to the nation, but failed to remember their own obligations to Him. They finally admitted that the **worthless idols** (cf. comments on 2:5) they had worshiped could not **bring rain** to quench the drought. **God** was **the** only **One** who could do **all this** (cf. 1 Kings 17:1; 18:18-46).

**15:1-4.** The chapter break between 14 and 15 should be disregarded. The first 4 verses of chapter 15 are God's answer to the apparent "confession" in 14:19-22. The nation's sin was so ingrained (cf. 13:23) that judgment was inevitable. **Even** the intercessory prayer of **Moses** or **Samuel** could not stop God's judgment. Mention of these two men was significant because Moses had interceded for the nation to turn away God's wrath (Ex. 32:9-14; Num. 14:11-20; Deut. 9:18-20, 25-29), and Samuel had interceded to defeat the nation's enemies and turn away God's wrath (1 Sam. 7:5-11; 12:19-25).

The fate of the people was sealed. **Four** options had been selected by God. Some were **destined** to **death**—probably meaning death by plague (cf. Jer. 14:12). Others would be cut down with **the sword,** while others would die from **starvation.** However, those not appointed to God's triad of terror (plague, sword, famine; cf. comments on 14:12) would escape death but would be taken into **captivity.** The scene of carnage continued (15:3) as Jeremiah pictured **dogs . . . birds,** and wild **beasts** devouring and destroying those who had been slain (cf. 16:4).

Judah had passed "the point of no return" in her dealings with God. That line was crossed through the actions of **Manasseh son of Hezekiah** (cf. 2 Kings 21:1-18; 2 Chron. 33:1-20). Manasseh so polluted **Jerusalem** with idolatry that her destruction was inevitable (2 Kings 21:10-15). Even Josiah's reforms could only postpone her certain destruction (2 Kings 22:16-20).

(3) The fate of Jerusalem (15:5-9). **15:5-7.** God asked **Jerusalem. . . . who**

would **pity** her or **mourn** for her when she was judged. The only One who had ever cared for her was God, but she had **rejected** Him. Therefore God vowed to **destroy** her without **compassion.** He would **winnow** her as a farmer winnowed his grain to remove the unbelievers who were like chaff.

**15:8-9.** The awesome effects of judgment touched all the people. **Widows** would become **more numerous than . . . sand** as the men were slaughtered by the Babylonians. Even **the mothers** would not escape. To be a **mother of seven** young men symbolized a zenith of happiness and security. But even seven able-bodied defenders would not be able to deflect the blow of God's judgment. That mother would **breathe her last** breath as the invading soldiers entered the city to kill **the survivors** of the siege. Though this "mother" could mean a physical mother, it is possible that Jeremiah was also picturing Jerusalem as a mother who felt secure. In either case, Babylon would shatter her security by destroying the city and those who lived in it.

(4) Jeremiah's complaint (15:10-21). **15:10-11.** Jeremiah lamented his own condition in life as he pictured **the whole land** against him. Though he had not **lent** or **borrowed,** actions which could cause tensions and conflicts (cf. Neh. 5:1-13; Prov. 22:7), Jeremiah was still being cursed by the people. God answered by assuring Jeremiah of vindication. Those who had been his **enemies** would **plead with** him when the **times of distress** finally arrived. This promise was fulfilled specifically in the requests of King Zedekiah to Jeremiah (cf. Jer. 21:1-7; 37:1-10, 17-20; 38:14-18).

**15:12-14.** God asked a rhetorical question to emphasize the inevitability of judgment. Just as **a man** cannot **break iron** or **bronze** with his bare hands, so the people of Judah would be unable to break the power of the Babylonian attack on their nation. Indeed all their **wealth** would be plundered (cf. 17:3; 20:5) by these invaders. The Babylonians would **enslave** the Judeans and deport them to **a land** they did **not know** (cf. 14:18; 15:2; 16:13; 17:4). This judgment was the result of God's **anger** which burned like **a fire . . . against** the people of Judah.

**15:15-18.** God had promised ultimately to deliver and vindicate Jeremiah (v. 11); but in light of the coming calamity (vv. 12-14) Jeremiah asked for a speedy settling of accounts. He wanted God to **avenge** him **on** his **persecutors.** Though God was **long-suffering,** Jeremiah hoped for swift justice; he wanted to be vindicated before God would **take** him **away** in death.

Jeremiah could make this request because of his relationship with God. In contrast with the people of Judah who despised God's Word (8:9), Jeremiah accepted **(ate)** it and claimed it as his **joy** and **delight** (cf. Ps. 1:2). Jeremiah refused to associate with **the company of revelers** (cf. Ps. 1:1), choosing instead to sit **alone** and be guided by God's **hand.** He shared God's **indignation** over the people's sin.

Jeremiah ended this address by painfully lamenting his pitiful condition. He wanted to know **why** his **pain** seemed **unending** and his **wound . . . incurable** (see comments on Jer. 6:14). He felt as though God was protracting his suffering. Worse yet, he wondered if the God who claimed to be a spring of Living Water (2:13) had become **like a deceptive brook** or **a spring that fails.** The disappointment of a dry wadi bed that only held water after a heavy rain was a depressing sight to those searching for water (cf. Job 6:15-20). Jeremiah hoped that God would not disappoint him.

**15:19-21.** God rebuked Jeremiah for his doubt and self-pity. Jeremiah needed to **repent** if he hoped to **serve** God. To be God's **spokesman** he had to **utter worthy, not worthless, words.** He was to remain steadfast before God so the **people** would **turn to** him; in no case was he to **turn to them.** If someone was to move, it was to be the people, not Jeremiah!

God ended His rebuke by restating the promises He made when He commissioned Jeremiah as a prophet (cf. 1:18-19). He would strengthen Jeremiah as a **wall of bronze** so that those opposing him could never **overcome** him. Though opposition would come, God promised to **rescue** Jeremiah **from** those who sought to kill him.

*g. Jeremiah's restrictions and Judah's sin (16:1–17:18)*

(1) Jeremiah's restrictions (16:1-9). **16:1-4.** God placed several restrictions on Jeremiah's personal life that were intended as object lessons for the people.

The first restriction was the command **not** to **marry and** raise a family. Jeremiah was denied this normal relationship that was cherished by all Israelites. God's purpose was to show that the coming catastrophe would disrupt all normal relationships. Many spouses and children would **die of deadly diseases.** Those who remained would **perish by sword and famine** (cf. 14:15-16; 15:2). The carnage would be so awesome that those killed would **not** even **be mourned or buried** (cf. 16:6). Instead they would remain **like refuse . . . on the ground** (cf. 25:33)— their lifeless bodies serving as **food for** wild animals (cf. 15:3).

**16:5-7.** The second restriction placed on Jeremiah was **not** to **enter a house where . . . a funeral meal** was being eaten, or **mourn or show sympathy** (cf. Ezek. 24:15-24). He was not to display the normal emotion of grief or to offer comfort when someone died. There were two purposes in this action. First, it was to show that God had **withdrawn** His **blessing . . . love,** and **pity.** Second, it served as a reminder that those who would **die** during the fall of Jerusalem would **not be buried or mourned** (cf. Jer. 16:4) and that the survivors would find no one **to console them** in their grief. The devastation would simply be too widespread. To **cut** oneself and to **shave** one's **head** were signs of grief (cf. 41:5; 47:5; 48:37) though cutting oneself was forbidden by the Law (Deut. 14:1) because of its pagan associations (cf. 1 Kings 18:28). On shaving one's head see comments on Job 1:20.

**16:8-9.** The third restriction placed on Jeremiah was **not** to **enter a house where there** was **feasting.** The purpose of this prohibition was to indicate that times of feasting and happiness would soon cease. God vowed to **bring an end to** Judah's **joy** and her present times of happiness (cf. 25:10).

(2) Judah's sin (16:10–17:18). **16:10-13.** As Jeremiah explained his behavior to the people, **they** asked **why** God had **decreed such a great disaster against** them. Naively they asked **what sin** they had **committed** to deserve such judgment. God's answer to these questions underscored the root problem throughout Israel's history. Though the previous generations (**fathers**) had abandoned the true God to follow **other gods,** the present

generation **behaved** even **more wickedly.** Instead of profiting from their ancestors' errors, the current generation was going further astray. **Each** person was **following the stubbornness** within **his evil heart** rather than **obeying** God.

Because of the continued rebellion of the people, God vowed to **throw** them **out of** the **land.** "Throw" (*tûl*) means to cast or hurl an object (cf. 1 Sam. 18:11; 20:33; Jer. 22:26-28). The people would be violently thrust into a country they had not **known** before (cf. 14:18; 15:2, 14; 17:4) where they would **serve other gods** (cf. 5:19). Because they rejected God He would **show** them **no favor** (cf. 16:5).

**16:14-15.** Once again God paused in His judgment to clarify His message. Lest the people interpret His previous words to mean that Israel would no longer have any place in His covenant program, God clearly indicated that this judgment was not permanent (cf. 4:27; 5:18). Ultimately Israel as a nation will be restored to her land and will enjoy God's blessing. This will happen during the millennial reign of Christ when the nation will experience the benefits of the New Covenant (31:31-34).

God promised that after Judah's coming Captivity there would be a new "Exodus." **No longer** would the people look back to the first Exodus when God **brought the Israelites . . . out of** bondage in **Egypt.** Instead they would point back to the time when God **brought** them from **the land of the north** (i.e., Babylon; cf. comments on 1:14) where they had earlier been **banished.** Thus God reaffirmed His promise ultimately to **restore** Israel to **the land.**

Since 16:14-15 is nearly identical to 23:7-8, some scholars think that 16:14-15 was placed here later by mistake, but such a view is unnecessary. Jeremiah used the same or similar wording in several places throughout his book (cf. 1:18-19 with 15:20; 6:13-15 with 8:10b-12; 7:31-32 with 19:5-6; 15:13-14 with 17:3-4).

**16:16-18.** After assuring the nation of her final restoration, God continued describing her impending judgment. Restoration could be expected in the future, **but now** the people were facing deportation. God first pictured the Babylonian invaders as **fishermen** who would **catch** the Judeans in their nets. Then he pictured the Babylonians as **hunters** who would **hunt . . . down** those who had managed to escape and were in hiding. No one could escape because God's **eyes** were **on all their ways.** Neither the refugees nor **their sin** were ever **concealed from** God. He would hunt the people down and **repay them** for the way they had **defiled** the **land** (ironically called His land, not theirs) **with their detestable idols.**

**16:19-21.** Jeremiah affirmed his trust in God as his **Strength . . . Fortress,** and **Refuge** (cf. comments on Ps. 18:2), three words that emphasized the protection God had provided for him. After affirming his trust in God, Jeremiah looked forward to the day when all the world would know God. Though Judah had turned to the false gods of the Gentiles, a time will come when the **nations will come** to the true God of Israel. They will admit that their former objects of worship were **nothing but false gods, worthless idols** (cf. comments on Jer. 2:5). At that **time** God **will teach them** of His **power and might** so they will understand His true character. **They will know** then **that** His **name is the LORD** (cf. Ezek. 36:22-23).

**17:1-4.** The Gentiles will one day forsake their idols and turn to God. However, in Jeremiah's day the people of Judah were permeated with idolatry. They were so entrenched in their ways that it was as if their **sin** were **engraved** or etched on **their hearts** with **an iron tool** or **a flint point.** Both iron and flint, being extremely hard, were used to chisel words into stone tablets (cf. Job 19:24). The sin of Judah, however, extended beyond their hearts and showed up **on the horns of their** idolatrous **altars.** The "horns" were stone projections at the top of each altar on the four corners.

Idolatry was so pervasive that **even . . . children** participated in worship at the **altars and Asherah poles.** Asherah was the Canaanite goddess of fertility. A carved image of Asherah had been placed in God's temple by Manasseh (2 Kings 21:7; cf. Deut. 16:21) though he later removed it (2 Chron. 33:13, 15). Evidently the image was put back in the temple after he died because Josiah took it out during his reforms and burned it in the Kidron Valley outside the city (2 Kings 23:6). After Josiah's death the people resumed their idolatry, and the

Asherah poles were again set up. Possibly the "idol of jealousy" (Ezek. 8:5) was a carved image of Asherah. These idols were being worshiped by **spreading trees and on the high hills,** traditional places of worship for false gods (cf. Ezek. 6:13).

Because of the people's sin God would **give** the city of Jerusalem (His **mountain in the land**) and the **wealth** of its inhabitants **as plunder** (cf. Jer. 15:13; 20:5) to the invaders. The people of Judah would **lose** the land (their **inheritance**) as God enslaved them **to** their **enemies** and deported them to **a land** they did **not know** (cf. 14:18; 15:2, 14; 16:13).

**17:5-8.** Jeremiah included a short poem contrasting the way of the wicked (vv. 5-6) with the way of the righteous (vv. 7-8). Judah had been turning to false gods and foreign alliances for protection, but God indicated that a person **who trusts in man** for protection is **cursed** because his **heart** has turned **away from** God. Instead of prospering, he will wither away **like a desert bush.** God would make him as unfruitful as the barren **salt land** around the Dead Sea, unable to support life.

A righteous person is **blessed** because his **confidence** (trust) is in God. Unlike the person in verses 5-6, a righteous person will flourish **like a tree planted by the water** (cf. Ps. 1:3). When difficulties (represented figuratively by **heat** and **drought**) come, he will **not fear.** Instead he will continue to prosper like a tree that bears **fruit** and whose **leaves** remain **green.**

**17:9-13.** If the ways of blessing and cursing are so clear (vv. 5-8), why would anyone choose the path of sin? The cause for such action is in the **heart.** It **is** so **deceitful** that Jeremiah wondered **who** could even **understand it.** God answered by informing Jeremiah that *He* can **search the heart and examine the mind.** God knows those innermost thoughts and motives that an individual might hide from all others. Therefore God could justly render to each person what **his deeds deserve.**

The principle of judgment was applied to those who had amassed **riches** by using **unjust means.** If **a partridge** hatched the **eggs** of another bird, the offspring would soon **desert** the mother and fly away. So wealth that had been acquired unjustly would be taken away, and the one who had been hoarding it would be exposed as **a fool.**

Jeremiah's solution to sin was to focus on the majesty of God. God was enthroned in His **sanctuary.** Those who chose to **forsake** God (**the Hope of Israel;** cf. 14:8) would **be written in the dust**—a possible reference to their lack of permanence (as opposed to being written in the book of life, Ex. 32:32-33; Ps. 69:28). They deserved such a fate **because they** had abandoned God, **the Spring of Living Water** (cf. Jer. 2:13).

**17:14-18.** Jeremiah concluded his message by calling on God to vindicate him. The message is in the form of an individual lament. Jeremiah contrasted his faithful devotion to God with the unbelief of those persecuting him. They scoffed at his predictions and demanded that those prophecies **now be fulfilled** if they were true. Yet, in spite of this opposition, Jeremiah had **not run away from** faithfully serving as God's **shepherd.** Therefore he asked God to **put** his **persecutors . . . to shame** by bringing **on them the day of disaster** Jeremiah had been predicting. Because they refused to accept his message, he asked God to bring the full measure of judgment against them (**double destruction;** cf. 16:18).

### h. The keeping of the Sabbath (17:19-27)

Jeremiah's previous messages dealt with the general sin and rebellion of the people. In these verses, however, he focused on one specific command in the Mosaic Law to show the nation how far they had departed from God (cf. Ex. 20:8-11). Again there is an explicit offer of repentance. Blessing will follow obedience, but judgment will follow disobedience.

**17:19.** God told Jeremiah to **stand at the gate of the people.** Which gate this was is unknown, though it is identified as the gate **through which the kings . . . go in and out.** The spot was selected because of the large number of people who passed by. Possibly this was the Eastern Gate that led from the temple mount to the Kidron Valley. Ezekiel pictured this gate as a place where Judah's leaders gathered (Ezek. 11:1). Or this may be the Benjamin Gate at the northern end of the city (cf. Jer. 37:13). It too was a place where a king would set up

his throne (38:7). Whatever the gate's location, Jeremiah did not stay there. He was to take his message to **all the other gates** so that the whole city would hear it.

**17:20-24.** His message to those who passed **through these gates** was to **keep the Sabbath Day holy.** In contrast with their **forefathers** who disobeyed, they were to honor the day God had set aside by **not doing any work on it.** This was one visible test of their faithfulness to God's covenant.

**17:25-27.** Faithfulness to the Law would bring blessing. If the people obeyed God's commandments, Jerusalem would be **inhabited forever. People** would flock to the city **from the** north (the **territory of Benjamin**), from the low, rolling hills of the Shephelah on the west (**western foothills**), from the rugged mountainous area between **Jerusalem** and the Jordan Valley and Dead Sea on the east (**hill country**), and from the semi-arid wilderness in the south (**Negev**). These people would bring their **offerings and sacrifices** to the temple. However, if they would **not obey** God's injunction on **the Sabbath,** He would **kindle** a **fire** of judgment that would **consume her fortresses** and leave her defenseless (cf. 49:27).

### i. The potter and the broken jar (chaps. 18–20)

Jeremiah's ninth message was a series of parables and events that climaxed the first section of the book. The Parable of the Potter (chap. 18) demonstrated God's sovereign dealings with Judah. This was followed by the symbolic breaking of a potter's jar to show God's impending judgment (chap. 19). Chapter 20 serves as a pivot in the book. It is connected chronologically with chapter 19, but it also prepares the reader for the open opposition and specific prophecies of judgment that follow.

(1) The message at the potter's house (chap. 18). **18:1-4.** God directed Jeremiah to **go down to the potter's house and** watch him molding **clay** into pots on his **wheel.** As Jeremiah watched, the potter discovered a flaw in **the pot he was shaping . . . in his hands. The potter** pressed the clay into a lump and **formed it into another pot.**

**18:5-12.** God announced that the

potter and the clay illustrated His relationship to His people. They were **like clay** in His **hand.** God has the right to tear **down** or build **up** a **nation** as He pleases. He had promised the **nation** blessing; but since she continued to do **evil,** He would **reconsider the good** He **had intended** and bring about judgment. However, if **Judah** would **turn from** her **evil ways** God would also revoke the **disaster** He promised to send.

The people of Judah would respond by saying that they were helpless to change (**it's no use**). They would stubbornly **continue** to follow the **plans** of their sinful hearts. The nation refused to turn from her idolatry to follow **the LORD.**

**18:13-17.** Judah stood alone **among the nations** in her stubborn refusal to follow her God (cf. 2:10-11). Even **the snow** on the slopes **of Lebanon** and the **cool waters** that **flow** from these majestic mountains were more dependable than fickle Judah. She had turned from God **to** worship **worthless idols** (cf. comments on 2:5) which only caused her to **stumble.** By abandoning **the ancient paths** of obedience to God (cf. 6:16), Judah found herself on **bypaths,** wandering aimlessly over rough **roads.**

God would judge the nation for her sin by having her **land . . . laid waste.** She would become **an object of . . . scorn** to those who were **appalled** at her stupidity in abandoning her God (cf. 19:8; Lam. 2:15). **The LORD** vowed to **scatter** the nation like the **wind from the east** (cf. Jer. 4:11-12; 13:24). They should expect God's judgment (His **back**), **not** His favor (His **face**).

**18:18-23.** Again the people responded by making **plans against Jeremiah.** They refused to accept his declaration of doom because it conflicted with their belief in the permanence of the then-present order. Their solution was to **attack him with** their **tongues** in an effort to slander and malign his message and also to **pay no attention** to his words, hoping to silence him by ignoring him. Evidently their plans were more sinister because Jeremiah told the LORD that they were plotting to take his life (**they have dug a pit,** vv. 20-21; cf. 11:18-21).

Jeremiah reacted to their threats by calling on God to **listen** to their accusations, to **remember** his (Jeremiah's) faithfulness, and to judge the plotters for their sin. Jeremiah had earlier asked God to **turn** His **wrath away** (18:20; cf. 7:16; 8:20-22), but now he called on God to **deal with them in** His **time of . . . anger** (18:23). They had rejected both God and His messenger; Jeremiah could do no more for them. They would experience **famine** and **the sword** (v. 21).

(2) The message of the broken jar (chap. 19). **19:1-6.** Probably chapter 19 was placed next to chapter 18 because both contained messages based on **a potter** and his wares. Jeremiah bought a narrow-necked pottery flask or vessel for carrying water. The word for **clay jar** is *baqbūq,* an onomatopoetic word suggesting the sound the water made as it was poured out. After gathering a group of **elders** and **priests,** he walked **to the Valley of Ben Hinnom** (see comments on 7:31) just outside **the Potsherd Gate.** The Hinnom Valley ran along the south and west of the city and served as Jerusalem's "community dump." The gate at the south of the city which opened into the valley was called the "Potsherd Gate" because people carried their potsherds (broken pieces of pottery) and other refuse through this gate to throw it in the Hinnom Valley. The Targum identifies the Potsherd Gate with the Dung Gate (cf. Neh. 2:13; 3:13-14). The modern Dung Gate in Jerusalem is also located on the south of the city, but the present walls are several hundred yards north of the walls in Jeremiah's day.

With the Hinnom Valley as a backdrop, Jeremiah delivered his message. God vowed to **bring a disaster on** Jerusalem because of her idolatry. The valley itself was a witness against the people because it contained **the high places of Baal** where people slaughtered **their sons** to offer them as sacrifices **in the fire.** Because of these wicked deeds God again (cf. Jer. 7:32-33) vowed to rename the place **the Valley of Slaughter** as He destroyed the people there.

**19:7-9.** Jeremiah elaborated on the coming catastrophe. The people would **fall by the sword before** Babylon, and **their carcasses** would serve **as food** for **the birds** and **beasts** (cf. 7:33; 16:4; 34:20; Deut. 28:26). The **city** itself would become **an object of scorn** (cf. Jer. 18:16) to those who observed her destruction. Those who sought refuge in the city would resort to cannibalism (**eat the flesh of their sons and daughters**) as Babylon's **siege** choked off the supply of food to the inhabitants (cf. Lev. 26:27-29; Deut. 28:53-57; Lam. 2:20; 4:10). All the curses promised by God would overtake the people because of their sin (cf. Lev. 26:14-39; Deut. 28:15-68; Jer. 11:1-8).

**19:10-13.** To dramatize the message to his audience God commanded Jeremiah to **break the jar** he had carried out to the valley. God said He would **smash** both the **nation** of Judah and the **city** of Jerusalem **just as** Jeremiah **smashed** the **potter's jar**. The **city** itself would become **like Topheth** (cf. comments on 7:31-32); its once-beautiful dwellings would be reduced to rubble and the entire area would **be defiled** with decaying bodies of the slain. The cause for the destruction was the sin of the people in burning **incense . . . to all the starry hosts** and in offering libations **to other gods.**

**19:14-15.** Returning **from Topheth** to the city Jeremiah went directly to **the** temple **court.** The message given to the leaders (cf. v. 1) was now repeated **to all the people.** God's judgment would come against Jerusalem **and the villages around** it **. . . because** the people refused to **listen to** His **words.**

(3) The response of Pashhur (20:1-6). **20:1-2.** Jeremiah's message of judgment was rejected by one of the priests, **Pashhur son of Immer.** This Pashhur was not the Pashhur in 21:1. The Pashhur in 20:1 was **the chief officer in the temple** and was probably assigned to maintain order within the temple area (cf. 29:26). **He** seized **Jeremiah** and **had** him **beaten,** or flogged with 40 lashes (cf. Deut. 25:2-3). Then he **put** Jeremiah **in the stocks** for public ridicule. These stocks were located **at the Upper Gate of Benjamin,** the northern gate of the city. This was the first of several instances of open opposition against Jeremiah's ministry.

**20:3-6.** When Jeremiah was **released** from his chains **the next day** he refused to change his message. Instead he changed Pashhur's name. God's new **name for Pashhur** was **Magor-Missabib** ("terror on every side"). Because **Pashhur** refused to heed God's message, he would **see** the outpouring of God's judgment. He would watch in terror as his own friends fell **by the sword,** and he

would see **Babylon** carry away **all the wealth of** Jerusalem **as plunder** (cf. 15:13; 17:3). **Pashhur** and his family would be exiled in **Babylon** where they would all **die.** The reason for this judgment was not only that he had Jeremiah beaten. Pashhur also **prophesied lies,** probably by denying the truth of Jeremiah's message. The exact fulfillment of the prophecy was not given, but it is possible that Pashhur was taken to Babylon during the second deportation in 597 B.C. along with the priest, Ezekiel (cf. 2 Kings 24:15-16; Ezek. 1:1-3).

(4) The complaint of Jeremiah (20:7-18). **20:7-10.** Jeremiah opened his heart to God and expressed the depth of his inner emotions. He felt that God had **deceived** him by letting him be **ridiculed** by the people for his message. He had faithfully warned them of the coming **violence and destruction;** but his reward was only their insults. Discouraged, Jeremiah considered withholding God's Word to avoid persecution. But when he did, the **Word** became **like a burning fire** (cf. 23:29) within him so that he was unable to contain it. To feel something in one's **bones** meant to feel it intensely (cf. Job 30:17; 33:19).

Jeremiah wanted to quit his ministry because the people plotted against him. The message of **terror on every side** that he was constantly proclaiming (Jer. 20:3-4; cf. 6:25; 17:18; 46:5; 49:29; Lam. 2:22) was now being hurled back at him (cf. Ps. 31:13). Even his **friends** were watching for him **to slip** up, perhaps by uttering a wrong prediction, so they could **take** their **revenge on him** as a false prophet (cf. Deut. 18:20).

**20:11-13.** Jeremiah continued his prayer by expressing his trust in God and by calling on God to avenge him (cf. 18:19-23). Though he had felt deceived (20:7), he still realized that God was **with** him **like a mighty warrior.** Since the LORD was fighting on Jeremiah's side, he was confident that those who were persecuting and mocking him would **stumble** and would ultimately be **disgraced.** Jeremiah asked to **see** the **vengeance** of the all-knowing God poured out on his opponents because he had **committed** his **cause** to God.

This assurance of vindication allowed Jeremiah to **sing** and **praise** God for His mighty acts. God could be praised because He would rescue Jeremiah **from . . . the wicked.**

**20:14-18.** In a sudden change of emotion Jeremiah again plunged from a height of confidence (vv. 11-13) to the depths of despair. Perhaps he realized that the vindication for which he sought could come only through the destruction of the city and nation which he dearly loved. His agony made him wish that the **day** he **was born** would have been **cursed.** By cursing the day of his birth, Jeremiah was wishing that he had never been **born** (cf. 15:10; Job 3:1-19). Had he died **in the womb,** he would not have **come out of the womb** in birth and been subject to the **trouble and sorrow** he was experiencing. Jeremiah's self-pity could not erase the fact that he had been selected "in the womb" for the task he was performing (cf. Jer. 1:5).

2. JEREMIAH'S FOUR SPECIFIC PROPHECIES OF JUDGMENT (CHAPS. 21–25)

The opposition of Pashhur (20:1-6) serves as a pivot or bridge in the Book of Jeremiah. Through a series of nine undated prophecies Jeremiah had denounced Judah's sin, threatened judgment, and offered hope if the people would repent. Though opposition had surfaced (11:18-23; 12:6; 15:10; 17:18; 18:19-23), he had not suffered any physical persecution. With the recording of Pashhur's response, however, Jeremiah's book took on a more personal note. His prophecies were now directed against specific individuals and groups, and Judah's hope of repentance was replaced with the certainty of God's judgment.

*a. The rebuke of the kings (21:1–23:8)*

The first group singled out by Jeremiah was the kings—those appointed by God to be shepherds of the flock of Judah (cf. 2:8; 10:21; 23:1-8; Ezek. 34:1-10). Jeremiah first rebuked the wicked kings who had ruled Judah (Jer. 21–22). Then he offered hope in the righteous King who would come to restore Judah (23:1-8).

Jeremiah's messages to the wicked kings were arranged in an unusual order. (See the chart "The Last Five Kings of Judah," near 2 Kings 24.) The first king listed was Zedekiah who was the last king chronologically (Jer. 21:1–22:9). The other kings were then arranged chrono-

logically beginning with Shallum (Jehoahaz, 22:10-12), continuing with Jehoiakim (22:13-23), and ending with Coniah (Jehoiachin/Jeconiah, 22:24-30). Why did Jeremiah place Zedekiah out of chronological order, putting him first and Coniah last? Perhaps for two reasons. First, by discussing Zedekiah at the beginning he was able to put the story of "Pashhur son of Malkijah" (21:1) next to the story of "Pashhur son of Immer" (20:1). The fact that these two individuals had the same name provides continuity. The vindication Jeremiah sought because of Pashhur son of Immer's ridicule was realized when Pashhur son of Malkijah was sent to Jeremiah to inquire of the Lord. Second, the accounts were arranged so that the prophecy against Coniah would climax God's judgments against the kings. The line of the wicked kings would be cut off (22:30) because God would raise a righteous Branch to rule the nation (23:1-8). So the arrangement of these prophecies provided both continuity and climax.

(1) The message to Zedekiah (21:1–22:9). **21:1-2.** This message was given some time between 588 B.C. and 586 B.C. **King Zedekiah sent . . . Pashhur son of Malkijah and . . . Zephaniah son of Maaseiah** to Jeremiah with a request. Pashhur, one of the king's officials, later petitioned the king to execute Jeremiah for treason (cf. 38:1-4). Zephaniah succeeded Jehoiada (29:25-26) as a **priest** second in rank to the high priest, Seraiah (52:24). So Zephaniah was the second highest religious leader in Judah. Later, after the fall of Jerusalem (52:24-27), Zephaniah was executed by Nebuchadnezzar.

These officials asked Jeremiah to **inquire . . . of the LORD** regarding Nebuchadnezzar's attack on Jerusalem. Though Jeremiah was to ask God what the outcome would be, they hoped that God would **perform wonders** as He had done **in times past so that Nebuchadnezzar** would **withdraw.** Probably Zedekiah and his advisers were thinking of King Hezekiah's day when the Assyrians had threatened Jerusalem (2 Kings 18:17–19:37; Isa. 36–37). Hezekiah responded to the crisis by sending his chief political and religious advisers to the Prophet Isaiah to ask for his intervention (Isa. 37:2-4). No doubt Zedekiah hoped that God's answer would be similar to that given by Isaiah (Isa. 37:5-7).

**21:3-7.** Unfortunately for **Zedekiah,** Jeremiah's message was one he did *not* wish to hear. Instead of rescuing Jerusalem, **God** would **turn against** her the very **weapons of war** she had **in** her **hands.** The armies **outside the wall** who were **besieging** the city would be gathered by God **inside** the **city.** Their siege would be successful. Rather than being Jerusalem's Deliverer, God would **fight against** her **with** His own **outstretched hand.** Those who were huddled for protection in the **city** would **die of a terrible plague**—one of the worst fears of a city under siege (cf. comments on 14:12).

Those who managed to **survive** the siege would not rejoice because God would **hand** them **over** to **Nebuchadnezzar.** They could expect **no mercy or pity or compassion** for he would kill them. This was fulfilled in 586 B.C. after the city fell. King Zedekiah was blinded and taken in chains to Babylon (39:5-7). The other leaders of the city were captured and sent to Riblah where they were executed (52:24-27).

**21:8-10.** The people had two clear choices: **the way of life and the way of death.** The "way of death" was selected by those who chose to remain **in** the **city.** They would die. The "way of life" was selected by those who deserted (surrendered) to the enemy besieging Jerusalem. This was the only hope for those still in the **city** because God had **determined** to harm Jerusalem by letting it fall to **Babylon.** The response to this message from Jeremiah is in 38:1-4.

**21:11-14.** Jeremiah again singled out **the royal house of Judah** and focused on their sin. The king was supposed to **administer justice** and to uphold the rights of those who were oppressed. Since he refused to heed God's warning, God's **wrath** would **burn like** an unquenchable **fire** (cf. 4:4; 17:4).

Evidently the king saw no need to obey God's injunction. He felt so secure in his well-protected city that he boasted, **Who can enter our refuge?** Because of this proud self-reliance, coupled with sinful disobedience, God would **punish** the king and his people. God's **fire** (cf. 21:12) of judgment would **consume everything around** them.

**22:1-5.** God instructed Jeremiah to go **down** from the temple to the king's **palace.** His message to **the king** and to the **officials** and **people** who were there was for them to **do what is just and right.** The content of this message was similar to 21:12, but certain consequences were attached to the actions. **If** the king would be **careful** to observe God's **commands** he could expect continued blessing. But if he disobeyed those **commands,** God vowed that the royal **palace** would **become a ruin.**

**22:6-9.** In these verses Jeremiah was referring to the royal **palace.** Both **Gilead** and **Lebanon** were known for their forests (Jud. 9:15; 1 Kings 4:33; 2 Chron. 2:8), and the royal palace in Jerusalem was known as the "Palace of the Forest of Lebanon" (1 Kings 7:2-5; Isa. 22:8). But after God's judgment the palace would be as desolate as **a desert.** The Babylonians would **cut up** the palace's **fine cedar beams** and cast **them into the fire** (cf. Jer. 52:13).

As **people from** other **nations** saw the destruction of this magnificent structure, they would **ask . . . why** God had **done such a thing. The answer** was simple. God had judged the city **because** the people had **forsaken the covenant** and had **worshiped . . . other gods.** God had judged the people with His promised curses because of their disobedience.

(2) The message to Shallum. **22:10-12. Shallum** was another name for Jehoahaz. He was a **son of Josiah,** and succeeded Josiah to the throne in 609 B.C. after Josiah was killed by Pharaoh Neco II (2 Kings 23:29-33). After a reign of only three months, Shallum was deposed by Pharaoh Neco. Jeremiah penned this prophecy in 609 after Shallum had **gone from** Jerusalem into captivity in Egypt (2 Kings 23:34). Jeremiah predicted that Shallum would **never return** to Jerusalem. Instead, he would **die in the place where** he had been deported as a **captive.**

(3) The message to Jehoiakim (22:13-23). **22:13-14.** After being appointed as king by Pharaoh Neco, Jehoiakim acted the part of a typical oriental despot. Judah needed a firm hand to guide the "ship of state," but instead she got a corrupt, petty king who cared only for personal gain. Jehoiakim sought to build a **palace** for himself, and did so at the expense of his subjects. They were forced

to **work for nothing** as Jehoiakim lavished his money on **panels** of **cedar** wood.

**22:15-17.** Jeremiah contrasted Jehoiakim with his **father,** King Josiah. Josiah had done **what was right and just** and had **defended the . . . poor and needy.** These were actions God expected of the king. As God's shepherd he was expected to nurture the flock, not decimate it. However, Jehoiakim inherited none of his father's godly traits. He cared **only** for **dishonest gain,** bloodshed, **oppression, and extortion.**

**22:18-19.** Because of Jehoiakim's heavy-handed oppression, the people would **not mourn for him** at his death. Instead of the lavish funeral normally given a monarch, Jehoiakim, Jeremiah predicted, would **have the burial of a donkey.** When an animal died in the city it was simply **dragged away** from the spot where it died and **thrown outside the gates.** Jehoiakim's body would be treated with the same contempt. Jehoiakim died in late 598 B.C. as Nebuchadnezzar was advancing on Jerusalem to punish the city for rebellion. Perhaps, as some suppose, Jehoiakim was assassinated in an attempt to appease Nebuchadnezzar and spare the city. The new king, Jehoiachin, surrendered and was taken to Babylon; but the city was spared (2 Kings 24:1-17).

**22:20-23.** Because of Jehoiakim's foolishness Jeremiah called on the city of Jerusalem to lament her fate. This passage should probably be dated in late 598 or early 597 B.C. since it focused on the coming invasion of Babylon in retaliation for Jehoiakim's rebellion. Jerusalem's **cry** would be heard throughout the land. From **Lebanon** in the north to **Bashan** in the northeast to **Abarim** (the mountains in Moab; cf. Num. 27:12; Deut. 32:49; Ezek. 39:11) in the southeast the lament would sound as Judah's **allies** would be **crushed** by Babylon.

God had **warned** Jerusalem of the consequences of disobedience **when** she **felt secure,** but she refused to **listen.** Now she could only watch in sorrow as her **shepherds** (kings) were taken **away** and her **allies** (possibly the Egyptians) also faced **exile** (cf. 2 Kings 24:7). In an ironic twist Jeremiah referred to the inhabitants of Jerusalem as those **who live in "Lebanon."** So much cedar had been imported to Jerusalem from Lebanon (cf. Jer. 22:6-7, 13-15) that living in Jerusalem was like dwelling among Lebanon's cedars. Yet those living in these majestic **cedar buildings** would **groan** when the **pangs** of God's judgment came on them (on a woman's **labor** pains cf. comments on 4:31).

(4) The message to Jehoiachin (22:24-30). **22:24-27.** Jehoiachin followed his father **Jehoiakim** to the throne. After a three-month reign Jehoiachin surrendered to Nebuchadnezzar and was deported to Babylon where he lived the rest of his life (cf. 52:31-34). God indicated that even if Jehoiachin were as valuable to Him as **a signet ring,** He **would still pull** him **off** because of his sins. A signet ring was most valuable because it was used to impress its owner's signature or seal on various documents. **Even if . . . Jehoiachin** were this important to God (and the clear implication is that he was not), God would rather remove him than allow him to continue sinning. (For a reversal of this judgment see the promise to Zerubbabel in Hag. 2:21-23.)

God vowed to **hand** Jehoiachin **over to the Babylonians.** He and his **mother** would be cast **into another country** (Babylon) where they **both** would **die.** Jehoiachin's mother was Nehushta, the widow of King Jehoiakim (2 Kings 24:8). This is Jeremiah's second prophecy of their deportation (cf. Jer. 13:18-19).

**22:28-30.** By a series of questions, Jeremiah indicated that God was responsible for Jehoiachin's judgment. The first question should be answered no. The people did *not* despise Jehoiachin as a **broken,** unwanted **pot.** In fact some hoped he would be restored as king (28:1-4), and some considered him to be the king even after Zedekiah was placed on the throne (cf. comments on Ezek. 7:27). But if Jehoiachin was so popular, **why** would **he and his children** be removed from office and **cast into** a foreign nation? (On the words, **a land they do not know;** cf. Jer. 14:18; 15:2, 14; 16:13; 17:4.) The answer is that God was in control, and He was responsible for Jehoiachin's fall. God called on the **land** (repeated three times for emphasis; cf. 7:4) to **hear** His **word** of judgment. Though King Jehoiachin did have children (22:28; cf. 1 Chron. 3:17), he was to be *considered* **childless** because **none of**

his offspring would be allowed to **sit on the throne of David** to **rule** as king of **Judah.**

This prophecy had both immediate and long-range significance. No offspring of Jehoiachin followed him to the throne. His uncle, Zedekiah, who replaced Jehoiachin, was Judah's last king. God "pruned away" that portion of the line of David from the kingly line. This prophecy also helps explain the genealogies of Christ in Matthew 1 and Luke 3. Matthew presented the legal line of Christ through his stepfather, Joseph. However, Joseph's line came through Shealtiel who was a son of Jehoiachin (Jeconiah, Matt. 1:12; cf. 1 Chron. 3:17). Had Christ been a physical descendant of Joseph and not virgin-born, He would have been disqualified as Israel's King. Luke presented the physical line of Christ through Mary, who was descended from David through the line of his son Nathan (Luke 3:31). In that way Christ was not under the "curse" of Jehoiachin. (For additional information see comments on Matt. 1:2-17; Luke 3:24-38.)

(5) The message concerning the righteous Branch (23:1-8). **23:1-4.** Jeremiah summarized the unrighteous kings as being like **shepherds** who were **destroying and scattering** God's **sheep. The shepherds** deserved **punishment** because of **the evil** they had **done** (cf. Ezek. 34:1-10). But if God removed them, whom would He appoint to regather His sheep? Jeremiah gave a twofold answer. First, God Himself would **gather the remnant** of the people who were dispersed and would **bring them back.** He would assume responsibility for Israel's regathering (cf. Jer. 31:10; Micah 2:12; 5:4; 7:14). Second, God would raise up new **shepherds over them who** would **tend** and care for the people the way God intended.

**23:5-6.** The branch of David through Jehoiachin had been "cut off." However, God promised to **raise up to David** another King who would be **a righteous Branch,** that is, another member of the Davidic line. Jesus Christ is the fulfillment of this prediction. As **King,** He **will reign wisely** and will **do what is just and right** (in contrast with God's condemnation of Jehoiachin, 22:25). Though Christ offered Himself as Israel's Messiah at His First Advent, the final fulfillment of this prophecy awaits His Second Advent immediately before His millennial reign. At that time the Southern Kingdom (**Judah**) and the Northern Kingdom (**Israel**) will again be delivered (cf. Rom. 11:26) from oppression and reunited as a single nation and will **live in safety** (cf. Ezek. 37:15-28).

The **name** of this coming King will be **the LORD Our Righteousness** (*Yahweh ṣidqēnû*). Unlike Zedekiah (*ṣidqîyāhû*, "my righteousness is Yahweh"), this coming King will live up to His name as Israel's righteous God.

**23:7-8.** Having already mentioned the future restoration of Judah and Israel (v. 6), Jeremiah now said the restoration will be so dramatic that the **people will no longer** look back to the time when God **brought** them **up out of Egypt.** The first Exodus will pale in comparison with this new Exodus when God will bring **the descendants of Israel . . . out of all the countries where** they have been and will restore them to **their own land** (cf. 16:14-15).

*b. The rebuke of the false prophets (23:9-40)*

Jeremiah turned from addressing Judah's kings to deliver God's verbal broadside against the prophets. These pseudo-seers opposed Jeremiah's declaration of doom (cf. 6:13-14; 8:10-11; 14:14-16; 28:1-4, 10-11; 29:8-9, 20-23, 31-32) and offered in its place a promise of peace.

(1) The character of the false prophets (23:9-15). **23:9-12.** Jeremiah's **heart** was **broken** and his body became weak when he thought of God's **holy words.** A prophet was God's spokesman, and his life and message reflected on the One who sent him. Thus the false prophets were impugning God's name because they claimed that their message came from Him and that He had authorized them to speak (cf. 28:2, 15-16). God had shown His displeasure on the physical and spiritual adulteries being done in Judah by bringing His **curse** of drought (cf. Deut. 28:23-24) so that the **land** was **parched** and **withered** (cf. Jer. 14:1-6, 22). Yet, instead of calling Judah back to her covenant with God, **the prophets** continued to lead the people on **an evil course,** implying that God was not using the drought to judge people for their sin.

The basic flaw of all Judah's spiritual leaders (**both prophet and priest**) was that they were **godless** (*ḥānap*). This Hebrew word does not mean that these leaders did not believe in God. On the contrary, they were quite "religious." Rather, it means "to be polluted or profaned." Jeremiah had used the word earlier to describe the "defilement" of the land (cf. 3:1-2, 9). These leaders had such a low view of God's holy character that they would even pollute His **temple** with **their wickedness.** Because of their sin God vowed to **bring disaster on them.**

**23:13-15.** Jeremiah compared **the prophets of Samaria** (v. 13) to **the prophets of Jerusalem** (v. 14). The prophets of the Northern Kingdom of Israel ("Samaria") had **prophesied by Baal** and **led** the nation **astray** (cf. 1 Kings 18:16-40; 2 Kings 10:18-29; 17:16). Because of their wickedness, God destroyed the Northern Kingdom.

The prophets of Judah followed in the same paths of sin. They continued to **commit adultery** and support **evildoers.** Their conduct was so repulsive that both they and the people of Jerusalem had become **like Sodom** and **Gomorrah** before God. The only alternative available to God was to judge them for their sin. God would **make** the false prophets **eat bitter food** (*la'ănâh*, "wormwood"; cf. Jer. 9:15; Lam. 3:15, 19) **and drink poisoned water.**

(2) The message of the false prophets (23:16-40). **23:16-22.** The message delivered by the false **prophets** was one of their own making. Their **visions** came **from their own minds** (cf. v. 26) instead of **from** God's **mouth.** They proclaimed **peace** (cf. 6:14; 8:11) and **no harm,** but they did not **hear** this **word** from God. God's message was that **a whirlwind** would destroy those in its path. God said His **anger** would **not turn back until** He had finished His judgment. Only then would the people **understand . . . clearly** that God had **not** sent **these prophets.** Had they been from God (cf. **council** in 23:18) **they would have proclaimed** His **words** to turn Judah **from** her **evil deeds.**

**23:23-32.** The false prophets misunderstood the character of God. He was not some localized God from whom a prophet could **hide** so God could not **see** him. Indeed, God in His omniscience fills **heaven and earth** so that no place is outside His realm. He had **heard what the prophets** said when they spoke **lies in** His **name.**

The prophets claimed that God had given them revelation in **a dream,** but their visions were only **delusions of their own minds** (cf. v. 16). These dreams were designed to **make** Judah **forget** God's **name** much as earlier prophets did **through Baal worship** (cf. v. 13). Their "dreams" were as worthless for meeting spiritual needs as was **straw** for meeting physical hunger. Their words had no force, while God's Word is as penetrating as **fire** (cf. 20:9) and as effective as **a hammer that breaks a rock in pieces.** Nothing can prevent God's Word from being fulfilled.

Because God had not spoken to these false **prophets** they were forced to **steal from one another** as they pronounced plagiarized prophecies that were **supposedly from** Him. God set Himself **against** those **prophets** because they were leading the **people astray with . . . reckless lies,** falsely claiming God's authority.

**23:33-40.** The people of Jerusalem were asking one another, **What is the oracle of the LORD?** The word "oracle" (*maśśā'*, from the verb *nāśā'*) means "to lift, carry, take" (see comments on Zech. 9:1). The noun referred to the load or burden that someone had to lift or carry (Ex. 23:5; Neh. 13:19). The "burden" the prophet had to carry was the message or oracle "laid on his heart" by God (Isa. 13:1; 14:28; Nahum 1:1; Hab. 1:1). Often the message was one of judgment (cf. Isa. 15:1; 17:1; 19:1; 21:1, 11, 13; 22:1; 23:1).

When the people sought for an oracle from God, Jeremiah was to announce that there was none. It had already been given; and the word from God was that He would **forsake** them. God said He would **punish** those who claimed any other **oracle.** The people were misusing the term so much in claiming divine authority for their own words that God told them **not** to **mention** the word **again.** Its misuse had caused the people to **distort the** true **words of the living God.** Those who continued to claim divine oracles would be judged. **God** vowed to **cast** them **out of** His **presence along with** the rest of Jerusalem. These false prophets faced the threat of unending **disgrace** and **shame** for their wicked words.

## c. The two baskets of figs (chap. 24)

(1) The vision of the two baskets of figs. **24:1-3.** The vision of the two baskets of figs was given Jeremiah **after Jehoiachin** and the other leaders of Jerusalem **were carried into exile** by the Babylonians (cf. 2 Kings 24:8-16). Thus this prophecy can be dated sometime in 597 B.C. at the beginning of the reign of Zedekiah. In the vision Jeremiah saw **two baskets of figs** that had been **placed in front of the temple.** The vision called to mind the offering of the firstfruits in a basket before **the LORD** (cf. Deut. 26:11). In **one** of the baskets the **figs** were **very good** and resembled **those that ripen early** (cf. Isa. 28:4; Hosea 9:10; Micah 7:1)—those firstfruits that were to be offered to God (Deut. 14:22). The second basket contained **very poor figs** that had deteriorated to the point where **they could not be eaten.** Such offerings were unacceptable to **the LORD** (cf. Mal. 1:6-9).

(2) The explanation of the good figs. **24:4-7. God** said the **good figs** represented **the exiles from Judah** who had been carried away to Babylon. This was a surprising answer because the people of Jerusalem believed that those in captivity had been taken away from **the LORD** (cf. Ezek. 11:14-15). Yet God promised to **watch over** the remnant in captivity and **bring them back** to the land (cf. Ezek. 11:16-17). He also promised to **give them a new heart** so they will **know** Him (cf. Jer. 4:22). At that time **they will be** His **people** (cf. comments on 30:22) and **will return** to Him **with all their heart.** Though God did restore a minority of the people to the land after the Babylonian Captivity, they never experienced the full blessings of fellowship promised by God (cf. 31:31-34; Ezek. 36:24-32). This awaits a still-future fulfillment when God again will regather Israel at the beginning of Christ's millennial reign on earth (Matt. 24:29-31).

(3) The explanation of the poor figs. **24:8-10.** The **poor figs** represented **Zedekiah** and the other **survivors** (cf. 29:17-19), including those in Israel and those who fled to **Egypt** (cf. 43:4-7). God vowed to **make them abhorrent . . . to all the kingdoms of the earth.** They would be ridiculed and cursed **wherever** they went. (Several times in the Book of Jer. the prophet predicted that the people would be cursed, ridiculed, and/or re-

proached and that others would be horrified at their desolate condition; cf. 25:9, 18; 26:6; 29:18; 42:18; 44:8, 12, 22. Also note 48:39; 49:13, 17; 51:37, about other countries.) God would send His instruments of judgment (**sword, famine, and plague;** cf. 14:12; 15:2-4) **until they** were all **destroyed.** These survivors had felt blessed of God, but in reality they were cursed.

## d. The 70-year Captivity in Babylon (chap. 25)

Jeremiah's 13 messages of judgment (chaps. 2–25) were arranged topically, not chronologically. Chapter 25 was placed last because it served as the capstone for all Jeremiah's previous messages.

(1) Warnings ignored (25:1-7). **25:1-3.** Jeremiah's final message concerned **all the people of Judah.** Because of the significance of the message, the time when it was given was recorded. It was delivered **in the fourth year of Jehoiakim . . . which was the first year of Nebuchadnezzar.** This has caused some confusion because the "first year" of Nebuchadnezzar's reign (after his accession year) would have begun on April 2, 604 B.C., while Jehoiakim's fourth year (using the Nisan [March-April]-to-Nisan dating system that Jeremiah usually employed) would have extended from April 12 (Nisan 1), 605 B.C. to April 2 (Nisan 1), 604 B.C. (not April 11, 604 B.C. because of the lunar calendar). So the two dates (Nebuchadnezzar's first year and Jehoiakim's fourth year) do not seem to occur in the same calendar year.

Two possible solutions have been suggested. First, it is possible that the word "first" (*ri'šōnî*) should be translated "beginning." This word is not the normal word used to describe the first year of a king's reign (cf. Jack Finegan, *Handbook of Bible Chronology.* Princeton, N.J.: Princeton University Press, 1964, p. 202). Thus the "beginning" year of Nebuchadnezzar could be equated with his accession year. This would place Jeremiah's prophecy sometime between September 7, 605 B.C. when Nebuchadnezzar ascended the throne and April 2, 604 B.C. when the first full year of his reign officially began.

Second, possibly Jeremiah was here using a Tishri (September-October)-to-

Tishri dating system for Jehoiakim. Thus Jehoiakim's fourth year extended from October 7 (Tishri 1), 605 B.C. to September 26 (Tishri 1), 604 B.C. (not October 6, 604 B.C. because of the lunar calendar). In this case Jeremiah's prophecy would have been given sometime between April 2, 604 B.C. (the start of Nebuchadnezzar's first full year) and September 25, 604 B.C. (the end of Jehoiakim's fourth year). Either solution allows the text to stand as it is written.

**Jeremiah** had been prophesying **for 23 years** (cf. 1:2)—a ministry that had spanned the reigns of three kings at the time of this prophecy. But though **Jeremiah** had **spoken to** the people **again and again,** they had **not listened** to his warnings to repent. God had given ample time for them to respond, but they refused.

**25:4-7.** God had also **sent** other **prophets** who warned the people to **turn** from their **evil ways** and **practices.** Had the people heeded the prophets' warnings, God would have graciously let them **stay in the land** and He would **not** have harmed them. Unfortunately the people **did not listen to** God. They continued in their idolatry and **brought harm to** themselves.

(2) Judgment described (25:8-14). **25:8-11.** **Because** the people had repeatedly rejected God's warnings, God would **summon** the Babylonians (**the peoples of the north;** cf. comments on 1:14). Their leader, **Nebuchadnezzar,** was called God's **servant** in the sense that he would do God's bidding in coming to destroy Jerusalem. God would use the Babylonians to **completely destroy** both Judah and her allies. **The sounds of joy and gladness** would cease (cf. 7:34; 16:9) in the nation because the **whole country** would **become a desolate wasteland** when **Babylon** was finished. God would deport Judah and the other rebellious people to **Babylon** to **serve** the Babylonians **70 years.**

Why did God predict that the Babylonian Exile would last 70 years? (605–536 B.C.) The answer seems to be that this was the number of years that the people had failed to observe God's Law of a "Sabbath rest" for the land. God had decreed that every seventh year the land was to lie fallow (Lev. 25:3-5). The people were not to sow their fields or prune

their vineyards. If the people would fail to follow this command, God would remove them from the land to enforce this "Sabbath rest" (Lev. 26:33-35). The writer of 2 Chronicles indicated that the 70-year Babylonian Captivity promised by Jeremiah allowed the land to enjoy its "Sabbath rest" (2 Chron. 36:20-21). Therefore the Captivity lasted 70 years probably because this was the number of Sabbath rests that had not been observed for the land.

**25:12-14.** After **the 70 years** were **fulfilled** God would also **punish . . . the Babylonians** because of the **guilt** they had incurred. He would fulfill **all the things . . . written in** Jeremiah's **book** against **Babylon.** The material to which God alluded is in chapters 50–51. Evidently at least part of chapters 50–51 was written about the same time as chapter 25. God would **repay** Babylon **according to** her **deeds.**

(3) Wrath promised (25:15-29). **25:15-26.** Jeremiah had a vision of **the LORD** holding in His **hand** a **cup.** The cup was **filled** with God's **wrath.** Jeremiah's task was to **make all the nations to whom** he was sent **drink it** (cf. Lam. 4:21; Ezek. 23:31-33; Rev. 16:19; 18:6). The first ones to drink of this bitter brew, God's "grapes of wrath," were **Jerusalem and the towns of Judah.**

Other nations would follow Judah in judgment. (For the locations of many of these nations see the map "The World of Jeremiah and Ezekiel," in the *Introduction.*) These included **Egypt,** whose feeble assistance prompted Judah to rebel against Babylon (cf. Ezek. 29:6-9). The location of **Uz** is somewhat uncertain, but it was probably east of Edom in northern Arabia (cf. comments on Job. 1:1). **The Philistines** occupied the coastal region on the shore of the Mediterranean just west of Judah, while **Edom, Moab, and Ammon** (listed from south to north) were the three nations just east of Judah on the other side of the Jordan River and the Dead Sea. Both **Tyre and Sidon** were north of Judah on the Mediterranean coast. **Dedan, Tema,** and **Buz** were cities in the northern part of the Arabian Peninsula, but the exact location of Buz is unknown. They are associated with **the kings of Arabia** who were bedouins **in the desert.** The identification of **Zimri** is uncertain, but it is associated with **Elam** and **Media** which were two countries east of the Tigris River. All these nations were conquered by Babylon.

All these nations would be judged at the hand of Babylon; but **after all of them,** God would make **the king of Sheshach . . . drink it too.** Who or what is Sheshach? Most scholars believe that the word is a cryptogram or *atbash* for Babylon. An *atbash* was a code in which the letters of a name counted from the end of the alphabet are substituted for the letters counted from the beginning. For example, in English the letter "z" would replace the letter "a," the letter "y" would replace the letter "b," etc. The word "Abby" as an *atbash* would become "zyyb." If "Sheshach" (*ššk*) is a Hebrew *atbash* the consonants become *bbl,* which is the spelling for Babylon (cf. Jer. 25:1). God would judge Babylon after judging the other nations. Because he had mentioned Babylon's judgment already (cf. vv. 12-14), it is unclear why Jeremiah would put such a message in code. Still this seems to be the best explanation of Sheshach.

**25:27-29.** The nations who **drink** from the cup of God's wrath will fall. Like a man who has become **drunk,** they will **vomit and fall.** Yet this collapse will be caused by **the sword** rather than strong drink. Some nations might try to **refuse** judgment, but God would make them partake of it. If God would **bring disaster on** His own **city** because of its sin, how could these heathen nations hope to **go unpunished?**

(4) Universal judgment affirmed (25:30-38). **25:30-33.** Switching from prose to poetry, Jeremiah continued the theme of God's judgment on the nations. Like a lion that would **roar mightily** before pouncing on its prey (cf. Amos 1:2; 3:4, 8), so God would shout **from His holy dwelling,** heaven, **against all who live on the earth.** God intended to **bring charges** (*rîb;* cf. comments on Jer. 2:9) **against** these **nations.** His **judgment** would extend beyond Judah to **all mankind.** This judgment was pictured as **a mighty storm** that would envelop all nations. In its wake the **slain** would be scattered **everywhere.** Their corpses would be **like refuse lying on the ground** in the same way that Judah's dead had remained unburied (cf. 8:2; 14:16; 16:4-6).

**25:34-38.** The **leaders of** these many nations (pictured as **shepherds**) would **weep and wail** and **roll in the dust** (signs of deep grief or mourning; cf. 6:26; Micah 1:10). They were mourning for their own lives because the **time** had **come** for them **to be slaughtered.** By briefly shifting his imagery from shepherds to pottery Jeremiah pictured the total destruction of these **leaders.** They would be **shattered** in pieces **like** a piece of **fine pottery** dropped on the floor. Jeremiah then returned to the pastoral image to complete his picture. The leaders (**shepherds**) would try **to flee,** but would have **no place to escape.** God would destroy **their** land (**pasture**) and would prowl around **like a lion** among the sheep (cf. Jer. 25:30). The **land** of all these nations would **become desolate.**

### B. Personal conflict with Judah (chaps. 26–29)

Though Jeremiah did record some opposition to his message (cf. 11:18-23; 15:10; 20:1-6), that was not his main point in chapters 1–25. The focus in those chapters was on God's coming judgment if the people refused to repent. But in chapters 26–29 Jeremiah zeroed in on the people's response to his message. Both he and his message were rejected by the leaders and the people.

1. CONFLICT WITH THE PEOPLE (CHAP. 26)

*a. Jeremiah's message (26:1-6)*

**26:1-3.** Jeremiah indicated that **this** message was delivered **early in the reign** of King **Jehoiakim.** Since Jehoiakim ascended the throne in 609 B.C., a date of 609–608 B.C. for this event seems probable. The message itself should probably be associated with the "temple address" of chapters 7–10. In those chapters Jeremiah focused on the content of the message, while in this chapter he focused on the response to the message. The purpose of the message was to get **the people** to **listen** to God's threatened judgment so they would **each . . . turn from his evil way.** If the people would repent, God promised that He would **not bring on them the disaster** He was **planning** (cf. 7:3-7).

**26:4-6.** The content of the message was one of judgment for disobedience. If the people refused to **follow** God's **Law** and to **listen to** God's **servants the prophets** (cf. 7:21-26), God would make the temple (**this house**) as desolate as the tabernacle that once stood at **Shiloh** (cf. 7:14). Also people would curse the **city** of Jerusalem (cf. comments on 24:9).

### b. Jeremiah's arrest and trial (26:7-15)

**26:7-11.** In chapters 7–10 Jeremiah did not record the response of the crowds to his message. When **the priests, the prophets, and all the people** who were in the temple courts **heard** Jeremiah's **words,** they **seized him** just as he finished his message and demanded that he **must die** for his words. The charge brought against **Jeremiah** was that he was a false prophet because he had claimed **in the Lord's name that** the temple and the **city** would become **desolate and deserted.** Obviously they believed that such a prophecy could never come from God.

The charges against Jeremiah had to be "tried in court," so Judah's **officials** (śārîm, lit., "princes," probably the high officials of the king; cf. 36:11-12) heard the case **at the entrance of the New Gate.** The city gate was where the leaders sat to administer justice and to conduct official business (cf. Deut. 21:18-19; Ruth 4:1-11; Jer. 39:3). The mob charged that Jeremiah **should be sentenced to death.** His crime was that he had **prophesied against** the **city** of Jerusalem.

**26:12-15.** Jeremiah gave a threefold defense on his own behalf. First, he announced that **the Lord** had **sent** him to deliver the message they had **heard.** He was not a false prophet. Second, he announced that his message was conditional. If the people would **reform** their **ways** (cf. 3:12; 7:3) God promised **not to bring** about **the disaster.** Thus Jeremiah's message did offer some hope for the city. Third, Jeremiah warned that if they **put** him **to death** they would **bring the guilt of innocent blood on** themselves. They would be guilty in God's sight of murdering an innocent man.

### c. Jeremiah's deliverance (26:16-24)

**26:16-19.** After hearing the case **the officials** along with **all the people** sided with Jeremiah against the religious establishment (**the priests and** false **prophets**). They declared that Jeremiah **should not be sentenced to death.** This verdict was supported by some **elders** who quoted from the Prophet **Micah.** By quoting

from Micah 3:12 they indicated that Micah had made similar statements against the city and **the temple** nearly 70 years earlier. Yet instead of seeking to **put** Micah **to death,** King **Hezekiah** listened to Micah's words and sought the **favor** of **the Lord.** In response to Hezekiah's request God **did not bring the disaster** predicted by Micah. Failure to follow Hezekiah's example was **to bring a terrible disaster on** Judah.

**26:20-23.** Though Jeremiah was spared, other prophets were not so fortunate. Another prophet during this time was **Uriah son of Shemaiah.** Nothing is known about this man apart from his hometown (**Kiriath Jearim**). He **prophesied the same things . . . as Jeremiah;** but when **the king** heard about it, he decided **to put** Uriah **to death.** Uriah was informed of the plot and **fled . . . to Egypt.** The king **sent** a delegation **to Egypt** to extradite him back to Judah. The delegation was led by **Elnathan son of Acbor.** Elnathan was one of the officials who heard the reading of Jeremiah's scroll (cf. 36:11-12), and his father, Acbor, may have been an earlier official of King Josiah (2 Kings 22:12-14). Uriah was convicted of treason and killed by **a sword.** He was given an ignoble burial, **his body** being **thrown into the burial place of the common people** (cf. 2 Kings 23:6).

**26:24.** **Jeremiah** had the support of **Ahikam son of Shaphan** who prevented the people from having Jeremiah **put to death.** The family of Shaphan played an important part in the final years of Judah (see the chart "The Line of Shaphan"). Shaphan was King Josiah's secretary who reported the finding of the Law to Josiah (2 Kings 22:3-13). Shaphan had at least four sons—three of whom were mentioned in a positive way by Jeremiah (Ahikam, Gemariah, and Elasah). The fourth son, Jaazaniah, was the "black sheep" of the family; his presence among the idol-worshipers in the temple caught Ezekiel by surprise (Ezek. 8:11). Ahikam's son, Gedaliah, was appointed governor of Judah by Nebuchadnezzar after the fall of Jerusalem in 586 B.C.

### 2. CONFLICT WITH THE FALSE PROPHETS IN JERUSALEM (CHAPS. 27–28)

### a. Jeremiah's prophecy (chap. 27)

(1) The message to the ambassadors (27:1-11). **27:1-7.** The events of chapter 27

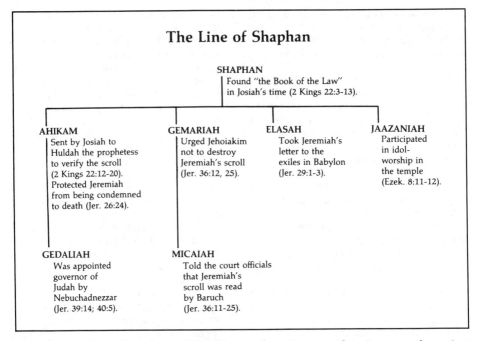

## The Line of Shaphan

**SHAPHAN**
Found "the Book of the Law"
in Josiah's time (2 Kings 22:3-13).

**AHIKAM**
Sent by Josiah to
Huldah the prophetess
to verify the scroll
(2 Kings 22:12-20).
Protected Jeremiah
from being condemned
to death (Jer. 26:24).

**GEMARIAH**
Urged Jehoiakim
not to destroy
Jeremiah's scroll
(Jer. 36:12, 25).

**ELASAH**
Took Jeremiah's
letter to the
exiles in Babylon
(Jer. 29:1-3).

**JAAZANIAH**
Participated
in idol-
worship in
the temple
(Ezek. 8:11-12).

**GEDALIAH**
Was appointed
governor of
Judah by
Nebuchadnezzar
(Jer. 39:14; 40:5).

**MICAIAH**
Told the court officials
that Jeremiah's
scroll was read
by Baruch
(Jer. 36:11-25).

took place **early in the reign of Zedekiah.** There is a textual problem here, and most Hebrew manuscripts name Jehoiakim (cf. KJV; NIV marg.) rather than Zedekiah. However, the internal evidence indicates that the chapter was written during the time of Zedekiah instead of Jehoiakim. Zedekiah is named as the king of Judah in verses 3 and 12, and 28:1 indicates that the prophecy of chapter 27 was given while he was king. Why then did most Hebrew manuscripts name Jehoiakim in this verse? No doubt it resulted from a later scribe's error in copying the manuscript. It is possible that a scribe mistakenly recopied 26:1 at the beginning of chapter 27. If so, the Septuagint (which omits 27:1) is preserving the text of the original manuscript. Or possibly a later scribe intentionally changed the king's name in 27:1 to make it conform to 26:1.

God commanded **Jeremiah** to **make a yoke** like those used to hitch together teams of oxen and to **put it on** his **neck. Then** he sent **word to the . . . envoys who** were in **Jerusalem** to meet with **Zedekiah.** These delegates were from **Edom, Moab,** and **Ammon** to the east of Judah and from **Tyre and Sidon,** Phoenician cities to the north. What were these delegates doing in Jerusalem? Most likely they were there to discuss the possibility

of uniting together in a revolt against Babylon. This meeting occurred sometime between May and August 593 B.C. (cf. 28:1). The Babylonian Chronicle recorded that just over a year earlier a rebellion had occurred in Babylon. Evidently Nebuchadnezzar had to defend himself against an attempted coup. Certainly such unrest within Babylon would cause the various vassal states to evaluate their chances of success for throwing off Babylon's yoke of domination.

Jeremiah's public pronouncement dashed any hope the delegates might have had of keeping their meeting secret. God's message was that He had **made the earth** and all life **on it** so He could **give it to anyone** He pleased. The one selected by God to subdue all nations was **Nebuchadnezzar king of Babylon.** God announced that **all nations** would **serve** Babylon until its **time** to be judged came. Only then would others be able to **subjugate** Babylon.

**27:8-11.** With the fact of Nebuchadnezzar's divine appointment clearly established, Jeremiah warned the ambassadors not to rebel. **Any nation** that refused to **bow its neck under** Babylon's **yoke** would be punished by **sword, famine, and plague** from God (cf. v. 13, and comments on 14:12). For the first of three times in chapter 27 Jeremiah warned his audience **not** to **listen to** the false **prophets** (cf. vv. 14, 16). Because he was addressing the representatives of heathen nations in verses 8-11, he also warned against listening to the methods of divination they might use to receive an answer. (On the word **diviners**; cf. 29:8 and see comments on *qāsam* in Deut. 18:10.) These false religious leaders were speaking **lies** when they promised a successful rebellion against Babylon because God vowed to **remove** any **nation** who rebelled. Only those nations that would submit to the authority of **Babylon** would be allowed to **remain in** their **own** lands.

(2) The message to Zedekiah. **27:12-15.** Jeremiah delivered **the same message** to the **king of Judah.** Again the prophet's word contained two parts. The first part was God's command to Zedekiah to **bow** his **neck under** Babylon's **yoke** and to continue to **serve** Babylon as a vassal king. If he refused to serve Babylon, the judgment God had **threatened** would come on Judah. The second part of Jeremiah's message was a warning not to trust **the** false **prophets.** Those predicting victory were **prophesying lies** because God had **not sent them.**

(3) The message to the priests and people. **27:16-22.** Jeremiah modified his message to **the priests** and the masses. He cautioned them **not** to **listen to the prophets.** These false prophets were predicting that **the articles from the LORD's house** that had been taken to Babylon (cf. 2 Kings 24:13; Dan. 1:1-2) would **soon** be **brought back.** In fact just the opposite would happen. The **furnishings** still **remaining in the house of the LORD** (along with those of the king's **palace**) which had not been removed during the deportation of **Jehoiachin** would **remain** in **Babylon** until God's judgment was complete. Only then would He **bring them back** (cf. 2 Kings 25:13-17; Ezra 1:7-11).

b. *Hananiah's opposition (chap. 28)*

(1) Jeremiah's conflict with Hananiah (28:1-11). **28:1-4.** Chapter 28 is a continuation of chapter 27. The specific time when Jeremiah gave his message was not given (cf. 27:1), but the exact month and year that his opponent spoke was recorded. It was **the fifth month** of **the fourth year** of King **Zedekiah.** The date was August-September 593 B.C. Jeremiah was careful in noting the date because of the

events that happened later (cf. 28:17).

Jeremiah's message was challenged by **Hananiah son of Azzur.** Perhaps Hananiah was a brother of "Jaazaniah son of Azzur" who was denounced by Ezekiel (Ezek. 11:1-3). Hananiah **was from Gibeon,** about six miles northwest of Jerusalem. Gibeon was another town that Joshua had assigned to the priests (cf. Josh. 21:17-18), so perhaps Hananiah, like Jeremiah, was from a priestly family.

Hananiah's message directly contradicted Jeremiah's prophecy. He stated that **God** promised to **break the yoke** of Babylonian oppression. So Hananiah was urging Judah and the nations to rebel against Babylon, not to submit to her (cf. Jer. 27:2, 8, 11-12, 17). Hananiah promised that the rebellion would be followed by restoration. **Within two years,** he said, God promised to **bring back** to Judah **all the articles of the LORD's house** (cf. 27:16-22). These would be accompanied by **Jehoiachin** and **all the other exiles.**

**28:5-11.** Two prophets had made conflicting claims, each one attributing his message to God. Though **Jeremiah** could have wished that **the LORD** would **fulfill the words** of Hananiah, **nevertheless** Hananiah's prophecy was false. The ultimate test for prophets was whether their prophecies were fulfilled. A **prophet** was known to be **sent by** God **only if his prediction** came **true** (cf. Deut. 18:20-22). Time would tell whether Jeremiah or Hananiah was the false prophet.

As if to convince the people that he was right, **Hananiah took the yoke off** Jeremiah's **neck** (cf. Jer. 27:2) **and broke it** apart. This dramatically visualized his prophecy that God would **break the yoke of Nebuchadnezzar . . . within two years.** Rather than opposing this open insult from Hananiah, **Jeremiah went on his way.**

(2) Jeremiah's message to Hananiah (28:12-17). **28:12-14.** God's word came to Jeremiah **shortly after . . . Hananiah** broke Jeremiah's **yoke.** God's message used Hananiah's actions to show the harshness of the coming judgment. **Hananiah** had **broken a wooden yoke, but** God would replace it with **a yoke of iron** that could not be broken. This **iron yoke,** figuratively speaking, would be fastened to **the necks of all these nations** who gathered in Jerusalem (27:3) to force

them to **serve Nebuchadnezzar.**

**28:15-17.** After answering Hananiah's predictions (vv. 12-14) **Jeremiah** attacked Hananiah's credentials as a **prophet.** God had **not sent** Hananiah as His spokesman, but through his eloquent speech he had **persuaded** the **nation** of Judah **to trust in lies.** As a judgment on **Hananiah** (and as a proof that Jeremiah was the true prophet of God) God said He would **remove** Hananiah **from the face of the earth.** His death would expose him as a false prophet. To emphasize the divine origin of this judgment, Jeremiah indicated that Hananiah's death would happen that **very year.** It was already the fifth month (28:1), so within the next seven months Hananiah would die. This was why Jeremiah took special care to state the exact month in verse 1. God fulfilled His word, and **in the seventh month**—less than two months after Jeremiah's prediction—**Hananiah . . . died.** God vindicated His true prophet, Jeremiah, and judged the false prophet, **Hananiah.**

3. CONFLICT WITH THE FALSE PROPHETS IN EXILE (CHAP. 29)

a. *Jeremiah's first letter to the exiles (29:1-23)*

(1) The introduction. **29:1-3. Jeremiah** inserted **the text of the letter** that he **sent** to those who had been **carried into exile from Jerusalem.** He identified the deportation as the one associated with the removal of **King Jehoiachin and the queen mother** (cf. 2 Kings 24:8-17; Jer. 13:18; 22:24-27; Dan. 1:1-2). This deportation occurred in 597 B.C., so Jeremiah's letter must have been written after that date.

(2) The announcement of a long exile (29:4-14). **29:4-9.** God's word to the exiles was to prepare for a long stay in **Babylon.** They were to **build houses and settle down.** They were also to **plant gardens** to sustain them during the period. Life was to go on as normal. The people were exhorted to **marry and have sons and daughters.** Instead of hoping for Babylon's quick demise they were encouraged to **seek** its **peace and prosperity.** Jeremiah even told them to **pray . . . for** Babylon! Those **prophets and diviners** (cf. 27:9) who were predicting a soon return to Judah were **prophesying lies.** They were **not sent** by God.

**29:10-14.** The restoration of the exiles to Judah would happen only **when** God's **70 years** of judgment were **completed** (cf. 25:11-12). Then God would **fulfill** His **gracious promise to** restore the exiles to their land. The 70-year Exile was a part of God's **plans** to give Judah **hope and a future.** The judgment prompted the exiles to **seek** God wholeheartedly (cf. Dan. 9:2-3, 15-19). Once they had turned back to their God He would **gather** them **from all the nations where** they had been **banished** and return them to their land. The larger purpose of the Exile was to force Israel back to her God (cf. Deut. 30:1-10).

(3) The warning against false prophets (29:15-23). **29:15-19.** The people disbelieved Jeremiah's message because it contradicted the message of the false Jewish **prophets . . . in Babylon.** Evidently these prophets were proclaiming the safety of Jerusalem and the swift return of those in captivity (cf. 28:2-4). Jeremiah shattered their optimistic forecasts by announcing that those who had **not** been exiled were destined for **the sword, famine, and plague** (cf. comments on 14:12). He shared with the exiles his vision of the two baskets of figs (cf. 24:1-2). Those remaining in Jerusalem were **like poor figs that** had to be thrown out. God would judge them for refusing to obey His words of warning (cf. 24:8-9). Unfortunately the **exiles** had **not listened** to God's words of warning **either.**

**29:20-23.** Jeremiah singled out two men who were evidently the ringleaders of the false prophets in Babylon. They were **Ahab son of Koliah and Zedekiah son of Maaseiah.** Nothing else is known about these men, but they were **prophesying lies** (v. 21) to the people and committing **adultery with their neighbors' wives** (v. 23). Such brazen lies and sinful actions would not go unpunished.

God vowed to judge these false prophets by handing **them over to Nebuchadnezzar.** Evidently they were predicting Nebuchadnezzar's and Babylon's downfall (cf. 28:2), and Nebuchadnezzar would hear of their rebellious remarks. He would **put them to death before the very eyes** of the exiles, to serve as an object lesson on the danger of fomenting rebellion. They were executed by being **burned** (*qālâh*, lit., "to roast") **in the fire,** a form of punishment often used in Babylon (cf. Dan. 3:6, 11, 15, 17, 19-23). Their death by fire would give rise to a **curse** that would be used by the captives. The curse probably developed as a play on words because the word for "curse" (*qᵉlālâh*) is similar to the word for "burned" (*qālâh*).

### b. Jeremiah's second letter to the exiles (29:24-32)

(1) The report of Shemaiah's letter to Jerusalem. **29:24-29.** The sequence of events is somewhat confusing here. Evidently after Jeremiah's first letter to the exiles (vv. 1-23) another prophet in Babylon, Shemaiah, wrote the leaders in Jerusalem urging them to punish Jeremiah (vv. 25-28). However, the letter was read to Jeremiah (v. 29) who then wrote a second letter to the exiles. He quoted the text of Shemaiah's letter (vv. 24-28) and delivered God's word of judgment against the false prophet (vv. 29-32).

**Shemaiah sent letters in his own name** to **Zephaniah son of Maaseiah** who had been **appointed** as **the priest** who was **in charge of the** temple. Possibly this Zephaniah was a brother of the false Prophet Zedekiah, who was in Babylon (assuming that Maaseiah, the name of each of their fathers, refers to the same man; cf. v. 21). Shemaiah exhorted **Zephaniah** that as guardian of the temple precincts he was to **put any madman who** was acting **like a prophet** (he was referring to Jeremiah) **into the stocks and neck-irons** (cf. 20:1-3). Shemaiah was upset that Zephaniah had **not reprimanded Jeremiah** for posing **as a prophet.** He cited the contents of Jeremiah's first letter to the exiles as proof that Jeremiah should be disciplined. But instead of attacking Jeremiah, **Zephaniah . . . read the letter** from Shemaiah to him. Evidently Zephaniah at this time accepted Jeremiah's authority as a prophet. He later consulted Jeremiah twice on behalf of King Zedekiah (cf. 21:1; 37:3). Zephaniah was captured and killed by Nebuchadnezzar after the fall of Jerusalem (52:24-27).

(2) The condemnation of Shemaiah. **29:30-32.** Under God's guidance **Jeremiah** sent a second **message to all the exiles** (cf. v. 1). This letter contained God's judgment against **Shemaiah** for claiming to be His prophet. God would **punish** both **Shemaiah . . . and his descendants.** Neither he nor his family would live to **see the good things** God promised

to **do for** His **people.** These "good things" are explained in chapters 30–33. **Shemaiah** forfeited his right to take part in these blessings because, by urging those in Jerusalem to oppose Jeremiah, he had **preached rebellion against** God.

### C. Future comfort for Israel and Judah (chaps. 30–33)

God had threatened Judah with judgment for her disobedience, but the nation refused to mend her ways. The stage was set and the curtain was about to rise on the final act of Judah's history as a nation. But before this sad scene of suffering started to unfold, Jeremiah inserted "The Book of Consolation," a collection of prophecies that offered hope in desperate times. These prophecies looked beyond Judah's imminent collapse and pointed to a new age when Israel and Judah would be returned to their land, reunited as a nation, and restored to their God.

1. THE RESTORATION OF ISRAEL AND JUDAH DECLARED (CHAPS. 30–31)

### a. The nation's physical deliverance (30:1-11)

(1) The nation's restoration to the land. **30:1-3.** God told **Jeremiah** to **write** His promises of comfort **in a book** so they would be available to the exiles after Jerusalem fell. This book would declare a note of hope that **the days are coming . . . when** God **will . . . restore** His **people.** Jeremiah's use of "the days" was significant because it described two different periods of time. The first "day" to which Jeremiah pointed was the day of destruction when God would judge Judah for her sin (cf. 5:18; 7:32; 9:25; 19:6). This day was fulfilled when Judah fell to Babylon. However, the second "day" to which Jeremiah pointed was a day of restoration when God will bring the nations of Judah and Israel into a new relationship with Him and when He will set straight His accounts with the Gentile nations (cf. 3:16, 18; 16:14; 23:5, 7, 20; 30:3, 24; 31:27, 29, 31, 33, 38; 33:14-16; 48:12, 47; 49:2, 39; 50:4, 20; 51:47, 52). This day has an eschatological perspective. It is the day when God will fulfill the blessings of restoration promised in Deuteronomy 30:1-10. However, as in all prophetic material one must keep in mind the principle of "foreshortening." That is, though Jeremiah saw all these predic-

tions as one continuous series of events, they were fulfilled over a long period, with intervening gaps of time. Thus, for example, prophecies about the suffering Messiah and the ruling Messiah appear together though they describe two different Advents of Christ (e.g., Isa. 9:6-7; 61:1-2). In the same way Jeremiah described the restoration of Judah after the Babylonian Captivity and the still-future restoration of Judah within some of the same passages. Therefore one should be cautious in interpreting the various parts of Jeremiah's predictions concerning "the coming days."

God's first promise was to **bring** the nations of **Israel and Judah back from captivity**. God promised to **restore them to the land** He had given them (cf. Deut. 30:3-5). This promised return of both the Northern and Southern Kingdoms served as an introduction to these chapters and provided hope to those who would soon be dispossessed from their land.

(2) The nation's distress. **30:4-7.** The return of **Israel and Judah** to the land will be preceded by a time of national distress. **Cries of fear** and **terror** will be **heard** among these captives instead of cries of **peace**. Jeremiah compared the anguish of men clutching themselves in fear to **a woman in labor** (cf. 4:31; 6:24; 13:21; 22:23; 49:24; 50:43). The coming calamity will be so **awful** that **none will be like it** in comparison. Jeremiah characterized it as **a time of trouble**. Yet all will not be lost because God guaranteed that the nation **will be saved out of it**. God will rescue His people in the midst of their distress.

To what "time of trouble" was Jeremiah referring? Some have felt that he was pointing to the coming fall of Judah to Babylon or to the later fall of Babylon to Medo-Persia. However, in both of these periods the Northern Kingdom of Israel was not affected. It had already gone into captivity (in 722 B.C.). A better solution is to see Jeremiah referring to the still-future Tribulation period when the remnant of Israel and Judah will experience a time of unparalleled persecution (Dan. 9:27; 12:1; Matt. 24:15-22). The period will end when Christ appears to rescue His elect (Rom. 11:26) and establish His kingdom (Matt. 24:30-31; 25:31-46; Rev. 19:11-21; 20:4-6).

(3) The Lord's deliverance (30:8-11). **30:8-9.** When God comes to rescue the nation, He **will break the yoke** of bondage He had placed on her neck. This deliverance did not come when the false prophets predicted it would (cf. 28:2, 10-11, 14), but God said it will come eventually (**in that day**). Instead of serving foreign powers the nation **will** once again **serve** the LORD. The people will also submit to the authority of **David their king** whom God **will raise up for them**. Many scholars view this as a reference to Christ who is from the line of David. However, there is no compelling reason not to take Jeremiah's reference in a literal sense (cf. comments on Ezek. 34:23-24). David is referred to by name elsewhere in passages that look to the future restoration of a united Israel (cf. Ezek. 34:23-24; 37:24-25; Hosea 3:5).

**30:10-11.** God's promise of restoration was designed to give **Israel** hope. She had no need to **fear** or **be dismayed** because God promised to **save** her **out of a distant place**. No country would be too far away for God to reach and rescue His people. When He brings them **back** to the land they will have the **peace and security** that was absent in Jeremiah's day (cf. 8:11). God will **completely destroy** the **nations** where Israel and Judah had been scattered. Though He would **discipline** Israel and Judah, He assured them that He would never **completely destroy** them. Any judgment would be mingled **with justice** (cf. 10:24; 46:28) so that the punishment for His Chosen People would not be overly severe.

*b. The nation's spiritual healing (30:12-17)*

(1) Israel's sin caused her wounds. **30:12-15.** Israel's condition was critical. Her **wound** appeared **incurable** (cf. comments on 6:14), and **no one** was available to provide a **remedy for** her **sore**. The **allies** in whom the nation had placed such great hope had **forgotten** her. Even God had **struck** her **as an enemy** and **punished** her **because** of her **guilt**.

(2) God would heal Israel's wounds. **30:16-17.** Israel's condition appeared hopeless, but God promised to reverse her misfortunes. Those who were devouring the nation would themselves be **devoured** by God. He would send her **enemies . . . into exile** and **plunder** those who sought to **make spoil of** her.

At the same time God promised to **restore** Israel to spiritual **health.** He would intervene for His **outcast** people.

### c. The nation's material blessing (30:18-22)

**30:18-22.** God's restoration will involve a physical rebuilding. (**Restore** Judah's **fortunes** is mentioned also in 32:44; 33:11, 26; cf. Deut. 30:3.) **The city** of Jerusalem **will be rebuilt on her ruins,** including **the** king's **palace. The** festive **sound of rejoicing** that had been silenced by Babylon (cf. Jer. 7:34; 16:19; 25:10) will once again be heard in the city, and God will increase Judah numerically (cf. Deut. 30:5). The nation **will be** secured and **established before** God, and He **will punish** anyone who tries to **oppress** her.

The **leader** of Israel will again **be one of their own** instead of some foreign despot (cf. Jer. 30:9). This ruler **will come close to** God as **the Lord** brings him into His service. Only at that future date when the city, its inhabitants, and their ruler have been restored to God will someone be able to declare that Israel is God's **people** and that He is her **God.** This ideal relationship between Israel and her God was expressed several times in the Old Testament (cf. Lev. 26:12; Deut. 7:6; 26:16-19; Jer. 7:23; 11:4; 24:7; 31:1, 33; Ezek. 11:20; 14:11; 34:30; 36:28; 37:23, 27; Hosea 2:23; Zech. 8:8; 13:9). Israel will finally experience the relationship with God that He had always intended.

### d. The judgment on the wicked (30:23–31:1)

**30:23-24.** Jeremiah repeated, with minor variations, the same words he had written in 23:19-20. Before God's blessing can be experienced He must judge sin. His **wrath** will **burst out** against **the wicked.** Though these words applied to false prophets in 23:19-20, Jeremiah may have been using them here to refer to God's judgment on the wicked nations who opposed Israel (cf. 30:16-20). God's **fierce anger** that had been poured out on Judah would **not turn back** till it also extended to the other nations of the earth.

**31:1.** This verse should be linked with the statements in 30:23-24. It explains the results of God's judgment on the earth and also serves to introduce the section on national restoration which follows. God promised that when He will

judge the world for its sins He will also restore all **Israel** to Himself. **All the clans,** not just the tribe of Judah, will be known as God's **people** (cf. 30:22).

### e. God's national restoration (31:2-40)

(1) The national restoration of Israel (31:2-22). **31:2-6.** God assured the Northern Kingdom that He will restore her. Those who had survived **the sword** (probably Assyria's destruction of **Israel**) will yet experience God's **favor** as He leads them into **the desert** for their new Exodus (cf. 16:14-15; 23:7-8; Hosea 2:14-15). The turmoil of their long years of exile will cease when God intervenes **to give rest to** the nation **Israel.**

The motivation for God's future restoration of the nation is His **everlasting love** (*'aḥăbâh*) which He will freely bestow on His people (cf. Hosea 11:4; 14:4; Zeph. 3:17) and His **loving-kindness** (*ḥesed;* cf. Jer. 9:24; 32:18; Lam. 3:32; Dan. 9:4). God had made a covenant with Abraham (Gen. 15:7-21) and another covenant with the nation Israel (Ex. 19:3-8; Lev. 26; Deut. 28:1–30:10), and He vowed to stay faithful to His commitments. Israel could look forward to experiencing God's blessing.

Jeremiah drew three word-pictures that will characterize God's restoration of Israel. First, it will be a time of renewed joy. Israel will once again **take up** her **tambourines** and **dance with the joyful.** The times of sadness will cease when the Captivity ends (cf. Ps. 137:1-4; Jer. 16:8-9; 25:10-11). Second, it will be a time of peace and prosperity as the people **plant** their **vineyards on the hills of Samaria.** Free from external threats, they will be able to **enjoy their fruit** (cf. Lev. 26:16; Deut. 28:33; Micah 4:4; Zech. 3:9-10). Third, it will be a time of renewed commitment to the Lord. The **watchmen** stationed **on the hills of Ephraim** will summon the people to **go up to Zion to** worship **the Lord.**

**31:7-9.** God's restoration will be accompanied by songs of **joy** and the **praises** of the people for His deliverance. No one will be too far away for the **Lord** to restore him; God will **gather** His people **from the ends of the earth.** Also no one will be too insignificant for the Lord to deliver him; God will restore **the blind and the lame** along with **expectant mothers.** As God leads these people on their new Exodus into Israel He will provide for their every need. He will guide the people **beside streams of water** (cf. Ex. 15:22-25; Num. 20:2-13; Ps. 23:2) and they will travel **on a level path** so they **will not stumble.** God will do all this because of His special relationship to Israel. He is **Israel's father** (Deut. 32:6), and **Ephraim** (emphasizing the Northern tribes of Israel) is his **firstborn son** (cf. Ex. 4:22). Jeremiah used the image of a father/son relationship to show God's deep love for His people (cf. Hosea 11:1, 8).

**31:10-14.** Israel's regathering (like a flock of sheep; cf. 23:3; Micah 2:12; 5:4; 7:14) will be accompanied by a renewal of God's material blessings. Those who will be restored to the land will **rejoice in the bounty of** crops (cf. Jer. 31:5) and **flocks.** Jeremiah compared Israel's material wealth to **a well-watered garden** that was producing in abundance (cf. Deut. 30:5, 9). This outpouring of blessing will produce **gladness . . . comfort, and joy** (cf. Jer. 31:4, 7).

**31:15-20.** The nation's future hope will contrast sharply with her present misery. The cry from **Ramah** was one of **mourning and great weeping** as Jeremiah pictured **Rachel weeping for her children.** To what was Jeremiah referring? Ramah was a town five miles north of Jerusalem, and Rachel was Joseph and Benjamin's mother. Joseph was the father of Ephraim and Manasseh, who became the two major tribes in the Northern Kingdom of Israel. Thus Jeremiah was picturing the weeping of the women of the Northern Kingdom as they watched their children being carried into exile in 722 B.C. However, Jeremiah could also have had the 586 B.C. deportation of Judah in view because Ramah was the staging point for Nebuchadnezzar's deportation (cf. 40:1). In all likelihood these women were crying because they would never see their **children** again. But as the women of Israel and Judah wept for their exiled children, God offered a word of comfort. There was **hope for** their **future** because their **children** would **return to their own land.** God would bring about a restoration.

In what sense was Herod's slaughter of the babies (Matt. 2:17-18) a "fulfillment" of Jeremiah 31:15? Jeremiah pointed to an Old Testament deportation of children from a town north of Jerusalem;

Matthew used the passage to explain the New Testament slaughter of children in a village south of Jerusalem. The answer to the problem hinges on Matthew's use of the word "fulfilled" (*plēroō*). Though Matthew did use the word to record an actual fulfillment of an Old Testament prediction (cf., e.g., Matt. 21:4-5 with Zech. 9:9), he also used the word to indicate that the full potential of something in the Old Testament had been realized (cf. Matt. 3:15; 5:17). In these latter instances there is no prophetic significance to the word "fulfill," which is how Matthew used the word to associate the slaughter in Bethlehem with the sadness in Ramah. Matthew used Jeremiah 31:15 in his book (Matt. 2:17-18) to explain the sadness of the mothers of Bethlehem. The pain of those mothers in Ramah who watched their sons being carried into exile found its full potential in the cries of the mothers of Bethlehem who cradled their sons' lifeless bodies in their arms.

Jeremiah ended this section by recording Israel's cry of contrition that she will recite when she returns to the land. Though she had **strayed** (Jer. 31:19) she will repent. When she returns to her God she will be **ashamed and humiliated because** of her sin. God in turn will express His **great compassion for** the wayward but returning nation (cf. Hosea 2:16-23).

**31:21-22.** God called on the captives to **set up road signs** and **guideposts** as they traveled to Babylon and to remember **the road** they would **take.** They would need this information during His promised restoration so they could **return to** their **towns.** This time of promised restoration will be so remarkable that it will be as if God **will create a new thing on earth.** That new event is described proverbially by the clause, **a woman will surround a man.** This is probably the most difficult verse to understand in the Book of Jeremiah. One possible idea is that a woman will seek, or court, a man (NIV marg.). In that culture a woman would not normally court a man, so this would indicate something unusual. The woman here is **Israel** (v. 21). She had been **unfaithful,** but in the future she will finally seek out her God and ask to be united with Him.

(2) The national restoration of Judah. **31:23-26.** When **God** will restore the nation of **Israel,** He will also reverse the

fortunes of **Judah.** Those living **in the land of Judah** will again invoke a blessing on Jerusalem (God's **righteous dwelling**) and the temple area (**the sacred mountain**; cf. Pss. 2:6; 43:3; Isa. 66:20). The land itself will be repopulated, and God will meet every need.

(3) The establishment of a new relationship with Israel and Judah (31:27-40). The rest of the chapter focuses on the new relationship God will establish with His people. Jeremiah used the same Hebrew phrase to introduce the three sections that form this unit. Each section begins with *hinnēh yāmîm bā'îm* (lit., "Behold, days are coming," vv. 27, 31, 38; cf. comments on 33:14). In the third occurrence the word for "coming" was omitted, but it is clear that Jeremiah intended for the reader to supply it. Jeremiah used this phrase to introduce three aspects of the Lord's new relationship with His people.

**31:27-30.** God vowed to provide a new beginning for His covenant people. In this new age God **will plant** the nations of **Israel** and **Judah with the offspring of men and animals.** Jeremiah again used agricultural and architectural metaphors to illustrate God's work (cf. comments on 1:10). God had judged Judah for her sin, but He will reverse that judgment.

God's work for the nation will silence a proverb that was common in Jeremiah's day (cf. comments on Ezek. 18:2-4). Those facing judgment in Jeremiah's day felt they were being unfairly punished by God for their ancestors' sins. Though the **fathers** had **eaten sour grapes,** it was the **children** who experienced the effects of having their **teeth . . . set on edge.** This proverb was false because it implied that God was unrighteous. God's justice will guarantee that each guilty person **will die for his own sin.**

**31:31-37.** In addition to a new beginning God promised to **make a New Covenant with** His people. This New Covenant was expressly for **the house of Israel** (the Northern Kingdom) and **the house of Judah** (the Southern Kingdom). It would **not be like the covenant** God had **made with** Israel's **forefathers** at the time of the Exodus because that covenant had been broken by the people (cf. 11:1-8). The earlier covenant God referred to

was the Mosaic Covenant contained in the Books of Exodus, Leviticus, Numbers, and Deuteronomy. Twice God had announced a series of punishments or "curses" that would be invoked on those who violated His Law (Lev. 26; Deut. 28). The final judgment would be a physical deportation from the land of Israel. With the destruction of Jerusalem in 586 B.C. this final "curse" was completed. God had set a holy standard of conduct before the people, but because of their sinful hearts they could not keep those standards. A change was needed.

God's New **Covenant** will involve an internalization of His Law. He **will put** His **Law in their minds** and **on their hearts,** not just on stones (Ex. 34:1). There will be no need to exhort people to **know the LORD because they will** already **all know** God (cf. Isa. 11:9; Hab. 2:14). God's New Covenant will give Israel the inner ability to obey His righteous standards and thus to enjoy His blessings. Ezekiel indicated that this change will result from God's bestowal of the Holy Spirit on these believers (cf. Ezek. 36:24-32). In Old Testament times the Holy Spirit did not universally indwell all believers. Thus one different aspect of the New Covenant is the indwelling of the Holy Spirit in all believers (cf. Joel 2:28-32).

A second aspect of the New Covenant will be God's provision for sin. The sins of the people resulted in the curses of the Old Covenant. However, as part of the New Covenant God will **forgive** Israel's **wickedness** and **remember their sins no more.** But how could a holy God overlook sin? The answer is that God did not "overlook" sin—its penalty was paid for by a Substitute (cf. Isa. 53:4-6). In the Upper Room Christ announced that the New Covenant was to be inaugurated through the shedding of His blood (cf. Matt. 26:27-28; Luke 22:20). Forgiveness of sin would be part of the New Covenant only because God provided a Substitute to pay the penalty required of man.

To underscore Israel's permanence because of this New Covenant, God compared her existence to that of the heavens and the earth. As God had appointed **the sun to shine by day** and **the moon and stars to shine by night** (cf. Gen. 1:14-19), so He had appointed Israel as His chosen nation. It would take a feat as fabulous as making **these** natural **decrees vanish from** nature to make **Israel . . . cease to be a nation.** The power God displayed in creating the universe was the power that He exercises in preserving Israel as a nation. Throughout history people have tried in vain to destroy Israel, but none have succeeded—and none ever will.

How is the church related to the New Covenant? Is the New Covenant being fulfilled in the church today? Ultimately the New Covenant will find its complete fulfillment during the Millennium when Israel is restored to her God. The New Covenant was made with Israel (Jer. 31:31, 33) just as the Mosaic Covenant had been (v. 32). One key element of the New Covenant is the preservation of Israel as a nation (vv. 35-37). However, though the ultimate fulfillment of this covenant awaits the millennial reign of Christ, the church today is participating in some of the benefits of that covenant. The covenant was inaugurated at Christ's death (Matt. 26:27-28; Luke 22:20), and the church, by her union with Christ, is sharing in many of the spiritual blessings promised to Israel (cf. Rom. 11:11-27; Eph. 2:11-22) including the New Covenant (2 Cor. 3:6; Heb. 8:6-13; 9:15; 12:22-24). But though the church's participation in the New Covenant is real, it is not the ultimate fulfillment of God's promise. The fact that believers today enjoy the spiritual blessings of the New Covenant (forgiveness of sins and the indwelling Holy Spirit) does *not* mean that spiritual *and* physical blessings will not be realized by Israel. That still awaits the day when Israel will acknowledge her sin and turn to the Messiah for forgiveness (Zech. 12:10–13:1). Some Bible scholars, however, take a slightly different view. They see one covenant (a covenant of grace), which God will apply to Israel in the Millennium and is now applying to the church in this present age. In both views the New Covenant is made possible by the blood of Christ.

**31:38-40.** The third aspect of God's new relationship will be the establishment of a new city for His people. Jerusalem, the city that symbolizes God's relationship with His people, was destroyed by Babylon. But even before that event took place God promised that the **city will be rebuilt. The Tower of Hananel**

was at the northeast corner of the city (cf. Neh. 3:1; 12:39; Zech. 14:10) and **the Corner Gate** was probably located on the northwest corner of the city (cf. 2 Kings 14:13; 2 Chron. 26:9; Zech. 14:10). Thus the northern wall will be restored. The locations of **the hill of Gareb** and **Goah** are unknown; but since Jeremiah 31:38 described the northern boundary and verse 40 describes the southern and eastern boundaries it may be assumed that Gareb and Goah detail the western boundary of the city. Perhaps Gareb referred to the hill west of the Tyropeon Valley that is today called Mount Zion. The southwestern and southern boundary will be the **valley** in which **dead bodies and ashes are thrown.** This is the Hinnom Valley (cf. 7:30-34; 19:1-6). The eastern boundary is **the terraces out to the Kidron Valley.** This boundary would extend to **the corner of the Horse Gate** on the southeast tip of the city, where the Kidron Valley and Hinnom Valley unite.

God described two characteristics of this new city. First, it **will be holy to the LORD** (cf. Zech. 14:20-21). The city and its inhabitants will be set apart to God who will dwell in her midst (Ezek. 48:35). Second, the city will no more **be uprooted or demolished.** The ravages of war will not be experienced in this new city. These verses were not fulfilled after the Babylonian Captivity ended. Since the postexilic period provides clear evidence that holiness was not a primary characteristic of the people in Jerusalem and Judah (cf. Mal. 1:6-14), so the city was destroyed again in A.D. 70 by the Romans. These promises (Jer. 31:31-40) await their future fulfillment during the Millennium.

2. THE RESTORATION OF ISRAEL AND JUDAH ILLUSTRATED (CHAP. 32)

a. *The illustration (32:1-12)*

(1) The circumstances (32:1-5). **32:1-2. Jeremiah** recorded the time frame in which this prophecy was given because of its significance to the message. The time was **the 10th year of Zedekiah which was** also **the 18th year of Nebuchadnezzar.** The 10th year of Zedekiah would have ended on October 17, 587 B.C. (using the Judean Tishri-to-Tishri year) while the 18th year of Nebuchadnezzar began on April 23, 587 (using the Babylonian Nisan-to-Nisan year). Thus this prophecy occurred sometime be-

tween April 23 and October 17, 587 B.C. During this time **Babylon** was **besieging Jerusalem**—a siege that lasted from January 15, 588 till July 18, 586—and Jeremiah was under arrest and **confined in the** palace **courtyard of the guard.**

**32:3-5.** The reason for Jeremiah's imprisonment is stated here. He had been **imprisoned** by Zedekiah for his "treasonous" prophecies. Jeremiah predicted Nebuchadnezzar's **capture** of both Jerusalem and **the king of Judah. Zedekiah** would **be handed over to** Nebuchadnezzar and taken **to Babylon.** Any attempt to oppose the Babylonians would **not succeed.** Such statements were not appreciated by those trying to hold out against Babylon's assault.

(2) The purchase of land (32:6-12). **32:6-9.** In this grim time God came to tell **Jeremiah** of an impending visit. Jeremiah's cousin, **Hanamel son of Shallum,** would visit Jeremiah in prison and ask him to **buy** his **field at Anathoth.** Hanamel was following the Mosaic Law which called for a person to redeem (purchase) the property of a relative who was forced to sell so that it would not leave the family (Lev. 25:25-28; Ruth 4:1-6). So **Hanamel** told Jeremiah it was his **right and duty to buy it.** Perhaps Hanamel was trying to sell the land to obtain money for food because of the siege. The village of Anathoth was already under Babylonian control so this purchase would appear to be foolish. Who would buy a parcel of land that had already fallen into enemy hands? Because of this apparent foolishness, God told Jeremiah in advance that Hanamel would come so Jeremiah would recognize God's hand in the request.

When **Hanamel** came, Jeremiah **bought the field** for **17 shekels of silver** (about 7 ounces; cf. NIV marg.). Ordinarily this would have been a small price for a field (cf. Gen. 23:12-16). But the size of the field is unknown and it was not really available at that time.

**32:10-12.** Following the legal customs of the day, Jeremiah **signed and sealed the deed** and **had it witnessed** before he paid **Hanamel.** Two copies of the **deed of purchase** were made. One was **sealed** by being bound with a piece of string or cord and then having Jeremiah's official seal stamped into a lump of clay placed over the string. The other

**copy** remained **unsealed** so it could later be examined. Jeremiah handed both copies of the **deed to Baruch,** Jeremiah's scribe and friend (cf. Jer. 36:4, 8, 26).

*b. The explanation (32:13-15)*

**32:13-15.** Jeremiah instructed **Baruch** to take both **documents** and **put them in a clay jar** for preservation. The documents had to **last a long time** because it would be many years before the people would be able to return from captivity and claim their land. Yet Jeremiah's purpose in buying the land and preserving the deeds was to show that **houses, fields, and vineyards** would **again be bought** by the people of Israel in the **land.**

*c. The prayer of Jeremiah (32:16-25)*

(1) His praise for God's greatness (32:16-23). **32:16-19.** Jeremiah began his prayer by focusing on the incomparable greatness and majesty of God's character. God's Creation of **the heavens and the earth** proves that **nothing** is **too hard for** Him (cf. v. 27). He is omnipotent, and He is also a God of love and justice. He shows **love** (ḥesed; cf. 9:24; 31:3) to many, but He also punishes sin (cf. Ex. 20:5; 34:7; Num. 14:18; Deut. 5:9-10). In God's omniscience He sees **all the ways of men.** Since nothing escapes His notice He can justly **reward everyone according to his conduct.**

**32:20-23.** God's character was displayed in His deeds throughout Israel's history. From the time of the Exodus God's **signs and wonders** (cf. Deut. 4:34; 26:8; 29:3; 34:11) had **continued** on Israel's behalf. God displayed His loyal love when He **brought . . . Israel out of Egypt** and **gave them** the **land** He had promised them. Unfortunately when Israel **took possession of** the land she refused to **obey . . . or follow** God's **Law.** She violated her covenant with Him. God was forced to display His power and justice as He **brought** the **disaster** of His curses (which included invasion and deportation) **upon them** (cf. Lev. 26:14-39; Deut. 28:15-68).

(2) His puzzlement over God's promise. **32:24-25.** After reminding God of His mighty character and deeds, Jeremiah expressed his continued perplexity at God's workings. In light of verses 17-23 it seems harsh to believe that Jere-

miah doubted God's ability to restore His people. Probably Jeremiah was expressing in verses 24-25 his bewilderment over *how* God would accomplish this restoration rather than doubting *if* God would accomplish it.

Babylon's **siege ramps** were already erected against Jerusalem, and the city's fate was sealed. Jerusalem would **be handed over to the Babylonians.** (On the **sword, famine, and plague**; cf. v. 36 and see comments on 14:12.) Everything that God had foretold through His prophets had **happened.** Yet as the army of Babylon stood poised to reduce Jerusalem to rubble, God had commanded Jeremiah to **buy** a **field** that was already under Babylon's control (32:6-12). Jeremiah did not understand how God's promised restoration related to Judah's present calamity.

*d. The answer of the Lord (32:26-44)*

(1) The city will be destroyed (32:26-35). **32:26-29.** God answered **Jeremiah** by first reminding him of His character. As Jeremiah had said, nothing is **too hard for** God (cf. v. 17). Jeremiah could depend on God's Word even if he did not understand how it would be accomplished. **Nebuchadnezzar** would indeed destroy Jerusalem. He would **set it on fire** and **burn it down** (cf. 21:10; 34:2, 22; 37:8, 10; 38:18, 23) because of the people's idolatry (cf. 19:13).

**32:30-35.** Evil had characterized both **Israel and Judah . . . from their youth**—it was a long-standing problem. All **the people** provoked God with their wicked conduct. Spiritually **they turned their backs** on God and refused to **listen or respond to discipline.** The temple was polluted with **abominable idols** (cf. 7:30; Ezek. 8:3-16), and **the Valley of Ben Hinnom** had become a slaughterhouse where the people would **sacrifice their sons and daughters** (cf. comments on Jer. 7:31-32; 19:5-6) **to Molech.** God would destroy Jerusalem because of her sin.

(2) The city will be restored (32:36-44). **32:36-41.** Jerusalem was **handed over to . . . Babylon** for **the sword, famine, and plague** (cf. v. 24 and see comments on 14:12), **but** that catastrophic event did not signal the end of God's covenant **people. God** offered hope in the midst of despair. First, He promised a regathering (cf. Ezek. 37:1-14). God will **gather** His people **from all the lands where** they had

been in exile and will **bring them back to** the land of Israel where they will **live in safety** (cf. Jer. 31:1-17). Second, He promised an everlasting covenant (cf. 31:31-34; Ezek. 36:24-32). Not only will the people of Israel be restored to their land, but also they will be restored to their God. **They will be** His **people and** He **will be their God** (see comments on Jer. 30:22). With **singleness of heart** they will follow the Lord as He makes **an everlasting covenant with them.** This "everlasting covenant" is another term for the "New Covenant" (see comments on 31:31-34). It was called "everlasting" (*'ôlām*) to stress its duration. Then God **will never stop doing good to** His people, and **they will never turn away from** Him.

**32:42-44.** Just as God had been faithful to His word in bringing **great calamity on** Israel because of her sin (Deut. 28:15-68), so He will also be faithful in providing **the prosperity** He had **promised them** (Deut. 30:1-10). Thus Jeremiah's purchase of the field (Jer. 32:1-15) was a symbolic act to show that **fields will** again **be bought for silver** throughout the land of Israel **because** God **will restore their fortunes** (cf. 30:18; 33:11, 26; Deut. 30:3).

3. THE RESTORATION OF ISRAEL AND JUDAH REAFFIRMED (CHAP. 33)

Chapter 33 concludes "The Book of Consolation." This chapter is structurally and chronologically related to chapter 32. Jeremiah 33:1-13 continued God's promise of blessing as He reaffirmed both the coming destruction and the future restoration of Jerusalem. God then reaffirmed His covenants with David and with the Levitical priests (vv. 14-26).

*a. The coming judgment and future restoration (33:1-13)*

(1) The judgment (33:1-5). **33:1-3.** Chapter 33 followed closely the message of chapter 32 as **Jeremiah was still confined in the courtyard of the guard** (cf. 32:1-2). God again identified Himself to Jeremiah by stressing both His power and His character. He is the God **who made the earth** (cf. 32:17). By revealing to Jeremiah that **the Lord** (*Yahweh*) **is His name,** God emphasized His covenant-keeping faithfulness on behalf of His people (cf. 32:18; Ex. 3:13-15). Jeremiah did not understand how God could re-

store a nation that was destined for doom (cf. Jer. 32:24-25), so God challenged the prophet to **call to** Him for understanding. God promised to **answer** by revealing **great and unsearchable things.** The word for "unsearchable" (*beṣurôṭ*) means something that is made inaccessible by fortifying it or enclosing it. It is used to describe heavily fortified cities (cf. Num. 13:28; Deut. 3:5; 28:52; Ezek. 21:20). God's plans for the future are inaccessible to ordinary people. Only God can unlock the secrets of the future, and He offered this knowledge to Jeremiah. God would share with Jeremiah "things" the prophet did **not know** or understand about Israel's future.

**33:4-5.** The first revelation focused on Jerusalem's impending fall. As Babylon's siege wore away at Jerusalem's outer defenses, **the houses** of Jerusalem along with **the royal palaces** were **torn down to** provide wood and stone to strengthen the walls **against the siege ramps.** The object of this frantic effort was to prevent Babylon's soldiers (**the sword**) from making a breach in the walls and entering the city.

God announced that Jerusalem's feeble attempts to shore up her defenses were futile. The partially dismantled houses would **be filled with the dead bodies of** those slain by **the Babylonians.** God would **hide** His **face from** the **city,** refusing to deliver it from this destruction (cf. 18:17; Ezek. 4:1-3). Jerusalem had to be destroyed **because of all its wickedness.**

(2) The restoration (33:6-13). **33:6-9.** The secret to understanding God's seemingly contradictory prophecies of judgment and blessing is to realize that the judgment was to be only temporary. After the time of judgment God will someday **bring health and healing to** His city and **people.** God spoke to Jeremiah about three elements of this blessing. First, the blessing will involve a restoration to the land (cf. 31:8-11; 32:37). God **will bring** both **Judah and Israel back from captivity.** Second, the blessing will involve a restoration to the Lord (cf. 31:31-34; 32:38-40). God **will cleanse** the people **from all** their **sin** and **forgive** them of their **rebellion.** Third, the blessing will involve a restoration to a special place of honor among the nations (cf. 31:10-14). Jerusalem will **bring . . . renown, joy,**

**praise, and honor** to God **before all nations.** Those nations **will be in awe and will tremble** as they marvel **at the abundant prosperity and peace** (cf. 33:6) God will lavish on His people.

**33:10-13.** God elaborated on the contrast between Israel's present judgment and her future blessing by drawing two pictures of the changes that would come. Each picture began with a similar phrase (vv. 10, 12) as God emphasized that **this is what the LORD** (or **LORD Almighty**) **says.** In each picture the scene in Jeremiah's day was similar (cf. vv. 10, 12). Jerusalem was **a desolate waste** that was **without men or animals** (cf. 32:43). Though the siege was still in progress, the fall of Jerusalem was so sure that God pictured it as if it had already happened. At this point the two pictures changed. In 33:10-11 God illustrated the joy and gladness that will again return to Jerusalem and Judah, and in verses 12-13 He illustrated the peace and prosperity that will again characterize Judah.

**The streets of Jerusalem** that were **deserted** after its destruction by Babylon (cf. Lam. 1:1-4) will again be filled with **the sounds of joy and gladness.** This joyful sound will be typified by **the voices of** a **bride and bridegroom** in a wedding ceremony (cf. Jer. 7:34; 16:9; 25:10) **and the voices of** worshipers as they **bring thank offerings to the house of the LORD** (cf. Ps. 100:1-2, 4). The song to be sung by the worshipers, recorded by Jeremiah, resembled the refrain of several psalms (cf. Pss. 100:4-5; 106:1; 107:1; 136:1-3). Joy will come when God restores Judah's **fortunes** (cf. Jer. 30:18; 32:44; 33:26; Deut. 30:3).

The **towns** of Judah that were destroyed by Babylon will also experience peace and prosperity. God **will again** provide safe **pastures** for **flocks.** This peace will extend from Jerusalem to **the hill country of** Judah in the east, **the western foothills** of the Shephelah in the west, **the Negev** in the south, and **the territory of Benjamin** in the north (cf. Jer. 17:26).

Throughout the land **flocks will again pass under the hand of the one who counts them** as a shepherd counts his sheep to be sure none is absent. Possibly Jeremiah was using shepherd and sheep in a metaphorical sense to refer to the leaders of Israel and the people. He had already compared the leaders to shepherds (cf. comments on 3:15) and the restored nation was compared to a re-gathered flock (cf. 23:3; 31:10). Jeremiah had also used this imagery to introduce his message on the righteous Branch from David (23:1-6), which is the subject of 33:14-26.

### b. The covenants with David and the Levitical priests (33:14-26)

(1) The covenants (33:14-18). **33:14-16.** The second section of this chapter is introduced with the phrase **the days are coming** (*hinnēh yāmîm bāʾîm*). Jeremiah used this phrase 16 times in his book. In a negative sense it referred to the coming destruction of Judah and the surrounding nations (cf. 7:32; 9:25; 19:6; 48:12; 49:2; 51:47, 52). However, in its remaining 9 occurrences it pointed to a future period of blessing for Israel when (a) the nation will be restored from captivity (16:14-15; 23:7-8; 30:3), (b) the righteous Branch of David will be ruling over a united monarchy (23:5-6; 33:14-15), (c) the nation will be experiencing peace and prosperity in the land (31:27-28; 33:14, 16), (d) the New Covenant with its cleansing from sin will be in effect ("The time is coming," 31:31-34), and (e) the city of Jerusalem will be rebuilt as a Holy City that will never again be destroyed (31:38-40). These promises transcend anything that Israel has experienced throughout her long history. They will find their ultimate fulfillment only in the Millennial Age when the kingdom of the Messiah is established. This will be when God **will fulfill the gracious promise** He **made to . . . Israel** and **Judah.**

The first aspect of this fulfillment will be the restoration of the monarchy (cf. 23:5). The **righteous Branch** that will **sprout from David's line** will rule as King over the nation. This was a prophecy about Jesus Christ who descended from the line of David and was promised David's throne (cf. Luke 1:31-33).

The second aspect of this fulfillment will be the restoration of **Jerusalem** as God's dwelling place. The city that was about to be destroyed by Babylon (Jer. 33:4-5) will someday **live in safety.** Though this verse is also found in 23:6, Jeremiah made a significant change in this passage to give it a new meaning. In 23:6 Jeremiah pictured the safety of Israel

and Judah through the ministry of the Messiah who was called "The LORD Our Righteousness." However, by changing "Israel" to "Jerusalem" and by changing the preposition "he" to "it" (*lāh,* lit., "to her") Jeremiah made the title, **The LORD Our Righteousness** apply to the city of Jerusalem instead of to the Messiah. The city will take on the same characteristics as the Lord who will dwell within her (cf. Ezek. 48:35).

It is significant that Jeremiah singled out the royal (Jer. 33:15) and religious (v. 16) aspects of God's restoration. Both were vital to Israel's existence as God's covenant community.

**33:17-18.** To emphasize the importance of both elements, God reiterated His covenants with the line of David and with the Levitical priests. The first covenant mentioned was God's covenant with David (cf. 2 Sam. 7:8-16; 1 Chron. 17:4-14). God vowed, **David will never fail to have a man to sit on** Israel's **throne.** Some have felt that this promise was incorrect because the throne did cease in 586 B.C. when Jerusalem fell. However, God did not promise an unbroken monarchy but an unbroken line of descendants from David who would be qualified to sit on that throne when it was reestablished. David's line would not fail before the righteous Branch came to claim His throne (cf. Luke 1:31-33). The genealogies of Matthew and Luke show that this promise was fulfilled as Christ was able to trace both His legal line through Joseph and His physical line through Mary back to David (Matt. 1:1-16; Luke 3:23-31).

The second covenant mentioned was God's covenant with **the priests, who are Levites.** This covenant was God's promise that the Levites would never **fail to have a man to stand before** Him **to offer burnt offerings . . . grain offerings,** and **sacrifices.** Again the promise was not that the sacrifices would continue unabated, because they did cease in 586 B.C. and were not resumed till 537 B.C. (cf. Ezra 3:1-6). The promise here was that the Levitical priesthood would not be extinguished. God was referring back to the promise He made to Phinehas (Num. 25:12-13). In other words neither the monarchy nor the priesthood would be abolished.

(2) The confirmation (33:19-26). God

gave two assurances that He would keep His covenant promises. Each assurance began with the same introductory phrase ("The word of the LORD came to Jeremiah," vv. 19, 23); and each used God's "covenant of day and night" to illustrate the permanence of these institutions (vv. 20, 25; cf. 31:35-37).

**33:19-22.** Only if man could **break** God's **covenant with the day and . . . the night** (cf. Gen. 1:14-19) could he break God's **covenant with David** and His **covenant with the Levites who are priests.** That is, God's covenants with these groups were as fixed as the natural order of the universe. They could not be overthrown by mere mortals. The word for "covenant" (*bᵉrîṯ*) referred to a treaty or agreement made between individuals or parties by which they bound themselves to a specific relationship or course of action. God had promised to preserve the kingly line of **David** (2 Sam. 7:8-16) and the priestly line of Phinehas (Num. 25:12-13), and He would not break His oath. Indeed, God promised to bless both lines so **the descendants** would become **as countless as the stars** and **the sand.**

**33:23-26.** God's second assurance (cf. vv. 19-22) to **Jeremiah** came because of external doubt and reproach. The group in question (**these people**) was not specified—they may have been doubting Israelites or Israel's heathen neighbors. Whoever they were, "these people" were claiming that God had so **rejected the two kingdoms** (*mišpāḥôṯ*, lit., "families or clans"; cf. 31:1) that He would **no longer regard them as a nation.** They felt that Israel's and Judah's sin had invalidated all God's covenant promises so that He was no longer obligated to fulfill them.

God responded to this argument by reaffirming His commitment to His covenant promises. The covenants with Abraham and **David** were not conditioned on the people's obedience but on God's character. They were as sure as His **covenant with day and night** and as immutable as **the fixed laws of heaven and earth.** Only if these natural laws could be undone would God **reject** Jacob's and David's **descendants.** The reference to **Abraham, Isaac, and Jacob** called to mind God's covenant promise to these patriarchs regarding His selection of Israel (cf. Gen. 15:7-21; 17:1-8; 26:1-6; 28:10-

15). God was bound to His promises and He would **restore** the nation's **fortunes** (cf. Jer. 30:18; 32:44; 33:11; Deut. 30:3) and **have compassion on** her. The greatest argument for the future restoration of Israel as a nation is the character of God. He made a series of covenants with the patriarchs, David, and the Levites; His character demands that He will ultimately fulfill these promises to their nation.

### D. Present catastrophe of Judah (chaps. 34-45)

After describing the future hope of Judah (chaps. 30–33), Jeremiah returned to discuss their present judgment. The collapse of the kingdom that he had been predicting (chaps. 2–29) would now come to pass. Chapters 34–36 continued the theme of rejection that began in 26–29. The judgment was sure because the people rejected God's word of warning. Chapters 37–45, arranged in chronological order, detailed the events that occurred during and after Jerusalem's fall to Babylon.

#### 1. BEFORE THE FALL (CHAPS. 34–36)

*a. The inconsistency of the people (chap. 34)*

(1) The warning to Zedekiah (34:1-7). **34:1-3.** When **Nebuchadnezzar** and **his army . . . were fighting against Jerusalem** God gave **Jeremiah** a message for King **Zedekiah.** This message was that Zedekiah's rebellion against Babylon would not succeed. **God** had already determined to **hand** the **city over to the** Babylonians, who would **burn it down** (cf. v. 22; 32:29; 37:8, 10; 38:18, 23). Though Zedekiah would try to flee, he would **not escape.** Instead he would be taken to Nebuchadnezzar and be required to meet with him **face to face** and be judged for his rebellion. Zedekiah would be taken captive **to Babylon** as punishment for his rebellion. Everything Jeremiah predicted came to pass (cf. 39:4-7; 52:7-11).

**34:4-5.** In the midst of judgment God did offer a **promise of** peace. Because of his rebellion **Zedekiah** could have been executed by Nebuchadnezzar, but God promised that he would **not die by the sword.** He would **die peacefully** and would receive a proper funeral befitting a king (in contrast with Jehoiakim; cf. 22:18-19). The **people** would kindle **a funeral fire** to **honor and lament** Zedekiah.

This fire does not refer to cremation because Israel and Judah buried dead bodies rather than cremating them. Instead it referred to the custom of lighting a large bonfire as a tribute to a dead king (cf. 2 Chron. 16:14; 21:19).

**34:6-7.** Jeremiah delivered his message to King Zedekiah as **the army . . . of Babylon** relentlessly continued its attack **against Jerusalem and the** two **other** fortified **cities** that remained **in Judah— Lachish and Azekah.** All the other Judean cities had already fallen. This grim picture of Judah's precarious position was illustrated by a tragic letter inscribed on a clay potsherd that was found in the ruins of Lachish. The letter was written to the commander at Lachish from an outpost that was close enough to Lachish and Azekah to see signal fires from both cities. Evidently Azekah had just fallen because the officer wrote, "And let my lord know that we are watching for the signals of Lachish, according to all the indications which my lord hath given, for we cannot see Azekah" (Lachish Letter No. 4; James B. Pritchard, ed., *Ancient Near Eastern Texts Relating to the Old Testament.* 3rd ed. Princeton, N.J.: Princeton University Press, 1969, p. 322).

(2) The warning to the people (34:8-22). **34:8-11.** Jeremiah raised the curtain of history on many social evils being practiced in his day. One such practice was the enslavement of Israelites by their own people. This violated God's Law (cf. Ex. 21:2-11; Lev. 25:39-55; Deut. 15:12-18). Perhaps in a desperate attempt to win God's favor during Babylon's siege of Jerusalem, the **king** proclaimed **freedom for the slaves,** a kind of "Emancipation Proclamation." **Everyone was to free his Hebrew slaves** in accordance with God's Law.

The slaves' freedom, however, was short-lived. All those who released their slaves **changed their minds . . . and enslaved them again.** What caused this reversal? Jeremiah placed at the end of the chapter (Jer. 34:21-22) the key that unlocks the puzzle. After the people had made the covenant and released the slaves, the army of Babylon broke off its siege of Jerusalem to repel an attack by the Egyptians (cf. 37:4-13). The people hoped for an Egyptian victory, which would force Babylon from Judah. But after so much destruction slaves would be needed to rebuild the cities and towns. So the people reneged on their promise to God when it seemed that life would return to normal.

**34:12-16.** God rebuked the people for their inconsistency by reminding them of the **covenant** He had **made with** their **forefathers when** He freed them from their **slavery in Egypt.** The Law required that **every seventh year** all Hebrew slaves were to **go free.** No Israelite was to be forced into permanent bondage again. Unfortunately the people **did not listen to** God's Word. But because of Babylon's attack the people finally **repented and did what** was **right** by granting **freedom to** their **countrymen.** When they rescinded their promise they **profaned** God's **name** (His reputation) because the covenant had been made before God in the temple.

**34:17-20.** God's punishment matched their sin. By revoking their covenant the people had **not proclaimed freedom** for those Israelites who were wrongfully enslaved. Therefore ironically God would give them **freedom** to die **by the sword, plague, and famine** (cf. comments on 14:12).

In making their **covenant** in the temple (cf. 34:15) the people had slaughtered a **calf . . . cut it in two,** and **walked between its pieces** to signify their commitment to the bargain. By walking through the parts of the animal they were symbolizing the judgment that should befall them if they violated the agreement. They were to be hacked to pieces like the calf. Significantly when God made His covenant with Abraham, the patriarch did not pass between the parts of the animal. Only God did; apparently the blazing torch symbolized Him (Gen. 15:4-18, esp. v. 17). The Abrahamic Covenant rested on God's character, not on man's obedience.

God promised to **treat** those who broke the covenant **like the calf they** had slaughtered. **All** who made the agreement would be handed **over to their enemies.** Like the parts of the calf, **their dead bodies** would lie on the ground as **food for** both **birds** and **beasts** (cf. Jer. 7:33; 15:3; 16:4; 19:7).

**34:21-22.** **Zedekiah** and **his officials** should have been models of godly leadership, but they were as vacillating as the people. Though the Babylonians had withdrawn from Jerusalem, God would give the order to bring them back. The siege would resume until the Babylonians would take Jerusalem and burn it down (cf. v. 2). The other towns would be devastated too so the whole country would be virtually deserted.

### b. The consistency of the Recabites (chap. 35)

(1) The fidelity of the Recabites (35:1-11). **35:1-5.** This prophecy was given **during the reign of Jehoiakim** (609–598 B.C.)—at least 11 years (and possibly 20 years) earlier than the prophecies in chapter 34. Jeremiah placed the chapter here to contrast the faithfulness of **the Recabite family** with the unfaithfulness of the people **of Judah.** The Recabites were a nomadic clan (35:7-10) descended from "Jonadab [or Jehonadab] son of Recab" (v. 6) who assisted Jehu in exterminating Baal worship from Israel (2 Kings 10:15-27). They were related to the Kenites (1 Chron. 2:54-55) who descended from Moses' father-in-law, Jethro (Jud. 1:16). Evidently Jonadab rejected a settled way of life for the life of a nomad, and his lifestyle became the norm for his clan (Jer. 35:6-10). They traveled in the wilderness of the Negev (Jud. 1:16; 1 Sam. 15:6), but were forced to move to Jerusalem when Nebuchadnezzar threatened Judah in 598 B.C. (Jer. 35:11).

Jeremiah invited **the Recabites,** including **Jaazaniah,** into **one of the side rooms** in the temple. These rooms surrounded the temple court and were used for meetings, storage, and as priests' residences (1 Kings 6:5; 1 Chron. 28:12; 2 Chron. 31:11; Neh. 13:7-9). The particular room Jeremiah entered beonged to **the sons of Hanan son of Igdaliah.** Nothing is known about Igdaliah except that he was a **man of God**—a term usually used to describe a prophet (cf. 1 Kings 12:22; 2 Kings 1:9-13; 4:21-22). The room occupied a prominent position, **next to the room of the officials** and **over** the room of **Maaseiah son of Shallum the doorkeeper.** Maaseiah was one of three "doorkeepers" for the temple. This was evidently a high position because those holding it were singled out by the Babylonians for judgment along with the chief priests (cf. 2 Kings 25:18-21; Jer. 52:24-27). Into this august company Jeremiah brought the rough, nomadic Recabites.

He **set bowls full of wine and some cups before the** Recabites and asked **them** to **drink some wine.**

**35:6-11.** The Recabites refused to drink the wine because their **forefather Jonadab** had prohibited it. The way of life chosen by Jonadab would not allow his **descendants . . . ever** to **drink wine.** Nor were they allowed to **build houses, sow seed, or plant vineyards,** that is, to settle down to a life of farming. Instead they were to **live** simple lives **in tents** as **nomads.**

Jonadab's descendants had **obeyed everything** he had **commanded.** They had never **drunk wine or built houses to live in,** nor had they ever cultivated **vineyards, fields, or crops.** In fact it was only because **Nebuchadnezzar** had **invaded** the **land** that they had come **to Jerusalem.**

(2) The example of the Recabites (35:12-17). **35:12-16.** Why did Jeremiah bring the Recabites into the temple and offer them wine when he knew they would refuse it? This was to provide **a lesson** to **Judah.** The Recabites consistently obeyed **their forefather's command.** They stood in sharp contrast with the people of Judah who had consistently **not obeyed** God.

**35:17.** The Recabites served as a visual reminder of Judah's sin. God vowed to **bring on Judah . . . every disaster** He had **pronounced against them.** This "disaster" could refer either to the curses of the covenant (cf. Lev. 26:14-39; Deut. 28:15-68) or, more probably, to the fall of Judah and Jerusalem predicted by Jeremiah (cf. Jer. 4:20; 6:19; 11:11-12; 17:18). Judah would be punished because she **did not listen** to God's words and **did not answer** God's summons.

(3) The reward of the Recabites. **35:18-19.** In contrast with faithless Judah the **Recabites** had consistently **obeyed the command of** their **forefather Jonadab.** God promised to reward their faithfulness, and assured them that they would **never fail to have a man to serve** Him. The phrase "serve Me" (*'ōmēd lepānay*) means literally, "to stand before Me." It was used of those who served the Lord as prophets (1 Kings 17:1; Jer. 15:19), of officials who served Solomon (1 Kings 10:8), and of priests in the temple (Deut. 4:10; 10:8; 2 Chron. 29:11). However, though God might have been

offering the Recabites a special place of service to Him in the covenant community, this interpretation is not required. The same phrase also described the people of **Israel** who stood before **the LORD** at the tabernacle and the temple (cf. Lev. 9:5; Deut. 4:10; Jer. 7:10). So God may have promised that the line of the Recabites would always have descendants who would be able to worship the Lord. The promise pointed to a continuing line rather than a specific place of ministry.

### c. Jehoiakim's scroll-burning (chap. 36)

(1) The writing of the scroll (36:1-7). **36:1-3.** The events of this chapter began **in the fourth year** of King **Jehoiakim** (605–604 B.C.; cf. 25:1). God commanded **Jeremiah** to **write on** a **scroll all the** prophecies God gave him about **Israel, Judah, and . . . other nations from the time** God **began speaking to** him **in the reign of Josiah** (627 B.C.; cf. 1:2; 25:3) until that day. This was the first formal compilation of Jeremiah's prophecies, and it was mentioned earlier (25:13). (See the chart "The Dating of Jeremiah's Prophecies," in the *Introduction*.) At least two additional stages of compilation are mentioned in the book (cf. 36:32; 51:64).

One purpose for recording these prophecies was so they could be read aloud to the people. The hope was that **the people** would **hear about every disaster** threatened by God and would **turn from** their **wicked way.** If the people would repent, God promised to **forgive their wickedness.**

**36:4-7. Jeremiah** summoned **Baruch,** his scribe (cf. 32:12-16; 36:26), and **dictated** to him **all the words.** It is not known whether Jeremiah recited all the prophecies from memory or if he read them from scrolls on which he had recorded them earlier. Both views allow for God's superintendence (cf. John 14:25-26). Jeremiah was **restricted,** or barred, from the **temple**—possibly because of his earlier unpopular addresses there (cf. Jer. 7:1-15; 26:1-19). Because of this restriction **Jeremiah told Baruch** to **go to the house of the LORD** in his place. **Baruch** was to go **on a day of fasting.** Prior to the fall of Jerusalem in 586 B.C. fast days were not specified but were called in times of emergency (cf. 36:9; 2 Chron. 20:3; Joel 1:14; 2:15). Only after the fall of Jerusalem were regular fast days instituted

(Zech. 7:3, 5; 8:19). **Jeremiah** hoped that as Baruch **read to the people from the scroll** they would repent of their sins.

(2) The reading of the scroll (36:8-19). **36:8-10.** Some time passed before a national emergency arose which prompted the leaders to call a fast. The scroll was written in Jehoiakim's fourth year (v. 1), but it was not **read** until **the ninth month of the fifth year.** This sounds like a gap of at least nine months, but because of the Hebrew method of dating it could have been a much shorter period of time. Assuming that **Jeremiah** employed the Tishri (September-October)-to-Tishri year for dating Judah's kings (see comments on 25:1), Jehoiakim's fourth year would have extended from October 7 (Tishri 1), 605 B.C. to September 25, 604 B.C. (not October 6 because of the lunar calendar); and his fifth year would have extended from September 26, 604 B.C. to October 14, 603 B.C. (including an intercalary month). However, when a specific month was given it was always reckoned by a Nisan (March-April)-to-Nisan year. Thus the "ninth month" was whatever ninth month from Nisan fell into the "fifth year" that began in Tishri. In the fifth year of Jehoiakim the ninth month extended from November 24, 604 B.C. through December 23, 604 B.C.—a date just three months after the end of Jehoiakim's fourth year. (For a more detailed discussion of these chronological problems see Edwin R. Thiele, *The Mysterious Numbers of the Hebrew Kings*. Rev. ed. Grand Rapids: Zondervan Publishing House, 1983; and Richard A. Parker and Waldo H. Dubberstein, *Babylonian Chronology: 626 B.C.–A.D. 75*. Providence, R.I.: Brown University Press, 1956.) The date was significant because the Babylonian Chronicle reports that at the same time Nebuchadnezzar was in Palestine collecting "vast tribute" from those nations he had conquered. In the same month the fast was called, Nebuchadnezzar captured the city of Ashkelon and plundered it (cf. Donald J. Wiseman, *Chronicles of Chaldean Kings (626–556 B.C.) in the British Museum*. London: Trustees of the British Museum, 1956, p. 69). It is possible that the fast was called to plead for deliverance from Babylon's harsh hand.

**Baruch** went to **the room of Gemariah son of Shaphan** (see the chart "The

Line of Shaphan," near 26:24) **which was in the upper courtyard** of the temple (cf. 26:10) **at the entrance of the New Gate.** Gemariah, like his brother Ahikam, supported Jeremiah's message and allowed **Baruch** to use his room from which he could **read** to **the people** gathered in the **temple** courtyard.

**36:11-19.** Gemariah did not remain in his room while Baruch read the scroll, but his son **Micaiah . . . heard all the words.** Micaiah **went** to **the royal palace** to report the contents of the scroll to **the officials.** Those gathered there included **Elishama the secretary** (cf. v. 21), **Delaiah son of Shemaiah** (cf. v. 25), and **Elnathan son of Acbor** (cf. v. 25). Though Acbor played a part in the recovery of the Law during the time of Josiah (2 Kings 22:12-14), his son Elnathan did not possess all his father's qualities. If he is the same Elnathan mentioned in 2 Kings 24:8, then he was King Jehoiakim's father-in-law. Though Elnathan did urge Jehoiakim not to burn Jeremiah's scroll (Jer. 36:25), he had also led an expedition to Egypt to extradite the Prophet Uriah back to Jerusalem to be executed (cf. 26:20-23). Also present in this meeting were **Gemariah** (36:10, 25), **Zedekiah son of Hananiah,** and **other officials.**

When **Micaiah** finished his report, **the officials sent Jehudi** to **Baruch** to summon him to appear before them. After **Baruch** entered the room they asked him to **sit down** and **read** the scroll **to** them. His reading caused the officials to look **at each other in fear** because they realized that they **must report all** its **words** to **King** Jehoiakim. They asked Baruch **how** the scroll was written, and he explained that **Jeremiah** had **dictated** the **words** and he **wrote them . . . on the scroll.**

Before the meeting adjourned, those present gave a word of warning **to Baruch.** Both he **and Jeremiah** were to **go and hide** and not **let anyone know where** they were. Jehoiakim's prior reaction against Uriah the prophet showed the wisdom of this advice (cf. 26:20-23).

(3) The burning of the scroll (36:20-26). **36:20-22.** Baruch's **scroll** was placed **in the room of Elishama,** and the officials **went to the king** and **reported** the incident **to him.** Jehudi was sent to retrieve **the scroll** and he **read it to the king** as

the officials watched. Jeremiah reemphasized that the events took place in **the ninth month** because that helped explain the story. The story happened between November 24 and December 23, 604 B.C.; the weather can be quite cold in Jerusalem during that time of year. Jehoiakim was **in** his **winter apartment,** which probably faced south to catch the winter sun, and he had **a fire burning in** a firepot, or brazier, to provide warmth.

**36:23-26.** The writing on **the scroll** was in vertical columns. After **Jehudi** would **read three or four columns,** Jehoiakim interrupted him to **cut** those columns **off** the scroll **with a scribe's knife.** He then **threw** those pieces **into the firepot until** he had burned **the entire scroll.** Jehoiakim, in contrast with his godly father Josiah (cf. 2 Kings 22:11-13), **showed no fear** of God's word of judgment **nor did** he and his counselors **tear their clothes** in a visible act of contrition or repentance. **Instead** Jehoiakim ordered the **arrest** of **Baruch** and **Jeremiah.** However, they were **hidden** by **the LORD** so the king's men could not find them.

(4) The rewriting of the scroll (36:27-32). **36:27-31.** Man can burn a **scroll,** but he cannot destroy the Word of God. Since Jehoiakim destroyed the first scroll, God told **Jeremiah** to **write** on **another scroll . . . all the words** of **the first scroll.** However, he was to include an additional word for King **Jehoiakim.** Because he had **burned** the **scroll** and refused to believe God's warning about **the king of Babylon,** God vowed to judge him. First, **no** descendant of his would permanently **sit on the throne of David.** Though his son, Jehoiachin, did follow him to the throne (cf. 2 Kings 24:8-17), he was deposed by Nebuchadnezzar after a reign of only three months. No other descendant of Jehoiakim ascended the throne (see comments on Jer. 22:24-30). Second, Jehoiakim would not receive a proper burial (cf. 22:18-19). Instead his **body** would **be thrown out** of the city and **exposed to** the elements. Third, Jehoiakim's **children and his attendants** would be judged **for their wickedness.** God would **bring** on them **every disaster** that He had **pronounced . . . because they** had **not listened.**

**36:32.** **Jeremiah** obeyed God's command and secured **another scroll.** He **dictated** while **Baruch wrote on** the new scroll **all the words of the** original **scroll.** Then **Jeremiah** added **many similar words,** most likely the contents of chapter 36 including the judgment on Jehoiakim.

### 2. DURING THE FALL (CHAPS. 37–39)

The events of chapters 37–39 are arranged chronologically. They trace Jeremiah's life and ministry during the final siege and fall of Jerusalem.

#### a. Jeremiah's message to Zedekiah (37:1-10)

**37:1-2.** The events in this section focus on **Zedekiah,** the last **king of Judah,** who was placed on the throne as a vassal king **by Nebuchadnezzar** (cf. 2 Kings 24:15-17). In these dark days Judah needed a strong and godly leader. Unfortunately Zedekiah possessed neither quality. From the king to the common **people,** no one **paid any attention to** Jeremiah's **words** of warning until it was too late.

**37:3-10.** But **Zedekiah** did send a delegation **to Jeremiah** asking him to **pray to the Lord** for Jerusalem. **Jeremiah was . . . not yet . . . in prison,** and Babylon had just lifted her siege of **Jerusalem** because **Pharaoh's army had marched** from **Egypt.** Perhaps Zedekiah hoped that Jeremiah's prayers would induce God to grant a victory to the Egyptians and force Babylon out of Palestine (cf. 21:1-7 for a similar request).

God's answer was not the one Zedekiah sought. The **army** of **Egypt** that had **marched out to support** Judah would be crushed by Babylon and forced to **go back to its own land. Then the** army of Babylon would **return and attack** Jerusalem. **They** would **capture it and burn it down** (cf. 21:10; 32:29; 34:2, 22; 37:10; 38:18, 23). Those who hoped for a Babylonian withdrawal were deceiving themselves. Even if **only wounded men** were in Nebuchadnezzar's army, God said that they still would **burn** Jerusalem **down** (cf. 37:8).

#### b. Jeremiah's imprisonment (37:11–38:28)

(1) Jeremiah's arrest and confinement in a dungeon. **37:11-16.** The withdrawal of **the Babylonian army** to fight the Egyptians produced a period of relative calm in Judah. **Jeremiah** used this lull **to leave the city** for a short journey into **the territory of Benjamin** (cf. 1:1). The purpose of his trip was to **get his**

**share of** some **property** belonging to his family. The word for "get his share" (*ḥālaq*) could also be translated "divide, share, apportion." Jeremiah was traveling to Anathoth to take care of personal business, either to secure some land or to divide up some land for sale to others. This land transaction probably does not relate to his purchase in chapter 32. By the time of the purchase in chapter 32 Jeremiah had already been arrested and confined to the courtyard of the guard (cf. 32:2). When he started toward Anathoth (chap. 37) he had not yet been arrested (cf. 37:4, 21; 38:13, 28). Therefore the events of chapter 37 took place before the events of chapter 32.

Just as Jeremiah **started** to leave, **the captain of the guard** seized **him. Irijah . . . arrested** Jeremiah and charged him with **deserting to** the enemy. **Jeremiah** denied the charge, but the captain **would not listen. Instead . . . Jeremiah** was taken **to the officials** who ordered **him beaten and imprisoned.** The prison was located **in the house of Jonathan the secretary** and was **a vaulted cell in a dungeon** (lit., "in the house of the cistern, in the vaulted rooms"). This was probably a complex of large, underground cisterns that had been converted into a prison. **Jeremiah . . . remained** there **a long time.**

(2) Jeremiah's first meeting with Zedekiah and transfer to the courtyard of the guard (37:17-21). **37:17-20.** Babylon **returned** to Jerusalem and renewed her siege of the city. **Zedekiah** secretly **sent** for Jeremiah and **brought** him **to the palace.** Because of Jeremiah's unpopularity with the people (cf. 26:10-11; 37:11-15; 38:4) Zedekiah met with **him privately** to ask if he had **any word from the Lord.** Jeremiah's word from the Lord was unaffected by his imprisonment. Jerusalem would fall and Zedekiah would **be handed over to the king of Babylon** (cf. 21:3-7).

**Jeremiah** used the opportunity of this appearance before **Zedekiah** to protest his innocence. He demanded to know **what crime** he had **committed.** The other **prophets** had **prophesied** lies by declaring that the Babylonians would **not attack. Jeremiah** petitioned Zedekiah **not to send** him **back to the** prison where he had been confined. As a man who was probably in his 60s, Jeremiah was concerned for his health in that dank, dark dungeon. If he were taken back to that hole he might **die there.**

**37:21.** Granting Jeremiah's request, **Zedekiah** had him transferred from the underground vaulted cistern to **the courtyard of the guard** in the royal palace (cf. 32:2). Here Zedekiah could better protect Jeremiah from his enemies—though Zedekiah was a weak-willed protector (cf. 38:4-10). Zedekiah also arranged **for Jeremiah** to be **given bread . . . each day** so he would not starve. This continued until the siege depleted the supply of grain so that **all the bread in the city was gone** (cf. 52:6).

(3) Jeremiah's confinement in a cistern (38:1-6). **38:1-3.** By being confined to the courtyard of the guard (37:21) Jeremiah had some freedom to meet with people (cf. 32:1-2, 6). He used this time as an opportunity to deliver God's message to any who would listen. His message was overheard by four high-ranking officials: **Shephatiah son of Mattan** (not mentioned elsewhere), **Gedaliah son of Pashhur** (possibly a son of the Pashhur who beat Jeremiah, 20:1-3), **Jehucal son of Shelemiah** (sent by Zedekiah to inquire about the lifting of Babylon's siege, 37:3), and **Pashhur son of Malkijah** (sent by Zedekiah to inquire about Babylon's initial attack on Jerusalem, 21:1-2). These four powerful officials **heard** Jeremiah speaking to **all the people.**

The contents of Jeremiah's message are summarized in 38:2-3. The message was the same one that Jeremiah gave before (21:3-10). Those who remained in Jerusalem would **die by the sword, famine, or plague** (cf. comments on 14:12). Only those who deserted **to the Babylonians** would **live.** Jerusalem's only hope was to surrender. Any thought of withstanding Babylon's siege was futile since God had said the **city** would be **handed over to** Nebuchadnezzar **who** would **capture it.**

**38:4-6.** **The officials** went to Zedekiah and demanded that Jeremiah **be put to death** for his words. His "treasonous" remarks were **discouraging** both **the soldiers** and **all the people.** In their twisted nationalistic logic these officials believed that Jeremiah was **seeking** the **ruin** of his **people** when, in fact, Jeremiah wanted just the opposite (v. 2). Zedekiah's weakness was most evident in his response to

these officials. Though earlier he had agreed to protect Jeremiah (37:18-21), Zedekiah now handed him over to those who sought his life. Zedekiah's lame excuse was that **the king** could **do nothing to oppose** them. Zedekiah was a political puppet, incapable of making strong, independent decisions. He was controlled either by Nebuchadnezzar (cf. 2 Kings 24:17) or by the city officials who urged him to rebel against Babylon and then influenced his decisions (Jer. 27:12-15; 38:5, 19, 24-28).

The officials **took Jeremiah** and **put him into** Malkijah's **cistern,** in **the courtyard of the guard.** A cistern was a large pit cut into rock and covered with plaster. It was used to gather rainwater in the winter for use during the dry summer (cf. 2:13). This **cistern** was so deep that they had to lower **Jeremiah** into it **by ropes.** Possibly because of the prolonged drought (cf. 14:1-4) the cistern **had no water in it.** All it contained was the **mud** that collected in the bottom of the pit from the dirt carried there by the rain. **Jeremiah** then **sank down into the mud.** His life was indeed threatened. Had the water or mud been deeper he would certainly have drowned or suffocated, and death by starvation was a near prospect. Also perhaps individuals threw stones at Jeremiah while he was in the cistern, hoping to kill him outright or to knock him unconscious so he would sink into the muddy water and die (cf. comments on Lam. 3:52-54).

(4) Jeremiah's rescue from the cistern (38:7-13). **38:7-9.** Many of Jeremiah's countrymen wanted him killed. The only official who cared enough to intercede on his behalf was **Ebed-Melech** (lit., "servant of the king") who was **a Cushite** from the area of upper Egypt (modern-day southern Egypt, Sudan, and northern Ethiopia). He was serving as **an official** (*sārîs,* lit., "a eunuch"; cf. comments on Dan. 1:7) in **the royal palace.** His exact position in the palace was not described, but he had access to the king.

**Ebed-Melech went** to **the Benjamin Gate** (cf. Jer. 20:2; 37:13) where **the king was sitting**—either conducting official business or supervising the strengthening of Jerusalem's defenses against the siege. His urgent message to **the king** was that the other officials had **acted wickedly** by throwing **Jeremiah . . . into**

a cistern where he would starve to death. Evidently Zedekiah had not known the officials' specific plan to kill Jeremiah or else he had not believed that they would carry it out. But now he knew Jeremiah's death was imminent.

**38:10-13.** Zedekiah ordered Ebed-Melech to take 30 men from there—possibly soldiers on duty at the gate—and lift Jeremiah from the cistern before he died. Thirty men would be needed to pull Jeremiah out of the mud and to stand guard against the officials who might oppose the rescue attempt. Ebed-Melech led the soldiers to a room under the treasury in the palace where the opening to the cistern was located. Old rags and worn-out clothes were passed down to Jeremiah to place under his arms to pad the ropes. Jeremiah was then pulled . . . up with the ropes and freed from the cistern. He was again put in the courtyard of the guard (cf. 37:21).

(5) Jeremiah's second meeting with Zedekiah (38:14-28). **38:14-16.** Zedekiah sent for Jeremiah again and met him in secret at the third entrance to the temple. This entrance, not mentioned elsewhere, may refer to a private entrance that connected the king's palace with the temple. Zedekiah wanted to ask Jeremiah something, and he told the prophet not to hide anything from him. Jeremiah voiced two objections. First, if he did answer with a message the king did not want to hear he had no guarantee that the king would not kill him. Second, any counsel Jeremiah gave was wasted because the king would not listen to him. Zedekiah answered the first objection but not the second. He promised that he would neither kill Jeremiah himself nor hand him over to people who were seeking his life. But the king made no promise to heed Jeremiah's message.

**38:17-23.** Jeremiah's message remained the same as before (cf. 21:1-10; 37:17; 38:1-3). If Zedekiah would surrender to the Babylonians his life would be spared, the city would not be burned down, and his family would live. However, if he would not surrender, the city would be handed over to the armies of Babylon who would burn it down (cf. 21:10; 32:29; 34:2, 22; 37:8, 10; 38:23); and Zedekiah would not escape from their hands.

Zedekiah refused to heed Jeremiah's advice because of fear. He was afraid of the Jews who had already gone over to the Babylonians because he thought the Babylonians would hand him over to those Jews who now opposed him. Given the opportunity, they would mistreat him for his past acts of cruelty to them. Jeremiah tried to assure Zedekiah that this would not happen. If he would obey the LORD by following Jeremiah's word, his life would be spared. But if he refused to surrender because of fear he would suffer the very ridicule and humiliation he sought to avoid. The women from his own palace (the royal harem) would scoff at Zedekiah as they were brought out to the officials of . . . Babylon. The theme of their song would be the gullibility of the king in trusting his advisers who had misled him while posing as his trusted friends. But when Zedekiah's feet had sunk in the mud of Babylon's pit (cf. 38:6) he would look around to discover that his friends who had brought him there had deserted him. If he refused to surrender to Babylon he would see his wives and children being led away (cf. 39:6). He himself would be captured and the city of Jerusalem would be burned down (cf. 38:18).

**38:24-28.** Zedekiah refused to follow Jeremiah's advice. Such a bold step was beyond the ability of this spineless monarch. Instead he warned Jeremiah not to let anyone know about their conversation. If word got out, the officials would try to kill Jeremiah. Palace spies were everywhere so Zedekiah gave Jeremiah an alibi in case he was questioned. If the officials asked Jeremiah what he said to the king and what the king said to him, he was to tell them that he was pleading with Zedekiah not to send him back to the dungeon in Jonathan's house (cf. 37:15). Jeremiah had indeed made such a request during his first meeting with Zedekiah (37:20).

Zedekiah's caution was well-founded because the officials did hear about the meeting and went to Jeremiah to question him. Jeremiah repeated the words Zedekiah told him to say; and since no one had heard the conversation, they accepted Jeremiah's story. Jeremiah remained in the courtyard of the guard (cf. 38:13) as a political prisoner till Jerusalem was captured by Nebuchadnezzar.

*c. Jerusalem's destruction (chap. 39)*

(1) The fate of the Jews (39:1-10).
**39:1-4.** Jeremiah's declarations of doom were ignored by the people of Jerusalem. His vindication came when God brought to pass Jerusalem's destruction just as he had predicted it. Jeremiah gave a detailed account of **how Jerusalem was taken.** The final conflict began **in the 9th year of** Zedekiah's reign **in the 10th month.** This event was so traumatic that it was recorded three other times in the Old Testament, even noting the day of the month (cf. 2 Kings 25:1; Jer. 52:4; Ezek. 24:1-2). The **siege** began on January 15, 588 B.C. and lasted until **the ninth day of the 4th month of Zedekiah's 11th year.** Using a Western method for reckoning of dates this would seem to give a siege of approximately 19 months (the last 3 months of the 9th year + the 12 months of the 10th year + the first 4 months of the 11th year). However, using the method for reckoning dates employed by the Hebrews, the length of the siege was much longer. For the *years* of the Hebrew kings were calculated on a Tishri (September-October)-to-Tishri calendar while the *months* of a year were calculated on a Nisan (March-April)-to-Nisan calendar (see comments on 36:9). Zedekiah's 11th year extended from October 18, 587 to October 6, 586. The 4th month from Nisan that coincided with his 11th year began on July 10, 586. The ninth day of that month was July 18, 586 B.C. Therefore the entire siege lasted just over 30 months, from January 15, 588 to July 18, 586 B.C.

After the 30-month siege the Babylonians broke **through** the **city wall. The officials of . . . Babylon** entered the city and **took seats in the Middle Gate.** The Middle Gate was probably on the north side of the city (where the Babylonians breached the walls) in the Central (or Tyropeon) Valley which separated the two quarters of the city. They "took seats" to establish their control over the city and to judge those taken captive (cf. comments on 38:7; Ezek. 11:1). One of these officials was **Nergal-Sharezer of Samgar** (also called Neriglissar) who was Nebuchadnezzar's son-in-law who ascended Babylon's throne in 560 B.C. after the death of Nebuchadnezzar's son, Evil-Merodach (cf. Jer. 52:31; also see the chart "Kings of the Neo-Babylonian Empire," in the *Introduction* to Dan.). The

other officials included **Nebo-Sarsekim** and **Nergal-Sharezer,** though the exact names and number of individuals listed are unclear (NIV marg.).

**Zedekiah** and his **soldiers saw** that the city had fallen. It would be only a matter of time till the Babylonians moved south through the city and captured them. In a desperate bid to escape **they fled** from **the city at night.** Their plan was to leave the city **by way of the king's garden,** located in the south near the Pool of Siloam (cf. Neh. 3:15). After passing **through the gate between the two walls,** the ragtag soldiers were in the steep ravine near where the Hinnom and Kidron Valleys unite. Climbing over the Mount of Olives the army **headed toward the Arabah,** probably hoping to cross the Jordan River and escape to Rabbah (modern Amman, Jordan), the capital of their allies, the Ammonites (cf. comments on Ezek. 21:18-23).

**39:5-7.** After waiting so long for this victory, the Babylonians were not about to let their prey escape. Pursuing **Zedekiah** and his soldiers, the Babylonians **overtook** them on the broad **plains of Jericho** just before the Jordan River. Zedekiah was **captured** and taken **to Nebuchadnezzar,** who had established his military headquarters **at Riblah in . . . Hamath** (see map "The World of Jeremiah and Ezekiel," in the *Introduction*). Nebuchadnezzar **pronounced sentence** on Zedekiah for rebelling against **Babylon. Zedekiah** was forced to watch as the Babylonians **slaughtered** his **sons . . . before his eyes** and **killed all the nobles of Judah.** To seal this sight of horror in Zedekiah's mind forever, Nebuchadnezzar **then . . . put out Zedekiah's eyes.** Finally he **bound** Zedekiah **with bronze shackles** to drag him in humiliation **to Babylon.** Zedekiah suffered the shame that he feared because he had ignored the warnings of the Lord (cf. 38:17-23).

**39:8-10.** Jerusalem too suffered the ignominious fate predicted by Jeremiah. The Babylonians **set fire** both to the magnificent **royal palace and the houses of the people** (cf. 21:10; 22:6-7; 32:29; 34:2, 22; 37:8-10; 38:18, 23). The soldiers also **broke down the walls of Jerusalem** so the city would remain defenseless (cf. Lam. 2:8-9; Neh. 1:3). **Nebuzaradan, commander of the imperial guard** (*rab-ṭabbāḥîm,* lit., "chief of the slaughterers";

cf. Gen. 37:36; Dan. 2:14), took as captives those who were still alive **in the city** (cf. Jer. 13:19; 15:2; Ezek. 5:8-12) **along with** the people who had defected (**gone over to him**) earlier (cf. Jer. 21:8-9; 38:1-4, 17-23). To insure loyalty, stability, and productivity, Babylon **left behind** a remnant of the extremely **poor—people who owned nothing. He gave them vineyards and fields.** No doubt he believed that those individuals would be grateful to the Babylonians for their newfound prosperity and would be unlikely to rebel. In return Babylon would receive income in the form of taxation on the produce of the land.

(2) The fate of Jeremiah (39:11-18). **39:11-14. Nebuchadnezzar** had evidently heard of **Jeremiah**—possibly either through the letters the prophet had sent to Babylon (cf. chap. 29) or through the testimony of those who had defected to the Babylonians (21:8-9; 38:1-3). Nebuchadnezzar issued **orders . . . through Nebuzaradan** to his soldiers to **take** Jeremiah **and look after him.** They were not to **harm him but** were to **do for him whatever** he desired. **Jeremiah** was released from **the courtyard of the guard** (cf. 38:28) and **turned . . . over to** Judahite **Gedaliah,** who was the **son of Ahikam** and the grandson **of Shaphan** (see the chart "The Line of Shaphan," near 26:24). Gedaliah was appointed as governor of those who remained in the land (40:7). Some have thought that the account of Jeremiah's kind treatment in 39:11-14 contradicts the account of his being in chains in 40:1. However, the accounts can be easily harmonized. Jeremiah was rounded up with the other survivors of Jerusalem and then taken five miles north to Ramah for processing (cf. 31:15). It was there that the prophet of God was identified and released (40:4-5).

**39:15-18. While Jeremiah** had waited for the city to fall, God gave him a message for **Ebed-Melech the Cushite** (cf. 38:7-13). God's **words against** Jerusalem would **be fulfilled before** Ebed-Melech's **eyes.** God promised that when Jerusalem fell He would **rescue** Ebed-Melech so that he would not be executed with all the other officials (cf. 39:6; 52:10, 24-27). He would **escape** because he had demonstrated his **trust in** God by helping Jeremiah.

### 3. AFTER THE FALL (CHAPS. 40–45)

One would think that the fall of Jerusalem would have taught Judah a lesson she would never forget. However, by recording the events that happened after the fall of the city, Jeremiah demonstrated that the basic character of the people who remained in the land was unchanged. They still refused to trust in God or to submit to Babylon (cf. Ezek. 33:23-29).

#### a. Jeremiah's ministry to the remnant in Palestine (chaps. 40–42)

(1) The governorship of Gedaliah (40:1-12). **40:1-6. Jeremiah** was **released** in **Ramah** where he had been taken **bound in chains** with the other **captives.** As **Nebuzaradan** let **Jeremiah** go he acknowledged his familiarity with Jeremiah's prophecies. No doubt some of those who had defected or who had been captured told the Babylonians about Jeremiah's messages. Nebuzaradan told **Jeremiah** that God brought **disaster** on Jerusalem as predicted because the **people** had **sinned against** Him. However, Nebuzaradan said he was **freeing** Jeremiah **from** his **chains** because he was innocent in Judah's revolt against **Babylon.**

**Jeremiah** was free **to go** wherever he wanted. If he went **to Babylon** with the other captives, Nebuzaradan promised to **look after** him (cf. 39:12). If he wished to stay in **Judah,** he could settle **wherever** he pleased. **However,** if he did stay in Judah **Nebuzaradan** suggested that he **go . . . to Gedaliah** and **live with him.** No doubt Governor **Gedaliah** could offer both the protection and the physical provisions that Jeremiah would need if he stayed. As Jeremiah left Ramah to make the three-mile journey to **Mizpah**—the administrative center for Judah after the destruction of Jerusalem—Nebuzaradan displayed his kindness by providing Jeremiah with **provisions and a present.**

**40:7-12.** As in many wars, scattered remnants of the army often still remain deployed in the field after the surrender of the main body of troops. The main forces of Judah, located in Jerusalem, Lachish, and Azekah, had been crushed; but groups of **army officers and their men** were still scattered **in the open country.** When these soldiers **heard** that **Gedaliah** was now **governor over the land** they **came to** him **at Mizpah.** Two of the leaders listed (v. 8) were worthy of special notice because of subsequent events. The one listed first was **Ishmael son of Nethaniah** (cf. vv. 14-15). He was from the royal line of David (cf. 41:1) and had served as one of King Zedekiah's officers. The second was **Johanan** who was one of two **sons of Kareah** (cf. 40:13-16). Nothing else is known about Johanan's background.

The commanders mentioned in verse 8 wanted to know what would happen if they would lay down their arms and surrender. **Gedaliah** reassured **them** that no harm would come to them if they surrendered. He encouraged them to **settle down in the land and serve . . . Babylon.** Gedaliah promised to **represent** them **before the Babylonians** while they concentrated on harvesting **the wine, summer fruit, and oil.** They would be free to **live in the towns** they had **taken over.**

In addition to reaching the scattered bands of Judah's resistance fighters, word of Gedaliah's appointment as governor also reached **the Jews in Moab, Ammon, Edom, and** elsewhere. These refugees **all came back to the land** to resettle, and helped in harvesting the **wine and summer fruit** (cf. v. 10).

(2) The assassination of Gedaliah (40:13–41:15). **40:13-16.** Judah's prospects looked bright. Peace and stability were returning to the land. The warring factions had submitted to Gedaliah's rule, and some refugees had returned. But just beneath the surface forces of intrigue and rebellion were churning and bubbling. It was only a matter of time before they broke to the surface.

The first report of trouble came from **Johanan son of Kareah** (cf. v. 8). He, along with **all the army officers,** reported to **Gedaliah** that **Baalis king of the Ammonites** had **sent Ishmael son of Nethaniah** (cf. v. 8) **to take** Gedaliah's **life.** Why would the king of Ammon conspire with Ishmael·to kill Gedaliah? The answer lies in understanding the relationship between Judah and Ammon. Both nations were vassals to Babylon and had participated in a secret meeting of nations in 593 B.C. to evaluate their prospects of uniting in rebellion against Babylon (cf. 27:1-11). That meeting did not produce any definite action; but in 588 B.C. Egypt's new Pharaoh (Hophra) per-

suaded Judah, Ammon, and Tyre to revolt against Babylon. Nebuchadnezzar had to decide which nation to attack first, and God directed him to Judah instead of to Ammon (cf. Ezek. 21:18-23). Judah and Ammon were still allies when Jerusalem fell, and Zedekiah was probably heading for Ammon when he was captured (Jer. 39:4-5). But in spite of their union as allies, Judah and Ammon did not care for each other. Their union was a "marriage of convenience." Ammon rejoiced over Jerusalem's fall because she knew that if Nebuchadnezzar committed his army against Jerusalem he would not be able to attack Ammon (cf. comments on 49:1-6; Ezek. 25:1-7). Thus Gedaliah's commitment to Babylon was unsettling to Ammon. If Judah did submit to Babylon, then after Nebuchadnezzar finished his siege of Tyre (cf. Ezek. 29:17-18) he would probably attack Ammon next. But a destabilized Judah could force Nebuchadnezzar to commit large numbers of troops there to maintain order, which would improve Ammon's chances for survival. So it was to Ammon's advantage to replace pro-Babylonian Gedaliah with an anti-Babylonian leader like Ishmael.

Unfortunately **Gedaliah . . . did not believe** these officers. **Johanan** met **privately** with **Gedaliah** and offered to **kill Ishmael.** He planned to do it secretly so **no one** would **know** who was responsible. Johanan thought Ishmael should be eliminated for the good **of Judah.** If Ishmael were allowed to **take** Gedaliah's **life,** it could **cause all the Jews** in the land **to be scattered** and **to perish. Gedaliah** ordered **Johanan** not to **do such a thing** because he was certain that the rumors **about Ishmael** were **not true.** Gedaliah was an honorable man who made a fatal mistake when he misjudged Ishmael's character.

**41:1-3.** Ishmael came to Gedaliah **in the seventh month** (September-October). Though the month was given, the year was not, so the exact dating of the assassination is uncertain. It would be difficult for all of these events to have occurred in 586 B.C. because the army of Babylon was still in Jerusalem as late as August 17 of that year (52:12). This would allow less than two months for the Babylonians to deport the people, establish a government, allot the land, and withdraw the main body of their forces. So the assassination must have happened in a later year. But which year would fit best? One suggestion focuses on a little-known deportation in 583–582 B.C. (cf. Jer. 52:30). Why did Nebuchadnezzar make another excursion into the land at that time? A likely answer would be to restore order after the assassination of the governor and the small contingent of Babylonian troops stationed in Judah (cf. 41:2-3). If these events are related, then the "seventh month" when Gedaliah was assassinated began on October 4, 583 B.C.

Ishmael . . . came to Gedaliah with 10 men for a "peaceful" meeting. As they sat together eating . . . Ishmael and his cohorts struck down Gedaliah. They also killed all the Jews (probably those attending the banquet) as well as the Babylonian soldiers who were stationed there (cf. 2 Kings 25:25).

41:4-9. The assassinations probably took place in the evening. The plot had gone so well that early the day after the assassination nobody knew about it. On that day 80 men in mourning (with shaved . . . beards, torn . . . clothes, and self-inflicted cuts; cf. comments on 16:6) were journeying to Jerusalem from Shechem, Shiloh, and Samaria—three cities that had been part of the Northern Kingdom of Israel. The fact that these men were from the Northern Kingdom implies that at least some of King Josiah's reforms (cf. 2 Kings 23:15-20; 2 Chron. 34:33) had a lasting impact. These men were carrying grain offerings and incense that they planned to offer at the temple. Though the temple had been destroyed (cf. Jer. 52:13, 17-23), people still worshiped at its site. No doubt these pilgrims were traveling to Jerusalem to celebrate one of the three feasts held during the seventh month (cf. Lev. 23:23-44).

Ishmael . . . went out to meet the pilgrims, weeping as he went. After feigning sympathy he invited them to come to Gedaliah. Certainly an offer to meet with the governor could not be refused so they went into the city. Once they were in the city Ishmael and his band of cutthroats slaughtered 70 of the 80 men and threw their bodies into a cistern. Why did Ishmael perform this savage act? Though not specifically stated, Jeremiah 41:8 implies that he intended to plunder his victims and seize their provisions. Certainly a caravan of 80 pilgrims would carry a fair amount of food and money. Ten of the 80 managed to bargain for their lives by announcing that additional supplies of wheat and barley, oil and honey were hidden in a field. If he would spare them, they would show him the location of this cache. Ishmael's greed got the better of him so he did not kill them.

In a sidelight Jeremiah explained the historical significance of the site where the slaughter occurred (v. 9). The cistern in which the bodies of the 70 men and Gedaliah had been cast had been constructed nearly 300 years earlier by King Asa. It had served as part of Asa's defense against Baasha when the king of Judah sought to stem the advances of the king of Israel (cf. 1 Kings 15:16-22). The cistern that had once helped preserve life was now filled . . . with the dead.

41:10-15. Ishmael had killed only a select group of those living in Mizpah (v. 2). He made captives of all the rest who lived there. These included the king's daughters and all the others who had been assigned to Gedaliah. No doubt Jeremiah was included among the captives (cf. 40:6). The group set out from Mizpah to go to Ammon, Ishmael's ally (40:14).

The slaughter could not go undetected indefinitely. Someone either happened on the scene or escaped from the group and reported the matter to the other commanders. When Johanan son of Kareah and the other army officers . . . heard about all the crimes . . . they mobilized all their men and set off to fight Ishmael. The band of soldiers caught up with the slower group of captives near the great pool in Gibeon (cf. 2 Sam. 2:12-16). Those taken captive were glad when they spotted their rescuers, and in the surprise and confusion they turned away from Ishmael and went over to Johanan. Ishmael along with 8 of his men escaped during the conflict and fled to the Ammonites. Two of Ishmael's 10 men must have been captured or killed (cf. Jer. 41:1).

(3) The leadership of Johanan (41:16–42:22). 41:16-18. Johanan . . . led away all the survivors they had rescued from Ishmael. This group included soldiers, women, children, and court officials. But instead of returning to Mizpah

they went on. Their first place of rest was at Geruth Kimham near Bethlehem, a journey of about 13 miles from Gibeon. The group was on its way to Egypt to escape the Babylonians because they were afraid Babylon would retaliate for the death of Gedaliah.

42:1-6. Before continuing, all the army officers, including both Johanan and Jezaniah (called Azariah in 43:2) son of Hoshaiah, and all the people decided to ask God's guidance for their journey. They asked Jeremiah to pray to . . . God on their behalf. They wanted God to tell them where they should go and what they should do. They had already decided to flee Israel, but their destination remained uncertain (though 42:14 and 43:7 imply that they were already planning to go to Egypt).

Jeremiah agreed to pray for the people, and promised to tell them everything God said. Summoning the LORD as their Witness the people promised to act in accordance with whatever God commanded, whether it was favorable or unfavorable. After watching God destroy their nation because of disobedience they were careful to agree that they would obey the LORD.

42:7-12. Jeremiah prayed for the people, and 10 days later God answered his request. Jeremiah called together the group and gave them God's answer. If they would stay in the land, God promised to build them up. They were not to be afraid of the Babylonians because God would deliver them from any harm from their hands. Indeed God vowed that Nebuchadnezzar would have compassion (rāḥam, "show tender concern"), a characteristic not usually associated with the Babylonians (cf. 6:23; 21:7). If the people submitted to the Babylonians, God promised that Nebuchadnezzar would restore them to their land.

42:13-18. Much like the blessings and cursings of Deuteronomy 28, Jeremiah followed his list of blessings for obedience with a list of judgments for disobedience. If the people refused to stay in the land and decided to disobey . . . God by going to live in Egypt, then they would experience God's judgment for violating their oath (Jer. 42:5-6). It is easy to understand their desire to move to Egypt where, in their understanding, they would no longer see war or hear the

trumpet announcing an impending attack (cf. 4:5, 19-21; 6:1). Also, in Egypt they would no longer be hungry for bread as they were during and after the siege of Jerusalem (cf. Lam. 1:11; 5:6, 9). Yet, warned Jeremiah, if they decided to disobey God and settle in Egypt, they would die by the sword, famine, or plague (cf. Jer. 14:12; 42:22). The very dangers they were wanting to avoid would come on them. No one would escape the disaster, and all those who left would never see the land of Israel again.

42:19-22. Jeremiah concluded his message by repeating God's command not to go to Egypt. God knew the people's hearts and warned them that they had made a fatal mistake when they asked Jeremiah to pray for them. For though they had vowed to do everything God said (cf. v. 6), when His word finally came they refused to obey it. Thus, Jeremiah warned them, the only thing they could be sure of was that they would die by the sword, famine, and plague (cf. v. 17) if they went to Egypt.

b. Jeremiah's ministry to the remnant in Egypt (chaps. 43–44)

(1) The remnant's flight to Egypt (43:1-7). 43:1-3. After Jeremiah finished telling the people God's answer to their request, both Azariah (called Jezaniah in 42:1) and Johanan, along with all the arrogant men, challenged his truthfulness. They said he was lying when he claimed God had said not to go to Egypt, and they accused Baruch of inciting Jeremiah to join a conspiracy to hand these former rebels over to the Babylonians who would then kill them or carry them into exile. It is not known why they singled out Baruch. But since he served as Jeremiah's confidant and companion, they might have assumed that he was responsible for Jeremiah's answer.

43:4-7. Instead of returning to Mizpah the group marched south from Geruth Kimham (41:17). In addition to the army officers and soldiers who had returned to Gedaliah (40:7-10) this band included the remnant who had returned to Judah from all the nations (41:11-12) and the men, women, and children and the king's daughters who had been entrusted to Gedaliah. The leaders also forced Jeremiah and Baruch to go along with them. They made their way to

Egypt and settled in **Tahpanhes,** a fortress city on the border of Lower (northern) Egypt (see the map "The World of Jeremiah and Ezekiel," in the *Introduction*).

(2) The prophecy of Nebuchadnezzar's invasion. **43:8-13.** As **the Jews** watched, **Jeremiah** performed another symbolic act to gain their attention (cf. 13:1-11). He gathered **some large stones** and buried **them in clay** under **the brick pavement** that covered the large courtyard **at the entrance to Pharaoh's palace.** Since Pharaoh's main residence during this time was at Elephantine in Upper (southern) Egypt, the "palace" mentioned by Jeremiah was probably a government building that served as Pharaoh's residence when he visited the city of **Tahpanhes.**

The purpose of the **stones** was to mark the spot where **Nebuchadnezzar** would **set his throne** when God brought him to Egypt. The king of Babylon would **spread his royal canopy** over the place Jeremiah indicated when he came to **attack Egypt.** The specters of **death . . . captivity,** and **the sword** which these exiles were fleeing (cf. 42:13-17) would follow them into Egypt. Nebuchadnezzar would **set fire to the temples** in Egypt and **take** her **gods captive. He** would **wrap up** Egypt and carry her away captive as easily **as a shepherd wraps his garment around him.** In **the temple of the sun** (*bêṭ šemeš,* a possible reference to the city of Heliopolis, also called On), Egypt's worship was centered (see the map "The World of Jeremiah and Ezekiel," in the *Introduction*). This city that was full of **sacred pillars** (obelisks) and **temples** would be demolished.

When did Nebuchadnezzar's attack on Egypt occur? Because the Babylonian Chronicles that have been discovered go only through 594 B.C., there is a general lack of extrabiblical sources that supply any information. However, one fragmentary text has been found which implies an invasion of Egypt by Nebuchadnezzar in 568–567 B.C. This would harmonize well with the prophecy of Nebuchadnezzar's invasion of Egypt in Ezekiel 29:19. That prophecy, given on April 26, 571 B.C., indicated that the invasion was still future. Therefore Nebuchadnezzar's attack on Egypt probably occurred sometime between 571 and 567 B.C.

(3) The warning of God's judgment (chap. 44). **44:1-10.** God's **word came to Jeremiah** a second time while he was in Egypt (cf. 43:8). This time the word concerned **all the Jews** who had traveled to Egypt. It applied to those **in Lower Egypt** which included the northern cities of **Migdol, Tahpanhes, and Memphis**; and it extended south to **Upper Egypt.** Jeremiah was using a figure of speech known as a merism in which, by listing the two extremes, he also included everything between them. Thus this message was for all Jews throughout the entire land of Egypt.

**God** reminded the Jews of the **disaster He brought** against **Jerusalem** and **all** Judah's **towns.** Their **ruins** stood as mute testimonies to God's judgment on **the evil they** had **done.** The particular sin to which God was referring was their worship of **other gods.** Though God had repeatedly warned the people through His **servants the prophets** to **turn from** their sin, they refused to **listen or pay attention.** God's **fierce anger** then **raged against . . . Judah** until only **desolate ruins** remained.

Jeremiah applied this "history lesson" to the Jews in Egypt. Instead of realizing the folly of idolatry they were **burning incense to other gods in** the land of **Egypt.** They were in danger of becoming **an object of cursing and reproach** (cf. comments on 24:9) by daring a holy God to judge them for their sin. It was as though they had **forgotten the wickedness** that both they and their ancestors had **committed** which had brought God's judgment. They had **not humbled themselves** before God or **followed** His **Law.** How quickly they seemed to have forgotten God's Word!

**44:11-14.** God would **bring disaster on** the **remnant in Egypt** for their sin just as He had the nation of **Judah. They** would **perish** by both **sword** and **famine** (cf. 42:22). This judgment would include nearly everyone. Those living **in Egypt** would experience the same judgments God used when He **punished Jerusalem.** Though these fugitives hoped to return home someday, God vowed that **none** would **return to the land of Judah.** All those who had fled to **Egypt** in violation of God's command would die there, **except** for **a few fugitives** whom God would allow to return.

**44:15-19.** Those who listened to Jeremiah's **message** refused to repent. The men, **who knew that their wives were** practicing idolatry, said they would continue to **do everything** just as they had in the past. These idolatrous practices included burning **incense to the Queen of Heaven** (see comments on 7:18). The widespread nature of that heathen practice is evident because it was done by the people, their ancestors (**fathers**), their **kings,** and their **officials.** In an ironic reversal of truth the people blamed their difficulties on their failure to continue these pagan rituals. As long as they sacrificed **to the Queen of Heaven,** so they said, **they had plenty of food.** They said that when they **stopped burning incense** they **had nothing** and began **perishing by sword and famine.** The people's hindsight was extremely myopic. They failed to remember that just the opposite was true in their history (cf. chap. 14; Hosea 2:5-9; Amos 4:4-12). Faithfulness and obedience to God brought blessing, and unfaithfulness and disobedience to God brought cursing (Lev. 26:1-45; Deut. 28). **The women** affirmed that their **husbands** knew (and evidently approved) of their idolatrous practices.

**44:20-23.** **Jeremiah** reminded **the people** that God knew **about the** idolatrous sacrifices that had been taking place. When He **could no longer endure** the sin, He judged the people and the **land** became **an object of cursing and a desolate waste.** Far from bringing blessing, Judah's worship of false gods had assured her doom. This failure to acknowledge and follow the Lord had produced the **disaster** in Judah which the remnant could **see** only too well.

**44:24-28.** The **actions** of **the people** revealed the sincerity of their pledge to continue worshiping **the Queen of Heaven** with **incense** and **drink offerings** (cf. v. 17). Since they were so determined to pursue their idolatry, God sarcastically told them to **go ahead** with the **vows** they had made to this false goddess. But as they worshiped her they were also to **hear** God's message of judgment. God took a solemn oath and swore **by His great name** that **no** Jew **living anywhere in Egypt** would **ever again invoke** His **name or swear** by Him in an oath. His judgment would pursue them till **all** were **destroyed.** Only a **very few** would

survive to return to **Judah.** They would **then . . . know** that only God's **word** would **stand**—a direct rebuke at their claim that idolatry brought prosperity (vv. 17-18).

**44:29-30.** God then gave a **sign** to validate the truth of His prophecy. The fulfillment of this sign would prove that God's **threats of harm** (cf. v. 27) **against** the idolatrous Jews in Egypt would **stand.** The sign was that **Pharaoh Hophra** would be handed **over to his enemies . . . just as . . . Zedekiah** was handed **over to Nebuchadnezzar.** According to historian Herodotus, Hophra lost his throne in 570 B.C. He sent Amasis, one of his generals, to quell a revolt among his army; but the army united behind Amasis and made him Pharaoh. Amasis defeated Hophra in battle and imprisoned him. Sometime later Amasis handed Hophra over to the Egyptians who were clamoring for Hophra's death, and they strangled him (Herodotus 2. 161-3, 169).

*c. Jeremiah's ministry to Baruch (chap. 45)*

**45:1-3.** This chapter was written **in the fourth year of Jehoiakim** (605–604 B.C.) **after Baruch had** recorded **on a scroll** the message **Jeremiah was then dictating.** The event in view was recorded in 36:1-8. Evidently Baruch was discouraged because of the content of the message. He felt that **God** had **added sorrow to** his **pain.** Much like Jeremiah earlier (cf. 8:21–9:2; 14:17-18; 15:10, 15-18), **Baruch** was **worn out with groaning** and could **find no rest.**

**45:4-5.** God's message to Baruch was intended to evoke a response of faith in the midst of judgment. God would indeed **overthrow what** He had **built and uproot what** He had **planted** (cf. 1:10). Baruch's discouragement came because the realities of judgment clashed with his personal aspirations of greatness. He was not to **seek great things for** himself because God was bringing **disaster.** Rather than being sad because God did not provide all he wanted, Baruch should have been thankful that God spared him. God did promise to **let** Baruch **escape with** his **life** despite the calamities happening all around. The response God expected of Baruch was the response of his contemporary, Habakkuk (cf. Hab. 3:16-19). The hope of a godly person in the midst of national judgment was to be fixed firmly on God. Probably Jeremiah placed this chapter last in his prophecies to Judah (Jer. 2–45) to emphasize the response that God wanted from godly Jews during the Exile.

## III. Prophecies concerning the Nations (chaps. 46–51)

Jeremiah had been commissioned as a prophet to the nations (cf. 1:5; 46:1). He grouped his prophecies concerning the nation of Judah first (chaps. 2–45) because Judah was God's covenant nation and because she consumed the largest amount of Jeremiah's prophetic activity. Yet other nations did not escape his prophetic eye. If God would judge His own covenant people for their sin, how could the heathen nations around Judah hope to escape when their sin was even more pronounced? In chapters 46–51 the spotlight of God's judgment shifted from Judah to her heathen neighbors.

### A. Prophecy against Egypt (chap. 46)

The first nation to be selected for judgment was Egypt, Judah's erstwhile ally. She had encouraged Judah's revolt against Babylon; but when it came time for Egypt to protect her partner in rebellion she proved incapable of meeting her commitments (cf. 37:4-10; Ezek. 29:6-7).

1. EGYPT TO BE DEFEATED AT CARCHEMISH (46:1-12)

**46:1-6.** Jeremiah's **message** was directed **against the army of Pharaoh Neco.** This **king of Egypt** killed King Josiah of Judah in 609 B.C. (2 Kings 23:29). **Jeremiah** penned his prophecy after the army of **Egypt** was **defeated at Carchemish** (see the map "The World of Jeremiah and Ezekiel," in the *Introduction*). This was the city **on the Euphrates River** where **Nebuchadnezzar** scored a major victory against the Egyptians. The battle took place in 605 B.C., **the fourth year of Jehoiakim.**

God sarcastically called the army of Egypt to **prepare** their **shields** and **march out for battle** against the Babylonians. **The horses** were to be harnessed and mounted, and infantry troops were to **take** their **positions** ready to fight. Their **spears** and **armor** were prepared, and the army of Egypt was poised for battle.

But the battle did not go Egypt's way. Babylon's swift attack left the Egyptians **terrified** as **their warriors** were **defeated.** The panic-stricken soldiers fled **in haste.** In the ensuing confusion the fleeing soldiers hindered their own retreat so that the **swift** were not able to **flee nor** were the **strong** able to **escape.** Babylon overtook them and destroyed them. The Babylonian Chronicle confirms this picture of hopeless confusion and defeat. The Egyptian army "withdrew" before the Babylonians, but the Babylonians "overtook and defeated them so that not a single man escaped to his own country" (Donald J. Wiseman, *Chronicle of Chaldean Kings (626–556 B.C.) in the British Museum.* London: Trustees of the British Museum, 1956, pp. 67-9).

**46:7-12.** God asked **who** this nation was that was trying to imitate **the Nile** River with its **surging waters** that overflowed their banks and inundated the countryside. The answer was **Egypt.** She was trying to rise **like the Nile** and **cover the earth** with her conquests. The nation was trying to take on the characteristics of her life-giving river.

The surge of Egypt's armies with her **horses** and **charioteers** would resemble the rushing of a mighty river. Egypt's army contained mercenary soldiers from **Cush** (present-day southern Egypt, Sudan, and northern Ethiopia) and **Put** (modern-day Libya) who carried **shields** as infantrymen, and soldiers from **Lydia** (the west coast of Asia Minor) who were archers (drew **the bow**). Ezekiel named these same groups of mercenaries (Ezek. 30:5).

Though Egypt amassed a mighty army, the **day** of battle belonged **to the Lord.** God would bring **vengeance on** Egypt until she was destroyed. Only then would His **sword** of judgment be **satisfied.** God compared this slaughter to the offering of a **sacrifice** as He destroyed the Egyptians at Carchemish **by the River Euphrates.**

Even if the Egyptians went **to Gilead** to **get balm** for their wounds (see comments on Jer. 8:22), their **remedies** would be **in vain** because God would permit **no healing for** them. Surrounding **nations** would **hear of** Egypt's **shame** as her **cries** of anguish and pain filled **the earth.** The mighty warriors would **stumble over another** (cf. 46:6) as they would **fall down together** in defeat.

## 2. EGYPT TO BE INVADED AND EXILED (46:13-26)

**46:13-19.** Nebuchadnezzar defeated the Egyptians at Carchemish in 605 B.C., but he did not invade the land of Egypt until approximately 571–567 B.C. (see comments on 43:8-13). In this undated prophecy (46:13-26) God supplied additional details of **the coming of Nebuchadnezzar . . . to attack Egypt.** The warning of Nebuchadnezzar's approach was to be sounded **in Migdol . . . Memphis, and Tahpanhes**—the same three cities Jeremiah mentioned in 44:1 to describe Lower (northern) Egypt. This was the area where Nebuchadnezzar's forces were urged to **take** their **positions** on the fortifications **and get ready.**

Jeremiah asked **why** Egypt's **warriors** would **be laid low** (v. 15). There is a textual problem here because the Septuagint reads, "Wherefore has Apis fled. . . ?" (LXX, 26:15; the LXX has rearranged the order of several chapters in Jer. so that 46:15 in Heb. is 26:15 in Gr.) The Septuagint has divided the Hebrew verb for "laid low" (*nishap*) into two words (*nis hap*, "Haf (i.e., Apis) fled." Apis was the bull god of Egypt. The defeat of a people was often symbolized by the defeat of their god (cf. Isa. 46:1-2; Jer. 50:2; 51:44). If the Septuagint reading is accepted, then Jeremiah was pointing to the inability of Egypt's god Apis to protect them from the Lord. However, 46:15 seems to flow better if one accepts the Hebrew text's reading of verse 15a, "Why are the warriors laid low?"

Jeremiah answered his own question. The warriors could not **stand** because God had pushed **them down.** As the mercenary army stumbled **over** one another in their effort to flee from Egypt they decided to return home to their **own people** and their **native lands.** Only by leaving Egypt could they escape **the sword of the oppressor. Pharaoh** Hophra had made bold claims about his ability to defeat the Babylonians, but these defeated soldiers realized now that his mighty words were **only a loud noise.** He could not deliver on his promises. He had already **missed his opportunity** to defeat Babylon.

God was sending someone to Egypt (i.e., Nebuchadnezzar) who towered above all others as Mount **Tabor** stood out **among the mountains.** This one would rise as impressively as Mount **Car-**mel does **by the sea.** What Pharaoh Hophra could not accomplish, Nebuchadnezzar could. The Egyptians were to **pack** their **belongings for exile** (cf. Ezek. 29:9-16) because Nebuchadnezzar would attack **Memphis** (cf. Jer. 46:14) and leave it **in ruins without inhabitant.**

**46:20-24.** Jeremiah used several similes and metaphors to picture Egypt's fall to Babylon. First, he compared **Egypt** to **a beautiful heifer.** This metaphor is especially striking since Apis, one of Egypt's gods, was a bull. However, **a gadfly . . . from the north** (Babylon) was **coming** to bite her. Second, he compared **the mercenaries** (cf. vv. 9, 16) in Egypt's **ranks** of soldiers to **fattened calves** who had been prepared for their slaughter. They would **turn and flee** when **the day of disaster** came. Third, Jeremiah compared **Egypt** to a **fleeing serpent** that could do little more than hiss at her **enemy** as she slithered away to avoid the **axes** of these mighty woodcutters who had come to **chop down her forest.** Fourth, he compared the size of Babylon's army to a swarm of **locusts** which were too numerous to **be counted.** The point of every simile and metaphor was the same: Egypt would **be put to shame** (cf. v. 12) because God had **handed** her **over to the people of the north.**

**46:25-26. God** would spare neither the gods nor the kings of Egypt. He would **bring punishment on Amon god of Thebes.** Amon was the chief god of Thebes (or No) in Upper (southern) Egypt. Thus God's judgment which began in the north (cf. vv. 14, 19) would extend to the south. It would encompass **Pharaoh,** all Egypt's **gods,** and all the people **who** relied **on Pharaoh.** They would be handed **over . . . to Nebuchadnezzar** (cf. Ezek. 29:17-20). However, Egypt's destruction would not be permanent. God promised that later . . . **Egypt** would **be inhabited as in times past.** This could refer to the return of Egypt's exiles from Babylon (cf. Jer. 46:19; Ezek. 29:10-16). However, the association of Egypt's fortunes with the still-future restoration of Israel (Jer. 46:27-28) and the future focus in some of Jeremiah's other prophecies to the nations (cf. 48:47; 49:39) suggests that the ultimate fulfillment will come during the millennial reign of Christ when Egypt will again be in her land.

3. ISRAEL TO BE REGATHERED (46:27-28)

**46:27-28.** In contrast with Egypt, who would be taken into exile, **Israel** was **not** to **fear** or **be dismayed.** She could rejoice because God promised to return her people **from . . . exile.** Israel could look forward to a time when she would enjoy **peace and security.** Though she too went into exile, God vowed that He would **not completely destroy** her. A remnant would survive to again receive God's blessings (cf. 31:1-6).

## B. Prophecy against Philistia (chap. 47)

**47:1.** Jeremiah's second prophetic broadside against the Gentile nations was directed toward **the Philistines.** Philistia occupied the coastal plain of Judah and had been a thorn in Israel's side since the time of the Conquest (cf. Jud. 3:1-4). Whenever the Philistines were strong, they tried to expand from the coastal plain into the hill country of Judah. These attempts were opposed by Shamgar (Jud. 3:31), Samson (Jud. 13–16), Samuel (1 Sam. 7:2-17), Saul (1 Sam. 13:1–14:23; 28:1-4; 29:1-2, 11; 31:1-10), and David (2 Sam. 5:17-25). David was finally able to subdue the Philistines (2 Sam. 8:1), and they remained a vassal of Israel through the reign of Solomon. During the time of the divided monarchy the balance of power shifted back and forth. Judah was in control during the reigns of Jehoshaphat (2 Chron. 17:10-11) and Uzziah, but Philistia regained dominion during the reigns of Jehoram (2 Chron. 21:16-17) and Ahaz (2 Chron. 28:16-18).

Jeremiah's message was delivered **before Pharaoh attacked Gaza.** The exact date for this event is uncertain though the two most likely times are either 609 B.C. when Pharaoh Neco marched north through Palestine to meet the Babylonians (2 Kings 23:29-30) or 601 B.C. when he defeated the armies of Babylon in a battle described only in the Babylonian Chronicle. Because of the reference to Ashkelon's still-future destruction, the 609 date is preferable. Ashkelon was destroyed by Nebuchadnezzar in late 604 B.C. (see comments on Jer. 36:9).

**47:2-7.** The Babylonians were pictured as **waters** that were **rising in the north.** They were about to **become an overflowing torrent** that would sweep away the Philistines. The Philistines would **cry out** in anguish as the swirl of **galloping steeds** and **enemy chariots** rushed through the land. **The people** would be so overcome by fear that **fathers** would **not** even **turn** back **to help their children.** Being destroyed, **the Philistines** would not be able to **help** their allies, **Tyre and Sidon** (cf. Ezek. 27–28).

**The Philistines** were **the remnant from the coasts of Caphtor,** that is, Crete (cf. Amos 9:7; Zeph. 2:5). They were one of the groups of sea peoples who made their way to the coast of Palestine (see the map "The World of Jeremiah and Ezekiel," in the *Introduction*). **Gaza** and **Ashkelon,** two of the five cities that formed the Philistine pentapolis (cf. Josh. 13:3; 1 Sam. 6:4, 18), were singled out for special mention. Gaza was attacked by the Egyptians (cf. Jer. 47:1), and Ashkelon was later destroyed by Nebuchadnezzar in November-December 604 B.C. (cf. comments on 36:9). God predicted that the Philistines would be caught in the middle of the struggle between Babylon and Egypt and would be destroyed. As a result, they were to **shave** their heads and **cut** themselves—both signs of mourning or grief (cf. comments on 16:6). God's **sword** of judgment would not **rest** till it had attacked **Ashkelon and the seacoast** and destroyed them (cf. Ezek. 25:15-17).

## C. Prophecy against Moab (chap. 48)

The country of Moab was east of the Dead Sea. It was separated from Edom on the south by the Zered River and from Ammon on the north by the Arnon River. Jeremiah listed many of the Moabite cities that God would destroy. Much of the imagery used by Jeremiah was borrowed from Isaiah 16:6-12.

1. MOAB'S LAND TO BE DESTROYED (48:1-10)

**48:1-5. Nebo,** mentioned here by Jeremiah, was not the mountain of the same name on which Moses viewed the Promised Land and died (cf. Deut. 32:48-50). It was a city inhabited by the tribe of Reuben (cf. Num. 32:37-38) that was later captured by Moab. The city of **Kiriathaim** was also inhabited by the tribe of Reuben (Josh. 13:19) and later captured by Moab. God was now predicting that it would be **captured** from **Moab** by others. **The stronghold** could be translated "Misgab" (NIV marg.) and might refer to an as-yet unknown city or fortress that was **shat-**

tered by these invaders. Heshbon was the capital of Sihon, king of the Amorites, during the Exodus (Num. 21:25-30). It was given to the tribe of Reuben that rebuilt it (Num. 32:37; Josh. 13:17), though it was on the border of the tribe of Gad (Josh. 13:26). The Moabite Stone (now in the British Museum, London) implies that Heshbon was later occupied by individuals from the tribe of Gad. It was eventually taken by Moab. In a play on words Jeremiah indicated that in Heshbon (bᵉḥešbôn) men will plot (ḥāšᵉbû) Moab's downfall.

Jeremiah then described God's judgment on the town of Madmen which would be silenced. The cries from Horonaim (cf. 2 Sam. 13:34) would reverberate throughout the hills of Moab as the fugitives who fled up the way to Luhith wept bitterly and those traveling down to Horonaim shouted anguished cries over the destruction that confronted them.

48:6-10. The people of Moab would flee and run for their lives to escape the coming judgment. They would become like a bush in the desert—deserted and forlorn. It is possible to translate "like a bush" as "like Aroer" (ka'ᵃrô'ēr), a city on the edge of the Arnon River gorge (cf. Deut. 2:36). The thought would be the same—the people of Moab would be like a deserted and forlorn city or a bush in the wilderness. Because Moab had trusted in her deeds and riches she too would be judged by being taken captive as was Judah. Her national god, Chemosh (cf. 1 Kings 11:7), would not be able to rescue her. Instead, he also would go into exile along with his priests and officials.

God's destruction would come on every town. The valley could refer to the many valleys in which the people lived, or it could refer to the Jordan Valley on Moab's western border. The plateau was the Transjordan highland where most of the cities of Moab were located. Moab's enemies would put salt on her land—a sign of destruction intended to show that the land was laid waste (cf. Jud. 9:45). God was so determined to assure Moab's destruction that He threatened to curse those nations appointed to destroy Moab who were lax in doing his work. These destroyers are not named, but Moab was destroyed by nomadic desert tribesmen from the East (cf. Ezek. 25:10).

2. MOAB'S COMPLACENCY TO BE SHATTERED (48:11-17)

48:11-13. Moab's history was one of relative peace. She had been at rest from her youth. Jeremiah compared her to wine left on its dregs that had not been poured from one jar to another. In making wine, first the grapes were stomped, then the juice was placed into bottles or skins and allowed to ferment. During this time the sediment, or dregs, would settle to the bottom. After 40 days the fermented wine was carefully poured into another container to separate it from the dregs. If the dregs were allowed to remain, the wine became too sweet and thick and was spoiled. This object lesson from nature was ultimately applied to people who had become too complacent (cf. Zeph. 1:12). Moab had never felt the harsh reality of exile so, like the unpoured wine, her aroma was unchanged.

God vowed that days were coming (cf. comments on Jer. 31:27), however, when He would arouse Moab from her complacency. He would send men to pour her out as wine that was no longer fit to drink. At that time Moab would be ashamed of Chemosh (cf. 48:7) just as Israel was ashamed when she had trusted in Bethel. Bethel was where one of the two golden calves was set up in the Northern Kingdom (cf. 1 Kings 12:26-30). Israel found out too late that her trust in the false god at Bethel could not prevent her destruction and deportation. Moab would learn the same lesson regarding her god.

48:14-17. Moab felt confident in her warriors who were valiant in battle. But these men would not be able to prevent her destruction. In fact they would go down in the slaughter which was at hand. Moab's calamity would come quickly. Jeremiah called for those nations surrounding Moab to come and console her at the time of her destruction. Together they could mourn the fact that her scepter (signifying her rule) had been broken.

3. MOAB'S CITIES TO EXPERIENCE CATASTROPHE (48:18-28)

48:18-25. The mighty city of Dibon was to humble herself because God vowed to come up against her. Those living in the remote city of Aroer (cf. comments on v. 6) were to stand by the road and **ask the** people **fleeing** past **what** had **happened.** They would be told that **Moab** had been **disgraced** and **shattered.** News of her fall would cause mourning even as far south as Aroer, **by the Arnon** River.

Jeremiah listed the cities of the Transjordan **plateau** that would be destroyed. Though the location of some is not certain, he seemed to follow a general movement from north to south. His point in naming these 11 cities was to show that **all the towns of Moab,** both **far and near,** would be destroyed.

Jeremiah used two symbols to show that Moab's power would be broken. First, he said **Moab's horn** would be **cut off.** An animal horn was a symbol of strength (cf. 1 Sam. 2:1, 10; Pss. 75:4-5; 89:17, 24; Micah 4:13; Zech. 1:19-21). Second, he said that Moab's **arm,** also a symbol of strength, would be **broken** (cf. comments on Ezek. 30:20-26).

**48:26-28.** Jeremiah pictured Moab's impending doom as someone becoming **drunk** (cf. 25:15-29). Because Moab had **defied** the Lᴏʀᴅ she would now **wallow in her vomit** and be ridiculed by **others.** She that had once treated **Israel** with the contempt of one **caught among thieves** would now experience the same **scorn** directed at her. She would be forced to **abandon** her **towns and dwell among the rocks** to hide from the invaders who sought her life.

4. MOAB'S PRIDE TO CEASE (48:29-39)

**48:29-33. Moab's** chief problem was her **pride** (cf. Isa. 16:6). Her physical security and history of relative peace had fed her **arrogance.** Unfortunately **her insolence** and **boasts** could do **nothing** to prevent her destruction. God expressed His concern for **Moab** as He mourned for **Kir Hareseth** (cf. Isa. 16:7, 11), another of her chief cities. Borrowing from Isaiah 16:9, Jeremiah indicated that God would **weep** along with the city of **Jazer** for the **vines of Sibmah** which had been destroyed. The country of Moab was known for its vineyards, and Jeremiah expanded the image to picture all Moab as a vineyard. Her **branches** had **spread as far as the** Dead Sea, but now **the destroyer** had **fallen on** her **ripened fruit and grapes.** Moab would be "harvested" much as a vine is plucked of its fruit. **Orchards and fields** would be devoid of

happiness, and the **flow of wine from the presses** would cease. When destruction came there would be **shouts** (cf. Jer. 48:3-5) but they would **not** be **shouts of joy** like those heard before.

**48:34-39.** The **cries** of Moab's mourners extended **from Heshbon . . . Elealeh, and Jahaz** in the northern part of the country to **Zoar . . . Horonaim . . . Eglath Shelishiyah,** and **the waters of Nimrim** in the southern part of the country. From north to south the land would be devastated. God would **put an end** to idolatrous practices at Moab's many **high places** where offerings were being made **to their gods.**

God raised a cry of lament **for Moab** that sounded **like** the high-pitched sound of **a flute. The wealth** that Moab had **acquired** was **gone,** and the people mourned their loss (cf. comments on 47:5). The once-proud country had **become an object of ridicule** and **horror,** that is, people mocked **Moab** and were also horrified at her desolate condition (cf. comments on 24:9).

5. MOAB'S DESTRUCTION TO BE COMPLETE (48:40-47)

**48:40-44.** Moab's enemies were like **an eagle** that would be **swooping down** and **spreading its wings over** her to seize her in its claws. The Moabites would be **captured,** and the **warriors** she depended on for protection (cf. v. 14) would be as fearful as **a woman in labor** (cf. 49:24; 50:43). Jeremiah repeated parts of 48:40-41 in 49:22 where he applied the message to Edom.

Lest **Moab** think her captivity was just accidental, God reminded her that her destruction would come **because she defied** Him. In view of her rebellion, none would escape; those who would try to flee God's **terror** would **fall into a pit.** Any who managed to get **out of the pit** would **be caught in a snare** (cf. Amos 5:18-20). God would make sure that all in **Moab** would take part in **the year of her punishment.**

**48:45-47.** Jeremiah ended his section on Moab by freely quoting an old song from **Heshbon** (cf. Num. 21:27-29). **The fugitives** who had escaped the destruction stood by **helpless** because God's **fire** of judgment had **gone out** into all **Moab** to burn those who had been **boasters.** Now the nation was **destroyed,** with her sons and **daughters** in **captivity**. Historically the people of Moab lost their national identity when they were overrun by the Arabians from the East (cf. Ezek. 25:10). Yet God still offered hope to Moab. He vowed to **restore the fortunes of Moab in days to come.** The use of "days to come" would imply that this restoration will occur during the millennial reign of Christ (cf. Deut. 4:30; Jer. 49:39; Dan. 2:28; 10:14).

### D. Prophecy against Ammon (49:1-6)

The Ammonites were located east of the Jordan River and north of Moab. They were allied with Judah against Babylon during Judah's final revolt, but throughout the history of both nations they had been in conflict (see comments on 40:14).

**49:1-3.** By asking four questions (though questions one and two are parallel and three and four are parallel) Jeremiah focused on Ammon's main problem. The Northern Kingdom of Israel had been taken captive in 722 B.C.; and Ammon, assuming **Israel** had **no sons** or **heirs** who would return to the land, seized it for herself. **Molech** (which could be translated "their king"; cf. NIV marg.) was the national god of Ammon that had found its way into Judah (cf. 32:35). Ammon had **taken possession of** the territory belonging to the Israelite tribe of **Gad**, and Ammonites were living **in its towns**.

God announced that **days** were **coming** (cf. comments on 31:27) **when** an enemy would attack Ammon's capital city of **Rabbah.** Rabbah would **become** nothing but **ruins,** and **Israel** would **drive out** the Ammonites who had settled in her villages. **Heshbon,** on the border between Moab and Ammon, was controlled by different countries at different periods of time (cf. Jud. 11:12, 26; Jer. 48:34, 45). This **Ai** was not the city by the same name in Israel (cf. Josh. 7:2). It was a city in Ammon whose location is not known today. The people of **Rabbah** would **put on sackcloth** (see comments on Jer. 4:8) **and mourn** (cf. 48:37) because their god **Molech** (or their king; cf. comments on 49:1) would **go into exile.**

**49:4-6.** Ammon's problem, like that of Moab, was pride (cf. 48:29). Ammon boasted of her **valleys** that were **so fruitful.** She trusted in her **riches** and felt secure enough to question **who** would

have the courage to **attack** her (cf. Ezek. 21:18-23). But God's judgment would shatter Ammon's complacency and pride when He brought His **terror on** her. Those who had been boasting of their security would be **driven away,** and **no** leader would be found to **gather the fugitives** to return and repossess their land. Yet in His grace God vowed that **afterward** He would **restore the fortunes of the Ammonites** (cf. Jer. 48:47; 49:39).

### E. Prophecy against Edom (49:7-22)

The country of Edom was located south of Moab and east of the Dead Sea. It had a history of conflict with Judah and came to symbolize all the heathen nations that sought Judah's harm (cf. Ezek. 35; 36:5; Obad. 15-16). Much of the imagery Jeremiah used to describe Edom was seemingly borrowed from Obadiah, though there is considerable debate on when the Book of Obadiah was written (see comments under "Date" in the *Introduction* to Obad.).

**49:7-13.** The association of **wisdom** with the men of **Teman** was as old as the Book of Job which spoke of Eliphaz the Temanite (cf. Job 2:11). In fact all of **Edom** was known for its wise men (cf. Obad. 8). Teman was in central Edom about three miles from Sela, later known as Petra. **Dedan,** a city in the northern part of the Arabian peninsula southeast of Edom, was known for its trading (cf. Jer. 25:23; Ezek. 25:13). Those Dedanites living in Edom were warned to **turn and flee** from the **disaster** God was about to bring on Edom. Two images were used to show the thoroughness of God's judgment. His judgment would be more thorough than **grape pickers** who at least **leave a few grapes** on the vine when they are done (cf. Obad. 5c; Deut. 24:21). God's judgment would also be more thorough than **thieves . . . during the night** who **steal only as much as they want** (cf. Obad. 5). Even a thief leaves something behind, but God would **strip Esau** (Edom) **bare.** Only the helpless **orphans** and **widows** would be spared by God.

Edom had to be judged because of her many crimes. If God made **those who do not deserve to drink the cup** of His wrath (i.e., those nations "unrelated" to Judah who boasted over her fall) **drink it** (cf. Jer. 25:15-29) how could a nation with close fraternal ties such as Edom's (cf. Deut. 23:7) hope to **go unpunished?** Sin against one's brother was a heinous crime. If nations unrelated to Judah were to be punished for their mistreatment of her, then nations closely related to Judah deserved greater condemnation (cf. Obad. 10). God would make the city of **Bozrah** in northern Edom **a ruin and an object of horror** (cf. comments on Jer. 24:9).

**49:14-18.** Borrowing language from international diplomacy used earlier by Obadiah (Obad. 1), Jeremiah pictured God sending **an envoy** to His allies among **the nations** asking them to **assemble** for an **attack** on Edom. Edom would become **small among the nations** and **despised** as God reduced her prestige and power (cf. Obad. 2). Edom's **pride** in her strong natural defenses made her feel secure, but God would **bring** her **down** (cf. Obad. 4) from her lofty perch and people would be horrified at her condition (cf. Jer. 49:13 and comments on 24:9). Edom would be destroyed **as were Sodom and Gomorrah** (cf. 50:40) so that no one would **dwell** there.

**49:19-22.** God would be as fierce as **a lion** when He rose up to **chase Edom from its land.** No one would be able to **challenge** God nor could a **shepherd . . . stand against** Him. The use of "shepherd" both continued the image of a shepherd trying to protect sheep from a marauding lion (cf. 1 Sam. 17:34-35) and implied God's judgment on the king who was the "shepherd" of the nation (cf. Jer. 23:1-4). God vowed to drag away **the young of the flock** and **destroy** the **pasture** of Edom. The **cry** of destruction would carry **to the Red** (Reed) **Sea**—the site of God's first destruction of a nation that threatened His Chosen People (cf. Ex. 14:21-31). God's prophet repeated (with slight modifications) Jeremiah 49:19-21 in 50:44-46 and applied the message to Babylon. Using an image He had earlier applied to Moab (48:40-41) God indicated that like **an eagle** He would **swoop down** in judgment **over Bozrah** in northern Edom. The **hearts** of the **warriors** on which Edom depended would be as afraid as **the heart of a woman in labor** (cf. 48:41; 49:24; 50:43). They would not be able to stop God's destruction.

Two points of interest may be noted. First, unlike Egypt, Moab, and Ammon

(cf. 46:26; 48:47; 49:6), Edom was given no promise of future restoration. Second, this prophecy was fulfilled in the intertestamental period when desert tribesmen called the Nabateans drove the Edomites from their land. The people of Edom were forced to migrate into southern Judah where they were called Idumeans. In 125 B.C. John Hyrcanus I, a Maccabean, subjugated the Idumeans and made them accept Judaism (Josephus *Antiquities* 13. 9. 1; 15. 4). The Edomites thus ceased to be a distinct national group.

### F. Prophecy against Damascus (49:23-27)

**49:23-27.** Three of the major cities of Syria—**Hamath . . . Arpad,** and **Damascus** (see the map "The World of Jeremiah and Ezekiel," in the *Introduction*)—were **dismayed** because of the **bad news** of Babylon's advance. Damascus' **pain** was **like that of a woman in labor** (cf. comments on 4:31). In Nebuchadnezzar's attack on Damascus the **soldiers** of Damascus were **silenced** (i.e., killed) and her fortifications burned (cf. Amos 1:4). God vowed to **consume the fortresses of Ben-Hadad.** "Ben-Hadad" (lit., "son of [the god] Hadad") was the name of the dynasty that ruled in Damascus in the ninth and eighth centuries B.C. (cf. 1 Kings 15:18, 20; 20:1-34; 2 Kings 6:24; 8:7; 13:3, 24; and see the chart "Kings of Aram in 1 and 2 Kings," near 1 Kings 11:23-25).

### G. Prophecy against Kedar and Hazor (49:28-33)

Kedar was a nomadic tribe of Ishmaelites (cf. Gen. 25:13) in the Arabian desert known for her skills in archery (Isa. 21:16-17), her flocks of sheep (Isa. 60:7; Jer. 49:28-29), her extensive trade (Ezek. 27:21), and her warlike nature (Ps. 120:5-6). "The kingdoms of Hazor" do not refer to the city of Hazor in Israel just north of the Sea of Galilee. Rather it was some as-yet unknown place in the Arabian desert. Jeremiah 49:28b-29 seems to picture Nebuchadnezzar's destruction of Kedar, and verses 30-33 view his destruction of Hazor.

**49:28-29.** God summoned **Nebuchadnezzar** to **attack Kedar,** destroying **their** black, goat-hair **tents** (cf. Song 1:5) and seizing **their flocks** along **with all their goods and camels.** Then these nomads would experience **terror on every side.**

**49:30-33.** The people of **Hazor** were urged to **flee** and hide in **deep caves** because **Nebuchadnezzar** had **plotted** to go **against** them in battle. As God had done against Kedar (v. 28), so here He summoned Nebuchadnezzar to **arise and attack** Hazor. These Arabian people felt so secure in their remote desert location that they did not even have city **gates** or **bars** to protect against attack. Nebuchadnezzar would take **their camels** (cf. v. 29) **and their large herds** as booty. The inhabitants would be scattered **to the winds** and the city itself would **become a haunt of jackals . . . forever**—a symbol of desolation (cf. 9:11; 10:22; 51:37 for Jeremiah's other uses of this phrase).

## H. Prophecy against Elam (49:34-39)

**49:34-39.** **Elam** was east of Babylon in what is today the country of Iran (see the map "The World of Jeremiah and Ezekiel," in the *Introduction*). This prophecy was given **early in the reign of Zedekiah,** about 597 B.C. God promised to **break the bow of Elam** which He called **the mainstay of their might.** This is significant because the Elamites were known for their archery skills (cf. Isa. 22:6). Her invaders would come from all directions (**the four winds** and **the four quarters of the heavens**) and would **scatter . . . Elam's exiles** throughout the earth.

Though there is some evidence that Nebuchadnezzar defeated the Elamites about 596 B.C., his subjugation at that time did not fulfill this message. Elam became a central part of the Persian Empire that later conquered Babylon (cf. Dan. 8:2). Jeremiah's statement about Elam's destruction seems to take on eschatological dimensions as God said He would **set** His **throne in Elam** to supervise her destruction. Yet Elam's destruction will not be total because God will **restore** her **fortunes . . . in days to come** (cf. Jer. 48:47; 49:6).

## I. Prophecy against Babylon (chaps. 50–51)

### 1. THE ANNOUNCEMENT OF JUDGMENT (50:1-10)

**50:1-5.** **Jeremiah** was commanded to **announce** to **the nations** the public humiliation of **Babylon.** She would **be cap-**

tured and her protecting god **Bel** (cf. 51:44; Isa. 46:1; the storm god Enlil), also known as **Marduk,** the chief deity of Babylon, would, figuratively speaking, **be put to shame** (cf. Jer. 46:24) and **filled with terror** because of his inability to protect her. Babylon would be destroyed by **a nation from the north** (cf. 50:9). Many see this as a reference to Babylon's fall to the Medo-Persian Empire, but several points do not fit historically. First, the Persians were from the east of Babylon, not from the north. Second, when Cyrus took Babylon he did not **lay waste her land** or destroy the city so that **no one** would **live in it.** Several times Jeremiah repeated this fact about Babylon being without any inhabitants (cf. vv. 39b-40; 51:29, 37, 43, 62). The city was spared and made one of the ruling centers for the Persian Empire with Daniel serving there in an administrative position (cf. Dan. 5:30; 6:1-3). Third, no one fled the city when it fell to Medo-Persia. In fact Daniel, who had access to Jeremiah's prophecies (cf. Dan. 9:1-2), remained in the city during and after its fall (cf. Dan. 5:28, 30-31; 6:1-3). Fourth, the promise that **in those days** and **at that time . . . the people of Israel** and **Judah** would again unite as a nation, return **to Zion,** and **bind themselves** to God **in an everlasting covenant** (cf. Jer. 31:31; 32:40) was not fulfilled after Babylon's fall in 539 B.C.

Jeremiah's prophecy looked beyond the destruction of Babylon in 539 to an eschatological destruction that will reverse the fortunes of Israel and Judah. Possibly this prophecy represents a blending of the near and the far. That is, the fall of Babylon and the return of the captives under Zerubbabel merged in the prophetic picture with the still-future destruction of Babylon and the final restoration of Israel and Judah. The destruction of Babylon will be the climax of God's judgment on the Gentile powers that have oppressed His people and will open the way for the fulfilling of God's promises to Israel. Other portions of Scripture also point to this still-future rebuilding of Israel and destruction of Babylon (cf. Zech. 5:5-11; Rev. 17–18). The city of Babylon will be rebuilt only to be destroyed at the end of the Tribulation period before Christ returns to establish His millennial reign.

**50:6-10.** Verses 6-7 are an editorial

comment on the restoration of Israel and Judah, announced in verses 4-5. Israel and Judah will need to be restored because they **have been lost sheep** wandering **over mountain and hill** (cf. 23:1-2; Ezek. 36:5-6). They have been **devoured** by **their enemies** because they have **sinned against** God. God summoned His sheep to **flee out of Babylon** because of the **alliance of great nations** coming **from the . . . North** (cf. comments on Jer. 50:3) against her to **plunder her.**

### 2. THE FALL OF BABYLON (50:11-16)

**50:11-13.** Babylon sinned in proudly destroying Judah. God will judge any nation that can **rejoice and** be **glad** as it pillages His **inheritance** (cf. comments on Deut. 4:20), frolicking **like a heifer** and neighing **like stallions.** He vowed to disgrace Babylon by making it **a desert** uninhabited, and **completely desolate.** The once-great city will be so thoroughly destroyed that **all who pass** by **will be horrified and scoff** (cf. Lam. 2:15) at **her wounds** (i.e., her physical devastation; cf. comments on Jer. 6:14).

**50:14-16.** The battle was graphically portrayed as the enemy taking their **positions around** the city and shooting their **arrows** at her defenders. When the city finally **surrenders,** her **towers** and **walls** will be **torn down** and God's **vengeance** will be poured out **on** those who remain. Because of this coming **sword** God warned the foreigners living in Babylon to **flee to** their **own land.** Again, this scene was not fulfilled when Cyrus attacked Babylon in 539 B.C. It awaits a future fulfillment.

### 3. THE RESTORATION OF ISRAEL (50:17-20)

**50:17-20. Israel,** here representing both the Northern and Southern Kingdoms, had become like **scattered** sheep (cf. vv. 6-7). The Northern Kingdom had been conquered by **Assyria** in 722 B.C., and the Southern Kingdom was crushed by **Babylon** in 586 B.C. **God** vowed to reverse the situation. He will **punish the** kings of **Babylon** and **Assyria** for their destruction of His people, **but** He **will bring Israel back to** her land. The majestic summit of **Carmel** and the fertile plains of **Bashan** east of the Sea of Kinnereth (Galilee; see the map "The World of Jeremiah and Ezekiel," in the *Introduction*) will once again belong to

Israel as will **the hills of Ephraim and Gilead** on the western and eastern banks of the Jordan River. (Cf. Bashan and Gilead in Micah 7:14.) For the second time in this chapter (cf. Jer. 50:4) God indicated that **in those days** and **at that time** He will also bring about a spiritual renewal within His people. Though some will **search** for **Israel's guilt** and **the sins of Judah,** they will not find any because God **will forgive** His **remnant** (cf. comments on 31:31-34).

### 4. THE ATTACK ON BABYLON (50:21-40)

**50:21-28.** Using two wordplays, God ordered the **attack** on **the land of Merathaim and** on the people **in Pekod.** "Merathaim" was the region of *Mat Marratim* in southern Babylon where the Tigris and Euphrates Rivers enter the Persian Gulf. However, the word in Hebrew (*merātayim*) means "double rebellion." "Pekod" referred to an Aramean tribe (*Pequdu*) in southern Babylon on the east bank of the Tigris River; but the word in Hebrew (*peqôd*) means "to punish" or "punishment." Thus God was saying He would attack the land of double rebellion and inflict His punishment on it.

The **noise of battle** signaled the **destruction** of **Babylon.** She who like a **hammer** had been shattering others would find herself **broken and shattered.** God spoke of Himself as a hunter to indicate that He had **set a trap** in which **Babylon** unknowingly found herself **caught.** He then referred to Himself as a warrior to show that He was bringing **out** His **weapons of . . . wrath** against her.

Babylon's enemies would **come . . . from afar** to **break** her **open** as one would break open **granaries.** The bodies of her slain inhabitants would be piled up **like heaps of grain,** and her soldiers (the **young bulls**) would be slaughtered. Those **fugitives and refugees** who had escaped (cf. vv. 8, 16) would travel to **Zion** and declare there that Babylon's destruction was God's **vengeance** for her destruction of **His temple** (cf. 52:13).

**50:29-32. Archers** were summoned to **encamp . . . around** Babylon to insure that **no one** would **escape.** The city had to be destroyed because **she** had **defied the LORD** with her haughtiness. Verse 30 is almost identical to 49:26 where Jeremiah applied the same message to Damascus. God emphasized Babylon's haughtiness by calling her the **arrogant one** (50:31-32). She would **be punished** for her pride as God vowed to **kindle a fire** that would **consume** her (cf. 15:14; Lam. 4:11; Amos 1:4, 7, 10, 12, 14; 2:2, 5).

**50:33-34.** The people of Israel and **Judah** were being held by **captors** who refused **to let them go.** How were they then to return to their own land? (vv. 4-5, 8, 19) The answer was that **their Redeemer,** none other than **the Lord Almighty,** would guarantee their return. He vowed to **defend their cause** by giving them rest in **their** own **land** while giving **unrest** (i.e., judgment) **to those** living **in Babylon.**

**50:35-38.** The threat of "unrest" (v. 34) was explained in verses 35-38 as God's bringing of **a sword against. . . . Babylon.** The word **a sword** (*ḥereḇ*) is used five times, and is followed by the announcement of **a drought** (*ḥōreḇ*) in verse 38. This **sword** of judgment will be directed **against** the **officials and wise men,** the **false prophets,** and the **warriors.** It will also be used against the **horses . . . chariots,** and **foreigners** serving as mercenaries **in** Babylon's **ranks.** The **sword** of judgment will even attack **her treasures** which **will be plundered.** Also **her waters . . . will dry up;** Babylon will become poor and unproductive.

**50:39-40.** The bustling metropolis of Babylon, Jeremiah said, will become a deserted wilderness where **desert creatures . . . hyenas,** and owls will live. After this destruction Babylon will **never again be inhabited** (cf. comments on v. 3); her desolation will be as complete as that of **Sodom and Gomorrah** (cf. 49:18). This prediction has not yet been fulfilled. Babylon has been inhabited throughout her history, and the government of Iraq has begun restoring some portions of the ancient city. Iraq's plans to restore Babylon are published in a pamphlet, *Archaeological Survival of Babylon Is a Patriotic, National, and International Duty* (Baghdad: State Organization of Antiquities and Heritage, 1982). The prophecy about Babylon's complete ruin awaits a future fulfillment during the Tribulation period.

5. THE ANGUISH OF BABYLON (50:41-46)

**50:41-46.** God told Babylon to **look** at the **army** which will come **from the north** (cf. v. 3). It will not be the ill-equipped

army of some vassal state trying to attack the might of Babylon. This army will come **from the ends of the earth. . . . armed with bows and spears** to attack. The character of this invading army will match that of the Babylonians (cf. 6:23). They will be **cruel and without mercy,** and the noise of the throng as it gallops to attack will **sound like the roaring sea.**

The **reports about** this approaching army will bring **anguish** to **the king of Babylon.** He will be as fearful as **a woman in labor** (cf. comments on 4:31). Jeremiah ended this section by applying to **Babylon** (50:44-46) the same judgment that he had earlier applied to Edom (49:19-21). **Like a lion** viciously and suddenly (**in an instant**) attacking lambs, God will attack **Babylon** (cf. 51:40). The rest of the world will **tremble** at His judgment of **Babylon.**

6. GOD'S VENGEANCE AGAINST BABYLON (51:1-14)

**51:1-10.** God will **stir up . . . a destroyer** and bring him **against Babylon** and **Leb Kamai.** "Leb Kamai" (*lēḇ qāmāy*) means "heart of my adversaries" but the expression is an *atbash* (see comments on 25:26) for Chaldea. The consonants for "heart of my adversary" (*lbqmy*), when reversed in the Hebrew alphabet, spell Chaldea (*ksdym*). **Foreigners** sent by God **to devastate her** will **completely destroy** Babylon's **army.**

God will destroy Babylon so that **Israel and Judah** will be free to return home (cf. 50:33-34). God called to His people to **flee from Babylon** to avoid being **destroyed** (cf. Rev. 18:4). **Babylon** had been God's **gold cup** of judgment from which He **made the whole earth** drink (cf. Jer. 25:15-29; Rev. 17:3-4; 18:6). However, **Babylon will** feel the sting of judgment. As she **suddenly** falls, her allies will try to find **balm for her pain** (cf. Jer. 8:22; 46:11) but they will search in vain for ways to heal her. She will not **be healed** so her allies will desert her to avoid the effects of **her judgment.** God's people, knowing that He **has vindicated** them, will raise a declarative song of praise in the temple **in Zion** to recount what He **has done.**

**51:11-14.** In an almost repetitive manner Jeremiah described the preparations of the armies poised to attack **Babylon.** This time he identified the attackers as **the kings of the Medes** (cf. v. 28). This could allude to the fall of Babylon in 539 B.C. to the Medo-Persians (cf. Dan. 5:31) or, more probably, it could indicate that one of the future kings who will invade Babylon will come from the area controlled by the Medes (i.e., what is today northern Iran). God will summon this army to **take vengeance** on **Babylon** for her having destroyed **His temple** (cf. 50:28). God **will carry out His purpose** to destroy the Babylonians (**who live by many waters**; i.e., near the Euphrates River) because He has taken an oath (**sworn by Himself**) that these invaders will completely cover **Babylon** like **a swarm of locusts** (cf. 51:27). God will personally assure Babylon's fall.

### 7. GOD'S SOVEREIGNTY OVER BABYLON (51:15-26)

**51:15-19.** Using language that is virtually synonymous with 10:12-16 (cf. comments there), Jeremiah stressed the sovereignty and power of the God who was guaranteeing Babylon's fall. God's **power** and **wisdom** were demonstrated in His Creation of the universe. Another visible demonstration of God's power is His control over a thunderstorm. In beautiful poetic language Jeremiah pictured the **clouds** with the **lightning . . . rain,** and **wind** as visible reminders of God's authority. In sorry contrast were the man-made **idols** (cf. comments on 2:5) that had **no breath in them.** Men made idols, but **the Portion of Jacob** (i.e., God, who in a sense is allotted to Israel; cf. 10:16) **is the Maker of all things, including** His Chosen People, **His inheritance** (cf. comments on Deut. 4:20).

**51:20-26.** Babylon had been God's **war club** used to **shatter** other **nations.** Jeremiah used the word **I shatter** nine times in verses 20-23 to indicate the extent to which God had used Babylon for judgment. (The form of the verb *nāpaṣ* means "to shatter to pieces.") Now, however, He said He will **repay Babylon** for **the wrong they** had done in **Zion.** God, being against the **mountain** (a symbol for a kingdom; cf. Dan. 2:35, 44-45) of Babylon, will make it **a burned-out mountain.** The judgment will be so complete that people will not even loot the ruins to find **a cornerstone** or a **stone for a foundation** to rebuild elsewhere. The ruins will lie **desolate forever.**

### 8. THE SUMMONS TO THE NATIONS AGAINST BABYLON (51:27-33)

**51:27-33.** For the third time God summoned the nations to **lift up** their **banner** and rally their troops **against** Babylon (cf. 50:2; 51:12). In addition to **the Medes,** mentioned both here (v. 28) and earlier (cf. v. 11), this invasion force will include the **kingdoms** of **Ararat, Minni, and Ashkenaz** (see the map "The World of Jeremiah and Ezekiel," in the *Introduction*). Ararat was located in present-day Armenia near Lake Van. Minni was located south of Lake Urmia in what is today western Iran, and Ashkenaz was located near Lake Urmia and Ararat. The people in all three areas were warlike.

God will send these invaders to accomplish His **purposes against Babylon,** namely, **to lay waste the land** and to remove its people (cf. comments on 50:3). Instead of offering resistance, the **warriors** of Babylon will stop **fighting** and withdraw to **their strongholds** (fortresses) for protection. The invaders will press their attack by setting Babylon's **dwellings . . . on fire.** Finally the **bars of her gates** holding out the attackers will be **broken.** Messengers will rush from the various quarters of the city **to announce to the** leader that the **entire city is captured.**

God then compared **Babylon** to a **threshing floor.** When an area for threshing was **trampled** down to prepare it for threshing and winnowing, then the people knew that **the time to harvest** would **soon come.** Likewise when the city of Babylon will be trampled down by these invaders, then the people will know that God's harvest of judgment has arrived.

### 9. GOD'S REVENGE ON BABYLON (51:34-44)

**51:34-35.** Jeremiah presented the complaint of the Jews against **Babylon.** Babylon had **devoured** them and set them aside like **an empty jar.** Or **Nebuchadnezzar . . . like a serpent,** had swallowed Judah whole. When **Babylon** was finished, she would vomit **out** the remains of the captives (i.e., release the exiles from captivity). The Jews called for God to act and to avenge **the violence done to** them. They wanted the **blood** (i.e., the guiltiness for their shed blood) to be required of **those who live in Babylonia.**

**51:36-44.** God answered Jerusalem's

request and vowed to **avenge** Judah. He will make **Babylon . . . a heap of ruins** and **a place where no one lives** (cf. comments on 50:3). And she will be scorned (cf. comments on 24:9). The Babylonians were fierce **like young lions. But** God **will** prepare **a feast for them to make them drunk.** As they drink from His cup of judgment they will fall asleep and never wake up (cf. 51:57). Using another figure, God compared the Babylonians to **lambs** (cf. 50:45) being led **to the slaughter.**

**Sheshach** was an *atbash* for Babylon (see comments on Sheshach in 25:26; also cf. 51:1). Babylon **will be captured** and destroyed. She will disappear as if **the sea** had risen **over** her to **cover her.** Or, to change images, **her towns will** become **desolate** (cf. comments on 50:3) like a **desert.** Swallowed by the sea or scorched by the sun, Jeremiah's point was that **Babylon** will be destroyed. God will **punish Bel,** a god of Babylon (cf. 50:2), by making **him spew out** the wealth he had **swallowed**—a direct answer to the complaint of the captives (51:34).

10. THE WARNING TO THE REMNANT IN BABYLON (51:45-48)

**51:45-48.** God ordered His people to **run for** their **lives** from **Babylon** to escape His **fierce anger.** They were not to **be afraid** of the many **rumors of** victory or **violence** floating through **the land.** Instead they were to remain confident that God **will surely** judge **Babylon.** At that time **heaven and earth . . . will shout for joy over** God's victory (cf. Rev. 18:20).

11. THE CERTAINTY OF BABYLON'S FALL (51:49-53)

**51:49-50.** God had ordained that **Babylon must fall because** she was responsible for killing many Israelites. God's promise to Abraham that those who cursed him would themselves be cursed (Gen. 12:2-3) was now applied to **Babylon.** When the Israelites escape from the future destruction of Babylon they should **not linger.** Instead they should **remember the LORD** and **think on Jerusalem.** Babylon's destruction will be the catalyst God uses to bring the Jews home.

**51:51-53.** As the remnant still in exile thought of Jerusalem, they were **dis-**graced . . . **insulted, and** full of **shame** because they remembered that **foreigners** had **entered the holy places of the** temple and desecrated it. God comforted these exiles by assuring them that **days are coming** when He **will** destroy Babylon's **idols** (cf. vv. 44, 47). No matter how exalted Babylon's position became or how much energy she devoted to fortifying her defenses, God still vowed to **send destroyers** (cf. v. 48) **against her** who would wipe her out.

12. GOD'S REPAYMENT OF BABYLON (51:54-58)

**51:54-58.** A **sound of great destruction** will be heard **from the land of** Babylon. The sound will come from **waves of** enemy soldiers attacking the city, the **roar of their voices** sounding forth over the other sounds of battle. These invaders will capture Babylon's **warriors** and destroy her military power (her **bows will be broken**). Every class of **officials** in **Babylon** will be forced to drink God's wine of judgment (cf. 25:15-29; 51:7-8) which will cause them to **sleep forever and not awake** (cf. v. 39). Again such wholesale destruction of Babylon's leaders and warriors did not occur when Babylon fell to Medo-Persia (cf. Dan. 5:29–6:2). It still awaits God's future fulfillment.

Jeremiah ended this message about Babylon's future fall by quoting a proverb (Jer. 51:58; also in Hab. 2:13) to show the futility of Babylon's attempts to resist God's judgment. Since God had already announced that **Babylon's . . . wall will be leveled and her . . . gates set on fire** (cf. Jer. 50:15; 51:30), any **labor** expended to prevent His judgment and shore up the defenses will only provide more **fuel** to feed **the flames** when they will finally come.

13. SERAIAH'S SYMBOLIC MISSION (51:59-64)

**51:59.** The capstone of Jeremiah's oracle against Babylon was a **message** he gave to **. . . Seraiah** who was a **staff officer** to the **king.** By noting that Seraiah was a **son of Neriah, the son of Mahseiah** Jeremiah indicated that Seraiah was the brother of Baruch, his scribe (cf. 32:12). Seraiah **went to Babylon with Zedekiah . . . in the fourth year** of Zedekiah's **reign.** Why did Zedekiah make a trip to Babylon in 594–593 B.C.? William Shea offers strong evidence to suggest that Nebuchadnezzar summoned all his vassal kings to Babylon in 594 B.C. to insure their loyalty after an attempted revolt in Babylon a little less than a year earlier. Shea believes that this gathering was recorded in Daniel 3 (William H. Shea, "Daniel 3: Extra-Biblical Texts and the Convocation on the Plain of Dura," *Andrews University Seminary Studies* 20. Spring 1982:29-52). Whatever the exact cause, Zedekiah was forced to make an official trip to Babylon, and brought Baruch's brother, Seraiah.

**51:60-64. Jeremiah** compiled **on a scroll . . . all** the prophecies he had **recorded concerning Babylon.** Very likely this scroll was a copy of chapters 50–51 of the present book. He gave the scroll **to Seraiah** and told him to **read** the **words aloud** when he got **to Babylon.** After affirming God's intention to **destroy** that **place,** Seraiah was to **tie a stone to** the scroll and **throw it into the Euphrates.** As the scroll and stone sank beneath the water, Seraiah was to announce that **Babylon,** like the scroll, would **sink to rise no more** (cf. Rev. 18:21).

The final note, **the words of Jeremiah end here,** helps in understanding the process by which the Book of Jeremiah was compiled. This note was probably made by the person who later added chapter 52 to the already-compiled work of Jeremiah. Because chapter 52 was written approximately 25 years after the rest of the book (see the chart "The Dating of Jeremiah's Prophecies," in the *Introduction*), the later editor included this note to distinguish between the portion of the book that had been compiled by Jeremiah and the portion that was added later. Who was this man? No one knows for sure except to say that whoever wrote chapter 52 was also responsible for completing the Book of 2 Kings. (Tradition states that Jeremiah wrote 1 and 2 Kings except for the final chapter, 2 Kings 25.) Likely candidates for Jeremiah 52 include Baruch or some other disciple of Jeremiah who lived long enough to see the events of chapter 52 take place. Whoever the individual, obviously the Holy Spirit guided him to include the chapter as a fitting ending to the book.

## IV. Conclusion (chap. 52)

Chapter 52 is nearly identical to 2 Kings 24:18–25:30 and was written

sometime after 561 B.C. when King Jehoiachin was released from prison in Babylon (Jer. 52:31). Much of the material is parallel to information recorded by Jeremiah in chapter 39. Why, then, was this chapter added to Jeremiah's prophecies? Most likely it was to show that Jeremiah's words of judgment against Jerusalem had been fulfilled and that his words about Judah's release from the Exile were about to be fulfilled. This final chapter served to vindicate the prophet and encourage the remnant still in captivity.

### A. The fate of Jerusalem (52:1-23)

1. THE FALL OF ZEDEKIAH (52:1-11)

**52:1-11.** The history of Judah's final king is again summarized (cf. 39:1-7). **Zedekiah . . . became king** when he **was 21 years old,** and **he reigned** for **11 years.** He **rebelled against** Nebuchadnezzar, and in **the 9th year of** his **reign, on the 10th day of the 10th month** (Jan. 15, 588 B.C.; cf. 2 Kings 25:1; Jer. 39:1; Ezek. 24:1-2) **Nebuchadnezzar** began the final **siege** of **Jerusalem.** In **the 11th year of . . . Zedekiah** on **the 9th** day of **the 4th month** (July 18, 586 B.C.) **the famine . . . had become so severe that** the **food** ran out. All resistance was gone, and on that day the Babylonians made a breach in **the city wall.** Zedekiah and his soldiers tried to flee, but they were **captured** as Jeremiah had predicted (cf. Jer. 38:14-23). **Zedekiah** was **taken to** Nebuchadnezzar, forced to watch the execution of his **sons,** blinded, **bound . . . with shackles,** and taken **to Babylon where** he remained imprisoned until he died.

2. THE DESTRUCTION OF THE CITY (52:12-16)

**52:12-16.** The city of **Jerusalem** fared no better than her king. By **the 10th day of the fifth month** which was in Nebuchadnezzar's **19th year** (August 17, 586 B.C.) the city had been cleared of rebels and sacked and was put to the torch. There is a problem here because 2 Kings 25:8 indicates that Nebuzaradan came on "the **7th** day of the fifth month." Two possible answers have been suggested. Some think that one of the two dates is the result of a later scribal error in copying the text. However, there is no textual or manuscript evidence to support this position. Others believe that "the 7th" indicates the day Nebuzaradan arrived in Jerusalem and "the 10th" indicates the day he began burning the city. **Nebu-zaradan. . . . set fire to the temple . . . the royal palace, and . . . the houses** as Jeremiah had predicted (cf. Jer. 22:7). **Every important building** was **burned down.** Those who survived the siege and **remained in the city** were **carried into exile.** Only **the poorest people** were left behind.

3. THE DESTRUCTION OF THE TEMPLE (52:17-23)

**52:17-23.** To understand this passage one must remember Jeremiah's conflict with the false prophet, Hananiah (cf. 27:16–28:17). Jeremiah had predicted that the furnishings still remaining in the temple would be taken to Babylon (27:19-22). Hananiah contradicted Jeremiah by promising that the furniture already taken to Babylon would be returned (28:3). Which prophet was correct? This additional chapter proves the truth of Jeremiah's prophecy. **The bronze pillars, the movable stands,** and the other furnishings named by Jeremiah were indeed **carried . . . to Babylon.** This was such an extensive undertaking that the author paused to explain the size of **the** bronze **pillars** which were removed (52:21).

*B. The fate of certain people (52:24-34)*

1. THE FATE OF THOSE IN THE CITY DURING ITS FALL (52:24-27)

**52:24-27. All** the city's leaders were rounded up by the Babylonians. These included **Seraiah the chief priest,** who was a grandson of Hilkiah, the high priest in King Josiah's time (1 Chron. 6:13-15), **Zephaniah the priest next in rank** (cf. Jer. 29:25-29; 37:3), **and the three doorkeepers** who were responsible for keeping order in the temple. Also captured were **the officer in charge of the fighting men** (secretary of defense), **seven royal advisers,** and the **chief officer** who was **in charge of conscripting the people** along with **60 of his men**—either lower officials or 60 conscripted soldiers. These were taken to **Riblah in the land of Hamath,** where Nebuchadnezzar had his headquarters (52:9), and **executed.**

2. THE FATE OF THE EXILES (52:28-30)

**52:28-30.** This section is not included in 2 Kings 25. The author added it here to show that other groups of exiles were taken to Babylon. The dates given for the first two deportations (Jer. 52:28-29) do not correspond with the dates of the two deportations given in 2 Kings 24:12-14; 25:8-12. Two possible solutions to this difficulty have been advanced. First, some have suggested that the deportations in 2 Kings and Jeremiah refer to the same events and should be harmonized. This is usually done by assuming that the writer of 2 Kings used a nonaccession-year method of dating the kings of Babylon while Jeremiah employed an accession-year method in Jeremiah 52:28-30 (see John Bright, *A History of Israel.* 3rd ed. Philadelphia: Westminster Press, 1981, p. 326, n. 45).

Second, others have suggested that the first two deportations listed in 52:28-30 were not the same as those in 2 Kings but were minor ones preceding the major deportations associated with Nebuchadnezzar's capture of the city in 597 and 586 B.C. Two arguments are said to support this second view. First, the years given (the **7th** and **18th** years of **Nebuchadnezzar**) are each one year earlier than the years given in 2 Kings for the two major assaults on Jerusalem by Babylon (the "8th," 2 Kings 24:12-14, and "19th," 2 Kings 25:8-12, years of Nebuchadnezzar). Second, the numbers of captives who were exiled in these deportations do not correspond with the numbers taken during the 597 and 586 deportations. In 597 about 10,000 people were taken (2 Kings 24:14), but Jeremiah 52:28 mentions only **3,023.** In 586 Nebuchadnezzar deported "the people who remained in the city, along with the rest of the populace and those who had gone over to the king" (2 Kings 25:11). The figure in Jeremiah 52:29 of **832** seems far too low to correspond to this final deportation. So according to this second view it seems reasonable to assume that these two deportations in verses 28-29 are secondary deportations. The author included them (along with a third minor deportation, v. 30) to show the full extent of Babylon's destruction of Judah. (See Alberto R. Green, "The Chronology of the Last Days of Judah: Two Apparent Discrepancies." *Journal of Biblical Literature* 101. 1982:57-73.)

The third deportation mentioned by Jeremiah possibly corresponds with Nebuchadnezzar's return to the land after Gedaliah's assassination (cf. chap. 41). Certainly such a threat to Babylon's control over Palestine did not go unnoticed. Perhaps Nebuchadnezzar sent a force to restore order and to remove anyone suspected of promoting rebellion. The small number of **745 Jews** would support the limited size of this action. The dates of these three deportations (based on a Tishri calendar) mentioned in 52:28-30 were then (a) **Nebuchadnezzar's** 7th year (598 B.C.), (b) his 18th year (587 B.C.), and (c) his **23rd year** (582 B.C.).

3. THE FATE OF JEHOIACHIN (52:31-34)

**52:31-34. Jehoiachin** became the "firstfruits" of those in captivity in Babylon. **In the 37th year of** Jehoiachin's **exile** (561–560 B.C.) **Evil-Merodach became king of Babylon.** As part of the festivities at the end of his accession year **he released Jehoiachin . . . from prison on the 25th day of the 12th month** (March 21, 560 B.C.). Jehoiachin was allowed to eat **regularly at the king's table.** Just as Jeremiah's prophecies of destruction had come true, so now his prophecies of future blessing were beginning. Jehoiachin's favor gave hope to the exiles that God's promised blessing and restoration would come.

# BIBLIOGRAPHY

Bright, John. *Jeremiah: A New Translation with Introduction and Commentary.* The Anchor Bible. Garden City, N.Y.: Doubleday & Co., 1965.

Cunliffe-Jones, H. *The Book of Jeremiah: Introduction and Commentary.* New York: Macmillan Co., 1961.

Feinberg, Charles L. *Jeremiah: A Commentary.* Grand Rapids: Zondervan Publishing House, 1982.

Freeman, H. *Jeremiah.* London: Soncino Press, 1949.

Harrison, R.K. *Jeremiah and Lamentations.* The Tyndale Old Testament Commentaries. Downers Grove, Ill.: InterVarsity Press, 1973.

Huey, F.B., Jr. *Jeremiah: Bible Study Commentary.* Grand Rapids: Zondervan Publishing House, 1981.

Jensen, Irving L. *Jeremiah and Lamentations.* Everyman's Bible Commentary. Chicago: Moody Press, 1974.

Kinsler, F. Ross. *Inductive Study of the Book of Jeremiah.* South Pasadena, Calif.: William Carey Library, 1971.

Laetsch, Theo. *Jeremiah.* Bible Commentary. St. Louis: Concordia Publishing House, 1952.

Orelli, C. von. *The Prophecies of Jeremiah.* Translated by J.S. Banks. Reprint. Minneapolis: Klock & Klock Christian Publishers, 1977.

Thompson, J.A. *The Book of Jeremiah.* The New International Commentary on the Old Testament. Grand Rapids: Wm. B. Eerdmans Publishing Co., 1980.

# LAMENTATIONS

## Charles H. Dyer

## INTRODUCTION

The Book of Lamentations is a mournful postscript to the Book of Jeremiah. Through the use of five dirges, or funeral laments, the author grieved over the fate of Jerusalem because of her sin. Yet the book contains more than just the backward glances of a vindicated prophet. "It is a mute reminder that sin, in spite of all its allurement and excitement, carries with it heavy weights of sorrow, grief, misery, barrenness, and pain. It is the other side of the 'eat, drink, and be merry' coin" (Charles R. Swindoll, *The Lamentations of Jeremiah*, "Introduction"). Lamentations both mourns the fall of the city and offers reproof, instruction, and hope to its survivors.

**Title.** The title of Lamentations is taken from the book's first word, *'êkâh*. This word may be translated "Alas!" or "How" and was a characteristic cry of lament or exclamation (cf. 2 Sam. 1:19; Jer. 9:19). Rabbinic and Talmudic writers referred to the book by this title or by the name *qînôt* which means "dirges" or "laments."

The Septuagint translators converted the Rabbinic title *qînôt* into *thrēnoi*, the Greek word for "dirges." This title was also adopted by the Latin Vulgate which named the book *threni*, or "Lamentations." The translators of the English Bible followed the pattern established by the Septuagint and Vulgate translators and named the book "Lamentations" after a description of its contents. Many also followed the Jewish tradition of ascribing the work to Jeremiah. Thus the title of the book in English is either "The Lamentations of Jeremiah" (KJV, ASV, NASB, RSV) or "Lamentations" (JB, NIV).

**Author and Date.** The book does not name its author, but Jewish tradition attributes it to Jeremiah. The Septuagint added the following words as an introduction to the book: "And it came to pass, after Israel was taken captive, and Jerusalem made desolate, that Jeremiah sat weeping, and lamented with this lamentation over Jerusalem, and said. . . . " The Aramaic Targum of Jonathan, the Babylonian Talmud, the Peshitta, and the Vulgate all made statements that attribute the work to Jeremiah.

Internal evidence also points to Jeremiah as the author. Several ideas used by Jeremiah in his prophecy reappear in Lamentations (cf. Jer. 30:14 with Lam. 1:2; and cf. Jer. 49:12 with Lam. 4:21). In both books the writer said his eyes flowed with tears (Jer. 9:1, 18; Lam. 1:16; 2:11); and in both the writer was an eyewitness of Jerusalem's fall to Babylon and pictured the atrocities that befell Jerusalem in her last days (Jer. 19:9; Lam. 2:20; 4:10).

Jeremiah's authorship of Lamentations was universally accepted till 1712 when Herman von der Hardt wrote a commentary which challenged this position. The objections raised by von der Hardt and others against Jeremiah's authorship have been answered (e.g., Gleason L. Archer, Jr., *A Survey of Old Testament Introduction*. Chicago: Moody Press, 1964, pp. 365-7; and Walter C. Kaiser, Jr., *A Biblical Approach to Personal Suffering*, pp. 24-30).

Assuming that Jeremiah was the author of the book, the book itself must have been composed within a narrow period of time. Jeremiah would have penned the poetic dirges after Jerusalem fell to Babylon in 586 B.C. (cf. 1:1-11) but before he was taken to Egypt after Gedaliah's assassination (ca. 583–582 B.C.; cf. Jer. 43:1-7). The vivid descriptions and deep emotions expressed in the Book of Lamentations argue for a composition shortly after the events occurred, possibly in late 586 B.C. or early 585 B.C.

## Lamentations

**Historical Background.** From 588 to 586 B.C. the army of Babylon ground away at the defenses of Jerusalem (for comments on these dates see information at 2 Kings 25:1-10). So Judah's early flush of excitement and euphoria following her rebellion against Babylon was replaced with uncertainty and fear. Her ally, Egypt, had been vanquished in battle as she tried in vain to rescue Judah from Babylon's grasp. One by one the other cities in Judah were crushed (cf. Jer. 34:6-7) till only Jerusalem remained before the Babylonian hordes.

Within the city the ever-tightening siege by Babylon's armies began unraveling the fabric of society. Starving mothers ate their own children (Lam. 2:20; 4:10). Idolatry flourished as the people cried out to any and every god for deliverance. Paranoia gripped the people until they were willing to kill God's prophet as a traitor and spy just because he spoke the truth.

The long siege ended abruptly on July 18, 586 B.C. The walls were then breached and the Babylonian army began entering the city (2 Kings 25:2-4a). King Zedekiah and the remaining men in his army tried to flee, but were captured (2 Kings 25:4b-7). It took several weeks for Nebuchadnezzar to secure the city and strip it of its valuables, but by August 14, 586 B.C. the task was completed and the destruction of the city began (2 Kings 25:8-10). (For support of the dates July 18 and August 14, 586 B.C., see Edwin R. Thiele, *The Mysterious Numbers of the Hebrew Kings.* Rev. ed. Grand Rapids: Zondervan Publishing House, 1983, p. 190.) The armies of Babylon burned the temple, the king's palace, and all the other major buildings in the city; and they tore down the walls of the city which provided her protection. When the Babylonians finally finished their destruction and departed with their prisoners, they left a jumbled heap of smoldering rubble.

Jeremiah witnessed the desecration of the temple and the destruction of the city (cf. Jer. 39:1-14; 52:12-14). The once-proud capital had been trampled in the dust. Her people were now under the harsh hand of a cruel taskmaster. With all these events stamped vividly on his mind Jeremiah sat down to compose his series of laments.

**Relationship to Deuteronomy 28.** A crucial, though often overlooked, characteristic of the Book of Lamentations is its relationship to Deuteronomy 28. As John A. Martin has noted, "The author of the Book of Lamentations was attempting to show the fulfillment of the curses presented in Deuteronomy 28" ("The Contribution of the Book of Lamentations to Salvation History." Th.M. thesis, Dallas Theological Seminary, 1975, p. 44). The following chart shows many of the parallels between Lamentations and Deuteronomy 28.

All the heartaches and hardships experienced by Jerusalem in the Book of Lamentations had been predicted about 900 years earlier by Moses. God had warned of the fearful consequences of disobedience and, as Jeremiah carefully noted, God faithfully carried out those curses. Yet this characteristic makes the Book of Lamentations a book of hope for Israel. God was *faithful* in discharging every aspect of the covenant He had made. Israel was punished for disobedience, but she was not consumed because God's covenant was still in force. The same covenant that promised judgment for disobedience also promised restoration for repentance (cf. Deut. 30:1-10). Thus Jeremiah could offer hope in the midst of despair (Lam. 3:21-32). Jeremiah's message to the Israelites in captivity was to learn the lessons of Deuteronomy 28 and turn back to their Lord. The prayer of Lamentations 5:21-22 was not a doubting cry from a discouraged remnant. Rather it was the response of faith from those captives who had mastered the lessons of Deuteronomy 28 and the Book of Lamentations. They were calling on God to fulfill the final part of His covenant and to restore them as a nation from captivity.

**Structure and Style.** The Book of Lamentations has at least three major structural or stylistic distinctives:

*1. Lament pattern.* Lamentations is a series of five laments, or funeral dirges; each chapter is a separate lament. A lament was a funeral poem or song written and recited for someone who had just died (cf. 2 Sam. 1:17-27). The song usually emphasized the good qualities of the departed and the tragedy or loss felt by those mourning his death. Jeremiah was

# Parallels between Lamentations and Deuteronomy

| Lamentations | | Deuteronomy | |
|---|---|---|---|
| 1:3 | She dwells among the nations; she finds no resting place. | 28:65 | Among those nations you will find no repose, no resting place for the sole of your foot. |
| 1:5 | Her foes have become her masters. | 28:44 | He will be the head, but you will be the tail. |
| 1:5 | Her children have gone into exile, captive before the foe. | 28:32 | Your sons and daughters will be given to another nation. |
| 1:6 | In weakness they have fled before the pursuer. | 28:25 | The LORD will cause you to be defeated before your enemies. You will come at them from one direction but flee from them in seven. |
| 1:18 | My young men and maidens have gone into exile. | 28:41 | You will have sons and daughters but you will not keep them, because they will go into captivity. |
| 2:15 | All who pass your way clap their hands at you; they scoff and shake their heads at the Daughter of Jerusalem. | 28:37 | You will become a thing of horror and an object of scorn and ridicule to all the nations where the LORD will drive you. |
| 2:20 | Should women eat their offspring, the children they have cared for? | 28:53 | Because of the suffering that your enemy will inflict on you during the siege, you will eat the fruit of the womb, the flesh of the sons and daughters the LORD your God has given you. |
| 2:21 | Young and old lie together in the dust of the streets. | 28:50 | . . . a fierce-looking nation without respect for the old or pity for the young. |
| 4:10 | With their own hands compassionate women have cooked their own children. | 28:56–57 | The most gentle and sensitive woman among you . . . will begrudge the husband she loves and her own son or daughter the afterbirth from her womb and the children she bears. For she intends to eat them secretly during the siege. |
| 5:2 | Our inheritance has been turned over to aliens, our homes to foreigners. | 28:30 | You will build a house, but you will not live in it. |
| 5:5 | We are weary and find no rest. | 28:65 | Among those nations you will find no repose. |
| 5:10 | Our skin is hot as an oven, feverish from hunger. | 28:48 | In hunger and thirst . . . you will serve the enemies the LORD sends against you. |
| 5:11 | Women have been ravished in Zion, and virgins in the towns of Judah. | 28:30 | You will be pledged to be married to a woman, but another will take her and ravish her. |
| 5:12 | Elders are shown no respect. | 28:50 | . . . a fierce-looking nation without respect for the old . . . |
| 5:18 | Mount Zion . . . lies desolate, with jackals prowling over it. | 28:26 | Your carcasses will be food for all the birds of the air and the beasts of the earth, and there will be no one to frighten them away. |

# Lamentations

lamenting the tragic "death" of the city of Jerusalem and the results of her demise which were being experienced by the people. Thus he used the form of a funeral lament to convey the feeling of sadness and loss being experienced by the survivors.

The lament pattern is emphasized by the use of two structural elements. The first is the repetition of the word "How" or "Alas" (*'êkâh*) to open three of the five chapters (cf. Lam. 1:1; 2:1; 4:1). As discussed earlier under "Title" the word *'êkâh* conveyed the idea of strong exclamation or lament. The second element that emphasizes the lament pattern is the frequent use of the *qînâh* meter in chapters 1–4. In this rhythmic pattern the second half of a line of verse has one less beat than the first half of a line. This forms a 3 + 2 "limping meter" which conveys a hollow, incomplete feeling to the reader. Both of these elements lend an air of sadness to the dirges and heighten their emotional intensity.

*2. Acrostic arrangement.* One key stylistic element that defies translation is the acrostic arrangement of chapters 1–4. An acrostic is a composition in which the first word of each sentence or line, when taken in order, forms a word, a connected group of words, or the regular sequence of the letters of the alphabet. In the Book of Lamentations each of the first

four chapters is arranged in an acrostic pattern. Thus verse 1 begins with the letter *'alep,* verse 2 with *bêt,* etc. Chapters 1, 2, and 4 each have 22 verses which begin with the 22 letters of the Hebrew alphabet. Chapter 3, the heart of the book, has 66 verses. In this chapter the first three verses begin with *'alep,* the next three begin with *bêt,* etc. Only chapter 5 is not arranged acrostically, though (like chaps. 1–2, and 4) it has 22 verses.

Before discussing the significance of the acrostics in the book, one variation should be noted. In each of chapters 2–4 two of the Hebrew letters are reversed. The normal order of the Hebrew alphabet for the 16th and 17th letters is *'ayin-pê* (cf. Ps. 119). This is the order given in Lamentations 1. However, in Lamentations 2–4 this order is *reversed,* giving a *pê-'ayin* sequence. This reversal perplexed scholars for many years, but recent archeological discoveries have helped clear up the difficulty. Several Hebrew abecedaries (alphabets scratched on pieces of broken pottery by Hebrew children learning to write) have been found by archeologists. Some of these alphabetical lists are in the normal order for the Hebrew letters but others are in the reverse *pê-'ayin* order. Evidently both arrangements of the alphabet were acceptable. Thus the writer of Lamentations was merely employing two forms of the Hebrew alpha-

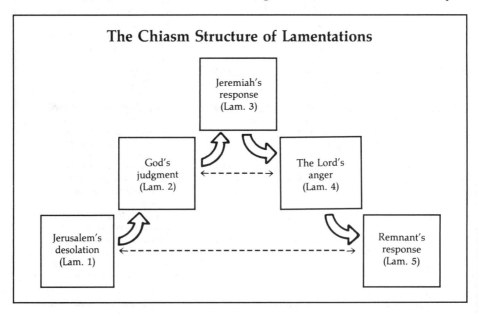

## The Chiasm Structure of Lamentations

Jeremiah's response (Lam. 3)

God's judgment (Lam. 2)

The Lord's anger (Lam. 4)

Jerusalem's desolation (Lam. 1)

Remnant's response (Lam. 5)

bet, both of which were used in his time.

*Why* was the acrostic form used? One possible reason was to help readers remember the words of the lament. Most schoolchildren today remember the musical acronyms "face" and "every good boy does fine" by which they were taught the notes on the spaces and lines of the musical treble clef. In the same way the acrostic pattern would serve as a memory device so that the Israelites would not forget any of the important lessons written in the Book of Lamentations.

A second possible reason for using the acrostic pattern was to emphasize to the readers the complete nature of their suffering because of sin. The alphabet was used to remind the people that Jerusalem's judgment was "from A to Z." Possibly Jeremiah had both reasons in mind when he arranged chapters 1–4 as acrostics. He broke the pattern, though, in chapter 5.

*3. Structural balance.* The Book of Lamentations has a definite structural balance. Chapters 1–2 and 4–5 parallel each other and are arranged in a chiasm pattern. Thus chapters 1 and 5 focus on the people while chapters 2 and 4 focus on the Lord. Chapter 3 provides the pivot for the book, pointing to Jeremiah's response in the midst of affliction. The arrangement may be diagramed as on the preceding page.

The structural symmetry is balanced by a definite progression in the book. The first four chapters are acrostics; chapter 5 is not. The first four chapters frequently use the *qînâh*, or limping meter; chapter 5 does not. Three of the first four chapters begin with *'êkâh* (chap. 3 is the only exception among the acrostic chaps.); chapter 5 does not. In many ways chapter 5 "breaks the mold" established in the other chapters and offers a response to the suffering. It is no accident that the chapter begins and ends as a prayer ("Remember, O LORD," 5:1; "Restore us to Yourself, O LORD," v. 21). In chapter 5 Jeremiah presented the response that the remnant needed to make to God. It thus formed a fitting ending to the book. God's chastisement was intended to lead to repentance.

# OUTLINE

# COMMENTARY

## I. First Dirge: Jerusalem's Desolation because of Her Sin (chap. 1)

Jeremiah's first dirge established the book's theme—the sorrow of sin. Five times in chapter 1 he noted that Jerusalem's cries for help after her fall went unanswered—"there is none to comfort her" (vv. 2, 9, 16-17, 21). The city had turned from the protective care of her God to pursue foreign alliances and lifeless idols; and now, at the time she needed the help of others most, she found herself alone—destitute and defenseless.

Jeremiah developed Jerusalem's plight by painting two pictures of the city. The first was that of an outside observer looking at the city (vv. 1-11). It is from the outside looking in. The second picture was that of Jerusalem personified calling out to those passing by to stop and observe her condition (vv. 12-22). This picture was from the inside looking out.

### A. Jeremiah's lament over Jerusalem's desolation (1:1-11)

As Jeremiah stood surveying the scene of destruction that had once been a thriving city, he began his lament over her desolation. In verses 1-7 he vividly described the extent of her destruction, and in verses 8-11 he explained the cause for her destruction.

**1:1.** Jerusalem had experienced a catastrophic metamorphosis. Jeremiah listed three ways in which the city had changed. First, her population had been decimated. The once-bustling **city** was now **deserted.** Second, her economic position had changed. The city that had **once** been **great among the nations** was now reduced to the status of **a widow.** The concept of widowhood is used throughout the Old Testament to depict a position of helpless despair; it is often linked with aliens and orphans as individuals who could not protect themselves (cf. Ex. 22:22; Deut. 10:18; 24:19-21; 26:13; 27:19; Isa. 1:17). Jerusalem was now destitute and defenseless. Third, her social position had changed. The **queen . . . has now become a slave.** The city that used to rule other nations was now forced to serve the nation of Babylon.

**1:2.** As Jeremiah continued his personification of Jerusalem, he described her response to her desolation. While other nations enjoyed the peaceful benefits of sleep, Jerusalem found herself "crying in her pillow," bitterly lamenting her sad state. She needed the **comfort** of her **lovers** and **friends,** but it did not come. She had forsaken her true Lover and Friend Yahweh, for false gods and foreign alliances. But in her hour of need her fickle friends were not to be found. **They** had **become her enemies.** She had no one to help ease her misery.

**1:3-6.** In these verses Jeremiah amplified the calamity that had befallen Judah and Jerusalem. Instead of dwelling securely in her own land, **Judah** had **gone into exile.** The Babylonian Captivity, which lasted from 605 B.C. to 538 B.C., forced most of the people to leave their homes and live in a strange country as slaves. **The roads** and gates of Jerusalem that had once been filled with pilgrims coming to worship at the **appointed feasts** at the temple were now deserted. The temple itself lay desolate (cf. v. 10),

the **priests** groaned, and the feasts had been discontinued. The **foes** and **enemies** of God's people had triumphed. Jerusalem's **maidens** grieved (v. 4), **her children** were captured (v. 5), and her leaders (**princes**) fled **like** hunted **deer** (v. 6).

The word **Zion** (vv. 4, 6) referred originally to the hill in Jerusalem on which the city of David was built (cf. 2 Sam. 5:7; 1 Kings 8:1). Later with the temple's construction on Mount Moriah and the ark's transfer from the city of David to the temple (cf. 2 Chron. 5:2, 7), the hill on which the temple stood began to be called Mount Zion (cf. Pss. 20:2; 48:2; 78:68-69). The word eventually was applied to the entire city of Jerusalem, which included the city of David, the temple mount, and the western hill on which the city later expanded (cf. Jer. 51:35). The term "Zion" is often associated with God's dwelling place whether the temple proper or the city where the temple was located. (On **the Daughter of Zion** see comments on Lam. 2:1.) So in 1:4-6 Jeremiah emphasized the religious desolation in Jerusalem after the temple and its associated sacrifices and feasts, which symbolized God's presence and fellowship with His people, were destroyed.

**1:7.** As if the physical trauma were not enough, mental anguish also beset the people of Jerusalem. **Jerusalem** remembered **all the treasures that were hers in days of old.** Her present state of ruin and ridicule contrasted sharply with her former glory—and Jerusalem found no solace in remembering what once was hers. Falling **into enemy hands** (cf. vv. 2-3, 5-6), she was **laughed at.**

**1:8-9.** After describing *what* had befallen Jerusalem (vv. 1-7) Jeremiah explained *why* (vv. 8-11). **Jerusalem** had **sinned greatly** (cf. v. 5). The catastrophe that overtook Jerusalem was not an action of a heartless God against an innocent people. Jerusalem brought about her own destruction because of her sin. She reaped what she had sown. When she turned from God to pursue her own idolatrous ways, **she did not consider her future.** As is true of many individuals, Jerusalem did not seem to realize that sin leads only to death and destruction (Ezek. 18:4; Rom. 6:23).

**1:10-11.** Jeremiah briefly sketched

two of the results that Jerusalem received because of her sin. First, Jerusalem saw her temple become desecrated—**pagan nations** entered **her sanctuary.** The building the people had falsely relied on for their security (cf. Jer. 7:2-15; 26:2-11) was now defiled before their eyes by Gentiles who were not supposed **to enter** it. Evidently the Jews viewed their temple as a giant talisman or good luck charm. They felt that Jerusalem was safe because God's house was there. He might let other places be destroyed, they argued, but surely not His own house. The people learned too late that God does not hold stones in higher regard than obedience. Disobedience brings destruction.

Second, because of her sin, Jerusalem experienced famine. During and after the siege, food was scarce. People were forced to **barter their treasures for food to keep themselves alive** (cf. Lam. 1:19; 2:20; 4:10). The futility of materialism became evident for those who had more silver and gold than bread.

### B. Jerusalem's plea for mercy (1:12-22)

The second half of this first lament now changed its focus. Instead of standing on the outside looking in, Jeremiah moved inside and looked out. Jerusalem herself called to those around to take note of her condition. Verses 12-19 contain Jerusalem's call to those who had observed her desolation. Verses 20-22 contain Jerusalem's call to the Lord.

**1:12-13.** Jerusalem called out to those passing by to stop and take note of her condition. First, she focused on God's judgment that had been poured out on her (vv. 12-17); then she explained that the judgment was deserved because of her sin (vv. 18-19).

Jerusalem's destruction was not a chance occurrence; it was a direct result of God's judgment. **The LORD brought** it (cf. 2:1-8; 4:11; 5:20). Jeremiah used four metaphors to describe God's work against Jerusalem. First, God's attack was like **fire** which **He sent . . . down into** Jerusalem's **bones.** This may refer to lightning bolts streaking down from the sky and striking people (cf. 1 Kings 18:38; 2 Kings 1:10, 12; Job 1:16; Ps. 18:12-14).

Second, God's attack was like that of a hunter who **spread a net for** Jerusalem's **feet.** Nets were used to trap numerous animals including birds (Prov.

1:17), fish (Ecc. 9:12), and antelope (Isa. 51:20). A net would entangle and trap an animal so that it could not escape.

**1:14.** Third, God's attack was like binding Jerusalem's **sins . . . into a yoke** which was placed over Jerusalem's **neck.** A yoke tied two draft animals together for pulling heavy loads. The heavy wooden crossbeam of the yoke referred metaphorically to slavery or to a burden or hardship someone had to bear (cf. Gen. 27:40; Lev. 26:13; Deut. 28:48; 2 Chron. 10:3-11; Isa. 9:4; 58:6, 9; Jer. 27:2, 6-11). Jerusalem's sins produced the yoke of judgment under which she was **bound** to serve Babylon. God **sapped** her **strength** and turned her **over to** her enemies.

**1:15.** Fourth, God's attack was compared to the treading of grapes. Like grapes, Jerusalem's **young men** were crushed. **In His winepress the LORD has trampled the Virgin Daughter of Judah.** Harvested grapes were placed in a winepress and trampled underfoot till the juice ran out into an adjoining pit. This action became associated with the thought of complete destruction (cf. Isa. 63:1-6; Joel 3:12-15; Rev. 14:17-20; 19:15). "The Virgin Daughter of Judah" referred to Jerusalem (cf. Lam. 2:2, 5) which felt the effects of God's judgment. God had **summoned an army against** her.

**1:16-17.** Jerusalem's explanation of God's judgment to those passing by ended in a cry of tragic despair. In a scene of touching sadness Jeremiah pictured Jerusalem as a broken, weeping widow (cf. v. 1) stretching out **her hands** to seek some condolence and aid. But **no one** was **near to comfort**; in fact **there** was **no one** at all **to comfort her** (cf. vv. 9, 21). The city was destitute and despised. Those **neighbors** to whom **Jerusalem** had turned for aid were now her **foes** (cf. v. 2) and viewed her as **an unclean thing.** The word used here (nidâh) referred to the ceremonial impurity associated with menstruation (cf. Lev. 15:19-20; Ezek. 18:6). Jerusalem was shunned and rejected by her erstwhile friends.

**1:18-19.** In Judah's confession of guilt, she acknowledged that judgment was caused by the righteous God disciplining an unrighteous people. **The LORD is righteous, yet I rebelled against His command.** God is not the author of evil nor is He a supreme sadist who delights in inflicting punishment on others (cf. Ezek. 33:11; 2 Peter 3:9). But God is righteous so He does not allow sin to continue unchecked. Sin exacts a horrible price from those who enjoy its temporary pleasures. Jerusalem abandoned her God to experience those "pleasures." Now Jerusalem was paying the cost—**suffering . . . exile** (cf. Lam. 1:3), betrayal by **allies,** and death by starvation.

**1:20-22.** Jerusalem had called to those passing by (vv. 12-19) but now she turned her cry to God. In baring her soul to the Lord, Jerusalem called on Him to notice her plight. **Outside, the sword bereaves; inside, there is only death.** While the city was under attack by Nebuchadnezzar's army, those who tried to escape to freedom by breaking through the siege were cut down by swords. Those who remained in the city died of starvation and plague.

After describing her plight, Jerusalem called on God to extend His judgment to her **enemies. May You bring the day You have announced so they may become like me.** The "day" was the "day of the LORD," which had already been announced by the prophets. This was the time when God's judgment would extend to all the earth to avenge injustice and bring about the Age of righteousness that had been promised (cf. comments on "the day of the LORD" under "Major Interpretive Problems," in the *Introduction* to Joel).

Jerusalem wanted God to judge the sins of her enemies as He had judged her sins: **deal with them as You have dealt with me because of all my sins** (cf. Lam. 4:21-22). This did not happen at that time, but God said He would judge all nations during and after the still-future Tribulation period (cf. Isa. 62:8–63:6; Ezek. 38–39; Joel 3:1-3, 9-21; Obad. 15-21; Micah 7:8-13; Zech. 14:1-9; Matt. 25:31-46; Rev. 16:12-16; 19:19-21.)

## II. Second Dirge: God's Punishment of Jerusalem's Sin (chap. 2)

Charles Swindoll has appropriately titled this chapter "Words from the Woodshed." The focus of Jeremiah's attention moved from the personified city of Jerusalem to the punishment inflicted by God. The first 10 verses depict the

anger of God as He systematically dismantled the city in judgment. Verses 11-19 contain (a) Jeremiah's anguished cry as he wept over the destruction of the city he had loved and (b) his call for the people to cry out to God. Verses 20-22 give the people's response, in which Jerusalem again cried out for the Lord to see her plight.

### A. God's anger (2:1-10)

The second dirge opens by focusing on the real cause for Jerusalem's calamity. God was the One who destroyed the city and its people. In these 10 verses Jeremiah hammered home the reality of God's judgment on Jerusalem because of her sin. The words Jeremiah used depict an image of God personally overseeing the dismantling of the city. The verb *bāla'* ("to swallow up" or "to engulf completely") was used four times (vv. 2, 5 [twice], 8 ["destroying"]), perhaps to picture the fire of God's judgment engulfing the city itself. Jeremiah used other vivid verbs as "hurled down" (v. 1), "torn down" (v. 2), "cut off" (v. 3), "burned" (v. 3), "destroyed" (vv. 5-6), "laid waste" (v. 6), "abandoned" (v. 7), "tear down" (v. 8), "broken and destroyed" (v. 9). These words describe the feeling of havoc and disarray in which Jerusalem found herself. God was the "one-man wrecking crew" responsible for the rubble.

**2:1-5.** Jeremiah explained that God's **anger** (vv. 1 [twice], 3; cf. 1:12; 2:6, 21-22; 3:43, 66; 4:11) and **wrath** (2:4; 3:1; 4:11) was directed against **the strongholds of the Daughter of Judah** (2:2). The "Daughter of Judah" referred specifically to the city of Jerusalem (cf. 1:15; 2:5). The city was also called the **Daughter of Zion** (1:6; 2:1, 4, 8, 10, 13, 18; 4:22) and the "Daughter of Jerusalem" (cf. 2:13, 15). This destruction included the physical **dwellings** (v. 2), **palaces** (v. 5; cf. v. 7), and **strongholds** (vv. 2, 5), but it also included the land's leaders. Thus God brought down **her kingdom and its princes** (v. 2). King Zedekiah and the royal family were ousted from their positions of leadership. The reference in verse 3 to **every horn of Israel** probably also meant the royal family. A "horn" was a symbol of strength; God removed all those to whom the people looked for guidance and leadership. Because of this destruction, in which God seemed to Judah **like a fire** (vv. 3-4) and **like an enemy** (vv. 4-5), the people were in **mourning and lamentation.**

**2:6-7.** God's anger was also directed against His temple: **He has laid waste His dwelling like a garden.** The word for "dwelling" (*sōk*) is a variant spelling of the word for "booth" (*sūkâh*). The thought expressed by Jeremiah is that God tore down His temple (**His place of meeting**) in the same way a farmer would tear down a temporary field hut or booth used to provide shade during a harvest. The **feasts,** Sabbath observances, all the sacrifices, and even the **altar** were affected by Jerusalem's fall. The **shout in the house of the LORD** was actually a wailing at the site of the destroyed temple.

**2:8-10.** Jeremiah again spoke of the leadership of Jerusalem which was devastated by Babylon. He pictured the leaders as being like a **wall around** Jerusalem which used to protect the people. But just as the physical **ramparts and walls** around Jerusalem were destroyed (vv. 8-9a), so her human wall of leadership was also dismantled (vv. 9b-10). The Davidic dynasty was ousted from its throne. The **king and her princes** (cf. v. 2) were **exiled among the nations.** Without the temple the function of the priests had been rendered ineffective (cf. v. 6) so that **the Law** was **no more.** Another group of leaders, the **prophets,** had been so corrupted by charlatans (cf. Jer. 23:9-32; 28; Ezek. 13) that they were **no longer** receiving communications (**visions**) from God or speaking in His name (cf. Lam. 2:14). Thus every group charged by God to lead the people—the king, the priests, and the prophets—was affected by Jerusalem's fall.

In response to their loss of leadership, the people mourned. The mourning extended from **the elders** to **the young women.** Possibly this is a figure of speech known as a merism, in which Jeremiah used two extremes (old men, young women) to show that *everyone*—young and old and all in between—was mourning the loss of leadership. In grief they were silent, sprinkling **dust on their heads,** and wearing **sackcloth,** both signs of sorrow and anguish (cf. Gen. 37:34; Job 2:12-13; Neh. 9:1). (On "sackcloth" see comments on Isa. 3:24, on "the Daughter of Zion" see comments on

Lam. 2:1, and on "Zion" see comments on 1:6.)

*B. Jeremiah's grief (2:11-19)*

Jeremiah cried out in anguish at the scene he had been surveying. He sketched five portraits of Jerusalem's condition which prompted his cry.

**2:11-12.** The first sketch highlighted the starvation that had decimated Jerusalem during the siege. The saddest scenes in any war or conflict are the sufferings experienced by children. Jeremiah wept so much from inner **torment** that tears blinded his **eyes** (cf. 3:48-49). For his **heart** (lit., "liver") to be **poured out on the ground** meant that he was fully drained emotionally. He captured the pathos of the moment as he described **children and infants,** who were **faint** (cf. 2:19), calling out for food **as their lives** ebbed **away in their mothers' arms.** Parents who loved their children could not provide even the necessities of life.

**2:13.** The city's hopeless condition prompted Jeremiah to address her directly. His second sketch was of a man trying desperately to offer **comfort** to a grieving friend. Unfortunately the judgment's magnitude was so severe that no comfort could be given.

**2:14.** The third sketch Jeremiah drew was of false **prophets** hastening rather than hindering Jerusalem's downfall. God had threatened to destroy Jerusalem because of her **sin,** and the prophets were supposed to announce this impending disaster and exhort the people to repent. Unfortunately, though Jeremiah and Ezekiel were faithful prophets of God, others were tickling the people's ears with rosy predictions of peace and prosperity (cf. Jer. 28:1-4, 10-11; 29:29-32). Jerusalem chose to ignore the true prophets' warnings and to listen to the flattering and therefore **misleading** lies of the **false** prophets.

**2:15-17.** The fourth sketch pictured the victorious enemy mocking the vanquished people. The once-majestic and secure **city** of **Jerusalem** was now the object of scoffing and derision. People taunted her, poking fun at her former **beauty** and **joy,** which were now gone, and her **enemies** scoffingly rejoiced in their victory (cf. 3:46).

However, lest Jerusalem begin to believe her enemies' boasts, Jeremiah reminded the Jews again that the destruction was the work of *God:* **He has let the enemy gloat over you; He has exalted the horn of your foes.** The "horn" (i.e., "strength"; cf. 2:3) exhibited by Jerusalem's enemies in their destruction of the city was not their own. *God* gave them the ability to take Jerusalem; thus *He* was the One who overthrew them. And **He** did so **without pity** (cf. vv. 2, 21; 3:43) because of His people's sin.

**2:18-19.** Jeremiah's fifth sketch pictured the remnant **of the people** ceaselessly wailing to God in despair because of their calamity. The phrase **pour out your heart like water** referred to sincere prayer. The people were to unleash their innermost thoughts and emotions and share them with God (cf. Pss. 42:4; 62:8; 142:2). There is a similarity between Jeremiah's exhortation to the people here and his own response (recorded in Lam. 2:11). In both cases (a) they were weeping and in torment, (b) they poured out their feelings in prayer to God, and (c) the heartrending scene of starving **children** was the focus of their grief.

### C. Jerusalem's pleas (2:20-22)

Jeremiah ended the expression of his personal grief (vv. 12-19) by calling on Jerusalem to respond to her calamity (v. 19) as he had. Then he recorded Jerusalem's plea to God.

**2:20a-b.** In a cry of pain and horror the city called on God to **look** and think about her calamity. The starving to death of children was a sickening twist. The siege against Jerusalem was so severe that all her inhabitants were in danger of starvation. In a shocking display of their self-preservation drive, some parents became cannibals and ate their own children. **Should women eat their offspring, the children they have cared for?** This action was predicted in graphic detail by Moses when he warned Israel of the consequences of disobedience to God's Law (cf. Lev. 26:27-29; Deut. 28:53-57). This reprehensible practice surfaced only during the most desperate times (cf. 2 Kings 6:24-31).

**2:20c-21b.** The slaughter moved beyond the children to encompass the religious leaders and people of all ages. **Priest and prophet** alike were slain inside the temple precincts as the Babylonian army rushed in for the conquest. As Jeremiah picked his way through the winding streets of Jerusalem, he saw bloated corpses strewn among the rubble: **young and old** lay **together in the dust of the streets.** When Babylon finally did break through Jerusalem's defenses, its soldiers were angry because Jerusalem had kept them at bay for 30 months. They made no distinction between age and sex; the bloodthirsty Babylonians butchered uncounted thousands.

**2:21c-22.** But lest anyone forget the ultimate Judge, Jeremiah again (cf. v. 17) reminded the people that God was the One wielding the sword of punishment. The Babylonians prevailed only because He let them prevail. God had warned Israel what He would do if she disobeyed Him (Lev. 26:14-39; Deut. 28:15-68) and He faithfully carried out His threat. Those whom He had loved were now **destroyed.**

## III. Third Dirge: Jeremiah's Response (chap. 3)

Chapter 3 is the heart of Jeremiah's short book. This chapter gives the book a positive framework around which the other chapters revolve. The black velvet of sin and suffering in chapters 1–2 and 4–5 serves as a fitting backdrop to display the sparkling brilliance of God's loyal love in chapter 3.

The chapter itself differs markedly from the first two. Instead of 22 verses it has 66—3 verses for each letter of the Hebrew alphabet. The chapter also begins without the familiar "How" (*'êkâh*) that stands guard over chapters 1 and 2. Instead, a first-person narrative unfolds as the writer describes his personal reaction to the suffering he has experienced.

The identity of the subject in chapter 3 has been disputed. Some feel that "I," "me," and "my" refer to Jerusalem personified (cf. 1:12-22; 2:22). However, while parts of chapter 3 could refer to the city, other parts of the chapter must refer to an individual (cf. 3:14, 52-54). In fact the parallels between this individual and Jeremiah are remarkable. Both were hated by their countrymen (Jer. 1:18-19; Lam. 3:52), were ridiculed by those they tried to help (Jer. 20:7-8; Lam. 3:63), had plots made against their lives (Jer. 11:18-19; Lam. 3:60), were cast into watery pits (Jer. 38:4-13; Lam. 3:53-58), and wept over the people's destruction (Jer. 9:1;

13:17; 14:17; Lam. 3:48-49).

Therefore it is probable that the person in question is Jeremiah himself. Yet his description goes beyond just one person to include all the people. This is most obvious in his switch from the singular to the plural ("we," "us," "our") within the chapter (cf. vv. 22, 40-46). The best solution is to see the individual in chapter 3 as Jeremiah representing all Israelites. He used his own experiences because the things he suffered represented things that many Israelites had suffered.

The chapter may be divided into three sections. Jeremiah detailed his afflictions during the time of Jerusalem's fall (vv. 1-18). But his knowledge of God's ways in the midst of his affliction produced hope, not despair (vv. 19-40). So Jeremiah could lead Israel in prayer to God for deliverance, restoration, and vindication (vv. 41-66).

## A. Jeremiah's afflictions (3:1-18)

**3:1-3.** In a long list of metaphors Jeremiah enumerated the many afflictions that he, as Judah's representative, suffered at the hand of God's **wrath** (cf. 2:2, 4; 4:11). Jeremiah was *confused* as he watched God seemingly reverse His past attitudes and actions. Instead of walking in the **light** of God's guidance he had been forced to stumble **in darkness** (cf. 3:6). God **turned His hand against** Jeremiah. This phrase is unique, but the concept of God's hand was known in the Old Testament (cf. 1 Sam. 5:6; Job 19:21). God's hand of favor had become a fist of adversity.

**3:4-6.** God's adversity resulted in *misery* for Jeremiah. God's afflictions had taken their toll on his health (cf. Ps. 38:2-3): his **skin** and **flesh** were **old** (probably wrinkled) and his **bones** were **broken** (figuratively speaking of his inner agony; cf. Ps. 42:10). These outward changes were matched by inner **bitterness** (cf. Lam. 3:15, 19). Jeremiah was broken in body and spirit.

**3:7-9.** Jeremiah could see no way out of his adversity. He was imprisoned and chained, so his freedom was gone. God refused to acknowledge his prayers **for help,** and all avenues of escape were blocked.

**3:10-13.** God's actions seemed designed to single out Jeremiah for punishment. God was **like a bear** or **lion in** hiding beside **the path** who attacked and mauled Jeremiah. Switching figures, Jeremiah said he felt like a **target** against which God was taking target practice (cf. Job 6:4; 7:20; 16:12-13). God had chosen him for adversity.

**3:14-18.** In a burst of vivid images Jeremiah concluded the description of his afflictions. He was mocked and laughed at by his compatriots, filled with bitterness (**bitter herbs** and **gall** [cf. v. 19], the most bitter-tasting plant in Judah), **trampled** underfoot, **deprived of peace** and **prosperity,** and led to despair.

## B. Jeremiah's hope (3:19-40)

**3:19-24.** Jeremiah's condition paralleled that of Judah. His outward **affliction** (v. 19a; cf. vv. 1-4) and inward turmoil (v. 19b; cf. vv. 5, 13, 15) pushed him toward despair (**my soul is downcast,** v. 20). However, one thought (**this I call to mind**) crowded out the hopelessness that threatened to overwhelm him: **Because of the LORD's great love we are not consumed, for His compassions never fail.** Judah was down, but not out. God was punishing Judah for her sin, but did not reject her as His covenant people. The word for "great love" is *ḥeseḏ,* which has the idea of loyal love. God was sticking by the people He had chosen. The covenant made with Israel in Deuteronomy 28 (see *Introduction*) had not been abrogated. In fact God's loyal love could be seen in His faithfulness in carrying out the curses He had promised while at the same time preserving a remnant. The judgment itself was a witness to the fact that God had not abandoned His people. God's "compassions" (from *reḥem,* "womb," and in the pl. for intensity) showed His gentle feeling of concern for those who belonged to Him.

Could Judah push God so far that He would finally abandon her forever? Was God's supply of loyal love and compassion limited? Jeremiah's answer was no. God's "loving-kindnesses" (NASB) **are new every morning.** God offered a fresh supply of loyal love every day to His covenant people. Much like the manna in the wilderness, the supply could not be exhausted. This truth caused Jeremiah to call out in praise, **Great is Your faithfulness.** He was taken back by the limitless supply of God's grace offered to him. Because of this, Jeremiah resolved to **wait** for God to act, bringing about restoration and blessing. He could trust God despite his circumstances because he now understood how inexhaustible was God's supply of loyal love.

**3:25-40.** The God who brought the cursings spoken of in Deuteronomy 28 would also bring about the restoration promised in Deuteronomy 30. In the meantime God's people needed to develop the proper attitude toward their afflictions. Jeremiah wrote seven principles about the nature of Israel's affliction: (1) Affliction should be endured with **hope** in God's **salvation,** that is, ultimate restoration (Lam. 3:25-30). (2) Affliction is only temporary and is tempered by God's **compassion** and **love** (vv. 31-32). (3) God **does not** delight in **affliction** (v. 33). (4) If affliction comes because of injustice, God sees it and does not approve of it (vv. 34-36). (5) Affliction is always in relationship to God's sovereignty (vv. 37-38; cf. Job 2:10). (6) Affliction ultimately came because of Judah's **sins** (Lam. 3:39). (7) Affliction should accomplish the greater good of turning God's people back to Him (v. 40).

Jeremiah was able to place his (and Israel's) affliction in proper perspective by remembering how it related to God's character and His covenant with His people. Judah's afflictions were not cruel acts of a capricious God who delighted in inflicting pain on helpless people. Rather the afflictions came from a compassionate God who was being faithful to His covenant. He did not enjoy making others suffer, but He allowed the afflictions as temporary means to force Judah back to Himself. So Jeremiah ended this section by exhorting the people, **Let us examine our ways . . . let us return to the LORD.** God's affliction was designed as a corrective measure to restore His wayward people (Deut. 28:15-68). It was designed to force the people to return to the Lord (Deut. 30:1-10).

### C. Jeremiah's prayer (3:41-66)

The condition of the prophet (vv. 1-18) and the character of God (vv. 19-40) prompted Jeremiah to pray. This next section is in two parts. In the first part (vv. 41-47) the prophet exhorted the people to confess their sins to God because of their suffering. This section was written in the plural ("we," "us," "our"). In

the second part (vv. 48-66) Jeremiah remembered God's personal deliverance after his cry; this prompted Jeremiah to call on God to judge his enemies. This section was written in the singular ("I," "me," "my"); it represented Jeremiah as the model for Judah. As God rescued Jeremiah and judged his enemies, so God would rescue Judah and judge her enemies if she would call on Him.

**3:41-47.** This prayer flows out of the exhortation in verse 40. Judah's return to the Lord would be accomplished through prayer. As she turned toward heaven she would acknowledge that she had **sinned and rebelled.** The nation's troubles—being under God's **anger** (cf. 2:1, 3, 6, 22; 3:43), having unanswered **prayer,** being rejected like **scum** by **the nations,** and being scoffed at (cf. 2:16)—stemmed from her disobedience **to God.** All her **terror and pitfalls, ruin and destruction** resulted from rebellion against God's covenant. When Judah would realize the awful consequences of her sin, she would finally admit her guilt.

**3:48-51.** In verse 48 Jeremiah abruptly shifted from the plural to the singular. Verses 48-51 provide a transition from the people's confession (vv. 41-47) to Jeremiah's example (vv. 52-66). As the people confessed their sin and then waited for God to respond, so Jeremiah continued to weep (cf. 2:11) and pray **until the LORD** would look **down from heaven and** see. God promised to restore Israel when she called on Him from her captivity (Deut. 30:2-3). So Jeremiah vowed to continue calling for God's restoration of His people till the event actually happened.

**3:52-55.** After vowing to pray for the people till God reversed their fortunes, Jeremiah related circumstances from his own life which were examples for them. As Judah was afflicted, Jeremiah was also afflicted. As she was to cry for relief, so Jeremiah had cried for relief. God's deliverance of Jeremiah was then a prelude to the deliverance He would bring the nation.

Jeremiah's ministry during Judah's final days created many **enemies.** The people from his own hometown plotted to kill him (Jer. 11:18-23), and everybody at the temple demanded that he be executed (Jer. 26:7-9). He was beaten and thrown into prison as a traitor (Jer. 37:11-16), and was later, near the end of Nebuchadnezzar's siege, lowered into a muddy cistern to starve to death (Jer. 38:1-6).

Jeremiah was probably referring to this last incident in Lamentations 3:53-55. He cried to God for deliverance from the **pit** where he was facing certain death. Some feel that the pit could also be a double reference to both the cistern and the grave or sheol (cf. 2 Sam. 22:5-6; Pss. 18:4-5; 69:1-2, 14-15; Jonah 2:5-6). Probably Jeremiah's experience in the physical **pit** brought to mind the Hebrew concept of the pit of death. One cannot push the metaphorical image too far, however, because the phrase **and threw stones at me** (Lam. 3:53) would be meaningless if the pit referred only to death. If one were sinking in the pit of death, why would he care if people were throwing stones at him? But if he were trapped in a physical cistern this could pose a real danger, as it did for Jeremiah.

**3:56-58.** Jeremiah's **plea** for deliverance from the pit was answered. **You came near when I called You.** God intervened on Jeremiah's behalf and rescued him from certain death in a muddy cistern (cf. Jer. 38:7-13). So Jeremiah was a living example to Judah of God's loyal love and faithfulness (cf. Lam. 3:22-23). God did deliver (**redeemed** here means "delivered") this man who called on Him for help.

**3:59-66.** Jeremiah then called on God to vindicate him before his **enemies,** those in Judah who opposed him. God had **seen . . . the wrong done to** Jeremiah—**their vengeance . . . their plots. . . . their insults,** and their mocking. Jeremiah also asked God to **pay them back what they deserve.** This was fulfilled historically when Nebuchadnezzar entered Jerusalem. The leaders responsible for rejecting and persecuting Jeremiah were punished by Babylon (cf. Jer. 39:4-7; 52:7-11, 24-27). The parallel to Jerusalem was

obvious. She too was persecuted by her enemies (Lam. 3:46-47); but she could be confident that God would vindicate her before her enemies if she would turn to Him.

## IV. Fourth Dirge: The Lord's Anger (chap. 4)

Chapter 4 parallels the judgment discussed in chapter 2. After describing the response of an individual in the midst of judgment (chap. 3), Jeremiah again returned to survey the scene of calamity in Jerusalem. He contrasted the conditions in Jerusalem before and after the siege (4:1-11), explained the causes for the siege, (vv. 12-20), and gave a call for vindication from Zion (vv. 21-22).

### A. Contrasts before and after the siege (4:1-11)

The stark reality of Jerusalem's judgment was brought into sharp focus by comparing her present condition with that before the fall. Several scholars have seen a parallelism between verses 1-6 and 7-11 (see the chart). Both sections are written to point to the same conclusion—Jerusalem's present calamity is God's punishment for her sin (vv. 6, 11).

**4:1-2.** Jeremiah compared Jerusalem to dull **gold** and cast-off **gems.** Then he explained his figurative language. The "gold" and "gems" were the **precious sons of Zion,** the inhabitants of Jerusalem.

In their former glory they had been as precious as **gold,** but they were **now considered as pots of clay.** Clay was common in Palestine; nearly all vessels were made from it. Clay pots were abundant and their value was little. If one broke, it was thrown out and a new one replaced it. Similarly the people of Jerusalem, God's precious people, had become worthless.

---

## Parallelism in Lamentations 4:1-11

| 4:1-6 | | 4:7-11 | |
|---|---|---|---|
| vv. 1-2 | The value of the sons of Zion has become despised. | vv. 7-8 | The value of the princes has become despised. |
| vv. 3-5 | The little children and adults suffer. | vv. 9-10 | The little children and adults suffer. |
| v. 6 | Conclusion: The calamity is God's punishment. | v. 11 | Conclusion: The calamity is God's punishment. |

**4:3-5.** Jeremiah then turned from the people in general to the children in particular. The treatment of children by their mothers during the siege was worse than that expected of loathsome animals. **Jackals**, found throughout the Mediterranean area, traveled in packs. They were associated with areas of desolation and destruction (cf. Isa. 35:7; Jer. 9:11; 10:22; 49:33; 51:37; Mal. 1:3). Yet even jackals nourished their offspring while the cries of **the children** of Jerusalem **for bread** and water went unheeded by their parents. The people of Jerusalem had **become** as **heartless** as wild **ostriches**. Mother ostriches seem unconcerned about their young, for they lay their eggs in the sand where they may be trampled (see comments on Job 39:14-18).

Infants and children were dying **of thirst** and starvation (cf. Lam. 2:19). Another constant in the siege was that those who used to eat well were now **destitute**, and princes (**those nurtured in purple**, royal clothing) were lying in **ash heaps**, probably in sickness (cf. Job 2:8).

**4:6.** Jeremiah ended the first stanza of this fourth dirge by comparing Jerusalem to **Sodom**. But Jerusalem's **punishment** was worse than Sodom's because (a) Jerusalem's punishment was protracted while Sodom's was short (**in a moment**), and (b) Jerusalem's came despite assistance from Egypt while Sodom had no assistance (**without a hand . . . to help**).

**4:7-9.** Jeremiah's second stanza (vv. 7-11) paralleled his first (vv. 1-6), but the illustrations here are heightened and narrowed for effect. The "sons of Zion" (v. 2) are now called the **princes** (cf. 2:2, 9). The leaders of the city suffered the same fate as everyone else. Their fine complexions and healthy **bodies** did not escape the ravages of Babylon. They too saw their skin darken (become **blacker than soot**) and grow taut (**shriveled**) as their bodies became **racked** by **hunger** and emaciated (cf. 5:10).

**4:10-11.** The children who had been starving (vv. 4-5) were now victimized by their parents. The gnawing pangs of hunger (cf. 1:11, 19) finally drove **compassionate women** into cannibalizing **their own children** (cf. comments on 2:20).

Jeremiah concluded this second stanza by again pointing to **the LORD** as

the source of Zion's punishment (cf. 1:12-17; 2:1-8; 5:20). Jerusalem was experiencing God's **wrath** (cf. 2:2, 4; 3:1) and **fierce anger** (cf. 1:12; 2:3, 6) for her sin. God's judgment was like **a fire** (cf. 2:3) that had raced out of control in Jerusalem, engulfing the entire city. Both the superstructure and foundations had been destroyed.

### B. Causes for the siege (4:12-20)

**4:12. Jerusalem** was a mighty fortress that had seemed secure. The city had been entered by invading armies on a few occasions previously (cf. 1 Kings 14:25-28; 2 Kings 14:13-14; 2 Chron. 21:16-17). But its defenses had been rebuilt and strengthened (cf. 2 Chron. 32:2-5; 33:14), and a water supply into the city was established with the digging of Hezekiah's tunnel. So by Jeremiah's time **the kings** considered the city impregnable. Yet God allowed it to be captured.

**4:13-16.** One cause of Jerusalem's siege and fall was **the sins of her prophets and the iniquities of her priests.** The leaders who had been placed as mediators between God and people had become corrupt. Instead of promoting righteousness and stressing faithfulness to God's covenant, these men had **shed . . . the blood** of innocent people and therefore were **defiled with blood.** They were so polluted with sin that they were treated like lepers. Amazingly the prophets and priests were actually shunned as **unclean** lepers and were forced out of the covenant community (cf. Lev. 13:45-46). God **scattered** Jerusalem's leaders (**priests** and **elders**) because they had led the people into sin.

**4:17-19.** If the first cause of Jerusalem's siege was the sin of the prophets and priests (vv. 13-16), the second cause was the futility of foreign alliances. Instead of trusting in God, Jerusalem had turned to Egypt for protection from Babylon. **In vain** she **watched for a nation that could not save** her. Both Jeremiah and Ezekiel had warned against the futility of trusting in Egypt for protection (Jer. 37:6-10; Ezek. 29:6-7). That false hope brought only bitter grief when Babylon's armies, **swifter than eagles** (cf. Hab. 1:8), finally captured Jerusalem, pursuing those who tried to escape, and the **end** came.

**4:20.** The third cause of Jerusalem's siege and fall was Zedekiah her king.

Zedekiah was **the Lord's anointed.** The word "anointed" (*māšîaḥ*) was used of the kings of Israel because oil was poured on their heads to indicate that they were set apart for their task by God (cf. 1 Sam. 10:1; 16:1; 1 Kings 1:39-45; 2 Kings 11:12). When Jerusalem fell, Zedekiah tried to escape toward the Jordan River and Ammon (Jer. 39:2-7) but he **was caught in** the enemy's **traps.** His children were killed and he was carried away in chains. The leader Jerusalem looked to for security (her **very life breath** and her **shadow**) was powerless to protect her.

### C. Call for vindication (4:21-22)

**4:21-22.** Because of God's covenant with Israel (Deut. 28–30) the people could hope for vindication. The last two verses in Lamentations 4 draw a contrast between Israel and her Gentile enemy Edom (see the chart).

**Edom** took an active role in promoting Jerusalem's fall to Babylon (cf. Ps. 137:7; Jer. 49:7-22; Ezek. 25:12-14; 35). (On **Uz** see comments on Job 1:1.) Edom's crimes against her "brother" Jacob (Deut. 23:7) represented the actions of all the nations that profited at Jerusalem's expense. God had noted their actions, and would punish those nations for their sin, exactly as He had said He would do (Deut. 30:7). Though Edom rejoiced and was **glad** over Jerusalem's calamity, **the** bitter **cup** would someday be **passed** to her (cf. Lam. 1:21-22). Drinking from a cup pictured being forced to undergo judgment (cf. Jer. 25:15-28). As God was judging Jerusalem in Jeremiah's day for her sin, so He would also judge Edom (and, by extension, all Gentile nations) for their sins. Jerusalem could look forward to restoration, but **Edom** could only expect judgment (cf. comments on Obad. 4, 15-18, 20-21).

## V. Fifth Dirge: The Remnant's Response (chap. 5)

The prophet's final dirge breaks the pattern established in his earlier laments. The acrostic pattern and *qînâh* meter are not used. In fact the entire chapter is more properly a prayer than a lament. Chapters 1–3 each close with a prayer to the Lord (1:20-22; 2:20-22; 3:55-66) but no prayer is included in chapter 4. Therefore it is possible to see chapter 5 functioning as the prayer following chapter 4 and

### Contrasts between Edom and Israel in Lamentations 4:21-22

| Present Condition | Future Condition |
|---|---|
| Edom rejoicing | Israel restored |
| Israel punished | Edom punished |

serving as the book's concluding prayer.

The prayer itself is composed of two sections, each of which summarizes the response the remnant needed to make. The first response is a call for God to *remember* their condition (5:1-18). This section also includes a confession of sin. After the call for God to *remember* is a call for God to *restore* Judah (vv. 19-22). In context this is a call to restore both the land of Israel and the blessings of the covenant (Deut. 30:1-10).

### A. The remnant's prayer for remembrance (5:1-18)

**5:1.** Verse 1 introduces the prayer. The remnant called on God to **remember** the indignities they had suffered and to **look** at their present **disgrace.** Jeremiah had already indicated that God notices such atrocities (3:34-36). Therefore the people's call was not just for God to **see** what had happened (for He sees everything: cf. Prov. 15:3), but rather that God see *and act* on their condition.

**5:2.** Through the use of the first person ("we," "us," "our") the people described (in vv. 2-10) the general conditions of suffering brought about by Babylon. The land of Judah had been parceled out **to foreigners.** Babylon assumed dominion over the land, and its occupying forces were stationed there (Jer. 40:10; 41:3). In addition, nations surrounding Judah appropriated or annexed some of her land for themselves (cf. Ezek. 35:10).

**5:3.** Besides losing their property, the people also lost their rights. Their new taskmasters were cruel despots who cared little for them. The men were as defenseless as the **orphans and fatherless** and the women were as vulnerable as **widows.** In Israel orphans and widows were the most helpless people in society (see comments on 1:1). They had no one to stand up for their rights or to insure that justice was done. Under Babylon's rule Judah had no rights or means of protection. She was the vanquished enemy, and Babylon her cruel overlord (cf. Hab. 1:6-11).

**5:4-5.** Babylon's rule over Judah was severe. The Jews now had to pay for the **water** they drank and the **wood** they used for cooking. Both in Judah and in Babylon the Jews found **no rest** from their pursuers. Persecution and fear dogged their every footstep (cf. Deut. 28:65-67; Ezek. 5:2, 12).

**5:6-8.** Still another reason accounted for Judah's calamity. She **submitted to Egypt and Assyria to get enough bread.** The words translated "submitted to" (*nāṯannû yāḏ*) literally mean "to give the hand to" or "to shake hands." The phrase implies the idea of establishing a pact or treaty (cf. 2 Kings 10:15) and often referred to one group surrendering or submitting to a more powerful group or person as part of a treaty (1 Chron. 29:24; 2 Chron 30:8; Jer. 50:15). Judah had pledged her allegiance both to Egypt and Assyria in her history, for the sake of national security (cf. Ezek. 16:26-28; 23:12, 21). Judah's past leaders (**fathers**) shifted their allegiance between countries, and their fickleness ultimately destroyed them. Their sin brought their death, and their survivors bore **their punishment.** The present generation was not claiming to be suffering unjustly for their forebears' sins (cf. Lam. 5:16), but saw their punishment as a logical conclusion to their ancestors' folly. Their forefathers' willing submission to godless nations was now bearing bitter fruit. Babylon appointed cruel taskmasters; men of low degree were exalted and the people of Judah were forced to submit to them: **Slaves rule over us.**

**5:9-10.** The severe conditions and scarcity of food prompted the people to take desperate means for survival. Probably **the sword** they had to brave was carried by the bands of roving **desert** nomads through whose area the people of Judah had to travel in order to buy **bread** (i.e., "food"). The Jews' **skin** was **feverish** because of their lack of adequate food (cf. 4:8).

**5:11-14.** In these verses the subject switches from the first person to the third person ("their"). After speaking of their general conditions of suffering (vv. 2-10),

the people described its effects on different groups of individuals. No element of society escaped the ravages of judgment.

The first group mentioned who suffered the horrors of foreign occupation were the **women** of Jerusalem (**Zion**) and the **virgins . . . of Judah.** Women who survived the Babylonian assault on their cities were mercilessly raped by the sadistic soldiers. In a scene of savage brutality, repeated by many conquering armies throughout history, the victors went on a wanton spree of lustful revenge against defenseless women.

The city's leaders also felt the fury of the Babylonians. **Princes** were **hung up by their hands.** Those responsible for leading Judah's rebellion against Babylon were tortured to death in this cruel way. Possibly this was a form of crucifixion since hanging and impaling victims on stakes was the usual method of execution used during that time. **Elders** were also tortured.

The **young men** who survived the Babylonian attack were enslaved. Because of the shortage of domestic animals in Palestine (probably because most had been eaten during the 30-month siege), men were forced to perform tasks usually done by animals. Men turned the **millstones** (as Samson also was forced to do, Jud. 16:21) to grind grain, and **boys** were forced to carry large **loads of wood** needed in the city. Those who were Judah's hope had been reduced to the status of slaves.

Wisdom, justice, and happiness had departed from the city. **The city gate** where **the elders** used to gather was the place of justice and wisdom. Disputes between individuals were taken to the wise elders. But with the departure of the elders (cf. Lam. 5:12) the wisdom and justice normally available to the Jews was gone. Even the **music** of **the young men** had ceased. Music was associated with joy and happiness (cf. Ps. 95:1-2); and Judah had nothing to rejoice about now as her people suffered under the harsh hand of Babylon.

**5:15-18.** A veil of gloom hung over Jerusalem. The **joy** and revelry that had once been there was replaced by sadness and **mourning.** The bustling activity of a once-thriving city had given way to **desolate** ruins inhabited only by wild animals. **The crown** figuratively represented the glory and majesty that had belonged to Jerusalem. That glory was now gone. It was lost because of sin. The people were **faint** from hunger, and their **eyes** were **dim** from tears (cf. 2:11; 3:48-49). Judah had only herself to blame for her present condition of desolation in which wild **jackals** (cf. 4:3) prowled.

### B. The remnant's prayer for restoration (5:19-22)

**5:19.** After describing her condition (vv. 1-18) Judah concluded her prayer by calling on God to act (vv. 19-22). The basis for this call was God's eternal sovereignty: **You, O LORD, reign forever.** Judah was not suffering because her God had been defeated by the stronger gods of Babylon. Judah's God was the only true God, and *He* had caused her calamity (cf. 1:12-17; 2:1-8; 4:11). Yet this same God who brought about her destruction also had the power to bring about her restoration—if He chose to do so.

**5:20.** The knowledge of God's ability to restore the nation prompted the people to ask two questions. Because of the nature of Hebrew parallelism these two questions should be viewed synonymously. To **forget** about Judah would be to **forsake** her to her present condition of suffering. The use of "forget" here is the opposite of "remember" in verse 1. God cannot "forget" anything. This figure of speech means to forsake or abandon the people *as though* He has forgotten them. The people were asking God **why** He had abandoned them for **so long.** Significantly Moses employed the figure of God remembering His covenant if His people would confess their sin (Lev. 26:40-42). So the people of Judah were calling on God to fulfill the remainder of His covenant promise.

**5:21-22.** The specific action the people requested was, **Restore us to Yourself . . . that we may return.** The people wanted to be restored to the blessings of God's covenant which included being restored to the land of Israel (Lev. 26:40-45; Deut. 3:1-10). Their ultimate hope for restoration was God's faithfulness to His covenant promises. **Unless** God had **utterly rejected** the nation (which He vowed never to do; Lev. 26:44; Jer. 31:31-37) the people could depend on Him to answer their request.

Thus the Book of Lamentations ends on a note of hope. In spite of severe suffering because of her sin, Judah had not been abandoned as a nation. God was still sovereign, and His covenant with Israel was still operative despite her disobedience. The hope for the nation was that if she would call on God and confess her sin He would protect her during her captivity (Lam. 3:21-30) and would ultimately restore her as a nation to covenant blessing (5:21).

# BIBLIOGRAPHY

Cohen, Abraham. *The Five Megilloth.* London: Soncino Press, 1946.

Gottwald, Norman K. *Studies in the Book of Lamentations.* London: SCM Press, 1962.

Harrison, R.K. *Jeremiah and Lamentations: An Introduction and Commentary.* The Tyndale Old Testament Commentaries. Downers Grove, Ill.: InterVarsity Press, 1973.

Hillers, Delbert R. *Lamentations.* The Anchor Bible. Garden City, N.Y.: Doubleday & Co., 1972.

Ironside, H.A. *Jeremiah: Prophecy & Lamentations.* New York: Loizeaux Brothers, 1950.

Jensen, Irving L. *Jeremiah and Lamentations.* Everyman's Bible Commentary. Chicago: Moody Press, 1974.

Kaiser, Walter C., Jr. *A Biblical Approach to Personal Suffering.* Chicago: Moody Press, 1982.

Laetsch, Theo. *Jeremiah.* St. Louis, Mo.: Concordia Publishing House, 1965.

Schaeffer, Francis A. *Death in the City.* Downers Grove, Ill.: InterVarsity Press, 1969.

Swindoll, Charles R. *The Lamentations of Jeremiah.* Bible Study Guide. Fullerton, Calif.: Insight for Living, 1977.

# EZEKIEL

## Charles H. Dyer

## INTRODUCTION

For the average reader of the Bible the Book of Ezekiel is mostly a perplexing maze of incoherent visions—a kaleidoscope of whirling wheels and dry bones that defy interpretation. This impression often causes readers to shy away from studying the book and to miss one of the great literary and spiritual portions of the Old Testament.

**Authorship and Date.** The author of this book is "Ezekiel the priest, the son of Buzi" (1:3). The name Ezekiel means "God will strengthen" or "God will harden."

Like Jeremiah (Jer. 1:1) and Zechariah (Zech. 1:1; cf. Neh. 12:4, 16), Ezekiel was a priest (Ezek. 1:3). Ezekiel's father Buzi is mentioned only in 1:3. Jeremiah, Zechariah, and Ezekiel were the only prophet-priests; and all three prophesied during the exilic or postexilic periods. Ezekiel's priestly background explains in part his emphasis on the temple in Jerusalem, the glory of the Lord, the actions of Jerusalem's priests, and God's future temple.

The date for Ezekiel's ministry can be determined by noting the chronological notations in his book (1:2; 8:1; 20:1; 24:1; 29:1, 17; 30:20; 31:1; 32:1, 17; 33:21; 40:1).

All Ezekiel's prophecies are arranged chronologically (starting with "the 5th year of the exile," 1:2, and ending with "the 25th year of our exile," 40:1, except the prophecies introduced in 29:1, 17). These two variations may be explained by the fact that they are grouped topically as part of the prophecies against Egypt in chapters 29–32.

Ezekiel's ministry began "in the fourth month on the fifth day" of "the fifth year of the exile of King Jehoiachin" (1:1-2). Jehoiachin came to the throne in December 597 B.C. after Jehoiakim died

(2 Kings 24:1-12). After a reign of only three months Jehoiachin was captured by Nebuchadnezzar and deported to Babylon. The fifth year of Jehoiachin's exile was 593 B.C., and the fourth month was the month Tammuz. According to Richard A. Parker and Waldo H. Dubberstein (*Babylonian Chronology: 626 B.C.–A.D. 75.* Providence, R.I.: Brown University Press, 1956) the month Tammuz (Akk., *Duzu*) began on July 27 in 593 B.C. Therefore Ezekiel began his ministry on July 31, 593 B.C. (the "fifth day" is inclusive, counting both July 27 and 31).

Ezekiel also said his ministry began "in the 30th year" (Ezek. 1:1). Scholars debate the exact meaning of this statement, but many feel it refers to Ezekiel's age. If so, he was commissioned as a prophet at the age he was qualified to enter the priesthood (cf. Num. 4:3).

The last dated prophecy in Ezekiel was "in the 27th year, in the first month on the first day" (Ezek. 29:17). Since Ezekiel began prophesying in 593 (the fifth year of Jehoiachin's exile, 1:2), this prophecy was 571 B.C. (March 26). So Ezekiel's prophetic activity spanned at least 22 years (593–571 B.C.), from age 30 to 52.

Till recently few Bible scholars had doubted the unity, authorship, or exilic date of Ezekiel. Arguments challenging these items have been satisfactorily answered by conservatives (e.g., Gleason L. Archer, Jr., *A Survey of Old Testament Introduction.* Rev. ed. Chicago: Moody Press, 1974, pp. 368-76; and John B. Taylor, *Ezekiel: An Introduction and Commentary,* pp. 13-20).

**Historical Background.** For a discussion of Judah's history in Ezekiel's time see "Historical Background" in the *Introduction* to Jeremiah.

The Book of Ezekiel was written during the time of Judah's bondage to Babylon under Nebuchadnezzar's rule. Ezekiel lived with a group of captives in Tel Aviv (not the modern-day city in Israel by that name), located beside the Kebar River (3:15) in Babylon. The exact site of this settlement is unknown, but the Kebar River has been identified with the Grand Canal (Akk., *naru kabaru*) in Babylon. This canal branched off from the Euphrates just above Babylon and flowed east of the city. It continued through the site of ancient Nippur and then reentered the Euphrates near Uruk (biblical Erech).

During these final years Ezekiel was ministering in Babylon, predicting the coming collapse of Jerusalem. His message fell on deaf ears till word of the city's destruction was received in Babylon. The fall of the city prompted a change in Ezekiel's prophetic message. Before Jerusalem fell, Ezekiel's message focused on Judah's forthcoming destruction because of her sin. After Jerusalem's fall, Ezekiel's message centered on Judah's future restoration.

**Structure and Style.** The structure and style of Ezekiel's book has at least four major characteristics.

1. *Chronological arrangement.* As noted earlier under "Authorship and Date" a definite chronological movement is evident within the book. Ezekiel is the only major prophet with such a precise chronological arrangement but the Books of Haggai and Zechariah have a similar arrangement.

2. *Structural balance.* In addition to its chronological arrangement Ezekiel's book also has a structural order and harmony. The first 24 chapters focus on the judgment of Judah; chapters 33–48 focus on the restoration of Judah. These two extremes are balanced by chapters 25–32 which deal with God's judgment on other nations. The glory of God departed from the temple in judgment (9:3; 10:4, 18-19; 11:22-25) and reappeared in the temple for blessing (43:1-5). Ezekiel was commissioned to deliver a message of judgment (chaps. 2–3) and later was recommissioned to give a message of deliverance (chap. 33).

3. *Focus on the glory and character of God.* Ezekiel emphasized the glory and character of God. Having received a vision of God's glory before he was commissioned, Ezekiel continued to refer to God's glory throughout the book (1:28;

3:12, 23; 8:4; 9:3; 10:4, 18-19; 11:22-23; 39:11, 21; 43:2-5; 44:4).

God's character determined His conduct throughout the book. Fifteen times God declared that He had acted for the sake of His name to keep it from being profaned (20:9, 14, 22, 39, 44; 36:20-23 [twice in v. 23]; 39:7 [twice], 25; 43:7-8). Over 60 times God said He had acted so that the people would "know that I am the LORD" (e.g., 6:7, 10, 13-14).

4. *Use of literary devices.* Ezekiel used unique literary devices to drive home his message to a "hardened and obstinate" people. These included proverbs (12:22-23; 16:44; 18:2-3); visions (chaps. 1–3; 8–11; 37; 40–48); parables (chap. 17; 24:1-14); symbolic acts (chaps. 4–5; 12; 24:15-27); and allegories (chaps. 16–17).

By these means Ezekiel presented his messages in dramatic and forceful ways, thus getting the people's attention so they would respond.

# OUTLINE

# COMMENTARY

## I. Judgment on Judah (chaps. 1–24)

The first half of the Book of Ezekiel focuses on God's coming judgment of Judah. God's sword was poised to strike, and Ezekiel was commissioned with the task of explaining to people already in captivity *what* God's judgment entailed and *why* it was coming.

## A. Ezekiel's preparation (chaps. 1–3)

The record of God's commissioning of Ezekiel is the longest such prophetic call in the Bible (cf. Isa. 6; Jer. 1). Ezekiel, like Isaiah and Jeremiah, was prepared for his ministry by receiving a vision of the glory and majesty of God before he was called to serve the Lord.

### 1. INTRODUCTION (1:1-3)

**1:1-2.** When God appeared to Ezekiel to inaugurate his prophetic ministry, it was **in the 30th year, in the fourth month on the fifth day**; it was also **the 5th year of the exile of King Jehoiachin.** As noted under "Authorship and Date" in the *Introduction* this was July 31, 593 B.C. "The 30th year" probably referred to Ezekiel's age. As a priest (v. 3) this was the age he would normally have entered the Lord's service.

Ezekiel had been taken into captivity with King Jehoiachin in March of 597. He was one of **the exiles** who had been resettled **by the Kebar River**—a canal off the Euphrates River that flowed to the east of Babylon (see "Historical Backgound" in the *Introduction*).

**I saw visions of God** was Ezekiel's summary of the visions which he then described in detail in 1:4–2:7. This view of God's glory profoundly influenced him.

**1:3. The word of the LORD** points to the *source* of Ezekiel's message. Ezekiel was to receive the message *God* wanted him to deliver. He then elaborated on this (2:8–3:11). **The hand of the LORD** described Ezekiel's *mandate* for his ministry. He was not acting on his own initiative but was constrained by God to minister, a fact detailed later (3:12-27).

### 2. THE VISIONS FOR THE WORK (1:4–2:7)

In this section Ezekiel discussed in detail the visions he mentioned briefly in 1:1. The prophet described the visions (1:4-28) and then stated their purpose (2:1-7).

#### a. The four living beings (1:4-14)

**1:4.** As Ezekiel peered to **the north** he noticed an approaching thunderstorm. In the storm were a big **cloud,** strong winds, and **flashing lightning.** As the cloud approached, though, Ezekiel's gaze shifted from the darkness of the storm to the **light** emanating from its **center.** This light **looked like glowing metal** (*ḥašmāl*). This word occurs in the Old Testament only in Ezekiel (here and in v. 27; 8:2). It seems to refer to some shining substance. In the other two occurrences it describes God's glowing splendor.

**1:5-8a.** Ezekiel spotted **four living creatures** in the midst of **the fire.** These beings are identified in chapter 10 as cherubim, a special order of angelic beings. They have special access to God (cf. 28:14, 16) and are bearers of God's throne-chariot. On the tabernacle's ark of the covenant, gold images of cherubim, with outstretched wings, guarded the mercy seat where the glory of the Lord dwelt (Ex. 25:17-22; Num. 7:89). God was "enthroned between the cherubim" of the ark of the covenant (1 Sam. 4:4; 2 Sam. 6:2; Pss. 80:1; 99:1; Isa. 37:16). This place where God was enthroned was called "the chariot" (1 Chron. 28:18). Since the earthly tabernacle and temple were a copy of the heavenly reality (Heb. 8:5), Ezekiel's vision was of the actual throne-chariot of God, borne by cherubim.

The general **appearance** of the living beings was somewhat like **a man.** However, they would not be mistaken for humans. They **each** had **four faces and four wings.** (The prophet explained these features in detail, Ezek. 1:10-11.) The cherubim's **legs were straight,** which implies that they were standing upright, but **their feet** were calf-like instead of human, and were **like burnished** (highly polished) **bronze.** Ezekiel said the four cherubim also had human-like **hands.**

**1:8b-9.** Ezekiel then explained how the **four** creatures functioned as a unit. Two of the four **wings** of each creature were outstretched so that **their wings touched one another,** forming a connecting square. Having four **faces** on four sides of their heads and being connected in a square, they were able to travel **straight** in any direction and to change direction without turning. Thus **they did not turn as they moved.**

**1:10.** In recording more details of the cherubim (vv. 10-14), Ezekiel first described **their faces.** The front of each cherub was **the face of a man, and on the right side** was **the face of a lion. The left** side was **the face of an ox,** and **the face of an eagle** was apparently in the back. Some interpreters feel that these represent intelligence (man), power (lion), service (ox), and swiftness (eagle). How-

ever, it seems better to see the faces as representing the highest forms of life in God's created realm. Man was mentioned first because he was the acme of God's creative work. He was followed by the lion, "king" among wild beasts; the ox, one of the strongest of domestic animals; and the eagle, the "lord" of the birds.

**1:11.** Ezekiel then described the cherubim's **wings. Two** of the four **wings** on each cherub **were spread out upward,** or extended out above the cherub and were **touching** a **wing of** a cherub **on either side.** The effect was to form a large "box" with a cherub at each corner. The other **two wings** on each cherub were for **covering its body.** Because these creatures were ministering before God's holy presence, they covered their bodies in reverence (cf. Isa. 6:1-3).

**1:12-14.** The motion of the cherubim was always **straight ahead.** They could go in any direction **without turning** their faces. They were directed in their motion by **the spirit,** probably God's Spirit.

These **creatures,** already described as "brilliant light. . . . glowing metal. . . . burnished bronze" (vv. 4, 7), were also said to look **like burning coals of fire or like torches.** The glowing embers were interspersed with **fire** that **moved back and forth among the creatures.** This seemed to presage Ezekiel's message of God's burning judgment on Judah.

*b. The four wheels (1:15-21)*

Looking below the cherubim, Ezekiel saw some wheels. He described the wheels generally (vv. 15-18) and then told how the wheels and the cherubim were related (vv. 19-21).

**1:15-18. On the ground beside each** cherub was **a wheel.** Each wheel **sparkled like chrysolite** (*taršîš*). This precious stone might be yellow jasper or some other gold-colored stone, or beryl which is commonly pale green, or chrysolite which is transparent yellow or green. The point is that the **wheels** sparkled with a yellow-green glow.

The two wheels for each cherub were unusual in shape; one **wheel** intersected another **wheel** at right angles. Thus they could roll in **four directions** without being turned and could move with the cherubim. Their great **awesome** (cf. v. 22) height added to their fearful design. This awesomeness was enhanced by the **rims** of the wheels being **full of eyes all around.** This unusual feature probably pictures divine omniscience (cf. 2 Chron. 16:9; Prov. 15:3), the eyes representing the all-seeing nature of the One who rides on this throne-chariot.

**1:19-21.** The statement, **the spirit of the living creatures was in the wheels,** may mean **the wheels** were like an extension of the cherubim on God's throne-chariot. Ezekiel envisioned the God of the universe on a mobile platform. As He directed the cherubim, **the wheels** responded and the chariot was propelled on its way.

### c. The expanse (1:22-24)

**1:22-24.** The outstretched **wings** of the cherubim joined together. **Above** their wings was an area that Ezekiel said **looked like an expanse** (*rāqîa'*). This was not an empty space. This same word was used to describe the expanse created by God on the second day of Creation (Gen. 1:6-7). That "expanse" was pictured there as something solid (*rāqîa'* is from *rāqa'*, "to beat, stamp, beat out, spread out"), which supported the waters above it.

The shining brilliance of the expanse above the cherubim reminded Ezekiel of **ice** crystals **sparkling** in the light of the sun. Interestingly the Apostle John said the expanse around God's throne is "clear as crystal" (Rev. 4:6).

**When** the **wings** of the cherubim **moved,** their **sound** was **like** water **rushing** down a mountain stream, and was as intense as **the voice of** God (possibly an allusion to thunder which sometimes depicts God's voice, Job 37:4-5; 40:9; Pss. 18:13; 104:7). This cacophony reminded Ezekiel of the din of **an army** in battle. When the cherubim stopped, **they lowered their wings.**

### d. The throne (1:25-28)

**1:25-28.** As the cherubim came to a halt and the sound of their **wings** stopped, Ezekiel became aware of another sound. It was **a voice from above the expanse over their heads.** This was the voice of God seated on the throne. As Ezekiel instinctively glanced upward in the direction of the voice, he saw above the expanse **what looked like a throne of sapphire.** "Sapphire" (*'eben-sappîr*) or,

more properly, *lapis lazuli* (NIV marg.) is an azure-blue stone, prized since ancient times. It is cut and polished for ornamental purposes.

Seated on this shining blue **throne** was Someone who looked like **a man.** Ezekiel's gaze was drawn first to the upper part of His body and then to the lower part. Though Ezekiel could describe the cherubim in detail, all he could say of God was that **He looked like glowing metal** and **fire.** The splendor of His glory was so bright that Ezekiel could see only His form before he was forced to look down. Ezekiel then noticed a **radiance** surrounding the vision. It looked **like . . . a rainbow.** The multisplendored colors of the rainbow were refracted from the blazing light of God's glory. The Apostle John described the same beauty in his vision of God's throne in heaven (Rev. 4:3).

Lest anyone doubt what Ezekiel saw, he stated clearly that it **was the appearance of the likeness of the glory of the LORD.** The Lord's glory is referred to 16 times in Ezekiel (1:28; 3:12, 23; 8:4; 9:3; 10:4, 18-19; 11:22-23; 39:21; 43:2 [twice], 4-5; 44:4; see comments under "Structure and Style" in the *Introduction*). Ezekiel had seen a theophany, as God had appeared to him in a visionary form. By using the terms "appearance" and "likeness" Ezekiel was pointing out that he had not seen God directly. That would have caused immediate death (cf. Ex. 33:18-23; John 1:18).

Ezekiel responded in humble submission; he **fell facedown** (cf. Ezek. 3:23). As he prostrated himself in awe before God's majesty, he **heard** God speak. This was probably the same **voice** mentioned in 1:25.

### e. The task for Ezekiel (2:1-7)

As God spoke (1:28), He provided power for Ezekiel (2:1-2), told Ezekiel of his assignment (vv. 3-5), and challenged him to be faithful (vv. 6-7).

**2:1-2.** God told Ezekiel to rise and receive His message. **Son of man** (*ben-'ādām*) occurs 93 times in the Book of Ezekiel to refer to that prophet. It emphasizes his humanity before God and seems to stress the distance that separates man from God. The word "son" expresses family and hereditary relationships, but often moves beyond the mere biological to denote association or identification with someone or something (cf. "sons of God," Gen. 6:2, 4; "son of the dawn," Isa. 14:12). By this title God was stressing Ezekiel's association with the human race.

When God told Ezekiel to **stand,** He also enabled him by **the** Holy **Spirit** to stand. In Old Testament times the Holy Spirit did not indwell all believers but indwelt selected persons temporarily for divine service (cf. Ex. 31:1-11; 1 Sam. 10:9-11; Ps. 51:11; Ezek. 3:24).

**2:3-5.** Ezekiel's assignment was difficult. His message was to be directed **to a rebellious nation** ("rebellious" occurs eight times in chaps. 2 and 3, and eight times elsewhere in Ezek.), **people** who were **obstinate** (cf. 3:7) **and stubborn.** Rather than acknowledging God's judgment and confessing their sins, the Jewish exiles viewed their time in Babylon as a temporary setback that would be alleviated by their soon return to Jerusalem. They refused to admit their sin or to believe the threat of impending judgment on their disobedient nation.

Ezekiel's task was to declare God's Word. **Whether they** responded was the people's own responsibility. But in the end (when the events did transpire), **they** (the **rebellious house;** cf. comments on 3:9) would **know that a prophet** had been in their midst.

As a prophet Ezekiel would be a channel for **the Sovereign LORD** (*'ăḏōnāy Yahweh*). Ezekiel used this title of God 217 times. Elsewhere in the Old Testament it occurs only 103 times (*Theological Dictionary of the Old Testament.* Grand Rapids: Wm. B. Eerdmans Publishing Co., s.v. *'āḏôn, 'ăḏōnāy,* 1:62-3). This name stesses both God's sovereign authority and His covenant-keeping faithfulness.

**2:6-7.** Three times God told Ezekiel, **Do not be afraid.** He needed this encouragement because the task was difficult (**briers and thorns are all around you**) and even dangerous (**you live among scorpions**). Ezekiel learned his lesson well. Nowhere does the book hint that he cowered in fear or hesitated to proclaim God's message.

God said Ezekiel was to **speak** His **words.** Verses 7-8 are a bridge between two major sections. The first section (1:4–2:7) reports the visions for the work.

The next section (2:8–3:11) gives the message for the work. This One who gave Ezekiel the word is the Sovereign Lord whom Ezekiel had just seen in the vision.

3. THE MESSAGE FOR THE WORK (2:8–3:11)

Ezekiel's vision of God's glory provided the perspective and motivation for his task. But he also needed a message, the content of which came from the Lord (cf. the "word of the LORD," 1:3). The prophet was told to receive God's word (2:8–3:3) and then to deliver it (3:4-11).

*a. The reception of God's word (2:8–3:3)*

**2:8.** Israel had chafed under the bit of divine instruction and rebelled (v. 3) against God and His word. But Ezekiel was to **open** his **mouth and eat what** God gave him. He was to be receptive and responsive to God's words.

**2:9-10.** The specific word was then revealed to Ezekiel. **A hand** (probably God's) **stretched out to** him from His throne with **a scroll.** This is supported by the fact that the One speaking, God, also gave Ezekiel the scroll (3:2).

The scroll had writing **on both sides.** Scrolls were the common means for recording and preserving God's Word in Israel. Leather, papyrus, or parchment sheets were joined together in long rolls. The writing was in vertical columns, and very seldom was writing done on both sides of a scroll (but cf. Rev. 5:1). Many interpretations of why the scroll was written on both sides have been given, but the best explanation seems to be that God had much that He wanted Ezekiel to communicate to Israel.

The message consisted of **words of lament and mourning and woe.** This accurately summarizes the contents of Ezekiel 4–32. It does not, however, reflect the latter part of the book, in which the prophet spoke of Israel's restoration. This could explain, in part, why Ezekiel was recommissioned (chap. 33)—the content of his message was substantially changed after his message of woe was fulfilled.

**3:1-3.** God had already told the prophet **to eat** what He would give him (2:8). Now God repeated the order, specifically telling him to **eat** the **scroll** he had just received. The purpose was so he could **then go and speak to the house of Israel** (cf. comments on 3:4 about "Israel"). His task as a prophet was to deliver God's word to God's people.

As Ezekiel **ate** the scroll, **it tasted as sweet as honey.** Though his message was one of judgment, it was still God's word. The sweetness came from the source of the words (God) rather than the content of the words (judgment). This same thought was expressed by David (Ps. 19:10), Jeremiah (Jer. 15:16), and the Apostle John (Rev. 10:9-11).

### b. The delivery of God's word (3:4-11)

**3:4.** After receiving God's word, Ezekiel was told to proclaim it. His hearers were to be **the house of Israel.** Does this refer to all Israel (including those still in Palestine) or only to those in exile in Babylon? The parallel command in verse 11 implies that only those Israelites "in exile" were in view. Yet the phrase "house of Israel" cannot be limited to them. In many of the 101 occurrences of this expression (or variations of it) in the Book of Ezekiel, more than Israelites in captivity were included (cf. 6:11; 8:11-12). Ezekiel's message was for the entire "house" (i.e., people) of Israel, though he specifically proclaimed it to a small portion of that household then in captivity.

God's specific task for Ezekiel was to **speak** God's **words to them** (Israel). At first these verses seem to repeat 2:3-7, but the focus of this passage is different. In 2:3-7 Ezekiel was commissioned as a prophet, and in 3:4-9 he was equipped for his task.

**3:5-6.** Ezekiel's task did not involve linguistic obstacles. He was **not being sent to a people of obscure speech and difficult language.** Obscure (lit., "deep") **speech** suggests words that are unfathomable or difficult to comprehend (e.g., the language of the Assyrians, Isa. 33:19). The words **difficult language** (lit., "heavy tongue") can denote speech that is thick or sluggish. Moses used this expression to describe his lack of eloquence (Ex. 4:10). In Ezekiel 3:5 it probably means **words** that are hard to **understand** because of a language barrier (v. 6). Ezekiel faced no such hurdle. His message was not for some distant land with an exotic language; it was for **Israel.** Though going to another culture and nation would have been difficult because of the language problem, the results elsewhere would have been more rewarding. Had

Ezekiel gone to another nation, **they would have listened to** him. Amazingly those who knew nothing of the true God of the universe would have been more responsive than those who claimed His name.

**3:7.** At the outset God warned Ezekiel not to expect dramatic results from his ministry (cf. Isa. 6:8-13; Jer. 1:11-19). In contrast with the open reception Ezekiel would receive from other nations, **Israel** was **not willing to listen to** him. She would reject him because she had rejected God. The people were not prepared to "listen to" or respond to Ezekiel **because they** were **not willing to listen to** God. Their spiritual deafness was acquired over long years of exposure to and rejection of God's word given by the prophets. Israel's response to God in the past was a harbinger of the response Ezekiel could expect.

The nation's malady extended to **the whole house of Israel.** This does not imply that every Israelite had rejected God, for Habakkuk, Jeremiah, Ezekiel, and Daniel were all ministering faithfully. God was referring to all parts of Israel rather than every Israelite. Rebellion had made its way into the royal household, the temple, the courts of justice, and into every city and town in the land. Though individuals here and there were still responding to the Lord, the nation as a whole had turned from Him.

**3:8.** Taking God's message of judgment to an unyielding people was a tough task. God encouraged Ezekiel by offering him the needed strength. The prophet need not worry about the weight of his assignment. God promised to **make** him as **unyielding and hardened as they** were. The word for "hardened" (ḥāzāq) is the same word that forms part of Ezekiel's name—yᵉḥezqēʾl, "God will strengthen" or "God will harden." When he heard his name he was reminded of God's promised strength.

**3:9.** God also said He would **make** Ezekiel's **forehead like the hardest stone, harder than flint.** Figuratively "forehead" expresses determination or defiance (cf. Isa. 48:4; 50:7, "face" is lit., "forehead"; Jer. 3:3, "the brazen look of a prostitute" is lit., "a harlot's forehead"; 48:45). Ezekiel's determination would not waver when beset by opposition. "Flint," the hardest stone in Palestine, was used by Israel for knives (cf. Josh. 5:2-3) and other implements. Ezekiel's God-given strength and determination would withstand any opposition (cf. Jer. 1:18).

Because of God's empowering of Ezekiel, He could command him **not** to **be afraid of them or terrified by them** (cf. Jer. 1:17). Though opposition was certain to come, Ezekiel had nothing to fear. God's power was more than adequate to overcome the expected resistance. **Rebellious house** is a term for Israel that Ezekiel used 12 times (Ezek. 2:5-6, 8; 3:9, 26-27; 12:3, 9, 25; 17:12; 24:3; 44:6), apparently to underscore the people's defiance against God.

**3:10-11.** To be an accurate channel of God's revelation Ezekiel was to **listen carefully and take to heart** God's word. The recipients of his message were his **countrymen in exile,** though the scope of his pronouncements went beyond that group to include all Israel.

Ezekiel was to proclaim to these exiles, **This is what the Sovereign LORD says.** In words that hearken back to 2:4-5 Ezekiel was reminded of his task. He was responsible to proclaim God's word accurately regardless of the response. Some would **listen,** that is, obey, and others would **fail to listen,** that is, refuse to obey (cf. 2:5).

4. THE MOTIVATION FOR THE WORK (3:12-27)

Ezekiel's vision of God's glory had provided the needed *perspective* for his task (1:4–2:7). The *message* he was to deliver was provided by God (2:8–3:11). Then he needed *motivation* to direct him in the task. That motivation was provided by the "hand of the LORD" (cf. 1:3). He was first guided by the Spirit to his place of ministry (3:12-15); he was then formally appointed as God's watchman to Israel (vv. 16-21); then the Lord imposed several physical restraints on Ezekiel (vv. 22-27).

a. The leading of the Spirit (3:12-15)

**3:12-14a.** After seeing the vision of God, Ezekiel was transported back to Tel Aviv (v. 15) by the Holy Spirit. (See comments on Tel Aviv under "Historical Background" in the *Introduction*.) The movement began when **the Spirit lifted** him **up.** The "Spirit" who transported Ezekiel was the same One who had entered into him (2:2). This was the Holy Spirit who divinely enabled God's servants in Old Testament times. Several times the Holy Spirit transported Ezekiel (mentally rather than physically; cf. 8:3; 11:1, 24; 37:1; 43:5) to various places to give him information.

Ezekiel began to describe the movement by the Holy Spirit (3:12), but did not return to that subject till later (v. 14) because he was distracted by **a loud rushing sound.** After an interjection of praise (v. 12b) Ezekiel explained that the rushing sound was **of the wings of the** cherubim **brushing against each other and . . . of the wheels.** Ezekiel was transported by the Spirit on God's throne-chariot, and the sound generated by its movement startled him (cf. 1:24).

In describing his transport by God's Spirit, Ezekiel interjected, **May the glory of the LORD** (cf. comments on 1:28) **be praised in His dwelling place.** The "rushing sound" before his expression of praise was made by the cherubim's wings and wheels. Overcome by the sight and sound of God's glory, Ezekiel responded with this spontaneous note of praise to God.

**3:14b-15.** As Ezekiel was returned by the Holy **Spirit,** his own spirit was churning. He said, **I went in bitterness and in the anger of my spirit.** "Bitterness" (*mar*) carries the ideas of anguish (Gen. 27:34), discontentment (1 Sam. 22:2), and fierce anger (2 Sam. 17:8). Of these possible nuances, the parallelism with "anger (*hēmâh*, 'heat, rage') of my spirit" points to fierce anger as Ezekiel's emotion. As he associated himself with God he felt the same emotions toward Israel's sin as God did.

Ezekiel was guided in his mission by **the strong hand of the LORD.** "The hand of the LORD" is also mentioned in Ezekiel 1:3; 3:22; 8:1; 33:22; 37:1. The idea of "the hand of the LORD" (or "of God")—occurring nearly 190 times in the Old Testament—refers to God's power or authority.

Ezekiel returned **to the exiles . . . at Tel Aviv near the Kebar River** (cf. 1:3 and see "Historical Background" in the *Introduction*). He **sat among them for seven days—overwhelmed.** The character of the vision he had just seen and the awesomeness of the task before him left the prophet stunned. Ezekiel needed time to collect his thoughts and prepare himself for his ministry.

### b. The appointment as a watchman (3:16-21)

**3:16-19.** After **seven days** of silence Ezekiel's solitude was shattered by God's words. God appointed him **a watchman for the house of Israel.** "Watchman" is used several times of prophets (cf. Isa. 56:10; Jer. 6:17; Hosea 9:8). Watchmen were stationed on city walls, hilltops, or specially designed watchtowers. A watchman was to be on the alert for approaching enemies and warn the city's people of any impending attack. This gave city dwellers outside the walls an opportunity to seek protection and gave the people time to secure the gates and man the defenses.

Similarly, as God's watchman, Ezekiel was responsible for sounding the **warning** of impending judgment to Israel. He was to warn both the **wicked** (Ezek. 3:18-19) and the righteous (vv. 20-21). **A wicked** person was to be warned to turn **from his evil ways in order to save his life.** Though both the Old and New Testaments clearly indicate the *spiritual* results of sin, the focus here is on the *physical* consequences. A wicked person who refuses to heed God's warnings **will die for his sin.** Since all are spiritually dead from birth, the obvious reference here is to physical death. As Nebuchadnezzar's armies approached, the **wicked** could expect death at the enemy's hands.

**3:20-21.** The **righteous man** also needed to be warned to prevent his turning **from his righteousness and** doing **evil.** If a righteous person had left the path of righteousness, he too was in danger of death. This is not referring to an individual losing his salvation. The "righteous" one described here was outwardly conforming to God's commandments, and the "death" spoken of here is physical death (cf. comments on vv. 18-19). The one obeying God's Law was to be protected during the approaching judgment, but those who broke the Law could expect death.

If Ezekiel failed to **warn** of approaching danger, God would **hold** him **accountable for** the **blood** of the people. The principle of blood accountability is expressed in Genesis 9:5-6. If Ezekiel did not **warn** the people, he would be held as

responsible for their murder as if he had killed them himself. However, if Ezekiel fulfilled his responsibility, then he would **have saved** himself (Ezek. 3:19, 21). The word "saved" (*nāṣal*, "to deliver, snatch away, rescue") should be translated here "delivered," as it does not refer to eternal salvation. Rather, by giving warning, Ezekiel would have delivered himself from any responsibility for the coming calamity. People who refused to heed his warning had only themselves to blame.

### c. The physical restraints of the Lord (3:22-27)

**3:22-23.** Ezekiel was called **out to the plain** to meet with God. "Plain" (*biq'āh*) means "valley" as it is translated in 37:1. The word refers to one of the many broad valleys or plains in the Mesopotamian basin (cf. Gen. 11:2). The location of the particular plain where Ezekiel went is unknown.

In the plain Ezekiel saw **the glory of the LORD** (cf. comments on Ezek. 1:28) for the second time. His response was again one of humble submission—he **fell facedown** (cf. 1:28).

**3:24. The Spirit** then **came into** him and made him stand up. In Old Testament times the Holy Spirit's indwelling was not continuous (cf. comments on 2:2). The Spirit again entered Ezekiel to give him strength for his ministry.

God then placed several restraints on the prophet. The first was a command to **shut** himself in his **house.** This does not imply that Ezekiel was never to leave his house (cf. 5:2; 12:3); instead he was to refrain from open fellowship with the people. Often the leaders came to him at his house to receive God's word (cf. 8:1; 14:1; 20:1).

**3:25.** The reason for Ezekiel's confinement was that if he did not stay in his house, people would **tie** him **with ropes . . . so that** he could not **go out among the people.** Some have suggested that God told Ezekiel to stay home out of concern for his physical safety, for those who opposed his ministry would physically try to keep him from proclaiming God's word. Yet there is no evidence that Ezekiel was ever physically bound or forcibly constrained. More likely this is a figure of speech. Ezekiel was **bound** from moving about among the people and was confined to his home because of their opposition to his message. It was a God-imposed restraint that would demonstrate to the people their rebellion.

**3:26.** God informed Ezekiel of another restriction: his **tongue** would **stick to the roof of** his **mouth.** Ezekiel experienced temporary dumbness so that he could not speak to the people. This dumbness, however, was not continuous (v. 27) or permanent (33:22). It was a sign to the **rebellious house** (cf. 3:27 and comments on 2:3 and 3:9) of their sin.

**3:27.** Some see a contradiction between Ezekiel's commission as a watchman (vv. 16-21) and his prohibition against speaking to the people (v. 26). The solution to the problem is in verse 27. Ezekiel's silence was placed on him as an individual. From then on, Ezekiel spoke only when God told him to. God said, **But when I speak to you, I will open your mouth.** When he was silent, it was because God had not spoken. When he spoke, it was because God had given him a message. As a watchman, he was to open his mouth to say, **This is what the Sovereign LORD says.**

The section closes, **Whoever will listen let him listen, and whoever will refuse let him refuse.** The first part of the sentence is literally, "Let the hearer hear" or "The one who hears will hear." The implication is that a person's reception or rejection of Ezekiel's message was determined by his openness or lack of it to God. One who was receptive to God would accept Ezekiel's message; one who rejected God would reject this message. These words are similar to Christ's words in His earthly ministry, "He who has ears, let him hear" (Matt. 11:15; 13:9, 43; Mark 4:9, 23; Luke 8:8; 14:35).

## B. Ezekiel's prophecies against Judah and Jerusalem (chaps. 4–24)

Ezekiel's ministry began with a personal encounter with God. Then God appeared to Ezekiel and gave him His word of judgment for Israel. He appointed Ezekiel as the watchman who was responsible to sound the alarm. Chapters 4–24 include the watchman's cry.

In chapters 4–11 Ezekiel focused on the need for judgment because of the people's disobedience. The prophet then attacked the futility of false optimism

(chaps. 12–19). Next Ezekiel placed their present disobedience and future judgment in perspective by reviewing the history of Judah's corruption (chaps. 20–24).

1. THE NECESSITY OF JUDGMENT BECAUSE OF DISOBEDIENCE (CHAPS. 4–11)

Ezekiel's task was to confront Israel with her sin and warn her (cf. 3:17) of impending destruction. Ezekiel employed several means to focus on the people's need for judgment. These included signs (chaps. 4–5), sermons (chaps. 6–7), and visions (chaps. 8–11). In each case the emphasis was on sin and its ensuing suffering.

### a. Four signs of coming judgment (chaps. 4–5)

Though Ezekiel was confined to his home (3:24), God still expected him to deliver His message of judgment. To arouse interest Ezekiel used objects and actions, possibly in his courtyard or at the entrance to his house. These were signs about the coming siege against Jerusalem.

(1) The sign of the brick (4:1-3). **4:1.** On **a clay tablet** Ezekiel drew an outline of **the city of Jerusalem.** The "clay tablet" (*lᵉḇēnâh*) could refer to a soft clay tablet used by the Babylonians for a writing pad, or it could refer to a large sun-baked brick, the major building material used in Babylon (cf. Gen. 11:3). It seems better to see the word used in its more normal sense of "brick." The shape of Jerusalem was distinctive so Ezekiel's sketch of it would be recognized immediately.

**4:2.** God then told Ezekiel to **lay siege to** the brick. Because Jerusalem was a well-fortified city, it would take Babylon months to capture it. The purpose of a siege was to starve out the enemies and wear them down by halting their flow of food, supplies, and weapons.

In depicting the attack on Jerusalem, Ezekiel may have used small wooden models or clods of dirt to represent the army of Babylon circling the city and laying siege to it. He first erected **siege works** (*dāyēq*) **against** his "city." These were earthen towers or walls of dirt erected all around Jerusalem (cf. 2 Kings 25:1; Jer. 52:4). They protected the offensive army from arrows fired from the wall and gave the attackers additional height from which to shoot arrows over the city wall.

Ezekiel was also to **build a ramp up to** the brick city. The ramp provided a relatively smooth incline up which siege towers and battering rams could be pushed. Also the ramp allowed the attackers to get above the bedrock and large foundation stones of the city so the smaller and more vulnerable upper stones could be reached by the battering rams.

To prevent reinforcements and supplies from coming in and to keep survivors from slipping out, an attacking army would **set up camps** around the besieged city. Ezekiel did the same on his small-scale model. Later Nebuchadnezzar's army surrounded Jerusalem during the siege and allowed the city no means of relief or escape. Once everything was positioned the **battering rams** were brought forward to begin their assault. Their constant hammering gradually weakened the city's walls.

**4:3.** As Nebuchadnezzar's **siege** (graphically pictured by Ezekiel) tightened its grip around Jerusalem, the people called to God for deliverance. Ezekiel pictured the futility of the people's cries by putting **an iron pan** like **an iron wall between** him and the city. The "pan" (*maḥăḇaṯ*) probably referred to an iron plate or griddle used by the Israelites for baking their bread or cakes (cf. Lev. 2:5). Some scholars believe the iron pan was positioned to represent the severity or irresistible nature of the siege, but the vivid description of the siege (Ezek. 4:2) makes such an understanding unnecessary. More likely the pan represented an impregnable barrier between God and Jerusalem because of her sin (Isa. 59:2; Lam. 3:44). As the siege progressed, Jerusalem would cry out for deliverance, but God would not answer her prayers.

(2) The sign of Ezekiel's lying on his sides. **4:4-8.** This is the most difficult sign in the book to interpret, partly because of the ambiguity of the text and partly because of a textual problem.

God told Ezekiel to **lie on** his **left side and put the sin of the house of Israel** on himself. If Ezekiel prostrated himself with his head toward Jerusalem (cf. Dan. 6:10), he was facing north when he lay on his left side (and south when he lay on his right side, Ezek. 4:6). His fac-

ing north, which represented Israel, the Northern Kingdom, was to be **for 390 days.** Ezekiel did not remain in this position 24 hours a day, because the very next sign (vv. 9-17) includes some other actions Ezekiel was to do in that time. He probably remained in this position for a portion of each day.

**After** remaining on his left side for 390 days, he was to **lie on** his **right side, and bear the sin of the house of Judah.** His facing toward the south, representing Judah, the Southern Kingdom, was to last for **40 days.** To symbolize the confinement of the siege, God had Ezekiel tied **up with ropes** (v. 8). Apparently Ezekiel was tied up only during the time each day when he lay on his side.

The meaning of Ezekiel's actions is somewhat obscure. The Septuagint (Gr. trans. of the OT) causes even more confusion by substituting 190 days (vv. 5, 9) for 390. This emending of the text was probably done so it would make more sense. If so, the translators of the Septuagint also had difficulty interpreting the passage.

The first sign (vv. 1-3) visualized the coming siege, and the third and fourth signs (vv. 9-17 and chap. 5) focused on the results of the siege. Therefore this second sign also probably refers in some way to the siege of Jerusalem. In fact at least two factors clearly indicate that this is its point: (1) The 390 days and 40 days are called **the days of your siege** (4:8). (2) In the third sign Ezekiel rationed his food and water during the time he was lying on his side to depict the scarcity of food during the time of the siege (vv. 9, 16-17).

But why did the Lord choose the numbers 390 and 40? The days represent **the years of their sin** (v. 5), that is, each day corresponds to a year in Israel's and Judah's history. But were the years *past* or *future*? If they refer to the past, Ezekiel was showing the number of years Israel and Judah had sinned before this judgment. If they refer to the future, Ezekiel was indicating the number of years the nation would be oppressed by Gentiles after falling to Babylon.

Those who say the sign pointed to the future have tried to determine some historical point of fullfillment. Others interpret the numbers "symbolically" as indicating the end of the Babylonian Captivity, but the specific numbers and their association with both Israel and Judah make such a view unlikely.

Other scholars have said the numbers refer to 430 years of Gentile domination beginning with Jehoiachin's exile in 597 B.C., ending in 167 B.C., the year the Maccabean revolt began. This view has several problems. First, there is no indication that 597 should be used as a starting point instead of 592 (the year Ezekiel began prophesying) or instead of 586 (the year the city actually fell). Second, this view does not explain why 390 years were assigned to Israel. They had gone into captivity (to Assyria in 722 B.C.) 125 years before 597, when the time assigned to them actually began. Third, it is not clear that 167 B.C. actually was the year Israel was freed from the yoke of Syria. That year was only the beginning of the struggle.

Perhaps the best solution is to see the numbers as referring to the past. The 390 days corresponded to "the years of their sin" (v. 5), not the years of their chastisement. Yet no specific years can be determined with any certainty. But while the details are unclear, the message is obvious—Babylon would lay siege to Jerusalem because of her sin, and in some way the length of the siege would correspond to the years of her sin.

(3) The sign of the unclean food (4:9-17). **4:9-14.** Ezekiel's third sign emphasized the severity of the siege of Jerusalem. God told him to **take wheat and barley, beans and lentils, millet and spelt.** These were common grains in Israel's diet (cf. 2 Sam. 17:27-29). But the fact that Ezekiel was told to **put them in a container and make them into bread for** himself indicates a scarcity of food. Normally each of these foods was in abundance. During the siege, however, supplies were so scarce that several foods had to be combined to provide enough for a meal.

Ezekiel had **to eat** the mixture of foods **during the 390 days** he was lying **on** his left **side.** He was to **weigh out 20 shekels of food to eat each day . . . at set times.** This daily ration weighed about eight ounces (NIV marg.). He was also allowed to drink **a sixth of a hin,** two-thirds of a quart, **of water.**

The purpose of his eating and drinking these meager rations was to show the scarcity of food and water in Jerusalem during the siege (cf. Ezek. 4:16-17). This sign also showed the pollution and defilement the people would experience. Ezekiel was to **bake** his bread **in the sight of the people, using human excrement for fuel.** The use of dung as fuel was practiced throughout the Middle East because of the scarcity of wood. Dung was mixed with straw and allowed to dry. The dried dung burned slowly and gave off an unpleasant odor. No stigma was associated with the use of animal dung, but using human dung was considered repulsive.

Ezekiel understood the symbolism of the sign, but the action was personally distasteful to him. He could not bring himself to do it. He responded, **Not so, Sovereign LORD! I have never defiled myself.** Ezekiel had always kept God's dietary laws (Deut. 14). As a priest (Ezek. 1:3) he was careful to keep himself undefiled (cf. Lev. 22:8; Ezek. 44:31). Though the Law did not specifically prohibit the use of human dung for cooking, its guideline regarding the disposal of human excrement suggests that it was considered improper (cf. Deut. 23:12-14). The LORD explained the symbolism of using human dung: **The people of Israel will eat defiled food among the nations where I will drive them** (Ezek. 4:13). The siege (and subsequent captivity) would force the Israelites to eat defiled food and thus become ceremonially unclean.

**4:15-17.** God graciously granted Ezekiel's request. **I will let you bake your bread over cow manure instead of human excrement.** Less of a stigma was associated with the use of cow dung, so God let Ezekiel use it.

The scarcity of **food** and **water** during Babylon's siege of Jerusalem (cf. Lam. 1:11; 2:11-12, 19; 4:4-5, 9), and the people's accompanying **anxiety** (cf. Ezek. 12:19) and emaciation (cf. Lam. 4:8), was all **because of their sin** (cf. Lam. 4:13; 5:16).

(4) The sign of the shaved head and divided hair (chap. 5). This fourth sign visualized Jerusalem's fate. The sign was given in verses 1-4 and explained in verses 5-17. After Ezekiel represented the *fact* of the siege (first sign), the *length* of the siege (second sign), and its *severity* (third sign), he demonstrated the *results* of the siege (fourth sign). To accomplish

this sign Ezekiel journeyed from the confines of his house—certainly an action which in itself caught the people's attention. He went "inside the city" (v. 2a) and "all around the city" (v. 2b).

**5:1.** God told Ezekiel to **shave** his **head** and **beard** with **a sharp sword.** "Sword" (*ḥereḇ*) is the common word for the weapon used by ancient armies. Ezekiel used the word 83 times in his book to speak of the means by which Jerusalem (cf. 6:11), Edom (25:13), Tyre (26:6, 8), Egypt (29:8-9; 30:4), and Gog (38:21) would be destroyed. Shaving one's head (and beard) was a sign of mourning (Job 1:20; Isa. 15:2-3; Jer. 7:29; 48:37; Ezek. 7:18), humiliation (2 Sam. 10:4-5), and possibly repentance (Jer. 41:5). No doubt all these were implied in Ezekiel's actions.

After Ezekiel shaved, he was to use **a set of scales** for weighing his **hair** in three equal piles with a few strands left over. He did this possibly sometime near the end of his previous two signs. But he did nothing else till the 430 days of his symbolic siege had ended.

**5:2.** The hair that had been set aside earlier was now put to use. Ezekiel carried **a third of** his **hair** to the middle of **the city** and set it on **fire.** The purpose of this action, explained in verse 12, was to illustrate that a third of the people would die by the plague or by famine. When Nebuchadnezzar's army finally broke through the city's walls, they found a population decimated by famine. The food shortage was so severe that the people had resorted to cannibalism (v. 10). Such horrors had been predicted by Moses (Deut. 28:52-57) and were verified by Jeremiah (Lam. 2:20; 4:10).

Those who survived the famine had to face the sword. After burning the first **third** of his hair, Ezekiel went through **the city** with the second **third** and chopped it up with his **sword.** This action meant that a third of the Jerusalemites would die by the sword (Ezek. 5:12).

The one-third of the inhabitants of Jerusalem who would survive the siege would still be in jeopardy. This was illustrated by the prophet's scattering **a third** of his hair **to the wind.** Those who survived Jerusalem's fall to Babylon would be taken away in captivity and would live in fear.

**5:3-4.** After Ezekiel had burned, chopped, and scattered his hair, **a few strands** remained. God told Ezekiel to **tuck them away in the folds of** his **garment.** Hiding these few hairs represented God's preserving a remnant in the midst of judgment. The "garment" was the long robe or tunic men wore. It was secured at the waist by a belt or sash. The bottom was pulled up and tucked into the belt to form a pouch for carrying things. This was probably where Ezekiel put those few hairs.

The **few** hairs in Ezekiel's garment did not remain undisturbed, for he was to toss some of them in **the fire.** Some scholars feel that this refers to a purifying judgment that would refine the remnant in captivity (cf. 6:8-10). However, the **fire** (5:4) probably refers (as in v. 2) to the suffering and death awaiting these people. This judgment was for **the whole house of Israel.** Even the remnant in exile would not escape the flames of oppression.

**5:5-7.** God was not capriciously inflicting this punishment on **Jerusalem.** It came because of her rebellion. God **set** Jerusalem **in the center of the nations, with countries all around her. Yet** in spite of this exalted position (possibly also referring to her central position geographically in the Middle East), Israel **rebelled** (cf. 2:3) **against** God's **laws and decrees more than the** surrounding **nations.** Jerusalem was the recipient of His word, the dwelling place of His glory, and the object of His love. The splendor of His favor only magnified the blackness of her deeds. Instead of honoring her God she rebelled against Him. Amazingly Israel's conduct was lower than **the standards of** Gentile **nations.**

**5:8-12.** God's anger was directed at **Jerusalem,** the nation's capital, because of her sin. She would suffer judgment **in the sight of the nations.** The object of God's special favor would soon become the object of His special judgment.

**5:13-17.** In three short vignettes Ezekiel indicated that God's judgment would last till the fury of His anger was spent. Ezekiel stressed the divine source of each judgment as God announced, **I the LORD have spoken** (vv. 13, 15, 17). In the first statement (v. 13) Ezekiel indicated that God's judgment would **cease** and

**subside** only after He had poured out His **wrath** on **them.**

The second statement (vv. 14-15) stressed the humiliation Jerusalem would feel because of God's judgment. Other **nations** would **reproach** and mock her (cf. Lam. 2:15). Yet those ridiculing nations would be horrified at what was happening to Jerusalem. In fact such carnage in the city would serve as **a warning** to them.

The third statement (Ezek. 5:16-17) pictured God as an attacking archer shooting His **destructive arrows** (cf. Deut. 32:23) against Jerusalem. God's "arrows" of judgment included **famine . . . wild beasts. . . . plague,** and **the sword**—calamities uniquely associated with divine judgment on God's disobedient nation (cf. Deut. 32:23-25; Ezek. 14:21).

*b. Two messages of coming judgment (chaps. 6–7)*

After giving his four dramatic signs, Ezekiel delivered two sermons, beginning the same way: "The word of the LORD came to me" (6:1; 7:1). God was the source of the words Ezekiel delivered. The first message (chap. 6) was on Israel's idolatry, the cause for judgment. The second message (chap. 7) depicted the nature of the judgment.

(1) Message on idolatry as the cause of judgment (chap. 6). **6:1-2.** God told the prophet to **set** his **face against the mountains of Israel.** The preposition "against" (*'el*) denotes movement toward something. The phrase "set your/his face toward" was used to denote direction (Gen. 31:21, "headed for"; Num. 24:1), determination or purpose (2 Kings 12:17, "turned to"), or hostile intentions (Lev. 17:10; 20:3, 5-6). Ezekiel used the phrase 14 times (Ezek. 4:3, 7; 6:2; 13:17; 14:8; 15:7 [twice]; 20:46; 21:2; 25:2; 28:21; 29:2; 35:2; 38:2). In each case the phrase means to turn one's face toward an object with hostile intentions. The instrument of God's judgment was being aimed at its intended target. Interestingly Ezekiel later prophesied to the "mountains of Israel" (36:1-15), but then he delivered a prophecy of coming blessing.

**6:3-7.** Ezekiel was also to speak against **Israel's ravines and valleys.** The significance of these words can be understood only in light of the Canaanite reli-

gious practices that permeated Israel (cf. Jer. 2:20-28; 17:1-3; 32:35). Israel was supposed to worship only the God of heaven in His temple in Jerusalem, but she set up shrines to false gods throughout the land (cf. 2 Kings 21:2-6, 10-15). Thus by addressing his message to the land itself, Ezekiel was focusing on the people's immoral use of the land.

God's **sword** (cf. 5:1, 12) would **destroy** Israel's **high places.** A "high place" (*bāmâh*) was usually (though not always; cf. 2 Kings 23:8) a place of worship located on a hill or mountain. The elevated site supposedly brought worshipers closer to their gods. While a high place could include a temple (1 Kings 12:31), most high places had only altars for offering sacrifices.

High places were in Canaan before Israel arrived, and God commanded Israel to destroy them (Num. 33:52). Israel was to worship only at the tabernacle, placed at Shiloh (cf. Deut. 12:2-14; 1 Sam. 1:3). After the destruction of Shiloh (probably by the Philistines) and before the construction of the temple in Jerusalem, Israel had no central place of worship. The altar and tabernacle were relocated at Gibeon (2 Chron. 1:1-3) and the ark was taken to Kiriath Jearim (1 Sam. 6:21–7:1). The table for the bread of the Presence was apparently at Nob (1 Sam. 21:1-6). During this time God permitted the use of high places as temporary worship centers (cf. 1 Kings 3:2). Both Samuel (1 Sam. 9:12-14) and Solomon (1 Kings 3:3) worshiped the Lord at high places.

After the temple in Jerusalem was completed, worshiping at high places was once again discouraged. Most high places remaining in the land were dedicated to false gods (1 Kings 11:7-10). The conflict between true worship and false worship often centered on these high places. Those kings who followed God tried to destroy the high places (e.g., Hezekiah, 2 Kings 18:3-4; Josiah, 2 Kings 23:8-9), and kings who did not follow God rebuilt them (e.g., Manasseh, 2 Kings 21:1-6).

By Ezekiel's time the high places were again flourishing in Judah. They included **altars** for sacrificing animals to false gods, **incense altars** for offering incense to the gods, and **idols** which were physical representations of the gods

(Ezek. 6:4). Israel's pernicious idolatry was a cancer that had to be eradicated.

God's judgment would be swift and sure. Both the false places of worship and those who built them and worshiped at them were to be destroyed. God vowed to intervene so that the **high places . . . altars . . . idols,** and **incense altars** would all be **wiped out.** Also **people** who built them would be killed, and their **dead bodies** would be strewn beside their crushed **idols** and **altars** (v. 5). Then the nation would realize that its gods were false. The people would **know,** God said, that **I am the LORD.** This phrase occurs 63 times in Ezekiel; by using Yahweh, God's covenant name, Ezekiel was focusing attention on the contrasting unfaithfulness and apostasy of the people.

**6:8-10.** In the midst of God's judgment came a promise of mercy. God vowed to **spare some** (cf. 5:3-5; 12:16). Not all Israelites would be destroyed, for **some** would **escape the sword when** Israel would be dispersed **among the . . . nations.** The impending defeat of Judah by Babylon did not signal the end of God's covenant promise to Israel. God was not turning away from His promises.

Some Israelites in captivity would **remember** God. They would call to mind His character—**how** He **grieved** for them in their idolatry. The words **their adulterous hearts** refer to their involvement in idol-worship, an act of unfaithfulness as terrible as a spouse's unfaithfulness in adultery. They would also remember God's faithfulness to His promises, especially those in which He promised to punish disobedience.

Those in exile would **loathe themselves** because of **all their detestable practices.** The sad consequences of sin produced a belated but necessary repentance. In acknowledging their sin and the justness of their judgment, they were again brought back to God—**they will know that I am the LORD.** Their personal knowledge of God would result from the **calamity** of exile. God **did not** bring captivity on Israel **in vain.**

**6:11-12.** The last section (vv. 11-14) of this sermon begins with God instructing Ezekiel to **strike** his **hands together . . . stamp** his **feet, and cry out, Alas!** Striking hands together, clapping, was a sign of rejoicing (2 Kings 11:12; Ps. 98:8) or

derision (Job 27:23; Lam. 2:15; Ezek. 21:14, 17; 22:13; 25:6, "clapped your hands"; Nahum 3:19). The phrase here was probably a symbol of derision (cf. Ezek. 25:6).

Ezekiel was to demonstrate this derisive behavior **because of all the wicked and detestable practices of the house of Israel.** Destruction **by the sword, famine, and plague** summarized the judgment already enacted by the prophet's fourth sign (chap. 5). Those in Jerusalem who escaped one calamity would only find another waiting to strike them down (6:12).

**6:13-14.** The imagery in verses 1-7 was repeated here as God promised He would slay the **people . . . among . . . their altars, on every high hill and . . . under every spreading tree and every leafy oak.** Often on the high places where altars were built were luxuriant trees, which represented growth and possibly fertility (cf. Hosea 4:13). The "oak" (*'ēlâh*) was the terebinth tree. It is a deciduous tree common to Palestine and grows to a height of 35-40 feet. The Elah Valley, where David slew Goliath, probably received its name because of the abundance of these trees (1 Sam. 17:2, 19).

God had given Israel a land luxurious with "spreading" trees and "leafy" oaks, but the people corrupted His gift, using these displays of His bounty as **places** to offer **fragrant incense to all their idols.** Therefore God would reduce their rich land to rubble—**a desolate waste from the desert to Diblah.** Instead of "Diblah" some manuscripts read "Riblah" (NIV marg.), a town on the Orontes River in Syria. If this reading is correct, Ezekiel was referring to all the land, from the desert in the south to Riblah in the north. This seems likely for two reasons. First, there is no record of a city in Judah named Diblah. (Though this is an argument from silence, it seems strange that Ezekiel would use a little-known city to indicate the extent of God's judgment.) Second, the change from Diblah to Riblah can be explained by the similar shape of the Hebrew letters *d* (ד) and *r* (ר). A copyist could easily have misread the manuscript and mistakenly changed the letters.

For the third time in this chapter Ezekiel stated that as a result of the judgment Israel would come to **know that** He is **the LORD** (cf. Ezek. 6:7, 10, 14), that is, acknowledge His supreme authority.

(2) Message on the nature of judgment (chap. 7). **7:1-4.** This message began in the same way as the first one (cf. 6:1): **The word of the LORD came to me.** This time the focus was not on idolatry (as in chap. 6), but on **the land,** which meant the people living in the land.

Ezekiel's message was that **the end had come upon the four corners of the land.** The word "end" is used five times at the beginning of this sermon (7:2 [twice], 3, 6 [twice]). The Prophet Amos used that word in a similar way to describe the fall of the Northern Kingdom in 722 B.C. (Amos 8:2, "the end has come," NASB). Ezekiel repeated the same message for the Southern Kingdom. "The four corners of the land" indicate that no portion would escape God's judgment.

The events about to unfold on Israel would bring a new revelation of God's character; the people would realize that God, being righteous, punishes sin. God vowed to **unleash** His **anger against** Israel (Ezek. 7:3) without **pity** (v. 4). He would judge her according to her **conduct** (cf. vv. 4, 8-9, 27) and **repay** her for her **detestable practices** (cf. vv. 8-9). These judgments were repeated (vv. 3-4) for emphasis. **Then** she would **know that** God is **the LORD.** This clause appears again at the end of the sermon (v. 27).

**7:5-6.** The **LORD** was like a herald who had raced to the city to shout breathlessly the warning of approaching calamity (vv. 5-9). In Hebrew the phrases are short and choppy, and the words "coming" or "came" occur six times in verses 5-7. The watchman first proclaimed, **Disaster! An unheard-of disaster is coming.** What was about to come on Jerusalem had no historical parallel.

The exact nature of Jerusalem's disaster was implied by the repetition of the words **the end has come** (v. 6). In Hebrew the two words translated in the first clause, **the end has come** are reversed in the second clause. In a wordplay Ezekiel announced that the end had **roused itself against you.** The words "end" (*qēṣ* and *haqqēṣ*) and "roused" (*hēqîṣ*) in verse 6 sounded so much alike that they drew attention to themselves. Disaster had been predicted for Jerusa-

lem by Micah (Micah 3:12), but that prophecy had remained unfulfilled for over 100 years. Now Jerusalem's end was about to come.

**7:7-9.** Ezekiel described Jerusalem's coming destruction as a time of **doom** (*haṣṣᵉpîrâh*; cf. v. 10). This word can mean "crown" or "diadem" (cf. Isa. 28:5), but not in this context. A similar word in Aramaic means "morning" which was the meaning adopted by the KJV translators. But neither does this fit because "morning" would imply blessing while the context speaks of disaster. Probably the word is related to the Akkadian *ṣabāru*, "destruction."

As the day of judgment would approach there would be **panic, not joy, upon the mountains.** Those who had been at ease in their idolatry on the high places (cf. comments on Ezek. 6:3) would be thrown into a state of apprehension when overtaken in judgment. Ezekiel repeated the theme of the impending calamity (7:8-9 is about the same as vv. 3-4). The destruction would come as predicted, so those affected would **know that . . . the LORD** had struck **the blow.** This is a variation of the other statements on knowing the Lord (6:7, 10, 14; 7:4, 27). Those who professed to know Him by other names (cf. Gen. 22:14; 33:20; Ex. 17:15) would now know Him by the name *Yahweh-makkeh*, "the LORD who strikes the blow."

**7:10.** The nearness of **the day** of judgment was compared to a budding rod. **Doom has burst forth, the rod has budded, arrogance has blossomed!** Ezekiel's imagery could be drawn from Aaron's rod that budded (Num. 17), or he could have been familiar with Jeremiah's picture of an almond tree in blossom (Jer. 1:11-12). If the allusion was to Aaron's rod, the point was that just as its budding indicated God had selected him for service, so the budding of Israel's rod of arrogance indicated God had selected Jerusalem for doom. If the prophet alluded to Jeremiah's almond tree in blossom, the point was that just as the budding of the almond tree indicated God's judgment was sure to follow so the budding of violence in Israel indicated God's judgment would follow.

**7:11-14.** In verse 10 the "rod" pictured the budding of Israel's wickedness, compared to the budding of a tree. But in verse 11 the rod became a rod of judgment used to flog the disobedient people: **a rod to punish wickedness.**

God's judgment would have economic consequences. When it struck, **none of the people** would **be left, none of that crowd** ("crowd," probably used derisively, occurs four times in vv. 11-14). **Nothing of value** would remain. Because of the Captivity, property and material possessions were worthless. Possessions would be confiscated and property owners torn from their land and carried to Babylon. Ezekiel exhorted, **Let not the buyer rejoice nor the seller grieve.** The buyer who normally rejoiced over a good business deal should not be happy because he would not be able to possess the land he had purchased. And one forced to sell his land should not grieve because he would have lost it anyway.

When land was sold in Israel, the transaction was always temporary. Every 50 years, during the Year of Jubilee, the property reverted to its original owners (Lev. 25:10, 13-17). However, God's coming judgment would prevent original owners from reclaiming their properties; they would be in exile along with the buyers.

No human effort could hinder God from accomplishing His plan. **Though they** would call soldiers to battle by **the trumpet, no one** would **go into battle.** Jerusalem would try to defend herself, but she would fall with little resistance.

**7:15-16.** Israel would find she had no defense *against* God's judgment and no escape *from* God's judgment. **Outside** would be **the sword, inside . . . plague and famine** (cf. 5:12). Those who sought **escape** outside Jerusalem's walls were hunted down and murdered by Babylon's armies. Those who sought protection within the city walls faced the dual enemies of famine and disease. The majority of the people would die, and even those who survived would pay a price. The pitiful wail of those hiding **in the mountains,** who were weeping over their **sins** and material losses, would sound like mourning **doves.**

**7:17-18.** Israel's response to God's onslaught is pictured in verses 17-19. Hands would **go limp, and** knees would **become as weak as water** (cf. similar words in 21:7; also cf. Jer. 6:24). The only

thing the defenders could do would be to lament their state (Ezek. 7:18) and remove the obstacle of materialism that had caused them to stumble (vv. 19-22). In their lament they would **put on sackcloth. . . . and their heads** would **be shaved.** "Sackcloth" was coarse cloth, woven from the long hair of goats or camels. Because of its dark color, sackcloth was considered appropriate for serious, somber occasions. To "put on sackcloth" was a sign of grief or mourning (Gen. 37:34; 1 Sam. 3:31; Job 16:15; Jer. 6:26) and repentance (Isa. 58:5; Dan. 9:3-4; Jonah 3:5-9; Matt. 11:21). Ezekiel was probably picturing the grief mixed **with terror** Israel would experience when the enemy destroyed her land. Shaving the head also pictured mourning, humiliation, and repentance (see comments on Ezek. 5:1).

**7:19-20.** In addition to lamenting their loss the people would remove the obstacles that had caused it (vv. 19-22). They would **throw their silver into the streets, and their gold** would **be an unclean thing.** Also their **idols** made from the metal of their **jewelry** would be **an unclean thing,** so items once deemed precious would be discarded. The word for "unclean thing" (*niddâh*) was used of the ceremonial impurity of menstruation (Lev. 15:19-33) and the touching of a corpse (Num. 19:13-21). It pictured the revulsion Israel would feel toward her wealth.

Why would the people suddenly loathe their material wealth? One reason was the inability of **silver and gold** to buy the security for which it was originally amassed. It would **not be able to save them.** God could not be "bought off." Another reason for the sudden revulsion of wealth was the inability of the silver and gold to buy food to **satisfy their hunger** in the famine.

**7:21-22.** Besides being useless as a means of deliverance, Israel's wealth was also temporary. All she had accumulated would be taken by Babylon; her wealth would be plundered by **foreigners.**

Even more disconcerting than the loss of wealth was God's pronouncement about the temple: **I will turn My face away from them, and they will desecrate My treasured place; robbers will enter it and desecrate it.** Many Israelites placed their hope of deliverance on God's temple in Jerusalem; they thought that surely He would not let His holy abode be destroyed (cf. Jer. 7:1-5). But Israel's sin was so serious that not even the temple would escape God's judgment (cf. Micah 3:12).

**7:23-24.** Chains would be used to carry into captivity the people, who were known for **bloodshed** and **violence** (cf. 8:17; 12:19). God's invasion plans were ready to be implemented: **I will bring the most wicked of the nations to take possession of their houses.** Babylon, a ruthless and cruel nation (cf. comments on 28:7), was selected by God to dispossess Israel (cf. Hab. 1:5-11). Israel's haughty **pride** and religious prostitution would be crushed under the heavy boot of Babylon's army.

**7:25-26.** Israel's response to the judgment portrayed the anguish, heartache, and despair that comes when sin is allowed to run its course. Israel felt she could never fall; but when she would finally realize the **terror** of her fate, it would be too late. Her desperate search for deliverance and **peace** would be in vain. God added, **Calamity upon calamity will come, and rumor upon rumor.** The blows of misfortune would pound relentlessly one after another without a break. The word for "calamity" (*hōwâh*), appearing only here and in Isaiah 47:11, conveys the idea of ruin or disaster. Like the catastrophes that hit Job (cf. Job 1:13-19), no sooner would one catastrophe be reported than word would come of another. Rumors spread through Jerusalem of alliances and deliverers and coups and reversals in Babylon—and each piece of gossip was eagerly received by a terrified people.

In addition to listening to the many false rumors racing through the city, the people would also seek out **the prophet . . . the priest,** and **the elders** to gain insight from God. But this too would be in vain. They had refused to heed the warnings from God's true spokesmen. So when they would desperately seek an answer, none would be available.

**7:27.** Because there would be no help from God, **the king,** Ezekiel said, would **mourn, the prince** would **be clothed with despair, and the hands of the people of the land** would **tremble.** Who are "the king" and "the prince"? Ezekiel generally used the word "prince" to refer to

Zedekiah (12:10, 12; 21:25), never giving him the title "king." The only Israelite Ezekiel called "king" was Jehoiachin, in captivity in Babylon (1:2).

"King" Jehoiachin was already in captivity mourning Jerusalem's certain fall, while "Prince" Zedekiah was in Jerusalem in despair over his plight. As a result the people were trembling in fear at their uncertain fate. God again said their punishment would be **according to their conduct** (a standard mentioned five times in chap. 7 [vv. 3-4, 8-9, 27]).

### c. A vision of coming judgment (chaps. 8–11)

Ezekiel had repeatedly stated that the coming judgment was prompted by the people's sins. But what had the people of Jerusalem done to deserve such punishment? God took Ezekiel back to Jerusalem in a vision to show him the wickedness there (chaps. 8–11).

This vision occurred "in the sixth year" (of Jehoiachin's exile; cf. comments on 1:2) "in the sixth month on the fifth day" (8:1). This date was September 17, 592 B.C. This was exactly 14 months after Ezekiel's first vision (1:1-2). In the interim Ezekiel had received a vision of God (chaps. 1–3), had acted out four signs (chaps. 4–5), and had given two messages on judgment (chaps. 6–7). Now God gave him a new vision.

The vision recorded in chapters 8–11 is a single unit. Yet four specific sections are within it. Ezekiel was first confronted with the wickedness of the people in the temple (chap. 8); then he was shown the slaughter of the people of Jerusalem (chap. 9). Jerusalem was so wicked that God's glory departed from the temple (chap. 10), and as it left the city, judgment was pronounced on her rulers (chap. 11).

(1) The wickedness in the temple (chap. 8). **8:1.** Ezekiel mentioned the date (see comments two pars. earlier) to identify when **the hand of the Sovereign LORD came upon** him (cf. 1:3; 3:14, 22). It was when he was in his **house and the elders of Judah were sitting** there with him. Ezekiel's outside ministry was still limited (cf. 3:24), so the elders of the community had to come to his house. They had probably gone to seek his advice, possibly on the fate of Jerusalem. The vision was God's answer which Eze-

kiel then reported to them (cf. 11:24-25).

**8:2-6.** As Ezekiel sat before the elders he **saw a figure like that of a man.** The figure was a manifestation or theophany of God like the one recorded in 1:26. From **His waist down He was like fire, and from there up His appearance was as bright as glowing metal** (cf. 1:27). As in chapter 1, Ezekiel's description of the vision was deliberately vague. Lest he be accused of picturing God as just a glorified man, Ezekiel carefully phrased his description as he wrote under the Holy Spirit's inspiration. God does not have the body of a man; His appearance was merely "a figure like that of a man." God did not extend an actual human hand down to Ezekiel; **He stretched out what looked like a hand.**

What Ezekiel described in chapters 8–11 took place **in visions,** that is, it did not physically transpire. As Ezekiel was transported to Jerusalem (cf. 3:14; 11:1, 24; 37:1; 43:5) his physical body remained in Babylon. The elders seated before him did not see the theophany **of God.** As the vision passed from Ezekiel (11:24b), he described it to the elders.

In the vision Ezekiel was **lifted . . . up between earth and heaven** and transported **to Jerusalem.** "Flown" from Babylon to Jerusalem, the prophet landed at **the entrance to the north gate of the inner court** (see the sketch "Plan of Solomon's Temple" near 1 Kings 6). The north gate was one of three gates that opened from the outer court to the inner court. The other two were located on the east and south sides. Since Ezekiel was at the "entrance" to the north gate, he was probably standing in the outer court looking south toward the inner court.

Beside the north entrance to the inner court was **the idol that provokes to jealousy.** Ezekiel also called it the **idol of jealousy** (Ezek. 8:5), probably because he viewed it as an affront to God. This idol violated the second of the Ten Commandments (Ex. 20:4; cf. Deut. 4:23-24). God was being provoked to jealousy because a foreign god was receiving the homage that should have been His alone. The god or goddess represented by this idol is not named, but it may have been Asherah, the Canaanite goddess of fertility. King Manasseh had placed a carved image of Asherah in the temple during his reign (2 Kings 21:7; cf. Deut. 16:21),

but later he removed it (2 Chron. 33:13, 15). After Manasseh's death an Asherah pole found its way back into the temple, and Josiah removed it during his reforms (2 Kings 23:6). He burned it in the Kidron Valley outside Jerusalem in the hope of eradicating this idolatrous worship forever. Unfortunately after Josiah's untimely death the people returned to their idolatry. Evidently a new Asherah pole was made to replace the destroyed one.

As Ezekiel stared at this idol, beside him **was the glory of the God of Israel** (cf. comments on Ezek. 1:28). God's moral outrage was expressed in His rhetorical question to Ezekiel: **Do you see what they are doing . . . detestable things . . . that will drive Me far from My sanctuary? God** will not share His glory with an idol (cf. Isa. 42:8). If the idol inhabited the temple, God would leave.

The shock of seeing the idol in the Lord's house must have unnerved Ezekiel. Yet this was not all Israel had done to provoke her Lord. Ezekiel would **see things . . . even more detestable** (cf. Ezek. 8:13, 15).

**8:7-13.** Then God led Ezekiel through the gateway **to the entrance to the court,** probably the inner court. Ezekiel then **saw a hole in the wall** that surrounded the court. In his visionary state God told him to **dig** through **the wall.** When he did so, he **saw a doorway there.** As Ezekiel entered the chamber and gazed about, he **saw portrayed all over the walls all kinds of crawling things and detestable animals and all the idols of the house of Israel.** Some have suggested these were idols of Egypt, or Canaan, or Babylon. Perhaps *all* those countries were represented in this pantheon of idolatry.

**Seventy elders . . . and Jaazaniah son of Shaphan** were standing with **incense** censers before the portrayals on the wall. These 70 elders were not the Sanhedrin which ruled in Israel after the Babylonian Captivity, but they did represent the leading men of Jerusalem. When Moses appointed assistants to aid in leading the people, the number whom God consecrated was 70 (Num. 11:16-17). Perhaps this tradition continued and the 70 elders Ezekiel saw were men of the city who had some official leadership capacity.

Among the 70 Ezekiel recognized Jaazaniah, a man whose relatives played important parts in the affairs of state during Judah's final years (see the chart "The Line of Shaphan" near Jer. 26:24). Jaazaniah's presence there surprised Ezekiel because everyone else in Jaazaniah's family had remained faithful to the Lord.

Sometimes incense was used to protect worshipers from the presence of God (cf. Lev. 16:12-13). In other instances incense represented worshipers' prayers being borne aloft to God (cf. Rev. 5:8). Whatever the exact purpose of the incense, these leaders of Israel had abandoned the true God and were worshiping idols—**each at the shrine of his own idol.** Evidently each elder had his own favorite god.

God, who knew their hearts, explained to Ezekiel that the elders sought to justify their sin by saying **The LORD does not see us; the LORD has forsaken the land.** The elders felt that what they did in their darkened chambers would escape God's notice. They thought He was only a petty god who had abandoned them. So they were courting other gods to protect them. These elders' attitude was soon transmitted to the people (cf. Ezek. 9:9).

The people's progression of idolatry went from open display of idols to secret worship of idols under the very shadow of the Almighty. Yet this was not the full extent of Israel's wickedness, for they were **doing things . . . even more detestable** (cf. 8:6, 15).

**8:14-15.** Ezekiel was taken out **to the entrance to the north gate of the** temple. This was probably the entrance to the temple's outer court. Beside this gate Ezekiel **saw women . . . mourning for Tammuz.** "Tammuz" is the Hebrew form of the name of the Sumerian god Dumuzi, the deity of spring vegetation. The apparent death of all vegetation in the Middle East during the hot, dry summer months was explained in mythology as caused by Tammuz's death and descent into the underworld. During that time his followers would weep, mourning his death. In the spring Tammuz would emerge victoriously from the underworld and bring with him the life-giving rains. The worship of Tammuz also involved fertility rites.

Worship of the true Giver of rain had

been supplanted by the debased adoration of a pagan deity. The worship of the Creator was replaced by the worship of the cycles of creation He had established. And yet Ezekiel was to **see things . . . even more detestable than these** (cf. vv. 6, 13).

**8:16.** When God again led Ezekiel **into the inner court,** he saw **at the entrance to the temple, between the portico and the altar . . . about 25 men.** They were between the portico, or covered entrance, to the temple building (cf. 1 Kings 6:2-3) and the bronze altar in the middle of the courtyard on which the sacrifices were offered. This was where God's priests should have been weeping and crying out to God for mercy because of their sin (cf. Joel 2:17).

Who were these 25 men? Later they were called "elders" (Ezek. 9:6), a term that applied to both civil and religious leaders. Because of their location, these men were probably priests. The people were allowed to approach the altar, but the approach to God from the altar to the holy of holies was through the mediation of the priests.

These priests should have been acting as Israel's mediators, crying to God for mercy. But instead, **they were bowing down to the sun in the east.** The entrance to God's temple faced the east, so that when a person stood at the altar and faced the entrance he was looking west. But these priests were facing east! They had turned **their backs** on God and were bowing in submission and worship to the sun. This expressed contempt for the God of Israel and implied that they had disowned Him. This directly violated God's command (Deut. 4:19).

**8:17-18.** The horrors Ezekiel had **seen** in the temple of God were disturbing. But the evil was not confined there. The wickedness being practiced in the temple by the priests and the people had spread through the nation. **Violence** filled the nation, which **continually** provoked God **to anger.**

The people were even **putting the branch to their nose.** Some feel this refers to a ritual act associated with worship of other gods. No such ritual is actually known, though some pictorial designs discovered on Assyrian reliefs could imply its existence. Early Jewish commentators translated "branch" as "stench." Some scholars feel that "their" was a later scribal change for an original reading of "my." In this case the phrase would read "putting the stench to My nose," that is, idolatry is a putrid, offensive smell to God. One cannot be dogmatic on which interpretation is correct, but in either case the general sense is clear: the gesture was a gross insult to God.

God's response was decisive: **I will deal with them in anger** and **not . . . with pity.** God would not allow such open rebellion to continue. Even a last-minute desperate effort on their part to get God to hear their cries would do no good. The stage was set for judgment.

(2) The slaughter in Jerusalem (chap. 9). **9:1-2.** The second part of Ezekiel's vision portrayed the execution of God's judgment (announced in 8:18) on Jerusalem's inhabitants. God summoned **the guards of the city . . . each with a weapon in his hand.** "Guards" comes from the verb "to attend to, visit, muster, appoint." The RSV and NASB translate it "executioners" here, but this seems too strong. Ezekiel used it again in 44:11 ("having charge of") to refer to the Levites who will serve as gatekeepers in the millennial temple.

The "guards" in 9:1 were probably angelic beings posted by God around His city. **Each** guard carried **a deadly weapon**—possibly a sword or a club.

The guards came into the inner court **from the direction of the upper gate, which faces north.** To reach Ezekiel they passed the four groups mentioned in chapter 8. **With** the **six** guards **was a** seventh **man clothed in linen who had a writing kit.** The linen clothing suggested dignity, purity, or divine origin (cf. Dan. 10:5; 12:6-7; Rev. 15:6). The "writing kit" was literally, a "case for the scribe." "Case" is an Egyptian loanword, meaning a case for carrying reed pens with an inkhorn attached.

**9:3-7.** As the guards and the scribe came through the temple, the vision of God's **glory** (cf. comments on 1:28) **went up from above the cherubim, where it had been, and moved to the threshold of the temple.** Similar wording in 10:4 dramatically illustrated God's departure from Jerusalem. Because this was a vision, events could happen in an otherwise unusual sequence. Thus one minute

God was personally guiding Ezekiel through the temple while the next minute He was seated on the cherubim in the holy of holies or on His throne-chariot.

God told the scribe dressed **in linen, Go throughout . . . Jerusalem and put a mark on the foreheads of those who grieve and lament over the detestable things** in **the city.** God knew those who had remained faithful to Him, and would spare them in His judgment (cf. God's marking of the 144,000 for preservation during the Tribulation, Rev. 7:3-4).

God then told the guards to **follow** the scribe **through the city and kill, without showing pity.** Those not receiving **the mark** were to be destroyed. There was to be no distinction by age or sex; the judgment would come on the **old** and **young,** on **men . . . women, and children.**

Then God ordered the guards, **Begin** at the **sanctuary.** Significantly the judgment first began in the house of God (cf. 1 Peter 4:17). Since the evil had spread from the temple throughout the land (Ezek. 8), the judgment would follow the same course. So the guards **began with the elders,** the priests whose backs were turned to God (8:16). Their slaughter would **defile the temple and fill the courts with the slain,** but the temple had already been defiled with their idolatrous practices. The historical fulfillment of this is seen in 2 Chronicles 36:17-19.

**9:8-10.** Overwhelmed by the magnitude of this judgment Ezekiel cried out, **Are You going to destroy the entire remnant of Israel?** (cf. 11:13) Ezekiel was a man of compassion who cared for his nation (cf. Abraham's intercession for Sodom, Gen. 18:20-33; and Amos' praying for Israel, Amos 7:1-9).

Though Ezekiel's appeal revealed his concern, the nation's **sin** had progressed too far to avert disaster. God had given Israel and Judah ample time to repent of her sin, but the people had used the time to grow more perverse in their ways of **bloodshed** (cf. "violence," Ezek. 8:17) and **injustice,** all the while thinking **the** LORD no longer cared for them or saw them (cf. 8:12). Without **pity** (cf. 7:4, 9; 8:18; 24:14) He would give them what they deserved.

**9:11.** Then the angelic scribe returned with his report: **I have done as**

**You commanded** (cf. v. 4). Those who were righteous and whose hearts grieved over the nation's sin had received God's mark of protection. They would be spared. The unrighteous who had rejected God and embraced evil did not receive the mark of protection. They would be killed. Each person's destiny was determined by his character.

(3) The departure of God's glory from the temple (chap. 10). **10:1-2.** God would not share His dwelling place with other "gods," and the sanctuary had been polluted with idolatry. God's worship center at Shiloh was removed shortly after His glory had departed from it (1 Sam. 4:1-4, 10-11, 19-23; Jer. 7:12-14); and the same fate awaited the Jerusalem temple.

Ezekiel, still standing beside the altar, **looked** at the sanctuary and **saw the likeness of a throne of sapphire above the expanse that was over the heads of the cherubim.** This was God's azure-blue throne on His throne-chariot (see comments on Ezek. 1:26). Though God was at the entrance to the sanctuary, His throne-chariot was "on the south side of the temple" (10:3).

God told the angelic scribe, **Go in among the wheels beneath the cherubim** and take **burning coals . . . and scatter them over the city.** The "burning coals" among the cherubim had been seen by Ezekiel earlier (1:13; cf. Isa. 6:6). Now God was going to use similar coals to purge His "holy" city.

**10:3-5.** Ezekiel's attention shifted back to God's throne-chariot beside the sanctuary. **A cloud filled the inner court,** signifying God's presence at the threshold of the sanctuary (cf. Ex. 33:9-10; 1 Kings 8:10-11; Isa. 6:1-4). Ezekiel repeated the fact that **the glory of the LORD** had **moved** from the throne-chariot **to the threshold** (Ezek. 10:4; cf. 9:3). As **the cloud filled the temple . . . the court was full of the radiance of the glory** (cf. comments on 1:28) **of the LORD.** The manifestation of God's glory pierced through the cloud to illuminate the plaza where Ezekiel stood. Along with this dazzling brightness was **the sound** of the cherubim's **wings,** so loud that it was **heard** in **the outer court** (cf. 1:24).

**10:6-7.** Ezekiel returned from his momentary digression to continue his account of **the man in linen.** The messenger approached God's throne-chariot and **stood beside** one of its four wheels and **the cherubim** (cf. 1:15-18). **One of the cherubim** then **took some of** the fire **and put it into the hands of the man in linen,** thus enacting the divine purification of Jerusalem.

God's judgment as a **fire** scattered on Jerusalem is interesting in light of her ultimate fate, for the Babylonian army destroyed her by fire (cf. 2 Kings 25:8-9). The man in linen **took** the fire **and went out.** Though Ezekiel did not write that the man scattered the fire over Jerusalem, it can be assumed. Possibly the prophet's eyes were still transfixed on God's throne-chariot.

**10:8-13.** Again Ezekiel described the **cherubim** and the **wheels** (vv. 8-11; cf. 1:15-21). However, Ezekiel noted some additional details (10:12-13). **Their entire bodies . . . were completely full of eyes.** Probably their eyes represent divine omniscience as did the eyes on the **wheels** (see comments on 1:15-18). The four creatures John saw surrounding God's throne were also covered with eyes (Rev. 4:8).

Then Ezekiel **heard the wheels** referred to as **whirling wheels.** "Whirling" (*hagalgal*) means rolling or revolving. Thus the wheels were named for their function: they set God's throne-chariot in motion by revolving. The naming of the wheels here seems to prepare the way for their departure (to be described in Ezek. 10:15-19). God's glory was about to whirl out of His temple on "the whirling wheels."

**10:14.** Ezekiel then described the faces of the **cherubim** a second time (see comments on 1:10). However, an apparent discrepancy exists between these two descriptions. In chapter 1 the cherubim had the faces of a man, a lion, an eagle, and an ox; but in chapter 10 they had the faces of **a cherub . . . a man . . . a lion,** and **an eagle.** Some have suggested that a later scribe mistakenly copied "a cherub" in place of "face of an ox." A second view is that the face of an ox was, in fact, the normal understanding of the face of a cherub. In Akkadian literature the *kuribu* (cognate of "cherub") appear to have nonhuman faces.

**10:15-22.** It was now time for God's glory to depart. **Then the cherubim rose upward.** God's throne ascended from the court of Israel into the air. Ezekiel's description of the movement of **the cherubim** and **wheels** (vv. 15-17) uses the same words he employed in chapter 1 (see comments on 1:19-20). God's **glory,** which had been standing at the entrance to the temple, **departed from over the threshold of the temple and stopped above the cherubim** (10:18). God was mounting His throne-chariot to ride out of His temple and city. The throne-chariot began moving toward the east; but as the cherubim approached the edge of the temple precincts, **they stopped at the entrance to the east gate of the LORD's house, and the glory** (cf. comments on 1:28) **of the God of Israel was above them.** These **creatures** (vv. 20-22) were unquestionably the same **cherubim** Ezekiel **had seen** earlier. Before **God** left both the temple and the city, there was a final pause. Once God passed from the gate, the inscription "Ichabod" ("the glory has departed") could be written over Jerusalem (cf. 1 Sam. 4:21-22). As if to delay this final movement in the departure of God's glory, Ezekiel inserted the story of 25 wicked rulers (Ezek. 11:1-21).

(4) The judgment on Jerusalem's rulers (chap. 11). This fourth portion of Ezekiel's vision completed his "tour" of the temple area in Jerusalem. Before God's glory departed from the city it stopped at the eastern gate and gave Ezekiel another glimpse of the sin of Jerusalem's inhabitants. Ezekiel received two messages from the Lord. The first emphasized judgment on the people who remained in Jerusalem (vv. 1-15), and the second emphasized the promised restoration of the people who were in captivity (vv. 16-21). Then Ezekiel recorded the final departure of God's glory (vv. 22-25).

**11:1.** As God's glory hovered over the eastern gate, **the Spirit lifted . . . up** (cf. 3:8, 14; 11:24; 37:1; 43:5) the prophet and took him **to the gate** facing **east** toward the Kidron Valley and the Mount of Olives. **At the entrance to the gate were 25 men,** not the same 25 who were worshiping the sun (8:16).

Among the 25 men at the entrance to the gate were **Jaazaniah son of Azzur and Pelatiah son of Benaiah.** The gate was the traditional place where the elders of a city sat to administer justice and oversee legal matters. It was a city's "courthouse" (cf. Gen. 23:10, 18; Deut.

21:19; Josh. 20:4; Ruth 4:1-2, 9, 11; Job 29:7, 14-17). "Jaazaniah son of Azzur" is not mentioned elsewhere in Scripture and should not be confused with three other Jaazaniahs living at the same time (cf. 2 Kings 25:23; Jer. 35:3; Ezek. 8:11). It is possible (though by no means certain) that this "Azzur" is the man named in Jeremiah 28:1. If so, then the Jaazaniah of Ezekiel 11 was a brother of Hananiah the false prophet who opposed Jeremiah and who delivered the same false message of hope just before Jerusalem's fall (cf. Jer. 28:1-4). Nothing else is known about Pelatiah. Both Jaazaniah and Pelatiah, **leaders of the people,** probably belonged to Israel's nobility.

**11:2-3.** These 25 were **plotting evil and giving wicked advice.** They should have been providing wise counsel and direction for Jerusalem, but instead were turning the people from the Lord.

Their wicked counsel was summarized for Ezekiel. **Will it not soon be time to build houses? This city is a cooking pot and we are the meat.** The elders were encouraging the Jerusalemites to forget the prophet's predictions of the coming Babylonian invasion. They were urging the people to build houses, a sign of peace and safety (28:26). After all, the people were safe in the city (Jerusalem) like meat in a kettle.

**11:4-5.** Because of this false optimism, God told Ezekiel to **prophesy against them.** The public statements of confidence only masked the people's underlying fears. They were seeking security from the ever-present danger of Babylon (by talking about building houses), but in their minds they feared such an attack and the consequences it would bring. God said He knew **what** they were thinking (vv. 5, 8).

**11:6-12.** Ezekiel then altered the elders' imagery of the meat and the pot. Those righteous men who had been murdered in the city (**you have killed many people in this city**) had been Jerusalem's hope for only they could have rescued the city. The elders thought they were safe as meat in a pot (v. 3). But the slain righteous were the "meat": **the bodies you have thrown there** (in the **streets,** v. 6) **are the meat and this city is the pot.** Though the elders felt secure within the "pot" of Jerusalem, God would **drive them out** and give them **over to foreign-**

ers. Instead of the **city** being a **pot** of safety with the people in it being "safe" like **meat** (v. 11) the city would be smashed and the people dragged away.

God's **judgment** by **the sword** would be executed **at the borders of Israel** (vv. 10-11). This was fulfilled literally when the captives of Jerusalem were deported to Riblah in Syria and killed (cf. 2 Kings 25:18-21; Jer. 52:8-11, 24-27).

**11:13-15.** As Ezekiel prophesied against those elders and the city, **Pelatiah son of Benaiah died.** This was a confirmation of Ezekiel's message and foreshadowed the judgment that would soon destroy all Jerusalem's wicked leaders. Ezekiel, understanding the significance of that event, responded by again pleading to God for mercy (cf. 9:8): **Ah, Sovereign LORD! Will You completely destroy the remnant of Israel?**

God's response to Ezekiel was twofold. First, He showed Ezekiel that the remnant would not be destroyed. Those already in exile would be preserved. They were his **brothers,** his **blood relatives.** The phrase "your blood relatives" (*ge'ullāteḵā*) is translated "fellow exiles" in the Septuagint and Syriac texts (which has *gālûteḵā*). This makes better sense in the context. Ezekiel's brothers in exile were the true remnant.

The second part of God's response was to show Ezekiel the need for judgment on Jerusalem. Jerusalem's moral compass needle was bent. They felt that those in exile (whom God had just said were the true remnant) were **far away from the LORD.** They localized God and thought in terms of geographical rather than spiritual proximity. They also assumed that their right to the land was absolute since it was **given to** them **as** their **possession.** This was a correct but incomplete statement. God had given Israel the land, but He had also threatened to remove them from it for disobedience (cf. Deut. 28:36, 64-68). God would spare a remnant (Ezek. 6:8; 12:16), as Ezekiel asked, but it would not include the smug, self-righteous leaders of Jerusalem.

**11:16.** God had emphasized the coming judgment of the people who remained in Jerusalem (vv. 1-12). He assured the prophet that He would preserve a remnant, but it would be comprised of those in captivity, not those in Jerusalem (vv. 13-15). As a sign of His faithfulness, God promised to restore the remnant to the land (vv. 16-21).

The proof of God's blessing on the remnant in captivity involved (a) what He had already done for them (v. 16) and (b) what He would do for them in the future (vv. 17-21). Though God had **sent** His people **far away among the nations,** He had not abandoned them. They had lost access to the "sanctuary," the temple in Jerusalem; but God Himself had been a **sanctuary for them in** those foreign **countries.** God was accessible to faithful Jews wherever they were geographically.

**11:17.** Yet there is to be a distinct future for Israel nationally. God promised, **I will gather you . . . from the countries where you have been scattered, and I will give you back the land of Israel again.** The remnant of Israel could look forward to a national restoration to the Promised Land. A partial restoration took place after the Babylonian Captivity (cf. Ezra; Neh.), but Ezekiel 11:17-21 goes beyond that return and points to a future gathering of Israel at the beginning of the Millennium (cf. 36:24-38; 37:11-28).

**11:18-19.** Israel's physical **return** will be accompanied by a spiritual renewal. When they come back to the land, **they will . . . remove all . . . vile images and detestable idols** (cf. v. 21). The land will be purged of idolatry, and the people will be purged too. For God said, **I will give them an undivided heart and put a new spirit in them.** Israel's external difficulties resulted from her internal condition. God promised to correct that.

Ezekiel's promise refers to the permanent indwelling of the Holy Spirit in Israel ("spirit" could read "Spirit"). Before the Church Age the Holy Spirit indwelt select individuals; this was generally a temporary enablement for a special task (see comments on 2:2). However, in the Millennium the Holy Spirit will indwell all believing Israelites (cf. 36:26-27; cf. Joel 2:28). The inauguration of the New Covenant, which includes this permanent indwelling (cf. Jer. 31:31-34), began with the death of Christ (cf. Matt. 26:28; Mark 14:24; Luke 22:20; Heb. 8:6-13; 9:15; 10:14-16; 12:24); but the ultimate fulfillment awaits the national regathering of Israel. The church today is participating in the *spiritual* (not the physical) benefits of the covenant through its association with Christ.

The results of the new "heart" (**a heart of flesh** instead of a **heart of stone**) for Israel will be new actions and a new relationship.

**11:20-21.** In their actions the people of Israel will be obedient; **they will follow** God's **decrees and . . . keep His laws.** Their new internal condition will produce righteous actions. Also it will result in a new relationship with God: **They will be My people, and I will be their God** (cf. 14:11; 36:28; 37:23, 27; Hosea 2:23).

God ended this discourse by bringing Ezekiel back to the reality of sin. The remnant in captivity could look forward to restoration and blessing, but those in Jerusalem **devoted to their vile images and detestable idols** (cf. Ezek. 11:18) could expect only judgment for their sin. This reminded Ezekiel of the sinful actions he had just witnessed that caused God's glory to depart from His city (chaps. 8–11).

**11:22-25.** God's glory then continued its departure. **The glory of the LORD** (cf. comments on 1:28) **went up from within the city and stopped above the mountain east of it.** As God's **glory** left Jerusalem, it passed over the Kidron Valley to the Mount of Olives. This departure signaled Jerusalem's doom. The city would be devoid of God's blessing till the glory will return via the Mount of Olives (cf. 43:1-3). It is no coincidence that Christ ascended to heaven from the Mount of Olives (Acts 1:9-12) and promised to return to the same place (Acts 1:11; cf. Zech. 14:4).

Ezekiel's vision ended and he was transported by **the Spirit** (cf. 3:14; 8:3; 11:1; 37:1; 43:5) back to **the exiles in Babylonia.** As **the vision . . . went up from** him he **told the exiles everything the LORD had shown** him.

2. THE FUTILITY OF FALSE OPTIMISM (CHAPS. 12–19)

Ezekiel's task (chaps. 4–11) had been to show the necessity of Jerusalem's judgment because of her disobedience. He had demonstrated the fact of the siege through a series of signs, and then he explained the reason for the siege through two messages and an extended vision. However, the people were still not ready to accept the fact of Jerusalem's fall. Therefore Ezekiel gave a new series of signs and messages. Any optimism would be futile; Jerusalem's fate had been sealed.

Ezekiel used the clause, "The word of the LORD came to me," in introducing 10 of the 11 signs, sermons, and proverbs in chapters 12–19 (12:1, 17, 21; 13:1; 14:2, 12; 15:1; 16:1; 17:1; 18:1). The only variation is the final section (19:1), but this is a lament which seems to sum up the entire section's theme.

*a. Two signs about impending captivity (12:1-20)*

Ezekiel gave two more action-signs because of the people's unbelief. He said, "They have eyes to see but do not see and ears to hear but do not hear." Israel's blindness and deafness was willful. They had the faculties for receiving God's message, but they chose not to receive it because they were "a rebellious house" (v. 3; cf. comments on 3:9). Blindness and deafness often indicate disobedience or disbelief (cf. Deut. 29:1-4; Isa. 6:9-10; Jer. 5:21; Matt. 13:13-15; Acts 28:26-28).

(1) The sign of the baggage and the hole in the wall (12:1-16). **12:1-6.** Here Ezekiel's sign to Israel involved two separate actions. In the first action he packed his **belongings** and went **to another place** as the exiles watched him. The people recognized the meaning of that action because six years earlier they had made similar preparations for their own deportation to Babylon.

This first action **in the daytime** was followed by a second action **in the evening.** While the people watched, Ezekiel was to pretend he was being taken captive and was to **dig through the wall and take** his **belongings** (cf. v. 4) **out through it,** carrying them **on his shoulder.** As Ezekiel pantomimed before the **people** a furtive escape attempt he was also to **cover his face so that** he could not **see the land.**

**12:7-11.** Ezekiel performed the actions as he **was commanded.** Next **morning** God spoke to him again, this time asking him if the exiles inquired **what** he was **doing.** Evidently the people's curiosity was aroused. Once Ezekiel had their attention he could deliver God's message.

God explained that **this oracle** (message) concerned **the prince in Jerusalem** (i.e., King Zedekiah) **and the whole house of Israel who** were **there** (i.e., in Jerusalem, v. 10). This first part of Ezekiel's sign pictured the inevitability of the exile: **they will go into exile as captives.** Those at ease in Jerusalem would soon be exiles whose only possessions could be held in small sacks flung over their backs.

**12:12-16.** The second part of Ezekiel's sign (in vv. 5-6) pictured Zedekiah's vain escape attempt. He would try to escape **at dusk** from Jerusalem through a breach **in the** city **wall.** However, **he** would **be caught in** God's **snare.** Zedekiah's escape attempt would fail because God would make sure he was captured. The final destiny of Zedekiah was grim. **I will bring him to Babylonia . . . but he will not see it, and there he will die. His troops** who would try to escape with him would be pursued and killed by the **sword.**

All this was dramatically and accurately fulfilled in 586 B.C. After a futile escape attempt Zedekiah was taken to Nebuchadnezzar, forced to watch the enemy kill his sons, and then blinded and carried off to Babylon where he spent the rest of his life in prison (cf. 2 Kings 25:1-7; Jer. 52:4-11).

Those in Jerusalem would ultimately realize the sovereignty of God (Ezek. 12:15-16), but that knowledge would come only after they were dispersed **among the nations.** And yet, as God had said, He would **spare a few of them** (cf. 6:8).

(2) The sign of trembling while eating and drinking. **12:17-20.** Ezekiel's second sign was briefer than the first, but it too was intended to convey a message about **those living in Jerusalem and in the land of Israel** (v. 19). Ezekiel was to **tremble as** he ate his **food, and shudder . . . as** he drank his **water** (v. 18).

Ezekiel's actions represented the terror Israel would experience. As he had said earlier (4:16) the people in Jerusalem would eat and drink **in anxiety** and in **despair.** The enemy would plunder the **land,** devastating the **towns** and making **the land . . . desolate. Fear** of the enemy would grip the people as they watched God's judgment decimate the land. Yet they brought the judgment on them-

selves by their **violence** (20:19; cf. 7:23; 8:17).

*b. Five messages on the certainty of judgments (12:21–14:23)*

Following Ezekiel's two signs (12:1-20), he delivered a series of five messages (12:21-25; 12:26-28; 13; 14:1-11; 14:12-23) to destroy the people's false optimism and to show the certainty of judgment.

(1) The first message on the certainty of judgment. **12:21-25.** The first two messages were attacks on two popular proverbs the people were quoting. This message began with God asking Ezekiel about the **proverb . . . The days go by and every vision comes to nothing.** A "proverb" (*māšāl*) was a terse expression of a commonly held or self-evident truth. The point of this proverb was the belief that Ezekiel's (and other prophets') predictions of doom would not take place. It had the effect of labeling those prophets doomsayers thus allowing the people to ignore their messages.

God said He would keep the people from quoting that **proverb** any **longer.** The people's smug assurance would end when the judgments arrived. The past days had not invalidated the earlier predictions as the people supposed. Instead, they had decreased the time remaining till the prophecies would be accomplished. **The days are near,** God said.

False prophets had been contradicting the claims of God's true messengers in both Jerusalem (cf. Jer. 28:1-4) and Babylon (cf. Jer. 29:1, 8-9). Their optimistic predictions would cease as God hastened to fulfill His word. He would remove **false visions** and **flattering divinations.** Ezekiel's cries of doom were not distant rumblings of some still-future storm. The judgment was imminent: **it shall be fulfilled without delay.** God would **fulfill whatever** He predicted (cf. Ezek. 12:28).

(2) The second message on the certainty of God's judgment. **12:26-28.** The first proverb attacked by Ezekiel expressed the people's doubts about the *fact* of God's judgment. The second proverb expressed their doubts about the *imminency* of God's judgment. This saying was not specifically called a proverb, but it was cast in the same mold as the first

proverb. It was another popular saying in Israel.

Even those Israelites who believed Ezekiel was a true prophet of God doubted the soon fulfillment of his oracles: **he prophesies about the distant future.** If God does act, their reasoning went, it will not be soon. Interestingly the Apostle Peter predicted that the same attitude would prevail in the last days regarding the second coming of Christ (2 Peter 3:3-10). God's delay is a sign of mercy, not uncertainty.

Ezekiel said the judgment was not distant; it was standing at Israel's very doorstep. God said, **None of My words will be delayed any longer** (cf. Ezek. 12:25). The second proverb, like the first, was giving false hope to a nation that needed a clear understanding of its dire condition.

(3) The third message on the certainty of judgment (chap. 13). Ezekiel's third message was directed against Israel's false prophets and prophetesses who were leading the nation astray. In a large measure they were responsible for the people's misplaced hope. Ezekiel denounced the prophets (vv. 1-16) and the prophetesses (vv. 17-23). For both groups he first condemned their sin and then pronounced judgment.

**13:1-3.** The message of the false prophets came from **their own imagination** (cf. v. 17), not from God. Ezekiel was challenging the source of their message. Since their message came from **their own spirit,** Ezekiel could rightfully claim that they had **seen nothing.**

**13:4.** Not only was the message of the false prophets untrue; it was also dangerous. The false **prophets were like jackals among ruins.** The word for "jackals" (*šû'ālîm*) may be rendered "foxes" (the normal Heb. word for jackal is *tan*). Though some feel Ezekiel emphasized the destructive nature of foxes, they are not generally known for their destruction. It is probably better to understand that Ezekiel was referring to the nature of the foxes' dwelling places. Just as foxes consider ruins to be a perfectly acceptable "home," so also the false prophets were able to flourish in a crumbling society.

**13:5.** The false prophets, Ezekiel said, had **not gone up to the breaks in the wall to repair it.** Israel's moral walls were ready to collapse, but the false

prophets did nothing to help. **The day of the Lord** has an eschatological meaning in most Old Testament passages where it refers to the Tribulation period, the second coming of Christ, or the Millennium (cf. comments on "Major Interpretive Problems" in the *Introduction* to Joel). But in this passage it seems to refer to the coming judgment by the Babylonians.

**13:6-9.** The false prophets claimed to represent God, but He did not claim them. **Because of** their **false words and lying visions,** He was **against** them. Ezekiel mentioned three aspects of their judgment. First, **they** would **not belong to the council of** God's **people.** The false prophets had enjoyed favor among Israel's leaders. They were in positions of influence both in Jerusalem and in the exile; but after their prophecies were proved false, they would lose this favor. Second, besides losing their places on the council, they would also not **be listed in** Israel's **records** (i.e., their names would not be recorded in the city's list of citizens). To be excluded from the list would deprive an individual of the rights of citizenship (cf. Ezra 2:62). These false prophets would be excommunicated from the fellowship of Israel. Third, the false prophets would never again **enter the land of Israel.** They would die as captives in a foreign land.

**13:10.** The false prophets were **saying, Peace,** whereas Ezekiel was predicting destruction. Their deceptive ministry was like **a flimsy wall** covered **with whitewash.** Instead of calling Israel's attention to the serious cracks in its moral foundation (v. 5), these prophets were "dabbing plaster" to hide the deficiencies. A white paste, formed from the chalk deposits in Israel, was used to plaster over the rocks that formed the walls of most houses. This plaster hid uneven rocks under a smooth surface. The prophets were compounding Israel's difficulties by hiding problems that needed to be exposed.

**13:11-12.** Since the false prophets had deceived the people by plastering over an unsafe wall (v. 10), they would be blamed **when the wall** collapsed. God's judgment would break down the flimsy wall of Israel. Heavy **rain . . . hailstones . . . and violent winds** (cf. v. 13) would beat against the wall and it would collapse. Then the people would ask the prophets, **Where is the whitewash you covered it with?** The "whitewash" was their false prophecies; and when Jerusalem was destroyed, this would be revealed.

**13:13-16.** When **wind . . . hailstones . . . and . . . rain** would cause **the wall** of Jerusalem **to fall** (cf. v. 11), the prophets would **be destroyed in it,** for God's **wrath** would be **against** them.

**13:17-19.** Ezekiel turned from the false prophets (vv. 1-16) to address the false prophetesses (vv. 17-23). They were called **the daughters of your people who prophesy out of their own imagination** (cf. v. 2). True prophetesses ministered in both Old and New Testament times (Ex. 15:20; Jud. 4:4-5; 2 Kings 22:14; Acts 21:8-9). However, the "prophetesses" Ezekiel denounced were like mediums or sorceresses.

These prophetesses sewed **magic charms on all their wrists and** made **veils of various lengths for their heads.** The Hebrew word for "magic charms" occurs in the Old Testament only in this passage (Ezek. 13:18, 20). This practice probably came from Babylonian magic rituals, in which magical knots and bands were bound to various parts of the body to ward off evil spirits or to heal diseases. These "good-luck charms" supposedly had magical powers. The "veils" were long drapes that were placed on "their heads" and that covered the prophetesses' bodies, possibly to convey the impression of mystery.

The purpose for the magic charms and mysterious veils was **to ensnare people.** Especially in times of uncertainty and turmoil, frauds and charlatans seem to prey on the fears of the gullible. These sorceresses would "tell the future" or provide a "good-luck spell" **for a few handfuls of barley and scraps of bread,** either as payment for the divination or as a means employed for divination. In some cultures barley was used in occult practices either as an offering to the spirits or as a means of trying to determine the future. Whatever the case, these prophetesses were employing fraudulent practices as a hoax and were making a living off the fears of others. God said they were really **lying to My people** (v. 19).

The results of the prophetesses' work ran counter to Israel's best inter-

ests. **You have killed those who should not have died and have spared those who should not live.** The prophetesses should have exposed and denounced evil practices in Jerusalem (cf. 2 Kings 22:13-20). But instead they let the wicked ("those who should not live") go free.

**13:20-21.** God said His anger would be vented against the false prophetesses and that He would neutralize their **power.** He would **tear** their **magic charms . . . from** their **arms** and would **set free the people** they ensnared **like birds.** Also God would **tear off** their **veils and save** His **people from** their **hands.** These sorceresses would then be exposed as charlatans, and their gullible clients would desert them.

**13:22-23.** The prophetesses had **disheartened the righteous with** their **lies** and **encouraged the wicked not to turn from** their **evil ways.** This directly opposed God's purposes for the people.

When God would judge the prophetesses the people would then realize that these women had lied. And the prophetesses themselves would be forced to admit their sin. God would banish **false visions** and **divination** (see comments on Deut. 18:10) from Israel and **save** His **people from** their terrible deception.

(4) *The fourth message on the certainty of judgment (14:1-11).* **14:1-6.** Ezekiel's fourth message was a condemnation of idolatry. **Some of the elders of Israel** went to see Ezekiel. Though he was still confined to his house (3:24) these exiles recognized him as a prophet and came to him for advice (cf. 8:1). Presumably the elders wanted to receive a message from God about Jerusalem or the length of their exile.

As the elders **sat** before Ezekiel, God informed him that those **men** had **set up idols in their hearts and put wicked stumbling blocks before their faces.** The idolatry in Jerusalem was openly displayed (chap. 8), but the idolatry in Babylon was more subtle—it was internal rather than external. Like **stumbling blocks,** this idolatry would cause the people to fall. Several times Ezekiel spoke of a stumbling block (*mikšôl*) to show the effects of idolatry on the people (cf. 7:19, "stumble"; 14:3-4, 7; 18:30, "downfall"; 44:12, "fall"). In the Book of

Ezekiel Israel's idolatry was seen as the major cause for God's judgment on His people.

These hypocritical elders came to the true God for answers while having another "god" in their hearts. God asked Ezekiel, **Should I let them inquire of Me at all?** God was not obligated to answer them when they refused to acknowledge His sovereignty. So instead of giving these elders the information they *desired,* God instructed Ezekiel to give them the information they *needed*—God's attitude toward their **idolatry.**

God informed the elders that **when any Israelite** came to God while harboring idolatry **in his heart,** God would deal with the idolatry. God would do this for the ultimate benefit of the nation, **to recapture the hearts of the people.** The message Israel needed to hear was not some oracle about Jerusalem or the Captivity. The urgent message was, **Repent! Turn from your idols and renounce all your detestable practices!**

**14:7-8.** Ezekiel then widened the scope of his message. Verse 7 is identical to verse 4b except that in verse 7 the warning applied also to **any alien living in Israel.** The "alien" (*gēr*) was a resident alien in Israel who had accepted Israel's ways and was responsible to obey God's Law (Lev. 16:29-30; 17:12-16; 18:26; Num. 15:13-16; Isa. 56:3-8; Ezek. 47:22-23).

If an **Israelite** or an alien dared to presume on God while harboring idolatry, God would answer in judgment. **I the LORD will answer him Myself** (cf. 14:4) and **make him an example and a byword.** He would be a "byword" in the sense that people would know about him and talk about him (cf. 23:10; Job 17:6; 30:9; Ps. 44:14; Jer. 24:9; Joel 2:17). God would **cut him off from** His **people.** God would respond with actions, not words. He would move against that idolatrous person to kill him. This harsh action would be an example to others.

**14:9-11.** God said He would not respond through His prophet to an inquirer who was harboring idolatry in his heart. Therefore if a **prophet** *did* give an answer, it meant he was a false prophet. The clause, **I the LORD have persuaded that prophet,** is somewhat enigmatic and at first glance seems to indicate that God *did* prompt the prophet to speak. However, "persuaded" (from *pātāh*) is better

translated with a negative connotation such as "entice" or "deceive" (cf. Ex. 22:16, "seduces"; 2 Sam. 3:25; Jer. 20:7). The best illustration of Ezekiel's meaning is the story of God's letting false prophets deceive Ahab, to bring him to his death (1 Kings 22:19-23).

If a false prophet in Ezekiel's day received a word to give an idolater, it would be a deceptive word that would lead to the destruction of both (**the prophet will be as guilty as the one who consults him**). God would hold both individuals responsible for their sin and would punish them accordingly.

**Then the people** would return to Him and **no longer . . . defile themselves** by **their sins.** God would remove the stumbling block of idolatry that had brought the nation to ruin. Then, God said, **they will be My people and I will be their God** (cf. Ezek. 11:20; 36:28; 37:23, 27; Hosea 2:23). God ultimately will restore Israel to her place of fellowship with Him.

(5) *The fifth message on the certainty of judgment* (14:12-23). Ezekiel again pointed up the inevitability of judgment on Israel. If God would spare the wicked city of Sodom for the sake of 10 righteous people (Gen. 18:22-33), the Israelites in Ezekiel's day thought that surely He would spare Jerusalem because of its righteous individuals. But Ezekiel's fifth message made it clear that the righteous few would not prevent God's judgment on Jerusalem.

**14:12-20.** In the first section of his message Ezekiel gave four "hypothetical" cases of judgment. A particular **country sins against** God **by being unfaithful and** He stretches **out His hand against it.** Being just, God could (a) **cut off its food supply and send famine** (v. 13), (b) **send wild beasts through that country** (v. 15), (c) **bring a sword** (v. 17), and/or (d) **send a plague** (v. 19). God could use any of these four means to punish the land and kill its people (cf. 5:17). In fact all four will be used during the Tribulation when God pours His judgment on the whole earth for her sin (cf. Rev. 6:8).

In his four hypothetical cases Ezekiel interjected another element: what if three of the most righteous men who ever lived inhabited this land? God's answer was that it would make no difference.

Even if these three men—Noah, Daniel, and Job—were in it, they could save only themselves by their righteousness (cf. Ezek. 14:20). Both **Noah** and **Job** are understood by most scholars to refer to the biblical characters with the same names, but there is some question on the identity of **Daniel.** Ezekiel's spelling of the name differs slightly from the statesman-prophet who wrote the Book of Daniel. Many scholars feel that Ezekiel was referring to the mythical *Dan'el* in Ugaritic texts who, as a righteous ruler and judge, could not protect his sons from the wrath of the goddess Anat.

But this identification should probably be rejected. The minor difference in spelling could be explained by the common practice of multiple spellings of a given name (cf. "Azariah" = "Uzziah," 2 Kings 15:1; 2 Chron. 26:1; "Jehoram" = "Joram," 2 Kings 3:1; 8:16). The Prophet Daniel, well known in Babylon, would have been familiar to Ezekiel and his audience. There is no indication in the Old Testament that the mythical character *Dan'el* was known to the Jews or accepted as a model of righteousness. It was Ezekiel's purpose (Ezek. 14:1-11) to lambast idolatry. Would he use an idolatrous myth as a model of righteousness? By contrast, the biblical Daniel is the perfect example of a man who refused to compromise his beliefs.

God mentioned Noah, Daniel, and Job because of their similar characteristics. Each was a man of **righteousness** who overcame adversity. Righteous Noah was able to save only his immediate family from judgment (Gen. 6:8–7:1). Daniel was a righteous man in Ezekiel's day whom God used to save his friends from judgment (Dan. 2:12-24). Job was a righteous man who interceded for his three friends to save them from God's wrath after his own trials (Job 42:7-9).

Even if these three pillars of righteousness prayed together for mercy in a land under judgment, their praying for others in that case would be of no avail; they could save only themselves. (Cf. Jeremiah's words about the ineffectiveness of Moses' and Samuel's praying, Jer. 15:1.) This was made even more poignant when God declared, **they could not save their own sons or daughters. They alone would be saved** (Ezek. 14:18; cf. v. 20). Noah had "saved" his family and Job's

family was restored after his calamities; but when God's judgment would come on Israel, they would be able to rescue **only themselves.**

**14:21-23.** Having established this general principle (vv. 12-20), Ezekiel applied it to Jerusalem. **How much worse it will be when** God sends **against Jerusalem** His **four dreadful judgments— sword and famine and wild beasts and plague** (cf. 5:17). It would be worse for Jerusalem because she did not have three giants of righteousness to intercede for her. If those righteous leaders could not save a wicked land, how could Jerusalem hope to escape with her paucity of righteous individuals?

In the midst of announcing judgment God included a note of consolation. God's judgment would be vindicated by the exiles in captivity when they observed the evil character of those who survived Jerusalem's fall. **Yet there** would **be some survivors—sons and daughters who** would **be brought out of it,** that is, some would live through Jerusalem's destruction and be brought to Babylon as captives. As that group of exiles went to Babylon, the exiles already there (the ones addressed by Ezekiel) would **see their conduct and their actions,** and **be consoled regarding the disaster** on **Jerusalem.**

Some have felt that the "conduct and actions" Ezekiel was referring to were the righteous deeds of this remnant which prompted God to spare them. But Ezekiel was probably referring to the wicked ways of the captives. The word for "conduct" (*derek*) was used 35 times in Ezekiel's book to refer to the people's *evil* actions (cf. 3:18-19; 7:3-4, 8-9, 27; 11:21; 13:22; 14:22-23; 16:27, 43, 47 [twice], 61; 18:23, 25, 29-30; 20:30, 43-44; 22:31; 23:31; 24:14; 33:8-9, 11, 17, 20; 36:17, 19, 31-32). The word for "actions" (*'ălîlôṯ*) is used 8 times in the book to refer to the *sinful* deeds of Israel (14:22-23; 20:43-44; 21:24; 24:14; 36:17, 19). These two words occur together 7 times, and in every occurrence the words convey sinful actions.

Those who questioned the severity of God's judgment would recognize its justice when they observed the evil character of the captives brought from Jerusalem. They would be forced to admit that these people did deserve to be punished and that God was not unjust.

*c. Three parables on judgment (chaps. 15–17)*

After his two signs (12:1-20) and five messages (12:21–14:23), Ezekiel delivered a series of three parables (chaps. 15–17) to show that there was no possibility of deliverance for Israel.

(1) The parable of the fruitless vine (chap. 15). **15:1-5.** God posed a question to Ezekiel. **Son of man, how is the wood of a vine better than that of a branch on any of the trees in the forest?** The obvious answer is that apart from its ability to bear fruit the wood of a tangled vine is inferior to the wood of a tree. God pressed His point by asking two additional questions. **Is wood ever taken from it to make anything useful? Do they make pegs from it to hang things on?** The wood of grapevines is useless as a building material. Its twisting, gnarled branches cannot even be fashioned into a stout peg for hanging objects.

If the vine by itself was nearly useless, how much more so would it be after it had been through **the fire?** The worthlessness of a **charred** branch with its crooked, blackened **ends** is obvious.

**15:6-8.** God then applied the parable to **Jerusalem.** She was the **vine** branch; since she had stopped bearing the fruit of righteousness, she was useless.

Israel thought of herself as the vine of God's blessing, but she had not produced the spiritual fruit God intended (cf. Ps. 80:8-18; Isa. 5:1-7; Jer. 2:21; Hosea 10:1). In fact Israel had become a wild vine of the forest that had tendrils expanding in all directions but with no fruit of any value. Its only use was as **fuel for the fire.** In the same way God would **treat** His **people** in Jerusalem.

God's judgment was certain: **I will set My face against them.** Jerusalem had surrendered to Babylon in 597 B.C.; and though they escaped total destruction then, God would bring Babylon back to finish the job. **Although they have come out of the fire, the fire will yet consume them.** There was no cause for optimism, for the judgment from Babylon had only been delayed.

(2) The parable of the adulterous wife (chap. 16). **16:1-5.** In this parable on Jerusalem's unfaithfulness Ezekiel pictured her as an unwanted child of a mixed union. **Your ancestry and birth were in the land of the Canaanites; your father was an Amorite and your mother a Hittite** (cf. v. 45). While Ezekiel had the *people* of Jerusalem in mind through most of this parable, this beginning seems to allude to the *city* of **Jerusalem** itself. Israel, of course, descended from Shem (Gen. 10:21-31); by contrast Jerusalem, before it was conquered by David (1 Chron. 11:4-9), was a Canaanite city (Canaan descended from Ham, not Shem, Gen. 10:6-20). The city's early inhabitants were called Jebusites (Jud. 19:10-12).

Why then did Ezekiel say that Jerusalem's father was an Amorite and mother a Hittite? Perhaps the pagan Jebusites were associated with and were apparently like the Amorites and Hittites. This association may be suggested in the Table of Nations, which lists the Jebusites *between* the Hittites and Amorites (Gen. 10:15-16; see comments on the Amorites in Gen. 14:13-16). A similar point of association but not actual blood relationship is evident in the reference to Sodom as a "sister" of Jerusalem (Ezek. 16:46).

The early beginnings of Jerusalem were like those of an unwanted child. Normally after a baby is **born** the umbilical **cord** is **cut.** In biblical times a newborn was then **washed** to remove the blood and vernix and was **rubbed with salt** to dry and firm the skin. Then the infant was **wrapped in cloth** for warmth and covering. But for Jerusalem these things were not done. **No one looked on** her **with pity or had compassion enough to do any of these things for** her.

Also the baby (Jerusalem) was **thrown out into the open field, for** she was **despised.** The cruel practice of infanticide was prevalent in the ancient world. Unwanted and deformed children were cast out at birth and left to die.

**16:6-7.** As God noticed the struggling infant wallowing helplessly (**kicking about in** her **blood**), He came to her aid. The life of the infant was hanging in the balance till God ordained her survival: **I said to you, Live!**

The child lived and **grew** to maturity **like a plant of the field.** The modern equivalent of that comparison is "She grew like a weed." As time went by, this baby grew into a young woman. Yet she was still **naked and bare,** in a destitute state.

**16:8.** God again passed by Jerusalem

and noticed that she was **old enough for love,** that is, of marriageable age. God then entered into a covenant of marriage with her. **I spread the corner of My garment over you and covered your nakedness. I gave you My solemn oath and entered into a covenant with you . . . and you became Mine.** The symbolic act of spreading the lower part of one's garment over another signified protection and betrothal (cf. Ruth 3:9). God pledged His fidelity to Jerusalem and took her as His own. The historical event to which this alludes could be the appointment of Jerusalem as Israel's capital and God's dwelling place.

**16:9-14.** God **clothed** His betrothed in splendor befitting a queen. The waif who had the stench of **blood** was **washed** and anointed with **ointments,** or expensive perfumes. The girl who was naked now received an **embroidered dress . . . leather sandals. . . . fine linen, and . . . costly garments.** God put **jewelry** on her, including **bracelets . . . a necklace,** a **ring on** her **nose, earrings,** and a **crown.** The "ring" was clipped to the outer part of a nostril and was worn as jewelry with bracelets and earrings (cf. Gen. 24:47; Isa. 3:21). All this suggests that under God's blessing during the reigns of David and Solomon Jerusalem became a magnificent city (cf. 1 Kings 10:4-5).

Besides receiving expensive jewelry and fine clothes Jerusalem also was given the choicest foods: **fine flour, honey, and olive oil.** Everything she could possibly need or want was lavished on her by her gracious, generous "Husband." Being **beautiful,** she became **a queen,** and her **beauty** was known throughout **the nations.**

Had Ezekiel's parable ended here, it would have been a beautiful rags-to-riches love story. But he added a bizarre twist to make the story correspond to the remainder of Jerusalem's history. He pictured the unfaithfulness of this woman who was made a queen (Ezek. 16:15-34).

**16:15-19.** Jerusalem's gaze turned from her Benefactor to her **beauty,** and she became proud (she **used** her **fame to become a prostitute**). Jerusalem forgot the One who had supplied her with her wealth, and turned away from Him (cf. Deut. 6:10-12; 8:10-20). Instead she basked in her **beauty** and prostituted herself to other gods. Beginning in Solo-

mon's reign (1 Kings 11:7-13), and continuing till her fall to Nebuchadnezzar, Jerusalem turned from God to idolatry. She had times of revival, but her general trend was downward.

The very blessings God had bestowed on the city were used to worship the false gods. She **took some of** her **garments to make gaudy high places,** false worship centers usually situated on high hills (see comments on Ezek. 6:3). God said, **You also took the fine jewelry I gave you** (cf. 16:11-13) **and you made for yourself male idols and engaged in prostitution with them.** Ezekiel used vivid imagery to drive home the truth of the vileness of Jerusalem's sin. He pictured her taking her jewelry to make a phallic image with which she engaged in sex. Similarly the people of Jerusalem took the material benefits given by God to make idols of false gods and committed spiritual adultery with them.

**16:20-22.** Jerusalem also offered up her own **sons and daughters** as human sacrifices (**as food**) to these false **idols.** The Canaanite practice of child sacrifice was forbidden to the Israelites (cf. Lev. 18:21; 20:2-5; Deut. 12:31). In Ammon, parents killed their **children** and offered them in fires to entreat the god Molech's favor. The practice crept into the nation of Israel, and by Ezekiel's time child sacrifice was practiced openly in Jerusalem (cf. 2 Kings 21:6; Jer. 7:30-31; 32:35). Jerusalem had strayed far from her "Husband"; she had forgotten all His blessings. In her pride she forgot who had saved her from her destitute state as a neglected newborn and had elevated her to her exalted position.

**16:23-29.** Jerusalem developed an ever-deepening lust for idols. Her harlotry moved from the "high places" to the highways as **shrines** to foreign gods were erected at every intersection (**in every public square**) and on **every street.** Her desire for idolatry drove her to seek out "lovers" promiscuously to satisfy her lust. Her whoredoms included Egypt (v. 26), Assyria (v. 28), and Babylon (v. 29). Mentioning these nations implies not only Jerusalem's desire for new foreign gods to worship but also her foreign intrigues and alliances.

God did not stand quietly by while His "wife" debased herself. He tried to curb her appetite by imposing judgment.

He **reduced** her **territory** (i.e., land governed by Jerusalem) and **gave** her **over to . . . the Philistines.** The Philistines attacked Judah and Jerusalem in the reigns of Jehoram (2 Chron. 21:16-17) and Ahaz (2 Chron. 28:16-19). Yet even the Philistines **were shocked by** Jerusalem's **lewd conduct.** The Philistines worshiped idols, but at least they remained faithful to their own gods.

**16:30-34.** Jerusalem was **like a brazen prostitute,** but with one major difference. **A prostitute** gets paid for her services, but Jerusalem **scorned payment.** She was an **adulterous wife** as well as a prostitute because she preferred **strangers to** her **own husband.** Jerusalem was a spiritual nymphomaniac. She had even resorted to paying bribes (rather than receiving **a fee)** to get the attention that earlier had been lavishly bestowed on her. Such a reversal was remarkably unusual, thus showing her debased commitment to idolatry and foreign alliances. As she departed from God, He then withheld His blessings that He had so freely given (cf. Deut. 28:15-23). Instead of realizing her sin and returning to the true God, she sought out still more gods and offered larger "bribes" to induce these other gods to bless her. Jerusalem was squandering her wealth on things that could not bless.

**16:35-43.** Jerusalem had degenerated from a queen to a tramp. Her beauty was gone; so she used her few remaining resources to try to bribe others into illicit relationships. God tried to stop her mad rush to destruction but she refused to heed His warnings. It was now time for Him to judge.

God's judgment on Jerusalem would fit her crime. She had **exposed** herself to all her **lovers;** now God would use her **lovers** to destroy her. He would bring the nations **against** her and **strip** her **in front of them,** so that they would all **see** her **nakedness.** Jerusalem would again be as defenseless before her enemies as she was before being espoused to the Lord (v. 8).

God said He would punish Jerusalem as **women** were punished **who commit adultery and who shed blood.** The sentence for adultery in the Old Testament was stoning (Lev. 20:10; cf. John 8:4-5). Jerusalem's "adultery" was her idolatry, and the punishment for idolatry

was the sword (Deut. 13:12-15). God actually employed both means of judgment—stoning and the sword—in Jerusalem's fall. **They will bring a mob against you, who will stone you and hack you to pieces with their swords** (cf. Ezek. 23:47). God had said that if a city in Israel became involved in idolatry its people were to be killed by the sword and the city was to be burned (Deut. 13:15-16). After Jerusalem's fall Babylon did in fact **burn down** her **houses and inflict punishment . . . in the sight of many women** (Ezek. 16:41).

God's judgment on Jerusalem would finally **put a stop to** her **prostitution.** Only after her destruction would His **wrath . . . subside.** God's **jealous anger** does not indicate pettiness or vindictiveness; instead it is an essential display of His holiness.

The root cause of Jerusalem's sin was her failure to **remember the days of** her **youth** (v. 43; cf. "you will remember" in vv. 61, 63). All her grandeur came as a result of the Lord's gracious favor. So when she turned from Him she was cutting herself off from the only true source of blessing and enraging the One who had raised her to greatness.

**16:44-45.** The first part of Ezekiel's parable (vv. 1-43) is an analogy between Jerusalem and an adulterous wife. The second part of the parable (vv. 44-63) is an analogy between Jerusalem and her **sisters** Samaria and Sodom. If Jerusalem's wicked sisters received judgment for their sin, how could Jerusalem, who was even more depraved, hope to escape?

Jerusalem had a proverb about her fate (see comments on 12:22), but God gave her a new **proverb: Like mother, like daughter.** This meant that the traits of the parents were seen in the **children.** Jerusalem's actions were characteristic of her family heritage. Her **mother** had **despised her husband and her children.**

For emphasis, Ezekiel repeated the ancestral background of Jerusalem, already stated in 16:3. The debauchery, petty rivalries, and heartless cruelties of the Canaanite tribes were well known. Jerusalem inherited these characteristics from her "parents" and displayed them in her abandoning God and in cruelly sacrificing her own children.

**16:46-48.** Ezekiel expanded his analogy by comparing Jerusalem to her sisters, both of whom had "despised their husbands and their children" (v. 45). These two sisters (**Samaria** and **Sodom**), who shared Jerusalem's family traits, were selected by Ezekiel to reinforce his point. Both cities—one **north** and one **south** of Jerusalem—were known for their gross sins and divine judgment.

Yet Jerusalem was even **more depraved than** both Samaria and Sodom. Not even **Sodom,** with its heinous sins, was guilty of some of Jerusalem's lewd ways! (v. 48)

**16:49-52.** Sodom's sin was her **haughty** unconcern for the needs of others in spite of her wealth. Also the Sodomites **did detestable things before** God. This could refer to their deviate sexual aberrations (cf. Gen. 19:4-5). The sin of Samaria, though not specifically stated, was her idolatry. But Jerusalem's sins were so vile that, in comparison, the sins of both **Sodom** and **Samaria** seemed almost like **righteous** deeds!

**16:53-58.** Having announced the sin of and judgment on Jerusalem, Ezekiel then offered consoling words for her. Verses 53-63 speak of the restoration of all three "sisters." **I will restore the fortunes** (blessings) **of Sodom . . . and of Samaria . . . and your fortunes along with them.** If God would restore Jerusalem, could He do any less for her more righteous sisters? Ezekiel was speaking of the national restoration of these cities in the Millennium. (Evidently Sodom will be rebuilt at that time.)

Once restored, Jerusalem will sense deep remorse. She will **bear** her **disgrace and be ashamed of all** she had **done in giving** Samaria and Sodom **comfort.** This statement is connected with verse 52. Jerusalem's shame would be deeper because the depths of her sins actually were a source of comfort to **Sodom** and **Samaria.** In other words, if God would restore (**return**) the wretched Jerusalem, certainly He would restore her **sisters.**

Jerusalem's sin became the subject of gossip. In her haughtiness, before her fall, she **would not even mention** the name of her "fallen" **sister Sodom.** However, after her exposure and sin Jerusalem would be the object of derision by surrounding nations, including **the daughters of Edom and all her neighbors and the daughters of the Philistines.**

Edom, south of the Dead Sea, was a constant rival of Judah (cf. 2 Kings 8:20-22; 2 Chron. 28:17; Obad.). Edom gloated over Judah's fall to Babylon and aided Babylon in her attack on Jerusalem (cf. Ps. 137:7; Ezek. 25:12-14; 35:5-6, 15). "The daughters" of Edom and Philistia probably were the cities located in those countries. Jerusalem would be restored—but she would first have to **bear the** shameful **consequences** of her sin.

**16:59-63.** Though Jerusalem's sin would be judged, God would restore her to fellowship with Him. Describing the certainty of Jerusalem's judgment, Ezekiel stressed that God was not abandoning His people forever. God had entered into a binding **covenant** with His people (cf. v. 8), and He would **remember** (i.e., keep) it. This **everlasting covenant** is the "New Covenant" spoken of by Jeremiah (Jer. 31:31-34) and Ezekiel (cf. Ezek. 11:18-20; 36:26-28; 37:26-28).

When this "everlasting covenant" is established, God will also change the relationship between Jerusalem and her restored **sisters.** They will become her **daughters,** that is, Jerusalem will assume responsibility for Samaria and Sodom when her kingdom is restored in the Millennium. God's **covenant** here (16:61) probably refers to the Mosaic Covenant established with Israel which she had broken (cf. vv. 59-60a).

In the Millennium, when God establishes the New Covenant and restores Jerusalem, she will **know that** God is **the LORD.** Jerusalem's problem had been her forgetting God's past deeds (v. 43). But God's final covenant will correct her problem of spiritual amnesia (v. 63). **Then,** God said, **when I make atonement for you . . . you will remember** (cf. v. 61) **and be ashamed** (cf. vv. 52, 54). God's judgment and subsequent restoration would have a humbling effect on the nation. Her problem of pride (v. 56) would be eliminated forever.

(3) The parable of the two eagles (chap. 17). This parable about two eagles pictures Zedekiah's rebellion against the king of Babylon and the judgment that would result.

**17:1-2.** God told Ezekiel to **set forth an allegory and tell the house of Israel a parable.** The Hebrew word for "allegory" (*ḥîḏâh*) refers to a riddle or an enigmatic saying that normally requires an explanation. It is used of the "riddle" Samson posed to the Philistines (Jud. 14:12-19) and the "hard questions" the Queen of Sheba asked Solomon (1 Kings 10:1; 2 Chron. 9:1).

Ezekiel was told to deliver a discourse or extended riddle that would require an explanation. The word for parable is *māšāl*, which is normally translated "proverb," a short, pithy statement (cf. Ezek. 12:22; 18:1) but which can also refer to a longer work involving extensive comparison(s). Ezekiel's riddle or parable was stated in 17:3-10 and explained in verses 11-21.

**17:3-4, 11-12.** The first of two eagles, **with powerful wings, long feathers, and full plumage of varied colors,** went **to Lebanon.**

As Ezekiel explained later (v. 12), the eagle symbolized Nebuchadnezzar, and Lebanon stood for Jerusalem: **Do you not know what these things mean? The king of Babylon went to Jerusalem** (on the **rebellious house** see comments on 3:9).

Then Ezekiel explained why the "eagle" had gone "to Lebanon." The eagle clipped **the top of a cedar** tree and replanted the bough **in a city** known for trade. This referred to Nebuchadnezzar's attack on Jerusalem in 597 B.C. when he reestablished his control over the city and deposed King Jehoiachin. As Ezekiel explained, Nebuchadnezzar **carried off her king** (17:12), the top **shoot** of the tree, **and her nobles, bringing them back with him** (cf. 2 Kings 24:8-16) and replanted the "shoot" in **Babylon.**

**17:5-6, 13-14.** The "eagle," Nebuchadnezzar, was not totally heartless. **He took some of the seed of the land and. . . . planted it like a willow by abundant water, and it sprouted and became a low, spreading vine.** Nebuchadnezzar weakened Jerusalem, but he did not destroy it at that time. Instead he set up Zedekiah as a vassal king. Jerusalem's military might was gone; but as long as she remained faithful to Nebuchadnezzar, her people could continue to live in peace. Zedekiah, **a member of the royal family,** by **a treaty** was put **under oath** (v. 13). Though Judah was **brought low,** weakened and humiliated, she could survive if she kept the **treaty** with Nebuchadnezzar.

**17:7-8, 15. Another . . . eagle** came along to "entice" **the vine** away from

**where it** had been **planted.** This new "eagle" was Egypt, which influenced Zedekiah to rebel against Babylon. Judah's **king** violated his oath of allegiance to Babylon and joined forces with Egypt, **sending . . . envoys to Egypt to get horses and a large army.** When Ezekiel penned this prophecy Zedekiah's final revolt had not yet happened. Assuming that the book was arranged chronologically, this prophetic parable was written sometime between 592 B.C. (8:1) and 591 B.C. (20:1). Zedekiah's final revolt against Babylon actually began in 588 B.C., so Ezekiel predicted Zedekiah's revolt about three years before it happened.

**17:9-10, 16-21.** The results for the "vine" (v. 8) would be disastrous. It would be **uprooted and stripped of its fruit** and wither. Because Zedekiah violated his **oath** to Nebuchadnezzar (an oath ordained by God; cf. Jer. 27), Nebuchadnezzar would not spare the city. As Ezekiel explained, this revolt meant that Zedekiah would **die in Babylon** for **Pharaoh** in Egypt would **be of no help.** In **breaking** his **oath** to Nebuchadnezzar, Zedekiah was also opposing God. **I will bring down on his head My oath that he despised and My covenant that he broke.** God would see that Zedekiah was caught by Nebuchadnezzar (in his **net** and **snare**) and brought **to Babylon,** with his **troops** killed **by the sword** (cf. 2 Kings 24:3-7).

**17:22-24.** Lest the people get overly discouraged about God's coming judgment, Ezekiel added an "addendum" to his prophecy against Jerusalem. Though not specifically calling God an "eagle," Ezekiel compared God's future actions to those of the two eagles (Babylon and Egypt) already mentioned. Neither of those eagles had been able to provide the security and prosperity Israel desperately longed for, but God would succeed where they had failed.

God said He (**I Myself) will take a shoot from the very top of a cedar and plant it.** The "shoot" was the Davidic line (cf. v. 4 with v. 12). God will replant a king from the line of David **on the mountain heights of Israel.** The kingdom will not be destroyed for God will restore it to the land of Israel. That kingdom **will produce branches and bear fruit and become a splendid cedar.** That is, it will prosper as it has never done before. Instead of plucking branches from it, **birds of every kind will nest in it.** This suggests that Israel will protect surrounding nations rather than being their pawn.

God's purpose in restoring Israel is to reveal His glory and plan for Israel to all nations. **All the trees . . . will know that I the LORD bring down the tall tree and make the low tree grow tall.** Israel's rise to prominence will be a catalyst to turn other nations to the Lord.

This prophecy was not fulfilled when Israel returned to the land after the Babylonian Captivity. The fulfillment of verses 22-24 awaits God's establishment of Israel in the Millennium under the Messiah, Jesus Christ. At that time God's kingdom will rule the world (cf. Dan. 2:44-45; Zech. 14:3-9, 16-17).

### d. The message on individual responsibility (chap. 18)

Ezekiel had delivered three parables to convict the nation of her sin (chaps. 15–17). He then returned to the bluntness of a direct message to drive home the fact of Israel's guilt. The message in chapter 18 is similar to that in 12:21-28, for they both answered the people's proverbs that denied their coming judgment.

**18:1-4.** God asked Ezekiel about a **proverb** being circulated. This proverb—**The fathers eat sour grapes, and the children's teeth are set on edge**—must have been well known in Israel because Jeremiah also quoted it (cf. Jer. 31:29-30). The proverb's point was that children were suffering because of their parents' sins. True, Jerusalem was suffering, but as stated in the proverb the people thought they were suffering not because of *their* sins but because of their *parents'* sins. So these people were blaming God for punishing them unjustly (cf. Ezek. 18:25).

God saw that this false **proverb** had to be refuted. Yet, as with all false doctrines, a kernel of truth in the teaching made it seem plausible. In the Ten Commandments God indicated that He was "a jealous God, punishing the children for the sin of the fathers to the third and fourth generation of those who hate Me" (Ex. 20:5). This same threat was repeated in Exodus 34:6-7 and Deuteronomy 5:9. Even Ezekiel had traced God's coming judgment back to the people's past ac-

tions (cf. Ezek. 16:15-29). But the point of these passages was that the *effects* of sin are serious and long-lasting, not that God capriciously punishes the innocent for their ancestors' evil ways.

Blaming others for their misfortunes, the people were denying their own guilt. This was wrong because every individual is personally responsible to God. **For every living soul belongs to Me, the father as well as the son.** Those who are guilty will receive their own deserved punishment. **The soul who sins is the one who will die** (cf. 18:20). The people of **Israel** could not rightly charge God with injustice.

**18:5-6a.** Ezekiel then presented three "cases" to prove the principle of individual responsibility. Each hypothetical situation begins with **Suppose** (vv. 5, 10, 14). The cases are those of a righteous man who does right (vv. 5-9), a violent son of a righteous father (vv. 10-13), and a righteous son of a violent father (vv. 14-18). In each Ezekiel described the individual's actions and God's response.

The first hypothetical case was that of a **man** who was **righteous** and who followed God's Law with all his heart (vv. 5-9). He was not guilty of idolatry. **He did not eat at the mountain shrines** (cf. 8:12; 16:24-25, 31, 39; 18:15; 22:9) **or look to the idols.** The "mountain shrines" were the high places scattered throughout Israel where idolatry was practiced (see comments on 6:3-7). The "idols" were the foreign images being worshiped by the people (cf. chap. 8; 16:20-25).

**18:6b-8a.** The righteous man was also careful to keep the portions of the Law pertaining to his fellow Israelites. He kept himself morally pure. Both adultery (Ex. 20:14; Lev. 20:10) and intercourse during the menstrual **period** (Lev. 18:19) were prohibited by the Mosaic Law. The righteous man in Ezekiel's hypothetical case faithfully maintained sexual purity.

Ezekiel's model Israelite was also careful **not** to **oppress** his fellow Israelites. He would not keep collateral **for a loan** which the borrower needed (cf. Ex. 22:26; Deut. 24:6). He would never **commit robbery,** or forcibly take anything from a fellow Israelite (Ex. 20:15). He did the opposite; he gave **food** and **clothing** to the needy. His concern was how he could help others, not what he could get from them.

If this righteous man loaned something to a fellow Israelite, he did not try to profit on the deal by **usury** (an exorbitant interest rate). **Take excessive interest** could be translated "take interest" (NIV marg.) in light of the first part of the sentence. The Law prohibited any charging of interest on loans made to fellow Israelites (Deut. 23:19-20); this man carefully followed the Law. He put God's Law ahead of financial gain.

**18:8b-9.** This righteous person was compassionate (not **doing wrong**) and fair (judging **fairly between man and man**). He faithfully kept the highest standards of conduct demanded by God's **laws** for His covenant people.

The **righteous** Israelite would **surely live.** He would be spared from judgment (cf. 14:12-20) and would not suffer for the sins of others. The vast majority of Jerusalem's inhabitants were *not* righteous. Therefore the implication is that they would be punished for their sins.

**18:10-13.** Ezekiel moved to his second hypothetical situation. **Suppose** the righteous man **has a** rebellious (**violent**) son who commits sins his **father** had avoided (cf. vv. 11-13a with vv. 8-9).

God's verdict on this man was unfavorable. He would **be put to death and his blood** would **be on his own head.** The father's righteousness would not benefit his son (cf. 14:16, 18). This confirmed the fallacy of the people's proverb (18:2) and the truth of God's principle (v. 4).

**18:14-20.** Ezekiel's third case continued to follow this hypothetical family. **Suppose** (cf. "suppose" in vv. 5, 10) **this** wicked **son has a son who sees all the sins of his father** but **does not do such things** himself. Instead of following in the sin of his father, this son followed in the righteous path of his grandfather (cf. vv. 15-16 with vv. 6-9).

God's conclusion is obvious: **He will not die for his father's sin; he will surely live.** A righteous son will not be punished for his father's evil deeds. **But his father will die for his own sin.** The proverb being quoted (v. 2) was incorrect. When the people were judged, it was not for the sins of someone in a former generation. Only those who remained faithful to God would be delivered (v. 19). (By

the word **live** Ezekiel meant escaping punishment in this life. See comments on v. 24.) Ezekiel then repeated his point: **The soul who sins is the one who will die** (v. 20; cf. v. 4).

**18:21-23.** However, escape from judgment was possible. Sinners could avoid judgment if they repented of their **sins** by turning **from** them (cf. Prov. 28:13) and kept God's **decrees.** Ezekiel was not teaching salvation by works. First, he was speaking of a temporal deliverance from Babylon's armies rather than eternal deliverance from the second death (Ezek. 18:13). Second, he clearly indicated that these righteous works would spring only from a "new heart and a new spirit" (v. 31). Good works result from a changed life; they do not bring about such a change.

Why would God allow a sinner who repented to avoid judgment? The answer lies in God's character. He takes no **pleasure in the death of the wicked** (cf. v. 32). Instead, He is **pleased when they turn from their ways.** God is not a petty despot who holds grudges and longs to inflict punishment on those who wrong Him. As a God of grace He longs for people to forsake their wickedness and turn to His righteous ways.

**18:24.** Though God forgives the sins of those who turn to righteousness, He does not excuse the sins of someone who has been walking in **righteousness** and then **turns** to wickedness. **Will** such a person **live? None of the righteous things he has done will be remembered.** God was not saying that a saved Israelite would lose his salvation if he fell into sin. Both the blessing and the judgment in view here are temporal, not eternal. The judgment was physical death (cf. vv. 4, 20, 26), not eternal damnation. An Israelite who had followed God's Law but who later turned to idolatry or immorality could not expect his past righteousness to negate his present **sins.** God does not balance an individual's good deeds against his bad deeds to determine his fate. An individual's relationship with God when the judgment arrives determines whether he will live or **die.**

**18:25-32.** Israel had charged God with unrighteousness, but God now turned the tables. **Is My way unjust? Is it not your ways that are unjust?** (cf. v. 29; Job 40:8)

Ezekiel reminded Israel of the responsibility for sin borne by each member of the nation. **I will judge you, each one according to his ways.** If Israel fell, it would be for the sins of her own generation. Because of this, the nation needed to **repent** if she hoped to escape. Israel needed spiritual renewal. The people needed to get **rid . . . of** their **offenses** and **get a new heart and a new spirit** (cf. Ezek. 11:19; 36:26). The life or death of the people depended on their individual responses to God. Those who continued to rebel would **die;** those who repented and turned from sin would **live.**

*e. The parable of lamentation for Israel's princes (chap. 19)*

Ezekiel concluded this section on the futility of false optimism (chaps. 12–19) with a lament or dirge for Israel and her leaders. This is the first of five laments in the book (cf. 26:17-18; 27; 28:12-19; 32:1-16). Three of the other laments were directed against Tyre, and the fourth (32:1-16) was for Egypt. A "lament" was a funeral song usually recited in honor of a dead person. The song generally stressed the good qualities of the departed and the tragedy or loss engendered by his death (cf. 2 Sam. 1:17-27).

**19:1-2.** This **lament** was for **the princes of Israel.** "Princes" was the title Ezekiel gave the kings residing in Jerusalem (see comments on 7:27). At the time of this lament Zedekiah was king. The date was 592 B.C., five years before the fall of Jerusalem. Thus Ezekiel was taking up a funeral dirge even though the city's "death" was still in the future. Jerusalem's fall was so certain that Ezekiel considered it inevitable. Part of this dirge traces the fate of Jehoahaz and Jehoiachin—two of the three kings who preceded Zedekiah. The dirge was not over one individual; it was being sung for the Davidic dynasty and the "death" of its rule.

In Ezekiel's lament he recalled with fondness the lioness who had produced the fallen lions. **What a lioness was your mother among the lions!** Since the "lions" were the kings, some scholars feel that the "lioness" was Hamutual, wife of Josiah and mother of Jehoahaz and Zedekiah (cf. 2 Kings 23:31; 24:18). However, this seems unlikely for two reasons. First, the "king" in Ezekiel 19:5-9 seems to be

Jehoiachin; and his mother was Nehushta, another wife of Josiah (cf. 2 Kings 24:8). Second, the "mother" of the kings, referred to throughout Ezekiel 19, seems to depict more than a physical mother. In verses 10-14 the nation herself is the "mother" of the kings. Verse 13 seems to allude to Israel's captivity. Therefore the lioness/mother in this chapter is the nation Israel. She was the one who set up her kings but saw them destroyed, and she was the one who would go into captivity.

**19:3-4.** The lioness, Israel, **brought up one of her cubs, and he became a strong lion** (a king). This lion was Jehoahaz who came to the throne after Josiah's untimely death (see "Historical Background" in the *Introduction*). After a reign of only three months he was deposed by Pharaoh Neco II, who **led him with hooks** (probably literal hooks in his nose attached to a rope-leash; cf. v. 9) **to the land of Egypt.** In Egypt Jehoahaz died in captivity (cf. 2 Kings 23:31-34; Jer. 22:11-12).

**19:5-9.** The king after Jehoahaz was Jehoiakim, but Ezekiel did not refer to him in this chapter. Ezekiel emphasized that Zedekiah would be taken into captivity, so he mentioned only those kings who suffered a similar fate, Jehoahaz and Jehoiachin. Jehoiakim died in Jerusalem, so he was not included in this lament. (See the chart "The Last Five Kings of Judah," near 2 Kings 24.)

Jehoiachin, **another of** Israel's **cubs** who became **a strong lion,** reigned for only three months before he was deposed by Nebuchadnezzar. His brief reign (described in Ezek. 19:5-7) was a time of terror and destruction. With lionlike ferocity Jehoiachin wrought havoc, breaking **down their strongholds and . . . their towns. The land,** Israel, **and all who were in it were terrified by his roaring.** The "terror" was removed only when he was dethroned and deported by Nebuchadnezzar. **With hooks** (cf. v. 4) **they pulled him into a cage** (perhaps *sûgar*, "cage," means a neck yoke, based on the Akk. *šigāru*) **and brought him to the king of Babylon.** Nebuchadnezzar imprisoned Jehoiachin in Babylon because of the revolt his father Jehoiakim had begun (2 Kings 24:8-17). Jehoiachin remained in prison for 37 years till he was released when Evil-Merodach

(Amel-Marduk) succeeded his father Nebuchadnezzar on the throne in Babylon (2 Kings 25:27-30; Jer. 52:31-34). However, Jehoiachin remained in Babylon; he never returned to the land he had ravaged.

**19:10-11.** In verses 10-14 Ezekiel addressed King Zedekiah directly. He is the subject of the rest of the dirge. The **mother,** Israel, **was like a vine.** Since vines were common in Israel, the writers of Scripture often referred to Israel and others as vines (cf. Isa. 5:1-7; Ezek. 15; 17:5-10; Matt. 21:33-41; John 15:1-8). In her past glory, Israel **was,** figuratively speaking, **fruitful and full of branches.** It had prospered under the blessing of God, and had produced many rulers. **Its branches were strong, fit for a ruler's scepter.** The exact identification of the ruler(s) intended by Ezekiel's metaphor is unknown. Possibly Ezekiel was not pointing to specific rulers in Israel's past, but was merely showing that Israel's past was glorious and that it included **many** mighty leaders.

**19:12-14.** The vine's past glory contrasted sharply with its condition in Ezekiel's day. Israel the vine **was uprooted in fury and thrown to the ground.** It was shriveled and its **branches** were burned. Ezekiel did not explain the cause for this judgment, but in chapters 16–17 he had already stated why Israel went from blessing to disaster. The vine forgot that God was her source of blessing. Therefore God "uprooted" the nation, deporting her from the land.

**The east wind** would have conveyed a double meaning to Israel. The prevailing winds in Israel are from the west and bring moisture-laden air from the Mediterranean Sea. The east wind, known as the sirocco, blows on Israel from the desert in the east, bringing severe problems. It can wither vegetation (Gen. 41:6), destroy houses (Job 1:19), and cause severe distress (Jonah 4:8). However, Ezekiel's east wind referred to more than the sirocco. Babylon was also east of Israel; and when she "blew in" from the east, the nation shriveled under the heat of her oppression.

Ultimately Israel fell to Babylon. Ezekiel's statement, **Now it is planted in the desert, in a dry and thirsty land,** probably refers to Babylon's destruction of Israel. As the sirocco destroyed vegetation in

its path, so Israel would languish under Babylon's attacks. However, Ezekiel was possibly alluding to the Babylonian Captivity which the nation would soon face. The luxuriant vine of the nation would be uprooted from her homeland and cast down on foreign soil.

God's judgment would also affect the royal line. **No strong branch is left on it fit for a ruler's scepter.** The nation which had produced mighty rulers in the past (Ezek. 19:11) now would have no king. After Zedekiah was overthrown by Babylon, no king from the Davidic dynasty replaced him. Not till Christ returns will a "ruler's scepter" again arise in the line of David and reign as Israel's king.

### 3. THE HISTORY OF JUDAH'S CORRUPTION (CHAPS. 20–24)

These prophecies against Judah and Jerusalem focus on Judah's history. Ezekiel had presented that history in a parable (chap. 16), but in this section he gave a more direct presentation, especially in chapters 20 and 23. Chapter 21 contains a series of four messages on the sword that would smite Jerusalem, and chapter 22 has three additional prophecies of judgment on Jerusalem. The entire section closes in chapter 24 with two prophecies about the city's fall.

### a. The message of Israel's past rebellion and restoration (20:1-44)

(1) Her past rebellion (20:1-31). **20:1-4.** This prophecy was given **in the seventh year, in the fifth month on the 10th day.** This was August 14, 591 B.C., almost 11 months after the last date given by Ezekiel (8:1). As in chapters 8 and 14, the message was given to Ezekiel when **some of the elders of Israel came to inquire of the LORD.** They again visited him to see if God had any new word for the nation.

The elders' question is not recorded, but it must have been inappropriate because God refused to respond: **I will not let you inquire of Me.** The answer God then gave was not a response to their question but a review of their history. To find an answer the people only needed to look into their past. The repetition of God's question **Will you judge them?** (20:4) conveyed His impatience with the people, and it has the force of a command, "Judge these people!" Ezekiel was to confront them regarding the detestable practices of their fathers. The court was to be opened and the evidence presented. Ezekiel was to act as the prosecuting attorney and present the evidence against the accused (cf. 22:2b).

**20:5-9.** When God sovereignly selected Israel to be His people He bound Himself to them as their God and Protector. The first evidence of His faithfulness was His self-revelation to them. He revealed Himself to them in Egypt and with uplifted hand He said to them, I am the LORD your God. This incident was at the burning bush when God appointed the people's deliverer (cf. Ex. 3:1-10). The uplifted hand (Ezek. 20:5 [twice], 15, 23, 42) was apparently a gesture used when one made an oath (cf. Ex. 6:8; Neh. 9:15; Ps. 106:26; Ezek. 36:7; 44:12; 47:14).

Why did God trace His selection of Israel only to the time of Moses? Was Ezekiel contradicting Genesis, which clearly indicates that God selected Israel when He made His covenant with Abraham? (cf. Gen. 12:1-3; 15; 17:1-8) No, Ezekiel was speaking of God's selection of Israel *as a nation.* When God made His covenant with Abraham, the patriarch did not even have an heir as the next recipient of the covenant. When the family of Joseph went into Egypt, they were only a small clan of nomadic herdsmen (cf. Gen. 46:1-27, 31-34). But in Moses' time Abraham's descendants had grown into a nation.

God also promised deliverance from bondage and provision for blessing. He assured Israel He would take her out of Egypt into a land . . . flowing with milk and honey, the most beautiful of all lands.

In His grace God asked the nation only to be faithful to Him, and to turn from the vile images and idols of Egypt. The Book of Exodus did not detail Israel's religious life before the Exodus, but Ezekiel implied that it was a time of apostasy.

But Israel refused to heed God's command. They did not remove the vile images . . . nor . . . forsake the idols of Egypt. This rebellion deserved judgment, so God was ready to pour out His wrath on them . . . in Egypt. Yet the wrath did not come; Israel was spared.

Israel's being spared from God's wrath was not because of any goodness on her part. It was only because of God's grace and mercy: for the sake of His name (cf. Ezek. 20:14, 22). The "name" of God expressed His revealed character. God's reputation among the nations was at stake in His covenant faithfulness to His people. Instead of giving them judgment, which they deserved, God gave deliverance.

**20:10-12.** Next Ezekiel traced Israel's history in the wilderness (vv. 10-26), discussing God's relationship to the first generation (vv. 10-17) and to the second generation (vv. 18-26).

The wilderness experience began with another outpouring of God's grace, by which He led them out of Egypt and . . . into the desert. Those listening to Ezekiel would remember hearing about the miracle at the Red Sea when God parted the waters for Israel and delivered them from Pharaoh's pursuing army. God did not rescue Israel only to abandon her in the heat of the desert. He saved her from Egypt so that He could set her apart to Himself as His special nation. The Books of Exodus and Leviticus contain God's Laws and statutes for His Chosen People.

God singled out one of His laws—the Sabbaths—as a visible manifestation of the Mosaic Covenant (cf. Isa. 56:1-8). It was a sign to the Israelites that they were God's special people and were obligated to keep His Law.

**20:13-17.** Instead of responding in obedience to God's gracious provision, the nation disobeyed and rebelled against His rule (cf. Num. 10:11–14:35) and kept on in idolatry (Ezek. 20:16).

God's response was the same as His response in Egypt. The people deserved to die, but for the sake of His name (cf. vv. 9, 22) He spared them. There was a temporal judgment, though. Those who had sinned were not allowed into the Promised Land (v. 15).

**20:18-26.** God repeated His opportunities of blessing to the second generation in the wilderness. But the same reaction developed. God gave the children the same orders He had given their parents (vv. 18-20; cf. vv. 11-12), but the children followed their parents in violating God's laws (v. 21a). Destruction was deserved, but once again God acted in grace **for the sake of** His **name** (vv. 21b-22; cf. vv. 9, 14).

God did not destroy the second generation of people for their sin, but He did impose some judgments on them. The first judgment was dispersion (v. 23). Just before Israel entered the land, God exhorted the people to obey His covenant. He delineated the blessings that would come through obedience and the problems that would result from disobedience (Deut. 28), including being scattered among the nations (Deut. 28:64-68).

God's second judgment was abandoning the people to their sin. He **gave them over to statutes that were not good and laws they could not live by.** Some have felt that God was referring here to the Mosaic Law, as if God imposed on the people stringent laws they could never keep. However, this view lowers the intrinsic quality of the Mosaic Law as an expression of God's righteousness. Paul declared that God's Law was "holy, righteous, and good" (Rom. 7:12). Even sinners must "agree that the Law is good" (Rom. 7:16). This view also neglects the chronology presented by Ezekiel. This judgment came *after* the second generation rebelled. The Mosaic Law was given to the first generation years earlier.

It is better to see the "statutes" and "laws" (Ezek. 20:25) as commandments of the pagan religions to which Israel had turned. These laws "required" the Israelites to offer **the sacrifice of every firstborn** (v. 26), a practice God strongly condemned (cf. Lev. 20:1-5).

God's "giving over" of the people to sin was His judicial act. Because they refused to follow His righteous ways, God would abandon them to the consequences of their actions. Paul expressed a similar judgment by God on the heathen (cf. Rom. 1:24, 26, 28).

**20:27-29.** Israel's new location in the land of promise did not change her sinful actions. In **the land** the people **offered their sacrifices** to idols on hills and under **leafy** trees, using the Promised Land as the setting for their idolatry. (On the "high place" see comments on 6:1-4.) With a wordplay Ezekiel emphasized the sin of the people by asking them, **What is this high place** (*mâh habāmâh*) **you go to?** (*habā'îm*) The similarity of these words underscored the point that Israel had turned to idol worship.

**20:30-31.** In Ezekiel's day **Israel** was still rebellious, just like her ancestors, and was involved in idolatry and child **sacrifice.** Therefore God refused to **let** them **inquire of** Him (cf. v. 3). He would not be a divine ouija board they could manipulate for an answer whenever they pleased.

(2) Her future restoration (20:32-44). **20:32-38.** After recounting Israel's past history of rebellion, God told of her future restoration. The people wanted **to be like** their idolatrous neighbors, **but** God would not let His people become totally divorced from Him: **What you have in mind will never happen.** He would remain their God, ruling **over** them **with a mighty hand and an outstretched arm and with outpoured wrath** (v. 33). The words "mighty hand" and "outstretched arm" would call to mind God's strength in delivering His people from Egypt (cf. Deut. 4:34; 5:15; 7:19; 11:2; Ps. 136:12; and cf. "outstretched arm" in Ex. 6:6 and "mighty hand" in Ex. 32:11). However, His hand and arm would now bring wrath, not deliverance.

Much as the Exodus brought Israel out of bondage into the wilderness, so God's new "Exodus" would **bring** Israel **from the countries where** she had **been scattered.** She would be brought into the wilderness, but this would be a **desert of . . . judgment.** In this "Exodus," like the one from Egypt, God repeated that He would use His **mighty hand and . . . outstretched arm** but in **outpoured wrath** (Ezek. 20:34).

As Israel gathered in the wilderness, God would begin the process of eliminating **those who** had rebelled. **I will take note of you as you pass under My staff, and I will bring you into the bond of the covenant** (v. 37). This pictures a shepherd holding out his rod and forcing the sheep to pass under it single file for counting (cf. Jer. 33:13). The shepherd would let those sheep that were actually his enter the fold, a place of protection. In this instance the fold was "the bond of the covenant." The "covenant" could refer to the Mosaic Covenant, which Israel had broken (cf. Ezek. 16:59), but this does not seem likely since Israel invalidated the Mosaic Covenant by her unbelief. Therefore God will make a New Covenant with her when He restores her to Himself (Jer. 31:31-33). Ezekiel seemed to make the same distinction (Ezek. 16:60) between the Old Covenant of Israel's "youth" and the "everlasting covenant" which will be enacted at the time of her restoration. God will again bring Israel into a covenant relationship with Him—but this covenant will be permanent.

As the sheep will pass under the rod of the Great Shepherd, those who do not belong to Him—unbelieving Israelites who **rebel against** God—will be removed. God will not allow those sheep to **enter** His **land**. God's process of purification will mean that only true sheep will enjoy the covenant of blessing.

This scene described by Ezekiel is yet future. At the end of the Tribulation God will regather Israel to the land of promise for the Millennium (cf. 36:14-38; 37:21-23). But first the Israelites will be required to stand before the Lord for judgment. Those who have placed their trust in Him will be allowed to enter the land and participate in His kingdom (cf. John 3:3). Those who are rebels will be judged for their sin and banished to everlasting punishment.

**20:39-41.** When Israel enters into the New Covenant she will really know the Lord (vv. 39-44). Though Israel was serving **idols** in Ezekiel's day (to her own defilement, vv. 25-26), in the future God will not permit such sin among His people (**you will . . . no longer profane My holy name**; cf. 39:7; 43:7).

God's ideal for Israel will finally be realized in the millennial kingdom. She will **serve** the Lord, He **will accept** her, and the people will offer Him their choicest **offerings . . . gifts,** and **sacrifices** in sincere worship. (For an explanation of sacrifices during the Millennium see the comments on 40:38-43.) As a result, God **will show** Himself **holy.** "Holy" (qōdēš) means "set apart," the opposite of "profaned" or "made common." Israel had profaned her God by debasing her worship with sin and idolatry (20:39). In the future, however, she will set God apart so all **the nations** will sense God's holiness.

**20:42-44.** God's restoration of Israel will produce several changes: (1) The first change will be a new *realization* of her God. God said that Israel **will know that I am the LORD.** "LORD" (*Yahweh*) is God's personal name, revealed to **Israel** (cf. Ex.

3:13-15). It stresses God's self-existence and His covenant-keeping faithfulness. Israel will come to understand the true meaning of God's name (and character) when He brings her into Palestine. This promise does not depend on her faithfulness, for she had been extremely unfaithful. The promise, made by God, depends on *His* faithfulness. He will demonstrate His covenant loyalty by fulfilling it (cf. Ezek. 20:44).

(2) The second result of Israel's restoration will be her *repentance*. She **will remember** her **conduct** and **will loathe** herself **for all the evil** she has **done.** The shame **Israel** should have felt (but didn't) in Ezekiel's day will finally be manifested when God restores her.

### b. The parable of the forest fire (20:45-49)

**20:45-49.** Ezekiel's long message (vv. 1-44) was followed by a short parable. In the Hebrew Bible 20:45 is actually the first verse of chapter 21, thus showing that this parable introduces the four messages in chapter 21. Ezekiel was to **face toward the south** (*têmānâh*) and **preach against the south** (*dārôm*) and **the southland** (*negeb*). The first of these three Hebrew words is literally "what is on the right hand" as an individual faces east. It was a poetic word, though when used as a proper name (Teman) it described a city in Edom, to Judah's south (cf. Amos 1:12; Jer. 49:7; Ezek. 25:13). Possibly the idea in 20:45 is that Ezekiel was to face toward Teman. The word *dārôm* was also poetic. Ezekiel used that word 12 other times, all in describing the millennial temple (cf. 40:24 [twice], 27 [twice], 28 [twice], 44-45; 41:11; 42:12-13, 18).

The third word used by Ezekiel (*negeb*, "southland" in the NIV) is also used as a proper name. Negev is the name of the southern portion of Palestine near Israel's border with Edom (cf. Josh. 15:21). Today the Negev is a semi-arid region with little rainfall and few sources of water. But since Ezekiel referred to the Negev **forest,** the land must have been more densely covered in those days. Major settlements in the Negev included Arad, Kadesh Barnea, and Beersheba.

In this prophecy against Judah, Ezekiel said God was going to devastate it by **fire** (probably a "fire" of judgment, not a literal fire).

The people saw Ezekiel's actions but

Ezekiel 21:1-13

refused to understand them. Ezekiel complained to God that the people were saying he was **just telling parables,** or perplexing riddles. Though he was predicting Judah's destruction, the people were only confused by his words.

*c. The four messages of the sword (chap. 21)*

Since the people refused to understand Ezekiel's message about the fire on the southland (20:45-49), he gave four messages to expand his parable's meaning. In these messages Ezekiel changed the "fire" to a "sword" and the "Negev" to Judah and Jerusalem.

(1) The sword drawn (21:1-7). **21:1-5.** In the parable (20:45-49) Ezekiel had "set" his "face toward the south," but now God told him to **set** his **face against Jerusalem and preach against the sanctuary** and **prophesy against the land of Israel.** The object of God's judgment was His land, His Holy City, and His dwelling place.

God said that by a **sword** He would **cut off . . . both the righteous and the wicked.** This seems to contradict Ezekiel's earlier prophecy (18:1-24) that only the **wicked** would die and the **righteous** would live. This problem so perplexed the translators of the Septuagint that they changed "righteous" to "unrighteous." One possible solution is that "the righteous and the wicked" may be viewed from the people's perspective. As far as the people could tell the judgment was indiscriminate. It affected those who were in open idolatry as well as those who claimed to be followers of God. Yet in God's eyes only the wicked were being punished since He had promised to deliver those who were truly righteous. Another solution is that the phrase "cut off" may refer to captivity, not physical death. Whatever the exact meaning, Ezekiel was stressing the extent of the coming judgment.

The judgment would extend from **south** to **north** (already stated in 20:47). In case anyone failed to understand the parable of the forest fire, Ezekiel repeated this phrase to stress that all Judah would be judged. When judgment came, **then** the **people** would **know that . . . the** LORD had **drawn** His **sword** (cf. 21:3). Though the people refused to acknowledge the meaning of the parable (20:49),

they could not claim ignorance when God's slaughter would actually begin.

**21:6-7.** Ezekiel was instructed to act out the grief the people would feel when Jerusalem fell. As he sobbed in anguish, the people would **ask** what was wrong. He was to answer that it was **because of the news that** was **coming.** The awful realization of their country's demise would devastate them (cf. 7:17). Yet there was no doubt it would happen. **It will surely take place,** declared **the Sovereign** LORD.

(2) The sword sharpened (21:8-17). **21:8-10.** Ezekiel's second message about the sword was a poetic song of judgment. Its theme was that God's **sword** was **sharpened,** ready **for the slaughter.** The song is in three stanzas (vv. 8-10a, 11-12, 14-17). These sections were divided by two interludes, each focusing on "the rod" (vv. 10b, 13).

In the first stanza God's **sword** of judgment was **sharpened** with a whetstone to give it a keen cutting edge and **polished** and scoured to remove all rust and give the blade a gleam. Much like a soldier preparing for battle, God had honed His weapon so it would be effective.

The sword was coming because Israel had **despised the rod and all advice.** Some feel that "rod" refers to the king's scepter (cf. Gen. 49:9-10). If so, the people were rejecting God's threat of judgment and relying instead on His promise of a continued line of rulers for Judah. But this interpretation seems foreign to the passage. Perhaps "rod" refers to the chastisement God had used to try to curb Israel's sin and bring her back to Himself. A rod was often used for discipline (cf. Prov. 10:13; 13:24; 23:13), and God used "the rod" to discipline His own (cf. 2 Sam. 7:14; Job 9:34; 21:9). Israel had despised God's earlier attempts to use a rod to correct her, so He now used the sword. In this interpretation the **son** in Ezekiel 21:10 was not Ezekiel but Israel and her king.

**21:11-13.** The second stanza revealed the victims against whom the **sword** was drawn: God's **people** and all Israel's **princes.** The leaders had rejected God's advice and chastisement so all they could expect was the sword. Because of the massive destruction God told Ezekiel, **Cry out and wail.**

**21:14-17.** The third stanza stressed the work of the sword. In derision both the prophet and God would **strike** their hands (vv. 14, 17; cf. 6:11; 22:13). As **the sword** would move swiftly against the people and princes, it would **strike and strike again** (**twice, even three times**), seemingly coming **from every side.** In fear the people's **hearts** would **melt** (cf. 21:7). The judgment moved to all sides (**to the right, then to the left**) as it relentlessly pursued the people. It would stop only when the judgment was complete.

(3) The sword directed toward Jerusalem (21:18-27). **21:18-23.** Ezekiel's third message on the sword showed God's directing the sword of Babylon against Jerusalem. In symbolic actions Ezekiel pictured God supernaturally guiding Nebuchadnezzar to Jerusalem to overthrow the city.

God told Ezekiel to **mark out two roads for the sword of the king of Babylon to take.** When Jerusalem rebelled against Babylon in 588 B.C., she was one of three cities or countries seeking independence. The other two were Tyre and Ammon. Nebuchadnezzar led his forces north and west from Babylon along the Euphrates River. When he reached Riblah (north of Damascus in Syria) he had to decide which nation he would attack first. He could head due west toward the coast and attack Tyre, or he could go south along one of two "highways" leading to Judah and Ammon. Tyre was the most difficult of the three cities to attack (cf. chap. 26; 29:17-20), so Nebuchadnezzar decided not to make it his first objective. His choice then was whether to head down the coastal highway and attack **Judah and . . . Jerusalem** or to head down the Transjordanian highway and attack Ammon and **Rabbah.** "Rabbah" was the capital of Ammon and is identified with the modern city of Amman in Jordan.

The war council met at Riblah, **at the fork in the road,** to decide which course of action to take. Apparently Nebuchadnezzar and his generals could not agree on which direction to go, so they consulted their gods.

Nebuchadnezzar used three means to determine his course of action: casting **lots with arrows,** consulting **his idols,** and examining **the liver.** Casting lots

with arrows was probably similar to today's practice of drawing straws. Two arrows were placed in a quiver, each one inscribed with the name of one of the cities being considered for attack. The arrow drawn or cast out first was the one the gods indicated should be attacked. The consulting of "idols" ($t^e r\bar{a}\hat{p}\hat{i}m$) involved the use of teraphim or household idols. The exact nature of this practice is unknown but perhaps the idols were used in an attempt to contact departed spirits and hear their advice. Examining the liver was a form of divination known as hepatoscopy. The shape and markings of the liver of a sacrificed animal were studied by soothsayers to see if a proposed plan was favorable or not.

These practices by themselves could do nothing, but God worked through them to accomplish His judgment. **Into** Nebuchadnezzar's **right hand** would **come the lot for Jerusalem.** As Nebuchadnezzar went through his procedures, God had all the signs point toward the coastal highway and Jerusalem. That would be where he decided to proceed.

The rulers of Judah had pledged **allegiance to** Babylon, but they had violated their oath by rebelling. Yet even as Nebuchadnezzar set up his **siege works** around the city, the people refused to believe he would succeed. They thought his **omen** was **false** and that he was doomed to failure—but they were wrong. Since they had broken their covenant with Nebuchadnezzar (cf. 17:11-21), he would **take them captive.**

**21:24-27.** God then pronounced judgment on the **people** (v. 24) and the prince (vv. 25-27). Because of **open rebellion,** Jerusalem's people would be **taken captive.** They felt secure in their city, but they would be forcibly torn from it and dragged in chains to Babylon.

The **profane and wicked prince of Israel** was King Zedekiah. Because he violated his oath of allegiance to Babylon, he would be deposed. Zedekiah was stripped of authority (his **turban** and **crown** were removed), blinded, and imprisoned for life in Babylon (2 Kings 25:4-7). The once-proud king was humbled (**the exalted will be brought low**). **The lowly** ("poorest people of the land," 2 Kings 25:12) who were allowed to remain took his place in managing the land for Babylon.

The right to rule in Israel was taken from Zedekiah, and the land was destroyed. Ezekiel's triple use of **ruin** stressed that Israel's throne was to be absolutely desolate. **It will not be restored until He comes to whom it rightfully belongs; to Him I will give it.** This prophecy recalls Genesis 49:10, which speaks of "the scepter" in the line of Judah. The line of David would not be restored till the righteous, God-appointed King would come. There were no valid claims till Christ rode into Jerusalem to claim His rightful rule (cf. Zech. 9:9; Matt. 21:1-11; Rev. 19:11-16; 20:4). Christ will fulfill Ezekiel's prophecy; *He* will be the King of Israel.

(4) The sword directed toward Ammon. **21:28-32.** Ezekiel's fourth prophecy about the **sword** was directed against **the Ammonites,** who thought they had escaped Nebuchadnezzar's attack (cf. vv. 20-22). Ammon and Jerusalem, though enemies, had allied against Babylon. When Nebuchadnezzar decided to attack Jerusalem, Ammon was relieved and happy. They were thankful that Jerusalem would suffer in their place. In fact after Jerusalem's fall the Ammonites organized a coup that caused the death of Gedaliah, the governor of the land appointed by Nebuchadnezzar (Jer. 40:13–41:10). The Ammonites tried to set up another government in Israel that would be opposed to Babylon—probably so Nebuchadnezzar would again attack Judah instead of Ammon!

The **sword** that had been **polished** for Jerusalem (Ezek. 21:9, 11) would also reach Ammon. The Ammonites thought they had escaped Nebuchadnezzar's judgment but they would be punished. In God's **wrath** and **fiery anger** He would **hand** Ammon **over to brutal men, men skilled in destruction.** These invaders are identified in 25:4 as "people of the East" (cf. comments on Job 1:3)—possibly a reference to nomadic invaders. The **fire** of judgment directed against Judah (cf. 20:45-49) would also consume Ammon.

*d. The three messages on the defilement and judgment of Jerusalem (chap. 22)*

(1) The cause of judgment (22:1-16). **22:1-5.** God asked Ezekiel, **Will you judge her? Will you judge this city of bloodshed?** This is similar to the questions God asked him at the beginning of this section on Jerusalem's sin (cf. 20:4). If Ezekiel was to function as a prosecuting attorney or judge, he had to declare the facts of the case. He needed to **confront** Jerusalem **with all her detestable practices.**

Then God gave Ezekiel two charges to present against the city: **shedding blood** and **making idols.** Ezekiel mentioned blood or bloodshed seven times in this message to drive home the city's sin of extreme violence (cf. "violence" in 7:23; 8:17; 12:19). These two sins opposed the Mosaic Law's standards for Israel's relationships with God and her fellow Israelites (cf. Matt. 22:34-40). Rather than loving God she had turned to idolatry; and her love for her fellow Israelites had been replaced by treachery.

Jerusalem's sin would be punished —**the end of** her **years had come.** When she fell, her neighbors would **mock** her. The pride of this **infamous city** would turn to shame as she would be exposed in her sin before others.

**22:6-12.** Ezekiel cited sins that specifically violated some of the Ten Commandments (cf. Ex. 20:1-17): social injustice (Ezek. 22:7), apostasy (v. 8), idolatry (v. 9), immorality (vv. 10-11), and greed (v. 12). The list concluded with another sin, the root problem behind the others: **you have forgotten Me** (cf. 23:35).

**22:13-16.** God would **strike** His **hands together** (cf. 6:11; 21:14, 17) in derision against Jerusalem. The proud and insolent people who treated God's commands lightly would not be able to dismiss His judgment. Their **courage** would vanish when God would **disperse** them **among the nations.** Moses had warned Israel that national disobedience would eventually lead to dispersion (cf. Lev. 26:27-39; Deut. 28:64-68). Israel had defiled God's Law; now she would be **defiled in the eyes of the nations.** After the nation was dispersed she would understand the character of the God she had scorned and forgotten: **you will know that I am the Lord.**

(2) The means of judgment (22:17-22). **22:17-19.** Ezekiel's second message stressed that Jerusalem would become a furnace of affliction—a smelting furnace of judgment that would melt those who remained in it.

Israel had become worthless to God, for she was **dross to** Him—like **the** scum of **copper, tin, iron, and lead left inside a furnace.** Metallurgy was a developed science throughout the ancient Near East (cf. Job 28:1-11). When metals are heated in furnaces, the residue left after the pure metal is poured is the **dross.** To God, Israel was like **dross**—worthless because of her sin.

**22:20-22.** The dross was the by-product of smelting, but God was going to resmelt the dross. Much as metals are **melted** in a **furnace,** so God would **gather** the people **inside the city and melt** them. This thought is stated three times (vv. 20-22). Judah retreated to Jerusalem when Nebuchadnezzar invaded the land. The city became the crucible as God's **fiery** blasts of **wrath** and judgment blew on the people. God's judgment and destruction forced the people to acknowledge Him: **And you will know that I the LORD have poured out My wrath upon you.**

(3) The recipients of judgment (22:23-31). **22:23-24.** This message names the recipients of the judgment: princes (v. 25), priests (vv. 26-27), prophets (v. 28), and people (v. 29).

In verse 24 the NIV has the Septuagint reading of **rain** instead of "cleansed" (see NIV marg.) because "rain" seems to match **showers** better than "cleansed." However, there is no compelling reason not to follow the Hebrew "cleansed." Because of her disobedience Israel had not experienced cleansing (from sin); she had not received rain (blessings) **in the day** God sent His **wrath.**

**22:25.** The sins of **her princes** (though possibly this should read "prophets," NIV marg.) were presented first. The "princes" probably referred to the royal family, including King Zedekiah (cf. 12:10-12; 19:1; 21:25). The leaders used their power for material gain, ravaging the people **like a . . . lion** (cf. 19:1-9). In their greed they took **treasures and precious things;** and they murdered, thus making many wives **widows.** Instead of being examples to the people, the leaders were corrupt despots.

**22:26-27.** The religious leaders were no better than the princes. **Her priests do violence to My Law and profane My holy things** (cf. Zeph. 3:4). They were not instructing the people in the ways of

God, or enforcing the Law's statutes. **They even shut their eyes to the keeping of** God's **Sabbaths** (cf. Ezek. 20:16, 21, 24). Abandoning God's precepts, they let sin run rampant among the people.

Other government **officials** besides those in the royal family (princes, 22:25) were also guilty of **unjust gain.** Instead of equitably dispensing justice and upholding the rights of the disadvantaged, they were **like wolves tearing their prey.**

**22:28-29.** The **prophets** should have been God's spokesmen and denounced these wicked **deeds;** but (except for men like Ezekiel and Jeremiah) the prophets ignored those sins and gave the people **false visions and lying divinations.** They claimed to be speaking for God **when the LORD** had **not spoken.**

Then Ezekiel denounced **the people,** the commoners who followed their leaders' example. The populace too was involved in **extortion and . . . robbery** (cf. vv. 25, 27), and in oppression of the **needy.** So rulers oppressed the common people, and the common people oppressed the helpless.

**22:30-31.** The corruption was so complete that when God searched **for a man** who could stem the tide of national destruction (**build up the wall and stand . . . in the gap), none** could be **found.** No one in a position of authority in Israel had the moral qualities to lead the nation aright. Obviously Jeremiah had these qualities, but he lacked the authority to lead the nation from the brink of disaster.

Israel's extensive decay demanded justice. God concluded this message against Jerusalem by vowing to **pour out** His **wrath** and **consume** the people with His **fiery anger** (cf. 21:31).

Israel would suffer because of her sins. She had rebelled against God's grace; now she would feel God's wrath.

*e. The parable of the two adulterous sisters (chap. 23)*

Ezekiel presented another parable to illustrate Judah's unfaithfulness and the certainty of her punishment. Chapter 23 seems to be a restatement of the parable in chapter 16 since both chapters deal with Judah's unfaithfulness to God. However, in chapter 16 Ezekiel focused on Judah's idolatry, whereas in chapter 23 he stressed Judah's illicit foreign alliances in addition to her idolatry. In chapter 16 her trust was in other gods; in chapter 23 it was in other nations.

(1) The infidelity of the sisters (23:1-21). **23:1-3.** Two sisters shared the same moral degradation for **they became prostitutes in Egypt, engaging in prostitution from their youth.** Ezekiel's reference to Egypt would call to mind the origins of the nation Israel in Egypt (cf. 20:4-12). The two sisters were sexually promiscuous women.

**23:4.** After describing their character Ezekiel gave their names and identities. **The older was named Oholah, and her sister was Oholibah.** These names are based on the Hebrew word for "tent" (*ʾōhel*). The first name means "her tent" and the second means "my tent is in her." Though one must be careful not to press a parable's details, probably these names have significance. The word "tent" implied a dwelling place or sanctuary. It was often used of God's sanctuary among Israel (cf. Ex. 29:4, 10-11, 30). The name Oholah ("her tent") could imply that the sanctuary associated with this sister was of her own making. By contrast, the name Oholibah ("my tent is in her") implies that God's sanctuary was in her midst.

**Oholah** represented **Samaria,** and **Oholibah** represented **Jerusalem.** These two "sisters," the capital cities of the kingdoms of Israel and Judah, represented the people of those two kingdoms.

Though God's covenant with these women was not explicitly stated, it was implied. **They were Mine and gave birth to sons and daughters.** The God of grace lavished His love on these undeserving sisters.

**23:5-10.** The sin of **Oholah,** the older sister, was her (Samaria's) association with **the Assyrians.** Samaria's alliance with Assyria ultimately led to her doom.

Israel's relationships with Assyria are well documented. The Black Obelisk of the Assyrian king Shalmaneser III (dated ca. 841 B.C.) mentions "Jehu son of Omri" and pictures him bowing down to the Assyrian monarch. This is not mentioned in the Bible, but it probably resulted from the Syrian threat to Israel. Syria was expanding into Israel's land in the Transjordan during Jehu's reign (2 Kings 10:32-34). To counter that threat Jehu allied Israel with Assyria and submitted himself as a vassal. The obelisk pictures

Jehu and his servants bringing tribute to the Assyrian king. Menahem and Hoshea, two later kings of Israel, also paid tribute to Assyria (2 Kings 15:19-20; 17:3-4). The Prophet Hosea (ca. 760–720 B.C.) rebuked Israel for her dependence on Assyria instead of on the Lord (cf. Hosea 5:13-14; 7:11; 8:9; 12:1).

After Israel became Assyria's vassal she could not disentangle herself. When she finally tried to break away by forming a coalition with both Syria and Egypt (cf. 2 Kings 17:4; Isa. 7:1), she felt Assyria's wrath. The very nation to which Samaria had turned for assistance would destroy her. God gave all Israel, including Samaria, **over to her lovers, the Assyrians, for whom she lusted** and who **killed her with the sword.** In 722 B.C. Samaria fell to Assyria (cf. 2 Kings 17:5-6, 18-20).

**23:11-18.** The judgment of the older sister Oholah (Samaria) should have been a warning to the younger sister **Oholibah** (Jerusalem). Unfortunately she failed to heed the warning. In fact **she was more depraved than her sister.**

Jerusalem followed the immoral course charted by her sister: **she too lusted after the Assyrians.** Judah curried the favor of Assyria rather than relying on her God. Possibly Ezekiel had in mind the disastrous political move of King Ahaz of Judah who willingly made Judah Assyria's vassal. Israel and Syria had banded together to oppose Assyria, and they sought to bring Judah into the alliance. When Ahaz refused, they attacked Judah hoping to dethrone Ahaz and to replace him with a king who would support their uprising. Rather than trusting in God for deliverance (as Isaiah the prophet urged him to do), Ahaz sent to Assyria to enlist her aid and protection. With that act Judah became a vassal of Assyria for the next century (cf. 2 Kings 16:5-9; Isa. 7).

But Jerusalem's political intrigues did not stop there; **she carried her prostitution still further.** After appealing to Assyria, Jerusalem turned to Babylon. Ezekiel described in some detail the garb of the Babylonian soldiers Jerusalem lusted after (Ezek. 23:15).

Jerusalem **sent messengers to them in Chaldea. Then the Babylonians came to her, to the bed of love, and in their lust they defiled her.** Jerusalem's respite from Assyria's domination was short-lived. King Josiah established her independence, but he was killed in battle as he tried to thwart an Egyptain incursion through his country (cf. 2 Kings 23:29-30). Judah became a vassal of Egypt for four years. Probably during that time King Jehoiakim contacted Babylon to request her aid. When Babylon defeated the Egyptians at Carchemish in 605 B.C., Jehoiakim willingly switched allegiances and became Nebuchadnezzar's vassal (2 Kings 24:1).

But when Babylon came, Jerusalem found that the lovers for whom she had lusted were brutal. **After she had been defiled by them, she turned away from them in disgust.** Babylon became a harsher taskmaster than either Assyria or Egypt, and Jerusalem sought to escape Babylon's dominance.

While Jerusalem turned from Babylon, God turned from Jerusalem. Jerusalem continued in the ways of her sister and even surpassed Samaria's unfaithfulness. God had finally rejected Samaria for her actions, and He now rejected Jerusalem.

**23:19-21.** Jerusalem's faithlessness cost her the only true protection she ever had. Yet instead of repenting of her sin, she sought additional human help, becoming **more and more promiscuous.** Her cycle of sin brought her back to the very nation with which she had originally been defiled and which had enslaved her—**Egypt** (vv. 3, 19, 21).

To show his absolute disgust in this course of action, Ezekiel used coarse language (v. 20), not to be vulgar, but to portray graphically the utter spiritual degradation to which Judah had fallen.

In the last 14 years of Judah's history (600–586 B.C.) she attempted to elicit Egypt's help in her revolt against Babylon. King Jehoiakim rebelled against Babylon in 600 B.C. after Egypt defeated Babylon (2 Kings 24:1). Judah eagerly grasped Egypt's hollow promises of aid. Zedekiah's final revolt against Babylon in 588 B.C. came with Egypt's promise of assistance (2 Kings 25:1; Jer. 37:5-8; Ezek. 29:6-7).

(2) The punishment of the sisters (23:22-35). **23:22-27.** Here Ezekiel gave four oracles, each beginning with the words, **This is what the Sovereign Lord says** (vv. 22, 28, 32, 35). The oracles all focused on Jerusalem's judgment. Those Jerusalem despised would be the ones who would punish her. God would bring her **lovers against** her, including **the Babylonians . . . the men of Pekod and Shoa and Koa, and all the Assyrians.** Perhaps Pekod, Shoa, and Koa were three Aramean tribes (*Puqûdû, Sutû,* and *Qutû*), near the mouth of the Tigris River. These three tribes, along with the Assyrians, were part of the Babylonian Empire and were represented in Babylon's army. Ezekiel was saying that the combined army of Babylon and her allies would descend on Jerusalem.

When the Babylonians would attack Jerusalem with military **officers . . . weapons,** and well-protected soldiers the city would not escape. The **punishment** God would inflict on her in His **anger** through Babylon would be like a mutilation. **They will cut off your noses and your ears, and those . . . who are left will fall by the sword.** In Mesopotamia facial mutilation was a frequent punishment for adultery. A guilty woman would be rendered so grotesque that she would be forever undesirable to anyone else; she would be forced to bear her shame and guilt publicly. Similarly Jerusalem would be rendered unattractive to any more potential lovers.

Also some of Jerusalem's children would be carried away as slaves, others would be burned **by fire,** and her possessions (**clothes** and **jewelry**) would be stripped away. God's punishment would cure Judah's lust; she would no longer look to **Egypt** for help.

**23:28-31.** This second oracle repeats (for emphasis) several points stated in verses 22-27, and adds that when the Babylonians were done, Jerusalem would be left **naked and bare.** Though ashamed, this punishment would come because of her **promiscuity** in seeking aid from other **nations** and becoming perverted by their idols. Since she had sinned like her **sister,** she would be punished in a similar way (**I will put her up into your hand**; cf. comments on vv. 32-34)—by the sword and exile.

**23:32-34.** This third oracle of judgment against Jerusalem differs from the others because it is a poem. The point of the poem, which might be titled "The Cup of God's Judgment," is that Jerusalem was to take part in Samaria's judgment because she had taken part in Samaria's sin. God said, **You will drink your sister's cup** (cf. v. 31), **a cup large and deep; it will bring scorn and derision, for it holds so much.**

The concept of imbibing a cup of judgment occurs throughout the Bible (cf. Ps. 75:8; Isa. 51:17-23; Jer. 25:15-19; 51:7; Hab. 2:16; Rev. 17:3-4; 18:6). The "contents" of the cup were the ruinous effects of sin—**sorrow . . . ruin, and desolation**—accumulated by the nation.

**23:35.** This fourth oracle presents the main reason Jerusalem was to be judged. She had **forgotten** God (cf. 22:12) **and thrust** Him **behind** her **back.** Jerusalem's illicit affairs with other nations came after she forgot her source of protection and openly rejected God. Because of this rejection, she **must bear the consequences of** her **lewdness.**

(3) Conclusion (23:36-49). In the final section of this chapter Ezekiel reviewed the sin and judgment of Samaria and Jerusalem. The history and judgment of both countries had been presented separately (vv. 1-35), but now they were combined for the sake of comparison. The sins of both nations were idolatry (vv. 36-39) and foreign alliances (vv. 40-44), and their judgments were the same (vv. 45-49).

**23:36-39.** Idolatry, though not the subject of verses 1-35, was common to Israel and Judah. The apex of their spiritual adultery was child sacrifice: **they even sacrificed their children, whom they bore to Me.** This, one of the most detestable practices of the Canaanite religions, had infiltrated both Israel and Judah (see comments on 16:20-22). The people were so hardened by sin that **on the very day they sacrificed their children to their idols, they entered** the temple with their children's blood on their hands and the smoky smell of burning flesh embedded in their clothes. Their very presence profaned and desecrated the **house** of God!

**23:40-44.** The spiritual adultery of the two nations was matched only by their political adultery. Both countries enticed foreign nations into illicit alliances. Ezekiel painted a vivid picture of the sisters preparing themselves for lovers (i.e., enticing other nations to help them). The harlot sisters **sent . . . for men** and **when they arrived** the girls **bathed** themselves **for them, painted** their **eyes, and put on . . . jewelry** (cf. Prov. 7:6-21).

The enticements of the two sisters drew **a carefree crowd** of **Sabeans . . . from the desert** and **men from the rabble.** The word "Sabeans" (*sābā'îm*) may also be translated "drunkards" (from *sābā'*, "to imbibe, drink largely"; cf. NIV marg.). Perhaps Ezekiel deliberately chose the word because of its double meaning. The wild nomadic Sabeans may have behaved like drunkards. The reputation of the sisters was so well known that even the lower elements of society knew where to find them. Ezekiel also employed two similar-sounding words to draw attention to the baser elements being attracted to the women. They **brought** in (*mûbā'îm*) "Sabeans/drunkards" (*sābā'îm*).

The sisters were using their charms to gain others' favors, so God reduced them to the status of prostitutes (cf. Ezek. 23:3). This appropriately pictures Israel and Judah turning to pagan nations for help and being molested by them.

**23:45-49.** God said that **righteous men** would **sentence them to the punishment** adulteresses deserved. Who were these "righteous men"? Certainly they were not the nations that ultimately destroyed the sisters, because those nations had previously committed adultery with them. Most likely the "righteous men" were the prophets of God raised up to denounce sin and pronounce judgment. They functioned like elders who decided the fate of someone accused of fornication (cf. Deut. 22:13-21).

The judgment for **adultery** was death (Lev. 20:10), generally by stoning (cf. Lev. 20:27; John 8:3-5); and the judgments for **idolatry** in a city were the sword and fire (Deut. 13:12-16). These judgments would be enacted against these "sisters." **The mob**—a derisive way of referring to the foreign nations— would **stone them and cut them down with . . . swords,** and flames would engulf **their houses.** These are the same judgments Ezekiel pronounced earlier (Ezek. 16:40-41). They would provide a **warning** to other nations.

*f. The parable of the boiling pot (24:1-14)*

Chapter 24 concludes the third series of judgments on Judah (chaps. 4–11; 12–

19; 20–24). Chapter 24 climaxes these prophecies with two additional messages that show the inevitability of judgment.

**24:1-2.** Ezekiel's final prophecies of doom against Jerusalem came **in the ninth year** (of King Jehoiachin's exile; cf. 1:2), **in the 10th month on the 10th day.** This was January 15, 588 B.C.—a day of national calamity for Jerusalem. **The king of Babylon** besieged **Jerusalem** that **very day.** This was the day Ezekiel had been pointing to for over four years. The date was so significant that it was also mentioned by the writer of 1 and 2 Kings (cf. 2 Kings 25:1) and by the Prophet Jeremiah (Jer. 39:1; 52:4).

**24:3-5.** Ezekiel told the **rebellious house** of Israel (cf. 3:9) **a parable** about a **cooking pot** being filled with **water** and **choice** cuts **of meat** being boiled. This was similar to his message in chapter 11, in which some leaders used the figure of a cooking pot to give Jerusalem false hope. The people thought that being in the pot (Jerusalem) would keep them safe; but here Ezekiel prophesied that the pot would be their place of destruction.

**24:6-8.** Ezekiel explained the parable through two similar statements (vv. 6-8, 9-14), each beginning with the words, **This is what the Sovereign LORD says: Woe to the city of bloodshed** (vv. 6, 9). These statements spoke of the city's blood-guiltiness (cf. 22:1-16).

Ezekiel said Jerusalem was like a **pot now encrusted, whose deposit will not go away!** "Encrusted" and "deposit" are from the Hebrew word *ḥel'âh* and could be translated "rusted" and "rust." In the fire of God's judgment Jerusalem's "impurities" floated to the surface. Her corruption could not be hidden. She was as unappealing as rusty scum floating on the surface of a meal being cooked.

The meal was ruined by the rusty scum, so the contents of the pot were dumped. People in Jerusalem who had felt secure from Babylon's onslaught would be dragged from the city into exile with no regard for their position in society (no **lots** would be cast **for them**).

The cause for the dispersion was repeated (24:7-8): bloodshed **poured** out openly on rocks, **not . . . where the dust would cover it.** Jerusalem had shed innocent blood and had not even bothered to hide her crimes. That blood was crying out, figuratively speaking, for vengeance

(cf. Gen. 4:10; Lev. 17:13-14; Job 16:18). Because Jerusalem had openly shed the blood of others, God would openly shed **her blood on the bare rock.**

**24:9-14.** Ezekiel's second statement of judgment dealt specifically with the rusty pot. **The meat** in the pot was to be cooked "**well** done," picturing the slaughter of the Jerusalemites by Babylon. But God's judgment would go beyond the inhabitants to encompass the city of Jerusalem itself. **The empty pot** (Jerusalem without its inhabitants) was to be **set . . . on the coals . . . its impurities** were **melted and its deposit,** or rust, **burned away.** The city itself had to be destroyed to remove its impurities.

God had **tried to cleanse** His people **from** their **impurities** but they resisted all such efforts. Therefore they would experience the purifying work of God's **wrath.** God's patience had run out; **the time** had **come** for Him to judge. He would **not hold back** or **have pity.** God's mercy prompts Him to withhold judgment as long as possible to enable people to repent (cf. 2 Peter 3:8-10), but He does not wait indefinitely. A time comes when God punishes wickedness.

*g. The sign of the death of Ezekiel's wife (24:15-27)*

**24:15-17.** Ezekiel acted out through his own heartbreaking experience the inner pain about to be felt by all those Israelites already in captivity.

God explained the sign to Ezekiel, possibly in a dream at night (v. 18). The tragedy of the death of Ezekiel's wife (**the delight of** his **eyes;** cf. v. 21) would normally produce an outpouring of grief and sadness. But God told him **not** to **lament or weep or shed any tears.** He was to **groan quietly** and **not mourn for the dead.** He had to keep his personal feelings of loss bottled up inside; he was not allowed to follow normal mourning procedures (v. 17b; cf. Jer. 16:5-7).

**24:18-19.** Next **morning** Ezekiel told **the people** about his vision, and that **evening** his **wife died. The next morning,** when his wife would have been buried, he followed God's instructions and did not mourn openly. Because the event had been explained to **the people** in advance, they realized that the action had some national significance. So they **asked** him to explain what it meant.

**24:20-24.** Ezekiel explained that the death of his wife symbolized the destruction of God's temple and the slaughter of the people of Jerusalem—people loved by those in exile. Ezekiel had lost the "delight" of his "eyes" (v. 16) and the exiles would lose Jerusalem, **the delight of** their **eyes** (cf. v. 25), to Babylon. **Just as** Ezekiel had experienced a great personal tragedy, so those already in captivity would feel the tragedy when they heard about Jerusalem's fall and the massacre of their loved ones (**sons and daughters**) there.

The Jews in captivity would be devastated by the news of Jerusalem's fall, and the magnitude of destruction would render all grief inadequate. Normally when a personal tragedy occurs, friends and relatives gather to share in the grief of the one affected and to support him in his time of anguish and loss. But when Jerusalem fell everyone was in anguish because everyone was affected. The tragedy would be so awesome that any public expression of grief would seem insignificant. The Jews already in Babylon were to avoid all public display of grief just as **Ezekiel** had **done**. They would simply **waste away because of** their **sins** while groaning **among** themselves. The catastrophe would send all the exiles into a state of shock and would force them to acknowledge their Lord: **When this happens, you will know that I am the Sovereign LORD.**

**24:25-27.** When **the news** of Jerusalem's fall reached the exiles, the prophet's **mouth** would **be opened**; he would no **longer be silent.** Ezekiel had been commanded to remain silent before his fellow exiles except to pronounce the prophecies God gave him (cf. 3:25-27). His part-time dumbness would end when the prophecies he had delivered were confirmed (cf. 33:21-22).

## II. Judgment on Gentile Nations (chaps. 25–32)

The siege of Jerusalem had begun; it was only a matter of time till her destruction would be complete. So Ezekiel turned from Jerusalem to give messages against those nations surrounding it. If God would not spare His own people because of their sin, how could the nations around her hope to escape His judgment? God's judgment began in Is-

rael (chaps. 4–24), but it would extend from there to other nations (chaps. 25–32).

God's judgment on these nations is based on the Abrahamic Covenant (cf. Gen. 12:1-3; 15). Those who bless the descendants of Abraham will be blessed, and those who curse the descendants of Abraham will be cursed. Ezekiel pronounced God's curse on seven countries that contributed to Judah's downfall.

The first three—Ammon, Moab, Edom—formed the eastern boundary of Judah; the fourth nation, Philistia, was on her western boundary. Tyre and Sidon, cities of Phoenicia, were the principal powers north of Judah; Egypt was the major power to the southwest. God's judgment would extend out from Judah in all directions.

Ezekiel's first four prophecies (against Ammon, Moab, Edom, and Philistia) each cited the sin that prompted God's judgment and then described that judgment. These two parts form a "because/therefore" pattern. "Because" (*ya'an*) the nation had sinned against God's people, "therefore" (*lākēn*) God would punish them. Each prophecy closes with a statement of the result of its judgment: then "they will know that I am the LORD."

### A. Judgment on Ammon (25:1-7)

**25:1-2.** Ezekiel had already pronounced judgment on Ammon (21:28-32). Now Ammon was singled out to head the list of nations that would feel the sting of divine judgment.

Ammon and Israel had been in conflict since the time of Jephthah during the period of the Judges (Jud. 10:6–11:33). Saul fought with the Ammonites to rescue Jabesh Gilead (1 Sam. 11:1-11), and David conquered Ammon (1 Chron. 19:1–20:3). Sometime after the death of Solomon the Ammonites regained their independence and renewed their hostilities with Judah. During Jehoshaphat's reign the Ammonites joined the Moabites and Edomites in an unsuccessful attack on Judah (2 Chron. 20:1-30). Ammon tried to expand her territory at Israel's expense (cf. Jer. 49:1), and she even sided initially with Nebuchadnezzar in an attempt to gain additional territory after Jehoiakim's revolt, about 600–597 B.C. (cf. 2 Kings 24:1-2).

In 593 B.C. Ammon joined a secret meeting of other potential conspirators to consider rebelling against Babylon (cf. Jer. 27:1-7). That plan did not materialize, but in 588 B.C. she did unite with Judah and Tyre against Babylon. So two ancient enemies, Judah and Ammon, were joined against a common foe.

When Nebuchadnezzar decided to attack Judah instead of Ammon (cf. Ezek. 21:18-27), Ammon was relieved that she had been spared. Instead of coming to Judah's aid, she rejoiced over Judah's misfortune, hoping to profit territorially from Judah's destruction.

**25:3-7.** Against this background Ezekiel gave this prophecy. Twice he repeated his "because/therefore/you will know" formula to show the destruction of Ammon (vv. 3-5, 6-8). Ammon rejoiced over the destruction of the temple (mockingly saying **Aha!**) and the decimation and exile of **the people of Judah.** The Ammonites gloated over Judah's misfortune (v. 6).

God's judgment would fit Ammon's sin. They rejoiced over Judah's downfall so *they* would fall. God would send them **to the people of the East,** nomadic desert tribesmen, **as a possession.** These nomads would overrun the Ammonites, turning **Rabbah,** Ammon's capital city, **into a pasture for camels and Ammon into a resting place for sheep.** Because of Ammon's **malice** against **Israel,** Ammon would be plundered by other **nations** and destroyed (**cut . . . off**).

## B. Judgment on Moab (25:8-11)

The hostility between Moab and Israel began when Balak, king of Moab, tried to oppose Israel as Moses was leading them to Palestine (cf. Num. 22–24). During the time of the Judges, Israel was oppressed by Eglon, king of Moab (Jud. 3:12-30). Relations between the countries improved slightly after that, and some Israelites went to Moab during a famine. Through this contact Ruth the Moabitess entered Israel's history and the royal line of David.

The relationship between Moab and Israel again deteriorated during Saul's reign (cf. 1 Sam. 14:47). David conquered Moab and made it a vassal of Israel (2 Sam. 8:2); it remained under Israel's control through Solomon's reign. Moab rebelled against Israel years after Israel

and Judah split, during Jehoshaphat's regime (cf. 2 Kings 3:4-27). Moab united with Ammon and Edom in an ill-fated attempt to defeat Judah also during Jehoshaphat's reign (2 Chron. 20:1-23). Later Moab supported Babylon and attacked Judah after Jehoiakim's revolt, possibly hoping to gain additional territory (cf. 2 Kings 24:2). Moab then joined other nations and considered revolting from Babylon in 593 B.C. (cf. Jer. 27:1-7), but no evidence indicates that she ever did.

**25:8-11.** Moab's sin, Ezekiel said, was her contempt for God's people. **Moab and Seir said, Look, the house of Judah has become like all the other nations.** Seir was the name of the mountain range south of the Dead Sea that encompassed the country of Edom. The word became synonymous with the land of Edom (cf. 2 Chron. 20:10 with Num. 20:14-21). Edom was included here with Moab (though her own judgment comes next) because she was guilty of the same sin of envy and contempt. In their scorn Moab and Edom were denying God's promises to Israel. By minimizing Judah's position of centrality among the nations, they were profaning the name of God who had promised Judah that position.

Because **Moab** treated Judah with contempt, God would remove Moab's **glory** by exposing its northern **flank** to attack. He would destroy three towns: **Beth Jeshimoth, Baal Meon, and Kiriathaim.** Beth Jeshimoth guarded the ascent to the Medeba Plateau from the Plains of Moab by the Jordan River. Baal Meon and Kiriathaim were important fortresses on the Medeba Plateau.

In addition to losing her defenses Moab would also lose her freedom. God said He would **give Moab . . . to the people of the East,** the same fate as Ammon (cf. v. 4). The nomadic desert tribesmen who would overrun Ammon would also overrun **Moab.**

## C. Judgment on Edom (25:12-14)

Like Ammon and Moab, Edom was involved in a long series of conflicts with Israel. The strife actually began when Edom refused to let Israel cross her territory during the time of the wilderness wanderings (cf. Num. 20:14-21). Saul fought the Edomites (1 Sam. 14:47), and David finally captured Edom and made it a vassal state to Israel (2 Sam. 8:13-14). Solomon further exploited Edom and established Elath in Edom as Israel's seaport (cf. 1 Kings 9:26-28); but Edom opposed Solomon during the latter part of his reign (1 Kings 11:14-18). The nation continued as a vassal state after Israel and Judah split, and it was controlled by a governor from Judah till after the time of Jehoshaphat (1 Kings 22:47-48).

In the days of Jehoram (ca. 845 B.C.) Edom successfully rebelled against Judah (2 Kings 8:20-22a) and regained her freedom. Thereafter Judah and Edom struggled to see who would control the vital caravan and shipping routes at the southern end of the Transjordanian highway. Both Amaziah (2 Kings 14:7) and Uzziah (or Azariah, 2 Kings 14:21-22) regained territory that had been lost to Edom, but Edom counterattacked during Ahaz's reign and inflicted a major loss on Judah (2 Chron. 28:17).

Edom became a vassal of Babylon after Nebuchadnezzar's stunning defeat of Egypt in 605 B.C. Then in 593 B.C. Edom joined the other conspirators in planning to revolt against Babylon (cf. Jer. 27:1-7), but did not carry out the plan. When Judah revolted in 588 B.C., Edom sided with Babylon and aided Babylon in her assaults on Judah (cf. Ps. 137:7; Jer. 49:7-22).

**25:12-14.** Ezekiel said Edom's sin was that she **took revenge on the house of Judah.** Edom saw in Judah's conflict with Babylon an opportunity to oppose her rival. If her foe were destroyed then Edom could achieve a place of power at the southern end of the Dead Sea.

Because Edom had aided in Judah's destruction, God said He would aid in her destruction. He would **kill** Edom's **men and their animals . . . from Teman to Dedan.** Teman was a city in central Edom about three miles from Sela, later known as Petra. Dedan was southeast of Edom in northern Arabia. Perhaps Dedan was mentioned here because some Edomites were living there. Edom was conquered by the Nabateans during the intertestamental period. The remnant of the Edomites (also called Idumeans) moved west to the Negev. Later they were forced to become Jewish converts (Josephus *The Antiquities of the Jews* 13. 9. 1). Thus the Edomites lost both their country and their national identity.

God said **Israel** would bring His **vengeance** against the Edomites. As a result the Edomites would come to **know** (experience) His **vengeance.** This differs from what He had said about Ammon and Moab (vv. 7, 11).

### D. Judgment on Philistia (25:15-17)

The Philistines had been Israel's enemy from the time of the Conquest. Israel had failed to take all the Promised Land because she disobeyed God and because of the Philistines' military superiority on the coastal plain (cf. Jud. 3:1-4). Then the Philistines moved into the hill country in an attempt to control all the territory of Israel. They were opposed by the judges Shamgar (Jud. 3:31), Samson (Jud. 13–16), and Samuel (1 Sam. 7:2-17). Saul's major battles in Israel were designed to check the Philistines' advances on the central Benjamin plateau (1 Sam. 13:1–14:23) and in the Jezreel Valley (1 Sam. 28:1-4; 29:1-2, 11; 31:1-3, 7-10).

David finally subdued the Philistines. After a series of battles early in his reign blunted a Philistine challenge to his kingdom (2 Sam. 5:17-25), David was able to go on the offensive and defeat the Philistines (2 Sam. 8:1). Philistia remained a vassal country through the reign of Solomon and into the divided monarchy.

The battle between Philistia and Judah was renewed during the divided monarchy as each country tried to control the other. Jehoshaphat was able to dominate Philistia as a vassal state (2 Chron. 17:10-11), but she revolted against his son Jehoram and sacked Judah and Jerusalem (2 Chron. 21:16-17). Uzziah reestablished Judah's control over Philistia (2 Chron. 26:6-7), but Philistia again gained the upper hand in Ahaz's reign (2 Chron 28:16-18).

The feud between Philistia and Judah was halted by Babylon's intervention. Nebuchadnezzar established control over both countries. Yet the rivalry remained. Philistia waited for an opportunity to try again to conquer Judah.

**25:15-17.** Ezekiel placed his finger on Philistia's underlying sin. She **acted in vengeance and took revenge** (cf. v. 12) **with malice** (cf. v. 6), **and with ancient hostility** she **sought to destroy Judah.** Philistia's history included a string of attacks on God's Chosen People as they tried to dispossess Israel of the Promised Land.

Because Philistia had tried to destroy Judah, God would destroy her. He would **stretch out** His **hand** (cf. v. 13) **against the Philistines, and** would **cut off the Kerethites and destroy those remaining along the seacoast.** "Kerethites" (*kᵉrēṯîm*) was a synonym for the Philistines (cf. 1 Sam. 30:1-14; Zeph. 2:5). The word might have come from "Crete" which was known as "Caphtor" in Old Testament times (cf. Amos 9:7). Ezekiel used "Kerethites" here instead of "Philistines" to produce an interesting wordplay: God would "cut off" (*hiḵraṯî*) the "Kerethites" (*kᵉrēṯîm*).

During the intertestamental period the Philistines disappeared as a nation. This nation that had tried to usurp God's people discovered God's true character (**they will know that I am the LORD**; cf. Ezek. 25:7, 11) when He judged them for their sin.

### E. Judgment on Tyre (26:1–28:19)

After four short prophecies against the nations east and west of Israel (chap. 25) Ezekiel delivered a long prophecy against the city/nation of Tyre to the north of Israel. This section is actually four separate oracles, each beginning with "The word of the LORD came to me" (26:1; 27:1; 28:1, 11). The first oracle (26:2-21) was a direct prophecy of Tyre's destruction; the second prophecy (chap. 27) was a lament or funeral dirge for the fallen city. The third and fourth messages were directed against the "ruler" of Tyre (28:1-10) and the "king" of Tyre (28:11-19).

#### 1. DESTRUCTION OF THE CITY (CHAP. 26)

**26:1-2.** All but the first of four divisions in this chapter are introduced with the clause, "This is what the Sovereign LORD says" (vv. 7, 15, 19). This prophecy was given **in the 11th year, on the first day of the month.** The 11th year of Jehoiakim's exile was the year 587–586 B.C., but Ezekiel did not state which month. Since Jerusalem fell to Babylon on July 18, 586 B.C., possibly Ezekiel's prophecy against Tyre was prompted by Jerusalem's imminent collapse.

In verses 1-6 Ezekiel followed the "Because/therefore/then you will know" format he used in chapter 25. Tyre's sin was her greedy rejoicing over Jerusalem's fall, saying **Aha!** (cf. 25:3) Now that **Jerusalem** was destroyed, her **doors** would be **swung open** to **Tyre,** and Tyre would **prosper.** Both Tyre and Jerusalem had vied for the lucrative trade routes between Egypt and the rest of the Middle East. Tyre dominated the sea routes, but Jerusalem controlled the caravan routes. Tyre responded to Jerusalem's fall like a greedy merchant gloating over a rival's catastrophe. Without Jerusalem being able to secure the overland caravan routes, more products would be shipped by sea. So Tyre saw Jerusalem's fall as an opportunity to "corner the market" for trade.

**26:3-6.** God's judgment against **Tyre** fit her crime. He said, **I will bring many nations against you, like the sea casting up its waves.** Tyre's pride was her seagoing prowess. She knew the Mediterranean Sea better than most nations. So Ezekiel used the image of a violent ocean storm to picture God's punishment. Like ocean **waves,** invading nations would pound against Tyre's defenses, smashing her **walls** and **towers.** God added that He would **scrape away her rubble and make her a bare rock.** In an interesting wordplay Ezekiel described Tyre's fate. "Tyre" (*ṣōr*) means "rock" or a "hard pebble." God would make the "rock" (*ṣōr*) a barren crag (*sela'*). No longer being the central city of commerce, she would **become a place to spread fishnets.** Fishermen generally spread out their nets to dry on barren rocks, to keep them from becoming tangled in trees or bushes. Tyre would be so decimated that the once-bustling city would be barren enough to use as a drying place for nets.

The city of **Tyre** included the mainland and an island about a half mile off the coast. The main city was supported by many satellite communities or suburbs around it. People in these **settlements** (*bᵉnôṯèhā*, lit., "her daughters") **on the mainland** would be **ravaged by the sword.**

**26:7-14.** God said He would bring **from the north . . . Nebuchadnezzar.** Tyre's gloating over Jerusalem's fall would be short-lived. The **king** who destroyed Jerusalem would also attack **Tyre.** After defeating Jerusalem, Nebuchadnezzar moved his army north to Tyre in 585 B.C. and besieged the city for

13 years till all **settlements on the mainland** were destroyed. Tyre could hold out for all those years because her navy brought in supplies that would otherwise have been depleted. Nebuchadnezzar destroyed mainland Tyre (depicted graphically by Ezekiel, vv. 8-12), but not the island stronghold. However, other evidence indicates that the island surrendered to Nebuchadnezzar in 573–572 B.C. That year Baal II succeeded Ethbaal III to the throne of Tyre. Most likely this was a political move by Nebuchadnezzar to remove the rebellious king and install a loyal vassal king. Some think Ethbaal III was deported to Babylon, but 28:8-9 seems to indicate that Nebuchadnezzar assassinated him.

Ezekiel switched from the singular **he** to the plural **they** (26:12). Probably this shift pointed to the "nations" (v. 3) that followed Nebuchadnezzar in attacking Tyre, completing the destruction he began. Alexander the Great devastated the city in 332 B.C. when it refused to submit to his advancing forces. Alexander destroyed the mainland city and then built a causeway out to the island fortress which he destroyed. In doing this, he threw **stones, timber, and rubble into the sea.** Though Tyre recovered from Nebuchadnezzar's and Alexander's onslaughts, she never regained the power she held before these attacks.

The final destruction of Tyre would be complete, for God predicted the city **will never be rebuilt.** Today this once-great commercial center lies in ruins. Though the surrounding area has been rebuilt, the original site is a mute testimony to God's awesome judgment.

**26:15-18.** The third section of this prophecy discusses the response of Tyre's neighbors to her **fall.** These coastal powers, dependent on Tyre for their trade and commerce, would be dismayed at Tyre's fall. Tyre's fall would send shock waves throughout the maritime community (**the coastlands would tremble**). **The princes of the seacoast** would remove their trappings of luxury (**robes** and **garments**) and **sit** in mourning, **trembling** and **appalled at** the unbelievable fate of their chief benefactor. Sitting in mourning was a common way to express grief for a loved one or friend (cf. Job 2:11-13).

As Tyre's allies came to sit and mourn her passing, they also sang a funeral **lament,** contrasting her present condition with her former glory. **Tyre** had been a formidable **power on the seas,** reigning supremely on the eastern Mediterranean shores. Her fall sent **terror** rippling to every shore she had touched. With their source of supplies gone, those nations would suffer great economic loss.

**26:19-21.** In Tyre's demise she would descend into the underworld never to rise again. Ezekiel had said Tyre's fate was like an ocean sweeping over it (v. 3). Now again he said **the ocean depths** would sweep **over** Tyre. The most fearful prospect facing ancient mariners was to be caught in a storm and be "lost at sea." Tyre would drown in the ocean and all traces of her would be lost. This same point was made again in 27:26-35.

Ezekiel then changed the imagery slightly. Instead of descending into the ocean depths, Tyre would **go down to the pit** (*bôr*), a figurative way of expressing death. "Pit" is synonymous with "sheol" or "the grave" (Prov. 1:12; Isa. 14:15, 19; 38:18). In Old Testament times death was a fearful event. Though the saints had some idea of resurrection (cf. Heb. 11:17-19), most viewed the grave as a place of no return. Ezekiel expressed this thought about Tyre: she would enter the place of the departed dead and never be able to **return** to **the land of the living.** People would long for her, but she would **never again be found.**

## 2. DIRGE OVER THE CITY (CHAP. 27)

**27:1-4.** Ezekiel's second message against **Tyre** was a lament over the city's fall (cf. comments on chap. 19 about a funeral lament). Tyre's destruction was so certain (chap. 26) that the funeral dirge could begin. Chapter 27, in which **Tyre** is compared to a ship, could be called "The Sinking of Tyre's Ship of State." The first section (vv. 1-9), written in poetry, pictures Tyre's former glory by describing her, appropriately, as a beautiful ship. The second section (vv. 10-25), in both poetry and prose, enumerates Tyre's many trading partners. The third section (vv. 26-36), again in poetry, describes Tyre's catastrophic shipwreck. This chapter focuses on the many countries and cities associated commercially with Tyre (see the map "The World of

Jeremiah and Ezekiel" in the *Introduction to Jer.*).

Ezekiel was told to recite his lament to **Tyre,** the city **situated at the gateway to the sea, merchant of peoples on many coasts.** The lament centered on Tyre's reputation as a major seaport and merchant power. Tyre was like a proud ocean vessel: **Your domain was on the high seas; your builders brought your beauty to perfection.** Focusing on Tyre's pride at the beginning of the lament (vv. 3-4) intimates that this was the reason for her downfall (cf. 28:2-10).

**27:5-9.** The materials used in constructing Tyre's "Ship of State" emphasized the city's sound construction. Her connections with other nations supposedly guaranteed her security. The **timbers** (probably for the ship's hull) had been selected from the finest **pine trees from Senir,** the Amorite name for Mount Hermon (Deut. 3:9) north of the Sea of Chinnereth, later named the Sea of Galilee. The ship's **mast** was made from **a cedar from Lebanon.** The Lebanon cedar trees, prized for their height and strength, were exported for use in construction (cf. 1 Kings 4:33; 5:6; 1 Chron. 17:1-6; Ezra 3:7; Isa. 2:13). The sturdy **oars** for the ship were crafted **of oaks from Bashan,** the area east of the Sea of Chinnereth, famous for its oak forests (cf. Isa. 2:13; Zech. 11:2).

The **deck** of the ship was made **of cypress wood from . . . Cyprus** and was **inlaid with ivory.** So Tyre used four kinds of wood: pine, cedar, oak, and cypress.

The **sail** of this vessel was sewn from **fine embroidered linen from Egypt.** Egypt was known for its fine linen cloth (cf. Gen. 41:42; Prov. 7:16). The **awnings,** colored with **blue and purple** dye **from the coasts of Elishah,** were possibly tentlike canopies that helped protect crewmen from bad weather. The location of Elishah is unknown though some scholars identify it with Alashia, the ancient name for Cyprus. Other suggestions are that Elishah was in Greece, Italy, or Syria. The dye industry was common throughout the Mediterranean.

The crewmen of the ship were the best available. **Men of Sidon and Arvad** (Ezek. 27:8) manned the oars and **men** of **Tyre** were the **seamen.** Sidon, another seaport 20 miles north of Tyre (cf. 28:20-

23), was one of the oldest maritime powers (cf. Gen. 10:15-19). Arvad was an island off the coast of Syria. Both cities were known for their shipping. The earliest Phoenician ships each had 50 oarsmen and were quite fast. The later commercial ships were much longer and had a crew of up to 200 with two or three banks of oars on each side.

Also **on board** the ship were experienced repairmen, **veteran craftsmen of Gebal.** Because the **ships** were woodenhulled, the **seams** between the wood were caulked with pitch to help make the vessel watertight (cf. Gen. 6:14). The friction of the ocean could work the caulking loose and let water seep into the hold, so **shipwrights** were on board to make necessary repairs. Gebal was the name of the modern city of Jebeil, located on Syria's Mediterranean coast. The craftsmen of Gebal were famous builders (cf. 1 Kings 5:18).

Ezekiel pictured Tyre as a strong, seaworthy vessel. She was the pride of the fleet, built with the best materials and manned by the best crews. **All the ships of the sea** (i.e., other countries) **and their sailors came alongside to trade for** her **wares.**

**27:10-11.** Ezekiel then described the military and commercial activity of this mighty city (vv. 10-25). Tyre was protected by the best mercenary army that could be mustered. The **soldiers** included **men** from **Persia, Lydia, and Put.** Persia, east of Babylon, ultimately defeated the Babylonians in 539 B.C. Lydia, on the west coast of Asia Minor, is sometimes translated Lud. The country of Put has sometimes been associated with "Punt" (Somalia) in East Africa, but the connection is tenuous. It is better to associate Put with the area of present-day Libya. Both Lydia and Put supplied mercenary soldiers for the Egyptian army (cf. Jer. 46:8-9). These mercenaries were joined by men from **Arvad** (cf. Ezek. 27:8), **Helech,** and **Gammad.** Helech was the Akkadian name for the region of Cilicia (where the city of Tarsus, Paul's birthplace, was located) in southeastern Asia Minor. The location of "Gammad" is unknown.

**27:12-25.** Tyre's partners in commerce (see the chart "Tyre's Trading Partners") spanned the limits of the then-known world, and their products represented numerous kinds of merchandise.

## Tyre's Trading Partners
### Ezekiel 27:12-25

| Name | Location | Merchandise |
|------|----------|-------------|
| 1. Tarshish | Spain (?) | Silver, iron, tin, lead |
| 2. Greece | Modern Greece | Slaves, bronze implements |
| 3. Tubal | Eastern Turkey | Slaves, bronze implements |
| 4. Meshech | Central Turkey | Slaves, bronze implements |
| 5. Beth Togarmah | Eastern Turkey | Work horses, war horses, mules |
| 6. Rhodes* | Modern Rhodes | Ivory tusks, ebony |
| 7. Aram (or Edom)† | Syria (or Jordan) | Turquoise, purple fabric, embroidered work, fine linen, coral, rubies |
| 8. Judah | Palestine | Wheat, olive oil, balm, confections, honey |
| 9. Israel | Palestine | Wheat, olive oil, balm, confections, honey |
| 10. Damascus | Syria | Wine, wool |
| 11. Danites‡ | Aden(?) | Wrought iron, cassia (a bark for perfume), calamus (an herb) |
| 12. Greeks§ from Uzal | Yemen (or southeastern Turkey) | Wrought iron, cassia, calamus |
| 13. Dedan | Arabia | Saddle blankets |
| 14. Arabia | Arabia | Lambs, rams, goats |
| 15. Kedar | Arabia | Lambs, rams, goats |
| 16. Sheba | Southern Arabia | Spices, precious stones, gold |
| 17. Raamah | Southern Arabia | Spices, precious stones, gold |
| 18.-23. Haran, Canneh, Eden, Sheba, Asshur, Kilmad | Mesopotamia | Blue fabric, embroidered work, multicolored rugs |

*The Hebrew has "Dedan" (*d'dān*) while the Septuagint has "Rhodes" (*rōdān*). The difference in the Hebrew consonants is between a "d" (ד) and an "r" (ר). Since "Dedan" occurs again in verse 20, it is better to see "Rhodes" here.

†Most Hebrew manuscripts have "Aram" (*'ărām*) but some Hebrew manuscripts and the Syriac read "Edom" (*'ĕdōm*), and the Septuagint reads "men" (*'ādām*). The difference in the Hebrew consonants is between an "r" (ר) and a "d" (ד).

‡The "Danites" are not the tribe of Dan which had already been taken into captivity. The NASB translates the word as "Vedan." The best conjecture is that it should be associated with the city of Aden on the Persian Gulf.

§"Greeks" is the translation of "Javan" (cf. v. 13), but the Javan in verse 19 must be different from that of verse 13. "Javan" could be referring to a tribe by that name in Yemen, or "Uzal" could refer to the city of Izalla in the Anatolian foothills of Asia Minor.

The fact that Tyre traded with about two dozen nations and cities shows her vast influence and commercial expertise. Tyre's trading was so brisk that **the ships of Tarshish** were the **carriers for** Tyre's **wares** (v. 25). Tarshish does not refer to the origin of the ships. "Ships of Tarshish" probably referred to large vessels carrying **cargo** on the open **sea.** This was the kind of ship Hiram and Solomon built to bring cargo to Israel (2 Chron. 9:21; cf. 2 Chron. 20:36-37; Isa. 2:16).

**27:26-27.** Ezekiel was building to a climax. He had described the beautiful construction of the ship (vv. 1-9) and its successful commerce (vv. 10-25). Then in a lament he described the ship's catastrophic sinking (vv. 26-36). Ezekiel reverted to poetry to accentuate the tragedy.

Tyre's destruction came in the element where she was most at home—the open sea. In **the high seas . . . the east wind** would **break** the ship **to pieces.** Most ships tried to stay close to the shore to avoid the rough storms. But Tyre's ship of state, venturing in her commercialism on "the high seas," was caught in a violent storm. During the fall and winter, weather on the Mediterranean becomes unpredictable and travel is hazardous (cf. Acts 27:9-26). A storm from the east or northeast would blow a ship away from the coast and out into the ocean where there was little chance of its survival. Ezekiel was again using the "east wind" in a dual meaning (cf. comments on Ezek. 19:12). Here the violent storm from the east referred to Babylon, east of Tyre. Tyre's ship of state was about to go down with the loss of all her people and her **wealth.** She would **sink into the heart of the sea.**

**27:28-32.** The surrounding countries would mourn the loss of Tyre. **They would cry . . . sprinkle dust on their heads, and roll in ashes.** Also they would **shave their heads** and **put on sackcloth.** These were signs of intense grief associated with personal loss (cf. Es. 4:1-3; Job 1:20; 2:8; Jer. 6:26). These people would bemoan their loss by taking **up a lament concerning . . . Tyre.** Ezekiel recorded a second lament within his larger lament: **Who was ever silenced like Tyre, surrounded by the sea?** Those who traded with the once-bustling city of Tyre would be appalled at her sudden loss and silence.

**27:33-36.** Tyre's commercial activity had enriched others. She had **satisfied many nations** and had **enriched . . . kings.** Having benefited immensely from her trade, those other countries would feel the loss. Those who had profited from her would be **appalled** and **their kings** would **shudder with horror** and **fear.** These rulers were fearful because if the great city of Tyre could be destroyed by the Babylonians, their hope of escape was dim. **The merchants** would also whistle through their teeth **(hiss)** in shock at Tyre's demise. This action does not necessarily indicate derision or scorn (cf. 1 Kings 9:8, where "scoff" is incorrectly substituted for "hiss"; Jer. 49:17; 50:13). It more often expressed astonishment. The businessmen would be astonished because the "pride of the fleet" had **come to a horrible end.**

### 3. DOWNFALL OF THE PRINCE OF THE CITY (28:1-19)

**28:1-5.** Ezekiel's third message against Tyre was directed specifically **to the ruler of Tyre.** "Ruler" (*nāgîḏ*) means "the man at the top" (cf. 1 Sam. 9:16; 10:1; 13:14; 2 Sam. 7:8). Ezekiel had prophesied against the whole city; he was now singling out the city's leader for

a special **word** from God. This ruler then was Ethbaal III, who ruled from 591-590 B.C. to 573-572 B.C.

The underlying sin of Tyre's king was his **pride,** which prompted him to view himself as **a god.** His claim to deity is referred to again in Ezekiel 28:6, 9. Evidently in Ezekiel's day the kings of Tyre believed they were divine.

The king's claims to deity were false. God said, **You are a man and not a god.** Ethbaal III was only a mortal. Evidently he felt he had wisdom that only a god could possess. In a statement dripping with irony Ezekiel asked the king, **Are you wiser than Daniel? Is no secret hidden from you?** The "Daniel" in view was probably the Prophet Daniel (see comments on 14:14, 20). He had already achieved a reputation for his wisdom in the courts of Nebuchadnezzar (cf. Dan. 1:19-20; 2:46-49). The irony was that Ethbaal III felt his wisdom exceeded that of even Daniel who served the country that would ultimately defeat Tyre. Daniel, who attributed all his wisdom to God (cf. Dan. 2:27-28), was much wiser than Ethbaal III, who claimed to be a god.

Ethbaal III had been able to use his **wisdom** and **skill** to acquire material possessions. His lucrative trade had produced great **wealth,** including **gold and silver,** but it also increased his pride (his **heart** had **grown proud**).

**28:6-10.** God would not let the pride (vv. 2, 5) of Tyre's ruler go unchallenged. The **foreigners** whom God would **bring against** Tyre had already been identified as the Babylonians (26:7-11). Babylon was **ruthless** (*'ārîṣ,* "terror-striking") in her treatment of others (cf. 30:11; 31:12; 32:12). Unimpressed with Ethbaal's **beauty and wisdom,** Babylon would destroy him in a **violent** way **in the heart of the seas** (cf. 27:26). When slain by his enemies, it would be evident that he was no **god.** Ethbaal III was removed from his throne by Nebuchadnezzar in 573-572 B.C. and Baal II was put in his place. Ethbaal III paid a high price for rebelling against Nebuchadnezzar. In fact Ethbaal would **die the death of the uncircumcised at the hands of foreigners.** While the Phoenicians practiced circumcision, Ezekiel's words conveyed a meaning that went beyond this cultural practice. To "die the death of the uncircumcised" meant to die in shame (cf. 32:30; 1 Sam.

17:26, 36). This king who claimed to be a god would suffer an ignoble death as a man.

**28:11-19.** Ezekiel's final prophecy against Tyre was **a lament concerning the king of Tyre.** The use of "king" (*melek*) instead of "ruler" (v. 2) was significant. Ezekiel used the word "king" sparingly. Apart from King Jehoiachin (1:2) he did not use the title "king" of any of Israel's monarchs.

The change from "ruler" to "king" was also significant in light of the content of these two prophecies. In 28:1-10 Ezekiel rebuked the *ruler* for claiming to be a god though he was just a man. But in verses 11-19 Ezekiel described the *king* in terms that could not apply to a mere man. This "king" had appeared in the Garden of Eden (v. 13), had been a guardian cherub (v. 14a), had possessed free access to God's holy mountain (v. 14b), and had been sinless from the time he was **created** (v. 15).

Some think Ezekiel was describing Ethbaal III in highly poetic language, comparing him with Adam (both had great potential, but sinned; both were judged, etc.). But some of the language does not apply to Adam. For example, Adam was not a guardian cherub and did not have free access to the mountain of God. Also the descriptions in verses 13 and 16 do not fit the first man in the Garden of Eden. When Adam sinned he was not cast from the mountain **of God** to the earth (vv. 16-17), and no **nations** existed to be **appalled** at his fall (v. 19).

Other scholars have held that Ezekiel was describing the "god" behind the king of Tyre (perhaps Baal). God judged the ruler of Tyre (vv. 1-10) and the god of the city who empowered the ruler (vv. 11-19). But it seems incongruous that Ezekiel would give credence to a mythological tale of a god supporting the ruler of Tyre when much in his book showed the falsehood of pagan beliefs. Also Ezekiel's imagery was drawn from the biblical account of Creation, not from pagan mythologies.

Ezekiel was not describing an ideal man or a false god in verses 11-26. But his switch from "ruler" to "king" and his allusions to the Garden of Eden do imply that the individual being described was more than human. The best explanation is that Ezekiel was describing Satan who

was the true "king" of Tyre, the one motivating the human "ruler" of Tyre. Satan was in the Garden of Eden (Gen. 3:1-7), and his chief sin was pride (1 Tim. 3:6). He also had access to God's presence (cf. Job 1:6-12). Speaking of God's judging the human "ruler" of Tyre for his pride (Ezek. 28:1-10), the prophet lamented the satanic "king" of Tyre who was also judged for his pride (vv. 11-19). Tyre was motivated by the same sin as Satan, and would suffer the same fate.

Ezekiel described the beauty and perfection of Satan as God originally created him (vv. 12-15a). He was **the model of perfection, full of wisdom, and perfect in beauty.** God did not create Satan as some prime minister of evil. As with all God's Creation, Satan was a perfectly created being—one of the crowning achievements in God's angelic realm.

Satan was given an exalted place; he was **in Eden, the garden of God.** Eden was the epitome of God's beautiful Creation on earth (cf. Gen. 2:8-14). Satan's beauty matched that of Eden: **every precious stone adorned** him. Ezekiel listed nine gemstones in describing Satan's beauty. These were 9 of the 12 kinds of stones worn in the breastplate of Israel's high priest (cf. Ex. 28:15-20; 39:10-13). The precious stones probably symbolized Satan's beauty and high position.

God had **anointed** Satan **as a guardian cherub** (Ezek. 28:14). The cherubim (pl. of cherub) were the "inner circle" of angels who had the closest access to God and guarded His holiness (cf. 10:1-14). Satan also had free access to God's **holy mount** (28:14), heaven, and he **walked among the fiery stones** (cf. v. 16). Some associate "the fiery stones" with the precious gems (v. 13), but the stones there were part of Satan's attire whereas the stones in verses 14 and 16 were part of the abode where Satan dwelt. Others have identified the "fiery stones" with God's fiery wall of protection (cf. Zech. 2:5). They see Satan dwelling *inside* or *behind* God's outer defenses in the "inner courts" of heaven itself. This view is possible, and the word translated "among" (*mitôk*) can have the idea of "between" or "inside." Whatever the exact identification, Ezekiel was stating that Satan had access to God's presence.

As originally created by God, Satan

was **blameless** . . . **till wickedness was found in** him (Ezek. 28:15) **and he sinned** (v. 16). The sin that corrupted Satan was self-generated. Created blameless, his sin was pride (1 Tim. 3:6) because of his **beauty**. Satan spoiled his **wisdom because of** his **splendor** (cf. Ethbaal's similar problem, Ezek. 28:1-2, 5, 7). Satan's pride led to his fall and judgment.

Though Ezekiel presented the fall of Satan as a single act, it actually occurred in stages. Satan's initial judgment was his expulsion from the position of God's anointed cherub before His throne. God expelled him **from the mount of God** (heaven, v. 16; cf. v. 14). Satan was cast from God's government in heaven (cf. Luke 10:18) but was still allowed access to God (cf. Job 1:6-12; Zech. 3:1-2). In the Tribulation Satan will be cast from heaven and restricted to the earth (Rev. 12:7-13); in the Millennium he will be in the bottomless pit (Rev. 20:1-3); and after his brief release at the end of the Millennium (Rev. 20:7-9) he will be cast into the lake of fire forever (Rev. 20:10).

One of the elements of Satan's sin was his widespread **dishonest trade**. The word for trade comes from the verb *rākal* which means "to go about from one to another." Ezekiel had used that noun in speaking of Tyre's commercial activities (Ezek. 28:5). Does this mean Satan was operating a business? Obviously not. Instead, Ezekiel was comparing the human "prince" of Tyre and his satanic "king." So Ezekiel used a word that could convey a broad meaning. Satan's position in heaven involved broad contact with many elements of God's creation much as the prince of Tyre's position enabled him to contact many nations.

Though Ezekiel was describing the "ultimate" ruler of Tyre, Satan, the purpose of the lament was to speak of the city's destruction. So he began to blend the characteristics of the satanic king with the human ruler. Satan would be cast **to the earth** (v. 17), and the king of Tyre would also be cast down **before** other **kings,** his enemies. Satan's ultimate destiny will be the lake of fire (cf. Rev. 21:10), and the defeat and death of the human ruler of Tyre was pictured as being **consumed** by **fire** (Ezek. 28:18). Both Satan's and Tyre's defeats would shock those nations who had followed them. They would be appalled because of

Satan's and Tyre's **horrible end** (cf. 27:35-36).

### F. Judgment on Sidon (28:20-26)

**28:20-24.** This judgment **against Sidon** begins the same way as the oracles against Tyre. **The word of the LORD came to me** (cf. 26:1; 27:1; 28:1, 11). Sidon, a sister city of Tyre (cf. Jer. 25:22; 47:4; Joel 3:4; Zech. 9:2; Luke 6:17; 10:13-14), was 20 miles farther up the Mediterranean coast. Because of their close association, Ezekiel may have used this same introductory formula to link the two cities in judgment. Sidon was so closely allied with Tyre that perhaps Ezekiel felt it unnecessary to cite the same sins. She had violated God's holy character and He would not allow her sin to remain unpunished. He would **gain glory within** Sidon and **show** Himself **holy.** God's judgment would be by **a plague** and **the sword.**

The judgment on Sidon would have two results: (1) It would force the Sidonians to acknowledge God's righteous character—**They will know that I am the LORD** (stated in Ezek. 28:22, repeated in v. 23). (2) The judgment would remove an obstacle to Israel's walk with God. Their **malicious neighbors** with their wicked influence on Israel had been like a pain in Israel's side (painful **briers and sharp thorns**). The sinful practices of Baal worship had entered Israel through "Jezebel daughter of Ethbaal king of the Sidonians" (1 Kings 16:31).

**28:25-26.** The second part of Ezekiel's prophecy against Sidon focused on the results of the destruction for **Israel.** As God would reveal His holiness by destroying Sidon (v. 22), so He would reveal His holiness by rescuing Israel **from the nations.** Several times in the Book of Ezekiel God said, **I will show Myself holy** (20:41; 28:22, 25; 36:23; 38:16; 39:27). God punished Israel for her sin, but He has not abandoned her. She is unique among all **nations** because God had established His covenant with her. Though all nations would be punished, only Israel was promised a restoration of fellowship. The land promise made to Abraham (Gen. 13:14-17; 15:17-21) and renewed to Jacob (Gen. 35:11-13) has not been revoked. Israel **will live in** her **own land,** because God has given it to **Jacob.** Restored to her land, Israel will enjoy God's blessings, including **safety** and prosperity. This promise, made through Ezekiel, has never been literally fulfilled; it awaits fulfillment in the millennial kingdom. After the Babylonian Captivity, some Israelites did go back to the land (cf. Neh. 1:3) but they did not **live there in safety.** When God finally punishes Israel's enemies and blesses His Chosen People, they will recognize their Lord: **they will know that** He is **the LORD their God.**

### G. Judgment on Egypt (chaps. 29–32)

The seventh and final nation Ezekiel prophesied against was Egypt. This prophecy was actually a series of seven oracles directed against Egypt and its Pharaoh. Each oracle is introduced by the clause, "The word of the LORD came to me"; and six of the seven oracles are dated (29:1, 17; 30:1 [undated], 20; 31:1; 32:1, 17). Though 29:1; 30:20; 31:1; 32:1; and 32:17 are in chronological order, 29:17 (the second oracle) is dated later than the others. This departure from his usual chronological arrangement is probably because Ezekiel wanted to arrange the oracles in a logical progression. He possibly placed 29:17-21 where he did to clarify his first prophecy (29:1-16). After predicting that the Pharaoh and Egypt would be destroyed (29:1-16), he then specified who would destroy them (29:17-21).

#### 1. THE SIN OF EGYPT (29:1-16)

This prophecy includes three sections, each of which closes with the words seen so often in Ezekiel, "then they will know that I am the LORD" (vv. 6a, 9, 16).

**29:1-6a.** This first of seven prophecies against Egypt was given **in the 10th year, in the 10th month on the 12th day.** That day, January 5, 587 B.C., was almost a year after the siege of Jerusalem began (cf. 24:1-2).

The **Pharaoh** in **Egypt** at that time was Hophra who reigned from 589 to 570 B.C. His promises of assistance prompted Judah to break with Babylon. Both Egypt and her leader were singled out for judgment.

Ezekiel compared **Pharaoh** to a **great monster** in Egypt's **streams.** "Monster" (*tannîm,* a variant spelling of *tannîn*) described reptiles, from large snakes (Ex. 7:9-10) to giant sea monsters (Gen. 1:21). It probably included crocodiles. This word was also used in Semitic mythology to describe the chaos-monster who was destroyed when the world was created. Possibly Ezekiel had both ideas in mind. Reptiles in the Nile (especially crocodiles) symbolized Egypt's strength and ferocity. Egyptians believed that Pharaoh could conquer the chaos-monster; but here, ironically, God called Pharaoh the monster! Pharaoh was considered a god; therefore he thought of himself as having created **the Nile** (cf. Ezek. 29:9). Pharaoh, however, would soon learn he was no match for the true Creator-God. God said He would drag Egypt away from her place of protection in the Nile and **leave** her **in the desert.** This depicts God's subduing a crocodile (or the mythological "god" who lived in the water) and dragging him to a barren place where he would soon perish. God would defeat **Egypt** despite her great strength.

**29:6b-9.** The second section of this prophecy deals with Egypt's basic sin: she had **been a staff of reeds for the house of Israel.** A "staff" was used as a cane or walking stick for support on the rough terrain in Israel (cf. Zech. 8:4; Mark 6:8; Heb. 11:21). Israel leaned on Egypt for support in her revolt against Babylon, but Egypt's support was as fragile as the reeds which grew abundantly on the Nile River's shores. When the pressure came, the reed snapped, and Israel found herself unable to stand. Possibly Ezekiel was quoting a proverb commonly applied to Egypt which had a reputation as an unreliable ally (cf. 2 Kings 18:20-21).

The time of this prophecy probably coincided with Egypt's halfhearted attempt to aid Jerusalem during Nebuchadnezzar's siege (cf. Jer. 37:4-8). Egypt backed out and Jerusalem suffered the consequences. Jerusalem learned too late that a slender reed could not give support. When she leaned on Egypt for deliverance from Babylon, Egypt let her down (like a reed, she **splintered** and **broke**).

Because of Egypt's false promises of support to Judah, God said He would punish the Egyptians by the **sword** and **Egypt** would **become a desolate wasteland.**

**29:10-16.** This portion of Ezekiel's

prophecy discusses the extent of God's judgment on **Egypt**. The desolation would extend **from Migdol to Aswan, as far as the border of Cush.** "Migdol" was in the Delta region in northern (lower) Egypt and "Aswan" (or "Syene") was at the first cataract in southern (upper) Egypt and was the southern boundary between Egypt and Cush. Cush corresponds to present-day southern Egypt, Sudan, and northern Ethiopia.

God's total devastation of **Egypt** would last **for 40 years.** Judah had been destroyed because she relied on Egypt; Egypt would suffer the same fate. God would **disperse** Egypt **among the nations**; she would also be carried into **captivity.**

No archeological finding has yet confirmed an Egyptian deportation similar to the one experienced by Israel. However, it is unwise to dismiss a clear statement of Scripture on the basis of incomplete archeological data. Nebuchadnezzar did attack Egypt (29:17-21; cf. Jer. 43:8-13; 46:1-25). Assuming that he conquered the country, one would expect him to deport people to Babylon as he did others he conquered. Presumably, then, the Egyptian captives would have been allowed to return home in the reign of Cyrus of Persia, who defeated Babylon in 539 B.C. (ca. 33 years after Nebuchadnezzar's attack). Allowing seven additional years for the people to return and rebuild, a 40-year period of desolation was entirely possible.

God would then take the Egyptians **back . . . to Pathros, the land of their ancestry.** "Pathros" (cf. 30:14) was a geographic region located in southern (upper) Egypt. Some feel that this was the traditional birthplace of the nation of Egypt. Perhaps "Pathros" was used here to represent the entire land of Egypt.

Though God would let **the Egyptians** return to their land, Egypt would not achieve the place of power she once held. Instead she would be **the lowliest of kingdoms.** After Persia's rise to power, Egypt never again in biblical times became a major international power. She tried to exert herself during the intertestamental period, but she was held in check by Greece, Syria, and Rome. Egypt's political weakness would be a continual object lesson to **Israel.** She would look at **Egypt** and remember her

folly of depending on men instead of God.

2. THE DEFEAT OF EGYPT BY BABYLON (29:17-21)

**29:17-21.** Ezekiel's second prophecy against Egypt came **in the 27th year, in the first month on the first day.** This is the latest dated prophecy in the Book of Ezekiel. The date was April 26, 571 B.C. As stated earlier, Ezekiel probably placed this prophecy out of chronological order to draw attention to his logical progression. He had just described Egypt's coming judgment (vv. 1-16); he placed verses 17-21 afterward to indicate who would bring the judgment. **Nebuchadnezzar** himself would attack Egypt.

This prophecy was written shortly after Tyre's surrender to Babylon in 572 B.C. For 13 years Nebuchadnezzar had besieged the city of Tyre (585-572 B.C.). The picture of heads **rubbed bare** because of the prolonged wearing of helmets and of shoulders that were **raw** from carrying wood and stone for building siege mounds is graphic. Nebuchadnezzar had worked hard for meager results. **Yet he . . . got no reward from** that **campaign . . . against Tyre.** Tyre surrendered to Nebuchadnezzar, but there were no vast spoils of war to distribute as booty to his army. Evidently Tyre shipped off her wealth before she surrendered.

**Nebuchadnezzar** needed money to pay his soldiers for their labor so he turned to **Egypt.** Prompted by economic necessity, Babylon attacked Egypt and plundered **its wealth** to **pay . . . his army.** Yet it was really God who was "paying" Babylon to attack Egypt: **I have given him Egypt as a reward for his efforts.**

Ezekiel's second prophecy against Egypt ended with a promise to Israel. **That day** is interpreted in various ways. Some see a reference to a still future day of the Lord when God will restore Israel to her land and judge the nations around her. However, such a jump seems foreign to the text. The "day" in question was probably the time when God would judge Egypt through Babylon and then restore Egypt to her land.

When God finally restored the nations of Israel and Egypt, He would **make a horn grow for . . . Israel.** A horn symbolized strength (cf. 1 Sam. 2:1; 2 Sam. 22:3; 1 Kings 22:11; Jer. 48:25) and was applied in an ultimate sense to the strength of the Messiah, Christ, who would deliver Israel (cf. Luke 1:69). However, here the "horn" probably refers to Israel's strength which Nebuchadnezzar had destroyed. When Egypt was restored, Israel would also be restored as a nation.

When Israel's strength as a nation was renewed, God said He would **open** Ezekiel's **mouth among them.** This cannot refer to the ending of Ezekiel's divine dumbness (cf. Ezek. 3:26) for two reasons: (1) Ezekiel's dumbness had already ended in the 12th year of Jehoiachin's exile (33:21-22), and this prophecy came in the 27th year (29:17). (2) This prophecy would take place **after** Israel was restored from captivity. Ezekiel was 30 years old in 592 B.C. (1:1-2), so he would have been 83 when Cyrus' edict to let Israel return to her land was issued. Perhaps an 83-year-old might not have survived such an arduous journey from Babylon to Israel. None of the postexilic records refer to Ezekiel returning to Israel. The best explanation is that Ezekiel's spoken prophecies which had perplexed the people would become clear when they were fulfilled. Israel would recognize God's character as He faithfully accomplished His promise.

3. THE DESTRUCTION OF EGYPT AND HER ALLIES (30:1-19)

**30:1-5.** Unlike Ezekiel's other prophecies against Egypt, he did not date this one, which stressed Babylon's judgment on Egypt and her allies. It has four sections, each beginning with **This is what the** "LORD" (or **Sovereign LORD**) **says** (vv. 2, 6, 10, 13).

In verses 2-5 Ezekiel discussed the day of the Lord. **Wail and say, Alas for that day! For the day is near, the day of the LORD is near—a day of clouds, a time of doom for the nations.** Clouds often pictured doom (cf. v. 18; 32:7-8; 34:12; Joel 2:2; Zeph. 1:15). Though some think this refers to the future day of the Lord when God will judge the world for her sin, that view divorces the phrase from its context. True, "the day of the LORD" usually refers to God's future judgment on the earth (cf. Isa. 13:6-16; 34:8; Mal. 4). It will be a time when Israel and the nations will be judged and when Israel will be restored to her place of national blessing. However, the "day" of the Lord can refer to any time God comes in judgment (cf. Lam. 2:21-22 and see comments under "Major Interpretive Problems" in the *Introduction* to Joel). Both Israel and Judah experienced a "day" of God's judgment when they were punished for their sins (cf. Ezek. 7:1-14, esp. vv. 7, 10, 12). Now God's "day" of judgment would extend to **Egypt,** who would be defeated by Babylon (cf. 30:10-12).

God's judgment—"a time of doom" —would lead to death and destruction. The **sword** drawn **against** Israel (21:1-17) would also overtake Egypt, and **anguish** would extend to **Cush,** adjoining Egypt on the south, out of fear that she would be attacked next (cf. 30:9). Egypt's people would be killed and her treasuries looted.

Egypt's allies would also be caught in her judgment. Egypt had many mercenary soldiers in her army (Jer. 46:8-9, 20-21). **Cush,** as stated earlier, refers to present-day southern Egypt, Sudan, and northern Ethiopia (Es. 1:1; Jer. 46:9; Ezek. 27:10). **Put** is modern-day Libya (Isa. 66:19; Jer. 46:9; Ezek. 27:10), and **Lydia** was on the west coast of Asia Minor (cf. 27:10). The words **all Arabia** could read "all the mixed people." Only one vowel in these Hebrew words makes this difference. Jeremiah used these same words to refer to all the foreigners residing in Egypt (cf. Jer. 25:20).

The Hebrew word translated **Libya** is actually "Cub" (*kûb,* NIV marg.). The normal Hebrew word for Libya is *lûb,* as in Nahum 3:9. No manuscript evidence warrants a change from *kûb* to *lûb.* It seems better to read "Cub" and to admit that the exact location of this nation is unknown. **The people of the covenant land** probably refers to those Israelites who fled to **Egypt** to avoid Nebuchadnezzar's attacks against Judah (cf. Jer. 42:19-22; 44:1-14).

**30:6-9.** Ezekiel continued to discuss the defeat of Egypt's mercenary **allies** within Egypt's borders. Throughout the land, **from Migdol to Aswan** (the northern and southern extremities of Egypt [see the map in the *Introduction* to Jer.]; cf. Ezek. 29:10). These allies would be crushed and the **cities** where they had settled would be ruined. The destruction would force these nations to acknowledge the God who predicted their downfall: **Then they will know that I am the LORD.**

The news of **Egypt's** destruction would spread rapidly, causing panic among her allies. **Messengers** would travel in ships up the Nile River south to **Cush** to announce Egypt's defeat. The news would cause panic in Cush because they, having sided with Egypt against Babylon, would now be vulnerable to attack. **Anguish** would **take hold of them** (cf. 30:4). "The day of the LORD" (v. 3) was now explained as **the day of Egypt's doom.** God's day of judgment on **Egypt** would surely take place.

**30:10-12.** The third section of this prophecy again zeroed in on the means of destruction against **the hordes of Egypt.** "Hordes" was mentioned 14 times in chapters 30–32 by Ezekiel, apparently to stress that proud nation's teeming populace. Egypt's judgment would come **by the hand of Nebuchadnezzar** (cf. 29:17-21). God selected Babylon, **the most ruthless of nations** (cf. 28:7; 30:10-11; 32:12), to accomplish His judgment. Babylon treated her captives cruelly. After King Zedekiah of Judah rebelled, Nebuchadnezzar forced him to watch soldiers kill all his sons. Then Zedekiah's eyes were put out so the last thing he ever saw was his sons' deaths (2 Kings 25:7). Ezekiel said that Babylon, after defeating Judah, would turn her cruel war machine against Egypt, killing the Egyptians with **swords** (cf. Ezek. 30:4).

In describing Babylon's attack, Ezekiel carefully pointed up the ultimate Source of destruction. Three times in verses 10-12 God said "I will" do this. Babylon was only a tool God used to accomplish His judgment. God declared that **by the hand of foreigners I will lay waste the land.** For the fifth time in this book God called the Babylonians "foreigners" (7:21; 11:9; 28:7, 10; 30:12).

**30:13-19.** In this fourth section of the prophecy Ezekiel enumerated the many places in Egypt that would be destroyed. No major city there would escape God's wrath. First, God said He would **destroy the idols and . . . put an end to the images in Memphis** (cf. v. 16). According to legend, Memphis was the first capital of united Egypt (ca. 3200 B.C.). But later, when Memphis was no longer the capital, the city still was important as a religious center. Numerous temples were built there. A colony of Jews had settled in Memphis (cf. Jer. 44:1).

Other cities would also feel the sting of judgment. **Pathros** was an area about midway between Cairo and Aswan. "Pathros" was a synonym for upper Egypt (cf. Jer. 44:1) and possibly for all Egypt (cf. Ezek. 29:14). **Zoan** was a royal residence in the Delta region (cf. Ps. 78:12, 43; Isa. 19:11, 13). Later Zoan was called Tanis by the Greeks. **Thebes** (or No), mentioned three times in this passage (Ezek. 30:14-16), was in southern (upper) Egypt about 400 miles south of Cairo at the site of modern Karnak and Luxor. For a long time it was the country's capital. The city was destroyed by the Assyrians in 663 B.C. (cf. Nahum 3:8-10) but was rebuilt. Jeremiah also predicted Thebes' destruction (cf. Jer. 46:25). **The hordes** of people there would be slain and the city would be **taken** suddenly **by storm.**

**Pelusium** would receive God's **wrath** (Ezek. 30:15), and when **fire** would spread through **Egypt, Pelusium** would **writhe in agony** (v. 16). Pelusium (or Sin) was in the Delta about a mile from the Mediterranean Sea. The city was a major military center and guarded the northern entrance to Egypt. Appropriately Ezekiel called it **the stronghold of Egypt.**

Ezekiel named the last three of the eight cities of Egypt in verses 17-18: **Heliopolis . . . Bubastis,** and **Tahpanhes.** Heliopolis (or On) was in northern (lower) Egypt just south of the Delta region. It was a major religious center during much of Egypt's ancient history. Possibly Jeremiah had Heliopolis in mind when he predicted the destruction of "the temple of the sun in Egypt" (cf. Jer. 43:13). Bubastis (or Pi Beseth) was northeast of the modern city of Cairo, in northern (lower) Egypt. Bubastis served briefly as a capital of Egypt, and it too was an important religious center. Tahpanhes was near the present Suez Canal. In Jeremiah's day Pharaoh had a palace in that city (Jer. 43:9) which may be why Ezekiel mentioned it last—for climactic effect. Jeremiah condemned that city along with Memphis (cf. Jer. 2:16). He was forced to go there after Gedaliah was assassinated (Jer. 43:7-8).

By naming Egypt's major cities God

was saying that the **strength** of the entire nation would be ended, like the breaking of a **yoke. She** would **be covered with clouds,** a figurative way to express doom and judgment (cf. Ezek. 30:3; 32:7-8; 34:12; cf. Joel 2:2; Zeph. 1:15). As gathering clouds herald an approaching storm, so covering Egypt with clouds would herald her coming judgment. Major cities would be destroyed, and people in the **villages** would be taken **into captivity.**

### 4. THE SCATTERING OF EGYPT (30:20-26)

**30:20-26.** Ezekiel's fourth of seven prophecies against Egypt was given **in the 11th year, in the first month on the seventh day.** That date was April 29, 587 B.C., almost four months after Ezekiel's first prophecy against Egypt (29:1). The first prophecy signified the time when the forces of Egypt went out to "rescue" Israel from Babylon (cf. Jer. 37:4-5); the fourth prophecy was recorded after the Babylonians defeated Egypt. The theme of the prophecy was Egypt's defeat by God: **I have broken the arm of Pharaoh king of Egypt.** This Pharaoh was Hophra, who ruled Egypt from 589 to 570 B.C. Possibly the days between the first and fourth prophecies were approximately the length of time the siege on Jerusalem was lifted as Babylon repositioned its army to meet the Egyptian attack.

Nebuchadnezzar broke the "arm" of Egypt so she was unable to defend Judah. In fact the damage done to Egypt was irreparable. Egypt's arm, symbolizing strength, was not even **put in a splint so as to become strong enough to hold a sword.**

Egypt "broke her arm" in her feeble attempt to rescue Israel, but this was only a prelude to God's full judgment. God said He would **break both** of Egypt's **arms, the good arm as well as the broken one.** In other words God would totally destroy Egypt's strength. Her ability to protect both others and herself would be eliminated.

Though God would destroy the power of Egypt, He would strengthen the power of Egypt's chief foe, **Babylon.** Nebuchadnezzar's **arms** would be strengthened by God, and **Pharaoh,** groaning **like a mortally wounded man,** would be utterly defenseless before the Babylonians.

Ezekiel's point was to contrast the recent defeat suffered by Egypt (her one "broken arm") with the still greater defeat she would suffer. She had been disarmed when she tried to intervene in Babylon's attack on Jerusalem, but she would later be destroyed by **Babylon.** When Nebuchadnezzar attacked **Egypt** herself, she would fall to him (cf. Ezek. 29:1-20). God would then **disperse** Egypt **among the nations** (a fact stated twice for emphasis; 30:23, 26; cf. 29:12). Egypt would follow Judah into exile.

### 5. THE SIMILARITY OF EGYPT AND ASSYRIA (CHAP. 31)

Ezekiel's fifth prophecy against Egypt is an allegory on Pharaoh's fall.

#### a. The allegory of Assyria as a cedar tree (31:1-9)

**31:1-9.** This prophecy was given **in the 11th year, in the third month on the first day.** This was June 21, 587 B.C., less than two months after the prophecy recorded in 30:20-26. Ezekiel addressed his message **to Pharaoh king of Egypt and to his hordes.** He ended it with the same words (31:18). This ruler (Hophra) and his mighty army obviously felt so secure in their military might and ability that Ezekiel responded rhetorically, **Who can be compared with you in majesty?** Obviously Egypt thought she was in a class by herself.

Ezekiel offered an example against whom Egypt could compare herself: **Consider Assyria.** Some scholars think that "Assyria" ('aššûr) should be emended to read "cypress tree" (or "pine tree") (te'aššûr) because of the difficulty in understanding why Ezekiel would mention Assyria in his prophecies against Egypt. However, there is no need to alter the text. Assyria would have had great significance to Egypt for two reasons. First, Assyria had been the only Mesopotamian nation to invade Egypt. In 633 B.C. Assyria had entered Egypt and destroyed the capital of Thebes (cf. Nahum 3:8-10). So the only nation that could be "compared" with Egypt was Assyria. Second, Assyria had been destroyed by Babylon, the same nation Ezekiel said would enter Egypt and destroy *it.*

Ezekiel compared Assyria to **a cedar in Lebanon.** (A lofty cedar also depicted the leaders of Israel; cf. Ezek. 17.) At the apex of her power Assyria dominated the Middle East, towering like a cedar **higher than all the trees of the field** (31:5). Several key cities of Assyria were situated at or near the Tigris River, which provided much-needed water. Thus situated, Assyria grew like a cedar nourished by **waters . . . deep springs** (v. 4), and **abundant waters** (vv. 5, 7). **Birds** in the cedar's **branches** and animals under its shade (v. 6; cf. vv. 12, 17) speak of Assyria, like a tall tree, overshadowing and protecting all her neighbors.

In a hyperbole Ezekiel stressed Assyria's grandeur: **The cedars in the garden of God** (Eden; cf. 28:13) **could not rival it.** This "tree" was unmatched by any of God's other "trees." In fact this tree was **the envy of all the trees of Eden.**

In Assyria's former exalted position, she had attained power and influence that far exceeded Egypt's. She was the perfect example to show Egypt the effects of God's judgment.

### b. The downfall of Assyria (31:10-14)

**31:10-14.** Assyria fell because of her pride. God judged the nation **because, like a cedar, it towered on high, lifting its top above the thick foliage, and because it was proud of its height.** Judah (16:56), Tyre (27:3; 28:2), and Egypt (30:6) would all be judged for their pride.

God judged Assyria by handing **it over to the ruler of the nations.** He was Nebuchadnezzar who, following in his father's footsteps, continued to expand the borders of Babylon at Assyria's expense. God ordained Assyria's fall (cf. Nahum). The city of Nineveh fell to Nabopolassar (Nebuchadnezzar's father) in 612 B.C., and the rest of the Assyrian army was crushed by Nebuchadnezzar in 609 B.C. at Haran (see "Historical Background" in the *Introduction* to Jer.).

**The most ruthless of foreign nations** (i.e., Babylon; cf. 28:7; 30:11; 32:12) **cut . . . down** Assyria, like felling a large tree. Then those who had sought protection **under** Assyria's **shade** (cf. 31:6, 17) abandoned her.

Assyria's fall was an object lesson to other nations. **No other trees so well-watered are ever to reach such a height** (v. 14). Egypt's desire to become a lasting great power in the Middle East was destined to failure. She and all other nations

were **destined for** the grave (**death** and **the pit**) instead of glory. (The "pit" is the place of the departed dead; see comments on 26:20-21.) No nation should exalt itself highly over others because they will all suffer Assyria's fate.

### c. The descent of Assyria into the grave (31:15-18)

**31:15-18.** Having mentioned death (v. 14), Ezekiel expanded and applied that fact by focusing on the reaction of other nations to Assyria's fall (vv. 15-18). The nations mourned her (the **springs** were held back by their **mourning**) and were alarmed (**the nations tremble**) that one as strong and mighty as Assyria could ever **fall.** If the strong "cedar" could fall, then how could any lesser "trees" (nations) hope to remain standing?

While the nations were alarmed, those that had already been destroyed (**all the trees of Eden**) were comforted and **consoled in the earth below** (in the grave). The lesser nations, their **allies** who had **lived in** Assyria's **shade** (cf. vv. 6, 12) and were now in the **grave**, could comfort themselves that even Assyria had descended to where they were. All were equal in death.

Assyria's "allies among the nations" brought the circle back to Egypt because she was Assyria's chief ally when Assyria fell to Babylon. Ezekiel drove home the point of his allegory (v. 18): **Which of the trees of Eden can be compared with you in splendor and majesty?** This was similar to the question in verse 2, but the answer was now obvious. Egypt, who was similar to Assyria, would suffer the same fate. She too would be **brought down with the trees of Eden to the earth below.** Egypt's end would be one of shame like that of **the uncircumcised** (see comments on 28:10; 32:19). And her fall would be fatal, **by the sword.** For emphasis Ezekiel repeated the subject of his story: **This is Pharaoh and all his hordes** (cf. 31:2).

### 6. THE LAMENT FOR PHARAOH (32:1-16)

**32:1-2a.** Ezekiel's sixth prophecy against Egypt was given **in the 12th year, in the 12th month on the first day.** That was March 3, 585 B.C.—two months after the news of Jerusalem's fall reached the captives in Babylon (cf. 33:21). The fall of

Egypt was now so certain that Ezekiel was told to **take up a lament concerning Pharaoh king of Egypt.** A lament, or funeral dirge, was usually delivered when one was buried. (For an explanation of a lament see the comments on chap. 19.) Ezekiel had already written laments for Judah (chap. 19), the city of Tyre (26:17-18; 27), and the king of Tyre (28:12-19). The lament against Egypt is in three parts (32:2b, 3-10, 11-16). The second and third sections each begin with, "This is what the Sovereign LORD says" (vv. 3, 11).

**32:2b.** Ezekiel said Pharaoh (Hophra), in his fierce power, was **like a lion** (cf. Judah's kings, 19:2-9) **among the nations** and **a monster in the seas** (cf. 29:2-5). The "monster" could refer to a crocodile or to the mythological chaos-monster, to picture Pharaoh's ferocity and seeming invulnerability. Possibly the crocodile is suggested as Ezekiel said Pharaoh was **churning** up the normally placid **water** (cf. Job 41:31-32). Pharaoh's actions were disturbing the international scene as he tried to blunt Babylon's power.

**32:3-10.** Ezekiel then spoke of Pharaoh's judgment. If Pharaoh were a crocodile, God would lead Pharaoh's enemies on a "crocodile hunt." **With a great throng of people I will cast My net over you, and they will haul you up in My net** (cf. 29:3-5). Pharaoh would be trapped by his enemies and removed from his sphere of power. This was an amazing statement, for in Egypt the Pharaoh supposedly could defeat a crocodile! (Cf. comments on Job 41.) God would drag Pharaoh from his place of power and **throw** him **on the land and hurl** him **on the open field.** Pharaoh's power would be broken and his people scattered.

The destruction of Pharaoh and Egypt was couched in terms that conjured up images of Egypt's judgment at the time of the Exodus. God said He would **drench the land** with Egypt's **flowing blood** (Ezek. 32:6). This recalled the first plague on Egypt in which the water turned to blood (Ex. 7:20-24). But this time, the blood would come from the slain in Egypt. God also said He would **darken** the **stars . . . sun,** and **moon,** bringing **darkness over** the **land** (Ezek. 32:7-8). Though these cataclysmic signs are similar to those that will accompany

the day of the Lord (Joel 2:30-31; 3:15), it seems Ezekiel was alluding here to the darkness of the ninth plague (Ex. 10:21-29).

In response to Egypt's fall the surrounding nations would **be appalled** (cf. Ezek. 26:16; 27:35; 28:19) **and their kings** would **shudder with horror.** God's revealing His holy character through Egypt's judgment would have a profound effect on other nations. If mighty Egypt could be destroyed, so could they.

**32:11-16.** This third section of Ezekiel's lament drops the figurative description of destruction (vv. 3-8) and portrays Egypt's fall to Babylon literally. **The sword of the king of Babylon will come against you.** Pharaoh's army would be crushed by the ruthless Babylonians (cf. 29:17-21; 30:10-12, 24) and the land of **Egypt** would be decimated. Egypt's **pride** would be shattered, **her hordes . . . overthrown** (cf. comments on "hordes" in 30:10), and **her cattle** by the Nile and streams destroyed. Both man and beast would be affected by the coming attack.

The waters that were once **stirred by the foot of man** and **muddied by the hoofs of cattle** would now be stilled. Figuratively Pharaoh had "muddied the waters" with his international intrigue (32:2); literally the Nile was muddied through the daily activities of man and beast (v. 13). But now the streams and rivers would **settle** because those activities would be curtailed through death and deportation. The **streams** would **flow like oil,** smoothly, undisturbed.

Like professional "chanters" the surrounding nations (**daughters of the nations;** cf. v. 18) would be "hired" as mourners to **chant** a dirge over Egypt's fall.

7. THE DESCENT OF EGYPT INTO SHEOL (32:17-32)

**32:17-21.** Ezekiel's last of seven prophecies against Egypt came **in the 12th year, on the 15th day of the month.** The month was not named, but many interpreters assume it was the same month as the previous prophecy (v. 1). If so, the date of this message was March 17, 585 B.C., exactly two weeks after the preceding message. The message's theme was the consignment of the hosts of **Egypt** to sheol. Since the language is highly poetic, Ezekiel's purpose was not to give a precise description of the after-life. However, he did indicate that after death a person has no opportunity to change his destiny.

In his own funeral dirge for Egypt, Ezekiel assigned her to sheol with her surrounding nations (**the daughters of mighty nations**; cf. v. 18), **with those who go down to the pit.** (On the "pit" as a figure for death see the comments on 26:19-21.) God's word of judgment was so sure that Egypt's appointment to the grave was already made.

Ezekiel derided both Pharaoh and his nation. **Are you more favored than others? Go down and be laid among the uncircumcised.** Egypt's pride would be shattered when her people were destroyed. She would be forced to take her place in death with "the uncircumcised." This phrase, used 10 times in chapter 32 (vv. 19, 21, 24-30, 32), described a death of shame and defeat (cf. comments on 28:10; 31:18). Every time Ezekiel used this phrase for death he associated it with defeat by **the sword** at the hands of one's enemies.

The descent of Egypt's defeated army **and her allies** into sheol would be derided by the military men already there. They would observe that she had **come down** to **lie with the uncircumcised, with those killed by the sword.** Egypt exulted in her military prowess, but would be humbled in death, taking her place with other defeated nations.

**32:22-32.** Ezekiel described the nations that Egypt would join in sheol. The descriptions are similar, for he spoke of each nation's being **slain . . . by the sword** and being in the **grave.** All (except Edom) were said to have caused **terror** among those they attacked. **Assyria is there with her whole army** (v. 22; cf. v. 23). Assyria had already been used as an object lesson by Ezekiel (chap. 31). All Assyria's soldiers killed in battle were buried **around her.**

The second country mentioned by Ezekiel was **Elam . . . with all her hordes around her grave** (32:24-25). Elam, east of Babylon, was a warlike nation (cf. Gen. 14:1-17). Though subdued by Assyria and conquered by Nebuchadnezzar (Jer. 49:34-39), Elam regained power and later became a major part of the Persian Empire. But Ezekiel was referring only to the defeated Elamites of

the past who were already in the **grave.**

The third group awaiting Egypt in the grave were the nations of **Meshech and Tubal** (Ezek. 32:26-27). "Meshech and Tubal," mentioned earlier (27:13), were probably located on the northern fringe of what is now eastern and central Turkey. They appear again in chapters 38–39 as Gog's allies. Aggressive Meshech and Tubal had carried on a long battle with the Assyrians for control of the area south of the Black Sea. **Do they not lie with the other uncircumcised warriors who have fallen?** Some scholars see this statement as a further judgment on Meshech and Tubal and translate it as an assertion ("they do not lie with . . ."). However, it seems better to view it as the NIV renders it. Meshech and Tubal are not being singled out from the other countries but are included with them in judgment. The once-awesome might **of these warriors** had vanished, and they were now suffering the judgment due their sin.

Ezekiel paused to state why he spoke of the grave. **You too, O Pharaoh, will be broken and will lie among the uncircumcised, with those killed by the sword** (32:28). The fate of these other nations was an object lesson to Egypt. Like those once-powerful nations that were now in the grave, Pharaoh and his powerful army could expect the same fate.

Then Ezekiel resumed listing other nations. **Edom is there, her kings and all her princes** (v. 29). Edom had already received notice of God's judgment (cf. 25:12-14). Her leaders who had died were in sheol awaiting Egypt's arrival.

The final group in the grave was **all the princes of the north and all the Sidonians** (32:30). These "princes of the north," connected with Sidon, were probably the Phoenician city-states. All these mighty maritime powers suffered the same humiliating fate: **slain in disgrace despite the terror caused by their power.** Their past exploits could not save them from the specter of death. They too were awaiting Egypt's appearance in sheol.

Ezekiel again mentioned Egypt's fate (vv. 31-32). **Pharaoh** would have a perverted sense of comfort (**be consoled**) when he and his hordes would finally arrive in sheol because **he** would **see** that he was not alone in his shame and humiliation.

## III. Blessings on Israel (chaps. 33–48)

This last major division of the book focuses on the restoration of Israel's blessing. Israel would be judged for her sin (chaps. 1–24) as would the surrounding nations (chaps. 25–32). But Israel will not remain under judgment forever. God had set her apart as His special people, and He will fulfill His promises to her.

### A. New life for Israel (chaps. 33–39)

The first step in Israel's restoration will be national renewal. Israel as a nation "died" when she went into captivity. Her homeland was gone, her temple destroyed, and her kings dethroned. Israel's enemies had triumphed. Her false leaders within had led the people astray, and her neighbors without had plundered and decimated the land. For Israel to experience God's blessing she will need to be "reborn" as a nation. The false leaders will be replaced with a true shepherd who will guide the people (chap. 34). The external enemies of Israel will be judged (chap. 35). The people will be restored both to the land and to their God (chaps. 36–37), and their security will be guaranteed by God Himself (chaps. 38–39).

#### 1. WATCHMAN EZEKIEL REAPPOINTED (CHAP. 33)

*a. Ezekiel's duties as a watchman (33:1-20)*

**33:1-20.** Ezekiel had been named God's **watchman** to **warn. . . . Israel** of coming judgment (see comments on 3:16-27). Ezekiel's first commissioning was to a ministry of judgment, but that ministry was now completed. God then appointed Ezekiel as a **watchman** for a second time, but this message was different. The focus was still on individual accountability and responsibility, but the message's thrust was God's restoration of **Israel.**

*b. The opening of Ezekiel's mouth (33:21-33)*

**33:21-22.** Ezekiel was primed for his new ministry, inaugurated when news of Jerusalem's fall reached the captives in Babylon. **In the 12th year of** their **exile, in the 10th month on the fifth day,** that is, on January 9, 585 B.C., news of the fall was delivered by one of Jerusalem's sur-

vivors, who had traveled several months and several hundred miles to tell Ezekiel. Only then did the awful reality of Ezekiel's prophecies strike home.

Now that Ezekiel's message was confirmed, there was no need for him to be silent. **So** his **mouth was opened** the night **before the** messenger **arrived.** Ezekiel had remained **silent** for seven years, only speaking to utter God's judgments (cf. 3:26-27).

**33:23-29.** In the rest of chapter 33 Ezekiel addressed two groups of people. First he condemned those Israelites who remained **in the land of Israel** and expected a soon end to the Babylonian Captivity (vv. 23-29). Then he rebuked those who gathered to hear him in Babylon (vv. 30-33).

The people who remained in Israel after Jerusalem's fall refused to acknowledge God's judgment. Comparing themselves to **Abraham,** they claimed to be the remnant left by God to possess His Promised Land. If the *one* man, Abraham, had a right to the land, certainly, they reasoned, the *many* Israelites remaining there had a right to it.

But there was one big difference between Abraham and those in **the land.** Abraham was righteous and they were wicked. They ate **meat with the blood still in it** (cf. Lev. 17:10-14), worshiped **idols** (Ex. 20:4-6), **and shed blood** (cf. Ex. 20:13). The right to **possess the land** depended on spiritual obedience, not numerical strength. Because of their sins these people had forfeited their rights to the Promised Land.

Those who felt a smug arrogance in their possession of **the land** would soon experience the pains of judgment. Those in the city's **ruins** would **fall by the sword,** those who fled to the countryside would be eaten by **wild animals,** and those who hid **in strongholds and caves** would **die of a plague.** Strikingly those were the same judgments the people of Jerusalem had experienced earlier (cf. Ezek. 5:17; 14:21). In addition, **the land** (Judah) would be **desolate.**

**33:30-33.** Ezekiel then spoke to the exiles in Babylon. He had developed a popular following among the people who recognized him as a prophet. They frequently gathered to **hear** his messages. The people liked to hear God's word, but neglected to obey it (cf. James 1:22-25):

they did not put the prophet's words into practice. They were paying lip service to God, but still harbored sin in their hearts. With their mouths they were expressing devotion, but their hearts were greedy. Ezekiel's words tantalized the people's ears much as beautiful love songs would do; but his message never penetrated their hearts.

But a day of reckoning would come. When all his words of prophecy would come true . . . then they would know that he was a prophet. Ezekiel was not referring to his prophecies about Jerusalem's fall because those had *already* "come true" (Ezek. 33:21). Some suggest he was referring to his prophecy against the remnant in Judah (vv. 23-29), but it is doubtful that a message of judgment on the remnant would have had any greater impact on those in captivity than the fall of the city. Therefore Ezekiel was probably referring to the fact of individual responsibility and judgment that God imposes on all people (cf. vv. 12-20). Each person would be held accountable for his actions and his responses to God's word. When their day of accountability came, then those "hearers of the Word" (James 1:22, KJV) would be forced to acknowledge the prophetic nature—and thus the truth—of Ezekiel's message.

2. THE PRESENT FALSE SHEPHERDS CONTRASTED WITH THE FUTURE TRUE SHEPHERD (CHAP. 34)

a. *The present false shepherds (34:1-10)*

34:1-6. God charged the prophet to prophesy against the shepherds of Israel. The rulers of the people were often called shepherds (cf. Ps. 78:70-72; Isa. 44:28; 63:11; Jer. 23:1-4; 25:34-38). They were to be strong, caring leaders who guarded their nation like a flock. Ezekiel first explained the sins of the shepherds (Ezek. 34:1-6), then pronounced judgment on them (vv. 7-10).

Israel's leaders did not serve their flock. Their first error was to put their own interests above those of the people (vv. 2-3). Woe to the shepherds of Israel who only take care of themselves! Israel's kings had added to their wealth at the expense of the common people. They viewed the flock as a source of wealth to be exploited rather than a trust to be protected.

The second error of the leaders was their harsh treatment of the people. A shepherd was to lead his sheep to food, protect them from attack, nurse to health the injured sheep, and search for any that strayed and got lost. However, Israel's shepherds did not gently nurture the people. They ruled . . . harshly and brutally.

The third error of the rulers was their flagrant disregard for the people, letting them be scattered without looking for them (vv. 5-6). Three times in verses 5-6 Ezekiel mentioned that the sheep were scattered. The chief job of a shepherd was to prevent such a catastrophe. Ezekiel was probably alluding to the Assyrian and Babylonian captivities which had scattered Israel and Judah among the nations. The shepherds had been unable to prevent the very thing they were appointed to guard against.

34:7-10. The shepherds had neglected their task, and the sheep were scattered. It was now time to call the shepherds to judgment for their actions. Holding the shepherds . . . accountable for His flock, God would judge the rulers and remove them from their positions of power. They would no longer have opportunities to profit at the people's expense. God said, I will rescue My flock from their mouths, and it will no longer be food for them, in the sense of the leaders taking advantage of the people. This statement was a bridge to the next section. The false shepherds had brought Israel to ruin. So God Himself would intercede and rescue His people.

b. *The future true shepherd (34:11-31)*

What the false shepherds failed to accomplish because of their greed (vv. 1-10), God would bring to pass. He would care for His flock (vv. 11-16), judge between His sheep (vv. 17-24), and establish a covenant of peace (vv. 25-31).

34:11-16. The flock was scattered because of cruel and indifferent shepherds (vv. 2-6). If the sheep were to be rescued and restored, the Great Shepherd would need to rescue them Himself. I Myself will search for My sheep and look after them. God would intervene personally on Israel's behalf.

God's first action would be to restore Israel to her land from the nations and to pasture her like sheep in good grazing land. God will do what the false shepherds had failed to do—**tend. . . . search . . . bring back. . . . strengthen,** and **shepherd . . . with justice.** This prophecy was not fulfilled when **Israel** returned to her **land** after the Babylonian Captivity. It still awaits future fulfillment in the Millennium.

**34:17-24.** In exercising His justice God said He would begin by judging between the individual sheep: **I will judge between one sheep and another, and between rams and goats.** Before the millennial kingdom begins, God will sort out the righteous from the unrighteous (cf. Matt. 25:31-46) and allow only the righteous into the Millennium.

But how will God differentiate one from the other? The character of the sheep is seen in their conduct (Ezek. 34:17-21). The wicked sheep are those that follow the conduct of the shepherds, oppressing the weaker sheep. They **trampled** the pasturelands and even **muddied** the streams so that other sheep were left with less-than-desirable vegetation and drinking water. These **fat sheep** were successful in brutalizing the **lean sheep.** The wicked sheep even butted **all the weak sheep with** their **horns,** to drive them away. God will not permit these wicked practices to continue. Instead He will rescue the oppressed and will judge the aggressors. He **will judge between one sheep and another** (v. 22; cf. v. 17).

After judging the individual sheep, God will exercise His leadership by appointing a new **shepherd** (vv. 23-24). This shepherd, God stated, will be His **servant David.** Many see this as an allusion to Christ, the Good Shepherd (cf. John 10:11-18), who descended from the line of David to be the King of Israel (cf. Matt. 1:1). However, nothing in Ezekiel 34:23 *demands* that Ezekiel was not referring to the literal King David who will be resurrected to serve as Israel's righteous prince. David is referred to by name elsewhere in passages that look to the future restoration of Israel (cf. Jer. 30:9; Ezek. 37:24-25; Hosea 3:5). Also Ezekiel indicated that **David will be** the **prince** (*nāśîʾ*) of the restored people (Ezek. 34:24; 37:25). This same "prince" will then offer sin offerings for himself during the millennial period (45:22; 46:4). Such actions would hardly be appropriate for the sinless Son of God, but they would be for David. So it seems this is a literal refer-

ence to a resurrected David. In place of the false shepherds God will resurrect a true **shepherd** to **tend** his **sheep.**

**34:25-31.** God's care and protection will result in peace for His people. **I will make a covenant of peace with them.** The peace that Israel has always longed for will be experienced. The uncertainties associated with desolate **places, wild animals,** other **nations,** and unpredictable weather will be alleviated. The **land** will enjoy peace and prosperity. **Trees** will bear **fruit and the ground will yield its crops,** and **the people will be secure in their land,** living **in safety.**

God's "covenant of peace" looks forward to the blessings **Israel** will experience in the Millennium. This covenant will establish Israel in her land permanently with David as her shepherd. Later Ezekiel stated that the covenant of peace will also involve the rebuilding of God's temple as a visible reminder of His presence (37:26-28).

God will restore Israel because of her unique relationship to Him. **You My sheep, the sheep of My pasture, are** My **people, and I am your God.**

3. THE ENEMY (EDOM) DESTROYED (CHAP. 35)

Why did Ezekiel devote a second prophecy to Edom (cf. 25:12-14), and why was it placed in this section on Israel's restoration? Most likely Edom was listed here to represent the judgment God would inflict on all nations who oppose Israel. Edom was the prototype of all Israel's later foes. The destruction of Edom would signal the beginning of God's judgment on the whole earth based on that nation's treatment of Israel (cf. Gen. 12:3).

The prophecy against Edom is in three parts, each ending with Ezekiel's common expression, "Then you/they will know that I am the LORD" (Ezek. 35:4, 9, 15).

**35:1-4** In a direct statement of judgment on Edom, God said, **I am against you, Mount Seir.** Seir, Edom's geographical name, was the mountain range east of the Wadi Arabah south of the Dead Sea. This was the mountainous homeland where the Edomites lived. God would **make** that people as **desolate** as their land.

**35:5-9.** Ezekiel's second section followed the "because/therefore" format (used in 25:1-17) in explaining why Edom would be judged. Edom's sin was her enmity against Israel. She had **harbored an ancient hostility and delivered the Israelites over to the sword** (cf. Obad. 10, 14). Edom hoped to profit from Israel's loss, and she abetted Israel's collapse.

Because Edom had assisted in Israel's slaughter, God would assist in her slaughter. Four times (in Heb.) in Ezekiel 35:6 God referred to **bloodshed** (*dām*, lit., "blood"). This may be a wordplay on Edom's name ('*ĕdōm*; from '*ādōm*, "to be red"). Edom, with its red mountains, was now red with blood. **Since you did not hate bloodshed, bloodshed will pursue you.** Edom would suffer the same fate she had tried to inflict on Israel (see comments on Obad.). Many people would be **slain** and her **towns** would become **desolate,** no longer **inhabited.**

**35:10-15.** Ezekiel again used the "because/therefore" formula. Edom also sinned in her desire to possess the land God had promised to Judah and Israel. Edom had said those **two nations** would become her **possession.** God severely chastised Israel and Judah for their sin, but He never abrogated His promises made to Abraham and his descendants. Edom was trying to usurp Israel's title deed to the land which had been guaranteed by God.

God's judgment corresponded to Edom's guilt: **I will treat you in accordance with the anger and jealousy you showed in your hatred of them** (v. 11). Edom had dared plot **against** God's Chosen People, so she would now experience the consequences. In her boast **against** God (v. 13) Edom **rejoiced when . . . Israel became desolate.** Therefore God would make Edom **desolate.** Her treatment of Israel determined her own fate.

Edom became an object lesson for all nations. When God restores Israel's fortunes in the future, He will judge the world's other nations based on their treatment of Israel (cf. Matt. 25:31-46). They will be measured by their actions toward Israel.

### 4. THE PEOPLE BLESSED (CHAP. 36)

Chapter 36 is set in antithesis to chapter 35. When God intervenes on Israel's behalf, the "mountains" of Israel's enemies will be judged (35:1-3, 8) but the "mountains of Israel" (cf. 35:12) will be blessed (36:1). In verses 1-7 Edom is again pictured as representing all nations who seek Israel's harm (cf. vv. 5, 7). The first section of the prophecy (vv. 1-15) uses the "because/therefore" format to compare the judgment on the nations with Israel's restoration. The second section of the prophecy (vv. 16-38) moves from the mountains of Israel to the people of Israel who will be the personal recipients of God's blessing.

The fact of Israel's future restoration seemed so remote after her fall to Babylon that God put great emphasis on His personal character (rather than external circumstances) as the basis for the fulfillment. Ten times the prophet stated, "This is what the Sovereign LORD says" (vv. 2-7, 13, 22, 33, 37).

### a. Israel's mountains to prosper (36:1-15)

Ezekiel contrasted Israel's present humiliation before her enemies with her future glorification.

**36:1-7.** God promised to punish Israel's enemies for their sin in hounding, slandering (v. 3), plundering (vv. 4-5), rejoicing over, and having **malice** against Israel. **Therefore** God swore with **uplifted hand** (a gesture accompanying an oath; cf. 20:5, 15, 23; 47:14) **that the nations** who had scorned her (36:6) **will also suffer scorn.** Surrounding **nations** seemed to have triumphed, but their victory was merely temporary. They would suffer for their sin.

**36:8-12.** In contrast with the judgment about to be inflicted on Israel's enemies, Israel herself could look forward to restoration and blessing. In a reversal of the catastrophe that God had earlier called against the **mountains of Israel** (6:1-7), He said the mountains **will produce branches and fruit for** His **people . . . will soon come home.** God will restore the land so that it can provide for the restored remnant.

God's blessing will involve numerical growth, for **the number of people** will be multiplied. The nation that had been decimated in the land (6:3, 5-7) will replenish it. Israel's latter state will be far superior to her former. When God finally restores the **people** to the land He will **prosper** the land; He guarantees the permanence of this arrangement. Once Israel is restored to the land her **inheritance** will be secure. The land **will never again**

**deprive** Israel of her **children.** Rather than being a cruel wilderness with drought, famine, and death (cf. Lev. 26:18-22; Num. 13:32; Deut. 28:20-24), it will be a place of blessing. This will take place when Israel possesses her land during Christ's millennial reign.

**36:13-15.** Besides punishing Israel's enemies (vv. 1-7) and restoring Israel's land (vv. 8-12), God will also remove Israel's reproach (vv. 13-15). The mockery and humiliation (**taunts** and **scorn**) Israel had been forced to endure (vv. 3-6) will cease (cf. 16:57-58). She will once again be restored to her position of prestige as God's Chosen People (cf. Deut. 28:13; Zech. 8:13, 20-23).

*b. Israel's people to be regathered (36:16-38)*

After discussing Israel's sinful past (vv. 16-21), Ezekiel discussed (in three parts, each beginning with "This is what the Sovereign LORD says," vv. 22, 33, 37) the nation's future restoration.

**36:16-21.** Before dwelling on Israel's future cleansing, Ezekiel reminded the exiles of their past sin which caused their judgment. **When** they **were . . . in the land, they defiled it by their conduct** and **actions** (cf. v. 19). This profaning was like a menstrual discharge that rendered a woman ceremonially unclean and defiled everything she touched (cf. Lev. 15:19-23). How did the people defile the land? By bloodshed and idolatry (cf. Ezek. 33:25). As a result God removed them from the defiled land. Yet even when **scattered** among other **nations,** they **profaned** God's **holy name.**

**36:22-23.** Other nations viewed the **sovereign** God through the actions **of Israel,** thus besmirching His holy name. Therefore God said He would restore **Israel . . . not for** her **sake . . . but for the sake of** His **holy name.** Israel had no intrinsic value which prompted God to act on her behalf. He would restore the nation because His character was at stake. He would **show the holiness of** His **great name** (cf. 20:41; 28:22, 25; 38:16; 39:27). God had shown His justice when He punished Israel for her sin; He will show His grace and faithfulness when He restores her and renews His covenant promises.

**36:24-32.** The means God will use to show His holiness are explained in these verses. He will first restore the nation

physically: He **will gather** her **from all the countries and bring** her **back into her own land** (v. 24). Headlining God's future program will be the restored nation of Israel.

However, Israel's restoration will be more than physical. God promised, **I will sprinkle clean water on you and you will be clean; I will cleanse you from all your impurities and from all your idols.** This did not refer to water baptism. In Old Testament times sprinkling or washing with water pictured cleansing from ceremonial defilement (cf. Lev. 15:21-22; Num. 19:17-19). Since Israel's sin was like the ceremonial impurity of menstruation (Ezek. 36:17) her cleansing was now compared to the ceremonial act of purification. The point is that God will purify Israel from her sins. This cleansing will be followed by the impartation of new life. God will give the converted nation **a new heart and . . . a new spirit.** In place of a **heart of stone** He will **give** Israel **a heart of flesh** (cf. 11:19). With God's **Spirit** indwelling them (cf. 37:14), they will be motivated to obey His **decrees** and **laws** (cf. 37:24). God's restoration will not simply be an undoing of Israel's sin to bring her to a state of neutrality. Rather it will involve the positive implanting of a new nature in Israel's people that will make them righteous. Jeremiah called this work of God the "New Covenant" (cf. comments on Jer. 31:31-33).

Implanting God's Spirit in believing Israelites will produce a new relationship between Israel and her God: **You will be My people, and I will be your God** (cf. Ezek. 11:20; 14:11; 37:23, 27). God will extend all His graciousness to His people. Being delivered from their sin, they will experience the bountiful provision of the land including **grain . . . fruit,** and **crops** (cf. 34:27) without **famine** (cf. 34:29).

When Israel reflects on God's grace and her former character (her **evil ways and wicked deeds**), she will realize she does not deserve His favor. In fact she **will loathe** herself because of her **detestable practices,** looking back in horror at them. The blackness of her past actions will contrast starkly with the light of God's grace. In the future, when Israel recalls her past actions, she will recognize that God had **not** saved her because of her merit. God will be **doing this** not **for** her **sake,** but to magnify His own name.

**36:33-36.** When Israel is restored and the **land . . . cultivated,** people will note that this wasteland will be **like the Garden of Eden.** Israel's **cities,** formerly **in ruins,** will be **fortified and inhabited.** To the surrounding nations Israel will become an object lesson of God's grace. They will be forced to acknowledge God's sovereign power in restoring His people: **they will know that I the LORD have rebuilt what was destroyed.**

**36:37-38.** God will also cause the nation to increase numerically. This was considered a sign of God's blessing (cf. Gen. 12:2; 15:1-6; 1 Sam. 1:5-6; 2:1-11; Zech. 8:4-5). Ezekiel, a priest, compared the swelling population of Israel to the **numerous . . . flocks** of sacrificial animals gathered for the **feasts** in **Jerusalem.** As tightly packed herds jostle for space because of their vast numbers, so Israel's **ruined cities,** then empty and desolate, will **be filled with flocks of people.**

5. THE NATION RESTORED (CHAP. 37)

Chapter 37 vividly illustrates the promise of chapter 36. God had just announced that Israel will be restored to her land in blessing under the leadership of David her king. However, this seemed remote in light of Israel's present condition. She was "dead" as a nation—deprived of her land, her king, and her temple. She had been divided and dispersed for so long that unification and restoration seemed impossible. So God gave two signs (37:1-14 and vv. 15-28) to Ezekiel to illustrate the fact of restoration and confirm the promises just made.

*a. The vision of the dry bones revived (37:1-14)*

Most Israelites may have doubted God's promise of restoration. Their present condition militated against the possibility of that being fulfilled. So God stressed the fact of His sovereign power and ability to carry out these remarkable promises. Their fulfillment depended on Him, not on circumstances. Ezekiel reported the vision (vv. 1-10) and then interpreted it (vv. 11-14).

**37:1-10.** God transported Ezekiel **by the Spirit** (cf. 3:14; 8:3; 11:1, 24; 43:5) to **a valley . . . full of bones.** There he no-

ticed that the **bones . . . were very dry,** bleached and baked under the hot sun.

God asked the prophet a remarkable question: **Son of man, can these bones live?** Was there potential for life in these lifeless frames? Ezekiel knew that humanly speaking it was impossible, so his answer was somewhat guarded. **O Sovereign LORD, You alone know.** Only God can accomplish such a feat.

God then directed Ezekiel to **prophesy to these bones.** The content of his message was God's promised restoration: **I will make breath enter you, and you will come to life.** "Breath" (*rûaḥ*) could also be translated "wind" or "spirit." In 37:14 the same word is translated "Spirit." Possibly God had in mind Genesis 2:7. In creating man, He transformed Adam into a living being by breathing into his nostrils "the breath of life." Whether God was referring to wind, physical breath, the principle of life, or the Holy Spirit is uncertain. However, the results were obvious. God gave life to these dead bones. As Ezekiel was giving this prophecy, he saw a remarkable thing. **The bones came together** (Ezek. 37:7), **flesh** developed, **skin covered them** (v. 8), **breath entered them,** and they **stood up** (v. 10).

**37:11-14.** To what did this vision refer? God said it was about the nation of Israel (**the whole house of Israel**) that was then in captivity. Like unburied skeletons, the people were pining away and saw no end to their judgment: **Our hope is gone; we are cut off.** The surviving Israelites felt their national hopes had been dashed. Israel had "died" in the flames of Babylon's attack, and had no hope of resurrection.

The reviving of the dry bones signified Israel's national restoration. The vision showed that Israel's new life depended on God's power, not outward circumstances: **I will open your graves . . . I will bring you back to the land of Israel.** Also when God restores Israel nationally, He will renew them spiritually. He **will put** His **Spirit in** Israel. The breath of life the corpses received symbolized the Holy Spirit, promised in Israel's New Covenant (cf. 36:24-28).

The Israelites residing in Palestine today are not the fulfillment of this prophecy. But it will be fulfilled when God regathers believing Israelites to the land (Jer. 31:33; 33:14-16), when Christ returns to establish His kingdom (cf. Matt. 24:30-31).

### b. The sign of the two sticks united (37:15-28)

Ezekiel's second sign in this chapter visualized God's restoration of the nation. First the sign was given (vv. 15-17), then explained (vv. 18-28).

**37:15-17.** Ezekiel was told to **take** two sticks **of wood** and to **write on** one of them the name of **Judah** and on the other the names of Ephraim and **Joseph.** Ezekiel was then to hold **them together** like **one stick.**

Some have claimed that the two sticks represent the Bible (the stick of Judah) and the Book of Mormon (the stick of Joseph). However, this assertion ignores the clear interpretation in verses 18-28 and seeks to impose a foreign meaning on the sticks.

After Solomon died the nation of Israel split asunder, in 931 B.C. The Southern Kingdom was known as Judah because Judah was its larger tribe and because the country was ruled by a king from that tribe (cf. 1 Kings 12:22-24). The Northern Kingdom was called Israel, or sometimes Ephraim (e.g., Hosea 5:3, 5, 11-14) either because Ephraim was the strongest and most influential tribe or because the first king of Israel, Jeroboam I, was an Ephraimite (1 Kings 11:26). Israel was taken into captivity by Assyria in 722 B.C., and Judah was taken into exile by Babylon in 605, 597, and 586 B.C.

**37:18-28.** The uniting of **the sticks** pictured God's restoring *and* reuniting His people in the **land** as a single nation (cf. Hosea 1:11). Cleansed from their **backsliding . . . they will be My people,** God said, **and I will be their God** (cf. Ezek. 11:20; 14:11; 36:28; 37:27).

When united, **Israel** will be led by King **David** himself (see comments on 34:23-24). As God's **servant,** he will be their **one shepherd.**

Then God repeated the blessings to be bestowed on the people **in the land.** They will have an eternal inheritance there and **David . . . will be their prince.** God's **covenant of peace** (cf. 36:15; Isa. 54:10) will be established **with them,** and His presence will remain with them **forever** (in contrast with the departing of His glory, Ezek. 9–11). The visible

reminder of God's presence will be His **sanctuary,** His **dwelling place.** Then again God added, **I will be their God, and they will be My people** (cf. 11:20; 14:11; 36:28; 37:23). These promises anticipate the detailed plans for God's new sanctuary (chaps. 40–43). This literal structure will serve as a visual object lesson to Israel and **the nations** of God's presence in the midst of His people.

### 6. THE ATTACK BY GOG REPULSED (CHAPS. 38–39)

Israel has been trampled underfoot by her enemies, but God will intervene in the future to insure her safety. He will defend His people and judge her enemies in distant countries (judgment on the nearby countries had already been cited, chaps. 25–32).

Some of the countries mentioned in Ezekiel 38 and 39 had already been identified as trading partners with Tyre. See the map "The World of Jeremiah and Ezekiel" in the *Introduction* to Jeremiah for the location of the places mentioned in Ezekiel 38:2-6.

Besides those place names another possible name must be considered. The NIV translates the word *rō'š* in 38:2 as "chief." However, other translations have taken the word as a proper noun and translated it "Rosh." Should the Hebrew word, which means "head," be taken as an adjective ("head prince," i.e., "chief prince") or as a proper noun ("Rosh")? The evidence seems to favor taking it as an adjective. "Rosh" never appears as a nation in any other biblical list of place names while all the other names are well attested (cf. Gen. 10:1-7; 1 Chron. 1:5-7; Ezek. 27:13-24; 32:26). One possible exception might be Isaiah 66:19 (NASB) but this is doubtful (see NIV).

Should these names be connected with the Soviet Union? One must first identify the areas against which Ezekiel prophesied and then determine the countries that occupy those land areas today. Ezekiel's *rō'š* does not point to "Russia" merely because the words sound similar. Neither should one identify "Meshech" with "Moscow" or "Tubal" with "Tobolsk." Ezekiel had historical places in mind (not modern-day names) and these areas must be located in Ezekiel's time. However, while one must avoid dogmatic assertions, three reasons suggest including the Soviet Union within Ezekiel's prophecy: (1) Some of the countries named by Ezekiel were located in what is now Russia. (2) The armies are said to come "from the far north" (Ezek. 38:6, 15; 39:2). This probably includes the land bridge between the Black and Caspian Seas, now part of the Soviet Union. (3) Ezekiel spoke of a coalition of several nations, many of whom are today aligned with or under the influence of the Soviet Union. These include Iran ("Persia"), Sudan and northern Ethiopia ("Cush"), Libya ("Put"), and Turkey ("Meshech," "Tubal," "Gomer," and "Beth Togarmah"). All these nations (see 38:2-3, 5-6), possibly led by the Soviet Union, will unite to attack Israel.

When will this prophecy be fulfilled? No past historical events match this prophecy, so it still awaits a future fulfillment. Some think this attack on Israel should be identified with the attack of Gog and Magog at the end of Christ's millennial reign (Rev. 20:7-9), but this identification has several flaws: (1) The results of Ezekiel's battle do not coincide with the events that follow the battle in Revelation 20. Why bury the dead for seven months after the battle (Ezek. 39:12-13) when the next prophetic event is the resurrection of the unsaved dead? (Rev. 20:11-13) Why would the people remain on earth after the battle to burn the weapons of war for seven years (Ezek. 39:9-10) instead of entering immediately into eternity? (Rev. 21:1-4) The events after each battle are so different that two separate battles must be assumed (see comments on Rev. 20:7-9). (2) The effect on the people is different. In Ezekiel the battle is the catalyst God will use to draw Israel to Himself (cf. Ezek. 39:7, 22-29) and to end her captivity. But the battle in Revelation 20 will occur after Israel has been faithful to her God and has enjoyed His blessings for 1,000 years.

If the battle of Ezekiel 38–39 is not at the end of the Millennium, could it be at the beginning of the Millennium? This also seems extremely doubtful. Everyone who enters the Millennium will be a believer (John 3:3), and will have demonstrated his faith by protecting God's Chosen People (cf. comments on Matt. 25:31-46). At the beginning of the Millennium all weapons of war will be destroyed (Micah 4:1-4). Thus it seems diffi-

cult to see a war occurring when the unsaved warriors have been eliminated and their weapons destroyed.

It seems best to place Ezekiel's battle of Gog and Magog in the Tribulation period. Other internal markers indicate that it should be placed in the first three and one-half years of the seven-year period. The attack will come when Israel is at peace (Ezek. 38:8, 11). When Israel's covenant with the Antichrist is in effect at the beginning of Daniel's 70th Week (Dan. 9:27a), she will be at peace. But after the covenant is broken at the middle of the seven-year period, the nation will suffer tremendous persecution (Dan. 9:27b; Matt. 24:15-22). This will provide the time needed to bury the dead (Ezek. 39:12-13) and to burn the weapons of war (39:9-10). So the battle described by Ezekiel may take place sometime during the first three and one-half years of the seven-year period before Christ's second coming. Possibly the battle will occur just before the midpoint of the seven-year period (see the "Outline of End-Time Events Predicted in the Bible," between Ezek. and Dan., point I.D.).

Ezekiel was describing a battle that will involve Israel's remotest neighbors. They will sense their opportunity to attack when Israel feels secure under the false protection of her covenant with the Antichrist sometime at the beginning of the seven-year period. The nations involved in the attack will include the Soviet Union, Turkey, Iran, Sudan, Ethiopia, and Libya. Ezekiel first pictured the invasion by Gog and his allies (38:1-16), and then described the judgment of Gog and his allies (38:17–39:29).

### a. The invasion by Gog (38:1-16)

**38:1-6.** On the identification of the proper names in these verses see the preceding paragraphs under "6. The Attack by Gog Repulsed (chaps. 38–39)." Gog's attack on Israel will actually be orchestrated by God. **The Lord said, I will turn you around, put hooks in your jaws, and bring you out with your whole army— your horses . . . horsemen . . . a great horde with . . . shields and swords.** On whether the horses and weapons are literal, see the comments on 39:9. God will use **Gog** and all his allies as pawns in His larger plans for Israel. Yet the idea for attacking Israel also will originate with

**Gog.** Gog will act freely to accomplish his own evil goals. He "will devise an evil scheme," 38:10.

**38:7-9.** This attack will be against **Israel, whose people** will be **gathered from many nations** and will be living **in safety.** Gog and his allies will **go** against Israel in massive strength, **advancing like a storm and a cloud** (cf. v. 16).

**38:10-13.** Gog's purpose in the attack will be to **plunder and loot** unwalled **and unsuspecting** Israel, which will be **rich in livestock and goods, living at the center of the land.** Israel's importance geographically, politically, and economically will be noticed. She will be a strategic target for any power wanting to control commerce between Asia and Africa.

**38:14-16.** Gog's attack against Israel will come from all sides. **Gog** will **come from** the **far north.** With him will come his allies from the east (Persia = Iran), the south (Cush = Sudan, southern Egypt, and northern Ethiopia), and the west (Put = Libya). They will **advance against . . . Israel like a cloud** (cf. v. 9) **that covers the land.** This awesome army will overrun all obstacles as effortlessly as a cloud sailing across the sky.

This attack will be another means of God's displaying to the nations His holy character and sovereign power. In going against Israel, **the nations** will come to **know** God for He will **show** Himself **holy** (cf. 20:41; 28:22, 25; 36:23; 39:27). As a result of the unsuccessful attack Israel will be delivered and God glorified.

*b. The judgment of Gog (38:17–39:29)*

(1) The defeat of Gog (38:17–39:8). **38:17-23.** Gog's attack will be crushed by God Himself. God asked Gog, **Are you not the one I spoke of in former days by My servants the prophets of Israel?** This has caused some confusion among interpreters because no direct reference to Gog is made by any of the previous writing prophets. Perhaps this means earlier prophets had predicted the coming of invading armies against Israel in the last days, which Ezekiel now associated specifically with Gog (cf. Joel 3:9-14; Zeph. 3:15-20).

When the armies reach **Israel,** God's **anger will be aroused** against them. He will cause a massive **earthquake in . . . Israel** that will interrupt Gog's invasion plans and spread fear and confusion throughout the ranks of the invading forces.

In the pandemonium, communication between the four invading armies will break down and they will begin attacking each other. **Every man's sword will be against his brother** (Ezek. 38:21). Fear and panic will sweep through the forces so each army will shoot indiscriminately at the others.

The slaughter of the armies will be aided by additional "natural" catastrophes, including **torrents of rain, hailstones, and burning sulphur** (v. 22). The rain will combine with dirt and debris from the earthquake to produce massive mud slides and floods. Large hailstones will pelt the survivors, killing many (cf. Josh. 10:11). The "burning sulphur" might be volcanic ash.

**39:1-8.** The invading armies will be totally destroyed by God. Having brought them **against the mountains of Israel** (v. 2; cf. 38:8), God will weaken them (39:3) and strike them down **on the mountains of Israel.** This once-mighty army will then be **food** for **birds and . . . wild animals.**

God will also punish the homelands of the invaders: **I will send fire on Magog and on those who live in safety in the coastlands.** Sending fire implies destruction and military devastation (30:8, 14, 16; cf. Hosea 8:14; Amos 1:4, 7, 10, 14; 2:2, 5). The nation that will spawn the invasion will herself be destroyed. The "coastlands," already mentioned several times by Ezekiel (cf. Ezek. 26:15, 18; 27:3, 6-7, 15, 35), imply the farthest reaches of the known world. Through all this God will teach Israel that He is **holy** and is not to **be profaned** by their sins (cf. 36:22). Also **the nations will** see that He is **the Holy One in Israel.**

(2) The aftermath of the battle (39:9-20). **39:9-11.** Those who will come to plunder Israel (38:12) will themselves be plundered. Israelites will **use the** fallen soldiers' **weapons for fuel. . . . for seven years.** Should the weapons of war—horses, **swords, shields . . . bows . . . arrows . . . clubs . . . and spears** (38:4-5; 39:9)—be understood literally or do they refer figuratively to modern-day weaponry? The text itself can allow for both interpretations, but the normal meaning of the words would lead one to see Ezekiel referring to literal horses, etc. With the

other worldwide catastrophies evident during the first three and one-half years of Daniel's 70th Week (Matt. 24:6-8; Rev. 6), a reversion to more primitive methods of warfare might become possible.

Throughout the remainder of the Tribulation period and into the beginning of the Millennium, as Israel will be burning those **weapons,** she will **not need to cut** down trees. This will be an amazing reversal of Gog's fortunes. Israel **will plunder those who plundered her and loot those who looted** her.

After the battle **Israel** will also bury Gog's dead. The burials will take place **in the valley of those who travel east toward the Sea.** This translation is somewhat confusing as "toward" was supplied by the translators, and the "east" (*qidmat*) should be translated "on the east of" (cf. Gen. 2:14; 1 Sam. 13:5). The valley where Gog's army will be buried is "on the east side of" the Dead Sea (NIV marg.) in what is today Jordan. The phrase "those who travel east" (*hāʿōbᵉrîm*) could be taken as a proper name. It might refer to the "mountains of Abarim" (*hāʿăbārîm*) east of the Dead Sea that Israel traversed on her way to the Promised Land (cf. Num. 33:48). If so, Gog's burial will be in the Valley of Abarim just across the Dead Sea from Israel proper in the land of Moab. Yet the burial will be in **Israel** because Israel controlled that area during some periods of her history (cf. 2 Sam. 8:2; Ps. 60:8).

The number of corpses will be so great that **the way of travelers** will be blocked. "The way of travelers" could again be translated "Abarim." The valley will be clogged with the bodies of soldiers. The name of the valley will be changed to **the Valley of Hamon Gog,** meaning "the Valley of the hordes of Gog."

**39:12-16.** The number of soldiers killed will be so great that **for seven months the house of Israel will be burying them.** Even after the initial cleanup, squads of men will be **employed** to search the land for additional remains. **As they go through the land and one of them sees a human bone, he will set up a marker beside it.** Then as **gravediggers** see the markers they will take the remains to **the Valley of Hamon Gog** for burial. The operation will be so vast that **a town** will be set up in the valley at the

gravesites to accommodate those cleansing **the land.** It will be named **Hamonah** —a form of the word "hordes."

**39:17-20.** Another result of Gog's defeat will be a feast for **the wild animals.** (These vv. expand v. 4 where God announced that the corpses of those who fall will be food for birds and beasts.) God will reverse the roles of animals and people. Usually people slaughtered and ate sacrificed animals. Here, however, the men of Gog's armies will be sacrifices; they will be eaten by animals. In addressing the birds and animals God said that at this **great sacrifice** they **will eat flesh and drink blood . . . as if they were . . . fattened animals from Bashan.** Bashan, east and northeast of the Sea of Kinnereth (later the Sea of Galilee) was known for its fertile land and fat cows (cf. Amos 4:1). **At** God's **table** the animals **will eat** their **fill of horses and riders, mighty men and soldiers of every kind.**

(3) The effects of the battle on Israel (39:21-29). **39:21-24.** Two results will come from the battle: (a) **the nations** will see God's glory (cf. comments on 1:28) and (b) Israel will turn back to her God (39:22; cf. v. 7). God's stunning defeat of Gog will force Israel to acknowledge His power.

**39:25-29.** The defeat of Gog will also hasten God's plans to restore the other Israelites from other nations. Verses 25-29 look ahead to the end of the Tribulation when God will restore the nation from her final dispersion. God will . . . **bring Jacob back from captivity and will have compassion on all the people of Israel.** God will **show** Himself **holy through them** (cf. 20:41; 28:22, 25; 36:23; 38:16), acknowledging them as His people. Also He **will pour out** His **Spirit on the house of Israel** (cf. 36:27; 37:14; Joel 2:28). The ultimate result of the battle with Gog will be Israel's national repentance and spiritual restoration. This will be fulfilled in the millennial kingdom.

*B. New order for Israel (chaps. 40–48)*

Chapters 33–39 dealt with the new life Israel will experience when she is gathered back into her land and restored to fellowship with God. The last nine chapters of the book explain how Israel's new order will be established. A new temple will be built as a sign of God's presence among His people (chaps.

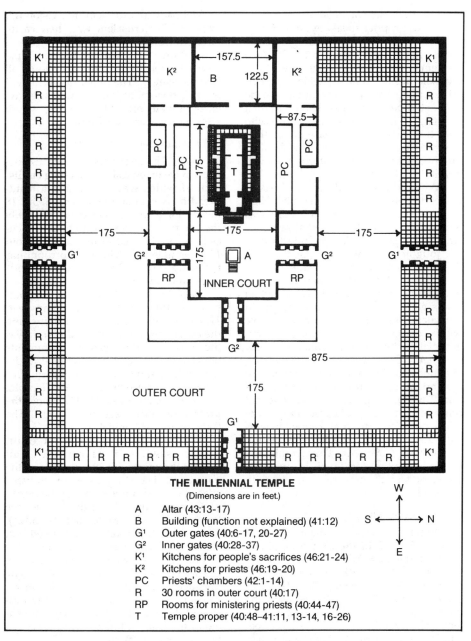

**THE MILLENNIAL TEMPLE**
(Dimensions are in feet.)

| | |
|---|---|
| A | Altar (43:13-17) |
| B | Building (function not explained) (41:12) |
| G¹ | Outer gates (40:6-17, 20-27) |
| G² | Inner gates (40:28-37) |
| K¹ | Kitchens for people's sacrifices (46:21-24) |
| K² | Kitchens for priests (46:19-20) |
| PC | Priests' chambers (42:1-14) |
| R | 30 rooms in outer court (40:17) |
| RP | Rooms for ministering priests (40:44-47) |
| T | Temple proper (40:48–41:11, 13-14, 16-26) |

40–43), and a new service of worship will be established so the people will have access to their God (chaps. 44–46). Then a new division of the land will be made for the people (chaps. 47–48).

### 1. A NEW TEMPLE (CHAPS. 40–43)

God had promised to rebuild His sanctuary among His people (37:26-28); chapters 44–46 give the plans for the tem-

ple to be rebuilt. Three interpretations of chapters 40–43 are held by Bible students: (1) Ezekiel predicted a rebuilding of Solomon's temple after the Babylonian Captivity. (2) Ezekiel was prophesying about the church in a figurative sense; he did not have a literal temple in mind. (3) A still-future literal temple will be built during the millennial kingdom. The first view must be eliminated because it suggests that Ezekiel was mistaken when he wrote. No prophet speaking under God's authority ever uttered a false prediction (Deut. 18:21-22; cf. Matt. 5:17-18). Also the remnant that returned to Israel after the Exile did not follow Ezekiel's specifications. The second view must also be eliminated because it violates the normal meaning of Ezekiel's words. Those who hold this view are inconsistent for they interpret Ezekiel's earlier, now-fulfilled prophecies literally, yet interpret his yet-unfulfilled prophecies symbolically.

Why did Ezekiel take so much space to describe the millennial temple? Here are two reasons: (1) The sanctuary was the visible symbol of God's presence among His people. The prelude to Israel's judgment began when God's glory departed from Solomon's temple in Jerusalem (Ezek. 8–11). The climax to her restoration as a nation will come when God's glory reenters the new temple in Jerusalem (43:1-5). (2) The new temple will become the visible reminder of Israel's relationship to God through His New Covenant. Since God gave detailed instructions for building the tabernacle to accompany His inauguration of the Mosaic Covenant (cf. Ex. 25–40), it is not unusual that He would also supply detailed plans for His new center of worship, to accompany the implementation of the New Covenant. This temple will be the focal point for the visible manifestation of Israel's new relationship with her God.

### a. Introduction (40:1-4)

**40:1-4.** The vision of the new temple came to Ezekiel **in the 25th year of . . . exile, at the beginning of the year, on the 10th of the month, in the 14th year after the fall of the city.** The date was sometime in 573 B.C. The phrase "the beginning of the year" poses some problems. The Israelite religious new year began in Nisan (April-May) and was established at the time of the Exodus (Ex. 12:1-2). However, in Israel's later history the seventh month, Tishri (October-November), became established as the first month of Israel's civil or regnal year. So the date would be either April 28, 573 B.C. or October 22, 573 B.C. The October date was also the Day of Atonement (cf. Lev. 23:27).

**On that very day. . . . God . . . took** Ezekiel back to Jerusalem in a vision (cf. Ezek. 8:1-3). Jerusalem was then vastly different from what it was before. Ezekiel was led on a "tour" of the future temple which he recorded in remarkable detail (see the sketch "The Millennial Temple," on the previous page). This tour was given by **a man,** probably an angel, **whose appearance was like bronze.**

### b. The outer court (40:5-27)

**40:5.** The angelic being with Ezekiel had a **measuring rod . . . six long cubits, each of which was a cubit and a handbreadth.** A common cubit was about 18 inches long and a long cubit (probably the one used in Ezek.) was about 21 inches long. So the measuring rod was about 10½ feet in length. **The wall** surrounding the temple was 10½ feet (**one . . . rod**) **thick** and 10½ feet (**one rod**) **high.**

**40:6-16.** Ezekiel passed into the outer court through **the gate facing east.** This was one of three gates leading into the outer court. Since it faced east, it was the most important gate (cf. comments on 44:1-3). He described the gate in detail, with **its steps . . . threshold,** guards' **alcoves. . . . portico facing the temple. . . . with palm trees** (40:16) along **the projecting walls** (see the sketch "The Gate to the Millennial Temple").

**40:17-19.** Entering **the outer court,** Ezekiel **saw . . . a pavement . . . all around the court** with **30 rooms along the pavement.** These rooms were probably spaced in even numbers along the north, east, and south walls of the temple (see the sketch "The Millennial Temple"). The use of these rooms is not stated, but they may have been storage rooms or meeting rooms for the people when they celebrated their feasts (cf. Jer. 35:2). **The distance from the inside of the lower gateway** (i.e., the east gate) **to the outside of the inner court** (i.e., to the threshold of the gate leading to the inner court) **was** 175 feet (**100 cubits**).

**40:20-27.** Ezekiel was then led from the **east** gate of **the outer court** to the **north** gate (vv. 20-23) and to the **south** gate (vv. 24-27). The design and dimensions of both gates were identical to those of the gate facing **east.**

### c. The inner court (40:28-47)

**40:28-37.** After measuring the outer court the angel measured **the inner court.**

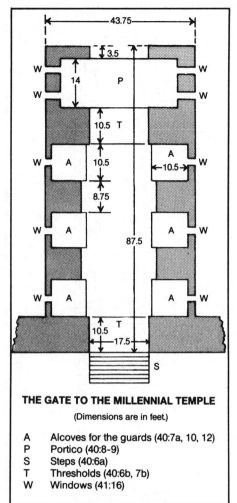

**THE GATE TO THE MILLENNIAL TEMPLE**

(Dimensions are in feet.)

| | |
|---|---|
| A | Alcoves for the guards (40:7a, 10, 12) |
| P | Portico (40:8-9) |
| S | Steps (40:6a) |
| T | Thresholds (40:6b, 7b) |
| W | Windows (41:16) |

He went from the south gate of the outer court **through the south gate** of the inner court. This gate **had the same measurements as the others.** The **south gate** (vv. 28-31), **east** gate (vv. 32-34), and **north gate** (vv. 35-37) of the inner court were identical and were also the same as the three gates of the outer court except that the porticos of the inner gates **faced the outer court.** The **portico** or vestibule was reversed on these gates (see the sketch "The Millennial Temple").

**40:38-43.** At the sides of **the inner** gates **tables** were set up for slaughtering the sacrifices. **Four tables** were **on one side of the** gate **and four on the other— eight tables in all.** The sacrifices prepared on these tables would then be offered on the altar in the inner court.

Many have objected to the thought

of animal sacrifices being reinstituted during the Millennium. Since these sacrifices, it is argued, revert back to the Levitical sacrificial system, they would seem to be out of place in the Millennium. This has caused some to take the passage symbolically rather than literally. However, no difficulty exists if one understands the proper function of these sacrifices. First, animal sacrifices *never* took away human sin; only the sacrifice of Christ can do that (Heb. 10:1-4, 10). In Old Testament times Israelites were saved by grace through faith, and the sacrifices helped restore a believer's fellowship with God. Second, even after the church began, Jewish believers did not hesitate to take part in the temple worship (Acts 2:46; 3:1; 5:42) and even to offer sacrifices (Acts 21:26). They could do this because they viewed the sacrifices as memorials of Christ's death.

Levitical sacrifices were connected with Israel's worship of God. When the church supplanted Israel in God's program (cf. Rom. 11:11-24) a new economy or dispensation began. The Levitical sacrificial system, which looked forward to Christ, was replaced by the Lord's Supper, which looked back to His death and forward to His second coming (1 Cor. 11:24, 26).

At Christ's second coming Israel will again assume her place of prominence in God's kingdom program (cf. Rom. 11:25-27). The Lord's Supper will be eliminated, because Christ will have returned. It will be replaced by animal sacrifices, which will be memorials or object lessons of the supreme sacrifice made by the Lamb of God. The slaughtering of these animals will be vivid reminders of the Messiah's suffering and death.

The millennial sacrifices will differ from the Levitical sacrifices though there are some similarities (see comments on Ezek. 45:18-25). Other passages also refer to a sacrificial system in the Millennium (Isa. 56:7; 66:20-23; Jer. 33:18; Zech. 14:16-21; Mal. 3:3-4).

**40:44-47.** As Ezekiel entered **the inner court** he again noticed **two rooms, one at the side of the north gate and facing south and another at the side of the south gate facing north** (see rooms designated "RP" in the sketch "The Millennial Temple"). **The room** on the north side was the one **facing south** (i.e., its

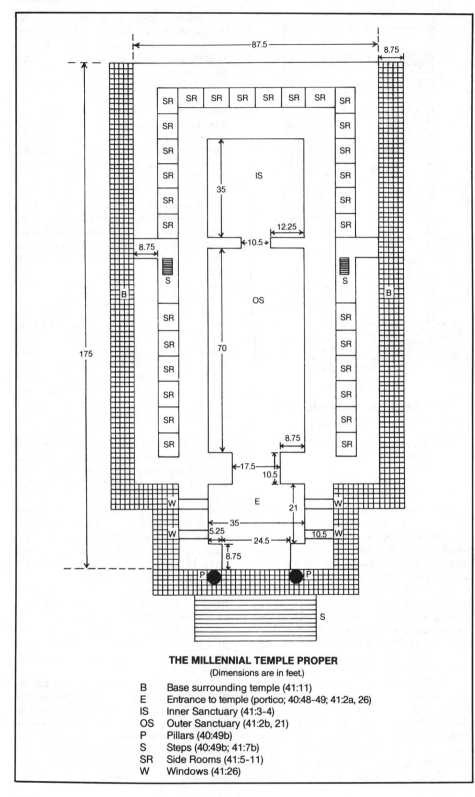

**THE MILLENNIAL TEMPLE PROPER**
(Dimensions are in feet.)

| | |
|---|---|
| B | Base surrounding temple (41:11) |
| E | Entrance to temple (portico; 40:48-49; 41:2a, 26) |
| IS | Inner Sanctuary (41:3-4) |
| OS | Outer Sanctuary (41:2b, 21) |
| P | Pillars (40:49b) |
| S | Steps (40:49b; 41:7b) |
| SR | Side Rooms (41:5-11) |
| W | Windows (41:26) |

entrance opened to the south into the inner court). This room was **for the priests** in **charge of the temple,** and the room on the south side was **for the priests** in **charge of the altar.** These rooms probably will serve as utility rooms and rest areas for the priests on duty. These priests will be descended from **Zadok** (cf. 43:19; 44:15; 48:11), the high priest in Solomon's day (1 Kings 1:26-27).

### d. The temple building (40:48–41:26)

**40:48–41:4.** Standing in the inner court, Ezekiel's gaze shifted to the temple building itself (see the sketch "The Millennial Temple Proper"). He described the structure in great detail as he was led through it. Ezekiel went first **to the portico** or entrance to **the temple** (40:48-49). This was the porch-like vestibule on the front of the temple. **A flight of stairs** led up to **the portico** and **pillars** were **on each side of the jambs.**

Ezekiel climbed the stairs and entered through the vestibule into **the outer sanctuary** (41:1). As one enters the building each gate or doorway is narrower than the one before it. Possibly this reflects God's restricting man's access into His holy presence. Ezekiel entered the outer sanctuary but not **the most holy place,** the inner sanctuary. Instead the angel **went into the inner sanctuary** to measure it. As a priest (1:3), Ezekiel was allowed into the outer sanctuary, but was barred from the most holy place (cf. Lev. 16; Heb. 9:6-7).

**41:5-11.** Surrounding **the temple** were **three levels** of **side rooms . . . one above another, 30 on each level** (see the rooms "SR" in the sketch "The Millennial Temple Proper"). These rooms were probably storerooms for the temple equipment and storage chambers for the people's tithes and offerings (cf. Mal. 3:8-10). These rooms were similar to those in Solomon's temple (cf. 1 Kings 6:5-10).

**41:12-26.** Ezekiel then recorded the overall dimensions of **the temple** proper (vv. 12-15) and described its decorations and furnishings (vv. 16-26). Immediately west of the temple was a structure described as **the building facing the temple courtyard on the west side** (v. 12). The function of this building (designated "B" in the sketch "The Millennial Temple") is not explained. The temple was 87½ feet wide and 175 feet (**100 cubits**) **long.**

**Carved cherubim and palm trees** were etched into the **wood** that covered the interior of the temple **building.** The carved cherubim represent the guardians of God's dwelling place (cf. 1:4-28; 10). Possibly the palm trees represent the fruitfulness and blessing provided by God. These decorations are similar to those Solomon included in his temple (cf. 1 Kings 6:29).

The only piece of furniture in the temple proper Ezekiel described **was a wooden altar three cubits** (5¼ feet) **high and two cubits** (3½ feet) **square,** called **the table that is before the LORD** (Ezek. 41:22). Was this the altar of incense in the holy place (cf. Ex. 30:1-3; 1 Kings 7:48) or the table that held the bread of the Presence? (Ex. 25:23-30) The proportions of the piece are closer to those of the altar of incense (cf. Ex. 25:23; 30:1-2). **Double doors** led to **the outer sanctuary** of the temple and to **the most holy place.** The doors to the outer sanctuary had **cherubim and palm trees . . . carved** on them (cf. Ezek. 41:17-20).

### e. The chambers in the inner court (42:1-14)

**42:1-12.** Leaving **the temple** proper, Ezekiel then described several adjacent structures for use by the priests (see rooms designated "PC" in the sketch "The Millennial Temple," near 40:1-4). This complex of rooms was connected with **the inner court,** with entrances from **the outer court.** There were two buildings on **the north side** with a common corridor 17½ feet (**10 cubits**) wide (v. 4). **The row of rooms . . . next to the outer court** was 87½ feet (**50 cubits**) **long.** The other **row** of rooms next to **the sanctuary** was twice as **long,** 175 feet (**100 cubits,** v. 8). These rooms were **three** stories high, with the rooms on the third level being **narrower** than those on the first and second floors (vv. 3-6). An identical group of **rooms** was on the temple's **south side** (vv. 10-12).

**42:13-14.** In those **rooms . . . the priests who approach the LORD will eat the most holy offerings** (cf. 46:20) and store their **garments** (44:19). According to the Mosaic Law the priests received a portion of some offerings (Lev. 2:3, 10; 6:16, 26-30; 7:7-10). A similar provision will be made for the millennial priests.

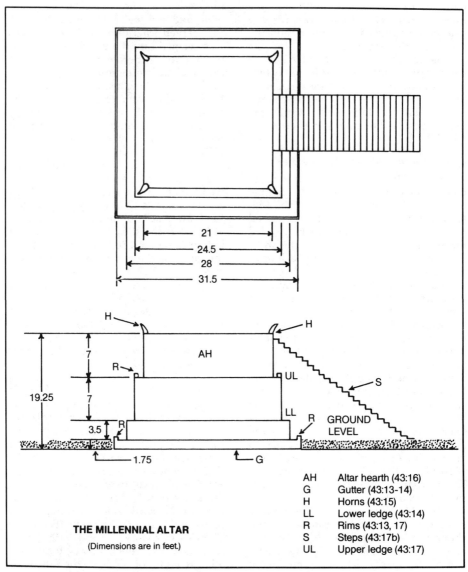

**THE MILLENNIAL ALTAR**

(Dimensions are in feet.)

| AH | Altar hearth (43:16) |
| G | Gutter (43:13-14) |
| H | Horns (43:15) |
| LL | Lower ledge (43:14) |
| R | Rims (43:13, 17) |
| S | Steps (43:17b) |
| UL | Upper ledge (43:17) |

*f. The outer walls of the temple (42:15-20)*

**42:15-20.** After the angel measured everything within **the temple** complex, **he led** Ezekiel outside to record the external dimensions of the temple. The complex was a square measuring 875 feet (**500 cubits**) on each side. The total area occupied by this temple area was 765,625 square feet—enough square feet for more than 13 football fields!

*g. The return of the Lord's glory (43:1-12)*

**43:1-5.** In a dramatic reversal of the departure of the Lord's glory (chaps. 10–11) Ezekiel saw **the glory of . . . God** returning **from the east** to dwell once again in His nation. **The glory of the LORD** (cf. comments on 1:28) **entered the temple through the gate facing east. Then the Spirit lifted** Ezekiel **up** (cf. 3:14; 8:3; 11:1, 24; 37:1) **and brought** him **into the inner court** in front of the temple proper, **and the glory of the LORD filled the temple.**

**43:6-9.** God said the new temple is to be **the place of** His **throne . . . the place. . . . where He will live among the Israelites forever** (v. 7; cf. v. 9). **The temple** will serve as God's earthly dwelling place among His people. God assured

Ezekiel that this home would be permanent. **Never again** would Israel **defile** His **holy name** (cf. 20:39; 39:7) by worshiping **lifeless idols,** bringing destruction on the nation (43:7-8).

**43:10-12.** The man (an angel, v. 6; cf. 40:3) standing next to Ezekiel told him to **describe the temple to the people of Israel, that they may be ashamed of their sins.** A clear vision of God's ideal **plan** would remind the people of the sins that had led to the destruction of the old temple. Another reason in sharing the **design** with the nation was to motivate the people to return to God and rebuild the temple: **so that they may be faithful to its design and follow all its regulations.** Though this prophecy was not fulfilled after the return from the Babylonian Captivity (and thus awaits a future fulfillment), the potentiality for fulfillment was there.

*h. The altar of burnt offering (43:13-27)*

When the millennial temple is established and God is enthroned in it, daily services will begin. Ezekiel was given a description of the altar (vv. 13-17) and regulations for consecrating it (vv. 18-27).

**43:13-17.** The height of **the altar** was 19¼ feet (11 **long cubits;** see the sketch "The Millennial Altar"), but part of this was below ground. The height of the altar above the ground (10 cubits) corresponds to the altar constructed by Solomon (2 Chron. 4:1). However, since Solomon used the shorter 18-inch cubit (2 Chron. 3:3), the total height of his altar was only 15 feet compared with an above-ground height of 17½ feet for the millennial altar. **The altar hearth,** 21 feet **square,** was reached by a flight of **steps** facing **east.**

**43:18-27.** A seven-day ritual will be employed by **the priests . . . of Zadok** (cf. 40:46) to set **the altar** apart to the **LORD.** This consecration service will be similar in some ways to the services followed by Moses (Ex. 40:10, 29) and Solomon (2 Chron. 7:8-9) to sanctify their houses of worship to God. After **seven days** of **offering** bulls, goats, and rams **the priests** will **present** the people's **burnt offerings and fellowship offerings on the altar.** This process will mark the full resumption of God's fellowship with His people, as then God **will accept** them. These sacrifices will point Israelites

to Christ who will have given them access to the Father (Heb. 10:19-25).

2. A NEW SERVICE OF WORSHIP (CHAPS. 44–46)

After the temple was described, its daily operation was explained to Ezekiel. A new way of life and worship will be practiced by the people during the Millennium. Yet in describing the holy standards in Israel's future worship, Ezekiel asked the people of his day to reevaluate their present practices. He explained the duties of the temple ministers (chap. 44), described the allocation of land for the temple priests (45:1-12), and then spoke of the offerings to be made to the Lord (45:13–46:24).

*a. The temple ministers (chap. 44)*

**44:1-3.** Ezekiel had been standing in the inner court of the temple, receiving instructions about the altar there (43:5). Now he was led out of the inner court to the **east** gate of the **outer** court, **and it was shut. This gate** at the outer court opened toward the Kidron Valley and the Mount of Olives. Ezekiel had just seen **the LORD** enter it on His return to His temple (43:4). God's presence had hallowed the gate. Therefore **it is to remain shut because the LORD, the God of Israel, has entered through it.** No one else will be allowed to tread through the gate which God Himself had entered.

Some have thought that the "Golden Gate" of Jerusalem, now sealed, is the gate spoken of here. However, the dimensions of the "Golden Gate" do not correspond with Ezekiel's gate, which is still future.

Only one person will be allowed to enter through the east gate complex: **the prince himself** (cf. 46:2). This "prince" has already been identified as King David (cf. 34:24; 37:24-25). He will be allowed **to eat in** the gate, possibly referring to the fellowship offerings which the worshipers will eat after offering them to the Lord (cf. Lev. 7:15-21). **The portico** (vestibule) faces the outer court (see the eastern G¹ in the sketch "The Millennial Temple," near Ezek. 40:1-4), so David, going east, will enter the gate complex from the outer court.

**44:4-9.** As Ezekiel went back into the inner court **by way of the north gate,** he saw the glory of the LORD (cf. comments on 1:28) **filling the temple of the LORD.**

Because of God's holiness Ezekiel told the nation, a **rebellious house** (cf. 2:5-6, 8; 3:9, 26-27; 12:3, 9, 25; 17:12; 24:3), that God said, **Enough of your detestable practices, O house of Israel!** God demanded holiness from His people, and a turning from the practice of allowing **uncircumcised** foreigners into the **temple** (44:9; cf. v. 7). The Jews who returned from the Babylonian Captivity stressed this prohibition (cf. Ezra 4:1-3; Neh. 13:1-9; cf. Acts 21:27-32).

**44:10-14.** The duties of **the Levites** for the new **temple** were explained to Ezekiel. Because of their sinful practices before Israel's fall to Babylon, their position will be downgraded in the new temple from ministers to servants. They will be allowed to **serve** as gatekeepers, slayers of the **sacrifices,** and to help the worshipers. However, they will not be allowed **to serve** the Lord **as priests or come near any of** His **holy things or . . . offerings.** The tasks of the Levites in Solomon's temple were more extensive (cf. 1 Chron. 15:16; 16:4; 23:28-31).

**44:15-19.** Then Ezekiel discussed the duties of **the priests . . . of Zadok.** The line of Zadok was one branch of the priestly line, a limited group of Levites. Zadok was appointed chief priest during Solomon's reign (and hence over the first temple) because he faithfully supported Solomon as king (cf. 1 Kings 1:32-35; 2:26-27, 35). Though the people had sinned, the priests in Zadok's line had remained faithful to God. So they will be restored to their position of honor. **They are . . . to offer sacrifices** (Ezek. 44:15) and **they alone are to enter** the **sanctuary** and **minister** there. These priests will serve as mediators between Israel and her God in much the same way as did the priests in Old Testament times.

Several Mosaic laws governing the priests were repeated by the Lord. The priestly vestments are to be made of **linen** (cf. Ex. 28:39-41). Linen is lighter than wool, which was not permitted because the priests **must not wear anything that makes them perspire.** Before the priests **go** among the **people** in **the outer court,** they will change from the vestments they wear in **ministering** before the Lord. This will help people distinguish between the holy and the common.

**44:20-23.** The priests **must not shave their heads or let their hair grow long.** Completely shaving one's head or letting one's hair go unkempt were signs of mourning (cf. Lev. 10:6; 21:5, 10). The priests will be prohibited from drinking **wine** before ministering lest they become drunk and not perform their duties properly (cf. Lev. 10:8-9). Also restrictions will be placed on whom they can **marry** (cf. Lev. 21:7, 13-15). These actions, designed to promote holiness, will help the **people** see **the difference between the holy and the common.**

**44:24-27. The priests** will **serve as judges,** and will follow God's regulations regarding the **feasts** and **Sabbaths.** Also the priests will avoid ritual defilement, by not **going near a dead person** (cf. Lev. 21:1-4). Even though death will be uncommon during the Millennium (cf. Isa. 65:20), provision was made for those instances when it will occur. An exception was made for close family members, but the priest will have to **wait seven days** and then **offer a sin offering** before reentering the temple service.

**44:28-31.** To emphasize the priests' position as the Lord's ministers, God will not let them possess land in Israel outside the allotment surrounding the temple (cf. 45:4). The reason is that He will **be the only inheritance the priests have.** He **will be their possession.** God will take care of those who minister before Him (cf. Deut. 18:1-5), by having them live off the sacrifices the people will bring to the temple.

*b. The land of the temple priests (45:1-12)*

Because Ezekiel had been speaking extensively about the priests and Levites (44:10-31), he then included their inheritance in the land (cf. 48:9-12). They will not have inheritances as will people in the other tribes (44:28). (The land for the priests is shown in the inset in the map "The Division of the Land during the Millennium" near 47:13-23.)

**45:1-6.** In the division of the land Israel is **to present to the Lord a portion of the land as a sacred district, 25,000 cubits** (about 8.3 miles) **long and 20,000 cubits** (about 6.6 miles) **wide.** Within this land **area** will be the temple complex Ezekiel had just described (chaps. 40–43). This rectangle of land will be divided into two equal portions, each about 8.3 miles long and about 3.3 miles wide. The first portion, in which will be located **the sanctuary,** will be allotted to **the priests. . . . for their houses as well as a holy place for the sanctuary.** The second portion will be allotted **to the Levites, who serve in the temple, as their possession for towns to live in.** Instead of being scattered throughout Israel as they were earlier (Josh. 21:1-42) the priests and Levites will reside near their place of ministry.

The rectangle formed by the priests' and Levites' portions was converted into a square with the addition of land for the city of Jerusalem itself. **The city** is to cover **an area 5,000 cubits** (about 1.7 miles) **wide and 25,000 cubits** (about 8.3 miles) **long, adjoining the sacred portion.** This will then be subdivided into the city proper, grazing land, and farmland (cf. Ezek. 48:15-18).

**45:7-8.** This square of land, 8.3 miles in each of its four dimensions, will be located at the present site of Jerusalem. A band of land will extend from the city to the east and **west. The prince** (i.e., David; cf. comments on 34:24) **will have the land bordering each side of the area formed by the sacred district and the property of the city.** This strip of land will extend on the east to the Jordan River and on the west to the Mediterranean Sea.

**45:9-12.** Ezekiel used the reality of God's promised future blessings as a springboard to exhort the princes in his day to repentance. **You have gone far enough, O princes of Israel!** (cf. 44:6) **Give up your violence and oppression and do what is just and right.** Israel's civil leaders had callously disregarded the rights of those they were to protect (cf. 19:1-9; 22:25; 34:1-10). Their basic problem was greed. So Ezekiel exhorted them to **use accurate scales, an accurate ephah, and an accurate bath.** An **ephah** was a measure of dry capacity and a **bath** was a **measure** of liquid capacity. They were each equivalent to approximately five gallons (see "Biblical Weights and Measures" before the commentary on Gen.). Each of these was **a 10th of a homer.** A **homer** was approximately 50 gallons or about 6 bushels. The Hebrew word *ḥōmer,* possibly related to *ḥămôr* ("donkey"), suggests that this was a "donkey load."

Ezekiel also defined the measure of weight (in addition to the measures of capacity): **the shekel is to consist of 20 gerahs.** A "shekel" weighed just under 11½ grams or about 2/5 of an ounce. The "gerah" was Israel's smallest unit of weight; it took 20 gerahs to make one shekel (cf. Ex. 30:13; Lev. 27:25; Num. 3:47). Ezekiel stated that 60 **shekels** (20 + 25 + 15) **equal one mina.** Some have felt that this was a deviation from the usual standard of 50 shekels to a mina, as in Ugaritic texts. However, there is evidence that the standard, at least in Babylon, was 60 shekels to a mina. This would make the mina about 24 ounces or 1½ pounds.

Weights found from Old Testament times vary to some extent. Apparently people used weights of differing sizes to cheat others. Ezekiel was exhorting Israel's leaders to establish honest standards for all Israelites.

### c. The offerings (45:13–46:24)

Having chastised the princes of Israel for using unjust weights, Ezekiel returned to discussing the Millennium, in which the future prince will use just weights to receive and offer gifts to God (45:13-17). This mention of offerings caused Ezekiel to describe briefly the future sacrificial system (45:18–46:24) before returning to the subject of the division of the land.

**45:13-17.** Ezekiel listed specific amounts of produce the people will give the prince (David; see comments on 34:24). **The prescribed portion** is to be proportionate to each individual's wealth or lack of it. They are each to give a 60th of their **wheat and . . . barley** (45:13), one percent of their olive **oil** (v. 14), and **1 sheep . . . from every . . . 200** of their flocks (v. 15). This tithe or tax will be required of **all the people** for use by **the prince in Israel.** As the people's representative, he will collect their gifts and use them to maintain the temple sacrifices, including **burnt offerings, grain offerings, and drink offerings at the festivals, the New Moons, and the Sabbaths.** (For a discussion on the use of sacrifices during the Millennium see the comments on 40:38-43.)

**45:18-25.** The festivals where the offerings will be given will include the New Year feast (vv. 18-20), the Passover/Unleavened Bread feast (vv. 21-24), and the seven-day Feast of Tabernacles (v. 25). The New Year's day celebration, on Nisan 1 (mid-April), will be to **purify the sanctuary** (v. 18). If someone **sins unintentionally,** a second purification will be offered **on the seventh day of the month** (v. 20). This offering and ceremonial cleansing possibly will replace the Day of Atonement (in the seventh month, Lev. 23:26-32).

This time of cleansing will be followed by the celebration of **the Passover** (Ezek. 45:21-24)/Unleavened Bread festival. The Passover will last **seven days, during which** the people will **eat bread made without yeast. The prince** will **provide** the sacrifices for that period (vv. 22-24). The fact that the prince is to make **a sin offering for himself** shows that he is not Christ.

The third **feast** will begin **in the seventh month on the 15th day.** This is the Festival of Tabernacles, also a seven-day celebration (Lev. 23:33-44), the last feast in Israel's yearly calendar.

Why did Ezekiel omit Israel's other national feasts, the Feast of Pentecost, the Feast of Trumpets, and the Day of Atonement? Two explanations may be given. First, he may have been signaling a change in God's program for Israel. The inauguration of the New Covenant and the fulfillment of Israel's kingdom promises may render those three feasts unnecessary. Thus only three of the six annual feasts under the Levitical system (cf. Lev. 23:4-44) will be followed: two feasts celebrating national cleansing (Passover and Unleavened Bread combined as one feast; see the chart "Calendrical Offerings," near Num. 28:1-8), which will point back to Christ's death, and the Feast of Tabernacles that will symbolize Israel's new position in God's millennial kingdom. Second, perhaps Ezekiel employed a figure of speech known as a merism to include all the feasts. By naming the first two feasts in Israel's festal calendar (Passover and Unleavened Bread) and the last one (Tabernacles), maybe he implied that all Israel's feasts would be reinstituted.

**46:1-10.** After speaking of selected feasts in Israel's religious year, Ezekiel provided information on the daily aspects of Israel's **worship.** He gave regulations for the Sabbath and New Moon sacrifices (vv. 1-10) and for the conduct and offerings of the people in the temple (vv. 11-15).

The **east** gate from the outer court to **the inner court** will be closed **six** days of the week, **but on the Sabbath Day and on the day of the New Moon it is to be opened. The prince,** David, will be allowed to **stand** at **the gatepost** of the east gate during these days as the sacrifice he brought on behalf of the people will be offered (cf. 44:3). He will also provide the sacrifices for the people **on the Sabbaths and New Moons** as well as on the major feast days.

The worshipers at the temple are given regulations to aid in their orderly assembly before **the LORD.** There is no entrance to the temple on the west, and the east gate will be permanently shut (cf. 44:1-2). Thus access into the temple will be from the north and the south. To avoid confusion the worshipers will be directed through the temple according to predesignated routes so that **whoever enters by the north gate to worship is to go out the south gate; and whoever enters by the south gate is to go out the north gate.** God is a God of order, and He wants orderliness to prevail in worship.

**46:11-15.** If the prince desires to make **a freewill offering to the LORD . . . the gate facing east is to be opened for him.** The regulation concerning the closing of the east gate to the inner court (cf. v. 1) will be suspended for this special **offering.** But after the prince leaves, **the gate** is to be closed again. Then Ezekiel mentioned the **morning** sacrifice, but not the evening sacrifice (cf. Ex. 29:38-41). This omission could be explained by the fact that he was giving only the highlights of the sacrificial system. So by listing the morning sacrifices he may have assumed that his readers would apply the same regulations to the evening sacrifice.

**46:16-18.** Another topic related to freewill gifts is the Year of Jubilee. Every 50 years property was to revert to its original owners (Lev. 25:10-13). Ezekiel posed two hypothetical cases based on the generosity of the prince to show that the Year of Jubilee will be in force during the Millennium. **If the prince** will give part of his estate **to one of his sons, it will also belong to his descendants.** Property given to a family member will not be returned in the Year of Jubilee.

However . . . **a gift** made to a servant will not be permanent; **the servant may keep it until the year of freedom; then it will revert to the prince.** Because the land will belong to God, He will apportion it to Israel as His stewards. This regulation assures that no one individual will gain permanent control of the land.

The prince will not be allowed to claim any land outside **his** allotted **inheritance.** In contrast with evil princes in Ezekiel's day (Ezek. 45:8-9), **the prince** during the Millennium will not oppress **the people** or take **their property.**

**46:19-24.** Ezekiel's angelic guide led him to the kitchens in the temple complex. He first described the priests' kitchens (vv. 19-20), then the kitchens for the people's sacrifices (vv. 21-24).

The kitchens for **the priests** are to be at the west **end** of the priests' chambers adjacent to the temple proper (see the sketch "The Millennial Temple," near 40:1-4). There **the priests will cook the guilt offering and the sin offering . . . to avoid bringing them into the outer court.** The priests will be allowed to eat a portion of the sacrifices brought to the temple.

**The kitchens** for the sacrifices **of the people** will be **in the four corners of the outer court.** When the people offer fellowship offerings to the Lord, they will be allowed to eat part of the sacrifice in a fellowship meal (cf. Lev. 7:15-18). Evidently at these four kitchens the priests **will cook** the people's **sacrifices.** This magnificent temple will be a place of fellowship as well as worship.

### 3. A NEW LAND (CHAPS. 47–48)

#### a. The river from the temple (47:1-12)

One feature in the Millennium will be a life-giving river flowing from the temple. Many think this refers *only* symbolically to the blessings that flow from God's presence. But nothing in the passage suggests that Ezekiel had anything in mind other than a literal river. The inclusion of details such as the fishermen (v. 10) and the salty swamps and marshes (v. 11) lend a touch of realism to the passage. These details become meaningless if the passage is only symbolic of spiritual blessing. Joel had mentioned this river before Ezekiel's time (cf. Joel 3:18), and Zechariah spoke of it after Israel returned from the Babylonian Captivi-

ty (cf. Zech. 14:8). In the Millennium this river will be another visible reminder of God's presence and blessing.

**47:1-6a.** Ezekiel was led from the kitchens in the temple's outer court back into the inner court **to the entrance** of **the temple** proper. There he **saw water coming out from under the threshold of the temple toward the east.** That stream of water, flowing out from God's presence, went eastward and passed **south of the altar.** Ezekiel left the temple complex by way of **the north gate** and saw **the water . . . flowing** out of the temple on **the south side** of the east gate into the Kidron Valley.

Zechariah recorded that the water flowing from Jerusalem will divide, with half flowing east toward the Dead Sea and half flowing west toward the Mediterranean (Zech. 14:8). Ezekiel followed only the branch that went toward the east.

The angelic being **led** Ezekiel toward the east along the riverbank. After 1,750 feet (**1000 cubits**) the **water . . . was ankle-deep**; in another 1,750 feet the river was **knee-deep.** The angel measured **another** 1,750 feet and the **water** reached Ezekiel's **waist.** A fourth measurement of 1,750 feet farther to the east revealed that **the water had risen and was deep enough to swim in—a river that no one could** walk across. Perhaps this rise in depth will come from additional streams feeding into this river, though Ezekiel did not mention them.

**47:6b-12.** Ezekiel went **back to the bank of the river** and **saw** many **trees on each side of the river.** These waters will produce beautiful vegetation along their banks.

The millennial river will flow **toward the eastern region and** will go **down into the Arabah, where it** will enter **the Sea.** The "Arabah" is the Jordan Valley running south from the Sea of Galilee to the Dead Sea and ultimately to the Gulf of Aqabah. The millennial river will merge with the Jordan River at the northern mouth of the Dead Sea.

As this new river enters the Dead Sea, **the water there** will become **fresh.** The Dead Sea, now some six times saltier than the ocean, will become completely salt-free—truly a miracle of God! This now-lifeless body of water will then support life so that **where the river flows**

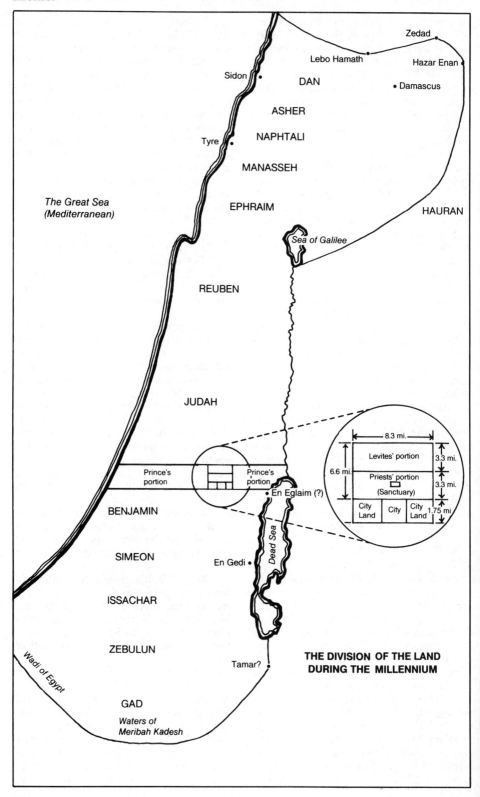

THE DIVISION OF THE LAND
DURING THE MILLENNIUM

everything will live. **Fishermen** will crowd the shores **from En Gedi to En Eglaim** (see the map "The Division of the Land during the Millennium") to catch **many kinds** of **fish** there. "En Gedi" is a settlement about midway down the western shore of the Dead Sea. The location of "En Eglaim" (lit., "Spring of the Two Calves") is uncertain. Suggested locations have included the southwestern shore of the Dead Sea near Zoar and an area on the northwestern shore south of Khirbet Qumran. Because of Ezekiel's focus on the water entering the Dead Sea at the northern end, the site near Qumran seems a possibility.

While the Dead Sea itself will be made fresh, **the swamps and marshes will not become fresh; they will be left for salt.** The lowlands near the Dead Sea will remain salt-crusted. Salt is essential to life, and the Dead Sea area is Israel's chief source of salt. God will provide for all of Israel's needs.

Another way God will provide for Israel is by the **trees** on the riverbanks that will bear **fruit** year-round. The **fruit will** provide **food and their leaves** will provide **healing.** How healing will come from the leaves is not clear, but sickness will be virtually eliminated. God will use these trees to meet people's physical needs.

### b. The boundaries of the land (47:13-23)

**47:13-14.** God promised Abraham (cf. Gen. 13:14-17; 15:17-21) and his descendants the land of Palestine, and that promise has never been rescinded. Israel's experiencing blessing in the land was conditioned on her obedience (Deut. 28), but her right to possess **the land** has never been revoked. When God inaugurates His New Covenant with **Israel** in the future, she will be restored to her place of blessing in the land (cf. Ezek. 36–37). To prepare the people for this new occupation, God defined the boundaries of the country. He said, **Because I swore with uplifted hand** (a gesture that often accompanied oath-taking; cf. Ex. 6:8; Neh. 9:15; Ps. 106:26; Ezek. 20:5, 15, 23, 42; 36:7; 44:12) **to give it to your forefathers, this land will become your inheritance.** Israel's borders during the Millennium will be similar to those promised her during the time of Moses (cf. Num. 34:1-12).

**47:15-17.** The northern **boundary of the land . . . will run** east **from the Great Sea,** the Mediterranean, starting somewhere north of Tyre and Sidon (more precisely, "Mount Hor," Num. 34:7). The boundary line will go **by the Hethlon road past Lebo Hamath to Zedad, Berothah, and Sibraim . . . as far as Hazer Hatticon . . . on the border of Hauran.** The location of Hethlon is unknown, but many associate it with the modern town of Heitela, northeast of Tripoli in modern Lebanon. Lebo Hamath has sometimes been identified with the city of Hamath on the Orontes River in modern Syria. The word "Lebo" is then taken to mean "by the way of" rather than as a proper name. However, this identification is problematic because Hamath is about 100 miles farther north than the other cities mentioned by Ezekiel. It is better to take "Lebo" as a proper name and to identify Lebo Hamath with the modern town of Al-Labwah in the Biqa Valley.

Zedad should probably be identified with the town of Sadad about 25 miles north of Damascus. The locations of the towns of Berothah and Sibraim are not known, but are said to lie **on the border between Damascus and Hamath.** Hamath (not the same as Lebo Hamath) is north of Damascus. So these cities are north of Damascus on the border between the territories held by Damascus and Hamath, probably near the town of Zedad.

Hazer Hatticon (Ezek. 47:16) is probably another name for **Hazer Enan** (v. 17). It is located on the border between Syrian Damascus and the province of Hauran. Hauran may possibly be identified with a district east of the Sea of Galilee north of the Yarmuk River. Some say Hazer Enan is modern-day Al-Qaryatayn, an important desert oasis northeast of Damascus. So the northern border will stretch east from the Mediterranean Sea north of the modern city of Tripoli and will include what was then the northern border of Syria.

**47:18.** The eastern border will extend **between Hauran and Damascus.** The edge of Israel's territory will arch back from Hazar Enan along the southern border of Syria till it reaches the Jordan River south of the Sea of Galilee. From there it will go **along the Jordan between Gilead and the land of Israel, to**

the eastern sea and as far as Tamar. The eastern border will be the Jordan River and the Dead Sea. Gilead and the Transjordan area to the east of the Jordan will not be included in Israel's future inheritance. The exact location of Tamar, to which the eastern **boundary** will continue, is uncertain, but it may be south of the Dead Sea.

**47:19.** The southern border of Israel's millennial kingdom will extend **from Tamar as far as the waters of Meribah Kadesh, then along the Wadi of Egypt to the Great Sea.** Since "the waters of Meribah Kadesh" were at Kadesh Barnea (cf. Num. 27:14), the southern border will stretch southwestward from Tamar to Kadesh Barnea. From there it will go to the "Wadi of Egypt." This is probably the Wadi el-Arish (cf. Num. 34:5), not the Nile River. The words "of Egypt," not in the Hebrew, are supplied as an explanatory addition.

**47:20.** The western border of the Promised Land will be **the Great Sea,** the Mediterranean. The border will go along the shoreline from the Wadi el-Arish in the south **to a point opposite Lebo Hamath** in the north.

**47:21-23.** The land will be distributed **according to the tribes of Israel.** This is the prelude to the division of the land (chap. 48). Ezekiel also included regulations for allotting land to resident **aliens** who will want to associate with Israel. Being considered **native-born Israelites . . . they are to be allotted an inheritance among the tribes of Israel.** Though foreigners had always been allowed to live in Israel (cf. Lev. 24:22; Num. 15:29), in the Millennium they will be allowed to enjoy other privileges previously granted only to Israelites (cf. Isa. 56:3-8). Though the Millennial Age will be a time of blessing for believing Israel, believing Gentiles will also enjoy God's blessing.

### c. The division of the land (48:1-29)

**48:1-7.** In dividing the millennial land among the people, God will give seven tribes portions in the northern part of the land. Proceeding from the north these tribes will be **Dan** (v. 1), **Asher** (v. 2), **Naphtali** (v. 3), **Manasseh** (v. 4), **Ephraim** (v. 5), **Reuben** (v. 6), and **Judah** (v. 7).

**48:8-22.** The central band of land was allotted **to the prince** (David, v. 21;

cf. 34:24), **the priests,** and **the Levites** (see comments on 45:1-8). That central **portion** will also include the city of Jerusalem and its suburbs. The city will be laid out as a square 7,875 feet (**4,500 cubits**) on each side and will cover approximately 2.2 square miles (48:16). Jerusalem will be surrounded by a band of land 437½ feet (**250 cubits**) wide, which will serve as **pastureland for** flocks and herds belonging to people living in **the city** (v. 17). On either side of the city proper will be two portions of land 3.3 miles (**10,000 cubits**) long (v. 18) and 1.65 miles (**5,000 cubits**) wide (cf. v. 15). This farmland will be cultivated to **supply food for the workers of the city.**

**48:23-29.** The lower part of the land will be allotted to the five remaining tribes. Proceeding southward these will be **Benjamin** (v. 23), **Simeon** (v. 24), **Issachar** (v. 25), **Zebulun** (v. 26), and **Gad** (v. 27). The locations of all 12 tribes will differ from their locations during Joshua's time to the captivities (Josh. 13–19).

### d. The gates of the city (48:30-35)

In describing the gates of the new city of Jerusalem, Ezekiel brought the city "full circle" from what it was at the beginning of his book. The city doomed for destruction will be restored to glory.

**48:30-31.** The new city of Jerusalem will have 12 gates, 3 on each side. Why these gates are grouped as they are is obscure. **The three gates on the north side** (closest to the sanctuary) **will be** named for **Reuben . . . Judah,** and **Levi.** Perhaps these three were listed first because of their preeminent positions among the tribes. Reuben was the firstborn of Jacob's 12 sons, Judah was the royal tribe, and Levi was the tribe of the priesthood. Also all three were children of Jacob's first wife Leah (cf. Gen. 29:31-35).

**48:32.** **On the east side** of Jerusalem the gates **will be** named for **Joseph . . . Benjamin,** and **Dan.** Because Levi was given a gate (v. 31) the tribes of Ephraim and Manasseh were combined as the one tribe of Joseph (cf. Gen. 48:1). Joseph and Benjamin were both sons of Rachel (Gen. 30:22-24; 35:16-18), and Dan was the first son of Rachel's servant Bilhah, who became Jacob's concubine (Gen. 30:4-6).

**48:33.** The gates **on the south** were named after **Simeon . . . Issachar,** and

**Zebulun.** These three were also born to Leah (Gen. 29:33; 30:17-20). Since each of these tribes was relocated in the southern portion of the land (cf. 48:24-26), the **gates** faced their inheritances.

**48:34.** The gates **on the west side** were named for **Gad . . . Asher,** and **Naphtali.** These three tribes descended from sons of Jacob's concubines. Gad and Asher were born to Zilpah (Gen. 30:9-13), and Naphtali was born to Bilhah (Gen. 30:7-8).

**48:35.** The most remarkable aspect of **the** new **city** of Jerusalem will be the presence of the Lord. God's glory had departed from the city as a prelude to its judgment (cf. chaps. 10–11), and His return will signal Jerusalem's blessing. This fact so impressed Ezekiel that he wrote that the city will be given a new name: THE LORD IS THERE. As the Prophet Ezekiel had stated repeatedly, God will return to dwell with His people. No longer worshiping lifeless idols and engaged in detestable practices, Israel will enjoy the Lord's holy presence in the Millennium.

# BIBLIOGRAPHY

Alexander, Ralph. *Ezekiel.* Everyman's Bible Commentary. Chicago: Moody Press, 1976.

Cooke, G.A. *A Critical and Exegetical Commentary on the Book of Ezekiel.* The International Critical Commentary. Edinburgh: T. & T. Clark, 1936.

Craigie, Peter C. *Ezekiel.* The Daily Study Bible (Old Testament). Philadelphia: Westminster Press, 1983.

Eichrodt, Walther. *Ezekiel.* The Old Testament Library. Philadelphia: Westminster Press, 1970.

Feinberg, Charles Lee. *The Prophecy of Ezekiel.* Chicago: Moody Press, 1969.

Fisch, S. *Ezekiel.* London: Soncino Press, 1950.

Greenberg, Moshe. *Ezekiel 1–20.* The Anchor Bible. Garden City, N.Y.: Doubleday & Co., 1983.

Hengstenberg, E.W. *The Prophecies of the Prophet Ezekiel Elucidated.* Translated by A.C. Murphy and J.G. Murphy. Edinburgh: T. & T. Clark, 1869. Reprint. Minneapolis: James Publications, 1976.

Keil, C.F. "Ezekiel." In *Commentary on the Old Testament in Ten Volumes.* Vol. 9. Reprint (25 vols. in 10). Grand Rapids: Wm. B. Eerdmans Publishing Co., 1982.

Tatford, Frederick A. *Dead Bones Live: An Exposition of the Prophecy of Ezekiel.* Eastbourne, East Sussex: Prophetic Witness Publishing House, 1977.

Taylor, John B. *Ezekiel: An Introduction and Commentary.* The Tyndale Old Testament Commentaries. Downers Grove, Ill.: InterVarsity Press, 1969.

Wevers, John W. *Ezekiel.* The New Century Bible Commentary. Grand Rapids: Wm. B. Eerdmans Publishing Co., 1969.

Zimmerli, Walther. *Ezekiel 1.* Translated by Ronald E. Clements. Philadelphia: Fortress Press, 1979.

_____. *Ezekiel 2.* Translated by James D. Martin. Philadelphia: Fortress Press, 1983.

# Outline of End-Time Events Predicted in the Bible*

I. Events Before, During, and After the Seven-Year End-Time Period (This seven-year period is the 70th "seven" of Daniel, Dan. 9:27.)
   A. Events immediately before the seven-year period
      1. Church raptured (John 14:1-3; 1 Cor. 15:51-52; 1 Thes. 4:16-18; Rev. 3:10)
      2. Restrainer removed (2 Thes. 2:7)
      3. Judgment seat of Christ (in heaven, 1 Cor. 3:12-15; 2 Cor. 5:10)
      4. Antichrist rises to power over the Roman confederacy (Dan. 7:20, 24)[1]
   B. Event at the beginning of the seven-year period
      Antichrist (the coming "ruler") makes a covenant with Israel (Dan. 9:26-27)
   C. Events in the first half of the seven-year period
      1. Israel living in peace in the land (Ezek. 38:8)
      2. Temple sacrifices instituted (Rev. 11:1-2)
      3. World church dominates religion and the Antichrist (Rev. 17)
   D. Events perhaps just before the middle of the seven-year period
      1. Gog and his allies invade Palestine from the north (Ezek. 38:2, 5-6, 22)[2]
      2. Gog and his allies destroyed by God (Ezek. 38:17-23)[2]
   E. Events at the middle of the seven-year period
      1. Satan cast down from heaven and energizes the Antichrist (Rev. 12:12-17)
      2. Antichrist breaks his covenant with Israel, causing her sacrifices to cease (Dan. 9:27)
      3. The 10 kings under the Antichrist destroy the world church (Rev. 17:16-18)
      4. The 144,000 Israelites saved and sealed (Rev. 7:1-8)[3]
   F. Events of the second half of the seven-year period
      These three-and-one-half years are called "the Great Tribulation" (Rev. 7:14; cf. "great distress," Matt. 24:21; "time of distress," Dan. 12:1; and "a time of trouble for Jacob," Jer. 30:7)
      1. Rebellion (apostasy) against the truth in the professing church (Matt. 24:12; 2 Thes. 2:3)[4]
      2. Antichrist becomes a world ruler (1st seal,[5] Rev. 6:1-2) with support of the Western confederacy (Rev. 13:5, 7; 17:12-13)
      3. Antichrist revealed as "the man of lawlessness," "the lawless one" (2 Thes. 2:3, 8-9)
      4. War, famine, and death (2nd, 3rd, and 4th seals,[5] Rev. 6:3-8)
      5. Converted multitudes from every nation martyred (5th seal,[5] Rev. 6:9-11; 7:9-14; Matt. 24:9)
      6. Natural disturbances and worldwide fear of divine wrath (6th seal,[5] Rev. 6:12-17)
      7. Antichrist's image (an "abomination") set up for worship (Dan. 9:27; Matt. 24:15; 2 Thes. 2:4; Rev. 13:14-15)
      8. Two witnesses begin their ministry (Rev. 11:3)[6]
      9. The false prophet promotes the Antichrist, who is worshiped by nations and unbelieving Israel (Matt. 24:11-12; 2 Thes. 2:11; Rev. 13:4, 11-15)
      10. Mark of the beast used to promote worship of the Antichrist (Rev. 13:16-18)
      11. Israel scattered because of the anger of Satan (Rev. 12:6, 13-17) and because of the "abomination" (Antichrist's image) in the temple (Matt. 24:15-26)
      12. Jerusalem overrun by

*Though premillenarians differ on the order of some of these events (see notes at the end of this outline) they do include all these events in the pattern of the end times.

Gentiles (Luke 21:24; Rev. 11:2)

13. Antichrist and false prophets deceive many people (Matt. 24:11; 2 Thes. 2:9-11)
14. The gospel of the kingdom proclaimed (Matt. 24:14)
15. Israel persecuted by the Antichrist (Jer. 30:5-7; Dan. 12:1; Zech. 13:8; Matt. 24:21-22)
16. Trumpet judgments (Rev. 8–9) and bowl judgments (Rev. 16) poured out by God on Antichrist's empire
17. Blasphemy increases as the judgments intensify (Rev. 16:8-11)

G. Events concluding the seven-year period
   1. Two witnesses slain by the Antichrist (Rev. 11:7)[7]
   2. Two witnesses resurrected (Rev. 11:11-12)[7]
   3. The king of the South (Egypt) and the king of the North fight against the Antichrist (Dan. 11:40a)[8]
   4. Antichrist enters Palestine and defeats Egypt, Libya, and Ethiopia (Dan. 11:40a-43)[8]
   5. Armies from the East and the North move toward Palestine (Dan. 11:44; Rev. 16:12)
   6. Jerusalem is ravaged (Zech. 14:1-4)
   7. Commercial Babylon is destroyed (Rev. 16:19; 18:1-3, 21-24)
   8. Signs appear in the earth and sky (Isa. 13:10; Joel 2:10, 30-31; 3:15; Matt. 24:29)
   9. Christ returns with the armies of heaven (Matt. 24:27-31; Rev. 19:11-16)
   10. Jews flee Jerusalem facilitated by topographical changes (Zech. 14:5)
   11. Armies unite at Armageddon against Christ and the armies of heaven (Joel 3:9-11; Rev. 16:16; 19:17-19)[8]
   12. Armies are destroyed by Christ (Rev. 19:19, 21)[8]
   13. The "beast" (Antichrist) and the false prophet are thrown

into the lake of fire (Rev. 19:20)

H. Events following the seven-year period
   1. Final regathering of Israel (Isa. 11:11-12; Jer. 30:3; Ezek. 36:24; 37:1-14; Amos 9:14-15; Micah 4:6-7; Matt. 24:31)
   2. A remnant of Israelites turn to the Lord and are forgiven and cleansed (Hosea 14:1-5; Zech. 12:10; 13:1)
   3. National deliverance of Israel from the Antichrist (Dan. 12:1b; Zech. 12:10; 13:1; Rom. 11:26-27)
   4. Judgment of living Israel (Ezek. 20:33-38; Matt. 25:1-30)
   5. Judgment of living Gentiles (Matt. 25:31-46)
   6. Satan cast into the abyss (Rev. 20:1-3)
   7. Old Testament saints resurrected (Isa. 26:19; Dan. 12:1-3)
   8. Tribulation saints resurrected (Rev. 20:4-6)
   9. Daniel 9:24 fulfilled
   10. Marriage supper of the Lamb (Rev. 19:7-9)
   11. Christ begins His reign on earth (Ps. 72:8; Isa. 9:6-7; Dan. 2:14-35, 44; 7:13-14; Zech. 9:10; Rev. 20:4)

II. Characteristics and Events of the Millennium
A. Physical characteristics
   1. Topography and geography of the earth changed (Isa. 2:2; Ezek. 47:1-12; 48:8-20; Zech. 14:4, 8, 10)
   2. Wild animals tamed (Isa. 11:6-9; 35:9; Ezek. 34:25)
   3. Crops abundant (Isa. 27:6; 35:1-2, 6-7; Amos 9:13; Zech. 14:8)
   4. Human longevity increased (Isa. 65:20-23)

B. Spiritual and religious characteristics and events
   1. Satan confined in the abyss (Rev. 20:1-3)
   2. Millennial temple built (Ezek. 40:5–43:27)
   3. Animal sacrifices offered as memorials to Christ's death (Isa. 56:7; 66:20-23;

Jer. 33:17-18;
Ezek. 43:18-27; 45:13–46:24;
Mal. 3:3-4)

4. Feasts of the New Year,
Passover, and Tabernacles
reinstituted (Ezek. 45:18-25;
Zech. 14:16-21)

5. Nations worship in Jerusalem
(Isa. 2:2-4; Micah 4:2; 7:12;
Zech. 8:20-23; 14:16-21)

6. Worldwide knowledge of God
(Isa. 11:9; Jer. 31:34; Micah 4:5;
Hab. 2:14)

7. Unparalleled filling of and
empowerment by the Holy
Spirit on Israel
(Isa. 32:15; 44:3; Ezek. 36:24-29;
39:29; Joel 2:28-29)

8. New Covenant with Israel
fulfilled (Jer. 31:31-34;
Ezek. 11:19-20; 36:25-32)

9. Righteousness and justice
prevails (Isa. 9:7; 11:4; 42:1-4;
Jer. 23:5)

C. Political characteristics and events
1. Israel reunited as a nation
(Jer. 3:18; Ezek. 37:15-23)

2. Israel at peace in the land
(Deut. 30:1-10; Isa. 32:18;
Hosea 14:5, 7; Amos 9:15;
Micah 4:4; 5:4-5a; Zech. 3:10;
14:11)

3. Abrahamic Covenant land-
grant boundaries established
(Gen. 15:18-21;
Ezek. 47:13–48:8, 23-27)

4. Christ in Jerusalem rules over
Israel (Isa. 40:11;
Micah 4:7; 5:2b)

5. Davidic Covenant fulfilled
(Christ on the throne of
David, 2 Sam. 7:11-16;
Isa. 9:6-7; Jer. 33:17-26;
Amos 9:11-12; Luke 1:32-33)

6. Christ rules over and judges
the nations (Isa. 11:3-5;
Micah 4:2-3a; Zech. 14:9;
Rev. 19:15)

7. Resurrected saints reign with
Christ (Matt. 19:28;
2 Tim. 2:12; Rev. 5:10; 20:6)

8. Universal peace prevails
(Isa. 2:4; 32:17-18; 60:18;
Hosea 2:18; Micah 4:2-4; 5:4;
Zech. 9:10)

9. Jerusalem made the world's
capital (Jer. 3:17;
Ezek. 48:30-35; Joel 3:16-17;

Micah 4:1, 6-8; Zech. 8:2-3)

10. Israel exalted above the
Gentiles (Isa. 14:1-2; 49:22-23;
60:14-17; 61:5-9)

11. The world blessed through
Israel (Micah 5:7)

D. Events following the Millennium
1. Satan released from the abyss
(Rev. 20:7)

2. Satan deceives the nations
(Rev. 20:8)

3. Global armies besiege
Jerusalem (Rev. 20:9a)

4. Global armies destroyed by
fire (Rev. 20:9b)

5. Satan cast into the lake of fire
(Rev. 20:10)

6. Evil angels judged (1 Cor. 6:3)

7. The wicked dead resurrected
(Dan. 12:2b; John 5:29b)

8. The wicked judged at the
Great White Throne
(Rev. 20:11-14)

9. The wicked cast into the lake
of fire (Rev. 20:14-15; 21:8)

III. Eternity
A. Christ delivers the mediatorial
(millennial) kingdom to God the
Father (1 Cor. 15:24)

B. Present heavens and earth
demolished (Rev. 21:1)

C. New heavens and new earth
created (2 Peter 3:10; Rev. 21:1)

D. New Jerusalem descends to the
new earth (Rev. 21:2, 10-27)

E. Christ rules forever in the eternal
kingdom (Isa. 9:6-7;
Ezek. 37:24-28; Dan. 7:13-14;
Luke 1:32-33; Rev. 11:15)

*Notes*

1. Some identify Antichrist's initial rise
to power with the first seal judgment
(Rev. 6:1-2)

2. Some place the battle of Gog and his
allies at the very middle of the seven-
year period; others place it later.

3. Some say the 144,000 will be saved
and sealed in the first half of the
seven-year period.

4. According to some, this apostasy will
begin in the first half of the seven-year
period.

5. Many premillenarians place the seal
judgments in the first half of
the seven-year period.

6. Some Bible scholars say the work of
the two witnesses will be in the
first half of the seven-year period.

7. Some suggest that the two witnesses will be slain and resurrected in the first half of the seven-year period.

8. Some equate these events with the battle of Gog and his allies.

# DANIEL

## J. Dwight Pentecost

## INTRODUCTION

Though the Book of Daniel is placed after the Prophet Ezekiel in English Bibles (as well as in the LXX and the Vulgate), the prophecy of Daniel is in a different place in the Hebrew Scriptures. The Hebrew Bible is divided into three portions. the first division is the Law, containing the five Books of Moses. The second is the Prophets, which includes Joshua, Judges, 1 and 2 Samuel (in Heb. 1 and 2 Sam. are one book), 1 and 2 Kings (also counted as one book), Isaiah, Jeremiah, Ezekiel, and the 12 Minor Prophets (which are counted as one book). The third classification is called the Writings. It contains 12 books: Psalms, Proverbs, Job, Song of Solomon, Ruth, Lamentations, Ecclesiastes, Esther, Daniel, Ezra, Nehemiah, 1 and 2 Chronicles (the latter two counted as one book). Thus the Book of Daniel is not included among the Prophets, the second major division. Nor is the man Daniel referred to in his book as a prophet. Also God did not deliver a message through Daniel *publicly* to the nation Israel. Yet Jesus called Daniel a prophet (Matt. 24:15). Certainly he was God's messenger with God's message to reveal truths God had disclosed to him.

**Author.** This book bears the simple title, "Daniel," not only because he is one of the chief characters portrayed in the book but more so because it follows a custom (though not a consistent one) of affixing the name of the author to the book he wrote. Little is known of Daniel's family background. From the testimony of his contemporaries he was known for his righteousness (Ezek. 14:14, 20) and his wisdom (Ezek. 28:3). He is mentioned in these passages with Noah and Job, who were historical people, so Daniel was also a historical person, not a fictional character.

Daniel was born into the royal family and was of noble birth (Dan. 1:3, 6). He was physically attractive and mentally sharp (1:4). He lived at least until the third year of Cyrus, that is, till 536 B.C. (10:1). Therefore he must have been a young man when he was taken captive by Nebuchadnezzar in 605 B.C. (In 1:4 Daniel was one of the "young" men of Israel.) If he were 16 when captured, he was 85 in Cyrus' third year.

**Literary Form.** The prophecy of Daniel is the first great book of apocalyptic literature in the Bible. The Greek word *apokalypsis,* from which comes the English "apocalypse," means an unveiling, a disclosing, or a revelation. Though all Scripture is revelation from God, certain portions are unique in the form by which their revelations were given and in the means by which they were transmitted.

Apocalyptic literature in the Bible has several characteristics: (1) In apocalyptic literature a person who received God's truths in visions recorded what he saw. (2) Apocalyptic literature makes extensive use of symbols or signs. (3) Such literature normally gives revelation concerning God's program for the future of His people Israel. (4) Prose was usually employed in apocalyptic literature, rather than the poetic style which was normal in most prophetic literature.

In addition to Daniel and Revelation, apocalyptic literature is found in Ezekiel 37–48 and Zechariah 1:7–7:8. In interpreting visions, symbols, and signs in apocalyptic literature, one is seldom left to his own ingenuity to discover the truth. In most instances an examination of the context or a comparison with a parallel biblical passage provides the Scriptures' own interpretation of the visions or the symbols employed. Apocalyptic literature then demands a careful comparison of Scripture with Scripture to arrrive at a correct understanding of the revelation being given.

**Languages.** The Book of Daniel is unusual in that it is written in two languages: 1:1–2:4a and chapters 8–12 are in Hebrew, and 2:4b–7:28 is in Aramaic, the lingua franca of the prophet's day. Hebrew was the language of God's covenant people Israel, and Aramaic was the language of the Gentile world.

Though the Book of Daniel is a single literary work, it has two major emphases. One has to do with God's program for the Gentile nations. This is contained in 2:4b–7:28. It was fitting that this prophecy concerning the Gentiles should be in their language. Hence the prophet used Aramaic in that portion of the book.

The second major emphasis is on the nation Israel and the influence or effect of the Gentiles on Israel. This theme is developed in 1:1–2:4a and chapters 8–12. Therefore it was fitting that Daniel wrote those portions in Hebrew, the language of the Jews.

**Unity.** Some scholars have questioned the unity of the Book of Daniel. They point out that chapters 1–6 record historical incidents in Daniel's lifetime, and that chapters 7–12 record prophetic visions given to Daniel. This observation, coupled with Daniel's use of two languages, has led some to infer a multiplicity of authors.

However, those observations do not support such a conclusion. As already pointed out, Daniel had reasons for employing two languages. Ancient literature often used different literary forms to heighten a contrast. The Book of Job, for instance, is mostly poetic but the prologue (chaps. 1–2) and epilogue (42:7-17) are in prose. Thus nothing in the literary style of the Book of Daniel demands more than one author.

The unity of Daniel's book is further supported by noting the interdependence of its two portions. The revelation in chapter 2 parallels closely the revelation in chapter 7. Further, some of the terms and theological concepts in the first half are similar to those in the second half. "Dream(s) and visions" are mentioned in 1:17; 2:28; 7:1. Lying "on (in) . . . bed" is referred to in 2:28; 4:10; 7:1. That God's "kingdom" is eternal is spoken of four times in the first half (2:44; 4:3, 34; 6:26) and three times in the second half (7:14, 18, 27). God's eternal "dominion" is extolled in 4:3, 34; 6:26; 7:14. And God is called "the Most High" or "the Most High God" nine times in the first half (3:26; 4:2, 17, 24-25, 32, 34; 5:18, 21) and four times in the second half (7:18, 22, 25, 27).

Also Daniel has a significant and unifying role in both portions of the book. Furthermore the message of the book is the same in both halves of the book. God is sovereign, rules over the nations, and controls them so that they fulfill His will. He is sovereignly preserving the nation Israel and bringing her to the fulfillment of the covenant He made with Abraham.

**Date and Authorship.** According to the contents of the Book of Daniel, it was written in the sixth century B.C. by Daniel who lived during its events. Daniel is referred to many times as the recipient of God's revelation. And he took part in many of the historical events recorded in the book. The Lord Himself attributed the authorship of the book to Daniel (Matt. 24:15). Daniel's familiarity with the individuals spoken of in the book and with the historical events and customs mentioned in the book necessitates a sixth-century date for the book.

The minute details included in the book could hardly have been retained accurately by oral tradition for some 400 years, as suggested by those who postulate a late date for the book. The fact that manuscript fragments from the Book of Daniel were found in Qumran, written perhaps in the second century B.C., preclude the notion that Daniel was written in 165 B.C., as many critics suggest. Not enough time would have been available for the book to have reached the Essene community in Qumran and for it to have been copied there. Also the fact that the Book of Daniel was accepted by the Jews into the canon of Scripture bears witness to its authenticity.

Critics reject an early date for the writing of Daniel mainly because they reject predictive prophecy. The book unfolds details concerning the history of Babylon, Medo-Persia, Greece, and Rome. Details recorded in Daniel 11:5-35 were fulfilled in the fourth to the second centuries B.C. Skeptics insist that Daniel could not have foreknown those details but must have written them *after* the events transpired and cast them in the form of prophecy to give credence to his writing. (Or they maintain that someone other than the Prophet Daniel wrote the book in the second century B.C. and used his name.) Such a view of course denies the power of God to reveal what He has predetermined.

A number of other objections have been raised against the early date for the book. For example, some argue that the several Persian and Greek words in the book indicate that it must have been written much later than the sixth century B.C. However, archeology has revealed that commerce existed between Greece and Babylon even *before* Daniel's day. This would explain the presence of Greek words. And the Persian words in the book were from an official or literary form of the Persian language which was in wide use throughout the Near East. (Cf. D.J. Wiseman et al., *Notes on Some Problems in the Book of Daniel*, pp. 23-7, 35-50.)

A further objection is based on the apocalyptic literature found in the book. Such literature appeared prolifically in Israel in the later time of the Maccabees (literature that is not part of the biblical canon); therefore many scholars infer that the book must have been written in that period (168–134 B.C.). However, as already noted (see "Literary Form"), apocalyptic literature is found in the Book of Ezekiel and he, like Daniel, was a sixth-century prophet.

Further objection is made to an early date because of the advanced theology in the book. Critics claim that frequent references to angels and a reference to the resurrection of the dead (12:2) necessitates a late postexilic date for the book. This, however, overlooks the fact that angels are frequently referred to throughout Israel's long history and that resurrection is mentioned in passages such as Psalm 16:10 and Isaiah 26:19, which certainly predate the time of Daniel.

Some have objected to Daniel's sixth-century date on the grounds that the book is included in the Writings, the third section of the Hebrew Bible, rather than among the Prophets, the second division. The last prophetic book (Malachi) was written in the fifth century B.C. Those arguing for a late date for Daniel

allege that if his book were written in the sixth century, it would have been included in the second division (the Prophets) rather than relegated to the third (the Writings). However, as previously noted, the prophets were set apart by God as His messengers with a special ministry to the nation Israel. Since Daniel was counted by his contemporaries as a governmental leader rather than a prophet, his writings were included in the third division rather than in the second. Thus the status of the author rather than the date of his book determined the division in which his book was included in the Hebrew Bible.

Some critics hold that since God's name Yahweh is not used by Daniel and since the name was commonly used in Daniel's day by others, the book must have been written at a later time. However, this objection fails to note that in chapter 9 this name *is* used eight times (Dan. 9:2, 4, 8, 10, 13-14 [thrice], 20). The name for God an author used in a given passage was determined by his content, not by popular custom.

Some have objected to Daniel's authorship because of supposed historical errors found in the book. Some have asserted, for instance, that Nebuchadnezzar was not the father of Belshazzar, as indicated in Daniel 5:2, 11, 13, 18 (cf. v. 22). They argue that if Daniel had written the book, he would not have made such an error. However, it has been demonstrated that a royal successor to the throne was called a "son" (5:22) even if he had no blood relationship to an earlier king. (See the chart "Kings of the Neo-Babylonian Empire.")

Again objection is made to Daniel's authorship because the writer refers in 1:21 to the time of Daniel's death. However, 1:21 does not state when Daniel died; it states that he "remained there" (in Babylon) till Cyrus' first year. Cyrus' decree liberated the Jews from their exile in Babylon, thus bringing the 70-year Captivity to a near end. Daniel 1:21 is simply pointing out that Daniel lived through the span of the Captivity. The verse does not specify the time of his death. In fact he lived on into at least Cyrus' third year (10:1).

**Historical Background.** Nineveh, the Assyrian capital, fell before the assault of

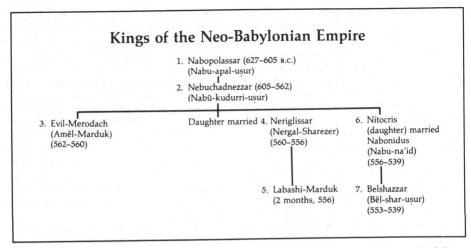

# Kings of the Neo-Babylonian Empire

1. Nabopolassar (627–605 B.C.)
   (Nabu-apal-uṣur)

2. Nebuchadnezzar (605–562)
   (Nabū-kudurri-uṣur)

3. Evil-Merodach
   (Amēl-Marduk)
   (562–560)

Daughter married 4. Neriglissar
   (Nergal-Sharezer)
   (560–556)

6. Nitocris
   (daughter) married
   Nabonidus
   (Nabu-na'id)
   (556–539)

5. Labashi-Marduk
   (2 months, 556)

7. Belshazzar
   (Bēl-shar-uṣur)
   (553–539)

the forces of Babylon and Media in 612 B.C. Under the leadership of Ashur-uballiṭ some Assyrians fled westward to Haran, from which they claimed authority over all of Assyria. Nabopolassar, the king of Babylon, moved in 611 B.C. against the Assyrian forces in Haran. The next year, 610 B.C., Babylon, allied with Media, attacked the Assyrians in Haran. Assyria withdrew from Haran westward beyond the Euphrates River and left Haran to the Babylonians.

In 609 B.C. the Assyrians sought the help of Egypt, and Pharaoh Neco II led an army from Egypt to join Assyria. Josiah, the king of Judah, hoping to incur favor with the Babylonians, sought to prevent the Egyptians from joining Assyria and met the Egyptian army at Megiddo. Josiah's army was defeated and he was killed in this attempt (2 Kings 23:28–30; 2 Chron. 35:24).

Pharaoh Neco proceeded to join the Assyrians and together they assaulted Babylon at Haran but were unsuccessful. Assyria seems to have passed from the scene at that time, but conflict continued between Egypt and Babylon.

In 605 B.C. Nebuchadnezzar led Babylon against Egypt in the Battle of Carchemish. Egypt was defeated, and Carchemish was destroyed by the Babylonians in May-June of that year. While pursuing the defeated Egyptians Nebuchadnezzar expanded his territorial conquests southward into Syria and toward Palestine. Learning of the death of his father Nabopolassar, Nebuchadnezzar returned from Riblah to Babylon in August 605 to receive the crown. Then he

returned to Palestine and attacked Jerusalem in September 605. It was on this occasion that Daniel and his companions were taken to Babylon as captives. Perhaps Nebuchadnezzar considered them hostages to warn the people in Judah against rebellion. Or the young men may have been taken to Babylon to prepare them for positions of administrative leadership there if Nebuchadnezzar should have to return to subjugate Judah. Returning to Babylon, Nebuchadnezzar reigned for 43 years (605–562).

Nebuchadnezzar returned to Judah a second time in 597 B.C. in response to Jehoiachin's rebellion. In this incursion Jerusalem was brought in subjection to Babylon, and 10,000 captives were taken to Babylon, among whom was the Prophet Ezekiel (Ezek. 1:1-3; 2 Kings 24:8-20; 2 Chron. 36:6-10).

Nebuchadnezzar returned to Judah a third time in 588 B.C. After a long siege against Jerusalem the city walls were breached, the city destroyed, and the temple burned in the year 586. Most of the Jews who were not killed in this assault were deported to Babylon (2 Kings 25:1-7; Jer. 34:1-7; 39:1-7; 52:2-11).

The restoration of the Jews back to their land was made possible when in 539 B.C. Cyrus overthrew Babylon and established the Medo-Persian Empire. Having a policy to restore displaced peoples to their lands, Cyrus issued a decree in 538 that permitted the Jews who so desired to return to Jerusalem (2 Chron. 36:22-23; Ezra 1:1-4). About 50,000 Jewish exiles returned to the land and began to rebuild the temple. This was in keeping with Daniel's prayer (Dan. 9:4-19). The temple was completed in 515 B.C. (Ezra 6:15). (See the chart "The Three Returns from Exile," in the *Introduction* to Ezra.) From the first subjugation of Jerusalem (605 B.C.) until the Jews returned and rebuilt the temple foundation (536) was approximately 70 years. From the destruction of the temple (586) until the temple was rebuilt (515) was also about 70 years. So Jeremiah's prophecy about the 70-year duration of the Babylon Exile was literally fulfilled (Jer. 25:11-12).

**Purposes.** The purposes of the book can be deduced from its contents:

1. Daniel's personal dedication to God (Dan. 1) would have been an example to the deportees on how they should live in a heathen society. Daniel served as an outstanding example of godliness to the exiles.

2. The book emphasizes God's sovereign authority over Gentile nations, how He establishes and deposes kings and empires to serve His purpose. It was this great truth that Nebuchadnezzar came to understand (4:35).

3. The book gives an example of God's faithfulness to His covenant people in protecting and preserving them even though they were under divine discipline for their disobedience. God does not cast off His covenant people; He deals patiently with them to bring them to blessing.

4. The book was also written to outline graphically the prophetic period known as "the times of the Gentiles" (Luke 21:24). The Book of Daniel marks the course of Gentile history through that extended period in which Israel was and is being disciplined by Gentiles. Also the consummation of God's program for the Gentiles will come to its conclusion in the coming Tribulation period. The book carefully and in detail shows the effect the Gentile nations will have on Israel while she is waiting for God's covenants to her to be fulfilled under the Messiah's reign.

5. Daniel's book also reveals Israel's future deliverance and the blessings she will enjoy in the coming Millennial Age. As God covenanted with Abraham, his descendants will occupy the land God promised them. Even though the nation must be disciplined because of her dis-

obedience, she will be brought to repentance, confession, and restoration. God remains faithful. He preserves His covenant people and guarantees them ultimate blessing in their covenanted kingdom on this earth.

**Importance of the Book.** The Book of Daniel is important historically. It bridges the gap between Israel's historical books and the New Testament. It records certain events in Israel's history in the 70-year Babylonian Captivity which are recorded nowhere else in Scripture (except for snatches of information in Ezek.). Daniel outlines the history of the times of the Gentiles and describes past and future empires that occupy Palestine and rule over Israel until the Messiah returns.

The prophecies in the book concerning God's program for the Gentiles, for the land of Palestine, and for the people of Israel, lay the foundation for His eschatological program. Some of the themes introduced in the Book of Daniel, with its emphasis on the Gentiles, are paralleled in the Book of Zechariah. And the themes introduced in these books come to their ultimate consummation in the Book of Revelation. To understand fully the culmination of God's program revealed to the Apostle John in Revelation, it is necessary to understand the inception of His program revealed to Daniel.

# OUTLINE

I. Personal History of Daniel (chap. 1)
  A. Daniel's deportation (1:1-7)
  B. Daniel's devotion to God (1:8-16)
    1. The request (1:8)
    2. The request granted (1:9-14)
    3. The result (1:15-16)
  C. Daniel's appointment (1:17-21)
II. Prophetic History of the Gentiles during the Times of the Gentiles (chaps. 2–7)
  A. The dream of Nebuchadnezzar (chap. 2)
    1. The dream of the king (2:1-16)
    2. The dream revealed to Daniel (2:17-23)
    3. The dream explained to

# COMMENTARY

## I. Personal History of Daniel (chap. 1)

### A. Daniel's deportation (1:1-7)

**1:1-2a.** The first two verses of the Book of Daniel state when and how the prophet was taken to Babylon. The events in the book began **in the third year of the reign of Jehoiakim king of Judah.** This seems to conflict with Jeremiah's statement that the first year of Nebuchadnezzar, king of Babylon, was in the *fourth* year of Jehoiakim's reign (Jer. 25:1). At least two explanations may be given for this apparent discrepancy. The first is the difference between Jewish and Babylonian reckoning. The Jewish calendar began the year in Tishri (September-October) while the Babylonian calendar began in the spring in the month of Nisan (March-April). If Babylonian reckoning were used, the year Nebuchadnezzar besieged Jerusalem was the fourth year of Jehoiakim's reign. But if the Jewish reckoning were used it was Jehoiakim's third year. Daniel, a Jew, may well have adopted the familiar Jewish calendar.

A second explanation is based on the Babylonian method of reckoning the dates of a king's reign. The portion of a king's reign that preceded the beginning of a new year in the month Nisan, that is, the year of accession, was called the first year even if it was of short duration. If Jeremiah followed that method of reckoning, he counted Jehoiakim's year of accession (which was only part of a full year) as the first year. And if Daniel used the Jewish method of reckoning (which did *not* count the first months of a king's reign before the new year) he then counted only the three full years of Jehoiakim's reign. The year was 605 B.C.

Daniel referred to **Nebuchadnezzar** (whose name means "Nabu has protected my inheritance") as **king of Babylon.** At that time (605) Nabopolassar was king in Babylon, and Nebuchadnezzar had not yet acceded to the throne. However, Nebuchadnezzar, while in battle, heard of the death of his father and hastened to Babylon to be enthroned (see "Historical Background" in the *Introduction*). Writing at a later date, Daniel referred to Nebuchadnezzar as king in anticipation of his occupation of the throne.

Nebuchadnezzar's besieging of **Jerusalem** took place during the reign of **Jehoiakim,** the 17th **king of Judah** and eldest son of Josiah (cf. 2 Chron. 36:2 with 2 Chron. 36:5). Jehoiakim's younger brother Jehoahaz had been placed on Judah's throne after Pharaoh Neco killed King Josiah in 609 B.C. (See the chart "The Last Five Kings of Judah," near 2 Kings 23:31-35.) But Neco dethroned Jehoahaz and placed Jehoiakim on the throne (2 Chron. 36:3-4).

Jeremiah had warned Jehoiakim of impending invasion by Babylon. And Jehoiakim had heard of the prophet's instruction to God's people to submit to Babylon without resistance. So when Nebuchadnezzar besieged the city, little or no resistance was offered, and Jehoiakim was captured and taken to Babylon. Thus Judah came under Nebuchadnezzar's authority.

With this incursion by Nebuchadnezzar an important prophetic time period —the times of the Gentiles (Luke 21:24)—began. The times of the Gentiles is that extended period of time in which the land given in covenant by God to Abraham and his descendants is occupied by Gentile powers and the Davidic throne is empty of any rightful heir in the Davidic line. The times of the Gentiles, beginning with Nebuchadnezzar's invasion of Jerusalem in 605 B.C., will continue till the Messiah returns. Then Christ will subdue nations, deliver the land of Israel from its Gentile occupants, and bring the nation Israel into her covenanted blessings in the millennial kingdom.

God had made a covenant with Israel in Moab (Deut. 28–30) just before she entered the land (Deut. 29:1). In this covenant God set forth the principle by which He would deal with His people. Their obedience to Him would bring blessing (Deut. 28:1-14) but disobedience to Him would bring discipline (Deut. 28:15-68). In this second portion God outlined the disciplines He would use to correct the people when their walk was out of line with His revealed Law. These disciplines would seek to conform them to His demands so they would be eligible for His blessings. The ultimate discipline He would use to correct His people was the invasion of Gentile nations who would subjugate them to their authority and disperse them from their land (Deut. 28:49-68).

Moses then stated when Israel would come under God's discipline, that discipline would not be lifted until the people forsook their sin, turned in faith to God, and obeyed His requirements (Deut. 30:1-10). The Northern Kingdom of Israel had gone into captivity to Assyria in 722 B.C. This was the outworking of the principles of Deuteronomy 28. From time to time (though not consistently) the Southern Kingdom (Judah), in light of the fall of the Northern Kingdom, had heeded the prophets' admonitions and turned to God. The Southern Kingdom continued for more than a century longer because of her repentance and obedience under her godly kings.

That condition, however, did not last. Judah also ignored God's covenant, neglected the Sabbath Day and the sabbatical year (Jer. 34:12-22), and went into idolatry (Jer. 7:30-31). Therefore, because of the covenant in Deuteronomy 28, judgment had to fall on Judah. God chose Nebuchadnezzar as the instrument to inflict discipline on God's disobedient people (cf. Jer. 27:6; Hab. 1:6).

**1:2b-3.** When Nebuchadnezzar returned to Babylon from this invasion of Judah, he brought spoils to signify Judah's submission to Babylon. First, he brought some valuable **articles from the temple** in Jerusalem which he placed in **the temple of his god in Babylonia** (cf. 2 Chron. 36:7). "His god" may have been Bel, also called Marduk, the chief god of the Babylonians (cf. comments on Dan. 4:8). (In Heb. the word rendered Babylonia is Shinar, NIV marg., an ancient name for that land; cf. Gen. 10:10; 11:2; 14:1;

Isa. 11:11, NIV marg.; Zech. 5:11, NIV marg.) This would signify the conquest of the God of Judah by the Babylonian deities.

Second, Nebuchadnezzar brought with him **some of the Israelites** (Jews) **from the royal family and the nobility.** As stated in the *Introduction*, these royal princes may have been considered hostages, to help assure Judah's continued submission to Babylon. Or they may have been taken to Babylon to prepare them to fulfill positions of administrative leadership there if Nebuchadnezzar should have to return to subjugate Judah. **Ashpenaz** was **chief of the court officials.** He is mentioned by name only here in the Old Testament but is called "the official" or "the chief official" six times (Dan. 1:7-11, 18). It is not clear whether the word for "official" (*sārîs*) means a eunuch or simply a courtier or court officer. Kitchen suggests it meant eunuch in Daniel's time (Kenneth A. Kitchen, *Ancient Orient and Old Testament.* Downers Grove, Ill.: InterVarsity Press, 1966, pp. 165-6).

**1:4-5.** These captives were choice **young men** both physically and mentally and as such, they could be an asset to **the king's palace.** An attempt was made to assimilate them into the culture of the court for they were compelled to learn both **the language and** the **literature** of the people among whom they now dwelt. They were to undergo a rigorous **three-**year course of training **after** which **they were to enter the king's service.** That educational program probably included a study of agriculture, architecture, astrology, astronomy, law, mathematics, and the difficult Akkadian language.

**1:6-7.** No mention was made of how many captives were taken but four are mentioned here by name because of their later significant role in Babylon. Because all four bore names that honored Yahweh, the God of Israel, their names were changed. *El* means God and *-iah* (or *-yah*) is an abbreviation for Yahweh, thus suggesting that the young men's parents were God-fearing people who gave them names that included references to God. **Daniel,** whose name means "God has judged" (or "God is my Judge"), was given the name **Belteshazzar** (*Bēlet-šar-uṣur* in Akk.), which means "Lady, pro-

tect the king." Eight of the 10 times "Belteshazzar" occurs in the Old Testament are in the Aramaic section of the Book of Daniel (2:26; 4:8-9, 18-19 [3 times]; 5:12). The other 2 occurrences are in 1:7 and 10:1.

**Hananiah** ("Yahweh has been gracious") became **Shadrach** probably from the Akkadian verb form *šādurāku*, meaning "I am fearful (of a god)."

**Mishael** ("Who is what God is?") was given the name **Meshach,** which possibly was from the Akkadian verb *mēšāku,* meaning "I am despised, contemptible, humbled (before my god)."

**Azariah** ("Yahweh has helped") was named **Abednego,** "Servant of Nebo" (Nego being a Heb. variation of the Babylonian name of the god Nebo). Nebo (cf. Isa. 46:1), son of Bel, was the Babylonian god of writing and vegetation. He was also known as Nabu (cf. comments on Dan. 1:1 on Nebuchadnezzar's name).

Thus **the chief court official** (Ashpenaz, v. 3) seemed determined to obliterate any testimony to the God of Israel from the Babylonian court. The names he gave the four men signified that they were to be subject to Babylon's gods.

## B. Daniel's devotion to God (1:8-16)

### 1. THE REQUEST (1:8)

**1:8.** Nebuchadnezzar had made abundant provision for the captives. Theirs was a life of luxury, not deprivation, for they were given a portion of **food and wine** daily from the king's own table. However, this food did not conform to the requirements of the Mosaic Law. The fact that it was prepared by Gentiles rendered it unclean. Also no doubt many things forbidden by the Law were served on the king's table, so to partake of such food would defile the Jewish youths. Further, without doubt this royal food had been sacrificed and offered to pagan gods before it was offered to the king. To partake of such food would be contrary to Exodus 34:15, where the Jews were forbidden to eat flesh sacrificed to pagan gods.

Similar problems would arise in drinking the wine. To abstain from the Old Testament prohibition against "strong drink" (e.g., Prov. 20:1, KJV; Isa. 5:11, "drinks"), Jews customarily diluted wine with water. Some added 3 parts of water to wine, others 6 parts, and some as much as 10 parts of water to 1 part of wine. The Babylonians did not dilute their wine. So both the food and the drink would have defiled these Jewish young men. **Daniel** knew the requirements of the Law governing what he should and should not eat and drink.

Daniel's desire was to please God in all he did. So he **resolved** that even though he was not in his own land but in a culture that did not follow God's laws, he would consider himself under the Law. **He** therefore **asked the chief** court **official** to be excused from eating and drinking the food and wine generously supplied by the king. Daniel was courageous, determined, and obedient to God.

2. THE REQUEST GRANTED (1:9-14)

**1:9-10.** The chief official's reticence to grant Daniel's request is understandable. He was responsible to oversee the young captives' physical and mental development so they would become prepared for the roles **the king** had in mind for them. Evidently these youths held a strategic place in the king's plans, so he wanted them well trained. If the men had been of little consequence to **the king,** their physical conditions would not have mattered and Ashpenaz would not have risked the loss of his life.

**Daniel** had trusted his situation to God who intervened on Daniel's behalf to move the official's heart **to show favor** (*ḥeseḏ,* "loyal love") **and sympathy** (*raḥămîm,* "compassion") **to Daniel.**

**1:11-14.** When Daniel's request seemed to have been denied by **the chief official . . .** Daniel approached **the guard whom** Ashpenaz placed over the four youths and requested a **10**-day trial period in which **Daniel** and his companions would be given only **vegetables . . . and water.** (The Heb. word for vegetables, meaning "sown things," may also include grains.) Since the Mosaic Law designated no vegetables as unclean, Daniel could eat any vegetables put before him without defiling himself. In so short a time (**10 days**) there could have been no marked deterioration that would jeopardize the life of anyone in authority. In fact Daniel hinted that their **appearance** would be better than that of the others who were on the king's diet.

Since the guard was under the chief official's authority he must have acted not on his own but with permission from Ashpenaz. This indicates that God intervenes on behalf of those who trust Him, and protects and preserves those who obey Him, even under pagan rule.

3. THE RESULT (1:15-16)

**1:15-16. At the** conclusion **of the 10 days,** the four who had lived on vegetables appeared **healthier** than those who had dined on the king's **food.** Since the four looked better—and not worse than the others, as Ashpenaz had feared (v. 10)—he did not object to the diet Daniel had requested for himself and his friends. So they were allowed to continue on a diet of **vegetables.**

Though God did not prohibit eating meat altogether (cf. Gen. 9:3; Rom. 14:14; 1 Cor. 10:25-26), the vegetable diet was superior to the king's food. Also this shows that God blesses those who obey His commands and prospers those who trust Him. This incident would have been a lesson for the nation Israel. God had demanded obedience to the Law. Punishment came because of disobedience but even during a time of discipline, God protects and sustains those who obey Him and trust Him for their sustenance.

## C. Daniel's appointment (1:17-21)

**1:17. These four . . . men** being prepared by Nebuchadnezzar for positions of responsibility in the royal court were actually being prepared by God. For **God gave** them **knowledge and understanding** in many realms. "Knowledge" has to do with reasoning skills and thought processes. They were able to think clearly and logically. "Understanding" has to do with insight. This points up their ability to discern the nature of things clearly and to interpret them in their true light. The **literature and learning** in which God gave them ability was broad (cf. comments on v. 4). By divine enablement and through his years of instruction under able teachers, **Daniel** gained a wide knowledge of arts and sciences.

Though the knowledge of others in Babylon in those subjects may have equaled that of Daniel, he was superior to them all in one area: he had the God-given ability to **understand visions and dreams.** People have always been curious about the future and have sought to predict coming events. For example, after Israel entered the land of Canaan, they encountered many who attempted to prognosticate the future by various means. But Israel was forbidden to follow any of these practices (Deut. 18:9-13), which were also prevalent in Babylon.

**1:18-21. At the end of the time set by the king** (i.e., at the end of the three years' training; cf. v. 5), **the king** examined **Daniel** and his three companions and **found** that **none** equaled them. In fact they were **10 times better than all** who practiced the arts of divination. (On **magicians** and **enchanters,** see comments on v. 17.) "Ten times" is an idiom meaning "many times" (cf. Gen. 31:7, 41; Num. 14:22; Job 19:3).

The king consulted magicians, enchanters, sorcerers, astrologers, wise men, and diviners. "Magicians" (*ḥarṭummîm*, Dan. 1:20; 2:2) was a general word referring to men who practiced the occult. (This word is also used in Gen. 41:8, 24; Ex. 7:11, 22; 8:7, 18-19; 9:11.) "Enchanters" (*'aššāpîm*, used only twice in the OT, Dan. 1:20; 2:21) may refer to those who used incantations in exorcisms. The word "sorcerers" (*mᵉkaššᵉpîm*, 2:2) probably is from the Akkadian verb *kašāpu*, "to bewitch, to cast a spell." (This participial noun, rendered "sorcerers," used only here in Dan., occurs only four other times in the OT: Ex. 7:11; 22:18; Deut. 18:10; Mal. 3:5.) "Astrologers" (Heb., *kaśdîm*, Dan. 2:2, 4; Aram., *kaśdā'în*, 2:5, 10 [twice]; 3:8; 5:7, 11) seems to refer to a priestly class in the Babylonian religion (misleadingly rendered "Chaldeans" in the KJV) who depended on revelation through the stars, which were objects of worship. "Diviners" (*gāzᵉrîn*, 2:27; 4:7; 5:7, 11) may be those who sought to ascertain or decree the fate of others.

The practices of these five groups may have overlapped extensively. Several times Daniel referred to these men under the general rubric of "wise men" (2:12-14, 18, 24 [twice], 48; 4:6, 18; 5:7-8, 15).

Daniel's ministry in the royal court of Babylon continued until the overthrow of the Babylonian Empire by **Cyrus** in 539 B.C. God had said, "Those who honor Me, I will honor" (1 Sam. 2:30). **Daniel** determined to honor God even though

he was living where people did not have the high standards God demanded. And God honored Daniel's obedience to the Law and promoted him in the king's court. This incident would have reminded Israel that obedience brings blessing and that righteousness is a prerequisite for enjoying the covenanted blessings.

The fact that God gave Daniel the ability to understand and interpret visions and dreams (Dan. 1:17) meant that throughout Nebuchadnezzar's long reign he depended on Daniel for understanding future events, revealed through dreams and visions. This anticipated the ministry Israel will one day fulfill. God had set Israel apart to be a kingdom of priests (Ex. 19:6). As such they were God's light to the world (Isa. 42:6; 49:6). They were to receive God's revelation and communicate it to nations that were ignorant of God. They were continually reminded of their role by the lampstand erected in the tabernacle. Daniel, during his tenure in the royal court in Babylon, fulfilled that function as God's spokesman to the Gentiles. When Israel will enter her millennial blessing under the reign of the Messiah, she will fulfill the role for which she was set apart by God and will then communicate God's truth to the Gentiles (Zech. 8:21-23).

## II. Prophetic History of the Gentiles during the Times of the Gentiles (chaps. 2–7)

### A. The dream of Nebuchadnezzar (chap. 2)

1. THE DREAM OF THE KING (2:1-16)

*a. The dream (2:1-3)*

**2:1.** Soon after Nebuchadnezzar's accession to the throne, he was plagued with a recurring dream. Since Daniel recalled and interpreted only a single dream (cf. vv. 24-26), the use of the plural here (**dreams**) seems to indicate a recurrence of the same dream. This dream evidently was perceived by **Nebuchadnezzar** as having great significance, for he **was troubled** (cf. v. 3) by the dream and so agitated that he was unable to **sleep.**

**2:2-3. The king summoned** the wise men of his realm. They professed to be able to foretell the future by one means or another (cf. comments on 1:17). If the method used by one failed to produce the desired result, hopefully the method employed by another would reveal the dream's significance. They were called collectively to exercise their enchantments in order to give the king an interpretation that would placate him. **The king** challenged the wise men, saying, **I want to know what it means.**

### b. The desperation of the wise men (2:4-11)

**2:4.** Evidently the request to interpret a dream (v. 3) had been made of the wise men on other occasions for they were not surprised. (As stated under "Languages" in the *Introduction, 1:1–2:4a* is in Heb., and beginning with the words **O king** in verse 4b the language is **Aramaic** through 7:28.) The wise men confidently asserted that when **the king** revealed **the dream** to them, they would **interpret it** to him. They were confident that with their collective wisdom, they could satisfy the king with an interpretation.

**2:5-6.** Though **the king** may have made such a demand on the wise men previously and been satisfied with their answers, he evidently had never asked them to interpret a dream that he discerned had such significance. So he decided to test them. If they could predict the future by interpreting dreams, they should be able to reconstruct the past and *recall* the king's **dream.** So he refused to share his dream with them. This does not mean he had forgotten it. Had he done so, the wise men, to save themselves from death, could easily have fabricated a dream and then interpreted it. The king reasoned that if they could not recall the past, their predictions concerning the future could not be trusted.

The king promised **rewards** and **honor** for the wise men's recalling and interpreting **the dream. But** he put them under a death penalty (they would be **cut into pieces**) and their **houses** would be burned to **rubble** if they proved to be false prognosticators who could not recall **the dream.**

**2:7-9.** Again the wise men (cf. v. 4) asked that **the king** share **the dream** with them, promising then to **interpret it. The king** complained that they were stalling for **time.** He again referred to the **penalty** (cf. v. 5) for failure to tell him **the dream.** He felt that the only way he could trust

their interpretation of the future was by having them first recall his dream. Otherwise he would conclude that they were conspiring **to tell** him **misleading and wicked things.** Also Nebuchadnezzar may have become impatient with the wise men who were presumably older than he as he had inherited them from his father. Another reason for the test may have been that he was suspicious of their claims to wisdom.

**2:10-11.** To defend themselves, the wise men asserted that **the king** was making an unreasonable request, one never asked by any other potentate. They attested that the future belongs to **the gods,** not to **men.** Interestingly this was an admission that they had deceived **the king** in their past interpretations, a startling revelation from those held in high esteem in the court.

### c. The decree of the king (2:12-13)

**2:12-13.** After the wise men revealed that they were unable to satisfy the king's demands, **the king** was **angry and furious** (cf. 3:13, 19). He issued an order for **the execution of all the wise men of Babylon. The decree** was not only for those currently serving the king's court, but on all who professed to be able to reveal the future. Since **Daniel and his** three **friends** were classified as **wise men,** the judgment also fell on them.

### d. The declaration of Daniel (2:14-16)

**2:14-16.** What had transpired in the royal court was unknown to **Daniel.** Perhaps he had refused to answer the king's summons (v. 2) to avoid contact with the pagan leaders. When word came that he was under a death sentence, he tactfully asked **Arioch, the commander of the king's guard,** for the reason. **Arioch . . . explained** the incident that had exposed the wise men's deception of **the king.**

**Daniel** boldly approached **the king** with the request that the executions be stayed for a while **so that he might interpret** the king's **dream.** This took boldness because the king had already accused the wise men of wanting more **time** (v. 8).

**Daniel** was evidently held in high esteem by the king because he was permitted access to the king's presence and was able to petition the king directly.

Though not recorded, Daniel had possibly interpreted dreams previously, though not necessarily for the king. So he was sure he could recall the dream and interpret it.

### 2. THE DREAM REVEALED TO DANIEL (2:17-23)

#### a. The petition (2:17-18)

**2:17-18.** In this time of testing **Daniel** was calm. He **returned to his house,** sought out his three **friends,** and together they prayed **for mercy from the God of heaven.** ("God of heaven" is a title used of God six times in Dan.: 2:18-19, 28, 37, 44; 5:23, nine times in Ezra, and four times in Neh. Elsewhere in the OT it occurs only in Gen. 24:3, 7; Ps. 136:26; Jonah 1:9.)

Mercy is God's response to a person's need. Daniel recognized his own inability in the circumstances and turned to God in confidence, expecting the Lord to meet his need.

#### b. The revelation (2:19a)

**2:19a.** In response to the prayer of the four, the dream **was revealed to Daniel,** evidently that same **night.**

#### c. The praise (2:19b-23)

**2:19b-23.** **Daniel** responded appropriately by offering praise to **God.** He acknowledged that God is a God of **wisdom,** knowing the end from the beginning, and a God of **power,** for whatever He determines, He can do. Daniel began and concluded His prayer speaking of God's **wisdom and power** (cf. v. 23).

Evidences of His *power* are seen in His control of events (**He changes times and seasons**) and of the destiny of nations (**He sets up kings and deposes them**). Nebuchadnezzar was on the throne because God determined to use him there to fulfill His will.

Evidences of God's *wisdom* are seen in His imparting **wisdom to the wise** (v. 21b) and in His revealing **deep** and dark **things** (v. 22). **Light dwells with** God in the sense that all things are clear to Him though people are surrounded by **darkness.** God knows and can reveal the future. God, not Daniel's insight, gave him **the dream** and its interpretation. Daniel's prayer of praise closed with thanks that **God** had revealed the king's dream to the four who had trusted Him.

### 3. THE DREAM EXPLAINED TO NEBUCHADNEZZAR (2:24-45A)

#### a. The explanation by Daniel (2:24-30)

**2:24-25.** Receiving from God the knowledge of the **dream** and its interpretation (v. 19) **Daniel went to Arioch,** the king's executioner (cf. v. 14), and informed him that he was ready to **interpret** the king's **dream.** Evidently the royal court knew of the king's agitation for **Arioch took Daniel . . . at once** to **the king.** Officer Arioch wrongly claimed credit for having **found** an interpreter for the king's dream. Actually it was Daniel who "went to Arioch." Arioch evidently expected to be highly rewardly for finding someone who could alleviate the king's agitation.

**2:26-28. The king** inquired whether **Daniel** was **able to tell** him **what** he had dreamed and then to **interpret it.** Daniel was subjected to the same test of his veracity the king had demanded of the wise men. They had previously said that only the gods could reveal the future to man (v. 11). Now **Daniel** asserted that what the wise men of Babylon could not do (v. 27) by consorting with their false deities, Daniel was able to do because **there is a God in heaven** (cf. comments on v. 18) **who reveals mysteries** (v. 28; cf. v. 47). Daniel took no credit to himself (cf. v. 23).

**2:29-30.** Daniel asserted at the outset that the king's dream was prophetic (cf. v. 45, "what will take place in the future"), about **things to come** and **what** was **going to happen.** Nebuchadnezzar's dream covered the prophetic panorama of Gentile history from his time till the forthcoming subjugation of Gentile powers to Israel's Messiah. This time period is called "the times of the Gentiles" (Luke 21:24). This dream was given to Nebuchadnezzar, the first of many Gentile rulers who would exert power by divine appointment during the times of the Gentiles. God was not revealing spiritual truth to Nebuchadnezzar but facts concerning the political dominion that Gentiles would exercise. Everything in the dream would be readily understandable to Nebuchadnezzar.

Again Daniel humbly affirmed that the **mystery** was not **revealed to** him **because** he was wiser than others (cf. Dan. 2:27-28).

### b. The recitation of the dream (2:31-35)

**2:31-33.** The king's dream was relatively simple. Daniel reported that the **king** had seen an enormously **large statue.** Its size and **appearance** were **awesome.** It made the king appear insignificant when he stood before it. The **statue** was **dazzling** because of the metals of which it was made. **The head of the** image was fashioned **of pure gold,** the **chest and arms** were **of silver,** the **belly and thighs of bronze,** and the **legs** were **of iron,** with **its feet partly . . . iron and partly . . . baked clay.** A casual glance would reveal the various parts of the statue.

**2:34-35. The statue** was not permanent; it was **struck** on **the feet** by **a rock (cut . . . not by human hands)** which reduced the whole statue **like chaff** that was blown away. Chaff was the light, unedible portion of grain stalks which blew away when the broken stalks were winnowed (tossed up in the air) on a windy **summer** day. **The rock that** destroyed **the statue** grew into **a huge mountain** that **filled the whole earth.** The dream itself was simple. It was the meaning of the dream that agitated the king.

### c. The interpretation of the dream (2:36-45a)

**2:36-38.** Daniel's interpretation makes it clear that the image revealed the course of Gentile kingdoms which in turn would rule over the land of Palestine and the people of Israel. Nebuchadnezzar, head of the Babylonian Empire, was represented by the **head of gold** (v. 38). His father had come to power in Babylon by military conquest, but Nebuchadnezzar received his **dominion and power and might and glory** from God (who sets up kings and deposes them, v. 21). (On **the God of heaven** see comments on v. 18.)

Nebuchadnezzar's rule was viewed as a worldwide empire, in which he ruled over all **mankind** as well as over **beasts** and **birds.** At the time of Creation the right to rule over the earth was given man who was to have dominion over it and all the creatures in it (Gen. 1:26). Here Nebuchadnezzar by divine appointment was helping fulfill what God had planned for man.

**2:39.** The second portion of the statue, the chest and arms of silver, represented the rise of the Medes and Persians

(cf. 5:28; 6:8; also cf. 5:31). The Medo-Persians conquered the Babylonians in 539 B.C. The arms of silver evidently represent the two nations of Media and Persia that together defeated Babylon. Though that **kingdom** lasted over 200 years (539–330 B.C.),longer than the Neo-Babylonian Empire of 87 years (626–539), the Medo-Persian Empire was **inferior to** it, as silver compared with gold.

The belly and thighs **of bronze** represented the third kingdom to arise. This was the Grecian Empire (cf. 8:20-21). Alexander the Great conquered the Medo-Persians between 334 and 330 B.C. and assumed authority over its peoples and territory. By Alexander's conquests he extended the Greek Empire as far east as the northwestern portion of India—an extensive empire that seemingly was **over the whole earth.**

**2:40.** The legs of **iron** represent the Roman Empire. This fourth kingdom conquered the Greek Empire in 63 B.C. Though the Roman Empire was divided into two legs and culminated in a mixture of iron and clay, it was one empire. This empire was characterized by its strength, as **iron** is stronger than bronze, silver, and gold. The Roman Empire was stronger than any of the previous empires. It crushed **all the** empires that had preceded it. Rome in its cruel conquest swallowed up the lands and peoples that had been parts of the three previous empires and assimilated those lands and peoples into itself.

**2:41-43.** The empire that began as **iron** regressed to a state of **clay** mixed with **iron.** This mixture speaks of progressive weakness and deterioration. Two metals together form an alloy which may be stronger than either of the metals individually. But **iron** and **clay** cannot be mixed. If iron and clay are put into a crucible, heated to the melting point, and poured into a mold, when the pour has cooled the iron and clay remain separate. The clay can be broken out which leaves a weak casting.

The Roman Empire was characterized by division (it was **a divided kingdom**) and deterioration (it was **partly strong and partly brittle**). Though Rome succeeded in conquering the territories that came under its influence, it never could unite the peoples to form a united empire. In that sense **the people** were **a** mixture and were not **united.** (Other views of this mixture of strength and weakness are suggested: [a] the empire was strong organizationally but weak morally; [b] imperialism and democracy were united unsuccessfully; [c] government was intruded by the masses, i.e., mob rule; [d] the empire was a mixture of numerous races and cultures.)

**2:44-45a.** Daniel then focused on the overthrow of those kingdoms. **The time of those kings** may refer to the four empires or, more likely, it refers to the time of the 10 toes (v. 42) since the first four kingdoms were not in existence at the same time as apparently the toes will be (cf. comments on the 10 horns of the fourth beast, 7:24). Nebuchadnezzar had seen a **rock** hit and smash the image (2:34). The statue was destroyed by the rock, **not by human hands.** In Scripture a rock often refers to Jesus Christ, Israel's Messiah (e.g., Ps. 118:22; Isa. 8:14; 28:16; 1 Peter 2:6-8). God, who had enthroned Nebuchadnezzar and would transfer authority from Babylon to Medo-Persia, then to Greece, and ultimately to Rome, will one day invest political power in a King who will rule over the earth, subduing it to His authority, thus culminating God's original destiny for man (Gen. 1:27).

In Nebuchadnezzar's dream the smiting rock became **a mountain** that filled the whole earth (Dan. 2:35). In Scripture a mountain is often a symbol for a kingdom. So Daniel explained that the four empires which would rule over the land and the people of Israel would not be destroyed by human means, but rather by the coming of the Lord Jesus Christ, the striking Stone. When He comes He will establish the messianic kingdom promised to Israel through David (2 Sam. 7:16). At His return He will subjugate **all . . . kingdoms** to Himself, thus bringing **them to an end** (cf. Rev. 11:15; 19:11-20). Then He will rule **forever** in the Millennium and in the eternal state.

Amillennialists hold that this kingdom was established by Christ at His *First* Advent and that now the church is that kingdom. They argue that: (a) Christianity, like the growing mountain, began to grow and spread geographically and is still doing so; (b) Christ came in the days of the Roman Empire; (c) the

Roman Empire fell into the hands of 10 kingdoms (10 toes); (d) Christ is the chief Cornerstone (Eph. 2:20).

Premillenarians, however, hold that the kingdom to be established by Christ on earth is yet future. At least six points favor that view: (1) The stone will become a mountain suddenly, not gradually. Christianity did not suddenly fill "the whole earth" (Dan. 2:35) at Christ's First Advent. (2) Though Christ came in the days of the Roman Empire, He did not destroy it. (3) During Christ's time on earth the Roman Empire did not have 10 kings at once. Yet Nebuchadnezzar's statue suggests that when Christ comes to establish His kingdom, 10 rulers will be in existence and will be destroyed by Him. (4) Though Christ is now the chief Cornerstone to the church (Eph. 2:20) and "a stone that causes [unbelievers] to stumble" (1 Peter 2:8), He is not yet a smiting Stone as He will be when He comes again. (5) The Stone (Messiah) will crush and end all the kingdoms of the world. But the church has not and will not conquer the world's kingdoms. (6) The church is not a kingdom with a political realm, but the future Millennium will be. Thus Nebuchadnezzar's dream clearly teaches premillennialism, that Christ will return to earth to establish His rule on the earth, thereby subduing all nations. The church is not that kingdom.

### 4. DANIEL HONORED (2:45B-49)

**2:45b.** Daniel had validated his interpretation by first recalling **the dream** (vv. 31-35) and had certified that **the interpretation** (vv. 36-45a) was **trustworthy** because it had come from **God** (cf. vv. 19, 23, 28, 30), who holds the destiny of nations in His own power. He knows **what will take place in the future** (cf. vv. 28-29).

**2:46-47.** The **king** was so moved at Daniel's interpretation that he prostrated himself **before Daniel** and **ordered that an offering** be made to **Daniel,** an honor that would normally have been given only to the gods of Babylon. Such was Nebuchadnezzar's recognition of Daniel's divine authority. Through Daniel's revelation and interpretation of the dream, Nebuchadnezzar was led to confess that Daniel's **God** is superior to all the **gods** of Babylon and that He is **Lord** over the earth's **kings.** Daniel's **God** was exalted in the eyes of **Nebuchadnezzar** because He through Daniel revealed the course of forthcoming history. God is, the king said, **a Revealer of mysteries,** as Daniel had said (cf. v. 28). Nebuchadnezzar apparently accepted the fact of his own appointment to power by Daniel's God (cf. vv. 37-38) and recognized His authority.

**2:48-49.** Nebuchadnezzar appointed **Daniel** to a **position** of responsibility in the government and rewarded him materially with royal **gifts.** Babylon was divided into many provinces, each one under the leadership of a satrap (3:2). Daniel was evidently made a satrap over the province in which the royal court was located (**the province of** [the city of] **Babylon**). Daniel did not forget his friends but asked that they be promoted too. So **the king** made **Shadrach** (Hananiah), **Meshach** (Mishael), and **Abednego** (Azariah) **administrators** to serve under Daniel in the same **province.** Daniel was able to remain in **the royal court,** perhaps as an adviser to Nebuchadnezzar.

In a remarkable way God elevated Daniel to a position in the royal court so that he could serve as a mediator between the king and the exiles from Judah who would shortly (in 597 and 586) be brought to Babylon.

## B. The image of Nebuchadnezzar (chap. 3)

### 1. THE ERECTION OF THE IMAGE (3:1-7)

**3:1.** The effect of the revelation given to **Nebuchadnezzar** about his significant role in Gentile history (2:37-38) is discerned from his response in the events recorded in chapter 3. Identified as the head of gold (2:38), Nebuchadnezzar then caused **an image of gold** to be erected! (3:1) When he erected this image is not known. It had to follow the events recorded in chapter 2 because Daniel's three companions were in a position of authority (3:12) to which they had been appointed (2:49).

The Septuagint adds in 3:1 that this event occurred in Nebuchadnezzar's 18th year (587), one year before the fall of Jerusalem (cf. 2 Kings 25:8). Since the final destruction of Jerusalem was the culmination of Nebuchadnezzar's conquests, that inference may well be true. However, a consideration of Daniel 3

seems to indicate that the events recorded there took place nearer the beginning of Nebuchadnezzar's long reign. The events associated with the king's erecting the image suggest that he wanted to unify his empire and consolidate his authority as ruler. The image was to become the unifying center of Nebuchadnezzar's kingdom.

The Aramaic word translated "image" ($s^e l\bar{e}m$) is related to the Hebrew word for image ($selem$). A general term, it allows for the image to have been in a human form (perhaps like the statue the king saw in his dream), though it does not require it. Perhaps sometime earlier Nebuchadnezzar had seen an Egyptian obelisk, on which were recorded the exploits of one of the pharaohs, and wanted to record his own conquests that way. The dimensions of the image would be fitting for an obelisk, for it was **90 feet high** (about the height of a present-day eight-story building) and only **9 feet wide.** This 10-to-1 ratio of height to width does not fit an image in human form, for it would be too slender. However, the Babylonians often distorted the human figure in constructing their images. Or perhaps the image was in proper human proportions but was set on a pedestal to make it more imposing.

Regardless of the image's form, it was an awesome sight (cf. 2:31), both because of its height and because of the gold of which it was constructed. The size and weight of the image seem to preclude that the image was of solid gold. It must have been overlaid with gold. Without doubt the use of gold in this image was inspired by Daniel's interpretation of the king's dream (2:32, 38).

The image was **set up . . . on the plain of Dura in the province of Babylon.** Dura was a common name in Mesopotamia for any place that was enclosed by mountains or a wall. "The province of Babylon" (cf. 2:48) seems to require a location close to the city of Babylon itself from which Nebuchadnezzar ruled his kingdom. Archeologists have uncovered a large square made of brick some six miles southeast of Babylon, which may have been the base for this image. Since this base is in the center of a wide plain, the image's height would have been impressive. Also its proximity to Babylon would have served as a suitable rallying point for the king's officials.

**3:2-3.** Nebuchadnezzar **summoned** eight classes of officials **to the dedication of the image.** This may suggest that the image was intended to symbolize the empire and its unity under Nebuchadnezzar's authority. The officers referred to in verse 2 are listed again in verse 3 and four of them in verse 27, thus emphasizing the political implications of this incident.

The **satraps** were chief representatives of the king, the **prefects** were military commanders, and the **governors** were civil administrators. The **advisers** were counselors to those in governmental authority. The **treasurers** administered the funds of the kingdom, the **judges** were administrators of the law, and the **magistrates** passed judgment in keeping with the law. The **other provincial officials** were probably subordinates of the satraps. This list of officers probably included all who served in any official capacity under **Nebuchadnezzar.**

On the possibility that Zedekiah, Judah's last king, was summoned to Babylon for this occasion see comments on Jeremiah 51:59.

To see so many officials stand before the image in Dura in Nebuchadnezzar's presence to swear their allegiance to him must have been impressive.

**3:4-6.** In demanding that these officials **fall down** before **the image of gold . . . Nebuchadnezzar** was demanding a public display of recognition and submission to his absolute authority in the kingdom.

The fact that the officials were commanded not only to fall down before the image, but also to **worship** it, indicates that the image had religious as well as political significance. Since no specific god is mentioned, it may be inferred that Nebuchadnezzar was not honoring one of the gods of Babylon, but rather was instituting a new form of religious worship with this image as the center. Nebuchadnezzar purposed to establish a unified government and also a unified religion. The king constituted himself as both head of state and head of religion. All who served under him were to recognize both his political and religious authority.

The officials summoned by Nebu-

chadnezzar to assemble in the plains of Dura had not been told why they were called. When they were all assembled, the king's **herald** then announced that the officials were to recognize Nebuchadnezzar's political and religious power. The herald addressed the officials as **peoples, nations, and men of every language** (cf. v. 7; 4:1; 5:19; 6:25; 7:14), apparently considering the officials as representatives of the peoples over whom they ruled. So the officials' act of obedience signified submission not only by the officials themselves, but also by those peoples they ruled.

Elaborate preparations in the construction of the image of gold made the occasion aesthetically appealing. To this was added musical accompaniment to make the occasion emotionally moving. The orchestra included wind instruments (the **horn** and **pipes**; cf. 3:10, 15), a reed instrument (the **flute**), and stringed instruments (**zither, lyre, harp**). Some critics argue that since the names of some of these instruments were Greek, the book was written later, in the time of the Grecian Empire. But communication between Greece and the Near East had been carried on for years before the Greek conquest by Alexander (see comments under "Date and Authorship" in the *Introduction*).

Failure to comply to the command to worship the image was penalized by sudden death, being **thrown into a blazing furnace.** The severity of the penalty indicates that submission on the part of every official was obligatory.

**3:7.** Overwhelmed by the king's command, the awesomeness of the image, and the sound of the **music,** the assembled officials **fell down and worshiped the image of gold.** In this way the officials and the peoples they represented recognized the political and religious authority of **Nebuchadnezzar.**

2. THE ACCUSATION AGAINST THE JEWS (3:8-12)

**3:8-12.** No indication is given of the size of the multitude that assembled on this occasion. But because it included all the kingdom's officials (vv. 2-3) it must have been huge. **Some** court advisers (**astrologers;** cf. comments on 1:17) were quick to bring an accusation against **the Jews.** The word translated **denounced** is strong, meaning "to tear in pieces." The accusation was severe, intended to destroy the accused. The accusers were evidently motivated by jealousy for they referred to the fact that **Nebuchadnezzar had set some Jews . . . over the affairs of the province of Babylon** (3:12; cf. 2:49). The jealousy evidently sprang from the king's recognition of the unusual ability of these men (1:20). Subjugated peoples, such as the Jewish captives, were normally relegated to positions of servitude, not elevated to authority in a realm. So the high positions of "some Jews" were resented.

The counselors evidently sought to curry favor from the **king** by contrasting the three Jews' refusal to bow to **the image** with their own **worship** of it. Interestingly they accused Daniel's three friends—**Shadrach, Meshach, and Abednego**—but not Daniel. Since Daniel was appointed to a higher office (2:48) he may not have been required to attend (cf. comments on 4:8) or perhaps he may have been elsewhere in the empire carrying out his duties. Or maybe the astrologers did not dare accuse Daniel, who was present but like the other three did not bow. Whatever the reason for his not being mentioned, Daniel's dedication to his God and submission to the Law certainly precluded his bowing before the image.

### 3. THE FAITH OF THE ACCUSED (3:13-18)

**3:13-15.** How significant this event was to **Nebuchadnezzar** is seen by his response to the astrologers' accusation of the three noncompliant Jews (vv. 9-12). When he heard that the three refused to bow, he became **furious with rage** (cf. v. 19; 2:12). The high esteem with which these men had previously been held by Nebuchadnezzar (1:20) did not exempt them from submission to his authority. Nebuchadnezzar did not pass an immediate judgment on the three but asked them if the accusation against them were **true.** He gave them another opportunity to bow before **the image.** By doing so they could prove the falsehood of the accusation (or show a changed attitude).

The king impressed on them the importance of such submission, warning them that the penalty for rebellion (being **thrown . . . into a blazing furnace**; cf. 3:6) would be carried out **immediately.**

Nebuchadnezzar considered himself above all gods, for he asked, **What god will be able to rescue you from my hand?** Again this shows that he claimed absolute authority in both political and religious realms. He was challenging any god to circumvent his authority. The matter then became a conflict between Nebuchadnezzar and Yahweh, the God of Daniel's companions.

**3:16-18.** The three showed absolute confidence in God, stating that their God was greater than **Nebuchadnezzar** and was **able to** deliver them from Nebuchadnezzar's judgment in a display of His superior power. Their words, **the God we serve** (cf. 6:16, 20), show they recognized that God's authority was greater than the authority claimed by Nebuchadnezzar. Though they were employed by Nebuchadnezzar (2:49), they "served" Yahweh.

Their God demanded implicit obedience and had forbidden them to worship any other gods. One who obeys God is not presuming when he expects God to protect and deliver him. Obeying God was more important than life to these three, so if God chose **not** to deliver them, they would still obey Him. Therefore they refused to **serve** Nebuchadnezzar's **gods (or worship the image** he made, possibly meaning to worship *him* as god) even if it meant they would die.

### 4. THE DELIVERANCE BY GOD (3:19-30)

**3:19.** In spite of the high regard with which **Nebuchadnezzar** had held these three (1:20), he determined to demonstrate his authority by ordering their immediate execution. This would serve as a lesson to any others who might consider rebelling against his political and religious authority. In a fit of anger (cf. 2:12; 3:13) Nebuchadnezzar had **the furnace heated seven times hotter than usual.** A low fire would have increased their torture by extending the duration of the punishment. A hotter fire would be expected to kill them instantly. Nebuchadnezzar wanted to display publicly the cost of rebelling against his authority.

**3:20-23.** The king ordered **some of his strongest soldiers . . . to tie up** the three **and throw them into the blazing furnace.** The furnace was probably constructed with an opening in the top, through which fuel could be fed, and an opening in the lower side from which ashes could be taken. **Soldiers** threw or lowered the **three . . . into the blazing furnace.** It was customary to remove the clothing of those being executed, but because of the haste in which the king wanted his command carried out (**the king's command was . . . urgent**) this practice was not followed this time. **The flames** leaping through the top opening of the furnace **killed the men who** had **thrown** the three into the fire.

**3:24-26a.** Nebuchadnezzar was watching the proceedings intently from a safe distance. As he peered into the furnace, probably through the lower opening, what he saw amazed him. The men who had been **tied up** were **walking around in the** furnace, **unbound.** And instead of seeing **three men** in the furnace, he saw **four,** and he said **the fourth was like a son of the gods.** This One was probably the preincarnate Christ (cf. comments on Gen. 16:13). Though Nebuchadnezzar did not know of the Son of God, he did recognize that the Person appearing with the three looked supernatural.

**Nebuchadnezzar . . . approached** as near as he dared to **the opening of the . . . furnace** so that his command could be heard. He ordered the three to **come out** of the furnace and to approach him. In giving this order he called them **servants of the Most High God.** Thus Nebuchadnezzar recognized that the God these three faithfully served (cf. Dan. 3:17) is truly God. The term "the Most High (lit., the Highest) God" or "the Most High" occurs 13 times in Daniel, more than in any other book except Psalms. Of those 13 occurrences 7 pertain to Nebuchadnezzar (3:26; 4:2, 17, 24-25, 32, 34) and 2 to Belshazzar (5:18, 21). The other 4 are in chapter 7 (7:18, 22, 25, 27).

This was a remarkable admission by Nebuchadnezzar. Up to then he had believed that his Babylonian gods were superior to Yahweh (though he had once acknowledged the greatness of Yahweh, 2:47). After all, he had taken captives from Judah and vessels from the Jews' temple. But his gods could not deliver anyone alive from a furnace! (cf. 3:29) As the three had predicted, their God (Yahweh) was able to deliver them from the furnace (v. 17). Though the king recognized the unusual nature of Yahweh, he did not acknowledge Him as *his* God.

**3:26b-27.** When the three walked **out of the fire** and were carefully examined, Nebuchadnezzar's officials (cf. comments on v. 2) saw that the **bodies** of the three men were unharmed, their clothing unaffected, and that the **smell of fire** was not even on their clothes.

**3:28-30.** In view of the evidence presented to him, **Nebuchadnezzar** declared that this was an act of **the God of Shadrach, Meshach, and Abednego who** had **sent His angel** (cf. v. 25) to rescue the three who served this God (cf. v. 17). Nebuchadnezzar was moved by the devotion of the three to their **God** (he knew **they trusted in Him**), even though it entailed their disobeying the king and jeopardizing **their** own **lives.**

As a result the king decreed that **the God** of the three young men was to be held in honor and that anyone who dishonored this God would lose his life (he would **be cut in pieces** and his house would be burned to **rubble**; cf. 2:5). **The king** then honored **Shadrach, Meshach, and Abednego** by promoting them to positions of greater honor and power in the kingdom.

This historical incident seems to have prophetic significance as well. In the coming Tribulation a Gentile ruler (7:8) will demand for himself the worship that belongs to God (2 Thes. 2:4; Rev. 13:8). Any who refuse to acknowledge his right to receive worship will be killed (Rev. 13:15). Assuming political and religious power, he will oppress Israel (Rev. 13:7). Most of the people in the world, including many in Israel, will submit to and worship him. But a small remnant in Israel, like the three in Daniel's day, will refuse. Many who will not worship the Antichrist will be severely punished; some will be martyred for their faithfulness to Jesus Christ. But a few will be delivered from those persecutions by the Lord Jesus Christ at His second coming.

In the forthcoming Tribulation period God will do for this believing remnant what He did for Daniel's three companions. They withstood the decree of the king, and though they were not exempted from suffering and oppression they were delivered out of it by the God they trusted. No doubt the remnant of believing Jews in that coming day will find great comfort, consolation, and instruction from this incident in the lives of Daniel's three companions, as those in Daniel's day must have found as they were living under Gentile rule.

## C. The second dream of Nebuchadnezzar (chap. 4)

### 1. THE KING'S PROCLAMATION (4:1-3)

Apparently a number of years transpired between the experience of Daniel's three friends in chapter 3 and Nebuchadnezzar's dream and period of insanity in chapter 4. Nebuchadnezzar reigned for 43 years (605–562 B.C.). His insanity lasted seven years and he returned to the throne for a short time afterward before he died. His last years did not take place until he had time to conclude his extensive building operations (v. 30). Thus this incident may have taken place about the 35th year of Nebuchadnezzar's rule, or about 570. This would be some 30 years after the experience of the three men in the fiery furnace, about the 50th year of Daniel's life.

**4:1-3.** Daniel recorded an official proclamation made by **Nebuchadnezzar** which was circulated throughout his realm. Daniel was led by the Holy Spirit's inspiration to include this official proclamation. God had shown the king that He is able to deliver and preserve those who trust and obey Him. But God's revelation of Himself to Nebuchadnezzar did not conclude there. For God further revealed Himself to the king through the circumstances recorded in this chapter. And in his proclamation to all the people in his empire (**peoples, nations, and men of every language;** cf. comments on 3:4), Nebuchadnezzar declared that through God's **miraculous signs** he had learned of His power and that **God** (**the Most High;** cf. comments on 3:26) is sovereign and exerts His will in **His . . . eternal kingdom.** Whereas earlier Nebuchadnezzar believed it was his own power and wisdom that had consolidated the kingdom under his authority, he learned that it is *God* who rules according to His will and uses those He chooses as His instruments.

### 2. THE KING'S TREE VISION (4:4-18)

#### a. The request for interpretation by the wise men (4:4-7)

**4:4-7.** For the second time a revelation was given to **Nebuchadnezzar**

through **a dream** (cf. 2:1, 27-29). This dream, like the one years before, **terrified** the king (cf. 2:1, 3). Though **contented and prosperous,** he was **afraid.** So he sought an interpretation of **the dream to** allay his fears. Though **all the wise men of Babylon** had been discredited previously because of their inability to interpret the king's first dream (2:10-12), counselors had been retained by the king. He summoned **the magicians, enchanters, astrologers, and diviners** (see comments on 1:17) and ordered them **to interpret the dream** which he revealed to **them.** However, they were unable to do so.

#### b. The dream explained to Daniel (4:8-18)

**4:8.** Then the king **told . . . the dream** to **Daniel.** Unable once again to be helped by his own conjurers, he had to consult one who worshiped Yahweh. However, the king still acknowledged his own **god** (perhaps Bel, alias Marduk) as he referred to Daniel by his Babylonian name (**Belteshazzar;** cf. comments on 1:7) which included Bel's name. The word **finally** suggests that some time passed before Daniel went **into** the king's **presence.** Obviously Daniel was not among the wise men who had first been summoned to interpret the dream (4:6). Apparently Daniel was in a position of significant governmental authority and not serving as a counselor to the king (cf. comments on 3:12). That would explain why he was not included in the invitation given previously to the wise men.

Because of the impression made on Nebuchadnezzar through Daniel's previous interpretation (cf. 2:46) it is not likely that the king had forgotten about Daniel's ability to interpret dreams. Possibly the king suspected the ominous message contained in his dream and hoped that the wise men could soften the message when they interpreted it to him. The king thought that Daniel operated by the **spirit of the holy gods** (cf. 4:9, 18; 5:11, 14) and that through Daniel the message would be unveiled. Obviously Nebuchadnezzar was still a polytheist though he had acknowledged Yahweh's sovereignty years before (2:47; 3:28-29).

**4:9-12.** Nebuchadnezzar referred to Daniel as **chief of the magicians,** not because he was in authority over the wise men but because he was wiser than all of them, capable of understanding and interpreting dreams. The king implored Daniel to **interpret** his **dream** for him. Nebuchadnezzar's dream was a simple one. He was perplexed not by what he had seen, but by his inability to understand its meaning.

Previously Nebuchadnezzar had traveled to Lebanon to watch the felling of the great cedars to provide timber for his construction projects in Babylon. So he had witnessed the felling of mighty trees. The **tree** he saw in his dream was significant because of its size (vv. 10-11), its beauty (v. 12), and its **fruit** (v. 12). It provided **food** and **shelter** for all the animals and **birds** who lived **under** it or **in** it.

**4:13-14.** The king then explained that he saw **a messenger, a holy one.** This holy messenger, unknown to Nebuchadnezzar, would have been known to the Jewish people as an angel sent **from heaven** with an announcement. The messenger said that **the tree** was to be **cut down,** the **branches** trimmed from the trunk, the **leaves** stripped off, and the **fruit** scattered. **The animals** and **birds** that found shelter under and in **its branches** were to scatter.

**4:15-16.** However, **the stump** was not to be removed but secured with bands of **iron and bronze.** The first part of the vision of the tree (vv. 10-12) probably would have caused Nebuchadnezzar no concern. It may have even produced pride as he recognized himself in the tree as the one who provided bountifully for the subjects in his realm. But this second part of the vision (vv. 13-15a), that the tree was to be cut down, must have greatly disturbed him.

The third part of the vision (vv. 15b-16) must have been even more terrifying—if Nebuchadnezzar recognized himself as represented by the tree—for sanity was to leave **him** and he would become demented, living among **the animals.** He would have no more mental ability than **an animal.** This condition would continue for an extended period of time (**till seven times pass by;** cf. vv. 23, 25, 32). The "seven times" were probably seven years because (a) seven days or months would have been inadequate for his hair to have grown to the length of feathers (v. 33), and (b) "times" in 7:25 means years (cf. comments there).

**4:17-18.** Several **messengers (holy ones)** announced the lesson to be learned through the vision: **so that the living may know that the Most High** (cf. comments on 3:26) **is sovereign over the kingdoms of men and gives them to anyone He wishes and sets over them the lowliest of men.** This vision was designed to be a part of God's revelation of Himself and His authority over **Nebuchadnezzar** who in pride had exalted himself above God. The **king** again (cf. 4:9) asked Daniel (**Belteshazzar;** cf. comments on v. 8) to **tell** him the meaning of **the dream.**

### 3. THE VISION INTERPRETED (4:19-27)

**4:19.** Whereas **Daniel** had had no reticence about interpreting Nebuchadnezzar's first dream to him (2:27-45), he now was reluctant to interpret this second **dream.** The first dream exalted Nebuchadnezzar; he was the head of gold (2:38). But this second dream debased him. When the **king** saw Daniel's reluctance, he encouraged Daniel not to be alarmed but to share its meaning with him. Daniel respectfully stated that he wished **the dream** pertained to the king's **enemies.**

**4:20-22.** Daniel repeated the description of the greatness of **the tree** (vv. 20-21) and then explained that the **tree** represented Nebuchadnezzar (v. 22). Daniel tactfully gave the good news first! Like the tree, Nebuchadnezzar had **become great and strong,** and his kingdom had been expanded and consolidated under his rule. His kingdom had become greater than any kingdom up to that time.

**4:23-25.** Then came the bad news. The cutting **down** of **the tree**—a **decree** from **the Most High**—meant that Nebuchadnezzar would be removed from his position of authority in the kingdom. He would be turned out of the palace (**driven away from people**) and would **live** like an animal among **the wild animals** until **seven times** (v. 23) would **pass by.** The word "times" is used again in 7:25 where it also means a year (cf. comments there). Thus Daniel predicted that Nebuchadnezzar would live in a demented state for seven years.

In the mental illness known as zoanthropy (an illness observed in modern times) a person thinks of himself as an animal and acts like one. This may have been the disease Nebuchadnezzar had. Daniel then referred to the purpose of this experience, which the messengers had announced in the dream (4:17). Through this illness Nebuchadnezzar would come to **acknowledge that the Most High is sovereign over the kingdoms of men and gives them to anyone He wishes.**

**4:26-27.** The fact that **the stump** was not to be uprooted (but was to be secured and left in the field, v. 15) indicates that the **king** would **be restored** to the throne. However, that restoration would not take place till Nebuchadnezzar acknowledged God's sovereign right to rule (**that heaven rules**).

Daniel concluded by exhorting the king to **renounce** his **sins.** This points out the principle that any announced judgment may be averted if there is repentance (cf. the Book of Jonah). Daniel urged Nebuchadnezzar to turn from his sinful pride and produce fruits of righteousness (**doing what is right** and **being kind to the oppressed**)—acts which stem from a heart that is submissive to God. Had Nebuchadnezzar done so, he would have averted his seven years of insanity.

## 4. THE VISION FULFILLED (4:28-33)

**4:28-33.** The revelation given **to . . . Nebuchadnezzar** through Daniel's interpretation was soon forgotten and Daniel's exhortation was ignored. Nebuchadnezzar continued in his sinful pride. He did not repent as Daniel had advised him to do (v. 27). The **king** was controlled by his great egotism. He considered the city of **Babylon** itself as his personal possession and as a reflection of his **power** and **glory** (v. 30).

God endured Nebuchadnezzar's pride for **12 months.** This may have been a period of grace in which God was giving Nebuchadnezzar an opportunity to turn to Him in repentance. But when Nebuchadnezzar ignored Daniel's exhortation God, who had given Nebuchadnezzar his authority, announced the interruption of his rule.

What had been predicted was no longer postponed and judgment came on **Nebuchadnezzar,** in keeping with Daniel's interpretation. As the king was boasting of his accomplishments while **walking on the roof** (apparently a flat roof, common in those days) **of** his **royal palace** (v. 29), **a voice . . . from heaven** (v. 31) announced his judgment.

As predicted, the king lived like an animal in the field, eating **grass like cattle.** (Later Daniel added that the king lived with wild donkeys, 5:21.) **His body was drenched with . . . dew . . . his hair grew** long like an eagle's **feathers . . . and his nails** grew **like** a bird's **claws.** He gave no attention to his bodily appearance. Perhaps, because of his royal position, Nebuchadnezzar was hidden in a secluded park so his true condition could be hidden from the populace. Also in the king's absence Daniel may have played a major role in preserving the kingdom and possibly in preventing anyone from killing the king.

## 5. THE KING'S RESTORATION (4:34-37)

**4:34-35.** When the seven years (cf. comments on v. 23) had transpired (**at the end of that time**) Nebuchadnezzar with his **sanity . . . restored . . . praised the Most High** (cf. comments on 3:26). The king who had sought honor and glory for himself now acknowledged that the Most High **lives forever.** The king confessed that God's **dominion is . . . eternal,** that **His kingdom endures** (cf. 6:26; 7:14, 27). Thus he acknowledged God's sovereign authority.

Nebuchadnezzar also acknowledged God's irresistible will: **He does as He pleases with the powers of heaven and the peoples of the earth.** Also the king confessed that man is answerable to God, not God to man, for no one can stop God and **no one** has a right to question Him (cf. Job 33:12b-13; Isa. 29:16; 45:9; Rom. 9:19-20).

**4:36-37.** The king's acknowledgment of God's right to rule (vv. 34-35) brought about the restoration of the king's **sanity** (cf. v. 34) and a restoration to his **throne.** Having been humbled before God, Nebuchadnezzar rose to **greater** heights of honor than he had known when he walked in pride. He said he praised, exalted, and glorified **the King of heaven** (cf. "honored" and "glorified" in v. 34). These verbs indicate continued action, suggesting that Nebuchadnezzar did these things habitually. These verbs embody the ideas of reverence, respect, honor, admiration, and worship.

Since Nebuchadnezzar said that these attitudes characterized his life, many have concluded that he experienced regeneration, becoming a child of God. Nebuchadnezzar did confess that what God had done in dealing with him was **right** and **just.** This is certainly not acknowledged by one who continues in rebellion against God. The king also admitted that he had walked **in pride** (cf. 5:20) but had been humbled by his experience. This too would testify to a transformation in Nebuchadnezzar's character through a newfound knowledge of God.

There seems to be prophetic significance in this incident as well as in the one in chapter 3. Even though God has appointed Gentiles to a place of prominence in His program during the times of the Gentiles, yet most nations and people walk in rebellion against God. This attitude is graphically described in Psalm 2:1-3. God will deal with the nations to humble them and bring them into subjection to Himself. One purpose of the Tribulation, which will immediately precede Christ's second coming, will be to humble the nations and bring them to the point of subjection to Christ's authority. At the conclusion of God's judgments, described in Revelation 6–19, Jesus Christ, the victorious Rider on the white horse, will descend from heaven and smite the nations. Then an angel will announce that "the kingdom of the world has become the kingdom of our Lord and of His Christ and He will reign forever and ever" (Rev. 11:15). God's judgment on Nebuchadnezzar, designed to subject him to God's authority, seems to prefigure God's judgment on the nations to subject them to the authority of the One who has been given the right to rule.

## D. The feast of Belshazzar (chap. 5)

### 1. THE REVELRY OF THE KING (5:1-4)

The events recorded in Daniel 1–4 pertained to the reign of Nebuchadnezzar, who expanded and united the Babylonian Empire. Nebuchadnezzar died in 562 B.C. after ruling 43 years. The ensuing years of Babylonian history till its overthrow by Cyrus in 539 B.C. were marked by progressive deterioration, intrigue, and murder. Nebuchadnezzar was succeeded by his son Evil-Merodach who ruled for two years (562–560 B.C., 2 Kings 25:27-30; Jer. 52:31-34). Evil-Merodach was murdered in August 560 by

Neriglissar, Nebuchadnezzar's son-in-law and Evil-Merodach's own brother-in-law. Neriglissar then ruled four years (560–556 B.C.). He is the Nergal-Sharezer mentioned in Jeremiah 39:3, 13. At his death, he was succeeded by his young son Labashi-Marduk, who ruled only two months (May and June 556) before he was assassinated and succeeded by Nabonidus, who reigned 17 years (556–539 B.C.). See the chart "Kings of the Neo-Babylonian Empire," in the *Introduction.*

Nabonidus did much to restore the glory that had belonged to Babylon under the reign of Nebuchadnezzar. Nabonidus' mother was the high priestess of the moon god at Haran. Perhaps because of her influence, he had great interest in restoring and expanding the Babylonian religion and did much to restore abandoned temples. He was absent from Babylon for 10 of his 17 years, from 554 through 545. In Haran he restored the temple of the moon god Sin, and then he attacked Edom and conquered parts of Arabia where he then lived for some time.

Belshazzar was Nabonidus' eldest son and was appointed by his father as his coregent. (Nebuchadnezzar is referred to as Belshazzar's father [Dan. 5:2, 11, 13, 18; cf. v. 22] in the sense that he was his ancestor or predecessor.) This coregency explains why Belshazzar was called king (v. 1) and why he exercised kingly authority even though Nabonidus actually held the throne.

**5:1.** Babylon was being besieged by the Persian army, led by Ugbaru, governor of Gutium, while **Belshazzar,** inside the city, was giving a **great banquet for 1,000 of his nobles.** Belshazzar's name means "Bel (another name for the god Marduk) has protected the king." Perhaps the banquet was given to show Belshazzar's contempt for the Persians and to allay his people's fears. Archeologists have excavated a large hall in Babylon 55 feet wide and 165 feet long that had plastered walls. Such a room would have been sufficient to house a gathering of this size. Belshazzar considered his city secure from assault because of its massive walls. Within the city were supplies that would sustain it for 20 years. Therefore the **king** felt he had little cause for concern.

**5:2-4.** The banquet itself showed Belshazzar's contempt for the power of men. Then, to show his contempt for the power of the true **God,** he ordered that **the gold and silver goblets that Nebuchadnezzar . . . had taken from the temple in Jerusalem** (cf. 1:1-2) be brought to the banquet hall so the assembled revelers **might drink from them.** In drinking, the people honored **the gods** of Babylon—idols made **of gold . . . silver . . . bronze, iron, wood, and stone.** Nabonidus, Belshazzar's father, had attempted to strengthen the Babylonian religion. In keeping with that, this act by his son may have been an attempt to undo the influence of Nebuchadnezzar's honoring the God of Israel (4:34-35). The polygamous king's **wives** and **concubines** were there too.

## 2. THE REVELATION TO THE KING (5:5-12)

**5:5-7.** **Suddenly** the hilarity of the revelry gave way to hushed fear. **Near** one of the lampstands that illuminated the banquet hall, **fingers of a human hand** were seen writing **on the** plastered **wall.** The terrified **king** (cf. 4:5) **watched** as **the hand . . . wrote** a message. The king had evidently arisen from the chair in which he had been seated to lead the festivities and stood to watch. **He** became **so frightened that . . . his legs gave way** and he fell to the floor. As was the custom (cf. 2:2; 4:6-7) Belshazzar summoned **the** wise men, **enchanters, astrologers, and diviners** (cf. comments on 1:17) and promised to reward **whoever** would interpret the meaning of this strange phenomenon.

The reward was great. The interpreter would **be clothed in purple** (cf. Mordecai's purple robe, Es. 8:15), that is, he would be given royal authority. Also he would receive **a gold chain** (cf. Gen. 41:42), which no doubt had great monetary value. And he would **be made the third highest ruler in the kingdom.** Since Nabonidus was king and Belshazzar his coregent, the highest office to be conferred was that of the third highest ruler. The king's offer shows the extremity of his fear.

**5:8-12.** The **wise men** were unable to **read** or interpret **the writing** on the wall. This fact produced even greater fear in **the king.** Their inability to interpret the message made it even more ominous.

Then all the guests who like the king had seen the writing on the wall were thrown into utter confusion (**his nobles were baffled**). The sound of confusion in the banquet hall came to the ears of **the queen.** Evidently she was not a wife of Belshazzar for his wives were with him in the hall (vv. 2-3). She was the king's mother, or perhaps even his grandmother. Her familiarity with both **Nebuchadnezzar** and **Daniel** seems to suggest that she was the king's grandmother. She evidently had previous contact with Daniel, **a man . . . who,** she said, **has the spirit of the holy gods** (cf. 4:8-9, 18; 5:14). She knew of his **insight . . . intelligence . . . wisdom** (v. 11), **knowledge . . . understanding and . . . ability to interpret dreams** (v. 12). (On Daniel's position as "chief of the magicians" and others, see comments on 4:9.) So she counseled Belshazzar to summon **Daniel** and let him interpret **the writing** on the plaster.

## 3. THE REQUEST OF THE KING (5:13-16)

**5:13-16.** Following the queen's suggestion, Belshazzar had **Daniel . . . brought in before** him. **The king** seemingly belittled Daniel, referring to him as **one of the exiles . . . from Judah.** He was from the same land whose God Belshazzar was holding in contempt! (vv. 2-3) The king told Daniel what he had **heard** from the queen (vv. 11-12) about Daniel's ability to do what **the wise men and enchanters** were unable to do. He promised Daniel the same rich rewards he had promised the wise men (v. 16; cf. v. 7) if Daniel could **read** the **writing** on the wall and interpret it. Though written in Aramaic, it was difficult to read, perhaps because it was in an unusual script.

## 4. THE REPLY BY DANIEL (5:17-28)

### a. The humbling of Nebuchadnezzar (5:17-21)

**5:17-19.** In his reply **Daniel** summarized God's dealing with Belshazzar's predecessor Nebuchadnezzar. He related lessons that Nebuchadnezzar had learned from God's dealings with him. God is sovereign and rules over nations and appoints kings according to His own will; Nebuchadnezzar was brought to his position of power in the Babylonian Empire by divine appointment. (**The Most High God**; cf. comments on 3:26, **gave . . . Nebuchadnezzar sovereignty.**) His authority was widely recognized (by **peoples and nations and men of every language**; cf. 3:4, 7; 4:1; 6:25; 7:14), and his decrees were unchangeable (5:19).

**5:20-21.** When Nebuchadnezzar failed to recognize that the power was God's and not his own, he **became arrogant** and proud (cf. 4:30). God then humbled him and **stripped** him of **his . . . throne** while he lived like **an animal . . . with the wild donkeys.** Through this discipline Nebuchadnezzar came to recognize the greatness of God's authority (4:34-35). Though the facts of Nebuchadnezzar's seven-year insanity may have been hidden from the populace, they were known by the royal family (cf. 5:22).

### b. The pride of Belshazzar (5:22-24)

**5:22-24.** Belshazzar . . . **knew** what his predecessor had experienced, and should have learned from it. However, Belshazzar had not done so; in fact he had openly challenged **the Lord of heaven** (cf. "the King of heaven," 4:37) by drinking from **the goblets** taken **from the temple** in Jerusalem (5:2-3) and by praising man-made **gods** (v. 4). They have no life, but by contrast the true **God** not only *has* **life,** but held *Belshazzar's* life **in His hand.** Perhaps Daniel intended an interesting wordplay by adding that God, who held Belshazzar's life in His *hand,* **sent** a *hand* to write him a message. Belshazzar, knowing about God, failed to **honor** Him.

### c. The judgment by God (5:25-28)

**5:25.** As God had judged Nebuchadnezzar's pride by removing him from the throne, so He would judge Belshazzar's pride by taking the kingdom from him and giving it to another people. **This** judgment **was written** in the words that appeared on the plaster. First Daniel read **the inscription** which the wise men were unable to read. It was brief, containing only three words with the first word repeated. *MENE* ($m^e n\bar{e}$) is an Aramaic noun referring to a weight of 50 shekels (a mina, equal to 1¼ pounds). It is from the verb $m^e n\hat{a}h$, "to number, to reckon." *TEKEL* ($t^e q\bar{e}l$) is a noun referring to a shekel (2/5 of an ounce). It is from the verb $t^e q\bar{a}l$, "to weigh." *PARSIN* (*parsîn*) is a noun meaning a half-mina (25 shekels, or about ⅔ of a pound). It is from the verb

$p^e ras$, "to break in two, to divide." The word on the wall was actually *Ûparsîn,* which means "and Parsin" (NIV marg.).

Even if the wise men could have read the words (which they couldn't), they could not have interpreted them for they had no point of reference as to what had been numbered, weighed, and divided.

**5:26-27.** Then Daniel proceeded to interpret the meaning of **these words.** He explained that *MENE* meant that **God** had **numbered** ($m^e n\hat{a}h$) the duration of **the days of** Belshazzar's kingdom and was about to bring **it to an end.** *TEKEL* meant that Belshazzar had **been** evaluated by God, **weighed** ($t^e q\hat{i}lt\hat{a}h$, from $t^e q\bar{a}l$) in a balance and had been **found wanting,** that is, he was too light. A balance was the normal device used in weighing payments. A payment was to meet a certain standard so if it did not meet that standard, it was rejected as unacceptable. Belshazzar's moral and spiritual character did not measure up to the standard of God's righteousness so he was rejected. "By Him [God] deeds are weighed" (1 Sam. 2:3).

**5:28.** In interpreting the third word Daniel changed the plural *parsîn* (v. 25) to the singular *PERES* ($p^e r\bar{e}s$). Belshazzar's **kingdom** was to be broken up (**divided,** $p^e r\hat{i}sat$) **and given to the Medes and Persians.** Apparently Daniel intended a play on words for a change in the vowels in $p^e r\bar{e}s$ gives the word "Persian" (*Pāras*). Thus the message was that because of the moral and spiritual degradation of the king and his kingdom, God would terminate the Babylonian Empire and give it to the Medes and Persians.

### 5. THE REVELATION FULFILLED (5:29-31)

**5:29-31.** One might have expected **Belshazzar's** wrath to fall on **Daniel** because of the message he brought. But instead the king, faithful to his word (cf. v. 16), rewarded Daniel. However, Daniel's enjoyment of those honors and the position to which he had been promoted was short-lived for **that very night Belshazzar was** killed **and Darius the Mede took over the kingdom.** (On the identity of Darius the Mede see comments on 6:1.)

The city had been under assault by Cyrus. In anticipation of a long siege the city had stored supplies to last for 20 years. The Euphrates River ran through the city from north to south, so the residents had an ample water supply. Belshazzar had a false sense of security, because the Persian army, led by Ugbaru, was outside Babylon's city walls. Their army was divided; part was stationed where the river entered the city at the north and the other part was positioned where the river exited from the city at the south. The army diverted the water north of the city by digging a canal from the river to a nearby lake.

With the water diverted, its level receded and the soldiers were able to enter the city by going under the sluice gate. Since the walls were unguarded the Persians, once inside the city, were able to conquer it without a fight. Significantly the defeat of Babylon fulfilled not only the prophecy Daniel made earlier that same night (5:28) but also a prophecy by Isaiah (Isa. 47:1-5). The overthrow of Babylon took place the night of the 16th of Tishri (October 12, 539 B.C.).

The rule of the Medes and Persians was the second phase of the times of the Gentiles (the silver chest and arms of the image in Dan. 2). The events in chapter 5 illustrate that God is sovereign and moves according to His predetermined plans. Those events also anticipate the final overthrow of all Gentile world powers that rebel against God and are characterized by moral and spiritual corruption. Such a judgment, anticipated in Psalm 2:4-6 and Revelation 19:15-16, will be fulfilled at the Second Advent of Jesus Christ to this earth.

## E. The edict of Darius (chap. 6)

### 1. THE PROMINENCE OF DANIEL (6:1-3)

**6:1a.** Critics have long questioned the historicity of Daniel. They challenge Daniel's reference to the accession of **Darius** (vv. 1, 28; 9:1; called Darius the Mede in 5:31) because there is no historical evidence outside the Bible for his reign. However, several explanations are possible: (1) Darius may have been another name for Cyrus. Daniel 6:28 may be translated, "So Daniel prospered during the reign of Darius, even the reign of Cyrus the Persian." It was common for ancient rulers to use different names in various parts of their realms. Thus Darius may have been a localized name for Cyrus. (This is the view of D.J. Wiseman,

"Some Historical Problems in the Book of Daniel," in *Notes on Some Problems in the Book of Daniel*, pp. 12-14.)

(2) A second explanation is that Darius was appointed by Cyrus to rule over Babylon, a comparatively small portion of the vast Medo-Persian Empire. According to Daniel 9:1 Darius "was *made* ruler over the Babylonian Kingdom." This suggests that he ruled by appointment, rather than by conquest and thus would have been subordinate to Cyrus, who appointed him. The historical situation leading to this appointment, based on the Nabonidus Chronicle, was that Babylon was conquered by Ugbaru, governor of Gutium, who entered the city of Babylon the night of Belshazzar's feast. After Ugbaru conquered Babylon on October 12, 539 B.C., Cyrus entered the conquered city on October 29 of that same year. Ugbaru was then appointed by Cyrus to rule on his behalf in Babylon. Eight days after Cyrus' arrival (Nov. 6) Ugbaru died. If Darius the Mede is another name for Ugbaru, as is entirely possible, the problem is solved. Since Darius was 62 years old when he took over Babylon (5:31), his death a few weeks later would not be unusual. According to this view (presented by William H. Shea, "Darius the Mede: An Update," *Andrews University Seminary Studies* 20. Autumn 1982, pp. 229-47), Gubaru is another spelling for Ugbaru, with the name Gobryas being a Greek form of the same name and appearing in Xenophon's *Cyropaedia* 4. 6. 1-9; 7. 5. 7-34.

(3) A third explanation is that Ugbaru, governor of Gutium, conquered Babylon, and that Gubaru, alias Darius, was the man Cyrus appointed to rule over Babylon. (This is the view of John C. Whitcomb, Jr., *Darius the Mede*. Nutley, N.J.: Presbyterian & Reformed Publishing Co., 1974.)

(4) Still others suggest Darius the Mede should be identified with Cambyses, Cyrus' son, who ruled Persia 530–522 B.C. (This view is held by Charles Boutflower, *In and Around the Book of Daniel*. Reprint. Grand Rapids: Kregel Publishing Co., 1977, pp. 142-55.) Any of these four views may be correct, but perhaps the second one is preferable.

**6:1b-3.** One of Darius' first responsibilities was to reorganize the newly conquered kingdom of Babylon. He appointed **120 satraps** (cf. 3:2) **to rule** over **the kingdom** of Babylon, and put them under **three administrators . . . one of whom was Daniel.** The satraps were responsible to the three administrators (perhaps 40 satraps to each administrator) **so that the king** was greatly aided in his administrative responsibilities. Daniel was an exceptional administrator, partly because of his extensive experience under Nebuchadnezzar (2:48) for about 39 years. So **the king planned to** make Daniel responsible for the administration of **the** entire **kingdom.** This of course created friction between Daniel and the other administrators and 120 satraps.

2. THE PLOT OF THE LEADERS (6:4-9)

**6:4-5.** The two **administrators** and 120 **satraps** sought some basis on which to accuse **Daniel in his** administrative work. They were probably jealous of his position and resented him because he was a Judean (cf. comments on 3:12). But they found that Daniel was not **corrupt;** he was **trustworthy** and diligent in discharging his responsibilities. They decided that they would have to find some **basis** for accusation in his religious practices, which obviously were well known to them.

**6:6-9.** So the 122 leaders devised a plot. (Daniel was certainly outnumbered!) They suggested to **King Darius** that he, **the king,** be made the sole object of worship for **30 days.** Either the 122 got others to agree to the plan (including **prefects . . . advisers, and governors)** or the 122 merely *said* the others agreed. Saying that they **all agreed** (v. 7) was wrong for they certainly had not discussed this with Daniel. All prayer was to be addressed to the **king** in recognition of his power in the religious realm. The penalty for rebelling against his religious authority was to be death by being **thrown into** a **den** of lions. **Darius,** no doubt flattered by the adulation he would receive, consented to the plot and signed it into law, which according to Medo-Persian custom was irrevocable.

3. THE PRAYER OF DANIEL (6:10-11)

**6:10-11. The decree** signed into law by Darius became public knowledge. But **Daniel,** knowing of the decree, followed his customary practice (**just as he had done before)** of going **to his** own **upstairs**

room. . . . **three times** each **day** to pray **to . . . God** (cf. Ps. 55:17). He prayed **toward Jerusalem** (cf. Ps. 5:7; 2 Chron. 6:21, 34, 38).

Daniel's prayer was first a prayer of thanksgiving (Dan. 6:10) as he acknowledged God's goodnesses to him. His prayer was also a prayer for guidance and **help** (v. 11). Doubtless the responsibility of high office rested heavily on **Daniel** and he sought God's wisdom in the decisions he had to make. Daniel was more than 80 years old at this time (539 B.C.); he was about 16 when he was taken captive 66 years earlier (605 B.C.). So because of his years he may have also sought **God** for physical strength to carry on his heavy duties. Daniel made no attempt to hide his devotion to or his dependence on God, even though it now meant disobeying a governmental decree (cf. Acts 5:29). Daniel would not and could not look to Darius for the guidance and strength he knew God alone could supply. Apparently his opponents knew where and when he prayed, so they **went** (lit., rushed) to his room at the time and, as expected, **found** him **praying.**

4. THE PROSECUTION OF DANIEL (6:12-18)

**6:12.** Accusation was soon made against Daniel by his opponents before Darius who had issued the **decree.** Darius found himself bound by his own law; he said, **the decree stands.** Nebuchadnezzar the Babylonian was above law, whereas Darius the Mede was bound by law. This was intimated in the contrast between the gold and the silver in the image in Nebuchadnezzar's dream (2:32, 39).

**6:13-16.** Hearing their accusation against **Daniel,** whom they derisively belittled as **one of the exiles from Judah** (as Arioch and Belshazzar had done; cf. 2:25; 5:13), Darius **was greatly distressed.** Interestingly three kings in the Book of Daniel were distressed (cf. 2:1; 3:13; 5:6, 9).

Though Darius knew he was bound by the law he had made, he sought some way **to rescue Daniel** from the penalty the law incurred. But finding it impossible to do so, he **gave the order** that **Daniel** be thrown **into the lions' den.**

As he was thrown in—to what seemed to be certain death—**the king said . . . May your God, whom you** serve continually (cf. 6:20; 3:17), rescue you. Whether Darius knew about God's deliverance of Daniel's three friends from the fiery furnace in Nebuchadnezzar's day is not known. Yet Darius' statement expressed a desire that **Daniel** be spared. He certainly *wanted* him spared, for he obviously appreciated his administrative abilities (cf. 6:2-3). Perhaps he had been impressed with Daniel's confidence in God.

**6:17-18.** So that Daniel could not escape from the lions' den, **a stone was . . . placed over the mouth of the den,** which was then **sealed** with a royal seal. Besides the side opening to the den (perhaps an underground cave) there may have been an opening at the top (cf. vv. 23-24). The seal, an impression made in clay by an image on a **ring,** would inform others that the stone was not to be tampered with in an effort to free Daniel. Reluctantly **the king** confined Daniel to the den.

**The king** was deeply agitated that he had been tricked by his administrators and satraps and that he was subject to his own laws. So he spent a sleepless **night** (cf. Xerxes' sleepless night, Es. 6:1).

5. THE PRESERVATION OF DANIEL (6:19-24)

**6:19-22.** At **dawn the king,** after a sleepless night (v. 18), **hurried to the lions' den.** In anguish over probably finding **Daniel** consumed, Darius hoped against hope (cf. v. 16) that the elderly statesman might have been rescued by **God, whom** he served (cf. 3:17; 6:16).

Daniel replied that **God** had in fact kept him unharmed because of his flawless life (v. 22) and **because he . . . trusted in . . . God** (v. 23). God's **Angel,** Daniel said, had kept the lions' **mouths** shut. Perhaps this Angel, like the One in the fiery furnace with the three young men (3:25), was the preincarnate Christ.

**6:23.** Discovering that **Daniel** was still alive, Darius **was overjoyed** and had him **lifted from the den** (cf. comments on v. 17). This experience illustrated for Darius the validity of faith in God and His power to control circumstances and deliver those who trust in Him. For 30 days Darius was addressed as God by the people in his realm (cf. v. 7). But **Daniel** served the true God, who did what Darius could never do: shut the mouths of lions to protect one who depended on Him.

**6:24.** Then the king ordered that Daniel's accusers and their families be **thrown into the . . . den.** The attempt by false accusation to exterminate this Jewish captive-turned-executive boomeranged (cf. Haman's similar fate, Es. 7:9-10). The accusers had persuaded Darius to put in effect a decree that was intended to eliminate **Daniel,** but ironically they could not dissuade **the king** from eliminating them!

6. THE PRONOUNCEMENT OF THE KING (6:25-28)

**6:25-28.** The one who by his **decree** was being revered for a month as god (v. 7) now made a proclamation that all subjects of his nation (**all the peoples, nations, and men of every language;** cf. 3:4, 7; 4:1; 5:19; 7:14) **must fear and reverence** Daniel's **God.** This was an amazing turnaround on Darius' part! The reason for this, **Darius wrote,** is that Daniel's God lives (**He is the living God;** cf. 6:20) whereas the gods of the Medes and Persians were dead idols. This God is eternal, **His kingdom** is indestructible (cf. 7:14), and He intervenes in people's affairs and delivers those who trust Him. He works by miraculous power (**signs and wonders;** cf. 4:2-3) to perform His will, including the miraculous delivery of **Daniel.** Such a God is truly to be reverenced and worshiped. In spite of the opposition of the satraps and administrators, **Daniel** was honored and lived **during** the reigns **of Darius** and **Cyrus.**

### F. The vision of the four beasts (chap. 7)

1. THE VISION (7:1-14)

*a. The four beasts (7:1-8)*

**7:1.** The vision recorded by the Prophet **Daniel** in this chapter was revealed to him **in the first year of** Belshazzar's reign, 553 B.C., when **Belshazzar** was made coregent with Nabonidus. Daniel's dream predated by 14 years his experience in the lions' den (chap. 6) which occurred in or soon after 539. When the **dream** came Daniel was about 68 years of age, for he was taken captive (at about the age of 16) 52 years earlier in 605 B.C.

The revelation was given Daniel in **a dream** through **visions** (cf. 2:28; 4:5, 10).

In referring to the experience as "a dream" (sing.) Daniel was emphasizing the unity of the revelation and in referring to it as "visions" (pl.) he emphasized the successive stages in which the revelation was given. (Five times in chap. 7 he said "looked" [vv. 2, 6-7, 13] and once "I kept looking" [v. 11].) The dream refers to his being asleep, and the visions refer to what he saw while dreaming. Sometimes, however, a person had a vision while he was awake (cf., e.g., 9:23). Because of the great significance of Daniel's dream, he immediately **wrote down** a summary of it.

Daniel had been the interpreter of two dreams by Nebuchadnezzar (chaps. 2; 4). Then the prophet-statesman became the recipient of four dreams or visions (chaps. 7; 8; 9:20-27; 10:1–12:5).

**7:2.** In the first six chapters, **Daniel** wrote in the third person; in the last six chapters he wrote in the first person. **In his vision** Daniel first saw **the great sea** churned by the action of **four winds.** The word translated "winds" may also be rendered "spirits," that is, angels. Elsewhere in Scripture this word is used to refer to God's providential actions in the affairs of men through angels (Jer. 23:19; 49:36; 51:1; Zech. 6:1-6; 7:14; Rev. 7:1-3). Throughout the Old Testament the Mediterranean Sea is referred to as the Great Sea (Num. 34:6-7; Josh. 1:4; 9:1; 15:12, 47; 23:4; Ezek. 47:10, 15, 20; 48:28). This vision then related specifically to the Mediterranean world.

**7:3-4.** The second thing Daniel saw in the vision was **four great beasts** emerging from **the** agitated **sea.** As explained to Daniel later (v. 17) the four beasts represented four kingdoms. **The first** beast **was like a lion,** an animal symbolizing power and strength. This lion had eagle **wings,** which speak of swiftness. Interestingly the lion and eagle were both symbols of Babylon (cf. Jer. 4:7, 13; Ezek. 17:3). The violent wrenching of the **wings** from the lion would deprive it of its great mobility. This could refer to Nebuchadnezzar's insanity or to his empire's deterioration after his death. The lion's rising up on **two feet** (its hind legs) made it look more **like a man.** The fact that it got a man's **heart** suggests that the animal lost its beastly nature and showed compassion. The lion's rising on its hind legs and

may refer to Nebuchadnezzar's humanitarian interests.

**7:5.** The **second beast** was **like a bear,** an animal of formidable strength (1 Sam. 17:34; Amos 5:19; Hosea 13:8). This represents Medo-Persia, the empire that followed Babylon. The Medo-Persian army was strong and fierce (Isa. 13:15-18). Unlike the grace of the manlike lion, the bear was ponderous and ungainly. It was evidently reclining with **one** side higher than the other. This suggests that though Persia rose later than Media, Persia soon overshadowed the Medes in their united kingdom. The **three ribs** in the bear's **mouth** may represent the kingdoms of Egypt, Assyria, and Babylon, which had preceded the empire represented by the bear. Or they may represent Babylon, Lydia, and Egypt, three nations conquered by the Medes and Persians. The bear **was told** to devour **flesh.** This command suggests that kingdoms operate by divine appointment, not their own authority. In devouring other kingdoms and extending its territory into a vast empire, the bear was fulfilling God's purpose.

**7:6.** The third **beast** Daniel saw was **like a leopard,** an animal noted for its swiftness (Hab. 1:8), cunning, and agility (Jer. 5:6; Hosea 13:7). This beast **had four wings like . . . a bird,** stressing a swiftness beyond its natural capacity. An additional feature of **this beast** is that it **had four heads.** Also **authority to rule** was **given** it. The kingdom that conquered Medo-Persia was Greece, which did so with great speed, conquering the entire empire between 334 and 330 B.C. A few years after Alexander died his kingdom was divided into four parts (cf. Dan. 8:8, 22).

**7:7a.** Daniel now described **a fourth beast.** Instead of likening it to some known animal Daniel simply called it a beast. Apparently it was a mongrel composed of parts of a lion, bear, and leopard (cf. the beast in Rev. 13:2). This fourth beast was more **terrifying** and **powerful** than the three preceding beasts, which were all ferocious and destructive. This beast **had large iron teeth** with which it was able to crush and devour its prey. The empire represented by this mongrel beast had **crushed** and assimilated into itself the three previous empires described by the lion, the bear, and the leopard (it **trampled underfoot whatever was left**; cf. Dan. 7:19).

**7:7b-8.** A significant feature of this fourth and **different** beast was that **it had 10 horns.** According to verse 24 they represent 10 kings. As Daniel focused his attention on **the horns,** he saw **another horn** begin to emerge among the 10. This **little** horn had an insignificant beginning but in its growth it was able to uproot **three of the** existing **horns.** This little horn was noted for its intelligence (it had **the eyes of a man**) and its blasphemous claims (it had **a mouth that spoke boastfully;** cf. vv. 11, 20, 25). (See vv. 19-26 for comments on the identity of this fourth beast and its little horn.)

### b. The Ancient of Days (7:9-12)

**7:9-10.** In this portion (vv. 9-12) of the vision Daniel saw **thrones** of judgment **set** up. One throne was occupied by **the Ancient of Days.** This is the sovereign God (cf. Isa. 43:13; 57:15a) who exercises control over men and nations. His white **clothing** and **hair** speak of His holiness (Rev. 1:14). Daniel's description of the glory surrounding the One seated on the flaming **throne** with **wheels** recalls the description of the glory of God which Ezekiel saw (Ezek. 1:4-28). The **thousands** who surrounded the throne were God's servants, angels who execute His will. When Daniel saw God the Judge take His seat, **the court** (cf. Dan. 7:26) was convened, **and the books were opened.** (Interestingly, as stated earlier, Daniel's name means "God has judged" or "God is my Judge"; cf. 1:7. Here Daniel saw God as the world's Judge.) In Revelation 20:12 the opening of books refers to a review and judging of one's stewardship. Thus God, who assigns power to kingdoms, will judge those kingdoms.

**7:11-12.** As Daniel was watching the little **horn** because of its boasting (cf. v. 8) he saw that the fourth **beast was slain** and consigned to **blazing fire.** This event will terminate "the times of the Gentiles" (Luke 21:24, 27). The kingdoms represented by the three preceding **beasts had** already **been stripped of their** power by military conquest. But the fourth beast will be relieved of its power not by being conquered militarily, but by divine judgment (cf. Dan. 9:27; Rev. 11:15; 19:15). Each of the three, however, had been

**allowed to live for a** short **time.** This may mean that the cultures of each of the first three conquered empires were assimilated into the conquering nations.

### c. The Son of Man (7:13-14)

**7:13-14.** In the third major portion of this **vision** Daniel saw the **Son of Man** approaching **the Ancient of Days.** Jesus Christ, taking the title "Son of Man" from this prophecy, frequently used it to refer to Himself (as recorded in the Gospels; cf. comments on Mark 8:31; John 1:51). When the Son of Man was brought **into** the **presence** of the Ancient of Days, all the **authority, glory, and sovereign power** that had been exercised by rulers in the four kingdoms over **all peoples, nations, and men of every language** (cf. Dan. 3:4, 7; 4:1; 5:19; 6:25) was conferred on Him and those peoples **worshiped Him.** This is in keeping with the Father's promise to the Son in Psalm 2:6-9, and will be fulfilled at Christ's Second Advent (Matt. 24:30; 25:31; Rev. 11:15).

The Son of Man will establish **an everlasting dominion** or kingdom (cf. Dan. 4:34; 7:27). That kingdom will **never be** conquered by another (cf. 6:26). His reign will be established on earth (Rev. 20:1-6). At the expiration of the 1,000 years of the Lord's millennial reign, He will surrender the kingdom to God the Father, after which Christ will be appointed as Ruler over God's eternal kingdom forever (1 Cor. 15:24-28).

### 2. THE INTERPRETATION (7:15-28)

### a. The four beasts explained (7:15-17)

**7:15-17.** Like Nebuchadnezzar before him (cf. 2:1; 4:4-5), **Daniel** was **disturbed** by his dream (cf. 7:28). Though he had demonstrated the ability to interpret dreams on previous occasions (chaps. 2; 4), he could not interpret this one or his next one (8:15). So he called on **one of those standing** nearby, apparently the angel later identified as Gabriel (8:16; 9:21), to interpret the vision to him. It was explained that **the four great beasts** represent **four kingdoms.** As stated earlier, the four kingdoms are Babylon, represented by the lion; Medo-Persia, represented by the bear raised up on one side; Greece, represented by the winged leopard with four heads; and Rome, represented by the mongrel beast. (See the maps of these four empires.)

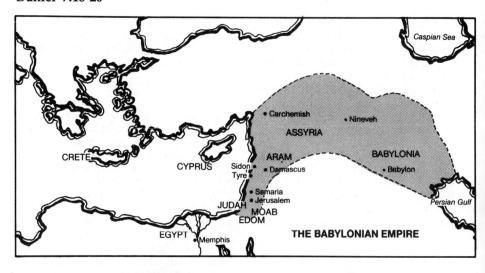

**THE BABYLONIAN EMPIRE**

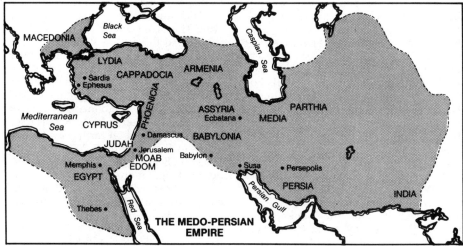

**THE MEDO-PERSIAN EMPIRE**

### b. The promise to Israel (7:18)

**7:18.** After the destruction of the fourth beast at the Second Advent, **the saints of the Most High** (cf. comments on "the Most High" at 3:26) **will receive the kingdom** (cf. 7:22, 27). The "saints" refer to the believing Jews (cf. comments on v. 25), not to believers of the Church Age. The existence of the church in the present Age was nowhere revealed in the Old Testament. The nation Israel has been set aside by divine discipline in the present "times of the Gentiles," which began with Nebuchadnezzar. During the "times of the Gentiles" four empires, Daniel was told, would rise and rule over the land and people of Israel. Yet God's covenant to David (2 Sam. 7:16; Ps. 89:1-4) stands and will ultimately be fulfilled.

The "saints" (believing Jews when Christ returns to earth) will enjoy the kingdom, the fulfillment of God's promise to Israel.

### c. The details of the fourth kingdom (7:19-28)

(1) The request. **7:19-20.** Daniel seems to have had no difficulty in interpreting the significance of the first three beasts. It was **the fourth beast** that caused him consternation, and he asked the angel (probably Gabriel; cf. 8:16; 9:21) to interpret the **meaning** of **the beast** and its **10 horns** and **the other horn that came up** among the 10 and was so **imposing.** What is represented by the 10 horns and particularly the little **horn** is of great significance. For from this point on to the end of the prophecy, Daniel concerned

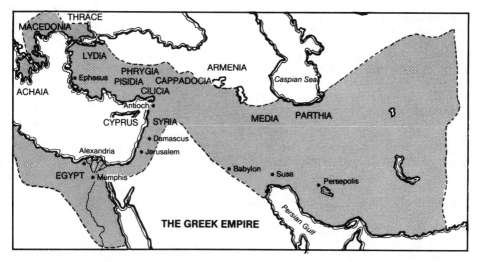

THE GREEK EMPIRE

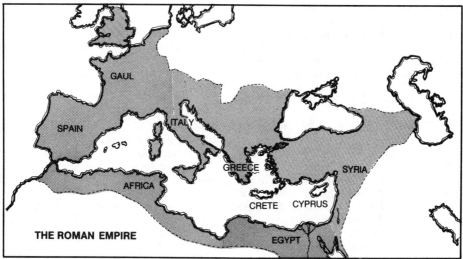

THE ROMAN EMPIRE

himself with the revelation about the person and work of the individual represented by this little horn.

(2) The judgment on the beast. **7:21-22.** Several facts about **this** little **horn** had already been revealed to Daniel (v. 8): (1) It came after the 10 horns (kings; cf. v. 24) were in existence and then was contemporaneous with them. (2) It uprooted 3 of the 10 horns (kings). (3) It was intelligent (it had the eyes of a man). (4) It was arrogant and boastful (cf. v. 11).

Now (vv. 21-22) three additional facts are given: (5) He will persecute **the saints of the Most High** (cf. v. 25; on "the Most High" see comments on 3:26). Obviously the horn represents a person. In 7:24 he is said to be a king. As in verse 18, **the saints** refer to the nation Israel.

His persecution of Israel will take place in the Tribulation. (6) He will overcome (he **was defeating**) the nation Israel and will bring that nation under his authority (Rev. 12:13-17; 17:7). (7) He will be judged by God (cf. Rev. 19:19-20), and Israel, no longer under the rule of the little horn, will enter into her covenanted blessings in **the kingdom** (cf. Dan. 7:18).

(3) The scope of the beast's kingdom. **7:23.** Though historically the sphere of **the fourth beast,** though greater than the extent of each of the previous three kingdoms, was limited, the sphere of this coming ruler in the **fourth kingdom** will be worldwide. Daniel was told that this empire **will devour the whole earth** (cf. Rev. 13:7). And it will be a ferocious conquest, in which that kingdom will tram-

ple and crush those who oppose it. This anticipates a coming one-world government under a worldwide dictator.

(4) The ten horns and the little horn (7:24-25). **7:24.** The angel then interpreted the meaning of **the 10 horns,** stating that they **are 10 kings** in **this kingdom.** The fourth empire, in spite of its great power (vv. 7, 23), will be characterized by progressive weakness, deterioration, and division (cf. comments on 2:41-43 on iron and clay in the fourth part of Nebuchadnezzar's image). When the hordes from the north conquered the Roman Empire in the fifth century A.D., they did not unite to form another empire. Instead individual nations emerged out of the old Roman Empire. Some of those nations and others stemming from them have continued till the present day. The present Age, then, is the 10-horned era of the fourth beast. (Other premillenarians, however, hold that the time of the 10 horns is yet future, that the present Church Age is not seen in this vision, and that 10 kings will coexist over a future revived [or realigned] Roman Empire.)

Sometime after the rise of the 10 horns—and no clue was given Daniel as to how much later—**another king** (the little horn, 7:8, 20) **will arise.** In his rise to power **he will subdue 3 kings** (called 3 horns in v. 8), that is, he will bring 3 of the 10 nations under his authority in his initial rise to power.

**7:25.** Besides several facts already given about this coming king (see comments on vv. 21-22), three additional ones are now revealed: (1) He will oppose God's authority. **He will speak against the Most High** (cf. Rev. 13:6). On "the Most High" see comments on Daniel 3:26. (2) He will **oppress His saints** (i.e., Israel; cf. comments on 7:21). (3) He will introduce an entirely new era in which he will abandon all previous **laws** and institute his own system. As in 9:27a, he will appear as Israel's friend, but will become Israel's persecutor (**the saints will be handed over to him**) and he will occupy Jerusalem as the capital of his empire (11:45) for three and one-half years (Rev. 12:6; 13:5). **A time, times, and half a time** (cf. Dan. 12:7; Rev. 12:14) refer to the three and one-half years of the Great Tribulation, with "a time" meaning one year, "times" two

years, and "half a time" six months. This equals the 1,260 days in Revelation 12:6 and the 42 months in Revelation 11:2; 13:5. (Cf. comments on "times" in Dan. 4:16.)

(5) The promise to Israel. **7:26-27.** When the Judge, God the Father, convenes **the court** (cf. v. 10), that is, when He judges the little horn, his **power will be** removed and he will be **destroyed** (cf. v. 11; 2 Thes. 2:8; Rev. 19:20). This will occur at the Second Advent of Christ. At the beginning of the Millennium the Son of Man will be given authority to rule (cf. Dan. 7:14), and He will rule over **the saints, the people of the Most High** (cf. comments on 3:26), that is, the nation Israel (cf. 7:18, 22), which has been bound to God by God's covenant with Abraham (Gen. 12:1-6; 13:14-17; 15:18-21). This **kingdom** will not be overthrown and superseded by another. It will continue in the Millennium and on forever (cf. Dan. 4:34; 6:26; 7:14). **All peoples and kings will worship and obey Him.**

(6) The response of Daniel. **7:28.** This prophetic panorama of the times of the Gentiles was so awesome to **Daniel** that he **was deeply** moved. He did not share the vision with anyone at the time. But later when he wrote the prophecies that bear his name, he recorded what had been revealed to him in the vision.

One cannot escape the parallels between the truths revealed to Daniel on this occasion and what was revealed to Nebuchadnezzar early in his reign (chap. 2). Both cover the span of the times of the Gentiles. Both dreams indicate that Israel and her land will be ruled over by four successive world empires. The first was Babylon, represented by the head of gold and the winged lion. The second was the Medo-Persian Empire, represented by the chest and arms of silver and the bear raised up on one side. The third was the Grecian Empire, represented by the belly and thighs of bronze and the four-headed winged leopard. The fourth was the Roman Empire, represented by the legs of iron with feet mixed with clay and by the mongrel beast. The iron-like strength of the fourth empire is seen in the iron legs (2:40) and the beast's iron teeth (7:7). Sovereignty passed from Assyria to Babylon in 609 B.C., from Babylon to Persia in 539 B.C., from Persia to Greece in 330

B.C., and from Greece to Rome in the first century B.C.

Toward the end of the times of the Gentiles, worldwide authority will be exercised by one called "a little horn" who will seek to prevent Christ's rule on the earth by destroying God's covenant people. His short reign of seven years (see comments on "one 'seven' " in 9:27) will be terminated by the Second Advent of Christ. At His coming Christ will establish His millennial kingdom on earth in fulfillment of God's covenant with Israel.

The amillenarian view that the "little horn" has already appeared sometime in the past (but since Christ's First Advent) is wrong because: (a) no such ruler has attained worldwide status (7:23), (b) no such ruler has subdued 3 of 10 kings who were ruling at once (v. 24), (c) no such ruler has persecuted Israel (v. 21) for three and one-half years (v. 25), and (d) no such ruler has been destroyed forever (v. 26) by Christ's return. Nor could this "little horn" be the Roman Catholic papacy because: (a) the "little horn" is a king, not a pope, (b) the papacy's power has not been limited to three and one-half years, (c) the papacy has not concentrated on persecuting the nation Israel, and (d) the papacy has not been destroyed by the return of Christ to the earth.

## III. The Prophetic History of Israel during the Times of the Gentiles (chaps. 8–12)

### A. The vision of the ram and the goat (chap. 8)

Chapters 8–12 (and 1:1–2:4a) are written in Hebrew, whereas 2:4b–7:28 are in Aramaic. For the significance of this, see "Languages" in the *Introduction*.

1. THE VISION (8:1-14)

*a. The preparation (8:1-2)*

**8:1-2.** The vision recorded by **Daniel** in chapter 8 came to him two years after the vision of chapter 7 (cf. Belshazzar's **third year,** 8:1, with his "first year," 7:1). In his **vision** Daniel **saw** himself **in the** palace in **Susa,** one of the Persian royal cities, more than 200 miles east of Babylon on **the Ulai Canal** (see map "The World of Jeremiah and Ezekiel" in the *Introduction* to Jer.). A century later the Persian king Xerxes built a magnificent palace there, which was where the events recorded in the Book of Esther took place (cf. Es. 1:2). And Nehemiah was King Artaxerxes' cupbearer in the Susa palace (Neh. 1:1).

*b. The vision of the ram (8:3-4)*

**8:3-4.** In his vision Daniel saw **a ram with two** long **horns** near the **canal.** The significant thing was that **one** horn **was longer than the other.** The horns did not arise simultaneously; the longer one arose after (**grew up later** than) the shorter one. The disparity between the ram's two horns recalls the bear raised up on one side (7:5). **The ram** that had been standing by the canal began to charge **toward the west . . . north and . . . south.** His charge was irresistible; **none could** escape his onslaught. Doing **as he** wished, the ram dominated all the territory against which he moved **and became great.**

*c. The vision of the goat (8:5-14)*

**8:5-8.** Daniel then saw **a goat with a** powerful single **horn** arise **suddenly . . . from the west.** His speed was so great that his feet did not touch **the ground.** The goat, determined to destroy **the two-horned ram,** went **at him in great rage . . . furiously** and broke the ram's **two horns.**

**The ram was powerless to** defend himself and the goat subjugated the ram. The greatness that had characterized **the ram** now belonged to **the goat.** Previously none could escape from the ram's power (v. 4); now **none could** escape from the goat (v. 7). As soon as **the goat** was elevated to great **power,** his **large** single **horn was broken off,** and **its place** was taken by **four prominent horns.**

The description of this goat is somewhat parallel to the third beast in 7:6, the leopard with wings. Both were rapid, and the leopard had four heads whereas the goat had four horns. The goat's horns probably represented kings (just as the horns on the fourth beast represented kings, 7:24).

**8:9-12. Out of one of** the four horns **came another horn.** It had an insignificant beginning but it exerted **power** southward and eastward **and toward the Beautiful Land,** that is, the land of Israel. He became a great persecutor of the people of Israel (**the host of the heaven;** cf. "host" in v. 13) and he subjugated that

## A Comparison of Daniel 2; 7; and 8

| Daniel 2 Metals | Daniel 7 Animals | Daniel 8 Animals | Nations |
|---|---|---|---|
| Gold | Winged lion | — | Babylon |
| Silver | Bear | Ram | Medo-Persia |
| Bronze | Winged leopard | Goat | Greece |
| Iron (and iron and clay) | Beast | — | Rome |

nation (**trampled on them**). He **set** himself **up** as Israel's king, calling himself **the Prince of the host.** He compelled the nation to worship him, as suggested by the fact that he prohibited Israel from following her religious practices (removing **the daily sacrifice**) and desecrated the temple (**brought** the **sanctuary . . . low**). The nation Israel (**the saints**; cf. comments on 7:18) acceded to this individual's wishes because of his rebellious attitude (cf. "rebellion" in 8:13). He **prospered** and so despised the truth contained in God's Word that **truth was** said to be **thrown to the ground.**

This part of the vision anticipated the rise of a ruler in the Greek Empire who subjugated the people and land of Israel, desecrated her temple, interrupted her worship, and demanded for himself the authority and worship that belongs to God.

**8:13-14.** For Daniel's benefit an angel (**a holy one**; cf. "holy ones" in 4:17) addressed the revealing angel (**another holy one**) and asked, **How long will it take for the vision to be fulfilled?** The answer was, **It will take 2,300 evenings and mornings.** (For the meaning of the "2,300 evenings and mornings" see the comments on 8:23-25.) At the conclusion of that time, **the sanctuary** that had been defiled would be cleansed and restored (**reconsecrated**) to its rightful place in the nation's life.

2. THE INTERPRETATION (8:15-27)

a. Gabriel's intervention (8:15-18)

**8:15-18.** Once again **Daniel,** though able to interpret Nebuchadnezzar's dreams (chaps. 2; 4), could not interpret this dream (cf. 7:16). **Gabriel** was sent to interpret **the meaning of the vision** to Daniel. Understandably Daniel **was terrified** (cf. 7:15) by the appearance of the glorious messenger **and fell prostrate** before him. Referring to Daniel as a **son of man** (cf. comments on Ezek. 2:1; not to be confused with Christ, the Son of Man), Gabriel explained that **the vision** pertained to **the time of the end** (cf. Dan. 8:19), that is, events future from Daniel's day, events concerning the nation Israel under the Greek Empire.

b. Gabriel's interpretation (8:19-26)

**8:19.** Gabriel stated that **the vision** pertained to events beyond Daniel's time (**what will happen later,** and **the appointed time of the end**; cf. v. 17). Significantly this later time, within the times of the Gentiles, was called **the time of wrath.** As stated earlier (chap. 2) the times of the Gentiles is the period from Nebuchadnezzar's reign to the second coming of Christ during which Israel is undergoing divine discipline. Her acts of disobedience brought forth God's disciplinary wrath on the nation.

**8:20-21.** Gabriel first interpreted the meaning of **the two-horned ram** (cf. vv. 3-7). This beast represented **Media and Persia,** the same empire represented by the bear raised up on one side (7:5). Though Persia rose later than Media (559 B.C. for Persia compared with centuries earlier for Media) the Persians overshadowed the Medes. So the second horn on the ram was larger than the first horn. Persia extended its empire to the west, north, and south with a vast army of more than 2 million soldiers.

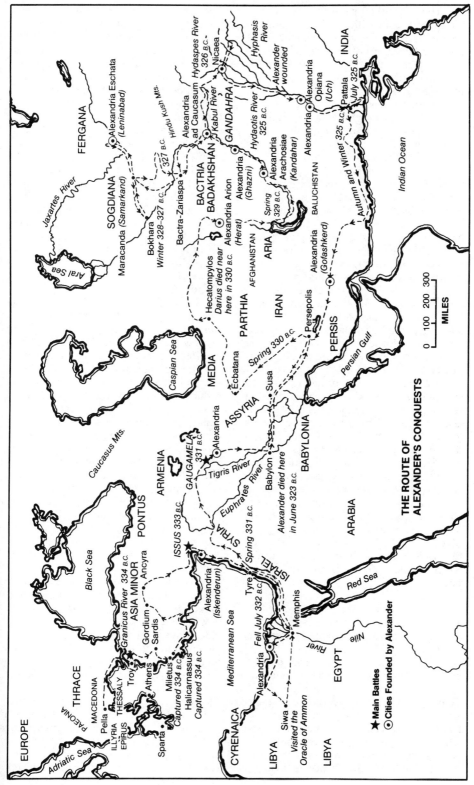

THE ROUTE OF
ALEXANDER'S CONQUESTS

★ Main Battles
◉ Cities Founded by Alexander

The angel then gave the meaning of **the shaggy goat** with **the large horn between his eyes.** The goat represented **the king** (or kingdom) **of Greece,** who in 7:6 was depicted by the winged leopard. (See the chart on p. 1356, "A Comparison of Daniel 2; 7; and 8.") The single horn represented Greece's **first king,** Alexander (cf. 11:3). Though his father Philip II of Macedonia had united all the Greek city-states except Sparta, Alexander is considered Greece's first king.

Alexander the Great (the prominent horn, 8:5) came from the west with a small but fast army. He was enraged (v. 6) at the Persians for having defeated the Greeks at the Battle of Marathon (490 B.C.) and the Battle of Salamis (481), Greek cities near Athens. He quickly conquered Asia Minor, Syria, Egypt, and Mesopotamia in a few years, beginning in 334 B.C. The Persians were helpless to resist him (v. 7). (See the map on p. 1357, "The Route of Alexander's Conquests.") Alexander died of malaria and complications from alcoholism in 323 B.C. at the age of 32 in Babylon. At the height of his power he was cut off (v. 8).

**8:22.** Since Alexander had no heirs to succeed him, the kingdom was divided several years later among his four generals, represented here by **the four horns** (cf. v. 8; cf. 11:4). But the divided kingdom of Greece never had **the same power** Greece had enjoyed under Alexander. To Ptolemy was given Egypt and parts of Asia Minor. Cassander was given the territory of Macedonia and Greece. Lysimachus was given Thrace and parts of Asia Minor (western Bithynia, Phrygia, Mycia, and Lydia). Seleucus was given the remainder of Alexander's empire which included Syria, Israel, and Mesopotamia.

**8:23-25.** Years later from among one of the four horns (kings) there would **arise,** Gabriel said, a severe (**stern-faced**) and cunning **king** (**a master of intrigue;** cf. **deceit,** v. 25). A powerful ruler, he would devastate property and **destroy** people in order to expand his kingdom. **The holy people,** the nation Israel (cf. "saints," 7:18, 22, 27), would be a special target of his oppression. In subjugating Israel, **many** would lose their lives just when they thought they were safe. His antagonism against Israel would also be **against** her God, **the Prince of princes.**

**Yet** this mighty conqueror himself would **be destroyed** by supernatural **power.** His rise was not his own doing (8:24) and his downfall was **not by human** means (he died insane in Persia in 163 B.C.).

The king referred to here is known as Antiochus IV Epiphanes. After murdering his brother, who had inherited the throne in the Seleucid dynasty, he came to power in 175 B.C. In 170 B.C. Ptolemy VI of Egypt sought to recover territory then ruled over by Antiochus. So Antiochus invaded Egypt and defeated Ptolemy VI and proclaimed himself king in Egypt. This was his growth "in power to the south" (v. 9). On his return from this conquest, trouble broke out in Jerusalem so he decided to subdue Jerusalem ("the Beautiful Land," v. 9; cf. 11:16, 41). The people were subjugated, the temple desecrated, and the temple treasury plundered.

From this conquest Antiochus returned to Egypt in 168 but was forced by Rome to evacuate Egypt. On his return he determined to make the land of Israel a buffer state between himself and Egypt. He attacked and burned Jerusalem, killing multitudes (cf. 8:10). The Jews were forbidden to follow the Mosaic Law in observing the Sabbath, their annual feasts, and traditional sacrifices, and circumcision of children (cf. v. 11). Altars to idols were set up in Jerusalem and on December 16, 167 B.C. the Jews were ordered to offer unclean sacrifices and to eat swine's flesh or be penalized by death. (Though his friends called him *Epiphanes* ["the Illustrious One"] no wonder the Jews called him *Epimanes* ["the Madman"].) (For more on the role of Antiochus IV Epiphanes see comments on 11:21-35.)

Antiochus' desecration of the temple was to last 2,300 evenings and mornings before its cleansing (8:14). Some take the 2,300 evenings and mornings to mean 2,300 days, that is, a little more than six years. In this interpretation, the six years were from Antiochus' first incursion into Jerusalem (170 B.C.) to the refurbishing and restoring of the temple by Judas Maccabeus in late 164. A second interpretation seems preferable. Rather than each evening and each morning representing a day, the reference may be to evening and morning sacrifices, which were interrupted by Antiochus' desecration (cf.

"the daily sacrifice," vv. 11-21). With two sacrifices made daily, the 2,300 offerings would cover 1,150 days or three years (of 360 days each) plus 70 days. This is the time from Antiochus' desecration of the temple (December 16, 167 B.C.) to the refurbishing and restoring of the temple by Judas Maccabeus in late 164 and on into 163 B.C. when all the Jewish sacrifices were fully restored and religious independence gained for Judah. Whichever interpretation it is that one accepts, the figure of 2,300 was a literal one and so the time period was literally fulfilled.

There is no question among expositors that Antiochus is in view in this prophecy. What was prophesied was fulfilled literally through him. However, the prophecy looks beyond Antiochus to a future person (the Antichrist) of whom Antiochus is only a foreshadowing. This coming one is said to "stand against the Prince of princes" (v. 25). This can be none other than the Lord Jesus Christ. Thus the prophecy must go beyond Antiochus and look forward to the coming of one whose ministry will parallel that of Antiochus.

From Antiochus certain facts can be learned about the forthcoming desecrator: (1) He will achieve great power by subduing others (v. 24). (2) He will rise to power by promising false security (v. 25). (3) He will be intelligent and persuasive (v. 23). (4) He will be controlled by another (v. 24), that is, Satan. (5) He will be an adversary of Israel and subjugate Israel to his authority (vv. 24-25). (6) He will rise up in opposition to the Prince of princes, the Lord Jesus Christ (v. 25). (7) His rule will be terminated by divine judgment (v. 25). So it may be concluded that there is a dual reference in this striking prophecy. It reveals Israel's history under the Seleucids and particularly under Antiochus during the time of Greek domination, but it also looks forward to Israel's experiences under Antichrist, whom Antiochus foreshadows.

**8:26.** Daniel was told to **seal up the vision** in the sense of concluding it, not in the sense of keeping it secret, because it needed to be preserved for the **future.** He kept it in his mind and later preserved it in writing when he wrote it down under the Holy Spirit's inspiration.

### c. Daniel's response (8:27)

**8:27. Daniel was** completely overcome (**exhausted and . . . ill**) by the interpretation of this **vision. For several days** he was unable to carry on his official **business.**

## B. The vision of the 70 "sevens" (chap. 9)

### 1. THE OCCASION OF THE VISION (9:1-2)

**9:1-2.** It was now **the first year** of the reign **of Darius** the **Mede.** (On the identity of this Darius see comments on 6:1.) This was 539 B.C., 66 years after Daniel had been exiled.

The overthrow of **the Babylonian Kingdom** by the Medo-Persians was indeed a momentous event. It had been revealed to Belshazzar through Daniel's interpretation of the writing on the wall (5:25-28, 30). The Babylonian overthrow prepared the way for liberation of the Jews who had been in exile since Nebuchadnezzar's first invasion **of Jerusalem** in 605 B.C. Besides predicting the overthrow of the people **Jeremiah** had also predicted that Israel's sojourn in Babylon was to **last 70 years** (Jer. 25:11-12).

Evidently moved by Darius' victory **Daniel** searched **the Scriptures** to understand the events of which he was a vital part. He **understood** Darius' victory meant that the termination of the 70-year Captivity was near. Thus these significant events became even more momentous for Daniel.

### 2. THE PRAYER OF DANIEL (9:3-19)

#### a. Confession (9:3-14)

**9:3-6.** Daniel's study of the Scriptures led him to turn to **God** and to pray a **prayer** of confession (vv. 3-14) and **petition** (vv. 15-19), with **fasting.** Wearing **sackcloth and**/or **ashes** was evidence of mourning in grief or repentance (cf. Gen. 37:34; Neh. 9:1; Es. 4:1, 3; Isa. 58:5; Jer. 49:3; Ezek. 7:18; Joel 1:8; Matt. 11:21).

Moses revealed the principle on which God would deal with His covenant people: obedience would bring blessing, and disobedience would bring discipline. One form of discipline was that Israel would be subjugated to Gentile powers (Deut. 28:48-57, 64-68). Israel's experience in Babylon was the outworking of this principle.

Then Moses revealed the basis on which the discipline would be lifted and the nation would be restored to blessing (Deut. 30). She would have to return to God and obey His voice; then **God** would turn back her Captivity and restore the people to the land from which they had been dispersed and shower blessings on them.

Daniel evidently was fully aware that the years in Babylon were a divine discipline on Israel. Knowing that confession was one requisite to restoration, he **confessed** the sin of his people, identifying himself with their sin as though he were personally responsible for it.

Daniel noted that blessing depends on obedience, for **God . . . keeps His covenant of love** (ḥeseḏ, "loyal love") **with all who love Him and obey** Him. Even a covenant people cannot be blessed if they disobey. Four times Daniel acknowledged that his people had **sinned** (Dan. 9:5, 8, 11, 15). Their sin was a sin of rebellion (cf. v. 9) against God and in turning **away** (cf. v. 11) **from** the Word of God (His **laws**; cf. vv 10-11) which they knew. God in grace had sent **prophets** (cf. v. 10) to exhort the people to return to Him but they had refused to heed their messages (**we have not listened**). **Kings** and **people** alike stood guilty before God.

**9:7-11a.** Daniel then acknowledged that God is **righteous** (cf. vv. 14, 16) and just in disciplining Israel for her **unfaithfulness,** for which she was **covered with shame** (vv. 7-8) and dispersed (**scattered**) into foreign **countries.** God's discipline did not mean that He had withheld mercy (cf. v. 18) and forgiveness from His people, but it meant that He, being righteous, must punish people's rebellion and disobedience (v. 10). They refused to keep God's **laws** (v. 10; cf. v. 5) for they **transgressed** His **Law** (v. 11) and **turned** from God (cf. v. 5), being obstinate in their disobedience (**refusing to obey**).

**9:11b-14.** Because of her rebellion and disobedience Israel was experiencing **the curses and . . . judgments written by** Moses (cf. v. 13) in Deuteronomy 28:15-68. In spite of the severity of the discipline, including **great** national **disaster** (Dan. 9:12), the nation was not **turning** from her **sins** and submitting to the authority of **the Law,** God's **truth. This disaster,** the fall of Jerusalem, was because **God is righteous** (cf. vv. 7, 16) and Israel had **not obeyed Him** (cf. vv. 10-11).

### b. Petition (9:15-19)

**9:15-16.** Daniel began his petition (v. 15) by mentioning two of the same things with which he began his confession (vv. 4-5): God's greatness and the people's sin. Daniel spoke of God's delivering Israel **out of Egypt** by His great power (**with a mighty hand**). God was glorified through the deliverance of His people. But because the nation had **sinned** (Daniel's fourth time to state that his people had sinned; cf. vv. 5, 8, 11) she had become **an object of scorn to** those nations **around** her. In prayer that God, **in keeping with** His **righteous acts** (cf. vv. 7, 14), would **turn away** His **anger and . . . wrath from Jerusalem,** Daniel was asking that God's discipline might be lifted and the people freed from their present bondage. (Jerusalem is God's **city;** cf. v. 24, and His **holy hill;** cf. v. 20; Joel 2:1; 3:17; Zeph. 3:11.)

Once again Daniel attributed the nation's present status to her past sin, the **sins and . . . iniquities of our fathers** (cf. Dan. 9:6, 8).

**9:17-19.** Having prayed for the negative, the removal of God's wrath (vv. 15-16), the prophet now prayed for the positive, God's favor, mercy, and forgiveness (vv. 17-19). Daniel asked that **God** would **hear** his **prayers** and restore (**look with favor on**) the **sanctuary** (the temple in Jerusalem) for His **sake** (cf. v. 19). And he wanted God to **hear** his request (**give ear**) and to **see** (**open Your eyes**) the city's **desolation.** Interestingly Daniel did not specify what God should do; he only asked that God "look" on the sanctuary and "see" the city, both in desolation for many years.

Daniel based his requests on God's **great mercy** (cf. v. 9), not on the nation's righteousness for she had none. But because God is merciful and forgiving, he prayed, **O Lord, listen! O Lord, forgive!** Concerned for God's reputation, Daniel wanted the **Lord** to **act** quickly (**do not delay**) on behalf of the **city** and **people** that bore His **name.** All this would bring glory to God for it was **for** His **sake** (cf. v. 17).

### 3. THE RESPONSE OF THE LORD (9:20-27)

### a. The message of Gabriel (9:20-23)

**9:20-21.** Daniel's prayer included confession of his **sin and the sin of** his **people,** and his **request** that **God** restore

Jerusalem (God's **holy hill**). The answer to Daniel's **prayer** was not delayed (cf. "do not delay," v. 19). For he was interrupted by the appearance of **Gabriel,** who had come to him **earlier** to interpret his **vision** of the ram and the goat (8:15-16). Gabriel **came** swiftly **about the time of the evening sacrifice.** This was one of the two daily sacrifices required in the Law (Ex. 19:38-39; Num. 28:3-4; cf. "evenings and mornings" in Dan. 8:14). Even though the temple was destroyed so the sacrifices could not be offered for those 66 years, Daniel still observed that time of day as an appointed time of worship. Perhaps this was one of the three times he prayed daily (6:10).

**9:22-23.** Though **Daniel** did not refer to it in his prayer, he was evidently concerned about God's program for Israel from that point on (cf. v. 2). Jeremiah's prophecy (Jer. 25:11-12) had revealed God's plan for the nation only up to the end of the 70-year Babylonian Captivity. Daniel wanted to know what would transpire after that. Daniel's previous two visions (Dan. 7–8) of forthcoming events dealt primarily with Gentile nations that would rise beginning with Babylon. So Gabriel was dispatched by God to satisfy Daniel's desire and to reveal God's program for His people until its consummation in the covenanted kingdom under Israel's Messiah. Gabriel would **give** Daniel **insight** into God's purposes for His people. Because the prophet was **highly esteemed** (cf. 10:11, 19) by God, Gabriel had received **an answer** for Daniel **as soon as** Daniel **began to pray.**

*b. The program in the 70 "sevens" (9:24)*

**9:24.** Daniel was first informed that God's program would be consummated in **70 "sevens."** Since Daniel had been thinking of God's program in terms of years (v. 1; cf. Jer. 25:11-12; 2 Chron. 36:21), it would be most natural for him to understand these "sevens" as years. Whereas people today think in units of tens (e.g., decades), Daniel's **people** thought in terms of sevens (heptads). Seven days are in one week. Every seventh year was a sabbath rest year (Lev. 25:1-7). Seven "sevens" brought them to the Year of Jubilee (Lev. 25:8-12). Seventy "sevens," then, is a span of 490 years. The 490 could not designate *days* (about 1⅓ years) for that would not be enough

time for the events prophesied in Daniel 9:24-27 to occur. The same is true of 490 weeks of seven days each (i.e., 3,430 days, about 9½ years). Also if days were intended one would expect Daniel to have added "of days" after "70 sevens" for in 10:2-3 he wrote literally, "three sevens of days" (NIV, "three weeks").

Also since Israel and Judah had failed to keep the sabbatical years (every seventh year the land was to lie fallow, Lev. 25:1-7) throughout her history, the Lord enforced on the land 70 "sabbaths" (cf. Lev. 26:34-35). Thus 490 years would be required to complete 70 sabbatical years with one occurring every seventh year.

This span of time was decreed for Daniel's people (cf. "your people" in Dan. 10:14; 11:14) and the Holy City (cf. 9:16, 24). This prophecy, then, is concerned not with world history or church history, but with the history of Israel and the city of Jerusalem. By the time these 490 years run their course, God will have completed six things for Israel. The first three have to do with sin, and the second three with the kingdom. The basis for the first three was provided in the work of Christ on the cross, but all six will be realized by Israel at the Second Advent of Christ.

1. At the end of the 490 years God will **finish** the **transgression** of Israel. The verb "to finish" (*kālā'*) means "to bring something to an end." Israel's sin of disobedience will be brought to an end at Christ's second coming when she repents and turns to Him as her Messiah and Savior. Then she will be restored to the land and blessed, in answer to Daniel's prayer.

In Old Testament days the highpoint in Israel's festival calendar was the Day of Atonement (Lev. 16). On that day the nation assembled before God, acknowledged her sin, and offered blood sacrifices to cover that sin. Though that sacrifice covered Israel's sin for 12 months, it did not permanently remove that sin (Heb. 10:1-3). It was necessary that a sacrifice be offered God that would permanently remove all the accumulated sins. This sacrifice was offered by Jesus Christ who by His death made payment for all sins that had not been removed in the past (cf. Rom. 3:25). So His atoning work on the cross has made possible His future "finishing" of Israel's transgression.

2. God will **put an end to sin.** The verb *ḥāṭam* has the idea of sealing up. Here the thought is sealing something up with a view to punishment (cf. Deut. 32:34; Job 14:17). This emphasized that Israel's sin which had gone unpunished would be punished—in or through Jesus Christ, her Substitute, who would bear the sins of the world on the cross. Then at Christ's second coming He will remove Israel's sin (Ezek. 37:23; Rom. 11:20-27).

3. God will **atone for wickedness.** The verb "to atone" (*kāpar*) means "to cover or expiate." This too relates to God's final atonement of Israel when she repents at Christ's second coming, as the provision for that atonement has already been made at the Cross. Israel's Day of Atonement should be kept in view here too, as in the first of these six accomplishments. On that day God provided a just basis on which He would deal with a guilty people. The blood applied to the mercy seat ("the atonement cover," Lev. 16:14) over the ark of the covenant enabled Him to dwell among His sinful people. Similarly Daniel's prophecy promised that because of Christ's blood shed on the cross God would deal with sinners, and here in particular, with sinners in Israel.

Being propitiated (i.e., satisfied) by Christ's blood, God can atone for or expiate sin. The Greek words for "atonement cover" (*hilasmos*; KJV, "mercy seat") and "propitiate" (*hilaskomai*) are related.

4. The second three accomplishments deal with positive aspects of God's program. Being satisfied by the death of Christ, God will **bring in everlasting righteousness.** The form of the verb "bring in" here means "to cause to come in." The word "everlasting" (here pl. in Heb.) means ages. Thus this phrase (lit., "to bring in righteousness of ages") is a prophecy that God will establish an age characterized by righteousness. This is a reference to the millennial kingdom (Isa. 60:21; Jer. 23:5-6).

5. God will **seal up vision and prophecy.** All that God through the prophets said He would do in fulfilling His covenant with Israel will be fully realized in the millennial kingdom. Until they are fulfilled, prophecies are "unsealed." ("Seal" translates the same verb,

*ḥāṭam,* used in the second of these six accomplishments.)

6. God will **anoint the Most Holy.** This may refer to the dedication of the most holy place in the millennial temple, described in Ezekiel 41–46. Or it may refer not to a holy place, but to the Holy One, Christ. If so, this speaks of the enthronement of Christ, "the Anointed One" (Dan. 7:25-27) as King of kings and Lord of lords in the Millennium.

These six accomplishments, then, anticipate the establishment of Israel's covenanted millennial kingdom under the authority of her promised King. The six summarize God's whole program to bring the nation Israel the blessings He promised through His covenants (Gen. 15:18-21; 2 Sam. 7:16; Jer. 31:31-34).

*c. The divisions of the 70 "sevens"
(9:25-27)*

**9:25.** Important revelation was then given Daniel about the inception of this important time period and its divisions. The 70 "sevens" would begin, Gabriel said, with **the issuing of the decree to restore and rebuild Jerusalem.** This decree was the fourth of four decrees made by Persian rulers in reference to the Jews. The first was Cyrus' decree in 538 B.C. (2 Chron. 36:22-23; Ezra 1:1-4; 5:13). The second was the decree of Darius I (522-486) in 520 B.C. (Ezra 6:1, 6-12). This decree actually was a confirmation of the first decree. The third was the decree of Artaxerxes Longimanus (464-424) in 458 B.C. (Ezra 7:11-26). The first two decrees pertain to the rebuilding of the temple in Jerusalem and the third relates to finances for animal sacrifices at the temple. These three say nothing about the rebuilding of the city itself. Since an unwalled city was no threat to a military power, a religious temple could be rebuilt without jeopardizing the military authority of those granting permission to rebuild it. No one of these three decrees, then, was the decree that formed the beginning of the 70 sevens.

The fourth decree was also by Artaxerxes Longimanus, issued on March 5, 444 B.C. (Neh. 2:1-8). On that occasion Artaxerxes granted the Jews permission to rebuild Jerusalem's city walls. This decree is the one referred to in Daniel 9:25.

The end or goal of the prophecy is the appearance of **the Anointed One, the**

# The 483 Years in the Jewish and Gregorian Calendars

**Jewish Calendar**
**(360 days per year\*)**

$(7 \times 7) + (62 \times 7)$ years = 483 years

$$
\begin{array}{r}
483 \text{ years} \\
\times \quad 360 \text{ days} \\
\hline
173,880 \text{ days}
\end{array}
$$

**Gregorian Calendar**
**(365 days a year)**

444 B.C. to A.D. 33 = 476 years†

$$
\begin{array}{r}
476 \text{ years} \\
\times \quad 365 \text{ days} \\
\hline
173,740 \text{ days} \\
+ \quad 116 \text{ days in leap years‡} \\
+ \quad 24 \text{ days (March 5–March 30)} \\
\hline
173,880 \text{ days}
\end{array}
$$

\*See comments on Daniel 9:27b for confirmation of this 360-day year.

†Since only one year expired between 1 B.C. and A.D. 1, the total is 476, not 477.

‡A total of 476 years divided by four (a leap year every four years) gives 119 additional days. But three days must be subtracted from 119 because centennial years are not leap years, though every 400th year is a leap year.

**Ruler.** This refers to Christ Himself. God the Father anointed Christ with the Spirit at the time of His water baptism (Acts 10:38), but the anointing referred to here is the anointing of Christ as the Ruler in His kingdom (cf. comments on "anoint the Most Holy" in Dan. 9:24). This prophecy of the 70 sevens, then, ends not with the First Advent of Christ, as some suggest, but rather with the Second Advent and the establishing of the millennial kingdom.

This 490-year period is divided into three segments; (a) 7 "sevens" (49 years), (b) 62 "sevens" (434 years), and (c) 1 "seven" (v. 27; 7 years). The first period of 49 years may refer to the time in which the rebuilding of the city of Jerusalem, permitted by Artexerxes' decree, was completed (444–395 B.C.). Though Nehemiah's wall construction project took only 52 days, many years may have been needed to remove the city's debris (after being desolate for many decades), to build adequate housing, and to rebuild the **streets and a trench.**

**9:26a. The 62 "sevens"** (434 years) extend up to the introduction of the Messiah to the nation Israel. This second period concluded on the day of the Triumphal Entry just before Christ was **cut off,** that is, crucified. In His Triumphal Entry, Christ, in fulfillment of Zechariah 9:9, officially presented Himself to the nation of Israel as the Messiah. He was evidently familiar with Daniel's prophecy when on that occasion He said, "If you, even you, had only known on this day what would bring you peace—but now it is hidden from your eyes" (Luke 19:42).

Thus the first two segments of the important time period—the 7 sevens (49 years) and the 62 sevens (434 years)—ran consecutively with no time between them. They totaled 483 years and extended from March 5, 444 B.C. to March 30, A.D. 33. How can 444 B.C. to A.D. 33 equal 483 years? For an answer see the chart "The 483 Years in the Jewish and Gregorian Calendars." (For more details see Harold W. Hoehner, *Chronological Aspects of the Life of Christ.* Grand Rapids: Zondervan Publishing House, 1977, and Alva J. McClain, *Daniel's Prophecy of the Seventy Weeks.* Grand Rapids: Zondervan Publishing House, 1969.)

According to Daniel 9:26 **the Anointed One** was not "cut off" *in* the 70th "seven"; He was cut off **after** the 7 and 62 "sevens" had run their course. This means that there is an interval between the 69th and 70th "sevens." Christ's crucifixion, then, was in that interval, right after His Triumphal Entry, which concluded the 69th "seven." This interval was anticipated by Christ when He prophesied the establishing of the church (Matt. 16:18). This necessitated the setting aside of the nation Israel for a season in order that His new program for the church might be instituted. Christ predicted the setting aside of the nation (Matt. 21:42-43). The present Church Age is the interval between the 69th and 70th "sevens."

Amillenarians teach that Christ's First Advent ministry was in the 70th "seven," that there was no interval between the 69th and 70th "sevens," and that the six actions predicted in Daniel 9:24 are being fulfilled today in the church. This view, however, (a) ignores the fact that verse 26 says *"after* the 62 'sevens,' " not *"in* the 70th 'seven,' " (b) overlooks the fact that Christ's ministry on earth was three and one-half years in length, not seven, and (c) ignores the fact that God's six actions pertain to Daniel's "people" (Israel) and His "Holy City" (Jerusalem), not the church.

When the Anointed One would be cut off, Daniel was told, he would **have nothing.** The word translated "cut off" is used of executing the death penalty on a criminal. Thus the prophecy clearly points to the crucifixion of Christ. At His crucifixion He would "have nothing" in the sense that Israel had rejected Him and the kingdom could not be instituted at that time. Therefore He did not then receive the royal glory as the King on David's throne over Israel. John referred to this when he wrote, "He came to that which was His own [i.e., the throne to which He had been appointed by the Father] but His own [i.e., His own people] did not receive Him" (John 1:11). Daniel's prophecy, then, anticipated Christ's offer of Himself to the nation Israel as her Messiah, the nation's rejection of Him as Messiah, and His crucifixion.

**9:26b.** The prophecy continues with a description of the judgment that would **come** on the generation that rejected the Messiah. **The city** which contains **the sanctuary,** that is, Jerusalem, would be destroyed by **the people of the ruler who will come.** The ruler who will come is that final head of the Roman Empire, the little horn of 7:8. It is significant that the *people* of the ruler, not the ruler himself, will destroy Jerusalem. Since he will be the final Roman ruler, the people of that ruler must be the Romans themselves. This, then, is a prophecy of the destruction of Jerusalem about which Christ spoke in His ministry.

When the leaders of the nation registered their rejection of Christ by attributing His power to Beelzebub, the prince of the demons (Matt. 12:24), Christ warned that if they persisted in that view they would be guilty of sin for which there would be no forgiveness (Matt. 12:31-32). He also warned the nation that Jerusalem would be destroyed by Gentiles (Luke 21:24), that it would be desolate (Matt. 23:38), and that the destruction would be so complete that not one stone would be left on another (Matt. 24:2). This destruction was accomplished by Titus in A.D. 70 when he destroyed the city of Jerusalem and killed thousands of Jews. But that invasion, awesome as it was, did not end the nation's sufferings, for **war,** Gabriel said, would **continue until the end.** Even though Israel was to be set aside, she would continue to suffer until the prophecies of the 70 "sevens" were completely fulfilled. Her sufferings span the entire period from the destruction of Jerusalem in A.D. 70 to Jerusalem's deliverance from Gentile dominion at the Second Advent of Christ.

**9:27a.** This verse unveils what will occur in the 70th seven years. This seven-year period will begin after the Rapture of the church (which will consummate God's program in this present Age). The 70th **"seven"** will continue till the return of Jesus Christ to the earth. Because Jesus said this will be a time of "great distress" (Matt. 24:21), this period is often called the Tribulation.

A significant event that will mark the beginning of this seven-year period is the confirming of **a covenant.** This covenant will be made **with many,** that is, with Daniel's people, the nation Israel. "The ruler who will come" (Dan. 9:26) will be this covenant-maker, for that person is the antecedent of the word **he** in verse 27. As a yet-future ruler he will be the final head of the fourth empire (the little horn of the fourth beast, 7:8).

The covenant he will make will evidently be a peace covenant, in which he will guarantee Israel's safety in the land. This suggests that Israel will be in her land but will be unable to defend herself for she will have lost any support she may have had previously. Therefore she will need and welcome the peacemaking role of this head of the confederation of 10 European (Roman) nations. In offering this covenant, this ruler will pose as a prince of peace, and Israel will accept his authority. **But** then **in the middle of that "seven,"** after three and one-half years, **he will** break the covenant. According to 11:45, he will then move from Europe into the land of Israel.

This ruler will **end . . . sacrifice and offering.** This expression refers to the entire Levitical system, which suggests that Israel will have restored that system in the first half of the 70th "seven." After this ruler gains worldwide political power, he will assume power in the religious realm as well and will cause the world to worship him (2 Thes. 2:4; Rev. 13:8). To receive such worship, he will terminate all organized religions. Posing as the world's rightful king and god and as Israel's prince of peace, he will then turn against Israel and become her destroyer and defiler.

**9:27b.** Daniel was told that "the ruler who will come" (v. 26) **will place abominations on a wing of the temple.** Christ referred to this incident: "You [will] see standing in the holy place the abomination that causes desolation" (Matt. 24:15). John wrote that the false prophet will set up an image to this ruler and that the world will be compelled to worship it (Rev. 13:14-15). But then his end will come (**the end that is decreed is poured out on him**). With his false prophet he will be cast into the lake of fire when Christ returns to the earth (Rev. 19:20; cf. Dan. 7:11, 26).

This covenant could not have been made or confirmed by Christ at His First Advent, as amillenarians teach, because: (a) His ministry did not last seven years, (b) His death did not stop sacrifices and offerings, (c) He did not set up "the abomination that causes desolation" (Matt. 24:15). Amillenarians suggest that Christ confirmed (in the sense of fulfilling) the Abrahamic Covenant but the Gospels give no indication He did that in His First Advent.

As stated, the Antichrist will break his covenant with Israel at the beginning of the second half of the 70th "seven," that is, it will be broken for three and one-half years. This is called "a time, times, and half a time" (Dan. 7:25; 12:7; Rev. 12:14). The fact that this is the same as the three and one-half years, which in turn are equated with 1,260 days (Rev.

11:3; 12:6) and with 42 months (Rev. 11:2; 13:5), means that in Jewish reckoning each month has 30 days and each year 360 days. This confirms the 360-day Jewish year used in the calculations in the chart, "The 483 Years in the Jewish and Gregorian Calendars" (near Dan. 9:26a). Since the events in the 69 sevens (vv. 24-26) were fulfilled literally, the 70th "seven," yet unfulfilled, must likewise be fulfilled literally.

## C. The final vision (chaps. 10–12)

### 1. THE PREPARATION OF THE PROPHET (10:1–11:1)

#### a. The occasion of the vision (10:1-3)

**10:1-3.** The final vision **given to Daniel** came **in the third year** of the reign of Cyrus which was 536 B.C. Exiles had returned from Babylon and had begun rebuilding the temple. (Perhaps Daniel had not returned with the exiles because of his age.) Israel's captivity had ended. Jerusalem was being reoccupied, and the nation seemed to be at peace. The **revelation** in the vision given to Daniel on this occasion shattered any hope the prophet might have had that Israel would enjoy her new freedom and peace for long. For God revealed that the nation would be involved in many conflicts (**a great war**). **Understanding** the significance of the **vision,** Daniel fasted **for three weeks** (lit., "three sevens of days"; cf. comments on 9:25). During this time of mourning he abstained from **choice** foods and apparently waited on God in prayer (cf. 10:12) concerning his people's destiny.

#### b. The heavenly messenger (10:4-11)

**10:4-11.** After three weeks (cf. v. 3) Daniel was visited by a messenger as the prophet **was standing** by the **Tigris** River (cf. 12:5). The messenger was an angel from heaven, not a human being. He was **dressed in linen** (cf. 12:7) and had a dazzlingly bright appearance. Since Gabriel previously had been sent by God to reveal truth to Daniel (8:16), probably Gabriel was also the visitor on this occasion. Angels, who dwell in the presence of God who is light, are themselves clothed with light, and Daniel saw something of heaven's glory reflected in this one who visited him (10:5-6).

Some Bible students say that the **man** was the preincarnate Christ because of (a) the similarity of the description here to that of Christ in Revelation 1:13-16, (b) the response of Daniel and his friends (Dan. 10:7-8), and (c) the fact that this "Man" may be the same as the "Son of Man" in 7:13 and the "Man" in 8:16. On the other hand, in favor of this messenger being an angel is the improbability of Christ being hindered by a prince (demon) of Persia (10:13) and needing the help of the angel Michael, and the fact that the person is giving a message from heaven.

Daniel's companions evidently **saw** the brilliance of the light without seeing the visitor and **they fled** to hide from its shining. Daniel remained **alone** in the angel's presence and, being weak, Daniel prostrated himself before the messenger. In that position Daniel **fell** asleep. He was then aroused from his **sleep** by the angel so he might receive the revelation the angel had come to deliver. The angel, calling the prophet **highly esteemed** (cf. 9:23; 10:19), declared, **I have now been sent to you** by God, who had heard Daniel's request for understanding.

*c. The explanation by the heavenly messenger (10:12-14)*

**10:12-14.** Encouraging Daniel **not to be afraid** (cf. v. 8), Gabriel explained the reason for the delay in God's answer to Daniel's prayer. When Daniel first began fasting and mourning in response to the vision of a great war (vv. 1-2), **God** had dispatched Gabriel with a message for him, but Gabriel was hindered by **the prince of the Persian kingdom** (cf. "the prince of Persia," v. 20). Since men cannot fight with angels (Jacob's wrestling was with God, not an angel; cf. comments on Gen. 32:22-32), the prince referred to here must have been a satanic adversary.

God has arranged the angelic realm in differing ranks referred to as "rule, authority, power, and dominion" (Eph. 1:21). Gabriel and Michael have been assigned authority over angels who administer God's affairs for the nation Israel (cf. Michael in Dan. 10:21; 12:1; Jude 9). In imitation Satan has also apparently assigned high-ranking demons to positions of authority over each kingdom. The prince of the Persian kingdom was a satanic representative assigned to Persia.

To seek to prevent Gabriel's message from getting to Daniel, the demonic prince attacked Gabriel as he embarked on his mission. This gives insight into the nature of the warfare fought in the heavenlies between God's angels and Satan's demons to which Paul referred (Eph. 6:12): "Our struggle is not against flesh and blood but against the rulers, against the authorities, against the powers of the dark world, and against spiritual forces of evil in heavenly realms."

The battle between Gabriel and the prince (demon) of Persia continued for three weeks until **Michael, one of the chief princes** of the angelic realm (cf. Dan. 10:21; 12:1), **came to** Gabriel's assistance. Such angelic-demonic conflict indicates something of Satan's power. While **the king of Persia** was fighting Michael, Gabriel was able to bring a message to Daniel concerning **the future** of Israel, Daniel's **people** (cf. "your people," 9:24). It was to be a revelation of the warfare (10:1) between Israel and her neighbors until Israel is given peace by the coming Prince of peace. This vision contains the most detailed prophetic revelation in the Book of Daniel.

*d. The strengthening of the prophet (10:15–11:1)*

**10:15-19.** Daniel had been weakened at the appearance of the messenger (v. 8; cf. 7:15; 8:27). Now he was also overwhelmed (**speechless**, 10:15) at learning of the angelic-demonic conflict that delayed the answer to his prayer. Moreover, he was **overcome with anguish** (v. 16) at the content of **the vision** of Israel's coming sufferings. He was left totally debilitated (cf. v. 8) and gasping for breath.

In addressing the messenger as **my lord** (cf. v. 19; 12:8) Daniel was using a title of respect something like the modern-day "Sir."

To meet the prophet's need, the angel first quieted the alarm in Daniel's heart (**Do not be afraid**; cf. 10:12, **O man highly esteemed**; cf. 9:23; 10:11), and **strengthened** him physically and emotionally. Daniel was then ready to receive the details of the message.

**10:20–11:1.** The messenger then stated that when he returned **to fight against the prince of Persia** (cf. "the prince of the Persian kingdom," 10:13),

## The Ptolemies and the Seleucids in Daniel 11:5-35

| Ptolemies (Kings "of the South," Egypt) | | Seleucids (Kings "of the North," Syria) | |
|---|---|---|---|
| Daniel 11:5 | Ptolemy I Soter (323–285 B.C.)* | Daniel 11:5 | Seleucus I Nicator (312–281 B.C.) |
| 11:6 | Ptolemy II Philadelphus (285–246) | | Antiochus I Soter† (281–262) |
| | | 11:6 | Antiochus II Theos (262–246) |
| 11:7-8 | Ptolemy III Euergetes (246–221) | 11:7-9 | Seleucus II Callinicus (246–227) |
| | | 11:10 | Seleucus III Soter (227–223) |
| 11:11-12, 14-15 | Ptolemy IV Philopator (221–204) | 11:10-11, 13, 15-19 | Antiochus III the Great (223–187) |
| 11:17 | Ptolemy V Epiphanes (204–181) | | |
| | | 11:20 | Seleucus IV Philopator (187–176) |
| 11:25 | Ptolemy VI Philometer (181–145) | 11:21-32 | Antiochus IV Epiphanes (175–163) |

*The years designate the rulers' reigns.
†Not referred to in Daniel 11:5-35.

**the prince of Greece** would **come.** These princes, as stated earlier (see comments on vv. 11-14), were demons, Satan's representatives assigned to nations to oppose godly forces. Persia and Greece were two major nations discussed in detail in chapter 11 (Persia, vv. 2-4; Greece, vv. 5-35).

What is **the Book of truth?** It was probably "God's record of truth in general, of which the Bible is one expression" (John F. Walvoord, *Daniel: The Key to Prophetic Revelation*, p. 250). The messenger was about to tell Daniel God's plans for Israel under Persia and Greece (11:2-35) and later in the Tribulation (vv. 36-45) and the Millennium (12:1-4).

The messenger told Daniel he was supported by **Michael** in his struggle with demons (cf. 10:13). Michael is **your** (Daniel's) **prince** in the sense that he has a special relationship to Israel (cf. 12:1), Daniel's people. When **Darius the Mede** (11:1; see comments on 6:1a; cf. 9:1) began his rule over Babylon, the messenger supported Darius in some way. Or if **him** refers to Michael then the thought is that the messenger supported Michael in return for Michael supporting the messenger.

2. THE DETAILS OF ISRAEL'S HISTORY UNDER THE SECOND AND THIRD EMPIRES (11:2-35)

*a. History under Persia (11:2)*

**11:2.** The angel informed Daniel that the present leadership in the Persian Empire would be succeeded by four rulers. The first was Cambyses, Cyrus' son, who came to the throne in 530 B.C. He was followed by Pseudo-Smerdis, who reigned a short period in 522 B.C. He was succeeded by Darius I Hystaspes who ruled from 521 to 486 B.C. He in turn was succeeded by Xerxes, known in the Book of Esther as Ahasuerus, who ruled from 485 to 465 B.C. (See the chart "Chronology of the Postexilic Period," near Ezra 1:1.) Xerxes was the most powerful, influential, and wealthy of the four. During his reign he fought wars against **Greece.**

*b. History under Greece (11:3-35)*

(1) The rise of Alexander (11:3-4). **11:3.** The **mighty king** was Alexander whose rise had been foreshadowed by (a) the bronze belly and thighs of Nebuchadnezzar's image (2:32, 39b), (b) the winged leopard (7:6), and (c) the prominent horn of the goat (8:5-8). Between 334 and 330

B.C. Alexander conquered Asia Minor, Syria, Egypt, and the land of the Medo-Persian Empire. His conquests extended as far as India (see the map "The Route of Alexander's Conquests," near 8:20-21) before Alexander's death at the age of 32 in 323 B.C. from malaria with complications from alcoholism.

**11:4.** A few years after Alexander's death, his kingdom was divided among his four generals (cf. 8:22): Seleucus (over Syria and Mesopotamia), Ptolemy (over Egypt), Lysimacus (over Thrace and portions of Asia Minor), and Cassander (over Macedonia and Greece). This division was anticipated through the four heads of the leopard (7:6) and the four prominent horns on the goat (8:8). Alexander founded no dynasty of rulers; since he had no heirs, his kingdom was divided and the **empire** was marked by division and weakness.

(2) The conflict between the Ptolemies and the Seleucids (11:5-20). The Ptolemies who ruled over Egypt, were called the kings "of the South." The Seleucids, ruling over Syria, north of Israel, were called the kings "of the North." This section (vv. 5-20) gives many details of the continuous conflict between the Ptolemies and the Seleucids during which the land of Israel was invaded first by one power and then by the other.

**11:5.** The strong **king of the South** was Ptolemy I Soter, a general who served under Alexander. He was given authority over Egypt in 323 B.C. and proclaimed king of Egypt in 304. The commander referred to in verse 5 was Seleucus I Nicator, also a general under Alexander, who was given authority to rule in Babylon in 321. But in 316 when Babylon came under attack by Antigonus, another general, Seleucus sought help from Ptolemy I Soter in Egypt. After Antigonus' defeat in 312, Seleucus returned to Babylon greatly strengthened. He ruled over Babylonia, Media, and Syria, and assumed the title of king in 305. Thus Seleucus I Nicator's **rule** was over far more territory than Ptolemy I Soter's.

**11:6.** Ptolemy I Soter died in 285 B.C. and Ptolemy II Philadelphus, Ptolemy's son, ruled in Egypt (285–246). Meanwhile Seleucus was murdered in 281 and his son Antiochus I Soter ruled till 262. Then Seleucus' grandson Antiochus II Theos

ruled in Syria (262–246). Ptolemy II and Antiochus II were bitter enemies but finally (**after some years**) they entered into an alliance in about 250. This alliance was sealed by the marriage of Ptolemy II's **daughter** Berenice to Antiochus II. This marriage, however, did **not last,** for Laodice, whom Antiochus had divorced in order to marry Berenice, had Berenice killed (she was **handed over**). Laodice then poisoned Antiochus II and made her son, Seleucus II Callinicus, king (246–227).

**11:7-8.** Berenice's brother, Ptolemy III Euergetes (246–221), succeeded his father and set out to avenge the death of his sister Berenice. He was **victorious** over the Syrian army (**the king of the North**), put Laodice to death, and returned **to Egypt** with many spoils.

**11:9-10.** After this humiliating defeat, Seleucus II Callinicus (**the king of the North**) sought to **invade** Egypt but was unsuccessful. After his death (by a fall from his horse) he was succeeded by his son, Seleucus II Soter (227–223 B.C.), who was killed by conspirators while on a military campaign in Asia Minor. Seleucus III's brother, Antiochus III the Great, became the ruler in 223 at 18 years of age and reigned for 36 years (till 187).

The two **sons** (Seleucus III and Antiochus III) had sought to restore Syria's lost prestige by military conquest, the older son by invading Asia Minor and the younger son by attacking Egypt. Egypt had controlled all the territory north to the borders of Syria which included the land of Israel. Antiochus III succeeded in driving the Egyptians back to the southern borders of Israel in his campaign in 219–217.

**11:11-13. The king of the South** in this verse was Ptolemy IV Philopator (221–204 B.C.). He was the one driven back by Antiochus III the Great (cf. comments on v. 10). Ptolemy IV came to meet Antiochus III at the southern borders of Israel. Ptolemy IV was initially successful in delaying the invasion of Antiochus (Ptolemy slaughtered **many thousands**). But after a brief interruption Antiochus returned with **another army** (much **larger**) and turned back **the king of the South.**

**11:14-17.** Syria was not Egypt's only enemy, for Philip V of Macedonia joined with Antiochus III against Egypt. Many

Jews (**your own people**, i.e., Daniel's people, the Jews; cf. "your people" in 9:24; 10:14) also joined Antiochus against Egypt. Perhaps the Jews hoped to gain independence from both Egypt and Syria by joining the conflict, **but** their hopes were not realized.

Antiochus then sought to consolidate control over Israel from which he had expelled the Egyptians. The **fortified city** seems to refer to Sidon which Antiochus captured in 203 B.C. Antiochus III continued his occupation and by 199 had established **himself in the Beautiful Land** (cf. 8:9; 11:41). Antiochus sought to bring peace between Egypt and Syria by giving his daughter to marry Ptolemy V Epiphanes of Egypt. But this attempt to bring a peaceful alliance between the two nations did not succeed (v. 17).

**11:18-19.** Antiochus III **then** turned **his attention** to Asia Minor in 197 B.C. and Greece in 192. However, Antiochus did not succeed because Cornelius Scipio (**a commander**) was dispatched from Rome to **turn** Antiochus **back**. Antiochus returned to **his own country** in 188 and died a year later. Antiochus III the Great had carried on the most vigorous military campaigns of any of Alexander's successors, **but** his dream of reuniting Alexander's empire under his authority was never realized.

**11:20.** Antiochus III's son Seleucus IV Philopator (187–176 B.C.) heavily taxed his people to pay Rome, but he was poisoned (**destroyed . . . not in . . . battle**) by his treasurer Heliodorus.

(3) Invasion by Antiochus IV Epiphanes (11:21-35). These verses describe Antiochus IV Epiphanes, a son of Antiochus III the Great. This one Seleucid who ruled from 175–163 B.C. is given as much attention as all the others before him combined. He is the little horn of Daniel 8:9-12, 23-25. A long section (11:21-35) is devoted to him not only because of the effects of his invasion on the land of Israel, but more so because he foreshadows the little horn (king) of 7:8 who in a future day will desecrate and destroy the land of Israel.

**11:21-22.** Antiochus IV is introduced as **a contemptible person.** He took to himself the name Epiphanes which means "the Illustrious One." But he was considered so untrustworthy that he was nicknamed Epimanes which means "the

Madman." The throne rightly belonged to Demetrius Soter, a son of Seleucus IV Philopator, but Antiochus IV Epiphanes seized the throne and had himself proclaimed king. Thus he did not come to the throne by rightful succession; he seized **it through intrigue.** He was accepted as ruler because he was able to turn aside an invading **army,** perhaps the Egyptians. He also deposed Onias III, the high priest, called here **a prince of the covenant.**

**11:23-24.** After his military victories, Antiochus Epiphanes' prestige and **power** rose with the help of a comparatively small number of **people.** He evidently sought to bring peace to his realm by redistributing **wealth,** taking from the rich and giving to **his followers.**

**11:25-27.** After Antiochus consolidated his kingdom, **he** moved **against** Egypt, **the king of the South,** in 170. Antiochus was able to move his army from his homeland to the very border of Egypt before he was met by the Egyptian army at Pelusium near the Nile Delta. In this battle the Egyptians had **a large . . . army but** were defeated and Antiochus professed friendship with Egypt. The victor and the vanquished sat at a **table** together as though friendship had been established, but the goal of both to establish peace was never realized for they both were deceptive.

**11:28.** Antiochus carried **great wealth** back to his homeland from his conquest. On his return he passed through the land of Israel. After his disappointment in Egypt (he had hoped to take all of Egypt but failed) he took out his frustrations on the Jews by desecrating the temple in Jerusalem. Evidently he opposed (set **his heart . . . against**) the entire Mosaic system (**the holy covenant**). After desecrating the temple, he returned **to his own country.**

**11:29-30a.** Two years later (in 168) Antiochus moved against Egypt (**the South**) **again.** As he moved into Egypt, he was opposed by the Romans who had come to Egypt in **ships** from **the western coastlands** (lit., "ships of Kittim"; cf. NIV marg., i.e., Cyprus). From the Roman senate Popillius Laenas took to Antiochus a letter forbidding him to engage in war with Egypt. When Antiochus asked for time to consider, the emissary drew a circle in the sand around Antiochus and demanded that he give his answer before he stepped out of the circle. Antiochus submitted to Rome's demands for to resist would be to declare war on Rome. This was a humiliating defeat for Antiochus Epiphanes (**he will lose heart**) but he had no alternative but to return to his own land.

**11:30b-32.** For a second time (cf. v. 28) Antiochus took out his frustration on the Jews, the city of Jerusalem, and their temple. He vented **his fury against the holy covenant,** the entire Mosaic system (cf. v. 28), favoring any renegade Jews who turned to help him (cf. v. 32). He desecrated **the temple** and abolished **the daily sacrifice.** Antiochus sent his general Apollonius with 22,000 soldiers into Jerusalem on what was purported to be a peace mission. But they attacked Jerusalem on the Sabbath, killed many people, took many women and children as slaves, and plundered and burned the city.

In seeking to exterminate Judaism and to Hellenize the Jews, he forbade the Jews to follow their religious practices (including their festivals and circumcision), and commanded that copies of the Law be burned. Then he **set up the abomination that causes desolation.** In this culminating act he erected on December 16, 167 B.C. an altar to Zeus on the altar of burnt offering outside the temple, and had a pig offered on the altar. The Jews were compelled to offer a pig on the 25th of each month to celebrate Antiochus Epiphanes' birthday. Antiochus promised apostate Jews (**those who . . . violated the covenant**; cf. v. 30) great reward if they would set aside the God of Israel and worship Zeus, the god of Greece. Many in Israel were persuaded by his promises (**flattery**) and worshiped the false god. However, a small remnant remained faithful to **God,** refusing to engage in those abominable practices. Antiochus IV died insane in Persia in 163 B.C. (Cf. comments on this Antiochus in 8:23-25.)

**11:33-35.** The Jews who refused to submit to Antiochus' false religious system were persecuted and martyred for their faith. The word **fall** (vv. 33-34), literally "stumble" (*kāšal*), refers to severe suffering on the part of many and death for others. This has in view the rise of the Maccabean revolt. Mattathias, a priest,

was the father of five sons. (One of them, Judas, became well known for refurbishing and restoring the temple in late 164 B.C. He was called Judas Maccabeus, "the Hammerer.") In 166, Mattathias refused to submit to this false religious system. He and his sons fled from Jerusalem to the mountains and began the Maccabean revolt. At first only a few Jews joined them. But as their movement became popular, **many** joined them, some out of **sincere** motives and some from false motives. The suffering that the faithful endured served to refine and purify them. This time of persecution was of short duration. It had previously been revealed to Daniel that the temple would be desecrated for 1,150 days (8:14; see comments on 8:23-25). Here Daniel was assured that this persecution would run its course and then be lifted, for its end **will still come at the appointed time.**

3. THE PROPHETIC HISTORY OF THE 70TH SEVEN (11:36–12:3)

*a. The king described (11:36-39)*

All the events described thus far in chapter 11 are past. The intricate details of the conflicts between the Seleucids and the Ptolemies were fulfilled literally, exactly as Daniel had predicted. So detailed are the facts that skeptics have denied that the book was written by Daniel in the sixth century B.C. They conclude that the book must have been written during the time of the Maccabees (168–134 B.C.) *after* the events took place. However, the God who knows the end from the beginning, was able to reveal details of forthcoming history to Daniel.

In verses 36-45 a leader is described who is introduced simply as "the king." Some suggest that this is Antiochus IV Epiphanes and that the verses describe additional incursions of his into Israel. However, the details given in these verses were not fulfilled by Antiochus. True, Antiochus was a foreshadowing of a king who will come (cf. comments on 8:25). But the two are not the same. One is past and the other is future. The coming king (the little "horn" of 7:8 and "the ruler" of 9:26) will be the final ruler in the Roman world. His rise to prominence by satanic power is described in Revelation 13:1-8 where he is called a "beast." According to John (Rev. 17:12-13), he will gain authority not by military conquest but by the consent of the 10 kings who will submit to him. Starting with Daniel 11:36 the prophecy moves from the "near" to the "far." The events recorded in verses 36-45 will occur during the final seven years of the 70 sevens (9:24).

**11:36.** This coming **king** will be independent of any authority apart from himself (he **will do as he pleases**). Midway during his seven-year reign he will exercise the political power given him by the 10 kings who will have elected him (Rev. 17:12-13). He will also take to himself absolute power in the religious realm, magnifying **himself above** all gods and defying and speaking blasphemously **against the God of gods.** "He opposes and exalts himself over everything that is called God or is worshiped, and even sets himself up in God's temple, proclaiming himself to be God" (2 Thes. 2:4). "He will speak against the Most High" (Dan. 7:25). The world will be persuaded to worship him as god by the miracles the false prophet will perform in his name (Rev. 13:11-15). He will succeed in spreading his influence around the world, both politically and religiously (Rev. 13:7-8).

The duration of this king's rule **has been determined** by God. **He will be successful** as the world ruler during **the time of wrath,** the three and one-half years of the Great Tribulation, but at the end of that period the judgment determined by God will be meted out to him (cf. Dan. 7:11, 26; 9:27; Rev. 19:19-20).

**11:37.** Because of the reference to **the gods** (or God, *'ĕlōhîm*) **of his fathers,** some have concluded that this ruler will be a Jew, since the Old Testament frequently uses the phrase "the God of your fathers" to refer to the God of Abraham, Isaac, and Jacob (e.g., Ex. 3:15). However, since this individual will be the final ruler in the Roman world, the little horn of the fourth beast (Dan. 7:8, 24b), he must be a Gentile. His showing **no regard** for the gods of his fathers means that in order to gain absolute power in the religious realm, this king will have no respect for his religious heritage. He will set aside all organized religion (**nor will he regard any god**) and will set himself up (**exalt himself**) as the sole object of worship. Instead of depending on gods, he will depend on his own power (received from Satan, Rev. 13:2) and by that

power he will demand worship of himself.

The fact that he has no regard **for the one desired by women** suggests he repudiates the messianic hope of Israel. Perhaps many an Israelite woman had longingly wondered if she would become the mother of the coming Messiah, the nation's Savior and King.

**11:38-39.** The Antichrist **will honor a god of fortresses,** that is, he will promote military strength. And because of his political and religious power he will be able to accumulate vast wealth. The **god unknown to his fathers** (ancestors), who will give him strength, may be Satan. Though this king will come to power offering peace through a covenant with Israel (cf. 9:27) he will not hesitate to use military power to expand his dominion. And he will be helped by **a foreign god.** Those who submit to his authority will be put in positions of power (he **will greatly honor** them), and his ability to dispense favors (**distribute the land at a** [reduced?] **price**) will gain him a great following.

*b. The king attacked (11:40-45)*

**11:40a.** The events in verses 40-45 will transpire **at the time of the end,** that is, they will occur in the second half of the 70th "seven" of years. **Him** refers back to the king introduced in verse 36. In verses 40-45 every occurrence of "he" (seven times), "him" (four times), and "his" (three times) refers to this coming king. He will have entered into a covenant with the people of Israel, binding that nation as a part of his domain (9:27). Any attack, then, against the land of Israel will be an attack against him with whom Israel will be joined by covenant.

**The king of the South will** attack Israel. Some suggest that this will occur at the middle of the 70th "seven" of years; more likely it will take place toward the end of the second half of that seven-year period. Since "the king of the South" in 11:5-35 referred to a king of Egypt, there seems to be no reason to relate *this* king of the South (v. 40) to some other nation. In fact Egypt is mentioned twice in verses 42-43. In this invasion Egypt will not come alone but will be joined by the Libyans and Nubians (v. 43). These nations, referred to elsewhere as Put and Cush, may be nations in Africa. However, it is more likely that Put refers to Arab nations in the Sinai area and Cush to nations in the Persian Gulf region (cf. Gen. 2:13 and comments there).

Simultaneous with the invasion of Israel by the king of the South (Egypt) will be an invasion by **the king of the North.** Some Bible scholars equate this invasion with the one by Gog and Magog, for Gog will "come from . . . the far north" (Ezek. 38:15). Others say the battle of Gog and Magog will occur in the first half of the 70th "seven" and thus *before* this two-pronged invasion in Daniel 11:40. They suggest that the battle of Gog and Magog will occur when Israel is at peace (Ezek. 38:11, 14). According to that view, a difference is made between Gog who will come from "the far north" (Ezek. 38:15) and a later invasion which will be headed by "the king of the North" (Dan. 11:40). Either way the king of the North in verse 40 is certainly not one of the *Seleucid* kings of the North in verses 5-35. This invasion has no correspondence to historical facts; it is yet future.

The king of the South and the king of the North will fight against the Antichrist. Israel will be occupied and many Jews will flee, seeking refuge among the Gentile nations (see comments on Rev. 12:14-16).

**11:40b-43.** When the Antichrist hears of this invasion, he will move his army from Europe into the Middle East, sweeping through **many countries . . . like a flood** (v. 40). He will move quickly into the land of Israel, **the Beautiful Land** (v. 41; cf. v. 16; 8:9). His first strike will be against **Egypt** (11:42-43a), for Egypt and her Arab allies (**Libyans and Nubians,** v. 43) are the ones who will initiate the invasion on Israel. On this occasion the king will not conquer the territory of **Edom, Moab, and . . . Ammon** (v. 41), now included in the present kingdom of Jordan. But he will gain control over "many countries."

**11:44-45.** Then the Antichrist will hear alarming reports **from the east** (probably referring to an invasion by a massive army of 200 million soldiers from east of the Euphrates River, Rev. 9:16) and from **the north** (perhaps another attack by the king of the North; cf. Dan. 11:40). Enraged, the Antichrist will set out to **destroy . . . many** of the invaders.

Then he will occupy Israel and **will pitch his royal tents between the seas,** that is, between the Dead Sea and the Mediterranean Sea, **at the beautiful holy mountain,** probably Jerusalem. Posing as Christ, the Antichrist will set up his headquarters in Jerusalem, the same city from which Christ will rule the world in the Millennium (Zech. 14:4, 17). The Antichrist will also pose as Christ by introducing a one-world government with himself as the ruler and a one-world religion in which he is worshiped as god. But God will destroy the kingdom of this king (**he will come to his end**; cf. Dan. 7:11, 26) at the personal appearance of Jesus Christ to this earth (Rev. 19:19-20).

### c. Israel delivered (12:1-3)

**12:1.** No doubt when the revelation contained in chapter 12 was given Daniel, he was concerned about his people's destiny. Now at the conclusion of this vision, the angel consoled Daniel by revealing two facts (vv. 1-3). First, the people of Israel (**your people**; cf. 9:24; 10:14) **will be delivered** by the intervention of **Michael** the angelic **prince** (cf. 10:13, 21), **who** is Israel's defender. In the Great Tribulation Satan will attempt to exterminate every descendant of Abraham (see comments on Rev. 12:15). This **will be a time of** great unprecedented **distress** for Israel (cf. Matt. 24:21). Satan's attack against the people of the kingdom will be part of his effort to prevent the return and reign of Christ.

The deliverance of Israel, Daniel's "people," refers not to individual salvation, though a remnant will be saved, but rather to national deliverance from subjugation to the Gentiles (cf. comments on "all Israel will be saved" in Rom. 11:26).

**12:2-3.** The second fact that consoled Daniel is the promise that those who sleep will be resurrected. Many Jews will lose their lives at the hands of Gentiles in the events revealed in chapter 11 (cf. Rev. 20:4). To **sleep in the dust of the earth** (cf. Ps. 7:5) does not mean unconscious existence in death. It simply means that a dead person *appears* to be asleep. The body is "asleep," not the soul (cf. comments on 1 Thes. 4:13). Unbelieving Jews will be resurrected **to shame and everlasting contempt** and will not partake in the covenanted blessings. Jews, however, who believe the Messiah will be resurrected bodily **to everlasting life** and to positions of honor in Christ's millennial kingdom. Being glorified in the kingdom, they **will shine like the brightness of the heavens.** (Cf. Matt. 13:43, "Then the righteous will shine like the sun in the kingdom of their Father.") They will be **wise,** for they will trust in the Messiah even though it will result in their suffering.

This message that God will remember His covenant and will fulfill all He promised to Israel (in spite of her sufferings at the hands of the Gentiles) will be a consolation that will in turn cause them to **lead** others **to righteousness** (cf. the "wise" in Dan. 12:10). No righteousness of God's people ever goes unrewarded so those who are faithful under persecution will shine **like the stars forever and ever.**

The resurrection of believers martyred in the Tribulation will occur at the second coming of Christ (cf. Rev. 20:4, "they came to life and reigned with Christ 1,000 years"). The unbelieving dead, however, will be resurrected to "everlasting contempt" and torment at the end of the 1,000-year reign of Christ (cf. Rev. 20:5; John 5:28-29).

4. CONCLUSION (12:4-13)

### a. Sealing of the book (12:4)

**12:4.** Understandably **Daniel** and his immediate readers could not have comprehended all the details of the prophecies given in this book (cf. v. 8). Not until history continued to unfold would many be able to understand these prophetic revelations. But God indicated that an increased understanding of what Daniel had written would come. People today, looking back over history, can see the significance of much of what Daniel predicted. And in **the time of the end** (cf. v. 9, and note " the end" and "the end of the days" in v. 13) the words of this book that have been sealed (kept intact) will be understood by **many** who will seek to gain **knowledge** from it. This will be in the Tribulation (cf. 11:40, "the time of the end"). Even though Daniel's people may not have fully understood this book's prophecies, the predictions did comfort them. They were assured that God will ultimately deliver Israel from the Gentiles

and bring her into His covenanted promises.

### b. Questions concerning the Great Tribulation (12:5-13)

**12:5-6.** This section (vv. 5-13) includes two requests (one by an angel and one by **Daniel**) and two angelic replies. The first request is in verses 5-6, and the first answer is in verse 7. The second question is in verse 8, and the second reply is in verses 9-13. Evidently **two** angels had attended the angelic messenger, who was probably Gabriel (cf. comments on 10:5). **One of** the angels across **the river** (the Tigris; cf. 10:4) called to an angel standing by Gabriel (the one **clothed in linen;** cf. 10:5) and asked, **How long will it be before these astonishing things are fulfilled?** "These astonishing things" probably refer to the events recorded in 11:36-45, which pertain to Israel's final occupation by the coming Gentile ruler.

**12:7.** Gabriel answered the inquiring angel that those events will be fulfilled in **a time, times, and half a time,** that is, in three and one-half years (cf. comments on 7:25). Though this final ruler will reign for seven years, the first half will be a time of comparative peace for Israel. They will be enjoying the benefits of the covenant this king will make with them (9:27). Israel will be "a land of unwalled villages," a land in which the people will be "without walls and without gates and bars" (Ezek. 38:11). But the Antichrist will break that covenant (Dan. 9:27) near the middle of the 70th "seven" of years. Then the king of the South and the king of the North will invade Israel (11:40). After destroying these two armies, this Gentile king (the Antichrist) will move into Israel, occupy the land, and set up his political and religious headquarters in Jerusalem (11:41, 45). He will reign in Jerusalem as king and god and will become the greatest persecutor Israel has ever known (Rev. 13:5-7). Israel's **power** will be **broken** by his ruthless power, and then at the end of the Tribulation **all these things** (the events in 11:40-45) **will be completed.**

**12:8.** Then Daniel addressed a question to Gabriel, whom he called **My lord** (a term of respect like "Sir"; cf. 10:16-17, 19). Daniel asked, **What will the outcome of all this be?** He wanted to know God's program for Israel beyond the Tribulation period. Little information about Israel's blessings in the millennial reign following the Second Advent of Christ had been given to Daniel, though he did know that God's eternal kingdom will be established (2:44; 7:14, 22, 27) and the saints will possess (rule in) that kingdom. Many such prophecies had been given through the prophets and more would be given through prophets who were yet to come (Haggai, Zechariah, Malachi).

**12:9-10.** As the angel already stated (v. 4), **the words are** to be **closed up and sealed** (kept intact and thus made available) **until the time of the end** (the second half of the 70th "seven" of years; cf. v. 7; also note "end" in vv. 4, 13). In that period of time **many** Jews will turn to the Savior (cf. v. 3), and as a result (**will be** spiritually **purified . . . spotless and refined. But the wicked will continue** in their ways, following and worshiping the Antichrist, the world ruler. What God revealed to Daniel will continue to be osbcure to them (cf. 1 Cor. 2:14), but **the wise** (i.e., the righteous; cf. "wise" and "righteousness" in Dan. 12:3) **will understand.**

**12:11.** The angel said that **1,290 days** will be measured off **from the time that the daily sacrifice is abolished** (cf. 9:27, "he will put an end to sacrifice") **and the abomination that causes desolation is set up** (cf. 9:27, "one who causes desolation will place abominations on a wing of the temple"). The last half of the 70th "seven" of years is "a time, times, and half a time" (7:25; Rev. 12:14), which is three and one-half years. It is also designated as 42 months (Rev. 11:2) or 1,260 days (Rev. 11:3). How then can the variance of 30 days (1,290 compared with 1,260) be explained? Some suggest that the 30 days will extend beyond the end of the Tribulation, allowing for the judgment of Israel and the judgment of the nations. Another possibility is that the 1,290 days will begin 30 days before the middle of the 70th "seven" of years when the world ruler will set up "the abomination that causes desolation" (Matt. 24:15). The 1,290 days could begin with an announcement (about the abomination) made 30 days before the abomination is introduced. This abomination, as stated earlier, will be an image of himself (Rev.

13:14-15) and will be the symbol of this religious system.

**12:12-13.** Blessing is pronounced on **one who waits for and** lives to see **the end of the 1,335 days.** This is an additional 45 days beyond the 1,290 days (v. 11). Forty-five days after the end of the Tribulation Israel's long-awaited blessings will be realized. This may mark the blessing of the Millennium; or it may be when Christ, who will have appeared in the *heavens* (Matt. 24:30) 45 days earlier, will actually descend to the *earth,* His feet touching down on the Mount of Olives (cf. Acts 1:11). For believers Christ's coming is a blessing and a glorious hope.

Daniel did not live to see many of his prophecies fulfilled. He, the angel said, would **rest,** that is, in death (cf. v. 2). But he will be resurrected (**you will rise at the end of the days**), and he will receive his **allotted inheritance** in the Millennium. Because of Daniel's faith in God he led a life of faithful service for Him, and for that faith and that obedience he will receive a glorious reward. All who like Daniel trust the Lord will share in the blessings of His millennial kingdom.

# BIBLIOGRAPHY

Anderson, Robert. *The Coming Prince.* London: Hodder & Stoughton, 1881. Reprint. Grand Rapids: Kregel Publications, 1975.

Baldwin, Joyce G. *Daniel: An Introduction and Commentary.* The Tyndale Old Testament Commentaries. Downers Grove, Ill.: Inter-Varsity Press, 1978.

Campbell, Donald K. *Daniel: Decoder of Dreams.* Wheaton, Ill.: SP Publications, Victor Books, 1977.

Culver, Robert D. *Daniel and the Latter Days.* Rev. ed. Chicago: Moody Press, 1977.

————. *The Histories and Prophecies of Daniel.* Winona Lake, Ind.: BMH Books, 1980.

McDowell, Josh. *Daniel in the Critic's Den.* San Bernardino, Calif.: Here's Life Publishers, 1979.

Price, Walter K. *In the Final Days.* Chicago: Moody Press, 1977.

Walvoord, John F. *Daniel: The Key to Prophetic Revelation.* Chicago: Moody Press, 1971.

Wilson, Robert Dick. *Studies in the Book of Daniel*. Grand Rapids: Baker Book House, 1979.

Wiseman, D.J., et al. *Notes on Some Problems in the Book of Daniel*. London: Tyndale Press, 1965.

Wood, Leon. *A Commentary on Daniel*. Grand Rapids: Zondervan Publishing House, 1973.

_____. *Daniel: A Study Guide*. Grand Rapids: Zondervan Publishing House, 1975.

# HOSEA

## Robert B. Chisholm, Jr.

## INTRODUCTION

**Authorship.** According to Hosea 1:1 the author of this prophecy was Hosea, son of Beeri. But several commentators have attributed some of the material in the book to later editorial activity. According to these scholars, the present form of the book is the product of an evolutionary process whereby original material by Hosea was reworked and supplemented (cf., e.g., William Rainey Harper, *A Critical and Exegetical Commentary on Amos and Hosea,* pp. clix-clxii; Hans Walter Wolff, *Hosea,* pp. xxix-xxxii). In particular, references to Judah and parallels to the language and theology of Deuteronomy have been offered as examples of redactional additions. However, it is unnecessary to deny the Judean passages to Hosea. Though his main target was the Northern Kingdom, his message encompassed the entire people of God. Like Hosea, other eighth-century B.C. prophets spoke to both kingdoms in the course of their prophecies (for a detailed discussion of the Judean passages in Hosea, see R.K. Harrison, *Introduction to the Old Testament.* Grand Rapids: Wm. B. Eerdmans Publishing Co., 1969, pp. 868-70). Hosea's parallels to Deuteronomy cannot be labeled later additions if Deuteronomy is correctly dated before, not after, Hosea.

**Date.** Hosea's ministry spanned several decades, beginning near the end of the reigns of Uzziah of Judah (ca. 790–739 B.C.) and Jeroboam II of Israel (ca. 793–753 B.C.) and concluding in the early years of Hezekiah's reign. The latter's rule began around 715 B.C. after a period of vice-regency with his father Ahaz. Since Israel was Hosea's primary audience, it seems strange that four Judean kings, but only one Israelite king, are mentioned in 1:1. The reason for the omission of the six Israelite kings who followed Jeroboam II is uncertain. Perhaps it suggests the legitimacy of the Davidic dynasty (cf. 3:5) in contrast with the instability and disintegration of the kingship in the North (cf. 7:3-7).

**Historical Background.** The events in the reigns of the kings mentioned in 1:1 are recorded in 2 Chronicles 26–32. Hosea began his ministry near the end of a period of military success and prosperity for both Israel and Judah (cf. 2 Kings 14:25-28; 2 Chron. 26:2, 6-15). During the first half of the eighth century Assyrian influence in the West had declined, allowing the kingdoms of Jeroboam II and Uzziah to flourish. However, the situation soon changed. As foreseen by Hosea the Assyrians under Tiglath-Pileser III (745–727 B.C.) revived their expansionist policy in the West. In 733–732 B.C. the Northern Kingdom was made a puppet state within the Assyrian Empire (2 Kings 15:29). After plotting revolt, Israel was defeated in 722 B.C. by the Assyrians and Israel's people were deported (2 Kings 17:1-6; 18:10-12). Also Judah was incorporated as a vassal state into the Assyrian Empire during Hosea's time (cf. 2 Kings 16:5-10).

**Purpose and Message.** The primary purpose of Hosea's prophecy, like that of his eighth-century contemporaries Amos, Isaiah, and Micah, must be understood against the background of the message and theology of Deuteronomy. The latter records the covenantal agreement between the Lord and Israel. Israel was to maintain loyalty to the Lord by worshiping Him alone and by obeying His commandments. Obedience to the covenant would result in blessing (cf. Deut. 28:1-14). Disobedience would bring judgment and eventually exile (cf. the covenant curses listed in Deut. 28:15-68). Hosea's role as a prophet was to expose the nation's breach of covenant and announce God's intention to implement the covenant curses. At the same time Hosea affirmed the Deuteronomic promise of Israel's ultimate restoration (cf. Deut. 30:1-10).

The major themes of Hosea's message can be summarized in three words: sin, judgment, and salvation. In exposing Israel's sin, Hosea emphasized its idolatry (e.g., Hosea 4:17; 8:4, 6; 10:5; 11:2; 13:2). He compared Israel's covenant relationship to the Lord with marriage and accused Israel (the Lord's "wife") of spiritual adultery. She had turned to Baal, the Canaanite storm and fertility god (cf. 2:8, 13; 11:2; 13:1), in an effort to promote agricultural and human fertility. To illustrate Israel's infidelity Hosea married a woman who would, like the nation, prove unfaithful to her husband. Many other sins are mentioned in the book, including social injustice (12:7), violent crime (4:2; 6:9; 12:1), religious hypocrisy (6:6), political revolt (7:3-7), foreign alliances (7:11; 8:9), selfish arrogance (13:6), and spiritual ingratitude (7:15).

Though Hosea's prophecy contains some calls to repentance, he did not expect a positive response. Judgment was inescapable. In implementing the curses, the Lord would cause the nation to experience infertility, military invasion, and exile. Several times Hosea emphasized the justice of God by indicating that His divine punishment fit the crimes perfectly.

However, the Lord would not abandon Israel totally. Despite its severity, each judgment was disciplinary and was intended to turn Israel back to God. Hosea's own reconciliation with his wayward wife illustrated Israel's ultimate restoration. The very structure of the book reflects this positive emphasis. One is able to discern five judgment-salvation cycles throughout the prophecy:

| | Judgment | Salvation |
|---|---|---|
| 1. | 1:2-9 | 1:10–2:1 |
| 2. | 2:2-13 | 2:14–3:5 |
| 3. | 4:1–5:14 | 5:15–6:3 |
| 4. | 6:4–11:7 | 11:8-11 |
| 5. | 11:12–13:16 | chap. 14 |

## OUTLINE

I. Hosea's Times (1:1)
II. Hosea's Experience: A Portrayal of God's Dealings with Israel (1:2–3:5)
  A. The symbolism of Hosea's family (1:2–2:1)
    1. Hosea's marriage: Israel's unfaithfulness (1:2–3a)
    2. Hosea's children: Israel's judgment (1:3b–9)
    3. The symbolism reversed (1:10–2:1)
  B. Restoration through punishment (2:2-23)
    1. The Lord's punishment of Israel (2:2-13)
    2. The Lord's restoration of Israel (2:14-23)
  C. The restoration of Hosea's marriage (chap. 3)
    1. The divine command (3:1)
    2. Hosea's obedient response (3:2-3)
    3. The illustration explained (3:4-5)
III. Hosea's Message: God's Judgment and Restoration of Israel (chaps. 4–14)
  A. The Lord's case against Israel (4:1–6:3)
    1. Israel's guilt exposed (chap. 4)
    2. Israel's judgment announced (5:1-14)
    3. Israel's restoration envisioned (5:15–6:3)
  B. The Lord's case against Israel expanded (6:4–11:11)
    1. Israel's guilt and punishment (6:4–8:14)
    2. Israel's guilt and punishment reiterated (9:1–11:7)
    3. The Lord's compassion renewed (11:8-11)
  C. The Lord's case against Israel concluded (11:12–14:9)
    1. A concluding indictment (11:12–13:16)
    2. A concluding exhortation (chap. 14)

## COMMENTARY

### I. Hosea's Times (1:1)

**1:1.** In Hebrew the name **Hosea** ("salvation") is the same as Hoshea, Israel's last king (2 Kings 17:1). Hoshea was also Joshua's original name (Num. 13:8, 16). Nothing is known of Hosea's family background except that he was a **son of Beeri.**

Hosea's ministry extended for a number of decades in the second half of the eighth century B.C. Four **kings of Judah (Uzziah, Jotham, Ahaz, and Hezekiah)** reigned when Hosea prophesied. Only one **king** of the north (**Jeroboam** II), is mentioned though Hosea's message was directed primarily to the Northern Kingdom. Six kings **of Israel** followed Jeroboam II during the reigns of the four Judean kings mentioned. Perhaps Hosea omitted those six (as stated under "Date" in the *Introduction*) to point up the legitimacy of the Davidic dynasty in Judah.

## II. Hosea's Experience: A Portrayal of God's Dealings with Israel (1:2–3:5)

The message of the first three chapters (and of the entire book) oscillates between judgment and salvation. Hosea's marital experiences, which included the heartbreak caused by his wife's unfaithfulness and the joy of their renewed relationship, provide the framework for this message.

### A. The symbolism of Hosea's family (1:2–2:1)

This opening section sets forth the major themes of the entire prophecy: Israel's unfaithfulness, the certainty of judgment, and the ultimate restoration of the nation. These ideas are introduced within the context of the Lord's command to Hosea to marry and have children.

1. HOSEA'S MARRIAGE: ISRAEL'S UNFAITHFULNESS (1:2-3A)

**1:2-3a.** At the outset of Hosea's ministry the LORD instructed him to marry **an adulterous** woman. This relationship, characterized by infidelity on the wife's part, was to portray Israel's unfaithfulness to its covenant with the Lord (cf. 2:2-23). In response to the divine command **Hosea. . . . married Gomer,** a **daughter of Diblaim.**

Much debate has centered on the circumstances of Hosea's marriage. Some have held that the marriage was only visionary or allegorical, not literal. This proposal was motivated by a desire to sidestep the supposed moral difficulty of the holy God commanding His servant to marry a woman of disreputable character. However, the account is presented as a straightforward narrative, not as a report of a vision or as a purely symbolic act (cf. chap. 3). The Lord sometimes required His prophets to carry out orders that many would consider over and above the call of duty (e.g., Isa. 20:1-4; Ezek. 4:1–5:4).

Those who hold to a literal marriage disagree over Gomer's status at the beginning of her relationship with Hosea. Some argue that Gomer was a prostitute at the time she was married. A modification of this is the view that she was a typical young Israelite woman who had participated in a Canaanite rite of sexual initiation in preparation for marriage (Wolff, *Hosea*, pp. 14-5). Others contend that Gomer was sexually pure at the time of marriage and later became an adulteress. The Book of Hosea does not provide information concerning Gomer's premarital sexual experience. The expression "adulterous wife" (lit., "wife of adultery") does not describe her condition at the time of marriage, but anticipates what she proved to be, a wife characterized by unfaithfulness. Any knowledge of Gomer's status at the time of marriage is thereby precluded.

Both the language of Hosea 1:2 and the following context support this interpretation. The expression is similar to others in Hebrew that describe a married woman's character (e.g., "wife of one's youth," "a quarrelsome wife" ["a wife of quarrelings"], "a wife of noble character"; for these and other examples see Francis I. Andersen and David Noel Freedman, *Hosea: A New Translation, Introduction and Commentary*, p. 159). The Hebrew word $z^e n \hat{u} n \hat{i} m$ (trans. here "adulterous") refers elsewhere in Hosea to the activity of Israel under the figure of a married woman (cf. 2:2, 4; 4:12; 5:4). Also the emphasis in the following context (1:2b; 2:2–3:5) is on the unfaithfulness that characterized both the Lord's and Hosea's marriages, not on the brides' premarital experiences. Thus the Lord's command should be understood as follows, "Go, take to yourself a wife who will prove to be unfaithful."

The Lord also told Hosea to **take . . .**

**children of unfaithfulness.** This does not refer to children born from another father before Gomer's marriage to Hosea. The Hebrew expression is elliptical with the second verb omitted. The command could be paraphrased, "Go, take to yourself an adulterous wife and have (NASB) children of unfaithfulness." The children are those mentioned in 1:3-9. "Unfaithfulness" does not necessarily imply they were the products of Gomer's illicit relationships. The fact that Hosea is not specifically mentioned in verses 6 and 8 as the children's father need not point to their illegitimacy. In Genesis 29:32-35 the same phrase which appears in Hosea 1:6, 8 ("she conceived again and gave birth") is used with no mention of the father (Jacob) because he is identified in the preceding context (as in Hosea, v. 3; cf. Andersen and Freedman, *Hosea,* p. 168). "Children of unfaithfulness" may simply point to their being born in the context of (but not as a direct result of) Gomer's infidelity. Also the phrase emphasizes the mother's character, not that of the children. Andersen and Freedman understand the phrase as elliptical: "children of (a wife of) promiscuity" (*Hosea,* p. 168). It is similar to other Hebrew expressions in which the descriptive term points primarily to a quality of the parent not of the offspring (cf. *$b^e n\hat{e}$ $hann^{e\cdot}\hat{u}r\hat{i}m$,* lit., "sons of youth," i.e., "sons born to a youthful parent," Ps. 127:4; and *ben $z^e q\bar{u}n\hat{i}m$,* lit., "son of old age," i.e., "a son born to an aged parent," Gen. 37:3).

In Hosea 1:2 **the land,** which stands for those living in it (cf. 4:1), is personified as a wife who **is guilty of the vilest adultery.** This Hebrew verbal expression is emphatic, highlighting the extent to which Israel had departed **from the LORD.**

### 2. HOSEA'S CHILDREN: ISRAEL'S JUDGMENT (1:3B-9)

The divinely chosen names for Hosea's three children served as reminders of the broken relationship between the Lord and Israel and pointed ahead to judgment. Each section on the children (vv. 3b-5, 6-7, 8-9) contains a birth notice (vv. 3b, 6a, 8), a divine word of instruction concerning the child's name (vv. 4a, 6b, 9a), and an explanation of the meaning of the name (vv. 4b-5, 6b, 9b). God's words (v. 7) are unique in that they qualify the announcement of judgment given (v. 6).

### a. Jezreel (1:3b-5)

**1:3b.** The first child (**a son**) was named Jezreel. At this point the significance of his name was not in its meaning ("God sows"), but in its association with past and future events at the place Jezreel (cf., however, v. 11; 2:22-23). Jezreel was the site of Jehu's ruthless massacre of the house of Ahab (1:4; cf. 2 Kings 9–10). In the future it would be the scene of Israel's military demise (Hosea 1:5).

**1:4.** The reason for the Lord's coming punishment on Jehu's dynasty (lit., **house**) was **the massacre** (lit., "bloodshed") **at Jezreel** (ca. 841 B.C.). Jehu's slaughter of Jezebel and Ahab's descendants had been prophesied by Elijah (1 Kings 21:21-24), commanded by Elisha (2 Kings 9:6-10), and commended by the Lord Himself (2 Kings 10:30). So many think the attitude expressed by the Lord (Hosea 1:4) contradicted that in the accounts in 1 and 2 Kings. But a closer examination of the historical record suggests a resolution to the problem. **Jehu** also killed Joram (2 Kings 9:24), Ahaziah, king of Judah (2 Kings 9:27-28), 42 of Ahaziah's relatives (2 Kings 10:12-14), and several functionaries of the Baal cult (2 Kings 10:18-28). Though the execution of Baal's servants was certainly in accord with the Lord's will (cf. 1 Kings 18:40), Jehu's attack on the house of David went too far. Despite the fact that Ahaziah's assassination could be attributed to God's providence (2 Chron. 22:7), it demonstrated an underlying lack of regard for the Lord's commands. This disregard subsequently came to the surface in other ways (cf. 2 Kings 10:29-31). So Hosea 1:4 probably refers to the slaughter of Ahaziah and his relatives. Though their deaths did not actually occur in Jezreel (cf. 2 Kings 9:27; 10:12-14), they were associated with the wholesale slaughter at that place.

The fulfillment of this prophecy came in 752 B.C. when Shallum assassinated Zechariah, the fourth of Jehu's descendants to rule the Northern Kingdom (2 Kings 15:10), thereby cutting off Jehu's dynasty forever.

**1:5.** God told Hosea that the demise of Jehu's dynasty was to be accompanied by the downfall of the Northern Kingdom. In a display of poetic justice the Lord would **break Israel's bow in the Valley of Jezreel,** the site of Jehu's sin. Breaking the bow refers to the destruction of the nation's military might (cf. 1 Sam. 2:4; Ps. 46:9; Jer. 49:35).

The general fulfillment of this prophecy came in 734–722 B.C. when the Assyrians overran Israel and reduced it to a province within their empire (2 Kings 15:29; 17:3-5). The Jezreel plain in particular was probably conquered in 733 B.C. by Tiglath-Pileser III. This valley, which had been the scene of a great military victory under Gideon (Jud. 6:33; 7), again became a symbol of national disgrace and defeat, as it had been after Saul's death (1 Sam. 29:1, 11; 31).

*b. Lo-Ruhamah: "Not loved" (1:6-7)*

**1:6.** The second child received the name **Lo-Ruhamah,** which means "she is not loved." Her name indicated that the Lord's **love** for **Israel** would be cut off for a time. "Ruhamah," from the verb *rāḥam,* describes tender feelings of compassion, such as those expressed by a parent for a child (cf. 1 Kings 3:26; Ps. 103:13; Isa. 49:15) or by a man for his younger brother (cf. Gen. 43:30). At Sinai the Lord described Himself (Ex. 34:6) as "the compassionate . . . God" (*'ēl raḥûm*) who is willing to forgive iniquity (Ex. 34:6). However, despite His gracious character, times come when He will no longer "leave the guilty unpunished" (Ex. 34:7). Such a time had come for the Northern Kingdom.

**1:7.** The light of God's grace shines through the gloom of impending judgment. **Judah,** the Southern Kingdom, in contrast with Israel, would experience the Lord's **love** in the form of deliverance from the Assyrians. This would **not** be accomplished through human military might (symbolized by the **bow, sword,** etc.), **but by the** Lord's intervention. This promise was fulfilled in 701 B.C. when God supernaturally annihilated 185,000 soldiers in the powerful Assyrian army in one night thereby ending its campaign against Judah (2 Kings 19:32-36).

*c. Lo-Ammi: "Not My people" (1:8-9)*

**1:8-9.** The third child, a **son,** was named **Lo-Ammi,** which means **not My people.** In the ancient covenant formula God declared, "I will walk among you

and be your God, and you will be My people" (Lev. 26:12; cf. Ex. 6:7; Deut. 26:17-18). But now that relationship was to be severed. The last clause of Hosea 1:9 (**I am not your God**) is literally, "and I [am] not I AM (*'ehyeh*) to you." The statement probably alludes to God's words to Moses, "I am (*'ehyeh*) who I am (*'ehyeh*). This is what you are to say to the Israelites: I AM (*'ehyeh*) has sent me to you" (Ex. 3:14). "I AM," which is closely related to the divine name Yahweh, points to God as the covenant **LORD** of Israel who watches over and delivers His people (cf. Ex. 3:16-17). However, through Lo-Ammi the Lord announced that Israel would no longer experience His special saving presence.

3. THE SYMBOLISM REVERSED (1:10–2:1)

In a remarkable shift of tone the Lord declared that the effects of judgment would someday be reversed. He promised a time of rich blessing accompanied by restoration of the covenant relationship and national unity.

**1:10.** Despite the demise of the Northern Kingdom (vv. 4-5), **the Israelites will** again **be like the sand on the seashore** in fulfillment of the Lord's irrevocable promise to Abraham (Gen. 22:17; 32:12). **In the** same **place where** Israel heard the words **not My people** (cf. Hosea 1:9) **they will be called sons of the living God.** The sonship reference points to restoration of the covenant relationship, pictured under the figure of a family setting (cf. 2:1-5). The divine title "living God" was used in Joshua 3:10 in reference to the Lord's mighty presence with Israel during the Conquest of the land. In the future Israel will again experience the benefits of a relationship with the living God as they reoccupy the Promised Land.

**1:11.** At the time of national restoration the two kingdoms (**Judah and . . . Israel**), which had divided under Solomon's son Rehoboam (1 Kings 12), **will be reunited** under **one Leader** (cf. Ezek. 37:22), the ideal Davidic Ruler of the Kingdom Age (cf. Hosea 3:5; Isa. 9:6-7; Amos 9:11; Micah 5:2). The promise to David of an everlasting throne will be fulfilled (cf. 2 Sam. 7:11b-16).

The united nation also **will come up out of the land.** This statement may refer to a return from exile, the "land" being

Egypt (cf. Hosea 2:15), which serves as a symbol of the future place(s) of captivity (cf. 8:13; 9:3, 6; 11:5; Deut. 28:68). However, "land" ('ereṣ) elsewhere in the Book of Hosea refers either to the land of Israel (cf. Hosea 1:2; 2:18, 23; 4:1, 3) or to the literal surface of the ground (cf. 2:21-22; 6:3) when used with the definite article and without a qualifying geographical term. The land of Egypt is specifically designated as such when mentioned in Hosea (2:15; 7:11, 16; 8:13; 9:3, 6; 11:1, 5, 11; 12:1, 9, 13; 13:4). So it is better to understand this as a comparison between Israel and a plant which grows up from the soil. "Land" can refer to the ground (as just noted), as "come up" ('ālâh) is used elsewhere of plant life sprouting forth from the soil (cf. "grow up," 10:8; "growing" Deut. 29:23). The following context also supports this view. According to Hosea 2:23, the Lord promised that He would "plant" (zāra', the same word used in the name Jezreel) the nation in the land as one sows seed on the ground (cf. 2:22, where the name Jezreel, "God sows," appears). Because the Lord Himself will be the One who sows, Israel will sprout forth and grow luxuriantly.

**The day of Jezreel** probably alludes to this time when God will plant His people in the land. If so, the literal meaning of the name Jezreel ("God sows") takes on significance at this point. It is also likely that it alludes to Gideon's victory over the Midianites in the Valley of Jezreel (Jud. 7). The future day of restoration will be ushered in by a great military triumph like that of Gideon (cf. Isa. 9:4-7; see also Isa. 41:8-16; Amos 9:11-12; Joel 3:9-17). Those who oppose the Lord's theocratic rule through the messianic King will be defeated (cf. Rev. 19:11-21). The greatness of this eschatological "day of Jezreel" will reverse the shame and defeat which Israel experienced there at the hands of the Assyrians (cf. Hosea 1:5).

**2:1.** These words were spoken to a segment of the restored nation of the future (cf. v. 23), viewed as a group of children (**say** and **your** are pl. in Heb.). They were told to proclaim to their **brothers** and **sisters** (other Israelites) that the nation's relationship with the Lord had been reestablished. The Lord then addressed them as **My people** ('ammî; cf. 1:9) and **My loved one** (ruḥāmâh; cf. 1:6). Long before Hosea, Moses had predicted

such a change in the Lord's attitude (Deut. 30:1-9). After describing the nation's future exile (Deut. 30:1), Moses promised that their repentance would result in a renewal of the Lord's compassion (Deut. 30:2-3, rāḥam) and a return to the land (Deut. 30:4-9). Long after Hosea, the Apostle Paul also foresaw this time of Israel's restoration (Rom. 11:25-32).

In summary, Hosea 1:10–2:1 contains a marvelous prophecy of Israel's future restoration, in which the effects of the Lord's judgment will be totally reversed. The nation that suffered defeat at Jezreel and was called "not loved" and "not My people" will take part in the great "day of Jezreel" and hear the Lord say, "My people" and "[My] loved one." The covenant promises to Abraham (of numerous descendants) and David (of eternal kingship) will be fulfilled when the covenant ideal predicted by Moses will be realized.

## B. Restoration through punishment (2:2-23)

Hosea's relationship with Gomer was designed to reflect the Lord's experience of being rejected by His covenant people Israel (cf. 1:2). In 2:2-23 the Lord described this rejection in detail, comparing Israel to an unfaithful wife who chased after lovers. In the process of confirming the nation's guilt, the Lord announced coming punishment. This judgment, however, would not be final, for God intended to draw Israel back and restore the broken covenantal relationship. Thus this section, like the preceding one (1:2–2:1) progresses from judgment (2:2-13) to salvation (2:14-23, along with chap. 3).

### 1. THE LORD'S PUNISHMENT OF ISRAEL (2:2-13)

Included in this section are an introductory summons (v. 2a), an appeal for repentance (v. 2b) accompanied by a threat of punishment (vv. 3-4), and two judgmental speeches (vv. 5-7, 8-13), each containing an accusation (vv. 5, 8) and an announcement of punishment (vv. 6-7, 9-13).

### a. Punishment threatened (2:2-4)

**2:2.** The section opens with the Lord calling for a formal accusation to be brought against Israel. The covenant relationship is likened to marriage, the Lord being the husband and Israel the wife. The children addressed (cf. **your mother**) need not represent any specific group within Israel. They are included for rhetorical effect and add to the realism of the figurative portrayal. The word translated **rebuke** (*rîḇ*) is used here of a formal legal accusation. A related noun often refers to a lawsuit (cf. Ex. 23:2-3, 6). In Hosea 4:1 this same noun is translated "charge." The reason for the accusation was the disrupted relationship between the covenant partners. The Lord, speaking as the Husband who had been severely wronged, declared, **She is not My wife, and I am not her Husband.** Some have interpreted this statement as a formal declaration of divorce, which is unlikely in this context. The Lord's ultimate purpose was to heal the relationship, not terminate it (cf. 2:2b, 6-7, 14-23). Thus the statement was probably an acknowledgment that "no reality remained in the relationship" (Derek Kidner, *Love to the Loveless*, p. 27). The Lord's wife, by her unfaithful behavior, had for all practical purposes severed the relationship with her Husband.

Rather than exercising His legal prerogative by having His wayward wife executed (cf. Lev. 20:10; Deut. 22:22), the Lord issued a call for repentance, urging the nation to abandon its **adulterous** activity (Hosea 2:2b).

**2:3.** The Lord's appeal (v. 2b) was strengthened by a severe threat containing three solemn warnings to Israel (**I will** occurs three times in vv. 3-4). First, the Lord threatened to **strip her naked**, making her an object of shame and ridicule (cf. v. 10; Ezek. 16:35-43). The punishment fit the crime. She who had exposed her nakedness to her lovers would be exposed publicly for all to see. This public act apparently preceded the execution of an adulteress (cf. Ezek. 16:38-40).

Second, the Lord threatened to **make her like** an arid **desert**, deprived of water (cf. **slay her with thirst**), incapable of producing or sustaining life. All her powers of fertility would be removed. Again the punishment fit the crime. She who had engaged in illicit sexual behavior would become incapable of reproduction.

**2:4.** The third threat involved the rejection of the wife's **children**. The reason was that **they** were **children of adultery.**

This may mean they were products of their mother's illicit relationships, though probably it simply indicates they were covered with shame by reason of their association with such a mother (cf. v. 5 and comments on 1:2). At any rate, the Lord announced they would not receive His **love** (*rāḥam*; cf. 1:6-8; 2:1), implying they would be disowned and become orphans. In this way any reminder of the relationship with their mother would be eliminated.

The harsh punishment threatened in verses 3-4 seems to imply complete termination of the marriage. The wayward wife would be executed and her children disowned. However, the context clearly demonstrates that this would not occur. This same anomaly occurs in Ezekiel 16 where Israel is executed as an adulteress (Ezek. 16:35-42) only to be eventually restored to favor (Ezek. 16:59-63). Apparently the harsh language was intended to emphasize the severity of the punishment without implying the absolute termination of the Lord's relationship with Israel.

### b. Punishment initiated (2:5-13)

The Lord's judgment, instead of bringing His relationship with Israel to a complete end, was designed to effect restoration. The first step in this process was to deprive the nation of its false gods and the prosperity it erroneously attributed to them.

(1) Israel deprived of her lovers. **2:5-7.** In verse 5 Israel's unfaithfulness is vividly pictured. She resolved to pursue her **lovers** (the Baals; cf. vv. 13, 17; 11:2) because she believed they supplied her physical nourishment (**food . . . water**), protection (**wool and . . . linen**; cf. 2:9), and pleasure (**oil and . . . drink**). In response the Lord declared that He would soon eliminate all means of access to these lovers. Israel would find familiar paths blocked with thorns and stone walls (v. 6). Her frantic efforts to find her **lovers** would be thwarted (v. 7a). As a last resort, she would resolve to return to her **Husband,** the Lord, opening the way for restoration. The reality behind this figurative portrayal of judgment probably included drought, invasion, and exile (cf. vv. 9, 11-12; Lev. 26:18-22).

(2) Israel deprived of the Lord's blessings (2:8-13). **2:8.** Israel's guilt was

established as the basis for her punishment. She had failed to acknowledge the Lord as the Source of her produce and wealth. Instead she used **silver and gold** to manufacture **Baal** idols (cf. 8:4; 13:2), for it was this Canaanite deity to whom she attributed her agricultural (**grain . . . new wine and oil**) and economic prosperity (2:5, 12-13).

Baal was the Canaanite god who supposedly controlled storms and was responsible for both agricultural and human fertility. The Canaanite "Legend of Keret" associated Baal's rain with agricultural blessing in the form of grain, bread, wine, and oil (cf. J.C.L. Gibson, *Canaanite Myths and Legends*. Edinburgh: T. & T. Clark, 1978, p. 98). By looking to Baal for these things Israel broke the first of the Ten Commandments (cf. Ex. 20:3; Deut. 5:7), rejecting one of the main principles of the Mosaic legislation. Moses taught that the Lord provided grain, wine, and oil (Deut. 7:13; 11:14). Each Israelite, when presenting his firstfruits in the harvest festival, was to recite the following words in the presence of the priest, "I bring the firstfruits of the soil that You, O LORD, have given me" (Deut. 26:10).

**2:9a.** In response to Israel's unfaithfulness, the Lord said He would deprive the nation of agricultural produce (**grain** and **new wine**), leaving it destitute. The Mosaic Law made agricultural prosperity dependent on loyalty to the Lord. Obedience to the covenant stipulations would result in the Lord's blessing in the form of plentiful harvests, numerous offspring, and security (cf. Lev. 26:3-13; Deut. 28:1-14). Disobedience would bring drought, pestilence, war, death, and exile (Lev. 26:14-39; Deut. 28:15-68). Thus the announcement in Hosea 2:9 revealed the Lord's intention to implement the covenant curses against Israel. Drought, blight, insect swarms, and invading armies would destroy the land's produce (cf. Deut. 28:51; Joel 1:4-12; Amos 4:6-9; 7:1).

**2:9b-10.** The figurative portrayal of Israel as the Lord's wife is carried along in these verses. Without **wool** and **linen** (cf. v. 5), which were used to make clothing (Lev. 13:47, 59; Deut. 22:11; Prov. 31:13; Ezek. 44:17), she would have no means of covering **her nakedness.** Through this deprivation the Lord would **expose her lewdness.** Her shameful behavior would become known to all through this public demonstration (cf. Hosea 2:3; Ezek. 16:36-37). "Lewdness" (*nablût*, which occurs only here in the OT) refers to a blatant breach of covenant which disgraces the entire community. A related term (*neḇālâh*) is used of Achan's sin (Josh. 7:15), as well as various prohibited sexual acts, including fornication (Deut. 22:21), incest (2 Sam. 13:12), rape (Jud. 19:23; 20:6), and adultery (Jer. 29:23). During this exhibition Israel's **lovers** would be forced to stand by helplessly, being unable to deliver her from the Lord's powerful grip. Then the Lord's superiority and the lovers' weakness (or apathy) would become apparent to her.

**2:11.** The coming judgment would also bring the cessation of Israel's joyous religious **celebrations,** including the great **yearly festivals** (Ex. 23:14-17), the monthly **New Moons** (i.e., New Moon sacrifices; Num. 10:10, 28:11-15), and the weekly **Sabbath** observances. These **feasts** had been corrupted by Baal worship (cf. Hosea 2:13) and were no longer desired by the Lord.

**2:12-13.** The themes in verses 5-9 are repeated in verses 12-13. In implementing the covenant curses the Lord would destroy the produce (**her vines and her fig trees**; cf. Deut. 28:38-42; Joel 1:7; Amos 4:9), which Israel erroneously regarded as the **pay** given by **her** paramours in exchange for her services (cf. Hosea 9:1; Micah 1:7). The vineyards would be reduced to an overgrown **thicket** inhabited by **wild animals.** This would be an effect of the depopulation which would accompany the nation's military defeat and exile (cf. Ps. 80:12-13; Isa. 5:5-6; 7:23-25; 17:9; 32:9-14; Micah 3:12).

In burning **incense to the Baals** Israel had, as it were, seductively chased **after her lovers** (cf. Hosea 2:5). The **rings and jewelry,** though sources of delight and signs of prestige in the proper context (cf. Prov. 25:12; Ezek. 16:12-14), here represent the unfaithful wife's efforts to attract her lovers. The plural "Baals" (cf. also Hosea 2:17; 11:2; Jud. 2:11 [see comments there]; 1 Sam. 7:4; Jer. 2:23; 9:14) in this context probably refer to various local manifestations of the one Canaanite deity (cf. the singular Baal in Hosea 2:8; 13:1), who was represented by images in Baal shrines scattered throughout the land (cf. 13:1-2). The plurality of idols naturally suggested the comparison to many lovers (cf. James Luther Mays, *Hosea: A Commentary*, p. 43).

The final statement in this section (2:2-13) summarizes Israel's basic sin and the reason for the coming judgment: she had forgotten (*šāḵaḥ*) **the Lord.** The verb here does not refer to a mental lapse or loss of knowledge; it describes a refusal to acknowledge the Lord's goodness and authority (cf. 8:14; 13:6). Moses had repeatedly urged the nation not to forget the Lord's gracious deeds (Deut. 4:9; 8:11) and His demand for exclusive worship (Deut. 4:23; 6:12; 8:19; cf. 2 Kings 17:38). However, in fulfillment of Moses' prediction (cf. Deut. 31:27-29 with Deut. 32:18) Israel throughout her history **forgot** the Lord and worshiped false gods (cf. Jud. 3:7; 1 Sam. 12:9-10; Ps. 78:9-11; Jer. 23:27).

2. THE LORD'S RESTORATION OF ISRAEL (2:14-23)

Having brought Israel to a place of desperation in which she would again look to Him (cf. v. 7), the Lord said He would take the next steps in restoring the relationship. Israel's positive response would lead to covenant renewal and blessing.

*a. Renewed love (2:14-15)*

In these verses the Lord described His overtures of love and Israel's future positive response.

**2:14.** The Lord promised to initiate reconciliation with His wayward wife by alluring **her. Allure** refers here to tender, even seductive, speech. Elsewhere the term describes a man's seduction of a virgin (Ex. 22:16) and a lover's attempt to entice a man (Samson) into divulging confidential information (Jud. 14:15; 16:5). The Lord said He **will lead** Israel **into the desert,** where she will be completely separated from past lovers and will be able to concentrate totally on His advances. The reference to the desert recalls Israel's 40 years of wandering in the wilderness after the Exodus. This was sometimes pictured as a time when Israel experienced the Lord's care in a special way (cf. Hosea 13:5) and when she, in return, loved Him with the devotion of a new bride (Jer. 2:2-3). The allusion to the wilderness also represents a remarkable reversal in the use of the desert motif in

this chapter. For the Lord had threatened to make Israel "like a desert" (Hosea 2:3). According to verse 14 the desert will become the site of His romantic overtures to her. There He will **speak tenderly to her** (lit., "speak to her heart"; cf. Isa. 40:2). This Hebrew idiom refers to gentle, encouraging words, such as a man speaks to his desired bride (cf. Gen. 34:3; Ruth 2:13). As Mays states, the boldly anthropomorphic language "is astonishing" especially in light of the Bible's "studied aversion for speaking of God in any sexual terms." He adds, "it is in this daring kind of portrayal that the passion of God becomes visible—a passion that does not hesitate at any condescension or hold back from any act for the sake of the beloved elect" (*Hosea*, pp. 44-5).

**2:15.** When the Lord leads Israel out of the desert back into the Promised Land, He will restore **her vineyards.** The words **There I will give** misinterpret the elliptical Hebrew text (which reads lit., "from there") by implying that vineyards will grow in the wilderness where Israel had wandered. The agricultural prosperity envisioned here will be in Israel (cf. vv. 22-23; Deut. 30:4-5, 9; Amos 9:13-15), not in the desert. When Israel enters the land she will again pass through the **Valley of Achor** (lit., "Valley of trouble"), the site of Achan's heinous sin which jeopardized the success of the Conquest (Josh. 7). However, this time the valley will be a symbol of better things to come, **a door of hope** leading to repossession of the Promised Land (cf. Isa. 65:10). The effects of the trouble caused by Israel's past unfaithfulness will have disappeared. Instead she will respond favorably to the Lord **as in the** days immediately after the Exodus (cf. Jer. 2:2). Admittedly this earlier period is idealized here, as even a cursory reading of the narratives in Exodus and Numbers reveals.

*b. Renewed marriage (2:16-20)*

**2:16-17. In that day,** when Israel is restored to the land, she will acknowledge **the Lord** as her husband. She will address Him as '*îšî,* **my Husband,** rather than *ba' ălî,* **my Master.** These two Hebrew words are essentially synonymous. They are used interchangeably in 2 Samuel 11:26, "Now when the wife of Uriah heard that Uriah her husband (*'îš*) was dead, she mourned for her husband (*ba'al*; NASB; cf. also Deut. 24:3-4). However, the word *ba'al* would be a reminder of Israel's former Baal worship. Therefore God will prohibit its use, and Israel will no longer use **the names of the Baals** (cf. the pl. "Baals" in Hosea 2:13; 11:2).

**2:18.** Israel's return to the land will be accompanied by peace. The Lord will mediate **a covenant** between the nation and the animal kingdom. **The** harmful **beasts of the field,** which had earlier devoured the vines and fig trees (v. 12; cf. Lev. 26:22), will no longer be hostile (cf. Ezek. 34:25). Isaiah also portrayed the Kingdom Age as one of harmony between man and animals (Isa. 11:6-8; 65:25). The Lord will also cause war (symbolized by **bow and sword and battle;** cf. Hosea 1:7) to cease in **the land** of Israel. The nation will dwell safely, free from the threat of foreign invasion. This marks the reversal of an earlier judgment (cf. 1:5) and the return of covenant blessing (cf. Lev. 26:5-6, where the same expressions, **lie down** and **in safety,** are used).

**2:19-20.** The restoration of the Lord's marriage to Israel is described in terms of a betrothal. Kidner points out that the word **betroth** marks "a new beginning, with all the freshness of first love, rather than the weary patching up of differences" (*Love for the Loveless,* p. 34). It will be as though the Lord and Israel had returned to the days of courtship. Betrothal in ancient Israel was much more binding than engagement is in contemporary Western society. The Law treated a betrothed couple as though they were legally married (Deut. 20:7; 22:23-24). At the time of the betrothal the man would pay a price to seal the agreement (cf. 2 Sam. 3:14). The Lord's price will consist of **righteousness. . . justice . . . love. . . compassion,** and **faithfulness.** These qualities will characterize His relationship with Israel, which will never again be disrupted (cf. Hosea 2:19).

"Righteousness" (*ṣeḍeq*) and "justice" (*mišpāṭ*) refer here to the maintenance of Israel's just cause, which includes vindication through deliverance. "Love" (*ḥeseḍ*) is an unswerving devotion which fulfills the responsibilities arising from a relationship. "Compassion" (*raḥămîm,* related to *rāḥam,* used in 1:6-7; 2:1, 4) is tender feeling which motivates

one to gracious action. "Faithfulness" (*'ĕmûnâh*) implies dependability and constant loyalty.

In response to the divine love showered on her, Israel **will acknowledge the Lord.** In contrast with her former tendency to forget (cf. v. 13) she will recognize His authority by demonstrating loyalty to Him. "Acknowledge" (*yāḏa',* "to know") often occurs in covenantal contexts with the sense of "recognize." For example, the Lord recognized (lit., "knew") Israel's special relationship to Him (cf. Amos 3:2, KJV). Israel in return was to recognize (lit., "know") only the authority of her Lord (cf. Hosea 13:4). In Hebrew thought, such recognition was not a mere mental exercise; it implied action (cf. Jer. 22:16). In Israel's case it meant obedience to the Lord's commandments (cf. Hosea 8:1-2). In the future all Israel will "know" the Lord because, as Jeremiah wrote, He will put His "Law in their minds and write it on their hearts" (Jer. 31:33). This is the promise of the New Covenant (Jer. 31:31-34), which corresponds to the new marriage pictured in Hosea 2:19-20.

### c. Renewed blessing (2:21-23)

**2:21-22.** The promise of restored agricultural blessing, mentioned briefly in verse 15, is expanded here. A series of cries and responses is envisioned as different elements of the natural world are pesonified. **Jezreel** (the nation of Israel here) will cry out **to the grain . . . wine, and oil. They** in turn **will respond** by calling **to the earth** from which they are produced. **The earth** in turn will look to the heavens, the source of the rain which makes the soil productive. The heavens will then call to the Lord, the One who ultimately controls the agricultural cycle. He will **respond** by providing the rain necessary for agricultural prosperity.

**2:23.** The Lord Himself is pictured as engaging in agricultural endeavors. He **will plant** Israel **in the land** (cf. comments on 1:2), where she will grow under His protective care. The nation called Lo-Ruhamah (**not . . . loved;** cf. 1:6) and Lo-Ammi (**not My people;** cf. 1:9) will experience God's compassion and will be addressed as His **people.** They will acknowledge that He, not Baal, is their **God.** This passage is parallel to 1:10–2:1, where the same reversal in the significance of the symbolic names is seen.

Hosea 2:23, along with 1:10, is quoted in Romans 9:25-26 and 1 Peter 2:10. Paul quoted those Hosea passages to say that both Jews and Gentiles will be converted during the Church Age (cf. Rom. 9:24). This does *not* mean, however, that he equated the Gentiles with Israel and regarded the conversion of Gentiles as a direct fulfillment of Hosea's prophecy. Paul clearly taught that national Israel would be saved as well (Rom. 11). Rather, Paul extracted from Hosea's prophecy a principle concerning God's gracious activity (cf. F.F. Bruce, *The Epistle of Paul to the Romans.* Grand Rapids: Wm. B. Eerdmans Publishing Co., 1963, p. 196).

According to Hosea, God will mercifully bring a previously rejected people into a relationship with Himself. Paul recognized this same pattern in God's dealings with the Gentiles. In Romans 9:25 Paul, then, was applying Hosea 2:23 to the Gentiles; he was not reinterpreting the verse (cf. comments on Rom. 9:24-26). Likewise Peter (1 Peter 2:10) saw the language of Hosea's prophecy as applicable to New Testament believers, who by divine mercy have been brought into a relationship with God (cf. 1 Peter 1:3).

## C. The restoration of Hosea's marriage (chap. 3)

As Hosea's experience with his unfaithful wife portrayed Israel's rejection of the Lord, so the recovery of his wayward wife pictured the Lord's love for and restoration of Israel.

### 1. THE DIVINE COMMAND (3:1)

**3:1.** The LORD told Hosea to demonstrate his **love to** his adulterous **wife** once more. This gracious act would serve as an object lesson of God's great love ('ahăḇâh) for Israel despite her gross unfaithfulness. Rather than responding favorably to the Lord, she was turning **to other gods** and loving ('āhaḇ) instead **the sacred raisin cakes,** delicacies apparently employed in feasts associated with Baal worship. Perhaps they were similar to the cakes offered to the goddess Astarte (cf. Jer. 7:18; 44:19).

### 2. HOSEA'S OBEDIENT RESPONSE (3:2-3)

**3:2.** Hosea responded obediently to the Lord's command (cf. 1:3). He **bought** his wife back for a substantial price. **A homer and lethek of barley** were probably valued together at **15 shekels** (Wolff, *Hosea,* p. 61). So the payment with the 15 shekels of silver was equivalent to 30 shekels, the price of a slave (cf. Ex. 21:32).

The circumstances surrounding this purchase are uncertain. Whether Hosea had legally divorced Gomer is unknown. She may have become a temple prostitute or was perhaps the legal property of someone who employed her as a concubine or hired her out as a prostitute. The phrase "loved by another" (Hosea 3:1) seems to suggest she was owned by another. However, the word "another" (rēa', "friend, fellow citizen") may refer to Hosea, not a paramour (cf. Jer. 3:20). The following statement concerning the Lord's love for Israel favors this. In this case one might translate, "Love a woman who is loved by her husband, yet [is] an adulteress" (Hosea 3:1, NASB).

**3:3.** After acquiring legal possession of Gomer, Hosea informed her that her adulterous lifestyle was over. She would remain at home *with* him, isolated from all potential lovers. The meaning of the final clause in verse 3 is unclear. The text literally reads, "and also I toward you." The NIV (**and I will live with you**) understands the expression to be analogous to the preceding **you are to live with me,** meaning that both parties would devote themselves entirely to each other. Others understand the clause to mean that Hosea would abstain from sexual relations with her for a prolonged period of time (NEB).

### 3. THE ILLUSTRATION EXPLAINED (3:4-5)

**3:4.** Gomer's lengthy period of isolation was designed to portray Israel's exile, when the nation would be separated from its illicit institutions and practices (cf. 2:6-7). The absence of **king** and **prince** implied loss of national sovereignty. The elimination of **sacrifice** and **sacred stones** meant the cessation of formal religious activity. Sacrifices, having been commanded by the Lord, were a legitimate aspect of worship when offered with an attitude of total devotion to God. However, in Israel sacrifices had become contaminated by their association with Baal worship (cf. 4:19) and by the people's failure to obey "the more important matters of the Law" (Matt. 23:23; cf. Hosea 6:6; 8:11-13). "Sacred stones" (*maṣṣēḇâh*) had been a legitimate part of patriarchal worship (cf. Gen. 28:18, 22; 31:13). However, because of those stones' association with pagan religion, Israel was forbidden to use them after entering Canaan (Lev. 26:1; Deut. 16:22). In direct violation of this covenant stipulation Israel had erected such stones as part of its Baal worship (2 Kings 3:2; 10:26-27; 17:10; Hosea 10:1; Micah 5:13).

**Ephod** and **idol** refer to methods of divination. In this context the ephod was not the garment worn by a priest, but a cultic object (cf. Jud. 8:27 and Roland de Vaux, *Ancient Israel*. 2 vols. New York: McGraw-Hill, 1965, 2:350). Idols (*tᵉrāp̄îm*), sometimes found in homes (Gen. 31:19; 1 Sam. 19:13, 16) or in a king's collection of divination devices (Ezek. 21:21), were despised by the Lord (1 Sam. 15:23; 2 Kings 23:24). These two items (ephod and idol) are also mentioned together in Judges (17:5; 18:14, 17-18, 20) as part of the belongings of an Ephraimite's personal priest. These instruments of divination were confiscated by the Danites and used in their unauthorized worship system (Jud. 18:27-31).

**3:5.** After Israel's period of isolation she will repent **and seek the LORD**, rather than false gods (2:7; 5:15; cf. Deut. 4:29). Israel will also recognize the authority of the Davidic monarchy, which it rejected at the time of Jeroboam I (cf. 1 Kings 12). The nation will approach the Lord with a healthy sense of fear (**trembling**), even in the context of blessing. In the past the nation had taken the Lord's gifts for granted and proudly turned away from His commandments (cf. Hosea 13:6; Deut. 8:10-18). The **blessings** (lit., "goodness") in view here are wealth and agricultural bounty (cf. Deut. 6:11; Isa. 1:19; Jer. 2:7; 31:12, 14 where the same word, *ṭûḇ*, is employed). The concluding phrase, **in the last days,** was used by the eighth-century prophets as a technical expression for the time of Israel's restoration predicted by Moses (Isa. 2:2; Micah 4:1; cf. Deut. 4:30, "in later days").

## III. Hosea's Message: God's Judgment and Restoration of Israel (chaps. 4–14)

The remainder of Hosea's prophecy expands the message of the first three chapters. Though emphasis is placed on Israel's guilt and impending doom, each of the three major sections (4:1–6:3; 6:4–11:11; 11:12–14:9) concludes on a positive note by referring to Israel's restoration (see "Purpose and Message" in the *Introduction*).

### A. The Lord's case against Israel (4:1–6:3)

This first judgment-salvation cycle is comprised of three parts. Chapter 4 focuses on the sins of the Northern Kingdom, while 5:1-15a establishes the guilt of the entire nation (Judah included) and announces judgment. In 5:15b–6:3 Israel's repentance is envisioned.

1. ISRAEL'S GUILT EXPOSED (CHAP. 4)

The guilt of the Northern Kingdom is the main theme of this opening judgment speech. The people and their leaders (prophets, rulers, and esp. priests) were the objects of God's displeasure. While most of the verses are accusatory in tone, announcements of forthcoming judgment are also scattered throughout (cf. vv. 6-10).

*a. Breach of covenant (4:1-3)*

**4:1-2.** Hosea began this section with an indictment (**charge**, *rîḇ*; cf. "charge" in 12:2 and the verb *rîḇ*, "rebuke," in 2:2) of the nation for breach of covenant. The people were devoid of the qualities that were to characterize life within God's covenant. They failed to exhibit **faithfulness** and **love** (*ḥesed*; cf. 2:19) and did not acknowledge **God** as their covenant Lord. (**Acknowledgment** translates *dā‘aṯ*, related to *yāḏa‘*, "to know"; cf. comments on 2:20.) Instead they blatantly disobeyed the Decalogue, which epitomized God's ideal for Israelite society. Violations of five of the Ten Commandments are specifically mentioned: **cursing, lying** (cf. 7:1; 12:1), **murder, stealing, and adultery** (commandments 3, 9, 6, 8, and 7, in that order). "Cursing" does not refer to improper speech as such, but to calling down a curse on another (cf. Job 31:30). Because such imprecations (for Israelites) entailed invoking God's name, they would be violating the third commandment when such an imprecation was unjustified (Ex. 20:7; Deut. 5:11; for an example of a justifiable curse invoking the Lord's name, see Num. 5:19-23).

**4:3.** Because of Israel's sin, severe drought would sweep over **the land** and people would die (**waste away**). The three verbs in this verse should be translated in the future tense (cf. Hosea 2:9, 12). Drought was one of the curses threatened by the Law for breaking the covenant (cf. Lev. 26:19; Deut. 28:23-24).

### b. The priests' guilt (4:4-11a)

The priests addressed in these verses shared the guilt of the people and therefore would not be exempt from punishment.

**4:4.** The guilt of the population as a whole is further established. The first two lines in this verse prohibit either lawsuits among the people (NIV) or formal opposition to God's charges (cf. Mays, *Hosea*, p. 67). In either case the reason for God's prohibition was that all the **people** were guilty of rebellion. They were **like those who** brazenly defy God's established human legal authorities (cf. Deut. 17:12).

**4:5a-b.** Here the accusation (v. 4) is extended to the religious leaders (NIV) or the demise of the religious leaders is announced (KJV, NASB). **Stumble** refers to their moral shortcomings (cf. 14:1, NASB; Isa. 3:8; Jer. 18:15; Mal. 2:8) or their coming downfall (cf. Hosea 5:5; Isa. 8:15; 28:13; 31:3; Jer. 6:21; 8:12; 20:11). These priests and **prophets** were attached to the official sanctuaries and royal court. Their allegiance was to their human king, not God (cf. 1 Kings 22:6-8; Amos 7:10-17), and they were characterized by self-gratification (cf. Isa. 28:7; Jer. 23:11) and greed (Jer. 6:13; Micah 3:11).

**4:5c-6.** The Lord held these leaders responsible for the people's **lack of knowledge** (cf. v. 1). The priests in particular had ignored their duty to communicate **the Law of . . . God** to the nation (cf. Deut. 31:9-13; 33:8-10; Mal. 2:7). So they would be severely but justly punished. Because of their part in the people's moral ruin mothers would be destroyed. This judgment, though unusual, appears elsewhere (cf. Jer. 22:26). In this way the source of the priestly line would be eliminated. As punishment for their rejection of knowledge, the **priests** themselves would be removed from their office by the Lord. Also because the priests ignored the Law, the Lord said He would ignore their **children,** apparently meaning they would not inherit their fathers' office (cf. 1 Sam. 2:27-35). In this way the future of the priestly line would be cut off.

The repetition of the verb in each cycle of the announcement of judgment (**destroy . . . destroyed. . . . rejected . . . reject . . . ignored . . . ignore**) emphasizes that each punishment fits each crime perfectly.

**4:7.** One would expect that an increase in the number of **priests** would have positive effects on the nation's moral climate. However, in Israel it only brought greater sin.

According to the NIV, verse 7b continues the accusation. This reading, which has some external support (cf. NIV marg.) suggests that the priests **exchanged their Glory,** the Lord, **for something disgraceful** (idols; cf. Ps. 106:20; Jer. 2:11). The Masoretic text, which reads, "I will change their glory into shame" (KJV, NASB, RSV), seems preferable. The Lord will take away the honor (*kābôd,* trans. here "glory," frequently carries this meaning) which they received because of their position.

**4:8.** In their greed the priests fed on **the sins of** the **people** by encouraging them to multiply the hypocritical sacrifices which the Lord hated (cf. 6:6; 8:11-13). The priests' underlying motive in doing this was greed, since they received portions of the offerings which were presented (cf. Lev. 7:7-10, 28-34; Num. 18:8-19; Deut. 18:1-5).

**4:9-10a.** Because the **priests** were no different from the other **people,** they also would experience the effects of the covenant curses. Despite their greedy schemes to accumulate food, their appetites would not be satisfied for drought would make food scarce (cf. 4:3; Lev. 26:26; Micah 6:14). Their efforts to promote fertility through cult **prostitution** would not succeed (cf. Hosea 2:13b; Deut. 28:18a).

**4:10b-11a.** The priests' sin is summarized here. They had **deserted the LORD** by breaking His covenant (cf. Deut. 28:20; 29:25; 31:16). The NIV puts the last three words of Hosea 4:10 with verse 11a, **to give themselves** (lit., "to keep or watch") **to prostitution** (RSV, "to cherish harlotry"). In this case prostitution was a sarcastic substitution for the Lord's commandments, which frequently appear as the object of the verb "to keep" (*šāmar*) in Deuteronomy (cf. Deut. 4:2; 5:10, 29; 6:2; etc.). The Hebrew reads literally, "for the Lord they have forsaken to obey" (KJV, NASB). In this case the clause must be understood as highly elliptical, the sense being, "they have forsaken the Lord, refusing to observe His commandments."

### c. The people's guilt (4:11b-19)

**4:11b-14.** The scope of the accusation widened to include the **people** in general. Sensual pleasures had robbed them of their senses, leaving them without **understanding.** They engaged in pagan worship practices, including divination (seeking answers **by a stick of wood**), sacrificed to false gods, and engaged in cult **prostitution** (cf. 5:4). The Canaanite shrines, which Moses had commanded Israel to destroy (cf. Deut. 12:2-3), were located on **hills** and/or **under** shady trees (**oak, poplar, and terebinth**) throughout the Northern Kingdom (cf. 2 Kings 17:10-11). Here many young women (**daughters**) of Israel took part in sexual rites with male cult **prostitutes** (cf. Deut. 23:17-18; 1 Kings 14:24). The intent of such acts was to ensure human and agricultural fecundity by making the fertility deities Baal and Asherah favorably inclined to their offerings and prayers. However, these women would not be singled out for divine punishment because **the men** frequented the shrines as well (Hosea 4:14). In response to such an obvious failure to grasp and apply the most basic principles of covenant life, the Lord cried out, **A people without understanding will come to ruin!** (cf. v. 11)

**4:15.** **Judah** was now warned to avoid the sins of her sister **Israel.** This need not mean that the people of Judah were in the habit of visiting northern cultic sites, such as **Gilgal** (cf. 9:15) and **Beth Aven.** Mays explains, "The exhortation . . . is simply bitter condemnation of their cult . . . for the ears of those who did worship in them" (*Hosea*, p. 77). The threefold warning (**Do not go . . . do not go . . . do not swear**) is a rhetorical device designed to accentuate Israel's guilt. To associate oneself with Israel's false, hypocritical worship would be contaminating. Even Bethel (lit., "house of God"), the site of Jacob's dream (Gen. 28:10-19), had become "Beth Aven" (lit.,

"house of wickedness"; cf. Hosea 10:5; Amos 5:5) because of the religious practices conducted there (1 Kings 12:28-30; 2 Kings 10:29; 23:15; Amos 4:4). In the midst of this idolatrous, immoral worship the Israelites even had the audacity to employ the Lord's name in oaths. The Law commanded Israel to swear by the Lord's name (Deut. 6:13; 10:20). However, to make a semblance of devotion to **the LORD** while serving other gods was the grossest hypocrisy.

**4:16.** Through her refusal to repent Israel had separated herself from the Lord's protective guidance. As long as the nation responded like a young cow, stubbornly resisting His leading, God would treat her appropriately (cf. Jer. 31:18), not like a lamb which is allowed to graze leisurely in broad pastures. **Stubborn** refers to a rebellious attitude which **the LORD** finds deplorable (cf. Deut. 21:18-21).

**4:17.** Because of her strong attachment to idolatry (**joined to idols**) Israel was to be left to herself and allowed to go to her doom. **Ephraim,** a prominent tribe in the Northern Kingdom, mentioned 36 times in the Book of Hosea, stands for Israel as a whole (cf. the parallelism in 5:3, 5; also cf. Isa. 7:2, 5, 8-9, 17).

**4:18.** The accusation concludes as it began by referring to the carousing and immorality which characterized the people and their rulers (cf. v. 11). **Rulers** is literally "shields," a term which suggests the positive, protective role which a nation's leaders should play (cf. Pss. 84:9, 11; 89:18). Israel's rulers failed miserably in this regard, loving only **shameful** deeds.

**4:19.** The result of Israel's sin would be judgment. The first line of this verse reads literally, "the wind has enveloped her with its wings," suggesting that she soon would be swept **away.** At that time the idolatrous **sacrifices** (or, perhaps, "altars," following the LXX) would prove to be only a source of disappointment and **shame** (cf. 10:5-6).

### 2. ISRAEL'S JUDGMENT ANNOUNCED (5:1-14)

The Northern Kingdom remains the primary target group in this section. However, Judah, which had been warned to avoid Israel's example (4:15), was now brought within the scope of

God's judgment (cf. 5:5, 8, 10, 13-14). The chapter begins with an accusation of guilt (vv. 1-5) which merges into an announcement of judgment (vv. 6-15a).

**5:1-2.** Though the accusation encompassed the entire nation (**you Israelites**), the priesthood (**priests**) and monarchy (**royal house**) were singled out for special consideration (cf. 4:4-10, 18). The leaders had encouraged the people to engage in false worship at cult sites such as **Mizpah** and **Tabor.** In so doing they were like **a snare** or **net** used to trap a bird (cf. 7:12; Amos 3:5). Mount Tabor was in northern Israel, about 12 miles southwest of the Sea of Galilee. Mizpah in this context refers to a site either in Gilead or in Benjamite territory. If the former, then the places mentioned represent areas of the Northern Kingdom west and east of the Jordan River. If the reference is to Mizpah of Benjamin, the idea is that all cult sites from south to north were involved. In either case the selection of place names was designed to emphasize how the false worship led by the priests had permeated the land.

The rebellious priesthood (**rebels**) had gone to great depths (**are deep**) as it were, to **slaughter** their prey (continuing the hunting imagery of Hosea 5:1b), the people of Israel.

Verse 2b can be taken in one of two ways. It refers either to approaching discipline (**I will discipline**; cf. NASB and 10:10) or to past divine efforts to correct rebellion ("I have been a Rebuker of them all," KJV; cf. Amos 4:6-12). In either case "discipline" (*mûsār*) refers here to severe punishment designed to restore one to proper behavior. As such, it is an expression of love that arises out of a close relationship (cf. Prov. 3:11; 13:24; 15:5). The positive goal of the Lord's judgment is evident (cf. Hosea 2:6-7; 5:15b).

**5:3-5.** The guilt of the nation as a whole is declared. **Israel** could not hide its sin from the omniscient **God.** The nation had become **corrupt** (*ṭāmā*, "to be unclean or defiled") through its spiritual adultery (cf. 6:10). This wording is probably drawn from Numbers 5:20, 27-28 where the same verb (*ṭāmā'*) describes the effects of adultery on the unfaithful party (cf. Lev. 18:20, 24). Sinful Israel had become so overpowered by **a spirit of prostitution** (Hosea 5:4; cf. 4:12) that any pos-

sibility of repentance and recognition of the Lord's authority was precluded for the time being. The nation's own **arrogance** served as a legal witness (**testifies;** cf. the same expression in 1 Sam. 12:3; 2 Sam. 1:16) to its guilt and, in accordance with the famous proverb (Prov. 16:18), had led to its fall (cf. **stumble** in Hosea 4:5). **Judah** had followed Israel's example and had come to mortal ruin as well.

**5:6.** The Lord's punishment of His people would be expressed in two ways: withdrawal of aid and blessing (vv. 6-7, 15a), and active warfare (vv. 8-14). In the days ahead Israel in desperation would **seek the LORD** through sacrifices of **flocks and herds.** However, this hypocritical ritualism, devoid of genuine covenant loyalty, would be ineffective (cf. 6:6; 8:11-13; Isa. 1:10-17).

**5:7.** God's people had been **unfaithful.** The Hebrew verb (*bāgad*) often refers to a failure to carry out the responsibilities of a natural (cf. Jer. 12:6) or contractual (cf. Jud. 9:6, 23; Mal. 2:14-16) relationship. Here marital infidelity provides the background (cf. Jer. 3:20). As in the preceding chapters, Hosea pictured Israel as the Lord's adulterous wife. Carrying on the figure, she had even given **birth to illegitimate children,** an inevitable result of her promiscuous activities. The reality behind the figure was perhaps those Israelite children whose birth was attributed to cultic sexual acts (cf. Hosea 4:13-15).

Such rituals only heightened the people's guilt. Participation in religious **festivals** (here represented by the **New Moon** celebrations; cf. 2:11) would actually hasten their destruction, not avert it. Rather than experiencing population growth, the people would ultimately be devoured by their own sins (cf. Lev. 26:21-22; Deut. 28:62-63). The **fields,** for which they sought fertility through Baal worship, would be destroyed by drought, blight, and insects, and would be overrun by invading armies (cf. Lev. 26:16, 19-20; Deut. 28:17, 22-24, 33, 38-42, 51).

**5:8-9.** The **sound** of battle trumpets was about to be heard in **Israel.** An invading force would sweep to the borders of the Southern Kingdom (cf. Kidner, *Love to the Loveless,* p. 61). **Gibeah** and **Ramah** were located a few miles north of Jerusalem in Benjamite territory in the

Southern Kingdom (cf. Josh. 18:25, 28). **Beth Aven** (probably Bethel; cf. Hosea 4:15), though originally a Benjamite town (Josh. 18:22), was then just inside Israel's southern border.

The significance of the last clause in Hosea 5:8, **lead on, O Benjamin** (lit., "behind you, O Benjamin") is not clear. The same expression appears in Deborah's song in reference to mustering Israel's troops (Jud. 5:14). At that time Benjamin went ahead of Ephraim into battle against the northern Canaanite forces (NASB). Perhaps this ancient song was given a sarcastic twist by Hosea. In the upcoming invasion **Ephraim** would be devastated. Rather than leading Ephraim into battle, Benjamin would be pursued by the same invader. The line might be paraphrased, "behind you, O Benjamin, Ephraim's conqueror advances."

The desolation of Ephraim was certain to take place because it had been announced by the Lord, whose word is inviolable (**I proclaim what is certain**). This coming judgment would fulfill the covenant curse in Leviticus 26:32-35.

**5:10.** Even Judah would not be spared ultimately (cf., however, 1:7). Its leaders were also guilty of breach of covenant. They were **like those who move boundary stones** for they showed no respect for God's commands. Moving boundary stones was clearly forbidden in the Law (Deut. 19:14) and carried a curse (Deut. 27:17). The act was tantamount to theft as it obscured the legal boundary between properties and was a way of taking some land that belonged to another. Perhaps this particular crime was cited in order to allude to the acts of social injustice being carried out by the Judean upper class (cf. Isa. 5:8; Micah 2:1-2). On **Judah's** sinful **leaders** the Lord would **pour out** His anger **like a flood of water** (lit., "like water"), possibly meaning like rainwater (cf. Amos 5:8; 9:6).

**5:11.** According to verses 11-14, judgment had already begun. **Ephraim** was **oppressed** and **trampled.** Again Hosea alluded to a covenant curse (cf. Deut. 28:33, NASB). This judgment may refer to the Assyrian invasion of 733 B.C. (cf. 2 Kings 15:29). However, Israel's troubles were ultimately attributable to her own sin, not to Assyrian imperialism. The word **idols** is a conjecture (cf. NIV marg.), for the Hebrew word ṣāw is obscure.

"Man's command" (NASB) is a highly unlikely translation. The word is possibly a corruption of "vanity" (šāw', RSV, following the LXX) or "filth" (ṣāw', i.e., "excrement"; cf. Andersen and Freedman, Hosea, pp. 409-10). The reference is probably to false gods (hence NIV's "idols"). The Hebrew literally reads, "for he persistently walked after vanity/filth (?)." The idiom "walk after," translated "follow(ed)(ing)," appears elsewhere with false gods as an object (cf. Deut. 4:3; 6:14; 8:19; 28:14; Jer. 2:5; etc.).

**5:12.** The Lord Himself was silently but effectively leading His people toward destruction. **To Ephraim** He was **like a moth,** which destroys clothing (cf. Job 13:28; Isa. 50:9; 51:8). **To . . . Judah** He was **like rot,** which progressively causes bones to decay (cf. Prov. 12:4; 14:30; Hab. 3:16). This unusual figurative language means that God was sovereignly in control of the international scene, which He was already manipulating to bring about Israel's demise.

**5:13.** The nation's response to its deteriorating condition (like a **sickness** with **sores**) was entirely misdirected. Following the path of political expediency, the Northern Kingdom **turned to** the invader himself, Tiglath-Pileser III of **Assyria,** in an effort to restore national stability. This probably refers to Hoshea's alliance with Assyria (2 Kings 17:3) at the time he usurped the throne of Israel (cf. 2 Kings 15:30). **Judah** had formed a similar alliance when threatened by Syria and Israel (2 Kings 16). Though Hosea 5:13b does not specifically mention Judah, the contextual references to her (vv. 13a, 14a) suggest that she was in Hosea's mind as well. These efforts to **heal** the nation's wounds would be futile. Assyria was a greedy overseer, not a physician. As soon as Hoshea withheld tribute, the Assyrians again invaded the land (2 Kings 17:3-6).

**5:14.** The moth (v. 12) is transformed into a raging **lion** which violently kills its prey. The use of six first-person forms (**I**) in the Hebrew emphasizes God's role in this judgment. In the final analysis the Lord Himself would be the attacker and destroyer, even though He would use foreign armies as His instruments.

For **Ephraim** this prophecy was fulfilled a few years later when Assyria conquered Samaria and carried the people into exile (2 Kings 17). **Judah** was overrun by the Assyrians in 701 B.C., but she experienced a miraculous deliverance after being severely ravaged (cf. comments on Hosea 1:7). The prophecy about Judah's fall and exile (5:14) was eventually fulfilled through Nebuchadnezzar (2 Kings 25).

### 3. ISRAEL'S RESTORATION ENVISIONED (5:15–6:3)

**5:15.** The ultimate purpose of the Lord's judgment on His people was to restore them (cf. 2:5-7). Having received the just punishment for their sins, God's people would turn to Him in repentance. The Hebrew word rendered **they admit their guilt** should be translated "they bear [their] punishment" (cf. its use in 10:2; 13:16). God would not hear their prayers. He would **go back** to His **place** like a lion returning to its lair (cf. 5:14) till the nation underwent its punishment. In contrast with their earlier hypocritical quest for the Lord through sacrificial ritual (cf. v. 6), the people will genuinely and earnestly **seek** Him.

**6:1-3.** These verses record the words the penitent generation of the future will declare as they seek **the LORD.** The message is constructed in two cycles, each containing an exhortation (vv. 1a, 3a) and a motivating promise (vv. 1b-2, 3b).

In contrast with her past folly (cf. 5:13), Israel will turn to **the LORD as** her source of healing and life (cf. Deut. 32:39). Assyria was not able to cure Israel (Hosea 5:13), but the Lord is able, even though like a lion (5:14) He had **torn** them **to pieces.** The people will confidently anticipate His forthcoming restoration of their national vitality. The equivalent expressions, **after two days** and **on the third day,** refer to a short period of time, indicating they expected the revival to occur soon. Israel will also resolve to **acknowledge** the Lord's authority (contrast 4:1, 6; 5:4). **Press on** is literally, "pursue or chase," which suggests the intensity of Israel's newfound devotion.

The Lord will surely respond favorably to such loyalty. His emergence from His hiding place (cf. 5:6, 15) will be as certain as the sunrise. He will pour out His blessings on His people, as the **winter** and **spring rains . . . water the**

**earth** and assure agricultural prosperity. The latter comparison was especially well chosen since the regularity of these rains was a sign of the Lord's favor (cf. Deut. 11:13-15).

### B. The Lord's case against Israel expanded (6:4–11:11)

The Lord's case against Israel is greatly expanded in these chapters. Emphasis is placed on the nation's guilt, especially for her ingratitude. As in the preceding section (cf. 5:15–6:3), judgment changes to restoration by the end of the unit (cf. 11:8-11). Each of the subunits is marked out formally by an introductory direct address (cf. 6:4; 9:1; 11:8). Both of the judgment cycles (6:4–8:14; 9:1–11:7) refer to a return to Egypt (cf. 8:13; 11:5) in their conclusions, while the brief salvation passage (11:8-11) pictures God's people returning from that land (cf. 11:11).

### 1. ISRAEL'S GUILT AND PUNISHMENT (6:4–8:14)

This first judgment cycle contains two parts (6:4–7:16; 8). Both refer to a breach of covenant in their opening verses (6:7; 8:1) and mention Egypt near the end (7:16; 8:13).

#### a. Israel's ingratitude punished (6:4–7:16)

These verses are primarily accusatory, though judgment is announced formally in the closing passage (cf. 7:12-13, 16). The Lord's attempts to restore His people contrast with their rebellion. The references to the Lord's gracious disposition toward the nation introduce the subunits of the section (cf. 6:4-11a; 6:11b–7:12; 7:13-16).

(1) The first subunit (6:4-11a). **6:4.** The Lord's argument here begins with a rhetorical question addressed both to **Ephraim** and **Judah.** The mood is one of despair and frustration. God's people had rejected all His attempts to bring them to their senses. Their **love** (ḥesed; cf. 2:19; 4:1) for the Lord was at best transitory (6:4b). **Like the** early **morning** fog or **dew,** any expression of loyalty quickly evaporated.

**6:5.** God's measures to bring His disloyal people to repentance had been extreme (cf. Amos 4:6-11). His **words** of judgment, spoken through the **prophets,** had brought sudden death and destruction on many people (cf. Jer. 1:10; 5:14).

**6:6.** The reason for such severe discipline is reiterated: God's people had failed to understand His true **desire.** He longed for devotion (*ḥesed*, **mercy**) and loyalty (**acknowledgment of God;** cf. 2:20; 4:1, 6) expressed through allegiance to the covenant demands. Unless offered in the context of obedience, sacrifices were meaningless and even offensive (cf. 1 Sam. 15:22; Isa. 1:11-20; Amos 5:21-24; Micah 6:6-8).

**6:7.** Rather than pleasing God, the people had **broken the covenant** and been **unfaithful** (*bāgaḏ*; cf. comments on 5:7) to God. The Hebrew word for **like Adam** has been translated variously. "At Adam" (RSV) requires a slight change in the Hebrew and suggests a geographical place near the Jordan River. The presence of the word **there** in the next line, as well as references to other places in 6:8-9, might support this reading. "Like men" (KJV) takes the Hebrew *'āḏām* in its widely attested generic sense, rather than as a proper name. In this case a comparison is made with fallen mankind, whose propensity to be unfaithful is well established (cf. Isa. 40:6-8, man's *ḥesed* ["glory," Isa. 40:6] is as transitory as grass and flowers that wither in the sun). On the other hand, the NIV and the NASB suggest a comparison with the first man, Adam, who blatantly violated God's requirement by eating from the forbidden tree.

**6:8.** Widespread physical violence was just one example of the people's unfaithfulness (vv. 8-9; cf. Ex. 20:13). Since **Gilead** was a district, not a city, the reference in Hosea 6:8a is probably to the **city** Ramoth Gilead, east of the Jordan. The town had become a center for **wicked men** (lit., "workers of iniquity"). In Psalm 5:5 this same expression is translated "who do wrong." It refers to the worst sort of men, who actively oppose righteousness and are the objects of God's hatred. In this case they were guilty of murder (Hosea 6:8b). The city streets are pictured as being tracked with **blood** from the murderers' sandals (cf. 1 Kings 2:5). The figurative language emphasizes both the extent and certainty of their guilt. Unfortunately the precise historical background for the crime cannot be determined. Perhaps oppression of the poor is in view. Elsewhere "workers

of iniquity" are said to be guilty of oppressing the poor which is only occasionally associated with murder (cf. Ps. 94:4-6; Isa. 1:21-23).

**6:9.** The background of this verse is equally obscure. Perhaps groups **of priests** were actually murdering travelers **to Shechem.** A more likely explanation is that the language is hyperbolic, perhaps pointing to the priests' false teaching and involvement in social exploitation. The references to (Ramoth) Gilead and Shechem are well chosen. Joshua had designated that both of these towns be cities of refuge, where manslayers could find asylum (Josh. 20:1-2, 7-8; see the map "The Six Cities of Refuge," near Num. 35). In this way the land would be spared outbreaks of bloodshed, and justice would be promoted. Ironically in Hosea's day these cities had become associated with bloodshed and injustice.

The priests' **crimes** were **shameful.** Elsewhere this word (*zimmâh*) is used of the vilest sexual sins, including incest (Lev. 18:17), cult prostitution (Lev. 19:29), rape (Jud. 20:5-6), and adultery (Job 31:9-11). This sexual connotation is probably applicable here because the priests' breach of covenant (Hosea 6:6-7) is likened to prostitution (v. 10).

**6:10-11a.** The nation's sin is described in powerful figurative language. The widespread breach of covenant (vv. 6-7) was a **horrible thing.** Jeremiah used a related term to describe rotten figs that are inedible (Jer. 29:17). **Israel** had become **defiled** by her prostitution, that is, her unfaithfulness to the Lord (cf. Hosea 5:3). The comparison of judgment to **a harvest** (cf. Jer. 51:33; Joel 3:13) emphasizes its certainty (**appointed**) and its thoroughness.

(2) The second subunit (6:11b–7:12). **6:11b–7:1.** The reference to the Lord's desire to **heal** (cf. 6:1) His people comes near the beginning of this subunit. God longed to restore **Israel** to a place of blessing, but His efforts were met with new outbreaks of **sin** and **crimes.** The people's widespread **deceit** and robbery epitomized their lack of regard for the covenant (cf. Ex. 20:15).

**7:2.** To make matters worse, they disregarded God's moral character by failing to **realize that** He was taking careful notice of **their** sin (cf. Ps. 50:16-21). Therefore like a wall **their sins** had completely surrounded (did **engulf**) **them,** making repentance improbable. (The Heb. word for "their sins" is trans. "their deeds" in Hosea 5:4.)

**7:3.** The rulers were no different from their subjects. A godly ruler was to oppose all forms of **wickedness** within his kingdom (cf. Ps. 101), but these leaders delighted in it.

**7:4.** Israel was a nation of **adulterers.** It is not clear whether general breach of covenant (cf. 6:10) or literal adultery (cf. 4:2, 13-14) is described here. In either case Israel's passion for disobedience was like a fire **burning** low in **an oven** while **the baker** kneads **the dough** and waits for the leavening process to be completed. Like an oven **fire,** Israel's passion might subside for a short time, but it was ever present, ready to blaze forth when kindled (cf. 7:6).

**7:5-6.** Between 752 and 732 B.C. four of Israel's rulers were assassinated (cf. 2 Kings 15). This political intrigue provides the background for Hosea 7:5-7. Here a description is given of how the conspirators characteristically carried out their plots.

**The day of the festival of our king** probably refers to a special celebration in which the ruler was the center of attention. The king caroused with his **princes,** who are called **mockers** probably because they were completely under the influence of **wine** (cf. Prov. 20:1). While they partied with the naive king, they plotted his overthrow.

The NIV rendering, **Their passion smolders,** which has some external support, requires a slight emendation of the Hebrew. The Masoretic text reads, "their baker sleeps" (cf. KJV). The latter, while certainly more difficult, is not impossible since it is similar in thought to Hosea 7:4 and carries along the comparison of their hearts to **an oven.** One might paraphrase verse 6: "When **they approach** the king **their hearts,** like **an oven,** contain a **fire.** Just as the fire burns lowly while the baker is inactive, so their scheme remains a secret. But when their time for action comes, the destructive plot is realized, just as a fire in an oven **blazes** forth when the time for baking arrives."

**7:7.** Because the royal court of Israel was filled with such murderers, the kingship frequently changed hands. Throughout this period of palace revolt

and regicide no one bothered to look to the Lord, the true King of Israel and her only Source of national stability.

**7:8.** Instead **Ephraim** launched a futile foreign policy (vv. 8-12). The baking metaphor continues in verse 8 (cf. vv. 4, 6-7). Israel had formed alliances with foreign **nations** (cf. v. 11; 8:9). This is compared to the mixing of flour with oil to form cakes (*bālal*, **mixes,** is frequently used in this sense). This policy had proven self-destructive. Israel had become like an unturned **cake** on hot stones— burned and soon to be discarded.

**7:9.** The negative effects of Israel's foreign policy are described further in this verse. The nation is compared to an elderly man who has failed to **notice** the gradual effects of the aging process (loss of physical **strength,** graying **hair**). Death is much closer than he expects. The point was probably that Israel was experiencing loss of political autonomy. This loss was epitomized by the tribute payments that were an excessive drain on its wealth and economy (cf. 2 Kings 15:19-20; 17:3).

**7:10.** Despite her weakened condition, Israel did **not** repent. The nation's refusal (**arrogance**) to acknowledge the covenant God was self-incriminating (cf. **testifies against him**; also see comments on 5:5).

**7:11.** In her efforts to arrange foreign alliances, Israel could be compared to **a dove,** which exhibits little sense (cf. comments on 11:11). Under Menahem (ca. 743 or 738 B.C.) Israel submitted to Assyrian suzerainty (2 Kings 15:19-20). Pekah (ca. 734 B.C.) joined a coalition against **Assyria,** which Tiglath-Pileser III violently crushed (2 Kings 15:29). Hoshea (ca. 732–722 B.C.), after acknowledging Assyrian rulership for a time, stopped tribute payments and sought an alliance with **Egypt** (2 Kings 17:3-4a). This act of rebellion led to the destruction of the Northern Kingdom (2 Kings 17:4b-6), the inevitable result of a foreign policy which for 20 years had been characterized by vacillating and expedient measures.

**7:12.** Worst of all, Israel's policy had no place for the Lord (cf. vv. 7, 10). Consequently He Himself would intervene in judgment. While Israel sought out alliances with all the naiveté of a dove (v. 11), the Lord would come like a wise and well-equipped fowler and trap them.

(3) The third subunit (7:13-16). **7:13.**

This brief unit begins on an ominous note. **Woe** (*'ôy*) suggests impending doom (cf. Num. 21:29; Jer. 4:13, 31, "alas"; 48:46), as the next sentence (cf. **Destruction to them**) clearly shows. The basis for judgment was Israel's rebellion (cf. Hosea 8:1; 13:16) against the Lord (**because they have strayed from Me** and **because they have rebelled against Me**). Despite His desire to save them (God said, **I long to redeem them**), they had spoken **lies against** Him. The word for "redeem" (*pādâh*) is used frequently to describe the deliverance from Egypt (cf. Deut. 7:8; 9:26; 13:5; 15:15; 24:18; 2 Sam. 7:23; Ps. 78:42; Micah 6:4). Mays aptly comments, "The God of the Exodus is unchanged in His will, but because of Israel's lies there will be no 'exodus' from the Assyrian danger" (*Hosea*, p. 111). In this context "lies" probably refers to Israel's practical denial of God's redemptive ability, expressed through her attempts to find security through other nations.

**7:14.** Israel's rejection of the Lord is illustrated here. The nation desired a plentiful crop (**grain and new wine**) but refused to exhibit the wholehearted devotion to God without which agricultural prosperity was impossible. They wailed (*yālal*; lit., "howled"; cf. Joel 1:11) and cut their bodies as they mourned over the crop failure. In the second sentence, the reading in the NIV margin ("They slash themselves," following the LXX and some Heb. mss.) seems better than **They gather together.** Cutting oneself was a sign of mourning (cf. Jer. 16:6; 41:5; 47:5) forbidden by the Law (Deut. 14:1) because of its pagan associations. The prophets of Baal cut themselves in an effort to arouse Baal, the storm god, to action (cf. 1 Kings 18:28).

**7:15.** Israel's rebellion also revealed her ingratitude. The Lord had **trained . . . and strengthened them** (lit., "their arms," NASB). Elsewhere the expression "strengthen the arms" can refer to divine bestowal of military might (Ezek. 30:24-25). Perhaps Israel's past military successes (including those of Jeroboam II; cf. 2 Kings 14:25-28) are in view. Despite experiencing divine aid in battle, Israel treated God like an enemy. The phrase **plot evil against Me** suggests intense hostility and ill will. Similar language is used to describe Joseph's brothers' schemes to destroy him (Gen. 50:20).

**7:16.** Israel's hostility toward the Lord was an expression of her unfaithfulness. Israel was **like a faulty bow.** Such a weapon is unreliable because it fails to respond properly to the archer. In the same way Israel's hostile response to God's grace demonstrated her unreliable, disloyal character (cf. Ps. 78:57). The nation's **leaders,** who had rejected their true source of strength (cf. Hosea 7:15), would be destroyed in battle **because of their** pride. **Insolent words** refers to a formal denunciation or curse. Israel's rejection of divine aid (cf. v. 13) in favor of foreign alliances is compared to a verbal reproach against God. Ironically Israel would become an object of derision among the Egyptians, whose aid they had foolishly sought (cf. v. 11).

### b. Israel's rebellion punished (chap. 8)

This section includes several specific illustrations of the nation's rebellious attitude and announces God's coming judgment.

**8:1.** The chapter begins with a note of alarm. A **trumpet** must be blown to signal an impending battle (cf. 5:8). An enemy (the Assyrians) was ready to swoop down on Israel like a powerful **eagle.** The announcement of judgment recalls the **covenant** curse of Deuteronomy 28:49. **The house of the LORD** refers here to the land of Israel (as in Hosea 9:15; cf. "the LORD's land," 9:3). Again Israel was said to be rebellious (cf. 7:13).

**8:2-3.** **Israel** made a pretense of devotion to the Lord, addressing Him as her own **God** and claiming to **acknowledge** His authority over her. This profession, however, was mere lip service (cf. 4:1, 6; 5:4). Her sinful actions spoke louder than her words. In reality she had **rejected what** was **good** (the Lord's moral and ethical requirements; cf. Amos 5:14-15; Micah 6:8). Consequently **an enemy** would soon **pursue** her. The swift retreat pictured here fulfills another covenant curse (cf. Deut. 28:45).

**8:4.** Two examples of Israel's sin are given in verses 4-6. She had appointed **kings** and other leaders **without** consulting the Lord. This alludes to the series of palace revolts that plagued the Northern Kingdom after Jeroboam II's reign (cf. 7:5-7). Israel had also made **idols for themselves** in direct violation of the second commandment (cf. Ex. 20:4).

**8:5.** The **calf-idol** of **Samaria** (cf. v. 6) was singled out because it epitomized Israel's idolatrous ways. Since there is no record of such an idol being erected in Samaria, the city may stand here for the Northern Kingdom as a whole (cf. 7:1; 10:7). If so, the calf-idol was probably the image set up by Jeroboam I at Bethel (cf. 1 Kings 12:28-30; Hosea 10:5). By setting up golden calves (one in Dan and one in Bethel), Jeroboam repeated the sins of an earlier generation (cf. Ex. 32:1-4). Probably the people associated these calves with the storm and fertility god Baal (cf. Hosea 13:1-2).

The words **Throw out** follow the Septuagint. However, the Hebrew is literally, "He has rejected your calf, O Samaria" (NASB). This third person reference to God within a divine speech is unusual, but is attested elsewhere (cf. 1:7, "the LORD"; 2:22, "the LORD"; 4:6, "your God"; 4:10, "the LORD"; 4:12, "their God"; 8:13, "the LORD" and "He"). "Rejected" (in the Heb. in v. 5) makes a striking wordplay with the word "rejected" in verse 3. Israel had rejected (zānaḥ) what is good and turned to idols. The Lord responded appropriately by rejecting (zānaḥ) Israel's idols. As Moses and Joshua had warned (Deut. 11:17; Josh. 23:16), the Lord's **anger** burned **against** the idolaters. In despair the Lord asked, **How long will they be incapable of purity?**

**8:6.** The calf-idol (v. 5) was a product of a human craftsman's skill; how, then, could it be considered a god? (Cf. Isa. 40:18-20; 44:9-20.) The words, **it is not God,** were probably meant to refute Jeroboam, who said of the calves, "Here are your gods, O Israel" (1 Kings 12:28; cf. Ex. 32:4). The destruction of this image would demonstrate the futility of idolatry.

**8:7.** The phrase **they sow the wind** is transitional. It alludes to the futility of both her idolatrous worship (vv. 4-6) and her foreign policy (vv. 8-10). "Wind" here represents that which lacks substance and is therefore worthless and of no assistance (cf. Prov. 11:29). Israel would **reap** in extra measure what she had sown. The futility (wind) which she had planted like seed would yield a crop of destruction (represented by **the whirlwind**). All her efforts directed toward

self-preservation would be self-destructive.

The agricultural metaphor continues. Israel's crop would be worthless, containing only stalks without **grain.** Even if she would produce grain, **foreigners would** take it away and the nation would not benefit from her labor.

**8:8.** Already **Israel** had been **swallowed up** by her foreign policy (cf. 7:8-12). Her involvement with foreigners was swiftly robbing the nation of its strength and identity as the Lord's people. Israel had become as worthless as a broken pot (cf. Jer. 22:28; 48:38). The words **worthless thing** are literally, "a pot in which no one delights" (NASB).

**8:9.** Israel's attempt to ally with **Assyria** could be compared to the **wandering** of **a wild donkey,** an animal well known for its desire to be independent of all restrictions (cf. Job 39:5-8). Israel's alliances were also compared to prostitution; like a harlot she had **sold herself to lovers** (i.e., foreign powers).

**8:10.** Despite Israel's desperate attempts to preserve herself, God's judgment was certain. The Lord is pictured as bringing her back from her wanderings to Assyria and Egypt so that He might oppress her (cf. 7:13). The instrument of judgment would be **the mighty King** (i.e., of Assyria; cf. 10:6) from whom, ironically, they had sought aid.

**8:11-13.** Another of Israel's sins was its hypocritical ritualism. The people had **built many altars for sin offerings.** But these altars had **become altars for sinning,** as the religious acts conducted there were hypocritical. Sacrifices are an offense to God when not combined with a wholehearted devotion to His commandments (cf. 6:6; Isa. 1:11). Israel had built many altars, but at the same time had treated **the many things of** God's **Law** (His covenant demands; cf. Hosea 8:1) **as something alien.** So the Lord would not accept the **sacrifices** she offered Him. Instead He would **punish** her for her **sins** by sending her into exile. **Egypt** stands here as a symbol for the place of future exile and bondage (cf. 9:3; 11:5; Deut. 28:68). This highlights the appropriateness of God's judgment. In the deliverance from Egyptian bondage Israel had experienced God's grace. Having spurned that grace, she would return to slavery.

**8:14.** A final illustration of the nation's unfaithfulness was her self-sufficiency. **Judah** is specifically included in the indictment at this point. Having **forgotten** (cf. 2:13) that her very existence depended on the Lord alone (cf. **his Maker**), God's people proudly sought prominence (**palaces**) and security (**fortified many towns. . . . fortresses**; cf. 10:14) through her own efforts. But the Lord was about to destroy (by **fire**) these sources of false security, fulfilling a covenant curse (cf. Deut. 28:52). God's judgment came through the Assyrians. Sennacherib "attacked all the fortified cities of Judah and captured them" (2 Kings 18:13).

### 2. ISRAEL'S GUILT AND PUNISHMENT REITERATED (9:1–11:7)

This judgment message contains four subunits. The first (9:1-9) begins with a direct address to Israel, which serves as a formal marker of a new section (cf. 6:4). Each of the other subunits begins with an allusion to Israel's early history (9:10; 10:1; 11:1).

#### a. Israel's hostility punished (9:1-9)

**9:1-2. Israel** was **not** to **rejoice** in expectation of a plentiful harvest (cf. v. 2) because her unfaithfulness had precluded any further divine blessing (v. 1; cf. 2:8-9). **At every threshing floor** Israel had erroneously attributed the prosperity of her harvests to Baal (cf. 2:5). She had become an adulteress, offering worship to Baal and receiving from Baal **the wages of a prostitute.** Those "wages" were wheat (at the threshing floor), vines and figs (2:12), and food, water, wool, linen, oil, and drink (2:5). That is, Israel believed that by prostituting herself in worship of Baal that Baal in turn blessed her crops and gave her other necessities of life.

The plentiful harvests were about to end (9:2; cf. 2:9-12). In fulfillment of several covenant curses (cf. Deut. 28:30, 38-42, 51) the Lord would take away her grain and **wine** (cf. Hosea 2:9; 7:14). **Winepresses** (*yeqeb*) were used for both grapes and olives (cf. Joel 2:24). Since wine is specifically mentioned (in the last line of Hosea 9:2), *yeqeb* may allude primarily to oil in this context (cf. grain, wine, and oil in 2:8, 22).

**9:3.** The judgment pictured in verse 2 would be accomplished ultimately through invasion and exile. The **land** belonged to the Lord (cf. Ex. 15:17; Lev. 25:23), who was responsible for its fertility (cf. Deut. 11:10-12). When the people attributed the produce of the land to Baal they forfeited the blessing of living on it in peace and prosperity (Deut. 11:8-21). **Egypt** is again mentioned as a symbol of the place of exile (cf. Hosea 7:16; 8:13; 11:5). **Assyria** would be the actual location (2 Kings 17:6). There in an unclean land (cf. Amos 7:17) Israel would be forced to **eat** ceremonially **unclean food** (cf. Ezek. 4:13), rather than the fruits of God's blessing. The punishment fit the crime. Israel had become defiled by her sin (cf. Hosea 5:3; 6:10). How appropriate, then, that she eat defiled food in a defiled land.

**9:4.** In exile, opportunity for legitimate worship **to the LORD** would end. Again the punishment was highly appropriate. Israel's Levitical worship had been corrupted by hypocrisy (cf. 6:6; 8:11-13). A nation that refused to conduct its formal worship in the proper spirit would be denied its privilege of worship. **Wine offerings,** which accompanied certain types of **sacrifices** (cf. Num. 15:1-12), would cease. **Sacrifices** offered in a foreign land would not be acceptable to the Lord. They would have the same effect on a worshiper as **bread** eaten by **mourners,** who made everything they touched ceremonially unclean because they had contacted a dead body (cf. Num. 19:14-15, 22). Such bread was not fit for use in worship.

Hosea 9:4b would be better translated, "**all who eat** it (i.e., the mourners' bread) become **unclean;** such bread can be used to satisfy one's appetite, but it may not enter the Lord's **temple.**" In this way verse 4b is understood as a general statement about the nature of mourners' bread rather than an additional prediction about the exilic worshipers and their sacrifices.

**9:5.** The rhetorical question in this verse emphasizes the exiles' plight. Israel would be unable to celebrate the most important **festival** (**feasts** and **days** in Heb. are both sing.) on her religious calendar. Perhaps the Feast of Tabernacles is specifically in view (cf. Lev. 23:39).

**9:6. Destruction** would sweep over

the land (cf. 7:13; 10:14). Those who happened to **escape** the sword of the invading army would face exile. The reference to **Egypt** probably has the same meaning as in preceding verses (cf. comments on 8:13; 9:3). **Memphis,** about 20 miles south of modern Cairo, was famous as a burial place. Here it symbolizes the ultimate destination of the exiles—a foreign graveyard. Few would ever return to their homeland (cf. Jer. 44:1-14). Meanwhile back in Israel the exiles' possessions (**treasures of silver**) and homes (**tents**) would lie in ruins and would be overgrown by **briers and thorns** (cf. Hosea 10:8).

**9:7.** The people's hostility toward the true prophets of God was one of several reasons for judgment (vv. 7-9). **Maniac** refers to one who is insane (cf. 1 Sam. 21:13-15). The term is used elsewhere by godless men who ridiculed true prophets (cf. 2 Kings 9:11; Jer. 29:26-27). **Hostility** (also used in Hosea 9:8) refers to intense animosity, such as Esau felt toward Jacob after Esau had been cheated of the paternal blessing (Gen. 27:41, "held a grudge").

**9:8.** The irony of the situation is that Israel tried to ensnare the prophets God had placed as watchmen **over** the nation. A **watchman** was responsible for warning a city of an approaching enemy (cf. Ezek. 33:6). In the same way God's prophets were to warn the people of coming judgment on sin (cf. Jer. 6:17; Ezek. 3:17; 33:7-9). **The house of his God** refers to the land of Israel (cf. Hosea 8:1; 9:15).

**9:9.** The depth of the people's sin against God is emphasized by Hosea's reference to **the days of Gibeah** (cf. 10:9). The phrase recalls the events that involved the brutal rape and murder of the Levite's concubine by some bisexual men of Gibeah (Jud. 19). On that occasion it was said, "Such a thing has never been seen or done, not since the day the Israelites came up out of Egypt" (Jud. 19:30). But Hosea said that black mark on Israel's history was now rivaled by Israel's blatant **sins** against the Lord.

*b. Israel's idolatry punished*
*(9:10-17)*

**9:10.** This section begins with a reference to Israel's origins, when the Lord **found** extreme delight in the nation (cf.

2:15). **Grapes in the desert** would be an unexpected source of surprise and delight. The delicious **early fruit on the fig tree** was irresistible (cf. Song 2:13; Isa. 28:4; Jer. 24:2; Micah 7:1).

However, the Lord's attitude toward His people soon changed. **When they** arrived at Peor they engaged in sexual immorality with Moabite and Midianite women as part of the fertility rites associated with the worship of **Baal Peor** (cf. Num. 25). This deity, which God called **that shameful idol,** may have been a local manifestation of the Canaanite fertility god Baal. This event in Moses' day was mentioned here because it set the pattern for Israel's subsequent history, characterized by unfaithfulness. In Hosea's day Israel had also defiled herself by making Baal her lover. Like the generation at Peor, they too had engaged in fertility rites (cf. Hosea 4:13-14).

**9:11-14.** As punishment for Israel's sin of involvement in the Baal fertility rites (v. 10), the Lord would bring the covenant curses of infertility (vv. 11, 14), death (vv. 12-13, 16), and exile (vv. 15, 17) on the nation. The name **Ephraim** is used in verses 11, 13, and 16 because it was associated with fertility and fruitfulness ("Ephraim" in Heb. sounds like "twice fruitful"; cf. Gen. 41:52).

**Ephraim's glory,** here associated with numerous offspring, would depart as swiftly as **a bird.** Appropriately many of those who had tried to secure fertility through Baal worship would become sterile and barren (cf. Hosea 4:10 and, in contrast, Deut. 7:14). Others would **miscarry** or watch their **children** die in the forthcoming invasion (Hosea 9:12-13; cf. v. 16b). The women's **breasts** would be **dry** for they would have no children to nurse (v. 14). The words **like Tyre, planted in a pleasant place** (v. 13) attempt to make sense of the difficult Hebrew text, which seems to contrast Ephraim's prosperous past (comparable to the Phoenician commercial center Tyre; cf. Ezek. 28) with its humiliating future. The RSV (following the LXX) translates Hosea 9:13a, "Ephraim's sons, as I have seen, are destined for a prey." This seems to provide better parallelism with verse 13b.

**9:15.** The **sinful** people were now the object of God's hatred, rather than His love. The language employed here should probably be seen against a domestic background. The Lord had become displeased with His wife, unfaithful Israel. Such displeasure is termed hatred (cf. Deut. 22:13; 24:3, where the same verb, *śānē'*, is used). God was prepared to drive her from the household (**drive them out of My house**), withdrawing His **love** (His devotion and protective care as her Husband; cf. Hosea 1:6; 2:4-5). The **rebellious** nation, whose opposition to the Lord's covenant was epitomized by the **Gilgal** fertility cult (cf. 4:15; 12:11), would be expelled from His "house" (i.e., the land; cf. 8:1; 9:8). "Drive . . . out" (*gāraš*) is used frequently of the conquest of Canaan, whereby the Lord gave Israel possession of His land (cf. Ex. 23:28, 31; Deut. 33:27). Now Israel was about to suffer the same fate as the Canaaanites, whose practices it had assimilated. Hosea may also be alluding here to the sinful couple's initial expulsion from God's presence (cf. Gen. 3:24).

**9:16-17.** Ironically, because of widespread sterility and infant mortality (vv. 11-14), **Ephraim,** once a symbol of fruitfulness, would be compared to a **withered** plant incapable of bearing **fruit.** Because of her disobedience Israel would be rejected by **God** (cf. 4:6). In exile Israel's people would become **wanderers among the nations.** "Wanderers" translates the same Hebrew word (*nādad*) as "strayed" in 7:13. Again the punishment fit the crime. Those who willfully strayed from the path of covenant loyalty were condemned to wander aimlessly among those outside the covenant (foreign nations). As in 9:15, the language in verse 17 may also allude to the Genesis account. The same verb (*nādad*) is used with respect to Cain (Gen. 4:12).

*c. Israel's "double sin" punished (chap. 10)*

**10:1.** As in 9:10 this prophecy employs a botanical metaphor in referring to Israel's earlier history. The Lord planted **Israel** like a **vine** in the land of Canaan and blessed her with **fruit** (i.e., prosperity; cf. Ps. 80:8-11; Jer. 2:21; Ezek. 19:10-11). However, as the nation prospered she erroneously attributed her success to false gods rather than the Lord (cf. Hosea 2:8; Deut. 8:8-20). At the same time the people attempted to maintain a semblance of devotion to the God of Israel. The **altars** mentioned here probably refer

to this hypocritical formalism (cf. Hosea 6:6; 8:11-13), while **sacred stones** allude to idolatry (cf. 3:4; 10:2).

**10:2.** Israel's unfaithfulness established her **guilt** (cf. 12:14, 13:12, 16) and necessitated her punishment. **Is deceitful** (*ḥālaq*) literally means "is slippery, smooth." Often the term is used of deceitful, unreliable speech (cf. Pss. 5:9; 12:2; 55:21). With **their heart** (or mind) as subject *ḥālaq* refers to the hypocrisy which characterized her approach to the Lord. Appropriately **the Lord** would **destroy** the sites of her hypocritical and false worship (cf. **sacred stones** in 3:4; 10:1).

**10:3.** As a result of the approaching invasion, the nation's political structure would be shattered and her **king** removed (cf. vv. 7, 15). In the aftermath of the calamity the people would recognize their own unfaithfulness (i.e., failure to **revere the Lord**) as the basis for judgment. The situation would become so hopeless that most would realize that **even . . . a king** could bring no remedy (cf. 13:10).

**10:4.** The people's lack of respect for the Lord was illustrated by their lack of regard for legal **agreements** they made with each other. Their attitude toward fellow Israelites (including frequently taking each other to court) simply reflected their lack of loyalty to God.

**10:5-6a.** Some details of the approaching judgment and exile are described in verses 5-8. **The calf-idol** (cf. comments on 8:5) located in **Beth Aven** (i.e., Bethel; cf. comments on 4:15) would be **carried** away by the victorious Assyrian army, causing great consternation among its worshipers. **Idolatrous priests** translates a rare term (*kᵉmārîm*), used only of priests of Baal (2 Kings 23:5; Zeph. 1:4). The reference to the Assyrian army carrying off the idols of defeated foes is abundantly illustrated in neo-Assyrian literature and art. **The great king** refers to Assyria's king (cf. Hosea 8:10).

**10:6b.** The NIV takes verse 6b as a reference to Israel's shame over the fate of her gods, called **wooden idols.** The text is better translated, "Israel will be shamed of its own *counsel*" (cf. KJV, NASB, NIV marg.), the reference being to the nation's unwise political policy of courting Assyria's favor (cf. 5:13; 7:8-9, 11; 8:9-10; in Isa. 30:1 the same word ['*ēṣâh*] is used of a political alliance with Egypt).

**10:7.** Israel's **king** (cf. vv. 3, 15), as well as her calf-idol, would be removed in the coming invasion. **Float away** (*dāmâh*) is literally, "be destroyed" (cf. 4:5-6; 10:15 where NIV translates the same word as "destroy"). **Like a twig** floating **on the . . . waters** the nation would be swept away by the current and brought to ruin.

**10:8.** The sites of idolatrous worship would **be destroyed** as well, the ruins becoming overgrown with **thorns** (cf. 9:6) **and thistles.** The reference to the destruction of **the high places** (*bāmôt*) is ironic (cf. Lev. 26:30-31). When Israel entered the land the Lord commanded her to destroy these worship centers (Num. 33:52; Deut. 12:2-3). Because of Israel's dismal failure in carrying out this charge, the Lord chose to use a foreign army to accomplish His purpose. In utter desperation the people would beg the **mountains** to **fall on** them. A similar plea will be made by unbelievers in the Tribulation in response to the terror of God's wrath in the seal judgments (Rev. 6:16).

**Wickedness** translates *'āwen*, which occurs, spelled slightly differently, in "Beth Aven," the derogatory name for Bethel (cf. Hosea 4:15; 5:8; 10:5).

**10:9.** Hosea referred again to the shameful incident at **Gibeah** (cf. 9:9). **Since** that time **Israel** had persisted in sin. The question in 10:9b is better translated with the future tense, *Will* **not war overtake the evildoers in Gibeah?** (cf. NASB; 5:8) How appropriate that judgment should "overtake" the city that had served as a pattern for Israel's sinful history!

**10:10.** At the time of the Lord's choosing (**When I please**) He would **punish** (lit., "discipline"; cf. 5:2) Israel by gathering the **nations . . . against** her. The translation and meaning of the final line in 10:10 are uncertain. The NIV takes the **bonds** as a reference to captivity and approaching exile. Probably a better translation is, "when they are *harnessed* to **their double sin.**" The imagery is that of plowing (cf. v. 11). Israel is pictured as yoked to her sin like a heifer (cf. Isa. 5:18). As Wolff suggests (*Hosea*, p. 184), "double sin" probably refers to Israel's former sin (at Gibeah) and her present guilt.

**10:11.** The comparison of Israel to a cow is continued (cf. comments on v. 10). Israel (**Ephraim** stands for the Northern Kingdom; see comments on 4:17) was like **a trained heifer that loves to thresh.** A heifer would like to thresh because "threshing was a comparatively light task, made pleasant by the fact that the creature was unmuzzled and free to eat . . . as it pulled the threshing sledge over the gathered corn" (Kidner, *Love for the Loveless*, pp. 97-8). However, Israel had abandoned this relatively easy task and had insisted on being yoked, as it were, to sin (cf. 10:10b).

So the Lord would place a different **yoke** on Israel's **neck** and force her to engage in the extremely arduous work of plowing (**so** is better trans. "but"). Even **Judah** was included in this judgment. **Jacob** referred to the Northern Kingdom (cf. 12:2). In this figurative portrayal the nation's threshing corresponded to the service the Lord required within the covenant relationship, whereas the plowing referred to the hardship that would accompany the exile.

**10:12.** A brief call to covenant loyalty is included here. Even in the midst of a message of condemnation and judgment God held out the possibility of repentance and blessing (cf. Isa. 1:18-20). Using agricultural imagery, He urged Israel to **seek the Lord** by cultivating **righteousness** (or justice) and reaping His **unfailing love** (*ḥeseḏ*, "loyalty"). The words **showers righteousness** compare God's future gift of righteousness (or just treatment in the form of **deliverance**; cf. Hosea 2:19) to abundant **rain** (cf. 6:3).

**10:13.** The exhortation in **verse 12** actually summarizes **the appeal** made by Israel's prophets throughout her history. **But** the sinful nation had not responded properly, producing instead **wickedness** (cf. v. 15), **evil, and deception.** Rather than relying on the power of God, the nation had **depended on** her **own** military might. **The contrast** between God's desires and Israel's response heightens her guilt. So **the call to repentance** (v. 12) had a twofold function: it testified to the Lord's grace **and contributed to the development of the prophet's accusation.**

**10:14-15.** In response to Israel's pride the Lord **said** He would destroy a source of her false confidence (**fortresses**; cf. 8:14). **The severity of the** judgment is emphasized **by a comparison** with a historical incident that was apparently well known to Hosea's contemporaries. But the identity of **Shalman** and the location of **Beth Arbel** are uncertain. The most popular identifications of Shalman have been: (a) Shalmaneser III (an Assyrian ruler who campaigned against the West in the ninth century B.C.), (b) Shalmaneser V (the Assyrian ruler from 727 to 722 B.C.; but his invasion of Israel postdates Hosea's prophecy), and (c) Salamanu (a Moabite king mentioned in a tribute list of the Assyrian king Tiglath-Pileser III and a contemporary of Hosea). Beth Arbel has been identified by some (e.g., Eusebius) with modern Irbid (Arbela) in the northern Transjordan region about 18 miles southeast of the Sea of Galilee and by others with modern Arbel two miles west of the Sea of Galilee (Arbela in the apocryphal 1 Maccabees 9:2, JB). At any rate this particular **battle** was vividly remembered for its atrocities, especially the wholesale slaughter of women and **children. Bethel,** which here represents the nation as a whole, would experience a similar fate because of her great sin (cf. Hosea 4:15; Amos 7:10-17). The fall of Israel's **king** would signal the conquest of the nation by Babylon (cf. Hosea 10:3, 7; 2 Kings 17:4-6).

*d. Israel's ingratitude punished (11:1-7)*

**11:1-2.** Once again the Lord recalled Israel's early history to contrast the past with the present (cf. 9:10; 10:1). At the beginning the Lord's relationship with **Israel** had been like that of a father to a **son** (cf. Ex. 4:22-23). (On the quotation of this passage, see comments on Matt. 2:15.) The Lord displayed His love toward the nation by summoning her from **Egypt** (cf. Deut. 7:8; also cf. Hosea 12:9, 13; 13:4). However, when God subsequently called them (11:2) to covenant obedience through His prophets, the people rejected Him (cf. Jer. 7:25-26) and turned instead to false gods (cf. 2 Kings 17:13-17) including **the Baals** (cf. Hosea 2:13, 17). Hosea 11:2a is literally, "The more they [i.e., the prophets] **called** them, the more they [the Israelites] **went from** them" (NASB; cf. KJV, NIV marg.).

**11:3-4.** The Lord's goodness to Israel is further illustrated. Like a father patiently teaching a young child **to walk,** the Lord had established and sustained Israel (cf. Deut. 1:31; Isa. 1:2). He also restored (**healed**) the nation's strength after times of judgment, though she failed to acknowledge His intervention.

In Hosea 11:4 Israel is compared to a work animal (cf. 10:11). The Lord is likened to a master who gently (in **kindness** and **love**; cf. 11:1) leads his animal and removes (or perhaps repositions) its **yoke** so that it might eat with greater ease the food he kindly provides. The Lord treated Israel with compassion and love.

**11:5-7.** Astonishingly Israel had responded to the Lord's kindness with ingratitude (cf. vv. 2, 3b). Even when the Lord called her to repentance through His prophets **they** refused **to repent** (cf. v. 7). Therefore inescapable judgment would fall in the form of military defeat and exile (vv. 5a, 6). Once again **Egypt is** named as a symbol of slavery and exile (cf. 8:13; 9:3, 6).

The wording **bars of their gates** (11:6) is supported by the parallel term **cities.** Another possible translation of the Hebrew for "bars of their gates" is "braggarts" (cf. Wolff, *Hosea*, p. 192). In favor of this is the following line (v. 6c) which literally reads, "on account of **their plans."** "Plans" refers to rebellious attitudes and practices (cf. Micah 6:16).

**Put an end** literally reads "eats, devours." The same Hebrew verb (*'āḵal*) appears in Hosea 11:4 ("**feed**"). The repetition of this **word in verses 4 and 6** emphasizes the **contrast between the** Lord's past blessing and His future judgment. In the past He had given Israel food to eat. Now, ironically, He was about to send **swords** to eat Israel! For a similar wordplay **involving the** same Hebrew term, see Isaiah 1:19-20.

The Hebrew text of Hosea 11:7b is so obscure that any translation must remain tentative. The problem is evidenced by the variations in the English versions. According to the NIV rendering, God refused to hear the desperate prayer of His obstinate people. But the NASB translates the text, "Though they call them to the One on high, none at all exalts Him," with "they" referring not to Israel but to the prophets. In that view Israel rejected the prophets' calls to repentance.

3. THE LORD'S COMPASSION RENEWED (11:8-11)

As in earlier sections of this prophecy, Hosea's message of judgment concludes with an abrupt shift to a message of salvation (cf. 1:10–2:1; 2:14–3:5; 5:15–6:3). These verses should not be understood as a decision to withhold the judgment threatened uncompromisingly throughout the book. Instead, the words are a divine response to Israel's suffering and exile. The Lord would not totally abandon Israel. The effects of His wrath would be tempered by His compassion, and He would ultimately call His people back from exile.

### a. The Lord's love for Israel (11:8-9)

**11:8-9.** One of the Bible's strongest expressions of divine emotion is in these verses. As God reflected on the severe judgment that His wrath would bring on **Israel,** He suddenly burst out with four rhetorical questions. They indicate that He would never completely desert His people. **Admah** and **Zeboiim,** which were annihilated along with Sodom and Gomorrah (Deut. 29:23; cf. Gen. 10:19; 14:2, 8), were symbols of complete divine destruction.

**Changed** (lit., "overturned") is the same word (*hāpak*) used to describe the overthrow of these cities (cf. Gen. 19:25; Deut. 29:23). Wolff comments on the wordplay, "Israel will not be completely 'overturned' as the cities mentioned here; rather, there will be an 'overturning,' that is, a change, in Yahweh's heart" (*Hosea*, p. 201).

Instead of carrying out His **fierce** (lit., "burning") **anger** to the fullest, God's **compassion** would be **aroused** (lit., "grow warm"; cf. "kindled" in KJV, NASB). The burning flame of God's anger would be replaced, as it were, by the fire of His compassion. **Ephraim** would never **again** experience the judgment of **God.** This promise is reliable because it was made by **the Holy One** (cf. Hosea 11:12) Himself, who condescends to dwell with His people (**among** them) and yet continues to transcend all that is human and fallible (He is **not man**; cf. 1 Sam. 15:29).

### b. Israel's return to the Lord (11:10-11)

**11:10-11.** In the day of national restoration Israel will **follow the LORD,** who will lead the people back to **their homes.** His lion-like **roar,** often associated with judgment and destruction (cf. 5:14; 13:7; Amos 1:2; 3:8), will become a summons

to return from exile. The people will again demonstrate a healthy respect for **the LORD;** they **will come trembling** (cf. Hosea 3:5 for a similar idea), as an earlier generation did when God appeared in theophanic might at Mount Sinai (cf. Ex. 19:16, where the same Heb. word is used).

The comparison to **doves** is significant in light of Hosea 7:11, where Israel's naiveté in seeking foreign alliances is likened to that of a dove. Here the force of the simile is positive, the reference being to the swiftness with which the dove returns to its nest (cf. Ps. 55:6-8; Isa. 60:8). Again **Egypt** represents exile (see comments on Hosea 8:13). Restoration **from Assyria** is also mentioned in Zechariah 10:10-11.

### C. The Lord's case against Israel concluded (11:12–14:9)

A hortatory and didactic tone characterizes the conclusion to Hosea's prophecy. As in earlier sections Hosea moves from judgment (11:12–13:16) to salvation (chap. 14).

#### 1. A CONCLUDING INDICTMENT (11:12–13:16)

Once more Israel's guilt is established and her punishment predicted.

### a. The nation's unfaithfulness (11:12–12:2)

These verses introduce the final section with a formal accusation (11:12–12:2a) and an announcement of judgment (12:2b).

**11:12.** The entire nation (**Judah** included) had broken her covenant with the Lord. **Lies** and **deceit** refer to hypocrisy and unfaithfulness. The latter (*mirmâh*; cf. comments on 12:7) is especially appropriate in light of the following comparison with the patriarch Jacob (cf. 12:3-4, 12). The same term was used to describe Jacob's deception in stealing Esau's blessing (cf. Gen. 27:35).

Ironically the nation was unfaithful to **the faithful Holy One,** who had always demonstrated fidelity to His covenant promises (cf. Hosea 12:9; 13:4-6). **Is unruly** (*rûd*) means to stray or roam restlessly, an apt picture of Israel's wandering off from God to Baal and to foreign nations for help. "Holy One" is plural here, emphasizing the magnitude of this divine characteristic. In this context

God's holiness refers primarily to His transcendence over fallible people (cf. 11:9).

**12:1-2.** Israel's unfaithfulness found expression in social injustice (she **multiplies lies and violence;** cf. 4:2; 7:1) and in foreign alliances with **Assyria** and **Egypt** (cf. 5:13; 7:8, 11; 8:8-9; 2 Kings 17:3-4). **Olive oil** was either used in the covenant-making ceremony or given as a token of allegiance. All this activity was futile and self-destructive, as the references to feeding on and pursuing **the wind** suggest (cf. Hosea 8:7; 13:15). **The LORD** had **a charge** (*rîb;* cf. 4:1; also see comments on 2:2) **against Judah** and was about to **punish** His people for their evil **ways.**

### b. A lesson from history (12:3-6)

Before further developing the themes of guilt and judgment (cf. 12:9–13:16), Hosea reminded the nation of her need to repent (12:5-6). In doing so he drew a lesson from the life of Jacob (vv. 3-4).

**12:3-4.** Jacob's birth gave a hint of the kind of person he would be. His grasping Esau's **heel** (cf. Gen. 25:26) foreshadowed his deception of his brother in stealing his birthright and blessing (cf. Gen. 27:35-36). However, Jacob eventually came to a turning point. When he faced the prospect of death at Esau's hand on his return to the land of Canaan he wrestled **with God,** refusing to let go till he received a blessing (Gen. 32:22-32). Later **at Bethel,** the site of his dream years before (cf. Gen. 28:10-22), God appeared to Jacob again. God changed his name to Israel, blessed him, and renewed His covenant promise (cf. Gen. 35:1-14).

**12:5-6.** Like Jacob, the deceitful nation (cf. 11:12) needed to **return** (12:6) **to** her covenant Ruler, **the LORD God Almighty** with tears and prayers (cf. v. 4). Genuine repentance would involve a commitment to **love** (*ḥeseḏ*) **and justice,** as well as a dependence on the Lord (**wait for your God always;** cf. Ps. 27:14), rather than on herself.

### c. The nation's pride (12:7-14)

**12:7-8.** Israel's repentance (v. 6) would necessitate a complete reversal in her dealings and attitudes. The nation was permeated by economic dishonesty

(*mirmâh;* cf. 11:12 for the same word), oppression (**defraud**), pride (**Ephraim boasts**), and insensitivity to her sin, thinking that her **wealth** would hide her **sin.** The Old Testament frequently spoke against using **scales** that were rigged to weigh out less merchandise than the buyer thought he was getting (cf. Lev. 19:36; Deut. 25:13-16; Prov. 11:1; 16:11; 20:10, 23; Amos 8:5; Micah 6:11).

**12:9.** The LORD, however, would not overlook such blatant disobedience and ingratitude. As their **God,** He had guided the nation since her days in **Egypt,** leading her through the wilderness to the Promised Land. As part of His coming judgment He would bring Israel into the wilderness **again,** making her **live in tents.** The wilderness experience, which the people commemorated in the Feast of Tabernacles (cf. Lev. 23:33-43), would be realized once more in the Exile.

**12:10-11.** Though the Lord had communicated His will to Israel through **the prophets,** the people had repudiated those messages (cf. 9:7 and comments on 11:2). The wickedness and hypocrisy manifested in **Gilead** (cf. 6:8) and **Gilgal** (cf. 4:15; 9:15) epitomized that of the nation. In the coming invasion the **altars** located there would be reduced to **piles of stones** (*gallîm;* cf. 10:8, "the high places . . . will be destroyed"). The use of this Hebrew word, which is a play on the name Gilgal facilitated by the repetition of the "g" and "l" sounds, is another example of Hosea's poetic techniques. Gilgal would become *gallîm.*

**12:12-13.** The Lord's past goodness is again recalled. Going back to Jacob's experience once more (cf. vv. 3-4), Hosea reminded the people of their humble beginnings. Their famous ancestor **was** once a refugee who had to tend **sheep in** order to acquire **a wife** (cf. Deut. 26:5). Later Jacob's descendants served **the** Egyptians till God delivered them **from Egypt** (cf. Hosea 11:1; 12:9; 13:4) and protected them through His **Prophet** Moses.

**12:14.** However, Israel had **provoked** the Lord **to anger** with her sin. Hosea probably was alluding here to idolatry because *kā'as,* the verb rendered "provoked to anger," is frequently used in reference to idols (cf., e.g., Deut. 4:25; 9:18; 31:29; 32:16, 21; Jud. 2:12; 1 Kings 14:9, 15). In response to this the LORD would not extend forgiveness (He would **leave upon** the nation its **guilt**; cf. Hosea 10:2; 13:12, 16); He would **repay** her for her evil.

### d. Impending doom (chap. 13)

**13:1-3.** Ephraim's prominent (**exalted**) place among the tribes of Israel was well known (cf. Gen. 48:13-20). Jeroboam I, who had led the Northern Kingdom's secession, was an Ephraimite (1 Kings 11:26; 12:25). However, this prominent tribe had also taken the lead in **Baal worship** and was as good as dead. As the Ephraimites (and the other Israelites they represent here) multiplied their **idols** and **images,** they added to their guilt. They debased themselves even further by kissing **the calf-idols** (cf. 1 Kings 19:18; also cf. "calf-idol" in Hosea 8:4-5; 10:5) in conjunction with their many sacrificial rites.

**They offer human sacrifice** literally reads, "sacrificers of men kiss calves." The Bible speaks of child sacrifice in conjunction with worship of the god Molech (cf. Lev. 18:21; 20:2-5; 2 Kings 23:10), which was apparently sometimes combined with Baal worship (cf. Jer. 32:35). However, the word used here, "men" (*'ādām*), does not suggest child sacrifice. A more likely interpretation is that "sacrificers of men" is idiomatic, meaning "sacrificers among men" or "men who sacrifice" (cf. KJV, NASB). One should compare this with the following expressions, "wild donkey of a man" (Gen. 16:12; i.e., a man who is like a wild donkey in character), "the poor of men" (Isa. 29:19, KJV; i.e., men who are poor), and "leaders (lit., princes) of men" (Micah 5:5; perhaps meaning men who are princes). In this case the prophet (Hosea 13:2) was emphasizing the absurdity of *men* kissing images of calves.

The judgment of God would make these idolaters quickly vanish (v. 3). Each of the four similes (**mist . . . dew**; cf. 6:4, **chaff . . smoke**) emphasizes the extremely transitory condition of the idolaters.

**13:4-9.** Once more **the LORD** reminded Israel of His gracious deeds at the beginning of their history (cf. 12:9a, 10, 12-13). He led them from **Egypt** (cf. 11:1; 12:9, 13), **cared for** (lit., "knew") them **in** the wilderness (13:5) and allowed them to feed in the Promised Land (v. 6).

**When I fed them** is literally, "when they pastured." It describes sheep or cattle grazing peacefully. In return for such blessings they should have acknowledged the Lord as their **God** and **Savior** (v. 4). Instead **they became proud** and **forgot** Him (v. 6; cf. comments on 2:13). **Like a** vicious and powerful wild beast (**lion . . . leopard,** or **bear**) the Lord would **attack** His people (still viewed here as a helpless flock or herd, 13:7-8; cf. 5:14). Ironically the **Helper** of **Israel** would become her Destroyer because she was **against** Him (13:9).

**13:10-11.** When the Lord would come to destroy (v. 9) no one would be able to **save** the people, not even the political leaders they had demanded from the Lord (v. 10; cf. 10:3, 7, 15). Hosea 13:11a (**in My anger I gave you a king**) probably refers to the Northern tribes' part in crowning Saul (1 Sam. 8:6-9; 12:12), as well as their secession under Jeroboam I (1 Kings 12:16). Hosea 13:11b refers to the cessation of Israel's kingship with Hoshea (2 Kings 17:1-6).

**13:12.** God had not overlooked Israel's **guilt** (cf. 10:2; 12:14; 13:16). Ephraim's sinful deeds were compared to a document which is bound up (NASB; cf. NIV's **stored up**) and a treasure which is stored up (NASB; cf. NIV's **kept on record**). Through both figures Israel's **sins** were pictured as something guarded carefully till the day of retribution when they would be brought forth as testimony against the nation.

**13:13.** Any basis for hope had all but disappeared. Israel had not responded to God's call for repentance during the period of grace He had extended. The procrastinating nation was compared to a baby which **does not come** out of its mother's **womb** despite her strenuous efforts in labor. Such a delay will **result** in death for both mother and child. Since the baby seemingly does not observe the proper **time** for his birth, he is referred to, figuratively, as **without wisdom** (cf. Ecc. 8:5).

**13:14.** Traditionally verse 14a has been interpreted as an expression of hope and a promise of salvation (NASB, NIV). However, this view is contextually problematic. Though Hosea's prophecy is characterized by abrupt changes in tone, such a shift appears to be premature here (the shift in this section appears to come in 14:1) and would leave 13:14a awkwardly connected with what follows (cf. v. 14b, **I will have no compassion**). The first two statements may be translated better as rhetorical questions implying a negative answer: "Shall I **ransom them from the power of** sheol? Shall I **redeem them from death?**" (RSV)

The next two questions (**Where, O death, are your plagues? Where, O grave, is your destruction?**) would then be appeals for death to unleash its "plagues" and "destruction" against Ephraim (cf. vv. 14b-16), not a triumphant cry of victory over death. Of course the Apostle Paul, writing under the inspiration of the Holy Spirit, applied the language of this text in the latter sense (cf. 1 Cor. 15:55-56). However, in that context Paul was drawing on the language of Scripture as traditionally understood (cf. the LXX); he was not offering a textual and exegetical analysis of Hosea 13:14.

**13:15-16.** With the Lord's compassion removed (v. 14; cf. 1:6), Israel's prosperity (**he thrives**) would come to an end. The LORD would **come** like a hot **east wind** which dries up everything in its path. The reality behind the figure is the Assyrian invasion, as the references to plundering and military atrocities make clear. Thus 13:15-16 correspond to the plagues and destruction of death mentioned in verse 14. The language is that of covenant curse (cf. Lev. 26:25; Deut. 28:21; 32:24-25; Amos 4:10). Again destruction would come, God said, because Israel had **rebelled against** Him (cf. Hosea 7:13; 8:1).

**2. A CONCLUDING EXHORTATION (CHAP. 14)**

**a. An appeal for repentance (14:1-3)**

**14:1-3.** Hosea's prophecy ends on a positive note with an exhortation to repentance (**Return . . . to the LORD**). Though this final appeal would surely be rejected by His arrogant and stubborn nation (cf. 10:12-15), it would instill hope in the hearts of a righteous remnant and provide the repentant generation of the future with a model to follow in returning to the Lord (cf. 3:5; 5:15b–6:3). True repentance would involve an acknowledgment of sin (**Say to Him, Forgive all our sins**) and a desire to praise the Lord (**that we may offer the fruit of our lips**), Israel's only Savior, God, and Helper

(contrast 5:13; 7:11; 8:4-5, 9; 13:2). No longer will **Israel** trust in **Assyria** or other nations, or will she call her hand-**made** idols **our gods.**

**b. A promise of restoration (14:4-8)**

**14:4-6.** In the day of Israel's repentance the Lord will turn from His **anger** and demonstrate His **love** by healing her (cf. 6:1). At that time the Lord's blessing will return **to Israel. Like . . . dew** it will cause the nation to **blossom like a lily** which was renowned for its beauty (cf. Song 2:2). This is a complete reversal of the imagery used in Hosea 13:15. Israel in her prosperity is also compared to **a cedar of Lebanon,** whose deep **roots,** luxuriant growth, and aromatic smell (cf. Song 4:11) were well known; and to **an olive tree,** widely recognized for its luxuriance (cf. Ps. 52:8; Jer. 11:16).

**14:7.** This verse is better translated: "Those who live in His shadow will again raise **grain,** and they **will blossom like** the vine. His** renown **will be like the wine** of Lebanon" (NASB). **His shade** (or shadow) could refer to the Lord's protection (cf. v. 8, where He is compared to a "pine tree"; also cf. Isa. 4:6). However, as Keil notes, it is more likely that "Israel is itself the tree beneath whose shade the members of the nation flourish with freshness and vigor" (C.F. Keil, "Minor Prophets," in *Commentary on the Old Testament in Ten Volumes,* 10:166). This seems more consistent with the imagery in Hosea 14:5-6, which compares Israel to trees. The picture of Israelites again growing grain points to the return of covenantal blessing (cf. Deut. 28:4, 8, 11; 30:9; Hosea 2:21-23; Amos 9:13-15). Once again Israel will be "like a" fruitful "vine" (cf. Hosea 10:1) which produces the best "wine."

**14:8.** The first statement is best translated, "**Ephraim** shall say, **What have I to do** any more **with idols?**" (KJV) The contrast with Ephraim's earlier attitude is stark (cf. 2:8; 4:17; 8:4-6; 13:2). The Lord speaks in the latter half of 14:8 (**I will answer** and **I am like**), proclaiming His concern for Israel. The words **care for** translate the same Hebrew word (*šûr*) as "lurk" in 13:7. The same God who stealthily watched Israel like a leopard ready to pounce on its prey will become the One who carefully watches over His people to protect them! Comparing Himself to **a green pine tree,** the Lord also asserted that He is the nation's source of prosperity: **your fruitfulness comes from Me.**

### c. A word of wisdom (14:9)

**14:9.** The book ends with a word on wisdom. One who **is wise** and **discerning** will learn a threefold lesson from Hosea's message. **The ways of the LORD** (i.e., His covenantal demands) **are right. The righteous walk in** (i.e., obey; cf. Deut. 8:6; 10:12; 11:22; 28:9; Jud. 2:17) **them** and experience the blessings of loyalty. **The rebellious** (cf. Hosea 7:13; 8:1; 13:16) **stumble** over (not **in**) **them** in the sense that destruction (stumbling) is the direct result of disobedience. The broken commandments become the ultimate reason for their downfall (cf. 5:5; 14:1). May all who read Hosea's words walk, not stumble!

# BIBLIOGRAPHY

Andersen, Francis I., and Freedman, David Noel. *Hosea: A New Translation, Introduction and Commentary.* The Anchor Bible. Garden City, N.Y.: Doubleday & Co., 1980.

Brueggemann, Walter. *Tradition for Crisis: A Study in Hosea.* Richmond, Va.: John Knox Press, 1968.

Cohen, Gary G., and Vandermey, H. Ronald. *Hosea/Amos.* Everyman's Bible Commentary. Chicago: Moody Press, 1981.

Feinberg, Charles L. *The Minor Prophets.* Chicago: Moody Press, 1976.

Harper, William Rainey. *A Critical and Exegetical Commentary on Amos and Hosea.* The International Critical Commentary. Edinburgh: T. & T. Clark, 1905.

Keil, C.F. "Minor Prophets." In *Commentary on the Old Testament in Ten Volumes.* Vol. 10. Reprint (25 vols. in 10). Grand Rapids: Wm. B. Eerdmans Publishing Co., 1982.

Kidner, Derek. *Love to the Loveless: The Message of Hosea.* The Bible Speaks Today. Downers Grove, Ill.: InterVarsity Press, 1981.

Mays, James Luther. *Hosea: A Commentary.* The Old Testament Library. Philadelphia: Westminster Press, 1969.

Pusey, E.B. *The Minor Prophets: A Commentary Explanatory and Practical.* 2 vols. Reprint. Grand Rapids: Baker Book House, 1950.

Riggs, Jack R. *Hosea's Heartbreak.* Neptune, N.J.: Loizeaux Brothers, 1983.

Tatford, Frederick A. *The Minor Prophets.* Vol. 1. Reprint (3 vols.). Minneapolis: Klock & Klock Christian Publishers, 1982.

Wolff, Hans Walter. *Hosea.* Translated by Gary Stansell. Philadelphia: Fortress Press, 1974.

# JOEL

## Robert B. Chisholm, Jr.

## INTRODUCTION

**Authorship and Date.** This book is attributed to Joel son of Pethuel (1:1). Unlike most other prophetic books, no information is given in the opening verse that establishes the time limits of his prophetic ministry. Thus one is forced to rely on internal evidence in determining a date of authorship.

Scholars have proposed various dates, ranging from the ninth to the second centuries B.C. Three views are surveyed here.

*1. An early preexilic date.* Those who support an early date (ninth century B.C.) for Joel point to its position in the Hebrew Old Testament (between Hosea and Amos) and its references to Tyre, Sidon, Philistia, Egypt, and Edom as enemies (Joel 3:4, 19). Hobart Freeman writes, "The very naming of these particular nations is strong evidence for a preexilic date for the book, inasmuch as they were the early preexilic enemies of Judah, not the later nations of Assyria, Babylonia, and Persia" (*An Introduction to the Old Testament Prophets.* Chicago: Moody Press, 1968, p. 148; see also Gleason L. Archer, Jr., *A Survey of Old Testament Introduction.* Chicago: Moody Press, 1974, p. 305).

Both of these arguments lack weight. The canonical position of the book is inconclusive, especially when one notes that the Septuagint places it differently in the canon. Even the Old Testament prophets in the Babylonian period delivered oracles against the nations mentioned (cf. Jer. 46–47; 49:7-22; Ezek. 27–30; Zeph. 2:4-7). One who contends for a late preexilic date could argue that Joel 2 pictures the Babylonians vividly enough to make formal identification unnecessary to a contemporary audience well aware of their ominous presence on the horizon.

Some seek to support an early date for Joel by appealing to the type of government reflected in the prophecy (elders, 1:2; 2:16; and priests ruling, 1:9, 13; 2:17, in view of Joash's crowning at age seven) and to verbal parallels in other prophetic books (Archer, *A Survey of Old Testament Introduction*, pp. 304-5). The inconclusive nature of these arguments is apparent as they are also used by proponents of a late date.

Several details of the text (cf. esp. 3:2, 6) seem to militate against an early date (in Joash's reign) for the prophecy (cf. S.R. Driver, *The Books of Joel and Amos*, pp. 14-15).

*2. A late preexilic date.* The view that the book comes from the late preexilic period has much to commend it. If one dates the prophecy between 597 and 587 B.C. (with Wilhelm Rudolph, *Joel-Amos-Obadja-Jona.* Gütersloh: Gütersloher Verlagshaus Gerd Mohn, 1971, pp. 24-8), Joel 3:2b (with its reference to scattering God's people and dividing the land) would refer to the Babylonian invasion of 597 B.C. when 10,000 of Judah's finest men were deported (cf. 2 Kings 24:10-16). This would also account for Joel's references to the temple (Joel 1:9, 13; 2:17), for it was not destroyed until 586 B.C. (cf. 2 Kings 25:9). At that same time such a dating would mean that Joel 1:15 and 2:1-11 anticipated the final destruction of Jerusalem (which indeed came in 586 B.C.; cf. 2 Kings 25:1-21).

Joel's prophecy would then fit nicely with several other passages which relate the "day of the LORD" (or "day of the LORD's wrath" or "day of the LORD's anger") to that event (cf. Lam. 1:12; 2:1, 21-22; Ezek. 7:19; 13:5; Zeph. 2:2-3). Joel's description (Joel 2:1-11) would also coincide with Jeremiah's description of the Babylonians (cf. Jer. 5:17). The reference in Joel 3:6 to slave trade between the Phoenicians and Greeks (or Ionians) harmonizes well with the late preexilic period. Ezekiel also referred to this economic arrangement (Ezek. 27:13). Arvid S. Kapelrud shows that Ionian trade flourished in the seventh and early sixth centuries B.C. (*Joel Studies,* pp. 154-8).

Despite the attractiveness of this view, problems arise in relation to Joel 2:18-19. This passage seems to record God's mercy to Joel's generation, implying they truly repented (see comments on those verses). If so, such a sequence of events is difficult to harmonize with the historical record of Judah's final days. Second Kings 23:26-27 indicates that even Josiah's revival did not cause the Lord to relent.

*3. A postexilic date.* Four arguments are used to suggest a postexilic date:

(1) Joel 3:1-2, 17 refer, it is argued, to the destruction of Jerusalem and the Babylonian Exile. In this case the references to the temple in 1:9, 13; 2:17 apply to the second temple, completed by the returning exiles in 515 B.C.

(2) The "elders" (cf. 1:2; 2:16), rather than the king, appear as the leaders of the community. This is more consistent with the postexilic period (cf. Ezra 10:14).

(3) Joel quotes other prophets, including Ezekiel (cf. Joel 2:3 with Ezek. 36:35; Joel 2:10 with Ezek. 32:7; Joel 2:27-28 with Ezek. 39:28-29).

(4) The reference to Greek slave trade (Joel 3:6) reflects the postexilic period.

Against these arguments the following responses may be made:

(1) Joel 3:1-2, 17 could refer to the deportation of 597 B.C., not that of 586 B.C. (but as noted previously under "2. A late preexilic date," this view poses problems). Some attempt to explain the language of Joel 3:1-2, 17 in light of the events recorded in 2 Chronicles 21:16-17 (Archer, *A Survey of Old Testament Introduction,* p. 305). However, the captivity of the royal sons and wives recorded there hardly satisfies the language of Joel 3:2.

(2) Though the omission of any reference to the monarchy is curious, it can carry little weight for it is an argument from silence. Also elders were prominent in Judean society *before* the Exile (2 Kings 23:1; Jer. 26:17; Lam. 5:12, 14; cf. Kapelrud, *Joel Studies,* pp. 187-9).

(3) In the case of literary parallels

with other prophetic passages, it is often difficult to determine in any given case who quoted from whom.

(4) Kapelrud has shown, as noted earlier, that Ionian slave trade flourished in the seventh century B.C.

In conclusion, it is impossible to be dogmatic about the date of the writing of Joel. The language of Joel 3:2b seems to favor a postexilic date. This verse suggests that nations in the future will be judged for having continued the policies of ancient Babylon in scattering the Israelites and dividing their land. Such a view is consistent with (but not proved by) several other observations (such as the reference to Phoenician-Ionian slave trade, the form of government implied in the book, and the literary parallels with other prophets). If one accepts a postexilic date, the references to the temple necessitate a date some time after 516 B.C. However, all this must remain tentative. Understandably, conservative scholars differ on the date of Joel.

## Major Interpretive Problems

*1. The nature of the army in 2:1-11.* Some contend that the locust plague in Joel 1, or an even more severe wave of locusts, is described in 2:1-11. Several factors support this position:

(1) Literary parallels exist between chapters 1 and 2 (cf. 2:2, 11 with 1:6; and 2:3 with 1:19).

(2) Several details in 2:1-11 suggest that locusts are in view—the great numerical size of the invader (2:2, 5), the destruction of the land (2:3), the leaping and scaling ability of the invaders (2:5, 7), and the darkening of the sky (2:10).

(3) A literary association apparently exists between 2:11 ("His army") and 2:25 ("My great army," which is equated with the locusts).

(4) The "army" is compared to a literal army in 2:4-5, 7. The words "appearance of horses," "like cavalry," "like . . . chariots," "like a mighty army," "like warriors," and "like soldiers" seemingly imply that an actual army cannot be in view since an army is employed as the object of comparison (cf. Leslie C. Allen, *The Books of Joel, Obadiah, Jonah and Micah,* p. 29; and Driver, *The Books of Joel and Amos,* p. 28).

A more likely interpretation is that a literal foreign army is envisioned. The account is patterned after that of chapter 1, the army being described in locust-like terms in many respects (cf. Hans W. Wolff, *Joel and Amos*, p. 42). In this way the close relationship and continuity between the plague of chapter 1 and the army of chapter 2 is emphasized. Both were instruments of the Lord's judgment—one past, the other future. Locusts had come—more "locusts" were coming!

Several observations may be made in support of this position.

(1) The locust plague of chapter 1 was past; the invasion of 2:1-11 was still future from Joel's vantage point (cf. also 1:15). Thus the two accounts cannot deal with the same event (Wolff, *Joel and Amos*, pp. 6-7, 42). Joel 2:25, where the locusts are called the Lord's "great army," refers to the judgment in chapter 1. Its effects could be reversed but not averted. Joel 2:11 refers to a judgment which was yet future and thus *could* be averted (cf. 2:20). So 2:25 cannot be used to interpret 2:11, despite the aforementioned literary parallel. The literary association does not equate the two forces; it merely suggests their close relationship. The locusts were an "army" *sent* by the Lord (2:25); the "northern army" (2:20) would be *led* by Him (2:11).

(2) The army in 2:1-11 is called in 2:20 "the northern army" (lit., "the northerner"). Locusts usually attack Palestine from the south or southeast, not the north (though invasions from the north or northeast are not unknown; cf. Allen, *The Books of Joel, Obadiah, Jonah and Micah*, p. 88). The designation "northerner" more likely refers to a literal foreign army, since historical or eschatological armies are often described as invading Palestine from that direction (including Assyria, Isa. 14:25, 31; Babylon, Jer. 6:1, 22; 15:12; Ezek. 26:7; and Gog, Ezek. 38:15).

(3) The use of locust imagery in the description of the army in Joel 2 has parallels in the ancient Near East (cf. John A. Thompson, "Joel's Locusts in the Light of Near Eastern Parallels," *Journal of Near Eastern Studies* 14. 1955:52-5).

(4) The Deuteronomic curses closely associate locusts (Deut. 28:38-42) with invading armies (Deut. 28:25, 32-33, 36-37, 49-52). This association was natural since both devoured agricultural produce

(Deut. 28:33, 51; Isa. 1:7; Jer. 5:17). This accounts for the similarity between Joel 1:19 and 2:3. An Assyrian inscription from the time of Sargon II (722–705 B.C.) vividly illustrates the effects of an invading army on a land: "The city of Aniashtania . . . together with 17 cities of its neighborhood, I [Sargon] destroyed, I leveled to the ground; the large timbers of their roots I set on fire, their crops [and] their stubble I burned, their filled-up granaries I opened and let my army devour the unmeasured grain. Like swarming locusts I turned the beasts of my camps into its meadows, and they tore up the vegetation on which it [the city] depended; they devastated its plain" (D.D. Luckenbill, *Ancient Records of Assyria and Babylonia*. 2 vols. Chicago: University of Chicago Press, 1926–1927, 2:85).

The comparisons with an army (in 2:4-5, 7) do not necessarily mean that a literal army is precluded. Two explanations for the similes are possible. One is that an army, if portrayed under the figure of locusts, could be compared to an army, the simile in this case hinting at the reality behind the figure. In this regard Freeman states that "the prophet, with the recent plague of chapter 1 as the background, uses *that* calamity as the basis of his imagery" (*An Introduction to the Old Testament Prophets*, p. 152). E.W. Bullinger gives another explanation. He suggests that a simile sometimes implies "not merely a resemblance but the actual thing itself" (*Figures of Speech Used in the Bible*. Grand Rapids: Baker Book House, 1968, pp. 728-9). In such cases the Hebrew preposition $k^e$, "like, as," indicates that a specific object is in every respect like another object, meaning that the former partakes of the latter's nature. For example, Isaiah 1:7b states that Judah was "laid waste *as* when overthrown by strangers" (i.e., it was indeed overthrown by strangers). Similarly, Isaiah 1:8b notes that Jerusalem was "*like* a city under siege" (i.e., it *was* under siege, probably by Sennacherib). (However, $k^e$ in Isa. 1:8-9 has its usual force: "like a shelter" and "like a hut," v. 8; and "like Sodom," v. 9.) Another example of the "identity" use of this preposition is in Joel 1:15, which states that "the day of the LORD . . . will come *like* a destruction from the Almighty" (i.e., it will indeed involve destruction brought about by God).

To summarize, the army in 2:1-11 is probably a literal northern army, described in locust-like terms to emphasize that it, like the locusts, was an instrument of the Lord which represented the culmination of the judgment initiated through the locust invasion.

2. *"The day of the LORD" in Joel.* Though the description of "the day of the LORD" was certainly influenced by traditions relating to the Lord's intervention in Israel's early wars (cf. Gerhard von Rad, "The Origin of the Concept of the Day of Yahweh," *Journal of Semitic Studies* 4. 1959:97-108), the expression itself is ultimately derived from the idea, prevalent in the ancient Near East, that a mighty warrior-king could consummate an entire military campaign in a single day (cf. Douglas Stuart, "The Sovereign's Day of Conquest," *Bulletin of the American Schools of Oriental Research* 220/21. December 1975, February 1976:159-64). So generally speaking, "the day of the LORD" is an idiom used to emphasize the swift and decisive nature of the Lord's victory over His enemies on any given occasion.

In the Old Testament "the day of the LORD" may refer to either a particular historical event or an eschatological battle which will culminate the present age. The following elements are associated with it:

(1) "The day of the LORD" sometimes involves the judgment of God's people, including the Northern Kingdom (at the hands of the Assyrians; cf. Amos 5:18, 20) and Judah (at the hands of the Babylonians; cf. Lam. 1:12; 2:1, 21-22; Ezek. 7:19; 13:5; Zeph. 2:2-3). Sometimes this judgment appears in the context of a more universal judgment on all nations (cf. Isa. 2:12; Zeph. 1:18).

(2) "The day of the LORD" often involves the judgment of foreign nations, including Babylon (at the hands of the Medes; cf. Isa. 13:6, 9), Egypt (at the hands of the Babylonians; cf. Jer. 46:10; Ezek. 30:3), Edom (cf. Isa. 34:8-9), and the eschatological northern coalition headed by Gog (Ezek. 39:8).

(3) "The day of the LORD" will bring purification and restoration for Israel (cf. Isa. 61:2; Mal. 4:5), but also intense suffering (Zech. 14:1-3).

"The day of the LORD," then, encompasses several specific past "days" or events (cf. A.J. Everson, "The Days of Yahweh," *Journal of Biblical Literature* 93. 1974:329-37). These include the destruction of the Northern Kingdom, the Babylonian Exile, Babylon's conquest of Egypt, and the fall of Babylon. These examples of the Lord's intervention in history prefigure that final time period when He will annihilate His enemies on a more universal scale and restore Israel (for a thorough development of this relationship between history and eschatology, see Isa. 13–27).

In Joel all three of the elements just listed appear in relationship to "the day of the LORD." Israel's judgment is threatened in Joel 1:15 and 2:1-11, Israel's deliverance is foreseen in 2:28-32, and universal judgment on the nations is depicted in chapter 3. Joel seemed to telescope events in his treatment of the Lord's "day." As he reported how his generation barely escaped "the day of the LORD," he envisioned Israel's ultimate deliverance from her enemies at the end of the age.

In discussing the day of the Lord in the end times, Joel focused on one major aspect of that "day," namely, the single event when the Lord will intervene in history to destroy His enemies and deliver His people Israel.

The day of the Lord, however, as other Scriptures show, will include other events:

(1) Before Israel's enemies will be destroyed they will plunder and devastate Israel (Zech. 14:1-2). This will be a time of anguish for Israel (Zeph. 1:7-18; cf. Dan. 12:1). Jesus called this time period (the Great Tribulation) a time of "great distress" (Matt. 24:21) for the nation.

(2) After the Lord will destroy His enemies (at Messiah's return) the day of the Lord will include a time of blessing for Israel (cf. Obad. 15 with Obad. 21), known as the Millennium.

(3) Then after the Millennium the day of the Lord will also include the destruction of the present heavens and earth and the making of new heavens and a new earth (2 Peter 3:10, 12-13).

Therefore, according to Scripture passages besides those in Joel, "the day of the LORD" will be a lengthy time period including both judgment and blessing. It will begin soon after the Rapture and will include the seven-year Tribulation, the return of the Messiah, the Millennium, and the making of the new heavens and new earth. Obviously this contradicts the view of some that at the end of the Great Tribulation the Rapture will occur and the day of the Lord will then begin (see comments on 1 Thes. 5:2; 2 Thes. 2:1-12 and the "Outline of End-Time Events Predicted in the Bible," between Ezek. and Dan.).

# OUTLINE

# COMMENTARY

## I. Introduction (1:1)

**1:1.** As stated in the *Introduction*, the only fact given about **Joel** is that he was a **son of Pethuel.** The prophet indicated that his message was God's **Word,** but did not date his prophecy in 1:1 in the reign of any king of Judah or Israel (cf. comments under "Authorship and Date" in the *Introduction*).

## II. The Locust Plague (1:2-20)

The opening chapter describes the effects of a severe locust plague which had swept over the land, destroying the agricultural produce on which both man and beast so heavily depended for survival. This disaster signaled an even worse calamity to come—the destructive day of the Lord.

### A. An opening appeal (1:2-4)

**1:2-3.** The prophet opened his message with an appeal to **all who** were living **in the land,** headed by the **elders,** to consider the uniqueness and significance of the disaster which had come on them. The elders were civil leaders who played a prominent part in the governmental and judicial systems (cf. 1 Sam. 30:26-31; 2 Sam. 19:11-15; 2 Kings 23:1; Prov. 31:23; Jer. 26:17; Lam. 5:12, 14).

The rhetorical question in Joel 1:2b anticipates an emphatic negative response. Nothing in the experience of Joel's generation or that of their ancestors was able to match the magnitude of this recent locust plague. The unique event would be spoken of throughout coming generations (**your children . . . their children,** and **the next generation**).

**1:4.** The event in view was a massive invasion by **locusts** which completely destroyed the land's vegetation. Four terms are used for locusts here (**locust swarm,** *gāzām;* **great locusts,** *'arbeh;* **young locusts,** *yeleq;* and **other locusts,** *ḥāsîl*). Some have proposed that the four terms correspond to the locust's phases of development from the pupa to full-grown stages (e.g., Thompson, "Joel's Locusts in the Light of the Near Eastern Parallels," pp. 52-5). However, several problems attend this position (see Wolff, *Joel and Amos,* pp. 27-8). More likely, the terms are synonymous, used for variety's sake and to emphasize the successive "waves" of locusts in the invasion.

The threefold reference to the leftovers of one wave of locusts being devoured by the next emphasizes the thorough nature of the destruction. (For records of eyewitness accounts of locust plagues, see Driver, *The Books of Joel and Amos,* pp. 40, 89-93; George Adam Smith, *The Book of the Twelve Prophets,* 2:391-5, and John D. Whiting, "Jerusalem's Locust Plague," *National Geographic Magazine* 28. December 1915, pp. 511-50.)

### B. A call to mourn (1:5-13)

Utilizing the form of a call to mourning, the prophet elaborated on the horrifying details and effects of the locust plague. This section contains four units (vv. 5-7, 8-10, 11-12, 13), each of which includes a call proper (vv. 5a, 8, 11a, 13a) followed by the reasons for sorrow (vv. 5b-7, 9-10, 11b-12, 13b). The personified land (or city?) as well as some of the groups most severely affected by the plague (drunkards, farmers, priests) were addressed.

1. DRUNKARDS SHOULD MOURN (1:5-7)

**1:5-7.** **Drunkards** were told to **weep** and **wail because** no **wine** would be available due to the destruction of the vineyards (v. 5; cf. vv. 7, 10, 12). Like a mighty **nation** an innumerable (**without number**) swarm of locusts had **invaded** the prophet's **land.** Their ability to devour was like that of **a lion,** which can rip and tear almost anything with its powerful **teeth** (likened to **fangs**). The locusts had destroyed the **vines** and **stripped** even the **bark** from the **fig trees. . . . leaving their branches white.** For photographs showing these effects of such an invasion, see *The Zondervan Pictorial Bible Dictionary.* Grand Rapids: Zondervan Publishing House, 1963, pp. 377, 435.

2. THE LAND SHOULD MOURN (1:8-10)

**1:8.** The grammatical form of **mourn** in verse 8 (fem. sing.) indicates that the

addressee is neither the drunkards in verse 5 nor the farmers in verse 11 (both of which are addressed with masc. pl. forms). The land itself (cf. 2:18) or Jerusalem (called Zion in 2:1, 15, 23, 32) is probably addressed here, being personified as **a virgin** or young woman (cf. 2 Kings 19:21, "the virgin Daughter of Zion," and Lam. 1:15, "The virgin Daughter of Judah"). She was told to mourn bitterly, as a bride or bride-to-be would mourn over the unexpected death of the man to whom she was betrothed or married.

There is some debate over the meaning of the term translated "virgin" (*bᵉṯûlâh*). If it refers to an actual virgin, then a betrothed woman, whose marriage had not been consummated, is in view. In this case the man could be called **the husband of her youth** because of the legally binding nature of betrothal. (Deut. 22:23-24 demonstrates that a betrothed woman could be referred to as both a "virgin" and a "wife.") However, possibly the word simply refers to a young woman (NIV marg.) regardless of her sexual status. If so, newlyweds are in view in Joel 1:8.

**Sackcloth** (cf. v. 13), a coarse, dark cloth, was worn in mourning rites as an outward expression of sorrow (cf. Gen. 37:34; 1 Kings 21:27; Neh. 9:1; Es. 4:1-4; Ps. 69:10-11; Isa. 22:12; 32:11; 37:1-2; Lam. 2:10; Dan. 9:3; Jonah 3:8).

**1:9-10.** The primary reason for mourning in this case was the plague's negative effect on the formal worship system (cf. v. 13). The destruction of the crops (**grain,** grapes, and olive **oil,** v. 10; cf. Hosea 2:22) had left the **priests** who served in **the house of the LORD** without the essentials for the daily **grain offerings** (*minḥâh*), which included flour and oil (cf. Num. 28:5), **and drink offerings** (*nesek*), which included **wine** (cf. Ex. 29:40; Num. 28:7).

3. FARMERS SHOULD MOURN (1:11-12)

**1:11-12.** The **farmers** and **vine growers** also had reason to mourn since the fruit of their labor had been **destroyed.** These included grains (**wheat** and **barley**) and five kinds of fruits (grapes, figs, pomegranates, dates from **palm** trees, and apples). Because of the destruction of their crops they did not experience **the joy** of the harvest (cf. Ps. 4:7).

### 4. PRIESTS SHOULD MOURN (1:13)

**1:13.** The **priests** were told to take part (**wail**) in this lament because, as already noted (v. 9), the ingredients for certain daily **offerings** were no longer available. (On **sackcloth,** see comments on v. 8.)

### C. A call to repentance (1:14)

**1:14.** The priests were told not only to mourn (v. 13) but also to **call a sacred assembly** at the temple for **all** the people. The nation was to **fast** and **cry out to the Lord.** Fasting was often associated with repentance (cf. 1 Sam. 7:6; Neh. 9:1-2; Jonah 3:5). The attitude that was to accompany this outward act is emphasized in Joel 2:12-17.

### D. The significance of the plague (1:15-20)

**1:15.** This locust plague was meaningful because of its role as a harbinger of **the day of the Lord** (see comments under "Major Interpretive Problems" in the *Introduction*). The locusts had destroyed the crops in the fields (see esp. v. 10, where the Heb. verb *šādad* is used twice and is trans. "ruined" and "destroyed" in the NIV). Similarly this coming **day** would be one of **destruction** (*šōd,* related to the verb *šādad*) **from the Almighty** (*šadday*; cf. comments on Gen. 17:1; this divine name was probably used here because of its similarity in sound to the word *šōd,* "destruction").

It was natural for the prophet to see this plague as an ominous sign of an extraordinary event. In Egypt a locust plague (Ex. 10:1-20) had preceded the final plagues of darkness (Ex. 10:21-29; cf. Joel 2:2) and death (Ex. 11; 12:29-30). The Deuteronomic curses threatened locust plagues (Deut. 28:38, 42) in conjunction with exile and death (Deut. 28:41, 48-57, 64-68).

**1:16-18.** Verses 16-20 contain a detailed description of the aftermath of the locust plague. By again concentrating on the unique nature of this particular event, the prophet supported his contention that the destructive day of the Lord was around the corner (cf. "near" in v. 15).

The people were all too aware (**before** their **very eyes**) that their **food** supply, and with it all reason to rejoice, had disappeared (v. 16). Drought had apparently set in as well, for the **seeds** had **shriveled. The clods** (v. 17) may be translated, "their (i.e., the farmers') shovels." When the farmers dug into the ground to investigate the absence of green life, the shovels uncovered seeds that had not germinated. With no harvest available, **the storehouses** and **granaries** had been left to deteriorate. The domesticated animals (**cattle. . . . herds . . . flocks of sheep**) were **suffering** from starvation.

**1:19-20.** The prophet, who clearly identified with his suffering nation (cf. "my" which occurs three times in vv. 6-7), cried out to the **Lord** in his anguish. He compared the locusts to a **fire** (in both vv. 19 and 20) which destroys everything in its path. Even **the streams** had **dried up,** causing the dehydrated **wild animals** to **pant** for **water.**

### III. The Coming Day of the Lord (2:1-11)

In this section the theme in 1:15 is more fully developed as details about the approaching day of the Lord are given. Joel spoke of the Lord as a mighty Warrior-King leading His powerful army into battle. If one posits a preexilic date, the Assyrians or Babylonians may be in view (cf. comments under "Authorship and Date" in the *Introduction*). Both are pictured in the Old Testament as instruments of the Lord's judgment (cf. Isa. 10:5-15 on Assyria; and Jer. 27:4-11; 51:20-25; Hab. 1:5-12 on Babylon). Other Bible scholars, who hold a preexilic date, say the army in Joel 2:1-11 is eschatological, possibly equated with the army in verse 20; 3:9, 12; Daniel 11:40; and Zechariah 14:2.

If a postexilic date is taken, it is uncertain to which nation the section alludes. The army would then take on a more indefinite, apocalyptic character (cf. Wolff, *Joel and Amos,* pp. 7, 42), perhaps representing Israel's enemies in general.

As noted under "Major Interpretive Problems" in the *Introduction,* this invading force is described in locust-like terms to establish continuity with Joel 1. At the same time the comparisons to a literal army (2:4-5, 7) hint at the reality in view.

Within this section, four units are discernible (vv. 1-2, 3-5, 6-9, 10-11), the last three being introduced by "before them" (vv. 3, 10) or "at the sight of them" (v. 6). Verses 1-2 correspond to verses 10-11 thematically, forming a bracket around the section. These two units focus on the fearful response caused by the approaching army (vv. 1b, 10a), the darkness which accompanies it (vv. 2a, 10b), and its extraordinary size (vv. 2b, 11a). Two of these motifs appear (in reverse order) at the center of the section. Verse 5c refers to the army's great size and verse 6 to the response of fear by people from many nations. Two motifs appear in verses 3-5a: the army is like a destructive fire (v. 3), and it charges relentlessly ahead (vv. 4-5a). Both ideas are repeated in verses 5b and 7-9, respectively.

### A. The nearness of the Lord's army (2:1-2)

**2:1.** The section begins with a call of **alarm,** emphasizing the nearness of the invader. **The trumpet** (*šôpār*) was a ram's horn, blown by a watchman to alert the people of great danger (cf. Jer. 4:5-6; Ezek. 33:2-6). The appropriate response was fear (**tremble;** cf. Amos 3:6), especially in this instance since **the day of the LORD** was **coming. Holy hill** (cf. Pss. 2:6; 3:4; 15:1; 24:3; 78:54; Dan. 9:16, 20; Obad. 16; Zeph. 3:11) refers to the temple mount.

**2:2a.** The day of the Lord is described as **a day of darkness and gloom . . . of clouds and blackness** (cf. Zeph. 1:15). The reference to intense darkness following the locust plague of Joel 1 recalls Exodus 10, where the same order of events appears. Darkness and clouds—often associated with the Lord in His role as the mighty victorious Warrior (cf. Deut. 4:11; 5:22-23; Pss. 18:9, 11; 97:2)—here symbolize both judgment and destruction (cf. Jer. 13:16; Ezek. 30:3, 18; 32:7-8; 34:12; Amos 5:18-20; Zeph. 1:15).

**2:2b.** The innumerable size of the invading force receives special attention. **Like** the rays of the morning sun (**dawn**) its hosts will cover the horizon. This **army** is said to be more awesome than any that had ever come or would come. The hyperbolic language may echo Exodus 10:14. If so, it emphasizes that the "locusts" of Joel 2:1-11 would be even more overwhelming than those that overran Egypt. Something even worse than the Egyptian plagues was about to engulf the land!

### B. The destructive power of the Lord's army (2:3-5)

**2:3.** The invaders, like the locusts in Joel 1, are compared to a **fire** that consumes everything in its path (cf. 1:19). Fruitful lands, whose lush growth was comparable to **the Garden of Eden** (cf. Gen. 2:8-9), would become **a desert waste.** The reality behind this figure is the devastating effect of a huge, invading army on the land (cf. Deut. 28:49-51; Isa. 1:7; Jer. 5:17; also note the Assyrian text cited under "Major Interpretive Problems" in the *Introduction*). The words **nothing escapes them** may allude to Exodus 10:5, 15.

**2:4-5.** In the context of the overall comparison to locusts, the invading force is likened to an **army** (v. 5b) consisting of **horses . . . cavalry,** and **chariots** (vv. 4-5a). Such an association is facilitated by three facts: (1) The heads of locusts and horses are similar in appearance. The German and Italian words for "locust" literally mean "hay-horse" and "little horse," respectively (Wolff, *Joel and Amos,* p. 45, n. 46; cf. also Driver, *The Books of Joel and Amos,* p. 52). (2) Both locusts and human armies advance swiftly. (3) The locusts' buzzing wings resemble the sound of chariot wheels (for accounts of the sounds made by locusts, see Driver, *The Books of Joel and Amos,* p. 52).

Nothing can impede the invaders' swift approach. They seemingly **leap over the mountaintops.** The Hebrew verb for "leap over" (*rāqaḏ*) suggests both flying locusts and speeding chariots (on the latter; cf. Nahum 3:2, where *rāqaḏ* is trans. "jolting").

### C. The relentless charge of the Lord's army (2:6-9)

**2:6.** The response to this awesome army was widespread terror, for it involved **nations. In anguish** (*ḥûl*) literally refers to writhing, as when a woman is overcome by labor pains (cf. *ḥûl* in Isa. 26:17; Jer. 4:31; Micah 4:10). This same response is seen elsewhere in contexts where the Lord comes to do battle (cf. Ex. 15:14; Deut. 2:25; Pss. 77:16; 97:4; Isa. 13:8; Hab. 3:10).

**2:7-9.** Once more the relentless advance of the army is emphasized (cf. vv. 4-5a). Again the language applies both to locusts (cf. Driver, *The Books of Joel and*

Amos, pp. 54-5; and Keil, "Joel," in *Commentary on the Old Testament in Ten Volumes,* 10:193, n. 1) and to a literal army. Both advance in orderly fashion (vv. 7-8a), **plunge through defenses** (v. 8b), and enter walled cities and homes. As elsewhere in this section (cf. v. 6), Joel seemingly alluded to Exodus 10.

### D. The invincibility of the Lord's army (2:10-11)

**2:10-11.** The army's approach is accompanied by cosmic disorder. The entire world, from **earth** below to **sky** above, quivers (cf. **shakes** and **trembles**) before the thunderous battle cry of the divine Commander. This cosmic response is a typical poetic description of the Lord's theophany as Warrior (cf. Jud. 5:4; Pss. 18:7; 77:18; Isa. 13:13; Joel 3:16). The darkening of the heavenly bodies (cf. 2:2, 30; 3:15) is another characteristic of the Lord's day (cf. Isa. 13:10; Ezek. 32:7; Zech. 14:6-7; also note Isa. 34:4). The prophet concluded with a rhetorical question (**Who can endure it?**), to suggest that no one can endure this **great** and **dreadful** day (cf. Mal. 3:2; 4:5). If the army in Joel 2:1-11 was in Joel's **day,** it may foreshadow the army in chapter 3.

### IV. Renewed Call to Repentance (2:12-17)

Before such an invincible army the nation's only hope was to turn immediately ("even now," v. 12) to the Lord in repentance. This section contains two formal appeals for repentance (vv. 12-14, 15-17). The first concludes with a motivational section (introduced by "for," vv. 13b-14).

### A. An appeal for a sincere change of heart (2:12-14)

#### 1. THE APPEAL (2:12-13A)

**2:12-13a.** The Lord Himself urged the people to repent with genuine sincerity (cf. **with all your heart** and **rend your heart and not your garments**) accompanied by **fasting and weeping and mourning.** Repentance is the desired outcome of the Lord's judgments (cf. Deut. 4:30; 30:1-2; Hosea 3:4-5; Amos 4:6-11).

#### 2. THE MOTIVATION (2:13B-14)

**2:13b.** A recognition of the nation's relationship to **the LORD** her **God** and of His gracious nature should have motivat-

ed His people to repent. The expression "the LORD your God" was well known to Israel (this phrase occurs 263 times in Deut.) and testified to the covenantal relationship between God and the nation. The words **gracious and compassionate, slow to anger and abounding in love** (*hesed,* "loyal love") recall Exodus 34:6 (cf. Neh. 9:17; Pss. 103:8; 143:8; Jonah 4:2), where the same affirmation preceded the renewal of the covenant after the sin of the golden calf. Because God's character is merciful, **He** often **relents from sending calamity.** Again the golden calf episode is recalled. On that occasion Moses begged the Lord to "relent" and "not bring disaster" on His people (Ex. 32:12). The Lord responded favorably to his request (Ex. 32:14).

**2:14.** The words **who knows** testify to the Lord's sovereignty in the matter (cf. 2 Sam. 12:22; Jonah 3:9). Even if sinful Israel repented, she could not presume on God's mercy as if it were something under their control which He had to grant automatically. They could only hope that **He** would **turn and have pity** (cf. Mal. 3:7) by averting the disaster (cf. Joel 2:20) and restoring their crops (cf. v. 25). Agricultural **blessing** would mark a reversal of the curse that had come on them (in the form of the locusts; cf. Deut. 28:38-42) and would make it possible for **grain . . . and drink offerings** to be presented again (cf. Joel 1:9, 13).

### B. An appeal for national involvement (2:15-17)

The second part of this call to repentance is an appeal to the nation to congregate for a formal ceremony of lamentation and prayer.

**2:15.** The opening words of verse 1, **Blow the trumpet in Zion,** are repeated. The fear elicited by the sound of the watchman's trumpet (v. 1) was to prompt another sound of the ram's horn, this time calling the people to **a holy fast** and **sacred assembly** (cf. 1:14). For the blowing of a ram's horn was also used to call religious convocations (cf. Lev. 25:9; Ps. 81:3).

**2:16.** The entire worshiping community (**assembly**) was to **gather,** from the oldest (**elders**) to the youngest (**those nursing at the breast**). Not even newlyweds were exempted (cf. Deut. 24:5).

**2:17. The priests** were to lead the

ceremony by weeping **before the Lord** in the court of the temple (i.e., **between the temple porch and the** bronze **altar** of burnt offering; cf. Ezek. 8:16) and by offering a prayer for deliverance.

The prayer was to include a twofold petition: (a) **spare** (*ḥûs*, "pity or have compassion on"; cf. Jonah 4:11 for the same word, where the NIV renders it "be concerned about") and (b) **do not make,** a question aimed at motivating **God** to action. The concern of the latter was God's reputation. If Israel, God's own **inheritance** (cf. Deut. 4:20; 9:26, 29; Pss. 28:9; 33:12; 78:62, 71; 79:1; 94:14; Micah 7:14, 18), were to become **an object of scorn** (cf. Joel 2:19), the nations might erroneously conclude that He lacked the power and/or love to save those who belonged to Him (cf. Ex. 32:12; Deut. 9:26-29; Ps. 79:4, 10).

The rendering, **a byword among the nations,** though not the only way to translate the Hebrew here (cf. KJV, "that the heathen should rule over them"), is favored by the poetic structure (cf. the parallel phrase "object of scorn"; also see Jer. 24:9).

## V. Forgiveness and Restoration (2:18-27)

This section marks a turning point in the argument of the book. It describes the divine response (v. 18) to the nation's repentance and records the Lord's comforting words to His people (vv. 19-27). The effects of the locust plague (chap. 1) are reversed (see esp. 2:25), and the threatened invasion (vv. 1-11) is averted (v. 20).

The divine message of verses 19-27 displays the following chiastic structure:

*a.* Verse 19
  *b.* Verse 20a
    *c.* Verses 20b-24
  *b.*¹ Verse 25
*a.*¹ Verses 26-27

Parts *a* and *a*¹ correspond as both parts promise a restoration of crops and a cessation of shame. Parts *b* and *b*¹ both refer to an elimination of enemies (or their effects). Part *c* contains two cycles (vv. 20b-21b; 21c-24), the second of which repeats and/or expands the three elements of the first (cf. v. 20b with v. 21c; v. 21a with v. 22; and v. 21b with vv. 23-24).

### A. The Lord's gracious response described (2:18)

The relationship between verses 18-19a and the preceding context is problematic. The NIV translation (cf. also NASB, KJV), which employs the future tense ("will be jealous," etc.), interprets these verses as a promise conditional on the people's positive response to the call to repentance in verses 12-17. However, that interpretation of the Hebrew verbal forms in this context is unlikely (cf. S.R. Driver, *A Treatise on the Use of the Tenses in Hebrew.* 3rd ed. Oxford: Clarendon Press, 1892, p. 95; Keil, "Joel," in *Commentary on the Old Testament in Ten Volumes,* 10:200). The forms seem better translated with the past tense (cf. NIV marg., NASB marg., RSV) and the text understood as a description of the Lord's turning to His people in Joel's time. This would, of course, imply they had responded positively to the appeal of verses 12-17 (cf. Allen, *The Books of Joel, Obadiah, Jonah and Micah,* p. 86).

**2:18.** In response to this genuine repentance, **the Lord** was **jealous for His land and** took **pity on His people.** The Lord's jealousy is His passionate loyalty toward what is His, a loyalty that prompts Him to lash out against anything that would destroy it (cf. Isa. 26:11; Ezek. 36:5-6; 38:19; Zech. 1:14; 8:2). The military protection described in Joel 2:20 is in view here.

### B. The Lord's promise of restored agricultural blessing (2:19-27)

**2:19-20a.** The Lord's promise began with a proclamation that the agricultural produce (**grain, new wine, and oil**) destroyed by the locusts (cf. 1:10) would be restored. He then announced that His people would **never again** be an **object of scorn to the nations** (cf. 2:17). Similarly (vv. 26-27) He promised they would "never again . . . be shamed."

The seemingly unconditional tone of these statements is problematic if verses 18-19a describe a historical event in Joel's day. Whether one posits a preexilic or postexilic date for the writing of Joel, history shows that Israel, after Joel's day, often did become an object of scorn. Perhaps the best solution to this difficulty is to understand that at least this aspect of the promise is eschatological in its ultimate fulfillment. Joel's prophecy deals with Israel's future apart from the chronological gaps which one sees so readily in retrospect. Consequently prophecies pertaining to his own generation are merged here with those that await future realization. This is common in Old Testament prophecies (e.g., Isa. 9:6-7; 61:1-2; Zech. 9:9-10).

The Lord next announced that the threat described in Joel 2:1-11 would be averted (v. 20a). He would turn against the very army He had been bringing against His disobedient people (cf. v. 11), driving it into the desert (**a parched and barren land**) and the seas (**the eastern sea** and **the western sea,** probably the Dead Sea and the Mediterranean Sea; cf. Zech. 14:8).

The carcasses' **stench** would permeate the air. As in Joel 2:1-11, the language, though alluding to a literal army (cf. Isa. 34:3; Amos 4:10), applies to locusts as well. Eyewitness accounts tell how dead locusts, having been driven into the sea and then washed ashore, gave out a foul odor (cf. Driver, *The Books of Joel and Amos,* pp. 62-3; Smith, *The Book of the Twelve Prophets,* 2:411).

As noted in the *Introduction,* the designation **northern army** (lit., "northerner") suggests that a literal army is ultimately in view. If "the northerner" is yet future (eschatological), the army is possibly the army in Joel 3:9, 12; Daniel 11:40; and Zechariah 14:2. But if the reference is strictly historical, any precise identification of the army is precluded by the uncertainty surrounding the date of authorship. So in this case it would not be clear to what extent, if any, Joel 2:20 was historically fulfilled in Joel's day. If the invasion threatened in 2:1-11 had not actually begun, the language of verse 20 need not refer to a historical event. It would simply be a vivid and concrete way of saying that the destruction planned by the Lord had been averted at the last moment.

**2:20b-21b.** The NIV understands the last line of verse 20 as a statement about the Lord (cf. v. 21b; in this case *kî* in v. 20b is taken as an emphatic assertion: **Surely**). Other translations (KJV, NASB, RSV) join the words to the preceding context, making the army the subject (cf. NASB, "For it has done great things"). The insolent pride of the invader would then be in view (cf. Isa. 10:5-19 for a

similar view). However, the NIV reading has much to commend it, especially the structural correspondence it produces (cf. note on Joel 2:18-27).

In the first two lines of verse 21 the personified **land,** which had been stripped of its produce (cf. 1:10), is encouraged to fear no longer but to **be glad and rejoice.**

**2:21c-24.** Each of the three elements in verses 20b-21b is repeated and/or expanded in these verses. The repeated affirmation that **the LORD has done great things** is followed by the expanded charges, **be not afraid** (v. 22) and **be glad and rejoice** (v. 23).

The first charge was directed to the **wild animals,** which had been affected so adversely by the locust invasion and accompanying drought (cf. 1:20). The effects of that judgment would be completely reversed. **The open pastures** (cf. 1:19) would again bring forth grass and vegetation. **The trees** and vines would again **yield their** fruit (cf. 1:7, 12, 19).

The second charge (2:23) was directed to the inhabitants **of Zion** (i.e., Jerusalem; cf. v. 1) who were earlier instructed to grieve over the destruction wrought by the locusts (cf. 1:5, 8, 11, 13). They could now "rejoice" because **the LORD** was prepared to restore fertility to their fields. As promised in Deuteronomy 11:14, the **autumn and spring rains** would come on schedule (in September-October and March-April), producing a bountiful harvest.

The phrase translated **a teacher for righteousness** (Joel 2:23) is better rendered, "in righteousness the autumn rains" (cf. NIV marg., NASB, KJV; see Allen, *The Books of Joel, Obadiah, Jonah and Micah,* pp. 92-3, n. 26; and Kapelrud, *Joel Studies,* p. 115). "Teacher" (*môreh*) is translated "autumn" later in the verse (cf. also Ps. 84:6). "For righteousness" would then probably mean, "according to justice" (i.e., in harmony with the covenantal principle that obedience is justly rewarded with agricultural blessing; see Kapelrud, *Joel Studies,* p. 116).

The abundance of the harvest will be evidenced by **the threshing floors** and **wine** and oil **vats** being filled to capacity (Joel 2:24).

**2:25-27.** Verse 25 nicely summarizes the overriding theme of verses 19-24. The effects of **the locusts** would be completely reversed. Speaking as though compelled by legal obligation, **the LORD** promised to **repay** (*šillēm*; cf. its use in Ex. 22:1; 2 Kings 4:7) the nation for the crops which His **great army** of locusts (cf. Joel 1:4) had devoured.

The agricultural abundance (2:26a) would prompt the people to **praise the name** (i.e., the revealed character) of their covenant **God,** who had **worked wonders for** them (v. 26b). This last expression placed the restoration of agricultural blessing in the mainstream of God's miraculous historical deeds on behalf of His people (cf. Ex. 3:15; 15:11; 34:10; Josh. 3:5; Jud. 6:13; Ps. 77:14).

The nation would also acknowledge (**know**) His active presence and His rightful place as their God (Joel 2:27). The words **I am in Israel** (lit., "I am in the midst of Israel") recall the Pentateuchal references to God being "among" (or, "in the midst of") His people (cf. Num. 11:20; 14:14; Deut. 7:21). The frequently used expression **you will know that . . . I am the LORD your God** also originated in the Pentateuch (cf. Ex. 6:7; 16:12). The association of that expression with the Lord's exclusive claim to be Israel's God (**there is no other**) reminds one of Deuteronomy 4:35, 39. Through these allusions to earlier traditions, the Lord affirmed that His relationship to His people was just as vital then as it had been in Moses' day.

## VI. Promises of a Glorious Future (2:28–3:21)

This concluding section of the Book of Joel develops more fully the eschatological element of the Lord's promise (cf. comments on 2:19-20a; "afterward" in 2:28; "in those days" in 3:1; "in that day" in 3:18). The deliverance experienced by Joel's generation foreshadowed that of the end times. The day of the Lord, so narrowly averted by Joel's repentant contemporaries, will come in full force against the enemies of God's people (perhaps foreshadowed by the northern army of 2:20). The promises of 2:19-27 will find their ultimate and absolute fulfillment as the Lord intervenes on Israel's behalf (2:28-32), decisively judges the nation's enemies (3:1-16a, 19), and securely establishes His people in their land (3:1, 16b-18, 20-21).

### A. Spiritual renewal and deliverance (2:28-32)

**2:28-29.** The Lord announced that His "day" (v. 31) would be accompanied by an outpouring of His **Spirit on all people** (lit., "all flesh"). The following context indicates that "all people" refers more specifically to all inhabitants of Judah (cf. the threefold use of **your** in v. 28, as well as the parallel passages in Ezek. 39:29; Zech. 12:10). This will be true regardless of age, gender, or social class (Joel 2:29 is better trans. "and even on the male and female servants"; cf. NASB).

At that time recipients of the divine **Spirit** will exercise prophetic gifts (**will prophesy . . . will dream dreams,** and **will see visions**) which in the past had been limited to a select few (cf. 1 Sam. 10:10-11; 19:20-24). This is probably an allusion to Numbers 11:29, where Moses, responding to Joshua's misguided zeal after an outpouring of the divine Spirit on the 72 elders (cf. Num. 11:24-28), declared, "I wish that all the LORD's people were prophets and that the LORD would put His Spirit on them!" This extensive outpouring of the Spirit will signal the advent of divine blessing (contrast 1 Sam. 3:1, where the absence of prophetic visions characterized a period of sin and judgment).

**2:30-31. The great and dreadful day of the LORD** will be preceded by ominous signs (**wonders**) of impending judgment (cf. v. 10; see also Ezek. 32:6-8 for literary parallels). **Blood and fire and billows of smoke** suggest the effects of warfare. The turning of **the moon to blood** refers in a poetic way to its being darkened (cf. the parallel line, **The sun will be turned to darkness,** and Joel 2:10; 3:15). Though such phenomena will signal doom for God's enemies, His people should interpret them as the precursors of their deliverance (cf. Matt. 24:29-31; Mark 13:24-27; Luke 21:25-28).

**2:32.** At this time of universal judgment, **everyone who calls on** (i.e., invokes) **the name of the LORD will be saved** (i.e., delivered from physical danger; cf. comments on Rom. 11:26). "Everyone" does not refer to all people, but the Spirit-empowered people of God mentioned in Joel 2:28-29. In Romans 10:13 Paul related this passage to Gentile (as well as Jewish) salvation, but he was suggesting a mere analogy, not a strict fulfillment of Joel 2:32, which pertains to Israel.

In the day of the Lord Jerusalem will be a place of refuge for **the survivors whom the LORD calls.** This remnant with whom the Lord initiates a special relationship (for the sense of "call" here, see Isa. 51:2) should probably be equated with the group described in Joel 2:28-29, 32a (cf. Wolff, *Joel and Amos*, pp. 68-9), though some (e.g., Driver, *The Books of Joel and Amos*, pp. 68-9) see this as referring to returning exiles.

On the day of Pentecost the Apostle Peter quoted Joel 2:28-32 in conjunction with the outpouring of the Holy Spirit (cf. Acts 2:17-21). His introductory words (cf. Acts 2:16, "this is what was spoken by the Prophet Joel") may seem to indicate that he considered Joel's prophecy as being completely fulfilled on that occasion. However, it is apparent that the events of that day, though extraordinary, did not fully correspond to those predicted by Joel.

In attempting to solve this problem one must recognize that in the early chapters of Acts the kingdom was being offered to Israel once more. Peter admonished the people to repent so that they might receive the promised Spirit (cf. Acts 2:38-39 where he alludes to Joel 2:32). Shortly thereafter Peter anticipated "times of refreshing" and the return of Christ in response to national repentance (cf. Acts 10:19-21). Not until later did Peter come to understand more fully God's program for the Gentiles in the present age (cf. Acts 10:44-48). When he observed the outpouring of the Spirit on the day of Pentecost he rightly viewed it as the first stage in the fulfillment of Joel's prophecy. Apparently he believed that the kingdom was then being offered to Israel and that the outpouring of the Holy Spirit signaled the coming of the Millennium. However, the complete fulfillment of the prophecy (with respect to both the extent of the Spirit's work and the other details) was delayed because of Jewish unbelief (for further discussion see comments on Acts 2:16-21; 3:19-21).

## B. The judgment of the nations (3:1-16)

### 1. JUDGMENT IS ANNOUNCED (3:1-8)

Verses 1-8 are a judgment speech against the nations. They contain accusatory elements (vv. 2b-3, 5-6), as well as an announcement of judgment (vv. 1-2a, 4, 7-8).

**3:1-3.** In the future day of the Lord Judah and her enemies will be carefully distinguished. The Lord will **restore the fortunes of Judah and Jerusalem,** in fulfillment of Moses' promise (cf. Deut. 30:3). At the same time God will **gather** the **nations** for **judgment.**

The site of the judgment will be **the Valley of Jehoshaphat,** mentioned only in Joel 3:2, 12. Whether such a geographical site was known by this name in ancient Israel is not certain. Some scholars suggest it is a yet-future valley, to be formed by the splitting of the Mount of Olives at the Messiah's return (Zech. 14:4). At any rate, the importance of the name is not in its geographical location, but in its meaning, "the Lord judges."

The reason for God's judgment is the nations' treatment of His covenant people (**My inheritance;** cf. comments on Joel 2:17), **My people.** The nations had **scattered** the Lord's **people,** sold them as slaves to distant lands, and **divided up** His **land.** "Scattered" (from *pāzar,* "to disperse") seems to refer to the Babylonian Exile (cf. Jer. 50:17). Even though the Lord Himself assigned the land to Israel's enemies (cf. Lam. 5:2; Micah 2:4), He still held these nations guilty for their failure to recognize His sovereignty and for their cruel treatment of His **people.**

**3:4-6.** In verses 4-8 the Lord spoke directly to the Phoenicians (**Tyre and Sidon**) and the Philistines, two groups that profited economically from Judah's demise (cf. Ezek. 25:15; 28:20-24). The Lord identified Himself with His people (note **Me** in Joel 3:4) and denied that these nations had any justification for their actions (this is the force of the rhetorical questions in v. 4).

God then announced that He would repay them for their offenses (v. 4b). These were specified as robbery (v. 5) and slave trade (v. 6). Since neither the Phoenicians nor the Philistines are mentioned as robbing the temple treasuries during the destruction of **Jerusalem** (cf. 2 Kings 25), Joel 3:5 may refer to Israel's wealth in general, not to the temple (cf. Wolff, *Joel and Amos,* p. 78).

Phoenician and Philistine involvement in slave trade (v. 6) is mentioned elsewhere (cf. Amos 1:6, 9). According to Kapelrud, the Greeks mentioned here are actually Ionians (*y*ᵉ*wānîm*), who populated the coasts of Asia Minor (*Joel Studies*, p. 154). Ionian commerce was at its peak in the seventh and sixth centuries B.C. Ezekiel 27:13, 19 mentions Tyrian trading arrangements (including slaves) with the Ionians (or Greece). The trading recalled in Joel may have occurred in conjunction with Judah's fall to the Babylonians.

**3:7-8.** The divine judgment on these nations would be perfectly appropriate. The Lord would **rouse** His dispersed people and put them in the position of slave traders. *They* would sell the **sons and daughters** of the Phoenicians and Philistines as slaves **to the Sabeans** (cf. Job 1:13-15), an Arabian people noted for their commercial activities (cf. "Sheba" in Ezek. 27:22-23).

The judgment threatened here probably was fulfilled, at least in part, in the fourth century B.C. Allen explains, "The people of Sidon were sold into slavery by Antiochus III in 345 B.C., while the citizens of Tyre and Gaza were enslaved by Alexander in 332 B.C." (*The Books of Joel, Obadiah, Jonah and Micah*, p. 114). Perhaps Jews were involved in some of the transactions.

In the context (cf. Joel 3:1) the passage also carries an eschatological significance which any historical fulfillment merely prefigures. From the eschatological perspective Philistia and Phoenicia represent all of Israel's enemies (much as do Moab in Isa. 25:10-12 and Edom in the Book of Obad.). At that time God's people will gain ascendancy over their enemies (cf. Isa. 41:11-12; Amos 9:12; Obad. 15-21; Micah 7:16-17; Zeph. 2:6-7).

2. A CALL TO WAR: JUDGMENT IS DESCRIBED (3:9-16)

In this section the judgment of the nations is described. It contains three subunits: (a) a call to the participants (the nations and the Lord) to assemble their forces (vv. 9-11), (b) a statement by the Lord (vv. 12-13), and (c) a description of the battle site (vv. 14-16).

**3:9-11.** Unidentified messengers are instructed to issue a call of **war** to **the nations** (cf. "all nations" in Isa. 34:2; Obad. 15; Zech. 14:2). The nations are to **beat** their farming implements **into** weapons (Joel 3:10; contrast Isa. 2:4; Micah 4:3) and **assemble** for battle (Joel 3:11a; cf. Zech. 12:9). The Lᴏʀᴅ is urged to **bring down** His **warriors.**

**3:12-13.** The Lord Himself now repeated the summons of the preceding verses, instructing **the nations** to enter **the Valley of Jehoshaphat** (cf. v. 2). Employing agricultural imagery, He then commanded His warriors to destroy His enemies. The first command (**Swing the sickle, for the harvest is ripe**) probably compares judgment to harvesting grain (cf. Isa. 17:5; Rev. 14:15). The second (**Come, trample the grapes**) compares the annihilation of the enemies to treading grapes in a **winepress** (cf. Isa. 63:1-6; Rev. 14:18-20). The underlying reason for the nations' demise is that **their wickedness** is **great.**

These verses (Joel 3:12-13) plainly indicate that the judgment mentioned in this chapter will actually take the form of divine warfare against Israel's enemies. So the event described here should be equated with Armageddon (cf. Rev. 14:14-20; 16:16; 19:11-21), rather than the judgment of the nations prophesied in Matthew 25:31-46.

**3:14-16.** An innumerable host will be assembled **in the valley of decision** (also called the Valley of Jehoshaphat, vv. 2, 12). Here the divine Judge's verdict will be executed on the nations. As in earlier passages (cf. 2:10, 31) the darkening of the heavenly bodies (3:15) serves as an ominous sign of **the** approaching **day of the Lᴏʀᴅ** (v. 14). **The Lᴏʀᴅ will** then emerge from His sanctuary in **Jerusalem** in theophanic splendor (v. 16; cf. Amos 1:2). His thunderous battle cry (cf. **will roar . . . and thunder**) will produce cosmic disorder (cf. Joel 2:10-11; Rev. 16:16, 18). He will then demonstrate that He is Israel's **Refuge** (cf. Pss. 46:1; 62:8; Isa. 25:4) and **Stronghold** (cf. Pss. 9:9; 18:2; 27:1; 37:39; 43:2; 144:2).

*C. Israel's ultimate restoration (3:17-21)*

**3:17.** After this awesome display of divine power, Israel will recognize (**know**) that **the Lᴏʀᴅ** truly dwells among them (cf. 2:27). **Jerusalem,** the site of the Lord's holy sanctuary (**My holy hill;** cf. comments on 2:1) **will be holy** in the sense that it will **never again** be defiled by foreign invaders (cf. Isa. 52:10-11; Nahum 1:15).

**3:18a.** At that time (**in that day,** when Messiah will reign over His people in the Millennium) the land will be a virtual paradise, enabling the Lord's people to enjoy His agricultural blessings to the fullest. The grape harvest will be so bountiful that **wine will** seemingly **drip** from **the mountains. Milk** will be just as plentiful. It too was a sign of prosperity; Canaan was described as a land "flowing with milk and honey" (see comments on Ex. 3:8; cf. Ex. 13:5; 33:3; Lev. 20:24; also note Isa. 55:1). The seasonal streams (**ravines,** or wadis) will no longer **run** dry. This abundance of wine, milk (implying the existence of extensive herds), and **water** represents a complete reversal of the effects of the locust plague (cf. Joel 1:5, 18, 20).

**3:18b. A fountain will flow out of the Lord's house,** the Jerusalem temple. Similar imagery is employed in Ezekiel 47:1-12 and Zechariah 14:8. This fountain (and the stream it produces) will be a tangible reminder that the Lord is the Source of the land's fertility (cf. Ezek. 47:8-10, 12). **The valley of acacias** is probably that portion of the Kidron Valley which runs through the arid wilderness to the Dead Sea (cf. Ezek. 47:8).

**3:19-20.** In contrast with the God-given abundance of Judah (v. 18), the lands of her enemies (represented by **Egypt** and **Edom**) will be infertile (**desolate** and **a desert waste**). The reason for this severe judgment is their mistreatment of **the people of Judah.** Israel's enemies are guilty of **violence** and of shedding **innocent blood.**

If the Book of Joel was written in the ninth century B.C., the reference to Egypt in Joel 3:19 may allude to her acts of violence committed during the invasion of the Egyptian Pharaoh Shishak (ca. 926 B.C.; cf. 1 Kings 14:25-26). But if the Book of Joel was written in the late preexilic or postexilic period, the invasion of Pharaoh Neco II may be in view (609 B.C.; cf. 2 Kings 23:29-35). Obadiah also referred to Edomite sins against the Lord's people (cf. Obad. 9-14).

The security and prosperity portrayed in Joel 3:17-18 will never again be interrupted. **Judah** and Jerusalem **will be inhabited forever** (cf. Ezek. 37:25; Amos 9:15; Zech. 14:11).

**3:21.** This verse has posed problems for interpreters. The NIV suggests that the first part of the verse is a declaration that Judah will be forgiven (**I will par-**

don). Against this is the fact that the sin of **bloodguilt** on the part of Judah is not mentioned elsewhere in the Book of Joel. A better reading is that of the NASB (following the LXX), which relates the passage to the judgment on the nations (cf. v. 19) by portraying the Lord as the Avenger of Judah's blood ("I will avenge their blood"). Another option is to translate, "And shall I leave their bloodshed [the Judean blood shed by the nations] go unpunished? I will not" (cf. Allen, *The Books of Joel, Obadiah, Jonah and Micah*, p. 117; for a similar rhetorical question and response using the same Hebrew verb, *niqqâh;* cf. Jer. 25:29).

The book ends with an affirmation of the Lord's presence **in Zion** (cf. Joel 3:17). It is this fact, above all else, which will assure the nation's glorious future, portrayed in verses 17-21.

# BIBLIOGRAPHY

Ahlström, G.W. *Joel and the Temple Cult of Jerusalem.* Supplements to *Vetus Testamentum.* Vol. 21. Leiden: E.J. Brill, 1971.

Allen, Leslie C. *The Books of Joel, Obadiah, Jonah and Micah.* The New International Commentary on the Old Testament. Grand Rapids: Wm. B. Eerdmans Publishing Co., 1976.

Driver, S.R. *The Books of Joel and Amos.* The Cambridge Bible for Schools and Colleges. Cambridge: University Press, 1915.

Feinberg, Charles L. *The Minor Prophets.* Chicago: Moody Press, 1976.

Kapelrud, Arvid S. *Joel Studies.* Uppsala: A.B. Lundequistska Bokhandeln, 1948.

Keil, C.F. "Joel." In *Commentary on the Old Testament in Ten Volumes.* Vol. 10. Reprint (25 vols. in 10). Grand Rapids: Wm. B. Eerdmans Publishing Co., 1982.

Price, Walter K. *The Prophet Joel and the Day of the Lord.* Chicago: Moody Press, 1976.

Smith, George Adam. *The Book of the Twelve Prophets.* 2 vols. Rev. ed. New York: Harper & Brothers, n.d.

Smith, John M.P.; Ward, William H.; and Bewer, Julius A. *A Critical and Exegetical Commentary on Micah, Zephaniah, Nahum, Habakkuk, Obadiah and Joel.* The International Critical Commentary. Edinburgh: T. & T. Clark, 1974.

# Joel

Tatford, Frederick A. *The Minor Prophets.* Vol. 1. Reprint (3 vols.). Minneapolis: Klock & Klock Christian Publishers, 1982.

Thompson, John. A. "The Date of Joel." In *A Light unto My Path: Old Testament Studies in Honor of Jacob M. Myers.* Philadelphia: Temple University Press, 1974.

Watts, John D.W. *The Books of Joel, Obadiah, Jonah, Nahum, Habakkuk and Zephaniah.* The Cambridge Bible Commentary. Cambridge: Cambridge University Press, 1975.

Wolff, Hans Walter. *Joel and Amos.* Translated by Waldemar Janzen, S. Dean McBride, Jr., and Charles A. Muenchow. Philadelphia: Fortress Press, 1977.

# AMOS

## Donald R. Sunukjian

## INTRODUCTION

**The Prophet.** Before Amos began prophesying, he had been one of the "shepherds" of Tekoa, a town in the hill country of Judah about 10 miles south of Jerusalem. The word used for "shepherds" in 1:1 is not the usual Hebrew word *rō'eh*, but the rare word *nōqēḏ*, suggesting instead "sheep breeders." The only other Old Testament occurrence of *nōqēḏ* is in 2 Kings 3:4 where Mesha, king of Moab, is said to have engaged in sheep-breeding on such a scale that he was able to supply the king of Israel with 100,000 lambs and the wool of 100,000 rams. Amos evidently managed or owned large herds of sheep and goats, and was in charge of other shepherds.

In Amos 7:14 the prophet further described himself as "a shepherd" and as one who "took care of sycamore-fig trees." This word for "shepherd," *bôqēr*, occurs only here in the Old Testament, and describes a "herdsman" or "cattleman."

Besides overseeing his livestock operations, Amos was also occupied in growing sycamore fruit, presumably as a sideline. The sycamore-fig tree was a broad heavy tree, 25 to 50 feet high, which produced a fig-like fruit three or four times a year. The sycamore did not grow in the heights of Tekoa, but only in the warmer lowlands, as the Jordan Valley and the fertile oases by the Dead Sea. Both of these places were near enough to Tekoa for Amos to supervise the taking care of the trees (7:14)—a technical term that describes the process of slitting or scratching the forming fruit so that some juice runs out, allowing the rest of the fig to ripen into a sweeter, more edible fruit.

The three terms together indicate that Amos, as a breeder, rancher, and farmer, was a substantial and respected man in his community.

**The Times.** Amos lived in times of material prosperity. The long reigns of Uzziah (790-739 B.C.) in Judah and of Jeroboam II (793-753 B.C.) in Israel (1:1) had brought stability, prosperity, and expansion to the two kingdoms.

The Southern Kingdom had subdued the Philistines to the west (see comments on 1:6; 6:2), the Ammonites to the east, and the Arab states to the south. Uzziah's political influence was felt as far as Egypt (cf. 2 Chron. 26:1-15).

The Northern Kingdom, to whom Amos' message was directed, was at the zenith of its power. Aram had not recovered from her defeat in 802 B.C. by Assyria under Adad-Nirāri III (811–783 B.C.). Assyria, however, had been unable to press her advantage further. A succession of inept rulers and the troublesome Urarteans to her north kept Assyria preoccupied until the accession of Tiglath-Pileser III in 745 B.C. Given a free hand, Jeroboam II was able to extend his borders northward into Aramean territory and to reclaim Israel's lands in Transjordan (cf. 2 Kings 14:23-29; Amos 6:13).

Because of the control this gave Israel over the trade routes, wealth began to accumulate in her cities. Commerce thrived (8:5), an upper class emerged (4:1-3), and expensive homes were built (3:15; 5:11; 6:4, 11). The rich enjoyed an indolent, indulgent lifestyle (6:1-6), while the poor became targets for legal and economic exploitation (2:6-7; 5:7, 10-13; 6:12; 8:4-6). Slavery for debt was easily accepted (2:6; 8:6). Standards of morality had sunk to a low ebb (2:7).

Meanwhile religion flourished. The people thronged to the shrines for the yearly festivals (4:4; 5:5; 8:3, 10), enthusiastically offering their sacrifices (4:5; 5:21-23). They steadfastly maintained that their God was with them, and considered themselves immune to disaster (5:14, 18-20; 6:1-3; 9:10).

**The Date.** For a period of probably no more than a year, Amos gave God's message to the Northern Kingdom. His ministry was two years before a notable earthquake (1:1; cf. Zech. 14:5). Josephus connects the quake with the events of 2 Chronicles 26:16-20 (*Antiquities of the Jews* 9. 10. 4). Archeological excavations at Hazor and Samaria have uncovered evidence of a violent earthquake in Israel about 760 B.C.

**The Message.** Amos, a man from Judah, was called to prophesy in Israel. This was possibly around 762 B.C. (see comments under "The Date"). The message God gave him was primarily one of judgment, though it ended with words of hope.

The Lord God Almighty, the sovereign Ruler of the universe, would come as a Warrior to judge the nations that had rebelled against His authority. Israel in particular would be punished for her covenant violations against Him.

Though the nation would be destroyed, God will preserve a repentant remnant from among the people. One day this remnant will be restored to political prominence and covenant blessing. And then, through them, God will draw all nations to His name.

# OUTLINE

I. Prologue (1:1-2)
   A. The author and date (1:1)
   B. The theme (1:2)
II. The Roar of Judgment (1:3–2:16)
   A. Judgment against the nations (1:3–2:5)
      1. Judgment against Damascus (1:3-5)
      2. Judgment against Gaza (1:6-8)
      3. Judgment against Tyre (1:9-10)
      4. Judgment against Edom (1:11-12)
      5. Judgment against Ammon (1:13-15)
      6. Judgment against Moab (2:1-3)
      7. Judgment against Judah (2:4-5)
   B. Judgment against Israel (2:6-16)
      1. The broken covenant (2:6-8)
      2. The spurned grace (2:9-12)
      3. The resulting judgment (2:13-16)
III. The Reasons for Judgment (chaps. 3–6)

A. The first message (chap. 3)
   1. The unique relationship (3:1-2)
   2. The inevitable judgment (3:3-8)
   3. The unparalleled oppression (3:9-10)
   4. The coming catastrophe (3:11-15)
B. The second message (chap. 4)
   1. Economic exploitation (4:1-3)
   2. Religious hypocrisy (4:4-5)
   3. Refusal to repent (4:6-13)
C. The third message (5:1-17)
   1. Description of certain judgment (5:1-3)
   2. Call for individual repentance (5:4-6)
   3. Accusation of legal injustice (5:7)
   4. Portrayal of a sovereign God (5:8-9)
   5. Accusation of legal injustice (5:10-13)
   6. Call for individual repentance (5:14-15)
   7. Description of certain judgment (5:16-17)
D. The fourth message (5:18-27)
   1. Description of certain judgment (5:18-20)
   2. Accusation of religious hypocrisy (5:21-22)
   3. Call for individual repentance (5:23-24)
   4. Accusation of religious hypocrisy (5:25-26)
   5. Description of certain judgment (5:27)
E. The fifth message (chap. 6)
   1. Their boastful complacency (6:1-3)
   2. Their luxurious indulgence (6:4-7)
   3. The complete devastation (6:8-14)
IV. The Results of Judgment (7:1–9:10)
   A. The swarming locusts (7:1-3)
   B. The devouring fire (7:4-6)
   C. The testing plumb line (7:7-17)
      1. The vision (7:7-9)
      2. The incident (7:10-17)
   D. The culminating fruit (chap. 8)
      1. The vision (8:1-3)
      2. The results (8:4-14)
   E. The avenging Lord (9:1-10)
      1. The inescapable sword (9:1-4)
      2. The universal Sovereign (9:5-6)
      3. The impartial shifting (9:7-10)

# COMMENTARY

## I. Prologue (1:1-2)

### A. The author and date (1:1)

**1:1.** These are **the words of Amos, one of the shepherds of Tekoa,** a town directly south of Jerusalem. These sayings or messages resulted from **what he saw** (i.e., his visions; cf. comments at 7:12) **concerning Israel.** They were delivered to the Northern Kingdom **two years before the earthquake,** during the prosperous reigns of **Uzziah** in **Judah** and **Jeroboam** in **Israel.** (For a discussion of the prophet, the date, and Kings Uzziah and Jeroboam, see the *Introduction.*)

### B. The theme (1:2)

**1:2.** Amos' theme is that Israel and the other nations were about to be violently judged for their sins. He pictured **the Lord** as a lion who had roared and begun His attack (cf. 3:4, 8; Jer. 25:30; Hosea 5:14; 11:10; 13:7). A lion's terrifying roar paralyzes its victim with fear, making it helpless before the lion's charge. Then the pounce, the tearing, and death are inevitable.

God's roar would have a similar paralyzing and withering effect. As the reverberating sound advanced **from Zion,** that is, **Jerusalem** (cf. Amos 6:1; see comments on Zech. 8:3) against the nations, it would shrivel and scorch the earth. To the south, **the pastures** near Bethlehem would **dry up** as the terrifying roar passed through Judah and continued toward Gaza (Amos 1:6-8), Edom (vv. 11-12), and Moab (2:1-3). Northward, the fertile south and west slopes of Mount **Carmel**—some of Israel's choicest farmland (Isa. 35:1-2; also note Isa. 33:9; Nahum 1:4)—would wither and die as the heat wave of God's wrath moved on to engulf Damascus (Amos 1:3-5), Tyre (vv. 9-10), and Ammon (vv. 13-15). Everywhere the sound passed, moisture would evaporate, the land would turn brown, and drought would crack the earth. With pastures dried up, sheep would die and shepherds would suffer economic loss. And with crops withered farmers would face severe hardships.

The picture of drought suggests the reason for the Lord's angry roar—the nations had violated their covenants with God. The treaty or covenant between a suzerain lord and a vassal people was common in Near Eastern societies. In exchange for the suzerain's protection and provision, the vassal would pledge loyalty and obedience. The terms of the covenant, spelled out and mutually agreed on, were binding on both parties. Failure of the vassals to abide by the terms would cause the curses or punishments written in the treaty to descend on them. The curse of drought appears frequently as a punishment for covenant disobedience (cf. Deut. 28:20-24 in the Mosaic Covenant; for other ancient treaties see James B. Pritchard, ed., *Ancient Near Eastern Texts Relating to the Old Testament.* 3rd ed. Princeton: Princeton University Press, 1969, pp. 539, 660).

Those who heard Amos' words would understand that the sovereign Lord of the universe was about to judge them for their covenant violations. (On the question of the covenant relationship of the surrounding Gentile nations to God, see comments on Amos 1:3.) The Northern tribes of Israel in particular would perceive this charge of covenant rebellion as they heard that the Lord's roar was originating from Zion, that central holy abode from which they had revolted. (On the meaning of Zion, see comments on Lam. 1:4; Zech. 8:3.)

## II. The Roar of Judgment (1:3–2:16)

The Lord's roar was first against seven nations surrounding Israel, then against Israel herself. A murmur of approval might have rippled among Amos' hearers as they heard the denunciation of Aram (1:3-5) and Philistia (vv. 6-8), Israel's historic and bitter enemies. But when the focus shifted to Tyre (vv. 9-10), a sometime ally (1 Kings 5), then in turn to Edom (Amos 1:11-12), Ammon (vv. 13-15), and Moab (2:1-3), blood relatives of Israel (cf. Gen. 19:36-38; 25:29-30), the encircling review might have seemed "a noose of judgment about to tighten round their throats" (J.A. Motyer, *The Day of the Lion,* p. 50). With the mention finally of Judah (2:4-5), Israel's own "brother," the conclusion was inescapable—God's judgment would be impartial. For the locations of these and other places in Amos see the map "Israel and Surrounding Nations in the Days of the Prophets," between Song of Songs and Isaiah.

For each nation the pronouncement of doom follows the same pattern: (a) a general declaration of irrevocable judgment, (b) a naming of the specific violation which caused the judgment, and (c) a description of God's direct and thorough punishment.

## A. Judgment against the nations (1:3–2:5)

### 1. JUDGMENT AGAINST DAMASCUS (1:3-5)

**1:3.** The general declaration of irrevocable judgment occurs through the repeated phrase, **For three sins of . . . even for four, I will not turn back My wrath** (cf. vv. 6, 9, 11, 13; 2:1, 4, 6). The use of a number followed by the next higher number is frequent in the Old Testament (Job 5:19; Ps. 62:11-12; Prov. 30:15-16, 18-19, 21-23, 29-31). Usually the higher number is enumerated in detail, with special emphasis given the final item. Here Amos cited only the last of the crimes, the one which had finally gone beyond God's patience. Meir Weiss argues that the phrase should be translated, "For three sins of . . . *even* for four," as a poetic way of expressing the number seven, "a clearly typological number which symbolizes completeness" ("The Pattern of Numerical Sequence in Amos 1–2, A Re-examination," *Journal of Biblical Literature* 86. 1967:418). If this is correct, it means irrevocable judgment was pronounced on each nation for its full and complete sin. In the case of the surrounding nations, only the final and culminating sin was named. But for Israel, the complete list of seven was given (Amos 2:6-8, 12—one in v. 6, two in v. 7, two in v. 8, two in v. 12). Israel's panic would likewise be sevenfold in the day God judged them (2:14-16).

The cause of judgment for each nation was its "sins," its covenant violations. The word for "sin" (*pešaʿ*) means "rebellion" or "revolt," and was used in secular treaties to describe a vassal's disobedience of the terms of a covenant (1 Kings 12:19; 2 Kings 1:1; 3:5, 7; 8:22; Prov. 28:2). The Old Testament prophets also used the noun *pešaʿ* or the verb *pāšaʿ* in denouncing Israel's rebellion against God's covenant with her (Isa. 1:2, 28; 46:8; 66:24; Jer. 2:8; Hosea 7:13; 8:1; Micah 1:5, 13).

Amos specifically viewed the sins of Judah (Amos 2:4-5) and Israel (2:6-16; cf. 3:14; 4:4; 5:12) as violations of the Mosaic Covenant. She had failed to observe the terms of God's Law.

But not only Israel had sinned against a covenant with God. The Gentile nations also were guilty of *pešaʿ*—rebellion against a divinely established and universally recognized agreement. Apparently Amos had in mind their rebellion against God's universal covenant with humanity made at the time of Noah (Gen. 9:5-17). In exchange for God's suzerain promise never again to destroy the earth with a flood (Gen. 9:11), the vassal peoples were to refrain from shedding blood because disregard for human life is an assault on God's own image in man (Gen. 9:5-6). Human life, rather than being destroyed or curtailed, was to multiply and increase on the earth (Gen. 9:7). This mutual agreement, whereby God would preserve the earth and people would honor and extend human life, was called an "everlasting covenant" (Gen. 9:16).

This is the covenant, Amos charged, that the Gentile nations had rebelled against. By their acts of barbarism (Amos 1:3), their wholesale deportations of slave populations (vv. 6, 9), their unnatural and stubborn hatreds (v. 11), their sickening atrocities (v. 13), and their desecrations of the dead (2:1), they had broken the covenant that forbade such inhuman acts. Because of these sins, the earth's sovereign Lord declared, "I will not turn back My wrath."

Similarly Isaiah (Isa. 24:4-6; 26:20-21) said that God would bring a "curse" of drought "to punish the people of the earth" because they had "broken the everlasting covenant" by shedding blood. As the New Testament confirms, though Gentiles may not have received the spoken or written Law, the requirements of human decency are nevertheless known to them, and their own accusing conscience tells them when they violate God's standard (Rom. 2:14-15).

The culminating sin of **Damascus,** the capital of Aram, is that **she threshed Gilead** (also mentioned in Amos 1:13) of Transjordanian Israel **with sledges having iron teeth.** Threshing (cutting and separating the grain from the husks) was done on a threshing floor by pulling a heavy sledge over the grain. The sledge was a pair of roughly shaped boards, bent upward at the front, studded with iron prongs or knives. The reference here could be quite literal, describing a method of torturing prisoners; it is also a figure for harsh and thorough conquest (cf. Isa. 41:15; Micah 4:13; Hab. 3:12). Aram's armies had raked across Gilead, slicing and crushing it as though it were grain on a threshing floor. This Israelite territory east of Jordan had suffered greatly during constant battles with the Arameans, particularly during the time of Hazael (841–801 B.C.) and his son and successor Ben-Hadad III (Amos 1:4; cf. 2 Kings 8:7-12; 10:32-33; 13:3-7; note the reference to "threshing" in 2 Kings 13:7).

**1:4-5.** In the judgment on each of the first seven nations God is pictured as a suzerain Lord who has brought his armies to punish a vassal city for its revolt. The attack begins in each case with a **fire** that would eventually **consume the** walls and/or **fortresses** of the city and leave it a smoldering ruin (vv. 4, 7, 10, 12, 14; 2:2, 5). In punishing Damascus God declared He would smash the bar of the city gate and **break down the gate,** stripping the city of its defenses. He would **destroy the** rebel **king who** reigned over the wicked and proud nations. **Valley of Aven** and **Beth Eden** may refer to other regions of Aram, Baalbek and Bit-Adini. More likely, they are derogatory references to the area and palace of **Damascus,** meaning "Valley of Wickedness" and "House of Pleasure." **The house** (dynasty) of **Hazael** would be terminated, and the Arameans would be exiled (cf. 1:15) back to their place of origin, a Mesopotamian site called **Kir.** In essence, this punishment would be a complete reversal of Aram's proud history. God, who had originally brought them out of Kir (9:7), would send them back, after obliterating all they had achieved. This judgment was carried out by the Assyrians under Tiglath-Pileser III in 732 B.C. (cf. 2 Kings 16:7-9).

2. JUDGMENT AGAINST GAZA (1:6-8)

**1:6.** In verses 6-8 four of the five cities comprising the Philistine pentapolis are mentioned—**Gaza,** Ashdod, Ashkelon, and Ekron. The omission of the fifth, Gath, may be due to its ruined condition at the time of Amos because of the batterings of Hazael in 815 B.C. and Uzziah in 760 B.C. (cf. 2 Kings 12:17; 2 Chron. 26:6; Amos 6:2). The Philistines' crime against humanity was that they captured **whole communities** in slave raids **and sold them** for commercial profit. Defenseless people were treated as mere objects and auctioned off in the slave markets of **Edom,** from which they were shipped to other parts of the world (cf. Joel 3:4-8).

**1:7-8.** For this sin, the Philistine cities would be completely annihilated—buildings, king, and people. God would **turn** His **hand against** them **till the last of the Philistines** was **dead.** This judgment was partially fulfilled in the subjugation of the Philistines to the Assyrians later in the eighth century B.C., and more completely during the Maccabean period (168–134 B.C.). **Sovereign LORD** (*'ăḏōnāy Yahweh*) occurs 19 times in Amos, but only 5 other times in all the Minor Prophets (Obad. 1; Micah 1:2; Hab. 3:19; Zeph. 1:7; Zech. 9:14). That title stresses both His lordship and His covenant relationship with His people.

3. JUDGMENT AGAINST TYRE (1:9-10)

**1:9.** The sin of **Tyre,** Phoenicia's leading city, was even more callous than Gaza's. Not only did **she** sell **whole communities of captives to Edom** (cf. v. 6), but she did so in violation of **a treaty of brotherhood,** a protective covenant between two partners. If Israel was the injured partner, the reference is probably to the pact between Solomon and Hiram (1 Kings 5) or perhaps to the later relations established through the marriage of Ahab and Jezebel (1 Kings 16:29-31).

**1:10.** Tyre's punishment is similar to that described in verse 7. Alexander the Great overran the city of **Tyre** in 332 B.C. after besieging it for seven months. Six thousand people were slain outright, 2,000 were crucified, and 30,000 were sold as slaves. Tyre had sold Israelites to Edom as captives; later many Tyrians became captives.

### 4. JUDGMENT AGAINST EDOM (1:11-12)

**1:11.** The sin **of Edom** was his persistent and unfeeling hostility against **his brother**. "Brother" could refer to some unknown treaty partner (cf. v. 9). But the frequent references in the Old Testament to Edom's brotherhood with Israel suggest that this refers to the physical kinship between the two nations that began with Esau and Jacob (Gen. 25:29-30; Num. 20:14; Deut. 2:4; 23:7). At some point in Israel's history Edom relentlessly **pursued his** defeated brother **with a sword** (cf. Obad. 10). Without any natural feelings of **compassion,** Edom let **his anger** rage **continually,** like a beast tearing its captured prey. He brooded over his **fury,** nourishing it so it **flamed unchecked.**

**1:12.** Because of this unnatural and vindictive hatred, God would **send fire upon Teman** and **Bozrah.** Teman was Edom's largest southern city; Bozrah was her fortress stronghold in the north. The two cities thus stand for the whole nation under God's wrath. Some scholars, however, say Teman was in the north near Bozrah. At any rate, both were major Edomite cities (cf. references to Teman in Jer. 49:7, 20; Ezek. 25:13; Obad. 9; Hab. 3:3). Edom was subjugated by the Assyrians in the eighth century B.C., turned into a desolate wasteland by the fifth century B.C. (Mal. 1:3), and overtaken by the Nabateans, an Arabian tribe, around 400–300 B.C.

### 5. JUDGMENT AGAINST AMMON (1:13-15)

**1:13.** The terrible cruelty of **Ammon** was that **he ripped open the pregnant women of Gilead** (cf. "Gilead" in v. 3). This atrocity, sometimes a feature of ancient warfare (cf. 2 Kings 8:12; 15:16; Hosea 13:16), was designed to terrorize and decimate an enemy. The Ammonites executed this crime against defenseless women and unborn children, not for self-preservation, but simply **in order to extend** their **borders.**

**1:14-15.** Because of this heartlessness God would **set fire to the walls** (cf. vv. 7, 10) **of Rabbah,** Ammon's capital city. **Amid** the engulfing flames the inhabitants would hear the **war cries** (cf. 2:2) of the attackers as they fell on their victims. **Violent winds,** symbolizing God's own awesome power (cf. Ps. 83:15; Jer. 23:19; 30:23), would lash at the city. And the enemy would take both **king** and **officials** (cf. Amos 2:3) **into exile** (cf. 1:5). This judgment was fulfilled through the Assyrian conquest under Tiglath-Pileser III in 734 B.C.

### 6. JUDGMENT AGAINST MOAB (2:1-3)

**2:1.** In ancient times much importance was placed on a dead man's body being peacefully placed in the family burial site, so that he could be "gathered to his fathers" and find rest in the grave. To rob, disturb, or desecrate a grave was an offense of the highest order. Many surviving tomb inscriptions utter violent curses against anyone who would commit such an outrage (G.A. Cooke, *A Textbook of North-Semitic Inscriptions.* Oxford: At the Clarendon Press, 1903, pp. 26-7, 30-2; Pritchard, *Ancient Near Eastern Texts Relating to the Old Testament,* p. 327). **Moab,** in a war against Edom (perhaps the incident referred to in 2 Kings 3:26-27), drove their opponents back to their own territory, opened the royal graves, and **burned, as if to lime, the bones of Edom's king.** This sacrilege was so thorough that bone ashes became as fine and white as powdered chalk.

**2:2-3.** Though this was not a crime against Israel, it was nevertheless a sin of rebellion (*peša';* see comments on 1:3) against the sovereign LORD of the universe, an assault against His own image in people. For such contempt and defilement, God would militarily annihilate **Moab.** A **fire** would **consume . . . Kerioth,** perhaps an alternate name for the capital Ar (cf. Num. 21:28; Isa. 15:1). In the **tumult** of battle, with **war cries** (cf. Amos 1:14) **and the blast of the trumpet** signaling her doom, **Moab** would **go down**—the people, **ruler,** and **all . . . officials** (cf. 1:15). Moab, like Ammon, fell to the Assyrians under Tiglath-Pileser III.

### 7. JUDGMENT AGAINST JUDAH (2:4-5)

**2:4.** The Gentile nations had rebelled against the "everlasting covenant" God made with them at the time of Noah (Gen. 9:5-17). But Judah's **sins** (*peša'*) were against the Mosaic Covenant. They had **rejected the Law of the LORD.** They had not observed the **decrees,** or stipulations, of His unique agreement with them. Instead of holding to His objective truth, they let themselves be **led astray by** the same **false gods** which had deceived many of **their ancestors.** The word for false god is *kāzāḇ,* "a lie or something deceptive." The idols were deceptive for they were unable to help the people. In Deuteronomy God constantly warned the Israelites not to follow false gods (Deut. 6:14; 7:16; 8:19; 11:16, 28; etc.).

**2:5.** The punishment for this faithlessness would be the destruction of the nation, fulfilled in 586 B.C. when Nebuchadnezzar, after a lengthy siege, broke through Jerusalem's defenses, slaughtered the royal family, burned the temple, the palace, and all houses in the city, and deported almost the entire population to Babylon (2 Kings 25:1-12).

### B. Judgment against Israel (2:6-16)

Having shown that the Lord is sovereign over the universe and holds all nations accountable for their rebellion against Him, Amos now addressed the Northern tribes of Israel. His message was that God would also judge them, because they had broken His covenant, despite His gracious acts on their behalf.

1. THE BROKEN COVENANT (2:6-8)

Israel had violated the Mosaic Covenant in several ways, including social injustice (v. 6b), legal perversion (v. 7a), sexual sin (v. 7b), abuse of collateral (v. 8a), and idolatry (v. 8b).

**2:6.** The first charge against the Israelites is that they callously sold into slavery the poor who could not pay their debts (cf. 2 Kings 4:1-7). Honest people **(the righteous)** who could be trusted to repay eventually, were sold **for** the **silver** they owed. The desperately poor **(the needy)** were enslaved because they could not pay back the insignificant sum they owed **for a pair of sandals** (cf. Amos 8:6). These sandals might refer to the custom of giving one's sandals as a kind of mortgage deed or title to confirm the legal transfer of land (cf. Ruth 4:7). The meaning would then be that the poor were being sold for either money or land. Such hardheartedness against Israel's *own* people, not against a foreign nation, was rebellion against God's covenant which called for generosity and openhandedness toward the poor (Deut. 15:7-11).

**2:7a.** Amos' second accusation against Israel was that legal procedures were being perverted to exploit **the poor.** Contrary to the covenant commands (Ex.

23:6; Deut. 16:19), the courts had gone into collusion with the creditors and were denying **justice to the oppressed.** This oppression was so terrible and painful it was like trampling **on** their **heads.**

**2:7b.** The third crime is that **father and son** were having sexual intercourse with **the same girl,** either a temple prostitute or a servant taken as a concubine (Ex. 21:7-9; Lev. 18:8, 15). By such promiscuity the men were showing their desregard for the Lord of the covenant and were profaning (i.e., treating as common) His **holy name.** God's "name" (see comments on Ex. 3:13-15) spoke of His character and His unique commitment to Israel. To flaunt His commandments openly was to mock His character and to disdain His special place in their lives.

**2:8a.** Fourth, God's Law placed restrictions on items which could be taken as collateral. Millstones were not to be taken since they were needed for grinding grain and thus were essential to sustaining life (Deut. 24:6). The cloak of a poor man was not to be kept as a pledge overnight (Ex. 22:26-27; Deut. 24:10-13; also note Job 22:6); a widow's garment could not be **taken in pledge** at all (Deut. 24:17). Yet the people openly and flagrantly were lying **down** with the forbidden **garments,** going so far in their contempt for the Law as to spread them at the sacrificial feasts by **every altar** (cf. 1 Sam. 9:12-13).

**2:8b.** Fifth, Israel had rebelled against the most basic covenant stipulation of all—they were worshiping other gods (as Judah was doing, v. 4). The **wine** they had unjustly extracted from the poor **as fines** was being raised in honor to a heathen **god.**

2. THE SPURNED GRACE (2:9-12)

**2:9.** Instead of announcing the punishment immediately after the accusation, as was done in the judgments against the seven other nations, God heightened Israel's guilt by setting her rebellion against the backdrop of His own gracious acts toward them. Israel's existence as a nation was only because of His intervention. By themselves they could never have conquered the Canaanites. **The Amorite** (cf. v. 10; note comments on Gen. 14:13-16), as the most formidable, stands for all the nations in Canaan at the time of the Conquest (cf.

Gen. 15:16-21; Josh. 24:8-15). The inhabitants of the land were the greatest of men, **tall as the cedars and strong as the oaks** (cf. Num. 13:28-33; Deut. 1:26-28). Yet God uprooted them, totally destroying them, both **fruit above** and **roots below.**

**2:10.** The Exodus from **Egypt** and God's preservation of Israel during **40 years in the desert** evidenced His kindness and good intentions toward her. (On **the Amorites** see comments on v. 9.)

**2:11.** God also **raised up** spiritual leaders for the nation. **Prophets from among** their own **sons** conveyed His words to them, and **Nazirites,** who consecrated themselves by vows for limited periods of time (cf. Num. 6:1-21), portrayed the depth of commitment that all Israel was supposed to share.

**2:12. But** despite these gracious acts Israel added two more sins to her account. She intimidated **the Nazirites** (cf. v. 11) to break their vows and **drink wine, and** she **commanded the prophets not to prophesy** (cf. 7:10-16). In so doing Israel revealed her own lack of commitment to God and her unwillingness to hear His Word.

3. THE RESULTING JUDGMENT (2:13-16)

**2:13-16.** Because of these sins God would not turn back His wrath (v. 6). He would **crush** rebellious Israel **as a cart crushes when loaded with grain.** There would be no hope in the devastating day of battle. Out of the entire army, none would be able to save his life—not (a) **the swift,** (b) **the strong,** (c) **the warrior,** (d) **the archer,** (e) **the fleet-footed soldier,** or (f) **the horseman.** So overpowering would be the onslaught that **even** (g) **the bravest warriors** would drop their weapons and cloaks in a futile attempt to **flee.** This wartime panic was sevenfold just as Israel's sins were seven (vv. 6b-8, 12).

The history of the Northern Kingdom came to an end only a few decades later with the Assyrian Captivity in 722 B.C. (2 Kings 17:1-23).

The roar of judgment ended. **The LORD,** the Sovereign of the earth, had spoken. He would come as a mighty Warrior to judge the surrounding nations for their rebellion against His authority. He would judge Israel too, because she also had broken His covenant despite His grace toward her.

## III. The Reasons for Judgment (chaps. 3–6)

After announcing the judgment that would come against the Northern Kingdom, Amos gave a series of five messages to explain more fully the reasons for God's judgment. The first three messages are marked by the phrase "Hear this word" (3:1; 4:1; 5:1); the last two begin with "Woe to you" (5:18; 6:1). Each message describes in more detail the religious, legal, political, and social rebellion which had brought God's wrath against the nation. Within the messages are appeals for repentance and instructions as to how individuals could escape the awful calamity that was coming.

### A. The first message (chap. 3)

In this message Amos declared that Israel would be punished because of her unique relationship with God. Her judgment was inevitable because of her unparalleled oppression of people. The message was addressed initially to both Israel and Judah (vv. 1-2), but then it was primarily directed to the Northern Kingdom (cf. vv. 9, 12).

1. THE UNIQUE RELATIONSHIP (3:1-2)

**3:1-2.** The reason God spoke **this word . . . against . . . Israel** and Judah —whom He **brought up out of Egypt**— was because they **only** had been **chosen of all the families of the earth.** "Chosen" (from *yāda*ʿ, lit., "to know") was used in ancient treaties to describe a sovereign's commitment to a vassal in a special covenant relationship (Herbert B. Huffmon, "The Treaty Background of Hebrew *Yāda*ʿ," *Bulletin of the American Schools of Oriental Research* 181. February 1966:31-7). They alone were God's people, the only nation He had ever really chosen to watch over and care for.

**Therefore** He would **punish** them **for** their **sins.** Because He had chosen them, intimately revealed Himself to them, and made available to them the greatest covenantal blessings a suzerain ever offered a vassal (Ex. 19:3-6; Deut. 28:1-14), they should have in return wanted to know Him and please Him. Because of His special commitment, their iniquities were even more terrible.

God's electing grace is always meant to influence one's conduct. His special commitments and blessings often contain special chastisements to discipline and to purge (Luke 12:47-48; 1 Cor. 11:27-32; Heb. 12:4-11; 1 Peter 1:7-9; 4:17). Because His love is so great, His people must be holy.

## 2. THE INEVITABLE JUDGMENT (3:3-8)

These verses show that Israel's punishment was inevitable. Much as there is often an inseparable link between two events in ordinary life, so there was an inseparable link between God's revelation to Amos and the inevitable appearance of judgment.

**3:3.** Through a series of seven rhetorical questions (in vv. 3-6) Amos reminded his listeners that certain events are inseparably connected (cf. Amos' other sevens in 2:6b-8, 11-12, 14-16). A second event does not happen unless it has been preceded by a necessary first event; once the first event has taken place the second is sure to follow.

First, **two** do not **walk together** along a road **unless they have** first met, chatted, and **agreed to** continue on together.

**3:4.** Second, **a lion,** does not **roar in the thicket** unless he has spotted his **prey** and begun his fearful charge (cf. Jud. 14:5). But once he has begun his savage rush, the paralyzing roar is inevitable (cf. comments on Amos 1:2). Third, in a similar way a lion's contented **growl in his den** is a sure sign that something has been **caught;** a successful hunt leads to his satisfied rumble.

**3:5.** Fourth, **a bird** does not **fall into a trap** unless a **snare** has first been baited and **set.** Nor, fifth, **does a trap spring up from the earth** unless something catchable has triggered it. A captured bird or wild animal usually means a trap was used.

**3:6.** Sixth, **people** do not **tremble** unless **a war trumpet** has been sounded **in a city;** but such an alarm always produces fear and apprehension. Nor does **disaster** finally come **to a city** unless **the Lord** has determined to cause **it** (cf. Isa. 45:7). But once His decision is made, the outcome is unavoidable. The "disaster" could be a plague, meager harvest, or hostile attack (cf. Amos 4:6-11), designed by God to lead the people to repent, acknowledge His sovereignty in their lives, and trust Him for deliverance (cf. Joel 1).

The seven examples of related events began innocuously, but become increasingly foreboding. The first example (Amos 3:3) had no element of force or disaster about it. The next two (v. 4), however, concerned the overpowering of one animal by another, and the two after that (v. 5) pictured man as the vanquisher of animal prey. In the final two examples (v. 6), people themselves were overwhelmed, first by other human instruments, then by God Himself. This ominous progression, to the point where God Himself is seen as the initiator of human calamity, brought Amos to a climactic statement (vv. 7-8).

**3:7-8.** Just as one event does not take place unless another necessary event has already happened, so **the sovereign Lord does nothing** regarding the history of Israel **without** first **revealing His plan to His servants the prophets.** But once this revelation has occurred—once **the lion has roared** and attacked (cf. 1:2; Hosea 5:14; 11:10; 13:7), once **the sovereign Lord has spoken**—Israel's judgment is sure to follow.

Major changes in Israel's history were preceded by revelations from God; He seldom acted without first giving warning through a prophet. Ahijah prophesied the schism in Solomon's empire (1 Kings 11:29-39; fulfilled in 1 Kings 12:15-20). An anonymous prophet forecast Josiah's reform (1 Kings 13:1-2; fulfilled in 2 Kings 23:15-20). Ahijah predicted the death of Abijah and the end of the dynasty of Jeroboam I (1 Kings 14:1-16; fulfilled in 1 Kings 14:17-18; 15:29). Elijah prophesied the deaths of Ahab and Jezebel, and the extermination of Ahab's descendants (1 Kings 21:17-24; fulfilled in 1 Kings 22:29-37; 2 Kings 9:30–10:11). Elijah also predicted the death of Ahaziah (2 Kings 1:2-4, 16; fulfilled in 2 Kings 1:17). Elisha forecast Moab's defeat by Jehoram and Jehoshaphat (2 Kings 3). Elisha repeated Elijah's prediction of the fall of Ahab's dynasty (2 Kings 9:7-10). Jeroboam II regained lost Israelite territory in fulfillment of an unrecorded prophecy by Jonah (2 Kings 14:25).

Isaiah predicted the collapse of the Assyrians in their invasion of Jerusalem (2 Kings 19:5-7, 20, 32-34; fulfilled in 2 Kings 19:35-37) and the extension of Hezekiah's life (2 Kings 20:1-11). Judah's exile to Babylon (fulfilled in 2 Kings 24–25) was repeatedly foretold—to Hezekiah by Isaiah (2 Kings 20:16-18), to Manasseh by anonymous prophets (2 Kings 21:10-15), and to Josiah by Huldah the prophetess (2 Kings 22:14-20). And Isaiah predicted that Cyrus would commission the rebuilding of the temple (Isa. 44:28; fulfilled in Ezra 1).

The Lord always revealed His major plans in advance to His servants the prophets. The prediction could precede the event by years or even centuries, but the fulfillment was always certain. Since the Lord had now roared His judgment like a lion, **who** could but **fear** the outcome? And since He had revealed His intentions to Amos, what could he do **but prophesy** God's message?

### 3. THE UNPARALLELED OPPRESSION (3:9-10)

**3:9-10.** Imaginary heralds were instructed to invite emissaries from **Ashdod** (in Philistia) and **Egypt** to **assemble . . . on the mountains** above **Samaria** and **see** what the city was like. These dignitaries, from countries where the art of injustice was well developed (cf. 1:6-8), would, ironically, be astonished at what they observed in Israel's capital. **Great unrest** was in the city. Instead of peace and order, panic and the terrifying disintegration of the rule of law prevailed. Instead of justice, violence and **oppression** were rampant. By means of threats and exploitation, the rich had amassed private fortunes, hoarding the results of **plunder and loot** in their homes. The words "plunder" and "loot" refer to acts of violence against persons and property, and stand essentially for "assault and robbery." Terrorizing had become so much a part of their lives that they no longer knew **how to do** what was **right** (i.e., what was straightforward, honest, and just).

The invitation was sent **to the fortresses** (3:9) of the neighboring states. A "fortress" was almost any building higher than an ordinary house. Containing several stories, it was constructed to be defensible, and often became part of a city's defense system. The king's palace usually included a fortress as part of its structure (cf. "citadel" in 1 Kings 16:18; 2 Kings 15:25); such buildings also served as residences of the rich and ruling class (Jer. 9:21). These residential strongholds were a national pride (Amos 6:8), a symbol of power and wealth, and therefore

the special focus of God's wrath (1:4, 7, 10, 14; 2:2, 5). Amos summoned leaders from the fortresses of Ashdod and Egypt to Samaria to see that the inhabitants of Israel's fortresses had outstripped even *them* in their ability to profit from oppression! Amos' accusation is similar to Paul's in 1 Corinthians 5:1—a level of sin was existing among God's people which did not even occur among pagans.

### 4. THE COMING CATASTROPHE (3:11-15)

In three progressive declarations Amos unfolded the catastrophe that would come on Israel because of her unparalleled oppression (cf. vv. 9-10).

**3:11.** An enemy, **the sovereign LORD** said, would invade and **overrun the land,** pulling **down** and plundering the nation's defenses. The **fortresses** (cf. v. 10) of the looters would themselves be looted.

**3:12.** Some of Amos' hearers might have objected to this announcement, insisting that somehow **the Israelites** would **be saved.** The word "saved" (usually trans. "rescued" or "delivered" in NIV) often described God's delivering or sparing of Israel (Ex. 3:8; 18:9-10; Pss. 54:7; 69:14; Jer. 15:21; Micah 4:10). This revealed the mistaken belief of Amos' hearers that God would surely rescue them from such a catastrophe. To dispel this false hope, Amos repeated **what the LORD** said: any "saving" of Israel would be like **a shepherd** saving a couple of **leg bones or** part **of an ear** from the jaws of a wild animal. These little bits of "rescued" evidence were to prove that a shepherd had not stolen or sold one of the sheep, but that it indeed had been torn by a beast of prey (Ex. 22:10-13; cf. Gen 31:39). The rescued shin bones and tip of an ear only proved that the rescue had come too late and that the animal was a total loss. **Those** Israelites in **Samaria** who dissolutely lounged on **their beds** and **couches** should not dismiss Amos' message with vague assurances of deliverance. Israel would be savagely and totally devoured.

**3:13-15.** God addressed the Northern Kingdom as **the house of Jacob,** using the patriarchal name (cf. 6:8; 7:2, 5; 8:7; 9:8) to remind them of His early commitment to their ancestors. In times past God had been a Warrior on their behalf. But now He would lead another army against them to **punish** them **for** their sins (on "sins," *pešaʿ*, as covenant violations, see comments on 1:3). **God Almighty** (lit., "God of hosts," i.e., "Head of armies") designates the most awesome Warrior. Throughout these chapters which describe Israel's violations (chaps. 3–6) **the LORD** is repeatedly presented (3:13; 4:13; 5:14-16, 27; 6:8, 14) as a mighty Suzerain who commands vast forces, whose power to punish rebels is both massive and irresistible.

In punishing them, God would **destroy the altars of Bethel** (cf. 9:1). Bethel was the royal sanctuary of Jeroboam II (7:10-13), the most popular religious center in Israel (cf. 4:4; 5:5). As the site of the golden calf erected by Jeroboam I (1 Kings 12:26-30; Hosea 10:5), its altars symbolized Israel's continued rebellion against God. **The horns of** these altars were projections on the altars' corners. Fugitives could grab these horns to claim asylum from their pursuers (1 Kings 1:50; 2:28; Ex. 21:12-13). Murderers, however, could not receive protection, but were torn by force from the altar (Ex. 21:14). Israel's sin was similarly so great that God Himself was going to **cut off** the means of claiming asylum. There would be no sanctuary from the enemy who was coming against them.

God would not only destroy their religious center; He would also **tear down** the luxurious **mansions** which resulted from their commercial exploitation. Once only kings could afford both a **winter house** and a **summer house.** For example, in the ninth century Ahab had a winter palace in the warmer plains of Jezreel (1 Kings 21:1) besides his Samaria residence. Luxury **houses adorned with ivory** inlay or furnishings (cf. Amos 6:4) were likewise the province of royalty (1 Kings 22:39; Ps. 45:8). Yet the ill-gotten prosperity (cf. Prov. 10:2) of Israel's upper classes had enabled them to build such dwellings. All these, however, would **be demolished** on the day God would punish Israel.

## B. The second message (chap. 4)

In the second message Amos declared that God would exile the upper-class women because of their economic exploitation, and judge the nation as a whole for its religious hypocrisy and obstinate refusal to repent, despite His repeated chastisements.

### 1. ECONOMIC EXPLOITATION (4:1-3)

**4:1.** The upper-class women were called **cows of Bashan.** Bashan, in Transjordan east of the Sea of Kinnereth (Galilee), was famous for its lush pastures (Jer. 50:19; Micah 7:14), and its well-fed cattle (Ezek. 39:18; Ps. 22:12). Amos accused the rich women of being equally pampered, insisting that their **husbands** continually supplied them with intoxicating **drinks.** The word for "husbands" is not one of the common Hebrew terms for husband, but a rare word meaning "master" or "lord" (cf. Gen. 18:12; Ps. 45:11). Amos scorned those husbands who were supposed to be "masters" but who in reality meekly obeyed like servants. The only way they could support their wives' expensive tastes was by ruthlessly exploiting **the poor** and **the needy** (cf. Amos 2:6-7; 5:11-12; 8:4-6). (Though the women are said in 4:1 to do the oppressing, apparently they did so by domineering their husbands.) The words **oppress** and **crush** describe threats and physical harassments used to squeeze money from the helpless.

**4:2-3.** In order to show the vehemence of His anger and the certainty of their punishment, **the sovereign LORD** had **sworn by His holiness** that every one of these society women would be dragged from the city either to captivity or to death. God had vowed the entire reality of His inmost being to this unchangeable sentence (cf. 6:8). An enemy would storm and capture the city. The destruction would be so thorough and the **breaks in the wall** so numerous that each woman, rather than going with others toward an exit gate, would simply be pushed **straight out** of the city. Once outside they would be fastened to ropes **with hooks** for a single-file march into Assyrian exile. Those who balked or refused to be led away would be forcibly snagged with large harpoons or **fishhooks,** much like fish pierced together and jerked over one's shoulder to be carried to market. Yanked in such manner, they eventually would be **cast out** as corpses as the march neared **Harmon.** (For the use of "cast out" to depict what is done with dead bodies; cf. 8:3; 1 Kings 13:24-25; Jer. 14:16.) "Harmon" may refer to Hermon, a mountain at the northern tip of the Bashan region on the way to Assyria. If so, an awful irony would at-

## The Covenant Chastenings

| Chastening | Amos | Leviticus | Deuteronomy | 1 Kings |
|---|---|---|---|---|
| Hunger/famine | 4:6 | 26:26, 29 | 28:17, 48 | 8:37 |
| Drought | 4:7-8 | 26:19 | 28:22-24, 48 | 8:35 |
| Blight/mildew | 4:9 | 26:20 | 28:18, 22, 30, 39-40 | 8:37 |
| Locusts | 4:9 | — | 28:38, 42 | 8:37 |
| Plagues | 4:10 | 26:16, 25 | 28:21-22, 27, 35, 59-61 | 8:37 |
| Military defeat | 4:10 | 26:17, 25, 33, 36-39 | 28:25-26, 49-52 | 8:33 |
| Devastation | 4:11 | 26:31-35 | 29:23-28 | — |

tach to their fate: the "cows of Bashan" (Amos 4:1) would end as carrion in Bashan!

### 2. RELIGIOUS HYPOCRISY (4:4-5)

**4:4-5.** Verse 4 is a parody of a priest's summons to pilgrims. The usual invitation was to "come into the sanctuary to worship" (Pss. 95:6; 96:8-9; 100:2-4). But with biting sarcasm Amos exhorted Israel to **go to Bethel** and **to Gilgal** in order to **sin** (i.e., to break their covenant with God; see Amos 1:3 for comments on "sin," *peša'*). Bethel was the chief sanctuary of the north, the place where the king worshiped (see comments on 3:14). Gilgal, with its memorial stones marking Israel's initial entrance into the land (Josh. 4), remained in the eighth century as a center for pilgrimage and sacrifice (Amos 5:5; Hosea 4:15; 9:15; 12:11).

Amos commanded the Israelites to bring the whole gamut of offerings to these shrines enthusiastically. **Sacrifices** were offerings in which an animal was slaughtered and consumed as part of a sacred meal (cf. 1 Sam. 1:3-5). **Tithes** of produce were set aside **every three years** in order to help the poor (Deut. 14:28-29). (A possible alternate trans. of Amos 4:4 refers to the custom of offering the regular tithes, Deut. 12:4-7; 14:22-27, on the third day after arriving at the sanctuary.) The purpose of the **thank** offerings was to express gratitude for blessings and answered prayers (Lev. 7:11-15). **Freewill offerings** were voluntary and spontaneous gifts, born of an inner devotion to God (Lev. 7:16; 22:17-19).

But all these offerings, Amos charged, had become a sham. The people's religious activities were carried out to impress others, not to fellowship with God. The Israelites would brag **about** their devotion, but their day-to-day conduct violated the spirit of their offerings.

Some of the produce they tithed came from stolen land. Some animals they sacrificed had been fattened on unjustly seized fields. Their very worship was an offense to God as it hypocritically offered the fruits of their rebellion against His covenant (cf. Isa. 1:10-20; Micah 6:6-8).

### 3. REFUSAL TO REPENT (4:6-13)

The people had persisted in their economic exploitation and religious hypocrisy despite God's repeated attempts to bring them back to Him (vv. 6-11). Therefore because they would not return to Him He would come to them in final judgment. They must prepare to meet their God (v. 12), whose terrible greatness was inescapable (v. 13).

**4:6.** Ancient Near Eastern covenants spelled out the curses or punishments the suzerain would bring against his vassals for disloyalty or disobedience. Verses 6-11 record how God had brought the chastisements of the Mosaic Covenant against His people in order to bring them back to Himself. Leviticus 26 and Deuteronomy 28–29 had warned that God would use famine (Amos 4:6), drought (vv. 7-8), crop failure (v. 9), plagues (v. 10), military defeat (v. 10), and even burning devastation (v. 11) to punish His people for covenant violations. Solomon also foretold (1 Kings 8:33-37) that God would use these means to turn the people from their sin. The chart "The Covenant Chastenings" compares the covenant chastenings of Amos

4:6-11 with those predicted in Leviticus 26, Deuteronomy 28–29, and 1 Kings 8.

With each chastisement God anticipated repentance. But Israel refused. The fivefold refrain—**yet you have not returned to Me** (Amos 4:6, 8-11)—underscores her continued obstinacy. This persistent refusal had now become an accumulated guilt. Final judgment, therefore, was inevitable.

God had given them **empty stomachs** (lit., "cleanness of teeth," i.e., nothing to chew on). Hunger and famine had afflicted the whole land—**every city** and **every town.** But the people did not turn to God.

**4:7-8.** Such famines were often caused by a prior drought, as God would withhold the spring **rain** so essential to the summer **harvest.** This discipline was often selective, so that **one town** had **rain** while **another** did not, **one field** was rained on but **another** was not. As the wells and cisterns in some localities **dried up** and its **people staggered** exhausted **from town to town** in search of limited drinking **water,** the contrast between their judgment and another town's favor should have caused them to ponder God's action. But they did not consider.

**4:9.** God **struck** the vegetables and fruit trees of their **gardens** and the grape clusters of their **vineyards.** The hot blasting wind of the Arabian desert blew relentlessly, causing **blight,** a premature drying and scorching of the grain (cf. Gen. 41:6, 23, 27; 2 Kings 19:26). Parasitic worms brought **mildew,** a yellowing of the tips of green grain. **Locusts devoured** the leaves of **fig and olive trees** (cf. Joel 1:1-7). But all this did not cause repentance.

**4:10.** Wars brought **plagues** and death to the nation. As populations were crowded into walled cities or assembled in camps, contagious diseases broke out and spread. The mention of **Egypt** has caused some to think that the "plagues" are similar to those that struck Egypt's livestock at the time of the Exodus (cf. Ex. 9:1-7). But because of the military scenes mentioned in Amos 4:10, and because the word "plague" can denote an epidemic pestilence among humans (cf. Ex. 5:3; 9:15; Lev. 26:25; Jer. 14:12; 21:7, 9; Ezek. 5:17; 14:19), the most likely one is the bubonic plague which spreads from rats to people by fleas. The mention of Egypt is best interpreted as "like those that happen in Egypt," a reference to the notorious human plagues which periodically swept that country (cf. Deut. 7:15; 28:27, 60).

During the battles God **killed** (i.e., caused the enemy to kill) their strong **young men,** the elite of their fighting force. Their **horses,** the strength of their chariot corps, were **captured.** Because of the carnage, **the stench** of diseased and decaying corpses filled their **camps.** But still Israel did **not** return to **the LORD.**

**4:11.** Finally, God totally **overthrew some of** their cities with the same burning devastation He had wreaked on **Sodom and Gomorrah** (cf. Gen. 19:23-29; Deut. 29:22-23). So thorough had been the destruction from a military siege that certain cities had ceased to exist. The whole nation had come perilously close to obliteration, barely escaping **like a burning stick snatched from the fire.** But this too had proved futile.

**4:12. Therefore,** because **Israel** had resisted these chastenings and had continued her sinful rebellion, God would pronounce her sentence of doom. **This is what I will do to you** refers to God's devastating sweep through the land as predicted in 3:11-15. The nation was commanded to get ready for this terrifying moment—**prepare to meet your God, O Israel.**

Some understand the word "prepare" as an invitation to repent before this final catastrophe. Since the word, however, was often used of war preparations (cf. Prov. 21:31; Jer. 46:14; Ezek. 38:7; Nahum 2:3, 5), "prepare to meet your God" is most likely a military summons to an awful confrontation. Israel was to face God's final judgment.

**4:13.** Amos likened God's terrifying approach in judgment to the darkening of a storm. The One who formed **the mountains** and created **the wind** now covered those **high places** with churning clouds. The early **dawn** turned back **to** eerie **darkness** as black swells unfolded to shroud **the earth.** The flash of lightning and the reverberation of thunder marked God's ominous "tread" from one hilltop to another as He approached the Northern capital (cf. Micah 1:3-5). God had revealed **His thoughts to man;** His intent to judge had been made known (Amos 3:7). Now, as **the LORD God Al-**

**mighty** (see comments on 3:13), Commander of all forces in heaven and earth, He advanced against them. Their judgment was inescapable.

## C. The third message (5:1-17)

Amos' third (vv. 1-17) and fourth (vv. 18-27) messages are structured and juxtaposed to highlight one overall truth: the nation would be judged by its mighty sovereign God, but individuals could yet repent and live.

Each message follows a chiastic structure in which the themes of the early paragraphs are repeated in reverse order in the later paragraphs:
a. Theme one
  b. Theme two
    c. Theme three
    c¹. Theme three (repeated)
  b¹. Theme two (repeated)
a¹. Theme one (repeated)
Sometimes the middle theme is unrepeated.

In chiastic structures the second or middle theme, whether repeated or not, emerges as the central focus of the whole message. In Amos' third message this central focus is the might and sovereignty of God:
a. Description of certain judgment (vv. 1-3)
  b. Call for individual repentance (vv. 4-6)
    c. Accusation of legal injustice (v. 7)
    d. Portrayal of a sovereign God (vv. 8-9)
    c¹. Accusation of legal injustice (vv. 10-13)
  b¹. Call for individual repentance (vv. 14-15)
a¹. Description of certain judgment (vv. 16-17)
The central focus of the fourth message is the call of individuals to repent:
a. Description of certain judgment (vv. 18-20)
  b. Accusation of religious hypocrisy (vv. 21-22)
    c. Call for individual repentance (vv. 23-24)
  b¹. Accusation of religious hypocrisy (vv. 25-26)
a¹. Description of certain judgment (v. 27)
Together these two messages present one overall truth: the mighty sovereign God would judge the nation as a whole for its legal injustice and religious hypocrisy, but He offered life to individuals within the nation who would yet repent and seek Him.

### 1. DESCRIPTION OF CERTAIN JUDGMENT (5:1-3)

**5:1.** Amos summoned the people to **hear** his **lament** over their death. A "lament" was ordinarily a poem of grief sung at the funeral of a relative, friend, or leader (cf. 2 Sam. 1:17-27; 3:33-34; 2 Chron. 35:25). Prophets, however, also used this poetic form to mourn the death of a city, people, or nation (cf. Jer. 7:29; 9:10-11, 17-22; Lam.; Ezek. 19; 26:17-18; 27:2, 32; 28:12; 32:2). Though **Israel** was at the height of prosperity under Jeroboam II, her judgment was so certain that Amos lamented her fall as though it had already happened. To his listeners, hearing this lament would be as jarring as reading one's own obituary in the newspaper.

**5:2. Virgin Israel** had **fallen.** This nation which had considered itself in the full bloom of youthful vigor had been cut off before her time in violent death. "Fallen" in funeral songs means "fallen by the sword" (cf. 2 Sam. 1:19, 25, 27; 3:34; Lam. 2:21). She had died in battle **in her own land.** Her corpse lay unattended, **deserted** by God Himself. The word "deserted" was often used of God's abandoning or forsaking His people (Jud. 6:13; 2 Kings 21:14; Isa. 2:6). There was **no one to lift her up,** no one to restore her to life. (Cf. 1 Sam. 2:6; Hosea 6:2; Amos 9:11 for the use of "to lift up," lit., "to raise up," to describe God's restoring to life.) Since the God who could help had Himself abandoned her, Israel had fallen, **never to rise again.**

**5:3.** Her armies had been decimated. **The city** or **town** that had detached a military unit of **a thousand** or **a hundred** (cf. 1 Sam. 17:18, NIV marg.; 18:13; 22:7; 2 Sam. 18:1, 4) saw only 10 percent return from war. An army could sustain a 50 percent loss and still fight (2 Sam. 18:3). But if 90 percent were slain, that nation had received its death sentence. Amos lamented an Israel that would cease to exist.

### 2. CALL FOR INDIVIDUAL REPENTANCE (5:4-6)

**5:4-5.** National judgment was certain, but individuals could yet **seek God**

and live (cf. v. 6). They should **not,** however, **seek** Him at the sanctuaries, for these were doomed. See comments on **Bethel** and **Gilgal** in 3:14; 4:4. **Beersheba** was in the southern part of Judah's territory. Evidently northern Israelites crossed over the border to worship at a shrine associated with the patriarchs (cf. Gen. 21:31-33; 26:23-25; 46:1-4). **Gilgal,** the memorial of entrance *into* the land (Josh. 4), was to become the symbol of **exile** *from* the land. And **Bethel,** the "house of God," was to become "Beth Aven" (Heb.), a "house of **nothing,**" a "house of spirits." In Hebrew, the last part of the city's name, "El," meaning "God," was changed by Amos to "Aven" (cf. NIV marg.; Hosea 4:15; 5:8; 10:5), meaning "nothing, empty, having no existence," a word often used to describe the powerless spirits of wickedness (cf. Isa. 41:22-24, 28-29). This sarcasm would have a stinging effect on the people.

**5:6.** The command to **seek** (cf. v. 4) **the LORD** meant to turn to Him, not in ritual worship, but by doing good and hating evil (cf. vv. 14-15). Those who did would **live:** when the unquenchable and devouring **fire** of the invader swept **through the house of Joseph** (the Northern Kingdom), the seekers would be the remnant spared in mercy (v. 15).

### 3. ACCUSATION OF LEGAL INJUSTICE (5:7)

**5:7.** Verse 7 connects in grammar and content with verses 10-13. Verses 8-9 are inserted to highlight God's awesome power to judge. See comments under "C. The third message (5:1-17)."

One reason for God's judgment was the corruption that permeated the courts. Court officials had turned **justice into bitterness and** had **cast righteousness to the ground.** "Justice" was the proper functioning of judicial procedures that enabled a court to declare who or what was right in a given case. "Righteousness" was the behavior of one who sought this end, who did "right" to those involved in the case. A righteous man was willing to speak in defense of an innocent person who had been wrongly accused. Righteousness was the action; justice was the end result.

To do what was "right" and "just" on behalf of the needy was a crowning gem of human behavior (Prov. 1:3; 2:9; 8:20; Isa. 1:21; 5:7; 28:17) and proved a

special relationship with God (Gen. 18:19; Ps. 72; Jer. 22:15-17). Justice and righteousness were more than essential sacrifice and ceremony (Prov. 21:3; Amos 5:23-24). And nowhere were righteousness and justice more crucial than in the courts. Here the weaker members of society, those without money or influence, could receive protection from their oppressors and find fairness under the Law.

But Israel, through the alchemy of greed, had turned justice into "bitterness"—literally, "wormwood," a small plant known for its bitter pulp, usually associated with poison (cf. 6:12; Deut. 29:18, NASB; Jer. 9:15; 23:15). The judicial system, instead of being like a medicinal herb to heal wrongs and restore the oppressed, had itself become a fatal poison within the nation. The description of the poison's spread is continued in 5:10-13.

### 4. PORTRAYAL OF A SOVEREIGN GOD (5:8-9)

**5:8-9.** In the midst of this denunciation of human perversity, Amos identified the God who controlled the workings of the physical universe and who surely, therefore, would overturn the injustice of men.

He who **made** the constellations **Pleiades and Orion** (cf. Job 9:9; 38:31—the rising of Pleiades before daybreak signaled the return of spring while the rising of Orion after sunset heralded the onset of winter), He **who** controls the 24-hour cycle of day and night, turning **blackness into dawn** and **day into night,** He who controls the elements of nature, gathering by evaporation **the waters of the sea** and draining **them out over . . . the land**—this great Sovereign of the universe is also Israel's covenant God. **The LORD** (Yahweh) **is His name.** And He would judge their covenant faithfulness.

This God whose dominion was unchallenged in heaven was also irresistible on earth. Nothing could withstand His **destruction**—not the mightiest **stronghold** or the most **fortified city.**

### 5. ACCUSATION OF LEGAL INJUSTICE (5:10-13)

**5:10-13.** Verses 10-13 continue the denunciation begun in verse 7. Within the larger chiasmus of verses 1-17, verses 10-13 form their own internal chiasmus:

*a.* Intimidation of the righteous (v. 10)
   *b.* Abuse of the poor (v. 11a)
      *c.* Judgment of covenant sin
         (vv. 11b-12a)
   *b¹.* Abuse of the poor (v. 12b)
*a¹.* Intimidation of the righteous (v. 13)

Because of their zeal to profit illegally through the courts, they hated any righteous judge who reproved their injustice, and despised any righteous witness who told **the truth** in defense of the innocent (v. 10; see comments on v. 7). Their venom and intimidation were so severe that many felt the **prudent** thing to do was to keep **quiet in such times** (v. 13).

The abusers, thus freed of any rebuke or opposition, found corrupt judges to **take bribes** and **deprive the poor of justice** (v. 12b; in contrast with the covenant Law of Ex. 23:8; Deut. 16:18-20; cf. 1 Sam. 12:3). Rich landowners successfully manipulated legal proceedings to **trample on the poor,** gain ownership of his fields, and **force him to give** a large fee of **grain** to remain a tenant on the land (Amos 5:11a; in violation of the covenant Law of Ex. 23:2, 6; cf. Amos 2:6-7; 4:1; Isa. 10:1-2).

But God knew **how many** were their **offenses** (*pešaʿ*, "covenant violations"; see comments on Amos 1:3). He knew **how great** were their **sins** (lit., their acts of "missing the mark" of His standard). **Therefore, though** they had **built stone mansions** fit for kings and had **planted lush vineyards** in the fields that once belonged to small farmers, they would neither **live in** the houses nor **drink** the **wine** (Amos 5:11b-12a). Their suzerain Lord would invoke the treaty punishments against covenant disobedience (Deut. 28:30, 38-40; cf. Micah 6:14; Zeph. 1:13; see comments on Amos 1:2; 4:6). Their greed would be met with poetic justice: as they had stripped the poor, so God would strip them.

6. CALL FOR INDIVIDUAL REPENTANCE
   (5:14-15)

**5:14-15.** The possibility still existed, however, for individuals to separate themselves from their guilty nation (cf. vv. 4-6). If people would **seek good, not evil,** they might yet **live.** If they would go counter to the prevailing corruption—if they would **hate evil** instead of hating the righteous (v. 10), if they would **main-**

tain justice in the courts instead of trampling it (vv. 11-12)—**then the LORD God Almighty,** the great suzerain Warrior (see comments on 3:13) would be their Defender instead of their Judge. He would indeed **be with** them, **just as** they were claiming **He** was.

"The LORD is with us" was Israel's ancient shout of assurance that their powerful God would fight for them in battle (Num. 23:21; Deut. 20:4; 31:8; Jud. 6:12; Isa. 8:10; Zeph. 3:15, 17) and defend them in adversity (Pss. 23:4; 46:7, 11). But in the time of Jeroboam II this shout had become an empty slogan. Their assurance, Amos insisted, was a delusion. God was no longer "with them." The guilty nation had been abandoned (cf. Amos 5:2). Their external prosperity was misleading; it had bred a false security (cf. 6:3; 9:10; Micah 3:11). In reality, there would be only a brief respite before their Sovereign would sweep them away in judgment.

If a handful, however, would turn and passionately seek the Lord, **perhaps** the great Suzerain would **have mercy on** that small repentant **remnant of** the Northern Kingdom, here called **Joseph** (see comments on Amos 9:8-15 for the fulfillment).

7. DESCRIPTION OF CERTAIN JUDGMENT
   (5:16-17)

**5:16-17.** Amos concluded his third message by returning to his opening lament and its staggering death statistics (vv. 1-3). After **the LORD God Almighty** (see comments on 3:13) had decimated their forces, the land would be full of funerals. There would **be wailing . . . and cries of anguish** throughout the cities (5:16) and the fields (v. 17). So many would be dead that there would not be enough professional **mourners to wail; the farmers** would have to **be summoned** from their fields **to weep.** (The poor who had suffered the injustice would be called in to bury their oppressors!) **The vineyards,** often places of laughter and harvest merriment (Isa. 16:10), would be silent except for the sound of **wailing** (cf. Amos 5:16). The mourning among **all the** buildings of the city and **all the** vineyards of the fields would fulfill the verdict of God's judgment (cf. v. 11).

Wailing would fill the land because God would **pass through** their **midst.**

Their God, who once "passed over" Israel in order to "pass through" Egypt (Ex. 11:4-7; 12:12-13), would now "pass through" them on a similar errand of death.

## D. The fourth message (5:18-27)

In this fourth message Amos declared that because of Israel's religious hypocrisy "the day of the LORD" would be a day of exile rather than exaltation. Repentant individuals, however, could escape this disaster. See the comments under "C. The third message (5:1-17)" on the chiastic structure of verses 18-27.

### 1. DESCRIPTION OF CERTAIN JUDGMENT (5:18-20)

**5:18.** Woe (hôy; cf. 6:1) was ordinarily the wail of grief over the dead (cf. 1 Kings 13:30 ["Oh"]; Jer. 22:18; 34:5 ["Alas"]). Pronounced over the living, "woe" was a prediction of death (cf. Amos 6:1; Isa. 5:8-24; 10:1-4; Micah 2:1-5; see comments on Amos 5:1) or an interjection of distress in the face of present or coming calamity (cf. comments on Isa. 3:9; 6:5).

The "woe" was addressed to those who were eagerly longing **for the day of the LORD.** Their earnest desire, Amos warned, was ill-founded, for **that day** would be a day of **darkness, not light** (cf. Amos 5:20).

In Israel's thinking, "the day of the LORD" was to be the time of God's culminating vengeance against her enemies, the day when their mighty Sovereign would fight on their behalf (Isa. 34:1-3, 8; Jer. 46:10). On that day, she thought, He would turn His wrath on the wicked nations, punishing with disaster and death those who had threatened His people (Zeph. 3:8; Zech. 14:1-3). On that day Israel would be permanently secured from danger, and exalted among all nations of the earth (Isa. 24:21-23; Joel 3).

Amos' hearers eagerly anticipated that day. They did not realize, however, that its horrors would fall, not only on the nations, but also on them. Israel mistakenly believed that their Sovereign was "with" her (see comments on Amos 5:14), and that on His day of conquest He would eradicate her enemies. The truth, Amos declared, was that Israel herself had become God's enemy. Her continual sins against His covenant had made her one of the adversaries. "The day of the

LORD," therefore, would not be the expected day of happiness. It would be instead the Suzerain's day of vengeance against the rebels within His kingdom (cf. 8:9-10; 9:1-10).

**5:19.** Their experience on that day would be like that of **a man** running **from a lion** who then meets **a bear.** Somehow eluding this second threat, he managed to flee to **his house** where he **rested his hand on the wall** in exhaustion and relief. But there, in the supposed safety of his home, a poisonous **snake** bit **him.** Similarly Israel would find no haven from God's judgment.

**5:20. The day of the LORD,** Amos repeated (cf. v. 18), would be a day of **darkness, not light** (Joel 2:1-2, 10-11; Zeph. 1:14-15), a day of **pitch-dark** gloom, **without a ray of brightness** or hint of hope.

The Old Testament prophets spoke of another brighter "day of the LORD," a day after the exile, when a chastened and impoverished remnant returned to the land, a day when God will restore His people's fortunes and turn their hearts toward Him (Jer. 30:8-11; Hosea 2:16-23; Amos 9:11-15; Micah 4:6-7; Zeph. 3:11-20).

### 2. ACCUSATION OF RELIGIOUS HYPOCRISY (5:21-22)

**5:21-22.** God's burning anger was directed mostly against Israel's religious hypocrisy. He hated, He despised (the repetition indicates vehemence and passion) their **religious feasts**—the three pilgrimage festivals of Unleavened Bread, Harvest (Weeks), and Ingathering (Tabernacles) which were celebrated annually at the sanctuary (Ex. 23:14-17; 34:18-24; Lev. 23; Deut. 16:1-17). He could not **stand** (lit., "smell") the offerings of their **assemblies. Though** they continually brought Him **burnt offerings** (Lev. 1) **and grain offerings** (Lev. 2), He would **not accept them** as legitimate sacrifices. **Though** they brought **choice fellowship offerings** (Lev. 3), He would **have no regard for** or awareness of **them.** He loathed every part of their religious worship (see comments on Amos 4:4-5).

### 3. CALL FOR INDIVIDUAL REPENTANCE (5:23-24)

In verses 23-24 the verbs "away" and "let . . . roll" are singular, whereas in verses 21-22 the pronouns "your" and "you" are plural. This indicates a shift from national accusation (vv. 21-22) to individual invitation (vv. 23-24).

**5:23.** God appealed to individuals to take **away** the burdensome **noise of** their praise **songs.** He would **not listen to the** accompanying **music of** their **harps.** Having shut His nostrils (as noted in v. 21b, "stand" means "smell"), He would also stop His ears.

**5:24.** Instead of ritual and performance, God wanted a relentless commitment to **justice** and **righteousness** (see comments on v. 7). He wanted a passionate concern for the rights of the poor, a concern that would **roll on like** an ever-flowing **river . . . like a never-failing stream** that did not run dry. God wanted a day-to-day life of surging integrity and goodness. Only this outer evidence of inner righteousness could offer the Israelites the possibility of survival in the day of the Lord (cf. vv. 6, 14-15).

4. ACCUSATION OF RELIGIOUS HYPOCRISY (5:25-26)

**5:25.** God returned to His denunciation of Israel's religious hypocrisy by reminding them that their sacrifices and rituals had been an affront to Him throughout their history. From the very beginning their worship had been falsely directed. It was often not to Him, but to a golden calf, to the sun, moon, and stars, and to Molech and other false gods that many of them brought **sacrifices and offerings** during their **40 years in the desert** (cf. Stephen's reference to Amos 5:25-27 in Acts 7:39-43).

**5:26.** Since then their worship had further degenerated as they began to honor "heavenly bodies" (Acts 7:42; 2 Kings 21:3-5; 23:4-5; Jer. 8:2; 19:13; Zeph. 1:5), in violation of their covenant Law (Deut. 4:19; 17:3). They **lifted up the shrine of** their false deity (their **king**), raised **the pedestal** on which their **idols** perched, and held high **the star** symbol of their **god.** The words "shrine" and "pedestal" could be translated as "Sakkuth" and "Kaiwan" (cf. NIV marg.), foreign deities associated with the starry heavens, especially the Planet Saturn.

5. DESCRIPTION OF CERTAIN JUDGMENT (5:27)

**5:27.** Because of this idolatry and hypocrisy in their worship, God said He would **send** Israel **into exile beyond Damascus,** toward the direction of Assyria (cf. 4:3). The horror of "exile" was more than the ruin of defeat and the shame of capture. For Israel, it meant being removed from the land of promise, the land of God's presence. Exile, in effect, was excommunication. Yet this was the judgment of their sovereign LORD, the mighty Suzerain whose covenant they had spurned (see 3:13 for comments on **God Almighty**).

E. The fifth message (chap. 6)

In his fifth message Amos pointed again to the reasons for Israel's judgment, declaring that God would completely devastate both the Southern and Northern Kingdoms (vv. 1, 14), partly because of their boastful complacency and luxurious indulgence.

1. THEIR BOASTFUL COMPLACENCY (6:1-3)

**6:1. Woe** was again uttered (see comments on 5:18), this time against those **who** were **complacent in Zion** and those **who** felt **secure on Mount Samaria.** Amos included Zion, capital of the South, in his opening lament, for they too were beginning to awaken God's wrath. The remainder of his message, however, was addressed to the careless pride of the Northern Kingdom.

The leaders of Samaria considered themselves the **notable men of the foremost nation.** Their nation was militarily and economically dominant, and they were its most distinguished citizens. All **the people of Israel** looked to them for guidance and for handling the nation's affairs.

**6:2.** But God directed these proud men to **go to** cities which once also considered themselves great, and to learn from their fall. **Calneh** (also called Calno, Isa. 10:9) and **Hamath** were city-states in northern Aram. They had been overrun by Assyria during Shalmaneser III's campaign in 854–846 B.C. **Gath in Philistia** had been devastated in 815 B.C. by Hazael, king of Aram, and again in 760 B.C. by Uzziah, king of Judah (2 Kings 12:17; 2 Chron. 26:6; cf. comments on Amos 1:6). Was Israel any **better** prepared to fend off an attack **than** were **those** powerful **kingdoms**? No. **Was their land larger than** Israel's? Yes. Those cities and their surrounding districts were greater in size than proud Samaria, yet they still were unable to stave off disaster.

**6:3.** Israel, arrogant and foolishly confident of its own prowess (cf. v. 13), **put off the evil day.** They scornfully dismissed any thought of coming calamity. But all the while, by their sinful actions, they were approaching **a reign of terror.** "A reign of terror" aptly describes the last years of Israel's history before her captivity by Assyria (2 Kings 15:8–17:6). In the 31 years after Jeroboam II, Israel had six kings, three of whom seized power by political coup and assassination. The fear and violence in this period is reflected in the atrocities of 2 Kings 15:16.

2. THEIR LUXURIOUS INDULGENCE (6:4-7)

**6:4-6.** Rather than heed the prophet's warnings of judgment, the leaders of Samaria instead gave themselves to a decadent hedonism. They reclined on expensive **beds** whose wood was **inlaid with ivory** (cf. 3:15). At their opulent feasts they "lounged" **on their couches.** The Hebrew word for **lounge** (*sāraḥ*) conveys a sprawled stupor of satiation and drunkenness, with arms and legs hanging over the side. They ate gourmet food—**choice lambs and fattened calves** —the tastiest and tenderest meat they could get. In their drunken revelry they imagined themselves strumming **like David** as they attempted to **improvise** music at their parties. Yet they were vastly different from David! Not content to **drink wine** from goblets, they consumed it **by the bowlful.** Only **the finest lotions** would do for their skin.

Their sole concern was for their own luxurious lifestyle. They did **not grieve over the** coming **ruin of Joseph,** the Northern Kingdom (cf. 5:6, 15). They had no concern for their nation's impending doom.

**6:7. Therefore** they, the first men of the first nation (v. 1), would **be among the first to go into exile.** Their festivities and drunken stupors would **end.** The sound of revelry would fade into bitter silence as they headed into captivity.

3. THE COMPLETE DEVASTATION (6:8-14)

**6:8.** Israel's **sovereign Lord** had **sworn by Himself,** binding the full force of His integrity to a solemn oath (cf. 4:2; 8:7), that He would utterly destroy the

land. He abhorred their **pride** as they said their national fortunes resulted from their own strength (6:1, 13). **Jacob,** like Joseph, is a synonym for the Northern Kingdom (see comments on 3:13). God detested the **fortresses** which were filled with the results of their oppression against the poor (see comments on 3:9-10). Therefore, as a great suzerain Warrior (see 3:13 for comments on **Lord God Almighty**), He would storm their **city,** and **deliver up** everyone **and everything in it.**

**6:9-10.** So completely would God "deliver up" the city that even **if 10 men** should huddle **in one house** to escape the sword, **they** would **die** of pestilence. **A relative who** came **to** take **the bodies** to burn them would be so afraid of death that if he discovered a survivor **hiding** in the house he would quickly beg him **not** even to **mention the** Lord's **name** in any way (not in lament or in anger for the slaughter or in praise for having survived). For in such a situation, to "mention the name" of Him who had so terribly destroyed the city might draw His attention to those whom He had overlooked, and cause Him to slay them also.

**6:11.** After killing the inhabitants, the conquering Suzerain would then **command** His forces to **smash . . . great** and **small** houses **into bits.** The dwellings of both rich and poor would be totally demolished. All that would remain would be a field of debris.

**6:12. Two** preposterous images expose the utter perversity of Israel's leaders. That **horses** would **run on the rocky crags,** or that **one** would **plow** those perpendicular cliffs **with oxen** was unimaginable. Israel, however, had done the unimaginable! They had **turned justice into poison and the fruit of righteousness into bitterness** (see comments on 5:7). The judicial process, designed to preserve the nation's health, had become a lethal "poison" within its body. The "fruit" of fairness and integrity, intended to refresh and delight, had become instead a corrupt bitter pulp.

**6:13.** Israel's leaders considered themselves immune to disaster, as the evidence of their might was obvious to them (vv. 1-3). Under Jeroboam II they had won an unbroken string of military victories (2 Kings 14:25). They had even recovered all their lands east of the Jordan. But Amos subtly and intentionally mispronounced the name of one of the captured towns, **Lo Debar** (a town east of the Jordan River, mentioned in 2 Sam. 9:4; 17:27), so that it came out in Hebrew as "Lo Dabar," which means "nothing." And with biting sarcasm he stressed the name of another subdued city, **Karnaim,** whose literal meaning of "horns" symbolized the "strength" of a bull. Amos scoffed that they were rejoicing over what was really "nothing," and were falsely imagining that they had seized "strength" by means of their **own strength.**

**6:14.** Their air of invincibility would be shattered by their mighty Suzerain (see 3:13 for comments on **Lord God Almighty**). God too would do the unimaginable—He would **stir up a nation against** His own vassal. He would raise a scourge against His own people Israel, and they would be "oppressed." The word **oppress** deliberately evoked and promised again the bitter experiences of Egypt (Ex. 3:9) and the time of the Judges (Jud. 2:18; 4:3; 6:9; 10:11-12; 1 Sam. 10:17-18); Israel would again descend into slavery. All the territory they so boastfully held—**from** the northern frontier of **Lebo Hamath to** the southern border of **the Arabah,** the valley extending from the Sea of Kinnereth to the Dead Sea (2 Kings 14:25)—would be swallowed by the invading foe. Then Israel would know whose "strength" really determined the destiny of nations.

## IV. The Results of Judgment (7:1–9:10)

In chapters 3–6 Amos had documented the reasons for God's judgment against Israel—legal injustice, economic exploitation, religious hypocrisy, luxurious indulgence, and boastful complacency. Because of these covenant violations "the Lord God Almighty," the great suzerain Warrior at the head of His armies, would crush His rebellious vassal. (Only in chaps. 3–6 does the title "the Lord God Almighty" occur in Amos.) Individuals who repented might yet be spared, but the nation as a whole was irrevocably doomed.

In chapter 7 Amos began to describe the results of this coming judgment. Through a series of five visions (7:1, 4, 7; 8:1; 9:1), he pictured God's total destruc-tion of the land, its buildings, and its people.

Throughout this section of the book (7:1–9:10), two phrases stand out—"sovereign Lord" (7:1-2, 4 [twice], 5-6; 8:1, 3, 9, 11; 9:8) and "My people" (7:8, 15; 8:2; 9:10). As the sovereign Lord over all nations, God has absolute freedom of action in His universe. He was especially at liberty to implement His will against the people who had spurned His special grace (cf. 3:2).

### A. The swarming locusts (7:1-3)

**7:1.** In the first of five visions Amos saw God actually **preparing swarms of locusts** at the nation's most vulnerable time of the year! (The Heb. expresses the prophet's amazement at such a thing; cf. "behold" in NASB.) The locusts were being loosed on the land **after the king's share had been harvested and just as the second crop was coming up.** The king had the right to claim the first cutting of the grain for his military animals (cf. 1 Kings 18:5). The "second crop"—either what grew after the first cutting or a separate late planting—was the final growth of the season before the summer's dryness. If it were lost the people would have nothing to eat until the next harvest.

A locust swarm was one of the most dreaded plagues of the ancient East. As a swarm made its ravenous way across the land, people despaired because it was an enemy against whom they were helpless. When the plague was past, suffering and death by famine followed. This misery was intensified in Israel, for locusts were recognized as God's instrument of punishment for covenant violations (Deut. 28:38, 42; cf. Amos 4:9; Joel 1:1-7).

**7:2.** In his vision Amos saw that the locusts **stripped the land clean** of all vegetation—both seeded crops and wild growth. Knowing that the nation would die if this vision became a reality, Amos begged the **sovereign Lord** to **forgive** the people of their sins. Though Israel was unrepentant, though her guilt was overwhelming, and though the punishment was just, Amos nevertheless pleaded with God not to bring this punishment on the nation. **Jacob** would never **survive** it. Jeroboam II's proud people might think themselves invulnerable (6:1-3, 8, 13; 9:10), but when viewed in the face of God's awesome might and wrath they were in reality **so small,** so helpless, so pitiable. By calling Israel "Jacob," Amos perhaps meant to remind God of His early commitment to the ancestor when he was at Bethel, a site still hallowed by his descendants (Gen. 28:10-22; Amos 3:14; 4:4; 5:5-6; 7:13). Jacob is mentioned in 3:13; 6:8; 7:2, 5; 8:7; 9:8.

**7:3.** Moved by the prophet's prayer, **the Lord relented** and promised that the swarm of locusts would **not happen.** (The word "relent" suggests a turning away and a relief from an earlier decision because one has been deeply stirred by the appeal of another; cf. comments on Ex. 32:11-14.)

The nation was not forgiven, but this particular punishment was withdrawn. Amos did not ask for forgiveness again (cf. Amos 7:2 with v. 5), for some judgment on Israel was inevitable. But by his prayers he was able to affect what form that judgment would take.

### B. The devouring fire (7:4-6)

**7:4.** In a second vision **the sovereign Lord** showed Amos a second terror—a **judgment by fire.** God intensified the blazing summer heat till all grasslands and trees became tinder dry. Then fires broke out and spread in every direction with incredible speed (cf. Joel 1:19-20). Attempts to combat the sweeping inferno were futile, for **the great deep,** the subterranean waters that fed all springs (Gen. 7:11; 49:25; Deut. 33:13), had **dried up.** With the source of all waters consumed, the rivers and streams disappeared, and the flames raged unchecked until they had **devoured the land** (cf. Deut. 32:22).

**7:5-6.** Again, distraught by the vision, Amos begged God to **stop,** and **the Lord relented** a second time. Neither would fire be the means by which He would punish the nation (see comments on v. 3).

### C. The testing plumb line (7:7-17)

1. THE VISION (7:7-9)

For the third time the prophet was shown a vision of judgment. This time the sentence was unalterable.

**7:7-8. The Lord** held **in His hand** a **plumb line. A plumb line** was a cord with a lead weight used by builders to

make sure that walls were constructed straight up and down. A plumb line was also used to test existing walls to see whether they had settled and tilted, needing to be torn down.

God was **setting a plumb line** (possibly the covenant Law and its requirements; cf. Isa. 28:17) **among** His **people Israel.** The nation had been built "true to plumb," but now was out of line and needed to be torn down.

God quickly precluded any appeal from His prophet. The matter was settled; He would **spare them no longer.** This was the form His judgment would take (see comments on Amos 7:3, 5-6).

**7:9.** Having failed the test of the plumb line, the nation's chief "structures"—both religious and political—would be demolished. **The** numerous **high places** (hilltop shrines) **of Isaac** would **be destroyed.** Like "Jacob" (see comments on 3:13) and "Joseph" (cf. 5:6, 15; 6:6) "Isaac" was a name for the Northern Kingdom. The larger official **sanctuaries of** worship, such as Bethel and Gilgal, would **be ruined** (cf. 3:14; 4:4; 5:5-6; 7:13). **And the house** (political dynasty) **of Jeroboam** II would crumble under the stroke of God's **sword** (cf. 2 Kings 14:29; 15:10).

2. THE INCIDENT (7:10-17)

The incident recorded in verses 10-17 is integrally tied to Amos' third vision (vv. 7-9) in two ways. First, it reveals the immediate historical reaction to the vision's content. The fact that certain words appear in both the vision and the incident, but nowhere else in the book after 1:1 (viz., "Isaac" in 7:9, 16; "sanctuaries" and "sanctuary" in vv. 9-11), indicates that the episode was an immediate response to the revelation.

Second, the historical incident is linked to the vision because it represents a concrete example of the "plumb line" in operation, this time as a test of individuals. The vision had revealed that Israel's institutions, both religious and political, had failed the test and would have to come down. Now, in the incident with Amaziah, the sovereign Lord drew near to measure two men—one a prophet, the other a priest. One was accepted; the other was not. One heard and obeyed the voice of the Lord; the other refused to hear.

## a. The challenge (7:10-13)

**7:10-13.** As **Amos** began publicly to recount his vision of ruined sanctuaries and dynastic demise, he was challenged by **Amaziah the priest of Bethel.**

Bethel was one of the two state sanctuaries established by Jeroboam I when in 931 B.C. he broke from Jerusalem and the kingdom there (1 Kings 12:26-33). In order to unite the 10 tribes around his rule, Jeroboam I created a new shrine and a duplicate religious system. The purpose of the calf, altar, priesthood, and festivals of Bethel was to give credence and stability to Jeroboam I's Northern Kingdom.

In Amos' day the shrine at Bethel was **the king's sanctuary and the temple** (lit., "house," but frequently used as a synonym for "temple"; cf. 1 Kings 6; 8:6-66; 2 Chron. 2:1) **of the kingdom** (Amos 7:13). Besides being the site where Jeroboam II worshiped, it was, more importantly, the religious symbol which rallied political commitment to the kingdom. As the temple in Jerusalem drew devotion to the lineage of David, so the existence of Bethel implied God's sanction and support of the Northern monarch. To denounce Bethel and its system of worship (cf. 3:14; 4:4-5; 5:5-6, 21-26; also note 7:9; 9:1) was to attack the very foundation of the kingdom.

Amaziah was evidently Bethel's chief priest, in charge of worship and personnel (cf. Jer. 20:1-2; 29:26). Hearing Amos' foreboding words against the sanctuary and the monarch, Amaziah **sent a message to Jeroboam** charging Amos with **raising a conspiracy against** the king **in the very heart of** the Northern Kingdom. He warned Jeroboam that **the land** could not **bear** such repeated messages of catastrophe: the people would be demoralized or sooner or later some dissident rebel would be prompted to fulfill the predictions. On previous occasions a prophet's words against a king had been followed by internal revolt and by a change in dynasties (1 Kings 11:29–12:24; 16:1-13; 2 Kings 8:7-15; 9).

Amaziah refused to acknowledge in any way the divine source of Amos' prophecies, choosing instead to view him as a political agitator. In his report to Jeroboam he prefaced the threatening quote (Amos 7:11) with, **This is what Amos is saying,** rather than with, "This

is what God has said." In quoting Amos, the priest deliberately omitted the prophet's words about God's claim of personal action, "with *My* sword *I* will rise against . . . Jeroboam" (v. 9). Amaziah substituted the simple fact, **Jeroboam will die.** He reported Amos' words in a form designed to incite the king, twisting the prediction of the dynasty's fall (v. 9) into a threat against Jeroboam himself (v. 11), and highlighting the announcements of national **exile** (v. 11; cf. 4:3; 5:5, 27; 6:7; cf. 7:17). Amaziah chose to see Amos as a menace to the status quo rather than as a messenger from the God of Israel.

Having dispatched his letter to the king, **Amaziah** then confronted **Amos** with the strong directive, **Get out, you seer!** Claiming authority over the activities **at Bethel,** the priest ordered Amos to **go back to** his home in **Judah** (cf. 1:1) and **do** his **prophesying there.**

A "seer" (7:12) was another name for a prophet (1 Sam. 9:9; 2 Sam. 24:11; Isa. 29:10). This title called attention to the prophet's activity of beholding or "seeing" visions (Isa. 1:1; 2:1; Obad. 1; Micah 1:1; Nahum 1:1; Amos 1:1). These visions were "seen" by the prophets mentally and spiritually. Amaziah, reacting to Amos' "visions" (7:1, 4, 7), used the word in a derogatory sense. His scornful advice to **earn your bread** in Judah implied that Amos was a professional predictor who made his living selling prophecies (Micah 3:5, 11; cf. the women of Ezek. 13:17-20 who prophesied "out of their own imagination. . . . for a few handfuls of barley and scraps of bread").

The stress in Amaziah's words fell on the location or geography of Amos' activity: "Go to *Judah,* earn your bread *there,* do your prophesying *there,* but don't prophesy anymore *at Bethel."* In his authority as the king's priest he commanded Amos, "Leave *Israel!"* Amos' response, however, was that a greater Authority had commanded him to prophesy *in Israel.*

## b. The response (7:14-17)

**7:14-15.** **Amos** denied that his ministry was self-generated, insisting that it was solely the result of God's initiative. Amos had not chosen the calling of **a prophet nor** had he trained for it by becoming **a prophet's son** (i.e., a member of a prophetic school under the tutelage of a "father"; cf. 2 Kings 2:1-15; 4:1, 38; 5:22; 6:1-7; 9:1). On the contrary, he had been profitably and contentedly occupied as **a shepherd, and** as a grower **of syca-more-fig trees.** (For a discussion of Amos' occupation, see "The Prophet" section in the *Introduction*.) **But** one day **the LORD took** him—the same verb is used for God's calling the Levites (Num. 18:6) and David (2 Sam. 7:8; Ps. 78:70)—**from tending the flock, and** the Lord (the words "the LORD" are repeated in Heb.) commissioned him to **Go, prophe-sy to My people Israel.** In the NASB the contrast is heightened between Amos' threefold denial of self-seeking ("I" . . . "I" . . . "I," Amos 7:14) and his three-fold assertion of "the LORD's" authority (vv. 15-16). God had commanded him not only what to say but also where to say it. The authority was not Amaziah's, but the Lord's. The place, therefore, would not be Judah, but Israel. The Lord had spoken, and Amos would prophesy as He directed (cf. 3:8; Acts 5:27-29).

**7:16-17.** Now this same **LORD** had a **word** for the priest who had dared to forbid what He had commanded (cf. 2:11-12). Because Amaziah had rejected God's word **against** the nation, he and his fam-ily would suffer the full fate of the na-tion. When the divine sentence of **exile** was carried out (cf. 5:5, 27; 6:7; 7:11; 9:4), he would be among those swept **away from their native land.** His **wife** would be forced to make a living as **a prostitute in the** very **city** where once she had been among the most distinguished women. His posterity and name would come to an end as **the sword** claimed the lives of his **sons and daughters.** His estate would **be measured and divided up** among for-eigners (cf. 2 Kings 17:24; Jer. 6:12), and he himself would **die in a pagan** (lit., "an unclean") **country.** He would be stripped of his office, bereft of a shrine, and de-filed by the unclean food of a heathen land (cf. Ezek. 4:13; Hosea 9:3-4).

Had Amaziah responded differently, had he repented at Amos' word, he might have been spared (Amos 5:4-6, 14-15). But instead he chose to align with an earthly monarch, to embrace the national mood of pride and security, and to assert his authority against God's messenger. So the Lord quietly withdrew the plumb line. He would spare Amaziah no longer.

## D. The culminating fruit (chap. 8)

### 1. THE VISION (8:1-3)

**8:1-2. The sovereign LORD** appeared a fourth time to **Amos,** this time asking him to identify an object. When Amos **answered** that it was **a basket of ripe fruit . . . the LORD** then replied, **The time is ripe** (lit., "The end has come") **for My people Israel.**

The meaning of the Lord's reply lay in the similar sound and significance of the words "ripe fruit" (v. 1) and "time is ripe" (v. 2). "Ripe fruit" (*qāyiṣ*) was "summer fruit" or "end-of-the-year fruit"—the last fruit of the season, fully ripened, with a short edible life. "Ripe time" (*qēṣ*) was "end time" or "cutting time"—the "reaping time" of death.

Israel was ripe for a dreadful harvest; her end had come. There would be no stay of execution, no last-minute re-prieve. The Lord would **spare them no longer.**

**8:3.** On the **day** (cf. vv. 9, 13; see 5:18-20 for comments on "the day of the LORD") when God would "end" Israel's life (cf. 5:2-3; 6:9-10), **the songs in the temple** would **turn to wailing** (cf. 8:10; 5:16-17). Hymns of joy and trust in the Lord would turn to howling chants of lamentation and disbelief at what His hand had done to them. The cause of their grief would be the **many, many** dead **bodies** lying **everywhere.** So great would be the **slaughter** that there would not be enough people or places to bury the dead. Innumerable corpses would lie on the ground, to be eaten by dogs and birds, or to become fertilizing dung for the fields (1 Kings 14:11; Jer. 8:2; 9:22; 16:4).

When the weary mourners would fi-nally cease their weeping, when they would lift wet eyes and questioning faces to seek a reason for the sorrow that en-gulfed them, they would find only **si-lence.** No answer would come. God would have no more words to say.

### 2. THE RESULTS (8:4-14)

These two results of God's judg-ment—human grief and divine silence—are described more fully in verses 4-14.

### a. Human grief (8:4-10)

Because of their greed and dishonest practices, God would cause an unprecedented mourning in the land.

**8:4-6.** Israel's businessmen single-mindedly pursued a profit, and did not care that they were trampling **the needy and** doing **away with the poor of the land** (cf. 2:6-7; 5:11). Preoccupied with making money, the businessmen begrudged the interruptions caused by the monthly feast of **the New Moon** and the weekly observance of **the Sabbath.** They impatiently fidgeted till these days of rest and worship (Ex. 20:8-11; 23:12; 31:14-17; 34:21; Num. 28:11-15; 2 Kings 4:23; Isa. 1:13-14; Ezek. 46:1-6; Hosea 2:11) were **over** so that they could resume their aggressive dealings.

They cunningly found ways to add to their profits—**skimping the** standard **measure** so that customers got less than they paid for, **boosting the price** by substituting heavier shekel-weights so that customers were overcharged, **and cheating with dishonest scales** by tampering with the cross beam of the balances. Not content with these covenant violations (Lev. 19:35-36; Deut. 25:13-16; cf. Prov. 11:1; 16:11; 20:10, 23; Hosea 12:7; Micah 6:10-11), they compounded their sin by deceptively **selling** an inferior product—**the sweepings** of soiled and trampled grain mixed and packaged **with the** clean pure **wheat.** They cared nothing about human suffering or the inability of **the poor** to pay their prices. Instead, they forced **the needy** into slavery in exchange for insignificant sums (see Amos 2:6 for comments on **a pair of sandals**).

**8:7-8.** The **LORD,** however, had **sworn by** Himself (see comments on 4:2; 6:8; unlike its use in 6:8, **the Pride of Jacob** occurs here as a title for God; cf. 1 Sam. 15:29). God swore that He would **never forget** any of the evil things **they** had **done.** Because of their heartless greed and dishonesty, because of these covenant violations, their Warrior-God would advance against them and **the land** would **tremble** under His steps. The quaking tremors would be so violent that **the whole land** would **rise . . . and then sink like the** annual swelling and receding of **the Nile . . . the river of Egypt.** The shattered ruins of farms and buildings would cause all who lived in the wake of His path to weep and to **mourn.**

**8:9-10. That day** of punishment would be a day of darkness (cf. comments on 5:18-20), for **the sovereign**

**LORD** would bring about eclipses; **the sun** would **go down at noon and darken the earth in broad daylight.** Eclipses in 784 B.C. and 763 B.C. would have enabled Amos' hearers to imagine the eerie fear and panic of such a time. Then in the midst of earthquake (8:8) and darkness the avenging Lord would begin His decimation of the people (cf. 5:2-3; 6:9-10; 8:3). The sword of their God would bring unprecedented grief on the land as He turned their **feasts into** funerals, **and all** their glad **singing into weeping** laments (cf. v. 3). The loss of life would be so widespread that every family would grieve and every home would observe the rites of mourning. God would cause **all of** them to **wear sackcloth** (a coarsely woven material, generally made of goats' hair) against their bodies (Gen. 37:34; 2 Sam. 3:31; 2 Kings 6:30; Job 16:15-16; Dan. 9:3) and **shave** their **heads** as a sign of sorrow (Job 1:20; Isa. 3:24; 15:2-3; Jer. 47:5; 48:37; Ezek. 7:18; 27:30-31; Micah 1:16). The intensity of their grief would be like the most tragic mourning of all—the **mourning for an only son,** whose death ended every hope for a family's future (Jer. 6:26; Zech. 12:10).

**The end** of that day would not be the end of their grief. Instead, its culmination would usher in another **bitter day**—the mourners' own "bitter day" of death. (For the day of one's death as a "bitter day"; cf. 1 Sam. 15:32; Job 21:25; Ecc. 7:26.) After a day of mourning for others, the mourners themselves would die.

*b. Divine silence (8:11-14)*

This agony of human grief would be even more unbearable in the face of God's awful silence (v. 3).

**8:11-12.** Since Israel had rejected all His words (2:11-12; 7:10-13, 16), they would hear His words no more. **The sovereign LORD** would **send a famine,** but this would **not** be **a famine of food** as before (cf. 4:6), **but a famine of hearing the words of the LORD.** They would desperately inquire of Him, but He would not answer—not by dreams, not by Urim, not by prophet (1 Sam. 28:6; cf. 1 Sam. 3:1). **Men** would **stagger** to every corner of the land, wandering in a complete circuit of Israel's territory (**from the** Dead Sea in the south **to the** Mediterranean **Sea** in the west, and from the **north to** the **east), searching for the word of the**

LORD—a word of explanation, of forgiveness, of hope. **But they** would **not find it.** When their grief would finally drive them to "seek the LORD" (Amos 5:4-6), the Lord would not be found. It would be too late.

**8:13-14. In that day** (cf. vv. 3, 9) even **lovely young women and strong young men**—those capable of enduring and persisting in the search the longest—would **faint because of** an unrelieved **thirst** to hear God's Word. Those who had perverted the worship of God, who had seen in the idol-calves **of Samaria** (Hosea 8:5-6) and **Dan** (1 Kings 12:28-30; 2 Kings 10:29) and in the image **of Beersheba** (Amos 5:5) a symbol of His power, would flock to the capital or traverse to the farthest points in a bravado appeal. Samaria's idol is called its **shame** or more literally, its guilt, because the idol-worship resulted in the Samaritans being guilty before God. (The expression "from Dan to Beersheba" encompasses the full extent of the land; Jud. 20:1; 1 Sam. 3:20; 2 Sam. 3:10; 17:11; 24:2, 15; 1 Kings 4:25; 2 Chron. 30:5.) But their imploring would be futile. God would remain silent. And **they** would **fall, never to rise again** (cf. Amos 5:2).

### E. The avenging Lord (9:1-10)

In a fifth and final vision, Amos witnessed the Sovereign of the universe wielding an inescapable sword against all the sinners among His people.

#### 1. THE INESCAPABLE SWORD (9:1-4)

**9:1.** At the autumn festival, when a large congregation had assembled at the sanctuary at Bethel, and the Northern monarch had approached the altar with his sacrifice (1 Kings 12:31-33), Amos **saw the LORD standing by the altar.** The Lord was indeed "with them" (Amos 5:14), but to destroy and to kill, not to bless. The "end" had come for the altar, the sanctuary, and the people (3:14; 5:5-6; 8:1-3).

The Lord commanded, **Smash the tops of the pillars so that** the crashing roof would cause even **the** great stone **thresholds to shake.** The thresholds were massive foundation stones on which the doorposts were fixed (Isa. 6:4; Ezek. 40:6).

In his vision Amos apparently saw the entire structure collapse, killing most of the gathered worshipers (cf. Jud. 16:29-30), for a second command came quickly, **Cut off the heads of all the people** who yet remain alive. The Lord was determined that **not one** would **get away; none** would **escape** (cf. 1 Kings 18:40). **Those who** survived and fled the disaster He would pursue and **kill with the sword** (cf. Amos 9:4, 10).

**9:2-4.** Even if they could flee to the outer reaches of the universe, He would find them and **slay them.** Neither **the depths of the grave** nor the heights of **the heavens** could separate them from the wrath of God (cf. Ps. 139:7-8; and note the contrast in Rom. 8:38-39). **Though they** hid in the dense forests of Mount **Carmel** (cf. Amos 1:2) or in some of its many limestone caves, He would **hunt them down and seize them.** If **they** somehow could **hide from** Him **at the bottom of the sea,** they would discover that **there** too He ruled, for **the serpent** would obey His command. This serpent is a sea monster, sometimes called Leviathan or Rahab, the personification of the sea's defeated power (cf. Job 26:12-13; Pss. 74:13-14; 89:9-10; Isa. 27:1; 51:9-10). Even if **enemies** captured them and herded them like cattle **into exile,** to be under the protection of a foreign king and god, no foreign power could shield them from God's relentless **sword** (cf. Amos 9:1, 10). Escape was impossible, for wherever they went God would **fix** His **eyes** on **them for evil and not for good.** He was determined to destroy them.

#### 2. THE UNIVERSAL SOVEREIGN (9:5-6)

**9:5-6.** The One Amos saw by the altar (v. 1) was **the LORD Almighty,** the great suzerain Warrior whose power was irresistible (cf. comments on 3:13). As the Sovereign, not only of Israel and the other nations (1:3–2:16; 3:9; 9:4, 7) but also of the vast universe, He could speak with certainty that there would be no escape for Israel anywhere in His universe. **He** whose finger merely **touches the earth,** causing the mountains to quake and "melt" (i.e., "flatten"; cf. Micah 1:3-4; Nahum 1:5), **the whole land** to undulate **like the Nile,** and the inhabitants to **mourn** (cf. Amos 8:8), would surely possess a powerful "hand" to "seize" (9:2-3) rebels from any spot on earth. **He who** built **His lofty palace in**

the heavens could not fail to reach any who sought refuge in "the heavens" (v. 2). He who controls the waters of the sea (cf. 5:8) would surely be obeyed by its denizens (9:3). The LORD is His name. His majesty and His power over creation means that they would not be able to escape Him. And as the Lord (Yahweh, the covenant-keeping God), He would keep His Word and judge those who had disobeyed Him. Interestingly the two verses in Amos that include the exclamation "The LORD is His name" speak of His sovereignty over the universe (5:8; 9:6).

### 3. THE IMPARTIAL SIFTING (9:7-10)

**9:7.** Israel's special position as His people would not save them from punishment (cf. 3:1-2). God would act toward them as toward any other nation within His universal domain. They would be the same to Him as the Cushites, who lived in what is today southern Egypt, all of Sudan, and northern Ethiopia. In Israel's thinking, the Cushites were a foreign and unimportant people living at the periphery of the known world.

God is the Sovereign of every nation. He had not only brought Israel up from Egypt (cf. 2:10; 3:1), but had also guided the historical migrations of their arch-enemies—the Philistines from Caphtor (cf. Jer. 47:4; Zeph. 2:5), probably another name for the island of Crete, and the Arameans from Kir (cf. Amos 1:5), a location in Mesopotamia. And as God had determined to reverse the destinies of those two nations (cf. 1:3-8), so He had determined to send Israel into exile (4:2-3; 5:5, 27; 6:7; 7:11, 17; 9:4). He would punish rebellion wherever it occurred.

**9:8-10.** Having declared that He would make no distinction between Israel and other nations, God then solemnly uttered His final edict of death. Verses 8-10 are the three final statements of judgment in the Book of Amos. They vow an impartial and certain death to all the sinners of the land.

Though these three statements seal the nation's doom, they also look forward to the final section of the book (vv. 11-15) where God speaks of a restoration after judgment. The first two statements (vv. 8-9) each conclude with a brief allusion to a spared remnant. The third statement (v. 10) is followed by God's full promise of renewal and covenant blessing.

The eyes (cf. v. 4) of the sovereign LORD were keeping close watch on the sinful kingdom (Israel) to make sure that the judgment came. His purpose was to destroy it from the face of the earth. Their Suzerain would fulfill the covenant curses until no trace of the nation remained (cf. comments on 1:2; 4:6; also note the use of "destroy" in the punishment sections of Israel's covenant; Deut. 28:20, 24 ["ruined"], 45, 48, 51, 61, 63). Yet God would not totally destroy the house of Jacob (i.e., the Northern Kingdom; cf. Amos 3:13-14; 6:8; 7:2, 5; 8:7). Some would be spared. The earlier possibility of a remnant (see "perhaps" in 5:15) was now made certain. God would indeed have mercy on those who repented (cf. 5:4-6, 14-15, 23-24).

Wherever His people were scattered among all the nations, God would impartially shake them as grain is shaken in a sieve. But not a kernel would fall to the ground. As a fine-meshed sieve lets the chaff and dust go through, but catches the good grain, so God would screen out and save any righteous among His people.

Others suggest that the sieve in view is the coarse-meshed sieve used at the beginning of the sifting process to screen out the stones and clods of earth, letting the smaller grains fall through (cf. the apocryphal Ecclesiasticus 27:5). If so, the "kernel" (lit., "pebble"; cf. the "piece" of a city wall in 2 Sam. 17:13) refers to a sinner who would not be allowed to escape through the screen of God's judgment.

In either interpretation the final point is the same: God's impartial sifting would separate the righteous from the sinners.

All the sinners among His people would then die by His inescapable sword (cf. Amos 9:1, 4). Their self-confident boasting would finally end (cf. 6:1-3, 13) for the promised disaster would destroy them.

## V. The Restoration after Judgment (9:11-15)

After all God's judgments are past, when the nation has received full punishment for her sins, the Lord will move in mercy to renew and refresh His people. God will restore David's kingdom over both the North and the South, and through it He will bless all nations of the earth. He will reverse the covenant curses and bring unprecedented prosperity to the land. Dispersed Israel will be returned to her land, there to dwell securely and enjoy its goodness. Then He who has always claimed them as "My people" (7:8, 15; 8:2; 9:10, 14; cf. Hosea 2:23; Zech. 8:8; 13:9) will once again take the title "your God" (Amos 9:15).

### A. Political renewal (9:11)

**9:11. In that day** (cf. Isa. 4:2; Micah 4:6; 5:10) God will **restore David's fallen tent.** Previous references in Amos to "that day" had spoken of it as a day of darkness and destruction (Amos 2:16; 3:14; 5:18-20; 8:3, 9, 11, 13). But when Israel's ordeal is finally over, "that day" will also become the day of her renewal.

God will reestablish David's "tent" over both the Northern and Southern Kingdoms. A "tent" (lit., "booth") or awning was made by setting up a simple frame and spreading branches over it. Its primary purpose was to shelter those under it, whether troops in the field (2 Sam. 11:11; 1 Kings 20:12-16), a watchman at post (Jonah 4:5), or pilgrims at the Feast of Booths (also called the Feast of Tabernacles, Lev. 23:33-42). David's dynasty, which had been a protective canopy over all the people of Israel, had "fallen" with the great schism of the 10 Northern tribes from the 2 Southern tribes (1 Kings 12). This booth had been broken in two. But God promised to unite the two kingdoms once again under Davidic rule (cf. Jer. 30:3-10; Ezek. 37:15-28; Hosea 3:4-5). He will restore the sheltering tent, **repair its broken places,** building **it as it used to be.** God will carry out His good promise to David that He would raise up a Descendant after him and establish His rule forever (2 Sam. 7:11-16, 25-29).

### B. National purpose (9:12)

**9:12.** The united kingdom under its Davidic King will then become the source of blessing to all Gentiles. **Edom,** a nation perpetually hostile toward God's people (cf. Num. 20:14-21; Ps. 137:7; Obad. 1; see comments on Amos 1:11-12), and therefore representative of all Israel's en-

emies, will become a sharer in the promises to David: Israel will **possess the remnant of** Edom (cf. Obad. 19). In fact, **all . . . nations** will be brought under the dominion of the Davidic King, for they too **bear** God's **name.** To "bear someone's name" meant to be under the suzerainty and protection of that individual (cf. Deut. 28:9-10; 2 Sam. 12:26-28; 1 Kings 8:43; Isa. 4:1; 63:19; Jer. 15:16; Dan. 9:18-19). All nations belong to God (cf. Amos 1:3–2:16; 3:9; 9:4, 7) and therefore will be included in the blessings of the future kingdom.

From the beginning, God's plan has been to provide salvation for the Gentile nations. His promise to Abraham was that through his descendants "all peoples on earth" will be blessed (Gen. 12:3; cf. Gen. 18:18; 22:17-18; 26:3-4; 28:13-14). Through Isaiah God continually affirmed that a united Israel under its Davidic King, the Messiah, will bring light, justice, and full knowledge of **the LORD** to all nations on the earth (Isa. 9:1-7; 11:1-13; 42:1-7; 45:22-25; 49:5-7; 55:1-5). When God restores the kingdom (the Millennium) under David's Son, both Jews and Gentiles will bear the name of the Lord.

At the Jerusalem Council, James cited Amos 9:11-12 as proof that the Gentiles of his day need not be circumcised and live as Jews in order to be saved (Acts. 15:1-20). James was aware that Israel's judgments were not yet over (cf. the Lord's statements regarding the coming destruction of the temple and renewed persecution and death, Matt. 24:1-22; Luke 21:5-24, and that the restoration had not yet begun; cf. Acts 1:6-7). But James also knew from Amos' succinct statement and from extended passages in other prophets (cf. "prophets" in Acts 15:15; also note Isa. 42:6; 60:3; Mal. 1:11) that when the promised kingdom would come, the Gentiles will share in it as Gentiles and not as quasi-Jews. Since this was God's millennial purpose, James concluded that the church should not require Gentiles to relinquish their identity and live as Jews. James was not saying the church fulfills the promises to Israel in Amos 9:11-12. He was saying that since Gentiles will be saved in the yet-to-come Millennium, they need not become Jews in the Church Age (see extended comments on Acts 15:15-18).

## C. Prosperity, peace, and permanence (9:13-15)

**9:13. The days are coming** when God will remove all curses (cf. the comments on 4:6 and the chart "The Covenant Chastenings") and restore covenant blessings to the land (cf. Lev. 26:3-10; Deut. 28:1-14).

Instead of drought and famine (Amos 1:2; 4:6-8), there will be unending prosperity (9:13; cf. Lev. 26:3-5, 10; Deut. 28:4-5, 8, 11-12).

Instead of the turmoil of war (Amos 2:13-16; 3:11, 15; 4:10-11; 5:2-3; 6:9-10; 7:17; 9:1, 10), there will be unbroken peace which will enable Israel to enjoy the fruit of her labor (v. 14; cf. Lev. 26:6; Deut. 28:6).

Instead of the fear of exile (Amos 4:2-3; 5:5, 27; 6:7; 7:11, 17; 9:4), Israel will confidently defend herself from every foe and remain in the land (v. 15; cf. Lev. 26:7-8; Deut. 28:7, 10).

In the days when God restores Israel, the land will be so productive (cf. Isa. 27:6) that **the plowman** who starts in October will have to wait for **the reaper** who should have finished in May. **The one** who treads **grapes** in July will find **the planter** still sowing new seed into the ground broken by the long-delayed plowman. The grapes will hang so heavy in the mountain vineyards that **the hills** will **drip** and **flow** (lit., "melt") with **new wine** (cf. Joel 3:18). So much juice will drip from the vines or overflow from the vats that **the mountains** will appear from a distance to be "dissolving" as softened mud will ooze down the slopes.

**9:14.** God's restored **people Israel** will live in peace and be able to enjoy lavish abundance. The frustration and insecurity of war will be a thing of the past (cf. Isa. 2:4: Micah 4:3). They will build houses (cf. Amos 5:11) and even whole **cities and live in them** (cf. Isa. 32:18). They will **drink** and **eat** and take pleasure in the labor of their hands.

**9:15.** God will **plant Israel in** her **own land, never again to be uprooted** and exiled **from the land** He has **given them** (cf. Gen. 13:14-15; 17:7-8; Deut. 30:1-5; 2 Sam. 7:10; Jer. 30:10-11; Joel 3:17-21; Micah 4:4-7). The land will be inhabited by Israel (cf. Ezek. 37:25; Joel 3:20; Zech. 14:11).

**The Lord** will certainly "do these things" (Amos 9:12), for He is the One who had been, was then, and always will be their **God.**

# BIBLIOGRAPHY

Barton, John. *Amos's Oracles against the Nations: A Study of Amos 1:3–2:5.* Cambridge: Cambridge University Press, 1980.

Cohen, Gary G., and Vandermey, H. Ronald. *Hosea/Amos.* Everyman's Bible Commentary. Chicago: Moody Press, 1981.

Cripps, Richard S. *A Critical and Exegetical Commentary on the Book of Amos.* 2nd ed. London: S.P.C.K., 1955. Reprint. Minneapolis: Klock & Klock Christian Publishers, 1981.

De Waard, Jan, and Smalley, William A. *A Translator's Handbook on the Book of Amos.* Stuttgart: United Bible Societies, 1979.

Feinberg, Charles L. *The Minor Prophets.* Chicago: Moody Press, 1976.

Hammershaimb, Erling. *The Book of Amos: A Commentary.* Translated by John Sturdy. New York: Schocken Books, 1970.

Harper, William Rainey. *A Critical and Exegetical Commentary on the Books of Amos and Hosea.* The International Critical Commentary. Edinburgh: T. & T. Clark, 1905.

Mays, James Luther. *Amos: A Commentary.* Philadelphia: Westminster Press, 1969.

Motyer, J.A. *The Day of the Lion: The Message of Amos.* Downers Grove, Ill.: InterVarsity Press, 1974.

Tatford, Frederick A. *The Minor Prophets.* Vol. 1. Reprint (3 vols.). Minneapolis: Klock & Klock Christian Publishers, 1982.

Veldkamp, Herman. *The Farmer from Tekoa.* St. Catherines, Ontario: Paideia Press, 1977.

Wolf, Hans Walter. *Joel and Amos.* Translated by Waldemar Janzen; S. Dean McBride, Jr.; and Charles A. Muenchow. Philadelphia: Fortress Press, 1977.

# OBADIAH

## Walter L. Baker

## INTRODUCTION

Obadiah, with its 21 verses, is the shortest Old Testament book. To many people this book has little appeal and is little known. Its message is primarily one of doom and judgment, and it is not quoted in the New Testament. Yet the Book of Obadiah merits careful study and reading for it contains a powerful message about the justice of God. His righteousness demanded vengeance on Edom, Israel's perennial enemy. Judgment against Edom is mentioned in more Old Testament books than it is against any other foreign nation (cf. Isa. 11:14; 34:5-17; 63:1-6; Jer. 9:25-26; 25:17-26; 49:7-22; Lam. 4:21-22; Ezek. 25:12-14; 35; Joel 3:19; Amos 1:11-12; 9:11-12; Obad.; Mal. 1:4).

In a sense Obadiah is a miniature profile of the message of all the writing prophets. In his thumbnail sketch, the Prophet Obadiah spoke of God's judgment on unbelieving Gentiles who oppressed the nation Israel. He also wrote of God's grace to believing Israel. This double thread is woven throughout the Major and Minor Prophets.

This small book speaks of the danger of the great sin of pride and arrogance, the feeling of superiority that often results from taking advantage of others. Obadiah graphically illustrates on a national scale the truth of Proverbs 16:18, "Pride goes before destruction, a haughty spirit before a fall."

**Authorship.** At least 12 Old Testament men were named Obadiah including an officer in David's army (1 Chron. 12:9), Ahab's servant (1 Kings 18:3), a Levite in the days of Josiah (2 Chron. 34:12), and a leader who returned from the Exile with Ezra (Ezra 8:9). Nothing is known of the author of this small prophetic profile except that his name means "Worshiper of Yahweh."

**Date.** Since the Bible gives no facts about the life or background of the man who wrote the Book of Obadiah, the date of its writing has been debated. Three suggestions for the date have been made: (a) in the reign of Jehoram (848–841 B.C.), son of Jehoshaphat, (b) in the reign of Ahaz (731–715 B.C.), and (c) in 585 B.C., soon after the destruction of Jerusalem by the Babylonians in 586.

Conservative scholars are about equally divided between the first and third views, and most liberal scholars hold the third view. A few hold the middle view because 2 Chronicles 28:17 speaks of the Edomites attacking Jerusalem and carrying off prisoners. Another argument used to suggest that the events in Obadiah (vv. 1-14) happened in Ahaz's reign (view b) is that the Edomites were able to move into Elath (at the southern tip of the Edomite territory) when Rezin drove out the Judahites in Ahaz's day (2 Kings 16:6). However, the Edomites' move into Elath does not correspond with the statements in Obadiah's book.

Arguments for the late date of the writing of Obadiah (after the fall of Jerusalem—view c) include the following:

1. The similarity of several verses in Obadiah to verses in Jeremiah 49 suggest that Obadiah quoted from Jeremiah.

| Obadiah | Jeremiah |
|---------|----------|
| v. 1 | 49:14 |
| v. 2 | 49:15 |
| vv. 3-4 | 49:16 |
| v. 5 | 49:9 |
| v. 6 | 49:10 |
| v. 8 | 49:7 |
| v. 9 | 49:22b |
| v. 16 | 49:12 |

2. The word "destruction" in Obadiah 12 speaks of Judah's fall to Babylon.

3. The word "exiles" (gālûṯ), used twice in Obadiah 20, refers to the Jewish

captives exiled in Babylon.

4. Obadiah's description of the Edomites' opposition to Jerusalem is similar to the statement in Psalm 137:7 about the Edomites tearing down Jerusalem. Also Obadiah 16-18 is similar to Lamentations 4:21-22.

These arguments, however, are answerable:

1. Jeremiah often quoted from or alluded to earlier prophets. Also several verses in Joel are similar to those in Obadiah. The words "as the LORD has said" (Joel 2:32) clearly indicate that the contents of that verse refer to Obadiah 17. So Obadiah must have been written before Joel which may have been written about 830 B.C. Obadiah may also have been referred to by Amos who wrote in the eighth century. The references or allusions to Obadiah in Joel and Amos (not always word for word) are:

| Obadiah | Joel | Obadiah | Amos |
|---------|------|---------|------|
| v. 10 | 3:19 | vv. 9-10, 18 | 1:11-12 |
| v. 11 | 3:3 | v. 14 | 1:6 |
| v. 15 | 1:15; 2:1; 3:3-4, 14 | v. 19 | 9:12 |
| v. 17 | 2:32; 3:17 | | |

2. The word "destruction" in Obadiah 12 need not mean Judah's total devastation by the Babylonians.

3. The word gālūṯ in Obadiah 20 can refer to a small group of exiles, not necessarily to the entire populace of Jewish captives taken to Babylon.

4. True, the Edomites abetted the Babylonians in their destruction of Jerusalem in 586 B.C. (Ps. 137:7). But the Book of Obadiah does not refer to the total destruction of the city by Nebuchadnezzar, which included pillaging and burning of the temple, burning of houses, and the demolition of the walls. Also no extrabiblical record indicates that the Babylonians "cast lots for Jerusalem" (Obad. 11), though admittedly this is an argument from silence. Therefore the casting of lots possibly occurred earlier.

The early date, sometime in the reign of Jehoram (848–841 B.C.), seems preferable for the following reasons:

1. The form of the Hebrew verbs in verses 12-14 ("you should not . . .") warned Edom against doing again what she had already done. Had Jerusalem already been destroyed, these commands would have had no meaning.

2. Verse 14 refers to "fugitives," people who escaped from Jerusalem, but when the Babylonians captured Jerusalem no Jerusalemites escaped (except King Zedekiah and a few with him, but they were soon captured).

3. Obadiah made no mention of the complete destruction of the city of Jerusalem, or the burning of its temple and houses or the destruction of its walls.

4. Edom's rebellion against Judah in the days of Jehoram (2 Kings 8:20-22) may have occurred at the same time the Philistines and Arabians attacked Jerusalem (2 Chron. 21:16-17). This best fits the statements in Obadiah 11-14. When the Philistines, Arabians, and Edomites entered the city, they cast lots to decide which portions of the city would be granted to each contingent for the purpose of plunder.

**Historical Background.** The animosity between the Edomites and the Israelites is one of the oldest examples of discord in human relationships. The conflict began with a struggle between Jacob and Esau in the womb of their mother Rebekah (Gen. 25:21-26). Years later, when Esau was hungry, he readily traded his birthright to Jacob for some red stew. For that reason Esau was also called Edom (Gen. 25:30), which means red. Also when Esau was born his skin appeared red (Gen. 25:25). Later Esau moved to the land of Seir (Gen. 36:8-9), the red sandstone area southeast of the Dead Sea. There his descendants, the Edomites, displaced the Horites (Deut. 2:12, 22). Interestingly the Hebrew word for Seir (śēʿîr) is similar to the word for "hairy" (śēʿār), the meaning of "Esau" (ʿēśāw). "Seir" and "Mount Seir" became synonyms for Edom (2 Chron. 20:10; 25:11; Ezek. 35:15).

Edom refused to let the Israelites pass through their land when Israel was on the way to the Promised Land (Num. 20:14-21). But God told Israel not to hate Edom since they were related (Deut. 23:7). However, hostility developed and continued for centuries (Ezek. 35:5). Saul (1 Sam. 14:47), David (2 Sam. 8:13-14),

Joab (1 Kings 11:16), and Solomon (1 Kings 11:17-22) all had problems with the sons of Edom. Jehoshaphat of Judah and Joram of Israel joined with Edom in an attack against Moab (2 Kings 3). Also in Jehoshaphat's reign Edom joined the Ammonites and the Moabites in an attack against Judah, but the attack ended with the Ammonites and Moabites defeating the Edomites (2 Chron. 20:1-2, 10-11, 22-26).

In the reign of Jehoram, Jehoshaphat's son, Edom revolted against Judah and crowned their own king (2 Kings 8:20-22; 2 Chron. 21:8). Later Amaziah, king of Judah, crushed Edom, and changed the name of the city Sela to Joktheel (2 Kings 14:7; 2 Chron. 25:11-12). Later Edom attacked Judah during Ahaz's reign (2 Chron. 28:17). In 586 B.C. Edom encouraged Babylon to destroy Jerusalem (Ps. 137:7).

In the late sixth or early fifth century B.C. the Nabateans, from northern Arabia, worshipers of gods and goddesses of fertility and the celestial bodies, drove out most of the Edomites (see comments on Obad. 7). Apparently some remained in Edom and were absorbed by the Nabatean Arabs. The Nabateans were the renowned stone-carvers of Petra. The expelled Edomites settled in Idumea, the Greek name for southern Judea. Later (ca. 120 B.C.) the Edomites there, then called Idumeans, were subdued by John Hyrcanus, a Maccabean, who forced them to be circumcised and to follow Judaism (Josephus *The Antiquities of the Jews* 13. 9. 1; 14. 7. 9). Herod the Great, king of Judea from 37 B.C. to 4 B.C., was an Idumean (Edomite).

The Idumeans joined the Jews in their rebellion against Rome in A.D. 70, but were almost obliterated by Titus, the Roman general. Only a few Idumean refugees escaped. The Edomites then faded from history.

# OUTLINE

# COMMENTARY

## I. Edom's Destruction (vv. 1-9)

*A. The call to the nations to destroy Edom (v. 1)*

**V. 1.** The word **vision** is also used in Isaiah 1:1, Micah 1:1, and Nahum 1:1 to introduce those prophetic books (cf. Dan. 1:17; 8:1; 9:24; Hosea 12:10). It suggests that the prophet "saw" (mentally and spiritually) as well as heard what God communicated to him. Nothing is known of the background or life and ministry of **Obadiah.** His name was a common one, meaning "Worshiper of Yahweh." This prophet received a direct communication from **the Sovereign** (*'ădônāy*) **LORD** (*Yahweh*). The word "Sovereign" stresses His rule over all nations and "LORD" speaks of His covenant relationship with Israel.

Concerning **Edom . . . the LORD** gave **a message** (or a report). It came through a representative He **sent to the nations,** telling them to unite in humiliating Edom. The nations that had a part in destroying the Edomites included the Nabateans, the Jews (under John Hyrcanus), and the Romans. This points up a truth seen throughout much of the Bible: God sovereignly employs nations to accomplish His will on earth.

*B. The prophecy of Edom's destruction (vv. 2-9)*

1. EDOM'S PRIDE TO BE DEBASED (VV. 2-4)

**V. 2.** Edom prided herself in her great wealth (obtained by trading, looting, and by iron and copper mining in the region) and in her almost impregnable position geographically.

Yet God said He would cause her to be made **small** (emphatic in the Heb.) in contrast with her self-exaltation, and to **be . . . despised** (also emphatic in the Heb.).

**Vv. 3-4.** Her **pride** would be her undoing, for it would deceive her into thinking that no one could conquer her. "Pride" translates z*e*dôn, from zîd, "to boil up, to be presumptuous." This recalls Jacob's cooking (zîd) the stew (nāzîd) which Esau bought with his birthright (Gen. 25:29). The Edomites' arrogance was presumptuous, whelming over their bounds, portrayed by the stew their ancestor ate.

Contributing to this self-deception was the supposed security of Edom's geographical location in the mountains of Seir. She trusted in the natural protection provided by **the clefts of the rocks.** Living in caves high (**on the heights**) above the ground level she felt totally safe from enemy attacks. Some of the Edomites had settled in such high caves and other places up in the mountains that it was as if they, hyperbolically speaking, were soaring **like the eagle** and nesting **among the stars.**

In response to Edom's self-confident, arrogant question, **Who can bring me down to the ground? . . . the LORD** answered that *He* would **bring** them **down!** God, like an eagle, would swoop down (Jer. 49:22) on those who thought they were safe as eagles. Though Edom was almost impregnable to man, she was not inaccessible to God.

2. EDOM'S WEALTH TO BE PLUNDERED
(VV. 5-7)

Edom prided herself in her wealth (v. 6), her alliances with her neighbors (v. 7), her wisdom (v. 8), and her soldiers (v. 9). Edom's fertile valleys had been developed through irrigation, and she had become a center in foreign trade routes.

**Vv. 5-6.** Obadiah now filled in details about Edom's coming judgment. First, he spoke of **thieves** stealing at **night . . . only as much as they** want. Second, he likened her humiliation to field workers gathering grapes, who **leave a few grapes** for the poor to glean.

By contrast, in Esau's **disaster** (cf. "disaster" for Jerusalem, v. 13) *nothing* would be left. Thieves and grape pickers normally do not take everything, **but** those who would plunder **Esau** would leave nothing. Esau is used here as a synonym for Edom, much as Jacob is often used as a synonym for Israel. The nation of Edom would **be ransacked,** and she would be stripped of her wealth. The invaders would find **treasures,** probably **hidden** in caves, and carry them all away, leaving her desolate.

**V. 7.** Edom prided herself in the alliances she had with her neighboring countries. Perhaps they became her allies to gain favorable trade relations with her. But those **allies,** in whom Edom trusted, would become her enemies. They would pursue her **to** her **border,** deceiving her and overpowering her. Ironically Edom, deceived by her own pride (v. 3), would then be deceived by her allies! What an alarming strategy—not an attack by a known enemy, but an ambush by an ally. **Those who eat your bread** refers to friends or allies (cf. Ps. 41:9).

Another point of irony in Obadiah 7 is that Edom, known for her wise men (cf. v. 8; Jer. 49:7), would be totally ignorant of her allies' deceptive scheme. The downfall referred to here probably occurred in the late sixth or early fifth century B.C. when the Nabateans (see "Historical Background" in the *Introduction*) went to the Edomites who took them in for a banquet. Once welcomed inside Edomite territory, the Nabateans turned against their ally and killed the guards.

3. EDOM'S PEOPLE TO BE SLAUGHTERED
(VV. 8-9)

**Vv. 8-9.** God had said He would debase Edom (v. 2), bringing her down from her pride (v. 4), and destroy her. Now He said He would **destroy the wise men of Edom** and her **men of understanding.** Her wise leaders would be unable to rescue her. Even Edom's **warriors** would be in complete dismay, and all Edomites who sought safety **in Esau's mountains** (cf. vv. 19, 21) would be slaughtered.

**Teman,** Edom's capital named for Esau's grandson (Gen. 36:10-11), represented the entire nation (cf. Amos 1:12). (See the location of Teman on the map "Israel and Surrounding Nations in the

Days of the Prophets," between Song and Isa.)

Edom's arrogance led to her complete humiliation. Her security and wealth would be gone, and her wise leaders, soldiers, and others would all fall under God's mighty hand. Nothing could render her safe—not her geographical position or military power or wisdom. What a false hope pride gives unbelievers who try to find security in their own strength apart from God.

## II. Edom's Crimes (vv. 10-14)

Obadiah, sensing the intensity of God's judgment on Esau's descendants, then stated the reasons for God's condemnation. The prophet spoke of the Edomites' sinful attitudes (vv. 10-12) and their actions against Judah (vv. 13-14).

### A. Violations in attitudes (vv. 10-12)

**V. 10.** Edom, God predicted, would **be covered with shame,** contrasting starkly with her arrogance (cf. v. 3), and she would **be destroyed** (cf. vv. 7-8), because of her violent, hurtful, oppressive cruelty (cf. Joel 3:19) **against** her **brother Jacob,** that is, Jacob's descendants. Obadiah intentionally spoke of the Judahites as Edom's "brother" to suggest the awfulness of **violence** against one's own blood relatives. Strikingly the Hebrew words for "violence" and "brother" are together in this verse.

**Vv. 11-12.** In verses 11-14 the phrases **on the day** and **in the day** occur 8 times (10 times in Heb.). When foreign forces went against Judah, they **cast lots** to see who would plunder which parts of **Jerusalem.** Edom, because of her indifference (she **stood aloof**) was no different from the **strangers** who went against her own relatives. (**You** is emphatic in Heb.) Then in a downward spiral, the indifference was followed by (a) gloating (looking **down;** cf. v. 13) over the misfortune of her **brother** (cf. v. 10), (b) rejoicing **over** Judah's **destruction,** and (c) boasting **of** her **trouble.** "Boast" is literally, "make your mouth large," talking big, another expression of arrogance.

### B. Violations in actions (vv. 13-14)

**Vv. 13-14.** Edom's crimes against Judah went beyond being spectators who rejoiced over Judah's misfortune. Because of wrong attitudes, sinful actions

followed. Edom even entered Jerusalem's **gates,** looking **down** (cf. v. 12) in arrogance on God's people **in their calamity.** Edom looted **their wealth,** killed those who tried to escape, and handed **over** any **survivors** to the attacking armies. The threefold repetition of **in the day of their disaster** (v. 13) heightens the effect of the calamity Judah experienced. (The Heb. for "disaster"; cf. v. 5, is *'êd,* similar to *'ĕdôm,* the Heb. for Edom.) Violence, harbored in the heart, gave birth to violent acts.

When did all this happen? This probably took place when the Philistines and Arabians attacked Jerusalem in the days of Jehoram, Jehoshaphat's son (2 Kings 8:20-22; 2 Chron. 21:16-17). Since Obadiah told Edom not to do such things (cf. "should not" in Obad. 12-14) again, he was probably writing about a time *before* Jerusalem's total destruction by Nebuchadnezzar (see additional comments in the *Introduction* under "Date" and "Historical Background").

## III. God's Judgment on Israel's Enemies (vv. 15-16)

**V. 15.** Edom illustrates God's judgment to come on **all nations** (cf. Isa. 34:2) who rebel in arrogance against God. **The day of the LORD** may refer to any time God judges by entering into world affairs (e.g., Ezek 30:3; see comments under "Major Interpretive Problems" in the *Introduction* to Joel). Most frequently, though, it refers to (a) God's judgments in the Great Tribulation and at the return of Jesus Christ in glory, and/or (b) God's establishing of the Millennium. In other words the Lord's "day" is when He will bring all things under His rule.

Edom's humiliation foreshadows what the Lord will do to all nations who similarly mistreat Israel. Besides her past humiliation, Edom will be repopulated in the future (see comments on Obad. 16) and with other nations will again come under God's wrath in the forthcoming day of the Lord when Christ returns to establish His reign.

God's judgments on Edom corresponded to her crimes. What she (**you** is sing.) had **done** to Judah would then be **done to** her: (1) She looted Jerusalem (v. 13), so she was looted (v. 6; cf. Jer. 49:10). (2) Edom killed Judean fugitives (Obad. 14; cf. Amos 1:11), so she was slaughtered (Obad. 8; cf. Isa. 34:5-8; Ezek. 32:29; 35:8). (3) She handed over Judean survivors to the enemy (Obad. 14; cf. Ezek. 35:5), so Edom's allies expelled her (Obad. 7). (4) Edom rejoiced over Judah's losses (Obad. 12; cf. Ezek. 35:15), so she was covered with shame and destroyed (Obad. 10).

**V. 16.** Edom had been involved in a drunken celebration in Jerusalem (**My holy hill**; cf. Pss. 2:6; 3:4; 15:1; 24:3; 78:54; Dan. 9:16, 20; Zeph. 3:11) when she entered the city (Obad. 13). Other **nations** that oppose Israel will also reap God's judgment, often pictured as a cup to **drink** (cf. Isa. 51:17, 21-23; Jer. 25:15-33; Hab. 2:16; Rev. 14:9-10; 16:19; also see Isa. 63:6). Those nations will be so completely destroyed when Jesus Christ returns to the earth (Rev. 19:15, 17-18, 21) that it will be **as if they had never** existed. Edom will be included in that judgment. For though Edom ceased to exist as a nation when the Romans conquered Idumea, some of the Edomites' descendants will again populate their land in the future. Even today that land, now a part of Jordan, is not totally desolate. But the Edomites will then be completely wiped out (cf. Obad. 18) and their land in the Millennium will be occupied by Israelites (vv. 19, 21).

## IV. God's Blessings on Israel's People (vv. 17-21)

### A. The deliverance of Israel (vv. 17-18)

**Vv. 17-18.** Though Esau will be destroyed by God's wrath, Israel in God's grace will experience **deliverance.** Israel will be freed from her enemies. **Mount Zion** (cf. v. 21), a synonym for Jerusalem (cf. comments on 2 Sam. 5:7; Lam. 1:4; Zeph. 3:14), though desecrated by Edom (Obad. 13), **will be holy** (cf. Isa. 52:1; Zech. 14:20-21), and the land promised to Israel (Gen. 15:18-21) will be occupied by **the house** (descendants) **of Jacob** (cf. Obad. 19-20). God's covenant people who trust Him will finally be delivered; they will be set apart to God. **Jacob** (the Southern Kingdom) and **Joseph** (the Northern Kingdom) will be united (cf. Ezek. 37:15-23), and will destroy Edom (**the house of Esau**; cf. Obad. 6) like **a flame** easily setting **stubble . . . on fire** (cf. Zech. 12:6; Mal. 4:1). Then the Edomites, Israel's longtime enemies, will finally be wiped out. Edom **will** have **no sur-**

vivors, in reprisal for her treatment of Judah's survivors (Obad. 14). The certainty of this truth is affirmed by the words, **The LORD has spoken.** Since He has said it, none should question it.

### B. The delineation of Israel's territories (vv. 19-20)

**Vv. 19-20.** Here Obadiah described some of the territories to be restored to God's people. (For locations of most of these places see the map "Israel and Surrounding Nations in the Days of the Prophets," between Song and Isa.) **People** in the southern desert portion of Israel (**the Negev**) **will** inherit Edom (**the mountains of Esau**; cf. Obad. 8, 21). This will fulfill the prophecies in Numbers 24:18, Isaiah 11:14, and Amos 9:11-12. Israelites in **the** western **foothills will** move south to **the land of the Philistines** with its coastal plains. Central Israel (**Ephraim and Samaria**) **will** be claimed, and small **Benjamin will** extend its borders to **Gilead,** east of the Jordan. **Exiles** sold into captivity will return and **possess the land as far** north **as Zarephath.** Others exiled **from Jerusalem** to **Sepharad, will possess . . . the** Negev. Suggestions on the location of Sepharad include two countries (Spain, Media) and two cities (Hesperides in Libya, and Sardis in Asia Minor). Sardis seems preferable. It may be the same as the Akkadian *Sapardu.* If Sepharad is to be identified with Sardis, then Jews there will be returning a distance of almost 400 miles to the Negev. At the beginning of the Millennium Israelites will return to their land from these and other lands, and their territory will be expanded.

### C. The establishment of the Lord's kingdom (v. 21)

**V. 21.** From Jerusalem (**Mount Zion;** cf. v. 17) **deliverers** (judges) **will . . . govern** the people who will have occupied **the mountains of Esau** (cf. vv. 8, 19). In the Millennium, **the kingdom will** belong to the Lord (cf. Zech. 14:9). Israel will be restored as a nation (Obad. 17), she will occupy the land (vv. 18-20), and she will be ruled by her King, the Lord Himself (v. 21).

The short Book of Obadiah presents a powerful message. It shows what happens to those who reject God's Word and His grace, rebelling in foolish pride. During Edom's prosperity many in Israel could have asked, "Why do the wicked prosper?" (cf. Ps. 73:3) But the voice of Obadiah comes thundering through the pages of the Old Testament, and is echoed in the New: "Do not be deceived: God cannot be mocked. A man reaps what he sows" (Gal. 6:7). Obadiah's words underscore the fact of God's justice. "For we know Him who said, 'It is Mine to avenge; I will repay.' . . . It is a dreadful thing to fall into the hands of the living God" (Heb. 10:30-31).

One who responds in obedience to the grace of God has everything to gain, but a person who spurns His grace in pride has everything to lose.

# BIBLIOGRAPHY

Allen, Leslie C. *The Books of Joel, Obadiah, Jonah and Micah*. The New International Commentary on the Old Testament. Grand Rapids: Wm. B. Eerdmans Publishing Co., 1976.

Feinberg, Charles L. *The Minor Prophets*. Chicago: Moody Press, 1976.

Gaebelein, Frank E. *Four Minor Prophets: Obadiah, Jonah, Habakkuk, and Haggai*. Chicago: Moody Press, 1977.

Keil, C.F. "Obadiah." In *Commentary on the Old Testament in Ten Volumes*. Vol. 10. Reprint (25 vols. in 10). Grand Rapids: Wm. B. Eerdmans Publishing Co., 1982.

Laetsch, Theo. *The Minor Prophets*. St. Louis: Concordia Publishing House, 1956.

Smith, J.M.P.; Ward, William H.; and Bewer, Julius A. *A Critical and Exegetical Commentary on Micah, Zephaniah, Nahum, Habakkuk, Obadiah and Joel*. The International Critical Commentary. Edinburgh: T. & T. Clark, 1974.

Tatford, Frederick A. *The Minor Prophets*. Vol. 2. Reprint (3 vols.). Minneapolis: Klock & Klock Christian Publishers, 1982.

Watts, John D.W. *Obadiah: A Critical Exegetical Commentary*. Winona Lake, Ind.: Alpha Publications, 1981.

# JONAH

## John D. Hannah

## INTRODUCTION

**Author.** Jonah, whose name means "dove," was a servant of the Lord from Gath Hepher (2 Kings 14:25), a town in the tribe of Zebulun (Josh. 19:10, 13). Jonah lived when Jeroboam II of the Northern Kingdom was king (2 Kings 14:23-25). The Prophet Jonah's prediction that Israel's boundaries (2 Kings 14:25) would extend under Jeroboam came true. This prophet, a Hebrew (Jonah 1:9) and the son of Amittai (1:1; Amittai means "[my] true one"), was the only Old Testament prophet to attempt to run from God.

Jonah was one of four Old Testament prophets whose ministries were referred to by Christ (cf. Matt. 12:41; Luke 11:32). The others were Elijah (Matt. 17:11-12), Elisha (Luke 4:27), and Isaiah (Matt. 15:7).

Jonah's ministry had some parallels to his immediate predecessors, Elijah (1 Kings 17–19; 21; 2 Kings 1–2) and Elisha (2 Kings 2–9; 13), who ministered to Israel and also were called to Gentile missions in Phoenicia and Aram.

Some have suggested that Jonah was not the author of the book because he is referred to in the third person (cf. Jonah 1:3, 5, 9, 12; 2:1; 3:4; 4:1, 5, 8-9). This, however, is not a strong argument. Moses, author of the Pentateuch, often used the third person when describing his own actions. Also Isaiah and Daniel sometimes wrote of themselves in the third person (e.g., Isa. 37:21; 38:1; 39:3-5; Dan. 1:1–7:1). However, since *all* of the Book of Jonah is in the third person some scholars believe this book was written by a prophet other than Jonah soon after the events.

**Date.** Since 2 Kings 14:25 relates Jonah to the reign of Jeroboam II, the events in the Book of Jonah took place some time in Jeroboam's reign (793–753 B.C.). Jonah's prophecy about Israel's boundaries being extended may indicate that he made that prophecy early in Jeroboam's reign. This makes Jonah a contemporary of both Hosea and Amos (cf. Hosea 1:1; Amos 1:1). Jonah's reference to Nineveh in the past tense (Jonah 3:3) has led some to suggest that Jonah lived later, after the city's destruction in 612 B.C. However, the tense of the Hebrew verb can just as well point to the city's existence in Jonah's day.

**Historical Setting.** Jeroboam II, in whose reign Jonah prophesied, was the most powerful king in the Northern Kingdom (cf. 2 Kings 14:23-29). Earlier the Assyrians had established supremacy in the Near East and secured tribute from Jehu (841–814 B.C.). (On the atrocious nature of the Assyrians, see the comments on the Book of Nahum.) However, after crushing the Arameans, the Assyrians suffered temporary decline because of internal dissension. In the temporary setback of Assyrian imperialistic hopes, Israel's Jeroboam was able to expand his nation's territories to their greatest extent since the time of David and Solomon by occupying land that formerly belonged to Aram (northeast toward Damascus and north to Hamath).

However, the religious life of Israel was such that God sent both Hosea and Amos to warn of impending judgment. Because of Israel's stubbornness, the nation would fall under God's chosen instrument of wrath, a Gentile nation from the east. Amos warned that God would send Israel "into exile beyond Damascus" (Amos 5:27). Hosea specifically delineated the ravaging captor as Assyria: "Will not Assyria rule over them because they refuse to repent?" (Hosea 11:5) So Assyria, then in temporary decline, would awake like a sleeping giant and devour the Northern Kingdom of Israel as its prey. This prediction was fulfilled in 722 B.C. when Sargon II carried the Northern Kingdom into captivity

(2 Kings 17). The prophecies of Hosea and Amos may explain Jonah's reluctance to preach in Nineveh. He feared he would be used to help the enemy that would later destroy his own nation.

Nineveh was located on the east bank of the Tigris River, about 550 miles from Samaria, capital of the Northern Kingdom. Nineveh was large and, like Babylon, was protected by an outer wall and an inner wall. The inner wall was 50 feet wide and 100 feet high. Before Jonah arrived at this seemingly inpregnable fortress-city, two plagues had erupted there (in 765 and 759 B.C.) and a total eclipse of the sun occurred on June 15, 763. These were considered signs of divine anger and may help explain why the Ninevites responded so readily to Jonah's message, around 759.

**Message.** This record of Jonah's episode and mission to Nineveh was addressed to Israel. The book was written not simply to record a historical narrative; in addition it conveyed a message to the Northern Kingdom. Also in one sense Jonah is not the principal person in the book; God is. The Lord had the first word (Jonah 1:1-2) and the last (4:11). God commanded the prophet twice (1:2; 3:2); He sent a violent storm on the sea (1:4); He provided a great fish to rescue Jonah (1:17); He commanded the fish to vomit Jonah onto dry land (2:10); He threatened Nineveh with judgment and relented in compassion (3:10); He provided a vine to shade His prophet (4:6); He commissioned a worm to destroy the plant (4:7); and He sent a scorching wind to discomfort Jonah (4:8).

What then is the message God was seeking to deliver to Israel through His dealings with Jonah, the Ninevites, and natural phenomena? (i.e., the sea, animal life, plant life, and the wind)

First, one apparent message to Israel is God's concern for Gentile peoples. The Lord's love for the souls of all people was supposed to be mediated through Israel, God's elect and covenant nation. Through Israel the blessing of His compassion was to be preached to the nations (Isa. 49:3). The Book of Jonah was a reminder to Israel of her missionary purpose.

Second, the book demonstrates the sovereignty of God in accomplishing His purposes. Though Israel was unfaithful in its missionary task, God was faithful in causing His love to be proclaimed. In praise to God for miraculously delivering him, Jonah confessed, "Salvation [deliverance] comes from the LORD" (Jonah 2:9). Israel failed to proclaim God's mercies, but His work gets done in spite of human weakness and imperfection.

Third, the response of the Gentiles served as a message of rebuke to God's sinful nation Israel (cf. John H. Stek, "The Message of the Book of Jonah," *Calvin Theological Journal* 4. 1969:42-3). The spiritual insight of the mariners (1:14-16) and their concern for the Jewish prophet contrast starkly with Israel's lack of concern for the Gentile nations. Jonah's spiritual hardness illustrated and rebuked Israel's callousness. Nineveh's repentance contrasted sharply with Israel's rejection of the warnings of Jonah's contemporaries, Hosea and Amos.

Fourth, Jonah was a symbol to Israel of her disobedience to God and indifference to the religious plight of other nations. Hosea, Jonah's contemporary, graphically portrayed the unending love of God for His people by loving a prostitute (who was a symbol of Israel's religious waywardness). Similarly Jonah symbolized Israel by his disobedience and disaffection. God's punishment of Jonah shows His wrath on Israel. Yet the Lord's gentle, miraculous dealings with Jonah also picture His tender love and slowness of anger with the nation. As Jonah wrote the book from a repentant heart, God desired that the nation would heed the lesson Jonah learned and repent as Jonah and Nineveh had done.

**Authenticity and Historicity.** Critical scholars, with their antisupernatural bias, have denied the authenticity of the Book of Jonah for several reasons. First, critics scoff at the miracle of a great fish swallowing the prophet. But scholars have demonstrated the validity of such an event (e.g., A.J. Wilson, "Sign of the Prophet Jonah and Its Modern Confirmations," *Princeton Theological Review* 25. October 1927, pp. 630-42; George F. Howe, "Jonah and the Great Fish," *Biblical Research Monthly*. January 1973, pp. 6-8). The "great fish" was possibly a mammal, a sperm whale (*Catodon Macrocephalus*). Sperm whales are known to

## Kings of Assyria in the Middle and New Assyrian Kingdoms

| | | | |
|---|---|---|---|
| Ashur-uballiṭ I | 1365–1330 | Shamshi-Adad V | 824–811 |
| Enlil-nirāri | 1329–1320 | Adad-nirāri III | 811–783 |
| Arik-dēn-ili | 1319–1308 | Shalmaneser IV | 783–772 |
| Adad-nirāri I | 1307–1275 | Ashur-dan III | 772–754 |
| Shalmaneser I | 1274–1245 | *(Jonah preached to the* | |
| Tukulti-Ninurta I | 1244–1208 | *Ninevites in this king's* | |
| Ashur-nādin-apli | 1207–1204 | *reign.)* | |
| Ashur-nirāri III | 1203–1198 | Ashur-nirāri V | 754–746 |
| Enlil-kudurri-uṣur | 1197–1193 | Tiglath-Pileser III | 745–727 |
| Ninurta-apil-Ekur | 1192–1180 | (Pul) | |
| Ashur-dan I | 1179–1134 | *(This king attacked* | |
| Ashur-rēsha-ishi | 1133–1116 | *Israel and Aram.)* | |
| Tiglath-Pileser I | 1115–1077 | Shalmaneser V | 727–722 |
| Ashared-apil-Ekur | 1076–1075 | *(This king besieged Samaria for* | |
| Ashur-bēl-kala | 1074–1057 | *three years, 725–722 and* | |
| Eriba-Adad II | 1056–1055 | *destroyed it in 722.)* | |
| Shamshi-Adad IV | 1054–1051 | Sargon II | 722–705 |
| Ashurnaṣirpal I | 1050–1032 | *(This king engaged in* | |
| Shalmaneser II | 1031–1020 | *mopping-up operations* | |
| Ashur-nirāri IV | 1019–1014 | *in Samaria in 721* | |
| Ashur-rabi II | 1013–973 | *after Shalmaneser V* | |
| Ashur-rēsha-ishi II | 972–968 | *died in 722.)* | |
| Tiglath-Pileser II | 967–935 | Sennacherib | 705–681 |
| Ashur-dan II | 935–912 | Esarhaddon | 681–669 |
| Adad-nirāri II | 912–889 | Ashurbanipal | 669–626 |
| Tukulti-Ninurta II | 889–884 | *(Nahum wrote of the* | |
| Ashurnasirpal II | 883–859 | *fall of Nineveh in the* | |
| Shalmaneser III | 859–824 | *reign of this king.)* | |
| *(This king attacked Israel* | | Ashur-etil-ilāni | 626–623 |
| *and received tribute from* | | Sin-shar-ishkun | 623–612 |
| *Jehu, king of Israel.)* | | Ashur-uballiṭ II | 612–609 |

have swallowed unusually large objects including even a 15-foot shark (Frank T. Bullen, *Cruise of the* Cachalot *Round the World after Sperm Whales.* London: Smith, 1898). Others have written that whale sharks (the *Rhineodon Typicus*) have swallowed men who later were found alive in the sharks' stomachs.

Second, some scholars have questioned the size of Nineveh (3:3) and its population (4:11). True, the circumference of Nineveh's inner wall, according to archeologists, was less than eight miles. So the diameter of the city, less than two miles, was hardly a three-day journey. (One day's journey in open territory was usually about 15-20 miles.)

However, two answers may be given to this objection: (1) "The city" probably included the surrounding towns that depended on Nineveh. Three such cities related to Nineveh are mentioned in Genesis 10:11-12. (2) Taking three days to go through such a city and its suburbs is

reasonable since Jonah stopped and preached along the way (Jonah 3:3-4). (On the population of Nineveh see comments on 4:11.) A city of two miles diameter was a colossal size in the ancient Near East. So it is not surprising that it was called a great city (1:2; 3:2-4, 7; 4:11).

Third, the reference to the king of Assyria as "the king of Nineveh" (3:6), has puzzled some, but to substitute a capital city (e.g., Nineveh) for the particular country (e.g., Assyria) is fairly common in the Old Testament. Ahab of Israel is called "king of Samaria" (1 Kings 21:1), Ahaziah of Israel is also called "the king of Samaria" (2 Kings 1:3), and Ben-Hadad of Aram is referred to as the "king of Damascus" (2 Chron. 24:23).

Fourth, some reject the Book of Jonah because of the sudden repentance of the Ninevites. This, however, denies the supernatural work of the Holy Spirit. If Jonah had gone to the city during the reign of the Assyrian king Ashur-dan III

(772–754 B.C.; see the chart "Kings of Assyria in the Middle and New Assyrian Kingdoms"), the prophet may have found the city psychologically prepared for his message by two foreboding famines (in 765 and 759) and a total solar eclipse on June 15, 763. People in those days often took such events as indicators of divine wrath.

Fifth, some scholars reject the authenticity of the book because of the rapid growth of the vine (Jonah 4:6). This plant, however, was probably the castor bean known for its rapid growth, tall height, and large leaves (also see the comments on 4:6).

Several arguments support the historicity of the book: (1) Known cities are mentioned in the book, including Nineveh (1:2; 3:2-4, 6-7; 4:11), Tarshish (1:3; 4:2), and Joppa (1:3). (2) Jonah is viewed as a historical person, not a fictional character. He was said to be a prophet from Gath Hepher (2 Kings 14:25) who lived in the reign of a historical person, Jeroboam II. (3) Jesus recognized the historicity of Jonah (Matt. 12:41; Luke 11:29-30, 32) and called him a prophet (Matt. 12:39), assenting to the great miracle of Jonah's recovery from the fish (Matt. 12:40). Jesus based His call to repentance in His day on the validity of Jonah's message of repentance (Matt. 12:41; Luke 11:29-32). If the story of Jonah is nonliteral (i.e., fiction, allegory, or parable), such a literary form is highly unusual, different from all the other prophetic books.

# OUTLINE

# COMMENTARY

## I. The Disobedience of Jonah (chaps. 1–2)

*A. The commission of the prophet (1:1-2)*

**1:1-2.** The God of Israel commanded **Jonah** (see comments under "Author" in the *Introduction*), a prophet (2 Kings 14:25; Matt. 12:39), to travel **to the great city of Nineveh and preach against it.** ("Great" and "greatly" occur frequently in the book: "great city," Jonah 1:2; 3:2; 4:11; "great wind," 1:4; "great storm," v. 12; "greatly feared," v. 16; "great fish," v. 17; "greatly displeased," 4:1; and "very [lit., 'greatly'] happy," 4:6.) The message he was to preach is stated in 3:4. Jonah had divine authority for this message because **the word of the LORD came to** him. It was authoritative because of its origin. The city of Nineveh was located on the east side of the Tigris River about 550 miles northeast of Samaria (see the map "The Assyrian Empire"). That distance required a journey of more than a month, if Jonah traveled the normal distance of 15-20 miles a day. The great city was second in size only to Babylon. (On Nineveh's size, see comments under "Authenticity and Historicity" in the *Introduction* and comments on 4:11.) It was in modern-day Iraq opposite the modern town of Mosul.

Nineveh was built by Nimrod (Gen. 10:11). After Jonah's day, it became the capital of the Assyrian Empire under Sennacherib (705–681 B.C.), the successor of Sargon II (722–705 B.C.) who destroyed the Northern Kingdom. The reason God sent Jonah to preach "against" Nineveh (i.e., to pronounce its doom under God's judgment) is that **its wickedness** had **come up before** Him, that is, the people were relentless and persistent in their sins. The Assyrian king acknowledged that his people's ways were "evil" and characterized by "violence" (Jonah 3:8). And they were "carefree" (Zeph. 2:15),

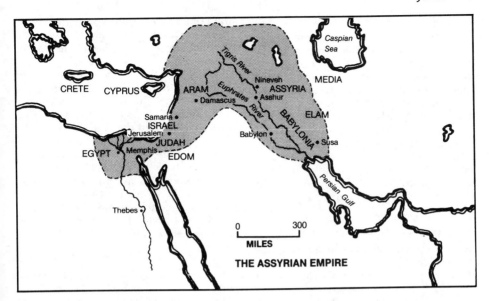

**THE ASSYRIAN EMPIRE**

thinking themselves invincible. The Prophet Nahum wrote about several of their crimes (Nahum 3:1, 4, 16). Nineveh was well known in the ancient Near East for the brutal atrocities it inflicted on its war captives. (For more on Nineveh's brutalities, see the *Introduction* to Nahum.) This city was also known for its idolatry; it had temples dedicated to the gods Nabu, Asshur, and Adad; the Ninevites also worshiped Ishtar, a goddess of love and war.

### B. The disobedience of the prophet (1:3)

**1:3.** Though **Jonah** apparently understood and appreciated God's wrath against Assyria, he was not nearly so compassionate as God was. Motivated by patriotic duty that clouded religious obligation, and knowing God's forgiving mercy (cf. 4:2), Jonah shirked his responsibility. It is strange that a prophet of God would not follow God's command to preach condemnation.

Instead of traveling northeast he fled by sea in the opposite direction. He boarded **a ship** at **Joppa** (modern Jaffa), on Israel's coast about 35 miles from Samaria and about the same distance from Jerusalem. The ship was bound **for Tarshish,** probably Tartessus in southern Spain, about 2,500 miles west of Joppa. Since Tarshish was a Phoenician colony, the ship's sailors may have been Phoenicians. Phoenicians were known for their seagoing vessels and skill on the seas.

### C. The consequences of the prophet's disobedience (1:4–2:10)

The structure of 1:4-16 is a chiasm, as seen in the following chart (adapted from Yehuda Radday, "Chiasmus in Hebrew Biblical Literature," in *Chiasmus in Antiquity: Structures, Analyses, Exegesis.* Hildesheim: Gerstenberg, 1981, p. 60).
*a.* The sailors' fright (vv. 4-5a)
  *b.* The sailors' prayer to their gods (v. 5b)
    *c.* The sailors' unloading the ship (v. 5c)
      *d.* The captain's speech to Jonah (v. 6)
        *e.* The sailors' word to each other (v. 7a)
          *f.* The sailors' question to Jonah, "Who are you?" (vv. 7b-8)
            *g.* Jonah's confession (v. 9)
          *f¹.* The sailors' question to Jonah, "What have you done?" (v. 10a)
        *e¹.* The sailors' question to Jonah, "What shall we do?" (vv. 10b-11)
      *d¹.* Jonah's words to the sailors (v. 12)
    *c¹.* The sailors' rowing of the ship (v. 13)
  *b¹.* The sailor's prayer to the Lord (v. 14)
*a¹.* The sailors' fear of the Lord (vv. 15-16)

1. THE GREAT WIND (1:4-16)

The principal person in the narrative was God, not Jonah. To accomplish His purposes, God sovereignly controlled various events recorded in the book, overcame Jonah's rebellion, and opened the Ninevites' hearts. Here He miraculously altered the direction of His servant's itinerary.

### a. The distress of the sailors (1:4-5a)

**1:4-5a.** God **sent** (*ṭûl*, "hurled") **a . . . wind on the** Mediterranean **Sea.** The wind was so **great** that it caused **a violent storm.** So terrible was the storm that **the sailors** thought **the ship** would **break up.** No wonder they were afraid! The fact that **each** sailor **cried out to his own god** suggests that many individual deities were worshiped by the Phoenicians. As seasoned seamen they also lightened **the ship** by tossing **the cargo** overboard (cf. Acts 27:17-18), hoping that the lighter ship would not sink.

### b. The complacency of Jonah (1:5b-6)

**1:5b-6.** In contrast with the concern of the mariners Jonah's reaction is amazing. He went **below deck** and fell asleep, undisturbed by the storm's tossing the ship. Perhaps he felt secure there. Obviously he was insensitive to the danger. Ironically a pagan ship **captain** had to call a man of God to prayer. The captain was desperate; every known **god** should be appealed to so that one might grant relief from their peril (cf. **we will not perish,** v. 6). The need was so great that the men despaired for their lives; yet God's servant slept. What an object lesson to God's people then and now to awaken from apathy as crying people perish on the sea of life.

### c. The reasons for the dilemma (1:7-9)

**1:7.** While the captain attempted to arouse Jonah (v. 6), **the sailors** concluded that the tragic storm was the result of divine wrath on the wrongdoing of some man on board. The casting of **lots** to determine a decision, in this case to find a culprit, was common in Israel and other countries in the ancient Near East (cf. Lev. 16:8; Josh. 18:6; 1 Sam. 14:42; Neh. 10:34; Es. 3:7; Prov. 16:33; Acts 1:26). Perhaps marked stones were put in a container, and one was taken out. God expressed His sovereignty over Jonah's affairs, causing **the lot** to "fall" on His disobedient prophet.

**1:8-9.** Though rebellious against God's command (cf. vv. 2-3) Jonah responded to the sailors' barrage of five questions by stating with no uncertainty his nationality (**I am a Hebrew**) and the worth and power of His God. Though disobedient to God, Jonah at least knew what He is like. Jonah said that God is **the LORD** (*Yahweh*), the covenant-making and covenant-keeping God of Israel. The prophet also said his God is **the God of heaven** (cf. Gen. 24:3, 7 and comments on Ezra 1:2), the one true Sovereign, in contrast with the sailors' many false gods (cf. Jonah 1:5). Jonah also affirmed that Yahweh is the Creator, the One **who made the sea and the land** (cf. Ex. 20:11; Ps. 95:5). As Creator of the world He can control nature, including storms on the sea (cf. Ps. 89:9). The sailors clearly acknowledged this fact in their question (Jonah 1:11). It may seem strange that Jonah claimed to worship this God when he did not obey Him, but this is often true of believers.

### d. The calming of the sea (1:10-16)

**1:10.** Hearing that Jonah's God controls the sea, and knowing that Jonah was rebelling against his God, the sailors concluded that the upheaval of the sea evidenced God's displeasure with him. This brought fear to the sailors, for they felt helpless in appeasing someone else's god. Perhaps too they sensed, superstitiously, that Jonah's God was holding them responsible as accomplices in Jonah's "crime." By their question, **What have you done?** the seamen chided the prophet for his senseless action. This question affirmed emphatically that he was responsible for their predicament. It was more a statement of horror at Jonah's disobedience than a question of inquiry. The pagan sailors seemed to grasp the seriousness of his disobedience more than the prophet did!

**1:11.** The sailors' perceptiveness is again evident. Believing that Jonah's God controls **the sea,** as he had told them (v. 9), they appealed to Jonah for a resolution to their heightening dilemma. They sensed that since he was responsible for the storm, they needed to do something **to** him. Only then would the storm be abated.

**1:12.** Jonah's response was penitent. Recognizing the gravity of his disobedience that resulted in the **great storm,** he was willing to endure punishment, even death. So he told them to **throw** him **into the sea.** Only then, when he was overboard, would the sea be **calm.** Perhaps Jonah also thought this would be a way out of his assignment (cf. 4:3, 8). But God had another plan!

**1:13-14.** The sailors, however, were not anxious to take human life for fear they would be held accountable for murder. This contrasts sharply with Jonah's lack of compassion for the Ninevites (cf. 4:1-2). So **the men** on the ship (except for Jonah) tried again to get **back to land.** But against the sovereign God, the sailors' meager efforts brought no relief. In fact the storm intensified. Recognizing the futility of their efforts, and believing that Jonah's God controls the sea, they realized Jonah's instructions had to be carried out. Yet those Gentiles, not having the Law of God, instinctively recognized the worth of human life and pleaded for His mercy on them **for killing an innocent man.** By their words, **You, O LORD, have done as You pleased,** the sailors were acknowledging His divine sovereignty and providence in the storm (1:4) and in the casting of the lots (v. 7).

**1:15-16.** Following the prophet's instructions (v. 12), the sailors **threw** Jonah into **the raging sea** and it became **calm.** This showed them the reality and power of the God of Israel. They stood in awe of (**feared**) **the LORD.** He had done what their gods could not do. The sudden calm was an answer to the sailors' prayers (v. 5). The calm also revealed that the storm had resulted from Jonah's disobedience and that an innocent life had not been snuffed out in casting him overboard. Utterly amazed at the sudden calm, **they offered a sacrifice** in praise **to the LORD** (*Yahweh*, Israel's God) and promised (**made vows**) to continue their praise. Again the sailors are seen in contrast with their former passenger. Whereas **Jonah** was disobedient to God, they were praising Him!

**2. THE GREAT FISH (1:17–2:10)**

*a. The swallowing of Jonah (1:17)*

**1:17.** The prophet's expected death did not occur. The sovereignty and centrality of God as the major figure in this historical narrative are evidenced in His providing a fish to swallow Jonah. This is the first of four things in this book He **provided** (cf. 4:6-8). The **great fish** was possibly a mammal, a sperm whale, or perhaps a whale shark (see "Authenticity and Historicity" under *Introduction*). God controls not only the sea but all that is in it. By means of the large sea monster God preserved **Jonah** alive and later deposited

him unhurt on land. The phrase **three days and three nights** need not be understood as a 72-hour period, but as one 24-hour day and parts of two other days (cf. Es. 4:16 with 5:1 and comments on Matt. 12:40, where Jesus said His burial would be the same length of time as Jonah's interment in the fish's stomach).

*b. The praise by Jonah (2:1-9)*

This prayer by Jonah was not a plea for deliverance for there were no petitions in it. The prayer is a psalm of thanksgiving (v. 9) to God for using the fish to save him from drowning. The prayer was made while Jonah was in the fish's stomach (v. 1) but it was written of course after he was expelled from the fish's stomach. Sensing that the great fish was God's means of delivering him, Jonah worshiped God for His unfathomable mercies. Jonah praised God for delivering him from death (cf. Ps. 30:3) in a watery grave (cf. Bernhard W. Anderson, *Out of the Depths.* Philadelphia: Westminster Press, 1974, pp. 84-6). The contents of Jonah 2 correspond in several ways to the contents in chapter 1:

| The Sailors | |
|---|---|
| 1:4 | Crisis on the sea |
| 1:14 | Prayer to Yahweh |
| 1:15b | Deliverance from the storm |
| 1:16 | Sacrifice and vows offered to God |
| **The Prophet** | |
| 2:3-6a | Crisis in the sea |
| 2:2, 7 | Prayer to Yahweh |
| 2:6b | Deliverance from drowning |
| 2:9 | Sacrifice and vows offered to God |

1. A summary of Jonah's experience. **2:1-2.** After noting the place (**inside the fish**) where he voiced this prayer, **Jonah** poetically recounted the story of his deliverance.

Though the sailors had sacrificed to **the LORD** (1:16), He was in a special sense Jonah's God. When the sailors cast him overboard, **in . . . distress** he prayed and **the LORD . . . answered** with a miraculous provision (the fish). The phrase **from the depths of the grave** refers to the fear of death that gripped the prophet. It does not mean he actually died. God **listened to** his **cry** for help and went to his rescue.

2. A description of Jonah's experience (2:3-7). Here the prophet recorded his watery horror and God's gracious deliverance.

**2:3.** Though the sailors had thrown him into the sea (1:15), actually God had **hurled** him **into the deep,** that is, He was behind their action. As **the currents** of the Mediterranean **swirled about** Jonah, he knew that God controls the **waves and breakers** (Jonah called them **Your**; cf. Ps. 88:7).

**2:4. Banished** by God because of his sin of disobedience, the prophet evidenced repentance and renewed faith, for he expressed confidence in approaching God (**I will look again toward Your holy temple**). The "holy temple" may be the Jerusalem temple or, perhaps more likely, God's heavenly abode (cf. Ps. 11:4), for the prophet said (Jonah 2:7) his prayer "rose" to God in His temple. Or verse 4 could refer to the Jerusalem temple and verse 7 to the heavenly temple.

**2:5-6a.** In his peril the **waters threatened** to take his life and the sea **surrounded** him. Ocean vegetation was bound about his **head** as if to imprison him. In the sea he **sank** to the bottoms **of the mountains,** and **the earth** was about to entrap him permanently. This is the prophet's description of his plunge into what appeared to be a watery grave.

**2:6b-7.** At the point of Jonah's hopelessness and utter despair, God used the fish to lift the prophet **up from the pit** ("pit" is a synonym for grave). Because God had saved his life, the repentant prophet confessed that the LORD was his **God** (cf. v. 1). Sensing that he was about to die by drowning and that his **life was ebbing away,** he turned to God, praying to Him (cf. v. 2) for deliverance (on the **holy temple**; cf. comments on v. 4). In the gravest of perils the prophet prayed and his petitions **rose** to heaven to be answered most uniquely.

3. An expression of Jonah's thankfulness. **2:8-9.** The statement concerning the folly of trusting **worthless idols** provides a dark background against which God's brilliant grace is evident. No lifeless idol could effect so great a deliverance as the God of heaven, who made the sea and the land (cf. 1:9). In contrast with those who trusted weak idols for deliverance (cf. 1:5) Jonah offered a **sacri-**

**fice** (cf. 1:16) of praise to the true God who effected such a wondrous provision. Also he **vowed** to obey the Lord because **salvation** (i.e., deliverance) **comes from the LORD.** Deliverance from perilous situations is a provision from a gracious God.

*c. The return of Jonah (2:10)*

**2:10.** After the deliverance of **Jonah** from the watery grave, **the LORD commanded the fish** to deposit the prophet safely on **dry land,** presumably on the coast of Palestine after the three-day return journey (cf. 1:17). Seven miracles have taken place already in this short narrative: God caused a violent storm (1:4), had the lot fall on Jonah (1:7), calmed the sea when Jonah was thrown overboard (1:15), commanded the fish to swallow Jonah (1:17), had the fish transport him safely, had the fish throw Jonah up on dry land, and perhaps greatest of all, melted the disobedient prophet's heart (evidenced by his thanksgiving prayer in chap. 2).

## II. The Obedience of Jonah (chaps. 3–4)

*A. The recommissioning of the prophet (3:1-2)*

**3:1-2.** After turning **Jonah** from willful disobedience **the LORD** again commanded the prophet to fulfill his appointed task (cf. 1:2). Three times Nineveh is described as a **great city** (1:2; 3:2; 4:11; cf. "very large city," 3:3). As noted in the *Introduction* the city was surrounded by an inner wall and an outer wall. The huge inner wall (50 feet wide and 100 feet high) was about eight miles in circumference while the outer wall encompassed fields and smaller towns (viz., Rehoboth Ir, Calah, and Resen; cf. Gen. 10:11-12). The words "great city" probably included the city of Nineveh proper and its administrative environs.

His instructions were simply to travel those 550 miles to **Nineveh** and preach **the message** the Lord would provide at the appropriate time (cf. Jonah 3:4). Interestingly in His recommissioning the prophet, God did not repeat the reason for the proclamation (cf. 1:2b).

*B. The obedience of the prophet (3:3-4)*

**3:3.** The prophet's response here differs from his response in chapter 1. Here he **obeyed the . . . LORD and** made his way northeast **to Nineveh.** Earlier (1:3) he disobeyed the Lord and went west.

**Jonah** again mentioned the great size of the **city,** commenting that **it took three days to go all through it,** that is, through Nineveh and its suburbs (see comments under "Authenticity and Historicity" in the *Introduction* and comments on 3:2).

**3:4. Going a day's journey** does not mean that Jonah traveled into the city for a whole day before preaching. Instead it means on the first day he entered the city he began preaching. The message God gave the prophet was the threat of complete destruction of **Nineveh** within **40 . . . days.** Perhaps this was a period of grace, giving the people an opportunity to repent before the judgment fell. Jonah continued this proclamation for three days before going "east of the city" (4:5).

### C. The conversion of the Ninevites (3:5-10)

1. THE ACTION OF THE PEOPLE (3:5)

**3:5.** The words of Jonah spread rapidly through every quarter of greater Nineveh. **The Ninevites** accepted Jonah's message and **believed God.** As the prophet preached doom, the people—ironically—changed. Earlier Jonah had repented, and now these Gentiles repented. As outward symbols of inward contrition and humiliation they fasted (cf. 1 Sam. 7:6; 2 Sam. 1:12; Neh. 1:4; Zech. 7:5) and **put on sackcloth** (coarse cloth; cf. Gen. 37:34; 1 Kings 21:27; Neh. 9:1; Es. 4:1-4; Lam. 2:10; Dan. 9:3; Joel 1:8). People in every social strata, **from the greatest to the least,** hoped that God might turn from His anger and spare them.

As previously noted, some scholars find such an extensive turning to God incredible. True, Assyrian records make no mention of this city-wide penitence, but official historical records often delete events, especially those that might embarrass them (e.g., Egyptian records do not refer to the Israelites' crossing the Red Sea or did the Assyrians record the loss of 185,000 soldiers in Jerusalem, 2 Kings 19:35).

Another question about the Ninevites is whether their conversion was genuine. Was their religious response superficial as in the case of Ahab? (1 Kings 21:27-29) If the Ninevites' conversion was genuine, it may be difficult to explain

why the Assyrians continued their violence and why they soon destroyed Israel (ca. 37 years later, in 722 B.C., the Assyrians destroyed the Northern Kingdom). Perhaps the next generation reverted to the Assyrians' typical violence.

Also Jonah's message concerned repentance from evil to avoid judgment; perhaps many believed Jonah's words without becoming genuinely converted. They could have believed the fact of God's threat of judgment without trusting in Yahweh as the *only* true God. C.F. Keil wrote, "But however deep the penitential mourning of Nineveh might be, and however sincere the repentance of the people . . . they acted according to the king's command; the repentance was not a lasting one, or permanent in its effects" ("Jonah," in *Commentary on the Old Testament in Ten Volumes,* 10:409). Apparently the Ninevites responded from fear (cf. Jonah 3:8-9) under the power of Jonah's proclamation. Though the people were outwardly contrite (fasting and wearing sackcloth) there may have been no enduring spiritual change. At any rate, the preaching of Jonah occasioned extensive and intensive, if not durative, religious effects.

2. THE ACTION OF THE KING (3:6-9)

*a. His repentance (3:6)*

**3:6.** Word of the religious humiliation of the people **reached the king of Nineveh** (probably Ashur-dan III). Though Nineveh did not become capital of the Assyrian Empire until some time in the reign of Sennacherib (705–681 B.C.), some of her kings did reside there. Such news of pending, almost immediate doom caused the king to respond in the way his people did (cf. v. 5). Wearing **sackcloth,** a coarse garment, and sitting in **dust** (cf. Isa. 47:1) showed he was contrite and believed the prophet's message.

*b. His proclamation (3:7-9)*

**3:7-8.** The king's remorse led him **and his nobles** to issue a royal **decree.** The decree instructed the people to fast (this decree may have been the reason for the fast referred to in v. 5), to wear **sackcloth** (cf. comments on v. 5), to **call urgently on God,** and to relinquish **their** wickedness (**evil ways;** cf. v. 10). Even the animals were not allowed to **eat,** and were draped with sackcloth. This practice was not strange in the Near East; it was another sign of the people's remorse.

**3:9. Who knows?** (cf. 2 Sam. 12:22; Joel 2:14) hints at the possibility of God's withdrawing His threat. By their contrition the king hoped that Jonah's **God** would **relent** of His judgment and **turn from His . . . anger,** thereby sparing the city. (Cf. **we will not perish,** in Jonah 1:6.) This fear of judgment from God is startling because the Assyrians were a cruel, violent nation (cf. Nahum 3:1, 3-4) fearing no one (cf. 2 Kings 18:33-35).

### 3. THE ACTION OF GOD (3:10)

**3:10.** The prophet's message may have included conditions whereby the threats of God could be rescinded. As an evidence of His mercy to the Ninevites God sent Jonah to them, told him what to proclaim to them, and opened the hearts of a vast population. Also, seeing their repentant actions, **God** relented of His threat of **destruction.** He had spared Jonah (chap. 2); now He spared Nineveh. God's mercies are always unmerited; His grace is never earned. Repentance is never a work to be rewarded. But this is not to say that God does not act in response to such repentance. Nineveh's repentance delayed God's destruction of the city for about 150 years. The people evidently fell into sin again, so that later the city was destroyed, in 612 B.C. (see the Book of Nahum).

**When** God **threatened** punishment He provided a dark backdrop on which to etch most vividly His forgiving mercies. This emphasized His grace most forcefully to the sinners' hearts. God's readiness to have **compassion** on a wicked but repentant people and to withhold threatened destruction showed Israel that *her* coming judgment at God's hand was not because of His unwillingness to forgive but because of her impenitence.

## D. The sorrow of the prophet (chap. 4)

### 1. THE DISPLEASURE OF JONAH (4:1-5)

#### a. Jonah's anger (4:1)

**4:1. Jonah** blatantly rejected and repudiated the goodness of God to the Ninevites. In that attitude he symbolized the nation Israel. Jonah's self-interests were a reminder to Israel of her lack of concern for the ways and mercies of God. The word **but** points up the contrast between God's compassion (3:10) and Jonah's displeasure, and between God's turning *from* His anger (3:9-10) and Jonah's turning *to* anger. Jonah's anger (**became angry** is lit., "became hot") at God for sparing Nineveh stemmed from his unbalanced patriotic fervor. Jonah probably knew from Amos and Hosea that Assyria would be Israel's destroyer. Jonah's fickle attitude toward God's dealings with him are remarkably abrupt and variegated (disobedience, chap. 1; thanksgiving, chap. 2; obedience, chap. 3; displeasure, chap. 4).

#### b. Jonah's prayer (4:2-3)

**4:2.** Out of anger and disgust the prophet rebuked his LORD, saying in essence, "I know **that You** are forgiving and now look what has happened!" Jonah admitted that he fled toward **Tarshish** because he did not want the Ninevites to be saved from judgment. (*He* wanted to be delivered from calamity, 2:2, 7, but he did not want the Ninevites to be kept from disaster.) The Ninevites were more ready to accept God's grace than Jonah was. Jonah, an object of God's compassion, had no compassion for Nineveh's people.

Jonah knew **God** is willing to forgive but he did not want his enemies to know it. Their threat of doom (3:4) could be diverted if his hearers turned to his forgiving God.

The prophet certainly had a clear grasp of God's character, as reflected in his near-quotation of Exodus 34:6. In fact Jonah's words about God are almost identical with Joel's description of Him (Joel 2:13; also cf. Neh. 9:17; Pss. 103:8; 145:8). **God** is **gracious** (i.e., He longs for and favors others) and **compassionate** (tender in His affection), **slow to anger** (He does not delight in punishing the wicked; cf. 2 Peter 3:9), **and abounding in love** (*ḥesed,* "loyal love, or faithfulness to a covenant"). The psalmists often spoke of God being "gracious" and "compassionate," though sometimes in reverse order (Pss. 86:15; 103:8; 111:4; 112:4; 145:8). Jonah also said He knew God **relents from sending calamity.** The prophet feared that all these attributes of God would be extended toward the despicable, cruel Ninevites—and it happened!

**4:3.** Jonah's anguish over what God

did led him to request that he might **die** (cf. Jonah 4:8; 1 Kings 19:4). Earlier he had prayed to live (Jonah 2:2). Perhaps now he was embarrassed that his threat was not carried out. Because God relented of His wrath and did not destroy the city, Jonah was so emotionally disappointed that he lost all reason for living. God was concerned about the city (4:11) but Jonah was not.

### c. Jonah's action (4:4-5)

**4:4-5.** Though Jonah knew that God is slow to anger (v. 2) he still wanted **the LORD** to execute His wrath swiftly. Yet God, hesitant to be angry with even His prophet, sought to reason with him. God asked the sulking messenger whether his anger was justified (cf. v. 9). This question implied a negative response: Jonah had no **right to be angry.** A person should never angrily question what God does, even when it differs from what he expects or wants.

**Jonah** was so distraught that he did not reply to God. Instead he left **the city** and built a crude **shelter,** perhaps from tree branches, and **sat** down (cf. the king's sitting in the dust, 3:6) **in its shade** (cf. Elijah under a broom tree, 1 Kings 19:4). Apparently Jonah had a clear view of the city. Why he **waited to see what would happen to the city** is difficult to understand. Perhaps he felt that God would answer his plea and judge the city anyway. Unable to imagine God not carrying out His justice on people who deserved it, Jonah was determined to wait till Nineveh was in fact judged. But he was wrong and his action was childish. Obviously he had forgotten that he, who also deserved death for disobedience, was delivered by God (chap. 2).

### 2. THE EXPLANATION OF THE LORD (4:6-11)

### a. The illustration prepared (4:6-8)

God, being slow to anger (v. 2), again attempted to reason with Jonah (cf. v. 4). This time God gave him a visual lesson. God erected an object of Jonah's affection (creaturely comfort) and contrasted it with the object of His own concern (the souls of people). God rebuked Jonah, not through a storm in this instance, but by exposing the selfishness of his likes and dislikes.

**4:6. God provided** (cf. "provided" in 1:17; 4:7-8) **a vine** to give the prophet

shade that his crude shelter (v. 5) could not provide. The God of the sea, who could provide a fish to swallow **Jonah,** is also the God of the land (cf. 1:9) and its vegetation. Here is evidence that God is compassionate (4:2)—even when His servants are upset and depressed.

As this plant grew it covered the prophet's hut. The shade from the green plant, covering his booth with its dense foliage, protected him from the rays of the desert sun. The plant (*qîqāyôn*) may have been a castor-bean plant (*Ricinus communis*), which grows rapidly in hot climates to a height of 12 feet and has large leaves. It easily withers if its stalk is injured. The fact that the plant grew overnight (cf. "at dawn the next day," v. 7, and note v. 10) shows that more-than-usual rapid growth was as much a miracle as God's providing the fish for Jonah. Delighted with this relief, **Jonah,** though he had been angry and depressed, was now overjoyed. Ironically he was glad for his own comfort but not for the Ninevites' relief from judgment.

**4:7-8.** Early **the next day God provided** (cf. "provided" in 1:17; 4:6) **a worm** that destroyed the plant that had brought joy to the prophet. Then the following day **God provided a scorching east wind** that left Jonah comfortless and **faint.** The prophet's own shelter was not enough to protect him from the terribly hot wind from the east. Strikingly in chapter 1 God intervened by a storm and a huge fish; now He intervened with a lowly worm and a sultry wind. Again the prophet was so discomforted—first by Nineveh's repentance and now by the loss of the shade from the vine—that he wanted **to die** (cf. 4:3).

### b. The explanation stated (4:9-11)

**4:9. God** asked **Jonah** the same question He posed earlier. **Do you have a right to be angry?** (cf. v. 4) But here He added the words **about the vine.** God was wanting Jonah to see the contrast between His sparing Nineveh and His destroying the vine—the contrast between Jonah's lack of concern for the *spiritual* welfare of the Ninevites and his concern for his own *physical* welfare. Both Jonah's unconcern (for Nineveh) and concern (for himself) were selfish. Jonah replied that his anger over the withered plant was justified, and that he was so

**angry** he wanted **to die.**

"Life for Jonah [is] a series of disconcerting surprises and frustrations. He tries to escape from God and is trapped. He then gives up, accepts the inevitability of perishing, and is saved. He obeys when given a second chance, and is frustratingly, embarrassingly successful. He blows up; his frustration is intensified" (Judson Mather, "The Comic Act of the Book of Jonah," *Soundings* 65. Fall 1982, p. 283).

**4:10-11.** God wanted Jonah to see that he had no right to be angry over Nineveh or the **vine** because Jonah did not give life to or sustain either of them. Nor was he sovereign over them. He had no control over the plant's growth or withering. The vine was quite temporal (**it sprang up overnight and died overnight**) and was of relatively little value. Yet Jonah grieved over it. Whereas Jonah had no part in making the plant **grow,** God had created the Ninevites. Jonah's affections were distorted; he cared more for a vine than for human lives. He cared more for his personal comfort than for the spiritual destiny of thousands of people. What a picture of Israel in Jonah's day.

God's words to the prophet indicate that Jonah had no right to be angry. Donald E. Baker paraphrases the Lord's response this way: "Let's analyze this anger of yours, Jonah. . . . It represents your concern over your beloved plant—but what did it really mean to you? Your attachment to it couldn't be very deep, for it was here one day and gone the next. Your concern was dictated by self-interest, not by genuine love. You never had the devotion of a gardener. If you feel as bad as you do, what would you expect a gardener to feel like, who tended a plant and watched it grow only to see it wither and die? This is how I feel about Nineveh, only much more so. All those people, all those animals—I made them; I have cherished them all these years. Nineveh has cost Me no end of effort, and it means the world to Me. Your pain is nothing compared to Mine when I contemplate their destruction" ("Jonah and the Worm," *His.* October 1983, p. 12).

Whereas Jonah had thought God was absurd in sparing the Assyrians, God exposed Jonah as the one whose thinking was absurd.

In contrast with an insignificant vine, greater **Nineveh** was significant; it had **more than 120,000 people.** The words, **who cannot tell their right hand from their left,** may refer to young children, in which case the population of Nineveh and its environs may have been, as some commentators state, about 600,000. But other commentators suggest that the 120,000 were adults, who were as undisciplined or undiscerning as children, thus picturing their spiritual and moral condition without God. (In that case the total population may have been about 300,000.) The figure of 120,000 for Nineveh *proper* accords with the adult population of Nimrod (Gen. 10:11-12; also known as Calah, a suburb of Nineveh). An inscription states that Ashurnaṣirpal II (883–859) invited 69,574 people of Nimrod to a feast (Leslie C. Allen, *The Books of Joel, Obadiah, Jonah and Micah,* p. 234, n. 27; Daniel David Luckenbill, *The Annals of Sennacherib.* Chicago: University of Chicago Press, 1924, p. 116). And according to Donald J. Wiseman, Nineveh's walls enclosed an area twice that of Calah ("Jonah's Nineveh," *Tyndale Bulletin* 30. 1979, p. 37).

Jonah is a remarkably tragic example of the plight of the nation Israel. Both Jonah and Israel were accused of religious disobedience and disaffection. What a tragedy when God's people care more for creaturely comforts than for the interests of God's will among men.

By contrast, God is unselfish. He has a right to **be concerned about** (*ḥûs,* "to spare"; cf. Joel 2:17) **that great city,** a city with many people who needed His grace.

The two Minor Prophets that deal almost exclusively with Nineveh—Jonah and Nahum—each end with a question (cf. Nahum 3:19). The question in Jonah 4:11 leaves the reader with a sense of uneasiness, for the curtain seems to drop abruptly. No response from Jonah is recorded. How is this silence to be understood? Most likely Jonah could not have written the book unless he had learned the point God was seeking to bring home to him. Apparently Jonah perceived his error and then wrote this historical-biographical narrative to urge Israel to flee from her disobedience and spiritual callousness.

As the book concludes, Jonah was angry, depressed, hot, and faint. And he was left to contemplate God's words about his own lack of compassion and God's depth of compassion. The Lord had made His points: (a) He is gracious toward all nations, toward Gentiles as well as Israelites; (b) He is sovereign; (c) He punishes rebellion; and (d) He wants His own people to obey Him, to be rid of religious sham, and to place no limits on His universal love and grace.

# BIBLIOGRAPHY

Allen, Leslie C. *The Books of Joel, Obadiah, Jonah and Micah.* The New International Commentary on the Old Testament. Grand Rapids: Wm B. Eerdmans Publishing Co., 1976.

Banks, William L. *Jonah, the Reluctant Prophet.* Chicago: Moody Press, 1966.

Blair, J. Allen. *Living Obediently: A Devotional Study of the Book of Jonah.* Neptune, N.J.: Loizeaux Brothers, 1963.

Draper, James T., Jr. *Jonah: Living in Rebellion.* Wheaton, Ill.: Tyndale House Publishers, 1971.

Fausset, A.R. *A Commentary: Critical, Experimental and Practical on the Old Testament.* Vol. 4. Grand Rapids: Wm. B. Eerdmans Publishing Co., 1945.

Feinberg, Charles L. *The Minor Prophets.* Chicago: Moody Press, 1976.

Gaebelein, Frank E. *Four Minor Prophets: Obadiah, Jonah, Habakkuk, and Haggai.* Chicago: Moody Press, 1977.

Keil, C.F. "Jonah." In *Commentary on the Old Testament in Ten Volumes.* Vol. 10. Reprint (25 vols. in 10). Grand Rapids: Wm. B. Eerdmans Publishing Co., 1982.

Kleinert, Paul. "The Book of Jonah." In *Commentary on the Holy Scriptures.* Reprint (24 vols. in 12). Grand Rapids: Zondervan Publishing House, 1960.

Kohlenberger, John R. III. *Jonah-Nahum.* Everyman's Bible Commentary. Chicago: Moody Press, 1984.

Laetsch, Theo. *The Minor Prophets.* St. Louis: Concordia Publishing House, 1956.

Pusey, E.B. *The Minor Prophets: A Commentary.* Vol. 1. Grand Rapids: Baker Book House, 1970.

Tatford, Frederick A. *The Minor Prophets.* Vol. 2. Reprint (3 vols.). Minneapolis: Klock & Klock Christian Publishers, 1982.

# MICAH

## John A. Martin

## INTRODUCTION

**Author and Date.** Little is known about the author of this book. His name Micah, a shortened form of the name Micaiah, means "Who is like Yahweh?" In Jeremiah's day the elders referred to Micah and quoted Micah 3:12 in defense of Jeremiah's message of judgment on the nation (Jer. 26:18).

Micah was from Moresheth (Micah 1:1; cf. 1:14), a Judean town about 25 miles southwest of Jerusalem near the Philistine city of Gath (see the map "Israel and the Surrounding Nations in the Days of the Prophets," between Song and Isa.). Moresheth, in Judah's fertile foothills, was also near Lachish, an important international trading point.

Like his contemporary Isaiah, Micah prophesied about the Assyrian destruction of the Northern Kingdom and the later defeat of the Southern Kingdom by the Babylonians. Micah prophesied in the eighth century B.C. during the reigns of Jotham, Ahaz, and Hezekiah (Micah 1:1; cf. the chart "Kings of Judah and Israel and the Preexilic Prophets," near 1 Kings 12).

**Message and Style.** The book has three messages (Micah 1:2–2:13; chaps. 3–5; chaps. 6–7), each beginning with the exhortation to "hear" or "listen" to what the Lord had to say to the nation. Though Micah mentioned the destruction coming on the Northern Kingdom of Israel, his main audience was the people of the Southern Kingdom of Judah. Micah's three messages showed that Judah was just as guilty as Israel. They too would be disciplined by God.

God's standard of measurement in the Book of Micah (as in all the prophetic writings) was the Mosaic Covenant God made with His people when the nation was redeemed from Egypt. The people were expected to live according to the covenant stipulations. If they did they would be blessed by God (Deut. 28:1-14). If they did not, they would be judged by God and eventually He would cast them out of the land of promise (Deut. 28:15-68). Micah pointed up how the people had failed to live up to the covenant stipulations. He announced that God was just in disciplining them. Actually God's discipline on the nation showed that He cared for them and would restore them.

Though the theme of judgment is prominent in each of Micah's three messages, the prophet also stressed restoration. Micah mentioned the "remnant" in each of his three messages (Micah 2:12; 4:7; 5:7-8; 7:18). He was confident that someday the Lord would restore the people of Israel to a place of prominence in the world under the Messiah. This emphasis would have greatly encouraged the righteous remnant in Micah's day.

Like many portions of the prophetic books, the Book of Micah is in poetry, not prose. Most of his statements therefore were in parallelism (see comments on parallelism under "Nature of the Psalms" in the *Introduction* to the Book of Pss.). His book includes several puns (see comments on Micah 1:10-15) and several probing questions. Micah is quoted twice in the New Testament (5:2 is quoted in Matt. 2:5-6, and Micah 7:6 is quoted in Matt. 10:35-36). Micah wrote about the Messiah's birthplace, lineage, and origin (Micah 5:4), and reign (4:1-7), and referred to Him as Israel's King (2:13) and Ruler (5:2).

## OUTLINE

I. First Message: Judgment Will Come
(chaps. 1–2)

# COMMENTARY

## I. First Message: Judgment Will Come (chaps. 1–2)

Here Micah foretold God's judgment on Israel and Judah. He also wrote that the nation will ultimately be restored to prominence and prosperity. The prophet was sure because of the promises God had given other writers. God had promised Abraham that he would have many descendants and they would dwell in Palestine (Gen. 12:2; 15:18-21; 17:1-8, 16, 19-20). Through Moses God promised the people they would enjoy great blessing in the land (Deut. 30:1-10). He told David that his offspring and throne would continue forever (2 Sam. 7:11b-16). The Major and Minor Prophets also wrote messages of consolation that God will ultimately bless the nation because of His promises. Isaiah, Micah's contemporary, also prophesied that God will restore the nation (see, e.g., Isa. 65–66).

The theme of judgment, voiced repeatedly in the prophetic books, can be traced back to Deuteronomy 27–28 when Moses warned the people about to enter the Promised Land about the dangers that awaited them there. The previous adult generation (except Caleb and Joshua) had died in the wilderness because of their refusal to follow God's command to possess the land. So Moses told the new generation that they had a choice. They could either follow the covenant given them by God and live in the land with prosperity (Deut. 28:1-14), or they could refuse and be cursed in the land with a lack of fertility and productivity (of people, animals, and crops) and ultimately be exiled from the land of promise. From that point on, much of the narrative and prophetic portions of the Old Testament focus on Israel's failure to live according to God's covenantal stipulations. Micah, along with Amos, especially pointed up the social failures of the nation in not keeping the covenant (see, e.g., Micah 2:1, 8-9; 3:11; 6:11).

### A. Introduction (1:1)

**1:1.** A number of important introductory points are made in this opening verse. **Micah** said the message of his book was **the word of the LORD.** This phrase, common to many of the prophets, is important in light of this revelation or "word" from the Lord to His people. God wanted Israel to react rationally to His word and to make proper decisions based on it. Her religious system contrasted directly with the contemporary pagan fertility religions in which sensory experience was the highest form of religious expression.

The prophet said he was from **Moresheth** (called Moresheth Gath in v. 14; perhaps modern Tell Judaiyideh). The town was about 25 miles southwest of Jerusalem, though its exact location has been disputed.

Micah prophesied **during the reigns of Jotham, Ahaz, and Hezekiah.** Micah prophesied about both the Northern and the Southern Kingdoms, but he mentioned only these three kings of Judah because the kings in the north were not in the Davidic line. The dates of these three kings means that Micah's ministry fell between 750 and 686, though scholars normally assume that Micah's ministry ended in the early part of Hezekiah's reign (perhaps before 700 B.C.).

Micah's book relays **the vision** (cf. Isa. 1:1; Obad. 1; Nahum 1:1) **he saw concerning Samaria,** capital of the Northern Kingdom (Israel), **and Jerusalem,** capital of the Southern Kingdom (Judah). The Hebrew word for "vision" suggests that God gave these passages to Micah who "saw" them mentally and spiritually. These cities obviously represented all 12 tribes of the nation. The prophet denounced evil which was rampant throughout the nation. The Northern Kingdom had long before strayed from the covenant given through Moses. And the people in the Southern Kingdom were acting like their brothers and sisters to the north, failing to live according to the covenant.

### B. Prediction of coming judgment (1:2-7)

**1:2.** Verses 2-7 form the backdrop for the rest of the book. After calling on the earth to **hear** God's lawsuit against His covenant people (v. 2), the prophet spoke of the results of God's punishment (vv. 3-4), the reason for the judgment (v. 5), and the certainty of judgment (vv. 6-7). In a kind of cosmic law court Micah asked **all** the **peoples** of the **earth,** like a jury, to "hear" what God as a **witness** would say about the nation's sins. Micah

implied that everyone, given the opportunity, would agree that God's judgment **against** His people was just.

Micah called God **the Sovereign** (*'ădōnāy*) **LORD** (*Yahweh*), and in the last line of verse 2 he used *'ădōnāy* (**Lord**) again. In 4:13 Micah used the shortened form *'ādôn.* On the title "Sovereign LORD" see comments on Ezekiel 2:4. Micah noted that the Lord would come **from His holy temple.** Of course the temple did not contain God; even all creation could not contain Him (1 Kings 8:27). His dwelling place (Micah 1:3) is in heaven (2 Chron. 6:21, 30, 33, 39). However, God had chosen to localize His presence in the tabernacle and later the temple above the atonement cover, the lid of the ark of the Testimony. Inside the ark were the two tablets on which were written the Ten Commandments, a portion of God's Word. As stated earlier, the Israelites were responsible to live according to the Mosaic Covenant. The sacrificial system and the temple were at the core of the covenantal system. Therefore to speak of the Lord going "from His holy temple" to witness against the nation meant He would judge them on the basis of the Mosaic Covenant which gave Him every right to do so.

**1:3-4.** Micah called on the people to look for God **coming** in judgment **from** heaven, **His dwelling place** (cf. comments on v. 2). The prophet pictured God treading or walking on **the high places** (the mountains; cf. v. 4) **of the earth.** In His majesty He was like a gigantic person stepping from one mountain peak to another. Thus God is capable of doing whatever He wants to do without being stopped by anyone. As God trod **the mountains** they melted **like wax before** a **fire** or **like water rushing down a slope** which cannot be stopped. Even **the valleys split,** disturbed by God's awesome power. These "high places" (v. 3) may have also subtly implied (by double entendre) the pagan altars on hilltops (cf. comments on v. 5).

**1:5.** The reason for this judgment was **Jacob's transgression** and **the sins of the house of Israel.** "Jacob" or "Jacob's" occurs 11 times in Micah. Nine times it refers to the entire nation of Israel (in the first question in v. 5 Jacob means the Northern Kingdom, and in 7:20 Jacob is the patriarch). "Jacob" and "Israel" are used together as synonyms in 1:5a; 2:12; 3:1, 8-9. **Transgression** and "sin(s)" occur together four times in Micah (1:5; 3:8; 6:7; 7:18).

The sins of the residents in **Samaria,** capital of Israel, and **Jerusalem,** capital of Judah, typified the sins of people throughout both nations. The capital cities apparently "set the pace" for the rest of Israel and Judah, with the worst sins being committed in the largest urban areas.

A **high place** was a place on a mountain or hill where people worshiped God (see, e.g., 2 Chron. 33:17) or idols. Pagan people in the land of Israel often worshiped on hilltops (perhaps to symbolize a closer relationship to their gods). Before David placed the central sanctuary in Jerusalem, the people worshiped the Lord at altars throughout the land. After the central sanctuary was set up the Israelites were then supposed to go to Jerusalem to worship God. But many of them, attracted to the nearby pagan high places, abandoned the worship of the Lord for pagan worship. This even took place in Jerusalem. No wonder that Micah sarcastically called Jerusalem the high place of Judah. The Jerusalemites were disobeying God outwardly as well as inwardly.

**1:6.** God's judgment was to come first on the Northern Kingdom (vv. 6-7) and then on the Southern Kingdom (vv. 9-16). The capital city of the North would be completely destroyed, even to its **foundations.** Samaria's ruins can still be seen today. Rather than a populated city, **Samaria** is only **a heap of rubble** (cf. 3:12), a field for **vineyards.** This prophecy was fulfilled in 722 B.C. when the Assyrian army captured the city after a three-year siege (2 Kings 17:1-5). The time leading up to the fall had been filled with political intrigue and assassinations (cf. comments on 2 Kings 15:8-31). Most of the people of Samaria and the Northern Kingdom were taken away and others were brought in to intermarry with the remaining people (cf. 2 Kings 17:6, 22-24).

**1:7.** Because much idolatrous worship had been going on in Samaria (**idols** and **images** were numerous) the Lord said He would bring it all to an end by a great destruction of the city. Samaria's idols would be smashed, the **temple gifts . . . burned,** and the images de-

stroyed. In Baalism, a pagan fertility religion, "sacred" **prostitutes** were set apart for the "worship" of pagan fertility deities. **Wages** paid to temple **prostitutes** were in turn given by them to the temple as "temple gifts." Apparently this practice had permeated Samaria. This illicit sexuality graphically pictured the illicit departure of the Northern Kingdom from their solemn covenant arrangement with the Lord. In effect, they were bound to God in a "marriage agreement" and to depart to other gods was tantamount to committing spiritual adultery (cf. comments on Hosea 4:10-15).

Since Israel had committed adultery with temple prostitutes, the temple gifts would be smashed by the Assyrians and used **again** by them in *their* prostitution. Becoming captives of Assyria the Israelites would be forced to continue in a prostituted relationship. They had sought out other gods so now God would send them away to lands where foreign gods were worshiped, giving them what they evidently wanted.

## C. Lament over the people (1:8-16)

Micah said he would lament because of Samaria's destruction (vv. 8-9); then through a clever use of several wordplays he called on certain towns of Judah to mourn for Samaria and for themselves because they too would feel the brunt of an Assyrian invasion (vv. 10-16).

### 1. MICAH'S LAMENT (1:8-9)

**1:8-9. Because of** the punishment to come on the Northern Kingdom, Micah was in a state of agitation. To **weep and wail** and to **go . . . barefoot and naked** were signs of extreme mourning (cf. 2 Sam. 15:30; Isa. 20:2; 22:12; Jer. 25:34). Identifying with the people, Micah felt as desolate as **a jackal** (a nighttime scavenger) and **an owl** (a nocturnal bird) who live in desolate places. Micah viewed the punishment as already having happened. It was as inevitable and **incurable** as a **wound.** In fact the sins of the Northern Kingdom had so influenced **Judah** that the "wound" (from God's judgment) would **come** on her too (cf. Isa. 1:5-6). Judgment would reach **the very gate** of **Jerusalem.** This happened in 701 B.C. when Sennacherib's Assyrian army destroyed 46 towns in Judah and then surrounded Jerusalem (2 Kings 18–19).

## 2. MICAH'S CALL FOR OTHERS TO MOURN (1:10-16)

Micah used several clever wordplays to describe the desolation the Assyrian invasion would bring to Judah's cities. (See the map "Israel and the Surrounding Nations in the Days of the Prophets," between Song and Isa.) Interestingly Sennacherib too used wordplays when recording *his* conquests.

**1:10. Tell it not in Gath** recalls 2 Samuel 1:20 where David made the same statement. In that case David did not want the Philistines to be glad about the demise of Saul, Israel's former ruler. In Micah's case he did not want the inhabitants of Gath to hear about the Assyrian attack on Judah. Nor should Gath **weep,** for then others would know about the desolation. "Gath" (*gat*) and "tell" (*taggîdû*) sounded something alike in Hebrew because of the letters "g" and "t."

However, Micah told the people of **Beth Ophrah** ("house of dust") to **roll in the dust,** in an expression of their grief (cf. Jer. 25:34; also note "roll in ashes," Jer. 6:26; Ezek. 27:20).

**1:11-12.** When attacked by Assyria, **Shaphir** ("beautiful or pleasant") would become the opposite of its name—a town of **nakedness and shame.** In Hebrew **Zaanan** (*ṣa'ănān*) and **come out** (*yaṣ'âh*) are related words; in contrast with their city's name, the Zaananites would not dare go outside their city walls because of the warfare. Nor would anyone go to **Beth Ezel** ("house of nearness or proximity") for **protection,** for that town would itself be **in mourning** and in need of help. In **Maroth** (which sounds in Heb. like the word for "bitterness") people would **writhe in pain** while **waiting for relief** from Jerusalem. But no relief would come because the destruction would go all the way **to the gate of Jerusalem** (cf. v. 9).

**1:13.** Sarcastically Micah urged the citizens of **Lachish** (*lākîš*), which sounds something like the word for a **team** (*rekeš*) of horses, to get a **chariot** ready for escaping from the Assyrians. (Lachish was known for its horses.) But their escape attempt would be in vain. Lachish was **the beginning of sin** to Jerusalem's inhabitants (**the Daughter of Zion;** cf. comments on 3:10; 4:8; Lam. 1:6). Perhaps this means that Lachish influenced Jerusalem toward idolatry. "Zion" occurs nine times in Micah (cf. comments on Zech. 8:3).

**1:14. Moresheth Gath** would be given **parting gifts,** perhaps by Jerusalem, if it is the city intended by the word **you.** "Parting gifts" means betrothal gifts, as a father gives his daughter when she marries. Similarly Jerusalem would "give" Moresheth Gath to the Assyrian king.

**The town of Aczib** (*'akzîb,* "deception") when conquered by the Assyrians, would become **deceptive** (*'akzāb*), unable to offer help **to** Israel's **kings.**

**1:15. A conqueror,** a reference to Sennacherib, would go **against . . . Mareshah,** another Judean town. The two words in Hebrew are similar ("conqueror" is *hayyōrēš,* and "Mareshah" is *mārēšâh*). Ironically Mareshah, which means possessor, would become the possession of Sennacherib. As David had escaped **to Adullam** (cf. 1 Sam. 22:1), so **the glory of Israel,** probably her leaders, would be shamed by becoming fugitives in Adullam.

**1:16.** Even **the children** in those Judean towns would be exiled by the Assyrians. This would cause the people of the area to mourn, one sign of which was to **shave** their **heads** (cf. Job 1:20; Isa. 15:2; Jer. 47:5; Ezek. 27:31; Amos 8:10). With heads shaved the mourners would look like **bald** vultures.

## D. Sins of Judah (2:1-11)

All the sins of Judah mentioned in these verses violate stipulations in the Mosaic Covenant. Therefore the destruction coming on them (cf. 1:9-16) was justified.

### 1. SINS OF THE PEOPLE (2:1-5)

**2:1.** Micah first noted that many of the people lay awake at night thinking up **evil** things to do the next day. On such people Micah pronounced **woe,** a term used by several prophets to announce guilt and coming judgment on the sinful people (cf., e.g., Isa. 3:9, 11; 5:8, 11, 18, 20-22; Jer. 13:27; Ezek. 13:3, 18; Hosea 7:13; 9:12; Amos 5:18; 6:1; Hab. 2:6, 9, 12, 15, 19; Zeph. 2:5; 3:1).

**2:2-3.** In their crass materialism, the people coveted others' **fields** and **houses and** took **them** simply because they wanted them. **They** would **defraud** another by stealing **his home** or **inheritance** (i.e., land). Micah was probably speaking against the influential people who had the power to do such things. Their sin, besides materialistic greed and theft, was wanton disregard for the rights of their **fellowman.**

The ancestors of the people Micah addressed had all been slaves in Egypt. In taking them out of Egypt, the Lord had freed them from slavery. Therefore the Israelites were not to enslave each other. Since God had given each tribe and each family its share of the land, the people were not to take away others' land. To take their financial holdings was to disregard the Law of God. As a result, God was **planning disaster** (cf. 1:12) **against** the **people.** They would be unable to **save** themselves from God's judgment because the **calamity,** when started, would not be stopped (cf. 1:3-4). Pride would be replaced with a debased condition.

**2:4-5.** Along with being unable to save themselves (v. 3) the people also would be derided by those around them. The people's enemies would mockingly sing to them what those in grief would normally have said about the loss of their **fields.** Ironically those Judahites who took away the land of others (v. 2) would have their own land taken **from** them. No longer would anyone be present to pass judgment about the division of **the land,** for their whole system would be destroyed. **The assembly of the LORD** referred to the covenant nation as a whole (cf. Deut. 23:1, 8).

### 2. SINS OF THE FALSE PROPHETS (2:6-11)

In much of her history, Israel in the Old Testament had both good (true) and bad (false) prophets. The true prophets spoke for God to the people, after urging them to return to the moral and ethical values of the covenantal Law. The false prophets often said that God would not harm the people so long as they were involved in the outward ceremonial aspects of the Law. True prophets urged the nation to follow the covenant, as outlined in Deuteronomy 27–28. A strong ethical dimension was in their messages. In fact their messages were often more ethical than eschatological. The yet-future peace and prosperity for the nation (promised in the Abrahamic Covenant; cf. Gen. 17:3-8; 22:17-18) will come only when the nation turns to the Lord

and follows His Word.

In contrast with the true prophets the false prophets spoke only what the people wanted to hear. Those messengers said God was for their nation and would not destroy it. This was of course partly true and partly false. God was for the nation of Israel, but He had said He would punish them if they did not obey Him.

**2:6-7a.** Apparently these false **prophets** were indignant that Micah mentioned coming disaster (vv. 3-5), so they enjoined him **not** to **prophesy** that the **disgrace** of judgment would come. They naively questioned whether **the Spirit of** God would ever be **angry** with His people, or that God would ever **do such things.** They were forgetting that a father often shows his love for his children by disciplining them. Had God not followed through on the discipline He would have been untrue to His own word.

**2:7b-9.** Micah answered the false prophets' objections by describing the situation in the nation at that time. He first reminded them that God's **words do good to him whose ways are upright.** God accurately judges human behavior. He blesses those whose ways are righteous.

In prophesying peace and not destruction, the false prophets were actually treating God's people as if they were the prophets' **enemy.** The false messengers robbed personal possessions (e.g., a **rich robe**) from people who were walking along oblivious to any danger. The victims were happy, carefree, and rich like soldiers **returning** with spoils **from** a victorious **battle.** Also the false prophets separated families by driving away mothers **from their . . . homes.**

By not telling the people to repent and return to the Lord, the prophets were neglecting the only thing that could save the people from the invading Assyrians. In effect, the prophets were opening the way for the Captivity by not warning the people to turn back to the Lord.

**2:10-11.** Partly because of the false prophets' perverted teaching, the land became irretrievably **defiled.** So the people would be exiled. Sarcastically Micah told the people to **go away,** that is, into exile (cf. Amos' sarcasm in Amos 4:4-5). The people's values were so degraded that they would readily respond to a false **prophet** who would deceptively predict not exile but continued prosperity, including **plenty of wine and beer.**

### E. Prediction of future regathering (2:12-13)

**2:12-13a.** Though the outlook was grim for Judah, the Prophet Micah voiced a ray of hope, based on God's covenant promises to Abraham. Each of the three sections of Micah's prophecy includes a promise of regathering and blessing on the nation (2:12-13; 4:1-8; 7:8-20). Here in chapter 2 the promise of blessing is brief. Two truths are stated in verses 12-13 which are expanded greatly in chapters 4–5. The first is that the Lord will regather and renew His people as their Shepherd (2:12-13a), and the second is that the Lord will lead His people as their King (v. 13b). **Jacob** and **Israel** are synonyms for the entire nation (cf. comments on 1:5). When God restores the believing remnant of Israel to their land, He will be like a shepherd leading his **flock** (cf. 5:4; 7:14). So great will be the regathering of the sheep that **the place** (i.e., the land) **will throng with people.** The Old Testament frequently spoke of God as a Shepherd and His people as sheep (cf. Pss. 23:1; 77:20; 78:52; 80:1; 100:3; Isa. 40:11; also note Jer. 23:3; 31:10). The people would be **like sheep** brought together **in a pen** for safekeeping.

That long-awaited time of blessing will come about for the nation of Israel in the Millennium. Some interpreters claim that this promise of blessing is being fulfilled now in the church, rather than in the future for Israel. However, if Micah 2:12 refers to spiritual blessings for the church, then Israel has been misled all these centuries since Abraham to think that she will inherit the land forever.

Much as a shepherd **breaks open** or clears the way for his sheep, going **before them** and leading them out **the gate** to pastures, so the Lord will remove all obstacles to blessing for His people Israel.

**2:13b.** A second fact about the forthcoming blessing is that **the Lord** will lead His people as **their King** (cf. Isa. 33:22; Zeph. 3:15; Zech. 14:9). He has not abandoned them. He will lead them, passing **through before them** as **their Head.** The

false prophets were partially correct when they stated that the Lord is for the covenant nation. He will fulfill His promises to Israel for, like a good king, He loves His people.

## II. Second Message: Blessing Will Follow Judgment (chaps. 3–5)

In Micah's first message (chaps. 1–2) he emphasized the people's sins and their failure to take seriously God's righteous demands on their lives. In only two verses (2:12-13) did Micah discuss God's future blessings on His nation. In this second message the emphasis is different. Two of the three chapters (chaps. 4–5) discuss God's blessing on Israel and Judah. (Chap. 3 details the sins of the *leaders* of Israel and Judah.) As is true throughout Scripture, God's plans for the future are given not simply to inform people of what will occur, but also—and more so—to motivate people to change their lives on the basis of God's plans for them. Certainly the promise of Israel's future blessings (chaps. 4–5) should have caused the nation—and first its leaders (chap. 3)—to turn to God in repentance and gratitude.

### A. Judgment on the nation's leaders (chap. 3)

1. JUDGMENT ON THE RULERS (3:1-4)

**3:1-2a.** In perverting justice the **leaders** and **rulers** (cf. v. 9) of the nation were acting like wild beasts. (On **Jacob** and **Israel** as synonyms for the 12-tribe nation, see comments on 1:5.) They were the ones who **should . . . know** and carry out **justice.** But instead of practicing justice they hated **good and** loved **evil.** Of course this is the opposite of the way leaders should act (cf. Amos 5:15). Their perverse standards (cf. Micah 3:9) showed that they did not love the Lord (cf. Ps. 97:10) or fear Him ("To fear the Lord is to hate evil," Prov. 8:13).

**3:2b-3.** Micah likened the unjust leaders to hunters who killed and ate (i.e., took undue advantage of) God's **people,** who were supposed to be under their care. The leaders were so harsh that they were not satisfied with tearing off **the skin** and eating **the flesh.** They even chopped up **their bones** as if they were preparing a stew. By unfair legal actions, by bribery (cf. v. 11; 7:3), by theft (cf. 2:8), by oppression (cf. 3:9), and even by bloodshed (cf. v. 10; 7:2), they left the people helpless.

By contrast faithful leaders protected their charges and looked out for their welfare. David, the epitome of a good leader for God, was taken from shepherding sheep (1 Sam. 17:15) to become a shepherd of the people (2 Sam. 5:2; 7:7). The people in Micah's day were being betrayed by their leaders, for if they really cared about the people, they would have turned them back to the Lord.

**3:4.** Because of Israel's sins a time would come when **they** would **cry out to the LORD but He** would **not answer them** (cf. v. 7). Micah was speaking of the **time** when Israel would be taken into captivity. The false prophets and leaders had refused to believe that the Lord would actually follow through and punish them for their behavior. However, when the Captivity came they would realize that God was actually punishing them. Then it would be too late for Him to deliver them. They would have to live with the consequences of their actions, enduring the punishment for their evil. Of course God listens to the prayers of His people, but sometimes He refuses to relieve them immediately from the consequences of their actions.

### 2. JUDGMENT ON THE FALSE PROPHETS (3:5-8)

**3:5.** Rather than serving as shepherds of the nation, caring for them, and leading them properly, the false **prophets** were leading the **people astray.** These leaders were giving the people false hope by telling them they would not be punished by God, that there would be no calamity. If someone paid the false shepherds well (**if one feeds them**) they would pronounce **peace** on him. In other words they told a person what he wanted to hear for a price (cf. v. 11). On the other hand if one did **not** feed them (i.e., pay the prophets their price) they were ready to oppose him (**to wage war against him**). The prophets were concerned with their own welfare rather than the nation's welfare. Materialism was their master (cf. v. 11).

**3:6-7.** Because the false prophets were not leading the people correctly and were taking advantage of them materially, these leaders would be shamed and humiliated. **Night** would **come over** them, **the sun** would **set for** those **prophets,** and **darkness** would come even in the daytime. Nightfall pictures impending doom. When that devastation would come, the prophets would have no **visions** or **divination.** They had been counseling the people to go on living as they had been, thinking that God surely would not judge His own nation. But suddenly judgment would come. And when it did, the people would ask the prophets why it came, and they would be unable to explain it. **The seers** (which corresponds in Heb. to "visions" in v. 6) would **be** totally **ashamed** (cf. Zech. 13:4). And **the diviners** (which corresponds in Heb. to "divination" in Micah 3:6; on the Heb. word *qāsam,* "to divine," see comments on Deut. 18:10) would be **disgraced** (cf. Micah 2:6). The prophets would **cover their faces** in humiliation, realizing they had **no answer from God** (cf. 3:4). The people would then see that the prophets were not true prophets after all. Because God would hide His face (v. 4) the false shepherds would "cover their faces"!

Micah warned the people and leaders about impending judgment so that they would see the folly of their ways and turn back to God. This true prophet warned them of the coming doom in hope that they would change their ways.

**3:8.** In contrast with the leaders (vv. 1-4) and false prophets (vv. 5-7), who had not been speaking God's message, Micah, **filled with** God's **power,** spoke **with** the authority of **the Spirit of the LORD** in denouncing the people's sins and predicting judgment. Micah's words, he said, were **with justice** because God is just in carrying out His judgment against the covenant people. And Micah's words had **might** because God is totally capable of carrying out His sentence against His people. The leaders, however, dealt unjustly (cf. vv. 9-10) and their prophets had no spiritual strength.

Micah declared the **transgression** and the **sin** (cf. 1:5; 6:7; 7:18) of the nation (on **Jacob** and **Israel** as synonyms; cf. 3:1, 9, for the entire nation, see comments on 1:5). Micah could see from God's perspective what was going on in the nation. Because she was not living according to God's covenant standards, He had to punish her.

## 3. JUDGMENT ON ALL THE NAIVE LEADERS (3:9-12)

**3:9-11.** Because Micah was filled with the Spirit of the Lord (v. 8), he boldly confronted the leaders about their sins and the eventual outcome. He first called on the **leaders** and **rulers** (cf. v. 1) to listen to him (**hear this**). Micah did not say if the leaders listened or responded to him, but apparently they did not, for no major change is recorded about them.

Micah then described what their leadership was like (vv. 9b-11). They despised (tā'ab, a strong word meaning "to abhor or regard as an abomination") **justice** (cf. vv. 1-3) and distorted ('āqaŝ, "twisted") **all that is right** (lit., "all that is straight"). Of course a ruler over God's people was supposed to be just and equitable, like God Himself. A leader was to desire righteous behavior in his own life and in the lives of his people. Instead of this, these rulers deliberately perverted uprightness. They even encouraged and took part in **bloodshed** and **wickedness** in the city of **Jerusalem,** where justice and righteousness should have reigned. **Zion** (cf. comments on 1:13) and Jerusalem are used together in Micah as synonyms four times (3:10, 12; 4:2, 8).

Micah noted that the **leaders . . . priests,** and **prophets** were always out **for money** (cf. 7:3) and yet had the audacity to say that God was still with them and that therefore the nation would not face destruction (cf. 2:6). (Tell **fortunes** translates, qāsam, "to divine"; cf. 3:6-7 and comments on Deut. 18:10.) To be influenced by bribery violated God's command in Deuteronomy 16:19.

**3:12.** Destruction would come on the nation **because of you,** that is, the leaders. This does not suggest that the *people* were guiltless, and that only the leaders were sinning. Probably the leaders were leading the people into wicked behavior and therefore the whole nation was guilty before God. **Zion** (Jerusalem; cf. 3:10; 4:2, 8) would **be plowed like a field,** turned over, and overthrown. It would be in ruins (**a heap of rubble;** cf. 1:6). Even **the temple hill** would be **overgrown with thickets** (weeds).

## B. Kingdom blessings for the nation (chaps. 4–5)

In these chapters Micah foretold the coming kingdom, which was announced by almost all the writing prophets. He spoke of the characteristics of the coming kingdom (4:1-8), events that will precede it (4:9–5:1), and the King who will establish it (5:2-15).

### 1. CHARACTERISTICS OF THE KINGDOM (4:1-8)

Micah 4:1-3 is similar to Isaiah 2:2-4. In Micah 4:1-8 Micah mentioned 11 characteristics of the kingdom.

#### a. The millennial temple will be prominent in the world (4:1a)

**4:1a.** The words **in the last days** denote the time when God will bring to consummation all the events in history (cf., e.g., Deut. 4:30, "in later days"; Ezek. 38:16, "in days to come"; Hosea 3:5). Usually "the last days" refers to the Tribulation and the Millennium (in the OT the word "kingdom" often referred to the Millennium). Micah did not state when "the last days" will occur, for Israel was supposed to be looking all the time for the consummation of the ages.

The **mountain of the LORD's temple**—Mount Zion where the millennial temple will be built (cf. Ezek. 40–43)—will become **chief among the mountains** (cf. Zech. 8:3). That is, the temple site will be the center of the millennial government, the place where Christ will rule. This fact contrasts sharply with the desolate condition of Jerusalem stated in Micah 3:12.

The religious and political systems will be closely related. From Moses' day, Israel's government was totally intertwined with her religious system. The king was anointed by God to govern the nation, and the priest was anointed to carry out the functions of worship.

Also in the Millennium, Israel's political-religious system, directed by the Messiah-King, will be predominant in the world. **It will be raised above the hills.** God's plan to bless the world through Israel (Gen. 12:3) was not nullified by her sin. Eventually Israel will be prominent above all other nations.

#### b. Peoples of the world will be attracted to Jerusalem (4:1b)

**4:1b.** In the Millennium people everywhere will realize the unique place Israel occupies in God's plans. No longer thinking of her as a small, insignificant nation, they will be attracted to her. In fact many **peoples will** travel **to** Jerusalem (cf. v. 2; 7:12) and her temple. "The verb **stream** may be a conscious play on the streams said to issue from the holy mount to water the earth (Ps. 46:4; see also Ps. 65:9; Isa. 33:21; Joel 3:18; Ezek. 47); a reverse flow of people begins toward the center" (James Luther Mays, *Micah: A Commentary*, pp. 96-7).

### c. Jerusalem will be the place of instruction for the entire world (4:2a)

**4:2a. The mountain of the LORD** (cf. "the mountain of the LORD's temple," v. 1) and **the house of** . . . **God** both refer to the temple complex. People from **many nations will** go to Jerusalem (cf. v. 1; 7:12) to be taught **His ways so that** they **may walk in His paths.** In the kingdom saved Gentiles will want to learn the ways of the Lord, whereas ironically Israel was *not* interested in obeying the Lord. What a rebuke this was to Micah's contemporaries.

### d. Revelation will go forth from Jerusalem (4:2b)

**4:2b.** This fact is closely related to the former one. **Law** (*tôrâh,* "instruction," not the Mosaic Law) will be given in **Zion** (i.e., **Jerusalem;** cf. 3:10, 12; 4:8), and God's **Word** (i.e., revelation about Him and His standards) will be communicated. Since God will be the Ruler (v. 3), it is natural that His Word should come from His place of rule.

### e. The Lord will be the Judge at Jerusalem (4:3a)

**4:3a. Many peoples** and even **strong nations** will bring their disputes to the Lord. They will submit to God's judgment, realizing that He will decide what and who is right. Micah's readers were chafing under the Word of God, not wanting to be told by Him or by His prophet that they were wrong. By contrast eventually the whole world will submit willingly to God's Word and His decisions.

### f. Peace will be universal (4:3b)

**4:3b.** Implements of warfare (**swords** and **spears**) will be changed into tools of agriculture (**plowshares** and **pruning hooks**). Neither will there be a need to **train** people for warfare because the na-

tions will be at peace. The Millennium is the kind of world people long for, a time when the earth's resources can be used for good instead of destruction. Justice and righteousness will be rewarded rather than scorned.

### g. Israel will dwell in security and peace (4:4)

**4:4.** Each person sitting **under his own vine** and **his own fig tree** depicts security (cf. 1 Kings 4:25; Zech 3:10). **No one** will fear losing his security, for **the LORD Almighty has** declared (cf. Obad. 18) that they will be secure. In Micah's day Israel's leaders were forecasting peace for those who could pay the price (Micah 3:5) but the only way to peace and security is to submit to God in trust.

### h. Israel will be spiritually sensitive to God (4:5)

**4:5. The nations** who were following **their gods** refer to pagan nations in Micah's day. They could not be the nations in the future Millennium because Micah had just written (vv. 2-3) that they will go to Jerusalem to learn of the Lord. Though pagan nations worshiped idols, Israel (**we**) in the Millennium **will walk** (cf. "walk" in v. 2) **in the name of the LORD,** that is, she will follow and obey His standards.

### i. Israel will be regathered (4:6)

**4:6. In that day** (i.e., at the beginning of the Millennium; cf. v. 1, "in the last days"; v. 7, "that day"; 5:10, "in that day") **the LORD** . . . **will** restore **the exiles,** those who had been removed from the land. Micah did not know when this regathering would be. In fact he might have supposed that when the coming Babylonian Exile was over the kingdom would begin. From books of the Bible written later it became clear that God's millennial kingdom did not come with the return from the Babylonian Exile (see the Books of Ezra, Neh., Es., Hag., Zech., and Mal.). Micah was certain, however, that in the kingdom Jewish exiles who had experienced **grief** will be restored. In the Tribulation, Jews will be persecuted (Dan. 7:25) and scattered (cf. Zech. 14:5); then when Christ returns they will be regathered (Matt. 24:31).

### j. Israel will be made strong (4:7)

**4:7.** In contrast with Israel's spiritual and moral weakness in Micah's day (spiritually they were **lame;** cf. Zeph. 3:19) and in contrast with Israel's being **driven away** into exile, the returned **remnant** (cf. Isa. 37:32; Micah 2:12; 5:7-8; 7:18; Rom. 9:27; 11:5) of believing Jews will become **a strong nation** (cf. "strong nations" in Micah 4:3). And **the LORD will rule over them** (cf. 5:2; Zeph. 3:15) **in Mount Zion** (Jerusalem) throughout the Millennium **and forever** (cf. Ps. 146:10; Luke 1:33; Rev. 11:15).

### k. Jerusalem will have dominion (4:8)

**4:8.** In this 11th characteristic of the millennial kingdom Micah returned to his thought in verse 1, namely, that Jerusalem and God's government centered there will be preeminent. Jerusalem's people are addressed as the **watchtower of the flock.** Much as a shepherd watches his sheep or a farmer views his crops from a tower, so Jerusalem will watch over the nation. ("Flock" refers to Israel in Isa. 40:11; Jer. 13:17, 20; Micah 5:4; Zech. 10:3.) **Daughter of Zion** (cf. Micah 4:10, 13) and **Daughter of Jerusalem** refer to the city's inhabitants (cf. Isa. 1:8; Jer. 4:31; Lam. 1:6; 2:13; Micah 1:13; Zech. 9:9). Jerusalem's **dominion will be restored** to her since the Messiah Himself will reign from Zion. The nation will no longer be under the domination of others, for "the times of the Gentiles" (Luke 21:24) will be ended.

### 2. EVENTS PRECEDING THE KINGDOM (4:9-5:1)

Here Micah spoke of four events that would occur before the millennial kingdom will be established.

### a. Israel would be exiled to Babylon (4:9-10a)

**4:9-10a.** Much as **a woman** in childbirth has tremendous **labor** pains, so the nation, carried away into exile, would **cry aloud** (*rûaʿ*, "cry out in distress"; cf. Isa. 15:4) in panic and **pain** (cf. Jer. 4:31; 6:24; 13:21; 22:23; 30:6; 49:24; 50:43). Then the nation would have **no king** or **counselor.** A king, making decisions in leading the nation, was like a counselor.

The Jews, being taken captive from their homeland, would **writhe in agony.**

(On **Daughter of Zion** see comments on Micah 1:13; 4:8.) But like a woman in labor pains they could do nothing to stop the agony; they had to go through the experience.

On the trek from their homeland the exiles were forced by their captors **to camp in the open field.** The prediction that they would be taken **to Babylon** was an amazing prophecy because in Micah's time Babylon was not the most powerful empire. It was still under Assyria.

### b. Israel would be rescued from Babylon (4:10b)

**4:10b.** Israel, Micah wrote, would **be rescued** and redeemed by the covenant God, who cares for her. The Exile, besides punishing the nation, was used to purge her and to encourage the people to more godly living. Captivity also was necessary because God had said that He would cast them out of the land if they did not obey Him. In a sense the Exile was a test of God's integrity.

### c. Nations will gather against the nation Israel (4:11-13)

**4:11-13. Many nations** (vv. 11a, 13) will unite **against** Jerusalem to try to conquer it. They will long to defile it by destroying it. But they will be ignorant of God's plans (**thoughts**) to defeat them. They will be devastated **like sheaves** of grain being broken up when threshed on a **threshing floor** (cf. Isa. 21:10; Jer. 51:33; Hosea 13:3).

Micah did not say when this would occur. Perhaps it was in Micah's day, for Israel certainly has had many enemies. If Micah 4:11 refers to Micah's time, then verses 12-13 seem to point ahead to a future time when other nations, gathered against Jerusalem, will be defeated. The **Daughter of Zion,** that is, the people of Jerusalem (cf. comments on v. 8) will **thresh** those **nations** (cf. Zech. 14:12-15), and **the LORD** will fight on Israel's behalf against them (Zech. 14:3). This battle—the Battle of Armageddon (Rev. 16:16; cf. Rev. 19:19)—will take place when the Messiah-King returns to establish the kingdom. The things Israel will capture in battle will be devoted (cf. comments on Josh. 6:17) **to the LORD,** whom Micah rightly calls **the LORD of all the earth** (cf. Ps. 97:5; Zech. 4:14; 6:5).

### d. The ruler of Israel will be humiliated (5:1)

**5:1.** Jerusalem, besieged by the Babylonians (2 Kings 25:1), was called a **city of troops** (lit., "daughter of troops"), that is, a city surrounded by marauding soldiers. Micah challenged the people to **marshal** their **troops,** though of course her defense efforts were in vain because of Nebuchadnezzar's **siege.** (This Heb. word for "siege" is used in the OT only of his siege of Jerusalem, 2 Kings 24:10; 25:2; Jer. 52:5; Ezek. 4:3, 7; 5:2.)

Micah did not identify the **ruler** of Israel except to say that he would be struck **on the cheek with a rod.** (To strike someone on the cheek was to humiliate him; cf. 1 Kings 22:24; Job 16:10; Lam. 3:30.) Some suggest this ruler was Christ, because (a) Christ was struck on the head (Matt. 27:30; Mark 15:19) and face (John 19:3) and (b) He is referred to in Micah 5:2. However, several factors show that the ruler is probably Judah's king Zedekiah: (1) The first part of verse 1 refers to the Babylonian attack on Jerusalem. (2) The word "ruler" translates *šōp̄ēṭ* ("judge"), whereas the word for ruler in verse 2, which does clearly refer to Christ, is *mōšēl.* (*Šōp̄ēṭ* forms an interesting wordplay on the similar-sounding word for "rod," *šēḇeṭ.*) (3) Christ was not smitten by troops of an enemy nation while Jerusalem was besieged. However, Nebuchadnezzar did capture Zedekiah and torture him (2 Kings 25:1-7). (4) A soon-coming event, not a distant-future one, seems to be suggested by the Hebrew word for "but now" in Micah 5:1 (not trans. in the NIV). This is followed by the distant future in verses 2-6. This pattern of present crisis followed by future deliverance is also seen in 4:11-13 in which the present (4:11) is introduced by "but now" and the distant future is discussed in 4:12-13.

### 3. THE RULER OF THE KINGDOM (5:2-15)

Micah described the birth of the Ruler (v. 2) and His work on behalf of the nation (vv. 3-15).

### a. The birth of Israel's Ruler (5:2)

**5:2.** The pattern of this verse is similar in some ways to that in 4:8. In each verse, a city is personified and addressed as **you;** the words **will come** are in both verses; and deliverance is suggested by

similar Hebrew words (trans. "dominion" in 4:8 and **Ruler** in 5:2). The "Ruler," Christ, will be from **Bethlehem Ephrathah,** about five miles from Jerusalem. Ephrathah, also called Ephrath (Gen. 35:16-19; 48:7), was an older name for Bethlehem or the name of the area around Bethlehem. David was born in Bethlehem (1 Sam. 16:1, 18-19; 17:12) as was His greatest Descendant, Jesus Christ (Matt. 2:1). The chief priests and teachers of the Law understood this verse in Micah to refer to the Messiah (Matt. 2:3-6). That confused some of the people in Jesus' day (John 7:42) for though He was born in Bethlehem He was raised in Nazareth, in Galilee.

The Messiah-Ruler, who will deliver His people, was born in an insignificant, **small** town (not even mentioned in the list of towns in Josh. 15 or Neh. 11) where **the clans of Judah** lived. And God said this One, who will minister on Yahweh's behalf (**for Me**), will be Israel's "Ruler" (cf. "rule" in Micah 4:7). Christ accomplished and will accomplish the Father's will (cf. John 17:4; Heb. 10:7).

This Ruler's **origins** (lit., "goings out," i.e., His victories in Creation, theophanies, and providential dealings) **are from of old, from ancient times.** The KJV renders "ancient times" as "everlasting," but the NIV translation is preferable for the Hebrew is literally, "days of immeasurable time." Other verses such as John 1:1; Philippians 2:6; Colossians 1:17; Revelation 1:8 point up the eternality of Jesus Christ.

### b. The work of Israel's Ruler (5:3-15)

Christ, Israel's Ruler, will accomplish several things for the nation during the Millennium:

1. He will reunite and restore the nation. **5:3.** As Micah had written earlier (4:9), Israel's spiritual pain in being dispersed (**abandoned**) was like a woman's physical pain **in labor.** But the time will come when the labor will end and **birth** will come. This refers not to Mary's giving birth to Jesus, but to Israel's national regathering (cf. 2:12; 4:6-7), likened here to a childbirth when **His brothers** (fellow Israelites; cf. Deut. 17:15) will **return** and **join** other **Israelites.** Christ will be one of them.

Micah 5:2-3 puts together the two

Advents of Christ, much as is done in Isaiah 9:6-7; 61:1-2.

2. He will care for His people and give them security. **5:4.** The Messiah **will . . . shepherd His flock** (cf. 2:12; 7:14; Zech. 10:3), something the nation's leaders in Micah's day were refusing to do (cf. comments on Micah 3:1-11). Christ's caring, guiding, and protecting role will be accomplished by the Lord's **strength** and for His sake. As He shepherds the nation they will have peace and security (cf. Zech. 14:11) because **His greatness will reach to the ends of the earth** (cf. Mal. 1:11a). Since He will rule over the entire world (Ps. 72:8; Zech. 14:9), all will know of His sovereign power, which will guarantee Israel's safety.

3. The Ruler will destroy Israel's enemies (5:5-9). **5:5-6.** This is one of Messiah's several accomplishments in bringing peace to Israel (vv. 5-15). **He will be** Israel's **peace** because He will subdue the hostile powers around that nation. Though **Assyria** will not exist as a nation in the future, it represents nations who, like Assyria in Micah's time, will threaten and attack Jerusalem (cf. Zech. 12:9; 14:2-3). **The land of Nimrod** (cf. Gen. 10:8-9; 1 Chron. 1:10) was a synonym for Assyria (cf. Assyria as a name for Persia in Ezra 6:22). Christ will enable Israel to defeat her foes, giving the nation a more-than-adequate number of **shepherds** or **leaders** (on the formula **seven . . . even eight;** cf. comments on "three . . . even four" in Amos 1:3). Whereas many nations have ruled Israel **with the sword,** in the Millennium the tables will be turned and Israel will rule over her foes because **He,** Messiah, **will deliver** her (cf. Zech. 14:3).

**5:7.** After Christ will destroy Israel's enemies **the remnant** (cf. 2:12; 4:7; 5:8; 7:18) of believing Israelites will be refreshing and influential (**like dew and showers**) among **many peoples.** Because the rainy season in Palestine was from October through March, nighttime dew in the other six months helped nourish the crops. As the dew and rain come from God in His timing (they **do not wait for man**), so God will refresh the nations in His own timing, apart from man's doings.

**5:8-9.** The remnant (cf. v. 7) of Israel will also be **like a lion.** Like a ferocious lion, domineering over other animals, Israel will be dominant and powerful over other nations of the world (cf. Deut. 28:13). God said He will lift **up** Israel's **hand . . . over** her **enemies,** and that **all** her **foes will be destroyed.**

4. The Ruler will also purge Israel of her reliance on military power. **5:10-11. In that day** (cf. 4:6 and comments on "in the last days" in 4:1), **the LORD . . . will destroy** the **horses** (cf. Zech. 9:10) and **chariots** in which she trusted (cf. God's prohibition in Deut. 17:16 against relying on horses). **Cities** in which Israel will build **strongholds** for protection will be demolished (cf. Micah 5:14).

5. The Ruler will destroy false worship from within Israel (5:12-14). **5:12.** Besides destroying enemies from outside Israel, the Messiah will purge the nation of every trace of occultic and idolatrous practices, which were "enemies" within. **Witchcraft** (*kešāpîm*, lit., "sorceries") is used in the Old Testament only here and in 2 Kings 9:22; Isaiah 47:9, 12; Nahum 3:4. In the last three of these verses the NIV renders the word "sorceries." The Hebrew word suggests seeking information from demonic sources. The casting of **spells** (from the verb *'ānan*) may refer to using demonic powers to exercise manipulative influences over others (in Lev. 19:26 and Deut. 18:10 the NIV translates this word "sorcery"; in Jer. 27:9 it is rendered "sorcerers"). Though prohibited in the Law, these and similar practices— common in the ancient Near East —were attractive to many Israelites throughout much of Israel's history. Occultism will be practiced in the Tribulation (cf. "magic arts" in Rev. 9:21), but it will be wiped out by the Lord.

**5:13-14. Carved images** (*pesîlîm*) were idols of foreign gods (cf. *pesel*, "idol," in Ex. 20:4). **Sacred stones** (or pillars) and **Asherah poles** (cf. 1 Kings 14:23; 2 Kings 17:10; 18:4; 23:14) were objects used in worshiping male and female Canaanite idols. God forbade their use by Israel (Deut. 16:21-22; cf. Ex. 34:13). Asherah was the Canaanite goddess of the sea and the consort of Baal. When the Ruler comes and banishes every evidence of idolatry from His people (cf. Zech. 13:2), they will no longer worship **the work of** their **hands** (cf. Hosea 14:3). Instead they will worship Yahweh, the true and living Creator. All the **cities** (cf. Micah 5:11) where Israel practiced idolatry or relied on her military strength will be demolished.

6. The Lord will judge the nations who oppose Him. **5:15. Nations** who refuse to obey the Lord will suffer God's **anger and wrath.** He will rule with an iron scepter (Ps. 2:9; Rev. 12:5; 19:15), that is, with firmness, strength, and justice.

## III. Third Message: An Indictment of Sin and a Promise of Blessing (chaps. 6–7)

This third main section of the book summarizes what has gone before and adds a plea from God's prophet on behalf of His people. The section focuses on the blessings that will come to the people because of God's goodness.

### A. An indictment by the Lord (6:1-5)

**6:1.** Again (cf. 1:2) **the LORD** called on witnesses to **listen to** His **case** (*rîḇ,* "lawsuit or litigation"; trans. "accusation" in 6:2a and "case" in v. 2b) against His covenant people. He then challenged Israel to **stand up . . . before the mountains** and give her side of the dispute with God. He was calling for outside witnesses to confirm that He had been just and righteous with His people and that Israel had been wrong in its attitudes and actions before God. The witnesses He appealed to were people everywhere, represented by "the mountains" (cf. v. 2) and **the hills.**

**6:2.** The **LORD** then began to set forth His **case against His people.** He repeated His call to the **mountains** (cf. v. 1) to listen to His **accusation** (*rîḇ*; cf. comments on v. 1) and "case" (*rîḇ*) against His people **Israel.**

**6:3-4.** In setting forth His case the Lord addressed the nation as **My people** (cf. v. 5). By a question (**What have I done to you?**) the Lord affirmed His innocence (cf. "What have I done?" in 1 Sam. 17:29; 20:1; 26:18; 29:8). He also asked the people to **answer** Him by naming some way in which He had **burdened** (lit., "wearied") them. Though the Israelites had often complained against God, they had no grounds for such complaints. For that reason they could not answer God's accusation.

God reminded the people of His goodness in leading them **out of Egypt** into the Promised Land. The prophets often reminded the people of their deliverance from Egyptian **slavery.** The Exodus was a great focal event in the life of Israel because by it God had delivered them from foreign domination and also because it was followed by the Lord's giving the Law to them through **Moses.** The word **redeemed** (*pāḏâh,* "to ransom"; cf. Deut. 7:8; 9:26; 13:5; 15:15; 24:18) would remind them of the slaying of the Passover lambs so that the oldest son of each Israelite family would not be killed (Ex. 12:3, 7, 12-13). God's mention of Moses would remind the people of the Law, and the name of **Aaron** would bring to mind the priesthood. Perhaps **Miriam** is mentioned because her name would bring to mind her song to the Lord (Ex. 15:21) and her role as a prophetess (Ex. 15:20). Because Moses represented God to man and Aaron represented man to God, the people had a unique relationship with the Lord.

**6:5.** Micah next reminded God's **people** (cf. "My people" in v. 3) of their forefathers' experience in the wilderness when **Balak . . . of Moab** tried to get **Balaam** to prophesy against the covenant people (Num. 22–24). Rather than cursing the people, Balaam blessed them. This was another evidence of God's goodness to them. Another great event in the nation's life was the **journey from Shittim,** the Israelites' last campsite east of the Jordan River (cf. Josh. 3:1), **to Gilgal,** the first encampment after the miraculous crossing of the Jordan River (cf. Josh. 4:18-19). In all these things God had not burdened His people. Rather He was their Protector and Defender, giving them grace over and over.

### B. The response of Micah for the nation (6:6-8)

In these well-known verses the prophet responded to the Lord's indictment. Micah spoke as a righteous person who understood his people's guilt. He was not like the many leaders who had refused to shepherd the people properly.

**6:6.** Speaking for the nation, Micah asked what he must take **before the LORD** in worship to regain His good favor. Micah asked if he should approach the Lord with **burnt offerings.** Should he go **with calves** ready to be sacrificed? By these questions the prophet was not downplaying the importance of the sacrificial system. The Lord had set up the Levitical system to provide, among other things, atonement for the people's sin. Micah, as a righteous member of the covenant community, was no doubt involved in the sacrificial system. He knew, however, that the sacrifices were meant to be outward expressions of inner trust and dependence on God for His grace and mercy.

**6:7.** Micah then asked in hyperbole if the LORD would want **thousands of rams,** or **10,000 rivers of oil,** or even his own **firstborn** child (**the fruit** of his **body**) to atone **for** his **transgression** and **sin** (cf. 1:5; 3:8; 7:18). He of course knew these would not appease God's wrath on the nation. Nor was Micah condoning the evil practice of child sacrifice, forbidden in the Law (cf. Lev. 18:21; 20:2-5; Deut. 12:31; 18:10). He asked those rhetorical questions to suggest to Israel that nothing—not even the most extreme sacrifice—could atone for what she had done. Also this emphasized that God did not want them to "pay" Him. Instead God wanted them to change their actions and attitudes.

**6:8.** Micah then told the nation (**O man** means any person in Israel) exactly what God did desire from them. God did not want them to be related to Him in only a ritualistic way. God wanted them to be related inwardly—to obey Him because they desired to, not because it was a burden on them. That relationship, which **is good** (beneficial), involves three things: that individuals (a) **act justly** (be fair in their dealings with others), (b) **love mercy** (ḥesed, "loyal love"; i.e., carry through on their commitments to meet others needs), and (c) **walk humbly with . . . God** (fellowship with Him in modesty, without arrogance). "Humbly" translates the verb ṣānaʿ (which occurs only here in the OT); it means to be modest. (The adjective ṣānûaʿ occurs only once, in Prov. 11:2.) The Lord had already told them of these demands (Deut. 10:12, 18). Doing justice "is a way of loving mercy, which in turn is a manifestation of walking humbly with God" (James Luther Mays, *Micah: A Commentary,* p. 142). Many people in Micah's day were *not* being just (Micah 2:1-2; 3:1-3; 6:11), or showing loyal love to those to whom they were supposed to be committed (2:8-9; 3:10-11; 6:12), or walking in

humble fellowship with God (2:3).

## C. The Lord's judgment because of sin (6:9-16)

Because of Israel's failure to meet God's requirements (v. 8), the Lord said He would have to punish the nation.

### 1. THE SINS (6:9-12)

These verses give a sampling of the sins in which Israel was involved. They are part of the reason for God's lawsuit (vv. 1-2). This list, though not complete, is sufficient to emphasize that the nation was guilty.

**6:9.** Again Micah told the people to **listen** (cf. 3:1; 6:1). In response to the Lord's **calling,** they should **heed the rod,** God's instrument of punishment. The second line, translated differently in various Bible versions, seems to mean (as the NIV has rendered it) that when the Lord speaks, it is wise to respond to Him in **fear** (reverence and obedience; cf. Prov. 1:7).

**6:10-12.** Not acting justly (cf. v. 8), the people were amassing wealth by devious means (**ill-gotten treasures;** cf. Prov. 10:2). They were being dishonest in their business practices by using a **short** (i.e., small) **ephah,** a dry-measure standard of about six gallons. In other words they were cheating their customers. Likewise, sellers used **dishonest scales** and **false weights** to give less merchandise than the buyers thought they were getting. God said He hates such unfair practices, that take advantage of others (cf. Lev. 19:35-36; Deut. 25:13-16; Prov. 11:1; 16:11; 20:23; Hosea 12:7; Amos 8:5). Obviously the people were not acting justly or loving mercy (Micah 6:8). Violence by **rich** people and lying by almost everyone were common (v. 12).

### 2. THE PUNISHMENT (6:13-16)

**6:13-15.** Because of the sins cited in verses 10-12 (and probably others as well), God's punishment had already **begun** to bring them **ruin** (cf. v. 16; Deut. 28:20). Their food would not satisfy them (the first line in Micah 6:14 quotes Lev. 26:26). What they would **store up** would be taken by their enemies (cf. Lev. 26:16-17; Deut. 28:33). Their planting would bring no **harvest** for them (cf. Deut. 28:30). Taken into captivity, they would not be allowed to enjoy the fruit of their labor (Micah 6:15; cf. Deut. 28:39-40). As God had stated (Deut. 28) these punishments resulted from the people's failure to obey Him.

**6:16.** Instead of following the Lord, the people **observed the statutes of Omri and all the practices of Ahab's house** (dynasty). Omri and Ahab were considered two of the worst kings in the Northern Kingdom for in their rule great apostasy flourished, including Baal worship (1 Kings 16:21–22:40). In Ahab's reign true prophets of the Lord were murdered (1 Kings 18:4). Judah (**you**) had **followed** those sinful **traditions.** As a result of such idolatry and violence, God said He would **give** Judah **over to ruin** (cf. Micah 6:13). Being taken captive, she would be ridiculed by **the nations** (cf. Lam. 2:15-16).

### D. Micah's pleading with the Lord (chap. 7)

1. MICAH'S BEMOANING OF THE NATION'S SINS (7:1-6)

**7:1-2.** Micah bemoaned his position in the midst of a people who were totally godless. He lamented the evil times in which he lived. He felt like a person who goes into the fields to pick **fruit** but finds it all gone. **No . . . grapes** or **early figs** were left for him to gather and eat (cf. 6:14). In like manner the nation was devoid of **godly** (ḥāsîd, "loyal or faithful," from ḥeseḏ, "loyal love") and **upright** people. It was as if each person were hunting **his brother,** trying to kill him (cf. 3:10; 6:12). This violence and lack of loyalty is described in 7:3-6.

**7:3-4a.** The only thing the people could do well was to sin! In their government **the ruler** ruled only in favor of those who gave him **gifts** even if justice were cast aside; in the courtroom **the judge** accepted **bribes** (cf. 3:11), and **the powerful** (rich and influential people) got whatever they wanted. The leaders even conspired **together** in taking advantage of others. Even **the best** of the leaders were **like a brier** and **worse than a thorn hedge,** entangling and injuring all who came in contact with them.

**7:4b.** What God's true prophets (the nation's **watchmen** warning of impending danger) had predicted would someday **come** true. **God** would "visit" the people in judgment and they would be confused, not knowing what to do.

**7:5-6.** The situation was so bad that even familiar relationships were distorted. Neighbors, friends, spouses, and children turned against each other. Treachery was so rampant that a person's own family members were his **enemies.**

2. MICAH'S CONFIDENCE IN THE LORD (7:7-13)

**7:7.** Speaking for himself and the godly remnant mentioned throughout the book, Micah said that even though the nation was in terrible shape he would continue to **watch** (cf. "watchmen," v. 4) and **wait in hope** for the Lord. Yes, judgment would come, but he knew also that salvation would follow. **God** would be Israel's **Savior** (cf. Isa. 59:20).

**7:8-10.** The prophet, still speaking as a representative of the nation (**me . . . my,** and **I** occur 15 times in vv. 8-10), expressed confidence in the fact that eventually God would reverse Israel's sad situation. Though the nation was in a depressed condition and would go into captivity, the **enemy** should **not gloat.** Though the situation was dark, **the Lord** would **be** her **light** (cf. v. 9), and would bring her out of her desperate circumstances. In the words **I have sinned** Micah identified himself with the people's sins (cf. Daniel's similar identification in his prayer, Dan. 9:5, 8, 11, 15). Because of their sins God's **wrath** would be tolerated for it would be His means of bringing them **into the light** (cf. Micah 7:8) and establishing **justice** (lit., "righteousness"). When God once again establishes Israel in her own land, the tables will be turned and her **enemy . . . will be** ashamed (cf. v. 16; Obad. 10). The enemy (pagan nations) taunted Israel with the question, **Where is the Lord your God?** (cf. Pss. 42:3, 10; 79:10; Joel 2:17) But God will vindicate His own, for Israel's enemies will fall and **be trampled** (be humiliated; cf. Micah 7:17).

**7:11-13.** When Israel will be restored to her land in the Millennium (when she will "rise," v. 8), she will rebuild her **walls** and expand her **boundaries.** Gāḏēr means a wall around a vineyard (cf. Num. 22:24; Isa. 5:5), not around a city. Jerusalem, established in peace by the Messiah, will need no protective wall (Zech. 2:4-5). (For specifics on Israel's boundary extensions see comments on Ezek. 47:13-23 and Obad. 19-20.) **Assyria**

and **Egypt,** enemies of Israel, will be inhabited by people who will travel to Jerusalem (cf. Isa. 19:23-25). In fact people from around the globe (**from sea to sea;** cf. Ps. 72:8; Zech. 9:10, **and from mountain to mountain**) will go to Jerusalem to learn of and worship the Lord (cf. Micah 4:2). Immediately before that glorious time, however, the nations, **because of** their sinful **deeds,** will be judged (Matt. 25:32-33, 46) and therefore **the earth will be desolate** (cf. Isa. 24:1).

### 3. MICAH'S PRAYER THAT GOD WOULD AGAIN SHEPHERD HIS FLOCK (7:14)

**7:14.** Is the speaker in this verse God or Micah? Probably the prophet is addressing God. Because of God's promise in 2:12 and 5:4, Micah asked the Lord to restore and provide for His people as a shepherd cares for his **flock.** The **staff** would be a rod (*šēbeṭ*) of blessing, not of judgment as in 6:9. Micah prayed that God's people (His **inheritance;** cf. 7:18 and comments on Deut. 4:20), then isolated like sheep **in a forest,** would enjoy prosperity and peace as they had **in Bashan and Gilead** (cf. Jer. 50:19) in former times (**in days long ago;** cf. Micah 7:20). Those two areas east of the Jordan River (see the map "Israel and Surrounding Nations in the Days of the Prophets," between Song and Isa.) were fertile grazing grounds for sheep and cattle. In 734 B.C. these areas were overrun by Tiglath-Pileser III, king of Assyria (745–727).

### 4. THE LORD'S PROMISE TO SHOW MIRACULOUS THINGS TO HIS PEOPLE (7:15-17)

**7:15.** In response to the prophet's request (v. 14) the Lord told the nation through Micah that a time would come when He would again be known as a miraculous God. **When** Israel **came out of Egypt,** God did **wonders** (cf. Ex. 3:20; 15:11; Jud. 6:13; Ps. 78:12-16) on her behalf, releasing her from Egypt, enabling her to cross the Red Sea on dry ground, and providing for her in the desert. Once again the nation will have a great "exodus" from its places of habitation and God will miraculously move the Israelites into their land. This will occur when the Messiah returns and sets up His millennial rule.

**7:16-17.** When God miraculously regathers Israel the **nations will see** it **and**

**be ashamed** (cf. 3:7; 7:10) for His **power** will be greater than theirs. Overwhelmed, they will be speechless and will refuse to hear about Israel's victories. In humiliation they will **lick** the **dust** like snakes (cf. Ps. 72:9; Isa. 49:23), and like animals coming **out of their** hiding places (**dens**) **they will** surrender **to the Lord** and will be fearful of Israel. These facts must have greatly encouraged the righteous remnant in Micah's day.

### 5. MICAH'S AFFIRMATION THAT GOD IS UNIQUE (7:18-20)

**7:18-20.** The author concluded his book by reminding himself and his readers about the goodness and uniqueness of their God (cf. Ex. 34:6-7a). Micah's final words of praise show that he had great faith in God's eventual out-working of His plans for His covenant people. Today orthodox Jews read these verses in their synagogues on the Day of Atonement, after they read the Book of Jonah.

The rhetorical question, **Who is a God like You?** (cf. Ex. 15:11; Pss. 35:10; 71:19; 77:13; 89:6; 113:5) may be a word-play on Micah's name which means, "Who is like Yahweh?" The obvious answer is that no one is like the Lord. The remainder of Micah 7:18-20 describes what He is like. God's acts on behalf of His people prove that He is completely trustworthy and merciful.

Micah affirmed six things about God: (1) He **pardons** the **sin** and **transgression** (cf. 1:5; 3:8; 6:7) **of the remnant** (cf. 2:12; 4:7; 5:7-8) **of His inheritance** (cf. 7:14).

(2) He does **not stay angry forever** (cf. Ps. 103:9) and (3) He likes **to show mercy** (*ḥesed;* cf. Micah 7:20). What encouragement these truths would have been for the godly remnant living in Israel's corrupt society. Confident that (4) the Lord **will again have compassion** (*reḥem,* "tender, heartfelt concern"; cf. Pss. 102:13; 103:4, 13; 116:5; 119:156; Hosea 14:3; Zech. 10:6) **on** Israel, Micah knew that (5) God would deal with her **sins** by, figuratively speaking, treading them **underfoot** (subduing them as if they were enemies) and hurling them **into . . . the sea** (thus completely forgiving them). Three Old Testament words for sin are used in Micah 7:18-19: sin(s), transgression, and iniquities.

Micah knew God would do these things because (6) He is **true** (faithful) **to**

# Micah

**Jacob** and shows **mercy** (*ḥesed*; cf. v. 18) **to Abraham.** God cannot lie; He is true to His Word and loyal to His commitments and His **oath.** Therefore Micah was trusting in God's promises to Abraham (Gen. 12:2-3; 15:18-21), which were confirmed to Jacob (Gen. 28:13-14), that He will bless their descendants.

Israel's peace and prosperity will be realized when the Messiah-King reigns. Christ will exercise justice over His and Israel's opponents and He will extend grace to His own. This promise gave Micah confidence in his dark days and is also a source of comfort to believers today.

## BIBLIOGRAPHY

Allen, Leslie C. *The Books of Joel, Obadiah, Jonah and Micah.* The New International Commentary on the Old Testament. Grand Rapids: Wm. B. Eerdmans Publishing Co., 1976.

Bennett, T. Miles. *The Book of Micah: A Study Manual.* Grand Rapids: Baker Book House, 1968.

Cohen, A. *The Twelve Prophets.* London: Soncino Press, 1948.

Feinberg, Charles L. *The Minor Prophets.* Chicago: Moody Press, 1976.

Hillers, Delbert R. *Micah.* Philadelphia. Fortress Press, 1984.

Keil, C.F. "Micah." In *Commentary on the Old Testament in Ten Volumes.* Vol 10. Reprint (25 vols. in 10). Grand Rapids: Wm. B. Eerdmans Publishing Co., 1982.

Laetsch, Theo. *The Minor Prophets.* St. Louis: Concordia Publishing House, 1956.

Mays, James Luther. *Micah: A Commentary.* Philadelphia: Westminster Press, 1976.

Pusey, E.B. *The Minor Prophets: A Commentary.* Vol. 2. Grand Rapids: Baker Book House, 1970.

Smith, John M.P., Ward, William H., and Bewer, Julius A. *A Critical and Exegetical Commentary on Micah, Zephaniah, Nahum, Habakkuk, Obadiah and Joel.* The International Critical Commentary. Edinburgh: T. & T. Clark, 1974.

Snaith, Norman H. *Amos, Hosea, and Micah.* London: Epworth Press, 1954.

Tatford, Frederick A. *The Minor Prophets.* Vol. 2. Reprint (3 vols.). Minneapolis: Klock & Klock Christian Publishers, 1982.

Wolff, Hans Walter. *Micah the Prophet.* Translated by Ralph D. Gehrke. Philadelphia: Fortress Press, 1981.

# NAHUM

## Elliott E. Johnson

## INTRODUCTION

**The Prophet Nahum.** Nothing is known of the human author of this brief prophecy except that he is Nahum the Elkoshite (Nahum 1:1). His name means "consolation" or "comfort," which is appropriate for his ministry to Judah. His message about the destruction of Nineveh, the enemy dreaded by many nations in that day, would have been a great comfort to Judah. "Elkoshite" suggests that Nahum's hometown was Elkosh, but the site of such a city is unknown. Jerome said it was in Galilee; others said it was on the Tigris River north of modern-day Mosul near Nineveh; some place Elkosh east of the Jordan River; others have suggested it was Capernaum. While no conclusive evidence exists, it seems best to locate Elkosh in southern Judah. This would help explain Nahum's concern for Judah (Nahum 1:12, 15) to whom his message was written.

**The City of Nineveh.** The subject of this prophecy is Nineveh (Nahum 1:1). A heavy weight of doom, a burden ("an oracle") rested on the Assyrian capital. Several other Old Testament passages refer to Assyria's fall (Isa. 10:12-19; 14:24-25; 30:31-33; 31:8-9; Ezek. 32:22-23; Zeph. 2:13-15; Zech. 10:11).

Nineveh is first mentioned in the Bible in Genesis 10:11-12. Nimrod built several cities in southern Mesopotamia (Gen. 10:8-10) and then "went to Assyria where he built Nineveh, Rehoboth Ir, Calah, and Resen." Inscriptions refer to Gudea restoring the temple of the goddess Ishtar in Nineveh, which he said was founded around 2300 B.C. Hammurabi, king of Babylon (ca. 1792–1750 B.C.), referred to Nineveh. The town was expanded by the Assyrian king Tiglath-Pileser I (1115–1071), who referred to himself as "king of the world." Ashurnaṣirpal II (883–859) and Sargon II (722–705) had their palace in Nineveh. In the ninth, eighth, and seventh centuries B.C. the Assyrian Empire became strong and repeatedly attacked nations to the east, north, and west, including Israel. (See the chart "The Kings of Assyria in the Middle and New Assyrian Kingdoms," in the *Introduction* to Jonah.)

Shalmaneser III (859–824 B.C.) made the city of Nineveh a base for military operations. During his reign Israel came into contact with Nineveh. He wrote that he fought a coalition of kings of Aram and others including "Ahab the Israelite" (in 853 B.C.). Later he wrote that he received tribute from "Jehu, son of Omri," who is pictured in the Black Obelisk of Shalmaneser. Neither of these events is mentioned in the Bible. Azariah, king of Judah (790–739), paid tribute to Tiglath-Pileser III (745–727). Menahem, king of Israel (752–742), did the same (2 Kings 15:14-23). In the reign of Ashur-dan III (772–754) Jonah preached to the Ninevites (see the *Introduction* to Jonah).

In 731 B.C. Ahaz, king of Judah (732–715), became a vassal of Tiglath-Pileser III, and Assyria invaded Damascus in the Syro-Ephraimite war. Shalmaneser V (727–722) besieged Samaria and defeated it in 722 B.C., thus defeating the Northern Kingdom (2 Kings 17:3-6; 18:9-10). Twenty-one years later (in 701), Sennacherib (705–681) invaded Judah and destroyed 46 Judean towns and cities. After encircling Jerusalem, 185,000 of Sennacherib's soldiers were killed overnight and Sennacherib returned to Nineveh (2 Kings 18:17-18; 19:32-36; Isa. 37:36). Esarhaddon (681–669) regarded Judah as a vassal kingdom, for he wrote in a building inscription, "I summoned the kings of the Hittite land [Aram] and [those] across the sea, Ba'lu, king of Tyre, Manasseh, king of Judah . . . " (Daniel David Luckenbill, *Ancient Records of Assyria and Babylonia*. 2 vols. Chicago: University of Chicago Press, 1926-7, 2:265).

In 669 B.C. Ashurbanipal succeeded his father Esarhaddon as king of Assyria. He may have been the king who released Manasseh king of Judah (2 Chron. 33:10-13). Ashurbanipal defeated Thebes in Egypt in 663 and brought treasures to Nineveh from Thebes, Babylon, and Susa. He established an extensive library at Nineveh.

The city of Nineveh fell to the Babylonians, Medes, and Scythians in August 612 B.C.

Nineveh was situated on the east bank of the Tigris River (see the map "The Assyrian Empire," near Jonah 1:1). Sennacherib fortified the city's defensive wall whose glory, he said, "overthrows the enemy." On the population of Nineveh, see "Authenticity and Historicity" in the *Introduction* to Jonah and comments on Jonah 4:11. Jonah called Nineveh "a great city" (Jonah 1:2; 3:2-4; 4:11).

The city's ruins are still evident today. The city was easily overtaken when the Khosr River, which flowed through it, overflowed its banks (see Nahum 1:8; 2:6, 8).

Nineveh was the capital of one of the cruelest, vilest, most powerful, and most idolatrous empires in the world. For example, writing of one of his conquests, Ashurnaṣirpal II (883–859) boasted, "I stormed the mountain peaks and took them. In the midst of the mighty mountain I slaughtered them; with their blood I dyed the mountain red like wool. . . . The heads of their warriors I cut off, and I formed them into a pillar over against their city; their young men and their maidens I burned in the fire" (Luckenbill, *Ancient Records of Assyria and Babylonia*, 1:148). Regarding one captured leader, he wrote, "I flayed [him], his skin I spread upon the wall of the city . . . " (ibid., 1:146). He also wrote of mutilating the bodies of live captives and stacking their corpses in piles.

Shalmaneser II (859–824) boasted of his cruelties after one of his campaigns: "A pyramid of heads I reared in front of his city. Their youths and their maidens I burnt up in the flames" (ibid., 1:213). Sennacherib (705–681) wrote of his enemies, "I cut their throats like lambs. I cut off their precious lives [as one cuts] a string. Like the many waters of a storm I made [the contents of] their gullets and entrails run down upon the wide earth.

. . . Their hands I cut off" (ibid., 2:127).

Ashurbanipal (669–626) described his treatment of a captured leader in these words: "I pierced his chin with my keen hand dagger. Through his jaw . . . I passed and made him occupy . . . a kennel" (ibid., 2:319). In his campaign against Egypt, Ashurbanipal also boasted that his officials hung Egyptian corpses "on stakes [and] stripped off their skins and covered the city wall(s) with them" (ibid., 2:295).

No wonder Nahum called Nineveh "the city of blood" (3:1), a city noted for its "cruelty"! (3:19)

Ashurbanipal was egotistic: "I [am] Ashurbanipal, the great [king], the mighty king, king of the universe, king of Assyria. . . . The great gods . . . magnified my name; they made my rule powerful" (ibid., 2:323-4). Esarhaddon was even more boastful. "I am powerful, I am all powerful, I am a hero, I am gigantic, I am colossal, I am honored, I am magnified, I am without equal among all kings, the chosen one of Asshur, Nabu, and Marduk" (ibid., 2:226).

Gross idolatry was practiced in Nineveh and throughout the Assyrian Empire. The religion of Assyria was Babylonian in origin but in Assyria the national god was Assur, whose high priest and representative was the king.

**Date of the Book.** The fall of Thebes (to Ashurbanipal) is mentioned in Nahum 3:8. Since that event occurred in 663 B.C. the book was written after that date. Then the fall of Nineveh, predicted in Nahum, occurred in 612 B.C. So the book was written between 663 and 612. Walter A. Maier suggests that Nahum gave his prophecy soon after Thebes fell, between 663 and 654 B.C. (*The Book of Nahum*, pp. 30, 34-7). His arguments include these:

1. The description of Nineveh (1:12; 3:1, 4, 16) does not match the decline of the Assyrian nation under Ashurbanipal's sons, Ashur-etil-ilāni (626–623 B.C.) and Sin-shar-ishkun (623–612 B.C.).

2. When Nahum prophesied, Judah was under the Assyrian yoke (1:13, 15; 2:1, 3). This fits with the reign of Manasseh over Judah (697–642) more than with the reign of Josiah (640–609).

3. The Medes rose in power around 645 B.C. as an independent nation, and

# Fulfillments of Nahum's Prophecies

| Nahum's Prophecies | Historical Fulfillments |
|---|---|
| 1. The Assyrian fortresses surrounding the city would be easily captured (3:12). | 1. According to the Babylonian Chronicle the fortified towns in Nineveh's environs began to fall in 614 B.C. including Tabris, present-day Sharif-Khan, a few miles northwest of Nineveh. |
| 2. The besieged Ninevites would prepare bricks and mortar for emergency defense walls (3:14). | 2. A.T. Olmstead reported: "To the south of the gate, the moat is still filled with fragments of stone and of mud bricks from the walls, heaped up when they were breached" (History of Assyria. Chicago: University of Chicago Press, 1951, p. 637). |
| 3. The city gates would be destroyed (3:13). | 3. Olmstead noted: "The main attack was directed from the northwest and the brunt fell upon the Hatamti gate at this corner. . . . Within the gate are traces of the counterwall raised by the inhabitants in their last extremity" (History of Assyria, p. 637). |
| 4. In the final hours of the attack the Ninevites would be drunk (1:10; 3:11). | 4. Diodorus Siculus (ca. 20 B.C.) wrote, "The Assyrian king . . . distributed to his soldiers meats and liberal supplies of wine and provisions. . . . While the whole army was thus carousing, the friends of Arbakes learned from some deserters of the slackness and drunkenness which prevailed in the enemy's camp and made an unexpected attack by night" (Bibliotheca Historica 2. 26. 4). |
| 5. Nineveh would be destroyed by a flood (1:8; 2:6, 8). | 5. Diodorus wrote that in the third year of the siege heavy rains caused a nearby river to flood part of the city and break part of the walls (Bibliotheca Historica 2. 26. 9; 2. 27. 13). Xenophon referred to terrifying thunder (presumably with a storm) associated with the city's capture (Anabasis, 3. 4. 12). Also the Khosr River, entering the city from the northwest at the Ninlil Gate and running through the city in a southwesterly direction, may have flooded because of heavy rains, or the enemy may have destroyed its sluice gate. |
| 6. Nineveh would be destroyed by fire (1:10; 2:13; 3:15). | 6. Archeological excavations at Nineveh have revealed charred wood, charcoal, and ashes. "There was no question about the clear traces of the burning of the temple (as also in the palace of Sennacherib), for a layer of ash about two inches thick lay clearly defined in places on the southeast side about the level of the Sargon pavement" (R. Campbell Thompson and R.W. Hutchinson, A Century of Exploration at Nineveh. London: Luzac, 1929, pp. 45, 77). |
| 7. The city's capture would be attended by a great massacre of people (3:3). | 7. "In two battles fought on the plain before the city the rebels defeated the Assyrians. . . . So great was the multitude of the slain that the flowing stream, mingled with their blood, changed its color for a considerable distance" (Diodorus, Bibliotheca Historica 2. 26. 6-7). |
| 8. Plundering and pillaging would accompany the overthrow of the city (2:9-10). | 8. According to the Babylonian Chronicle, "Great quantities of spoil from the city, beyond counting, they carried off. The city [they turned] into a mound and ruin heap" (Luckenbill, Ancient Records of Assyria and Babylonia, 2:420). |
| 9. When Nineveh would be captured its people would try to escape (2:8). | 9. "Sardanapalus [another name for King Sin-shar-ishkun] sent away his three sons and two daughters with much treasure into Paphlagonia, to the governor of Kattos, the most loyal of his subjects" (Diodorus, Bibliotheca Historica, 2. 26. 8). |
| 10. The Ninevite officers would weaken and flee (3:17). | 10. The Babylonian Chronicle states that "[The army] of Assyria deserted [lit., ran away before] the king" (Luckenbill, Ancient Records of Assyria and Babylonia, 2:420). |
| 11. Nineveh's images and idols would be destroyed (1:14). | 11. R. Campbell Thompson and R.W. Hutchinson reported that the statue of the goddess Ishtar lay headless in the debris of Nineveh's ruins ("The British Museum Excavations on the Temple of Ishtar at Nineveh, 1930-1," Annals of Archaeology and Anthropology. 19, pp. 55-6). |
| 12. Nineveh's destruction would be final (1:9, 14). | 12. Many cities of the ancient Near East were rebuilt after being destroyed (e.g., Samaria, Jerusalem, Babylon) but not Nineveh. |

the Neo-Babylonian Empire began in 626. If Nahum had written shortly before Nineveh's fall to those nations in 612, mention of them would be expected. But since Nahum does not mention the Medes or the Babylonians, he probably wrote his prophecy before 645.

4. Most important, however, is the fact that nine years after Thebes was destroyed, it was restored (in 654). Nahum's rhetorical question in 3:8 would have had little or no force if it had been written after 654.

**Unity of the Text.** Some scholars have suggested that Nahum wrote most of 2:4–3:19 with some phrases having been inserted later by some other writer(s), and that 1:1–2:3 was written by someone other than Nahum. Some have even questioned the authenticity of 1:1 because, they say, it is a double title: "An oracle concerning Nineveh. The book of the vision of Nahum the Elkoshite." But these phrases supplement each other; the first indicates the subject and the second the author. This is similar in form to Isaiah 13:1; Amos 1:1; Micah 1:1 (in Isa. 13:1 and Amos 1:1 "saw" means "saw in a vision"). Other scholars have sought to establish the notion that Nahum 1:2-10 is not original but was an acrostic psalm added years after Nahum. It is questionable that these verses constitute an acrostic, but even if they do this does not prove that someone other than Nahum wrote them.

**Literary Form of the Text.** Some writers have tried to prove that the Book of Nahum was not a prophecy but was a liturgy for the annual "enthronement festival" of the Lord held in Jerusalem after the fall of Nineveh in 612 B.C. According to this analysis the book consists of fragments of various literary categories and features, questions and responses, passages given by soloists and choruses antiphonally—all of which form a liturgy commemorating Nineveh's destruction. But this theory contradicts the title which identifies the contents as "an oracle" and a "vision." The liturgy view destroys the prophetic nature of the book.

Though the book is a literary unit written by one author, it does use several literary forms. These include an introduction extolling God's attributes (1:2-8), a series of announcement oracles addressed to both Nineveh and Judah (1:9-15), a vivid prophetic description of Nineveh's fall (chap. 2), and a denunciation of Nineveh for her guilt (chap. 3). These parts are laced together with a series of rhetorical questions (1:6; 3:7-8, 19). In metaphors and similes Nineveh is likened to dry stubble (1:10), lions (2:12), and a harlot and a sorcerer (3:4). The city's fortresses are said to be like ripe figs (3:12), and its guards and officials like locusts (3:17). Nahum wrote tersely as he described the battle leading to the city's conquest (2:8-10; 3:2-3, 14).

**Purpose of the Book.** The initial clue to the book's purpose is in the title "oracle" (or burden; see comments on 1:1 and those prior to Zech. 9:1). Nahum placed a burden on Nineveh; he wrote a prophetic word of a threatening nature. Though the prophet primarily addressed Nineveh (Nahum 1:8, 11, 14; 2:1, 8; 3:7), he also addressed Judah (1:12, 15; 2:2) in comfort. The coming judgment on Nineveh (in return for her terrible atrocities on various nations including Israel, the Northern Kingdom, in 722 B.C.) would bring great comfort to the afflicted Judah (1:12). Judah had felt the threat of the Assyrian Empire breathing down her neck. In fact Assyria had defeated much of Judah and had even surrounded Jerusalem in 701 B.C. And during much of Manasseh's reign Judah had to pay tribute to Assyria. So the purpose of Nahum's book is to announce the fall of Nineveh and thereby comfort Judah with the assurance that God is in control.

# OUTLINE

I. The Title (1:1)
II. The Certainty of God's Judgment on Nineveh (1:2-15)
  A. God's wrath to be extended to Nineveh and His goodness to His own (1:2-8)
  B. Nineveh's plotting against the Lord to come to an end (1:9-11)
  C. Judah's affliction to end because of Nineveh's destruction (1:12-15)
III. The Description of God's Judgment on Nineveh (chap. 2)
  A. The attack (2:1-6)

B. The defeat and the plundering
(2:7-13)
IV. The Reasons for God's Judgment on
Nineveh (chap. 3)
  A. Her violence and deceit to
result in shame (3:1-7)
  B. Her treatment of Thebes to result
in her own defeat (3:8-11)
  C. Her defense efforts to be useless
(3:12-19)

# COMMENTARY

## I. The Title (1:1)

**1:1.** The book was **an oracle** against
**Nineveh.** As an oracle it was a burden
(*maśśā'*; see comments on Isa. 13:1 and
those prior to Zech. 9:1), a threatening
message about Nineveh's doom. It was a
**vision** (*ḥāzôn*), that is, a message which
the prophet "saw" mentally and spiritually (cf. Isa. 1:1; Obad. 1; Micah 1:1;
Zech. 1:8). On **Nahum the Elkoshite** see
"The Prophet Nahum" in the *Introduction.*

## II. The Certainty of God's Judgment on Nineveh (1:2-15)

Nahum wrote that Nineveh's end
would certainly come. Because Nineveh
had plotted against the Lord (vv. 9-11)
she would receive His wrath (vv. 2-6, 8).
Yet God remains a refuge for those who
trust Him (v. 7). Nineveh's destruction
would comfort Judah who had been afflicted by the Assyrian threat (vv. 12-15).

### A. God's wrath to be extended to Nineveh and His goodness to His own (1:2-8)

**1:2.** The LORD is righteous in relation
to His covenant people and in relation to
her wicked oppressors. As a righteous
God, He is **jealous,** that is, zealous to
protect what belongs to Him (see comments on Deut. 6:15; cf. Deut. 4:24; 5:9;
32:16, 21), namely, Judah. He will allow
no rivals. He is also an **avenging God.**
This fact is strongly emphasized, for the
word *nōqēm* ("avenging") occurs three
times in this verse (twice trans. **takes
vengeance**). God said, "It is Mine to
avenge" and "I will take vengeance on
My adversaries and repay those who
hate Me" (Deut. 32:35, 41). God avenges
His people in the sense that He champions their cause against their enemies. He

does so because He is jealous or protective of His people. While God is avenging *for* or on behalf of His people, He is
avenging **against** His adversaries. Judah's enemies were **His enemies. He is
filled with wrath** (lit., "He is baal [i.e.,
master] of fury"). *Ḥēmâh*, related to the
verb meaning "to be hot," speaks of
God's burning rage or intense fury
against sin.

**1:3a.** Though God takes vengeance
on His enemies, He **is slow to anger** (lit.,
"long of anger"), that is, He withholds
His judgment for a long time (cf. Ex. 34:6;
Num. 14:18; Neh. 9:17; Pss. 86:15; 103:8;
145:8; Joel 2:13; Jonah 4:2). Such "length
of anger" accounts for the apparent delay, from Judah's perspective, which allowed Assyria to act in such lustful freedom. But this does not suggest that God
is weak. He is long-suffering and patient
(2 Peter 3:9) because of His desire that
people repent. This was exhibited in His
sending Jonah to Nineveh, about 100
years before Nahum prophesied.

Also **the** LORD is **great in power.**
Though He may prolong His mercy, His
omnipotence remains. The word for
power is *kōaḥ,* which suggests the ability
to endure or the capacity to produce, and
from there comes the idea of the ability to
cope with situations (e.g., Deut. 8:17-18).
That ability is seen in God's acts of judgment. For, the prophet added, **He will
not leave the guilty unpunished** (cf.
Num. 14:18). He would serve as the
Ninevites' Judge because of their guilt.
He would not treat them as if they were
innocent. Though the Ninevites had repented under Jonah's preaching, the city
had gone into iniquity again, and therefore would not escape His wrath.

**1:3b-5.** The greatness of God's power (v. 3a) is evident in His control over
nature. Because He is powerful over inanimate nature, He certainly would be
able to cope with and judge Nineveh. He
causes **the whirlwind and the** threatening **storm** (cf. Job 9:17a), two awesome
and often destructive forces of nature. In
His dealings with Nineveh, He would be
as destructive as a devastating whirlwind
and storm. He is so great that the **clouds
are** like **dust** under **His feet** (cf. 2 Sam.
22:10; Ps. 18:9). "His strides cover the
vast areas of extenuated clouds. His
movements are marked by the darkening
of the heavens as the whirlwind sweeps

and the tempest howls" (Maier, *The Book of Nahum: A Commentary,* pp. 158-9).

In His power He merely speaks (**rebukes**) **the sea,** and **the rivers . . . dry** up. This refers to His delivering Israel from Egyptian bondage (cf. Ex. 14:21; Pss. 66:6; 106:9; Isa. 50:2; 51:10; also note Ps. 18:15). Since He could defeat Egypt in that way, certainly He is powerful enough to destroy Nineveh. **Bashan,** a region east of the Sea of Kinnereth (Galilee), **Carmel,** a mountain range near present-day Haifa, and **Lebanon,** north of Israel, were fertile areas (cf. Isa. 33:9; also note Carmel in Amos 1:2 and Bashan in Micah 7:14). God's ability to dry up verdant areas shows He could judge Nineveh. Even **the mountains,** symbolic of stability, shake under His power, as did Mount Sinai (Ex. 19:18) and **the hills melt** (cf. Micah 1:4). Even the entire **earth** and its people, including the Ninevites, will tremble before His awesome power.

**1:6.** The two rhetorical questions (**Who can withstand. . . ? Who can endure. . . ?**) forcefully affirm that no one can stand before the Lord, angered by man's wickedness. Sennacherib's field commander (2 Kings 18:17) had challenged Hezekiah with the questions, "Who of all the gods of these countries has been able to save his land from me? How then can the LORD deliver Jerusalem from my hand?" (2 Kings 18:35) Assyria was soon to learn that *God,* not Assyria, has the last word! **Indignation** translates *za'am,* which means to be enraged like foam on water. Two synonyms of indignation were already used (**anger** in Nahum 1:3 and **wrath,** *ḥēmâh,* in v. 2). God's wrath is destructive and devastating **like fire.** When He comes in judgment even **the rocks** shatter **before Him** (cf. 1 Kings 19:11).

**1:7-8.** Though **the LORD** is wrathful and powerful against those who oppose Him, He **is good** (cf. Ex. 34:6; Pss. 106:1; 107:1; 136:1; Jer. 33:11) to **those who trust in Him.** He is good in the sense that He is faithful and merciful, protecting (**a refuge in times of trouble**), helpful, and caring. The Hebrew word for "refuge" is *mā'ôz.* Translated "stronghold" in Psalms 27:1; 37:39; 43:2; 52:7, it means a strong, fortified place. The people of Nineveh thought they were safe in their fortifications, but their security was short-lived

compared with the comfort and safety God provides for His people.

On the other hand God's enemies will experience His judgment. By **an overwhelming flood** God would **make an end** (cf. Nahum 1:9) **of Nineveh.** "Nineveh" is literally, "its site" (cf. "the place," KJV), but Nineveh is clearly intended. ("Nineveh" is also supplied in vv. 11, 14; 2:1.) This reference to a flood could suggest figuratively an unrestrained army invasion (cf. Isa. 8:7-8; Jer. 47:2; Dan. 9:26; 11:40). Or it may refer to a literal destruction by water, the Tigris and Khosr rivers overflowing and destroying part of the city walls (cf. Nahum 2:6, 8; see the chart "Fulfillments of Nahum's Prophecies," in the *Introduction*).

Nahum added that God **will pursue His foes into darkness.** Darkness symbolizes the spiritual condition of persons without God, their defeat, and ultimately eternal judgment (Job 17:13; Pss. 82:5; 88:12; Prov. 4:19; 20:20; Isa. 8:22; 42:7; Jer. 23:12; Matt. 4:16; 8:12; John 3:19; Col. 1:13; 1 Peter 2:9; Jude 6; Rev. 16:10).

### B. Nineveh's plotting against the Lord to come to an end (1:9-11)

In affirming Nineveh's end, Nahum made a forthright prediction about Nineveh (vv. 9-10), a promise to Judah (vv. 12-13), a command and prediction to Nineveh (v. 14), and a call to Judah (v. 15).

**1:9.** Though Sennacherib, king of Assyria, had failed in his attempt to destroy Jerusalem, the Ninevites continued to **plot** ways to overcome the city. In plotting evil or calamity against His people they were actually plotting **against the LORD** (cf. v. 11). But their schemes would fail for God would keep those plans from being carried out (cf. **end** in v. 8). Assyria in fact never got a second chance to attack Jerusalem; just as God said, **trouble** to the holy city did **not come** from Assyria **a second time.** Any challenge to the Lord's declaration about Nineveh's end (cf. v. 8) would be thwarted.

**1:10-11.** Nineveh's being **entangled among thorns** has been interpreted in various ways: (a) the thorns symbolize wicked enemies, as in Ezekiel 2:6, but this does not fit; (b) the thorns (i.e., thornbushes) refer to the habitat of lions, but nothing in the text suggests this; (c) the entanglement of thorns refers to the confusion of the Ninevites when they were attacked in 612 b.c. This third view is preferable. This confusion, because of their drunkenness, resulted in complete disaster: the people were **consumed** quickly and fully **like** the burning of **dry stubble** (cf. Isa. 10:12, 17). A wordplay is suggested by the similarity in sound between the Hebrew words for "entangled" (*sᵉbûkîm*) and "drunk" (*sᵉbû'îm*). The **one** who was plotting **evil** (i.e., calamity) **against the Lord** (Nahum 1:11; cf. v. 9) was an Assyrian king (Sennacherib or someone after him). **Wickedness** translates *bᵉliyya'al*, "worthlessness" (trans. "wicked" in v. 15). His plans were both worthless and wicked (cf. Job 34:18). In 2 Samuel 16:7 and Proverbs 16:27 the word is rendered "scoundrel."

### C. Judah's affliction to end because of Nineveh's destruction (1:12-15)

**1:12-13.** The promise to Judah in these two verses is introduced by the statement **This is what the Lord says.** This clause, occurring in Nahum only here, guarantees that what He predicted would indeed be fulfilled. For centuries Nineveh had gone **unscathed**; no enemy had penetrated her walls. And her inhabitants were many, presumably well able to defend the city. Yet God promised that Nineveh would be **cut down** (defeated) **and** would **pass away** (vanish). God had used Assyria to afflict **Judah** in several ways: by Sennacherib's attack in 701 b.c., by Judah's having to pay tribute to Assyria during much of Manasseh's reign, and by Judah's King Manasseh being taken captive (2 Chron. 33:11). But that Assyrian oppression, like a **yoke** on an animal's **neck**, would be broken when Nineveh fell.

**1:14-15.** Whereas Nineveh would have no heirs or places of worship (v. 14), Judah was called on to worship **the Lord** in view of her coming deliverance (v. 15). The Lord's **command** (*ṣāwâh*) to **Nineveh** indicates that she was subject to God's decrees. The Lord's judgment on the city would touch her prosperity and her false worship. **No** one would be left to worship and no idols would be left to be worshiped. Many times Nineveh had desecrated the altars and temples of her defeated foes and carried off their **images** and **idols.** Assyria thought this meant

her gods were superior. But now Nineveh would experience the same fate it had placed on others. **The temple of** her **gods** was either the temple of Ishtar or of Nabu.

God would see that Nineveh was buried (**I will prepare your grave**; cf. Ezek. 32:22-23) because she was **vile** (*qālal*, "to be of no account, to be unworthy"; cf. Job 40:4).

In contrast with Nineveh's fall (Nahum 1:14), **Judah** would experience freedom (v. 15). The prophet spoke as if the fall of Nineveh had already occurred and as if a messenger were arriving **on the mountains** around Jerusalem to bring the **good news.** And the fall of the capital of Assyria, the ruthless nation, would indeed be a message of **peace.** Therefore Judah could resume her worship, keeping her festivals (the Feast of Unleavened Bread, the Feast of Harvest or Pentecost, and the Feast of Ingathering or Tabernacles, Ex. 23:14-17) to express her gratitude to God and to keep her vows (cf. Lev. 22:21; 27:2, 8). **The wicked** one (*bᵉliyya'al*; see comments on Nahum 1:11) would **no** longer **invade** Judah (cf. v. 9) because he would be **completely destroyed** (cf. v. 10). Nineveh was never rebuilt. So complete was its destruction that when Xenophon passed by the site about 200 years later, he thought the mounds were the ruins of some other city. And Alexander the Great, fighting in a battle nearby, did not realize that he was near the ruins of Nineveh.

### III. The Description of God's Judgment on Nineveh (chap. 2)

Chapter 1 includes more or less general statements about the Lord's judgment on His enemy, but now the book moves to more specific descriptions of the attack and plundering of the city. Nineveh would be attacked (2:1, 3-6), defeated (vv. 7-8), and plundered (vv. 9-13), but Judah's glory will be restored (v. 2). Associated with this change in emphasis is a shift in tone—from calmness and dignity to increasing emotion and vivid descriptions. Concerning some of these tense, graphic descriptions of action in battle Raymond Calkins wrote, "Nahum portrays [the] siege, reproduces its horrors and its savagery, its cruelties and mercilessness, in language so realistic that one is able to see it and feel it. First comes the fighting in the suburbs. Then the assault upon the walls. Then the capture of the city and its destruction" (*The Modern Message of the Minor Prophets*. New York: Harper & Brothers, 1947, p. 82).

## A. The attack (2:1-6)

**2:1.** Under attack, Nineveh was called on to defend itself. In an alternating pattern Nahum had addressed Nineveh in 1:11, 14 and now in 2:1; he had addressed Judah in 1:12-13, 15. The advance of **an** unnamed **attacker** (*mēpîṣ*, "scatterer or disperser"; cf. 2:8b; 3:18) **against . . . Nineveh** was so certain that Nahum spoke of it in the present tense. The verb **advances** is literally "goes up" (*ʿālâh*), a word used of hostile military operations (e.g., Jud. 1:1, "go up"; 1 Sam. 7:7, "came up"; 1 Kings 20:22, "attack"; Isa. 7:1, "marched up"; Isa. 7:6, "invade"; Isa. 21:2, "attack"). The attacker was Nabopolassar, the Babylonian who, with Cyaxeres the Mede, conquered Nineveh.

Then a series of four terse commands follows. They reflect the Ninevites' scurry of activity to defend their great city. In bitter irony, a subtle form of ridicule, Nahum urged the city to prepare for the approaching siege by guarding **the fortress,** watching **the road** for invaders, bracing themselves (lit., **brace** "the loins," i.e., exert strength physically and mentally), and marshaling **all** their **strength** (*kōaḥ*; see comments on Nahum 1:3). The prophet knew that such precautions could not hold back the siege or change its outcome. All Nineveh's efforts to defend itself would be futile because, as God said (1:15), the city would be destroyed.

**2:2.** The description of the attack is interrupted by a word about Jacob and Israel. Perhaps **Jacob** and **Israel** are synonyms for the entire nation, though possibly Jacob refers to the Southern Kingdom and Israel the Northern Kingdom. The destruction of Nineveh makes it possible for God's people to be taken out of their humbled, debased condition and to have their **splendor** (*gāʾôn*, "excellence or majesty") restored. This will not be fully realized till Israel is in the land in the millennial kingdom which the Messiah will establish. This will contrast with her

having been **laid . . . waste** by Assyria (the defeat of the Northern Kingdom in 722 B.C.), which included the ruining of her grape **vines.**

**2:3-4.** Nahum spoke of the equipment and speed of the "attacker" (v. 1) and his soldiers and chariots. **His** in the first line of verse 3 probably refers not to the defending Assyrian king but to the unidentified "attacker." **The shields of** the Medes and Babylonians were **red** either from blood, or from red-dyed leather over the wooden shields, or by being covered with copper. The warriors' **scarlet**-colored attire (cf. "red" in Ezek. 23:14) would make them awesome in appearance. (Xenophon wrote about the Persians in Cyrus' army being dressed in scarlet, *Cyropaedia* 6. 4. 1.) **The metal on the chariots** glistened in the sun, as the soldiers' wooden **spears** were **brandished** (swung) in their wild attack.

The charging **chariots** of the besieging enemy seemed to bolt furiously in wild frenzy (cf. Jer. 46:9). They moved so quickly that they looked **like lightning. The streets** "may include the avenues and suburban highways about Nineveh and leading to the city, for the context describes an attack that gradually leads to the city's walls" (Maier, *The Book of Nahum: A Commentary*, p. 243). **The squares** were the wider open spaces within a city (cf. streets and squares in Prov. 5:16; 7:12; Jer. 5:1; 9:21).

**2:5-6.** **He** in verse 5 probably refers to the Assyrian king because he summoned **his . . . troops** to defend **the city wall** and set up **the protective shield.** The exact nature of this protective covering is unknown but somehow it protected the defenders against the attackers' stones, spears, and arrows.

Several possible interpretations of **the river gates** have been suggested: (a) fortified bridges, (b) city gates near the banks of the Tigris River, (c) sluice gates in dams in the city moats (but no archeological evidence supports this), (d) breaches made in the wall by the torrential rush of water, (e) floodgates to control the flow of the Khosr River that passed through the city.

The fifth view is supported by the most natural sense of the language and by archeological remains. "Sennacherib . . . dammed the . . . Khosr [River], outside the city, and thus made a reservoir.

Thompson and Hutchinson report that the water was restrained by a magnificent double dam with two massive river walls at some distance from Nineveh itself. In the ruins they found traces of the original dam gates, or sluices, by which the water flow to the city could be increased or reduced" (Maier, *The Book of Nahum: A Commentary,* p. 253). So perhaps at the beginning of the siege the enemy closed the floodgates. When the reservoirs were completely full, they threw **open** the gates **and the palace** collapsed. The waters may have also been increased by heavy rains as Diodorus Siculus wrote (see point 5 in the chart "Fulfillments of Nahum's Prophecies," in the *Introduction*). The palace may have been Ashurbanipal's palace in the north part of the city. The nation that had ruined many enemy palaces now found its own palace devastated.

### B. The defeat and the plundering (2:7-13)

**2:7.** Nineveh's destiny was **decreed** by God: she would be taken into exile. The word translated "decreed" is *ḥuṣṣab.* The KJV renders this "Huzzab" and translates the first part of the verse, "And Huzzab shall be led away captive." This is supposedly the capture of the queen by that name. However, no queen by this name is known in extrabiblical records. The NIV rendering "It is decreed" is preferred. Though this seemingly interrupts the flow of thought, it does so to affirm that such an event as Nineveh's exile was established by God. Such words of divine purpose occur repeatedly (1:13-14; 2:2, 13; 3:5-6). The **slave girls** wailed **like doves,** whose cooing resembled lamenting (cf. Isa. 38:14; 59:11), and in sorrow **beat . . . their breasts,** knowing they were to **be exiled.**

**2:8-10.** With their city flooded, the Ninevites would flee, leaving their possessions behind. The word **pool,** perhaps meaning a reservoir, aptly describes Nineveh as an inundated area (cf. comments on v. 6). The people, like **water** flowing out of a tank, would flee rapidly from the city. As they would leave in panic, some would shout for them to **stop . . . but no one** would turn **back.** Who shouted **stop** is not stated. Perhaps they were the city leaders, or army officers, or perhaps even the attacking enemy.

Nahum now encouraged the victorious invaders to gather the spoils. For many years Nineveh had exacted huge booties from her foes, so that her **supply** of **silver** and **gold** was almost limitless. She also acquired **wealth** by tribute and by trading. In his annals Ashurbanipal mentioned silver and gold together 27 times in his inventories of booty taken from other nations. Luckenbill records the reports of vast amounts of wealth acquired by several Assyrian kings, including Ashurnaṣirpal, Shalmaneser III, Adad-nirari, Tiglath-Pileser III, Sargon II, Sennacherib, and Esarhaddon (*Ancient Records of Assyria and Babylonia,* 1:181, 211, 263, 276; 2:20, 133, 205). The words **pillaged, plundered,** and **stripped** render three similar-sounding Hebrew words: *bûqâh,* *mᵉbûqâh,* and *mᵉḇullāqâh.* Because their wealth was being plundered and their lives were endangered, the Ninevites were frightened and terror-stricken.

**2:11-12.** Nahum responded to the envisioned destruction of the city with a taunt, **Where now is the lions' den?** His rhetorical question implied that the capital no longer existed. The symbolism of the lions' den (and the **lion . . . lioness,** and **cubs;** cf. "young lions," v. 13) is uniquely appropriate. Like a **lion** hunting for his lioness and **cubs,** Assyria had plundered other nations. Assyrian kings prided themselves in their ability to kill lions in lion hunts. And the kings likened their own ferocity and fearlessness to that of lions. For example, Sennacherib boasted of his military fury by saying, "Like a lion I raged." Lions were frequently pictured in Assyrian reliefs and decorations. No wonder Nahum likened Nineveh to a lions' den! But now the **lairs** would be empty. No longer would there be lions, cubs, and ripped carcasses.

**2:13.** God's hostility against Nineveh is stated in forceful words: **I am against you** (cf. 3:5; Jer. 21:13; 50:31; 51:25; Ezek. 5:8; 13:8; 26:3; 28:22; 39:1). Fire would destroy her **chariots;** the **sword** would cut down her soldiers (**young lions**); and Nineveh would **no longer** be permitted to pounce on defenseless nations (**prey**) and helpless vassals. Nor would the haughty city be able to send any more **messengers** or heralds (as Sennacherib's field commander, 2 Kings 18:17-25) to demand submission, or to exact tribute (or to blaspheme the Lord; cf. 2 Kings 19:22; Isa. 37:4, 6).

## IV. The Reasons for God's Judgment on Nineveh (chap. 3)

This final section of the book continues the vigorous emotion and intensified tones of the second chapter. But the focus turns from the fact of judgment to the reasons for it. The prophet showed the spiritually depraved condition of the once-haughty and prosperous city.

### A. Her violence and deceit to result in shame (3:1-7)

**3:1.** **Woe** is an interjection pronouncing either grief or, as here, impending death (cf. comments on Isa. 3:9). Nineveh was truly a **city of blood**—blood spilled by her uncontrolled lust and murder. She earned this title by her "atrocious practice of cutting off hands and feet, ears and noses, gouging out eyes, lopping off heads, and then binding them to vines or heaping them up before city gates [and] the utter fiendishness by which captives could be impaled or flayed alive through a process in which their skin was gradually and completely removed" (Maier, *The Book of Nahum: A Commentary*, p. 292). It was also a city of deception (**lies**). The tactics Assyria followed when surrounding Jerusalem clearly display this characteristic (2 Kings 18:31). On Nineveh's plundering see comments on Nahum 2:9.

**3:2-4.** Nahum's accusation of Nineveh's guilt (v. 1) is followed by several terse descriptions of the final assault on the city. These statements are a progression from **whips,** to **wheels** and **horses** of **chariots,** to **cavalry** with **swords** and **spears,** to widespread slaughter and carnage (**bodies without number**). These describe the attack on Nineveh (cf. 2:3-4), which was surprisingly like Nineveh's own war tactics. She had piled up many dead bodies, but now the *Ninevites'* **corpses** would be piled up.

The reason for this terror is that she had lusted for power like the lusting **of a harlot.** Nineveh sold her military aid and power in order to lure **nations** under her control. By this statement Nahum may have also subtly alluded to Ishtar, the Assyrian-Babylonian goddess of sex and war, who was called a harlot and some of

whose exploits were acts of savagery. Nineveh's control over others was exercised by **sorceries** and **witchcraft.** The Assyrians used hundreds of incantations in order to seek to foretell the future and influence others' lives; they also read omens in the movements of birds, animals, clouds, and in dreams.

**3:5-7.** Her shameless actions against others would be matched by shameless exposure. God was **against** her (cf. comments on 2:13) and is against every nation, no matter how wealthy, powerful, or self-sufficient it may be, that disregards divine authority and tramples on human life. God said He would uncover what the privacy of her **skirts** had once covered (cf. the similar fate of Babylon, Isa. 47:1-3; and Jerusalem, Ezek. 16:37). She had caused others disgrace and **shame** by her prostitution, but now *she* would be shamed. Added to this indignity would be the disgrace of being pelted **with filth** (human excrement) and **contempt.** The Hebrew word for filth (*šiqqûṣ*) is used of anything that is detestable. It often refers to idols (e.g., Deut. 29:17; Jer. 4:1; Ezek 20:7-8). Nineveh's glory would turn into filth.

Nineveh's shame would reach a climax when she would be **in ruins,** and have no one **to comfort** her. Her cruelties had irreconcilably estranged her victims. The once-attractive harlot would be exposed in shame and would no longer be attractive to anyone.

### B. Her treatment of Thebes to result in her own defeat (3:8-11)

**3:8.** Nineveh's strength, God said, would be no greater than that of the Egyptian city of **Thebes,** which Assyria had conquered in 663 B.C. Before that date Jeremiah (Jer. 46:25) and Ezekiel (Ezek. 30:14, 16) had predicted Thebes' fall. The Hebrews called the city No-Amon (city of the god Amun). Thebes was at the site of modern-day Karnak and Luxor, 400 miles south of Cairo. The city was built on the eastern bank of **the Nile** River but its suburbs were on both shores. One strength of Thebes was her strategic location. **Water** was all **around her,** that is, moats, canals, and water channels flowed throughout much of the city. These helped defend the city as enemy soldiers would find it difficult to cross numerous canals to get to the heart of the city. The **waters** were thus like a **wall.** In this way Nineveh and Thebes were similar (cf. Nahum 2:8).

**3:9.** Another strength of Thebes was her support by notable alliances and their almost limitless resources. Nineveh, by contrast, had no allies. Thebes was the most prominent city in **Cush,** the region of the upper Nile River, which corresponds to present-day southern Egypt, Sudan, and northern Ethiopia. The lower Nile region was known as **Egypt,** and at that time this territory was subjugated by Cush. While **Put** is sometimes identified as **Libya,** the mention of both here favors a location for Put on the coast of the Red Sea as far south as present-day Somaliland. The Libyans inhabited the territory west of Egypt. So Thebes' **allies** were south, north, east, and west of her. Yet their combined help was unable to defend her against Nineveh.

**3:10.** In spite of her strength, Thebes endured an ignominious end. Assyrian records describe in detail the conquest of Thebes. Most of the people of Thebes were **taken . . . into exile.** (Similarly many Ninevites would be exiled, 2:7.) Rather than taking Thebian **infants** into captivity, the Assyrians ruthlessly massacred them (cf. Hosea 13:16; other nations did the same: Ps. 137:9; Isa. 13:16, 18; Hosea 10:14). The Assyrians did this in full view of many Thebians **at the** intersection **(head) of every street.** This created maximum fear and agony among the people and also helped wipe out a future generation of Thebians. Such terrible atrocities added to Nineveh's deep guilt. While many of the people of the great city of Thebes were herded into captivity, the nobility were bid for by casting **lots,** perhaps to become the Ninevites' slaves, a humbling experience.

**3:11.** Nineveh's treatment of Thebes would be turned back on Nineveh. Like **drunk** persons, the Ninevites would be bereft of sense and direction under attack, frantically seeking to hide. Also the people of Nineveh literally became drunk (cf. 1:10) with intoxicants, which contributed to their aimless tottering and inability to defend themselves.

### C. Her defense efforts to be useless (3:12-19)

**3:12.** Under attack by the Medes, Scythians, and Babylonians, Nineveh

would find that its **fortresses** were weak. The initial yield on **fig trees** (cf. Num. 13:20) in the spring (which is followed by a later crop; see comments on Song 2:13) falls easily to the ground when the tree is **shaken.** The figs **fall,** as it were, **into the mouth of the eater** with the slightest effort. Similarly Nineveh's defenses would easily and quickly succumb to the attackers. This was actually the case in 612 B.C.

**3:13.** Seeing the attackers, the men trying to defend the city would lose their courage and become like **women,** afraid and defenseless (cf. Isa. 19:16; Jer. 50:37; 51:30). The dreaded Assyrians, ferocious as lions, would become weak.

Because of the destructive effect of the floodwaters on the city (see comments on 2:6), enemy soldiers were able to enter it. Then they set **fire** to the city **gates** and their **bars** (cf. Isa. 10:16-17) and rushed headlong into the city.

**3:14.** Nineveh's efforts at defense would be no match for the Lord's judgment. The scene of the destruction moves from the fortresses and gates (vv. 12-13) to within the city itself (vv. 14-17).

In ridiculing irony (cf. 2:1; also see 3:15) Nahum again ordered the Ninevites to defend themselves. When a city is under **siege,** one of its most urgent needs is an adequate supply of clean drinking **water.** And when the enemy would tear off some of the bricks of the city's wall (as the Assyrians often did), the city under attack would need to **repair** those weakened places in the walls with new bricks and **mortar.** In Nehemiah 3:19 the past tense of the Hebrew word here translated **strengthen** is rendered "repaired." Nineveh's ruins include traces of a counterwall built by the inhabitants to defend the city near places where the enemy had broken down some of the city's **defenses.**

**3:15-17.** When those defense efforts would prove futile, then disaster would strike with fire and **sword.** On destruction by **fire** see point 6 on the chart "Fulfillments of Nahum's Prophecies," in the *Introduction.* The attacking soldiers entered the city, killing many of the people with swords. The soldiers were like **grasshoppers,** consuming and destroying entire crops for miles (on devastation caused by grasshoppers and locusts, see comments on Joel 1:2-13). Nahum's command to **multiply like grasshoppers** and like locusts may be directed to the Ninevites to increase their numbers (as if they could!) to defend themselves more adequately. Or it may be addressed to the enemy to increase themselves (to be successful) in their conquest of Nineveh.

Again the prophet spoke of locusts (Nahum 3:16). The city had increased its wealth by commercial trading with numberless merchants, but they would become like countless locusts stripping the land of its vegetation. Nineveh had acquired vast amounts of wealth by trading (probably often done deceptively; see comments on v. 4), but now those merchants by looting would take back much merchandise. Neither military power (v. 15) nor wealth (v. 16) could deliver the Ninevites.

The locusts provided still another point of comparison (v. 17). When Nineveh would be attacked her military guards and national officials would be so afraid (cf. v. 13a) that they would escape overnight. In the cool of the evening, locusts settle on walls but when the warmth of the sun comes in the morning, they fly away. Similarly, in panic the guards on the walls would also suddenly vanish.

3:18. The final dirge-like words in verses 18-19 may be addressed to Sin-shar-ishkun, the king who was ruling Nineveh when it was destroyed in 612 B.C. or, perhaps more likely, to King Ashur-uballiṭ (612–609 B.C.) who tried to hold together the Assyrian Empire in the city of Haran, until it finally crumbled completely in 609, three years after Nineveh's fall. In surveying his devastated empire, he would realize that his leaders (shepherds and nobles) were dead (spoken of as if they were sheep; cf. Pss. 13:3; 76:6; Dan. 12:2) and that people who were not taken as captives were scattered, never again to be gathered. This empire that for centuries had been invincible would be totally disintegrated.

3:19. The devastation of the burned and looted city of Nineveh would look like a wound (cf. Isa. 1:6-7). So fatal and final was her fall that she would never be rebuilt. Archeology has confirmed this fact. Peoples who had been oppressed by the brutally atrocious Ninevites would now rejoice in her demise. Judah especially would be greatly comforted by the fact that Nineveh's fall would mean the end (cf. Nahum 1:8-9) of the seemingly endless cruelty that had lasted for centuries. In this way the Lord would pour out His wrath (cf. 1:2-3, 6) on Nineveh and demonstrate His care for those who trust in Him (1:7). Readers today know from the Book of Nahum that God's wrath will eventually fall on inveterate sinners, and can be comforted by knowing that those who turn to Him are safe.

# BIBLIOGRAPHY

Bennett, T. Miles. *The Books of Nahum and Zephaniah*. Grand Rapids: Baker Book House, 1968.

Feinberg, Charles L. *The Minor Prophets*. Chicago: Moody Press, 1976.

Freeman, Hobart E. *Nahum, Zephaniah, Habakkuk: Minor Prophets of the Seventh Century B.C.* Chicago: Moody Press, 1973.

Keil, C.F. "Nahum." In *Commentary on the Old Testament in Ten Volumes*. Vol. 10. Reprint (25 vols. in 10). Grand Rapids: Wm. B. Eerdmans Publishing Co., 1982.

Kohlenberger, John R., III. *Jonah-Nahum*. Everyman's Bible Commentary. Chicago: Moody Press, 1984.

Laetsch, Theo. *The Minor Prophets*. St. Louis: Concordia Publishing House, 1956.

Maier, Walter A. *The Book of Nahum: A Commentary*. St. Louis: Concordia Publishing House, 1959. Reprint. Grand Rapids: Baker Book House, 1980.

Tatford, Frederick A. *The Minor Prophets*. Vol. 2. Reprint (3 vols.). Minneapolis: Klock & Klock Christian Publishers, 1982.

Watts, John D.W. *The Books of Joel, Obadiah, Jonah, Nahum, Habakkuk, and Zephaniah*. New York: Cambridge University Press, 1975.

# HABAKKUK

## J. Ronald Blue

## INTRODUCTION

Planet Earth may look marvelous from a satellite, but for those who live on the dusty globe things tend to look rather grim. Increased turmoil, rising terrorism, mounting tragedies, unprecedented trauma, increasing pollution, deepening trials, and unparalleled tensions cast dark shadows over earthlings. The world looks more and more like some ominous black sphere with a very short fuse, a time bomb sizzling to explode.

It is little wonder thinking people begin to ask questions. Why is there so much oppression? Why all the injustice? Why do evil men prosper? Why do the righteous suffer? Why doesn't God do something? Why doesn't God clean up this mess? Why? Why? Why?

These penetrating questions are hardly new. Centuries before Christ visited this planet, an ancient prophet looked around at the violence and wickedness of the world and cried out to God, "Why do You make me look at injustice? Why do You tolerate wrong? . . . Why are You silent while the wicked swallow up those more righteous than themselves?" (Hab. 1:3, 13) The prophet not only asked the mysterious whys that plague mankind; he also received answers to his questions. The answers given by the Creator of the universe are carefully recorded in the little book called Habakkuk.

Habakkuk is a unique book. Unlike other prophets who declared God's message to people this prophet dialogued with God about people. Most Old Testament prophets proclaimed divine judgment. Habakkuk pleaded for divine judgment. In contrast with the typical indictment, this little book records an intriguing interchange between a perplexed prophet and his Maker.

This is not merely a little on-the-street interview with God, however. Habakkuk went beyond that. The *dialogue*

developed in chapter 1. The prophet's complaints were then met with the Lord's command, "Write down the revelation," in chapter 2. God's declaration included a lengthy *dirge*, or taunt-song, of five woes on the evil Babylonians. Chapter 3 climaxes with a magnificent *doxology* of praise. The ever-present "Why?" is best answered by the everlasting "Who!" Though the outlook may elicit terror, the uplook elicits trust. The prophet's complaints and fears were resolved in confidence and faith. This is the heart of the message of Habakkuk: "The righteous will live by his faith" (2:4).

**The Author.** Little is known of Habakkuk the prophet. The book simply records his name and his profession. His name has meaning, and conjecture about that meaning runs free. Most scholars trace the name "Habakkuk" to the Hebrew verb *ḥābaq*, "to fold one's hands or to embrace." But is it to be considered active or passive? Is he an "embracer" or the "embraced"? Luther took it in the active sense and saw Habakkuk as one who embraced his people to comfort and uphold them. Jerome saw Habakkuk as one who embraced the problem of divine justice in a wicked world. Others prefer the passive sense and picture Habakkuk as one embraced by God as His child and messenger. More recently the word *ḥambaququ* has been found in Akkadian literature in texts from Mesopotamia which indicate it was the name of a garden plant. So some scholars contend that the prophet's name shows the influence of Assyria and Babylonia on the Israelites, or that Habakkuk was of a mixed Israelite and Assyrian marriage.

Whatever the meaning of his name, Habakkuk was a prophet. In the title of other prophetic books various items of information are given: the name of the prophet's father (Isa. 1:1), the names of the kings contemporary with the prophet

# Habakkuk

(Hosea 1:1), the prophet's hometown (Amos 1:1). But only three times is the writer designated as a "prophet" in the title of his book: Habakkuk, Haggai, and Zechariah. Habakkuk, therefore, is the only *preexilic* prophet to be so designated.

Though Habakkuk is specifically called a prophet, his book resembles the literary style of the Psalms and the Wisdom books. The concluding note in his book, "For the director of music. On my stringed instruments" (Hab. 3:19), suggests that Habakkuk may have been a musician of the Levitical office. In the apocryphal book, Bel and the Dragon, Habakkuk is described as the son of Jeshua, of the tribe of Levi, in a legend of fantasy in which the prophet supposedly was commanded by an angel to take a meal to Daniel, who had been cast a second time into a lions' den. When Habakkuk complained that he did not know the location of the lions' den, the angel allegedly transported the prophet by a lock of his hair on the appointed journey.

It has been suggested by Rabbinic tradition that Habakkuk was the son of the Shunammite woman mentioned in 2 Kings 4, whom Elisha restored to life. This is apparently based solely on the meaning of Habakkuk's name, "embrace," and Elisha's words to the Shunammite, "You shall embrace a son" (2 Kings 4:16, NASB).

All conjecture and speculation aside it is safe, and perhaps sufficient, to say that Habakkuk was an officially ordained prophet who took part in temple liturgical singing. He was well educated, deeply sensitive, and in his literary style was as much a poet as he was a prophet. Above all, he was God's choice servant who penned one of the most penetrating books of the Old Testament.

**The Date.** It is generally accepted that the reference to the Babylonians (Hab. 1:6) places the book within the seventh century B.C. More precise dating of the prophecy has provoked controversy. The dates proposed fall into three time periods: the reign of Manasseh (697–642), the reign of Josiah (640–609), and the reign of Jehoiakim (609–598).

Those who date Habakkuk's prophecy in the reign of Manasseh say that the statement of 1:5, "I am going to do something in your days that you would not

believe, even if you were told," indicates a time before Babylon's rise as a world power. The date, then, would have to be before the battle of Carchemish in 605 B.C., when Nebuchadnezzar defeated Pharaoh Neco II of Egypt and Babylon rose to become a formidable nation making its bid for world power, and most likely before 612 B.C., when Babylon overthrew Nineveh. However, if the fulfillment of Habakkuk's prophecy (v. 5) is the fall of Jerusalem at the hands of the Babylonians in 586 B.C., the book definitely was not written early in the reign of Manasseh. The prophecy is said to be fulfilled "in your days" (v. 5) and those who heard the prophecy in Manasseh's early days would probably have died before its fulfillment.

A date in the latter years of Manasseh's reign or during the reign of Josiah might fit, but Habakkuk's complaint (vv. 2-4) points to a period in the history of Judah when lawlessness and violence were rampant. The reforms in the latter part of Manasseh's reign (2 Chron. 33:15-16) and the extensive reforms of Josiah (2 Chron. 34) do not fit Habakkuk's dire description.

It seems far better to understand the disbelief referred to in Habakkuk 1:5 as a reaction to God's use of such a sinful nation to judge Israel rather than the surprise that a nation as yet unrecognized would emerge in power. That the Babylonians had already attained renown for their power seems evident from the description recorded by Habakkuk in verses 7-11. Thus the most likely date falls between 606 and 604 B.C., sometime around Babylon's victory at the battle of Carchemish (605).

**The Setting.** Habakkuk wrote in a time of international crisis and national corruption. Babylonia had just emerged as a world power. When the Babylonians rebelled against Assyria, Judah found a brief period of relief reflected in the reforms initiated by Josiah. The Assyrians were forced to devote their energies to stop the Babylonian rebellion. The Babylonians finally crushed the Assyrian Empire and quickly proceeded to defeat the once-powerful Egyptians. A new world empire was stretching across the world. Soon the Babylonians would overtake Judah and carry its inhabitants away into captivity. On the eve of pending destruction, a period of uncertainty and fear, Habakkuk wrote his message.

The crisis internationally was serious. But of even greater concern was the national corruption. Great unrest stirred within Judah. Josiah had been a good king. When he died, Josiah's son Jehoahaz rose to the throne. In only three months, the king of Egypt invaded Judah, deposed Jehoahaz, and placed his brother Jehoiakim on the throne. Jehoiakim was evil, ungodly, and rebellious (2 Kings 23:36–24:7; 2 Chron. 36:5-8). Shortly after Jehoiakim ascended to power, Habakkuk wrote his lament over the decay, violence, greed, fighting, and perverted justice that surrounded him.

No wonder Habakkuk looked at all the corruption and asked, "Why doesn't God do something?" Godly men and women continue to ask similar "whys" in a world of increasing international crises and internal corruption. Nation rises up against nation around the world and sin abounds at home. World powers aim an ever-increasing array of complex nuclear weapons at each other while they talk of peace. World War III seems incredibly imminent.

While the stage is set for a global holocaust, an unsuspecting home audience fiddles a happy tune. The nation's moral fiber is being eaten away by a playboy philosophy that makes personal pleasure the supreme rule of life. Hedonism catches fire while homes crumble. Crime soars while the church sours. Drugs, divorce, and debauchery prevail and decency dies. Frivolity dances in the streets. Faith is buried. "In God We Trust" has become a meaningless slogan stamped on corroding coins.

In such a world of crisis and chaos, Habakkuk speaks with clarity. This little book is as contemporary as the morning newspaper.

**The Message.** In the dark days of Jehoiakim's reign just before the Babylonian Captivity, the Prophet Habakkuk penned an unusual message of hope and encouragement for God's people. Though doubts and confusion reign when sin runs rampant, an encounter with God can turn those doubts into devotion and all confusion into confidence.

Habakkuk's book begins with an interrogation of God but ends as an intercession to God. Worry is transformed into worship. Fear turns to faith. Terror becomes trust. Hang-ups are resolved with hope. Anguish melts into adoration.

What begins with a question mark ends in an exclamation point. The answer to Habakkuk's "Why?" is "Who!" His confusion, "Why all the conflict?" is resolved with his comprehension of who is in control: God!

# OUTLINE

B. God's presence of majesty
   (3:3-15)
   1. God's arrival (3:3a)
   2. God's appearance (3:3b-7)
   3. God's actions (3:8-15)
C. Habakkuk's peace in ministry
   (3:16-19)

# COMMENTARY

## I. A Dialogue with God: Habakkuk Previewed God's Discipline of Judah (chap. 1)

The prophet was perplexed. Wickedness and violence seemed to go unchecked. Would there be no end to the rising tide of sin? Habakkuk took his complaint to God. "Why don't You do something?" God answered, "I am doing something. Judah will be punished by Babylon." Then the prophet was *more* perplexed. Habakkuk's distress deepened to a profound dilemma. So he continued his conversation with God. "Why would You use those wretched Babylonian barbarians to judge Judah?"

### A. Habakkuk's distress (1:1-4)

1. WHY IS GOD INDIFFERENT TO
   SUPPLICATION? (1:1-2)

**1:1.** Little wonder the book was titled **The oracle that Habakkuk the prophet received.** The prophet called his writing a *maśśā'*, a "burden." This Hebrew noun is derived from a verb meaning "to lift up," and consequently signifies "what is lifted up," and thus "a burden." The message Habakkuk presented is indeed a weighty one. However, *maśśā'* was not always used to preface a burdensome message. It was used, for example, as a title for the rather nonthreatening sayings recorded in Proverbs 30 and 31 (where the NIV renders *maśśā'* "oracle" in 30:1; 31:1). Nonetheless, if there ever was a heavy message, Habakkuk had one.

The title here might be more literally translated, "The burden that Habakkuk the prophet saw." The same two Hebrew words, "burden" and "saw," are used in Isaiah 13:1. The word "saw" (*ḥāzâh*), when used of the prophets, often means to see in a vision (cf. Isa. 1:1; 2:1; Ezek. 12:27; Amos 1:1; Micah 1:1). Receiving glimpses from God into the future (i.e., "visions," *ḥāzôn*) the prophets were

sometimes called God's "seers" (*ḥōzeh*).

**1:2.** The prophet's long-standing concern which finally erupted into a volcanic complaint was twofold. First, he wanted to know why God seemed so indifferent: Why doesn't God hear? Second, he wanted to know why God seemed so insensitive: Why doesn't God **help?**

Habakkuk's words **How long** show his agony over God's seeming delay in responding to the prophet's concerns. Many Christians today sense the same problem. They wonder why God seems silent when they pray. Like several psalmists (David, Pss. 13:1-4; 22:1, 11, 19-20; Asaph, Ps. 74:1-2, 10-11; the sons of Korah, Ps. 88), Habakkuk went to God to complain about his troubles and the troubles of his people. He described the injustice that was rampant around him and then asked "How long?" (Hab. 1:2) and "Why?" (v. 3) Later he used these same words again: "Why?" (twice in v. 13) and "How long?" (2:6)

This prophet sounded more like a singer than a seer. Part of Israel's worship involved making impassioned pleas to God for help in times of desperate trouble. Israel did not normally complain about its troubles in "letters to the editor." They took their pleas directly to God in worship.

Habakkuk's concern was not only that his cries went unheeded but that the corruption continued unchecked. He cried out to God, **Violence!** but God seemed to do nothing. The stark word "violence" sums up all the chaos Habakkuk witnessed around him. The word is sprinkled throughout the book (1:2-3, 9; 2:17) like inkblots on a crumpled page in history.

2. WHY IS GOD INSENSITIVE TO SIN AND
   SUFFERING? (1:3-4)

**1:3.** Sin was abounding and God seemed both indifferent and idle. Habakkuk put the blame on God with his penetrating question, **Why do You make me look at injustice?** Then he asked an even greater question: **Why do You tolerate wrong?** God caused Habakkuk to witness injustice (lit., "iniquity"), but He Himself also tolerated (lit., "beholds"), the very same wrong. It is bad enough that a weak *sinner* should have to behold wickedness. But to have a righteous *God* see the evil and do nothing about it seemed beyond comprehension (cf. v. 13).

The picture was bleak indeed. **Destruction and violence** were coupled with **strife and conflict** (cf. "violence" in vv. 2, 9; 2:17). "Destruction" (*šōḏ*, "violent treatment causing desolation") and "violence" (*ḥāmās*, "malicious conduct intended to injure another") frequently appear together (e.g., Jer. 6:7; 20:8; Ezek. 45:9, "violence and oppression"; Amos 3:10, "plunder and loot"; in each case here the two words in Heb. are in the reverse order from their order in Hab. 1:3). Habakkuk described the scene well.

**1:4.** The greatest tragedy, however, was the people's neglect of God's Law. Habakkuk described the consequence: **Therefore the Law is paralyzed** (lit., "becomes cool, numbed"). The divine Law appeared to have suffered a knockout; also civic **justice,** Habakkuk said, **never prevails,** or never came forth to fight (cf. "injustice," v. 3). It appears that wickedness was the uncontested victor. **The wicked hem in the righteous.** The righteous were locked up and the wicked vigilantes had thrown away the key. Therefore **justice** was **perverted** (from *'āqal*, "to bend or twist out of shape," a word used only here in the OT). With wicked men in power, justice was twisted and turned till it came out injustice! The situation in Habakkuk's day was perilous.

## B. God's disclosure (1:5-11)

Though the prophet was engaged in a typical Jewish lament and was asking essentially rhetorical questions, God answered his complaint. The Lord was neither indifferent nor insensitive. God was not idle; He was already at work on specific plans to discipline erring Judah. He revealed those plans to the distressed prophet.

1. GOD'S INTENTION OF DISCIPLINE (1:5)

**1:5. Look at the nations and watch** was God's reply. The change in speakers is apparent from the verbs "look" and "watch," which in Hebrew include the plural "you." God addressed both the prophet and the people. Habakkuk had complained about being made to look at injustice. But the prophet and people suffered from myopia. They were too nearsighted. God instructed them to get their eyes off the immediate havoc and look

out on the international horizons. They needed to develop a world view that included "the nations." As they did so, they would **be utterly amazed.** The political developments about to be revealed to Habakkuk and the people would stun them (the verb *tāmâh* means "to be astounded, bewildered, or dumbfounded"). In fact Habakkuk *was* dumbfounded (vv. 12, 17). What God was about to perform would be hard for them to **believe, even** though God would reveal it to them.

2. GOD'S INSTRUMENT OF DISCIPLINE (1:6-11)

Judah's sin would not go unchecked. Justice was not dead, nor did it sleep. Discipline was forthcoming; correction was on the way. But the surprise was not the anticipated discipline but the dispenser of that discipline. It was not coming correction that was unbelievable but the channel of correction that seemed so incredible.

### a. Destruction by the Babylonians (1:6)

**1:6.** God dropped a bombshell: **I am raising up the Babylonians.** Granted, sin had abounded all too long in Judah. But the sinners of Judah were but soiled saints next to the barbaric Babylonians. Babylon was a nation known for its violent impulses. Its people readily committed atrocities without forethought or remorse. The historical records present the Babylonians as a fierce and pitilessly cruel people. And God affirmed it to Habakkuk by calling them **that ruthless** (*mar,* "bitter," i.e., bitter in temper, or fierce) **and impetuous** (lit., "swift") **people.** Ezekiel too called Babylon a ruthless nation (though he used the Heb. word *'ārîṣ,* meaning "terror-striking," Ezek. 28:7; 30:11; 31:12; 32:12). Furthermore, their conduct matched their character. They swept **across the whole earth** to plunder and possess. No doubt "the whole earth" meant much of the then-known world, for Babylon did conquer many of the nations including Assyria, Judah, Egypt, and Edom. Judah was just a speck of loose dust before this gigantic vacuum cleaner.

### b. Description of the Babylonians (1:7-11)

The Babylonians, also known as Chaldeans, lived in southern Mesopotamia and were called "an ancient . . . nation" (Jer. 5:15), a primeval people. Abram, of course, migrated from Ur of the Chaldees to Canaan. God had called a people out of this increasingly savage populace. Now this nation had burst out of the Tigris-Euphrates Valley and like some awesome lava flow it spilled across the world. Its quiet little cousin, Judah, would soon lie in its wake.

(1) Their status. **1:7.** Babylon apparently was without rival. This terrible and dreadful people were **a law to themselves. They** promoted **their own honor,** that is, they lifted themselves up. They recognized no law or judge but themselves and their superiority and authority was gained by their own ruthless conquests.

(2) Their speed. **1:8.** In vivid and awesome imagery, the Lord further described the foe as a people with **horses . . . swifter than leopards, fiercer than wolves at dusk.** Both leopards and wolves are fierce, fast, and excellent hunters. At dusk, wolves are hungry and ready to pounce on prey. The Babylonians' voracious speed in conquest was also likened to **a vulture swooping to devour.** This "vulture" (*nešer*) may have been the great griffon vulture, a majestic bird often seen in Palestine circling higher and higher and then rapidly swooping down on its prey. Jeremiah wrote about the Babylonians devouring everything in their path, including fields, people, animals, trees, and cities (Jer. 5:17; also cf. Lam. 4:19). Certainly the Babylonians, likened to ferocious beasts and birds, were a terrible enemy.

(3) Their success. **1:9.** There was no hope of stopping the Babylonians. Collectively **they all** came **bent on violence.** The nation's entire military force would be engaged in the invasion and would be irresistibly victorious. The second line in this verse, **their hordes advance like a desert wind,** consists of three words in Hebrew and is variously interpreted. The first word in the clause occurs nowhere else and is variously rendered "resisting," "striving," "eagerness," "assembling," and a "gathering host," "troops," or "horde." The last Hebrew word "desert wind" is also the word for the East. Here it means a wind that comes from the East. Such fierce scorching winds moving across the desert from the East often devastated vegetation (cf. Jer.

18:17; Ezek. 17:10; 19:12; Jonah 4:8). The enemy was coming like a whirlwind and would **gather prisoners like sand,** a figure expressing numbers too vast to calculate.

(4) Their scoffing. **1:10.** Confident in their strength, the Babylonians scoffed at **kings** and ridiculed **rulers.** It was their custom to exhibit captive rulers as public spectacles. Their brutality is seen in the way they treated Zedekiah after Jerusalem fell. They killed his sons before his eyes and then, with that awesome sight burned into his memory, they put out his eyes, bound him in shackles, and took him prisoner to Babylon (2 Kings 25:7).

But not only did the Babylonians scoff at their foes; **they** also laughed **at all fortified cities** (lit., "every fortress"). They poured derision on the strongholds which their victims considered impregnable. **They** simply built **earthen ramps** (lit., "heaped up earth") against the walls of cities built on mounds, and raced up those ramps, attacked the cities easily, and seized the fortified strongholds. This practice was fairly common in ancient warfare, but the "siege ramp" (2 Kings 19:32; cf. Ezek. 4:2) was more developed by the Babylonians.

(5) Their sacrilege. **1:11.** The first part of this verse is difficult to translate. The KJV has, "Then shall his mind (*rûaḥ*, 'spirit' or 'wind') change, and he shall pass over." That is, the Babylonians changed their minds and went beyond all restraint to their own destruction. However, it is unlikely that *rûaḥ* is the subject; the verb "change" can better be translated in its normal sense "to pass through." The NIV has a more likely rendering, **Then they sweep past like the wind** (cf. "desert wind," v. 9). Their major offense was clearly recorded. They considered their **own strength** as **their god.** They treated their might as their master. For them, "might was right" became "might was divine." It is little wonder that God declared them **guilty** for such sacrilege.

## C. Habakkuk's dilemma (1:12-17)

God's amazing disclosure left the prophet even more perplexed and bewildered. Habakkuk's complaint about the sin and lawlessness in Judah (vv. 2-4) was met by God's response that He was not ignorant of His people's conduct. Judgment was on its way. The Babylonians would soon take these erring people captive. The prophet was astonished, just as God said he would be (v. 5). He was appalled that Yahweh would employ so evil an instrument to punish Judah. Habakkuk expressed his deep concern; he questioned God's plan.

1. WHY WOULD GOD EMPLOY A PEOPLE OF INIQUITY? (1:12-13)

However devastating the divine judgment may sound, the prophet drew consolation and hope from God's holiness and faithfulness. In a sea of confusion, Habakkuk clung to the life buoy of God's holy character. In a chaotic storm, the prophet grasped the rock of his steadfast Lord.

**1:12.** In Hebrew, the form of the question—**O LORD, are You not from everlasting?**—requires an affirmative reply. It is as much a declaration as an interrogation. The prophet's confidence in the living, eternal God, Yahweh, contrasts starkly with the previous verse in which the Babylonians considered their own strength to be their god.

Humanly speaking, of course, Babylon could very easily extinguish the people of Judah. But the prophet found utterly unthinkable the extinction of God's people and thereby the destruction of their covenant relationship with Yahweh. Habakkuk based his conclusion on two truths: (a) the immutable and everlasting Lord (cf. 3:6) who will not break His covenant with Israel, and (b) the holy (cf. 3:3) and righteous God who will not allow sin to go unpunished in Israel or in her foes. The prophet rightly concluded, **My God, my Holy One, we will not die.**

Habakkuk reminded himself that the LORD had **appointed** the Babylonians **to execute judgment** (i.e., discipline), not total destruction on Judah. The enemy was God's instrument **to punish,** not to demolish. The prophet referred to his Lord as the **Rock** (*ṣûr*), a term first applied to Yahweh in Deuteronomy 32:4 to indicate the Almighty's stability and security (cf. Deut. 32:15, 18, 30-31).

**1:13.** A burning question remained in Habakkuk's heart. Why would the everlastingly preeminent Yahweh, the absolutely Holy One, the immutably permanent Rock, utilize so wicked a people to administer discipline on Judah? **Your eyes are too pure to look on evil,** complained the prophet. **You cannot tolerate wrong.** In his first address Habakkuk questioned why he was forced to look on injustice and why God seemed to be less contentious and more comprehensive than the thought he expressed in verses 2-4. His focus seemed to be shifting from the sin problems to the sovereign Person in control.

In light of Yahweh's character, however, it seemed fair to Habakkuk to ask, **Why** (cf. v. 3) **do You tolerate the treacherous? Why** would God allow such a **wicked** nation to devour **those** who were **more righteous?** That seemed like a perversion of justice. Sinful though Judah had been, her wickedness was dwarfed by the atrocities committed by the Babylonians. Habakkuk was in a dilemma. Certainly his concern over God's seeming silence has concerned many of God's people (cf. Job 19:7).

2. WHY WOULD GOD ENDORSE A PEOPLE OF INJUSTICE? (1:14-15)

**1:14.** Habakkuk said that God **made men like fish in the sea, like sea creatures that have no ruler.** Helpless as fish, Judah's people were easy prey for powerful invaders. So helpless were they that they lacked the ability to organize themselves for self-protection. They were like sea creatures that are on their own, with no leader to guide them.

**1:15. The wicked** (cf. v. 13) Babylonians were pictured catching unsuspecting men, like fish, **with hooks,** sweeping them into a **net,** and gathering them in a large seine or **dragnet** (cf. v. 16). The imagery is vivid. Jeremiah used a similar analogy of fishermen, coupling it with that of hunters (Jer. 16:16). The evil Babylonians had as little regard for the welfare of humanity as fishermen have for unprotesting fish. The victorious Babylon foe rejoiced and was **glad.** It was hard to understand why God would permit such blatant injustice. Habakkuk was in a dilemma.

3. WHY WOULD GOD EXCUSE A PEOPLE OF IDOLATRY? (1:16-17)

**1:16.** The hooks and nets brought **food** and plenty to the Babylonians. Their conquests provided not only a livelihood but also **luxury.** So these barbaric people paid homage to the instruments that contributed to their prosperity. The enemy sacrificed to their nets and burned **incense to** their dragnets. (This word for **dragnet** occurs in the OT only here and in v. 15). The metaphor is potent. The Babylonians worshiped the means that brought them military success. Already God had declared that the Babylonians saw their might as their god (v. 11). Now Habakkuk added that their military power brought monetary profit.

Idolatry is not limited to those who bring sacrifices or burn incense to inanimate objects. People of position, power, or prosperity often pay homage to the business or agency that provided them their coveted status. It becomes their constant obsession, even their "god."

**1:17.** The prophet asked the fat fisherman Babylon if **he** was **to keep on emptying his net, destroying nations** (cf. 2:8, 17) **without mercy?** The action depicted signified a seemingly perpetual operation. They emptied their net so they could fill it again, again, and again. When would God put a stop to the Babylonians' greed for conquest? How could He let a people continue in power when they so openly worshiped that very power as their god? Habakkuk was confused.

## II. A Dirge from God: Habakkuk Pronounced God's Destruction of Babylon (chap. 2)

The prophet's dilemma deepened. Why should God use an ungodly nation such as Babylon as the instrument of judgment on His own people Judah? Habakkuk had boldly lodged his contentions and now he waited for God's reply. Surely some logical explanation would be given.

### A. Habakkuk's anticipation: "Watch" (2:1)

**2:1.** Like a sentinel standing in a watchtower to detect the first signs of an approaching enemy, Habakkuk stationed himself **on the ramparts . . . to see what** God would **say to** him. He had made his complaint and now he resolved to position himself so he might obtain the earliest and clearest information and then, like a watchman, inform his waiting brethren. It is likely that the **watch** (*mišmeret*, "observation station") and the ramparts (*māṣôr*, "watchtower or fortress") refer to the prophet's attitude of expectation rather than his physical location. This vivid imagery was common in Habakkuk's society (2 Sam. 18:24; Isa. 21:6). The prophet or seer, like a lookout, waited to *see* more than *hear* what God would say.

The prophet was also concerned about what He would reply **to this complaint.**

Probably Habakkuk referred to his own complaint lodged in his dialogue with God (Hab. 1:2-4, 12-17). Some translators, however, say that the "complaint" (*tôkaḥat*, "correction, rebuke, or argument") was *against* the prophet rather than *by* the prophet. Thus they render the phrase, "what to answer when I am rebuked" (NIV marg.). Whether or not Habakkuk anticipated reproof in God's response one thing is certain: the prophet anxiously anticipated God's answer.

### B. God's admonition: "Write" (2:2-5)

True to his profession, Habakkuk was a spokesman for God's revelation. He waited for God's message, not simply for his own satisfaction. He was ready to carry God's message to his people. Habakkuk waited; God spoke.

1. GOD'S CLEAR REVELATION (2:2)

**2:2.** God does not mumble. He speaks with clarity and forthrightness. He told Habakkuk, **Write down the revelation and make it plain on tablets.** The revelation (lit., "vision") was to be recorded on tablets of baked clay so God's Word would be preserved and, even more important, publicized—**so that a herald** could **run with it.** This phrase has been mistaken by some to signify that the messenger should be able to read the tablet on the run. On the contrary, the point is that the messenger would read it and then run to spread the news to others.

2. GOD'S CERTAIN REVELATION (2:3)

**2:3.** Every prophetic revelation demands a certain degree of patience. One must **wait for** its fulfillment. God's words to Habakkuk were reassuring: **the revelation awaits an appointed time.** The prophecy pointed toward a future goal (lit., "it pants toward the end," like a runner toward the finish line). Reference to **the end** seems to signify not only the coming destruction of evil Babylonia but the broader fulfillment of the messianic judgment in the fall of "Babylon the Great" at the close of the Tribulation (Rev. 17–18).

One thing is certain: God's revelation **will not prove false. Though** the fulfillment seems delayed, **it will . . . come** to pass in accord with His perfect plan. For those in Judah about to experience the awesome Babylonian invasion and Captivity, this assurance of fulfillment should have been a great comfort. Their barbaric captors would themselves in God's due time suffer divine judgment!

The writer of Hebrews referred to this verse in his appeal for persecuted believers to persevere (Heb. 10:37). In his quote, he stressed the messianic significance of this passage in Habakkuk. The day is coming when the King of kings will reign on earth with perfect justice.

3. GOD'S CONDEMNATORY REVELATION (2:4-5)

**2:4.** As an introduction to the woeful taunt-songs Habakkuk was instructed to record, God gave His summary condemnation of the conceited character of the Babylonian: **He is puffed up.** Like a bloated toad, these arrogant people hopped along toward destruction. They were swollen (the Heb. verb *'āpal* is used only here in the OT) with evil passions. Their **desires** were **not upright.**

Yahweh then declared that a **righteous** person, by stark contrast, **will live by his faith** (*ĕmûnâh*, "steadfastness or faithfulness"). A righteous Israelite who remained loyal to God's moral precepts and was humble before the Lord enjoyed God's abundant life. To "live" meant to experience God's blessing by enjoying a life of security, protection, and fullness. Conversely, an apparently victorious but proud and perverse Babylonian would die. Faithfulness (NIV marg.) and faith are related. One who trusts in the Lord is one who relies on Him and is faithful to Him.

The key clause "the righteous will live by his faith" sparkles like a diamond in a pile of soot. In the midst of God's unrelenting condemnations of Babylon stands a bright revelation of God's favor that is quoted three times in the New Testament (Rom. 1:17; Gal. 3:11; Heb. 10:38). In those passages the words "will

live" have a broader meaning than in Habakkuk. In the New Testament they mean to enjoy salvation and eternal life. In contrast with the self-reliant, boastful ways of the unrighteous, the righteous are found to be reliant on God and faithful to Him.

**2:5.** The general description of the Babylonians' wickedness is made more specific. They were betrayed by **wine.** (They also used wine to betray others, v. 15.) The Babylonians were said to be very addicted to wine. For example, Babylon was conquered while Belshazzar and his leaders were feasting at a riotous banquet (Dan. 5). The treachery of wine is described in Proverbs 23:31-32. It looks so inviting in the glass but "in the end it bites like a snake and poisons like a viper."

As God continued His condemnation, He said the typical Babylonian **is arrogant** (*yāhîr,* "haughty," occurs only here and in Prov. 21:24) **and never at rest.** These proud, restless people were **as greedy as the grave.** Just as **death** and the grave are not **satisfied** till all come into their grasp, so the Babylonians sought to take **captive all the peoples** (cf. Hab. 1:17). Like some hideous monster, the grave devours the nations. Likewise, Babylon opened wide her insatiable jaws to devour all peoples. But this evil nation would not continue unpunished. God's judgment would fall!

*C. Habakkuk's annotation: "Woe" (2:6-20)*

The destruction of Babylon intimated in God's comments to Habakkuk was announced in fuller detail in a song of woe in five stanzas of three verses each ("woe" occurs in vv. 6, 9, 12, 15, 19). All those nations conquered and plundered by the Babylonians would in due time witness the fall of their conqueror and join in a song of derision and denunciation. Habakkuk recorded a satirical outburst or taunt-song. The NIV's rendering, "Will not all of them taunt him?" (v. 6a) is literally, "Will not all of them take up against him a taunt-song?" The song (*māšāl*) is any form of poetical composition in which parallelism is the principle of construction. It may denote a parable, proverb, ode, or a dirge such as the doleful lamentation recorded here. Five woes follow.

## 1. WOE FOR INTIMIDATION (2:6-8)

**2:6. Woe** is an interjection of distress pronounced in the face of disaster or in view of coming judgment (e.g., Isa. 3:11; 5:11; 10:5) because of certain sins. "Woe" was used frequently by the prophets (22 times by Isaiah, 10 times in Jer. and Lam., 7 times by Ezekiel, and 14 times in the Minor Prophets). The first woe compares the Babylonians to an unscrupulous pawnbroker who lends on extortionate terms. As spoil for their own gain they had been merciless in heaping up the wealth of the nations. It was, of course, sheer theft. The valuables taken were not the property of the invaders. **How long must this go on?** How long would these evil aggressors be permitted to retain their ill-gained plunder? (Cf. Habakkuk's "How long?" about Judah's violence, Hab. 1:2.)

**2:7.** The question in verse 6 was answered by two other questions. **Will not your debtors suddenly arise?** The victimized nations would suddenly arise in revolt. The debtors (lit., "biters") would unexpectedly strike back. They would not only get their bite of the stolen goods but also give their aggressors a good shakedown. **Will they not wake up and make you tremble?** That shake would not be a handshake. With hurricane force the evil creditor would be shaken as a violent wind shakes the leaves and branches off a tree. Babylon would **become their victim,** the victim of the very nations she had victimized. Babylon who had attacked (cf. 1:6, 8-10) and extorted (1:6, 16) would now herself be attacked and extorted.

**2:8.** The spoiler would be spoiled, for the **plundered** would suddenly rise to **plunder.** The **nations** subdued by Babylon but not destroyed, **the peoples who are left,** would lead the encounter. The boomerang would spin back. Babylon's intimidation and inhumanity would recoil on their own heads. They would reap what they had sown (Prov. 22:8; Gal. 6:7). They had ruthlessly **shed man's blood** and had recklessly ravaged (cf. Hab. 1:17; 2:17) both **lands and cities** (lit., "land and city," in the collective sense). "Blood" is literally "bloods." "Bloodshed" in verse 12 and "blood" in verse 17 are also "bloods" (pl.). Now Babylon would suffer the penalty for her crimes (cf. 1:12).

## 2. WOE FOR INTEMPERANCE (2:9-11)

**2:9.** Not only were the Babylonians guilty of **unjust gain** (vv. 6-8), but they also used that plunder for self-aggrandizement. They sought their own exaltation. Like an eagle setting **his nest** inaccessible to all predators by building it **high** on a mountainside, the Babylonians sought to make their empire free from harm (**to escape the clutches of ruin**). From the low-lying valley of their homeland, these conquerors used their illegal gain to build a towering world empire.

**2:10.** To elevate themselves, the Babylonians trampled others down. Their building plans included **the ruin** (lit., "cutting off") **of many peoples** (cf. "nations" in 1:17; "nations" and "peoples" in 2:5; and "many nations" in v. 8). But their plan to destroy others in order to make themselves secure failed. A **house** built of tortured bodies and stark skeletons is not too habitable. In the fray to erect a monument, they constructed their own shameful (cf. "shame" in v. 16) mausoleum. Death became their due.

**2:11.** Intriguing witnesses in the trial that would yield the eventual death sentence were **the stones of the wall . . . and the beams of the woodwork.** Even if every single enemy were exterminated, the very stones and lumber would testify against the rapacious and cruel hands of the Babylonians that had fashioned these building materials to show off their empire's strength and glory. The stones and timber with which the houses and palaces were built had been obtained through plunder and injustice.

The exalted nest (v. 9) would be knocked from its lofty perch and the lavish palace would seal the deaths of its builders. The proud, intemperate building plans only served as evidence of God's forthcoming judgment on wicked Babylon.

## 3. WOE FOR INIQUITY (2:12-14)

**2:12.** The plunder mentioned in the first woe (vv. 6-8) and the pride exposed in the second woe (vv. 9-11) were both fed by the sin-sick perversity revealed in the third woe (vv. 12-14). It is as though the stones and timbers of Babylon's vast building projects took up the song here. **Woe to him who builds a city with bloodshed and establishes a town by crime!** The cities of the Babylonian Empire were built by the blood and sweat of enslaved peoples. Murder, bloodshed, oppression, and tyranny were the tools employed in this building project. (The word trans. "bloodshed" is the pl. of the Heb. noun "blood" and always signifies the guilt of murder; cf. the Heb. "bloods" in vv. 8, 17.)

**2:13.** In each of the previous stanzas of this dirge, the sins introduced by the woe exclaimed in the first verse of each stanza were further exposed in the two verses that followed. Here, however, attention is diverted to **the LORD Almighty** and His penetrating assessment of the sordid scene. It is a welcome break in the midst of the five distressing stanzas. The Lord Almighty, the Sovereign of the universe, declared that their ambitious work had been done in vain: **the people's labor is only fuel for the fire** (cf. Jer. 51:58). Their carefully hewn stones would serve as the altar and their ornately carved wood as kindling for the giant sacrificial fire that would leave Babylon in ashes. Habakkuk added **that the nations exhaust themselves for nothing.** All their work—the labor of Babylon or any nation like it—is a waste if it is wrought with bloodshed and crime.

**2:14.** By contrast, **the** entire **earth will** one day **be filled with the knowledge of the glory of the LORD, as the waters cover the sea.** The wearisome toil of a whole generation of boasting Babylonians provided a little fire and ended up as a heap of ashes in one corner of the earth. But God's everlasting glory will fill the entire earth! This verse is based on the declaration in Isaiah 11:9 with only minor alterations. (The earth filled with God's glory is also spoken of in Num. 14:21; Ps. 72:19; and Isa. 6:3.) Isaiah closed his description of the messianic kingdom (Isa. 11:1-9) by stating that the earth would be full of the knowledge of *the Lord.* Habakkuk stated that the earth would be filled with the knowledge of *His glory.* Isaiah dealt with the essence of the kingdom, Habakkuk with the establishment of the kingdom. Isaiah presented the fact, Habakkuk the act. God will overthrow and judge future Babylon (Rev. 17–18) and all ungodly powers (Rev. 19:19) represented by Babylon. The Lord's glory (Matt. 24:30) and majesty (2 Thes. 1:9) will be made evident in the Millennium and thereby acknowledged

throughout the earth.

When the Messiah rules in His kingdom, knowledge of the Lord will be worldwide. Everyone will know of Him (cf. Jer. 31:34). So extensive and abundant will be that knowledge that it will be like water covering the sea. The jagged rocks of injustice and the slimy seaweed of sin will be covered with the smooth surface of God's righteousness.

4. WOE FOR INDIGNITY (2:15-17)

**2:15.** The fourth woe turns back to the sordid scene of the Babylonians' barbaric actions. The focus here is on the inhumanity and the indignity of the conqueror to his subjects. He is pictured as a drunkard giving **his neighbors** wine to intoxicate them so that he may indulge in some evil wantonness and expose his victims to shame. So the Babylonians added lust to their violence and drunkenness. Such action is severely condemned by God (Gen. 9:21-25). An alternate rendering of the phrase **pouring it from the wineskin** is "joining (to it) your wrath." In other words the Babylonians poured out more than wine. With the wine they mixed "wrath," a word related to "heat," signifying any violent passion. This was indeed a "mixed drink." Hate and passion were poured out together. The nations that were enticed, or more often forced, to partake of the Babylonians' poisonous mix fell like drunks and lay prostrate in shame and subjugation.

**2:16.** Those who gloated over the shame of their drunken victims would someday **be filled with shame** (cf. "shaming" in v. 10). Their glory was their shame. This perverted "glory" of the Babylonians contrasted sharply with God's preeminent glory (v. 14). Far from glory, the Babylonians reveled in shame and soon they would **drink,** fall down intoxicated, **and be exposed** as one who is "uncircumcised" (literal Heb.). To be uncircumcised was, to the Jews, to be scorned. The Babylonians had caused others to drink and be shamefully exposed (v. 15); later the tables would be turned (cf. v. 7) and *they* would be drunk and naked.

**The cup** that they must drink was **from the LORD's right hand,** a figure of divine retribution (cf. Isa. 51:17-23; Jer. 25:15-17; Lam. 4:21). On drinking God's judgment, Babylon would be covered with **disgrace.** "Shame" in the first line of Habakkuk 2:16 and "disgrace" in the last line translate similar Hebrew words, but the second of these is in an emphatic form in Hebrew (used only here in the OT). It signifies extreme contempt. The once-glorious Babylon was pictured as a disgraceful, contemptible drunk.

**2:17.** The reason for Babylon's abject shame was her **violence** (cf. 1:9) **done to Lebanon.** Lebanon, a nation north of Israel, was known for its abundance of cedar trees and wild **animals.** It had suffered the ruthless removal of timber for Babylonian buildings and the destructive slaughter of beasts that lived in the forests. The violence done to the forests would weigh on Babylon and its senseless hunting and killing of the fauna would **terrify** it.

The worst charge, however, was that of human bloodshed, already leveled against the Babylonians twice (2:8, 12). They had not only wrecked the forests and ravaged the hillsides, but had also ruined **lands and cities** (cf. v. 8) **and everyone in them.** The indignities on God's creation and His creatures would bring Babylon from apparent world glory to everlasting shame. God's great judgment would **overwhelm** her.

5. WOE FOR IDOLATRY (2:18-20)

**2:18.** The final stanza does not open with the hollow and ominous "Woe!" (That comes in v. 19.) Rather it begins with the penetrating question, **Of what value is an idol?** The answer is obvious. An idol (lit., "graven image," i.e., an idol carved out of wood or hewn from stone) and **an image** (lit., "molten image," i.e., an idol made by melting metal and casting it into a shape of a false god) were of no benefit. Whatever form or seeming beauty those objects may have had, they were still only blocks of wood or masses of metal. To trust in such an idol was to trust in an object **that teaches lies,** for people were deceived and deluded by it, thinking it could help them. But **idols** and images were lifeless. Since they were the worshipers' own creations, idols could not aid them (cf. v. 19). **Carved** or cast, they were dumb objects. The oracles attributed to them were obvious lies, for idols **cannot speak.**

**2:19.** God expressed His condemnation of the insidious sin of idolatry. **Woe**

to him who says to wood, Come to life! Or to lifeless stone, Wake up! How absurd it is to stand before a piece of wood or some cold stone and cry out, "Arise! Awake!" The scene is like the prophets of Baal when they were taunted by Elijah (1 Kings 18:26-29).

No help or **guidance** comes from a lifeless object even if it is encased in **gold and silver** (cf. Isa. 40:19). It has **no breath** or spirit and therefore no life (cf. Gen. 2:7). Isaiah frequently taunted the Babylonians for their trust in numerous false gods, which were nothing but man-made idols (Isa. 41:7; 44:9-20; 45:16, 20; 46:1-2, 6-7; cf. Jer. 10:8-16). Idols are valueless for they cannot talk, come alive, guide, or breathe. And idolatry—worshiping man's carvings rather than the Creator—stands condemned under God's woe.

**2:20.** The last verse of this stanza is unique. In the other four "woe" stanzas each concluding verse starts in the Hebrew with "for" (*kî,* vv. 8, 11, 14, 17). However, verse 20 opens with "but." The contrast is marked and the climax is marvelous: **But the LORD is in His holy temple.** From dumb, man-carved idols, attention shifts to the living Lord, the self-existent, eternal (cf. 1:12; 3:6), holy (cf. 1:12; 3:3) Sovereign who rules the universe from His holy temple, that is, heaven (cf. Pss. 11:4; 18:6, 9; Micah 1:2-3). Instead of shouting, "Arise! Awake," the whole **earth** must stand in **silent** awe and worship **before Him.** The Hebrew word *hāsâh,* rendered "be silent," means "hush" (also used in Zeph. 1:7, "Be silent," and Zech. 2:13, "Be still").

For Habakkuk, the message was clear. Stop complaining! Stop doubting! God is not indifferent to sin. He is not insensitive to suffering. The Lord is neither inactive nor impervious. He is in control. In His perfect time Yahweh will accomplish His divine purpose. Habakkuk was to stand in humble silence, a hushed expectancy of God's intervention. The closing verse of this woeful dirge recorded by Habakkuk serves as a link to the song of worship that follows in Habakkuk 3.

## III. A Doxology to God: Habakkuk Praised God's Design of Creation (chap. 3)

The distressed prophet, who complained over the unchecked sin in his country, was amazed at God's disclosure that He had already prepared an instrument to judge Judah, namely, Babylon. Habakkuk was shocked. He expressed his dilemma tó God and waited for an answer. That answer came in the form of a dirge, or taunt-song, that Habakkuk was instructed to record. Learning of God's just plan to destroy Babylon, Habakkuk bowed in humble adoration. His majestic prayer and hymn of praise followed.

Chapter 3 is the culmination and climax of Habakkuk's book, contrary to the contentions of some scholars who would make this chapter a separate entity that he wrote much later. Others consider this chapter a document written by some other author, a second person also named Habakkuk or a second person who assumed Habakkuk's name.

Despite the arguments about change of style and a separate title, the third chapter fits well in the flow of the book. The new style fits the new subject, just as the shift from the dialogue in chapter 1 to the dirge in chapter 2 indicated a changing emphasis. Furthermore, the title in 3:1 provides a clear break in the change, as "the ramparts" announced the shift at chapter 2.

When the Dead Sea Scrolls Commentary on Habakkuk, which included only chapters 1 and 2, was discovered at Qumran, those who held to the disjointed theory felt they had won their case. But the issue is not so easily conceded. The ancient commentator may well have used only the parts of the book that suited his purpose. This scroll is not proof that a chapter 3 did not exist. It is more reasonable to see the thematic unity of Habakkuk. Chapter 3 is not a postscript; it is a pinnacle of praise. It is the mountaintop destination of a journey that began in a valley of distress.

## A. Habakkuk's prayer for mercy (3:1-2)

**3:1.** At the opening of chapter 2, Habakkuk had positioned himself to await God's reply and to determine how he might respond to the Lord concerning his complaint (2:1). He then recorded God's extensive reply (2:2-20). Now the prophet gave his response to God. It was no protest, however. It was a prayer of praise as indicated by its simple title: **A prayer of Habakkuk the prophet.**

This heading resembles that of several psalms, in which the contents, the author, and the poetical character of the song are indicated (cf., e.g., Pss. 16; 30; 45; 88; 102; 142). Habakkuk again identified himself as a prophet, as he had done at the beginning of his book (Hab. 1:1).

The word *shigionoth* is somewhat obscure. In Hebrew it is the plural of the noun that appears elsewhere only in the title to Psalm 7 where it is in a slightly different form rendered "*shiggaion*" in the NIV. It seems to be related to a verb meaning "to reel to and fro." Thus some see this as an erratic song of enthusiastic irregularity sometimes used in songs of triumph or victory, or an elegy or plaintive song of variant chords. It is unlikely that it refers to the content of the song, even though the Hebrew root verb may also mean "to transgress or err." But the theme is not directed to the transgressions or wanderings of Babylon and Judah; the song centers on the majesty of God. Therefore it is much more reasonable to see *shigionoth* as having a musical-liturgical significance. Another musical notation is found at the end of Habakkuk 3. Possibly this song became a part of the temple worship.

**3:2.** Habakkuk had **heard** God's purposes to discipline Judah and destroy Babylon. The report filled him with **awe.** God's plans were beyond human understanding and God's preeminence beyond comprehension. The reaction to what he "heard" (lit., "Yahweh I have heard the hearing of You") was to fear God (lit., "I am afraid").

The prophet then expressed two petitions. He prayed for a fresh manifestation of God's power (**Renew them,** i.e., **Your deeds**) and a full measure of God's pardon. Both might and **mercy** were requested. These were the only petitions in his entire prayer.

The first request for renewal or revival of God's intervention was twice linked to time: **in our day** and **in our time** (lit., "in the midst of the years" on both occasions). It seems that the prophet desired a prompt fulfillment. God had, of course, already promised it (1:5).

The prophet's second request evolved from the first. In these acts of judgment (**wrath;** cf. 3:8, 12) Habakkuk pleaded for mercy.

After he expressed the two petitions

he wrote what is more appropriately considered a hymn of praise than a prayer (vv. 3-19). In it Habakkuk recalled the awesome deeds the Lord had performed in bringing His people from Egypt through the wilderness and into the Promised Land. Recounting those deeds gave the prophet confidence that God could also deliver His people from Babylon.

## B. God's presence of majesty (3:3-15)

Habakkuk's telephone-like conversation with God in chapter 1 became more like a closed-circuit television hookup in chapter 2. The audio connection (chap. 1) was enhanced by visuals witnessed from Habakkuk's ramparts (2:1). Then suddenly the prophet was ushered into the very presence of the Creator with whom he had spoken so boldly from a distance. The prophet stood face-to-face, so to speak, with the sovereign Lord (cf. Job 42:5).

### 1. GOD'S ARRIVAL (3:3A)

**3:3a.** As God came down to His people at Sinai to establish His covenant with them, so He would come to liberate His people and reaffirm His covenant with them. Habakkuk wrote of God's earlier visitation at Sinai: **God came from Teman, the Holy One** (cf. 1:12) **from Mount Paran.** Moses had said the Lord's appearance was like a light shining "from Seir . . . and from Mount Paran" (Deut. 33:2).

Teman was a desert oasis in Edom but it might also represent the entire region south of the Dead Sea. "Seir," used by Moses, was a poetic name for the mountainous region referred to as Teman. Paran lies west of Edom across the valley Ghor, between the Sinai Peninsula to the south and Kadesh Barnea to the north, another mountainous area.

It may be of some significance that God's appearance to Moses was in the region south of Judah while the Babylonians invaded from the north. Furthermore, it was in this area to the south that God performed many wonders as He led His people into the Promised Land from Egypt.

The term normally used for "God," the plural 'ĕlōhîm, is used in this verse in the singular, 'ĕlôah, which may stress the essential unity of the divine Deliverer, "the Holy One."

What is generally considered another musical notation, **Selah** (Hab. 3:3, 9, 13), probably indicates a pause in the song. (In the NIV "Selah" is in the right-hand marg., whereas in other versions it is within the verses.) "Selah" is used elsewhere only in the Psalms, where it occurs 71 times. The Hebrew verb from which the term comes means "to exalt, to lift up." It may mean a pause (a) to elevate to a higher key or increase the volume, (b) to reflect on what has been sung and exalt the Lord in praise, or (c) to lift up certain instruments for something like a trumpet fanfare. Whatever its meaning, an obvious break was intended in the middle of Habakkuk 3:3.

### 2. GOD'S APPEARANCE (3:3B-7)

**3:3b.** At Sinai God had come like an awesome thunderstorm sweeping down from the mountainous region in the south. As **His glory covered the heavens,** the sun and the moon appeared pale in comparison. God's shimmering glory not only filled the heavens but **His praise filled the earth.** "Praise" probably refers not to the response of mankind but to the reality of God's fame. God's revelation of Himself encompassed the heavens and penetrated to the uttermost parts of the earth.

**3:4.** The prophet indicated a progressive quality to God's appearance by comparing **His splendor** to a **sunrise.** The heavens are first tinted with early **rays** of the hidden sun, then the earth is illuminated as the ball of fire appears over the horizon, and finally everything is flooded with brilliant, glorious light. Just as rays of light streak across the morning sky, so rays **flashed from** God's **hand.** As God advanced, the all-pervading light was traced to its source, the hand of the Lord. The rays (lit., "horns") emanated from God as they do from the sun. People often illustrate a sunrise by drawing a circle surrounded by lines, cones, or horns, a rather crude but nevertheless effective way of depicting radiance. Interestingly the Hebrew verb "to send out rays," related to the Hebrew noun for "horns," was used to describe Moses' countenance after he had come down from Mount Sinai: "his face was radiant" (lit., "his face sent out rays of light," Ex. 34:29-30, 35). This accounts for the strange horns emanating from Michelangelo's famed statue of Moses.

God's radiance is both emanating and concealing. It reveals His glory but veils **His power.** It is easy to forget that the light and warmth which showers the earth with blessing comes from a ball of fire that could consume the globe in a moment. So God's power is **hidden** in His glory. His revelation is restrained lest it consume its beholders.

**3:5.** God is fully capable of exercising His might. He is a terrifying God to those who oppose Him. Habakkuk saw that as God moved across the land, **plague** preceded **Him** and **pestilence** (lit., "burning heat" or "bolts of fire") lay in **His** wake. At His will God can strike down His enemies with plagues (as in the 10 plagues on Egypt, Ex. 7:14–11:10) or with pestilence (cf. Deut. 32:24). The pestilence here may refer to some disease that is accompanied with a burning fever or to the charring of the earth by lightning bolts. God is not a little old man upstairs who dotes on people with sweetness and light. He is all-powerful as He is all-loving. His grace and glory are coupled with might and majesty.

**3:6.** Habakkuk's vision of God coming from the distance and marching across the land rose to a climax. Having reached the place from which He would execute judgment, God stopped, **stood, and shook the earth.** His very presence caused the earth to shake. Furthermore, by a mere glance at **the nations** He caused them to **tremble** (lit., "leap in terror") and even the framework of nature was shattered. **The** primeval **mountains** and **age-old hills,** the firmest constituents of the globe, **crumbled** into dust. He came down on Mount Sinai with thunder, lightning, and fire amidst shaking mountains (Ex. 19:16-19). Though the age-old (lit., "eternal") hills **collapsed,** God's everlasting **ways** go on. Here is a stark warning to those who honor the creation over the Creator! (Cf. Hab. 2:19-20.)

**3:7.** Witnesses to God's appearance at the Exodus and in the wilderness wanderings were **Cushan** and **Midian,** nations that lay on either side of the Red Sea (or Cushan may be another name for Midian). God's wondrous acts at the Red Sea (when He led His people from Egyp-

tian captivity) threw neighboring nations into terror and they experienced **distress** (fear) and **anguish.** Other nations too heard of God's mighty acts and were in fear (Ex. 15:14-16; Deut. 2:25; Josh. 2:9; 5:1). Reference to the people's **tents** and **dwellings** (lit., "tent hangings") seems to emphasize their precarious state. If the mountains melted away, what hope was there for those who huddled under canvas?

### 3. GOD'S ACTIONS (3:8-15)

Habakkuk's attention was now drawn from the awesome appearance of God to a description of God's acts on earth. This section of the ode is introduced in verse 8 by a series of questions that serve as a literary interruption to give life and vitality to the message and to provoke the reader to think about its implications. The questions are in a poetic style that expects no answer. They are thought-questions.

#### a. In nature (3:8-11)

**3:8.** Three questions center on God's motive for His appearance: Was God showing His wrath at **the rivers?** And at **the streams?** And at **the sea?** In other words, was God **angry** with nature? While direct answers are not given, a no answer was implied. God is not displeased with nature. He was using nature as a tool to demonstrate His power (cf. vv. 12-13). God had exhibited His power by smiting the Nile River (Ex. 7:20-21), the Red Sea (Ex. 14:15-28; 15:8-10; cf. Ps. 78:13), and the Jordan River (Josh. 3:14-17). Similarly God would smite the nations. His motive was to destroy His enemies and deliver His people. God was seen as a victor riding forth **with** His **horses** (cf. Hab. 3:15) and **chariots** in majestic power. What a contrast with the Babylonians' horses (1:8-9) that would eventually be stopped when Babylon fell a few decades later, in 539 B.C. (cf. 2:6-8).

**3:9.** God **uncovered** His **bow,** that is, He pulled it from its sheath for ready action. The statement translated **You called for many arrows** is an enigma in Hebrew. One scholar claimed he found more than 100 translations of this short phrase of three Hebrew words (*šebuʿôt maṭṭôt ʾōmer*). The first word may be rendered "seventh" (related to Sabbath), "oath," or "sworn." *Maṭṭôṯ* may be "branches," "rods," "staves," or "tribes." (The NIV has "arrows," in parallel with the word "bow.") *'Ōmer*, a word used exclusively in poetry, denotes "a discourse," "a word," or "an affair or occasion." (NIV has "You called.") Perhaps a reasonable and somewhat literal translation is, "Staves [arrows] are sworn by a word." There is a certain seriousness about God's action here. By solemn oath He affirmed that His weapons were employed. The NIV captures this thought of God's confirming His use of arrows by saying He "called for" them.

The parallel between this verse and parts of Deuteronomy 32 is striking. The Song of Moses speaks of a consuming fire (Deut. 32:22), pestilence and plagues (Deut. 32:24), and arrows drunk with blood (Deut. 32:42) as part of His oath for vengeance against His adversaries (Deut. 32:41).

Whatever the translation of this rather minor phrase in Habakkuk's ode, there is another call by the word *Selah* to stop and meditate. God's motive and His majestic power were seen in His actions in nature, among the nations, and against His enemies. The effect of God's power is seen in the way He creases the earth's surface **with rivers.**

**3:10.** In personifying **the mountains,** Habakkuk said they added their reaction to God's presence and power, for they **saw** God **and writhed.** The Hebrew verb translated "writhed" depicts a person twisting or turning while seized with pangs like a woman in childbirth. Earlier (v. 6) the prophet had said that mountains crumble before God; now he said they writhe. Mount Sinai had quaked when God appeared to Moses (Ex. 19:18; Ps. 114:4, 6-7). To the witness of rivers (Hab. 3:9) and mountains (v. 10a), flooding waters moved in recognition of God's power. Underground waters of the abyss (**the deep**) were personified as speaking (**roared** is lit., "gave their voice") and its high waves were personified as having hands: the deep **lifted its waves** (lit., "hands") **on high.** God's power can cause tremendous upheaval in nature! The Red Sea and the Jordan River had both responded to God's command (cf. Pss. 77:16, 19; 114:3, 5).

**3:11.** In the chorus of nature, the **sun and moon stood still** (cf. Josh. 10:12-13), eclipsed by the dazzling majesty of God. They were pictured as being **in the heavens** (lit., "high or elevated dwelling places").

While all nature shook, the **arrows** and spears of God's wrath (His flashes of **lightning;** cf. Pss. 18:14; 77:17) sped to their targets. Sun and moon paled before the brilliance of the lightning flashes, which perhaps accompanied the hail that destroyed Israel's enemies near Gilgal (Josh. 10:11). In His wrath God often used and controlled the forces of nature.

### b. Among the nations (3:12-15)

**3:12.** Habakkuk envisioned God as being like a thundering giant who **strode through the earth.** God was hardly "tip-toeing through the tulips." **In wrath** (cf. vv. 2, 8) He had **threshed the nations.** As an ox treads the grain to beat out and crush the chaff, so God marched across the earth to crush sinful people and bring salvation to Israel. And the prophet was confident God would do it again.

**3:13.** The motive of God's judgment is clear. His anger was not vented toward nature (cf. v. 8) or against everybody. His purpose was to crush **wickedness** and **deliver** His own. Special deliverance was the goal behind God's destruction. Salvation was for God's people, but it was also for the **anointed One,** a term never used in the Old Testament for the nation Israel. The term probably refers to the coming Messiah (cf. Ps. 2:2; Dan. 9:26). By preserving the people of Israel (delivering them from Egypt and then later from Babylonian Captivity), God maintained the line for the Messiah.

God, Habakkuk said, **crushed the leader of the land** (lit., "head of the house") and **stripped him.** The figure in the Hebrew is that of a building from which the gable is ripped off and then the entire structure demolished, so that the foundations are laid bare. God had destroyed Pharaoh's horsemen who pursued Israel (Ex. 14:23-28) and other leaders (Num. 21:23-25; Josh. 6:2; 8:28-29; 10-11). If God could do this, He could destroy Babylon. Belshazzar, also a "leader" in a "land of wickedness," was stripped of his power (Dan. 5:26-28, 30-31).

Again, the musical score of this dreadful ode called for a pause. The third and final *Selah* is inserted (cf. comments on Hab. 3:3). The utter and absolute ruin of those who oppose God elicits meditation. Before God charged in for the final slaughter of the wicked people, He called for a moment of reflection while the dust settled from the devastating blow that crushed the Babylonian fortress.

**3:14.** These final two verses of this ode on God's awesome self-revelation speak of the ultimate destruction of the enemy. Thrown into panic, those who sought to destroy Israel would destroy each other with their own weapons, as the **warriors** (lit., "village hoards") **stormed** into battle. Apparently the prophet had identified himself with those the Babylonians sought **to scatter,** for he referred to the enemies' target (Judah) as **us** (lit., "me").

The barbaric hordes were also described as bandits who were **gloating** (a word meaning "rejoicing or exulting," used only here in the OT) over the helpless, **wretched** victims they were about to rob. Their gloating would turn to gore, their pride to panic, and they would suddenly attack one another in deadly confusion. It is not clear which event in Israel's history this refers to.

**3:15.** The awesome recital of God's acts came to a crashing conclusion with a reference to one of the most spectacular of His miracles. He took His people through the Red Sea and then delivered the pursuing Egyptians to their watery grave (Ex. 14:15-18; 15:8-10). God's victory over Egypt's horsemen was pictured figuratively as if He Himself had **trampled the sea with** His own **horses** and chariots (cf. Hab. 3:8). In this victory God had churned **the great waters** (cf. v. 10).

## C. Habakkuk's peace in ministry (3:16-19)

Obviously anyone who witnessed this amazing display of God's power would be left in awe. Habakkuk was no exception. He had asked for a show of God's might (v. 2). Little did he realize what a display it would be.

**3:16.** The prophet's **heart pounded,** his **lips quivered,** and his **legs trembled.** Habakkuk was about to collapse from this amazing encounter with God. He felt as though his **bones** were in a state of **decay** and his nervous system was all unraveled. In his weakened state, however, his confidence and hope were re-

newed. He found a new sense of peace and purpose in his prophetic ministry. He said he would **wait patiently** (lit., "rest") **for the day of calamity to come on the nation invading** Judah. The prophet was determined to wait for that day which would be filled with destruction and yet be a day of victory and vindication over wicked Babylon. God's deeds on Israel's behalf in Egypt, at the Red Sea, at Mount Sinai, at the Jordan River, and in the Conquest of Canaan were unquestionably awe-invoking. This review of God's power in the past assured the prophet that God would provide a similar deliverance for Israel from Babylon. Habakkuk was confident that someday God would again "renew" (v. 2) those acts of power, with "wrath" on Babylon and "mercy" (v. 2) on Judah.

**3:17.** The prophet's weakened physical state contrasted with his incredibly strong spiritual state. Habakkuk outlined the worst possible consequences: complete failure of crops (figs, **grapes,** olives, and grain—on which the nation depended for food) and total loss of **sheep** and **cattle.** Even in the midst of absolute ruin and abject famine (which came when the Babylonians captured Jerusalem, Lam. 2:12, 20, 4:4, 9-10; 5:17-18), the prophet was prepared to trust God. He realized that inner peace did not depend on outward prosperity.

**3:18.** Habakkuk did not state that he would merely endure in the hour of distress. He said he would **rejoice in the LORD** and **be joyful.** God is the inexhaustible source and infinite supply of joy. **God my Savior** is literally, "the God of my salvation" ('ĕlōhê yiš'i; the same Heb. words are in Pss. 18:46; 25:5). Far too many people keep trying to buy joy, but happiness is not found in circumstances. Joy is available to everyone, even to those stripped of every material possession, for joy is to be found in a Person. It comes through an intimate and personal relationship with the Lord, so that even those in the worst circumstances can smile.

**3:19.** The unfailing source of **strength** and confidence necessary to satisfaction and contentment is **the Sovereign** ('ădōnāy) **LORD** (Yahweh) Himself. The strength He gives is like the power found in **the feet of a deer,** a gazelle, or any active, swift-footed animal. Much as a deer can quickly bound through a dark forest, so the prophet said he could move joyfully through difficult circumstances. Though his legs trembled (v. 16) at the awesome theophany of God, that same Lord was His joy (v. 18), strength (v. 19), and assurance. Furthermore, God enabled the prophet to walk **on the heights.** Not only would he bound through trials; he would also climb to the mountaintops of victory and triumph. The poetic language of this verse is common in other passages (e.g., Deut. 32:13; 2 Sam. 22:34; Ps. 18:33). A deer or gazelle pictures strength, surefootedness, beauty, and speed.

The concluding words, **For the director of music. On my stringed instruments,** serve as an addendum and are related to the heading of the prophet's doxological ode (Hab. 3:1). They refer to the use of this song in worship. The prophet appointed his psalm for use in public worship accompanied by players with stringed instruments. The sour drone of Habakkuk's complaining (1:2-4, 12–2:1) was replaced by vibrant chords of hope and happiness.

The Sovereign Lord gives triumph over circumstances to those who trust Him. The way to get out from under the load is to get right under the Lord. To be under the Lord is to be over the circumstances. That lesson is worth the price of the book, especially when the world seems like a cesspool of quicksand.

Habakkuk was about to "go under" when he started this book. Destruction, violence, strife, conflict, injustice, and wickedness were all he could see. But he cried out to God and his cry did not go unheeded. The Lord not only answered his complaint but also provided the confidence needed to lift him from the quagmire. Habakkuk started in the pits, but ended on the mountaintop. His journey was not exactly an easy one, but it was certainly worth it.

God directed Habakkuk through the *dialogue* (chap. 1) in which He revealed His plans for disciplining Judah and destroying Babylon. Then at God's command Habakkuk recorded a woeful *dirge* (chap. 2) that further justified God's judgment on Babylon. Finally, the prophet reached a pinnacle of praise in which God revealed Himself in all His glory and power. The *doxology* (chap. 3)

concluded with Habakkuk's unwavering trust in the Lord.

The prophet's complaints were swallowed up by confidence. His fear turned to faith. Habakkuk was transformed from a sour, jittery prophet weighed down with burdens to a secure, joyous preacher bouyed up with blessing. The just, the upright, the happy, the contented, the victorious live by their faith. Yes, faith *is* the victory that overcomes the world! (1 John 5:4)

# BIBLIOGRAPHY

Eaton, J.H. *Obadiah, Nahum, Habakkuk and Zephaniah.* Torch Bible Commentaries. London: SCM Press, 1961.

Feinberg, Charles L. *The Minor Prophets.* Chicago: Moody Press, 1976.

Freeman, Hobart E. *Nahum, Zephaniah, Habakkuk: Minor Prophets of the Seventh Century B.C.* Everyman's Bible Commentary. Chicago: Moody Press, 1973.

Fuerbringer, L. *The Eternal Why.* St. Louis: Concordia Publishing House, 1947.

Gaebelein, Frank E. *Four Minor Prophets: Obadiah, Jonah, Habakkuk, and Haggai.* Chicago: Moody Press,1977.

Gowan, Donald E. *The Triumph of Faith in Habakkuk.* Atlanta: John Knox Press, 1976.

Ironside, H.A. *Notes on the Minor Prophets.* Neptune, N.J.: Loizeaux Brothers, 1909.

Keil, C.F. "Habakkuk." In *Commentary on the Old Testament in Ten Volumes.* Vol. 10. Reprint (25 vols. in 10). Grand Rapids: Wm. B. Eerdmans Publishing Co., 1982.

Lloyd-Jones, D. Martin. *From Fear to Faith.* Reprint. Grand Rapids: Baker Book House, 1982.

Pusey, E.B. *The Minor Prophets: A Commentary.* Vol. 2. Grand Rapids: Baker Book House, 1950.

Stoll, John H. *The Book of Habakkuk.* Grand Rapids: Baker Book House, 1972.

Tatford, Frederick A. *The Minor Prophets.* Vol. 2. Reprint (3 vols.). Minneapolis: Klock & Klock Christian Publishers, 1982.

Ward, William Hayes. "Habakkuk." In *A Critical and Exegetical Commentary on Micah, Zephaniah, Nahum, Habakkuk, Obadiah, and Joel.* The International Critical Commentary. Edinburgh: T. & T. Clark, 1911.

# ZEPHANIAH

## John D. Hannah

## INTRODUCTION

**Title.** The name "Zephaniah," which is also borne by three other men in the Old Testament, means "Yahweh hides," "Yahweh has hidden," or "Yahweh treasured." This may point to God's protection of His people during the impending difficulties in Zephaniah's day, or to God's protection of Zephaniah in his childhood during Manasseh's wicked reign (2 Kings 21:16).

**Author.** Beyond the information given in Zephaniah 1:1, little is known about this prophet. His ancestry is traced back four generations, which is unique among the prophets. This implies he was a man of prominence and even of royalty. As the great-great-grandson of Hezekiah, king of Judah, Zephaniah was the only known Old Testament prophet with such high social standing. He was thus a distant relative of King Josiah in whose reign he prophesied. Also the prophet may have been a resident of Jerusalem because of his words "from this place" (v. 4) and his familiarity with the city (vv. 10-11).

**Date.** According to 1:1, Zephaniah's ministry was during the reign of King Josiah (640–609 B.C.). Scholars differ on whether the prophet ministered before or after the recovery of the Law by Hilkiah and the subsequent religious revival in 622 B.C. (2 Kings 22–23; 2 Chron. 34). Probably Zephaniah's prophecy was given after Josiah's revival, for these reasons: (1) Cutting off the remnant of Baal worship (Zeph. 1:4) implied that a religious awakening was in progress. (2) Jeremiah, who prophesied long after 622 (as well as before), described Judah's religious and moral condition much as did Zephaniah (cf. Jer. 8:2; 19:13 with Zeph. 1:5; cf. Jer. 5:2, 7 with Zeph. 1:5b; and cf. Jer. 8:8-9 with Zeph. 3:4). (3) The fact that the king's sons wore foreign apparel (1:8)

suggests that they were old enough to make their own choices. (4) Zephaniah's frequent quotations of the Law suggest that he was using the sources discovered by Hilkiah (cf. v. 13 with Deut. 28:30, 39; cf. Zeph. 1:15 with Deut. 4:11; cf. Zeph. 1:17 with Deut. 28:29; and cf. Zeph. 2:2 with Deut. 28:15-62). (5) Zephaniah's message of impending judgment would be appropriate for those who spurned the religious revival under Josiah. Thus his prophecy was given sometime after the time of Josiah's revival in 622, but before the destruction of Nineveh in 612—which Zephaniah indicated was still in existence then (Zeph. 2:13) as the capital of the Assyrian Empire.

**Setting.** Politically Judah was benefiting from a power vacuum among the superpowers of the day, so much so that King Josiah extended his influence militarily as far north as Naphtali. At that time Assyria—which had carried off the 10 Northern tribes in 722 B.C., under Sargon II— was rapidly suffering eclipse. When Sin-shar-ishkun (623–612 B.C.), Ashurbanipal's son, was reigning over Assyria, the Neo-Babylonian Empire began to emerge under Nabopolassar in 626. Also the Medes, under Cyaxares II in 625, pulled out from under Assyrian authority. So Josiah was encouraged to remove Assyrian religious practices from Judah. As a result Judah prospered politically. The collapse of the Assyrian Empire was delayed as the Egyptians under Psamtik I (664–609) allied with them, but a coalition of Medes and Babylonians destroyed Assyria's capital city, Nineveh, in 612.

Before Josiah's reign, Manasseh (695–642) and Manasseh's son Amon (642–640) had introduced wicked practices into Judah. Manasseh built altars to Baal and worshiped the sun, moon, and stars. He built altars to these stellar objects and placed them in the temple courts (2 Kings 21:4-5) and he made a carved Asherah pole (an image of the goddess Asherah) and placed it in the temple (2 Kings 21:7). Child sacrifice and astrology prospered (2 Kings 21:6; 23:10-11). King Amon, who may have been named after an Egyptian deity, continued his father's policies until his assassination (2 Kings 21:19-26; 2 Chron. 33:21-25). Josiah succeeded Amon in 640 at the age of 8. In 632, at age 16, Josiah began to seek after the God of his forefather David. In 628, Josiah started a reform movement in which much of the idolatry was purged from Jerusalem and Judah. About that time Jeremiah (627) commenced his ministry and Judah moved toward independence from Assyria with a possible revival of the idea of an undivided kingdom like that of David and Solomon. Then in the 18th year of Josiah's reign (622) a copy of the Law was discovered by Hilkiah the high priest (2 Kings 22:3-8). This accentuated the religious renewal including a new enthusiasm for celebrating the Passover (2 Kings 23:1-25). Unfortunately the promising reform movement was superficial for it did not deeply affect the politico-religious life of the nation. Worship of Yahweh was reestablished, but idolatry was not entirely removed. Both Zephaniah and Jeremiah prophesied to a politically prospering people of coming judgment because Josiah's reform movement still went unheeded.

**Theme.** "The day of the LORD" is an expression used more frequently in this prophecy than in any other Old Testament book. Thus the theme of the book is the impending judgment of God on Judah for its disobedience. A corollary of the judgment motif within Zephaniah and the other prophets is the preservation of the true remnant by the mercies of the covenant-keeping God. Though judgment was sure, God's promise to protect His people and fulfill His promises was steadfast and everlasting. The book's theme is capsuled in Zephaniah 1:7a: "Be silent before the Sovereign LORD, for the day of the LORD is near."

# OUTLINE

# COMMENTARY

## I. Introduction (1:1)

**1:1.** Zephaniah's introductory words, **The word of the LORD that came,** were also used by Hosea, Joel, and Micah at the beginnings of their books. (In the NIV Micah begins, "The word of the LORD given," but the Heb. is the same as in the other books mentioned.) This introduction along with the words **to Zephaniah** make the reader aware of both the Source of the message and the messenger; though the messenger is human, the message is from God and has His authority.

The biographical note on Zephaniah traces his lineage back four generations. Most prophets are traced only to their fathers (e.g., Jonah son of Amittai [Jonah 1:1]; Joel son of Pethuel [Joel 1:1]), though Zechariah's lineage is traced to his grandfather (Zech. 1:1). Zephaniah's careful delineation of his pedigree which included **Hezekiah** has led many scholars to assume Zephaniah's royalty (not all hold to this inference, however; cf. Laetsch, *The Minor Prophets,* p. 354).

## II. The Day of Yahweh's Judgment (1:2–3:8)

Zephaniah's prophecy has two major themes: (a) the bold declaration of God's imminent wrath, which implies a serious call to repentance, and (b) the comforting words of the prophet that even in judgment God will not forget his covenantal mercies but will restore His people at a future time. In his initial section Zephaniah sounded a stern warning of doom. He began by pronouncing judgment on the earth (1:2-3) and concluded with the same theme (3:8). In the interim he dealt twice with Judah and/or Jerusalem (1:4–2:3; 3:1-7) and once with the surrounding nations (2:4-15). This is an interesting introversion pattern (*a, b, c, b¹, a¹*) illustrated in this way:

*a* Judgment on all the earth (1:2-3)
   *b* Judgment on Judah and Jerusalem (1:4–2:3)
      *c* Judgment on the surrounding nations (2:4-15)
   *b¹* Judgment on Jerusalem (3:1-7)
*a¹* Judgment on all the earth (3:8)

### A. Judgment on all the earth (1:2-3)

**1:2-3.** With horrifying abruptness Zephaniah set forth the Lord's proclamation of universal judgment. Isaiah also wrote about God's worldwide judgment (Isa. 24:1-6, 19-23). In Zephaniah 1:2 the prophet spoke in general about judgment and in verse 3 he gave details of that judgment. God would bring about this judgment, in which He would **sweep away everything.** "Sweep away" (used three times in vv. 2-3) means "to gather

and take away, to remove, to destroy." This impending judgment on **the earth** would extend, Zephaniah said, to life on the land (**men and animals**), in the **air** (**birds**), and in the **sea** (**the fish**). Interestingly these four are in reverse order from Creation: fish (Gen. 1:20a), birds (Gen. 1:20b), livestock and wild animals (Gen. 1:24), and man (Gen. 1:26). So this destruction which Zephaniah saw is a kind of reversal of Creation. When God would **cut off** (cf. Zeph. 1:4; 3:6) **man,** the only thing left on **earth** would be ruins (**heaps of rubble**) of a once-prosperous past. Since Zephaniah later wrote that a remnant would be delivered (3:9-13), the universal destruction of mankind referred to in 1:2-3 would apparently be limited to **the wicked.** Jeremiah made this clear (Jer. 25:31-33).

### B. Judgment on Judah and Jerusalem (1:4–2:3)

Having set forth in broad terms the major premise of impending doom, the prophet then focused on Judah and Jerusalem. In the Old Testament a generalized statement is often followed by detailed particulars (cf. Gen. 1:1 with Gen. 1:2-31).

This section (Zeph. 1:4–2:3) clearly indicates that Judah's wicked people would be destroyed at the Babylonian invasion of Jerusalem in 586 B.C. But how could Zephaniah at the same time write about *universal* judgment? (1:2-3) How could he turn so quickly from Judah's destruction in 586 to speak of the "day of the LORD" (v. 14), a yet-future event separated from that devastation in 586 by many centuries? When Babylon conquered Judah, judgment was not universal; so how could the two be related? One common answer is that every instance of divine judgment is called the day of the Lord. Another answer is that verses 2-3 and 3:8 refer not to universal judgment but to the Babylonian invasion described in words of hyperbole. Perhaps a better explanation is that Zephaniah saw Judah's destruction and universal judgment as *two parts of one grand event,* "the great day of the LORD" (1:14). The destruction of the prophet's own people would be so terrible that it was envisioned as ushering in God's day of wrath (v. 15; 2:2) on all the world's wicked. Later Zephaniah again associated God's judgment on the nations (3:6) and the whole world (3:8) with His judgment on Judah (3:1-5). The Babylonian destruction of Judah was thus a step in God's work of wrath on His people.

The day of the Lord (see comments under "Major Interpretive Problems" in the *Introduction* to Joel) was referred to by many of the prophets (Isa. 2:12; 13:6, 9; Jer. 46:10; Ezek. 13:5; 30:3; Joel 1:15; 2:1, 11, 31, 3:14; Obad. 15; Amos 5:18, 20; Zech. 14:1; Mal. 4:5). In several of these verses and in verses immediately before or after them the day of the Lord is associated with universal judgment (cf. Isa. 24).

1. THE OBJECTS OF JUDGMENT (1:4-13)

a. The idolaters (1:4-7)

**1:4.** The prophet informed his hearers that the Lord was about to **stretch out** His **hand** in judgment and wrath (cf. 2:13) on the Southern Kingdom and its capital, **Jerusalem.** Every aspect of **Baal** worship would be removed. Baal was the Canaanite god of fertility whom many in Israel had worshiped in the time of the Judges (Jud. 2:13) and in the time of Ahab (1 Kings 16:32). Baal worship involved terrible sexual acts. Manasseh, wicked king of Judah, had erected Baal altars (2 Chron. 33:3, 7), but his grandson Josiah destroyed them (2 Chron. 34:4). But this "revival" of Josiah's in 622 B.C. had no lasting effect. Baal was again being worshiped (cf. Jer. 19:5; 32:35). However, the time would come, Zephaniah wrote, when God would remove every last vestige of that pagan worship.

Zephaniah referred to two classes of priests. One group was **the pagan . . . priests,** non-Levitical appointees by the kings of Judah (2 Kings 23:5; cf. **idolatrous** "priests," the same Heb. word, in Hosea 10:5). The Hebrew word for "pagan priests" is *kᵉmārîm,* which means idol-priests, priests who prostrated themselves before idols. The other group was the idolatrous priests, Levitical priests who had defected from the worship of the true God to a superstitious faith.

**1:5-6.** After Zephaniah said that God would remove the false priests, he then referred to three forms of idolatrous worship, introducing each of them by the phrase **those who.** First, he noted the worshipers of stellar bodies, people **who bow down on** flat **housetops** (cf. Jer. 19:13; 2:29) as star-worshipers—through which the powers of nature were supposedly harnessed. The sun, moon, and stars were regarded as deities. Though God had clearly warned against this practice (Deut. 4:19), Manasseh led the way in this perversion also (2 Kings 21:3, 5; cf. 2 Kings 23:4-5).

Second, Zephaniah mentioned **those who** attempted to combine the worship of Yahweh with the worship of **Molech,** a form of religious syncretism. Molech was the chief god of the Ammonites (1 Kings 11:33), a people east of the Dead Sea (cf. Zeph. 2:8-9). Jeremiah, a contemporary of Zephaniah, said the Jews were sacrificing children to Molech (Jer. 32:35; cf. 2 Kings 16:3; 21:6). The Hebrew *Malkām* (Zeph. 1:5, NIV marg.) is a variant spelling of "Molech." To **swear by** a deity meant to pronounce an oath under the threat of punishment by that deity if one failed to carry out his oath.

Third, the prophet spoke of others who were religiously indifferent and unconcerned about worshiping the true God (v. 6), though they may not have been worshiping other gods.

**1:7.** After citing three types of idolatry in Judah—the overtly pagan, the syncretistic, and the religiously indifferent—the prophet called on all of them to be **silent before** God (cf. Hab. 2:20) because of the imminence of **the day of the LORD.** This is the first of 19 references in Zephaniah to "the day," "that day," "a day," "the day of the LORD's wrath," and similar phrases referring to "the day of the LORD." (See comments on Zeph. 1:4–2:3 and 1:14.) Such impending judgment ought to evoke fear and silence. No more calling on Baal; no more invoking the stars; no more swearing by Molech—for now Yahweh, the only God, would act. They may have forgotten Him, but He would not forget them! In fact God **prepared** Judah like **a sacrifice,** that is, He prepared her for slaughter much as sacrificial animals were prepared to be eaten (cf. Isa. 34:6; Jer. 46:10). The **invited** guests, the Babylonians, were God's chosen instrument (cf. Jer. 10:25; Hab. 1:6) to eat the sacrifice; they had been **consecrated** or set apart to be the agent of God's judgment on His chosen nation.

### b. The princes (1:8)

**1:8.** In addition to the idolaters (vv. 4-7) Judah's royalty were also the objects of God's scorn. They included **princes** (officers of the king's court; cf. Jer. 36:12; Hosea 8:4), Josiah's **sons,** and the aristocracy who evidenced their disobedience by wearing the latest fashions from Nineveh and Babylon (**foreign clothes**). Adopting foreign dress outwardly most likely implied that they also had absorbed foreign values and practices inwardly. Josiah's sons were certainly punished. His son Jehoahaz reigned only three months and then was captured by Pharaoh Neco II and taken to Egypt (2 Kings 23:31-34). Josiah's wicked son Jehoiakim, who reigned for 11 years (2 Kings 23:36), was defeated by Nebuchadnezzar (2 Kings 24:1-2). Jehoiakim's son Jehoiachin reigned only three months in 597 and was taken captive to Babylon (2 Kings 24:8-16). Then 11 years later Judah's last king, Zedekiah, another of Josiah's sons, was blinded by Nebuchadnezzar and taken to Babylon (2 Kings 24:18–25:7).

### c. The oppressors (1:9)

**1:9.** God said He would **punish** not only false worshipers (vv. 4-6) and sinful political leaders (v. 8), but also those who plundered for material gain. **All who avoid stepping on the threshold** refers either to people who followed the Philistines' superstition about not stepping on a threshold (1 Sam. 5:5) or perhaps more likely to those who suddenly leaped into others' homes to pillage and steal. This is paralleled by the words **violence and deceit.** The gain of such robbery was then offered to pagan deities as objects of sacred worship. It was strange that pagan religious leaders condoned such violence and plundering.

### d. The merchants (1:10-11)

**1:10.** To emphasize the thought that God's judgment would fall on every segment of Jewish society, Zephaniah noted that lamentations would arise from every quarter of Jerusalem (cf. the words "all who live in Jerusalem," v. 4). **The Fish Gate,** located in the northern sector, was the gate through which Nebuchadnezzar entered the city. It was given its name because of its proximity to the fish market. **The New Quarter** was northwest of the temple area. The meaning of **the hills** is uncertain. They could refer to the whole city, or the hills on which Jerusalem was erected, or the hills surrounding the lower portion of the city (cf. Jer. 31:39). **A cry** and **wailing . . . and a loud crash** would go up from these areas because of the loss of lives as Nebuchadnezzar progressed through the city.

**1:11.** Zephaniah then singled out one area in the city—**the market** (or business) **district**—and said that those who **live** there would **wail** (cf. v. 10) because their businessmen (**merchants**) would **be wiped out** (lit., "will be silenced"). In the Tyropean Valley, running north to south and separating the city east and west, the merchants plied their **trade with silver** and grew rich through usury. Because they took advantage of others, God would judge them and they would **be ruined** (lit., "be cut off, killed"; cf. "cut off" in vv. 3-4).

### e. The indifferent (1:12-13)

**1:12.** The Lord declared that He would make a diligent, comprehensive **search** throughout **Jerusalem** so that none would go unpunished. Josephus wrote about a later invasion in which the city's aristocracy were literally dragged from the sewer system where they hid for fear of death. Probably something like this also occurred when the Babylonians attacked Jerusalem. The analogy of **wine left on its dregs** suggests that the nation had become spiritually polluted. Wine allowed to ferment for a long time forms a hard crust and the liquid becomes syrupy, bitter, and unpalatable. Instead of removing the dregs of daily pollution, Judah had become hardened and indifferent to God. So great was her degeneration that the people did not even believe that Yahweh did as much as their self-made images. Pagan idolaters accorded their numerous deities the power of judging wrong and vindicating right. But the Jews at that time had such a low view of Yahweh that they believed He could not keep either His promises or His threats: He **will do nothing, either good or bad.** Their own spiritual complacency led them to think **the Lord** was complacent.

**1:13.** Zephaniah stated that Yahweh is not so weak and uninterested as the Jews thought because judgment is within both His power and His will. In this three-part verse the prophet first stated that God will cause the Jews' enemies to plunder the people's **wealth** and demolish **their houses.** This would be as God had predicted (Deut. 28:30). With both their money and their residences gone, they would have no physical security. God then stated that their effort to rebuild their **houses** and **plant** their **vineyards** would be futile. They would **not live** long enough to enjoy them.

### 2. THE DESCRIPTION OF JUDGMENT (1:14-18)

Having boldly pronounced Yahweh's impending judgment on the land of Judah by delineating the objects of His wrath, the prophet then described the devastation of that judgment.

#### a. The nearness (1:14a)

**1:14a.** To awaken the complacent (cf. v. 12) nation to its peril the prophet returned to the theme stated in verse 7, **the great day of the LORD.** Grammatically the verse stresses the word **near,** which is first in the sentence in Hebrew (cf. "near" in v. 7, where it also appears in this emphatic position). The fearful wrath of God was to come on the nation **quickly.** Since Zephaniah wrote shortly after 622 B.C., the year of Josiah's partial revival, the day of the Lord was in fact imminent. In 605, only 17 years after Josiah's revival, Judah under Jehoiakim became a vassal of Babylon and many of Judah's best young men were deported. Under Jehoiakim's equally wicked successor, Jehoiachin, the city was again besieged by Nebuchadnezzar in 597 and some 10,000 Jews were deported. Under Zedekiah the city was under a long siege by Nebuchadnezzar and was finally destroyed in the summer of 586. (For the relationship of this event to the day of the Lord see the comments under "B. Judgment on Judah and Jerusalem [1:4–2:3].")

#### b. The horror (1:14b-18)

Verses 14b-16 describe the physical characteristics of that awful day, while verses 17-18 describe the personal trauma of that judgment.

**1:14b-16.** The prophet began by calling the nation to hear his words (**Listen!**) for the **day** of Babylonian terror would cause the people to **cry** in bitterness and even the mighty Jewish **warrior** would retreat in fear and horror. The **wrath** of Almighty God on sinners (cf. v. 18; 2:2-3; 3:8) is depicted by such words as **distress . . . anguish . . . trouble . . . ruin . . . darkness . . . gloom . . . clouds, and blackness.** When the Babylonian soldiers did barge into the city, the Jerusalemites were distressed and in anguish; their houses were ruined, and the sky was dark from the smoke of the buildings set on fire. As the Babylonian hordes rushed to conquer, kill, and ravish, they sounded the **trumpet** and shouted in **battle** in their moves **against** not only Jerusalem but also other **fortified cities** in Judah. Soldiers at **the corner towers,** normally strongholds of defense against attacking enemies, were defenseless.

**1:17.** So great would be God's judgment, Zephaniah said, that the Jews in **distress** would wander about **like** helplessly **blind** people (cf. Deut. 28:28-29), unable to find any safe quarter. Such **distress** was not because of God's impersonal cruelty; it was retribution for their having **sinned against the LORD.** The inhabitants of Judah would be viciously killed; so much of **their blood** would be shed that it would be **like dust** on the streets. And their bodies would be cruelly ravished, with their innards piled up **like the filth** of dung piles.

**1:18.** They would have no hope of deliverance; their wealth (**silver** [cf. "silver" in v. 11] and **gold**) would not **be able to** buy off their attackers (cf. Ezek. 7:19). Zephaniah then returned to the theme of universal judgment (cf. Zeph. 1:2-3). **The whole world will be** destroyed and **all** its inhabitants will quickly (**He will make a sudden end**) be subjected to the wrath of God. All this will stem from **His jealousy,** His consuming passion and concern that His own people follow Him, not false gods.

### 3. THE DETERRENT TO JUDGMENT (2:1-3)

Having described the awful day of God's wrath on Judah, the prophet at last brought his readers to his purpose. His goal was not to bring the people to despair, but to repentance and obedience. As Matthew Henry so appropriately stated, Zephaniah intended "not to frighten them out of their wits, but to frighten them out of their sins" (*Commentary on the Whole Bible in One Volume*, p. 1168).

## a. A summons to the nation: Repent (2:1-2)

**2:1.** Zephaniah urged the people, **Gather together,** perhaps to come collectively to repent as a nation. Repeating the command stressed the urgency of his appeal. The words **O shameful nation** are literally, "O nation not shamed." ("Shamed" is *niḵsāp̄*, from *kāsap̄*, "to be pale or white with shame." A related word *kesep̄* means "silver," the pale-colored metal mentioned in 1:11, 18.) Judah, because of her sin, was without shame (cf. 3:5); her face was not blushing or white or pale with embarrassment. Sin had hardened her sensitivity to sin (cf. 1:12).

**2:2.** The urgency of the prophet's summons is seen in this verse. The three phrases introduced by the word **before** emphasize the point. If the nation did not repent, it would soon be too late. The nation could prevent the impending judgment if their repentance, like that of Nineveh's, were immediate. The words **and that day sweeps on like chaff** function as a parenthesis to strengthen the first of the three clauses. Imminent repentance was imperative because the day of God's wrath was rapidly approaching, like light chaff driven forcefully by the wind. The words **anger** and **wrath** translate the same Hebrew word *'ap̄* (lit., "nostril," thus anger evident in hard breathing). **Fierce** (*ḥārôn*) means "burning," from *ḥārâh,* "to burn, to kindle" (cf. "fierce anger" in 3:8).

## b. A summons to the humble: Seek God (2:3)

**2:3.** The prophet urged those who already know the Lord (as evidenced by their humble obedience to Him) to continue steadfast in their walk with Him. They were commanded to strive for three things: **the LORD . . . righteousness,** and **humility** (cf. 3:12). The last two result from following the Lord. If the remnant would seek the Lord, then they would **be sheltered** (lit., "hidden, concealed," from *sāṯar,* a synonym of *ṣāp̄an,* from which comes the name "Zephaniah") from the impending doom of God's **anger** (*'ap̄;* cf. 2:2). Though many died in the Babylonian invasions, others were spared and some were exiled to Babylon (2 Kings 24:14-16). God sheltered or protected His remnant.

## C. Judgment on the surrounding nations (2:4-15)

Zephaniah turned from warning Judah to prophesy similar wrath on her equally idolatrous neighbors. God is the God of all the nations, and those nations that led Judah to stumble would not escape the fury of His wrath. Since He would punish Judah, He surely would not overlook the sins of others. Zephaniah began with the nation to Judah's west, Philistia (vv. 4-7), then moved east to Moab and Ammon (vv. 8-11), then south to Ethiopia (v. 12), and north to Assyria (vv. 13-15).

### 1. ON PHILISTIA (2:4-7)

**2:4.** The prophet predicted the destruction of four of Philistia's five major cities—**Gaza . . . Ashkelon . . . Ashdod,** and **Ekron,** mentioned in order from south to north (see the map "Israel and Surrounding Nations in the Days of the Prophets" before Isa.). The reason for Gath's being omitted is uncertain, but most scholars feel that the city had not recovered from Uzziah's devastation of it (2 Chron. 26:6). Or it may be that four rather than five are mentioned in order to maintain the literary symmetry of the verse's structure. (Amos 1:6-8 omits Gath also.) Fittingly the Hebrew words for "Gaza" (*'azzâh*) and **abandoned** (*'āzûḇâh*) are similar in sound, as are the words for "Ekron" (*'eqrôn*) and **uprooted** (*tēʿāqēr*). Ashdod would be destroyed **at midday,** when many people would be eating or resting, not alert for an invasion.

**2:5.** The identity of the **Kerethite people** (cf. "Kerethites" in v. 6) is uncertain. The words are literally "nation of the Cretans," thus referring to some Cretans who migrated eastward and settled on the Mediterranean coastal plains, **by the sea.** (Kerethites are also mentioned in 1 Sam. 30:14; 2 Sam. 8:18; 20:23; 1 Chron. 18:17; Ezek. 25:16.) "Caphtor" in Jeremiah 47:4 and Amos 9:7 is another name for Crete. The name **Canaan** in the same verse also refers to the coastal plains. The Lord's pronouncement is as horrifying as it is clear—complete destruction was coming! **None** of the inhabitants on Palestine's coastal plain would **be left.** That destruction was initially inflicted by Pharaoh Neco II of Egypt (609–594), the succesor of Psamtik I, as he attempted to consolidate the area west of the Euphrates against the Babylonians (Jer. 47).

**2:6-7.** Zephaniah wrote that Philistia, **the land by the sea, where the Kerethites dwell,** would be so depopulated that it would become pastures for the herding of **sheep.** In fact it would be acquired by **the remnant of . . . Judah,** those whom God would rescue from the judgment (v. 3). The survivors of the day of wrath would become sheepherders, would occupy the land of their once-hated enemy, and would derive sustenance from it. The explanation for this gracious provision for God's remnant is given in the last sentence of verse 7. The remnant is the object of the love and providential concern of **the LORD their God** who cares for and restores His people. (**Restore their fortunes**; cf. 3:20, renders the lit. "bring back their captives"; cf. NIV marg.) Judah's future occupancy of this territory is guaranteed by the Abrahamic Covenant (Gen. 15:18-20).

### 2. ON MOAB AND AMMON (2:8-11)

**2:8.** Zephaniah turned from the Philistines in the west to the two tribes to the east, **Moab** and Ammon, that were descended from Lot's daughters (Gen. 19:30-38) and therefore were blood relatives of Judah. The sin of these tribes was their verbal hostility (**insults . . . taunts . . . threats**) toward God's Chosen **People** (cf. Zeph. 2:10). These tribes had consistently been Israel's enemies. The Moabite king Balak tried to destroy the nation with Balaam's curses (Num. 22), for which God pronounced extermination (Num. 24:17). In the era of the Judges both Moab and Ammon repeatedly attempted to subjugate Israel (Jud. 3:12-14; 10:7-9; 11:4-6). Both Saul and David defeated **the Ammonites** (1 Sam. 11:1-11; 2 Sam. 10:1-14), and Joram and Jehoshaphat routed the rebelling Moabites (2 Kings 3). Other prophets noted that Moab and Ammon haughtily violated Judah's borders and ridiculed their distant Jewish relatives (cf. Isa. 16:6; 25:10-11; Jer. 48:29-30; Ezek. 25:1-3, 6; Amos 1:13).

**2:9.** Following God's indictment (v. 8) His punishment was pronounced (v. 9), intensified by the twice-repeated word **surely.** The Almighty God made a solemn oath (**as surely as I live**) that those arrogant oppressors would **become like Sodom** and Gomorrah, key cities destroyed in the day of their ancestor Lot (Gen. 19:23-29). This analogy meant that those nations would be reduced to complete ruin. The **land** would be taken from them and would become so barren that it would grow only **weeds** (prickly plants) and be covered with **salt pits** (cf. Jer. 48:9). As a sterile **wasteland** it would no longer be fruitful. Being near the Dead Sea, much of Moab and Ammon is salty, barren land, though the final fulfillment of the prophecies in Zephaniah 2:8-10 is yet future in view of the words in verse 11.

Zephaniah added that the Moabites and Ammonites will be enslaved by the Jews and that the Jewish remnant (**the remnant of My people . . . the survivors**) will possess those territories (cf. Isa. 11:14).

**2:10-11.** Zephaniah repeated the reasons for the judgments described in verse 9. The sin of Moab and Ammon was **their pride** (cf. Isa. 16:6; Jer. 48:29), evidenced by their **insulting and mocking** of God's **people** (cf. Zeph. 2:8; Ezek. 25:5-6, 8). Again after the indictment God spelled out the penalty (cf. the similar pattern in Zeph. 2:8 followed by v. 9). **The LORD will** judge **them** with His power and will destroy all their idols. Then the prophet made another statement that awaits future fulfillment. In the Millennium people in all **nations . . . will worship** the true God (cf. Mal. 1:11), **everyone in his own land.** The removal of all idolatry will pave the way for worldwide worship when Christ rules as King on the earth.

In this section (Zeph. 2:8-11) the prophet repeated his message in a three-fold argument: reasons for judgment (vv. 8, 10), nature of the judgment (vv. 9a, 11a), and the ultimate provision of blessing (vv. 9b, 11b).

### 3. ON ETHIOPIA (2:12)

**2:12.** The **Cushites** or Ethiopians are descendants of Cush, a son of Ham (Gen. 10:6; 1 Chron. 1:8). These people, residing in the upper Nile region (today's southern Egypt, Sudan, and northern Ethiopia), were the southernmost people known to Judah. Zephaniah's words concerning them were few and one wonders if his choice of them, rather than, say, the troublesome Edomites, was simply to stretch the points of the compass to the known extremes. Cushite kings dominated Egypt until their defeat by the Assyrian king Esarhaddon in 670 B.C. King Asa of Judah defeated a large Cushite expedition under Zerah that threatened Judah (2 Chron. 14:9-13). The Lord's judgment on Cushites is that they, like all Israel's enemies, would be killed in battle (**slain**). The fulfillment of this prophecy was at least partially realized by the Babylonians under Nebuchadnezzar in 586 B.C. (cf. Ezek. 30:4-5, 9). Since the Babylonians were God's instrument, God called the attackers' swords **My sword.**

### 4. ON ASSYRIA (2:13-15)

**2:13.** Though Assyria lay to the distant northeast of Judah, Zephaniah designated them as from **the north** because invaders from that area followed the Fertile Crescent westward and then proceeded southward. Zephaniah predicted that the Lord would **destroy Assyria** and leave **Nineveh,** Assyria's capital and a city well known for its impregnability, a wasteland. This was the nation that conquered the Northern Kingdom of Israel in 722 B.C. Assyria was a much-feared nation because of its merciless atrocities on its captives. An alliance of Babylonians and Medes destroyed Nineveh in 612 B.C., with the Assyrian king Sin-sharishkun dying while trying to defend his city. A remnant of the Assyrians escaped the fall of the city under their new king, Ashur-uballit II. Though aided by an alliance with Pharaoh Neco II of Egypt, the Assyrian Empire was crushed in 609 B.C. Zephaniah's prediction was fulfilled. (Another prophetic description of the fall of Nineveh is given in Nahum 3.) Zephaniah's words that Nineveh would become **dry as the desert** were fitting because the city had many irrigation canals! Nahum's words were equally appropriate (Nahum 1:8; 2:6, 8).

**2:14.** Having stated the fact of Assyria's destruction (v. 13), Zephaniah then elaborated on the nature of that nation's utter demise (v. 14). **Flocks and herds** may refer to hordes of wild animals (cf. v. 15), not domesticated ones, that require extensive vegetation. Animals, the prophet said, would find their abode (**lie down**) in the city, and the noise of a busy city would be replaced by the sounds of the beasts and birds. Eerily, owls would occupy the **columns** and call **through the windows** of deserted buildings. (The exact identification of the birds **desert owl** and **screech owl** is uncertain, as noted in the NIV marg. to Isa. 34:11.) **Doorways** of homes would be deserted; only **rubble** would lie there (cf. "rubble" in Zeph. 1:3). **The beams of cedar,** lying under more elaborate wall and ceiling coverings, would **be exposed** because of the soldiers' ransacking of homes. The image that emerges is one of depopulation, destruction, and ruin.

**2:15.** The picture of Nineveh's destruction is completed as the prophet reiterated that the city, though apparently quite secure, would be shamed. Its king was arrogant (cf. Isa. 10:12) because of its supposed impregnability. It was known as **the carefree city,** as its populace felt it **lived in** complete **safety.** The city was quite large, having with its suburban areas a circumference of 60 miles and a population of at least 120,000 (cf. comments on Jonah 3:3; 4:11). In addition to an extensive outer wall there was an inner wall with an 8-mile circumference, 50 feet thick and 100 feet high. Between the two walls was enough farmland to support the huge population. Nineveh's claim (**there is none besides me**) was no idle boast! For approximately 200 years she was superior in strength to any other city of her time.

An attack on the outer wall, begun in 614 B.C. by the Medes and Babylonians, was initially withstood by the Ninevites, but a combination of trickery by the attackers, carelessness by the attacked, and a natural disaster, finally brought victory to the attackers (cf. Nahum 1:10; 2:3-5; 3:11). The great inner wall collapsed because of an unexpected deluge that swelled the Tigris River in a normally dry season of the year and inundated the wall. Thus the city was unexpectedly defeated (cf. Nahum 1:8; 2:6-8; 3:12). The carefree boasting of the city was hushed by her enemies, and all who later saw its ruins scoffed at her former haughtiness (cf. Nahum 3:19). To **scoff and** to **shake their fists** were signs of contempt. God reduced the city miraculously and gave it to the **wild beasts!**

### D. Judgment on Jerusalem (3:1-7)

Having described God's impending judgment on the countries surrounding Judah, the Prophet Zephaniah again returned to the theme of Jerusalem's doom (cf. 1:4–2:3). He emphasized the need for the wicked Jews to seek repentance. The prophet listed God's grievances against His people (3:1-5), and then pronounced God's inevitable judgment (vv. 6-7).

### 1. THE PROPHET'S INDICTMENT (3:1-5)

**3:1-2.** The prophet made a general statement about Jerusalem's wickedness: she had sunk to the level of the heathen nations (cf. Hab. 1:2-4). Though Jerusalem is not named in Zephaniah 3:1, verse 2 shows that it was meant. **Woe** was a pronouncement of an indictment, an indictment that was here threefold: a **city of oppressors** (cf. Nineveh, which Nahum called "the city of blood," Nahum 3:1), **rebellious and defiled.** This general threefold indictment was then elaborated in Zephaniah 3:2-5: they *oppressed* their own people (v. 3), were *rebellious* against God (v. 2), and were *defiled* religiously (v. 4). The Jerusalemites failed to heed the **correction** provided by the Law and the Prophets. Such rebellion was a failure to **trust in the Lord** and to be **near** Him in fellowship and worship (cf. 1:6).

**3:3-4.** The prophet then indicted both the civil leaders (cf. 1:8) and the religious leaders (cf. 1:4-5). The **officials** were compared to voracious, hungry **lions**; the **rulers** (judges) were insatiable **wolves** who completely devoured an evening prey by **morning** (cf. Ezek. 22:27; Micah 3:1-3). Judah's leaders robbed the citizenry in order to appease their own lust for power and plenty (cf. Micah 3:9-10).

Jerusalem's religious leaders were equally debauched! The **prophets** were self-styled, **arrogant** religionists who, with the treachery of the priests, twisted and perverted the Law of God in order to fill their bulging purses (cf. Ezek. 22:28; Micah 3:5, 11). The **priests** (cf. Zeph. 1:4) profaned **the sanctuary** probably by their idolatry and astrology (1:4-5) and by offering blemished animal sacrifices. Since they violated **the Law** by their disobedience (cf. Ezek. 22:26), no wonder their people were not teachable (Zeph. 3:2).

**3:5.** The **Lord**—in contrast with the people in general (v. 2), their civil leaders (v. 3), and their religious leaders (v. 4)— **is righteous . . . does no wrong,** exercises **justice,** and never fails. Certainly, then, He would uphold the oppressed

and punish the wicked! The nation evidenced the depth of its debauchery by its callous conscience: **the unrighteous know no shame** (cf. 2:1). The word "unrighteous" (*'awwāl*) is related to the word "wrong" (*'awlâh*) in the first part of 3:5. It means "to distort, to turn aside, to be wicked."

### 2. THE LORD'S JUDGMENT (3:6-7)

**3:6-7.** The Lord's words recorded in verses 6-13 point up Judah's dire situation. The Lord rehearsed His past actions against other **nations** (v. 6), and then cited both the reasons for and the actuality of a near-future judgment (v. 7). God had acted in conformity with His righteousness by judging nations for their wickedness, leaving them **demolished . . . deserted,** and **destroyed.** A classic example for Judah would be the 10 Northern tribes dispersed by Sargon II of Assyria in 722 B.C. God pleaded with His people to follow in His ways, accepting His **correction** (cf. v. 2) in order to avoid being **cut off** (cf. 1:3-4) and having to face His **punishments** (cf. 1:9-13; 2:1-3). The word **but** in the last sentence of 3:7 has a sad implication. Instead of responding to the Lord's unceasing mercies, Judah consciously and purposely repudiated Him and was even **eager** to continue in her corrupt ways. Complacency (1:12) and rebellion (3:1) led to an enthusiasm for corruption! (v. 7) What a cameo of human history!

### E. Judgment on all the earth (3:8)

**3:8.** The prophet concluded the "judgments" portion of his prophecy by reverting to the universal theme with which he introduced the section. He began with a summary statement of universal judgment (1:2-3); then he delineated God's judgment on Judah and Jerusalem (1:4–2:3) and on other **nations** (2:4-15). Then for emphasis he repeated the judgment on Jerusalem (3:1-7). Now he ended this long section with another general summary of universal judgment. In the Lord's impending universal judgment on the nations, His cup of wrath was about to be poured out; at that time His grace would take second place to His anger! At the end of the yet-future Tribulation, God will cause the nations' armies to assemble toward Jerusalem, and in the Battle of Armageddon (cf. Zech. 14:2; Rev.

16:14, 16) He will **pour out** on them His **wrath** (za'am, from "foam"), **all His fierce anger** (cf. comments on Zeph. 2:2), and **the fire of His jealous anger** (lit., "jealousy").

## III. The Day of Yahweh's Restoration (3:9-20)

The word "then" in verse 9 signifies a major pivot in the prophet's message both in tone and in content; he shifted from frightful predictions of destruction to prophecies of blessing and peace. After destroying the nations' armies, God will restore the nations to His favor. Instead of horrifying threats, here are comforting promises of love, mercy, and restoration. These promises look forward to the Millennium when Christ will rule as King on the earth.

### A. The restoration of the nations (3:9-10)

**3:9.** Zephaniah predicted that the nations will be renewed both morally (v. 9) and spiritually (v. 10). The purifying of **the lips of the peoples** does not mean they will speak a new language (as the KJV seems to imply by its trans. "a pure language"). Instead it means the renewal of once-defiled speech. One's lips represent what he says (the words spoken by his lips), which in turn reflect his inner life (cf. Isa. 6:5-7). The nations, formerly perverted by the blasphemy of serving idols, will be cleansed by God for true worship. As a result the nations, turning to reverential trust in God, will **call on the name of the LORD and** will evidence their dependence on Him by their united service (**shoulder to shoulder**).

**3:10.** As an example of the unanimity of their spiritual service the prophet mentioned those **beyond the rivers of Cush** (the upper Nile region—southern Egypt, Sudan, and northern Ethiopia; cf. 2:12), the most distant land to his knowledge. In their converted state the nations, represented by Cush, **will bring . . . offerings** to the Lord in Jerusalem (cf. Isa. 66:18, 20). This will be a marvelous reversal of the Gentiles' policies during Zephaniah's day! This stream of **worshipers** going to Jerusalem will include Israel—**My scattered people.** Zephaniah then elaborated on this fact (Zeph. 3:11-20).

### B. The restoration of Israel (3:11-20)

When God restores the nations to Himself, He will also turn from wrath to bless His chosen nation Israel. This grand prophetic theme is both the high point of prophetic promise for the nation and the climax of Zephaniah's message. Israel's regathering to Jerusalem was promised by God in words given to Moses (Deut. 30:1-10). Though God must punish sin, He is full of mercies and is always true to His promises. Though national judgment is assured, God will not forsake His people. He is the covenant-keeping Sovereign! This closing section of Zephaniah's message is comforting to Israel because of the reassurance of God's faithfulness to His promises.

#### 1. THE REDEMPTION OF THE NATION (3:11-13)

**3:11-13.** At the beginning of the Millennium (**that day**) Israel will be cleansed and restored. She will have no **shame** before God because of her sins (**wrongs** renders a Heb. word that means "terrible deeds") for God will have removed **from** the **city** all **those** guilty of **pride** or haughtiness. This will occur in the judgment of Israel (Ezek. 20:34-38; Matt. 25:1-13). Evildoers, full of shame, will be judged, and God's **holy hill** (Jerusalem; cf. Pss. 2:6; 3:4; 15:1; 24:3; 78:54; Dan. 9:16, 20; Joel 2:1; 3:17; Obad. 16) will be inhabited only by a pure people—**the meek and humble** (cf. Zeph. 2:3)—those trusting in the . . . LORD. All iniquity—**wrong** ('awlâh, lit., "injustice"; cf. 3:5, God "does no wrong"), **lies,** and **deceit**—will be purged away, and in that cleansed condition they will find peace and security. The closing line of verse 13 brings to mind the promises of the shepherd psalm, Psalm 23. Israel, so long defiled, turbulent, and ravished, will at last be at rest among the nations and without fear (cf. Zeph. 3:15-16).

#### 2. THE JOY OF THE NATION (3:14)

**3:14.** The tone of this verse is clearly that of exultation and joy: **Sing . . . shout aloud. . . . Be glad and rejoice.** Israel will be joyful in that millennial day because she will have been redeemed by God. Though the immediate prospect for the nation was one of sorrow and torment (vv. 1, 5-7), a day will come when the remnant's fears will give way to shouts of praise.

3. THE RULER OF THE NATION (3:15-17)

**3:15.** Shouts of joy will arise because Israel's Redeemer, the Messiah King, will be in her midst (cf. Isa. 9:7; Zech. 14:9). The long-promised Deliverer will protect them. Wrath from God's hand (Zeph. 3:8) and oppression by her **enemy** (cf. v. 19) will be gone, and **the LORD, the King of Israel,** will be **with** her (cf. v. 17), and she will have no **fear** (cf. v. 13).

**3:16-17.** Verse 16 amplifies the theme of calm from fear in the last line of verse 15. **They** (apparently converted Gentiles) will encourage Israel not to be fearful or in despair. **Hands** that **hang limp** picture despair through alarm and anxiety (cf. Jer. 47:3). Instead, Israel will lift her hands, symbolic of triumph, because of the Lord's presence (He will be **with you;** cf. Zeph. 3:15) and power (**He is mighty to save**). In addition to being with His redeemed remnant and delivering them, **He will . . . delight in** them. The nation will again be the object of God's great **love,** not His wrath. The Millennium will indeed be a time of peace for His troubled people; Israel will rejoice (v. 14). But more than that, God **will rejoice!** (v. 17) In fact He will be **singing** with delight and joy because His Chosen People will be in the land under His blessing.

4. THE REWARD OF THE NATION (3:18-20)

Seven times in these concluding verses, the Lord said, "I will." He wanted to place a strong hope before the believing remnant in Zephaniah's day, since His judgment was imminent and His restoration mercies remote. The prophet, in spite of dark days, wanted the repentant to grasp firmly God's promises for comfort and strength.

**3:18.** Many Jews, scattered from their homeland, had **sorrows** because they were unable to take part in **the appointed feasts.** But the Lord **will remove** those sorrows when He regathers His people to Jerusalem where they will enjoy His blessings. No longer will their feasts be **a burden,** something they hate to do, **and a reproach,** a cause for God's displeasure because of their sinful ways.

**3:19.** As Zephaniah had already stated (2:4-15; 3:8-15), God will remove Israel's foreign oppressors (cf. Gen. 12:3, "whoever curses you I will curse"), **gather** His people **scattered** in other lands,

and give them a favorable reputation (**praise and honor;** cf. Deut. 26:19; Zeph. 3:20) in all places where they are held in disrepute (cf. v. 11).

**3:20.** This verse summarizes Israel's yet-future blessings: regathering in the Promised Land (**home**), a favorable reputation (**honor and praise;** cf. v. 19) **among all the** nations, and a restoring of her **fortunes** (or a bringing back of her captives; cf. 2:7). This will all happen **before** her **very eyes.** In the Millennium, Israel will possess her land as God promised (Gen. 12:1-7; 13:14-17; 15:7-21; 17:7-8), and the Messiah, Israel's King, will establish His kingdom and will reign (2 Sam. 7:16; Ps. 89:3-4; Isa. 9:6-7; Dan. 7:27; Zeph. 3:15).

To emphasize the divine authority of his message as well as the certainty of God's comfort, Zephaniah ended his book with the words, **says the LORD!**

# BIBLIOGRAPHY

Baxter, J. Sidlow. *Explore the Book.* Reprint (6 vols. in 1). Grand Rapids: Zondervan Publishing House, 1970.

Calvin, John. *Commentaries on the Twelve Minor Prophets.* Vol. 4. Grand Rapids: Baker Book House, 1981.

Fausset, A.R. "Zephaniah." In *A Commentary Critical, Experimental and Practical on the Old and New Testaments.* Vol. 2. Reprint (6 vols. in 3). Grand Rapids: Wm. B. Eerdmans Publishing Co., 1978.

Feinberg, Charles L. *The Minor Prophets.* Chicago: Moody Press, 1976.

Freeman, Hobart E. *Nahum, Zephaniah, Habakkuk: Minor Prophets of the Seventh Century B.C.* Chicago: Moody Press, 1973.

Henry, Matthew. *Commentary on the Whole Bible in One Volume.* Reprint (6 vols. in 1). Grand Rapids: Zondervan Publishing House, 1966.

Keil, C.F. "Minor Prophets." In *Commentary on the Old Testament in Ten Volumes.* Vol. 10. Reprint (25 vols. in 10). Grand Rapids: Wm. B. Eerdmans Publishing Co., 1982.

Kleisert, Paul. "The Book of Zephaniah." In *Commentary on the Holy Scriptures Critical, Doctrinal and Homiletical.* Vol. 7. Reprint (24 vols. in 12). Grand Rapids: Zondervan Publishing House, 1960.

Laetsch, Theo. *The Minor Prophets.* St. Louis: Concordia Publishing House, 1956.

Poole, Matthew. *A Commentary on the Holy Bible.* Vol. 2. 1685. Reprint. London: Banner of Truth Trust, 1979.

Pursey, E.B. *The Minor Prophets: A Commentary.* Vol. 2. Reprint. Grand Rapids: Baker Book House, 1950.

Tatford, Frederick A. *The Minor Prophets.* Vol. 3. Reprint (3 vols.). Minneapolis: Klock & Klock Christian Publishers, 1982.

# HAGGAI

## F. Duane Lindsey

## INTRODUCTION

**Significance.** The Book of Haggai is the second shortest book in the Old Testament; only Obadiah is shorter. The literary style of Haggai is simple and direct. The content of the book is a report of four messages by a seemingly insignificant postexilic prophet whose ministry was apparently of limited duration.

Nonetheless the significance of his message and of his role in encouraging the rebuilding of the temple should not be underestimated. "The truth is that few prophets have succeeded in packing into such brief compass so much spiritual common sense as Haggai did" (Frank E. Gaebelein, *Four Minor Prophets: Obadiah, Jonah, Habakkuk, and Haggai*, p. 199). Notable in Haggai's ministry is his self-awareness of the divine origin of his messages. No less than 25 times in his two short chapters Haggai affirmed the divine authority of his messages. Not only did he introduce his sermons with, "This is what the LORD Almighty says," but also he concluded them with a similar formula ("declares the LORD Almighty"), and sprinkled those expressions throughout his messages. He was fully aware he was God's messenger (1:13).

**Haggai the Prophet.** The life and ministry of Haggai are wrapped in comparative obscurity. He was the first prophet through whom God spoke to the postexilic Judean community. His four messages are all dated in the second year of Darius I (520 B.C.). He was soon joined by the Prophet Zechariah who continued and completed the task of encouraging the people to rebuild the temple (cf. Ezra 5:1-2; 6:14). (See the chart in the *Introduction* to the Book of Zech. for a comparison of dates mentioned in the Books of Hag. and Zech.)

Haggai referred to himself simply as "the Prophet Haggai" (Hag. 1:1, etc.; cf. Ezra 5:1; 6:14). Nothing is known of his parentage or genealogy. His name apparently means "festive" or "festival," derived from the Hebrew word *ḥāg* ("a festival"). A few scholars therefore suppose that he was born on a feast day, but nothing in the text supports this. Some believe his reference to the Solomonic temple in Haggai 2:3 shows he was one of the exiles who saw it destroyed in 586 B.C. If so, he may have been an elderly prophet.

It is interesting that some ancient versions of the Old Testament attribute the authorship of certain psalms to Haggai and/or Zechariah: Psalms 137 and 145–148 in some manuscripts of the Septuagint (Gr. trans. of OT); Psalms 125–126; and 145–147 in the Latin Vulgate. This probably erroneous tradition apparently arose from the close connection these prophets had with the temple where these psalms were sung.

**Historical Background.** The destruction of the temple in Jerusalem by the Babylonian armies in 586 B.C. marked the end of an era in Jewish national and religious life. As exiles in Babylon, the Jews were without a temple and without their sacrifices. Though they could direct their prayers toward Jerusalem (1 Kings 8:48; Dan. 6:10), it was only under the generous policies of Cyrus the Great, king of Persia, that almost 50,000 Jews were allowed to return to Jerusalem with Zerubbabel (Ezra 1:2-4; cf. Isa. 44:28), accompanied by Joshua the high priest and the Prophets Haggai and Zechariah. Levitical sacrifices were soon reinstituted on a rebuilt altar for burnt offerings (Ezra 3:1-6), and in the second year of the return the foundation of the temple was laid (Ezra 3:8-13; 5:16). However, Samaritan harassment and eventual Persian pressure brought a halt to the rebuilding of the temple. Then spiritual apathy set in; and for about 16 more years—until the rule of the Persian king, Darius Hystaspes (521–486 B.C.)—the construction of the temple was discontinued. In the second year of Darius (520 B.C.) God raised up Haggai the prophet to encourage the Jews in the rebuilding of the temple (Ezra 5:1-2; Hag. 1:1). His task was to arouse the leaders and the people of Judah from their spiritual lethargy and to encourage them to continue working on the temple. The initial success of Haggai in his mission (cf. 1:12-15) was supplemented by the continued efforts of Zechariah until the temple reconstruction was finished in 515 B.C. (The critical problems relating to the Book of Hag. are minor and are reviewed by Hobart E. Freeman, *An Introduction to the Old Testament Prophets.* Chicago: Moody Press, 1968, pp. 330-2).

## OUTLINE

## COMMENTARY

Haggai, the Lord's messenger (1:13), delivered four dated messages from the Lord which encouraged the leaders and the people of Judah to rebuild the temple. (See the comments on vv. 12-15 for the view of some scholars that the book contains five messages.)

### I. The First Message: A Judgmental Call to Rebuild the Temple (chap. 1)

*A. The superscription (1:1)*

**1:1.** This superscription identifies the date, the prophet, and the addressees. That the prophecy is dated **in the second year of** the Persian **King Darius** rather than in a regnal year of a king of Judah is a vivid reminder that Haggai was ministering during "the times of the Gentiles" when Israel had no king of her own (cf. Zech. 1:1; Dan. 2; Luke 21:24). In Judah's postexilic calendar, adopted from the Babylonian system of beginning the new year in the spring rather than in the fall (cf. Ex. 23:16; 34:22), this date was 1 Elul (August 29), 520 B.C. Since this was the **day** of the new moon, it was probably a holy festival day in Jerusalem (cf. Isa. 1:14; Hosea 2:11). This provided **the Prophet Haggai** with a ready audience to listen to **the** first **word of the LORD** that broke the postexilic prophetic silence. The instrumental role of Haggai as a prophet, "the LORD's messenger" (Hag. 1:13), is stressed throughout this brief book. The book is virtually punctuated with the "messenger formula" ("This is what the LORD Almighty says," and similar expressions, vv. 2, 7, 13; 2:4, 6-9, 11, 14, 23). In addition, each message is identified as "the word of the LORD" (1:1; 2:1, 10, 20). There is no doubt about the divine origin of Haggai's messages.

The people were included in the implied address of 1:3 but this first message is initially directed **to** the two leaders, **Zerubbabel** the **governor of Judah** and **Joshua . . . the high priest.** Zerubbabel was the heir apparent to the throne of David, being the grandson of King Jehoiachin (1 Chron. 3:17-19; cf. Matt. 1:12, where Jehoiachin is called Jeconiah). That Zerubbabel was called both the **son of Shealtiel** and the son of Shealtiel's brother Pedaiah (1 Chron. 3:17-19) is probably due to a levirate marriage (cf. Deut. 25:5-10). After Pedaiah died his brother Shealtiel may have taken Pedaiah's widow to be his wife and to them was born Zerubbabel. Joshua's father **Jehozadak** was the high priest who was deported to Babylon from Jerusalem in 586 B.C. (1 Chron. 6:15).

### B. The accusation of procrastination (1:2-6)

**1:2.** Haggai's addressing the leaders first (v. 1) emphasizes their responsibility. The message is from **the LORD Almighty** (lit., "the LORD [*Yahweh*] of armies"). Haggai used this title of God, "the LORD Almighty," 14 times! The reference to Judah as **these people** rather than "My people" implies a divine rebuke because they did not act like the Lord's people. Their excuse for not building the temple (**the time has not yet come**) is laid bare in the next verses which describe their misplaced priorities.

**1:3-4. The word of the LORD** was now addressed to the people (**you** is pl.) mentioned in verse 2, and not just to the leaders. **Haggai** rebuked the people for their selfish indifference and negligence. They had built their own houses while neglecting to rebuild the **house** of God (cf. v. 9). The term **paneled houses** may only mean that they had roofs over their heads, though the word can also refer to luxurious paneling which may have adorned the houses of the leaders and the more well-to-do people.

**1:5-6. The LORD** exhorted the people to reflect on their conduct in view of their present poverty. **Give careful thought to your ways** is literally, "Set your hearts on your ways." Four other times Haggai wrote, "Give careful thought to" (v. 7; 2:15, 18 [twice]). They needed to reappraise their perverted priorities and give preeminence to God and their relationships with Him. What they had done was deplorable; and it was also fruitless. Their self-centeredness had not produced economic stability. Their abundant

plantings had resulted in only meager harvests (cf. 1:10-11; 2:15-17, 19). The simplest necessities of life—food, **drink,** and clothing—were not being met. The resulting inflation is pictured graphically: **You earn wages, only to put them in a purse with holes in it.** The implication is strong that these economic conditions were divine chastening for disobedience (cf. Lev. 26:18-20; Deut. 28:38-40). All their efforts at farming and wage-earning availed nothing because they had not put the Lord first. Their ancestors who had gone into captivity had experienced the same retribution (cf. Deut. 28:41), but God wanted better things of the returned exiles.

### C. The exhortation to rebuild the temple (1:7-8)

**1:7-8. The LORD** again (cf. v. 5) exhorted the people to reflection and challenged them to action. Having rebuked them for what they had *not* done and having shown the fruitlessness of what they *had* done, **the LORD** challenged them concerning what they *should* do—rebuild the temple to the glory of God. The implicit message of verses 2-4 is now made explicit: **Build the house** (i.e., God's temple). The need for bringing **timber** down from **the mountains** may imply that they had used up for their own houses the lumber purchased for rebuilding the temple a few years before (cf. Ezra 3:7). Also it appears that sufficient stone was available from the desolated temple and that they needed only timber for finishing the walls and roof. The completion of the temple would be pleasing to God (**so that I may take pleasure in it**). It would also bring Him honor or glory, showing the nations that Israel's God was worthy of worship in such a place by His servants.

### D. The explanation of the people's impoverishment (1:9-11)

The divine judgment referred to in verses 5-7 is now made more specific. Failure to do what they should—rebuild the temple—resulted in economic ruin and poverty.

**1:9a.** Two steps led them downward to poverty: (a) their harvest was much smaller than **expected,** for while their hopes were high, the yield was low, and (b) what they did receive appeared to vanish at once, graphically pictured as God's doing: **What you brought home I blew away.**

**1:9b.** God then explained that the reason for this chastening was their selfish neglecting to rebuild the temple. These words emphatically restated the thought in verse 4 (the temple remained **a ruin while** the people were **busy with** building their **own** houses). While laboriously involved with their own affairs the people were neglecting their spiritual responsibilities.

**1:10-11.** Their economic impoverishment resulted from a divinely designed drought. **Because of** their disobedience **the heavens . . . withheld their dew and the earth its crops.** In the dry season (April-October) morning dew, often heavy in Palestine, was essential to the growth of summer crops. So the absence of dew was devastating. The **drought,** brought about by God, affected the three basic crops of Palestine—**the grain, the new wine,** and **the oil** (from olive trees)—as well as **whatever** else **the ground** produced (cf. 2:16-17, 19). The absence of rain and dew indicates God's curse on the land and its people because of their disobedience to the covenant (cf. Lev. 26:19-20; Deut. 28:22-24). This in turn deprived **men and cattle** of food provisions. **The labor of** the people's **hands** in the fields would all be for naught.

### E. The response of leaders and people to the prophetic message (1:12-15)

Because of God's word of encouragement in verse 13 and the mention of a different date in verse 15, some scholars regard this section (vv. 12-15) as a separate prophetic message, making five in all. However, the date in verse 15 relates to the actual resumption of construction which probably followed the word of encouragement, so the whole section best fits the structure of the book as the response motif within this first of four messages.

**1:12.** Haggai reported the obedient and reverent attitude of both the leaders and **the people.** It was rare for a prophet of God to receive rapid and favorable response to a message he had given them from God. But this was the case regarding Haggai's simple and straightforward

message. The response of the leaders and **the people** was demonstrated in two ways: (a) they **obeyed the voice of the LORD their God and the message of the Prophet Haggai** (their recognizing the words of Haggai as God's word caused an effective change in their attitudes and actions), and (b) they **feared the LORD** (they had a new awe and reverence for God as they pondered the significance of their past disobedience and self-centeredness and their new sense of obedience to divine priorities). Haggai referred to the people as a **remnant** (here and also in v. 14 and in 2:2), not merely because they were survivors of the Babylonian Exile but also because they were becoming what the remnant of God's people should always be—those who are obedient within their covenant relationship to the Lord (cf. Isa. 10:21).

**1:13.** This verse, more than any other in his book, describes Haggai's role as **the LORD's messenger** and his words as the **message of the LORD.** The divine origin of all Haggai's recorded words is affirmed throughout this prophetic book (cf. v. 1). Here Haggai conveyed a word of encouragement from the Lord **to the people** as they anticipated rebuilding the temple: **I am with you** (repeated in 2:4; cf. 2:5 and Isa. 43:5). This assurance of God's presence to guide and empower them should have cast out all fear and apprehension about accomplishing their designated task of rebuilding.

**1:14.** **The LORD stirrred up the spirit of Zerubbabel . . . Joshua . . . and . . . the whole remnant** to rebuild the temple, just as He had moved their hearts to leave Babylon about 18 years earlier (cf. Ezra 1:5). Thus aroused by God and enabled for the task, **they . . . began to work on the house of the LORD Almighty, their God.**

**1:15.** The date when the actual rebuilding was resumed was 24 Elul (September 21), 520 B.C. There had been a delay of 23 days between the original prophecy (v. 1) and the resumption of the work (v. 15). This delay is explained by two factors: (a) the harvest of figs, grapes, and pomegranates was in Elul, the same **sixth month,** and (b) a period of planning and gathering of materials probably preceded the actual reconstruction.

## II. The Second Message: A Prophetic Promise of the Future Glory of the Temple (2:1-9)

### A. The superscription (2:1-2)

**2:1-2.** Like the superscription of the first message (1:1), this superscription identifies the date, the prophet, and the addressees. The date of this message was 21 Tishri (October 17), 520 B.C. This was nearly a **month** after the people had resumed the rebuilding of the temple (1:15). In this period the progress in rebuilding was slow, no doubt because of the laborious task of cleaning up 60 years of rubble and the cessation of work during the numerous festivals **of the seventh** month—the weekly Sabbaths, the Feast of Trumpets on the first day, the Day of Atonement on the 10th, and the Feast of Booths (or Tabernacles) from Tishri 15 to 21, with Tishri 22 also being a rest day (Lev. 23). This second message by **the Prophet Haggai** was delivered on the last ordinary day of the Feast of Booths. It was addressed to those who had begun to rebuild: **Zerubbabel . . . Joshua . . . and . . . the remnant of the people** (cf. Hag. 1:12).

### B. The promise of the Lord's enabling presence as an encouragement for rebuilding the temple (2:3-5)

**2:3.** The Lord surfaced their unfavorable comparison of the temple then under construction with the preexilic temple. Even in the initial stages of reconstruction the people were apparently making insidious comparisons between the restored temple and the glories of Solomon's temple which had been dedicated centuries before at the same time of year (1 Kings 8:2).

Before Haggai gave a solution to the people's discouragement, God told Haggai to ask three questions to surface the people's unfavorable comparison: **Who of you . . . saw this house in its former glory? How does it look to you now? Does it not seem to you like nothing?** These questions are essentially rhetorical, causing the people to face openly the fact that their temple was not going to be as splendid as Solomon's. Implied is the fact that some of those present, perhaps even Haggai himself, had seen the glories of the Solomonic edifice prior to its destruction 66 years before (in 586 B.C.). (A similar phenomenon occurred when

the foundation of the temple was laid a few years earlier; Ezra 3:10-13; cf. Zech. 4:10.)

**2:4a.** The LORD then encouraged the people by urging the two leaders and their people to take firm action. The thrice-repeated exhortation, **Be strong** (or "Take courage"), is followed by the single command, **and work.** Interestingly David had used both expressions when he committed the original temple project to Solomon (1 Chron. 28:10, 20), along with the promise of divine enablement. God had motivated the people (Hag. 1:14) and now He strengthened them. The expression, **all you people of the land,** does not refer to the adversaries of Judah as in Ezra 4:4, but is synonymous with "the remnant of the people" (Hag. 2:2; cf. 1:12, 14).

**2:4b-5.** The LORD forthrightly reaffirmed His presence with them: **I am with you** (cf. 1:13). As the **Spirit** of God was with the Israelites **when** they **came out of Egypt** (cf. Isa. 63:11-14), so He would be **among** them in rebuilding the temple, a task associated with the "Exodus" from Babylon. The covenant relationship between God and His people was also recalled in order to encourage them in their rebuilding.

The Lord then reassured them by encouraging them not to be fearful. Since He was with them (Hag. 1:13; 2:4) and since His Holy **Spirit** was with them, they could be calm and assured. The expression, **Do not fear,** is a common motif in an oracle of salvation (e.g., Isa. 41:10; 43:1).

### C. The proclamation of the future glory of the temple (2:6-9)

The people's unfavorable comparison of the restored temple with Solomon's temple (v. 3) was counteracted by God's assurance of ultimate success because of the future glory of the millennial temple. This proclamation about coming glory was given to encourage present success.

**2:6-7a.** The words **in a little while** suggest not chronological immediacy but the impending or imminent it-could-occur-anytime character of God's action indicated here. This future divine judgment (**I will once more shake the heavens and the earth, the sea and the dry land**) is depicted in terms of an earthquake as a symbol of God's supernatural intervention (cf. Isa. 2:12-21; 13:13; Ezek. 38:20; Amos 8:8; Hag. 2:21-22). When Jesus Christ returns to earth, "the earth and the sky will tremble" (Joel 3:16; Matt. 24:29-30). This event will affect not only the natural order (Hag. 2:6) but also people (**I will shake all nations,** v. 7). This "shaking" of the nations may refer to God's gathering the nations for the Battle of Armageddon (Zech. 14:1-4).

The writer to the Hebrews quoted Haggai 2:6 in Hebrews 12:26 and then added that the kingdom of God, which "cannot be shaken" (Heb. 12:28), will survive all divine judgments. This divine judgment was impending in Haggai's day since the Old Testament prophets did not see the valley of time lying between the First and Second Advents of Jesus Christ (cf. Isa. 61:1-2; Luke 4:18-21).

**2:7b.** The adornment of the future temple will be provided by the nations' wealth. **The desired of all nations** should probably be understood as a collective noun ("desirable things," i.e., treasures) to correspond with its plural verb (in the Heb.) **will come,** suggesting that surrounding nations will gladly give up their treasures to adorn the temple in Jerusalem (cf. Isa. 60:5; Zech. 14:14). The rendering, "the desire of all nations" (KJV), has been usually understood as a messianic prophecy referring to the coming of the One desired by all nations. The trend of recent translations and commentators has been away from this personal reference to the impersonal "desired things." However, the evidence is not all one-sided, and a case can be made for retaining a personal messianic reference. Perhaps Haggai deliberately selected a term that had exactly the ambiguity he wanted in order to include both an impersonal and personal reference (see Herbert Wolf, *Haggai and Malachi,* pp. 34-7).

**2:7c.** The future millennial temple (**this house**) **will** be filled **with glory.** This too could refer to material splendor (cf. Isa. 60:7, 13) but elsewhere the only "glory" that is said to **fill** the temple is the Shekinah glory of God's presence (cf. Ex. 40:34-35; 1 Kings 8:10-11). Though the ultimate reference is to the glory of God in the millennial temple (cf. Ezek. 43:1-12), Christ's bodily presence in the temple at His first coming may also be implied in Luke 2:32. Simeon referred to

Jesus as "the Glory of Thy people Israel" (NASB).

**2:8.** Some of the Lord's inexhaustible natural resources (**silver** and **gold**) will be available for use in constructing the temple, for He has ultimate providential control of the wealth of all nations.

**2:9a.** The restoration temple (**this present house**), Haggai said, would have a **glory** greater than the Solomonic temple (**the former house**) because during Herodian times the presence of the Messiah would adorn it (cf. Matt. 12:6; John 2:13-22). (The Herodian temple was a continuation, in a sense, of the postexilic "second" temple, not a "third" temple.) In addition, the ultimate fulfillment of this **greater glory** will be in the millennial temple. By building this postexilic temple the people would help advance God's program of manifesting Himself in a central place of worship: the Solomonic temple, and the yet-future millennial temple. So their work was more than merely constructing a building; it was a spiritual work which would ultimately culminate in God's millennial program.

**2:9b.** The blessings of the Messianic Age are summed up in a word—**peace. This place** probably refers to Jerusalem, not just the temple. Lasting peace in Jerusalem will result only from the presence of the Prince of Peace (cf. Isa. 9:6; Zech. 9:9-10).

## III. The Third Message: A Priestly Decision to Illustrate the Present Blessings of Obedience (2:10-19)

### A. The superscription (2:10)

**2:10.** The superscription of the third message specifies the date as 24 Kislev (December 18), 520 B.C., and once again **the Prophet Haggai** received **the word of the LORD.** During the two months since the second sermon (v. 1, "seventh month"; v. 10, **ninth month**), the Prophet Zechariah had begun his ministry (Zech. 1:1).

### B. A ritual comparison showing the corrupting effect of sin (2:11-14)

**2:11-13. The LORD** commanded Haggai to **ask the priests what the Law says,** that is, he was to seek an official priestly ruling on a ceremonial matter. Haggai's question regarding the transmission of ritual holiness was answered in the negative by **the priests. Consecrated meat** was meat set apart for a specific sacrificial purpose (cf. Lev. 6:25; Num. 6:20). While the **garment** that might contain such meat would also be holy (cf. Lev. 6:27), that holiness of the garment could not be transferred to **bread . . . stew . . . wine, oil, or** any **other food.** But this is not true of ritual defilement, as indicated by the priests' positive reply to Haggai's question regarding the transmission of ritual uncleanness (Hag. 2:13). A person's ceremonial defilement (e.g., **by contact with a dead body**) is as transferable to other things as is a contagious disease (cf. Lev. 11:28; 22:4-7).

**2:14.** **Haggai** then applied to the **people** of Judah the priests' answer in verse 13—disobedience renders even sacrificial worship unacceptable. This defilement of the **nation** Israel probably looked back to the period before the temple rebuilding began (cf. 1:2-4), because the defilement contrasts with the changed situation "from this day on" (2:15).

*C. A promise of present blessing in contrast with previous chastening (2:15-19)*

**2:15-17.** Haggai called on the people to remember their previous economic disaster which came because they disobeyed by not rebuilding the **temple.** For the third of five times (1:5, 7; 2:15, 18 [twice]) the people were challenged to **give careful thought to** (lit., "set their hearts on") their disobedience (**before** they started rebuilding) and the consequences of their sins. As stated in 1:6, their harvests were again (2:16) said to be short in quantity. Grain had decreased 50 percent (from **20 measures** to **10**) and the grape harvest had decreased 60 percent (from **50** to **20** measures of juice in the **wine vat;** cf. 1:10-11; 2:19). Again God claimed responsibility for this condition: **I struck . . . the work of your hands** (cf. 1:9, "I blew [it] away"). **Blight** (crop disease) and **mildew** are linked in several passages that deal with divine judgment for disobedience (cf. Deut. 28:22; 1 Kings 8:37; 2 Chron. 6:28; Amos 4:9). **Hail** also occurs in many judgment passages (Ex. 9:25; Isa. 28:2; 30:30). For an agricultural society such punishments were catastrophic to the economy and to survival. **The LORD** reminded the nation of its

failure to respond to His chastening hand (**you did not turn to Me**) just like the failure of an earlier generation (Amos 4:9).

**2:18-19.** After citing God's present chastening on Israel for her past disobedience, Haggai urged the people to remember the renewed temple construction as the beginning of present blessing. They were to **give careful thought to** (lit., "set your hearts on"; cf. 1:5, 7; 2:15) **the day when** they laid the temple's **foundation.** From the day of this third message (**in the ninth month**) they were to look back three months ("the sixth month," 1:14-15). The drought of divine judgment had already affected the year's harvest so that their barns were already emptied of the sparse harvest. They had neither staples (**seed,** or grapes, or olives) nor luxuries (figs and pomegranates). To this too they were to **give careful thought.** But things would now be different, for the Lord promised, **From this day on I will bless you.** Their faithful obedience in continuing to rebuild would enable them to experience God's blessing.

**IV. The Fourth Message: A Messianic Prophecy concerning Zerubbabel (2:20-23)**

*A. The superscription (2:20-21a)*

**2:20-21a.** The final message begins with the mention of the prophet, the date, and the addressee. As in the previous messages, Haggai said he was merely the Lord's messenger bringing **the word of the LORD.** This message **came to Haggai** on the same **day** as the third message, that is, 24 Kislev (December 18), 520 B.C. This message, however, was addressed only to **Zerubbabel governor of Judah.** As the people had needed encouragement to rebuild, perhaps Zerubbabel needed encouragement to lead this seemingly insignificant group of Jews who resided in a corner of the vast Persian Empire.

*B. A proclamation of the future overthrow of the Gentile kingdoms (2:21b-22)*

**2:21b.** God told Haggai to tell Zerubbabel that He would **shake the heavens and the earth.** As in the second message (vv. 6-7), the earthquake motif highlights divine judgment and introduces the subject of God's judgment on Gentile world powers.

**2:22.** Zerubbabel learned from Haggai that God would **overturn royal thrones and shatter the power of the foreign kingdoms.** This is reminiscent of the destruction of Gentile world powers represented in the great image in Daniel 2. There the worldwide messianic kingdom will replace the Gentile kingdoms (Dan. 2:34-35, 44-45). The overthrowing of **chariots** and the **fall** of **horses and their riders** indicate that this change in world government will be military as well as political. In the confusion of this great Battle of Armageddon (Rev. 16:16-18) at the Lord's second coming (Rev. 19:11-21) many a man will turn **the sword** against **his** own **brother** (cf. Zech. 12:2-9; 14:1-5).

## C. A proclamation of the restoration of the Davidic kingdom (2:23)

**2:23.** Three facts are prominent in this verse: (a) **the LORD** will fulfill this prophecy **on** the future **day** of Gentile judgment (cf. vv. 21-22); (b) the Lord will make **Zerubbabel . . . like My signet ring;** and (c) **the LORD** had **chosen** Zerubbabel as the channel of the Davidic line and therefore representative or typical of the Messiah. The title **My servant** frequently marked out the Davidic king (cf. the "Servant songs" in Isa. [42:1-9; 49:1-13; 50:4-11; 52:13–53:12] and also cf. 2 Sam. 3:18; 1 Kings 11:34; Ezek. 34:23-24; 37:24-25). Haggai's contemporary, Zechariah, used the messianic title "Branch" to refer to Zerubbabel (Zech. 3:8; 6:12; cf. Isa. 11:1; Jer. 23:5-6; 33:14-16).

The significance of comparing Zerubbabel to a "signet ring" (a seal of royal authority or personal ownership) is clarified by the imagery in Jeremiah 22:24-25. God said that if Jehoiachin (Zerubbabel's grandfather) were His signet ring, He would pull him off His hand and give him over to Nebuchadnezzar. Possibly Haggai was saying that in Zerubbabel God was reversing the curse pronounced on Jehoiachin. At any rate, Zerubbabel's place in the line of messianic descent (Matt. 1:12) confirmed his representative role in typifying the Messiah. Since the words "on that day" point to a yet-future fulfillment in the Messianic Age, it is wrong to suggest that Zerubbabel would actually rule as the anointed one on the Davidic throne in Haggai's day. This was not intended any more than the crowning of Joshua the high priest (Zech. 3:1-

10) indicated he would have political rule over Israel. The crowning of Joshua was clearly symbolic of things yet to be fulfilled by the Messiah (Zech. 6:9-15). Joshua was portrayed in Zechariah's vision in his official capacity as high priest rather than in his own person. Similarly Zerubbabel was owned as the Lord's "signet ring" in his representative position as the son of David, not for personal fulfillment in his own lifetime but for messianic fulfillment in the kingdom of the final Son of David (cf. Luke 1:32-33). An alternate interpretation sees Zerubbabel exercising delegated authority with David during the future millennial reign of Christ.

Appropriately the last words in Haggai's book are **the LORD Almighty** (cf. comments on Hag. 1:2). The sovereign covenant-God is able to bring about all He promised through Haggai. The temple will be rebuilt and filled with the glory of the Lord. The final Son of David will rule the earth in peace and righteousness. Therefore God's people are to be faithful now to the task to which He has called them.

# BIBLIOGRAPHY

Baldwin, Joyce G. *Haggai, Zechariah, Malachi: An Introduction and Commentary.* Downers Grove, Ill.: InterVarsity Press, 1972.

Feinberg, Charles L. "Haggai." In *The Wycliffe Bible Commentary.* Chicago: Moody Press, 1962.

————. *The Minor Prophets.* Chicago: Moody Press, 1976.

Gaebelein, Frank E. *Four Minor Prophets: Obadiah, Jonah, Habakkuk, and Haggai.* Chicago: Moody Press, 1970.

Keil, C.F. "Minor Prophets." In *Commentary on the Old Testament in Ten Volumes.* Vol. 10. Reprint (24 vols. in 10). Grand Rapids: Wm. B. Eerdmans Publishing Co., 1982.

Laetsch, Theo. *The Minor Prophets.* St. Louis: Concordia Publishing House, 1956.

Tatford, Frederick A. *The Minor Prophets.* Vol. 3. Reprint (3 vols.). Minneapolis: Klock & Klock Christian Publishers, 1982.

Wolf, Herbert. *Haggai and Malachi.* Chicago: Moody Press, 1976.

Wolff, Richard. *The Book of Haggai.* Grand Rapids: Baker Book House, 1967.

# ZECHARIAH

## F. Duane Lindsey

## INTRODUCTION

In an often-quoted statement, George L. Robinson has called the Book of Zechariah "the most messianic, the most truly apocalyptic and eschatological of all the writings of the Old Testament" (*International Standard Bible Encyclopedia.* Grand Rapids: Wm. B. Eerdmans Publishing Co., 1956, 5:3136). The messianic emphasis of Zechariah accounts for its frequent citation by New Testament authors. Nestle and Aland list 41 New Testament citations or allusions to Zechariah's book (Eberhard Nestle and Kurt Aland, eds., *Novum Testamentum Graece.* New York: American Bible Society, 1950, pp. 670-1).

**Zechariah the Prophet.** The postexilic Prophet Zechariah was a Levite born in Babylon (Neh. 12:1, 16). He was the son of Berekiah and the grandson of Iddo the priest (Zech. 1:1). Ezra and Nehemiah referred to him as "a descendant of Iddo" (Ezra 5:1; 6:14; cf. Neh. 12:4, 16), implying perhaps that his father had died young and Zechariah became the successor of his grandfather (cf. Neh. 12:4, 16). So, like Jeremiah and Ezekiel before him, Zechariah was both a prophet and a priest. Zechariah's name, which he shared with about 30 other men in the Old Testament, means "Yahweh (NIV, 'the LORD') remembers."

Zechariah was a contemporary of Haggai the prophet, Zerubbabel the governor, and Joshua the high priest (Ezra 5:1-2; Zech. 3:1; 4:6; 6:11). Zechariah returned to Jerusalem from Babylon with almost 50,000 other Jewish exiles. He was probably a relatively young man at the beginning of his prophetic ministry (cf. 2:4) while Haggai might have been considerably older.

**The Historical Background of Zechariah.** The fall of Jerusalem to the armies of Nebuchadnezzar in 586 B.C. marked the finale of the kingdom of Judah, much as the earlier defeat at the hands of the Assyrians in 722 B.C. brought to an end the Northern Kingdom of Israel. Most of Jerusalem's inhabitants were deported to Babylon for a period of about 70 years, as prophesied by the Prophet Jeremiah (Jer. 25:11; 29:10). During this Exile the Prophet Daniel received the revelation that Gentile kingdoms would be dominant over Judah and Israel until God would set up His kingdom on the earth under the rule of the Messiah (Dan. 2; 7). This period was referred to by Jesus Christ as "the times of the Gentiles" (Luke 21:24).

When the Babylonian Empire fell to the Persian Empire (539 B.C.), Cyrus the Great decreed that the Jews could return to Jerusalem to rebuild their temple (Ezra 1:2-4; cf. Isa. 44:28). However, only a small minority of about 50,000 Jews (including Haggai and Zechariah) returned under the leadership of Zerubbabel the governor and Joshua the high priest (Ezra 2). Levitical sacrifices were soon reinstituted on a rebuilt altar of burnt offering (Ezra 3:1-6), and in the second year of their return the foundation of the temple was laid (Ezra 3:8-13; 5:16). However, external oppression and internal depression halted the rebuilding of the temple for about 16 more years of spiritual apathy till the rule of the Persian King Darius Hystaspis (522–486 B.C.). In the second regnal year of Darius (520 B.C.) God raised up Haggai the prophet to encourage the Jews in rebuilding (Ezra 5:1-2; Hag. 1:1). Haggai preached four sermons in four months and then disappeared from the scene. Two months after Haggai delivered his first sermon, Zechariah began his prophetic ministry (cf. Hag. 1:1; Zech. 1:1), encouraging the people to spiritual renewal and motivating them to rebuild the temple by revealing to them God's plans for Israel's future. With this prophetic encouragement the people completed the temple reconstruction in 515 B.C. (Ezra 6:15). The dated portions of Zechariah's prophecy fall within the period of the rebuilding of the temple. The undated prophecies of Zechariah 9–14 were probably written much later in his ministry.

The following summary compares significant dates in the ministries of Haggai and Zechariah (cf. the chart "Chronology of the Postexilic Period," near Ezra 1:1):

## Dates of Key Events in Haggai's and Zechariah's Time

| | |
|---|---|
| August 29, 520 B.C. | Haggai's first sermon (Hag. 1:1-11; Ezra 5:1) |
| September 21, 520 | Temple building resumed (Hag. 1:12-15; Ezra 5:2) |
| October 17, 520 | Haggai's second sermon (Hag. 2:1-9) |
| October-November 520 | Zechariah's ministry begun (Zech. 1:1-6) |
| December 18, 520 | Haggai's third and fourth sermons (Hag. 2:10-23) |
| February 15, 519 | Zechariah's eight visions (Zech. 1:7–6:8) |
| December 7, 518 | Delegation from Bethel (Zech. 7) |
| March 12, 515 | Temple dedicated (Ezra 6:15-18) |

**The Unity of the Book of Zechariah.** The unity of the Book of Zechariah was first questioned by those who attributed chapters 9–14 to a preexilic writer such as Jeremiah (cf. Zech. 11:12-13; Matt. 27:9-10). However, the higher critical tradition has generally argued for a composition date for those chapters long after Zechariah (about the third century B.C.). The arguments for a later date generally emphasize stylistic differences and alleged historical discrepancies. Such arguments have been answered satisfactorily by conservative scholars who have demonstrat-

ed that the entire Book of Zechariah was indeed written by the prophet (e.g., Hobart E. Freeman, *An Introduction to the Old Testament Prophets.* Chicago: Moody Press, 1968, pp. 337-44; Merrill F. Unger, *Commentary on Zechariah,* pp. 12-4). The differences in subject matter, literary style, and probably a later period in Zechariah's life account adequately for the stylistic differences found in chapters 9–14. The reference to Greece in 9:13 does not require a late date if one accepts the reality of predictive prophecy.

**The Style and Literary Genre of the Book of Zechariah.** The style of Zechariah is characterized by epitome and also much figurative language. Zechariah showed much dependence on his predecessors and summarized many of their prophetic themes. However, he also displayed creative individuality of both thought and expression as the Spirit of God guided the recording of the divine revelation communicated to him.

Zechariah's prophetic book embraces several types of literary genres. Following the opening exhortation (call to repentance, 1:2-6), Zechariah gave a series of eight prophetic dream-visions he saw in a single night (1:7–6:8). These visions are in the form of apocalyptic ("revelatory") literature—highly figurative descriptions of eschatological encouragement. Chapters 9–14 are composed of two prophetic oracles (see comments on 9:1), which consist primarily of promises of Israel's future salvation.

# OUTLINE

I. The Eight Symbolic Visions (chaps. 1–6)
 A. The introduction to the visions (1:1-6)
  1. Preface to the call to repentance (1:1)
  2. Particulars of the call to repentance (1:2-6)
 B. The communication of the visions (1:7–6:8)
  1. The vision of the red-horse rider among the myrtles (1:7-17)
  2. The vision of the four horns and the four craftsmen (1:18-21)

3. The vision of the surveyor with the measuring line (chap. 2)
4. The vision of the cleansing and crowning of Joshua (chap. 3)
5. The vision of the gold lampstand and the two olive trees (chap. 4)
6. The vision of the flying scroll (5:1-4)
7. The vision of the woman in the ephah (5:5-11)
8. The vision of the four chariots (6:1-8)

C. The symbolic act concluding the vision (6:9-15)
1. The symbolic crowning (6:9-11)
2. The prophetic message (6:12-13)
3. The visible memorial (6:14)
4. The universal significance (6:15)

II. The Four Explanatory Messages (chaps. 7–8)
A. The messages required by the question about fasting (7:1-3)
B. The messages declared as the answer from the Lord (7:4–8:23)
1. A message of rebuke (7:4-7)
2. A message of repentance (7:8-14)
3. A message of restoration (8:1-17)
4. A message of rejoicing (8:18-23)

III. Two Revelatory Oracles (chaps. 9–14)
A. The anointed King rejected (chaps. 9–11)
1. The intervening judgments on nations surrounding Israel (9:1-8)
2. The blessings of the Messiah (9:9–10:12)
3. The rejection of the Good Shepherd and its consequences for Israel (chap. 11)
B. The rejected King enthroned (chaps. 12–14)
1. The redemption of Israel (chaps. 12–13)
2. The return of the King (chap. 14)

# COMMENTARY

## I. The Eight Symbolic Visions (chaps. 1–6)

### A. The introduction to the visions (1:1-6)

This preface to the entire book appropriately introduces Zechariah's series of eight apocalyptic visions. Its clarion call to repentance establishes the prerequisite for the spiritual blessings promised to Israel in the eight visions to follow. God would not bestow comfort on unrepentant hearts. God's covenants with Abraham (cf. Gen. 12:2-3; 15:5-21) and David (cf. 2 Sam. 7:8-16) rendered certain the fulfillment of His purposes for Israel. But those covenants did not nullify the need for each generation of Israelites to be obedient to God in order to experience His promised blessings.

1. PREFACE TO THE CALL TO REPENTANCE (1:1)

**1:1.** This verse relates the time, source, and agent of the opening call to repentance. The specific day of **the eighth month** (which began October 27, 520 B.C.) is not mentioned as it is apparently unimportant. More significant is the fact that a Jewish prophet dated his prophecy according to the reign of a Gentile monarch. This was a vivid reminder to all of Zechariah's hearers that "the times of the Gentiles" (cf. Luke 21:24; Dan. 2; 7) were in progress and that no descendant of David was sitting on the throne in Jerusalem (cf. Hosea 3:4-5). (See the *Introduction* for a list of dates mentioned in Ezra, Hag., and Zech.)

**Zechariah** was merely the agent of this prophecy and not its source, for **the word of the LORD came to** him as it did to other true prophets before him (e.g., Hosea 1:1; Joel 1:1; et al.). As a **prophet** Zechariah was merely a servant and spokesman called to bring God's efficacious word to the people. Regarding Zechariah's lineage, the same three generations are mentioned in Zechariah 1:7, but in Ezra 5:1; 6:14, Zechariah is called the "descendant" (lit., **son**) of **Iddo.** (In Heb. the word "son" often means a descendant.) In this way the prophet was seen in relation to his better-known grandfather. (A comparison of Jehu's lineage in 2 Kings 9:2, 14 with that in

1 Kings 19:16 and 2 Kings 9:20 illustrates the same phenomenon.)

### 2. PARTICULARS OF THE CALL TO REPENTANCE (1:2-6)

This solemn warning not to repeat the errors of their fathers (cf. Paul's analogous warning in 1 Cor. 10:11) was intended to destroy any false security that Zechariah's contemporaries might develop in view of the great things God intended to do for Israel in the future. This warning for the present, which emphasized divine anger (Zech. 1:2) and extended divine grace (v. 3), drew its severity from a threefold lesson from the past—a warning against disobedience (v. 4), delay (v. 5), and doubt (v. 6).

**1:2.** Zechariah affirmed that the destruction of Jerusalem and the Exile experienced by the previous generations were an expression of divine anger. In fact **the LORD was very angry** (lit., "angry with anger"), a phrase indicating extreme displeasure. The Lord ("Yahweh"), who had entered into personal covenant relationship with the nation Israel, was intensely angry **with** their **forefathers,** especially the last generation before the Captivity (but cf. 2 Kings 21:14-15), because of their rebellion against Him.

**1:3.** Whereas the sins of their forefathers were responsible for the desolation of the temple, their own sins had resulted in delay in rebuilding the temple. Nevertheless **the LORD Almighty** now extended to them a gracious invitation to repent. The threefold repetition of the divine name stresses the divine imperative conveyed in this call to repentance. The condition for their receiving divine blessing was not simply to resume building the temple, but to **return to** Him—not just to the Lord's Law or to His ways but to **the LORD** Himself. Their repentance two months before (cf. Hag. 1:12-15) apparently involved an incomplete commitment, resulting in delay in rebuilding the temple. Now a complete return to **the LORD** would bring divine blessing, expressed by the words, **I will return to you.**

**1:4.** The warning against disobedience features the bad example of their **forefathers** who not only rebelled against the Lord but also refused to respond to the preexilic prophets' preaching. These **earlier prophets** were separated from Zechariah and his contemporaries by the years of Exile in Babylon. One major feature (but not the whole content) of the preexilic preaching was a call to repentance—**Turn from your evil ways and your evil practices.** This illustrates the "*forth*telling" aspect of a prophet's message to his own generation (cf. Jer. 3:12-13; 18:11; 25:5-6; Ezek. 33:11; Hosea 14:1; Joel 2:12-13; Amos 5:4-6). Another aspect of prophecy ("*fore*telling") is prominent in Zechariah's own ministry (cf. Zech. 9–14). The negative response of the forefathers (**they would not listen or pay attention to Me**) was already apparent to the earlier prophets (e.g., Jer. 17:23; 29:19; 36:31).

**1:5.** The warning against delay was conveyed by two striking rhetorical questions which call attention to the brevity of human life. Zechariah asked, **Where are your forefathers now?** They were dead from sword, famine, pestilence, and natural causes, as predicted by the earlier prophets. Zechariah's second question was, **The prophets, do they live forever?** The implied answer was, no; their ministries were also brief, so the opportunity for repentance which they offered should not be ignored.

**1:6.** A warning against doubt was implied in Zechariah's affirming the effectiveness and certain fulfillment of God's message of judgment. This message consisted of **My words** (of threatened punishment; e.g., Jer. 39:16) **and My decrees** (i.e., judicial decisions; e.g., Zeph. 2:2; Isa. 10:1). Though **the prophets** died, God's words live on to be fulfilled. The certainty of fulfillment is indicated in that God's words and decrees did **overtake** their **forefathers.** The Hebrew word for "overtake" is a hunting term implying that the threatened judgment of God pursued and caught the evildoers. "Overtake" is used in Deuteronomy 28 of both judgment (Deut. 28:15, 45) and blessing (Deut. 28:2), and is illustrated in the action of the avenger of blood (Deut. 19:6). That the forefathers **repented** does not necessarily mean that they returned to God, but perhaps only that they came to their senses and recognized that they deserved punishment and that God had justly accomplished what He had purposed in sending them into Exile (Lam. 2:17). On the other hand many could have repented sincerely dur-

## Zechariah's Eight Night Visions

| Vision | Reference | Meaning |
|---|---|---|
| The Red-horse Rider among the Myrtles | 1:7-17 | God's anger against the nations and blessing on restored Israel |
| The Four Horns and the Four Craftsmen | 1:18-21 | God's judgment on the nations that afflict Israel |
| The Surveyor with a Measuring Line | Chapter 2 | God's future blessing on restored Israel |
| The Cleansing and Crowning of Joshua the High Priest | Chapter 3 | Israel's future cleansing from sin and reinstatement as a priestly nation |
| The Golden Lampstand and the Two Olive Trees | Chapter 4 | Israel as the light to the nations under Messiah, the King-Priest |
| The Flying Scroll | 5:1-4 | The severity and totality of divine judgment on individual Israelites |
| The Woman in the Ephah | 5:5-11 | The removal of national Israel's sin of rebellion against God |
| The Four Chariots | 6:1-8 | Divine judgment on Gentile nations |

ing the Exile, resulting in the forgiveness and restoration to the land that followed.

Thus the prerequisite for experiencing the spiritual blessings revealed in Zechariah's further visions and prophecies was a genuine and wholehearted turning to **the LORD.** They were not to be disobedient as were those of the former generation who were taken into Exile as a result of God's certain judgment.

### B. The communication of the visions (1:7–6:8)

In a single night Zechariah saw a series of eight visions which were interpreted by an angel and which described the future of the nation Israel. God's program of spiritual blessing set forth in the visions bridges the centuries from the rebuilding of the temple in Zechariah's day to the restoration of the kingdom to Israel under the Messiah (still future in Acts 1:6, to be fulfilled at Christ's Second Advent; cf. Acts 15:16). Joyce Baldwin has

correctly observed a "standard pattern" in the record of Zechariah's visions: (a) introductory words, (b) a description of the things seen, (c) a question by Zechariah to the angel for the meaning, and (d) the explanation by the angel. She also notes that four of the visions are accompanied by summarizing oracles which usually follow the vision (Zech. 1:14-17; 2:6-13; 6:9-15), except for one oracle within a vision (4:6-10) (*Haggai, Zechariah, Malachi,* pp. 92-3).

### 1. THE VISION OF THE RED-HORSE RIDER AMONG THE MYRTLES (1:7-17)

This vision established the general theme of hope for dispersed and downtrodden Israel. Gentile oppression was offset by comforting promises of divine blessing.

**1:7a.** The day the visions came was **the 24th day of the 11th** (Jewish) **month** of Darius' **second** regnal **year** (February 15, 519 B.C.). **Shebat** was the Babylonian name of the 11th **month,** adopted by the Jews after the Exile. This date was five months after the building of the temple was resumed (Hag. 1:14-15; 2:15), three months after Zechariah's first prophecy (Zech. 1:1), and two months after Haggai's last prophecy (Hag. 2:20—a prophecy regarding the destruction of world powers before the millennial rule of the Messiah; cf. Hag. 2:21-23).

**1:7b-8a.** The source of Zechariah's visions is clearly denoted by the clause **the Word of the LORD came** (cf. v. 1), a kind of prophetic "formula" indicating divine revelation. The visions, with partial interpretations, were seen in the spirit, had the significance of verbal revelation, and were supplemented by additional words of God. The words **I had a vision** (KJV, "I saw") denote the means by which divine revelation was conveyed to **Zechariah.** The expression does not refer to a dream, much less to a mere literary form. Zechariah was awake, as is apparent from his questions (e.g., v. 9) and interruptions (e.g., 3:5).

**1:8b.** The vision included three things: (a) a description of what Zechariah saw (v. 8), (b) an explanation of the same (vv. 9-11), and (c) intercession by the Angel of the Lord (v. 12).

Throughout the vision the primary focus on the **man riding a red horse** suggests that he was the leader of the horsemen. **He was standing** (i.e., astride his horse) as though stationed to await the report of his reconnaissance patrol. He is identified in verse 11 as "the Angel of the LORD." This Messenger (cf. comments on v. 11) was located **among the myrtle trees in a ravine,** possibly in the Kidron Valley east or southeast of Jerusalem where these fragrant evergreen shrubs were probably abundant. Riders sat on the horses **behind him** (because the riders were to report, v. 11), but the more important fact here is the colors of the horses: **red** (bay or reddish brown), **brown** (sorrel), **and white.** The significance of the colors is not stated, and this is complicated by the fact that the Hebrew word translated "brown" (NIV) or "speckled" (KJV) is found only here in the Old Testament, so that its meaning is not sure.

**1:9-11.** When Zechariah **asked** about the vision's meaning (**What are these?** cf. v. 19; 4:4, 11; 6:4; also cf. 5:6) an interpreting angel answered. In the fifth and sixth

visions the angel asked Zechariah if he knew the meaning (4:2, 5, 13; 5:2). Apparently this was to rouse his curiosity. This angel referred to in the visions as **the angel who was talking with me** (1:11, 13-14, 19; 2:3; 4:1, 4-5; 5:10; 6:4), was not **the Angel of the LORD** (1:11-12; 3:1-6). The interpreting angel showed Zechariah the meaning of the vision by allowing its actors to speak. The first speaker was the central figure astride the red horse, who referred to the other riders as **the ones the LORD has sent to go throughout the earth.** The phrase "to go throughout" seems to be used here in the military sense of patrolling or reconnoitering. Just as the Persian kings had mounted messengers to send throughout the empire, so the Angel of the Lord had sent out angelic horsemen to reconnoiter the world scene. The patrol reported to their Leader, now called "the Angel of the LORD." That this "Angel" (lit., "Messenger") is a manifestation of the preincarnate Christ is established in chapter 3 where He is specifically called "the LORD" who yet refers to "the LORD" as another Person (3:2). Also He is seen exercising the divine prerogative of forgiving sins (3:4). (Cf. comments on "the Angel of the LORD" in Gen. 16:7.) The patrol had completed its assignment of searching **throughout the earth, and** had **found** the earth peacefully inhabited, **at rest** from war, but Israel was not at **peace** and rest. Was this report good news or bad news? If the reference is to the peace that existed during the second year of Darius, it was the result of Persian oppression and injustice, so this was bad news to Israelites who were under Gentile domination. Perhaps the vision has a more eschatological reference in anticipation of the worldwide kingdom of Messiah, since the patrol covered not only the vast Persian Empire, but also **the whole world**—though perhaps "the whole world" is a figure of speech (synecdoche) for the Persian Empire.

**1:12.** The intercession of **the Angel of the LORD** is unusual, for this divine Messenger is usually seen representing God to people rather than functioning in an intercessory role representing people to God. That the divine Messenger addressed the LORD **Almighty** in prayer supports a distinction of Persons in the Godhead, and contributes to the implicit doctrine of the Trinity in the Old Testament. The lament formula **How long?** expresses the deep need of Israel to have the Lord act on her behalf. The **70 years** of promised Captivity were over (cf. Jer. 25:12; 29:10), but the city was still not rebuilt.

**1:13.** The preceding vision unveiled God's controlling activity in the world, but a verbal message was now added to convey comfort to Israel. This message from **the LORD** (this may or may not be "the Angel of the LORD" of v. 12) was communicated to and through the interpreting angel to Zechariah so that he might proclaim it to the people. The message conveys (a) God's love for Israel (vv. 13-14), (b) God's wrath on the nations (v. 15), and (c) God's blessings on Israel (vv. 16-17).

The content of the **kind . . . words** which promised good and the **comforting** words which produced consolation is found in verses 14-17.

**1:14.** God's love for His people (**Jerusalem and Zion**) is expressed in the words **very jealous** (lit., "jealous with great jealousy"). This speaks of His burning zeal (cf. 8:2) to protect His covenant love with Israel. This burning zeal was expressed against Judah for 70 years (1:12), but His anger now turned toward the nations, which is the theme of the second vision (vv. 18-21).

**1:15.** God's anger with **the nations** was doubly emphatic (**very angry**; lit., "with great anger I am angry"; cf. v. 2) because of the false security which they so precariously enjoyed. His extensive wrath on the nations resulted from their immoderate, prolonged, and intensified punishment of Israel when God **was only a little angry,** that is, when He desired moderate punishment of His people. The nations **added to the calamity** by overstepping the limits God had intended for Israel's punishment (cf. Isa. 47:6).

**1:16-17.** Because of (**therefore**) God's love for Israel and His anger toward the Gentiles, He now promised six blessings for Israel: (a) the presence of God in **Jerusalem** (**I will return . . . with mercy**; cf. Ezek. 43:5; 48:35) in contrast with the departure of the divine glory from the preexilic temple (Ezek. 10:18-19; 11:22-23); (b) the rebuilding of the temple (**My house will be rebuilt;** cf. Ezek. 40–48); (c)

the rebuilding of the city (**the measuring line will be stretched out over Jerusalem;** cf. Jer. 31:38-40); (d) Israel will be enriched (**towns will again overflow** with the wealth of divine blessings which the city walls will be unable to contain; cf. Isa. 60:4-9); (e) the inhabitants of Jerusalem (**Zion**) will be comforted by the fulfillment of God's gracious promises (cf. Deut. 13:17; 30:3; Isa. 14:1; 49:15); and (f) they will be chosen (cf. Zech. 2:12; 3:2), referring to God's focusing His sovereign love on them and perhaps also referring to God's inaugurating the New Covenant with Israel (Jer. 31:31-40; cf. Rom. 11:26-27).

The complete fulfillment of these blessings from a New Testament perspective relates to the Second Advent of Christ, the millennial temple, and the blessings of the millennial kingdom, as suggested in the parallel Scripture passages mentioned above. Though the restoration temple was completed about four years after this prophecy (Ezra 6:15) and a partial rebuilding of the city about 80 years later (Neh. 6:15), the passages noted from Ezekiel indicate that the divine glory will be absent from the temple until millennial times. Nevertheless the Jews of Zechariah's day may have felt that those promised blessings were imminent, and this probably encouraged them in rebuilding the temple.

Several salient features from this first vision are elaborated on in the next two visions, in which God's displeasure with the nations is visualized in the second vision and God's causing Israel to prosper with the blessing of His presence is pictured in the third vision.

2. THE VISION OF THE FOUR HORNS AND THE FOUR CRAFTSMEN (1:18-21)

The consolation and comfort spoken of in verses 13 and 17 are displayed panoramically in the contrasting features of the second and third visions. The second vision on the one hand shows God's judgment on the nations that afflict Israel (vv. 18-21). The third vision on the other hand shows God's blessing in prospering Israel (chap. 2). The vision of the four horns and the four craftsmen shows *how* God will execute His displeasure, mentioned in 1:15, on the Gentiles. The nations that scattered Israel will themselves be crushed.

### a. The four horns observed (1:18)

**1:18.** Zechariah **looked up** to see a new scene portrayed **before** his eyes (cf. 2:1; 5:1, 9; 6:1; Dan. 8:3; 10:5). He observed **four horns** such as those of a ram or a goat (cf. Dan. 8:3-8). However, since no reference is made to any animals their presence should not be presumed.

### b. The four horns identified (1:19)

**1:19.** Again Zechariah asked, **What are these?** (cf. v. 9; 4:4, 11; 6:4; also cf. 5:6) A horn when used symbolically indicates invincible strength (cf. Micah 4:13) or often a Gentile king who represents his kingdom (Dan. 7:24; Rev. 17:12). Here the four **horns** symbolize proud Gentile powers ("horns of the nations," Zech. 1:21) **that scattered Judah, Israel, and Jerusalem** (an all-inclusive designation to denote God's people in Exile). Some writers understand these four horns to be the four Gentile empires envisioned in Daniel 2 and 7 (Babylon, Medo-Persia, Greece, and Rome). In that view the four craftsmen are the empires that succeeded them, respectively, with the fourth craftsman being the messianic kingdom from heaven (Dan. 2:44). However, in Zechariah's vision the angel said the horns "scattered" Israel (past tense, Zech. 1:19) and that was before any craftsmen arrived on the scene. It seems better either to regard the number four as a number of completeness, the totality of Israel's opposition, or to refer the four horns to four nations that had scattered Israel before Zechariah saw the vision (perhaps Assyria, Egypt, Babylonia, and Medo-Persia).

### c. The four craftsmen introduced (1:20)

**1:20.** The Hebrew word for **craftsmen** (ḥārāšîm) indicates workmen skilled in wood, stone, or metal. Since the material of which the horns are composed is not mentioned, the general translation "craftsmen" is appropriate. (The RSV translates the word "smiths," apparently assuming the horns were iron.)

### d. The four craftsmen explained (1:21)

**1:21.** The identity of **the craftsmen** depends on the identity of **the horns.** If the **horns** are the succeeding kingdoms in Daniel's visions (Dan. 2; 7), then the craftsmen are Medo-Persia, Greece, Rome, and the messianic kingdom. Otherwise they were probably **nations,** including Persia, which God used to overthrow Israel's past oppressors (see comments on Zech. 1:19). In any case, the vision shows that God raises up instruments of judgment to deliver His people Israel from all her enemies.

3. THE VISION OF THE SURVEYOR WITH THE MEASURING LINE (CHAP. 2)

### a. The content of the vision (2:1-2)

**2:1.** The expression, **Then I looked up** (cf. 1:18; 5:1, 9; 6:1) reflects not only the transition to a new vision, but also its continuity with the preceding one. The divine judgment on the Gentile nations will be followed by God's enlarging and protecting Jerusalem. This basic message of the vision is clear, but the details are less certain because of ambiguity in answering three key interpretive questions: Who are the persons mentioned in the vision? What is the position and movement of each person? Who is speaking in 2:4-13?

The man's occupation as a surveyor is identified by the **measuring line in his hand.** There is no necessary reason to regard this man as more than an unidentifiable man in the vision. Some interpreters, however, identify the "young man" (v. 4) with the "man with a measuring line" (v. 1). According to this view the "interpreting angel" left Zechariah's side and met another angel who urged him to recall the surveyor who had a mistaken notion about Jerusalem needing rebuilt walls. However, it seems better to regard this young man as Zechariah himself who was given the message of Jerusalem's enlargement (vv. 4-13) as an explanation of the surveyor's activity.

The identity of the surveyor is not given in the passage, but there is merit to the view which identifies him with the Angel of the Lord (1:11; 3:1; cf. Ezek. 40:3). Comparing this vision with Zechariah's first vision (Zech. 1:7-17) supports this view that the surveyor is the divine Angel of the Lord who is conveying divine revelation to Zechariah. At any rate the words in 2:4-13 are a message (or series of messages) from the Lord Himself, addressed first to the young man (vv. 4-5), then to Israel (vv. 6-12), and finally to "all mankind" (v. 13).

**2:2.** The surveyor's purpose, as indicated in his response to Zechariah's question, was to mark out the boundaries of **Jerusalem,** probably to indicate the present boundaries of the city from which the future overflowing would progress.

*b. The communication of the message (2:3-13)*

**2:3-4a. Another angel,** possibly coming from the surveyor, gave a message to Zechariah's interpreting **angel** to be conveyed to the prophet.

**2:4b.** That **Jerusalem will be a city without walls** indicates that the city will overflow its boundaries because of divine blessing. It will need no fortification or protection because of God's presence (cf. v. 5; Ezek. 38:11).

**2:5. The Lord** will be Jerusalem's protection without and **glory within** (cf. Isa. 60:19). This promise looks forward to the Lord's personal presence through the Messiah in the millennial kingdom on earth. Ezekiel envisioned the future return of the divine glory to the temple (Ezek. 43:2-5) but Zechariah was granted a vision of the glory extending to the entire city (Zech. 2:5) and to the whole land (v. 12; cf. 14:20-21).

**2:6-9.** This divine oracle seems to be a practical application of the preceding vision(s) addressed to Zechariah's contemporaries (**Zion** refers to Jews) who are still in **Babylon,** urging them to return to Jerusalem. The last part of verse 6 should probably be translated **I have scattered you**—not to **the four winds,** but—"*as the four winds*" **of heaven.** This may suggest a violent scattering, or it may be a figurative way of describing any significant dispersion of the Jews from their land. The exiles were intact in Babylon, **the land of the north,** so-called because invasions from Babylon came on Israel from the north. **The Lord** Himself (i.e., as the Angel of the Lord or as the Messiah) speaks in verses 8-9, though some interpreters refer parts of this statement to Zechariah's explanation of his prophetic call. **After He has honored Me and has sent Me** is the NIV translation of a difficult Hebrew phrase, translated in the KJV, "After the glory hath He sent Me." The idea seems to be that God will send the Messiah who will judge **the nations that . . .** plundered Israel and will display His glory. This will be fulfilled in the judgment of the Gentiles at Messiah's Second Advent (Matt. 25:31-46). **The ap-**

**ple of His eye** is a figure taken from Deuteronomy 32:10, the "apple" (lit., "gate or opening") probably referring to the pupil of the eye, that part of the eye most easily injured, the most demanding of protection. Here it symbolizes Israel under God's protective care.

**2:10-12.** This oracle is possibly aimed at the remnant which had already returned to Jerusalem. But again the reason for the call to praise is messianic, looking forward to the time when the earth will be prepared for the reign of Christ. **Shout and be glad** is a typical call to praise in songs and is linked with the rule of Yahweh (NIV, **the Lord**) as King in Jerusalem (cf. Pss. 93; 96; 98; Isa. 52:7-10; Zeph. 3:14-15). The Lord's **coming** to **live among** Israel is messianic, referring to the time when the Messiah will come to rule on the throne of David. Possibly, however, both of Christ's advents are in view here as in passages such as Isaiah 9:6-7; 61:1-2. But the emphasis here is on the Second Advent when God's blessings on Israel will overflow to the nations. **That day** is a shortened way of referring to the future "day of the Lord" when He will come to judge the nations and fulfill His covenants with Israel in the millennial kingdom. In the Millennium people from **many nations** will worship **the Lord** (cf. Zech. 8:20-23; 14:16; Isa. 2:3). **The holy land**—a phrase found only here in the Bible—will be the Lord's inheritance (cf. Zech. 8:3), and **Jerusalem** will be God's choice (cf. 1:17; 3:2) for the world's capital (Isa. 2:1-2).

**2:13.** The entire human race is to bow in silence and awe before the Almighty God.

4. THE VISION OF THE CLEANSING AND CROWNING OF JOSHUA (CHAP. 3)

Topographically the setting of Zechariah's visions apparently shifted from a valley outside Jerusalem (first two visions, 1:7-21) to an observation point within the city (third vision, chap. 2) to the courts of the temple itself (fourth and fifth visions, chaps. 3–4). Symbolically the first three visions pictured Israel's external deliverance from Captivity, her expansion, and the material prosperity of the land, whereas the fourth vision (chap. 3) sets forth Israel's internal cleansing from sin and reinstatement into her priestly office and functions.

### a. The symbolic action (3:1-5)

The Lord introduced the vision to Zechariah ("He showed me"), who clearly perceived the identity of the actors in the vision and the significance of their actions. Therefore this fourth vision differs from the preceding ones by the absence of questions by Zechariah and explanations by the interpreting angel. The actors or participants are (a) Joshua the son of Jehozadak, the high priest of the restoration who returned with Zerubbabel from Babylon; (b) the Angel of the Lord, the preincarnate Christ, already introduced in 1:11-12; (c) Satan, the accuser (cf. Rev. 12:10); (d) attending angels ("those who were standing before" Joshua, Zech. 3:4); and (e) the Prophet Zechariah, who became a vocal participant in the vision (v. 5).

**3:1-2.** The first significant feature in the vision is the position of **Joshua ... standing before the Angel of the Lord.** Here the word "standing" is practically a technical word for priestly ministry (cf. Deut. 10:8; 2 Chron. 29:11). This implication concerning the deity of the Angel of the Lord and His identity as the preincarnate Christ is more explicitly indicated in Zechariah 3:2 where He speaks under the title of "Lord" and yet distinguishes Himself *from* **the Lord** in addressing **Satan** (cf. comments on 1:11). This identification is further supported in 3:4 where His action is virtually that of forgiving sins.

Satan's resistance changed the scene from a priestly one to a judicial one where Joshua was the object of Satan's accusations. Then the Angel of the Lord rebuked **Satan** and proceeded to acquit Joshua, not because Satan's accusations were false, but because of God's gracious love for and choice of His people Israel. Joshua was functioning here in his high priestly capacity as representative of the nation Israel. God's choice of **Jerusalem,** not Joshua, was the basis of the **rebuke** (v. 2). Later the sin was removed from the land, not just from Joshua (v. 9). Joshua and his priestly companions were said to be "men symbolic of things to come" (v. 8). Therefore much as the high priest represented the entire nation on the Day of Atonement (cf. Lev. 16:1-10), so here Joshua the high priest was accused and acquitted on behalf of the nation Israel.

**3:3-5.** The acquittal took the form of removing Joshua's **filthy clothes,** representative of his sin and guilt and that of the nation. Joshua was then **clothed** with festal or **rich garments,** speaking of the purity associated with his forgiveness, and **a clean turban,** possibly suggesting the joy of his reinstatement into the priesthood. This symbolized the forgiveness and restoration of the nation Israel as a priestly nation (cf. Ex. 19:6).

### b. The significant communication (3:6-10)

This communication includes a charge to Joshua (vv. 6-7) and an explanation of the vision's symbolism (vv. 8-10).

**3:6-7.** The **charge to Joshua** embodied two conditions and three results of divine blessing. To **walk in** God's **ways** describes the personal attitude of the priests (and ultimately the nation) toward God, and keeping God's **requirements** (cf. 1 Kings 2:3) refers to the faithful performance of priestly duties. If Joshua met these conditions he would enjoy three things: (a) **govern My house** —have continued service in the temple; (b) **have charge of My courts**—guard the temple from idolatry and other religious defilement; and (c) receive **a place among these standing here**—perhaps referring to Joshua's free access to God (cf. Zech. 3:1) comparable to that of the angels (those who are "standing" are distinguished from Joshua's fellow priests who are "seated," v. 8).

**3:8-10.** The Lord next affirmed the point of the vision—that **Joshua** and his priestly companions were **symbolic of things to come.** In their official priestly cleansing from sin they prefigured the future cleansing of the nation Israel. This future cleansing was linked with the coming of the Sin-Remover who was given three messianic titles—**My Servant, the Branch,** and **the Stone.** As the Servant of the Lord, Christ is the One who comes to do the will of the Father (Isa. 42:1; 49:3-4; 50:10; 52:13; 53:11). As the Branch of David, Christ is the Davidic Descendant who will rise to power and glory out of the humiliation into which the line of David had fallen (Isa. 4:2; 11:1; Jer. 23:5; 33:15; Zech. 6:12-13). As the Stone (cf. Ps. 118:22; Matt. 21:42; 1 Peter 2:6) He will bring judgment on the Gentiles (Dan. 2:44-45) and be a stone of stumbling for unbelieving Israel (Rom. 9:31-33). But ultimately He will bring cleansing to Israel and **remove the sin of this land in a single day.** Some say this refers to the day of Christ's crucifixion, but it is more likely a reference to the day of His Second Advent when at the end of the future Tribulation period the merits of His death will be applied to believing Israel (Zech. 13:1).

The **seven eyes** on the **stone** probably symbolize the Messiah's full intelligence with which He will judge. This may also allude to the Holy Spirit (Isa. 11:2; Rev. 5:6). **That day** (Zech. 3:10) seems to refer to the whole period of millennial blessing which will follow the return of Christ. Sitting under one's own **vine and fig tree** refers to conditions of peace and prosperity (1 Kings 4:25; Isa. 36:16; Micah 4:4).

5. THE VISION OF THE GOLD LAMPSTAND AND THE TWO OLIVE TREES (CHAP. 4)

*a. The description of the vision (4:1-4)*

**4:1-4.** The interpreting **angel** aroused Zechariah **from . . . sleep** and directed his attention (by a question; cf. vv. 5, 13; 5:2) to **a solid gold lampstand,** the exact appearance of which is subject to controversy. Appearing in a context of priestly temple ministry (cf. the previous vision), this lampstand was apparently similar to the lampstand placed in Israel's tabernacle (cf. Ex. 25:31-40), and the 10 lampstands of Solomon's temple (1 Kings 7:49). However, the tabernacle lampstand had to be filled with oil by the priests, but this lampstand was automatically filled with an endless supply of oil without human agency. This is indicated by three significant and peculiar features: (a) **a bowl** for storing oil was suspended over the lampstand (Zech. 4:2); (b) oil was transported by gravity from the bowl through **seven channels** or conduits to each of the **seven lights** of the lampstand, apparently 49 conduits in all (v. 2); and (c) the lampstand was flanked by **two olive trees** which were tapped by "two gold pipes" through which "golden oil" flowed constantly into **the bowl** (vv. 3, 11-12). (Baldwin gives an alternate description of the construction of this lampstand; *Zechariah,* pp. 119-20.) Zechariah's inquiry **What are these?** (cf. 1:9, 19; 4:11; 6:4; also cf. 5:6) possibly referred to the "seven lights" (i.e., lamps). (See com-

ments on 4:10b.) But, more likely, "these" referred to the two olive trees. The prophet's question was seemingly put off by the angel and repeated later by Zechariah (v. 12), when again the prophet received a delayed answer. The two delays by the angel focused attention on the answer which was finally given in verse 14.

*b. The significance of Zerubbabel (4:5-10a)*

**4:5-10a.** Before identifying the "two olive trees" (v. 3) with "the two who are anointed" (v. 14), the angel prepared for this conclusion by relating the vision **to Zerubbabel,** the governor of Judah (cf. Hag. 1:1, 12, 14; 2:21). The angel suggested that he would finish the **temple** (Zech. 4:9) through the abundant supply of the **Spirit** of God. Thus the oil for the lamp is associated with the Holy Spirit. By His enabling the temple would be completed (v. 6) and every obstacle (**mighty mountain,** v. 7) to rebuilding would be removed. Military strength (**might**) and human manpower (**power**) could not accomplish the task, but Spirit-empowered workers under the direction and leadership of **Zerubbabel** would do so.

The LORD explained to Zechariah (vv. 8-10) that Zerubbabel's finishing the restoration temple would drive the critics to silence for they would **know** God had **sent** the prophet and the reconstructionists (**God bless it!** [v. 7] **Men will rejoice** [v. 10]). (Because Joshua the high priest was the subject of the preceding vision, no specific mention is made of him in this vision, but the two visions go together).

As **Zerubbabel . . . laid the foundation of this temple** (v. 9; i.e., he began the work of rebuilding on the ancient foundations), so he would **also complete it,** epitomized by his laying **the capstone** (v. 7). The word translated **plumb line** (v. 10) is disputed and possibly refers to this final crowning stone (cf. Baldwin, *Zechariah,* pp. 122-3). Others say it symbolizes Zerubbabel's supervising the rebuilding project. Those who despised **the day of small things** may have been older Jews who thought this temple was insignificant compared with the former temple of preexilic times (cf. Ezra 3:12-13; Hag. 2:3).

### c. The interpretation of the two olive trees (4:10b-14)

**4:10b-14.** The words about the **seven** being **the eyes of the LORD** are possibly a delayed answer to Zechariah's question in verse 4. Like "eyes" the seven lights (lamps, v. 2) symbolize God's worldwide scrutiny, for nothing is hidden from Him. Others understand the "seven" to refer back to the seven eyes in the previous vision (3:9).

The **two olive branches** and **two gold pipes** are mentioned for the first time in the vision in 4:12. The two branches with olives poured their oil into the gold pipes, which flowed into the bowl and then through the 49 channels to the seven lamps. The interpreting angel removed Zechariah's confusion regarding the **two olive trees** (vv. 3, 11) by indicating that their two oil-supplying branches represent **the two who are anointed to serve the LORD of all the earth** (v. 14). The branches refer to the anointing of priests and kings, with particular allusion to Joshua and Zerubbabel who typify the Messiah as both Priest and King. **The lampstand,** then, seems to represent Israel as a light to the nations (cf. Isa. 42:6; 49:6), potentially in Zechariah's time, but will be actually so during the millennial reign of Christ. Another fulfillment, partial at least, of Zechariah 4:11-14 is found in the two witnesses in the future Tribulation period (Rev. 11:3-6, esp. v. 4).

### 6. THE VISION OF THE FLYING SCROLL (5:1-4)

The last three visions have to do with the administration of judgment. This vision of the flying scroll is both simple and severe.

**5:1.** This vision is introduced with the words **I looked again** (cf. v. 9), similar to the second and third visions ("Then I looked up," 1:18; 2:1; cf. "I looked up again," 6:1).

**5:2.** Again (cf. 4:2, 5, 13) the interpreting angel asked Zechariah, **What do you see?** to bring out the features and to communicate the significance of the vision. Zechariah said he saw a huge **flying scroll, 30 feet long and 15 feet wide.** The scroll was not rolled up; it was spread out like a large sheet so it could be read on both sides (cf. 5:3). Its large size was coincidentally or intentionally the exact size of the tabernacle, perhaps suggesting that the judgments contained on the scroll were in harmony with God's holy presence in the midst of Israel. The suspended position of the scroll as "flying" or floating facilitates its function of rapid entrance into and judgment on the houses of thieves and perjurers.

**5:3.** That the scroll had writing **on one side** and **on the other** is reminiscent of language describing the two tablets of the Law (Ex. 32:15). In fact **the curse** of the scroll is directed toward violators of the middle command of each of the two tablets—the eighth commandment against stealing (Ex. 20:15) and the third commandment against swearing **falsely** by (misusing) the **name** of the Lord (Ex. 20:7). Thus the specified objects of the curse probably represent all those who violate the Law of God.

**5:4.** The severity ("banished," v. 3, purged out of the covenant community) and the totality (**remain in his house and destroy it**) of the judgments suggest a fulfillment in the Millennium because only then will divine judgment on sin be so rapid and so complete.

### 7. THE VISION OF THE WOMAN IN THE EPHAH (5:5-11)

### a. The appearance of the ephah (5:5-6)

**5:5-6.** The interpreting **angel** directed Zechariah's attention to another object in flight, this time **a measuring basket** (Heb., *'êpâh*, a large barrel or basket used for a common household measure). Estimates of the capacity of an ephah, the largest dry measure used by the Jews, range from approximately 5 to 10 gallons. Since this would be much too small a container to enclose a woman, the ephah was apparently greatly enlarged in the vision, as the scroll was in the previous vision.

The angel indicated that the basket represented **the iniquity of the people throughout the land.** The NIV marginal translation for "iniquity of the people" is "appearance," which is closer to the Hebrew word which is literally "eye." The clause could be translated, "This is the appearance (or resemblance, i.e., of the ephah) in all the land," which gives good sense. However, the term "iniquity" is attested by the Greek and Syriac versions and also makes sense in this passage (cf. Baldwin, *Zechariah*, p. 128).

The use of a measuring basket to

symbolize the corporate evil of the land of Israel was appropriate in view of the common perversity of making false measures (cf. Amos 8:5). The sins associated with commercial preoccupation were gripping Israel at this time (Neh. 5:1-13; cf. Mal. 3:8-9). However, it is probably too specific to identify the basket only with godless commercialism. The rest of the vision seems to include the concept of false worship.

### b. The woman in the ephah (5:7-8)

**5:7-8.** The material of which the measuring **basket** was made is not identified, but it had a **cover of lead** to assure the security of its contents. When the cover was lifted, **a woman** was observed inside and was identified as **wickedness.** The woman (probably because the Heb. word for wickedness is in the fem. gender) was wickedness personified, a term denoting civil, ethical, and religious evil. The interpreting angel had to keep the woman (wickedness) in confinement. Not only must the wicked in Israel be punished (the vision of the flying scroll, vv. 1-4) but also wickedness itself must be removed from the land.

### c. The removal of the ephah (5:9-11)

**5:9-11.** Two unidentified **women** with great **wings like those of a stork** transported the ephah of wickedness **to the country of Babylonia** (lit., Shinar), the recent place of Israel's Exile but also the site of ancient and future idolatry and rebellion against God (Gen. 11:2; Rev. 17:3-5). This lends support to the view that the city of Babylon on the Euphrates River will be rebuilt (cf. comments on Rev. 17–18). Unger identifies these women with demonic forces that seek to protect the woman of wickedness and enshrine her for worship in Babylon (*Zechariah*, p. 98). Others see them as agents of divine power or providence.

Israel's corporate sin, associated with idolatry, will be removed from her land. The phrases in Zechariah 5:11—**to build a house for it,** and **be set there in its place** (i.e., on an idol pedestal)—suggest that the ephah of wickedness will be erected in a temple as an idol. Such idols of Babylon were powerlessness personified, as indicated in Isaiah's many idol satires (Isa. 44:9-20; 46:1-2; etc.). Returning the wickedness of idolatry to its place

of origin in Babylon apparently will set the stage for final judgment on Babylon (Rev. 17–18). Its removal from Israel will prepare the way for Christ's second coming and millennial kingdom (Rev. 19–20).

### 8. THE VISION OF THE FOUR CHARIOTS (6:1-8)

This eighth vision concludes the messages which Zechariah saw in one night and which outline the future history of the nation Israel. It is reminiscent of the first vision, with horses going out from the presence of the Lord throughout the whole earth. However, these horses are harnessed to chariots and come on the scene from between two mountains of bronze. The judgment determined by God on the Gentiles in the first vision is executed by divinely commissioned war chariots in this final vision. No mention is made of any riders or charioteers. Except for the divine words in verses 7b-8, the conversation is limited to the normal dialogue between Zechariah and the interpreting angel.

### a. The description of the vision (6:1-3)

**6:1-3.** The chariots' place of departure is identified as **two mountains** which were made **of bronze** (an alloy of copper and tin), the ancient counterpart to brass (an alloy of copper and zinc). Bronze seems to symbolize righteous divine judgment against sin (cf. Rev. 1:15; 2:18). Since the Hebrew text has the definite article ("*the* two mountains"), some see a reference to the two well-known mountains, Zion (cf. Joel 3:16) and Olivet (cf. Zech. 14:4). Though the association of Olivet with the second coming of Christ may support this view, it is doubtful that actual mountains are intended since these were made of bronze. The **four chariots** with different-colored **horses** speak of the universality of divine judgment which will go in all directions throughout the earth. If the colors are significant, perhaps **red** symbolizes war and bloodshed, **black** designates death and famine, **white** speaks of triumph and victory, and **dappled** denotes pestilence and plagues (see comments on Rev. 6:1-8). For a discussion on problems regarding the Hebrew words for the various colors of the horses in both this and the first vision see Baldwin, *Zechariah*, pages 138-40.

### b. The explanation of the vision (6:4-8)

**6:4-7a.** At Zechariah's request (**What are these?** cf. 1:9, 19; 4:4, 11; also cf. 5:6) the interpreting **angel** explained the significance of the horses with their chariots. **The four spirits** (or "winds") **of heaven** may refer to angels of divine judgment or to the power of God to accomplish His judicial purposes (cf. Ps. 148:8; Jer. 49:36; Dan. 7:2; Rev. 7:1). The divine title, **the Lord** (*'ăḏôn*) **of the whole world**, is a millennial designation describing the universal rule of Messiah over the earth during the future Kingdom Age (cf. Micah 4:13, "Lord [*'ăḏôn*] of all the earth"). **The north country** refers to Babylon whose invasions came on Israel from the north. **The south,** of course, refers to Egypt. Rather than the NIV text, **the one with the white horses toward the west,** the Hebrew may read "the one with the white horses after them" (cf. NIV marg. and NASB), that is, after **the black horses** going to the north. If that translation is followed, then north and south are the only directions mentioned. This would be appropriate to Israel's location.

**6:7b-8.** The speaker in these verses is the Lord, introduced simply as **He. My Spirit** probably refers here to divine wrath (hence the NIV marg., "spirit"; cf. God's wrath subsiding, as recorded in Ezek. 5:13; 16:42; 24:13). God's wrath, after being executed on the wickedness transplanted to Babylon (Zech. 5:5-11; cf. Rev. 18:2, 10, 21; 19:1-3) will then come to **rest.** In the first vision God was angry with the nations that felt secure (Zech. 1:15); in this vision He was satisfied with their just judgment (cf. Rev. 19:2, 15-19).

### C. The symbolic act concluding the visions (6:9-15)

The eight night visions were brought to a conclusion with a divine oracle to Zechariah. God instructed him to perform a symbolic act by crowning Joshua the high priest. Joshua hereby represented "the Branch," the Messiah, who will rebuild the future temple and will be both a Priest and a King.

#### 1. THE SYMBOLIC CROWNING (6:9-11)

**6:9-11.** By **the word of the LORD** (this formula, indicating direct prophetic revelation, assumes that the night visions had terminated) Zechariah was instructed to crown **Joshua** the **high priest** with a **crown** made of **silver and gold.** The precious metals were received from a small, otherwise unknown delegation of Jewish **exiles** from Babylon—**Heldai** (the Heb. text calls him Helem in v. 14), **Tobijah, and Jedaiah**—who probably brought **the silver and gold to** aid in the rebuilding of the temple. They were apparently visiting at the home of an also otherwise unknown Jew—**Josiah son of Zephaniah** (nicknamed Hen, meaning "gracious one," in v. 14). The "crown" is singular though the Hebrew word for it is plural, perhaps indicating a "plural of majesty" or the fact that it might have had several parts, or tiers (made of *two* precious metals). The crowning of the high priest Joshua, rather than Zerubbabel the governor (Hag. 1:1, 12, 14; 2:21; cf. Zech. 4:6-10) safeguards the symbolic significance of the crowning. The crowning of Zerubbabel could have been misunderstood by some as the crowning of the messianic Son of David, since Zerubbabel, like the promised Messiah, was both a descendant of David and a political leader.

#### 2. THE PROPHETIC MESSAGE (6:12-13)

**6:12-13.** God told Zechariah to convey to Joshua that he would represent or typify **the Branch** who will rebuild the millennial temple. The crowning had a typical significance pointing forward to the Messiah as King-Priest, like Melchizedek centuries earlier (Gen. 14:18-20; Ps. 110:4; cf. Heb. 7:11-21). The title "Branch" is a messianic title, as already indicated (Zech. 3:8). Since the promise to rebuild the postexilic temple in Zechariah's day was given to Zerubbabel (4:9), any role Joshua himself had was apparently minor. So the promise that the Branch will **build the temple of the LORD** is probably limited to Messiah's role in establishing the millennial temple (cf. Isa. 2:2-4; 56:6-7; Ezek. 40–46; Micah 4:1-2).

The messianic Branch **will be clothed with majesty**; this refers to Christ as the Bearer of the essential glory of God (cf. Isa. 4:2; John 1:14). Christ will also **sit and rule on His throne** (Isa. 9:7; Jer. 23:5; Micah 4:3, 7; Zeph. 3:15; Zech. 14:9) as a **Priest** (Heb. 4:15; 5:6; 7:11-21) **on His throne.** A Levitical priest could never become a king and sit on a throne. But Christ will unite in Himself the offices of priest and king, as also indicated in the statement, **there will be harmony between the two** (i.e., the two offices of priest and king).

### 3. THE VISIBLE MEMORIAL (6:14)

**6:14.** God told Zechariah to give **the crown** to the delegation from Babylon **as a memorial** of the significant and typical crowning of Joshua. Apparently after Joshua was crowned, the three were to place the crown **in the temple of the LORD,** after it would be built.

### 4. THE UNIVERSAL SIGNIFICANCE (6:15)

**6:15.** Imperceptibly the divine instructions to Zechariah to perform the symbolic crowning seem to have merged with a prophecy spoken by the Branch or the Angel of the Lord (who are One and the same), who is sent by the Lord (**the LORD Almighty has sent Me to you**). The deputation from Babylon, though consisting of Jews, appears to be typical of all **those who are far away** who will **help to build the** millennial **temple.** People from many nations around the world will bring their wealth for the temple (Isa. 60:5, 9, 11; 61:6b; Hag. 2:7-8).

## II. The Four Explanatory Messages (chaps. 7–8)

### A. The messages required by the question about fasting (7:1-3)

**7:1-2.** Nearly two years after the night visions (December 7, 518 B.C.; cf. v. 1 with 1:7) and about halfway through the period of temple rebuilding (520–516) **Zechariah** gave four messages. Three of the messages were introduced by the clause "the word of the LORD Almighty came to me" (7:4; 8:1, 18). The second message was introduced similarly: "The word of the LORD came again to Zechariah" (7:8). These messages were given in response to a delegation that came to Jerusalem to ask whether the nation should continue to fast in remembrance of Jerusalem's destruction. The delegates were evidently Jews (in spite of their foreign names, apparently acquired in Babylon) who came from **Bethel** (cf. Ezra 2:28), the Israelite city 12 miles north of Jerusalem that had been the center of apostate worship for the Northern 10 tribes of Israel (cf. 1 Kings 12:28-29; 13:1; Amos 7:13). (The KJV reads, "When they had sent unto the house of God Sherezer and Regemmelech." This trans. does not

specify who sent them or where they came from. For a discussion of this and other views on the grammatical problem in the sentence, see Baldwin, *Zechariah,* pp. 141-3.)

**7:3.** The question raised by the Bethelites implied a desire to discontinue the self-imposed religious observance of fasting **in the fifth month** (July-August, the month Ab), which commemorated the burning to the ground of the city and the temple by Nebuchadnezzar (2 Kings 25:8-10).

### B. The messages declared as the answer from the Lord (7:4–8:23)

### 1. A MESSAGE OF REBUKE (7:4-7)

**7:4-7.** The answer to the delegates' question was not given till the fourth message (8:18-19). Meanwhile the first divine message reminded the people that God warned their fathers **through the earlier prophets** that He wanted reality, not ritual (e.g., Isa. 1:11-17; Hosea 6:6; Amos 5:21-24). The question provided an occasion to rebuke self-imposed fasts that not only were antiquated by God's present blessing on the returned remnant but also were observed without proper motivation and spiritual attitude. Thus the rebuke was against empty formalism devoid of spiritual reality, for whether fasting or **feasting,** they were doing it not for the Lord (Zech. 7:5) but for themselves (v. 6).

The exiles had observed two fasts during the Babylonian Captivity, one in the **fifth** month (see comments on v. 3) and one in the **seventh** month. This seventh-month fast was not the divinely instituted fast on the annual Day of Atonement (Lev. 16:29, 31; 23:26-32), which was also in the seventh month, but a fast commemorating the murder of Gedaliah, governor of Judah, during a time of civil strife after the fall of **Jerusalem** (Jer. 41:2). The feasting probably included both the national feasts of Leviticus 23 and the family feasts associated with Levitical sacrifices (cf. Deut. 12:5-7).

### 2. A MESSAGE OF REPENTANCE (7:8-14)

**7:8-10.** The second message from **the LORD** centered on the conduct of the earlier generation that resulted in the Exile. In preexilic times, as in Zechariah's own day, God desired inner spiritual reality rather than external formalism. **True**

justice (cf. Isa. 1:17; Amos 5:24) along with **mercy and compassion** (cf. Zech. 8:16-17; Micah 6:8) should be demonstrated toward all, but especially toward **the widow . . . the fatherless, the alien,** and **the poor** (cf. Deut. 15:7-11; 24:14-15, 19-21; 26:12-13), who were in no position to stand up for themselves, and so are often mentioned in the Bible as objects of God's care. In addition God's people were not even to **think evil of each other.**

**7:11-14.** The previous generation had been disobedient; **they turned their backs** (lit., "shoulder") **and** plugged **up their ears** (cf. Isa. 6:10). **They made their hearts as hard as flint** (KJV, "an adamant stone," i.e., diamond) and neither listened to nor obeyed **the words that the LORD Almighty had sent by His Spirit through the earlier prophets.** This statement not only places the words of the preexilic prophets on a par with the Mosaic Law but also identifies the Spirit of God as the Source of prophetic inspiration who spoke through human agents (cf. 2 Tim. 3:16; 2 Peter 1:21). The people's disobedience to revealed truth resulted in divine anger, the results of which are indicated in Zechariah 7:13-14: (a) a denial of response to prayer (v. 13), (b) a dispersion **among . . . the nations** (v. 14a), (c) a desolation of the **land** (v. 14b).

### 3. A MESSAGE OF RESTORATION (8:1-17)

As chapter 7 resembles the call to repentance in 1:2-6, so chapter 8 reflects the promised blessings pictured throughout the night visions (1:7–6:8). Thus the third and fourth messages view the restoration from Exile in Zechariah's day as a precursor of future blessing and prosperity in the Millennial Age. They also place emphasis on that future time when righteousness, justice, and peace will fill the earth.

**8:1.** Zechariah again identified this message as a revelation from God (cf. 7:4, 8; 8:18). The message is divided into seven parts by the recurring phrase, "This is what the LORD Almighty [or LORD] says" (vv. 2-4, 6-7, 9, 14). Whether each of these sections summarizes more lengthy messages which Zechariah delivered orally but did not record cannot be determined from the passage.

**8:2.** God's zeal on behalf of **Zion** (i.e., the people of Jerusalem) is affirmed in superlative terms (cf. 1:14; Joel 2:18).

**8:3.** God's resumed presence with His people when He will **return to Zion and dwell in Jerusalem** (cf. 2:12) anticipates millennial fulfillment through the personal reign of Christ on the throne of David. At that time His **truth** and holiness (cf. Joel 3:17; Obad. 17) will be imparted in **the city** and throughout the earth. Zion was originally the name of the mound where the Jebusites lived, whose fortress David conquered (2 Sam. 5:7). Later Zion (and Mount Zion) were names for the temple site in Jerusalem (Ps. 2:6; Isa. 8:18; Joel 2:1). Also Zion became a synonym for the entire city of Jerusalem (Isa. 2:3; 4:3; 33:20; Amos 1:2; Micah 3:10, 12). Zion and Jerusalem are mentioned together several times by Zechariah (Zech. 1:14, 17; 8:3; 9:9).

**8:4-5. Jerusalem** will be secure and safe for senior citizens and children alike (cf. Isa. 65:20-22).

**8:6.** Such future blessings **may seem marvelous to the remnant of this people at that time,** in contrast with the destruction that will precede it (cf. Matt. 24:15-25), but such miraculous performances are not difficult for God (cf. Gen. 18:14; Matt. 19:26).

**8:7-8.** Once again **the LORD** promised to regather Israel and Judah in the future. **The countries of the east and the west** is probably a merism for countries in all directions, all over the earth (cf. Isa. 11:11-12; 43:5-6). The worldwide scope of this restoration suggests that **Jerusalem** represents the land of Israel as a whole. This regathering will institute a restored relationship between God and Israel (**They will be My people;** cf. Zech. 13:9; Hosea 2:21-23) in which God's faithfulness and righteousness will be most evident (cf. Hosea 2:19-20).

**8:9-13.** The people who heard **these words spoken by the prophets** (Zechariah and Haggai) were to be encouraged (**let your hands be strong;** cf. Hag. 2:4) to complete the rebuilding of **the temple.** God's promises of future blessing should always encourage His people in their present tasks.

**Before that time,** when the people started to rebuild the temple, their work had little results (Hag. 1:6, 9-11; 2:16-19) and enemies kept them unsafe. Israel's future blessings relate not only to the productivity of the land (Zech. 8:12) but also to a reversed role among the nations (v. 13). Now **an object of cursing among the nations** (cf. Deut. 28:37), **Judah and Israel . . . will be a blessing** (cf. Micah 5:7; Zech. 8:22-23). Therefore the people should **not be afraid** (cf. v. 15).

**8:14-17.** The Lord then affirmed the certainty of the fulfillment of His divine purpose for future blessing. He contrasted that forthcoming blessing with the already fulfilled promises of **disaster** which He brought on their sinning **fathers** (vv. 14-15; cf. 7:11-14). In view of the options of disaster and blessing, God offered His people an agenda that reflected spiritual reality rather than the hypocritical formalism that had characterized their fathers and was threatening them. **Truth,** justice, mercy, and honesty should characterize them in both personal and civil spheres (cf. 7:9-10). In short, the message is, "Do the things God loves (cf. 8:19) and avoid the things God hates."

### 4. A MESSAGE OF REJOICING (8:18-23)

**8:18.** Like the preceding **word of the Lord** through Zechariah, this one is also divided into several sections by the repeated phrase, "This is what the Lord Almighty says" (vv. 19-20, 23).

**8:19.** The Lord waited till now to answer the question raised by the Bethel delegates (7:2-3) about the commemorative fasts. He said **the fasts** would **become joyful and glad occasions and happy festivals.** Two additional fasts are included which were not previously mentioned (cf. 7:3, 5)—one on the 10th day of the **10th** month to remember the commencement of the siege of Jerusalem (2 Kings 25:1-2; Jer. 39:1), and one on the 9th day of the **4th** month to recall the capture of Jerusalem by Nebuchadnezzar (the 9th day of the 4th month was the day the city wall was breached, 2 Kings 25:3-4; Jer. 39:2). These fasts were all self-imposed and had been observed for 70 years (Zech. 7:5) with sorrowful hearts and misdirected motives (cf. 7:5-7). These fasts are still observed by some Jews today. But at the Lord's Second Advent these fasts will be turned into feasts, symbolizing millennial joy. Therefore again the people in Zechariah's day were encouraged by their future hope to **love** what God loves (cf. 8:16-17), in this case, **truth and peace.**

**8:20-23.** In the future day of blessing, peoples of the whole earth will join with Jews because of their relationship with the Lord. People will know **that God is with** Israel and that they are His people (v. 8). As a result, many **nations will come to Jerusalem** to worship during the Millennium (cf. 14:16-19; Isa. 2:3).

## III. Two Revelatory Oracles (chaps. 9–14)

The final division of the book consists of two oracles (see comments on 9:1-8) that look forward to the messianic King and kingdom. Chapters 9–11 refer (for the most part) to the First Advent of Christ, stressing the theme of His rejection but also outlining Israel's prophetic history to the end times. Chapters 12–14 focus on Messiah's Second Advent and emphasize His enthronement as the commencement of the grand finale of Israel's history.

These two oracles contain numerous passages which are counterparts to major themes of the eight visions, thus giving testimony to the unity of the entire Book of Zechariah. The future prosperity of Israel and Jerusalem (first vision, 1:7-17) parallels 10:6-9 (in the first oracle) and 12:6-8 and 14:11 (in the second oracle). The destruction of the nations (second vision, 1:18-21) is reaffirmed in 9:1-8 (first oracle) and in 12:1-6 and 14:1-3 (second oracle). The divine protection and exaltation of Jerusalem (third vision, chap. 2) are further developed in 9:9-17 (first oracle) and in 12:7-9 and 14:4-11 (second oracle). The spiritual cleansing of Israel (fourth vision, chap. 3) is clarified in 10:2-3 (first oracle) and in 12:10-14 and 14:8 (second oracle). The divine enablement of Israel (fifth vision, chap. 4) is explained in 10:1-6 (first oracle) and in 13:1-6 (second oracle). Divine judgment on sinners (sixth vision, 5:1-4) is elaborated in chapter 11 (first oracle) and in 13:7-9 and 14:12-15 (second oracle). The removal of iniquity from the land of Israel (seventh vision, 5:5-11) results in a condition of holiness in Jerusalem and Judah (14:20-21, second oracle). God's judgment on and rule of the whole world (eighth vision, 6:1-8) are reflected in 14:16-19 (second oracle).

## A. The anointed King rejected (chaps. 9–11)

### 1. THE INTERVENING JUDGMENTS ON NATIONS SURROUNDING ISRAEL (9:1-8)

The NIV regards the term "An oracle" ("burden," KJV) as a heading separated from verse 1, which begins with, "the word of the LORD" (cf. 12:1). This is probably more accurate than the redundant translation of the KJV, "The burden of the word of the LORD." The Hebrew word *maśśā'* ("oracle") is derived from the verb *nāśā'* which has two meanings— "to bear" and "to lift up." Though some translations (KJV, ASV) and scholars (e.g., Baldwin, *Zechariah*, pp. 162-3) have understood the word *maśśā'* to mean "burden," an ominous message of judgment which was borne by the prophetic messenger, the word is more likely based on the other nuance of the verb—"to lift up (the voice)" (cf. Jud. 9:7, "shouted"; Isa. 3:7; 42:2, "cry out"). The noun is used this way ("oracle," not "burden") in Numbers 23:7; 24:3, 15-16. So the noun in Zechariah 9:1 and 12:1 should be translated "oracle"—what is lifted up (by the voice), whether a threat or a promise. In this context in Zechariah the two oracles are primarily promises of salvation.

Most conservative commentators regard 9:1-8 as a prophecy of the conquests of Alexander the Great throughout the area of Palestine after the battle of Issus in 333 B.C. Zechariah, living in the days of the Medo-Persian Empire, predicted the coming Grecian Empire (9:1-8, 13), the Roman Empire (11:4-14), and Israel's future in the last days (chaps. 12–14).

**9:1-2.** Alexander the Great was probably the human cause of the destruction set forth in these and the following verses (the order of the cities seems to correspond generally with Alexander's line of march). But his involvement is bypassed in this prophecy to stress the ultimate divine cause of the judgment on certain cities and countries beginning north of Israel. The northernmost location, **Hadrach,** was probably Hatarikka, a city and country lying north of Hamath and mentioned in Assyrian cuneiform inscriptions. **Damascus** was the capital of Aram (Syria). The words, **the eyes of men and all the tribes of Israel are on the** LORD indicate the awe of all peoples at the divine judgment brought on their cities. **Hamath** was an Aramean (Syrian)

city north of Damascus on the Orontes River. Westward on the coast were the Phoenician cities of **Tyre and Sidon.**

**9:3-4. Tyre** was **a stronghold,** a citadel of defense which had withstood a 5-year siege by the Assyrians under Shalmaneser V and, years later, a 13-year siege by the Babylonian army of Nebuchadnezzar. Her commercial and economic self-sufficiency is reflected in figures of speech which speak of **silver** being as common as **dust and gold** as common as **the dirt** (cf. Ezek. 28:4-5; 27:33). Her impoverishment and destruction by Alexander's relatively brief five-month siege are ascribed to God's ultimate action in destroying **her power on the sea** (NASB, "cast her wealth into the sea"; cf. Ezek. 26:17-21; 27:27, 34).

**9:5-7.** Four of the five principal Philistine cities (Gath is omitted) are next on the judgment march (cf. Amos 1:6-8; Zeph. 2:4; Jer. 25:20). **The blood** and **the forbidden food** (from idolatrous sacrifices) removed from the very **mouths** and clenched **teeth** of some Philistines indicate their removal from idolatry to **belong** to the **God** of Israel and even **become leaders in Judah. Like the Jebusites,** they will be absorbed into the population of God's people. Since there is no evidence that this was fulfilled in the invasion of Alexander, it apparently awaits future fulfillment as part of the blessing that will result from the messianic rule (Zech. 9:10).

**9:8.** The Macedonian armies of Alexander passed and repassed the city of Jerusalem without laying siege to it. The ultimate cause of this was the divine protection of the city (**I will defend My house**). This defense foreshadows God's final protection of the city in the Millennium, when **never again will** enemies invade Jerusalem (cf. Joel 3:17).

### 2. THE BLESSINGS OF THE MESSIAH (9:9–10:12)

#### a. The coming of the Prince of Peace (9:9)

**9:9.** The inhabitants of Jerusalem were personified as the **Daughter of Zion** (cf. 2:10; Isa. 1:8) and the **Daughter of Jerusalem** who, representing the whole nation of Israel, were exhorted to welcome the coming King not with fear but with glad rejoicing. The announcement that **your King comes to you** refers to the long-awaited King and Messiah (cf. Isa. 9:5-7; Micah 5:2-4; Luke 1:32-33). **Righteous** describes both His character and His reign (cf. Ps. 45:6-7; Isa. 11:1-5; 32:17; Jer. 23:5-6; 33:15-16). The phrase **having salvation** denotes that He will come as a Deliverer, as One to give salvation to others (cf. Isa. 62:11). His peaceful entrance—**riding on a donkey**—was fulfilled when He presented Himself to Israel in the Triumphal Entry (Matt. 21:1-5). In the ancient Near East, if a king came in peace, he would ride on a donkey instead of on a war stallion. Christ rode **on a colt, the foal** (lit., "son") **of a donkey.** (On the question of whether Christ rode one or two donkeys see comments on Matt. 21:2.) Like some other Old Testament prophecies this one (Zech. 9:9-10) blends two events into one perspective—events that the New Testament divides into two distinct advents of Christ separated by the present Church Age (cf. Isa. 9:6-7; 61:1-2; Luke 4:18-21). In His First Advent He rode on a donkey and presented Himself to the nation Israel but they rejected Him as their King. So His universal rule (Zech. 9:10) will be established when He comes again.

*b. The kingdom of the Prince of Peace (9:10–10:12)*

(1) Messiah will establish peace. **9:10.** God's destruction of war instruments—removing **the chariots,** the **war horses,** and **the battle bow**—signifies the end of war in the Millennium (cf. Isa. 2:4; Micah 4:3). This peaceful **rule** of the coming messianic King **will extend from sea to sea and from the River** (the Euphrates; cf. Micah 7:12; Isa. 7:20) **to the ends of the earth.** These expressions clearly indicate the worldwide extent of the messianic kingdom.

(2) Messiah will deliver Israel (9:11-17). **9:11-12.** God's faithfulness to His covenants with Israel is His basis for delivering her from worldwide dispersion. The immediate addressees in these verses may have been Jewish exiles still in Babylon, but the covenant-fulfillment theme suggests an ultimate reference to Israel's end-time regathering. At least the nation's future hope (messianic deliverance) was the basis for contemporary encouragement in Zechariah's day. **The blood of My covenant with you** may refer to the sacrifices of the Mosaic Covenant (cf. Ex. 24:8), but could as well relate back to the foundational Abrahamic Covenant which was confirmed with a blood sacrifice (Gen. 15:8-21). **The waterless pit** (an empty cistern used for a dungeon) is probably a figure for the place of exile. The **fortress** refers to Jerusalem. The exiles in Babylon were called **prisoners of hope** because they had God's promise of being regathered. God **will restore twice as much,** that is, His blessings in the Millennium will far exceed anything Israel has ever known.

**9:13.** At least this verse, and perhaps the rest of the chapter, refer to the conflict of the Maccabees (169–135 B.C.) with Antiochus IV Epiphanes (cf. Dan. 11:32; see comments on Dan. 8:9-14), Antiochus V Eupator, Antiochus VI, and Antiochus VII Sidetes, Greek rulers of Syria. This Jewish victory foreshadowed Israel's final conflict and victory when God will bring them into millennial blessing. As the **bow** and arrow (that which "fills" the bow) are each essential to the other, so **Judah** and **Ephraim** (Ephraim represents the 10 Northern tribes of Israel) will be reunited. The reference to these weapons of warfare (including the **warrior's sword**) indicates that God will empower His people to defeat the enemy, the **sons** of **Greece.**

**9:14-15.** The description of a thunderstorm controlled by God (v. 14) pictures poetically Israel's empowerment for victory over her enemies (v. 15). The divine appearance was through providential means in the Maccabean period but will be literal and visible when Christ appears victoriously at His Second Advent. The last part of verse 15 pictures Israel's unrestrained joy and fullness of rejoicing because of God's mighty deliverance.

**9:16-17.** The divine deliverance predicted here will come **on that day,** a reference to the end time. **God will** care for them as a shepherd cares for his **flock** (cf. 10:3). Then Israel **will sparkle in His land like jewels in a crown.** This is a beautiful cameo of the fulfilled promises concerning the people in the land (cf. Amos 9:11-15). They will be **attractive and beautiful** symbols of all God has done for them. Divine blessing on nature will produce conditions of plenty (cf. Joel 2:21-27) so that physical health will also be assured (Zech. 9:17).

(3) Messiah will destroy the false shepherds at His coming. **10:1-5.** The exhortation in verse 1 is transitional, indicating that the source of natural blessings (**rain** and **plants of the field**) is **the LORD,** not idolatrous and deceptive false **shepherds** (vv. 2-3). As a result of the deception by the false (and apparently foreign) prophets and **diviners,** God's **people wander like sheep.** Therefore God announced that He would bring wrath and judgment on the false shepherds and victory to **His flock** (cf. Micah 5:4). The remedy for the nation's deception focuses on the coming of the Messiah who is described in a fourfold way as **the Cornerstone** (cf. Isa. 28:16), **the Tent Peg . . . the Battle Bow** (cf. Ps. 45:5), and the **Ruler** (cf. Gen. 49:10; Micah 5:2). These terms emphasize the strong, stable, victorious, and trustworthy nature of Messiah's rule. The Lord will not do all the fighting but will empower His people to conquer **like mighty men.** His presence (He will be **with them**) will enable them to be victorious.

(4) Messiah will regather all Israel (10:6-12). The worldwide scope of this prophecy relating to both Israel and Judah and God's activity on behalf of His Chosen People indicate that the final regathering of Israel just before the Second Advent of the Messiah is in view.

**10:6-7.** God announced that He **will strengthen** (cf. v. 12) and deliver all Israel (**Joseph** was the father of two major Northern tribes, Ephraim and Manasseh). **Because** of His **compassion** they will be restored and reunited (cf. Hosea 1:11), with their sins forgiven and forgotten—**as though I had not rejected them,** enjoying communion with God (**I will answer them**). The name of the northern tribe of Ephraim was sometimes used for the Northern Kingdom (cf. Hosea 10:6; 11:8, 12). Israelites will **be glad** and **joyful** and will **rejoice in the LORD** because of God's blessings on them.

**10:8-10.** Israel will be regathered from present worldwide dispersion. God announced, **I will signal for them.** The term "signal" means "whistle" (as in gathering a swarm of insects; cf. Isa. 7:18) or "pipe" (as a shepherd using a reed pipe to gather his flocks; cf. Jud. 5:16). The latter meaning seems more appropriate in view of the shepherd/sheep imagery in the general context (Zech. 9:16;

10:2-3; 11:4-16; 13:7). Their regathering will be accompanied by redemption and multiplication (10:8b; cf. Hosea 1:10). On the human side their **return** will involve the fact that **they will remember** God. On the divine side God said, **I will bring them back. Egypt** and **Assyria** are representative of all the countries of Israel's dispersion (cf. Hosea 11:11; Zech. 10:11). **Gilead and Lebanon** are probably named to indicate the northern and eastern extents of Israel's occupancy of the land promised to Abraham (Gen. 15:18; cf. Deut. 30:3-5).

**10:11-12.** In regathering Israel to the land, God will remove every obstacle to restoration, pictured in terms of the ancient deliverance when He brought Israel **through the sea** on dry land. Again Assyria and Egypt were mentioned to represent all Israel's enemies (cf. v. 10). The prophecy closes with its opening phrase, **I will strengthen them,** so that Israel's behavior (**walk**) will be **in His name** (i.e., she will glorify Him by obeying Him).

3. THE REJECTION OF THE GOOD SHEPHERD AND ITS CONSEQUENCES FOR ISRAEL (CHAP. 11)

This dark chapter conveys the cause for the delay in Israel's realizing the blessings of chapter 10.

*a. The coming of wrath introduced (11:1-3)*

**11:1-3.** This lamentation portrays the impending devastation that will result from the people rejecting the Messiah as the True and Good Shepherd (vv. 4-14). The language obviously involves personification, but the references to the **cedars** of **Lebanon . . . oaks of Bashan,** and **lush thicket of the Jordan** suggest devastation of the entire land of Israel from the north to the south, including of course its inhabitants. All three areas—Lebanon, Bashan, and the Jordan—were heavily forested. **Shepherds** would **wail** because their **pastures** would be devastated. Even **lions** who lived in the thick woods around the Jordan River would **roar** because of the destruction of their living areas.

The general description of the devastation is to be taken literally. However, some writers have viewed the trees as representing the glory of Jerusalem, particularly the temple which was constructed, in part, of lumber. While this is doubtful, the general period of the destruction, whether literal or figurative, probably includes the destruction of Jerusalem by the Romans in A.D. 70.

### b. The cause of devastation indicated (11:4-14)

In this difficult but messianically significant passage, Zechariah was directed by God to portray Israel's true Shepherd-Messiah. Then (vv. 15-17) Zechariah was required to portray the wicked shepherd, pointing to the end-time Antichrist. The passage (vv. 4-14) is probably not intended to be a strict dramatic portrayal, for this would require the unlikely cooperation of other actors in the narrative. The passage focuses attention on Israel's spiritual condition at the time of Christ's ministry and the consequences of her rejection of Christ, the True Shepherd.

**11:4.** God told Zechariah, **Pasture the flock marked for slaughter.** To "pasture" includes not only feeding but also directing and defending. The "flock" was the nation Israel which God had designated for slaughter by the Romans.

**11:5.** There is debate whether the **buyers** of the flock and **those who sell them** were Jewish leaders or foreign oppressors. However, **their own shepherds** are Jewish leaders who would fail in their responsibilities to care for their people (cf. 10:3).

**11:6.** The climactic phase of Israel's apparently pitiable condition was God's withholding of pity: **I will no longer have pity on the people of the land.** This divine withdrawal seemed to result from the people's rejection of their true Shepherd-Messiah, stated in verses 8-13. The **king** to whom God would hand over Israel was apparently the Roman emperor (cf. John 19:15, "We have no king but Caesar"). God would not deliver them from the Roman armies.

**11:7.** As commanded, Zechariah portrayed the work of a shepherd tending **the flock marked for slaughter** (cf. v. 4), especially **the oppressed of the flock.** This perhaps refers to the believing remnant at Messiah's First Advent. Like any good shepherd, Zechariah **took two staffs** to use in directing and protecting the flock. The staffs were given the symbolic names of **Favor** (or beauty, grace, pleasantness) and **Union** (lit., bands or

"ties"). They depicted God's gracious benefits toward His people (cf. 9:14-17) and the internal union of Israel and Judah as a nation (cf. Hosea 1:11).

**11:8-9.** The identity of **the three shepherds** disowned by the True Shepherd is not indicated (accounting for the more than 40 interpretations of v. 8!). Most likely, the shepherds refer to three kinds of Jewish leaders—prophets (custodians of the Law), priests, and kings (or civil magistrates)—all of them inadequate. Closely linked to the disowning of the three shepherds is the flock's disowning of their True Shepherd whom they **detested,** a word (used only here in the OT) that means to loathe to the point of nausea. The Messiah (portrayed by Zechariah) repudiated His role as Shepherd (**I will not be your Shepherd**), and He relegated the flock to their doom, involving foreign oppression (**Let the dying die and the perishing perish**) and internal civil strife (**Let those who are left eat one another's flesh**). An alternate interpretation sees this last clause as speaking of the cannibalism that occurred in the Roman siege of Jerusalem in A.D. 70.

**11:10-11.** The revoked **covenant** (symbolized by breaking the **staff called Favor**) had been **made with all the nations,** apparently to secure God's providential protection of Israel. The divine disfavor on Israel because of her rejection of the True Shepherd resulted in spiritual blindness (Rom. 11:25) and national destruction and dispersion. Only the believing remnant (**the afflicted of the flock**) who recognized Jesus as the true Messiah understood His true origin in God.

**11:12-13.** Israel's appraisal of the True Shepherd's worth was **30 pieces of silver,** the compensation price for a slave gored by an ox (Ex. 21:32). Baldwin thinks 30 pieces of silver for a slave indicates the "high value set on human life" in the Mosaic Law (*Zechariah*, p. 184). Whether or not this is correct, the choice of the slave price was probably intended as an insult to the Shepherd, worse than a direct refusal to pay Him any wage. Throwing this **handsome price** (an obvious use of irony) **to the potter** shows its trifling worth (**the potter** was one of the lowest of the laboring class). This prophecy was fulfilled in Judas' betrayal of Christ (Matt. 26:14-16; 27:3-10; for a survey of problems relating to Matthew's citation of this passage, cf. Hobart E. Freeman, *An Introduction to the Old Testament Prophets.* Chicago: Moody Press, 1968, pp. 340-2).

**11:14.** Zechariah then **broke** the **second staff called Union** to picture the dissolving of the national solidarity of **Judah and Israel.** Discord within the nation was one of the factors that led to the destruction of Jerusalem in A.D. 70 and a new wave of worldwide dispersion.

### c. The consequences of rejecting the True Shepherd (11:15-17)

After rejecting the True Shepherd, the flock of Israel will accept a foolish and worthless shepherd. This is a prophecy of the end-time Antichrist who will do the very opposite of Christ the True Shepherd (cf. John 5:43).

**11:15-16.** Zechariah was called on to portray a second prophetic role, this time **a foolish shepherd.** The Hebrew word rendered "foolish" (*'ĕwîl*) suggests a person who is a coarse, hardened fool. This **shepherd** will have no concern for the flock and its needs; he will be interested only in his own gluttony. Instead of defending the flock, the foolish shepherd will destroy it (cf. Rev. 13:7).

**11:17.** Thus the foolish shepherd is also a **worthless shepherd who** rightfully deserves the condemnation pronounced (**Woe**). The **arm** indicates his strength and the **eye** his intelligence. The foolish plottings of the worthless shepherd will be annulled when the True Shepherd returns (cf. 12:10; Rev. 19:19-20).

## B. The rejected King enthroned (chaps. 12–14)

Chapters 12–14 are one "oracle" (KJV, "burden"; cf. 9:1) concerning God's people Israel. The events predicted deal with one future time period (except for 13:7) and center in the city of Jerusalem. Thus the prophecies of these chapters rank among the most significant in the Old Testament.

### 1. THE REDEMPTION OF ISRAEL (CHAPS. 12–13)

Two conditions are necessary for the establishment of Israel's future messianic kingdom: (a) the overthrow of the Gentile world powers that oppose the establishment of this kingdom and (b) the re-

generation of individual Jews who will constitute the nation when God fulfills the Abrahamic and Davidic Covenants. Both of these conditions will be accomplished by the Lord, as seen in chapters 12–13. He will deliver Israel physically from her enemies (12:1-9) and He will deliver her spiritually (12:10–13:9).

### a. Israel's physical deliverance (12:1-9)

**12:1-3.** The future siege of **Jerusalem** by the nations (cf. 14:1-5) is revealed through **the word of the LORD,** who is identified as the great Preserver of His Creation (portrayed in 12:1 by **stretches out . . . lays . . . forms,** which are pres. participles in Heb.). This almighty power of the Lord is mentioned to confirm His ability to fulfill the deliverance predicted in the following verses.

An introductory summary is given in figurative language (v. 2) and a concluding summary is given in literal language (v. 9). God will destroy **the surrounding peoples** (i.e., **all the nations of the earth,** v. 3) who besiege **Judah** and **Jerusalem . . . on that day.** "That day" (mentioned five times in vv. 3-4, 6, 8-9, three times in chap. 13 [vv. 1-2, 4], and seven times in chap. 14 [vv. 4, 6, 8-9, 13, 20-21]) refers to the future Battle (or better, Campaign) of Armageddon, in which the nations' armies will gather against Jerusalem (cf. 14:1-3; Rev. 16:16; 19:19). Some think that Judah will be on the side of the nations till they recognize that God is empowering the Jerusalemites (Zech. 12:5). Two metaphors describe how God will use Jerusalem as a foil to destroy the nations: (1) Jerusalem will be **a cup** of **reeling** (v. 2). This common prophetic phrase describes divine judgment (cf. Isa. 51:17, 21-22; Jer. 25:15-28). (2) **Jerusalem** will be **an immovable rock** (Zech. 12:3). The defeat of the Armageddon armies is thus likened to a man who drinks more than he can hold, or tries to move a weight heavier than he can lift. Those who attack Jerusalem will do so to their own ruin.

**12:4-5.** In verses 4-9 Judah's future deliverance by the Lord is described more fully in terms not only of the defeat of the nations but also of the victories first for Judah and then for Jerusalem.

The characteristic chaos of a cavalry defeat is here ascribed to divine intervention. God will cause **every horse** to **panic** and every **rider** to go mad, and **the horses** will be blinded (cf. 14:15; see comments on Ezek. 39:9-11 on whether literal horses will be involved in battles in the last days). In contrast, God's protective care for **Judah** is anthropomorphically attributed to His **watchful eye**. The leaders of Judah will recognize in faith the divine source of the empowerment for victory, so they will be encouraged also to trust **God** for triumph over their enemies.

**12:6-7.** Judah's future military triumph is described in two similes: **like a firepot in a woodpile, like a flaming torch among sheaves.** The armies of the nations will be devastated quickly and thoroughly as **Jerusalem** watches (**intact in her place**). Elsewhere Judah's enemies are said to be consumed like stubble burned by fire (e.g., Isa. 47:14; Obad. 18; Mal. 4:1). Judah's victory will come from the Lord (**the LORD will save . . . Judah first**). The priority of Judah's deliverance over that of Jerusalem will assure the entire nation's unity with the inhabitants of the capital city.

**12:8-9.** God will protect Jerusalem like a **shield** and will also give divine enablement to all **those who live in Jerusalem,** from the weakest to the greatest. This empowerment will be so great that the most feeble weakling **will be** a great warrior **like David,** and the leaders of the city (**the house of David**) **will be** granted superhuman strength. Some scholars believe the reference to "the house of David" is a personal reference to Christ at His Second Advent, but this is not likely since "the house of David" in verse 10 and 13:1 apparently refers simply to the political leaders of Israel. So 12:9 is a concluding summary regarding the defeat of **the nations** gathered against **Jerusalem** (cf. the introductory summary in v. 2).

*b. Israel's spiritual deliverance (12:10–13:9)*

Israel's spiritual deliverance at the Second Advent of Christ will be accomplished only by a divinely provided fountain of cleansing (13:1) and the outpouring of the Holy Spirit to lead individual Israelites to repentant faith in Jesus as their Messiah (12:10-14).

(1) The outpouring of the Holy Spirit. **12:10a.** Both leaders (**the house of David**) and commoners (**the inhabitants of Jerusalem**)—thus excluding no Israelites (cf. 13:1)—will be the objects of the outpouring of the divine **spirit of grace and supplication.** This is most probably a reference to the Holy Spirit (see NIV marg.), so called because He will minister graciously to Israel in her sinful condition and will lead her to supplication and repentance.

(2) The mourning of the nation Israel (12:10b-14). **12:10b.** Thus Israelites will receive divine enablement to **look on Me, the One they have pierced.** The Lord refers to the nation's action of piercing Him, a term usually indicating "piercing to death." The piercing evidently refers to the rejection of Christ (as God Incarnate) and crucifying Him, though the word does not specifically refer to the Crucifixion. The "looking" could be either physical vision (sight) or spiritual vision (faith). Probably it refers here to both, for this will occur at the Second Advent of Christ when Israel will recognize her Messiah and turn to Him. The change to the third person (**mourn for Him,** rather than "mourn for Me") is common in prophetic literature. The mourning for sin that is prompted by the outpoured Spirit is illustrated by a private act of mourning (v. 10) and a public act of mourning (v. 11). The loss of **an only child** or of **a firstborn son** was aggravated by the felt curse associated with childlessness and the lack of an heir to continue the family name and property.

**12:11.** The future mourning of Israel over her Messiah is likened, in the second place (cf. v. 10), to **the weeping** on the day when godly King Josiah, the last hope of the fading Judean nation, was slain by Pharaoh Neco II, **at Hadad Rimmon,** traditionally identified as a village near Jezreel, **in the plain of Megiddo** (cf. 2 Chron. 35:20-27). Thus the greatness of the mourning at this final outpouring of the Holy Spirit can be compared only to the weeping of a most extreme individual (Zech. 12:10) and to corporate (v. 11) catastrophes of the nation.

**12:12-14.** These verses picture the universality and intensity of the nation's future mourning. David had a son named Nathan (2 Sam. 5:14) and Levi had a grandson named Shimei (Num. 3:17-18). There was also a Nathan who was a prophet in David's time (cf. 2 Sam.

7:1-17). Thus the mention of **the house of David . . . the house of Nathan . . . the house of Levi,** and **clan of Shimei** may refer to the repentance (and guilt) of kings, prophets, and priests; or if the Nathan referred to is David's son, then just the royal and priestly families are specified. The phrase **each clan by itself, with their wives by themselves** seems to indicate the individuality and thus the sincerity of the mourning rather than a mere outward conformity.

(3) The cleansing of the nation Israel (13:1-6). This section discusses the provision for Israel's cleansing (v. 1) and the removal of idolatry and false prophecy (vv. 2-6).

**13:1. That day** refers to the future day of the Lord (cf. 14:1). The phrase "on that day" occurs 16 times in these three closing chapters (12:3-4, 6, 8-9, 11; 13:1-2, 4; 14:4, 6, 8-9, 13, 20-21). On the day of Christ's crucifixion the fountain was opened *potentially* for all Israel and the whole world. At the Second Advent of Christ, the **fountain will be opened** *experientially* for the Jewish nation. This spiritual cleansing of the nation is associated in other passages of Scripture with Israel's spiritual regeneration and the inauguration of the New Covenant (e.g., Jer. 31:31-37; Ezek. 36:25-32; Rom. 11:26-27). **The house of David** (political leaders) and **the inhabitants of Jerusalem** include all the people of the land (cf. Zech. 12:10) who need cleansing. The terms **sin and impurity** can refer specifically to idolatry (cf. "impurity" in 13:2; Ezek. 7:19-20 speaks of gold being "unclean" and of idols being "detestable"), but they probably have a broader reference here to the total sinful condition of the people.

**13:2a.** The Lord announced His intention to **banish the names of the idols from the land** (cf. Micah 5:13-14). He will overcome all factors that detract from His worship and all idolatry will become extinct. Idolatry near the time of the Second Advent of Christ will include worship of the image of the beast in the temple in Jerusalem (Dan. 9:27; 11:31; Matt. 24:15; 2 Thes. 2:4; Rev. 13:4), though other types of idolatry will also be present (Rev. 9:20).

**13:2b-3.** Associated with the extinction of idolatry will be the extinguishing of false prophecy, which includes human false **prophets** and the (superhuman)

**spirit of impurity** (cf. v. 1), probably to be understood as a personal agency of evil, in contrast with the Spirit of grace, that will inspire false prophets. The death penalty enjoined against false prophets in Deuteronomy 18:20 (cf. Deut. 13:6-11) will be exacted by the nearest of kin, one's **parents,** to remove false prophets **from the land.**

**13:4-6.** This prevalence of justice will cause false prophets to disavow all associations with their prophetic trade. They will forego the deception of wearing **a prophet's** garb. Some true prophets did wear a **garment of hair** (e.g., Elijah, 2 Kings 1:8, and later John the Baptist, Matt. 3:4). Also to avoid detection, the alleged prophets will claim to have been involved in the lifelong occupation of farming. Further, false prophets will lie about the source of **wounds** or scars on their bodies. This probably means on the chest (though the Heb. phrase, lit., "between your hands," NIV marg., could also refer to the back). These scars no doubt will be from self-inflicted wounds associated with idol-worship. To answer the accusation that they were involved in idol-worship, the false prophets will claim they were disciplined by those who love them, either loving parents or brawling companions. Some scholars relate Zechariah 13:6 to verses 7-9, and say that verse 6 refers to the Messiah. However, that makes the thought shift rather abruptly from verses 5 to 6. The thought in verse 6 fits better with the preceding verses on false prophets.

(4) The provision of the True Shepherd (13:7-9). In contrast with false prophets (vv. 2-6) the Lord presented His True Prophet, the Messiah, whom He calls My Shepherd. This poetic unit (vv. 7-9) highlights aspects of the *preceding* prophecy, including the piercing of the Messiah (12:10; cf. 11:7-8), the abandoning of the sheep (cf. 11:9), and the restoration of covenant relationship (13:1-2). This passage (vv. 7-9) speaks of the smitten Shepherd (v. 7a), the scattered sheep (vv. 7b-8), and the saved remnant (v. 9).

**13:7a.** This highly poetic utterance by **the Lord Almighty** combines a number of figures of speech. The abrupt turning aside to address a nonpresent agent (**Awake, O sword**) combines two figures of speech—apostrophe (a direct address to an impersonal object as if it were a person) and personification. These words ascribe to an inanimate object the ability to hear, respond, and arouse out of sleep. The "sword," as a synecdoche (mention of a specific object to represent the more general), represents any instrument causing death (cf. 2 Sam. 11:24; 12:9 where Uriah's death by arrows is ascribed to the sword). The basic idea, then, is that the Lord will direct the death of His **Shepherd.** He is the True Shepherd, the Messiah (cf. Zech. 11:4-14; John 10:11, 14, "the Good Shepherd"; Heb. 13:20, "the Great Shepherd"; 1 Peter 5:4, "the Chief Shepherd").

The Lord added that this Shepherd is **the Man who is close to Me.** The Hebrew word translated "who is close to Me" is found elsewhere only in Leviticus (6:2; 18:20; etc.) where it refers to a "near relative" (though it is trans. "neighbor" in the NIV). In Zechariah 13:7 the Lord is claiming identity of nature or unity of essence with His Shepherd, thus strongly affirming the Messiah's deity.

**13:7b-8.** Calling on the wielder of the sword to **strike the Shepherd,** the Lord then indicated the consequences: **the sheep will be scattered.** In His crucifixion Christ was smitten (Isa. 53:4, 7, 10). His own disciples abandoned Him like scattered sheep (Matt. 26:31, 56). The reference to God's turning His **hand against the little ones** may refer to His allowing the persecutions against Jewish Christians in the Book of Acts. The scattering of the sheep also seems to refer to the scattering of the Jewish nation when Jerusalem was destroyed by the Romans in A.D. 70. Just as the Olivet Discourse (Matt. 24–25; Mark 13; Luke 21) telescopes prophecies of the scattering of the Jewish nation fulfilled in A.D. 70 with those to be fulfilled in the last half of the future Tribulation period, so Zechariah here combines into one focus the same two periods and scatterings of the Jewish nation. Thus Zechariah 13:8-9 probably will see its final and complete fulfillment in Israel's dispersion in the Tribulation (cf. Rev. 12:6, 13-17). At that time **two-thirds** of the Jewish nation **will be struck down and perish,** but the surviving remnant will be restored, at least for the most part, to their covenant relationship with the Lord.

**13:9.** The surviving remnant will have been purged and purified by the persecutions in the Tribulation, as well as by God's judgment on living Israel at the Second Advent (cf. Ezek. 20:33-38; Matt. 25:1-30). They will **call on** the **name** of the Lord in faith (Zech. 12:10–13:1) and become a restored nation (Rom. 11:26-27). Their renewed covenant relationship with the Lord (Hosea 1–2; Jer. 32:38-41; Ezek. 37:23-28) will be reflected in God's words, **They are My people** (cf. Zech. 8:8), and the people's response, **The Lord is our** (lit., "my") **God** (cf. Hosea 2:21-23).

### 2. THE RETURN OF THE KING (CHAP. 14)

This chapter pictures the triumphant return of Israel's Messiah as the divine King. Thus it portrays the fulfillment of eschatological psalms—such as Psalms 93, 96–97, 99—which envision the universal earthly reign of the Lord. This reign is known from other Scriptures as the personal reign of the Messiah on the throne of David. Zechariah 14 progresses from the initial plundering of Jerusalem near the end of the future Tribulation, through the catastrophic judgment on the Gentile armies at Messiah's Second Advent and the establishment of His millennial reign, to a description of the worship in Jerusalem during the Millennium. The fact that these events have not yet occurred points to a premillennial return of Christ, that is, His return *before* the Millennium.

### a. The deliverance of Jerusalem from the nations (14:1-3)

**14:1.** This summary verse announces the sack of Jerusalem in the **day of the Lord,** a theme occurring many times in the Old Testament, in relation to the severe judgments in the Tribulation period (e.g., Zeph. 1:14-18), as well as those accompanying the Second Advent (as here). The New Testament (2 Peter 3:10) makes it clear that the Millennial Age is also included within "the day of the Lord." The **plunder** which **will be divided** refers to the valuables in Jerusalem that will be taken and shared by the Gentile armies "in your midst" (better than NIV's **among you**), that is, within the city itself. This speaks of the self-assurance and seeming security of the conquerors.

**14:2.** This siege of **Jerusalem** by **all the nations** (i.e., their representative armies) is an early stage of the siege by the confederated Gentile armies described in 12:2-9 (cf. Isa. 34:2; Obad. 15; Rev. 16:14, 16) and known as the Battle (or better, Campaign) of Armageddon. Before the peoples of Judah and Jerusalem will be empowered for victory (Zech. 12:6-8; 14:14) and before the Lord brings about the destruction of the Gentile armies (12:9; 14:12-15), the Gentiles will at first obtain an initial but fleeting taste of victory in Jerusalem, including the typical characteristics of conquest described in verse 2. Either **half** of the population of Jerusalem will be left in **the city** (perhaps under occupational troops), or the Lord will return to destroy the enemies before their job is more than half completed.

**14:3.** Concerning the military intervention of the Messiah, Zechariah announced that **the Lord will go out and fight against those nations.** In military context the term "go out" is a technical term for a king going out to **battle,** which is the clear meaning here. The Lord will "fight" as a warrior (cf. Ex. 15:3; Isa. 42:13; Rev. 19:11-21).

*b. The return of the Deliverer (14:4-5)*

**14:4-5.** After affirming the fact of Messiah's military intervention, Zechariah explained the details of its accomplishment. It will begin with the personal appearance of the Messiah when **His feet will stand on the Mount of Olives,** the very place from which He ascended (Acts 1:11-12). Interestingly God's glory in Ezekiel's vision (Ezek. 11:23) departed from Jerusalem at a mountain **east of Jerusalem.** The apparent earthquake which will **split** the **Mount of Olives . . . in two from east to west** seems to be a direct intervention by the divine King. It will form **a great valley** eastward from Jerusalem as far as **Azel,** an unknown location, through which the remnant of Jews **will flee.** This may be the Valley of Jehoshaphat, spoken of by Joel, where God will judge the Gentiles (see comments on Joel 3:2, 12). The Lord will call the valley **My mountain valley.**

**The earthquake in the days of Uzziah** is mentioned in Amos 1:1 but not in the historical books. Josephus regarded it as a divine judgment on Uzziah for his intrusion into the temple to assume the priest's function (2 Chron. 26:16). When **the Lord** returns He will be accompanied

by **all the holy ones,** probably angels as well as the souls of the redeemed (cf. 1 Thes. 3:13).

*c. The establishment of the messianic kingdom (14:6-11)*

At the heart of this section is the affirmation that "the Lord will be King over the whole earth" and that He will be accepted as the "one Lord" (v. 9). This great pronouncement is set in the context of changes in illumination, climate, and topography which God will bring on Jerusalem, Palestine, and no doubt the whole earth during the Millennium.

(1) The phenomena in the kingdom (14:6-8). **14:6-7.** The **unique day, without daytime or nightime,** may refer to the actual day of the Lord's return when the celestial darkness accompanying the divine judgments will be replaced by light **when evening comes.** At any rate the time of Christ's Second Advent will be accompanied by unparalleled natural phenomena (Isa. 13:10; 34:4; Joel 2:10, 30-31; 3:15; Matt. 24:29).

**14:8.** A perennial spring of water (**living water** as opposed to rainwater) will erupt in **Jerusalem** dividing its water flow between **the eastern sea** (the Dead Sea) and **the western sea** (the Mediterranean). This year-round provision apparently will promote unsurpassed fertility throughout the land (cf. Isa. 27:6; 35:1-3, 6-7; Amos 9:13-14).

(2) The absolute lordship of the Messiah-King. **14:9.** The Messiah will not only reign as King of Israel but He **will** also **be King over the whole earth.** The worldwide scope of His reign is supported by Zechariah's description of Him elsewhere as "the Lord of all the earth" (4:14; 6:5; cf. Micah 4:13). This is confirmed by the Apostle John's identification of Him as the "Lord of lords and King of kings" (Rev. 17:14; 19:16). He has always been the one Lord (Deut. 6:4) in His unique, solitary, incomparable Being (cf. Isa. 37:16; 45:5-6, 14, 18, 22; 46:9). When He establishes His millennial kingdom, He will be universally recognized as such and worshiped as the one true God (Rev. 21:3). With idolatry and false worship cut off from the land (Zech. 13:1-2) **His name** will be **the only name** (cf. Acts 4:12) recognized in worship by people.

(3) The renovation of Judah and the

security of Jerusalem. **14:10-11. The whole land** of Judah—**from Geba** on its northern border (Josh. 21:17) **to Rimmon,** probably on its southern border, 35 miles southwest of **Jerusalem** (Josh. 15:32)— will be miraculously leveled to a broad valley **like the Arabah,** the low plain stretching from below Mount Hermon down the Jordan River Valley and the Dead Sea on to the Gulf of Aqabah. This will help make **Jerusalem** more prominent (cf. Isa. 2:2), as the capital city of the great King. Mention of the city's gates indicate the whole city. **The Benjamin Gate** (cf. Jer. 37:13; 38:7) may have been near the east part of the northern wall; **the site of the First Gate** is unknown; **the Corner Gate** was on the west wall; and **the Tower of Hannanel** (cf. Neh. 3:1) was on the north wall (see the map "Jerusalem in the time of Nehemiah," near Neh. 3:1-5). **The royal winepresses** were probably south of the city. Not only will **Jerusalem** be fully **inhabited** (cf. Joel 3:20); it will also be free of the curse or ban to destruction associated with holy war. It **will be** eternally **secure** (cf. Isa. 32:18; 33:20; Amos 9:15; Micah 4:4; Zech. 3:10).

*d. The destruction of Israel's enemies (14:12-15)*

**14:12-15.** In this parenthetical flashback (the words **the nations that fought against Jerusalem** look back to v. 2), Zechariah described the second phase of the invasion of Jerusalem by the confederated Gentile armies. In this phase the Gentile armies will be destroyed around Jerusalem (as previously described in 12:2-9). This section in chapter 14 summarizes: (a) the divine **plague** on the enemies, both man and beast (vv. 12, 15; cf. 12:4); (b) the **panic** from **the LORD** (14:13); and (c) the plunder taken from the Gentile armies (v. 14), much of which no doubt will be plunder that the Gentiles have just taken from Jerusalem (vv. 1-2).

*e. The worship of Messiah-King by the nations (14:16-19)*

**14:16.** After **Jerusalem** becomes secure and Messiah's worldwide reign has been established (vv. 9-11), **then the survivors from all the nations** will **worship** annually in Jerusalem. "The survivors" are not the Jewish remnant that had been scattered among "all the nations," for the Jewish remnant will already have been

regathered to the land at the time of the Second Advent. Rather, these survivors are from nonmilitary personnel of those nations whose armies were destroyed by Messiah in the attack on Jerusalem (vv. 1-5; cf. Rev. 19:19). The armies in the Campaign of Armageddon will be destroyed, but not the people of the nations they will represent. Futhermore, they will be the survivors of the divine judgment on the Gentile nations who will enter the kingdom of Christ as "sheep," the "goats" having been barred from entrance into the Millennium (Matt. 25:31-46).

That Gentiles will go to Jerusalem (cf. Isa. 2:2; 14:1; 66:23; Zech. 8:23) to worship does not mean they will become Jewish proselytes, as in Old Testament times. Millennial religious worship will not be a restored Judaism but a newly instituted worldwide religious order embracing both Jews and Gentiles. It will center in Jerusalem and will incorporate some features identical with or similar to certain aspects of Old Testament worship. One of these aspects is the annual celebration of **the Feast of Tabernacles** (cf. Lev. 23:33-43; Zech. 14:18-19). The need to go to Jerusalem is partially explained by the presence there of the object of worship—**the King, the LORD Almighty,** that is, Jesus Christ who will be ruling on the throne of David (2 Sam. 7:13, 16; Luke 1:32) in Jerusalem (Isa. 24:23).

**14:17-19.** Worshiping annually in Jerusalem will be necessary for the people to enjoy fertility of crops. Those nations that neglect or refuse such opportunities for **worship** will forfeit their water supply. For most nations this simply means **they will have no rain.** But **Egypt,** whose irrigation depends not on rain (at least not directly) but rather on the flooding of the Nile, will still experience **the plague** of drought as **punishment** from **the LORD,** as will **all the nations that do not go up to celebrate the Feast of Tabernacles.**

*f. The holiness of Judah and Jerusalem during Messiah's reign (14:20-21)*

**14:20-21.** In **that day** holiness will characterize millennial life (cf. 8:3) whether it be in public life (**the bells of the horses**), religious life (**the cooking pots in the LORD's house,** the millennial temple, Ezek. 40–43), or private life (**every pot in Jerusalem and Judah**). Perhaps the general thought is the removal of a dichotomy between secular and sacred. In the Old Testament **a Canaanite** had become symbolic of anything ceremonially unclean and ungodly (the dishonest "merchant" in Hosea 12:7 is lit., "the Canaanite"). In the millennial temple no such defilement will occur. Thus Zechariah's prophetic book which began with a call to repentance (Zech. 1:2-6) concludes with an affirmation that all will be **holy to the Lord** (14:20-21). Because He is **the Lord Almighty** and the Holy One, He will establish holiness throughout the glorious Millennium!

# BIBLIOGRAPHY

Baldwin, Joyce G. *Haggai, Zechariah, Malachi: An Introduction and Commentary.* The Tyndale Old Testament Commentaries. Downers Grove, Ill.: InterVarsity Press, 1972.

Baron, David. *The Visions and Prophecies of Zechariah.* Reprint. Grand Rapids: Kregel Publications, 1972.

Feinberg, Charles L. *The Minor Prophets.* Chicago: Moody Press, 1976.

Keil, C.F. "Zechariah." In *Commentary on the Old Testament in Ten Volumes.* Vol. 10. Reprint (25 vols. in 10). Grand Rapids: Wm. B. Eerdmans Publishing Co., 1982.

Laney, J. Carl. *Zechariah,* Everyman's Bible Commentary. Chicago: Moody Press, 1984.

Leopold, H.C. *Exposition of Zechariah.* Grand Rapids: Baker Book House, 1965.

Luck, G. Coleman. *Zechariah.* Chicago: Moody Press, 1969.

Moore, T.V. *A Commentary on Haggai, Zechariah, Malachi.* London: Banner of Truth Trust, 1960.

Robinson, George L. *The Prophecies of Zechariah.* Chicago: University of Chicago Press, 1896. Reprint. Grand Rapids: Baker Book House, 1926.

Tatford, Frederick A. *The Minor Prophets.* Vol. 3. Reprint (3 vols). Minneapolis: Klock & Klock Christian Publishers, 1982.

Unger, Merrill F. *Commentary on Zechariah.* Grand Rapids: Zondervan Publishing House, 1962.

# MALACHI

## Craig A. Blaising

## INTRODUCTION

**Historical Setting.** Malachi ministered in the fifth century B.C., about 100 years after Cyrus had issued the decree in 538 B.C. which permitted Jews to return from exile to Judah. In response to the prophetic ministries of Haggai and Zechariah, the repatriated Jews had rebuilt the temple, completing it in 515 B.C. Houses had been reconstructed. Most likely in Malachi's day the wall of Jerusalem was being rebuilt or had been completed (by Nehemiah's crew).

Life was not easy. The Jews were under the political dominion of Persia (*peḥâh*, "governor," Mal. 1:8, was a Persian title, also used in Ezra 5:3, 6, 14; 6:6-7, 13; Dan. 3:2-3, 27; 6:7). Harvests were poor and subject to locust damage (Mal. 3:11). Most hearts were indifferent or resentful toward God. Both the priests and the people were violating the stipulations of the Mosaic Law regarding sacrifices, tithes, and offerings. The people's hope in God's covenant promises had dimmed, as evidenced by their (a) intermarriages with pagans, (b) divorces, and (c) general moral ambivalence.

**Date.** Malachi's reference to a Persian governor (Mal. 1:8) shows that the book was written *after* 538 B.C. Most scholars agree that the Book of Malachi was written around 450–430 B.C., for these reasons: (1) Malachi's rebuke of the priests' malpractice in the temple shows that the temple had been rebuilt and the priesthood reestablished. (2) The moral and spiritual conditions Malachi addressed were similar to those encountered by Ezra, who returned in 458, and Nehemiah, who returned in 444. These included intermarriages with Gentiles (2:10-11; cf. Ezra 9:1-2; Neh. 13:1-3, 23-28), lack of the people's support for the Levites (Mal. 3:10; cf. Neh. 13:10), and oppression of the poor (Mal. 3:5; cf. Neh. 5:4-5). Either Malachi was addressing the same generation that Ezra and Nehemiah spoke to, or Malachi spoke to a later generation some time after Ezra's and Nehemiah's corrections.

**Author.** Traditionally Malachi (*mal'āḵî*, lit., "My messenger") has been viewed as the last prophet of the Old Testament period before John the Baptist, whose ministry Malachi predicted (Mal. 3:1). Many, however, have argued that the word *mal'āḵî* is an anonymous designation, not a personal name. They give four reasons to support that view: (1) *Mal'āḵî* is not properly a name form. However, no other prophetic book in the Bible is anonymous. Possibly *mal'āḵî* is a contraction of a longer form *mal'āḵiyyâh* (cf. *'ăḇî* in 2 Kings 18:2, NIV marg. with *'ăḇiyyâh* in 2 Chron. 29:1, and *'ûrî* in 1 Kings 4:19 with *'ûriyyâh* in 1 Chron. 11:41). (2) The Targum (Aram. trans. and paraphrase of the OT) does not consider "Malachi" in Malachi 1:1 as a personal name. However, the Targum adds that this messenger was Ezra, a view that has little support. (3) Since *mal'āḵî* is an anonymous designation in Malachi 3:1 it therefore ought to be the same in 1:1. However, it is more likely that the anonymous *mal'āḵî* in 3:1 is a wordplay on the name of the prophet in 1:1.

(4) Another suggestion by some scholars is that the Book of Malachi was one of three anonymous oracles (the other two being Zech. 9–11 and 12–14) appended to the end of the Minor Prophets. The basis for this view is that the word *maśśā'* ("burden or oracle") introduces each of these three portions of Scripture (Zech. 9:1; 11:1; Mal. 1:1). However, the way Malachi introduces his book (lit., "The oracle of the word of the LORD to Israel by the hand of Malachi") differs from the way Zechariah introduced his two oracles (see Brevard Childs, *Introduction to the Old Testament as*

1573

*Scripture*. Philadelphia: Fortress Press, 1979, pp. 489-92).

The contents of the Book of Malachi clearly indicate that it was written by a prophet. Nothing is known of his family line and he is not mentioned by name elsewhere in the Bible.

**Style.** Malachi's style differs from that of the other writing prophets. Rather than making direct proclamations, Malachi used a dialectical or disputational style. In this style he introduced each of his six messages (see points II–VII in the *Outline*) by a charge or command addressed to the people. Malachi then characterized the people as questioning five of the six charges (each one except the third one, point IV in the *Outline*). Then he offered proof that each charge was correct. This style was an appropriate way to confront the apathetic Israelites.

**Message.** Malachi's message is similar to that of the other prophets: covenant blessing requires covenant faithfulness. As people in each generation obeyed the requirements of the Mosaic Covenant, they participated in the blessings founded in the unconditional Abrahamic Covenant. Obedience to the Law was rewarded with blessing in the land of promise. Disobedience, on the other hand, brought a curse on the people and eventually exile. This covenant regulated Israel's relationship with God throughout the old dispensation.

Malachi's message applied the Mosaic Covenant to the problems of postexilic Israel—problems of neglect, expediency, and outright disobedience. Underlying these problems was a lack of proper perspective on God's covenant faithfulness, and the loss of the hope that the kingdom would be established. This led to widespread unfaithfulness, affecting the people's worship in the temple and marital relations in their homes. Malachi pointed to God's past, present, and future dealings with Israel in order to renew their perspective, reestablish their hope, and motivate them to proper covenant faithfulness.

# OUTLINE

I. Introduction: The Burden of Malachi (1:1)

II. First Oracle: Respond to God's Love (1:2-5)
   A. The claim of God's love for Israel (1:2a)
   B. Israel's question of the claim (1:2b)
   C. The vindication of God's claim (1:2c-5)
      1. The election of Israel over Edom (1:2c-3a)
      2. The judgment of Edom (1:3b-5)

III. Second Oracle: Honor God (1:6–2:9)
   A. The charge of disrespect (1:6a)
   B. Israel's question of the charge (1:6b)
   C. The proof of God's charge: Contemptible sacrifices (1:7-14)
   D. A warning to the priests (2:1-9)
      1. The warning stated (2:1-4)
      2. The standard for priests (2:5-9)

IV. Third Oracle: Be Faithful as God's Covenant People (2:10-16)
   A. The charge of unfaithfulness (2:10)
   B. The first evidence: Illegal intermarriage (2:11-12)
      1. The sin (2:11)
      2. The consequence (2:12)
   C. The second evidence: Divorce (2:13-16a)
      1. The consequence (2:13)
      2. The sin (2:14-16a)
   D. The charge to faithfulness (2:16b)

V. Fourth Oracle: Hope in God (2:17–3:6)
   A. The charge of wearisome speech (2:17a)
   B. Israel's question of the charge (2:17b)
   C. The proof of the charge: No hope for God's justice (2:17c)
   D. The warning by God (3:1-5)
      1. The coming of the messenger in preparation (3:1a)
      2. The coming of the Lord in judgment (3:1b-5)
   E. The basis for hope in God (3:6)

VI. Fifth Oracle: Obey God (3:7-12)
   A. The charge of disobedience (3:7a)
   B. Israel's question of the charge

(3:7b)
  C. The specification of the charge: Robbery (3:8a)
  D. Israel's repeated question of the charge (3:8b)
  E. The proof of the charge (3:8c-9)
    1. The sin: Failure to give tithes and offerings (3:8c)
    2. The curse (3:9)
  F. The promise of blessing (3:10-12)
VII. Sixth Oracle: Fear God (3:13–4:3)
  A. The charge of blasphemy (3:13a)
  B. Israel's question of the charge (3:13b)
  C. The proof of the charge: The endorsement of evil (3:14-15)
  D. The response of the believing remnant (3:16)
  E. The warning and promise of God (3:17–4:3)
VIII. Conclusion: Be Prepared for God's Coming (4:4-6)
  A. The present preparation (4:4)
  B. The future preparation (4:5-6)

# COMMENTARY

## I. Introduction: The Burden of Malachi (1:1)

**1:1.** The word *maśśā'* ("burden"), with which the book begins, sets a sober mood. The NIV translates this word **An oracle.** In the prophetic books *maśśā'* introduces messages of a threatening nature 27 times (e.g., Isa. 13:1; 14:28; 15:1; Nahum 1:1; Hab. 1:1; Zech. 9:1; 12:1). (See comments on *maśśā'* at Zech. 9:1-8.) Standing alone at the beginning of Malachi, the word *maśśā'* gives this prophet's entire message a sense of anxiety and foreboding.

The phrase **the word of the LORD** frequently appears as an introduction to a prophecy, to identify it as a revelation from God that carries His authority. "The LORD" (*Yahweh*) is of course the name of God which recalls His association with the covenant He made with Israel at Sinai. Since the word is addressed **to Israel,** the burden of this discourse concerns problems in the covenant relationship between God and Israel. And since Yahweh is the faithful, loyal, covenant-keeping God, trouble in the covenant relationship can only be because of *Israel's* unfaithfulness. The fact that this burden from the Lord came **through Malachi** must have heightened the sense of imminent rebuke in the minds of the original readers. The priests were supposed to be God's messengers (cf. Mal. 2:7), but now *they* were to listen to one whose name means "My messenger."

## II. First Oracle: Respond to God's Love (1:2-5)

People who read these verses today may feel a little uncomfortable and yet somewhat fascinated, like one who is in the presence of an intensely personal conversation between two parties who have long known each other. By introducing the prophecy as a burden (v. 1) Malachi had already prepared his readers to anticipate accusation and rebuke. However, this first oracle begins not with a charge of wrongdoing but with a claim of God's unrequited love.

### A. The claim of God's love for Israel (1:2a)

**1:2a.** The words **I have loved you** are not a general statement about God's love for all people. The God of *Israel* was speaking: He is the One who called her into existence and who ruled over her and raised her (cf. v. 6) for more than 1,000 years on the basis of His covenant with her. And she was the object of His love (v. 2c).

Considerable pathos is in the words, "I have loved you." This was not the first time **the LORD** had said this. One is reminded of Hosea 11:1, 3-4, 8-9, and God's tender words in Isaiah 43:4. But His love for Israel antedated her existence; He loved her in that He sovereignly and graciously elected her to be His own possession. This was clearly revealed at the time He gave the covenant (Deut. 4:37; 5:10; 7:6-9). Love was the heart of this covenant relationship. This is clear from the exhortations that follow these declarations of divine love (Deut. 4:39-40; 7:9-15). Acknowledging God's love for her, Israel should have responded by loving Him and obeying His commands (Deut. 6:4-9).

### B. Israel's question of the claim (1:2b)

**1:2b.** Israel asked God, **How have You loved us?** (Cf. Israel's similar questioning in vv. 6-7; 2:17; 3:7-8, 13.) By questioning God's claim, Israel was betraying a distrust of God, a lack of faith in His Word—not only a lack of trust in Malachi's statement (1:2a) but also a distrust of God's faithfulness to His covenant. Israel's failure to believe God's Word caused her to fail to love Him and also caused her to be hostile toward Him.

Perhaps Israel thought her complaint was legitimate. After all, about 100 years had passed since the people had returned from the Exile; yet the kingdom predicted by God's prophets had still not come. Instead the people continued to be dominated by foreign governors (v. 8) and experienced hard times economically (2:2; 3:9, 11). If they had carefully read the covenant in Deuteronomy they would have known that such misfortunes were the *result*—not the *cause*—of their disobedience. While Malachi later indicated that a righteous remnant, which feared God, did exist at that time (3:16-18), the nation as a whole needed to repent from the sin of unbelief and fall in love wholeheartedly with the Lord.

## C. The vindication of God's claim (1:2c-5)

### 1. THE ELECTION OF ISRAEL OVER EDOM (1:2C-3A)

**1:2c-3a.** The Lord's claim over Israel was vindicated by two considerations. First was His love expressed in His free choice, His election of **Jacob** and his descendants (including this generation which had questioned Him) to inherit the promise. This was contrary to the normal practice of choosing the oldest son. **Esau,** also named Edom and the father of the Edomites (Gen. 36:1), was the firstborn of the twins. Yet even before birth God freely elected Jacob, later named Israel, as the heir (Gen. 25:21-34; Rom. 9:10-13). The Hebrew words for **loved** and **hated** refer not to God's emotions but to His choice of one over the other for a covenant relationship (cf. Gen. 29:31-35; Deut. 21:15, 17; Luke 14:26). To hate someone meant to reject him and to disavow any loving association with him (cf. Ps. 139:21). Nor do these words by themselves indicate the eternal destinations of Jacob and Esau. The verbs refer to God's acts in history toward both of the two nations which descended from the two brothers.

### 2. THE JUDGMENT OF EDOM (1:3B-5)

**1:3b-4a.** The verbs "I have loved" and "I have hated" (vv. 2b-3a) are in the perfect tense and therefore express not only God's past relationship with Israel and Edom but also His historical and present dealings (in Malachi's day) with these peoples. This provided the second consideration which vindicated God's claim. Israel needed to consider what her lot would have been if she, like Edom, had not been elected to a covenant relationship with Yahweh. Both Israel and Edom received judgment from God at the hands of the Babylonians in the sixth century (Jer. 27:2-8). Yet God repeatedly promised to restore Israel (because of His covenant promises, Deut. 4:29-31; 30:1-10), but He condemned Edom to complete destruction, never to be restored (Jer. 49:7-22; Ezek. 35).

Thus the Lord **turned** Edom's **mountains into a wasteland** and only **the desert jackals** would have that land to pass on to their "descendants." Even Edom's greatest efforts to **rebuild** its **ruins** would be frustrated by **the LORD Almighty** (a title Malachi used 24 times in his short book). In the fifth century, the Nabateans, an Arabian tribe, occupied Edom (located south and east of Judea) and forced the Edomites westward into a desert area later known as Idumea. In the fourth century, the Nabateans took over Idumea as well.

**1:4b-5. The Wicked Land** contrasts with "the holy land" (Zech. 2:12) so that Israel's borders were also the borders of blessing. On the one side was Israel whom God loved and chose to set apart ("holy" means set apart) for covenant blessings. On the other side was Edom whom God had not chosen. Rather she would be destroyed by Him in His **wrath.** (On Edom's wickedness, see Obad. 8-14.) Israel, seeing God's sovereign dealings with Edom, would have a better understanding not only of God's love for her, but also of His greatness over all the earth: **Great is the LORD— even beyond the borders of Israel!**

## III. Second Oracle: Honor God (1:6–2:9)

The first oracle ended with a statement about God's greatness both in and beyond Israel. In sharp contrast the second oracle addressed Israel's failure to honor God properly. Since Israel was supposed to love God wholeheartedly (Deut. 6:5) and to fear Him (Deut. 6:3), the seriousness of her condition was clear.

### A. The charge of disrespect (1:6a)

**1:6a.** Malachi spoke of proper relationships in society, relationships Israel certainly would have insisted on. **A son honors his father, and a servant his master.** The question follows, Which set of relationships would Israel have considered comparable to her relationship with the Lord? Some Israelites might have suggested that God was like a father to Israel, for this analogy had been used before (Ex. 4:22; Isa. 63:16; 64:8; Hosea 11:1). The fifth of the Ten Commandments states that children are to honor their parents (Ex. 20:12; Deut. 5:16). Disobedient children who rebelled against discipline were to be stoned (Deut. 21:18-21).

Therefore should the nation which considered itself a "son" of the Lord be less obedient? So God's question was sharply presented, **If I am a Father, where is the honor** or glory **due Me?** (Cf. Isa. 1:2.) The Hebrew word for "honor" (*kābôd*) also means "glory." The glory of God is spoken of frequently throughout the Scriptures (He is even called "the King of glory," Ps. 24:7-10), and the fact that glory and honor are due Him is beyond dispute.

Perhaps some Israelites might consider the Lord the Master of Israel. Certainly Scripture presents Israel as the Lord's servant (Isa. 44:1-2). Therefore how could the nation that was the Lord's servant be disrespectful to Him? The Lord's second question was ominous, **If I am a Master, where is the respect due Me?** The word "respect" may also be translated "fear." There is no contradiction between the admonition to love God (implied in the first oracle, Mal. 1:2-5) and the exhortation to fear Him. Both appear together in the covenant (cf. Deut. 6:5 with Deut. 6:13). Fear of God does not mean being terrified of Him; it means a proper respect and reverence for Him, a reverence that leads to worship and obedience.

**It is you, O priests, who despise My name.** This charge is doubly sad because after the return from the Exile, the priests were responsible to teach the people God's covenant and turn their hearts to God (Neh. 9:38–10:39; cf. Ezra 6:16-22; 7:10). If the *priests* failed to honor God, what could be expected of the people? The words "My name" stand for God Himself. (In Mal., reference to God's "name" occurs 10 times: 1:6 [twice], 11 [thrice], 14; 2:2, 5; 3:16; 4:2.) They despised *Him*, the One who is **the LORD Almighty.**

### B. Israel's question of the charge (1:6b)

**1:6b.** Malachi cast the priests in the rhetorical role of questioning God: **How have we despised Your name?** From the specific nature of the charge that follows (vv. 7-14), the priests were extremely insensitive to their sin, seemingly—and surprisingly—unaware that they had despised God.

### C. The proof of God's charge: Contemptible sacrifices (1:7-14)

**1:7.** The Lord's reference to **defiled food** should have been enough to cause the priests to repent. They had specific instructions on what constituted defective sacrifices (Lev. 22:17-30). They were warned against offering such sacrifices lest the priests thereby profane and defile God's name (Lev. 22:2, 32). Yet the priests were guilty of that very sin—despising His name (Mal. 1:6) by offering "defiled food" (v. 7). But why did Malachi call the sacrifices "food"? Because all the offerings were called "the food of . . . God" (Lev. 21:6).

The priests asked, **How have we defiled You?** They did not say "We have not defiled You," for they could not really plead ignorance of the Law. So they asked *how* they had profaned the Lord. The fact that they saw the charge of improper sacrifices as a defilement of God Himself showed that they were familiar with Leviticus 22:2, 32. Apparently they had become so hardened and had so rationalized their sin that Malachi could portray them as daring God to spell out their wrongs.

Malachi answered that they had defiled God **by saying that the LORD's table is contemptible.** Malachi 1:7, 12 are the only two verses in the Old Testament where the phrase "the LORD's table" is found. It probably does not refer to the table on which the bread of the Presence was placed (Ex. 25:23-30; 1 Kings 7:48; 2 Chron. 13:10-11). Possibly it refers to the altar of burnt offering (cf. Ex. 38:1; 40:6) because Malachi had already mentioned it (Mal. 1:7) and he spoke of animal sacrifices (v. 8). Or the table may refer metaphorically to the whole spread of offerings sacrificed on the altar (cf. Ezek. 44:15-16).

The charge that the priests were calling the Lord's table contemptible was substantiated by their actions (Mal. 1:8). They were treating it with contempt by disregarding God's requirements concerning the kinds of sacrifices that should be placed on it. This made them guilty, deserving of death (Lev. 22:9). Also their contempt was deepened as they ate some of those unacceptable sacrifices (the priests received their food from the offerings, Lev. 24:5-9).

**1:8-10.** Malachi pointed out that the priests brought **blind animals** and **crippled** and **diseased animals** as sacrifices (cf. v. 13). He asked if **that** was **wrong.** Their answer, according to Leviticus 22:18-25 and Deuteronomy 15:21, should have been yes. It was to their shame that these things had to be pointed out to them. Ironically Malachi suggested, **Try offering them to your governor!** The governor's "table" was a lavishly prepared banquet (cf. Neh. 5:17) including "offerings" from the people. Certainly the governor (*peḥâh,* a Persian title) would not have been **pleased with** the meat of blind, crippled, or diseased animals; in fact he would not have accepted it. How much more absurd it was to expect the favor of **the Lord Almighty** (cf. Mal. 1:4) with such offerings. He did not accept such sacrifices, nor did He **accept** (vv. 8-9) the priests. To emphasize this point, Malachi said the whole **temple** service might as well be **shut** down. It was even useless to light the **fires on** the **altar** of burnt offering. God was **not pleased**; He would **accept** no **offerings from** them.

**1:11.** In the Hebrew, this verse begins with *kî* ("for, because"), not translated in the NIV. It indicates that what follows is the reason the Lord refused to accept the priests' offerings (v. 10). Scholars differ on whether the Hebrew passive participle *mûggāš* should be rendered **will be brought** (future tense, as in KJV, NASB, NIV or "is brought" (pres. tense as

in RSV and many commentaries). If the present tense is followed, then Malachi was referring to practices in his day. In that case the offerings refer either to those brought by Jews who were still dispersed among the nations or to offerings made by Gentiles. The first of these is rejected because the phrases **from the rising to the setting of the sun** and **in every place** indicate a practice more universal than the limited extent of the Jewish dispersion. Also the sacrifices given by Jews in the Dispersion could not be called **pure offerings** since they could be made only in Jerusalem. (Furthermore there is no evidence that Jews in the Dispersion offered any sacrifices.)

Those who accept a present-tense rendering of the verb *mûggāš* usually choose the second of the options just described. In this view God was endorsing pagan worship. However, this view must be rejected for several reasons. If it were adopted, it would be the only place in the Bible where pagan worship is considered legitimate, which would directly contradict numerous references that specifically condemn such worship (e.g., Ex. 23:24, 32-33; Deut. 13:6-11; 29:17; 1 Kings 18:19-46; Ps. 96:5; Isa. 48:5; 66:3; Hab. 2:18-20). Not even Paul's reference to the Athenean worship of an unknown god (Acts 17:22-31) supports this interpretation that pagans worship God's "name" with "pure offerings." Also such an interpretation does not accord with the rest of Malachi, which strongly emphasizes strict obedience to the Mosaic Covenant.

Taking *mûggāš* as future ("will be brought"), however, corresponds with other Old Testament prophecies and with the Book of Malachi itself. The prophets predicted a time when Gentiles will see the light and become worshipers of the Lord (Isa. 45:22-25; 49:5-7; 59:19). The Messiah will become King over the entire earth. Believers in all nations will worship Him (Isa. 11:3-4, 9; Dan. 7:13-14, 27-28; Zeph. 2:11; 3:8-11; Zech. 14:9, 16). Malachi also spoke of the coming of the future day when the Lord will return and will bring about pure worship in Israel (Mal. 3:1-4). It seems preferable then to associate the "pure" Gentile worship mentioned in 1:11 with Israel's pure worship. But will Gentiles in the kingdom give offerings "in every place"? No. This problem is alleviated if the preposition *bᵉ* (usually meaning "in") before "every place" is rendered "from," as in Isaiah 21:1 (cf. *Theological Wordbook of the Old Testament*. 2 vols. Chicago: Moody Press, 1980, s.v. "*b^e*," 1:87).

**1:12-13.** After speaking of the pure offerings in the future kingdom (v. 11), Malachi referred again to the immediate condition of the priests in his day. He repeated the charge that they were profaning God's name (cf. v. 6). In verses 7-8 the *actions* of the priests were condemned; here their *attitude* was condemned. Their attitude was one of contempt. Apparently the priests recognized that these sacrificial practices were irregular, for they said that **the Lord's table** (cf. v. 7) **is defiled** and that **its food . . . is contemptible.** But they did not care to take the trouble to set things straight. Being involved in offering the sacrifices was just **a burden.** Such a response was a form of contempt (cf. James 4:17).

That the priests brought unacceptable **animals** was repeated in Malachi 1:13 (cf. v. 8), and God's refusal to **accept them** was repeated from verses 8-10.

**1:14.** Here Malachi moved from speaking of sacrifices in general to discussing the payment of vows. Making a vow to the Lord was not mandatory, but if a person did so he was required to pay it (Deut. 23:21-23). Moses (Lev. 22:17-25) gave the priests specific instructions about the kinds of sacrifices acceptable for payments of vows. The vow to give an **acceptable** animal and then bring a **blemished animal** was wrong. Certainly no one would try to cheat a king or governor, for fear of being reprimanded and punished by that authority. Nor should one try to cheat *the* **great King,** the One whose **name is to be feared among the nations.** Malachi 1 ends by emphasizing God's supreme authority.

## D. A warning to the priests (2:1-9)

### 1. THE WARNING STATED (2:1-4)

**2:1-2.** After giving and substantiating a charge against the priests, Malachi gave them a command (**admonition;** cf. v. 4): they were to **honor** God (**My name** stands for **Me**). How they were to honor Him is clear from the ways they had failed Him (1:6-14) and from the portrayal of a true priest (2:7). Failure to honor Him would result in their experiencing **a curse** (hardships). The Mosaic Covenant

had included curses for those who disobeyed the Law (see Deut. 27:15-26; 28:15-68). These curses were concerned with the people's physical, mental, and material welfare. The curse Malachi referred to would affect the priests' **blessings,** either their own blessings (as income from people's tithes and offerings) or blessings they pronounced on the people (Num. 6:22-27). Because of their hearts' condition, the curse was **already** in effect.

**2:3-4.** The priests were then warned of a rebuke that would fall against their seed. *Zera'* ("seed") refers to grain (NIV marg.) or to physical **descendants.** The following threat of the removal of the priests from office makes the latter option more probable. Some have suggested that instead of *zera'*, the text should read *z^erōa'* which means "arm." To rebuke one's arm was a metaphor for rendering one powerless (1 Sam. 2:31, "strength" in the NIV is lit., "arm"). This would correlate with the interpretation (cf. Mal. 2:1-2) that the curse concerned the blessings pronounced by the priests on the people.

The Lord said He would **spread on** their **faces** the waste matter **from** the **sacrifices,** which ironically were described as festive. "Spread," from the verb *zārâh*, is a pun on the word *zera'* ("seed"), the descendants who were the object of God's rebuke (v. 3). The priests would be made as unclean as **the offal.** Much as it was discarded, so they would be disposed of as well. In other words they would be cast out of service. Then they would realize that **the Lord** was speaking to them. His purpose in admonishing them was to purify the priesthood **so that** His **covenant with Levi** could **continue.**

### 2. THE STANDARD FOR PRIESTS (2:5-9)

**2:5-6.** The **covenant** with Levi (v. 4), is now discussed in more detail. The tribal name Levi is used for the descendants of Levi who made up the priestly class. The covenant mentioned here refers to what may be called a covenant of grant (Num. 18:7-8, 19-21), a covenant made with an individual (and sometimes his descendants) because of some service the recipient performed. God made a similar covenant of grant with Phinehas (Num. 25:10-13). The phrase **a covenant of life and peace** seems to recall how Phinehas' zeal for the Lord turned away God's wrath from the people (cf. Num. 25:11 with Mal. 2:6, **He . . . turned many from sin**). Most important, **he revered** God (v. 5), the point of exhortation in this oracle. Besides, Levi's teaching was **true,** and his conduct was in **uprightness.**

**2:7-9.** The word **instruction** is *tôrâh,* also the word for "Law." The priests were to teach the Law (Deut. 33:10). As teachers, each priest was to be a **messenger** (*mal'ak*). However, since they were not giving true instruction, they were rebuked by the prophet whose very name, ironically, means "My messenger." Their **teaching . . . caused many to stumble** because they themselves had **turned from the way.** Saying that defiled sacrifices were accepted **violated** God's **covenant with Levi** (see Num. 18:19, 21). So the priests were **despised and humiliated before all the people.** This actually was a light sentence, for their penalty should have been death (Num. 18:32).

## IV. Third Oracle: Be Faithful as God's Covenant People (2:10-16)

### A. The charge of unfaithfulness (2:10)

**2:10.** The style of the third oracle differs from the others. Instead of an initial statement or charge followed by a question of feigned innocence, this oracle begins with three questions asked by the prophet. However, as at the beginning of each of the other oracles, the point is presented at the outset. The reference to **one Father** is probably parallel to **one God** so that "Father" refers to God (cf. 1:6), not to Abraham, as some suggest. Israel was like God's firstborn son (Ex. 4:22; Hosea 11:1). The fact that God had created Israel to be a distinct people on the earth (cf. Amos 3:2) formed the background for the problem Malachi now discussed (Mal. 2:10-16).

**Breaking faith** (cf. vv. 11, 14-16) renders the word *bāgad,* "to act unfaithfully with respect to a prior agreement or covenant." This word is often translated "to act treacherously." The concern of this oracle is the people's unfaithful activity in their relationships **with one another.** This activity was another way (in addition to the charge in the previous oracle) in which **the covenant** was being profaned.

### B. The first evidence: Illegal intermarriage (2:11-12)

#### 1. THE SIN (2:11)

**2:11.** What had been charged in the form of a question (v. 10) was then stated as a fact and explained. The unfaithfulness Malachi had in mind (v. 10) is called **a detestable thing** (lit., "an abomination"), something abhorrent to God. Furthermore this abominable unfaithfulness involved a profaning of holiness. The word for "holiness" (*qōdeš,* "apartness, separateness") may refer to **the sanctuary** (as in the NIV), the covenant, the people, or simply the quality of holiness itself. Since the concern of this oracle is the uniqueness and unity of the people ("Did not one God create us?" [v. 10]), holiness may refer here to the quality of distinctiveness or separateness that the Lord desired **in Israel.**

The abominable unfaithfulness that profaned Israel's holiness was intermarriage with pagans. **Daughter of a foreign god** refers to pagan women who worshiped false gods. (If *qōdeš* refers to the "sanctuary," then possibly the profanation referred to the involvement of these women in temple worship.) Such marriages had been expressly forbidden because they would lead the people into idolatry (Ex. 34:11-16; Deut. 7:3-4; Josh. 23:12-13). Intermarrying was a big problem after the return from the Exile (cf. Ezra 9:1-2, 10-12; Neh. 13:23-27). The Jews were supposed to marry within their own nation. Failures to do so were acts of unfaithfulness among themselves as well as to God. They involved both a disregard for the nation's corporate nature and disobedience to God.

#### 2. THE CONSEQUENCE (2:12)

**2:12.** The prophet invoked a curse on any Jew who had committed or would commit this sin of marrying a pagan. To be **cut . . . off from the tents of Jacob** meant either that **the man** would die or that his line would cease and he would have no descendants in Israel. The phrase *'ēr wᵉʿōneh* is difficult to translate. The NIV translates it **whoever he may be.** The NASB, which is more literal, reads, "everyone who awakes and answers," and the KJV has "the master and the scholar." Some translate it "who gives testimony" (NIV marg.). Perhaps this was a proverbial expression, whose meaning is not clear today.

The last clause—**even though he brings offerings to the LORD Almighty**—emphasizes the hypocritical and insensitive attitude of those who committed this sin of intermarrying. One is shocked to read that despite the abomination such a person committed he still brought offerings to seek the Lord's favor.

## C. The second evidence: Divorce (2:13-16a)

### 1. THE CONSEQUENCE (2:13)

**2:13.** The two lines of evidence in this oracle are arranged chiastically so that the sin-consequence structure in the foregoing (v. 12) is reversed here. The consequence or symptom of the sin is presented first (v. 13); then the sin is stated (vv. 14-16a). Malachi said some people **flood the LORD's altar with tears.** Whose tears do these refer to? Some have suggested that these were the tears of divorced wives who were seeking justice from the Lord. But the second half of verse 13 indicates that these were the tears of the men who (after divorcing their Israelite wives to marry pagans, v. 14) found that the Lord **no longer** received their **offerings.** This fits naturally with verse 12.

### 2. THE SIN (2:14-16A)

**2:14.** Again Malachi stressed the Israelites' spiritual insensitivity. Since they—surprisingly—could not imagine what the problem was (**You ask, Why?**), the prophet had to spell it out for them. **The LORD** was **acting as the witness between** such a man **and** his **wife** with whom he had **broken faith** (cf. vv. 10-11, 15-16), that is, whom he had divorced. This "witness" may have been in a legal sense or in a general sense, depending on the covenant referred to. If it is to be taken in a legal sense, then the Lord was called on to be a witness and a judge in a legal agreement, as was sometimes done among the ancients (cf. Gen. 31:50, 53). If *bᵉrîṭekā* means **your marriage covenant** (NIV) then the Lord's witness would have this legal sense. He was the witness of the marriage covenant between the man and woman.

However, the word *bᵉrîṭekā* (lit., "your covenant") could conceivably refer to the covenant between God and Israel (cf. Mal. 2:10). In that case the Lord was a witness in the general sense that He knows all that happens. Then "the wife of your marriage covenant" would refer to the fact that she was chosen from among the covenant people. While the preceding context seems to support this second interpretation, the statement **she is your partner** (v. 14) seems to emphasize the marriage relationship itself (cf. Prov. 2:17). Most likely the word "covenant" (Mal. 2:14) refers to both the national covenant between God and Israel and the marriage covenant of individuals.

**2:15.** This is the most difficult verse in Malachi to translate. The first phrase could be either, "Did not One make them?" or "Did not He [the LORD] make one?" The first rendering emphasizes the creative and sovereign work of the one God (v. 10). The second has several possibilities. It may refer to one wife, one child of Abraham (Isaac), one flesh (man and woman made one in marriage), or one covenant nation.

The second sentence in verse 15 is even more difficult. Literally it reads, "And a remnant of the Spirit [or spirit] to him." The NIV follows the view of many commentators and reads **flesh** in place of remnant. However, the primary motivation for this is the opinion that the first phrase alludes to Genesis 2:24, which speaks of man and woman becoming one in marriage. This view is possible because marriage is being discussed in Malachi 2:10-16.

Probably a better view is that the prophet was contrasting the Lord's faithfulness to Israel (His one covenant people) with the marital unfaithfulness of individual Israelites. This contrast had already been drawn in verse 10 and was involved in the discussion of the sin of intermarriage (v. 11).

In this view the **one** in the first clause in verse 15 refers to Israel as one people. The stress on oneness would have special significance in the postexilic period, as the former division between Israel and Judah was removed. (In v. 11 "Judah" and "Israel" are used interchangeably.) Therefore the first phrase might have an intended double reference: "Has He not made one people?" *and* "Has He not made the people one?" The second phrase could read, "and made them His spiritual remnant." They could be His "spiritual" remnant only because He would fill them with His Spirit. Though Judah and Israel were united in Malachi's day, the granting of the Holy Spirit to the remnant is still future (Ezek. 37). But it was described from God's standpoint as if it had already taken place. Why was God concerned about the unity of His people? (**And why one?**) God is **seeking** a **godly offspring** (lit., "a seed of God"). "Seed" refers to the people corporately as the heir of His covenant promise (cf. Gen. 17:7) and parallels the phrase "spiritual remnant."

Malachi's command, **So guard yourself in your spirit** (repeated in Mal. 2:16) means to have the same desire for covenant unity that the Holy Spirit seeks, which would mean **not** violating the marriage covenant. Because the nation is one, no husband, Malachi said, should **break faith** (vv. 10-11, 14, 16) **with the wife of** his **youth** (cf. v. 14) by divorcing her (cf. v. 16).

**2:16a.** Malachi used strong language to emphasize God's displeasure with divorce. He said, **I hate divorce.** "Hate" (from *śānē'*) means to detest. (This differs from the Heb. word for "hate" used in 1:3.) To underscore his point, Malachi said that this pronouncement was made by **the LORD God of Israel.** This recalls the fact that He is the sovereign Lawgiver and Judge of Israel. If God despises a practice, certainly it ought not be done.

**A man's covering himself . . . with his garment** symbolizes marriage (cf. Ruth 3:9; Ezek. 16:8). But covering himself **with violence** describes violating the marriage relationship, which is what divorce does. The fact that this is the Lord's view is repeated for emphasis (**says the LORD Almighty**).

This verse is the most explicit statement in the Old Testament on God's feelings about divorce. Divorce was allowed but actually the instructions in that passage (Deut. 24:1-4) were given to protect the wife if a divorce should occur. Jesus taught that those concessions by Moses were given because of the hardness of people's hearts, but He emphasized that God does not approve of divorce (Matt. 19:7-9), though some Bible scholars see some bases for exceptions to this ideal. (Cf. comments on Matt. 5:31-32; 19:1-12; Mark 10:1-12; and 1 Cor. 7:10-24.)

### D. The charge to faithfulness (2:16b)

**2:16b.** The charge in verse 15b is repeated in verse 16b: **So guard yourself in your spirit, and do not break faith** (cf. vv. 10-11, 14). The Israelites were not to break faith with one another by divorcing their Jewish wives and intermarrying with pagans (v. 11). Such activity profaned the covenant promise God gave to Israel. By guarding their spirits they would be acting in accord with God's purpose and would help preserve the unity of the nation as well as their individual marriages.

## V. Fourth Oracle: Hope in God (2:17-3:6)

### A. The charge of wearisome speech (2:17a)

**2:17a.** This oracle has a striking contrast between its first and last verses. Though the people had changed in their views on God's justice (2:17) God Himself had not changed (3:6). Because He does not change, neither do His covenant promises. Therefore Israel's faith and hope should have been stabilized. However, she was acting and talking as if she had no God to believe in or hope for. Therefore, ironically, the God whose word to people of faith is that He does not change or grow weary (cf. Isa. 40:28) is now said to be wearied with this people's faithless and hopeless **words** (cf. Isa. 43:24).

### B. Israel's question of the charge (2:17b)

**2:17b.** Again the people were portrayed as being oblivious to their sin (cf. 1:6-7; 2:14): **How have we wearied Him?** (cf. Isa. 44:24)

### C. The proof of the charge: No hope for God's justice (2:17c)

**2:17c.** The apparent prosperity of the wicked (**All who do evil are good in the eyes of the LORD**) and the suffering of the righteous is an age-old problem. In the Old Testament the problem was more pronounced than it is today because God promised Israel material prosperity as a reward for obedience to His Law (Deut. 28). However, many of these promises were intended for the entire nation, and in a society in which the righteous and wicked were mixed, there was opportunity for confusion and misunderstanding in individual cases. Added to this is the fact that God in His providence blesses the wicked as well as the righteous as a testimony to Himself (Matt. 5:45; Acts 14:17). Also the righteous as well as the wicked suffer because of the Fall (Gen. 3:16-19; Ecc. 2:17-23). The Book of Job adds to the dilemma of human suffering the extra dimension of God's dealing with Satan. All of this makes it difficult, apart from known sin in one's life, to determine why a righteous person suffers.

The prosperity of the wicked was equally perplexing and was discussed by at least five biblical writers (Job 21:7-26; 24:1-17; Ps. 73:1-14; Ecc. 8:14; Jer. 12:1-4; Hab. 1). Though answers to this problem are not given in these passages, in each case questions about God's justice are removed by a futuristic perspective: God will come in judgment and punish the wicked (Job 24:22-24; 27:13-23; Ps. 73:16-20; Ecc. 8:12-13; Jer. 12:7-17; Hab. 2:3; 3:2-19) and establish the righteous in His kingdom forever.

The Jews in Malachi's day had failed to learn such hope from the Scriptures. They questioned God's justice by saying that He delights in evil people and by asking, **Where is the God of justice?** Yet *they* were the guilty ones; they were the ones who were unfaithful to Him. Here too God responded by referring to His forthcoming judgment (Mal. 3:1-5). However, unlike the answers by the righteous biblical writers mentioned earlier, the judgment which Malachi referred to was to be against the hypocritical questioners as well.

## D. The warning by God (3:1-5)

### 1. THE COMING OF THE MESSENGER IN PREPARATION (3:1A)

**3:1a.** Malachi directed the attention of the faithless and hopeless questioners (2:17) to the future. Though some have taken **My messenger** (*mal'ākî*) as the writer of this book or as an angel, it seems best to see him as a future prophet. Jesus explicitly identified this person as John the Baptist (Matt. 11:7-10). The fact that this messenger will prepare His way harmonizes with Isaiah 40:3 (cf. John 1:23). The coming of this messenger was to be the first of a twofold eschatological event. The second step would be the coming of the Lord in His day.

### 2. THE COMING OF THE LORD IN JUDGMENT (3:1B-5)

**3:1b.** After the preparation by God's messenger, **suddenly the LORD . . . will come to His temple.** The coming of the Lord in His day is a much-discussed theme among the prophets. Zechariah said He will come to Zion and dwell there (Zech. 8:3). Ezekiel predicted the return of the glory of God to the temple (Ezek. 43:1-5). Malachi's two preceding oracles identified serious problems in the practice of temple worship, so the coming of the Lord to His temple would answer the questions about His justice (Mal. 2:17) and would have an ominous significance for the priests.

The title **the messenger of the covenant** occurs only here in the Bible. This individual is not the same as "My messenger" in 3:1, for the messenger of the covenant comes *after* the earlier messenger. Most likely the messenger here should be identified with **the LORD** Himself. The word "messenger" can be translated "angel," and the Angel of the Lord, a manifestation of God Himself, had been quite active in Israel's earlier history (cf. Gen. 16:10; 22:15-18; Ex. 3:2; 33:14 with Isa. 63:9; and Jud. 13:21-22). The parallel phrases, **the LORD you are seeking** and **whom you desire,** reflect the general expectation of the Lord's coming, as predicted by many other prophets. But these phrases also carry a note of sarcasm. That Israel's hope was superficial was indicated by her question (Mal. 2:17). However, though their hope was superficial, He **will come.**

**3:2-4.** The day of the Lord will be a day of judgment on the whole world, a day of disaster and death (Isa. 2:12; Joel 3:11-16; Amos 5:18-21; Zech 1:14-18). Later Malachi spoke of this day as coming like fire to burn up the wicked (Mal. 4:1). So the answer to both questions, **Who can endure the day of His coming?** and **Who can stand when He appears?** is that none of the wicked will endure. The Lord's coming will **purify** Israel by purging out the wicked.

Often the prophets spoke of the day of the Lord in connection with the judgment that would be poured on the nations and would effect Israel's deliverance (see comments under "Major Interpretive Problems" in the *Introduction* to Joel; and cf. Zech. 14). Malachi, however, made no mention of the other nations. He concentrated on this day as a time of judgment on Israel and especially on the Levites, her leaders and teachers.

The figures of **a refiner's fire** (that burned out the dross from metal ores) and **launderer's soap** emphasize the effectiveness of God's spiritual purging of the nation (cf. Isa. 1:25; Jer. 6:29-30; Ezek. 22:17-22). The result would be a pure class of **Levites.** Refined **like gold and silver,** they **will bring offerings in righteousness . . . as in days gone by.** This will contrast with Israel's unacceptable offerings of which Malachi wrote (Mal. 2:12-13). Following the return of **the Lord** and the judgment of Israel, **offerings** will be sacrificed in the kingdom (cf. Isa. 56:7; 66:20-23; Jer. 33:18; Ezek. 40:38-43; 43:13-27; Zech. 14:16-21).

**3:5.** The judgment of Israel will not be limited to Levites; it will include the whole nation (cf. Ezek. 20:34-38). God **will come near** Israel **for judgment.** He will purge the nation of those who are involved in sorcery (cf. Micah 5:12), adultery, perjury, depriving workers **of their wages,** oppressing **widows** and orphans, and mistreating **aliens**—all those who **do not fear** Him. All these crimes were prohibited in the Mosaic Law. God's removing these sinners from Israel will be His answer to the nation's question about His justice (Mal. 2:17).

### E. The basis for hope in God (3:6)

**3:6.** But will this judgment bring about the end of Israel? Will the people be consumed by the refiner's fire? No, for as other prophets had predicted, Malachi stated that Israel will be delivered in the day of **the Lord.** The **descendants of Jacob** will **not** be **destroyed.** This is because of God's covenant promise. A promise is only as good as the person who makes it. God will keep His promise to the nation of Israel—it will **not change**—because His Word, like Himself, is immutable. This is the basis for Israel's hope (cf. Deut. 4:31; Ezek. 36:22-32). Significantly the Apostle Paul gives the same reason for expecting a future for national Israel (Rom. 3:3-4; 9:6; 11:1-5, 25-29).

## VI. Fifth Oracle: Obey God (3:7-12)

### A. The charge of disobedience (3:7a)

**3:7a.** Malachi's fifth oracle begins with a blanket condemnation of Israel's disobedience to God's **decrees** throughout her history. (This contrasts with the positive note of God's unchanging faithfulness which concluded the preceding oracle, v. 6.) This calls to mind God's comments about Israel's stubbornness at Sinai (Ex. 32:7-9), which Moses repeated before the nation entered Canaan (Deut. 9:6-8, 13, 23-24; 31:27-29). Certainly the history of Israel from that day to Malachi's substantiated the prophet's charge. Malachi then voiced the Lord's appeal and a promise. If Israel would **return to** Him (in faith and obedience), then He would respond and would **return to** her. This promise was based on the covenant God made with Israel (cf. Deut. 4:30-31; 30:1-10).

### B. Israel's question of the charge (3:7b)

**3:7b.** Again Malachi placed Israel in the rhetorical role of questioning God's charge: **How are we to return?** Only one who is aware of the path he has taken can retrace his steps. But Israel pretended to be ignorant of her waywardness.

### C. The specification of the charge: Robbery (3:8a)

**3:8a.** Bluntly stated, Israel was accused of being a thief. Thievery against people was bad enough, but only a fool would try to **rob God. Yet** this was the charge against Israel.

### D. Israel's repeated question of the charge (3:8b)

**3:8b.** The fifth oracle is parallel to the second, having two questions, "How are we to return?" (v. 7b) and **How do we rob You?** (v. 8) This literary device helped represent the general and the specific natures of the charge.

### E. The proof of the charge (3:8c-9)

1. THE SIN: FAILURE TO GIVE TITHES AND OFFERINGS (3:8C)

**3:8c.** Again, the nation's problem had to do with offerings. The second oracle (1:6–2:9) dealt with the attitude of disrespect (1:6) which led to a profaning of the offerings (1:7-14). There the *quality* of the sacrifices was in question. Here the *quantity* was the issue (cf. "the whole tithe," 3:10).

The nation, God answered, was robbing God by not bringing **tithes and offerings.** The tithe was literally a 10th of all produce and livestock which the people possessed (Lev. 27:30, 32). A tithe was to be given to the Levites who in turn were to give a tithe of the tithe to the priests (Num. 18:21-32). The Israelites were also to bring a tithe of their produce and animals and eat it with the Levites before the Lord in Jerusalem as an act of festal worship (Deut. 12:5-18; 14:22-26). Also every third year a tithe was to be stored up in the towns for Levites, strangers, widows, and orphans (Deut. 14:27-29). While the word "offerings" may refer to offerings in general, it seems to refer here (Mal. 3:8c) to those portions of the offerings (as well as those portions of the tithes) designated for the priests (*Theological Wordbook of the Old Testament,* s.v. "*t^erûmâh,*" 2:838). If the Levites and priests would not receive the tithes and offerings, they would have to turn to other means of supporting themselves. As a result, the temple ministry would suffer.

2. THE CURSE (3:9)

**3:9.** Since the temple was God's house (v. 10), failure to support its ministry was considered equal to **robbing** God Himself. The nature of the **curse** on the **nation** can be determined from verse 11: famine due to pests (locusts) eating the vegetation, and vines without grapes (cf. Deut. 28:38-40).

*F. The promise of blessing (3:10-12)*

**3:10-12.** This promise was a reaffirmation of the obedience-blessing relationship specified in the Mosaic Law (Deut. 28:1-14). What the people were experiencing was the disobedience-curse arrangement also given in that covenant (Deut. 28:15-68). This covenant was a gracious provision for Israel. No other nation had such promises from God. Since the Word of God is sure, God's part of the covenant arrangement would definitely be carried out. Israel could attest to this because she was experiencing certain curses in return for her disobedience to God's Law about the tithe. The Lord then appealed to His covenant promises in challenging Israel to **bring the whole tithe into the storehouse** so there would be adequate **food** for the priests. "Storehouse" refers to a special room or rooms in the temple for keeping tithed grain (cf. 1 Kings 7:51; Neh. 10:38; 13:12). By doing

this, the people would see that God would **open** heaven's **floodgates** and **pour out . . . blessing** on them. These blessings would include agricultural prosperity—good **crops** not destroyed by **pests,** and undamaged **vines** (Mal. 3:11) —and a good reputation among **all the nations** (v. 12). These blessings simply awaited their obedience.

One must be careful in applying these promises to believers today. The Mosaic Covenant, with its promises of material blessings to Israel for her obedience, is no longer in force (Eph. 2:14-15; Rom. 10:4; Heb. 8:13). However, the New Testament speaks about generosity and giving. While not requiring a tithe of believers today, the New Testament does speak of God's blessing on those who give generously to the needs of the church and especially to those who labor in the Word (Acts 4:31-35; 2 Cor. 9:6-12; Gal. 6:6; Phil. 4:14-19).

## VII. Sixth Oracle: Fear God (3:13–4:3)

*A. The charge of blasphemy (3:13a)*

**3:13a.** In contrast with the blessings the Lord extended to Israel (v. 12), the sixth oracle charged the people with speaking **harsh things against . . . the Lord.** This was more than a contrast in tone, for the people's harsh words contradicted the promises reaffirmed in verses 10-12.

*B. Israel's question of the charge (3:13b)*

**3:13b.** Again, typical of Malachi's style, the spiritually insensitive people were portrayed as ignorant of the sin. They asked God, **What have we said against You?**

*C. The proof of the charge: The endorsement of evil (3:14-15)*

This sixth oracle is parallel in many respects to the fourth one (2:17–3:6). Questions concerning God's justice, because of the suffering of the apparently righteous and the seeming prosperity of the wicked (cf. 2:17), now reached a climax.

**3:14.** The people **said, It is futile to serve God.** "Futile" (*šāw^e*) may also be translated "vain." Ironically the people, in a sense, were indicting themselves, saying their own worship and service of the Lord was empty, useless, and without result. Hence they felt they gained no benefits from serving Him. They asked, **What did we gain. . . ?** They presumed they had been faithful to God, **carrying out His requirements.** And they presumed they had repented of their misdeeds, **going about like mourners before the LORD Almighty.** They thought all that remained was for God to fulfill His part of His bargain and bless them. They were subtly suggesting that God was *not* keeping His promises.

The problem, of course, was not on God's side. Malachi had already demonstrated that God was responding to them in accord with the covenant. However, His response was not in the form of blessing, which they desired. Two reasons explain this: (1) The people's hearts were not right with God; they were disobedient. (2) Some of the people who made the complaint (3:14) were guilty of the myopic legalism that eventually led to Jewish pharisaism in the first century A.D. This legalism concentrated on performing certain rigorous activities and not doing other things as the means of vindicating themselves before God. But this actually stifled the full expression of inner righteousness required by God (Matt. 5:20-48; 23:1-36). Thus their works would not be accepted as proper covenant obedience. God requires external obedience, but it must stem from the heart, and this obedience is not to vindicate one's own righteousness but to manifest God's righteousness. Believers today are in a much better position than Old Testament saints because those in the body of Christ have received the permanently indwelling Spirit who can overcome the flesh in manifesting the righteousness of God (Rom. 8:1-17; Gal. 5:16-26; Phil. 2:12-13).

**3:15.** Israel was still concerned that sinners were not punished. **The arrogant were blessed. . . . evildoers were prospering,** and those who confronted **God escaped judgment.** However, as Malachi pointed out later (4:1), the arrogant and the evildoers **will** be punished. (On this problem of the prosperity of the wicked, see comments on 2:17c.)

### D. The response of the believing remnant (3:16)

**3:16.** The word **then** (*'āz*) is emphatic, indicating that the action described in

this verse was a consequence of the preceding confrontation. It is difficult to tell whether this remnant (**those who feared the LORD**) differs from the preceding questioners (vv. 13-15), is the same, or is a part of them. If the two groups are in some way identical, then the righteous repented of their harsh words and were then strengthened in their faith. But if they are unrelated, then their attitude and speech contrasted with the people in verses 13-15. What they said to **each other** is unknown, but it probably concerned a renewed perspective of God's faithfulness as was true in other similar struggles over these issues (cf. Ps. 73; Ecc. 12:13-14). Their fear of God exemplifies the response which God desired from this oracle. The **scroll of remembrance** means that a permanent remembrance of their faithful and reverent response is kept in heaven. This provides assurance that when God deals with these individuals He will not forget their submission to Him.

### E. The warning and promise of God (3:17–4:3)

**3:17-18.** Those who fear the Lord (v. 16) will become His **in the day** He makes **up His treasured possession.** "The day" (also mentioned in 3:2 and 4:1; cf. "that . . . day" in 4:5) is the day of the Lord. It will be a day of judgment on the wicked and of deliverance for the righteous (God **will spare them**). As a result Israel **will again see the distinction between the righteous and the wicked.** In previous times Israel had seen God intervene decisively in judgment and deliverance (e.g., the Exodus, the Exile, and the return). Those events pointed up a distinction between the righteous and the wicked. The future day of the Lord, however, will bring about a much more extensive judgment on the wicked, and through physical deliverance and bodily resurrection, the righteous will be His "treasured possession" in the kingdom, fulfilling God's original intention for Israel (Ex. 19:5-6; Deut. 7:6; 14:2; 26:18; Ps. 135:4). This hope renews the righteous and strengthens their fear of God.

**4:1.** Malachi here elaborated on **the day** of the Lord. As in 3:2-3, the judgment on that day is described as a judgment of **fire.** The fact that **it will burn like a furnace** stresses not only its intensity but also its judgmental purpose; it is not a fire that burns out of control. Unlike 3:2-3, which emphasized the purification of Israel (in particular, the Levites), this passage emphasizes the destruction of the wicked (cf. Isa. 66:15; Zeph. 1:18; 3:8). So complete will be the judgment that the wicked (**the arrogant and every evildoer**; cf. Mal. 3:15), compared to **stubble**, will **not** have **a root or a branch** remaining. This does not mean annihilation in the sense of cessation of being (the wicked will be resurrected, Dan. 12:2), but rather the complete exclusion of the wicked from God's kingdom (cf. Matt. 25:46).

**4:2.** The day of the Lord, which will be like a fire to the wicked, will in contrast be like sunshine to God's people. The phrase **the sun of righteousness** appears only here in Scripture. Though many commentators have taken these words to refer to Christ, the phrase seems to refer to the day of the Lord in general. In the kingdom, righteousness will pervade like the sun. **Healing** (*marpē*, "health or restoration") **in its wings** (or rays) refers to the restorative powers of righteousness, which are like the healthful rays of the sun. God's people will be spiritually restored and renewed.

The righteous are described as **you who revere My name** (cf. comments on "My name" in 1:6). "Revere" translates the same Hebrew word rendered "fear" in 3:5 and "feared" in 1:14; 3:16. Revering God contrasts with saying "harsh things" against God (3:13). The fact that the righteous rather than the wicked are personally addressed indicates the Lord's contempt for the wicked as much as His love for His own. The figure of **calves** enjoying open pasture after being cooped up in a pen (**stall**) expresses the future satisfaction and joy of the righteous (cf. Isa. 65:17-25; Hosea 14:4-7; Amos 9:13-15; Zeph. 3:19-20).

**4:3.** The righteous will **trample down the wicked,** who **will be** like **ashes under the . . . feet** of the righteous. This not only indicates the finality of the judgment on the wicked, but it also brings to a sharp conclusion the answer in this oracle to the cynical question asked by the unfaithful Israelites, "What do we gain by carrying out His requirements?" (3:14)

## VIII. Conclusion: Be Prepared for God's Coming (4:4-6)

### A. The present preparation (4:4)

**4:4.** In light of all that has been said about the Mosaic Covenant and Malachi's concern for the people's covenant faithfulness and obedience, this concluding exhortation was appropriately direct and to the point. The verb **remember** (*zāḵar*) is used 14 times in Deuteronomy as an exhortation to Israel concerning this covenant **Law.** This command can refer to: (a) mental acts of remembering or paying attention to something, or to (b) mental acts combined with appropriate external actions (in other words, recalling and obeying), or to (c) acts of reciting or repeating something verbally (*Theological Wordbook of the Old Testament*, s.v. "*zāḵar*," 1:241). In light of Malachi's insistence on obedience, meaning (b) seems to be the force of this command: "Recall it to mind and do it!"

The reference to **My servant Moses** not only speaks of Moses' faithfulness (Heb. 3:5) but also reminds the reader that the Lord Almighty (Mal. 4:3) is the same God who powerfully displayed His judgments and His salvation at the time of the Exodus. And He is the Living God who gave the Ten Commandments to the people **at Horeb** (the ancient name for Mount Sinai; Ex. 3:1; Deut. 5:2; Ps. 106:19). He graciously accepted Moses' role as prophetic mediator in the giving of the entire Law (Deut. 5:23-31). The people in Malachi's time needed a renewed fear of God; they needed to repent and be faithful to God's covenant. Such repentance would cause them to benefit from rather than suffer in the coming day of the Lord.

### B. The future preparation (4:5-6)

**4:5-6.** God promised through Malachi that **the Prophet Elijah** would come and minister **before** the day of the Lord. (See comments under "Major Interpretive Problems" in the *Introduction* to Joel.) This is the only passage in the Prophets that speaks of a future ministry for Elijah. Many commentators have linked this prophecy to 3:1 which speaks of a messenger who prepares the way for the Lord's coming. However, Matthew (Matt. 11:7-10) specifically states that John the Baptist was the messenger (Mal. 3:1) who prepared the way for the Lord.

But should John the Baptist also be considered the fulfillment of the prophecy about Elijah? (Mal. 4:5-6) Before John the Baptist was born an angel of the Lord predicted that he would minister "in the spirit and power of Elijah, to turn the hearts of the fathers to their children and the disobedient to the wisdom of the righteous—to make ready a people prepared for the Lord" (Luke 1:17). This would seem to put together the two prophecies (Mal. 3:1 and 4:5-6) and to see John as fulfilling both of them.

However, while he freely admitted that he was the one who prepared the way for the Lord (Isa. 40:3; Mal. 3:1), John expressly denied that he was Elijah (John 1:21-23). Even when Jesus called John "the Elijah who was to come," He conditioned that designation with the phrase, "if you are willing to accept it" (Matt. 11:14). A solution to the problem seems to be offered in Matthew 17. After Elijah appeared with Christ in His transfiguration, the disciples asked about Elijah's future coming. Jesus, speaking apparently after John's death (cf. Matt. 14:1-2), affirmed that "Elijah comes and will restore all things" (Matt. 17:11). This future expectation indicates that Malachi 4:5-6 was *not* fulfilled in the ministry of John. Israel did not accept John the Baptist as the Elijah-like restorer of all things, so another Elijah-like forerunner is yet to come before the day of the Lord.

However, Jesus went on to say, "Elijah has already come, and they did not recognize him" (Matt. 17:12), and the disciples understood He was talking about John the Baptist (Matt. 17:13). The solution to all this seems to be that though John did not fulfill Malachi 4:5-6 (for Elijah is yet to come), Elijah was a type of John in that there is a great deal of similarity between Elijah in 4:5-6 and the messenger (John the Baptist) in 3:1.

It is difficult to determine whether the Elijah to come is Elijah himself (as possibly indicated in Matt. 17:11) or someone in the spirit and power of Elijah (as John was, so that Christ referred to him as simply Elijah, Matt. 17:12). The latter seems preferable. The most likely New Testament reference to this future Elijah-like ministry is Revelation 11:1-13, which speaks of the two witnesses in the Tribulation. Possibly the Apostle John was expanding the Elijah expectation into an Elijah-Elisha ministry (cf. comments on Rev. 11:3-6.) As a result of the ministry of the two witnesses many people will repent, thus uniting **the hearts of . . . fathers** with **their children.** This repentance will mean that they will not experience God's judgment in the day of the Lord.

The last words of the Old Testament are Malachi's ominous anticipation of the **great and dreadful day of the Lord.** This event of judgment, a climactic event in history, was a major theme of the prophets. The force of the warnings and appeals in Malachi's book hinges as much on the certainty of this coming judgment as on the covenant-based offer of grace. The Book of Revelation renders the same expectation of judgment and repentance at the end of the New Testament (Rev. 22:12-17) but with greater details about the One who will return.

# BIBLIOGRAPHY

Baldwin, Joyce G. *Haggai, Zechariah, Malachi.* The Tyndale Old Testament Commentaries. Downers Grove, Ill.: InterVaristy Press, 1972.

Feinberg, Charles L. *The Minor Prophets.* Chicago: Moody Press, 1976.

Freeman, Hobart E. *Introduction to the Old Testament Prophets.* Chicago: Moody Press, 1968.

Isbell, Charles D. *Malachi: A Study Guide Commentary.* Grand Rapids: Zondervan Publishing House, 1980.

Kaiser, Walter C., Jr. *Malachi: God's Unchanging Love.* Grand Rapids: Baker Book House, 1984.

Keil, C.F. "Minor Prophets." In *Commentary on the Old Testament in Ten Volumes.* Vol. 10. Reprint (25 vols. in 10). Grand Rapids: Wm. B. Eerdmans Publishing Co., 1982.

Morgan, G. Campbell. *Malachi's Message for Today.* Reprint. Grand Rapids: Baker Book House, 1972.

Oswalt, John. *Where Are You, God?* Wheaton, Ill.: SP Publications, Victor Books, 1982.

Smith, J.M.P. *A Critical and Exegetical Commentary on the Book of Malachi.* The International Critical Commentary. New York: Charles Scribner, 1912.

Tatford, Frederick A. *The Minor Prophets.* Vol. 3. Reprint (3 vols.). Minneapolis: Klock & Klock Christian Publishers, 1982.

Wolf, Herbert. *Haggai and Malachi.* Chicago: Moody Press, 1976.